GENERAL MOTORS

LUMINA/GRAND PRIX/CUTLASS SUPREME/REGAL 1988-92 REPAIR MANUAL

President, Chilton Enterprises	David S. Loewith
Senior Vice President	Ronald A. Hoxter
Publisher and Editor-In-Chief	Kerry A. Freeman, S.A.E.
Managing Editors	Peter M. Conti, Jr. □ W. Calvin Settle, Jr., S.A.E.
Assistant Managing Editor	Nick D'Andrea
Senior Editors	Debra Gaffney □ Ken Grabowski, A.S.E., S.A.E. Michael L. Grady □ Richard J. Rivele, S.A.E. Richard T. Smith □ Jim Taylor Ron Webb
Director of Manufacturing	Mike D'Imperio
Editor	Steven Morgan

CHILTON BOOK COMPANY

*ONE OF THE **DIVERSIFIED PUBLISHING COMPANIES**, A PART OF **CAPITAL CITIES/ABC, INC.***

Manufactured in USA

Chilton Way, Radnor, PA 19089
ISBN 0–8019–8258–8
Library of Congress Catalog Card No. 91–058824
2345678901 3210987654

Contents

Contents

SAFETY NOTICE

Proper service and repair procedures are vital to the safe, reliable operation of all motor vehicles, as well as the personal safety of those performing repairs. This manual outlines procedures for servicing and repairing vehicles using safe, effective methods. The procedures contain many NOTES, CAUTIONS and WARNINGS which should be followed along with standard safety procedures to eliminate the possibility of personal injury or improper service which could damage the vehicle or compromise its safety.

It is important to note that the repair procedures and techniques, tools and parts for servicing motor vehicles, as well as the skill and experience of the individual performing the work vary widely. It is not possible to anticipate all of the conceivable ways or conditions under which vehicles may be serviced, or to provide cautions as to all of the possible hazards that may result. Standard and accepted safety precautions and equipment should be used when handling toxic or flammable fluids, and safety goggles or other protection should be used during cutting, grinding, chiseling, prying, or any other process that can caus material removal or projectiles.

Some procedures require the use of tools specially designed for a specific purpose. Before substituting another tool or procedure, you must be completely satisfied that neither your personal safety, nor the performance of the vehicle will be endangered.

Although information in this manual is based on industry sources and is complete as possible at the time of publication, the possibility exists that some car manufacturers made later changes which could not be included here. While striving for total accuracy, Chilton Book Company cannot assume responsibility for any errors, changes or omissions that may occur in the compilation of this data.

PART NUMBERS

Part numbers listed in this reference are not recommendations by Chilton for any product by brand name. They are references that can be used with interchange manuals and aftermarket supplier catalogs to locate each brand supplier's discrete part number.

SPECIAL TOOLS

Special tools are recommended by the vehicle manufacturer to perform their specific job. Use has been kept to a minimum, but where absolutely necessary, they are referred to in the text by the part number of the tool manufacturer. These tools can be purchased, under the appropriate part number, from your GM dealer or regional distributor, or an equivalent tool can be purchased locally from a tool supplier or parts outlet. Before substituting any tool for the one recommended, read the SAFETY NOTICE at the top of this page.

ACKNOWLEDGMENTS

The Chilton Book Company expresses appreciation to General Motors Corp., Detroit, Michigan for their generous assistance.

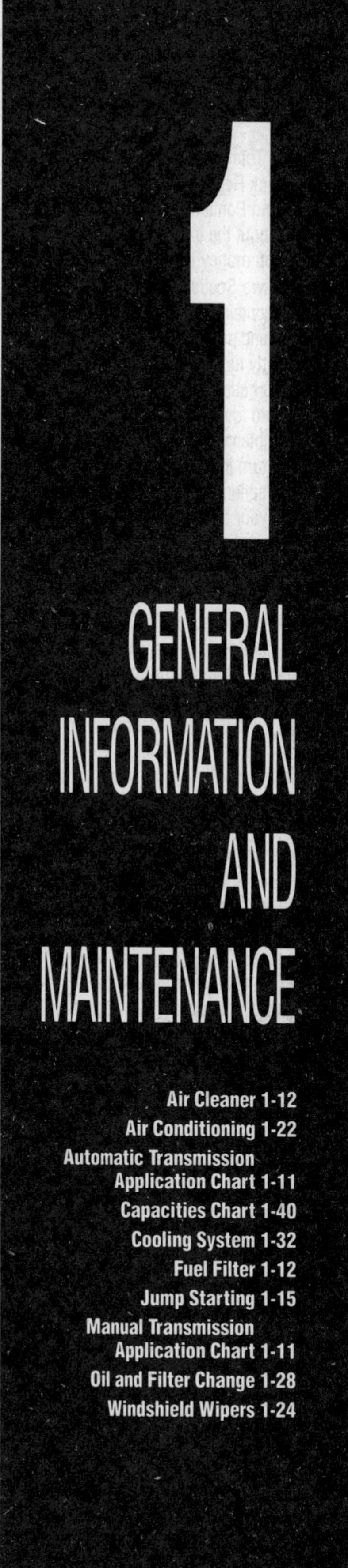

1 GENERAL INFORMATION AND MAINTENANCE

HOW TO USE THIS BOOK

Chilton's Total Car Care for the Chevrolet Lumina, Buick Regal, Oldsmobile Cutlass Supreme, and Pontiac Grand Prix is intended to teach you about the inner workings of your car and save you money on its upkeep.

The first two Sections will be the most used, since they contain maintenance and tune-up information and procedures. Studies have shown that a properly tuned and maintained car can get at least 10% better gas mileage (which translates into lower operating costs) and periodic maintenance will catch minor problems before they turn into major repair bills. The remaining Sections deal with more complex systems of your car. Operating systems from engine through brakes are covered to the extent that the average do-it-yourselfer becomes mechanically involved.

A secondary purpose of this book is a reference guide for owners who want to understand their car and/or their mechanics better. In this case, no tools at all are required. Knowing just what a particular repair job requires in parts and labor time will allow you to evaluate whether or not you're getting a fair price quote and help decipher itemized bills from a repair shop.

Before attempting any repairs or service on your car, read through the entire procedure outlined in the appropriate Section. This will give you the overall view of what tools and supplies will be required. There is nothing more frustrating than having to walk to the bus stop on Monday morning because you were short one gasket on Sunday afternoon. So read ahead and plan ahead. Each operation should be approached logically and all procedures thoroughly understood before attempting any work. Some special tools that may be required can often be rented from local automotive jobbers or places specializing in renting tools and equipment. Check the yellow pages of your local phone book.

All Sections contain adjustments, maintenance, removal and installation procedures, and overhaul procedures. When overhaul is not considered practical, you will learn how to remove the failed part and then how to install its replacement. In this way, you at least save the labor costs. Backyard overhaul of some components (such as the alternator or water pump) is just not practical, but the removal and installation procedure is often simple and well within the capabilities of the average car owner.

Two basic mechanic's rules should be mentioned here. First, whenever the LEFT side of the car or engine is referred to, it is meant to specify the DRIVER'S side of the car. Conversely, the RIGHT side of the car means the PASSENGER'S side. Second, all screws and bolts are removed by turning counterclockwise, and tightened by turning clockwise.

Safety is always the most important rule. Constantly be aware of the dangers involved in working on or around an automobile and take proper precautions to avoid the risk of personal injury or damage to the vehicle. See "SERVICING YOUR VEHICLE SAFELY" in this Section, and the SAFETY NOTICE on the acknowledgment page before attempting any service procedures and pay attention to the instructions provided. There are 3 common mistakes committed when working mechanically:

1. Incorrect order of assembly, disassembly or adjustment. When taking something apart or putting it together, doing things in the wrong order usually just costs you extra time; however it CAN break something. Read the entire procedure before beginning disassembly. Do everything in the order in which the instructions say you should do it, even if you can't immediately see a reason for it. When you're taking apart something that is fairly complex, you might want to draw a picture of (or photograph) how it looks at points during disassembly in order to make sure you get everything back in its proper position. Exploded views are supplied whenever possible, but sometimes the job requires more attention to detail than an illustration provides. When making adjustments (especially tune-up adjustments), do them in order. One adjustment often affects another and you cannot expect satisfactory results unless each adjustment is made only when it cannot be changed by any other.

2. Over-torquing (or under-torquing) nuts and bolts. While it is more common for over-torquing to cause damage, under-torquing can cause a fastener to vibrate loose and cause serious damage, especially when dealing with aluminum parts. Pay attention to torque specifications and utilize a torque wrench when assembling. If a torque figure is not available remember that, if you are using the right tool to do the job, you will probably not have to strain yourself to get a fastener tight enough. The pitch of most threads is so slight that the tension you put on the wrench will be multiplied many times in actual force on what you are tightening. A good example of how critical torque is can be seen in the case of spark plug installation, especially where you are putting the plug into an aluminum cylinder head. Too little torque can fail to crush the gasket, causing leakage of combustion gases and consequent overheating of the plug and engine parts. Too much torque can damage the threads or distort the plug, which changes the spark gap at the electrode. Since more and more manufacturers are using aluminum in their engine and chassis parts to save weight, a torque wrench should be in any serious do-it-yourselfer's tool box.

Incidentally, there are various commercial chemical products available for ensuring that fasteners won't come loose; a common brand is Loctite®. Read the label on the package and make sure the product is compatible with the materials, fluids, etc. involved before choosing one.

3. Crossthreading. This occurs when a threaded fastener is screwed into a nut or casting at the wrong angle and forced, causing the threads to become damaged. Crossthreading is more likely to occur if access is difficult. It helps to clean and lubricate fasteners, and to start threading with the part to be installed going straight in, using just your fingers initially. If you encounter resistance, unscrew the part and start over again at a different angle until it can be inserted and turned several times without much effort. Keep in mind that many parts, especially spark plugs, use tapered threads so that gentle turning will automatically bring the part you're threading to the proper angle if you don't force it or resist a change in angle. Don't put a wrench on the part until it's been turned in a couple of times by hand. If you suddenly encounter resistance and the part has not seated fully, don't force it. Pull it back out and make sure it's clean and threading properly. Always take your time and be patient; once you have some experience, working on your car will become an enjoyable hobby.

TOOLS AND EQUIPMENT

➧ SEE FIG. 1

Naturally, without the proper tools and equipment, it is impossible to properly service your vehicle. It would be impossible to catalog each tool that you would need to perform each or every operation in this book. It would also be unwise for the amateur to rush out and buy an expensive set of tools and the theory that he may need one or more of them at sometime.

The best approach is to proceed slowly, gathering together a good quality set of those tools that are used most frequently. Don't be misled by the low cost of bargain tools. It is far better to spend a little more for better quality. Forged wrenches, 6- or 12-point sockets and fine-tooth ratchets are by far preferable to their less expensive counterparts. As any good mechanic can tell you, there are few worse experiences than trying to work on a car with bad tools. Your monetary savings will be far outweighed by frustration and mangled knuckles.

Certain tools, plus a basic ability to handle tools, are required to get started. A basic mechanics tool set, a quality torque wrench, and a Torx® bit set should start you off. Torx® and inverted Torx® bits are hexagonal drivers which fit both inside and outside Torx® head fasteners used in various places on many of today's cars. Begin accumulating those tools that are used most frequently: those associated with routine maintenance and tune-up.

In addition to the normal assortment of screwdrivers and pliers you should have the following tools for routine maintenance jobs (your car, depending on the model year, uses both SAE and metric fasteners).

1. SAE/Metric wrenches, sockets and combination open end/box end wrenches in sizes from $^1/_8$ in. (3mm) to $1^1/_4$ in. (32mm), and a spark plug socket ($^5/_8$ in. and $^{13}/_{16}$ in.). If possible, buy various-length socket drive extensions. Metric sockets will fit the ratchet handles and extensions you may already have ($^1/_4$, $^3/_8$, and $^1/_2$ in. drive).
2. Quality jackstands for support. Make sure the jackstands are rated for the vehicle that you are supporting.
3. Oil filter wrenches. These come in lots of different styles. Take advantage of the selection to make things easier on yourself.
4. Oil filler spout or funnel.
5. Grease gun for chassis lubrication.
6. Hydrometer for checking the battery.
7. A low flat pan for draining oil.
8. Lots of rags for wiping up the inevitable mess.

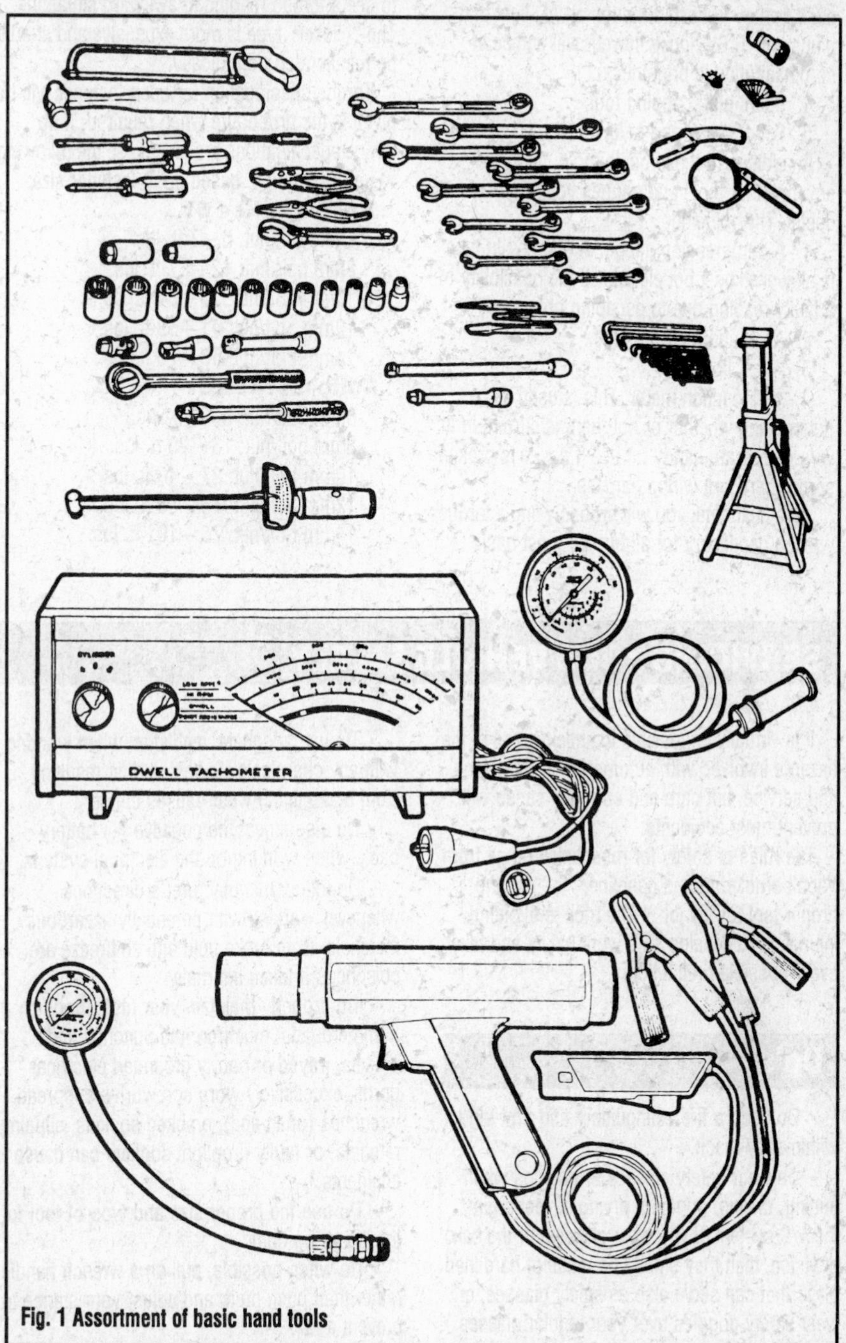

Fig. 1 Assortment of basic hand tools

In addition to the above items, there are several others that are not absolutely necessary, but handy to have around. These include oil dry, a long transmission fluid funnel and the usual supply of lubricants, antifreeze and fluids, although these can be purchased as needed. This is a basic list for routine maintenance, but only your personal needs and desires can accurately determine your list of necessary tools.

The second list of tools is for tune-ups. While the tools involved here are slightly more sophisticated, they need not be outrageously expensive. There are several inexpensive tach/dwell meters on the market that are every bit as good for the average mechanic as a $100 professional model. Just be sure that it goes to at least 1,200–1,500 rpm on the tach scale and that it works on 4, 6 and 8 cylinder engines. A basic list of tune-up equipment could include:

1. Tachometer.
2. Spark plug wrench.
3. Timing light (a DC light that works from the car's battery is best, although an AC light that plugs into 110V house current will suffice at some sacrifice in brightness).
4. Spark plug gapping tool.
5. Set of brass and steel feeler blades.

In addition to these basic tools, there are several other tools and gauges you may find useful. These include:

1. A compression gauge. The screw-in type is slower to use, but eliminates the possibility of a faulty reading due to escaping pressure.
2. A vacuum pump/gauge.
3. A test light.
4. An induction meter. This is used for determining whether or not there is current in a wire. These are handy for use if a wire is broken somewhere in a wiring harness.

As a final note, you will probably find a torque wrench necessary for all but the most basic work. The beam type models are usually adequate, but the newer "clicker" type is more precise, and you don't have to crane your neck to see a torque reading in awkward situations. The "clicker" type is more expensive and should be recalibrated periodically.

Torque specification for each fastener will be given in the procedure when required. If no torque specifications are given, use the following values as a guide, based upon fastener size:

Bolts marked 6T

6mm bolt/nut: 5–7 ft. lbs.
8mm bolt/nut: 12–17 ft. lbs.
10mm bolt/nut: 23–34 ft. lbs.
12mm bolt/nut: 41–59 ft. lbs.
14mm bolt/nut: 56–76 ft. lbs.

Bolts marked 8T

6mm bolt/nut: 6–9 ft. lbs.
8mm bolt/nut: 13–20 ft. lbs.
10mm bolt/nut: 27–40 ft. lbs.
12mm bolt/nut: 46–69 ft. lbs.
14mm bolt/nut: 75–101 ft. lbs.

Special Tools

Normally, the use of special factory tools is avoided for repair procedures, since these are not readily available for the do-it-yourselfer mechanic. When it is possible to perform the job with more commonly available tools, it will be pointed out, but occasionally, a special tool was designed to perform a specific function and really should be used. Before substituting another tool, you should be convinced that neither your safety nor the quality of the repair will be compromised.

Some special tools are available commercially from major tool manufacturers. Others for your car can be purchased from you dealer or from Special Tool Division, Kent-Moore 29784 Little Mack, Roseville, MI 48066-2298.

SERVICING YOUR VEHICLE SAFELY

It is virtually impossible to anticipate all of the hazards involved with automotive maintenance and service, but care and common sense will prevent most accidents.

The rules of safety for mechanics range from "don't smoke around gasoline," to "use the proper tool for the job." The trick to avoiding injuries is to develop safe work habits and take every possible precaution.

Do's

- Do keep a fire extinguisher and first aid kit within easy reach.
- Do wear safety glasses or goggles when cutting, drilling, grinding, prying or recharging the A/C system. If you wear glasses for the sake of vision, then they should be made of hardened glass that can serve also as safety glasses, or wear safety goggles over your regular glasses.
- Do shield your eyes whenever you work around the battery. Batteries contain sulfuric acid. In case of contact with the eyes or skin, flush the area with water or a mixture of water and baking soda and get medical attention immediately.
- Do use safety stands (jackstands) for any under-car service. Jacks are for raising vehicles; safety stands are for making sure the vehicle stays raised until you want it to come down. Whenever the vehicle is raised, block the wheels remaining on the ground and set the parking brake.
- Do use adequate ventilation when working with any chemicals. Asbestos dust resulting from brake lining wear causes cancer.
- Do disconnect the negative (–) battery cable when working on the electrical system.
- Do follow manufacturer's directions whenever working with potentially hazardous materials. Both brake fluid and antifreeze are poisonous if taken internally.
- Do properly maintain your tools. Loose hammerheads, mushroomed punches and chisels, frayed or poorly grounded electrical cords, excessively worn screwdrivers, spread wrenches (open end), cracked sockets, slipping ratchets, or faulty droplight sockets can cause accidents.
- Do use the proper size and type of tool for the job being done.
- Do when possible, pull on a wrench handle rather than push on it, and adjust your stance to prevent a fall.
- Do be sure that adjustable wrenches are tightly adjusted on the nut or bolt and pulled so that the face is on the side of the fixed jaw.
- Do select a wrench or socket that fits the nut or bolt. The wrench or socket should sit straight, not cocked.
- Do strike squarely with a hammer; avoid glancing blows.
- Do set the parking brake and block the wheels if the work requires that the engine be running.

Don'ts

- Don't run an engine in a garage or anywhere else without proper ventilation EVER! Carbon monoxide is poisonous. It is absorbed by the body 400 times faster than oxygen. It takes a long time to leave the human body and you can build up a deadly supply of it in your system by simply breathing in a little every day. You may not realize you are slowly poisoning yourself. Always use power vents, windows, fans or open the garage doors.
- Don't work around moving parts while wearing a necktie or other loose clothing. Short sleeves are much safer than long, loose sleeves. Hard-toed shoes with neoprene soles protect your toes and give a better grip on slippery surfaces. Jewelry such as watches, fancy belt buckles, rings, beads, or body adornment of any kind is not safe while working around a car. Long hair should be hidden under a hat or cap.
- Don't use pockets for toolboxes. A fall or bump can drive a screwdriver deep into you body. Even a wiping cloth hanging from the back pocket can wrap around a spinning shaft or fan.
- Don't smoke when working around gasoline, cleaning solvent or other flammable material. In fact, it's a good idea to extinguish all smoking materials when working on your car at all.
- Don't smoke when working around the battery. When the battery is being charged, it gives off explosive hydrogen gas.

• Don't use gasoline to wash your hands. There are excellent soaps available. Gasoline may contain lead, and lead can enter the body through a cut, accumulating in the body until you are very ill. Gasoline also removes all the natural oils from the skin so that bone dry hands will suck up oil and grease.

• Don't service the air conditioning system unless you are equipped with the necessary tools and training. The refrigerant (R-12) is extremely cold and when exposed to the air, will instantly freeze any surface it comes in contact with, including your eyes. Always wear safety glasses when servicing the A/C system. Although the refrigerant is normally non-toxic, R-12 becomes a deadly poisonous gas in the presence of an open flame. One good whiff of the vapors from burning refrigerant can be fatal.

SERIAL NUMBER IDENTIFICATION

➧ SEE FIGS. 2–14

Vehicle Identification Number (VIN)

The vehicle identification plate is located on the left upper corner of the instrument panel and is visible through the windshield.

Engine

The engine identification letter is the eighth (8th) digit of the vehicle identification number. See the accompanying illustrations for engine code stamping locations.

Transaxle

For transaxle identification plate locations, see the accompanying illustrations.

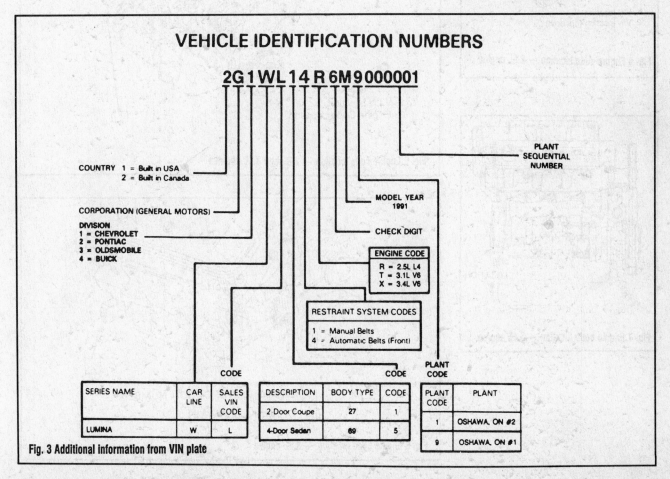

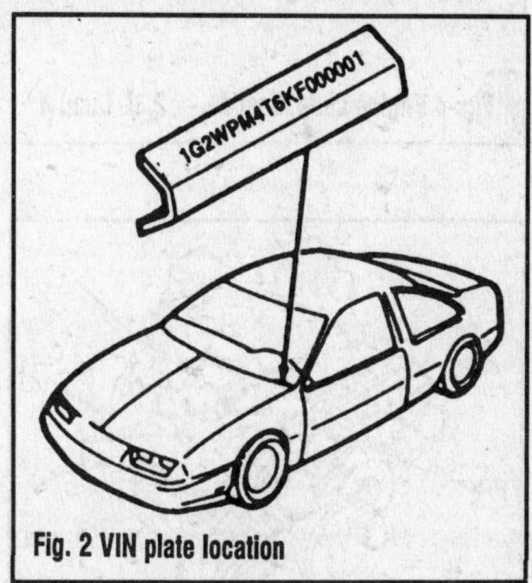

Fig. 2 VIN plate location

VEHICLE IDENTIFICATION NUMBERS

2G1WL14R6M9000001

COUNTRY 1 = Built in USA
2 = Built in Canada

CORPORATION (GENERAL MOTORS)

DIVISION
1 = CHEVROLET
2 = PONTIAC
3 = OLDSMOBILE
4 = BUICK

PLANT SEQUENTIAL NUMBER

MODEL YEAR 1991

CHECK DIGIT

ENGINE CODE
R = 2.5L L4
T = 3.1L V6
X = 3.4L V6

RESTRAINT SYSTEM CODES
1 = Manual Belts
4 = Automatic Belts (Front)

CODE

SERIES NAME	CAR LINE	SALES VIN CODE
LUMINA	W	L

CODE

DESCRIPTION	BODY TYPE	CODE
2-Door Coupe	27	1
4-Door Sedan	69	5

PLANT CODE

PLANT CODE	PLANT
1	OSHAWA, ON #2
9	OSHAWA, ON #1

Fig. 3 Additional information from VIN plate

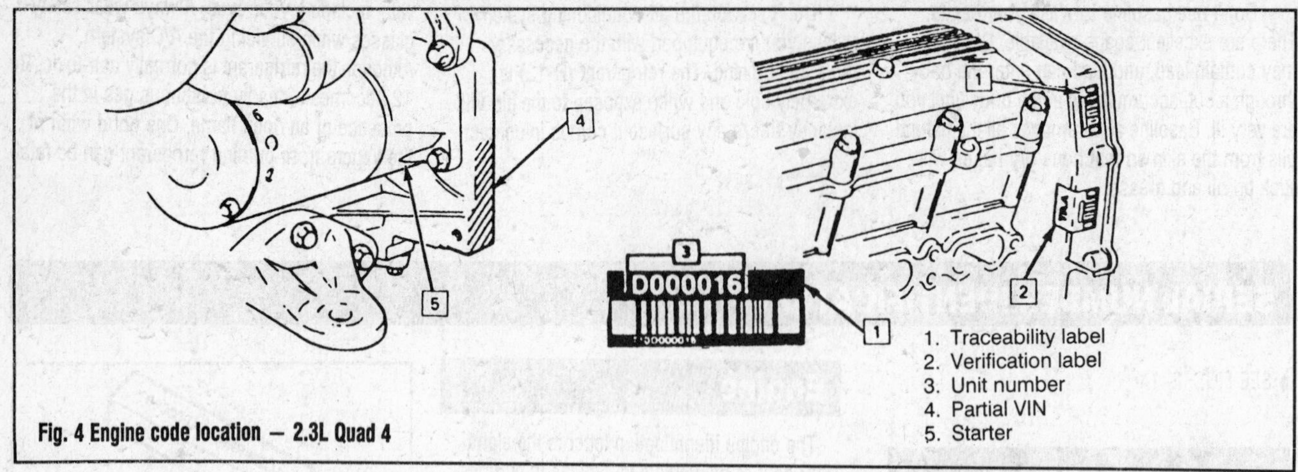

Fig. 4 Engine code location — 2.3L Quad 4

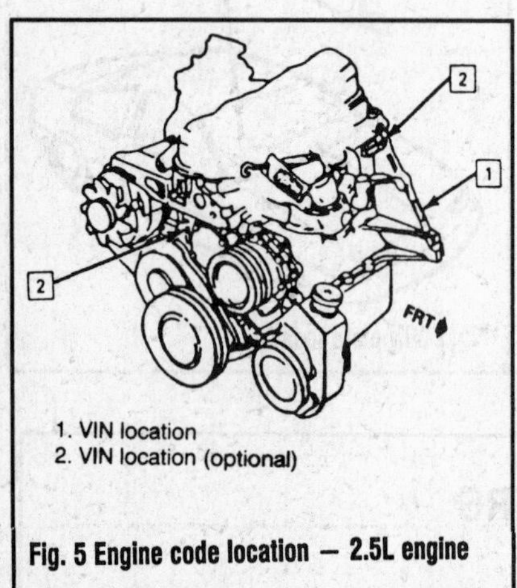

Fig. 5 Engine code location — 2.5L engine

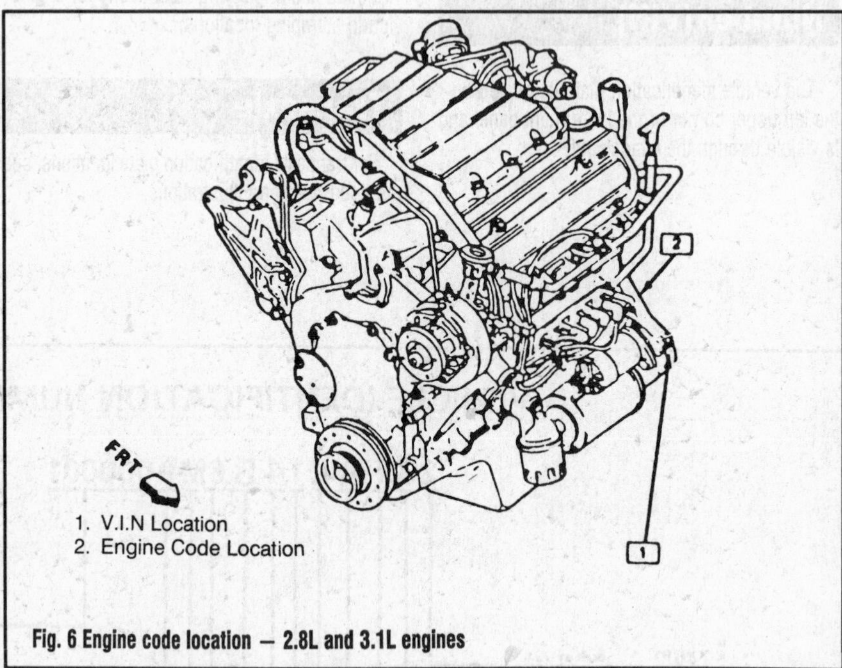

Fig. 6 Engine code location — 2.8L and 3.1L engines

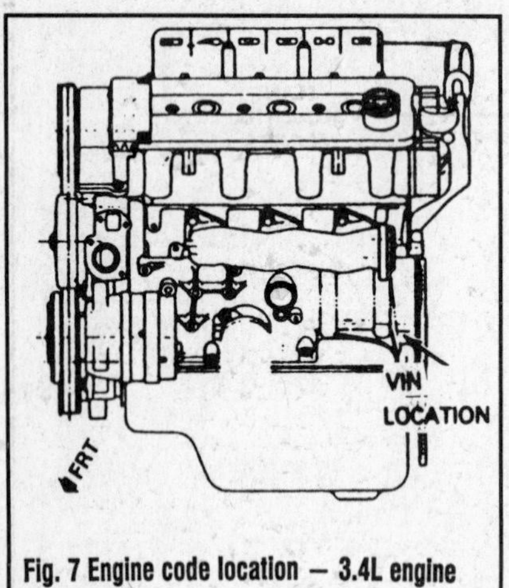

Fig. 7 Engine code location — 3.4L engine

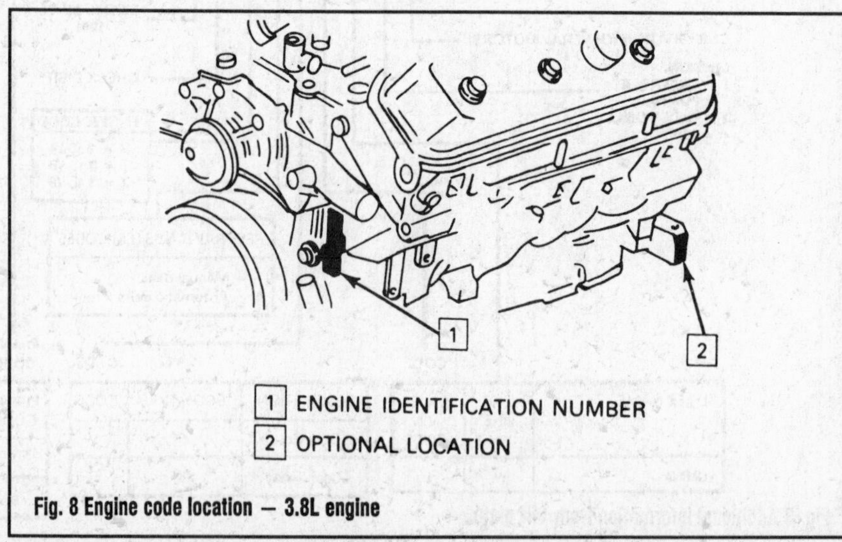

Fig. 8 Engine code location — 3.8L engine

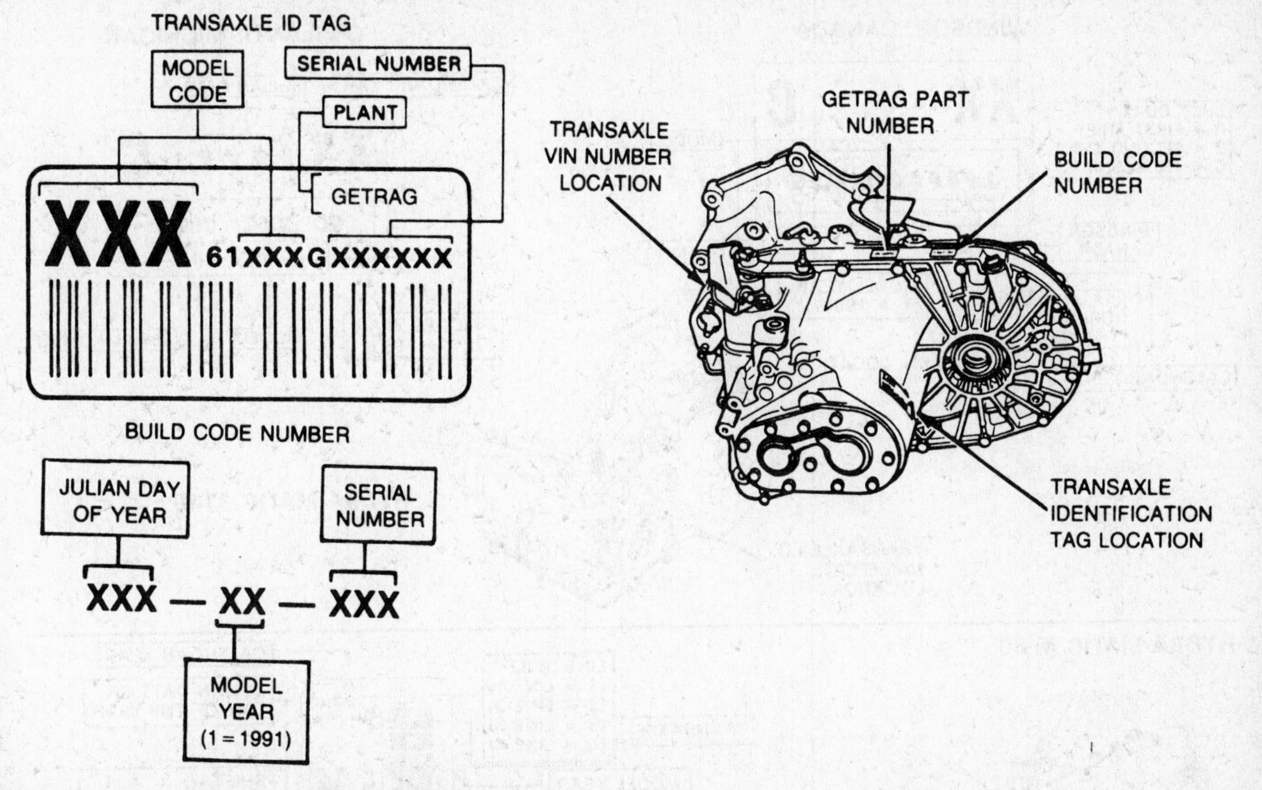

TRANSAXLE ID TAG
MODEL CODE
SERIAL NUMBER
PLANT
GETRAG
XXX 61XXXGXXXXXX

BUILD CODE NUMBER
JULIAN DAY OF YEAR
SERIAL NUMBER
XXX — XX — XXX
MODEL YEAR (1 = 1991)

TRANSAXLE VIN NUMBER LOCATION
GETRAG PART NUMBER
BUILD CODE NUMBER
TRANSAXLE IDENTIFICATION TAG LOCATION

Fig. 10 Transaxle code location — Getrag 284 manual transaxle

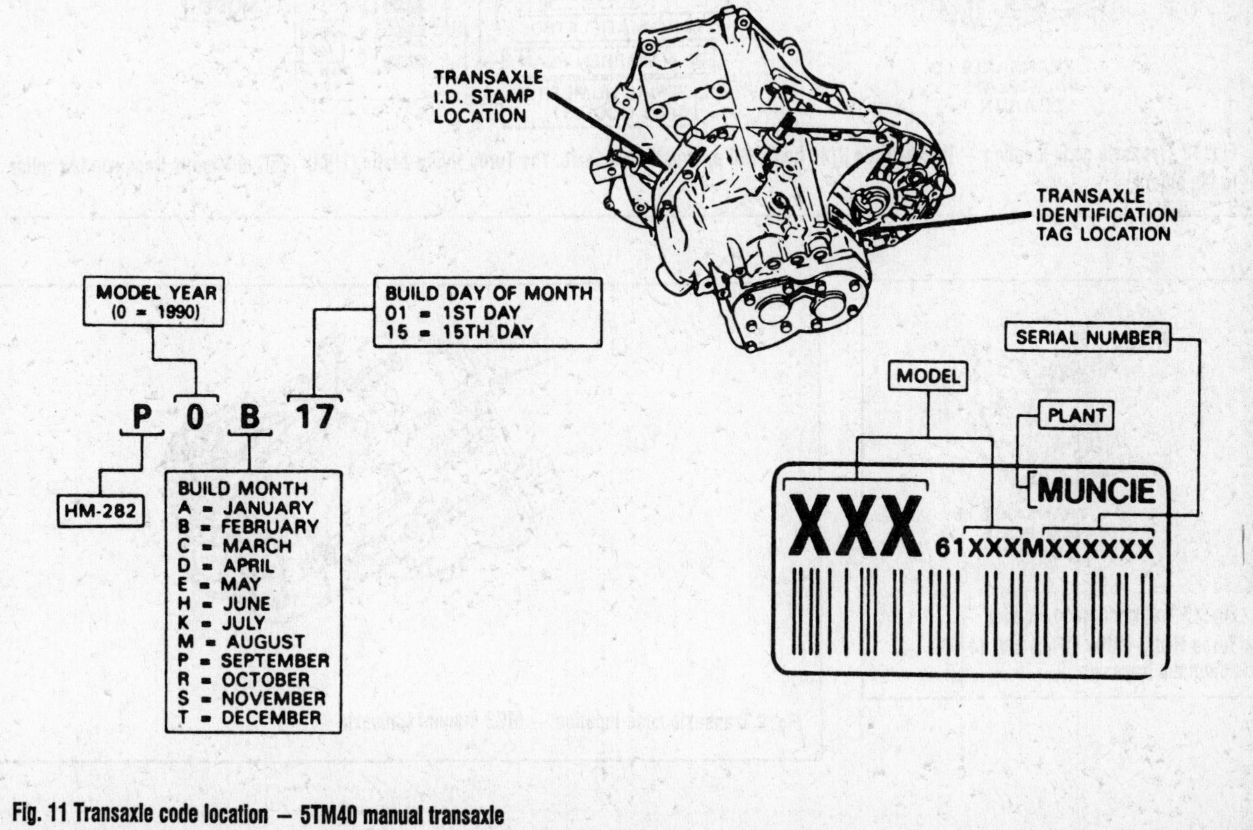

TRANSAXLE I.D. STAMP LOCATION
TRANSAXLE IDENTIFICATION TAG LOCATION

MODEL YEAR (0 = 1990)
BUILD DAY OF MONTH
01 = 1ST DAY
15 = 15TH DAY
P 0 B 17
HM-282

BUILD MONTH
A = JANUARY
B = FEBRUARY
C = MARCH
D = APRIL
E = MAY
H = JUNE
K = JULY
M = AUGUST
P = SEPTEMBER
R = OCTOBER
S = NOVEMBER
T = DECEMBER

SERIAL NUMBER
MODEL
PLANT
MUNCIE
XXX 61XXXMXXXXXX

Fig. 11 Transaxle code location — 5TM40 manual transaxle

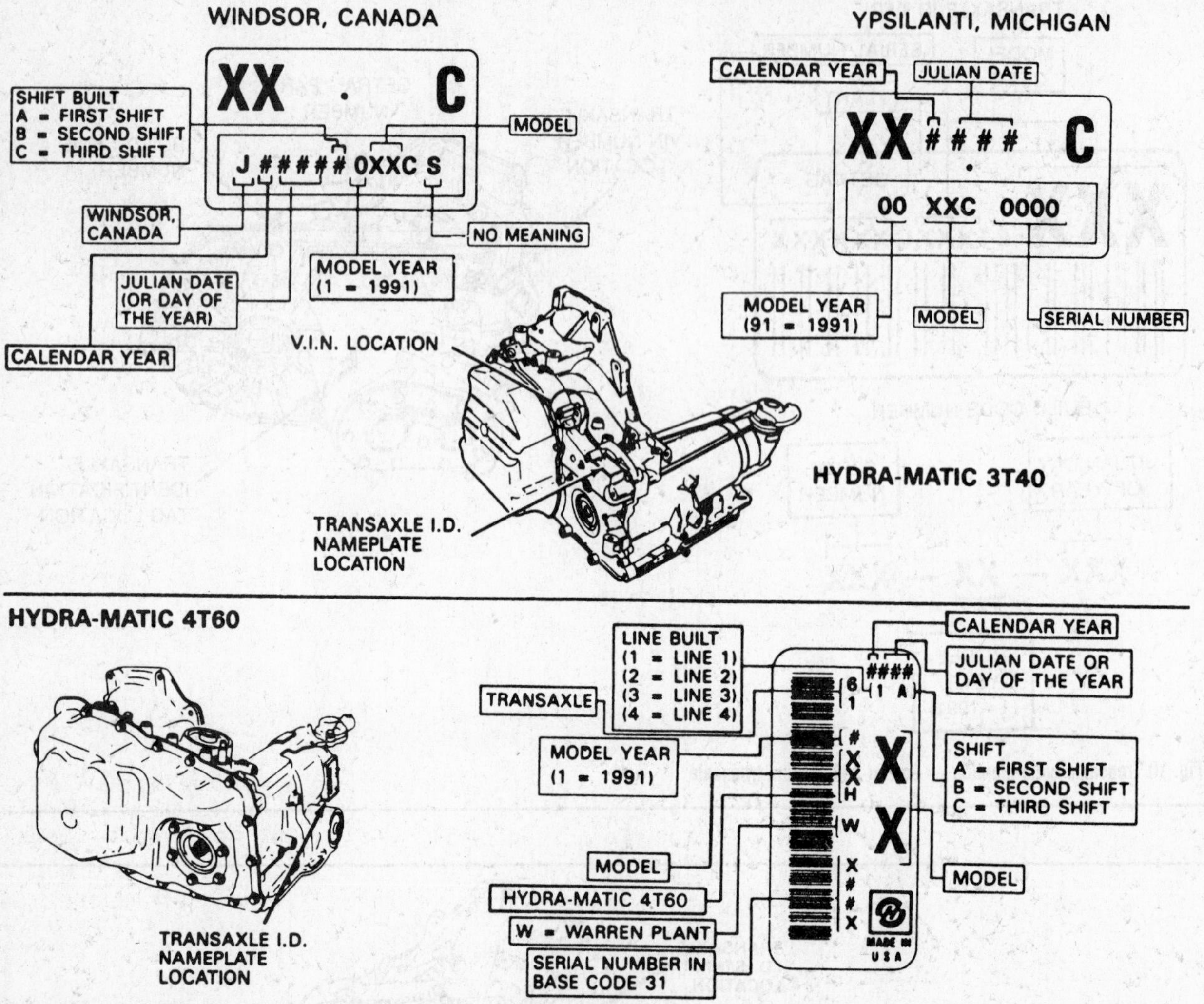

WINDSOR, CANADA
XX . C
J ##### 0XXC S
SHIFT BUILT
A = FIRST SHIFT
B = SECOND SHIFT
C = THIRD SHIFT
MODEL
WINDSOR, CANADA
NO MEANING
MODEL YEAR (1 = 1991)
JULIAN DATE (OR DAY OF THE YEAR)
CALENDAR YEAR
V.I.N. LOCATION
TRANSAXLE I.D. NAMEPLATE LOCATION
YPSILANTI, MICHIGAN
CALENDAR YEAR
JULIAN DATE
XX #### C
00 XXC 0000
MODEL YEAR (91 = 1991)
MODEL
SERIAL NUMBER
HYDRA-MATIC 3T40
HYDRA-MATIC 4T60
TRANSAXLE I.D. NAMEPLATE LOCATION
LINE BUILT
(1 = LINE 1)
(2 = LINE 2)
(3 = LINE 3)
(4 = LINE 4)
TRANSAXLE
MODEL YEAR (1 = 1991)
MODEL
HYDRA-MATIC 4T60
W = WARREN PLANT
SERIAL NUMBER IN BASE CODE 31
CALENDAR YEAR
JULIAN DATE OR DAY OF THE YEAR
SHIFT
A = FIRST SHIFT
B = SECOND SHIFT
C = THIRD SHIFT
MODEL
MADE IN U S A

Fig. 12 Transaxle code location — Hydra-Matic 3T40 and 4T60 automatic transaxle. The Turbo Hydra-Matic (THM) 125C automatic transaxle is similar to the others

TRANSAXLE I.D. NAMEPLATE LOCATION

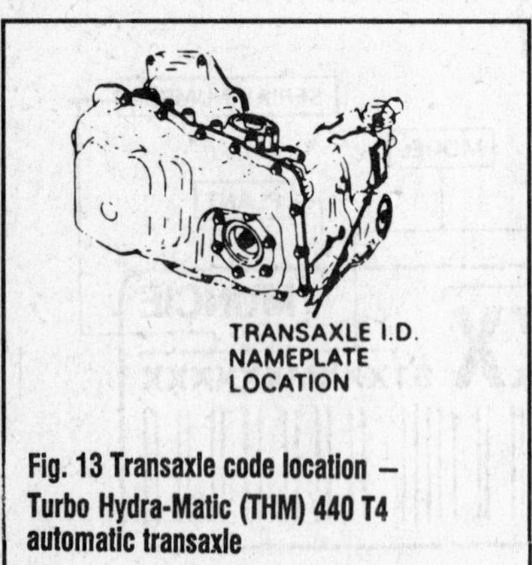

Fig. 13 Transaxle code location — Turbo Hydra-Matic (THM) 440 T4 automatic transaxle

V.I.N. LOCATION

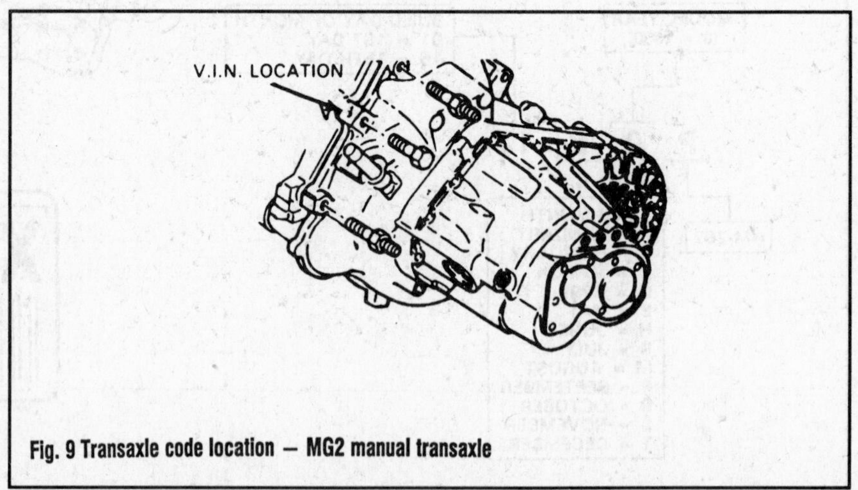

Fig. 9 Transaxle code location — MG2 manual transaxle

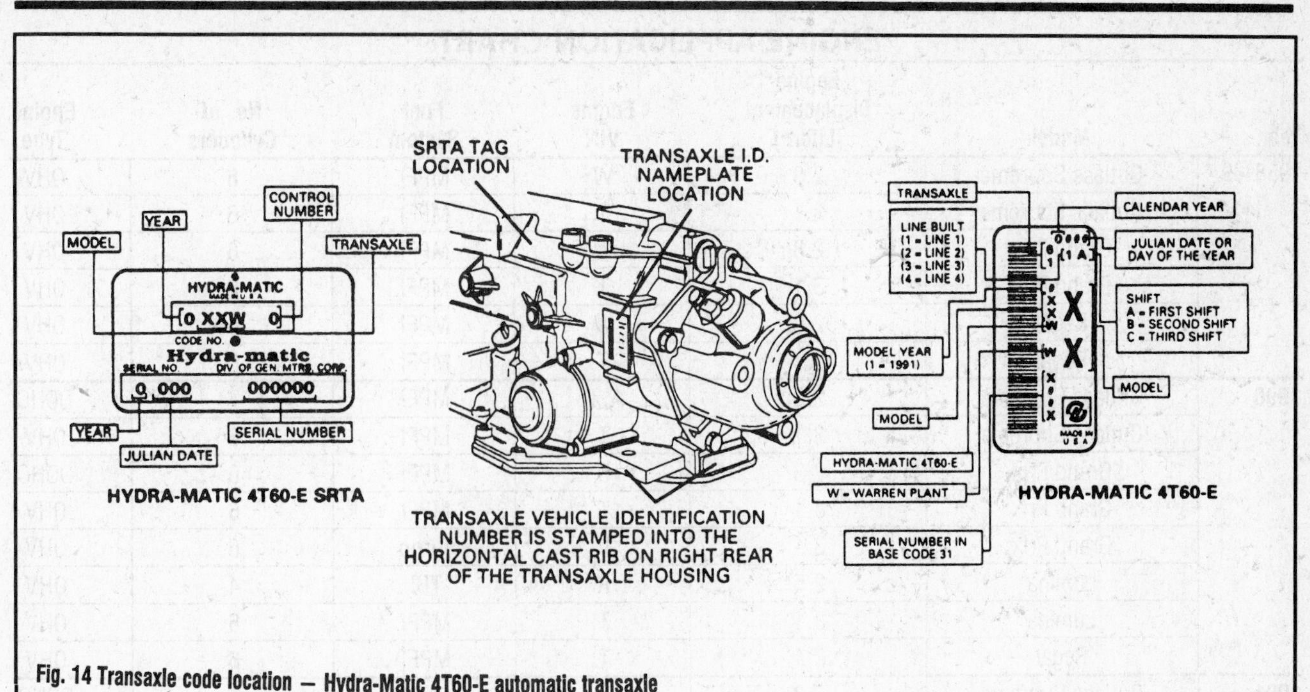

Fig. 14 Transaxle code location – Hydra-Matic 4T60-E automatic transaxle

VEHICLE IDENTIFICATION CHART

It is important for servicing and ordering parts to be certain of the vehicle and engine identification. The VIN (vehicle identification number) is a 17 digit number visible through the windshield on the driver's side of the dash and contains the vehicle and engine identification codes. The tenth digit indicates model year and the eighth digit indicates engine code. It can be interpreted as follows:

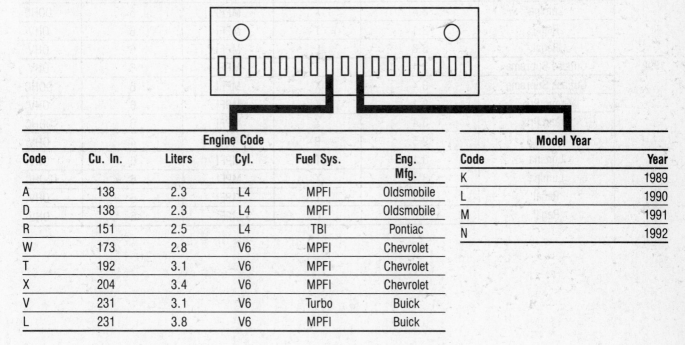

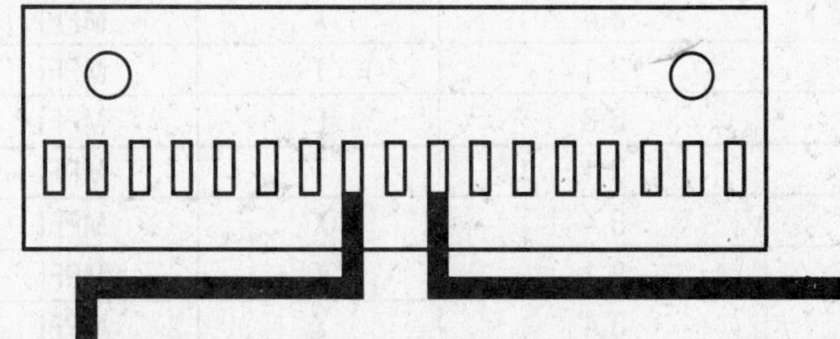

Engine Code

Code	Cu. In.	Liters	Cyl.	Fuel Sys.	Eng. Mfg.
A	138	2.3	L4	MPFI	Oldsmobile
D	138	2.3	L4	MPFI	Oldsmobile
R	151	2.5	L4	TBI	Pontiac
W	173	2.8	V6	MPFI	Chevrolet
T	192	3.1	V6	MPFI	Chevrolet
X	204	3.4	V6	MPFI	Chevrolet
V	231	3.1	V6	Turbo	Buick
L	231	3.8	V6	MPFI	Buick

Model Year

Code	Year
K	1989
L	1990
M	1991
N	1992

ENGINE APPLICATION CHART

Year	Model	Engine Displacement (Liters)	Engine VIN	Fuel System	No. of Cylinders	Engine Type
1988-89	Cutlass Supreme	2.8	W	MPFI	6	OHV
	Cutlass Supreme	3.1	T	MPFI	6	OHV
	Grand Prix	2.8	W	MPFI	6	OHV
	Grand Prix	3.1	T	MPFI	6	OHV
	Regal	2.8	W	MPFI	6	OHV
	Regal	3.1	T	MPFI	6	OHV
1990	Cutlass Supreme	2.3	A, D	MPFI	4	DOHC
	Cutlass Supreme	3.1	T	MPFI	6	OHV
	Grand Prix	2.3	D	MPFI	6	DOHC
	Grand Prix	3.1	T	MPFI	6	OHV
	Grand Prix	3.1	V	Turbo	6	OHV
	Lumina	2.5	R	TBI	4	OHV
	Lumina	3.1	T	MPFI	6	OHV
	Regal	3.1	T	MPFI	6	OHV
1991	Cutlass Supreme	2.3	D	MPFI	4	DOHC
	Cutlass Supreme	3.1	T	MPFI	6	OHV
	Cutlass Supreme	3.4	X	MPFI	6	DOHC
	Grand Prix	2.3	D	MPFI	4	DOHC
	Grand Prix	3.1	T	MPFI	6	OHV
	Grand Prix	3.4	X	MPFI	6	DOHC
	Lumina	2.5	R	TBI	4	OHV
	Lumina	3.1	T	MPFI	6	OHV
	Lumina	3.4	X	MPFI	6	DOHC
	Regal	3.1	T	MPFI	6	OHV
	Regal	3.8	L	MPFI	6	OHV
1992	Cutlass Supreme	3.1	T	MPFI	6	OHV
	Cutlass Supreme	3.4	X	MPFI	6	DOHC
	Grand Prix	3.1	T	MPFI	6	OHV
	Grand Prix	3.4	X	MPFI	6	DOHC
	Lumina	2.5	R	TBI	4	OHV
	Lumina	3.1	T	MPFI	6	OHV
	Lumina	3.4	X	MPFI	6	DOHC
	Regal	3.1	T	MPFI	6	OHV
	Regal	3.8	L	MPFI	6	OHV

TRANSMISSION APPLICATION CHART

Year	Model	Engine Displacement (Liters)	Engine VIN	Manual Transaxle	Automatic Transaxle
1988-89	Cutlass Supreme	2.8	W	MG2	440 T4
	Cutlass Supreme	3.1	T	—	440 T4
	Grand Prix	2.8	W	MG2	440 T4
	Grand Prix	3.1	T	—	440 T4
	Regal	2.8	W	—	440 T4
	Regal	3.1	T	—	440 T4
1990	Cutlass Supreme	2.3	A	—	3T40
	Cutlass Supreme	2.3	D	5TM40	—
	Cutlass Supreme	3.1	T	—	4T60
	Grand Prix	2.3	D	—	3T40
	Grand Prix	3.1	T	5TM40	4T60
	Grand Prix	3.1	V	5TM40	—
	Lumina	2.5	R	—	THM 125C
	Lumina	3.1	T	MG2	4T60
	Regal	3.1	T	—	4T60
1991	Cutlass Supreme	2.3	D	—	3T40
	Cutlass Supreme	3.1	T	—	3T40 or 4T60
	Cutlass Supreme	3.4	X	Getrag 284	4T60-E
	Grand Prix	2.3	D	—	3T40
	Grand Prix	3.1	T	—	3T40 or 4T60
	Grand Prix	3.4	X	Getrag 284	4T60-E
	Lumina	2.5	R	—	3T40
	Lumina	3.1	T	—	3T40 or 4T60
	Lumina	3.4	X	Getrag 284	4T60-E
	Regal	3.1	T	—	4T60
	Regal	3.8	L	—	4T60
1992	Cutlass Supreme	3.1	T	—	3T40 or 4T60
	Cutlass Supreme	3.4	X	Getrag 284	4T60-E
	Grand Prix	3.1	T	—	3T40 or 4T60
	Grand Prix	3.4	X	Getrag 284	4T60-E
	Lumina	2.5	R	—	3T40
	Lumina	3.1	T	—	3T40 or 4T60
	Lumina	3.4	X	Getrag 284	4T60-E
	Regal	3.1	T	—	4T60
	Regal	3.8	L	—	4T60

ROUTINE MAINTENANCE

Air Cleaner

➧ SEE FIGS. 15A–15B

REMOVAL & INSTALLATION

1. Remove the air cleaner cover and hold-down fasteners.
2. Remove the cover and the element itself.
3. Clean any dirt from the housing and cover.
4. Install the new element, cover and hold-down nut or clips.

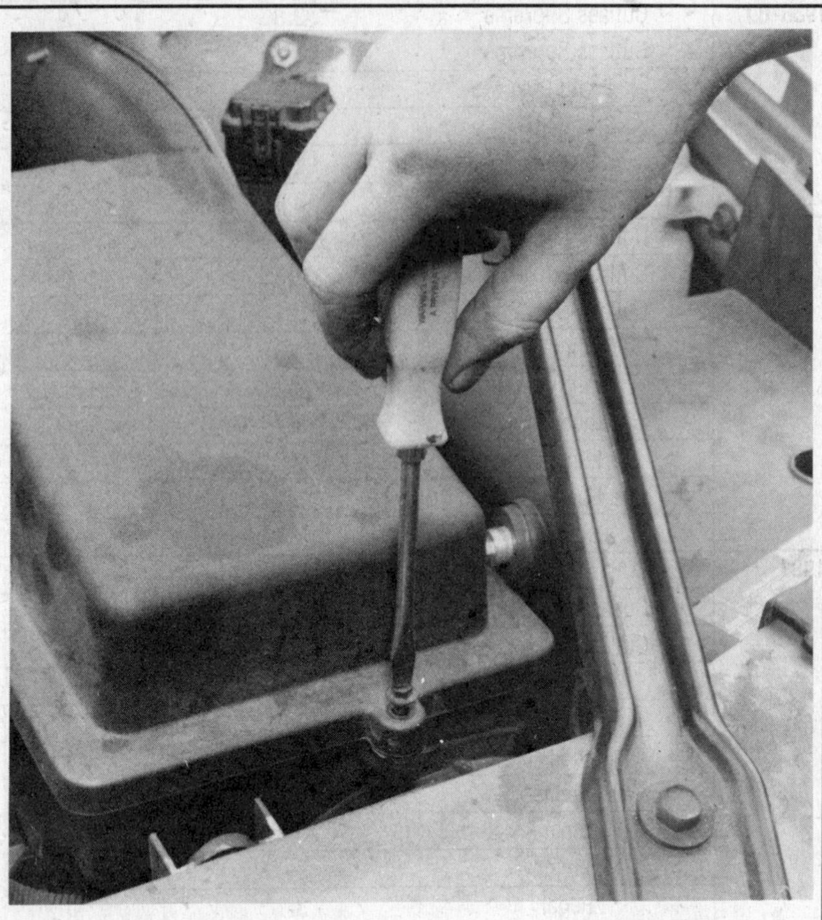

FIG. 15A. Remove the screws around the perimeter of the air cleaner box to expose the element

Fuel Filter

CAUTION

To reduce the risk of fire and personal injury, it is necessary to relieve the fuel system pressure before servicing any fuel system component. If this procedure is not performed, fuel may be sprayed out of the connection under pressure. Cover fuel hose connections with a shop towel before disconnecting to catch any residual fuel that may still be in the line. Always keep a dry chemical (Class B) fire extinguisher near the work area.

RELIEVING FUEL PRESSURE

2.3L and 2.5L Engines

1. Remove the fuel filler cap to relieve fuel tank vapor pressure.
2. From under the vehicle, disconnect the fuel pump electrical connector. It should be the only connector coming from the fuel tank.
3. Start the engine and run until the engine stalls. Engage the starter an additional 3 seconds to assure complete relief.
4. Install the fuel filler cap.
5. Disconnect the negative battery cable and continue with fuel system work.

2.8L, 3.1L , 3.4L and 3.8L Engines

1. Disconnect the negative (–) battery cable.
2. Loosen the fuel filler cap to relieve fuel tank vapor pressure.
3. Connect fuel pressure valve J 34730-1 or equivalent to the fuel pressure relief connection at the fuel rail.
4. Wrap a shop towel around the fittings while connecting the tool to prevent fuel spillage.
5. Install a bleed hose into an approved container and open the valve to bleed the system pressure.
6. Install the fuel filler cap.

REMOVAL & INSTALLATION

➧ SEE FIG. 15

The fuel filter is located in the fuel feed line attached to the left frame rail, at the rear of the vehicle.

1. Relieve the fuel system pressure.
2. Raise the vehicle and support with jackstands.
3. Disconnect the fuel lines from the filter. To reduce fuel spillage, place a shop towel over the fuel lines before disconnecting.
4. Remove the filter from its bracket.

To install:

5. Position the new filter in the bracket. Using new O-rings, install the fuel lines to the filter. Use a backup wrench to prevent the filter from turning. Torque the fittings to 16 ft. lbs. (22 Nm).
6. Lower the vehicle.
7. Connect the negative (–) battery cable, and check for leaks.

PCV Valve

The PCV valve should be inspected every 30,000 miles (50,000 km) for proper operation. A rough idle or oil consumption may result from improper operation or vacuum leak. To maintain proper idle control, the PCV valve restricts the flow when the intake manifold vacuum is high. The system is designed to allow excess blow by gases to be vented into the intake manifold to be burned, reducing hydrocarbon emissions.

To remove the PCV valve, pull the valve out of the rocker arm cover and disconnect the rubber hose. Insert the new valve into the hose and the rocker cover.The 2.3L QUAD 4 is not equipped with a PCV valve.

FIG. 15B. Lift the cover and remove the element from the air cleaner box

Evaporative Canister

The evaporative canister is not a serviceable unit. If found to be defective, replace the entire unit.

Battery

✲✲ CAUTION

Keep flame or sparks away from the battery; it gives off explosive hydrogen gas. Battery electrolyte contains sulphuric acid. If you should splash any on your skin or in your eyes, flush the affected area with plenty of clear water. If it lands in your eyes, get medical help immediately.

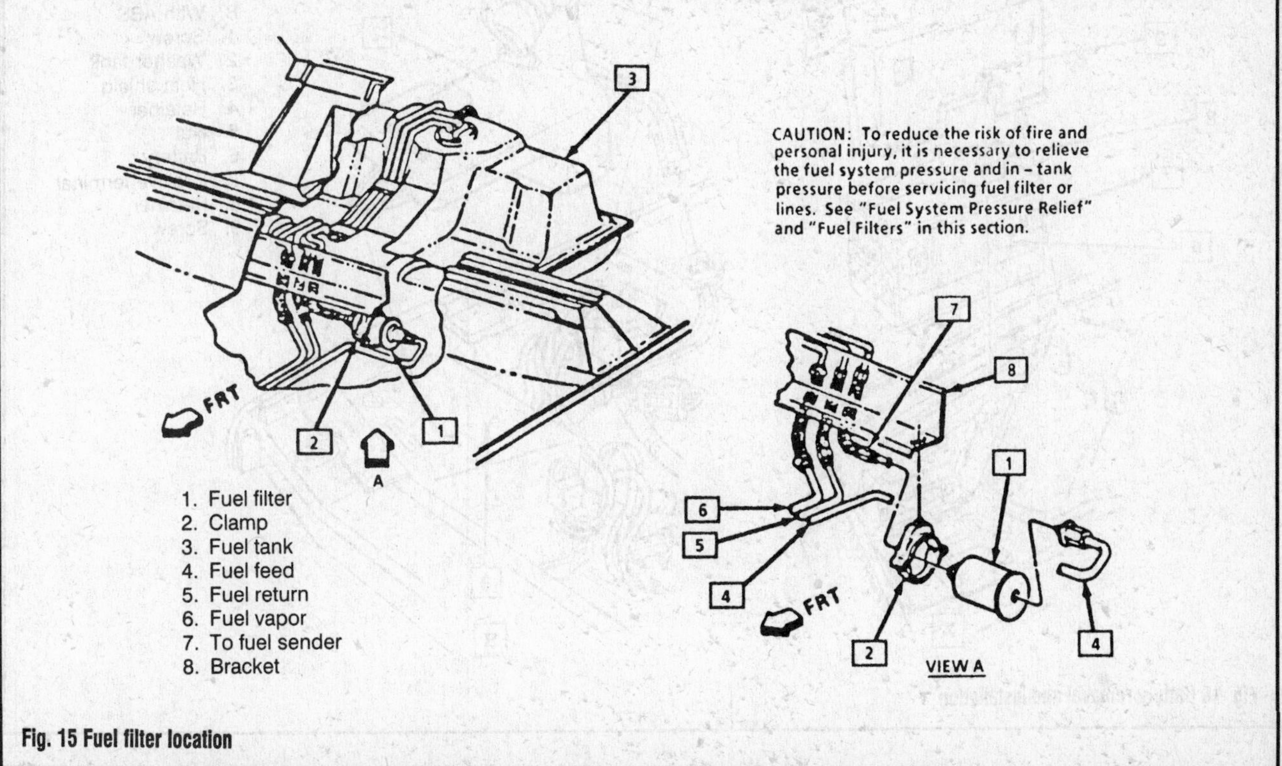

CAUTION: To reduce the risk of fire and personal injury, it is necessary to relieve the fuel system pressure and in - tank pressure before servicing fuel filter or lines. See "Fuel System Pressure Relief" and "Fuel Filters" in this section.
FRT
A
VIEW A
1. Fuel filter
2. Clamp
3. Fuel tank
4. Fuel feed
5. Fuel return
6. Fuel vapor
7. To fuel sender
8. Bracket

Fig. 15 Fuel filter location

GENERAL MAINTENANCE

Once a year, the battery should be removed and cleaned with baking soda and water. Replace any cable that shows signs of fraying or imbedded corrosion. Terminals and the cable clamps should also be cleaned. Many various types of tools for this operation are available. It is especially important to clean the inside of the clamp thoroughly, since a small deposit of foreign material or oxidation there will prevent a sound electrical connection and inhibit either starting or charging. Also, it's a good idea to remove the battery and check the battery tray. Clear it of any debris, and check it for soundness.

After everything is clean, install the battery and cables, negative cable last; do not hammer on the clamps to install. Tighten the clamps securely, but do not distort them. Give the clamps and terminals a thin external coat of grease after installation, to retard corrosion.

BUILT-IN HYDROMETER

A sealed battery is standard on all vehicles; fluid level cannot be checked. Instead, use the built-in hydrometer on the top of the battery to check the condition of the battery. When checking, be sure to clean off the top of the hydrometer and tap it lightly to dislodge any air bubbles that may be present.

If the green dot is visible, the battery is probably in good shape. If the indicator is dark, but the green dot is not visible, the battery may simply need a good charge. If the indicator is clear or light yellow, the battery should be replaced.

CABLES

Whenever you replace a battery cable, be sure to use a replacement cable that is the same gauge and length. Be sure to replace all additional feed wires and/or ground leads. Also, make sure that the replacement cable is routed in exactly the same way that the original was.

TESTING

1. Connect a voltmeter and battery load tester to the battery terminals.
2. Apply a 300-ampere load for 15 seconds to remove surface charge from the battery. Remove the load.
3. Wait 15 seconds to allow the battery to recover. Then apply the load specified on the battery's label. After 15 seconds, read the voltage and remove the load.
4. If the voltage does not drop below 9.5 volts, the battery can be judged as good.
5. If the voltage is less than 9.5 volts, you can try to charge it, but replacement is recommended.

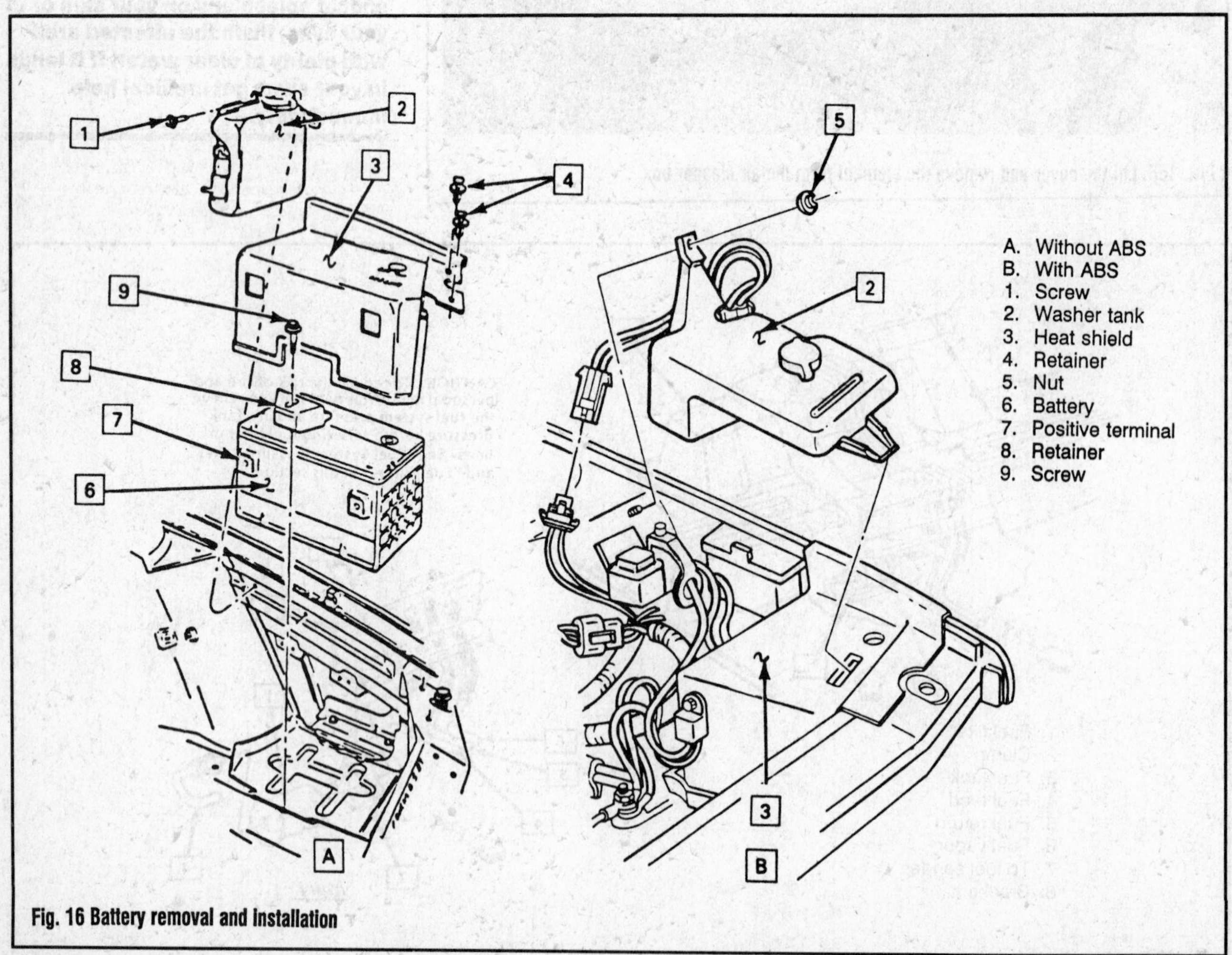

Fig. 16 Battery removal and installation

JUMP STARTING A DEAD BATTERY

The chemical reaction in a battery produces explosive hydrogen gas. This is the safe way to jump start a dead battery, reducing the chances of an accidental spark that could cause an explosion.

Jump Starting Precautions

1. Be sure both batteries are of the same voltage.
2. Be sure both batteries are of the same polarity (have the same grounded terminal).
3. Be sure the vehicles are not touching.
4. Be sure the vent cap holes are not obstructed.
5. Do not smoke or allow sparks around the battery.
6. In cold weather, check for frozen electrolyte in the battery. Do not jump start a frozen battery.
7. Do not allow electrolyte on your skin or clothing.
8. Be sure the electrolyte is not frozen.

CAUTION: Make certin that the ignition key, in the vehicle with the dead battery, is in the OFF position. Connecting cables to vehicles with on-board computers will result in computer destruction if the key is not in the OFF position.

Jump Starting Procedure

1. Determine voltages of the two batteries; they must be the same.
2. Bring the starting vehicle close (they must not touch) so that the batteries can be reached easily.
3. Turn off all accessories and both engines. Put both vehicles in Neutral or Park and set the handbrake.
4. Cover the cell caps with a rag—do not cover terminals.
5. If the terminals on the run-down battery are heavily corroded, clean them.
6. Identify the positive and negative posts on both batteries and connect the cables in the order shown.
7. Start the engine of the starting vehicle and run it at fast idle. Try to start the car with the dead battery. Crank it for no more than 10 seconds at a time and let it cool for 20 seconds in between tries.
8. If it doesn't start in 3 tries, there is something else wrong.
9. Disconnect the cables in the reverse order.
10. Replace the cell covers and dispose of the rags.

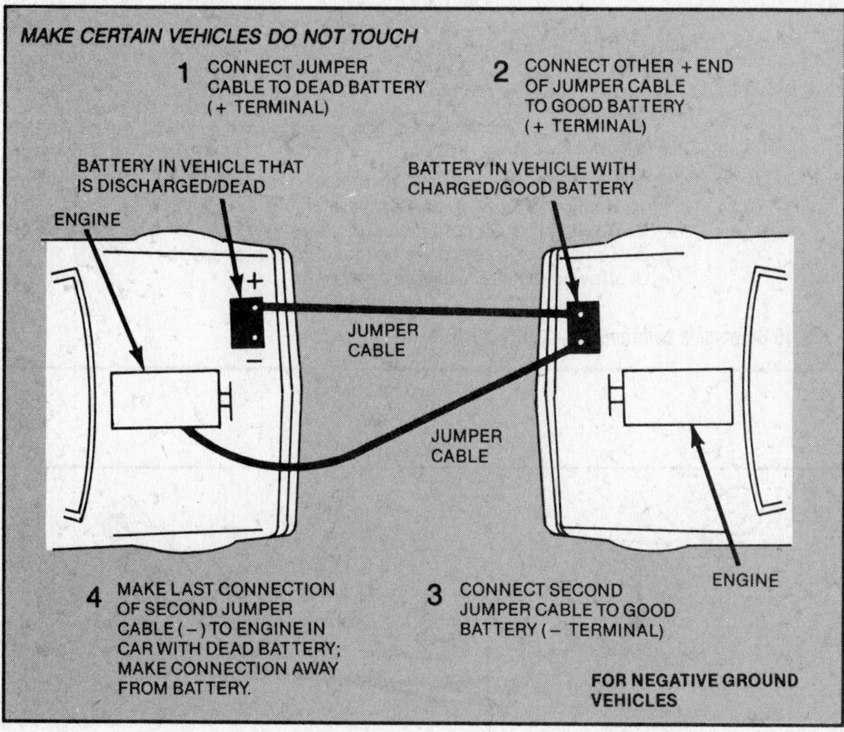
MAKE CERTAIN VEHICLES DO NOT TOUCH
1 CONNECT JUMPER CABLE TO DEAD BATTERY (+ TERMINAL)
2 CONNECT OTHER + END OF JUMPER CABLE TO GOOD BATTERY (+ TERMINAL)
BATTERY IN VEHICLE THAT IS DISCHARGED/DEAD
BATTERY IN VEHICLE WITH CHARGED/GOOD BATTERY
ENGINE
+
−
JUMPER CABLE
JUMPER CABLE
ENGINE
4 MAKE LAST CONNECTION OF SECOND JUMPER CABLE (−) TO ENGINE IN CAR WITH DEAD BATTERY; MAKE CONNECTION AWAY FROM BATTERY.
3 CONNECT SECOND JUMPER CABLE TO GOOD BATTERY (− TERMINAL)
FOR NEGATIVE GROUND VEHICLES

Side terminal batteries occasionally pose a problem when connecting jumper cables. There frequently isn't enough room to clamp the cables without touching sheet metal. Side terminal adaptors are available to alleviate this problem and should be removed after use

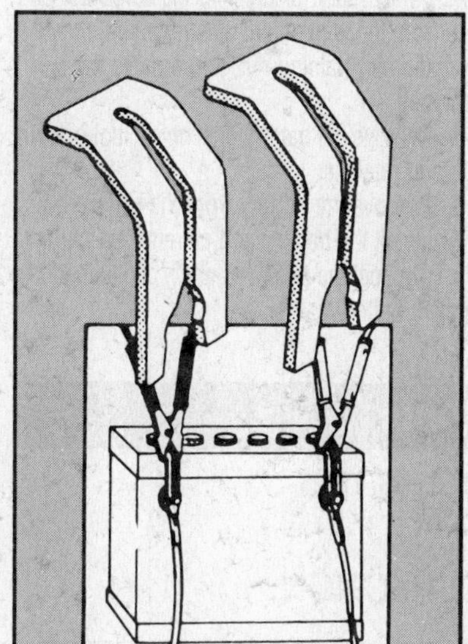

CHARGING

If charging the battery while is installed in the vehicle, be sure the ignition switch is off. Failing to do so may damage on board computers and other electrical components. It is best to remove the battery and charge it slowly with a trickle charger, following the instructions provided with the charger. Some important points to remember when charging a battery:

- Do not attempt to charge a battery with clear or light yellow hydrometer.
- Do not attempt to charge a frozen battery.
- Charge the battery at room temperature.
- During the charge, monitor the battery at least hourly. Discontinue the process if the battery temperature exceeds 125°F (52°C) or if any fluid or visible gas is spewing from the vapor holes.
- Charge until the green dot appears, then load test it to ensure a full charge.

REPLACEMENT

SEE FIG. 16

1. Make sure the ignition is off. Remove the air cleaner assembly if necessary, and disconnect the negative battery cable, then the positive cable.
2. Remove the cross brace.
3. If equipped with Anti-Lock Brakes (ABS), remove the relay center and bracket.
4. If necessary, disconnect the connector and hose from the windshield washer pump, remove the reservoir retaining nut, and remove the reservoir.
5. Remove the battery heat shield, hold-down bolt, and retainer.
6. Remove the battery from the battery tray.
7. Install the battery and all removed parts.
8. Connect the positive battery cable, then the negative battery cable.

Belts

SEE FIGS. 17–25

INSPECTION

Once a year or at 12,000 mile intervals, the tension and condition of the drive belts should be checked, and, if necessary, adjusted. Loose accessory drive belts can lead to poor engine cooling and diminish alternator, power steering pump, air conditioning compressor or Thermactor air pump output. A belt that is too

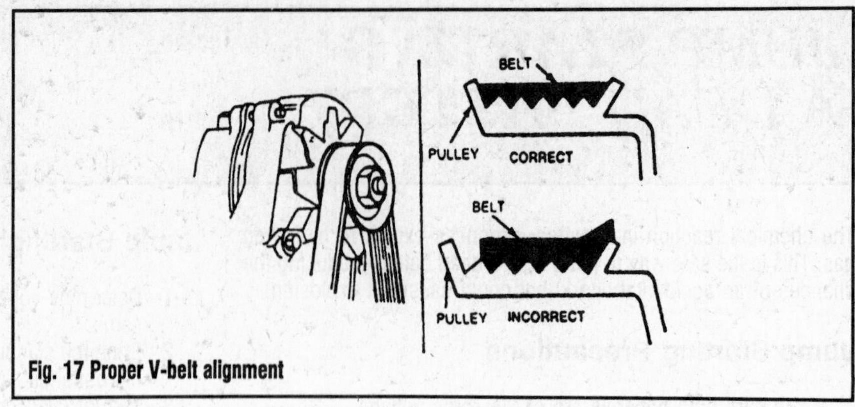

Fig. 17 Proper V-belt alignment

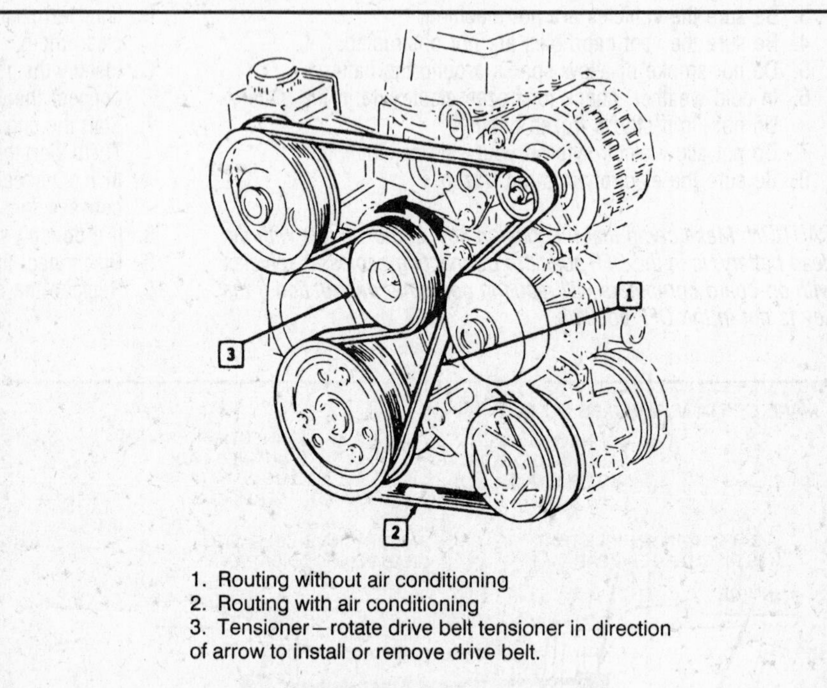

Fig. 18 Serpentine belt routing — 2.5L engine

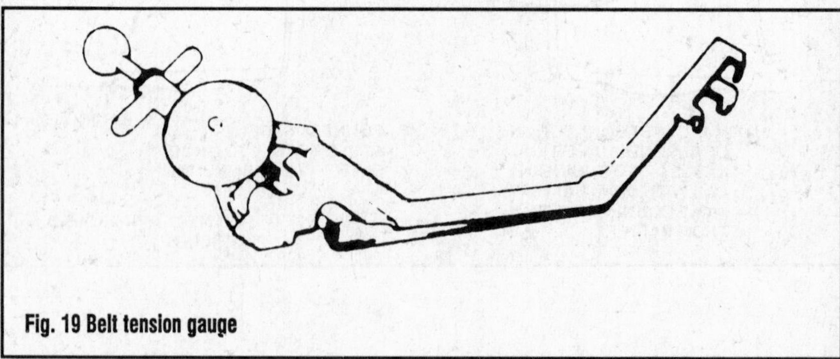

Fig. 19 Belt tension gauge

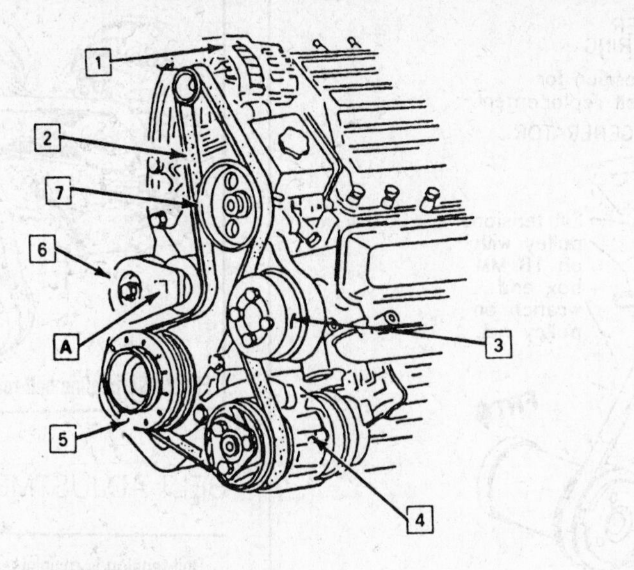

A. Insert breaker bar here
1. Generator
2. Serpentine belt
3. Water pump
4. Air conditioning compressor
5. Crankshaft
6. Belt tensioner
7. Power steering pump

Fig. 20 Serpentine belt routing — 2.8L and 3.1L engines

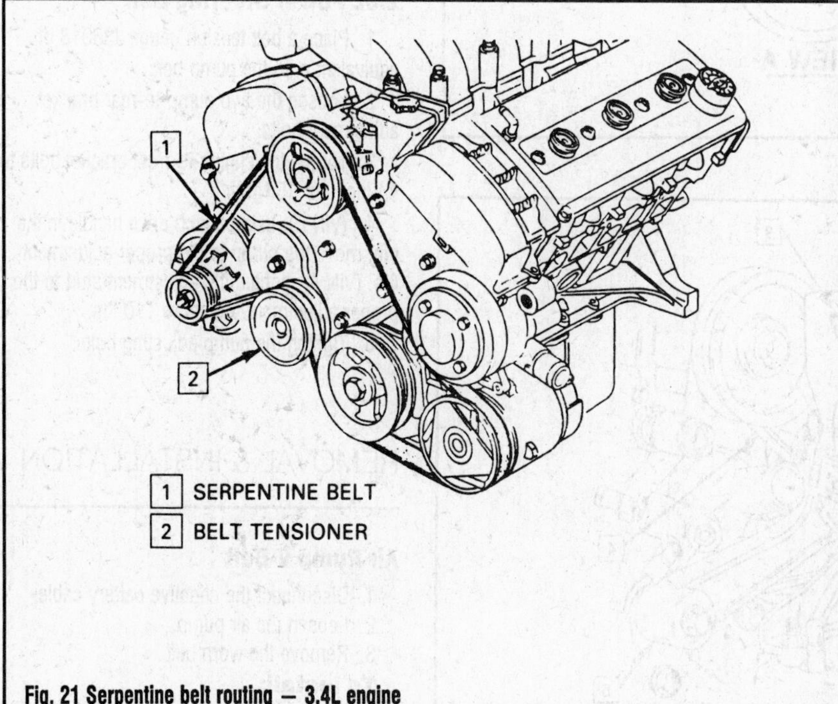

1 SERPENTINE BELT
2 BELT TENSIONER

Fig. 21 Serpentine belt routing — 3.4L engine

tight places a severe strain on the water pump, alternator, power steering pump, compressor or air pump bearings. Inspection of the belt may reveal cracks in the belt ribs. The cracks will not impair belt performance and should not considered a problem requiring belt replacement. Belts should be replaced if sections of the belt ribs are missing or if the belt is outside the tensioners operating range. The material used in late-model drive belts is such that the belts do not show wear. Replace belts at least every three years.

A single serpentine belt is used to drive all engine accessories formerly driven by multiple drive belts. The accessories are rigidly mounted with the belt tension maintained automatically by a spring loaded tensioner (all engines except 2.8L and 3.1L engines with manual transaxle). The manual transaxle engines use a separate belt to drive the thermactor air pump.

The 2.3L QUAD 4 engine uses two drive belts, one to drive the power steering pump and the second to drive the A/C compressor and alternator. The power steering belt is not self-adjusting and has to be adjusted manually. The A/C and alternator belt is automatically adjusted by a spring loaded belt tensioner, requiring no periodic adjustment. QUAD 4 engine without air conditioning has an idler pulley in place of the compressor, consequently the A/C and non-A/C belts are the same.

Tension Measurement

1. Run the engine with no accessories ON until the engine is warmed up. Shut the engine OFF. Using a belt tension gauge No. J23600B or equivalent, measure tension between the alternator and power steering pump. Note the reading.
2. With the accessories OFF, start the engine and allow to stabilize for 15 seconds. Turn the engine OFF. Using a 15mm socket, apply clockwise force to the tensioner pulley bolt. Release the tension and record the tension.
3. Using the 15mm socket, apply counterclockwise force to the tensioner pulley bolt and raise the pulley to eliminate all tension. Slowly lower the pulley to the belt and take a tension reading without disturbing the belt tensioner position.
4. Average the three readings. If the average is not between 50–70 lbs. (225–315 N) and the belt is within the tensioner's operating range, replace the belt.

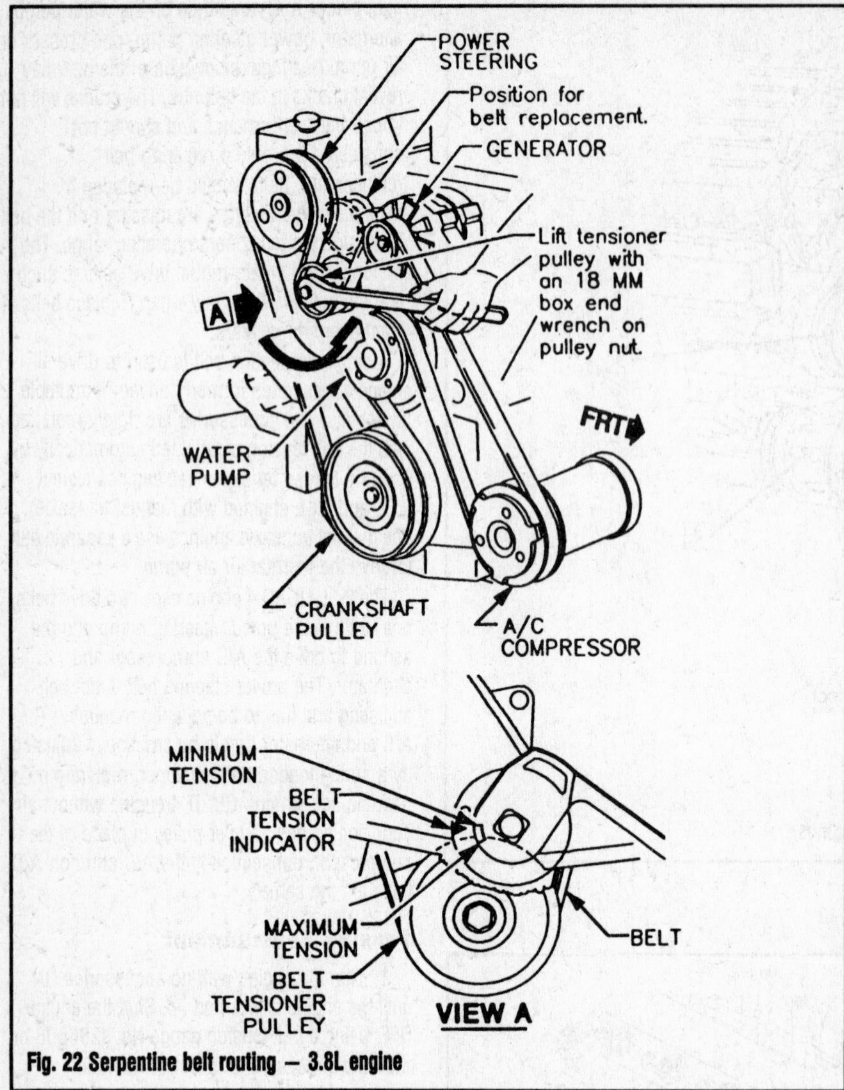

Fig. 22 Serpentine belt routing — 3.8L engine

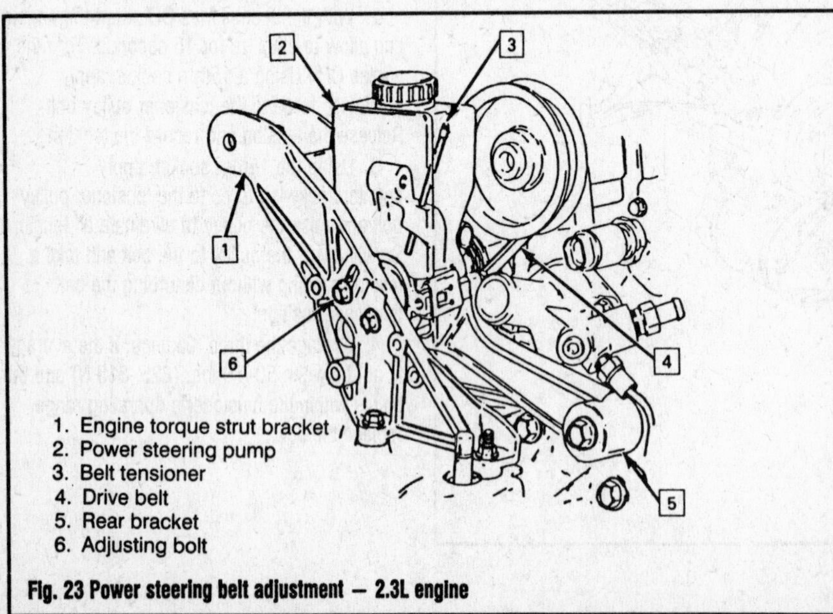

Fig. 23 Power steering belt adjustment — 2.3L engine

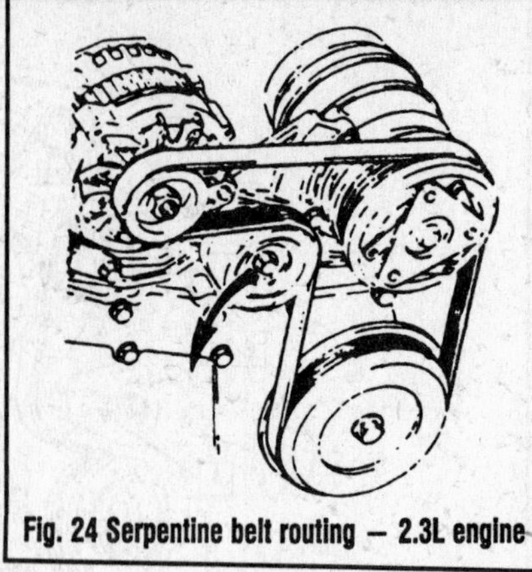

Fig. 24 Serpentine belt routing — 2.3L engine

BELT ADJUSTMENT

Belt tension is maintained by the automatic tensioner and is NOT adjustable except on the following:

2.8L and 3.1L Air Pump Belt

1. Loosen the air pump mounting bolts.
2. Using a suitable pry bar, move the air pump until the belt deflection at the center of the longest span of the belt is about $^1/_4$ inch. Be careful not to damage the aluminum pump housing.
3. Tighten the air pump bolts.

2.3L Power Steering Belt

1. Place a belt tension gauge J36018 or equivalent onto the pump belt.
2. Loosen the two pump-to-rear bracket adjustment bolts.
3. Torque the engine-to-front bracket bolts to 44 inch lbs. (5 Nm).
4. (VIN D), using a inch drive handle in the tab, move the pump to the proper adjustment lbs. (VIN A), tighten the adjustment stud to the proper adjustment. Adjust to 110 lbs.
5. Tighten the pump adjusting bolts.

REMOVAL & INSTALLATION

Air Pump V-Belt

1. Disconnect the negative battery cable.
2. Loosen the air pump.
3. Remove the worn belt.

To install:

4. Wrap the new belt around the pump.
5. Adjust the belt to specifications and tighten the pump mounting bolts.

HOW TO SPOT WORN V-BELTS

V–Belts are vital to efficient engine operation – they drive the fan, water pump and other accessories. They require little maintenance (occasional tightening) but they will not last forever. Slipping or failure of the V–belt will lead to overheating. If your V–belt looks like any of these, it should be replaced.

Cracking or Weathering

This belt has deep cracks, which cause it to flex. Too much flexing leads to heat build–up and premature failure. These cracks can be caused by using the belt on a pulley that is too small. Notched belts are available for small diameter pulleys.

Softening (Grease and Oil)

Oil and grease on a belt can cause the belt's rubber compounds to soften and separate from the reinforcing cords that hold the belt together. The belt will first slip, then finally fail altogether.

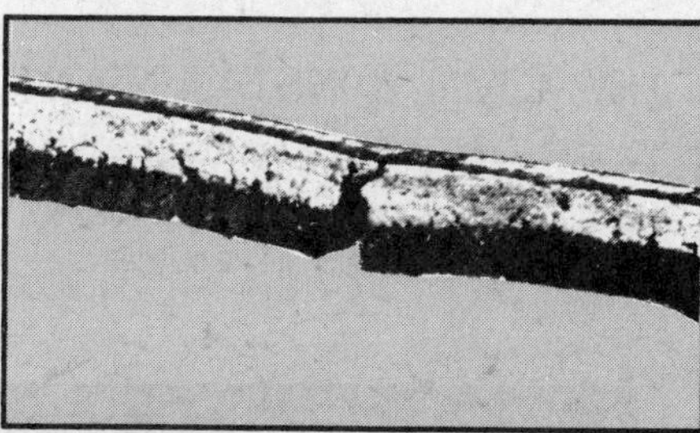

Glazing

Glazing is caused by a belt that is slipping. A slipping belt can cause a run-down battery, erratic power steering, overheating or poor accessory performance. The more the belt slips, the more glazing will be built up on the surface of the belt. The more the belt is glazed, the more it will slip. If the glazing is light, tighten the belt.

Worn Cover

The cover of this belt is worn off and is peeling away. The reinforcing cords will begin to wear and the belt will shortly break. When the belt cover wears in spots or has a rough jagged appearance, check the pulley grooves for roughness.

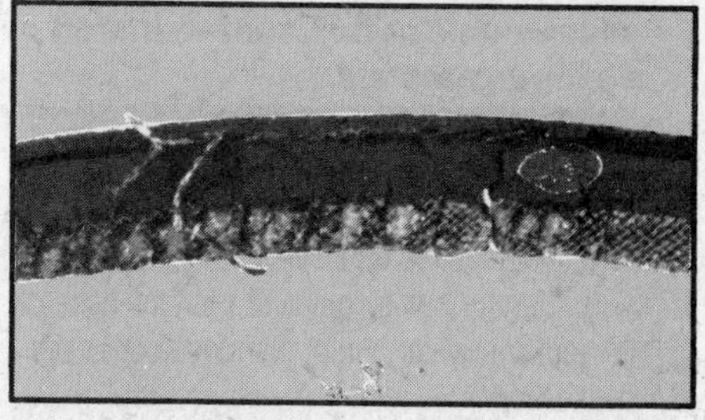

Separation

This belt is on the verge of breaking and leaving you stranded. The layers of the belt are separating and the reinforcing cords are exposed. It's just a matter of time before it breaks completely.

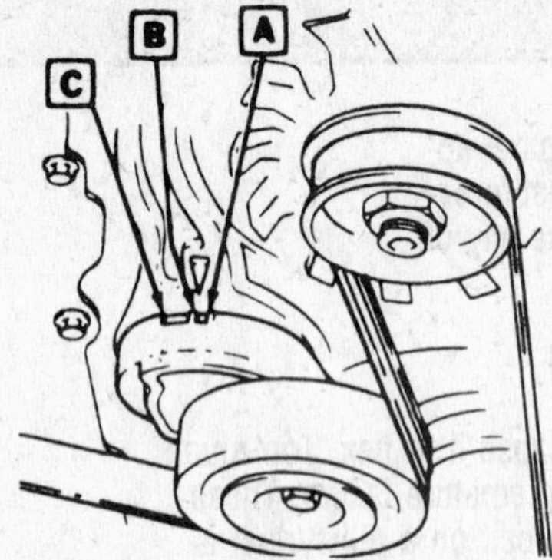

THE INDICATOR MARK ON THE STATIONARY PORTION OF THE TENSIONER MUST BE WITHIN THE LIMITS OF THE SLOTTED AREA ON THE MOVEABLE PORTION OF THE TENSIONER. ANY READING OUTSIDE THESE LIMITS INDICATES EITHER A FAULTY BELT OR TENSIONER.
A
B
C
A MINIMUM BELT LENGTH
B NORMAL BELT LENGTH
C MAXIMUM (REPLACE) BELT LENGTH

Fig. 25 Belt tensioner adjustment positions — 2.3L engine

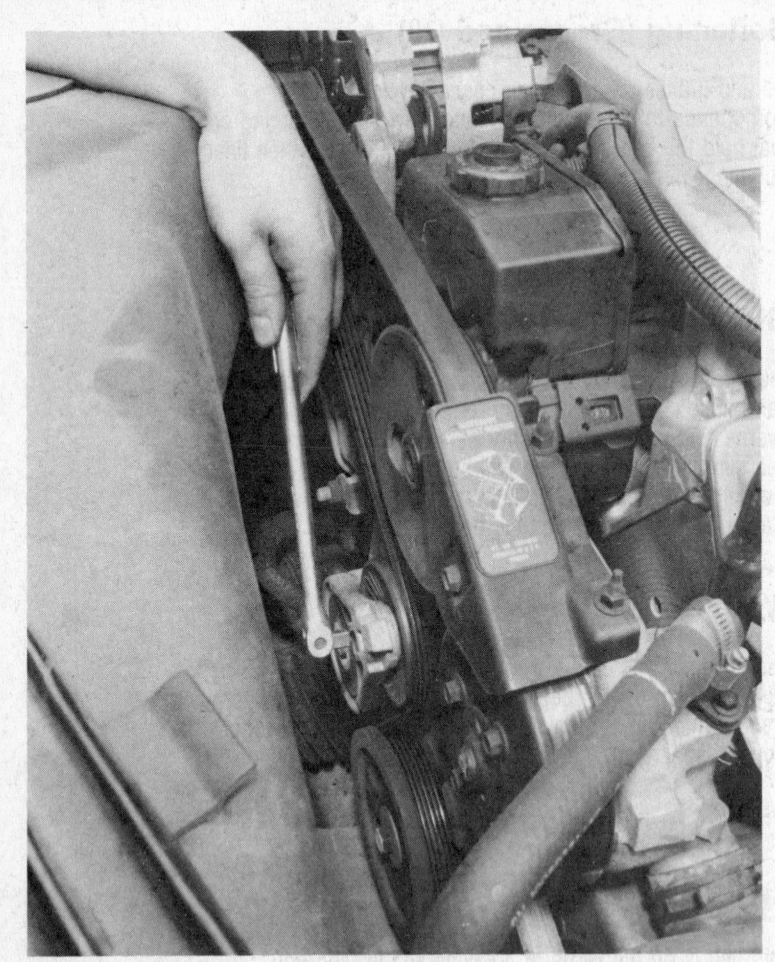

FIG. 20A. Insert the breaker bar here to rotate the tensioner–2.8L and 3.1L engines

Serpentine Belt

1. Disconnect the negative battery cable.
2. Remove the belt guard or coolant recovery reservoir as required.
3. Take note of the belt's routing. Lift or rotate the tensioner using a breaker bar in the square opening or box end wrench on the pulley nut. Loosen the pump-to-engine bracket bolts and adjusting stud to remove the power steering pump belt on the 2.3L QUAD 4 engines.
4. Remove the belt.

To install:

5. Lift the tensioner, and install the belt onto pulleys. Make sure the belt is routed properly.
6. Install the belt guard or reservoir.

Hoses

✱✱ CAUTION

On models equipped with an electric cooling fan, disconnect the negative battery cable or fan motor wiring harness connector before replacing any radiator/heater hose. The fan may come on even though the ignition has been turned off.

REMOVAL & INSTALLATION

1. Disconnect the negative battery cable. Drain the cooling system into a suitable container.

✱✱ CAUTION

When draining the coolant, keep in mind that cats and dogs are attracted by the ethylene glycol antifreeze, and are quite likely to drink any that is left in an uncovered container or in puddles on the ground. This will prove fatal in sufficient quantity. Always drain the coolant into a sealable container. Coolant should be reused unless it is contaminated or several years old.

2. Loosen the hose clamps at each end of the hose that requires replacement.
3. Carefully twist, pull and slide the hose off the radiator, water pump, thermostat or heater connection.

HOW TO SPOT BAD HOSES

Both the upper and lower radiator hoses are called upon to perform difficult jobs in an inhospitable environment. They are subject to nearly 18 psi at under hood temperatures often over 280°F, and must circulate nearly 7500 gallons of coolant an hour—3 good reasons to have good hoses.

Swollen Hose

A good test for any hose is to feel it for soft or spongy spots. Frequently these will appear as swollen areas of the hose. The most likely cause is oil soaking. This hose could burst at any time, when hot or under pressure.

Cracked Hose

Cracked hoses can usually be seen but feel the hoses to be sure they have not hardened; a prime cause of cracking. This hose has cracked down to the reinforcing cords and could split at any of the cracks.

Frayed Hose End (Due to Weak Clamp)

Weakened clamps frequently are the cause of hose and cooling system failure. The connection between the pipe and hose has deteriorated enough to allow coolant to escape when the engine is hot.

Debris in Cooling System

Debris, rust and scale in the cooling system can cause the inside of a hose to weaken. This can usually be felt on the outside of the hose as soft or thinner areas.

To install:

4. Clean the hose mounting connections. Position the hose clamps on the new hose.
5. Coat the connection surfaces with a water-resistant sealer and slide the hose into position. Make sure the hose clamps are located beyond the raised bead of the connector and centered in the clamping area of the connection.
6. Tighten the clamps to 20–30 inch lbs. Do not overtighten.
7. Fill the cooling system.
8. Start the engine and allow it to reach normal operating temperature. Check for leaks.

Air Conditioning System

SAFETY WARNINGS

Because of the importance of the necessary safety precautions that must be exercised when working with air conditioning systems and R12 refrigerant, a recap of the safety precautions are outlined.

1. Avoid contact with a charged refrigeration system, even when working on another part of the air conditioning system or vehicle. If a heavy tool comes into contact with a section of copper tubing or a heat exchanger, it can easily cause the relatively soft material to rupture.
2. When it is necessary to apply force to a fitting which contains refrigerant, as when checking that all system couplings are securely tightened, use a wrench on both parts of the fitting involved, if possible. This will avoid putting torque on the refrigerant tubing. (It is advisable, when possible, to use tube or line wrenches when tightening these flare nut fittings.)
3. Do not attempt to discharge the system by merely loosening a fitting, or removing the service valve caps and cracking these valves. Precise control is possibly only when using the service gauges. Place a rag under the open end of the center charging hose while discharging the system to catch any drops of liquid that might escape. Wear protective gloves when connecting or disconnecting service gauge hoses.
4. Never start a system without first verifying that both service valves are backseated, if equipped, and that all fittings are throughout the system are snugly connected.
5. Avoid applying heat to any refrigerant line or storage vessel. Charging may be aided by using water heated to less than 125°F (52°C) to warm the refrigerant container. Never allow a refrigerant storage container to sit out in the sun, or near any other source of heat, such as a radiator.
6. Always wear safety goggles when working on a system to protect the eyes. If refrigerant contacts the eye, it is advisable in all cases to see a physician as soon as possible.
7. Frostbite from liquid refrigerant should be treated by first gradually warming the area with cool water, and then gently applying petroleum jelly. A physician should be consulted.
8. Always keep refrigerant can fittings capped when not in use. Avoid sudden shock to the can which might occur from dropping it, or from banging a heavy tool against it. Never carry a refrigerant can in the passenger compartment of a car.
9. Always completely discharge the system before painting the vehicle (if the paint is to be baked on), or before welding anywhere near the refrigerant lines.

GENERAL INFORMATION

The most important aspect of air conditioning service is the maintenance of pure and adequate charge of refrigerant in the system. A refrigeration system cannot function properly if a significant percentage of the charge is lost. Leaks are common because the severe vibration encountered in an automobile can easily cause a sufficient cracking or loosening of the air conditioning fittings. As a result, the extreme operating pressures of the system force refrigerant out.

The problem can be understood by considering what happens to the system as it is operated with a continuous leak. Because the orifice tube regulates the flow of refrigerant to the evaporator, the level of refrigerant there is fairly constant. The accumulator-drier stores any excess of refrigerant, and so a loss will first appear there as a reduction in the level of liquid. As this level nears the bottom of the vessel, some refrigerant vapor bubbles will begin to appear in the stream of liquid supplied to the orifice tube. This vapor decreases the capacity of the orifice tube verv little as the valve opens to compensate for its presence. As the quantity of liquid in the condenser decreases, the operating pressure will drop there and throughout the high side of the system. As the R-12 continues to be expelled, the pressure available to force the liquid through the orifice tube will continue to decrease, and, eventually, the orifice will prove to be too much of a restriction for adequate flow.

At this point, low side pressure will start to drop, and severe reduction in cooling capacity, marked by freeze-up of the evaporator coil, will result. Eventually, the operating pressure of the evaporator will be lower than the pressure of the atmosphere surrounding it, and air will be drawn into the system wherever there are leaks in the low side.

Because all atmospheric air contains at least some moisture, water will enter the system and mix with the R-12 and the oil. Trace amounts of moisture will cause sludging of the oil, and corrosion of the system. Saturation and clogging of the accumulator-drier, and freezing of the orifice will eventually result. As air fills the system to a greater and greater extend, it will interfere more and more with the normal flows of refrigerant and heat.

A list of general precautions that should be observed while doing this follows:

1. Keep all tools as clean and dry as possible.
2. Thoroughly purge the service gauges and hoses of air and moisture before connecting them to the system. Keep them capped when not in use.
3. Thoroughly clean any refrigerant fitting before disconnecting it, in order to minimize the entrance of dirt into the system.
4. Plan any operation that requires opening the system beforehand in order to minimize the length of time it will be exposed to open air. Cap or seal the open ends to minimize the entrance of foreign material.
5. When adding oil, pour it through an extremely clean and dry tube or funnel. Keep the oil capped whenever possible. Do not use oil that has not been kept tightly sealed.
6. Use only refrigerant 12 (R-12). Purchase refrigerant intended for use in only automotive air conditioning system. Avoid the use of refrigerant 12 that may be packaged for another use, such as cleaning, or powering a horn, as it is impure.
7. Completely evacuate any system that has been opened to replace a component, other than when isolating the compressor, or that has leaked sufficiently to draw in moisture and air. This requires evacuating air and moisture with a good vacuum pump for at least one hour. If a system has been open for a considerable length of time it may be advisable to evacuate the system for up to 12 hours (overnight).
8. Use a wrench on both halves of a fitting that is to be disconnected, so as to avoid placing torque on any of the refrigerant lines.

Additional Checks

ANTIFREEZE

In order to prevent heater core freeze-up during A/C operation, it is necessary to maintain permanent type antifreeze protection of +15°F (9°C) or lower. A reading of +15°F (26°C) is ideal since this protection also supplies sufficient corrosion inhibitors for the protection of the engine cooling system.

RADIATOR CAP

For efficient operation of an air conditioned car's cooling system, the radiator cap should have a holding pressure which meets

RELATIVE HUMIDITY (%)	AMBIENT AIR TEMP °F	°C	MAXIMUM LOW SIDE PRESSURE PSIG	kPaG	ENGINE SPEED (rpm)	MAXIMUM RIGHT CENTER AIR OUTLET TEMPERATURE °F	°C	MAXIMUM HIGH SIDE PRESSURE PSIG	kPaG
20	70	21	32	221	2000	43	6	175	1207
	80	27	32	221		44	7	225	1551
	90	32	32	221		50	10	275	1896
	100	38	33	228		51	11	275	1896
30	70	21	32	221	2000	45	7	190	1310
	80	27	32	221		47	8	235	1620
	90	32	34	234		54	12	290	2000
	100	38	38	262		57	14	310	2137
40	70	21	32	221	2000	46	8	210	1448
	80	27	32	221		50	10	255	1758
	90	32	37	255		57	14	305	2103
	100	38	44	303		63	17	345	2379
50	70	21	32	221	2000	48	9	225	1551
	80	27	34	234		53	12	270	1862
	90	32	41	283		60	16	325	2241
	100	38	49	338		69	21	380	2620
60	70	21	32	221	2000	50	10	240	1655
	80	27	37	255		56	13	290	2000
	90	32	44	303		63	17	340	2344
	100	38	55	379		75	24	395	2724
70	70	21	32	221	2000	52	11	255	1758
	80	27	40	276		59	15	305	2103
	90	32	48	331		67	19	355	2448
80	70	21	36	248	2000	53	12	270	1862
	80	27	43	296		62	17	320	2206
	90	32	52	356		70	21	370	2551
90	70	21	40	276	2000	55	13	285	1965
	80	27	47	324		65	18	335	2310

LC0001-1B-W-RA

Fig. 26 Air conditioning performance test chart

manufacturer's specifications. A cap which fails to hold these pressure should be replaced.

CONDENSER

Any obstruction of or damage to the condenser configuration will restrict the air flow which is essential to its efficient operation. It is therefore, a good rule to keep this unit clean and in proper physical shape. Bug screens with lots of dead bugs can become obstructions.

CONDENSATION DRAIN TUBE

This single molded drain tube expels the condensation, which accumulates on the bottom of the evaporator housing, into the engine compartment. If this tube is obstructed, the air conditioning performance can be restricted and condensation buildup can spill over onto the vehicle's floor.

SYSTEM INSPECTION

➧ SEE FIG. 26

These cars are not equipped with a sight glass. The only way to properly check the system is by using a manifold gauge set and comparing the pressures and temperatures with those on the accompanying performance test chart. Be sure to follow all safety warnings above when working with air conditioning systems.

Performance Test

1. Vent the vehicle's interior. Install manifold gauge set.
2. Record outside temperature and humidity.
3. Close all doors and windows.
4. Set mode control to **A/C** with blower on its highest speed and the temperature on full cold.
5. Place a thermometer in the right center vent.
6. Start the engine and run the engine for about 3 minutes.
7. Record the outlet temperature and high side and low side pressures.
8. Turn the engine off and compare the readings with the chart.

DISCHARGING THE SYSTEM

➡ R-12 refrigerant is a chlorofluorocarbon which, when released into the atmosphere, can contribute to the depletion of the ozone layer in the upper atmosphere. Ozone filters out harmful radiation from the sun. If possible, an approved R-12 Recovery/Recycling machine that meets SAE standards should be employed when discharging the system. Follow the operating instructions provided with the equipment exactly to properly discharge the system.

1. Remove the caps from the high and low pressure charging valves in the high and low pressure lines.
2. Connect an approved R-12 Recovery/ Recycling machine to the valves and follow the instructions provided with the unit.
5. Open the low pressure gauge valve slightly and allow the system pressure to bleed off.
6. When the system is just about empty, open the high pressure valve very slowly to avoid losing an excessive amount of refrigerant oil. Do not allow any refrigerant to escape.

EVACUATING THE SYSTEM

1. Discharge the system.
2. Connect the proper service hose to the inlet fitting of the vacuum pump.
3. Turn both gauge valves to the wide open position.

4. Start the pump and note the low side gauge reading.

5. Operate the pump until the low pressure gauge reads 28 inch Hg. Continue running the vacuum pump for at Least 10 minutes. If you have replaced some component in the system, run the pump for an additional 20 or 30 minutes.

6. Close the valves and turn the pump off. The needle should remain stationary at the point at which the pump was turned off. If the needle drops to zero rapidly, there is a leak in the system which must be repaired.

CHARGING THE SYSTEM

✻✻ CAUTION

NEVER OPEN THE HIGH PRESSURE SIDE WITH A CAN OF REFRIGERANT CONNECTED TO THE SYSTEM! OPENING THE HIGH PRESSURE SIDE WILL OVER-PRESSURIZE THE CAN, CAUSING IT TO EXPLODE! Always wear safety goggles when working on a system to protect the eyes. If refrigerant contacts the eye, it is advisable in all cases to see a physician as soon as possible.

1. Connect a manifold gauge set (engine not running).

2. Close (clockwise) both gauge set valves.

3. Connect the center hose to the refrigerant can opener valve.

4. Make sure the can opener valve is closed, that is, the needle is raised, and connect the valve to the can. Open the valve, puncturing the can with the needle.

5. Loosen the center hose fitting at the pressure gauge, allowing refrigerant to purge the hose of air. When the air is bled, tighten the fitting.

✻✻ CAUTION

IF THE LOW PRESSURE GAUGE SET HOSE IS NOT CONNECTED TO THE ACCUMULATOR/DRIER, KEEP THE CAN IN AN UPRIGHT POSITION!

6. Open the low side gauge set valve, then the can valve.

7. Allow refrigerant to be drawn into the system. To help speed the process, the can may be placed, upright, in a pan of warm water.

8. When no more refrigerant is drawn into the system, start the engine and run it at about 1,500 rpm. Turn on the system and operate it at the full high position. The compressor will operate and pull refrigerant into the system.

9. If more than one can of refrigerant is needed, close the can valve and gauge set low side valve when the can is empty and connect a new can to the opener. R-12 charge is 2.25 lbs. for the VDOT system and 2.75 lbs. for the CCOT system. Follow capacity stickers if they differ from the above.

✻✻ CAUTION

NEVER ALLOW THE HIGH PRESSURE SIDE READING TO EXCEED 240 psi!

10. When the charging process has been completed, close the gauge set valve and can valve.

11. Turn the engine OFF before removing the manifold gauges.

12. Loosen both service hoses at the gauges to allow any refrigerant to escape. Remove the gauge set and install the dust caps on the service valves.

LEAK TESTING

Look for trails left where refrigerant has flowed and test the suspect fitting with soapy water. There must be at least a 1 lb. charge in the system for a leak to be detected. The most extensive leak tests are performed an electronic leak tester. Follow the instruction provided with the unit when using the leak checker.

Windshield Wipers

➧ SEE FIG. 27

For maximum effectiveness and longest element lift, the windshield and wiper blades should be kept clean. Dirt, tree sap, road tar and so on will cause streaking, smearing and blade deterioration if left on the glass. It is advisable to wash the windshield carefully with a commercial glass cleaner at least once a month. Wipe off the rubber blades with the wet rag afterwards. Do not attempt to move the wipers by hand; damage to the motor and drive mechanism will result.

If the blades are found to be cracked, broken or torn, they should be replaced immediately. Replacement intervals will vary with usage, although ozone deterioration usually limits blade life to about one year. If the wiper pattern is smeared or streaked, or if the blade chatters across the glass, the elements should be replaced. It is easiest and most sensible to replace the elements in pairs.

There are basically three different types of refills, which differ in their method of replacement. One type has two release buttons, approximately of the way up from the ends of the blade frame. Pushing the buttons down releases a lock and allows the rubber filler to be removed from the frame. The new filler slides back into the frame and locks in place.

The second type of refill has two metal tabs which are unlocked by squeezing them together. The rubber filler can then be withdrawn from the frame jaws. A new refill is installed by inserting the refill into the front frame jaws and sliding it rear ward to engage the remaining frame jaws. There are usually four jaws. Be certain when installing that the refill is engaged in all of them. At the end of its travel, the tabs will lock into place on the front jaws of the wiper blade frame.

The third type is a refill made from polycarbonate. The refill has a simple locking device at one end which flexes downward out of the groove into which the jaws of the holder fit, allowing easy release. By sliding the new refill through all the jaws and pushing through the slight resistance when it reaches the end of its travel, the refill will lock into position.

Regardless of the type of refill used, make sure that all of the frame jaws are engaged as the refill is pushed into place and locked. The metal blade holder and frame will scratch the glass if allowed to touch it.

Tires and Wheels

TIRE INFLATION

The inflation should be checked at least once per month and adjusted if necessary. The tires must be cold (driven less than one mile) or an inaccurate reading will result. Do not forget to check the spare.

The correct inflation pressure for your vehicle can be found on a decal located at the driver's door, the passenger's door or the glove box. If you cannot find the decal a local automobile tire dealer can furnish you with information. If the tires are not OEM, refer to the sidewall of the tire for correct inflation pressures.

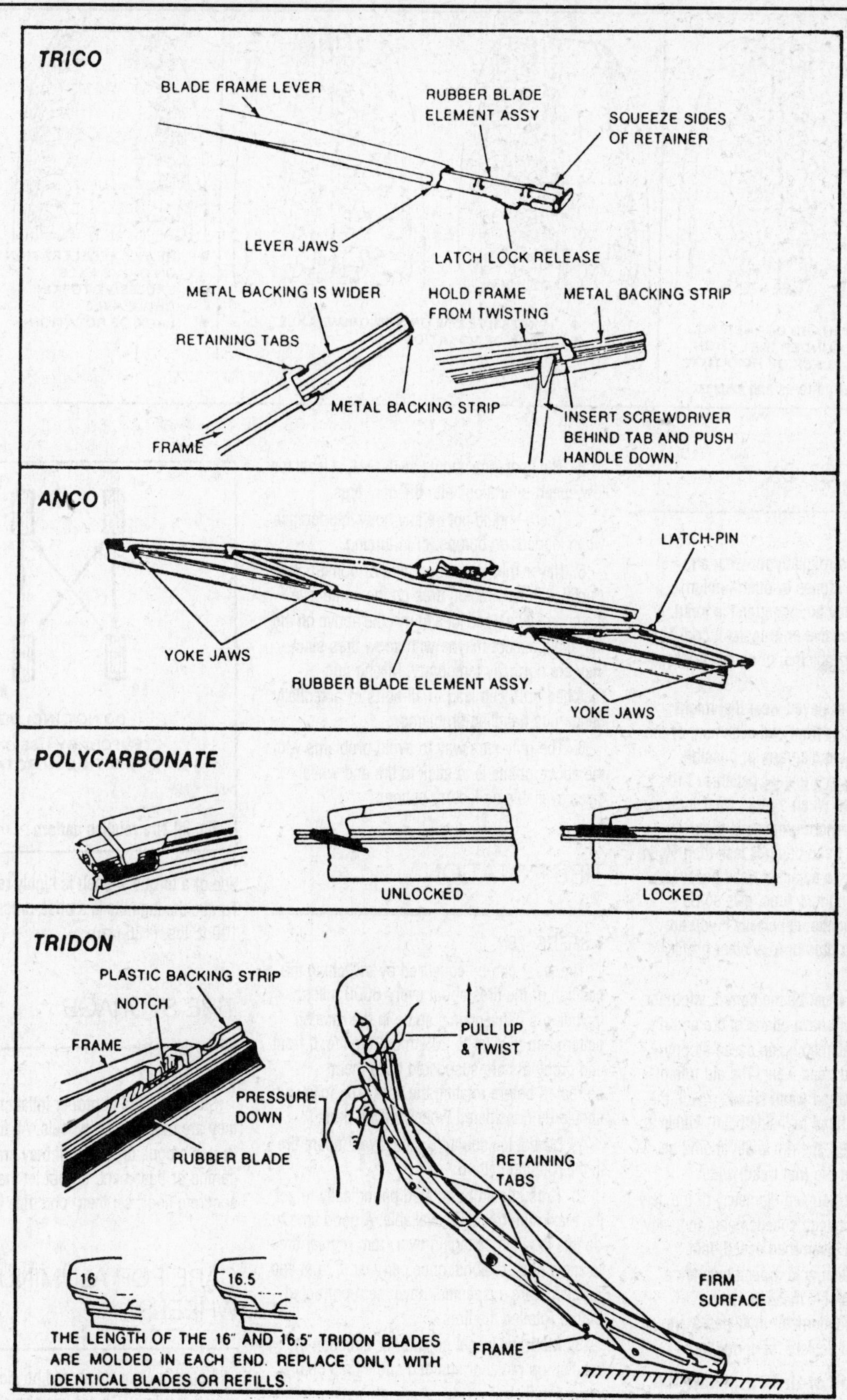

Fig. 27 Windshield wiper refills

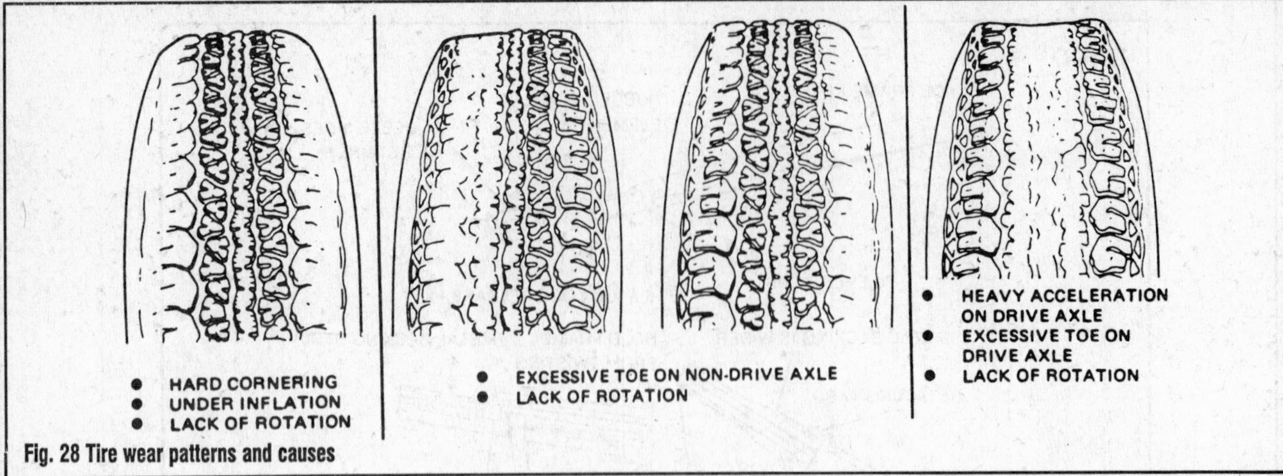

Fig. 28 Tire wear patterns and causes

TIRE INSPECTION

➧ SEE FIG. 28

Inspect the tires regularly for wear and damage. Remove stones or other foreign particles which may be lodged in the tread. If tread wear is excessive or irregular it could be a sign of front end problems, or simply improper inflation.

Inspect tires for uneven wear that might indicate the need for front end alignment or tire rotation. Refer to the diagram for possible causes according to tire wear patterns. Tires should be replaced when a tread wear indicator appears in two or more grooves in three locations or if the tread depth is less than $\frac{1}{16}$ in. (1.6mm) on any two adjacent tread grooves.

When purchasing new tires, give some thought to these points, especially if you are switching to larger tires or to another profile series:

1. The wheels must be the correct width for the tire. Tire dealers have charts of tire and rim compatibility. A mismatch can cause sloppy handling and rapid tread wear. The old rule of thumb is that the tread width should match the rim width (inside bead to inside bead) within an inch. For radial tires, the rim width should be 80% or less of the tire (not tread) width.
2. The height (mounted diameter) of the new tires can greatly change speedometer accuracy, engine speed at a given road speed, fuel mileage, acceleration, and ground clearance. Tire makers furnish full measurement specifications. Speedometer drive gears are available from GM dealers for correction.

➡ **Dimensions of tires marked the same size may vary significantly, even among tires from the same maker.**

3. The spare tire should be usable, at least for low speed operation, with the new tires.
4. There should not be any body interference when loaded, on bumps, or in turning.
5. Never mix size, tread type or construction (radial with non-radial) tires on the same axle. It's not really a good idea to mix the above on the car at all, except maybe with snow tires since they are normally temporary. Mixing non-matched tires can lead to all sorts of potentially dangerous handling problems.
6. The only sure way to avoid problems with the above points is to stick to tire and wheel sizes available as factory options.

TIRE ROTATION

➧ SEE FIG. 29

Tire wear can be equalized by switching the position of the tires about every 6000 miles. Including a conventional spare in the rotation pattern can give up to 20% more tire life. If front end problems are suspected have them corrected before rotating the tires. The following should be considered when rotating tires:

1. Do not include a "Spacesaver" spare tire in the rotation pattern.
2. Tires should be rotated periodically to get the maximum tread life available. A good time to do this is when changing over from regular tires to snow tires, or about once per year. If front end problems are suspected, have them corrected before rotating the tires.
3. Mark the wheel position or direction of rotation on radial or studded snow tires before removing them.
4. Avoid overtightening the lug nuts to prevent damage to the brake disc or drum. Alloy wheels can also be cracked by overtightening.

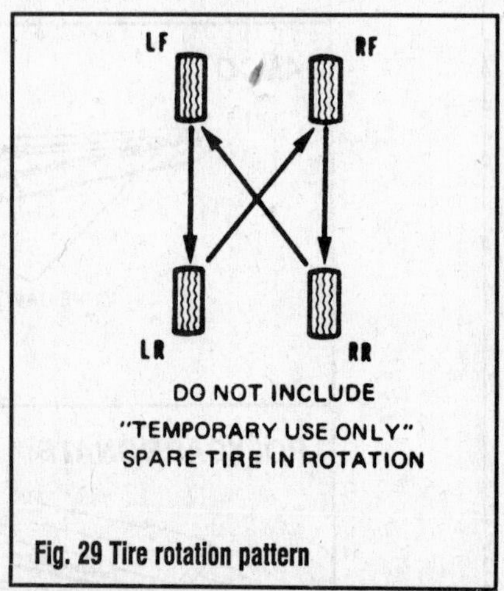

Fig. 29 Tire rotation pattern

Use of a torque wrench is highly recommended. Torque the lug nuts in a criss-cross sequence to 100 ft. lbs. (136 Nm).

TIRE STORAGE

➧ SEE FIG. 30

Store the tires at proper inflation pressure if they are mounted on wheels. All tires should be kept in a cool, dry place. If they are stored in the garage or basement, do not let them stand on a concrete floor; set them on strips of wood.

CARE FOR ALUMINUM WHEELS

Aluminum wheels should be cleaned and waxed regularly. Do not use abrasive cleaners because they may damage the protective coating.

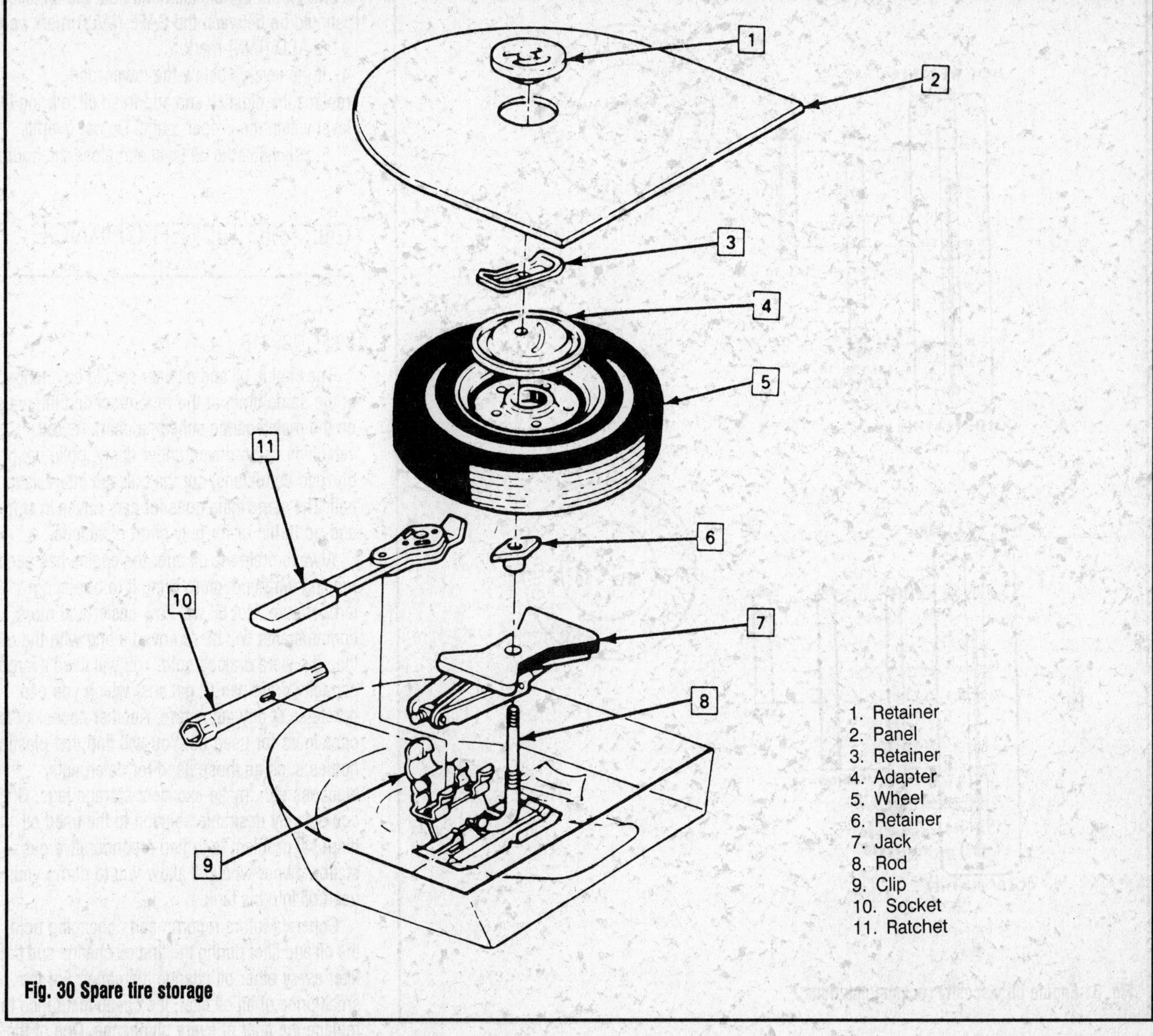

Fig. 30 Spare tire storage

FLUIDS AND LUBRICANTS

Fuel and Engine Oil Recommendations

➧ SEE FIG. 31

It is important to use fuel of the proper octane rating in your car. Octane rating is based on the quantity of anti-knock compounds added to the fuel and it determines the speed at which the gas will burn. The lower the octane rating, the faster it burns. The higher the octane, the slower the fuel will burn and a greater percentage of compounds in the fuel prevent spark ping (knock), detonation and preignition (dieseling).

Using leaded gasoline can damage the emission control system by decreasing the effectiveness of the catalyst in the catalytic converter and by damaging the oxygen sensor which is part of the "Computer Command Control System". UNLEADED GASOLINE ONLY must be used in your vehicle to prevent damage to these components.

Do not use gasolines containing more than 5 percent methanol even if they contain cosolvents and corrosion inhibitors.

All engines except the 2.3L engine and 3.1L turbo engine are designed to use only unleaded gasoline, with an Research Octane Number (RON) rating of at least 91, or an Antiknock Index of 87. The 2.3L QUAD 4 and 3.1L Turbo is designed to use only unleaded gasoline with an Antiknock Index of 91. Higher octane fuels will help keep your fuel system clean and may add some performance.

Engine oils are labeled on the containers with various API (American Petroleum Institute) designations of quality. Always use SF/CC or SF/CD quality energy conserving oils of the proper viscosity. A new quality designation, SG will protect the engine even better than the previous oils. The SG designation may be shown alone or in combination with other designations such as SG/CC, SG/CD, SF, SG or CC.

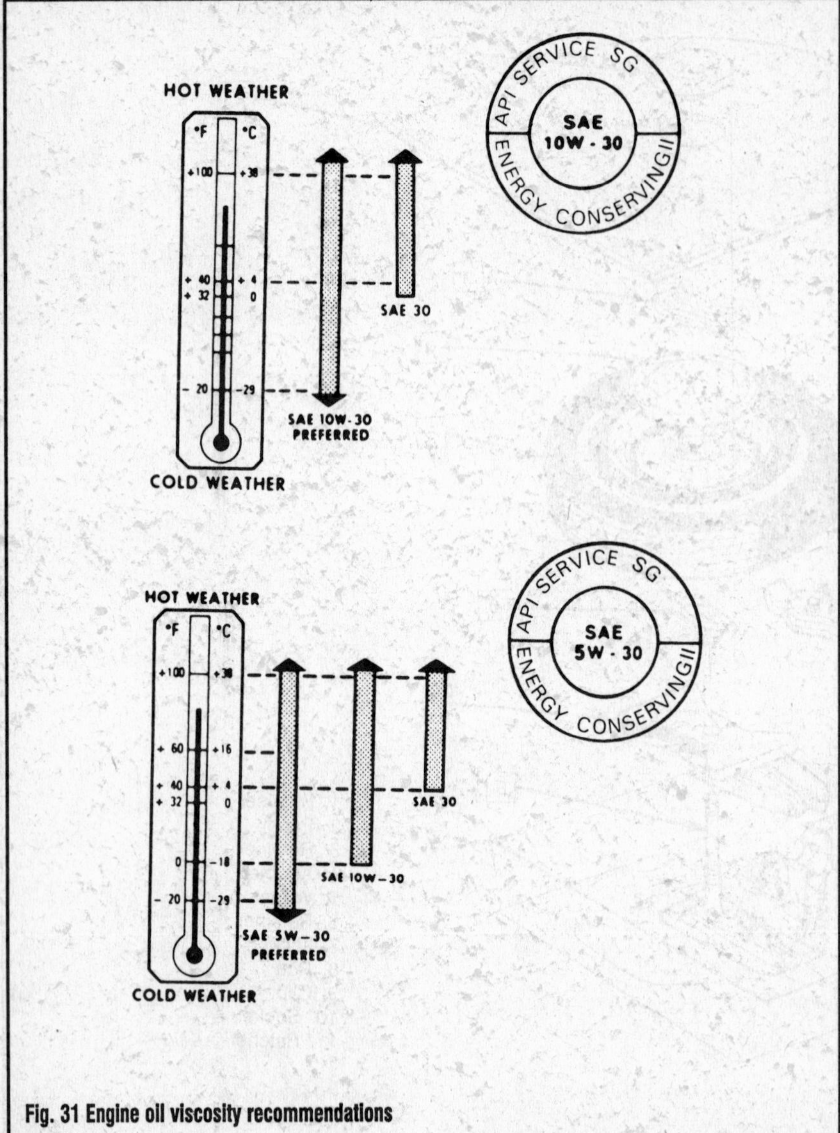

Fig. 31 Engine oil viscosity recommendations

Engine oil viscosity (thickness) has an effect on fuel economy and cold weather starting. The lower viscosity oil can provide better fuel economy and cold weather performance, but if used in hot weather condition, may not provide adequate engine lubrication.

CAUTION

Using oils of any viscosity other than those recommended may cause engine damage.

When choosing an engine oil, consider the range of temperature the vehicle will be operated in before the next oil change. Refer to the "Engine Oil Viscosity Recommendations" chart in this section.

Engine

OIL LEVEL CHECK

SEE FIG. 31A

The engine oil level should be checked frequently. For instance, at each refueling stop. Be sure that the vehicle is parked on a level surface with the engine off. Also, allow a few minutes after turning off the engine for the oil to drain into the pan or an inaccurate reading will result.

1. Open the hood and remove the engine oil dipstick.
2. Wipe the dipstick with a clean, lint-free rag and reinsert it. Be sure to insert it all the way.
3. Pull out the dipstick and note the oil level. It should be between the SAFE (MAX) mark and the ADD (MIN) mark.
4. If the level is below the lower mark, replace the dipstick and add fresh oil to bring the level within the proper range. Do not overfill.
5. Recheck the oil level and close the hood.

OIL AND FILTER CHANGE

SEE FIG. 31B

The engine oil and oil filter should be changed at the same time, at the recommended intervals on the maintenance schedule chart. If your vehicle is being driven under dusty, polluted, or off road conditions, cut the mileage intervals in half. The same thing goes for cars driven in stop-and-go traffic or for only short distances.

Always drain the oil after the engine has been running long enough to bring it to operating temperature. Hot oil will flow easier and more contaminants will be removed along with the oil than if it were drained cold. You will need a large capacity drain pan (2 gallons) which you can purchase at any auto store. Another necessity is containers for used oil. You will find that plastic bottles such as those used for detergents, bleaches etc., make excellent storage jugs. One ecologically desirable solution to the used oil disposal problem is to find a cooperative gas station owner who will allow you to dump your used oil into his tank.

General Motors recommends changing both the oil and filter during the first oil change and the filter every other oil change thereafter. For the small price of an oil filter, it's cheap insurance to replace the filter at every oil change. One of the larger filter manufacturers points out in its advertisements that not changing the filter leaves a quantity of dirty oil in the engine, which could be as much as a quart on some models. This claim is true and should be kept in mind when changing your oil.

Always properly dispose of used engine oil. You can take it to most service stations that recycle. Give a hoot. Don't pollute!

Change your oil as follows:

1. Run the engine to normal operating temperature.
2. after the engine has reached operating temperature, shut it off, firmly apply the parking brake, and block the wheels.
3. Raise and support the front end on jackstands.
4. Place a drip pan beneath the oil pan and remove the drain plug.

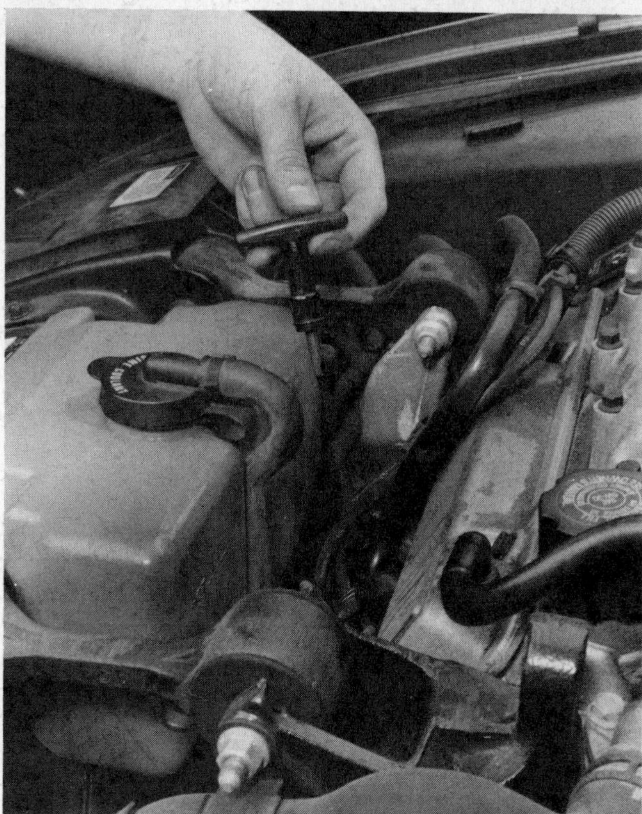

FIG. 31A. Dipstick location–2.8L and 3.1L engines

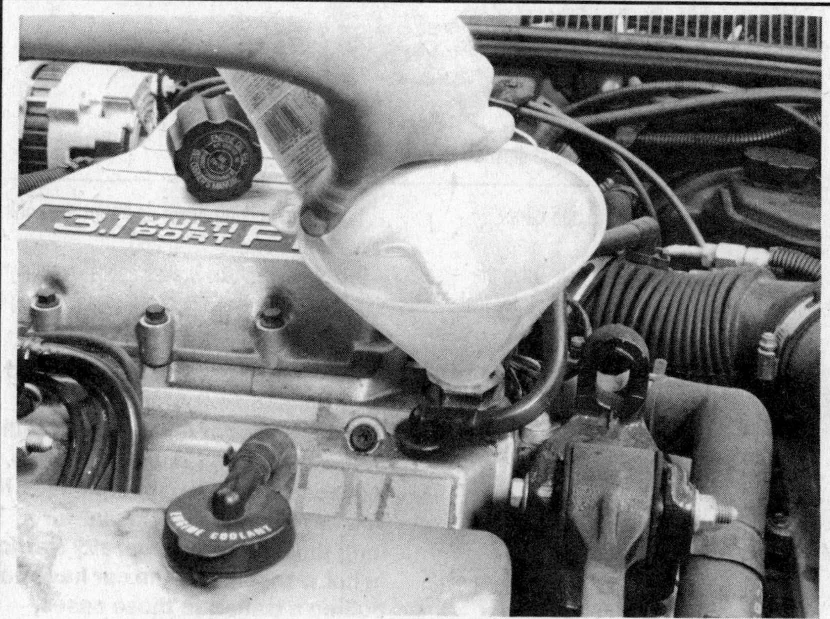

FIG. 31B. Pour in fresh oil here when filling the crankcase

5. Allow the engine to drain thoroughly.
6. While the oil is draining, replace the filter as described below.
7. When the oil has completely drained, clean the threads of the plug and coat them with non-hardening sealer or Teflon tape and install the plug. Tighten it snugly.

**** WARNING**

The threads in the oil pan are easily stripped! Do not overtighten the plug! Torque to 25 ft. lbs. (34 Nm).

8. Fill the crankcase with the proper amount of oil shown in the Capacities Chart in this Section.
9. Start the engine and check for leaks.

Replacing the Oil Filter

➧ SEE FIG. 32

1. Place the drip pan beneath the oil filter.
2. Using an oil filter wrench, turn the filter counterclockwise to remove it. Keep in mind that it's holding dirty, hot oil. Remove the oil filter through the hole in the oil pan directly above the oil drain plug on the 2.5L L4 Lumina engines. Pull the filter through with a pliers. Refer to the "Force Balancer Assembly" in Section 3 for filter location.

**** CAUTION**

The oil could be very hot! Protect yourself by using rubber gloves if necessary.

4. Wipe the contact surface of the new filter clean and coat the rubber gasket with clean engine oil.
5. Clean the mating surface of the adapter on the block.
6. Screw the new filter into position on the block using hand pressure only. Do not use a strap wrench to install the filter! Then hand-turn the filter additional turn. Do not overtighten or you may squash the gasket and cause it to leak.
7. Refill the engine with the correct amount of fresh oil.
8. Check the oil level on the dipstick. It is normal for the level to be a bit above the full mark. Start the engine and allow it to idle a few minutes. Do not run the engine above idle speed until it has built up oil pressure, indicated when the oil light goes out.
9. Shut off the engine, allow the oil to drain for a minute, and check the oil level. Check around the filter and drain plug for any leaks, and correct as necessary.

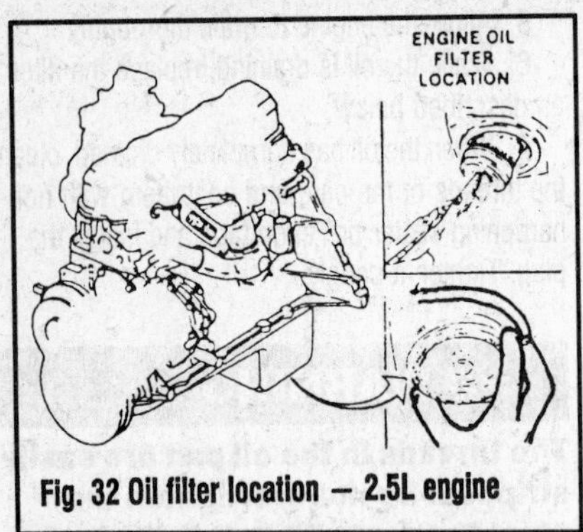

Fig. 32 Oil filter location — 2.5L engine

Manual Transaxle

FLUID RECOMMENDATION

According to General Motors, manual transaxle fluid should be checked every 15,000 miles to make sure the level is full. The transaxle fluid does not have to be changed at a regular interval. The manufacturer recommends no need manual transaxle fluid change, but after 100,000 miles the fluid should be changed.

The proper manual transaxle fluid for all manual transaxles is Manual Transaxle Oil No. 12345349 or equivalent. Do NOT use any other fluid because damage may occur.

FLUID LEVEL CHECK

➧ SEE FIGS. 34 AND 35

To check for proper fluid level on the MG2 or 5TM40, remove the fluid level dipstick located on the driver's side (left) in the transaxle case. The dipstick is located on the top of the Differential housing on the Getrag 284 transaxle. With the engine warm, add enough fluid to bring the level to the proper level.

DRAIN AND REFILL

1. Raise the vehicle and support with jackstands.
2. Position a drain pan under the transaxle drain plug. Remove the drain plug/magnet and allow to drain completely.
3. Clean and install the drain plug and torque to 18 ft. lbs. (24 Nm).
4. Using a long thin funnel, refill with the proper amount of 2 qts. of Manual Transaxle Oil No. 12345349 or equivalent.

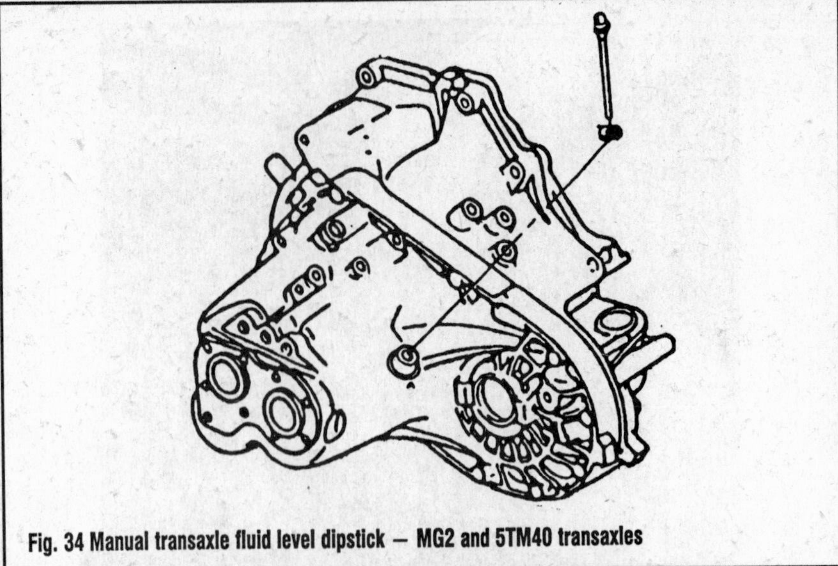
Fig. 34 Manual transaxle fluid level dipstick — MG2 and 5TM40 transaxles

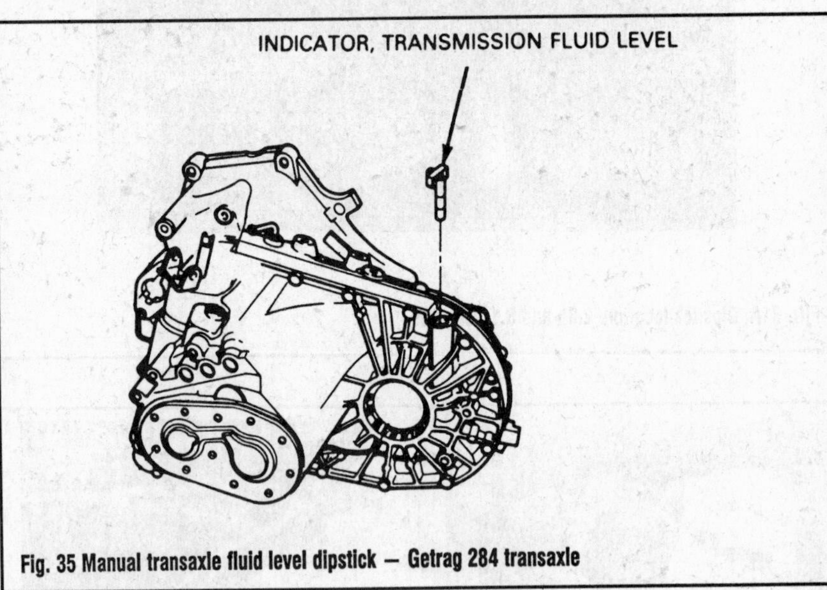

Fig. 35 Manual transaxle fluid level dipstick — Getrag 284 transaxle

5. Check the fluid level and add oil as required.
6. Install the fluid level dipstick. Drive the vehicle for a mile and stop and check for leaks.

Automatic Transaxle

FLUID RECOMMENDATION AND LEVEL CHECK

➧ SEE FIG. 35A

The automatic transaxle fluid level should be checked at each engine oil change. When adding or changing the automatic transaxle fluid use only fluid labeled Dexron®II.

1. Set the parking brake and start the engine with the transaxle in "P" (Park).
2. With the service brakes applied, move the shift lever through all the gear ranges, ending in "P" (Park).

➡ The fluid level must be checked with the engine running at slow idle, with the car level, and the fluid at least at room temperature. The correct fluid level cannot be read if you have just driven the car for a long time at high speed, city traffic in hot weather or if the car has been pulling a trailer. In these cases, wait at least 30 minutes for the fluid to cool down.

3. Remove the dipstick located at the rear end of the engine compartment, wipe it clean, then push it back in until the cap seats.

FIG. 35A. Automatic transaxle dipstick location–2.8L and 3.1L engines

1 FLUID LEVEL INDICATOR (125C)
2 LEVEL TO BE IN CROSS-HATCHED AREA ON FLUID LEVEL INDICATOR BLADE. CHECK AT OPERATING TEMPERATURE.
3 COLD LEVEL ENGINE OFF

Fig. 36 Automatic transaxle fluid level dipstick — THM 125C and 3T40 transaxles

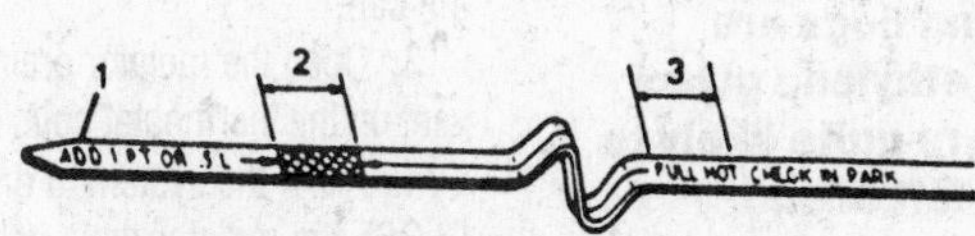

1 FLUID LEVEL INDICATOR (440-T4)
2 LEVEL TO BE IN CROSS-HATCHED AREA ON FLUID LEVEL INDICATOR BLADE. CHECK AT OPERATING TEMPERATURE.
3 COLD LEVEL ENGINE OFF

Fig. 37 Automatic transaxle fluid level dipstick — 440 T4 and 4T60 transaxles

4. Pull the dipstick out and read the fluid level. The level should be in the cross-hatched area of the dipstick.

5. Add fluid using a long plastic funnel in the dipstick tube. Keep in mind that it only takes one pint of fluid to raise the level from "ADD" to "FULL" with a hot transaxle.

✻✻ WARNING

Damage to the automatic transaxle may result if the fluid level is above the "FULL" mark. Remove excess fluid by threading a small rubber hose into the dipstick tube and pump the fluid out with a siphon pump.

FLUID DRAIN AND REFILL

➧ SEE FIGS. 36–39

According to General Motors, under normal operating conditions the automatic transmission fluid only needs to be changed every 100,000 miles unless one or more of the following driving conditions is encountered. In the following cases the fluid and filter should be changed every 15,000 miles:

1. Driving in heavy traffic when the outside temperature reaches 90°F.
2. Driving regularly in hilly or mountainous areas.
3. Towing a trailer.
4. Using a vehicle as a taxi or police car or for delivery purposes.

➡ Remember, these are factory recommendations and are considered to be minimum. You must determine a change interval which fits your driving habits. If your vehicle is never subjected to these conditions, a 100,000 mile change interval is adequate. If you are a normal driver, a two-year/30,000 mile interval will be more than sufficient to maintain the long life for which your automatic transaxle was designed.

✻✻ CAUTION

Use only fluid labeled Dexron®II. Use of other fluids could cause erratic shifting and transaxle damage.

1. Jack up your vehicle and support it safely with jackstands.
2. Disconnect the negative (–) battery cable.
3. Remove the bottom pan bolts.
4. Loosen the rear bolts about four turns.
5. Carefully pry the oil pan loose and allow the fluid to drain.
6. Remove the remaining bolts, the pan, and the gasket or RTV sealant. Discard the old gasket.
7. Clean the pan with solvent and dry it thoroughly.
8. Remove the filter and O-ring seal.
9. Install a new transaxle filter and O-ring seal, locating the filter against the dipstick stop. Always replace the filter with a new one. Do not attempt to clean the old one!
10. Install a new gasket or RTV sealant. Thoroughly clean and dry all bolts and bolt holes. Install the pan and tighten the bolts in a crisscross manner, starting from the middle and working outward.
11. Lower the car and add about 4 quarts of Dexron®II transmission fluid.
12. Start the engine and let it idle. Block the wheels and apply the parking brake.
13. At idle, move the shift lever through the ranges. With the lever in "PARK", check the fluid level and add as necessary.

Differential

The differential assembly is integral with the transaxle assembly and is lubricated by the transaxle fluid. Fluid checks or changes are not possible.

Cooling System

The engine is kept cool by a liquid circulating through the engine to a radiator. In the radiator, the liquid is cooled by air passing through the radiator tubes. The the coolant is circulated by a rotating water pump driven by the engine crankshaft. The complete engine cooling system consists of a radiator, recovery system, cooling fan, thermostat, water pump and serpentine belt.

FLUID RECOMMENDATION AND LEVEL CHECK

A see-through plastic reservoir called a coolant recovery bottle, is located in the front compartment near the radiator assembly. This bottle is connected to the radiator by a hose. As the car is driven, the coolant is heated and expands, the portion of the fluid displaced by this expansion flows from the radiator into the recovery bottle. When the car is stopped and the coolant cools and contracts, the displaced coolant is drawn back into the radiator by vacuum. Thus, the radiator is kept filled with coolant to the desired level at all times. The coolant level should be between the "ADD" and "FULL" marks on the recovery bottle. If coolant is needed, add it to the recovery bottle, not the radiator. The "ADD" and "FULL" marks on the recovery bottle are approximately one quart apart so that a 50/50 mixture can be added. (i.e. 50% ethylene glycol antifreeze and 50% water, which is the ideal mixture).

CAUTION

Do not remove the radiator cap or the thermostat housing cap while the engine and radiator are still hot. This also includes the recovery bottle cap if coolant in the recovery bottle is boiling. Scalding fluid and steam can be blown out under pressure if any cap is taken off too soon. The engine cooling fan is Electric and can come on whether or not the engine is running. The fan can start automatically in response to a heat sensor when the ignition is in "Run". Remember to keep hands, tools and clothing away from the cooling fan when working under the hood.

DRAIN AND REFILL

➧ SEE FIG. 40

CAUTION

When draining the coolant, keep in mind that cats and dogs are attracted by the ethylene glycol antifreeze, and are quite likely to drink any that is left in an uncovered container or in puddles on the ground. This will prove fatal in sufficient quantity. Always drain the coolant into a sealable container. Coolant should be reused unless it is contaminated or several years old.

Fig. 38 Oil pan, gasket, and filter — THM 125C and 3T40 transaxles

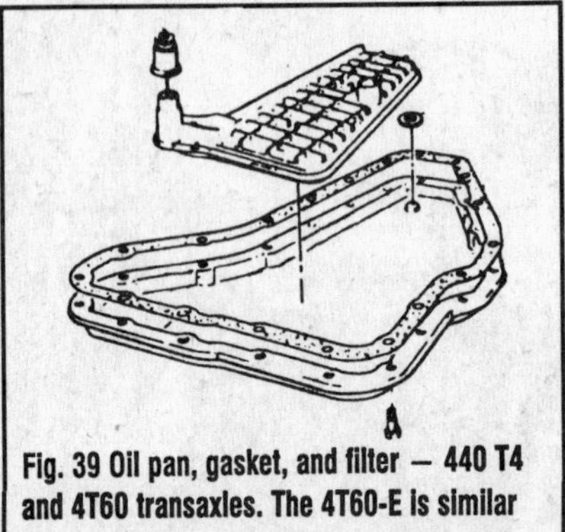

Fig. 39 Oil pan, gasket, and filter — 440 T4 and 4T60 transaxles. The 4T60-E is similar

The cooling system should be drained and refilled every 24 months or 30,000 miles. Please observe all cautions when working with antifreeze.:

➡ Use a good quality antifreeze with water pump lubricants, rust inhibitors and other corrosion inhibitors along with acid neutralizers. Use a permanent type coolant that meets manufacturer's specifications.

1. When the engine is cool, open the engine compartment lid and turn the thermostat housing cap slowly counter-clockwise (without pushing down) until it reaches a stop.
2. Wait until any remaining pressure is released, then press down on the cap and continue turning it counter-clockwise. Remove the cap.
3. Open the radiator drain valve and air bleed vent on the thermostat housing and bypass pipe.
4. Allow the system to drain completely, then CLOSE the radiator drain valve tightly.
5. Remove the coolant recovery bottle and clean with tap water. Reinstall the recovery bottle.
6. Using a 50/50 solution of antifreeze and water, fill the radiator through the radiator neck until the coolant reaches the neck.

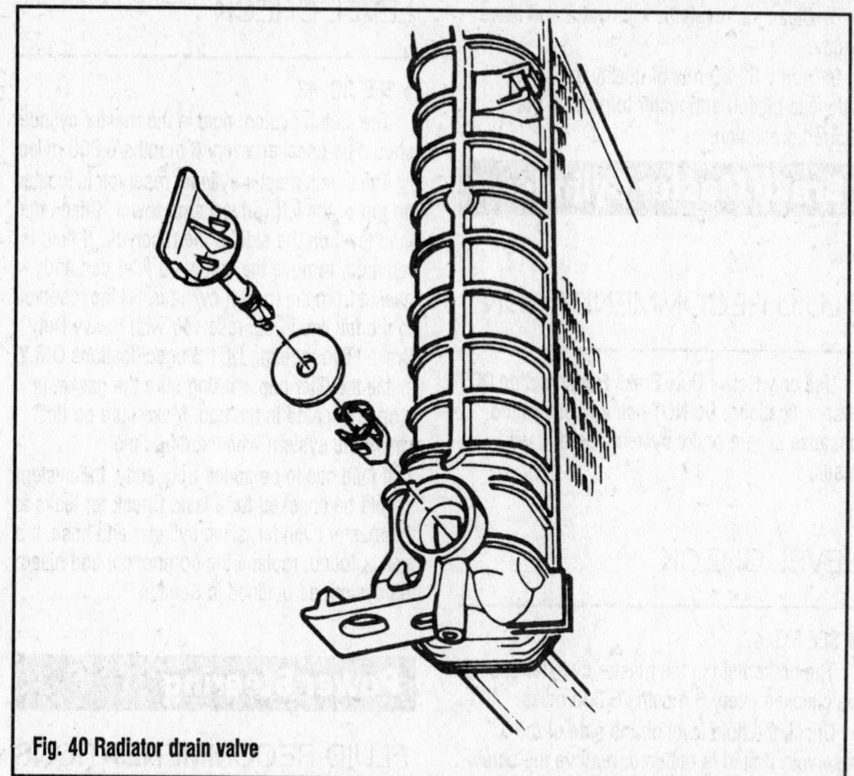

Fig. 40 Radiator drain valve

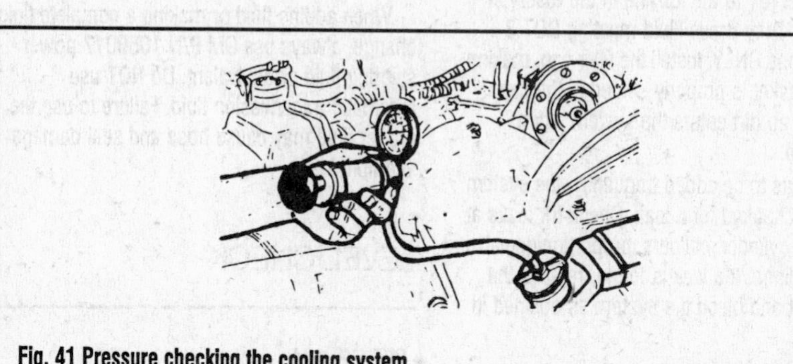

Fig. 41 Pressure checking the cooling system

7. Start the engine and let idle for five minutes; keep adding coolant until the coolant lever is to the radiator neck.
8. Install the radiator cap. Add coolant to the recovery bottle after the engine has warmed up. The coolant level should be at the HOT mark.

➡ The low coolant light may come on after this procedure. After operating the vehicle so that the engine heats up and cools down two times, if the low coolant indicator light does not go out, check and refill the recovery bottle.

CHECKING SYSTEM PROTECTION

A 50/50 mix of coolant concentrate and water will usually provide protection to 35°F (37°C). Freeze protection may be checked by using a cooling system hydrometer. Inexpensive hydrometers (floating ball types) may be obtained from a local department store (automotive section) or an auto supply store. Follow the directions packaged with the coolant hydrometer when checking protection.

COOLING SYSTEM PRESSURE TESTING

➧ SEE FIG. 41

⁂ CAUTION

When draining the coolant, keep in mind that cats and dogs are attracted by the ethylene glycol antifreeze, and are quite likely to drink any that is left in an uncovered container or in puddles on the ground. This will prove fatal in sufficient quantity. Always drain the coolant into a sealable container. Coolant should be reused unless it is contaminated or several years old.

1. Tighten the radiator and heater hose clamps.

⁂ CAUTION

To avoid being burned, do not remove the radiator cap while the engine is at normal operating temperature. The scalding coolant is under pressure and may be forced out of the filler neck, causing personal injury. Allow the engine to cool down and use a large shop towel to turn the cap.

2. Remove the radiator cap.
3. Fill the system to the base of the filler neck with antifreeze.
4. Connect a cooling system pressure tester to the filler neck.
5. Build up pressure to NO more than 20 psi (138 kPa). The system should hold the pressure for at least two minutes.
6. If the system will not hold the pressure, check for leaks.
7. Repair the leak and recheck the system.

FLUSHING AND CLEANING

CAUTION

When draining the coolant, keep in mind that cats and dogs are attracted by the ethylene glycol antifreeze, and are quite likely to drink any that is left in an uncovered container or in puddles on the ground. This will prove fatal in sufficient quantity. Always drain the coolant into a sealable container. Coolant should be reused unless it is contaminated or several years old. Do not remove the radiator cap or the thermostat housing cap while the engine and radiator are still hot. This also includes the recovery bottle cap if coolant in the recovery bottle is boiling. Scalding fluid and steam can be blown out under pressure if any cap is taken off too soon. The engine cooling fan is electric and can come on whether or not the engine is running. The fan can start automatically in response to a heat sensor when the ignition is in "Run." Remember to keep hands, tools and clothing away from the cooling fan when working under the hood.

1. Drain the existing antifreeze and coolant. Open the radiator and engine drain petcocks (models equipped), or disconnect the bottom radiator hose, at the radiator outlet. Set the heater temperature controls to the full HOT position.
2. Close the drain plug or reconnect the lower hose and fill the system with water.
3. Add a can of quality radiator flush. Make sure the flush is safe to use in engines having aluminum components.
4. Idle the engine until the upper radiator hose gets hot.
5. Drain the system again.
6. Repeat this process until the drained water is clear and free of scale.
7. Close all drain plugs and connect all the hoses.
8. Clean the reservoir with water and leave empty.
9. Add a 50/50 mix of quality antifreeze (ethylene glycol) and water to provide the desired protection.

Brake Master Cylinder

FLUID RECOMMENDATION

Use only Heavy Duty Brake Fluid meeting DOT 3 specifications. Do NOT use any other fluid because severe brake system damage will result.

LEVEL CHECK

➧ SEE FIG. 42

The brake fluid in the master cylinder should be checked every 6 months/6,000 miles.

Check the fluid level on the side of the reservoir. If fluid is required, remove the screw on filler cap and gasket from the master cylinder. Fill the reservoir to the full line in the reservoir with Heavy Duty Brake Fluid meeting DOT 3 specifications ONLY. Install the filler cap, making sure the gasket is properly seated in the cap. Make sure no dirt enters the system when adding fluid.

If fluid has to be added frequently, the system should be checked for a leak. Check for leaks at the master cylinder, calipers, proportioning valve and brake lines. If a leak is found, replace the component and bleed the system as outlined in Section 9.

Clutch Master Cylinder

FLUID RECOMMENDATION

Use only Heavy Duty Brake Fluid meeting DOT 3 specifications. Do NOT use any other fluid because severe clutch system damage will result.

LEVEL CHECK

➧ SEE FIG. 43

The clutch system fluid in the master cylinder should be checked every 6 months/6,000 miles.

The clutch master cylinder reservoir is located on top of the left (driver) strut tower. Check the fluid level on the side of the reservoir. If fluid is required, remove the screw on filler cap and gasket from the master cylinder. Fill the reservoir to the full line in the reservoir with Heavy Duty Brake Fluid meeting DOT 3 specifications ONLY. Install the filler cap, making sure the gasket is properly seated in the cap. Make sure no dirt enters the system when adding fluid.

If fluid has to be added frequently, the system should be checked for a leak. Check for leaks at the master cylinder, slave cylinder and hose. If a leak is found, replace the component and bleed the system as outlined in Section 7.

Power Steering

FLUID RECOMMENDATIONS

When adding fluid or making a complete fluid change, always use GM P/N 1050017 power steering fluid or equivalent. Do NOT use automatic transmission fluid. Failure to use the proper fluid may cause hose and seal damage and fluid leaks.

LEVEL CHECK

➧ SEE FIG. 43A

The power steering fluid reservoir is directly above the steering pump. The pump is located on top of the engine on the right (passenger's) side.

Power steering fluid level is indicated either by marks on a see through reservoir or by marks on a fluid level indicator on the reservoir cap.

If the fluid is warmed up (about 150°F), the level should be between the HOT and COLD marks.

If the fluid is cooler than above, the level should be between the ADD and COLD marks.

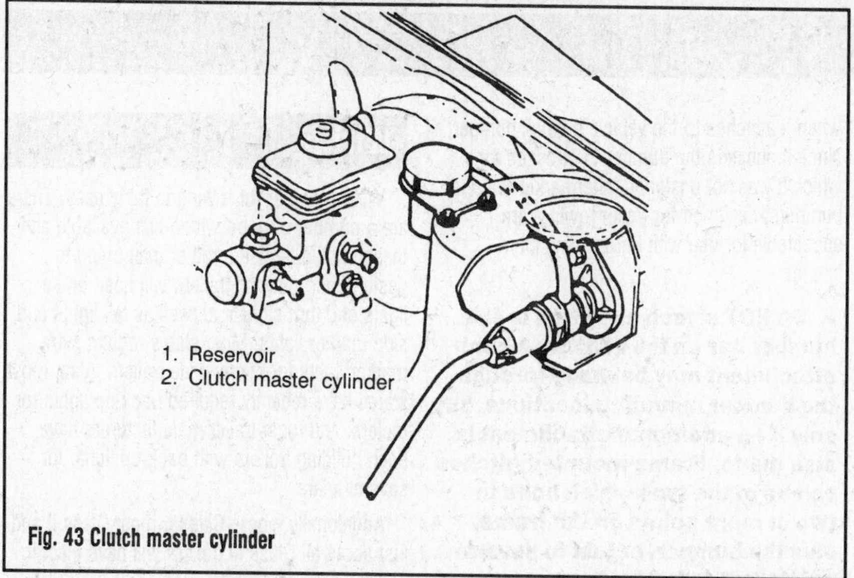

Fig. 43 Clutch master cylinder

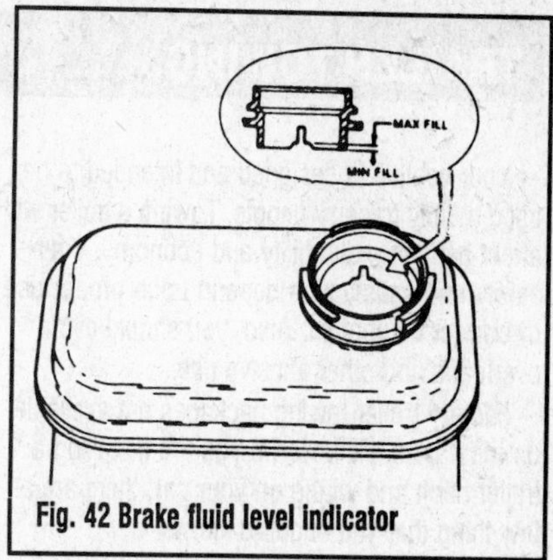

Fig. 42 Brake fluid level indicator

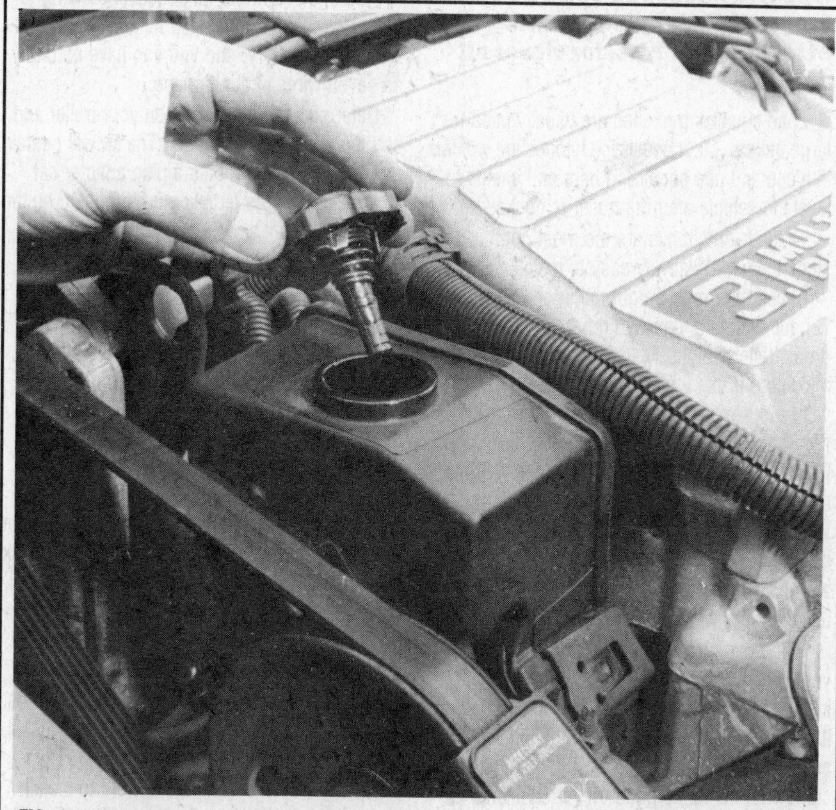
FIG. 43A. Checking the power steering fluid level

Chassis Greasing

Lubricate the chassis lubrication points every 7,500 miles or 12 months. If your vehicle is equipped with grease fittings, lubricate the suspension and steering linkage with heavy duty chassis grease. Lubricate the transaxle shift linkage, parking cable guides, under body contact points and linkage with white lithium grease.

Body Lubrication and Maintenance

Lock Cylinders

Apply graphite lubricant sparingly though the key slot. Insert the key and operate the lock several times to be sure that the lubricant is worked into the lock cylinder.

Door Hinges and Hinge Checks

Spray a silicone lubricant on the hinge pivot points to eliminate any binding conditions. Open and close the door several times to be sure that the lubricant is evenly and thoroughly distributed.

Trunk lid or Tailgate

Spray a silicone lubricant on all of the pivot and friction surfaces to eliminate any squeaks or binds. Work the tailgate to distribute the lubricant

Body Drain Holes

Be sure that the drain holes in the doors and rocker panels are cleared of obstruction. A small screwdriver can be used to clear them of any debris.

Wheel Bearings (Rear)

✲✲ CAUTION

Some brake pads contain asbestos, which has been determined to be a cancer causing agent. Never clean the brake surfaces with compressed air! Avoid inhaling any dust from any brake surface! When cleaning brake surfaces, use a commercially available brake cleaning fluid.

The W body models are equipped with sealed hub and bearing assemblies. The hub and bearing assemblies are nonserviceable. If the assembly is damaged, the complete unit must be replaced.

TRAILER TOWING

Your vehicle is designed and intended to be used mainly to carry people. Towing a trailer will affect handling, durability and economy. Your safety and satisfaction depend upon proper use of correct equipment. Also, you should avoid overloads and other abusive use.

Factory trailer towing packages are available on most cars. However, if you are installing a trailer hitch and wiring on your car, there are a few thing that you ought to know.

Information on trailer towing, special equipment and optional equipment is available at your local dealership. You can write to Oldsmobile Customer Service Department, P.O. Box 30095, Lansing, MI 48909. In Canada, General Motors of Canada Limited, Customer Service Department, Oshawa, Ontario L1J 5Z6.

Trailer Weight

Trailer weight is the first, and most important, factor in determining whether or not your vehicle is suitable for towing the trailer you have in mind. The horsepower-to-weight ratio should be calculated. The basic standard is a ratio of 35:1. That is, 35 pounds of GVW (gross vehicle weight) for every horsepower.

To calculate this ratio, multiply you engine's rated horsepower by 35, then subtract the weight of the vehicle, including passengers and luggage. The resulting figure is the ideal maximum trailer weight that you can tow. One point to consider: a numerically higher axle ratio can offset what appears to be a low trailer weight. If the weight of the trailer that you have in mind is somewhat higher than the weight you just calculated, you might consider changing your rear axle ratio to compensate, depending on parts availability.

Hitch Weight

There are three kinds of hitches: bumper mounted, frame mounted, and load equalizing.

Bumper mounted hitches are those which attach solely to the vehicle's bumper. Many states prohibit towing with this type of hitch, when it attaches to the vehicle's stock bumper, since it subjects the bumper to stresses for which it was not designed. aftermarket rear step bumpers, designed for trailer towing, are acceptable for use with bumper mounted hitches.

➡ Do NOT attach any hitch to the bumper bar on the vehicle. A hitch attachment may be made through the bumper mounting locations, but only if an additional attachment is also made. Frame mounted hitches can be of the type which bolts to two or more points on the frame, plus the bumper, or just to several points on the frame. Frame mounted hitches can also be of the tongue type, for Class I towing, or, of the receiver type, for classes II and III.

Load equalizing hitches are usually used for large trailers. Most equalizing hitches are welded in place and use equalizing bars and chains to level the vehicle after the trailer is hooked up.

The bolt-on hitches are the most common, since they are relatively easy to install.

Check the gross weight rating of your trailer. Tongue weight is usually figured as 10% of gross trailer weight. Therefore, a trailer with a maximum gross weight of 2,000 lbs. (907kg) will have a maximum tongue weight of 200 lbs. (90.7kg). Class I trailers fall into this category. Class II trailers are those with a gross weight rating of 2,000–03,500 lbs. (907–1588kg), while Class III trailers fall into the 3,500–6,000 lbs. (1588–2722kg) category. Class IV trailers are those over 6,000 lbs. (2722kg) and are for use with fifth wheel trucks, only.

When you have determined the hitch that you'll need, follow the manufacturer's installation instructions, exactly, especially when it comes to fastener torques. The hitch will subjected to a lot of stress and good hitches come with hardened bolts. Never substitute an inferior bolt for a hardened bolt.

Wiring

Wiring the car for towing is fairly easy. There are a number of good wiring kits available and these should be used, rather than trying to design your own. All trailers will need brake lights and turn signals as well as tail lights and side marker lights. Most states require extra marker lights for overly wide trailers. Also, most states have recently required back-up lights for trailers, and most trailer manufacturers have been building trailers with back-up lights for several years.

Additionally, some Class I, most Class II and just about all Class III trailers will have electric brakes.

Add to this number an accessories wire, to operate trailer internal equipment or to charge the trailer's battery, and you can have as many as seven wires in the harness.

Determine the equipment on your trailer and buy the wiring kit necessary. The kit will contain all the wires needed, plus a plug adapter set which included the female plug, mounted on the bumper or hitch, and the male plug, wired into, or plugged into the trailer harness.

When installing the kit, follow the manufacturer's instructions. The color coding of the wires is standard throughout the industry.

One point to note is that some domestic vehicles, and most imported vehicles, have separate turn signals. On most domestic vehicles, the brake lights and rear turn signals operate with the same bulb. For those vehicles with separate turn signals, you can purchase an isolation unit so that the brake lights won't blink whenever the turn signals are operated, or, you can go to your local electronics supply house and buy four diodes to wire in series with the brake and turn signal bulbs. Diodes will isolate the brake and turn signals. The choice is yours. The isolation units are simple and quick to install, but far more expensive than the diodes. The diodes, however, require more work to install properly, since they require the cutting of each bulb's wire and soldering in place of the diode.

One final point, the best kits are those with a spring loaded cover on the vehicle mounted socket. This cover prevents dirt and moisture from corroding the terminals. Never let the vehicle socket hang loosely. Always mount it securely to the bumper or hitch.

PUSHING AND TOWING

✲✲ CAUTION

Push starting is not recommended for cars equipped with a catalytic converter. Raw gas collecting in the converter may cause damage. Jump starting is recommended.

To push start your manual-transmission-equipped car (automatic transmission models cannot be push started), make sure of bumper alignment. If the bumper of the car pushing does not match with your car's bumper, it would be wise to tie an old tire either on the back of your car, or on the front of the pushing car. Switch the ignition to ON and depress the clutch pedal. Shift the transaxle to third gear and hold the accelerator pedal about halfway down. Signal the push car to proceed, when the car speed reaches about 10 mph, gradually release the clutch pedal. The engine should start; if not have the car towed.

If the transaxle is in proper working order, the car can be towed with the front wheels on the ground for distances under 15 miles at speeds no greater then 30 mph. If the transaxle is known to be damaged or if the car has to be towed over 15 miles or over 30 mph the car must be dollied or towed with the rear wheels raised and the steering wheel secured so that the front wheels remain in the straight-ahead position. The steering wheel must be clamped with a special clamping device designed for towing service. If the key controlled lock is used damage to the lock and steering column may occur.

JACKING

➧ SEE FIGS. 44–44B

✲✲ CAUTION

The jack that is furnished with the vehicle is ONLY to be used in an emergency to remove a flat tire. Never get beneath the car or, start or run the engine while the vehicle is supported by the jack. Front wheel drive cars have a center line of gravity that is far forward. Take the proper precautions to make sure the car does not fall forward while it is suspended. Personal injury may result if these procedures are not followed exactly.

When using floor jack to lift the front of the car, lift from the center of the front crossmember. When using floor jack to lift the rear of the car, lift from the center of the rear jack pad.

After lifting the car, place jackstands under the body side pinch welds or similar strong and stable structure. Lower the car onto the jackstands slowly and carefully and check for stability before getting under the car.

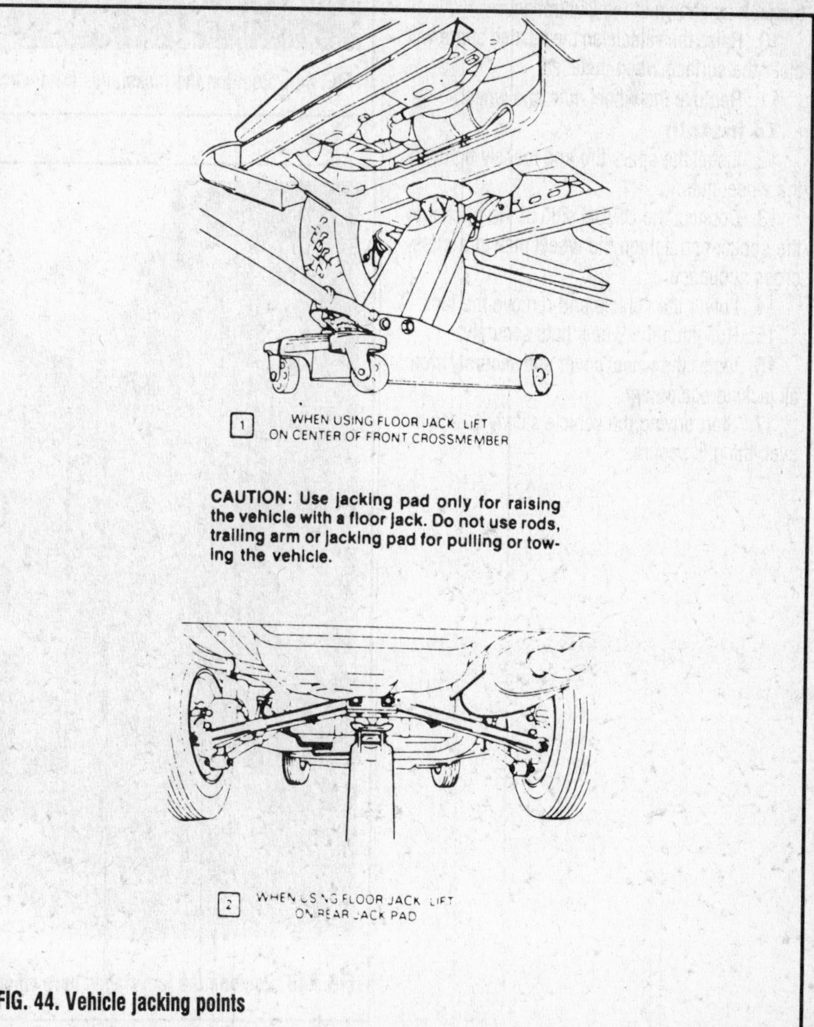

1 WHEN USING FLOOR JACK LIFT ON CENTER OF FRONT CROSSMEMBER
CAUTION: Use jacking pad only for raising the vehicle with a floor jack. Do not use rods, trailing arm or jacking pad for pulling or towing the vehicle.
2 WHEN USING FLOOR JACK LIFT ON REAR JACK PAD

FIG. 44. Vehicle jacking points

CHANGING A FLAT TIRE

1. Park on a level surface and apply the parking brake firmly.
2. If you are in a public or in a potentially dangerous location, turn the 4-way hazard flashers on.
3. Shift the transaxle gear selector into the PARK position.
4. Remove the jacking tools and spare tire from the stowage area.
5. Connect the socket with side of ratchet marked UP/ON. Raise the jack slowly.
6. Position the jack head under the vehicle closest to the tire to be changed.
7. Raise the jack until the lift head mates with the vehicle notches as shown in the jacking previous illustration. Do NOT raise the vehicle.
8. Remove the wheel cover using the wedge end of ratchet. Connect the DOWN/OFF side of the ratchet to the socket and loosen, but do not remove the wheel nuts.
9. Connect the UP/ON side of the ratchet to the jack as shown in the illustration.
10. Raise the vehicle so the inflated spare will clear the surface when installed.
11. Remove the wheel nuts and wheel.

To install:

12. Install the spare tire and loosely tighten the wheel nuts.
13. Connect the UP/ON side of the ratchet to the socket and tighten the wheel nuts in a criss-cross sequence.
14. Lower the vehicle and remove the jack.
15. Retighten the wheel nuts securely.
16. Install the wheel cover and securely store all jacking equipment.
17. Start driving the vehicle slowly to see if everything is secure.

FIG. 44A. Position the jackstands here when supporting the front of the car

FIG. 44B. Position the jackstands here when supporting the rear of the car

MAINTENANCE INTERVAL SCHEDULE — NORMAL DRIVING CONDITIONS

ITEM NO.	TO BE SERVICED	WHEN TO PERFORM MILES (KILOMETERS) OR MONTHS, WHICHEVER OCCURS FIRST	THE SERVICES SHOWN IN THIS SCHEDULE UP TO 45,000 MILES (75 000 km) ARE TO BE PERFORMED AFTER 45,000 MILES AT THE SAME INTERVALS					
		MILES (000)	7.5	15	22.5	30	37.5	45
		KILOMETER (000)	12.5	25	37.5	50	62.5	75
1	Engine Oil Change*	Every 7,500 mi. (12 500 km) or 12 mos.	●	●	●	●	●	●
	Filter Change*	At first and every other oil change or 12 mos.	●		●		●	
2	Chassis Lubrication	Every 7,500 mi. (12 500 km) or 12 mos.	●	●	●	●	●	●
3	Throttle Body Mount Bolt Torque (Some Models)*	At 7,500 mi. (12 500 km) only	●					
4	Tire & Wheel Insp. and Rotation	At 7,500 mi. (12 500 km) and then every 15,000 mi. (25 000 km)	●		●		●	
5	Engine Accessory Drive Belt(s) Insp.*	Every 30,000 mi. (50 000 km) or 24 mos.				●		
6	Cooling System Service*					●		
7	Transmission/Transaxle Service	See explanation for service interval						
8	Spark Plug Replacement*	Every 30,000 mi (50 000 km)				●		
9	Spark Plug Wire Insp. (Some Models)*					●		
10	PCV Valve Insp. (Some Models)*††					●		
11	EGR System Insp.*††	Every 30,000 mi. (50 000 km) or 36 mos.				●		
12	Air Cleaner & PCV Filter Repl.*					●		
13	Fuel Tank, Cap & Lines Insp.*††	Every 30,000 mi. (50 000 km)				●		

FOOTNOTES: * An Emission Control Service

†† The U.S. Environmental Protection Agency has determined that the failure to perform this maintenance item will not nullify the emission warranty or limit recall liability prior to the completion of vehicle useful life. General Motors, however, urges that all recommended maintenance services be performed at the indicated intervals and the maintenance be recorded in Section C of the Owner's Maintenance Schedule.

MC0002-0B-W-RA

MAINTENANCE INTERVAL SCHEDULE — SEVERE DRIVING CONDITIONS

ITEM NO.	TO BE SERVICED	WHEN TO PERFORM MILES (Kilometers) OR MONTHS, WHICHEVER OCCURS FIRST	THE SERVICES SHOWN IN THIS SCHEDULE UP TO 48,000 MILES (80 000 km) ARE TO BE PERFORMED AFTER 48,000 MILES AT THE SAME INTERVALS															
		MILES (000)	3	6	9	12	15	18	21	24	27	30	33	36	39	42	45	48
		KILOMETER (000)	5	10	15	20	25	30	35	40	45	50	55	60	65	70	75	80
1	Engine Oil & Oil Filter Change*	Every 3,000 (5 000 km) or 3 mos.	•	•	•	•	•	•	•	•	•	•	•	•	•	•	•	•
2	Chassis Lubrication	Every other oil change		•		•		•		•		•		•		•		•
3	Throttle Body Mount Bolt Torque (Some Models)*	At 6,000 mi. (10 000 km) only		•														
4	Tire & Wheel Insp. and Rotation	At 6,000 mi. (10 000 km) and then every 15,000 mi. (25 000 km)		•					•					•				
5	Engine Accessory Drive Belt(s) Insp.*	Every 30,000 mi. (50 000 km) or 24 mos.										•						
6	Cooling System Service*											•						
7	Transmission/Transaxle Service	See explanation for service interval																
8	Spark Plug Replacement*	Every 30,000 mi (50 000 km)										•						
9	Spark Plug Wire Insp. (Some Models)*											•						
10	PCV Valve Insp. (Some Models)*††											•						
11	EGR System Insp.*††	Every 30,000 mi. (50 000 km) or 36 mos.										•						
12	Air Cleaner & PCV Filter Repl.*											•						
13	Fuel Tank, Cap & Lines Insp.*††	Every 30,000 mi. (50 000 km)										•						

FOOTNOTES: * An Emission Control Service

†† The U.S. Environmental Protection Agency has determined that the failure to perform this maintenance item will not nullify the emission warranty or limit recall liability prior to the completion of vehicle useful life. General Motors, however, urges that all recommended maintenance services be performed at the indicated intervals and the maintenance be recorded in Section C of the Owner's Maintenance Schedule.

** Trailering is not recommended for some models, see the Owner's Manual for details.

MC0001-0B-W-RA

CAPACITIES

Year	Model	VIN	No. Cylinder Displacement cu. in. (liter)	Engine Crankcase with Filter ④	Transmission (pts.) 4-Spd	5-Spd	Auto.	Drive Axle (pts.)	Fuel Tank (gal.)	Cooling System (qts.)
1988-89	Grand Prix	W	6-173 (2.8)	4.0	—	5	12.0③	—	16.0	12.6
	Grand Prix	T	6-192 (3.1)	4.0	—	5	12.0③	—	16.0	12.6
	Cutlass Supreme	W	6-173 (2.8)	4.0	—	5	12.0③	—	16.0	12.6
	Cutlass Supreme	T	6-192 (3.1)	4.0	—	5	12.0③	—	16.0	12.6
	Regal	W	6-173 (2.8)	4.0	—	—	12.0③	—	16.0	12.6
	Regal	T	6-192 (3.1)	4.0	—	—	12.0③	—	16.0	12.6
	Lumina	R	4-151 (2.5)	4.0	—	—	12.0③	—	16.0	12.6
	Lumina	T	6-192 (3.1)	4.0	—	—	12.0③	—	16.0	12.6

CAPACITIES

Year	Model	VIN	No. Cylinder Displacement cu. in. (liter)	Engine Crankcase with Filter ④	Transmission (pts.) 4-Spd	5-Spd	Auto.	Drive Axle (pts.)	Fuel Tank (gal.)	Cooling System (qts.)
1990	Grand Prix	A	4-138 (2.3)	4.0	—	4.2	⑤	—	16.5	8.9
	Grand Prix	D	4-138 (2.3)	4.0	—	4.2	⑤	—	16.5	9.2
	Grand Prix	T	6-192 (3.1)	4.0	—	4.2	⑤	—	16.5	12.5
	Grand Prix	V	6-192 (3.1)	4.0	—	4.2	⑤	—	16.5	13.2
	Cutlass Supreme	A	4-138 (2.3)	4.0	—	4.4	⑤	—	16.5	8.9
	Cutlass Supreme	D	4-138 (2.3)	4.0	—	4.4	⑤	—	16.5	9.2
	Cutlass Supreme	T	6-192 (3.1)	4.0	—	4.4	⑤	—	16.5	12.5
	Regal	T	6-192 (3.1)	4.0	—	—	⑤	—	16.5	12.5
	Regal	L	6-231 (3.8)	4.0	—	—	⑤	—	16.5	11.1
	Lumina	R	4-151 (2.5)	4.0	—	—	⑤	—	16.0	9.4
	Lumina	T	6-192 (3.1)	4.0	—	—	⑤	—	16.0	12.6
1991	Grand Prix	D	4-138 (2.3)	4.0	—	4.2	⑤	—	16.5	9.2
	Grand Prix	T	6-192 (3.1)	4.0	—	4.2	⑤	—	16.5	12.5
	Grand Prix	X	6-204 (3.4)	5.0	—	4.0	⑤	—	16.5	12.7
	Cutlass Supreme	D	4-138 (2.3)	4.0	—	4.4	⑤	—	16.5	9.2
	Cutlass Supreme	T	6-192 (3.1)	4.0	—	4.4	⑤	—	16.5	12.5
	Cutlass Supreme	X	6-204 (3.4)	5.0	—	4.0	⑤	—	16.5	12.7
	Regal	T	6-192 (3.1)	4.0	—	—	⑤	—	16.5	12.5
	Regal	L	6-231 (3.8)	4.0	—	—	⑤	—	16.5	11.1
	Lumina	R	4-151 (2.5)	4.0	—	—	⑤	—	16.0	9.4
	Lumina	T	6-192 (3.1)	4.0	—	—	⑤	—	16.0	12.6
	Lumina	X	6-204 (3.4)	5.0	—	4.0	⑤	—	16.5	12.7
1992	Grand Prix	T	6-192 (3.1)	4.0	—	4.2	⑤	—	16.5	12.5
	Grand Prix	X	6-204 (3.4)	5.0	—	4.0	⑤	—	16.5	12.7
	Cutlass Supreme	T	6-192 (3.1)	4.0	—	4.4	⑤	—	16.5	12.5
	Cutlass Supreme	X	6-204 (3.4)	5.0	—	4.0	⑤	—	16.5	12.7
	Regal	T	6-192 (3.1)	4.0	—	—	⑤	—	16.5	12.5
	Regal	L	6-231 (3.8)	4.0	—	—	⑤	—	16.5	11.1
	Lumina	R	4-151 (2.5)	4.0	—	—	⑤	—	16.0	9.4
	Lumina	T	6-192 (3.1)	4.0	—	—	⑤	—	16.0	12.6
	Lumina	X	6-204 (3.4)	5.0	—	4.0	⑤	—	16.5	12.7

① Drain and refill only.
Completely overhaul—22 pts.

② Without air conditioning—12.3 qts.
With air conditioning—12.6 qts.

③ Drain and refill only.
Compelte overhaul—16 pts.

④ Add fluid as necessary to bring to appropriate level.

⑤ Hydra-matic 3T40: drain and refill only—14 pts., complete overhaul—18 pts.
Hydra-matic 4T60: drain and refill only—12 pts., complete overhaul—16 pts.

Troubleshooting Basic Air Conditioning Problems

Problem	Cause	Solution
There's little or no air coming from the vents (and you're sure it's on)	• The A/C fuse is blown • Broken or loose wires or connections • The on/off switch is defective	• Check and/or replace fuse • Check and/or repair connections • Replace switch
The air coming from the vents is not cool enough	• Windows and air vent wings open • The compressor belt is slipping • Heater is on • Condenser is clogged with debris • Refrigerant has escaped through a leak in the system • Receiver/drier is plugged	• Close windows and vent wings • Tighten or replace compressor belt • Shut heater off • Clean the condenser • Check system • Service system
The air has an odor	• Vacuum system is disrupted • Odor producing substances on the evaporator case • Condensation has collected in the bottom of the evaporator housing	• Have the system checked/repaired • Clean the evaporator case • Clean the evaporator housing drains
System is noisy or vibrating	• Compressor belt or mountings loose • Air in the system	• Tighten or replace belt; tighten mounting bolts • Have the system serviced
Sight glass condition		
Constant bubbles, foam or oil streaks	• Undercharged system	• Charge the system
Clear sight glass, but no cold air	• No refrigerant at all	• Check and charge the system
Clear sight glass, but air is cold	• System is OK	
Clouded with milky fluid	• Receiver drier is leaking dessicant	• Have system checked
Large difference in temperature of lines	• System undercharged	• Charge and leak test the system
Compressor noise	• Broken valves • Overcharged • Incorrect oil level • Piston slap • Broken rings • Drive belt pulley bolts are loose	• Replace the valve plate • Discharge, evacuate and install the correct charge • Isolate the compressor and check the oil level. Correct as necessary. • Replace the compressor • Replace the compressor • Tighten with the correct torque specification
Excessive vibration	• Incorrect belt tension • Clutch loose • Overcharged • Pulley is misaligned	• Adjust the belt tension • Tighten the clutch • Discharge, evacuate and install the correct charge • Align the pulley
Condensation dripping in the passenger compartment	• Drain hose plugged or improperly positioned • Insulation removed or improperly installed	• Clean the drain hose and check for proper installation • Replace the insulation on the expansion valve and hoses

Troubleshooting Basic Air Conditioning Problems (cont.)

Problem	Cause	Solution
Frozen evaporator coil	• Faulty thermostat • Thermostat capillary tube improperly installed • Thermostat not adjusted properly	• Replace the thermostat • Install the capillary tube correctly • Adjust the thermostat
Low side low—high side low	• System refrigerant is low • Expansion valve is restricted	• Evacuate, leak test and charge the system • Replace the expansion valve
Low side high—high side low	• Internal leak in the compressor—worn	• Remove the compressor cylinder head and inspect the compressor. Replace the valve plate assembly if necessary. If the compressor pistons, rings or
Low side high—high side low (cont.)		cylinders are excessively worn or scored replace the compressor
	• Cylinder head gasket is leaking • Expansion valve is defective • Drive belt slipping	• Install a replacement cylinder head gasket • Replace the expansion valve • Adjust the belt tension
Low side high—high side high	• Condenser fins obstructed • Air in the system • Expansion valve is defective • Loose or worn fan belts	• Clean the condenser fins • Evacuate, leak test and charge the system • Replace the expansion valve • Adjust or replace the belts as necessary
Low side low—high side high	• Expansion valve is defective • Restriction in the refrigerant hose	• Replace the expansion valve • Check the hose for kinks—replace if necessary
Low side low—high side high	• Restriction in the receiver/drier • Restriction in the condenser	• Replace the receiver/drier • Replace the condenser
Low side and high normal (inadequate cooling)	**• Air in the system** **• Moisture in the system**	**• Evacuate, leak test and charge the system** **• Evacuate, leak test and charge the system**

Troubleshooting Basic Wheel Problems

Problem	Cause	Solution
The car's front end vibrates at high speed	• The wheels are out of balance • Wheels are out of alignment	• Have wheels balanced • Have wheel alignment checked/adjusted
Car pulls to either side	• Wheels are out of alignment • Unequal tire pressure • Different size tires or wheels	• Have wheel alignment checked/adjusted • Check/adjust tire pressure • Change tires or wheels to same size
The car's wheel(s) wobbles	• Loose wheel lug nuts • Wheels out of balance • Damaged wheel • Wheels are out of alignment • Worn or damaged ball joint • Excessive play in the steering linkage (usually due to worn parts) • Defective shock absorber	• Tighten wheel lug nuts • Have tires balanced • Raise car and spin the wheel. If the wheel is bent, it should be replaced • Have wheel alignment checked/adjusted • Check ball joints • Check steering linkage • Check shock absorbers
Tires wear unevenly or prematurely	• Incorrect wheel size • Wheels are out of balance • Wheels are out of alignment	• Check if wheel and tire size are compatible • Have wheels balanced • Have wheel alignment checked/adjusted

Troubleshooting Basic Tire Problems

Problem	Cause	Solution
The car's front end vibrates at high speeds and the steering wheel shakes	• Wheels out of balance • Front end needs aligning	• Have wheels balanced • Have front end alignment checked
The car pulls to one side while cruising	• Unequal tire pressure (car will usually pull to the low side) • Mismatched tires • Front end needs aligning	• Check/adjust tire pressure • Be sure tires are of the same type and size • Have front end alignment checked
Abnormal, excessive or uneven tire wear See "How to Read Tire Wear"	• Infrequent tire rotation • Improper tire pressure • Sudden stops/starts or high speed on curves	• Rotate tires more frequently to equalize wear • Check/adjust pressure • Correct driving habits
Tire squeals	• Improper tire pressure • Front end needs aligning	• Check/adjust tire pressure • Have front end alignment checked

Tire Size Comparison Chart

"Letter" sizes			Inch Sizes	Metric-inch Sizes		
"60 Series"	"70 Series"	"78 Series"	1965–77	"60 Series"	"70 Series"	"80 Series"
			5.50-12, 5.60-12	165/60-12	165/70-12	155-12
		Y78-12	6.00-12			
		W78-13	5.20-13	165/60-13	145/70-13	135-13
		Y78-13	5.60-13	175/60-13	155/70-13	145-13
			6.15-13	185/60-13	165/70-13	155-13, P155/80-13
A60-13	A70-13	A78-13	6.40-13	195/60-13	175/70-13	165-13
B60-13	B70-13	B78-13	6.70-13	205/60-13	185/70-13	175-13
			6.90-13			
C60-13	C70-13	C78-13	7.00-13	215/60-13	195/70-13	185-13
D60-13	D70-13	D78-13	7.25-13			
E60-13	E70-13	E78-13	7.75-13			195-13
			5.20-14	165/60-14	145/70-14	135-14
			5.60-14	175/60-14	155/70-14	145-14
			5.90-14			
A60-14	A70-14	A78-14	6.15-14	185/60-14	165/70-14	155-14
	B70-14	B78-14	6.45-14	195/60-14	175/70-14	165-14
	C70-14	C78-14	6.95-14	205/60-14	185/70-14	175-14
D60-14	D70-14	D78-14				
E60-14	E70-14	E78-14	7.35-14	215/60-14	195/70-14	185-14
F60-14	F70-14	F78-14, F83-14	7.75-14	225/60-14	200/70-14	195-14
G60-14	G70-14	G77-14, G78-14	8.25-14	235/60-14	205/70-14	205-14
H60-14	H70-14	H78-14	8.55-14	245/60-14	215/70-14	215-14
J60-14	J70-14	J78-14	8.85-14	255/60-14	225/70-14	225-14
L60-14	L70-14		9.15-14	265/60-14	235/70-14	
	A70-15	A78-15	5.60-15	185/60-15	165/70-15	155-15
B60-15	B70-15	B78-15	6.35-15	195/60-15	175/70-15	165-15
C60-15	C70-15	C78-15	6.85-15	205/60-15	185/70-15	175-15
	D70-15	D78-15				
E60-15	E70-15	E78-15	7.35-15	215/60-15	195/70-15	185-15
F60-15	F70-15	F78-15	7.75-15	225/60-15	205/70-15	195-15
G60-15	G70-15	G78-15	8.15-15/8.25-15	235/60-15	215/70-15	205-15
H60-15	H70-15	H78-15	8.45-15/8.55-15	245/60-15	225/70-15	215-15
J60-15	J70-15	J78-15	8.85-15/8.90-15	255/60-15	235/70-15	225-15
	K70-15		9.00-15	265/60-15	245/70-15	230-15
L60-15	L70-15	L78-15, L84-15	9.15-15			235-15
	M70-15	M78-15				255-15
		N78-15				

NOTE: Every size tire is not listed and many size comaprisons are approximate, based on load ratings. Wider tires than those supplied new with the vehicle should always be checked for clearance

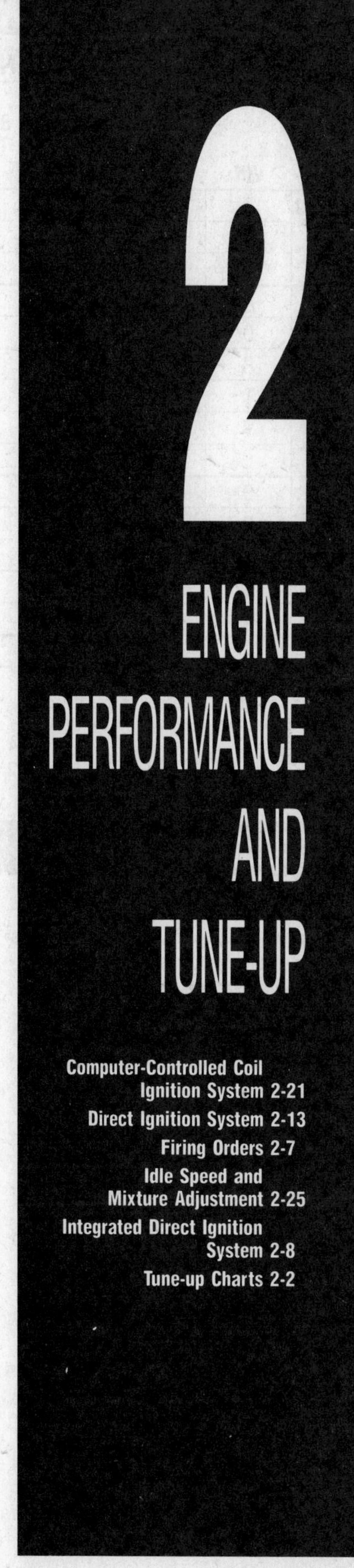
2
ENGINE PERFORMANCE AND TUNE-UP

ENGINE TUNE-UP SPECIFICATIONS

Year	VIN	Engine Displacement (liter)	Spark Plugs Gap (in.)	Ignition Timing (deg.) MT	Ignition Timing (deg.) AT	Fuel Pump (psi)	Idle Speed (rpm) MT	Idle Speed (rpm) AT	Valve Clearance In.	Valve Clearance Ex.
1988-89	R	(2.5)	0.060	①	①	26–32	①	①	Hyd.	Hyd.
	W	(2.8)	0.045	①	①	40–47	①	①	Hyd.	Hyd.
	T	(3.1)	0.045	①	①	40–47	①	①	Hyd.	Hyd.
1990	A	(2.3)	0.035	①	①	40.5–47	①	①	Hyd.	Hyd.
	D	(2.3)	0.035	①	①	40.5–47	①	①	Hyd.	Hyd.
	R	(2.5)	0.060	①	①	26–32	①	①	Hyd.	Hyd.
	T	(3.1)	0.045	①	①	40.5–47	①	①	Hyd.	Hyd.
	V	(3.1)	0.045	①	①	40.5–47	①	①	Hyd.	Hyd.
	L	(3.8)	0.060	①	①	40–47	①	①	Hyd.	Hyd.
1991	D	(2.3)	0.035	①	①	40.5–47	①	①	Hyd.	Hyd.
	R	(2.5)	0.060	①	①	26–32	①	①	Hyd.	Hyd.
	T	(3.1)	0.045	①	①	40.5–47	①	①	Hyd.	Hyd.
	L	(3.8)	0.060	①	①	40–47	①	①	Hyd.	Hyd.
	X	(3.4)	0.045	①	①	41–47	①	①	Hyd.	Hyd.
1992	SEE UNDERHOOD SPECIFICATION STICKER									

Hyd.—Hydraulic
① Ignition timing and idle speed are controlled by the Electronic Control Module. No adjustment is necessary

TUNE-UP PROCEDURES

In order to extract the full measure of performance and economy from your engine it is essential that it is properly tuned at regular intervals. A regular tune-up will keep your vehicle's engine running smoothly and will prevent annoying minor breakdowns and poor performance associated with an untuned engine.

The tune-up should be performed every 30,000 miles (48,300km). This interval should be halved if the vehicle is operated under severe conditions, such as trailer towing, prolonged idling, continual stop and start driving, or if starting or running problems are noticed. It is assumed that the routine maintenance described in Section 1 has been kept up, as this will have a decided effect on the results of a tune-up. All of the applicable steps of a tune-up should be followed in order, as the result is a cumulative one.

If the specifications on the tune-up sticker in the engine compartment disagree with the Tune-Up Specifications chart in this Section, the figures on the sticker must be used. The sticker often reflects changes made during the production run.

Spark Plugs

A typical spark plug consists of a metal shell surrounding a ceramic insulator. A metal electrode extends downward through the center of the insulator and protrudes a small distance. Located at the end of the plug and attached to the side of the outer metal shell is the side electrode. The side electrode bends in at a 90 angle so that its tip is even with, and parallel to, the tip of the center electrode. The distance between these two electrodes (measured in thousandths of an inch) is called the spark plug gap.

The spark plug in no way produces a spark but merely provides a gap across which the current can arc. The coil produces 20,000–40,000 volts or more, which travels from the coils, through the spark plug wires to the spark plugs. The current passes along the center electrode and jumps the gap to the side electrode, and, in so doing, ignites the air/fuel mixture in the combustion chamber.

SPARK PLUG HEAT RANGE

Spark plug heat range is the ability of the plug to dissipate heat. The longer the insulator (or the farther it extends into the engine), the hotter the plug will operate; the shorter the insulator the cooler it will operate. A plug that absorbs little heat and remains too cool will quickly accumulate deposits of oil and carbon since it is not hot enough to burn them off. This leads to plug fouling and consequently to misfiring. A plug that absorbs too much heat will have deposits also, but due to the excessive heat, the electrodes will burn away quickly and in some instances, pre-ignition may result. Preignition takes place when plug tips get so hot that they glow sufficiently to ignite the fuel/air mixture before the actual spark occurs. This early ignition will usually cause pinging during low speeds and heavy loads.

The general rule of thumb for choosing the correct heat range when picking a spark plug is, if most of your driving is long distance, high speed travel, use a colder plug; if most of your driving is stop and go, use a hotter plug. Original equipment plugs are compromise plugs, but most people never have occasion to change their plugs from the factory recommended heat range. The best rule of thumb is to use the factory recommended spark plug.

A set of spark plugs usually requires replacement after about 30,000 miles (48,300km) on cars with electronic ignition, depending on your style of driving. In normal operation, plug gap increases about 0.001 inch (0.0254mm) for every 1,000–2,500 miles (1600–4000km). As the gap increases, the plug's voltage requirement also increases. It requires a greater voltage to jump the wider gap and about two to three times as much voltage to fire a plug at high speeds than at idle.

REMOVAL & INSTALLATION

➧ SEE FIGS. 1–5

➡ To avoid engine damage, do NOT remove spark plugs when the engine is warm; the spark plug threads may be stripped if removed on a hot engine. When you're removing spark plugs, you should work on one at a time. Don't start by removing the plug wires all at once, because unless you number them, they may become mixed up. Take a minute before you begin and number the wires with tape. The best location for numbering is near where the wires come out of the cap.

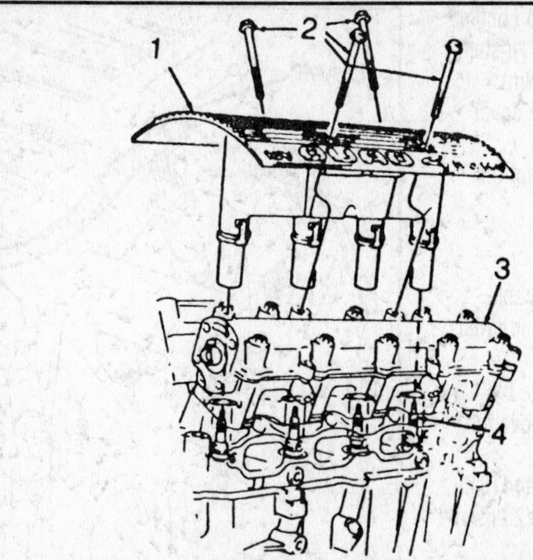

FIG. 1 Remove the entire ignition cover to gain access to the spark plugs — 2.3L engine

2.3L Engine

The spark plugs on this engine are located under the ignition coil and module assembly. To gain access to the spark plugs, the coil and module assembly has to be removed.

1. Disconnect the negative battery cable.
2. Remove the air cleaner assembly.
3. Remove the four ignition cover-to-cylinder head bolts.
4. If the spark plug boot sticks, use a spark plug connector removing tool J-36011 or equivalent to remove with a twisting motion.
5. Remove the ignition cover and set aside.
6. Clean any dirt away from the spark plug recess area.
7. Remove the spark plugs with a spark plug socket.

To install:

8. The 2.3L engine uses AC Type FR3LS plugs. Properly gap them to 0.035 in. (0.89mm) prior to installation.
9. Lubricate the threads lightly with penetrating oil and install the four spark plugs. Torque the plugs to 17 ft. lbs. (23 Nm).
10. If removed, install the plug boots and retainers-to-ignition cover.
11. Apply dielectric compound to the plug boot.
12. Install the ignition cover-to-engine while carefully aligning the boots with the spark plug terminals.

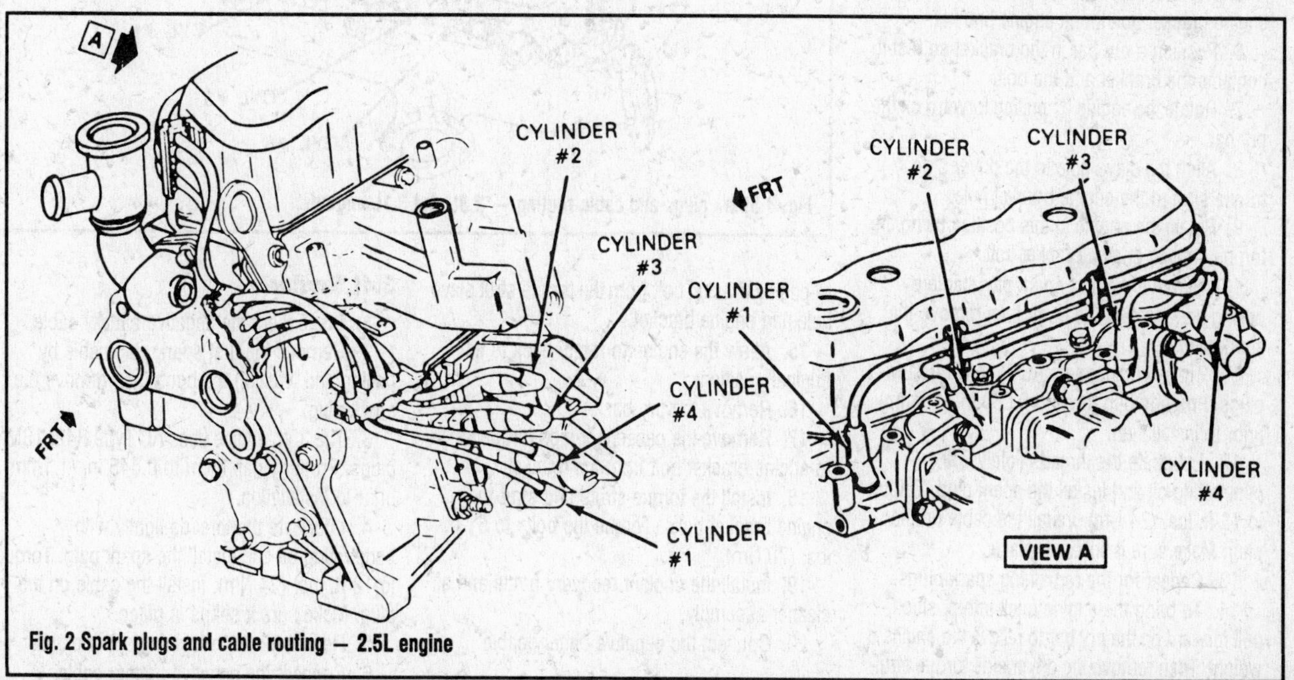

Fig. 2 Spark plugs and cable routing — 2.5L engine

13. Apply thread locking compound Loctite® or equivalent to the ignition cover bolts. Install the bolts and torque to 15 ft. lbs. (20 Nm).
14. If removed, connect the ignition cover electrical connectors.
15. Install the air cleaner and connect the negative battery cable.

2.5L Engine

1. Disconnect the negative battery cable.
2. Remove air cleaner components in order to gain access to the spark plugs.
3. Remove the first spark plug cable by pulling and twisting the boot; then remove the spark plug.
4. The 2.5L engine uses AC Type R44TSX plugs. Properly gap them to 0.080 in. (2.0mm) prior to installation.
5. Lubricate the threads lightly with penetrating oil and install the spark plug. Torque to 20 ft. lbs. (27 Nm). Install the cable on the plug. Make sure it snaps in place.
6. Repeat for the remaining spark plugs.
7. Install the air cleaner components.
8. Connect the negative battery cable.

2.8L and 3.1L Engines

➡ **In order to gain access to the spark plugs, the engine must first be rotated.**

1. Disconnect the negative battery cable.
2. Place the transaxle in Neutral.
3. Remove the air cleaner assembly and coolant recovery bottle.
4. Remove the torque strut-to-engine bracket bolts and swing the torque struts aside.
5. Replace the passenger side torque strut-to-engine bracket bolt in the engine bracket.
6. Position a pry bar in the bracket so that it contacts the bracket and the bolt.
7. Rotate the engine by pulling forward on the pry bar.
8. Align the slave hole in the driver side torque strut to the engine bracket hole.
9. Retain the engine in this position using the torque strut-to-engine bracket bolt.
10. Remove the first spark plug cable by pulling and twisting the boot; then remove the spark plug.
11. These engines use AC Type R44LTSM plugs. Properly gap them to 0.060 in. (1.5mm) prior to installation.
12. Lubricate the threads lightly with penetrating oil and install the spark plug. Torque to 18 ft. lbs. (24 Nm). Install the cable on the plug. Make sure it snaps in place.
13. Repeat for the remaining spark plugs.
14. To bring the engine back into position, pull forward on the pry bar to relieve the engine's weight. Then remove the driver side torque strut-to-engine bracket bolt from the torque strut slave hole and engine bracket.
15. Allow the engine to rotate back to its original position.
16. Remove the pry bar.
17. Remove the passenger side torque strut-to-engine bracket bolt from the bracket.
18. Install the torque struts and strut-to-engine bracket bolts. Torque the bolts to 51 ft. lbs. (70 Nm).
19. Install the coolant recovery bottle and air cleaner assembly.
20. Connect the negative battery cable.

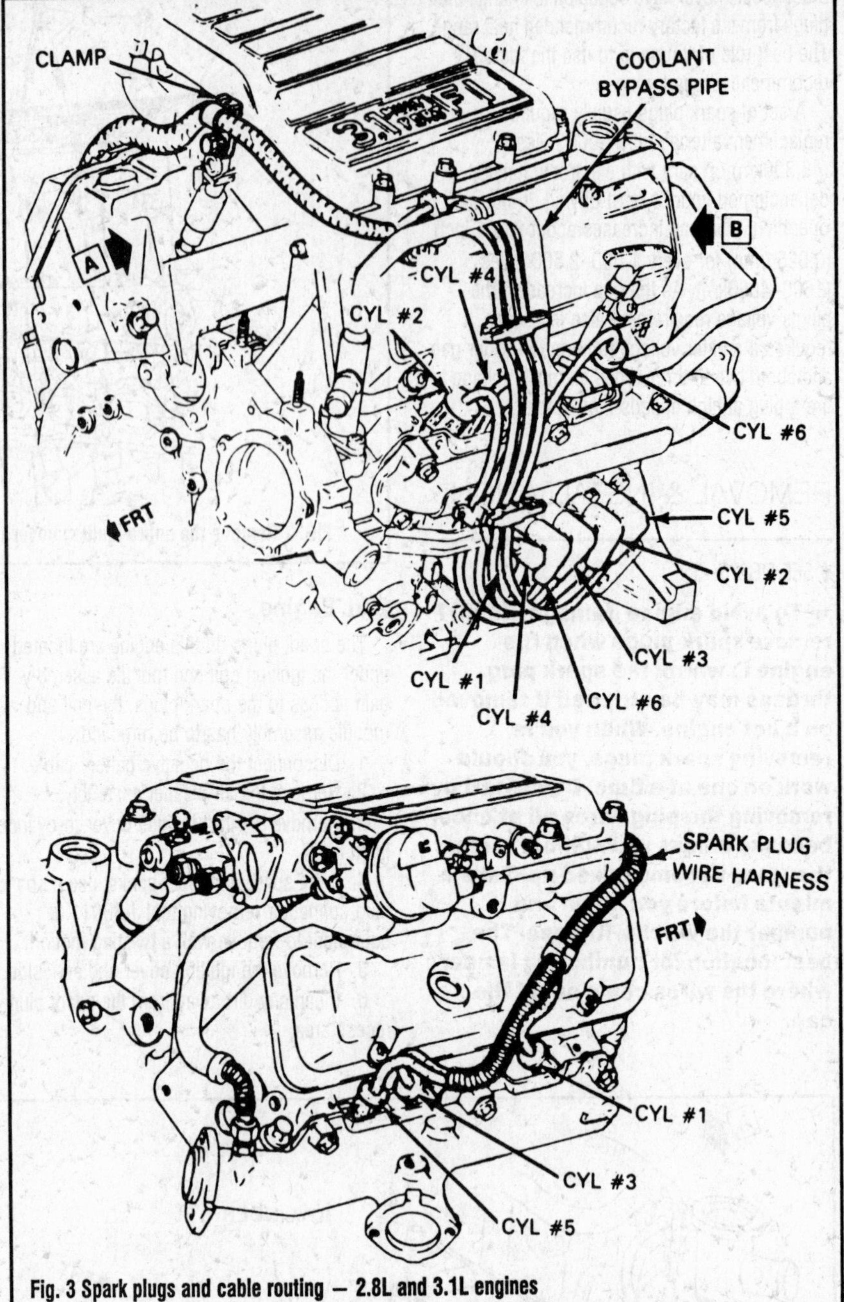

Fig. 3 Spark plugs and cable routing — 2.8L and 3.1L engines

3.4L Engine

1. Disconnect the negative battery cable.
2. Remove the first spark plug cable by pulling and twisting the boot; then remove the spark plug.
3. The 3.4L engine uses AC Type R42LTSMX plugs. Properly gap them to 0.045 in. (1.1mm) prior to installation.
4. Lubricate the threads lightly with penetrating oil and install the spark plug. Torque to 18 ft. lbs. (24 Nm). Install the cable on the plug. Make sure it snaps in place.
5. Repeat for the remaining spark plugs.
6. Connect the negative battery cable.

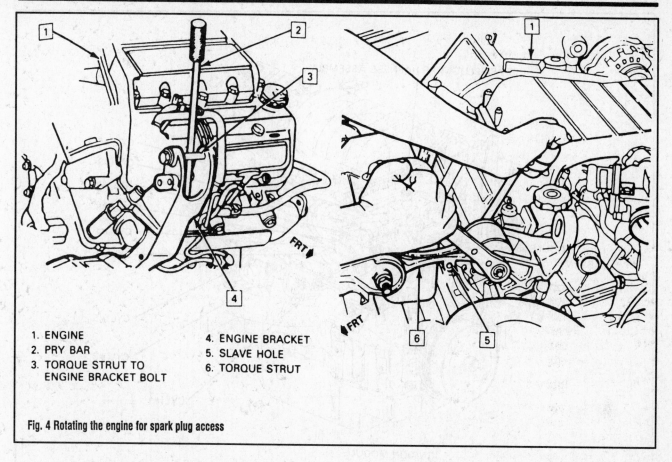

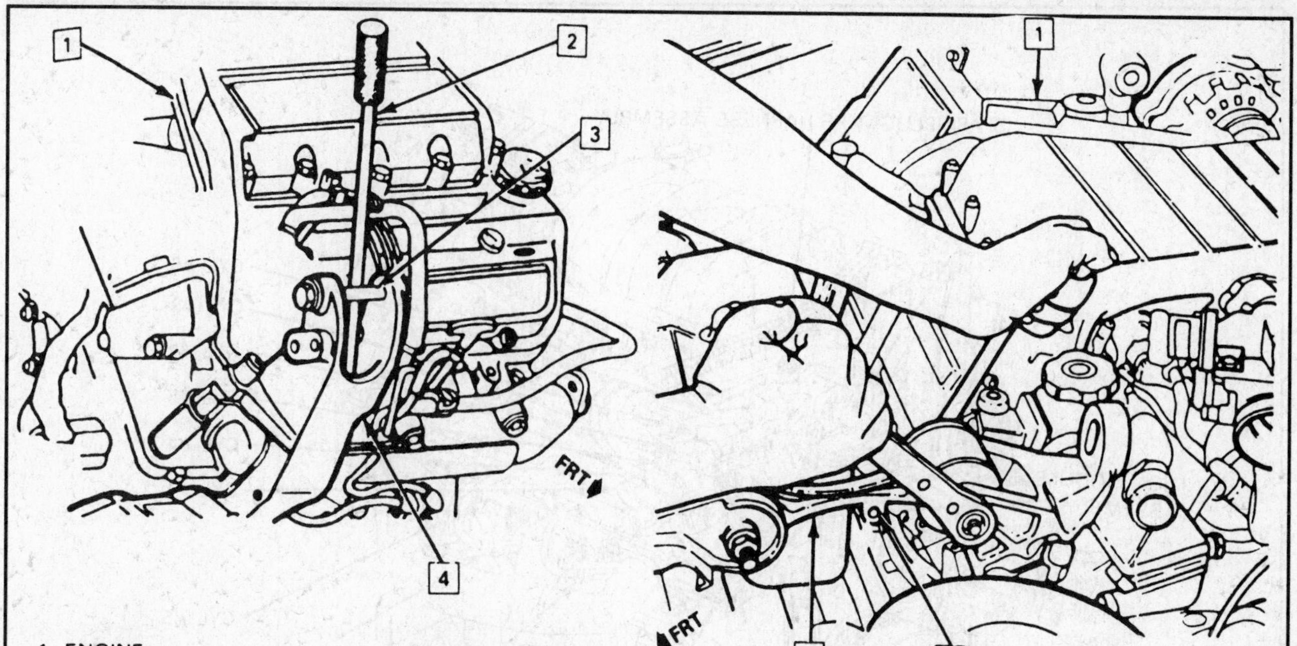

1. ENGINE
2. PRY BAR
3. TORQUE STRUT TO ENGINE BRACKET BOLT
4. ENGINE BRACKET
5. SLAVE HOLE
6. TORQUE STRUT

Fig. 4 Rotating the engine for spark plug access

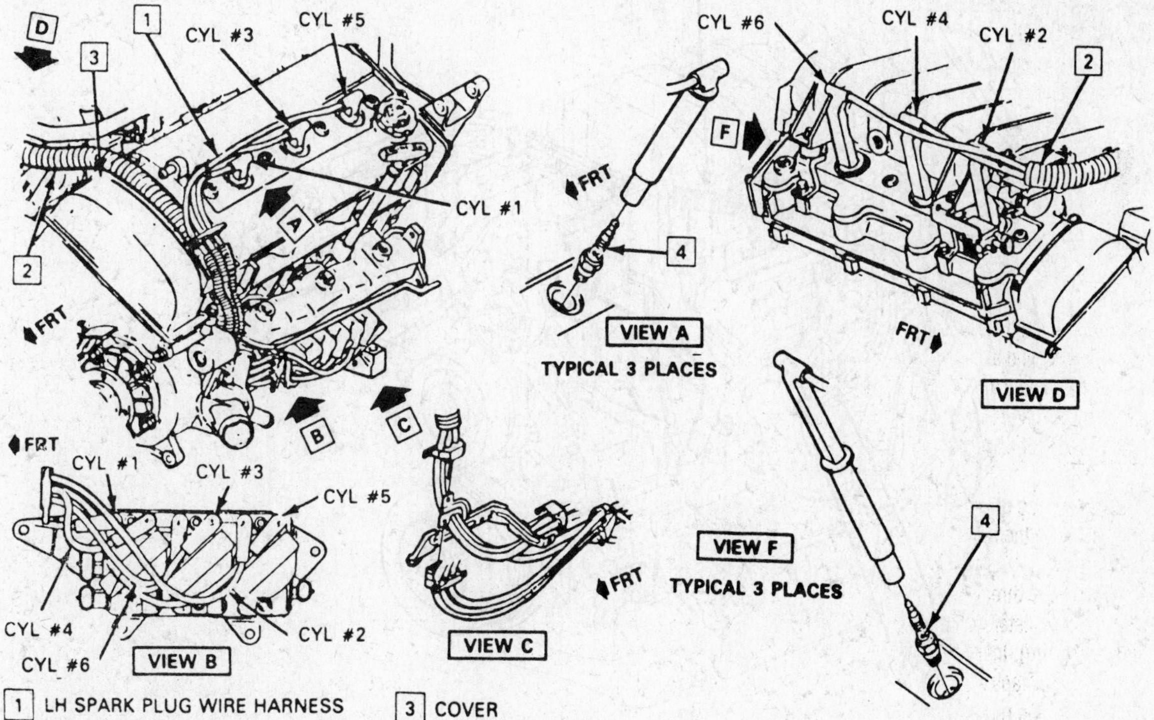

1 LH SPARK PLUG WIRE HARNESS
2 RH SPARK PLUG WIRE HARNESS
3 COVER
4 SPARK PLUG

Fig. 5 Spark plugs and cable routing — 3.4L engine

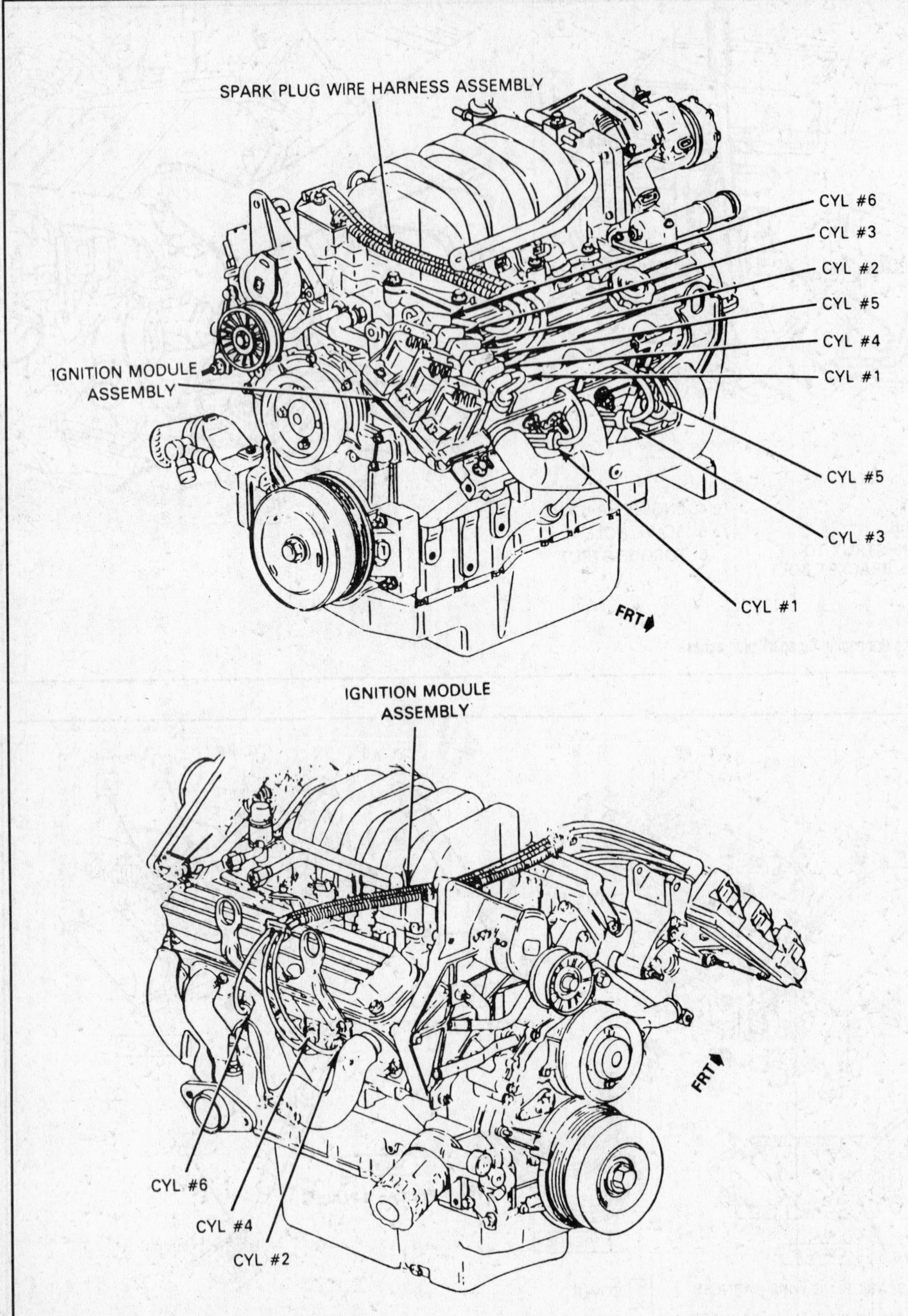

Fig. 6 Spark plugs and cable routing with heat shield shown — 3.8L engine

3.8L Engine

1. Disconnect the negative battery cable.
2. Use a small prying tool to remove the heat shields on the rear cylinders.
3. Remove the first spark plug cable by twisting the boot half a turn, then pulling up. Then remove the spark plug.
4. The 3.8L engine uses AC Type R44LTS6 plugs. Properly gap them to 0.060 in. (1.5mm) prior to installation.
5. Lubricate the threads lightly with penetrating oil and install the spark plug. Torque to 20 ft. lbs. (27 Nm). Install the cable to the plug and snap it in place.
6. When installing the heat shields, make sure they are seated against the bump stop and the lower tabs extend over the spark plug's hex.
7. Repeat for the remaining spark plugs.
8. Connect the negative battery cable.

CHECKING AND REPLACING SPARK PLUG CABLES

Your vehicle is equipped with an electronic ignition system which utilizes 8mm wires to conduct the hotter spark produced (except 2.3L QUAD 4). The boots on these wires are designed to cover the spark plug cavities on the cylinder head. The 2.3L QUAD 4 doesn't use spark plug wires. The coil assembly is connected directly to the spark plug with rubber connectors.

Visually inspect the spark plug cables for burns, cuts, or breaks in the insulation. Check the spark plug boots and the nipples on the distributor cap and coil. Replace any damaged wiring. If no physical damage is obvious, the wires can be checked with an ohmmeter for excessive resistance or an open. The resistance specification is 30,000 ohms or less. Always coat the terminals of any wire removed or replaced with a thin layer of dielectric compound.

When installing a new set of spark plug cables, replace the cables one at a time so there will be no mix-up. Start by replacing the longest cable first. Install the boot firmly over the spark plug. Route the wire exactly the same as the original, through all convolute tubing and clamped in all holders. Make sure ends snap into place. Repeat the process for each cable.

FIRING ORDERS

➧ SEE FIGS. 7–10

➡ **To avoid confusion, label, remove, and replace spark plug cables one at a time.**

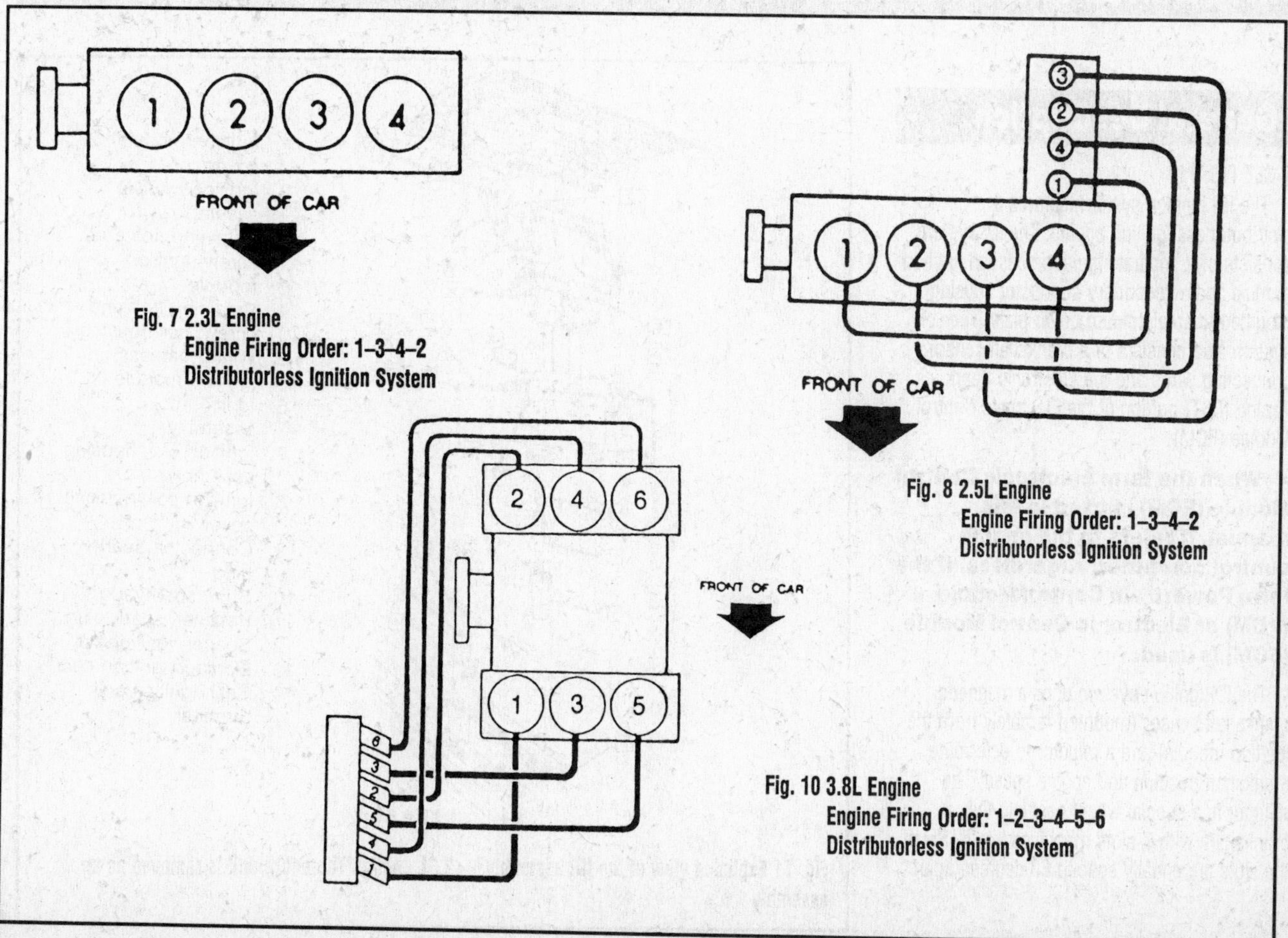

Fig. 7 2.3L Engine
Engine Firing Order: 1–3–4–2
Distributorless Ignition System

Fig. 8 2.5L Engine
Engine Firing Order: 1–3–4–2
Distributorless Ignition System

Fig. 10 3.8L Engine
Engine Firing Order: 1–2–3–4–5–6
Distributorless Ignition System

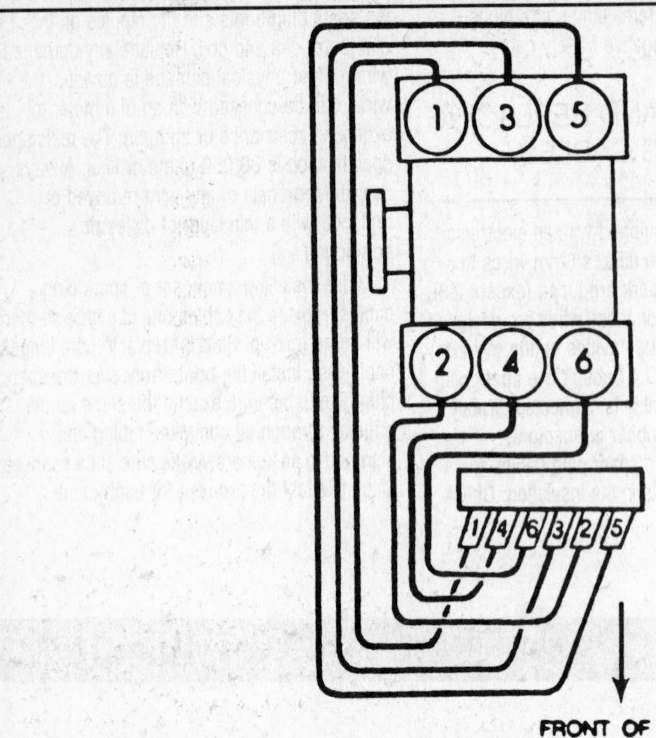

Fig. 9 2.8L, 3.1L and 3.4L Engines Engine Firing Order: 1–2–3–4–5–6 Distributorless Ignition System

INTEGRATED DIRECT IGNITION SYSTEM (IDI) 2.3L QUAD 4 ENGINE

General Description

➧ SEE FIG. 11

The IDI ignition system features a distributorless ignition engine. The IDI system consists of 2 separate ignition coils, an ignition module and a secondary conductor housing mounted to an aluminum cover plate. The system also consists of a crankshaft sensor, connecting wires and the Electronic Spark Timing (EST) portion of the Electronic Control Module (ECM).

➡ When the term Electronic Control Module (ECM) is used in this manual, it refers to the engine control computer; regardless, if the term Powertrain Control Module (PCM) or Electronic Control Module (ECM) is used.

The IDI ignition system uses a magnetic crankshaft sensor (mounted remotely from the ignition module) and a reluctor to determine crankshaft position and engine speed. The reluctor is a special wheel cast into the crankshaft, with 7 slots machined into it. Six of the slots are equally spaced 60 degrees apart

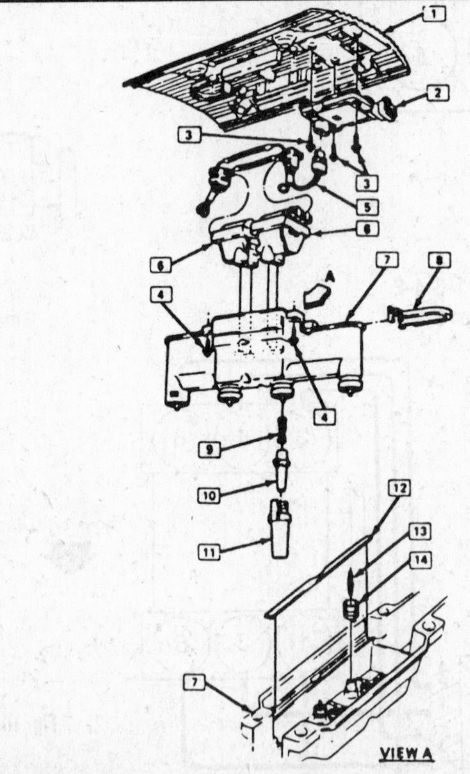

1. Ignition module cover
2. Ignition module assembly
3. Retaining bolt and screw, ignition module
4. Retaining bolt and screw, coil housing
5. Wiring harness, ignition module
6. Ignition coil assembly
7. Ignition coil, housing assembly
8. Ignition coil, housing cover
9. Connector, spark plug
10. Boot, spark plug
11. Retainer, spark plug
12. Spacer, ignition coil
13. Contact, ignition coil
14. Seal, ignition coil terminal

Fig. 11 Exploded view of the IDI assembly — 2.3L engine. The entire unit is removed as an assembly

and the seventh slot is spaced 10 degrees from 1 of the other slots. This seventh slot is used to generate a sync-pulse.

The IDI system uses the same Electronic Spark Timing (EST) circuits as the distributor-type ignition. The ECM uses the EST circuit to control spark advance and ignition dwell, when the ignition system is operating in the EST mode.

To control spark knock and to use maximum spark advance to improve driveability and fuel economy, an Electronic Spark Control (ESC) system is used. This system is consists of a knock sensor and an ESC module (part of Mem-Cal). The ECM monitors the ESC signal to determine when engine detonation occurs.

System Operation

The IDI ignition system uses a waste spark distribution method. Each cylinder is paired with the cylinder opposite it (i.e. 1–4, 2–3). The ends of each coil secondary is attached to a spark plug. These 2 plugs are on companion cylinders, cylinders that are at top dead center at the same time. The one that is on compression is said to be the event cylinder and the one on the exhaust stroke, the waste cylinder. When the coil discharges, both plugs fire at the same time to complete the series circuit.

Since the polarity of the primary and the secondary windings are fixed, one plug always fires in a forward direction and the other in reverse. This is different than a conventional system firing all plugs the same direction each time. Because of the demand for additional energy; the coil design, saturation time and primary current flow are also different. This redesign of the system allows higher energy to be available from the distributorless coils, greater than 40 kilovolts at all rpm ranges.

The IDI ignition system uses a magnetic crankshaft sensor mounted remotely from the ignition module. It protrudes into the block at approximately 0.050 inch of the crankshaft reluctor. As the crankshaft rotates, the slots of the reluctor causes a changing magnetic field at the crankshaft sensor, creating an induce voltage pulse.

The IDI module sends reference signal to the ECM, based on the crankshaft sensor pulses, which are used to determine crankshaft position and engine speed. Reference pulses to the ECM occurs at a rate of 1 per each 180 degrees of crankshaft rotation. This signal is called the 2X reference because it occurs 2 times per crankshaft revolution.

A second reference signal is sent to the ECM which occurs at the same time as the sync-pulse, from the crankshaft sensor. This signal is called the 1X reference because it occurs 1 time per crankshaft revolution.

By comparing the time between the 1X and 2X reference pulses, the ignition module can recognize the sync-pulse (the seventh slot) which starts the calculation of the ignition coil sequencing. The second crank pulse following the sync-pulse signals the ignition module to fire No. 2–3 ignition coil and the fifth crank pulse signals the module to fire the No. 1–4 ignition coil.

During cranking, the ignition module monitors the sync-pulse to begin the ignition firing sequence and below 700 rpm the module controls spark advance by triggering each of the 2 coils at a pre-determined interval based on engine speed only. Above 700 rpm, the ECM controls the spark timing (EST) and compensates for all driving conditions. The ignition module must receive a sync-pulse and then a crank signal in that order to enable the engine to start.

To control EST the ECM uses the following inputs:

- Crankshaft position
- Engine speed (rpm)
- Engine coolant temperature
- Manifold air temperature
- Engine load (manifold pressure or vacuum)

The ESC system is designed to retard spark timing up to 15 degrees to reduce spark knock in the engine. When the knock sensor detects spark knocking in the engine, it sends an A/C voltage signal to the ECM, which increases with the severity of the knock. The ECM then adjusts the EST to reduce spark knock.

SYSTEM COMPONENTS

Crankshaft Sensor

The crankshaft sensor, mounted remotely from the ignition module on an aluminum cover plate, is used determine crankshaft position and engine speed.

Ignition Coil

The ignition coil assemblies are mounted inside the module assembly housing. Each coil distributes the spark for 2 plugs simultaneously.

Electronic Spark Timing (EST)

The EST system is basically the same EST to ECM circuit use on the distributor type ignition systems with EST. This system includes the following circuits:

- Reference circuit — provides the ECM with rpm and crankshaft position information from the IDI module. The IDI module receives this signal from the crank sensor.
- Bypass signal — above 700 rpm, the ECM applies 5 volts to this circuit to switch spark timing control from the IDI module to the ECM.
- EST signal — reference signal is sent to the ECM via the DIS module during cranking. Under 700 rpm, the IDI module controls the ignition timing. Above 700 rpm, the ECM applies 5 volts to the bypass line to switch the timing to the ECM control.
- Reference ground circuit — this wire is grounded through the module and insures that the ground circuit has no voltage drop between the ignition module and the ECM which could affect performance.

ESC Sensor

The ESC sensor, mounted in the engine block near the cylinders, detects abnormal vibration (spark knock) in the engine.

Diagnosis and Testing

SERVICE PRECAUTIONS

➡ To avoid damage to the ECM or other ignition system components, do not use electrical test equipment such as battery or AC powered voltmeter, ohmmeter, etc. or any type of tester other than specified.

- When performing electrical tests on the system, use a high impedance multimeter, digital voltmeter (DVM) J-34029-A or equivalent. Use of a 12 volt test light is not recommended.
- To prevent Electrostatic Discharge damage, when working with the ECM, do not touch the connector pins or soldered components on the circuit board.
- When handling a PROM, CAL-PAK or MEM-CAL, do not touch the component leads. Also, do not remove the integrated circuit from the carrier.
- Never pierce a high tension lead or boot for any testing purpose; otherwise, future problems are guaranteed.
- Leave new components and modules in the shipping package until ready to install them.
- Never disconnect any electrical connection with the ignition switch **ON** unless instructed to do so in a test.

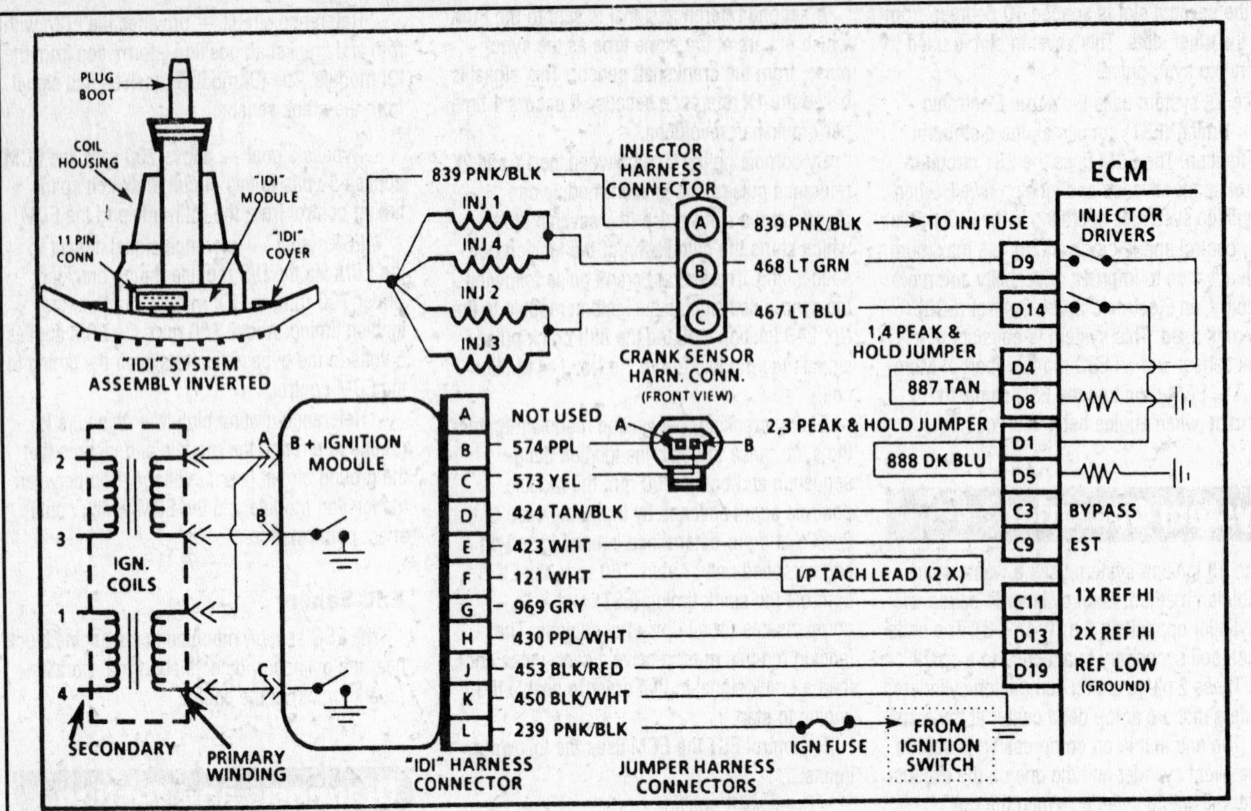

INTEGRATED DIRECT IGNITION (IDI) MISFIRE DIAGNOSIS 2.3L (VIN D) "W" CARLINE (PORT)

Circuit Description:

The "Integrated Direct Ignition" (IDI) system uses a waste spark method of distribution. In this type of system the ignition module triggers the #1-4 coil pair resulting in both #1 and #4 spark plugs firing at the same time. #1 cylinder is on the compression stroke at the same time #4 is on the exhaust stroke, resulting in a lower energy requirement to fire # 4 spark plug. This leaves the remainder of the high voltage to be used to fire #1 spark plug. On this application, the crank sensor is mounted to, and protrudes through the block to within approximately 0.050" of the crankshaft reluctor. Since the reluctor is a machined portion of the crankshaft and the sensor is mounted in a fixed position on the block, timing adjustments are not possible or necessary.

Test Description: Numbers below refer to circled numbers on the diagnostic chart.

1. This checks for equal relative power output between the cylinders. Any injector which when disconnected did not result in an rpm drop approximately equal to the others, is located on the misfiring cylinder.
2. If a plug boot is burned, the other plug on that coil may still fire at idle. This step tests the system's ability to produce at least 25,000 volts at each spark plug.
3. No spark, on one coil, may be caused by an open secondary circuit. Therefore, the coil's secondary resistance should be checked. Resistance readings above 20,000 ohms, but not infinite, will probably not cause a no start but may cause an engine miss under certain conditions.
4. If the no spark condition is caused by coil connections, a coil or a secondary boot assembly, the test light will blink. If the light does not blink, the fault is module connections or the module.
5. Checks for ignition voltage feed to injector and for an open injector driver circuit.
6. An injector driver circuit shorted to ground would result in the test light "ON" steady, and possibly a flooded condition which could damage engine. A shorted injector (less than 2 ohms) could cause incorrect ECM operation.

Diagnostic Aid:

Verify IDI connector terminal "K", CKT 450 resistance to ground is less than .5 ohm.

Fig. 12 Ignition system diagnosis — 2.3L engine

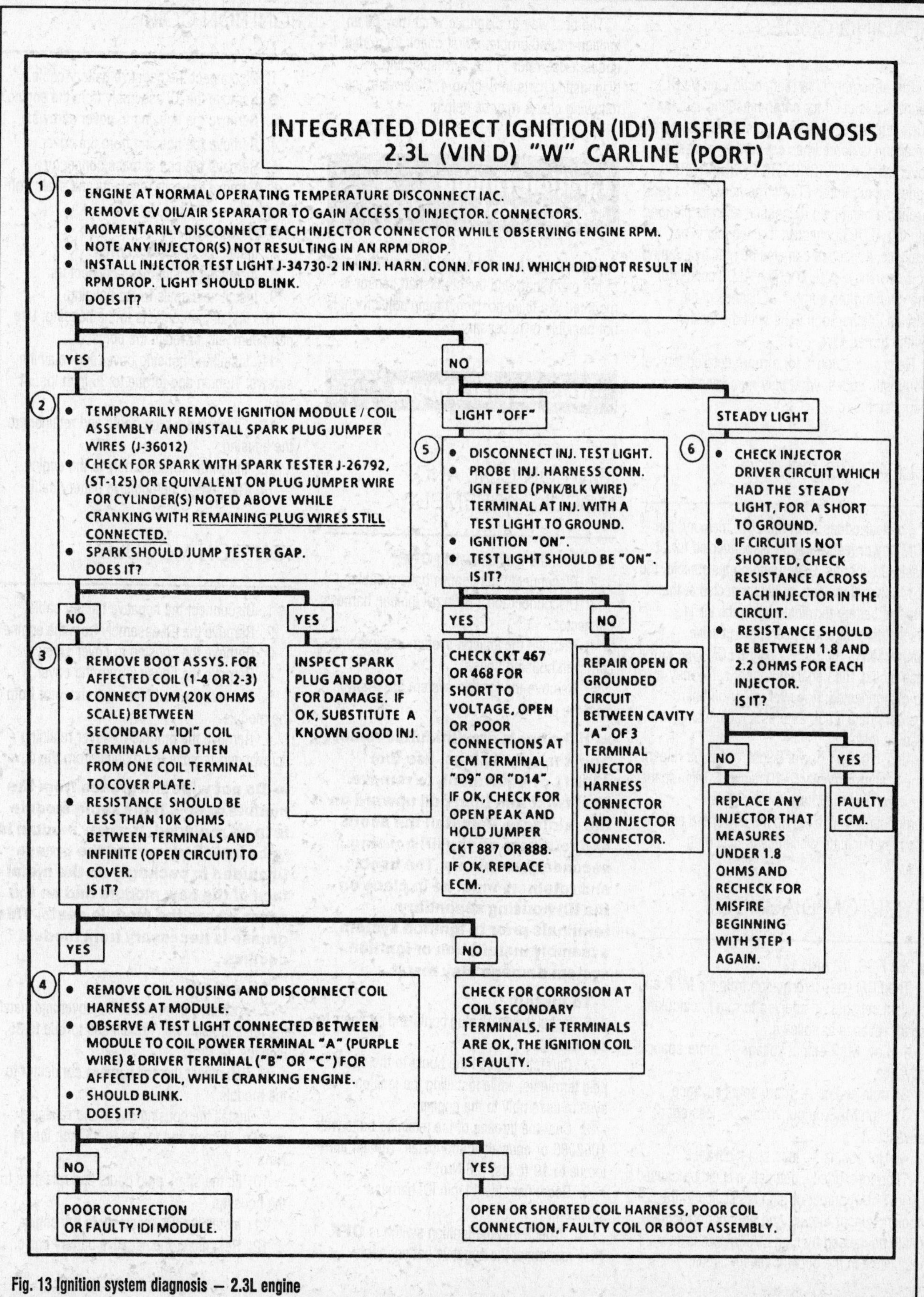

INTEGRATED DIRECT IGNITION (IDI) MISFIRE DIAGNOSIS
2.3L (VIN D) "W" CARLINE (PORT)
1
• ENGINE AT NORMAL OPERATING TEMPERATURE DISCONNECT IAC.
• REMOVE CV OIL/AIR SEPARATOR TO GAIN ACCESS TO INJECTOR. CONNECTORS.
• MOMENTARILY DISCONNECT EACH INJECTOR CONNECTOR WHILE OBSERVING ENGINE RPM.
• NOTE ANY INJECTOR(S) NOT RESULTING IN AN RPM DROP.
• INSTALL INJECTOR TEST LIGHT J-34730-2 IN INJ. HARN. CONN. FOR INJ. WHICH DID NOT RESULT IN RPM DROP. LIGHT SHOULD BLINK.
DOES IT?
YES
NO
2
• TEMPORARILY REMOVE IGNITION MODULE / COIL ASSEMBLY AND INSTALL SPARK PLUG JUMPER WIRES (J-36012)
• CHECK FOR SPARK WITH SPARK TESTER J-26792, (ST-125) OR EQUIVALENT ON PLUG JUMPER WIRE FOR CYLINDER(S) NOTED ABOVE WHILE CRANKING WITH REMAINING PLUG WIRES STILL CONNECTED.
• SPARK SHOULD JUMP TESTER GAP.
DOES IT?
LIGHT "OFF"
5
• DISCONNECT INJ. TEST LIGHT.
• PROBE INJ. HARNESS CONN. IGN FEED (PNK/BLK WIRE) TERMINAL AT INJ. WITH A TEST LIGHT TO GROUND.
• IGNITION "ON".
• TEST LIGHT SHOULD BE "ON".
IS IT?
STEADY LIGHT
6
• CHECK INJECTOR DRIVER CIRCUIT WHICH HAD THE STEADY LIGHT, FOR A SHORT TO GROUND.
• IF CIRCUIT IS NOT SHORTED, CHECK RESISTANCE ACROSS EACH INJECTOR IN THE CIRCUIT.
• RESISTANCE SHOULD BE BETWEEN 1.8 AND 2.2 OHMS FOR EACH INJECTOR.
IS IT?
NO
YES
YES
NO
3
• REMOVE BOOT ASSYS. FOR AFFECTED COIL (1-4 OR 2-3)
• CONNECT DVM (20K OHMS SCALE) BETWEEN SECONDARY "IDI" COIL TERMINALS AND THEN FROM ONE COIL TERMINAL TO COVER PLATE.
• RESISTANCE SHOULD BE LESS THAN 10K OHMS BETWEEN TERMINALS AND INFINITE (OPEN CIRCUIT) TO COVER.
IS IT?
INSPECT SPARK PLUG AND BOOT FOR DAMAGE. IF OK, SUBSTITUTE A KNOWN GOOD INJ.
CHECK CKT 467 OR 468 FOR SHORT TO VOLTAGE, OPEN OR POOR CONNECTIONS AT ECM TERMINAL "D9" OR "D14". IF OK, CHECK FOR OPEN PEAK AND HOLD JUMPER CKT 887 OR 888. IF OK, REPLACE ECM.
REPAIR OPEN OR GROUNDED CIRCUIT BETWEEN CAVITY "A" OF 3 TERMINAL INJECTOR HARNESS CONNECTOR AND INJECTOR CONNECTOR.
NO
YES
REPLACE ANY INJECTOR THAT MEASURES UNDER 1.8 OHMS AND RECHECK FOR MISFIRE BEGINNING WITH STEP 1 AGAIN.
FAULTY ECM.
YES
NO
4
• REMOVE COIL HOUSING AND DISCONNECT COIL HARNESS AT MODULE.
• OBSERVE A TEST LIGHT CONNECTED BETWEEN MODULE TO COIL POWER TERMINAL "A" (PURPLE WIRE) & DRIVER TERMINAL ("B" OR "C") FOR AFFECTED COIL, WHILE CRANKING ENGINE.
• SHOULD BLINK.
DOES IT?
CHECK FOR CORROSION AT COIL SECONDARY TERMINALS. IF TERMINALS ARE OK, THE IGNITION COIL IS FAULTY.
NO
YES
POOR CONNECTION OR FAULTY IDI MODULE.
OPEN OR SHORTED COIL HARNESS, POOR COIL CONNECTION, FAULTY COIL OR BOOT ASSEMBLY.

Fig. 13 Ignition system diagnosis — 2.3L engine

READING CODES

The Assembly Line Diagnostic Link (ALDL) connector is used for communicating with the ECM. It is usually located under the instrument panel and is sometimes covered by a plastic cover labeled "DIAGNOSTIC CONNECTOR." Codes stored in the ECM's memory can be read through a hand held diagnostic scanner plugged into the ALDL connector. If a scanner is not available, the codes can also be read by jumping from terminals **A** to **B** of the ALDL connector and counting the number of flashes of the Service Engine Soon light, with the ignition switch turned **ON**.

Refer to Section 4 for a more detailed look at diagnostic codes, what they mean and how to diagnose them.

CLEARING CODES

To clear codes from the ECM memory, the ECM power feed must be disconnected for at least 30 seconds. Depending on the vehicle, the ECM power feed can be disconnected at the positive battery terminal pigtail, the inline fuseholder that originates at the positive connection at the battery or the ECM fuse in the fuse block. The negative battery cable may also be disconnected; however, other on-board memory data, such as preset radio tuning, will also be lost.

Also, if battery power is lost, computer relearn time is approximately 5–10 minutes. This means the computer may have to re-calibrate components which set up the idle speed and the idle may fluctuate while this is occurring.

SYMPTOM DIAGNOSIS

➧ SEE FIGS. 12 AND 13

The ECM uses information from the MAP and coolant sensors, in addition to rpm to calculate spark advance as follows:

1. Low MAP output voltage — more spark advance
2. Cold engine — more spark advance
3. High MAP output voltage — less spark advance
4. Hot engine — less spark advance

Therefore, briefly, detonation could be caused by low MAP output or high resistance in the coolant sensor circuit. And poor performance could be caused by high MAP output or low resistance in the coolant sensor circuit.

The best way to diagnose what may be an ignition-related problem, first check for codes. If codes, exist, refer to the corresponding diagnostic charts in Section 4. Otherwise, the following charts may be helpful.

Ignition Timing Adjustment

Because the reluctor wheel is an integral part of the crankshaft and the crankshaft sensor is mounted in a fixed position, timing adjustment is not possible or necessary.

Parts Replacement

IGNITION COIL AND MODULE ASSEMBLY

1. Turn the ignition switch **OFF**.
2. Disconnect the negative battery cable.
3. Disconnect the 11-pin IDI ignition harness connector.
4. Remove the ignition system assembly-to-camshaft housing bolts.
5. Remove the ignition system assembly from the engine.

➡ If the boots are difficult to remove from the spark plugs, use tool J36011 or equivalent, to remove. First twist and then pull upward on the retainers. Reinstall the boots and retainers on the IDI housing secondary terminals. The boots and retainers must be in place on the IDI housing secondary terminals prior to ignition system assembly installation or ignition system damage may result.

To install:

6. Install the spark plug boots and retainers to the housing.
7. Carefully aligned the boots to the spark plug terminals, while installing the ignition system assembly to the engine.
8. Coat the threads of the retaining bolts with 1052080 or equivalent and install. Tighten and torque to 19 ft. lbs. (26 Nm).
9. Reconnect the 11-pin IDI harness connector.
10. Check that the ignition switch is **OFF**. Then reconnect the negative battery cable.

IGNITION COIL

1. Disconnect the negative battery cable.
2. Remove the IDI assembly from the engine.
3. Remove the housing to cover screws.
4. Remove the housing from the cover.
5. Remove the coil harness connector.
6. Remove the coils, contacts and seals from the cover.

To install:

7. Install the coil to the cover.
8. Install the coil harness connectors.
9. Install new seals to the housing.
10. Install the contacts to the housing. Use petroleum jelly to retain the contacts.
11. Install the housing cover and retaining screws. Tighten and torque to 35 inch lbs. (4 Nm).
12. Fit the spark plug boots and retainers to the housing.
13. Install the IDI assembly to the engine.
14. Reconnect the negative battery cable.

IGNITION MODULE

1. Disconnect the negative battery cable.
2. Remove the IDI assembly from the engine.
3. Remove the housing to cover screws.
4. Remove the housing from the cover.
5. Remove the coil harness connector from the module.
6. Remove the module-to-cover retaining screws and remove the module from the cover.

➡ Do not wipe the grease from the module or coil, if the same module is to be replaced. If a new module is to be installed, spread the grease (included in package) on the metal face of the new module and on the cover where the module seats. This grease is necessary from module cooling.

To install:

7. Position the module to the cover and install the retaining screws. Tighten and torque to 35 inch lbs. (4 Nm).
8. Reconnect the coil harness connector to the module.
9. Install the housing cover and retaining screws. Tighten and torque to 35 inch lbs. (4 Nm).
10. Fit the spark plug boots and retainers to the housing.
11. Install the IDI assembly to the engine.
12. Reconnect the negative battery cable.

CRANKSHAFT SENSOR

SEE FIG. 14

1. Disconnect the negative battery cable.
2. Disconnect the sensor harness connector at the sensor.
3. Remove the sensor retaining bolts and pull the sensor from the engine.

To install:

4. Fit a new O-ring to the sensor and lubricate with engine oil. Install the sensor into the engine.
5. Install the sensor retaining bolt. Tighten and torque to 88 inch lbs. (10 Nm).
6. Reconnect the sensor harness connector.
7. Reconnect the negative battery cable.

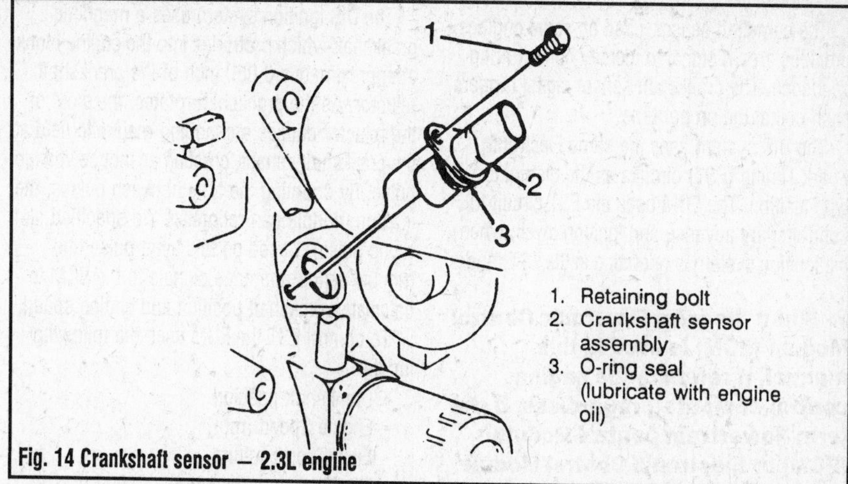

Fig. 14 Crankshaft sensor — 2.3L engine

ELECTRONIC CONTROL MODULE (ECM) OR MEM-CAL

1. Turn the ignition switch **OFF**.
2. Disconnect the negative battery cable.
3. Remove the right side hush panel.
4. Disconnect the harness connectors from the ECM.
5. Remove the ECM-to-bracket retaining screws and remove the ECM.

Before replacement of a defective ECM/PCM first check the resistance of each ECM controlled solenoid. This can be done at the ECM connector, using an ohmmeter and the ECM connector wiring diagram. Any ECM controlled device with low resistance will damage the replacement ECM due to high current flow through the ECM internal circuits.

6. If replacement of the Mem-Cal is required, remove the access cover retaining screws and cover from the ECM. Note the position of the Mem-Cal for proper installation in the new ECM. Using 2 fingers, carefully push both retaining clips back away from the Mem-Cal. At the same time, grasp it at both ends and lift it up out of the socket. Do not remove the cover of the Mem-Cal.

To install:

7. Fit the replacement Mem-Cal into the socket.

The small notches in the Mem-Cal must be aligned with the small notches in the socket. Press only on the ends of the Mem-Cal until the retaining clips snap into the ends of the Mem-Cal. Do not press on the middle of the Mem-Cal, only the ends.

8. Install the access cover and retaining screws.
9. Position the ECM in the vehicle and install the ECM-to-bracket retaining screws.
10. Reconnect the ECM harness connectors.
11. Install the hush panel.
12. Check that the ignition switch is **OFF**. Then reconnect the negative battery cable.

Functional Check

1. Turn the ignition switch **ON**.
2. Enter diagnostics.
   a. Allow Code 12 to flash 4 times to verify no other codes are present. This indicates the Mem-Cal is installed properly and the ECM is functioning.
   b. If trouble Codes 42, 43 or 51 occur, or if the Service Engine Soon light is ON constantly with no codes, the Mem-Cal is not fully seated or is defective.
   c. If it is not fully seated, press firmly on the ends of the Mem-Cal.

ESC KNOCK SENSOR

1. Disconnect the negative battery cable.
2. Raise and support the vehicle safely.
3. Disconnect the harness connector from the knock sensor.
4. Remove the sensor from the engine block.

To install:

5. Clean the threads on the engine block, where the sensor was installed. Install the sensor. Tighten to 11–16 ft. lbs. (15–22 Nm).
6. Reconnect the harness connector to the knock sensor.
7. Lower the vehicle.
8. Reconnect the negative battery cable.

DIRECT IGNITION SYSTEM (DIS) 2.5L, 2.8L, 3.1L AND 3.4L ENGINES

General Description

The DIS ignition system features a distributorless ignition engine. The DIS system consists of 2 separate ignition coils on the 2.5L engines or 3 separate coils on the V6 engines, a DIS ignition module, a crankshaft sensor, crankshaft reluctor ring, connecting wires and the Electronic Spark Timing (EST) portion of the Electronic Control Module (ECM). A camshaft sensor may also be incorporated on some engines.

The DIS ignition system uses a magnetic crankshaft sensor and a reluctor to determine crankshaft position and engine speed. The reluctor is a special wheel cast into the crankshaft with several machined slots. A specific slot, on the reluctor wheel, is used to generate a sync-pulse.

The camshaft sensor, used on some engines, provides a cam signal to identify correct firing sequence. The crankshaft sensor signal triggers each coil at the proper time.

The DIS system uses the same Electronic Spark Timing (EST) circuits as the distributor-type ignition. The ECM uses the EST circuit to control spark advance and ignition dwell, when the ignition system is operating in the EST mode.

➡ **When the term Electronic Control Module (ECM) is used in this manual, it refers to the engine control computer; regardless, if the term Powertrain Control Module (PCM) or Electronic Control Module (ECM) is used.**

To control spark knock and to use maximum spark advance to improve driveability and fuel economy, an Electronic Spark Control (ESC) system is used on some engines. This system is consists of a knock sensor and an ESC module (part of the Mem-Cal). The ECM monitors the ESC signal to determine when engine detonation occurs.

System Operation

The DIS ignition system uses a waste spark distribution method. Each cylinder is paired with the cylinder opposite it (i.e. 1–4, 2–3 on a 4-cylinder engine or 1–4, 2–5, 3–6 on the V6 engines.) The ends of each coil secondary is attached to a spark plug. These 2 plugs are on companion cylinders, cylinders that are at top dead center at the same time. The one that is on compression is said to be the event cylinder and the one on the exhaust stroke, the waste cylinder. When the coil discharges, both plugs fire at the same time to complete the series circuit.

Since the polarity of the primary and the secondary windings are fixed, one plug always fires in a forward direction and the other in reverse. This is different than a conventional system firing all plugs the same direction each time. Because of the demand for additional energy; the coil design, saturation time and primary current flow are also different. This redesign of the system allows higher energy to be available from the distributorless coils, greater than 40 kilovolts at all rpm ranges.

The DIS ignition system uses a magnetic crankshaft which protrudes into the engine block at approximately 0.050 inch of the crankshaft reluctor. As the crankshaft rotates, the slots of the reluctor causes a changing magnetic field at the crankshaft sensor, creating an induce voltage pulse. By counting the time between pulses, the ignition module can recognize the specified slot (sync pulse). Based on this sync pulse, the module sends reference signals to the ECM to calculate crankshaft position and engine speed.

To control EST the ECM uses the following inputs:

- Crankshaft position
- Engine Speed (rpm)
- Engine temperature
- Manifold air temperature
- Atmospheric (barometric) pressure
- Engine load (manifold pressure or vacuum)

The ESC system is designed to retard spark timing up to 10 degrees to reduce spark knock in the engine. When the knock sensor detects spark knocking in the engine, it sends an A/C voltage signal to the ECM, which increases with the severity of the knock. The ECM then adjusts the EST to reduce spark knock.

SYSTEM COMPONENTS

Crankshaft Sensor

The crankshaft sensor is mounted on the bottom of the DIS module on 2.5L engine. The sensor is located toward the bottom of the rear (right side) of the engine block on V6 engines. It is used determine crankshaft position and engine speed.

Ignition Coils

The ignition coil assemblies are mounted on the DIS module on the 2.5L engine. The coils are located on the front of the engine (where the spark plug cables lead) on V6 engines. Each coil distributes the spark for 2 plugs simultaneously.

Electronic Spark Timing (EST)

The EST system is basically the same EST to ECM circuit use on the distributor type ignition systems with EST. This system includes the following circuits:

- DIS reference circuit — provides the ECM with rpm and crankshaft position information from the DIS module. The DIS module receives this signal from the crank sensor.
- Bypass signal — above 400 rpm, the ECM applies 5 volts to this circuit to switch spark timing control from the DIS module to the ECM.
- EST signal — reference signal is sent to the ECM via the DIS module during cranking. Under 400 rpm, the DIS module controls the ignition timing. Above 400 rpm, the ECM applies 5 volts to the bypass line to switch the timing to the ECM control.
- Reference ground circuit — this wire is grounded through the module and insures that the ground circuit has no voltage drop between the ignition module and the ECM which could affect performance.

Diagnosis and Testing

SERVICE PRECAUTIONS

➡ **To avoid damage to the ECM or other ignition system components, do not use electrical test equipment such as battery or AC powered voltmeter, ohmmeter, etc. or any type of tester other than specified.**

- When performing electrical tests on the system, use a high impedance multimeter or quality digital voltmeter (DVM). Use of a 12 volt test light is not recommended.
- To prevent electrostatic discharge damage, when working with the ECM, do not touch the connector pins or soldered components on the circuit board.
- When handling a PROM, CAL-PAK or MEM-CAL, do not touch the component leads. Also, do not remove the integrated circuit from the carrier.
- When performing electrical tests on the system, use a high impedance multimeter, digital voltmeter (DVM) J-34029-A or equivalent.
- Never pierce a high tension lead or boot for any testing purpose; otherwise, future problems are guaranteed.
- Leave new components and modules in the shipping package until ready to install them.
- Never disconnect any electrical connection with the ignition switch **ON** unless instructed to do so in a test.

READING CODES

➧ SEE FIG. 15

The Assembly Line Diagnostic Link (ALDL) connector is used for communicating with the ECM. It is usually located under the instrument panel and is sometimes covered by a plastic cover labeled "DIAGNOSTIC CONNECTOR."

F E D C B A
G M

TERMINAL IDENTIFICATION

A	GROUND	E	SERIAL DATA
B	DIAGNOSTIC TERMINAL	F	TCC (IF USED)
C	A.I.R. (IF USED)	G	FUEL PUMP (IF USED)
D	SERVICE ENGINE SOON LIGHT (IF USED)	M	SERIAL DATA (IF USED)

Fig. 15 ALDL connector terminals

Codes stored in the ECM's memory can be read through a hand held diagnostic scanner plugged into the ALDL connector. If a scanner is not available, the codes can also be read by jumping from terminals **A** to **B** of the ALDL connector and counting the number of flashes of the Service Engine Soon light, with the ignition switch turned **ON**.

Refer to Section 4 for a more detailed look diagnostic codes, what they mean and how to diagnose them.

CLEARING CODES

To clear codes from the ECM memory, the ECM power feed must be disconnected for at least 30 seconds. Depending on the vehicle, the ECM power feed can be disconnected at the positive battery terminal pigtail, the inline fuseholder that originates at the positive connection at the battery or the ECM fuse in the fuse block. The negative battery cable may also be disconnected; however, other on-board memory data, such as preset radio tuning, will also be lost.

Also, if battery power is lost, computer relearn time is approximately 5–10 minutes. This means the computer may have to re-calibrate components which set up the idle speed and the idle may fluctuate while this is occurring. If you own a Tech 1 scan tool or equivalent tool and you are working on 3.1L or 3.4L engine, follow the Idle Learn Procedure at the end of this Section for quicker relearn time.

SYMPTOM DIAGNOSIS

➧ SEE FIGS. 16–19

The ECM uses information from the MAP and coolant sensors, in addition to rpm to calculate spark advance as follows:

1. Low MAP output voltage — more spark advance
2. Cold engine — more spark advance
3. High MAP output voltage — less spark advance
4. Hot engine — less spark advance

Therefore, briefly, detonation could be caused by low MAP output or high resistance in the coolant sensor circuit. And poor performance could be caused by high MAP output or low resistance in the coolant sensor circuit.

The best way to diagnose what may be an ignition-related problem, first check for codes. If codes, exist, refer to the corresponding diagnostic charts in Section 4. Otherwise, the following charts may be helpful.

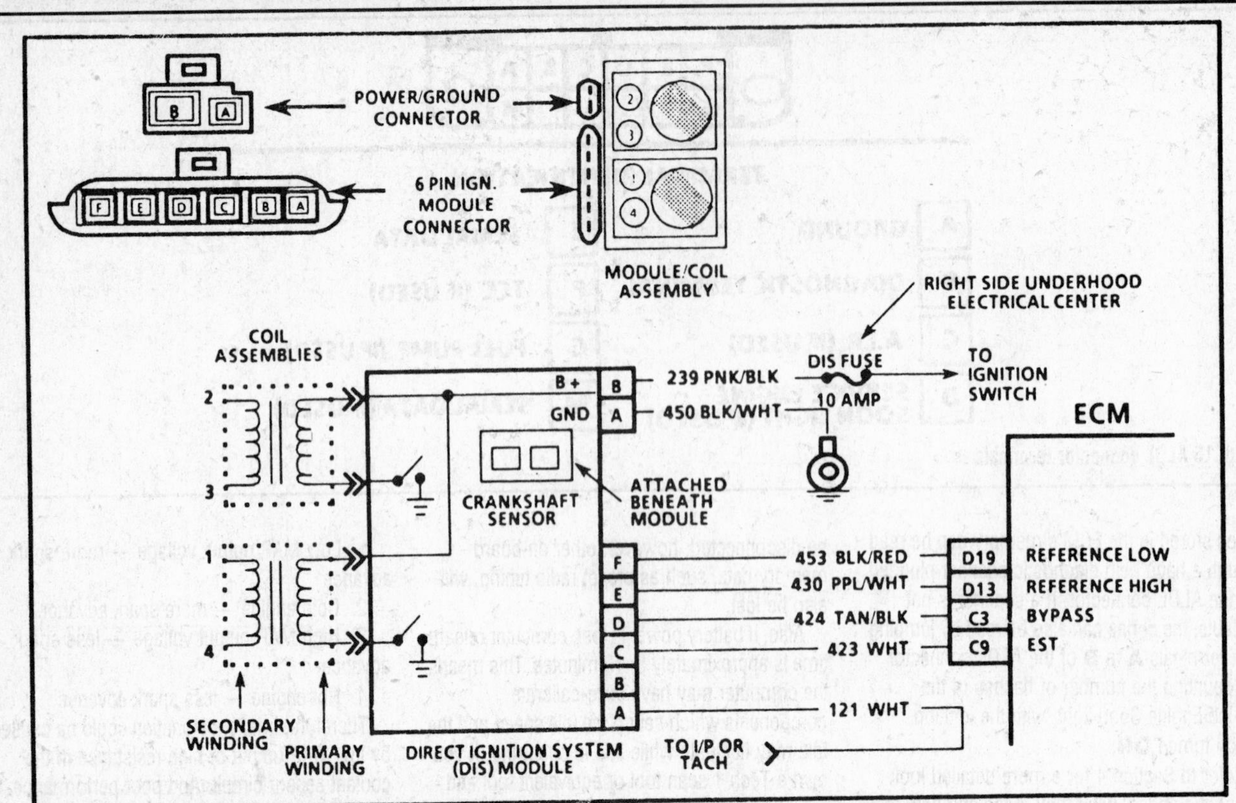

"DIS" MISFIRE UNDER LOAD
2.5L (VIN R) "W" CARLINE (TBI)

Circuit Description:

The Direct Ignition System (DIS) uses a waste spark method of distribution. In this type of system, the ignition module triggers a dual coil, resulting in both connected spark plugs firing at the same time. One cylinder is on its compression stroke at the same time that the other is on the exhaust stroke, resulting in a lower energy requirement to fire the spark plug in the cylinder on its exhaust stroke. This leaves the remainder of the high voltage to be used to fire the spark plug which is in the cylinder on its compression stroke. On this application, the crank sensor is mounted to the bottom of the coil/module assembly and protrudes through the block to within approximately .050" of the crankshaft reluctor. Since the reluctor is a machined portion of the crankshaft and the crank sensor is mounted in a fixed position on the block, timing adjustments are not possible or necessary.

Test Description: Number(s) below refer to circled number(s) on the diagnostic chart.

1. If the "Misfire" complaint exists <u>at idle only</u>, CHART C-4D-1 must be used. Engine rpm should drop approximately equally on all plug leads. A spark tester such as a ST-125 must be used because it is essential to verify adequate available secondary voltage at the spark plug (25,000 volts).
2. If the spark jumps the test gap after grounding the opposite plug wire, it indicates excessive resistance in the plug which was bypassed. A faulty or poor connection at that plug could also result in the miss condition. Also check for carbon deposits inside the spark plug boot.
3. If carbon tracking is evident, replace coil and be sure plug wires relating to that coil are clean and tight. Excessive wire resistance or faulty connections could have caused the coil to be damaged.
4. If the no spark condition follows the suspected coil, that coil is faulty. Otherwise, the ignition module is the cause of no spark. This test could also be performed by substituting a known good coil for the one causing the no spark condition.

Fig. 16 Ignition system diagnosis — 2.5L engine

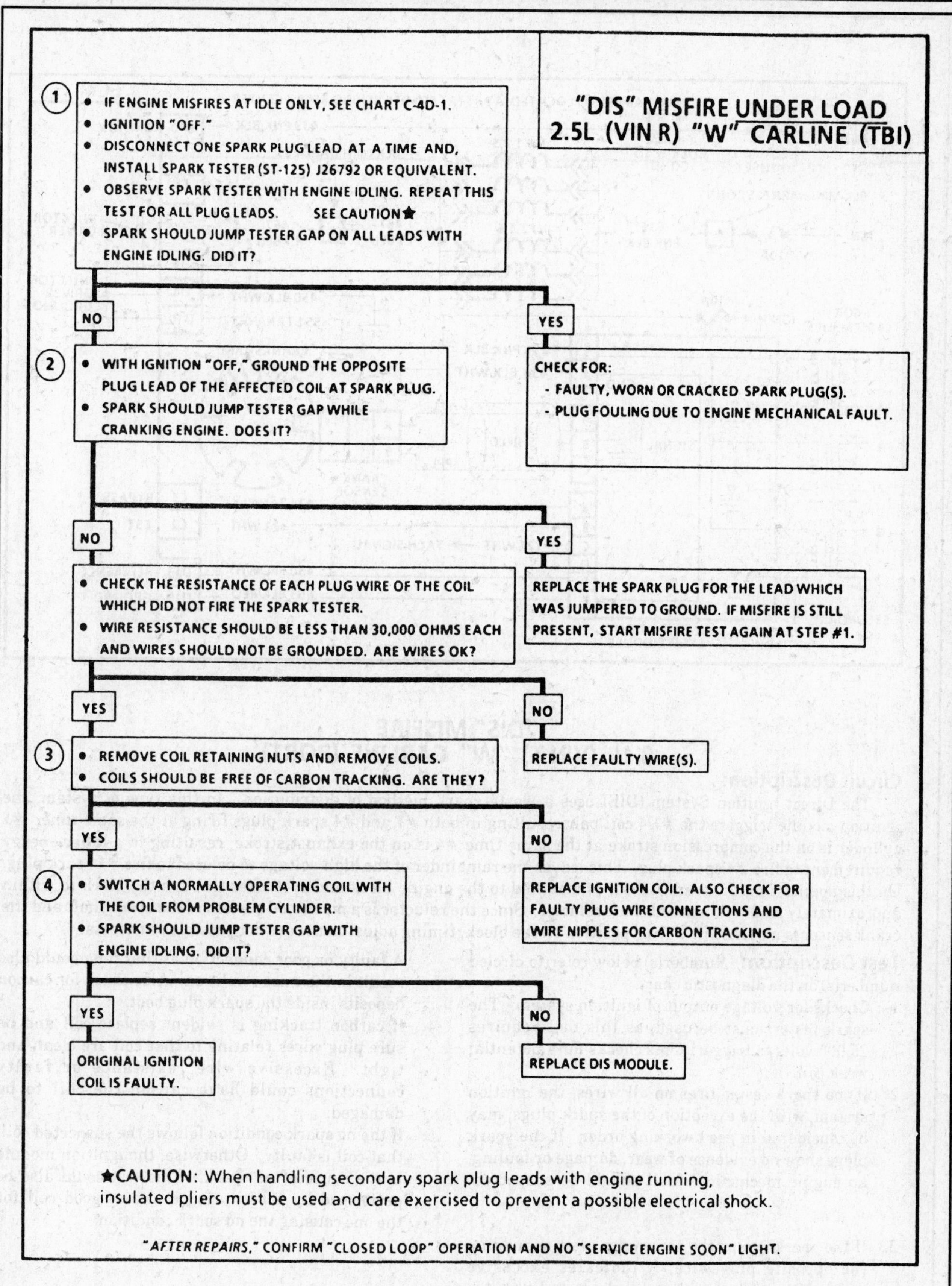

"DIS" MISFIRE UNDER LOAD
2.5L (VIN R) "W" CARLINE (TBI)
1
• IF ENGINE MISFIRES AT IDLE ONLY, SEE CHART C-4D-1.
• IGNITION "OFF."
• DISCONNECT ONE SPARK PLUG LEAD AT A TIME AND, INSTALL SPARK TESTER (ST-125) J26792 OR EQUIVALENT.
• OBSERVE SPARK TESTER WITH ENGINE IDLING. REPEAT THIS TEST FOR ALL PLUG LEADS. SEE CAUTION★
• SPARK SHOULD JUMP TESTER GAP ON ALL LEADS WITH ENGINE IDLING. DID IT?
NO
YES
2
• WITH IGNITION "OFF," GROUND THE OPPOSITE PLUG LEAD OF THE AFFECTED COIL AT SPARK PLUG.
• SPARK SHOULD JUMP TESTER GAP WHILE CRANKING ENGINE. DOES IT?
CHECK FOR:
- FAULTY, WORN OR CRACKED SPARK PLUG(S).
- PLUG FOULING DUE TO ENGINE MECHANICAL FAULT.
NO
YES
• CHECK THE RESISTANCE OF EACH PLUG WIRE OF THE COIL WHICH DID NOT FIRE THE SPARK TESTER.
• WIRE RESISTANCE SHOULD BE LESS THAN 30,000 OHMS EACH AND WIRES SHOULD NOT BE GROUNDED. ARE WIRES OK?
REPLACE THE SPARK PLUG FOR THE LEAD WHICH WAS JUMPERED TO GROUND. IF MISFIRE IS STILL PRESENT, START MISFIRE TEST AGAIN AT STEP #1.
YES
NO
3
• REMOVE COIL RETAINING NUTS AND REMOVE COILS.
• COILS SHOULD BE FREE OF CARBON TRACKING. ARE THEY?
REPLACE FAULTY WIRE(S).
YES
NO
4
• SWITCH A NORMALLY OPERATING COIL WITH THE COIL FROM PROBLEM CYLINDER.
• SPARK SHOULD JUMP TESTER GAP WITH ENGINE IDLING. DID IT?
REPLACE IGNITION COIL. ALSO CHECK FOR FAULTY PLUG WIRE CONNECTIONS AND WIRE NIPPLES FOR CARBON TRACKING.
YES
NO
ORIGINAL IGNITION COIL IS FAULTY.
REPLACE DIS MODULE.
★CAUTION: When handling secondary spark plug leads with engine running, insulated pliers must be used and care exercised to prevent a possible electrical shock.
"AFTER REPAIRS," CONFIRM "CLOSED LOOP" OPERATION AND NO "SERVICE ENGINE SOON" LIGHT.

Fig. 17 Ignition system diagnosis — 2.5L engine

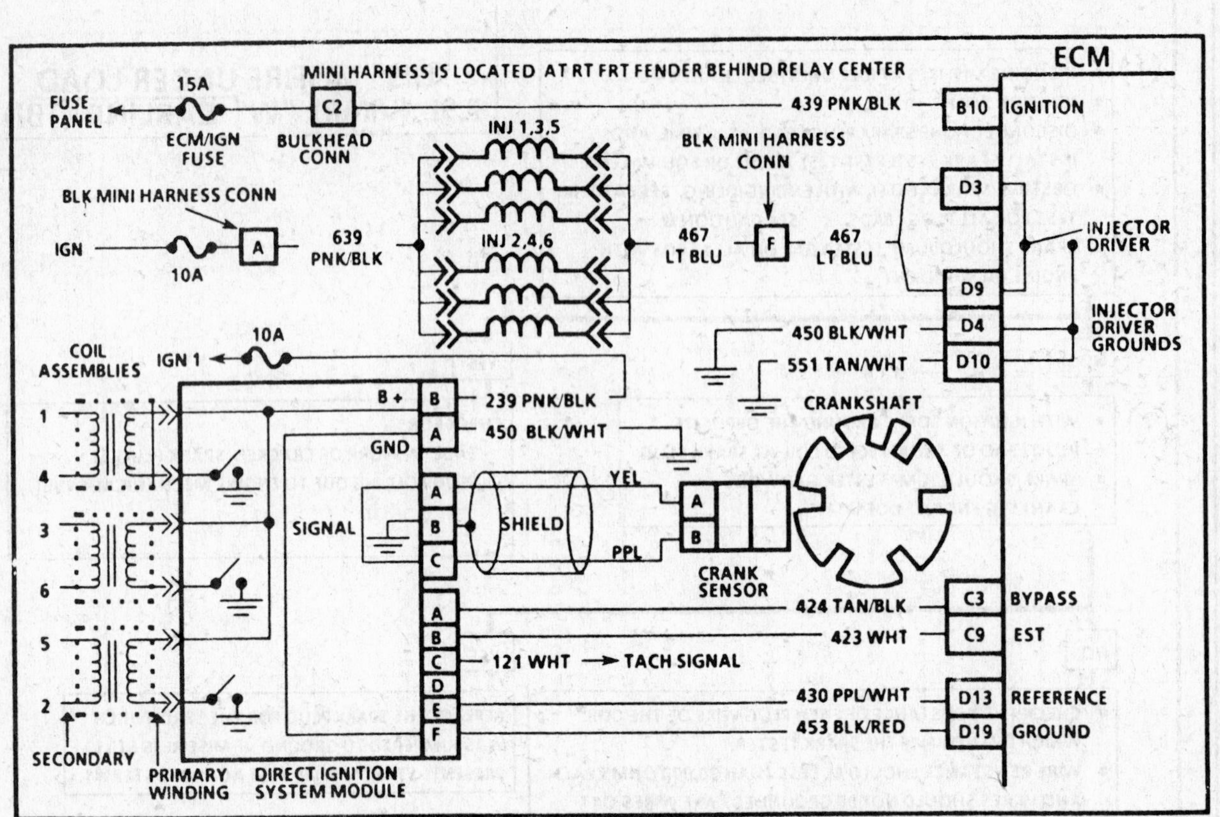

"DIS" MISFIRE
3.1L (VIN T) "W" CARLINE (PORT)

Circuit Description:

The Direct Ignition System (DIS) uses a waste spark method of distribution. In this type of system, the ignition module triggers the #1/4 coil pair resulting in both #1 and #4 spark plugs firing at the same time. #1 cylinder is on the compression stroke at the same time #4 is on the exhaust stroke, resulting in a lower energy requirement to fire #4 spark plug. This leaves the remainder of the high voltage to be used to fire #1 spark plug. On this application, the crank sensor is mounted to the engine block and protrudes through the block to within approximately .050" of the crankshaft reluctor. Since the reluctor is a machined portion of the crankshaft and the crank sensor is mounted in a fixed position on the block, timing adjustments are not possible or necessary.

Test Description: Number(s) below refer to circled number(s) on the diagnostic chart.

1. Checks for voltage output of ignition system. The spark tester must be used, as this tool requires 25,000 volts to trigger. This checks for a potential weak coil.
2. If the spark tester fires on all wires, the ignition system, with the exception of the spark plugs, may be considered in good working order. If the spark plugs show no evidence of wear, damage or fouling, an engine mechanical fault should be suspected.
3. If the spark jumps the tester gap after grounding the opposite plug wire, it indicates excessive resistance in the plug which was bypassed. A faulty or poor connection at that plug could also result in the miss condition. Also check for carbon deposits inside the spark plug boot.
4. If carbon tracking is evident replace coil and be sure plug wires relating to that coil are clean and tight. Excessive wire resistance or faulty connections could have caused the coil to be damaged.
5. If the no spark condition follows the suspected coil, that coil is faulty. Otherwise, the ignition module is the cause of no spark. This test could also be performed by substituting a known good coil for the one causing the no spark condition.

Fig. 18 Ignition system diagnosis — 2.8L, 3.1L and 3.4L engines

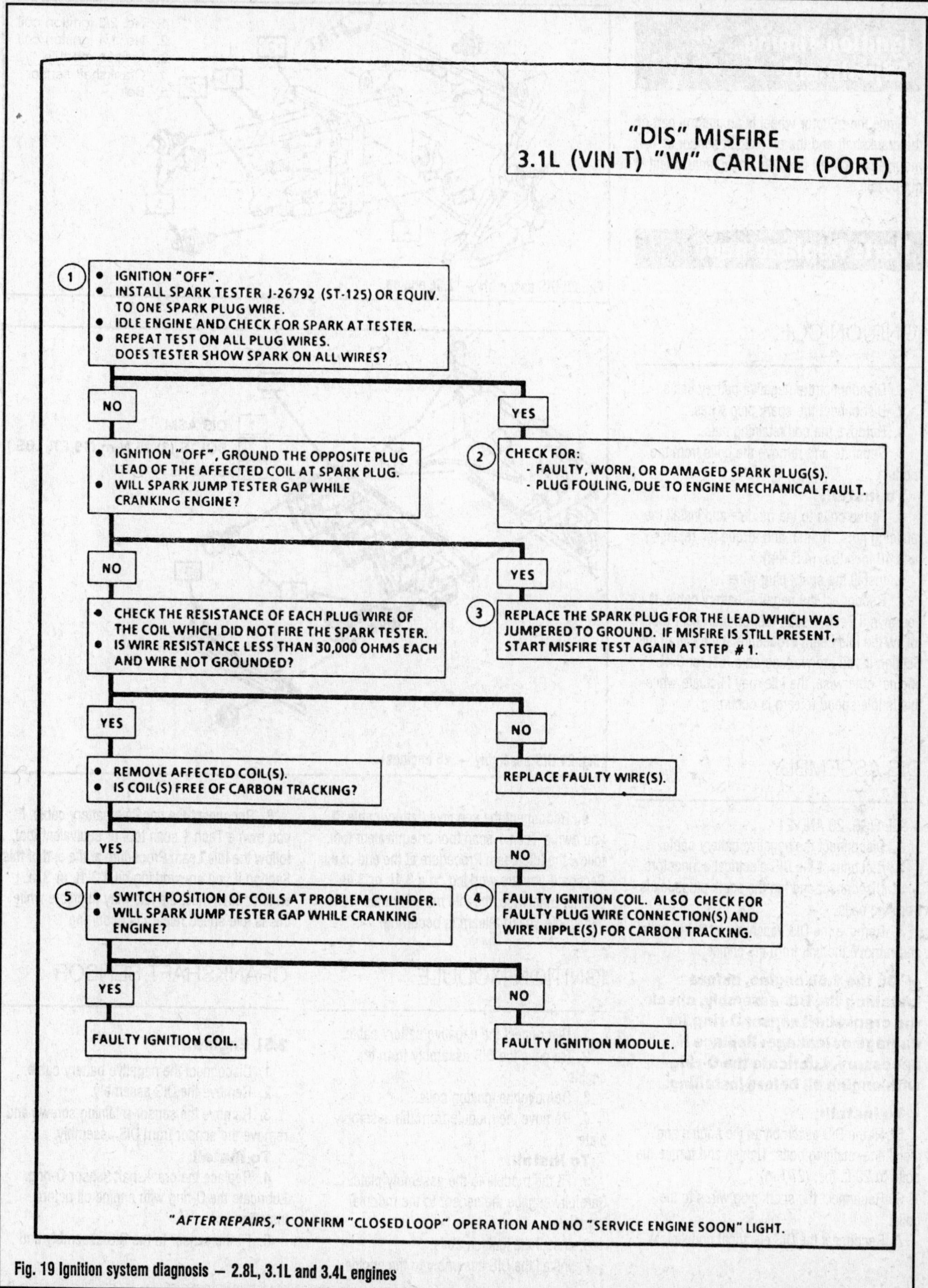
"DIS" MISFIRE
3.1L (VIN T) "W" CARLINE (PORT)
1
• IGNITION "OFF".
• INSTALL SPARK TESTER J-26792 (ST-125) OR EQUIV. TO ONE SPARK PLUG WIRE.
• IDLE ENGINE AND CHECK FOR SPARK AT TESTER.
• REPEAT TEST ON ALL PLUG WIRES.
DOES TESTER SHOW SPARK ON ALL WIRES?
NO
YES
• IGNITION "OFF", GROUND THE OPPOSITE PLUG LEAD OF THE AFFECTED COIL AT SPARK PLUG.
• WILL SPARK JUMP TESTER GAP WHILE CRANKING ENGINE?
2
CHECK FOR:
- FAULTY, WORN, OR DAMAGED SPARK PLUG(S).
- PLUG FOULING, DUE TO ENGINE MECHANICAL FAULT.
NO
YES
• CHECK THE RESISTANCE OF EACH PLUG WIRE OF THE COIL WHICH DID NOT FIRE THE SPARK TESTER.
• IS WIRE RESISTANCE LESS THAN 30,000 OHMS EACH AND WIRE NOT GROUNDED?
3
REPLACE THE SPARK PLUG FOR THE LEAD WHICH WAS JUMPERED TO GROUND. IF MISFIRE IS STILL PRESENT, START MISFIRE TEST AGAIN AT STEP # 1.
YES
NO
• REMOVE AFFECTED COIL(S).
• IS COIL(S) FREE OF CARBON TRACKING?
REPLACE FAULTY WIRE(S).
YES
NO
5
• SWITCH POSITION OF COILS AT PROBLEM CYLINDER.
• WILL SPARK JUMP TESTER GAP WHILE CRANKING ENGINE?
4
FAULTY IGNITION COIL. ALSO CHECK FOR FAULTY PLUG WIRE CONNECTION(S) AND WIRE NIPPLE(S) FOR CARBON TRACKING.
YES
NO
FAULTY IGNITION COIL.
FAULTY IGNITION MODULE.
"AFTER REPAIRS," CONFIRM "CLOSED LOOP" OPERATION AND NO "SERVICE ENGINE SOON" LIGHT.

Fig. 19 Ignition system diagnosis — 2.8L, 3.1L and 3.4L engines

Ignition Timing Adjustment

Since the reluctor wheel is an integral part of the crankshaft and the crankshaft sensor is mounted in a fixed position, timing adjustment is not possible.

Parts Replacement

IGNITION COIL

1. Disconnect the negative battery cable.
2. Disconnect the spark plug wires.
3. Remove the coil retaining nuts.
4. Separate and remove the coils from the module.

To install:

5. Fit the coils to the module and install the retaining nuts. Tighten and torque the retaining nuts 40 inch lbs. (4.5 Nm).
6. Install the spark plug wires.
7. Reconnect the negative battery cable. If you own a Tech 1 scan tool or equivalent tool, follow the Idle Learn Procedure at the end of this Section if you are working on a 3.1L or 3.4L engine; otherwise, the idle may fluctuate while this is idle speed relearn is occurring.

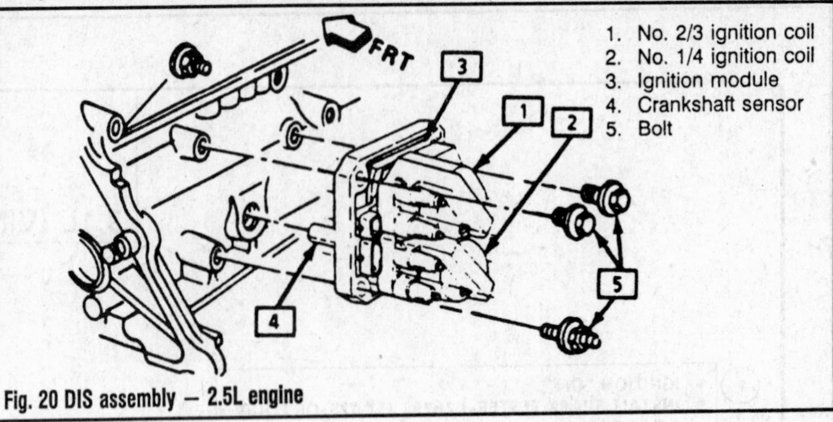

Fig. 20 DIS assembly — 2.5L engine

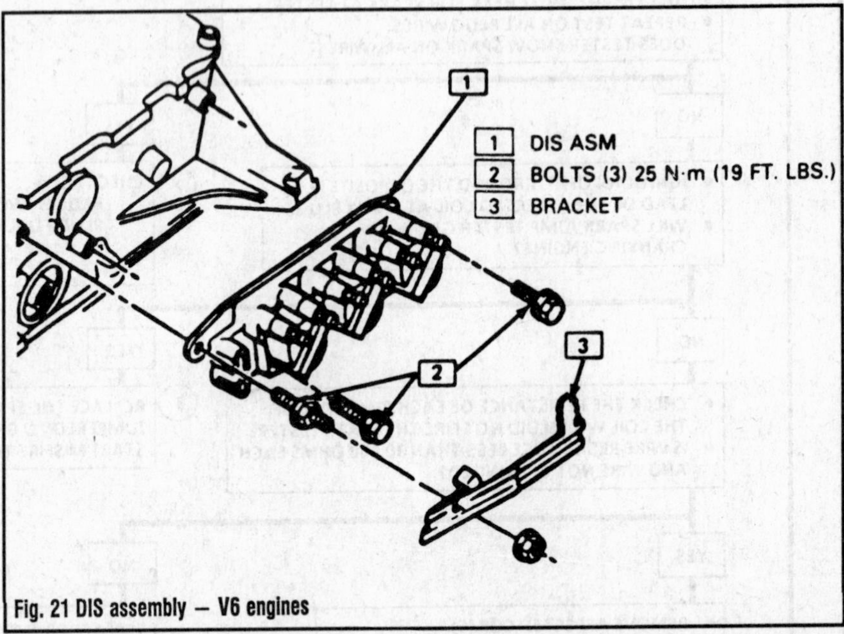

Fig. 21 DIS assembly — V6 engines

DIS ASSEMBLY

➧ SEE FIGS. 20 AND 21

1. Disconnect the negative battery cable.
2. Disconnect the DIS electrical connectors.
3. Disconnect and tag the spark plugs leads from the coils.
4. Remove the DIS assembly retaining bolts and remove the unit from the engine.

➡ On the 2.5L engine, before installing the DIS assembly, check the crankshaft sensor O-ring for damage or leakage. Replace if necessary. Lubricate the O-ring with engine oil before installing.

To install:

5. Fit the DIS assembly to the engine and install the retaining bolts. Tighten and torque the bolts to 20 ft. lbs. (27 Nm).
6. Reconnect the spark plug wires to the coils.
7. Reconnect the DIS electrical connectors.
8. Reconnect the negative battery cable. If you own a Tech 1 scan tool or equivalent tool, follow the Idle Learn Procedure at the end of this Section if you are working on a 3.1L or 3.4L engine; otherwise, the idle may fluctuate while this is idle speed relearn is occurring.

IGNITION MODULE

1. Disconnect the negative battery cable.
2. Remove the DIS assembly from the engine.
3. Remove the ignition coils.
4. Remove the module from the assembly plate.

To install:

5. Fit the module to the assembly plate. Carefully engage the sensor to the module terminals.
6. Install the ignition coils.
7. Install the DIS assembly to the engine.
8. Reconnect the negative battery cable. If you own a Tech 1 scan tool or equivalent tool, follow the Idle Learn Procedure at the end of this Section if you are working on a 3.1L or 3.4L engine; otherwise, the idle may fluctuate while this is idle speed relearn is occurring.

CRANKSHAFT SENSOR

2.5L Engine

1. Disconnect the negative battery cable.
2. Remove the DIS assembly.
3. Remove the sensor retaining screws and remove the sensor from DIS assembly.

To install:

4. Replace the crankshaft sensor O-ring. Lubricate the O-ring with engine oil before installing.
5. Fit the sensor to the DIS assembly and

5. Fit the sensor to the DIS assembly and install the retaining screws. Tighten and torque the retaining screws 20 inch lbs. (2.3 Nm).
6. Install the DIS assembly to the engine.
7. Reconnect the negative battery cable.

V6 Engines

1. Disconnect the negative negative battery cable.
2. Disconnect the sensor electrical connector.
3. Remove the sensor mounting screw and bracket.
4. Remove the sensor from the engine.

To Install:

5. Replace the crankshaft sensor O-ring. Lubricate the O-ring with engine oil and install to the engine.
6. Install the bracket and retaining screw. Torque to 71 inch lbs. (8 Nm).
7. Connect the connector.
8. Connect the negative battery cable. If you own a Tech 1 scan tool or equivalent tool, follow the Idle Learn Procedure at the end of this Section if you are working on a 3.1L or 3.4L engine; otherwise, the idle may fluctuate while this is idle speed relearn is occurring.

ELECTRONIC CONTROL MODULE (ECM) OR PROM

Removal and Installation

1. Turn the ignition switch **OFF**.
2. Disconnect the negative battery cable.
3. Remove the interior access panel.
4. Disconnect the harness connectors from the ECM.
5. Remove the ECM-to-bracket retaining screws and remove the ECM.
6. If PROM replacement is required, remove the access cover retaining screws and cover from the ECM. Carefully remove the PROM carrier assembly from the ECM, using the rocker type PROM removal tool.

To install:

7. Fit the replacement PROM carrier assembly into the PROM socket.

➡ **The small notch of the carrier should be aligned with the small notch in the socket. Press on the PROM carrier until if is firmly seated in the socket. Do not press on the PROM, only the carrier.**

8. Install the access cover and retaining screws.
9. Position the ECM in the vehicle and install the ECM-to-bracket retaining screws.
10. Reconnect the ECM harness connectors.
11. Install the interior access panel.

➡ **Before replacement of a defective ECM/PCM first check the resistance of each ECM controlled solenoid. This can be done at the ECM connector, using an ohmmeter and the ECM connector wiring diagram. Any ECM controlled device with low resistance will damage the replacement ECM due to high current flow through the ECM internal circuits.**

12. Check that the ignition switch is **OFF**. Then, reconnect the negative battery cable. If you own a Tech 1 scan tool or equivalent tool, follow the Idle Learn Procedure at the end of this Section if you are working on a 3.1L or 3.4L engine; otherwise, the idle may fluctuate while this is idle speed relearn is occurring.

COMPUTER CONTROLLED COIL IGNITION (C^3I) SYSTEM 3.8L ENGINE

General Description

The computer controlled coil (C^3I) ignition system features a distributorless ignition engine. The C^3I system consists of 3 ignition coils, a C^3I ignition module, a dual crank sensor, camshaft sensor, connecting wires, and the Electronic Spark Timing (EST) portion of the Electronic Control Module (ECM)/Powertrain Control Module (PCM).

The C^3I system uses the same Electronic Spark Timing (EST) circuits as the distributor-type ignition. The ECM/PCM uses the EST circuit to control spark advance and ignition dwell, when the ignition system is operating in the EST mode. There are 2 modes of ignition system operation. These modes are as follow:

- Module mode — the ignition system operates independently of the ECM/PCM, with module mode spark advance always at 10 degrees BTDC. The ECM/PCM have no control of the ignition system when in this mode.
- EST mode — the ignition spark timing and ignition dwell time is fully controlled by the ECM. EST spark advance and ignition dwell is calculated by the ECM.

To control spark knock, and to use maximum spark advance to improve driveability and fuel economy, an Electronic Spark Control (ESC) system is used. This system is consists of a knock sensor and an ESC module (part of Mem-Cal). The ECM/PCM monitors the ESC signal to determine when engine detonation occurs.

System Operation

The C^3I ignition system uses a waste spark distribution method. Each cylinder is paired with the cylinder opposite it (i.e. 1–4, 2–5, 3–6). The ends of each coil secondary is attached to a spark plug. These 2 plugs are on companion cylinders, cylinders that are at top dead center at the same time. The one that is on compression is said to be the event cylinder and the one on the exhaust stroke, the waste cylinder. When the coil discharges, both plugs fire at the same time to complete the series circuit.

Since the polarity of the primary and the secondary windings are fixed, one plug always fires in a forward direction and the other in reverse. This is different than a conventional system firing all plugs the same direction each time. Because of the demand for additional energy; the coil design, saturation time and primary current flow are also different. This redesign of the system allows higher energy to be available from the distributorless coils, greater than 40 kilovolts at all rpm ranges.

During cranking, when the engine speed is beneath 400 rpm, the C^3I module monitors the dual crank sensor sync signal. The sync signal is used to determine the correct pair of cylinders to be sparked first. Once the sync signal has been processed by the ignition module, it sends a fuel control reference pulse to the ECM/PCM.

During the cranking period, the ECM/PCM will also receive a cam pulse signal and will operate the injectors sequentially, based on true camshaft position only.

➡ **When the term Electronic Control Module (ECM) is used in this manual, it refers to the engine control computer; regardless, if the term Powertrain Control Module (PCM) or Electronic Control Module (ECM) is used.**

The sync signal is used only by the ignition module. It is used for spark synchronization at start-up only.

When the engine speed is beneath 400 rpm (during cranking), the C³I module controls the spark timing. Once the engine speed exceeds 400 rpm (engine running) spark timing is controlled by the EST signal from the ECM. To control EST the ECM/PCM uses the following inputs:

- Crankshaft position
- Engine speed (rpm)
- Engine coolant (Coolant Temperature Sensor — CTS)
- Intake air (Mass Air Flow — MAF)
- Throttle valve position (Throttle Position Sensor — TPS)
- Gear shift lever position (Park/Neutral Switch — P/N)
- Vehicle speed (Vehicle Speed Sensor — VSS)
- ESC signal (Knock Sensor)

The C³I ignition module provides proper ignition coil sequencing during both the module and the EST modes.

The ESC system is designed to retard spark timing up to 10 degrees to reduce spark knock in the engine. When the knock sensor detects spark knocking in the engine, it sends an A/C voltage signal to the ECM, which increases with the severity of the knock. The ECM/PCM then adjusts the EST to reduce spark knock.

SYSTEM COMPONENTS

C³I Module

The C³I module monitors the sync-pulse and the crank signal. During cranking the C³I module monitors the sync-pulse to begin the ignition firing sequence. During this time, each of the 3 coils are fired at a pre-determined interval based on engine speed only. Above 400 rpm, the C³I module is only use as a reference signal.

Ignition Coil

The ignition coil assemblies are mounted on the C³I module. Each coil distributes the spark for 2 plugs simultaneously.

Electronic Spark Control (ESC)

The ESC system incorporates a knock sensor and the ECM. The knock sensor detects engine detonation. When engine detonation occurs, the ECM receives the ESC signal and retards EST to reduce detonation.

Electronic Spark Timing (EST)

The EST system is basically the same EST to ECM circuit use on the distributor type ignition systems with EST. This system includes the following circuits:

- Reference circuit — provides the ECM with rpm and crankshaft position information from the C³I module. The C³I module receives this signal from the crank sensor hall-effect switch.
- Bypass signal — above 400 rpm, the ECM applies 5 volts to this circuit to switch spark timing control from the C³I module to the ECM.
- EST signal — reference signal is sent to the ECM via the C³I module during cranking. Under 400 rpm, the C³I module controls the ignition timing. Above 400 rpm, the ECM applies 5 volts to the bypass line to switch the timing to the ECM control.

Electronic Control Module (ECM) or Powertrain Control Module (PCM)

The ECM/PCM is responsible for maintaining proper spark and fuel injection timing for all driving conditions.

Dual Crank Sensor

The dual crank sensor is mounted in a pedestal on the front of the engine near the harmonic balancer. The sensor consists of 2 hall-effect switches, which depend on 2 metal interrupter rings mounted on the balancer to activate them. Windows in the interrupters activate the hall-effect switches as they provide a path for the magnetic field between the switches transducers and magnets.

Camshaft Sensor

The camshaft sensor sends signal to the ECM/PCM which is used as a sync-pulse to trigger the injectors in the proper sequence.

Diagnosis and Testing

SERVICE PRECAUTIONS

✱✱ CAUTION

The ignition coil's secondary voltage output capabilities can exceed 40,000 volts. Avoid body contact with the C³I high voltage secondary components when the engine is running, or personal injury may result.

➡ To avoid damage to the ECM/PCM or other ignition system components, do not use electrical test equipment such as battery or AC-powered voltmeter, ohmmeter, etc. or any type of tester other than specified.

- To properly diagnosis the ignition systems and their problems, it will be necessary to refer to the diagnostic charts in the fuel injection section. Locate the charts that apply to the vehicle in question and follow them from start to stop.
- When performing electrical tests on the system, use a high impedance multimeter or quality digital voltmeter (DVM). Use of a 12 volt test light is not recommended.
- To prevent electrostatic discharge damage, when working with the ECM, do not touch the connector pins or soldered components on the circuit board.
- When handling a PROM, CAL-PAK or MEM-CAL, do not touch the component leads. Also, do not remove the integrated circuit from the carrier.
- Never pierce a high tension lead or boot for any testing purpose; otherwise, future problems are guaranteed.
- Do not allow extension cords for power tools or droplights to lie on, near or across any vehicle electrical wiring.
- Leave new components and modules in the shipping package until ready to install them.

READING CODES

The Assembly Line Diagnostic Link (ALDL) connector is used for communicating with the ECM. It is usually located under the instrument panel and is sometimes covered by a plastic cover labeled "DIAGNOSTIC CONNECTOR." Codes stored in the ECM's memory can be read through a hand held diagnostic scanner plugged into the ALDL connector. If a scanner is not available, the codes can also be read by jumping from terminal **A** to **B** of the ALDL connector and counting the number of flashes of the Service Engine Soon light, with the ignition switch turned **ON**.

Refer to Section 4 for a more detailed look diagnostic codes, what they mean and how to diagnose them.

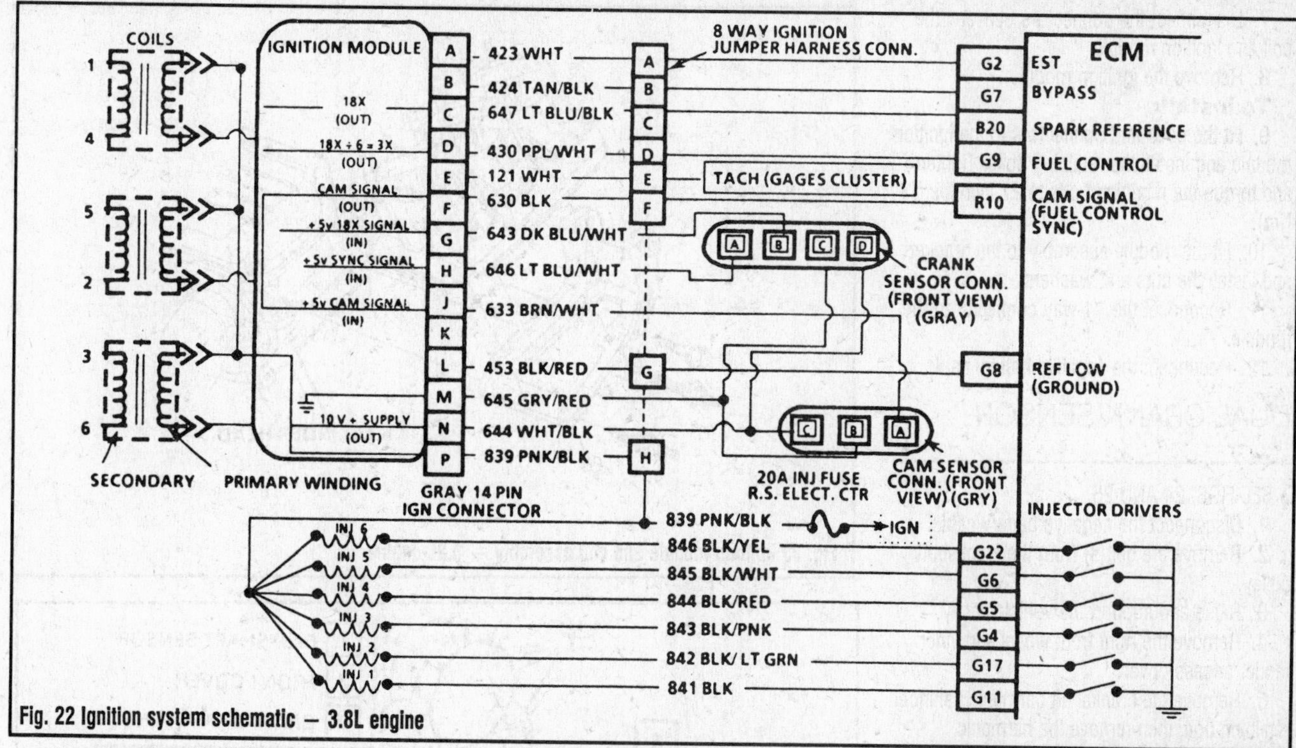

Fig. 22 Ignition system schematic — 3.8L engine

CLEARING CODES

To clear codes from the ECM memory, the ECM power feed must be disconnected for at least 30 seconds. Depending on the vehicle, the ECM power feed can be disconnected at the positive battery terminal pigtail, the inline fuseholder that originates at the positive connection at the battery or the ECM fuse in the fuse block. The negative battery cable may also be disconnected; however, other on-board memory data, such as preset radio tuning, will also be lost.

Also, if battery power is lost, computer relearn time is approximately 5–10 minutes. This means the computer may have to re-calibrate components which set up the idle speed and the idle may fluctuate while this is occurring.

BASIC IGNITION SYSTEM CHECK

➧ SEE FIG. 22

1. Check for codes. If any are found, refer to the appropriate chart in Section 4.
2. Turn the ignition switch **ON**. Verify that the Service Engine Soon light is ON.
3. Install the scan tool and check the following:

Throttle Position Sensor (TPS) — if over 2.5 volts, at closed throttle, check the TPS and circuit.

Coolant — if not between −30°C and 130°C, check the sensor and circuit.

4. Disconnect all injector connectors and install injector test light (J-34730-2 or equivalent) in injector harness connector. Test light should be OFF.

➡ **Perform this test on 1 injector from each bank.**

5. Connect spark checker, (J–26792 or equivalent), and check for spark while cranking. Check at least 2 wires.

a. If spark occurs, reconnect the spark plug wires and check for fuel spray at the injector(s) while cranking.

b. If no spark occurs, check for battery voltage to the ignition system. If OK, substitute known good parts for possible faulty ignition parts. If not, refer to the wiring diagrams to track down loss of voltage.

Ignition Timing Adjustment

Because the C³I system uses a crank sensor for EST, ignition timing is not adjustable. However, positioning of the interrupter ring is very important. A clearance of 0.025 inch is required on either side of the interrupter ring.

Parts Replacement

IGNITION COIL

➧ SEE FIG. 23

1. Disconnect the negative battery cable.
2. Disconnect the spark plug wires.
3. Remove the 2 retaining screws securing the coil to the ignition module.
4. Remove the coil assembly.

To install:

5. Fit the coil assembly to the ignition module.
6. Install the retaining screws and torque to 40 inch lbs. (4–5 Nm).
7. Install the spark plug wires.
8. Reconnect the negative battery cable.

C³I MODULE

1. Disconnect the negative battery cable.
2. Disconnect the 14-way connector at the ignition module.
3. Disconnect the spark plug wires at the coil assembly.
4. Remove the nuts and washers that retains the module to the bracket.
5. Remove the coil-to-module retaining bolts.
6. Note the lead colors or mark for reassembly.

7. Disconnect the connectors between the coil and ignition module.
8. Remove the ignition module.

To install:

9. Fit the coils and connectors to the ignition module and install the retaining bolts. Tighten and torque the retaining bolts to 27 inch lbs. (3 Nm).
10. Fit the module assembly to the bracket and install the nuts and washers.
11. Reconnect the 14-way connector to the module.
12. Reconnect the negative battery cable.

DUAL CRANK SENSOR

➧ SEE FIGS. 24 AND 25

1. Disconnect the negative battery cable.
2. Remove the belt(s) from the crankshaft pulley.
3. Raise and support the vehicle safely.
4. Remove the right front wheel and inner fender access cover.
5. Remove the crankshaft harmonic balancer retaining bolt, then remove the harmonic balancer.
6. Disconnect the sensor electrical connector.
7. Remove the sensor and pedestal from the engine block, then separate the sensor from the pedestal.

To install:

8. Loosely install the crankshaft sensor to the pedestal.
9. Using tool J-37089 or equivalent, position the sensor with the pedestal attached, on the crankshaft.
10. Install the pedestal-to-block retaining bolts. Tighten and torque to 14–28 ft. lbs. (20–40 Nm).
11. Torque the pedestal pinch bolt 30–35 inch lbs. (20–40 Nm).
12. Remove tool J-37089 or equivalent.
13. Place tool J-37089 or equivalent, on the harmonic balancer and turn. If any vane of the harmonic balancer touches the tool, replace the balancer assembly.

➡ A clearance of 0.025 inch is required on either side of the interrupter ring. Be certain to obtain the correct clearance. Failure to do so will damage the sensor. A misadjusted sensor of bent interrupter ring could cause rubbing of the sensor, resulting in potential driveability problems, such as rough idle, poor performance, or a no start condition.

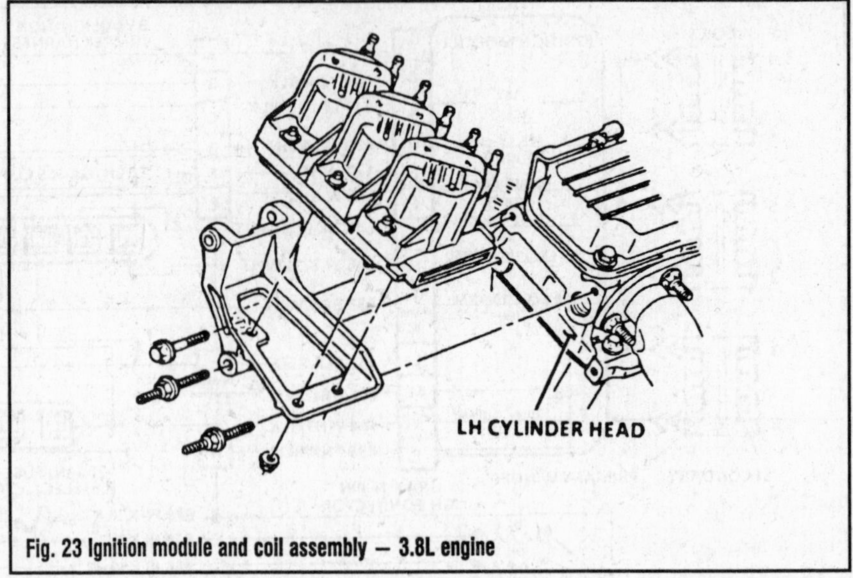

Fig. 23 Ignition module and coil assembly — 3.8L engine

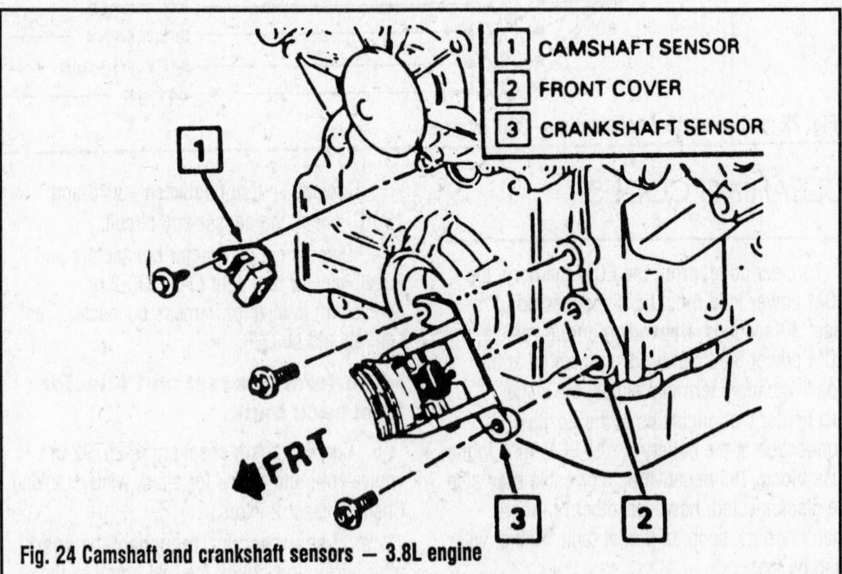

Fig. 24 Camshaft and crankshaft sensors — 3.8L engine

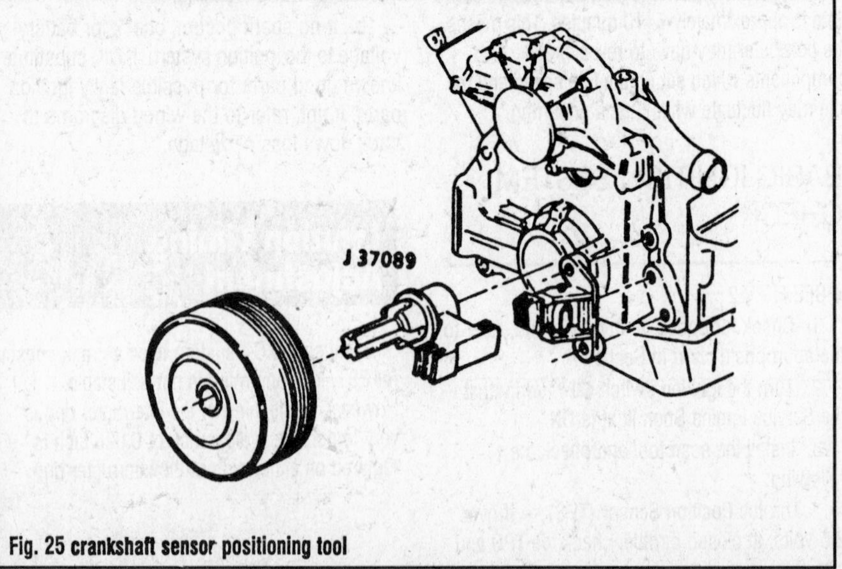

Fig. 25 crankshaft sensor positioning tool

14. Install the balancer on the crankshaft. Install the balancer retaining bolt. Tighten and torque the retaining bolt to 200–239 ft. lbs. (270–325 Nm).
15. Install the inner fender shield.
16. Install the right front wheel assembly. Tighten and torque the wheel nuts to 100 ft. lbs. (140 Nm).
17. Lower the vehicle.
18. Install the belt(s).
19. Reconnect the negative battery cable.

ESC KNOCK SENSOR

1. Disconnect the negative battery cable.
2. Raise and support the vehicle safely.
3. Disconnect the harness connector from the knock sensor.
4. Remove the sensor from the engine block.

To install:

5. Clean the threads on the engine block, where the sensor was installed. Install the sensor. Tighten to 11–16 ft. lbs. (15–22 Nm).
6. Reconnect the harness connector to the knock sensor.
7. Lower the vehicle.
8. Reconnect the negative battery cable.

ELECTRONIC CONTROL MODULE (ECM) AND/OR MEM-CAL

1. Turn the ignition switch **OFF**.
2. Disconnect the negative battery cable.
3. Remove the right side hush panel.
4. Disconnect the harness connectors from the control unit.
5. Remove the control unit-to-bracket retaining screws and remove the control unit.
6. If replacement of the Mem-Cal is required, remove the access cover retaining screws and cover from the control unit. Note the position of the Mem-Cal for proper installation in the new ECM. Using 2 fingers, carefully push both retaining clips back away from the Mem-Cal. At the same time, grasp it at both ends and lift it up out of the socket. Do not remove the cover of the Mem-Cal.

To install:

7. Fit the replacement Mem-Cal into the socket.

➡ The small notches in the Mem-Cal must be aligned with the small notches in the socket. Press only on the ends of the Mem-Cal until the retaining clips snap into the ends of the Mem-Cal. Do not press on the middle of the Mem-Cal, only the ends.

8. Install the access cover and retaining screws.
9. Position the control unit in the vehicle and install the control unit-to-bracket retaining screws.
10. Reconnect the control unit harness connectors.
11. Install the hush panel.
12. Check that the ignition switch is **OFF**. Then reconnect the negative battery cable.

Functional Check

1. Turn the ignition switch **ON**.
2. Enter diagnostics.
   a. Allow Code 12 to flash 4 times to verify no other codes are present. This indicates the Mem-Cal is installed properly and the control unit is functioning.
   b. If trouble Codes 42, 43 or 51 occur, or if the Service Engine Soon light is ON constantly with no codes, the Mem-Cal is not fully seated or is defective.
   c. If it is not fully seated, press firmly on the ends of the Mem-Cal.

IDLE SPEED AND MIXTURE ADJUSTMENTS

All engines' idle speed and mixture is electronically controlled by the computerized fuel injection system. Adjustment are neither necessary nor possible. All threaded throttle stop adjusters are factory set and capped to discourage any tampering; in some areas, tampering is illegal. In most cases, proper diagnosis and parts replacement will straighten out any problems concerning this subject.

IDLE LEAN PROCEDURE (3.1L AND 3.4L ENGINES)

Any time the battery is disconnected, the programmed position of the IAC (idle air control) valve pintle is lost and replaced with a default value. This condition may cause the engine idle to fluctuate for approximately 5–10 minutes. To return the IAC valve pintle to the proper position, perform the following:

1. Place the transaxle in **P** or **N**.
2. Install the Tech 1 scan tool or equivalent.
3. Turn the ignition switch **ON**, engine OFF.
4. Select "IAC System", then "Idle Learn" in the "Misc. Test" mode.
5. Proceed with the Idle Learn as directed by the scan tool.

TORQUE SPECIFICATIONS

Component	U S	Metric
C^3I ignition coil retaining bolts	40 inch lbs.	4 5 Nm
C^3I module retaining bolts	27 inch lbs.	3 Nm
DIS ignition coil retaining bolts	40 inch lbs.	4 5 Nm
DIS assembly retaining bolts	20 ft lbs.	27 Nm
DIS crankshaft sensor 2.5L engine	20 inch lbs.	2 3 Nm
DIS crankshaft sensor V6 engines	71 inch lbs.	8 Nm
IDI coil and module assembly retaining bolts	19 ft lbs.	26 Nm
IDI ignition coil retaining bolts	35 inch lbs.	4 Nm
IDI ignition module retaining bolts	35 inch lbs.	4 Nm

TORQUE SPECIFICATIONS

Component	U S	Metric
IDI crankshaft sensor retaining bolt	88 inch lbs.	10 Nm
Spark Plugs		
2.3L engine	17 ft lbs.	23 Nm
2.5L engine	20 ft lbs.	27 Nm
2.8L, 3.1L, and 3.4L engines	18 ft lbs.	24 Nm
3.8L engine	20 ft lbs.	27 Nm
Torque strut-to-engine bracket bolts	51 ft lbs.	70 Nm

Diagnosis of Spark Plugs

Problem	Possible Cause	Correction
Brown to grayish-tan deposits and slight electrode wear.	• Normal wear.	• Clean, regap, reinstall.
Dry, fluffy black carbon deposits.	• Poor ignition output.	• Check distributor to coil connections.
Wet, oily deposits with very little electrode wear.	• "Break-in" of new or recently overhauled engine. • Excessive valve stem guide clearances. • Worn intake valve seals.	• Degrease, clean and reinstall the plugs. • Refer to Section 3. • Replace the seals.
Red, brown, yellow and white colored coatings on the insulator. Engine misses intermittently under severe operating conditions.	• By-products of combustion.	• Clean, regap, and reinstall. If heavily coated, replace.
Colored coatings heavily deposited on the portion of the plug projecting into the chamber and on the side facing the intake valve.	• Leaking seals if condition is found in only one or two cylinders.	• Check the seals. Replace if necessary. Clean, regap, and reinstall the plugs.
Shiny yellow glaze coating on the insulator.	• Melted by-products of combustion.	• Avoid sudden acceleration with wide-open throttle after long periods of low speed driving. Replace the plugs.
Burned or blistered insulator tips and badly eroded electrodes.	• Overheating.	• Check the cooling system. • Check for sticking heat riser valves. Refer to Section 1. • Lean air-fuel mixture. • Check the heat range of the plugs. May be too hot. • Check ignition timing. May be over-advanced. • Check the torque value of the plugs to ensure good plug-engine seat contact.
Broken or cracked insulator tips.	• Heat shock from sudden rise in tip temperature under severe operating conditions. Improper gapping of plugs.	• Replace the plugs. Gap correctly.

3 ENGINE AND ENGINE OVERHAUL

ENGINE ELECTRICAL SYSTEMS

Understanding the Engine Electrical System

The engine electrical system can be broken down into three separate and distinct systems:

1. The starting system.
2. The charging system.
3. The ignition system.

BATTERY AND STARTING SYSTEM

Basic Operating Principles

The battery is the first link in the chain of mechanisms which work together to provide cranking of the automobile engine. In most modern cars, the battery is a lead/acid electrochemical device consisting of six 2V subsections connected in series so the unit is capable of producing approximately 12V of electrical power. Each subsection, or cell, consists of a series of positive and negative plates held a short distance apart in a solution of sulfuric acid and water. The two types of plates are of dissimilar metals. This causes a chemical reaction to be set up, and it is this reaction which produces current flow from the battery when its positive and negative terminals are connected to an electrical appliance such as a lamp or motor. The continued transfer of electrons would eventually convert the sulfuric acid in the electrolyte to water, and make the two plates identical in chemical composition. An electrical energy is removed from the battery, its voltage output tends to drop. Thus, measuring battery voltage and battery electrolyte composition are two ways of checking the ability of the unit to supply power. During the starting of the engine, electrical energy is removed from the battery. However, if the charging circuit is in good condition and the operating conditions are normal, the power removed from the battery will be replaced by the generator (or alternator) which will force electrons back through the battery, reversing the normal flow, and restoring the battery to its original chemical state.

The battery and starting motor are linked by very heavy electrical cables designed to minimize resistance to the flow of current. Generally, the major power supply cable that leaves the battery goes directly to the starter, while other electrical system needs are supplied by a smaller cable. During starter operation, power flows from the battery to the starter and is grounded through the car's frame and the battery's negative (–) ground strap.

The starting motor is a specially designed direct current electric motor capable of producing a very great amount of power for its size. One thing that allows the motor to produce a great deal of power is its tremendous rotating speed. It drives the engine through a tiny pinion gear (attached to the starter's armature), which drives the very large flywheel ring gear at a greatly reduced speed. Another factor allowing it to produce so much power is that only intermittent operation is required of it. This little allowance for air circulation is required, and the winding can be built into a very small space.

The starter solenoid is a magnetic device which employs the small current supplied by the starting switch circuit of the ignition switch. This magnetic action moves a plunger which mechanically engages the starter and electrically closes the heavy switch which connects it to the battery. The starting switch circuit consists of the starting switch contained within the ignition switch, a transmission neutral safety switch or clutch pedal switch, and the wiring necessary to connect these in series with the starter solenoid or relay.

A pinion, which is a small gear, is mounted to a one-way drive clutch. This clutch is splined to the starter armature shaft. When the ignition switch is moved to the START position, the solenoid plunger slides the pinion toward the flywheel ring gear via a collar and spring. If the teeth on the pinion and flywheel match properly, the pinion will engage the flywheel immediately. If the gear teeth butt on another, the spring will be compressed and will force the gears to mesh as soon as the starter turns far enough to allow them to do so. As the solenoid plunger reaches the end of its travel, it closes the contacts that connect the battery and starter and then the engine is cranked.

As soon as the engine starts, the flywheel ring gear begins turning fast enough to drive the pinion at an extremely high rate of speed. At this point, the one-way clutch begins allowing the pinion to spin faster than the starter shaft so that the starter will not operate at excessive speed. When the ignition switch is released from the starter position, the solenoid is de-energized, and a spring contained within the solenoid assembly pulls the gear out of mesh and interrupts the current flow to the starter.

Some starters employ a separate relay, mounted away from the starter, to switch the motor and solenoid current on and off. The relay thus replaces the solenoid electrical switch, but does not eliminate the need for a solenoid mounted on the starter used to mechanically engage the starter drive gears. The relay is used to reduce the amount of current the starting switch must carry.

CHARGING SYSTEM

Basic Operating Principles

The automobile charging system provides electrical power for operation of the vehicle's ignition and starting systems and all the electrical accessories. The battery services as an electrical surge or storage tank, storing (in chemical form) the energy originally produced by the engine driven alternator. The system also provides a means of regulating alternator output to protect the battery from being overcharged and to avoid excessive voltage to the accessories.

The storage battery is a chemical device incorporating parallel lead plates in a tank containing a sulfuric acid/water solution. Adjacent plates are slightly dissimilar, and the chemical reaction of the two dissimilar plates produces electrical energy when the battery is connected to a load such as the starter motor. The chemical reaction is reversible, so that when the alternator is producing a voltage (electrical pressure) greater than that produced by the battery, electricity is forced into the battery, and the battery is returned to is fully charged state.

The vehicle's alternator is driven mechanically, through serpentine belts, by the engine crankshaft. It consists of two coils of find wire, one stationary (the stator), and one movable (the rotor). The rotor may also be known as the armature, and consists of fine ware wrapped around an iron core which is mounted on a shaft. The electricity which flows through the two coils of wire (provided initially by the battery in some cases) creates an intense magnetic field around both rotor and stator, and the interaction between the two fields creates voltage, allowing the alternator to power the accessories and charge the battery.

Newer automobiles use alternating current generators or alternators, because they are more efficient, can be rotated at higher speeds, and have fewer brush problems, In an alternator, the field rotates while all the current produced passes only through the stator winding. The brushes bear against continuous slip rings rather than a commutator. This causes the current produced to periodically reverse the direction of its flow. Diodes (electrical one-way switches) block the flow of current from traveling in the wrong direction. A series of diodes is wired together to permit the alternating flow of the stator to be converted to a pulsating, but unidirectional flow at the alternator output. The alternator's field is wired in series with the voltage regulator.

The regulator consists of several circuits. Each circuit has a core, or magnetic coil of wire, which operates a switch. Each switch is connected to ground through one or more resistors. The coil of wire responds directly to system voltage. When the voltage reaches the required level, the magnetic field created by the winding of wire closes the switch and inserts a resistance into the generator field circuit, thus reducing the output. The contacts of the switch cycle open and close many times each second to precisely control voltage.

While alternators are self-limiting as far as maximum current is concerned, DC generators employ a current regulating circuit which responds directly to the total amount of current flowing through the generator circuit rather than to the output voltage. The current regulator is similar to the voltage regulator except that all system current must flow through the energizing coil on its way to the various accessories.

Alternator

The alternator charging system consists of the alternator, voltage regulator, warning light, battery, and fuse link wire.

A failure of any component of the charging system can cause the entire system to stop functioning. Because of this, the charging system can be very difficult to troubleshoot when problems occur.

When the ignition key is turned on, current flows from the battery, through the charging system indicator light on the instrument panel, to the voltage regulator, and to the alternator. Since the alternator is not producing any current, the alternator warning light comes on. When the engine is started, the alternator begins to produce current and turns the alternator light off. As the alternator turns and produces current, the current is divided in two ways: part to the battery to charge the battery and power the electrical components of the vehicle, and part is returned to the alternator to enable it to increase its output. In this situation, the alternator is receiving current from the battery and from itself. A voltage regulator is wired into the current supply to the alternator to prevent it from receiving too much current which would cause it to put out too much current. Conversely, if the voltage regulator does not allow the alternator to receive enough current, the battery will not be fully charged and will eventually go dead.

The battery is connected to the alternator at all times, whether the ignition key is turned on or not. If the battery were shorted to ground, the alternator would also be shorted. This would damage the alternator. To prevent this, a fuse link is installed in the wiring between the battery and the alternator. If the battery is shorted, the fuse link will melt, protecting the alternator.

ENGINE ELECTRICAL

Ignition System

Refer to Section 2, Engine Performance and Tune-Up" for an in-depth look at all ignition systems, their components, and proper diagnosis.

Alternator

ALTERNATOR PRECAUTIONS

✲✲ CAUTION

To prevent damage to the alternator and possible to yourself, the following precautions should be taken when working with the electrical system.

1. Never reverse the battery connections.
2. Booster batteries for starting must be connected properly: positive-to-positive (+) and negative-to-negative (–).
3. Disconnect the battery cables before using a fast charger; the charger has a tendency to force current through the diodes in the opposite direction for which they were designed. This burns out the diodes.
4. Never use a fast charger as a booster for starting the vehicle.
5. Never disconnect the voltage regulator while the engine is running.
6. Avoid long soldering times when replacing diodes or transistors. Prolonged heat is damaging to AC (alternating current) generators.
7. Do not use test lamps of more than 12 volts (V) for checking diode continuity.
8. Do not short across or ground any of the terminals of the AC (alternating current) generator.
9. The polarity of the battery, generator, and regulator must be matched and considered before making any electrical connections within the system.
10. Never operate the alternator on an open circuit. Make sure that all connections within the circuit are clean and tight.
11. Disconnect the battery terminals when performing any service on the electrical system. This will eliminate the possibility of accidental reversal of polarity.
12. Disconnect the battery ground cable if arc welding is to be done on any part of the car.

BELT TENSION ADJUSTMENT

All alternators used have a rated output of 100–105 amps. If the charging system is inadequate, check the serpentine belt and tensioner.

➡ The drive belt tensioner can control the belt tension over a wide range of belt lengths; however, there are limits to the tensioners ability to compensate for various belt lengths. Installing the wrong size belt and using the tensioner outside of its operating range can result in poor tension control and damage to the tensioner, drive belt and driven components.

REMOVAL & INSTALLATION

➧ SEE FIGS. 1–5

2.3L ENGINE

1. Disconnect the negative battery cable.
2. Remove the electrical center fuse block shield.
3. Remove the serpentine belt, by removing the belt guard, and lifting or rotating the tensioner, using a breaker bar.
4. Label and remove the alternator electrical connectors.
5. Remove the alternator brace bolt, rear bolt and front bolt.

➡ **Use extreme care when removing the alternator, not to damage the air conditioning compressor and condenser hose.**

6. Lift the alternator out between the engine lifting eyelet and the air conditioning compressor.

To install:

7. Install the alternator, front, rear and brace retaining bolts.
8. Torque the long bolt to 40 ft. lbs. (54 Nm), the short bolt to 19 ft. lbs. (26 Nm) and the brace bolt to 18 ft. lbs. (25 Nm).
9. Connect the alternator electrical connectors, serpentine belt and fuse block shield.
10. Connect the negative battery cable and check for proper operation.

2.5L ENGINE

1. Disconnect the negative battery cable.
2. Remove the serpentine belt.
3. Remove the electrical connectors from the back of the alternator.
4. Remove the rear (first), front attaching bolts and heat shield.
5. Remove the alternator assembly carefully making sure all wires are disconnected.

To install:

6. Position the alternator into the mounting bracket.
7. Install the front and rear mounting bolts but do not tighten.
8. Install the heat shield with the rear mounting bolts.
9. Install the electrical connectors and tighten the battery cable nut.
10. Torque the mounting bolts to 18 ft. lbs. (25 Nm).
11. Install the serpentine belt.
12. Reconnect the negative battery cable.

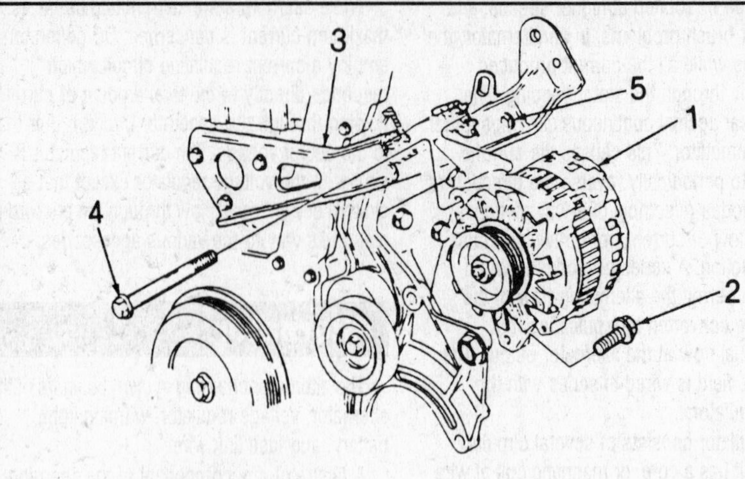

Fig. 1 Alternator mounting — 2.3L engine

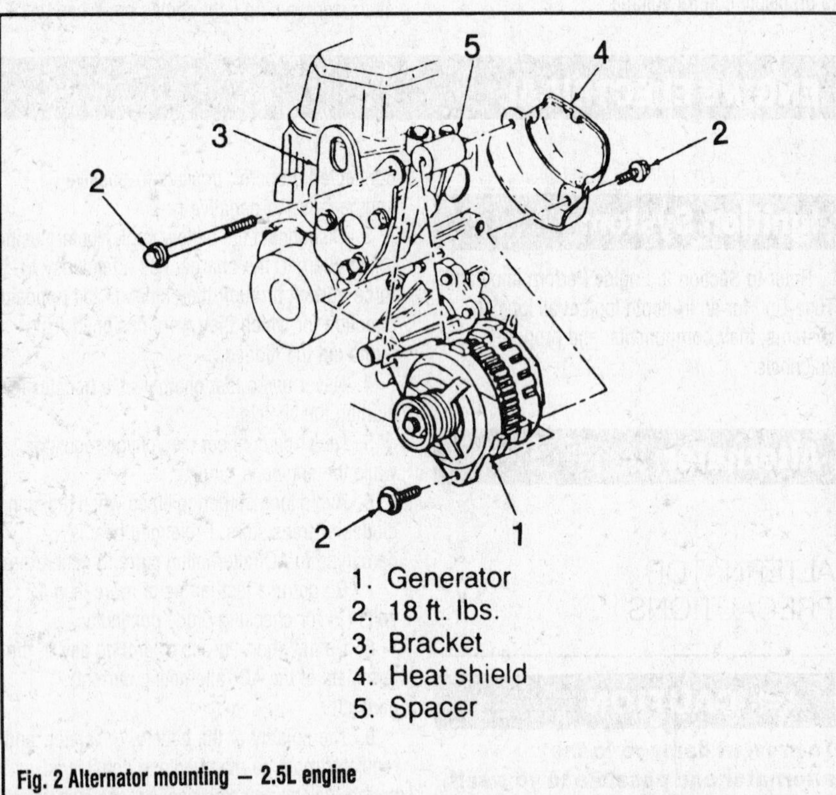

Fig. 2 Alternator mounting — 2.5L engine

2.8L AND 3.1L ENGINES

1. Disconnect the negative battery cable. Remove the air cleaner assembly.
2. Remove the serpentine belt.
3. Remove the electrical connectors from the back of the alternator.
4. Remove the rear and front attaching bolts,and bolt from brace to alternator.
5. Remove the alternator assembly carefully making sure all wires are disconnected.

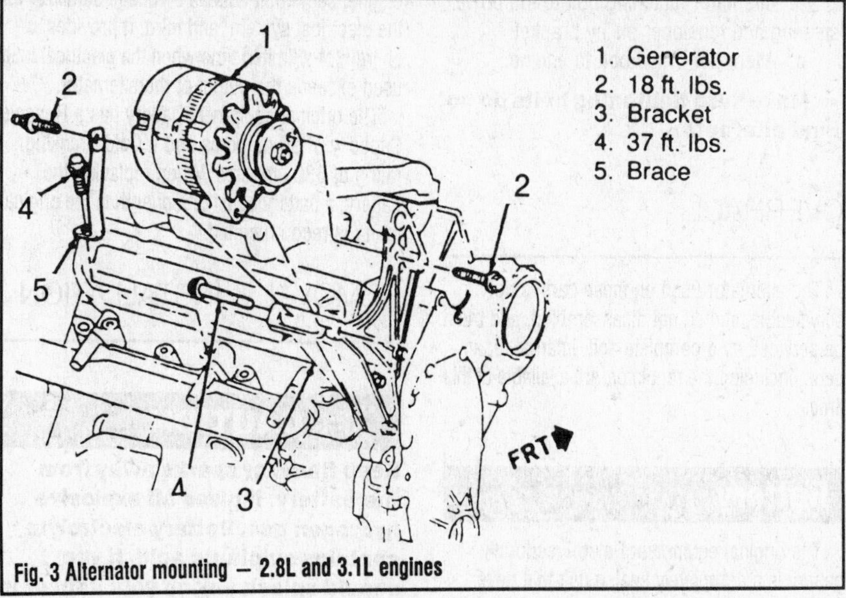

Fig. 3 Alternator mounting — 2.8L and 3.1L engines

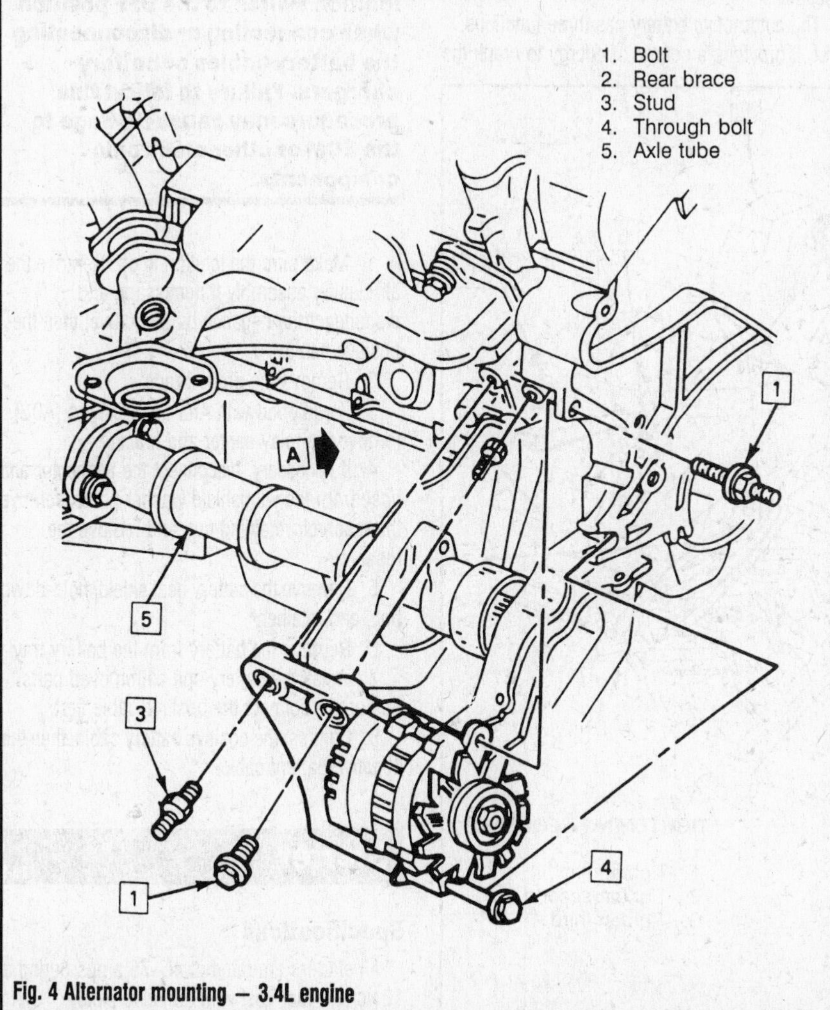

Fig. 4 Alternator mounting — 3.4L engine

➡ **If alternator brace is removed, studs must be retightened before installation or damage to the brace may result.**

To install:

6. Position the alternator into the mounting bracket.
7. Install brace to alternator bolt but do not tighten.
8. Install the front and rear mounting bolts. Torque the mounting bolts as follows:
   a. Long bolt to 35 ft. lbs. (47 Nm)
   b. Short bolt to 18 ft. lbs. (25 Nm)
   c. Bracket bolt to 18 ft. lbs. (25 Nm)
9. Check that tightening of the brace bolts did not bind alternator.
10. Install the electrical connectors and tighten the battery cable nut.
11. Install the serpentine belt.
12. Install the air cleaner and negative battery cable.

3.4L ENGINE

➡ **Vehicles with the 3.4L engine will also be equipped with an alternator cooling fan behind the right side headlight, used to cool the unit through a duct hose.**

1. Disconnect the negative battery cable.
2. Remove air cleaner assembly.
3. Remove coolant recovery reservoir and set aside.
4. Remove serpentine belt.
5. Raise and safely support vehicle.
6. Remove power steering pipe retaining clip nut from upper alternator stud and remove alternator stud.
7. Remove right front tire and wheel assembly.
8. Separate lower ball joint from lower control arm.
9. Remove halfshaft from transaxle.
10. Remove right hand engine splash shield.
11. Disconnect connectors and wires from alternator.
12. Remove brace bolt from alternator and loosen brace at engine block.
13. Remove alternator lower mounting bolt and alternator.

To install:

14. Install alternator and loosely install all mounting bolts.

If replacement alternator does not fit into mounts, remove adhesive-backed shim from rear of alternator bracket.

15. Tighten alternator lower mounting bolts to 61 ft. lbs. (83 Nm).
16. Install connectors and wires to alternator.
17. Install right hand engine splash shield.

18. Reinstall halfshaft.
19. Install lower ball joint to lower control arm.
20. Reinstall tire and wheel assembly and lower vehicle.
21. Install upper alternator stud and power steering pipe retaining clip nut.
22. Reinstall serpentine belt and coolant recovery reservoir.
23. Reinstall negative battery cable.
24. Install air cleaner assembly.

3.8L ENGINE

1. Disconnect the negative battery cable.
2. Remove the serpentine belt.
3. Remove the electrical connectors from the back of the alternator.
4. Remove the nut and the positive battery connector from the **BAT** terminal.
5. Remove the alternator mounting bolts and remove the alternator from the vehicle.

To install:

6. Installation is the reverse of removal. Tighten all mounting bolts to 20 ft. lbs. using the following sequence:
   a. Alternator attaching bolt to the direct fire mounting bracket/rear brace.
   b. Alternator attaching bolt to the power steering and tensioner pulley bracket.
   c. Alternator brace bolt to engine.

➡ **Make sure tightening bolts do not bind alternator.**

OVERHAUL

The alternator used on these cars is not serviceable, should not disassembled, and must be serviced as a complete unit. Internal repair parts, including the regulator, are available at this time.

Battery

The original equipment Delco Freedom® battery is a completely sealed unit that never requires the addition of water or acid. The only openings in the battery are vent holes located on the sides of the battery case. The vents allow the small amount of gas produced in the battery to escape.

The automotive battery has three functions: first, it provides a source of energy to crank the engine; second, it acts as a voltage stabilizer for the electrical system; and third, it provides energy for a limited time when the electrical load used exceeds the output of the alternator.

The original equipment battery has a Reserve Capacity of 90 amperes and a Cold Cranking rating of 630 amperes. When replacing the battery, a battery equal or higher than the original rating is recommended.

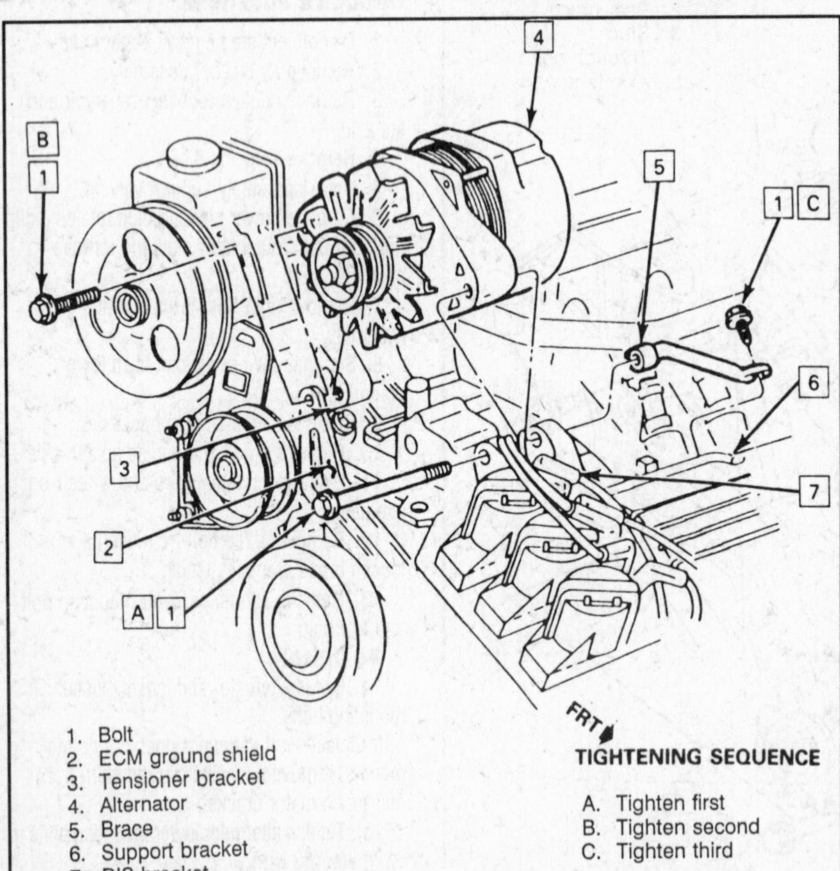

Fig. 5 Alternator mounting — 3.8L engine

REMOVAL & INSTALLATION

⁂ CAUTION

Keep flame or sparks away from the battery; it gives off explosive hydrogen gas. Battery electrolyte contains sulphuric acid. If you should splash any on your skin or in your eyes, flush the affected area with plenty of clear water. If it lands in your eyes, get medical help immediately. Also, always turn the ignition switch to the OFF position when connecting or disconnecting the battery cables or battery chargers. Failure to follow this procedure may cause damage to the ECM or other electronic components.

1. Make sure the ignition is off. Remove the air cleaner assembly if necessary, and disconnect the negative battery cable, then the positive cable.
2. Remove the cross brace.
3. If equipped with Anti-Lock Brakes (ABS), remove the relay center and bracket.
4. If necessary, disconnect the connector and hose from the windshield washer pump, remove the reservoir retaining nut, and remove the reservoir.
5. Remove the battery heat shield, hold-down bolt, and retainer.
6. Remove the battery from the battery tray.
7. Install the battery and all removed parts. Be sure to connect the positive cable first.
8. Connect the positive battery cable, then the negative battery cable.

Starter

Specifications

All starters are rated at 45–75 amps during a 10 volt no-load test with the drive pinion spinning at 6,000–12,000 rpm.

**** CAUTION**

Never operate the starter motor motor than 30 seconds at a time without pausing to allow it to cool for at least two minutes. Overheating, caused by excessive cranking, will seriously damage the starter motor.

REMOVAL & INSTALLATION

➧ SEE FIGS. 6–9

2.3L ENGINE

1. Disconnect the negative battery cable.
2. Remove the air cleaner and inlet hose from the throttle body.
3. Remove and plug the coolant reservoir hose at the radiator filler neck.
4. Remove the coolant reservoir.
5. Remove the intake manifold brace bolts.
6. Place a drain pan under the oil filter and remove the filter.
7. Remove the starter retaining bolts, lower the starter onto the frame member and disconnect the starter electrical connectors.

To install:

8. Position the starter into the vehicle, connect the electrical connectors and torque the retaining bolts to 32 ft. lbs. (43 Nm).
9. Install a new oil filter and add engine oil, as needed.
10. Install the intake manifold brace, coolant reservoir and hoses.
11. Add coolant, if needed.
12. Install the air cleaner and inlet hose.
13. Connect the negative battery cable and check for proper operation.

2.5L ENGINE

1. Disconnect the negative battery cable.
2. Raise and support the vehicle safely.
3. Remove the flywheel inspection cover bolts and cover.
4. Remove the stud from the starter support bracket.
5. Remove the 2 starter mounting bolts and shim, if equipped.
6. Remove the starter motor. Be careful not to damage the starter wires by letting the starter hang.
7. While holding the starter motor, disconnect the starter electrical connectors from the starter solenoid.

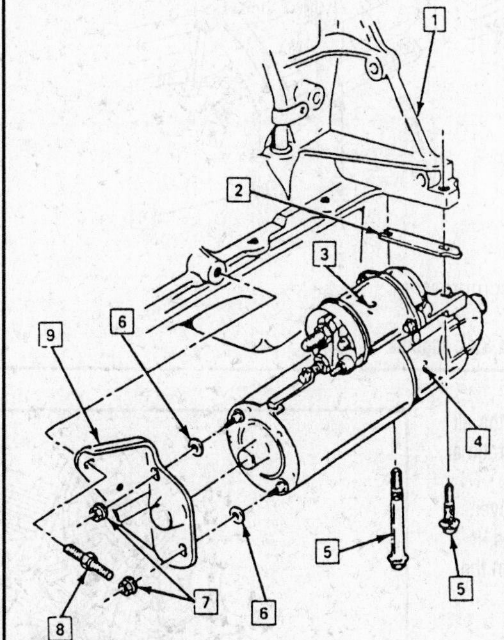

Fig. 7 Starter mounting – 2.5L engine

8. Remove the starter from the rear bracket.

To install:

9. Install the support bracket to the starter.
10. Install the starter adjustment shims, if equipped.
11. Position the starter to the engine mounting flange and torque the bolts to 32 ft. lbs. (43 Nm).
12. Install the bracket-to-engine and torque the stud to 18 ft. lbs. (25 Nm).
13. Install the inspection cover.
14. Lower the vehicle and connect the starter electrical wires. Reconnect the negative battery cable.

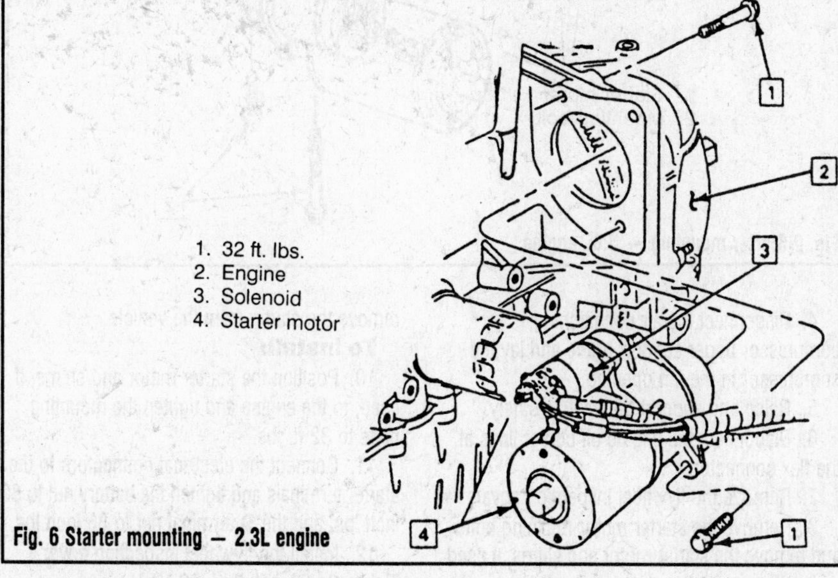

Fig. 6 Starter mounting – 2.3L engine

2.8L, 3.1L AND 3.4L ENGINES

1. Remove the air cleaner.
2. Disconnect the negative battery cable.
3. Raise the vehicle and support it safely.
4. If equipped with an engine oil cooler, remove the engine oil, oil filter and position the hose next to the starter motor to the side.

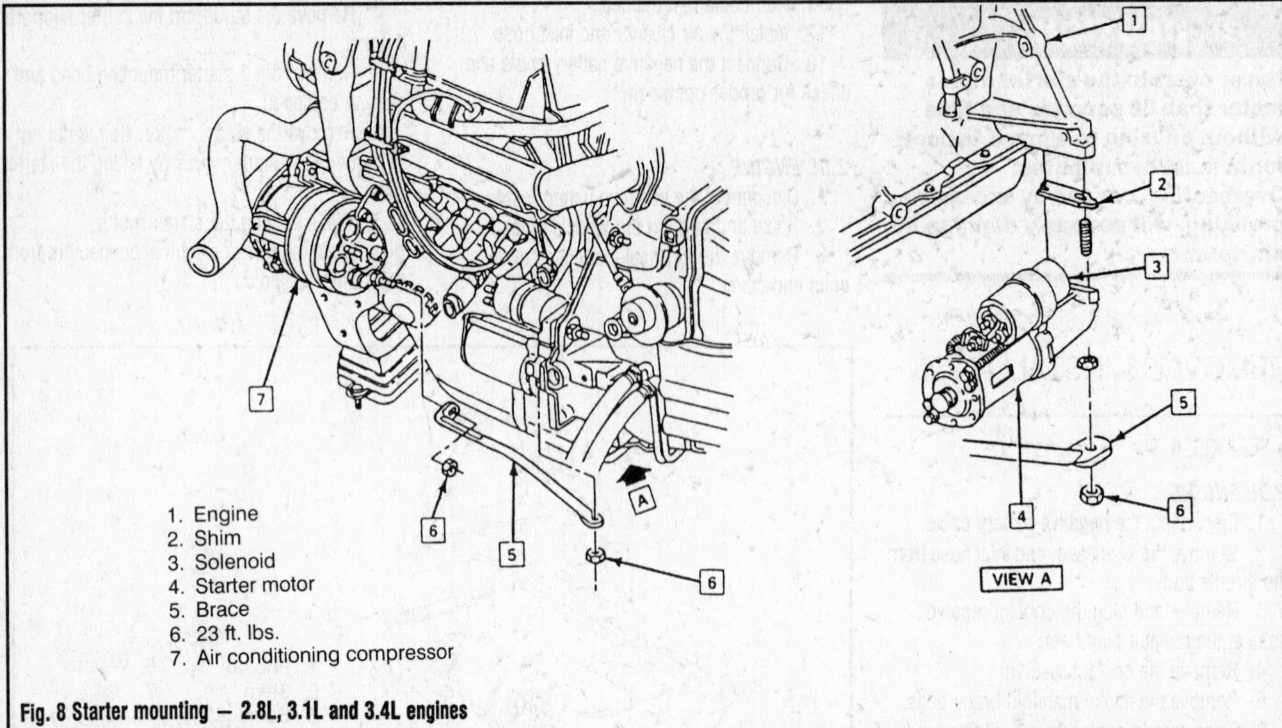

Fig. 8 Starter mounting — 2.8L, 3.1L and 3.4L engines

5. Remove the nut from the brace at the air conditioning compressor, nut from the brace at the engine and the brace.

6. Remove the flywheel inspection cover.

7. Remove the starter bolts and shims, if equipped. Do not let the starter hang from the starter wires.

8. Remove the starter wires from the solenoid and remove the starter.

To install:

9. While supporting the starter, connect the starter wires at the solenoid.

10. Install the starter motor-to-engine mount with the shims, if equipped, and the mounting bolts. Torque the bolts to 32 ft. lbs. (43 Nm).

11. If equipped with an engine oil cooler, reposition the hose next to the starter motor, install the oil filter and refill the engine with the proper amount of engine oil.

12. Install the flywheel inspection cover and tighten the bolts.

13. Install the starter support brace to the air conditioning compressor and torque the nut to 23 ft. lbs. (31 Nm).

14. Lower the vehicle, reconnect the negative battery cable and install the air cleaner assembly.

3.8L ENGINE

1. Disconnect the negative battery cable.

2. If necessary, remove the right side cooling fan.

3. Remove the serpentine drive belt.

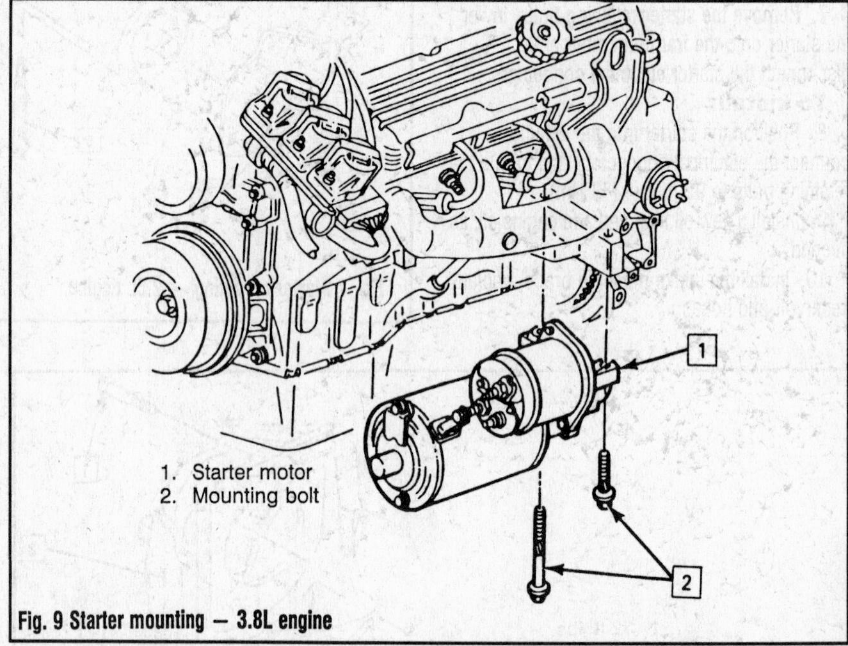

Fig. 9 Starter mounting — 3.8L engine

4. Disconnect the air conditioning compressor upper support brace and lay the compressor in the fan opening.

5. Raise and support the vehicle safely.

6. Disconnect the engine oil cooler lines at the flex connector.

7. Remove the flywheel inspection cover.

8. Remove the starter motor retaining bolts and remove the starter motor and shims, if used.

9. Disconnect the starter motor wiring and remove the starter from the vehicle.

To install:

10. Position the starter motor and shims, if used, to the engine and tighten the mounting bolts to 32 ft. lbs.

11. Connect the electrical connectors to the starter terminals and tighten the battery nut to 80 inch lbs. and the **S** terminal nut to 35 inch lbs.

12. Install the flywheel inspection cover. Tighten to 89 inch lbs. (10 Nm).

13. Connect the engine oil cooler lines at the flex connector.
14. Lower the vehicle and install the air conditioner compressor.
15. Install the serpentine drive belt, cooling fan and negative battery cable.

STARTER ALIGNMENT

While the starter is engages, if a high pitch whine, low pitch whoop or rumble occurs, the starter may have to be aligned or serviced with the proper shims that can be purchased at the dealer or local parts distributors. Measure the distance between the pinion gear and the flywheel ring gear.

STARTER OVERHAUL

➧ SEE FIGS. 10–12

1. To remove the solenoid, remove the screw from the field coil connector and solenoid mounting screws. Rotate the solenoid 90° and remove it along with the plunger return spring.
2. For further service, remove the two through-bolts, then remove the commutator end frame and washer.
3. To replace the clutch and drive assembly proceed as follows:
   a. Remove the thrust washer or the collar from the armature shaft.
   b. Slide a 5/8 in. deep socket or a piece of 16mm dia. pipe over the shaft and against the retainer as a driving too. Tap the tool to remove the retainer off the snap ring.
   c. Remove the snap ring from the groove in the shaft. Check and make sure the snap ring is not distorted. If it is, it will be necessary to replace it with a new one upon reassembly.
   d. Remove the retainer and clutch assembly from the armature shaft.
4. The shift lever may be disconnected from the plunger at this time by removing the roll pin.
5. On models with the standard starter, the brushes may be removed by removing the brush holder pivot pin which positions one insulated and one grounded brush. Remove the brush and spring and replace the brushes as necessary.
6. On models with the smaller 5MT starter, remove the brush and holder from the brush support, then remove the screw from the brush holder and separate the brush and holder. Replace the brushes as necessary.

To assemble:

1. Lubricate the drive end of the armature shaft and slide the clutch assembly onto the armature shaft with the pinion away from the armature.
2. Slide the retainer onto the shaft with the cupped side facing the end of the shaft.
3. Install the snap ring into the groove on the armature shaft.
4. Install the thrust washer on the shaft.

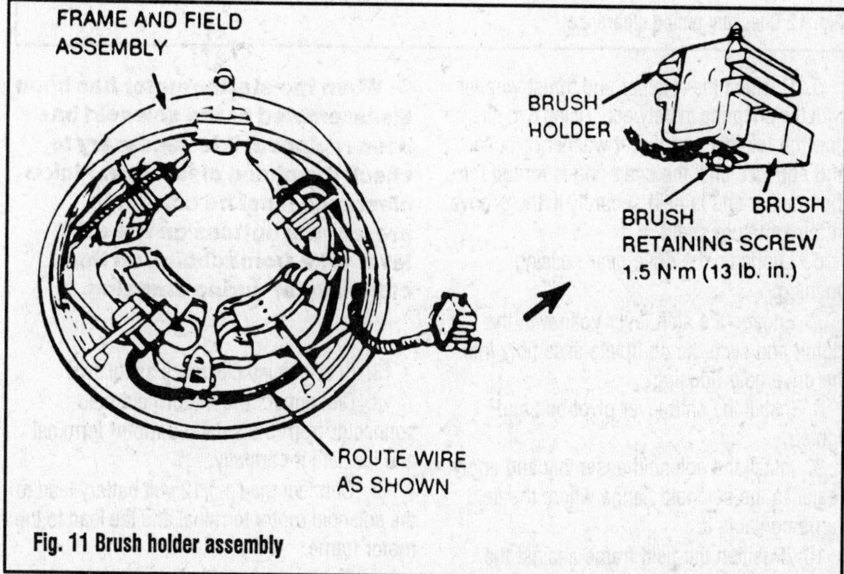

Fig. 11 Brush holder assembly

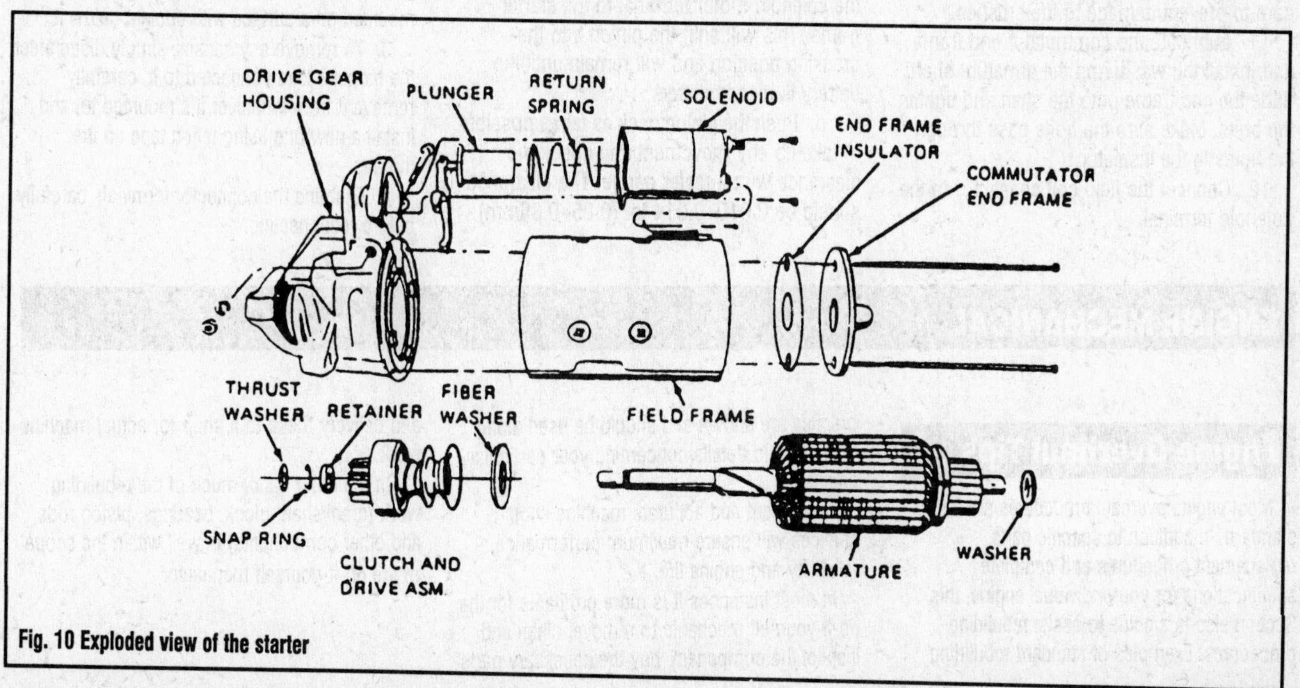

Fig. 10 Exploded view of the starter

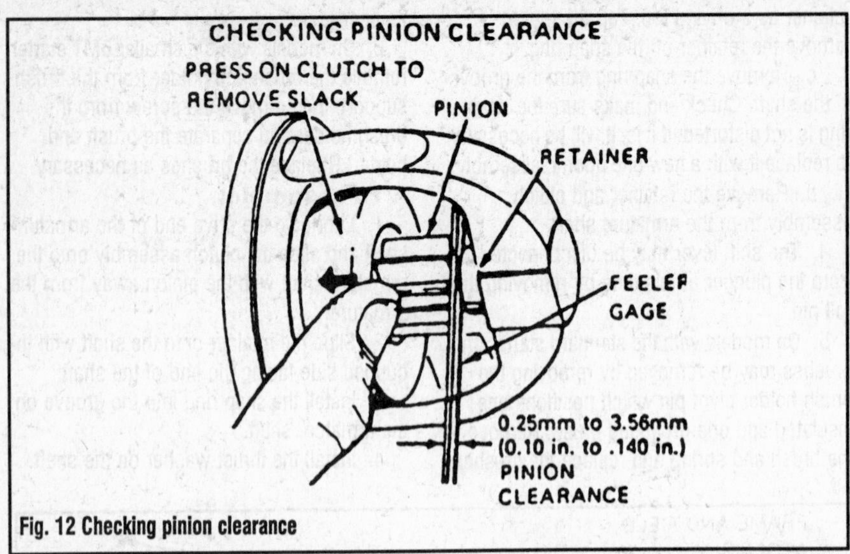

Fig. 12 Checking pinion clearance

5. Position the retainer and thrust washer with the snapring in between. Using two pliers, grip the retainer and thrust washer or collar and squeeze until the snap ring is forced into the retainer and is held securely in the groove in the armature shaft.
6. Lubricate the drive gear housing bushing.
7. Engage the shift lever yoke with the clutch and slide the complete assembly into the drive gear housing.
8. Install the shift lever pivot bolt and tighten.
9. Install the solenoid assembly and apply sealer to the solenoid flange where the field frame contacts it.
10. Position the field frame against the drive gear housing on the alignment pin using care to prevent damage to the brushes.
11. Lubricate the commutator end frame and install the washer on the armature shaft. Slide the end frame onto the shaft and tighten the bolts. Make sure the bolts pass through the holes in the insulator.
12. Connect the field coil connector to the solenoid terminal.

➡ When the starter motor has been disassembled or the solenoid has been replaced, it is necessary to check the pinion clearance. Pinion clearance must be correct to prevent the buttons on the shift lever yoke from rubbing on the clutch collar during cranking.

13. Check pinion clearance as follows
   a. Disconnect the motor field coil connector from the solenoid motor terminal and insulate it carefully.
   b. Connect the (+) 12 volt battery lead to the solenoid motor terminal and the lead to the motor frame.
   c. Flash a jumper lead momentarily from the solenoid motor terminal to the starter frame. This will shift the pinion into the cranking position and will remain until the battery is disconnected.
   d. Push the pinion back as far as possible to take up any movement and check the clearance with a feeler gauge. The clearance should be 0.010–0.014 in. (0.25–0.35mm).
   e. Means for adjusting pinion clearance is not provided on the starter motor. If the clearance is not within specifications, check for improper installation or worn parts.

Sending Units and Sensors

Preceding each engine's engine code charts in Section 4 is a diagram identifying all engine sensors and sending units. To locate any sensor, refer to the appropriate diagram for your engine.

REMOVAL & INSTALLATION

1. Disconnect the negative battery cable.

CAUTION

When draining the coolant, keep in mind that cats and dogs are attracted by the ethylene glycol antifreeze, and are quite likely to drink any that is left in an uncovered container or in puddles on the ground. This will prove fatal in sufficient quantity. Always drain the coolant into a sealable container. Coolant should be reused unless it is contaminated or several years old.

2. Drain the coolant if removing a switch mounted on a surface with coolant below it.
3. To remove any sensor, simply disconnect the harness lead connected to it, carefully remove it from whatever it's mounted to, and install a new one using teflon tape on the threads.
4. Examine the connector terminals carefully before reconnecting.

ENGINE MECHANICAL

Engine Overhaul Tips

Most engine overhaul procedures are fairly standard. In addition to specific parts replacement procedures and complete specifications for your individual engine, this Section also is a guide to assist rebuilding procedures. Examples of standard rebuilding practice are shown and should be used along with specific details concerning your particular engine.

Competent and accurate machine shop services will ensure maximum performance, reliability and engine life.

In most instances it is more profitable for the do-it-yourself mechanic to remove, clean and inspect the component, buy the necessary parts and delivery these to a shop for actual machine work.

On the other hand, much of the rebuilding work (crankshaft, block, bearings, piston rods, and other components) is well within the scope of the do-it-yourself mechanic.

TOOLS

The tools required for an engine overhaul or parts replacement will depend on the depth of your involvement. With a few exceptions, they will be the tools found in a mechanic's tool kit (see Section 1). More in-depth work will require any or all of the following.

- dial indicator (reading in thousandths) mounted on a universal base
- micrometers and telescope gauges
- jaw and screw-type pullers
- scraper
- valve spring compressor
- ring groove cleaner
- cylinder hone or glaze breaker
- Plastigage®
- engine hoist and stand

The use of most of these tools is illustrated in this Section. Many can be rented for a one-time use from a local parts jobber or tool supply house specializing in automotive work.

Occasionally, the use of special tools is called for. See the information on Special Tools and Safety. Notice in the front of this book before substituting another tool.

INSPECTION TECHNIQUES

Procedures and specifications are given in this Section for inspecting, cleaning and assessing the wear limits of most major components. Other procedures such as Magnaflux® and Zyglo® can be used to locate material flaws and stress cracks. Magnaflux® is a magnetic process applicable only to ferrous materials. The Zyglo® process coats the material with a fluorescent dye penetrant and can be used on any material. Check for suspected surface cracks can be more readily made using spot check dye. The dye is sprayed onto the suspected area, wiped off and the area sprayed with a developer. Cracks will show up brightly.

OVERHAUL TIPS

Aluminum has become extremely popular for use in engines, due to its low weight. Observe the following precautions when handling aluminum parts:

- Never hot tank aluminum parts (the caustic hot tank solution will disintegrate the aluminum.
- Remove all aluminum parts (identification tag, etc.) from engine parts prior to the tanking.
- Always coat threads lightly with engine oil or anti-seize compounds before installation, to prevent seizure.
- Never overtorque bolts or spark plugs especially in aluminum threads.
- Stripped threads in any component can be repaired using any of several commercial repairs kits (Heli-Coil®, Microdot®, Keenserts®, etc.
- When assembling the engine, any parts that will be frictional contact must be prelubed to provide lubrication at initial start-up. Any product specifically formulated for this purpose can be used, but engine oil is not recommended as a prelube.
- When semi-permanent (locked, but removable) installation of bolts or nuts is desired, threads should be cleaned and coated with Loctite® or other similar, commercial non-hardening sealant.

REPAIRING DAMAGED THREADS

Several methods of repairing damaged threads are available. Heli-Coil®, Keenserts® and Microdot® are among the most widely used. All involve basically the same principle-drilling out stripped threads, tapping the hole and installing a prewound insert-making welding, plugging and oversize fasteners unnecessary.

Two types of thread repair inserts are usually supplied: a standard type for most Inch Coarse, Inch Fine, Metric Course and Metric Fine thread sizes and a spark lug type to fit most spark plug port sizes. Consult the individual manufacturer's catalog to determine exact applications. Typical thread repair kits will contain a selection of prewound threaded inserts, a tap (corresponding to the outside diameter threads of the insert) and an installation tool. Spark plug inserts usually differ because they require a tap equipped with pilot threads and a combined reamer/tap section. Most manufacturers also supply blister-packed thread repair inserts separately in addition to a master kit containing a variety of taps and inserts plus installation tools. Be sure to follow the instructions provided with the kit you purchased to attain a successful repair.

Before effecting a repair to a threaded hole, remove any snapped, broken or damaged bolts or studs. Penetrating oil can be used to free frozen threads. The offending item can be removed with locking pliers or with a screw or stud extractor. After the hole is clear, the thread can be repaired.

Checking Engine Compression

A noticeable lack of engine power, excessive oil consumption and/or poor fuel mileage measured over an extended period are all indicators of internal engine wear. Worn piston rings, scored or worn cylinder bores, blown head gaskets, sticking or burnt valves and worn valve seats are all possible culprits here. A check of each cylinder's compression will help you locate the problems.

As mentioned in the Tools and Equipment section of Section 1, a screw-in type compression gauge is more accurate that the type you simply hold against the spark plug hole, although it takes slightly longer to use. It's worth it to obtain a more accurate reading. Follow the procedures given:

1. Warm up the engine to normal operating temperature.
2. Make the spark plug wires and remove all the spark plugs.
3. Disconnect the BAT terminal from the ignition module.
4. Remove the air cleaner assembly and fully open the throttle plates by operating the throttle linkage by hand or by having an assistant floor the accelerator pedal.
5. Coat the gauge threads with oil and screw the compression gauge into the no. 1 spark plug hole until the fitting is snug.

**** CAUTION**

Be careful not to crossthread the plug hole. On aluminum cylinder heads use extra care, as the threads in these heads are easily ruined.

6. Ask an assistant to depress the accelerator pedal fully. Then, while you read the compression gauge, ask the assistant to crank the engine two or three times in short bursts using the ignition switch. There should be four puffs per cylinder.
7. Read the compression gauge at the end of each series of cranks, and record the highest of these readings. Repeat this procedure for each of the engine's cylinders. Compare the highest

reading of each cylinder to the compression pressure specification. The lowest cylinder reading should not be less than 70% of the highest reading. Examples follow:

a. NORMAL: Compression builds up quickly and evenly to the specified compression on each cylinder.

b. PISTON RINGS: Compression low on the first stroke, tends to build up on the following strokes, but does not reach normal. This reading should be tested with the addition of a few shots of engine oil into the cylinder. If the compression increases considerably, the rings are leaking compression.

c. VALVES: Low on the first stroke, does not tend to build up on following strokes. This reading will stay around the same with a few shots of engine oil.

d. HEAD GASKET: The compression reading is low between two adjacent cylinders. the head gasket between the two cylinders may be blown. If there is the sign of white smoke coming from the exhaust while the engine is running may indicate water leaking into the cylinder.

8. If a cylinder is unusually low, shoot about a tablespoon of clean engine oil into the cylinder through the spark plug hole and repeat the compression test. If the compression comes up after adding the oil, it appears that the cylinder's piston rings or bore are damaged or worn. If the pressure remains low, the valves may not be seating properly (a valve job is needed), or the head gasket may be blown near that cylinder. If compression in any two adjacent cylinders is low, and if the addition of oil does not help the compression, there is leakage past the head gasket. Oil and coolant water in the combustion chamber can result from this problem. There may be evidence of water droplets on the engine dipstick when a head gasket has blown.

GENERAL ENGINE SPECIFICATIONS

Year	VIN	No. Cylinder Displacement (liter)	Fuel System Type	Net Horsepower @ rpm	Net Torque @ rpm (ft. lbs.)	Bore × Stroke (in.)	Com-pression Ratio	Oil Pressure @ rpm
1988-89	R	2.5	TBI	98 @ 4500	134 @ 2800	4.000 × 3.000	8.3:1	26 @ 800
	W	2.8	MFI	125 @ 4500	160 @ 3600	3.500 × 2.990	8.9:1	15 @ 1100
	T	3.1	MFI	140 @ 4500	185 @ 3600	3.500 × 3.310	8.8:1	15 @ 1100
1990	A	2.3 ①	MFI	180 @ 6200	160 @ 5200	3.620 × 3.350	10.0:1	30 @ 2000
	D	2.3	MFI	160 @ 6200	155 @ 5200	3.620 × 3.350	9.5:1	30 @ 2000
	R	2.5	TBI	98 @ 4500	134 @ 2800	4.000 × 3.000	8.3:1	35 @ 2000
	T	3.1	MFI	140 @ 4400	185 @ 3200	3.500 × 3.310	8.8:1	15 @ 1100
	V	3.1	MFI ②	205 @ 4800	220 @ 3000	3.500 × 3.310	8.9:1	15 @ 1100
	L	3.8	MFI	165 @ 4800	210 @ 2000	3.800 × 3.400	8.5:1	60 @ 1850
1991	D	2.3	MFI	160 @ 6200	155 @ 5200	3.620 × 3.350	9.5:1	30 @ 2000
	R	2.5	TBI	98 @ 4500	134 @ 2800	4.000 × 3.000	8.3:1	35 @ 2000
	T	3.1	MFI	140 @ 4400	180 @ 3600	3.500 × 3.310	8.8:1	15 @ 1100
	L	3.8	MFI	170 @ 4800	220 @ 3200	3.800 × 3.400	8.5:1	60 @ 1850
	X	3.4	MFI	③	215 @ 4000	3.622 × 3.312	9.25:1	15 @ 1100
1992	R	2.5	TBI	98 @ 4500	134 @ 2800	4.000 × 3.000	8.3:1	35 @ 2000
	T	3.1	MFI	140 @ 4400	180 @ 3600	3.500 × 3.310	8.8:1	15 @ 1100
	L	3.8	MFI	170 @ 4800	220 @ 3200	3.800 × 3.400	8.5:1	60 @ 1850
	X	3.4	MFI	③	215 @ 4000	3.622 × 3.312	9.25:1	15 @ 1100

MFI—Multi Point Fuel Injection
TBI—Throttle Body Injection
① High output (H.O.)
② Turbocharged
③ Manual—210 @ 5200
Auto—200 @ 5000

VALVE SPECIFICATIONS

Year	VIN	No. Cylinder Displacement (liter)	Seat Angle (deg.)	Face Angle (deg.)	Spring Test Pressure (lbs.)	Spring Installed Height (in.)	Stem-to-Guide Clearance (in.)		Stem Diameter (in.)	
							Intake	Exhaust	Intake	Exhaust
1988-89	R	2.5	46	45	75 @ 1.68 ①	1.68	0.0010–0.0026	0.0013–0.0041	NA	NA
	W	2.8	46	45	90 @ 1.70 ①	1.57	0.0010–0.0027	0.0010–0.0027	NA	NA
	T	3.1	46	45	90 @ 1.70 ①	1.57	0.0010–0.0027	0.0010–0.0027	NA	NA
1990	A	2.3	45	②	76 @ 1.43 ①	NA	0.0010–0.0027	0.0015–0.0032	NA	NA
	D	2.3	45	②	76 @ 1.43 ①	NA	0.0010–0.0027	0.0015–0.0032	NA	NA
	R	2.5	45	46	75 @ 1.68	1.68	0.0010–0.0026	0.0013–0.0041	NA	NA
	V	3.1	46	45	90 @ 1.70 ①	1.57	0.0010–0.0027	0.0010–0.0027	NA	NA
	T	3.1	46	45	90 @ 1.70 ①	1.57	0.0010–0.0027	0.0010–0.0027	NA	NA
	L	3.8	46	45	80 @ 1.75 ①	1.70	0.0015–0.0035	0.0015–0.0032	NA	NA
1991	D	2.3	45	②	76 @ 1.43 ①	NA	0.0010–0.0027	0.0015–0.0032	NA	NA
	R	2.5	45	46	75 @ 1.68	1.68	0.0010–0.0026	0.0013–0.0041	NA	NA
	T	3.1	46	45	90 @ 1.70 ①	1.57	0.0010–0.0027	0.0010–0.0027	NA	NA
	X	3.4	46	45	75 @ 1.400 ①	1.66	0.0011–0.0026	0.0014–0.0031	NA	NA
	L	3.8	46	45	80 @ 1.75 ①	1.70	0.0015–0.0035	0.0015–0.0032	NA	NA
1992	R	2.5	45	46	75 @ 1.68	1.68	0.0010–0.0026	0.0013–0.0041	NA	NA
	T	3.1	46	45	90 @ 1.70 ①	1.57	0.0010–0.0027	0.0010–0.0027	NA	NA
	X	3.4	46	45	75 @ 1.400 ①	1.66	0.0011–0.0026	0.0014–0.0031	NA	NA
	L	3.8	46	45	80 @ 1.75 ①	1.70	0.0015–0.0035	0.0015–0.0032	NA	NA

NA—Not available
① Valve closed
② Intake—44 degrees
Exhaust—44.5 degrees

CAMSHAFT SPECIFICATIONS

All measurements given in inches.

Year	VIN	No. Cylinder Displacement (liter)	Journal Diameter 1	2	3	4	5	Lobe Lift In.	Lobe Lift Ex.	Bearing Clearance	Camshaft End Play
1988-89	R	2.5	1.869	1.869	1.869	1.869	—	0.248	0.248	0.0010–0.0030	0.0014–0.0050
	W	2.8	1.867–1.881	1.867–1.881	1.867–1.881	1.867–1.881	—	0.262	0.273	0.0010–0.0040	—
	T	3.1	1.867–1.881	1.867–1.881	1.867–1.881	1.867–1.881	—	0.262	0.273	0.0010–0.0040	—
1990	A	2.3	1.5728–1.5720	1.3751–1.3760	1.3751–1.3760	1.3751–1.3760	1.3751–1.3760	0.410	0.410	0.0019–0.0043	0.0009–0.0088
	D	2.3	1.5728–1.5720	1.3751–1.3760	1.3751–1.3760	1.3751–1.3760	1.3751–1.3760	0.375	0.375	0.0019–0.0043	0.0009–0.0088
	R	2.5	1.869	1.869	1.869	1.869	—	0.248	0.248	0.0010–0.0027	0.0014–0.0050
	T	3.1	1.8677–1.8815	1.8677–1.8815	1.8677–1.8815	1.8677–1.8815	—	0.262	0.273	0.0010–0.0040	—
	V	3.1	1.8677–1.8815	1.8677–1.8815	1.8677–1.8815	1.8677–1.8815	—	0.262	0.273	0.0010–0.0040	—
	L	3.8	1.785–1.786	1.785–1.786	1.785–1.786	1.785–1.786	—	0.250	0.255	0.0005–0.0035	—
1991	D	2.3	1.5728–1.5720	1.3751–1.3760	1.3751–1.3760	1.3751–1.3760	1.3751–1.3760	0.375	0.375	0.0019–0.0043	0.0009–0.0088
	R	2.5	1.869	1.869	1.869	1.869	—	0.248	0.248	0.0007–0.0027	0.0014–0.0050
	T	3.1	1.8677–1.8815	1.8677–1.8815	1.8677–1.8815	1.8677–1.8815	—	0.262	0.273	0.0010–0.0040	—
	X	3.4	2.165–2.166	2.165–2.166	2.165–2.166	2.165–2.166	—	0.370	0.370	0.0015–0.0035	—
	L	3.8	1.785–1.786	1.785–1.786	1.785–1.786	1.785–1.786	—	0.250	0.255	0.0005–0.0035	—
1992	R	2.5	1.869	1.869	1.869	1.869	—	0.248	0.248	0.0007–0.0027	0.0014–0.0050
	T	3.1	1.8677–1.8815	1.8677–1.8815	1.8677–1.8815	1.8677–1.8815	—	0.262	0.273	0.0010–0.0040	—
	X	3.4	2.165–2.166	2.165–2.166	2.165–2.166	2.165–2.166	—	0.370	0.370	0.0015–0.0035	—
	L	3.8	1.785–1.786	1.785–1.786	1.785–1.786	1.785–1.786	—	0.250	0.255	0.0005–0.0035	—

CRANKSHAFT AND CONNECTING ROD SPECIFICATIONS

All measurements are given in inches.

Year	VIN	No. Cylinder Displacement (liter)	Crankshaft Main Brg. Journal Dia.	Crankshaft Main Brg. Oil Clearance	Crankshaft Shaft End-play	Crankshaft Thrust on No.	Connecting Rod Journal Diameter	Connecting Rod Oil Clearance	Connecting Rod Side Clearance
1988-89	R	2.5	2.3000	0.0005–0.0022	0.0005–0.0180	5	2.0000	0.0005–0.0030	0.0060–0.0240
	W	2.8	2.6473–2.6483	0.0012–0.0027	0.0024–0.0083	3	1.9994–1.9983	0.0014–0.0036	0.0140–0.0270
	T	3.1	2.6473–2.6483	0.0024–0.0027	0.0012–0.0083	3	1.9994–1.9983	0.0014–0.0036	0.0140–0.0270
1990	A	2.3	2.0470–2.0480	0.0005–0.0023	0.0034–0.0095	3	1.8887–1.8897	0.0005–0.0020	0.0054–0.0177
	D	2.3	2.0470–2.0480	0.0005–0.0023	0.0034–0.0095	3	1.8887–1.8897	0.0005–0.0020	0.0054–0.0177
	R	2.5	2.3000	0.0005–0.0022	0.0005–0.0180	5	2.0000	0.0005–0.0003	0.0060–0.0240
	T	3.1	2.6473–2.6483	0.0012–0.0030	0.0024–0.0083	3	1.9983–1.9994	0.0016–0.0034	0.0140–0.0270
	V	3.1	2.6473–2.6483	0.0012–0.0030	0.0024–0.0083	3	1.9983–1.9994	0.0011–0.0034	0.0140–0.0270
	L	3.8	2.4988–2.4998	0.0018–0.0030	0.0030–0.0110	3	2.2487–2.2499	0.0003–0.0026	0.0030–0.0150
1991	D	2.3	2.0470–2.0480	0.0005–0.0023	0.0034–0.0095	3	1.8887–1.8897	0.0005–0.0020	0.0054–0.0177
	R	2.5	2.3000	0.0005–0.0022	0.0005–0.0180	5	2.0000	0.0005–0.0003	0.0060–0.0240
	T	3.1	2.6473–2.6483	0.0012–0.0030	0.0024–0.0083	3	1.9983–1.9994	0.0016–0.0034	0.0140–0.0270
	X	3.4	2.6473–2.6479	0.0013–0.0030	0.0024–0.0083	3	1.9987–1.9994	0.0011–0.0032	0.0140–0.0250
	L	3.8	2.4988–2.4998	0.0018–0.0030	0.0030–0.0110	3	2.2487–2.2499	0.0003–0.0026	0.0030–0.0150
1992	R	2.5	2.3000	0.0005–0.0022	0.0005–0.0180	5	2.0000	0.0005–0.0003	0.0060–0.0240
	T	3.1	2.6473–2.6483	0.0012–0.0030	0.0024–0.0083	3	1.9983–1.9994	0.0016–0.0034	0.0140–0.0270
	X	3.4	2.6473–2.6479	0.0013–0.0030	0.0024–0.0083	3	1.9987–1.9994	0.0011–0.0032	0.0140–0.0250
	L	3.8	2.4988–2.4998	0.0018–0.0030	0.0030–0.0110	3	2.2487–2.2499	0.0003–0.0026	0.0030–0.0150

PISTON AND RING SPECIFICATIONS

All measurements are given in inches.

Year	VIN	No. Cylinder Displacement cu. in. (liter)	Piston Clearance	Ring Gap Top Compression	Ring Gap Bottom Compression	Ring Gap Oil Control	Ring Side Clearance Top Compression	Ring Side Clearance Bottom Compression	Ring Side Clearance Oil Control
1988-89	R	2.5	0.0014–0.0022	0.010–0.020	0.010–0.020	0.020–0.060	0.002–0.003	0.001–0.003	0.015–0.055
	W	2.8	0.0009–0.0022	0.010–0.020	0.010–0.020	0.020–0.055	0.002–0.003	0.002–0.003	0.001–0.008
	T	3.1	0.0009–0.0022	0.010–0.020	0.010–0.028	0.010–0.030	0.002–0.003	0.002–0.003	0.001–0.008
1990	A	2.3	0.0007–0.0020	0.013–0.023	0.015–0.025	0.015–0.055	0.002–0.004	0.001–0.003	0.019–0.026
	D	2.3	0.0007–0.0020	0.013–0.023	0.015–0.025	0.015–0.055	0.002–0.003	0.001–0.003	0.019–0.026
	R	2.5	0.0014–0.0022	0.010–0.020	0.010–0.020	0.020–0.060	0.002–0.003	0.001–0.003	0.015–0.055
	V	3.1	0.0009–0.0022	0.010–0.020	0.020–0.028	0.010–0.030	0.002–0.003	0.002–0.003	0.001–0.008
	T	3.1	0.0009–0.0022	0.010–0.020	0.010–0.028	0.010–0.030	0.002–0.003	0.002–0.003	0.001–0.008
	L	3.8	0.0004–0.0022	0.010–0.025	0.010–0.025	0.015–0.055	0.001–0.003	0.001–0.003	0.001–0.008
1991	D	2.3	0.0007–0.0020	0.013–0.023	0.015–0.025	0.015–0.055	0.002–0.003	0.001–0.003	0.019–0.026
	R	2.5	0.0014–0.0022	0.010–0.020	0.010–0.020	0.020–0.060	0.002–0.003	0.001–0.003	0.015–0.055
	T	3.1	0.0009–0.0022	0.010–0.020	0.010–0.028	0.010–0.030	0.002–0.003	0.002–0.003	0.001–0.008
	X	3.4	0.0009–0.0023	0.012–0.022	0.019–0.029	0.010–0.030	0.001–0.003	0.001–0.003	0.002–0.008
	L	3.8	0.0004–0.0022	0.010–0.025	0.010–0.025	0.015–0.055	0.001–0.003	0.001–0.003	0.001–0.008
1992	R	2.5	0.0014–0.0022	0.010–0.020	0.010–0.020	0.020–0.060	0.002–0.003	0.001–0.003	0.015–0.055
	T	3.1	0.0009–0.0022	0.010–0.020	0.010–0.028	0.010–0.030	0.002–0.003	0.002–0.003	0.001–0.008
	X	3.4	0.0009–0.0023	0.012–0.022	0.019–0.029	0.010–0.030	0.001–0.003	0.001–0.003	0.002–0.008
	L	3.8	0.0004–0.0022	0.010–0.025	0.010–0.025	0.015–0.055	0.001–0.003	0.001–0.003	0.001–0.008

TORQUE SPECIFICATIONS

All readings in ft. lbs.

Year	VIN	No. Cylinder Displacement cu. in. (liter)	Cylinder Head Bolts	Main Bearing Bolts	Rod Bearing Bolts	Crankshaft Pulley Bolts	Flywheel Bolts	Manifold Intake	Manifold Exhaust	Spark Plugs
1988-89	R	2.5	②	65	29	162	55	25	④	18
	W	2.8	①	70	37	76	46	③	18	18
	T	3.1	①	70	37	76	46	③	18	18
1990	A	2.3	⑤	⑥	⑦	⑧	⑨	18	27	17
	D	2.3	⑤	⑥	⑦	⑧	⑨	18	27	17
	R	2.5	②	65	29	162	55	25	④	18
	V	3.1	①	73	39	76	44	③	18	18
	T	3.1	①	73	39	76	44	③	18	18
	L	3.8	⑩	⑪	⑫	⑬	⑭	⑮	41	20
1991	D	2.3	⑤	⑥	⑦	⑧	⑨	18	27	17
	R	2.5	②	65	29	162	55	25	④	18
	V	3.1	①	73	39	76	44	③	18	18
	T	3.1	①	73	39	76	44	③	18	18
	X	3.4	⑯	⑰	39	37	61	18	⑱	11
	L	3.8	⑩	⑪	⑫	⑬	⑭	⑮	41	20
1992	R	2.5	②	65	29	162	55	25	④	18
	V	3.1	①	73	39	76	44	③	18	18
	T	3.1	①	73	39	76	44	③	18	18
	X	3.4	⑯	⑰	39	37	61	18	⑱	11
	L	3.8	⑩	⑪	⑫	⑬	⑭	⑮	41	20

① Torque in 2 steps:
1st step—33 ft. lbs.
2nd step—Turn an additional 90 degrees (1/4) turn

② Torque in 3 steps:
1st step—18 ft. lbs.
2nd step—Bolts "A" through "J" except "I" to 26 ft. lbs. Tighten bolt "I" to 18 ft. lbs.
3rd step—Turn an additional 90 degrees (1/4) turn

③ Torque in 2 steps:
1st step—15 ft. lbs.
2nd step—24 ft. lbs.

④ Torque inner bolts to 37 ft. lbs. and outer bolts to 26 ft. lbs.

⑤ Torque in 2 steps:
1st step—Torque all bolts in sequence to 26 ft. lbs.
2nd step—Torque in sequence bolts number 7 and 9 an additional 100 degrees and the remaining bolts 110 degrees

⑥ 15 ft. lbs. plus an additional 90 degree turn

⑦ 18 ft. lbs. plus an additional 80 degree turn

⑧ 74 ft. lbs. plus an additional 90 degree turn

⑨ 22 ft. lbs. plus an additional 45 degree turn

⑩ Torque in 3 steps:
1st step—Tighten all bolts in sequence to 35 ft. lbs.
2nd step—Tighten all bolts in sequence an additional 130 degrees
3rd step—Tighten the center 4 bolts an additional 30 degrees

⑪ 26 ft. lbs. plus an additional 45 degree turn

⑫ 20 ft. lbs. plus an additional 50 degree turn

⑬ 105 ft. lbs. plus an additional 56 degree turn

⑭ 89 inch lbs. plus an additional 90 degree turn

⑮ Intake manifold to cylinder head (lower)—89 inch lbs.

⑯ Torque in 2 steps:
1st step—Torque all bolts in sequence to 37 ft. lbs.
2nd step—Turn an additinal 90 degrees (1/4) turn

⑰ 37 ft. lbs. plus an additinoal 75 degree turn

⑱ Torque to 115 inch lbs.

Relieving Fuel System Pressure

2.5L Engine

1. Remove the fuel filler cap.
2. Remove the fuel pump fuse from the fuse block located in the passenger compartment.
3. Start the engine and run until the engine stops due to the lack of fuel.
4. Crank the engine for 3 seconds to ensure all pressure is relieved.
5. Make sure the negative battery cable is disconnected.

2.3L, 2.8L, 3.1L, 3.4L, and 3.8L Engines

1. Disconnect the negative battery cable. Loosen fuel filler cap.
2. Connect fuel pressure gauge J–34730–1 or equivalent, to the fuel pressure connection.
3. Wrap a shop cloth around the fitting while connecting the gauge to catch any leaking fuel.
4. Install the bleed hose into an approved container and open the valve. Connect the negative battery cable.
5. When the repair to the fuel system is complete check all of the fittings for leaks.

Engine

REMOVAL & INSTALLATION

**** CAUTION**

When draining the coolant, keep in mind that cats and dogs are attracted by the ethylene glycol antifreeze, and are quite likely to drink any that is left in an uncovered container or in puddles on the ground. This will prove fatal in sufficient quantity. Always drain the coolant into a sealable container. Coolant should be reused unless it is contaminated or several years old.

The EPA warns that prolonged contact with used engine oil may cause a number of skin disorders, including cancer! You should make every effort to minimize your exposure to used engine oil. Protective gloves should be worn when changing the oil. Wash your hands and any other exposed skin areas as soon as possible after exposure to used engine oil. Soap and water, or waterless hand cleaner should be used.

**** WARNING**

2.3L Engine

➧ SEE FIG. 13

1. Disconnect the negative battery cable.
2. Release the fuel system pressure.
3. Mark the hood hinges and remove the hood with an assistant. Drain the engine coolant into a suitable drain pan.
4. Remove the heater hoses at the heater core and thermostat housing.
5. Remove the radiator upper hose.
6. Remove the air cleaner and inlet hose from the vehicle.
7. If equipped with air conditioning, discharge the system.
8. Remove the air conditioning compressor and condenser hose at the compressor, if equipped.
9. Disconnect and label engine the vacuum lines.
10. Disconnect and label the electrical connectors from the alternator, air conditioning compressor, fuel injection harness, starter solenoid, engine ground strap, ignition assembly, coolant sensor, oil pressure sensor, knock sensor, oxygen sensor, Idle Air Control (IAC) valve and Throttle Position Sensor (TPS). The last 2 sensors are located at the throttle body.
11. Disconnect the power brake vacuum hose and throttle cable.
12. Remove the power steering pump and position aside. Do not remove the pump hoses, unless necessary.
13. Release the fuel pressure, if not already done and remove the fuel lines.
14. Remove the engine torque strut mounts.
15. Remove the transaxle fill tube, auto transaxle only.
16. Remove the exhaust heat shield and exhaust pipe-to-manifold.
17. Remove the upper transaxle-to-engine bolts.
18. Raise the vehicle and support it safely.
19. Remove the remaining lower transaxle-to-engine bolts.
20. Remove the exhaust-to-transaxle bracket.
21. Remove the lower radiator hose.
22. Remove the flywheel or converter cover.
23. Scribe a mark on the torque converter and flywheel. Remove the torque converter nuts.
24. Remove the transaxle-to-engine bracket.
25. Lower the vehicle.
26. Install the engine lifting fixture and remove the engine. Place the engine on a workstand.

To install:

➡ Make sure all the engine mounting bolts are in their correct location to prevent transaxle and engine damage.

27. Install the engine to a lifting fixture and position the engine in the vehicle. With an assistant, align the engine-to-transaxle.
28. Raise the vehicle and support it safely.
29. Install the transaxle-to-engine bracket

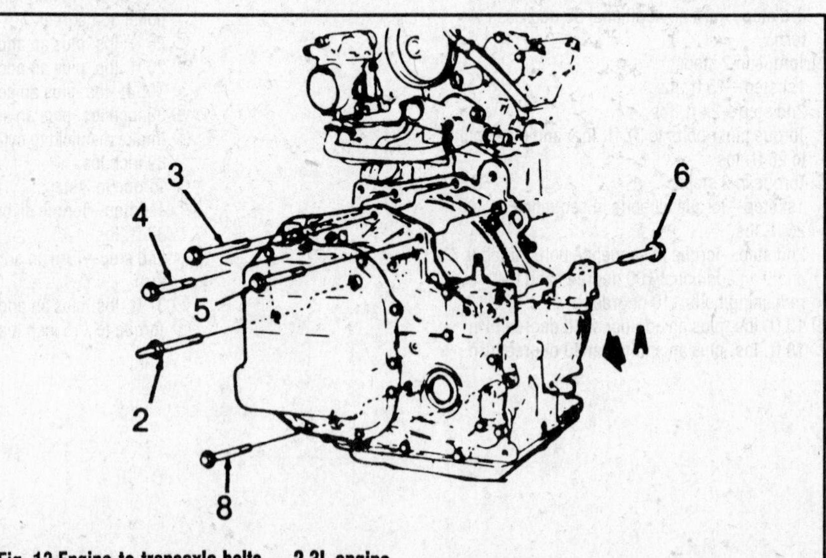

Fig. 13 Engine-to-transaxle bolts — 2.3L engine

and bolts. Torque the engine-to-transaxle bolts to:

a. Positions No. 2, 3, 4, 5, 6 — 71 ft. lbs. (96 Nm).

b. Positions No. 7, 8 — 41 ft. lbs. (56 Nm).

30. Apply thread locking compound and install the torque converter-to-flywheel bolts. Torque the bolts to 46 ft. lbs. (63 Nm). Install the flywheel cover.
31. At the right side of the vehicle, install the engine mount bolt.
32. Install the lower radiator hose and engine ground wires.
33. Install the air conditioning compressor and CONDENSER hose. Connect the compressor and alternator electrical harnesses.
34. Install the heater hoses at the heater core and throttle body.
35. Install the exhaust-to-transaxle bracket.
36. Lower the vehicle.
37. Install the exhaust pipe-to-manifold and heat shield. Torque the exhaust bolts to 22 ft. lbs. (30 Nm).
38. Install the upper engine mounts.
39. Connect the fuel lines.
40. Install the power steering pump, lines and drive belt.
41. Install the throttle cable and power brake vacuum hose.
42. Connect the electrical connectors to the oxygen sensor, knock sensor, oil pressure sensor, coolant sensor, ignition assembly, TPS sensor, IAC sensor and starter solenoid.
43. Connect all engine vacuum hoses.
44. Install the upper radiator hose and fill the radiator with the specified amount of antifreeze.
45. Refill the engine with the specified amount of engine oil.
46. Evacuate and recharge the air conditioning system.
47. Install the air cleaner and inlet hose.
48. Install the hood assembly with the help of an assistant.
49. Recheck all procedures for completion of repair.
50. Recheck all fluid levels.
51. Connect the negative battery cable. Start the engine and check for fluid leaks.

2.5L Engine

1. Disconnect the negative battery cable.
2. Place a suitable drain pan under the radiator drain valve and drain the engine coolant.
3. Remove the air cleaner assembly. Release fuel system pressure.
4. Mark the hood hinges with a scribe and remove the hood assembly.
5. Mark and remove all engine wiring. Place all the wire assemblies out of the way.
6. Remove the vacuum, heater and radiator hoses labeling for location.
7. Remove the air conditioning compressor from the engine and place to the side with a piece of rope or wire. Do not disconnect the hoses from the compressor.
8. Remove the alternator and bracket.
9. Remove the engine torque strut.
10. Remove the throttle and transaxle linkage.
11. Remove the transaxle-to-engine bolts except the 2 upper bolts.
12. Raise the vehicle and support it safely.
13. Remove the engine mount-to-frame bolts.
13. Remove the exhaust pipe from the manifold.
14. Remove the torque converter-to-flywheel bolts.
15. Remove the starter motor.
16. Remove the power steering pump and attach to the inner fender with a piece of rope or wire. Do not disconnect the hoses.
17. Release fuel pressure, if not done prior, and remove the fuel lines at the throttle body assembly.
18. Remove the rear engine support bracket.
19. Support the transaxle assembly with a transaxle holding fixture.
20. Disconnect the transaxle from the engine and support with a jack.
21. Attach an suitable engine lifting device.
22. Remove the engine assembly. Use care not to get under the engine assembly in case of lift failure.
23. Place the engine on a workstand.

To Install:

24. Place the engine assembly onto a lifting device.
25. With an assistant, install the engine into the vehicle.
26. Position the engine into the engine mounts and engage the transaxle with the engine.
27. Remove the engine lifting device.
28. Install the torque converter bolts and engine-to-transaxle mounting bolts. Torque the torque converter bolts to 55 ft. lbs. (75 Nm).
29. Remove the transaxle holding fixture.
30. Install the rear support bracket bolts.
31. Install the engine mount nuts and torque to 32 ft. lbs. (43 Nm).
32. Install the rear transaxle mount bracket bolts and torque to 35 ft. lbs. (47 Nm).
33. Install the fuel lines to the throttle body assembly.
34. Install the power steering pump.
35. Install the starter motor assembly.
36. Install the flywheel cover plate.
37. Install the exhaust pipe-to-manifold.
38. Install the engine torque strut.
39. Install the alternator and bracket.
40. Install the air conditioning compressor.
41. Install the heater, radiator and vacuum hoses.
42. Install the throttle and transaxle linkages.
43. Install and reconnect all engine wiring harnesses.
44. Install the hood assembly to its original position with an assistant.
45. Refill the cooling system with engine coolant.
46. Reconnect the negative battery cable.
47. Install the air cleaner assembly.
48. Inspect for proper fluid levels.
49. Recheck every procedure for proper reinstallation.
50. Start the vehicle and check for any fluid leaks.

2.8L, 3.1L and 3.4L Engines

ENGINE REMOVED FROM BELOW

1. Remove the air cleaner assembly and ground wire near cleaner bracket.
2. Disconnect the negative battery cable and body ground.
3. Drain the engine coolant into a suitable drain pan. On 3.4L engine, it will be necessary to remove the coolant recovery tank.
4. Remove the battery remote jump start terminal from the body but leave the cables attached.
5. Disconnect the cooling fan electrical connectors and remove fans. Remove wiring harness cover and upper engine wire connectors at right strut tower, if equipped.
6. Remove the transaxle cooler lines at the radiator and the fluid level indicator.
7. Remove the upper and lower radiator hoses.
8. Remove the heater inlet and outlet hoses. On 3.4L engine, disconnect heater hose quick connect at intake manifold.
9. Release the fuel pressure. Disconnect fuel lines at fuel rail.
10. Remove the serpentine belt from the engine.
11. Remove the shift cable linkage and cable from the mounting bracket.
12. Remove the accelerator and cruise control from the throttle linkage, if equipped.
13. Remove the air conditioning pressure switch wire connector.
14. Remove the vacuum check valve from the power brake booster.
15. Remove the canister purge vacuum line at the engine.

16. Remove the torque struts from the engine.

17. Remove all electrical connectors at the right side cowl.

18. Remove the upper bolts securing the wiring harness plastic bracket-to-body side rail.

19. Remove the ECM and fuse block and set on top of the engine. If equipped with CONVENIENCE center, remove center, wiring harness cover, harness clips and low coolant sensor electrical connector.

20. Remove the strut-to-body mounting nuts.

21. Remove the vacuum hose from the vacuum reservoir.

22. Raise the vehicle and support it safely.

23. Remove the front wheel and tire assemblies.

24. Remove both side engine splash shields. On models with Anti-Lock Brakes (ABS), disconnect front brake ABS electrical sensors.

25. Remove the oil from the crankcase and remove the oil filter.

26. Remove the air conditioning compressor and hang from the body with the hoses still connected. On 3.4L engine, the factory recommends to discharge the air conditioner system and remove the lines near the accumulator.

27. Remove the exhaust crossover pipe and converter assembly.

CAUTION

Failure to disconnect the intermediate shaft from the rack and pinion stub shaft can result in damage to steering gear and/or intermediate shaft. This damage can result in loss of steering control which could cause personal injury.

28. Remove the steering gear pinch bolt.

29. Remove the brake hose from the strut.

30. Remove the brake calipers and support to body.

31. Lower the vehicle far enough to place the engine/transaxle table under the frame.

32. Remove the frame bolts.

33. Lower the table with the engine/transaxle attached.

34. Raise the vehicle and remove the engine/transaxle from the vehicle.

35. Separate the engine from the transaxle and place the engine on a workstand.

To install:

36. Attach the transaxle and engine together and tighten. Slowly lower the body onto the drivetrain.

37. Install the strut bolts to the shock towers.

38. Install the frame bolts.

39. Remove the engine/transaxle table from under the vehicle.

40. Install the brake calipers.

41. Install the brake hoses at the struts.

➡ When installing the intermediate shaft make sure the shaft is seated prior to pinch bolt installation. If the pinch bolt is inserted into the coupling before shaft installation, the 2 mating shafts may disengage.

42. Install the steering pinch bolt.

43. Install the exhaust crossover pipe and converter assembly.

44. Install the air conditioning compressor and hoses as required.

45. Install the oil filter and splash shields. Reconnect ABS electrical connector.

46. Install the tire and wheel assemblies and torque the lug nuts to 100 ft. lbs. (136 Nm).

47. Install the wiring harness bracket to body side rail.

48. Lower the vehicle.Add engine oil to correct level.

49. Install the vacuum hose at the vacuum reservoir.

50. Install the ECM and the fuse block.

51. Install the remaining bolts securing the wiring harness bracket to the body side rail.

52. Install the torque struts at engine.

53. Reconnect the canister purge vacuum line and vacuum check valve at the power brake booster.

54. Reconnect the air conditioning pressure switch electrical connector. Recharge air conditioning system as required.

55. Reconnect the accelerator and cruise control cables to the mounting bracket.

56. Install the serpentine belt and fuel lines to fuel rail.

57. Install the heater inlet and outlet hoses. Reconnect heater hose quick connect at intake manifold.

58. Install the radiator upper and lower hoses and coolant recovery tank.

59. Install the transaxle fluid indicator and cooler lines at the radiator.

60. Install radiator fans and reconnect the fan electrical connectors.

61. Install the battery remote jump start terminal to body.

62. Refill all necessary fluids, engine oil, coolant, transaxle fluid.

63. Install the battery cables and all body grounds.

64. Install the air cleaner assembly.

65. Recheck all procedures for proper reinstallation.

66. Turn ignition **ON** for 3 seconds and turn **OFF**. Check for fuel leaks. Repeat this procedure a second time and recheck for fuel leaks.

67. Start the engine and check for any fluid leaks.

68. Test drive vehicle, recheck for fluid leaks.

2.8L, 3.1L and 3.4L Engines

ENGINE REMOVED FROM TOP

1. Remove the air cleaner and duct assembly.

2. Disconnect the negative battery cable.

3. Mark the hood hinges to ensure proper reinstallation. With an assistant, remove the hood assembly.

4. Mark and remove all necessary engine wiring and place the harnesses out of the way.

5. Remove the throttle, TV and cruise control cables, if equipped, from the throttle body assembly.

6. Release the fuel pressure and remove the fuel lines at engine.

7. Remove the AIR pump and serpentine belt.

8. Position a suitable drain pan under the radiator drain valve and drain the engine coolant. Remove coolant recovery tank.

9. Remove the upper and lower radiator hoses and heater hose quick connect at intake manifold.

10. Remove the air conditioning compressor mounting bolts at the front mounting bracket.

11. Remove the power steering pump and move to the side. Attach to the body with a piece of wire or rope. Do not disconnect the pump hoses.

12. Remove the heater hoses from the engine and move out of the way.

13. Remove the brake booster vacuum hose.

14. Remove the EGR hose from the exhaust manifold. Remove pipe from EGR valve, if equipped.

15. Raise the vehicle and support it safely.

16. Remove the air conditioning compressor from the engine and attach to the body with a piece of rope or wire. The factory recommends removal of the air conditioning manifold from compressor.

17. Remove the right front tire and wheel.

18. Disconnect right ball joint nut and separate from control arm.

19. Remove halfshaft assembly.

20. Remove the flywheel cover, starter motor and torque converter bolts.

21. Remove the transaxle bracket and front engine mount nuts.

22. Remove the exhaust pipe and converter assembly from manifold.

23. Lower the vehicle.
24. Remove the torque struts.
25. Remove the left crossover pipe-to-manifold clamp.
26. Disconnect the bulkhead electrical connector and quick connects near Electronic Control Module (ECM).
27. Remove the right crossover pipe-to-manifold clamp.
28. Support the transaxle with a suitable floor jack or equivalent.
29. Remove the remaining transaxle-to-engine bolts.
30. Attach an engine lifting device and remove the engine from the vehicle. Check for connected wires and hoses as the engine is coming out of the body.
31. Place the engine on a workstand.

To install:

32. With an assistant, install a lifting device onto the engine and position into the vehicle.
33. Remove the lifting device.
34. Install the transaxle-to-engine bolts.
35. Remove the transaxle support.
36. Reconnect the right crossover pipe-to-manifold clamp.
37. Reconnect the bulkhead electrical connector.
38. Reconnect electrical connector at ECM.
39. Install the left crossover pipe-to-manifold clamp.
40. Install the coolant recovery bottle and torque struts.
41. Raise the vehicle and support it safely.
42. Reinstall halfshaft assembly.
43. Reconnect ball joint to control arm.
44. Reinstall tire and wheel. Torque to 100 ft. lbs.
45. Reconnect ABS electrical connector if equipped.
42. Install the crossover pipe and converter assembly.
43. Install the front engine mount retaining nuts and torque to 32 ft. lbs. (43 Nm).
44. Install the transaxle bracket, torque converter bolts and starter motor.
45. Install the flywheel cover.
46. Install the air conditioning compressor to engine.
47. Lower the vehicle.
48. Install the EGR pipe and hose to valve.
49. Reconnect the brake booster vacuum supply, heater hoses and power steering pump.
50. Install the air conditioning compressor front mounting bracket bolts.
51. Install the radiator hoses and fans, serpentine and AIR pump belts. Recharge as required.
52. Reconnect the fuel lines. Install coolant recovery tank.
53. Install the throttle, TV and cruise control linkage to the throttle body.
54. Reconnect all necessary engine electrical and ground wiring.
55. Install the hood assembly with an assistant.
56. Reconnect the battery cables.
57. Turn the ignition **ON** for 3 seconds and then return to **OFF** position. Check for fuel leaks. Repeat this procedure a second time.
58. Install the air cleaner and duct assembly.
59. Recheck all procedures for proper reinstallation and correct if necessary.
60. Refill the engine with engine oil, coolant and transaxle fluid, if needed.
61. Inspect vehicle for fluid leaks before and after starting the engine.
62. Road test the vehicle and recheck for fluid leaks.

3.8L Engine

1. Disconnect the negative battery cable.
2. Remove the air cleaner assembly.
3. Release the fuel system pressure.
4. Disconnect the fuel lines from the rail and mounting brackets.
5. Drain the engine coolant and remove the recovery bottle.
6. Remove the inner fender electrical cover and the fuel injector sight cover.
7. Disconnect the throttle cables from the throttle body and mounting bracket.
8. Remove the rear heat shield from the crossover pipe.
9. Remove the throttle cable mounting bracket and vacuum line as an assembly.
10. Disconnect the exhaust crossover from the manifolds.
11. Disconnect the engine torque strut bolt and strut from the engine.
12. Remove the right side engine cooling fan.
13. Disconnect the vacuum line to the transaxle module.
14. Remove the serpentine belt.
15. Remove the power steering pump and alternator assemblies.
16. Tag and disconnect all electrical connections from the engine.
17. Disconnect the upper and lower radiator, and heater hoses from the engine.
18. Remove the transaxle to engine bolts and ground wire harness.
19. Raise and support the vehicle safely.
20. Remove the right front wheel and inner splash shield.
21. Remove the flywheel cover, scribe a mark on the torque converter and flywheel and remove the flywheel to torque converter bolts.
22. Disconnect the wire harness clamps from the frame near the radiator.
23. Remove the air conditioner compressor from the bracket and lay aside and secure to the frame.
24. Disconnect the wires and remove the starter motor assembly.
25. Safely support the transaxle and remove the transaxle to engine bolt, through the wheel well, using a long extension.
26. Attach a lifting device and remove the engine mount to frame nuts.
27. Drain the engine oil and remove the oil filter.
28. Disconnect the oil cooler pipes from the hose connections.
29. Disconnect the exhaust pipe from the manifold.
30. Lower the vehicle and remove the engine assembly from the vehicle.

To install:

31. With an assistant, install a lifting device onto the engine and position into the vehicle.
32. Support the transaxle, install the transaxle-to-engine bolts and ground wire harness and torque to 46 ft. lbs.
33. Install the heater and upper and lower radiator hoses to the engine.
34. Install all electrical connections to the engine.
35. Install the alternator, power steering pump and serpentine belt.
36. Install the vacuum line to the transaxle module.
37. Install the engine torque strut and bolt and torque to 41 ft. lbs.
38. Install the exhaust crossover pipe.
39. Install the throttle cable mounting bracket and vacuum lines.
40. Install the heat shield to the crossover pipe and the throttle cables to the throttle body and mounting bracket.
41. Install the inner fender electrical cover and the coolant recovery bottle.
42. Install the fuel hoses to the fuel rail and mounting brackets.
43. Raise and support the vehicle safely.
44. Connect the front exhaust pipe to the manifold.
45. Install the oil filter and oil cooler pipes.
46. Install the engine mount nuts to the frame and torque to 32 ft. lbs.
47. Install the transaxle to engine bolt through the wheel well and torque to 46 ft. lbs.
48. Install the starter motor assembly and connect the electrical connectors.
49. Install the air conditioner compressor to the bracket.
50. Install the wire harness clamps to the frame near the radiator.
51. Align the scribe marks, install the torque converter to flywheel bolts and torque to 46 ft. lbs.

52. Install the flywheel cover and the inner fender splash shield.
53. Install the right front wheel assembly and lower the vehicle.
54. Refill the cooling system and bleed the power steering system.
55. Install the right side cooling fan.
56. Install the fuel injector sight shield and the air cleaner assembly.
57. Connect the negative battery cable and install the hood.
58. Check and add fluids as required. Test drive vehicle and recheck for leaks and correct levels.

Engine Mounts

REMOVAL & INSTALLATION

2.5L Engine

1. Disconnect the negative battery cable.
2. Raise and safely support the vehicle.
3. Remove the engine-to-chassis nuts.
4. Disconnect the engine torque struts.
5. Install an engine support fixture J–28467–A or equivalent.
6. Remove the upper mount-to-engine bracket nuts and remove the mount.

To install:

7. Install the mount and mount-to-engine bracket. Tighten the nuts to 32 ft. lbs. (43 Nm).
8. Install and tighten the torque strut nuts to 32 ft. lbs. (43 Nm).
9. Lower the vehicle and remove the engine support fixture.
10. Reconnect negative battery cable.

2.3L, 2.8L and 3.1L Engines

1. Disconnect the negative battery cable. Raise and safely support the vehicle.
2. Remove the engine mount retaining nuts from below the cradle mounting bracket.
3. Raise the engine slightly to provide clearance and remove the engine mount-to-bracket nuts.
4. Remove the engine mount.

To install:

5. Install the mount in position and tighten the mount-to-bracket nuts to 32 ft. lbs. Lower the engine into position.
6. Install the mounting bracket-to-cradle nuts and tighten to 63 ft. lbs.
7. Lower the vehicle and connect the negative battery cable.

3.4L Engine

FRONT MOUNT

1. Disconnect the negative battery cable.
2. Remove the air cleaner assembly.
3. Remove the engine torque strut.
4. Position engine support tools J–284678–A, J–28647–90 and J–36462 or equivalents, to support engine.
5. Raise and safely support vehicle.
6. Remove right front tire and wheel assembly.
7. Remove right front engine splash shield and halfshaft splash shield.
8. Remove engine oil filter.
9. Remove engine mount nuts on frame.
10. Remove engine mount nuts on bracket.
11.Install a halfshaft boot protector and raise engine. Remove mount.

To install:

12. Install mount in place and lower engine. Remove halfshaft boot protector.
13. Install engine mount nuts at bracket.
14. Install engine mount nuts at frame.
15. Install oil filter and right front splash shield.
16. Install right front wheel assembly.
17. Lower vehicle and remove engine supports.
18. Install engine torque strut, air cleaner assembly and negative battery cable.

REAR MOUNT

1. Disconnect the negative battery cable.
2. Remove the air cleaner assembly.
3. Remove the engine torque strut.
4. Position engine support tools J–284678–A, J–28647–90 and J–36462 or equivalents, to support engine.
5. Raise and safely support vehicle.
6. Remove right front tire and wheel assembly.
7. Remove right front engine splash shield and halfshaft splash shield.
8. Remove engine oil filter.
9. Remove engine mount nuts on frame.
10. Raise engine. Remove rack and pinion mounting bolts and secure to frame.
11. Remove right ball joint at control arm. Install support under right side of frame.
12. Remove right frame mounting bolts, loosen left side frame mounting bolts and lower right side of frame 2–3 in. (51–76mm).
13. Install halfshaft boot protector. Remove upper engine mount nuts at mount. Remove mount.

To install:

14. Install mount in place.
15. Install upper engine mount nuts at mount.
16. Install halfshaft splash shield.
17. Raise right side frame. Install and tighten right side frame and left frame mounting bolts to 103 ft. lbs.
18. Install right side ball joint and rack and pinion assembly.
19. Lower engine into position.
20. Install engine mount nuts at frame, torque to 32 ft. lbs.
21. Install oil filter and right front splash shield. Remove halfshaft boot protector.
22. Install right front wheel assembly.
23. Lower vehicle and remove engine supports.
24. Install engine torque strut, air cleaner assembly and negative battery cable.

3.8L Engine

1. Disconnect the negative battery cable. Raise and safely support the vehicle.
2. Remove the mount retaining nuts from below the frame mounting bracket.
3. Raise the engine slightly to provide clearance and remove the engine mount-to-bracket nuts using engine support and lifting fixtures J–28467–A, J–28467–90 and J–35953 or equivalent.
4. Remove the engine mount nuts and the mounts.

To install:

5. Install the mount and mount to engine bracket and remove the engine support and lifting fixtures.
6. Install the engine mount to frame nuts and torque to 32 ft. lbs., the engine mount to frame nuts to 32 ft. lbs. and the engine bracket to engine bolts to 70 ft. lbs.
7. Connect the negative battery cable.

Rocker Arm (or Valve) Cover

REMOVAL & INSTALLATION

CAUTION

When draining the coolant, keep in mind that cats and dogs are attracted by the ethylene glycol antifreeze, and are quite likely to drink any that is left in an uncovered container or in puddles on the ground. This will prove fatal in sufficient quantity. Always drain

the coolant into a sealable container. Coolant should be reused unless it is contaminated or several years old.

2.3L ENGINE

➡ The camshaft housing covers and cylinder heads use the same retaining bolts. When the bolts are removed to service the camshaft cover, the cylinder head gasket MUST be replaced also. Refer to "Cylinder Head" for procedures.

2.5L ENGINE

1. Remove the air cleaner assembly.
2. Remove the PCV valve and hose.
3. Remove the accelerator and throttle valve TV cables.
4. Remove the valve cover.
5. Disconnect and mark the wires from the spark plugs and clips.
6. Remove the valve cover by using the Rocker Arm Cover Removing tool No. J34144-A or equivalent and lightly tap with a rubber hammer.

➡ Prying on the cover could cause damage to the sealing surfaces.

To install:

7. Clean the rocker arm cover with solvent and dry with a clean rag.
8. Apply a continuous $^{3}/_{16}$ in. (5mm) diameter bead of RTV sealant or equivalent around the cylinder head sealing surfaces inboard at the bolt holes.
9. Install the rocker arm cover and torque the attaching bolts to 80 inch lbs. (9 Nm).
10. Install the spark plug wires and clips, PCV valve and hose, accelerator and TV cable and air cleaner assembly.

2.8L and 3.1L ENGINES

Front Rocker Cover

1. Remove the air cleaner assembly.
2. Disconnect the negative battery cable.
3. Drain the engine coolant from the radiator.
4. Remove the ignition wire clamps and guide from the coolant tube.
5. Remove the coolant tube mount at the cylinder head, coolant tube at each end, coolant tube at the water pump and coolant tube.
6. Remove the tube from the rocker cover to the air inlet.
7. Remove the four rocker cover retaining bolts and remove the cover.

➡ Prying on the cover could cause damage to the sealing surfaces.

To install:

8. Clean all sealing surfaces on the cylinder head and rocker cover with degreaser and a gasket scraper.
9. Install a new gasket and bolt grommets. Make sure the gasket is properly seated in the Rocker cover groove.
10. Apply a continuous $^{3}/_{16}$ in. (5mm) diameter bead of RTV sealant surfaces inboard at the bolt holes.
11. Install the rocker cover and torque the retaining bolts to 89 inch lbs. (10 Nm).
12. Install the ignition wire guide.
13. Install the tube from the rocker arm cover to the air inlet.
14. Reconnect the coolant tube, coolant tube hose at the water pump, coolant tube at each end and coolant tube mount at the cylinder head.
15. Install the ignition wire clamp at the coolant tube.

Rear Rocker Cover

1. Remove the air cleaner assembly.
2. Disconnect the negative battery cable.
3. Drain the engine coolant from the radiator.
4. Remove the vacuum hoses at the intake plenum.
5. Remove the EGR tube at the crossover pipe.
6. Remove the ignition wire guide and harness at the intake plenum and at spark plugs.
7. Remove the coolant hoses at the throttle base and electrical wiring from the intake plenum.
8. Remove the throttle, TV and cruise control cables from the throttle body assembly.
9. Remove the bracket from the right side of the intake plenum.
10. Remove the brake booster vacuum hose from the plenum.
11. Remove the serpentine belt.
12. Remove the coolant recovery bottle, exhaust pipe at the crossover and engine struts at the engine.
13. Rotate the engine as outlined in the "Ignition Coil" section in this Section.
14. Remove the alternator and set aside.
15. Remove the PCV valve from the rocker cover.
16. Remove the four rocker cover retaining bolts and remove the cover.

➡ Prying on the cover could cause damage to the sealing surfaces.

To install:

17. Clean all sealing surfaces on the cylinder head and rocker cover with degreaser and a gasket scraper.
18. Install a new gasket and bolt grommets. Make sure the gasket is properly seated in the rocker cover groove.
19. Apply a continuous $^{3}/_{16}$ in. (5mm) diameter bead of RTV sealant or equivalent around the cylinder head sealing surfaces inboard at the bolt holes.
20. Install the rocker cover and torque the retaining bolts to 89 inch lbs. (10 Nm).
21. Install the PCV valve to the rocker cover.
22. Install the alternator.
23. Return the engine to the proper position.
24. Install the torque struts to the engine, exhaust pipe at the crossover and the coolant recovery bottle.
25. Install the serpentine belt.
26. Reconnect the brake booster vacuum hose and support bracket in the intake plenum.
27. Reconnect the throttle, TV and cruise control linkage to the intake plenum.
28. Reconnect all necessary electrical wiring to the intake plenum.
29. Install the coolant hoses to the throttle base and ignition wire harness.
30. Install the EGR tube at the crossover pipe.
31. Refill the cooling system with the specified engine coolant.
32. Reconnect the negative battery cable.
33. Install the air cleaner assembly.
34. Recheck all procedures to ensure proper reinstallation.
35. Start the vehicle and check for oil, coolant, vacuum and exhaust leaks.

3.4L ENGINE (CAM CARRIER COVERS)

Left Side (Front Cover)

1. Disconnect the negative battery cable.
2. Remove the oil/air breather hose.
3. Disconnect the spark plug cable from the spark plugs.
4. Remove the rear spark plug cables cover.
5. Remove the cam carrier cover retaining bolts and remove the cover with a light tap with a rubber mallet.
6. The installation is the reverse of the removal procedure. Be sure to thoroughly clean and dry all parts prior to installing them.
7. Replace the gasket and O-rings and torque the retaining bolts to 89 inch lbs. (10 Nm).
8. Run the engine and check for leaks.

Right Side (Rear Cover)

1. Disconnect the negative battery cable.
2. Remove the intake plenum assembly.
3. Remove the right side timing belt cover.
4. Disconnect the spark plug cables.
5. Disconnect the oil/air separator hose from the cover.
6. Remove the cam carrier cover retaining bolts and remove the cover with a light tap with a rubber mallet.

7. The installation is the reverse of the removal procedure. Be sure to thoroughly clean and dry all parts prior to installing them.

8. Replace all gasket and O-rings and torque the cover retaining bolts to 89 inch lbs. (10 Nm).

9. Run the engine and check for leaks.

3.8L ENGINE

Left Side (Front Cover)

1. Disconnect the negative battery cable.
2. Remove the engine lift bracket from the exhaust manifold studs.
3. Remove the fuel injector sight shield.
4. Disconnect the spark plug cables and remove the cover from the valve cover.
5. Remove the valve cover retaining bolts and remove the cover with a light tap with a rubber mallet.
6. The installation is the reverse of the removal procedure. Be sure to thoroughly clean and dry all parts prior to installing them.
7. Replace the gasket, apply thread-locking compound to the threads, and torque the retaining bolts to 89 inch lbs. (10 Nm).
8. Run the engine and check for leaks.

Right Side (Rear Cover)

1. Disconnect the negative battery cable.
2. Remove the coolant recovery bottle.
3. Remove the serpentine drive belt.
4. Without disconnecting the hoses, remove the power steering pump and position aside.
5. Remove the fuel injector sight shield.
6. Remove the canister purge sensor valve from the bracket and remove the power steering pump support braces.
7. Disconnect the spark plug cables.
8. Remove the engine lift brackets from the exhaust manifold studs.
9. Remove the valve cover retaining bolts and remove the cover with a light tap with a rubber mallet.

To install:

10. Be sure to thoroughly clean and dry all parts prior to installing them.
11. Replace the gasket, apply thread-locking compound to the threads, and torque the retaining bolts to 89 inch lbs. (10 Nm).
12. Install the engine lift brackets to the exhaust manifold studs.
13. Connect the spark plug cables.
14. Install the power steering pump support braces.
15. Install the canister purge sensor valve from the bracket.
16. Install the fuel injector sight shield.
17. Install the power steering pump.
18. Install the serpentine drive belt.
19. Install coolant recovery bottle.
20. Run the engine and check for leaks.

Pushrod Cover

➧ SEE FIG. 14

REMOVAL & INSTALLATION

✻✻ CAUTION

When draining the coolant, keep in mind that cats and dogs are attracted by the ethylene glycol antifreeze, and are quite likely to drink any that is left in an uncovered container or in puddles on the ground. This will prove fatal in sufficient quantity. Always drain the coolant into a sealable container. Coolant should be reused unless it is contaminated or several years old.

2.5L ENGINE

1. Disconnect the negative battery cable.
2. Remove the intake manifold as outlined in the "Intake Manifold" procedures in this Section.
3. Remove the four push rod cover attaching nuts.

➡ Do not pry on the cover or damage to the sealing surface may result.

4. To remove the push rod cover, proceed as follows:

a. Unscrew the four nuts from the cover attaching studs, reverse the two nuts so the washers face outward and screw them back onto the inner two studs. Assembly the remaining nuts to the same two inner studs with washers facing inward.

b. Using a small wrench on the inner nut, on each stud, jam the two nuts tightly together. Again using the small wrench, on the inner nut, unscrew the studs until the cover breaks loose.

c. After breaking the cover loose, remove the jammed nuts from each stud. Remove the cover from the studs. Examine the stud and rubber washer assembly and replace if either stud or washer is damaged.

To install:

5. Clean the sealing surfaces on the cover and cylinder block.
6. Apply a continuous $^{3}/_{16}$ in. (5mm) bead of RTV sealer or equivalent around the push rod cover.
7. Install the cover and torque the bolts to 90 inch lbs. (10 Nm).
8. Install the intake manifold as outlined in the "Intake Manifold" installation procedures in this Section.

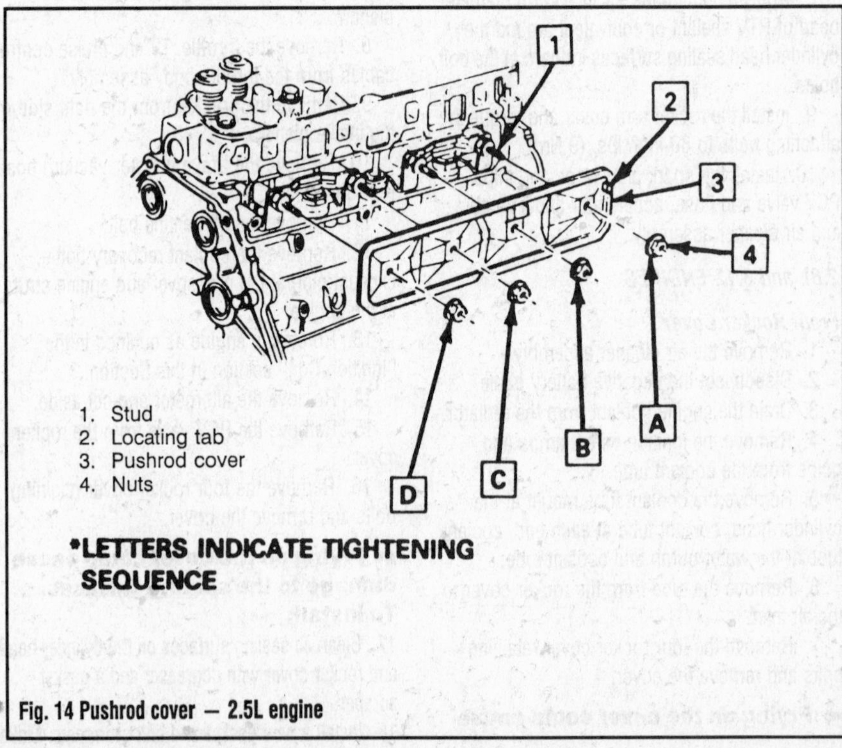

Fig. 14 Pushrod cover — 2.5L engine

Rocker Arms and/or Push Rods

REMOVAL & INSTALLATION

➧ SEE FIGS. 15 AND 16

CAUTION

When draining the coolant, keep in mind that cats and dogs are attracted by the ethylene glycol antifreeze, and are quite likely to drink any that is left in an uncovered container or in puddles on the ground. This will prove fatal in sufficient quantity. Always drain the coolant into a sealable container. Coolant should be reused unless it is contaminated or several years old.

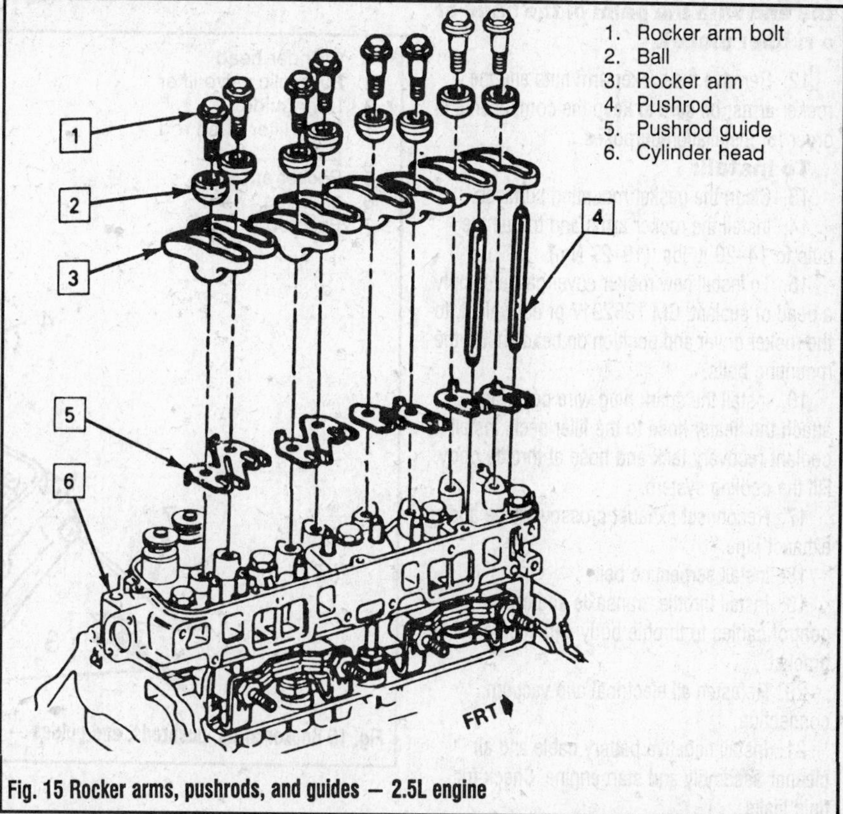

Fig. 15 Rocker arms, pushrods, and guides – 2.5L engine

2.5L ENGINE

1. Disconnect the negative battery cable.
2. Remove the rocker arm cover.

➡ **Mark all valve components so they are reinstalled in their original locations.**

3. Remove the rocker arm bolt and ball.
4. Remove the rocker arm, guide, and push rod.
5. If removed, install the pushrod through the cylinder head and into the lifter seat.
6. Install the guide, rocker arm, ball and bolt. Tighten the rocker arm bolts to 24 ft. lbs. (32 Nm)
7. Install the rocker arm cover.

2.8L AND 3.1L ENGINES

➡ **The intake pushrods and exhaust pushrods are different lengths. To distinguish the different pushrods, paint has been used, although this paint may be hard to identify after prolonged use. The intake pushrods are color-coded orange and are 6 in. (152mm) long. The exhaust pushrods are color-coded blue and are 6$^3/_8$ in. (162mm) long.**

Left Side

1. Disconnect the negative battery cable. Remove the air cleaner assembly.
2. Remove the ignition wire clamps from coolant tube. Disconnect the bracket tube from the rocker cover.
3. Remove the spark plug wire cover. Drain the cooling system and remove the heater hose from the filler neck. Remove the coolant hose at the coolant pump and the coolant tube.
4. Remove the EGR valve if equipped.
5. Remove the rocker arm cover-to-cylinder head bolts and the rocker cover.

➡ **If the rocker arm cover will not lift off the cylinder head easily, strike the end with the palm of the hand or a rubber mallet.**

6. Remove the rocker arm nuts and remove the rocker arms; keep the components in order for installation purposes.
7. Clean the gasket mounting surfaces.

To install:

8. Install the rocker arms and torque the nuts to 14–20 ft. lbs. (19–27 Nm).
9. To install new rocker cover gaskets, apply a bead of sealant, GM 1052917 or equivalent, to the rocker cover and position on head. Install the mounting bolts.
10. Install the spark plug wire cover. Install EGR valve, if removed.
11. Attach the heater hose to the filler neck. Attach the coolant hose at the coolant pump. Fill the cooling system.
12. Install negative battery cable and air cleaner assembly. Start vehicle and check for leaks.

Right Side

1. Disconnect the negative battery cable. Disconnect the brake booster vacuum line from the bracket.
2. Disconnect the cable bracket from the plenum. Disconnect throttle, cruise control and transaxle cable from throttle body.
3. Drain cooling system and remove coolant hose at throttle body. Remove coolant recovery tank.
4. Remove serpentine belt. Remove EGR tube at crossover pipe and disconnect crossover pipe from exhaust pipe.
5. Disconnect the vacuum line bracket from the cable bracket.
6. Disconnect the lines from the alternator brace stud.
7. Remove the rear alternator brace and the serpentine drive belt.
8. Remove the alternator and support it out of the way.
9. Remove the PCV valve.
10. Loosen the alternator bracket.
11. Disconnect the spark plug wires from the spark plugs. Remove the rocker cover-to-cylinder head bolts and the rocker cover.

➡ **If the rocker arm cover will not lift off the cylinder head easily, strike**

the end with the palm of the hand or a rubber mallet.

12. Remove the rocker arm nuts and the rocker arms; be sure to keep the components in order for installation purposes.

To install:

13. Clean the gasket mounting surfaces.
14. Install the rocker arms and torque the nuts to 14–20 ft. lbs. (19–27 Nm).
15. To install new rocker cover gaskets apply a bead of sealant, GM 1052917 or equivalent, to the rocker cover and position on head. Install the mounting bolts.
16. Install the spark plug wire cover and attach the heater hose to the filler neck. Install coolant recovery tank and hose at throttle body. Fill the cooling system.
17. Reconnect exhaust crossover pipe and exhaust pipe.
18. install serpentine belt.
19. Install throttle, transaxle and cruise control cables to throttle body and secure cable bracket.
20. Refasten all electrical and vacuum connection.
21. Install negative battery cable and air cleaner assembly and start engine. Check for fluid leaks.

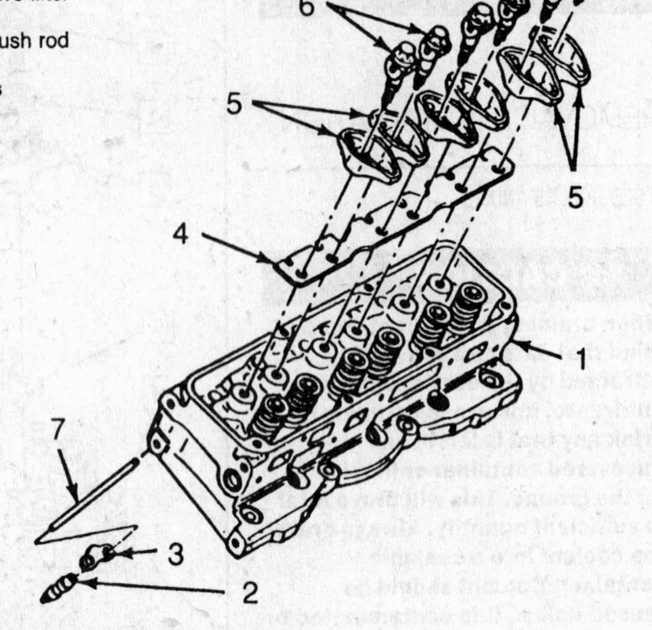

Fig. 16 Rocker arms, pushrods, and guides — 3.8L engine

3.8L ENGINE

1. Disconnect the negative battery cable.
2. Remove the valve cover.
3. Remove the rocker arm pedestal retaining bolts and remove the pedestal and rocker arm assembly.
4. Remove the pushrods.

➡ **Intake and exhaust pushrods are the same length. Store components in order so they can reassembled in the same location.**

To install:

5. Install the pushrods and make sure they seat in the lifter.
6. Apply a thread lock compound to the bolt threads before reassembly.
7. Install the pedestal and rocker arm assemblies and tighten the retaining bolts to 28 ft. lbs.
8. Install the valve covers and connect the negative battery cable.
9. Start engine and check for fluid leaks.

Thermostat

➧ SEE FIGS. 17–21

The thermostat is used to control the flow of engine coolant. When the engine is cold, the thermostat is closed to prevent coolant from circulating through the engine. As the engine begins to warm up, the thermostat opens to allow the coolant to flow through the radiator and cool the engine to its normal operating temperature. Fuel economy and engine durability is increased when operated at normal operating temperature.

REMOVAL & INSTALLATION

✲✲ CAUTION

Never open the cooling system when the engine is hot. The system is under pressure and will release scalding hot coolant and steam which can cause severe burns and other bodily harm. When draining the coolant, keep in mind that cats and dogs are attracted by the ethylene glycol antifreeze, and are quite likely to drink any that is left in an uncovered container or in puddles on the ground. This will prove fatal in sufficient quantity. Always drain the coolant into a sealable container. Coolant should be reused unless it is contaminated or several years old.

2.3L ENGINE

1. Disconnect the negative battery cable.
2. Remove the air cleaner assembly and partially drain the engine coolant into a drain pan.
3. Remove the radiator and heater hoses from the coolant outlet.
4. Remove the electrical connectors from the coolant outlet.
5. Remove the pipe and retaining bolts from the outlet.
6. Remove the outlet and thermostat.

To install:

7. Clean the gasket mating surfaces.
8. Using a new gasket and RTV sealant, install the thermostat and outlet.
9. Torque the bolts to 19 ft. lbs. (26 Nm).
10. Install the pipe, electrical connectors and hoses to the coolant outlet.
11. Refill the radiator with the specified amount of engine coolant, connect the negative battery cable and install the air cleaner.
12. Start the engine and check for leaks.

2.5L ENGINE

1. Partially drain engine coolant from the radiator. Disconnect negative battery cable.
2. Remove the thermostat housing cap.
3. Remove the thermostat by using the wire handle to lift it out of the housing.

To install:

4. Insert the thermostat and seal into the housing.

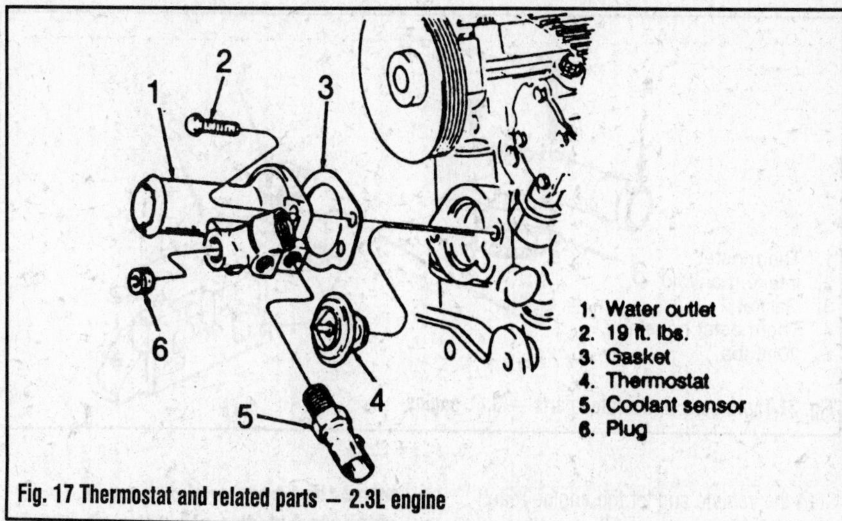

Fig. 17 Thermostat and related parts — 2.3L engine

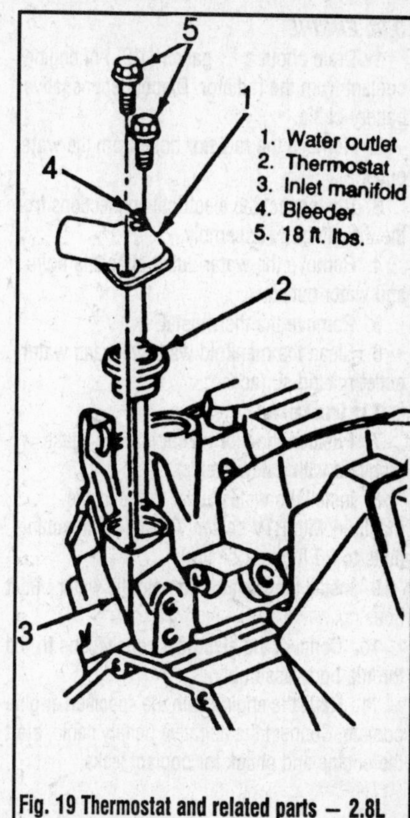

Fig. 19 Thermostat and related parts — 2.8L and 3.1L engines

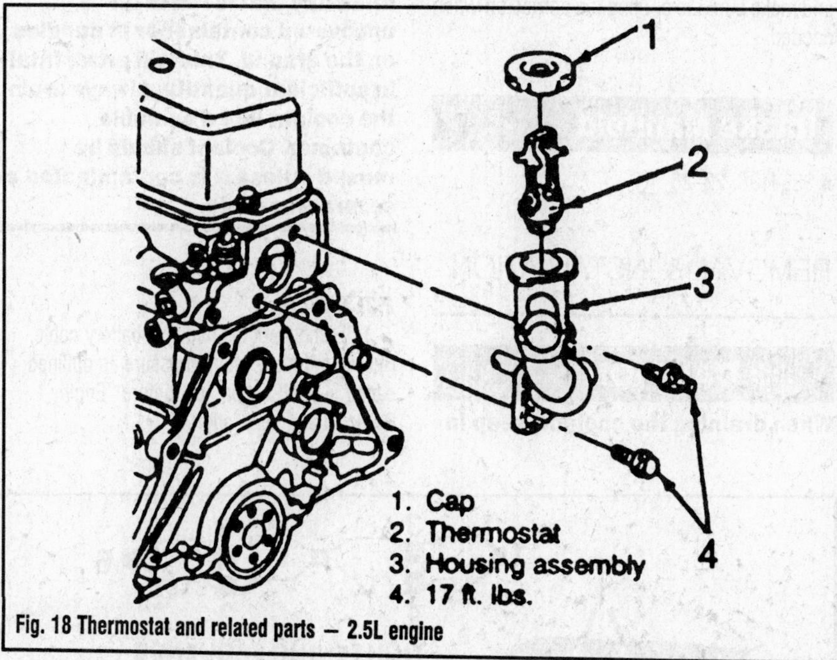

Fig. 18 Thermostat and related parts — 2.5L engine

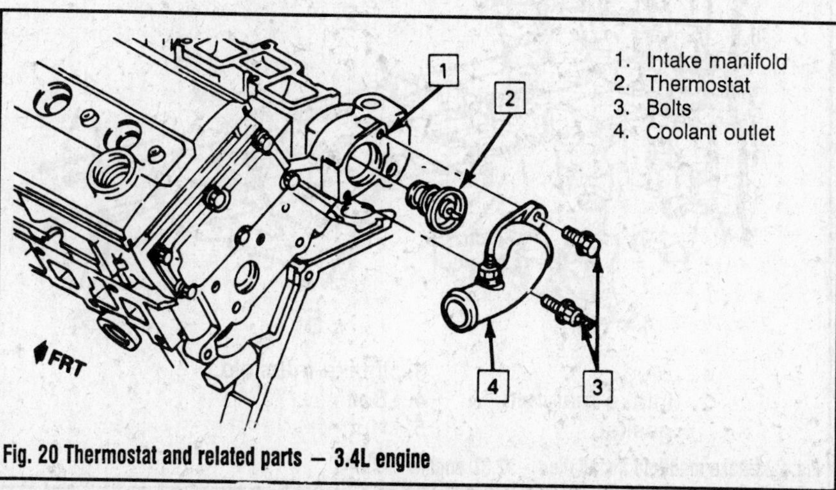

Fig. 20 Thermostat and related parts — 3.4L engine

5. Install the thermostat housing cap and refill the engine with the proper amount of engine coolant. Reconnect negative battery cable.

6. Start engine and check for leaks.

2.8L, 3.1L AND 3.4L ENGINES

1. Disconnect the negative battery cable. Drain 1 gallon (3.8L) of engine coolant from the radiator.

2. Remove the radiator hose from the water outlet.

3. Remove the water outlet attaching bolts and water outlet.

4. Remove the thermostat.

5. Clean the manifold water inlet and water outlet mating surfaces.

To install:

6. Position the thermostat into the inlet manifold.

7. Apply a 0.125 in. (3mm) bead of RTV sealer to the thermostat housing.

8. Install the water outlet to the inlet manifold. Torque the attaching bolts to 18 ft. lbs. (23 Nm).

9. Install the radiator hose to the water outlet housing.

10. Refill the engine with the specified engine coolant. Reconnect negative battery cable, start the engine and check for coolant leaks.

3.8L ENGINE

1. Drain about a 1/2 gallon (1.9L) of engine coolant from the radiator. Disconnect negative battery cable.
2. Remove the radiator hose from the water outlet.
3. Disconnect the electrical connections from the throttle body assembly.
4. Remove the water outlet attaching bolts and water outlet.
5. Remove the thermostat.
6. Clean the manifold water inlet and water outlet mating surfaces.

To install:

7. Position the thermostat into the intake manifold with a new gasket.
8. Install the water outlet to the intake manifold with RTV sealer. Torque the attaching bolts to 20 ft. lbs. (27 Nm).
9. Install the radiator hose to the water outlet housing.
10. Connect the electrical connections to the throttle body assembly.
11. Refill the engine with the specified engine coolant. Connect the negative battery cable, start the engine and check for coolant leaks.

COOLING SYSTEM BLEEDING

To ensure complete filling of the cooling system, it is necessary to bleed the system.

1. Disconnect the negative battery cable.
2. Park vehicle on level surface.
3. Remove thermostat housing cap and thermostat or open bleed vents:
   a. On 2.5L engine, remove the thermostat housing cap and thermostat.
   b. On 2.3L and 2.8L engines open bleed valve on thermostat housing 2–3 turns.
   c. On 3.1L engine, open the air bleed vents on the thermostat housing and the throttle body return pipe above coolant pump. Open vents 2–3 turns.
   d. On 3.4L engine, open the air bleed vents on the thermostat housing and the heater coolant inlet pipe by the master brake cylinder. Open vents 2–3 turns.
   e. On 3.8L engine, open air bleed vent on thermostat housing. Open 2–3 turns.
4. Fill cooling system with coolant to base of radiator neck.
5. Reinstall or replace the thermostat and housing and close air vents.
6. Fill the coolant reservoir to proper level with a 50/50 blend of ethylene glycol and water.
7. Reconnect the negative battery cable.

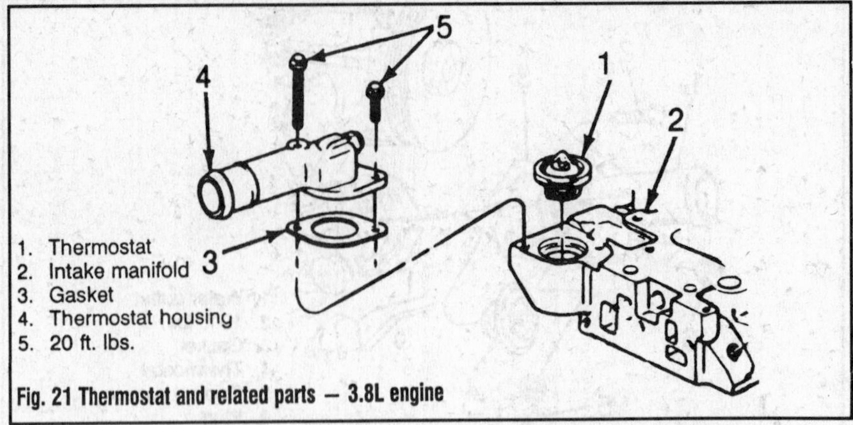

Fig. 21 Thermostat and related parts — 3.8L engine

Start the vehicle and let the engine reach operating temperature adding coolant as needed. Check the cooling system for leaks and make sure the cooling fan comes on when needed.

Intake Manifold

SEE FIGS. 22–28

REMOVAL & INSTALLATION

CAUTION

When draining the coolant, keep in mind that cats and dogs are attracted by the ethylene glycol antifreeze, and are quite likely to drink any that is left in an uncovered container or in puddles on the ground. This will prove fatal in sufficient quantity. Always drain the coolant into a sealable container. Coolant should be reused unless it is contaminated or several years old.

2.3L ENGINE

1. Disconnect the negative battery cable. Relieve the fuel system pressure as outlined earlier in this Section, just before "Engine Removal and Installation."

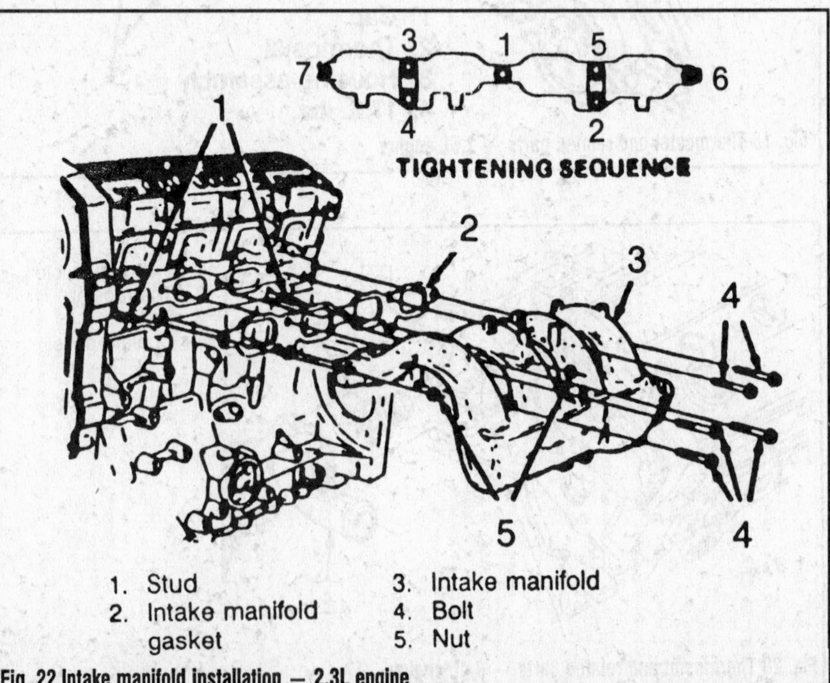

Fig. 22 Intake manifold installation — 2.3L engine

2. Remove the coolant fan shroud, vacuum hose and electrical connector from the MAP sensor.

3. Disconnect the throttle body to air cleaner duct.

4. Remove the throttle cable bracket.

5. Remove the power brake vacuum hose, including the retaining bracket to power steering bracket and position it to the side.

6. Remove the throttle body from the intake manifold with electrical harness, coolant hoses, vacuum hoses and throttle cable attached. Position these components aside.

7. Remove the oil/air separator bolts and hoses. Leave the hoses attached to the separator, disconnect from the oil fill, chain housing and the intake manifold. Remove as an assembly.

8. Remove the oil fill cap and oil level indicator stick.

9. Pull the oil tube fill upward to unseat from block and remove.

10. Disconnect the injector harness connector.

11. Remove the fill tube, rotating as necessary to gain clearance for the oil/air separator nipple between the intake tubes and fuel rail electrical harness.

12. Remove the intake manifold support bracket bolts and nut. Remove the intake manifold retaining nuts and bolts.

13. Remove the intake manifold.

To install:

14. Thoroughly clean and dry the mating surfaces. Install new gaskets and place the intake manifold in position.

15. Tighten the intake manifold bolts/nuts, in sequence, to 18 ft. lbs. (25 Nm). Tighten intake manifold brace and retainers hand tight. Tighten to specifications in the following order:

a. Nut to stud bolt — 18 ft. lbs. (25 Nm)

b. Bolt to intake manifold — 40 ft. lbs. (55 Nm)

c. Bolt to cylinder block — 40 ft. lbs. (55 Nm)

16. Lubricate a new oil fill tube ring seal with engine oil and install tube between No. 1 and 2 intake tubes. Rotate as necessary to gain clearance for oil/air separator nipple on fill tube.

17. Locate the oil fill tube in its cylinder block opening. Align the fill tube so it is approximately in its installed position. Press straight down to seat fill tube and seal into cylinder block.

18. Lubricate the hoses and install the oil/air separator assembly.

19. Install throttle body to intake manifold using a new gasket.

20. Install the power brake vacuum hose and the retaining bracket to power steering bracket.

21. Install the throttle cable bracket.

22. Connect the throttle body to air cleaner duct.

23. Install the coolant fan shroud, vacuum hose and electrical connector to the MAP sensor.

24. Fill all fluids to their proper levels.

25. Connect the negative battery cable and check for leaks.

2.5L ENGINE

1. Disconnect the negative battery cable.

2. Remove the air cleaner assembly.

3. Remove the PCV valve and hose at the throttle body assembly.

4. Drain the engine coolant at the radiator.

5. Relieve the fuel system pressure as outlined earlier in this Section, just before "Engine Removal and Installation." Remove the fuel lines from the throttle body.

6. Remove the vacuum lines and brake booster hose from the throttle body.

7. Remove all linkage and wiring from the TBI assembly.

8. Remove the power steering pump and position aside.

9. Remove the heater hose.

10. Remove the seven intake manifold retaining bolts and the manifold.

To install:

11. Clean all gasket surfaces on the cylinder head and intake manifold.

12. Install the intake manifold with a new gasket.

13. Install all the retaining bolts and washers hand tight.

14. Tighten the bolts, in proper sequence, to 25 ft. lbs. (34 Nm)

15. Install power steering pump assembly.

16. Install all heater hoses, vacuum hoses, throttle linkages and wiring.

17. Install the fuel lines.

18. Refill the engine coolant.

19. Install the PCV valve and hose to the TBI assembly.

20. Install the air cleaner assembly and connect the negative battery cable. Check for fluid leaks.

2.8L AND 3.1L ENGINES

1. Relieve fuel system pressure as outlined earlier in this Section, just before "Engine Removal and Installation."

2. Disconnect the TV and accelerator cables from the plenum.

3. Remove the throttle body-to-plenum bolts and the throttle body. Remove the EGR valve.

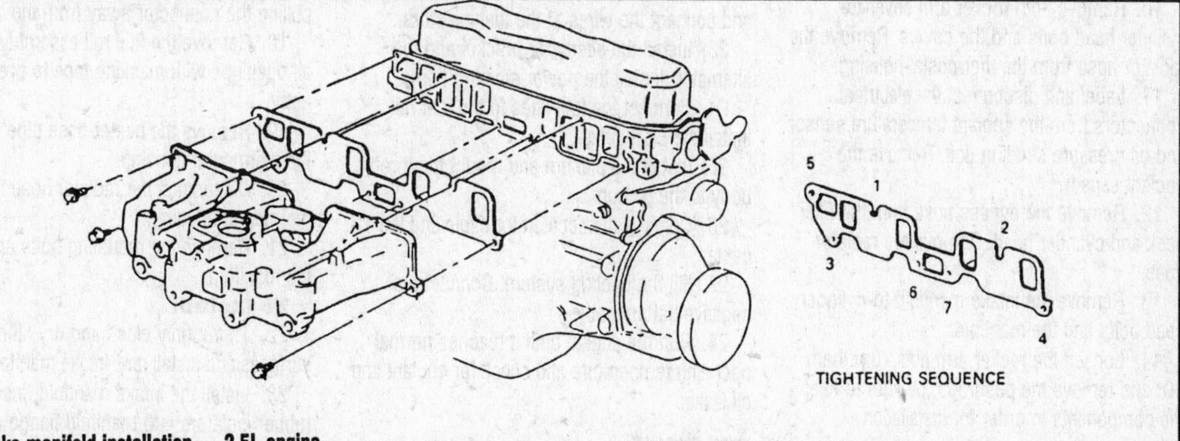

Fig. 23 Intake manifold installation — 2.5L engine

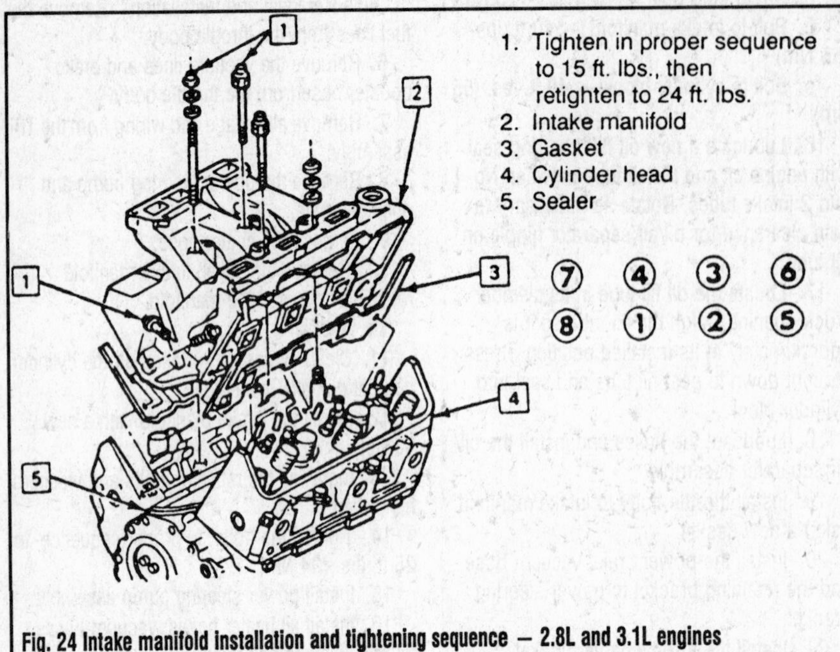

Fig. 24 Intake manifold installation and tightening sequence — 2.8L and 3.1L engines

4. Remove the plenum-to-intake manifold bolts and the plenum. Disconnect and plug the fuel lines and return pipes at the fuel rail.
5. Remove the serpentine drive belt. Remove the power steering pump-to-bracket bolts and support the pump out of the way; do not disconnect the pressure hoses.
6. Remove the alternator-to-bracket bolts and support the alternator out of the way.
7. Loosen the alternator bracket. From the throttle body, disconnect the idle air vacuum hose.
8. Label and disconnect the electrical connectors from the fuel injectors. Remove the fuel rail.
9. Remove the breather tube. Disconnect the runners.
10. Remove both rocker arm cover-to-cylinder head bolts and the covers. Remove the radiator hose from the thermostat housing.
11. Label and disconnect the electrical connectors from the coolant temperature sensor and oil pressure sending unit. Remove the coolant sensor.
12. Remove the bypass hose from the filler neck and cylinder head. Remove top radiator hose.
13. Remove the intake manifold-to-cylinder head bolts and the manifold.
14. Loosen the rocker arm nuts, turn them 90° and remove the pushrods; be sure to keep the components in order for installation purposes.
15. Clean all of the gasket mounting surfaces.

To install:

16. Place a bead of RTV sealer or equivalent on each ridge where the intake manifold and block meet. Install the intake manifold gasket in place on the block.
17. Install the pushrods and reposition the rocker arms, tighten the rocker arm nuts to 18 ft. lbs. (25 Nm).
18. Mount the intake manifold on the engine and tighten the bolts to 23 ft. lbs. (29 Nm)
19. Connect the heater inlet pipe to the manifold. Install and connect the coolant sensor.
20. Attach the radiator hoses. Connect the wire at the oil sending switch.
21. Install the rocker covers, tighten the retaining bolts to 90 inch lbs. (10 Nm)
22. Install the runners, breather tube, fuel rail and connect the wires at the fuel injectors.
23. Install the alternator bracket and the alternator. Install the power steering pump.
24. Connect the fuel lines to the fuel rail. Install the EGR valve.
25. Install the plenum and mount the throttle body to the plenum.
26. Connect the accelerator cable and the TV cable.
27. Fill the cooling system. Connect the negative battery cable.
28. Run the engine until it reaches normal operating temperature and check for coolant and oil leaks.

3.4L ENGINE

➡ Much of this procedure involves servicing the Intake Plenum. Do not confuse it with the Intake Manifold. They are separate entities and are separately serviceable, although the Intake Plenum must first be removed to gain access to the fuel rail and Intake Manifold.

1. Relieve the fuel system pressure as outlined earlier in this Section, just before "Engine Removal and Installation."
2. Disconnect the negative battery cable and remove the air cleaner assembly.
3. Disconnect the control cables from the connections from the throttle body portion of the plenum.
4. Remove the fuel rail cover and disconnect the fuel feed line and return line from the fuel rail assembly; be sure to use a backup wrench on the inlet fitting to prevent turning.
5. Disconnect the heater hose from the intake manifold.
6. Disconnect the PCV valve and vacuum line from the throttle body portion of the plenum.
7. Disconnect the AIR solenoid, EGR valve, and TPS connectors.
8. Remove the EGR valve.
9. Remove the fuel line bracket from the throttle body portion of the plenum.
10. Loosen the throttle body hose clamp.
11. Disconnect the canister purge solenoid and MAP sensor connectors.
12. Carefully disconnect the vacuum hoses from the vacuum tee on the plenum.
13. Remove the wiring loom bracket for the rear spark plug cables.
14. Remove the plenum support bracket nuts.
15. Remove the plenum mounting bolts and remove the intake plenum.
16. Remove the vacuum line at the pressure regulator. Remove the fuel rail assembly retaining bolts.
17. Push in the wire connector clip, while pulling the connector away from the injector.
18. Remove the fuel rail assembly and cover all openings with masking tape to prevent dirt entry.
19. Remove the heater hose pipe bracket at the thermostat housing.
20. Disconnect the radiator hose from thermostat housing.
21. Remove the mounting bolts and remove the manifold.

To install:

22. Thoroughly clean and dry all mating surfaces and install new intake manifold gaskets.
23. Install the intake manifold. Insert new rubber isolators into manifold flange and tighten mounting bolts to 18 ft. lbs. (25 Nm). Start with center bolts and work outwards in a circular pattern.

24. Connect the radiator hose to thermostat housing.

25. Install the heater hose pipe bracket to the thermostat housing.

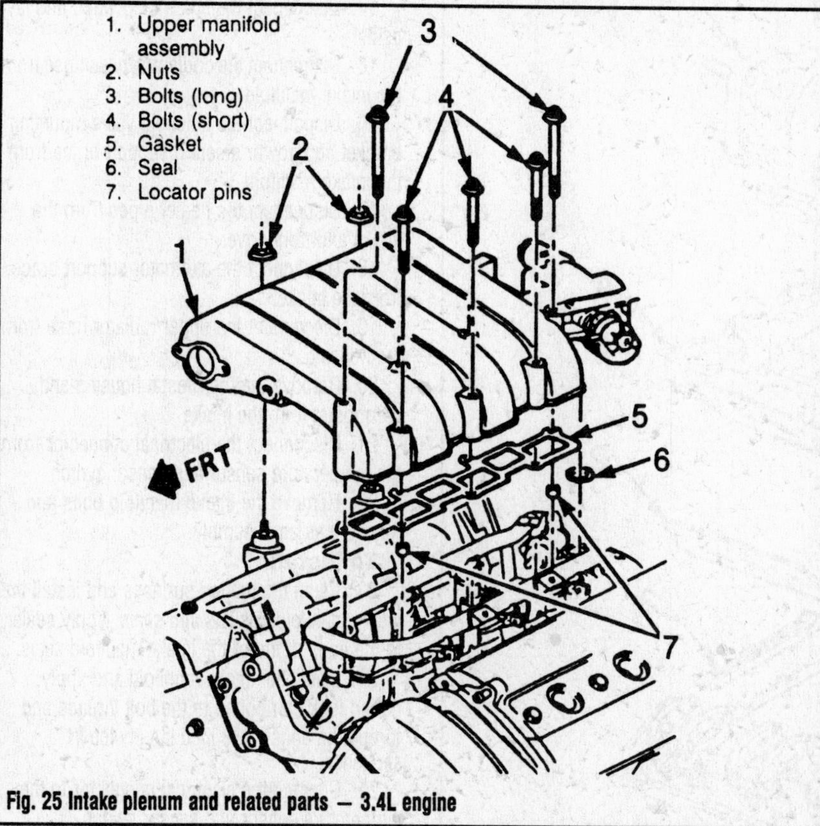

Fig. 25 Intake plenum and related parts — 3.4L engine

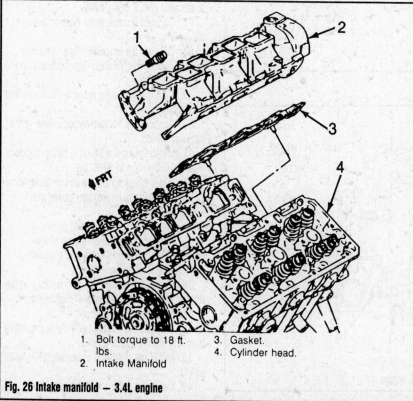

1. Bolt torque to 18 ft. lbs.
2. Intake Manifold
3. Gasket.
4. Cylinder head.

Fig. 26 Intake manifold — 3.4L engine

26. Install the fuel rail assembly.

27. Install the fuel rail assembly retaining bolts.

28. Connect the vacuum line to the pressure regulator.

29. Install the intake plenum and install the bolts. Torque them to 18 ft. lbs. (25 Nm) starting in the center and working outwards in a circular pattern.

30. Install the plenum support bracket nuts.

31. Install the wiring loom bracket for the rear spark plug cables.

32. Carefully connect the vacuum hoses to the vacuum tee on the plenum.

33. Connect the canister purge solenoid and MAP sensor connectors.

34. Tighten the throttle body hose clamp.

35. Install the fuel line bracket to the throttle body portion of the plenum.

36. Install the EGR valve.

37. Connect the AIR solenoid, EGR valve, and TPS connectors.

38. Connect the PCV valve and vacuum line to the throttle body portion of the plenum.

39. Connect the heater hose from the intake manifold.

40. Connect the fuel feed line and return line to the fuel rail assembly and install the fuel rail cover.

41. Connect the control cables to the throttle body portion of the plenum.

42. Install the air cleaner assembly. Connect the negative battery cable.

3.8L ENGINE

1. Relieve the fuel system pressure as outlined earlier in this Section, just before "Engine Removal and Installation."

2. Disconnect the negative battery cable. Place a clean drain pan under the radiator, open the drain cock and drain the cooling system.

3. Remove the air cleaner assembly and the fuel injector sight shield.

4. Disconnect the cables from the throttle body and mount bracket.

5. Remove the coolant recovery reservoir.

6. Remove the inner fender electrical cover on the right side.

7. Remove the right rear crossover pipe heat shield.

8. Disconnect the fuel lines from the fuel rail and from the cable bracket.

9. Remove the alternator and brace.

10. Remove the throttle body cable mounting bracket with the vacuum lines and disconnect the vacuum lines.

11. Tag and disconnect the electrical connections at the throttle body and both banks of fuel injectors.

12. Disconnect the vacuum hoses from the canister purge solenoid valve and transaxle

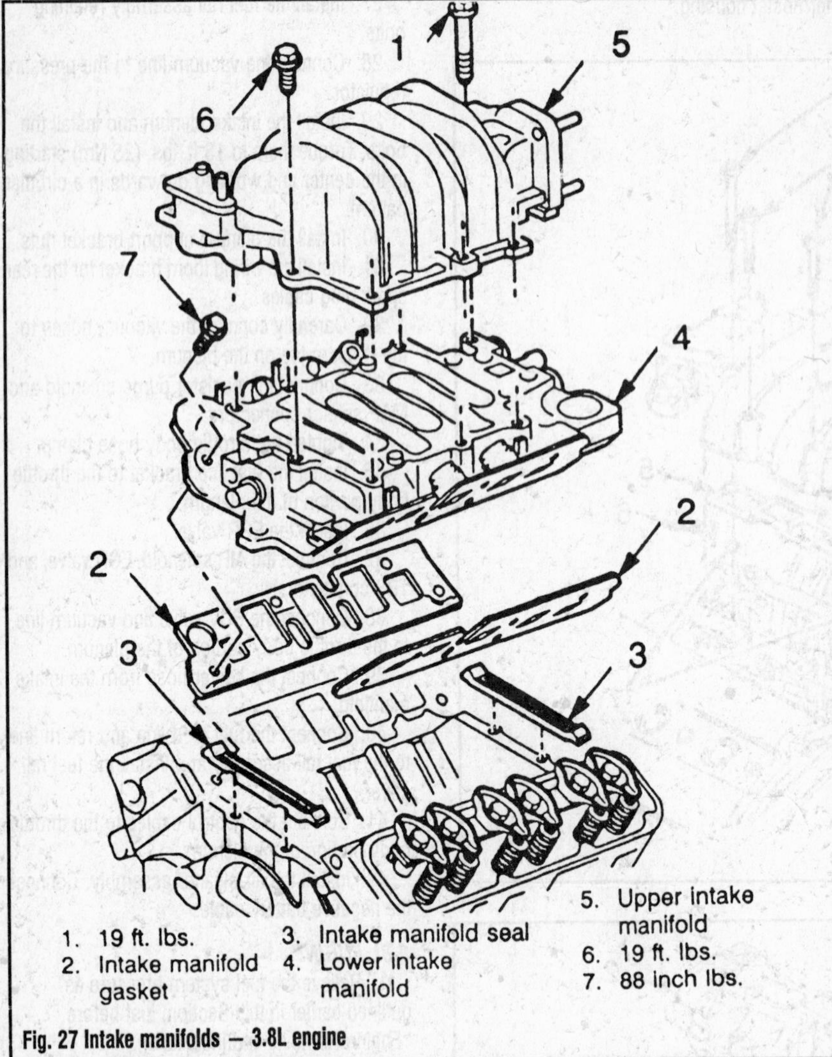

Fig. 27 Intake manifolds — 3.8L engine

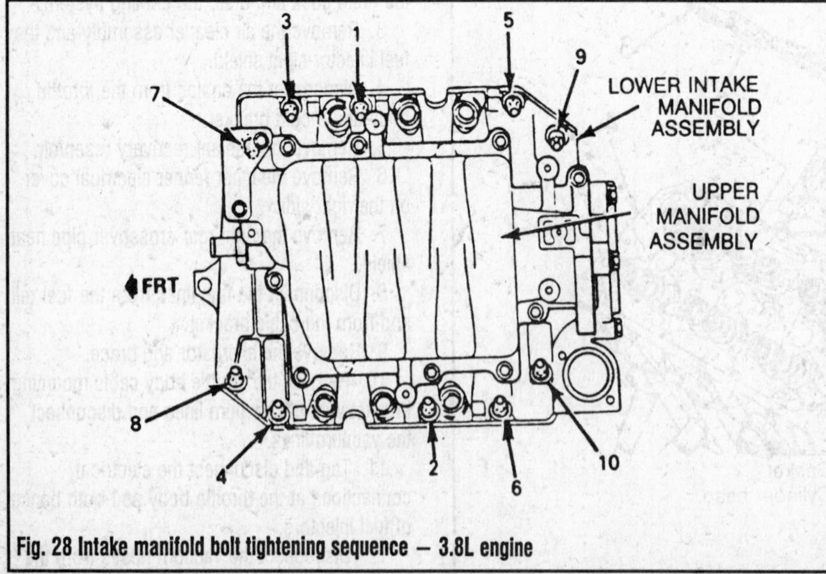

Fig. 28 Intake manifold bolt tightening sequence — 3.8L engine

module and intake connection.

13. Disconnect the power steering pump and move forward.

14. Disconnect the spark plug wires and lay aside.

15. Disconnect the coolant bypass hose from the intake manifold.

16. Disconnect the solenoid valve mounting bracket and power steering support brace from the intake manifold.

17. Disconnect the heater pipes from the intake and front cover.

18. Disconnect the alternator support brace from the intake.

19. Disconnect the upper radiator hose from the housing.

20. Remove the thermostat housing and thermostat from the intake.

21. Disconnect the electrical connector from the temperature sensor and sensor switch.

22. Remove the intake manifold bolts and manifold as an assembly.

To install:

23. Clean the mating surfaces and install the intake manifold gaskets and seals. Apply sealer to the ends of the of the intake manifold seals.

24. Install the intake manifold and apply thread lock compound to the bolt threads and torque the bolts to 88 inch lbs., twice in sequence.

25. Connect the electrical connector to the temperature sensor and sensor switch.

26. Install the thermostat housing and thermostat with a new gasket.

27. Connect the alternator support brace to the intake.

28. Connect the solenoid valve mounting bracket and power steering support brace to the intake manifold.

29. Connect the heater pipes to the intake and front cover.

30. Connect the coolant bypass hose to the intake manifold.

31. Install the power steering pump support bracket and torque to 37 ft. lbs.

32. Install the spark plug wires on both sides.

33. Install the belt tensioner pulley and tighten to 33 ft. lbs.

34. Install the power steering pump.

35. Connect the vacuum hoses to the canister purge solenoid valve and transaxle module and intake connection.

36. Connect the electrical connections at the throttle body and both banks of fuel injectors.

37. Install the alternator and brace.

38. Connect the throttle body cable mounting bracket with the vacuum lines.

39. Install the right rear crossover pipe heat shield.

40. Install the cables to the throttle body.

41. Connect the fuel lines to the fuel rail and mount bracket.

42. Install the inner fender electrical cover on the right side.

43. Install the coolant recovery reservoir and upper radiator hose. Fill the cooling system.

44. Install the air cleaner assembly and the fuel injector sight shield.

45. Connect the negative battery cable.

Exhaust Manifold

➧ SEE FIGS. 29–33

REMOVAL & INSTALLATION

2.3L ENGINE

1. Disconnect the negative battery cable and oxygen sensor connector.
2. Remove the upper and lower exhaust manifold heat shields.
3. Remove the bolt that attaches the exhaust manifold brace to the manifold.
4. Break loose the manifold to exhaust pipe spring loaded bolts using a 13mm box wrench.
5. Raise the vehicle and support safely.

➡ It is necessary to relieve the spring pressure from 1 bolt prior to removing the second bolt. If the spring pressure is not relieved it will cause the exhaust pipe to twist and bind up the bolt as it is removed.

6. Remove the manifold to exhaust pipe bolts from the exhaust pipe flange as follows:
   a. Unscrew either bolt clockwise 4 turns.
   b. Remove the other bolt.
   c. Remove the first bolt.
7. Pull down and back on the exhaust pipe to disengage it from the exhaust manifold bolts.
8. Lower the vehicle.
9. Remove the exhaust manifold mounting bolts and remove the manifold.
10. The installation is the reverse of the removal procedure. Torque the mounting bolts in sequence to 27 ft. lbs. (37 Nm). Install the exhaust pipe flange bolts evenly and gradually to avoid binding.
11. Connect the negative battery cable and check for leaks.

2.5L ENGINE

1. Disconnect the negative battery cable.
2. Remove the torque strut bolts at the radiator panel and cylinder head.
3. Disconnect the oxygen sensor and remove the oil level indicator tube.
4. Raise and safely support the vehicle.
5. Remove the exhaust pipe from the manifold and lower the vehicle.
6. Bend the locking tabs away from the bolts and remove the retaining bolts and washers.
7. Remove the exhaust manifold and gasket.

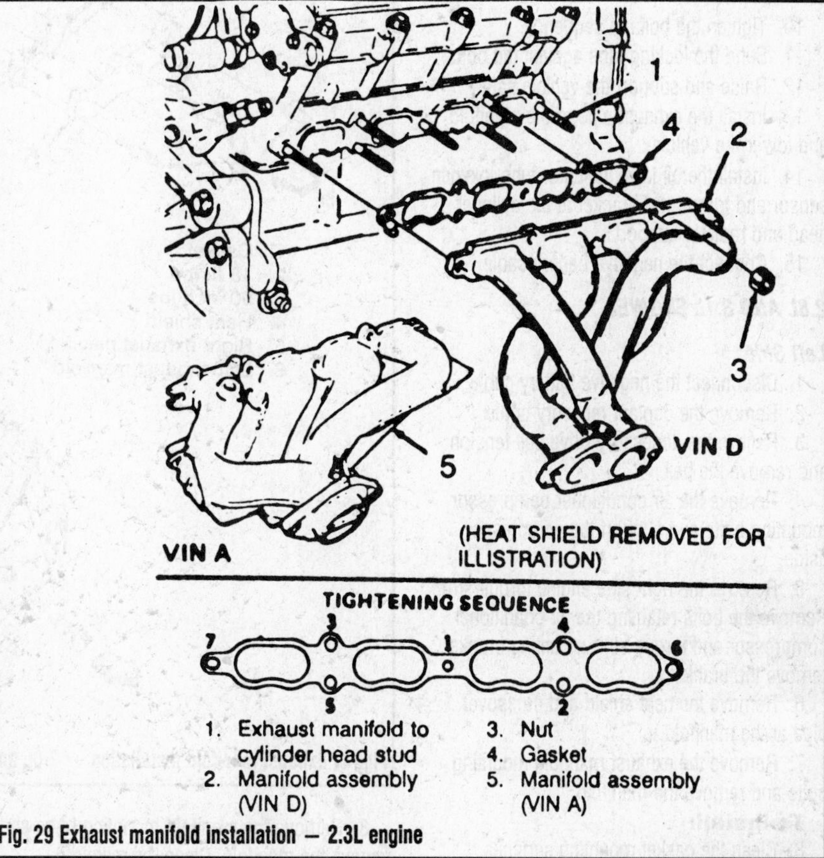

Fig. 29 Exhaust manifold installation — 2.3L engine

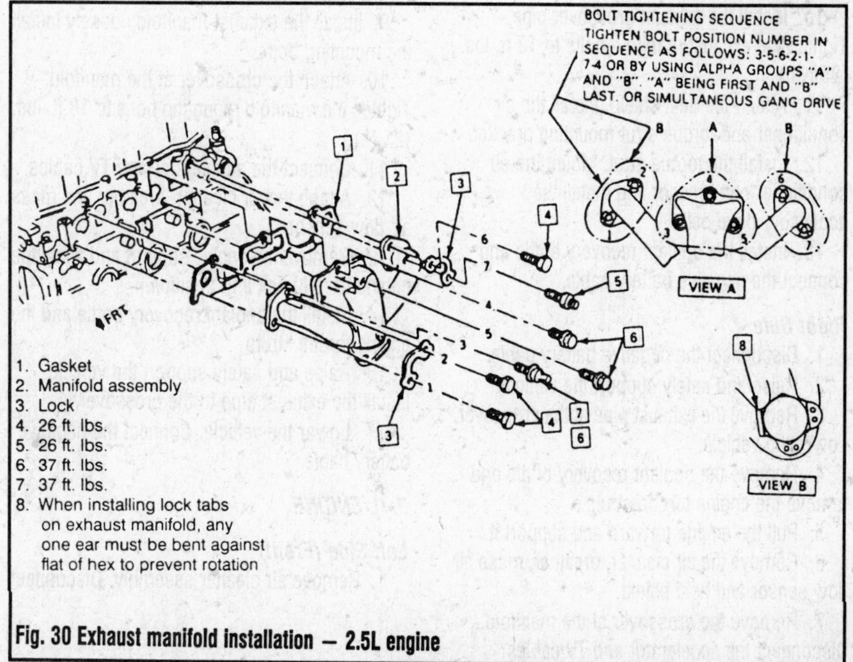

Fig. 30 Exhaust manifold installation — 2.5L engine

To install:

8. Clean the sealing surfaces of the cylinder head and manifold.
9. Lubricate the bolt threads with anti-seize compound and install the exhaust manifold with a new gasket.
10. Tighten the bolts in sequence.
11. Bend the locking tabs against the bolts.
12. Raise and support the vehicle safely.
13. Install the exhaust pipe to the manifold and lower the vehicle.
14. Install the oil level indicator tube, oxygen sensor and torque rod bracket at the cylinder head and radiator support.
15. Connect the negative battery cable.

2.8L AND 3.1L ENGINES

Left Side

1. Disconnect the negative battery cable.
2. Remove the coolant recovery bottle.
3. Relieve the accessory drive belt tension and remove the belt.
4. Remove the air conditioner compressor mounting bolts and support the compressor aside.
5. Remove the right side engine torque strut. Remove the bolts retaining the air conditioner compressor and torque strut mounting bracket, remove the bracket.
6. Remove the heat shield and crossover pipe at the manifold.
7. Remove the exhaust manifold mounting bolts and remove the manifold.

To install:

8. Clean the gasket mounting surfaces.
9. Install the exhaust manifold to the engine, loosely install the mounting bolts.
10. Install the exhaust crossover pipe. Tighten the exhaust manifold bolts to 18 ft. lbs. (25 Nm)
11. Attach the heat shield. Install the air conditioner and torque strut mounting bracket.
12. Install the torque strut. Mount the air conditioner compressor and install the accessory drive belt.
13. Install the coolant recovery bottle and connect the negative battery cable.

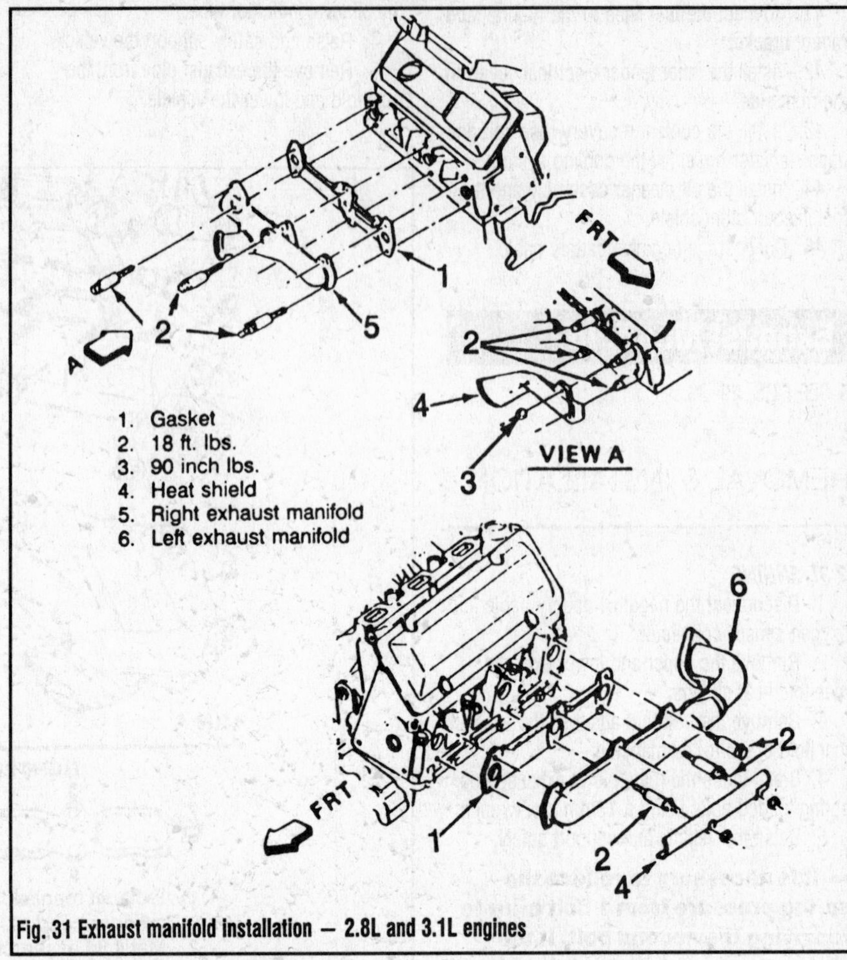

Fig. 31 Exhaust manifold installation — 2.8L and 3.1L engines

Right Side

1. Disconnect the negative battery cable.
2. Raise and safely support the vehicle.
3. Remove the exhaust pipe at the crossover. Lower the vehicle.
4. Remove the coolant recovery bottle and remove the engine torque struts.
5. Pull the engine forward and support it.
6. Remove the air cleaner, breather, mass air flow sensor and heat shield.
7. Remove the crossover at the manifold. Disconnect the accelerator and TV cables.
8. Remove the manifold mounting bolts and remove the manifold. Clean the manifold mounting surfaces.

To install:

9. Install the exhaust manifold, loosely install the mounting bolts.
10. Attach the crossover at the manifold. Tighten the manifold mounting bolts to 18 ft. lbs. (25 Nm).
11. Connect the accelerator and TV cables.
12. Attach the air cleaner, breather and mass air flow sensor.
13. Remove the engine support and allow the engine to roll back into position.
14. Install the coolant recovery bottle and the engine torque struts.
15. Raise and safely support the vehicle. Install the exhaust pipe to the crossover.
16. Lower the vehicle. Connect the negative battery cable.

3.4L ENGINE

Left Side (Front)

1. Remove air cleaner assembly. Disconnect the negative battery cable.
2. Remove exhaust crossover.
3. Remove the engine torque strut bracket at frame and position out of the way.
4. Remove the upper radiator shroud. Remove right side cooling fan.
5. Remove front hose from air pipe for manual transaxle only.
6. Remove exhaust retaining nuts and manifold. Remove old gasket and discard.

To install:

7. Install a new gasket, heat shields and the manifold.
8. Install manifold nuts and torque to 115 inch lbs. (14 Nm).
9. Install cooling fan, radiator shroud and torque strut into position and secure.
10. Install the exhaust crossover.
11. Install the air cleaner assembly. Connect the negative battery cable and check for leaks.

Right Side (Rear) With Automatic Transaxle

1. Disconnect the negative battery cable.
2. Remove right side cam carrier as follows:
   a. Remove intake plenum and right timing belt cover.
   b. Remove right spark plug wires.

c. Remove air/oil separator hose at cam carrier cover.

d. Remove cam carrier cover bolts and lift of cover. Remove gasket and O-rings from cover.

e. Remove secondary timing belt by removing secondary timing belt actuator and tensioner assembly and sliding belt from pulleys.

f. Install 6 sections of fuel line hoses under cam shaft and between lifters. This will hold lifters in carrier. For this procedure use $^5/_{16}$ in. (8mm) fuel line hose for exhaust valves and $^7/_{32}$ in. (5.5mm) fuel line hose for the intake valves.

g. Remove exhaust crossover pipe and torque strut.

h. Remove torque strut bracket at engine. Remove front engine lift hook.

i. Remove cam carrier mounting bolts and nuts and remove cam carrier.

j. Remove cam carrier gasket from cylinder head.

3. Remove exhaust manifold to crossover pipe nuts.

4. Raise and safely support vehicle.

5. Remove front exhaust pipe at manifold. Lower vehicle.

6. Remove electrical connector from oxygen sensor.

7. Remove exhaust manifold nuts, heat shield and manifold.

To install:

8. Clean all mating surfaces, then install manifold gasket and heat shields.

9. Install exhaust manifold. Torque nuts to 116 inch lbs. (14 Nm).

10. Install electrical connector at oxygen sensor.

11. Raise and safely support vehicle.

12. Install exhaust pipe at manifold.Lower vehicle.

13. Install exhaust crossover pipe.

14. Install right cam carrier as follows:

a. Install new gasket on cam carrier to cylinder mounting surface.

b. Install cam hold-down tool J-38613 or equivalent, to carrier assembly.

c. Install cam carrier to cylinder head. Install mounting bolts and nuts. Torque bolts and nuts to 18 ft. lbs.

d. Remove lifter hold-down hoses and cam hold-down tool.

e. Install torque strut bracket to engine and install torque strut.

f. Install engine crossover pipe and engine lift hook.

g. Install secondary timing belt and cam carrier cover and gasket.

h. Install spark plug wires and cover.

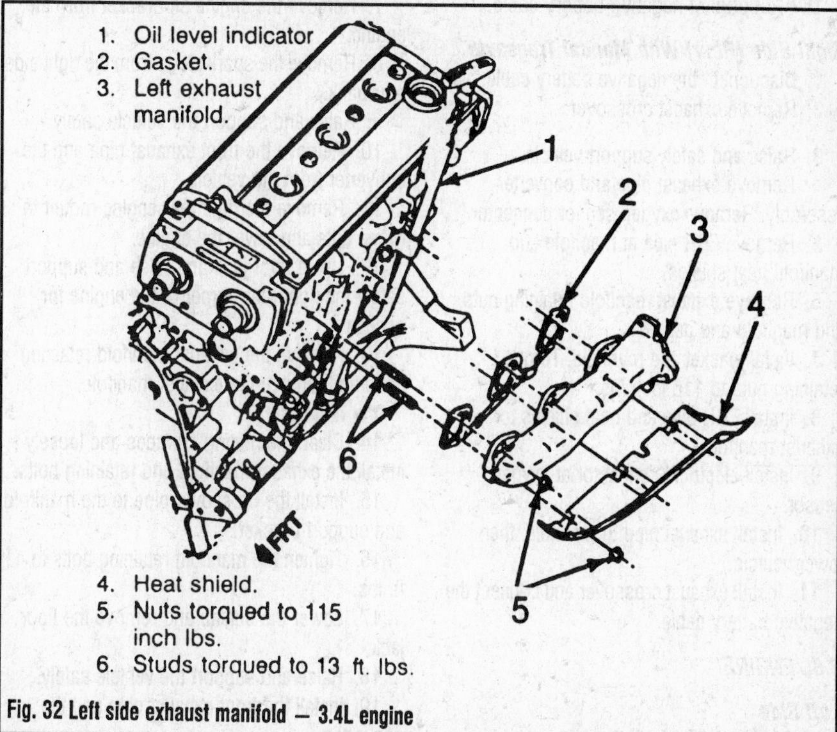

Fig. 32 Left side exhaust manifold — 3.4L engine

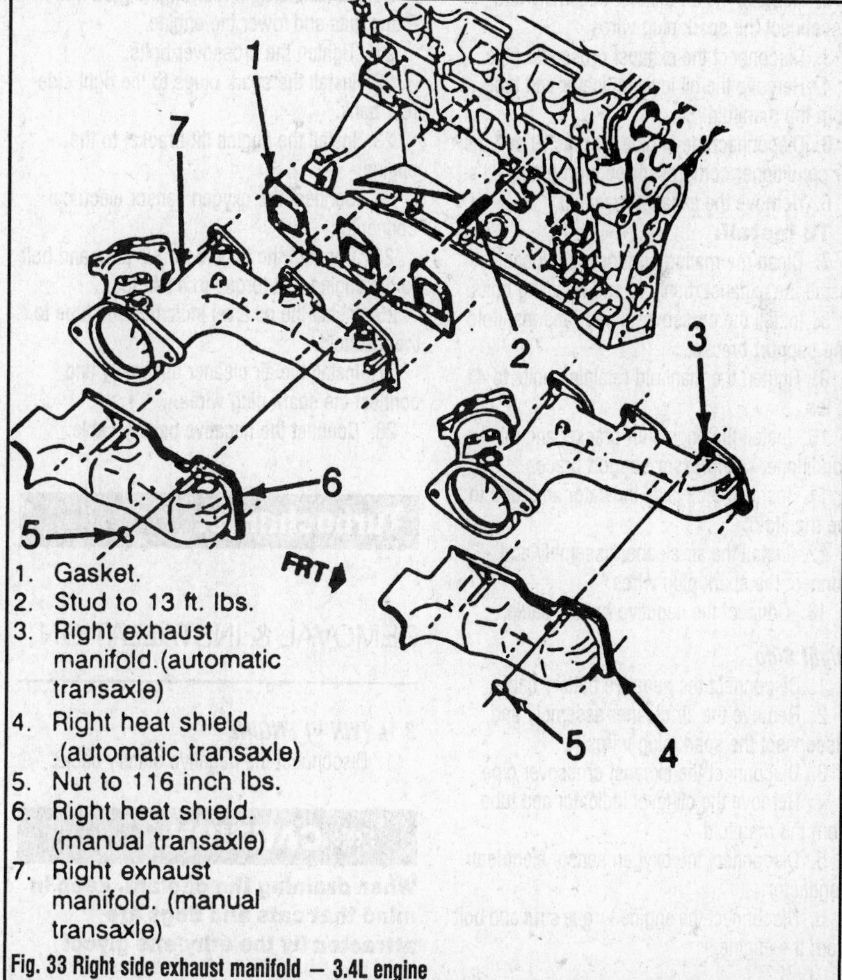

Fig. 33 Right side exhaust manifold — 3.4L engine

15. Reconnect negative battery cable.

Right Side (Rear) With Manual Transaxle

1. Disconnect the negative battery cable.
2. Remove exhaust crossover.
3. Raise and safely support vehicle.
4. Remove exhaust pipe and converter assembly. Remove oxygen sensor connector.
5. Remove EGR pipe at manifold and manifold heat shields.
6. Remove exhaust manifold retaining nuts and manifold and gasket.
7. Install gasket and manifold. Torque retaining nuts to 116 inch lbs.
8. Install EGR pipe and heat shields to exhaust manifold.
9. Install electrical connector at oxygen sensor.
10. Install exhaust pipe to manifold, then lower vehicle.
11. Install exhaust crossover and connect the negative battery cable.

3.8L ENGINE

Left Side

1. Disconnect the negative battery cable.
2. Remove the air cleaner assembly and disconnect the spark plug wires.
3. Disconnect the exhaust crossover pipe.
4. Remove the oil level indicator and tube from the manifold.
5. Disconnect the engine lift bracket and the air conditioner compressor support brace.
6. Remove the exhaust manifold.

To install:

7. Clean the mating surfaces and loosely install the exhaust manifold and retaining bolts.
8. Install the crossover pipe to the manifold and support bracket.
9. Tighten the manifold retaining bolts to 41 ft. lbs.
10. Install the engine lift bracket and the air conditioner compressor support brace.
11. Install the oil level indicator and tube to the manifold.
12. Install the air cleaner assembly and connect the spark plug wires.
13: Connect the negative battery cable.

Right Side

1. Disconnect the negative battery cable.
2. Remove the air cleaner assembly and disconnect the spark plug wires.
3. Disconnect the exhaust crossover pipe.
4. Remove the oil level indicator and tube from the manifold.
5. Disconnect the oxygen sensor electrical connector.
6. Disconnect the engine torque strut and bolt from the engine.
7. Remove the engine lift bracket from the engine.
8. Remove the spark plugs from the right side rear bank.
9. Raise and support the vehicle safely.
10. Remove the front exhaust pipe and the converter from the vehicle.
11. Remove the right rear engine mount to frame nuts and lower the engine.
12. Use a floor jack and raise and support safely the right rear corner of the engine for access.
13. Remove the exhaust manifold retaining bolts and remove the exhaust manifold.

To install:

14. Clean the mating surfaces and loosely install the exhaust manifold and retaining bolts.
15. Install the crossover pipe to the manifold and support bracket.
16. Tighten the manifold retaining bolts to 41 ft. lbs.
17. Lower the engine and remove the floor jack.
18. Raise and support the vehicle safely.
19. Install the front exhaust pipe and the converter.
20. Install the right rear engine mount to frame nuts and lower the engine.
21. Tighten the crossover bolts.
22. Install the spark plugs to the right side rear bank.
23. Install the engine lift bracket to the engine.
24. Connect the oxygen sensor electrical connector.
25. Connect the engine torque strut and bolt to the engine and torque to 41 ft. lbs.
26. Install the oil level indicator and tube to the manifold.
27. Install the air cleaner assembly and connect the spark plug wires.
28. Connect the negative battery cable.

Turbocharger

REMOVAL & INSTALLATION

3.1L (VIN V) ENGINE

1. Disconnect the negative battery cable.

CAUTION

When draining the coolant, keep in mind that cats and dogs are attracted by the ethylene glycol antifreeze, and are quite likely to drink any that is left in an uncovered container or in puddles on the ground. This will prove fatal in sufficient quantity. Always drain the coolant into a sealable container. Coolant should be reused unless it is contaminated or several years old.

2. Drain the coolant from the radiator.
3. Remove the intercooler to intake manifold duct attaching bolt at the thermostat housing and remove the intercooler to intake manifold duct.
4. Disconnect the air cleaner to turbocharger duct at the turbo.
5. Disconnect the air cleaner inlet duct.
6. Remove the air cleaner and duct assembly.
7. Disconnect the turbocharger to intercooler duct at the turbocharger.
8. Remove the turbocharger heat covers.
9. Disconnect the oxygen sensor electrical connector and remove the oxygen sensor.
10. Disconnect the turbo water and oil lines at the turbocharger.
11. Disconnect the vacuum lines at the turbocharger compressor outlet and actuator assembly.
12. Disconnect the actuator arm from the wastegate.
13. Disconnect the wastegate actuator from the turbocharger.
14. Remove the cruise control servo and set aside.
15. Disconnect the turbocharger downpipe at the turbocharger.
16. Disconnect the the water supply clamp and rubber hose.
17. Disconnect the turbocharger drain hose at the drain pipe.
18. Remove the turbocharger to exhaust crossover attaching bolts and remove the turbocharger from the engine.

To install:

19. Install the turbocharger to the engine compartment and tighten the turbocharger to exhaust crossover bolts to 17 ft. lbs. (23 Nm)
20. Connect the turbocharger drain hose at the drain pipe.
21. Connect the the water supply clamp and rubber hose.
22. Connect the turbocharger downpipe at the turbocharger and tighten to 17 ft. lbs. (23 Nm)
23. Install the cruise control servo.
24. Connect the wastegate actuator to the turbocharger.
25. Connect the actuator arm to the wastegate.

26. Connect the vacuum lines at the turbocharger compressor outlet and actuator assembly.
27. Connect the turbo water line and tighten to 21 ft. lbs.
28. Connect the oil line at the turbocharger and tighten to 15 ft. lbs.
29. Install the oxygen sensor and tighten to 31 ft. lbs. Install the electrical connector.
30. Install the turbocharger heat covers.
31. Connect the turbocharger to intercooler duct at the turbocharger.
32. Install the air cleaner and duct assembly.
33. Install the air cleaner to turbocharger duct at the turbo.
34. Install the intercooler to intake manifold duct attaching bolt at the thermostat housing and tighten to 17 ft. lbs. (23 Nm)
35. Fill the radiator with coolant.
36. Connect the negative battery cable.

➡ **Prime the turbocharger with oil before running the engine. Crank the engine with the fuel pump fuse removed until normal operating oil pressure is achieved.**

37. Perform the idle learn procedure to allow the ECM memory to be updated with the correct IAC valve pintle position and provide for a stable idle speed.
   a. Install a Tech 1 scan tool.
   b. Turn the ignition to the **ON** position, engine not running.
   c. Select **IAC SYSTEM**, then **IDLE LEARN** in the **MISC TEST** mode.
   d. Proceed with idle learn as directed by the scan tool.

Intercooler

REMOVAL & INSTALLATION

3.1L (VIN V) ENGINE

1. Disconnect the negative battery cable.
2. Remove the air cleaner-to-turbocharger duct at the turbocharger.
3. Remove the air cleaner assembly along with all adjoining duct work.
4. Remove the intercooler-to-intake manifold duct assembly.
5. Remove the turbocharger-to-intercooler duct.
6. Remove the upper intercooler attaching bolts and remove the intercooler.
7. The installation is the reverse of the removal procedure.
8. Make sure that no duct work is leaking when reassembling.

Radiator

➧ SEE FIG. 34

REMOVAL & INSTALLATION

1. Disconnect the negative battery cable.
2. Remove the air cleaner, mounting stud and duct.

✲✲ CAUTION

When draining the coolant, keep in mind that cats and dogs are attracted by the ethylene glycol antifreeze, and are quite likely to drink any that is left in an uncovered container or in puddles on the ground. This will prove fatal in sufficient quantity. Always drain the coolant into a sealable container. Coolant should be reused unless it is contaminated or several years old. To avoid being burned, do NOT remove the thermostat housing cap while the engine is at normal operating temperature. The cooling system will release scalding fluid and steam under pressure if the cap is removed while the engine is still hot.

3. Drain the engine coolant from the radiator.
4. Remove the coolant recovery bottle.
5. Remove the engine strut brace bolts from the upper tie bar and rotate the struts and brace rearward.

➡ **To prevent shearing of the rubber bushing, loosen the bolts on the engine strut before swinging the struts.**

6. Remove the air intake resonator mounting nut, upper radiator mounting panel bolts and clamps.
7. Disconnect the cooling fan electrical connectors.

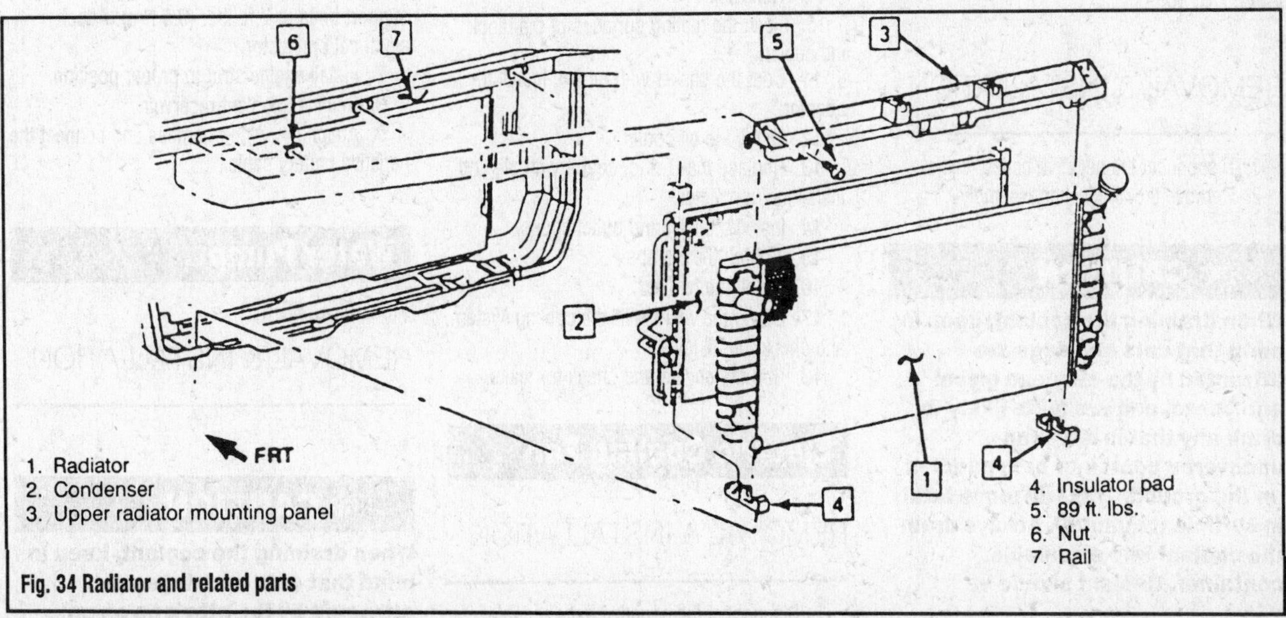

Fig. 34 Radiator and related parts

8. Remove the upper radiator mounting panel with the fans attached.
9. Remove the upper and lower radiator hoses.
10. Remove low coolant sensor and electrical connector, if used.
11. Remove the automatic transaxle cooler lines from the radiator.
12. Remove the radiator.

To install:

➡ **If a new radiator is being used, transfer all necessary fittings from the old radiator to the new one.**

13. Position the radiator into the lower insulator pads
14. Install the automatic transaxle cooler lines to radiator.
15. Install low coolant sensor and electrical connector.
16. Install the upper and lower radiator hoses and tighten the clamps.
17. Install the upper radiator mounting panel with the fans attached and connect the fan wires.
18. Install the mounting panel bolts and clamps. Torque the bolts to 89 inch lbs. (10 Nm).
19. Install the coolant recovery bottle.
20. Swing the engine strut to the proper position and tighten the bolts.
21. Refill the engine with the specified amount of engine coolant.
22. Install the air cleaner and negative battery cable. Start the engine and check for coolant leaks.

Engine Oil Cooler

➧ SEE FIG. 35

REMOVAL & INSTALLATION

1. Disconnect the negative battery cable.
2. Remove the air cleaner assembly.

✻✻ CAUTION

When draining the coolant, keep in mind that cats and dogs are attracted by the ethylene glycol antifreeze, and are quite likely to drink any that is left in an uncovered container or in puddles on the ground. This will prove fatal in sufficient quantity. Always drain the coolant into a sealable container. Coolant should be reused unless it is contaminated or several years old.

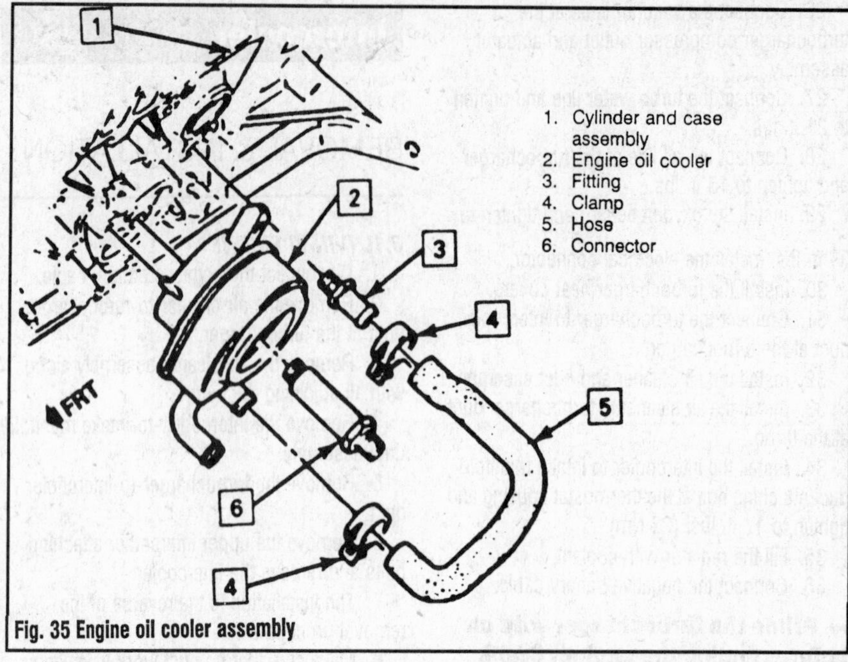

Fig. 35 Engine oil cooler assembly

3. Drain the cooling system.
4. Raise the vehicle and safely support.
5. Place a drain pan under the oil filter and remove the filter.
6. Disconnect the outlet hose a position it aside.
7. Disconnect the inlet hose a position it aside.
8. Remove the connector piece.
9. Remove the oil cooler and adaptor.

To install:

10. Clean the mating surfaces of the block and cooler.
11. Coat the gasket with oil and install the adaptor.
12. Install the oil cooler.
13. Replace the O-ring, coat it with oil, and install the connector.
14. Install the inlet and outlet hoses.
15. Tighten the clamps.
16. Install the oil filter.
17. Lower the vehicle, fill the cooling system, and check the oil level.
18. Run the engine and check for leaks.

Electric Cooling Fan

REMOVAL & INSTALLATION

1. Disconnect the negative battery cable.
2. Remove the coolant reservoir.
3. Remove engine strut brace bolts from upper tie bar and rotate strut and brace rearward.

➡ **To prevent shearing of the rubber bushing, loosen the bolts on the engine strut before swinging the struts.**

4. Disconnect the electrical wiring harness from the cooling fan frame.
5. Remove the fan assembly from the radiator support.

To install:

6. Install the fan assembly to the radiator support. Torque the fan assembly-to-radiator support bolts to 7 ft. lbs. (9.5 Nm). Attach electrical connector.
7. Install engine strut to proper position.
8. Reinstall coolant reservoir.
9. Attach the wiring harness and connect the negative battery cable.

Water Pump

➧ SEE FIGS. 36–40

REMOVAL & INSTALLATION

✻✻ CAUTION

When draining the coolant, keep in mind that cats and dogs are attracted by the ethylene glycol

antifreeze, and are quite likely to drink any that is left in an uncovered container or in puddles on the ground. This will prove fatal in sufficient quantity. Always drain the coolant into a sealable container. Coolant should be reused unless it is contaminated or several years old.

2.3L ENGINE

1. Disconnect the negative battery cable.
2. Disconnect the upper engine torque strut and rotate the engine rearward.
3. Disconnect and remove the oxygen sensor, if needed.
4. Remove the exhaust heat shield and EGR valve, if equipped.
5. Remove the exhaust pipe from manifold.
6. Remove the exhaust manifold.
7. Partially drain the engine coolant.
8. Remove the coolant return hose and lower coolant pipe from the pump.
9. Remove the pump retaining bolts and pump.

To install:

10. Clean the gasket mating surfaces.
11. Install the pump, retaining bolts and torque to 10 ft. lbs. (25 Nm).
12. Install the lower coolant pipe and torque to 124 inch lbs. (14 Nm).
13. Install the coolant return hose.
14. Install the exhaust manifold and pipe, oxygen sensor, EGR valve and heat shield.
15. Return the engine to its proper position and install the torque strut.
16. Refill the engine with coolant, connect the negative battery cable, start the engine and check for coolant leaks.

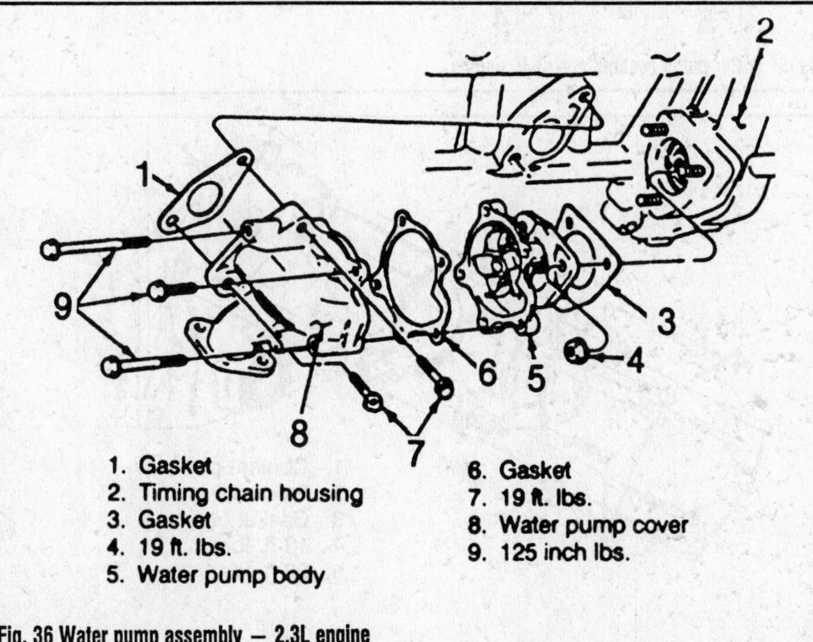

Fig. 36 Water pump assembly — 2.3L engine

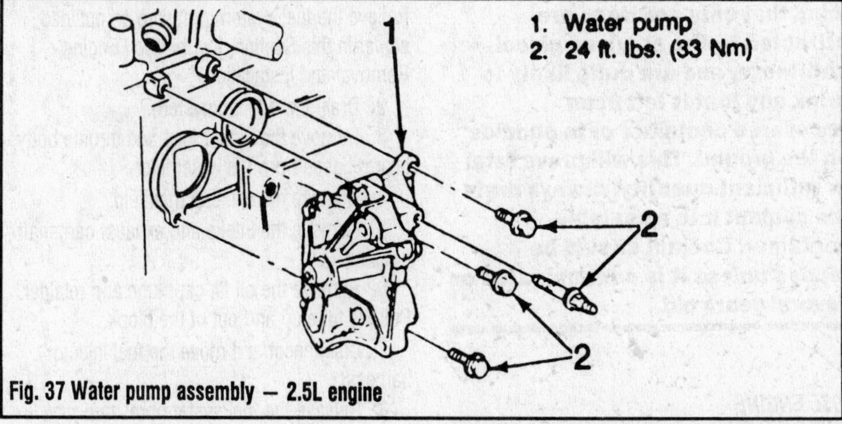

Fig. 37 Water pump assembly — 2.5L engine

2.5L ENGINE

1. Disconnect the negative battery cable.
2. Remove the alternator.
3. Remove the convenience center heat shield.
4. Drain about a gallon of engine coolant from the radiator. Enough to be below the water pump level.
5. Remove the 4 water pump-to-engine attaching bolts.
6. Remove the water pump and gasket.
7. Remove the pulley from the old pump, if a new pump is being installed.

To install:

8. Clean the water pump mating surfaces.
9. Install the pump and pulley assembly onto the engine with a new gasket.
10. Install the water pump attaching bolts and torque to 24 ft. lbs. (33 Nm).
11. Install the convenience center heat shield, alternator and negative battery cable.
12. Refill the cooling system with the specified amount of engine coolant.
13. Start the engine and check for coolant leaks.

2.8L, 3.1L AND 3.4L ENGINES

1. Disconnect the negative battery cable.
2. Remove the air cleaner assembly.
3. Drain about a gallon of engine coolant from the radiator. The level must be below the water pump level.
4. Remove the serpentine belt.
5. Remove the pulley.
6. Remove the 5 water pump attaching bolts.
7. Remove the water pump and gasket.

To install:

8. Clean the water pump mounting surfaces.
9. Install the water pump with a new gasket.
10. Install the attaching bolts and torque to 89 inch lbs. (10 Nm).
11. Install the pulley and serpentine belt.
12. Refill the cooling system with the specified amount of engine coolant.
13. Install the air cleaner and negative battery cable.
14. Start the engine and check for coolant leaks.

3.8L ENGINE

1. Disconnect the negative battery cable.
2. Drain the engine coolant from the radiator.

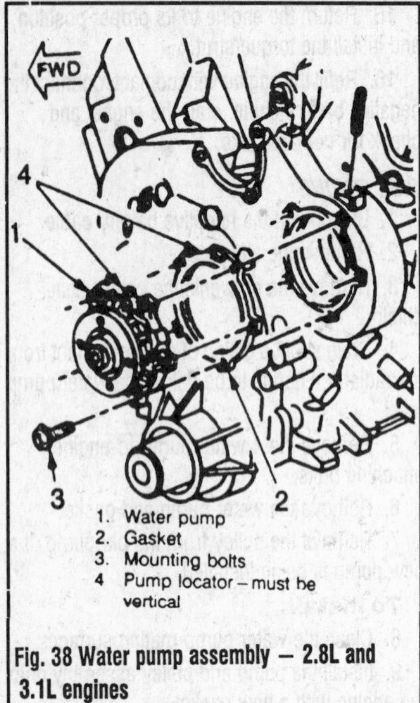

Fig. 38 Water pump assembly — 2.8L and 3.1L engines

1. Locator must be in vertical position
2. Front cover
3. Gasket
4. Coolant pump
5. 89 inch lbs. (10 Nm)

Fig. 39 Water pump assembly — 3.4L engine

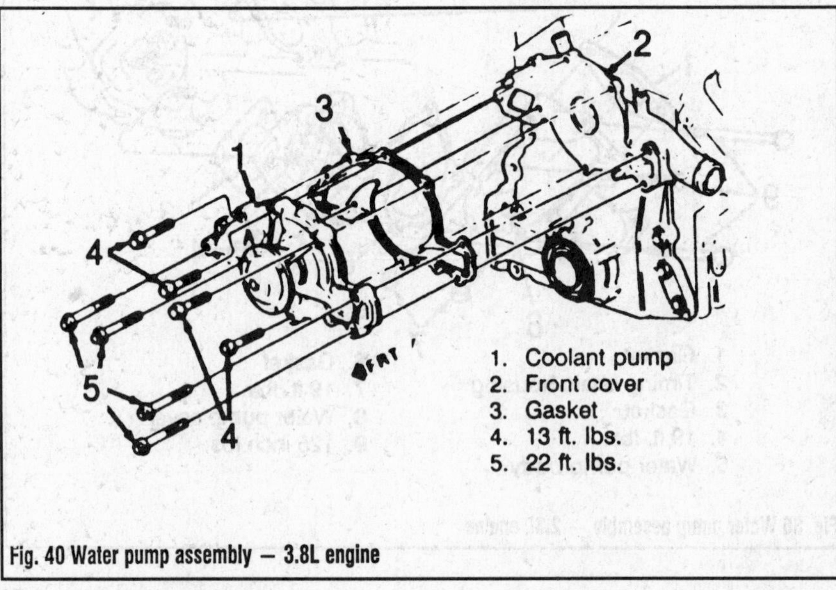

Fig. 40 Water pump assembly — 3.8L engine

3. Disconnect the coolant recovery reservoir.
4. Remove the serpentine belt.

➡ **If more access is needed, remove the inner fender electrical cover.**

5. Remove the pulley.
6. Remove the 8 water pump attaching bolts.
7. Remove the water pump and gasket.

To install:

8. Clean the water pump mounting surfaces.
9. Install the water pump with a new gasket.
10. Install the attaching bolts and torque the long bolts to 22 ft. lbs. (30 Nm) and the short bolts to 13 ft. lbs. (18 Nm).
11. Install the pulley and serpentine belt. Tighten the pulley to 115 inch lbs.
12. Reconnect the coolant recovery reservoir.
13. Refill the cooling system with the specified amount of engine coolant.
14. Install the negative battery cable.
15. Start the engine and check for coolant leaks.

Cylinder Head

REMOVAL & INSTALLATION

✻✻ CAUTION

When draining the coolant, keep in mind that cats and dogs are attracted by the ethylene glycol antifreeze, and are quite likely to drink any that is left in an uncovered container or in puddles on the ground. This will prove fatal in sufficient quantity. Always drain the coolant into a sealable container. Coolant should be reused unless it is contaminated or several years old.

2.3L ENGINE

1. Disconnect the negative battery cable.

Relieve the fuel system pressure as outlined earlier in this Section, just before "Engine Removal and Installation."

2. Drain the cooling system.
3. Remove the heater inlet and throttle body heater hoses from the water inlet.
4. Remove the exhaust manifold.
5. Remove the intake and exhaust camshaft housing.
6. Remove the oil fill cap, tube and retainer. Pull the tube up and out of the block.
7. Disconnect and move the fuel injector harness.
8. Release the fuel system pressure.
9. Remove the throttle body and air inlet tube with the hoses and cables still connected.

Position the assembly out of the way.

10. Remove the power brake booster hose and throttle cable bracket.

11. Remove the MAP sensor vacuum hose and all electrical connectors from the intake manifold and cylinder head.

12. Remove the radiator inlet hose and coolant sensor connectors.

13. In the reverse order of installation, remove the cylinder head-to-block retaining bolts.

14. Gently tap the outer edges of the cylinder head with a rubber hammer to dislodge the head gasket. Do not pry a screwdriver between the 2 surfaces.

15. Remove the cylinder head and intake manifold as an assembly.

To install:

16. Clean all gasket mating surfaces with a plastic scraper and solvent. Remove all dirt from the bolts with a wire brush.

17. Clean and inspect the oil flow check valve but do not remove the valve.

18. Check the cylinder head mating surface for flatness using a straight edge and a feeler gauge. Resurface the head, if the warpage exceeds 0.010 in. (0.25mm).

19. Check to see if the dowel pins are installed properly, and replace if necessary.

➡ To avoid damage, install new spark plugs after the cylinder head has been installed on the engine. In the mean time, plug the holes to prevent dirt from entering the combustion chamber during reinstallation.

20. Do not use any sealing compounds on the new cylinder head gasket. Match the new gasket with the old one to ensure a perfect match.

21. Install the cylinder head and camshaft housing covers.

22. Torque all bolts to 26 ft. lbs. (35 Nm) plus an additional 100° for bolts No. 7 and 9. Torque an additional 110° for all bolts except No. 7 and 9.

23. Install the throttle body heater hoses, upper radiator hose and intake manifold bracket.

24. Install cylinder head and intake manifold electrical connectors and vacuum hoses.

25. Install the throttle body-to-intake manifold with a new gasket. Install the throttle cable, MAP sensor vacuum hose and air cleaner duct.

26. Lubricate the new oil fill tube O-ring and install the fill tube. Make sure the tube is fully seated in the block.

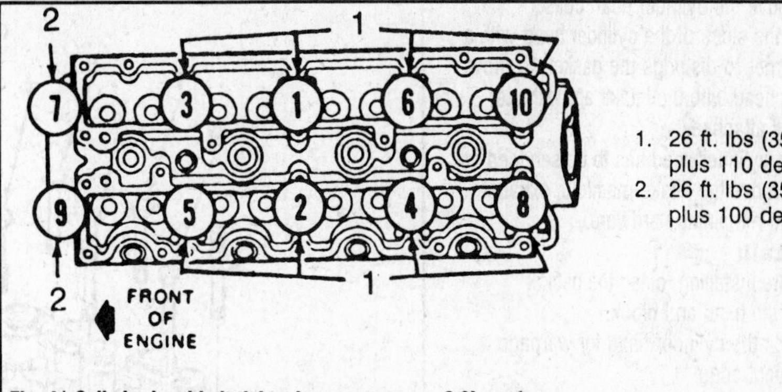

Fig. 41 Cylinder head bolt tightening sequence — 2.3L engine

Fig. 42 Camshaft housing cover bolt tightening sequence — 2.3L engine

27. Install and torque the exhaust manifold.

28. Fill the radiator with the specified amount of engine coolant.

29. Recheck all procedures to ensure completion of repair.

30. Connect the negative battery cable, start the engine and check for fluid leaks.

2.5L ENGINE

1. Disconnect the negative battery cable. Relieve the fuel system pressure as outlined earlier in this Section, just before "Engine Removal and Installation."

2. Drain the cooling system.

3. Raise and safely support the vehicle.

4. Remove the exhaust pipe and oxygen sensor.

5. Lower the vehicle.

6. Remove the oil level indicator tube and auxiliary ground cable.

7. Remove the air cleaner assembly.

8. Disconnect the EFI electrical connections and vacuum hoses.

9. Release the fuel pressure. Remove the wiring connectors, throttle linkage and fuel lines.

10. Remove the heater hose from the intake manifold.

11. Remove the wiring connectors from the manifold and cylinder head.

12. Remove the vacuum hoses, serpentine belt and alternator bracket.

13. Remove the radiator hoses.

14. Remove the rocker arm cover.

15. Loosen the rocker arm nuts and move the rocker arms to the side enough to remove the pushrods.

16. Mark each pushrod and remove from the engine.

➡ Mark each valve component to ensure that they are replaced in the same location as removed.

17. Remove the cylinder head bolts.

18. Tap the sides of the cylinder head with a plastic hammer to dislodge the gasket. Remove the cylinder head with the intake and exhaust manifold still attached.

19. If the cylinder head has to be serviced or replaced, remove the intake manifold, exhaust manifold and remaining hardware.

To install:

20. Before installing, clean the gasket surfaces of the head and block.

21. Check the cylinder head for warpage using a straight edge.

22. Match up the old head gasket with the new one to ensure the holes are exact. Install a new gasket over the dowel pins in the cylinder block.

23. Install the cylinder head in place over the dowel pins.

24. Coat the cylinder head bolt threads with sealing compound and install finger tight.

25. Torque the cylinder head bolts, in sequence, in 3 steps.

a. Torque all bolts to 18 ft. lbs.

b. Torque bolts "A" through "J" except "I" to 26 ft. lbs. Torque bolt "I" to 18 ft. lbs.

c. Turn all bolts an additional 90° (1/4 turn).

26. Install the pushrods, rocker arms and nuts (or bolts) in the same location as removed. Tighten the nuts (or bolts) to 24 ft. lbs. (32 Nm).

27. Install the rocker arm cover.

28. Install the radiator hoses, alternator bracket and serpentine belt.

29. Connect all intake manifold and cylinder head wiring.

30. Install the vacuum hoses and heater hose at manifold.

31. Install the wiring, throttle linkage and fuel lines to the throttle body assembly.

32. Install the oil level indicator tube-to-exhaust manifold.

33. Install the air cleaner assembly and refill the cooling system.

34. Raise and safely support the vehicle.

35. Install the exhaust pipe and oxygen sensor.

36. Lower the vehicle and connect the negative battery cable.

37. Start the engine and check for leaks.

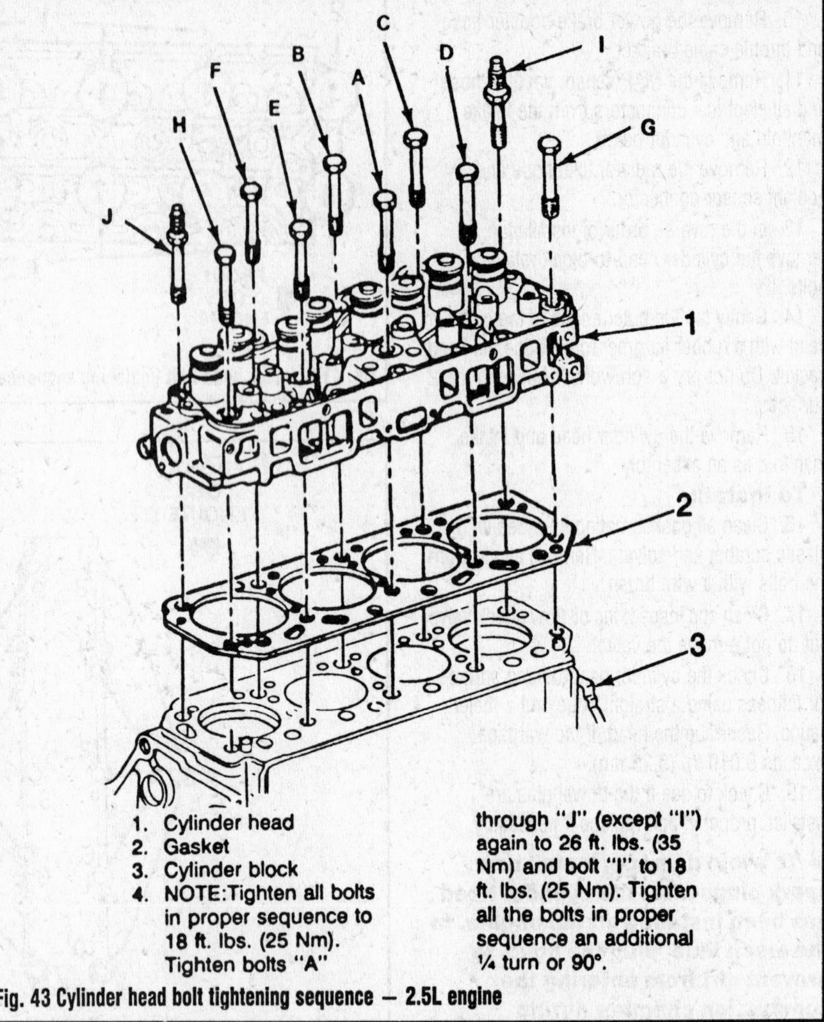
A
B
C
D
E
F
G
H
I
J
1
2
3
1. Cylinder head
2. Gasket
3. Cylinder block
4. NOTE:Tighten all bolts in proper sequence to 18 ft. lbs. (25 Nm). Tighten bolts "A" through "J" (except "I") again to 26 ft. lbs. (35 Nm) and bolt "I" to 18 ft. lbs. (25 Nm). Tighten all the bolts in proper sequence an additional ¼ turn or 90°.

Fig. 43 Cylinder head bolt tightening sequence — 2.5L engine

2.8L AND 3.1L ENGINES

Left Side

1. Disconnect the negative battery cable. Drain the cooling system. Remove the rocker cover. Relieve the fuel system pressure as outlined earlier in this Section, just before "Engine Removal and Installation."

2. Remove the intake manifold-to-cylinder head bolts and the intake manifold.

3. Disconnect the exhaust crossover and manifold bolts and remove left exhaust manifold.

4. Disconnect the oil level indicator tube bracket.

5. Loosen the rocker arms nuts, turn the rocker arms and remove the pushrods. Intake and exhaust pushrods are different lengths and are color coded for identification; intake pushrods are marked orange and exhaust pushrods are marked blue in color.

➡ **Be sure to keep the parts in order for installation purposes.**

6. Remove spark plug wires.

7. Remove the cylinder head-to-engine bolts; start with the outer bolts and work toward the center. Remove the cylinder head with the exhaust manifold as an assembly.

To install:

8. Clean the gasket mounting surfaces. Inspect the surfaces of the cylinder head, block and intake manifold for damage and/or warpage. Clean the threaded holes in the block and the cylinder head bolt threads.

9. Use new gaskets, align the new cylinder head gasket over the dowels on the block with the note **THIS SIDE UP** facing the cylinder head.

10. Install the cylinder head and exhaust manifold crossover assembly on the engine.

11. Using GM sealant 1052080 or equivalent, coat the cylinder head bolts and install the bolts hand tight.

12. Using the correct sequence, torque the bolts to 33 ft. lbs. (45 Nm). After all bolts are torqued to 33 ft. lbs. (45 Nm), rotate the torque wrench another 90° or 1/4 turn. This will apply the correct torque to the bolts.

13. Install the pushrods in the same order that they were removed. Torque the rocker arm nuts to 14–20 ft. lbs. (19–27 Nm).

14. Install the intake manifold using a new gasket and following the correct sequence, torque the bolts to the correct specification.

15. Install the oil level indicator tube and

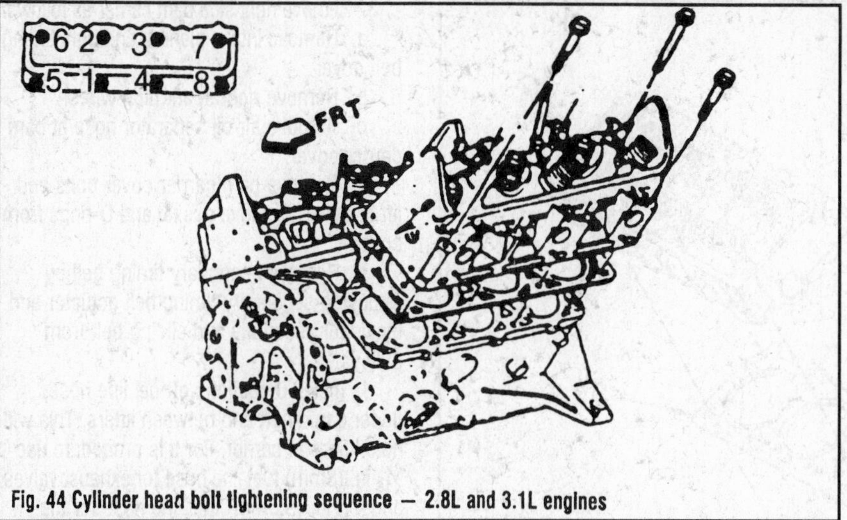

Fig. 44 Cylinder head bolt tightening sequence — 2.8L and 3.1L engines

install the rocker cover. Install the air inlet tube and spark plug wires.

16. Reinstall engine strut bracket and exhaust manifold.

17. Connect the negative battery cable. Refill the cooling system. Start the engine and check for leaks.

Right Side

1. Disconnect the negative battery cable. Drain the cooling system. Remove air cleaner assembly. Remove the torque strut at engine. Relieve the fuel system pressure as outlined earlier in this Section, just before "Engine Removal and Installation."

2. Raise and safely support the vehicle. Remove the exhaust manifold-to-exhaust pipe bolts and separate the pipe from the manifold.

3. Lower the vehicle. Remove coolant recovery tank.

4. Remove the exhaust manifold-to-cylinder head bolts and the manifold.

5. Remove exhaust crossover heat shield and crossover pipe at right exhaust manifold.

6. Remove right side spark plug wires at cylinder head.

7. Remove the rocker arm cover. Remove the intake manifold-to-cylinder head bolts and the intake manifold.

8. Loosen the rocker arms nuts, turn the rocker arms and remove the pushrods. Intake and exhaust pushrods are different lengths and are color coded for identification; intake pushrods are marked orange and exhaust pushrods are marked blue in color.

➡ **Be sure to keep the components in order for reassembly purposes.**

9. Remove the cylinder head-to-engine bolts, starting with the outer bolts and working toward the center and the cylinder head.

To install:

10. Clean the gasket mounting surfaces. Inspect the parts for damage and/or warpage.

11. Clean the engine block's threaded holes and the cylinder head bolt threads.

12. To install, use new gaskets and reverse the removal procedures. Using GM sealant 1052080 or equivalent, coat the cylinder head bolts and install the bolts hand tight.

13. Place the cylinder head gasket on the engine block dowels with the note **THIS SIDE UP** facing the cylinder head.

14. Using the torquing sequence, torque the bolts to 33 ft. lbs. (45 Nm). After all bolts are torqued to 33 ft. lbs. (45 Nm), rotate the torque wrench another 90° or 1/4 turn. This will apply the correct torque to the bolts.

15. Install the pushrods in the same order as they were removed. Torque the rocker arm nuts to 14–20 ft. lbs. (19–27 Nm).

16. Follow the torquing sequence, use a new gasket and install the intake manifold.

a. Install spark plug wires to cylinder head.

b. Install right side exhaust crossover pipe, heat shield and manifold.

c. Install exhaust pipe to manifold.

17. Install the oil level indicator tube and install the rocker cover. Install the air inlet tube.

18. Install coolant recovery tank. Refill the cooling system. Start the engine, allow it to reach normal operating temperatures and check for leaks.

3.4L ENGINE

Left Side (Front)

1. Disconnect the negative battery cable. Relieve the fuel system pressure as outlined earlier in this Section, just before "Engine Removal and Installation."

2. Drain cooling system. Remove the intake manifold.

3. Remove left side cam carrier as follows:

a. Disconnect oil/air breather hose from cam carrier cover. Remove spark plug wires from plugs and remove rear spark plug wire cover.

b. Remove cam carrier cover bolts and lift off cover. Remove gasket and O-rings from cover.

c. Remove secondary timing belt by removing secondary timing belt actuator and tensioner assembly and sliding belt from pulleys.

d. Install 6 sections of fuel line hoses under cam shaft and between lifters. This will hold lifters in the carrier. For this procedure use 5/16 inc. fuel line hose for exhaust valves and 7/32 in. (5.5mm) fuel line hose for the intake valves.

e. Remove exhaust crossover pipe and torque strut.

f. Remove torque strut bracket at engine.

g. Remove cam carrier mounting bolts and nuts and remove cam carrier.

h. Remove cam carrier gasket from cylinder head.

4. Remove front air hose on manual transaxle only.

5. Remove right cooling fan.

6. Remove exhaust mounting bolts and manifold.

7. Remove oil level indicator tube bolt and tube.

8. Disconnect electrical connector from temperature sending unit.

9. Remove cylinder head bolts and remove cylinder head.

To install:

10. Clean the gasket mounting surfaces. Inspect the parts for damage and/or warpage.

11. Clean the engine block threaded holes and the cylinder head bolt threads. Remove oil from threaded holes in block.

12. Install new cylinder head gasket to block with tabs between cylinders facing up.

13. Install cylinder head and bolts and torque in proper sequence. Torque bolts to 33 ft. lbs. (45 Nm) plus an additional 1/4 turn.

14. Connect electrical connector to coolant temperature sending unit.

15. Install oil level tube and bolt. Tighten to 89 inch lbs. (10 Nm).

16. Install exhaust manifold and nuts. Tighten to 116 inch lbs. (13 Nm).

17. Install front air pipe, manual transaxle. Install cooling fan.

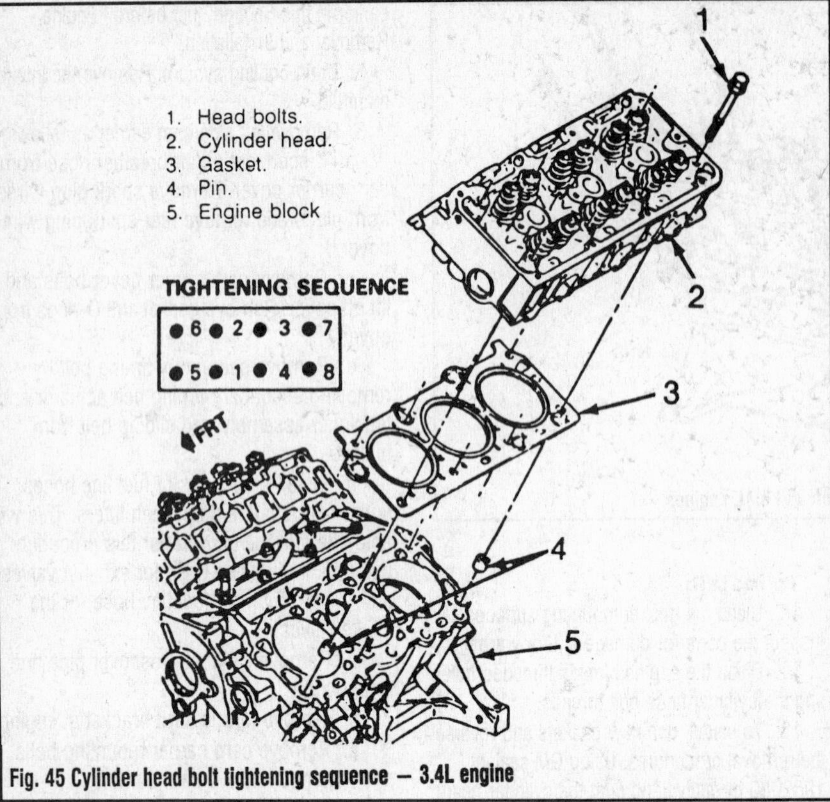

Fig. 45 Cylinder head bolt tightening sequence — 3.4L engine

18. Install cam carrier following these steps:

a. Install new gasket on cam carrier to cylinder mounting surface.

b. Install cam hold-down tool J-38613 or equivalent, to carrier assembly.

c. Install cam carrier to cylinder head. Install mounting bolts and nuts. Torque bolts and nuts to 18 ft. lbs. (25 Nm).

d. Remove lifter hold-down hoses and cam hold-down tool.

e. Install torque strut bracket to engine and install torque strut.

f. Install engine crossover pipe.

g. Install secondary timing belt and cam carrier cover.

19. Install the intake manifold.

20. Refill fluid levels as required. Connect negative battery cable.

21. Start the engine and check for fluid leaks.

Right Side (Rear)

1. Disconnect the negative battery cable. Relieve the fuel system pressure as outlined earlier in this Section, just before "Engine Removal and Installation."

2. Drain cooling system. Remove intake manifold.

3. Remove right side cam carrier as follows:

a. Remove intake plenum and right timing belt cover.

b. Remove right spark plug wires.

c. Remove air/oil separator hose at cam carrier cover.

d. Remove cam carrier cover bolts and lift of cover. Remove gasket and O-rings from cover.

e. Remove secondary timing belt by removing secondary timing belt actuator and tensioner assembly and sliding belt from pulleys.

f. Install 6 sections of fuel line hoses under cam shaft and between lifters. This will hold lifters in carrier. For this procedure use $^{5}/_{16}$ in. (8mm) fuel line hose for exhaust valves and $^{7}/_{32}$ in. (5.5mm) fuel line hose for the intake valves.

g. Remove exhaust crossover pipe and torque strut.

h. Remove torque strut bracket at engine. Remove front engine lift hook.

i. Remove cam carrier mounting bolts and nuts and remove cam carrier.

j. Remove cam carrier gasket from cylinder head.

4. Raise and support vehicle safely.

5. Remove front exhaust pipe at manifold.

6. Remove rear air hose from air pipe on manual transaxle only.

7. Lower vehicle and disconnect electrical connector from oxygen sensor.

8. Remove rear timing belt tensioner bracket.

9. Remove cylinder head bolts and remove cylinder head.

To install:

10. Clean the gasket mounting surfaces. Inspect the parts for damage and/or warpage.

11. Clean the engine block threaded holes and the cylinder head bolt threads. Remove oil from threaded holes in block.

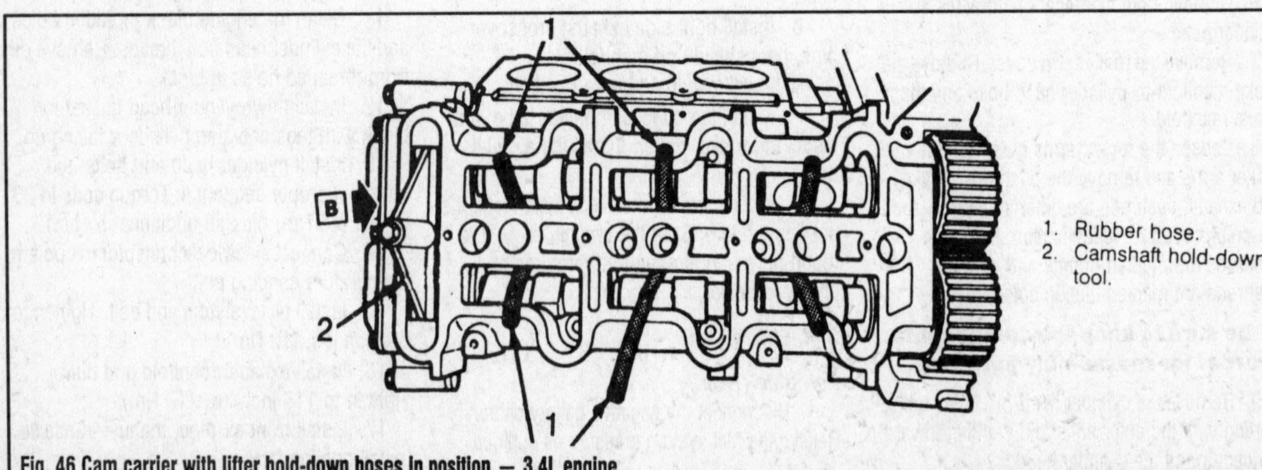

Fig. 46 Cam carrier with lifter hold-down hoses in position — 3.4L engine

12. Install new cylinder head gasket to block with tabs between cylinders facing up.

13. Install cylinder head and bolts and torque in proper sequence. Torque bolts to 33 ft. lbs. (45 Nm) plus an additional 1/4 turn.

14. Install rear timing belt tensioner bracket.

15. Connect electrical connector to oxygen sensor.

16. Raise vehicle and support safely.

17. Connect rear air hose to air pipe for manual transaxle.

18. Install front exhaust pipe to manifold. Lower vehicle.

19. Install cam carrier following these steps:

a. Install new gasket on cam carrier to cylinder mounting surface.

b. Install cam hold-down tool J-38613 or equivalent, to carrier assembly.

c. Install the cam carrier to the cylinder head. Install mounting bolts and nuts. Torque bolts and nuts to 18 ft. lbs. (26 Nm).

d. Remove lifter hold-down hoses and cam hold-down tool.

e. Install torque strut bracket to engine and install torque strut.

f. Install engine crossover pipe and engine lift hook.

g. Install secondary timing belt and cam carrier cover.

h. Install spark plug wires and cover.

20. Install intake manifold.

21. Refill fluid levels as required. Connect negative battery cable.

22. Start vehicle and check for fluid leaks.

3.8L ENGINE

Left Side (Front)

1. Disconnect the negative battery cable and remove the air cleaner assembly.Relieve the fuel system pressure as outlined earlier in this Section, just before "Engine Removal and Installation."

2. Drain the cooling system and remove the intake manifold.

3. Remove the valve covers and remove the rocker arm assemblies.

4. Disconnect the torque strut from the bracket at cylinder head.

5. Disconnect the vacuum line from the transaxle.

6. Remove the left exhaust manifold.

7. Disconnect the spark plug wires and remove the spark plugs.

8. Remove the alternator front mount bracket and ignition module with bracket.

9. Remove the cylinder head bolts and remove the cylinder head.

10. Clean all gasket mating surfaces and the cylinder head bolt holes in the block.

To install:

11. Place the cylinder head gasket on the engine block dowels with the note **THIS SIDE UP** facing the cylinder head and the arrow facing the front of the engine.

12. Install the cylinder head bolts and tighten as follows:

a. Tighten the cylinder head bolts, in sequence, to 35 ft. lbs. (47 Nm).

b. Rotate each bolt 130°, in sequence.

c. Rotate the center 4 bolts an additional 30°, in sequence.

13. Install the rocker arm assemblies and valve covers.

14. Install the intake and exhaust manifolds.

15. Install the alternator front mount bracket and ignition module with bracket.

16. Install the spark plugs and wires.

17. Install the torque strut to the bracket, at the head and torque to 41 ft. lbs.

18. Fill the cooling system, connect the negative battery cable and install the air cleaner assembly.

Right Side (Rear)

1. Disconnect the negative battery cable and remove the air cleaner assembly. Relieve the fuel system pressure as outlined earlier in this Section, just before "Engine Removal and Installation."

2. Drain the cooling system and disconnect the exhaust crossover pipe.

3. Remove the intake manifold.

4. Raise and support the vehicle safely.

5. Disconnect the front exhaust pipe from the manifold.

6. Remove the valve covers.

7. Remove the belt tensioner pulley.

8. Disconnect the heater hose from the engine.

9. Remove the power steering pump mounting bracket and lay the pump to 1 side.

10. Remove the spark plug wires and remove the spark plugs.

11. Disconnect the exhaust manifold and leave in place.

12. Disconnect the electrical connection from the oxygen sensor.

13. Remove the rocker arm assemblies.

14. Remove the cylinder head bolts and remove the cylinder head.

15. Clean all gasket mating surfaces and the cylinder head bolt holes in the block.

To install:

16. Place the cylinder head gasket on the engine block dowels with the note **THIS SIDE UP** facing the cylinder head and the arrow facing the front of the engine.

17. Install the cylinder head bolts and tighten as follows:

a. Tighten the cylinder head bolts, in sequence, to 35 ft. lbs. (47 Nm).

b. Rotate each bolt 130°, in sequence.

c. Rotate the center 4 bolts an additional 30°, in sequence.

18. Connect the electrical connection to the oxygen sensor.

19. Install the exhaust manifold and intake manifold.

20. Install the rocker arm assemblies.

21. Install the valve cover.

22. Install the spark plugs and wires.

23. install the power steering pump bracket and torque the bolts to 37 ft. lbs. (50 Nm).

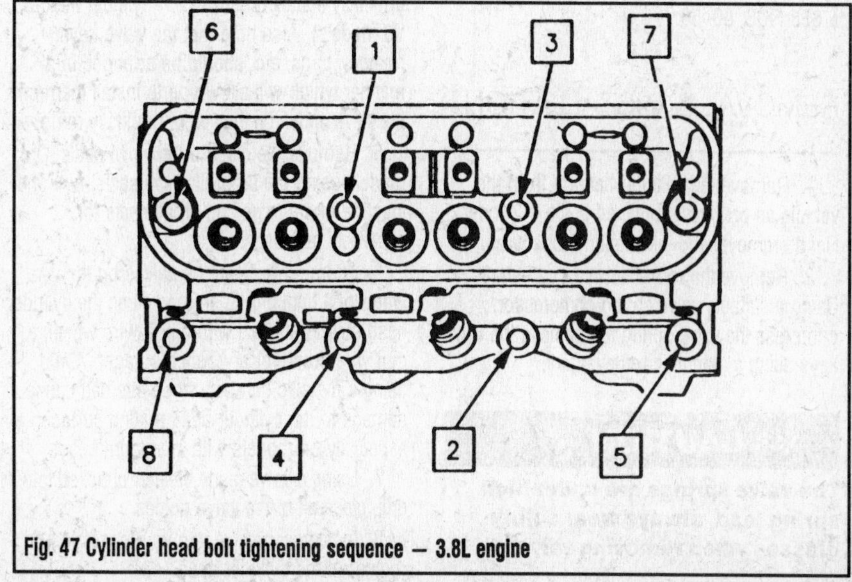

Fig. 47 Cylinder head bolt tightening sequence — 3.8L engine

24. Install the belt tensioner pulley.
25. Install the heater hose to the engine.
26. Install the exhaust crossover pipe.
27. Raise and support the vehicle safely.
28. Install the front exhaust pipe to the manifold and lower the vehicle.
29. Fill the cooling system, connect the negative battery cable and install the air cleaner assembly.

CLEANING AND INSPECTION

➧ SEE FIGS. 48 AND 49

✲✲ CAUTION

To avoid personal injury ALWAYS wear safety glasses when using a power drill and wire brush.

1. Remove all traces of carbon from the head, using a decarbon-type wire brush mounted in an electric drill. Do not use a motorized brush on any gasket mating surface.
2. Lay a straight edge across the cylinder head face and check between the straight edge and the head with feeler gauges. Make the check at at least six points. Cylinder head flatness should be within 0.003–0.006 in. (0.076–0.152mm). These surfaces may be reconditioned by parallel grinding. This procedure must be done by a qualified machine shop. If more than 10% must be removed, the head should be replaced.

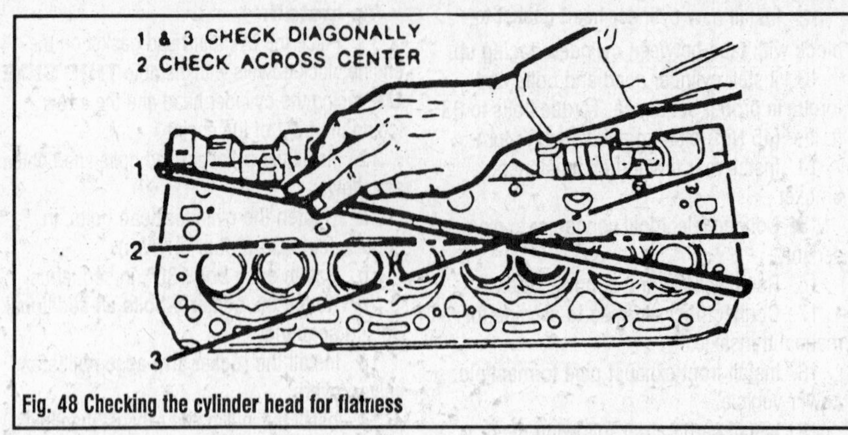

Fig. 48 Checking the cylinder head for flatness

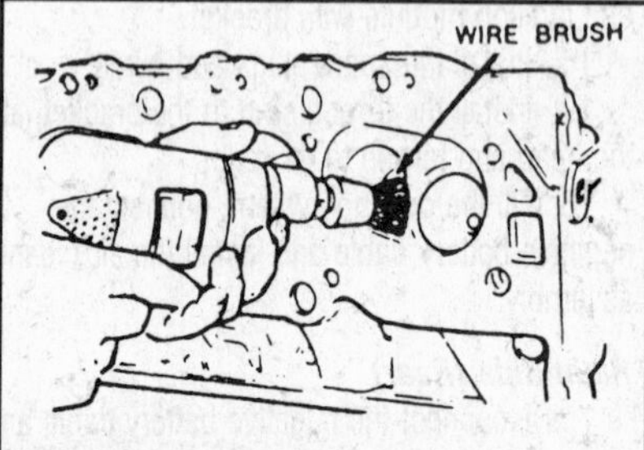

Fig. 49 Removing carbon from the cylinder head

Valves

➧ SEE FIGS. 50–55

REMOVAL & INSTALLATION

1. Remove the cylinder head(s) from the vehicle as previously outlined in the "Cylinder Head" removal and installation procedures.
2. Remove the rocker arms or camshafts. Using a suitable valve spring compressor, compress the valve spring and remove the valve keys using a magnetic retrieval tool.

✲✲ CAUTION

The valve springs are under high spring load, always wear safety glasses when removing valve springs. Decompressing a valve spring quickly may cause personal injury.

3. Slowly release the compressor and remove the valve spring caps (or rotors) and the valve springs.
4. Fabricate a valve arrangement board (piece of cardboard with holes punched through) to use when you remove the valves, which will indicate the port in which each valve was originally installed (and which cylinder head on V6 models). Also note that the valve keys, rotators, caps, etc. should be arranged in a manner which will allow you to install them on the valve on which they were originally removed.
5. Remove the discard the valve seals. On models using the umbrella type seals, note the location of the large and small seals for assembly purposes.
6. Thoroughly clean the valves on the wire wheel of a bench grinder, then clean the cylinder head mating surface with a soft wire wheel, a soft wire brush, or a wooden scraper. Avoid using a metallic scraper, since this can cause damage to the cylinder head mating surface, especially on models with aluminum heads.
7. Using a valve guide cleaner chucked into a drill, clean all of the valve guides.
8. Install each valve into its respective port (guide) of the cylinder head.
9. Mount a dial indicator so that the stem is at 90° to the valve stem, as close to the valve guide as possible.
10. Move the valve off its seat, and measure the valve guide-to-stem clearance by rocking the stem back and forth to actuate the dial indicator.
11. Measure the valve stems using a micrometer, and compare to specifications to determine whether stem or guide wear is responsible for excessive clearance. Consult the machine shop for valve guide reconditioning.

REFACING

1. Using a valve grinder, resurface the valves according to specifications in this Section.

➡ All machine work should be performed by a competent, professional machine shop.

2. Valve face angle is not always identical to valve seat angle. Consult the specifications chart in this Section.
3. A minimum margin of $\frac{1}{32}$ in. (0.8mm) should remain after grinding the valve. The valve stem top should also be squared and resurfaced, by placing the stem in the V-block of the grinder, and turning it while pressing lightly against the grinding wheel.
4. Be sure to chamfer the edge of the tip so that the squared edges don't dig into the rocker arm.

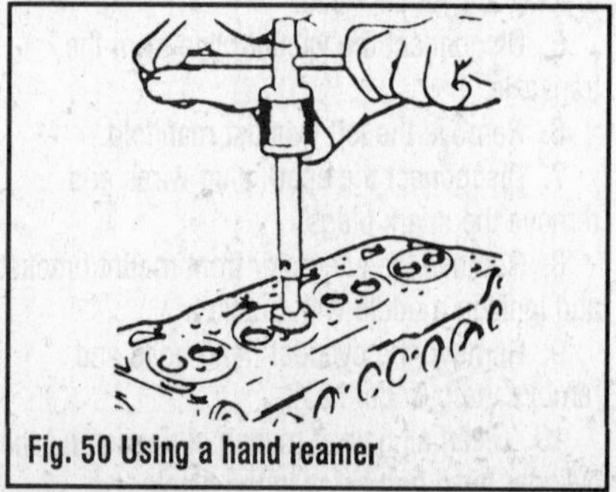
Fig. 50 Using a hand reamer

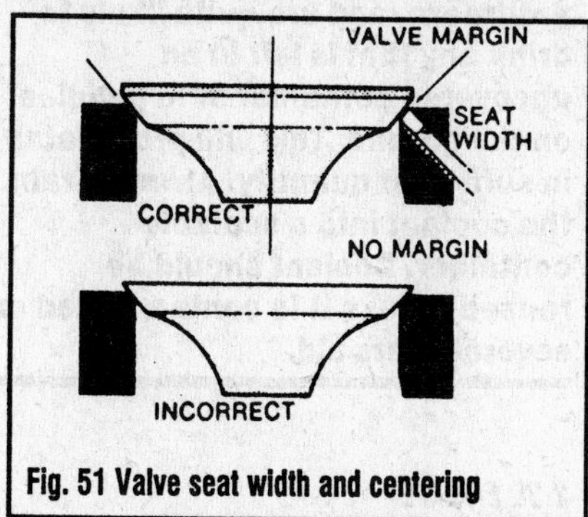

Fig. 51 Valve seat width and centering

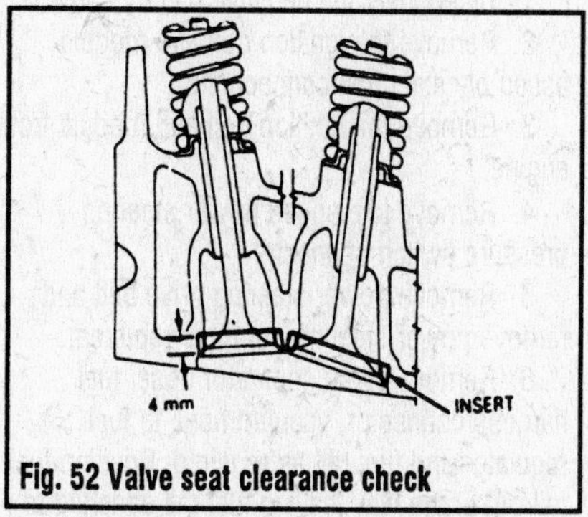

Fig. 52 Valve seat clearance check

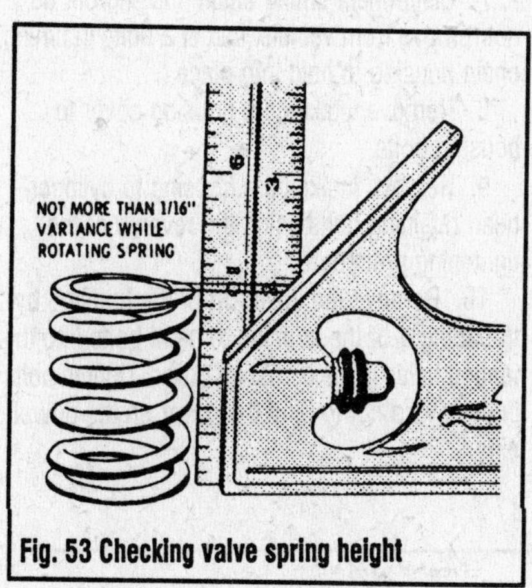

Fig. 53 Checking valve spring height

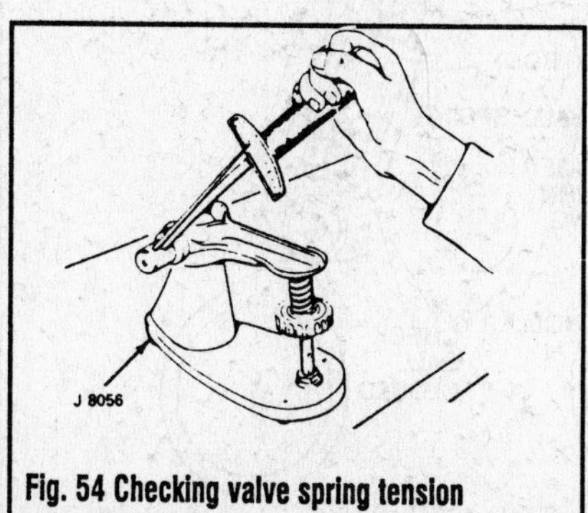

Fig. 54 Checking valve spring tension

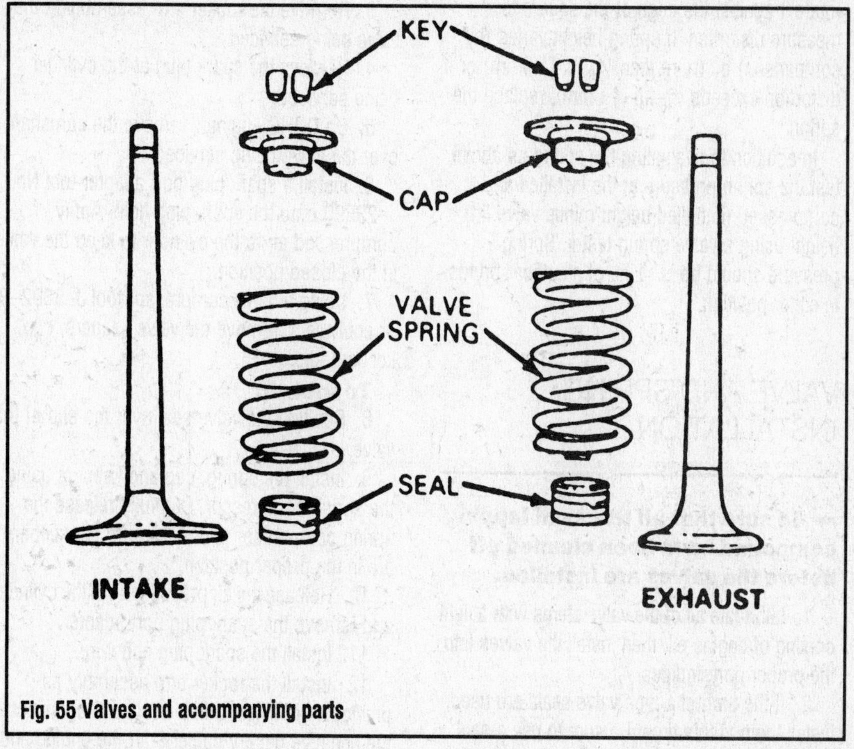

Fig. 55 Valves and accompanying parts

LAPPING

This procedure should be performed after the valves and seats have been machined, to ensure that each valve mates to each seat precisely.

1. Invert the cylinder head, lightly lubricate the valve stems, and install the valves in the head as numbered.
2. Coat valve seats with find grinding compound, and attach the lapping tool suction cup to a valve head.

➡ **Moisten the suction cup.**

3. Rotate the tool between your palms, changing position and lifting the tool often to prevent grooving.
4. Lap the valve until a smooth and uniform wear pattern exists.
5. Remove the valve and tool, and rinse away all traces of grinding compound.

Valve Guide Service

The valve guides used in these engines are integral with the cylinder head, that is, they cannot be replaced.

Valve guides are most accurately repaired using the bronze wall rebuilding method. In this operation, "threads" are cut into the bore of the valve guide and bronze wire is turned into the threads. The bronze "wall" is then reamed to the proper diameter. This method is well received for a number of reasons: it is relatively inexpensive, it offers better valve lubrication (the wire forms channels which retain oil), it offers less valve friction, and it preserves the original valve guide-to-seat relationship.

Another popular method of repairing valve guides is to have the guides "knurled." The knurling entails cutting into the bore of the valve guide with a special tool. The cutting "raises" metal off of the guide bore which actually narrows the inner diameter of the bore, thereby reducing the clearance between the valve guide bore and the valve stem. This method offers the same advantages as the bronze wall method, but will generally wear faster.

Either of the above services must be performed by a professional machine shop which has the specialized knowledge and tools necessary to perform the service.

Valve Seat Service

The valve seats are integral with the cylinder head on all engines. On all engines the seats are machined into the cylinder head casting itself.

Valve Spring Testing

Place the spring on a flat surface next to a square. Measure the height of the spring, and rotate it against the edge of the square to measure distortion. If spring height varies (by comparison) by more than $\frac{1}{16}$ in. (1.6mm) or if distortion exceeds $\frac{1}{16}$ in. (1.6mm), replace the spring.

In addition to evaluating the spring as above, test the spring pressure at the installed and compressed (installed height minus valve lift) height using a valve spring tester. Spring pressure should be ± 1 lb. of all other springs in either position.

VALVE AND SPRING INSTALLATION

➡ **Be sure that all traces of lapping compound have been cleaned off before the valves are installed.**

1. Lubricate all of the valve stems with a light coating of engine oil, then install the valves into the proper ports/guides.
2. If the umbrella-type valve seals are used, install them at this time. Be sure to use a seal protector to prevent damage to the seals as they are pushed over the valve keeper grooves. If O-ring seals are used, don't install them yet.
3. Install the valve springs and the spring retainers (or rotators), and using the valve compressing tool, compress the springs.
4. If umbrella-type seals are used, just install the valve keepers (white grease may be used to hold them in place) and release the pressure on the compressing tool. If O-ring type seals are used, carefully work the seals into the second groove of the valve (closest to the head), install the valve keepers and release the pressure on the tool.

➡ **If the O-ring seals are installed BEFORE the springs and retainers are compressed, the seal will be destroyed.**

5. After all of the valves are installed and retained, tap each valve spring retainer with a rubber mallet to seat the keepers in the retainer.

Valve Seals

REMOVAL & INSTALLATION

1. Disconnect the negative battery cable.
2. Remove the rocker arm cover as previously outlined in this Section.
3. Remove the rocker arm assembly at the valve being serviced.
4. Remove the spark plug at the cylinder being serviced.
5. On DOHC engines, remove the camshaft over the valve being serviced.
6. Install a spark plug port adapter tool No. J-23590 onto the spark plug hole. Apply compressed air to the cylinder to keep the valve in the closed position.
7. Using a valve compressor tool J-5892-B or equivalent, remove the valve keepers, cap, keepers and seal.

To install:

8. Position the valve seal over the end of the valve.
9. Install the spring, cap and keepers using the spring compressor. Carefully release the spring compressor and make sure the keepers are in the proper position.
10. Release the air pressure from the cylinder and remove the spark plug port adapter.
11. Install the spark plug and wire.
12. Install the rocker arm assembly as previously outlined in this Section. Reconnect the negative battery cable. Start the engine and check for oil leaks.

Valve Lifters

➧ SEE FIG. 56

REMOVAL & INSTALLATION

❄❄ CAUTION

When draining the coolant, keep in mind that cats and dogs are attracted by the ethylene glycol antifreeze, and are quite likely to drink any that is left in an uncovered container or in puddles on the ground. This will prove fatal in sufficient quantity. Always drain the coolant into a sealable container. Coolant should be reused unless it is contaminated or several years old.

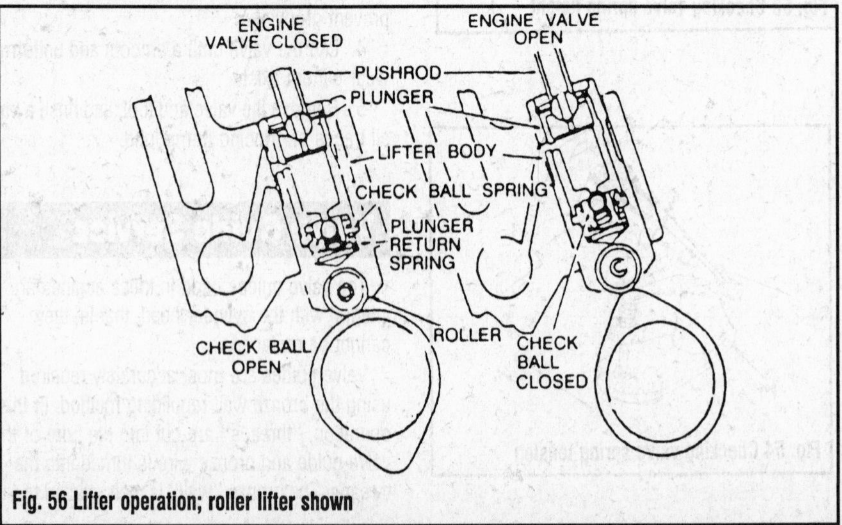

Fig. 56 Lifter operation; roller lifter shown

2.3L ENGINE

Intake Camshaft and Lifters

1. Disconnect the negative battery cable.
2. Remove the ignition coil and module assembly electrical connections.
3. Remove the ignition coil and module from engine.
4. Remove idle speed power steering pressure switch connector.
5. Remove power steering drive belt and remove power steering pump as required.
6. Remove oil/air separator hose, fuel harness connector, vacuum hose to fuel regulator and fuel rail as required. Position fuel rail out of the way leaving fuel rail attached to fuel lines.
7. Disconnect timing chain housing but do not remove from vehicle. Install 2 bolts in timing chain housing to hold into place.
8. Remove intake cam housing cover to housing bolts.
9. Remove intake cam housing to cylinder head retaining bolts using the reverse of the tightening procedure.
10. Remove the cover off of the housing by threading 4 of the housing to head bolts into the tapped holes in the camshaft cover. Tighten bolts in evenly so not to bind the cover on the dowel pins.

11. Remove 2 loosely installed bolts in cover and remove cover. Discard gasket from cover.

12. Note position of chain sprocket dowel pin for reassembly. Remove camshaft.

13. Remove valve lifters keeping in order of removal.

To install:

14. Install lifters into bores. Used lifters must be returned to their original position. Replace all lifters if new camshaft is being installed.

15. Prelube camshaft lobes and journals and install into same position as when removed.

16. Install new camshaft housing to camshaft housing cover seals into cover. Remove bolts holding housing into place and install cover and retaining bolts. Coat housing and cover retaining bolts with pipe sealer prior to installing. Torque bolts 82A, in proper sequence, to 11 ft. lbs. plus an additional 75°; on 82B bolts, torque to 11 ft. lbs. plus an additional 25°.

17. Install timing chain and housing.

18. Install new O-rings on injectors and install fuel rail into cylinder head. Install fuel rail to camshaft housing bolts and tighten to 19 ft. lbs.

19. Install injector wiring harness, vacuum hose to fuel pressure regulator and oil/air separator assembly.

20. Lube inner sealing surface of intake camshaft seal with clean engine oil and install seal into housing using tool J-36009 or equivalent.

21. Install drive pulley onto intake camshaft using tool J-36015 or equivalent.

22. Install power steering pump and drive belt.

23. Install idle speed power steering switch connector.

24. Install ignition module and coil assembly with retainer bolts and reconnect electrical connector.

25. Connect negative battery cable, start engine and check for oil leaks.

Exhaust Camshaft and Lifters

1. Disconnect the negative battery cable.

2. Disconnect electrical connection from ignition coil and module assembly.

3. Remove ignition coil and module assembly from camshaft housing.

4. Disconnect electrical connector from oil pressure switch.

5. Remove transaxle fluid level indicator tube from exhaust camshaft cover and set aside for automatic transaxle only.

6. Remove exhaust camshaft cover and gasket.

7. Disconnect timing chain housing but do not remove from vehicle.

8. Remove exhaust housing to cylinder head bolts reversing the order of tightening. Leave 2 bolts loosely in place while removing cover from housing.

9. Remove the cover off of the housing by threading 4 of the housing to head retaining bolts into the tapped holes in the camshaft cover. Tighten bolts in evenly so not to bind the cover on the dowel pins.

10. Remove 2 loosely installed bolts in cover and remove cover.

11. Note position of chain sprocket dowel pin for reassembly. Remove camshaft.

12. Remove valve lifters keeping in order of removal.

13. Remove camshaft housing.

To install:

14. Install camshaft housing to cylinder head with a new gasket. Loosely install one bolt to hold into place.

15. Install lifters into bores. Used lifters must be returned to their original position. Replace all lifters if new camshaft is being installed.

16. Prelube camshaft lobes and journals and install into same position as when removed.

17. Install new camshaft housing to camshaft housing cover seals into cover. Remove bolt holding housing into place and install cover and retaining bolts. Coat housing and cover retaining bolts with pipe sealer prior to installing. Torque bolts, in proper sequence, to 11 ft. lbs. plus an additional 75°.

18. Install timing chain and housing.

19. Install exhaust camshaft housing cover with new gasket in place.

20. Install transaxle level indicator tube to exhaust camshaft cover.

21. Install electrical connection to oil pressure switch.

22. Install ignition coil and module assembly and connect electrical connector.

23. Install negative battery cable and start vehicle. Inspect for leaks.

2.5L ENGINE

1. Disconnect the negative battery cable.
2. Remove the rocker arm cover.
3. Remove the intake manifold.
4. Remove the pushrod cover.
5. Loosen the rocker arms and move to the side.
6. Mark and remove the pushrods, retainer and lifter guides.
7. Mark and remove the lifters.

➡ Mark each valve component location for reassembly.

8. Lubricate all bearing surfaces and lifters with engine oil and install the lifters.

9. Install the lifter guides, retainers and pushrods.

10. Position the rocker arms over the pushrods and tighten the rocker arm nuts to 24 ft. lbs. (32 Nm) with the lifter at the base circle of the camshaft.

11. Install the pushrod cover, intake manifold and rocker arm cover.

12. Connect the negative battery cable.

2.8L AND 3.1L ENGINES

1. Disconnect the negative terminal from the battery.

2. Drain the cooling system.

3. Remove the rocker arm covers and intake manifold.

4. Loosen the rocker arms nuts enough to move the rocker arms to 1 side and remove the pushrods.

5. Remove the lifters from the engine.

6. Using Molykote® or equivalent, coat the base of the new lifters and install them into the engine.

7. Position the pushrods and the rocker arms correctly into their original positions. Torque the rocker arm nuts to 18 ft. lbs. (25 Nm)

8. Install the intake manifold and tighten the intake manifold-to-cylinder head bolts to specification.

9. Install the rocker cover. Connect the negative battery cable.

10. Fill the cooling system.

3.4L ENGINE

Left Side (Front)

1. Disconnect the negative battery cable.

2. Remove left side cam carrier as follows:

a. Disconnect oil/air breather hose from cam carrier cover. Remove spark plug wires from plugs and remove rear spark plug wire cover.

b. Remove cam carrier cover bolts and lift off cover. Remove gasket and O-rings from cover.

c. Remove secondary timing belt by removing secondary timing belt actuator and tensioner assembly and sliding belt from pulleys.

d. Install 6 sections of fuel line hoses under cam shaft and between lifters. This will hold lifters in the carrier. For this procedure use $^{5}/_{16}$ in. (8mm) fuel line hose for exhaust valves and $^{7}/_{32}$ in. (5.5mm) fuel line hose for the intake valves.

e. Remove exhaust crossover pipe and torque strut.

f. Remove torque strut bracket at engine.

g. Remove cam carrier mounting bolts and nuts and remove cam carrier.

h. Remove cam carrier gasket from cylinder head.

3. Remove the 6 lifter hold-down hoses. Remove the lifters.

To install

4. Lubricate lifters with clean engine oil and install lifters into original position.

5. Install lifter hold-down hoses to cam carrier.

6. Install cam carrier following these steps:

a. Install new gasket on cam carrier to cylinder mounting surface.

b. Install cam hold-down tool J–38613 or equivalent, to carrier assembly.

c. Install cam carrier to cylinder head. Install mounting bolts and nuts. Torque bolts and nuts to 18 ft. lbs.

d. Remove lifter hold-down hoses and cam hold-down tool.

e. Install torque strut bracket to engine and install torque strut.

f. Install engine crossover pipe.

g. Install secondary timing belt and cam carrier cover.

h. Reconnect spark plug cover and wires.

i. Connect breather hose to cam carrier cover.

7. Add fluids as required, reconnect negative battery cable. Start engine and recheck for leaks.

Right Side (Rear)

1. Disconnect the negative battery cable. Drain cooling system.

2. Remove right side cam carrier as follows:

a. Remove intake plenum and right timing belt cover.

b. Remove right spark plug wires.

c. Remove air/oil separator hose at cam carrier cover.

d. Remove cam carrier cover bolts and lift of cover. Remove gasket and O-rings from cover.

e. Remove secondary timing belt by removing secondary timing belt actuator and tensioner assembly and sliding belt from pulleys.

f. Install 6 sections of fuel line hoses under cam shaft and between lifters. This will hold lifters in carrier. For this procedure use $^5/_{16}$ in. (8mm) fuel line hose for exhaust valves and $^7/_{32}$ in. (5.5mm) fuel line hose for the intake valves.

g. Remove exhaust crossover pipe and torque strut.

h. Remove torque strut bracket at engine. Remove front engine lift hook.

i. Remove cam carrier mounting bolts and nuts and remove cam carrier.

j. Remove cam carrier gasket from cylinder head.

3. Remove 6 lifter hold-down hoses.

4. Remove lifters.

To install

5. Lubricate lifters with clean engine oil and install lifters into original position.

6. Install lifter hold-down hoses to cam carrier.

7. Install cam carrier following these steps:

a. Install new gasket on cam carrier to cylinder mounting surface.

b. Install cam hold-down tool J–38613 or equivalent, to carrier assembly.

c. Install cam carrier to cylinder head. Install mounting bolts and nuts. Torque bolts and nuts to 18 ft. lbs.

d. Remove lifter hold-down hoses and cam hold-down tool.

e. Install torque strut bracket to engine and install torque strut.

f. Install engine crossover pipe and engine lift hook.

g. Install secondary timing belt and cam carrier cover.

h. Install spark plug wires and cover.

8. Add fluids as required. Connect negative battery cable. Start engine and check for fluid leaks.

3.8L ENGINE

1. Disconnect the negative terminal from the battery.

2. Drain the cooling system.

3. Remove the rocker arm covers and intake manifold.

4. Remove the rocker arm assemblies.

5. Remove the guide retainer bolts and retainer.

6. Remove the valve lifter guides and and valve lifters.

To install:

7. Prelube (dip) the valve lifters with oil before installation.

8. Install the lifter guides, guide retainer and bolts and torque to 27 ft. lbs.

9. Install the rocker arm assemblies, intake manifold and valve covers.

10. Fill the cooling system and connect the negative battery cable.

Oil Pan

➧ SEE FIGS. 57 AND 58

REMOVAL & INSTALLATION

✲✲ CAUTION

The EPA warns that prolonged contact with used engine oil may cause a number of skin disorders, including cancer! You should make every effort to minimize your exposure to used engine oil. Protective gloves should be worn when changing the oil. Wash your hands and any other exposed skin areas as soon as possible after exposure to used engine oil. Soap and water, or waterless hand cleaner should be used.

2.3L ENGINE

1. Disconnect the negative battery cable.

2. Raise and support the vehicle safely.

3. Remove the flywheel inspection cover.

4. Remove the splash shield-to-suspension support bolt. Remove the exhaust manifold brace, if equipped.

5. Remove the radiator outlet pipe-to-oil pan bolt.

6. Remove the transaxle-to-oil pan nut and stud using a 7mm socket.

7. Gently pry the spacer out from between oil pan and transaxle.

8. Remove the oil pan bolts. Rotate the crankshaft if necessary and remove the oil pan and gasket from the engine.

9. Inspect the silicone strips across the top of the aluminum carrier at the oil pan-cylinder block-seal housing 3-way joint. If damaged, these strips must be repaired with silicone sealer. Use only enough sealer to restore the strips to their original dimension; too much sealer could cause leakage.

To install:

10. Thoroughly clean and dry the mating surfaces, bolts and bolt holes. Install the oil pan with a new gasket; do not uses sealer on the gasket. Loosely install the pan bolts.

11. Place the spacer in its approximate installed position but allow clearance to tighten the pan bolt above it.

12. Torque the pan to block bolts to 17 ft. lbs. (24 Nm) and the remaining bolts to 106 inch lbs. (12 Nm)

13. Install the spacer and stud.

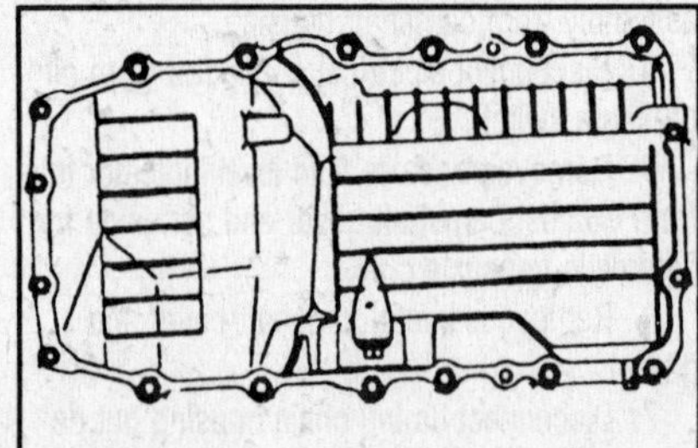

Fig. 57 Oil pan – 2.3L engine; the block bolts are different from the others

14. Install the oil pan transaxle nut and bolt.
15. Install the slash shield to suspension support.
16. Install the radiator outlet pipe bolt.
17. Install the exhaust manifold brace, if removed.
18. Install the flywheel inspection cover.
19. Fill the crankcase with the proper oil.
20. Connect the negative battery cable and check for leaks.

2.5L ENGINE

1. Disconnect the negative battery cable.
2. Remove the coolant recovery bottle, engine torque strut, air cleaner and the air inlet.
3. Remove the serpentine belt, loosen and move the air conditioning compressor from the bracket.
4. Remove the oil level indicator and fill tube.
5. Support the engine using an engine support tool J-28467-A and J-36462.
6. Raise and safely support the vehicle, drain the engine oil and remove the oil filter.
7. Remove the starter motor, flywheel cover and turn the front wheels to full right.
8. Remove the engine wiring harness retainers under the oil pan on the right and left sides.
9. Remove the right engine splash shield, front engine mount bracket bolts and nuts.
10. Remove the transaxle mount nuts.
11. Using the engine support fixture tool J-28467-A and J-36462, raise the engine about 2 in. (51mm).
12. Remove the front engine mount, bracket and loosen the frame bolts.
13. Remove the oil pan retaining bolts and oil pan.

To install:

14. Clean all gasket surfaces and apply RTV sealer to the oil pan and engine surfaces.
15. Install the oil pan and retaining bolts and tighten to 89 inch lbs. (10 Nm)
16. Install the frame bolts and tighten to 103 ft. lbs. (140 Nm)
17. Install the engine mount, bracket, lower the engine into position and install the transaxle mount nuts.
18. Install the engine mount nuts and bracket bolts.
19. Install the engine splash shield, wiring harness to the oil pan, flywheel cover and the starter motor.
20. Lower the vehicle and remove the engine support fixtures.
21. Install the oil level indicator and tube assembly.
22. Reinstall the air conditioning compressor to its original location and serpentine belt.

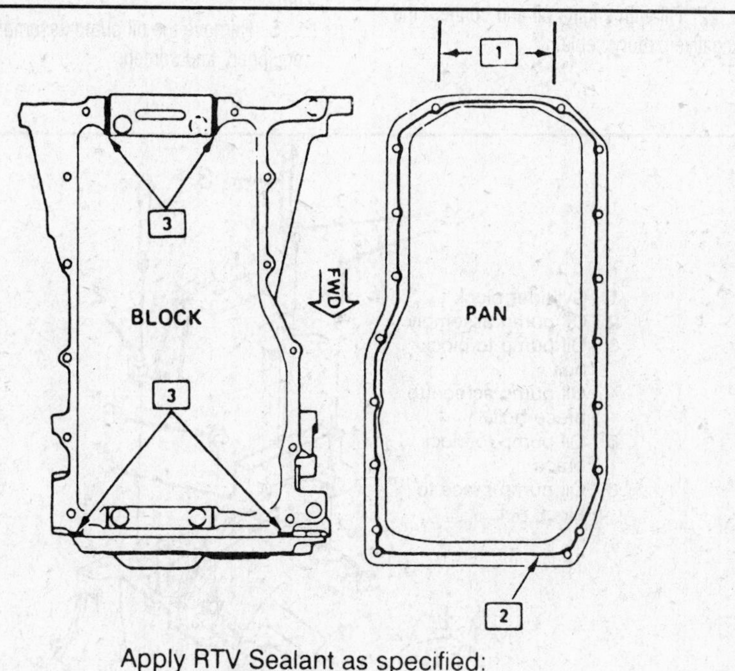

Fig. 58 Oil pan sealer locations — 2.5L engine

23. Install the air inlet, air cleaner, torque strut and coolant recovery bottle.
24. Connect the negative battery cable and fill the engine with oil.

2.8L AND 3.1L ENGINES

1. Disconnect the negative battery cable.
2. Remove the serpentine belt and the tensioner.
3. Support the engine with tool J-28467 or equivalent.
4. Raise and safely support the vehicle. Drain the engine oil.
5. Remove the right tire and wheel assembly. Remove the right inner fender splash shield.
6. Remove the steering gear pinch bolt. Remove the transaxle mount retaining bolts. Failure to disconnect intermediate shaft from rack and pinion stub shaft can result in damage to the steering gear and/or intermediate shaft. This could cause a loss of steering control which could result in personal injury.
7. Remove the engine-to-cradle mounting nuts. Remove the front engine collar bracket from the block.
8. Remove the starter shield and the flywheel cover. Remove the starter.
9. Loosen, but do not remove the rear engine cradle bolts. Remove electrical connector at DIS sensor.
10. Remove the front cradle bolts and lower front of frame. Remove the oil pan retaining bolts and nuts. Remove the oil pan.

To install:

11. Clean the gasket mating surfaces.
12. Install a new gasket on the oil pan. Apply silicon sealer to the portion of the pan that contacts the rear of the block.
13. Install the oil pan, nuts and retaining bolts. Tighten rear bolts to 18 ft. lbs. (18–25 Nm), and remaining nuts and bolts to 89 inch lbs. (10 Nm).
14. Install the front cradle bolts and tighten the rear cradle bolts. Install DIS connector. Install the starter and splash shield. Install the flywheel shield.
15. Attach the collar bracket to the block, install the engine-to-cradle nuts. Install the transaxle mount nuts.
16. Install the steering pinch bolt. Install the right inner fender splash shield and tire assembly. Lower the vehicle.
17. Remove the engine support tool. Install the serpentine belt and tensioner.
18. Fill the crankcase to the correct level. Connect the negative battery cable. Run the engine to normal operating temperature and check for leaks.

3.4L ENGINE

1. Disconnect the negative battery cable.
2. Raise and safely support vehicle. Drain engine oil,
3. Remove right front wheel assembly and steering gear heat shield.
4. Remove steering gear retaining bolts and support steering gear to body.
5. Separate right and left lower ball joints.
6. Disconnect power steering cooler line clamps at frame.
7. Support frame and remove engine mount nuts at frame.
8. Remove frame retaining bolts and remove frame assembly.
9. Remove starter assembly and flywheel cover.
10. Remove oil pan retaining nuts and bolts and remove oil pan.
11. Remove old pan gasket. Clean all mating surfaces.

To install:

12. Install new gasket adding sealer to gasket next to rear main bearing cap.Install oil pan and secure rear retaining bolts to 18 ft. lbs. (24 Nm) and all other bolts and nuts to 89 inch lbs. (10 Nm).
13. Install flywheel cover and starter motor.
14. Install frame assembly and secure all bolts.
15. Install engine mount nuts at frame. Remove frame support.
16. Install power steering cooler lines at frame.
17. Install lower ball joints. Install steering gear to steering gear mounts.
18. Install steering gear retainer bolts and heat shield.
19. Install tire assembly and lower vehicle.
20. Connect negative battery cable and add engine oil.
21. Start vehicle and check for leaks.

3.8L ENGINE

1. Disconnect the negative battery cable.
2. Disconnect the engine torque strut from the engine.
3. Raise and support the vehicle safely.
4. Disconnect the front exhaust pipe from the manifold.
5. Remove the right front wheel and the inner fender splash shield.
6. Drain the engine oil and remove the oil filter.
7. Disconnect the oil cooler pipes and allow to hang loose for access.
8. Remove both front engine mounts from the frame.
9. Remove the flywheel cover.
10. Raise the engine assembly safely, using a suitable jack and remove the oil pan retaining bolts.
11. Lower the oil pan and disconnect the oil pump screen assembly.
12. Remove the oil pan and pump screen assembly.

To install:

13. Clean the gasket mating surfaces.
14. Use a new oil pan gasket and install the oil pan and screen assembly to the engine.

➡ If the rear main bearing cap is being installed, then RTV sealant must be placed on the oil pan gasket tabs that insert into the gasket groove of the outer surface on the rear main bearing cap.

15. Tighten the screen assembly bolts to 115 inch lbs. (13 Nm) and the oil pan retaining bolts to 124 inch lbs. (14 Nm). Do not overtighten.
16. Lower the engine and install the transaxle converter cover.
17. Install the engine mount nuts to the frame and tighten to 32 ft. lbs. (43 Nm).
18. Install the oil cooler pipes and oil filter.
19. Install the inner fender splash shield and wheel assembly.
20. Install the front exhaust pipe to the manifold.
21. Lower the vehicle and install the engine torque strut to the engine.
22. Fill with engine oil and connect the negative battery cable.

Oil Pump

➧ SEE FIGS. 59–63

REMOVAL

✻✻ CAUTION

The EPA warns that prolonged contact with used engine oil may cause a number of skin disorders, including cancer! You should make every effort to minimize your exposure to used engine oil. Protective gloves should be worn when changing the oil. Wash your hands and any other exposed skin areas as soon as possible after exposure to used engine oil. Soap and water, or waterless hand cleaner should be used.

2.3L ENGINE

1. Disconnect the negative battery cable.
2. Raise and support the vehicle safely.
3. Drain the engine oil and remove the oil pan.
4. Remove the oil pump retaining bolts and nut.
5. Remove the oil pump assembly, shims, if equipped, and screen.

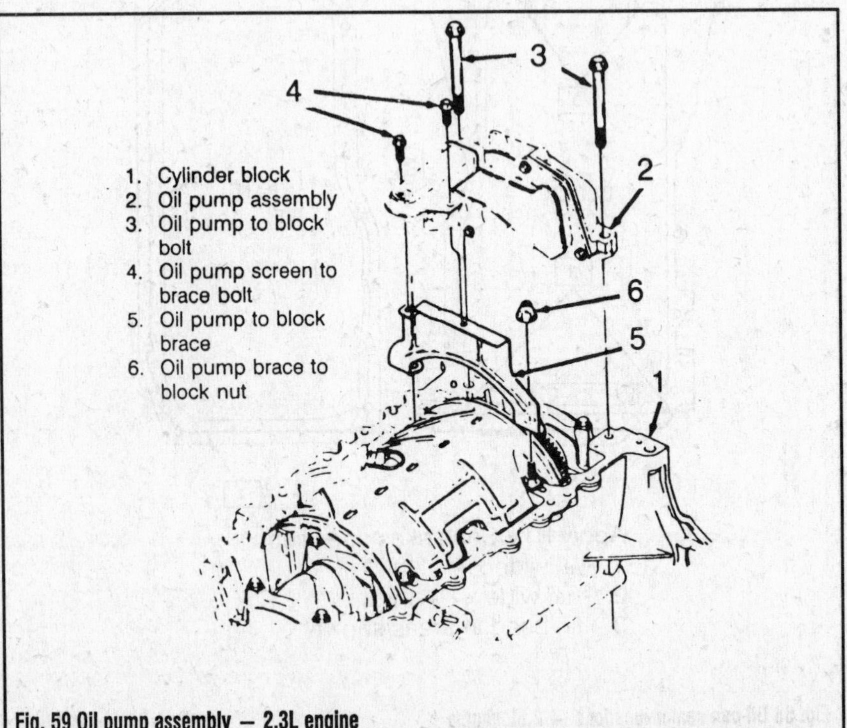

Fig. 59 Oil pump assembly — 2.3L engine

2.5L, 2.8L, 3.1L AND 3.4L ENGINES

➡ **On the 2.5L engine, the force balancer assembly does not have to be removed to service the oil pump or pressure regulator assemblies.**

1. Disconnect the negative battery cable.
2. Raise and safely support the vehicle.
3. Drain the engine oil.
4. Remove the oil pan.
5. On 3.4L engine, it will be necessary to remove the oil pan baffle by extracting the nuts and rotating the oil pick up tube out of the way.
6. Remove the oil pump retaining bolts and remove the oil pump and pump driveshaft.

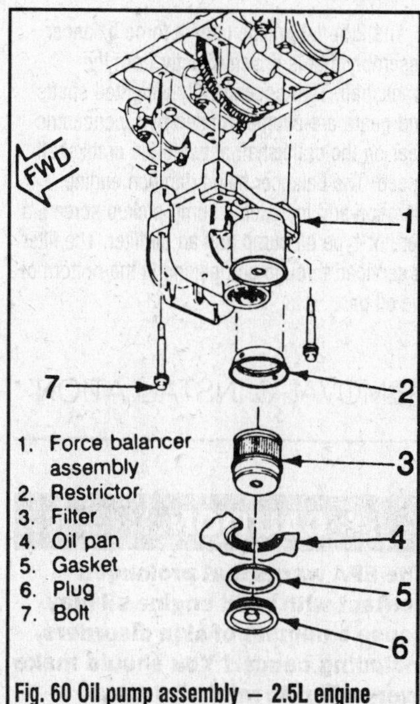

Fig. 60 Oil pump assembly — 2.5L engine

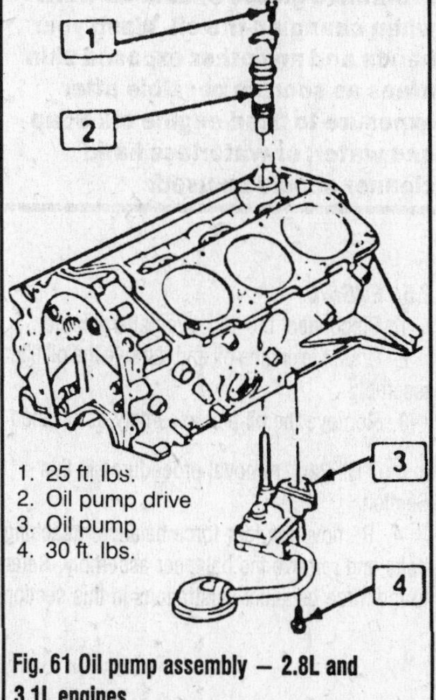

Fig. 61 Oil pump assembly — 2.8L and 3.1L engines

3.8L ENGINE

1. Disconnect the negative battery cable.
2. Raise and safely support the vehicle.
3. Drain the engine oil.
4. Remove the front cover assembly.
5. Remove the oil filter adapter, pressure regulator valve and spring.
6. Remove the oil pump cover attaching screws and remove the cover.
7. Remove the oil pump gears.

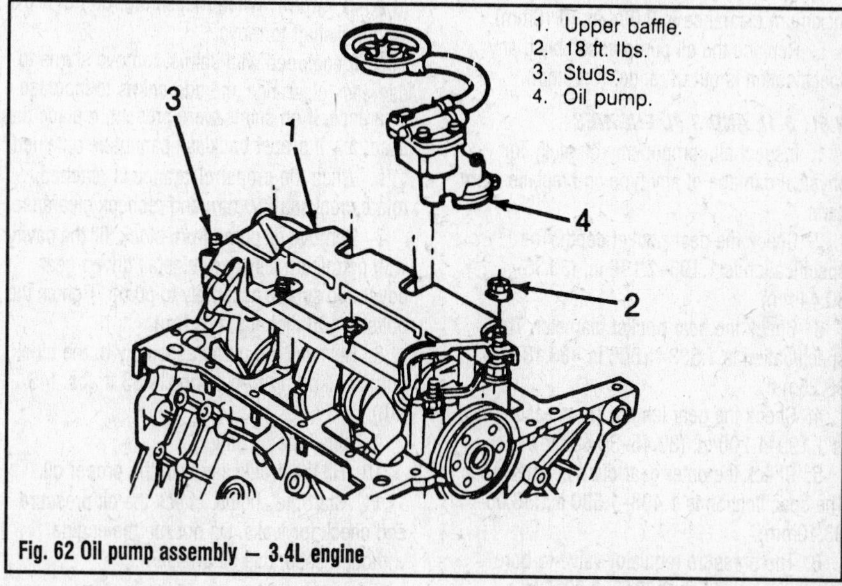

Fig. 62 Oil pump assembly — 3.4L engine

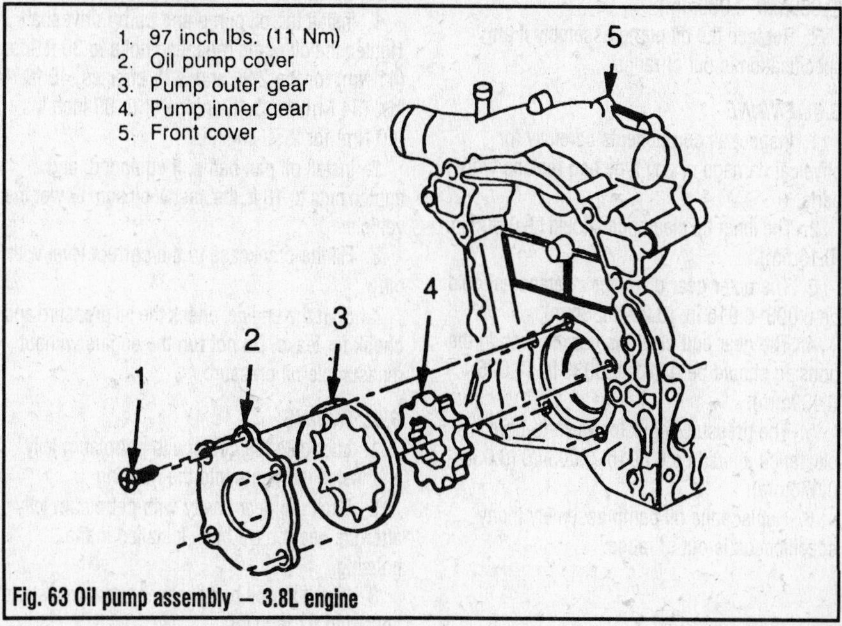

Fig. 63 Oil pump assembly — 3.8L engine

INSPECTION

2.3L ENGINE

1. Inspect all components carefully for physical damage of any type and replace worn parts.
2. Check the gerotor cavity depth. The specification is 0.674–0.676 in. (17.11–17.16mm).
3. Check the gerotor cavity diameter. The specification is 2.127–2.129 in. (53.95–54.00mm).
4. Check the inner gerotor tip clearance. The maximum clearance is 0.006 in. (0.15mm).

5. Check the outer gerotor diameter clearance. The specification is 0.010–0.014 in. (0.254–0.354mm).

6. Replace the oil pump assembly if any specification is out of range.

2.5L ENGINE

1. Inspect all components carefully for physical damage of any type and replace worn parts.

2. Check the gerotor cavity depth. The specification for 1988 is 0.995–0.998 in. (25.27–25.35mm). The specification for 1989–92 is 0.514–0.516 in. (13.05–13.10mm).

3. Check the gear lash. The specification is 0.009–0.015 in. (0.23–0.38mm).

4. Check the clearance of both gears. The maximum clearance is 0.004 in. (0.10mm).

5. Replace the oil pump assembly if any specification is out of range. (0.10mm).

2.8L, 3.1L AND 3.4L ENGINES

1. Inspect all components carefully for physical damage of any type and replace worn parts.

2. Check the gear pocket depth. The specification is 1.195–1.198 in. (30.36–30.44mm).

3. Check the gear pocket diameter. The specification is 1.503–1.506 in. (38.18–38.25mm).

4. Check the gear length. The measurement is 1.199–1.200 in. (30.45–30.48mm).

5. Check the outer gear diameter clearance. The specification is 1.498–1.500 in. (38.05–38.10mm).

6. The pressure regulator valve-to-bore clearance should be 0.0015–0.0035 in. (0.038mm–0.089mm).

7. Replace the oil pump assembly if any specification is out of range.

3.8L ENGINE

1. Inspect all components carefully for physical damage of any type and replace worn parts.

2. The inner tip clearance should be 0.006 in. (0.15mm).

3. The outer gear diameter clearance should be 0.008–0.015 in. (0.20–0.38mm).

4. The gear end clearance or the drop in the housing should be 0.001–0.0035 in. (0.025–0.089mm).

5. The pressure regulator valve-to-bore clearance should be 0.0015–0.003 in. (0.038–0.076mm).

6. Replace the oil pump assembly if any specification is out of range.

INSTALLATION

2.3L ENGINE

1. With oil pump assembly off engine, remove 3 retaining bolts and separate the driven gear cover and screen assembly from the oil pump.

2. Install the oil pump on the block using the original shims, if equipped. Tighten the bolts to 33 ft. lbs. (45 Nm).

3. Mount a dial indicator assembly to measure backlash between oil pump to drive gear.

4. Record oil pump drive to driven gear backlash. Proper backlash is 0.010–0.018 in. (0.25–0.45mm). When measuring, do not allow the crankshaft to move.

5. If equipped with shims, remove shims to decrease clearance and add shims to increase clearance. If no shims were present, replace the assembly if proper backlash cannot be obtained.

6. When the proper clearance is reached, rotate crankshaft 1/2 turn and recheck clearance.

7. Remove oil pump from block, fill the cavity with petroleum jelly and reinstall driven gear cover and screen assembly to pump. Tighten the bolts to 106 inch lbs. (13 Nm).

8. Reinstall the pump assembly to the block. Torque oil pump-to-block bolts 33 ft. lbs. (45 Nm).

9. Install the oil pan.

10. Fill the crankcase with the proper oil.

11. Start the engine, check the oil pressure and check for leaks. Do not run the engine without measurable oil pressure.

2.5L, 2.8L, 3.1L AND 3.4L ENGINES

1. Install the oil pump and pump driveshaft. Tighten the oil pump mounting bolts to 30 ft. lbs. (41 Nm) for the 2.8L and 3.1L engines, 40 ft. lbs. (54 Nm) for 3.4L engine or to 89 inch lbs. (10 Nm) for 2.5L engine.

2. Install oil pan baffle, if equipped, and tighten nuts to 18 ft. lbs. Install oil pan. Lower the vehicle.

3. Fill the crankcase to the correct level with oil.

4. Start the engine, check the oil pressure and check for leaks. Do not run the engine without measurable oil pressure.

3.8L ENGINE

1. Lubricate the gears with petroleum jelly and install the gears into the housing.

2. Pack the gear cavity with petroleum jelly after the gears have been installed in the housing.

3. Install the oil pump cover and screws and tighten to 97 inch lbs.

4. Install the oil filter adapter with new gasket, pressure regulator valve and spring.

5. Install the front cover assembly.

6. Fill with clean engine oil. Start the engine, check the oil pressure and check for leaks. Do not run the engine without measurable oil pressure.

Force Balancer Assembly

The 2.5L L4 engine uses a force balancer assembly that is driven directly from the crankshaft. Two eccentrically weighted shafts and gears are counter rotated by a concentric gear on the crankshaft at twice the crankshaft speed. The balancer helps dampen engine vibration and includes a sump pickup screen, a gerotor-type oil pump and an oil filter. The filter is serviced through an opening in the bottom of the oil pan.

REMOVAL & INSTALLATION

**** CAUTION**

The EPA warns that prolonged contact with used engine oil may cause a number of skin disorders, including cancer! You should make every effort to minimize your exposure to used engine oil. Protective gloves should be worn when changing the oil. Wash your hands and any other exposed skin areas as soon as possible after exposure to used engine oil. Soap and water, or waterless hand cleaner should be used.

2.5L ENGINE

1. Disconnect the negative battery cable.

2. Drain the engine oil and remove the oil filter assembly.

3. Remove the oil pan assembly as outlined in the "Oil Pan" removal procedures in this Section.

4. Remove the four force balancer attaching bolts and remove the balancer assembly. Refer to the force balancer illustrations in this section.

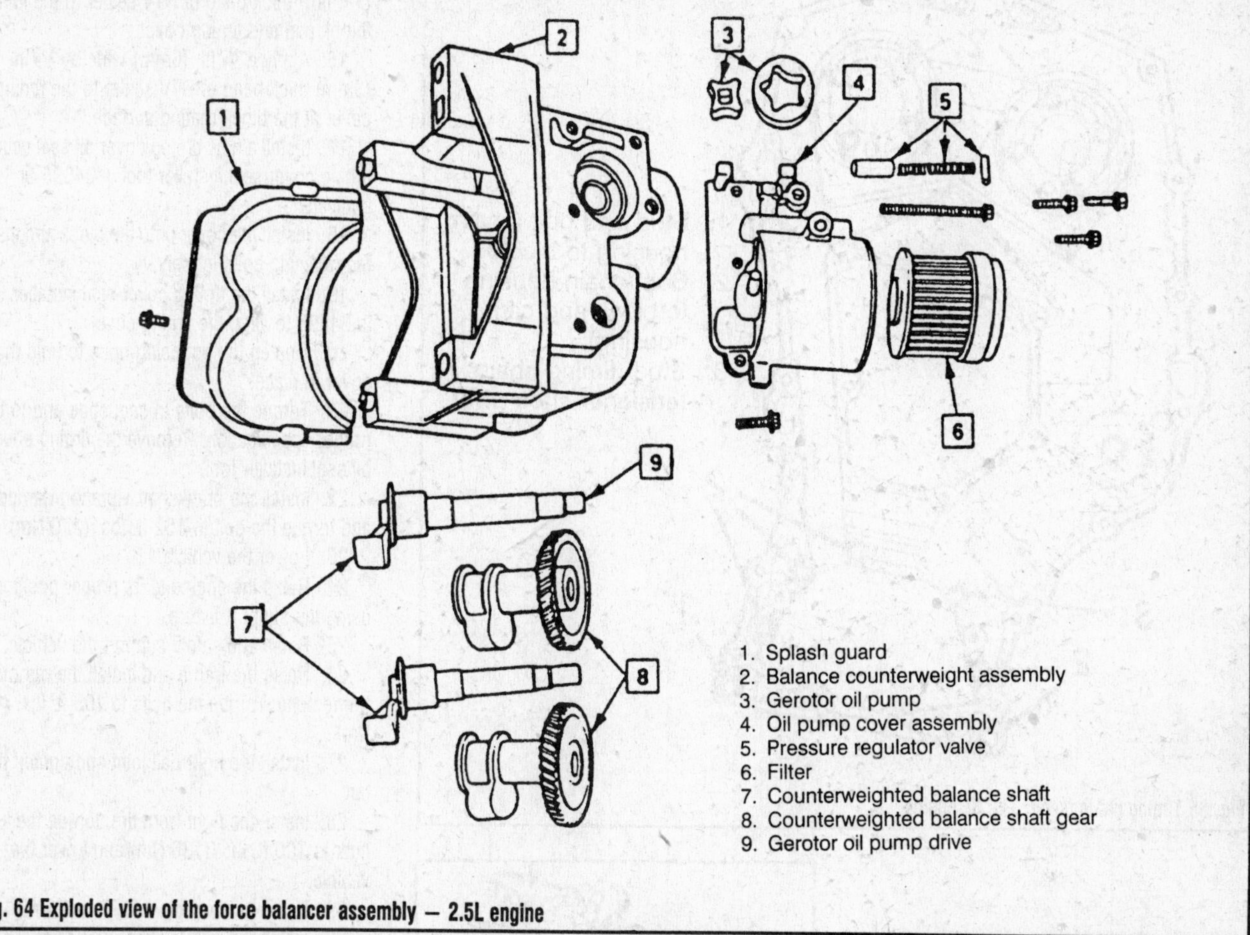

Fig. 64 Exploded view of the force balancer assembly — 2.5L engine

➡ When installing the balancer, the end of the housing without the dowel pins MUST remain in contact with the block surface. If it loses contact, gear engagement may be lost and permanent damage to either the crank or balancer gears may result.

a. Rotate the engine to Top Dead Center (TDC) on the No. 1 and No. 4 cylinders.

b. Position the balancer assembly onto the crankshaft with the balancer weights at BDC (bottom dead center), plus or minus one half of a gear tooth.

c. Torque the bolts in the following sequence in two steps, 3–1–2–4.

d. The first torque step to 107 inch lbs. (12 Nm). The second torque step to 11 ft. lbs. (15 Nm) plus 75° (1 flat) for the short bolts. And 11 ft. lbs. (15 Nm) plus 90° (1½ flats) for the long bolts.

5. Install the oil pan assembly as outlined in the "Oil Pan" installation procedures in this Section.

6. Refill the crankcase with the specified engine oil. Start the engine and check for oil leaks.

Timing Chain/Gear Front Cover

➧ SEE FIGS. 65–68

REMOVAL & INSTALLATION

✲✲ CAUTION

When draining the coolant, keep in mind that cats and dogs are attracted by the ethylene glycol antifreeze, and are quite likely to drink any that is left in an uncovered container or in puddles on the ground. This will prove fatal in sufficient quantity. Always drain the coolant into a sealable container. Coolant should be reused unless it is contaminated or several years old.

✲✲ WARNING

The EPA warns that prolonged contact with used engine oil may cause a number of skin disorders, including cancer! You should make every effort to minimize your exposure to used engine oil. Protective gloves should be worn when changing the oil. Wash your hands and any other exposed skin areas as soon as possible after exposure to used engine oil. Soap and water, or waterless hand cleaner should be used.

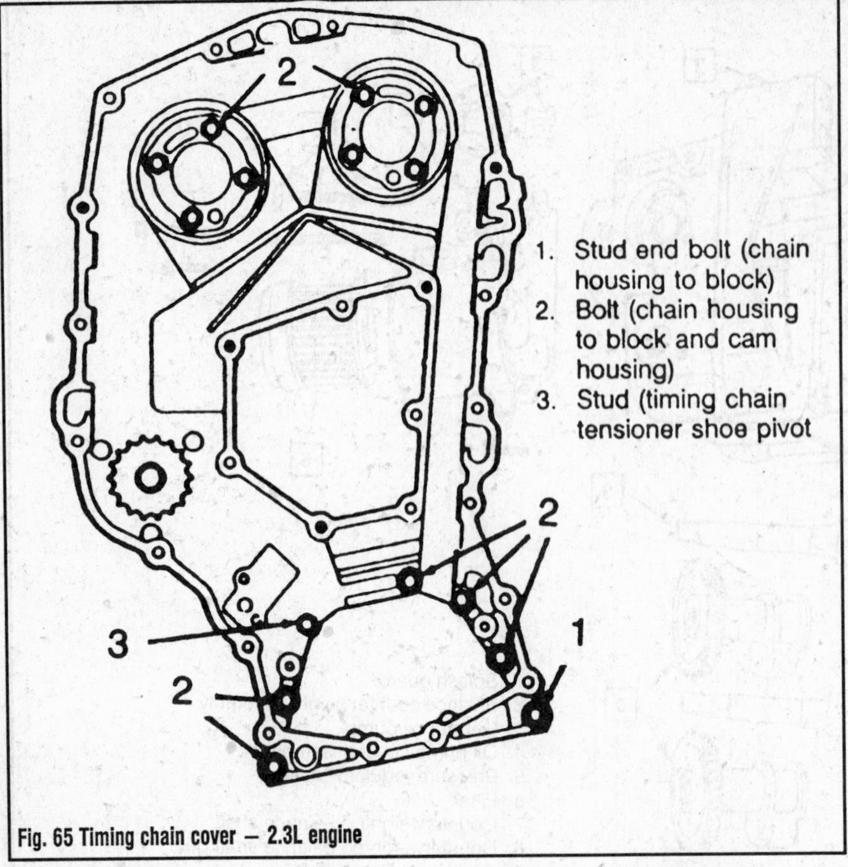

Fig. 65 Timing chain cover — 2.3L engine

2.3L ENGINE

1. Disconnect the negative battery cable. Remove the coolant recovery reservoir.
2. Remove the serpentine drive belt using a 13mm wrench that is at least 24 in. (61cm) long.
3. Remove upper cover fasteners.
4. Raise the vehicle and support safely.
5. Remove the right front wheel assembly and lower splash shield.
6. Remove the crankshaft balancer assembly.
7. Remove lower cover fasteners and lower the vehicle.
8. Remove the front cover.
9. The installation is the reverse of the removal procedure. Torque the balancer retaining bolt to 74 ft. lbs. (100 Nm) plus an additional 90° turn.

2.5L ENGINE

1. Disconnect the negative battery cable.
2. Remove the torque strut bolt at the cylinder head bracket and move the strut out of the way.
3. Remove the serpentine belt.
4. Install the engine support fixture tool J-28467-A and J-36462.

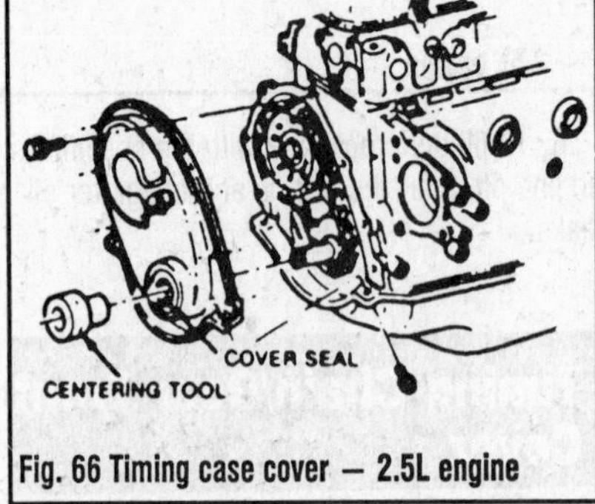

Fig. 66 Timing case cover — 2.5L engine

5. Raise and safely support the vehicle.
6. Remove the right front tire assembly.
7. Disconnect the right lower ball joint from the knuckle.
8. Remove the 2 right frame attaching bolts.
9. Loosen the 2 left frame attaching bolts but do not remove.
10. Lower the vehicle.
11. Lower the engine on the right side. Raise and safely support the vehicle.
12. Remove the engine vibration dampener using a dampener puller.
13. Remove the timing cover retaining bolts and cover.

To install:

14. Clean all gasket mating surfaces with solvent and a gasket scraper.
15. Apply a 3/8 in. (10mm) wide by 1/16 in. (1.6mm) thick bead of RTV sealer to the joint at the oil pan and timing cover.
16. Apply a 1/4 in. (6mm) wide by 1/8 in. (3mm) thick bead of RTV sealer to the timing cover at the block mating surface.
17. Install a new timing cover oil seal using a timing cover seal installer tool J-34995 or equivalent.
18. Install the cover onto the block and install the retaining bolts loosely.
19. Install the timing cover seal installer tool J-34995 to align the timing cover.
20. Tighten the opposing bolts to hold the cover in place.
21. Torque the bolts in sequence and to the proper specification. Remove the timing cover oil seal installer tool.
22. Install the crankshaft vibration dampener and torque the bolt to 162 ft. lbs. (220 Nm)
23. Lower the vehicle.
24. Raise the engine to its proper position using the support fixture.
25. Raise and safely support the vehicle.
26. Raise the frame and install the removed frame bolts. Torque the bolts to 103 ft. lbs. (140 Nm)
27. Install the right ball joint and tighten the nut.
28. Install the right front tire, torque the lug nuts to 100 ft. lbs. (136 Nm) and lower the vehicle.
29. Remove the engine support fixture.
30. Install the torque strut and bolt to the cylinder head bracket.
31. Install the serpentine belt, connect the negative battery cable and check for oil leaks.

2.8L AND 3.1L ENGINES

1. Disconnect the negative terminal from the battery. Drain the cooling system.
2. Remove the serpentine belt and the belt tensioner.
3. Remove the alternator-to-bracket bolts and remove the alternator, with the wires attached, support it out of the way.
4. Remove the power steering pump-to-bracket bolts and support it out of the way. Do not disconnect the pressure hoses.
5. Raise and safely support the vehicle.
6. Remove the right side inner fender splash shield. Remove the flywheel dust cover.
7. Using a crankshaft pulley puller tool, remove the crankshaft damper.
8. Label and disconnect the starter wires, and remove the starter.
9. Drain the engine oil and remove the oil pan. Remove the lower front cover bolts.
10. Lower the vehicle. Disconnect the radiator hose from the water pump.

11. Disconnect the heater coolant hose from the cooling system filler pipe.

12. Remove the bypass and overflow hoses.

13. Remove the water pump pulley. Disconnect the canister purge hose.

14. Remove the spark plug wire shield from the water pump.

15. Remove the upper front cover-to-engine bolts and remove the front cover.

16. Clean front cover mounting surfaces.

To install:

17. Apply a thin bead of silicone sealant on the front cover mating surface and using a new gasket, install the front cover on the engine with the top bolts to hold it in place.

18. Raise and safely support the vehicle.

19. Install the oil pan. Install the lower front cover bolts, tighten all of the front cover bolts to 26–35 ft. lbs. (35–48 Nm)

20. Install the serpentine belt and idler pulley. Install the damper on the engine using tool J-29113 or equivalent. Install the starter.

21. Install the inner fender splash shield. Lower the vehicle.

22. Attach the radiator hose too the water pump and attach the heater hoses.

23. Install the power steering pump and the alternator.

24. Attach the spark plug wire shield. Fill the cooling system.

25. Connect the negative battery cable. Check for coolant and oil leaks.

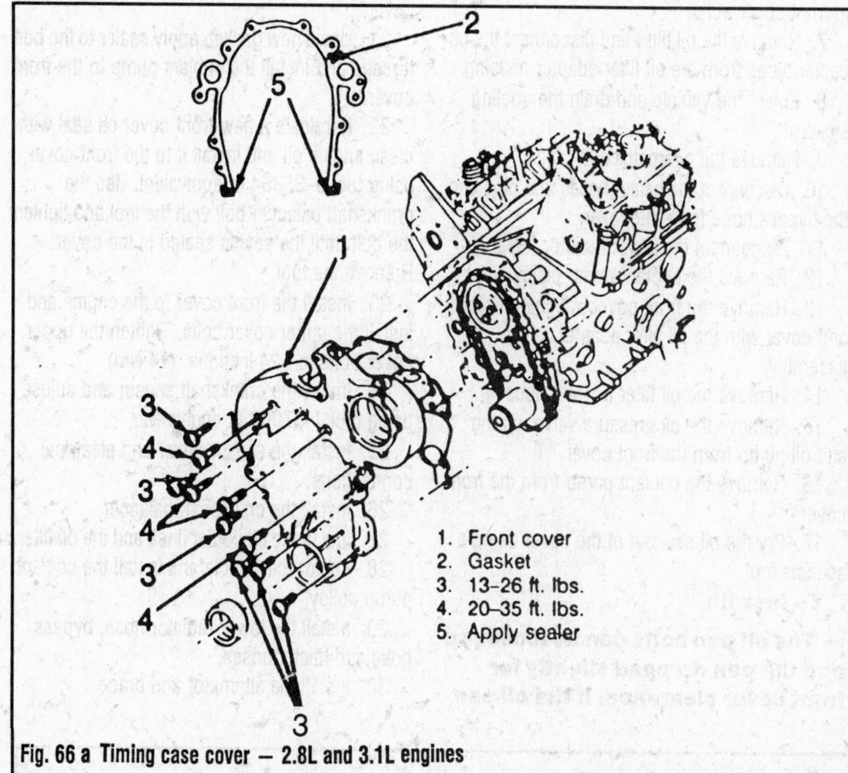

Fig. 66 a Timing case cover — 2.8L and 3.1L engines

3.4L ENGINE

1. Disconnect the negative battery cable.

2. Remove secondary timing belt tensioner mounting bracket and gasket by removing tensioner pulley and mounting bracket bolts.

3. Remove secondary timing belt idler pulleys.

4. Remove the front engine lift hook.

5. Remove engine torque strut mount bracket to frame bolts and position strut out of the way.

6. Remove the upper radiator support, cooling fan bolts and right side cooling fan.

7. Drain cooling system and remove lower radiator hose from coolant pump inlet pipe.

8. Remove the heater hose at the front cover and the heater pipe bracket retainer bolts at frame.

9. Raise and safely support vehicle.

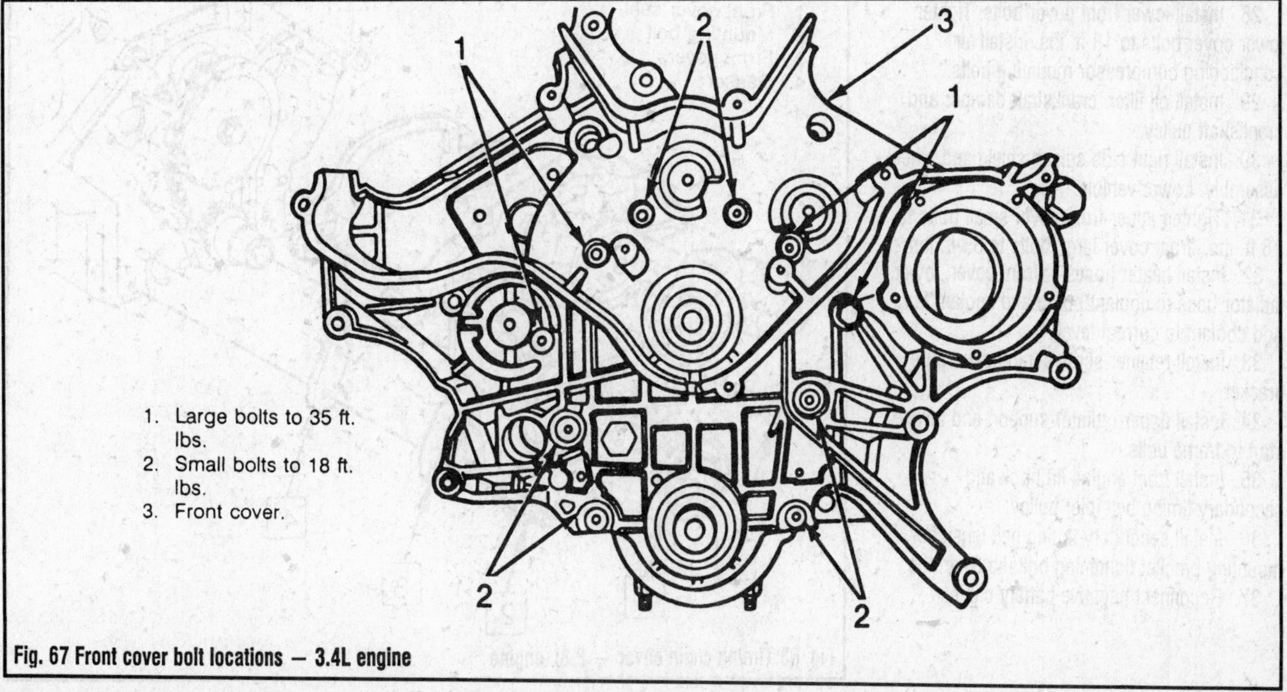

Fig. 67 Front cover bolt locations — 3.4L engine

10. Remove right front tire and wheel assembly. Remove right splash shield.
11. Remove crankshaft pulley and damper.
12. Remove oil filter.
13. Remove air conditioner compressor mounting bracket bolts.
14. Remove lower front cover bolts.
15. On automatic transaxle vehicles remove the halfshaft.
16. Remove the rear alternator bracket and starter motor. Lower vehicle.
17. Remove the camshaft drive belt sprocket retaining bolt and extract camshaft drive belt sprocket using tool J-38616 or equivalent.
18. Remove upper alternator retaining bolts. Remove the forward light relay center screws and position relay center aside.
19. Remove oil cooler hose at front cover and coolant pump pulley.
20. Remove upper front cover bolts and front cover. Remove the old gasket and clean mating surfaces of front cover and block.

To install:

21. Apply GM sealer 1052080 or equivalent, to lower edges of the sealing surface of the front cover and install. Apply thread sealant to large bolts and tighten cover into place.
22. Install the water pump pulley. Install oil cooler coolant hose to front cover.
23. Install forward light relay center and upper alternator retaining bolts.
24. Install camshaft drive belt sprocket and retaining bolt.
25. Raise and safely support vehicle.
26. Install starter motor.
27. Reinstall halfshaft and rear alternator bracket.
28. Install lower front cover bolts. Tighten lower cover bolts to 18 ft. lbs. Install air conditioning compressor mounting bolts.
29. Install oil filter, crankshaft damper and crankshaft pulley.
30. Install right side splash shield and wheel assembly. Lower vehicle.
31. Tighten upper front cover small bolts to 18 ft. lbs., front cover large bolts to 35 ft. lbs.
32. Install heater hoses at front cover, lower radiator hose to coolant pump and coolant fan. Add coolant to correct level.
33. Install retainer screws into heater pipe bracket.
34. Install upper radiator support and torque strut to frame bolts.
35. Install front engine lift hook and secondary timing belt idler pulley.
36. Install secondary timing belt tensioner mounting bracket tightening bolts to 37 ft. lbs.
37. Reconnect negative battery cable.

3.8L ENGINE

1. Disconnect the negative battery cable.
2. Remove the crankshaft balancer.
3. Remove the crankshaft sensor cover.
4. Disconnect the electrical connections at the camshaft, crankshaft and oil pressure sensors.
5. Raise and support the vehicle safely.
6. Drain the engine oil and remove the oil pan to front cover bolts.
7. Remove the oil filter and disconnect the oil cooler pipes from the oil filter adapter housing.
8. Lower the vehicle and drain the cooling system.
9. Remove the alternator and brace.
10. Disconnect the heater hoses and pipe and the bypass hose from the cover.
11. Disconnect the lower radiator hose.
12. Remove the coolant pump pulley.
13. Remove the front cover attaching bolts and cover with the oil filter adapter as an assembly.
14. Remove the oil filter adapter housing.
15. Remove the oil pressure valve, spring and oil pump from the front cover.
16. Remove the coolant pump from the front cover.
17. Pry the oil seal out of the cover using a suitable tool.

To install:

➡ **The oil pan bolts can be loosened and the pan dropped slightly for front cover clearance. If the oil pan gasket is excessively swollen, the oil pan must be removed and the gasket replaced.**

18. Clean the mating surfaces of the front cover and cylinder block with a degreaser.
19. Install the oil filter and adapter housing with the oil pressure valve and spring to the cover. Tighten the bolts to 24 ft. lbs.
20. Install the oil pump assembly to the cover.
21. Use a new gasket, apply sealer to the bolt threads and install the coolant pump to the front cover.
22. Lubricate a new front cover oil seal with clean engine oil and install it to the front cover, using tool J-35354 or equivalent. Use the crankshaft balancer bolt with the tool and tighten the bolt until the seal is seated in the cover. Remove the tool.
23. Install the front cover to the engine and install the upper cover bolts. Tighten the upper cover bolts to 124 inch lbs. (14 Nm)
24. Install the crankshaft sensor and adjust, using tool J-37089 or equivalent.
25. Install the sensor cover and electrical connections.
26. Install the crankshaft balancer.
27. Install the oil cooler lines and the oil filter.
28. Lower the vehicle and install the coolant pump pulley.
29. Install the lower radiator hose, bypass hose and heater hoses.
30. Install the alternator and brace.

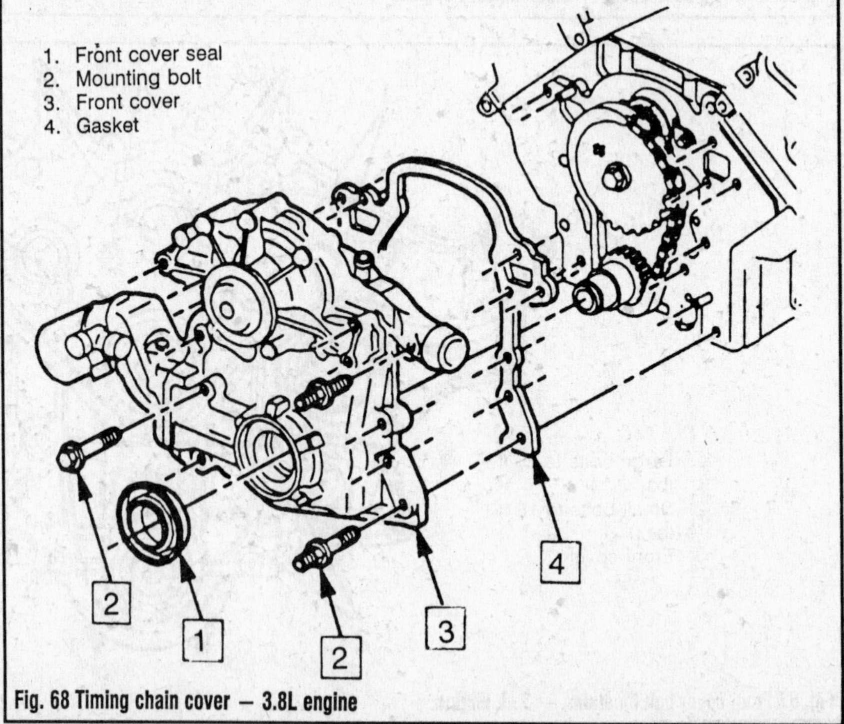

Fig. 68 Timing chain cover — 3.8L engine

31. Add engine coolant, oil and connect the negative battery cable.

Front Cover Oil Seal

REPLACEMENT

1. Disconnect the negative terminal from the battery. Remove the serpentine belt.
2. Raise and safely support the vehicle. Remove the right side inner fender splash shield.
3. Remove the damper retaining bolt.
4. Using a crankshaft pulley puller tool, press the damper pulley from the crankshaft.
5. Using a small prybar, pry out the seal in the front cover.

➡ **Use care not to damage the seal seat or the crankshaft while removing or installing the seal. Inspect the crankshaft seal surface for signs of wear.**

6. Coat the new seal with oil. Using a seal installer tool, drive the new seal in the cover with the lip facing towards the engine.
7. Using a crankshaft pulley installer tool, press the crankshaft pulley onto the crankshaft. Torque the damper bolt to 67–85 ft. lbs. (90–115 Nm) for 2.8L and 3.1L engines, 95 ft. lbs (130 Nm) for 3.4L engine, 162 ft. lbs. (220 Nm) for 2.5L engine, 105 ft. lbs. plus an additional 56° turn for 3.8L engine or 74 ft. lbs. plus an additional 90° turn for 2.3L engine.
8. Install the inner fender splash shield. Lower the vehicle.
9. Install the serpentine belt. Connect the negative battery cable. Run the engine to normal operating temperature and check for leaks.

Timing Chain and Gears

➧ SEE FIGS. 70–77

REMOVAL & INSTALLATION

2.3L ENGINE

➡ **It is recommended that the entire procedure be reviewed before attempting to service this timing chain.**

1. Disconnect the negative battery cable.
2. Remove the front timing chain cover and crankshaft oil slinger.

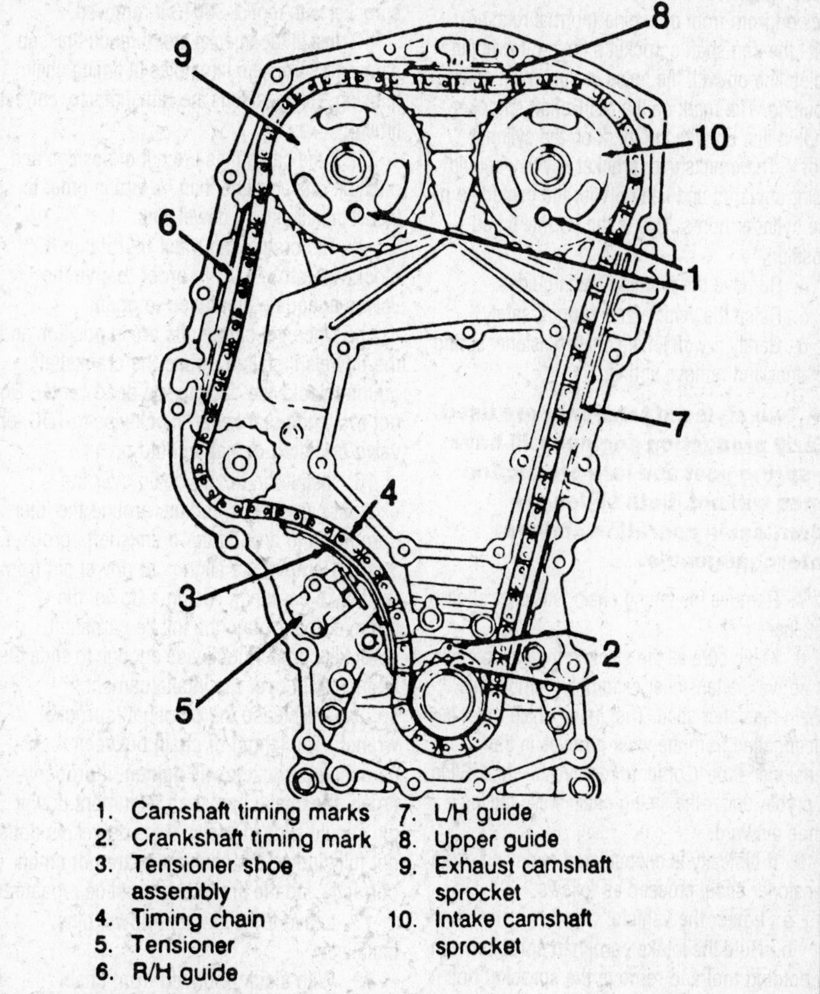

Fig. 70 Timing chain properly installed — 2.3L engine

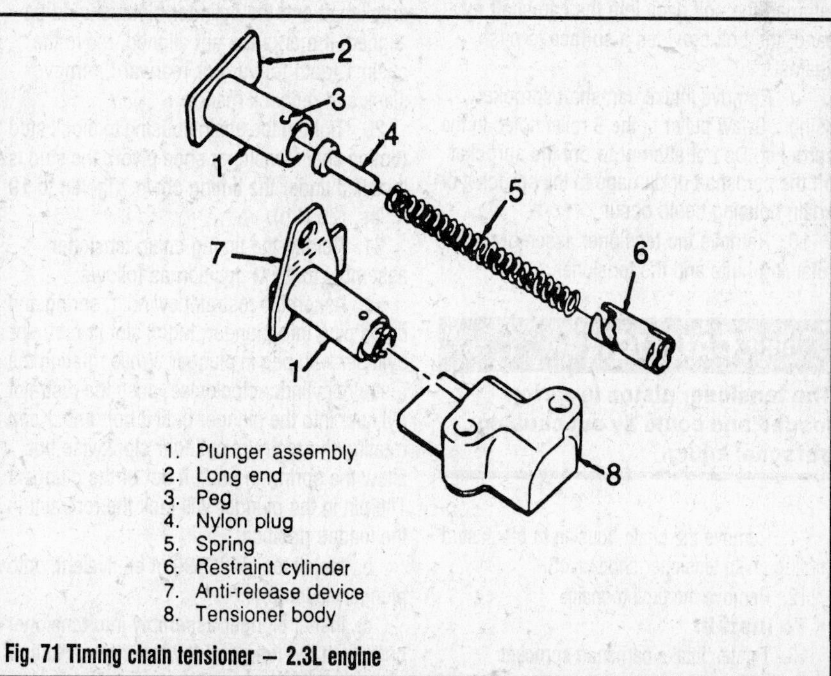

Fig. 71 Timing chain tensioner — 2.3L engine

3. Rotate the crankshaft clockwise, as viewed from front of engine (normal rotation) until the camshaft sprocket's timing dowel pin holes line up with the holes in the timing chain housing. The mark on the crankshaft sprocket should line up with the mark on the cylinder block. The crankshaft sprocket keyway should point upwards and line up with the centerline of the cylinder bores. This is the normal timed position.

4. Remove the 3 timing chain guides.

5. Raise the vehicle and support safely.

6. Gently pry off timing chain tensioner spring retainer and remove spring.

➡ Two styles of tensioner are used. Early production engines will have a spring post and late production ones will not. Both styles are identical in operation and are interchangeable.

7. Remove the timing chain tensioner shoe retainer.

8. Make sure all the slack in the timing chain is above the tensioner assembly; remove the chain tensioner shoe. The timing chain must be disengaged from the wear grooves in the tensioner shoe in order to remove the shoe. Slide a prybar under the timing chain while pulling shoe outward.

9. If difficulty is encountered removing chain tensioner shoe, proceed as follows:

a. Lower the vehicle.

b. Hold the intake camshaft sprocket with a holding tool and remove the sprocket bolt and washer.

c. Remove the washer from the bolt and rethread the bolt back into the camshaft by hand, the bolt provides a surface to push against.

d. Remove intake camshaft sprocket using a 3-jaw puller in the 3 relief holes in the sprocket. Do not attempt to pry the sprocket off the camshaft or damage to the sprocket or chain housing could occur.

10. Remove the tensioner assembly retaining bolts and the tensioner.

✱✱ CAUTION

The tensioner piston is spring loaded and could fly out causing personal injury.

11. Remove the chain housing to block stud (timing chain tensioner shoe pivot).

12. Remove the timing chain.

To install:

13. Tighten intake camshaft sprocket retaining bolt and washer, while holding the sprocket with tool J-36013 if removed.

14. Install the special tool through holes in camshaft sprockets into holes in timing chain housing. This positions the camshafts for correct timing.

15. If the camshafts are out of position and must be rotated more than 1/8 turn in order to install the alignment dowel pins:

a. The crankshaft must be rotated 90° clockwise off of TDC in order to give the valves adequate clearance to open.

b. Once the camshafts are in position and the dowels installed, rotate the crankshaft counterclockwise back to top dead center. Do not rotate the crankshaft clockwise to TDC, or valve or piston damage could occur.

16. Install the timing chain over the exhaust camshaft sprocket, around the idler sprocket and around the crankshaft sprocket.

17. Remove the alignment dowel pin from the intake camshaft. Using a dowel pin remover tool, rotate the intake camshaft sprocket counterclockwise enough to slide the timing chain over the intake camshaft sprocket. Release the camshaft sprocket wrench. The length of chain between the 2 camshaft sprockets will tighten. If properly timed, the intake camshaft alignment dowel pin should slide in easily. If the dowel pin does not fully index, the camshafts are not timed correctly and the procedure must be repeated.

18. Leave the alignment dowel pins installed.

19. With slack removed from chain between intake camshaft sprocket and crankshaft sprocket, the timing marks on the crankshaft and the cylinder block should be aligned. If marks are not aligned, move the chain 1 tooth forward or rearward, remove slack and recheck marks.

20. Tighten the chain housing to block stud (timing chain tensioner shoe pivot). the stud is installed under the timing chain. Tighten to 19 ft. lbs. (26 Nm).

21. Reload the timing chain tensioner assembly to its **O** position as follows:

a. Assemble restraint cylinder, spring and nylon plug into plunger. Index slot in restraint cylinder with peg in plunger. While rotating the restraint cylinder clockwise, push the restraint cylinder into the plunger until it bottoms. Keep rotating the restraint cylinder clockwise but allow the spring to push it out of the plunger. The pin in the plunger will lock the restraint in the loaded position.

b. Install tool J-36589 or equivalent, onto plunger assembly.

c. Install plunger assembly into tensioner body with the long end toward the crankshaft when installed.

22. Install the tensioner assembly to the chain housing. Recheck plunger assembly installation. It is correctly installed when the long end is toward the crankshaft.

23. Install and tighten timing chain tensioner bolts and tighten to 10 ft. lbs. (14 Nm)

24. Install the tensioner shoe and tensioner shoe retainer.

25. Remove special tool J-36589 and squeeze plunger assembly into the tensioner body to unload the plunger assembly.

26. Lower vehicle and remove the alignment dowel pins. Rotate crankshaft clockwise 2 full rotations. Align crankshaft timing mark with mark on cylinder block and reinstall alignment dowel pins. Alignment dowel pins will slide in easily if engine is timed correctly.

➡ If the engine is not correctly timed, severe engine damage could occur.

27. Install the 3 timing chain guides and crankshaft oil slinger.

28. Install the timing chain front cover.

29. Connect the negative battery cable and check for leaks.

2.5L, 2.8L AND 3.1L ENGINES

1. Disconnect the negative battery cable.

2. Remove the front cover assembly.

3. Place the No. 1 piston at TDC with the marks on the crankshaft and the camshaft aligned (No. 4 firing position).

4. Remove the camshaft sprocket and the timing chain.

➡ If the camshaft sprocket does not come off easily, a light blow on the lower edge of the sprocket with a rubber mallet should loosen the sprocket.

5. Remove the crankshaft sprocket with a suitable prybar.

To install:

6. Install the crankshaft sprocket. Apply a coat of Molykote® or equivalent, to the sprocket thrust surface.

7. Hold the camshaft sprocket with the chain hanging down, and align the marks on the camshaft and crankshaft sprockets.

8. Align the dowel in the camshaft with the dowel hole in the camshaft sprocket. Install the camshaft sprocket and chain, use the camshaft sprocket bolts to draw the sprocket on to the camshaft. Tighten the sprocket bolts to 18 ft. lbs. (25 Nm).

9. Lubricate the timing chain with engine oil. Install the front cover assembly.

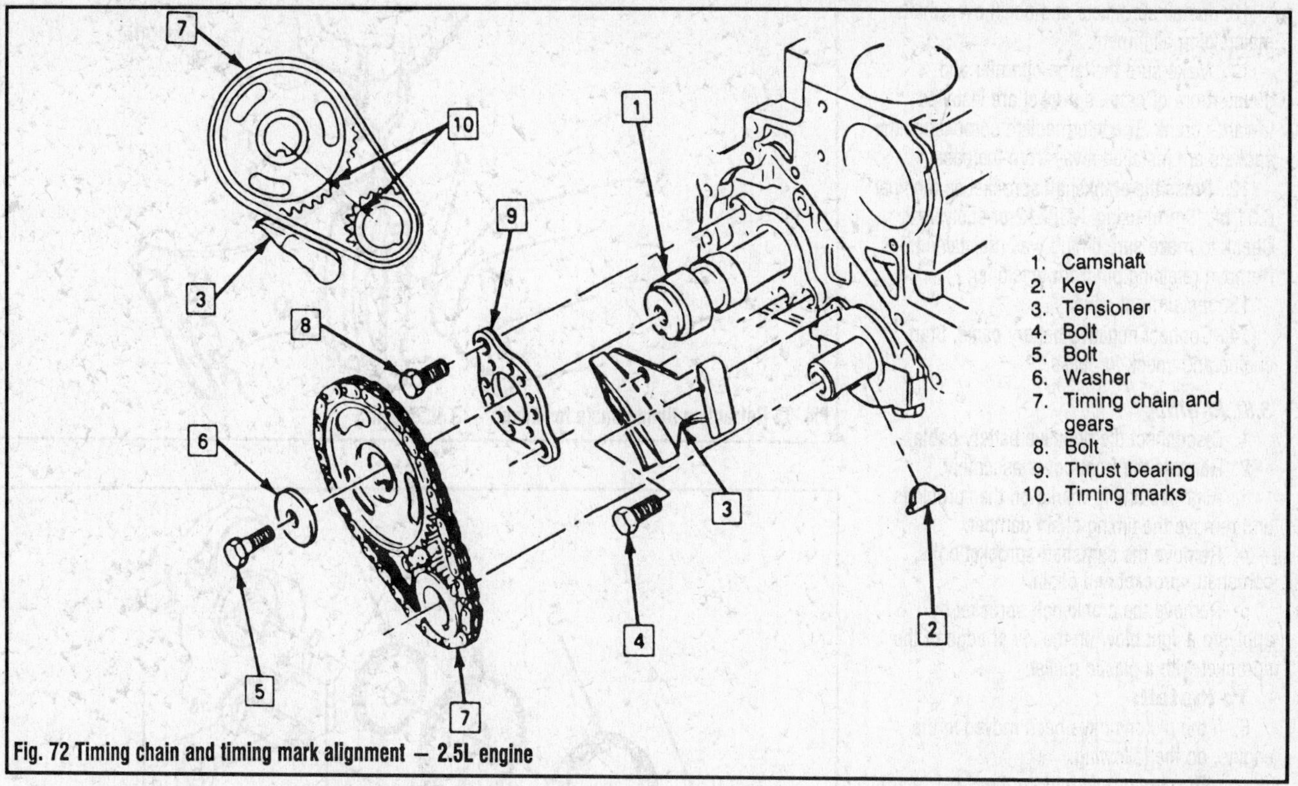

Fig. 72 Timing chain and timing mark alignment — 2.5L engine

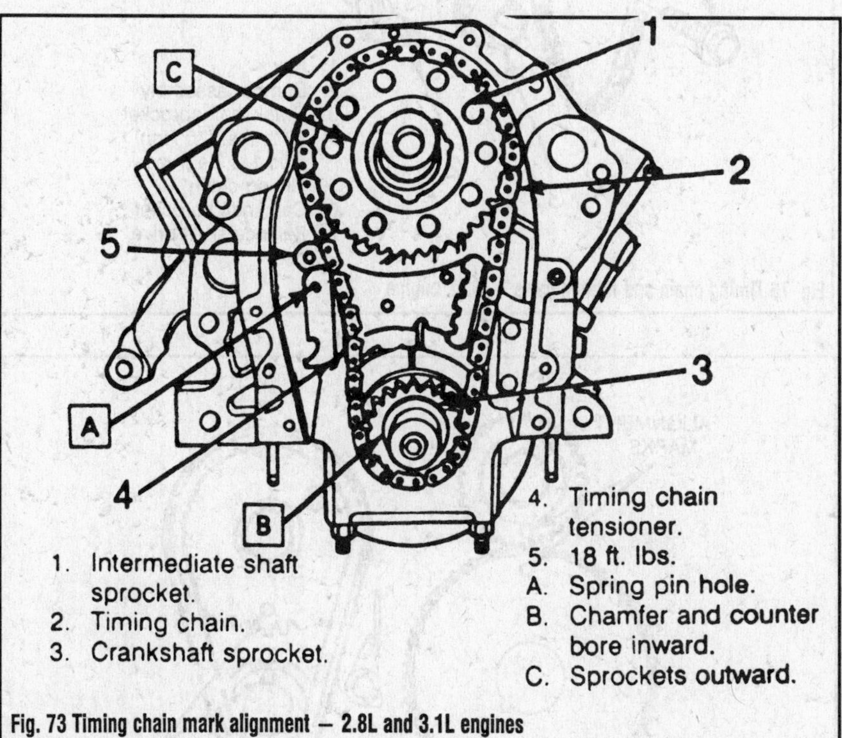

Fig. 73 Timing chain mark alignment — 2.8L and 3.1L engines

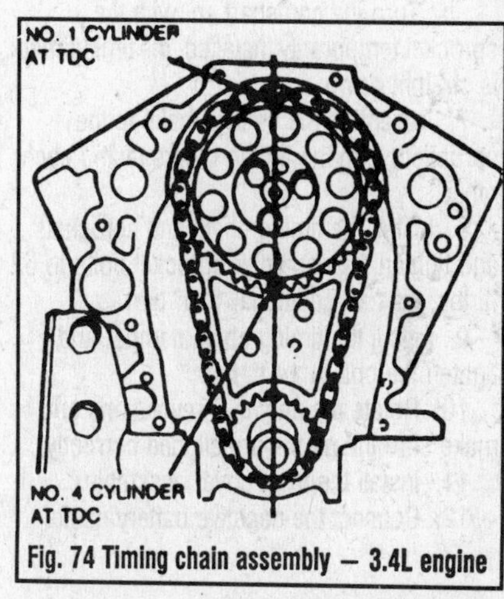

Fig. 74 Timing chain assembly — 3.4L engine

3.4L ENGINE

1. Disconnect the negative battery cable.
2. Raise and safely support vehicle.
3. Remove starter motor and flywheel cover.
4. Remove oil pan retaining nuts and bolts. Remove lower frame and powertrain onto transmission table.
5. Remove front cover.
6. Mark intermediate sprocket, chain link, front face of cylinder and crank sprocket for reference.
7. Retract the timing chain tensioner shoe by using J-33875 or equivalent, on both sides of the tensioner and pulling on the thru pin in the tensioner arm to retract the spring. While spring is retracted, insert a holding tool to hold it.
8. Remove the timing chain and crankshaft sprocket using gear puller. If the intermediate gear does not slide off easily with the timing chain assembly, rotate the crankshaft back and forth to loosen tight fit.

To install:

9. Check to ensure that crankshaft key is fully seated and chain tensioner is fully seated and retracted.

10. Install sprockets and chain over shafts maintaining alignment.
11. Make sure the large chamfer and counterbore of crank sprocket are installed towards crank. The intermediate sprocket spline sockets are installed away from the case.
12. Press the crankshaft sprocket on the final 0.31 in. (8mm) using J–38612 or equivalent. Check to make sure timing was maintained. Remove retaining pin from tensioner.
13. Install front cover.
14. Connect negative battery cable. Start engine and check for leaks.

3.8L ENGINE

1. Disconnect the negative battery cable.
2. Remove the front cover assembly.
3. Align the timing marks on the sprockets and remove the timing chain damper.
4. Remove the camshaft sprocket bolts, camshaft sprocket and chain.
5. Remove the crankshaft sprocket by applying a light blow on the lower edge of the sprocket with a plastic mallet.

To install:

6. If the pistons have been moved in the engine, do the following:
   a. Turn the crankshaft so the No. 1 piston is at Top Dead Center (TDC).
   b. Turn the camshaft so, with the sprocket temporarily installed, the timing mark is straight down.
7. Assemble the timing chain on the sprockets with the timing marks facing each other.
8. Install the timing chain and sprockets and tighten the camshaft sprocket bolts to 52 ft. lbs. plus an additional 110° turn.
9. Install the timing chain damper and tighten the bolt to 14 ft. lbs.
10. Rotate the engine 2 revolutions and make sure the marks are aligned correctly.
11. Install the front cover assembly.
12. Connect the negative battery cable.

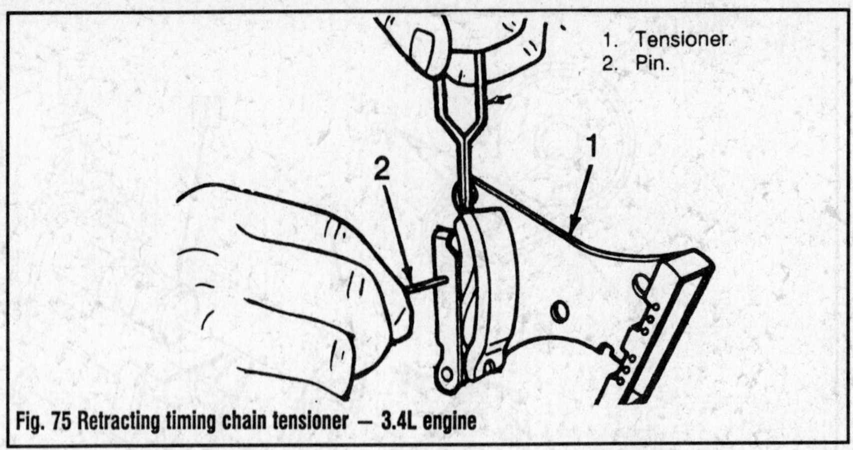

Fig. 75 Retracting timing chain tensioner — 3.4L engine

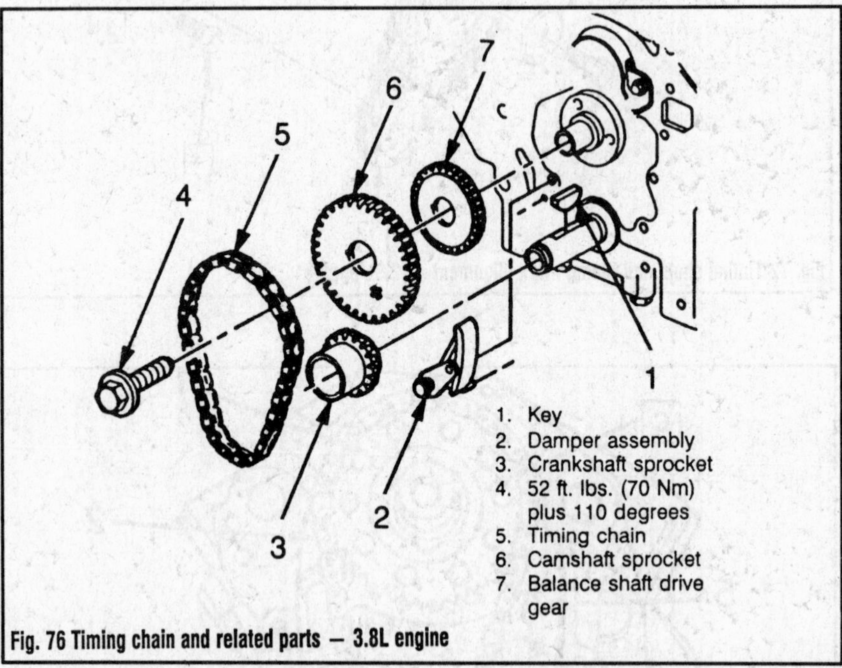

Fig. 76 Timing chain and related parts — 3.8L engine

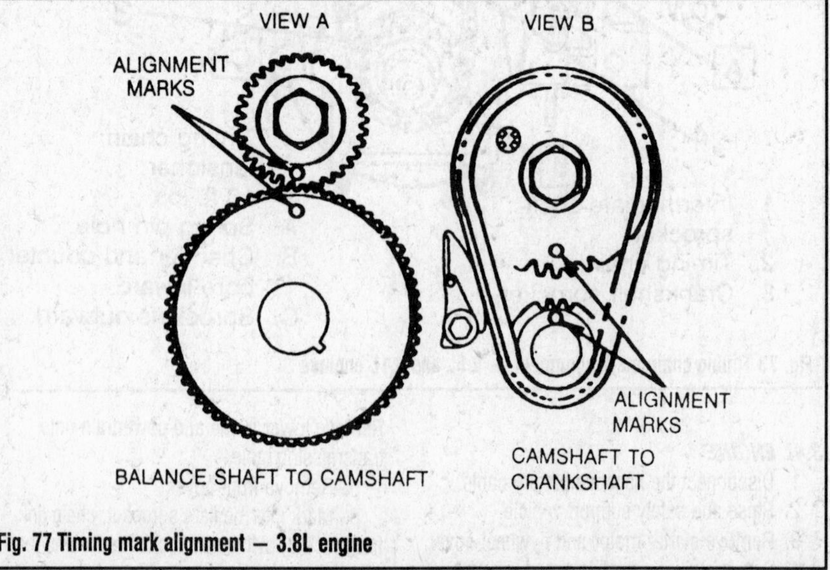

Fig. 77 Timing mark alignment — 3.8L engine

Secondary Timing Belt Cover

REMOVAL & INSTALLATION

3.4L ENGINE

Right Side

1. Disconnect negative battery cable.
2. Remove retaining bolts and remove cover.

3. To install, position cover and install retaining bolts.

Left Side

1. Disconnect the negative battery cable.
2. Remove spark plug wire cover.
3. Remove retaining bolts and cover.
4. To install, position cover and secure with retaining bolts.
5. Install spark plug wire cover.

Center Cover

1. Disconnect the negative battery cable.
2. Disconnect Electronic Control Module (ECM) harness cover.
3. Remove serpentine belt tensioner.
4. Remove right and left side timing belt covers.
5. Remove power steering pipe retaining clip nut at alternator stud.
6. Remove center timing belt cover bolts and remove cover.

To Install:

7. Position cover on engine and secure with retainer bolts. Tighten bolts to 89 inch lbs.
8. Reinstall power steering pipe retaining clip nut to alternator stud.
9. Install right and left side covers.Install serpentine belt.
10. Install Electronic Control Module (ECM) harness cover. Reconnect negative battery cable.

Secondary Timing Belt and Tensioner

➧ SEE FIG. 78

REMOVAL & INSTALLATION

1. Disconnect the negative battery cable.
2. Remove secondary timing belt actuator.
3. If belt is to be reused mark direction of rotation.
4. Remove tensioner and pulley arm assembly.
5. Remove timing belt by sliding off of pulleys. Do not bend, twist, or kink belt or damage to the belt may occur.
6. Install new belt or old belt taking note of direction of rotation.
7. Install tensioner pulley to mounting base. Tighten bolt to 37 ft. lbs.
8. Rotate the tensioner pulley counterclockwise into the belt using the cast square lug on body and engage ball end of the actuator into socket on pulley arm.
9. Remove tensioner lock pin allowing tensioner shaft to extend and the pulley to move into the belt.
10. Rotate the tensioner pulley counterclockwise applying 12–15 ft. lbs. torque.
11. Rotate the engine clockwise 3 times to seat belt. Align the crankshaft reference marks during final rotation to TDC. Do not allow crankshaft to spring back or reverse direction of rotation.
12. Seat lock ring on the right exhaust and right intake camshaft into the bore by threading in the attaching bolts.
13. Hold sprocket from turning using tool J–38614 or equivalent. Tighten attaching bolt to 81 ft. lbs. taking note of running torque; torque

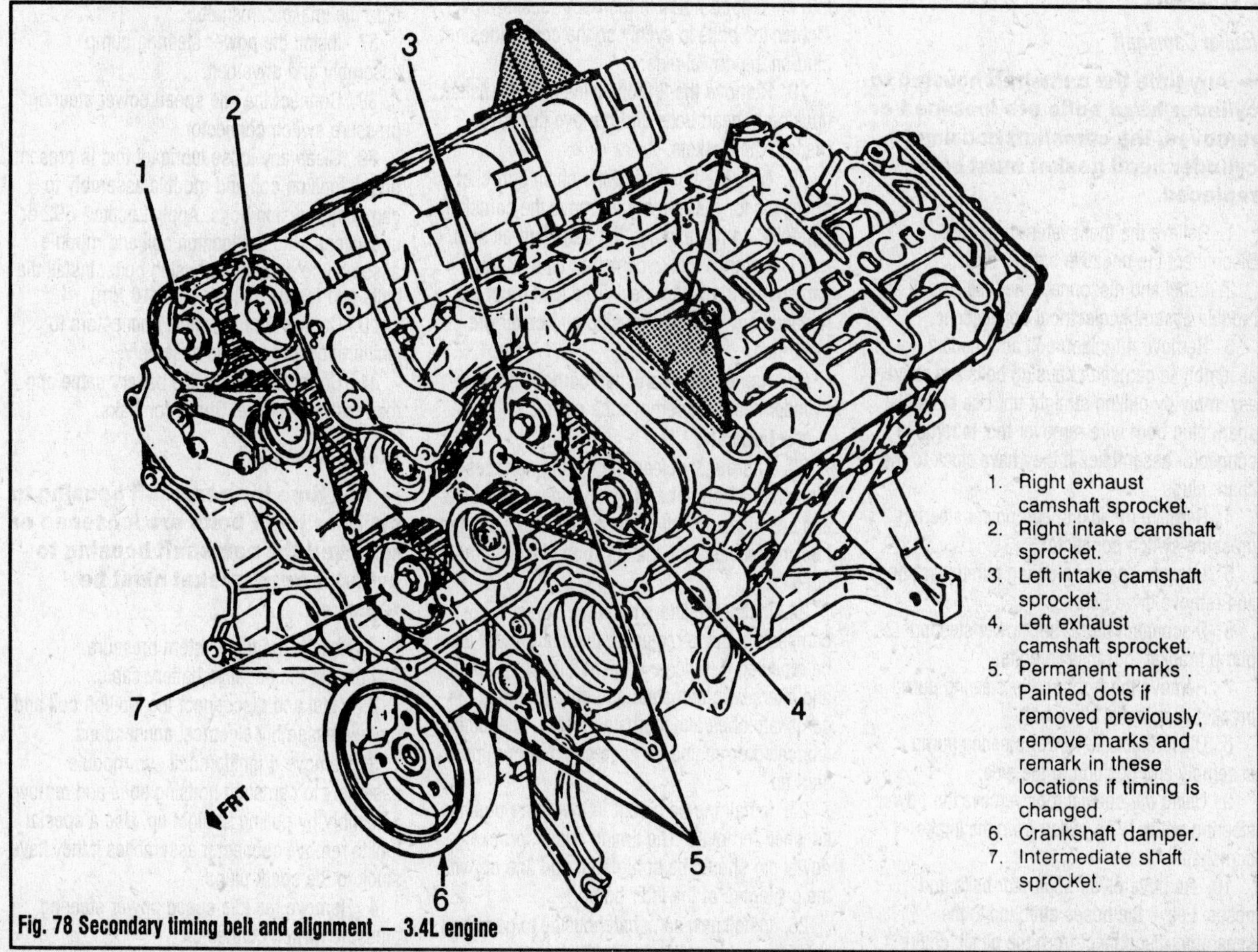

Fig. 78 Secondary timing belt and alignment – 3.4L engine

required to turn bolt before seating. Running torque of bolt should be 44–66 ft. lbs. If less torque is required, replace the shim and lock rings and inspect the nose of the camshaft for brinelling. If more torque is required than replace the shim and lock rings and check the attaching bolt threads for burrs or foreign material.

14. Rotate engine clockwise 1 revolution and realign the balancer marks at TDC. Make sure timing mark on damper lines up with front cover timing mark.

15. Repeat steps 7–13 starting with left intake then left exhaust camshaft.

16. Install secondary timing belt covers and retaining bolts.

17. Reconnect negative battery cable.

Camshaft

SEE FIGS. 79–81

REMOVAL & INSTALLATION

2.3L ENGINE

Intake Camshaft

➡ Any time the camshaft housing to cylinder head bolts are loosened or removed, the camshaft housing to cylinder head gasket must be replaced.

1. Relieve the fuel system pressure. Disconnect the negative battery cable.
2. Label and disconnect the ignition coil and module assembly electrical connections.
3. Remove 4 ignition coil and module assembly to camshaft housing bolts and remove assembly by pulling straight up. Use a special spark plug boot wire remover tool to remove connector assemblies if they have stuck to the spark plugs.
4. Remove the idle speed power steering pressure switch connector.
5. Loosen 3 power steering pump pivot bolts and remove drive belt.
6. Disconnect the 2 rear power steering pump bracket to transaxle bolts.
7. Remove the front power steering pump bracket to cylinder block bolt.
8. Disconnect the power steering pump assembly and position to the side.
9. Using the special tool, remove the power steering pump drive pulley from the intake camshaft.
10. Remove oil/air separator bolts and hoses. Leave the hoses attached to the separator, disconnect from the oil fill, chain housing and intake manifold. Remove as an assembly.
11. Remove vacuum line from fuel pressure regulator and disconnect the fuel injector harness connector.
12. Disconnect fuel line retaining clamp from bracket on top of intake camshaft housing.
13. Remove fuel rail to camshaft housing retaining bolts.
14. Remove the fuel rail from the cylinder head. Cover injector openings in cylinder head and cover injector nozzles. Leave fuel lines attached and position fuel rail aside.
15. Disconnect the timing chain and housing but do not remove from the engine.
16. Remove intake camshaft housing cover to camshaft housing retaining bolts.
17. Remove the intake camshaft housing to cylinder head retaining bolts. Use the reverse of the tightening sequence when loosening camshaft housing to cylinder head retaining bolts. Leave 2 bolts loosely in place to hold the camshaft housing while separating camshaft cover from housing.
18. Push the cover off the housing by threading 4 of the housing to head retaining bolts into the tapped holes in the cam housing cover. Tighten the bolts in evenly so the cover does not bind on the dowel pins.
19. Remove the 2 loosely installed camshaft housing to head bolts and remove the cover. Discard the gaskets.
20. Note the position of the chain sprocket dowel pin for reassembly. Remove the camshaft carefully; do not damage the camshaft oil seal.
21. Remove intake camshaft oil seal from camshaft and discard seal. This seal must be replaced any time the housing and cover are separated.
22. Remove the camshaft carrier from the cylinder head and remove the gasket.

To install:

23. Thoroughly clean the mating surfaces of the camshaft carrier and the cylinder head, bolts and bolt holes. Install a new gasket and place the housing on the head. Install 1 bolt loosely to hold in place.
24. Install the lifters into their bores. If the camshaft is being replaced, the lifters must also be replaced. Lubricate camshaft lobes, journals and lifters with camshaft and lifter prelube. The camshaft lobes and journals must be adequately lubricated or engine damage could occur upon start up.
25. Install the camshaft in the same position as when removed. The timing chain sprocket dowel pin should be straight up and line up with the centerline of the lifter bores.
26. Install new camshaft housing to camshaft housing cover seals into cover; do not use sealer. Make sure the correct color seal is placed in each groove. Install the cover to the housing.
27. Apply thread locking compound to the camshaft housing and cover retaining bolt threads.
28. Install bolts and torque to 11 ft. lbs. Rotate the bolts (except the 2 rear bolts that hold fuel pipe to camshaft housing) an additional 75° in sequence. Rotate the excepted bolts an additional 25°.
29. Install timing chain housing and timing chain.
30. Uncover fuel injectors and install new fuel injector ring seals lubricated with oil. Install the fuel rail.
31. Install the fuel line retaining clamp and retainer to bracket on top of the intake camshaft housing.
32. Connect the vacuum line to the fuel pressure regulator.
33. Connect the fuel injectors harness connector.
34. Install the oil/air separator assembly.
35. Lubricate the inner sealing surface of the intake camshaft seal with oil and install the seal to the housing.
36. Install the power steering pump pulley onto the intake camshaft.
37. Install the power steering pump assembly and drive belt.
38. Connect the idle speed power steering pressure switch connector.
39. Clean any loose lubricant that is present on the ignition coil and module assembly to camshaft housing bolts. Apply Loctite® 592 or equivalent, onto the ignition coil and module assembly to camshaft housing bolts. Install the bolts and torque to 13 ft. lbs. (18 Nm)
40. Connect the electrical connectors to ignition coil and module assembly.
41. Connect the negative battery cable and road test the vehicle. Check for leaks.

Exhaust Camshaft

➡ Any time the camshaft housing to cylinder head bolts are loosened or removed the camshaft housing to cylinder head gasket must be replaced.

1. Relieve the fuel system pressure. Disconnect the negative battery cable.
2. Label and disconnect the ignition coil and module assembly electrical connections.
3. Remove 4 ignition coil and module assembly to camshaft housing bolts and remove assembly by pulling straight up. Use a special tool to remove connector assemblies if they have stuck to the spark plugs.
4. Remove the idle speed power steering pressure switch connector.
5. Remove the transaxle fluid level indicator

tube assembly from exhaust camshaft cover and position aside.

6. Remove exhaust camshaft cover and gasket.

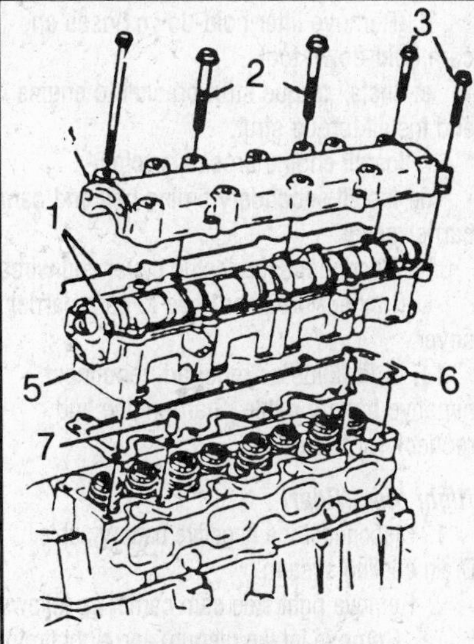

Fig. 79 Camshaft housing assembly — 2.3L engine

7. Disconnect the timing chain and housing but do not remove from the engine.

8. Remove exhaust camshaft housing to cylinder head bolts. Use the reverse of the tightening procedure when loosening camshaft housing while separating camshaft cover from housing.

9. Push the cover off the housing by threading 4 of the housing to head retaining bolts into the tapped holes in the camshaft cover. Tighten the bolts evenly so the cover does not bind on the dowel pins.

10. Remove the 2 loosely installed camshaft housing to cylinder head bolts and remove cover, discard gaskets.

11. Loosely install 1 camshaft housing to cylinder head bolt to retain the housing during camshaft and lifter removal.

12. Note the position of the chain sprocket dowel pin for reassembly. Remove camshaft being careful not to damage the camshaft or journals.

13. Remove the camshaft carrier from the cylinder head and remove the gasket.

To install:

14. Thoroughly clean the mating surfaces of the camshaft carrier and the cylinder head, bolts and bolt holes. Install a new gasket and place the housing on the head. Install 1 bolt loosely to hold in place.

15. Install the lifters into their bores. If the camshaft is being replaced, the lifters must also be replaced. Lubricate camshaft lobes, journals and lifters with camshaft and lifter prelube. The camshaft lobes and journals must be adequately lubricated or engine damage could occur upon start up.

16. Install camshaft in same position as when removed. The timing chain sprocket dowel pin should be straight up and align with the centerline of the lifter bores.

17. Install new camshaft housing to camshaft housing cover seals into cover; do not use sealer. Make sure the correct color seal is placed in each groove. Install the cover to the housing.

18. Apply thread locking compound to the camshaft housing and cover retaining bolt threads.

19. Install bolts and torque in sequence to 11 ft. lbs. Then rotate the bolts an additional 75°, in sequence.

20. Install timing chain housing and timing chain.

21. Install the transaxle fluid level indicator tube assembly to exhaust camshaft cover.

22. Connect the idle speed power steering pressure switch connector.

23. Clean any loose lubricant that is present on the ignition coil and module assembly to camshaft housing bolts. Apply Loctite® 592 or equivalent, onto the ignition coil and module assembly to camshaft housing bolts. Install the bolts and torque to 13 ft. lbs. (18 Nm)

24. Connect the electrical connectors to ignition coil and module assembly.

25. Connect the negative battery cable and road test the vehicle. Check for leaks.

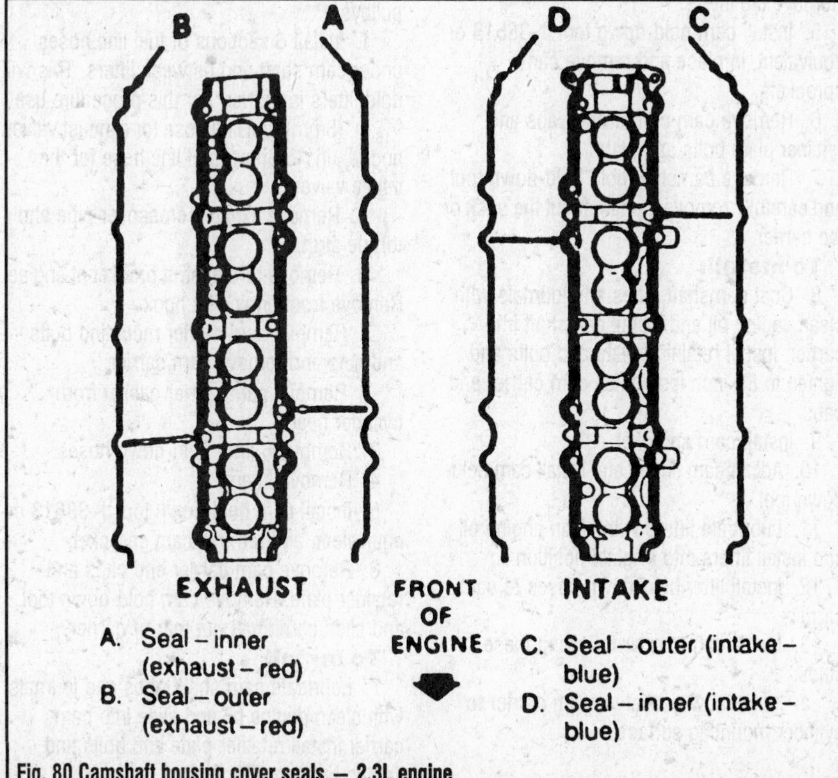

Fig. 80 Camshaft housing cover seals — 2.3L engine

2.5L ENGINE

➡ **For the removal of the camshaft, the engine assembly must be removed from the vehicle.**

1. Disconnect the negative battery cable.
2. Remove the engine assembly from the vehicle.
3. Remove the rocker arm cover and pushrods.
4. Remove the pushrod cover and valve lifters.
5. Remove the serpentine belt, crankshaft pulleys and vibration dampener.
6. Remove the front cover.
7. Remove the camshaft thrust plate screws.

➡ **The camshaft journals are the same diameter. Care must be taken when removing the camshaft to avoid damage to the cam bearings.**

8. Carefully slide the camshaft and gear through the front of the block.

9. To remove the camshaft gear, use a arbor press and adapter.

10. Old and new camshafts should be cleaned with solvent and compressed air before being installed.

To install:

11. Install the camshaft gear onto the camshaft with an arbor press.

12. Measure the end clearance with a feeler gauge between the cam journal and thrust plate. The measurement should be between 0.0015–0.0050 in. (0.038–0.127mm). If the measurement is less than 0.0015 in. (0.127mm), replace the spacer ring. If the measurement is more than 0.0050 in. (0.038mm), replace the thrust plate.

➡ Always apply assembly lube, GM Engine Oil Supplement (E.O.S) or equivalent, to the cam journals and lobes. If this procedures is not done, cam damage may result.

13. Carefully install the camshaft into the engine block by rotating and pushing forward until seated.

14. Install the thrust plate screws and torque to 89 inch lbs. (10 Nm).

15. Install the front cover, vibration dampener and serpentine belt.

16. Install the valve lifter and pushrod cover.

17. Install the pushrods and rocker arm cover.

18. Install the engine into the vehicle.

19. Refill all necessary fluids.

20. Start the engine and check for leaks.

2.8L, 3.1L AND 3.8L ENGINES

➡ For the removal of the camshaft the engine assembly must be removed from the vehicle.

1. Remove the engine assembly from the vehicle.

2. Remove the rocker covers and remove the valve lifters.

3. Remove the front cover assembly, timing chain and sprockets.

4. Remove the camshaft by sliding it from the block.

To install:

5. Coat the camshaft journals with engine oil. Coat the camshaft lobes with GM Engine Oil Supplement (E.O.S) or equivalent.

6. Slide the camshaft into the block.

7. Install the timing chain and sprockets, making sure to align the timing marks.

8. Install the front cover assembly. Install the valve lifters.

9. Install the engine assembly into the vehicle. Run the engine and check for leaks.

3.4L ENGINE

Left Side

1. Disconnect the negative battery cable.

2. Drain cooling system.

3. Remove left side cam carrier as follows:

a. Disconnect oil/air breather hose from cam carrier cover. Remove spark plug wires from plugs and remove rear spark plug wire cover.

b. Remove cam carrier cover bolts and lift off cover. Remove gasket and O-rings from cover.

c. Remove secondary timing belt by removing secondary timing belt actuator and tensioner assembly and sliding belt from pulleys.

d. Install 6 sections of fuel line hoses under cam shaft and between lifters. This will hold lifters in the carrier. For this procedure use $^{5}/_{16}$ in. (8mm) fuel line hose for exhaust valves and $^{7}/_{32}$ in. (5.5mm) fuel line hose for the intake valves.

e. Remove exhaust crossover pipe and torque strut.

f. Remove torque strut bracket at engine.

g. Remove cam carrier mounting bolts and nuts and remove cam carrier.

h. Remove cam carrier gasket from cylinder head.

4. Remove the 6 lifter hold-down hoses. Remove the lifters.

5. Install cam hold-down tool J–38613 or equivalent, in place and remove cam sprockets.

6. Remove cam carrier end caps and retainer plate bolts and plate.

7. Remove camshaft hold hold-down tool and carefully remove camshaft out the back of the carrier.

To install:

8. Coat camshaft lobes and journals with clean engine oil and install camshaft into carrier. Install retaining plate and bolts and tighten to 89 inch lbs. Install cam carrier end caps.

9. Install cam sprocket.

10. Adjust cam timing and install cam hold-down tool.

11. Lubricate lifters with clean engine oil and install lifters into original position.

12. Install lifter hold-down hoses to cam carrier.

13. Install cam carrier following these steps:

a. Install new gasket on cam carrier to cylinder mounting surface.

b. Install cam hold-down tool J–38613 or equivalent, to carrier assembly.

c. Install cam carrier to cylinder head. Install mounting bolts and nuts. Torque bolts and nuts to 18 ft. lbs.

d. Remove lifter hold-down hoses and cam hold-down tool.

e. Install torque strut bracket to engine and install torque strut.

f. Install engine crossover pipe.

g. Install secondary timing belt and cam carrier cover.

h. Reconnect spark plug cover and wires.

i. Connect breather hose to cam carrier cover.

14. Add fluids as required, reconnect negative battery cable. Start engine and recheck for leaks.

Right Side (Rear)

1. Disconnect the negative battery cable. Drain cooling system.

2. Remove right side cam carrier as follows:

a. Remove intake plenum and right timing belt cover.

b. Remove right spark plug wires.

c. Remove air/oil separator hose at cam carrier cover.

d. Remove cam carrier cover bolts and lift of cover. Remove gasket and O-rings from cover.

e. Remove secondary timing belt by removing secondary timing belt actuator and tensioner assembly and sliding belt from pulleys.

f. Install 6 sections of fuel line hoses under cam shaft and between lifters. This will hold lifters in carrier. For this procedure use $^{5}/_{16}$ in. (8mm) fuel line hose for exhaust valves and $^{7}/_{32}$ in. (5.5mm) fuel line hose for the intake valves.

g. Remove exhaust crossover pipe and torque strut.

h. Remove torque strut bracket at engine. Remove front engine lift hook.

i. Remove cam carrier mounting bolts and nuts and remove cam carrier.

j. Remove cam carrier gasket from cylinder head.

3. Remove 6 lifter hold-down hoses.

4. Remove lifters.

5. Install cam hold-down tool J–38613 or equivalent, and remove cam sprocket.

6. Remove cam carrier end caps and retainer plate. Remove cam hold-down tool and slide cam shaft out rear of carrier.

To install

7. Lubricate cam shaft lobes and journals with clean engine oil and slide into cam carrier.Install retainer plate and bolts and tighten bolts to 89 inch lbs.

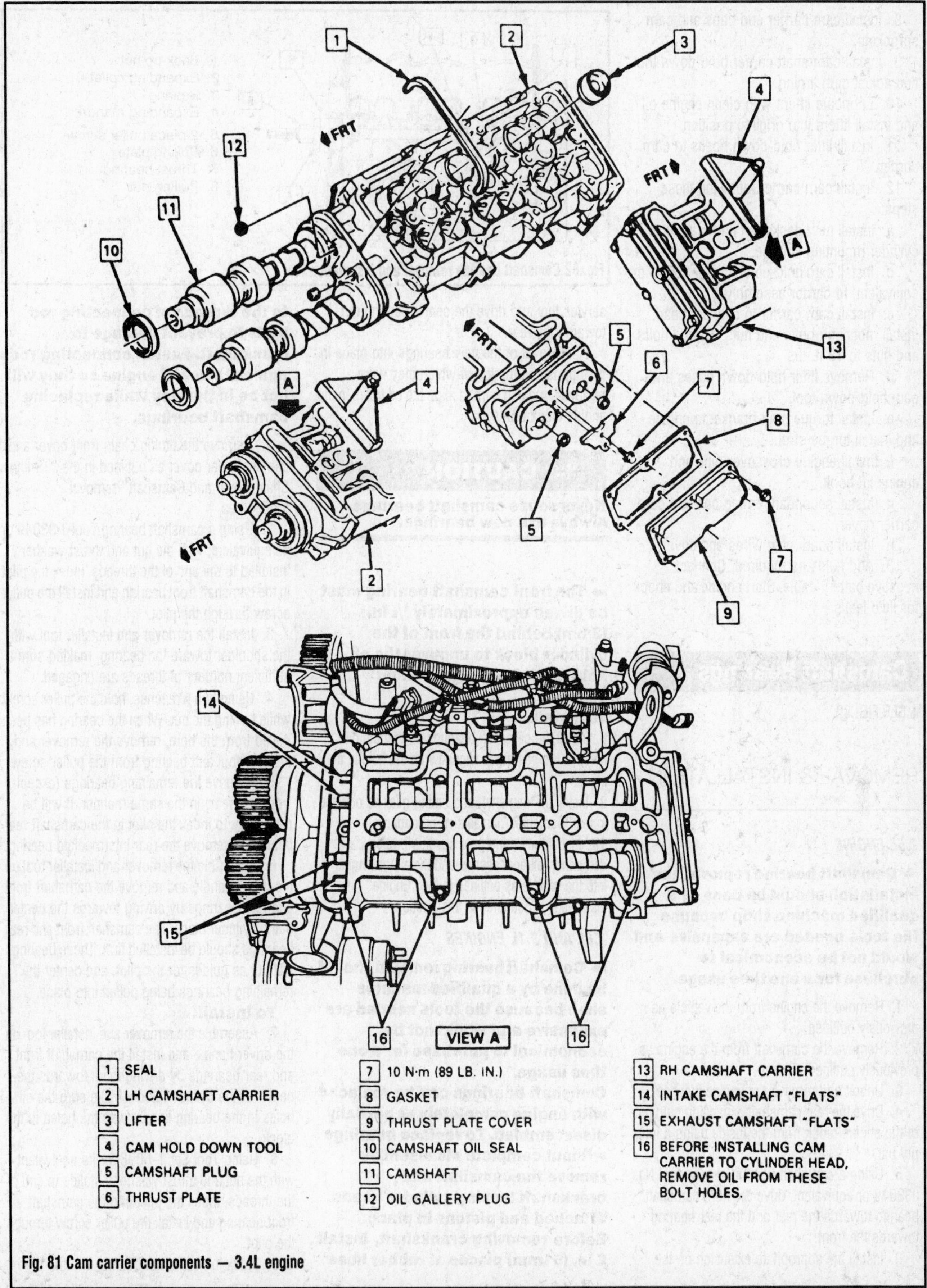

Fig. 81 Cam carrier components — 3.4L engine

8. Install cam carrier end caps and cam sprockets.
9. Install cam shaft carrier hold-down tool and adjust cam timing.
10. Lubricate lifters with clean engine oil and install lifters into original position.
11. Install lifter hold-down hoses to cam carrier.
12. Install cam carrier following these steps:
   a. Install new gasket on cam carrier to cylinder mounting surface.
   b. Install cam hold-down tool J–38613 or equivalent, to carrier assembly.
   c. install cam carrier to cylinder head. Install mounting bolts and nuts. Torque bolts and nuts to 18 ft. lbs.
   d. Remove lifter hold-down hoses and cam hold-down tool.
   e. Install torque strut bracket to engine and install torque strut.
   f. Install engine crossover pipe and engine lift hook.
   g. Install secondary timing belt and cam carrier cover.
   h. Install spark plug wires and cover.
13. Add fluids as required. Connect negative battery cable. Start engine and check for fluid leaks.

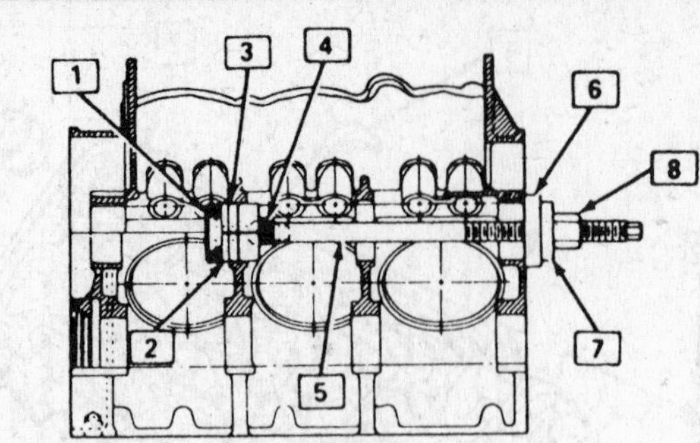

Fig. 82 Camshaft bearing removal and installation tool

Camshaft Bearings

➧ SEE FIG. 82

REMOVAL & INSTALLATION

2.5L ENGINE

➡ Camshaft bearing removal and installation should be done by a qualified machine shop because the tools needed are expensive and would not be economical to purchase for a one time usage.

1. Remove the engine from the vehicle as previously outlined.
2. Remove the camshaft from the engine as previously outlined.
3. Unbolt and remove the engine flywheel.
4. Drive the rear camshaft expansion plug out of the engine block from the inside using a long pry bar.
5. Using a camshaft bearing service tool No. J33049 or equivalent, drive the front camshaft bearing towards the rear and the rear bearing towards the front.
6. Install the appropriate extension on the service tool and drive the center bearing out towards the rear.
7. Drive all of the new bearings into place in the opposite direction of which they were removed, making sure to align the oil holes in the engine block bores.

✲✲ CAUTION

Never reuse camshaft bearings. Always use new bearings.

➡ The front camshaft bearing must be driven approximately 1/8 in. (3mm) behind the front of the cylinder block to uncover the oil hole to the timing gear oiling nozzle.

To install:

8. Install the camshaft bearings so that the oil holes in the bearing is aligned with the hole in the block.
9. Install the camshaft and timing gear as outlined in the "Camshaft" installation procedures.
10. Install the timing gear cover, vibration dampener, all accessories and install the engine into the vehicle as outlined in the "Engine" installation procedures in this Section.

2.8L AND 3.1L ENGINES

➡ Camshaft bearing removal should be done by a qualified machine shop because the tools needed are expensive and would not be economical to purchase for a one time usage.
Camshaft bearings can be replaced with engine completely or partially disassembled. To replace bearings without complete disassembly remove the camshaft and crankshaft leaving cylinder heads attached and pistons in place. Before removing crankshaft, install 2 in. (51mm) pieces of rubber hose to the threads of connecting rod bolts to prevent damage to crankshaft. Fasten connecting rods against sides of engine so they will not be in the way while replacing camshaft bearings.

1. Remove the timing chain front cover and camshaft rear cover as outlined in the "Timing Chain Cover and Camshaft" removal procedures.
2. Using a camshaft bearing Tool J-33049 or its equivalent, with the nut and thrust washer installed to the end of the threads, index the pilot in the camshaft front bearing and install the puller screw through the pilot.
3. Install the remover and installer tool with the shoulder toward the bearing, making sure a sufficient number of threads are engaged.
4. Using two wrenches, hold the puller screw while turning the nut. When the bearing has been pulled from the bore, remove the remover and installer tool and bearing from the puller screw.
5. Remove the remaining bearings (except front and rear) in the same manner. It will be necessary to index the pilot in the camshaft rear bearing to remove the rear intermediate bearing.
6. Assemble the remover and installer tool on the driver handle and remove the camshaft front and rear bearings by driving towards the center of the cylinder block. The camshaft front and rear bearings should be installed first. These bearings will act as guides for the pilot, and center the remaining bearings being pulled into place.

To install:

7. Assemble the remover and installer tool on the driver handle and install the camshaft front and rear bearings by driving them towards the center of the cylinder block. Make sure the oil holes in the bearing line up with the holes in the block.
8. Using Tool Set J–6098, or its equivalent with the nut and thrust washer installed to end of the threads, index the pilot into the camshaft front bearing and install the puller screw through the pilot.
9. Index the camshaft bearing into the bore

(with oil hole aligned as outlined below), then install the remover and installer tool on the puller screw with the shoulder toward the bearing.

10. Using two wrenches, hold the puller screw while turning the nut. After the bearing has been pulled into the bore, remove the remover and installer tool from the puller screw and check the alignment of the oil holes in the camshaft bearings.

11. Install the remaining bearings in the same manner. It will be necessary to index the pilot in the camshaft rear bearing to install the rear intermediate bearing.

12. Clean the rear cover mating surfaces and apply a 1/8 in. (3mm) bead of RTV to the cover. Install the rear cover using the appropriate size core plug installer.

13. Install the camshaft as outlined in the "Camshaft" installation procedures. Install the timing gear cover, all accessories and install the engine into the vehicle.

INSPECTION

1. Check the camshaft sprocket, keyway and threads, bearing journals and lobes for wear, galling, gouges or overheating. If any of these conditions exist, replace the camshaft.

➡ Do NOT attempt to repair the camshaft. Always replace the camshaft and lifters as an assembly. Old valve lifters will destroy a new camshaft in less time than it tool you to replace the camshaft.

2. Camshaft Lift Measurement:

a. Lubricate the camshaft bearings with Assembly Lube 1051396 or equivalent.

b. Carefully install the camshaft into the block. If the cam bearings are damaged badly, set the camshaft on "V" blocks instead.

c. Install a dial indicator J–8520 and measure the camshaft lift as shown in the illustration in this section.

d. Measure the bearing journals with a micrometer. Take measurements for run-out and diameter. If not within specification in the "Camshaft" chart in the beginning of this Section, replace the camshaft.

✲✲ CAUTION

Always apply Assembly Lube (GM E.O.S 1052367 or equivalent) to the cam journals and lobes. If this procedure is not done, cam damage may result.

Balance Shaft/ Intermediate Shaft

REMOVAL & INSTALLATION

INTERMEDIATE SHAFT

(3.4L ENGINE)

1. Disconnect the negative battery cable.
2. Remove engine from vehicle.
3. Remove right side cylinder head and oil pump drive assembly.
4. Remove the timing chain assembly.
5. Remove thrust plate screws and plate.
6. Remove intermediate using care not to damage journals or bearings.

To install:

7. Lubricate intermediate shaft journals and gear with engine oil. Install shaft, thrust plate and retainer screws. Tighten screws to 89 inch lbs.
8. Replace O-ring after sprocket is installed and install timing chain and gear assembly.
9. Install oil pump drive assembly and cylinder head.
10. Install engine assembly.

BALANCE SHAFT (3.8L ENGINE)

➧ SEE FIG. 83

1. Disconnect the negative battery cable. Remove the engine and secure it to a workstand.
2. Remove the flywheel-to-crankshaft bolts and the flywheel.
3. Remove the timing chain cover-to-engine bolts and the cover.
4. Remove the camshaft sprocket-to-camshaft gear bolts, the sprocket, the timing chain and the gear.
5. To remove the balance shaft, perform the following procedures:

a. Remove the balance shaft gear-to-shaft bolt and the gear.

b. Remove the balance shaft retainer-to-engine bolts and the retainer.

c. Using the slide hammer tool, pull the balance shaft from the front of the engine.

To install:

6. If replacing the rear balance shaft bearing, perform the following procedures:

a. Drive the rear plug from the engine.

b. Using the camshaft remover/installer tool, press the rear bearing from the rear of the engine.

c. Dip the new bearing in clean engine oil.

d. Using the balance shaft rear bearing installer tool, press the new rear bearing into the rear of the engine.

e. Install the rear cup plug.

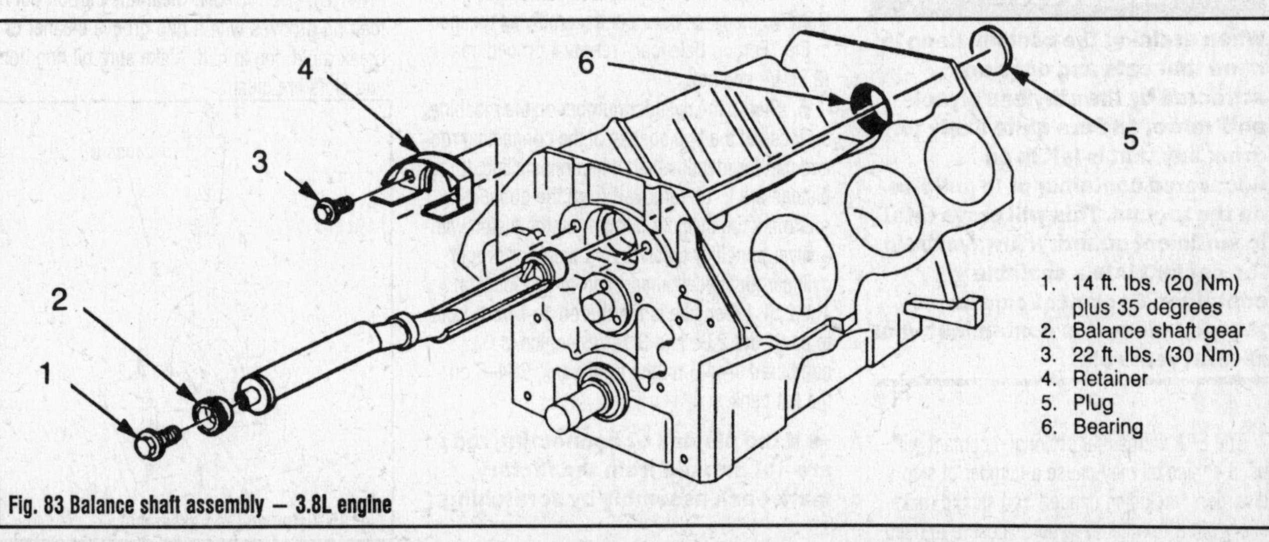

Fig. 83 Balance shaft assembly — 3.8L engine

7. Using the balance shaft installer tool, screw it into the balance shaft and install the shaft into the engine; remove the installer tool.

8. Clean the gasket mounting surfaces. Inspect the parts for wear and/or damage; replace the parts, if necessary.

9. Install the balance shaft retainer. Torque the balance shaft retainer-to-engine bolts to 27 ft. lbs.

10. Align the balance shaft gear with the camshaft gear timing marks. Install the balance shaft gear onto the balance shaft. Torque the balance gear-to-balance shaft bolt to 15 ft. lbs, then using a torque angle meter tool, rotate another 35°.

11. Align the marks on the balance shaft gear and the camshaft gear by turning the balance shaft.

12. Turn the crankshaft so the No. 1 piston is at TDC.

13. Install the timing chain and sprocket.

14. Replace the balance shaft front bearing retainer and bolts. Tighten the bolts to 26 ft. lbs.

15. Install the front timing cover and the lifter guide retainer.

16. Install the intake manifold and flywheel assembly. Tighten the flywheel bolts to 89 inch lbs., plus an additional 90° turn.

17. Install the engine assembly and connect the negative battery cable. Start the engine and check for leaks.

Pistons and Connecting Rods

➧ SEE FIGS. 84–99

✲✲ CAUTION

When draining the coolant, keep in mind that cats and dogs are attracted by the ethylene glycol antifreeze, and are quite likely to drink any that is left in an uncovered container or in puddles on the ground. This will prove fatal in sufficient quantity. Always drain the coolant into a sealable container. Coolant should be reused unless it is contaminated or several years old.

The EPA warns that prolonged contact with used engine oil may cause a number of skin disorders, including cancer! You should make every effort to minimize your exposure to used engine oil. Protective gloves should be worn when changing the oil. Wash your hands and any other exposed skin areas as soon as possible after exposure to used engine oil. Soap and water, or waterless hand cleaner should be used.

✲✲ WARNING

REMOVAL

The engine does not have to be removed to remove a piston and connecting rod assembly. The cylinder head and oil pan has to be removed to access the connecting rod bolts. If more than one assembly needs to be serviced, it is easier to remove the engine from the vehicle.

1. Remove the engine assembly from the vehicle, see "Engine" removal and installation procedures.

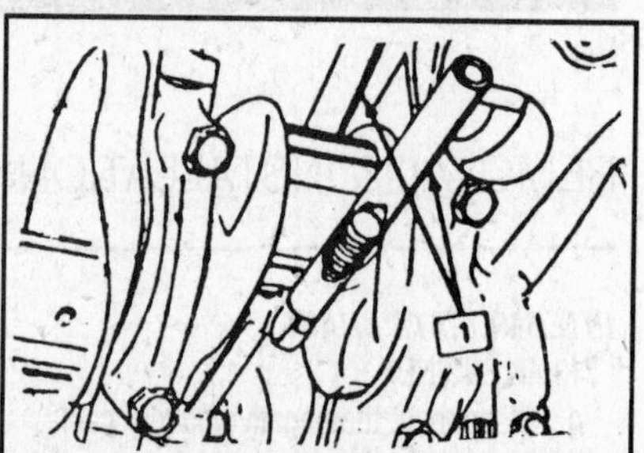

Fig. 84 To protect the connecting rod journal, use short pieces of rubber hose

2. On 6 cylinder engines: remove the intake manifold and the cylinder head over piston assembly being removed. On 4 cylinder engines: remove the cylinder head and manifolds as an assembly.

3. Drain the oil and remove the oil pan.

4. Remove the oil pump and sump assembly. Remove the force balancer assembly as outlined in the "Forced Balancer" removal procedures (2.5L L4 engine).

5. Stamp the cylinder number on the machine surfaces of the bolt bosses of the connecting rod and cap for identification when reinstalling. If the pistons are to be removed from the connecting rod, mark the cylinder number on the piston with a silver pencil or quick drying paint for proper cylinder identification and cap-to-rod location. The 2.5L L4 engine is numbered 1–4 from front to back; the 2.8L and 3.1L V6 engine is numbered 1–3–5 on the right bank, 2–4–6 on the left bank.

➡ If the pistons or connecting rods are not marked from the factory, mark each assembly by scratching the number in the part with a scribe.

6. Examine the cylinder bore above the ring travel. If a ridge exists, remove the ridge with a ridge reamer before attempting to remove the piston and rod assembly. This tool can be purchased at your local parts distributor or rented at a tool rental.

7. Remove the rod bearing cap and bearing. Tap on the lower cap to dislodge it from the connecting rod.

8. Install a guide hose over threads of rod bolts. This is to prevent damage to bearing journal and rod bolt threads. Use two pieces of 3/8 in. (10mm) fuel hose.

9. Remove the rod and piston assembly through the top of the cylinder bore by lightly tapping the connecting rod with a wooden hammer handle. Do NOT use any metal tools to remove the piston and connecting rod assembly.

➡ If the piston rings will not clear the top of the cylinder, check to see if the ridge is completely removed.

10. Remove all other rod and piston assemblies in the same manner.

CLEANING AND INSPECTION

Connecting Rods

Wash connecting rods in cleaning solvent and dry with compressed air. Check for twisted or bent rods and inspect for nicks or cracks. Also check the length of the rods and replace connecting rods that are damaged.

Pistons

Clean varnish from piston skirts and pins with a cleaning solvent. DO NOT WIRE BRUSH ANY PART OF THE PISTON. Clean the carbon out of the ring grooves with a ring groove cleaner or break a old ring in half. Make sure oil ring holes and slots are clean.

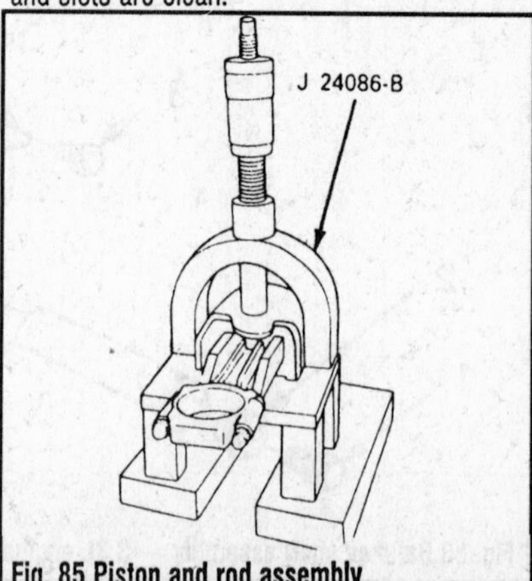

Fig. 85 Piston and rod assembly

Inspect the piston for cracked ring lands, skirts or pin bosses, wavy or worn ring lands, scuffed or damaged skirts, eroded areas at the top of the piston. Replace pistons that are damaged or show signs of excessive wear. Inspect the grooves for nicks or burrs that might cause the rings to hang up.

Measure piston skirt (across center line of piston pin) and check piston clearance.

PISTON PIN REMOVAL AND INSTALLATION

Use care at all times when handling and servicing connecting rods and pistons. To prevent possible damage to these units, do not clamp the rod or piston in a vise since they may become distorted. Do not allow the pistons to strike against one another, against hard objects or bench surfaces, since distortion of the piston contour or nicks in the soft aluminum material may result.

Removing the piston from the connecting rod requires the use of expensive tools that would not be practical to purchase for a one time basis (except 2.3L QUAD 4). This procedure should be performed by a qualified engine machine shop.

2.3L ENGINE

The piston pin is held in by retaining clips on either side of the pin, requiring no special tools to remove. Remove the retaining clips and push out the piston pin. Reuse the old retainers if not damaged. Make sure the clips are fully seated before installing into cylinder block.

All Other Engines

1. Remove the piston rings using a suitable piston right remover.
2. Install the guide bushing of the piston pin removing and installing tool.
3. Install the piston and connecting rod assembly on a support, and place the assembly in an arbor press. Press the pin out of the connecting rod, using the appropriate piston pin tool.
4. When installing the new piston, apply clean engine oil to the pin and press in with a piston pin installing tool. Make sure the connecting rod moves freely without binding after pin in installed. If not, reaming the pin hole may have to be performed.

MEASURING THE OLD PISTONS

Check used piston-to-cylinder bore clearance as follows:

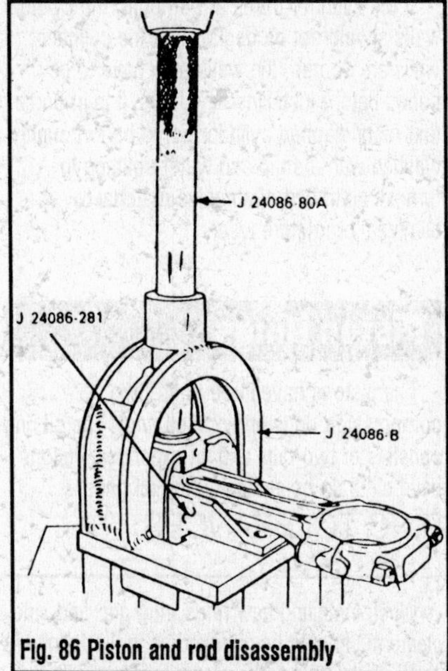

Fig. 86 Piston and rod disassembly

1. Measure the cylinder bore diameter with a telescope gauge.
2. Measure the piston diameter. When measuring the pistons for size or taper, measurements must be made with the picton pin removed.
3. Subtract the piston diameter from the cylinder bore diameter to determine piston-to-bore clearance.
4. Compare the piston-to-bore clearances obtained with those clearances recommended in the "Piston and Connecting Rod" chart in the beginning of this Section. Determine if the piston-to-bore clearance is in the acceptable range.
5. When measuring taper, the largest reading must be at the bottom of the skirt.
6. If the measurement is not within specifications, the cylinders should be bored and new oversize pistons should be installed.

SELECTING NEW PISTONS

1. If the used piston is not acceptable, check the service piston size and determine if a new piston can be selected. (Service pistons are available in standard high limit and standard 0.254mm (0.010 in.) oversize.
2. If the cylinder bore must be reconditioned, measure the new piston diameter, then hone the cylinder bore to obtain the preferred clearance.
3. Select a new piston and mark the piston to identify the cylinder for which it was fitted. (On some cars, oversize pistons may be found. This pistons will be 0.254mm (0.010 in.) oversize).

Aftermarket piston manufacturers supply oversized pistons 0.030 in. (0.762mm), 0.040

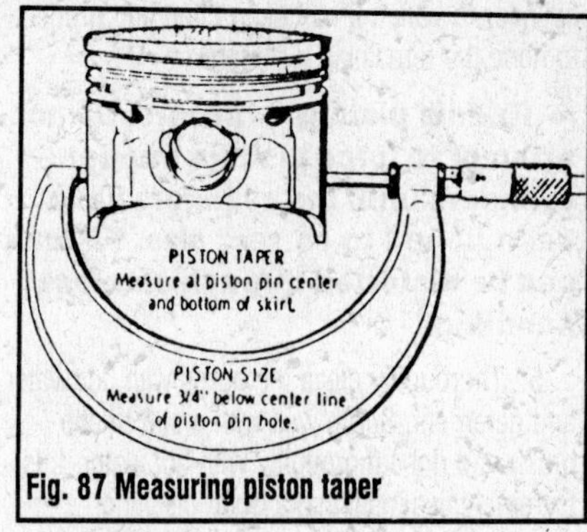

Fig. 87 Measuring piston taper

in. (1.016mm), and 0.060 in. (1.524mm) in most cases.

4. After the cylinder has been reconditioned and new pistons purchased, remeasure bore and piston to ensure proper piston fit.

CYLINDER HONING

1. When cylinders are being honed, follow the manufacturer's recommendations for the use of the hone.
2. Occasionally during the honing operation, the cylinder bore should be thoroughly cleaned and the selected piston checked for correct fit.
3. When finish-honing a cylinder bore, the hone should be moved up and down at a sufficient speed to obtain a very find uniform surface finish in a cross-hatch pattern of approximately 45–65° included angle. The finish marks should be clean but not sharp, free from imbedded particles and torn or folded metal.
4. Permanently mark the piston for the

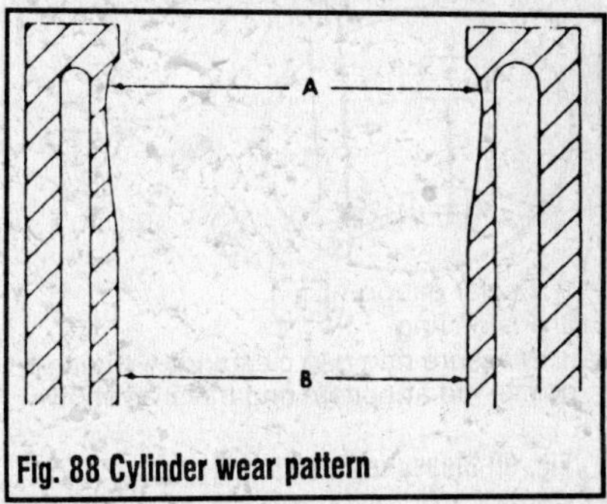

Fig. 88 Cylinder wear pattern

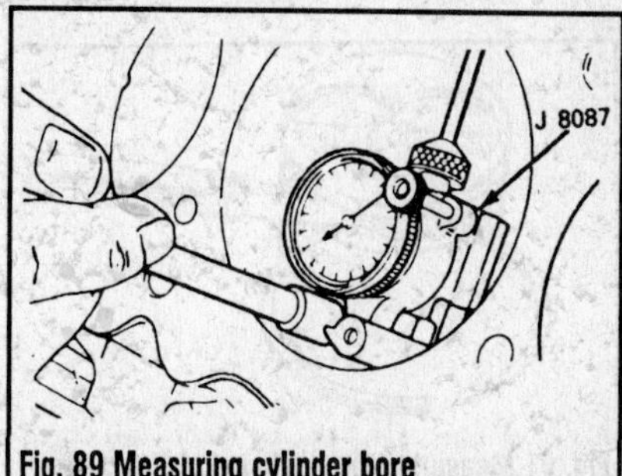

Fig. 89 Measuring cylinder bore

cylinder to which it has been fitted and proceed to hone the remaining cylinders.

➡ Handle pistons with care. Do not attempt to force pistons through cylinders until the cylinders have been honed to correct size. Pistons can be distorted through careless handling.

5. Thoroughly clean the bores with hot water and detergent. Scrub well with a stiff bristle brush and rinse thoroughly with hot water. It is extremely essential that a good cleaning operation be performed. If any of the abrasive material is allowed to remain in the cylinder bores, it will rapidly wear the new rings and cylinder bores. The bores should be swabbed several times and light engine oil with a clean cloth and then wiped with a clean dry cloth. CYLINDERS SHOULD NOT BE CLEANED WITH KEROSENE OR GASOLINE. Clean the remainder of the cylinder block to remove the excess material spread during the honing operation.

CHECKING CYLINDER BORE

Cylinder bore size can be measured with inside micrometers or a cylinder gauge. The most wear will occur at the top of the ring travel.

Reconditioned cylinder bores should be held to not more than 0.025mm (0.001 in.) taper.

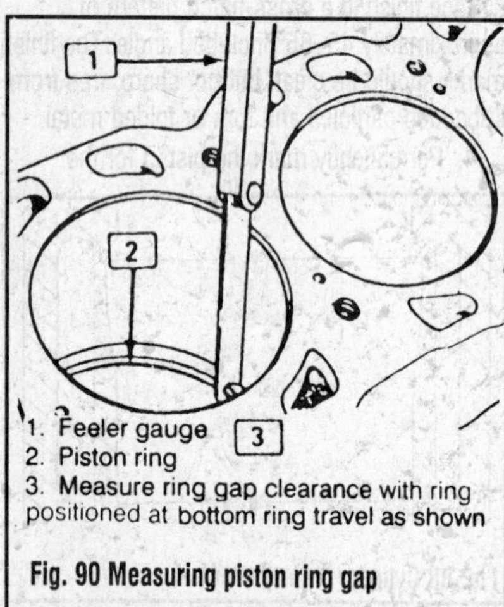

Fig. 90 Measuring piston ring gap

Fig. 91 Measuring piston ring side clearance

If the cylinder bores are smooth, the cylinder walls should not be deglazed. If the cylinder walls are scored, the walls may have to be honed before installing new rings. It is important that reconditioned cylinder bores be thoroughly washed with a soap and water solution to remove all traces of abrasive material to eliminate premature wear.

Piston Rings

The pistons have three rings (two compression rings and one oil ring). The oil ring consists of two rails and an expander. Pistons have oil drain holes behind the oil rings.

RING TOLERANCES

When installing new rings, ring gap and side clearance should be checked as in the following illustrations. Check the measurements with the specifications in the "Piston and Rings" chart in the beginning of the Section.

Piston Ring and Rail Gap

Each ring and rail gap must be measured with the ring or rail positioned squarely and at the bottom of the ring-travel area of the bore.

Piston Ring and Rail Gap

Each ring and rail gap must be measured with the ring or rail positioned squarely and at the bottom of the ring-travel area of the bore.

Side Clearance

Each ring must be checked for side clearance in its respective piston groove by inserting a feeler gauge between the ring and its upper land. The piston grooves must be cleaned before checking the ring for side clearance specifications. To check oil ring side clearance, the oil rings must be installed on the piston.

RING INSTALLATION

For service ring specifications and detailed installation productions, refer to the instructions furnished with the parts package. If oversized pistons are being used, make sure to select the proper oversize piston rings to fit the oversized pistons.

1. Using your fingers, install the oil expander.

➡ Use care when installing the piston rings so not to scratch the piston skirt.

2. Install the lower oil control ring and position the gaps as shown in the "Piston Ring Gap Location" illustration in this section. Install the upper oil control ring.

➡ Use a piston ring expander to install the compression rings. Avoid expanding the rings more than necessary, which may cause ring damage or breakage.

3. Using a piston ring installer (expander), install the second compression ring with manufacturers mark facing UP. Install the top compression ring with manufacturers mark facing UP. Position the gaps as shown in the ring gap illustration.

Connecting Rod Bearings

If you have already removed the connecting rod and piston assemblies from the engine, follow only Steps 3–7 of the following procedure.

✲✲ CAUTION

When draining the coolant, keep in mind that cats and dogs are attracted by the ethylene glycol antifreeze, and are quite likely to drink any that is left in an uncovered container or in puddles on the ground. This will prove fatal in sufficient quantity. Always drain the coolant into a sealable container. Coolant should be reused unless it is contaminated or several years old.

✲✲ WARNING

The EPA warns that prolonged contact with used engine oil may cause a number of skin disorders, including cancer! You should make every effort to minimize your exposure to used engine oil. Protective gloves should be worn when changing the oil. Wash your hands and any other exposed skin areas as soon as possible after exposure to used engine oil. Soap and water, or waterless hand cleaner should be used.

REMOVAL, INSPECTION AND INSTALLATION

The connecting rod bearings are designed to have a slight projection above the rod and cap

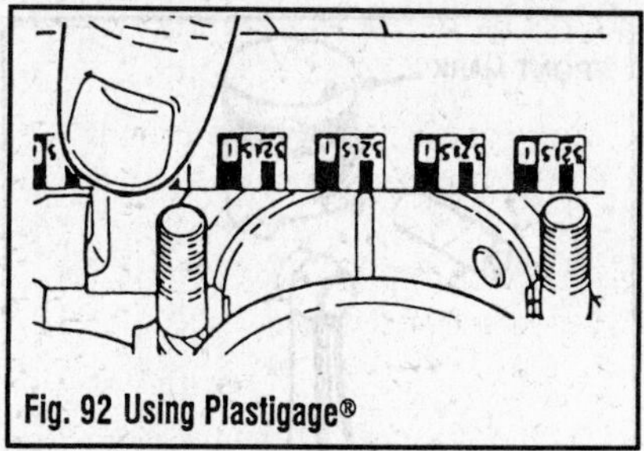
Fig. 92 Using Plastigage®

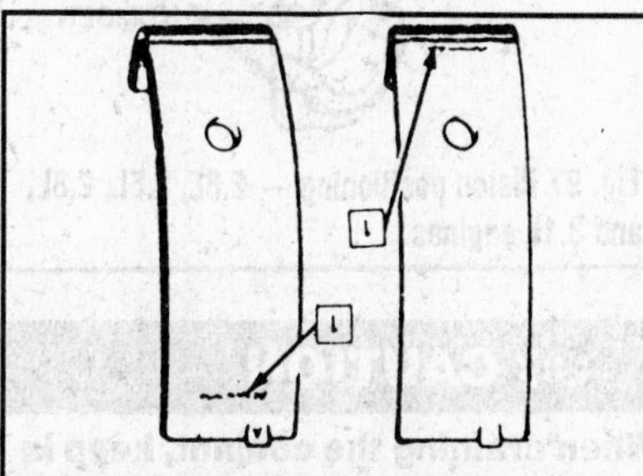
Fig. 93 Main bearing insert markings. Undersize markings are located at either end

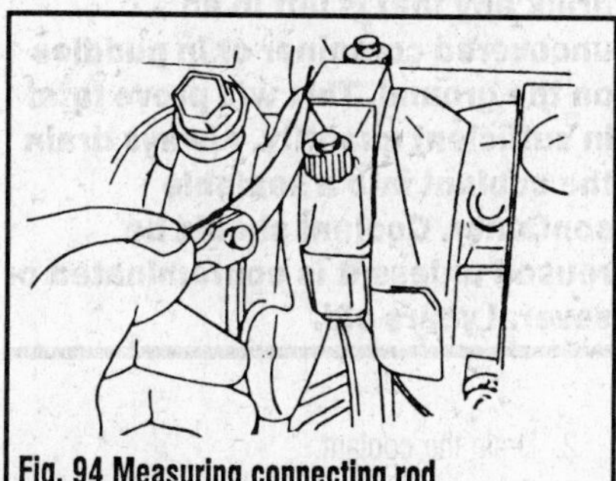
Fig. 94 Measuring connecting rod side clearance

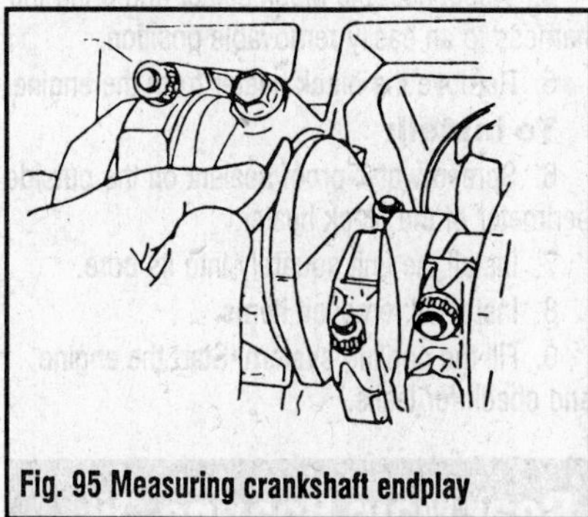
Fig. 95 Measuring crankshaft endplay

faces to insure a positive contact. The bearings can be replaced without removing the rod and piston assemblies from the engine.

1. Drain the engine oil and remove the oil pan. See the "Oil Pan" removal procedures. It may be necessary to remove the oil pump to provide access to rear connecting rod bearings.
2. With the connecting rod journal at the bottom of the travel, stamp the cylinder number on the machined surfaces of the connecting rod and cap for identification when installing, then remove the rod nuts and caps.
3. Inspect journals for roughness and wear. Slight roughness may be removed with a fine grit polishing cloth saturated with engine oil. Burrs may be removed with a fine oil stone by moving the stone on the journal circumference. Do not move the stone back and forth across the journal. If the journals are scored or ridged, the crankshaft must be reconditioned or replaced.
4. The connecting rod journals should be checked for out-of-round and correct size with a micrometer.

➡ Crankshaft rod journals will normally be standard size. If any undersized bearings are used, all will be 0.254mm undersize and 0.254mm will be stamped on the number 4 counterweight.

If PLASTIGAGE® material is to be used:

5. Clean oil from the journal bearing cap, connecting rod and outer and inner surfaces of the bearing inserts. Position the insert so that the tang is properly aligned with the notch in the rod and cap.
6. Place a piece of Plastigage® material in the center of lower bearing shell as shown in the illustration.
7. Install the bearing cap onto the connecting rod and torque to specifications. Remove the bearing cap and determine the bearing clearances by comparing the width of the flattened plastic gauging material at its widest point with the graduation on the Plastigage® package. The number within the graduation on the envelope indicates the clearance in thousandths of an inch or millimeters. If this clearance is excessive, replace the bearing and recheck the clearance with the Plastigage® material. Lubricate the bearing with Assembly Lube or engine oil before installation. Repeat Steps 2-7 on the remaining connecting rod bearings.

➡ All rods must be connected to their journals when rotating the crankshaft, to prevent engine damage.

Piston and Connecting Rod Assembly

INSTALLATION

1. Make sure all parts are clean. Install some lengths of rubber tubing over the connecting rod bolts to prevent damage to the crankshaft journals.
2. Apply engine oil to the pistons, rings and cylinder walls, then install a piston ring compressing tool on the piston.
3. Install the assembly in its respective cylinder bore with the notch in the top of the piston facing towards the FRONT of the engine.
4. Lubricate the crankshaft journal with Assembly Lube and install the connecting rod bearing cap, with the bearing index tang in rod and cap on same side.

➡ When more than one rod and piston assembly is being installed, the connecting rod cap attaching nuts should be tightened only enough to keep each rod in position until all have been installed. This will aid installation of the remaining piston assemblies.

5. Torque the rod cap nuts to the specifications in the "Torque Specifications" chart in the beginning of this Section.
6. Install all other parts in reverse order of removal.
7. Install the engine in the vehicle. See "Engine" removal and installation.

Freeze Plugs

REMOVAL & INSTALLATION

1. Disconnect the negative battery cable.

**** CAUTION**

When draining the coolant, keep in mind that cats and dogs are attracted by the ethylene glycol antifreeze, and are quite likely to drink any that is left in an uncovered container or in puddles on the ground. This will prove fatal in sufficient quantity. Always drain the coolant into a sealable container. Coolant should be reused unless it is contaminated or several years old.

2. Drain the coolant.
3. Remove all necessary items in order to gain access to the affected freeze plug.
4. Use a freeze plug removal tool and thread it into the center of the freeze plug.

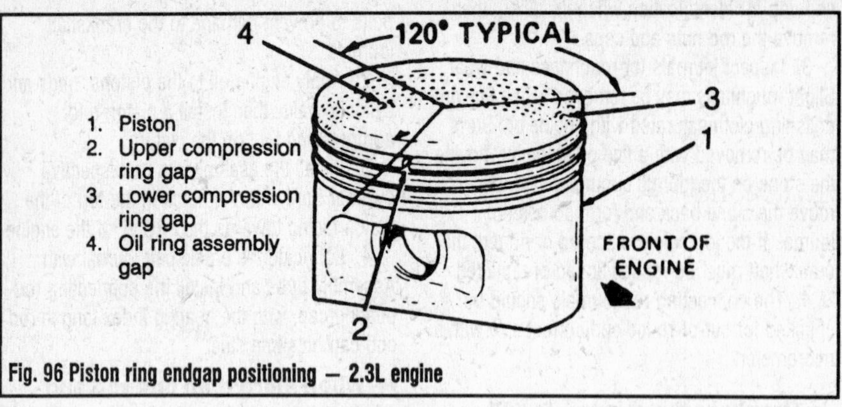

Fig. 96 Piston ring endgap positioning — 2.3L engine

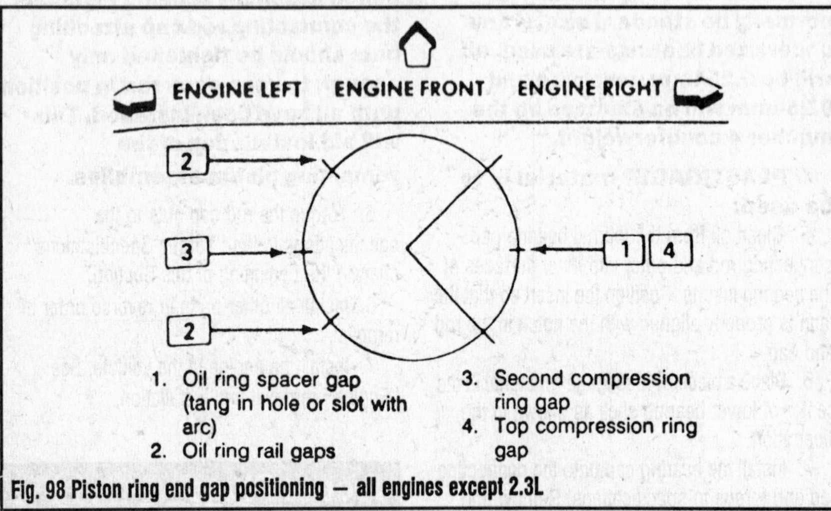

Fig. 98 Piston ring end gap positioning — all engines except 2.3L

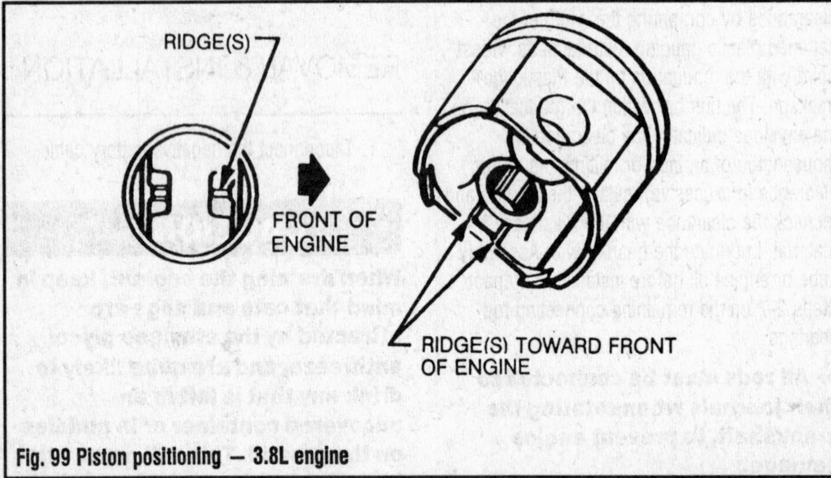

Fig. 99 Piston positioning — 3.8L engine

5. Remove the freeze plug from the engine.

To install:

6. Spread water-proof sealant on the outside perimeter and back face of the new plug.
7. Use an installing tool to install the plug squarely into its bore.
8. Install all removed items.
9. Fill the cooling system. Start the engine and check for leaks.

Block Heaters

REMOVAL & INSTALLATION

1. Disconnect the negative battery cable.

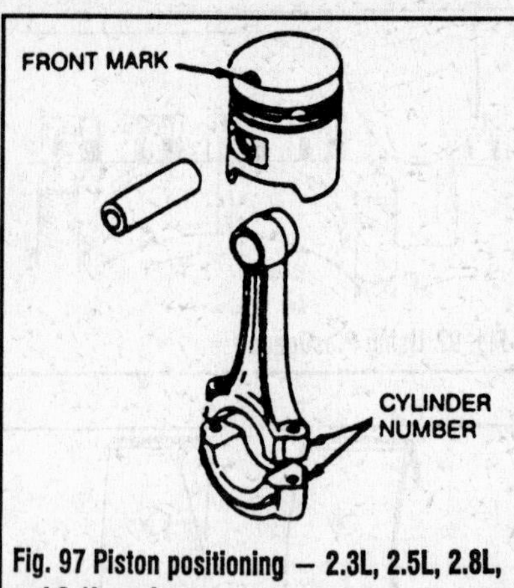

Fig. 97 Piston positioning — 2.3L, 2.5L, 2.8L, and 3.1L engines

CAUTION

When draining the coolant, keep in mind that cats and dogs are attracted by the ethylene glycol antifreeze, and are quite likely to drink any that is left in an uncovered container or in puddles on the ground. This will prove fatal in sufficient quantity. Always drain the coolant into a sealable container. Coolant should be reused unless it is contaminated or several years old.

2. Drain the coolant.
3. Remove all necessary items in order to gain access to the block heater.
4. Disconnect the block heater and bring the harness to an easily removable position.
5. Remove the block heater from the engine.

To install:

6. Spread water-proof sealant on the outside perimeter of the block heater.
7. Install the unit squarely into its bore.
8. Install all removed items.
9. Fill the cooling system. Start the engine and check for leaks.

Rear Main Bearing Oil Seal

➧ SEE FIGS. 100 AND 101

REMOVAL & INSTALLATION

2.3L ENGINE

1. Disconnect the negative battery cable.
2. Remove the transaxle.

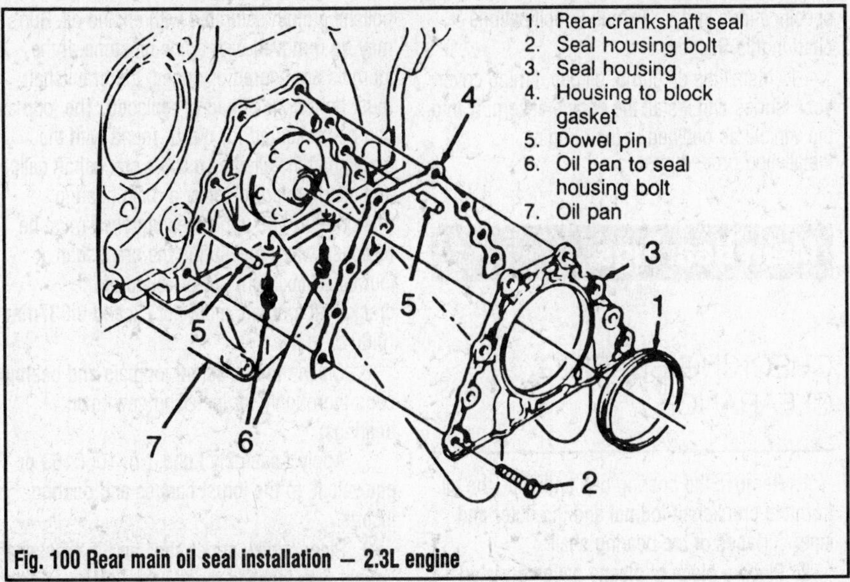

Fig. 100 Rear main oil seal installation — 2.3L engine

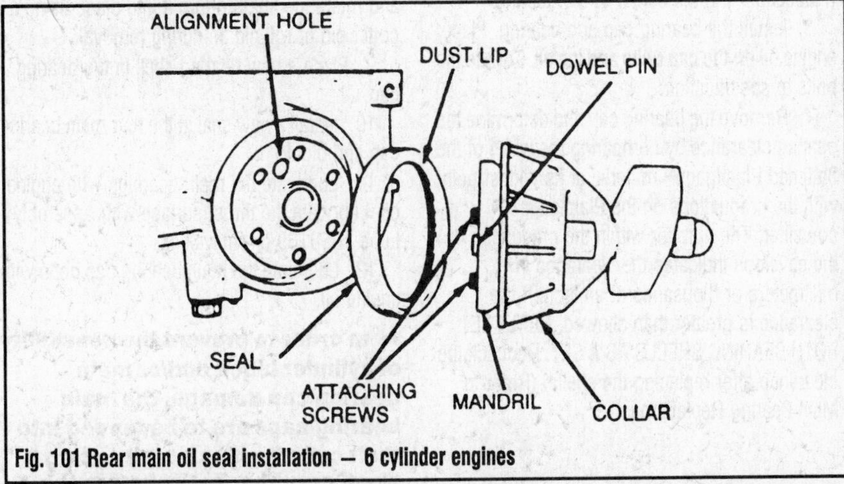

Fig. 101 Rear main oil seal installation — 6 cylinder engines

3. Remove the flywheel-to-crankshaft bolts and the flywheel.
4. Remove the oil pan-to-seal housing bolts and the block-to-seal housing bolts.
5. Remove the seal housing from the engine.
6. Place 2 blocks of equal thickness on a flat surface and position the seal housing on the 2 blocks. Remove the seal from the housing.
7. The installation is the reverse of the removal procedure. Use new gaskets when installing.
8. Connect the negative battery cable and for leaks.

2.5L ENGINE

1. Disconnect the negative battery cable.
2. Remove the transaxle assembly.
3. Remove the flywheel.
4. Carefully pry out the seal, using a suitable tool.

To install:

5. Clean the the block and crankshaft to seal mating surfaces.
6. Apply engine oil to the inside and outside diameter of the new seal.
7. Press the new seal evenly into place, using tool J-34924-A or equivalent.
8. Install the flywheel and transaxle and check for leaks.

2.8L, 3.1L, 3.4L AND 3.8L ENGINES

➡ **These engines use a round rear oil seal that requires removal of the transaxle and flywheel.**

1. Support the engine with tool J-28467 or equivalent. Raise and safely support the vehicle.
2. Remove the transaxle assembly. Remove the flywheel.
3. Using a small prybar or equivalent, insert it through the dust lip at an angle and pry the old seal from the block.
4. Inspect the seal bore and the crankshaft end for any damage.
5. Coat the inside lip of the seal with engine oil and install it on the seal installation tool J-34686 or equivalent.
6. Align the dowel pin of the tool with the dowel pin of the crankshaft. Install the tool on the crankshaft and turn the wing nut until the tool and seal are fully seated on the crankshaft.
7. Loosen the wing nut and remove the tool. Check the seal to make sure it is properly seated.
8. Install the flywheel and the transaxle.
9. Remove the engine support tool. Run the engine and check for leaks.

Crankshaft

REMOVAL & INSTALLATION

1. Remove the engine assembly as previously outlined in the "Engine" removal procedures.
2. Remove the engine front timing cover.
3. Remove the timing chain and sprockets.
4. Remove the oil pan as outlined in the "Oil Pan" removal procedures.
5. Remove the oil pump, (remove the force balancer assembly on the 2.5L L4 engine).
6. Stamp the cylinder number on the machined surfaces of the bolt hoses of the connecting rods and caps, if not done by the factory, for identification when installing. If the pistons are to be removed from the connecting rod, mark the cylinder number on each piston with an indelible marker, silver pencil or quick drying paint for proper cylinder identification and cap to rod location.
7. Remove the connecting rod caps and store them so that they can be installed in their original positions. Put pieces of rubber fuel hose on the rod bolts before removal to protect the connecting rod journals.
8. Mark and remove all the main bearing caps.
9. Note the position of the keyway in the crankshaft so it can be installed in the same position.
10. With an assistant, lift the crankshaft out of the block. The rods will pivot to the center of the engine when the crankshaft is removed.
11. Remove both halves of the rear main oil seal.

To install:

12. Measure the crankshaft journals with a micrometer to determine the correct size rod and main bearings to be used. Whenever a new or reconditioned crankshaft is installed, new connecting rod bearings and main bearings must be installed. The bearing undersize are usually 0.010 (0.254mm), 0.020 (0.501mm) and 0.030

in. (0.762mm). Do not go any further undersize than 0.030 in. (0.762mm). See Main Bearings and Rod Bearings in the beginning of this Section.

13. Clean all oil passages in the block (and crankshaft if it is being reused).

➡ **A new rear main seal should be installed any time the crankshaft is removed or replaced.**

14. Install sufficient oil pan bolts in the block to align with the connecting rod bolts. Use rubber bands between the bolts to position the connecting rods as required. Connecting rod position can be adjusted by increasing the tension on the rubber bands with additional turns around the pan bolts or thread protectors. Install if not already don, pieces of rubber hose on the connecting rod bolts to protect the crankshaft journals during installation.

15. Position the upper half of main bearings in the block and lubricate them with Assembly Lube. Position crankshaft keyway in the same position as removed, with an assistant, lower the crankshaft into the block. The connecting rods will follow the crank pins into the correct position as the crankshaft is lowered.

16. Lubricate the thrust flanges with Assembly Lube 10501609 or equivalent. Install rod caps with the lower half of the bearings lubricated with Assembly Lube. Lubricate the cap bolts with Assembly Lube and install, but do not tighten.

17. With a block of wood, bump the crankshaft in each direction to align the thrust flanges of the main bearing. After bumping the shaft in each direction, wedge the shaft to the front and hold it while torquing the thrust bearing cap bolts.

➡ **In order to prevent the possibility of cylinder block and/or main bearing cap damage, the main bearing caps are to be tapped into their cylinder block cavity using a wood or rubber mallet before the bolts are installed. Do not use attaching bolts to pull the main bearing caps into their seats. Failure to observe this information may damage the cylinder block or a bearing cap.**

18. Torque all main bearing caps to specification in the "Torque Specifications" chart in this Section.

19. Remove the connecting rod bolt thread protectors and lubricate the connecting rod bearings with Assembly Lube.

20. Install the connecting rod bearing caps in their original position. Torque the nuts to specifications in the "Torque Specifications" chart in this Section.

21. Install the oil pump, oil pan, timing cover, accessories and install the engine assembly into the vehicle as outlined in the "Engine" installation procedures.

Main Bearings

CHECKING BEARING CLEARANCE

1. Remove the bearing cap and wipe the oil from the crankshaft journal and the outer and inner surfaces of the bearing shell.

2. Place a piece of plastic gauging material (Plastigage®) in the center of the bearing.

3. Install the bearing cap and bearing. Place engine oil on the cap bolts and install. Torque the bolts to specification.

4. Remove the bearing cap and determine the bearing clearance by comparing the width of the flattened Plastigage® material at its widest point with the graduations on the Plastigage® container. The number within the graduation on the envelope indicates the clearance in millimeters or thousands of an inch. If the clearance is greater than allowed, REPLACE BOTH BEARING SHELLS AS A SET. Recheck the clearance after replacing the shells. (Refer to Main Bearing Replacement).

REPLACEMENT

Main bearing clearances must be corrected by the use of selective upper and lower shells. UNDER NO CIRCUMSTANCES should the use of shims behind the shells to compensate for wear be attempted. To install the main bearing shells, proceed as follows:

1. Remove the oil pan as outlined below. On some models, the oil pump may also have to be removed.

2. Loosen all main bearing caps.

3. Remove the bearing caps and remove the lower shell.

4. Insert a flattened cotter pin or roll pin in the oil passage hole in the crankshaft, then rotate the crankshaft in the direction opposite to cranking rotation. The pin will contact the upper shell and roll it out.

5. The main bearing journals should be checked for roughness and wear. Slight roughness may be removed with a fine grit polishing cloth saturated with engine oil. Burrs may be removed with a fine oil stone. If the journals are scored or ridged, the crankshaft must be reconditioned or replaced. The journals can be measured for out-of-round with the crankshaft installed by using a crankshaft caliper and inside micrometer or a main bearing micrometer. The upper bearing shell must be removed when measuring the crankshaft journals. Maximum out-of-round of the crankshaft journals must not exceed 0.037mm (0.0015 in.).

6. Clean the crankshaft journals and bearing caps thoroughly for installing new main bearings.

7. Apply Assembly Lube, No. 1050169 or equivalent, to the thrust flanges and bearing inserts.

8. Place a new upper shell on the crankshaft journal with locating tang in the correct position and rotate the shaft to turn it into place using a cotter pin or roll pin as during removal.

9. Place a new bearing shell in the bearing cap.

10. Install a new seal in the rear main bearing cap and block.

11. Lubricate the main bearings with engine oil. Lubricate the thrust surface with Assembly Lube 1050169 or equivalent.

12. Lubricate the main bearing cap bolts with engine oil.

➡ **In order to prevent the possibility of cylinder block and/or main bearing cap damage, the main bearing caps are to be tapped into their cylinder block cavity using a wood or rubber ballet before the attaching bolts are installed. Do not use attaching bolts to pull the main bearing caps into their seats. Failure to observe this information may damage the cylinder block or a bearing cap.**

13. Torque the main bearing cap bolts to the specification in the "Torque Specifications" chart in the beginning of this Section.

Flywheel

REMOVAL & INSTALLATION

All Engines

1. Disconnect the negative battery cable.

2. Remove the transaxle assembly as

outlined in the "Transaxle" removal procedures in Section 7.

3. Remove the six flywheel attaching bolts and remove the flywheel for automatics. Remove the pressure plate and disc before removing the six flywheel attaching bolts for manuals.

4. To install: position the flywheel onto the crankshaft. Apply GM Thread Lock compound to the bolt threads and torque the bolts to the specifications in the "Torque Specifications" chart in this Section. Install the pressure plate and clutch disc for a manual transaxle. Install the transaxle assembly as outlined in the "Transaxle" installation procedures in Section 7.

EXHAUST SYSTEM

➧ SEE FIGS. 102–108

⁂ CAUTION

Do NOT service the exhaust system while the engine is warm. Extreme heat is generated by engine and may cause severe burns if not allowed to completely cool before servicing.

Rubber straps, rubber rings and block type hangers are used to support the complete exhaust system. It is very important that they be installed properly to avoid annoying vibrations which are difficult to diagnose.

Front Exhaust Pipe

REMOVAL & INSTALLATION

1. Support the catalytic converter with a floor jack and a piece of wood.
2. Cut the front exhaust pipe at the manifold.
3. Remove the pipe.

To install:

4. Insert the front pipe into the converter and install an approved exhaust system clamp.
5. Torque the clamp nuts to 37 ft. lbs. (50 Nm).
6. Start the engine and check the entire system carefully for leaks.

Catalytic Converter

REMOVAL & INSTALLATION

1. Cut the front exhaust pipe at the manifold.
2. Support the converter and cut the intermediate pipe as close to the weld as possible.
3. Remove the converter.

To install:

4. Place the clamps over the converter but do not tighten clamps.
5. Install the converter and torque the clamps to 37 ft. lbs. (50 Nm).
6. Start the engine and check the entire system carefully for leaks.

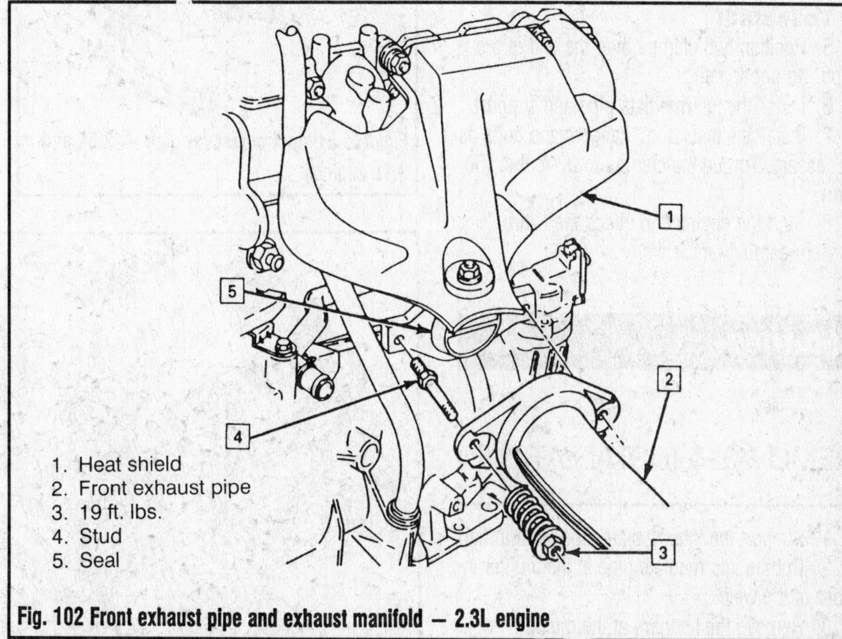

Fig. 102 Front exhaust pipe and exhaust manifold — 2.3L engine

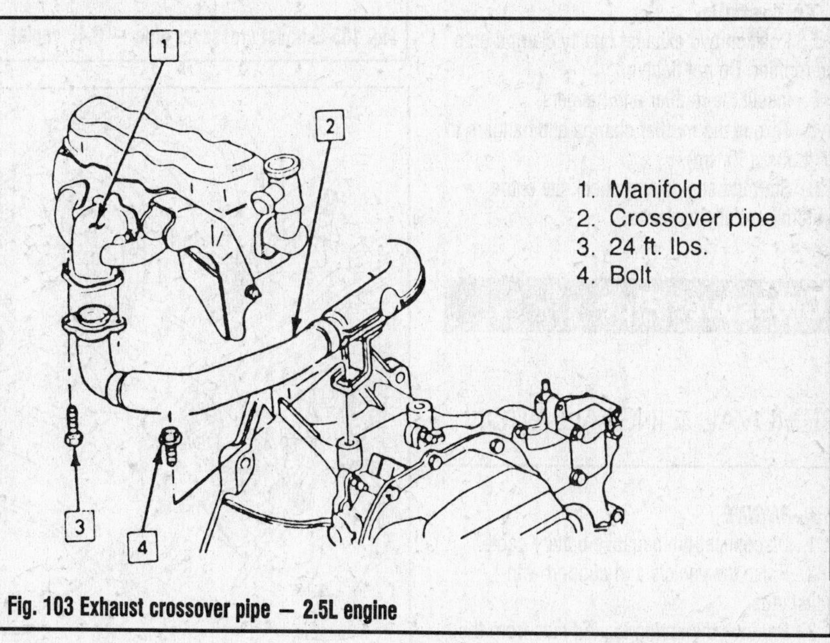

Fig. 103 Exhaust crossover pipe — 2.5L engine

Intermediate Pipe

REMOVAL & INSTALLATION

1. Support the muffler and catalytic converter with a floor jack and a piece of wood.
2. Cut the intermediate pipe at the muffler.
3. Support the intermediate pipe and cut the pipe at the converter.
4. Remove the pipe.

To install:

5. Position two clamps over the end of the pipe. Do not tighten.
6. Install the intermediate pipe and support.
7. Install the insulators, hangers and bolts as necessary. Torque the clamps to 37 ft. lbs. (50 Nm).
8. Start the engine and check the entire system carefully for leaks.

Muffler

REMOVAL & INSTALLATION

1. Support the intermediate pipe and muffler.
2. Cut the intermediate pipe at the muffler in front of the weld.
3. Remove the hangers at the muffler.
4. Remove the muffler assembly.

To install:

5. Position two exhaust quality clamps onto the muffler. Do not tighten.
6. Install the muffler and hangers.
7. Torque the muffler clamps and hangers to 37 ft. lbs. (50 Nm).
8. Start the engine and check the entire system carefully for leaks.

Crossover Pipe

REMOVAL & INSTALLATION

2.3L ENGINE

1. Disconnect the negative battery cable.
2. Raise the vehicle and support with jackstands.
3. Remove the spring loaded nuts from the exhaust manifold and pipe.
4. Support the catalytic converter. Cut the front pipe at the converter as close to the welds as possible to ensure an adequate overlap for clamping.

To install:

5. Position the front pipe to the manifold.
6. Torque the bolts to 19 ft. lbs. (26 Nm).

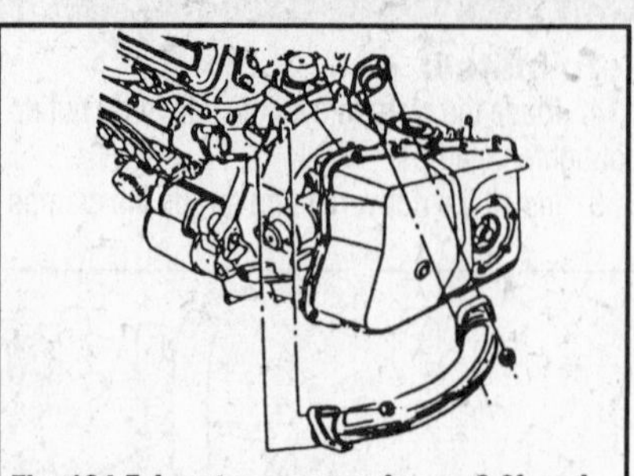

Fig. 104 Exhaust crossover pipe — 2.8L and 3.1L engines

7. Insert the pipe into the converter and install a clamp. Torque the clamp to 37 ft. lbs. (50 Nm).
8. Lower the vehicle.
9. Start the engine and check the entire system carefully for leaks.

2.5L ENGINE

1. Disconnect the negative battery cable.
2. Remove the bolts from the transaxle.
3. Raise the vehicle and support with jackstands.
4. Remove the bolts from the exhaust manifold and pipe. Remove the crossover pipe.

To install:

5. Position the crossover to the manifold.
6. Torque the bolts to 24 ft. lbs. (32 Nm).
7. Lower the vehicle.
8. Install the bolt to transaxle and tighten.
9. Start the engine and check the entire system carefully for leaks.

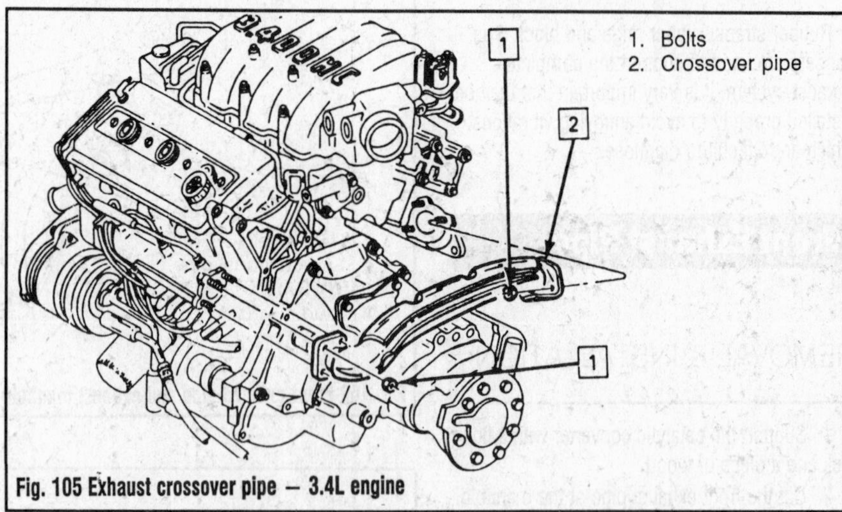

Fig. 105 Exhaust crossover pipe — 3.4L engine

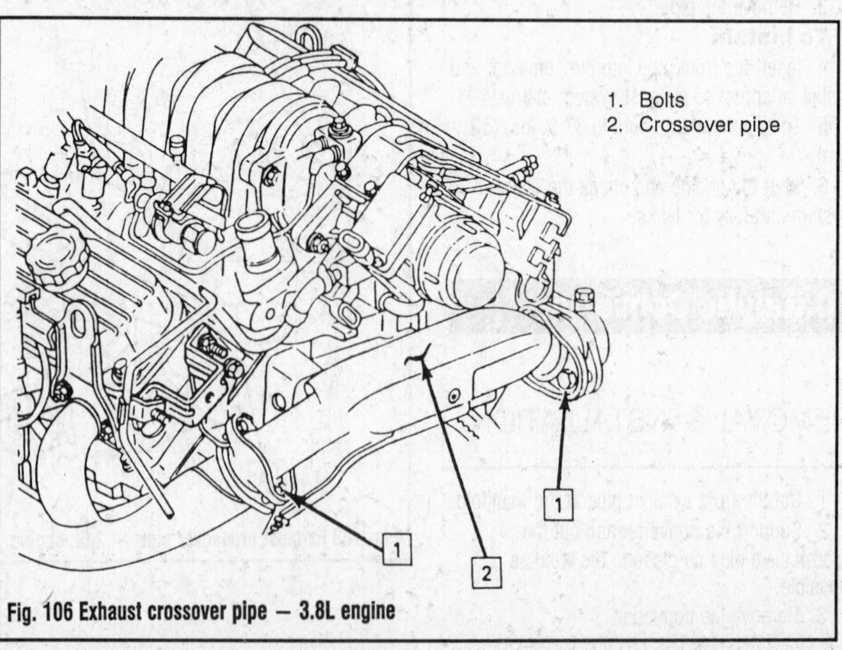

Fig. 106 Exhaust crossover pipe — 3.8L engine

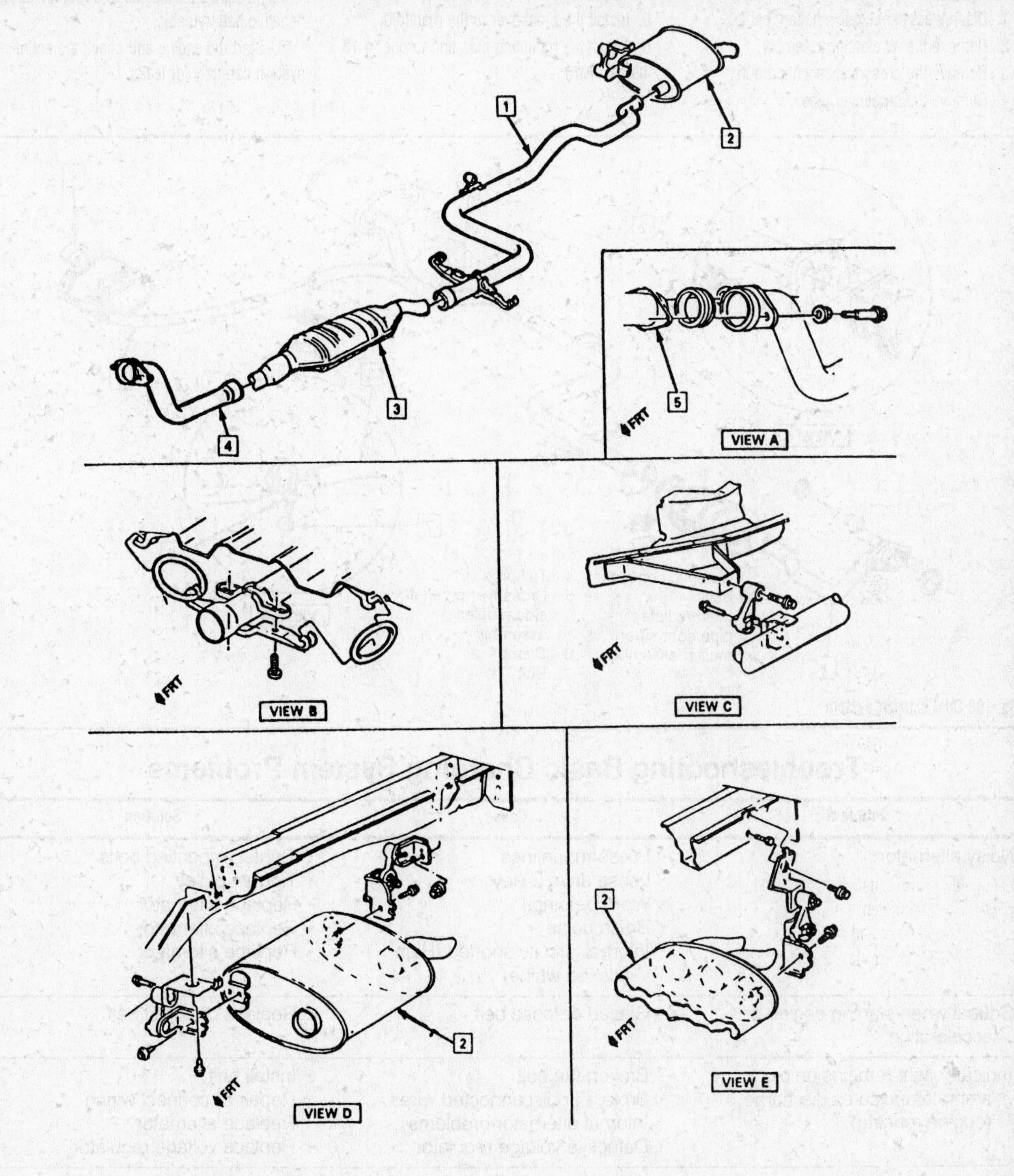

1. Intermediate pipe assembly
2. Muffler assembly
3. Converter
4. Front pipe assembly
5. Crossover pipe

Fig. 107 Single exhaust system components

V6 ENGINES

1. Disconnect the negative battery cable.
2. Remove the air cleaner assembly.
3. Remove the crossover mounting nuts.
4. Remove the crossover pipe.

To install:

5. Install the crossover to the manifold.
6. Install the mounting nuts and torque to 18 ft. lbs. (25 Nm).
7. Install the air cleaner and reconnect the negative battery cable.
8. Start the engine and check the entire system carefully for leaks.

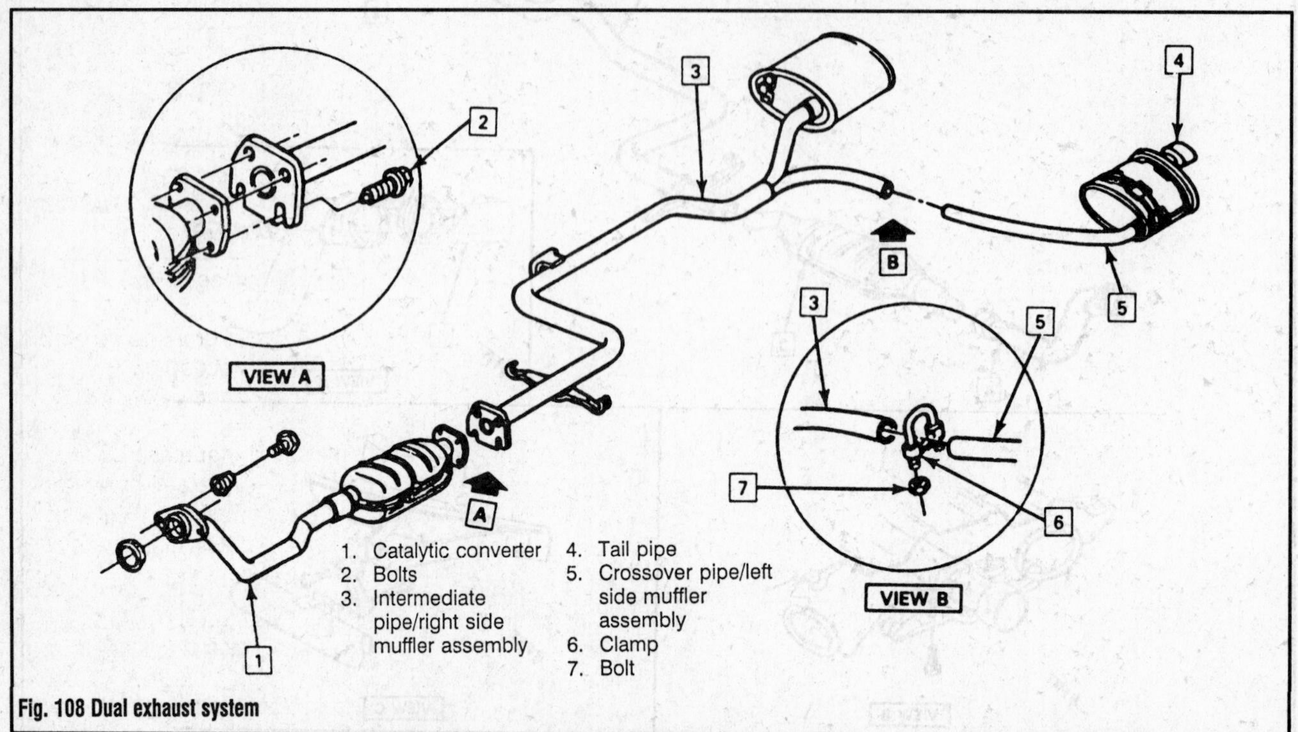

Fig. 108 Dual exhaust system

Troubleshooting Basic Charging System Problems

Problem	Cause	Solution
Noisy alternator	• Loose mountings • Loose drive pulley • Worn bearings • Brush noise • Internal circuits shorted (High pitched whine)	• Tighten mounting bolts • Tighten pulley • Replace alternator • Replace alternator • Replace alternator
Squeal when starting engine or accelerating	• Glazed or loose belt	• Replace or adjust belt
Indicator light remains on or ammeter indicates discharge (engine running)	• Broken fan belt • Broken or disconnected wires • Internal alternator problems • Defective voltage regulator	• Install belt • Repair or connect wiring • Replace alternator • Replace voltage regulator
Car light bulbs continually burn out—battery needs water continually	• Alternator/regulator overcharging	• Replace voltage regulator/alternator
Car lights flare on acceleration	• Battery low • Internal alternator/regulator problems	• Charge or replace battery • Replace alternator/regulator
Low voltage output (alternator light flickers continually or ammeter needle wanders)	• Loose or worn belt • Dirty or corroded connections • Internal alternator/regulator problems	• Replace or adjust belt • Clean or replace connections • Replace alternator or regulator

Troubleshooting Basic Starting System Problems

Problem	Cause	Solution
Starter motor rotates engine slowly	• Battery charge low or battery defective	• Charge or replace battery
	• Defective circuit between battery and starter motor	• Clean and tighten, or replace cables
	• Low load current	• Bench-test starter motor. Inspect for worn brushes and weak brush springs.
	• High load current	• Bench-test starter motor. Check engine for friction, drag or coolant in cylinders. Check ring gear-to-pinion gear clearance.
Starter motor will not rotate engine	• Battery charge low or battery defective	• Charge or replace battery
	• Faulty solenoid	• Check solenoid ground. Repair or replace as necessary.
	• Damage drive pinion gear or ring gear	• Replace damaged gear(s)
	• Starter motor engagement weak	• Bench-test starter motor
	• Starter motor rotates slowly with high load current	• Inspect drive yoke pull-down and point gap, check for worn end bushings, check ring gear clear-ance
	• Engine seized	• Repair engine
Starter motor drive will not engage (solenoid known to be good)	• Defective contact point assembly	• Repair or replace contact point assembly
	• Inadequate contact point assembly ground	• Repair connection at ground screw
	• Defective hold-in coil	• Replace field winding assembly
Starter motor drive will not disengage	• Starter motor loose on flywheel housing	• Tighten mounting bolts
	• Worn drive end busing	• Replace bushing
	• Damaged ring gear teeth	• Replace ring gear or driveplate
	• Drive yoke return spring broken or missing	• Replace spring
Starter motor drive disengages prematurely	• Weak drive assembly thrust spring	• Replace drive mechanism
	• Hold-in coil defective	• Replace field winding assembly
Low load current	• Worn brushes	• Replace brushes
	• Weak brush springs	• Replace springs

Troubleshooting Engine Mechanical Problems

Problem	Cause	Solution
External oil leaks	• Fuel pump gasket broken or improperly seated	• Replace gasket
	• Cylinder head cover RTV sealant broken or improperly seated	• Replace sealant; inspect cylinder head cover sealant flange and cylinder head sealant surface for distortion and cracks
	• Oil filler cap leaking or missing	• Replace cap
External oil leaks	• Oil filter gasket broken or improperly seated	• Replace oil filter
	• Oil pan side gasket broken, improperly seated or opening in RTV sealant	• Replace gasket or repair opening in sealant; inspect oil pan gasket flange for distortion
	• Oil pan front oil seal broken or improperly seated	• Replace seal; inspect timing case cover and oil pan seal flange for distortion
	• Oil pan rear oil seal broken or improperly seated	• Replace seal; inspect oil pan rear oil seal flange; inspect rear main bearing cap for cracks, plugged oil return channels, or distortion in seal groove
	• Timing case cover oil seal broken or improperly seated	• Replace seal
	• Excess oil pressure because of restricted PCV valve	• Replace PCV valve
	• Oil pan drain plug loose or has stripped threads	• Repair as necessary and tighten
	• Rear oil gallery plug loose	• Use appropriate sealant on gallery plug and tighten
	• Rear camshaft plug loose or improperly seated	• Seat camshaft plug or replace and seal, as necessary
	• Distributor base gasket damaged	• Replace gasket
Excessive oil consumption	• Oil level too high	• Drain oil to specified level
	• Oil with wrong viscosity being used	• Replace with specified oil
	• PCV valve stuck closed	• Replace PCV valve
	• Valve stem oil deflectors (or seals) are damaged, missing, or incorrect type	• Replace valve stem oil deflectors
	• Valve stems or valve guides worn	• Measure stem-to-guide clearance and repair as necessary
	• Poorly fitted or missing valve cover baffles	• Replace valve cover
	• Piston rings broken or missing	• Replace broken or missing rings
	• Scuffed piston	• Replace piston
	• Incorrect piston ring gap	• Measure ring gap, repair as necessary
	• Piston rings sticking or excessively loose in grooves	• Measure ring side clearance, repair as necessary
	• Compression rings installed upside down	• Repair as necessary
	• Cylinder walls worn, scored, or glazed	• Repair as necessary

Troubleshooting Engine Mechanical Problems (cont.)

Problem	Cause	Solution
	• Piston ring gaps not properly staggered	• Repair as necessary
	• Excessive main or connecting rod bearing clearance	• Measure bearing clearance, repair as necessary
No oil pressure	• Low oil level	• Add oil to correct level
	• Oil pressure gauge, warning lamp or sending unit inaccurate	• Replace oil pressure gauge or warning lamp
	• Oil pump malfunction	• Replace oil pump
	• Oil pressure relief valve sticking	• Remove and inspect oil pressure relief valve assembly
	• Oil passages on pressure side of pump obstructed	• Inspect oil passages for obstruction
	• Oil pickup screen or tube obstructed	• Inspect oil pickup for obstruction
	• Loose oil inlet tube	• Tighten or seal inlet tube
Low oil pressure	• Low oil level	• Add oil to correct level
	• Inaccurate gauge, warning lamp or sending unit	• Replace oil pressure gauge or warning lamp
	• Oil excessively thin because of dilution, poor quality, or improper grade	• Drain and refill crankcase with recommended oil
	• Excessive oil temperature	• Correct cause of overheating engine
	• Oil pressure relief spring weak or sticking	• Remove and inspect oil pressure relief valve assembly
	• Oil inlet tube and screen assembly has restriction or air leak	• Remove and inspect oil inlet tube and screen assembly. (Fill inlet tube with lacquer thinner to locate leaks.)
	• Excessive oil pump clearance	• Measure clearances
	• Excessive main, rod, or camshaft bearing clearance	• Measure bearing clearances, repair as necessary
High oil pressure	• Improper oil viscosity	• Drain and refill crankcase with correct viscosity oil
	• Oil pressure gauge or sending unit inaccurate	• Replace oil pressure gauge
	• Oil pressure relief valve sticking closed	• Remove and inspect oil pressure relief valve assembly
Main bearing noise	• Insufficient oil supply	• Inspect for low oil level and low oil pressure
	• Main bearing clearance excessive	• Measure main bearing clearance, repair as necessary
	• Bearing insert missing	• Replace missing insert
	• Crankshaft end play excessive	• Measure end play, repair as necessary
	• Improperly tightened main bearing cap bolts	• Tighten bolts with specified torque
	• Loose flywheel or drive plate	• Tighten flywheel or drive plate attaching bolts
	• Loose or damaged vibration damper	• Repair as necessary

Troubleshooting Engine Mechanical Problems (cont.)

Problem	Cause	Solution
Connecting rod bearing noise	• Insufficient oil supply	• Inspect for low oil level and low oil pressure
	• Carbon build-up on piston	• Remove carbon from piston crown
	• Bearing clearance excessive or bearing missing	• Measure clearance, repair as necessary
	• Crankshaft connecting rod journal out-of-round	• Measure journal dimensions, repair or replace as necessary
	• Misaligned connecting rod or cap	• Repair as necessary
	• Connecting rod bolts tightened improperly	• Tighten bolts with specified torque
Piston noise	• Piston-to-cylinder wall clearance excessive (scuffed piston)	• Measure clearance and examine piston
	• Cylinder walls excessively tapered or out-of-round	• Measure cylinder wall dimensions, rebore cylinder
	• Piston ring broken	• Replace all rings on piston
	• Loose or seized piston pin	• Measure piston-to-pin clearance, repair as necessary
	• Connecting rods misaligned	• Measure rod alignment, straighten or replace
	• Piston ring side clearance excessively loose or tight	• Measure ring side clearance, repair as necessary
	• Carbon build-up on piston is excessive	• Remove carbon from piston
Valve actuating component noise	• Insufficient oil supply	• Check for: (a) Low oil level (b) Low oil pressure (c) Plugged push rods (d) Wrong hydraulic tappets (e) Restricted oil gallery (f) Excessive tappet to bore clearance
	• Push rods worn or bent	• Replace worn or bent push rods
	• Rocker arms or pivots worn	• Replace worn rocker arms or pivots
	• Foreign objects or chips in hydraulic tappets	• Clean tappets
	• Excessive tappet leak-down	• Replace valve tappet
	• Tappet face worn	• Replace tappet; inspect corresponding cam lobe for wear
	• Broken or cocked valve springs	• Properly seat cocked springs; replace broken springs
	• Stem-to-guide clearance excessive	• Measure stem-to-guide clearance, repair as required
	• Valve bent	• Replace valve
	• Loose rocker arms	• Tighten bolts with specified torque
	• Valve seat runout excessive	• Regrind valve seat/valves
	• Missing valve lock	• Install valve lock
	• Push rod rubbing or contacting cylinder head	• Remove cylinder head and remove obstruction in head
	• Excessive engine oil (four-cylinder engine)	• Correct oil level

Troubleshooting the Cooling System

Problem	Cause	Solution
High temperature gauge indication—overheating	• Coolant level low	• Replenish coolant
	• Fan belt loose	• Adjust fan belt tension
	• Radiator hose(s) collapsed	• Replace hose(s)
	• Radiator airflow blocked	• Remove restriction (bug screen, fog lamps, etc.)
	• Faulty radiator cap	• Replace radiator cap
	• Ignition timing incorrect	• Adjust ignition timing
	• Idle speed low	• Adjust idle speed
	• Air trapped in cooling system	• Purge air
	• Heavy traffic driving	• Operate at fast idle in neutral intermittently to cool engine
	• Incorrect cooling system component(s) installed	• Install proper component(s)
	• Faulty thermostat	• Replace thermostat
	• Water pump shaft broken or impeller loose	• Replace water pump
	• Radiator tubes clogged	• Flush radiator
	• Cooling system clogged	• Flush system
	• Casting flash in cooling passages	• Repair or replace as necessary. Flash may be visible by removing cooling system components or removing core plugs.
	• Brakes dragging	• Repair brakes
	• Excessive engine friction	• Repair engine
	• Antifreeze concentration over 68%	• Lower antifreeze concentration percentage
	• Missing air seals	• Replace air seals
	• Faulty gauge or sending unit	• Repair or replace faulty component
	• Loss of coolant flow caused by leakage or foaming	• Repair or replace leaking component, replace coolant
	• Viscous fan drive failed	• Replace unit
Low temperature indication—undercooling	• Thermostat stuck open	• Replace thermostat
	• Faulty gauge or sending unit	• Repair or replace faulty component
Coolant loss—boilover	• Overfilled cooling system	• Reduce coolant level to proper specification
	• Quick shutdown after hard (hot) run	• Allow engine to run at fast idle prior to shutdown
	• Air in system resulting in occasional "burping" of coolant	• Purge system
	• Insufficient antifreeze allowing coolant boiling point to be too low	• Add antifreeze to raise boiling point
	• Antifreeze deteriorated because of age or contamination	• Replace coolant
	• Leaks due to loose hose clamps, loose nuts, bolts, drain plugs, faulty hoses, or defective radiator	• Pressure test system to locate source of leak(s) then repair as necessary

Troubleshooting the Cooling System (cont.)

Problem	Cause	Solution
Coolant loss—boilover	• Faulty head gasket • Cracked head, manifold, or block • Faulty radiator cap	• Replace head gasket • Replace as necessary • Replace cap
Coolant entry into crankcase or cylinder(s)	• Faulty head gasket • Crack in head, manifold or block	• Replace head gasket • Replace as necessary
Coolant recovery system inoperative	• Coolant level low • Leak in system • Pressure cap not tight or seal missing, or leaking • Pressure cap defective • Overflow tube clogged or leaking • Recovery bottle vent restricted	• Replenish coolant to FULL mark • Pressure test to isolate leak and repair as necessary • Repair as necessary • Replace cap • Repair as necessary • Remove restriction
Noise	• Fan contacting shroud • Loose water pump impeller • Glazed fan belt • Loose fan belt • Rough surface on drive pulley • Water pump bearing worn • Belt alignment	• Reposition shroud and inspect engine mounts • Replace pump • Apply silicone or replace belt • Adjust fan belt tension • Replace pulley • Remove belt to isolate. Replace pump. • Check pulley alignment. Repair as necessary.
No coolant flow through heater core	• Restricted return inlet in water pump • Heater hose collapsed or restricted • Restricted heater core • Restricted outlet in thermostat housing • Intake manifold bypass hole in cylinder head restricted • Faulty heater control valve • Intake manifold coolant passage restricted	• Remove restriction • Remove restriction or replace hose • Remove restriction or replace core • Remove flash or restriction • Remove restriction • Replace valve • Remove restriction or replace intake manifold

NOTE: *Immediately after shutdown, the engine enters a condition known as heat soak. This is caused by the cooling system being inoperative while engine temperature is still high. If coolant temperature rises above boiling point, expansion and pressure may push some coolant out of the radiator overflow tube. If this does not occur frequently it is considered normal.*

Troubleshooting the Serpentine Drive Belt

Problem	Cause	Solution
Tension sheeting fabric failure (woven fabric on outside circumference of belt has cracked or separated from body of belt)	• Grooved or backside idler pulley diameters are less than minimum recommended • Tension sheeting contacting (rubbing) stationary object • Excessive heat causing woven fabric to age • Tension sheeting splice has fractured	• Replace pulley(s) not conforming to specification • Correct rubbing condition • Replace belt • Replace belt
Noise (objectional squeal, squeak, or rumble is heard or felt while drive belt is in operation)	• Belt slippage • Bearing noise • Belt misalignment • Belt-to-pulley mismatch • Driven component inducing vibration • System resonant frequency inducing vibration	• Adjust belt • Locate and repair • Align belt/pulley(s) • Install correct belt • Locate defective driven component and repair • Vary belt tension within specifications. Replace belt.
Rib chunking (one or more ribs has separated from belt body)	• Foreign objects imbedded in pulley grooves • Installation damage • Drive loads in excess of design specifications • Insufficient internal belt adhesion	• Remove foreign objects from pulley grooves • Replace belt • Adjust belt tension • Replace belt
Rib or belt wear (belt ribs contact bottom of pulley grooves)	• Pulley(s) misaligned • Mismatch of belt and pulley groove widths • Abrasive environment • Rusted pulley(s) • Sharp or jagged pulley groove tips • Rubber deteriorated	• Align pulley(s) • Replace belt • Replace belt • Clean rust from pulley(s) • Replace pulley • Replace belt
Longitudinal belt cracking (cracks between two ribs)	• Belt has mistracked from pulley groove • Pulley groove tip has worn away rubber-to-tensile member	• Replace belt • Replace belt
Belt slips	• Belt slipping because of insufficient tension • Belt or pulley subjected to substance (belt dressing, oil, ethylene glycol) that has reduced friction • Driven component bearing failure • Belt glazed and hardened from heat and excessive slippage	• Adjust tension • Replace belt and clean pulleys • Replace faulty component bearing • Replace belt
"Groove jumping" (belt does not maintain correct position on pulley, or turns over and/or runs off pulleys)	• Insufficient belt tension • Pulley(s) not within design tolerance • Foreign object(s) in grooves	• Adjust belt tension • Replace pulley(s) • Remove foreign objects from grooves

Troubleshooting the Serpentine Drive Belt (cont.)

Problem	Cause	Solution
"Groove jumping" (belt does not maintain correct position on pulley, or turns over and/or runs off pulleys)	• Excessive belt speed • Pulley misalignment • Belt-to-pulley profile mismatched • Belt cordline is distorted	• Avoid excessive engine acceleration • Align pulley(s) • Install correct belt • Replace belt
Belt broken (Note: identify and correct problem before replacement belt is installed)	• Excessive tension • Tensile members damaged during belt installation • Belt turnover • Severe pulley misalignment • Bracket, pulley, or bearing failure	• Replace belt and adjust tension to specification • Replace belt • Replace belt • Align pulley(s) • Replace defective component and belt
Cord edge failure (tensile member exposed at edges of belt or separated from belt body)	• Excessive tension • Drive pulley misalignment • Belt contacting stationary object • Pulley irregularities • Improper pulley construction • Insufficient adhesion between tensile member and rubber matrix	• Adjust belt tension • Align pulley • Correct as necessary • Replace pulley • Replace pulley • Replace belt and adjust tension to specifications
Sporadic rib cracking (multiple cracks in belt ribs at random intervals)	• Ribbed pulley(s) diameter less than minimum specification • Backside bend flat pulley(s) diameter less than minimum • Excessive heat condition causing rubber to harden • Excessive belt thickness • Belt overcured • Excessive tension	• Replace pulley(s) • Replace pulley(s) • Correct heat condition as necessary • Replace belt • Replace belt • Adjust belt tension

ENGINE MECHANICAL SPECIFICATIONS

Component	U.S.	Metric
Camshaft		
2.3L Engine		
End Play	0.0009-0.0088 in.	0.025-0.225mm
Bearing Diameter		
No. 1	1.572-1573 in.	39.93-39.95mm
Nos. 2-5	1.375-1376 in.	34.93-34.95mm
Bearing Clearance	0.0019-0.0043 in.	0.50-0.110mm
Lobe Lift (VIN D)		
Intake	0.375 in.	9.525mm
Exhaust	0.375 in.	9.5252m
Lobe Lift (VIN A)		
Intake	0.410 in.	10.414mm
Exhaust	0.410 in.	10.414mm
2.5L Engine		
End Play	0.0015-0.005 in.	0.0381-0.127mm
Bearing Diameter	1.869 in.	47.4726mm
Bearing Clearance	0.0007-0.0027 in.	0.01778-0.0685mm
Lobe Lift (1989)		
Intake	0.232 in.	5.8882mm
Exhaust	0.232 in.	5.8882mm

ENGINE MECHANICAL SPECIFICATIONS

Component	U.S.	Metric
Lobe Lift (1990-92)		
Intake	0.248 in.	6.302mm
Exhaust	0.248 in.	6.302mm
2.8L Engine		
End Play	NA	NA
Bearing Diameter	1.8678-1.8815 in.	47.44-47.79mm
Bearing Clearance	0.001-0.004 in.	0.026-0.101mm
Lobe Lift		
Intake	0.2626 in.	6.67mm
Exhaust	0.2732 in.	6.94mm
3.1L Engine		
End Play	NA	NA
Bearing Diameter	1.8678-1.8815 in.	47.44-47.79mm
Bearing Clearance	0.001-0.004 in.	0.026-0.101mm
Lobe Lift		
Intake	0.2626 in.	6.67mm
Exhaust	0.2732 in.	6.94mm
3.4L Engine		
End Play	NA	NA
Bearing Diameter	1.871-1.872 in.	47.516-47.541mm
Bearing Clearance	0.0015-0.0035 in.	0.037-0.088mm
Lobe Lift	0.370 in.	9.398mm
3.8L Engine		
End Play	NA	NA
Bearing Diameter	1.786-1.789 in.	45.377-45.428mm
Bearing Clearance	0.0005-0.0035 in.	0.0127-0.0889mm
Valves		
2.3L Engine		
Face Angle		
Intake	44°	44°
Exhaust	44.5°	44.5°
Seat Angle	45°	45°
Seat Runout	0.002 in.	0.05mm
Seat Width	0.037-0.748 in.	0.940-1.900mm
Stem Clearance		
Intake	0.001-0.0028 in.	0.028-0.071mm
Exhaust	0.0015-0.0032 in.	0.038-0.081mm
2.5L Engine		
Face Angle	45°	45°
Seat Angle	46°	46°
Seat Runout	0.002 in.	0.05mm
Seat Width		
Intake	0.035-0.075 in.	0.889-1.905mm
Exhaust (1982-89)	0.058-0.097 in.	1.473-2.642mm
Exhaust (1990-92)	0.058-0.105 in.	1.473-2.667mm
Stem Clearance		
Intake	0.001-0.0028 in.	0.028-0.071mm
Exhaust (1982-89)	0.0013-0.0041 in.	0.033-0.1040mm
Exhaust (1990-92)	0.0013-0.0041 in.	0.033-0.1040mm
2.8L Engine		
Face Angle	45°	45°
Seat Angle	46°	46°
Seat Runout	0.001 in.	0.25mm
Seat Width		
Intake	0.061-0.073 in.	1.550-1.850mm
Exhaust	0.067-0.079 in.	1.70-2.0mm
Stem Clearance		
Intake	0.001-0.0027 in.	0.026-0.068mm
Exhaust	0.001-0.0027 in.	0.026-0.068mm
3.1L Engine		
Face Angle	45°	45°

ENGINE MECHANICAL SPECIFICATIONS

Component	U.S.	Metric
Seat Angle	46°	46°
Seat Runout	0.001 in.	0.25mm
Seat Width		
Intake	0.061-0.073 in.	1.550-1.850mm
Exhaust	0.067-0.079 in.	1.70-2.0mm
Stem Clearance		
Intake	0.001-0.0027 in.	0.026-0.068mm
Exhaust	0.001-0.0027 in.	0.026-0.068mm
3.4L Engine		
Face Angle	45°	45°
Seat Angle	46°	46°
Seat Runout	0.002 in.	0.05mm
Seat Width		
Intake	0.049-0.059 in.	1.250-1.500mm
Exhaust	0.063-0.075 in.	1.600-1.900mm
Stem Clearance		
Intake	0.0011-0.0026 in.	0.028-0.066mm
Exhaust	0.0014-0.0031 in.	0.035-0.078mm
3.8L Engine		
Face Angle	45°	45°
Seat Angle	46°	46°
Seat Runout	0.002 in.	0.05mm
Seat Width		
Intake	0.0600-0.0800 in.	1.530-2.030mm
Exhaust	0.0900-0.1100 in.	2.290-2.790mm
Stem Clearance		
Intake	0.0015-0.0035 in.	0.038-0.089mm
Exhaust	0.0015-0.0032 in.	0.038-0.081mm
Valve Spring		
2.3L Engine	NA	NA
2.5L Engine		
Free Length	2.01 in.	51mm
Installed Height	1.68 in.	42.64mm
2.8L Engine		
Free Length	1.91 in.	48.5mm
Installed Height	1.5748 in.	40.0mm
3.1L Engine		
Free Length	1.91 in.	48.5mm
Installed Height	1.5748 in.	40.0mm
3.4L Engine		
Free Length	1.66 in.	42.04mm
3.8L Engine		
Free Length	1.98 in.	50mm
Installed Height	1.70 in.	43.18mm
Spring Load		
2.3L Engine		
Closed	75 ft.lbs. @ 1.44 in.	332 Nm @ 36.50mm
Open	200 ft.lbs. @ 1.04 in.	900 Nm @ 26.08mm
2.5L Engine		
Closed	75 ft.lbs. @ 1.68 in.	332 Nm @ 42.64mm
Open	173 ft.lbs. @ 1.24 in.	770 Nm @ 31.46mm
2.8L Engine		
Closed	90 ft.lbs. @ 1.70 in.	400 Nm @ 43.0mm
Open	215 ft.lbs. @ 1.29 in.	956 Nm @ 33.0mm
3.1L Engine		
Closed	90 ft.lbs. @ 1.701 in.	400 Nm @ 43.0mm
Open	215 ft.lbs. @ 1.291 in.	956 Nm @ 33.0mm
3.4L Engine		
Closed	75 ft.lbs. @ 1.40 in.	334 Nm @ 42.64mm
Open	180 ft.lbs. @ 1.03 in.	800 Nm @ 31.46mm
3.8L Engine		
Closed	80 ft.lbs. @ 1.750 in.	356 Nm @ 43.7mm
Open	210 ft.lbs. @ 1.320 in.	935 Nm @ 33.4mm

ENGINE MECHANICAL SPECIFICATIONS

Component	U.S.	Metric
Lifter		
2.3L Engine		
Bore Clearance	0.0006-0.024 in.	0.014-0.060mm
2.5L Engine		
Body Diameter	0.841-0.843 in.	21.3668-21.4046mm
Bore Diameter	0.844-0.845 in.	21.425-21.450mm
Bore Clearance	0.002-0.0006 in.	0.06-0.016mm
Plunger Travel	0.022 in.	5.3mm
2.8L Engine	NA	NA
3.1L Engine	NA	NA
3.4L Engine	NA	NA
3.8L Engine	NA	NA
Oil Pump		
2.3L Engine		
Gear Pocket Depth	0.674-0.676 in.	17.11-17.16mm
Gear Thickness	0.6727-0.6731 in.	17.087-17.099mm
2.5L Engine		
Gear Pocket Depth	0.514-0.516 in.	13.05-13.10mm
Gear Thickness	0.511-0.512 in.	12.973-12.998mm
2.8L Engine		
Gear Pocket Depth	1.195-1.198 in.	30.36-30.44mm
Gear Clearance	1.498-1.500 in.	38.05-38.10mm
3.1L Engine		
Gear Pocket Depth	1.195-1.198 in.	30.36-30.44mm
Gear Clearance	1.498-1.500 in.	38.05-38.10mm
3.4L Engine		
Gear Pocket Depth	1.195-1.198 in.	30.36-30.44mm
Gear Clearance	1.498-1.500 in.	38.05-38.10mm
3.8L Engine		
Inner tip clearance	0.006 in.	0.1524mm
Outer clearance	0.008-0.015 in.	0.203-0.381mm
Cylinder Bore		
2.3L Engine		
Diameter	3.620 in.	92.0mm
Out of Round	0.0004 in.	0.10mm
Taper	0.0003 in.	0.008mm
2.5L Engine		
Diameter	4.0 in 101.6mm	
Out of Round	0.001 in.	0.02mm
Taper	0.005 in.	0.13mm
2.8L Engine		
Diameter	3.5046-3.5033 in.	89.016-89-034mm
Out of Round	0.0005 in.	0.13mm
Taper	0.0005 in.	0.13mm
3.1L Engine		
Diameter	3.5046-3.5033 in.	89.016-89-034mm
Out of Round	0.0005 in.	0.13mm
Taper	0.0005 in.	0.13mm
3.4L Engine		
Diameter	3.6224-3.6231 in.	92.010-92.028mm
Out of Round	0.0003 in.	0.0072mm
Taper	NA	NA
3.8L Engine		
Diameter	3.8 in.	96.52mm
Out of Round	0.001 in.	0.02mm
Taper	0.001 in.	0.02mm

ENGINE MECHANICAL SPECIFICATIONS

Component	U.S.	Metric
Piston		
2.3L Engine		
Clearance	0.0007-0.0020 in.	0.019-0.051mm
2.5L Engine		
Clearance	0.0014-0.0022 in.	0.036-0.056mm
2.8L Engine		
Clearance	0.00093-0.00222 in.	0.0235-0.0565mm
3.1L Engine		
Clearance	0.0022-0.0028 in.	0.057-0.072mm
3.4L Engine		
Clearance	0.0009-0.0023 in.	0.022-0.058mm
3.8L Engine		
Clearance	0.0004-0.0022 in.	0.102-0.056mm
Piston Rings		
2.3L Engine		
Gap (top)	0.013-0.023 in.	0.35-0.56mm
Gap (second)	0.015-0.025 in.	0.40-0.65mm
Gap (oil)	0.015-0.055 in.	0.40-1.40mm
Side Clearance		
Top	0.002-0.004 in.	0.05-0.10mm
Second	0.001-0.003 in.	0.04-0.08mm
Oil Control	0.019-0.026 in.	0.48-0.66mm
2.5L Engine		
Gap (top)	0.01-0.02 in.	0.30-0.50mm
Gap (second)	0.01-0.02 in.	0.30-0.50mm
Gap (oil)	0.02-0.06 in.	0.50-1.50mm
Side Clearance		
Top	0.002-0.003 in.	0.05-0.08mm
Second	0.001-0.003 in.	0.03-0.08mm
Oil Control	0.015-0.055 in.	0.38-1.40mm
2.8L Engine		
Gap (top)	0.01-0.02 in.	0.30-0.50mm
Gap (second)	0.01-0.02 in.	0.30-0.50mm
Gap (oil)	0.02-0.55 in.	0.50-1.40mm
Side Clearance		
Top	0.001-0.003 in.	0.03-0.08mm
Second	0.001-0.003 in.	0.03-0.08mm
Oil Control	0.008 in.	0.20mm
3.1L Engine		
Gap (top)	0.01-0.02 in.	0.30-0.50mm
Gap (second)	0.01-0.02 in.	0.30-0.50mm
Gap (oil)	0.01-0.50 in.	0.25-1.27mm
Side Clearance		
Top	0.002-0.0035 in.	0.05-0.09mm
Second	0.002-0.0035 in.	0.05-0.09mm
Oil Control	0.008 in.	0.20mm
3.4L Engine		
Gap (top)	0.012-0.022 in.	0.30-0.56mm
Gap (second)	0.019-0.029 in.	0.48-0.74mm
Gap (oil)	0.010-0.030 in.	0.25-0.76mm
Side Clearance		
Top	0.001-0.003 in.	0.04-0.09mm
Second	0.001-0.003 in.	0.04-0.09mm
Oil Control	0.002-0.008 in.	0.05-0.20mm
3.8L Engine		
Gap (top)	0.010-0.025 in.	0.254-0.635mm
Gap (second)	0.010-0.025 in.	0.254-0.635mm
Gap (oil)	0.015-0.550 in.	0.381-1.397mm
Side Clearance		
Top	0.001-0.003 in.	0.03-0.08mm
Second	0.001-0.003 in.	0.03-0.08mm
Oil Control	0.001-0.008 in.	0.03-0.20mm

ENGINE MECHANICAL SPECIFICATIONS

Component	U.S.	Metric
Piston Pins		
2.3L Engine		
Diameter	0.8659-0.8661 in.	21.995-22.000mm
Piston clearance	0.0003-0.0006 in.	0.008-0.017mm
Rod clearance	0.00027-0.0012 in.	0.007-0.031mm
2.5L Engine		
Diameter	0.927-0.928 in.	23.546-23.561mm
Fit in piston	0.0003-0.0005 in.	0.008-0.013mm
Fit in rod	press	press
2.8L Engine		
Diameter	0.9052-0.9056 in.	22.937-23.001mm
Clearance	0.00025-0.0037 in.	0.0065-0.091mm
Fit in rod	0.00078-0.0021 in.	0.020-0.0515mm
3.1L Engine		
Diameter	0.9052-0.9054 in.	22.937-22.964mm
Clearance	0.0004-0.0008 in.	0.0096-0.0215mm
Fit in rod	0.00078-0.0021 in.	0.020-0.0515mm
3.4L Engine		
Diameter	0.9052-0.9054 in.	22.992-22.996mm
Fit in piston	0.0005-0.0009 in.	0.012-0.024mm
Fit in rod	press	press
3.8L Engine		
Diameter	0.9053-0.9055 in.	22.995-23.000mm
Fit in piston	0.0004-0.0007 in.	0.0100-0.0177mm
Fit in rod	0.0007-0.0017 in.	0.017-0.0432mm
Crankshaft		
2.3L Engine		
Main Journal		
Diameter	2.0470-2.0480 in.	51.99-52.02mm
Taper	0.0005 in.	0.013mm
Out of Round	0.0005 in.	0.013mm
Clearance	0.0005-0.0022 in.	0.013-0.056mm
End-play	0.0034-0.0095 in.	0.0864-0.241mm
Crankpin		
Diameter	1.8887-1.8897 in.	47.97-48.00mm
Taper	0.0005 in.	0.013mm
Out of Round	0.0005 in.	0.013mm
Clearance		
Bearing	0.0005-0.0020 in.	0.013-0.05mm
Side	0.0054-0.018 in.	0.137-0.457mm
2.5L Engine		
Main Journal		
Diameter	2.3 in.	58.399-58.400mm
Taper	0.0005 in.	0.013mm
Out of Round	0.0005 in.	0.013mm
Clearance	0.0005-0.0022 in.	0.013-0.056mm
End-play	0.0051-0.010 in.	0.13-0.26mm
Crankpin		
Diameter	2.0 in.	50.708-50.805mm
Taper	0.0005 in.	0.013mm
Out of Round	0.0005 in.	0.013mm
Clearance		
Bearing	0.0005-0.003 in.	0.013-0.07mm
Side	0.006-0.024in.	0.015-0.06mm
2.8L Engine		
Main Journal		
Diameter	2.6473-2.6483 in.	67.241-67.265mm
Taper	0.0002 in.	0.005mm
Out of Round	0.0002 in.	0.005mm
Clearance	0.0012-0.0027 in.	0.032-0.069mm
Thrust	0.0016-0.0031 in.	0.042-0.079mm

ENGINE MECHANICAL SPECIFICATIONS

Component	U.S.	Metric
End-play	0.0024-0.0083 in.	0.06-0.21mm
Crankpin		
Diameter	1.9994-1.9983 in.	50.784-50.758mm
Taper	0.0002 in.	0.005mm
Out of Round	0.0002 in.	0.005mm
Clearance		
Bearing	0.0015-0.0036 in.	0.038-0.083mm
Side	0.014-0.027in.	0.360-0.680mm
3.1L Engine		
Main Journal		
Diameter	2.6473-2.6483 in.	67.241-67.265mm
Taper	0.0003 in.	0.008mm
Out of Round	0.0002 in.	0.005mm
Clearance	0.0012-0.0027 in.	0.032-0.069mm
Thrust	0.0012-0.0027 in.	0.032-0.069mm
End-play	0.0024-0.0083 in.	0.06-0.21mm
Crankpin		
Diameter	1.9994-1.9983 in.	50.784-50.758mm
Taper	0.0003 in.	0.008mm
Out of Round	0.0002 in.	0.005mm
Clearance		
Bearing	0.0013-0.0031 in.	0.032-0.079mm
Side	0.014-0.027in.	0.360-0.680mm
3.4L Engine		
Main Journal		
Diameter	2.6473-2.6479 in.	67.241-67.257mm
Taper	0.0002 in.	0.005mm
Out of Round	0.0002 in.	0.005mm
Clearance	0.0013-0.0030 in.	0.032-0.077mm
End-play	0.0024-0.0083 in.	0.06-0.21mm
Crankpin		
Diameter	1.9987-1.9994 in.	50.768-50.784mm
Diameter	2.6473-2.6479 67.241-67.257mm	
Taper	0.0002 in.	0.005mm
Clearance		
Bearing	0.0011-0.0032 in.	0.028-0.82mm
Side	0.014-0.025 in.	0.36-0.64mm
3.8L Engine		
Main Journal		
Diameter	2.4988-2.4998 in.	63.47-63.50mm
Taper	0.0003 in.	0.008mm
Out of Round	0.0003 in.	0.008mm
Clearance	0.0018-0.0030 in.	0.008-0.045mm
End-play	0.003-0.0011 in.	0.08-0.2794mm
Crankpin		
Diameter	NA	NA
Taper	0.0003 in.	0.008mm
Out of Round	0.0003 in.	0.008mm
Clearance	0.0003-0.0026 in.	0.008-0.066mm
End-play	0.003-0.015 in.	0.0762-0.381mm

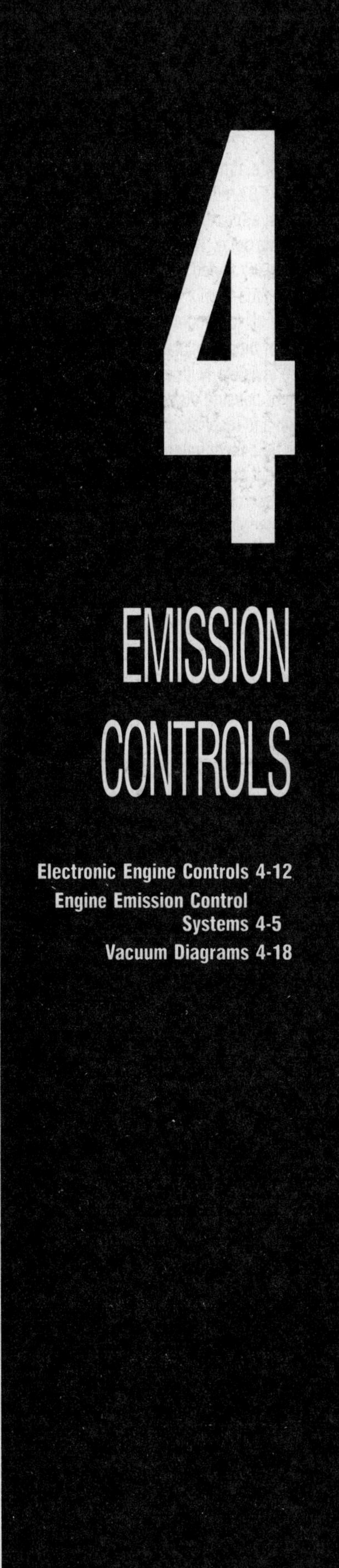

4 EMISSION CONTROLS

AIR POLLUTION

The earth's atmosphere, at or near sea level, consists of 78% nitrogen, 21% oxygen and 1% other gases, approximately. If it were possible to remain in this state, 100% clean air would result. However, many varied causes allow other gases and particulates to mix with the clean air, causing the air to become unclean or polluted.

Certain of these pollutants are visible while others are invisible, with each having the capability of causing distress to the eyes, ears, throat, skin and respiratory system. Should these pollutants be concentrated in a specific area and under the right conditions, death could result due to the displacement or chemical change of the oxygen content in the air. These pollutants can cause much damage to the environment and to the many man made objects that are exposed to the elements.

To better understand the causes of air pollution, the pollutants can be categorized into 3 separate types, natural, industrial and automotive.

Natural Pollutants

Natural pollution has been present on earth before man appeared and is still a factor to be considered when discussing air pollution, although it causes only a small percentage of the present overall pollution problem existing in our country. It is the direct result of decaying organic matter, wind born smoke and particulates from such natural events as plains and forest fires (ignited by heat or lightning), volcanic ash, sand and dust which can spread over a large area of the countryside.

Such a phenomenon of natural pollution has been recent volcanic eruptions, with the resulting plume of smoke, steam and volcanic ash blotting out the sun's rays as it spreads and rises higher into the atmosphere, where the upper air currents catch and carry the smoke and ash, while condensing the steam back into water vapor. As the water vapor, smoke and ash traveled on their journey, the smoke dissipates into the atmosphere while the ash and moisture settle back to earth in a trail hundred of miles long. In many cases, lives are lost and millions of dollars of property damage result, and ironically, man can only stand by and watch it happen.

Industrial Pollution

Industrial pollution is caused primarily by industrial processes, the burning of coal, oil and natural gas, which in turn produces smoke and fumes. Because the burning fuels contain much sulfur, the principal ingredients of smoke and fumes are sulfur dioxide (SO_2) and particulate matter. This type of pollutant occurs most severely during still, damp and cool weather, such as at night. Even in its less severe form, this pollutant is not confined to just cities. Because of air movements, the pollutants move for miles over the surrounding countryside, leaving in its path a barren and unhealthy environment for all living things.

Working with Federal, State and Local mandated rules, regulations and by carefully monitoring the emissions, industries have greatly reduced the amount of pollutant emitted from their industrial sources, striving to obtain an acceptable level. Because of the mandated industrial emission clean up, many land areas and streams in and around the cities that were formerly barren of vegetation and life, have now begun to move back in the direction of nature's intended balance.

Automotive Pollutants

The third major source of air pollution is the automotive emissions. The emissions from the internal combustion engine were not an appreciable problem years ago because of the small number of registered vehicles and the nation's small highway system. However, during the early 1950's, the trend of the American people was to move from the cities to the surrounding suburbs. This caused an immediate problem in the transportation areas because the majority of the suburbs were not afforded mass transit conveniences. This lack of transportation created an attractive market for the automobile manufacturers, which resulted in a dramatic increase in the number of vehicles produced and sold, along with a marked increase in highway construction between cities and the suburbs. Multi-vehicle families emerged with much emphasis placed on the individual vehicle per family member. As the increase in vehicle ownership and usage occurred, so did the pollutant levels in and around the cities, as the suburbanites drove daily to their businesses and employment in the city and its fringe area, returning at the end of the day to their homes in the suburbs.

It was noted that a fog and smoke type haze was being formed and at times, remained in suspension over the cities and did not quickly dissipate. At first this "smog", derived from the words "smoke" and "fog", was thought to result from industrial pollution but it was determined that the automobile emissions were largely to blame. It was discovered that as normal automobile emissions were exposed to sunlight for a period of time, complex chemical reactions would take place.

It was found the smog was a photo chemical layer and was developed when certain oxides of nitrogen (NOx) and unburned hydrocarbons (HC) from the automobile emissions were exposed to sunlight and was more severe when the smog would remain stagnant over an area in which a warm layer of air would settle over the top of a cooler air mass at ground level, trapping and holding the automobile emissions, instead of the emissions being dispersed and diluted through normal air flows. This type of air stagnation was given the name "Temperature Inversion".

Temperature Inversion

In normal weather situations, the surface air is warmed by the heat radiating from the earth's surface and the sun's rays and will rise upward, into the atmosphere, to be cooled through a convection type heat expands with the cooler upper air. As the warm air rises, the surface pollutants are carried upward and dissipated into the atmosphere.

When a temperature inversion occurs, we find the higher air is no longer cooler but warmer than the surface air, causing the cooler surface air to become trapped and unable to move. This warm air blanket can extend from above ground level to a few hundred or even a few thousand feet into the air. As the surface air is trapped, so are the pollutants, causing a severe smog condition. Should this stagnant air mass extend to a few thousand feet high, enough air movement with the inversion takes place to allow the smog layer to rise above ground level but the pollutants still cannot dissipate. This inversion can remain for days over an area, with only the smog level rising or lowering from ground level to a few hundred feet high. Meanwhile, the pollutant levels increases, causing eye irritation, respirator problems, reduced visibility, plant damage and in some cases, cancer type diseases.

This inversion phenomenon was first noted in the Los Angeles, California area. The city lies in a basin type of terrain and during certain weather conditions, a cold air mass is held in the basin while a warmer air mass covers it like a lid.

Because this type of condition was first documented as prevalent in the Los Angeles area, this type of smog was named Los Angeles Smog, although it occurs in other areas where a large concentration of automobiles are used and the air remains stagnant for any length of time.

Internal Combustion Engine Pollutants

Consider the internal combustion engine as a machine in which raw materials must be placed so a finished product comes out. As in any machine operation, a certain amount of wasted material is formed. When we relate this to the internal combustion engine, we find that by putting in air and fuel, we obtain power from this mixture during the combustion process to drive the vehicle. The by-product or waste of this power is, in part, heat and exhaust gases with which we must concern ourselves.

HEAT TRANSFER

The heat from the combustion process can rise to over 4000°F (2204°C). The dissipation of this heat is controlled by a ram air effect, the use of cooling fans to cause air flow and having a liquid coolant solution surrounding the combustion area and transferring the heat of combustion through the cylinder walls and into the coolant. The coolant is then directed to a thin-finned, multi-tubed radiator, from which the excess heat is transferred to the outside air by 1 or all of the 3 heat transfer methods, conduction, convection or radiation.

The cooling of the combustion area is an important part in the control of exhaust emissions. To understand the behavior of the combustion and transfer of its heat, consider the air/fuel charge. It is ignited and the flame front burns progressively across the combustion chamber until the burning charge reaches the cylinder walls. Some of the fuel in contact with the walls is not hot enough to burn, thereby snuffing out or Quenching the combustion process. This leaves unburned fuel in the combustion chamber. This unburned fuel is then forced out of the cylinder along with the exhaust gases and into the exhaust system.

Many attempts have been made to minimize the amount of unburned fuel in the combustion chambers due to the snuffing out or "Quenching", by increasing the coolant temperature and lessening the contact area of the coolant around the combustion area. Design limitations within the combustion chambers prevent the complete burning of the air/fuel charge, so a certain amount of the unburned fuel is still expelled into the exhaust system, regardless of modifications to the engine.

EXHAUST EMISSIONS

Composition Of The Exhaust Gases

The exhaust gases emitted into the atmosphere are a combination of burned and unburned fuel. To understand the exhaust emission and its composition review some basic chemistry.

When the air/fuel mixture is introduced into the engine, we are mixing air, composed of nitrogen (78%), oxygen (21%) and other gases (1%) with the fuel, which is 100% hydrocarbons (HC), in a semi-controlled ratio. As the combustion process is accomplished, power is produced to move the vehicle while the heat of combustion is transferred to the cooling system. The exhaust gases are then composed of nitrogen, a diatomic gas (N_2), the same as was introduced in the engine, carbon dioxide (CO2), the same gas that is used in beverage carbonation and water vapor (H_2O). The nitrogen (N_2), for the most part passes through the engine unchanged, while the oxygen (O_2) reacts (burns) with the hydrocarbons (HC) and produces the carbon dioxide (CO_2) and the water vapors (H_2O). If this chemical process would be the only process to take place, the exhaust emissions would be harmless. However, during the combustion process, other pollutants are formed and are considered dangerous. These pollutants are carbon monoxide (CO), hydrocarbons (HC), oxides of nitrogen (NOx) oxides of sulfur (SOx) and engine particulates.

Lead (Pb), is considered 1 of the particulates and is present in the exhaust gases whenever leaded fuels are used. Lead (Pb) does not dissipate easily. Levels can be high along roadways when it is emitted from vehicles and can pose a health threat. Since the increased usage of unleaded gasoline and the phasing out of leaded gasoline for fuel, this pollutant is gradually diminishing. While not considered a major threat lead is still considered a dangerous pollutant.

HYDROCARBONS

Hydrocarbons (HC) are essentially unburned fuel that have not been successfully burned during the combustion process or have escaped into the atmosphere through fuel evaporation. The main sources of incomplete combustion are rich air/fuel mixtures, low engine temperatures and improper spark timing. The main sources of hydrocarbon emission through fuel evaporation come from the vehicle's fuel tank and carburetor bowl.

To reduce combustion hydrocarbon emission, engine modifications were made to minimize dead space and surface area in the combustion chamber. In addition the air/fuel mixture was made more lean through improved carburetion, fuel injection and by the addition of external controls to aid in further combustion of the hydrocarbons outside the engine. Two such methods were the addition of an air injection system, to inject fresh air into the exhaust manifolds and the installation of a catalytic converter, a unit that is able to burn traces of hydrocarbons without affecting the internal combustion process or fuel economy.

To control hydrocarbon emissions through fuel evaporation, modifications were made to the fuel tank and carburetor bowl to allow storage of the fuel vapors during periods of engine shut-down, and at specific times during engine operation, to purge and burn these same vapors by blending them with the air/fuel mixture.

CARBON MONOXIDE

Carbon monoxide is formed when not enough oxygen is present during the combustion process to convert carbon (C) to carbon dioxide (CO_2). An increase in the carbon monoxide (CO) emission is normally accompanied by an increase in the hydrocarbon (HC) emission because of the lack of oxygen to completely burn all of the fuel mixture.

Carbon monoxide (CO) also increases the rate

at which the photo chemical smog is formed by speeding up the conversion of nitric oxide (NO) to nitrogen dioxide (NO_2). To accomplish this, carbon monoxide (CO) combines with oxygen (O_2) and nitrogen dioxide (NO_2) to produce carbon dioxide (CO_2) and nitrogen dioxide (NO_2). ($CO + O_2 + NO = CO_2 + NO_2$).

The dangers of carbon monoxide, which is an odorless, colorless toxic gas are many. When carbon monoxide is inhaled into the lungs and passed into the blood stream, oxygen is replaced by the carbon monoxide in the red blood cells, causing a reduction in the amount of oxygen being supplied to the many parts of the body. This lack of oxygen causes headaches, lack of coordination, reduced mental alertness and should the carbon monoxide concentration be high enough, death could result.

NITROGEN

Normally, nitrogen is an inert gas. When heated to approximately 2500°F (1371°C) through the combustion process, this gas becomes active and causes an increase in the nitric oxide (NOx) emission.

Oxides of nitrogen (NOx) are composed of approximately 97–98% nitric oxide (NO2). Nitric oxide is a colorless gas but when it is passed into the atmosphere, it combines with oxygen and forms nitrogen dioxide (NO2). The nitrogen dioxide then combines with chemically active hydrocarbons (HC) and when in the presence of sunlight, causes the formation of photo chemical smog.

OZONE

To further complicate matters, some of the nitrogen dioxide (NO_2) is broken apart by the sunlight to form nitric oxide and oxygen. (NO_2 + sunlight = NO + O). This single atom of oxygen then combines with diatomic (meaning 2 atoms) oxygen (O_2) to form ozone (O_3). Ozone is 1 of the smells associated with smog. It has a pungent and offensive odor, irritates the eyes and lung tissues, affects the growth of plant life and causes rapid deterioration of rubber products. Ozone can be formed by sunlight as well as electrical discharge into the air.

The most common discharge area on the automobile engine is the secondary ignition electrical system, especially when inferior quality spark plug cables are used. As the surge of high voltage is routed through the secondary cable, the circuit builds up an electrical field around the wire, acting upon the oxygen in the surrounding air to form the ozone. The faint glow along the cable with the engine running that may be visible on a dark night, is called the "corona discharge." It is the result of the electrical field passing from a high along the cable, to a low in the surrounding air, which forms the ozone gas. The combination of corona and ozone has been a major cause of cable deterioration. Recently, different types and better quality insulating materials have lengthened the life of the electrical cables.

Although ozone at ground level can be harmful, ozone is beneficial to the earth's inhabitants. By having a concentrated ozone layer called the 'ozonosphere', between 10 and 20 miles (16–32km) up in the atmosphere much of the ultra violet radiation from the sun's rays are absorbed and screened. If this ozone layer were not present, much of the earth's surface would be burned, dried and unfit for human life.

There is much discussion concerning the ozone layer and its density. A feeling exists that this protective layer of ozone is slowly diminishing and corrective action must be directed to this problem. Much experimenting is presently being conducted to determine if a problem exists and if so, the short and long term effects of the problem and how it can be remedied.

OXIDES OF SULFUR

Oxides of sulfur (SOx) were initially ignored in the exhaust system emissions, since the sulfur content of gasoline as a fuel is less than $\frac{1}{10}$ of 1%. Because of this small amount, it was felt that it contributed very little to the overall pollution problem. However, because of the difficulty in solving the sulfur emissions in industrial pollutions and the introduction of catalytic converter to the automobile exhaust systems, a change was mandated. The automobile exhaust system, when equipped with a catalytic converter, changes the sulfur dioxide (SO_2) into the sulfur trioxide (SO_3).

When this combines with water vapors (H_2O), a sulfuric acid mist (H_2SO_4) is formed and is a very difficult pollutant to handle and is extremely corrosive. This sulfuric acid mist that is formed, is the same mist that rises from the vents of an automobile storage battery when an active chemical reaction takes place within the battery cells.

When a large concentration of vehicles equipped with catalytic converters are operating in an area, this acid mist will rise and be distributed over a large ground area causing land, plant, crop, paints and building damage.

PARTICULATE MATTER

A certain amount of particulate matter is present in the burning of any fuel, with carbon constituting the largest percentage of the particulates. In gasoline, the remaining percentage of particulates is the burned remains of the various other compounds used in its manufacture. When a gasoline engine is in good internal condition, the particulate emissions are low but as the engine wears internally, the particulate emissions increase. By visually inspecting the tail pipe emissions, a determination can be made as to where an engine defect may exist. An engine with light gray smoke emitting from the tail pipe normally indicates an increase in the oil consumption through burning due to internal engine wear. Black smoke would indicate a defective fuel delivery system, causing the engine to operate in a rich mode. Regardless of the color of the smoke, the internal part of the engine or the fuel delivery system should be repaired to a "like new" condition to prevent excess particulate emissions.

Diesel and turbine engines emit a darkened plume of smoke from the exhaust system because of the type of fuel used. Emission control regulations are mandated for this type of emission and more stringent measures are being used to prevent excess emission of the particulate matter. Electronic components are being introduced to control the injection of the fuel at precisely the proper time of piston travel, to achieve the optimum in fuel ignition and fuel usage. Other particulate after-burning components are being tested to achieve a cleaner particular emission.

Good grades of engine lubricating oils should be used, meeting the manufacturers specification. "Cut-rate" oils can contribute to the particulate emission problem because of their low "flash" or ignition temperature point. Such oils burn prematurely during the combustion process causing emissions of particulate matter.

The cooling system is an important factor in the reduction of particulate matter. With the cooling system operating at a temperature specified by the manufacturer, the optimum of combustion will occur. The cooling system must be maintained in the same manner as the engine oiling system, as each system is required to perform properly in order for the engine to operate efficiently for a long time.

Other Automobile Emission Sources

Before emission controls were mandated on the internal combustion engines, other sources of engine pollutants were discovered, along with the exhaust emission. It was determined the engine combustion exhaust produced 60% of the total emission pollutants, fuel evaporation from the fuel tank and carburetor vents produced 20%, with the another 20% being produced through the crankcase as a by-product of the combustion process.

CRANKCASE EMISSIONS

Crankcase emissions are made up of water, acids, unburned fuel, oil fumes and particulates. The emissions are classified as hydrocarbons (HC) and are formed by the small amount of unburned, compressed air/fuel mixture entering the crankcase from the combustion area during the compression and power strokes, between the cylinder walls and piston rings. The head of the compression and combustion help to form the remaining crankcase emissions.

Since the first engines, crankcase emissions were allowed to go into the air through a road draft tube, mounted on the lower side of the engine block. Fresh air came in through an open oil filler cap or breather. The air passed through the crankcase mixing with blow-by gases. The motion of the vehicle and the air blowing past the open end of the road draft tube caused a low pressure area at the end of the tube. Crankcase emissions were simply drawn out of the road draft tube into the air.

To control the crankcase emission, the road draft tube was deleted. A hose and/or tubing was routed from the crankcase to the intake manifold so the blow-by emission could be burned with the air/fuel mixture. However, it was found that intake manifold vacuum, used to draw the crankcase emissions into the manifold, would vary in strength at the wrong time and not allow the proper emission flow. A regulating type valve was needed to control the flow of air through the crankcase.

Testing, showed the removal of the blow-by gases from the crankcase as quickly as possible, was most important to the longevity of the engine. Should large accumulations of blow-by gases remain and condense, dilution of the engine oil would occur to form water, soots, resins, acids and lead salts, resulting in the formation of sludge and varnishes. This condensation of the blow-by gases occur more frequently on vehicles used in numerous starting and stopping conditions, excessive idling and when the engine is not allowed to attain normal operating temperature through short runs. The crankcase purge control or PCV system will be described in detail later in this section.

FUEL EVAPORATIVE EMISSIONS

Gasoline fuel is a major source of pollution, before and after it is burned in the automobile engine. From the time the fuel is refined, stored, pumped and transported, again stored until it is pumped into the fuel tank of the vehicle, the gasoline gives off unburned hydrocarbons (HC) into the atmosphere. Through redesigning of the storage areas and venting systems, the pollution factor has been diminished but not eliminated, from the refinery standpoint. However, the automobile still remained the primary source of vaporized, unburned hydrocarbon (HC) emissions.

Fuel pumped form an underground storage tank is cool but when exposed to a warner ambient temperature, will expand. Before controls were mandated, an owner would fill the fuel tank with fuel from an underground storage tank and park the vehicle for some time in warm area, such as a parking lot. As the fuel would warm, it would expand and should no provisions or area be provided for the expansion, the fuel would spill out the filler neck and onto the ground, causing hydrocarbon (HC) pollution and creating a severe fire hazard. To correct this condition, the vehicle manufacturers added overflow plumbing and/or gasoline tanks with built in expansion areas or domes.

However, this did not control the fuel vapor emission from the fuel tank and the carburetor bowl. It was determined that most of the fuel evaporation occurred when the vehicle was stationary and the engine not operating. Most vehicles carry 5–25 gallons (19–95 liters) of gasoline. Should a large concentration of vehicles be parked in one area, such as a large parking lot, excessive fuel vapor emissions would take place, increasing as the temperature increases.

To prevent the vapor emission from escaping into the atmosphere, the fuel system is designed to trap the fuel vapors while the vehicle is stationary, by sealing the fuel system from the atmosphere. A storage system is used to collect and hold the fuel vapors from the carburetor and the fuel tank when the engine is not operating. When the engine is started, the storage system is then purged of the fuel vapors, which are drawn into the engine and burned with the air/fuel mixture.

The components of the fuel evaporative system will be described in detail later in this section.

EMISSION CONTROLS

Positive Crankcase Ventilation System

➧ SEE FIGS. 1–3

OPERATION

The Positive Crankcase Ventilation (PCV) system is used on all vehicles to evacuate the crankcase vapors. Fresh air from the air cleaner or intake duct is supplied to the crankcase, mixed with blow-by gases and then passed through a Positive Crankcase Ventilation valve into the intake manifold (2.5L) or the Air Plenum (V6 engines).

When manifold vacuum is high, such as at idle, the orifice or valve restricts the flow of blow-by gases allowed into the manifold. If abnormal operating conditions occur, the system will allow excessive blow-by gases to back flow through the hose into the air cleaner. These blow-by gases will then be mixed with the intake air in the air cleaner instead of in the manifold. The air cleaner has a small filter attached to the inside wall that connects to the breather hose to trap impurities flowing in either direction.

A plugged PCV valve, orifice or hose may cause rough idle, stalling or slow idle speed, oil

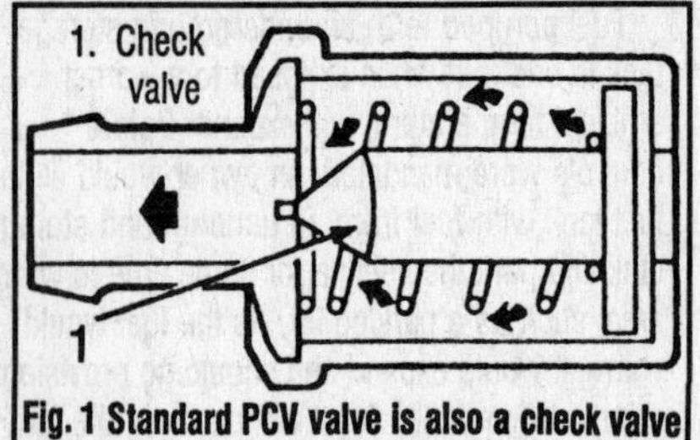

Fig. 1 Standard PCV valve is also a check valve

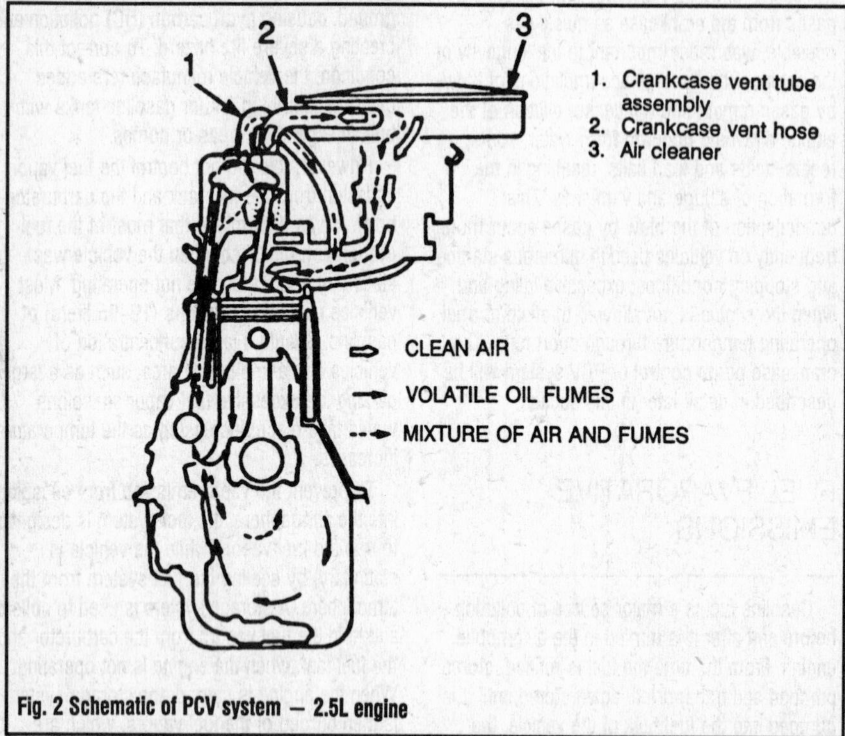

Fig. 2 Schematic of PCV system — 2.5L engine

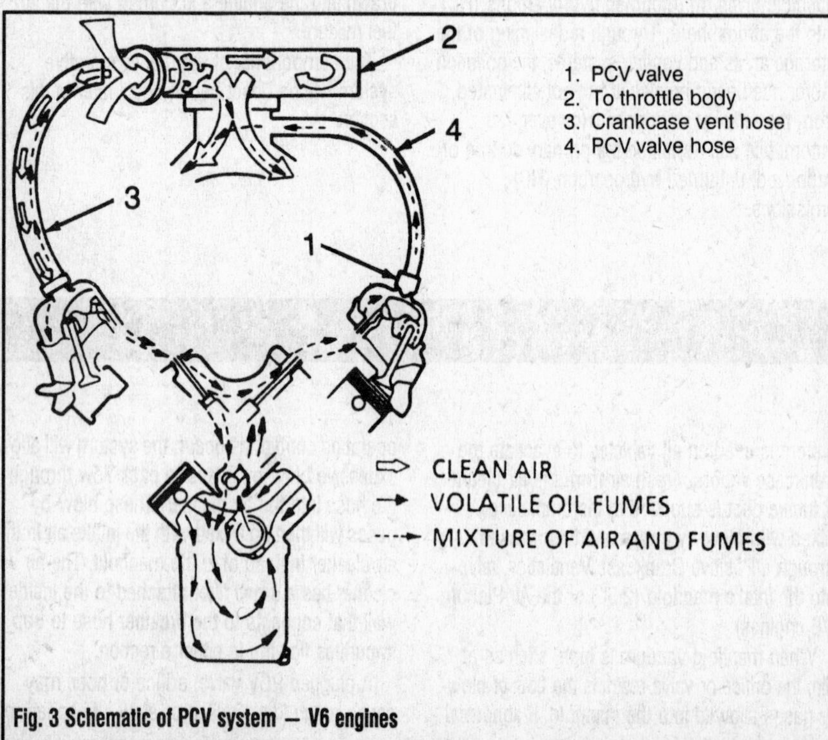

Fig. 3 Schematic of PCV system — V6 engines

leaks, oil in the air cleaner or sludge in the engine. A leak could cause rough idle, stalling or high idle speed. The condition of the grommets in the valve cover will also affect system and engine performance.

TESTING

PCV VALVE

1. Remove the PCV valve from the rocker arm cover.
2. With the engine at normal operating temperature, run at idle.
3. Remove the PCV valve or orifice from the grommet in the valve cover and place thumb over the end to check if vacuum is present. If vacuum is not present, check for plugged hoses or manifold port. Repair or replace as necessary.
4. If the engine is equipped with a PCV valve, stop the engine and remove the valve. Shake and listen for the rattle of the check valve needle. If no rattle is heard, replace the valve.

PCV SYSTEM

1. Check to make sure the engine has the correct PCV valve or bleed orifice.
2. Start the engine and bring to normal operating temperature.
3. Block off PCV system fresh air intake passage.
4. Remove the engine oil dipstick and install a vacuum gauge on the dipstick tube.
5. Run the engine at 1500 rpm for 30 seconds then read the vacuum gauge with the engine at 1500 rpm.

- If vacuum is present, the PCV system is functioning properly.
- If there is no vacuum, the engine may not be sealed and/or is drawing in outside air. Check the grommets and valve cover or oil pan gasket for leaks.
- If the vacuum gauge registers a pressure or the vacuum gauge is pushed out of the dipstick tube, check for the correct PCV valve or bleed orifice, a plugged hose or excessive engine blow-by.

Fuel Evaporative Emission Control System

➧ SEE FIGS. 4 AND 5

OPERATION

The Evaporative Emission Control System is designed to prevent fuel tank vapors from being emitted into the atmosphere. When the engine is not running, gasoline vapors from the tank are stored in a charcoal canister, mounted under the hood. The charcoal canister absorbs the gasoline vapors and stores them until certain engine conditions are met and the vapors can be purged and burned by the engine. In some vehicles with fuel injection, any liquid fuel entering the canister goes into a reservoir in the bottom of the canister to protect the integrity of the carbon element in the canister above. Three different methods are used to control the purge cycle of the charcoal canister.

First, the charcoal canister purge cycle is controlled by throttle position without the use of a valve on the canister. A vacuum line connects the canister to a ported vacuum source on the throttle body. When the throttle is at any position above idle, fresh air is drawn into the bottom of the canister and the fuel vapors are carried into the throttle body at that port. The air/vapor flow volume is only what can be drawn through the vacuum port and is fairly constant.

Second, the flow volume is modulated with throttle position through a vacuum valve. The ported vacuum from the throttle body is used to open a diaphragm valve on top of the canister. When the valve is open, air and vapors are drawn into the intake manifold, usually through the same manifold port as the PCV system. With this method, the purge valve cycle is slaved to the throttle opening; more throttle opening, more purge air flow.

And third, the charcoal canister purge valve cycle is controlled by the ECM through a solenoid valve on the canister. When the solenoid is activated, full manifold vacuum is applied to the top of the purge valve diaphragm to open the valve all the way. A high volume of fresh air is drawn into the canister and the gasoline vapors are purged quickly. The ECM

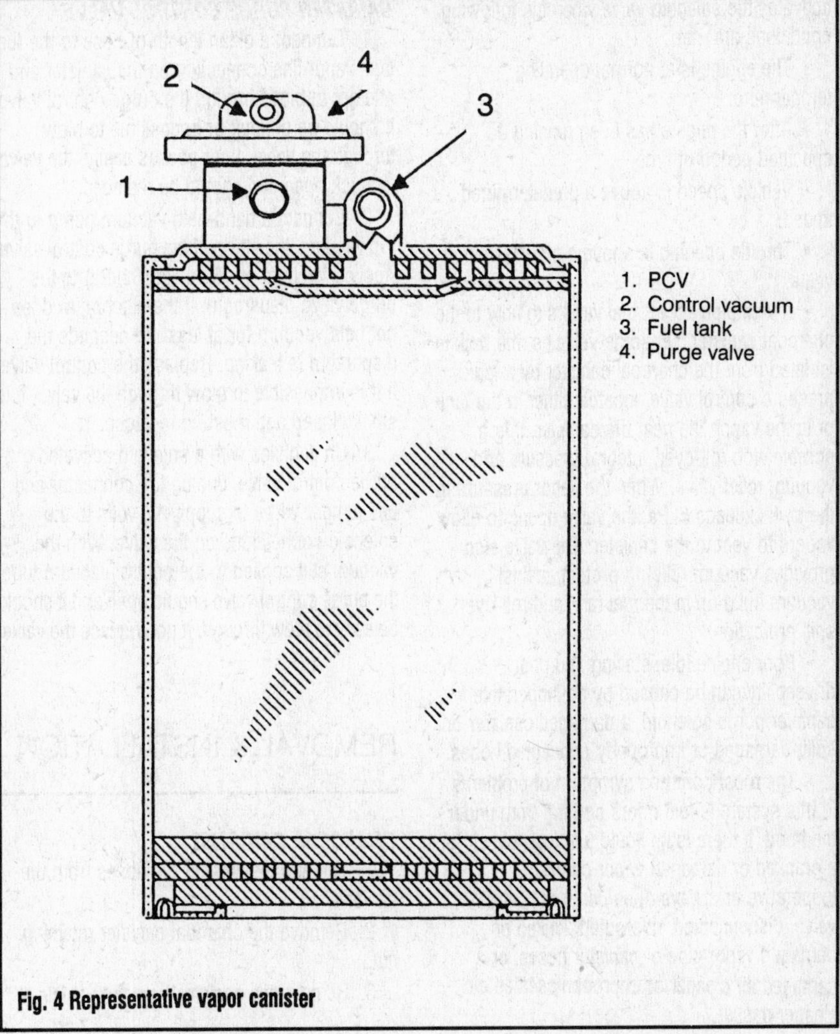

Fig. 4 Representative vapor canister

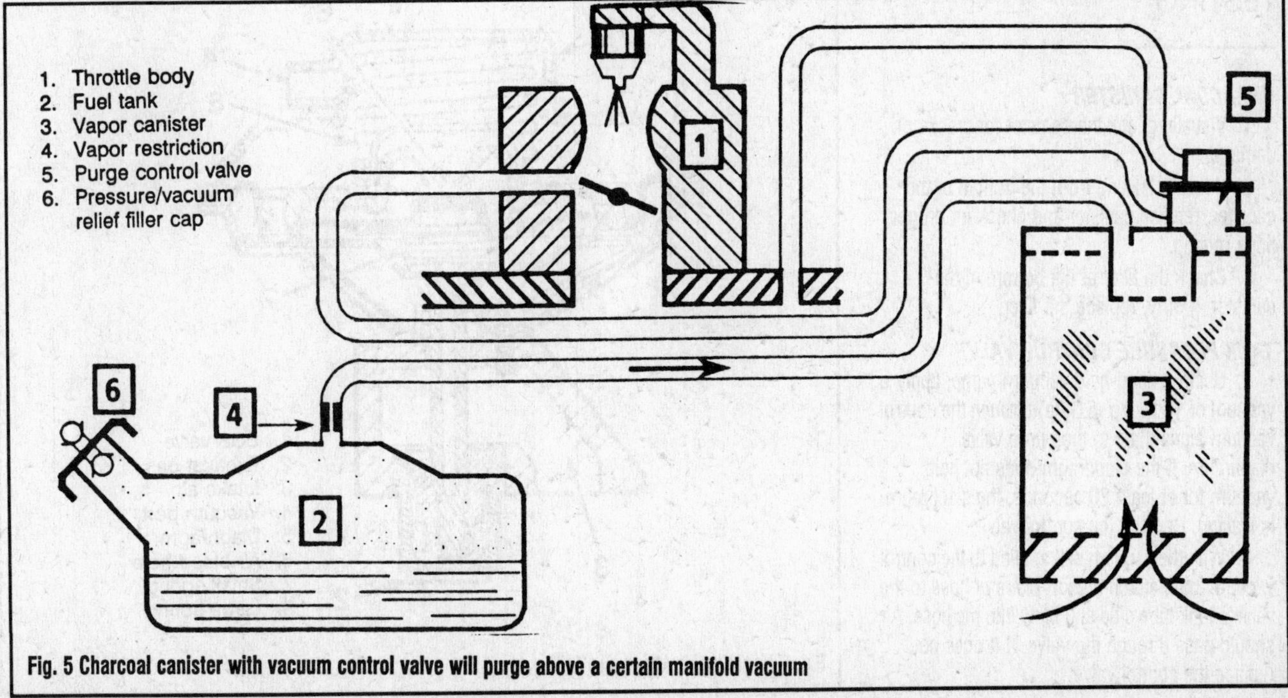

Fig. 5 Charcoal canister with vacuum control valve will purge above a certain manifold vacuum

activates the solenoid valve when the following conditions are met:

• The engine is at normal operating temperature.

• After the engine has been running a specified period of time.

• Vehicle speed is above a predetermined speed.

• Throttle opening is above a predetermined value.

• A vent pipe allows fuel vapors to flow to the charcoal canister. On some vehicles, the tank is isolated from the charcoal canister by a tank pressure control valve, located either in the tank or in the vapor line near the canister. It is a combination roll-over, integral pressure and vacuum relief valve. When the vapor pressure in the tank exceeds 5kPa, the valve opens to allow vapors to vent to the canister. The valve also provides vacuum relief to protect against vacuum build-up in the fuel tank and roll-over spill protection.

• Poor engine idle, stalling and poor driveability can be caused by an inoperative canister purge solenoid, a damaged canister or split, damaged or improperly connected hoses.

• The most common symptom of problems in this system is fuel odors coming from under the hood. If there is no liquid fuel leak, check for a cracked or damaged vapor canister, inoperative or always open canister control valve, disconnected, misrouted, kinked or damaged vapor pipe or canister hoses; or a damaged air cleaner or improperly seated air cleaner gasket.

TESTING

CHARCOAL CANISTER

1. Visually check the canister for cracks or damage.
2. If fuel is leaking from the bottom of the canister, replace canister and check for proper hose routing.
3. Check the filter at the bottom of the canister. If dirty, replace the filter.

TANK PRESSURE CONTROL VALVE

1. Using a hand-held vacuum pump, apply a vacuum of 15 in. Hg (51kPa) through the control vacuum signal tube to the purge valve diaphragm. If the diaphragm does not hold vacuum for at least 20 seconds, the diaphragm is leaking. Replace the control valve.
2. With the vacuum still applied to the control vacuum tube, attach a short piece of hose to the valve's tank tube side and blow into the hose. Air should pass through the valve. If it does not, replace the control valve.

CANISTER PURGE CONTROL VALVE

1. Connect a clean length of hose to the fuel tank vapor line connection on the canister and attempt to blow through the purge control valve. It should be difficult or impossible to blow through the valve. If air passes easily, the valve is stuck open and should be replaced.
2. Connect a hand-held vacuum pump to the top vacuum line fitting of the purge control valve. Apply a vacuum of 15 in. Hg (51kPa) to the purge valve diaphragm. If the diaphragm does not hold vacuum for at least 20 seconds the diaphragm is leaking. Replace the control valve. If it is impossible to blow through the valve, it is stuck closed and must be replaced.
3. On vehicles with a solenoid activated purge control valve, unplug the connector and use jumper wires to supply 12 volts to the solenoid connections on the valve. With the vacuum still applied to the control vacuum tube, the purge control valve should open and it should be easy to blow through. If not, replace the valve.

REMOVAL & INSTALLATION

CHARCOAL CANISTER

1. Tag and disconnect the hoses from the canister.
2. Remove the charcoal canister retaining nut.
3. Remove the canister from the vehicle.
4. Installation is the reverse of the removal procedure. Torque the retainers to 25 inch lbs. (2.8 Nm). Refer to the Vehicle Emission Control Information label, located in the engine compartment, for proper routing of the vacuum hoses.

TANK PRESSURE CONTROL VALVE

1. Disconnect the hoses from the control valve.
2. Remove the mounting hardware.
3. Remove the control valve from the vehicle.
4. Installation is the reverse of the removal procedure. Refer to the Vehicle Emission Control Information label, located in the engine compartment, for proper routing of the vacuum hoses.

Exhaust Gas Recirculation System

➧ SEE FIGS. 6–13

OPERATION

The EGR system is used to reduce oxides of nitrogen (NOx) emission levels caused by high

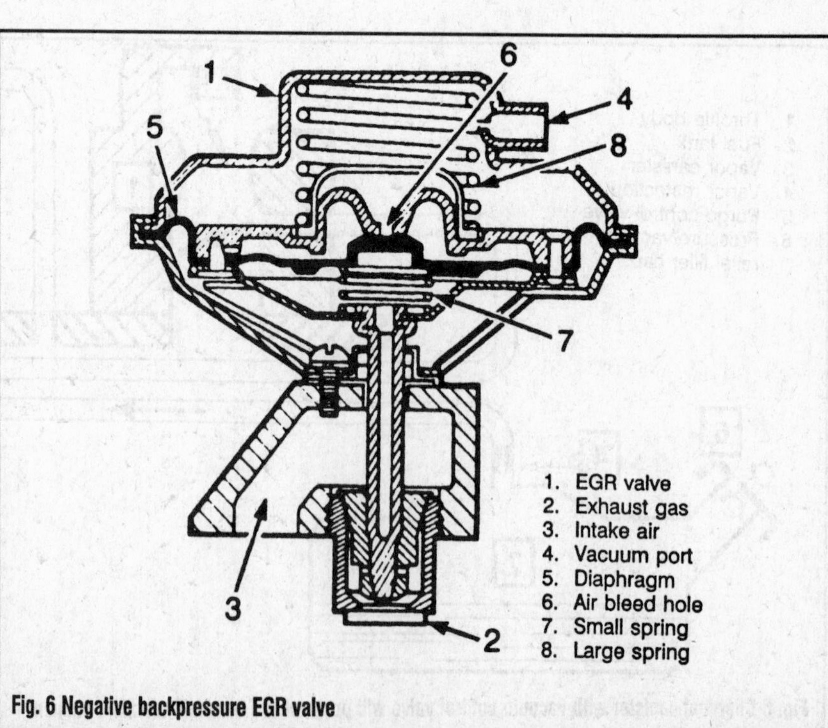

Fig. 6 Negative backpressure EGR valve

combustion chamber temperatures. This is accomplished by the use of an EGR valve which opens, under specific engine operating conditions, to admit a small amount of exhaust gas into the intake manifold, below the throttle plate. The exhaust gas mixes with the incoming air charge and displaces a portion of the oxygen in the air/fuel mixture entering the combustion chamber. The exhaust gas does not support combustion of the air/fuel mixture but it takes up volume, the net effect of which is to lower the temperature of the combustion process. This lower temperature also helps control detonation. **The 2.3L (VIN A) and 3.8L engines do not use an EGR valve.**

The EGR valve is a mounted on the intake manifold and has an opening into the exhaust manifold. Except for the Digital version, the EGR valve is opened by manifold vacuum to permit exhaust gas to flow into the intake manifold. With the Digital version, the EGR valve is purely electrical and uses solenoid valves to open the flow passage. If too much exhaust gas enters, combustion will not occur. Because of this, very little exhaust gas is allowed to pass through the valve. The EGR system will be activated once the engine reaches normal operating temperature and the EGR valve will open when engine operating conditions are above idle speed and below Wide Open Throttle (WOT). On California vehicles equipped with a Vehicle Speed Sensor (VSS), the EGR valve opens when the VSS signal is greater than 2 mph. The EGR system is deactivated on vehicles equipped with a Transmission Converter Clutch (TCC) when the TCC is engaged.

Too much EGR flow at idle, cruise, or during cold operation may result in the engine stalling after cold start, the engine stalling at idle after deceleration, vehicle surge during cruise and rough idle. If the EGR valve is always open, the vehicle may not idle. Too little or no EGR flow allows combustion temperatures to get too high which could result in spark knock (detonation), engine overheating and/or emission test failure.

There are three basic types of systems as described below, differing in the way EGR flow is modulated.

NEGATIVE BACKPRESSURE EGR VALVE

The negative backpressure EGR valve, used on the 2.5L engine, varies the amount of exhaust gas flow into the intake manifold depending on manifold vacuum and variations in exhaust backpressure. An air bleed valve, located inside the EGR valve assembly acts as a vacuum regulator. The bleed valve controls the amount of vacuum in the vacuum chamber by bleeding vacuum to outside air during the open phase of the cycle. The diaphragm on the valve has an internal air bleed hole which is held closed by a small spring when there is no exhaust backpressure. Engine vacuum opens the EGR valve against the pressure of a spring. When manifold vacuum combines with negative exhaust backpressure, the vacuum bleed hole opens and the EGR valve closes. This valve will open if vacuum is applied with the engine not running.

INTEGRATED ELECTRONIC EGR VALVE

The integrated electronic EGR valve, used on 1989 engines, functions like a port valve with a remote vacuum regulator, except the regulator and a pintle position sensor are sealed in the black plastic cover. The regulator and position sensor are not serviceable items; there is a serviceable filter that provides fresh air to the regulator, along side the vacuum tube.

This valve has a vacuum regulator, to which the ECM provides variable current. This current produces the desired EGR flow using inputs from the MAT and coolant temperature sensors and engine rpm.

DIGITAL EGR VALVE

The digital EGR valve, used on all 1990 and later EGR-equipped engines except 2.5L, is designed to control the flow of EGR independent of intake manifold vacuum. The valve controls EGR flow through 3 solenoid-opened orifices, which increase in size, to produce 7 possible combinations. When a solenoid is energized, the armature with attached shaft and swivel pintle, is lifted, opening the orifice.

The digital EGR valve is opened by the ECM, grounding each solenoid circuit individually. The flow of EGR is regulated by the ECM which uses information from the Coolant Temperature Sensor (CTS), Throttle Position Sensor (TPS) and Manifold Absolute Pressure (MAP) sensor to determine the appropriate rate of flow for a particular engine operating condition.

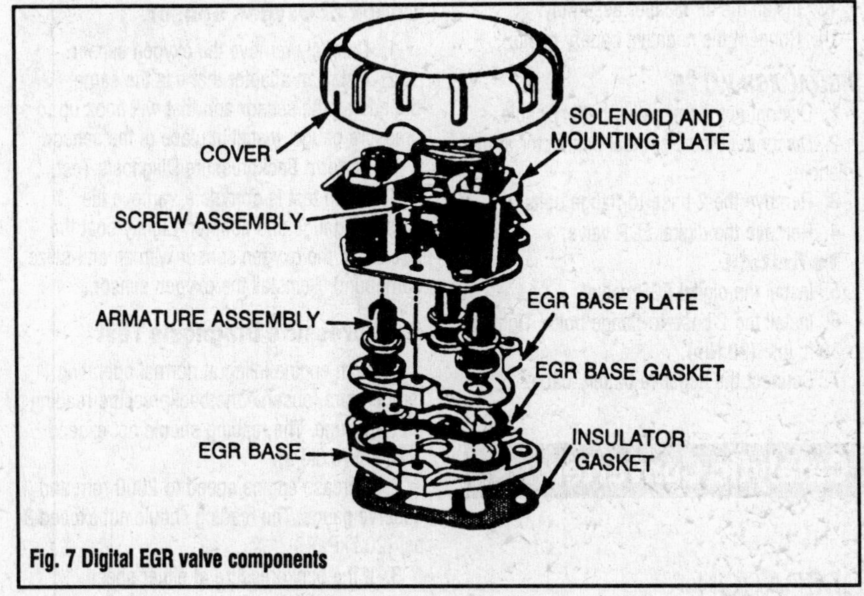

Fig. 7 Digital EGR valve components

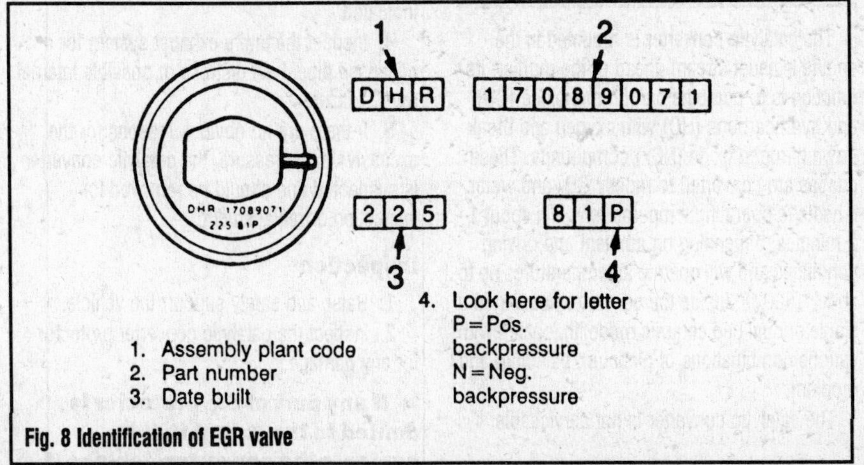

Fig. 8 Identification of EGR valve

TESTING

NEGATIVE BACKPRESSURE EGR VALVE

1. Inspect all passages and moving parts for plugging, sticking and deposits.
2. Inspect the entire system (hoses, tubes, connections, etc.) for leakage. Replace any part that is leaking, hardened, cracked, or melted.
3. Run the engine to normal operating temperature, and allow the engine to idle for 2 minutes. Quickly accelerate the engine to 2,500 rpm. Visible movement of the EGR stem should occur indicating proper system function. If no movement occurs, check the vacuum source and hose.
4. To determine if gas is flowing through the system, connect a vacuum pump to the valve.
5. With the engine idling, slowly apply vacuum. Engine speed should start to decrease when applied vacuum reaches 3 in. Hg. The engine speed may drop quickly and could even stall; this indicated proper function.
6. If engine speed does not drop off, remove the EGR valve and check for plugged passages. If everything checks out, replace the valve.

DIGITAL EGR VALVE

➡ This system must be checked using a Scan tool, or similar device. Steps 4, 5 and 6 must be done very quickly, as the ECM will adjust the idle air control valve to adjust idle speed.

1. Using a Scan tool or equivalent, check for trouble codes and solve those problems first, referring to appropriate chart elsewhere in this Section.
2. Using the Scan tool, select "EGR CONTROL."
3. Run the engine to normal operating temperature, and allow the engine to idle for 2 minutes.
4. Energize EGR SOL #1; engine rpm should drop slightly.
5. Energize EGR SOL #2; the engine should have a rough idle.
6. Energize EGR SOL #3; the engine should idle rough or stall.
7. If all tests were as specified, the system is functioning properly.
8. If not, check the EGR valve, pipe, adaptor, gaskets, fittings, and all passages for damage, leakage or plugging. If all is OK, replace the EGR valve assembly.

INTEGRATED ELECTRONIC EGR VALVE

To check this system, refer to Chart C-7 for 2.8L engines. This check is the same even if you have a 1989 car with a 3.1L engine.

REMOVAL & INSTALLATION

EXCEPT DIGITAL VERSION

1. Disconnect the negative battery cable.
2. Remove the air cleaner assembly.
3. Tag and disconnect the necessary hoses and wiring to gain access to the EGR valve.
4. Remove the EGR valve retaining bolts.
5. Remove the EGR valve. Discard the gasket.
6. Buff the exhaust deposits from the mounting surface and around the valve using a wire wheel.
7. Remove deposits from the valve outlet.
8. Clean the mounting surfaces of the intake manifold and valve assembly.

To install:

9. Install a new EGR gasket.
10. Install the EGR valve to the manifold.
11. Install the retaining bolts and torque to 16 ft. lbs. (22 Nm).
12. Connect the wiring and hoses.
13. Install the air cleaner assembly.
14. Connect the negative battery cable.

DIGITAL EGR VALVE

1. Disconnect the negative battery cable.
2. Disconnect the electrical connector at the solenoid.
3. Remove the 2 base-to-flange bolts.
4. Remove the digital EGR valve.

To install:

5. Install the digital EGR valve.
6. Install the 2 base-to-flange bolts. Tighten to 22 ft. lbs. (30 Nm).
7. Connect the negative battery cable.

Catalytic Converter

OPERATION

The catalytic converter is mounted in the engine exhaust stream ahead of the muffler. Its function is to combine carbon monoxide (CO) and hydrocarbons (HC) with oxygen and break down nitrogen oxide (NOx) compounds. These gasses are converted to mostly CO_2 and water. It heats to operating temperature within about 1–2 minutes, depending on ambient and driving conditions and will operate at temperatures up to about 1500 °F. Inside the converter housing is a single or dual bed ceramic monolith, coated with various combinations of platinum, paladium and rhodium.

The catalytic converter is not serviceable. If tests and visual inspection show the converter to be damaged, it must be replaced. There are 2 types of failures: melting or fracturing. The most common failure is melting, resulting from unburned gasoline contacting the monolith, such as when a cylinder does not fire. Usually when the monolith melts, high backpressure results. When it cracks, it begins to break up into small particles that get blown out the tail pipe.

Poor fuel mileage and/or a lack of power can often be traced to a melted or plugged catalytic converter. The damage may be the result of engine malfunction or the use of leaded gasoline in the vehicle. Proper diagnosis for a restricted exhaust system is essential before any components are replaced. The following procedure that can be used to determine if the exhaust system is restricted.

TESTING

Check at Oxygen Sensor

1. Carefully remove the oxygen sensor.
2. Install an adapter that has the same threads as the sensor and that will hook up to a pressure gauge. Install in place of the sensor.
3. Perform Backpressure Diagnosis Test.
4. When test is complete, remove the pressure gauge and adapter. Lightly coat the threads of the oxygen sensor with an anti-seize compound. Reinstall the oxygen sensor.

Backpressure Diagnosis Test

1. With engine idling at normal operating temperature, observe the backpressure reading on the gauge. The reading should not exceed 1.25 psi (8.6kPa).
2. Increase engine speed to 2000 rpm and observe gauge. The reading should not exceed 3 psi (20.7kPa).
3. If the backpressure at either speed exceeds specification, a restricted exhaust is indicated.
4. Inspect the entire exhaust system for a collapsed pipe, heat distress or possible internal muffler failure.
5. If there are no obvious reasons for the excessive backpressure, the catalytic converter is suspected and should be removed for inspection or replacement.

Inspection

1. Raise and safely support the vehicle.
2. Inspect the catalytic converter protector for any damage.

➡ If any part of the protector is dented to the extent that is contacts the converter, replace it.

3. Check the heat insulator for adequate clearance between the converter and the heat insulator. Repair or replace any damaged components.

REMOVAL & INSTALLATION

1. Raise and safely support the vehicle.
2. Remove the retaining bolts at the front and the rear and remove the converter.
3. On units with a ceramic monolith, it should be possible to look into the end of the housing and see light through the other end. If it is melted enough to cause high exhaust backpressure, it will be obvious.
4. Installation is the reverse of the removal procedure. Lower the vehicle, start the engine and check for exhaust leaks.

Air Injection Reaction (AIR) System V6 with Manual Transaxle

➧ SEE FIG. 12

OPERATION

The Air Injection Reaction (AIR) system is used to reduce carbon monoxide (CO), hydrocarbon (HC) and oxides of nitrogen (NOx) emissions. The system also heats up the catalytic converter on engine start-up so the exhaust gases will be converted more quickly.

The system consists of an air pump, belt driven off the crankshaft. The pump has an in line filter to remove any foreign material. The control valve regulates air from the pump to the check valve at the exhaust ports. A check valve prevents back flow of exhaust into the pump in the event of an exhaust backfire.

INSPECTION

1. Check the pump for a seized condition.
2. Check hoses, tubes, and connections for leaks and proper routing.
3. Check for air flow from control/divert valve.
4. Check the pump for proper mounting.
5. If no irregularities exist and the pump is noisy, replace the pump assembly.
6. Do not attempt to lubricate the pump.
7. Further diagnostics can be found in the Chart C-6, in the "Diagnostic Charts", portion of this Section.

1. Digital EGR valve
2. EGR gasket
3. Adapter
4. Adapter seal

Fig. 11 Digital EGR valve — 2.3L engine

AIR PUMP REMOVAL AND INSTALLATION

1. Disconnect the negative battery cable.
2. Hold the pump pulley from turning by compressing the drive belt, then loosen the pump pulley bolts.
3. Loosen the pump mounting bracket bolts and release the tension from the belt.
4. Move the belt out of the way.
5. Remove the hoses, vacuum and electrical connections from the pump.
6. Remove the pulley from the pump.
7. If required, insert needle nose pliers and pull the filter fan from the hub.
8. Install the air pump to the mounting brackets and torque bolts as shown in the illustration.
9. Install the hoses, vacuum and electrical connections to the pump.
10. Install the control valve.
11. Install a new filter fan onto the pump hub.
12. Install the spacer and pump pulley against the centrifugal filter fan.
13. Torque the pulley bolts to 10 ft. lbs. (13 Nm).

➡ The preceding procedure will compress the centrifugal filter fan onto the pump hole. Do NOT drive the filter fan on with a hammer. There might be a slight amount of interference with the housing bore, this is normal. After the new filter has been installed, it may squeal upon initial operation until the outside diameter sealing lip has worn in. This may require a short period of pump operation at various engine speeds.

14. Install the pump drive belt and adjust.
15. Reconnect the negative battery cable.
16. Start the engine and check for air injection system operation.

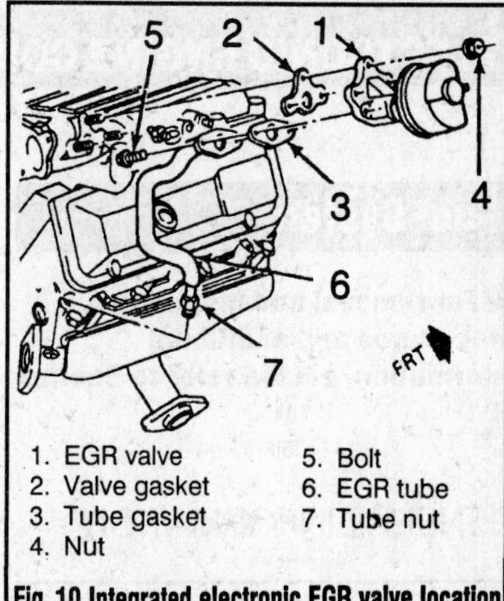

1. EGR valve
2. Valve gasket
3. Tube gasket
4. Nut
5. Bolt
6. EGR tube
7. Tube nut

Fig. 10 Integrated electronic EGR valve location

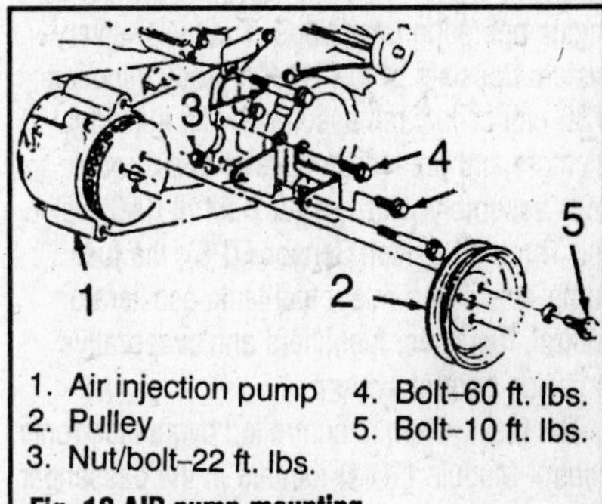

1. Air injection pump
2. Pulley
3. Nut/bolt-22 ft. lbs.
4. Bolt-60 ft. lbs.
5. Bolt-10 ft. lbs.

Fig. 12 AIR pump mounting

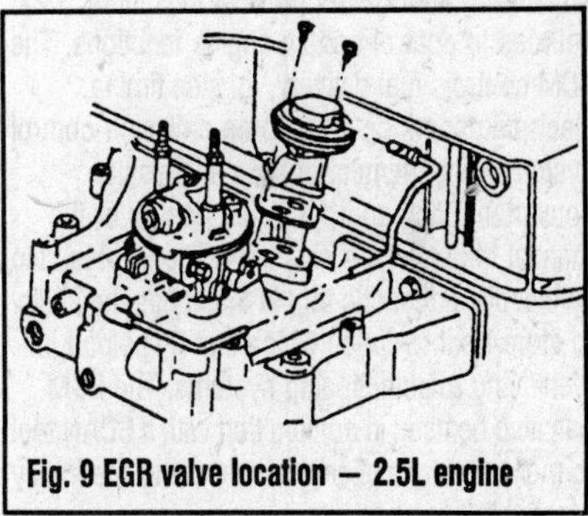

Fig. 9 EGR valve location — 2.5L engine

ELECTRONIC ENGINE CONTROLS

Fuel System

➡ **For removal and installation procedures and additional information, please refer to Section 5.**

GENERAL INFORMATION

The basic function of the fuel metering system is to control the delivery of fuel to the meet all engine operating conditions. The fuel delivery system consists of the Throttle Body Injection (TBI) unit or fuel rail assembly with individual injectors and pressure regulator and throttle body assembly with Idle Air Control (IAC) valve and Throttle Position Sensor (TPS); the fuel pump, fuel pump relay, fuel tank, accelerator control, fuel lines, fuel filters and evaporative emission control system.

The fuel system is controlled by an Electronic Control Module (ECM) located in the passenger compartment. The ECM is the control center of the computer command control system processing information from various input sources to control certain engine functions. The ECM controls fuel delivery, ignition timing, electronic spark control, some emission control systems, engagement of the transmission converter clutch and downshift control or the manual transmission shift light. The ECM is also a valuable diagnostic tool in that it has the ability to store trouble codes which can by helpful in identifying malfunctioning systems. The ECM can also be used in conjunction with a SCAN tool to monitor values of engine sensors to see if they are within specification.

The ECM operates in 2 running mode conditions: open and closed loop. When the engine is cold and engine rpm is above a specified value, the ECM ignores any signal it may be receiving from the oxygen sensor and stays in open loop. The ECM will go into closed loop when the following conditions are met: the oxygen sensor is sending a fluctuating signal to the ECM (indicating that it is hot enough to operate properly and respond to changes in the oxygen content in the exhaust gas), the engine is at normal operating temperature and a specific amount of time has elapsed since engine start. When operating in closed loop, the ECM varies the injector on-time in order to maintain the ideal stoichiometric ratio of 14.7:1. This mixture ratio provides optimum fuel economy and engine performance as well as minimizing exhaust emissions.

Fuel Injection System

OPERATION

The fuel injection system uses solenoid-operated fuel injector(s) mounted either on the throttle body (2.5L engine) or at the intake valve port of each cylinder (all other engines). The ECM controls the flow of fuel to the cylinders by varying the injector duty cycle or length of time the electrical solenoid is energized.

The TBI system uses model 700 fuel injector units. The model 700 unit, used on the 2.5L engine, consists of 2 major castings: the fuel meter assembly with pressure regulator and fuel injector and the throttle body with the IAC valve and TPS.

MPFI systems deliver fuel to the intake port of each cylinder by a fuel injector which is controlled by the ECM.

Coolant Temperature Sensor

OPERATION

Most engine functions are affected by the coolant temperature. Determining whether the engine is hot or cold is largely dependent on the temperature of the coolant. An accurate temperature signal to the ECM is supplied by the coolant temperature sensor. The coolant temperature sensor is a thermistor mounted in the engine coolant stream. A thermistor is an electrical device that varies its resistance in relation to changes in temperature. Low coolant temperature produces a high resistance (100,000Ω at –40°F/–40°C) and high coolant temperature produces low resistance (70Ω at 266°F/130°C). The ECM supplies a signal of 5 volts to the coolant temperature sensor through a resistor in the ECM and measures the voltage. The voltage will be high when the engine is cold and low when the engine is hot.

Fuel Filters

OPERATION

The inline fuel filter is a paper element filter designed to trap particles that may damage the fuel injection system. The filter element must be replaced periodically. The fuel system pressure must be relieved before opening the system to replace the filter.

Fuel Injector Assembly

➧ SEE FIG. 13

OPERATION

The fuel injector(s) are mounted on the fuel meter assembly or at the intake port of each cylinder. The fuel injector is a solenoid-operated device, controlled by the ECM. The ECM energizes the solenoid, which lifts a normally-closed ball valve off its seat. The fuel, which is under pressure, is injected in a conical spray pattern at the walls of the throttle body bore above the throttle valve. The amount of fuel sprayed is determined by the length of time the ECM energizes the injector solenoid, known as the pulse width.

The fuel which is not used by the injectors is cycled through the pressure regulator and back to the fuel tank; cycling the fuel helps prevent vapor lock.

Fuel Pressure Regulator

➧ SEE FIG. 14

OPERATION

The fuel pressure regulator keeps the fuel available to the injectors within a specified pressure range. The pressure regulator is a diaphragm-operated relief valve with fuel pump pressure on one side and air cleaner pressure in vehicles equipped with TBI or intake manifold vacuum in others, acting on the other side. On some engines, the pressure regulator and fuel rail are serviced as an assembly, and the regulator cannot be removed from the fuel rail.

Idle Air Control (IAC) Valve

➧ SEE FIG. 15

OPERATION

Engine idle speeds are controlled by the ECM through the IAC valve mounted on the throttle body. The ECM sends voltage pulses to the IAC motor windings causing the IAC motor shaft and pintle to move **IN** or **OUT** a given distance (number of steps) for each pulse (called counts). The movement of the pintle controls the airflow around the throttle plate, which in turn, controls engine idle speed. IAC valve pintle position counts can be observed using a Scan tool. Zero (0) counts correspond to a fully closed passage, while 140 counts or more correspond to full flow.

Idle speed can be categorized in 2 ways: actual (controlled) idle speed and minimum idle speed. Controlled idle speed is obtained by the ECM positioning the IAC valve pintle. Resulting idle speed is determined by total air flow (IAC/passage + PCV + throttle valve + calibrated vacuum leaks). Controlled idle speed is specified at normal operating conditions, which consists of engine coolant at normal operating temperature, air conditioning compressor **OFF**, manual transmission in neutral or automatic transmission in **D**.

Minimum idle air speed is set at the factory with a stop screw. This setting allows enough air flow by the throttle valves to cause the IAC valve pintle to be positioned a calibrated number of steps (counts) from the seat during normal controlled idle operation.

The idle speed is controlled by the ECM through the IAC valve. No adjustment is required during routine maintenance. Tampering with the minimum idle speed adjustment is highly discouraged and may result in premature failure of the IAC valve.

Manifold Absolute Pressure (MAP) Sensor

OPERATION

The MAP sensor measures the changes in intake manifold pressure, which result from engine load and speed changes and converts this information to a voltage output. The MAP sensor reading is the opposite of a vacuum gauge reading: when manifold pressure is high, MAP sensor value is high and vacuum is low. A MAP sensor will produce a low output on engine coast down with a closed throttle while a wide open throttle will produce a high output. The high output is produced because the pressure inside the manifold is the same as outside the manifold, so 100% of the outside air pressure is measured.

The MAP sensor is also used to measure barometric pressure under certain conditions,

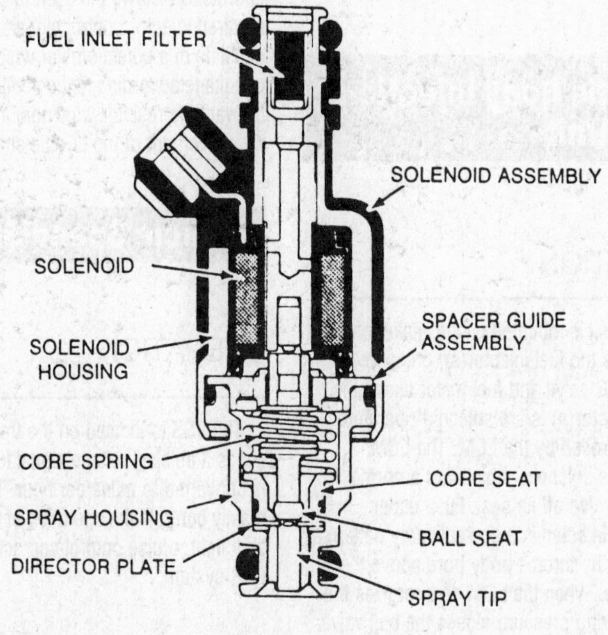

Fig. 13 Cutaway view of MPFI fuel injector assembly

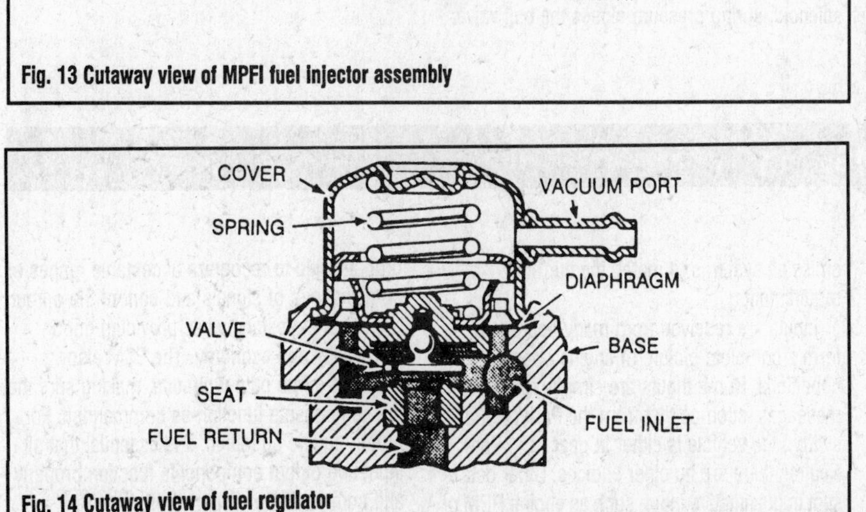

Fig. 14 Cutaway view of fuel regulator

1. Terminal pins
2. Ball bearing assembly
3. Stator assembly
4. Rotor assembly
5. Spring
6. Pintle
7. Lead screw

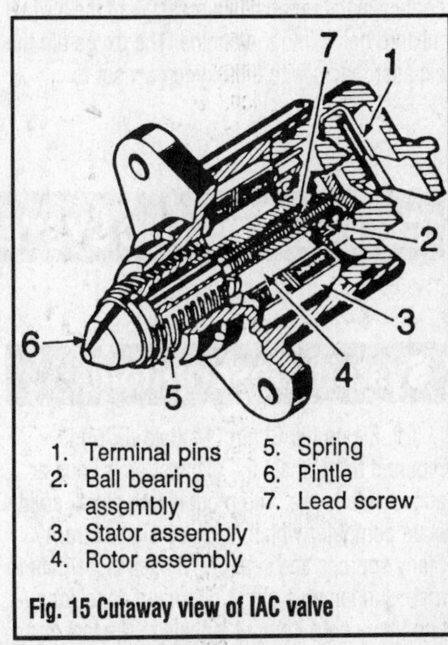

Fig. 15 Cutaway view of IAC valve

which allows the ECM to automatically adjust for different altitudes.

The MAP sensor changes the 5 volt signal supplied by the ECM, which reads the change and uses the information to control fuel delivery and ignition timing.

Manifold Air Temperature (MAT) Sensor

OPERATION

The MAT sensor is a thermistor which supplies manifold air temperature information to the ECM. The MAT sensor produces high resistance (100,000Ω at –40°F/–40°C) at low temperatures and low resistance of 70Ω at 266°F (130°C) at high temperatures. The ECM supplies a 5 volt signal to the MAT sensor and measures MAT sensor output voltage. The voltage signal will be high when the air is cold and low when the air is hot.

Oxygen Sensor

OPERATION

The exhaust oxygen sensor or O_2 sensor, is mounted in the exhaust stream where it monitors oxygen content in the exhaust gas. The oxygen content in the exhaust is a measure of the air/fuel mixture going into the engine. The oxygen in the exhaust reacts with the oxygen sensor to produce a voltage which is read by the ECM. The voltage output is very low, ranging from 0.1 volt in a high oxygen-lean mixture condition to 0.9 volt in a low oxygen-rich mixture condition.

Precautions:

- Careful handling of the oxygen sensor is essential.
- The electrical pigtail and connector are permanently attached and should not be removed from the oxygen sensor.
- The inline electrical connector and louvered end of the oxygen sensor must be kept free of grease, dirt and other contaminants.
- Avoid using cleaning solvents of any type on the oxygen sensor.
- Do not drop or roughly handle the oxygen sensor.
- The oxygen sensor may be difficult to remove if the engine temperature is below 120°F (48°C). Excessive force may damage the threads in the exhaust manifold or exhaust pipe.

Throttle Body Injection (TBI) Unit

OPERATION

The TBI unit is mounted on the intake manifold and contains the fuel injector(s), pressure regulator, IAC valve and fuel meter assembly. The fuel injector(s) is/are solenoid-operated device, controlled by the ECM. The ECM energizes the solenoid, which lifts a normally closed ball valve off its seat. Fuel, under pressure, is injected in a conical spray pattern at the walls of the throttle body bore above the throttle valve. When the ECM de-energizes the solenoid, spring pressure closes the ball valve. The amount of fuel sprayed is determined by the length of time the injector is energized (pulse width) which is controlled by the ECM. The longer the injector solenoid is energized (greater the pulse width), the more fuel is injected.

Throttle Position Sensor (TPS)

OPERATION

The TPS is mounted to the throttle body, opposite the throttle lever and is connected to the throttle shaft. Its function is to sense the current throttle valve position and relay that information to the ECM. Throttle position information allows the ECM to generate the required injector control signals. The TPS consists of a potentiometer which alters the flow of voltage according to the position of a wiper on the variable resistor windings, in proportion to the movement of the throttle shaft.

Vehicle Speed Sensor

OPERATION

The VSS is located on the transmission and sends a pulsing voltage signal to the ECM which is converted to miles per hour. This sensor mainly controls the operation of the TCC system, shift light, cruise control and activation of the EGR system.

SELF-DIAGNOSTIC SYSTEMS

System Description

The Electronic Control Module (ECM) is required to maintain the exhaust emissions at acceptable levels. The module is a small, solid state computer which receives signals from many sources and sensors; it uses these data to make judgements about operating conditions and then control output signals to the fuel and emission systems to match the current requirements.

Inputs are received from many sources to form a complete picture of engine operating conditions. Some inputs are simply Yes or No messages, such as that from the Park/Neutral switch; the vehicle is either in gear or in Park/Neutral; there are no other choices. Other data is sent in quantitative input, such as engine RPM or coolant temperature. The ECM is pre-programmed to recognize acceptable ranges or combinations of signals and control the outputs to control emissions while providing good driveability and economy. The ECM also monitors some output circuits, making sure that the components function as commanded. For proper engine operation, it is essential that all input and output components function properly and communicate properly with the ECM.

Since the control module is programmed to

recognize the presence and value of electrical inputs, it will also note the lack of a signal or a radical change in values. It will, for example, react to the loss of signal from the vehicle speed sensor or note that engine coolant temperature has risen beyond acceptable (programmed) limits. Once a fault is recognized, a numeric code is assigned and held in memory. The dashboard warning lamp — CHECK ENGINE or SERVICE ENGINE SOON — will illuminate to advise the operator that the system has detected a fault.

More than one code may be stored. Although not every engine uses every code, possible codes range from 12 to 100. Additionally, the same code may carry different meanings relative to each engine or engine family.

In the event of an ECM failure, the system will default to a pre-programmed set of values. These are compromise values which allow the engine to operate, although possibly at reduced efficiency. This is variously known as the default, limp-in or back-up mode. Driveability is almost always affected when the ECM enters this mode.

Learning Ability

The ECM can compensate for minor variations within the fuel system through the block learn and fuel integrator systems. The fuel integrator monitors the oxygen sensor output voltage, adding or subtracting fuel to drive the mixture rich or lean as needed to reach the ideal air fuel ratio of 14.7:1. The integrator values may be read with a scan tool; the display will range from 0–255 and should center on 128 if the oxygen sensor is seeing a 14.7:1 mixture.

The temporary nature of the integrator's control is expanded by the block learn function. The name is derived from the fact that the entire engine operating range (load vs. rpm) is divided into 16 sections or blocks. Within each memory block is stored the correct fuel delivery value for that combination of load and engine speed. Once the operating range enters a certain block, that stored value controls the fuel delivery unless the integrator steps in to change it. If changes are made by the integrator, the new value is memorized and stored within the block. As the block learn makes the correction, the integrator correction will be reduced until the integrator returns to 128; the block learn then controls the fuel delivery with the new value.

The next time the engine operates within the block's range, the new value will be used. The block learn data can also be read by a scan tool; the range is the same as the integrator and should also center on 128. In this way, the systems can compensate for engine wear, small air or vacuum leaks or reduced combustion.

Any time the battery is disconnected, the block learn values are lost and must be relearned by the ECM. This loss of corrected values may be noticed as a significant change in driveability. To reteach the system, make certain the engine is fully warmed up. Drive the vehicle at part throttle using moderate acceleration and idle until normal performance is felt.

Dashboard Warning Lamp

The primary function of the dash warning lamp is to advise the operator and that a fault has been detected, and, in most cases, a code stored. Under normal conditions, the dash warning lamp will illuminate when the ignition is turned **ON**. Once the engine is started and running, the ECM will perform a system check and extinguish the warning lamp if no fault is found.

Additionally, the dash warning lamp can be used to retrieve stored codes after the system is placed in the Diagnostic Mode. Codes are transmitted as a series of flashes with short or long pauses. When the system is placed in the Field Service Mode, the dash lamp will indicate open loop or closed loop function to the technician.

Intermittents

If a fault occurs intermittently, such as a loose connector pin breaking contact as the vehicle hits a bump, the ECM will note the fault as it occurs and energize the dash warning lamp. If the problem self-corrects, as with the terminal pin again making contact, the dash lamp will extinguish after 10 seconds but a code will remain stored in the ECM memory.

When an unexpected code appears during diagnostics, it may have been set during an intermittent failure that self-corrected; the codes are still useful in diagnosis and should not be discounted.

Tools and Equipment

SCAN TOOLS

Although stored codes may be read with only the use of a small jumper wire, the use of a hand-held scan tool such as GM's TECH 1 or equivalent is recommended. There are many manufacturers of these tools; a purchaser must be certain that the tool is proper for the intended use. If you own a Scan type tool, it probably came with comprehensive instructions on proper use. Be sure to follow the instructions that came with your unit if they differ from what is given here; this is a general guide with useful information included.

The scan tool allows any stored codes to be read from the ECM memory. The tool also allows the operator to view the data being sent to the ECM while the engine is running. This ability has obvious diagnostic advantages; the use of the scan tool is frequently required by the diagnostic charts. Use of the scan tool provides additional data but does not eliminate the need for use of the charts. The scan tool makes collecting information easier; the data must be correctly interpreted by an operator familiar with the system.

An example of the usefulness of the scan tool may be seen in the case of a temperature sensor which has changed its electrical characteristics. The ECM is reacting to an apparently warmer engine (causing a driveability problem), but the sensor's voltage has not changed enough to set a fault code. Connecting the scan tool, the voltage signal being sent to the ECM may be viewed; comparison to either a chart of normal values or a known good vehicle reveals the problem quickly.

The ECM is capable of communicating with a scan tool in 3 modes:

Normal or Open Mode

This mode is not applicable to all engines. When engaged, certain engine data can be observed on the scanner without affecting engine operating characteristics. The number of items readable in this mode varies with engine family. Most scan tools are designed to change automatically to the ALDL mode if this mode is not available.

ALDL Mode

Also referred to as the 10K or SPECIAL mode, the scanner will present all readable data as available. Certain operating characteristics of the engine are changed or controlled when this mode is engaged. The closed loop timers are bypassed, the spark (EST) is advanced and the PARK/NEUTRAL restriction is bypassed. If applicable, the IAC controls the engine speed to 1000 rpm ± 50, and, on some engines, the canister purge solenoid is energized.

Factory Test

Sometimes referred to as BACK-UP mode, this level of communication is primarily used during vehicle assembly and testing. This mode will confirm that the default or limp-in system is working properly within the ECM. Other data obtainable in this mode has little use in diagnosis.

➡ **A scan tool that is known to display faulty data should not be used for diagnosis. Although the fault may be believed to be in only one area, it can possibly affect**

many other areas during diagnosis, leading to errors and incorrect repair.

To properly read system values with a scan tool, the following conditions must be met. All normal values given in the charts will be based on these conditions:

- Engine running at idle, throttle closed
- Engine warm, upper radiator hose hot
- Vehicle in park or neutral
- System operating in closed loop
- All accessories **OFF**

ELECTRICAL TOOLS

The most commonly required electrical diagnostic tool is the Digital Multimeter, allowing voltage, ohmage (resistance) and amperage to be read by one instrument. The multimeter must be a high-impedance unit, with 10 megohms of impedance in the voltmeter. This type of meter will not place an additional load on the circuit it is testing; this is extremely important in low voltage circuits. The multimeter must be of high quality in all respects. It should be handled carefully and protected from impact or damage. Replace batteries frequently in the unit.

Other necessary tools include an unpowered test light, a quality tachometer with an inductive (clip-on) pick up, and the proper tools for releasing GM's Metri-Pack, Weather Pack and Micro-Pack terminals as necessary. The Micro-Pack connectors are used at the ECM connector. A vacuum pump/gauge may also be required for checking sensors, solenoids and valves.

Diagnosis and Testing

TROUBLESHOOTING

Diagnosis of a driveability and/or emissions problems requires attention to detail and following the diagnostic procedures in the correct order. Resist the temptation to perform any repairs before performing the preliminary diagnostic steps. In many cases this will shorten diagnostic time and often cure the problem without electronic testing.

The proper troubleshooting procedure for these vehicles is as follows:

Visual/Physical Underhood Inspection

This is possibly the most critical step of diagnosis. A detailed examination of connectors, wiring and vacuum hoses can often lead to a repair without further diagnosis. Performance of this step relies on the skill of the technician performing it; a careful inspector will check the undersides of hoses as well as the integrity of hard-to-reach hoses blocked by the air cleaner or other component. Wiring should be checked carefully for any sign of strain, burning, crimping, or terminal pull-out from a connector. Checking connectors at components or in harnesses is required; usually, pushing them together will reveal a loose fit.

Diagnostic Circuit Check

This step is used to check that the on-board diagnostic system is working correctly. A system which is faulty or shorted may not yield correct codes when placed in the Diagnostic Mode. Performing this test confirms that the diagnostic system is not failed and is able to communicate through the dash warning lamp.

If the diagnostic system is not operating correctly, or if a problem exists without the dash warning lamp being lit, refer to the specific vehicle's A-Charts. These charts cover such conditions as Engine Cranks but Will Not Run or No Service Engine Soon Light.

Reading Codes and Use of Scan Tool

➧ SEE FIG. 16

Once the integrity of the system is confirmed, enter the Diagnostic Mode and read any stored codes. To enter the diagnostic mode:

1. Turn the ignition switch **OFF**. Locate the Assembly Line Diagnostic Link (ALDL), usually under the instrument panel. It may be within a plastic cover or housing labeled DIAGNOSTIC CONNECTOR. This link is used to communicate with the ECM.
2. The code(s) stored in memory may be read either through the flashing of the dashboard warning lamp or through the use of a hand-held scan tool. If using the scan tool, connect it correctly to the ALDL.
3. If reading codes via the dash warning lamp, use a small jumper wire to connect Terminal B of the ALDL to Terminal A. As the ALDL connector is viewed from the front, Terminal A is on the extreme right of the upper row; Terminal B is second from the right on the upper row.
4. After the terminals are connected, turn the ignition switch to the **ON** position but do not start the engine. The dash warning lamp should begin to flash Code 12. The code will display as one flash, a pause and two flashes. Code 12 is not a fault code. It is used as a system acknowledgement or handshake code; its presence indicates that the ECM can communicate as requested. Code 12 is used to begin every diagnostic sequence. Some vehicles also use Code 12 after all diagnostic codes have been sent.
5. After Code 12 has been transmitted 3 times, the fault codes, if any, will each be transmitted 3 times. The codes are stored and transmitted in numeric order from lowest to highest.

➡ **The order of codes in the memory does not indicate the order of occurrence.**

6. If there are no codes stored, but a driveability or emissions problem is evident, refer to the Symptoms and Intermittents Chart for the specific fuel system.
7. If one or more codes are stored, record them. At the end of the procedure, refer to the applicable Diagnostic Code chart.
8. If no fault codes are transmitted, connect the scan tool (if not already connected). Use the scan functions to view the values being sent to the ECM. Compare the actual values to the typical or normal values for the engine.
9. Switch the ignition **OFF** when finished with code retrieval or scan tool readings.

F E D C B A
G M

TERMINAL IDENTIFICATION

A GROUND	E SERIAL DATA
B DIAGNOSTIC TERMINAL	F TCC (IF USED)
C A.I.R. (IF USED)	G FUEL PUMP (IF USED)
D SERVICE ENGINE SOON LIGHT (IF USED)	M SERIAL DATA (IF USED)

Fig. 16 ALDL connector terminal identification

Circuit/Component Diagnosis and Repair

Using the appropriate chart(s) based on the Diagnostic Circuit Check, the fault codes and the scan tool data will lead to diagnosis and checking of a particular circuit or component. It is important to note that the fault code indicates a fault or loss of signal in an ECM-controlled system, not necessarily in the specific component. Detailed procedures to isolate the problem are included in each code chart; these procedures must be followed accurately to insure timely and correct repair. Following the procedure will also insure that only truly faulty components are replaced.

DIAGNOSTIC MODE

The ECM may be placed into the diagnostic mode by turning the ignition switch from **OFF** to **ON**, then grounding ALDL Terminal B to Terminal A. When in the Diagnostic Mode, the ECM will:

- Display Code 12, indicating the system is operating correctly.
- Display any stored fault codes 3 times in succession.
- Energize all the relays controlled by the ECM except the fuel pump relay. This will allow the relays and circuits to be checked in the shop without recreating certain driving conditions.
- Move the IAC valve to its fully extended position, closing the idle air passage.

➡ **Due to increased battery draw, do not allow the vehicle to remain in the Diagnostic Mode for more than 30 minutes. If longer periods are necessary, connect a battery charger.**

FIELD SERVICE MODE

If ALDL terminal B is grounded to terminal A with the engine running, the system enters the Field Service Mode. In this mode, the dash warning lamp will indicate whether the system is operating in open loop or closed loop.

If working in open loop, the dash warning lamp will flash rapidly 2½ times per second. In closed loop, the flash rate slows to once per second. Additionally, if the system is running lean in closed loop, the lamp will be off most of the cycle. A rich condition in closed loop will cause the lamp to remain lit for most of the 1 second cycle.

When operating in the Field Service Mode, additional codes cannot be stored by the ECM. The closed loop timer is bypassed in this mode.

CLEARING THE TROUBLE CODES

Stored fault codes may be erased from memory at any time by removing power from the ECM for at least 30 seconds. It may be necessary to clear stored codes during diagnosis to check for any recurrence during a test drive, but the stored codes must be written down when retrieved. The codes may still be required for subsequent troubleshooting. Whenever a repair is complete, the stored codes must be erased and the vehicle test driven to confirm correct operation and repair.

➡ **The ignition switch must be OFF any time power is disconnected or restored to the ECM. Severe damage may result if this precaution is not observed.**

Depending on the electric distribution of the particular vehicle, power to the ECM may be disconnected by removing the ECM fuse in the fusebox, disconnecting the inline fuse holder near the positive battery terminal or disconnecting the ECM power lead at the battery terminal. Disconnecting the negative battery cable to clear codes is not recommended as this will also clear other memory data in the vehicle such as radio presets or seat memory.

DIAGNOSTIC CHARTS

➡ **Following are charts that should help solve most emission-related problems. When checking the system, codes may appear that are not covered here; they are probably not emission-related. For additional information on those codes, etc. please refer to Chilton's Guide to Fuel Injection and Electronic Engine Controls – 1988–1990 General Motors Cars and Trucks (Book No. 7954)** and/or **Chilton's Guide to Fuel Injection and Electronic Engine Controls – 1990–1992 General Motors Cars and Trucks (Book No. 8173).**

DIAGNOSTIC CHARTS — 2.8L engine

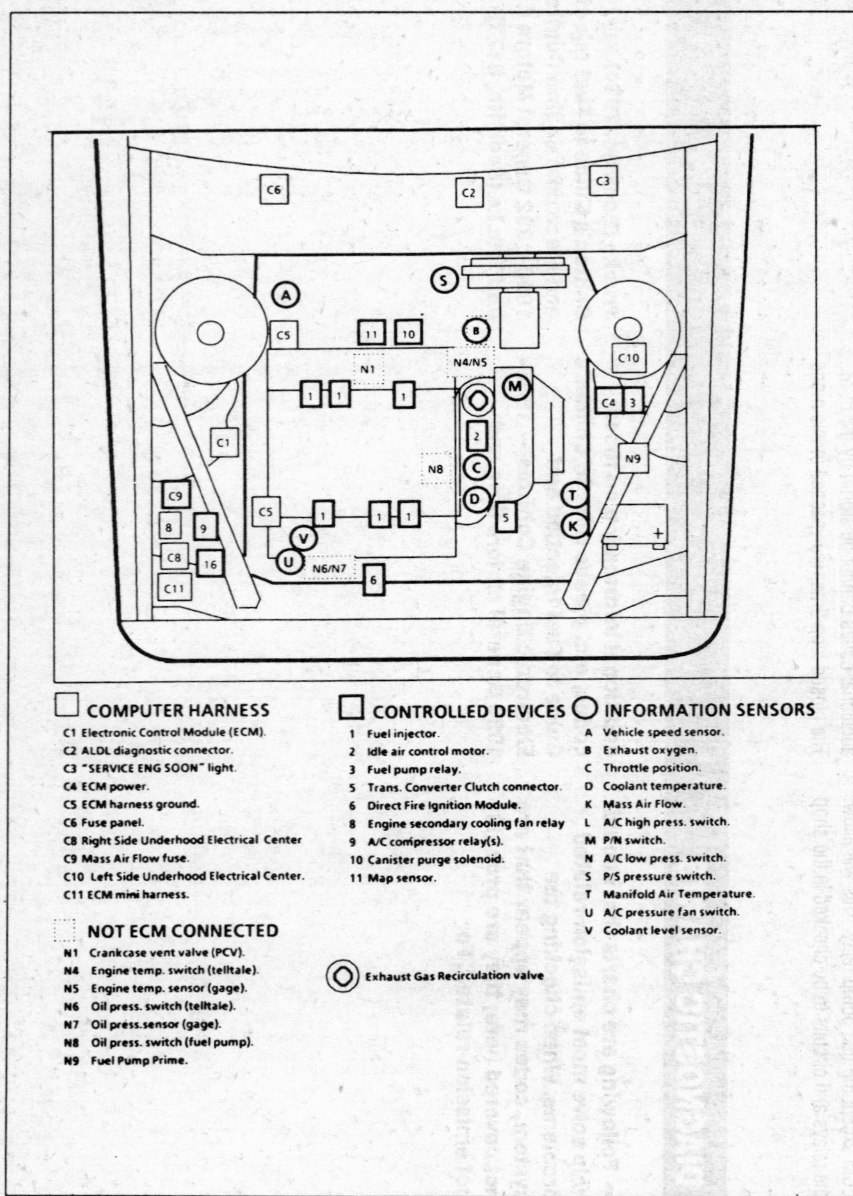

ECM
451 WHT/BLK — B3 DIAGNOSTIC TEST
450 BLK/WHT
F E D C B A M
ALDL CONNECTOR
461 ORN — B5 SERIAL DATA INPUT
AUTOMATIC TRANS. TORQUE CONVERTER CLUTCH SOLENOID
D B C A
422 TAN/BLK — B7 A/T TCC CONTROL
446 LT BLU — D22 4TH GEAR SIGNAL (IF APPLICABLE)
108 DK GRN — D6 3RD GEAR SIGNAL
P/N SWITCH (N.O.)
A B
434 ORN/BLK — D11 PARK/NEUTRAL SWITCH (A/T)
450 BLK
420 PPL
VEHICLE SPEED SENSOR (TRANS. MOUNTED)
B A
401 PPL — C2 VSS (INPUT)
400 YEL — C8 VSS (INPUT)
BRAKE SWITCH (N.C.)
10A
SES
CLUSTER MODULE
CL
419 BRN/WHT — B1 SERVICE ENGINE SOON LIGHT CONTROL
39 PNK/BLK
68 YEL/BLK — A13 COOLANT LIGHT CONTROL
389 DK GRN — B8 BUFFERED SPEED OUTPUT
IGN.
10A
839 PNK/BLK
CPC SOLENOID
C
428 DK GRN/YEL — A10 CANISTER PURGE CONTROL
BLK MINI HARNESS CONN
10A
639
D
EGR SOLENOID
GRY MINI HARNESS CONN
C
435 GRY/RED — A4 EXHAUST GAS RECIRCULATION CONTROL
EGR CONTROLLER AND POSITION FEEDBACK ASSEMBLY
A B E C
GRY MINI HARNESS CONN
D
416 GRY — C12 +5V REFERENCE
E
357 RED — C18 EGR POSITION SIGNAL
452 BLK — C5 SENSOR GROUND
MAP SENSOR
C B A
B
432 LT GRN — C22 MANIFOLD ABSOLUTE PRESSURE SENSOR SIGNAL
GRY MINI HARNESS CONN
COOLANT LEVEL SENSOR
A C B
416 GRY — C7 +5V REFERENCE
69 GRY/RED — C14 COOLANT LEVEL SENSOR SIGNAL
COOLANT TEMPERATURE SENSOR
A B
K
410 YEL — C16 COOLANT TEMP. SIGNAL
GRY MINI HARNESS CONN

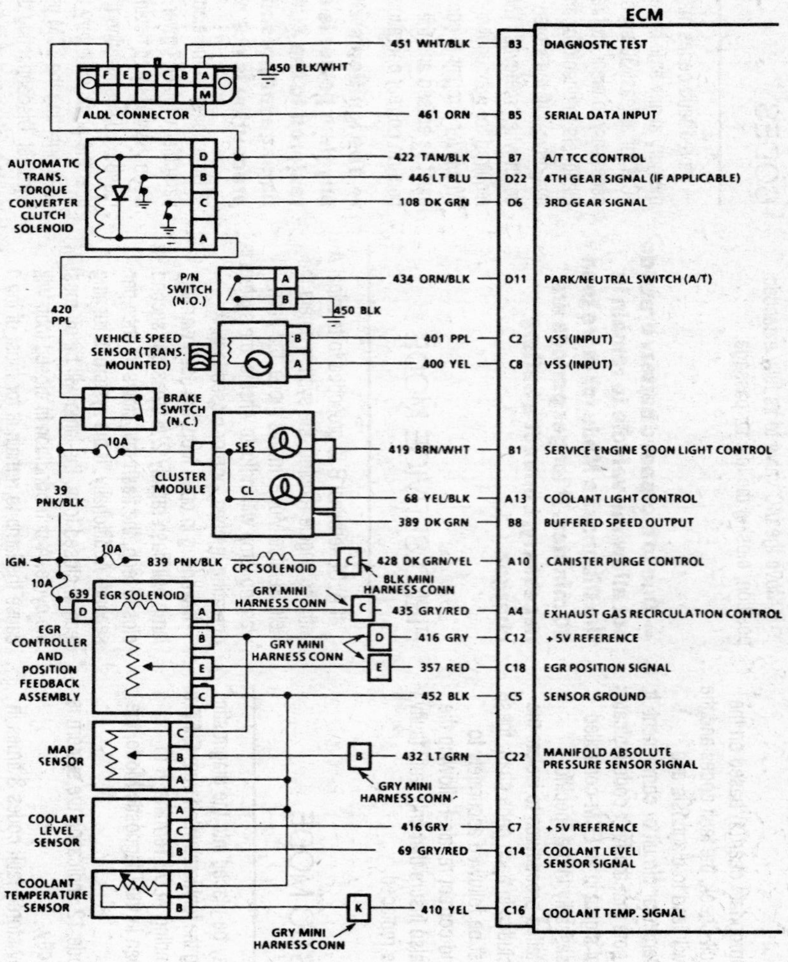

DIAGNOSTIC CHARTS — 2.8L engine

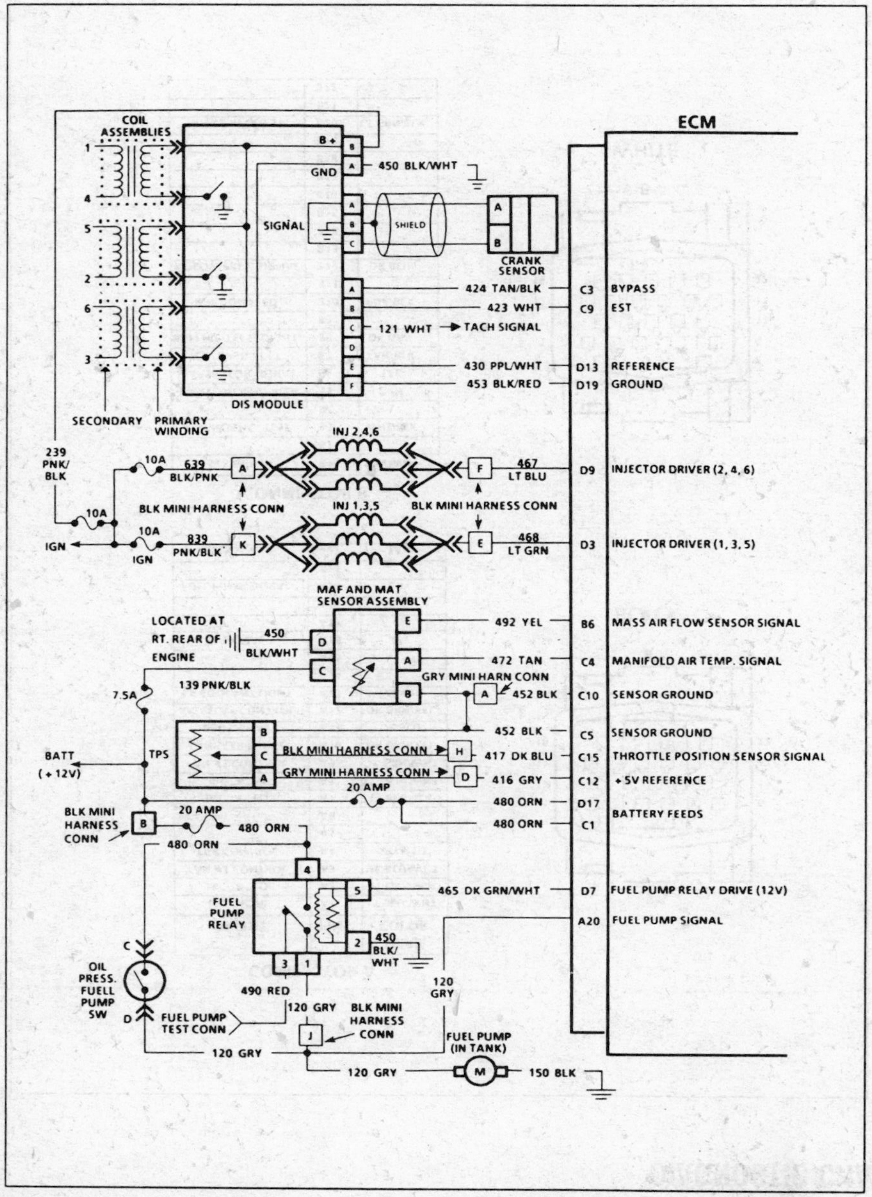

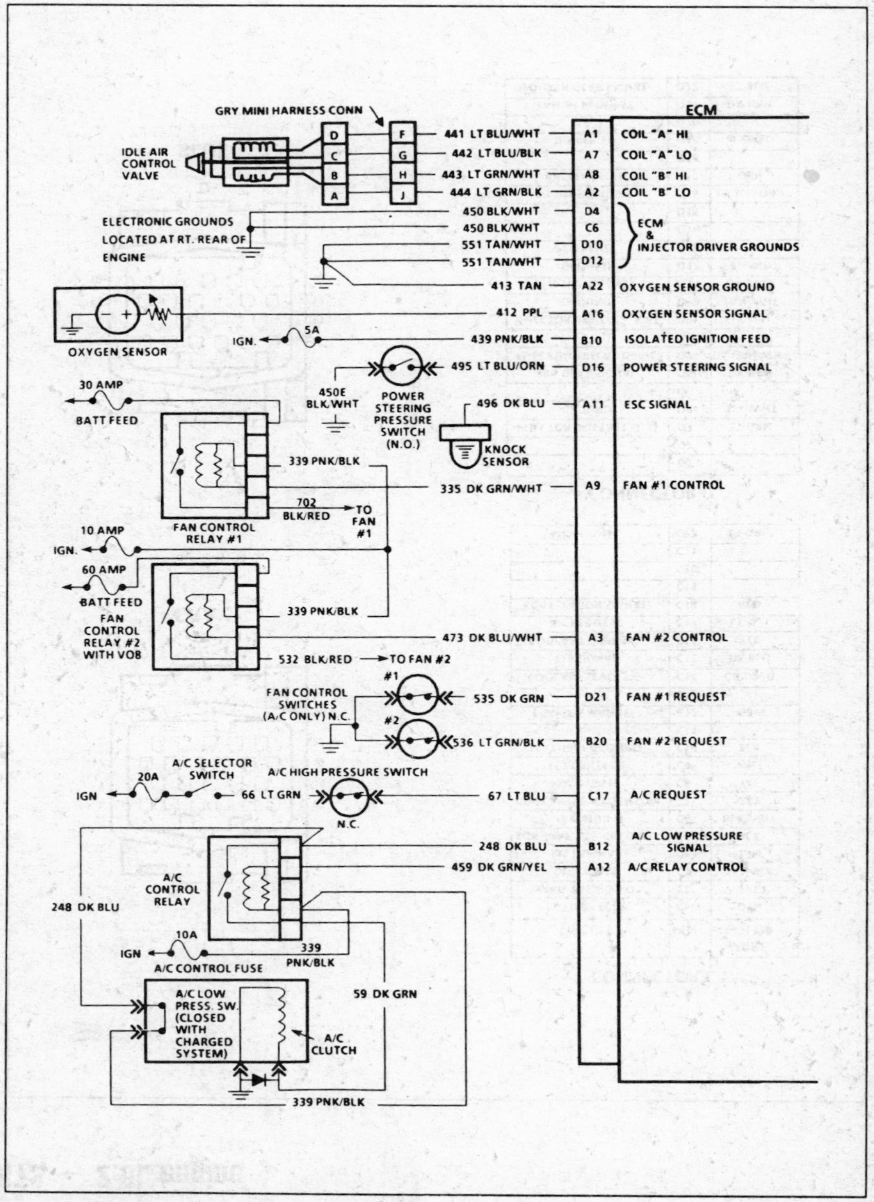

ECM

COIL ASSEMBLIES
1 4 5 2 6 3
SECONDARY
PRIMARY WINDING
DIS MODULE
B+ GND SIGNAL
450 BLK/WHT
SHIELD
CRANK SENSOR
424 TAN/BLK — C3 BYPASS
423 WHT — C9 EST
121 WHT → TACH SIGNAL
430 PPL/WHT — D13 REFERENCE
453 BLK/RED — D19 GROUND
239 PNK/BLK
10A 639 BLK/PNK
INJ 2,4,6
BLK MINI HARNESS CONN
467 LT BLU — D9 INJECTOR DRIVER (2, 4, 6)
INJ 1,3,5
10A IGN 839 PNK/BLK
468 LT GRN — D3 INJECTOR DRIVER (1, 3, 5)
MAF AND MAT SENSOR ASSEMBLY
LOCATED AT RT. REAR OF ENGINE 450 BLK/WHT
492 YEL — B6 MASS AIR FLOW SENSOR SIGNAL
472 TAN — C4 MANIFOLD AIR TEMP. SIGNAL
GRY MINI HARN CONN
452 BLK — C10 SENSOR GROUND
139 PNK/BLK
7.5A
452 BLK — C5 SENSOR GROUND
BATT (+12V)
TPS
BLK MINI HARNESS CONN 417 DK BLU — C15 THROTTLE POSITION SENSOR SIGNAL
GRY MINI HARNESS CONN 416 GRY — C12 +5V REFERENCE
20 AMP
480 ORN — D17
480 ORN — C1 BATTERY FEEDS
BLK MINI HARNESS CONN
20 AMP 480 ORN
480 ORN
FUEL PUMP RELAY
465 DK GRN/WHT — D7 FUEL PUMP RELAY DRIVE (12V)
A20 FUEL PUMP SIGNAL
450 BLK/WHT
120 GRY
OIL PRESS. FUELL PUMP SW
490 RED
120 GRY
BLK MINI HARNESS CONN
FUEL PUMP TEST CONN
120 GRY
FUEL PUMP (IN TANK)
120 GRY
150 BLK

ECM

GRY MINI HARNESS CONN
IDLE AIR CONTROL VALVE
441 LT BLU/WHT — A1 COIL "A" HI
442 LT BLU/BLK — A7 COIL "A" LO
443 LT GRN/WHT — A8 COIL "B" HI
444 LT GRN/BLK — A2 COIL "B" LO
ELECTRONIC GROUNDS LOCATED AT RT. REAR OF ENGINE
450 BLK/WHT — D4
450 BLK/WHT — C6
551 TAN/WHT — D10
551 TAN/WHT — D12
ECM & INJECTOR DRIVER GROUNDS
413 TAN — A22 OXYGEN SENSOR GROUND
OXYGEN SENSOR
412 PPL — A16 OXYGEN SENSOR SIGNAL
IGN. 5A
439 PNK/BLK — B10 ISOLATED IGNITION FEED
495 LT BLU/ORN — D16 POWER STEERING SIGNAL
30 AMP BATT FEED
450E BLK/WHT
POWER STEERING PRESSURE SWITCH (N.O.)
496 DK BLU — A11 ESC SIGNAL
KNOCK SENSOR
339 PNK/BLK
335 DK GRN/WHT — A9 FAN #1 CONTROL
FAN CONTROL RELAY #1
702 BLK/RED → TO FAN #1
10 AMP IGN.
60 AMP BATT FEED
FAN CONTROL RELAY #2 WITH VO8
339 PNK/BLK
473 DK BLU/WHT — A3 FAN #2 CONTROL
532 BLK/RED → TO FAN #2
FAN CONTROL SWITCHES (A/C ONLY) N.C.
#1 535 DK GRN — D21 FAN #1 REQUEST
#2 536 LT GRN/BLK — B20 FAN #2 REQUEST
A/C SELECTOR SWITCH
A/C HIGH PRESSURE SWITCH
IGN 20A 66 LT GRN
N.C.
67 LT BLU — C17 A/C REQUEST
248 DK BLU — B12 A/C LOW PRESSURE SIGNAL
459 DK GRN/YEL — A12 A/C RELAY CONTROL
A/C CONTROL RELAY
248 DK BLU
IGN 10A A/C CONTROL FUSE
339 PNK/BLK
59 DK GRN
A/C LOW PRESS. SW. (CLOSED WITH CHARGED SYSTEM)
A/C CLUTCH
339 PNK/BLK

DIAGNOSTIC CHARTS — 2.8L engine

CONNECTOR A

CIRCUIT	PIN	WIRE COLOR
IAC "A" HI	A1	LT BLU/WHT
IAC "B" LO	A2	LT GRN/BLK
FAN #2 CONTROL	A3	DK BLU/WHT
EGR CONTROL	A4	GRY/RED
	A5	
	A6	
IAC "A" LO	A7	LT BLU/BLK
IAC "B" HI	A8	LT GRN//WHT
FAN #1 CONTROL	A9	DK GRN/WHT
CANISTER PURGE	A10	DK GRN/YEL
ESC SIGNAL	A11	DK BLU
A/C RELAY CONTROL	A12	DK GRN/YEL
CK COOLANT LIGHT	A13	YEL/BLK
	A14	
	A15	
O_2 SIGNAL	A16	PPL
	A17	
	A19	
FUEL PUMP SIGNAL	A20	GRY
	A21	
O_2 SENSOR LO	A22	TAN

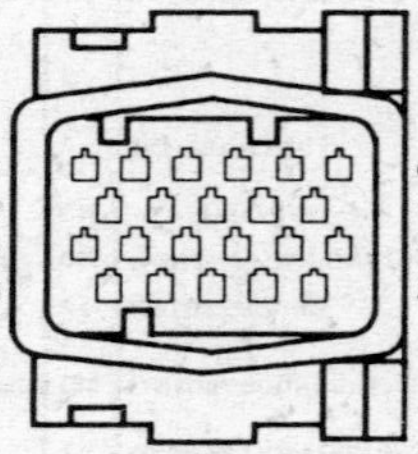

CONNECTOR B

CIRCUIT	PIN	WIRE COLOR
SES LIGHT	B1	BRN/WHT
	B2	
DIAGNOSTIC / TEST	B3	WHT/BLK
	B4	
SERIAL DATA IN / ALDL	B5	ORN
MAF SENSOR SIGNAL	B6	YEL
TCC / UPSHIFT LT.	B7	TAN/BLK
BUFFERED SPEED OUT.	B8	DK GRN
	B9	
IGNITION FEED	B10	PNK/BLK
	B11	
A/C LOW PRES. SIGNAL	B12	DK BLU
	B13	
	B14	
	B15	
	B16	
	B17	
	B18	
	B19	
FAN #2 REQUEST	B20	LT GRN/BLK
	B21	
	B22	

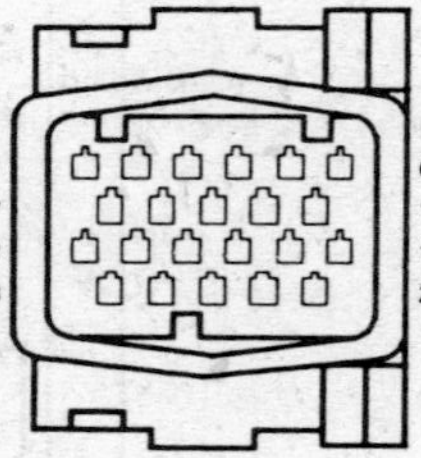

A BLACK

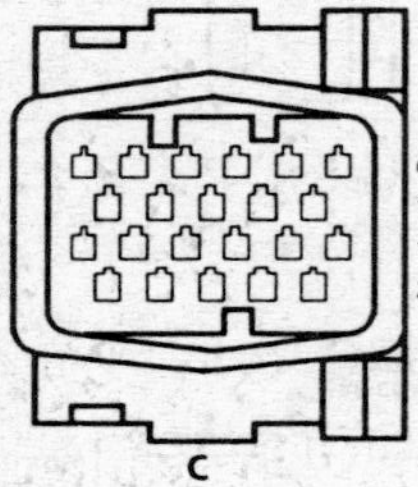

B WHITE

C GRAY

D BLUE

CONNECTOR C

CIRCUIT	PIN	WIRE COLOR
BATTERY FEED	C1	ORN
MAG. VSS SIG. LO	C2	PPL
DIS BYPASS	C3	TAN/BLK
MAT SIGNAL	C4	TAN
EGR, MAP, CTS, CLS GND.	C5	BLK
GROUND	C6	BLK/WHT
COOLANT LEVEL SENSOR	C7	GRY
MAG. VSS HI	C8	YEL
EST CONTROL	C9	WHT
MAT, MAF GROUND	C10	BLK
	C11	
EGR, TPS, MAP REF.	C12	GRY
	C13	
COOLANT LEVEL SIG.	C14	GRY/RED
TPS SIGNAL	C15	DK BLU
COOLANT TEMP SIG.	C16	YEL
A/C REQUEST	C17	LT BLU
EGR POSITION SIGNAL	C18	RED
	C19	
	C20	
	C21	
MAP SIGNAL	C22	LT GRN

CONNECTOR D

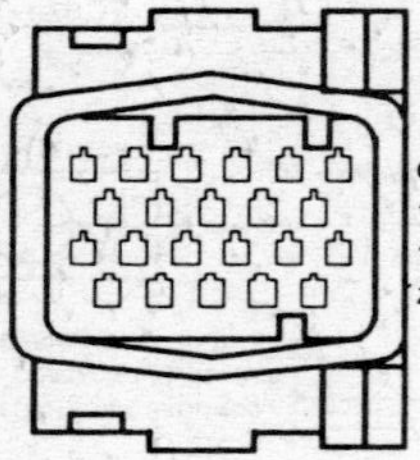

CIRCUIT	PIN	WIRE COLOR
	D1	
	D2	
INJECTOR DRIVER (1, 3, 5)	D3	LT GRN
GROUND	D4	BLK/WHT
	D5	
3RD GEAR SIGNAL	D6	DK GRN
FUEL PUMP RELAY DRIVE	D7	DK GRN/WHT
	D8	
INJECTOR DRIVER (2, 4, 6)	D9	LT BLU
GROUND	D10	TAN/WHT
P/N SWITCH (A/T)	D11	ORN/BLK
GROUND	D12	TAN/WHT
REFERENCE	D13	PPL/WHT
	D14	
	D15	
P/S PRESSURE SIG.	D16	LT BLU/ORN
BATTERY FEED	D17	ORN
	D18	
DIS REF. LO	D19	BLK/RED
	D20	
FAN #1 REQUEST	D21	DK GRN
FOURTH GEAR SIGNAL	D22	LT BLU

DIAGNOSTIC CHARTS — 2.8L engine

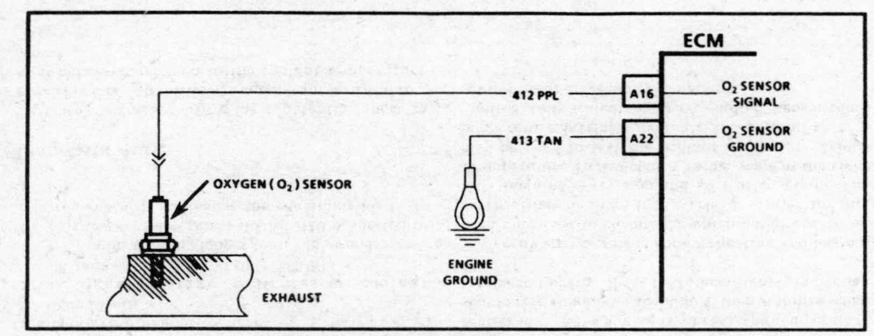

CODE 13

OXYGEN SENSOR CIRCUIT (OPEN CIRCUIT) 2.8L (VIN W) "W" SERIES (PORT)

Circuit Description:

The ECM supplies a voltage of about .45 volt between terminals "A16" and "A22". (If measured with a 10 megohm digital voltmeter, this may read as low as .32 volts.) The O_2 sensor varies the voltage within a range of about 1 volt if the exhaust is rich, down through about .10 volt if exhaust is lean.

The sensor is like an open circuit and produces no voltage when it is below 315°C (600°F). An open sensor circuit or cold sensor causes "Open Loop" operation.

Test Description: Numbers below refer to circled numbers on the diagnostic chart.

1. Code 13 will set under the following conditions:
   - Engine running at least 2 minutes after start.
   - Coolant temperature at least 50°C.
   - No Code 21 or 22.
   - O_2 signal voltage steady between .35 and .55 volts.
   - Throttle position sensor signal above 6% for more time than TPS was below 6%. (About .3 volts above closed throttle voltage)
   - All conditions must be met and held for at least 60 seconds.

   If the conditions for a Code 13 exist the system will not go "Closed Loop".
2. This will determine if the sensor is at fault or the wiring or ECM is the cause of the Code 13.
3. In doing this test use only a high impedence digital volt ohmmeter. This test checks the continuity of CKTs 412 and 413 because if CKT 413 is open the ECM voltage on CKT 412 will be over .6 volts (600 mV).

Diagnostic Aids:

Normal "Scan" voltage varies between 100 mV to 999 mV (.1 and 1.0 volt) while in "Closed Loop". Code 13 sets in one minute if voltage remains between .35 and .55 volts, but the system will go "Open Loop" in about 15 seconds. Refer to "Intermittents" in Section "B".

CODE 13

OXYGEN SENSOR CIRCUIT (OPEN CIRCUIT) 2.8L (VIN W) "W" SERIES (PORT)

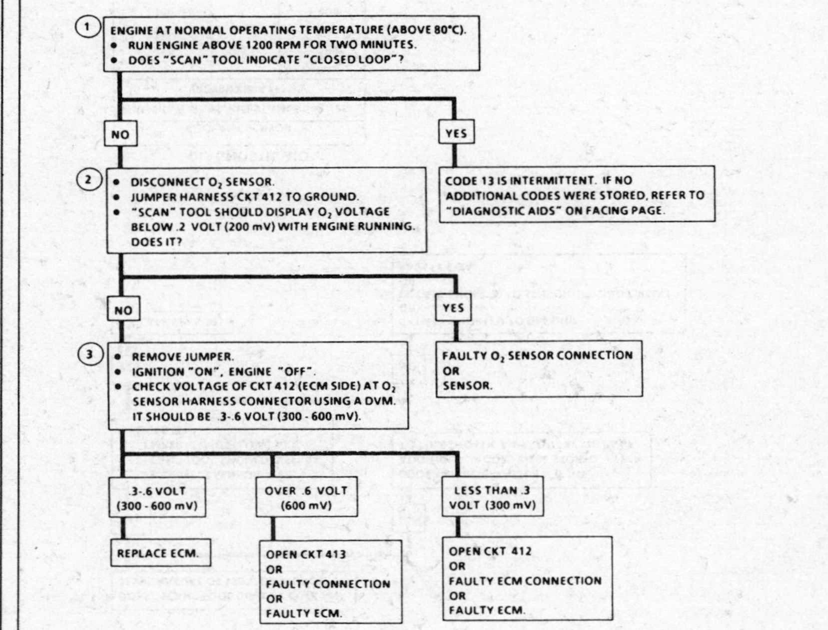

1
ENGINE AT NORMAL OPERATING TEMPERATURE (ABOVE 80°C).
• RUN ENGINE ABOVE 1200 RPM FOR TWO MINUTES.
• DOES "SCAN" TOOL INDICATE "CLOSED LOOP"?
NO
YES
2
• DISCONNECT O_2 SENSOR.
• JUMPER HARNESS CKT 412 TO GROUND.
• "SCAN" TOOL SHOULD DISPLAY O_2 VOLTAGE BELOW .2 VOLT (200 mV) WITH ENGINE RUNNING. DOES IT?
CODE 13 IS INTERMITTENT. IF NO ADDITIONAL CODES WERE STORED, REFER TO "DIAGNOSTIC AIDS" ON FACING PAGE.
NO
YES
3
• REMOVE JUMPER.
• IGNITION "ON", ENGINE "OFF".
• CHECK VOLTAGE OF CKT 412 (ECM SIDE) AT O_2 SENSOR HARNESS CONNECTOR USING A DVM. IT SHOULD BE .3-.6 VOLT (300 - 600 mV).
FAULTY O_2 SENSOR CONNECTION OR SENSOR.
.3-.6 VOLT (300 - 600 mV)
OVER .6 VOLT (600 mV)
LESS THAN .3 VOLT (300 mV)
REPLACE ECM.
OPEN CKT 413 OR FAULTY CONNECTION OR FAULTY ECM.
OPEN CKT 412 OR FAULTY ECM CONNECTION OR FAULTY ECM.

CLEAR CODES AND CONFIRM "CLOSED LOOP" OPERATION AND NO "SERVICE ENGINE SOON" LIGHT.

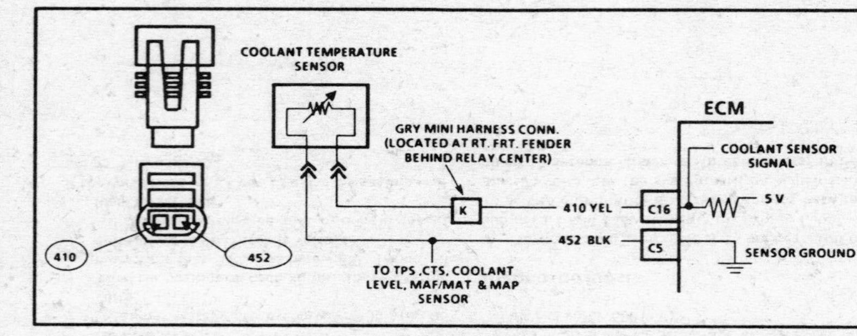

CODE 14

COOLANT TEMPERATURE SENSOR CIRCUIT
(HIGH TEMPERATURE INDICATED)
2.8L (VIN W) "W" SERIES (PORT)

Circuit Description:

The coolant temperature sensor uses a thermistor to control the signal voltage to the ECM. The ECM applies a voltage on CKT 410 to the sensor. When the engine is cold the sensor (thermistor) resistance is high, therefore the ECM will see high signal voltage.

As the engine warms, the sensor resistance becomes less, and the voltage drops. At normal engine operating temperature the voltage will measure about 1.5 to 2.0 volts at the ECM terminal "C16".

Coolant temperature is one of the inputs used to control:

- Fuel delivery
- Engine spark timing (EST)
- Idle (IAC)
- Converter clutch (TCC)
- Canister purge (CCP)
- EGR
- Cooling fan

Test Description: Numbers below refer to circled numbers on the diagnostic chart.

1. Code 14 will set if:
   - Signal voltage indicates a coolant temperature above 140°C (285°F).
   - Engine running longer than 128 seconds
2. This test will determine if CKT 410 is shorted to ground which will cause the conditions for Code 14.

Diagnostic Aids:

Check harness routing for a potential short to ground in CKT 410. CKT is routed from the ECM to a mini harness, and then to the coolant temperature sensor.

"Scan" tool displays engine temperature in degrees centigrade. After engine is started, the temperature should rise steadily to about 90°C then stabilize when thermostat opens. Refer to "Intermittents" in Section "B".

Verify that engine is not overheating and has not been subjected to conditions which could create an overheating condition (i.e. overload, trailer towing, hilly terrain, heavy stop and go traffic, etc.). The "Temperature To Resistance Value" scale at the right may be used to test the coolant sensor at various temperature levels to evaluate the possibility of a "shifted" (mis-scaled) sensor. A "shifted" sensor could result in poor driveability complaints.

CODE 14

COOLANT TEMPERATURE SENSOR CIRCUIT
(HIGH TEMPERATURE INDICATED)
2.8L (VIN W) "W" SERIES (PORT)

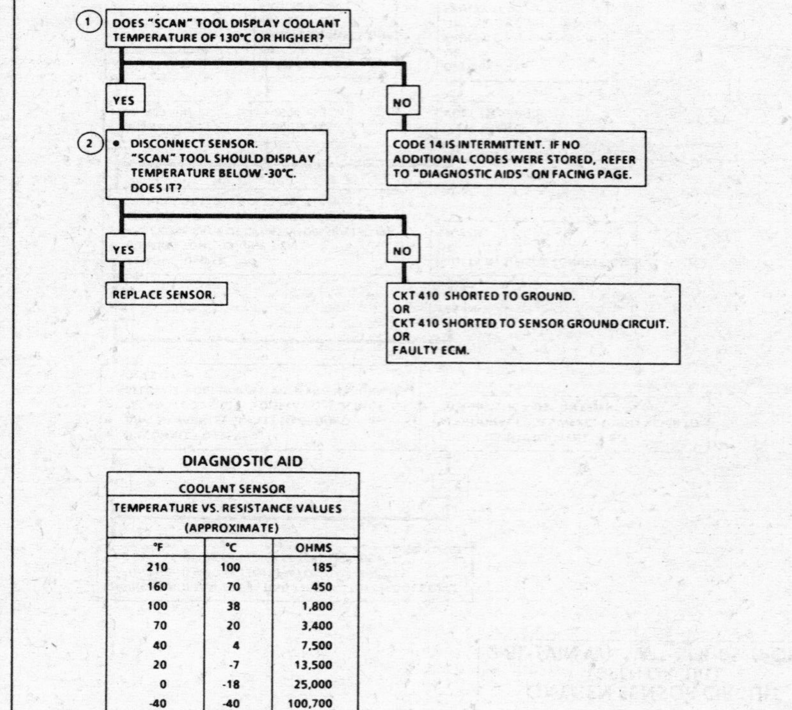

1
DOES "SCAN" TOOL DISPLAY COOLANT TEMPERATURE OF 130°C OR HIGHER?
YES
NO
2
• DISCONNECT SENSOR.
"SCAN" TOOL SHOULD DISPLAY TEMPERATURE BELOW -30°C.
DOES IT?
CODE 14 IS INTERMITTENT. IF NO ADDITIONAL CODES WERE STORED, REFER TO "DIAGNOSTIC AIDS" ON FACING PAGE.
YES
NO
REPLACE SENSOR.
CKT 410 SHORTED TO GROUND.
OR
CKT 410 SHORTED TO SENSOR GROUND CIRCUIT.
OR
FAULTY ECM.

DIAGNOSTIC AID

COOLANT SENSOR TEMPERATURE VS. RESISTANCE VALUES (APPROXIMATE)		
°F	°C	OHMS
210	100	185
160	70	450
100	38	1,800
70	20	3,400
40	4	7,500
20	-7	13,500
0	-18	25,000
-40	-40	100,700

CLEAR CODES AND CONFIRM "CLOSED LOOP" OPERATION AND NO "SERVICE ENGINE SOON" LIGHT.

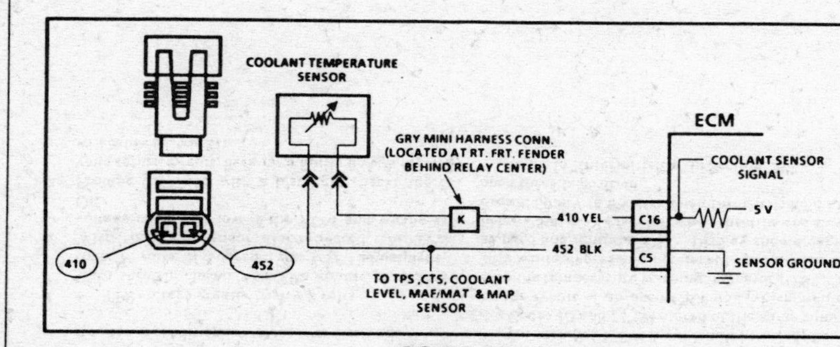

CODE 15

COOLANT TEMPERATURE SENSOR CIRCUIT
(LOW TEMPERATURE INDICATED)
2.8L (VIN W) "W" SERIES (PORT)

Circuit Description:

The coolant temperature sensor uses a thermistor to control the signal voltage to the ECM. The ECM applies a voltage on CKT 410 to the sensor. When the engine is cold the sensor (thermistor) resistance is high, therefore the ECM will see high signal voltage.

As the engine warms, the sensor resistance becomes less, and the voltage drops. At normal engine operating temperature the voltage will measure about 1.5 to 2.0 volts at the ECM terminal "C16".

Coolant temperature is one of the inputs used to control:

- Fuel delivery
- Engine spark timing (EST)
- Idle (IAC)
- Converter clutch (TCC)
- Canister purge (CCP)
- EGR
- Cooling fan

Test Description: Numbers below refer to circled numbers on the diagnostic chart.

1. Code 15 will set if:
   - Signal voltage indicates a coolant temperature less than -44°C (-47°F) for 20 seconds.
2. This test simulates a Code 14. If the ECM recognizes the low signal voltage, (high temperature) and the "Scan" reads 130°C, the ECM and wiring are OK.
3. This test will determine if CKT 410 is open. There should be 5 volts present at sensor connector if measured with a DVM.

Diagnostic Aids:

A "Scan" tool reads engine temperature in degrees centigrade.

After engine is started the temperature should rise steadily to about 95°C then stabilize when thermostat opens. CKT 410 is routed from the ECM to a mini harness, and then to the coolant temperature sensor.

A faulty connection, or an open in CKT 410 or 452 will result in a Code 15.

If Code 23 is also set, check CKT 452 for faulty wiring or connections. Check terminals at sensor for good contact.

Codes 15 and 21 are stored at the same time could be the result of an open CKT 452 which would also turn the temperature warning indicator "ON." The "Temperature to Resistance Value" scale at the right may be used to test the coolant sensor at various temperature levels to evaluate the possibility of a "shifted" (mis-scaled) sensor. A "shifted" sensor could resut in poor driveability complaints.

Refer to "Intermittents" in Section "B".

CODE 15

COOLANT TEMPERATURE SENSOR CIRCUIT
(LOW TEMPERATURE INDICATED)
2.8L (VIN W) "W" SERIES (PORT)

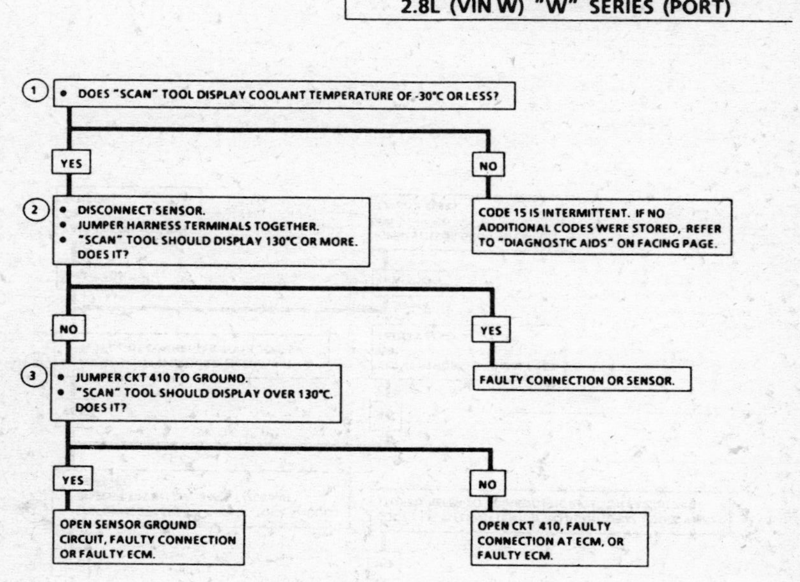

1
• DOES "SCAN" TOOL DISPLAY COOLANT TEMPERATURE OF -30°C OR LESS?
YES
NO
CODE 15 IS INTERMITTENT. IF NO ADDITIONAL CODES WERE STORED, REFER TO "DIAGNOSTIC AIDS" ON FACING PAGE.
2
• DISCONNECT SENSOR.
• JUMPER HARNESS TERMINALS TOGETHER.
• "SCAN" TOOL SHOULD DISPLAY 130°C OR MORE. DOES IT?
NO
YES
FAULTY CONNECTION OR SENSOR.
3
• JUMPER CKT 410 TO GROUND.
• "SCAN" TOOL SHOULD DISPLAY OVER 130°C. DOES IT?
YES
NO
OPEN SENSOR GROUND CIRCUIT, FAULTY CONNECTION OR FAULTY ECM.
OPEN CKT 410, FAULTY CONNECTION AT ECM, OR FAULTY ECM.

DIAGNOSTIC AID

COOLANT SENSOR TEMPERATURE TO RESISTANCE VALUES (APPROXIMATE)		
°F	°C	OHMS
210	100	185
160	70	450
100	38	1,800
70	20	3,400
40	4	7,500
20	-7	13,500
0	-18	25,000
-40	-40	100,700

CLEAR CODES AND CONFIRM "CLOSED LOOP" OPERATION AND NO "SERVICE ENGINE SOON" LIGHT.

DIAGNOSTIC CHARTS — 2.8L engine

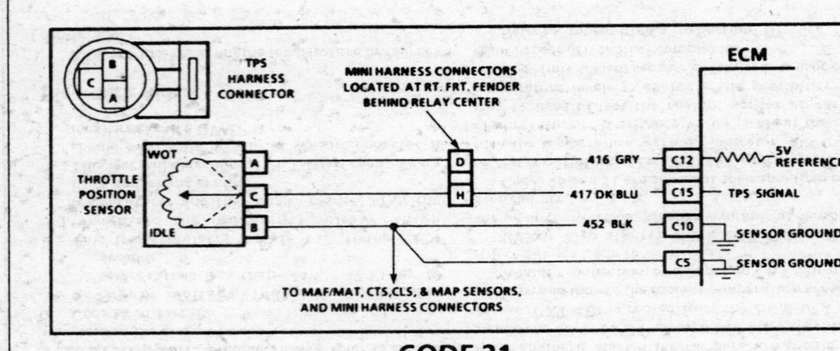
TPS HARNESS CONNECTOR
MINI HARNESS CONNECTORS LOCATED AT RT. FRT. FENDER BEHIND RELAY CENTER
ECM
THROTTLE POSITION SENSOR
WOT
IDLE
A
C
B
D
H
416 GRY
417 DK BLU
452 BLK
C12
C15
C10
C5
5V REFERENCE
TPS SIGNAL
SENSOR GROUND
SENSOR GROUND
TO MAF/MAT, CTS,CLS, & MAP SENSORS, AND MINI HARNESS CONNECTORS

CODE 21

THROTTLE POSITION SENSOR (TPS) CIRCUIT
(SIGNAL VOLTAGE HIGH)
2.8L (VIN W) "W" SERIES (PORT)

Circuit Description:

The throttle position sensor (TPS) provides a voltage signal that changes relative to the throttle blade. Signal voltage will vary from about .5 at idle to about 5 volts at wide open throttle.

The TPS signal is one of the most important inputs used by the ECM for fuel control and for most of the ECM control outputs.

Test Description: Numbers below refer to circled numbers on the diagnostic chart.

1. Code 21 will set if:
   - Engine is running
   - No Code 33 or 34
   - MAF less than 12 gm/sec
   - TPS voltage greater than 4.9 volts.
   - Above conditions exist for over 5 seconds.

   OR

   - TPS voltage greater than 4.9 volts.

   With throttle closed, the TPS should read less than .70 volts. If it doesn't, check TPS adjustment.
2. With the TPS sensor disconnected, the TPS voltage should go low if the ECM and wiring is OK.
3. Probing CKT 452 with a test light checks the 5 volts return circuit, because a faulty 5 volts return will cause a Code 21.

Diagnostic Aids:

A "Scan" tool reads throttle position in volts. Voltage should increase at a steady rate as throttle is moved toward WOT.

Also some "Scan" tools will read throttle angle 0% = closed throttle 100% = WOT.

An open in CKT 452 will result in a Code 21.

Codes 15 and 21 are stored at the same time could be the result of an open CKT 452 which would also turn the temperature warning indicator "ON". "Scan" TPS while depressing accelerator pedal with engine stopped and ignition "ON". Display should vary from below 2500 mV (2.5 volts) when throttle was closed, to over 4500 mV (4.5 volts) when throttle is held at wide open throttle position.

Refer to "Intermittents" in Section "B".

CODE 21

THROTTLE POSITION SENSOR (TPS) CIRCUIT
(SIGNAL VOLTAGE HIGH)
2.8L (VIN W) "W" SERIES (PORT)

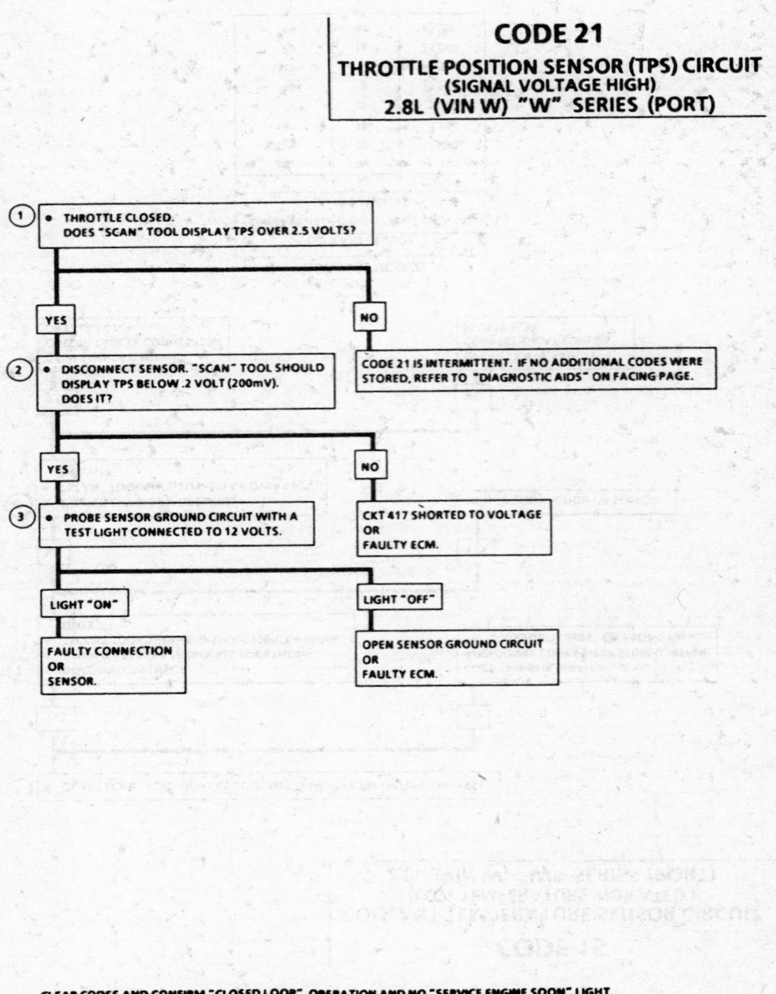
1
• THROTTLE CLOSED. DOES "SCAN" TOOL DISPLAY TPS OVER 2.5 VOLTS?
YES
NO
CODE 21 IS INTERMITTENT. IF NO ADDITIONAL CODES WERE STORED, REFER TO "DIAGNOSTIC AIDS" ON FACING PAGE.
2
• DISCONNECT SENSOR. "SCAN" TOOL SHOULD DISPLAY TPS BELOW .2 VOLT (200mV). DOES IT?
YES
NO
CKT 417 SHORTED TO VOLTAGE OR FAULTY ECM.
3
• PROBE SENSOR GROUND CIRCUIT WITH A TEST LIGHT CONNECTED TO 12 VOLTS.
LIGHT "ON"
LIGHT "OFF"
FAULTY CONNECTION OR SENSOR.
OPEN SENSOR GROUND CIRCUIT OR FAULTY ECM.

CLEAR CODES AND CONFIRM "CLOSED LOOP" OPERATION AND NO "SERVICE ENGINE SOON" LIGHT.

DIAGNOSTIC CHARTS — 2.8L engine

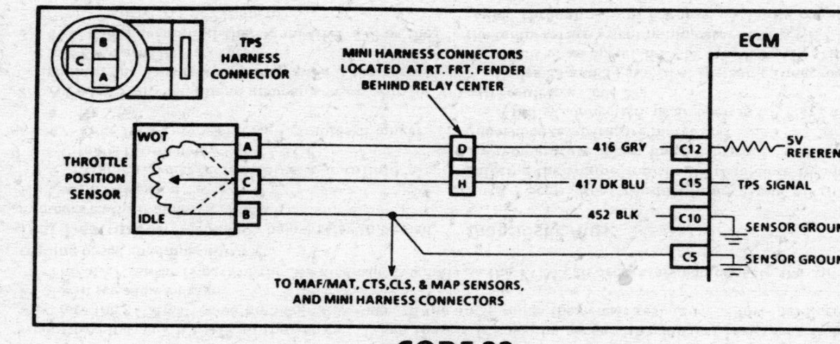

CODE 22

THROTTLE POSITION SENSOR (TPS) CIRCUIT
(SIGNAL VOLTAGE LOW)
2.8L (VIN W) "W" SERIES (PORT)

Circuit Description:

The throttle position sensor (TPS) provides a voltage signal that changes relative to the throttle blade. Signal voltage will vary from about .5 at idle to about 5 volts at wide open throttle.

The TPS signal is one of the most important inputs used by the ECM for fuel control and for most of the ECM control outputs.

Test Description: Numbers below refer to circled numbers on the diagnostic chart.

1. Code 22 will set if:
   - Engine running
   - TPS signal voltage is less than about .25volt for 3 seconds.
2. Simulates Code 21: (High Voltage) If the ECM recognizes the high signal voltage the ECM and wiring are OK.
3. TPS check: The TPS has an auto zeroing feature. If the voltage reading is within the range of 0.35 to 0.70 volts, the ECM will use that value as closed throttle. If the voltage reading is out of the auto zero range on an existing or replacement TPS, the TPS should be adjusted.
4. This simulates a high signal voltage to check for an open in CKT 417.
5. CKTs 416 and 432 share a common 5volts buffered reference signal. If either of these circuits is shorted to ground, Code 22 will set. To determine if the MAP sensor is causing the 22 problem disconnect it to see if Code 22 resets. Be sure TPS is connected and clear codes before testing.

Diagnostic Aids:

A "Scan" tool reads throttle position in volts. Voltage should increase at a steady rate as throttle is moved toward WOT.

Also some "Scan" tools will read throttle angle 0% = closed throttle 100% = WOT.

An open or short to ground in CKTs 416 or 417 will result in a Code 22.

CKTs 416 and 417 are routed through a mini harness. CKT 416 is connected to terminal "D" at the gray connector, CKT 417 is connected to terminal "H" at the black connector.

"Scan" TPS while depressing accelerator pedal with engine stopped and ignition "ON" Display should vary from below 500 mV (.5V) when throttle was closed, to over 4500 mV (4.5V) when throttle is held at wide open throttle position.

Also some "Scan" tools will read throttle angle.
0% = closed throttle.
100% = open throttle.

If Code 22 is set, check CKT 416 for faulty wiring or connections.

Refer to "Intermittents" in Section "B".

CODE 22

THROTTLE POSITION SENSOR (TPS) CIRCUIT
(SIGNAL VOLTAGE LOW)
2.8L (VIN W) "W" SERIES (PORT)

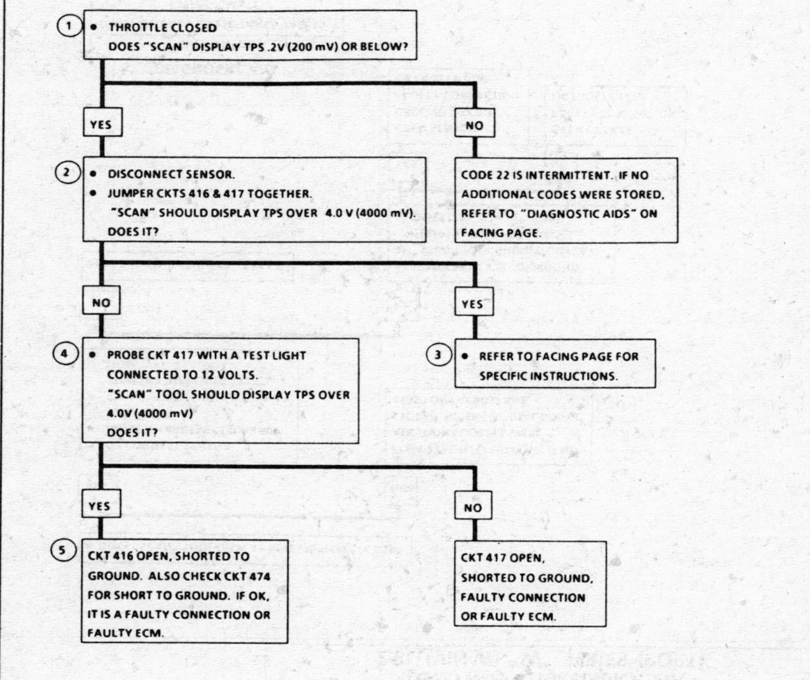

1 • THROTTLE CLOSED
DOES "SCAN" DISPLAY TPS .2V (200 mV) OR BELOW?
YES
NO
2 • DISCONNECT SENSOR.
• JUMPER CKTS 416 & 417 TOGETHER.
"SCAN" SHOULD DISPLAY TPS OVER 4.0 V (4000 mV).
DOES IT?
CODE 22 IS INTERMITTENT. IF NO ADDITIONAL CODES WERE STORED, REFER TO "DIAGNOSTIC AIDS" ON FACING PAGE.
NO
YES
4 • PROBE CKT 417 WITH A TEST LIGHT CONNECTED TO 12 VOLTS.
"SCAN" TOOL SHOULD DISPLAY TPS OVER 4.0V (4000 mV)
DOES IT?
3 • REFER TO FACING PAGE FOR SPECIFIC INSTRUCTIONS.
YES
NO
5 CKT 416 OPEN, SHORTED TO GROUND. ALSO CHECK CKT 474 FOR SHORT TO GROUND. IF OK, IT IS A FAULTY CONNECTION OR FAULTY ECM.
CKT 417 OPEN, SHORTED TO GROUND, FAULTY CONNECTION OR FAULTY ECM.

CLEAR CODES AND CONFIRM "CLOSED LOOP" OPERATION AND NO "SERVICE ENGINE SOON" LIGHT

DIAGNOSTIC CHARTS — 2.8L engine

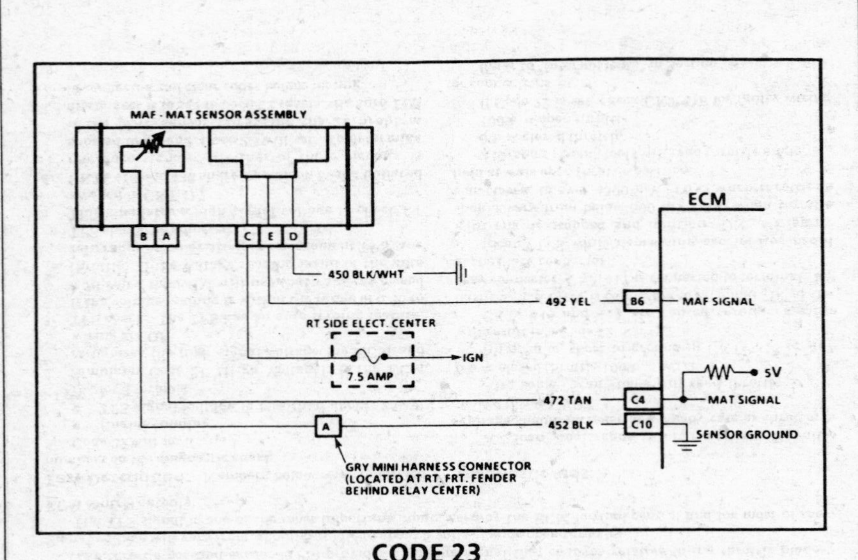

CODE 23

MANIFOLD AIR TEMPERATURE (MAT) SENSOR CIRCUIT
(LOW TEMPERATURE INDICATED)
2.8L (VIN W) "W" SERIES (PORT)

Circuit Description:

The MAT sensor uses a thermistor to control the signal voltage to the ECM. The ECM applies a voltage (about 5 volts) on CKT 472 to the sensor. When the air is cold the sensor (thermistor) resistance is high, therefore the ECM will see a high signal voltage. If the air is warm the sensor resistance is low therefore the ECM will see a low voltage.

The MAT sensor is part of the MAF sensor assembly so the ECM can accurately compensate the air flow reading based on temperature.

Test Description: Numbers below refer to circled numbers on the diagnostic chart.

1. Code 23 will set if:
   - A signal voltage indicates a manifold air temperature below -35°C (-31°F).
   - Time since engine start is 4 minutes or longer.
   - No VSS.
2. A Code 23 will set, due to an open sensor, wire, or connection. This test will determine if the wiring and ECM are OK.
3. This will determine if the signal CKT 472 or the 5volts return CKT 452 is open.

Diagnostic Aids:

A "Scan" tool reads temperature of the air entering the engine and should read close to ambient air temperature when engine is cold, and rises as underhood temperature increases.

A faulty connection, or an open in CKT 472 or 452 will result in a Code 23.

Codes 23 and 34 stored at the same time, could be the result of an open CKT 452 which would also turn the temperature warning indicator "ON". CKT 452 is routed through a mini harness. A faulty connection could result in intermittent failures. The "Temperature to Resistance Values" scale at the right may be used to test the MAT sensor at various temperature levels to evaluate the possibility of a "shifted" (mis-scaled) sensor. A "slewed" sensor could result in poor driveability complaints.

Refer to "Intermittents" in Section "B"

CODE 23

MANIFOLD AIR TEMPERATURE (MAT) SENSOR CIRCUIT
(LOW TEMPERATURE INDICATED)
2.8L (VIN W) "W" SERIES (PORT)

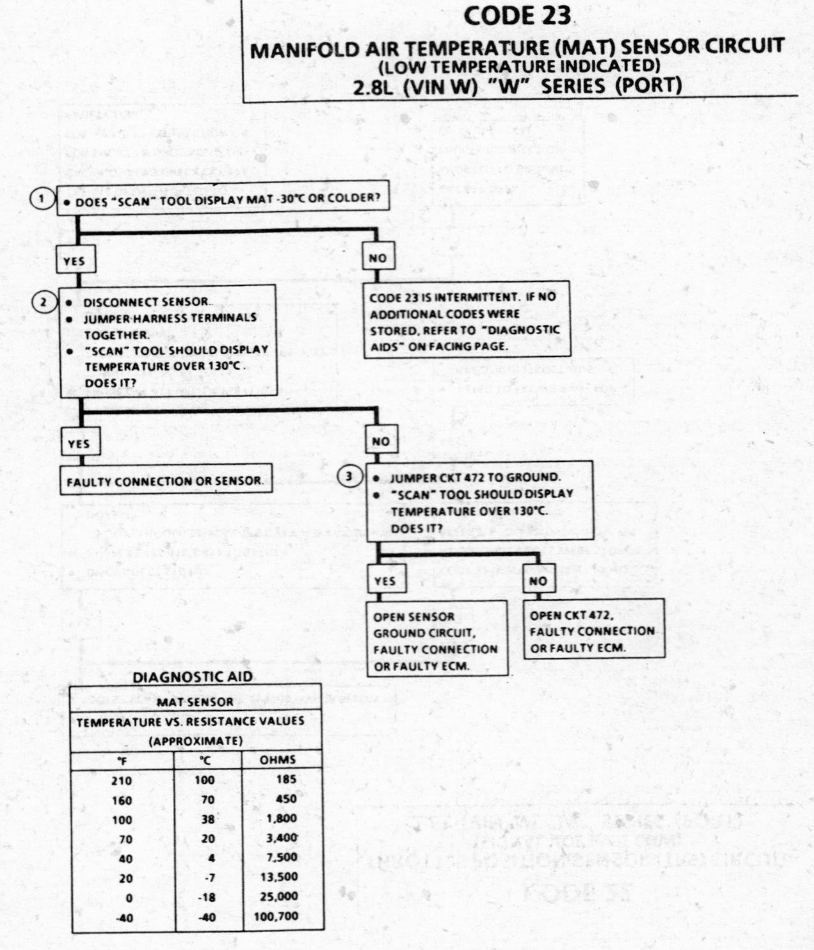

1 • DOES "SCAN" TOOL DISPLAY MAT -30°C OR COLDER?
YES
NO
CODE 23 IS INTERMITTENT. IF NO ADDITIONAL CODES WERE STORED, REFER TO "DIAGNOSTIC AIDS" ON FACING PAGE.
2 • DISCONNECT SENSOR.
• JUMPER HARNESS TERMINALS TOGETHER.
• "SCAN" TOOL SHOULD DISPLAY TEMPERATURE OVER 130°C.
DOES IT?
YES
FAULTY CONNECTION OR SENSOR.
NO
3 • JUMPER CKT 472 TO GROUND.
• "SCAN" TOOL SHOULD DISPLAY TEMPERATURE OVER 130°C.
DOES IT?
YES
OPEN SENSOR GROUND CIRCUIT, FAULTY CONNECTION OR FAULTY ECM.
NO
OPEN CKT 472, FAULTY CONNECTION OR FAULTY ECM.

DIAGNOSTIC AID

MAT SENSOR
TEMPERATURE VS. RESISTANCE VALUES (APPROXIMATE)

°F	°C	OHMS
210	100	185
160	70	450
100	38	1,800
70	20	3,400
40	4	7,500
20	-7	13,500
0	-18	25,000
-40	-40	100,700

CLEAR CODES AND CONFIRM "CLOSED LOOP" OPERATION AND NO "SERVICE ENGINE SOON" LIGHT.

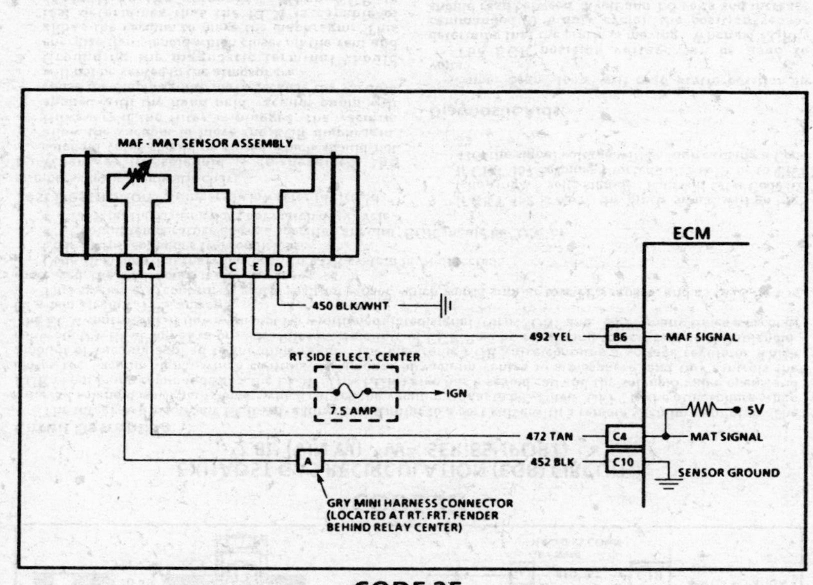

CODE 25

MANIFOLD AIR TEMPERATURE (MAT) SENSOR CIRCUIT
(HIGH TEMPERATURE INDICATED)
2.8L (VIN W) "W" SERIES (PORT)

Circuit Description:

The MAT sensor uses a thermistor to control the signal voltage to the ECM. The ECM applies a voltage (about 5 volts) on CKT 472 to the sensor. When the air is cold the sensor (thermistor) resistance is high, therefore the ECM will see a high signal voltage. If the air is warm the sensor resistance is low therefore the ECM will see a low voltage.

The MAT sensor is part of the MAF sensor assembly so the ECM can accurately compensate the air flow reading based on temperature.

Test Description: Numbers below refer to circled numbers on the diagnostic chart.

Code 25 will set if:

- Signal voltage indicates a manifold air temperature greater than 135°C (293°F) for 3 seconds.
- Time since engine start is 8 minutes or longer.
- A vehicle speed over 3 mph is present.

Due to the conditions necessary to set a Code 25 the "Service Engine Soon" light will remain "ON" while the signal is low and vehicle speed is present.

Diagnostic Aids:

A "Scan" tool reads temperature of the air entering the engine and should read close to ambient air temperature when engine is cold, and rises as underhood temperature increases.

A short to ground in CKT 472 will result in a Code 25.

The "Temperature to Resistance Values" scale at the right may be used to test the MAT sensor at various temperature levels to evaluate the possibility of a "shifted" (mis-scaled) sensor. A "slewed" sensor could result in poor driveability complaints.

Refer to "Intermittents" in Section "B".

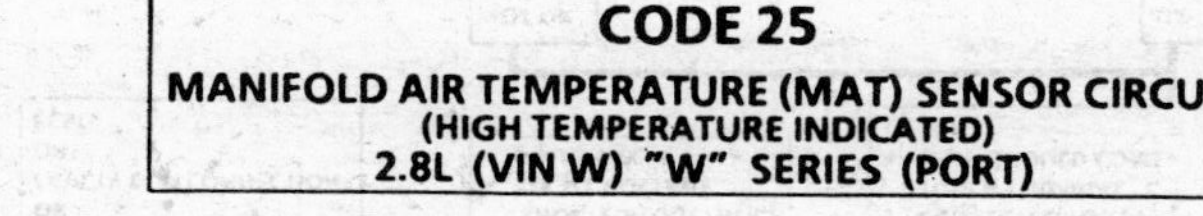

CODE 25

MANIFOLD AIR TEMPERATURE (MAT) SENSOR CIRCUIT
(HIGH TEMPERATURE INDICATED)
2.8L (VIN W) "W" SERIES (PORT)

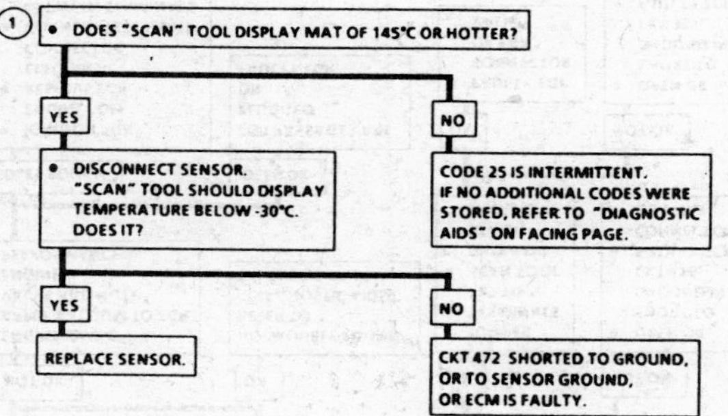

DIAGNOSTIC AID

MAT SENSOR		
TEMPERATURE VS. RESISTANCE VALUES (APPROXIMATE)		
°F	°C	OHMS
210	100	185
160	70	450
100	38	1,800
70	20	3,400
40	4	7,500
20	-7	13,500
0	-18	25,000
-40	-40	100,700

CLEAR CODES AND CONFIRM "CLOSED LOOP" OPERATION AND NO "SERVICE ENGINE SOON" LIGHT.

CODE 32

EXHAUST GAS RECIRCULATION (EGR) CIRCUIT 2.8L (VIN W) "W" SERIES (PORT)

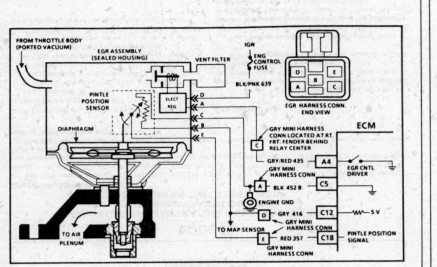

Circuit Description:

The integrated electronic EGR valve functions similar to a port valve with a remote vacuum regulator. The internal solenoid is normally open, which causes the vacuum signal to be vented "OFF" to the atmosphere when EGR is not being commanded by the ECM. This EGR valve has a sealed cap and the solenoid valve opens and closes the vacuum signal which controls the amount of vacuum vented to atmosphere, and this controls the amount of vacuum applied to the diaphragm. The electronic EGR valve contains a voltage regulator which converts the ECM signal to provide different amounts of EGR flow by regulating the current to the solenoid. The ECM controls EGR flow with a pulse width modulated signal (turns "ON" and "OFF" many times a second) based on air flow, TPS, and rpm.

This system also contains a pintle position sensor which works similar to a TPS sensor, and as EGR flow is increased, the sensor output also increases.

Code 32 means that there has been an EGR system fault detected.

Code 32 will set under two conditions:

- Coolant temperature above a specified amount, EGR should be "ON" or:
- EGR pintle position does not match duty cycle.

Test Description: Numbers below refer to circled numbers on the diagnostic chart.

1. Whenever the solenoid is de-energized, the solenoid valve should be closed which should not allow the vacuum to move the EGR diaphragm. However, if the filter is plugged, the vacuum applied with the hand held vacuum pump will cause the diaphragm to move because the vacuum will not be vented to the atmosphere.
2. Grounding the diagnostic terminal should energize the solenoid which closes off the vent and allows the vacuum to move the diaphragm. This test determines that the ECM is capable of controlling the solenoid. When EGR is commanded on by the ECM, the test light should be "ON."
3. If CKT 452 is open, the pintle signal will go high (showing a 5 volts signal). This will set a Code 32. If CKT 357 becomes shorted to 12 volts or to CKT 416, the signal voltage will go high causing a Code 32.

Diagnostic Aids:

Some "Scan" tools will read pintle position in volts.

The EGR position voltage can be used to determine that the pintle is moving. When no EGR is commanded (0-% duty cycle), the position sensor should read between .5 volt and 1.5 volts and increase with the commanded EGR duty cycle. If system operates correctly, refer to "Intermittents" in Section "B".

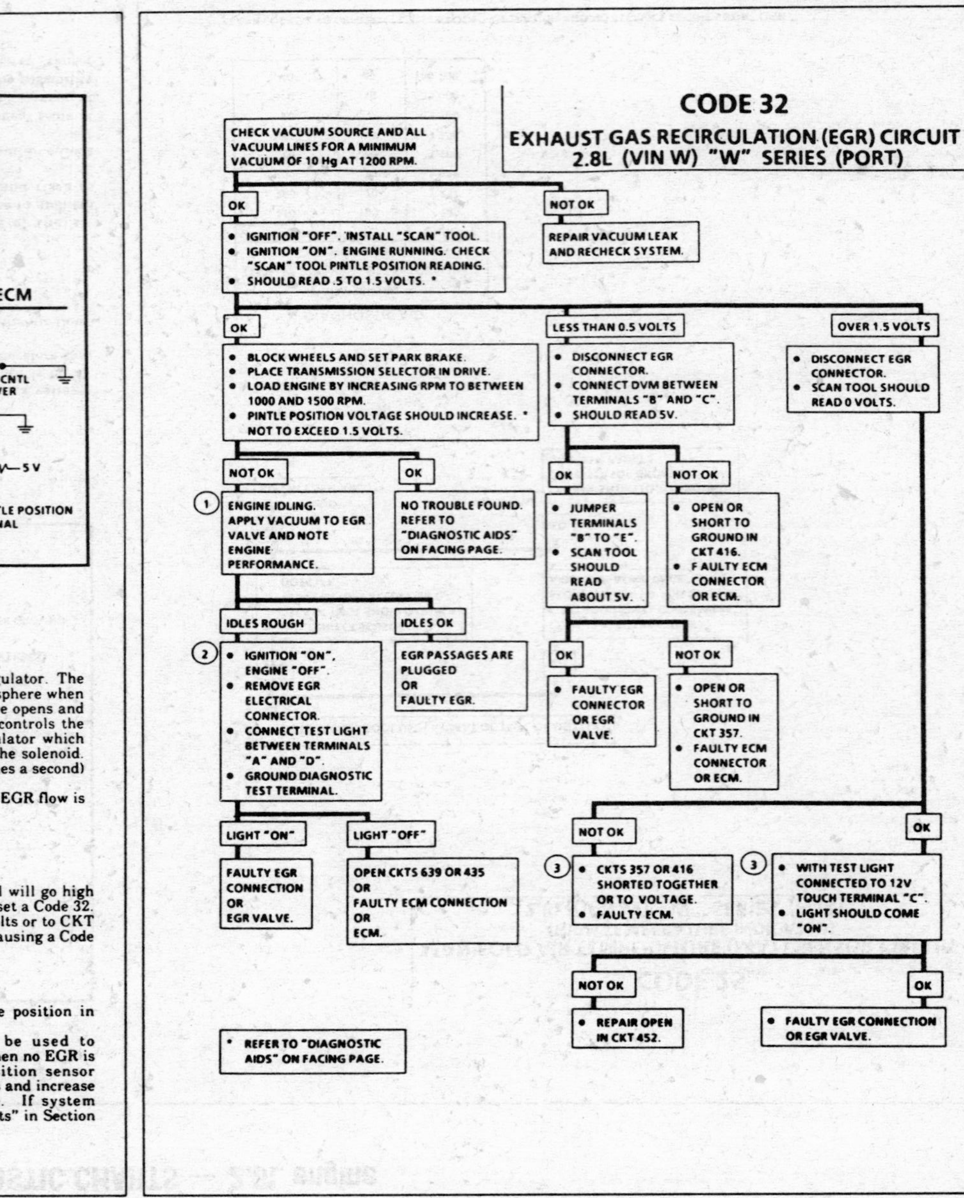

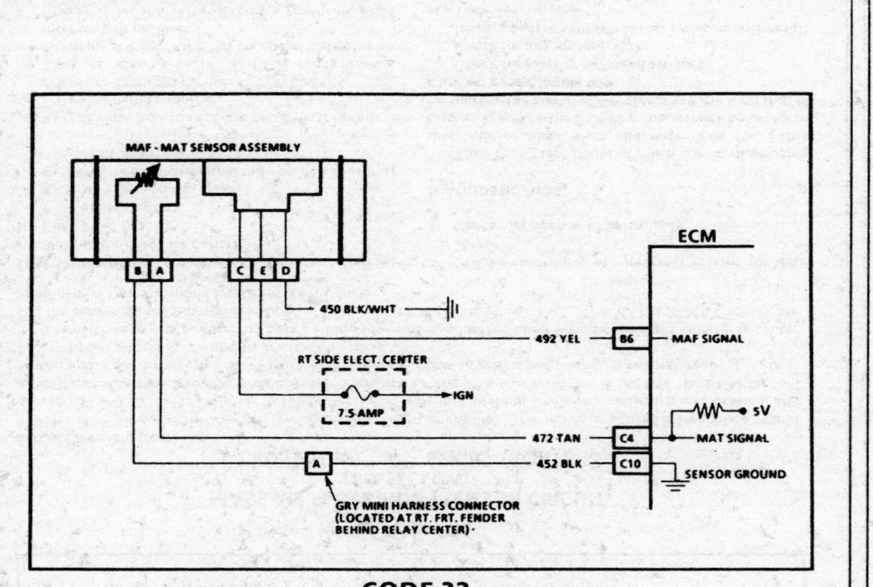

CODE 33

MASS AIR FLOW (MAF) SENSOR CIRCUIT
(GM/SEC HIGH)
2.8L (VIN W) "W" SERIES (PORT)

Circuit Description:

The MAF sensor measures the flow of air entering the engine. The sensor produces a frequency output between 32 and 150 hertz (3gm/sec to 150gm/sec.). A large quantity (high frequency) indicates acceleration, and a small quantity (low frequency) indicates deceleration or idle. This information is used by the ECM for fuel control and is converted by a "Scan" tool to read out the air flow in grams per second. A normal reading is about 4-7 grams per second at idle and increases with rpm.

The MAF sensor is powered up by a 7.5 amp fuse which is located underhood in the right side relay center and the sensor should have power supplied to it anytime the ignition is "ON." The MAF and MAT sensor are combined into one assembly located in the air duct.

Test Description: Numbers below refer to circled numbers on the diagnostic chart.

Code 33 will set if:

- Ignition "ON," engine "OFF," and air flow exceeds 20 gm/sec.

OR

- Engine is running at less than 1300 rpm.
- TPS is 8% or less.
- Air flow greater than 20 gm/sec. (high frequency).
- The above three conditions are met for 2 seconds.

Diagnostic Aids:

The "Scan" tool is not of much use in diagnosing this code because when the code sets, the value displayed will be the default value. However, it may be useful in comparing the signal of a problem vehicle with that of a known good running one.

Refer to "Intermittents" in Section "B".

Inspect wire routing of high voltage wires such as spark plug wires. Such wires routed too closely to MAF wiring harness could possibly cause an intermittent Code 33.

CODE 33

MASS AIR FLOW (MAF) SENSOR CIRCUIT
(GM/SEC HIGH)
2.8L (VIN W) "W" SERIES (PORT)

(1)
- CLEAR CODES.
- IDLE ENGINE FOR 1 MINUTE OR UNTIL CODE 33 SETS.

DOES CODE 33 SET?

YES → REPLACE MAF SENSOR

NO → CODE 33 IS INTERMITTENT. REFER TO "DIAGNOSTIC AIDS" ON FACING PAGE.

CLEAR CODES AND CONFIRM "CLOSED LOOP" OPERATION AND NO "SERVICE ENGINE SOON" LIGHT.

DIAGNOSTIC CHARTS — 2.8L engine

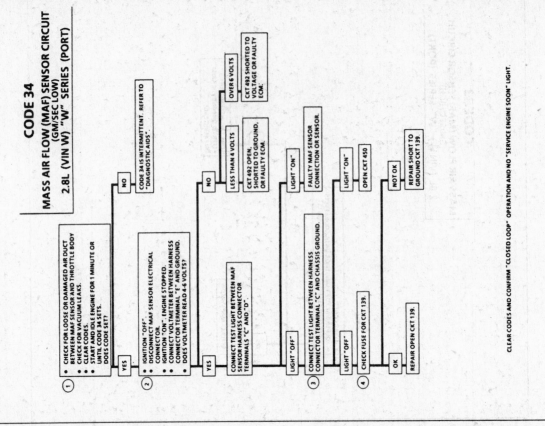

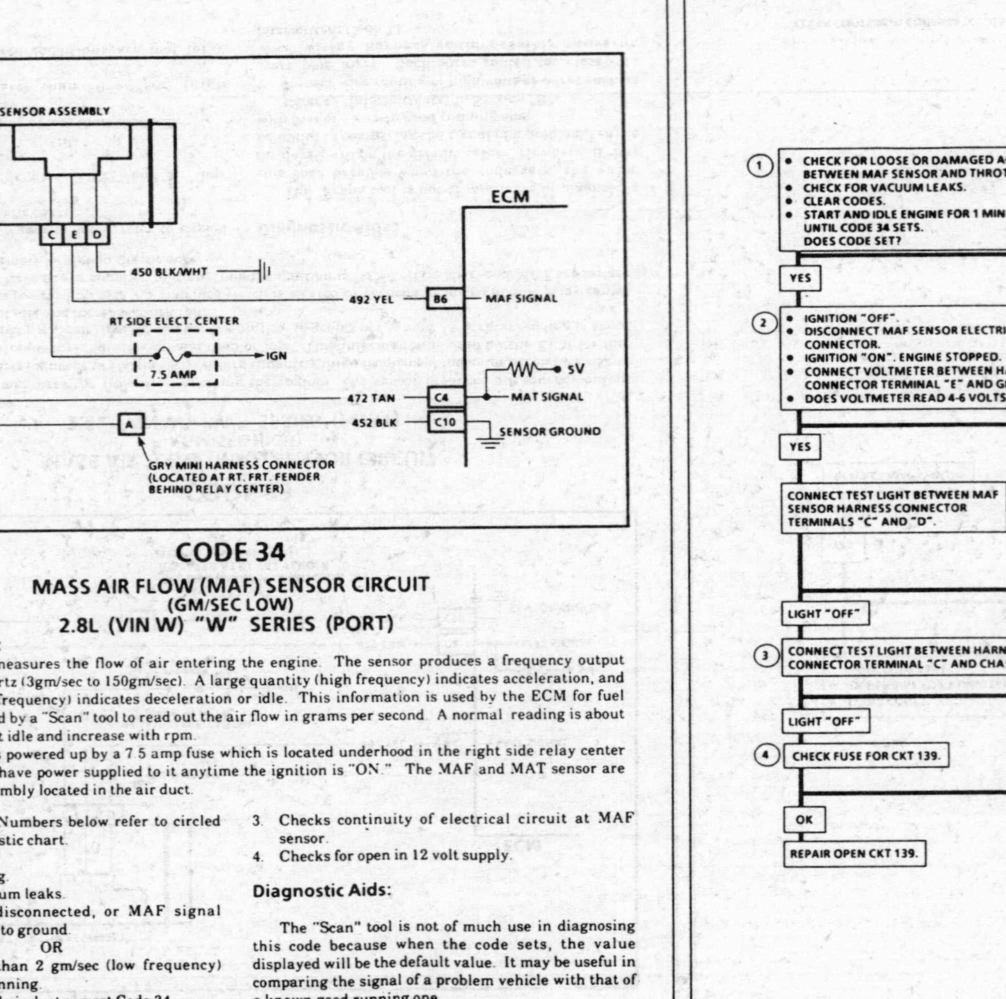

CODE 34

MASS AIR FLOW (MAF) SENSOR CIRCUIT
(GM/SEC LOW)
2.8L (VIN W) "W" SERIES (PORT)

Circuit Description:

The MAF sensor measures the flow of air entering the engine. The sensor produces a frequency output between 32 and 150 hertz (3gm/sec to 150gm/sec). A large quantity (high frequency) indicates acceleration, and a small quantity (low frequency) indicates deceleration or idle. This information is used by the ECM for fuel control and is converted by a "Scan" tool to read out the air flow in grams per second. A normal reading is about 4-7 grams per second at idle and increase with rpm.

The MAF sensor is powered up by a 7.5 amp fuse which is located underhood in the right side relay center and the sensor should have power supplied to it anytime the ignition is "ON." The MAF and MAT sensor are combined into one assembly located in the air duct.

Test Description: Numbers below refer to circled numbers on the diagnostic chart.

1. Code 34 will set if:
   - Engine running.
   - Check for vacuum leaks.
   - MAF sensor disconnected, or MAF signal circuit shorted to ground.

     OR
   - Air flow less than 2 gm/sec (low frequency) with engine running.

   A loose or damaged air duct can set Code 34.

   This test checks to see if ECM recognizes a problem. A light "OFF" at this point indicates an intermittent problem.
2. Checks to see if 5 volt reference signal from ECM is at MAF sensor harness connector.
3. Checks continuity of electrical circuit at MAF sensor.
4. Checks for open in 12 volt supply.

Diagnostic Aids:

The "Scan" tool is not of much use in diagnosing this code because when the code sets, the value displayed will be the default value. It may be useful in comparing the signal of a problem vehicle with that of a known good running one.

Check for loose or damaged air duct.

Check for any vacuum leaks.

Inspect sensor connections as an open will result in a Code 34.

Refer to "Intermittents" in Section "B".

CODE 34

MASS AIR FLOW (MAF) SENSOR CIRCUIT
(GM/SEC LOW)
2.8L (VIN W) "W" SERIES (PORT)

(1)
- CHECK FOR LOOSE OR DAMAGED AIR DUCT BETWEEN MAF SENSOR AND THROTTLE BODY
- CHECK FOR VACUUM LEAKS.
- CLEAR CODES.
- START AND IDLE ENGINE FOR 1 MINUTE OR UNTIL CODE 34 SETS. DOES CODE SET?

NO: CODE 34 IS INTERMITTENT. REFER TO "DIAGNOSTIC AIDS".

YES:

(2)
- IGNITION "OFF".
- DISCONNECT MAF SENSOR ELECTRICAL CONNECTOR.
- IGNITION "ON". ENGINE STOPPED.
- CONNECT VOLTMETER BETWEEN HARNESS CONNECTOR TERMINAL "E" AND GROUND.
- DOES VOLTMETER READ 4-6 VOLTS?

NO:
- LESS THAN 4 VOLTS: CKT 492 OPEN, SHORTED TO GROUND, OR FAULTY ECM.
- OVER 6 VOLTS: CKT 492 SHORTED TO VOLTAGE OR FAULTY ECM.

YES: CONNECT TEST LIGHT BETWEEN MAF SENSOR HARNESS CONNECTOR TERMINALS "C" AND "D".

LIGHT "ON": FAULTY MAF SENSOR CONNECTION OR SENSOR.

LIGHT "OFF":

(3) CONNECT TEST LIGHT BETWEEN HARNESS CONNECTOR TERMINAL "C" AND CHASSIS GROUND.

LIGHT "ON": OPEN CKT 450

LIGHT "OFF":

(4) CHECK FUSE FOR CKT 139.

OK: REPAIR OPEN CKT 139.

NOT OK: REPAIR SHORT TO GROUND CKT 139.

CLEAR CODES AND CONFIRM "CLOSED LOOP" OPERATION AND NO "SERVICE ENGINE SOON" LIGHT.

DIAGNOSTIC CHARTS — 2.8L engine

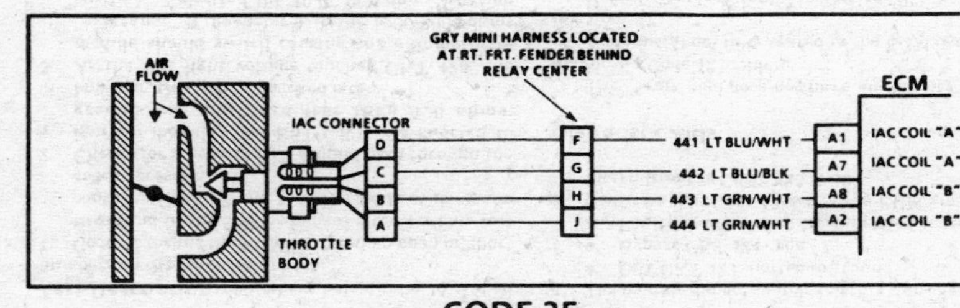
GRY MINI HARNESS LOCATED AT RT. FRT. FENDER BEHIND RELAY CENTER
AIR FLOW
IAC CONNECTOR
D
C
B
A
THROTTLE BODY
F
G
H
J
441 LT BLU/WHT
442 LT BLU/BLK
443 LT GRN/WHT
444 LT GRN/WHT
ECM
A1
A7
A8
A2
IAC COIL "A" HI
IAC COIL "A" LO
IAC COIL "B" HI
IAC COIL "B" LO

CODE 35

IDLE SPEED CONTROL (ISC) CIRCUIT 2.8L (VIN W) "W" SERIES (PORT)

Circuit Description:

Code 35 will set when the closed throttle engine speed is 100 rpm above or below the desired (commanded) idle speed for 45 seconds.

Test Description: Numbers below refer to circled numbers on the diagnostic chart.

1. Continue with test even if engine will not idle. If idle is too low, "Scan" will display 80 or more counts, or steps. If idle is high it will display "0" counts.
   Occasionally an erratic or unstable idle may occur. Engine speed may vary 200 rpm or more up and down. Disconnect IAC. If the condition is unchanged, the IAC is not at fault. There is a system problem. Proceed to diagnostic aids below.
2. When the engine was stopped, the IAC valve retracted (more air) to a fixed "park" position for increased air flow and idle speed during the next engine start. A "Scan" will display 80 or more counts.
3. Be sure to disconnect the IAC valve prior to this test. The test light will confirm the ECM signals by a steady or flashing light on all circuits.
4. There is a remote possibility that one of the circuits is shorted to voltage which would have been indicated by a steady light. Disconnect ECM and turn the ignition "ON" and probe terminals to check for this condition.
5. IAC wiring is routed from the ECM through a mini harness. Faulty connection or shorted wires could result in poor IAC operation.

Diagnostic Aids:

A slow unstable idle may be caused by a system problem that cannot be overcome by the IAC. "Scan" counts will be above 80 counts if idle is too low and "0" counts if it is too high.

If idle is too high, stop engine. Ignition "ON". Ground diagnostic terminal. Wait a few seconds for IAC to seat then disconnect IAC. Start engine. If idle speed is above rpm listed above, locate and correct vacuum leak.

- <u>System too lean (high air/fuel ratio)</u>
  Idle speed may be too high or too low. Engine speed may vary up and down, disconnecting IAC does not help. This may set Code 44.
  "Scan" and/or voltmeter will read an oxygen sensor output less than 300 mV(.3volt). Check for low regulated fuel pressure or water in fuel. A lean exhaust with an oxygen sensor output fixed above 800 mV (.8volt) will be a contaminated sensor, usually silicone. This may also set a Code 45 or 61.
- <u>System too rich (low air/fuel ratio)</u>
  Idle speed too low. "Scan" counts usually above 80. System obviously rich and may exhibit black smoke exhaust.
  "Scan" tool and/or voltmeter will read an oxygen sensor signal fixed above 800 mV (.8volt).
  Check:
  - For fuel in pressure regulator hose
  - High fuel pressure
  - Injector leaking or sticking.
- <u>MAF sensor</u> If idle is rough or unstable, disconnect MAF sensor. If idle improves, check for Code 34.
- <u>Throttle body</u> Remove IAC and inspect bore for foreign material or evidence of IAC valve dragging the bore.
- <u>A/C compressor or relay failure</u> See CHART C-10 if the A/C control relay drive circuit is shorted to ground or, if the relay is faulty, an idle problem may exist.
- Refer to "Rough, Unstable, Incorrect Idle or Stalling" in "Symptoms" in Section "B".

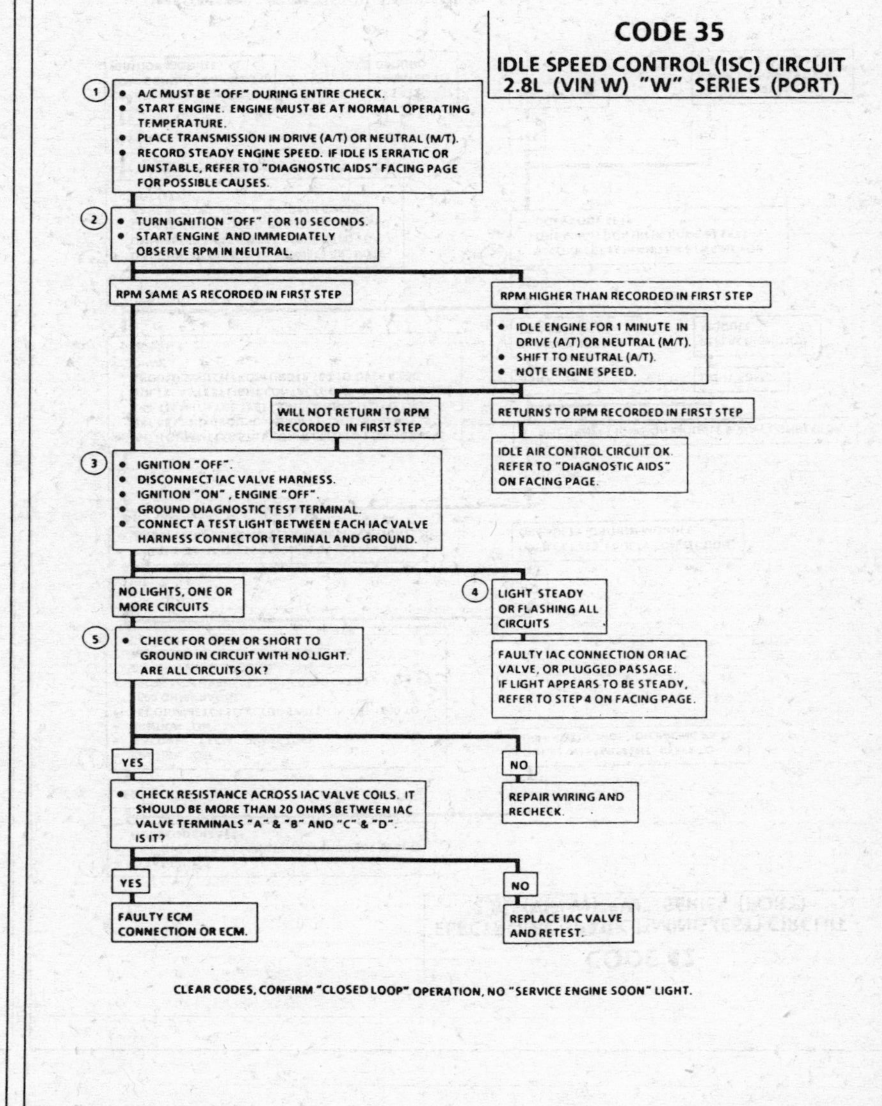
CODE 35
IDLE SPEED CONTROL (ISC) CIRCUIT 2.8L (VIN W) "W" SERIES (PORT)
1
• A/C MUST BE "OFF" DURING ENTIRE CHECK.
• START ENGINE. ENGINE MUST BE AT NORMAL OPERATING TEMPERATURE.
• PLACE TRANSMISSION IN DRIVE (A/T) OR NEUTRAL (M/T).
• RECORD STEADY ENGINE SPEED. IF IDLE IS ERRATIC OR UNSTABLE, REFER TO "DIAGNOSTIC AIDS" FACING PAGE FOR POSSIBLE CAUSES.
2
• TURN IGNITION "OFF" FOR 10 SECONDS.
• START ENGINE AND IMMEDIATELY OBSERVE RPM IN NEUTRAL.
RPM SAME AS RECORDED IN FIRST STEP
RPM HIGHER THAN RECORDED IN FIRST STEP
• IDLE ENGINE FOR 1 MINUTE IN DRIVE (A/T) OR NEUTRAL (M/T).
• SHIFT TO NEUTRAL (A/T).
• NOTE ENGINE SPEED.
WILL NOT RETURN TO RPM RECORDED IN FIRST STEP
RETURNS TO RPM RECORDED IN FIRST STEP
IDLE AIR CONTROL CIRCUIT OK. REFER TO "DIAGNOSTIC AIDS" ON FACING PAGE.
3
• IGNITION "OFF".
• DISCONNECT IAC VALVE HARNESS.
• IGNITION "ON", ENGINE "OFF".
• GROUND DIAGNOSTIC TEST TERMINAL.
• CONNECT A TEST LIGHT BETWEEN EACH IAC VALVE HARNESS CONNECTOR TERMINAL AND GROUND.
NO LIGHTS, ONE OR MORE CIRCUITS
4
LIGHT STEADY OR FLASHING ALL CIRCUITS
FAULTY IAC CONNECTION OR IAC VALVE, OR PLUGGED PASSAGE. IF LIGHT APPEARS TO BE STEADY, REFER TO STEP 4 ON FACING PAGE.
5
• CHECK FOR OPEN OR SHORT TO GROUND IN CIRCUIT WITH NO LIGHT. ARE ALL CIRCUITS OK?
YES
NO
REPAIR WIRING AND RECHECK.
• CHECK RESISTANCE ACROSS IAC VALVE COILS. IT SHOULD BE MORE THAN 20 OHMS BETWEEN IAC VALVE TERMINALS "A" & "B" AND "C" & "D". IS IT?
YES
NO
FAULTY ECM CONNECTION OR ECM.
REPLACE IAC VALVE AND RETEST.
CLEAR CODES, CONFIRM "CLOSED LOOP" OPERATION, NO "SERVICE ENGINE SOON" LIGHT.

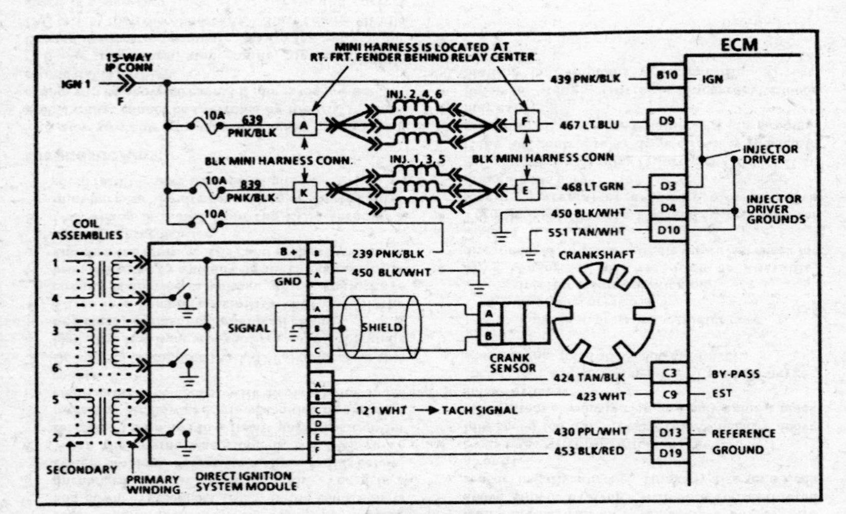

CODE 42

ELECTRONIC SPARK TIMING (EST) CIRCUIT 2.8L (VIN W) "W" SERIES (PORT)

Circuit Description:

When the system is running on the ignition module, that is, no voltage on the bypass line, the ignition module grounds the EST signal. The ECM expects to see no voltage on the EST line during this condition. If it sees a voltage, it sets Code 42 and will not go into the EST mode.

When the rpm for EST is reached (about 400 rpm), and bypass voltage applied, the EST should on longer be grounded in the ignition module so the EST voltage should be varying.

If the bypass line is open or grounded, the ignition module will not switch to EST mode so the EST voltage will be low and Code 42 will be set.

If the EST line is grounded, the ignition module will switch to EST, but because the line is grounded there will be no EST signal. A Code 42 will be set.

Test Description: Numbers below refer to circled numbers on the diagnostic chart.

1. Code 42 means the ECM has seen an open or short to ground in the EST or bypass circuits. This test confirms Code 42 and that the fault causing the code is present.
2. Checks for a normal EST ground path through the ignition module. An EST CKT 423 shorted to ground will also read less than 500 ohms; however, this will be checked later.
3. As the test light voltage touches CKT 424, the module should switch causing the ohmmeter to "overrange" if the meter is in the 1000-2000 ohms position. Selecting the 10-20,000 ohms position will indicate above 5000 ohms. The important thing is that the module "switched".
4. The module did not switch and this step checks for:
   - EST CKT 423 shorted to ground.
   - Bypass CKT 424 open.
   - Faulty ignition module connection or module.
5. Confirms that Code 42 is a faulty ECM and not an intermittent in CKTs 423 or 424.

Diagnostic Aids:

The "Scan" tool does not have any ability to help diagnose a Code 42 problem.

A Mem-Cal not fully seated in the ECM can result in a Code 42.

Refer to "Intermittents" in Section "B".

CODE 42

ELECTRONIC SPARK TIMING (EST) CIRCUIT 2.8L (VIN W) "W" SERIES (PORT)

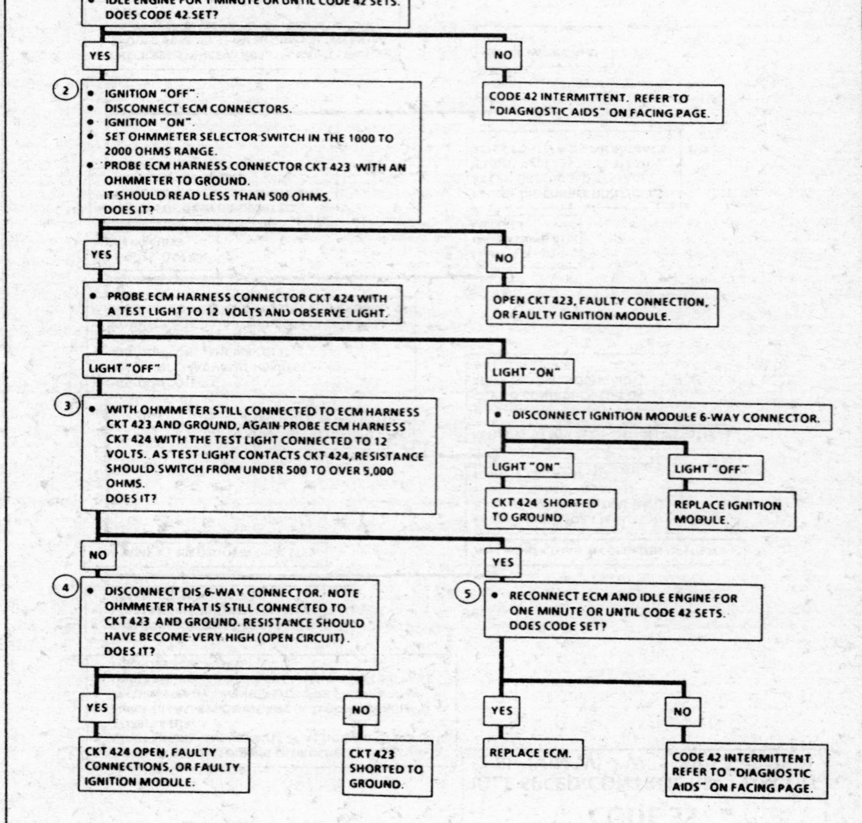

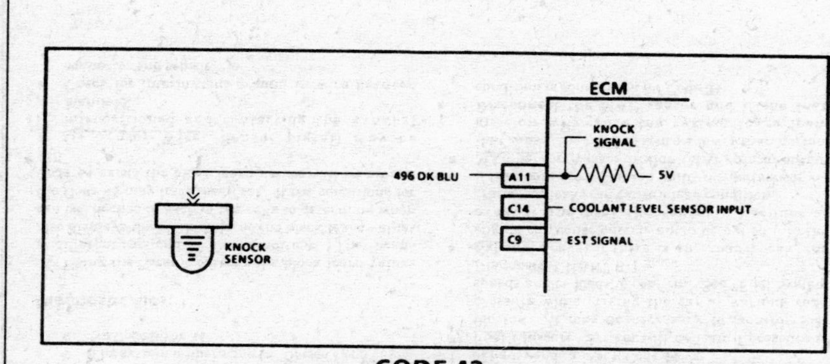
ECM
KNOCK SIGNAL
5V
496 DK BLU
A11
C14
COOLANT LEVEL SENSOR INPUT
C9
EST SIGNAL
KNOCK SENSOR

CODE 43

ELECTRONIC SPARK CONTROL (ESC) CIRCUIT 2.8L (VIN W) "W" SERIES (PORT)

Circuit Description:

The knock sensor is used to detect engine detonation and the ECM will retard the electronic spark timing based on the signal being received. The circuitry within the knock sensor causes the ECM 5 volts to be pulled down so that under a no knock condition, CKT 496 would measure about 2.5 volts. The knock sensor produces an AC signal which rides on the 2.5volts DC voltage. The amplitude and signal frequency is dependent upon the knock level.

There are two tests run on this circuit to determine if it is operating correctly. If either of the tests fail, a Code 43 will be set.

43A. If CKT 496 becomes open or shorted to ground the voltage will either go above 3.5 volts or below 1.5 volts. If either of these conditions are met for about ½ second a Code 43 will be stored.

43B. This system also performs a functional test to determine if the knock sensor is responding to engine detonation. To perfom this test, the ECM will advance the spark under certain load conditions and look for a knock signal response. If knock is detected before conditions are met to run the test, the test is bypassed, but if the test is run and no knock detected the Code 43 will be set.

The test is performed when:

Coolant temperature is over 90°C.
MAT temperature is over 0°C.
High engine load based on air flow and rpm between 3400 and 4400.

Test Description: Numbers below refer to circled numbers on the diagnostic chart.

1. If the conditions for the A test, as described above, are being met the "Scan" tool will always indicate "yes" when the knock signal position is selected. If an audible knock is heard from the engine, repair the internal engine problem, as normally no knock should be detected at idle.
2. If tapping on the engine lift hook does not produce a knock signal, try tapping engine closer to sensor before proceeding.
3. The ECM has a 5 volt pull-up resistor which should be present at the knock sensor terminal.
4. This test determines if the knock sensor is faulty or if the ESC portion of the Mem-Cal is faulty.

Diagnostic Aids:

Check CKT 496 for a potential open or short to ground.

Also check for proper installation of Mem-Cal. Refer to "Intermittents" in Section "B".

If the customer's complaint is the "Service Engine Soon" light comes "ON" when in acceleration, the B portion of the code is failing. There is a possibility that the direct ignition system was in bypass mode when the 43 test was run. An intermittent open in the EST circuit will put the DIS module in bypass which will not allow the spark to be advanced so the 43B test would fail. If ECM also had a 42 stored, then the EST circuit is likely the cause of the Code 43.

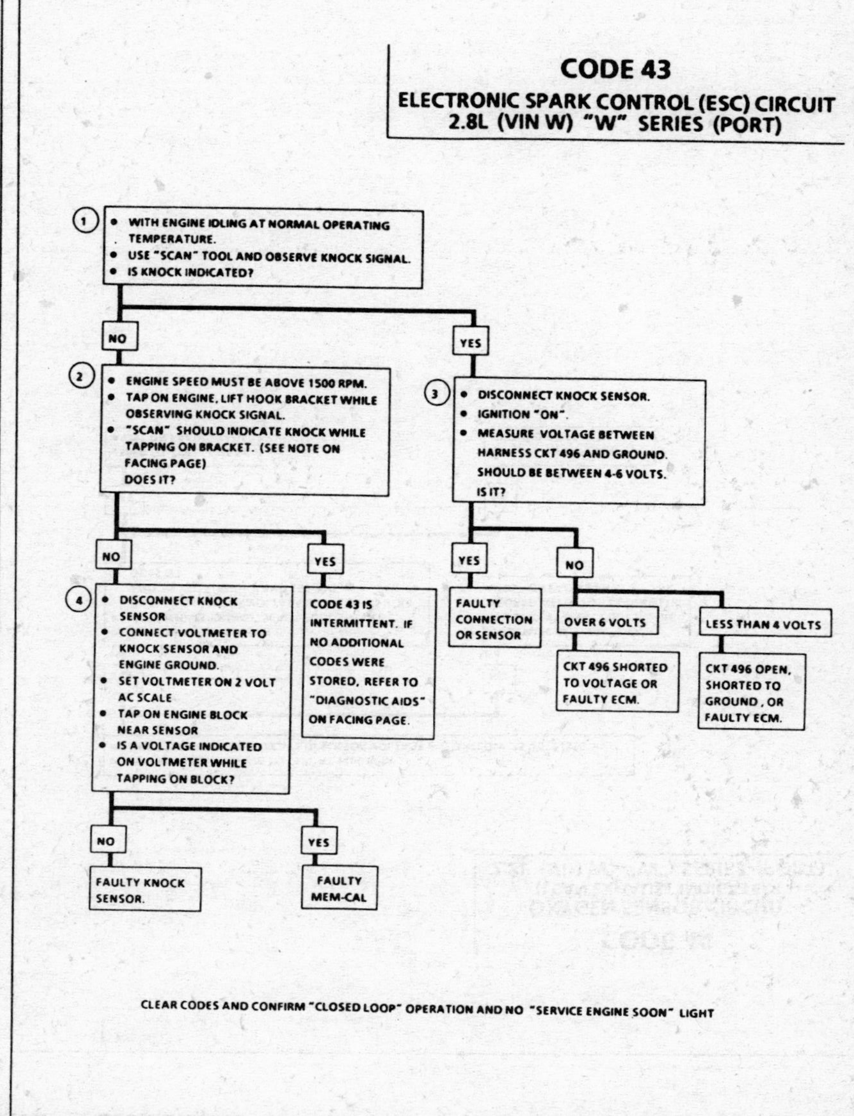
CODE 43
ELECTRONIC SPARK CONTROL (ESC) CIRCUIT
2.8L (VIN W) "W" SERIES (PORT)
1
• WITH ENGINE IDLING AT NORMAL OPERATING TEMPERATURE.
• USE "SCAN" TOOL AND OBSERVE KNOCK SIGNAL.
• IS KNOCK INDICATED?
NO
YES
2
• ENGINE SPEED MUST BE ABOVE 1500 RPM.
• TAP ON ENGINE, LIFT HOOK BRACKET WHILE OBSERVING KNOCK SIGNAL.
• "SCAN" SHOULD INDICATE KNOCK WHILE TAPPING ON BRACKET. (SEE NOTE ON FACING PAGE)
DOES IT?
3
• DISCONNECT KNOCK SENSOR.
• IGNITION "ON".
• MEASURE VOLTAGE BETWEEN HARNESS CKT 496 AND GROUND. SHOULD BE BETWEEN 4-6 VOLTS.
IS IT?
NO
YES
YES
NO
4
• DISCONNECT KNOCK SENSOR
• CONNECT VOLTMETER TO KNOCK SENSOR AND ENGINE GROUND.
• SET VOLTMETER ON 2 VOLT AC SCALE
• TAP ON ENGINE BLOCK NEAR SENSOR
• IS A VOLTAGE INDICATED ON VOLTMETER WHILE TAPPING ON BLOCK?
CODE 43 IS INTERMITTENT. IF NO ADDITIONAL CODES WERE STORED, REFER TO "DIAGNOSTIC AIDS" ON FACING PAGE.
FAULTY CONNECTION OR SENSOR
OVER 6 VOLTS
LESS THAN 4 VOLTS
CKT 496 SHORTED TO VOLTAGE OR FAULTY ECM.
CKT 496 OPEN, SHORTED TO GROUND, OR FAULTY ECM.
NO
YES
FAULTY KNOCK SENSOR.
FAULTY MEM-CAL
CLEAR CODES AND CONFIRM "CLOSED LOOP" OPERATION AND NO "SERVICE ENGINE SOON" LIGHT

DIAGNOSTIC CHARTS — 2.8L engine

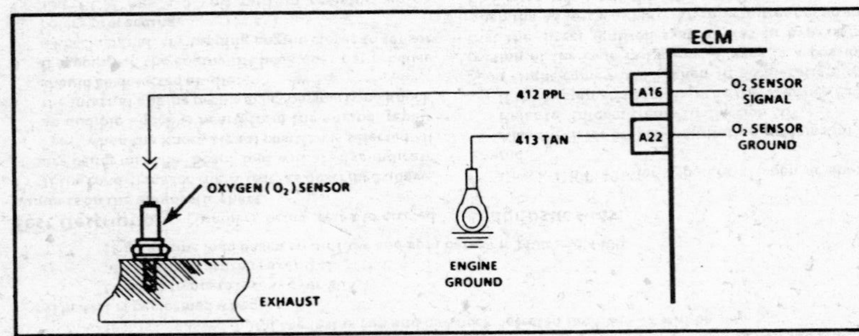

CODE 44

OXYGEN SENSOR CIRCUIT
(LEAN EXHAUST INDICATED)
2.8L (VIN W) "W" SERIES (PORT)

Circuit Description:

The ECM supplies a voltage of about .45 volt between terminals "A16" and "A22". (If measured with a 10 megohm digital voltmeter, this may read as low as .32 volt.) The O_2 sensor varies the voltage within a range of about 1 volt if the exhaust is rich, down through about .10 volt if exhaust is lean.

The sensor is like an open circuit and produces no voltage when it is below about 315°C (600°F). An open sensor circuit or cold sensor causes "Open Loop" operation.

Test Description: Numbers below refer to circled numbers on the diagnostic chart.

Code 44 will set if:

- Voltage on CKT 412 remains below .2 volt for 60 seconds or more;
- The system is operating in "Closed Loop".
- No Code 33 or 34.

Diagnostic Aids:

Using the "Scan", observe the block learn values at different rpm and air flow conditions. The "Scan" also displays the block cells, so the block learn values can be checked in each of the cells to determine when the Code 44 may have been set. If the conditions for Code 44 exists the block learn values will be around 150.

- O_2 Sensor Wire Sensor pigtail may be mispositioned and contacting the exhaust manifold.
- Check for intermittent ground in wire between connector and sensor.
- Lean Injector(s) Perform injector balance test CHART C-2A.
- Fuel Contamination Water, even in small amounts, near the in-tank fuel pump inlet can be delivered to the injectors. The water causes a lean exhaust and can set a Code 44.
- Fuel Pressure System will be lean if pressure is too low. It may be necessary to monitor fuel pressure while driving the car at various road speeds and/or loads to confirm. See "Fuel System Diagnosis" CHART A-7.
- Exhaust Leaks If there is an exhaust leak, the engine can cause outside air to be pulled into the exhaust and past the sensor. Vacuum or crankcase leaks can cause a lean condition.
- If the above are OK, it is a faulty oxygen sensor.
- MAF Sensor A mass air flow (MAF) sensor output that causes the ECM to sense a lower than normal air flow will cause the system to go lean. Disconnect the MAF sensor and if the lean condition is gone, check for Code 34.

CODE 44

OXYGEN SENSOR CIRCUIT
(LEAN EXHAUST INDICATED)
2.8L (VIN W) "W" SERIES (PORT)

(1)
- RUN WARM ENGINE (75 TO 95)°C AT 1200 RPM.
- DOES "SCAN" TOOL INDICATE O_2 SENSOR VOLTAGE FIXED BELOW .35 VOLT (350 mV)?

YES:
- DISCONNECT O_2 SENSOR.
- WITH ENGINE IDLING, "SCAN" TOOL SHOULD DISPLAY O_2 SENSOR VOLTAGE BETWEEN .35 VOLT AND .55 VOLT (350 mV AND 550 mV). DOES IT?

  YES: REFER TO "DIAGNOSTIC AIDS" ON FACING PAGE.

  NO: CKT 412 SHORTED TO GROUND OR FAULTY ECM.

NO: CODE 44 IS INTERMITTENT. IF NO ADDITIONAL CODES WERE STORED, REFER TO "DIAGNOSTIC AIDS" ON FACING PAGE.

CLEAR CODES AND CONFIRM "CLOSED LOOP" OPERATION AND NO "SERVICE ENGINE SOON" LIGHT.

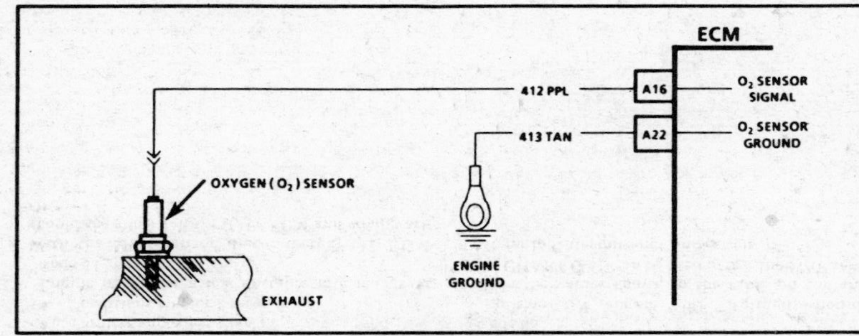
ECM
412 PPL
A16
O_2 SENSOR SIGNAL
413 TAN
A22
O_2 SENSOR GROUND
OXYGEN (O_2) SENSOR
ENGINE GROUND
EXHAUST

CODE 45

OXYGEN SENSOR CIRCUIT (RICH EXHAUST INDICATED) 2.8L (VIN W) "W" SERIES (PORT)

Circuit Description:

The ECM supplies a voltage of about .45 volt between terminals "A16" and "A22". (If measured with a 10 megohm digital voltmeter, this may read as low as .32 volt.) The O_2 sensor varies the voltage within a range of about 1 volt if the exhaust is rich, down through about .10 volt if exhaust is lean.

The sensor is like an open circuit and produces no voltage when it is below about 315°C (600°F). An open sensor circuit or cold sensor causes "Open Loop" operation.

Test Description: Numbers below refer to circled numbers on the diagnostic chart.

Code 45 will set if:

- Voltage on CKT 412 remains above .7 volt for 30 seconds.
- Engine time after start is 1 minute or more.
- Throttle angle between 3% and 45%.
- Operation is in "Closed Loop".

Diagnostic Aids:

Using the "Scan", observe the block learn values at different rpm and air flow conditions. The "Scan" also displays the block cells, so the block learn values can be checked in each of the cells to determine when the Code 45 may have been set. If the conditions for Code 45 exists, the block learn values will be around 115.

- Fuel Pressure. System will go rich if pressure is too high. The ECM can compensate for some increase. However, if it gets too high, a Code 45 may be set. See fuel system diagnosis CHART A-7.
- Rich Injector Perform injector balance test CHART C-2A.
- Leaking Injector See CHART A-7.
- Check for fuel contaminated oil.
- O_2 Sensor Contamination Inspect oxygen sensor for silicone contamination from fuel, or use of improper RTV sealant. The sensor may have a white, powdery coating and result in a high but false signal voltage (rich exhaust indication).

The ECM will then reduce the amount of fuel delivered to the engine, causing a severe surge driveability problem.

- HEI Shielding An open ground CKT 453 (ignition system reflow) may result in EMI, or induced electrical "noise". The ECM looks at this "noise" as reference pulses. The additional pulses result in a higher than actual engine speed signal. The ECM then delivers too much fuel, causing system to go rich. Engine tachometer will also show higher than actual engine speed, which can help in diagnosing this problem.
- Canister Purge Check for fuel saturation. If full of fuel, check canister control and hoses.
- Check for leaking fuel pressure regulator diaphragm by checking vacuum line to regulator for fuel.
- TPS An intermittent TPS output will cause the system to go rich, due to a false indication of the engine accelerating.
- EGR An EGR staying open (especially at idle) will cause the O_2 sensor to indicate a rich exhaust, and this could result in a Code 45.
- MAF Sensor An output that causes the ECM to sense a higher than normal airflow can cause the system to go rich. Disconnecting the MAF sensor will allow the ECM to set a fixed value for the sensor. Substitute a different MAF sensor if the the rich condition is gone while the sensor is disconnected, check for a Code 34.

CODE 45

OXYGEN SENSOR CIRCUIT (RICH EXHAUST INDICATED) 2.8L (VIN W) "W" SERIES (PORT)

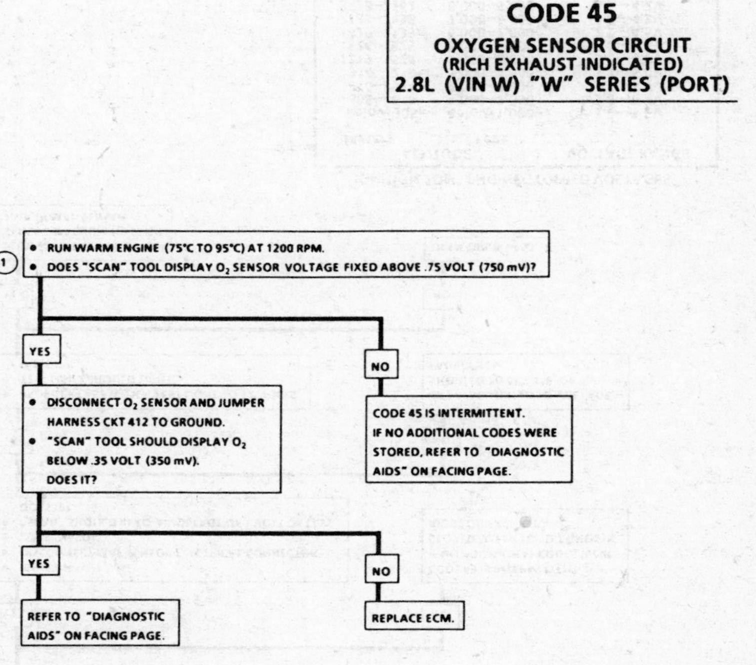
1
• RUN WARM ENGINE (75°C TO 95°C) AT 1200 RPM.
• DOES "SCAN" TOOL DISPLAY O_2 SENSOR VOLTAGE FIXED ABOVE .75 VOLT (750 mV)?
YES
NO
• DISCONNECT O_2 SENSOR AND JUMPER HARNESS CKT 412 TO GROUND.
• "SCAN" TOOL SHOULD DISPLAY O_2 BELOW .35 VOLT (350 mV).
DOES IT?
CODE 45 IS INTERMITTENT.
IF NO ADDITIONAL CODES WERE STORED, REFER TO "DIAGNOSTIC AIDS" ON FACING PAGE.
YES
NO
REFER TO "DIAGNOSTIC AIDS" ON FACING PAGE.
REPLACE ECM.
CLEAR CODES AND CONFIRM "CLOSED LOOP" OPERATION AND NO "SERVICE ENGINE SOON" LIGHT.

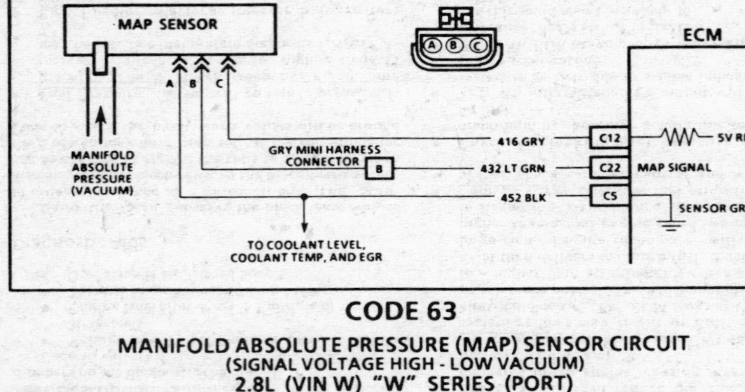

CODE 63

MANIFOLD ABSOLUTE PRESSURE (MAP) SENSOR CIRCUIT
(SIGNAL VOLTAGE HIGH - LOW VACUUM)
2.8L (VIN W) "W" SERIES (PORT)

Circuit Description:

The manifold absolute pressure sensor (MAP) responds to changes in manifold pressure (vacuum). The ECM recieves this information as a signal voltage that will vary from about 1/1.5 volts at idle (high vacuum) to 4/4.5 volts at wide open throttle (low vacuum).

Test Description: Numbers below refer to circled numbers on the diagnostic chart.

1. Code 63 will set when:
   - Engine running
   - Manifold pressure greater than 75.3 kPa (A/C "OFF") 81.2 kPa (A/C "ON")
   - Throttle angle less than 2%
   - Conditions met for 2 seconds

   Engine misfire or a low unstable idle may set Code 63.
2. With the MAP sensor disconnected, the ECM should see a low voltage if the ECM and wiring are OK.

Diagnostic Aids:

If idle is rough or unstable, refer to "Symptoms" in Section "B" for items which can cause an unstable idle.

An open in CKT 452 or the connection will result in a Code 63.

Ignition "ON" engine "OFF," voltages should be within the values shown in the table on the chart. Also CHART C-1D can be used to test the MAP sensor.

Refer to "Intermittents" in Section "B".

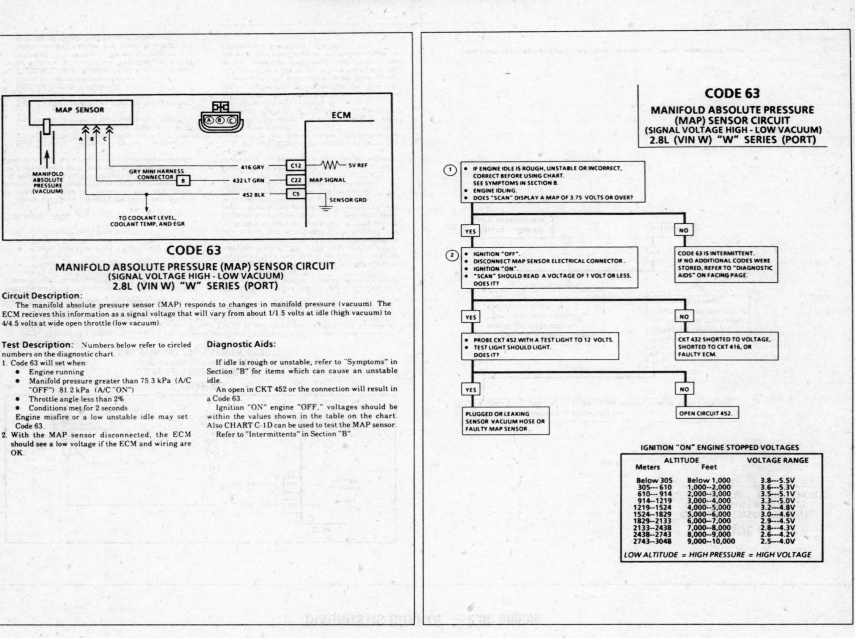

CODE 63

MANIFOLD ABSOLUTE PRESSURE (MAP) SENSOR CIRCUIT
(SIGNAL VOLTAGE HIGH - LOW VACUUM)
2.8L (VIN W) "W" SERIES (PORT)

(1)
- IF ENGINE IDLE IS ROUGH, UNSTABLE OR INCORRECT, CORRECT BEFORE USING CHART. SEE SYMPTOMS IN SECTION B.
- ENGINE IDLING.
- DOES "SCAN" DISPLAY A MAP OF 3.75 VOLTS OR OVER?

NO → CODE 63 IS INTERMITTENT. IF NO ADDITIONAL CODES WERE STORED, REFER TO "DIAGNOSTIC AIDS" ON FACING PAGE.

YES ↓

(2)
- IGNITION "OFF".
- DISCONNECT MAP SENSOR ELECTRICAL CONNECTOR.
- IGNITION "ON".
- "SCAN" SHOULD READ A VOLTAGE OF 1 VOLT OR LESS. DOES IT?

NO → CKT 432 SHORTED TO VOLTAGE, SHORTED TO CKT 416, OR FAULTY ECM.

YES ↓

- PROBE CKT 452 WITH A TEST LIGHT TO 12 VOLTS.
- TEST LIGHT SHOULD LIGHT. DOES IT?

YES → PLUGGED OR LEAKING SENSOR VACUUM HOSE OR FAULTY MAP SENSOR.

NO → OPEN CIRCUIT 452.

IGNITION "ON" ENGINE STOPPED VOLTAGES

ALTITUDE Meters	ALTITUDE Feet	VOLTAGE RANGE
Below 305	Below 1,000	3.8---5.5V
305--- 610	1,000--2,000	3.6---5.3V
610--- 914	2,000--3,000	3.5---5.1V
914--1219	3,000--4,000	3.3---5.0V
1219--1524	4,000--5,000	3.2---4.8V
1524--1829	5,000--6,000	3.0---4.6V
1829--2133	6,000--7,000	2.9---4.5V
2133--2438	7,000--8,000	2.8---4.3V
2438--2743	8,000--9,000	2.6---4.2V
2743--3048	9,000--10,000	2.5---4.0V

LOW ALTITUDE = HIGH PRESSURE = HIGH VOLTAGE

MAP SENSOR
A B C
MANIFOLD ABSOLUTE PRESSURE (VACUUM)
GRY MINI HARNESS CONNECTOR B
416 GRY C12 5V REF
432 LT GRN C22 MAP SIGNAL
452 BLK C5 SENSOR GRD
ECM
TO COOLANT LEVEL, COOLANT TEMP, AND EGR

CODE 64

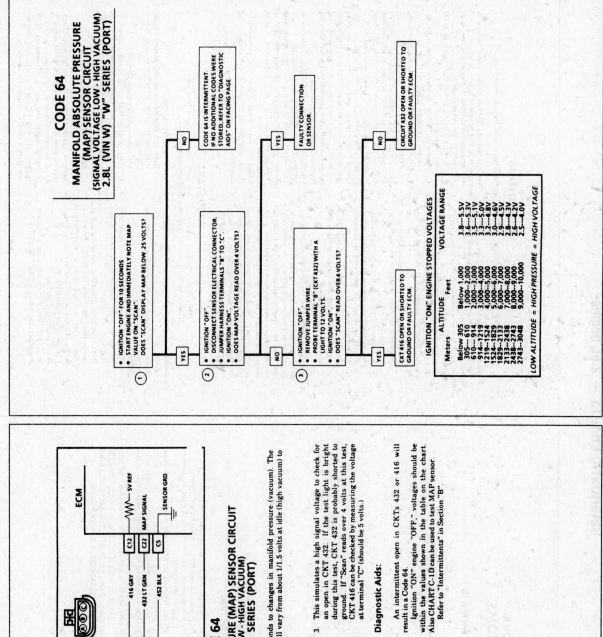

MANIFOLD ABSOLUTE PRESSURE (MAP) SENSOR CIRCUIT (SIGNAL VOLTAGE LOW - HIGH VACUUM) 2.8L (VIN W) "W" SERIES (PORT)

Circuit Description:

The manifold absolute pressure sensor (MAP) responds to changes in manifold pressure (vacuum). The ECM recieves this information as a signal voltage that will vary from about 1/1.5 volts at idle (high vacuum) to 4/4.5 volts at wide open throttle (low vacuum).

Test Description: Numbers below refer to circled numbers on the diagnostic chart.

1. Code 64 will set if:
   - Engine rpm less than 600
   - Manifold pressure reading less than 13 kPa
   - Conditions met for 1 second

   or
   - Engine rpm greater than 600
   - Throttle angle over 20%
   - Manifold pressure less than 13 kPa
   - Conditions met for 1 second
2. This test to see if the sensor is at fault for the low voltage, or if there is an ECM or wiring problem.
3. This simulates a high signal voltage to check for an open in CKT 432. If the test light is bright during this test, CKT 432 is probably shorted to ground. If "Scan" reads over 4 volts at this test, CKT 416 can be checked by measuring the voltage at terminal "C" (should be 5 volts.)

Diagnostic Aids:

An intermittent open in CKTs 432 or 416 will result in a Code 64.

Ignition "ON" engine "OFF," voltages should be within the values shown in the table on the chart. Also CHART C-1D can be used to test MAP sensor.

Refer to "Intermittents" in Section "B".

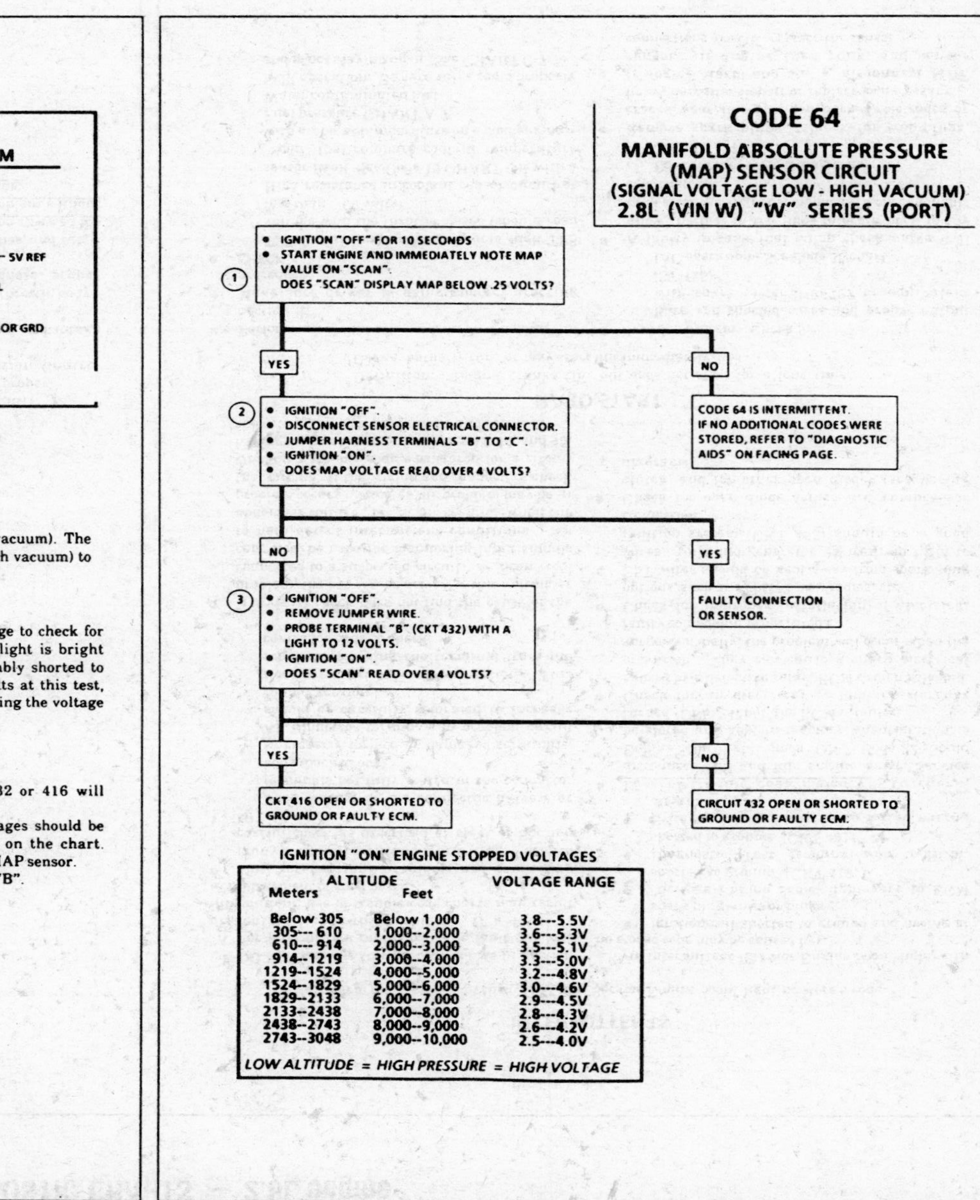
CODE 64
MANIFOLD ABSOLUTE PRESSURE (MAP) SENSOR CIRCUIT
(SIGNAL VOLTAGE LOW - HIGH VACUUM)
2.8L (VIN W) "W" SERIES (PORT)
1
• IGNITION "OFF" FOR 10 SECONDS
• START ENGINE AND IMMEDIATELY NOTE MAP VALUE ON "SCAN".
DOES "SCAN" DISPLAY MAP BELOW .25 VOLTS?
YES
NO
CODE 64 IS INTERMITTENT. IF NO ADDITIONAL CODES WERE STORED, REFER TO "DIAGNOSTIC AIDS" ON FACING PAGE.
2
• IGNITION "OFF".
• DISCONNECT SENSOR ELECTRICAL CONNECTOR.
• JUMPER HARNESS TERMINALS "B" TO "C".
• IGNITION "ON".
• DOES MAP VOLTAGE READ OVER 4 VOLTS?
NO
YES
FAULTY CONNECTION OR SENSOR.
3
• IGNITION "OFF".
• REMOVE JUMPER WIRE.
• PROBE TERMINAL "B" (CKT 432) WITH A LIGHT TO 12 VOLTS.
• IGNITION "ON".
• DOES "SCAN" READ OVER 4 VOLTS?
YES
CKT 416 OPEN OR SHORTED TO GROUND OR FAULTY ECM.
NO
CIRCUIT 432 OPEN OR SHORTED TO GROUND OR FAULTY ECM.

IGNITION "ON" ENGINE STOPPED VOLTAGES

ALTITUDE Meters	Feet	VOLTAGE RANGE
Below 305	Below 1,000	3.8---5.5V
305--- 610	1,000--2,000	3.6---5.3V
610--- 914	2,000--3,000	3.5---5.1V
914--1219	3,000--4,000	3.3---5.0V
1219--1524	4,000--5,000	3.2---4.8V
1524--1829	5,000--6,000	3.0---4.6V
1829--2133	6,000--7,000	2.9---4.5V
2133--2438	7,000--8,000	2.8---4.3V
2438--2743	8,000--9,000	2.6---4.2V
2743--3048	9,000--10,000	2.5---4.0V

LOW ALTITUDE = HIGH PRESSURE = HIGH VOLTAGE

DIAGNOSTIC CHARTS — 2.8L engine

SECTION B
SYMPTOMS

TABLE OF CONTENTS

BEFORE STARTING

Before using this section you should have performed the DIAGNOSTIC CIRCUIT CHECK and found out that:

1. The ECM and "Service Engine Soon" light are operating.
2. There are no trouble codes.

Verify the customer complaint, and locate the correct SYMPTOM below. Check the items indicated under that symptom.

If the ENGINE CRANKS BUT WILL NOT RUN, see CHART A-3.

Several of the symptom procedures below call for a careful visual check. This check should include:

- ECM grounds for being clean and tight
- Vacuum hoses for splits, kinks, and proper connections, as shown on Emission Control Information label.
- Air leaks at throttle body mounting and intake manifold.
- Air leaks between MAF sensor and throttle body.
- Ignition wires for cracking, hardness, proper routing, and carbon tracking.
- Wiring for proper connections, pinches, and cuts.

The importance of this step cannot be stressed too strongly - it can lead to correcting a problem without further checks and can save valuable time.

INTERMITTENTS

Problem may or may not turn "ON" the "Service Engine Soon" light, or store a code.

DO NOT use the trouble code charts in Section "A" for intermittent problems. The fault must be present to locate the problem. If a fault is intermittent, use of trouble code charts may result in replacement of good parts.

- Most intermittent problems are caused by faulty electrical connections or wiring. Perform careful check as described at start of Section "B". Check for:
  - Poor mating of the connector halves, or terminals not fully seated in the connector body (backed out).
  - Improperly formed or damaged terminals. All connector terminals in problem circuit should be carefully reformed to increase contact tension.
  - Poor terminal to wire connection. This requires removing the terminal from the connector body to check.
- If a visual check does not find the cause of the problem, the car can be driven with a voltmeter connected to a suspected circuit. A "Scan" tool can, also, be used for monitoring input signals to help detect intermittent conditions. An abnormal voltage, or "Scan" reading, when the problem occurs, indicates the problem may be in that circuit. If the wiring and connectors check OK and a trouble code was stored for a circuit having a sensor, except for Codes 43, 44, and 45, substitute a known good sensor and recheck.

An intermittent "Service Engine Soon" light with no stored code may be caused by:

- Ignition coil shorted to ground and arcing at spark plug wires or plugs.
- "Service Engine Soon" light wire to ECM shorted to ground. (CKT 419)
- Diagnostic "Test" terminal wire to ECM, shorted to ground. (CKT 451)
- ECM power grounds. See ECM wiring diagrams.
- Loss of trouble code memory. To check, disconnect TPS and idle engine until "Service Engine Soon" light comes "ON." Code 22 should be stored and kept in memory when ignition is turned "OFF." If not, the ECM is faulty.
- Check for an electrical system interference caused by a defective relay, ECM driven solenoid, or switch. They can cause a sharp electrical surge. Normally, the problem will occur when the faulty component is operated.
- Check for improper installation of electrical options, such as lights, 2-way radios, etc.
- EST wires should be kept away from spark plug wires, coils and generator. Wire from ECM to ignition system (CKT 453) should be a good connection.
- Check for open diode across A/C compressor clutch, and for other open diodes (see wiring diagrams).

HARD START

Definition: Engine cranks OK, but does not start for a long time. Does eventually run, or may start but immediately dies.

- Perform careful check as described at start of Section "B".
- Make sure driver is using correct starting procedure.
- **CHECK:**
  - TPS for sticking or binding or a high TPS voltage with the throttle closed (should read less than .700 volts).
  - High resistance in coolant sensor circuit or sensor itself. See Code 15 CHART OR with a "Scan" tool compare coolant temperature with ambient temperature on a cold engine.
  - Fuel pressure CHART A-7.
  - Water contaminated fuel.
  - EGR operation. Be sure valve seats properly and is not staying open. See CHART C-7.
- Ignition system - Check for:
  - Bare and shorted wires and proper output with spark tester J-26792 or equivalent (ST-125).
  - IAC operation - See Code 35 chart.
- A faulty in-tank fuel pump check valve will allow the fuel in the lines to drain back to the tank after the engine is stopped. To check for this condition:

  Perform fuel system diagnosis, CHART A-7.
- Remove spark plugs. Check for wet plugs, cracks, wear, improper gap, burned electrodes, or heavy deposits. Repair or replace as necessary.
- If engine starts and stalls, disconnect MAF sensor. If engine then runs, and sensor connections are OK, replace the sensor.

DIAGNOSTIC CHARTS — 2.8L engine

HESITATION, SAG, STUMBLE

Definition: Momentary lack of response as the accelerator is pushed down. Can occur at all car speeds. Usually most severe when first trying to make the car move, as from a stop sign. May cause the engine to stall if severe enough.

- Perform careful visual check as described at start of Section "B".
- CHECK:
  - Fuel pressure. See CHART A-7. Also check for water contaminated fuel.
  - Air leaks at air duct between MAF sensor and throttle body.
  - Spark plugs for being fouled or faulty wiring.
  - Mem-Cal number and Service Bulletins for latest Mem-Cal.
  - TPS for binding or sticking. Voltage should increase at a steady rate as throttle is moved toward W.O.T.
  - Generator output voltage. Repair, if less than 9 or more than 16 volts.
  - Ignition system ground, CKT 453.
  - Canister purge system for proper operation. See CHART C-3.
  - EGR - See CHART C-7.
  - MAP sensor - See CHART C-1D
- Perform injector balance test, CHART C-2A.

SURGES AND/OR CHUGGLE

Definition: Engine power variation under steady throttle or cruise. Feels like the car speeds up and slows down with no change in the accelerator pedal.

- Be sure driver understands transmission/ transaxle converter clutch and A/C compressor operation in Owner's Manual.
- Perform careful visual inspection as described at start of Section "B".
- To help determine if the condition is caused by a rich or lean system, the car should be driven at the speed of the complaint. Monitoring block learn at the complaint speed will help identify the cause of the problem. If the system is running lean (block learn greater than 138), refer to "Diagnostic Aids" on facing page of Code 44. If the system is running rich (block learn less than 118), refer to "Diagnostic Aids" on facing page of Code 45.
- CHECK:
  - Loose or leaking air duct between MAF sensor and throttle body.
  - Generator output voltage. Repair if less than 9 or more than 16 volts.
  - EGR (2.8L) - There should be no EGR at idle. See CHART C-7
  - EGR filter for being plugged (2.8L). See CHART C-7.
  - Vacuum lines for kinks or leaks.
  - In-line fuel filter. Replace if dirty or plugged.
  - Fuel pressure while condition exists. See CHART A-7.
- Remove spark plugs. Check for cracks, wear, improper gap, burned electrodes, or heavy deposits. Also check condition of spark plug wires and check for proper output voltage using spark tester (ST-125) J-26792 or equivalent.

LACK OF POWER, SLUGGISH, OR SPONGY

Definition: Engine delivers less than expected power. Little or no increase in speed when accelerator pedal is pushed down part way.

- Perform careful visual check as described at start of Section "B".
- Compare customer's car to similar unit. Make sure the customer's car has an actual problem.
- Remove air filter and check air filter for dirt, or for being plugged. Replace as necessary.
- CHECK:
  - For loose or leaking air duct between MAF Sensor and throttle body.
  - Restricted fuel filter, contaminated fuel or improper fuel pressure. See CHART A-7
  - ECM power grounds, see wiring diagrams.
  - EGR operation for being open or partly open all the time - See CHART C-7.
  - Exhaust system for possible restriction: See CHART B-1.
    - Inspect exhaust system for damaged or collapsed pipes.
    - Inspect muffler for heat distress or possible internal failure.
  - Generator output voltage. Repair if less than 9 or more than 16 volts.
  - Engine valve timing and compression.
  - Engine for proper or worn camshaft.
  - Secondary voltage using a shop ocilliscope or a spark tester J-26792 (ST-125) or equivalent.
  - Check A/C operation. A/C clutch should cut out at WOT. See A/C CHART C-10.

DETONATION /SPARK KNOCK

Definition: A mild to severe ping, usually worse under acceleration. The engine makes sharp metallic knocks that change with throttle opening. Sounds like popcorn popping.

- Check for obvious overheating problems:
  - Low coolant.
  - Loose belt.
  - Restricted air flow to radiator, or restricted water flow through radiator.
  - Inoperative electric cooling fan circuit. See CHART C-12.
- To help determine if the conditions is caused by a rich or lean system, the car should be driven at the speed of the complaint. Monitoring block learn, at the complaint speed, will help identify the cause of the problem. If the system is running lean (block learn greater than 138), refer to diagnostic aids on facing page of Code 44. If the system is running rich (block learn less than 118), refer to facing page of Code 45.
- CHECK:
  - EGR system for not opening or plugged EGR passages - See CHART C-7.
  - ESC system for no retard - See CHART C-5.
  - Park/Neutral switch. Be sure "Scan" indicates drive with gear selector in drive or overdrive. See CHART C-1A.
  - TCC operation, TCC applying too soon - see CHART C-8.
- Fuel system pressure - See CHART A-7.
- Remove carbon with top engine cleaner. Follow instructions on can.
  - Check for correct Mem-Cal.
  - Check for excessive oil in combustion chamber.
  - Check for incorrect basic engine parts such as cam, heads, pistons, etc.
  - Check for poor fuel quality, proper octane rating.

DIAGNOSTIC CHARTS — 2.8L engine

CUTS OUT, MISSES

Definition: Steady pulsation or jerking that follows engine speed, usually more pronounced as engine load increases. Not normally felt above 1500 rpm or 30 mph (48 km/h). The exhaust has a steady spitting sound at idle or low speed.

- Perform careful visual check as described at start of Section "B".
- Check for missing cylinder by:
  1. Disconnect IAC motor. Start engine. Remove one spark plug wire at a time using insulated pliers.
  2. If there is an rpm drop on all cylinders (equal to within 50 rpm), go to ROUGH, UNSTABLE, OR INCORRECT IDLE, STALLING symptom. Reconnect IAC motor.
  3. If there is no rpm drop on one or more cylinders, or excessive variation in drop, check for spark on the suspected cylinder(s) with J-26792 (ST-125) spark gap tool or equivalent. If no spark, see Section "6D" for Intermittent Operation or Miss. If there is spark, remove spark plug(s) in these cylinders and check for:
     - Cracks
     - Wear
     - Improper Gap
     - Burned Electrodes
     - Heavy Deposits
- Perform compression check on questionable cylinder(s) found above. If compression is low, repair as necessary.
- Disconnect all injector harness connectors. Connect J-34730-2 injector test light or equivalent 6 volt test light between the harness terms. of each injector connector and note light while cranking. If test light fails to blink at any connector, it is a faulty injector drive circuit harness, connector, terminal, or ECM.
- Perform the injector balance test. See CHART C-2A.
- Check spark plug wires by connecting ohmmeter to ends of each wire in question. If meter reads over 30,000 ohms, replace wire(s).
- Spray plug wires with fine water mist to check for shorts.
- Check for restricted fuel filter. Also check fuel tank for water.
- Check for low fuel pressure. See CHART A-7.
- Remove rocker covers. Check for bent pushrods, worn rocker arms, broken valve springs, worn camshaft lobes. Repair as necessary. See Section "6A".
- Check for proper valve timing.
- Check secondary voltage using a shop oscilliscope or a spark tester J-26792 (ST-125) or equivalent.

BACKFIRE

Definition: Fuel ignites in intake manifold, or in exhaust system, making a loud popping noise.

- **CHECK**:
  - Loose wiring connector or air duct at MAF Sensor.
  - Compression - Look for sticking or leaking valves.
  - EGR operation for being open all the time. See CHART C-7.
  - EGR gasket for faulty or loose fit.
  - Output voltage of ignition coils, using a shop ocilliscope or spark tester J-26792 (ST-125), or equivalent.
  - Valve timing.
  - Spark plugs, spark plug wires, and proper routing of plug wires.
  - AIR check valve (manual trans. "A" Series only).
  - Intermittent condition in ignition system.

POOR FUEL ECONOMY

Definition: Fuel economy, as measured by an actual road test, is noticeably lower than expected. Also, economy is noticeably lower than it was on this car at one time, as previously shown by an actual road test.

- **CHECK**:
  Engine thermostat for faulty part (always open) or for wrong heat range. Using a "Scan" tool, monitor engine temperature. A "Scan" displays engine temp. in degrees centigrade. After engine is started, the temperature should rise steadily to about 90°C, then stabilize, when thermostat opens.
  - Fuel Pressure. See CHART A-5.
- Check owner's driving habits.
  - Is A/C "ON" full time (Defroster mode "ON")?
  - Are tires at correct pressure?
  - Are excessively heavy loads being carried?
  - Is acceleration too much, too often?
  - Suggest driver read "Important Facts on Fuel Economy" in Owner's Manual.
- Check air cleaner element (filter) for dirt or being plugged.
- Check for proper calibration of speedometer.
- Visually (physically) check:
  - Vacuum hoses for splits, kinks, and proper connections as shown on Vehicle Emission Control Information label.
  - Ignition wires for cracking, hardness, and proper connections.
- Remove spark plugs. Check for cracks, wear, improper gap, burned electrodes, or heavy deposits. Repair or replace as necessary.
- Check compression.
- Check TCC for proper operation. See CHART C-8. A "Scan" should indicate an rpm drop, when the TCC is commanded "ON".
- Suggest owner fill fuel tank and recheck fuel economy.
- Check for exhaust system restriction. See CHART B-1.

DIESELING, RUN-ON

Definition: Engine continues to run after key is turned "OFF," but runs very roughly. If engine runs smoothly, check ignition switch and adjustment.

- Check injectors for leaking. See CHART A-7.

ROUGH, UNSTABLE, OR INCORRECT IDLE, STALLING

Definition: The engine runs unevenly at idle. If bad enough, the car may shake. Also, the idle may vary in rpm (called "hunting"). Either condition may be bad enough to cause stalling. Engine idles at incorrect speed.

- Perform careful visual check as described at start of Section "B".
- **CHECK:**
  - Throttle linkage for sticking or binding.
  - TPS for sticking or binding, and be sure output is stable at idle.
  - IAC system. See Code 35 Chart.
  - Generator output voltage. Repair if less than 9 or more than 16 volts.
  - P/N switch circuit. See CHART C-1A, or use "Scan" tool, and be sure tool indicates vehicle is in drive with gear selector in drive (125C), or overdrive (440-T4).
  - Injector balance. See CHART C-2A.
  - PCV valve for proper operation by placing finger over inlet hole in valve end several times. Valve should snap back. If not, replace valve.
  - Evaporative Emission Control System. CHART C-3.
  - Power steering pressure switch input. The state of the switch should only change when wheels are turned up against the stops. See CHART C-1E.
  - Minimum Idle Speed.
  - ECM ground circuits.
  - EGR valve: There should be no EGR at idle.
- Monitoring block learn values may help identify the cause of the problem. If the system is running lean (block learn greater than 138) refer to "Diagnostic Aids" on facing page of Code 44. If the system is running rich (block learn values less than 118) refer to "Diagnostic Aids" on facing page of Code 45.
- Run a cylinder compression check.
- Check for fuel in pressure regulator hose. If present, replace regulator assembly.
- Check ignition system; wires and plugs.
- Check for loose or damaged MAF duct between sensor and throttle body.
- Disconnect MAF sensor and if condition is corrected, replace sensor. "Scan" tool should read about 4-8 grams per second at idle.
- If problem exists with A/C "ON," check A/C system operation CHART C-10.
- M/T "A" series - check AIR system for intermittent air to exhaust ports, while in "Closed Loop." See CHART C-6.
- Inspect oxygen sensor for silicon contamination from fuel, or use of improper RTV sealant. The sensor will have a white, powdery coating, and will result in a high but false signal voltage (rich exhaust indication). The ECM will then reduce the amount of fuel delivered to the engine causing a severe driveability problem.

EXCESSIVE EXHAUST EMISSIONS OR ODORS

Definition: Vehicle fails an emission test. Vehicle has excessive "rotten egg" smell. Excessive odors do not necessarily indicate excessive emissions.

- Perform "Diagnostic Circuit Check."
- IF TEST SHOWS EXCESSIVE CO AND HC, (or also has excessive odors):
  - Check items which cause car to run RICH.
    - Make sure engine is at normal operating temperature.
- **CHECK:**
  - Fuel pressure. See CHART A-7.
  - Canister for fuel loading. See CHART C-3.
  - Injector balance. See CHART C-2A.
  - PCV valve for being plugged, stuck, or blocked PCV hose, or fuel in the crankcase.
  - Spark plugs, plug wires, and ignition components.
  - Check for lead contamination of catalytic converter (look for removal of fuel filler neck restrictor).
  - Check for properly installed fuel cap.
- If the system is running rich, (block learn less than 118), refer to "Diagnostic Aids" on facing page of Code 45.
- IF TEST SHOWS EXCESSIVE NOx:
  - Check items which cause car to run LEAN, or to run too hot.
    - EGR valve for not opening. See CHART C-7.
    - Vacuum leaks.
    - Coolant system and coolant fan for proper operation. See CHART C-12.
    - Remove carbon with top engine cleaner. Follow instructions on can.
- If the system is running lean, (block learn greater than 138), refer to "Diagnostic Aids" on facing page of Code 44.

CHART B-1
RESTRICTED EXHAUST SYSTEM CHECK
ALL ENGINES

Proper diagnosis for a restricted exhaust system is essential before any components are replaced. Either of the following procedures may be used for diagnosis, depending upon engine or tool used:

CHECK AT A. I. R. PIPE:

1. Remove the rubber hose at the exhaust manifold A.I.R. pipe check valve. Remove check valve.
2. Connect a fuel pump pressure gauge to a hose and nipple from a Propane Enrichment Device (J26911) (see illustration).
3. Insert the nipple into the exhaust manifold A.I.R. pipe.

OR CHECK AT O_2 SENSOR:

1. Carefully remove O_2 sensor.
2. Install Borroughs exhaust backpressure tester (BT 8515 or BT 8603) or equivalent in place of O_2 sensor (see illustration).
3. After completing test described below, be sure to coat threads of O_2 sensor with anti-seize compound P/N 5613695 or equivalent prior to re-installation.

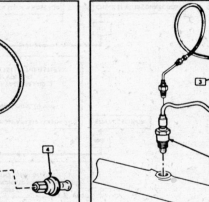

1 GAGE
2 HOSE AND NIPPLE ADAPTER
3 A.I.R. PIPE (EXHAUST PORT)
4 CHECK VALVE

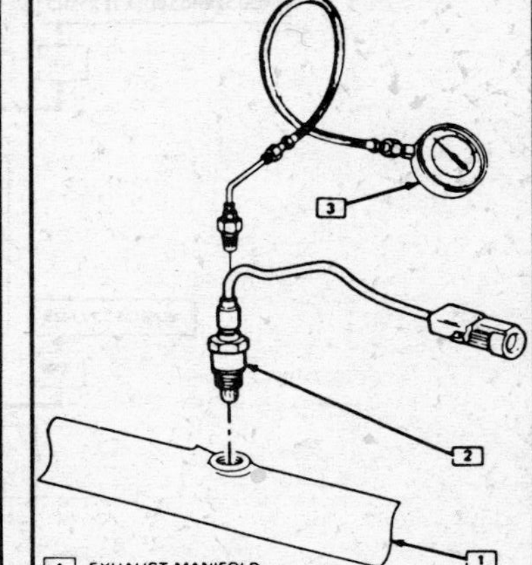

DIAGNOSIS:

1. With the engine idling at normal operating temperature, observe the exhaust system backpressure reading on the gauge. Reading should not exceed 8.6 kPa (1.25 psi).
2. Increase engine speed to 2000 rpm and observe gauge. Reading should not exceed 20.7 kPa (3 psi).
3. If the backpressure at either speed exceeds specification, a restricted exhaust system is indicated.
4. Inspect the entire exhaust system for a collapsed pipe, heat distress, or possible internal muffler failure.
5. If there are no obvious reasons for the excessive backpressure, the catalytic converter is suspected to be restricted and should be replaced using current recommended procedures.

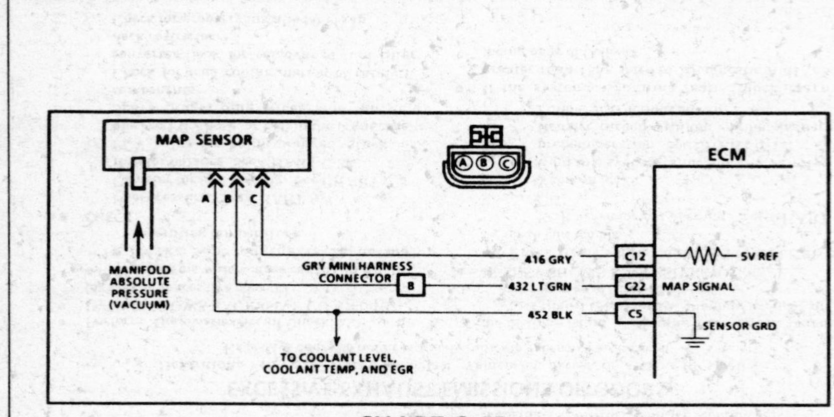
MAP SENSOR
A B C
MANIFOLD ABSOLUTE PRESSURE (VACUUM)
GRY MINI HARNESS CONNECTOR
B
A B C
ECM
416 GRY
432 LT GRN
452 BLK
C12
C22
C5
5V REF
MAP SIGNAL
SENSOR GRD
TO COOLANT LEVEL, COOLANT TEMP, AND EGR

CHART C-1D

MANIFOLD ABSOLUTE PRESSURE (MAP) OUTPUT CHECK 2.8L (VIN W) "W" SERIES (PORT)

Circuit Description:

The manifold absolute pressure (MAP) sensor measures manifold pressure (vacuum) and sends that signal to the ECM. The MAP sensor is mainly used for fuel calculation when the ECM is running in the throttle body backup mode. The MAP sensor is also used to determine the barometric pressure and to help calculate fuel delivery.

Test Description: Numbers below refer to circled numbers on the diagnostic chart.

1. Checks MAP sensor output voltage to the ECM. This voltage, without engine running, represents a barometer reading to the ECM.
2. Applying 34 kPa (10 inches Hg) vacuum to the MAP sensor should cause the voltage to be 1.2 volts less than the voltage at Step 1. Upon applying vacuum to the sensor, the change in voltage should be instantaneous. A slow voltage change indicates a faulty sensor.

   The engine must be running in this step or the "scanner" will not indicate a change in voltage. It is normal for the "Service Engine Soon" light to come "ON" and for the system to set a Code 63 during this step. Make sure the code is cleared when this test is completed.
3. Check vacuum hose to sensor for leaking or restriction. Be sure no other vacuum devices are connected to the MAP hose.

CHART C-1D

MANIFOLD ABSOLUTE PRESSURE (MAP) OUTPUT CHECK 2.8L (VIN W) "W" SERIES (PORT)

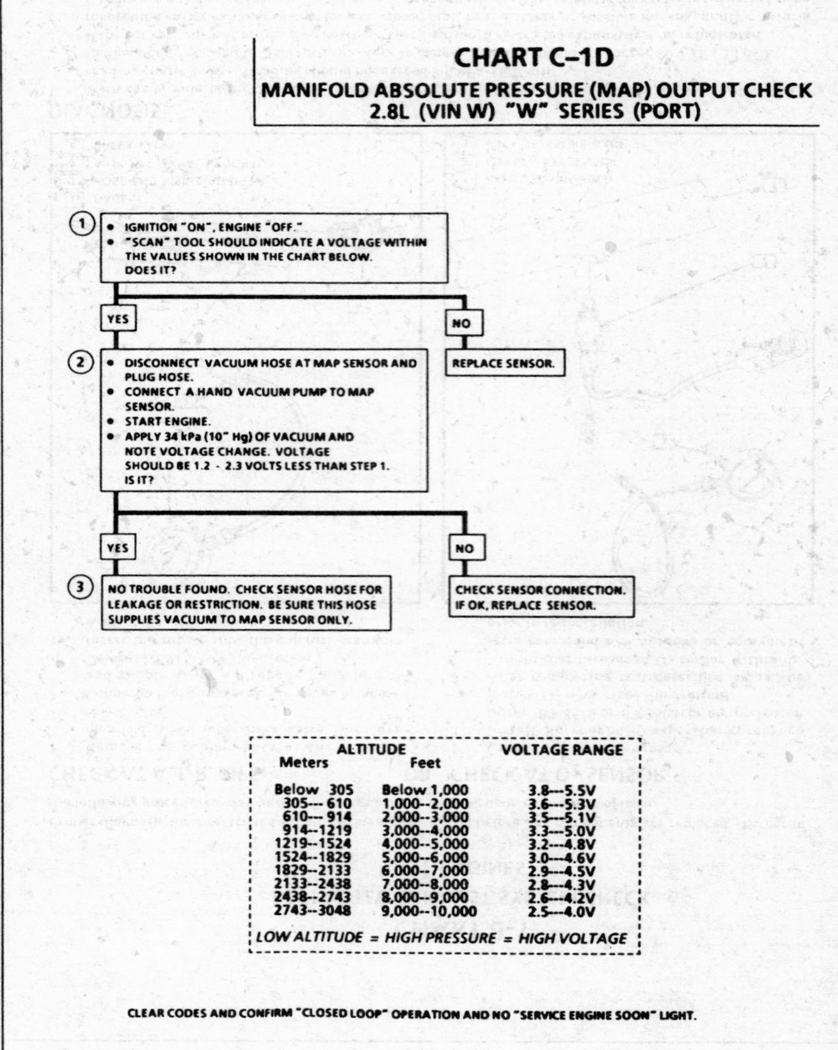
1
• IGNITION "ON", ENGINE "OFF."
• "SCAN" TOOL SHOULD INDICATE A VOLTAGE WITHIN THE VALUES SHOWN IN THE CHART BELOW.
DOES IT?
YES
NO
REPLACE SENSOR.
2
• DISCONNECT VACUUM HOSE AT MAP SENSOR AND PLUG HOSE.
• CONNECT A HAND VACUUM PUMP TO MAP SENSOR.
• START ENGINE.
• APPLY 34 kPa (10" Hg) OF VACUUM AND NOTE VOLTAGE CHANGE. VOLTAGE SHOULD BE 1.2 - 2.3 VOLTS LESS THAN STEP 1.
IS IT?
YES
NO
3
NO TROUBLE FOUND. CHECK SENSOR HOSE FOR LEAKAGE OR RESTRICTION. BE SURE THIS HOSE SUPPLIES VACUUM TO MAP SENSOR ONLY.
CHECK SENSOR CONNECTION. IF OK, REPLACE SENSOR.

ALTITUDE Meters	Feet	VOLTAGE RANGE
Below 305	Below 1,000	3.8—5.5V
305—610	1,000—2,000	3.6—5.3V
610—914	2,000—3,000	3.5—5.1V
914—1219	3,000—4,000	3.3—5.0V
1219—1524	4,000—5,000	3.2—4.8V
1524—1829	5,000—6,000	3.0—4.6V
1829—2133	6,000—7,000	2.9—4.5V
2133—2438	7,000—8,000	2.8—4.3V
2438—2743	8,000—9,000	2.6—4.2V
2743—3048	9,000—10,000	2.5—4.0V

LOW ALTITUDE = HIGH PRESSURE = HIGH VOLTAGE

CLEAR CODES AND CONFIRM "CLOSED LOOP" OPERATION AND NO "SERVICE ENGINE SOON" LIGHT.

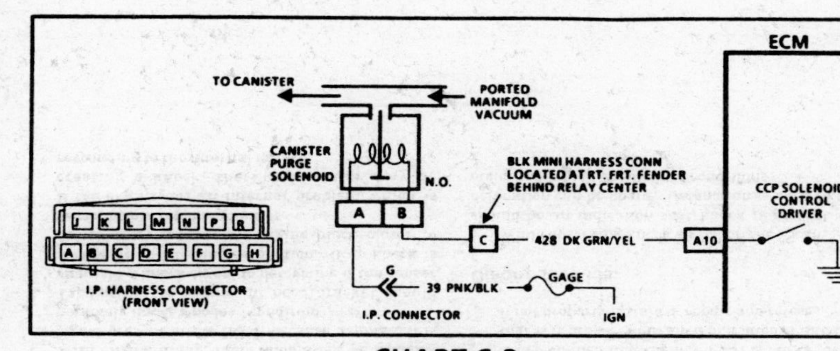
ECM
TO CANISTER
PORTED MANIFOLD VACUUM
CANISTER PURGE SOLENOID
N.O.
A
B
BLK MINI HARNESS CONN LOCATED AT RT. FRT. FENDER BEHIND RELAY CENTER
CCP SOLENOID CONTROL DRIVER
C
428 DK GRN/YEL
A10
G
39 PNK/BLK
GAGE
IGN
I.P. CONNECTOR
J K L M N P R
A B C D E F G H
I.P. HARNESS CONNECTOR (FRONT VIEW)

CHART C-3

CANISTER PURGE VALVE CHECK
2.8L (VIN W) "W" SERIES (PORT)

Circuit Description:

Canister purge is controlled by a solenoid that allows manifold vacuum to purge the canister when de-energized. The ECM supplies a ground to energize the solenoid (purge "OFF"). The purge solenoid control by the ECM is pulse width modulated (turned "ON" and "OFF" several times a second). The duty cycle (pulse width) is determined by the amount of air flow, and the engine vacuum as determined by the MAP sensor input. The duty cycle is calculated by the ECM and the output commanded when the following conditions have been met:

- Engine run time after start more than 3 minutes.
- Coolant temperature above 80°C.
- Vehicle speed above 15 mph.
- Throttle off idle (about 3%).

Also, if the diagnostic test terminal is grounded with the engine stopped, the purge solenoid is de-energized (purge "ON").

Test Description: Numbers below refer to circled numbers on the diagnostic chart.

1. Checks to see if the solenoid is opened or closed. The solenoid is normally energized in this step; so it should be closed.
2. Checks for a complete circuit. Normally there is ignition voltage on CKT 39 and the ECM provides a ground on CKT 428.
3. Completes functional check by grounding test terminal. This should normally de-energize the solenoid opening the valve which should allow the vacuum to drop (purge "ON").

CHART C-3

CANISTER PURGE VALVE CHECK
2.8L (VIN W) "W" SERIES (PORT)

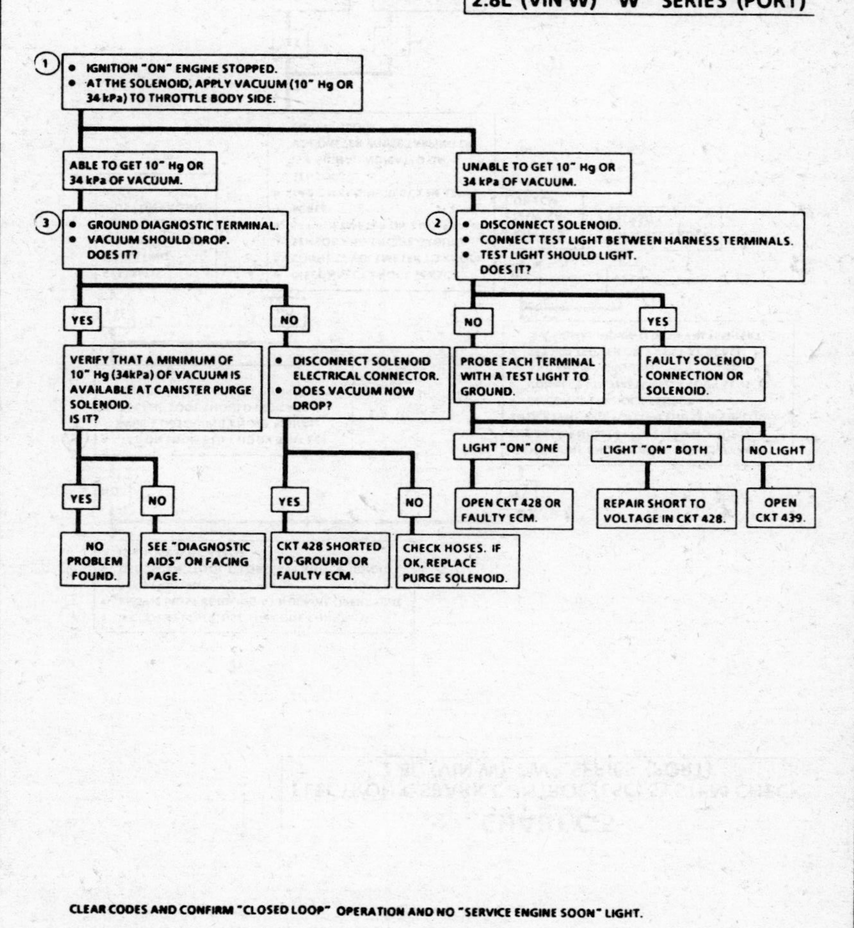
1
• IGNITION "ON" ENGINE STOPPED.
• AT THE SOLENOID, APPLY VACUUM (10" Hg OR 34 kPa) TO THROTTLE BODY SIDE.
ABLE TO GET 10" Hg OR 34 kPa OF VACUUM.
UNABLE TO GET 10" Hg OR 34 kPa OF VACUUM.
3
• GROUND DIAGNOSTIC TERMINAL.
• VACUUM SHOULD DROP.
DOES IT?
2
• DISCONNECT SOLENOID.
• CONNECT TEST LIGHT BETWEEN HARNESS TERMINALS.
• TEST LIGHT SHOULD LIGHT.
DOES IT?
YES
NO
NO
YES
VERIFY THAT A MINIMUM OF 10" Hg (34kPa) OF VACUUM IS AVAILABLE AT CANISTER PURGE SOLENOID.
IS IT?
• DISCONNECT SOLENOID ELECTRICAL CONNECTOR.
• DOES VACUUM NOW DROP?
PROBE EACH TERMINAL WITH A TEST LIGHT TO GROUND.
FAULTY SOLENOID CONNECTION OR SOLENOID.
LIGHT "ON" ONE
LIGHT "ON" BOTH
NO LIGHT
YES
NO
YES
NO
OPEN CKT 428 OR FAULTY ECM.
REPAIR SHORT TO VOLTAGE IN CKT 428.
OPEN CKT 439.
NO PROBLEM FOUND.
SEE "DIAGNOSTIC AIDS" ON FACING PAGE.
CKT 428 SHORTED TO GROUND OR FAULTY ECM.
CHECK HOSES. IF OK, REPLACE PURGE SOLENOID.

CLEAR CODES AND CONFIRM "CLOSED LOOP" OPERATION AND NO "SERVICE ENGINE SOON" LIGHT.

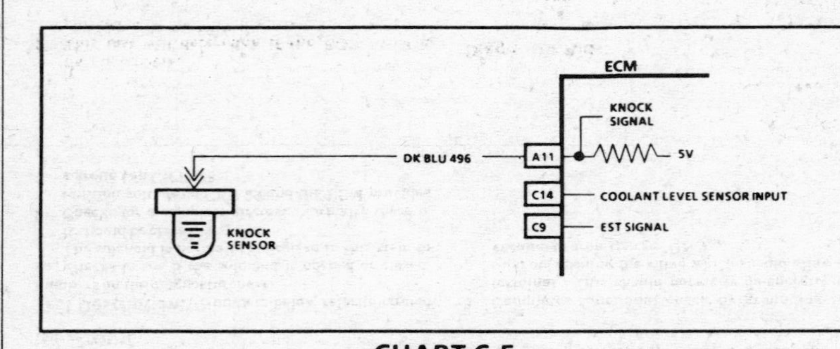

CHART C-5

ELECTRONIC SPARK CONTROL (ESC) SYSTEM CHECK 2.8L (VIN W) "W" SERIES (PORT)

Circuit Description:

The knock sensor is used to detect engine detonation and the ECM will retard the electronic spark timing based on the signal being received. The circuitry within the knock sensor causes the ECM's 5 volts to be pulled down so that under a no knock condition, CKT 496 would measure about 2.5 volts. The knock sensor produces an AC signal which rides on the 2.5 volt DC voltage. The amplitude and frequency are dependent upon the knock level.

The Mem-Cal used with this engine, contains the functions which were part of remotely mounted ESC modules used on other GM vehicles. The ESC portion of the Mem-Cal, then sends a signal to other parts of the ECM which adjusts the spark timing to retard the spark and reduce the detonation.

Test Description: Numbers below refer to circled numbers on the diagnostic chart.

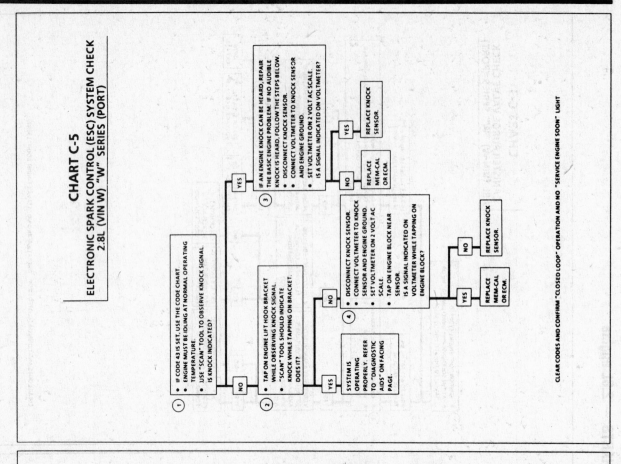

1. **With engine idling, there should not be a knock signal present at the ECM, because detonation is not likely under a no load condition.**
2. **Tapping on the engine lift hood bracket should simulate a knock signal to determine if the sensor is capable of detecting detonation. If no knock is detected, try tapping on engine block closer to sensor before replacing sensor.**
3. **If the engine has an internal problem which is creating a knock, the knock sensor may be responding to the internal failure.**
4. This test determines if the knock sensor is faulty or if the ESC portion of the Mem-Cal is faulty. If it is determined that the Mem-Cal is faulty, be sure that is is properly installed and latched into place. If not properly installed, repair and retest.

Diagnostic Aids:

While observing knock signal on the "Scan," there should be an indication that knock is present when detonation can be heard. Detonation is most likely to occur under high engine load conditions.

CHART C-5

ELECTRONIC SPARK CONTROL (ESC) SYSTEM CHECK 2.8L (VIN W) "W" SERIES (PORT)

(1)
- IF CODE 43 IS SET, USE THE CODE CHART.
- ENGINE MUST BE IDLING AT NORMAL OPERATING TEMPERATURE.
- USE "SCAN" TOOL TO OBSERVE KNOCK SIGNAL. IS KNOCK INDICATED?

NO → (2)
- TAP ON ENGINE LIFT HOOK BRACKET WHILE OBSERVING KNOCK SIGNAL.
- "SCAN" TOOL SHOULD INDICATE KNOCK WHILE TAPPING ON BRACKET. DOES IT?

YES → SYSTEM IS OPERATING PROPERLY. REFER TO "DIAGNOSTIC AIDS" ON FACING PAGE.

NO → (4)
- DISCONNECT KNOCK SENSOR.
- CONNECT VOLTMETER TO KNOCK SENSOR AND ENGINE GROUND.
- SET VOLTMETER ON 2 VOLT AC SCALE.
- TAP ON ENGINE BLOCK NEAR SENSOR. IS A SIGNAL INDICATED ON VOLTMETER WHILE TAPPING ON ENGINE BLOCK?

YES → REPLACE MEM-CAL OR ECM.

NO → REPLACE KNOCK SENSOR.

YES → (3) IF AN ENGINE KNOCK CAN BE HEARD, REPAIR THE BASIC ENGINE PROBLEM. IF NO AUDIBLE KNOCK IS HEARD, FOLLOW THE STEPS BELOW.
- DISCONNECT KNOCK SENSOR.
- CONNECT VOLTMETER TO KNOCK SENSOR AND ENGINE GROUND.
- SET VOLTMETER ON 2 VOLT AC SCALE. IS A SIGNAL INDICATED ON VOLTMETER?

NO → REPLACE MEM-CAL OR ECM.

YES → REPLACE KNOCK SENSOR.

CLEAR CODES AND CONFIRM "CLOSED LOOP" OPERATION AND NO "SERVICE ENGINE SOON" LIGHT

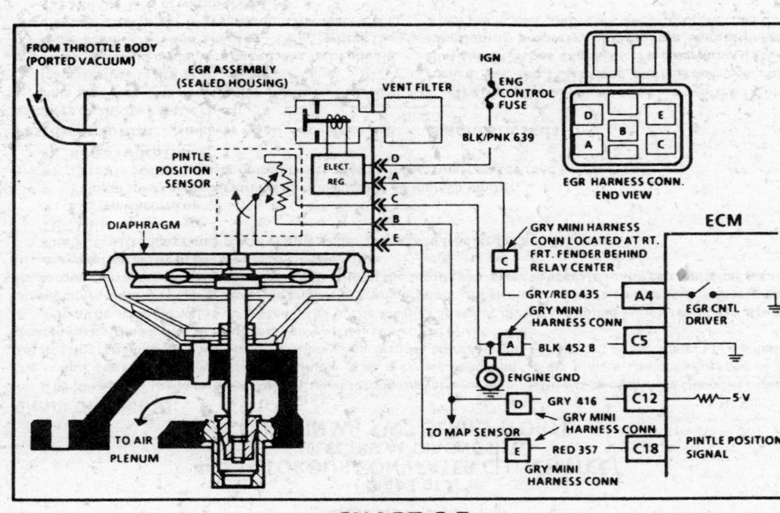

CHART C-7

EXHAUST GAS RECIRCULATION (EGR) VALVE CHECK 2.8L (VIN W) "W" SERIES (PORT)

Circuit Description:

The integrated electronic EGR valve functions similar to a port valve with a remote vacuum regulator. The internal solenoid is normally open, which causes the vacuum signal to be vented "OFF" to the atmosphere when EGR is not being commanded by the ECM. This EGR valve has a sealed cap and the solenoid valve opens and closes the vacuum signal which controls the amount of vacuum vented to atmosphere, and this controls the amount of vacuum applied to the diaphragm. The electronic EGR valve contains a voltage regulator which converts the ECM signal to provide different amounts of EGR flow by regulating the current to the solenoid. The ECM controls EGR flow with a pulse width modualted signal (turns "ON" and "OFF" many times a second) based on airflow, TPS, and rpm.

This system also contains a pintle position sensor which works similar to a TPS sensor, and as EGR flow is increased, the sensor output also increases.

Test Description: Numbers below refer to circled numbers on the diagnostic chart.

1. Whenever the solenoid is denergized, the solenoid valve should be closed which should not allow the vacuum to move the EGR diaphragm. However, if the filter is plugged, the vacuum applied with the hand held vacuum pump will cause the diaphragm to move because the vacuum will not be vented to the atmosphere.
2. This test will determine if the EGR filter is plugged or if the EGR itself is faulty. Use care when removing the filter to avoid damaging the EGR assembly.
3. If the valve moves in this test, it's probably due to CKT 435 being shorted to ground.
4. Grounding the diagnostic terminal should energize the solenoid which closes off the vent and allows the vacuum to move the diaphragm.
5. The EGR assembly is designed to have some leak and therefore, 7" of vacuum is all that should be able to be held on the assembly. However, if toomuch of a leak exists (less than 3") the EGR assembly is leaking and must be replaced.

Diagnostic Aids:

The EGR position voltage can be used to determine that the pintle is moving. When no EGR is commanded (0% duty cycle), the position sensor should read between .5 volts and 1.5 volts, and increase with the commanded EGR duty cycle.

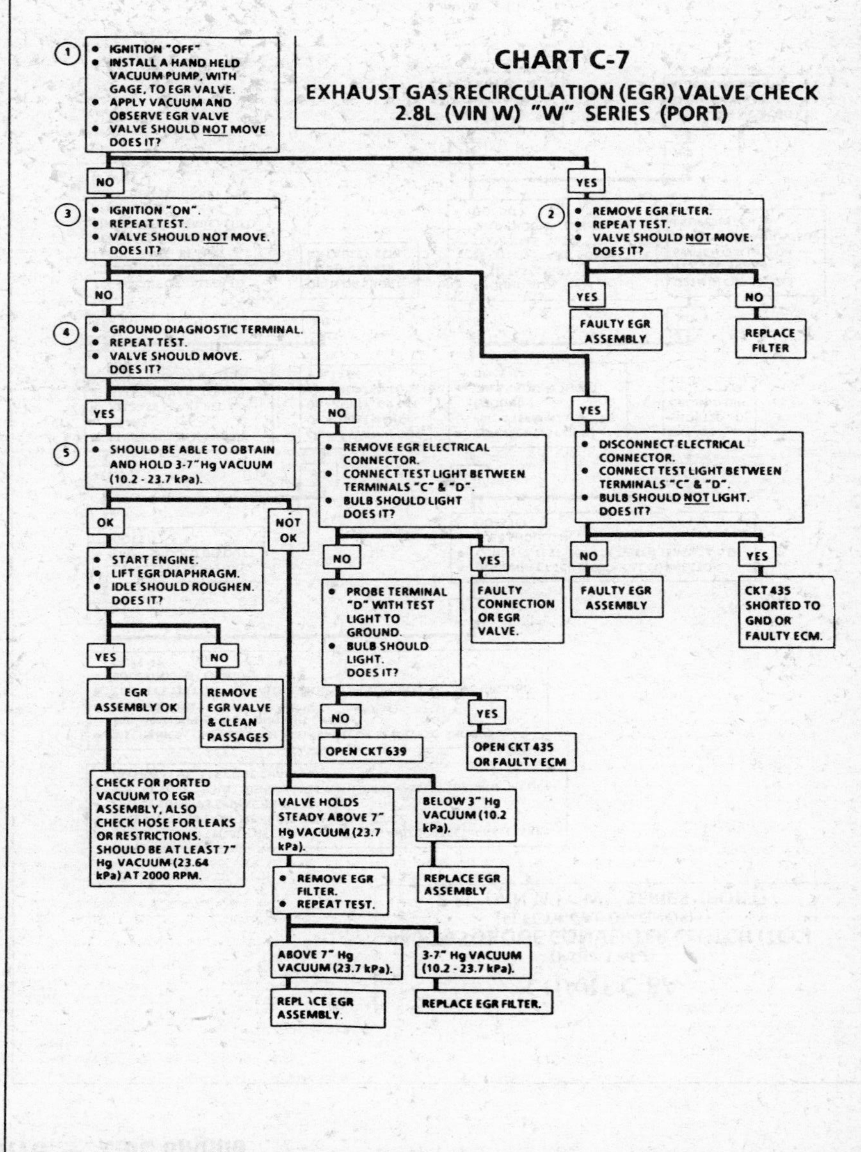

CHART C-8A

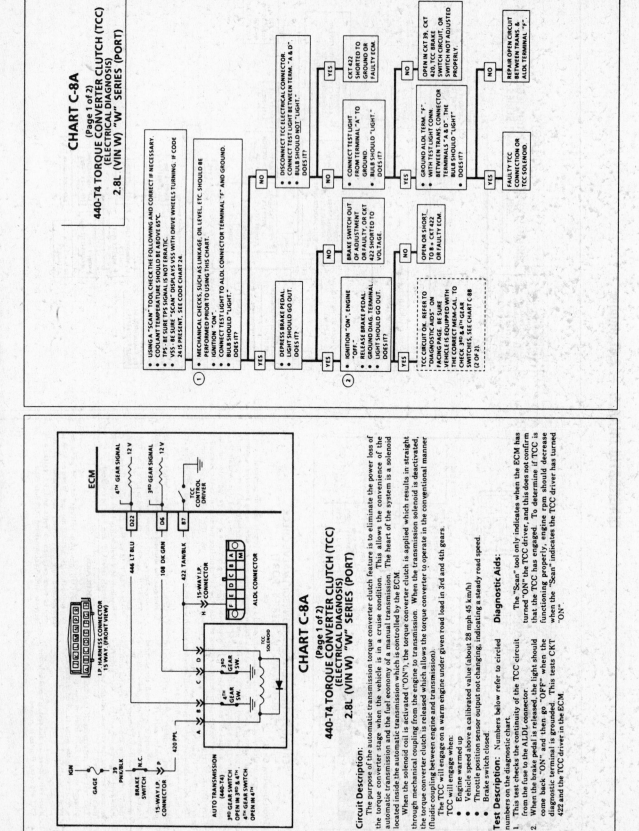

(Page 1 of 2)
440-T4 TORQUE CONVERTER CLUTCH (TCC)
(ELECTRICAL DIAGNOSIS)
2.8L (VIN W) "W" SERIES (PORT)

Circuit Description:

The purpose of the automatic transmission torque converter clutch feature is to eliminate the power loss of the torque converter stage when the vehicle is in a cruise condition. This allows the convenience of the automatic transmission and the fuel economy of a manual transmission. The heart of the system is a solenoid located inside the automatic transmission which is controlled by the ECM.

When the solenoid coil is activated ("ON"), the torque converter clutch is applied which results in straight through mechanical coupling from the engine to transmission. When the transmission solenoid is deactivated, the torque converter clutch is released which allows the torque converter to operate in the conventional manner (fluidic coupling between engine and transmission).

The TCC will engage on a warm engine under given road load in 3rd and 4th gears.
TCC will engage when:

- Engine warmed up
- Vehicle speed above a calibrated value (about 28 mph 45 km/h)
- Throttle position sensor output not changing, indicating a steady road speed.
- Brake switch closed.

Test Description: Numbers below refer to circled numbers on the diagnostic chart.

1. This test checks the continuity of the TCC circuit from the fuse to the ALDL connector.
2. When the brake pedal is released, the light should come back "ON" and then go "OFF" when the diagnostic terminal is grounded. This tests CKT 422 and the TCC driver in the ECM.

Diagnostic Aids:

The "Scan" tool only indicates when the ECM has turned "ON" the TCC driver, and this does not confirm that the TCC has engaged. To determine if TCC is functioning properly, engine rpm should decrease when the "Scan" indicates the TCC driver has turned "ON".

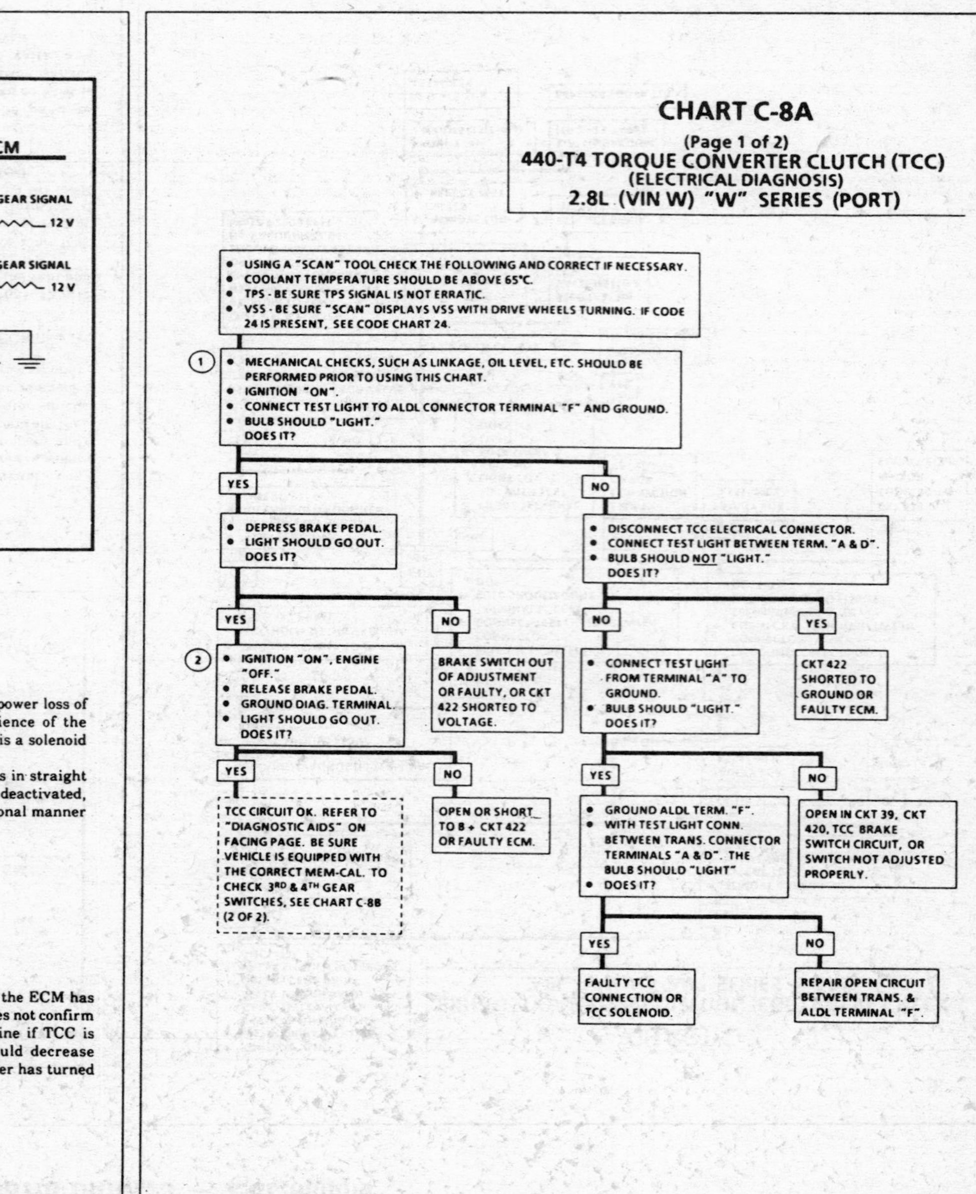

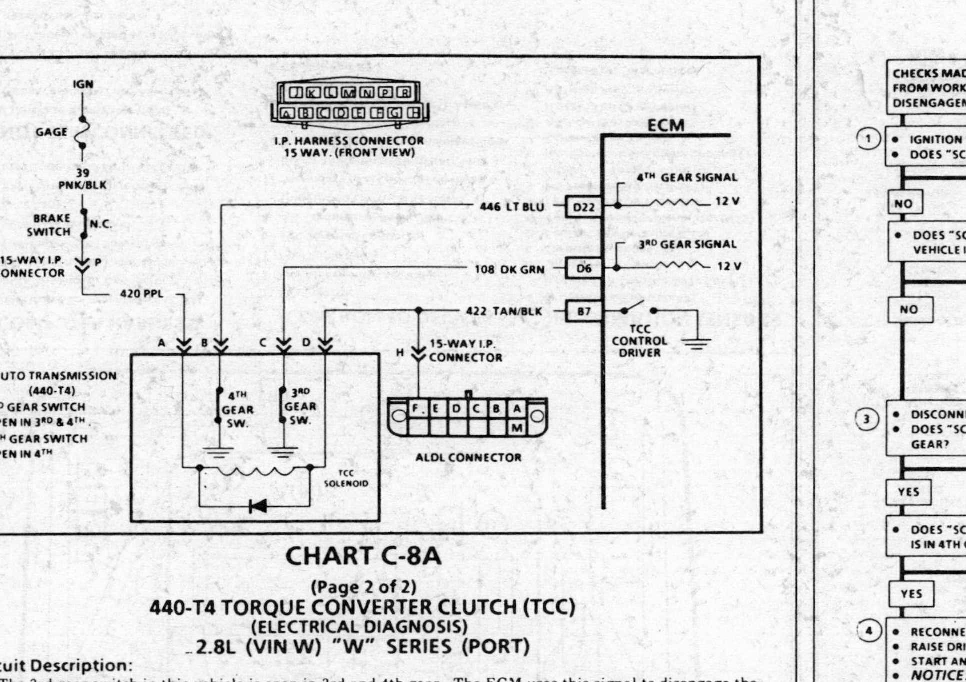

CHART C-8A

(Page 2 of 2)
440-T4 TORQUE CONVERTER CLUTCH (TCC)
(ELECTRICAL DIAGNOSIS)
2.8L (VIN W) "W" SERIES (PORT)

Circuit Description:

The 3rd gear switch in this vehicle is open in 3rd and 4th gear. The ECM uses this signal to disengage the TCC when going into a downshift.

The fourth gear switch is open in fourth gear.

Test Description: Numbers below refer to circled numbers on the diagnostic chart.

1. Some "Scan" tools display the state of these switches in different ways. Be familiar with the type of tool being used. Since both switches should be in the closed state during this test, the tool should read the same for either the 3rd or 4th gear switch.
2. Determines whether the switch or signal circuit is open. The circuit can be checked for an open by measuring the voltage (with a voltmeter) at the TCC connector. Should be about 12 volts.
3. Because the switch(es) should be grounded in this step, disconnecting the TCC connector should cause the "Scan" switch state to change.
4. The switch state should change when the vehicle shifts into 3rd gear.

Diagnostic Aids:

If vehicle is road tested because of a TCC related problem, be sure the switch states do not change while in 4th gear because the TCC will disengage. If switches change state, carefully check wire routing and connections.

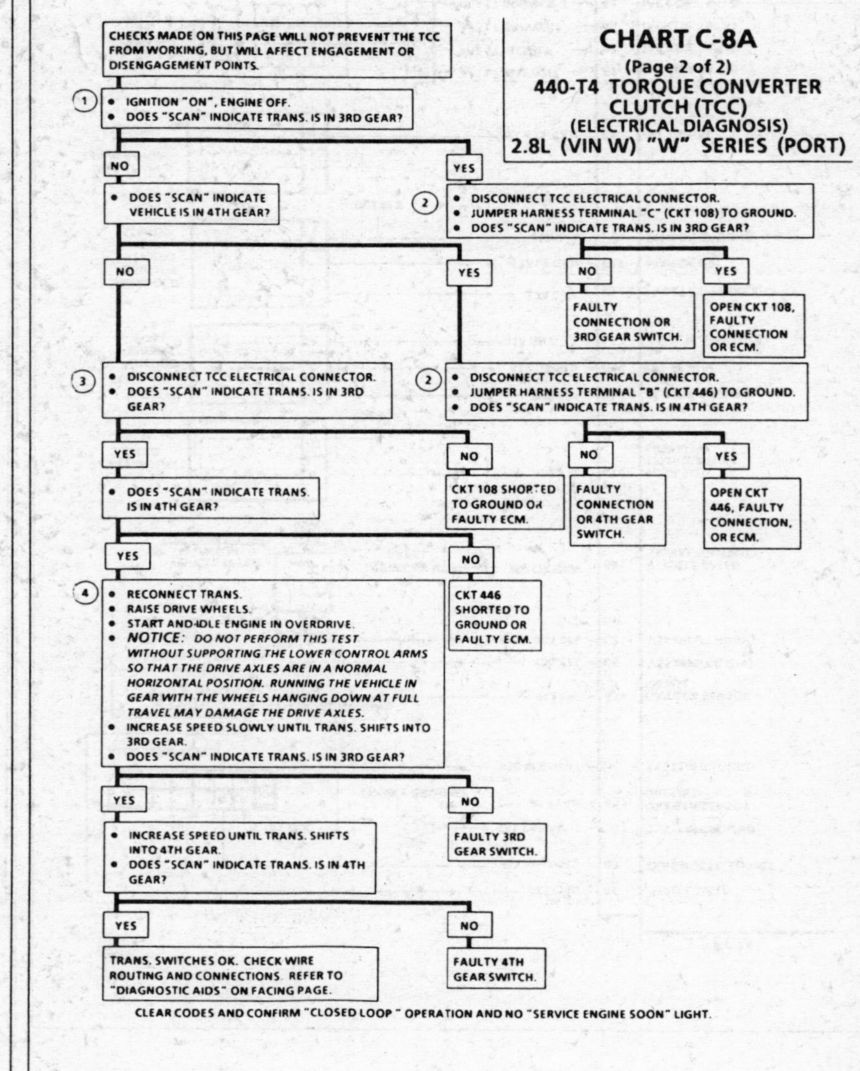

DIAGNOSTIC CHARTS — 2.5L engine

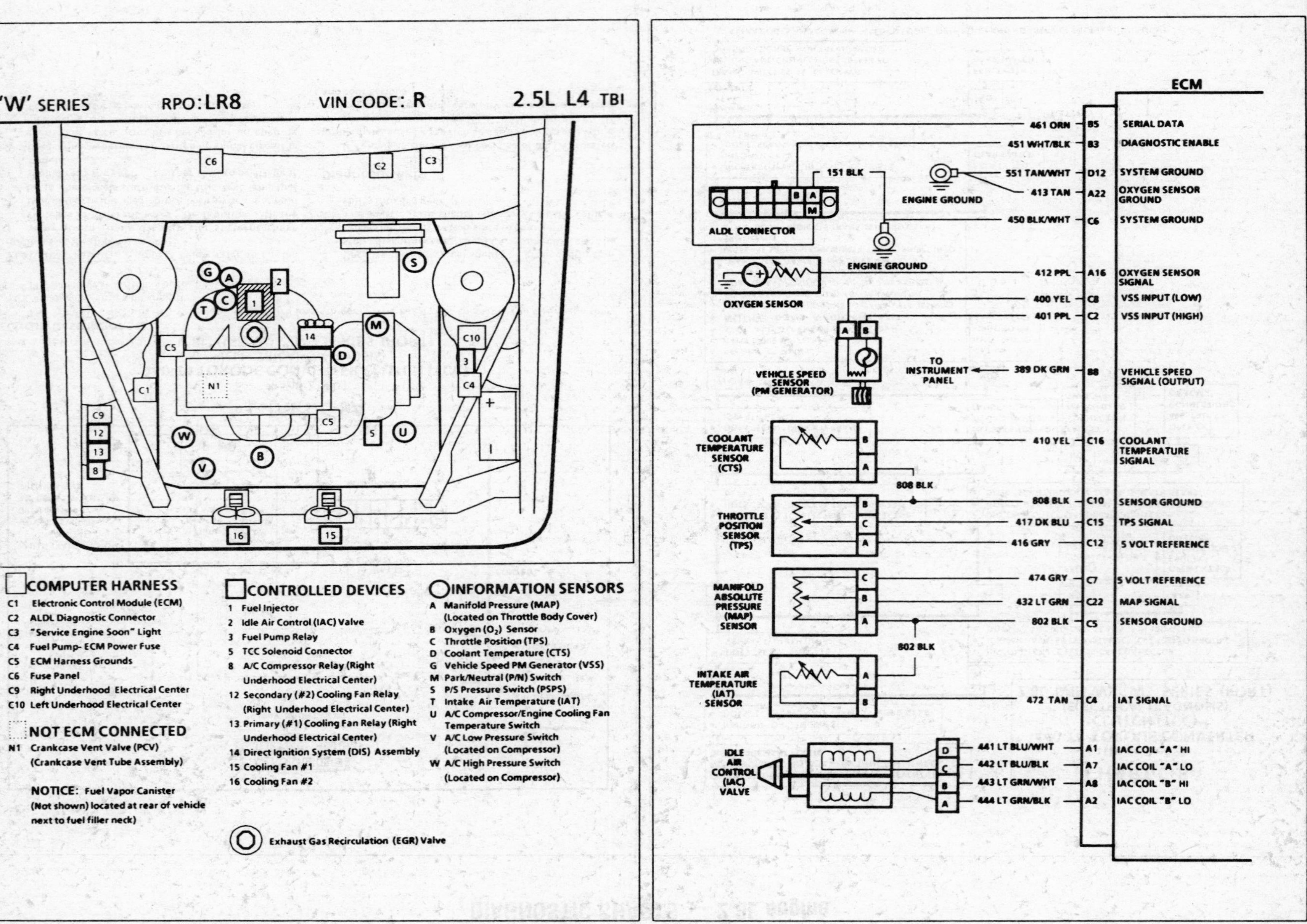
'W' SERIES
RPO: LR8
VIN CODE: R
2.5L L4 TBI
COMPUTER HARNESS
C1 Electronic Control Module (ECM)
C2 ALDL Diagnostic Connector
C3 "Service Engine Soon" Light
C4 Fuel Pump- ECM Power Fuse
C5 ECM Harness Grounds
C6 Fuse Panel
C9 Right Underhood Electrical Center
C10 Left Underhood Electrical Center
NOT ECM CONNECTED
N1 Crankcase Vent Valve (PCV) (Crankcase Vent Tube Assembly)
NOTICE: Fuel Vapor Canister (Not shown) located at rear of vehicle next to fuel filler neck)
CONTROLLED DEVICES
1 Fuel Injector
2 Idle Air Control (IAC) Valve
3 Fuel Pump Relay
5 TCC Solenoid Connector
8 A/C Compressor Relay (Right Underhood Electrical Center)
12 Secondary (#2) Cooling Fan Relay (Right Underhood Electrical Center)
13 Primary (#1) Cooling Fan Relay (Right Underhood Electrical Center)
14 Direct Ignition System (DIS) Assembly
15 Cooling Fan #1
16 Cooling Fan #2
Exhaust Gas Recirculation (EGR) Valve
INFORMATION SENSORS
A Manifold Pressure (MAP) (Located on Throttle Body Cover)
B Oxygen (O_2) Sensor
C Throttle Position (TPS)
D Coolant Temperature (CTS)
G Vehicle Speed PM Generator (VSS)
M Park/Neutral (P/N) Switch
S P/S Pressure Switch (PSPS)
T Intake Air Temperature (IAT)
U A/C Compressor/Engine Cooling Fan Temperature Switch
V A/C Low Pressure Switch (Located on Compressor)
W A/C High Pressure Switch (Located on Compressor)
ECM
461 ORN B5 SERIAL DATA
451 WHT/BLK B3 DIAGNOSTIC ENABLE
551 TAN/WHT D12 SYSTEM GROUND
413 TAN A22 OXYGEN SENSOR GROUND
450 BLK/WHT C6 SYSTEM GROUND
412 PPL A16 OXYGEN SENSOR SIGNAL
400 YEL C8 VSS INPUT (LOW)
401 PPL C2 VSS INPUT (HIGH)
389 DK GRN B8 VEHICLE SPEED SIGNAL (OUTPUT)
410 YEL C16 COOLANT TEMPERATURE SIGNAL
808 BLK C10 SENSOR GROUND
417 DK BLU C15 TPS SIGNAL
416 GRY C12 5 VOLT REFERENCE
474 GRY C7 5 VOLT REFERENCE
432 LT GRN C22 MAP SIGNAL
802 BLK C5 SENSOR GROUND
472 TAN C4 IAT SIGNAL
441 LT BLU/WHT A1 IAC COIL "A" HI
442 LT BLU/BLK A7 IAC COIL "A" LO
443 LT GRN/WHT A8 IAC COIL "B" HI
444 LT GRN/BLK A2 IAC COIL "B" LO
151 BLK
ALDL CONNECTOR
ENGINE GROUND
OXYGEN SENSOR
VEHICLE SPEED SENSOR (PM GENERATOR)
TO INSTRUMENT PANEL
COOLANT TEMPERATURE SENSOR (CTS)
808 BLK
THROTTLE POSITION SENSOR (TPS)
MANIFOLD ABSOLUTE PRESSURE (MAP) SENSOR
802 BLK
INTAKE AIR TEMPERATURE (IAT) SENSOR
IDLE AIR CONTROL (IAC) VALVE

DIAGNOSTIC CHARTS — 2.5L engine

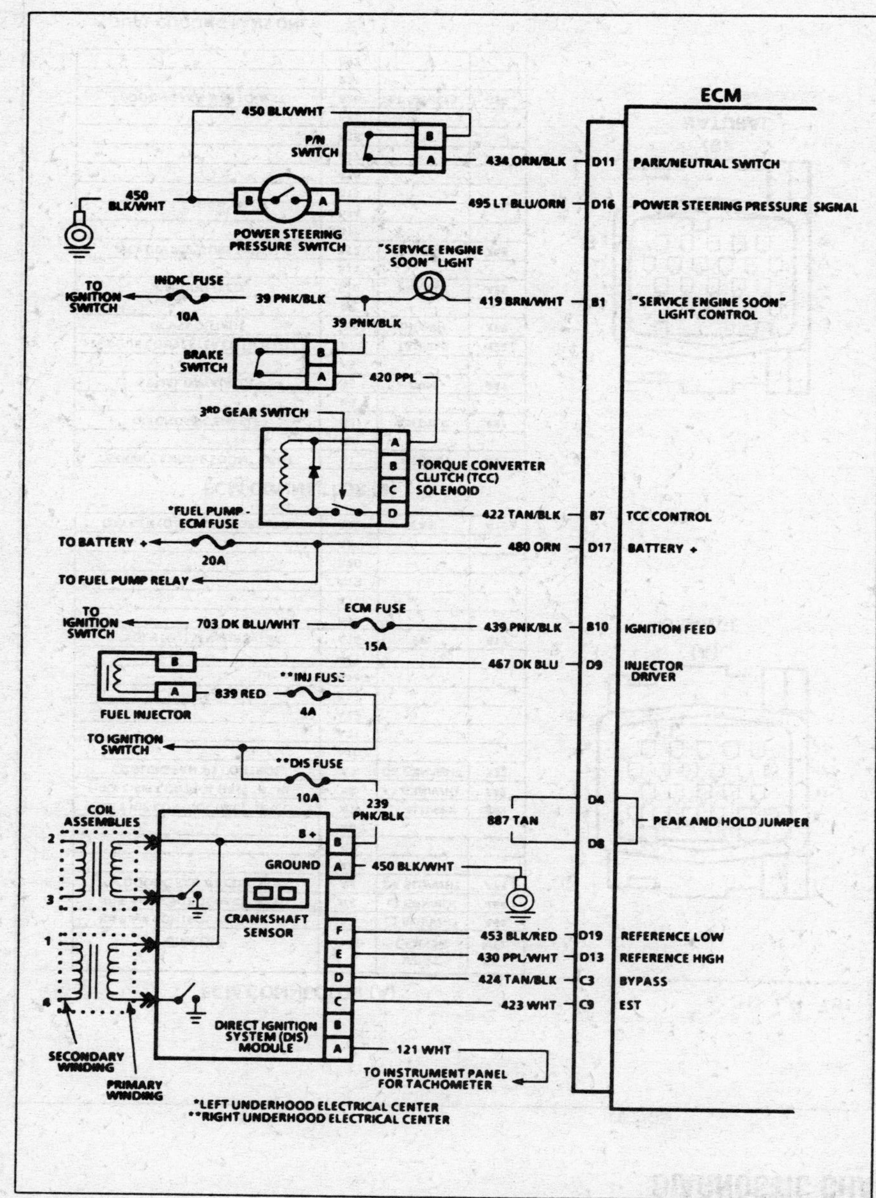

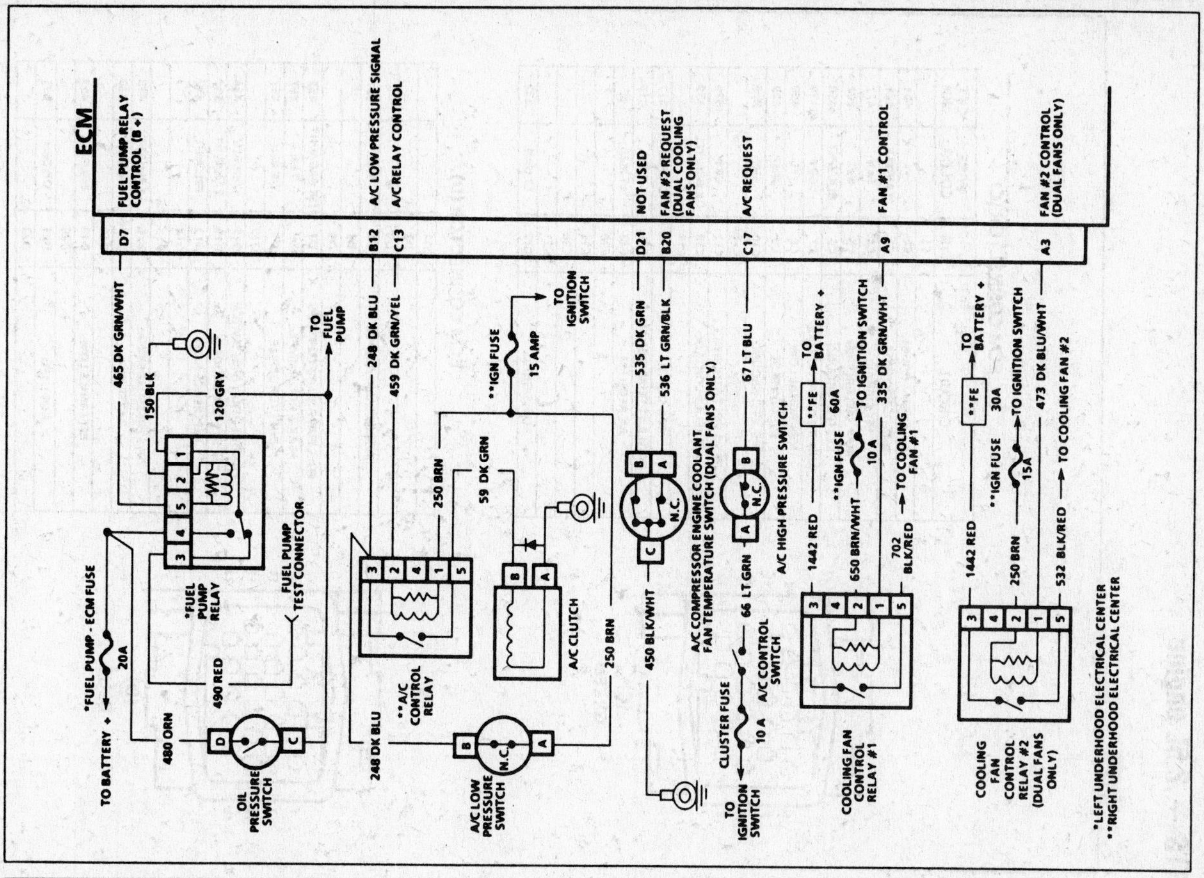

DIAGNOSTIC CHARTS — 2.5L engine

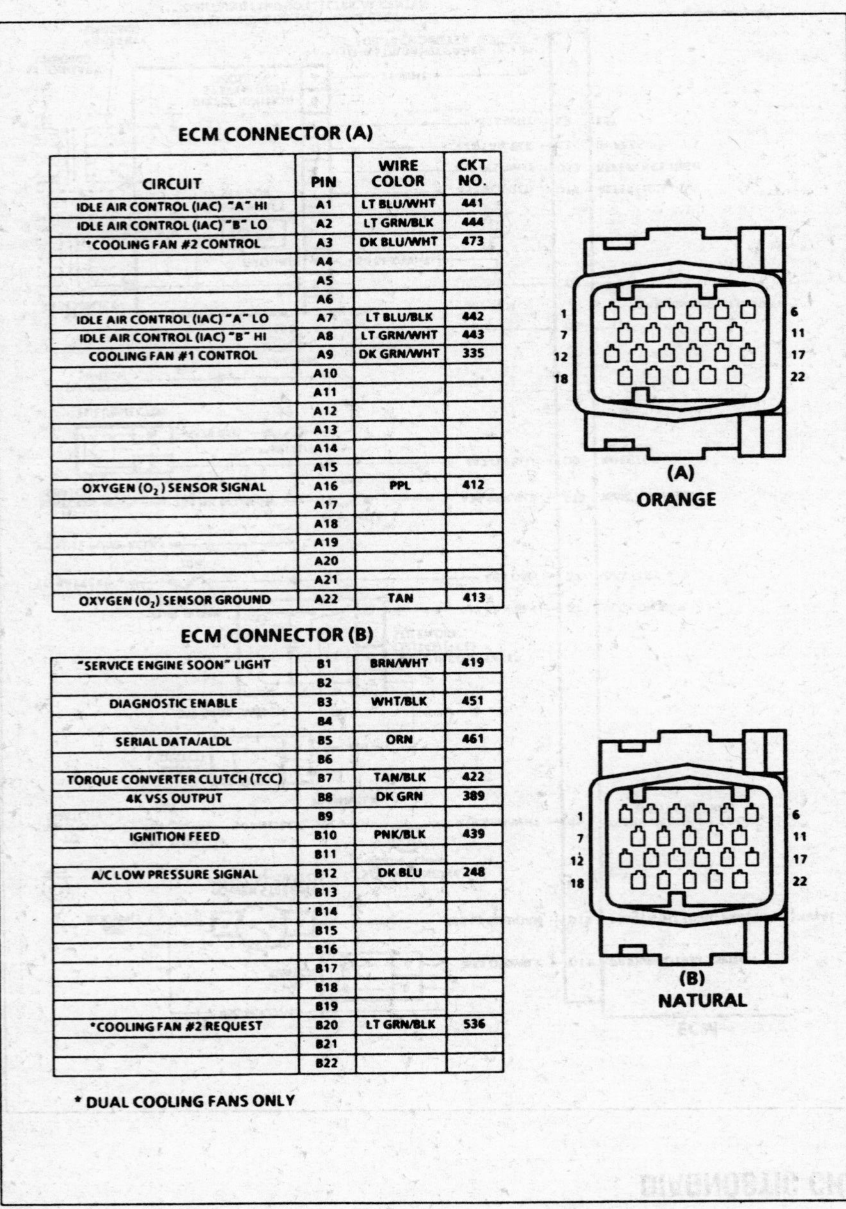

ECM CONNECTOR (A)

CIRCUIT	PIN	WIRE COLOR	CKT NO.
IDLE AIR CONTROL (IAC) "A" HI	A1	LT BLU/WHT	441
IDLE AIR CONTROL (IAC) "B" LO	A2	LT GRN/BLK	444
*COOLING FAN #2 CONTROL	A3	DK BLU/WHT	473
	A4		
	A5		
	A6		
IDLE AIR CONTROL (IAC) "A" LO	A7	LT BLU/BLK	442
IDLE AIR CONTROL (IAC) "B" HI	A8	LT GRN/WHT	443
COOLING FAN #1 CONTROL	A9	DK GRN/WHT	335
	A10		
	A11		
	A12		
	A13		
	A14		
	A15		
OXYGEN (O_2) SENSOR SIGNAL	A16	PPL	412
	A17		
	A18		
	A19		
	A20		
	A21		
OXYGEN (O_2) SENSOR GROUND	A22	TAN	413

ECM CONNECTOR (B)

CIRCUIT	PIN	WIRE COLOR	CKT NO.
"SERVICE ENGINE SOON" LIGHT	B1	BRN/WHT	419
	B2		
DIAGNOSTIC ENABLE	B3	WHT/BLK	451
	B4		
SERIAL DATA/ALDL	B5	ORN	461
	B6		
TORQUE CONVERTER CLUTCH (TCC)	B7	TAN/BLK	422
4K VSS OUTPUT	B8	DK GRN	389
	B9		
IGNITION FEED	B10	PNK/BLK	439
	B11		
A/C LOW PRESSURE SIGNAL	B12	DK BLU	248
	B13		
	B14		
	B15		
	B16		
	B17		
	B18		
	B19		
*COOLING FAN #2 REQUEST	B20	LT GRN/BLK	536
	B21		
	B22		

* DUAL COOLING FANS ONLY

1 7 12 18 — 6 11 17 22

(C)
GREEN

1 7 12 18 — 6 11 17 22

(D)
BLUE

ECM CONNECTOR (C)

CIRCUIT	PIN	WIRE COLOR	CKT. NO.
	C1		
VSS SIGNAL (HIGH)	C2	PPL	401
IGNITION BYPASS	C3	TAN/BLK	424
IAT SIGNAL	C4	TAN	472
MAP, IAT, GROUND	C5	BLK	802
SYSTEM GROUND	C6	BLK/WHT	450
MAP 5 VOLT REFERENCE	C7	GRY	474
VSS SIGNAL LOW	C8	YEL	400
EST CONTROL	C9	WHT	423
TPS, CTS, GROUND	C10	BLK	808
	C11		
TPS 5 VOLT REFERENCE	C12	GRY	416
A/C RELAY CONTROL	C13	DK GRN/YEL	459
	C14		
TPS SIGNAL	C15	DK BLU	417
COOLANT TEMP SIGNAL	C16	YEL	410
A/C REQUEST	C17	LT BLU	67
	C18		
	C19		
	C20		
	C21		
MAP SIGNAL	C22	LT GRN	432

ECM CONNECTOR (D)

	D1		
	D2		
	D3		
PEAK & HOLD JUMPER	D4	TAN	887
	D5		
	D6		
FUEL PUMP RELAY CONTROL	D7	DK GRN/WHT	465
PEAK & HOLD JUMPER	D8	TAN	887
INJECTOR DRIVER	D9	DK BLU	467
	D10		
PARK/NEUTRAL (P/N) SWITCH	D11	ORN/BLK	434
SYSTEM GROUND	D12	TAN/WHT	551
REFERENCE HIGH	D13	PPL/WHT	430
	D14		
	D15		
P/S PRESSURE SIGNAL	D16	LT BLU/ORN	495
BATTERY +	D17	ORN	480
	D18		
REFERENCE LOW	D19	BLK/RED	453
	D20		
NOT USED	D21	DK GRN	535
	D22		

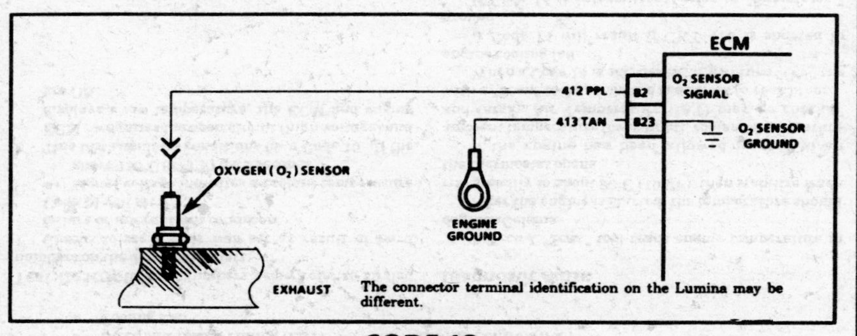

The connector terminal identification on the Lumina may be different.

CODE 13
OXYGEN (O_2) SENSOR CIRCUIT (OPEN CIRCUIT)

Circuit Description:

The ECM supplies a voltage of about .45 volt between terminals "B2" and "B23". (If measured with a 10 megohm digital voltmeter, this may read as low as .32 volt).

When the O_2 sensor reaches operating temperature, it varies this voltage from about .1 volt (exhaust is lean) to about .9 volt (exhaust is rich).

The sensor is like an open circuit and produces no voltage when it is below 316°C (600°F). An open sensor circuit, or cold sensor, causes "Open Loop" operation.

Test Description: Numbers below refer to circled numbers on the diagnostic chart.

1. Code 13 will set under the following conditions:
   - Engine at normal operating temperature.
   - At least 40 seconds have elapsed since engine start-up.
   - O_2 signal voltage is steady between .35 and .55 volt.
   - Throttle angle is above 7%.
   - All above conditions are met for about 4 seconds.

   If the conditions for a Code 13 exist, the system will not operate in "Closed Loop."
2. This test determines if the O_2 sensor is the problem or if the ECM and wiring are at fault.
3. In doing this test, use only a 10 megohm digital voltmeter. This test checks the continuity of CKTs 412 and 413. If CKT 413 is open, the ECM voltage on CKT 412 will be over .6 volt (600 mV).

Diagnostic Aids:

Normal "Scan" tool O_2 sensor voltage varies between 100 mV to 999 mV (.1 and 1.0 volt) while in "Closed Loop." Code 13 sets in one minute if sensor signal voltage remains between .35 and .55 volt, but the system will go to "Open Loop" in about 15 seconds.

Verify a clean, tight ground connection for CKT 413. Open CKT(s) 412 or 413 will result in a Code 13. If Code 13 is intermittent, refer to "Symptoms,"

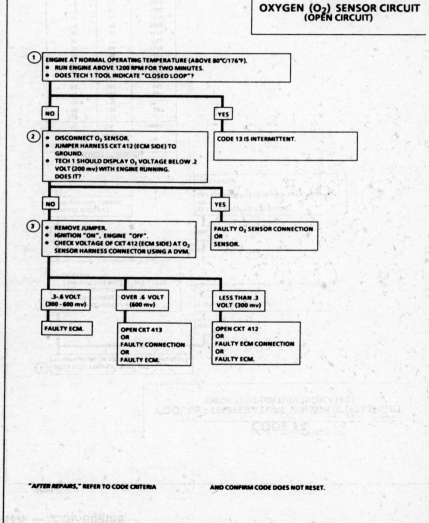

CODE 13
OXYGEN (O_2) SENSOR CIRCUIT (OPEN CIRCUIT)

(1) ENGINE AT NORMAL OPERATING TEMPERATURE (ABOVE 80°C/176°F).
- RUN ENGINE ABOVE 1200 RPM FOR TWO MINUTES.
- DOES TECH 1 TOOL INDICATE "CLOSED LOOP"?

YES → CODE 13 IS INTERMITTENT.

NO →

(2)
- DISCONNECT O_2 SENSOR.
- JUMPER HARNESS CKT 412 (ECM SIDE) TO GROUND.
- TECH 1 SHOULD DISPLAY O_2 VOLTAGE BELOW .2 VOLT (200 mv) WITH ENGINE RUNNING. DOES IT?

YES → FAULTY O_2 SENSOR CONNECTION OR SENSOR.

NO →

(3)
- REMOVE JUMPER.
- IGNITION "ON", ENGINE "OFF".
- CHECK VOLTAGE OF CKT 412 (ECM SIDE) AT O_2 SENSOR HARNESS CONNECTOR USING A DVM.

.3-.6 VOLT (300 - 600 mv) → FAULTY ECM.

OVER .6 VOLT (600 mv) → OPEN CKT 413 OR FAULTY CONNECTION OR FAULTY ECM.

LESS THAN .3 VOLT (300 mv) → OPEN CKT 412 OR FAULTY ECM CONNECTION OR FAULTY ECM.

"AFTER REPAIRS," REFER TO CODE CRITERIA AND CONFIRM CODE DOES NOT RESET.

DIAGNOSTIC CHARTS — 2.5L engine

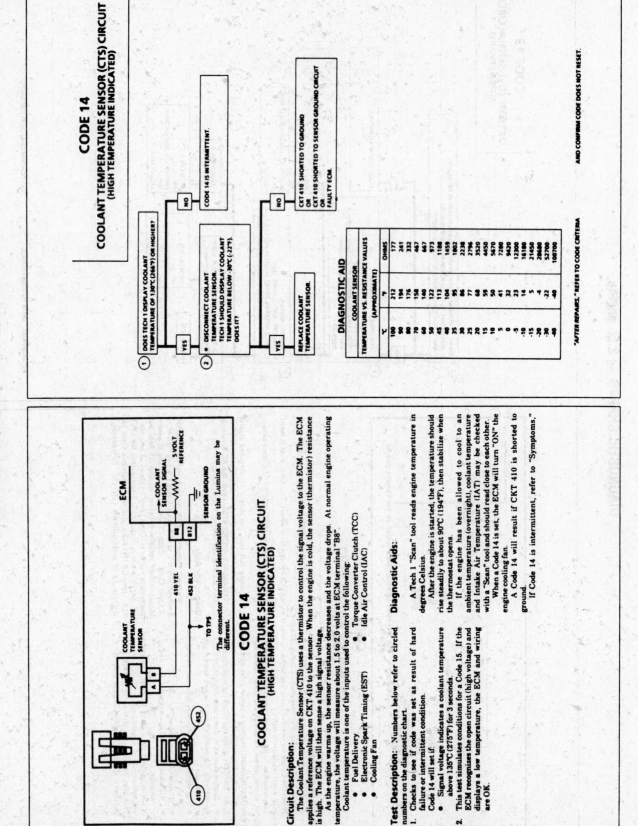

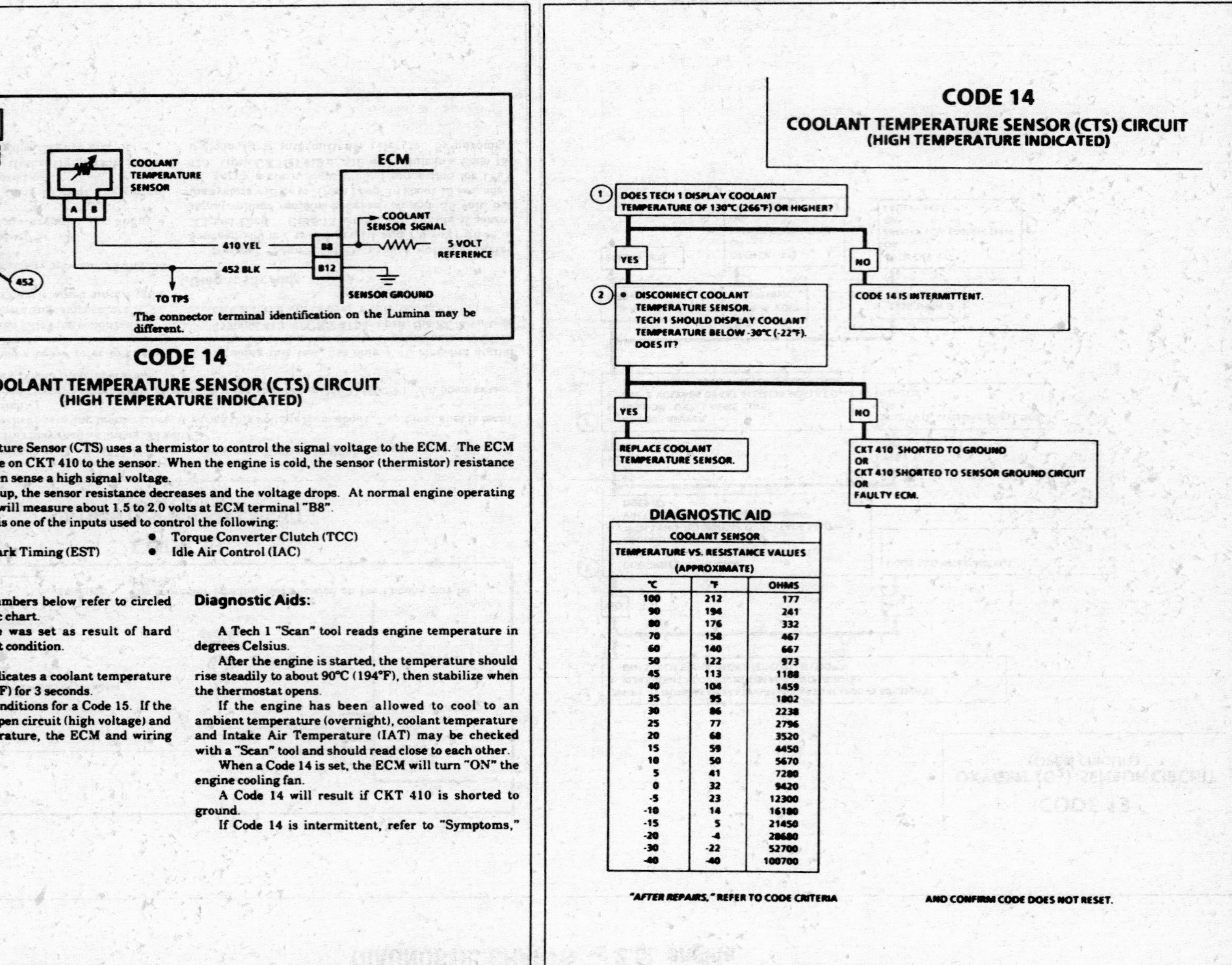

The connector terminal identification on the Lumina may be different.

CODE 14

COOLANT TEMPERATURE SENSOR (CTS) CIRCUIT (HIGH TEMPERATURE INDICATED)

Circuit Description:

The Coolant Temperature Sensor (CTS) uses a thermistor to control the signal voltage to the ECM. The ECM applies a reference voltage on CKT 410 to the sensor. When the engine is cold, the sensor (thermistor) resistance is high. The ECM will then sense a high signal voltage.

As the engine warms up, the sensor resistance decreases and the voltage drops. At normal engine operating temperature, the voltage will measure about 1.5 to 2.0 volts at ECM terminal "B8".

Coolant temperature is one of the inputs used to control the following:

- Fuel Delivery
- Electronic Spark Timing (EST)
- Cooling Fan
- Torque Converter Clutch (TCC)
- Idle Air Control (IAC)

Test Description: Numbers below refer to circled numbers on the diagnostic chart.

1. Checks to see if code was set as result of hard failure or intermittent condition.
   Code 14 will set if:
   - Signal voltage indicates a coolant temperature above 135°C (275°F) for 3 seconds.
2. This test simulates conditions for a Code 15. If the ECM recognizes the open circuit (high voltage) and displays a low temperature, the ECM and wiring are OK.

Diagnostic Aids:

A Tech 1 "Scan" tool reads engine temperature in degrees Celsius.

After the engine is started, the temperature should rise steadily to about 90°C (194°F), then stabilize when the thermostat opens.

If the engine has been allowed to cool to an ambient temperature (overnight), coolant temperature and Intake Air Temperature (IAT) may be checked with a "Scan" tool and should read close to each other.

When a Code 14 is set, the ECM will turn "ON" the engine cooling fan.

A Code 14 will result if CKT 410 is shorted to ground.

If Code 14 is intermittent, refer to "Symptoms,"

CODE 14

COOLANT TEMPERATURE SENSOR (CTS) CIRCUIT (HIGH TEMPERATURE INDICATED)

(1) DOES TECH 1 DISPLAY COOLANT TEMPERATURE OF 130°C (266°F) OR HIGHER?

- YES → (2) • DISCONNECT COOLANT TEMPERATURE SENSOR. TECH 1 SHOULD DISPLAY COOLANT TEMPERATURE BELOW -30°C (-22°F). DOES IT?
  - YES → REPLACE COOLANT TEMPERATURE SENSOR.
  - NO → CKT 410 SHORTED TO GROUND OR CKT 410 SHORTED TO SENSOR GROUND CIRCUIT OR FAULTY ECM.
- NO → CODE 14 IS INTERMITTENT.

DIAGNOSTIC AID

COOLANT SENSOR
TEMPERATURE VS. RESISTANCE VALUES
(APPROXIMATE)

°C	°F	OHMS
100	212	177
90	194	241
80	176	332
70	158	467
60	140	667
50	122	973
45	113	1188
40	104	1459
35	95	1802
30	86	2238
25	77	2796
20	68	3520
15	59	4450
10	50	5670
5	41	7280
0	32	9420
-5	23	12300
-10	14	16180
-15	5	21450
-20	-4	28680
-30	-22	52700
-40	-40	100700

"AFTER REPAIRS," REFER TO CODE CRITERIA AND CONFIRM CODE DOES NOT RESET.

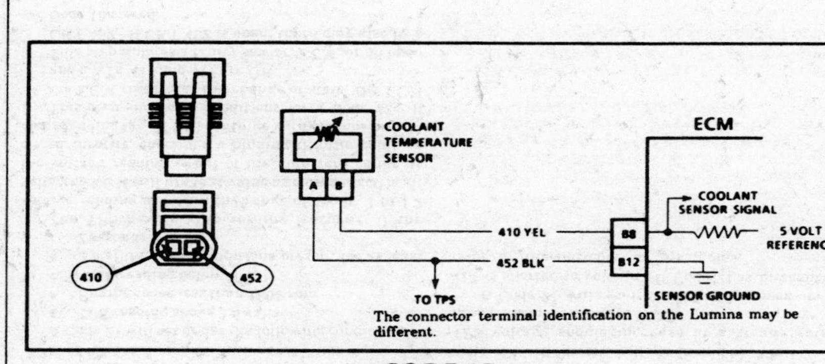

The connector terminal identification on the Lumina may be different.

CODE 15

COOLANT TEMPERATURE SENSOR (CTS) CIRCUIT (LOW TEMPERATURE INDICATED)

Circuit Description:

The Coolant Temperature Sensor (CTS) uses a thermistor to control the signal voltage to the ECM. The ECM applies a reference voltage on CKT 410 to the sensor. When the engine is cold, the sensor (thermistor) resistance is high. The ECM will then sense a high signal voltage.

As the engine warms up, the sensor resistance decreases and the voltage drops. At normal engine operating temperature, the voltage will measure about 1.5 to 2.0 volts at ECM terminal "B8".

Coolant temperature is one of the inputs used to control the following:

- Fuel Delivery
- Electronic Spark Timing (EST)
- Cooling Fan
- Torque Convertor Clutch (TCC)
- Idle Air Control (IAC)

Test Description: Numbers below refer to circled numbers on the diagnostic chart.

1. Checks to see if code was set as result of hard failure or intermittent condition.
   Code 15 will set if:
   - Signal voltage indicates a coolant temperature below -30°C (-22°F) for 60 seconds.
2. This test simulates conditions for a Code 14. If the ECM recognizes the grounded circuit (low voltage) and displays a high temperature, the ECM and wiring are OK.
3. This test will determine if there is a wiring problem or a faulty ECM. If CKT 452 is open, there may also be a Code 21 stored.

Diagnostic Aids:

A Tech 1 "Scan" tool reads engine temperature in degrees Celsius. After the engine is started, the temperature should rise steadily to about 90°C (194°F), then stabilize when the thermostat opens.

If the engine has been allowed to cool to an ambient temperature (overnight), coolant temperature and Intake Air Temperature (IAT) may be checked with a "Scan" tool and should read close to each other.

When a Code 15 is set, the ECM will turn "ON" the engine cooling fan.

A Code 15 will result if CKTs 410 or 452 are open.

If Code 15 is intermittent, refer to "Symptoms,"

CODE 15

COOLANT TEMPERATURE SENSOR (CTS) CIRCUIT (LOW TEMPERATURE INDICATED)

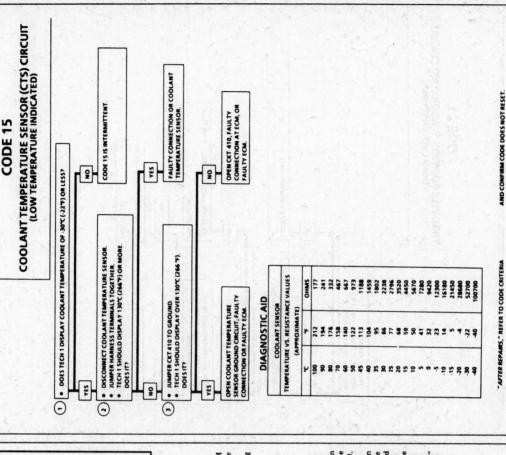

(1) • DOES TECH 1 DISPLAY COOLANT TEMPERATURE OF -30°C (-22°F) OR LESS?

- NO → CODE 15 IS INTERMITTENT.
- YES → (2) • DISCONNECT COOLANT TEMPERATURE SENSOR. • JUMPER HARNESS TERMINALS TOGETHER. • TECH 1 SHOULD DISPLAY 130°C (266°F) OR MORE. DOES IT?
  - YES → FAULTY CONNECTION OR COOLANT TEMPERATURE SENSOR.
  - NO → (3) • JUMPER CKT 410 TO GROUND. • TECH 1 SHOULD DISPLAY OVER 130°C (266°F). DOES IT?
    - YES → OPEN COOLANT TEMPERATURE SENSOR GROUND CIRCUIT, FAULTY CONNECTION OR FAULTY ECM.
    - NO → OPEN CKT 410, FAULTY CONNECTION AT ECM, OR FAULTY ECM.

DIAGNOSTIC AID

COOLANT SENSOR
TEMPERATURE VS. RESISTANCE VALUES (APPROXIMATE)

°C	°F	OHMS
100	212	177
90	194	241
80	176	332
70	158	467
60	140	667
50	122	973
45	113	1188
40	104	1459
35	95	1802
30	86	2238
25	77	2796
20	68	3520
15	59	4450
10	50	5670
5	41	7280
0	32	9420
-5	23	12300
-10	14	16180
-15	5	21450
-20	-4	28680
-30	-22	52700
-40	-40	100700

"AFTER REPAIRS," REFER TO CODE CRITERIA AND CONFIRM CODE DOES NOT RESET.

DIAGNOSTIC CHARTS — 2.5L engine

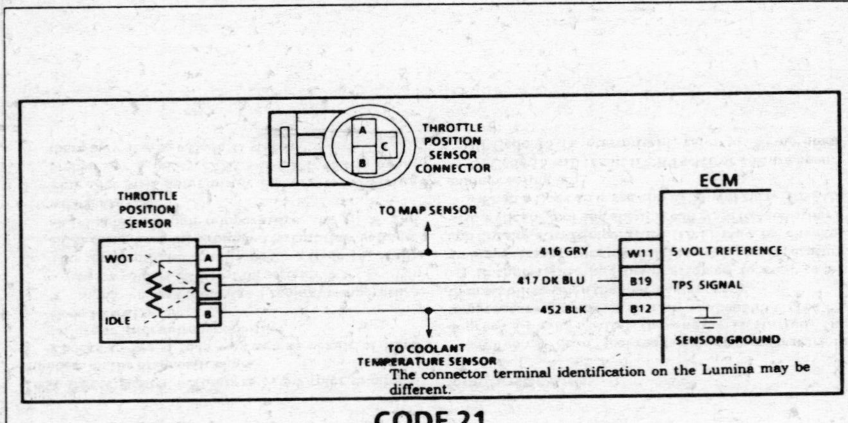
THROTTLE POSITION SENSOR CONNECTOR
A
B
C
THROTTLE POSITION SENSOR
WOT
IDLE
TO MAP SENSOR
ECM
416 GRY
417 DK BLU
452 BLK
W11
B19
B12
5 VOLT REFERENCE
TPS SIGNAL
SENSOR GROUND
TO COOLANT TEMPERATURE SENSOR
The connector terminal identification on the Lumina may be different.

CODE 21

THROTTLE POSITION SENSOR (TPS) CIRCUIT (SIGNAL VOLTAGE HIGH)

Circuit Description:

The Throttle Position Sensor (TPS) provides a voltage signal that changes relative to the throttle valve. Signal voltage will vary from about .3 to 1.3 volts at idle to about 5 volts at Wide Open Throttle (WOT).

The TPS signal is one of the most important inputs used by the ECM for fuel control and for many of the ECM controlled outputs.

Test Description: Numbers below refer to circled numbers on the diagnostic chart.

1. This step checks to see if Code 21 is the result of a hard failure or an intermittent condition.
   A Code 21 will set under the following conditions:
   - TPS reading above 2.5 volts
   - Engine speed less than 1800 rpm
   - MAP reading below 60 kPa
   - All of the above conditions present for at least 2 seconds.

   The TPS has an auto zeroing feature. If the voltage reading is within the range of about .3 to 1.3 volts, the ECM will use that value as closed throttle. If the voltage reading is out of the auto zero range at closed throttle, check for a binding throttle cable or damaged linkage. If OK, continue with diagnosis.
2. This step simulates conditions for a Code 22. If the ECM recognizes the change of state, the ECM and CKTs 416 and 417 are OK.
3. This step isolates a faulty sensor, ECM, or an open CKT 452. If CKT 452 is open, there may also be a Code 15 stored.

Diagnostic Aids:

A Tech 1 "Scan" tool displays throttle position in volts. Closed throttle voltage should be .3 to 1.3 volts. TPS voltage should increase at a steady rate as throttle is moved toward WOT.

A Code 21 will result if CKT 452 is open or CKT 417 is shorted to voltage. If Code 21 is intermittent, refer to "Intermittents" in "Symptoms."

CODE 21

THROTTLE POSITION SENSOR (TPS) CIRCUIT (SIGNAL VOLTAGE HIGH)

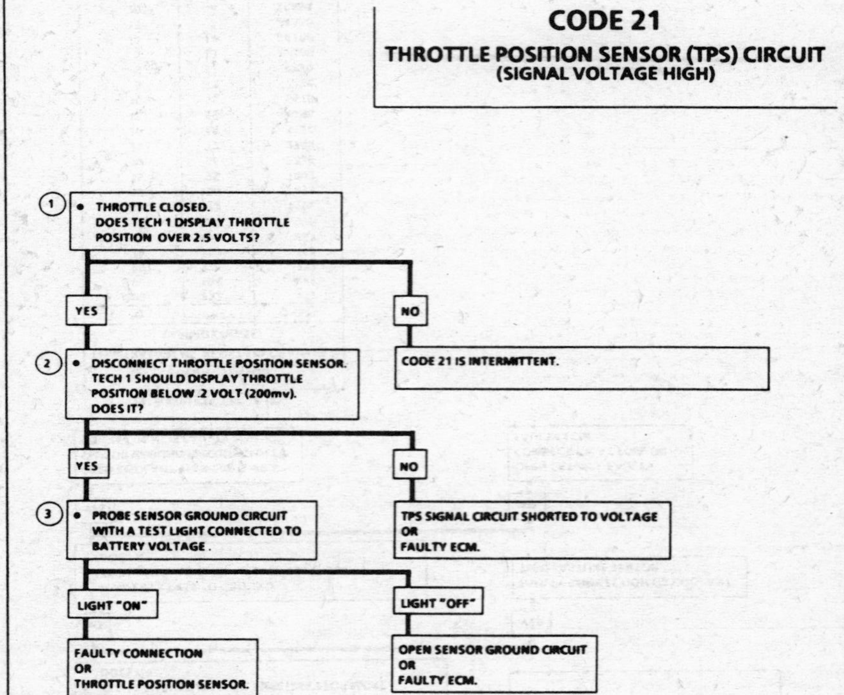
1 • THROTTLE CLOSED. DOES TECH 1 DISPLAY THROTTLE POSITION OVER 2.5 VOLTS?
YES
NO
CODE 21 IS INTERMITTENT.
2 • DISCONNECT THROTTLE POSITION SENSOR. TECH 1 SHOULD DISPLAY THROTTLE POSITION BELOW .2 VOLT (200mv). DOES IT?
YES
NO
TPS SIGNAL CIRCUIT SHORTED TO VOLTAGE OR FAULTY ECM.
3 • PROBE SENSOR GROUND CIRCUIT WITH A TEST LIGHT CONNECTED TO BATTERY VOLTAGE.
LIGHT "ON"
LIGHT "OFF"
FAULTY CONNECTION OR THROTTLE POSITION SENSOR.
OPEN SENSOR GROUND CIRCUIT OR FAULTY ECM.
"AFTER REPAIRS," REFER TO CODE CRITERIA AND CONFIRM CODE DOES NOT RESET.

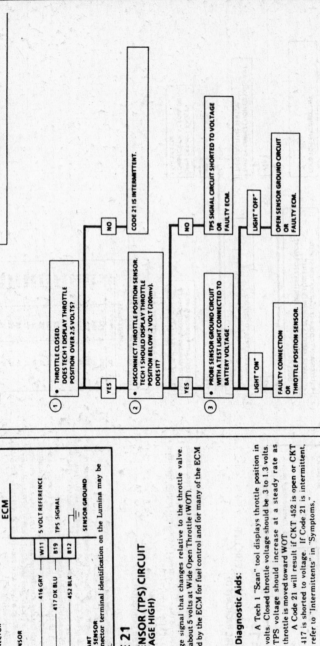

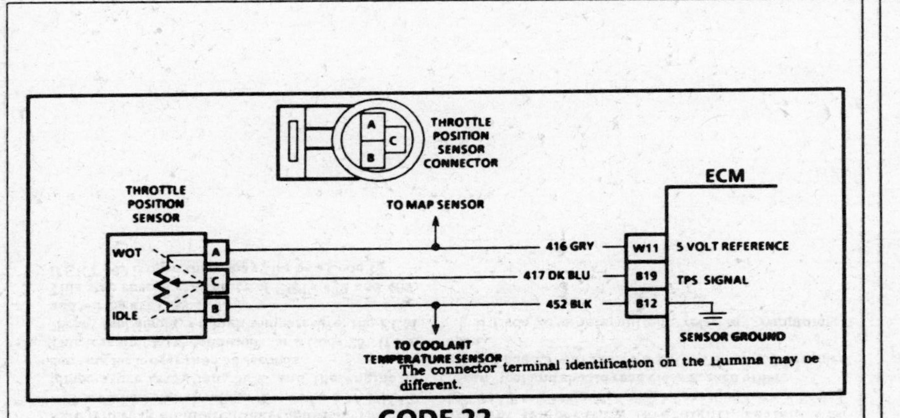

The connector terminal identification on the Lumina may be different.

CODE 22

THROTTLE POSITION SENSOR (TPS) CIRCUIT (SIGNAL VOLTAGE LOW)

Circuit Description:

The Throttle Position Sensor (TPS) provides a voltage signal that changes relative to the throttle valve. Signal voltage will vary from about .3 to 1.3 volts at idle to about 5 volts at Wide Open Throttle (WOT).

The TPS signal is one of the most important inputs used by the ECM for fuel control and for many of the ECM controlled outputs.

Test Description: Numbers below refer to circled numbers on the diagnostic chart.

1. Code 22 will set if:
   - Engine is running
   - TPS signal voltage is less than .20 volt.

   The TPS has an auto zeroing feature. If the voltage reading is within the range of about .3 to 1.3 volts, the ECM will use that value as closed throttle. If the voltage reading is out of the auto zero range at closed throttle, check for a binding throttle cable or damaged linkage, if OK, continue with diagnosis.
2. Simulates Code 21: (high voltage). If the ECM recognizes the high signal voltage then the ECM and wiring are OK.
3. Check for good sensor connection. If connection is good, replace TPS.
4. This simulates a high signal voltage to check for an open in CKT 417. The "Scan" tool will not read up to 12 volts, but what is important is that the ECM recognizes the signal on CKT 417.

Diagnostic Aids:

A Tech 1 "Scan" tool reads throttle position in volts. With ignition "ON" or at idle, TPS signal voltage should read from about .3 to 1.3 volts with the throttle closed and increase at a steady rate as throttle is moved toward WOT.

An open or short to ground in CKT 416 or CKT 417 will result in a Code 22.

If Code 22 is intermittent, refer to "Intermittents" in "Symptoms,"

CODE 22

THROTTLE POSITION SENSOR (TPS) CIRCUIT (SIGNAL VOLTAGE LOW)

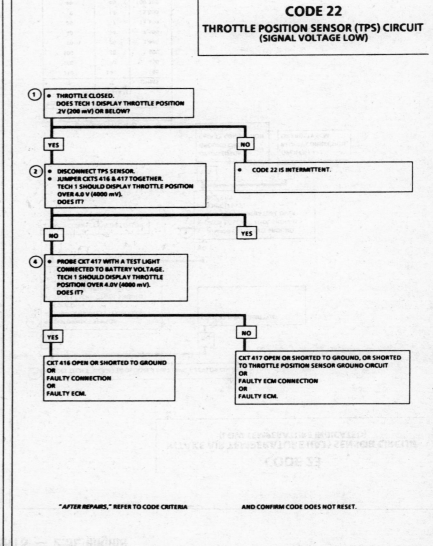

(1)
- THROTTLE CLOSED.
  DOES TECH 1 DISPLAY THROTTLE POSITION .2V (200 mV) OR BELOW?

YES → (2)

NO →
- CODE 22 IS INTERMITTENT.

(2)
- DISCONNECT TPS SENSOR.
- JUMPER CKTS 416 & 417 TOGETHER.
  TECH 1 SHOULD DISPLAY THROTTLE POSITION OVER 4.0 V (4000 mV).
  DOES IT?

NO → (4)

YES

(4)
- PROBE CKT 417 WITH A TEST LIGHT CONNECTED TO BATTERY VOLTAGE.
  TECH 1 SHOULD DISPLAY THROTTLE POSITION OVER 4.0V (4000 mV).
  DOES IT?

YES → CKT 416 OPEN OR SHORTED TO GROUND OR FAULTY CONNECTION OR FAULTY ECM.

NO → CKT 417 OPEN OR SHORTED TO GROUND, OR SHORTED TO THROTTLE POSITION SENSOR GROUND CIRCUIT OR FAULTY ECM CONNECTION OR FAULTY ECM.

"*AFTER REPAIRS*," REFER TO CODE CRITERIA AND CONFIRM CODE DOES NOT RESET.

DIAGNOSTIC CHARTS — 2.5L engine

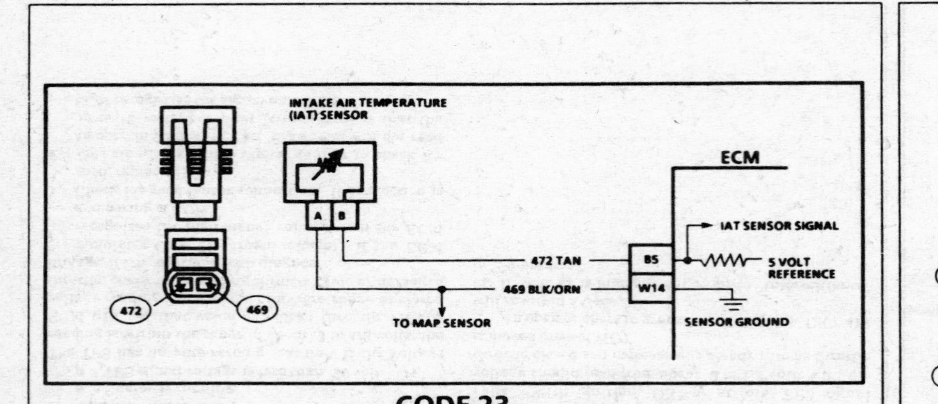

CODE 23

INTAKE AIR TEMPERATURE (IAT) SENSOR CIRCUIT (LOW TEMPERATURE INDICATED)

Circuit Description:

The Intake Air Temperature (IAT) sensor, located on the intake manifold, uses a thermistor to control the signal voltage to the ECM. The ECM applies a reference voltage (4-5.5 volts) on CKT 472 to the sensor. When intake air is cold, the sensor (thermistor) resistance is high. The ECM will then sense a high signal voltage. As the air warms, the sensor resistance becomes less and the voltage drops.

Test Description: Numbers below refer to circled numbers on the diagnostic chart.

1. This step determines if Code 23 is the result of a hard failure or an intermittent condition. Code 23 will set when signal voltage indicates a IAT/MAT temperature less than -30°C and the engine is running for longer than 58 seconds.
2. This test simulates conditions for a Code 25. If the "Scan" tool displays a high temperature, the ECM and wiring are OK.
3. This step checks continuity of CKTs 472 and 469. If CKT 469 is open there may also be a Code 33.

Diagnostic Aids:

If the engine has been allowed to cool to an ambient temperature (overnight), coolant and IAT/MAT temperatures may be checked with a Tech 1 "Scan" tool and should read close to each other.

A Code 23 will result if CKT 472 or 469 becomes open.

If Code 23 is intermittent, refer to "Symptoms,"

CODE 23

INTAKE AIR TEMPERATURE (IAT) SENSOR CIRCUIT (LOW TEMPERATURE INDICATED)

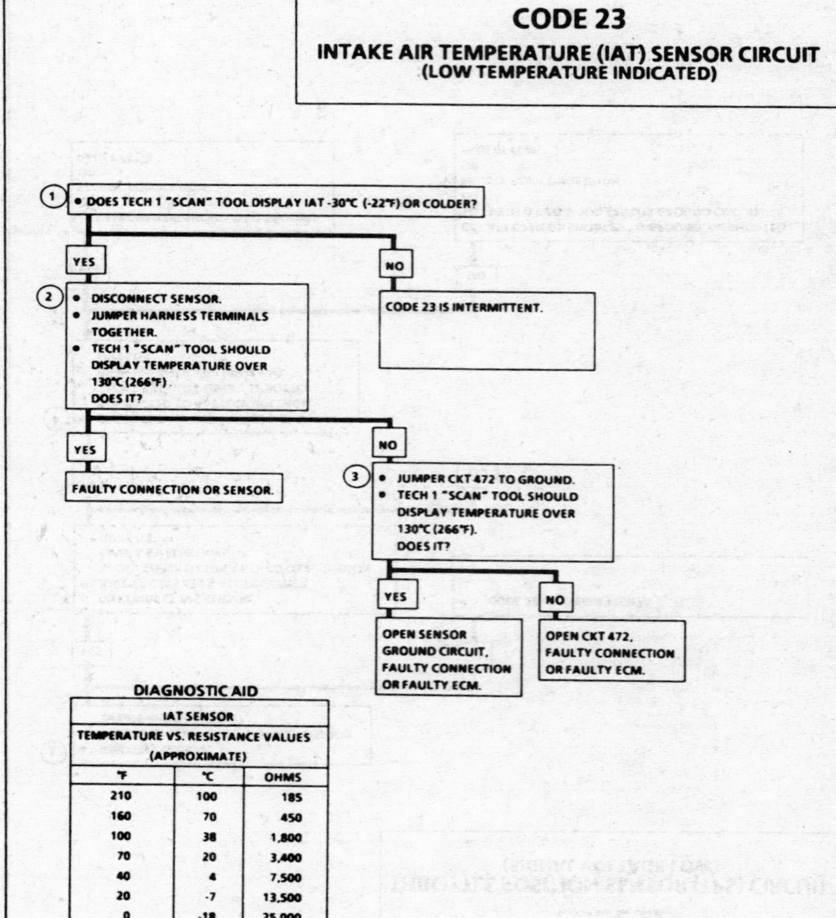

1
• DOES TECH 1 "SCAN" TOOL DISPLAY IAT -30°C (-22°F) OR COLDER?
YES
NO
2
• DISCONNECT SENSOR.
• JUMPER HARNESS TERMINALS TOGETHER.
• TECH 1 "SCAN" TOOL SHOULD DISPLAY TEMPERATURE OVER 130°C (266°F). DOES IT?
CODE 23 IS INTERMITTENT.
YES
NO
FAULTY CONNECTION OR SENSOR.
3
• JUMPER CKT 472 TO GROUND.
• TECH 1 "SCAN" TOOL SHOULD DISPLAY TEMPERATURE OVER 130°C (266°F). DOES IT?
YES
NO
OPEN SENSOR GROUND CIRCUIT, FAULTY CONNECTION OR FAULTY ECM.
OPEN CKT 472, FAULTY CONNECTION OR FAULTY ECM.

DIAGNOSTIC AID

IAT SENSOR
TEMPERATURE VS. RESISTANCE VALUES (APPROXIMATE)

°F	°C	OHMS
210	100	185
160	70	450
100	38	1,800
70	20	3,400
40	4	7,500
20	-7	13,500
0	-18	25,000
-40	-40	100,700

"*AFTER REPAIRS*," REFER TO CODE CRITERIA AND CONFIRM CODE DOES NOT RESET.

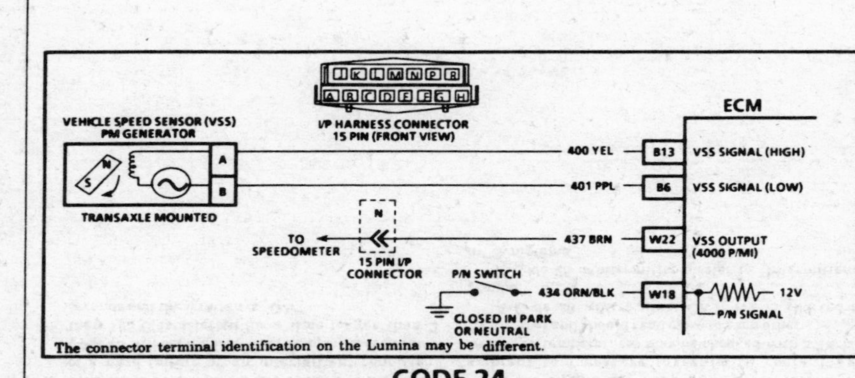

The connector terminal identification on the Lumina may be different.

CODE 24

VEHICLE SPEED SENSOR (VSS) CIRCUIT

Circuit Description:

Vehicle speed information is provided to the ECM by the Vehicle Speed Sensor (VSS). The VSS is a Permanent Magnet (PM) generator located in the transmission. The PM generator produces a pulsing voltage whenever vehicle speed is over about 3 mph. The A/C voltage level and the number of pulses increases with vehicle speed. The ECM converts the pulsing voltage to miles per hour. This data is used for calculations and can be displayed on a Tech 1 "Scan" tool.

The function of VSS buffer used in past model years has been incorporated into the ECM. The ECM supplies the necessary signal for the instrument panel (4000 pulses per mile) for operating the speedometer and the odometer.

Test Description:

Code 24 will set if vehicle speed equals 0 mph when:

- Engine speed is between 1500 and 4400 rpm
- TPS is less than 2%
- Low load condition (low MAP voltage, high manifold vacuum)
- Transmission not in park or neutral
- All above conditions are met for 4 seconds.

These conditions are met during a road load deceleration.

Disregard a Code 24 that sets when the drive wheels are not turning. This can be caused by a faulty park/neutral switch circuit.

The PM generator only produces a signal if the drive wheels are turning greater than 3 mph.

Diagnostic Aids:

A "Scan" tool should indicate a vehicle speed whenever the drive wheels are turning greater than 3 mph.

A problem in CKT 437 will not affect the VSS input or the readings on a "Scan" tool.

Check CKTs 400 and 401 for proper connections to be sure they are clean and tight and the harness is routed correctly. Refer to "Intermittents" in "Symptoms,"

(A/T) - A faulty or misadjusted park/neutral switch can result in a false Code 24. Use a "Scan" tool and check for the proper signal while in a drive range. Refer to CHART C-1A for the P/N switch check.

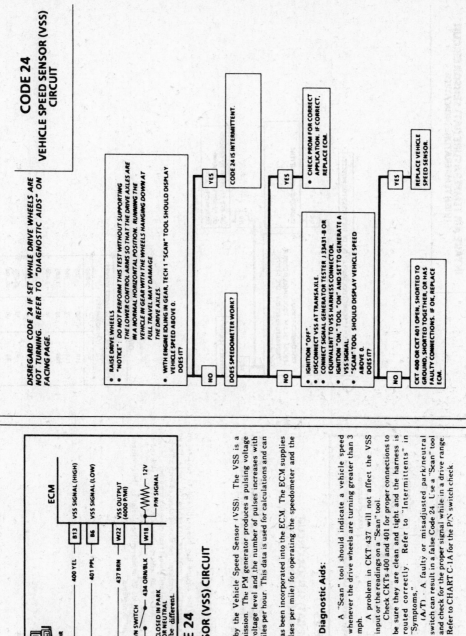

CODE 24
VEHICLE SPEED SENSOR (VSS) CIRCUIT

DISREGARD CODE 24 IF SET WHILE DRIVE WHEELS ARE NOT TURNING. REFER TO "DIAGNOSTIC AIDS" ON FACING PAGE.

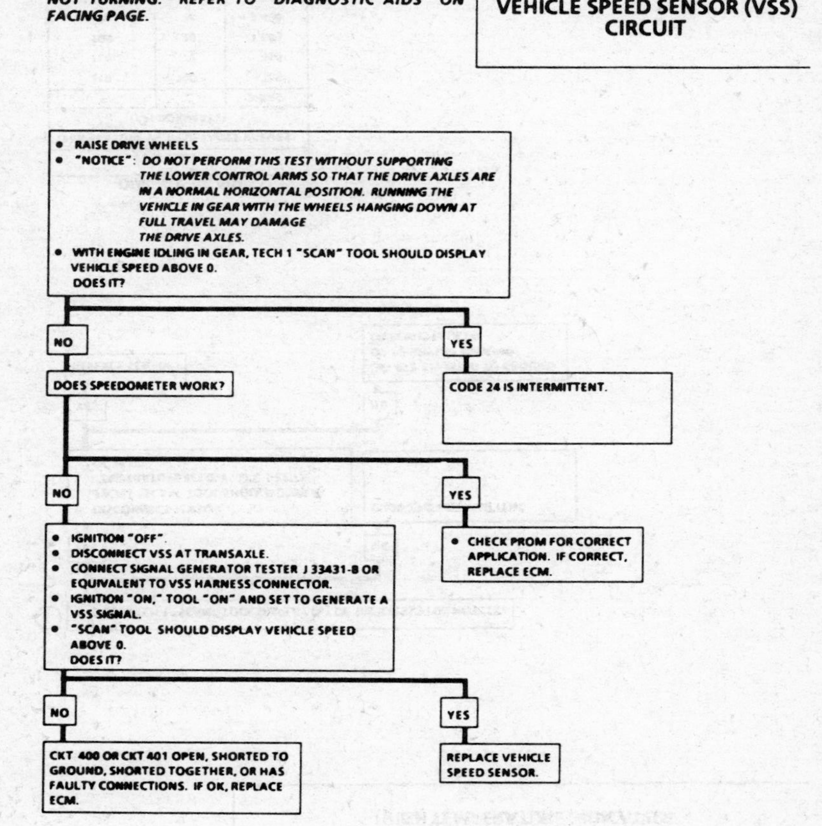

• RAISE DRIVE WHEELS
• "NOTICE": DO NOT PERFORM THIS TEST WITHOUT SUPPORTING THE LOWER CONTROL ARMS SO THAT THE DRIVE AXLES ARE IN A NORMAL HORIZONTAL POSITION. RUNNING THE VEHICLE IN GEAR WITH THE WHEELS HANGING DOWN AT FULL TRAVEL MAY DAMAGE THE DRIVE AXLES.
• WITH ENGINE IDLING IN GEAR, TECH 1 "SCAN" TOOL SHOULD DISPLAY VEHICLE SPEED ABOVE 0. DOES IT?
NO
YES
DOES SPEEDOMETER WORK?
CODE 24 IS INTERMITTENT.
NO
YES
• IGNITION "OFF".
• DISCONNECT VSS AT TRANSAXLE.
• CONNECT SIGNAL GENERATOR TESTER J 33431-B OR EQUIVALENT TO VSS HARNESS CONNECTOR.
• IGNITION "ON," TOOL "ON" AND SET TO GENERATE A VSS SIGNAL.
• "SCAN" TOOL SHOULD DISPLAY VEHICLE SPEED ABOVE 0. DOES IT?
• CHECK PROM FOR CORRECT APPLICATION. IF CORRECT, REPLACE ECM.
NO
YES
CKT 400 OR CKT 401 OPEN, SHORTED TO GROUND, SHORTED TOGETHER, OR HAS FAULTY CONNECTIONS. IF OK, REPLACE ECM.
REPLACE VEHICLE SPEED SENSOR.

"*AFTER REPAIRS*," REFER TO CODE CRITERIA AND CONFIRM CODE DOES NOT RESET.

DIAGNOSTIC CHARTS — 2.5L engine

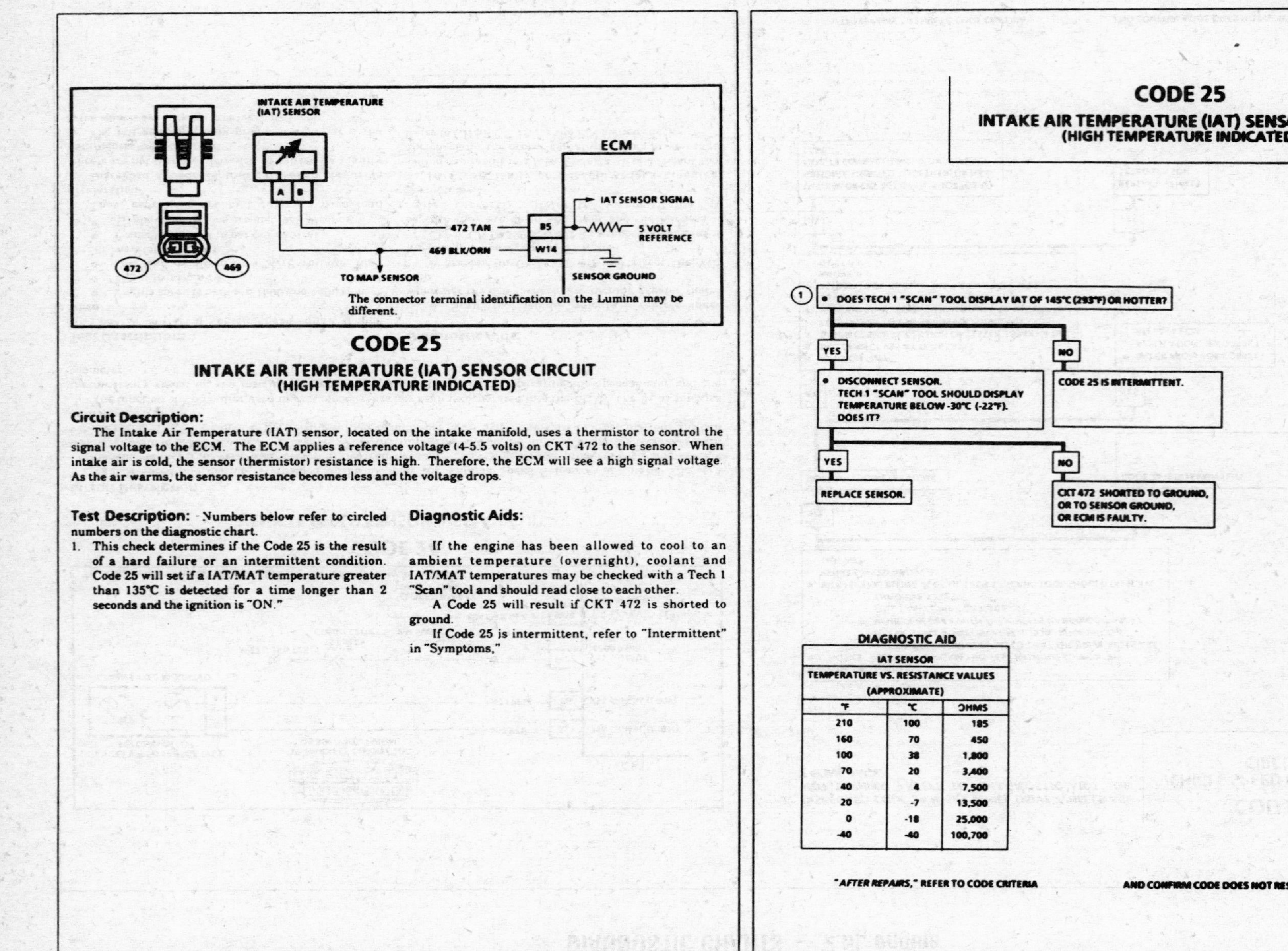
INTAKE AIR TEMPERATURE (IAT) SENSOR
A B
472
469
472 TAN
469 BLK/ORN
TO MAP SENSOR
B5
W14
ECM
IAT SENSOR SIGNAL
5 VOLT REFERENCE
SENSOR GROUND

The connector terminal identification on the Lumina may be different.

CODE 25

INTAKE AIR TEMPERATURE (IAT) SENSOR CIRCUIT (HIGH TEMPERATURE INDICATED)

Circuit Description:

The Intake Air Temperature (IAT) sensor, located on the intake manifold, uses a thermistor to control the signal voltage to the ECM. The ECM applies a reference voltage (4-5.5 volts) on CKT 472 to the sensor. When intake air is cold, the sensor (thermistor) resistance is high. Therefore, the ECM will see a high signal voltage. As the air warms, the sensor resistance becomes less and the voltage drops.

Test Description: Numbers below refer to circled numbers on the diagnostic chart.

1. This check determines if the Code 25 is the result of a hard failure or an intermittent condition. Code 25 will set if a IAT/MAT temperature greater than 135°C is detected for a time longer than 2 seconds and the ignition is "ON."

Diagnostic Aids:

If the engine has been allowed to cool to an ambient temperature (overnight), coolant and IAT/MAT temperatures may be checked with a Tech 1 "Scan" tool and should read close to each other.

A Code 25 will result if CKT 472 is shorted to ground.

If Code 25 is intermittent, refer to "Intermittent" in "Symptoms,"

CODE 25

INTAKE AIR TEMPERATURE (IAT) SENSOR CIRCUIT (HIGH TEMPERATURE INDICATED)

1
• DOES TECH 1 "SCAN" TOOL DISPLAY IAT OF 145°C (293°F) OR HOTTER?
YES
NO
• DISCONNECT SENSOR. TECH 1 "SCAN" TOOL SHOULD DISPLAY TEMPERATURE BELOW -30°C (-22°F). DOES IT?
CODE 25 IS INTERMITTENT.
YES
NO
REPLACE SENSOR.
CKT 472 SHORTED TO GROUND, OR TO SENSOR GROUND, OR ECM IS FAULTY.

DIAGNOSTIC AID

IAT SENSOR		
TEMPERATURE VS. RESISTANCE VALUES (APPROXIMATE)		
°F	°C	OHMS
210	100	185
160	70	450
100	38	1,800
70	20	3,400
40	4	7,500
20	-7	13,500
0	-18	25,000
-40	-40	100,700

"AFTER REPAIRS," REFER TO CODE CRITERIA AND CONFIRM CODE DOES NOT RESET.

DIAGNOSTIC CHARTS — 2.5L engine

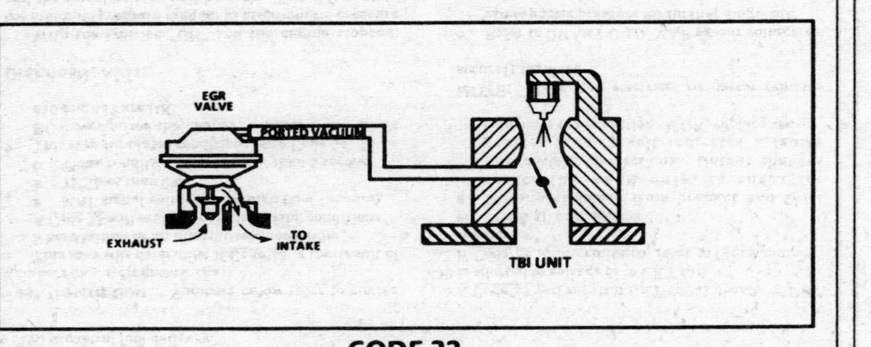

CODE 32

EXHAUST GAS RECIRCULATION (EGR) SYSTEM FAILURE

Circuit Description:

A properly operating EGR system will directly affect the air/fuel requirements of the engine. Since the exhaust gas introduced into the air/fuel mixture is an inert gas (contains very little or no oxygen), less fuel is required to maintain a correct air/fuel ratio. If the EGR system were to become inoperative, the inert exhaust gas would be replaced with air and the air/fuel mixture would be leaner. The ECM would compensate for the lean condition by adding fuel, resulting in higher block learn values.

The engine control system operates within two block learn cells, a closed throttle cell, and an open throttle cell. Since EGR is not used at idle, the closed throttle cell would not be affected by EGR system operation. The open throttle cell is affected by EGR operation and, when the EGR system is operating properly, the block learn values in both cells should be close to being the same. If the EGR system was inoperative, the block learn value in the open throttle cell would change (become higher) to compensate for the resulting lean system, but the block learn value in the closed throttle cell would not change.

This change or difference in block learn values is used to monitor EGR system performance. When the change becomes too great, a Code 32 is set.

Diagnostic Aids:

The Code 32 chart is a functional check of the EGR system. If the EGR system works properly, but a Code 32 has been set, check other items that could result in high block learn values in the open throttle cell, but not in the closed throttle cell.

CHECK:

EGR Passages
Restricted or blocked

MAP Sensor
A MAP sensor may shift in calibration enough to affect fuel delivery. Use CHART C-1D, "Manifold Absolute Pressure (MAP) Output Check."

CODE 32

EXHAUST GAS RECIRCULATION (EGR) SYSTEM FAILURE

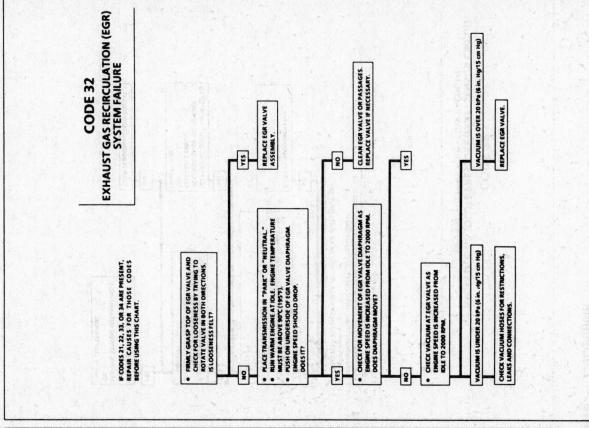

IF CODES 21, 22, 33, OR 34 ARE PRESENT, REPAIR CAUSES FOR THOSE CODES BEFORE USING THIS CHART.

- FIRMLY GRASP TOP OF EGR VALVE AND CHECK FOR LOOSENESS BY TRYING TO ROTATE VALVE IN BOTH DIRECTIONS. IS LOOSENESS FELT?

YES → REPLACE EGR VALVE ASSEMBLY.

NO →

- PLACE TRANSMISSION IN "PARK" OR "NEUTRAL."
- RUN WARM ENGINE AT IDLE. ENGINE TEMPERATURE MUST BE ABOVE 90°C (195°F).
- PUSH ON UNDERSIDE OF EGR VALVE DIAPHRAGM. ENGINE SPEED SHOULD DROP. DOES IT?

NO → CLEAN EGR VALVE OR PASSAGES. REPLACE VALVE IF NECESSARY.

YES →

- CHECK FOR MOVEMENT OF EGR VALVE DIAPHRAGM AS ENGINE SPEED IS INCREASED FROM IDLE TO 2000 RPM. DOES DIAPHRAGM MOVE?

YES

NO →

- CHECK VACUUM AT EGR VALVE AS ENGINE SPEED IS INCREASED FROM IDLE TO 2000 RPM.

VACUUM IS UNDER 20 kPa (6 in. Hg/15 cm Hg) → CHECK VACUUM HOSES FOR RESTRICTIONS, LEAKS AND CONNECTIONS.

VACUUM IS OVER 20 kPa (6 in. Hg/15 cm Hg) → REPLACE EGR VALVE.

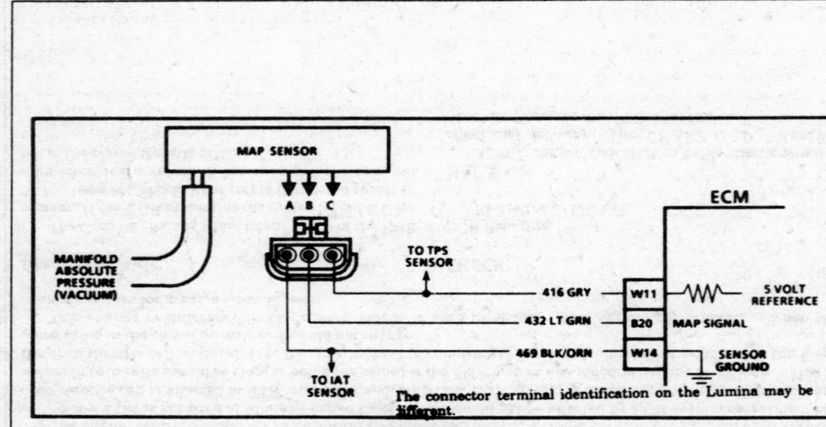

CODE 33

MANIFOLD ABSOLUTE PRESSURE (MAP) SENSOR CIRCUIT
(SIGNAL VOLTAGE HIGH - LOW VACUUM)

Circuit Description:

The Manifold Absolute Pressure (MAP) sensor, located on the air cleaner assembly, responds to changes in manifold pressure (vacuum). The ECM receives this information as a signal voltage that will vary from about 1 to 1.5 volts at closed throttle (idle) to 4.5-4.8 volts at wide open throttle (low vacuum).

If the MAP sensor fails, the ECM will substitute a fixed MAP value and use the Throttle Position Sensor (TPS) to control fuel delivery.

Test Description: Numbers below refer to circled numbers on the diagnostic chart.

1. This step will determine if Code 33 is the result of a hard failure or an intermittent condition.
   A Code 33 will set under the following conditions:
   - MAP signal voltage is too high (low vacuum).
   - TPS less than 2%.
   - These conditions exist longer than 5 seconds.
2. This step simulates conditions for a Code 34. If the ECM recognizes the change, the ECM and CKTs 416 and 432 are OK.

Diagnostic Aids:

With the ignition "ON" and the engine stopped, the manifold pressure is equal to atmospheric pressure and the signal voltage will be high. This information is used by the ECM as an indication of vehicle altitude. Comparison of this reading with a known good vehicle with the same sensor is a good way to check accuracy of a "suspect" sensor. Readings should be the same ± .4 volt.

A Code 33 will result if CKT 469 is open or if CKT 432 is shorted to voltage or to CKT 416.

If Code 33 is intermittent, refer to "Intermittent" in "Symptoms,"

- Check all connections.
- Disconnect sensor from bracket and twist sensor (**by hand only**) to check for intermittent connections. Output changes greater than .1 volt indicates a faulty connector or connection. If OK, replace sensor.

NOTE: Make sure electrical connector remains securely fastened.

- Refer to CHART C-1D, MAP sensor voltage vs. atmospheric pressure for further diagnosis.

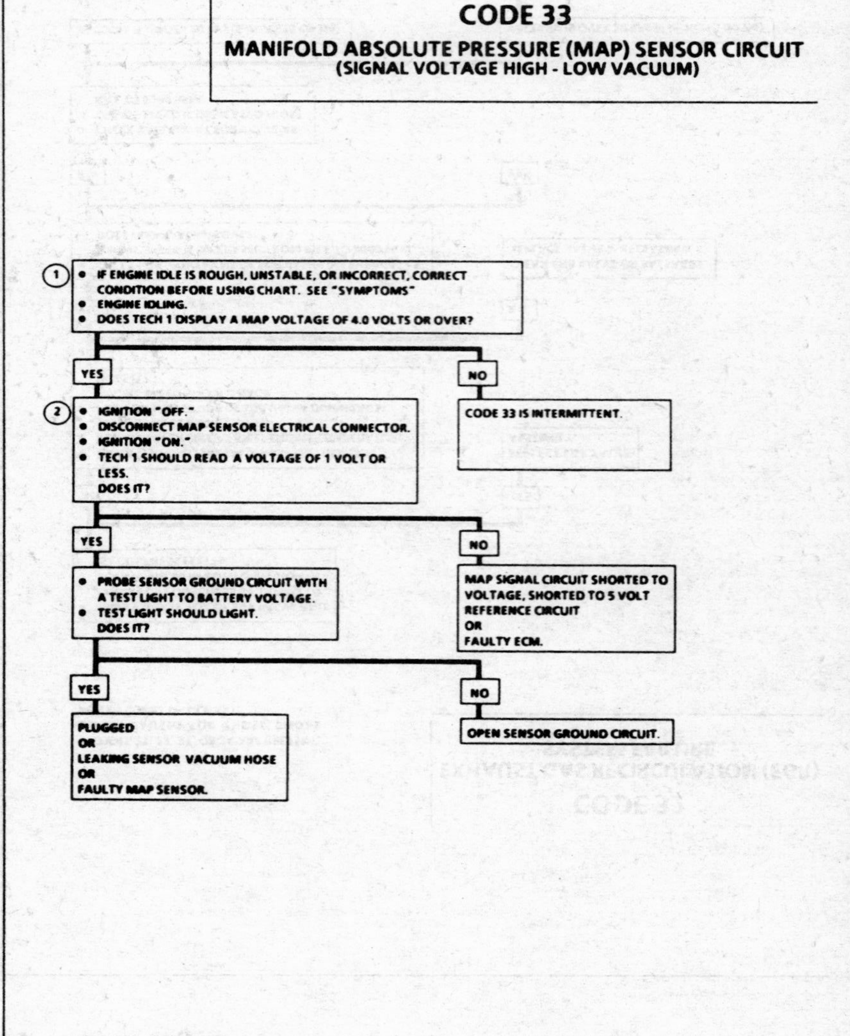

CODE 33
MANIFOLD ABSOLUTE PRESSURE (MAP) SENSOR CIRCUIT
(SIGNAL VOLTAGE HIGH - LOW VACUUM)
1
• IF ENGINE IDLE IS ROUGH, UNSTABLE, OR INCORRECT, CORRECT CONDITION BEFORE USING CHART. SEE "SYMPTOMS"
• ENGINE IDLING.
• DOES TECH 1 DISPLAY A MAP VOLTAGE OF 4.0 VOLTS OR OVER?
YES
NO
CODE 33 IS INTERMITTENT.
2
• IGNITION "OFF."
• DISCONNECT MAP SENSOR ELECTRICAL CONNECTOR.
• IGNITION "ON."
• TECH 1 SHOULD READ A VOLTAGE OF 1 VOLT OR LESS.
DOES IT?
YES
NO
MAP SIGNAL CIRCUIT SHORTED TO VOLTAGE, SHORTED TO 5 VOLT REFERENCE CIRCUIT OR FAULTY ECM.
• PROBE SENSOR GROUND CIRCUIT WITH A TEST LIGHT TO BATTERY VOLTAGE.
• TEST LIGHT SHOULD LIGHT.
DOES IT?
YES
NO
OPEN SENSOR GROUND CIRCUIT.
PLUGGED OR LEAKING SENSOR VACUUM HOSE OR FAULTY MAP SENSOR.

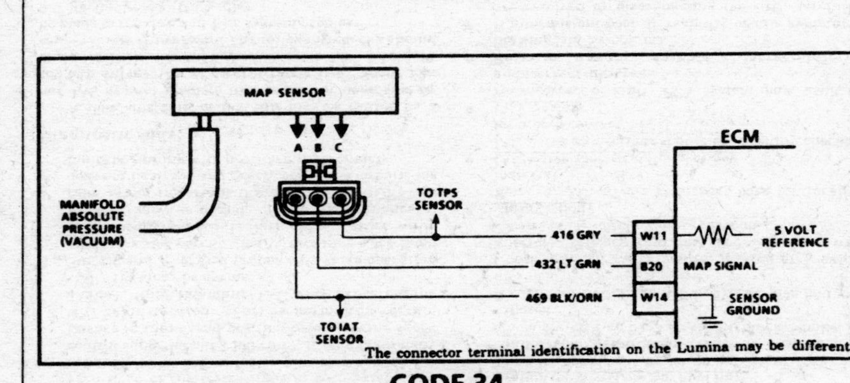
MAP SENSOR
A B C
MANIFOLD ABSOLUTE PRESSURE (VACUUM)
TO TPS SENSOR
TO IAT SENSOR
416 GRY
432 LT GRN
469 BLK/ORN
W11
B20
W14
ECM
5 VOLT REFERENCE
MAP SIGNAL
SENSOR GROUND

The connector terminal identification on the Lumina may be different

CODE 34

MANIFOLD ABSOLUTE PRESSURE (MAP) SENSOR CIRCUIT (SIGNAL VOLTAGE LOW - HIGH VACUUM)

Circuit Description:

The Manifold Absolute Pressure (MAP) sensor, located on the air cleaner assembly, responds to changes in manifold pressure (vacuum). The ECM receives this information as a signal voltage that will vary from about 1 to 1.5 volts at closed throttle (idle) to 4.5- 4.8 volts at wide open throttle (low vacuum).

If the MAP sensor fails, the ECM will substitute a fixed MAP value and use the Throttle Position Sensor (TPS) to control fuel delivery.

Test Description: Numbers below refer to circled numbers on the diagnostic chart.

1. This step determines if Code 34 is the result of a hard failure or an intermittent condition. A Code 34 will set under the following conditions:
   - Code 21 is not detected.
   - MAP signal voltage is too low.
   - Engine speed is less than 1200 rpm.
     OR
   - Engine speed is greater than 1200 rpm and throttle angle is greater than 20%.
   - All conditions above have been present for a period of time greater than .02 second.
2. Jumpering harness terminals "B" to "C" (5 volts to signal circuit) will determine if the sensor is at fault, or if there is a problem with the ECM or wiring.
3. The "Scan" tool may not display 5 volts. The important thing is that the ECM recognizes the voltage as more than 4 volts, indicating that the ECM and CKT 432 are OK.

Diagnostic Aids:

An intermittent open in CKT 432 or CKT 416 will result in a Code 34. If CKT 416 is open or shorted to ground, there may also be a stored Code 22.

With the ignition "ON" and the engine "OFF," the manifold pressure is equal to atmospheric pressure and the signal voltage will be high. This information is used by the ECM as an indication of vehicle altitude.

Comparison of this reading with a known good vehicle with the same sensor is a good way to check accuracy of a "suspect" sensor. Readings should be the same ± .4 volts. Also CHART C-1D can be used to test the MAP sensor. Refer to "Intermittents" in "Symptoms,"

- Check all connections.
- Disconnect sensor from bracket and twist sensor (**by hand only**) to check for intermittent connections. Output changes greater than .1 volt indicates a faulty connector or connection. If OK, replace sensor.

NOTE: Make sure electrical connector remains securely fastened.

- Refer to CHART C-1D, MAP sensor voltage vs. atmospheric pressure for further diagnosis.

CODE 34

MANIFOLD ABSOLUTE PRESSURE (MAP) SENSOR CIRCUIT (SIGNAL VOLTAGE LOW - HIGH VACUUM)

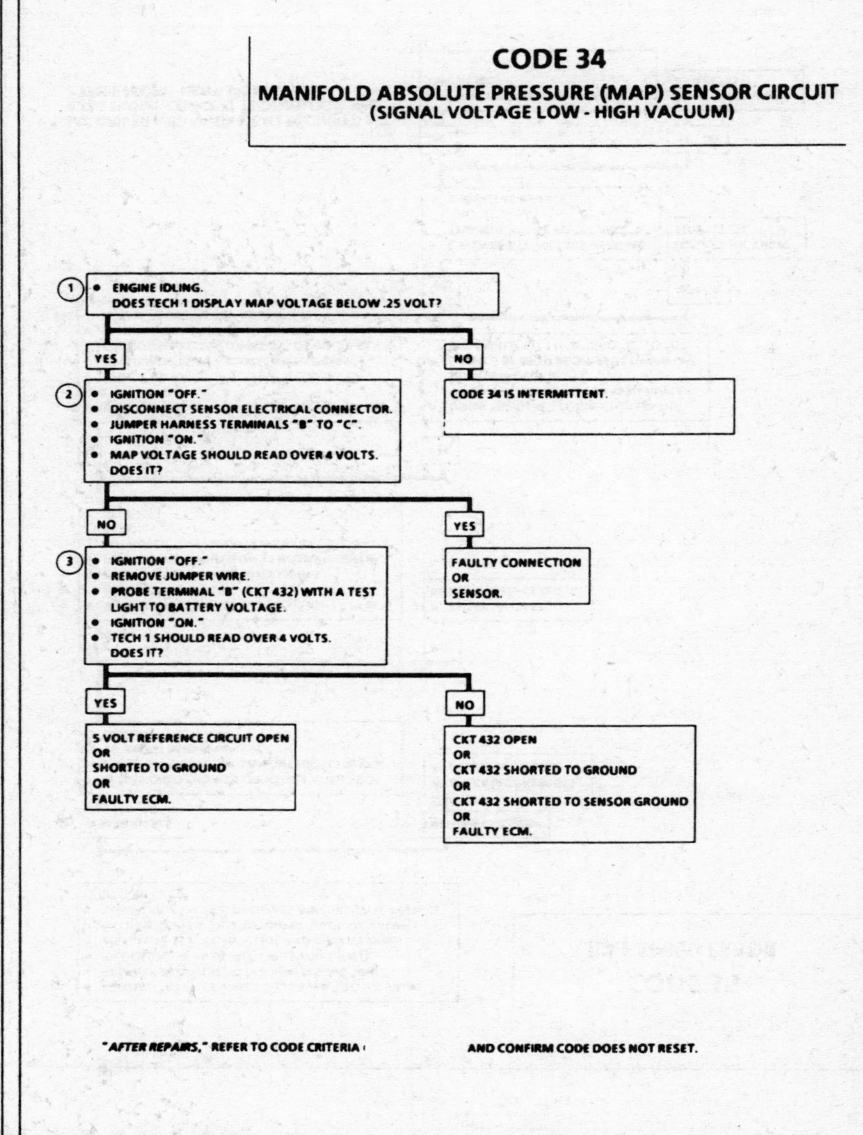
1
• ENGINE IDLING.
DOES TECH 1 DISPLAY MAP VOLTAGE BELOW .25 VOLT?
YES
NO
CODE 34 IS INTERMITTENT.
2
• IGNITION "OFF."
• DISCONNECT SENSOR ELECTRICAL CONNECTOR.
• JUMPER HARNESS TERMINALS "B" TO "C".
• IGNITION "ON."
• MAP VOLTAGE SHOULD READ OVER 4 VOLTS.
DOES IT?
NO
YES
FAULTY CONNECTION
OR
SENSOR.
3
• IGNITION "OFF."
• REMOVE JUMPER WIRE.
• PROBE TERMINAL "B" (CKT 432) WITH A TEST LIGHT TO BATTERY VOLTAGE.
• IGNITION "ON."
• TECH 1 SHOULD READ OVER 4 VOLTS.
DOES IT?
YES
NO
5 VOLT REFERENCE CIRCUIT OPEN
OR
SHORTED TO GROUND
OR
FAULTY ECM.
CKT 432 OPEN
OR
CKT 432 SHORTED TO GROUND
OR
CKT 432 SHORTED TO SENSOR GROUND
OR
FAULTY ECM.

"AFTER REPAIRS," REFER TO CODE CRITERIA AND CONFIRM CODE DOES NOT RESET.

DIAGNOSTIC CHARTS — 2.5L engine

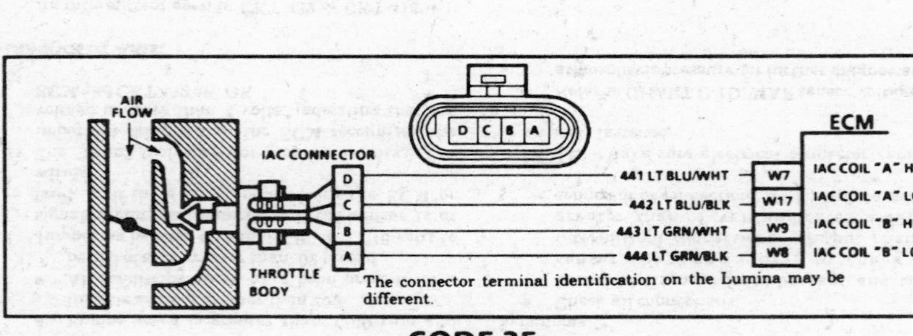

The connector terminal identification on the Lumina may be different.

CODE 35
IDLE SPEED ERROR

Circuit Description:

The ECM controls engine idle speed with the IAC valve. To increase idle speed, the ECM retracts the IAC valve pintle away from its seat, allowing more air to bypass the throttle bore. To decrease idle speed, it extends the IAC valve pintle towards its seats, reducing bypass air flow. A Tech 1 "Scan" tool wil! read the ECM commands to the IAC valve in counts. Higher the counts indicate more air bypass (higher idle). The lower the counts indicate less air is allowed by bypass (lower idle.) Code 35 will be set when the closed throttle speed is 100 rpm above or below the desired idle speed for 2.5 seconds.

Test Description: Numbers below refer to circled numbers on the diagnostic chart.

1. The IAC tester is used to extend and retract the IAC valve. Valve movement is verified by an engine speed change. If no change in engine speed occurs, the valve can be retested when removed from the throttle body.
2. This step checks the quality of the IAC movement in step 1. Between 700 rpm and about 1500 rpm, the engine speed should change smoothly with each flash of the tester light in both extend and retract. If the IAC valve is retracted beyond the control range (about 1500 rpm), it may take many flashes in the extend position before engine speed will begin to drop. This is normal on certain engines, fully extending IAC may cause engine stall. This may be normal.
3. Steps 1 and 2 verified proper IAC valve operation while this step checks the IAC circuits. Each lamp on the node light should flash red and green while the IAC valve is cycled. While the sequence of color is not important if either light is "OFF" or does not flash red and green, check the circuits for faults beginning with poor terminal contacts.

Diagnostic Aids:

A slow, unstable, or fast idle may be caused by a non-IAC system problem that cannot be overcome by the IAC valve. Out of control range IAC "Scan" tool counts will be above 60 if idle is too low, and zero counts if idle is too high. The following checks should be made to repair a non-IAC system problem:

- Vacuum Leak (High Idle)
  If idle is too high, stop the engine. Fully extend (low) IAC with tester. Start engine. If idle speed is above 800 rpm, locate and correct vacuum leak including PCV system. Also check for binding of throttle blade or linkage.
- System too lean (High Air/Fuel Ratio)
  The idle speed may be too high or too low. Engine speed may vary up and down and disconnecting the IAC valve does not help. Code 44 may be set. "Scan" O_2 voltage will be less than 300 mV (.3 volt). Check for low regulated fuel pressure, water in the fuel or a restricted injector.
- System too rich (Low Air/Fuel Ratio)
  The idle speed will be too low. "Scan" tool IAC counts will usually be above 80. System is obviously rich and may exhibit black smoke in exhaust.
  "Scan" tool O_2 voltage will be fixed above 800 mV (.8 volt).
  Check for high fuel pressure, leaking or sticking injector. Silicone contaminated O_2 sensor will "Scan" an O_2 voltage slow to respond.
- Throttle Body
  Remove IAC valve and inspect bore for foreign material.
- IAC Valve Electrical Connections
  IAC valve connections should be carefully checked for proper contact.
- PCV System
  An incorrect or faulty PCV system may result in an incorrect idle speed.
- Refer to "Rough, Unstable, Incorrect Idle or Stalling" in "Symptoms."
- If intermittent poor driveability or idle symptoms are resolved by disconnecting the IAC, carefully recheck connections, valve terminal resistance, or replace IAC.

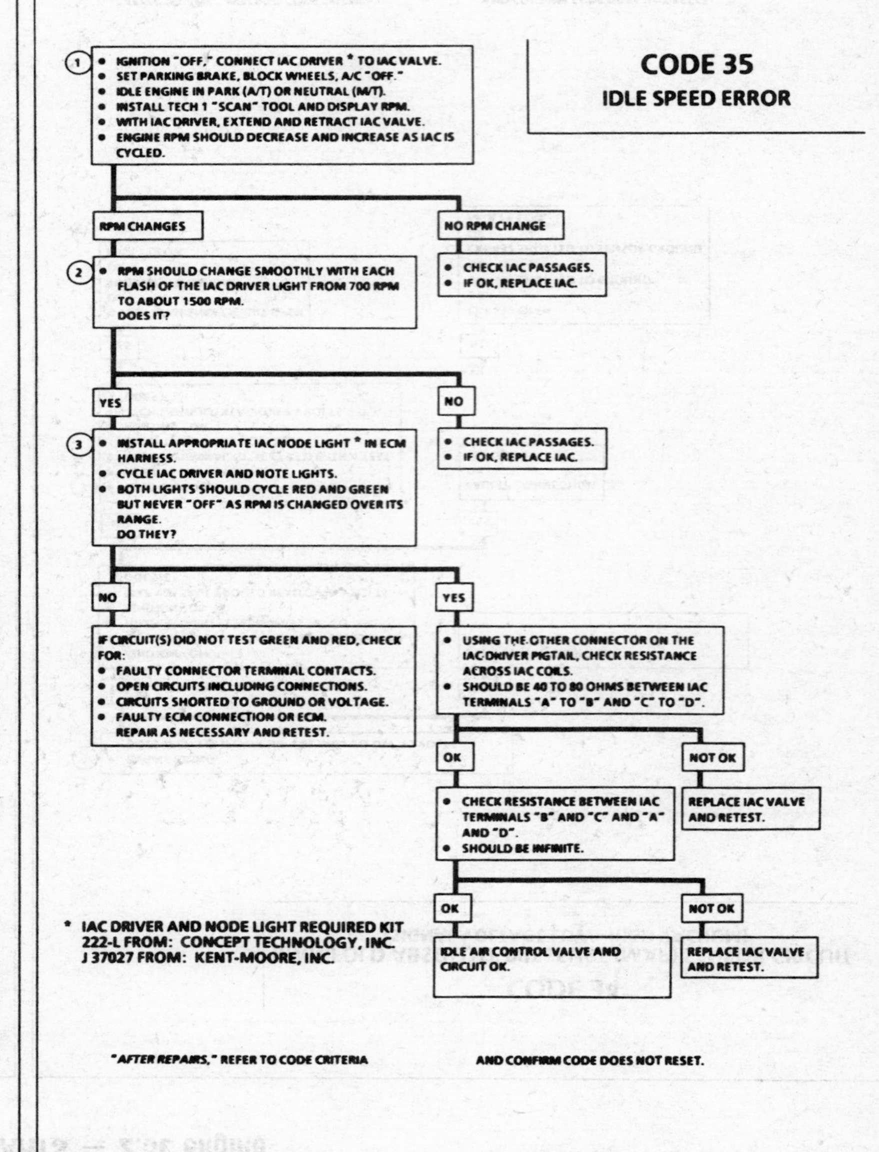

CODE 35
IDLE SPEED ERROR
1
• IGNITION "OFF," CONNECT IAC DRIVER * TO IAC VALVE.
• SET PARKING BRAKE, BLOCK WHEELS, A/C "OFF."
• IDLE ENGINE IN PARK (A/T) OR NEUTRAL (M/T).
• INSTALL TECH 1 "SCAN" TOOL AND DISPLAY RPM.
• WITH IAC DRIVER, EXTEND AND RETRACT IAC VALVE.
• ENGINE RPM SHOULD DECREASE AND INCREASE AS IAC IS CYCLED.
RPM CHANGES
NO RPM CHANGE
• CHECK IAC PASSAGES.
• IF OK, REPLACE IAC.
2
• RPM SHOULD CHANGE SMOOTHLY WITH EACH FLASH OF THE IAC DRIVER LIGHT FROM 700 RPM TO ABOUT 1500 RPM.
DOES IT?
YES
NO
• CHECK IAC PASSAGES.
• IF OK, REPLACE IAC.
3
• INSTALL APPROPRIATE IAC NODE LIGHT * IN ECM HARNESS.
• CYCLE IAC DRIVER AND NOTE LIGHTS.
• BOTH LIGHTS SHOULD CYCLE RED AND GREEN BUT NEVER "OFF" AS RPM IS CHANGED OVER ITS RANGE.
DO THEY?
NO
YES
IF CIRCUIT(S) DID NOT TEST GREEN AND RED, CHECK FOR:
• FAULTY CONNECTOR TERMINAL CONTACTS.
• OPEN CIRCUITS INCLUDING CONNECTIONS.
• CIRCUITS SHORTED TO GROUND OR VOLTAGE.
• FAULTY ECM CONNECTION OR ECM.
REPAIR AS NECESSARY AND RETEST.
• USING THE OTHER CONNECTOR ON THE IAC DRIVER PIGTAIL, CHECK RESISTANCE ACROSS IAC COILS.
• SHOULD BE 40 TO 80 OHMS BETWEEN IAC TERMINALS "A" TO "B" AND "C" TO "D".
OK
NOT OK
• CHECK RESISTANCE BETWEEN IAC TERMINALS "B" AND "C" AND "A" AND "D".
• SHOULD BE INFINITE.
REPLACE IAC VALVE AND RETEST.
OK
NOT OK
IDLE AIR CONTROL VALVE AND CIRCUIT OK.
REPLACE IAC VALVE AND RETEST.
* IAC DRIVER AND NODE LIGHT REQUIRED KIT
222-L FROM: CONCEPT TECHNOLOGY, INC.
J 37027 FROM: KENT-MOORE, INC.
"AFTER REPAIRS," REFER TO CODE CRITERIA AND CONFIRM CODE DOES NOT RESET.

DIAGNOSTIC CHARTS — 2.5L engine

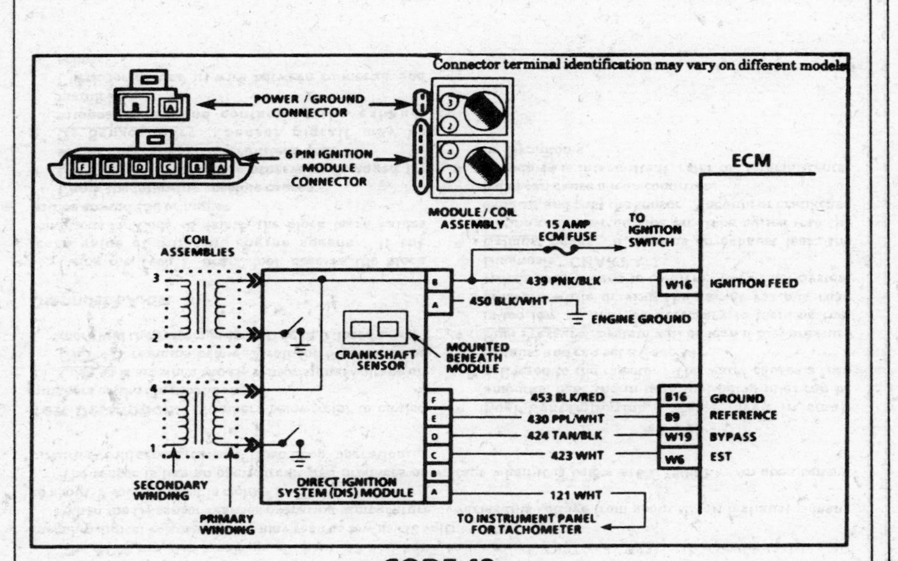
Connector terminal identification may vary on different models
POWER / GROUND CONNECTOR
6 PIN IGNITION MODULE CONNECTOR
MODULE / COIL ASSEMBLY
ECM
COIL ASSEMBLIES
15 AMP ECM FUSE
TO IGNITION SWITCH
439 PNK/BLK
W16
IGNITION FEED
450 BLK/WHT
ENGINE GROUND
CRANKSHAFT SENSOR
MOUNTED BENEATH MODULE
453 BLK/RED
430 PPL/WHT
424 TAN/BLK
423 WHT
B16
B9
W19
W6
GROUND
REFERENCE
BYPASS
EST
SECONDARY WINDING
PRIMARY WINDING
DIRECT IGNITION SYSTEM (DIS) MODULE
121 WHT
TO INSTRUMENT PANEL FOR TACHOMETER

CODE 42

ELECTRONIC SPARK TIMING (EST) CIRCUIT

Circuit Description:

The DIS module sends a reference signal to the ECM when the engine is cranking. While the engine speed is under 400 rpm, the DIS module controls the ignition timing. When the system is running on the ignition module (no voltage on the bypass line), the ignition module grounds the EST signal. The ECM expects to sense no voltage on the EST line during this condition. If it senses a voltage, it sets Code 42 and will not enter the EST mode.

When the engine speed exceeds 400 rpm, the ECM applies 5 volts to the bypass line to switch the timing to ECM control (EST). If the bypass line is open or grounded, once the rpm for EST control is reached, the ignition module will not switch to EST mode. This results in low EST voltage and the setting of Code 42. If the EST line is grounded, the ignition module will switch to EST, but because the line is grounded, there will be no EST signal. A Code 42 will be set.

Test Description: Numbers below refer to circled numbers on the diagnostic chart.

1. Code 42 means the ECM has sensed an open or short to ground in the EST or bypass circuits. This test confirms Code 42 and that the fault causing the code is present.
2. Checks for a normal EST ground path through the ignition module. An EST CKT 423, shorted to ground, will also read less than 500 ohms, but this will be checked later.
3. As the test light voltage contacts CKT 424, the module should switch, causing the ohmmeter to "overrange" if the meter is in the 1000-2000 ohms position. Selecting the 10-20,000 ohms position will indicate a reading above 5000 ohms. The important thing is that the module "switched."
4. The module did not switch and this step checks for:
   - EST CKT 423 shorted to ground
   - Bypass CKT 424 open
   - Faulty ignition module connection or module.
5. Confirms that Code 42 is a faulty ECM and not an intermittent in CKT(s) 423 or 424.

Diagnostic Aids:

The "Scan" tool does not have any ability to help diagnose a Code 42 problem.

If Code 42 is intermittent, refer to "Intermittent" in "Symptoms,"

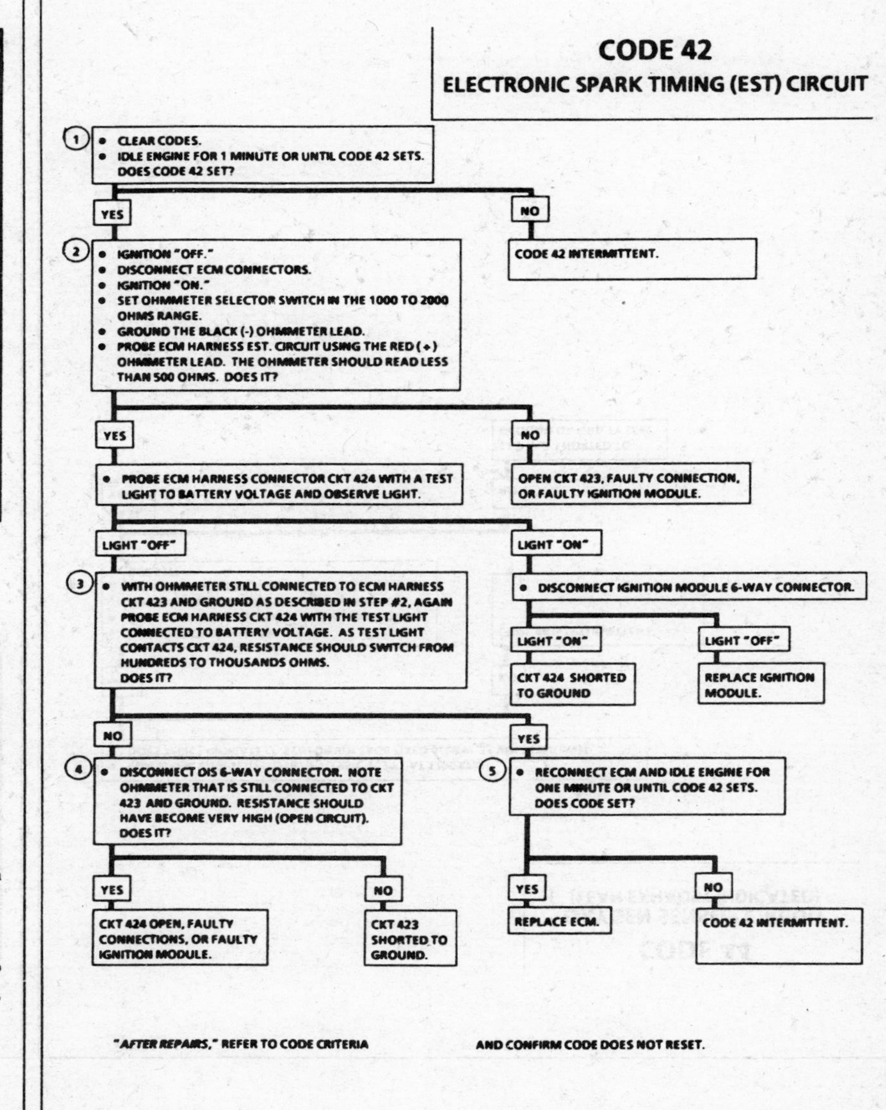
CODE 42
ELECTRONIC SPARK TIMING (EST) CIRCUIT
1
• CLEAR CODES.
• IDLE ENGINE FOR 1 MINUTE OR UNTIL CODE 42 SETS. DOES CODE 42 SET?
YES
NO
CODE 42 INTERMITTENT.
2
• IGNITION "OFF."
• DISCONNECT ECM CONNECTORS.
• IGNITION "ON."
• SET OHMMETER SELECTOR SWITCH IN THE 1000 TO 2000 OHMS RANGE.
• GROUND THE BLACK (-) OHMMETER LEAD.
• PROBE ECM HARNESS EST. CIRCUIT USING THE RED (+) OHMMETER LEAD. THE OHMMETER SHOULD READ LESS THAN 500 OHMS. DOES IT?
YES
NO
• PROBE ECM HARNESS CONNECTOR CKT 424 WITH A TEST LIGHT TO BATTERY VOLTAGE AND OBSERVE LIGHT.
OPEN CKT 423, FAULTY CONNECTION, OR FAULTY IGNITION MODULE.
LIGHT "OFF"
LIGHT "ON"
3
• WITH OHMMETER STILL CONNECTED TO ECM HARNESS CKT 423 AND GROUND AS DESCRIBED IN STEP #2, AGAIN PROBE ECM HARNESS CKT 424 WITH THE TEST LIGHT CONNECTED TO BATTERY VOLTAGE. AS TEST LIGHT CONTACTS CKT 424, RESISTANCE SHOULD SWITCH FROM HUNDREDS TO THOUSANDS OHMS. DOES IT?
• DISCONNECT IGNITION MODULE 6-WAY CONNECTOR.
LIGHT "ON"
LIGHT "OFF"
CKT 424 SHORTED TO GROUND
REPLACE IGNITION MODULE.
NO
YES
4
• DISCONNECT DIS 6-WAY CONNECTOR. NOTE OHMMETER THAT IS STILL CONNECTED TO CKT 423 AND GROUND. RESISTANCE SHOULD HAVE BECOME VERY HIGH (OPEN CIRCUIT). DOES IT?
5
• RECONNECT ECM AND IDLE ENGINE FOR ONE MINUTE OR UNTIL CODE 42 SETS. DOES CODE SET?
YES
NO
YES
NO
CKT 424 OPEN, FAULTY CONNECTIONS, OR FAULTY IGNITION MODULE.
CKT 423 SHORTED TO GROUND.
REPLACE ECM.
CODE 42 INTERMITTENT.
"AFTER REPAIRS," REFER TO CODE CRITERIA AND CONFIRM CODE DOES NOT RESET.

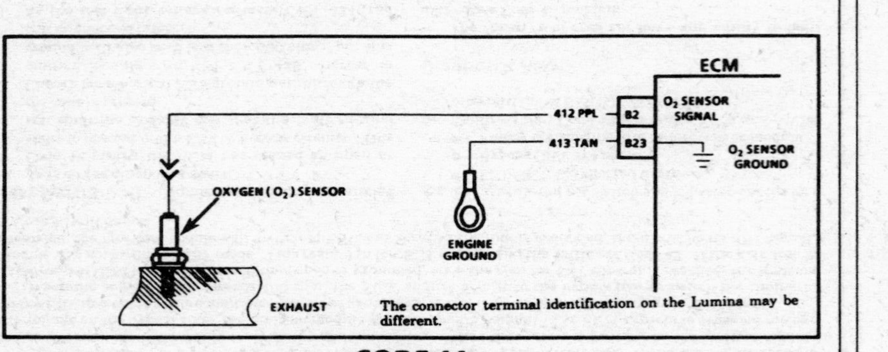

The connector terminal identification on the Lumina may be different.

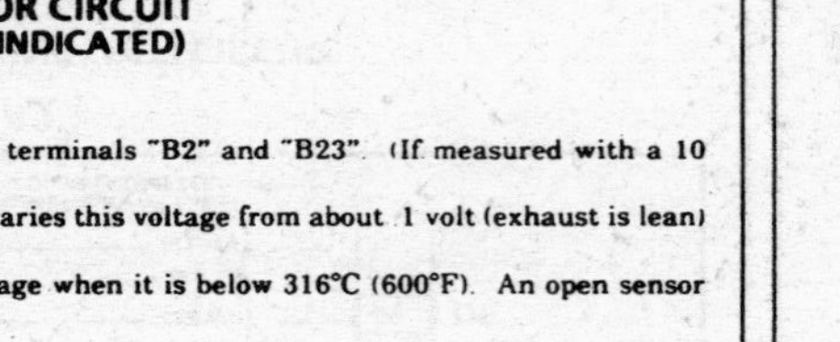

CODE 44

OXYGEN SENSOR CIRCUIT (LEAN EXHAUST INDICATED)

Circuit Description:

The ECM supplies a voltage of about .45 volt between terminals "B2" and "B23". (If measured with a 10 megohm digital voltmeter, this may read as low as .32 volt).

When the O_2 sensor reaches operating temperature, it varies this voltage from about .1 volt (exhaust is lean) to about .9 volt (exhaust is rich).

The sensor is like an open circuit and produces no voltage when it is below 316°C (600°F). An open sensor circuit, or cold sensor, causes "Open Loop" operation.

Test Description: Numbers below refer to circled numbers on the diagnostic chart.

1. Code 44 is set when the O_2 sensor signal voltage on CKT 412 remains below .2 volt for 60 seconds or more and the system is operating in "Closed Loop."

Diagnostic Aids:

Using the Tech 1 "Scan" tool, observe the block learn value at different engine speeds. If the conditions for Code 44 exists, the block learn values will be around 150 or higher.

Check the following possible causes:

- O_2 Sensor. A cracked or otherwise damaged O_2 sensor may cause an intermittent Code 44.
- O_2 Sensor Wire. Sensor pigtail may be mispositioned and contacting the exhaust manifold.

  Check for ground in wire between connector and sensor.
- Fuel Contamination. Water, even in small amounts, near the in-tank fuel pump inlet can be delivered to the injector. The water causes a lean exhaust and can set a Code 44.
- Fuel Pressure. System will be lean if fuel pressure is too low. It may be necessary to monitor fuel pressure while driving the car at various road speeds and/or loads to confirm. See "Fuel System Diagnosis," CHART A-7.
- Exhaust Leaks. If there is an exhaust leak, the engine can cause outside air to be pulled into the exhaust and past the sensor. Vacuum or crankcase leaks can cause a lean condition.
- If Code 44 is intermittent, refer to "Intermittents" in "Symptoms,"

CODE 44

OXYGEN SENSOR CIRCUIT (LEAN EXHAUST INDICATED)

(1)
- RUN WARM ENGINE (75°C/167°F TO 95°C/203°F) AT 1200 RPM.
- DOES TECH 1 INDICATE O_2 SENSOR VOLTAGE FIXED BELOW .35 VOLT (350 mv)?

NO → CODE 44 IS INTERMITTENT.

YES →
- DISCONNECT O_2 SENSOR.
- WITH ENGINE IDLING, TECH 1 SHOULD DISPLAY O_2 SENSOR VOLTAGE BETWEEN .35 VOLT AND .55 VOLT (350 mV AND 550 mv). DOES IT?

YES

NO → CKT 412 SHORTED TO GROUND OR FAULTY ECM.

"AFTER REPAIRS," REFER TO CODE CRITERIA AND CONFIRM CODE DOES NOT RESET.

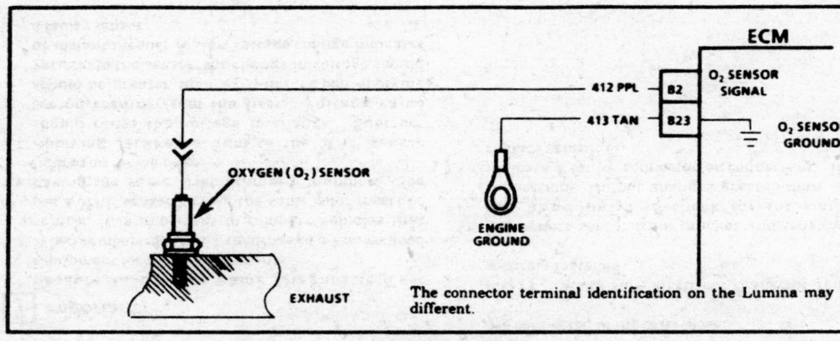
ECM
412 PPL
413 TAN
B2
B23
O_2 SENSOR SIGNAL
O_2 SENSOR GROUND
OXYGEN (O_2) SENSOR
ENGINE GROUND
EXHAUST

The connector terminal identification on the Lumina may be different.

CODE 45

OXYGEN SENSOR CIRCUIT (RICH EXHAUST INDICATED)

Circuit Description:

The ECM supplies a voltage of about .45 volt between terminals "B2" and "B23". (If measured with a 10 megohm digital voltmeter, this may read as low as .32 volt.)

When the O_2 sensor reaches operating temperature, it varies this voltage from about 1 volt (exhaust is lean) to about .9 volt (exhaust is rich).

The sensor is like an open circuit and produces no voltage when it is below 316°C (600°F). An open sensor circuit, or cold sensor, causes "Open Loop" operation.

Test Description: Numbers below refer to circled numbers on the diagnostic chart.

1. Code 45 is set when the O_2 sensor signal voltage on CKT 412 remains above .7 volt under the following conditions:
   - 50 seconds or more.
   - System is operating in "Closed Loop."
   - Engine run time after start is 1 minute or more.
   - Throttle angle is between 3% and 45%.

Diagnostic Aids:

Code 45, or rich exhaust, is most likely caused by one of the following:

- Fuel Pressure. System will go rich, if pressure is too high. The ECM can compensate for some increase. However, if it gets too high, a Code 45 will be set. See "Fuel System Diagnosis," CHART A-7.
- Leaking Injector. See CHART A-7.
- HEI Shielding. An open ground CKT 453 may result in EMI, or induced electrical "noise." The ECM looks at this "noise" as reference pulses. The additional pulses result in a higher than actual engine speed signal. The ECM then delivers too much fuel causing the system to go rich. The engine tachometer will also show higher than actual engine speed, which can help in diagnosing this problem.
- Canister Purge. Check for fuel saturation. If full of fuel, check canister hoses. See "Evaporative Emission Control System (EECS)."
- MAP Sensor. An output that causes the ECM to sense a higher than normal manifold pressure (low vacuum) can cause the system to go rich. Disconnecting the MAP sensor will allow the ECM to set a fixed value for the MAP sensor. Substitute a different MAP sensor if the rich condition is gone, while the sensor is disconnected.
- TPS. An intermittent TPS output will cause the system to operate richly due to a false indication of the engine accelerating.
- O_2 Sensor Contamination. Inspect oxygen sensor for silicone contamination from fuel, or use of improper RTV sealant. The sensor may have a white, powdery coating and result in a high but false signal voltage (rich exhaust indication). The ECM will then reduce the amount of fuel delivered to the engine causing a severe surge driveability problem.
- EGR Valve. EGR sticking open at idle is usually accompanied by a rough idle and/or stall condition. If Code 45 is intermittent, refer to "Symptoms,"
- Engine Oil Contamination. Fuel fouled engine oil could cause the O_2 sensor to sense a rich air/fuel mixture and set a Code 45.

CODE 45

OXYGEN SENSOR CIRCUIT (RICH EXHAUST INDICATED)

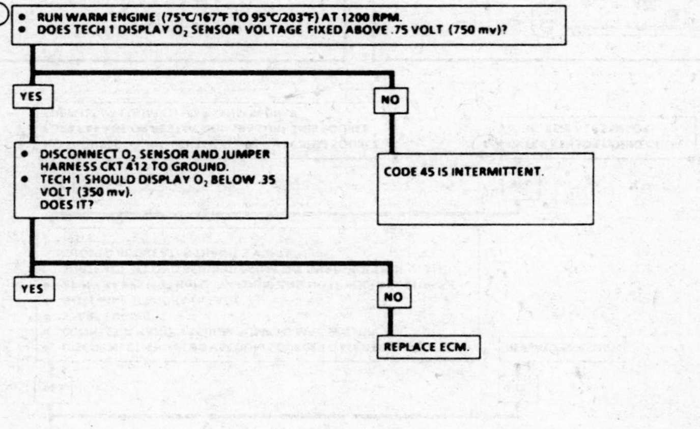
1
• RUN WARM ENGINE (75°C/167°F TO 95°C/203°F) AT 1200 RPM.
• DOES TECH 1 DISPLAY O_2 SENSOR VOLTAGE FIXED ABOVE .75 VOLT (750 mv)?
YES
NO
• DISCONNECT O_2 SENSOR AND JUMPER HARNESS CKT 412 TO GROUND.
• TECH 1 SHOULD DISPLAY O_2 BELOW .35 VOLT (350 mv). DOES IT?
CODE 45 IS INTERMITTENT.
YES
NO
REPLACE ECM.

"AFTER REPAIRS," REFER TO CODE CRITERIA AND CONFIRM CODE DOES NOT RESET.

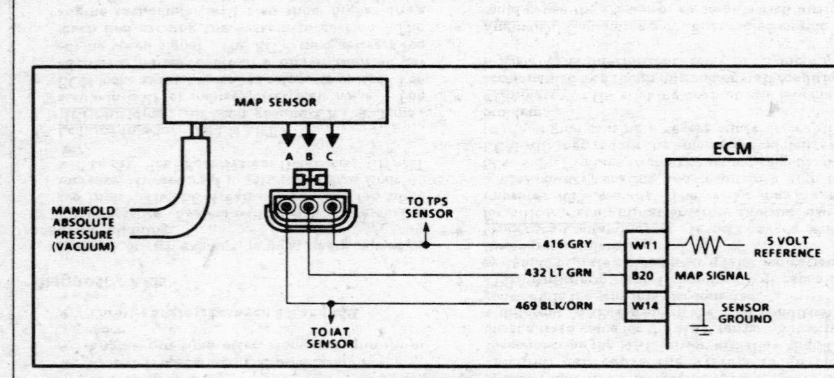

CHART C-1D

MANIFOLD ABSOLUTE PRESSURE (MAP) OUTPUT CHECK

Circuit Description:

The Manifold Absolute Pressure (MAP) sensor measures the changes in the intake manifold pressure which result from engine load (intake manifold vacuum) and rpm changes; and converts these into a voltage output. The ECM sends a 5 volt reference voltage to the MAP sensor. As the manifold pressure changes, the output voltage of the sensor also changes. By monitoring the sensor output voltage, the ECM knows the manifold pressure. A lower pressure (low voltage) output voltage will be about 1 - 2 volts at idle. While higher pressure (high voltage) output voltage will be about 4 - 4.8 at Wide Open Throttle (WOT). The MAP sensor is also used, under certain conditions, to measure barometric pressure, allowing the ECM to make adjustments for different altitudes. The ECM uses the MAP sensor to control fuel delivery and ignition timing.

Test Description: Numbers below refer to circled numbers on the diagnostic chart.

Important

- Be sure to use the same Diagnostic Test Equipment for all measurements.

1. When comparing Tech 1 readings to a known good vehicle, it is important to compare vehicles that use a MAP sensor having the same color insert or having the same "Hot Stamped" number. See figures on facing page.
2. Applying 34 kPa vacuum to the MAP sensor should cause the voltage to change. Subtract second reading from the first. Voltage value should be greater than 1.5 volts. Upon applying vacuum to the sensor, the change in voltage should be instantaneous. A slow voltage change indicates a faulty sensor.
3. Check vacuum hose to sensor for leaking or restriction. Be sure that no other vacuum devices are connected to the MAP hose.

NOTE: Make sure electrical connector remains securely fastened.

4. Disconnect sensor from bracket and twist sensor (**by hand only**) to check for intermittent connection. Output changes greater than .1 volt indicate a faulty connector or connection. If OK, replace sensor.

CHART C-1D

MANIFOLD ABSOLUTE PRESSURE (MAP) OUTPUT CHECK

NOTE: THIS CHART ONLY APPLIES TO MAP SENSORS HAVING GREEN OR BLACK COLOR KEY INSERT (SEE BELOW).

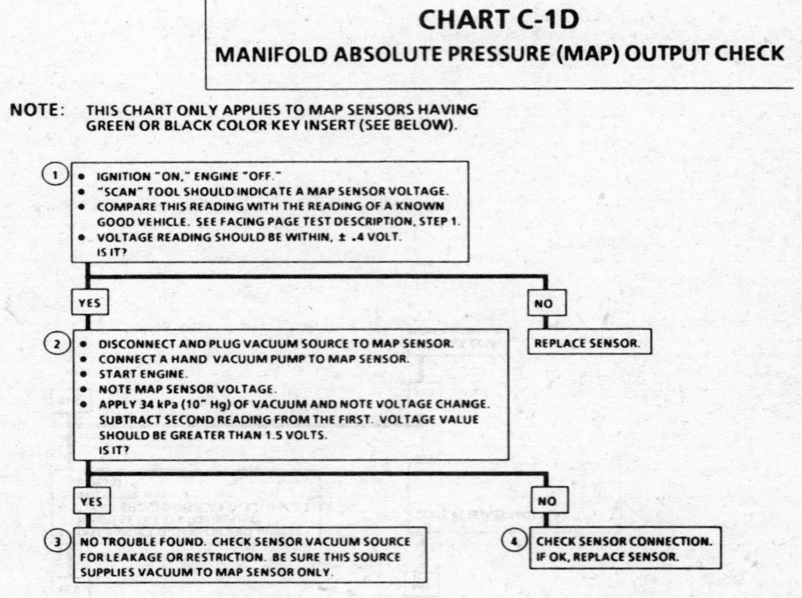

1
IGNITION "ON," ENGINE "OFF."
"SCAN" TOOL SHOULD INDICATE A MAP SENSOR VOLTAGE.
COMPARE THIS READING WITH THE READING OF A KNOWN GOOD VEHICLE. SEE FACING PAGE TEST DESCRIPTION, STEP 1.
VOLTAGE READING SHOULD BE WITHIN, ± .4 VOLT.
IS IT?
YES
NO
REPLACE SENSOR.
2
DISCONNECT AND PLUG VACUUM SOURCE TO MAP SENSOR.
CONNECT A HAND VACUUM PUMP TO MAP SENSOR.
START ENGINE.
NOTE MAP SENSOR VOLTAGE.
APPLY 34 kPa (10" Hg) OF VACUUM AND NOTE VOLTAGE CHANGE.
SUBTRACT SECOND READING FROM THE FIRST. VOLTAGE VALUE SHOULD BE GREATER THAN 1.5 VOLTS.
IS IT?
YES
NO
3
NO TROUBLE FOUND. CHECK SENSOR VACUUM SOURCE FOR LEAKAGE OR RESTRICTION. BE SURE THIS SOURCE SUPPLIES VACUUM TO MAP SENSOR ONLY.
4
CHECK SENSOR CONNECTION. IF OK, REPLACE SENSOR.

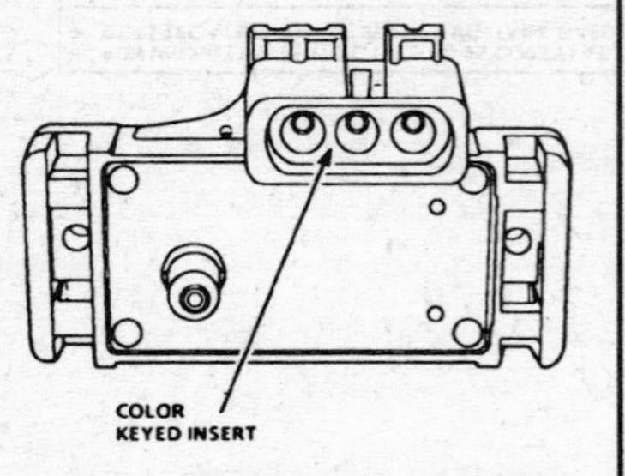

Figure 1 - Color Key Insert

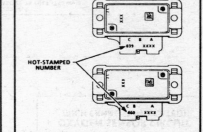

HOT-STAMPED NUMBER

Figure 2 - Hot-Stamped Number

***"AFTER REPAIRS,"* CONFIRM "CLOSED LOOP" OPERATION AND NO "SERVICE ENGINE SOON" LIGHT.**

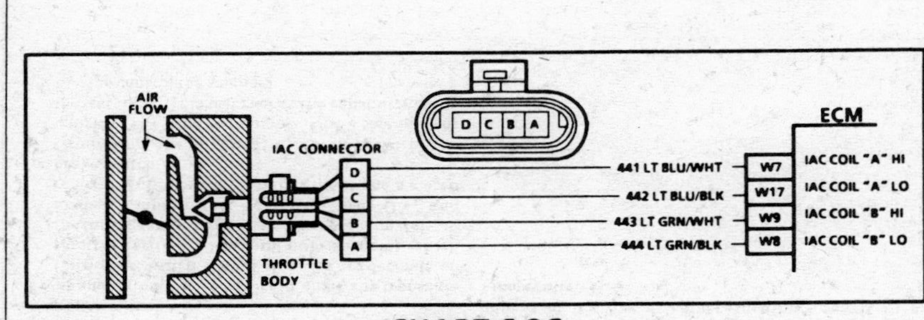
AIR FLOW
IAC CONNECTOR
THROTTLE BODY
D C B A
441 LT BLU/WHT
442 LT BLU/BLK
443 LT GRN/WHT
444 LT GRN/BLK
W7
W17
W9
W8
ECM
IAC COIL "A" HI
IAC COIL "A" LO
IAC COIL "B" HI
IAC COIL "B" LO

CHART C-2C

IDLE AIR CONTROL (IAC) SYSTEM CHECK

Circuit Description:

The ECM controls engine idle speed with the IAC valve. To increase idle speed, the ECM retracts the IAC valve pintle away from its seat, allowing more air to bypass the throttle bore. To decrease idle speed, it extends the IAC valve pintle towards its seat, reducing bypass air flow. A Tech 1 "Scan" tool will read the ECM commands to the IAC valve in counts. Higher the counts indicate more air bypass (higher idle). The lower the counts indicate less air is allowed to bypass (lower idle).

Test Description: Numbers below refer to circled numbers on the diagnostic chart.

1. The IAC tester is used to extend and retract the IAC valve. Valve movement is verified by an engine speed change. If no change in engine speed occurs, the valve can be retested when removed from the throttle body.
2. This step checks the quality of the IAC movement in step 1. Between 700 rpm and about 1500 rpm, the engine speed should change smoothly with each flash of the tester light in both extend and retract. If the IAC valve is retracted beyond the control range (about 1500 rpm), it may take many flashes in the extend position before engine speed will begin to drop. This is normal on certain engines, fully extending IAC may cause engine stall. This may be normal.
3. Steps 1 and 2 verified proper IAC valve operation while this step checks the IAC circuits. Each lamp on the node light should flash red and green while the IAC valve is cycled. While the sequence of color is not important if either light is "OFF" or does not flash red and green, check the circuits for faults, beginning with poor terminal contacts.

Diagnostic Aids:

A slow, unstable, or fast idle may be caused by a non-IAC system problem that cannot be overcome by the IAC valve. Out of control range IAC "Scan" tool counts will be above 60 if idle is too low, and zero counts if idle is too high. The following checks should be made to repair a non-IAC system problem:

- Vacuum Leak (High Idle)
  If idle is too high, stop the engine. Fully extend (low) IAC with tester.
  Start engine. If idle speed is above 800 rpm, locate and correct vacuum leak including PCV system. Also check for binding of throttle blade or linkage.
- System too lean (High Air/Fuel Ratio)
  The idle speed may be too high or too low. Engine speed may vary up and down and disconnecting the IAC valve does not help. Code 44 may be set. "Scan" O_2 voltage will be less than 300 mv (.3 volt). Check for low regulated fuel pressure, water in the fuel or a restricted injector.
- System too rich (Low Air/Fuel Ratio)
  The idle speed will be too low. "Scan" tool IAC counts will usually be above 80. System is obviously rich and may exhibit black smoke in exhaust.
  "Scan" tool O_2 voltage will be fixed above 800 mv (.8 volt).
  Check for high fuel pressure, leaking or sticking injector. Silicone contaminated O_2 sensors "Scan" voltage will be slow to respond.
- Throttle Body
  Remove IAC valve and inspect bore for foreign material.
- IAC Valve Electrical Connections
  IAC valve connections should be carefully checked for proper contact.
- PCV System
  Incorrect or faulty PCV system components may result in an incorrect idle speed.
- Refer to "Rough, Unstable, Incorrect Idle or Stalling" in "Symptoms,"
- If intermittent poor driveability or idle symptoms are resolved by disconnecting the IAC, carefully recheck connections, valve terminal resistance, or replace IAC.

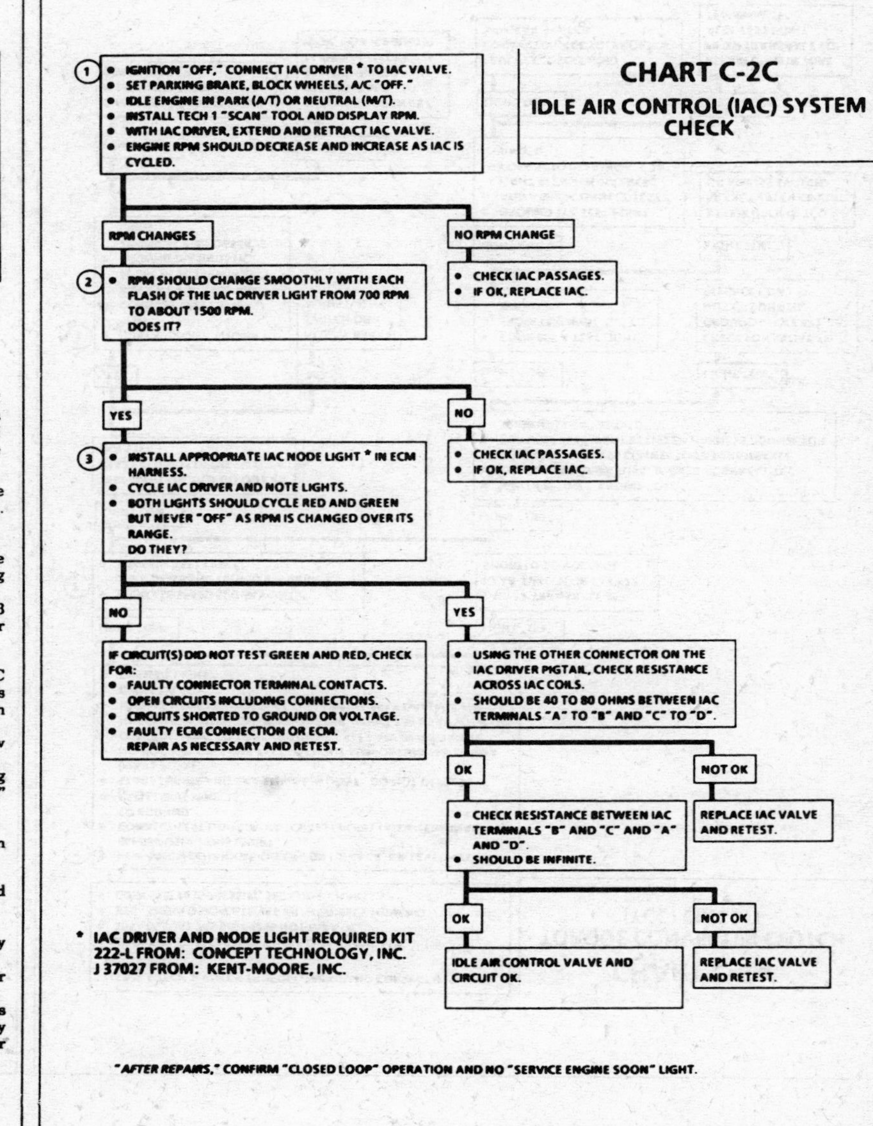
CHART C-2C
IDLE AIR CONTROL (IAC) SYSTEM CHECK
1
• IGNITION "OFF," CONNECT IAC DRIVER * TO IAC VALVE.
• SET PARKING BRAKE, BLOCK WHEELS, A/C "OFF."
• IDLE ENGINE IN PARK (A/T) OR NEUTRAL (M/T).
• INSTALL TECH 1 "SCAN" TOOL AND DISPLAY RPM.
• WITH IAC DRIVER, EXTEND AND RETRACT IAC VALVE.
• ENGINE RPM SHOULD DECREASE AND INCREASE AS IAC IS CYCLED.
RPM CHANGES
NO RPM CHANGE
2
• RPM SHOULD CHANGE SMOOTHLY WITH EACH FLASH OF THE IAC DRIVER LIGHT FROM 700 RPM TO ABOUT 1500 RPM. DOES IT?
• CHECK IAC PASSAGES.
• IF OK, REPLACE IAC.
YES
NO
3
• INSTALL APPROPRIATE IAC NODE LIGHT * IN ECM HARNESS.
• CYCLE IAC DRIVER AND NOTE LIGHTS.
• BOTH LIGHTS SHOULD CYCLE RED AND GREEN BUT NEVER "OFF" AS RPM IS CHANGED OVER ITS RANGE. DO THEY?
• CHECK IAC PASSAGES.
• IF OK, REPLACE IAC.
NO
YES
IF CIRCUIT(S) DID NOT TEST GREEN AND RED, CHECK FOR:
• FAULTY CONNECTOR TERMINAL CONTACTS.
• OPEN CIRCUITS INCLUDING CONNECTIONS.
• CIRCUITS SHORTED TO GROUND OR VOLTAGE.
• FAULTY ECM CONNECTION OR ECM.
REPAIR AS NECESSARY AND RETEST.
• USING THE OTHER CONNECTOR ON THE IAC DRIVER PIGTAIL, CHECK RESISTANCE ACROSS IAC COILS.
• SHOULD BE 40 TO 80 OHMS BETWEEN IAC TERMINALS "A" TO "B" AND "C" TO "D".
OK
NOT OK
• CHECK RESISTANCE BETWEEN IAC TERMINALS "B" AND "C" AND "A" AND "D".
• SHOULD BE INFINITE.
REPLACE IAC VALVE AND RETEST.
OK
NOT OK
IDLE AIR CONTROL VALVE AND CIRCUIT OK.
REPLACE IAC VALVE AND RETEST.
* IAC DRIVER AND NODE LIGHT REQUIRED KIT 222-L FROM: CONCEPT TECHNOLOGY, INC. J 37027 FROM: KENT-MOORE, INC.
"AFTER REPAIRS," CONFIRM "CLOSED LOOP" OPERATION AND NO "SERVICE ENGINE SOON" LIGHT.

DIAGNOSTIC CHARTS — 2.5L engine

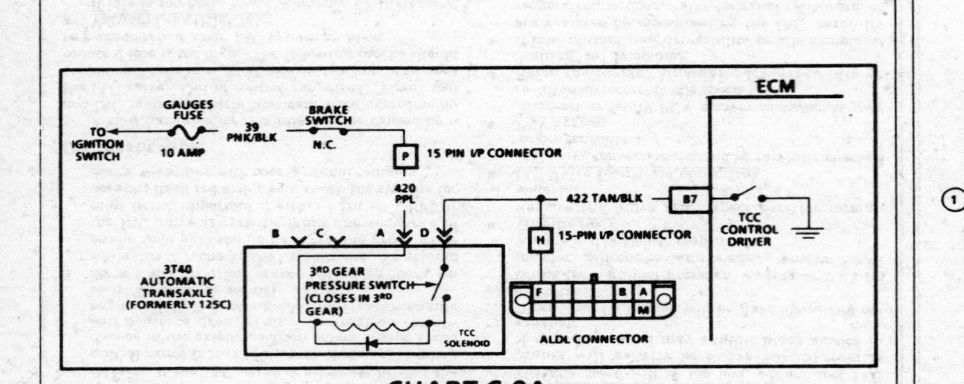

CHART C-8A

TORQUE CONVERTER CLUTCH (TCC) CIRCUIT

Circuit Description:

The purpose of the automatic transaxle torque converter clutch is to eliminate the power loss of the torque converter when the vehicle is in a cruise condition. This allows the convenience of the automatic transaxle and the fuel economy of a manual transaxle.

Fused ignition voltage is supplied to the TCC solenoid through the brake switch and transaxle third gear apply switch. The ECM will engage TCC by grounding CKT 422 to energize the solenoid.

TCC will engage under the following conditions:

- Vehicle speed is above 56 km/h (35 mph) with A/C "OFF," or above 70 km/h (44 mph) with A/C "ON."
- Engine at normal operating temperature (above 70°C/158°F).
- Throttle position sensor output not changing, indicating a steady road speed.
- Transaxle third gear switch closed.
- Brake switch closed.

Test Description: Numbers below refer to circled numbers on the diagnostic chart.

1. Light "OFF" confirms transaxle third gear apply switch is open.
2. At approximately 48 km/h (30 mph), the transaxle third gear switch should close. This depends on throttle position. The minimum speed at which the third gear switch will close is approximately 34 km/h (21 mph). Test light will turn "ON" and confirm ignition voltage in the circuit and a closed brake switch.
3. Grounding the diagnostic terminal with the ignition "ON" and the engine "OFF" should light the test light. This test checks the capability of the ECM to control the solenoid.

Diagnostic Aids:

An engine coolant thermostat that is stuck open or opens at too low a temperature may result in an inoperative TCC.

CHART C-8A

TORQUE CONVERTER CLUTCH (TCC) CIRCUIT

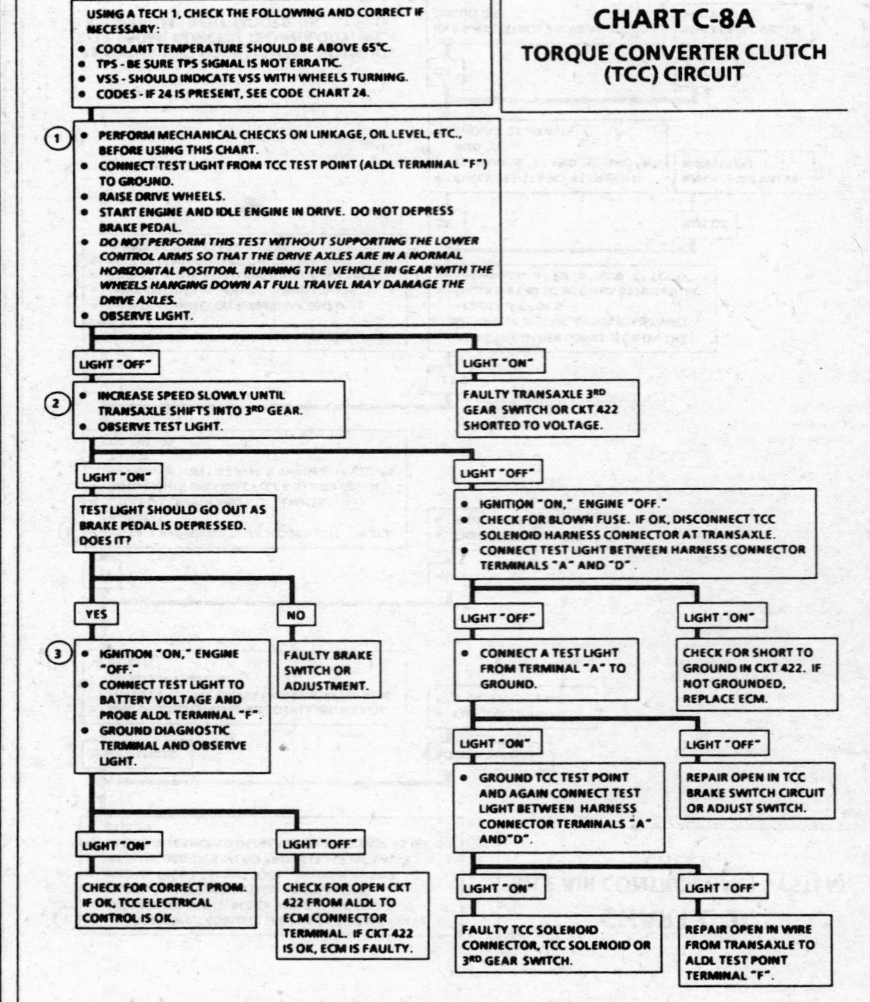

USING A TECH 1, CHECK THE FOLLOWING AND CORRECT IF NECESSARY:
• COOLANT TEMPERATURE SHOULD BE ABOVE 65°C.
• TPS - BE SURE TPS SIGNAL IS NOT ERRATIC.
• VSS - SHOULD INDICATE VSS WITH WHEELS TURNING.
• CODES - IF 24 IS PRESENT, SEE CODE CHART 24.
1
• PERFORM MECHANICAL CHECKS ON LINKAGE, OIL LEVEL, ETC., BEFORE USING THIS CHART.
• CONNECT TEST LIGHT FROM TCC TEST POINT (ALDL TERMINAL "F") TO GROUND.
• RAISE DRIVE WHEELS.
• START ENGINE AND IDLE ENGINE IN DRIVE. DO NOT DEPRESS BRAKE PEDAL.
• DO NOT PERFORM THIS TEST WITHOUT SUPPORTING THE LOWER CONTROL ARMS SO THAT THE DRIVE AXLES ARE IN A NORMAL HORIZONTAL POSITION. RUNNING THE VEHICLE IN GEAR WITH THE WHEELS HANGING DOWN AT FULL TRAVEL MAY DAMAGE THE DRIVE AXLES.
• OBSERVE LIGHT.
LIGHT "OFF"
LIGHT "ON"
2
• INCREASE SPEED SLOWLY UNTIL TRANSAXLE SHIFTS INTO 3RD GEAR.
• OBSERVE TEST LIGHT.
FAULTY TRANSAXLE 3RD GEAR SWITCH OR CKT 422 SHORTED TO VOLTAGE.
LIGHT "ON"
LIGHT "OFF"
TEST LIGHT SHOULD GO OUT AS BRAKE PEDAL IS DEPRESSED. DOES IT?
• IGNITION "ON," ENGINE "OFF."
• CHECK FOR BLOWN FUSE. IF OK, DISCONNECT TCC SOLENOID HARNESS CONNECTOR AT TRANSAXLE.
• CONNECT TEST LIGHT BETWEEN HARNESS CONNECTOR TERMINALS "A" AND "D".
YES
NO
LIGHT "OFF"
LIGHT "ON"
3
• IGNITION "ON," ENGINE "OFF."
• CONNECT TEST LIGHT TO BATTERY VOLTAGE AND PROBE ALDL TERMINAL "F".
• GROUND DIAGNOSTIC TERMINAL AND OBSERVE LIGHT.
FAULTY BRAKE SWITCH OR ADJUSTMENT.
• CONNECT A TEST LIGHT FROM TERMINAL "A" TO GROUND.
CHECK FOR SHORT TO GROUND IN CKT 422. IF NOT GROUNDED, REPLACE ECM.
LIGHT "ON"
LIGHT "OFF"
• GROUND TCC TEST POINT AND AGAIN CONNECT TEST LIGHT BETWEEN HARNESS CONNECTOR TERMINALS "A" AND "D".
REPAIR OPEN IN TCC BRAKE SWITCH CIRCUIT OR ADJUST SWITCH.
LIGHT "ON"
LIGHT "OFF"
CHECK FOR CORRECT PROM. IF OK, TCC ELECTRICAL CONTROL IS OK.
CHECK FOR OPEN CKT 422 FROM ALDL TO ECM CONNECTOR TERMINAL. IF CKT 422 IS OK, ECM IS FAULTY.
LIGHT "ON"
LIGHT "OFF"
FAULTY TCC SOLENOID CONNECTOR, TCC SOLENOID OR 3RD GEAR SWITCH.
REPAIR OPEN IN WIRE FROM TRANSAXLE TO ALDL TEST POINT TERMINAL "F".
"AFTER REPAIRS," CONFIRM "CLOSED LOOP" OPERATION AND NO "SERVICE ENGINE SOON" LIGHT.

DIAGNOSTIC CHARTS — 2.3L engine

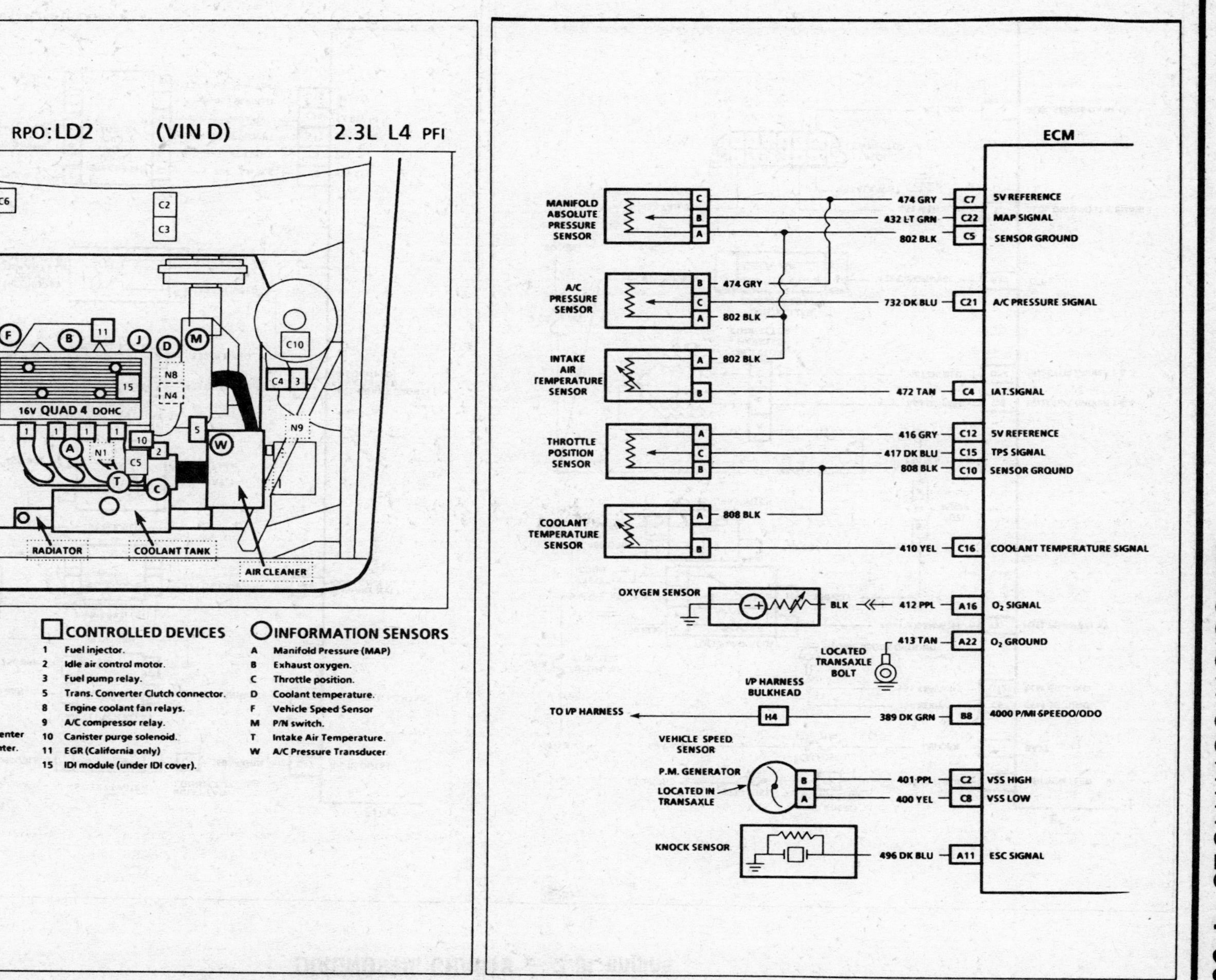
"W" CARLINE RPO: LD2 (VIN D) 2.3L L4 PFI
C6
C2
C3
C1
C10
C4
3
N9
N8
N4
16V QUAD 4 DOHC
15
11
5
10
2
C5
N1
8
9
C8
RADIATOR
COOLANT TANK
AIR CLEANER
COMPUTER HARNESS
C1 Electronic Control Module (ECM).
C2 ALDL diagnostic connector.
C3 "Service Engine Soon" light.
C4 ECM power.
C5 ECM harness ground.
C6 Fuse panel.
C8 Right Side Underhood Electrical Center
C10 Left Side Underhood Electrical Center.
CONTROLLED DEVICES
1 Fuel injector.
2 Idle air control motor.
3 Fuel pump relay.
5 Trans. Converter Clutch connector.
8 Engine coolant fan relays.
9 A/C compressor relay.
10 Canister purge solenoid.
11 EGR (California only)
15 IDI module (under IDI cover).
INFORMATION SENSORS
A Manifold Pressure (MAP)
B Exhaust oxygen.
C Throttle position.
D Coolant temperature.
F Vehicle Speed Sensor
M P/N switch.
T Intake Air Temperature.
W A/C Pressure Transducer
NOT ECM CONNECTED
N1 Crankcase vent oil/air separator.
N4 Engine temp. switch (telltale) Sensor (gage).
N8 Oil press. switch (fuel pump).
N9 Fuel pump prime.
ECM
MANIFOLD ABSOLUTE PRESSURE SENSOR
474 GRY C7 5V REFERENCE
432 LT GRN C22 MAP SIGNAL
802 BLK C5 SENSOR GROUND
A/C PRESSURE SENSOR
474 GRY
802 BLK
732 DK BLU C21 A/C PRESSURE SIGNAL
INTAKE AIR TEMPERATURE SENSOR
802 BLK
472 TAN C4 IAT SIGNAL
THROTTLE POSITION SENSOR
416 GRY C12 5V REFERENCE
417 DK BLU C15 TPS SIGNAL
808 BLK C10 SENSOR GROUND
COOLANT TEMPERATURE SENSOR
808 BLK
410 YEL C16 COOLANT TEMPERATURE SIGNAL
OXYGEN SENSOR
BLK
412 PPL A16 O_2 SIGNAL
413 TAN A22 O_2 GROUND
LOCATED TRANSAXLE BOLT
I/P HARNESS BULKHEAD
TO I/P HARNESS
H4
389 DK GRN B8 4000 P/MI SPEEDO/ODO
VEHICLE SPEED SENSOR
P.M. GENERATOR
LOCATED IN TRANSAXLE
401 PPL C2 VSS HIGH
400 YEL C8 VSS LOW
KNOCK SENSOR
496 DK BLU A11 ESC SIGNAL

DIAGNOSTIC CHARTS — 2.3L engine

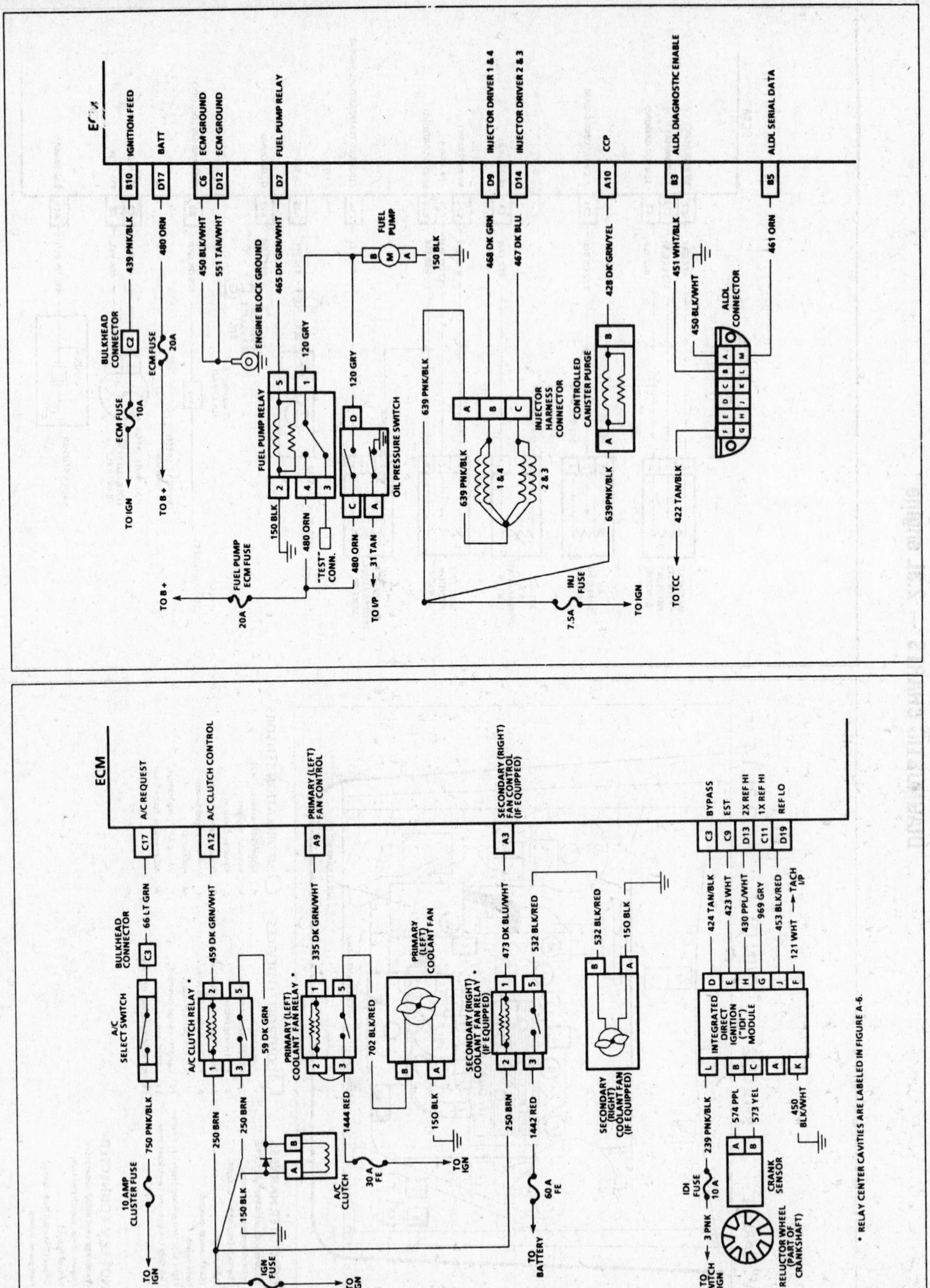

ECM
B10 IGNITION FEED
D17 BATT
C6 ECM GROUND
D12 ECM GROUND
D7 FUEL PUMP RELAY
D9 INJECTOR DRIVER 1 & 4
D14 INJECTOR DRIVER 2 & 3
A10 CCP
B3 ALDL DIAGNOSTIC ENABLE
B5 ALDL SERIAL DATA
439 PNK/BLK
480 ORN
450 BLK/WHT
551 TAN/WHT
465 DK GRN/WHT
150 BLK
468 DK GRN
467 DK BLU
428 DK GRN/YEL
451 WHT/BLK
461 ORN
BULKHEAD CONNECTOR
C2
ECM FUSE 10A
ECM FUSE 20A
TO IGN
TO B +
ENGINE BLOCK GROUND
FUEL PUMP
FUEL PUMP RELAY
120 GRY
OIL PRESSURE SWITCH
"TEST" CONN.
480 ORN
31 TAN
TO I/P
FUEL PUMP ECM FUSE
20A
639 PNK/BLK
1 & 4
2 & 3
INJECTOR HARNESS CONNECTOR
CONTROLLED CANISTER PURGE
INJ FUSE
7.5A
TO IGN
422 TAN/BLK
TO TCC
450 BLK/WHT
ALDL CONNECTOR

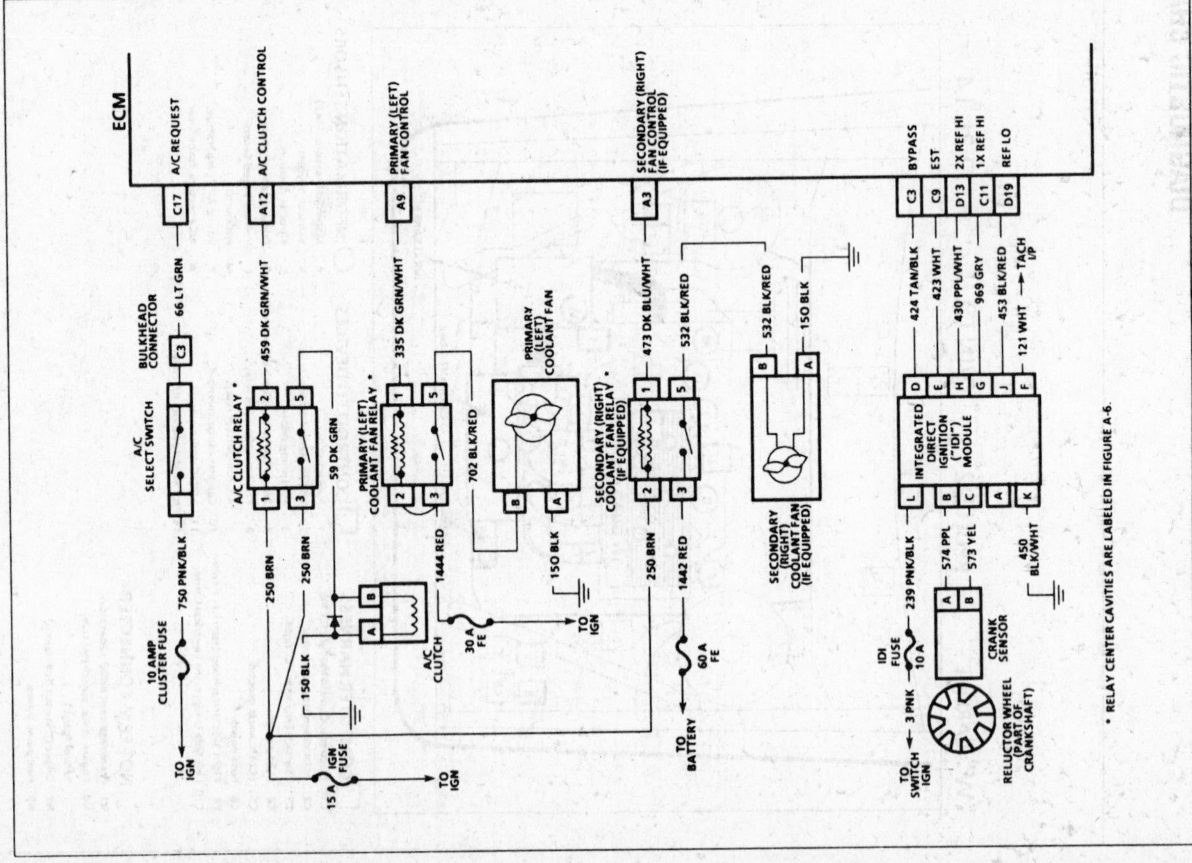

* RELAY CENTER CAVITIES ARE LABELED IN FIGURE A-6.

DIAGNOSTIC CHARTS — 2.3L engine

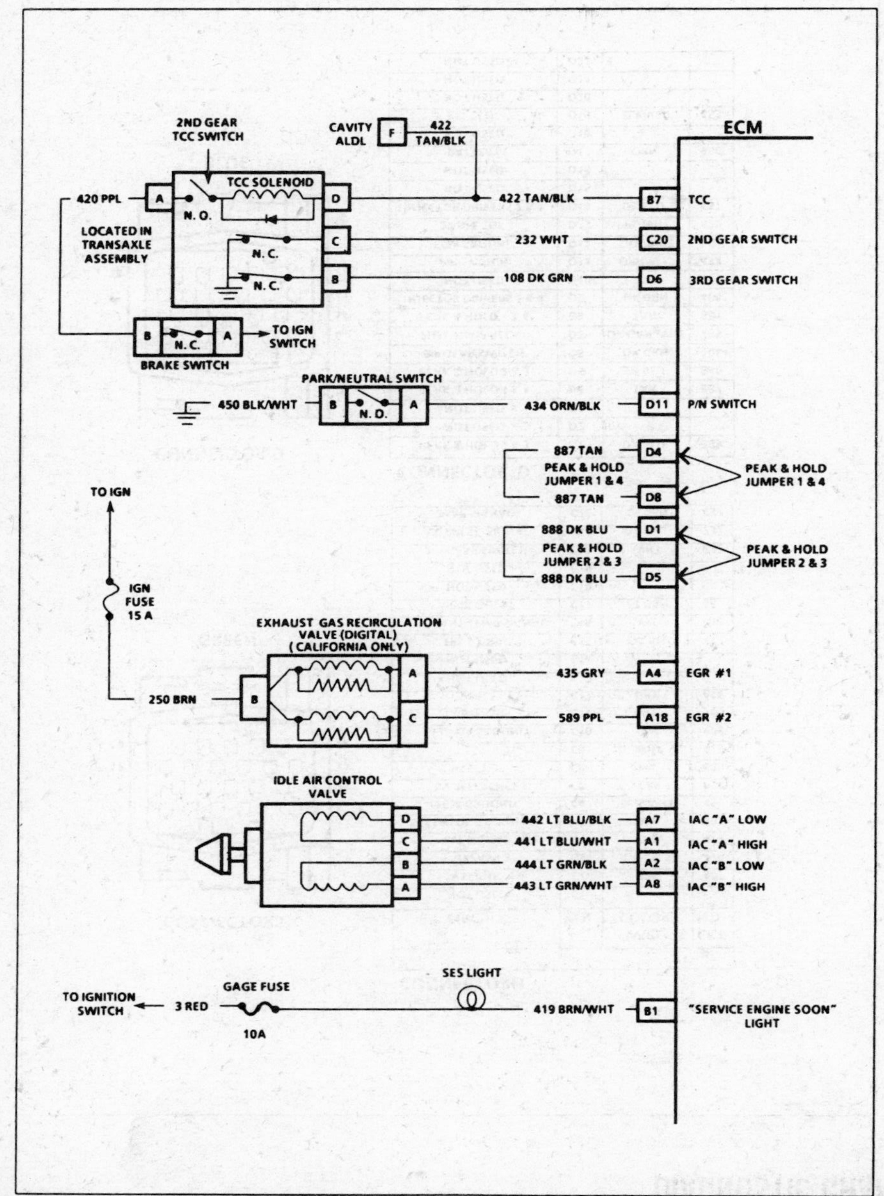

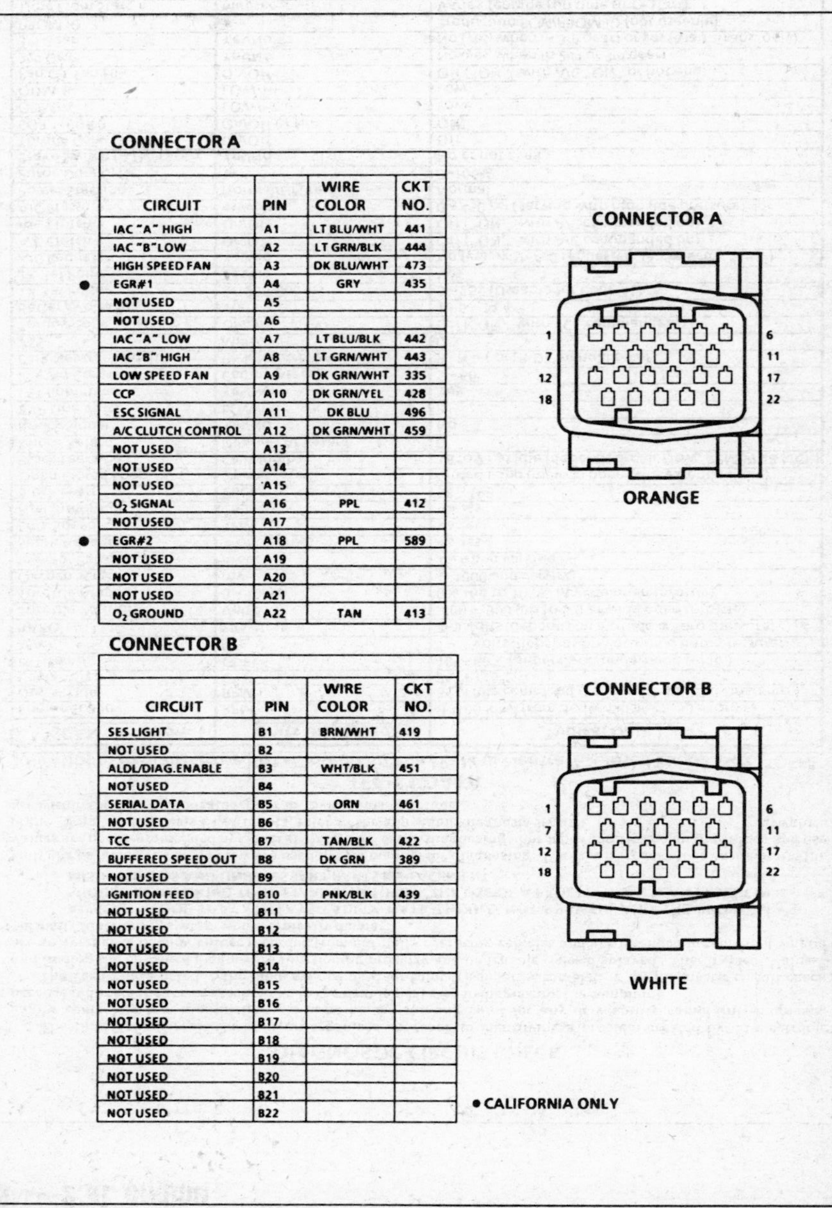

CONNECTOR A

	CIRCUIT	PIN	WIRE COLOR	CKT NO.
	IAC "A" HIGH	A1	LT BLU/WHT	441
	IAC "B" LOW	A2	LT GRN/BLK	444
	HIGH SPEED FAN	A3	DK BLU/WHT	473
●	EGR#1	A4	GRY	435
	NOT USED	A5		
	NOT USED	A6		
	IAC "A" LOW	A7	LT BLU/BLK	442
	IAC "B" HIGH	A8	LT GRN/WHT	443
	LOW SPEED FAN	A9	DK GRN/WHT	335
	CCP	A10	DK GRN/YEL	428
	ESC SIGNAL	A11	DK BLU	496
	A/C CLUTCH CONTROL	A12	DK GRN/WHT	459
	NOT USED	A13		
	NOT USED	A14		
	NOT USED	A15		
	O_2 SIGNAL	A16	PPL	412
	NOT USED	A17		
●	EGR#2	A18	PPL	589
	NOT USED	A19		
	NOT USED	A20		
	NOT USED	A21		
	O_2 GROUND	A22	TAN	413

CONNECTOR B

CIRCUIT	PIN	WIRE COLOR	CKT NO.
SES LIGHT	B1	BRN/WHT	419
NOT USED	B2		
ALDL/DIAG.ENABLE	B3	WHT/BLK	451
NOT USED	B4		
SERIAL DATA	B5	ORN	461
NOT USED	B6		
TCC	B7	TAN/BLK	422
BUFFERED SPEED OUT	B8	DK GRN	389
NOT USED	B9		
IGNITION FEED	B10	PNK/BLK	439
NOT USED	B11		
NOT USED	B12		
NOT USED	B13		
NOT USED	B14		
NOT USED	B15		
NOT USED	B16		
NOT USED	B17		
NOT USED	B18		
NOT USED	B19		
NOT USED	B20		
NOT USED	B21		
NOT USED	B22		

● CALIFORNIA ONLY

DIAGNOSTIC CHARTS — 2.3L engine

CONNECTOR C

GREEN

CONNECTOR C

CIRCUIT	PIN	WIRE COLOR	CKT NO.
NOT USED	C1		
VSS "HI"	C2	PPL	401
BYPASS	C3	TAN/BLK	424
IAT SIGNAL	C4	TAN	472
SENSOR GROUND	C5	BLK	802
ECM GROUND	C6	BLK/WHT	450
5V REFERENCE	C7	GRY	474
VSS "LO"	C8	YEL	400
EST	C9	WHT	423
SENSOR GROUND	C10	BLK	808
1X REF "HI"	C11	GRY	969
5V REF	C12	GRY	416
NOT USED	C13		
NOT USED	C14		
TPS SIGNAL	C15	DK BLU	417
COOLANT TEMP SIGNAL	C16	YEL	410
A/C REQUEST	C17	LT GRN	66
NOT USED	C18		
NOT USED	C19		
2nd GEAR SWITCH	C20	WHT	232
A/C PRESS. SIGNAL	C21	DK BLU	732
MAP SIGNAL	C22	LT GRN	432

CONNECTOR D

BLUE

CONNECTOR D

CIRCUIT	PIN	WIRE COLOR	CKT NO.
PEAK & HOLD 2 & 3	D1	DK BLU	888
NOT USED	D2		
NOT USED	D3		
PEAK & HOLD 1 & 4	D4	TAN	887
PEAK & HOLD 2 & 3	D5	DK BLU	888
3rd GEAR SWITCH	D6	DK GRN	108
FUEL PUMP RELAY	D7	DK GRN/WHT	465
PEAK & HOLD 1 & 4	D8	TAN	887
INJECTOR DRIVERS 1 & 4	D9	DK GRN	468
NOT USED	D10		
P/N SWITCH	D11	ORN/BLK	434
ECM GROUND	D12	TAN/WHT	551
2X REF "HI"	D13	PPL/WHT	430
INJECTOR DRIVERS 2 & 3	D14	DK BLU	467
NOT USED	D15		
NOT USED	D16		
BATTERY	D17	ORN	480
NOT USED	D18		
REF "LO"	D19	BLK/RED	453
NOT USED	D20		
NOT USED	D21		
NOT USED	D22		

DIAGNOSTIC CIRCUIT CHECK

The Diagnostic Circuit Check is an organized approach to identifying a problem created by an electronic engine control system malfunction. It must be the starting point for any driveability complaint diagnosis, because it directs the service technician to the next logical step in diagnosing the complaint.

The Tech 1 data listed in the table may be used for comparison, after completing the diagnostic circuit check and finding the on-board diagnostics functioning properly and no trouble codes displayed. The "Typical Values" are an average of display values recorded from normally operating vehicles and are intended to represent what a normally functioning system would typically display.

A "SCAN" TOOL THAT DISPLAYS FAULTY DATA SHOULD NOT BE USED, AND THE PROBLEM SHOULD BE REPORTED TO THE MANUFACTURER. THE USE OF A FAULTY "SCAN" CAN RESULT IN MISDIAGNOSIS AND UNNECESSARY PARTS REPLACEMENT.

Only the parameters listed below are used in this manual for diagnosing. If a "Scan" reads other parameters, the values are not recommended by General Motors for use in diagnosing. For more description on the values and use of the "Scan" to diagnosis ECM inputs, refer to the applicable diagnosis section If all values are within the range illustrated, refer to "Symptoms," Section

TECH 1 DATA

Idle / Upper Radiator Hose Hot / Closed Throttle / Park or Neutral / "Closed Loop" / Acc. "OFF"

"SCAN" Position	Units Displayed	Typical Data Value
Engine Speed	RPM	± 100 RPM from desired RPM (± 50 in drive)
Desired Idle	RPM	ECM idle command (varies with calibration. temp.)
Coolant Temp.	C° F°	85° - 115°C
IAT Temp.	C° F°	10° - 80°C (depends on underhood temp.)
MAP	kPa, V	1 - 3 Volts (depends on Vacuum & Baro pressure)
BARO	kPa, V	3-5 Volts (depends on altitude & Baro pressure)
Throttle Position	Volts	.400 - .900 (up to 5.0 at wide open throttle)
Throttle Angle	0 - 100%	0% (up to 100% at wide open throttle)
Oxygen Sensor	mV	1-1000 and varying
Injector Pulse Width	m Sec.	1 - 4 and varying
Spark Advance	# of Degrees	Varies
Eng. Speed	RPM	Varies
Fuel Integrator	Counts	Varies
Block Learn	Counts	58 - 198
Open/Closed Loop	Open/Closed	Closed Loop (may go open with extended idle)
Block Learn Cell	Cell Number	18 to 21 at idle (depends on Air Flow, RPM, P/N&A/C)
Knock Retard	Degrees of Retard	0
Knock Signal	Yes/No	No
BYP Line Volts	LOW/HI	HI
EST Command	Yes/No	Yes
Idle Air Control	Counts (steps)	5 - 60
Park Neutral Switch	Park Neutral and RDL	P - N -- (or -R-DL manual only)
VSS	MPH/KPH	0
Torque Conv. Cl (TCC)	On/Off	Off ("ON," with TCC commanded)
Battery Voltage	Volts	13.5 - 14.5
1X Ref Pulse	0 - 255 Counts	0 - 255 (Useable for Code 41)
2X Ref Pulse	Yes/No	Yes
A/C Request	Yes/No	No (yes, with A/C requested, ie: selector "ON")
A/C Clutch	On/Off	Off ("ON," with A/C commanded on)
A/C Clutch	On/Off	Off ("ON," with A/C commanded on)
A/C Pressure	psi/volts	0 - 450 psi (varying with high side pressure)
Power Steering	Normal/Hi Press.	Normal
Purge Duty Cycle	%	0-100%
Brake Switch (AT)	Yes/No	No or not avail.
Torque Conv Clutch	On/Off	Off
EGR 1 EGR 2	On/Off or N/A	Off
QDM A	LOW/HI	Low
QDM B	LOW/HI	Low
Fan LO Fan HI	On/Off	Off ("ON," with A/C "ON" or hot eng)
2nd Gear	Yes/No	No (yes, when in 2nd or 3rd gear)
3rd Gear	Yes/No	No (yes, when in 3rd gear) or yes (Man. Trans. only)
PROM ID	#	Production ECM/PROM ID (not useable)
Time From Start	min/sec	Varies (engine run time since start)

ECM

412 PPL — A16 — O_2 SENSOR SIGNAL

413 TAN — A22 — O_2 SENSOR GROUND

OXYGEN (O_2) SENSOR

ENGINE GROUND

EXHAUST

CODE 13

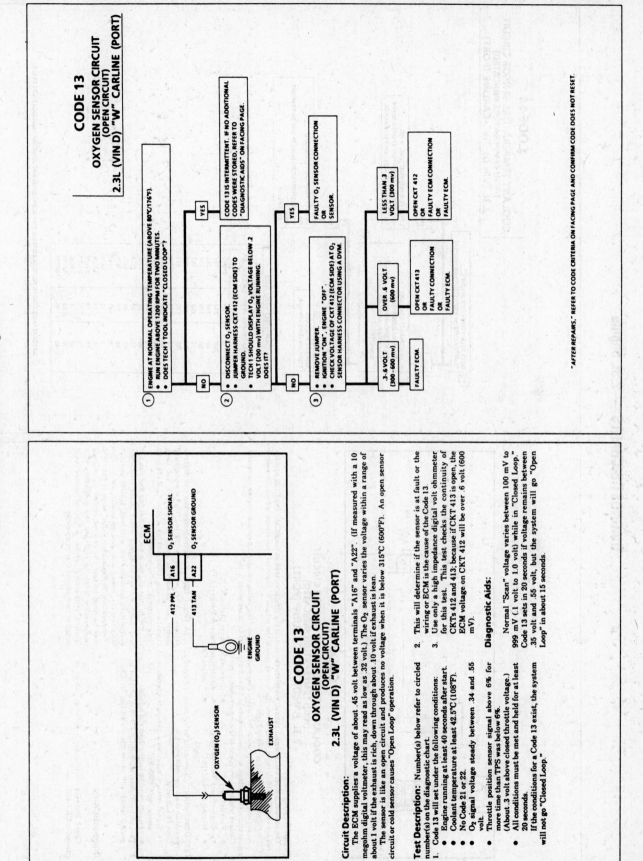

OXYGEN SENSOR CIRCUIT (OPEN CIRCUIT) 2.3L (VIN D) "W" CARLINE (PORT)

Circuit Description:

The ECM supplies a voltage of about .45 volt between terminals "A16" and "A22". (If measured with a 10 megohm digital voltmeter, this may read as low as .32 volt.) The O_2 sensor varies the voltage within a range of about 1 volt if the exhaust is rich, down through about .10 volt if exhaust is lean.

The sensor is like an open circuit and produces no voltage when it is below 315°C (600°F). An open sensor circuit or cold sensor causes "Open Loop" operation.

Test Description: Number(s) below refer to circled number(s) on the diagnostic chart.

1. Code 13 will set under the following conditions:
   - Engine running at least 40 seconds after start.
   - Coolant temperature at least 42.5°C (108°F).
   - No Code 21 or 22.
   - O_2 signal voltage steady between .34 and .55 volt.
   - Throttle position sensor signal above 6% for more time than TPS was below 6%. (About .3 volt above closed throttle voltage.)
   - All conditions must be met and held for at least 20 seconds.

   If the conditions for a Code 13 exist, the system will not go "Closed Loop."
2. This will determine if the sensor is at fault or the wiring or ECM is the cause of the Code 13.
3. Use only a high impedance digital volt ohmmeter for this test. This test checks the continuity of CKTs 412 and 413; because if CKT 413 is open, the ECM voltage on CKT 412 will be over .6 volt (600 mV).

Diagnostic Aids:

Normal "Scan" voltage varies between 100 mV to 999 mV (.1 volt to 1.0 volt) while in "Closed Loop." Code 13 sets in 20 seconds if voltage remains between .35 volt and .55 volt, but the system will go "Open Loop" in about 15 seconds.

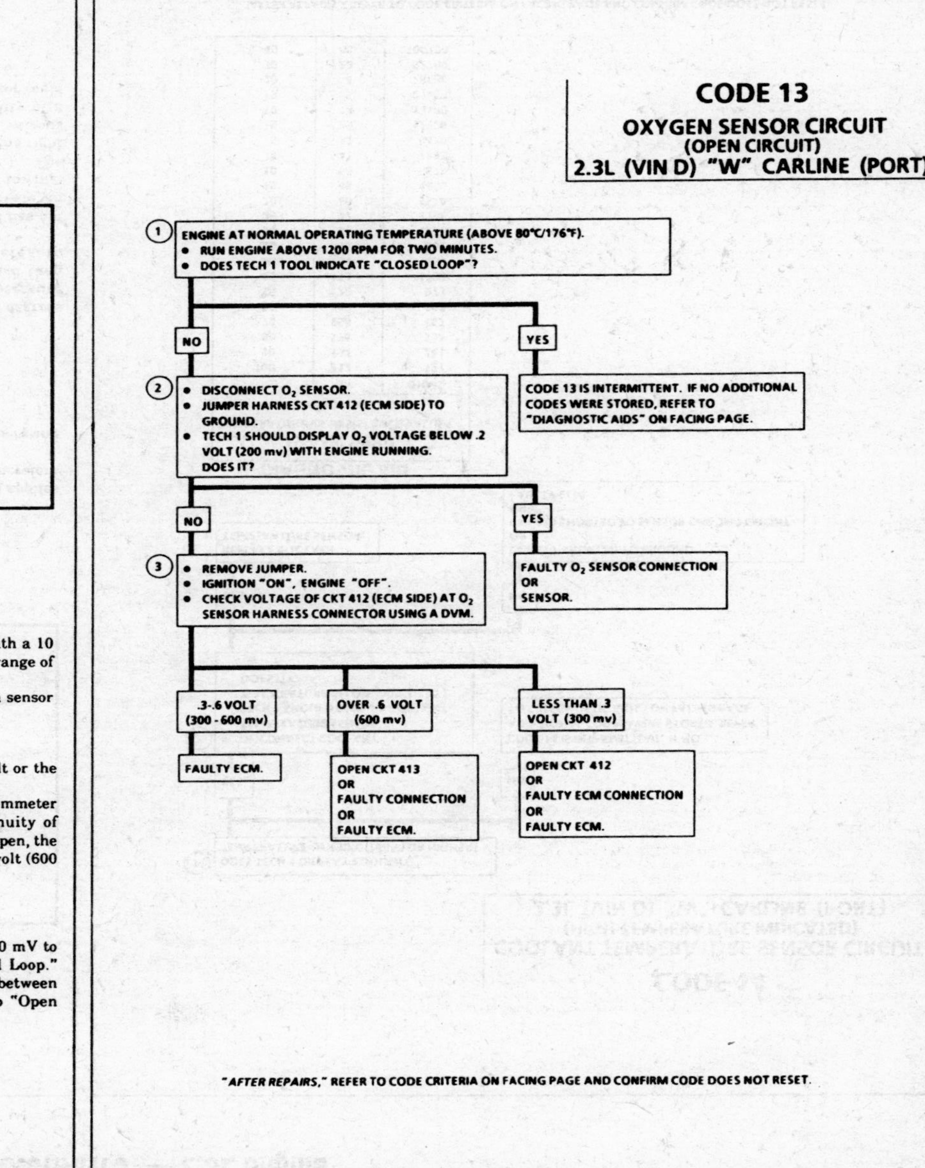

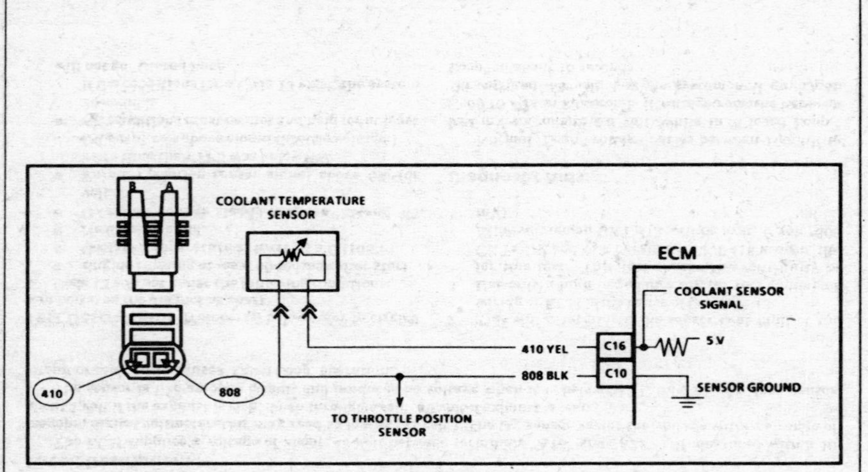

CODE 14

COOLANT TEMPERATURE SENSOR CIRCUIT (HIGH TEMPERATURE INDICATED) 2.3L (VIN D) "W" CARLINE (PORT)

Circuit Description:

The coolant temperature sensor uses a thermistor to control the signal voltage at the ECM. The ECM applies a voltage on CKT 410 to the sensor. When the engine is cold the sensor (thermistor) resistance is high, therefore ECM terminal "C16" voltage will be high.

As the engine warms, the sensor resistance becomes less, and the voltage drops. At normal engine operating temperature, the voltage will measure about 1.5 to 2.0 volts at ECM terminal "C16".

Coolant temperature is one of the inputs used to control:

- Fuel delivery
- Engine Spark Timing (EST)
- Idle Air Control (IAC)
- Torque Convertor Clutch (TCC)
- Controlled Canister Purge (CCP)
- Coolant Fan

Test Description: Number(s) below refer to circled number(s) on the diagnostic chart.

1. Code 14 will set if:
   - Signal voltage indicates a coolant temperature above 140°C (285°F).
   - Engine running longer than 128 seconds.
2. This test will determine if CKT 410 is shorted to ground which will cause the conditions for Code 14.

Diagnostic Aids:

Check harness routing for a potential short to ground in CKT 410.

A Tech 1 displays engine temperature in degrees celsius. After engine is started, the temperature should rise steadily to about 90°C (194°F), and then stabilize when thermostat opens. Refer to "Intermittents" in "Symptoms,"

Verify that engine is not overheating and has not been subjected to conditions which could create an overheating condition (i.e. overload, trailer towing, hilly terrain, heavy stop and go traffic, etc.). The "Temperature To Resistance Value" scale at the right may be used to test the coolant sensor at various temperature levels to evaluate the possibility of a "shifted" (mis-scaled) sensor. A "shifted" sensor could result in poor driveability complaints.

CODE 14

COOLANT TEMPERATURE SENSOR CIRCUIT (HIGH TEMPERATURE INDICATED) 2.3L (VIN D) "W" CARLINE (PORT)

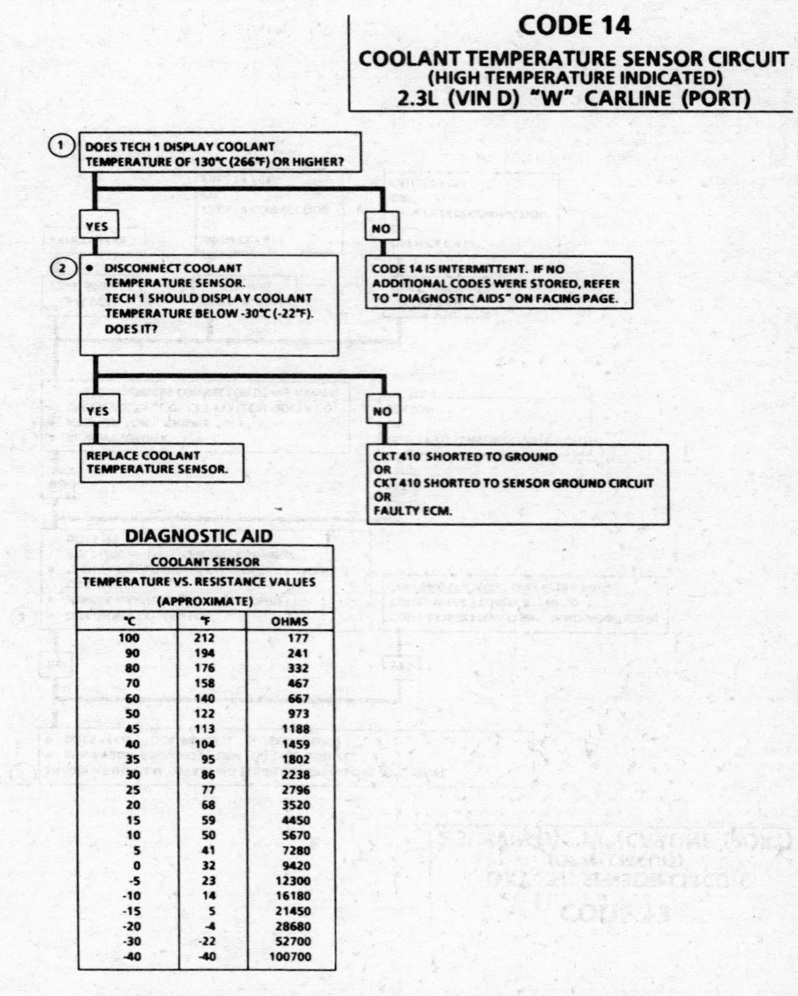

1 DOES TECH 1 DISPLAY COOLANT TEMPERATURE OF 130°C (266°F) OR HIGHER?
YES
NO
CODE 14 IS INTERMITTENT. IF NO ADDITIONAL CODES WERE STORED, REFER TO "DIAGNOSTIC AIDS" ON FACING PAGE.
2 • DISCONNECT COOLANT TEMPERATURE SENSOR. TECH 1 SHOULD DISPLAY COOLANT TEMPERATURE BELOW -30°C (-22°F). DOES IT?
YES
NO
REPLACE COOLANT TEMPERATURE SENSOR.
CKT 410 SHORTED TO GROUND OR CKT 410 SHORTED TO SENSOR GROUND CIRCUIT OR FAULTY ECM.

DIAGNOSTIC AID

COOLANT SENSOR
TEMPERATURE VS. RESISTANCE VALUES (APPROXIMATE)

°C	°F	OHMS
100	212	177
90	194	241
80	176	332
70	158	467
60	140	667
50	122	973
45	113	1188
40	104	1459
35	95	1802
30	86	2238
25	77	2796
20	68	3520
15	59	4450
10	50	5670
5	41	7280
0	32	9420
-5	23	12300
-10	14	16180
-15	5	21450
-20	-4	28680
-30	-22	52700
-40	-40	100700

"AFTER REPAIRS," REFER TO CODE CRITERIA ON FACING PAGE AND CONFIRM CODE DOES NOT RESET.

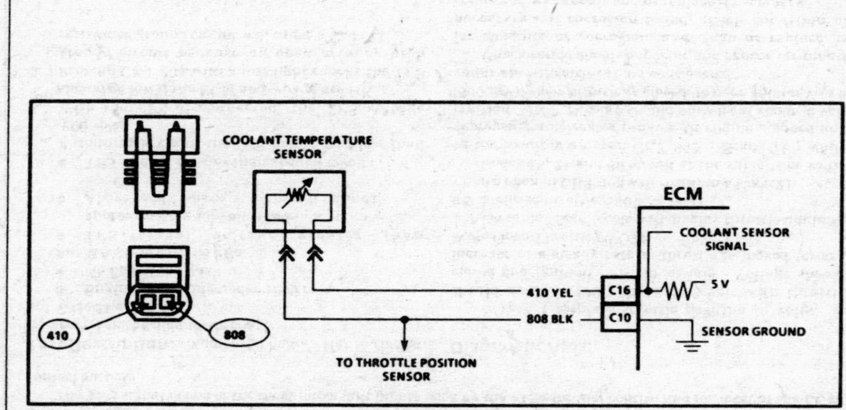

CODE 15

COOLANT TEMPERATURE SENSOR CIRCUIT
(LOW TEMPERATURE INDICATED)
2.3L (VIN D) "W" CARLINE (PORT)

Circuit Description:

The coolant temperature sensor uses a thermistor to control the signal voltage at the ECM. The ECM applies a voltage on CKT 410 to the sensor. When the engine is cold, the sensor (thermistor) resistance is high, therefore, ECM terminal "C16" voltage will be high.

As the engine warms, the sensor resistance becomes less, and the voltage drops. At normal engine operating temperature the voltage will measure about 1.5 to 2.0 volts at ECM terminal "C16".

Coolant temperature is one of the inputs used to control:

- Fuel delivery
- Engine Spark Timing (EST)
- Idle Air Control (IAC)
- Torque Convertor Clutch (TCC)
- Controlled Canister Purge (CCP)
- Coolant Fan

Test Description: Number(s) below refer to circled number(s) on the diagnostic chart.

1. Code 15 will set if:
   - Signal voltage indicates a coolant temperature less than -39°C (-38°F) for 60 seconds.
2. This test simulates a Code 14. If the ECM senses the low signal voltage (high temperature) and the "Scan" reads 130°C (266°F), the ECM and wiring are OK.
3. This test will determine if CKT 410 is open. There should be 5 volts present at sensor connector if measured with a DVM.

Diagnostic Aids:

A Tech 1 displays engine temperature in degrees celsius. After the engine is started the temperature should rise steadily to about 95°C (203°F), and then stabilize when the thermostat opens. It is normal for coolant temperature to fluctuate slightly around 95°C (203°F).

A faulty connection, or an open in CKT 410 or CKT 808 can result in a Code 15.

Codes 15, 21 and 66 stored at the same time could be the result of an open CKT 808.

The "Temperature to Resistance Value" scale at the right may be used to test the coolant sensor at various temperature levels to evaluate the possibility of a "shifted" (mis-scaled) sensor. A "shifted" sensor could result in poor driveability complaints.

CODE 15

COOLANT TEMPERATURE SENSOR CIRCUIT
(LOW TEMPERATURE INDICATED)
2.3L (VIN D) "W" CARLINE (PORT)

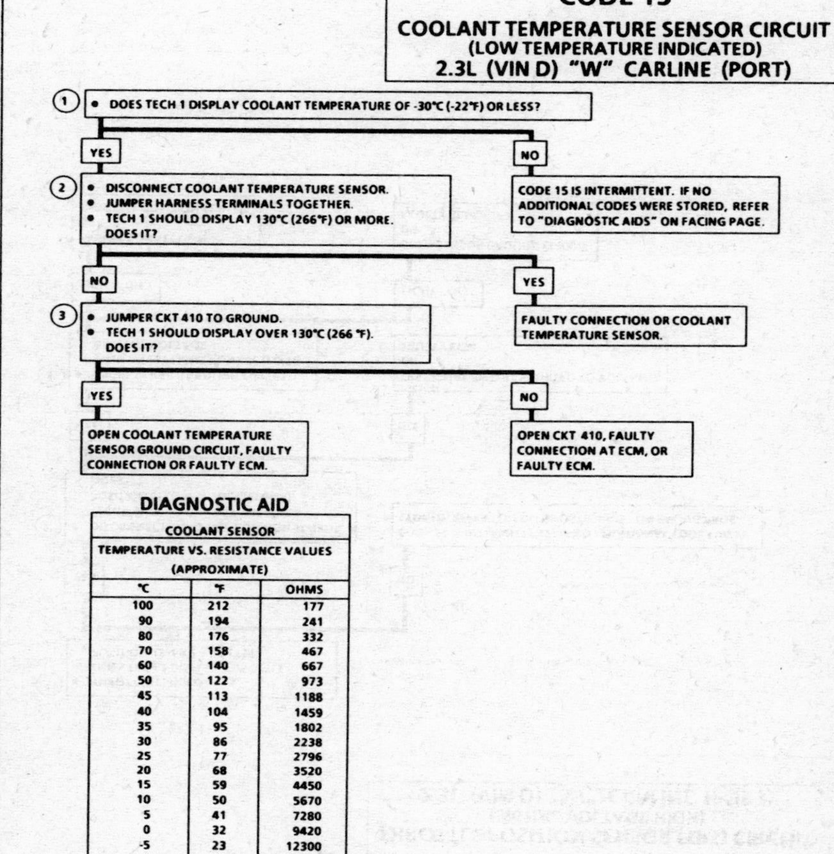

1
• DOES TECH 1 DISPLAY COOLANT TEMPERATURE OF -30°C (-22°F) OR LESS?
YES
NO
CODE 15 IS INTERMITTENT. IF NO ADDITIONAL CODES WERE STORED, REFER TO "DIAGNOSTIC AIDS" ON FACING PAGE.
2
• DISCONNECT COOLANT TEMPERATURE SENSOR.
• JUMPER HARNESS TERMINALS TOGETHER.
• TECH 1 SHOULD DISPLAY 130°C (266°F) OR MORE. DOES IT?
NO
YES
FAULTY CONNECTION OR COOLANT TEMPERATURE SENSOR.
3
• JUMPER CKT 410 TO GROUND.
• TECH 1 SHOULD DISPLAY OVER 130°C (266 °F). DOES IT?
YES
NO
OPEN COOLANT TEMPERATURE SENSOR GROUND CIRCUIT, FAULTY CONNECTION OR FAULTY ECM.
OPEN CKT 410, FAULTY CONNECTION AT ECM, OR FAULTY ECM.

DIAGNOSTIC AID

COOLANT SENSOR
TEMPERATURE VS. RESISTANCE VALUES
(APPROXIMATE)

°C	°F	OHMS
100	212	177
90	194	241
80	176	332
70	158	467
60	140	667
50	122	973
45	113	1188
40	104	1459
35	95	1802
30	86	2238
25	77	2796
20	68	3520
15	59	4450
10	50	5670
5	41	7280
0	32	9420
-5	23	12300
-10	14	16180
-15	5	21450
-20	-4	28680
-30	-22	52700
-40	-40	100700

"AFTER REPAIRS," REFER TO CODE CRITERIA ON FACING PAGE AND CONFIRM CODE DOES NOT RESET.

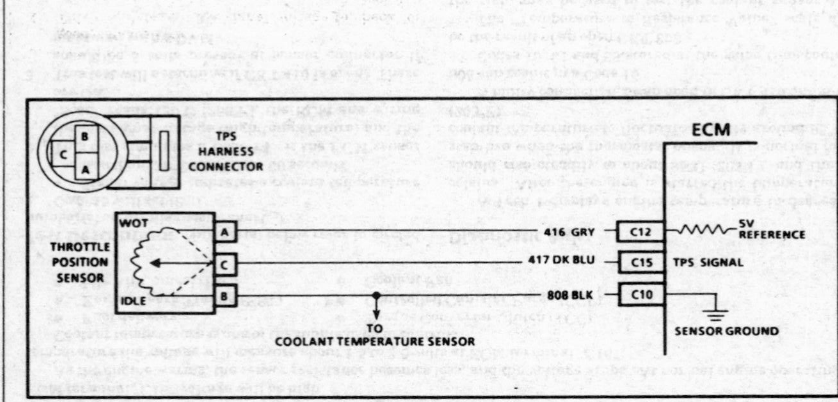

CODE 21

THROTTLE POSITION SENSOR (TPS) CIRCUIT
(SIGNAL VOLTAGE HIGH)
2.3L (VIN D) "W" CARLINE (PORT)

Circuit Description:

The Throttle Position Sensor (TPS) provides a voltage signal that changes relative to the throttle opening. Signal voltage will vary from about .5 volt at idle to about 4.9 volts at Wide Open Throttle (WOT).

The TPS signal is one of the most important inputs used by the ECM for fuel control and for most of the ECM control outputs.

Test Description: Number(s) below refer to circled number(s) on the diagnostic chart.

1. Code 21 will set if:
   - Engine is running under 1500 rpm.
   - No Code 33 or 34.
   - MAP less than 65 kPa.
   - TPS signal voltage greater than approximately 4.0 volts (78%).
   - Above conditions exist for over 5 seconds.

   OR
   - TPS voltage greater than about 4.8 volts.

   With throttle closed the TPS should read less than .900 volt.
2. With the TPS disconnected, the TPS voltage should go low if the ECM and wiring are OK.
3. Probing CKT 808 with a test light checks the TPS ground circuit because an open or very high resistance ground circuit will cause a Code 21.

Diagnostic Aids:

A Tech 1 displays throttle position in volts. It should display .400 volt to .900 volt with throttle closed and ignition "ON" or at idle. Voltage should increase at a steady rate as throttle is moved toward Wide Open Throttle (WOT).

Also some "Scan" tools will display throttle angle %, 0% = closed throttle 100% = WOT.

An open in CKT 808 will result in a Code 21.

Codes 15, 21 and 66 stored at the same time could be the result of an open CKT 808. "Scan" TPS while depressing accelerator pedal with engine stopped and ignition "ON." Display should vary from about .5 volt (500 mV) when throttle is closed, to over 4500 mV (4.5 volts) when throttle is held wide open.

Check condition of connector and sensor terminals for moisture or corrosion, and clean or replace as necessary. If corrosion found, check condition of connector seal, repair and/or replace if necessary.

CODE 21

THROTTLE POSITION SENSOR (TPS) CIRCUIT
(SIGNAL VOLTAGE HIGH)
2.3L (VIN D) "W" CARLINE (PORT)

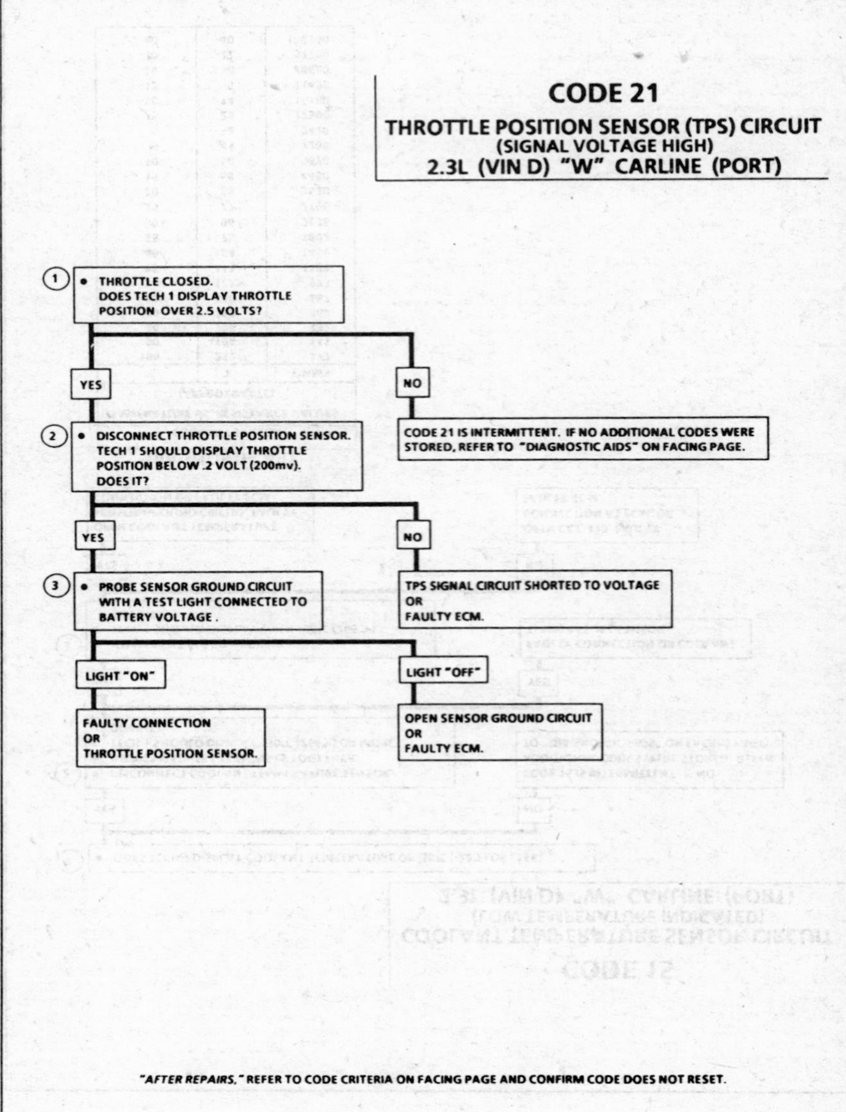

"AFTER REPAIRS," REFER TO CODE CRITERIA ON FACING PAGE AND CONFIRM CODE DOES NOT RESET.

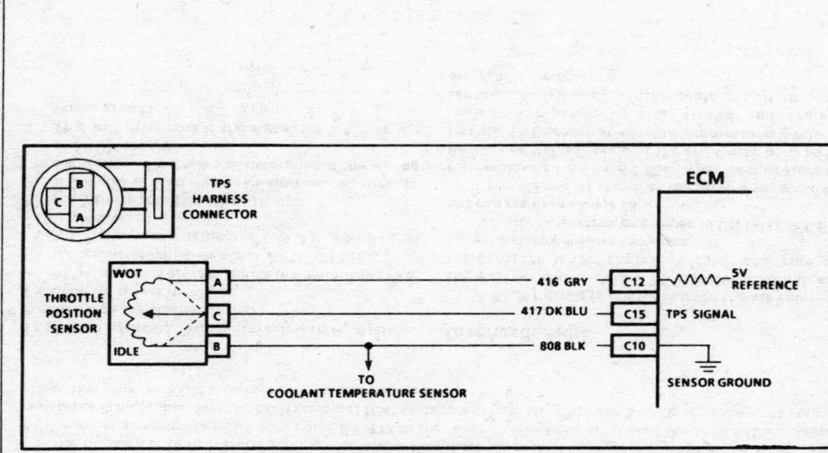

CODE 22

THROTTLE POSITION SENSOR (TPS) CIRCUIT
(SIGNAL VOLTAGE LOW)
2.3L (VIN D) "W" CARLINE (PORT)

Circuit Description:

The Throttle Position Sensor (TPS) provides a voltage signal that changes relative to the throttle opening. Signal voltage will vary from about .5 volt at idle to about 4.9 volts at Wide Open Throttle (WOT).

The TPS signal is one of the most important inputs used by the ECM for fuel control and for most of the ECM control outputs.

Test Description: Number(s) below refer to circled number(s) on the diagnostic chart.

1. Code 22 will set if:
   - Engine is running.
   - TPS signal voltage is less than .20 volt.

   The TPS has an auto zeroing feature. If the voltage reading is within the range of about .4 to .9 volt, the ECM will use that value as closed throttle. If the voltage reading is out of the auto zero range at closed throttle, check for a binding throttle cable or damaged linkage, if OK, continue with diagnosis.
2. Simulates Code 21: (high voltage). If the ECM recognizes the high signal voltage, then the ECM and wiring are OK.
3. Check for good sensor connection. If connection is good, replace TPS.
4. This simulates a high signal voltage to check for an open in CKT 417. The Tech 1 "Scan" tool will not read up to 12 volts, but what is important is that the ECM recognizes the signal on CKT 417.

Diagnostic Aids:

"Scan" TPS while depressing accelerator pedal with engine stopped and ignition "ON." Display should vary from about 500 mV (.5 volt) when throttle is closed, to over 4500 mV (4.5 volts) when throttle is held wide open.

Also, some "Scan" tools will display throttle angle %: 0% = closed throttle; 100% = WOT.

If Code 22 and 66 are set, check CKT 416 for faulty wiring or connections.

Should check condition of connector and sensor terminals for moisture or corrosion, and clean and/or replace as necessary. If corrosion is found, check condition of connector seal and repair or replace if necessary.

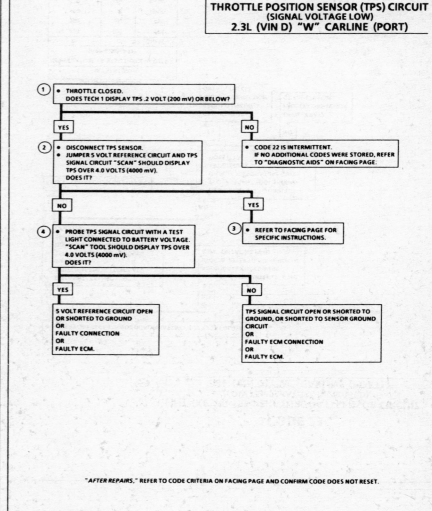

CODE 22

THROTTLE POSITION SENSOR (TPS) CIRCUIT
(SIGNAL VOLTAGE LOW)
2.3L (VIN D) "W" CARLINE (PORT)

(1)
- THROTTLE CLOSED.
  DOES TECH 1 DISPLAY TPS .2 VOLT (200 mV) OR BELOW?

YES → (2)
- DISCONNECT TPS SENSOR.
- JUMPER 5 VOLT REFERENCE CIRCUIT AND TPS SIGNAL CIRCUIT "SCAN" SHOULD DISPLAY TPS OVER 4.0 VOLTS (4000 mV).
  DOES IT?

NO →
- CODE 22 IS INTERMITTENT.
  IF NO ADDITIONAL CODES WERE STORED, REFER TO "DIAGNOSTIC AIDS" ON FACING PAGE.

(2) YES → (3)
- REFER TO FACING PAGE FOR SPECIFIC INSTRUCTIONS.

(2) NO → (4)
- PROBE TPS SIGNAL CIRCUIT WITH A TEST LIGHT CONNECTED TO BATTERY VOLTAGE. "SCAN" TOOL SHOULD DISPLAY TPS OVER 4.0 VOLTS (4000 mV).
  DOES IT?

(4) YES →
5 VOLT REFERENCE CIRCUIT OPEN OR SHORTED TO GROUND
OR
FAULTY CONNECTION
OR
FAULTY ECM.

(4) NO →
TPS SIGNAL CIRCUIT OPEN OR SHORTED TO GROUND, OR SHORTED TO SENSOR GROUND CIRCUIT
OR
FAULTY ECM CONNECTION
OR
FAULTY ECM.

"AFTER REPAIRS," REFER TO CODE CRITERIA ON FACING PAGE AND CONFIRM CODE DOES NOT RESET.

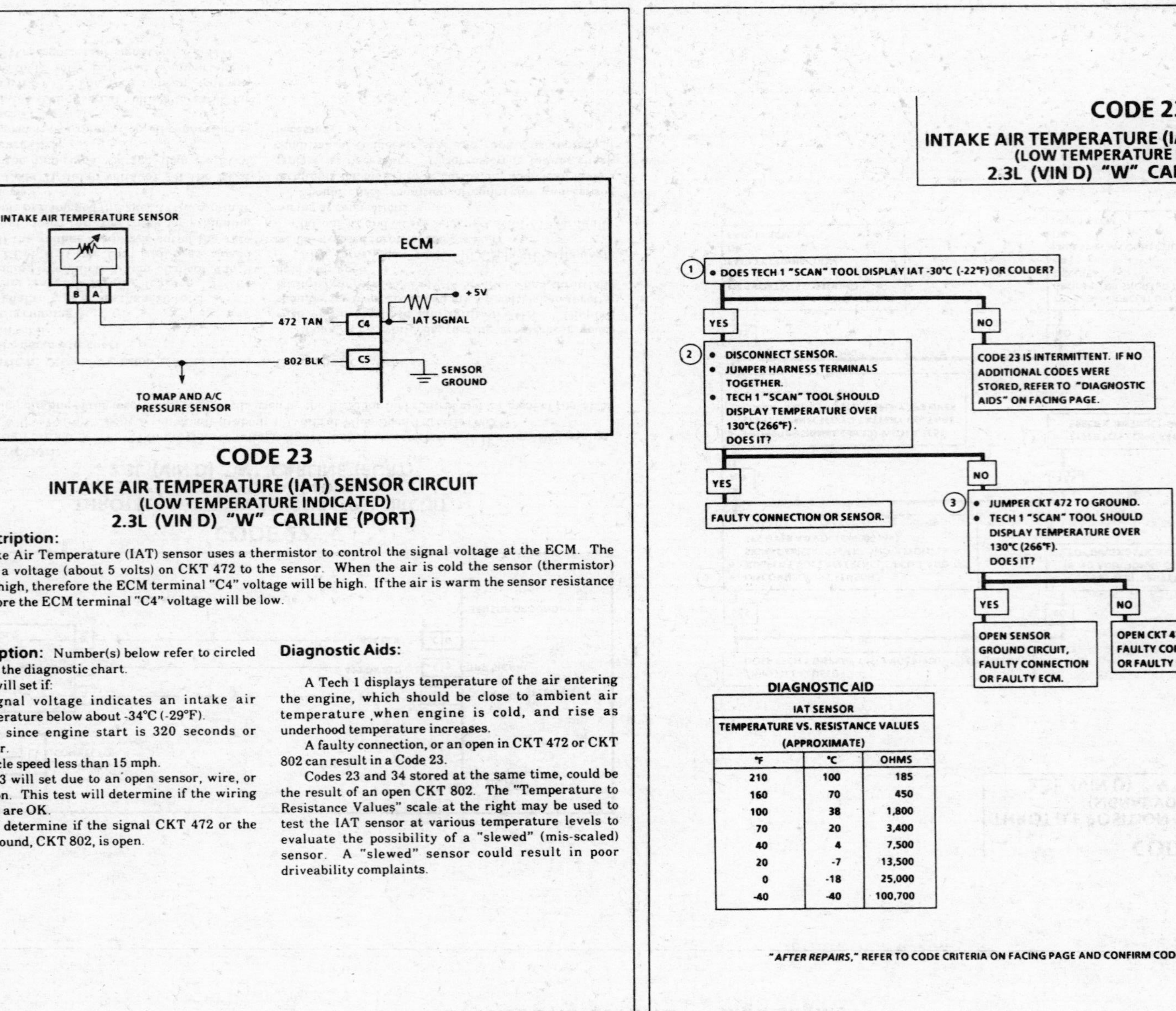
INTAKE AIR TEMPERATURE SENSOR
B
A
ECM
+5V
IAT SIGNAL
472 TAN
C4
802 BLK
C5
SENSOR GROUND
TO MAP AND A/C PRESSURE SENSOR
1 • DOES TECH 1 "SCAN" TOOL DISPLAY IAT -30°C (-22°F) OR COLDER?
YES
NO
CODE 23 IS INTERMITTENT. IF NO ADDITIONAL CODES WERE STORED, REFER TO "DIAGNOSTIC AIDS" ON FACING PAGE.
2 • DISCONNECT SENSOR.
• JUMPER HARNESS TERMINALS TOGETHER.
• TECH 1 "SCAN" TOOL SHOULD DISPLAY TEMPERATURE OVER 130°C (266°F).
DOES IT?
YES
NO
FAULTY CONNECTION OR SENSOR.
3 • JUMPER CKT 472 TO GROUND.
• TECH 1 "SCAN" TOOL SHOULD DISPLAY TEMPERATURE OVER 130°C (266°F).
DOES IT?
YES
NO
OPEN SENSOR GROUND CIRCUIT, FAULTY CONNECTION OR FAULTY ECM.
OPEN CKT 472, FAULTY CONNECTION OR FAULTY ECM.
"AFTER REPAIRS," REFER TO CODE CRITERIA ON FACING PAGE AND CONFIRM CODE DOES NOT RESET.

CODE 23

INTAKE AIR TEMPERATURE (IAT) SENSOR CIRCUIT
(LOW TEMPERATURE INDICATED)
2.3L (VIN D) "W" CARLINE (PORT)

Circuit Description:

The Intake Air Temperature (IAT) sensor uses a thermistor to control the signal voltage at the ECM. The ECM applies a voltage (about 5 volts) on CKT 472 to the sensor. When the air is cold the sensor (thermistor) resistance is high, therefore the ECM terminal "C4" voltage will be high. If the air is warm the sensor resistance is low, therefore the ECM terminal "C4" voltage will be low.

Test Description: Number(s) below refer to circled number(s) on the diagnostic chart.

1. Code 23 will set if:
   - A signal voltage indicates an intake air temperature below about -34°C (-29°F).
   - Time since engine start is 320 seconds or longer.
   - Vehicle speed less than 15 mph.
2. A Code 23 will set due to an open sensor, wire, or connection. This test will determine if the wiring and ECM are OK.
3. This will determine if the signal CKT 472 or the sensor ground, CKT 802, is open.

Diagnostic Aids:

A Tech 1 displays temperature of the air entering the engine, which should be close to ambient air temperature when engine is cold, and rise as underhood temperature increases.

A faulty connection, or an open in CKT 472 or CKT 802 can result in a Code 23.

Codes 23 and 34 stored at the same time, could be the result of an open CKT 802. The "Temperature to Resistance Values" scale at the right may be used to test the IAT sensor at various temperature levels to evaluate the possibility of a "slewed" (mis-scaled) sensor. A "slewed" sensor could result in poor driveability complaints.

DIAGNOSTIC AID

IAT SENSOR
TEMPERATURE VS. RESISTANCE VALUES (APPROXIMATE)

°F	°C	OHMS
210	100	185
160	70	450
100	38	1,800
70	20	3,400
40	4	7,500
20	-7	13,500
0	-18	25,000
-40	-40	100,700

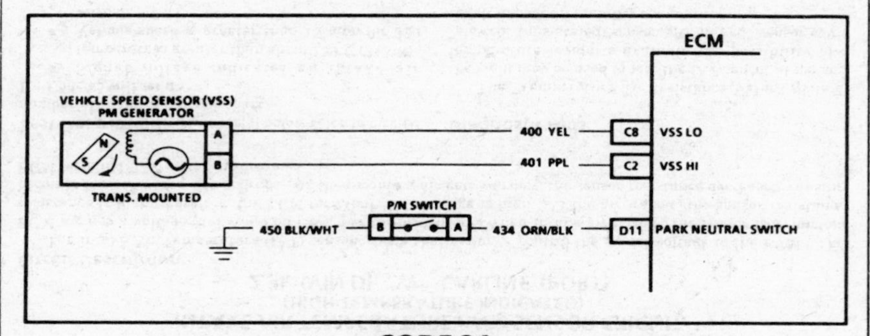

CODE 24

VEHICLE SPEED SENSOR (VSS) CIRCUIT 2.3L (VIN D) "W" CARLINE (PORT)

Circuit Description:

Vehicle speed information is provided to the ECM by the Vehicle Speed Sensor (VSS) which is a Permanent Magnet (PM) generator that is mounted in the transaxle. The PM generator produces a pulsing voltage whenever vehicle speed is over about 3 mph (5 km/h). The AC voltage level and the number of pulses increases with vehicle speed. The ECM then converts the pulsing voltage to mph which is used for calculations, and the mph can be displayed with a Tech 1. Output of the generator can also be seen by using a digital voltmeter on the AC scale while rotating the generator.

The function of VSS buffer used in past model years has been incorporated into the ECM. The ECM then supplies the necessary signal for the instrument panel for operating the speedometer, the odometer, and for the cruise control module.

Test Description: Number(s) below refer to circled number(s) on the diagnostic chart.

1. Code 24 will set if the vehicle speed input to the ECM is less than 2 mph under the following conditions:
   - Engine speed is between 1500 and 3600 rpm.
   - TPS is less than 2%.
   - MAP sensor input is between 11.8 and 30 kPa.
   - P/N switch indicates drive. No Code 21, 22, 33 or 34.
   - All conditions are met for 5 seconds. (These conditions occur on a road load deceleration.)
2. Check MEM-CAL for correct application before replacing ECM.

Diagnostic Aids:

Tech 1 should indicate a vehicle speed whenever the drive wheels are turning greater than 3 mph (5 km/h).

A problem in CKT 434 will not affect the VSS input or the speed display on a Tech 1, but will affect park/neutral display.

Check CKT 400 and 401 for proper connections. Be sure they are clean and tight and the harness is routed correctly.

A faulty or misadjusted park/neutral switch can result in a false Code 24. Use a Tech 1 and check for proper signal while in drive (3T40). Refer to CHART C-1A for P/N switch diagnosis check.

CODE 24

VEHICLE SPEED SENSOR (VSS) CIRCUIT 2.3L (VIN D) "W" CARLINE (PORT)

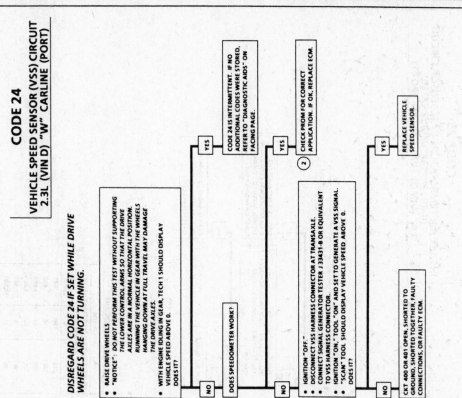

DISREGARD CODE 24 IF SET WHILE DRIVE WHEELS ARE NOT TURNING.

(1)
- RAISE DRIVE WHEELS
- "NOTICE": *DO NOT PERFORM THIS TEST WITHOUT SUPPORTING THE LOWER CONTROL ARMS SO THAT THE DRIVE AXLES ARE IN A NORMAL HORIZONTAL POSITION. RUNNING THE VEHICLE IN GEAR WITH THE WHEELS HANGING DOWN AT FULL TRAVEL MAY DAMAGE THE DRIVE AXLES.*
- WITH ENGINE IDLING IN GEAR, TECH 1 SHOULD DISPLAY VEHICLE SPEED ABOVE 0.

DOES IT?

YES → CODE 24 IS INTERMITTENT. IF NO ADDITIONAL CODES WERE STORED, REFER TO "DIAGNOSTIC AIDS" ON FACING PAGE.

NO → DOES SPEEDOMETER WORK?

YES → (2) CHECK PROM FOR CORRECT APPLICATION. IF OK, REPLACE ECM.

NO →
- IGNITION "OFF."
- DISCONNECT VSS HARNESS CONNECTOR AT TRANSAXLE.
- CONNECT SIGNAL GENERATOR TESTER J 33431-B OR EQUIVALENT TO VSS HARNESS CONNECTOR.
- IGNITION "ON," TOOL "ON" AND SET TO GENERATE A VSS SIGNAL.
- "SCAN" TOOL SHOULD DISPLAY VEHICLE SPEED ABOVE 0.

DOES IT?

YES → REPLACE VEHICLE SPEED SENSOR.

NO → CKT 400 OR 401 OPEN, SHORTED TO GROUND, SHORTED TOGETHER, FAULTY CONNECTIONS, OR FAULTY ECM.

"AFTER REPAIRS," REFER TO CODE CRITERIA ON FACING PAGE AND CONFIRM CODE DOES NOT RESET.

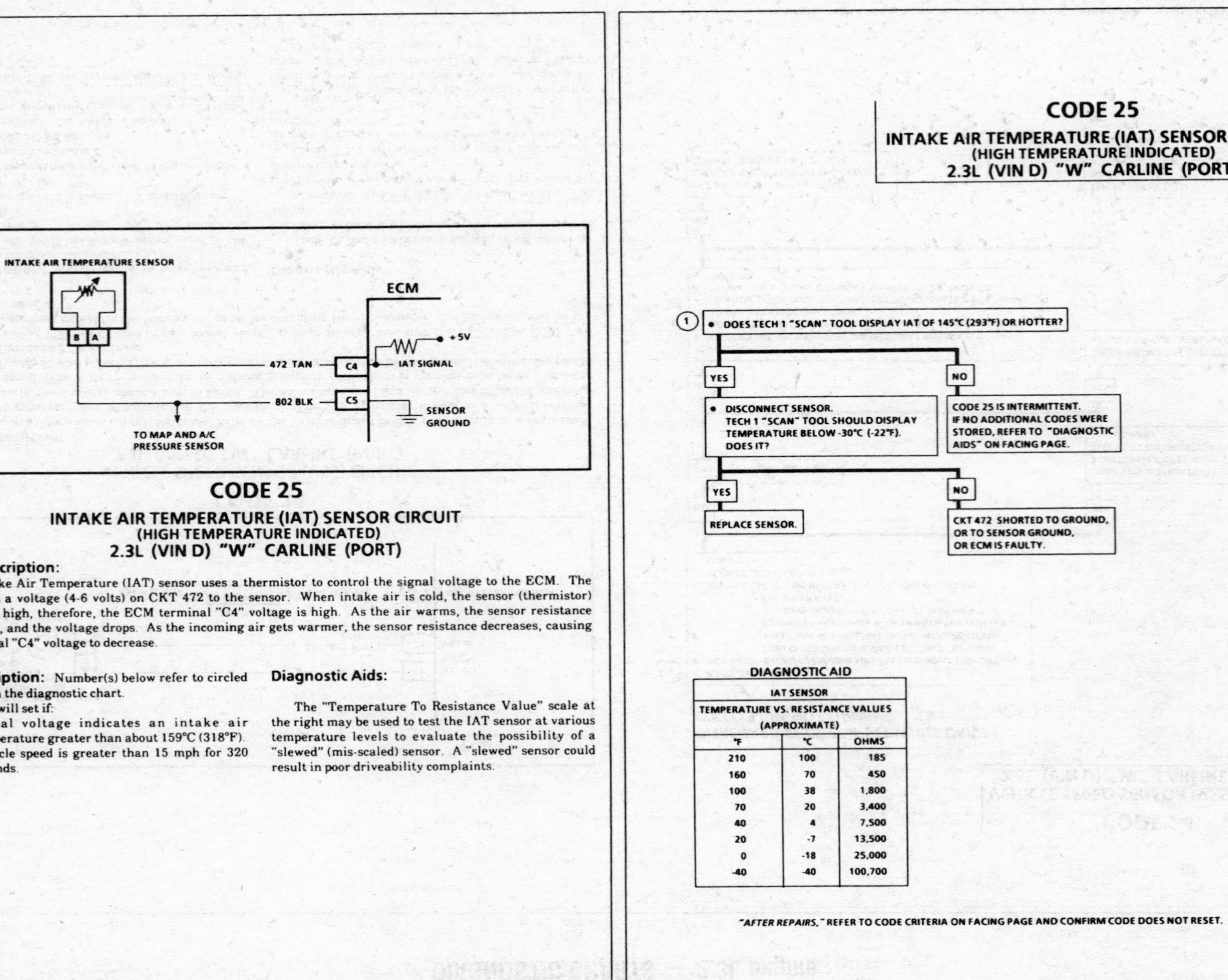

CODE 25

INTAKE AIR TEMPERATURE (IAT) SENSOR CIRCUIT
(HIGH TEMPERATURE INDICATED)
2.3L (VIN D) "W" CARLINE (PORT)

Circuit Description:

The Intake Air Temperature (IAT) sensor uses a thermistor to control the signal voltage to the ECM. The ECM applies a voltage (4-6 volts) on CKT 472 to the sensor. When intake air is cold, the sensor (thermistor) resistance is high, therefore, the ECM terminal "C4" voltage is high. As the air warms, the sensor resistance becomes less, and the voltage drops. As the incoming air gets warmer, the sensor resistance decreases, causing ECM terminal "C4" voltage to decrease.

Test Description: Number(s) below refer to circled number(s) on the diagnostic chart.

1. Code 25 will set if:
   - Signal voltage indicates an intake air temperature greater than about 159°C (318°F).
   - Vehicle speed is greater than 15 mph for 320 seconds.

Diagnostic Aids:

The "Temperature To Resistance Value" scale at the right may be used to test the IAT sensor at various temperature levels to evaluate the possibility of a "slewed" (mis-scaled) sensor. A "slewed" sensor could result in poor driveability complaints.

CODE 25

INTAKE AIR TEMPERATURE (IAT) SENSOR CIRCUIT
(HIGH TEMPERATURE INDICATED)
2.3L (VIN D) "W" CARLINE (PORT)

(1) • DOES TECH 1 "SCAN" TOOL DISPLAY IAT OF 145°C (293°F) OR HOTTER?

YES:
• DISCONNECT SENSOR.
TECH 1 "SCAN" TOOL SHOULD DISPLAY TEMPERATURE BELOW -30°C (-22°F).
DOES IT?

- YES: REPLACE SENSOR.
- NO: CKT 472 SHORTED TO GROUND, OR TO SENSOR GROUND, OR ECM IS FAULTY.

NO:
CODE 25 IS INTERMITTENT.
IF NO ADDITIONAL CODES WERE STORED, REFER TO "DIAGNOSTIC AIDS" ON FACING PAGE.

DIAGNOSTIC AID

IAT SENSOR		
TEMPERATURE VS. RESISTANCE VALUES (APPROXIMATE)		
°F	°C	OHMS
210	100	185
160	70	450
100	38	1,800
70	20	3,400
40	4	7,500
20	-7	13,500
0	-18	25,000
-40	-40	100,700

"AFTER REPAIRS," REFER TO CODE CRITERIA ON FACING PAGE AND CONFIRM CODE DOES NOT RESET.

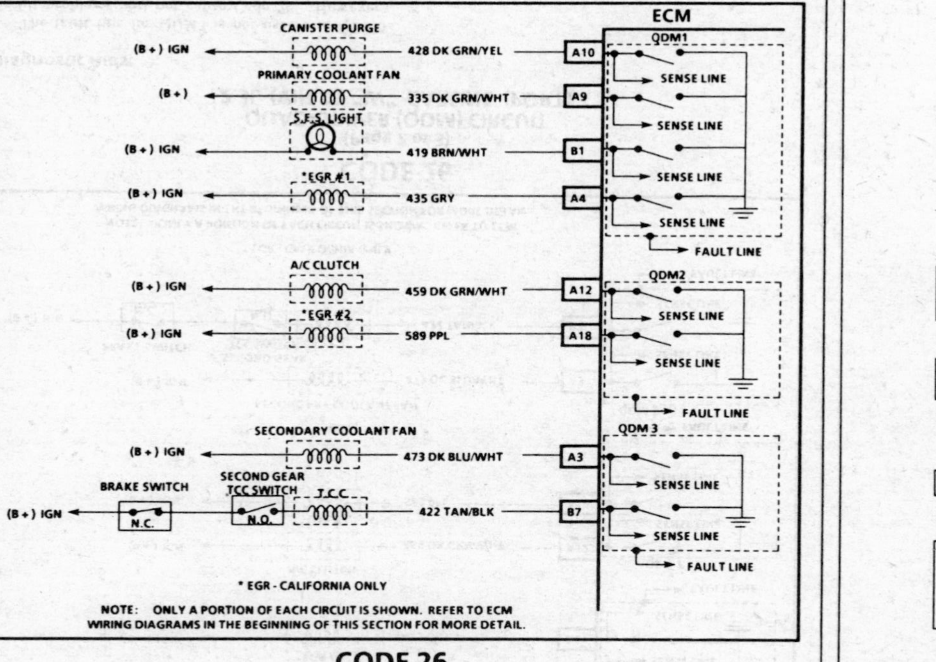

CODE 26

(Page 1 of 3)

QUAD-DRIVER (QDM) CIRCUIT
2.3L (VIN D) "W" CARLINE (PORT)

Circuit Description:

The ECM controls most components with electronic switches which complete a ground circuit when turned "ON." These switches are arranged in groups of 4, called Quad-Driver Modules (QDMs), which can independently control up to 4 outputs (4 ECM terminals, although not all outputs are used). When an output is "ON," the terminal is grounded and its voltage should be low. When an output is "OFF," its terminal voltage should be high, except for the TCC control, which should also be low if the brake or 2nd gear TCC switches are open.

QDMs are fault protected. If a relay or solenoid coil is shorted to voltage, it would allow too much current. The QDM senses this, and its internal resistance increases to limit current and to protect the QDM. The result is high output terminal voltage when it should be low. If the circuit from B+ or the component is open, or the driver side of the circuit is shorted to ground, terminal voltage will be low, even when output is commanded "OFF." Either of these faults will send a fault signal, indicating Code 26. The ECM ignores the fault line signal from QDM 3 to prevent false setting of Code 26 due to brake and second gear TCC series switches. As a result, QDM 3 circuit problems will not cause Code 26, although the circuits are fault protected and operate in the same way as QDM 1 and QDM 2.

CODE 26

(Page 1 of 3)

QUAD-DRIVER (QDM) CIRCUIT
2.3L (VIN D) "W" CARLINE (PORT)

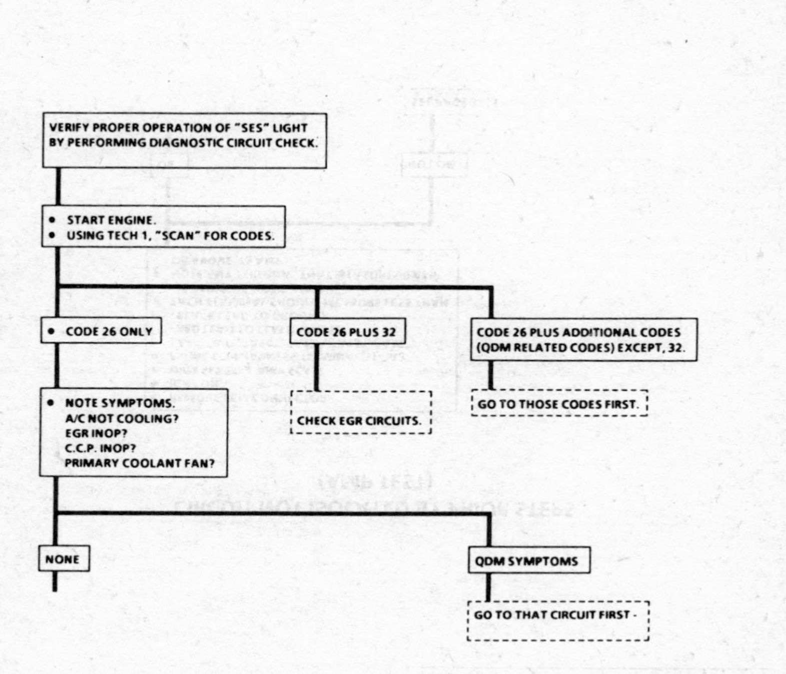

"AFTER REPAIRS," REFER TO CODE CRITERIA ON FACING PAGE AND CONFIRM CODE DOES NOT RESET.

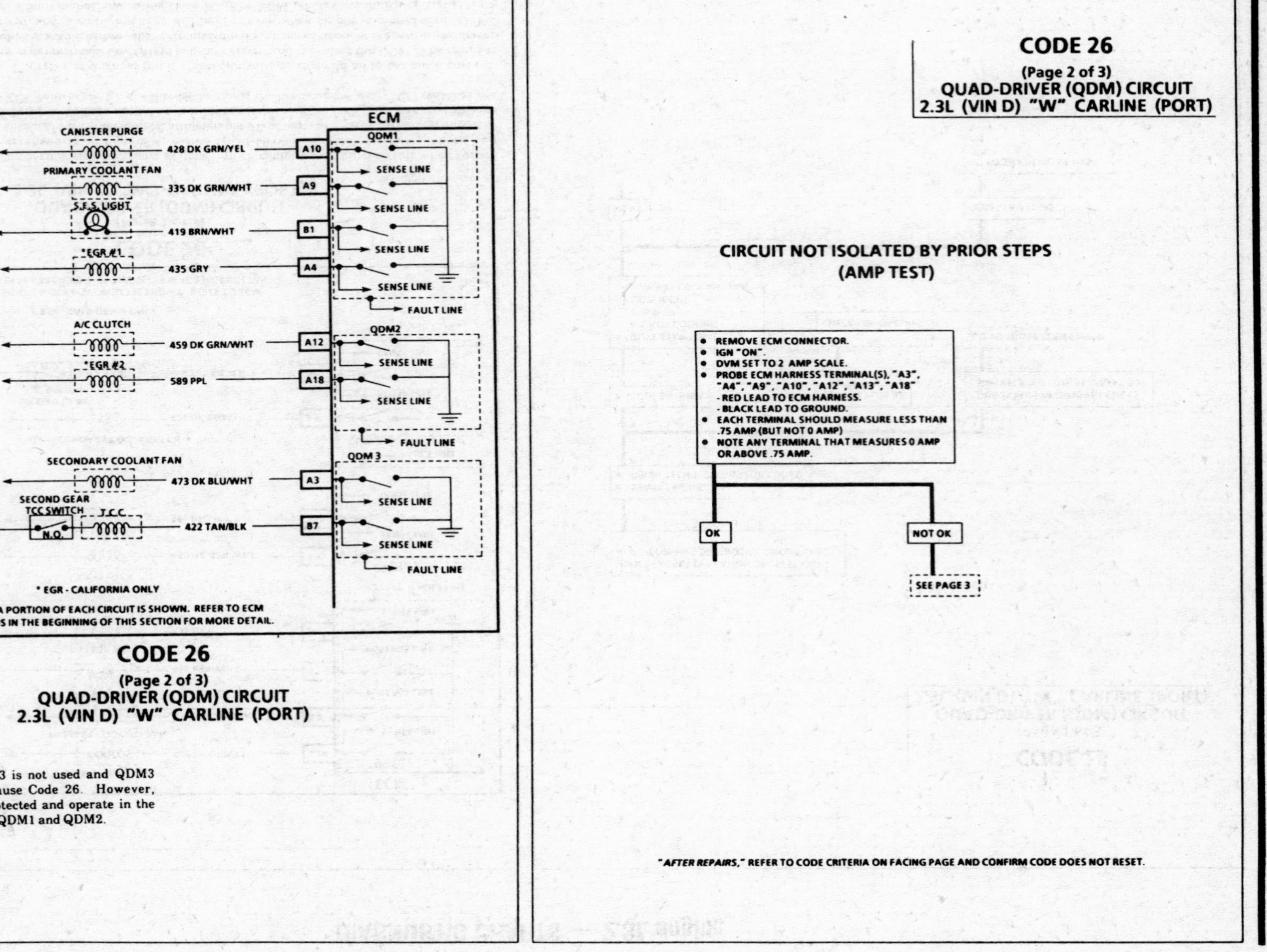

CODE 26

(Page 2 of 3)

QUAD-DRIVER (QDM) CIRCUIT
2.3L (VIN D) "W" CARLINE (PORT)

Diagnostic Aids:

The fault line for QDM3 is not used and QDM3 circuit problems will not cause Code 26. However, QDM3 circuits are fault protected and operate in the same way as the circuits for QDM1 and QDM2.

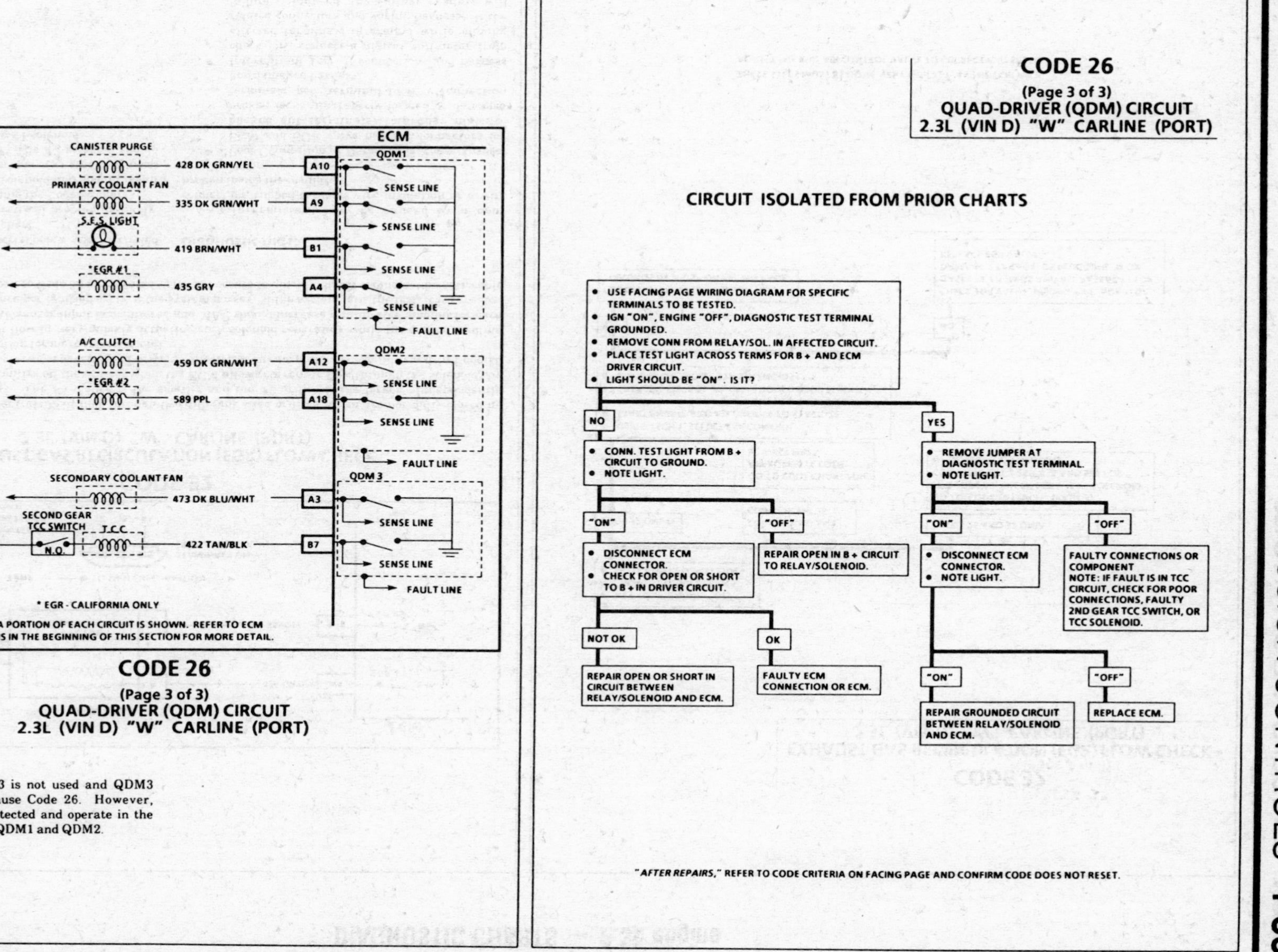
CODE 26
(Page 3 of 3)
QUAD-DRIVER (QDM) CIRCUIT
2.3L (VIN D) "W" CARLINE (PORT)
CIRCUIT ISOLATED FROM PRIOR CHARTS
• USE FACING PAGE WIRING DIAGRAM FOR SPECIFIC TERMINALS TO BE TESTED.
• IGN "ON", ENGINE "OFF", DIAGNOSTIC TEST TERMINAL GROUNDED.
• REMOVE CONN FROM RELAY/SOL. IN AFFECTED CIRCUIT.
• PLACE TEST LIGHT ACROSS TERMS FOR B + AND ECM DRIVER CIRCUIT.
• LIGHT SHOULD BE "ON". IS IT?
NO
YES
• CONN. TEST LIGHT FROM B + CIRCUIT TO GROUND.
• NOTE LIGHT.
• REMOVE JUMPER AT DIAGNOSTIC TEST TERMINAL.
• NOTE LIGHT.
"ON"
"OFF"
• DISCONNECT ECM CONNECTOR.
• CHECK FOR OPEN OR SHORT TO B + IN DRIVER CIRCUIT.
REPAIR OPEN IN B + CIRCUIT TO RELAY/SOLENOID.
• DISCONNECT ECM CONNECTOR.
• NOTE LIGHT.
FAULTY CONNECTIONS OR COMPONENT
NOTE: IF FAULT IS IN TCC CIRCUIT, CHECK FOR POOR CONNECTIONS, FAULTY 2ND GEAR TCC SWITCH, OR TCC SOLENOID.
NOT OK
OK
REPAIR OPEN OR SHORT IN CIRCUIT BETWEEN RELAY/SOLENOID AND ECM.
FAULTY ECM CONNECTION OR ECM.
REPAIR GROUNDED CIRCUIT BETWEEN RELAY/SOLENOID AND ECM.
REPLACE ECM.
"AFTER REPAIRS," REFER TO CODE CRITERIA ON FACING PAGE AND CONFIRM CODE DOES NOT RESET.
ECM
QDM1
QDM2
QDM 3
CANISTER PURGE
PRIMARY COOLANT FAN
S.E.S. LIGHT
EGR #1
A/C CLUTCH
EGR #2
SECONDARY COOLANT FAN
SECOND GEAR TCC SWITCH
T.C.C.
BRAKE SWITCH
N.C.
N.O.
(B +) IGN
(B +)
428 DK GRN/YEL
335 DK GRN/WHT
419 BRN/WHT
435 GRY
459 DK GRN/WHT
589 PPL
473 DK BLU/WHT
422 TAN/BLK
A10
A9
B1
A4
A12
A18
A3
B7
SENSE LINE
FAULT LINE
* EGR - CALIFORNIA ONLY
NOTE: ONLY A PORTION OF EACH CIRCUIT IS SHOWN. REFER TO ECM WIRING DIAGRAMS IN THE BEGINNING OF THIS SECTION FOR MORE DETAIL.

CODE 26
(Page 3 of 3)
QUAD-DRIVER (QDM) CIRCUIT
2.3L (VIN D) "W" CARLINE (PORT)

Diagnostic Aids:

The fault line for QDM3 is not used and QDM3 circuit problems will not cause Code 26. However, QDM3 circuits are fault protected and operate in the same way as the circuits for QDM1 and QDM2.

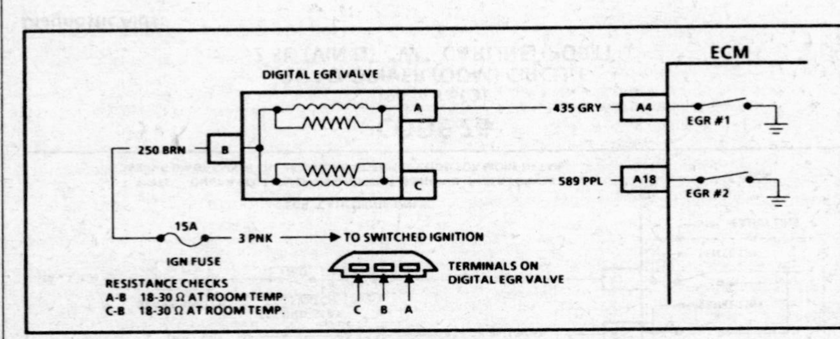

CODE 32

EXHAUST GAS RECIRCULATION (EGR) FLOW CHECK 2.3L (VIN D) "W" CARLINE (PORT)

Circuit Description:

The digital EGR valve controls EGR flow through two different sized orifices which are normally closed by pintles held down by springs. The #1 orifice is the smaller and the #2 orifice is the larger. Independently controlled solenoids lift the pintles off the orifices when the ECM allows current to flow through the solenoids by creating ground paths through two separate quad-drivers. Electrical circuit problems should result in Code 26 setting. (See Code 26 description for more information.)

The ECM also tests EGR flow by very quickly actuating each solenoid separately while the engine is idling under stable conditions. MAP sensor input is monitored and MAP should increase a calibrated amount for each solenoid. This test is done once per ignition cycle, if the system passes. If the system fails the test, it is repeated and must fail several times before Code 32 is indicated. The test occurs so quickly that it should not be noticeable to the driver.

Test Description: Number(s) below refer to circled number(s) on the diagnostic chart.

1. Code 26 indicates an electrical problem is likely. This can be diagnosed using the Code 26 chart.
2. This step actuates each solenoid and should result in a a momentary drop in rpm or engine roughness if the EGR flows at idle. The #2 solenoid should have more effect than the #1 solenoid.

Diagnostic Aids:

An intermittent may be caused by a poor connection, rubbed-through wire insulation or a wire broken inside the insulation.

Check for:

- Poor Connection or Damaged Harness Inspect ECM and EGR valve harness connectors for backed out terminals, improper mating, broken locks, improperly formed or damaged terminals, poor terminal to wire connection and damaged harness.
- Intermittent Test If connections and harness check OK, connect a digital voltmeter from effected terminals to ground while moving related connectors and wiring harness. If the failure is induced, the voltage reading will change.

CODE 32

EXHAUST GAS RECIRCULATION (EGR) FLOW CHECK 2.3L (VIN D) "W" CARLINE (PORT)

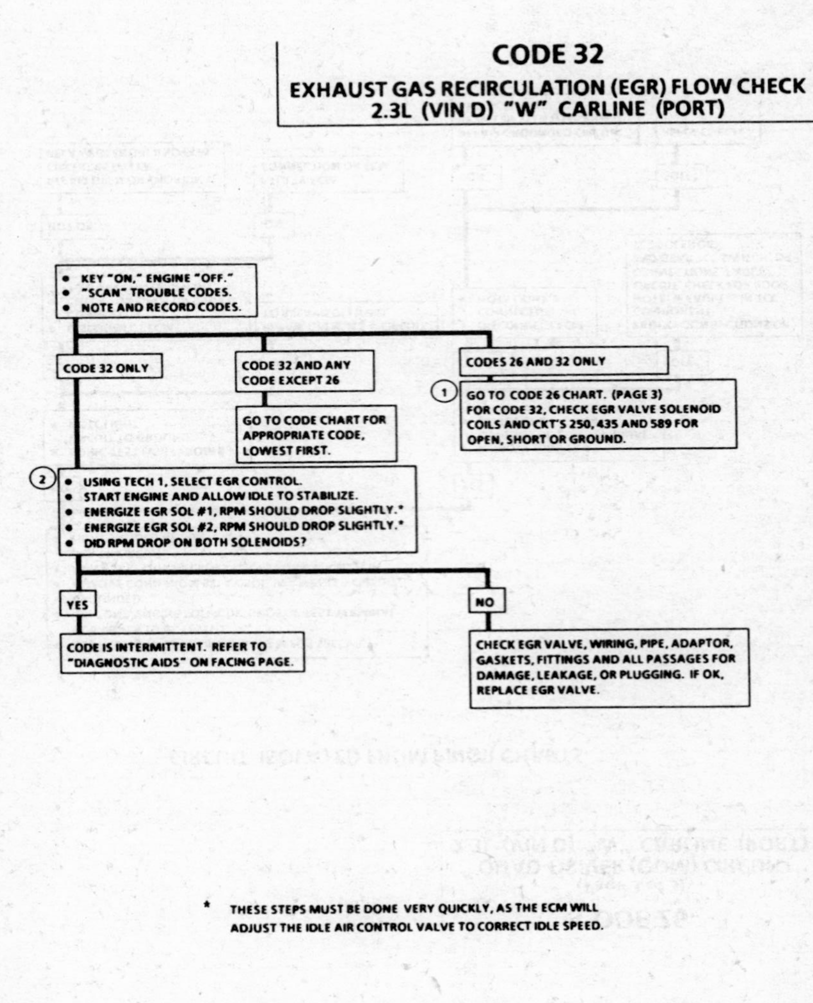

• KEY "ON," ENGINE "OFF."
• "SCAN" TROUBLE CODES.
• NOTE AND RECORD CODES.
CODE 32 ONLY
CODE 32 AND ANY CODE EXCEPT 26
CODES 26 AND 32 ONLY
GO TO CODE CHART FOR APPROPRIATE CODE, LOWEST FIRST.
1
GO TO CODE 26 CHART. (PAGE 3) FOR CODE 32, CHECK EGR VALVE SOLENOID COILS AND CKT'S 250, 435 AND 589 FOR OPEN, SHORT OR GROUND.
2
• USING TECH 1, SELECT EGR CONTROL.
• START ENGINE AND ALLOW IDLE TO STABILIZE.
• ENERGIZE EGR SOL #1, RPM SHOULD DROP SLIGHTLY.*
• ENERGIZE EGR SOL #2, RPM SHOULD DROP SLIGHTLY.*
• DID RPM DROP ON BOTH SOLENOIDS?
YES
NO
CODE IS INTERMITTENT. REFER TO "DIAGNOSTIC AIDS" ON FACING PAGE.
CHECK EGR VALVE, WIRING, PIPE, ADAPTOR, GASKETS, FITTINGS AND ALL PASSAGES FOR DAMAGE, LEAKAGE, OR PLUGGING. IF OK, REPLACE EGR VALVE.

* THESE STEPS MUST BE DONE VERY QUICKLY, AS THE ECM WILL ADJUST THE IDLE AIR CONTROL VALVE TO CORRECT IDLE SPEED.

"*AFTER REPAIRS,*" REFER TO CODE CRITERIA ON FACING PAGE AND CONFIRM CODE DOES NOT RESET.

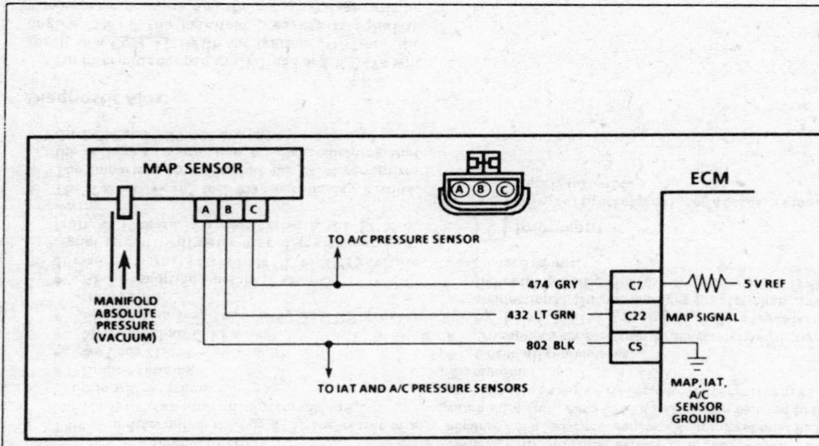

TO A/C PRESSURE SENSOR

TO IAT AND A/C PRESSURE SENSORS

474 GRY
432 LT GRN
802 BLK

ECM

C7 — 5 V REF
C22 — MAP SIGNAL
C5 — MAP, IAT, A/C SENSOR GROUND

CODE 33

MANIFOLD ABSOLUTE PRESSURE (MAP) SENSOR CIRCUIT
(SIGNAL VOLTAGE HIGH - LOW VACUUM)
2.3L (VIN D) "W" CARLINE (PORT)

Circuit Description:

The Manifold Absolute Pressure (MAP) sensor responds to changes in manifold pressure (vacuum). The ECM receives this information as a signal voltage that will vary from about 1 to 3 volts at closed throttle (idle) to 4-4.5 volts at wide open throttle (low vacuum).

If the MAP sensor fails, the ECM will substitute a fixed MAP value and use the Throttle Position Sensor (TPS) to control fuel delivery.

Test Description: Number(s) below refer to circled number(s) on the diagnostic chart.

1. This step will determine if Code 33 is the result of a hard failure or an intermittent condition.
   Code 33 will set when:
   - Code 21 or 22 not present.
   - MAP signal greater than 80 kPa.
   - TPS less than 12%.
   - VSS less than 1 mph.
   - Above conditions met for 5 seconds.
2. This step simulates conditions for a Code 34. If the ECM recognizes the change, the ECM and CKT 474 and CKT 432 are OK. If CKT 802 is open, there may also be a stored Code 23.

A Code 33 will result if CKT 802 is open or if CKT 432 is shorted to voltage or to CKT 474.

If Code 33 is intermittent, refer to "Symptoms," Section

- Check all connections.
- Disconnect sensor from bracket and twist sensor by hand (only) to check for intermittent connections. Output changes greater than .1 volt indicates a bad connector or connection. If OK, replace sensor.

Important

- Make sure electrical connector remains securely fastened.

Diagnostic Aids:

With the ignition "ON" and the engine stopped, the manifold pressure is equal to atmospheric pressure and the signal voltage will be high. This information is used by the ECM as an indication of vehicle altitude. Comparison of this reading with a known good vehicle with the same sensor is a good way to check accuracy of a "suspect" sensor. Readings should be the same ± .4 volt.

CODE 33

MANIFOLD ABSOLUTE PRESSURE (MAP) SENSOR CIRCUIT
(SIGNAL VOLTAGE HIGH - LOW VACUUM)
2.3L (VIN D) "W" CARLINE (PORT)

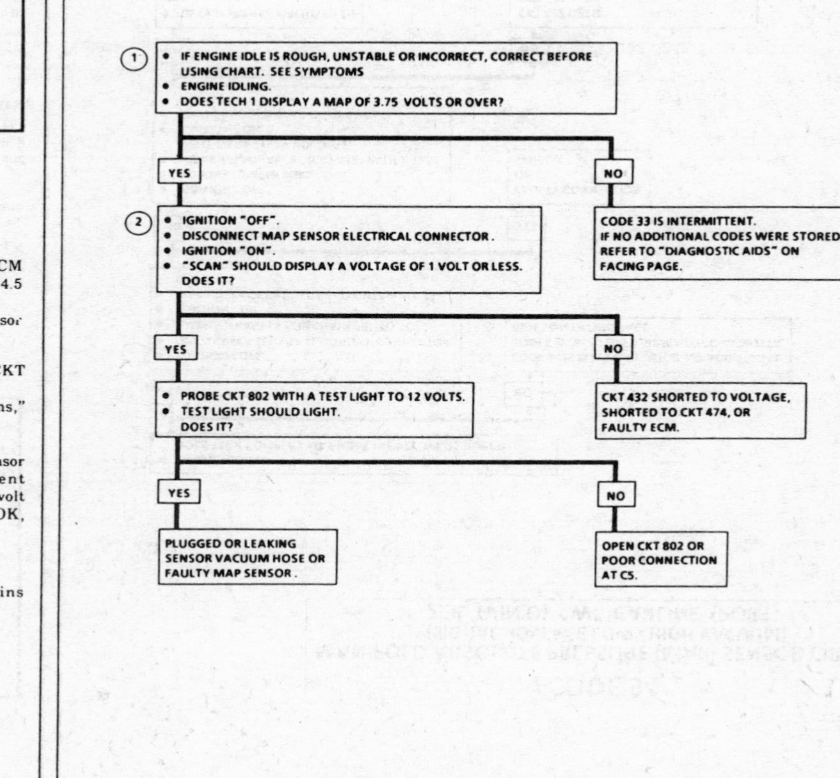

1
• IF ENGINE IDLE IS ROUGH, UNSTABLE OR INCORRECT, CORRECT BEFORE USING CHART. SEE SYMPTOMS
• ENGINE IDLING.
• DOES TECH 1 DISPLAY A MAP OF 3.75 VOLTS OR OVER?
YES
NO
2
• IGNITION "OFF".
• DISCONNECT MAP SENSOR ELECTRICAL CONNECTOR.
• IGNITION "ON".
• "SCAN" SHOULD DISPLAY A VOLTAGE OF 1 VOLT OR LESS. DOES IT?
CODE 33 IS INTERMITTENT. IF NO ADDITIONAL CODES WERE STORED, REFER TO "DIAGNOSTIC AIDS" ON FACING PAGE.
YES
NO
• PROBE CKT 802 WITH A TEST LIGHT TO 12 VOLTS.
• TEST LIGHT SHOULD LIGHT. DOES IT?
CKT 432 SHORTED TO VOLTAGE, SHORTED TO CKT 474, OR FAULTY ECM.
YES
NO
PLUGGED OR LEAKING SENSOR VACUUM HOSE OR FAULTY MAP SENSOR.
OPEN CKT 802 OR POOR CONNECTION AT C5.

"AFTER REPAIRS," REFER TO CODE CRITERIA ON FACING PAGE AND CONFIRM CODE DOES NOT RESET.

DIAGNOSTIC CHARTS — 2.3L engine

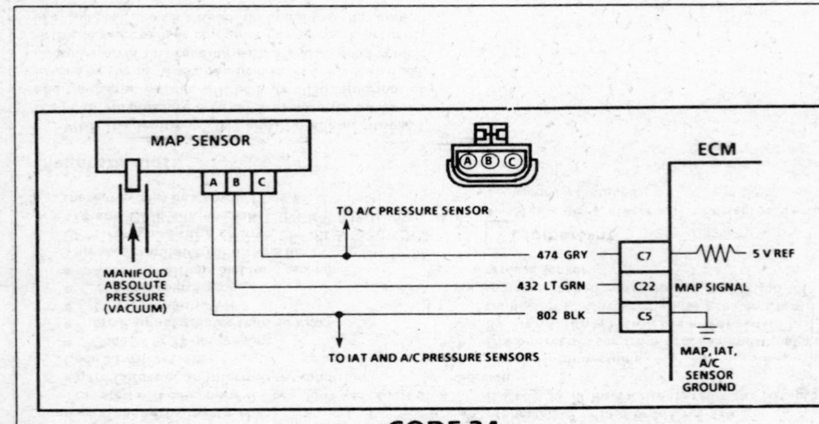

CODE 34

MANIFOLD ABSOLUTE PRESSURE (MAP) SENSOR CIRCUIT
(SIGNAL VOLTAGE LOW - HIGH VACUUM)
2.3L (VIN D) "W" CARLINE (PORT)

Circuit Description:

The Manifold Absolute Pressure (MAP) sensor responds to changes in manifold pressure (vacuum). The ECM receives this information as a signal voltage that will vary from about 1 to 3 volts at closed throttle (idle) to 4- 4.5 volts at wide open throttle (low vacuum).

If the MAP sensor fails, the ECM will substitute a fixed MAP value and use the Throttle Position Sensor (TPS) to control fuel delivery.

Test Description: Number(s) below refer to circled number(s) on the diagnostic chart.

1. This step determines if Code 34 is the result of a hard failure or an intermittent condition.
   Code 34 will set when:
   - Engine running.
   - No Code 21.
   - MAP less than 14 kPa.
   - Engine rpm less than 1200 or TPS greater than 15.2%.
   - Above conditions met for .2 seconds.
2. Jumpering harness terminals "B" to "C" (5 volts to signal circuit) will determine if the sensor is at fault, or if there is a problem with the ECM or wiring.
3. The Tech 1 "Scan" tool may not display 5 volts. The important thing is that the ECM recognizes the voltage as more than 4 volts, indicating that the ECM and CKT 432 are OK.

Diagnostic Aids:

An intermittent open in CKT 432 or CKT 474 will result in a Code 34. With the ignition "ON" and the engine "OFF," the manifold pressure is equal to atmospheric pressure and the signal voltage will be high. This information is used by the ECM as an indication of vehicle altitude.

Comparison of this reading with a known good vehicle with the same sensor is a good way to check accuracy of a "suspect" sensor. Readings should be the same ± .4 volt. Also CHART C-1D can be used to test the MAP sensor. Refer to "Intermittents" in "Symptoms,"

- Check all connections.
- Disconnect sensor from bracket and twist sensor by hand (only) to check for intermittent connections. Output changes greater than .1 volt indicates a bad connector or connection. If OK, replace sensor.

Important

- Make sure electrical connector remains securely fastened.

CODE 34

MANIFOLD ABSOLUTE PRESSURE (MAP) SENSOR CIRCUIT
(SIGNAL VOLTAGE LOW - HIGH VACUUM)
2.3L (VIN D) "W" CARLINE (PORT)

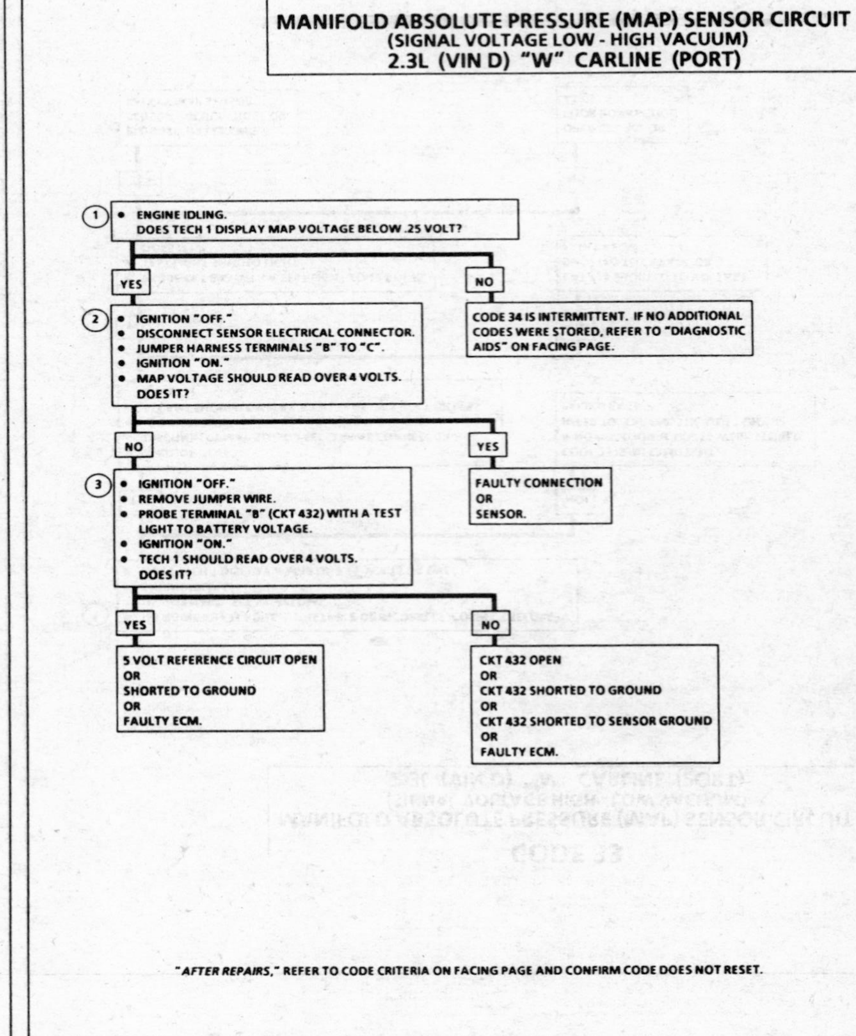

1
• ENGINE IDLING.
DOES TECH 1 DISPLAY MAP VOLTAGE BELOW .25 VOLT?
YES
NO
CODE 34 IS INTERMITTENT. IF NO ADDITIONAL CODES WERE STORED, REFER TO "DIAGNOSTIC AIDS" ON FACING PAGE.
2
• IGNITION "OFF."
• DISCONNECT SENSOR ELECTRICAL CONNECTOR.
• JUMPER HARNESS TERMINALS "B" TO "C".
• IGNITION "ON."
• MAP VOLTAGE SHOULD READ OVER 4 VOLTS.
DOES IT?
NO
YES
FAULTY CONNECTION OR SENSOR.
3
• IGNITION "OFF."
• REMOVE JUMPER WIRE.
• PROBE TERMINAL "B" (CKT 432) WITH A TEST LIGHT TO BATTERY VOLTAGE.
• IGNITION "ON."
• TECH 1 SHOULD READ OVER 4 VOLTS.
DOES IT?
YES
NO
5 VOLT REFERENCE CIRCUIT OPEN OR SHORTED TO GROUND OR FAULTY ECM.
CKT 432 OPEN OR CKT 432 SHORTED TO GROUND OR CKT 432 SHORTED TO SENSOR GROUND OR FAULTY ECM.

"AFTER REPAIRS," REFER TO CODE CRITERIA ON FACING PAGE AND CONFIRM CODE DOES NOT RESET.

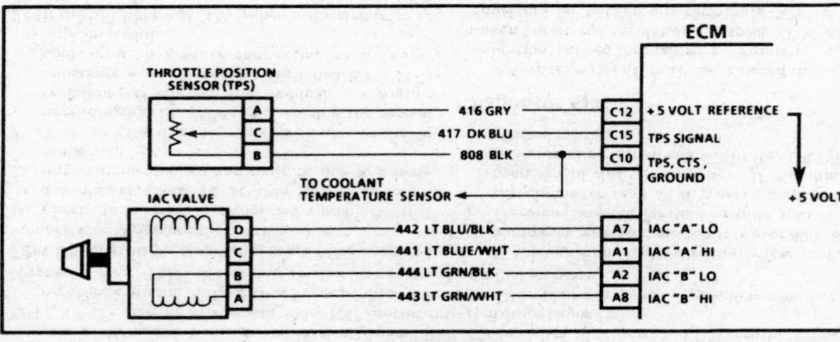
ECM
THROTTLE POSITION SENSOR (TPS)
A
C
B
416 GRY
417 DK BLU
808 BLK
C12
C15
C10
+5 VOLT REFERENCE
TPS SIGNAL
TPS, CTS, GROUND
TO COOLANT TEMPERATURE SENSOR
+5 VOLT
IAC VALVE
D
C
B
A
442 LT BLU/BLK
441 LT BLUE/WHT
444 LT GRN/BLK
443 LT GRN/WHT
A7
A1
A2
A8
IAC "A" LO
IAC "A" HI
IAC "B" LO
IAC "B" HI

CODE 35

IDLE AIR CONTROL
2.3L (VIN D) "W" CARLINE (PORT)

Circuit Description:

The ECM controls idle speed to a calculated, "desired" rpm based on sensor inputs and actual engine rpm, determined by the time between successive 2X ignition reference pulses from the ignition module. The ECM uses 4 circuits to move an Idle Air Control (IAC) valve, which allows varying amounts of air flow into the intake manifold, controlling idle speed. A detailed description of the IAC system may be found in "Fuel Metering System,"

Code 35 sets when:

- Engine speed is at least 175 rpm more or less than "desired."
- TPS voltage indicates throttle is open less than 1%.
- VSS indicates vehicle speed is less than 3 mph.
- All above conditions are continuously met for 5 seconds or more.
- IAC steps must be less than 10.

Test Description: Number(s) below refer to circled number(s) on the diagnostic chart.

1. The Tech 1 is used to extend and retract the IAC valve. Valve movement is verified by an engine speed change. If no change in engine speed occurs, the valve can be retested when removed from the throttle body.
   This step checks the quality of the IAC movement. Between 700 rpm and about 1500 rpm, the engine speed should change smoothly with each flash of the tester light in both extend and retract. If the IAC valve is retracted beyond the control range (about 1500 rpm), it may take many flashes in the extend position before engine speed will begin to drop. This is normal on certain engines, fully extending IAC may cause engine stall. This may be normal.
2. Step 1 verified proper IAC valve operation while this step checks the IAC circuits. Each lamp on the node light should flash red and green while the IAC valve is cycled. While the sequence of color is not important if either light is "OFF" or does not flash red and green, check the circuits for faults, beginning with poor terminal contacts.

Diagnostic Aids:

Check for vacuum leaks, disconnected or brittle vacuum hoses, cuts, etc. Examine manifold and throttle body gaskets for proper seal. Check for cracked intake manifold. Check open, shorts, or poor connections to IAC valve in CKTs 441, 442, 443 and 444.

Check for poor connections at ECM terminals "A1", "A2", "A7" and "A8". An open, short, or poor connection in CKTs 441, 442, 443 or 444 will result in improper idle control and may cause Code 35.

An IAC valve which is stopped and cannot respond to the ECM, a throttle stop screw which has been tampered with, or a damaged throttle body or linkage could cause Code 35. If no problem is found and code resets, replace ECM.

CODE 35

IDLE AIR CONTROL
2.3L (VIN D) "W" CARLINE (PORT)

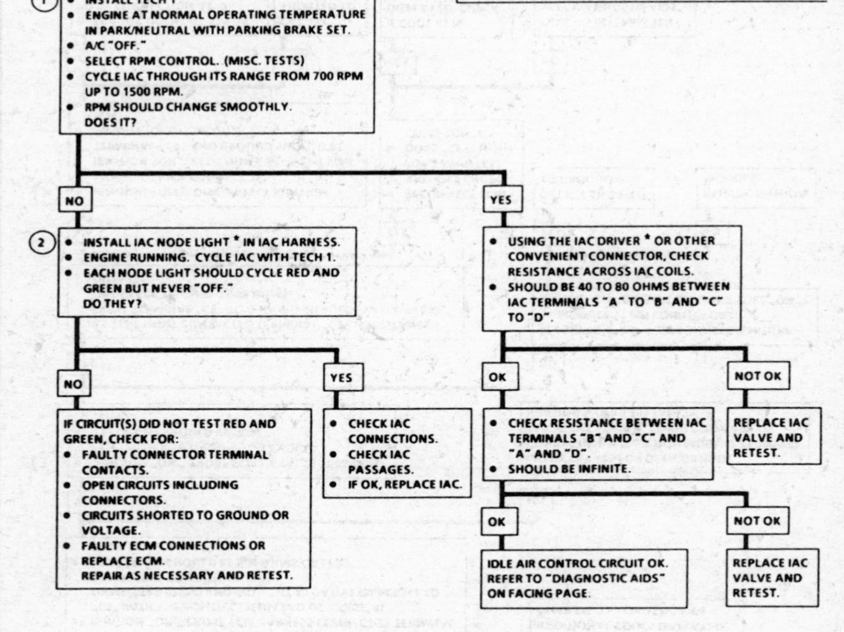
1
• INSTALL TECH 1
• ENGINE AT NORMAL OPERATING TEMPERATURE IN PARK/NEUTRAL WITH PARKING BRAKE SET.
• A/C "OFF."
• SELECT RPM CONTROL. (MISC. TESTS)
• CYCLE IAC THROUGH ITS RANGE FROM 700 RPM UP TO 1500 RPM.
• RPM SHOULD CHANGE SMOOTHLY. DOES IT?
NO
YES
2
• INSTALL IAC NODE LIGHT * IN IAC HARNESS.
• ENGINE RUNNING. CYCLE IAC WITH TECH 1.
• EACH NODE LIGHT SHOULD CYCLE RED AND GREEN BUT NEVER "OFF." DO THEY?
• USING THE IAC DRIVER * OR OTHER CONVENIENT CONNECTOR, CHECK RESISTANCE ACROSS IAC COILS.
• SHOULD BE 40 TO 80 OHMS BETWEEN IAC TERMINALS "A" TO "B" AND "C" TO "D".
NO
YES
OK
NOT OK
IF CIRCUIT(S) DID NOT TEST RED AND GREEN, CHECK FOR:
• FAULTY CONNECTOR TERMINAL CONTACTS.
• OPEN CIRCUITS INCLUDING CONNECTORS.
• CIRCUITS SHORTED TO GROUND OR VOLTAGE.
• FAULTY ECM CONNECTIONS OR REPLACE ECM.
REPAIR AS NECESSARY AND RETEST.
• CHECK IAC CONNECTIONS.
• CHECK IAC PASSAGES.
• IF OK, REPLACE IAC.
• CHECK RESISTANCE BETWEEN IAC TERMINALS "B" AND "C" AND "A" AND "D".
• SHOULD BE INFINITE.
REPLACE IAC VALVE AND RETEST.
OK
NOT OK
IDLE AIR CONTROL CIRCUIT OK. REFER TO "DIAGNOSTIC AIDS" ON FACING PAGE.
REPLACE IAC VALVE AND RETEST.

* IAC DRIVER AND NODE LIGHT REQUIRED KIT
222-L FROM: CONCEPT TECHNOLOGY, INC.
J 37027 FROM: KENT-MOORE, INC.

CLEAR CODES, CONFIRM "CLOSED LOOP" OPERATION, NO "SERVICE ENGINE SOON" LIGHT, PERFORM IAC RESET PROCEDURE PER APPLICABLE SERVICE MANUAL AND VERIFY CONTROLLED IDLE SPEED IS CORRECT.

"AFTER REPAIRS," REFER TO CODE CRITERIA ON FACING PAGE AND CONFIRM CODE DOES NOT RESET.

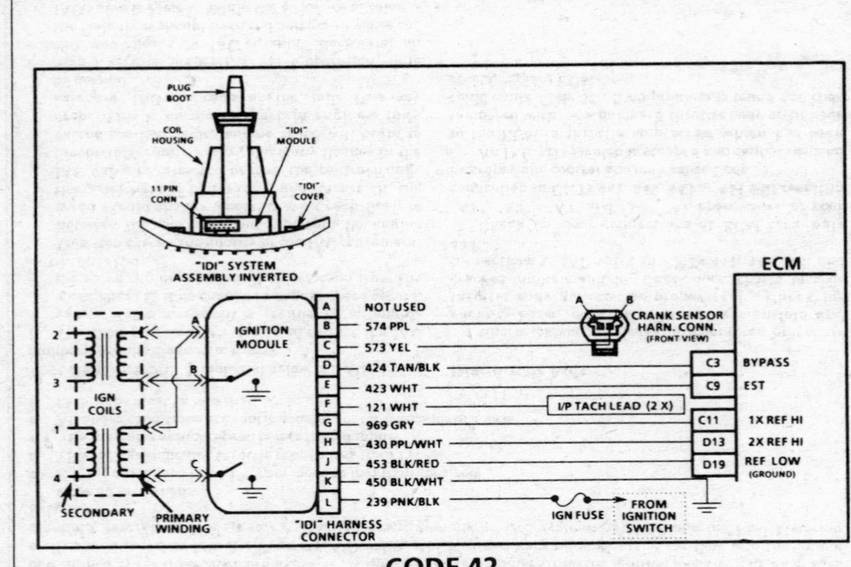
PLUG BOOT
COIL HOUSING
"IDI" MODULE
11 PIN CONN
"IDI" COVER
"IDI" SYSTEM ASSEMBLY INVERTED
IGN COILS
SECONDARY
PRIMARY WINDING
IGNITION MODULE
A NOT USED
B 574 PPL
C 573 YEL
D 424 TAN/BLK
E 423 WHT
F 121 WHT
G 969 GRY
H 430 PPL/WHT
J 453 BLK/RED
K 450 BLK/WHT
L 239 PNK/BLK
"IDI" HARNESS CONNECTOR
CRANK SENSOR HARN. CONN. (FRONT VIEW)
I/P TACH LEAD (2 X)
ECM
C3 BYPASS
C9 EST
C11 1X REF HI
D13 2X REF HI
D19 REF LOW (GROUND)
IGN FUSE
FROM IGNITION SWITCH

CODE 42

ELECTRONIC SPARK TIMING (EST) CIRCUIT 2.3L (VIN D) "W" CARLINE (PORT)

Circuit Description:

The ignition module sends a reference signal to the ECM when the engine is cranking or running. While the engine is under 700 rpm, the ignition module controls the ignition timing. When the engine speed exceeds 700 rpm, the ECM sends a 5 volts signal on the "bypass" CKT 424 to switch the timing to ECM control through the EST CKT 423. Engine will remain under EST control until rpm drops below 150.

An open or ground in the EST or "bypass" circuit will set a Code 42 and cause the engine to run on module or "bypass" timing. This will result in poor performance and poor fuel economy.

Test Description: Number(s) below refer to circled number(s) on the diagnostic chart.

1. Checks to see if ECM recognizes a problem. If it doesn't set Code 42 at this point, it is an intermittent problem and could be due to a loose connection.
2. With the ECM disconnected, the ohmmeter should be reading less than 500 ohms, which is the normal resistance of the ignition module. A higher resistance would indicate a fault in CKT 423, a poor ignition module connection or a faulty ignition module.
3. If the test light was "ON" when connected from 12 volts to ECM harness terminal "C3", either CKT 423 is shorted to ground or the ignition module is faulty.
4. Checks to see if ignition module switches when the bypass circuit is energized by 12 volts through the test light. If the ignition module actually switches, the ohmmeter reading should shift to over 8000 ohms.
5. Disconnecting the ignition module should make the ohmmeter read as if it were monitoring an open circuit (infinite reading). If the ohmmeter has a reading other than infinite, CKT 423 is shorted to ground.

Diagnostic Aids:

An intermittent may be caused by a poor connection, rubbed through wire insulation, or a wire broken inside the insulation. Inspect ECM harness connectors for backed out terminals "C3" or "C9", improper mating, broken locks, improperly formed or damaged terminals, poor terminal to wire connection, and damaged harness. A detailed description of the EST circuits operation and Code 42 causes may be found "Integrated Direct Ignition System (IDI)/EST,"

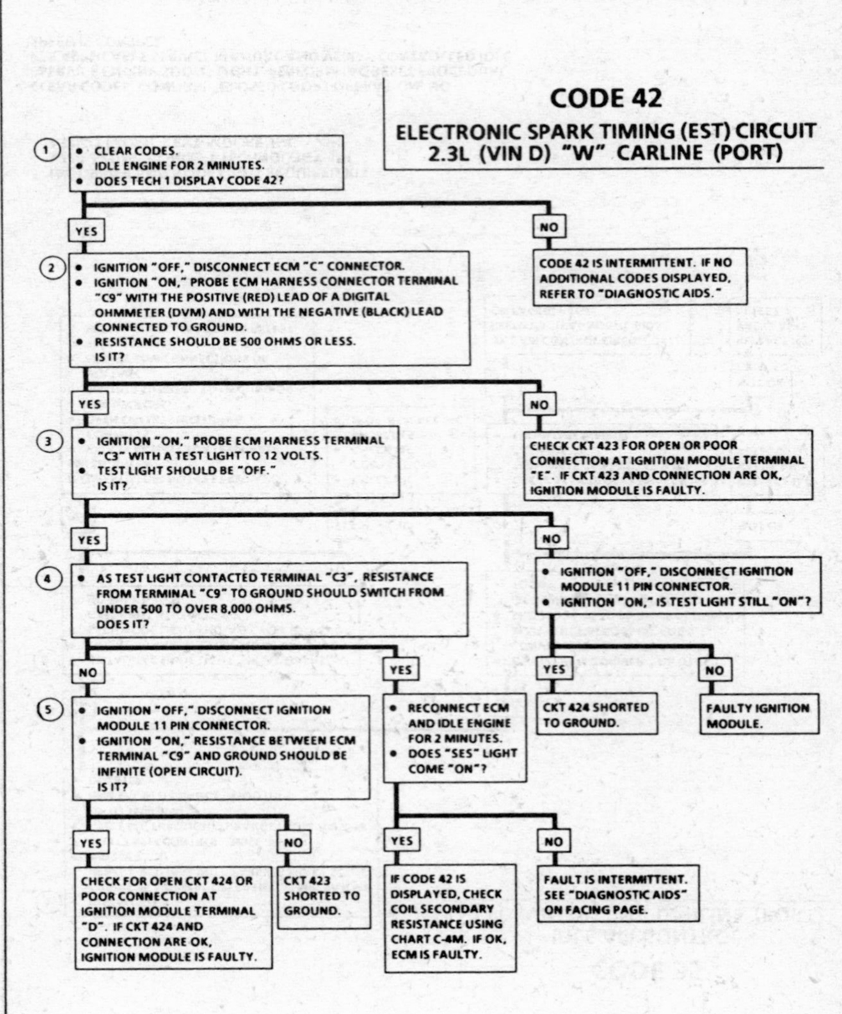
CODE 42
ELECTRONIC SPARK TIMING (EST) CIRCUIT 2.3L (VIN D) "W" CARLINE (PORT)
1 • CLEAR CODES. • IDLE ENGINE FOR 2 MINUTES. • DOES TECH 1 DISPLAY CODE 42?
YES
NO
CODE 42 IS INTERMITTENT. IF NO ADDITIONAL CODES DISPLAYED, REFER TO "DIAGNOSTIC AIDS."
2 • IGNITION "OFF," DISCONNECT ECM "C" CONNECTOR. • IGNITION "ON," PROBE ECM HARNESS CONNECTOR TERMINAL "C9" WITH THE POSITIVE (RED) LEAD OF A DIGITAL OHMMETER (DVM) AND WITH THE NEGATIVE (BLACK) LEAD CONNECTED TO GROUND. • RESISTANCE SHOULD BE 500 OHMS OR LESS. IS IT?
YES
NO
CHECK CKT 423 FOR OPEN OR POOR CONNECTION AT IGNITION MODULE TERMINAL "E". IF CKT 423 AND CONNECTION ARE OK, IGNITION MODULE IS FAULTY.
3 • IGNITION "ON," PROBE ECM HARNESS TERMINAL "C3" WITH A TEST LIGHT TO 12 VOLTS. • TEST LIGHT SHOULD BE "OFF." IS IT?
YES
NO
• IGNITION "OFF," DISCONNECT IGNITION MODULE 11 PIN CONNECTOR. • IGNITION "ON," IS TEST LIGHT STILL "ON"?
YES
CKT 424 SHORTED TO GROUND.
NO
FAULTY IGNITION MODULE.
4 • AS TEST LIGHT CONTACTED TERMINAL "C3", RESISTANCE FROM TERMINAL "C9" TO GROUND SHOULD SWITCH FROM UNDER 500 TO OVER 8,000 OHMS. DOES IT?
NO
YES
5 • IGNITION "OFF," DISCONNECT IGNITION MODULE 11 PIN CONNECTOR. • IGNITION "ON," RESISTANCE BETWEEN ECM TERMINAL "C9" AND GROUND SHOULD BE INFINITE (OPEN CIRCUIT). IS IT?
YES
CHECK FOR OPEN CKT 424 OR POOR CONNECTION AT IGNITION MODULE TERMINAL "D". IF CKT 424 AND CONNECTION ARE OK, IGNITION MODULE IS FAULTY.
NO
CKT 423 SHORTED TO GROUND.
• RECONNECT ECM AND IDLE ENGINE FOR 2 MINUTES. • DOES "SES" LIGHT COME "ON"?
YES
IF CODE 42 IS DISPLAYED, CHECK COIL SECONDARY RESISTANCE USING CHART C-4M. IF OK, ECM IS FAULTY.
NO
FAULT IS INTERMITTENT. SEE "DIAGNOSTIC AIDS" ON FACING PAGE.
"AFTER REPAIRS," REFER TO CODE CRITERIA ON FACING PAGE AND CONFIRM CODE DOES NOT RESET.

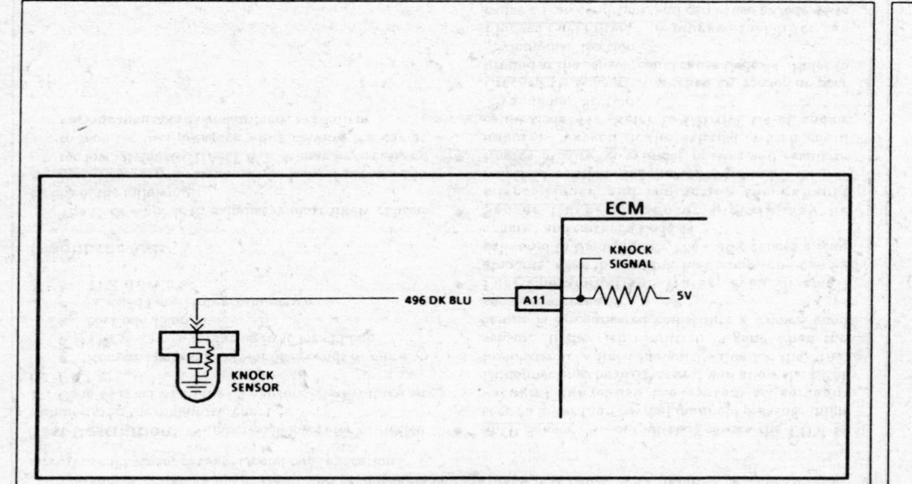

CODE 43

ELECTRONIC SPARK CONTROL (ESC) CIRCUIT 2.3L (VIN D) "W" CARLINE (PORT)

Circuit Description:

The knock sensor detects engine detonation and the ECM retards the electronic spark timing based on the signal being received. The circuitry within the knock sensor causes the ECM 5 volts to be pulled down so that, under a no knock condition, CKT 496 would measure about 2.5 volts. The knock sensor produces an AC signal which rides on the 2.5 volts DC voltage. The amplitude and signal frequency are dependent upon the knock level.

The ECM performs two tests on this circuit to determine if it is operating correctly. If either of the tests fail, a Code 43 will be set.

- If there is an indication of knock for 3.67 seconds over a 3.9 second interval with the engine running.
- If ECM terminal "A11" voltage is either above about 3.75 volts (indicating open CKT 496), or below about 1.25 volts (indicating CKT 496 is shorted to ground) for 5 seconds or more.

Test Description: Number(s) below refer to circled number(s) on the diagnostic chart.

1. If the conditions for the test, as described above, are being met, the Tech 1 "Scan" tool will always indicate "Yes" when the knock signal position is selected. If an audible knock is heard from the engine, repair the internal engine problem, because normally, no knock should be detected at idle.
2. If tapping on the engine lift hook does not produce a knock signal, try tapping engine closer to sensor before proceeding.
3. The ECM has a 5 volts signal through a pull-up resistor which should be present at the knock sensor terminal.
4. This test determines if the knock sensor is faulty or if the ESC portion of the MEM-CAL is faulty.

Diagnostic Aids:

Check CKT 496 for a potential open or short to ground.

Also check for proper installation of MEM-CAL.

Mechanical engine knock can cause a knock sensor signal. Abnormal engine noise must be corrected before using this chart.

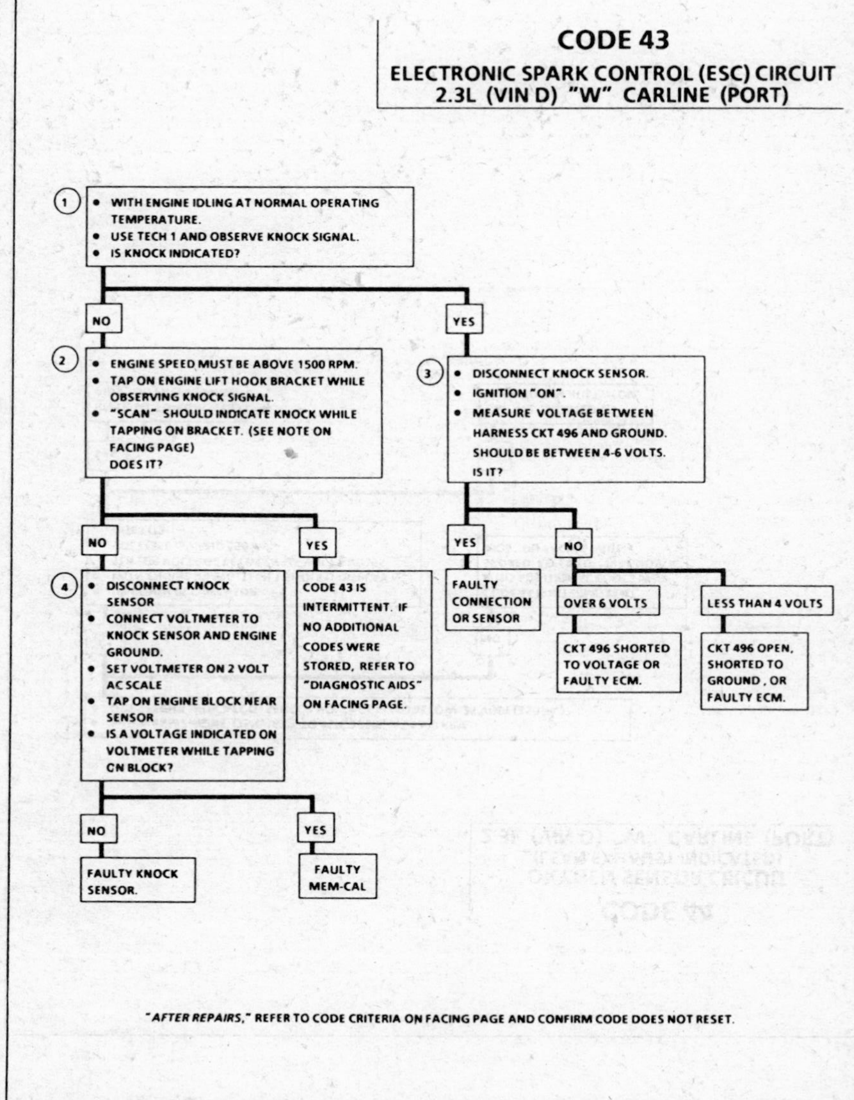

CODE 43
ELECTRONIC SPARK CONTROL (ESC) CIRCUIT
2.3L (VIN D) "W" CARLINE (PORT)
1
• WITH ENGINE IDLING AT NORMAL OPERATING TEMPERATURE.
• USE TECH 1 AND OBSERVE KNOCK SIGNAL.
• IS KNOCK INDICATED?
NO
YES
2
• ENGINE SPEED MUST BE ABOVE 1500 RPM.
• TAP ON ENGINE LIFT HOOK BRACKET WHILE OBSERVING KNOCK SIGNAL.
• "SCAN" SHOULD INDICATE KNOCK WHILE TAPPING ON BRACKET. (SEE NOTE ON FACING PAGE)
DOES IT?
3
• DISCONNECT KNOCK SENSOR.
• IGNITION "ON".
• MEASURE VOLTAGE BETWEEN HARNESS CKT 496 AND GROUND. SHOULD BE BETWEEN 4-6 VOLTS. IS IT?
NO
YES
YES
NO
4
• DISCONNECT KNOCK SENSOR
• CONNECT VOLTMETER TO KNOCK SENSOR AND ENGINE GROUND.
• SET VOLTMETER ON 2 VOLT AC SCALE
• TAP ON ENGINE BLOCK NEAR SENSOR
• IS A VOLTAGE INDICATED ON VOLTMETER WHILE TAPPING ON BLOCK?
CODE 43 IS INTERMITTENT. IF NO ADDITIONAL CODES WERE STORED, REFER TO "DIAGNOSTIC AIDS" ON FACING PAGE.
FAULTY CONNECTION OR SENSOR
OVER 6 VOLTS
LESS THAN 4 VOLTS
CKT 496 SHORTED TO VOLTAGE OR FAULTY ECM.
CKT 496 OPEN, SHORTED TO GROUND, OR FAULTY ECM.
NO
YES
FAULTY KNOCK SENSOR.
FAULTY MEM-CAL
"AFTER REPAIRS," REFER TO CODE CRITERIA ON FACING PAGE AND CONFIRM CODE DOES NOT RESET.

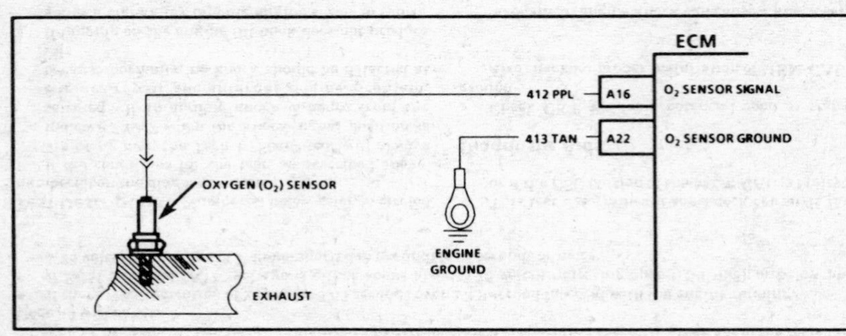
ECM
412 PPL
A16
O_2 SENSOR SIGNAL
413 TAN
A22
O_2 SENSOR GROUND
OXYGEN (O_2) SENSOR
ENGINE GROUND
EXHAUST

CODE 44

OXYGEN SENSOR CIRCUIT
(LEAN EXHAUST INDICATED)
2.3L (VIN D) "W" CARLINE (PORT)

Circuit Description:

The ECM supplies a voltage of about .45 volt between terminals "A16" and "A22". (If measured with a 10 megohm digital volt meter, this may read as low as .32 volt.) The O_2 sensor varies the voltage within a range of about 1.0 volt if the exhaust is rich, down through about .10 volt if exhaust is lean.

The sensor is like an open circuit and produces no voltage when it is below 315°C (600°F). An open sensor circuit or cold sensor causes "Open Loop" operation.

Test Description: Number(s) below refer to circled number(s) on the diagnostic chart.

1. Code 44 is set when the O_2 sensor signal voltage on CKT 412:
   - Remains below .3 volt for 50 seconds or more.
   - The system is operating in "Closed Loop."
   - No Code 33 or 34.
   - "Closed Loop" integrator active.
   - TPS above 5%.

Diagnostic Aids:

The Code 44 or lean exhaust is most likely caused by one of the following:

- Fuel Pressure System will be lean if pressure is too low. Refer to CHART A-7. It may be necessary to monitor fuel pressure while driving the car at various road speeds and/or loads to confirm.
- MAP Sensor An output that causes the ECM to sense a lower than normal manifold pressure (high vacuum) can cause the system to go lean. Disconnecting the MAP sensor will allow the ECM to substitute a fixed (default) value for the MAP sensor. If the rich condition is gone when the sensor is disconnected, substitute a known good sensor and recheck.
- Fuel Contamination Water, even in small amounts, near the in-tank fuel pump inlet can be delivered to the injector. The water causes a lean exhaust and can set a Code 44.
- Sensor Harness Sensor pigtail may be mispositioned and contacting the exhaust manifold, or otherwise shorted to ground.
- Engine Misfire A cylinder misfire will result in unburned oxygen in the exhaust, which could cause Code 44. Refer to CHART C4-M and/or "Symptoms," Section
- Cracked O_2 Sensor A cracked O_2 sensor or poor ground at the sensor, could cause Code 44. Refer to "Symptoms," Section
- Plugged Fuel Filter A plugged fuel filter can cause a lean condition, and can cause a Code 44 to set.

CODE 44

OXYGEN SENSOR CIRCUIT
(LEAN EXHAUST INDICATED)
2.3L (VIN D) "W" CARLINE (PORT)

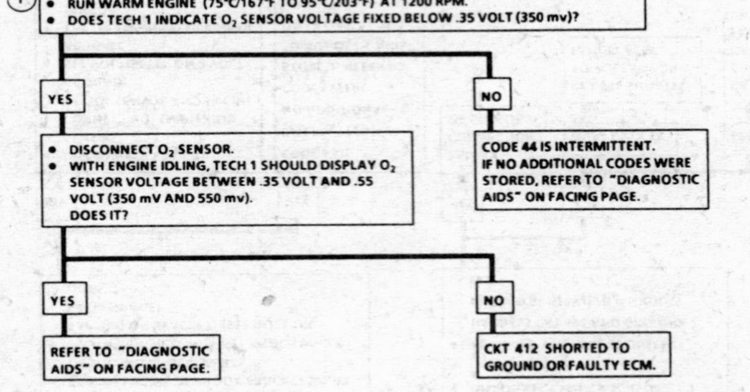
1
• RUN WARM ENGINE (75°C/167°F TO 95°C/203°F) AT 1200 RPM.
• DOES TECH 1 INDICATE O_2 SENSOR VOLTAGE FIXED BELOW .35 VOLT (350 mv)?
YES
NO
• DISCONNECT O_2 SENSOR.
• WITH ENGINE IDLING, TECH 1 SHOULD DISPLAY O_2 SENSOR VOLTAGE BETWEEN .35 VOLT AND .55 VOLT (350 mV AND 550 mv). DOES IT?
CODE 44 IS INTERMITTENT. IF NO ADDITIONAL CODES WERE STORED, REFER TO "DIAGNOSTIC AIDS" ON FACING PAGE.
YES
NO
REFER TO "DIAGNOSTIC AIDS" ON FACING PAGE.
CKT 412 SHORTED TO GROUND OR FAULTY ECM.

"AFTER REPAIRS," REFER TO CODE CRITERIA ON FACING PAGE AND CONFIRM CODE DOES NOT RESET.

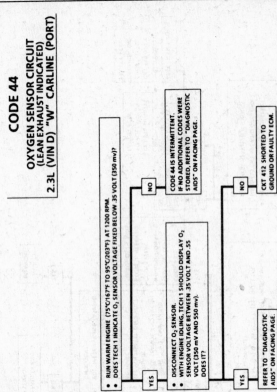

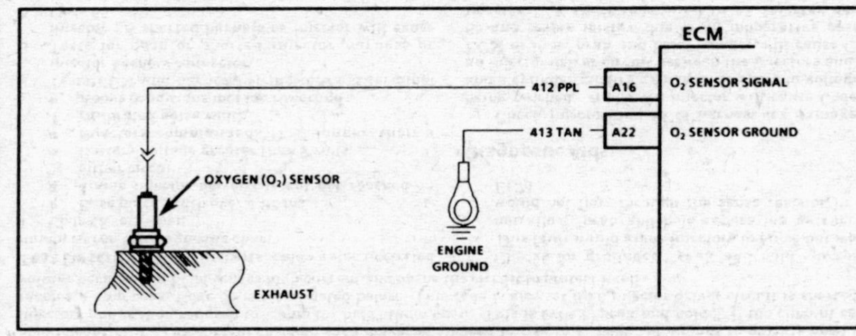
ECM
412 PPL
A16
O_2 SENSOR SIGNAL
413 TAN
A22
O_2 SENSOR GROUND
OXYGEN (O_2) SENSOR
ENGINE GROUND
EXHAUST

CODE 45

OXYGEN SENSOR CIRCUIT
(RICH EXHAUST INDICATED)
2.3L (VIN D) "W" CARLINE (PORT)

Circuit Description:

The ECM supplies a voltage of about .45 volt between terminals "A16" and "A22". (If measured with a 10 megohm digital voltmeter, this may read as low as .32 volt.) The O_2 sensor varies the voltage within a range of about 1.0 volt if the exhaust is rich, down through about .10 volt if exhaust is lean.

The sensor is like an open circuit and produces no voltage when it is below 315°C (600°F). An open sensor circuit or cold sensor causes "Open Loop" operation.

Test Description: Number(s) below refer to circled number(s) on the diagnostic chart.

1. Code 45 is set when:
   - O_2 voltage is above .75 volt.
   - No Code 33 or 34.
   - Fuel system in "Closed Loop."
   - TPS above 5%
   - Above conditions met for 30 seconds or over 1 volt for 5 seconds.

Diagnostic Aids:

The Code 45 or rich exhaust is most likely caused by one of the following:

- Fuel Pressure System will go rich if pressure is too high. The ECM can compensate for some increase. However, if it gets too high, a Code 45 will be set. See "Fuel System Diagnosis," CHART A-7.
- Leaking Injector See CHART A-7.
- HEI Shielding An open ground CKT 453 may result in EMI or induced electrical noise. The ECM looks at this noise as reference pulses. The additional pulses result in a higher than actual engine speed signal. The ECM then delivers too much fuel causing system to go rich. Engine tachometer will also show higher than actual engine speed which can help in diagnosing this problem.
- Canister Purge Check for fuel saturation. If full of fuel, check canister control and hoses. See "Canister Purge,"
- MAP Sensor An output that causes the ECM to sense a higher than normal manifold pressure (low vacuum) can cause the system to go rich. Disconnecting the MAP sensor will allow the ECM to set a fixed value for the MAP sensor. Substitute a different MAP sensor if the rich condition is gone while the sensor is disconnected.
- Pressure Regulator Check for leaking fuel pressure regulator diaphragm by checking for the presence of liquid fuel in the vacuum line to the regulator.
- TPS An intermittent TPS output will cause the system to go rich due to a false indication of the throttle being opened.
- O_2 Sensor Contamination Inspect oxygen sensor for silicone contamination from fuel or use of improper RTV sealant. The sensor may have a white powdery coating and result in a high but false signal voltage (rich exhaust indication). The ECM will then reduce the amount of fuel delivered to the engine causing a severe surge driveability problem.

CODE 45

OXYGEN SENSOR CIRCUIT
(RICH EXHAUST INDICATED)
2.3L (VIN D) "W" CARLINE (PORT)

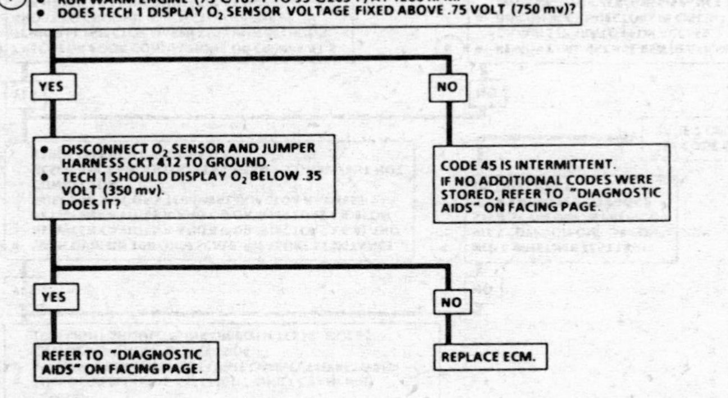
1
• RUN WARM ENGINE (75°C/167°F TO 95°C/203°F) AT 1200 RPM.
• DOES TECH 1 DISPLAY O_2 SENSOR VOLTAGE FIXED ABOVE .75 VOLT (750 mv)?
YES
NO
• DISCONNECT O_2 SENSOR AND JUMPER HARNESS CKT 412 TO GROUND.
• TECH 1 SHOULD DISPLAY O_2 BELOW .35 VOLT (350 mv).
DOES IT?
CODE 45 IS INTERMITTENT.
IF NO ADDITIONAL CODES WERE STORED, REFER TO "DIAGNOSTIC AIDS" ON FACING PAGE.
YES
NO
REFER TO "DIAGNOSTIC AIDS" ON FACING PAGE.
REPLACE ECM.

CODE 51

MEM-CAL ERROR
(FAULTY OR INCORRECT MEM-CAL)
2.3L (VIN D) "W" CARLINE (PORT)

CHECK THAT ALL PINS ARE FULLY INSERTED IN THE SOCKET AND THAT MEM-CAL IS PROPERLY LATCHED. IF OK, REPLACE MEM-CAL, CLEAR MEMORY, AND RECHECK. IF CODE 51 REAPPEARS, REPLACE ECM.

NOTICE: TO PREVENT POSSIBLE ELECTROSTATIC DISCHARGE DAMAGE TO THE ECM OR MEM-CAL, DO NOT TOUCH THE COMPONENT LEADS, AND DO NOT REMOVE THE MEM CAL COVER OR THE INTEGRATED CIRCUIT FROM CARRIER.

"AFTER REPAIRS," REFER TO CODE CRITERIA ON FACING PAGE AND CONFIRM CODE DOES NOT RESET.

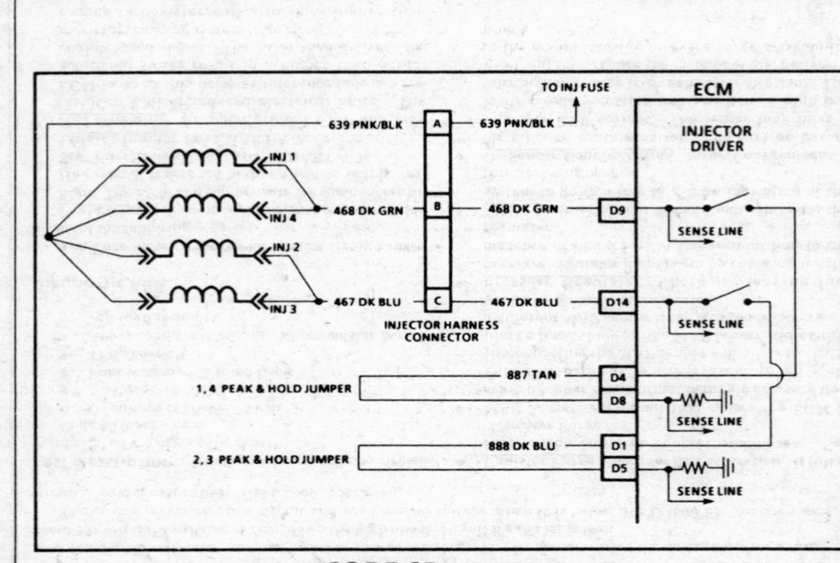

CODE 65 (Page 1 of 2)

FUEL INJECTOR CIRCUIT (LOW CURRENT)
2.3L (VIN D) "W" CARLINE (PORT)

Circuit Description:

The ECM has two injector driver circuits, each of which controls a pair of injectors (1 and 4 or 2 and 3). The ECM monitors the current in each driver circuit by measuring voltage drop through a fixed, sense resistor and is able to control it. The current through each driver is allowed to rise to a "peak" of 4 amps to quickly open the injectors and is then reduced to 1 amp to "hold" them open. This is called "peak and hold." If the current can't reach a 4 amp peak, Code 65 is set as noted below. This code is also set if an injector driver circuit is shorted to voltage because the ECM senses high current and opens the circuit to protect itself.

Test Description: Number(s) below refer to circled number(s) on the diagnostic chart.

1. Code 65 sets when:
   - Base pulse width over 1.98 ms.
   - 4 amp injector driver current not reached on either circuit.
   - Battery voltage greater than 9 volts.
   - Injectors commanded "ON" longer than a calibrated pulse width.
   - Above conditions met for 10 seconds.
2. Tests ECM and harness wiring to the 3 terminal injector harness connector.
3. Tests for open or shorted injector harness or injector. A shorted harness or injector will cause Code 65.
4. Results of Step 2 will determine which branch to follow on Page 2.
5. Checks remainder of circuit from injectors to ECM as both harnesses were confirmed OK in Steps 2 and 3.
6. Determines cause of high resistance found in Step 3. A shorted injector will cause a Code 65.
7. Checks for grounded "peak and hold" jumpers. This fault would allow injectors to pulse but would not allow "peak and hold" operation as current would not flow through the sense resistor in the ECM.

Diagnostic Aids:

Check injector and ECM harness for damage or being pinched. A shorted injector will cause Code 65 and a cylinder misfire. An open or short to voltage in an injector driver circuit between the injectors and the ECM or in a "peak and hold" jumper will cause Code 65 and severe misfire due to an inoperative pair of injectors. A short to ground in an injector driver circuit between the injectors and the ECM will also cause Code 65 and severe misfire due to a pair of injectors being open continuously. However, a short to ground in a "peak and hold" jumper will cause Code 65 with <u>no</u> noticeable effect on engine performance. An intermittent problem must be continuously present for at least 10 seconds to set Code 65.

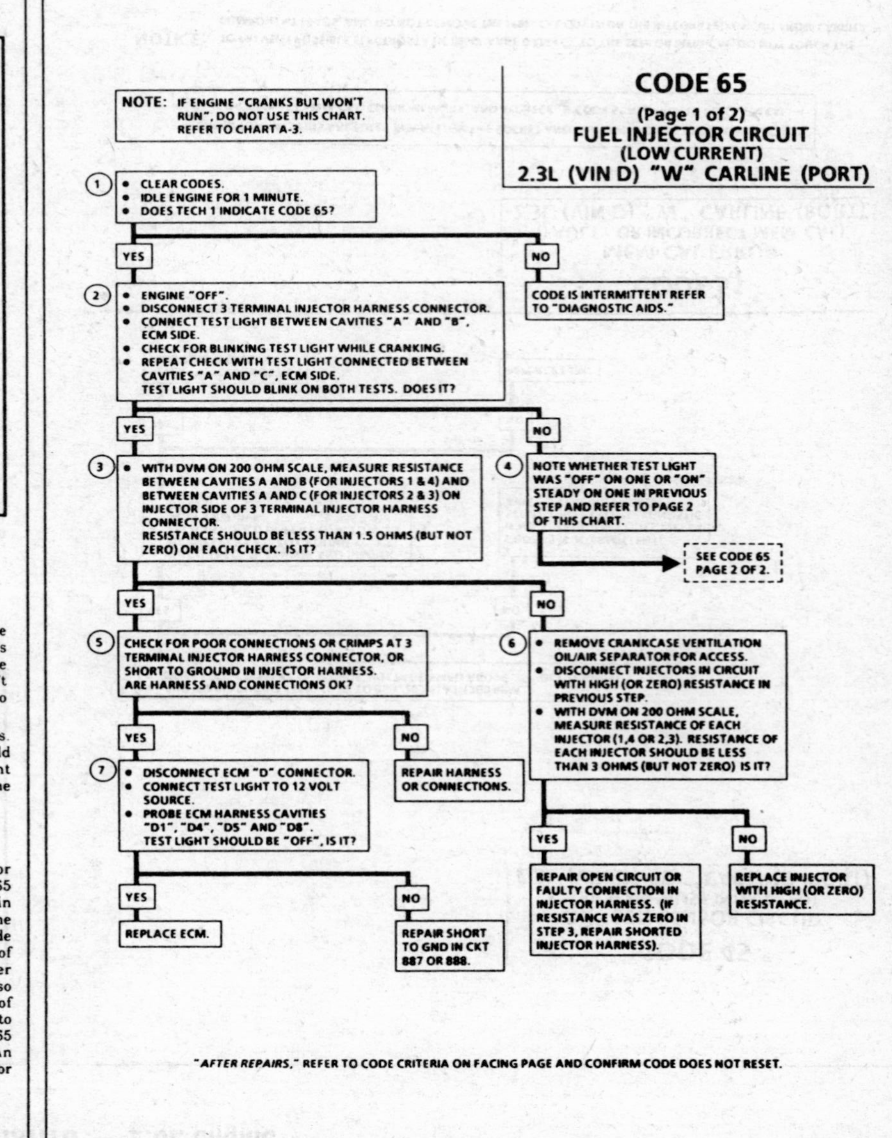

TO INJ FUSE
ECM
INJECTOR DRIVER
639 PNK/BLK — A — 639 PNK/BLK
INJ 1
INJ 4
468 DK GRN — B — 468 DK GRN — D9
SENSE LINE
INJ 2
INJ 3
467 DK BLU — C — 467 DK BLU — D14
SENSE LINE
INJECTOR HARNESS CONNECTOR
1, 4 PEAK & HOLD JUMPER — 887 TAN — D4 / D8
SENSE LINE
2, 3 PEAK & HOLD JUMPER — 888 DK BLU — D1 / D5
SENSE LINE

CODE 65

(Page 2 of 2)
FUEL INJECTOR CIRCUIT
(LOW CURRENT)
2.3L (VIN D) "W" CARLINE (PORT)

Circuit Description:

The ECM has two injector driver circuits, each of which controls a pair of injectors (1 and 4 or 2 and 3). The ECM monitors the current in each driver circuit by measuring voltage drop through a fixed resistor and is able to control it. The current through each driver is allowed to rise to a "peak" of 4 amps to quickly open the injectors and is then reduced to 1 amp to "hold" them open. This is called "peak and hold." If the current can't reach a 4 amp peak, Code 65 is set. This code is also set if an injector driver circuit is shorted to voltage.

Test Description: Number(s) below refer to circled number(s) on the diagnostic chart.

8. This checks for short to voltage in injector driver circuits.
9. Determines whether injector driver CKTs 467 and 468 are shorted to ground.
10. This determines if problem is CKT 467 or 468 or poor connection at ECM.
11. Checks for good continuity of "peak and hold" jumpers CKTs 887 and 888.

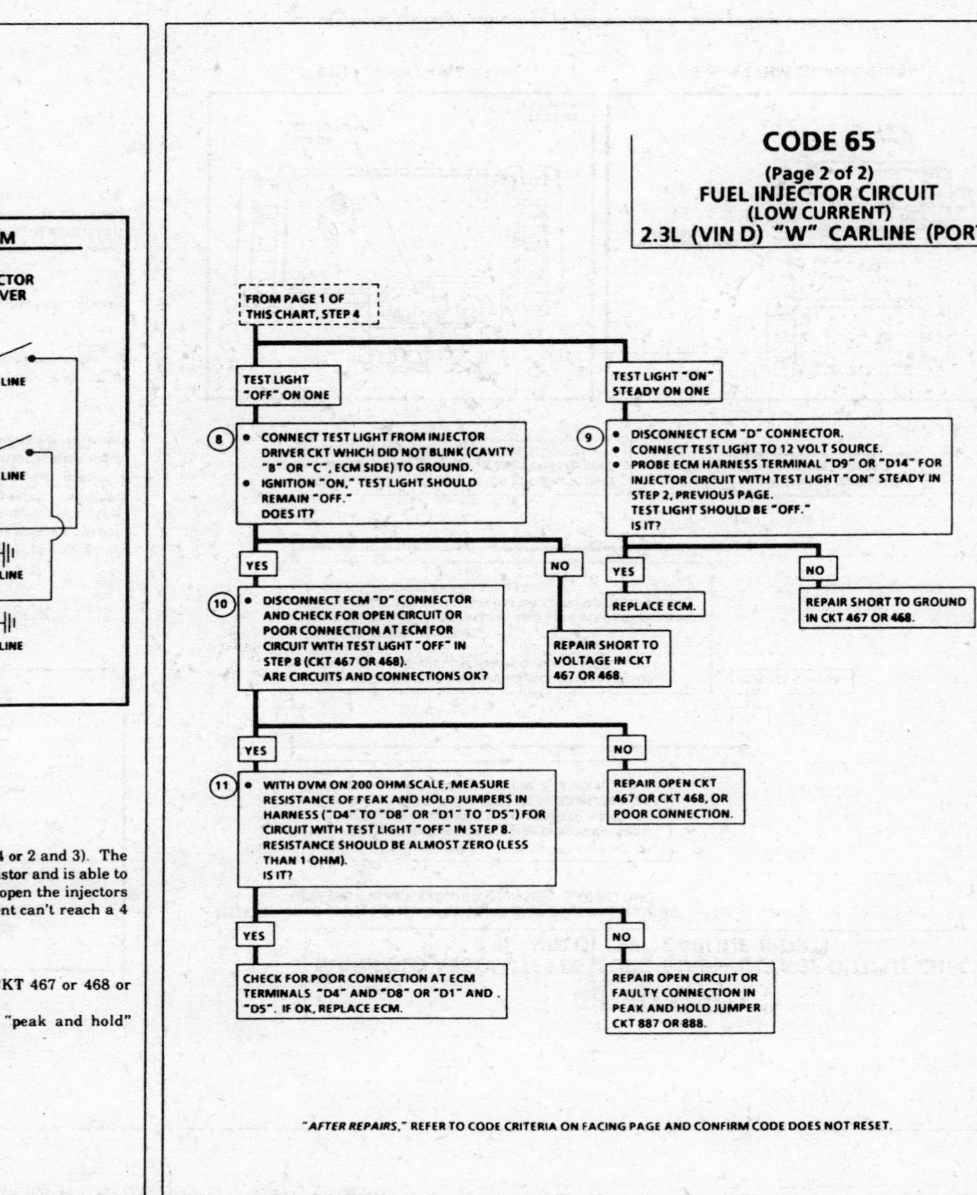

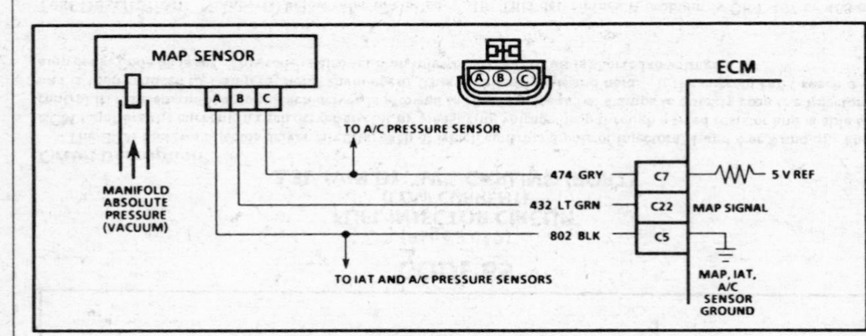

MAP SENSOR
A B C
MANIFOLD ABSOLUTE PRESSURE (VACUUM)
TO A/C PRESSURE SENSOR
474 GRY
432 LT GRN
802 BLK
TO IAT AND A/C PRESSURE SENSORS
ECM
C7
C22
C5
5 V REF
MAP SIGNAL
MAP, IAT, A/C SENSOR GROUND

CHART C-1D

MANIFOLD ABSOLUTE PRESSURE (MAP) VOLTAGE OUTPUT CHECK 2.3L (VIN D) "W" CARLINE (PORT)

Circuit Description:

The Manifold Absolute Pressure (MAP) sensor measures the changes in the intake manifold pressure which result from engine load (intake manifold vacuum) and rpm changes; and converts these into a voltage output. The ECM sends a 5 volts reference voltage to the MAP sensor. As the manifold pressure changed, the output voltage of the sensor also changes. By monitoring the sensor output voltage, the ECM knows the manifold pressure. A lower pressure (low voltage) output voltage will be about 1 - 2 volts at idle. While higher pressure (high voltage) output voltage will be about 4 - 4.8 at Wide Open Throttle (WOT). The MAP sensor is also used, under certain conditions, to measure barometric pressure, allowing the ECM to make adjustments for different altitudes. The ECM uses the MAP sensor to control fuel delivery and ignition timing.

Test Description: Number(s) below refer to circled number(s) on the diagnostic chart.

Important

- Be sure to use the same diagnostic test equipment for all measurements.

1. When comparing "Scan" readings to a known good vehicle, it is important to compare vehicles that use a MAP sensor having the same color insert or having the same "Hot Stamped" number. See figures on facing page.
2. Applying 34 kPa (10" Hg) vacuum to the MAP sensor should cause the voltage to change. Subtract second reading from the first. Voltage value should be greater than 1.5 volts. Upon applying vacuum to the sensor, the change in voltage should be instantaneous. A slow voltage change indicates a faulty sensor.
3. Check vacuum hose to sensor for leaking or restriction. Be sure that no other vacuum devices are connected to the MAP hose.

   NOTE: Make sure electrical connector remains securely fastened.

4. Disconnect sensor from bracket and twist sensor by hand (only) to check for intermittent connection. Output changes greater than .1 volt indicate a bad connector or connection. If OK, replace sensor.

CHART C-1D

MANIFOLD ABSOLUTE PRESSURE (MAP) VOLTAGE OUTPUT CHECK 2.3L (VIN D) "W" CARLINE (PORT)

NOTE: THIS CHART ONLY APPLIES TO MAP SENSORS HAVING GREEN OR BLACK COLOR KEY INSERT (SEE BELOW).

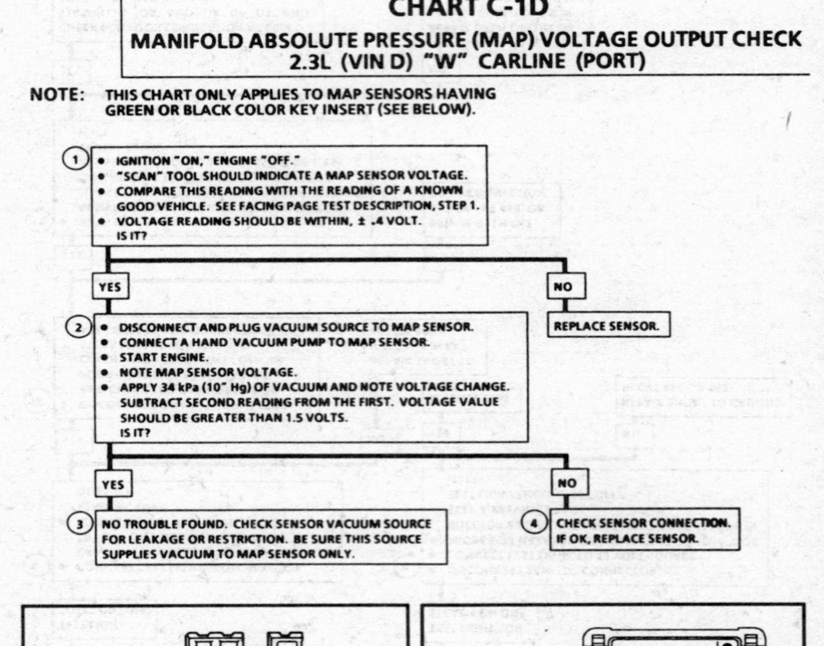

1
• IGNITION "ON," ENGINE "OFF."
• "SCAN" TOOL SHOULD INDICATE A MAP SENSOR VOLTAGE.
• COMPARE THIS READING WITH THE READING OF A KNOWN GOOD VEHICLE. SEE FACING PAGE TEST DESCRIPTION, STEP 1.
• VOLTAGE READING SHOULD BE WITHIN, ± .4 VOLT. IS IT?
YES
NO
REPLACE SENSOR.
2
• DISCONNECT AND PLUG VACUUM SOURCE TO MAP SENSOR.
• CONNECT A HAND VACUUM PUMP TO MAP SENSOR.
• START ENGINE.
• NOTE MAP SENSOR VOLTAGE.
• APPLY 34 kPa (10" Hg) OF VACUUM AND NOTE VOLTAGE CHANGE. SUBTRACT SECOND READING FROM THE FIRST. VOLTAGE VALUE SHOULD BE GREATER THAN 1.5 VOLTS. IS IT?
YES
NO
3
NO TROUBLE FOUND. CHECK SENSOR VACUUM SOURCE FOR LEAKAGE OR RESTRICTION. BE SURE THIS SOURCE SUPPLIES VACUUM TO MAP SENSOR ONLY.
4
CHECK SENSOR CONNECTION. IF OK, REPLACE SENSOR.

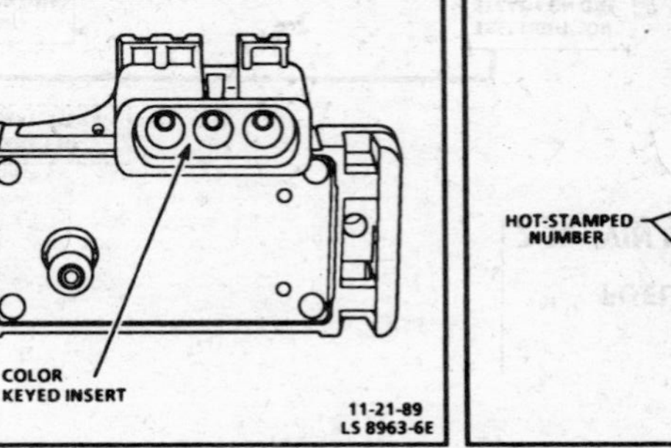

COLOR KEYED INSERT
11-21-89
LS 8963-6E

Figure 1 - Color Key Insert

Figure 2 - Hot-Stamped Number

"*AFTER REPAIRS*," CONFIRM "CLOSED LOOP" OPERATION AND NO "SERVICE ENGINE SOON" LIGHT.

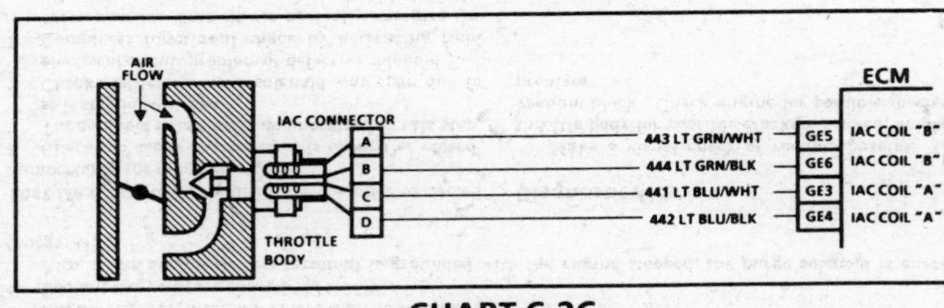
AIR FLOW
IAC CONNECTOR
A
B
C
D
THROTTLE BODY
443 LT GRN/WHT
444 LT GRN/BLK
441 LT BLU/WHT
442 LT BLU/BLK
ECM
GE5 IAC COIL "B" HI
GE6 IAC COIL "B" LO
GE3 IAC COIL "A" HI
GE4 IAC COIL "A" LO

CHART C-2C

IDLE AIR CONTROL (IAC) VALVE CHECK 2.3L (VIN D) "W" CARLINE (PORT)

Circuit Description:

The ECM controls idle rpm with the IAC valve. To increase idle rpm, the ECM moves the IAC valve out, allowing more air to bypass the throttle plate. To decrease rpm, it moves the IAC valve in, reducing air flow by-passing the throttle plate. A Tech 1 will read the ECM commands to the IAC valve in counts. The higher the counts, the more air allowed (higher idle). The lower the counts, the less air allowed (lower idle).

Test Description: Number(s) below refer to circled number(s) on the diagnostic chart.

1. The Tech 1 is used to extend and retract the IAC valve. Valve movement is verified by an engine speed change. If no change in engine speed occurs, the valve can be retested when removed from the throttle body.
   This step checks the quality of the IAC movement. Between 700 rpm and about 1500 rpm, the engine speed should change smoothly with each flash of the tester light in both extend and retract. If the IAC valve is retracted beyond the control range (about 1500 rpm), it may take many flashes in the extend position before engine speed will begin to drop. This is normal on certain engines, fully extending IAC may cause engine stall. This may be normal.
2. Step 1 verified proper IAC valve operation while this step checks IAC circuits. Each lamp on the node light should flash red and green while the IAC valve is cycled. While the sequence of color is not important if either light is "OFF" or does not flash red and green, check the circuits for faults, beginning with poor terminal contacts.

Diagnostic Aids:

A slow, unstable, or fast idle may be caused by a non-IAC system problem that cannot be overcome by the IAC valve. Out of control range IAC "Scan" tool counts will be above 60 if idle is too low, and zero counts if idle is too high. The following checks should be made to repair a non-IAC system problem.

- Vacuum Leak (High Idle) - If idle is too high, stop the engine. Fully extend (low) IAC with tester. Start engine. If Idle speed is above 800 rpm, locate and correct vacuum leak including CV system. Also check for binding of throttle blade or linkage.
- System too lean (High Air/Fuel Ratio) - Idle speed may be too high or too low. Engine speed may vary up and down and disconnecting IAC does not help. Code 44 may be set. "Scan" O_2 voltage will be less than 300 mV (.3 volt.) Check for low regulated fuel pressure, water in the fuel or a restricted injector.
- System too rich (Low Air/Fuel Ratio) - The idle speed will be too low. "Scan" tool IAC counts will usually be above 80. System is obviously rich and may exhibit black smoke exhaust.
  "Scan" tool O_2 voltage will be fixed above 800 mV (.8 volt). Check for high fuel pressure, leaking or sticking injector. Silicone contaminated O_2 sensor will "Scan" an O_2 voltage slow to respond.
- Throttle Body - Remove IAC and inspect bore for foreign material.
- Refer to "Rough, Unstable, Incorrect Idle or Stalling" in "Symptoms," Section
- If intermittent poor driveability or idle symptoms are resolved by disconnecting the IAC, carefully recheck connections, valve terminal resistance, or replace IAC.

CHART C-2C

IDLE AIR CONTROL (IAC) VALVE CHECK 2.3L (VIN D) "W" CARLINE (PORT)

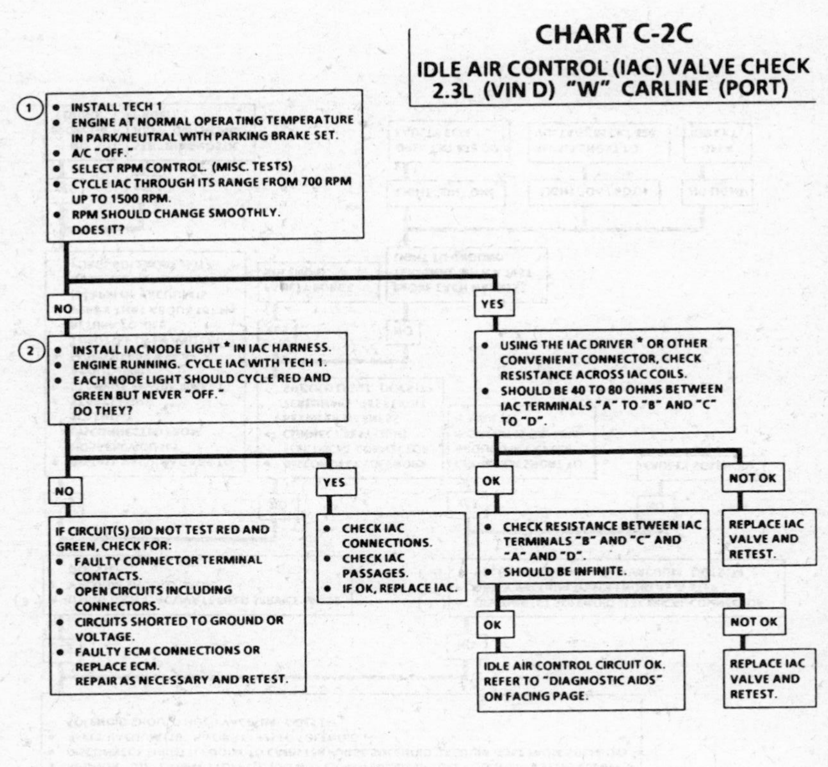
1
• INSTALL TECH 1
• ENGINE AT NORMAL OPERATING TEMPERATURE IN PARK/NEUTRAL WITH PARKING BRAKE SET.
• A/C "OFF."
• SELECT RPM CONTROL (MISC. TESTS)
• CYCLE IAC THROUGH ITS RANGE FROM 700 RPM UP TO 1500 RPM.
• RPM SHOULD CHANGE SMOOTHLY.
DOES IT?
NO
YES
2
• INSTALL IAC NODE LIGHT * IN IAC HARNESS.
• ENGINE RUNNING. CYCLE IAC WITH TECH 1.
• EACH NODE LIGHT SHOULD CYCLE RED AND GREEN BUT NEVER "OFF."
DO THEY?
• USING THE IAC DRIVER * OR OTHER CONVENIENT CONNECTOR, CHECK RESISTANCE ACROSS IAC COILS.
• SHOULD BE 40 TO 80 OHMS BETWEEN IAC TERMINALS "A" TO "B" AND "C" TO "D".
NO
YES
OK
NOT OK
IF CIRCUIT(S) DID NOT TEST RED AND GREEN, CHECK FOR:
• FAULTY CONNECTOR TERMINAL CONTACTS.
• OPEN CIRCUITS INCLUDING CONNECTORS.
• CIRCUITS SHORTED TO GROUND OR VOLTAGE.
• FAULTY ECM CONNECTIONS OR REPLACE ECM.
REPAIR AS NECESSARY AND RETEST.
• CHECK IAC CONNECTIONS.
• CHECK IAC PASSAGES.
• IF OK, REPLACE IAC.
• CHECK RESISTANCE BETWEEN IAC TERMINALS "B" AND "C" AND "A" AND "D".
• SHOULD BE INFINITE.
REPLACE IAC VALVE AND RETEST.
OK
NOT OK
IDLE AIR CONTROL CIRCUIT OK. REFER TO "DIAGNOSTIC AIDS" ON FACING PAGE.
REPLACE IAC VALVE AND RETEST.

* IAC DRIVER AND NODE LIGHT REQUIRED KIT
222-L FROM: CONCEPT TECHNOLOGY, INC.
J 37027 FROM: KENT-MOORE, INC.

CLEAR CODES, CONFIRM "CLOSED LOOP" OPERATION, NO "SERVICE ENGINE SOON" LIGHT, PERFORM IAC RESET PROCEDURE PER APPLICABLE SERVICE MANUAL AND VERIFY CONTROLLED IDLE SPEED IS CORRECT.

"*AFTER REPAIRS,*" CONFIRM "CLOSED LOOP" OPERATION AND NO "SERVICE ENGINE SOON" LIGHT.

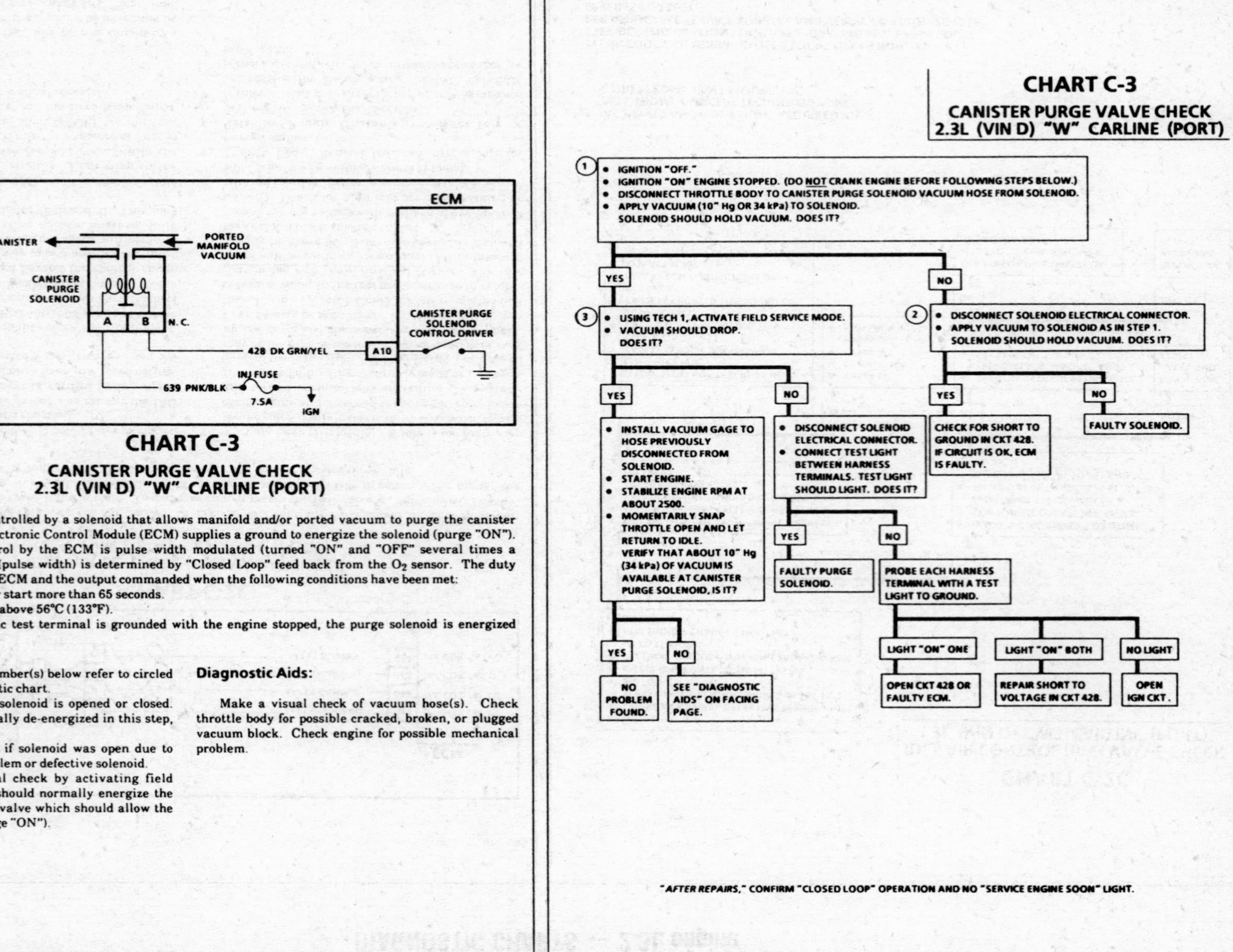

ECM
TO CANISTER
PORTED MANIFOLD VACUUM
CANISTER PURGE SOLENOID
A
B
N.C.
CANISTER PURGE SOLENOID CONTROL DRIVER
428 DK GRN/YEL
A10
INJ FUSE
639 PNK/BLK
7.5A
IGN
CHART C-3
CANISTER PURGE VALVE CHECK
2.3L (VIN D) "W" CARLINE (PORT)
1
• IGNITION "OFF."
• IGNITION "ON" ENGINE STOPPED. (DO NOT CRANK ENGINE BEFORE FOLLOWING STEPS BELOW.)
• DISCONNECT THROTTLE BODY TO CANISTER PURGE SOLENOID VACUUM HOSE FROM SOLENOID.
• APPLY VACUUM (10" Hg OR 34 kPa) TO SOLENOID.
SOLENOID SHOULD HOLD VACUUM. DOES IT?
YES
NO
3
• USING TECH 1, ACTIVATE FIELD SERVICE MODE.
• VACUUM SHOULD DROP.
DOES IT?
2
• DISCONNECT SOLENOID ELECTRICAL CONNECTOR.
• APPLY VACUUM TO SOLENOID AS IN STEP 1.
SOLENOID SHOULD HOLD VACUUM. DOES IT?
YES
NO
YES
NO
• INSTALL VACUUM GAGE TO HOSE PREVIOUSLY DISCONNECTED FROM SOLENOID.
• START ENGINE.
• STABILIZE ENGINE RPM AT ABOUT 2500.
• MOMENTARILY SNAP THROTTLE OPEN AND LET RETURN TO IDLE.
VERIFY THAT ABOUT 10" Hg (34 kPa) OF VACUUM IS AVAILABLE AT CANISTER PURGE SOLENOID, IS IT?
• DISCONNECT SOLENOID ELECTRICAL CONNECTOR.
• CONNECT TEST LIGHT BETWEEN HARNESS TERMINALS. TEST LIGHT SHOULD LIGHT. DOES IT?
CHECK FOR SHORT TO GROUND IN CKT 428. IF CIRCUIT IS OK, ECM IS FAULTY.
FAULTY SOLENOID.
YES
NO
FAULTY PURGE SOLENOID.
PROBE EACH HARNESS TERMINAL WITH A TEST LIGHT TO GROUND.
YES
NO
NO PROBLEM FOUND.
SEE "DIAGNOSTIC AIDS" ON FACING PAGE.
LIGHT "ON" ONE
LIGHT "ON" BOTH
NO LIGHT
OPEN CKT 428 OR FAULTY ECM.
REPAIR SHORT TO VOLTAGE IN CKT 428.
OPEN IGN CKT.
"AFTER REPAIRS," CONFIRM "CLOSED LOOP" OPERATION AND NO "SERVICE ENGINE SOON" LIGHT.

CHART C-3

CANISTER PURGE VALVE CHECK
2.3L (VIN D) "W" CARLINE (PORT)

Circuit Description:

Canister purge is controlled by a solenoid that allows manifold and/or ported vacuum to purge the canister when energized. The Electronic Control Module (ECM) supplies a ground to energize the solenoid (purge "ON"). The purge solenoid control by the ECM is pulse width modulated (turned "ON" and "OFF" several times a second). The duty cycle (pulse width) is determined by "Closed Loop" feed back from the O_2 sensor. The duty cycle is calculated by the ECM and the output commanded when the following conditions have been met:

- Engine run time after start more than 65 seconds.
- Coolant temperature above 56°C (133°F).

Also, if the diagnostic test terminal is grounded with the engine stopped, the purge solenoid is energized (purge "ON").

Test Description: Number(s) below refer to circled number(s) on the diagnostic chart.

1. Checks to see if the solenoid is opened or closed. The solenoid is normally de-energized in this step, so it should be closed.
2. Checks to determine if solenoid was open due to electrical circuit problem or defective solenoid.
3. Completes functional check by activating field service mode. This should normally energize the solenoid opening the valve which should allow the vacuum to drop (purge "ON").

Diagnostic Aids:

Make a visual check of vacuum hose(s). Check throttle body for possible cracked, broken, or plugged vacuum block. Check engine for possible mechanical problem.

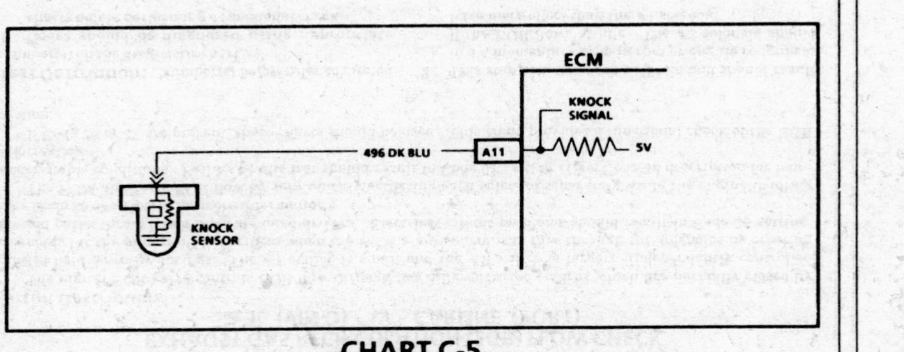
ECM
KNOCK SIGNAL
496 DK BLU
A11
5V
KNOCK SENSOR

CHART C-5

ELECTRONIC SPARK CONTROL (ESC) SYSTEM CHECK
2.3L (VIN D) "W" CARLINE (PORT)

Circuit Description:

The knock sensor is used to detect engine detonation and the ECM will retard the electronic spark timing based on the signal being received. The circuitry within the knock sensor causes the ECMs 5 volts to be pulled down so that CKT 496 would measure about 2.5 volts. The knock sensor produces an AC signal which rides on the 2.5 volts DC voltage. The amplitude and frequency are dependent upon the knock level.

The MEM-CAL used with this engine contains the functions which were part of remotely mounted ESC modules used on other GM vehicles. The ESC portion of the MEM-CAL then sends a signal to other parts of the ECM which adjusts the spark timing to retard the spark and reduce the detonation.

Test Description: Number(s) below refer to circled number(s) on the diagnostic chart.

1. With engine idling, there should not be a knock signal present at the ECM because detonation is not likely under a no load condition.
2. Tapping on the engine lift hook bracket should simulate a knock signal to determine if the sensor is capable of detecting detonation. If no knock is detected, try tapping on engine block closer to sensor before replacing sensor.
3. If the engine has an internal problem which is creating a knock, the knock sensor may be responding to the internal failure.
4. This test determines if the knock sensor is faulty or if the ESC portion of the MEM-CAL is faulty. If it is determined that the MEM-CAL is faulty, be sure that is is properly installed and latched into place. If not properly installed, repair and retest.

Diagnostic Aids:

While observing knock signal on the Tech 1, there should be an indication that knock is present when detonation can be heard. Detonation is most likely to occur under high engine load conditions.

CHART C-5

ELECTRONIC SPARK CONTROL (ESC) SYSTEM CHECK
2.3L (VIN D) "W" CARLINE (PORT)

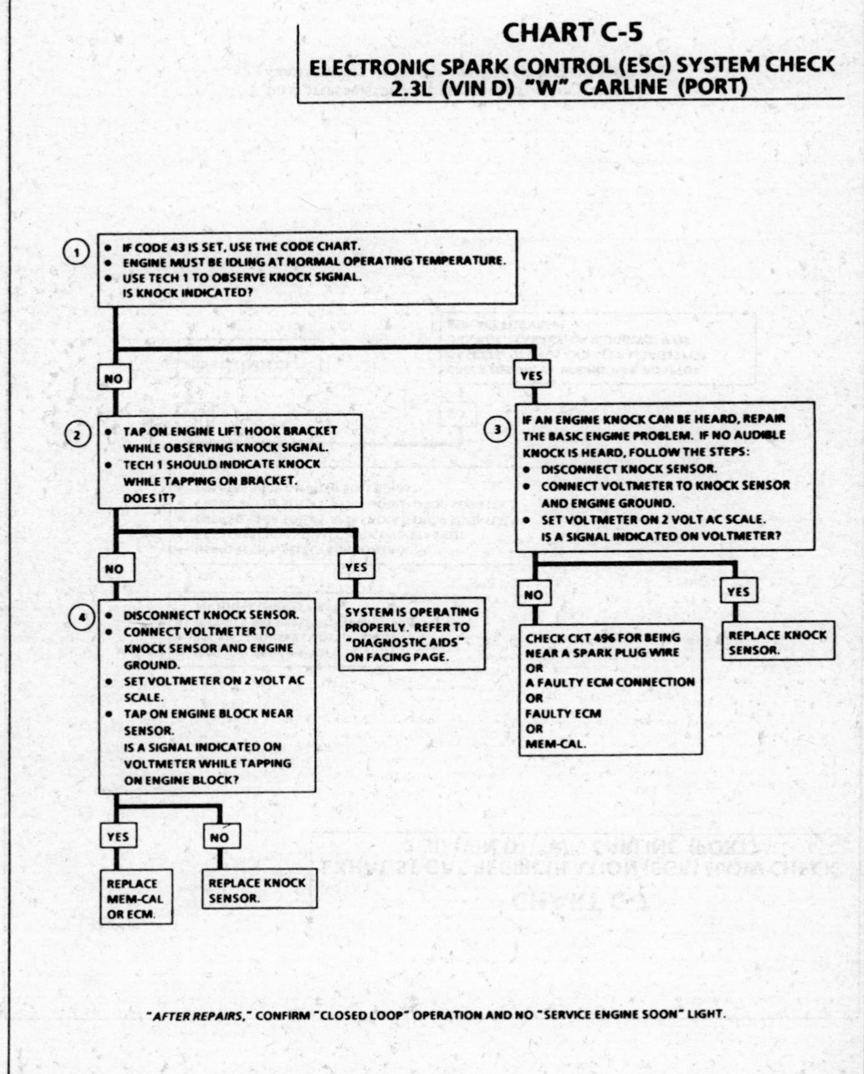
1
• IF CODE 43 IS SET, USE THE CODE CHART.
• ENGINE MUST BE IDLING AT NORMAL OPERATING TEMPERATURE.
• USE TECH 1 TO OBSERVE KNOCK SIGNAL.
IS KNOCK INDICATED?
NO
YES
2
• TAP ON ENGINE LIFT HOOK BRACKET WHILE OBSERVING KNOCK SIGNAL.
• TECH 1 SHOULD INDICATE KNOCK WHILE TAPPING ON BRACKET.
DOES IT?
3
IF AN ENGINE KNOCK CAN BE HEARD, REPAIR THE BASIC ENGINE PROBLEM. IF NO AUDIBLE KNOCK IS HEARD, FOLLOW THE STEPS:
• DISCONNECT KNOCK SENSOR.
• CONNECT VOLTMETER TO KNOCK SENSOR AND ENGINE GROUND.
• SET VOLTMETER ON 2 VOLT AC SCALE.
IS A SIGNAL INDICATED ON VOLTMETER?
NO
YES
SYSTEM IS OPERATING PROPERLY. REFER TO "DIAGNOSTIC AIDS" ON FACING PAGE.
NO
YES
CHECK CKT 496 FOR BEING NEAR A SPARK PLUG WIRE OR A FAULTY ECM CONNECTION OR FAULTY ECM OR MEM-CAL.
REPLACE KNOCK SENSOR.
4
• DISCONNECT KNOCK SENSOR.
• CONNECT VOLTMETER TO KNOCK SENSOR AND ENGINE GROUND.
• SET VOLTMETER ON 2 VOLT AC SCALE.
• TAP ON ENGINE BLOCK NEAR SENSOR.
IS A SIGNAL INDICATED ON VOLTMETER WHILE TAPPING ON ENGINE BLOCK?
YES
NO
REPLACE MEM-CAL OR ECM.
REPLACE KNOCK SENSOR.

"AFTER REPAIRS," CONFIRM "CLOSED LOOP" OPERATION AND NO "SERVICE ENGINE SOON" LIGHT.

DIAGNOSTIC CHARTS — 2.3L engine

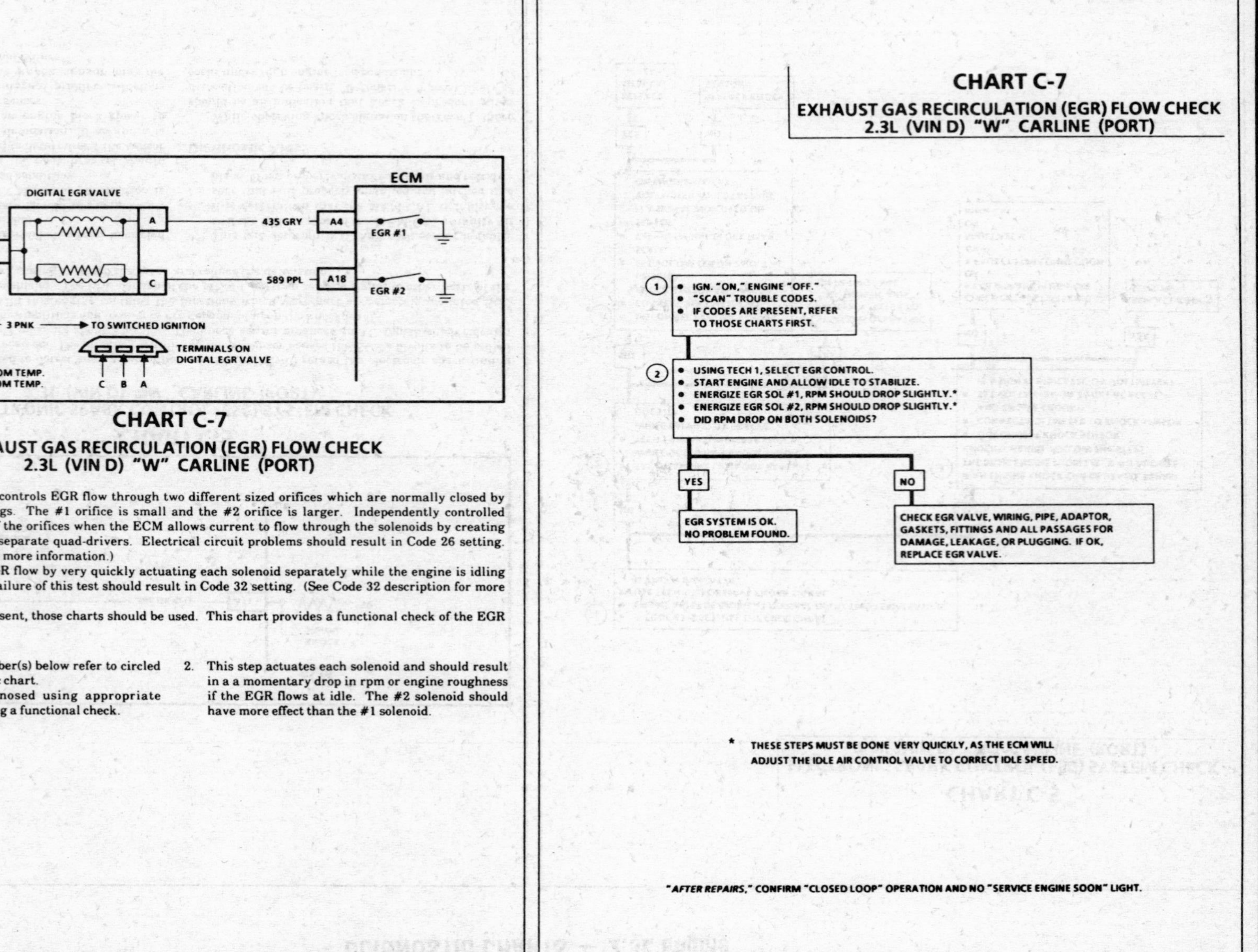
DIGITAL EGR VALVE
ECM
250 BRN
B
A
C
435 GRY
A4
EGR #1
589 PPL
A18
EGR #2
15A
IGN FUSE
3 PNK
TO SWITCHED IGNITION
TERMINALS ON DIGITAL EGR VALVE
C B A
RESISTANCE CHECKS
A-B 18-39 Ω AT ROOM TEMP.
C-B 18-30 Ω AT ROOM TEMP.
CHART C-7
EXHAUST GAS RECIRCULATION (EGR) FLOW CHECK
2.3L (VIN D) "W" CARLINE (PORT)
1
• IGN. "ON," ENGINE "OFF."
• "SCAN" TROUBLE CODES.
• IF CODES ARE PRESENT, REFER TO THOSE CHARTS FIRST.
2
• USING TECH 1, SELECT EGR CONTROL.
• START ENGINE AND ALLOW IDLE TO STABILIZE.
• ENERGIZE EGR SOL #1, RPM SHOULD DROP SLIGHTLY.*
• ENERGIZE EGR SOL #2, RPM SHOULD DROP SLIGHTLY.*
• DID RPM DROP ON BOTH SOLENOIDS?
YES
NO
EGR SYSTEM IS OK. NO PROBLEM FOUND.
CHECK EGR VALVE, WIRING, PIPE, ADAPTOR, GASKETS, FITTINGS AND ALL PASSAGES FOR DAMAGE, LEAKAGE, OR PLUGGING. IF OK, REPLACE EGR VALVE.
* THESE STEPS MUST BE DONE VERY QUICKLY, AS THE ECM WILL ADJUST THE IDLE AIR CONTROL VALVE TO CORRECT IDLE SPEED.
"AFTER REPAIRS," CONFIRM "CLOSED LOOP" OPERATION AND NO "SERVICE ENGINE SOON" LIGHT.

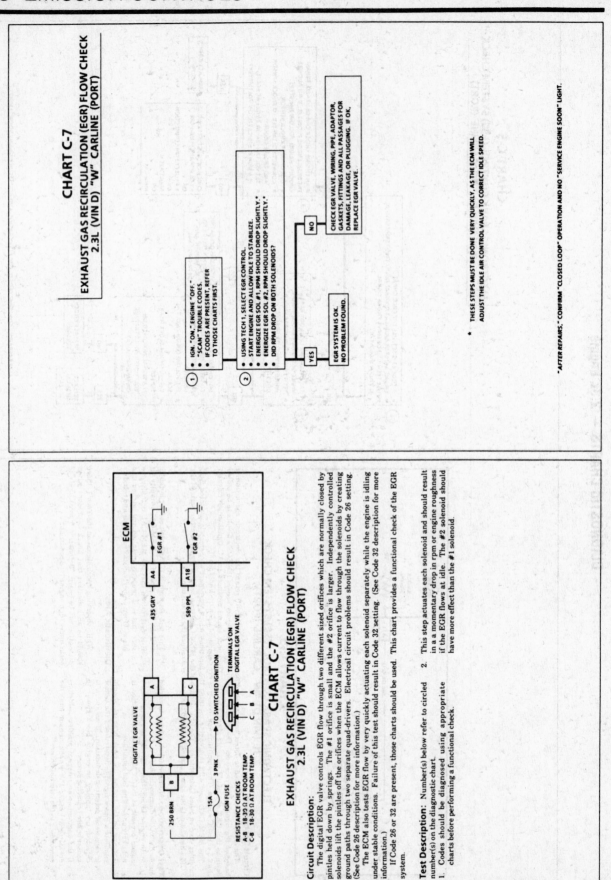

CHART C-7
EXHAUST GAS RECIRCULATION (EGR) FLOW CHECK
2.3L (VIN D) "W" CARLINE (PORT)

Circuit Description:

The digital EGR valve controls EGR flow through two different sized orifices which are normally closed by pintles held down by springs. The #1 orifice is small and the #2 orifice is larger. Independently controlled solenoids lift the pintles off the orifices when the ECM allows current to flow through the solenoids by creating ground paths through two separate quad-drivers. Electrical circuit problems should result in Code 26 setting. (See Code 26 description for more information.)

The ECM also tests EGR flow by very quickly actuating each solenoid separately while the engine is idling under stable conditions. Failure of this test should result in Code 32 setting. (See Code 32 description for more information.)

If Code 26 or 32 are present, those charts should be used. This chart provides a functional check of the EGR system.

Test Description: Number(s) below refer to circled number(s) on the diagnostic chart.

1. Codes should be diagnosed using appropriate charts before performing a functional check.
2. This step actuates each solenoid and should result in a a momentary drop in rpm or engine roughness if the EGR flows at idle. The #2 solenoid should have more effect than the #1 solenoid.

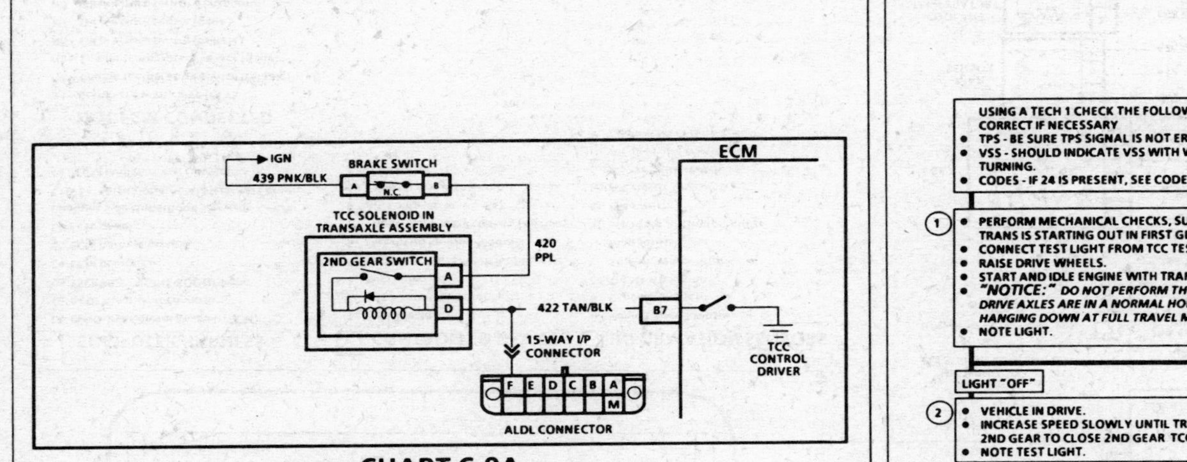

CHART C-8A

3T40 TORQUE CONVERTER CLUTCH (TCC)
(ELECTRICAL DIAGNOSIS)
2.3L (VIN D) "W" CARLINE (PORT)

Circuit Description:

The purpose of the torque converter clutch feature is to eliminate the power loss of the transaxle converter stage when the vehicle is in a cruise condition. This allows the convenience of the automatic transaxle and the fuel economy of a manual transaxle.

Fused battery ignition is supplied to the TCC solenoid through the brake switch, and transaxle second gear apply switch. The ECM will engage TCC by grounding CKT 422 to energize the solenoid.

TCC will engage when:

- Vehicle speed above a calibrated value (about 34 mph) (55 km/h).
- Throttle position sensor output not changing, indicating a steady road speed.
- Transaxle second gear switch closed.
- Brake switch closed.

Test Description: Number(s) below refer to circled number(s) on the diagnostic chart.

1. Light "OFF" confirms transaxle second gear apply switch is open.
2. By 25 mph, the transaxle second gear TCC switch should close. Test light will come "ON" and confirm battery supply and closed brake switch.
3. Grounding the diagnostic terminal with ignition "ON," engine "OFF," should energize the TCC solenoid by grounding CKT 422. This test checks the ability of the ECM to supply a ground to the TCC solenoid. The test light connected from 12 volts to ALDL terminal "F" will turn "ON" as CKT 422 is grounded.

Diagnostic Aids:

A Tech 1 only indicates when the ECM has turned "ON" the TCC driver and this does not confirm that the TCC has engaged. To determine if TCC is functioning properly, engine rpm should decrease when the "Scan" indicates the TCC driver has turned "ON."

CHART C-8A

3T40 TORQUE CONVERTER CLUTCH (TCC)
(ELECTRICAL DIAGNOSIS)
2.3L (VIN D) "W" CARLINE (PORT)

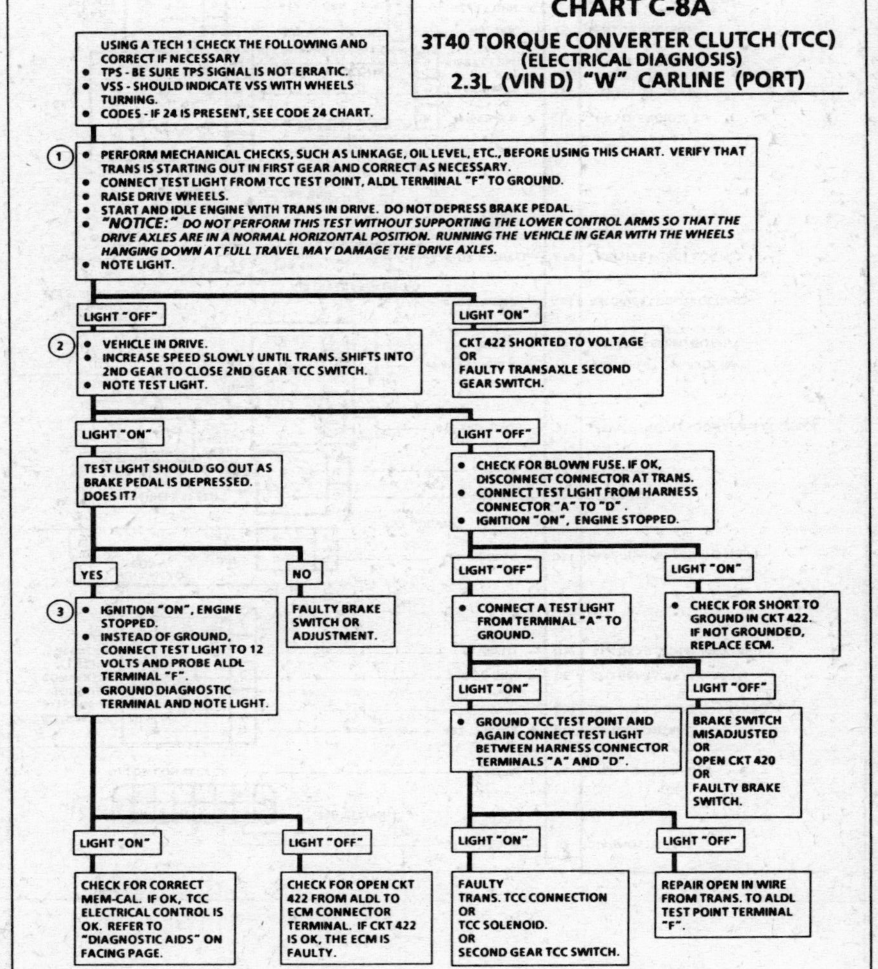

USING A TECH 1 CHECK THE FOLLOWING AND CORRECT IF NECESSARY
• TPS - BE SURE TPS SIGNAL IS NOT ERRATIC.
• VSS - SHOULD INDICATE VSS WITH WHEELS TURNING.
• CODES - IF 24 IS PRESENT, SEE CODE 24 CHART.
1
• PERFORM MECHANICAL CHECKS, SUCH AS LINKAGE, OIL LEVEL, ETC., BEFORE USING THIS CHART. VERIFY THAT TRANS IS STARTING OUT IN FIRST GEAR AND CORRECT AS NECESSARY.
• CONNECT TEST LIGHT FROM TCC TEST POINT, ALDL TERMINAL "F" TO GROUND.
• RAISE DRIVE WHEELS.
• START AND IDLE ENGINE WITH TRANS IN DRIVE. DO NOT DEPRESS BRAKE PEDAL.
• "NOTICE:" DO NOT PERFORM THIS TEST WITHOUT SUPPORTING THE LOWER CONTROL ARMS SO THAT THE DRIVE AXLES ARE IN A NORMAL HORIZONTAL POSITION. RUNNING THE VEHICLE IN GEAR WITH THE WHEELS HANGING DOWN AT FULL TRAVEL MAY DAMAGE THE DRIVE AXLES.
• NOTE LIGHT.
LIGHT "OFF"
LIGHT "ON"
2
• VEHICLE IN DRIVE.
• INCREASE SPEED SLOWLY UNTIL TRANS. SHIFTS INTO 2ND GEAR TO CLOSE 2ND GEAR TCC SWITCH.
• NOTE TEST LIGHT.
CKT 422 SHORTED TO VOLTAGE OR FAULTY TRANSAXLE SECOND GEAR SWITCH.
LIGHT "ON"
LIGHT "OFF"
TEST LIGHT SHOULD GO OUT AS BRAKE PEDAL IS DEPRESSED. DOES IT?
• CHECK FOR BLOWN FUSE. IF OK, DISCONNECT CONNECTOR AT TRANS.
• CONNECT TEST LIGHT FROM HARNESS CONNECTOR "A" TO "D".
• IGNITION "ON", ENGINE STOPPED.
YES
NO
LIGHT "OFF"
LIGHT "ON"
3
• IGNITION "ON", ENGINE STOPPED.
• INSTEAD OF GROUND, CONNECT TEST LIGHT TO 12 VOLTS AND PROBE ALDL TERMINAL "F".
• GROUND DIAGNOSTIC TERMINAL AND NOTE LIGHT.
FAULTY BRAKE SWITCH OR ADJUSTMENT.
• CONNECT A TEST LIGHT FROM TERMINAL "A" TO GROUND.
• CHECK FOR SHORT TO GROUND IN CKT 422. IF NOT GROUNDED, REPLACE ECM.
LIGHT "ON"
LIGHT "OFF"
• GROUND TCC TEST POINT AND AGAIN CONNECT TEST LIGHT BETWEEN HARNESS CONNECTOR TERMINALS "A" AND "D".
BRAKE SWITCH MISADJUSTED OR OPEN CKT 420 OR FAULTY BRAKE SWITCH.
LIGHT "ON"
LIGHT "OFF"
LIGHT "ON"
LIGHT "OFF"
CHECK FOR CORRECT MEM-CAL. IF OK, TCC ELECTRICAL CONTROL IS OK. REFER TO "DIAGNOSTIC AIDS" ON FACING PAGE.
CHECK FOR OPEN CKT 422 FROM ALDL TO ECM CONNECTOR TERMINAL. IF CKT 422 IS OK, THE ECM IS FAULTY.
FAULTY TRANS. TCC CONNECTION OR TCC SOLENOID. OR SECOND GEAR TCC SWITCH.
REPAIR OPEN IN WIRE FROM TRANS. TO ALDL TEST POINT TERMINAL "F".
"AFTER REPAIRS," CONFIRM "CLOSED LOOP" OPERATION AND NO "SERVICE ENGINE SOON" LIGHT.

DIAGNOSTIC CHARTS — 3.1L engine

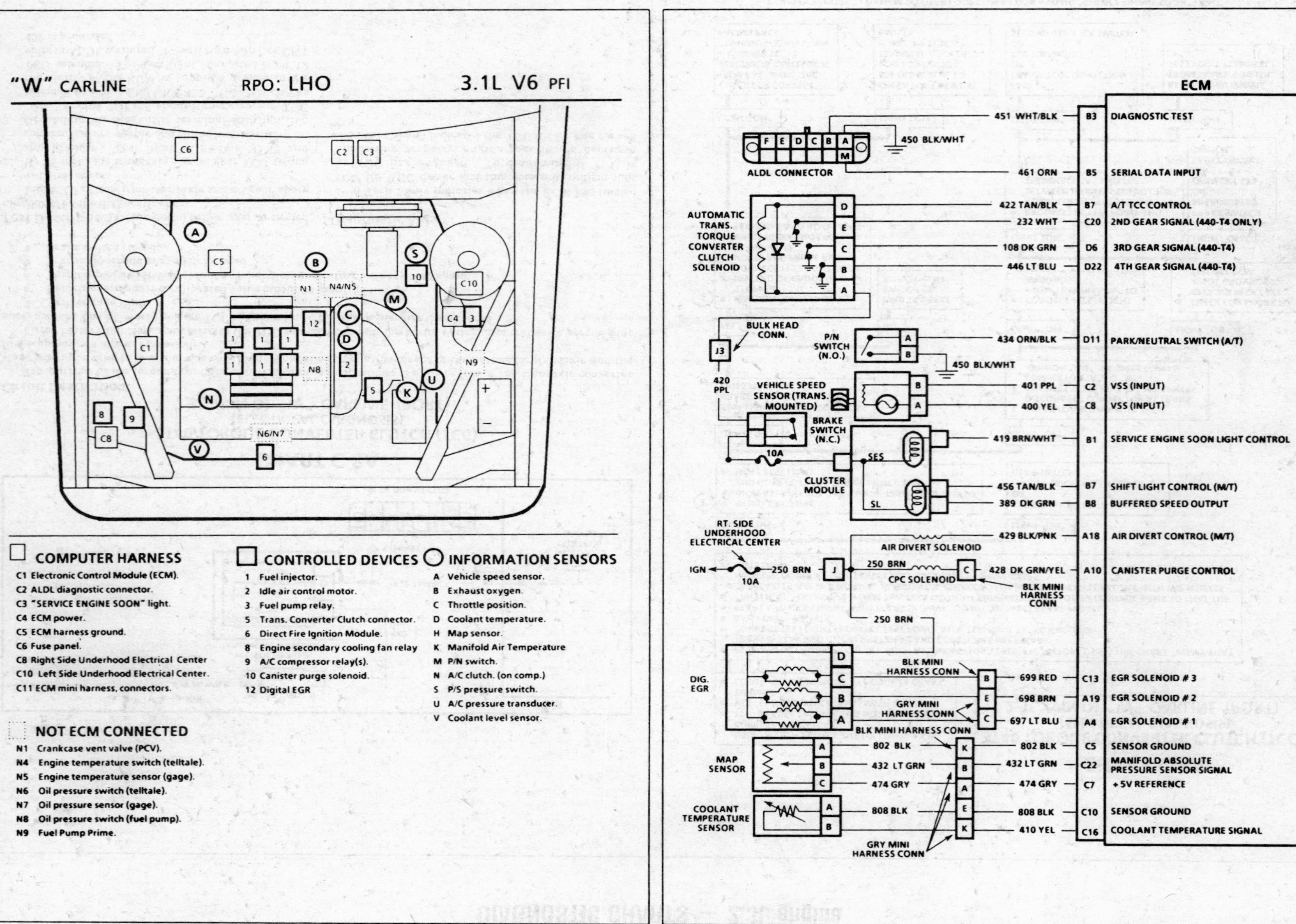
"W" CARLINE
RPO: LHO
3.1L V6 PFI
COMPUTER HARNESS
C1 Electronic Control Module (ECM).
C2 ALDL diagnostic connector.
C3 "SERVICE ENGINE SOON" light.
C4 ECM power.
C5 ECM harness ground.
C6 Fuse panel.
C8 Right Side Underhood Electrical Center
C10 Left Side Underhood Electrical Center.
C11 ECM mini harness, connectors.
CONTROLLED DEVICES
1 Fuel injector.
2 Idle air control motor.
3 Fuel pump relay.
5 Trans. Converter Clutch connector.
6 Direct Fire Ignition Module.
8 Engine secondary cooling fan relay
9 A/C compressor relay(s).
10 Canister purge solenoid.
12 Digital EGR
INFORMATION SENSORS
A Vehicle speed sensor.
B Exhaust oxygen.
C Throttle position.
D Coolant temperature.
H Map sensor.
K Manifold Air Temperature
M P/N switch.
N A/C clutch. (on comp.)
S P/S pressure switch.
U A/C pressure transducer.
V Coolant level sensor.
NOT ECM CONNECTED
N1 Crankcase vent valve (PCV).
N4 Engine temperature switch (telltale).
N5 Engine temperature sensor (gage).
N6 Oil pressure switch (telltale).
N7 Oil pressure sensor (gage).
N8 Oil pressure switch (fuel pump).
N9 Fuel Pump Prime.
ECM
451 WHT/BLK B3 DIAGNOSTIC TEST
450 BLK/WHT
ALDL CONNECTOR
461 ORN B5 SERIAL DATA INPUT
AUTOMATIC TRANS. TORQUE CONVERTER CLUTCH SOLENOID
422 TAN/BLK B7 A/T TCC CONTROL
232 WHT C20 2ND GEAR SIGNAL (440-T4 ONLY)
108 DK GRN D6 3RD GEAR SIGNAL (440-T4)
446 LT BLU D22 4TH GEAR SIGNAL (440-T4)
BULK HEAD CONN.
P/N SWITCH (N.O.)
434 ORN/BLK D11 PARK/NEUTRAL SWITCH (A/T)
450 BLK/WHT
420 PPL
VEHICLE SPEED SENSOR (TRANS. MOUNTED)
401 PPL C2 VSS (INPUT)
400 YEL C8 VSS (INPUT)
BRAKE SWITCH (N.C.)
10A
SES
419 BRN/WHT B1 SERVICE ENGINE SOON LIGHT CONTROL
CLUSTER MODULE
SL
456 TAN/BLK B7 SHIFT LIGHT CONTROL (M/T)
389 DK GRN B8 BUFFERED SPEED OUTPUT
RT. SIDE UNDERHOOD ELECTRICAL CENTER
AIR DIVERT SOLENOID
429 BLK/PNK A18 AIR DIVERT CONTROL (M/T)
IGN
250 BRN
10A
CPC SOLENOID
428 DK GRN/YEL A10 CANISTER PURGE CONTROL
BLK MINI HARNESS CONN
250 BRN
DIG. EGR
BLK MINI HARNESS CONN
699 RED C13 EGR SOLENOID # 3
GRY MINI HARNESS CONN
698 BRN A19 EGR SOLENOID # 2
697 LT BLU A4 EGR SOLENOID # 1
BLK MINI HARNESS CONN
MAP SENSOR
802 BLK
802 BLK C5 SENSOR GROUND
432 LT GRN
432 LT GRN C22 MANIFOLD ABSOLUTE PRESSURE SENSOR SIGNAL
474 GRY
474 GRY C7 +5V REFERENCE
COOLANT TEMPERATURE SENSOR
808 BLK
808 BLK C10 SENSOR GROUND
410 YEL C16 COOLANT TEMPERATURE SIGNAL
GRY MINI HARNESS CONN

DIAGNOSTIC CHARTS — 3.1L engine

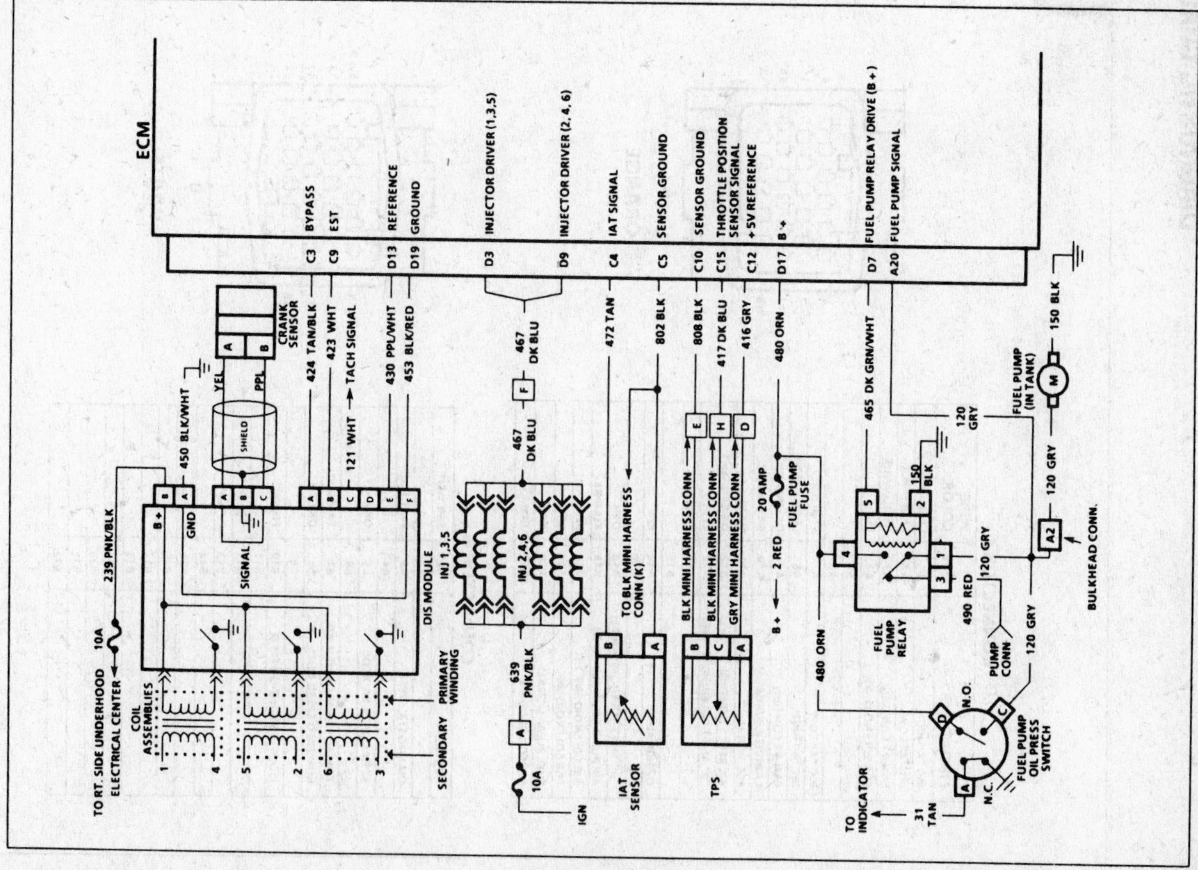

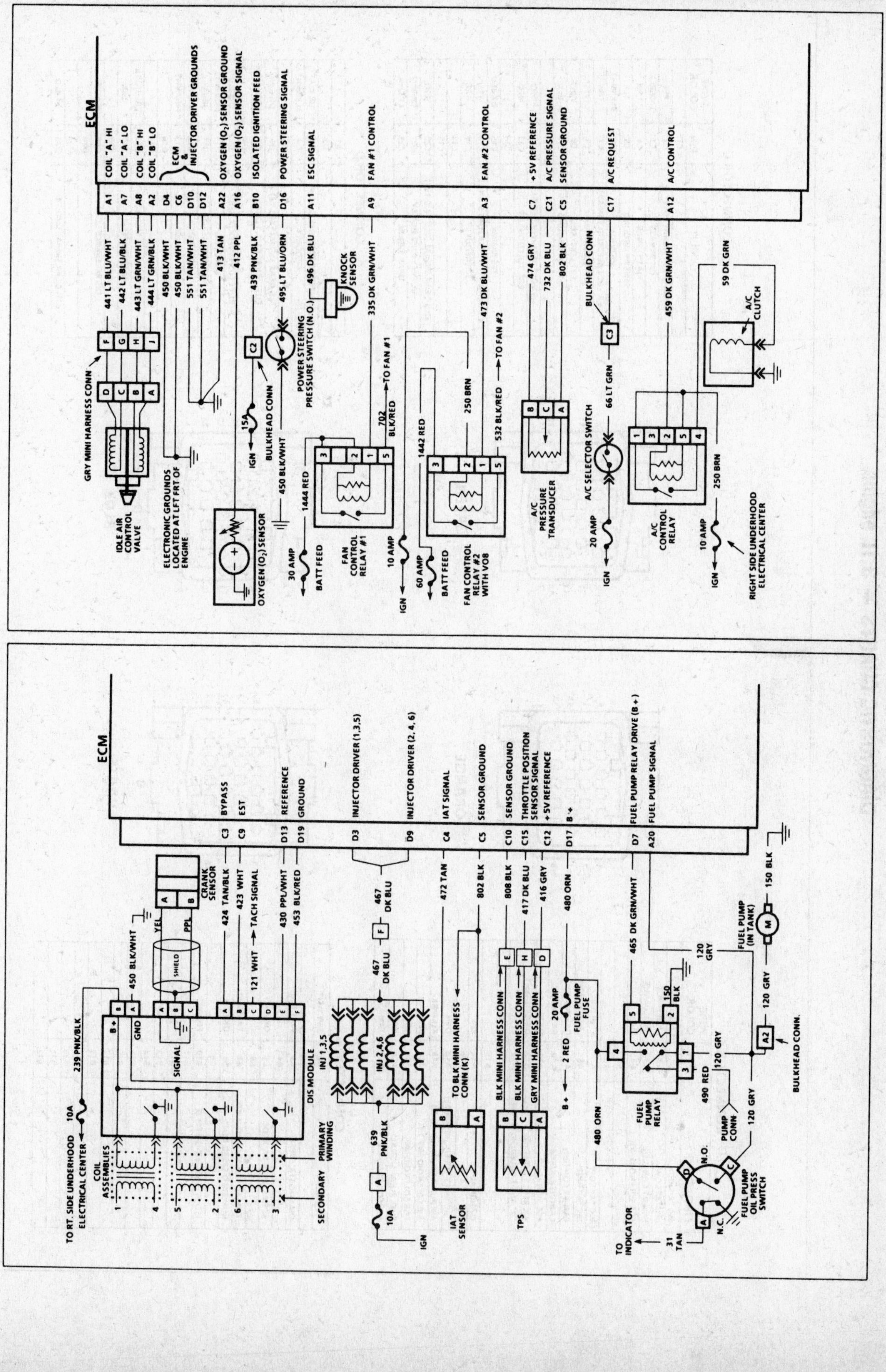

DIAGNOSTIC CHARTS — 3.1L engine

CONNECTOR A

CIRCUIT	PIN	WIRE COLOR
IAC "A" HIGH	A1	LT BLU/WHT
IAC "B" LOW	A2	LT GRN/BLK
FAN #2 CONTROL	A3	DK BLU/WHT
EGR SOLENOID #1	A4	BLU
	A5	
	A6	
IAC "A" LOW	A7	LT BLU/BLK
IAC "B" HIGH	A8	LT GRN/WHT
FAN #1 CONTROL	A9	DK GRN/WHT
CANISTER PURGE	A10	DK GRN/YEL
ESC SIGNAL	A11	DK BLU
A/C RELAY CONTROL	A12	DK GRN/WHT
"B" SHIFT SOLENOID (4T60E)	A13	LT BLU
	A14	
	A15	
O_2 SIGNAL	A16	PPL
	A17	
"A" SHIFT SOLENOID (4T60E)	A18	ORN
AIR PUMP RELAY (M/T 3.4L)	A18	BLK/PNK
AIR SOLENOID M/T 3.1L	A18	BLK/PNK
EGR SOLENOID #2	A19	BRN
FUEL PUMP SIGNAL	A20	GRY
SENSOR GROUND	A22	TAN

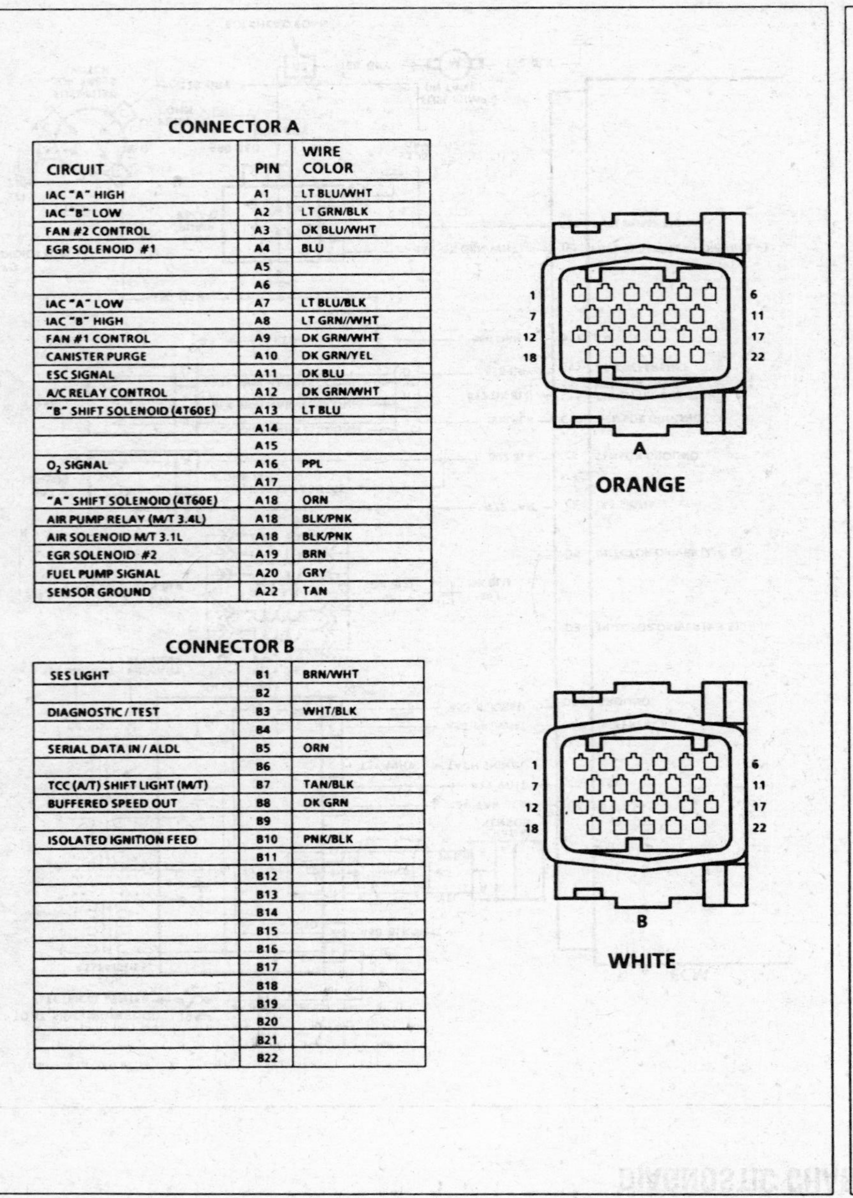

CONNECTOR B

SES LIGHT	B1	BRN/WHT
	B2	
DIAGNOSTIC/TEST	B3	WHT/BLK
	B4	
SERIAL DATA IN/ALDL	B5	ORN
	B6	
TCC (A/T) SHIFT LIGHT (M/T)	B7	TAN/BLK
BUFFERED SPEED OUT	B8	DK GRN
	B9	
ISOLATED IGNITION FEED	B10	PNK/BLK
	B11	
	B12	
	B13	
	B14	
	B15	
	B16	
	B17	
	B18	
	B19	
	B20	
	B21	
	B22	

CONNECTOR C

CIRCUIT	PIN	WIRE COLOR
	C1	
MAG. VSS SIGNAL LOW	C2	PPL
DIS BYPASS	C3	TAN/BLK
IAT SIGNAL	C4	TAN
SENSOR GROUND	C5	BLK
GROUND	C6	BLK/WHT
+5 VOLT REFERENCE (MAP)	C7	GRY
MAG. VSS HIGH	C8	YEL
EST CONTROL	C9	WHT
SENSOR GROUND	C10	BLK
	C11	
+5 VOLT REFERENCE (TPS)	C12	GRY
EGR SOLENOID #3	C13	RED
	C14	
TPS SIGNAL	C15	DK BLU
COOLANT TEMPERATURE SIGNAL	C16	YEL
A/C REQUEST	C17	GRN
	C18	
	C19	
2ND GEAR SIGNAL (440-T4 ONLY)	C20	WHT
A/C PRESSURE SIGNAL	C21	DK BLU
MAP SIGNAL	C22	LT GRN

CONNECTOR D

	D1	
	D2	
INJECTOR DRIVER (1, 3, 5)	D3	DK BLU
GROUND	D4	BLK/WHT
	D5	
3RD GEAR SIGNAL (440-T4)	D6	DK GRN
FUEL PUMP RELAY DRIVE	D7	DK GRN/WHT
	D8	
INJECTOR DRIVER (2, 4, 6)	D9	DK BLU
GROUND	D10	TAN/WHT
P/N SWITCH (A/T)	D11	ORN/BLK
GROUND	D12	TAN/WHT
REFERENCE	D13	PPL/WHT
	D14	
	D15	
P/S PRESSURE SIGNAL	D16	LT BLU/ORN
BATTERY FEED	D17	ORN
	D18	
DIS REFERENCE LOW	D19	BLK/RED
	D20	
	D21	
4TH GEAR SIGNAL (440-T4)	D22	LT BLU

DIAGNOSTIC CHARTS — 3.1L engine

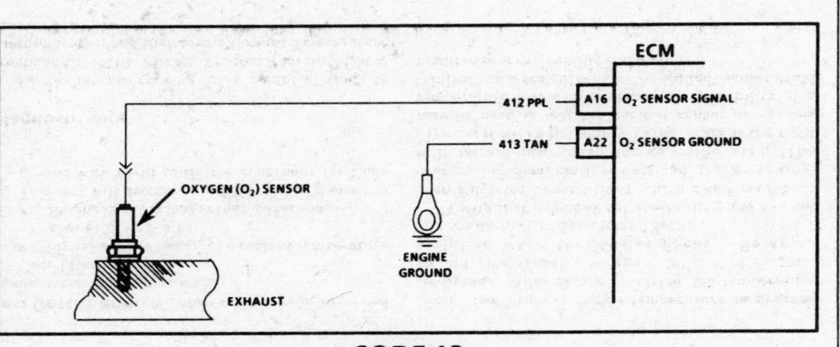
ECM
412 PPL
A16
O_2 SENSOR SIGNAL
413 TAN
A22
O_2 SENSOR GROUND
OXYGEN (O_2) SENSOR
ENGINE GROUND
EXHAUST

CODE 13

OXYGEN (O_2) SENSOR CIRCUIT (OPEN CIRCUIT) 3.1L (VIN T) "W" CARLINE (PORT)

Circuit Description:

The ECM supplies a voltage of about .55 volt between terminals "A16" and "A22". (If measured with a 10 megohm digital voltmeter, this may read as low as .35 volt.) The Oxygen (O_2) sensor varies the voltage within a range of about 1 volt if the exhaust is rich, down through about .10 volt if exhaust is lean.

The sensor is like an open circuit and produces no voltage when it is below 315°C (600°F). An open sensor circuit or cold sensor causes "Open Loop" operation.

Test Description: Number(s) below refer to circled number(s) on the diagnostic chart.

1. Code 13 will set under the following conditions:
   - Engine running at least 2 minutes after start.
   - Coolant temperature at least 50°C (122°F).
   - No Code 21 or 22.
   - O_2 signal voltage steady between .35 and .55 volt.
   - Throttle position sensor signal above 4% for more time than TPS was below 4%. (About .3 volt above closed throttle voltage.)
   - All conditions must be met and held for at least 25 seconds.

   If the conditions for a Code 13 exist, the system will not go "Closed Loop."
2. This will determine if the sensor is at fault or the wiring or ECM is the cause of the Code 13.
3. In doing this test use only a high impedance digital volt ohmmeter. This test checks the continuity of CKT 412 and CKT 413 because if CKT 413 is open the ECM voltage on CKT 412 will be over .6 volt (600 mV).

Diagnostic Aids:

Normal "Scan" voltage varies between 100 mV to 999 mV (.1 and 1.0 volt) while in "Closed Loop." Code 13 sets if voltage remains between .35 and .55 volt, but the system will go "Open Loop" in about 15 seconds. Refer to "Intermittents" in "Symptoms,"

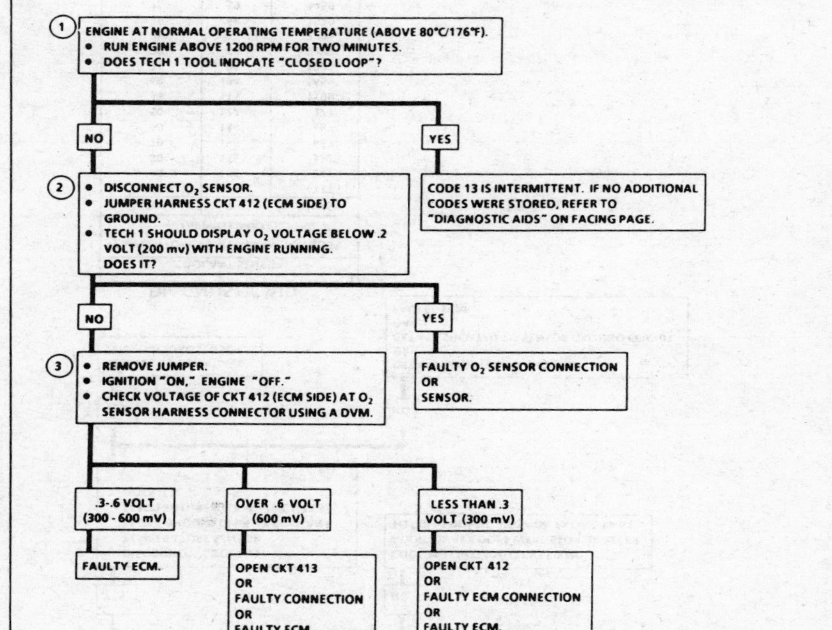
CODE 13
OXYGEN (O_2) SENSOR CIRCUIT
(OPEN CIRCUIT)
3.1L (VIN T) "W" CARLINE (PORT)
1
ENGINE AT NORMAL OPERATING TEMPERATURE (ABOVE 80°C/176°F).
• RUN ENGINE ABOVE 1200 RPM FOR TWO MINUTES.
• DOES TECH 1 TOOL INDICATE "CLOSED LOOP"?
NO
YES
CODE 13 IS INTERMITTENT. IF NO ADDITIONAL CODES WERE STORED, REFER TO "DIAGNOSTIC AIDS" ON FACING PAGE.
2
• DISCONNECT O_2 SENSOR.
• JUMPER HARNESS CKT 412 (ECM SIDE) TO GROUND.
• TECH 1 SHOULD DISPLAY O_2 VOLTAGE BELOW .2 VOLT (200 mv) WITH ENGINE RUNNING. DOES IT?
NO
YES
FAULTY O_2 SENSOR CONNECTION OR SENSOR.
3
• REMOVE JUMPER.
• IGNITION "ON," ENGINE "OFF."
• CHECK VOLTAGE OF CKT 412 (ECM SIDE) AT O_2 SENSOR HARNESS CONNECTOR USING A DVM.
.3-.6 VOLT (300 - 600 mV)
FAULTY ECM.
OVER .6 VOLT (600 mV)
OPEN CKT 413 OR FAULTY CONNECTION OR FAULTY ECM.
LESS THAN .3 VOLT (300 mV)
OPEN CKT 412 OR FAULTY ECM CONNECTION OR FAULTY ECM.
"AFTER REPAIRS," REFER TO CODE CRITERIA ON FACING PAGE AND CONFIRM CODE DOES NOT RESET.

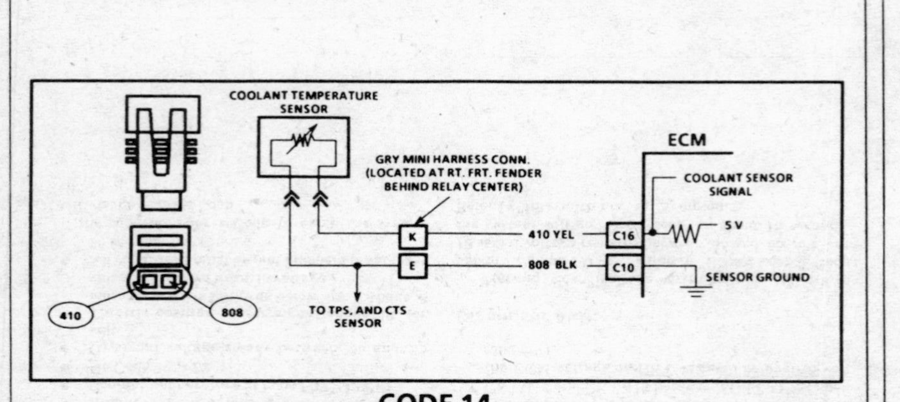
COOLANT TEMPERATURE SENSOR
GRY MINI HARNESS CONN.
(LOCATED AT RT. FRT. FENDER
BEHIND RELAY CENTER)
ECM
COOLANT SENSOR SIGNAL
5 V
K
E
410 YEL
808 BLK
C16
C10
SENSOR GROUND
410
808
TO TPS, AND CTS SENSOR

CODE 14

COOLANT TEMPERATURE SENSOR (CTS) CIRCUIT
(HIGH TEMPERATURE INDICATED)
3.1L (VIN T) "W" CARLINE (PORT)

Circuit Description:

The Coolant Temperature Sensor (CTS) uses a thermistor to control the signal voltage to the ECM. The ECM applies a voltage on CKT 410 to the sensor. When the engine is cold, the sensor (thermistor) resistance is high, therefore the ECM will see high signal voltage.

As the engine warms, the sensor resistance becomes less, and the voltage drops. At normal engine operating temperature, the voltage will measure about 1.5 to 2.0 volts at the ECM terminal "C16".

Coolant temperature is one of the inputs used to control:

- Fuel delivery
- Electronic Spark Timing (EST)
- Idle Air Control (IAC)
- Torque Converter Clutch (TCC)
- Controlled Canister Purge (CCP)
- Exhaust Gas Recirculation (EGR)
- Cooling fan

Test Description: Number(s) below refer to circled number(s) on the diagnostic chart.

1. Code 14 will set if:
   - Signal voltage indicates a coolant temperature above 135°C (270°F).
   - Engine running longer than 20 seconds.
2. This test will determine if CKT 410 is shorted to ground which will cause the conditions for Code 14.

Diagnostic Aids:

Check harness routing for a potential short to ground in CKT 410. Circuit is routed from the ECM to a mini harness, and then to the Coolant Temperature Sensor (CTS).

"Scan" tool displays engine temperature in degrees centigrade. After engine is started, the temperature should rise steadily to about 90°C (194°F) then stabilize when thermostat opens. Refer to "Intermittents" in "Symptoms," Section

Verify that engine is not overheating and has not been subjected to conditions which could create an overheating condition (i.e. overload, trailer towing, hilly terrain, heavy stop and go traffic, etc.). The "Temperature To Resistance Value" scale at the right may be used to test the coolant sensor at various temperature levels to evaluate the possibility of a "shifted" (mis-scaled) sensor. A "shifted" sensor could result in poor driveability complaints.

CODE 14

COOLANT TEMPERATURE SENSOR (CTS) CIRCUIT
(HIGH TEMPERATURE INDICATED)
3.1L (VIN T) "W" CARLINE (PORT)

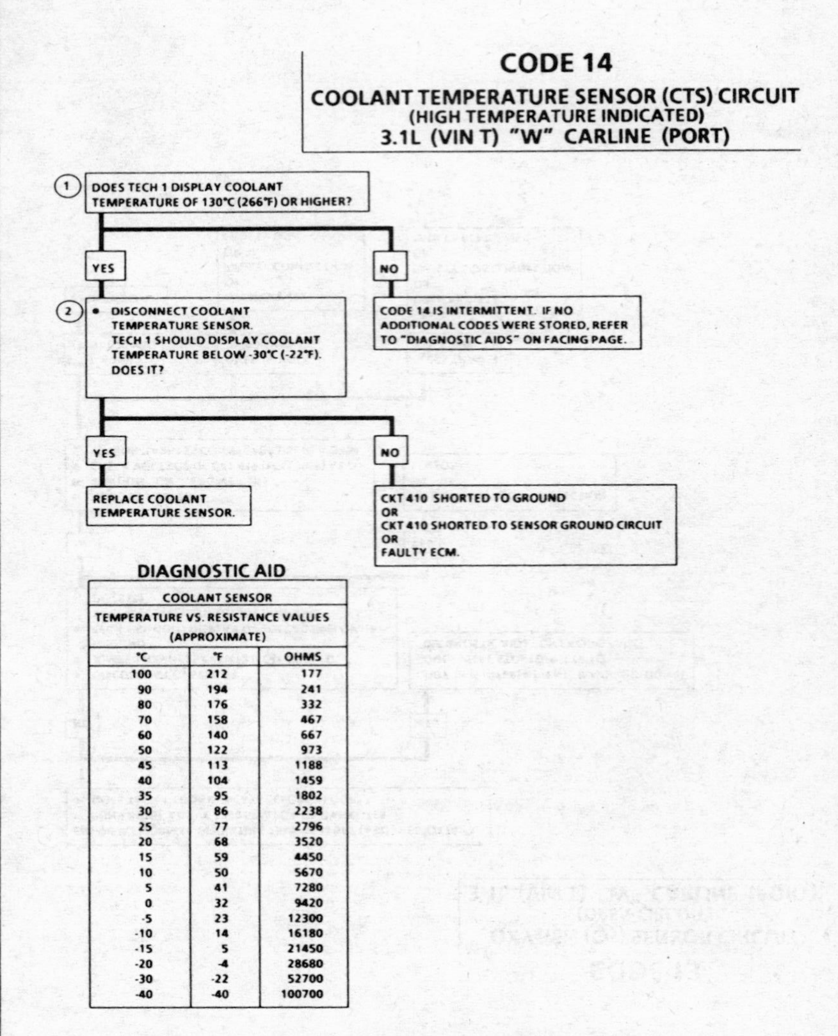
1 DOES TECH 1 DISPLAY COOLANT TEMPERATURE OF 130°C (266°F) OR HIGHER?
YES
NO
CODE 14 IS INTERMITTENT. IF NO ADDITIONAL CODES WERE STORED, REFER TO "DIAGNOSTIC AIDS" ON FACING PAGE.
2 • DISCONNECT COOLANT TEMPERATURE SENSOR. TECH 1 SHOULD DISPLAY COOLANT TEMPERATURE BELOW -30°C (-22°F). DOES IT?
YES
NO
REPLACE COOLANT TEMPERATURE SENSOR.
CKT 410 SHORTED TO GROUND OR CKT 410 SHORTED TO SENSOR GROUND CIRCUIT OR FAULTY ECM.

DIAGNOSTIC AID

COOLANT SENSOR

TEMPERATURE VS. RESISTANCE VALUES (APPROXIMATE)

°C	°F	OHMS
100	212	177
90	194	241
80	176	332
70	158	467
60	140	667
50	122	973
45	113	1188
40	104	1459
35	95	1802
30	86	2238
25	77	2796
20	68	3520
15	59	4450
10	50	5670
5	41	7280
0	32	9420
-5	23	12300
-10	14	16180
-15	5	21450
-20	-4	28680
-30	-22	52700
-40	-40	100700

"*AFTER REPAIRS*," REFER TO CODE CRITERIA ON FACING PAGE AND CONFIRM CODE DOES NOT RESET.

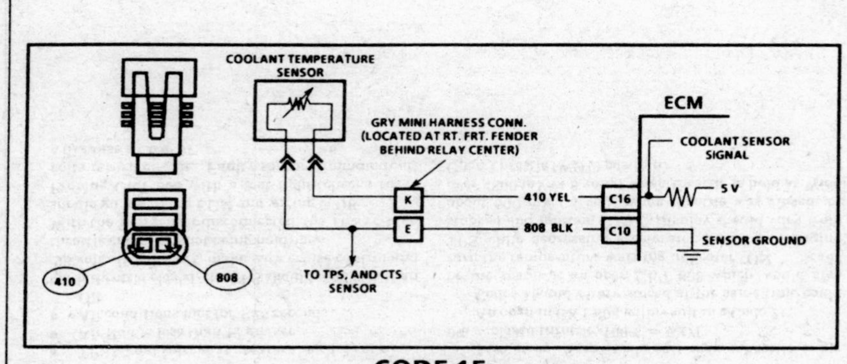
COOLANT TEMPERATURE SENSOR
GRY MINI HARNESS CONN. (LOCATED AT RT. FRT. FENDER BEHIND RELAY CENTER)
ECM
COOLANT SENSOR SIGNAL
5 V
K
E
410 YEL
808 BLK
C16
C10
SENSOR GROUND
TO TPS, AND CTS SENSOR
410
808

CODE 15

COOLANT TEMPERATURE SENSOR (CTS) CIRCUIT
(LOW TEMPERATURE INDICATED)
3.1L (VIN T) "W" CARLINE (PORT)

Circuit Description:

The Coolant Temperature Sensor (CTS) uses a thermistor to control the signal voltage to the ECM. The ECM applies a voltage on CKT 410 to the sensor. When the engine is cold the sensor (thermistor) resistance is high, therefore the ECM will see high signal voltage.

As the engine warms, the sensor resistance becomes less, and the voltage drops. At normal engine operating temperature the voltage will measure about 1.5 to 2.0 volts at the ECM terminal "C16".

Coolant temperature is one of the inputs used to control:

- Fuel delivery
- Engine Spark Timing (EST)
- Idle Air Control (IAC)
- Torque Converter Clutch (TCC)
- Controlled Canister Purge (CCP)
- Electronic Gas Recirculation (EGR)
- Cooling fan

Test Description: Number(s) below refer to circled number(s) on the diagnostic chart.

1. Code 15 will set if:
   - Signal voltage indicates a coolant temperature less than -38.5°C (-37.30°F).
2. This test simulates a Code 14. If the ECM recognizes the low signal voltage, (high temperature) and the "Scan" reads 130°C (266°F), the ECM and wiring are OK.
3. This test will determine if CKT 410 is open. There should be 5 volts present at sensor connector if measured with a DVM.

Diagnostic Aids:

A "Scan" tool reads engine temperature in degrees centigrade. After engine is started the temperature should rise steadily to about 95°C (203°F) then stabilize when thermostat opens. CKT 410 is routed from the ECM to a mini harness, and then to the Coolant Temperature Sensor (CTS).

A faulty connection, or an open in CKT 410 or 808 will result in a Code 15.

Codes 15 and 21 are stored at the same time could be the result of an open CKT 808 which would also turn the temperature warning indicator "ON." The "Temperature to Resistance Value" scale at the right may be used to test the coolant sensor at various temperature levels to evaluate the possibility of a "shifted" (mis-scaled) sensor. A "shifted" sensor could result in poor driveability complaints.

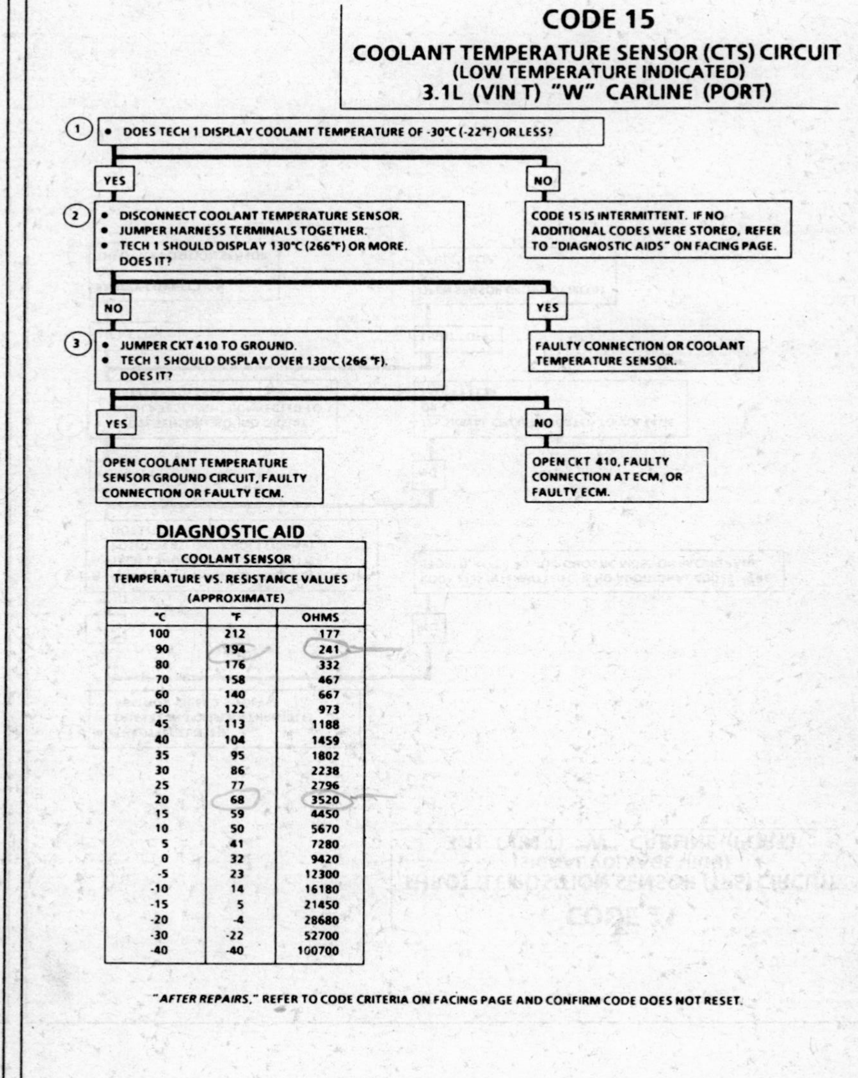
CODE 15
COOLANT TEMPERATURE SENSOR (CTS) CIRCUIT
(LOW TEMPERATURE INDICATED)
3.1L (VIN T) "W" CARLINE (PORT)
1 • DOES TECH 1 DISPLAY COOLANT TEMPERATURE OF -30°C (-22°F) OR LESS?
YES
NO
CODE 15 IS INTERMITTENT. IF NO ADDITIONAL CODES WERE STORED, REFER TO "DIAGNOSTIC AIDS" ON FACING PAGE.
2 • DISCONNECT COOLANT TEMPERATURE SENSOR. • JUMPER HARNESS TERMINALS TOGETHER. • TECH 1 SHOULD DISPLAY 130°C (266°F) OR MORE. DOES IT?
NO
YES
FAULTY CONNECTION OR COOLANT TEMPERATURE SENSOR.
3 • JUMPER CKT 410 TO GROUND. • TECH 1 SHOULD DISPLAY OVER 130°C (266 °F). DOES IT?
YES
NO
OPEN COOLANT TEMPERATURE SENSOR GROUND CIRCUIT, FAULTY CONNECTION OR FAULTY ECM.
OPEN CKT 410, FAULTY CONNECTION AT ECM, OR FAULTY ECM.

DIAGNOSTIC AID

COOLANT SENSOR
TEMPERATURE VS. RESISTANCE VALUES
(APPROXIMATE)

°C	°F	OHMS
100	212	177
90	194	241
80	176	332
70	158	467
60	140	667
50	122	973
45	113	1188
40	104	1459
35	95	1802
30	86	2238
25	77	2796
20	68	3520
15	59	4450
10	50	5670
5	41	7280
0	32	9420
-5	23	12300
-10	14	16180
-15	5	21450
-20	-4	28680
-30	-22	52700
-40	-40	100700

"AFTER REPAIRS," REFER TO CODE CRITERIA ON FACING PAGE AND CONFIRM CODE DOES NOT RESET.

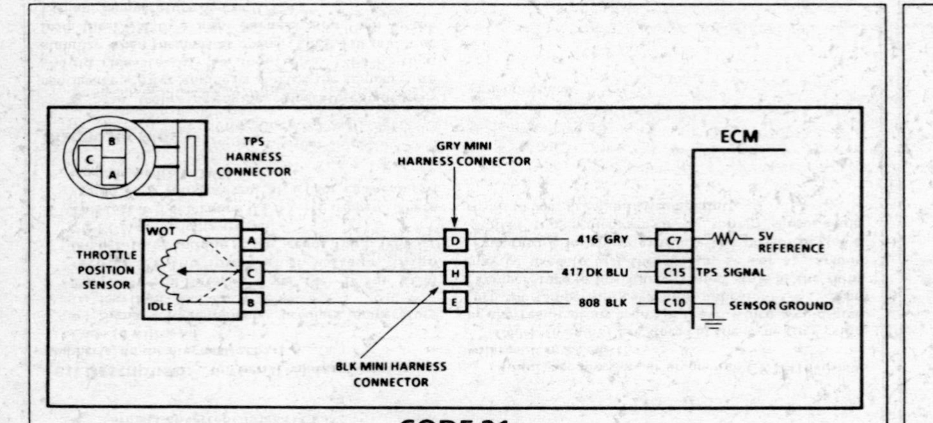

CODE 21

THROTTLE POSITION SENSOR (TPS) CIRCUIT (SIGNAL VOLTAGE HIGH) 3.1L (VIN T) "W" CARLINE (PORT)

Circuit Description:

The Throttle Position Sensor (TPS) provides a voltage signal that changes relative to the throttle blade. Signal voltage will vary from about .5 at idle to about 4.8 volts at Wide Open Throttle (WOT).

The TPS signal is one of the most important inputs used by the ECM for fuel control and for most of the ECM control outputs.

Test Description: Number(s) below refer to circled number(s) on the diagnostic chart.

1. Code 21 will set if:
   - No Code 33 or Code 34.
   - Engine is running.
   - TPS signal voltage is greater than 4.3 volts.
   - Air flow is less than 17 gm/sec.
   - All conditions met for 1.25 seconds.

   OR

   With throttle closed, the TPS should read less than .98 volt. If it doesn't, make sure cruise control and throttle cables are not being held open.
2. With the TPS sensor disconnected, the TPS voltage should go low, if the ECM and wiring is OK.
3. Probing CKT 808 with a test light, checks the 5 volts return circuit. Faulty sensor ground circuit will cause a Code 21.

Diagnostic Aids:

A "Scan" tool reads throttle position in volts. Voltage should increase at a steady rate as throttle is moved toward WOT.

Also some "Scan" tools will read: throttle angle 0% = closed throttle, 100% = WOT.

An open in CKT 808 will result in a Code 21.

Codes 15 and 21 are stored at the same time could be the result of an open CKT 808 which would also turn the temperature warning indicator "ON." "Scan" TPS while depressing accelerator pedal with engine stopped and ignition "ON." Display should vary from about 500 mV (.5 volt) when throttle was closed, to over 4800 mV (4.8 volts) when throttle is held at Wide Open Throttle (WOT) position.

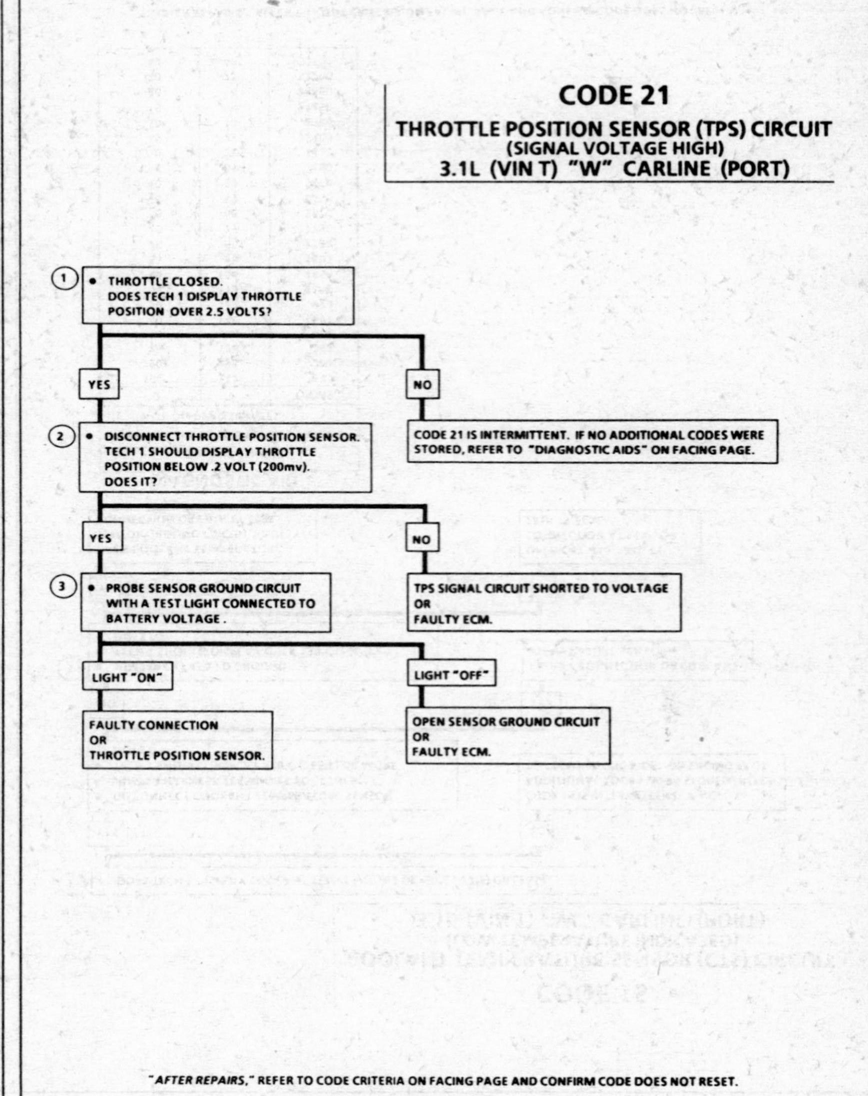

CODE 21
THROTTLE POSITION SENSOR (TPS) CIRCUIT
(SIGNAL VOLTAGE HIGH)
3.1L (VIN T) "W" CARLINE (PORT)
1 • THROTTLE CLOSED. DOES TECH 1 DISPLAY THROTTLE POSITION OVER 2.5 VOLTS?
YES
NO
CODE 21 IS INTERMITTENT. IF NO ADDITIONAL CODES WERE STORED, REFER TO "DIAGNOSTIC AIDS" ON FACING PAGE.
2 • DISCONNECT THROTTLE POSITION SENSOR. TECH 1 SHOULD DISPLAY THROTTLE POSITION BELOW .2 VOLT (200mv). DOES IT?
YES
NO
TPS SIGNAL CIRCUIT SHORTED TO VOLTAGE OR FAULTY ECM.
3 • PROBE SENSOR GROUND CIRCUIT WITH A TEST LIGHT CONNECTED TO BATTERY VOLTAGE.
LIGHT "ON"
LIGHT "OFF"
FAULTY CONNECTION OR THROTTLE POSITION SENSOR.
OPEN SENSOR GROUND CIRCUIT OR FAULTY ECM.
"AFTER REPAIRS," REFER TO CODE CRITERIA ON FACING PAGE AND CONFIRM CODE DOES NOT RESET.

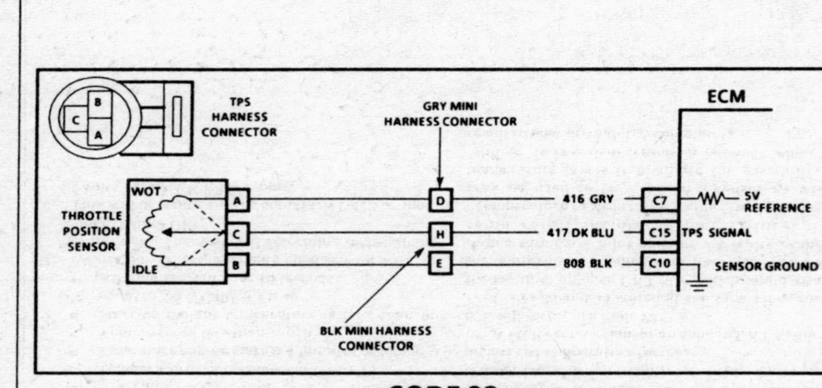
TPS HARNESS CONNECTOR
GRY MINI HARNESS CONNECTOR
ECM
WOT
THROTTLE POSITION SENSOR
IDLE
A
C
B
D
H
E
416 GRY
417 DK BLU
808 BLK
C7
C15
C10
5V REFERENCE
TPS SIGNAL
SENSOR GROUND
BLK MINI HARNESS CONNECTOR

CODE 22

THROTTLE POSITION SENSOR (TPS) CIRCUIT (SIGNAL VOLTAGE LOW) 3.1L (VIN T) "W" CARLINE (PORT)

Circuit Description:

The Throttle Position Sensor (TPS) provides a voltage signal that changes relative to the throttle blade. Signal voltage will vary from about .5 at idle to about 4.8 volts at Wide Open Throttle (WOT).

The TPS signal is one of the most important inputs used by the ECM for fuel control and for most of the ECM control outputs.

Test Description: Number(s) below refer to circled number(s) on the diagnostic chart.

1. Code 22 will set if:
   - Engine running.
   - TPS signal voltage is less than about .25 volt for 3 seconds.
2. Simulates Code 21: (High Voltage) If the ECM recognizes the high signal voltage, the ECM and wiring are OK.
3. TPS check: The TPS has an auto zeroing feature. If the voltage reading is within the range of 0.29 to 0.98 volt, the ECM will use that value as closed throttle. If the voltage reading is out of the auto zero range on an existing or replacement TPS; check for cruise control and throttle cables for being held open.
4. This simulates a high signal voltage to check for an open in CKT 417.
5. CKT 416 and CKT 474 share a common 5 volts buffered reference signal. If either of these circuits is shorted to ground, Code 22 will set. To determine if the MAP sensor is causing the Code 22 problem, disconnect it to see if Code 22 resets. Be sure TPS is connected and clear codes before testing.

Diagnostic Aids:

A "Scan" tool reads throttle position in volts. Voltage should increase at a steady rate as throttle is moved toward WOT.

Also some "Scan" tools will read: throttle angle 0% = closed throttle 100% = WOT.

An open or short to ground in CKTs 416 or 417 will result in a Code 22.

CKTs 416 and 417 are routed through a mini harness. CKT 416 is connected to terminal "D" at the gray connector, CKT 417 is connected to terminal "H" at the black connector.

"Scan" TPS while depressing accelerator pedal with engine stopped and ignition "ON." Display should vary from about 500 mV (.5 volt) when throttle was closed, to over 4800 mV (4.8 volts) when throttle is held at Wide Open Throttle (WOT) position.

Also some "Scan" tools will read throttle angle.

0% = closed throttle.

100% = open throttle.

If Code 22 is set, check CKT 416 for faulty wiring or connections.

CODE 22

THROTTLE POSITION SENSOR (TPS) CIRCUIT (SIGNAL VOLTAGE LOW) 3.1L (VIN T) "W" CARLINE (PORT)

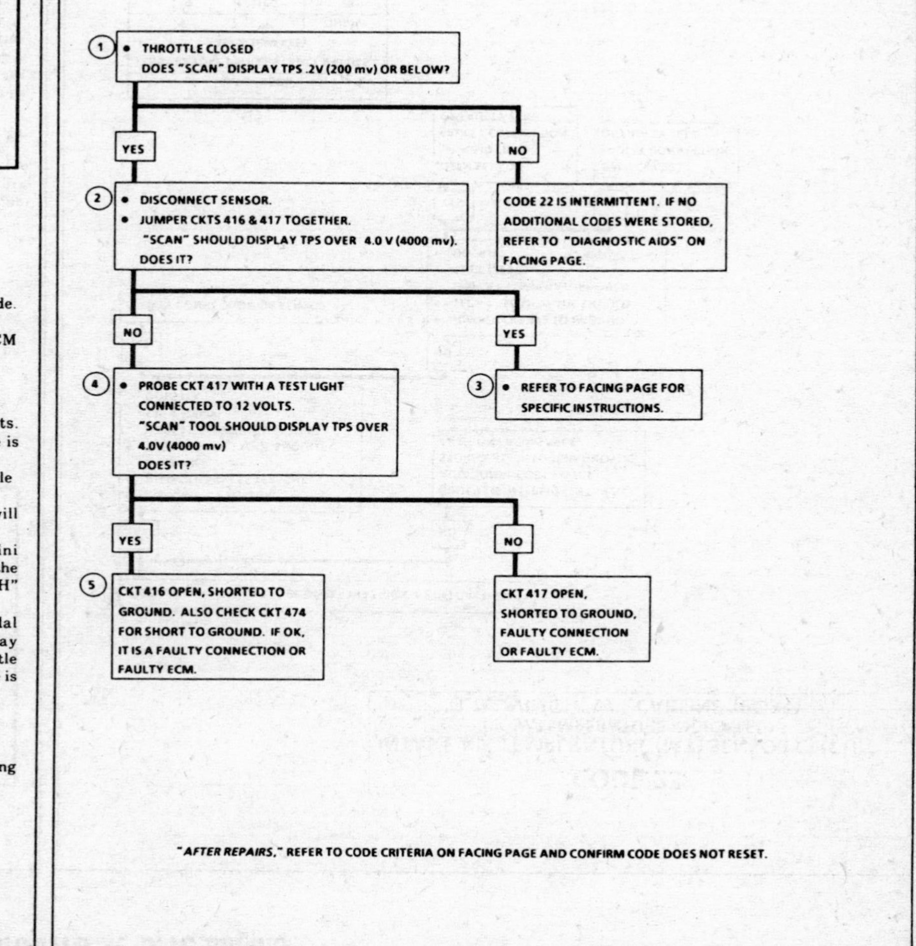
1
• THROTTLE CLOSED
DOES "SCAN" DISPLAY TPS .2V (200 mv) OR BELOW?
YES
NO
2
• DISCONNECT SENSOR.
• JUMPER CKTS 416 & 417 TOGETHER.
"SCAN" SHOULD DISPLAY TPS OVER 4.0 V (4000 mv).
DOES IT?
CODE 22 IS INTERMITTENT. IF NO ADDITIONAL CODES WERE STORED, REFER TO "DIAGNOSTIC AIDS" ON FACING PAGE.
NO
YES
4
• PROBE CKT 417 WITH A TEST LIGHT CONNECTED TO 12 VOLTS.
"SCAN" TOOL SHOULD DISPLAY TPS OVER 4.0V (4000 mv)
DOES IT?
3
• REFER TO FACING PAGE FOR SPECIFIC INSTRUCTIONS.
YES
NO
5
CKT 416 OPEN, SHORTED TO GROUND. ALSO CHECK CKT 474 FOR SHORT TO GROUND. IF OK, IT IS A FAULTY CONNECTION OR FAULTY ECM.
CKT 417 OPEN, SHORTED TO GROUND, FAULTY CONNECTION OR FAULTY ECM.

"*AFTER REPAIRS,*" REFER TO CODE CRITERIA ON FACING PAGE AND CONFIRM CODE DOES NOT RESET.

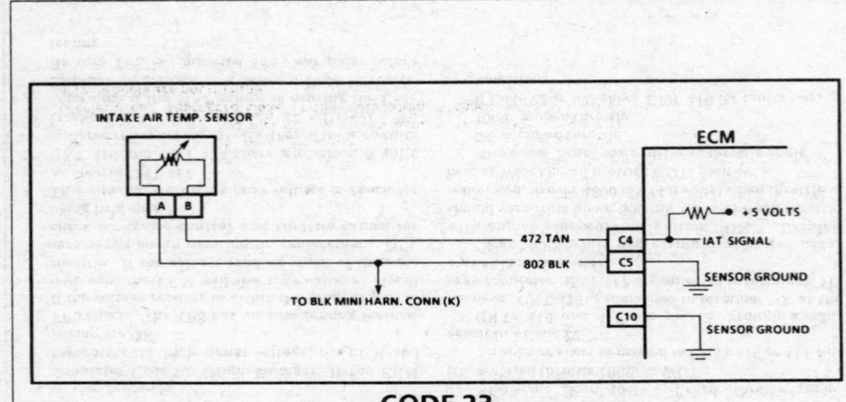
INTAKE AIR TEMP. SENSOR
A
B
ECM
+5 VOLTS
472 TAN
C4
IAT SIGNAL
802 BLK
C5
SENSOR GROUND
TO BLK MINI HARN. CONN (K)
C10
SENSOR GROUND

CODE 23

INTAKE AIR TEMPERATURE (IAT) SENSOR CIRCUIT
(LOW TEMPERATURE INDICATED)
3.1L (VIN T) "W" CARLINE (PORT)

Circuit Description:

The Intake Air Temperature (IAT) sensor uses a thermistor to control the signal voltage to the ECM. The ECM applies a voltage (about 5 volts) on CKT 472 to the sensor. When the air is cold the sensor (thermistor) resistance is high, therefore, the ECM will see a high signal voltage. If the air is warm the sensor resistance is low, therefore, the ECM will see a low voltage.

The IAT sensor is located in the air cleaner.

Test Description: Number(s) below refer to circled number(s) on the diagnostic chart.

1. Code 23 will set if:
   - A signal voltage indicates an Intake Air Temperature (IAT) below -35°C (-31°F).
   - Time since engine start is 4 minutes or longer.
   - Vehicle speed less than 1 mph.
   - Start-up coolant temperature is less than or equal to -35.5°C (31.9°F).
   - All conditions met for 10 seconds.
2. A Code 23 will set, due to an open sensor, wire, or connection. This test will determine if the wiring and ECM are OK.
3. This will determine if the signal CKT 472 or the 5 volts return CKT 802 is open.

Diagnostic Aids:

A "Scan" tool reads temperature of the air entering the engine and should read close to ambient air temperature when engine is cold, and rises as underhood temperature increases.

A faulty connection, or an open in CKT 472 or CKT 802 will result in a Code 23.

Codes 23 and 34 stored at the same time, could be the result of an open CKT 802, which would also turn the temperature warning indicator "ON." CKT 802 is routed through a mini harness. A faulty connection could result in intermittent failures. The "Temperature to Resistance Values" scale at the right may be used to test the IAT sensor at various temperature levels to evaluate the possibility of a "shifted" (mis-scaled) sensor. A "slewed" sensor could result in poor driveability complaints.

CODE 23

INTAKE AIR TEMPERATURE (IAT) SENSOR CIRCUIT
(LOW TEMPERATURE INDICATED)
3.1L (VIN T) "W" CARLINE (PORT)

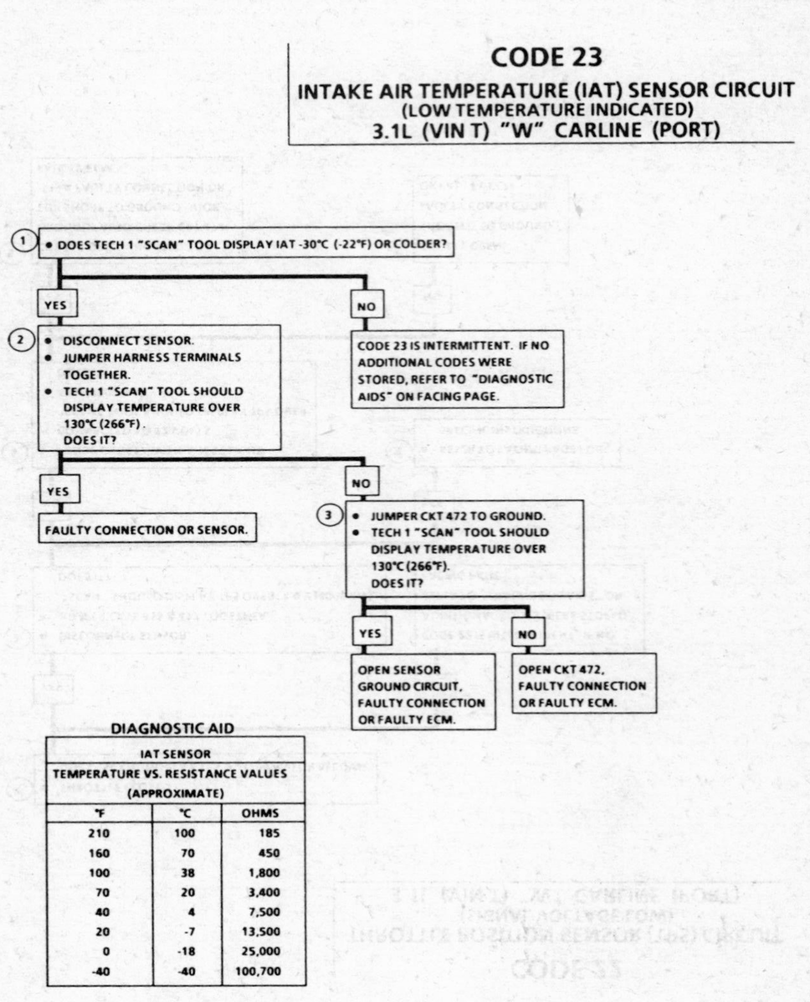
1
• DOES TECH 1 "SCAN" TOOL DISPLAY IAT -30°C (-22°F) OR COLDER?
YES
NO
2
• DISCONNECT SENSOR.
• JUMPER HARNESS TERMINALS TOGETHER.
• TECH 1 "SCAN" TOOL SHOULD DISPLAY TEMPERATURE OVER 130°C (266°F).
DOES IT?
CODE 23 IS INTERMITTENT. IF NO ADDITIONAL CODES WERE STORED, REFER TO "DIAGNOSTIC AIDS" ON FACING PAGE.
YES
NO
FAULTY CONNECTION OR SENSOR.
3
• JUMPER CKT 472 TO GROUND.
• TECH 1 "SCAN" TOOL SHOULD DISPLAY TEMPERATURE OVER 130°C (266°F).
DOES IT?
YES
NO
OPEN SENSOR GROUND CIRCUIT, FAULTY CONNECTION OR FAULTY ECM.
OPEN CKT 472, FAULTY CONNECTION OR FAULTY ECM.

DIAGNOSTIC AID

IAT SENSOR		
TEMPERATURE VS. RESISTANCE VALUES (APPROXIMATE)		
°F	°C	OHMS
210	100	185
160	70	450
100	38	1,800
70	20	3,400
40	4	7,500
20	-7	13,500
0	-18	25,000
-40	-40	100,700

"*AFTER REPAIRS*," REFER TO CODE CRITERIA ON FACING PAGE AND CONFIRM CODE DOES NOT RESET.

DIAGNOSTIC CHARTS — 3.1L engine

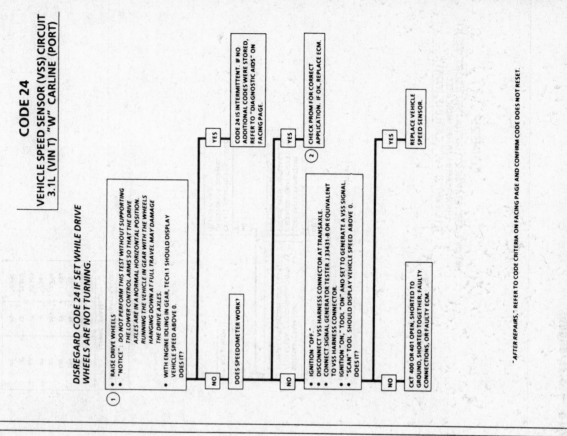

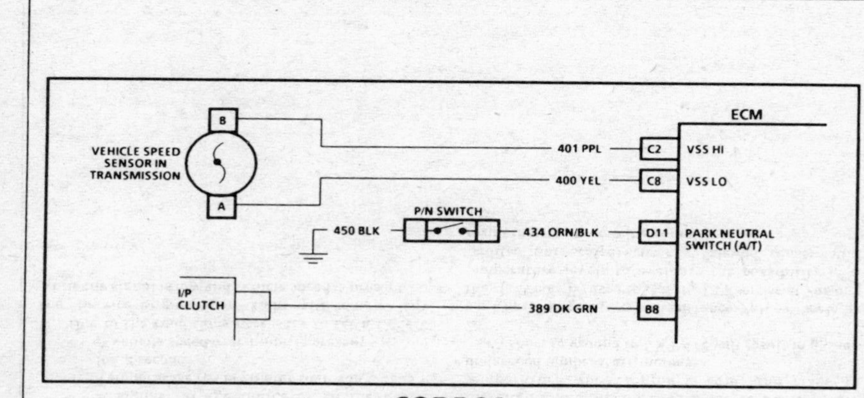

CODE 24

VEHICLE SPEED SENSOR (VSS) CIRCUIT 3.1L (VIN T) "W" CARLINE (PORT)

Circuit Description:

Vehicle speed information is provided to the ECM by the vehicle speed sensor which uses a Permanent Magnet (PM) generator and it is mounted in the transaxle. The PM generator produces a pulsing voltage whenever vehicle speed is over about 3 mph. The AC voltage level and the number of pulses increases with vehicle speed. The ECM then converts the pulsing voltage to mph which is used for calculations, and the mph can be displayed with a "Scan" tool. Output of the generator can also be seen by using a digital voltmeter on the AC scale while rotating the generator.

The function of VSS buffer used in past model years has been incorporated into the ECM. The ECM then supplies the necessary signal for the instrument panel (4000 pulses per mile) for operating the speedometer and the odometer. If the vehicle is equipped with cruise control, the ECM also provides a signal (2000 pulses per mile) to the cruise control module.

NOTE: To prevent misdiagnosis, the technician should review ELECTRICAL DIAGNOSIS or the Electrical Troubleshooting Manual and identify the type of vehicle speed sensor used prior to using this chart. Disregard a Code 24 set when drive wheels are not turning.

Test Description: Number(s) below refer to circled number(s) on the diagnostic chart.

1. Code 24 will set if vehicle speed equals 0 mph when:
   - VSS indicates less than 2 mph.
   - MAP is less than 30 kPa.
   - Engine speed is between 2200 and 4400 rpm.
   - TPS is less than 2%.
   - Not in park or neutral.
   - No Code 21, 22, 33 or 34.
   - All conditions met for 3 seconds.

   These conditions are met during a road load deceleration. Disregard Code 24 that sets when drive wheels are not turning.
   - The PM generator only produces a signal if drive wheels are turning greater than 3 mph.
2. If CKTs 400, 401 and 389 are OK, and if the speedometer works properly, Code 24 is being caused by a faulty ECM, faulty MEM-CAL or an incorrect MEM-CAL.

Diagnostic Aids:

"Scan" should indicate a vehicle speed whenever the drive wheels are turning greater than 3 mph.

A problem in CKT 389 will not affect the VSS input or the readings on a "Scan."

Check CKT 400 and CKT 401 for proper connections to be sure there clean and tight and the harness is routed correctly. Refer to "Intermittents" in "Symptoms," Section "6E3-B".

(A/T) A faulty or misadjusted Park/Neutral (P/N) switch can result in a false Code 24. Use a "Scan" and check for proper signal while in overdrive (440-T4).

CODE 24

VEHICLE SPEED SENSOR (VSS) CIRCUIT 3.1L (VIN T) "W" CARLINE (PORT)

DISREGARD CODE 24 IF SET WHILE DRIVE WHEELS ARE NOT TURNING.

(1)
- RAISE DRIVE WHEELS
- "NOTICE": *DO NOT PERFORM THIS TEST WITHOUT SUPPORTING THE LOWER CONTROL ARMS SO THAT THE DRIVE AXLES ARE IN A NORMAL HORIZONTAL POSITION. RUNNING THE VEHICLE IN GEAR WITH THE WHEELS HANGING DOWN AT FULL TRAVEL MAY DAMAGE THE DRIVE AXLES.*
- WITH ENGINE IDLING IN GEAR, TECH 1 SHOULD DISPLAY VEHICLE SPEED ABOVE 0. DOES IT?

YES: CODE 24 IS INTERMITTENT. IF NO ADDITIONAL CODES WERE STORED, REFER TO "DIAGNOSTIC AIDS" ON FACING PAGE.

NO: DOES SPEEDOMETER WORK?

YES: (2) CHECK PROM FOR CORRECT APPLICATION. IF OK, REPLACE ECM.

NO:
- IGNITION "OFF."
- DISCONNECT VSS HARNESS CONNECTOR AT TRANSAXLE.
- CONNECT SIGNAL GENERATOR TESTER J 33431-B OR EQUIVALENT TO VSS HARNESS CONNECTOR.
- IGNITION "ON," TOOL "ON" AND SET TO GENERATE A VSS SIGNAL.
- "SCAN" TOOL SHOULD DISPLAY VEHICLE SPEED ABOVE 0. DOES IT?

YES: REPLACE VEHICLE SPEED SENSOR.

NO: CKT 400 OR 401 OPEN, SHORTED TO GROUND, SHORTED TOGETHER, FAULTY CONNECTIONS, OR FAULTY ECM.

"*AFTER REPAIRS,*" REFER TO CODE CRITERIA ON FACING PAGE AND CONFIRM CODE DOES NOT RESET.

DIAGNOSTIC CHARTS — 3.1L engine

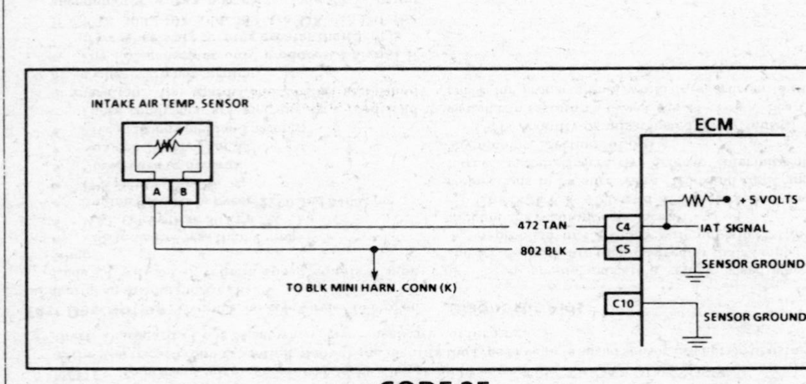
INTAKE AIR TEMP. SENSOR
A
B
ECM
+5 VOLTS
472 TAN
C4
IAT SIGNAL
802 BLK
C5
SENSOR GROUND
TO BLK MINI HARN. CONN (K)
C10
SENSOR GROUND

CODE 25

INTAKE AIR TEMPERATURE (IAT) SENSOR CIRCUIT
(HIGH TEMPERATURE INDICATED)
3.1L (VIN T) "W" CARLINE (PORT)

Circuit Description:

The Intake Air Temperature (IAT) sensor uses a thermistor to control the signal voltage to the ECM. The ECM applies a voltage (about 5 volts) on CKT 472 to the sensor. When the air is cold the sensor (thermistor) resistance is high, therefore the ECM will see a high signal voltage. If the air is warm the sensor resistance is low therefore the ECM will see a low voltage.

The IAT sensor is located in the air cleaner.

Test Description: Number(s) below refer to circled number(s) on the diagnostic chart.

1. Code 25 will set if:
   - A signal voltage indicates an Intake Air Temperature (IAT) greater than 135°C (293°F) for .2 seconds.
   - A vehicle speed over 1 mph is present.

Due to the conditions necessary to set a Code 25 the "Service Engine Soon" light will remain "ON" while the signal is low and vehicle speed is present.

Diagnostic Aids:

A "Scan" tool reads temperature of the air entering the engine and should read close to ambient air temperature when engine is cold, and rises as underhood temperature increases.

A short to ground in CKT 472 will result in a Code 25.

The "Temperature to Resistance Values" scale at the right may be used to test the IAT sensor at various temperature levels to evaluate the possibility of a "shifted" (mis-scaled) sensor. A "slewed" sensor could result in poor driveability complaints.

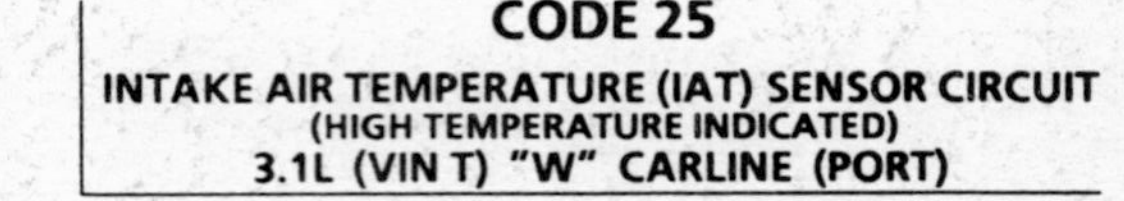

CODE 25

INTAKE AIR TEMPERATURE (IAT) SENSOR CIRCUIT
(HIGH TEMPERATURE INDICATED)
3.1L (VIN T) "W" CARLINE (PORT)

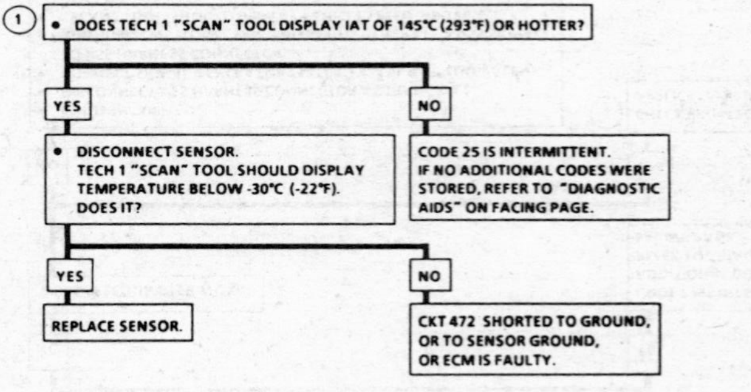
1
• DOES TECH 1 "SCAN" TOOL DISPLAY IAT OF 145°C (293°F) OR HOTTER?
YES
NO
• DISCONNECT SENSOR.
TECH 1 "SCAN" TOOL SHOULD DISPLAY TEMPERATURE BELOW -30°C (-22°F).
DOES IT?
CODE 25 IS INTERMITTENT.
IF NO ADDITIONAL CODES WERE STORED, REFER TO "DIAGNOSTIC AIDS" ON FACING PAGE.
YES
NO
REPLACE SENSOR.
CKT 472 SHORTED TO GROUND, OR TO SENSOR GROUND, OR ECM IS FAULTY.

DIAGNOSTIC AID

IAT SENSOR		
TEMPERATURE VS. RESISTANCE VALUES (APPROXIMATE)		
°F	°C	OHMS
210	100	185
160	70	450
100	38	1,800
70	20	3,400
40	4	7,500
20	-7	13,500
0	-18	25,000
-40	-40	100,700

"*AFTER REPAIRS*," REFER TO CODE CRITERIA ON FACING PAGE AND CONFIRM CODE DOES NOT RESET.

DIAGNOSTIC CHARTS — 3.1L engine

TOP VIEW OF EGR VALVE
A C B D
699 RED
697 BLU
698 BRN/WHT
250 BRN
BLK MINI HARN. CONN.
B C E J
GRY MINI HARN. CONN.
BLK MINI HARNESS CONNECTOR
10A
RT SIDE UNDERHOOD ELECT CTR
699 RED C13
697 BLU A4
698 BRN A19
ECM
EGR 3
EGR 1
EGR 2

CODE 32
DIGITAL EGR
EXHAUST GAS RECIRCULATION (EGR) CIRCUIT
(ELECTRICAL DIAGNOSIS)
3.1L (VIN T) "W" CARLINE (PORT)

Circuit Description:

Code 32 represents an EGR flow test failure. The ECM, on a closed throttle coast down, will cycle the solenoids "ON" and "OFF" individually and look for a resulting change in engine rpm and Oxygen (O_2) sensor activity.

Test Description: Number(s) below refer to circled number(s) on the diagnostic chart.

1. This test determines if there is power to the EGR valve.
2. This test will determine if there is an open circuit in the EGR wiring or if the EGR valve is at fault.
3. This test will determine if there is a short to ground in any circuit going to the EGR valve or if the ECM is at fault.

Diagnostic Aids:

An intermittent may be caused by a poor connection, rubbed-through wire insulation, or a wire broken inside the insulation.

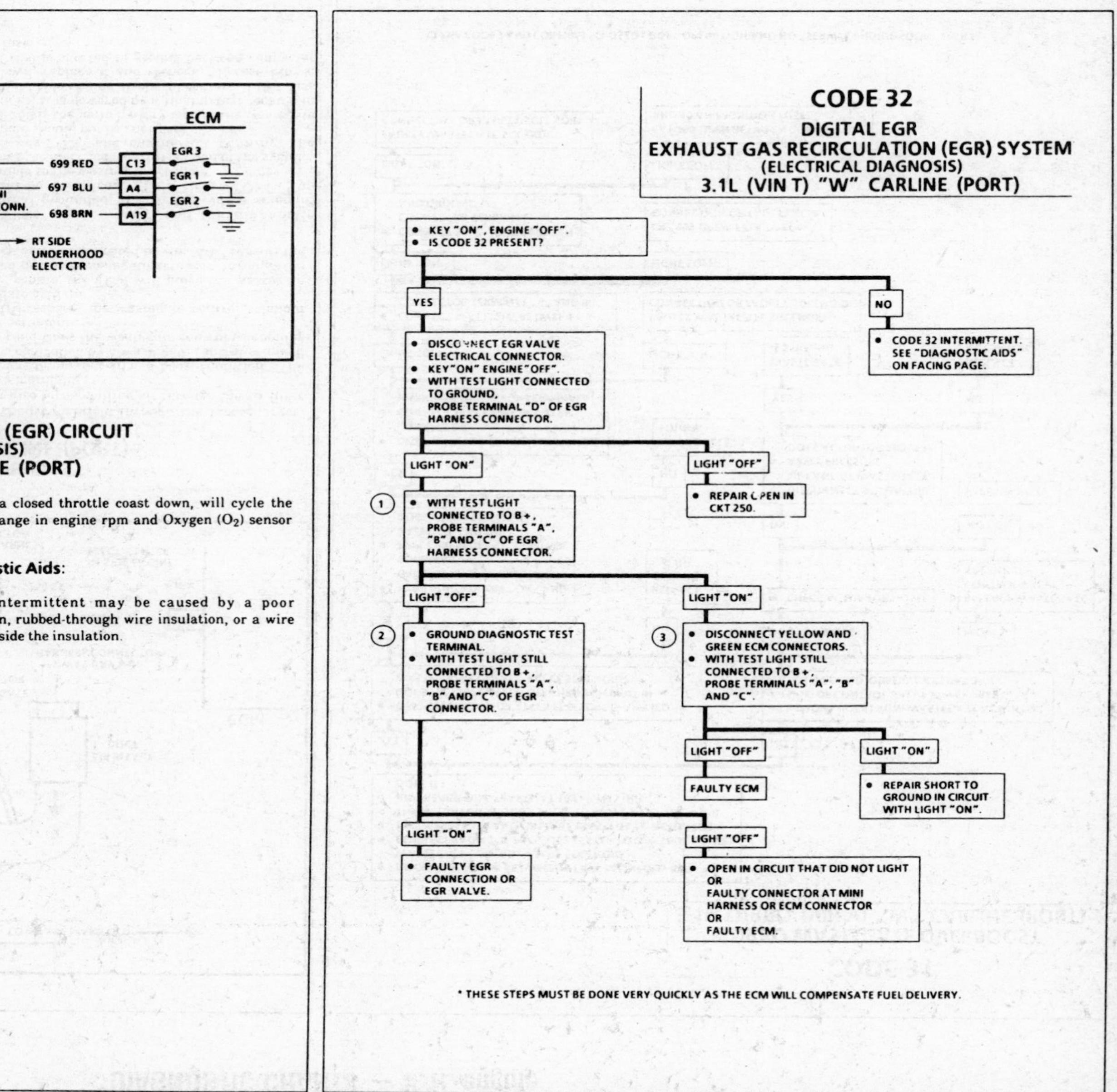
CODE 32
DIGITAL EGR
EXHAUST GAS RECIRCULATION (EGR) SYSTEM
(ELECTRICAL DIAGNOSIS)
3.1L (VIN T) "W" CARLINE (PORT)
• KEY "ON", ENGINE "OFF".
• IS CODE 32 PRESENT?
YES
NO
• CODE 32 INTERMITTENT. SEE "DIAGNOSTIC AIDS" ON FACING PAGE.
• DISCONNECT EGR VALVE ELECTRICAL CONNECTOR.
• KEY "ON" ENGINE "OFF".
• WITH TEST LIGHT CONNECTED TO GROUND, PROBE TERMINAL "D" OF EGR HARNESS CONNECTOR.
LIGHT "ON"
LIGHT "OFF"
• REPAIR OPEN IN CKT 250.
1
• WITH TEST LIGHT CONNECTED TO B+, PROBE TERMINALS "A", "B" AND "C" OF EGR HARNESS CONNECTOR.
LIGHT "OFF"
LIGHT "ON"
2
• GROUND DIAGNOSTIC TEST TERMINAL.
• WITH TEST LIGHT STILL CONNECTED TO B+, PROBE TERMINALS "A", "B" AND "C" OF EGR CONNECTOR.
3
• DISCONNECT YELLOW AND GREEN ECM CONNECTORS.
• WITH TEST LIGHT STILL CONNECTED TO B+, PROBE TERMINALS "A", "B" AND "C".
LIGHT "OFF"
FAULTY ECM
LIGHT "ON"
• REPAIR SHORT TO GROUND IN CIRCUIT WITH LIGHT "ON".
LIGHT "ON"
• FAULTY EGR CONNECTION OR EGR VALVE.
LIGHT "OFF"
• OPEN IN CIRCUIT THAT DID NOT LIGHT OR FAULTY CONNECTOR AT MINI HARNESS OR ECM CONNECTOR OR FAULTY ECM.
* THESE STEPS MUST BE DONE VERY QUICKLY AS THE ECM WILL COMPENSATE FUEL DELIVERY.

DIAGNOSTIC CHARTS — 3.1L engine

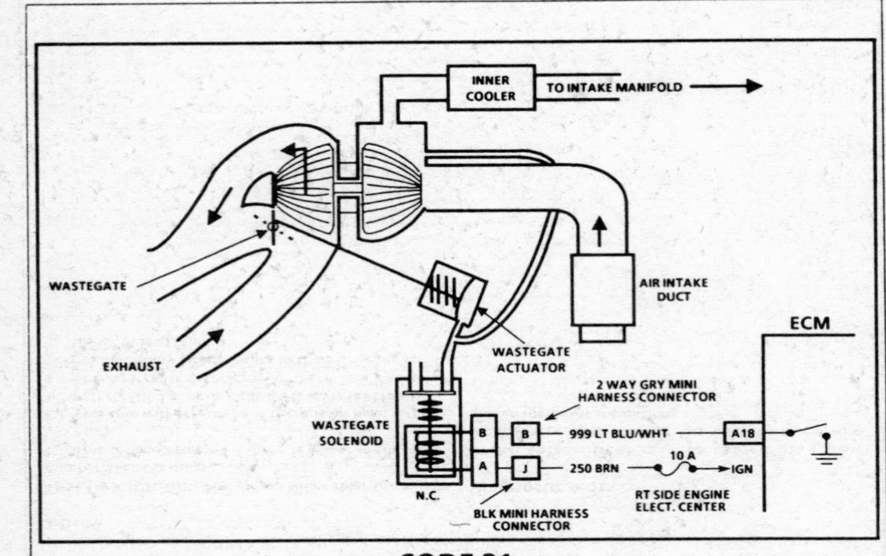
INNER COOLER
TO INTAKE MANIFOLD
WASTEGATE
EXHAUST
AIR INTAKE DUCT
ECM
WASTEGATE ACTUATOR
2 WAY GRY MINI HARNESS CONNECTOR
WASTEGATE SOLENOID
B
A
B
J
999 LT BLU/WHT
250 BRN
A18
10 A
IGN
N.C.
BLK MINI HARNESS CONNECTOR
RT SIDE ENGINE ELECT. CENTER

CODE 31

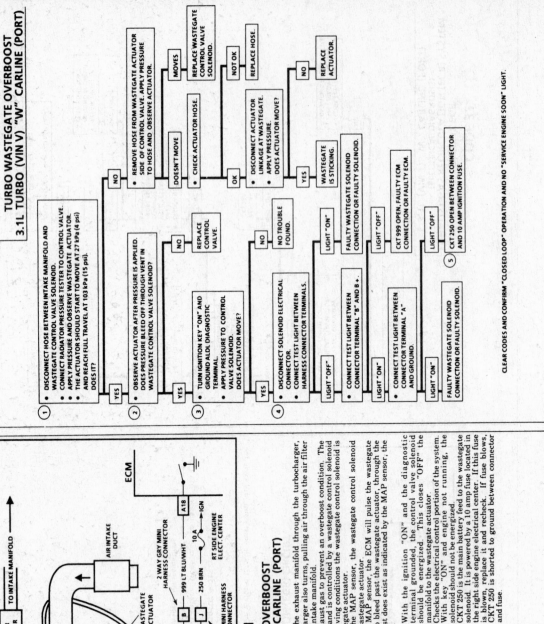

TURBO WASTEGATE OVERBOOST
3.1L TURBO (VIN V) "W" CARLINE (PORT)

Circuit Description:

On turbocharged engines, the exhaust gases pass from the exhaust manifold through the turbocharger, turning the turbine blades. The compressor side of the turbocharger also turns, pulling air through the air filter and pushing the air into the intake manifold, pressurizing the intake manifold.

The wastegate is normally closed, but opens to bypass exhaust gas to prevent an overboost condition. The wastegate will open when pressure is applied to the actuator, and is controlled by a wastegate control solenoid valve pulsed "ON" and "OFF" by the ECM. Under normal driving conditions the wastegate control solenoid is not energized, which allows MAP pressure directly to the wastegate actuator.

As a boost (or MAP) pressure increase is detected, by the MAP sensor, the wastegate control solenoid remains closed, and MAP pressure only will be applied to the wastegate actuator.

If a boost (or MAP) pressure decrease is detected, by the MAP sensor, the ECM will pulse the wastegate control solenoid valve. MAP pressure will then be allowed to bleed past the wastegate actuator, through the solenoid valve, allowing the wastegate to close. If an overboost does exist as indicated by the MAP sensor, the ECM will reduce fuel delivery to prevent damage to the engine.

Test Description: Numbers below refer to circled numbers on the diagnostic chart.

1. A Code 31 will set when the manifold pressure exceeds 65 kPa (9.5 psi) of boost for .5 seconds, and a Code 33 has not previously been set. Code 31 will set, but the "Service Engine Soon" light will stay "ON" only while the overboost exists. The light will stay "ON" for 10 seconds after the condition exists and then go "OUT."
   An overboost condition could be caused by
   - CKT 999 shorted to ground
   - A sticking wastegate actuator or wastegate
   - A control valve stuck in the open position
   - A cut or pinched hose
   - A faulty ECM
   - An extremely dirty air filter

   With ignition shut "OFF," the control valve solenoid is open.
2. With the ignition "ON" and the diagnostic terminal grounded, the control valve solenoid should be energized. This closes "OFF" the manifold to the wastegate actuator.
3. Checks the electrical control portion of the system. With key "ON" and engine not running, the solenoid should not be energized.
4. CKT 250 is the main battery feed to the wastegate solenoid. It is powered by a 10 amp fuse located in the right side engine electrical center. If this fuse is blown, replace it and recheck. If fuse blows, CKT 250 is shorted to ground between connector and fuse.

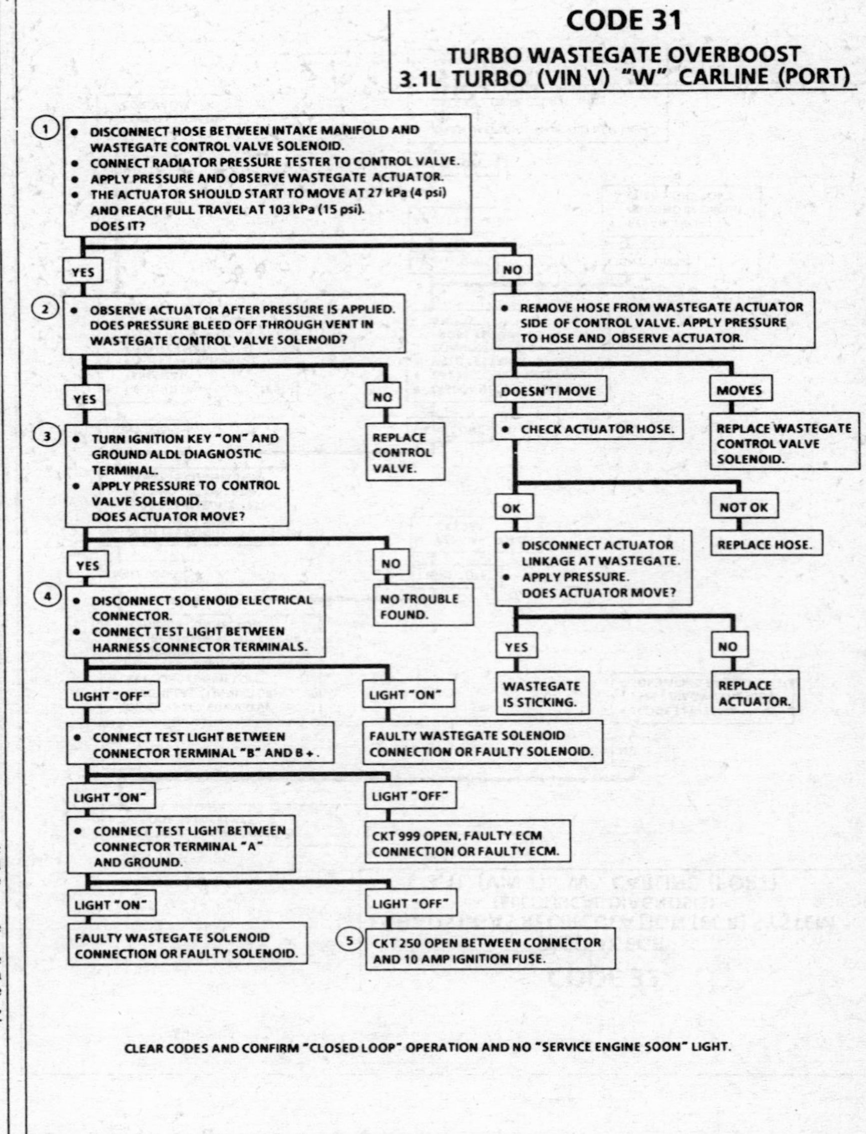
CODE 31
TURBO WASTEGATE OVERBOOST
3.1L TURBO (VIN V) "W" CARLINE (PORT)
1
• DISCONNECT HOSE BETWEEN INTAKE MANIFOLD AND WASTEGATE CONTROL VALVE SOLENOID.
• CONNECT RADIATOR PRESSURE TESTER TO CONTROL VALVE.
• APPLY PRESSURE AND OBSERVE WASTEGATE ACTUATOR.
• THE ACTUATOR SHOULD START TO MOVE AT 27 kPa (4 psi) AND REACH FULL TRAVEL AT 103 kPa (15 psi).
DOES IT?
YES
NO
2
• OBSERVE ACTUATOR AFTER PRESSURE IS APPLIED. DOES PRESSURE BLEED OFF THROUGH VENT IN WASTEGATE CONTROL VALVE SOLENOID?
• REMOVE HOSE FROM WASTEGATE ACTUATOR SIDE OF CONTROL VALVE. APPLY PRESSURE TO HOSE AND OBSERVE ACTUATOR.
YES
NO
DOESN'T MOVE
MOVES
3
• TURN IGNITION KEY "ON" AND GROUND ALDL DIAGNOSTIC TERMINAL.
• APPLY PRESSURE TO CONTROL VALVE SOLENOID.
DOES ACTUATOR MOVE?
REPLACE CONTROL VALVE.
• CHECK ACTUATOR HOSE.
REPLACE WASTEGATE CONTROL VALVE SOLENOID.
OK
NOT OK
YES
NO
• DISCONNECT ACTUATOR LINKAGE AT WASTEGATE.
• APPLY PRESSURE.
DOES ACTUATOR MOVE?
REPLACE HOSE.
4
• DISCONNECT SOLENOID ELECTRICAL CONNECTOR.
• CONNECT TEST LIGHT BETWEEN HARNESS CONNECTOR TERMINALS.
NO TROUBLE FOUND.
YES
NO
LIGHT "OFF"
LIGHT "ON"
WASTEGATE IS STICKING.
REPLACE ACTUATOR.
• CONNECT TEST LIGHT BETWEEN CONNECTOR TERMINAL "B" AND B+.
FAULTY WASTEGATE SOLENOID CONNECTION OR FAULTY SOLENOID.
LIGHT "ON"
LIGHT "OFF"
• CONNECT TEST LIGHT BETWEEN CONNECTOR TERMINAL "A" AND GROUND.
CKT 999 OPEN, FAULTY ECM CONNECTION OR FAULTY ECM.
LIGHT "ON"
LIGHT "OFF"
FAULTY WASTEGATE SOLENOID CONNECTION OR FAULTY SOLENOID.
5
CKT 250 OPEN BETWEEN CONNECTOR AND 10 AMP IGNITION FUSE.
CLEAR CODES AND CONFIRM "CLOSED LOOP" OPERATION AND NO "SERVICE ENGINE SOON" LIGHT.

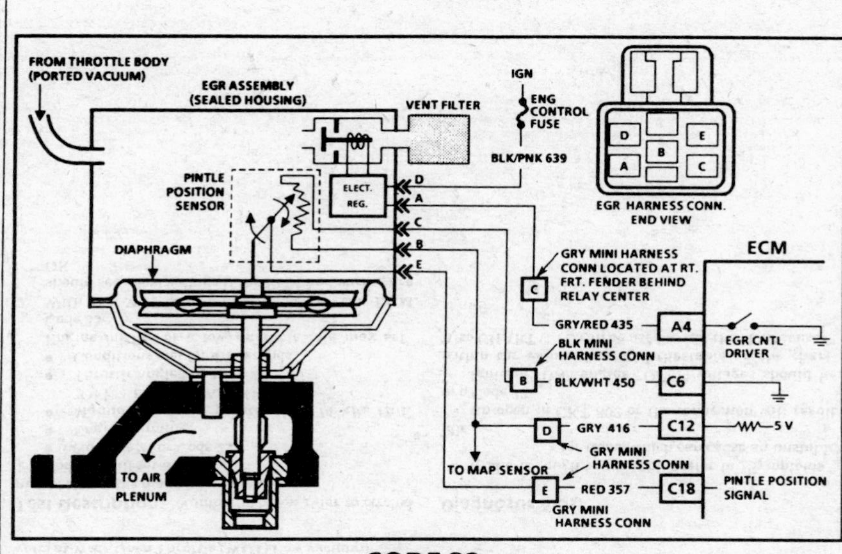

CODE 32

WITH E.V.R.V.

EXHAUST GAS RECIRCULATION (EGR) CIRCUIT 3.1L TURBO (VIN V) "W" CARLINE (PORT)

Circuit Description:

The integrated electronic EGR valve functions similar to a port valve with a remote vacuum regulator. The internal solenoid is normally open, which causes the vacuum signal to be vented "OFF" to the atmosphere when EGR is not being commanded by the ECM. This EGR valve has a sealed cap and the solenoid valve opens and closes the vacuum signal which controls the amount of vacuum vented to atmosphere, and this controls the amount of vacuum applied to the diaphragm. The electronic EGR valve contains a voltage regulator which converts the ECM signal to provide different amounts of EGR flow by regulating the current to the solenoid. The ECM controls EGR flow with a pulse width modulated signal (turns "ON" and "OFF" many times a second) based on air flow, TPS, and rpm.

This system also contains a pintle position sensor which works similar to a TPS sensor, and as EGR flow is increased, the sensor output also increases.

Code 32 means that there has been an EGR system fault detected.

Code 32 will set under two conditions:

- Coolant temperature above a specified amount, EGR should be "ON" or;
- EGR pintle position does not match duty cycle.

Test Description: Numbers below refer to circled numbers on the diagnostic chart.

1. With the engine running and the transmission in gear, with brakes applied, increasing engine rpm will put a load on the engine. Engine vacuum will be applied to the EGR diaphragm and cause the EGR pintle to open increasing pintle position voltage.
2. Grounding the diagnostic terminal should energize the solenoid which closes off the vent and allows the vacuum to move the diaphragm. This test determines that the ECM is capable of controlling the solenoid. When EGR is commanded on by the ECM, the test light should be "ON."
3. If CKT 452 is open, the pintle signal will go high (showing a 5 volts signal). This will set a Code 32. If CKT 357 becomes shorted to 12 volts or to CKT 416, the signal voltage will go high causing a Code 32.

Diagnostic Aids:

Some "Scan" tools will read pintle position in volts.

The EGR position voltage can be used to determine that the pintle is moving. When no EGR is commanded (0-% duty cycle), the position sensor should read between .5 volt and 1.5 volts and increase with the commanded EGR duty cycle. If system operates correctly, refer to "Intermittents" Section

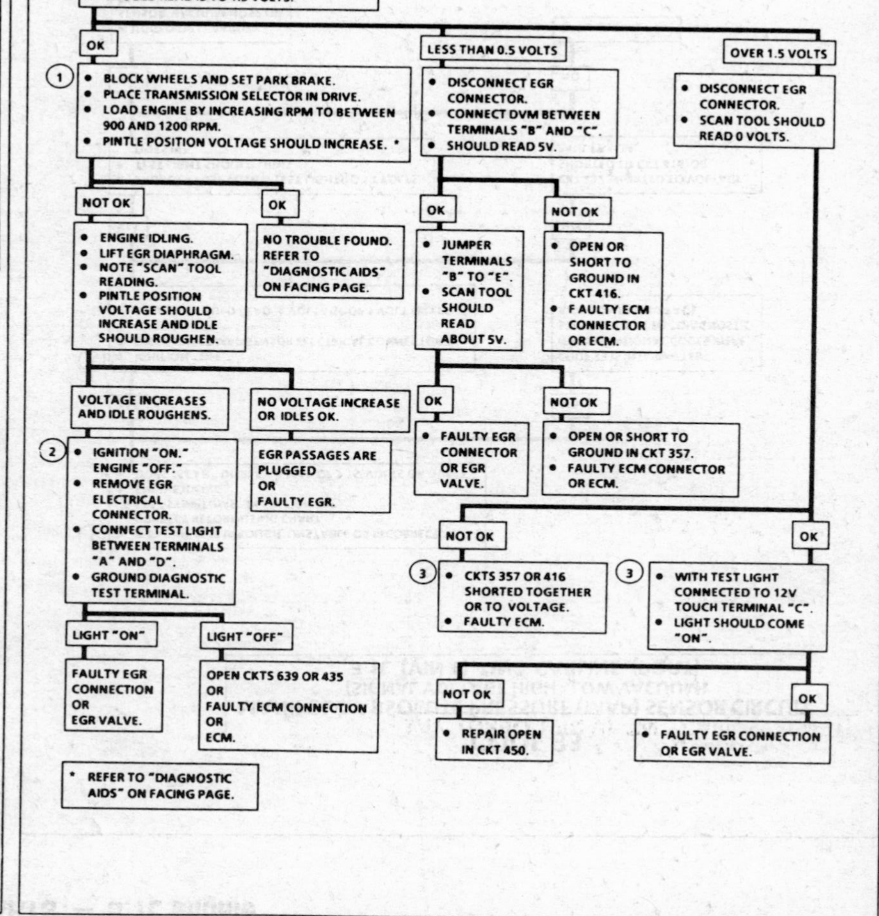

DIAGNOSTIC CHARTS — 3.1L engine

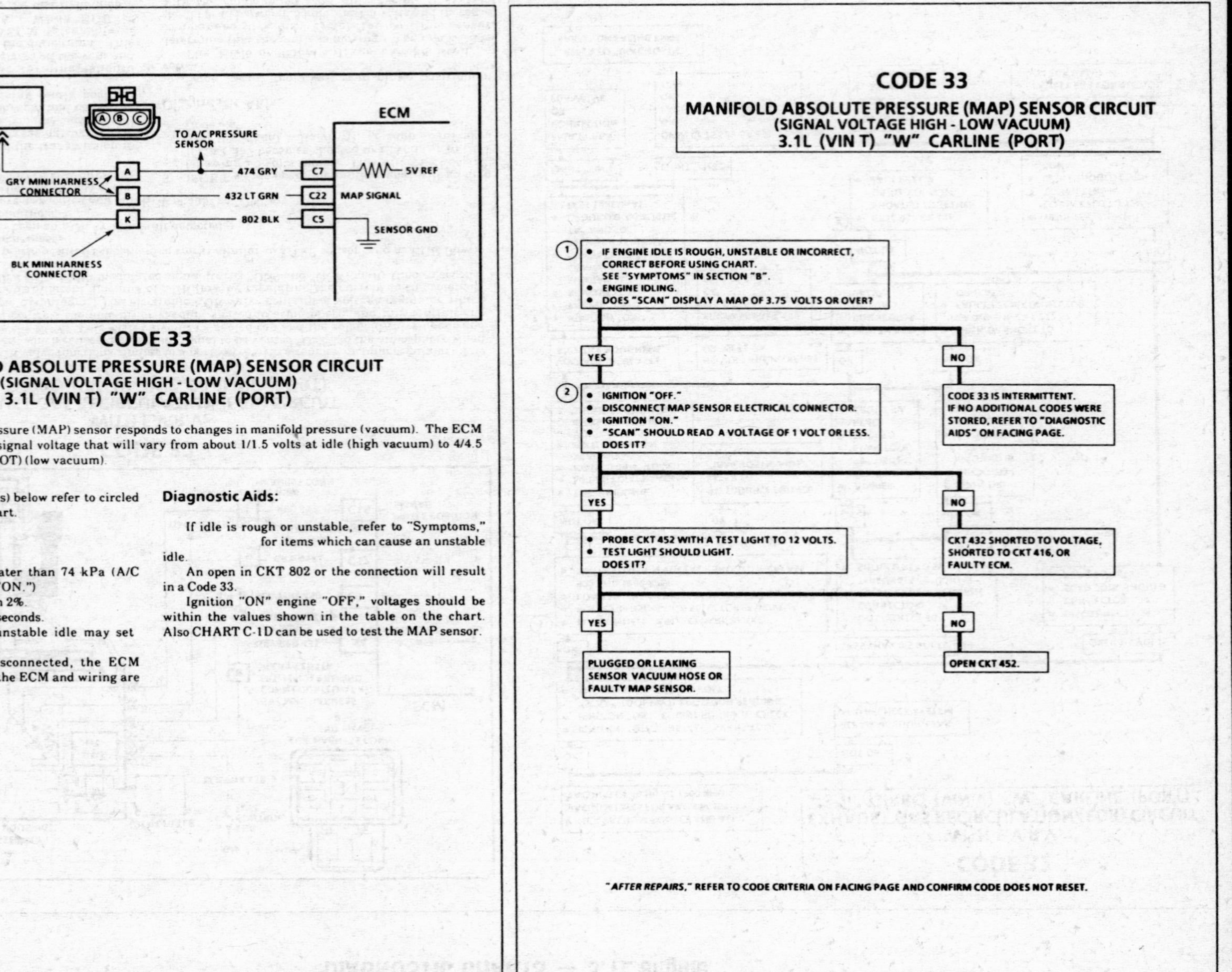
MAP SENSOR
A B C
MANIFOLD ABSOLUTE PRESSURE (VACUUM)
GRY MINI HARNESS CONNECTOR
BLK MINI HARNESS CONNECTOR
TO A/C PRESSURE SENSOR
A
B
K
474 GRY
432 LT GRN
802 BLK
C7
C22
C5
ECM
5V REF
MAP SIGNAL
SENSOR GND
① • IF ENGINE IDLE IS ROUGH, UNSTABLE OR INCORRECT, CORRECT BEFORE USING CHART. SEE "SYMPTOMS" IN SECTION "B".
• ENGINE IDLING.
• DOES "SCAN" DISPLAY A MAP OF 3.75 VOLTS OR OVER?
YES
NO
② • IGNITION "OFF."
• DISCONNECT MAP SENSOR ELECTRICAL CONNECTOR.
• IGNITION "ON."
• "SCAN" SHOULD READ A VOLTAGE OF 1 VOLT OR LESS. DOES IT?
CODE 33 IS INTERMITTENT. IF NO ADDITIONAL CODES WERE STORED, REFER TO "DIAGNOSTIC AIDS" ON FACING PAGE.
YES
NO
• PROBE CKT 452 WITH A TEST LIGHT TO 12 VOLTS.
• TEST LIGHT SHOULD LIGHT. DOES IT?
CKT 432 SHORTED TO VOLTAGE, SHORTED TO CKT 416, OR FAULTY ECM.
YES
NO
PLUGGED OR LEAKING SENSOR VACUUM HOSE OR FAULTY MAP SENSOR.
OPEN CKT 452.
"AFTER REPAIRS," REFER TO CODE CRITERIA ON FACING PAGE AND CONFIRM CODE DOES NOT RESET.

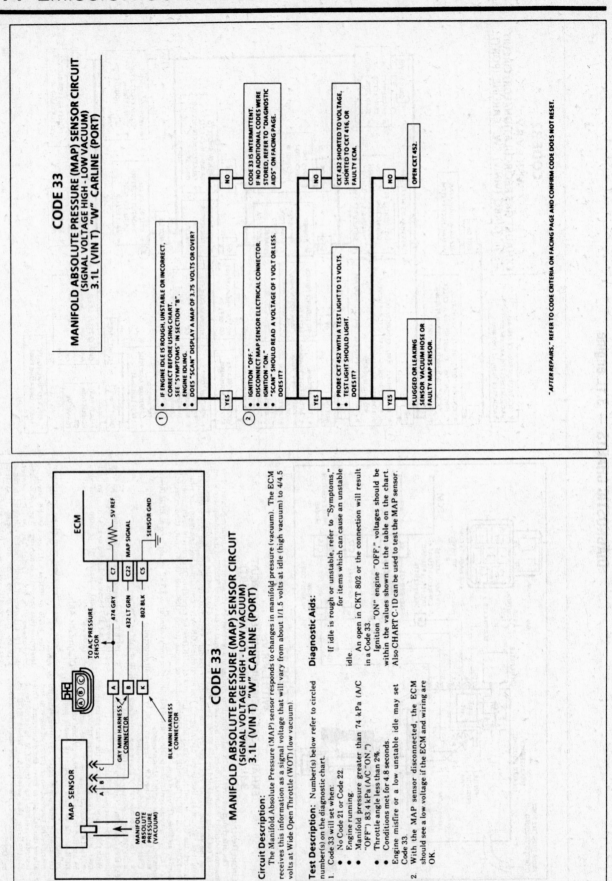

CODE 33
MANIFOLD ABSOLUTE PRESSURE (MAP) SENSOR CIRCUIT
(SIGNAL VOLTAGE HIGH - LOW VACUUM)
3.1L (VIN T) "W" CARLINE (PORT)

Circuit Description:

The Manifold Absolute Pressure (MAP) sensor responds to changes in manifold pressure (vacuum). The ECM receives this information as a signal voltage that will vary from about 1/1.5 volts at idle (high vacuum) to 4/4.5 volts at Wide Open Throttle (WOT) (low vacuum).

Test Description: Number(s) below refer to circled number(s) on the diagnostic chart.

1. Code 33 will set when:
   - No Code 21 or Code 22.
   - Engine running.
   - Manifold pressure greater than 74 kPa (A/C "OFF") 83.4 kPa (A/C "ON.")
   - Throttle angle less than 2%.
   - Conditions met for 4.8 seconds.

   Engine misfire or a low unstable idle may set Code 33.
2. With the MAP sensor disconnected, the ECM should see a low voltage if the ECM and wiring are OK.

Diagnostic Aids:

If idle is rough or unstable, refer to "Symptoms," for items which can cause an unstable idle.

An open in CKT 802 or the connection will result in a Code 33.

Ignition "ON" engine "OFF," voltages should be within the values shown in the table on the chart. Also CHART C-1D can be used to test the MAP sensor.

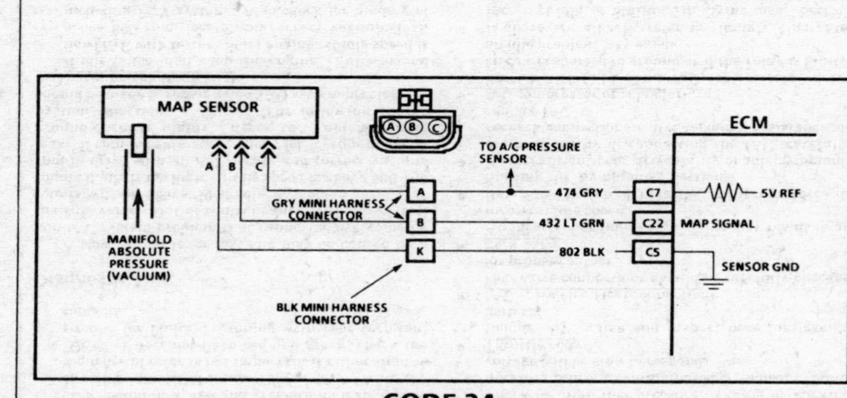

CODE 34

MANIFOLD ABSOLUTE PRESSURE (MAP) SENSOR CIRCUIT
(SIGNAL VOLTAGE LOW - HIGH VACUUM)
3.1L (VIN T) "W" CARLINE (PORT)

Circuit Description:

The Manifold Absolute Pressure (MAP) sensor responds to changes in manifold pressure (vacuum). The ECM receives this information as a signal voltage that will vary from about 1/1.5 volts at idle (high vacuum) to 4/4.5 volts at Wide Open Throttle (WOT) (low vacuum).

Test Description: Number(s) below refer to circled number(s) on the diagnostic chart.

1. Code 34 will set if:
   - Engine rpm less than 700.
   - Manifold pressure reading less than 13 kPa.
   - Conditions met for .22 second.

   OR
   - Engine rpm greater than 700.
   - Throttle angle over 20%.
   - Manifold pressure less than 13 kPa.
   - Conditions met for .22 second.
2. This test to see if the sensor is at fault for the low voltage, or if there is an ECM or wiring problem.
3. This simulates a high signal voltage to check for an open in CKT 432. If the test light is bright during this test, CKT 432 is probably shorted to ground. If "Scan" reads over 4 volts at this test, CKT 474 can be checked by measuring the voltage at terminal "C" (should be 5 volts).

Diagnostic Aids:

An intermittent open in CKT 432 or CKT 474 will result in a Code 34.

Ignition "ON" engine "OFF," voltages should be within the values shown in the table on the chart. Also CHART C-1D can be used to test MAP sensor.

CODE 34

MANIFOLD ABSOLUTE PRESSURE (MAP) SENSOR CIRCUIT
(SIGNAL VOLTAGE LOW - HIGH VACUUM)
3.1L (VIN T) "W" CARLINE (PORT)

(1)
- IGNITION "OFF" FOR 10 SECONDS.
- START ENGINE AND IMMEDIATELY NOTE MAP VALUE ON "SCAN."

DOES "SCAN" DISPLAY MAP BELOW .25 VOLTS?

NO → CODE 34 IS INTERMITTENT. IF NO ADDITIONAL CODES WERE STORED, REFER TO "DIAGNOSTIC AIDS" ON FACING PAGE.

YES →

(2)
- IGNITION "OFF."
- DISCONNECT SENSOR ELECTRICAL CONNECTOR.
- JUMPER HARNESS TERMINALS "B" TO "C".
- IGNITION "ON."
- DOES MAP VOLTAGE READ OVER 4 VOLTS?

YES → FAULTY CONNECTION OR SENSOR.

NO →

(3)
- IGNITION "OFF."
- REMOVE JUMPER WIRE.
- PROBE TERMINAL "B" (CKT 432) WITH A LIGHT TO 12 VOLTS.
- IGNITION "ON."
- DOES "SCAN" READ OVER 4 VOLTS?

YES → CKT 416 OPEN OR SHORTED TO GROUND OR FAULTY ECM.

NO → CKT 432 OPEN OR SHORTED TO GROUND OR FAULTY ECM.

"AFTER REPAIRS," REFER TO CODE CRITERIA ON FACING PAGE AND CONFIRM CODE DOES NOT RESET.

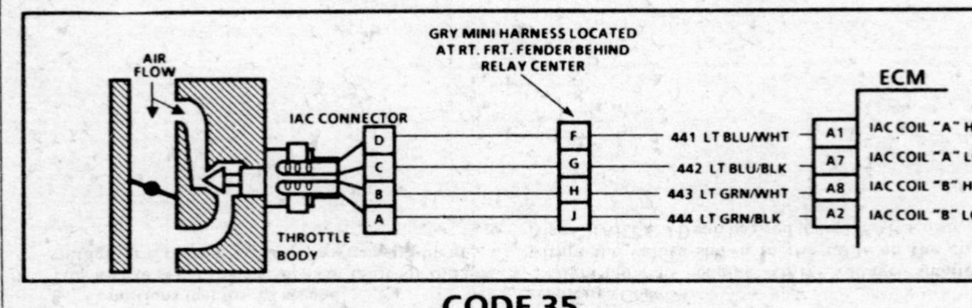

GRY MINI HARNESS LOCATED AT RT. FRT. FENDER BEHIND RELAY CENTER
AIR FLOW
IAC CONNECTOR
D
C
B
A
THROTTLE BODY
F
G
H
J
441 LT BLU/WHT
442 LT BLU/BLK
443 LT GRN/WHT
444 LT GRN/BLK
A1
A7
A8
A2
ECM
IAC COIL "A" HI
IAC COIL "A" LO
IAC COIL "B" HI
IAC COIL "B" LO

CODE 35

IDLE AIR CONTROL (IAC) CIRCUIT
3.1L (VIN T) "W" CARLINE (PORT)

Circuit Description:

Code 35 will set when the closed throttle engine speed is 200 rpm above or below the desired (commanded) idle speed for 50 seconds. Review the "General Description" of the IAC operation in "Fuel Metering System," Section "6E3-C2".

Test Description: Number(s) below refer to circled number(s) on the diagnostic chart.

1. The Tech 1 rpm control mode is used to extend and retract the IAC valve. The valve should move smoothly within the specified range. If the idle speed is commanded (IAC extended) too low (below 700 rpm), the engine may stall. This may be normal and would not indicate a problem. Retracting the IAC beyond its controlled range (above 1500 rpm) will cause a delay before the rpm's start dropping. This too is normal.
2. This test uses the Tech 1 to command the IAC controlled idle speed. The ECM issues commands to obtain commended idle speed. The node lights each should flash red and green to indicate a good circuit as the ECM issues commands. While the sequence of color is not important if either light is "OFF" or does not flash red and green, check the circuits for faults, beginning with poor terminal contacts.

Diagnostic Aids:

A slow, unstable, or fast idle may be caused by a non-IAC system problem that cannot be overcome by the IAC valve. Out of control range IAC "Scan" tool counts will be above 60 if idle is too low, and zero counts if idle is too high. If idle speed is above 600-700 rpm in drive with an A/T, locate and correct vacuum leak. If rpm is below spec., check for foreign material around throttle plates. Refer to "Fuel Metering System," Section   The following checks should be made to repair a non-IAC system problem.

- Vacuum leak (high idle)
  If idle is too high, stop the engine. Fully extend (low) IAC with tester. Start engine. If idle speed is above 800 rpm, locate and correct vacuum leak including PCV system. Also check for binding of throttle blade or linkage.
- System too lean (high air/fuel ratio)
  The idle speed may be too high or too low. Engine speed may vary up and down and disconnecting the IAC valve does not help. Code 44 may set. "Scan" O_2 voltage will be less than 300 mV (.3 volt). Check for low regulated fuel pressure, water in the fuel or a restricted injector.
- System too rich (low air/fuel ratio)
  The idle speed will be too low. "Scan" tool IAC counts will usually be above 80. System is obviously rich and may exhibit black smoke in exhaust.
  "Scan" tool O_2 voltage will be fixed above 800 mV (.8 volt).
  Check for high fuel pressure, leaking or sticking injector. Silicone contaminated O_2 sensors "Scan" voltage will be slow to respond.
- Throttle body
  Remove IAC valve and inspect bore for foreign material.
- IAC valve electrical connections
  IAC valve connections should be carefully checked for proper contact.
- PCV valve
  An incorrect or faulty PCV valve may result in an incorrect idle speed.
- Refer to "Rough, Unstable, Incorrect Idle, or Stalling" in "Symptoms," Section
- If intermittent poor driveability or idle symptoms are resolved by disconnecting the IAC, carefully recheck connections, valve terminal resistance, or replace IAC.
- A/C compressor or relay failure
  See CHART C-10 if the A/C control relay drive circuit is shorted to ground or if the relay is faulty, an idle problem may exist.
- If above are all OK, refer to "Rough, Unstable, Incorrect Idle, or Stalling" in "Symptoms," Section

CODE 35

IDLE AIR CONTROL (IAC) CIRCUIT
3.1L (VIN T) "W" CARLINE (PORT)

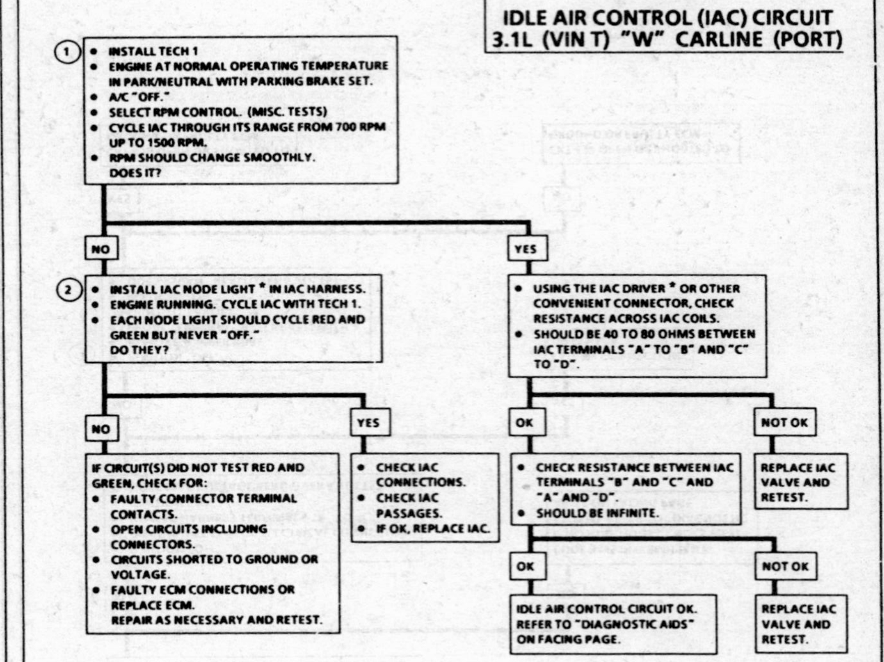

1
• INSTALL TECH 1
• ENGINE AT NORMAL OPERATING TEMPERATURE IN PARK/NEUTRAL WITH PARKING BRAKE SET.
• A/C "OFF."
• SELECT RPM CONTROL. (MISC. TESTS)
• CYCLE IAC THROUGH ITS RANGE FROM 700 RPM UP TO 1500 RPM.
• RPM SHOULD CHANGE SMOOTHLY. DOES IT?
NO
YES
2
• INSTALL IAC NODE LIGHT * IN IAC HARNESS.
• ENGINE RUNNING. CYCLE IAC WITH TECH 1.
• EACH NODE LIGHT SHOULD CYCLE RED AND GREEN BUT NEVER "OFF." DO THEY?
• USING THE IAC DRIVER * OR OTHER CONVENIENT CONNECTOR, CHECK RESISTANCE ACROSS IAC COILS.
• SHOULD BE 40 TO 80 OHMS BETWEEN IAC TERMINALS "A" TO "B" AND "C" TO "D".
NO
YES
OK
NOT OK
IF CIRCUIT(S) DID NOT TEST RED AND GREEN, CHECK FOR:
• FAULTY CONNECTOR TERMINAL CONTACTS.
• OPEN CIRCUITS INCLUDING CONNECTORS.
• CIRCUITS SHORTED TO GROUND OR VOLTAGE.
• FAULTY ECM CONNECTIONS OR REPLACE ECM.
REPAIR AS NECESSARY AND RETEST.
• CHECK IAC CONNECTIONS.
• CHECK IAC PASSAGES.
• IF OK, REPLACE IAC.
• CHECK RESISTANCE BETWEEN IAC TERMINALS "B" AND "C" AND "A" AND "D".
• SHOULD BE INFINITE.
REPLACE IAC VALVE AND RETEST.
OK
NOT OK
IDLE AIR CONTROL CIRCUIT OK. REFER TO "DIAGNOSTIC AIDS" ON FACING PAGE.
REPLACE IAC VALVE AND RETEST.

* IAC DRIVER AND NODE LIGHT REQUIRED KIT
222-L FROM: CONCEPT TECHNOLOGY, INC.
J 37027 FROM: KENT-MOORE, INC.

CLEAR CODES, CONFIRM "CLOSED LOOP" OPERATION, NO "SERVICE ENGINE SOON" LIGHT, PERFORM IAC RESET PROCEDURE PER APPLICABLE SERVICE MANUAL AND VERIFY CONTROLLED IDLE SPEED IS CORRECT.

"*AFTER REPAIRS*," REFER TO CODE CRITERIA ON FACING PAGE AND CONFIRM CODE DOES NOT RESET.

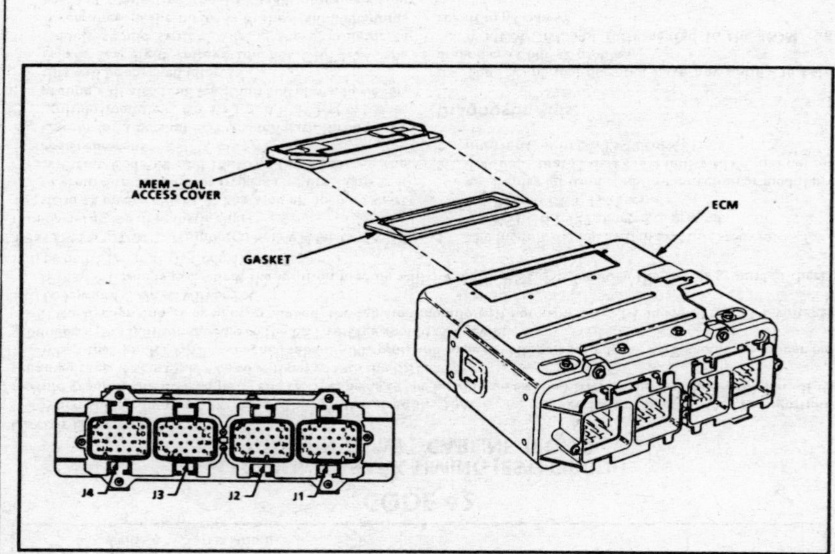

CODE 41

CYLINDER SELECT ERROR
(FAULTY OR INCORRECT MEM-CAL)
3.1L (VIN T) "W" CARLINE (PORT)

Test Description: Number(s) below refer to circled number(s) on the diagnostic chart.

1. The ECM used for this engine can also be used for other engines and the difference is in the MEM-CAL. If a Code 41 sets, the incorrect MEM-CAL has been installed or it is faulty and it must be replaced.

Diagnostic Aids:

Check MEM-CAL to be sure locking tabs are secure.

CODE 41

CYLINDER SELECT ERROR
(FAULTY OR INCORRECT MEM-CAL)
3.1L (VIN T) "W" CARLINE (PORT)

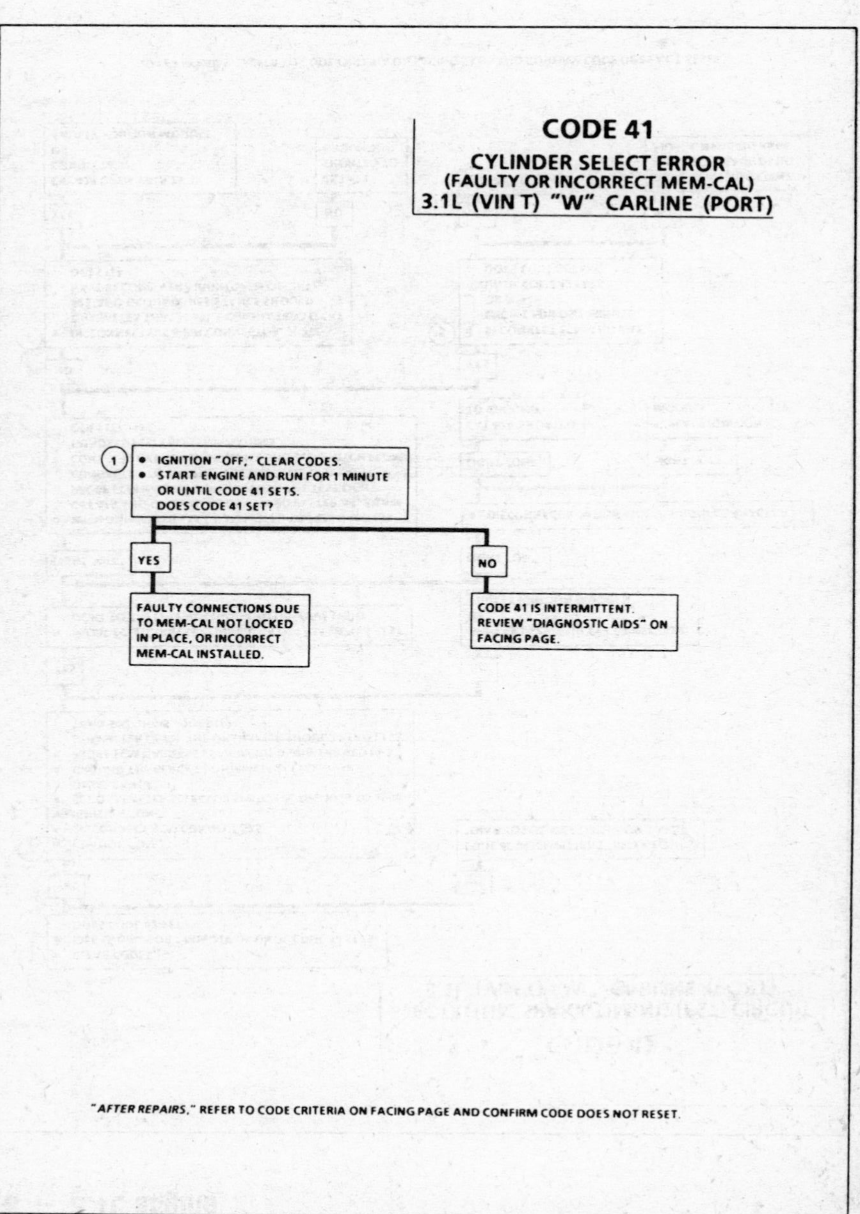

1
• IGNITION "OFF," CLEAR CODES.
• START ENGINE AND RUN FOR 1 MINUTE OR UNTIL CODE 41 SETS.
DOES CODE 41 SET?
YES
NO
FAULTY CONNECTIONS DUE TO MEM-CAL NOT LOCKED IN PLACE, OR INCORRECT MEM-CAL INSTALLED.
CODE 41 IS INTERMITTENT. REVIEW "DIAGNOSTIC AIDS" ON FACING PAGE.

"*AFTER REPAIRS,*" REFER TO CODE CRITERIA ON FACING PAGE AND CONFIRM CODE DOES NOT RESET.

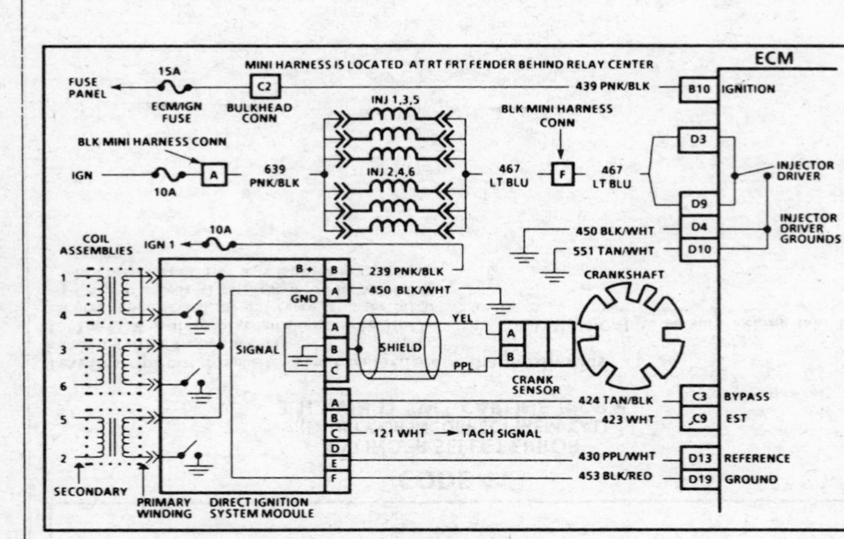

CODE 42

ELECTRONIC SPARK TIMING (EST) CIRCUIT 3.1L (VIN T) "W" CARLINE (PORT)

Circuit Description:

When the system is running on the ignition module, that is, no voltage on the bypass line, the ignition module grounds the EST signal. The ECM expects to see no voltage on the EST line during this condition. If it sees a voltage, it sets Code 42 and will not go into the EST mode.

When the rpm for EST is reached (about 400 rpm), and bypass voltage applied, the EST should on longer be grounded in the ignition module so the EST voltage should be varying.

If the bypass line is open or grounded, the ignition module will not switch to EST mode so the EST voltage will be low and Code 42 will be set.

If the EST line is grounded, the ignition module will switch to EST, but because the line is grounded there will be no EST signal. A Code 42 will be set.

Test Description: Number(s) below refer to circled number(s) on the diagnostic chart.

1. Code 42 means the ECM has seen an open or short to ground in the EST or bypass circuits. This test confirms Code 42 and that the fault causing the code is present.
2. Checks for a normal EST ground path through the ignition module. An EST CKT 423 shorted to ground will also read less than 500 ohms; however, this will be checked later.
3. As the test light voltage touches CKT 424, the module should switch causing the ohmmeter to "overrange" if the meter is in the 1000-2000 ohms position. Selecting the 10-20,000 ohms position will indicate above 5000 ohms The important thing is that the module "switched."
4. The module did not switch and this step checks for:
   - EST CKT 423 shorted to ground.
   - Bypass CKT 424 open.
   - Faulty ignition module connection or module.
5. Confirms that Code 42 is a faulty ECM and not an intermittent in CKTs 423 or 424.

Diagnostic Aids:

The "Scan" tool does not have any ability to help diagnose a Code 42 problem.

A MEM-CAL not fully seated in the ECM can result in a Code 42.

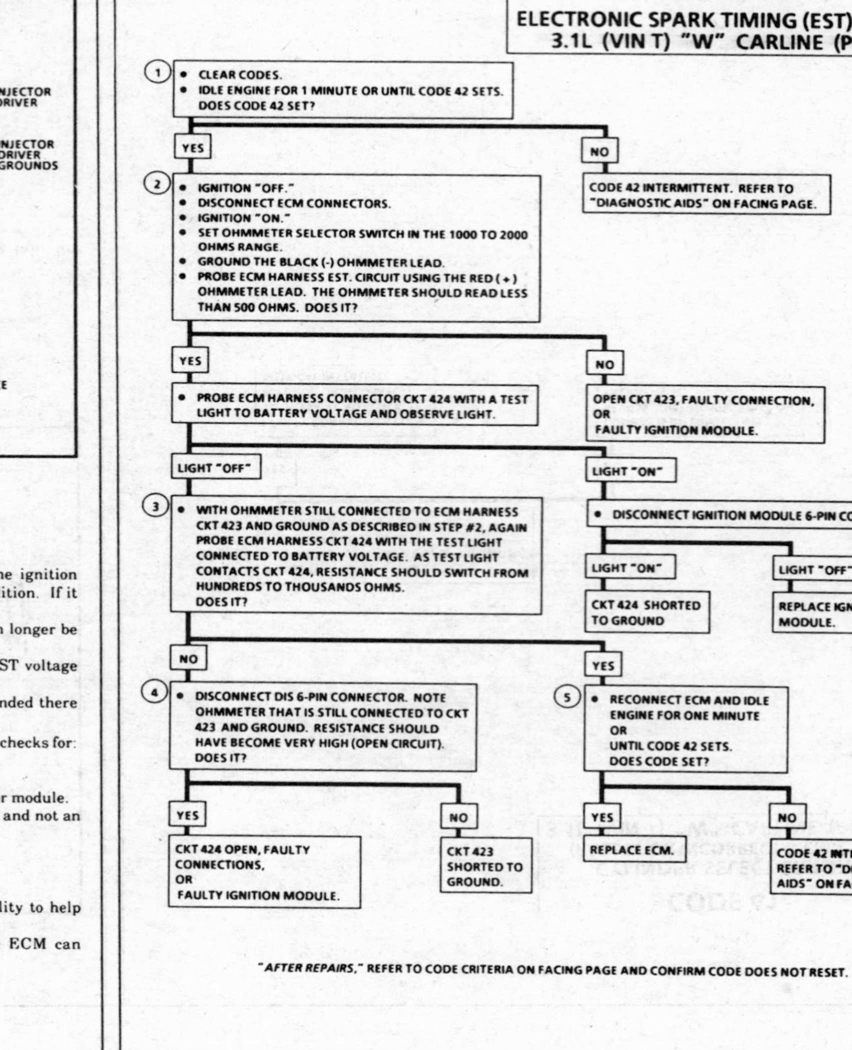

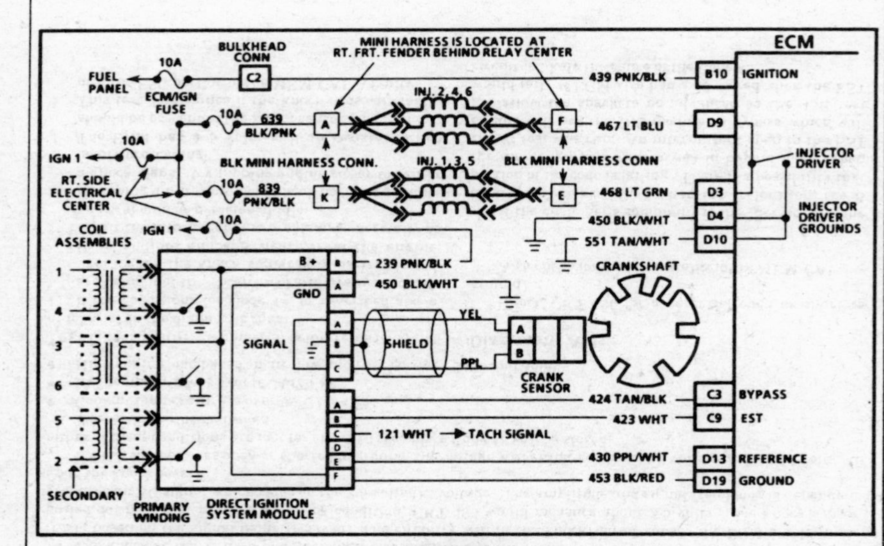

CODE 42

ELECTRONIC SPARK TIMING (EST) CIRCUIT 3.1L TURBO (VIN V) "W" CARLINE (PORT)

Circuit Description:

When the system is running on the ignition module, that is, no voltage on the bypass line, the ignition module grounds the Electronic Spark Timing (EST) signal. The ECM expects to see no voltage on the EST line during this condition. If it sees a voltage, it sets Code 42 and will not go into the EST mode.

When the rpm for EST is reached (about 400 rpm), and bypass voltage applied, the EST should on longer be grounded in the ignition module so the EST voltage should be varying.

If the bypass line is open or grounded, the ignition module will not switch to EST mode so the EST voltage will be low and Code 42 will be set.

If the EST line is grounded, the ignition module will switch to EST, but because the line is grounded there will be no EST signal. A Code 42 will be set.

Test Description: Numbers below refer to circled numbers on the diagnostic chart.

1. Code 42 means the ECM has seen an open or short to ground in the EST or bypass circuits. This test confirms Code 42 and that the fault causing the code is present.
2. Checks for a normal EST ground path through the ignition module. An EST CKT 423 shorted to ground will also read less than 500 ohms; however, this will be checked later.
3. As the test light voltage touches CKT 424, the module should switch causing the ohmmeter to "overrange" if the meter is in the 1000-2000 ohms position. Selecting the 10-20,000 ohms position will indicate above 5000 ohms. The important thing is that the module "switched."
4. The module did not switch and this step checks for:
   - EST CKT 423 shorted to ground
   - Bypass CKT 424 open
   - Faulty ignition module connection or module
5. Confirms that Code 42 is a faulty ECM and not an intermittent in CKTs 423 or 424.

Diagnostic Aids:

The "Scan" tool does not have any ability to help diagnose a Code 42 problem.

A Mem-Cal not fully seated in the ECM can result in a Code 42.

Refer to "Intermittents" Section

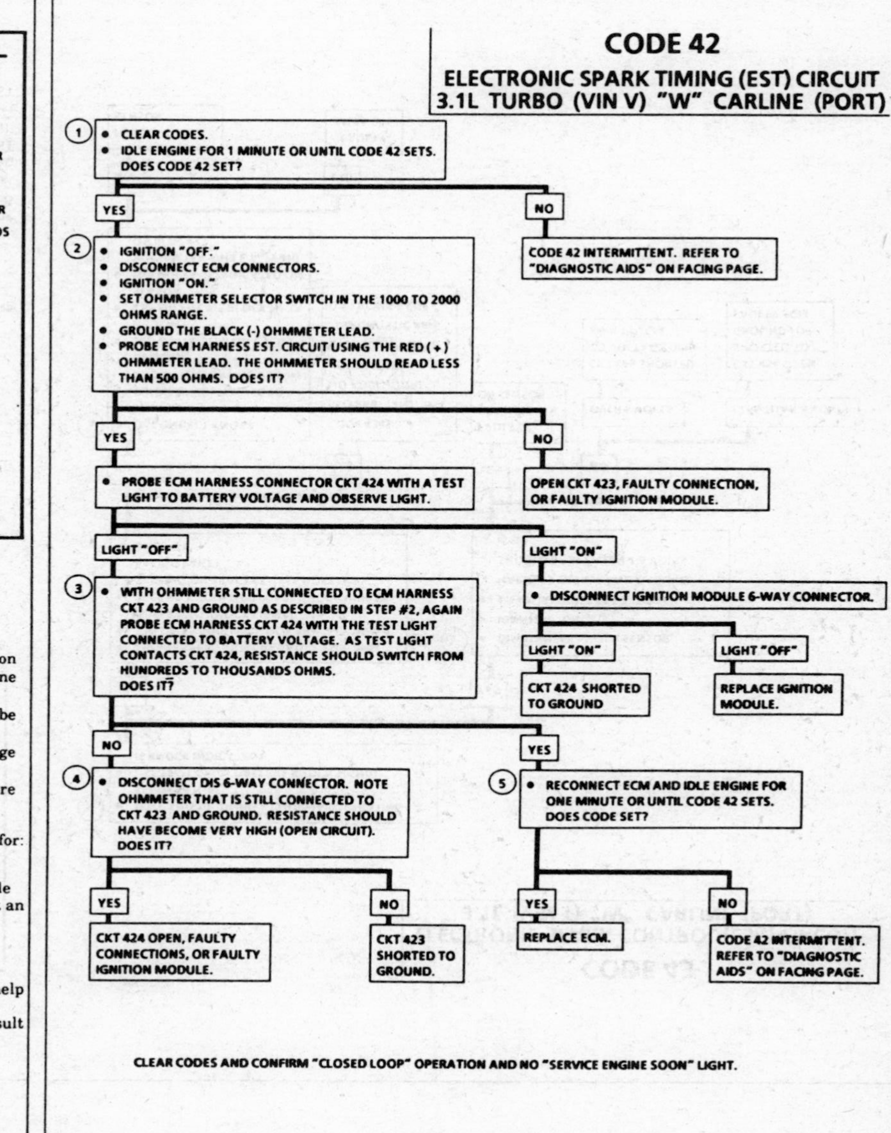

DIAGNOSTIC CHARTS — 3.1L engine

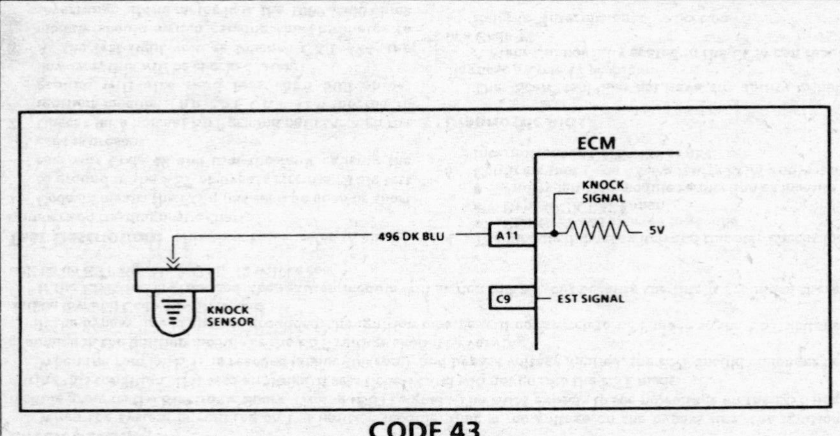
ECM
KNOCK SIGNAL
5V
496 DK BLU
A11
C9
EST SIGNAL
KNOCK SENSOR

CODE 43

ELECTRONIC SPARK CONTROL (ESC) CIRCUIT 3.1L (VIN T) "W" CARLINE (PORT)

Circuit Description:

The knock sensor is used to detect engine detonation and the ECM will retard the Electronic Spark Timing (EST) based on the signal being received. The circuitry within the knock sensor causes the ECM 5 volts to be pulled down so that under a no knock condition, CKT 496 would measure about 2.5 volts. The knock sensor produces an AC signal which rides on the 2.5 volts DC voltage. The amplitude and signal frequency is dependent upon the knock level.

If CKT 496 becomes open or shorted to ground, the voltage will either go above 4.8 volts or below .64 volts. If either of these conditions are met for about 10 seconds, a Code 43 will be stored.

The test is performed when:

- Coolant temperature is over 90°C (194°F).
- IAT temperature is over 0°C (32°F).
- High engine load based on air flow and rpm between 3400 and 4400.

Test Description: Number(s) below refer to circled number(s) on the diagnostic chart.

1. If the conditions for Code 43, as described above, are being met the "Scan" tool will always indicate "Yes" when the knock signal position is selected. If an audible knock is heard from the engine, repair the internal engine problem, as normally no knock should be detected at idle.
2. If tapping on the engine lift hook does not produce a knock signal, try tapping engine closer to sensor before proceeding.
3. The ECM has a 5 volts pull-up resistor which should be present at the knock sensor terminal.
4. This test determines if the knock sensor is faulty or if the ESC portion of the MEM-CAL is faulty.

Diagnostic Aids:

Check CKT 496 for a potential open or short to ground.

Also check for proper installation of MEM-CAL.

If the customer's complaint is the "Service Engine Soon" light comes "ON" when in acceleration, the B portion of the code is failing. There is a possibility that the direct ignition system was in bypass mode when the 43 test was run. An intermittent open in the EST circuit will put the DIS module in bypass which will not allow the spark to be advanced so the 43B test would fail. If ECM also had a 42 stored, then the EST circuit is likely the cause of the Code 43.

CODE 43

ELECTRONIC SPARK CONTROL (ESC) CIRCUIT 3.1L (VIN T) "W" CARLINE (PORT)

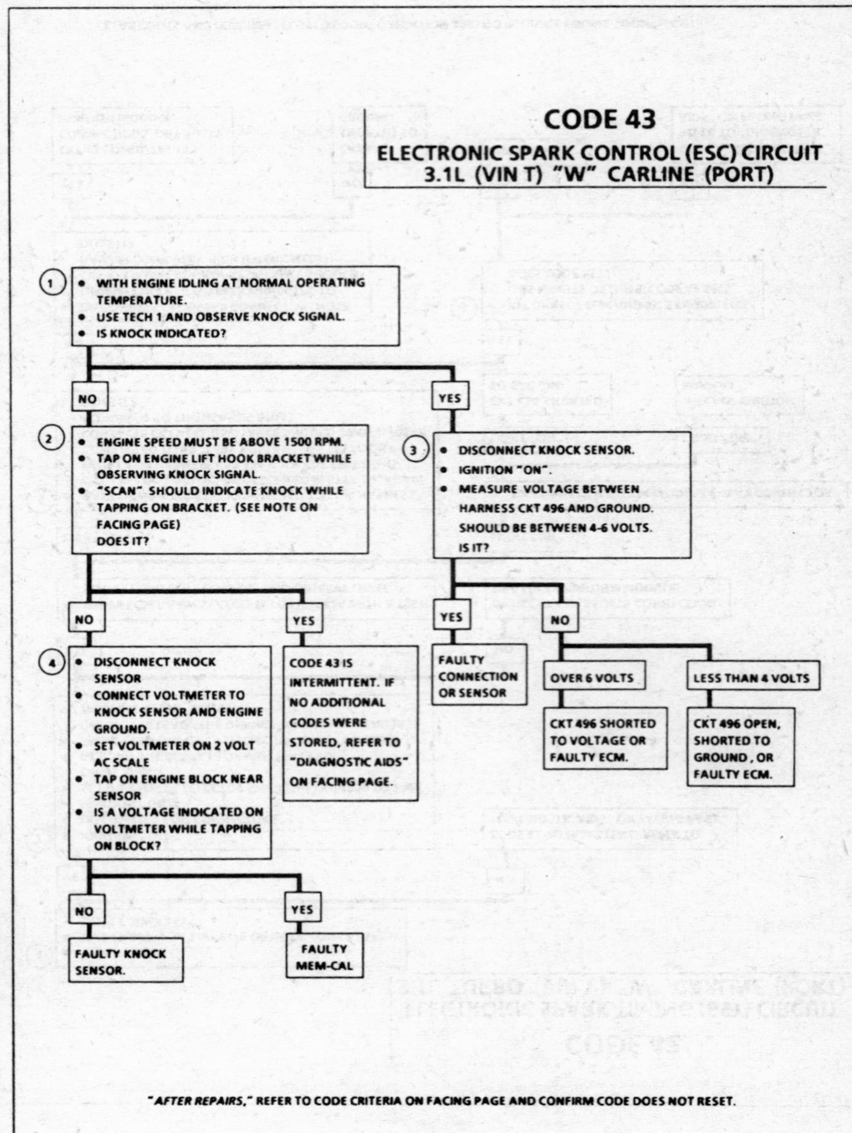
1
• WITH ENGINE IDLING AT NORMAL OPERATING TEMPERATURE.
• USE TECH 1 AND OBSERVE KNOCK SIGNAL.
• IS KNOCK INDICATED?
NO
YES
2
• ENGINE SPEED MUST BE ABOVE 1500 RPM.
• TAP ON ENGINE LIFT HOOK BRACKET WHILE OBSERVING KNOCK SIGNAL.
• "SCAN" SHOULD INDICATE KNOCK WHILE TAPPING ON BRACKET. (SEE NOTE ON FACING PAGE)
DOES IT?
3
• DISCONNECT KNOCK SENSOR.
• IGNITION "ON".
• MEASURE VOLTAGE BETWEEN HARNESS CKT 496 AND GROUND. SHOULD BE BETWEEN 4-6 VOLTS.
IS IT?
NO
YES
YES
NO
4
• DISCONNECT KNOCK SENSOR
• CONNECT VOLTMETER TO KNOCK SENSOR AND ENGINE GROUND.
• SET VOLTMETER ON 2 VOLT AC SCALE
• TAP ON ENGINE BLOCK NEAR SENSOR
• IS A VOLTAGE INDICATED ON VOLTMETER WHILE TAPPING ON BLOCK?
CODE 43 IS INTERMITTENT. IF NO ADDITIONAL CODES WERE STORED, REFER TO "DIAGNOSTIC AIDS" ON FACING PAGE.
FAULTY CONNECTION OR SENSOR
OVER 6 VOLTS
LESS THAN 4 VOLTS
CKT 496 SHORTED TO VOLTAGE OR FAULTY ECM.
CKT 496 OPEN, SHORTED TO GROUND, OR FAULTY ECM.
NO
YES
FAULTY KNOCK SENSOR.
FAULTY MEM-CAL
"AFTER REPAIRS," REFER TO CODE CRITERIA ON FACING PAGE AND CONFIRM CODE DOES NOT RESET.

DIAGNOSTIC CHARTS — 3.1L engine

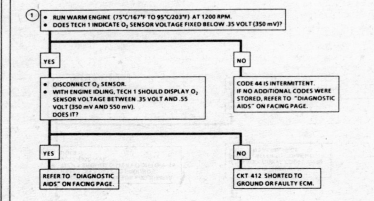

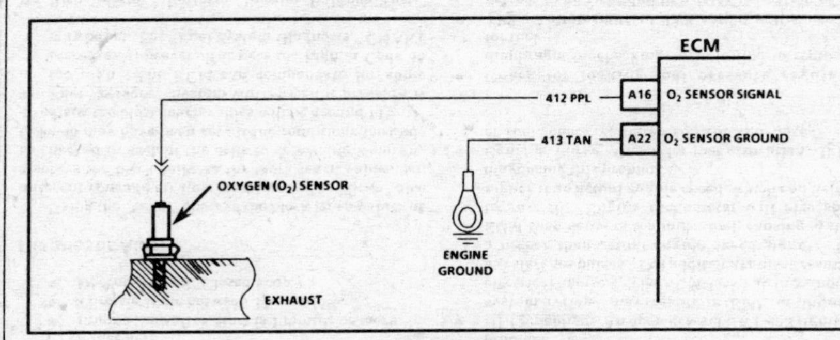

CODE 44

OXYGEN (O_2) SENSOR CIRCUIT
(LEAN EXHAUST INDICATED)
3.1L (VIN T) "W" CARLINE (PORT)

Circuit Description:

The ECM supplies a voltage of about .55 volt between terminals "A16" and "A22". (If measured with a 10 megohm digital voltmeter, this may read as low as .35 volt.) The Oxygen (O_2) sensor varies the voltage within a range of about 1 volt if the exhaust is rich, down through about .10 volt if exhaust is lean.

The sensor is like an open circuit and produces no voltage when it is below about 315°C (600°F). An open sensor circuit or cold sensor causes "Open Loop" operation.

Test Description: Number(s) below refer to circled number(s) on the diagnostic chart.

1. Code 44 will set if:
   - No Code 33 or Code 34.
   - Voltage on CKT 412 remains below .2 volt for 60 seconds or more.
   - The system is operating in "Closed Loop."

Diagnostic Aids:

Using the "Scan," observe the block learn values at different rpm and air flow conditions. The "Scan" also displays the block cells, so the block learn values can be checked in each of the cells to determine when the Code 44 may have been set. If the conditions for Code 44 exists the block learn values will be around 150.

- O_2 Sensor Wire. Sensor pigtail may be mispositioned and contacting the exhaust manifold.
- Check for intermittent ground in wire between connector and sensor.
- Lean Injector(s). Perform injector balance test CHART C-2A.
- Fuel Contamination. Water, even in small amounts, near the in-tank fuel pump inlet can be delivered to the injectors. The water causes a lean exhaust and can set a Code 44.
- Fuel Pressure. System will be lean if pressure is too low. It may be necessary to monitor fuel pressure while driving the car at various road speeds and/or loads to confirm. See "Fuel System Diagnosis," CHART A-7.
- Exhaust Leaks. If there is an exhaust leak, the engine can cause outside air to be pulled into the exhaust and past the sensor. Vacuum or crankcase leaks can cause a lean condition.
- If the above are OK, it is a faulty Oxygen (O_2) sensor.

CODE 44

OXYGEN (O_2) SENSOR CIRCUIT
(LEAN EXHAUST INDICATED)
3.1L (VIN T) "W" CARLINE (PORT)

(1)
- RUN WARM ENGINE (75°C/167°F TO 95°C/203°F) AT 1200 RPM.
- DOES TECH 1 INDICATE O_2 SENSOR VOLTAGE FIXED BELOW .35 VOLT (350 mV)?

YES:
- DISCONNECT O_2 SENSOR.
- WITH ENGINE IDLING, TECH 1 SHOULD DISPLAY O_2 SENSOR VOLTAGE BETWEEN .35 VOLT AND .55 VOLT (350 mV AND 550 mV). DOES IT?

  YES: REFER TO "DIAGNOSTIC AIDS" ON FACING PAGE.

  NO: CKT 412 SHORTED TO GROUND OR FAULTY ECM.

NO: CODE 44 IS INTERMITTENT. IF NO ADDITIONAL CODES WERE STORED, REFER TO "DIAGNOSTIC AIDS" ON FACING PAGE.

"AFTER REPAIRS," REFER TO CODE CRITERIA ON FACING PAGE AND CONFIRM CODE DOES NOT RESET.

DIAGNOSTIC CHARTS — 3.1L engine

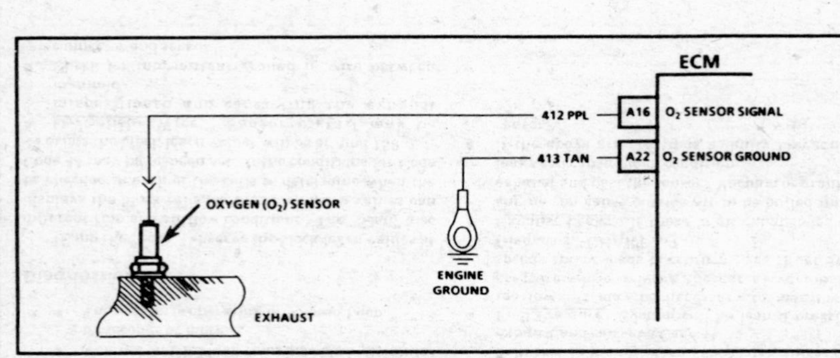

CODE 45

OXYGEN (O_2) SENSOR CIRCUIT
(RICH EXHAUST INDICATED)
3.1L (VIN T) "W" CARLINE (PORT)

Circuit Description:

The ECM supplies a voltage of about .55 volt between terminals "A16" and "A22". (If measured with a 10 megohm digital voltmeter, this may read as low as .35 volt.) The Oxygen (O_2) sensor varies the voltage within a range of about 1 volt if the exhaust is rich, down through about .10 volt if exhaust is lean.

The sensor is like an open circuit and produces no voltage when it is below about 315°C (600°F). An open sensor circuit or cold sensor causes "Open Loop" operation.

Test Description: Number(s) below refer to circled number(s) on the diagnostic chart.

1. Code 45 will set if:
   - Voltage on CKT 412 remains above .7 volt for 50 seconds.
   - Engine time after start is 1 minute or more.
   - Throttle angle between 3% and 45%.
   - Operation is in "Closed Loop."

Diagnostic Aids:

Using the "Scan," observe the block learn values at different rpm and air flow conditions. The "Scan" also displays the block cells, so the block learn values can be checked in each of the cells to determine when the Code 45 may have been set. If the conditions for Code 45 exists, the block learn values will be around 115.

- Fuel Pressure. System will go rich if pressure is too high. The ECM can compensate for some increase. However, if it gets too high, a Code 45 may be set. See "Fuel System Diagnosis," CHART A-7.
- Rich Injector. Perform "Injector Balance Test," CHART C-2A.
- Leaking Injector. See CHART A-7.
- Check for fuel contaminated oil.
- O_2 Sensor Contamination. Inspect Oxygen (O_2) sensor for silicone contamination from fuel, or use of improper RTV sealant. The sensor may have a white, powdery coating and result in a high but false signal voltage (rich exhaust indication). The ECM will then reduce the amount of fuel delivered to the engine, causing a severe surge driveability problem.
- HEI Shielding. An open ground CKT 453 (ignition system reflow) may result in EMI, or induced electrical "noise." The ECM looks at this "noise" as reference pulses. The additional pulses result in a higher than actual engine speed signal. The ECM then delivers too much fuel, causing system to go rich. Engine tachometer will also show higher than actual engine speed, which can help in diagnosing this problem.
- Canister Purge. Check for fuel saturation. If full of fuel, check canister control and hoses.
- Check for leaking fuel pressure regulator diaphragm by checking vacuum line to regulator for fuel.
- TPS. An intermittent TPS output will cause the system to go rich, due to a false indication of the engine accelerating.
- EGR. An EGR staying open (especially at idle) will cause the Oxygen (O_2) sensor to indicate a rich exhaust, and this could result in a Code 45.

CODE 45

OXYGEN (O_2) SENSOR CIRCUIT
(RICH EXHAUST INDICATED)
3.1L (VIN T) "W" CARLINE (PORT)

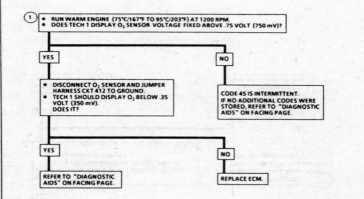

(1)
- RUN WARM ENGINE (75°C/167°F TO 95°C/203°F) AT 1200 RPM.
- DOES TECH 1 DISPLAY O_2 SENSOR VOLTAGE FIXED ABOVE .75 VOLT (750 mV)?

YES:
- DISCONNECT O_2 SENSOR AND JUMPER HARNESS CKT 412 TO GROUND.
- TECH 1 SHOULD DISPLAY O_2 BELOW .35 VOLT (350 mV). DOES IT?

  YES: REFER TO "DIAGNOSTIC AIDS" ON FACING PAGE.

  NO: REPLACE ECM.

NO: CODE 45 IS INTERMITTENT. IF NO ADDITIONAL CODES WERE STORED, REFER TO "DIAGNOSTIC AIDS" ON FACING PAGE.

"*AFTER REPAIRS,*" REFER TO CODE CRITERIA ON FACING PAGE AND CONFIRM CODE DOES NOT RESET.

DIAGNOSTIC CHARTS — 3.1L engine

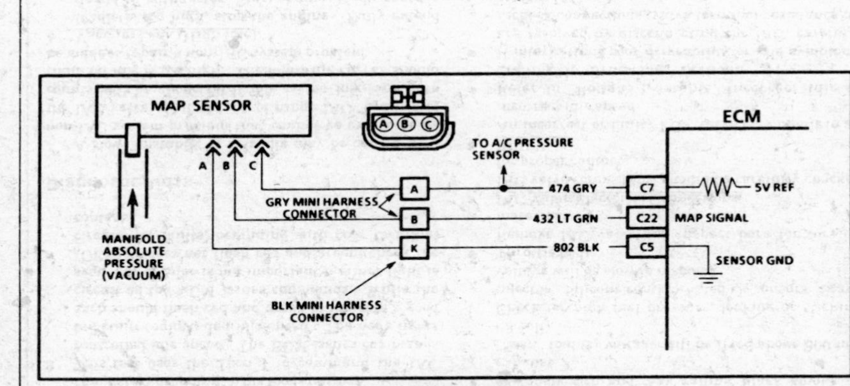

CHART C-1D
MANIFOLD ABSOLUTE PRESSURE (MAP) OUTPUT CHECK
3.1L (VIN T) "W" CARLINE (PORT)

Circuit Description:

The Manifold Absolute Pressure (MAP) sensor measures manifold pressure (vacuum) and sends that signal to the ECM. The MAP sensor is mainly used for fuel calculation when the ECM is running in the throttle body backup mode. The MAP sensor is also used to determine the barometric pressure and to help calculate fuel delivery.

Test Description: Number(s) below refer to circled number(s) on the diagnostic chart.

1. Checks MAP sensor output voltage to the ECM. This voltage, without engine running, represents a barometer reading to the ECM.
2. Applying 34 kPa (10 inch Hg) vacuum to the MAP sensor should cause the voltage to be 1.2 volts less than the voltage at Step 1. Upon applying vacuum to the sensor, the change in voltage should be instantaneous. A slow voltage change indicates a faulty sensor.

   The engine must be running in this step or the "scanner" will not indicate a change in voltage. It is normal for the "Service Engine Soon" light to come "ON" and for the system to set a Code 33 during this step. Make sure the code is cleared when this test is completed.
3. Check vacuum hose to sensor for leaking or restriction. Be sure no other vacuum devices are connected to the MAP hose.
4. A poor connection at that MAP sensor could cause faulty readings on the Tech 1.

CHART C-1D
MANIFOLD ABSOLUTE PRESSURE (MAP) OUTPUT CHECK
3.1L (VIN T) "W" CARLINE (PORT)

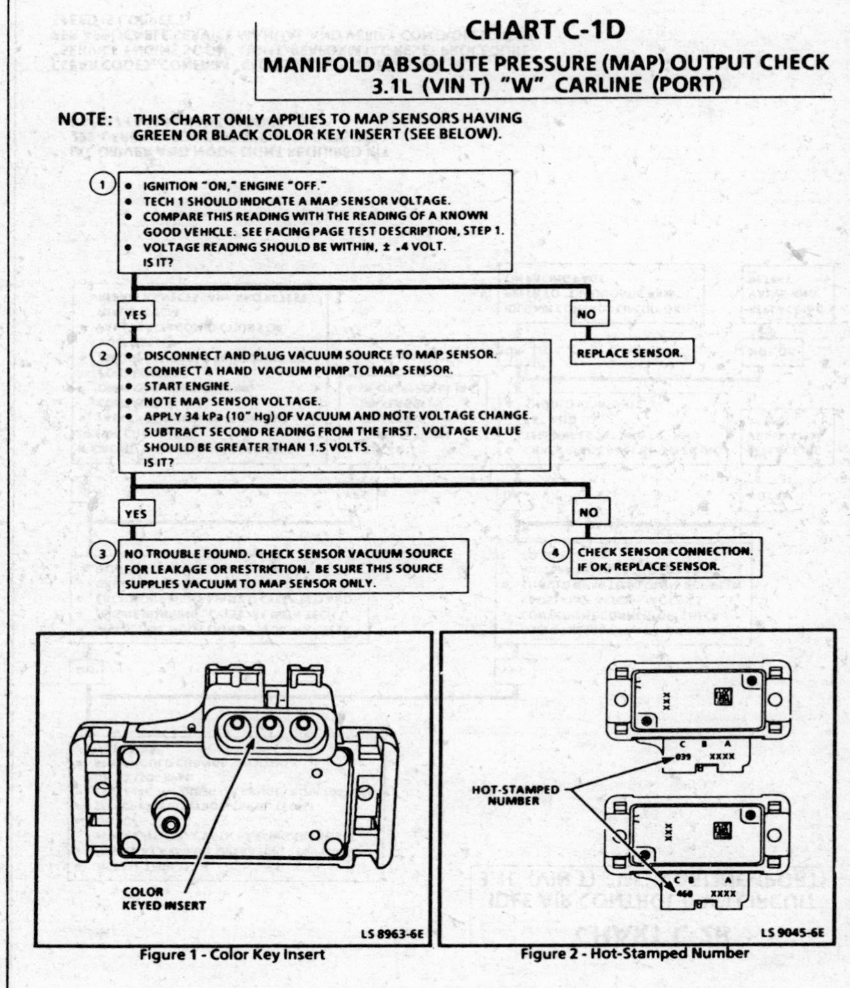

NOTE: THIS CHART ONLY APPLIES TO MAP SENSORS HAVING GREEN OR BLACK COLOR KEY INSERT (SEE BELOW).
1
• IGNITION "ON," ENGINE "OFF."
• TECH 1 SHOULD INDICATE A MAP SENSOR VOLTAGE.
• COMPARE THIS READING WITH THE READING OF A KNOWN GOOD VEHICLE. SEE FACING PAGE TEST DESCRIPTION, STEP 1.
• VOLTAGE READING SHOULD BE WITHIN, ± .4 VOLT.
IS IT?
YES
NO
REPLACE SENSOR.
2
• DISCONNECT AND PLUG VACUUM SOURCE TO MAP SENSOR.
• CONNECT A HAND VACUUM PUMP TO MAP SENSOR.
• START ENGINE.
• NOTE MAP SENSOR VOLTAGE.
• APPLY 34 kPa (10" Hg) OF VACUUM AND NOTE VOLTAGE CHANGE. SUBTRACT SECOND READING FROM THE FIRST. VOLTAGE VALUE SHOULD BE GREATER THAN 1.5 VOLTS.
IS IT?
YES
NO
3
NO TROUBLE FOUND. CHECK SENSOR VACUUM SOURCE FOR LEAKAGE OR RESTRICTION. BE SURE THIS SOURCE SUPPLIES VACUUM TO MAP SENSOR ONLY.
4
CHECK SENSOR CONNECTION. IF OK, REPLACE SENSOR.
COLOR KEYED INSERT
LS 8963-6E
HOT-STAMPED NUMBER
XXX
C B A
039 XXXX
460 XXXX
LS 9045-6E

Figure 1 - Color Key Insert

Figure 2 - Hot-Stamped Number

"*AFTER REPAIRS*," CONFIRM "CLOSED LOOP" OPERATION AND NO "SERVICE ENGINE SOON" LIGHT.

DIAGNOSTIC CHARTS — 3.1L engine

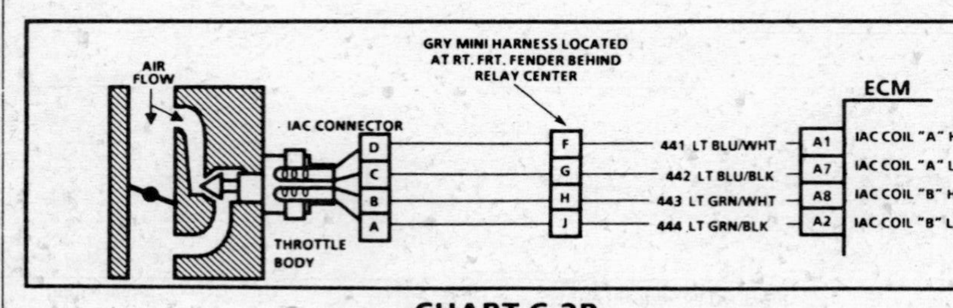
AIR FLOW
IAC CONNECTOR
D
C
B
A
THROTTLE BODY
GRY MINI HARNESS LOCATED AT RT. FRT. FENDER BEHIND RELAY CENTER
F
G
H
J
441 LT BLU/WHT
442 LT BLU/BLK
443 LT GRN/WHT
444 LT GRN/BLK
ECM
A1
A7
A8
A2
IAC COIL "A" HI
IAC COIL "A" LO
IAC COIL "B" HI
IAC COIL "B" LO

CHART C-2B

IDLE AIR CONTROL (IAC) CIRCUIT 3.1L (VIN T) "W" CARLINE (PORT)

Circuit Description:

The ECM controls engine idle speed with the IAC valve. To increase idle speed, the ECM retracts the IAC valve pintle away from its seat, allowing more air to bypass the throttle bore. To decrease idle speed, it extends the IAC valve pintle towards its seat, reducing bypass air flow. A "Scan" tool will read the ECM commands to the IAC valve in counts. Higher the counts indicate more air bypass (higher idle). The lower the counts indicate less air is allowed to bypass (lower idle).

Test Description: Number(s) below refer to circled number(s) on the diagnostic chart.

1. The Tech 1 rpm control mode is used to extend and retract the IAC valve. The valve should move smoothly within the specified range. If the idle speed is commanded (IAC extended) too low (below 700 rpm), the engine may stall. This may be normal and would not indicate a problem. Retracting the IAC beyond its controlled range (above 1500 rpm) will cause a delay before the rpm's start dropping. This too is normal.
2. This test uses the Tech 1 to command the IAC controlled idle speed. The ECM issues commands to obtain commended idle speed. The node lights each should flash red and green to indicate a good circuit as the ECM issues commands. While the sequence of color is not important if either light is "OFF" or does not flash red and green, check the circuits for faults, beginning with poor terminal contacts.

Diagnostic Aids:

A slow, unstable, or fast idle may be caused by a non-IAC system problem that cannot be overcome by the IAC valve. Out of control range IAC "Scan" tool counts will be above 60 if idle is too low, and zero counts if idle is too high. The following checks should be made to repair a non-IAC system problem:

- Vacuum Leak (High Idle).
  If idle is too high, stop the engine. Fully extend (low) IAC with tester. Start engine. If idle speed is above 800 rpm, locate and correct vacuum leak including PCV system. Also check for binding of throttle blade or linkage.
- System too lean (High Air/Fuel Ratio).
  The idle speed may be too high or too low. Engine speed may vary up and down and disconnecting the IAC valve does not help. Code 44 may be set. "Scan" O_2 voltage will be less than 300 mV (.3 volt). Check for low regulated fuel pressure, water in the fuel or a restricted injector.
- System too rich (Low Air/Fuel Ratio).
  The idle speed will be too low. "Scan" tool IAC counts will usually be above 80. System is obviously rich and may exhibit black smoke in exhaust.
  "Scan" tool O_2 voltage will be fixed above 800 mV (.8 volt).
  Check for high fuel pressure, leaking or sticking injector. Silicone contaminated O_2 sensors "Scan" voltage will be slow to respond.
- Throttle body.
  Remove IAC valve and inspect bore for foreign material.
- IAC Valve Electrical Connections.
  IAC valve connections should be carefully checked for proper contact.
- PCV Valve.
  An incorrect or faulty PCV valve may result in an incorrect idle speed.
- Refer to "Rough, Unstable, Incorrect Idle or Stalling" in "Symptoms," Section
- If intermittent poor driveability or idle symptoms are resolved by disconnecting the IAC, carefully recheck connections, valve terminal resistance, or replace IAC.

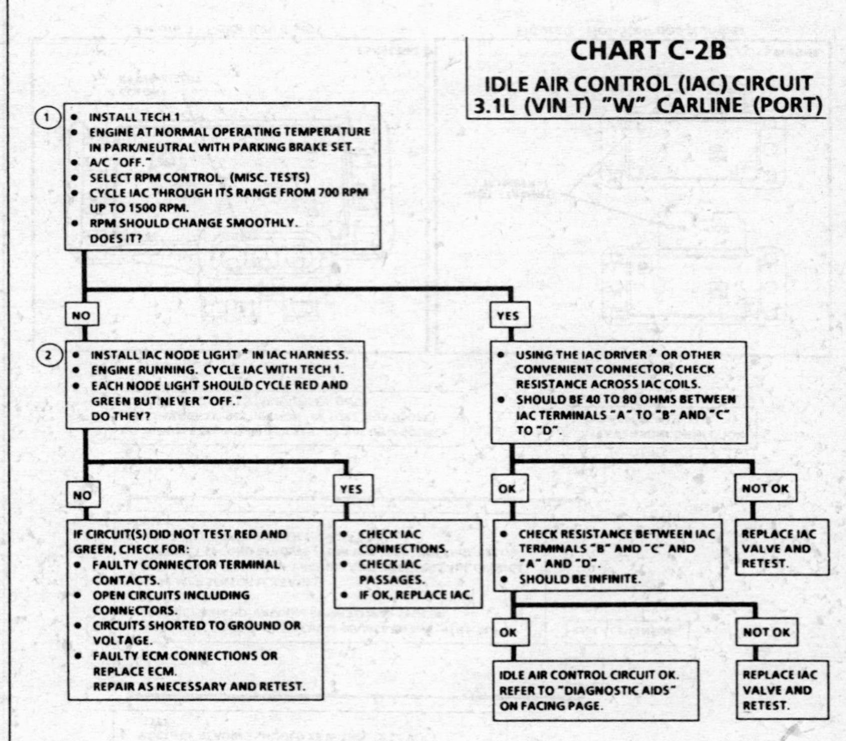
CHART C-2B
IDLE AIR CONTROL (IAC) CIRCUIT
3.1L (VIN T) "W" CARLINE (PORT)
1
• INSTALL TECH 1
• ENGINE AT NORMAL OPERATING TEMPERATURE IN PARK/NEUTRAL WITH PARKING BRAKE SET.
• A/C "OFF."
• SELECT RPM CONTROL. (MISC. TESTS)
• CYCLE IAC THROUGH ITS RANGE FROM 700 RPM UP TO 1500 RPM.
• RPM SHOULD CHANGE SMOOTHLY. DOES IT?
NO
YES
2
• INSTALL IAC NODE LIGHT * IN IAC HARNESS.
• ENGINE RUNNING. CYCLE IAC WITH TECH 1.
• EACH NODE LIGHT SHOULD CYCLE RED AND GREEN BUT NEVER "OFF." DO THEY?
• USING THE IAC DRIVER * OR OTHER CONVENIENT CONNECTOR, CHECK RESISTANCE ACROSS IAC COILS.
• SHOULD BE 40 TO 80 OHMS BETWEEN IAC TERMINALS "A" TO "B" AND "C" TO "D".
NO
YES
OK
NOT OK
IF CIRCUIT(S) DID NOT TEST RED AND GREEN, CHECK FOR:
• FAULTY CONNECTOR TERMINAL CONTACTS.
• OPEN CIRCUITS INCLUDING CONNECTORS.
• CIRCUITS SHORTED TO GROUND OR VOLTAGE.
• FAULTY ECM CONNECTIONS OR REPLACE ECM.
REPAIR AS NECESSARY AND RETEST.
• CHECK IAC CONNECTIONS.
• CHECK IAC PASSAGES.
• IF OK, REPLACE IAC.
• CHECK RESISTANCE BETWEEN IAC TERMINALS "B" AND "C" AND "A" AND "D".
• SHOULD BE INFINITE.
REPLACE IAC VALVE AND RETEST.
OK
NOT OK
IDLE AIR CONTROL CIRCUIT OK. REFER TO "DIAGNOSTIC AIDS" ON FACING PAGE.
REPLACE IAC VALVE AND RETEST.

* IAC DRIVER AND NODE LIGHT REQUIRED KIT
222-L FROM: CONCEPT TECHNOLOGY, INC.
J 37027 FROM: KENT-MOORE, INC.

CLEAR CODES, CONFIRM "CLOSED LOOP" OPERATION, NO "SERVICE ENGINE SOON" LIGHT, PERFORM IAC RESET PROCEDURE PER APPLICABLE SERVICE MANUAL AND VERIFY CONTROLLED IDLE SPEED IS CORRECT.

"*AFTER REPAIRS*," CONFIRM "CLOSED LOOP" OPERATION AND NO "SERVICE ENGINE SOON" LIGHT.

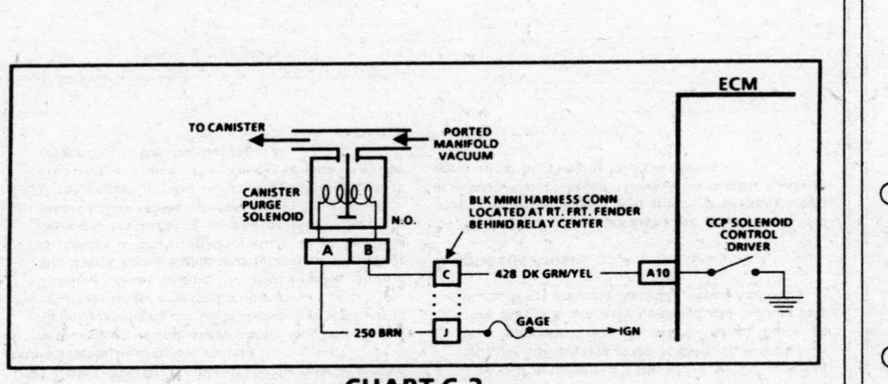
ECM
TO CANISTER
PORTED MANIFOLD VACUUM
CANISTER PURGE SOLENOID
N.O.
A
B
BLK MINI HARNESS CONN LOCATED AT RT. FRT. FENDER BEHIND RELAY CENTER
CCP SOLENOID CONTROL DRIVER
C
428 DK GRN/YEL
A10
J
250 BRN
GAGE
IGN

CHART C-3

CANISTER PURGE VALVE CHECK 3.1L (VIN T) "W" CARLINE (PORT)

Circuit Description:

Canister purge is controlled by a solenoid that allows manifold vacuum to purge the canister when de-energized. The ECM supplies a ground to energize the solenoid (purge "OFF"). The purge solenoid control by the ECM is pulse width modulated (turned "ON" and "OFF" several times a second). The duty cycle (pulse width) is determined by the amount of air flow, and the engine vacuum as determined by the MAP sensor input. The duty cycle is calculated by the ECM and the output commanded when the following conditions have been met:

- Engine run time after start more than 3 minutes.
- Coolant temperature above 80°C (176°F).
- Vehicle speed above 15 mph.
- Throttle of idle (about 3%).

Also, if the diagnostic "test" terminal is grounded with the engine stopped, the purge solenoid is de-energized (purge "ON").

Test Description: Number(s) below refer to circled number(s) on the diagnostic chart.

1. Checks to see if the solenoid is opened or closed. The solenoid is normally energized in this step; so it should be closed.
2. Checks for a complete circuit. Normally there is ignition voltage on CKT 250 and the ECM provides a ground on CKT 428.
3. Completes functional check by grounding "test" terminal. This should normally de-energize the solenoid opening the valve which should allow the vacuum to drop (purge "ON").

CHART C-3

CANISTER PURGE VALVE CHECK 3.1L (VIN T) "W" CARLINE (PORT)

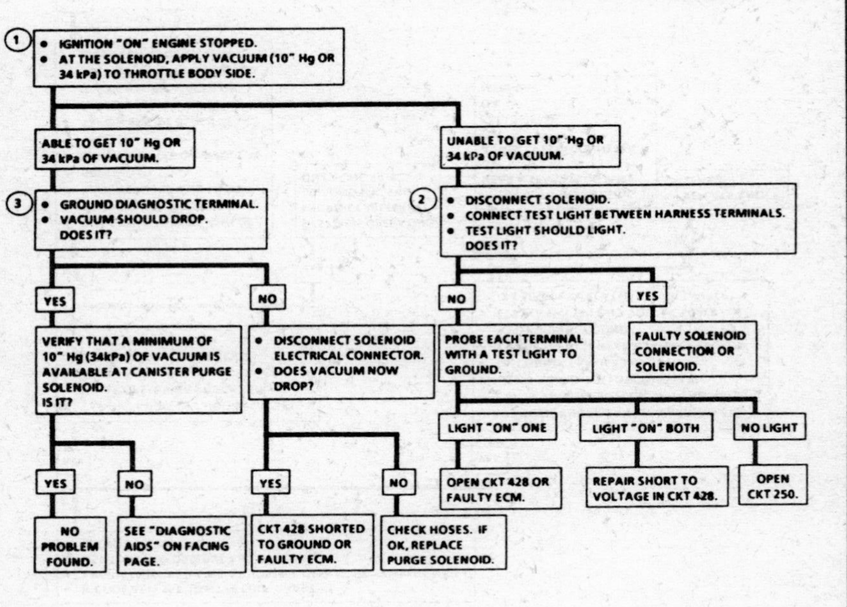
1
• IGNITION "ON" ENGINE STOPPED.
• AT THE SOLENOID, APPLY VACUUM (10" Hg OR 34 kPa) TO THROTTLE BODY SIDE.
ABLE TO GET 10" Hg OR 34 kPa OF VACUUM.
UNABLE TO GET 10" Hg OR 34 kPa OF VACUUM.
3
• GROUND DIAGNOSTIC TERMINAL.
• VACUUM SHOULD DROP.
DOES IT?
2
• DISCONNECT SOLENOID.
• CONNECT TEST LIGHT BETWEEN HARNESS TERMINALS.
• TEST LIGHT SHOULD LIGHT.
DOES IT?
YES
NO
NO
YES
VERIFY THAT A MINIMUM OF 10" Hg (34kPa) OF VACUUM IS AVAILABLE AT CANISTER PURGE SOLENOID. IS IT?
• DISCONNECT SOLENOID ELECTRICAL CONNECTOR.
• DOES VACUUM NOW DROP?
PROBE EACH TERMINAL WITH A TEST LIGHT TO GROUND.
FAULTY SOLENOID CONNECTION OR SOLENOID.
LIGHT "ON" ONE
LIGHT "ON" BOTH
NO LIGHT
YES
NO
YES
NO
OPEN CKT 428 OR FAULTY ECM.
REPAIR SHORT TO VOLTAGE IN CKT 428.
OPEN CKT 250.
NO PROBLEM FOUND.
SEE "DIAGNOSTIC AIDS" ON FACING PAGE.
CKT 428 SHORTED TO GROUND OR FAULTY ECM.
CHECK HOSES. IF OK, REPLACE PURGE SOLENOID.

"*AFTER REPAIRS,*" CONFIRM "CLOSED LOOP" OPERATION AND NO "SERVICE ENGINE SOON" LIGHT.

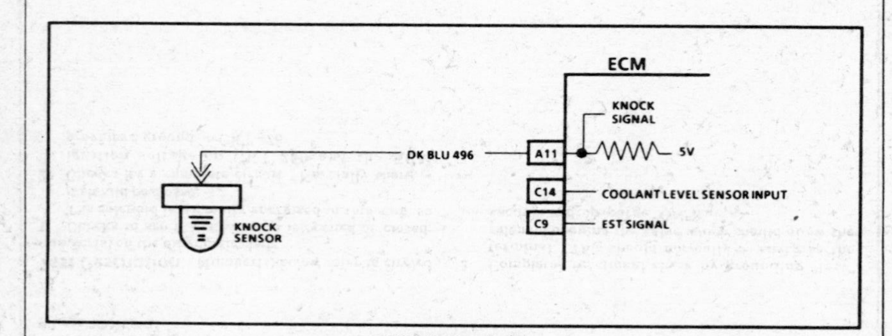
ECM
KNOCK SIGNAL
DK BLU 496
A11
5V
C14
COOLANT LEVEL SENSOR INPUT
C9
EST SIGNAL
KNOCK SENSOR

CHART C-5

ELECTRONIC SPARK CONTROL (ESC) SYSTEM CHECK 3.1L (VIN T) "W" CARLINE (PORT)

Circuit Description:

The knock sensor is used to detect engine detonation and the ECM will retard the electronic spark timing based on the signal being received. The circuitry, within the knock sensor, causes the ECM's 5 volts to be pulled down so that under a no knock condition, CKT 496 would measure about 2.5 volts. The knock sensor produces an AC signal which rides on the 2.5 volts DC voltage. The amplitude and frequency are dependent upon the knock level.

The MEM-CAL used with this engine, contains the functions which were part of remotely mounted ESC modules used on other GM vehicles. The ESC portion of the MEM-CAL, then sends a signal to other parts of the ECM which adjusts the spark timing to retard the spark and reduce the detonation.

Test Description: Number(s) below refer to circled number(s) on the diagnostic chart.

1. With engine idling, there should not be a knock signal present at the ECM, because detonation is not likely under a no load condition.
2. Tapping on the engine lift hood bracket should simulate a knock signal to determine if the sensor is capable of detecting detonation. If no knock is detected, try tapping on engine block closer to sensor before replacing sensor.
3. If the engine has an internal problem which is creating a knock, the knock sensor may be responding to the internal failure.
4. This test determines if the knock sensor is faulty or if the ESC portion of the MEM-CAL is faulty. If it is determined that the MEM-CAL is faulty, be sure that is is properly installed and latched into place. If not properly installed, repair and retest.

Diagnostic Aids:

While observing knock signal on the "Scan," there should be an indication that knock is present when detonation can be heard. Detonation is most likely to occur under high engine load conditions.

CHART C-5

ELECTRONIC SPARK CONTROL (ESC) SYSTEM CHECK 3.1L (VIN T) "W" CARLINE (PORT)

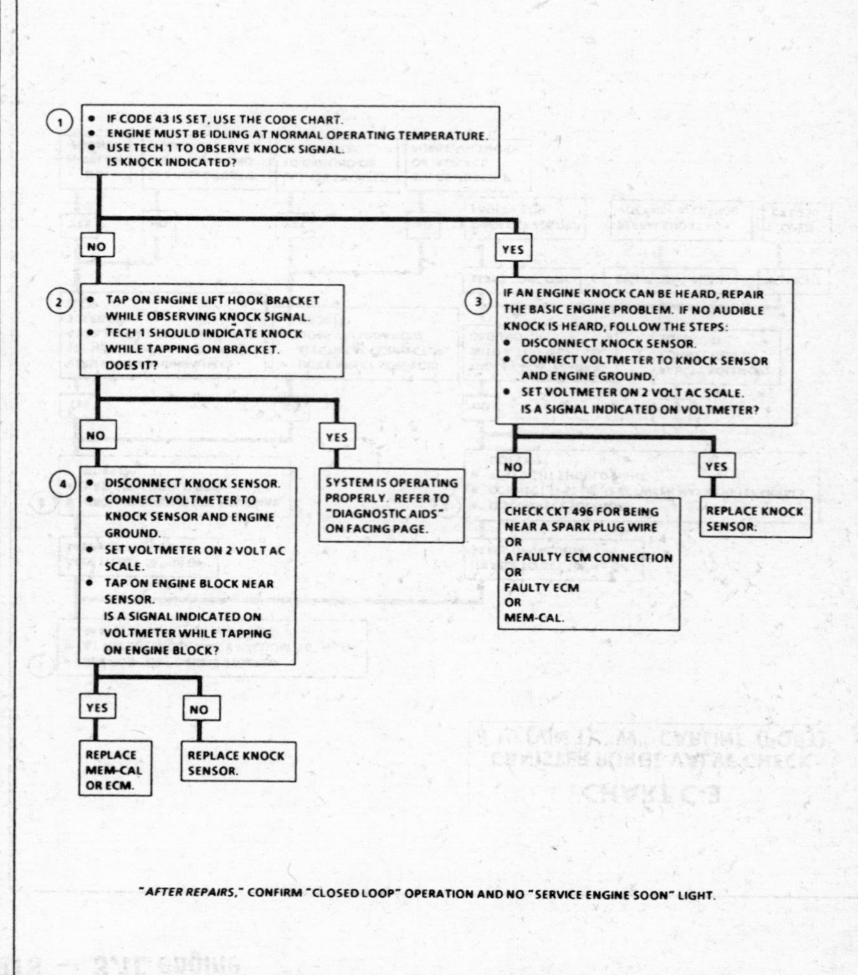
1
• IF CODE 43 IS SET, USE THE CODE CHART.
• ENGINE MUST BE IDLING AT NORMAL OPERATING TEMPERATURE.
• USE TECH 1 TO OBSERVE KNOCK SIGNAL.
IS KNOCK INDICATED?
NO
YES
2
• TAP ON ENGINE LIFT HOOK BRACKET WHILE OBSERVING KNOCK SIGNAL.
• TECH 1 SHOULD INDICATE KNOCK WHILE TAPPING ON BRACKET.
DOES IT?
3
IF AN ENGINE KNOCK CAN BE HEARD, REPAIR THE BASIC ENGINE PROBLEM. IF NO AUDIBLE KNOCK IS HEARD, FOLLOW THE STEPS:
• DISCONNECT KNOCK SENSOR.
• CONNECT VOLTMETER TO KNOCK SENSOR AND ENGINE GROUND.
• SET VOLTMETER ON 2 VOLT AC SCALE.
IS A SIGNAL INDICATED ON VOLTMETER?
NO
YES
4
• DISCONNECT KNOCK SENSOR.
• CONNECT VOLTMETER TO KNOCK SENSOR AND ENGINE GROUND.
• SET VOLTMETER ON 2 VOLT AC SCALE.
• TAP ON ENGINE BLOCK NEAR SENSOR.
IS A SIGNAL INDICATED ON VOLTMETER WHILE TAPPING ON ENGINE BLOCK?
SYSTEM IS OPERATING PROPERLY. REFER TO "DIAGNOSTIC AIDS" ON FACING PAGE.
NO
YES
CHECK CKT 496 FOR BEING NEAR A SPARK PLUG WIRE OR A FAULTY ECM CONNECTION OR FAULTY ECM OR MEM-CAL.
REPLACE KNOCK SENSOR.
YES
NO
REPLACE MEM-CAL OR ECM.
REPLACE KNOCK SENSOR.

"AFTER REPAIRS," CONFIRM "CLOSED LOOP" OPERATION AND NO "SERVICE ENGINE SOON" LIGHT.

DIAGNOSTIC CHARTS — 3.1L engine

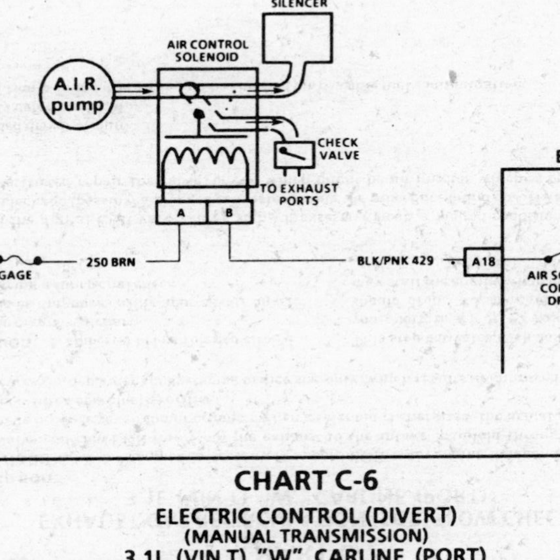
DIVERT SILENCER
AIR CONTROL SOLENOID
A.I.R. pump
CHECK VALVE
TO EXHAUST PORTS
A
B
ECM
IGNITION
GAGE
250 BRN
BLK/PNK 429
A18
AIR SOLENOID CONTROL DRIVER

CHART C-6
ELECTRIC CONTROL (DIVERT)
(MANUAL TRANSMISSION)
3.1L (VIN T) "W" CARLINE (PORT)

Circuit Description:

This system uses a single bed converter and air management is controlled by an air control valve (divert valve).

When grounded by the ECM, the solenoid causes the valve to direct air to the exhaust ports. When de-energized air diverts to the atmosphere. Air will go to the ports provided the valve has a ground to the ECM and good manifold vacuum.

Test Description: Number(s) below refer to circled number(s) on the diagnostic chart.

1. This is a system performance test. When vehicle goes to "Closed Loop," air will switch from the ports to divert.
2. Tests for a grounded electric divert circuit. Normal system light will be "OFF."
3. Checks for an open control circuit. Grounding "test" terminal will energize the solenoid if ECM and circuits are normal. In this step, if test light is "ON," circuits are normal and faulty is in valve connections or valve.

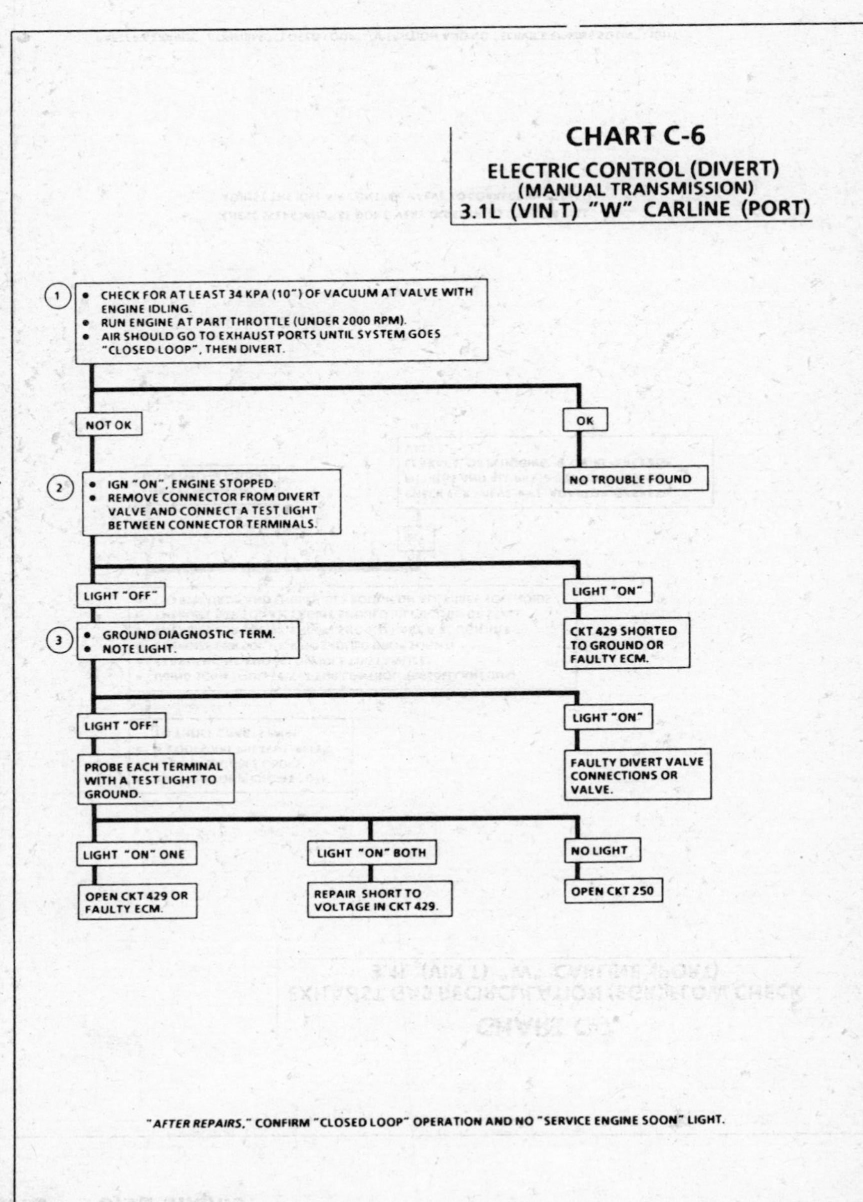
CHART C-6
ELECTRIC CONTROL (DIVERT)
(MANUAL TRANSMISSION)
3.1L (VIN T) "W" CARLINE (PORT)
1
• CHECK FOR AT LEAST 34 KPA (10") OF VACUUM AT VALVE WITH ENGINE IDLING.
• RUN ENGINE AT PART THROTTLE (UNDER 2000 RPM).
• AIR SHOULD GO TO EXHAUST PORTS UNTIL SYSTEM GOES "CLOSED LOOP", THEN DIVERT.
NOT OK
OK
NO TROUBLE FOUND
2
• IGN "ON", ENGINE STOPPED.
• REMOVE CONNECTOR FROM DIVERT VALVE AND CONNECT A TEST LIGHT BETWEEN CONNECTOR TERMINALS.
LIGHT "OFF"
LIGHT "ON"
CKT 429 SHORTED TO GROUND OR FAULTY ECM.
3
• GROUND DIAGNOSTIC TERM.
• NOTE LIGHT.
LIGHT "OFF"
LIGHT "ON"
FAULTY DIVERT VALVE CONNECTIONS OR VALVE.
PROBE EACH TERMINAL WITH A TEST LIGHT TO GROUND.
LIGHT "ON" ONE
LIGHT "ON" BOTH
NO LIGHT
OPEN CKT 429 OR FAULTY ECM.
REPAIR SHORT TO VOLTAGE IN CKT 429.
OPEN CKT 250
"AFTER REPAIRS," CONFIRM "CLOSED LOOP" OPERATION AND NO "SERVICE ENGINE SOON" LIGHT.

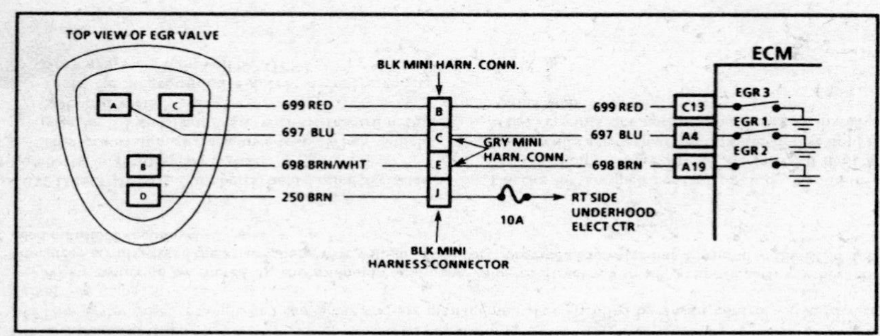
TOP VIEW OF EGR VALVE
A
C
B
D
699 RED
697 BLU
698 BRN/WHT
250 BRN
BLK MINI HARN. CONN.
B
C
E
J
GRY MINI HARN. CONN.
BLK MINI HARNESS CONNECTOR
10A
RT SIDE UNDERHOOD ELECT CTR
699 RED
697 BLU
698 BRN
C13
A4
A19
ECM
EGR 3
EGR 1
EGR 2

CHART C-7

EXHAUST GAS RECIRCULATION (EGR) FLOW CHECK 3.1L (VIN T) "W" CARLINE (PORT)

Circuit Description:

The digital (EGR) valve is designed to accurately supply EGR to an engine independent of intake manifold vacuum. The valve controls EGR flow from the exhaust to the intake manifold through three orifices which increment in size to produce seven combinations. When a solenoid is energized, the armature with attached shaft and swivel pintle is lifted opening the orifice.

The flow accuracy is dependent on metering orifice size only, which results in improved control.

Test Description: Number(s) below refer to circled number(s) on the diagnostic chart.

1. Codes should be diagnoses using appropriate chart before preparing a functional check.
2. This step activates each solenoid individually. As you energize #1 or #2 solenoid, the engine rpm should drop. #3 solenoid has the large port and may stall the engine when energized.

NOTE: If the digital EGR valve shows signs of excessive heat, a melted condition. Check the exhaust system for blockage (possibly a plugged converter) using the procedure found on CHART B-1. If the exhaust system is restricted repair the cause, one of which might be an injector which is open due to one of the following:

a. Stuck.
b. Grounded driver circuit.
c. Possibly defective ECM.

If this condition is found, the oil should be checked for possible fuel contamination.

CHART C-7

EXHAUST GAS RECIRCULATION (EGR) FLOW CHECK 3.1L (VIN T) "W" CARLINE (PORT)

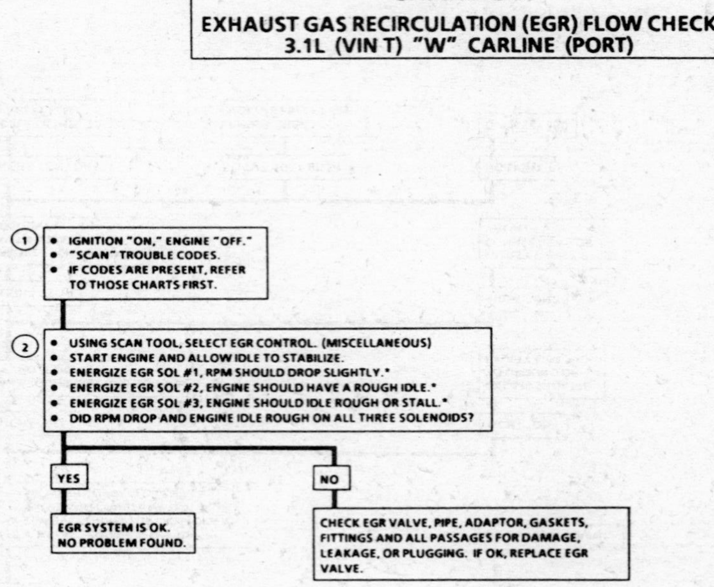
1
• IGNITION "ON," ENGINE "OFF."
• "SCAN" TROUBLE CODES.
• IF CODES ARE PRESENT, REFER TO THOSE CHARTS FIRST.
2
• USING SCAN TOOL, SELECT EGR CONTROL. (MISCELLANEOUS)
• START ENGINE AND ALLOW IDLE TO STABILIZE.
• ENERGIZE EGR SOL #1, RPM SHOULD DROP SLIGHTLY.*
• ENERGIZE EGR SOL #2, ENGINE SHOULD HAVE A ROUGH IDLE.*
• ENERGIZE EGR SOL #3, ENGINE SHOULD IDLE ROUGH OR STALL.*
• DID RPM DROP AND ENGINE IDLE ROUGH ON ALL THREE SOLENOIDS?
YES
NO
EGR SYSTEM IS OK. NO PROBLEM FOUND.
CHECK EGR VALVE, PIPE, ADAPTOR, GASKETS, FITTINGS AND ALL PASSAGES FOR DAMAGE, LEAKAGE, OR PLUGGING. IF OK, REPLACE EGR VALVE.

* THESE STEPS MUST BE DONE VERY QUICKLY, AS THE ECM WILL ADJUST THE IDLE AIR CONTROL VALVE TO CORRECT IDLE SPEED.

"AFTER REPAIRS." CONFIRM "CLOSED LOOP" OPERATION AND NO "SERVICE ENGINE SOON" LIGHT.

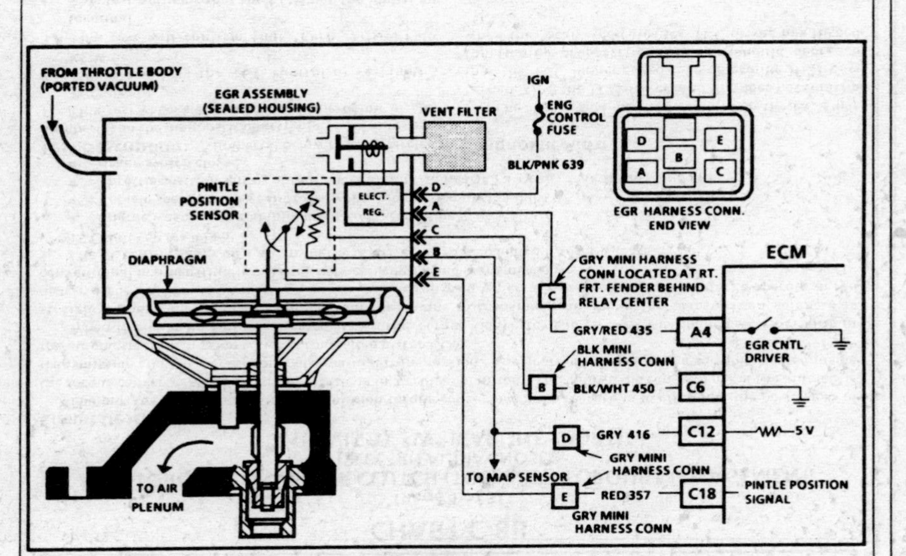

CHART C-7

EXHAUST GAS RECIRCULATION (EGR) VALVE CHECK 3.1L TURBO (VIN V) "W" CARLINE (PORT)

Circuit Description:

The integrated electronic EGR valve functions similar to a port valve with a remote vacuum regulator. The internal solenoid is normally open, which causes the vacuum signal to be vented "OFF" to the atmosphere when EGR is not being commanded by the ECM. This EGR valve has a sealed cap and the solenoid valve opens and closes the vacuum signal which controls the amount of vacuum vented to atmosphere, and this controls the amount of vacuum applied to the diaphragm. The electronic EGR valve contains a voltage regulator which converts the ECM signal to provide different amounts of EGR flow by regulating the current to the solenoid. The ECM controls EGR flow with a pulse width modulated signal (turns "ON" and "OFF" many times a second) based on airflow, TPS, and rpm.

This system also contains a pintle position sensor which works similar to a TPS sensor, and as EGR flow is increased, the sensor output also increases.

Test Description: Numbers below refer to circled numbers on the diagnostic chart.

1. Whenever the solenoid is de-energized, the solenoid valve should be open which should not allow the vacuum to move the EGR diaphragm. However, if the filter is plugged, the vacuum applied with the hand held vacuum pump will cause the diaphragm to move because the vacuum will not be vented to the atmosphere.
2. This test will determine if the EGR filter is plugged or if the EGR itself is faulty. Use care when removing the filter to avoid damaging the EGR assembly. See "On-Vehicle Service" for procedure.
3. If the valve moves in this test, it's probably due to CKT 435 being shorted to ground.
4. Grounding the diagnostic terminal should energize the solenoid which closes "OFF" the vent and allows the vacuum to move the diaphragm.
5. The EGR assembly is designed to have some leak and therefore, 7" of vacuum is all that should be able to be held on the assembly. However, if too much of a leak exists (less than 3") the EGR assembly is leaking and must be replaced.

Diagnostic Aids:

The EGR position voltage can be used to determine that the pintle is moving. When no EGR is commanded (0% duty cycle), the position sensor should read between .5 volt and 1.5 volts, and increase with the commanded EGR duty cycle.

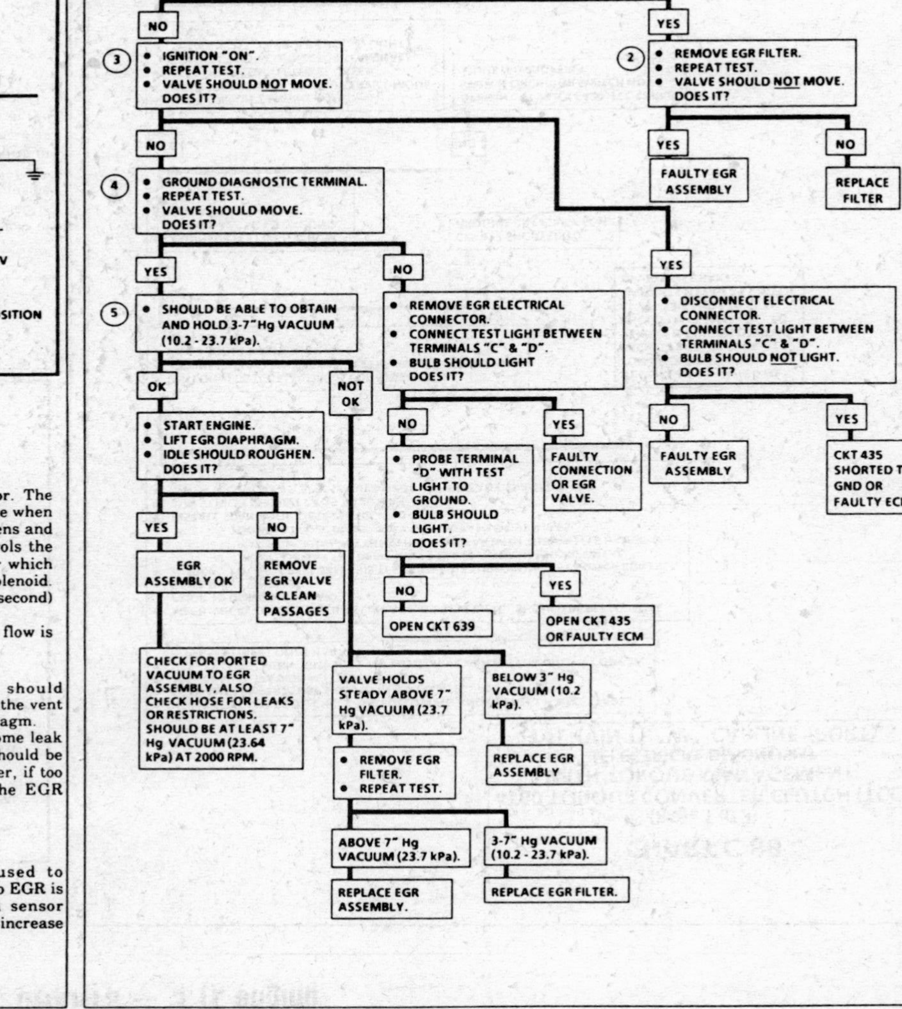

IGN
GAGE
39 PNK/BLK
BRAKE SWITCH
N.C.
BULK HEAD CONN
J3
420 PPL
A B C E D
AUTO TRANSMISSION (4T60) W.T.M. 2ND GEAR OPENS IN 2ND & 3RD GEAR. 3RD GEAR OPENS IN 3RD & 4TH. 4TH GEAR OPENS IN 4TH GEAR.
4TH GEAR SW.
3RD GEAR SW.
2ND GEAR SW.
ECM
446 LT BLU — D22 — 4TH GEAR SIGNAL — B+
108 DK GRN — D6 — 3RD GEAR SIGNAL — B+
232 WHT — C20 — 2ND GEAR SIGNAL — B+
422 TAN/BLK — B7 — TCC CONTROL DRIVER

CHART C-8B

(Page 1 of 3)

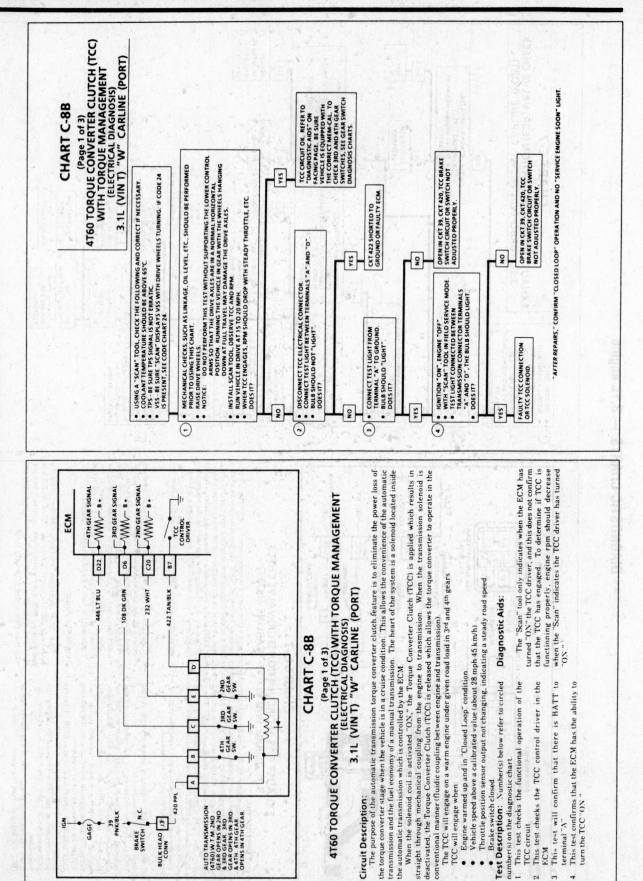

4T60 TORQUE CONVERTER CLUTCH (TCC) WITH TORQUE MANAGEMENT

(ELECTRICAL DIAGNOSIS)

3.1L (VIN T) "W" CARLINE (PORT)

Circuit Description:

The purpose of the automatic transmission torque converter clutch feature is to eliminate the power loss of the torque converter stage when the vehicle is in a cruise condition. This allows the convenience of the automatic transmission and the fuel economy of a manual transmission. The heart of the system is a solenoid located inside the automatic transmission which is controlled by the ECM.

When the solenoid coil is activated "ON," the Torque Converter Clutch (TCC) is applied which results in straight through mechanical coupling from the engine to transmission. When the transmission solenoid is deactivated, the Torque Converter Clutch (TCC) is released which allows the torque converter to operate in the conventional manner (fluidic coupling between engine and transmission).

The TCC will engage on a warm engine under given road load in 3rd and 4th gears.

TCC will engage when:

- Engine warmed up and in "Closed Loop" condition.
- Vehicle speed above a calibrated value (about 28 mph 45 km/h).
- Throttle position sensor output not changing, indicating a steady road speed.
- Brake switch closed.

Test Description: Number(s) below refer to circled number(s) on the diagnostic chart.

1. This test checks the functional operation of the TCC circuit.
2. This test checks the TCC control driver in the ECM.
3. This test will confirm that there is BATT to terminal "A".
4. This test confirms that the ECM has the ability to turn the TCC "ON."

Diagnostic Aids:

The "Scan" tool only indicates when the ECM has turned "ON" the TCC driver, and this does not confirm that the TCC has engaged. To determine if TCC is functioning properly, engine rpm should decrease when the "Scan" indicates the TCC driver has turned "ON."

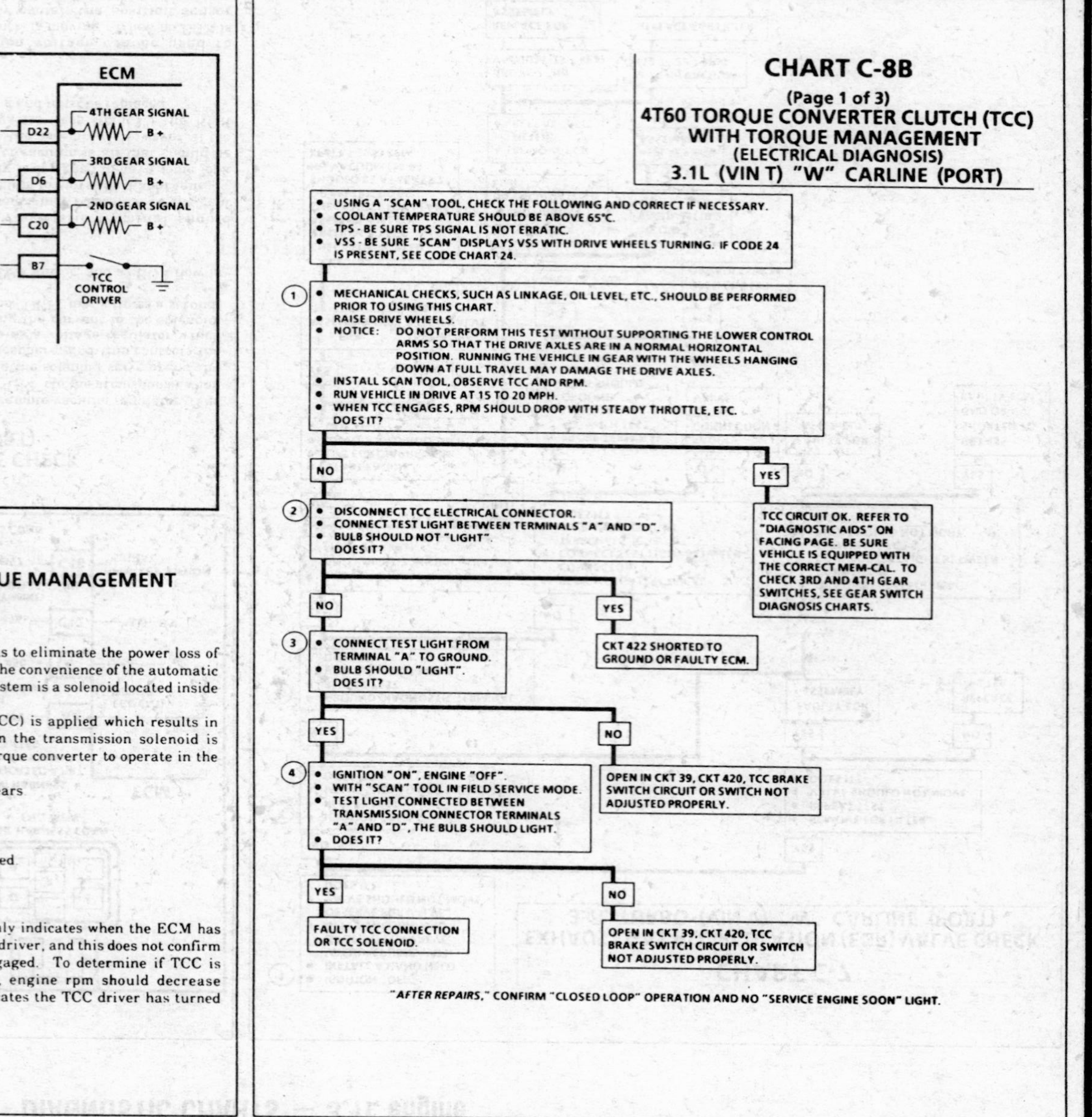

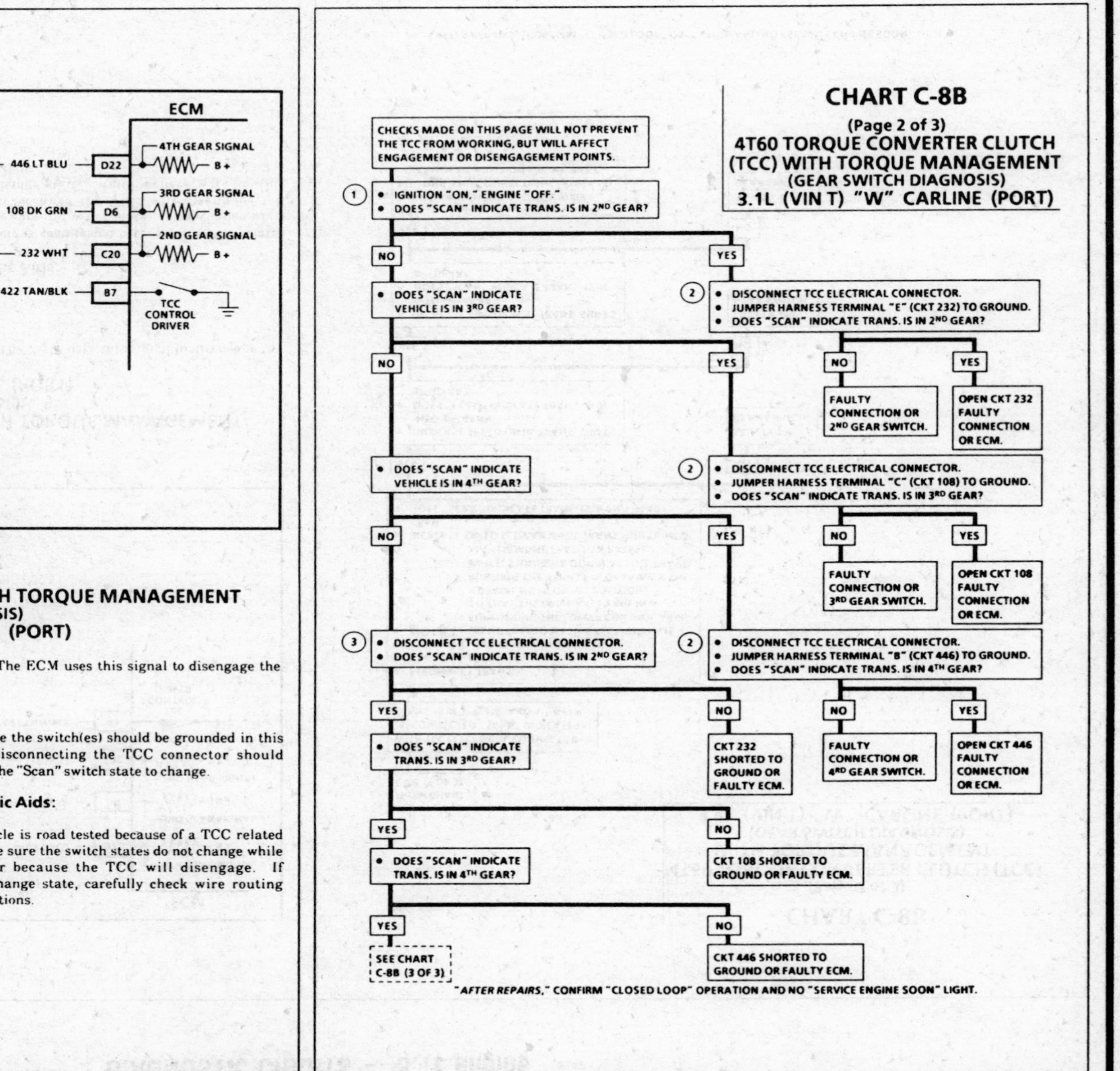

CHART C-8B

(Page 2 of 3)

4T60 TORQUE CONVERTER CLUTCH (TCC) WITH TORQUE MANAGEMENT (GEAR SWITCH DIAGNOSIS) 3.1L (VIN T) "W" CARLINE (PORT)

Circuit Description:

The 2nd gear switch in this vehicle is open in 3rd and 4th gear. The ECM uses this signal to disengage the Torque Converter Clutch (TCC) when going into a downshift.

The fourth gear switch is open in fourth gear.

Test Description: Number(s) below refer to circled number(s) on the diagnostic chart.

1. Some "Scan" tools display the state of these switches in different ways. Be familiar with the type of tool being used. Since both switches should be in the closed state during this test, the tool should read the same for either the 2nd, 3rd or 4th gear switch.
2. Determines whether the switch or signal circuit is open. The circuit can be checked for an open by measuring the voltage (with a voltmeter) at the TCC connector. Should be about 12 volts.
3. Because the switch(es) should be grounded in this step, disconnecting the TCC connector should cause the "Scan" switch state to change.

Diagnostic Aids:

If vehicle is road tested because of a TCC related problem, be sure the switch states do not change while in 4th gear because the TCC will disengage. If switches change state, carefully check wire routing and connections.

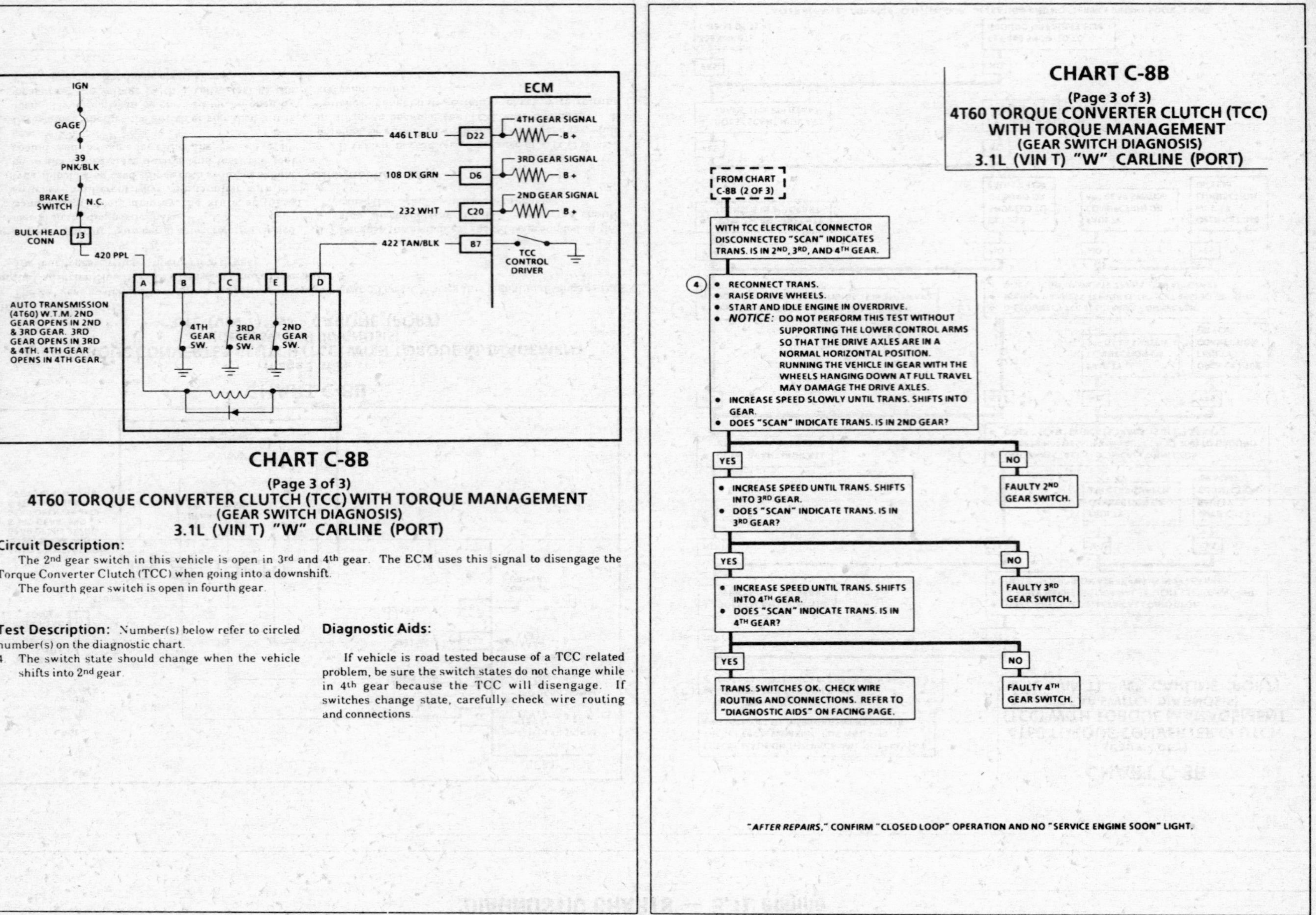

CHART C-8B

(Page 3 of 3)

4T60 TORQUE CONVERTER CLUTCH (TCC) WITH TORQUE MANAGEMENT (GEAR SWITCH DIAGNOSIS) 3.1L (VIN T) "W" CARLINE (PORT)

Circuit Description:

The 2nd gear switch in this vehicle is open in 3rd and 4th gear. The ECM uses this signal to disengage the Torque Converter Clutch (TCC) when going into a downshift.

The fourth gear switch is open in fourth gear.

Test Description: Number(s) below refer to circled number(s) on the diagnostic chart.

4. The switch state should change when the vehicle shifts into 2nd gear.

Diagnostic Aids:

If vehicle is road tested because of a TCC related problem, be sure the switch states do not change while in 4th gear because the TCC will disengage. If switches change state, carefully check wire routing and connections.

DIAGNOSTIC CHARTS — 3.4L engine

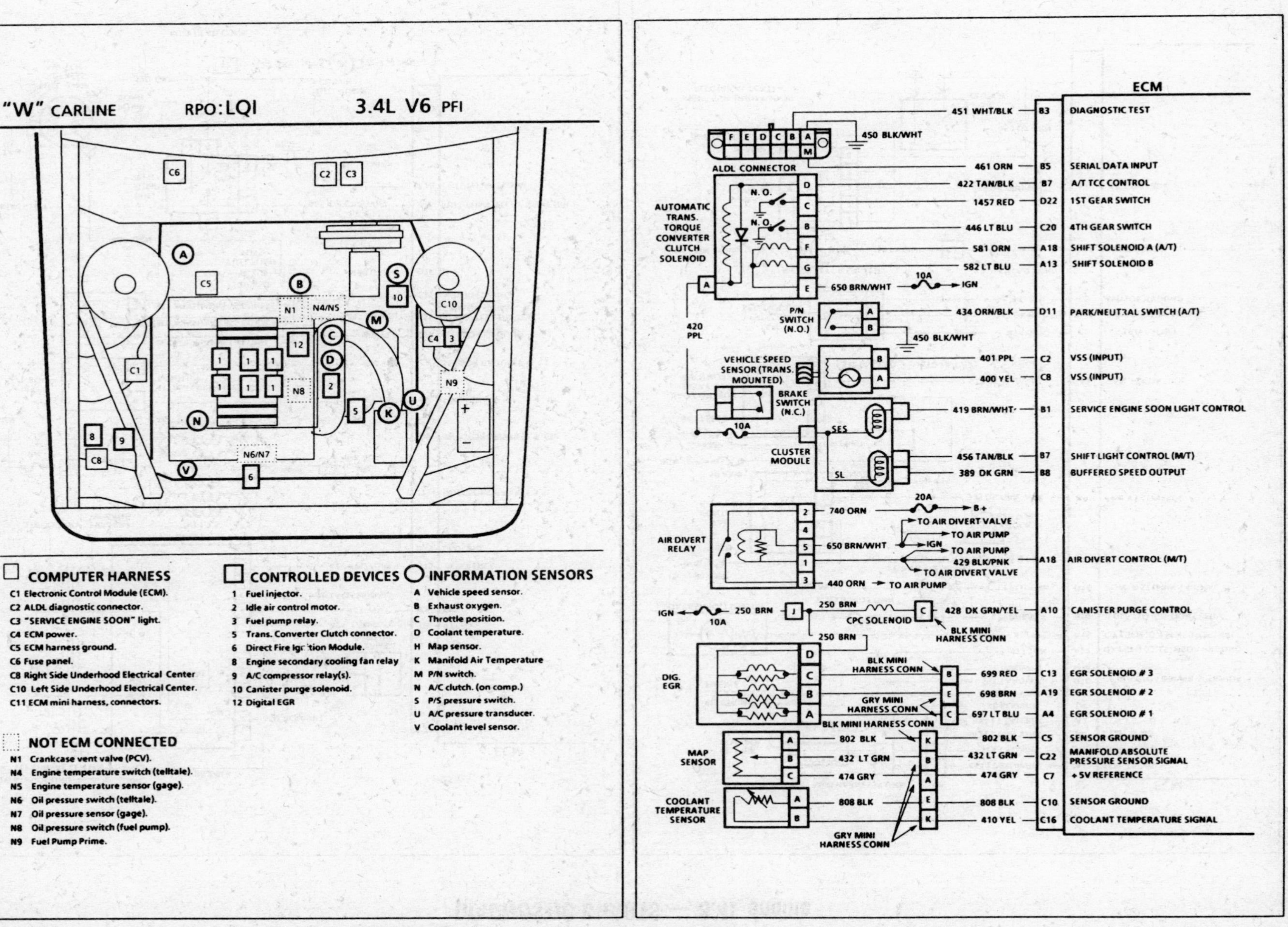
"W" CARLINE
RPO: LQI
3.4L V6 PFI
COMPUTER HARNESS
C1 Electronic Control Module (ECM).
C2 ALDL diagnostic connector.
C3 "SERVICE ENGINE SOON" light.
C4 ECM power.
C5 ECM harness ground.
C6 Fuse panel.
C8 Right Side Underhood Electrical Center
C10 Left Side Underhood Electrical Center.
C11 ECM mini harness, connectors.
CONTROLLED DEVICES
1 Fuel injector.
2 Idle air control motor.
3 Fuel pump relay.
5 Trans. Converter Clutch connector.
6 Direct Fire Ignition Module.
8 Engine secondary cooling fan relay
9 A/C compressor relay(s).
10 Canister purge solenoid.
12 Digital EGR
INFORMATION SENSORS
A Vehicle speed sensor.
B Exhaust oxygen.
C Throttle position.
D Coolant temperature.
H Map sensor.
K Manifold Air Temperature
M P/N switch.
N A/C clutch. (on comp.)
S P/S pressure switch.
U A/C pressure transducer.
V Coolant level sensor.
NOT ECM CONNECTED
N1 Crankcase vent valve (PCV).
N4 Engine temperature switch (telltale).
N5 Engine temperature sensor (gage).
N6 Oil pressure switch (telltale).
N7 Oil pressure sensor (gage).
N8 Oil pressure switch (fuel pump).
N9 Fuel Pump Prime.
ECM
ALDL CONNECTOR
AUTOMATIC TRANS. TORQUE CONVERTER CLUTCH SOLENOID
P/N SWITCH (N.O.)
VEHICLE SPEED SENSOR (TRANS. MOUNTED)
BRAKE SWITCH (N.C.)
CLUSTER MODULE
AIR DIVERT RELAY
DIG. EGR
MAP SENSOR
COOLANT TEMPERATURE SENSOR
451 WHT/BLK — B3 DIAGNOSTIC TEST
450 BLK/WHT
461 ORN — B5 SERIAL DATA INPUT
422 TAN/BLK — B7 A/T TCC CONTROL
1457 RED — D22 1ST GEAR SWITCH
446 LT BLU — C20 4TH GEAR SWITCH
581 ORN — A18 SHIFT SOLENOID A (A/T)
582 LT BLU — A13 SHIFT SOLENOID B
650 BRN/WHT 10A IGN
420 PPL
434 ORN/BLK — D11 PARK/NEUTRAL SWITCH (A/T)
450 BLK/WHT
401 PPL — C2 VSS (INPUT)
400 YEL — C8 VSS (INPUT)
419 BRN/WHT — B1 SERVICE ENGINE SOON LIGHT CONTROL
SES
SL
10A
456 TAN/BLK — B7 SHIFT LIGHT CONTROL (M/T)
389 DK GRN — B8 BUFFERED SPEED OUTPUT
740 ORN 20A B+
650 BRN/WHT
TO AIR DIVERT VALVE
TO AIR PUMP
IGN
TO AIR PUMP
429 BLK/PNK — A18 AIR DIVERT CONTROL (M/T)
TO AIR DIVERT VALVE
440 ORN TO AIR PUMP
IGN 10A 250 BRN
250 BRN
CPC SOLENOID
428 DK GRN/YEL — A10 CANISTER PURGE CONTROL
BLK MINI HARNESS CONN
250 BRN
BLK MINI HARNESS CONN
699 RED — C13 EGR SOLENOID # 3
698 BRN — A19 EGR SOLENOID # 2
GRY MINI HARNESS CONN
697 LT BLU — A4 EGR SOLENOID # 1
BLK MINI HARNESS CONN
802 BLK — C5 SENSOR GROUND
432 LT GRN — C22 MANIFOLD ABSOLUTE PRESSURE SENSOR SIGNAL
474 GRY — C7 +5V REFERENCE
808 BLK — C10 SENSOR GROUND
410 YEL — C16 COOLANT TEMPERATURE SIGNAL
GRY MINI HARNESS CONN

DIAGNOSTIC CHARTS — 3.4L engine

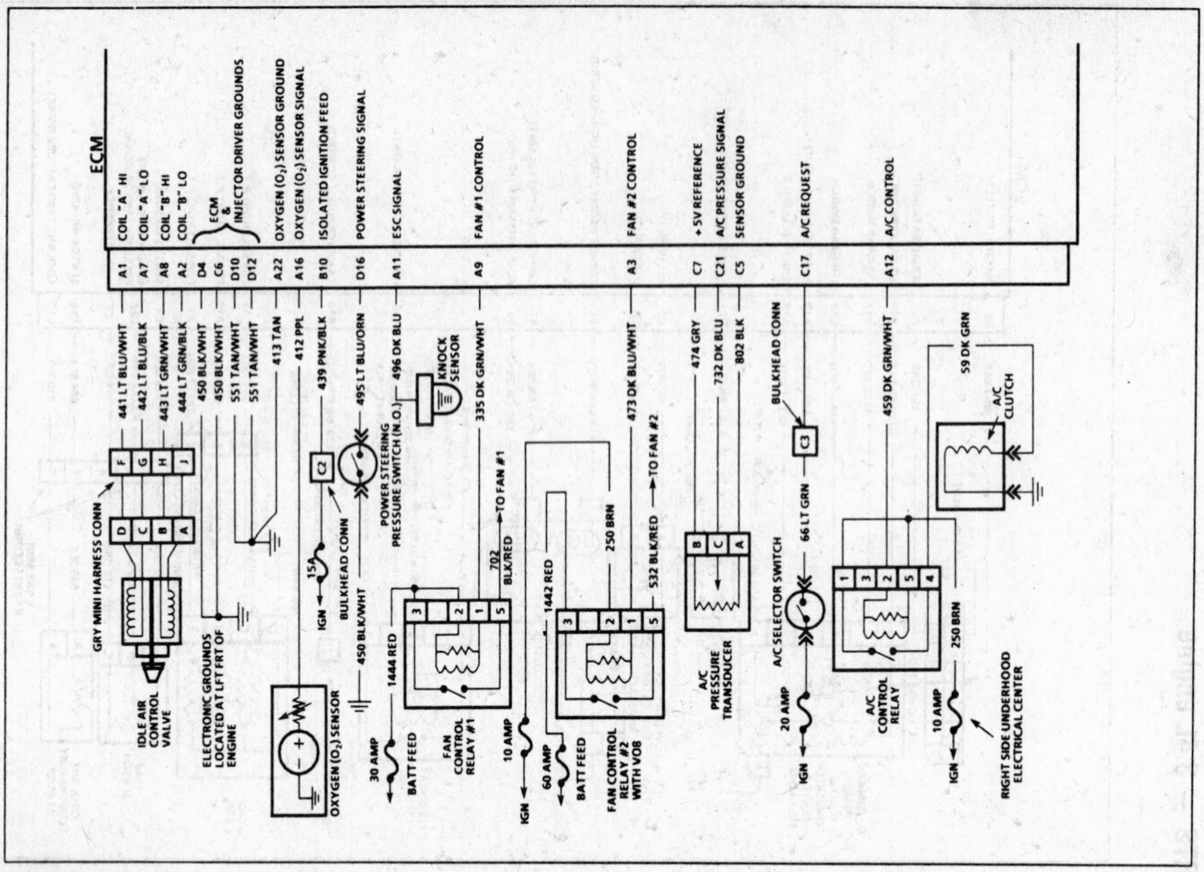

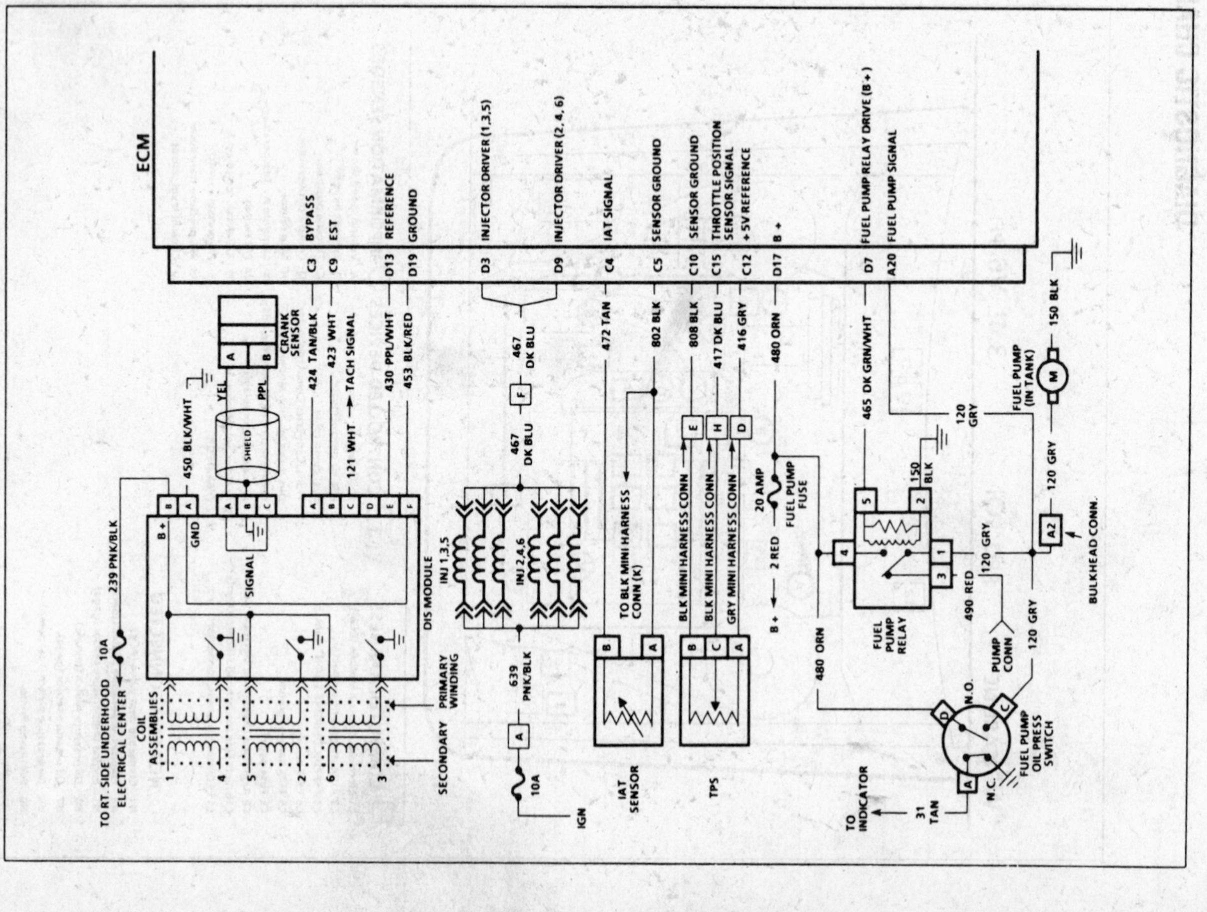

TO RT. SIDE UNDERHOOD ELECTRICAL CENTER
10A
239 PNK/BLK
COIL ASSEMBLIES
1
4
5
2
6
3
SECONDARY
PRIMARY WINDING
DIS MODULE
B+
GND
450 BLK/WHT
SIGNAL
SHIELD
YEL
PPL
CRANK SENSOR
424 TAN/BLK
423 WHT
121 WHT → TACH SIGNAL
430 PPL/WHT
453 BLK/RED
INJ 1,3,5
INJ 2,4,6
639 PNK/BLK
10A
IGN
467 DK BLU
IAT SENSOR
TO BLK MINI HARNESS CONN (K)
472 TAN
802 BLK
TPS
BLK MINI HARNESS CONN
BLK MINI HARNESS CONN
GRY MINI HARNESS CONN
808 BLK
417 DK BLU
416 GRY
B+ ← 2 RED
20 AMP
FUEL PUMP FUSE
480 ORN
480 ORN
TO INDICATOR
31 TAN
N.C.
N.O.
FUEL PUMP OIL PRESS SWITCH
FUEL PUMP RELAY
465 DK GRN/WHT
150 BLK
120 GRY
490 RED
120 GRY
PUMP CONN
120 GRY
FUEL PUMP (IN TANK)
120 GRY
150 BLK
BULKHEAD CONN.

ECM
C3 BYPASS
C9 EST
D13 REFERENCE
D19 GROUND
D3 INJECTOR DRIVER (1,3,5)
D9 INJECTOR DRIVER (2, 4, 6)
C4 IAT SIGNAL
C5 SENSOR GROUND
C10 SENSOR GROUND
C15 THROTTLE POSITION SENSOR SIGNAL
C12 +5V REFERENCE
D17 B+
D7 FUEL PUMP RELAY DRIVE (B+)
A20 FUEL PUMP SIGNAL

GRY MINI HARNESS CONN
IDLE AIR CONTROL VALVE
441 LT BLU/WHT
442 LT BLU/BLK
443 LT GRN/WHT
444 LT GRN/BLK
ELECTRONIC GROUNDS LOCATED AT LFT FRT OF ENGINE
450 BLK/WHT
450 BLK/WHT
551 TAN/WHT
551 TAN/WHT
413 TAN
OXYGEN (O_2) SENSOR
412 PPL
IGN
15A
BULKHEAD CONN
439 PNK/BLK
450 BLK/WHT
POWER STEERING PRESSURE SWITCH (N.O.)
495 LT BLU/ORN
496 DK BLU
KNOCK SENSOR
30 AMP
BATT FEED
1444 RED
FAN CONTROL RELAY #1
335 DK GRN/WHT
702 BLK/RED → TO FAN #1
10 AMP
IGN
60 AMP
BATT FEED
1442 RED
FAN CONTROL RELAY #2 WITH V08
250 BRN
473 DK BLU/WHT
532 BLK/RED → TO FAN #2
A/C PRESSURE TRANSDUCER
474 GRY
732 DK BLU
802 BLK
20 AMP
IGN
A/C SELECTOR SWITCH
66 LT GRN
BULKHEAD CONN
A/C CONTROL RELAY
459 DK GRN/WHT
10 AMP
IGN
250 BRN
RIGHT SIDE UNDERHOOD ELECTRICAL CENTER
59 DK GRN
A/C CLUTCH

ECM
A1 COIL "A" HI
A7 COIL "A" LO
A8 COIL "B" HI
A2 COIL "B" LO
D4, C6, D10, D12 ECM & INJECTOR DRIVER GROUNDS
A22 OXYGEN (O_2) SENSOR GROUND
A16 OXYGEN (O_2) SENSOR SIGNAL
B10 ISOLATED IGNITION FEED
D16 POWER STEERING SIGNAL
A11 ESC SIGNAL
A9 FAN #1 CONTROL
A3 FAN #2 CONTROL
C7 +5V REFERENCE
C21 A/C PRESSURE SIGNAL
C5 SENSOR GROUND
C17 A/C REQUEST
A12 A/C CONTROL

DIAGNOSTIC CHARTS — 3.4L engine

CONNECTOR A

CIRCUIT	PIN	WIRE COLOR
IAC "A" HIGH	A1	LT BLU/WHT
IAC "B" LOW	A2	LT GRN/BLK
FAN #2 CONTROL	A3	DK BLU/WHT
EGR SOLENOID #1	A4	BLU
	A5	
	A6	
IAC "A" LOW	A7	LT BLU/BLK
IAC "B" HIGH	A8	LT GRN//WHT
FAN #1 CONTROL	A9	DK GRN/WHT
CANISTER PURGE	A10	DK GRN/YEL
ESC SIGNAL	A11	DK BLU
A/C RELAY CONTROL	A12	DK GRN/WHT
"B" SHIFT SOLENOID (4T60E)	A13	LT BLU
	A14	
	A15	
O_2 SIGNAL	A16	PPL
	A17	
"A" SHIFT SOLENOID (4T60E)	A18	ORN
AIR PUMP RELAY (M/T 3.4L)	A18	BLK/PNK
AIR SOLENOID M/T 3.1L	A18	BLK/PNK
EGR SOLENOID #2	A19	BRN
FUEL PUMP SIGNAL	A20	GRY
SENSOR GROUND	A22	TAN

A

ORANGE

CONNECTOR B

CIRCUIT	PIN	WIRE COLOR
SES LIGHT	B1	BRN/WHT
	B2	
DIAGNOSTIC / TEST	B3	WHT/BLK
	B4	
SERIAL DATA IN / ALDL	B5	ORN
	B6	
TCC (A/T) SHIFT LIGHT (M/T)	B7	TAN/BLK
BUFFERED SPEED OUT	B8	DK GRN
	B9	
ISOLATED IGNITION FEED	B10	PNK/BLK
	B11	
	B12	
	B13	
	B14	
	B15	
	B16	
	B17	
	B18	
	B19	
	B20	
	B21	
	B22	

B

WHITE

C

GREEN

D

BLUE

CONNECTOR C

CIRCUIT	PIN	WIRE COLOR
	C1	
MAG. VSS SIGNAL LOW	C2	PPL
DIS BYPASS	C3	TAN/BLK
IAT SIGNAL	C4	TAN
SENSOR GROUND	C5	BLK
GROUND	C6	BLK/WHT
+ 5 VOLT REFERENCE (MAP)	C7	GRY
MAG. VSS HIGH	C8	YEL
EST CONTROL	C9	WHT
SENSOR GROUND	C10	BLK
	C11	
+ 5 VOLT REFERENCE (TPS)	C12	GRY
EGR SOLENOID #3	C13	RED
	C14	
TPS SIGNAL	C15	DK BLU
COOLANT TEMPERATURE SIGNAL	C16	YEL
A/C REQUEST	C17	LT BLU
	C18	
	C19	
4TH GEAR SIGNAL	C20	LT BLU
A/C PRESSURE SIGNAL	C21	DK BLU
MAP SIGNAL	C22	LT GRN

CONNECTOR D

CIRCUIT	PIN	WIRE COLOR
	D1	
	D2	
INJECTOR DRIVER (1, 3, 5)	D3	DK GRN
GROUND	D4	BLK/WHT
	D5	
	D6	
FUEL PUMP RELAY DRIVE	D7	DK GRN/WHT
	D8	
INJECTOR DRIVER (2, 4, 6)	D9	DK BLU
GROUND	D10	TAN/WHT
P/N SWITCH (A/T)	D11	ORN/BLK
GROUND	D12	TAN/WHT
REFERENCE	D13	PPL/WHT
	D14	
	D15	
P/S PRESSURE SIGNAL	D16	LT BLU/ORN
BATTERY FEED	D17	ORN
	D18	
DIS REFERENCE LOW	D19	BLK/RED
	D20	
	D21	
1ST GEAR SIGNAL	D22	RED

DIAGNOSTIC CHARTS — 3.4L engine

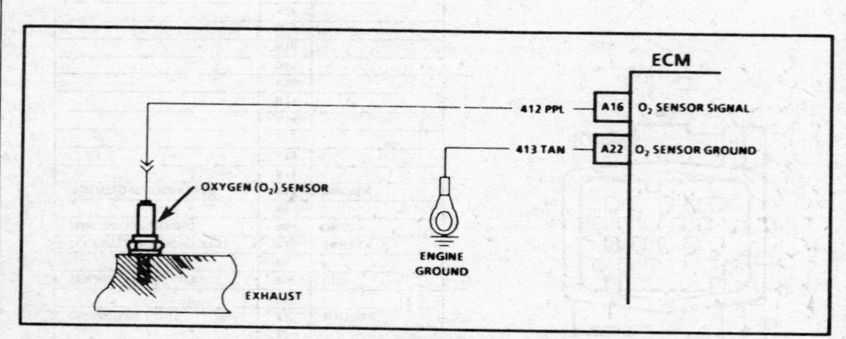
ECM
412 PPL
A16
O₂ SENSOR SIGNAL
413 TAN
A22
O₂ SENSOR GROUND
OXYGEN (O₂) SENSOR
ENGINE GROUND
EXHAUST

CODE 13

OXYGEN (O_2) SENSOR CIRCUIT (OPEN CIRCUIT) 3.4L (LQ1) "W" CARLINE (PORT)

Circuit Description:

The ECM supplies a voltage of about .55 volt between terminals "A16" and "A22" (If measured with a 10 megohm digital voltmeter, this may read as low as .35 volt.) The Oxygen (O_2) sensor varies the voltage within a range of about 1 volt if the exhaust is rich, down through about .10 volt if exhaust is lean.

The sensor is like an open circuit and produces no voltage when it is below 315°C (600°F). An open sensor circuit or cold sensor causes "Open Loop" operation.

Test Description: Number(s) below refer to circled number(s) on the diagnostic chart.

1. Code 13 will set under the following conditions:
   - Engine running at least 2 minutes after start.
   - Coolant temperature at least 50°C.
   - No Code 21 or 22.
   - O_2 signal voltage steady between .35 and .55 volt.
   - Throttle position sensor signal above 4% for more time than TPS was below 4%. (About .3 volt above closed throttle voltage.)
   - All conditions must be met and held for at least 25 seconds.

   If the conditions for a Code 13 exist, the system will not go "Closed Loop."
2. This will determine if the sensor is at fault or the wiring or ECM is the cause of the Code 13.
3. In doing this test use only a high impedance digital volt ohmmeter. This test checks the continuity of CKT 412 and CKT 413 because if CKT 413 is open the ECM voltage on CKT 412 will be over .6 volt (600 mV).

Diagnostic Aids:

Normal "Scan" voltage varies between 100 mV to 999 mV (.1 and 1.0 volt) while in "Closed Loop." Code 13 sets if voltage remains between .35 and .55 volt, but the system will go "Open Loop" in about 15 seconds. Refer to "Intermittents" in "Symptoms," Section

CODE 13

OXYGEN (O_2) SENSOR CIRCUIT (OPEN CIRCUIT) 3.4L (LQ1) "W" CARLINE (PORT)

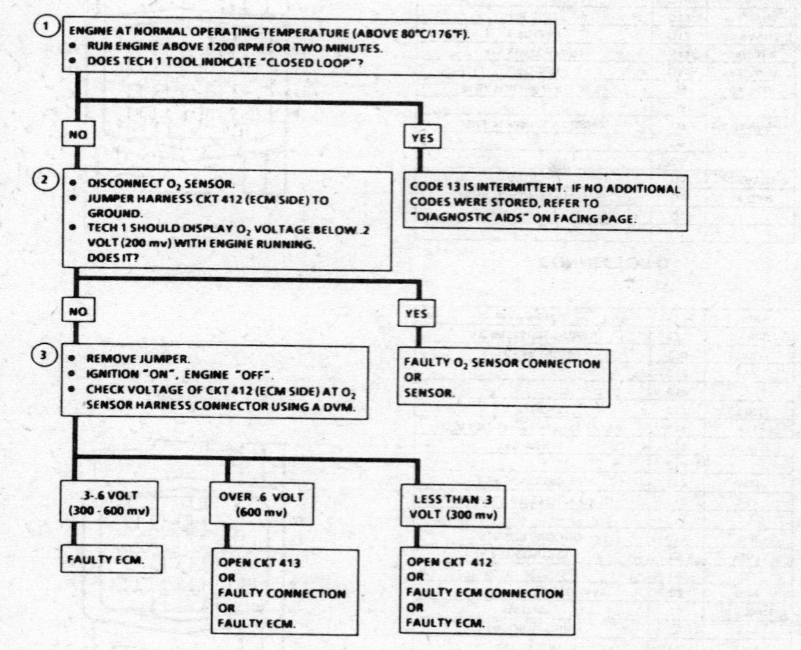
1
ENGINE AT NORMAL OPERATING TEMPERATURE (ABOVE 80°C/176°F).
• RUN ENGINE ABOVE 1200 RPM FOR TWO MINUTES.
• DOES TECH 1 TOOL INDICATE "CLOSED LOOP"?
NO
YES
CODE 13 IS INTERMITTENT. IF NO ADDITIONAL CODES WERE STORED, REFER TO "DIAGNOSTIC AIDS" ON FACING PAGE.
2
• DISCONNECT O₂ SENSOR.
• JUMPER HARNESS CKT 412 (ECM SIDE) TO GROUND.
• TECH 1 SHOULD DISPLAY O₂ VOLTAGE BELOW .2 VOLT (200 mv) WITH ENGINE RUNNING.
DOES IT?
NO
YES
FAULTY O₂ SENSOR CONNECTION OR SENSOR.
3
• REMOVE JUMPER.
• IGNITION "ON", ENGINE "OFF".
• CHECK VOLTAGE OF CKT 412 (ECM SIDE) AT O₂ SENSOR HARNESS CONNECTOR USING A DVM.
.3-.6 VOLT (300 - 600 mv)
OVER .6 VOLT (600 mv)
LESS THAN .3 VOLT (300 mv)
FAULTY ECM.
OPEN CKT 413 OR FAULTY CONNECTION OR FAULTY ECM.
OPEN CKT 412 OR FAULTY ECM CONNECTION OR FAULTY ECM.

CLEAR CODES AND CONFIRM "CLOSED LOOP" OPERATION AND NO "SERVICE ENGINE SOON" LIGHT.

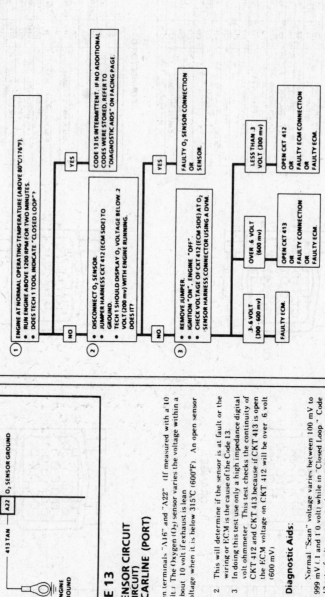

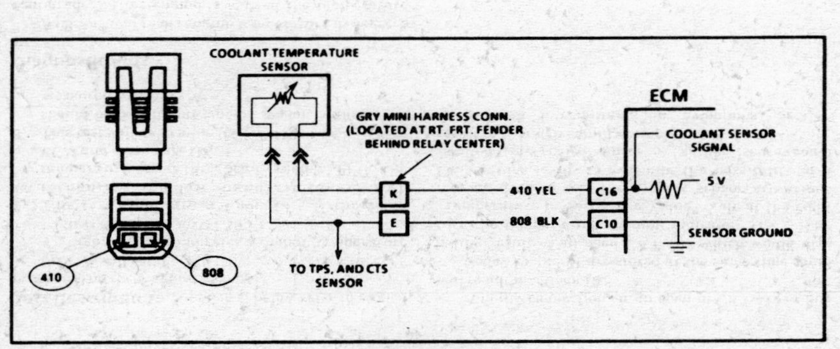
COOLANT TEMPERATURE SENSOR
GRY MINI HARNESS CONN. (LOCATED AT RT. FRT. FENDER BEHIND RELAY CENTER)
ECM
COOLANT SENSOR SIGNAL
5 V
K
E
410 YEL
808 BLK
C16
C10
SENSOR GROUND
TO TPS, AND CTS SENSOR
410
808

CODE 14

COOLANT TEMPERATURE SENSOR (CTS) CIRCUIT
(HIGH TEMPERATURE INDICATED)
3.4L (LQ1) "W" CARLINE (PORT)

Circuit Description:

The Coolant Temperature Sensor (CTS) uses a thermistor to control the signal voltage to the ECM. The ECM applies a voltage on CKT 410 to the sensor. When the engine is cold, the sensor (thermistor) resistance is high, therefore the ECM will see high signal voltage.

As the engine warms, the sensor resistance becomes less, and the voltage drops. At normal engine operating temperature, the voltage will measure about 1.5 to 2.0 volts at the ECM terminal "C16".

Coolant temperature is one of the inputs used to control:

- Fuel delivery
- Electronic Spark Timing (EST)
- Idle Air Control (IAC)
- Torque Converter Clutch (TCC)
- Controlled Canister Purge (CCP)
- Exhaust Gas Recirculation (EGR)
- Cooling fan

Test Description: Number(s) below refer to circled number(s) on the diagnostic chart.

1. Code 14 will set if:
   - Signal voltage indicates a coolant temperature above 135°C (270°F).
   - Engine running longer than 20 seconds.
2. This test will determine if CKT 410 is shorted to ground which will cause the conditions for Code 14.

Diagnostic Aids:

Check harness routing for a potential short to ground in CKT 410. Circuit is routed from the ECM to a mini harness, and then to the Coolant Temperature Sensor (CTS).

"Scan" tool displays engine temperature in degrees centigrade. After engine is started, the temperature should rise steadily to about 90°C then stabilize when thermostat opens. Refer to "Intermittents" in "Symptoms," Section

Verify that engine is not overheating and has not been subjected to conditions which could create an overheating condition (i.e. overload, trailer towing, hilly terrain, heavy stop and go traffic, etc.). The "Temperature To Resistance Value" scale at the right may be used to test the coolant sensor at various temperature levels to evaluate the possibility of a "shifted" (mis-scaled) sensor. A "shifted" sensor could result in poor driveability complaints.

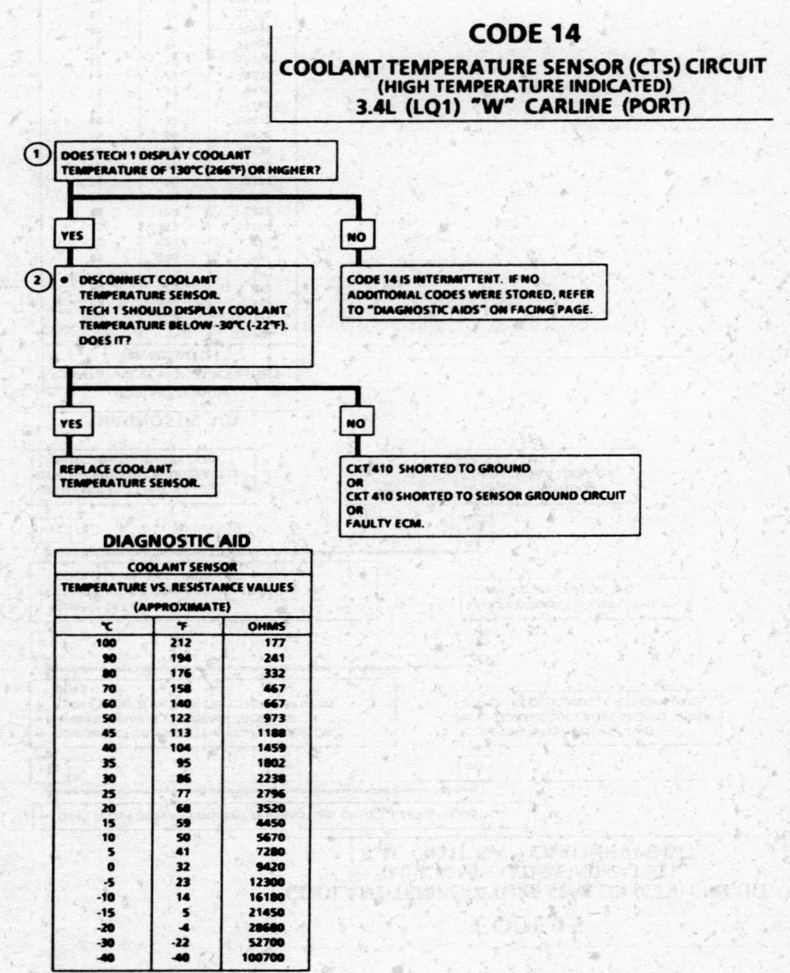
CODE 14
COOLANT TEMPERATURE SENSOR (CTS) CIRCUIT
(HIGH TEMPERATURE INDICATED)
3.4L (LQ1) "W" CARLINE (PORT)
1 DOES TECH 1 DISPLAY COOLANT TEMPERATURE OF 130°C (266°F) OR HIGHER?
YES
NO
CODE 14 IS INTERMITTENT. IF NO ADDITIONAL CODES WERE STORED, REFER TO "DIAGNOSTIC AIDS" ON FACING PAGE.
2 • DISCONNECT COOLANT TEMPERATURE SENSOR. TECH 1 SHOULD DISPLAY COOLANT TEMPERATURE BELOW -30°C (-22°F). DOES IT?
YES
NO
REPLACE COOLANT TEMPERATURE SENSOR.
CKT 410 SHORTED TO GROUND OR CKT 410 SHORTED TO SENSOR GROUND CIRCUIT OR FAULTY ECM.
CLEAR CODES AND CONFIRM "CLOSED LOOP" OPERATION AND NO "SERVICE ENGINE SOON" LIGHT. BE SURE TRANSAXLE IS FUNCTIONING PROPERLY

DIAGNOSTIC AID

COOLANT SENSOR

TEMPERATURE VS. RESISTANCE VALUES (APPROXIMATE)

°C	°F	OHMS
100	212	177
90	194	241
80	176	332
70	158	467
60	140	667
50	122	973
45	113	1188
40	104	1459
35	95	1802
30	86	2238
25	77	2796
20	68	3520
15	59	4450
10	50	5670
5	41	7280
0	32	9420
-5	23	12300
-10	14	16180
-15	5	21450
-20	-4	28680
-30	-22	52700
-40	-40	100700

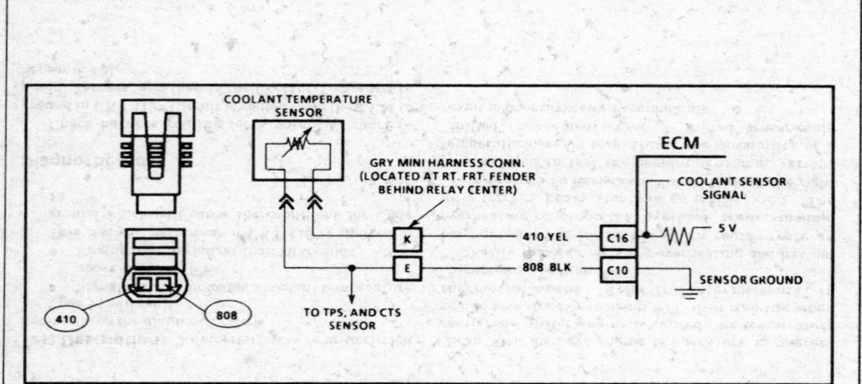
COOLANT TEMPERATURE SENSOR
ECM
GRY MINI HARNESS CONN. (LOCATED AT RT. FRT. FENDER BEHIND RELAY CENTER)
COOLANT SENSOR SIGNAL
5 V
K
E
410 YEL
808 BLK
C16
C10
SENSOR GROUND
410
808
TO TPS, AND CTS SENSOR

CODE 15

COOLANT TEMPERATURE SENSOR (CTS) CIRCUIT (LOW TEMPERATURE INDICATED) 3.4L (LQ1) "W" CARLINE (PORT)

Circuit Description:

The Coolant Temperature Sensor (CTS) uses a thermistor to control the signal voltage to the ECM. The ECM applies a voltage on CKT 410 to the sensor. When the engine is cold the sensor (thermistor) resistance is high, therefore the ECM will see high signal voltage.

As the engine warms, the sensor resistance becomes less, and the voltage drops. At normal engine operating temperature the voltage will measure about 1.5 to 2.0 volts at the ECM terminal "C16".

Coolant temperature is one of the inputs used to control:

- Fuel delivery
- Engine Spark Timing (EST)
- Idle Air Control (IAC)
- Torque Converter Clutch (TCC)
- Controlled Canister Purge (CCP)
- Electronic Gas Recirculation (EGR)
- Cooling fan

Test Description: Number(s) below refer to circled number(s) on the diagnostic chart.

1. Code 15 will set if:
   - Signal voltage indicates a coolant temperature less than 38.5°C (-37.30°F).
2. This test simulates a Code 14. If the ECM recognizes the low signal voltage, (high temperature) and the "Scan" reads 130°C, the ECM and wiring are OK.
3. This test will determine if CKT 410 is open. There should be 5 volts present at sensor connector if measured with a DVM.

A faulty connection, or an open in CKT 410 or 808 will result in a Code 15.

Codes 15 and 21 are stored at the same time could be the result of an open CKT 808 which would also turn the temperature warning indicator "ON." The "Temperature to Resistance Value" scale at the right may be used to test the coolant sensor at various temperature levels to evaluate the possibility of a "shifted" (mis-scaled) sensor. A "shifted" sensor could result in poor driveability complaints.

Refer to "Intermittents" in "Symptoms," Section

Diagnostic Aids:

A "Scan" tool reads engine temperature in degrees centigrade. After engine is started the temperature should rise steadily to about 95°C then stabilize when thermostat opens. CKT 410 is routed from the ECM to a mini harness, and then to the Coolant Temperature (CTS) Sensor.

CODE 15

COOLANT TEMPERATURE SENSOR (CTS) CIRCUIT (LOW TEMPERATURE INDICATED) 3.4L (LQ1) "W" CARLINE (PORT)

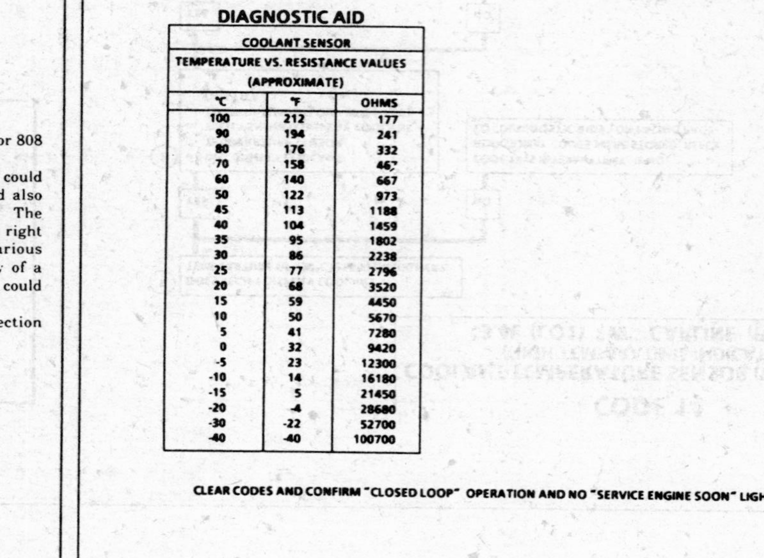
1
DOES TECH 1 DISPLAY COOLANT TEMPERATURE OF -30°C (-22°F) OR LESS?
YES
NO
CODE 15 IS INTERMITTENT. IF NO ADDITIONAL CODES WERE STORED, REFER TO "DIAGNOSTIC AIDS" ON FACING PAGE.
2
DISCONNECT COOLANT TEMPERATURE SENSOR.
JUMPER HARNESS TERMINALS TOGETHER.
TECH 1 SHOULD DISPLAY 130°C (266°F) OR MORE.
DOES IT?
NO
YES
FAULTY CONNECTION OR COOLANT TEMPERATURE SENSOR.
3
JUMPER CKT 410 TO GROUND.
TECH 1 SHOULD DISPLAY OVER 130°C (266 °F).
DOES IT?
YES
NO
OPEN COOLANT TEMPERATURE SENSOR GROUND CIRCUIT, FAULTY CONNECTION OR FAULTY ECM.
OPEN CKT 410, FAULTY CONNECTION AT ECM, OR FAULTY ECM.

DIAGNOSTIC AID

COOLANT SENSOR
TEMPERATURE VS. RESISTANCE VALUES (APPROXIMATE)

°C	°F	OHMS
100	212	177
90	194	241
80	176	332
70	158	467
60	140	667
50	122	973
45	113	1188
40	104	1459
35	95	1802
30	86	2238
25	77	2796
20	68	3520
15	59	4450
10	50	5670
5	41	7280
0	32	9420
-5	23	12300
-10	14	16180
-15	5	21450
-20	-4	28680
-30	-22	52700
-40	-40	100700

CLEAR CODES AND CONFIRM "CLOSED LOOP" OPERATION AND NO "SERVICE ENGINE SOON" LIGHT.

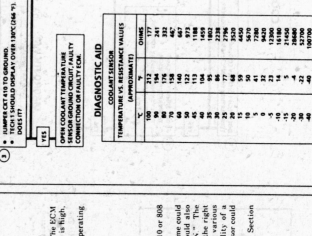

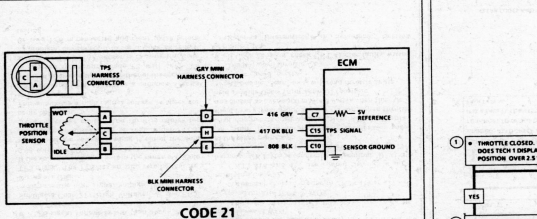

CODE 21

THROTTLE POSITION SENSOR (TPS) CIRCUIT
(SIGNAL VOLTAGE HIGH)
3.4L (LQ1) "W" CARLINE (PORT)

Circuit Description:

The Throttle Position Sensor (TPS) provides a voltage signal that changes relative to the throttle blade. Signal voltage will vary from about .5 at idle to about 4.8 volts at Wide Open Throttle (WOT).

The TPS signal is one of the most important inputs used by the ECM for fuel control and for most of the ECM control outputs.

Test Description: Number(s) below refer to circled number(s) on the diagnostic chart.

1. Code 21 will set if:
   - No Code 33 or Code 34.
   - Engine is running.
   - TPS signal voltage is greater than 4.3 volts.
   - Air flow is less than 17 gm/sec.
   - All conditions met for 1.25 seconds.

   OR

   With throttle closed, the TPS should read less than .98 volt. If it doesn't, make sure cruise control and throttle cables are not being held open.
2. With the TPS sensor disconnected, the TPS voltage should go low, if the ECM and wiring is OK.
3. Probing CKT 808 with a test light, checks the 5 volts return circuit. Faulty sensor ground circuit will cause a Code 21.

Diagnostic Aids:

A "Scan" tool reads throttle position in volts. Voltage should increase at a steady rate as throttle is moved toward WOT.

Also some "Scan" tools will read throttle angle 0% = closed throttle, 100% = WOT.

An open in CKT 808 will result in a Code 21.

Codes 15 and 21 are stored at the same time could be the result of an open CKT 808 which would also turn the temperature warning indicator "ON." "Scan" TPS while depressing accelerator pedal with engine stopped and ignition "ON." Display should vary from about 500 mV (.5 volt) when throttle was closed, to over 4800 mV (4.8 volts) when throttle is held at Wide Open Throttle (WOT) position.

Refer to "Intermittents" in "Symptoms," Section

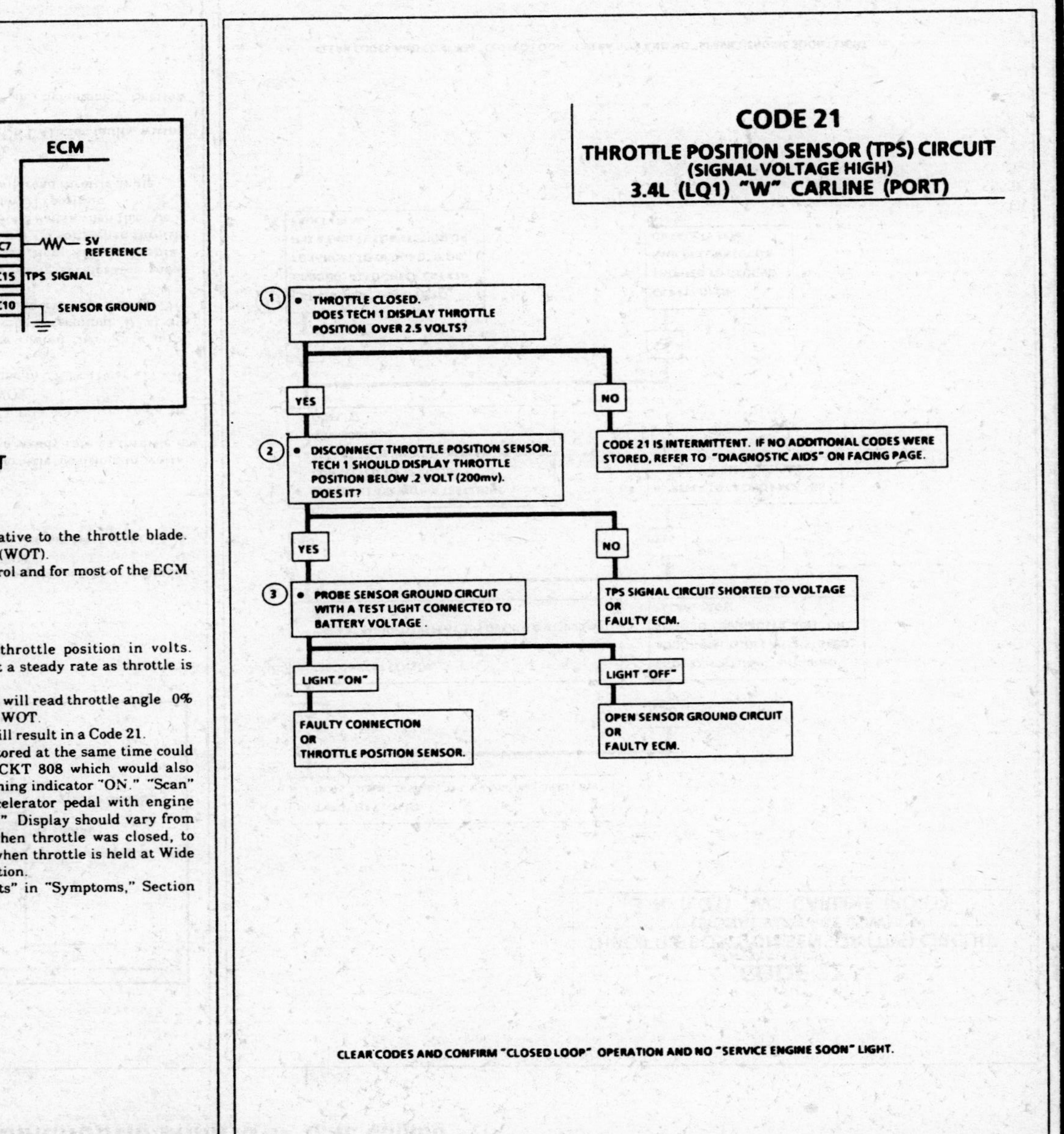
CODE 21
THROTTLE POSITION SENSOR (TPS) CIRCUIT
(SIGNAL VOLTAGE HIGH)
3.4L (LQ1) "W" CARLINE (PORT)
1
• THROTTLE CLOSED.
DOES TECH 1 DISPLAY THROTTLE POSITION OVER 2.5 VOLTS?
YES
NO
CODE 21 IS INTERMITTENT. IF NO ADDITIONAL CODES WERE STORED, REFER TO "DIAGNOSTIC AIDS" ON FACING PAGE.
2
• DISCONNECT THROTTLE POSITION SENSOR. TECH 1 SHOULD DISPLAY THROTTLE POSITION BELOW .2 VOLT (200mv). DOES IT?
YES
NO
TPS SIGNAL CIRCUIT SHORTED TO VOLTAGE OR FAULTY ECM.
3
• PROBE SENSOR GROUND CIRCUIT WITH A TEST LIGHT CONNECTED TO BATTERY VOLTAGE.
LIGHT "ON"
LIGHT "OFF"
FAULTY CONNECTION OR THROTTLE POSITION SENSOR.
OPEN SENSOR GROUND CIRCUIT OR FAULTY ECM.
CLEAR CODES AND CONFIRM "CLOSED LOOP" OPERATION AND NO "SERVICE ENGINE SOON" LIGHT.

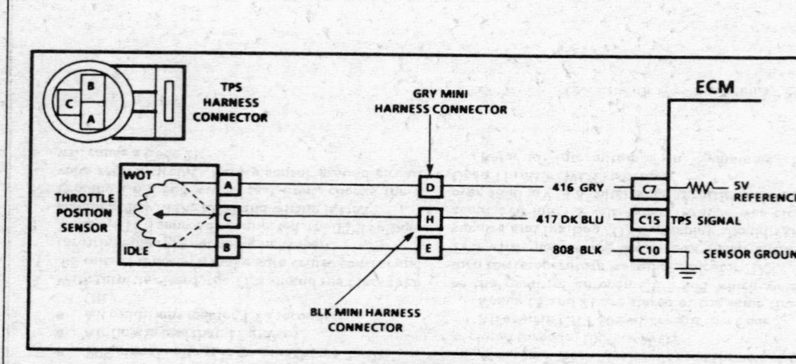

TPS HARNESS CONNECTOR
GRY MINI HARNESS CONNECTOR
ECM
THROTTLE POSITION SENSOR
WOT
IDLE
A
C
B
D
H
E
416 GRY
417 DK BLU
808 BLK
C7
C15
C10
5V REFERENCE
TPS SIGNAL
SENSOR GROUND
BLK MINI HARNESS CONNECTOR

CODE 22

THROTTLE POSITION SENSOR (TPS) CIRCUIT (SIGNAL VOLTAGE LOW) 3.4L (LQ1) "W" CARLINE (PORT)

Circuit Description:

The Throttle Position Sensor (TPS) provides a voltage signal that changes relative to the throttle blade. Signal voltage will vary from about .5 at idle to about 4.8 volts at Wide Open Throttle (WOT).

The TPS signal is one of the most important inputs used by the ECM for fuel control and for most of the ECM control outputs.

Test Description: Number(s) below refer to circled number(s) on the diagnostic chart.

1. Code 22 will set if:
   - Engine running
   - TPS signal voltage is less than about .25 volt for 3 seconds.
2. Simulates Code 21: (High Voltage) If the ECM recognizes the high signal voltage, the ECM and wiring are OK.
3. TPS check: The TPS has an auto zeroing feature. If the voltage reading is within the range of 0.29 to 0.98 volt, the ECM will use that value as closed throttle. If the voltage reading is out of the auto zero range on an existing or replacement TPS, check for cruise control and throttle cables for being held open.
4. This simulates a high signal voltage to check for an open in CKT 417.
5. CKT 416 and CKT 432 share a common 5 volts buffered reference signal. If either of these circuits is shorted to ground, Code 22 will set. To determine if the MAP sensor is causing the Code 22 problem, disconnect it to see if Code 22 resets. Be sure TPS is connected and clear codes before testing.

Diagnostic Aids:

A "Scan" tool reads throttle position in volts. Voltage should increase at a steady rate as throttle is moved toward WOT.

Also some "Scan" tools will read throttle angle 0% = closed throttle 100% = WOT.

An open or short to ground in CKTs 416 or 417 will result in a Code 22.

CKTs 416 and 417 are routed through a mini harness. CKT 416 is connected to terminal "D" at the gray connector, CKT 417 is connected to terminal "H" at the black connector.

"Scan" TPS while depressing accelerator pedal with engine stopped and ignition "ON." Display should vary from about 500 mV (.5 volt) when throttle was closed, to over 4800 mV (4.8 volts) when throttle is held at Wide Open Throttle (WOT) position.

Also some "Scan" tools will read throttle angle.
0% = closed throttle.
100% = open throttle.

If Code 22 is set, check CKT 416 for faulty wiring or connections.

Refer to "Intermittents" in "Symptoms," Section

CODE 22

THROTTLE POSITION SENSOR (TPS) CIRCUIT (SIGNAL VOLTAGE LOW) 3.4L (LQ1) "W" CARLINE (PORT)

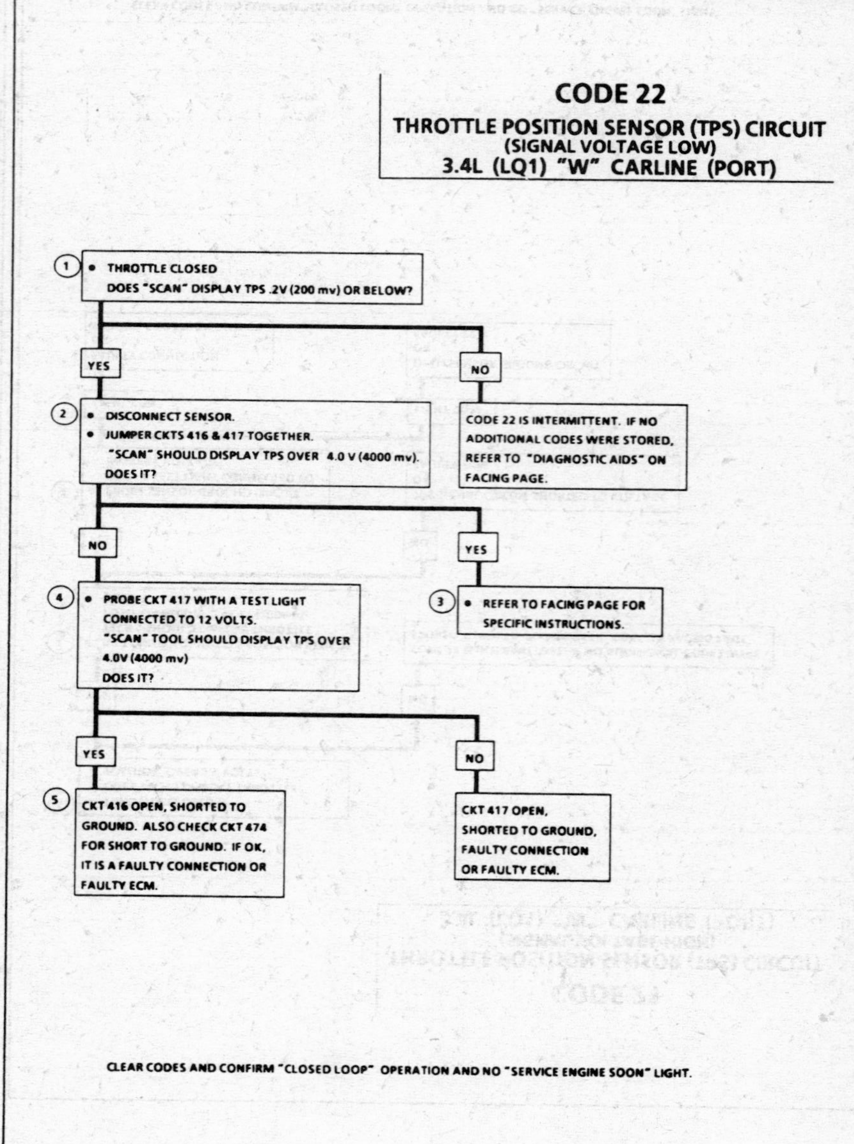

1 • THROTTLE CLOSED
DOES "SCAN" DISPLAY TPS .2V (200 mv) OR BELOW?
YES
NO
CODE 22 IS INTERMITTENT. IF NO ADDITIONAL CODES WERE STORED, REFER TO "DIAGNOSTIC AIDS" ON FACING PAGE.
2 • DISCONNECT SENSOR.
• JUMPER CKTS 416 & 417 TOGETHER.
"SCAN" SHOULD DISPLAY TPS OVER 4.0 V (4000 mv).
DOES IT?
NO
YES
3 • REFER TO FACING PAGE FOR SPECIFIC INSTRUCTIONS.
4 • PROBE CKT 417 WITH A TEST LIGHT CONNECTED TO 12 VOLTS.
"SCAN" TOOL SHOULD DISPLAY TPS OVER 4.0V (4000 mv)
DOES IT?
YES
NO
5 CKT 416 OPEN, SHORTED TO GROUND. ALSO CHECK CKT 474 FOR SHORT TO GROUND. IF OK, IT IS A FAULTY CONNECTION OR FAULTY ECM.
CKT 417 OPEN, SHORTED TO GROUND, FAULTY CONNECTION OR FAULTY ECM.
CLEAR CODES AND CONFIRM "CLOSED LOOP" OPERATION AND NO "SERVICE ENGINE SOON" LIGHT.

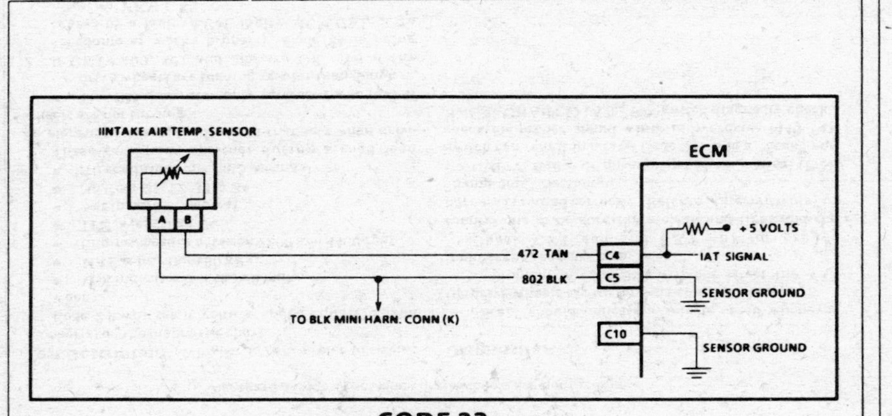
INTAKE AIR TEMP. SENSOR
A
B
ECM
+5 VOLTS
472 TAN
C4
IAT SIGNAL
802 BLK
C5
SENSOR GROUND
TO BLK MINI HARN. CONN (K)
C10
SENSOR GROUND

CODE 23

INTAKE AIR TEMPERATURE (IAT) SENSOR CIRCUIT
(LOW TEMPERATURE INDICATED)
3.4L (LQ1) "W" CARLINE (PORT)

Circuit Description:

The Intake Air Temperature (IAT) sensor uses a thermistor to control the signal voltage to the ECM. The ECM applies a voltage (about 5 volts) on CKT 472 to the sensor. When the air is cold the sensor (thermistor) resistance is high, therefore, the ECM will see a high signal voltage. If the air is warm the sensor resistance is low, therefore, the ECM will see a low voltage.

The IAT sensor is located in the air cleaner.

Test Description: Number(s) below refer to circled number(s) on the diagnostic chart.

1. Code 23 will set if:
   - A signal voltage indicates a manifold air temperature below -35°C (-31°F).
   - Time since engine start is 4 minutes or longer.
   - Vehicle speed less than 1 mph
   - Start-up coolant temperature is less than or equal to -35.5°C (31.9°F).
   - All conditions met for 10 sec.
2. A Code 23 will set, due to an open sensor, wire, or connection. This test will determine if the wiring and ECM are OK.
3. This will determine if the signal CKT 472 or the 5 volts return CKT 802 is open.

Diagnostic Aids:

A "Scan" tool reads temperature of the air entering the engine and should read close to ambient air temperature when engine is cold, and rises as underhood temperature increases.

A faulty connection, or an open in CKT 472 or CKT 802 will result in a Code 23.

Codes 23 and 34 stored at the same time, could be the result of an open CKT 802, which would also turn the temperature warning indicator "ON." CKT 802 is routed through a mini harness. A faulty connection could result in intermittent failures. The "Temperature to Resistance Values" scale at the right may be used to test the IAT sensor at various temperature levels to evaluate the possibility of a "shifted" (mis-scaled) sensor. A "slewed" sensor could result in poor driveability complaints.

Refer to "Intermittents" in "Symptoms," Section

CODE 23

INTAKE AIR TEMPERATURE (IAT) SENSOR CIRCUIT
(LOW TEMPERATURE INDICATED)
3.4L (LQ1) "W" CARLINE (PORT)

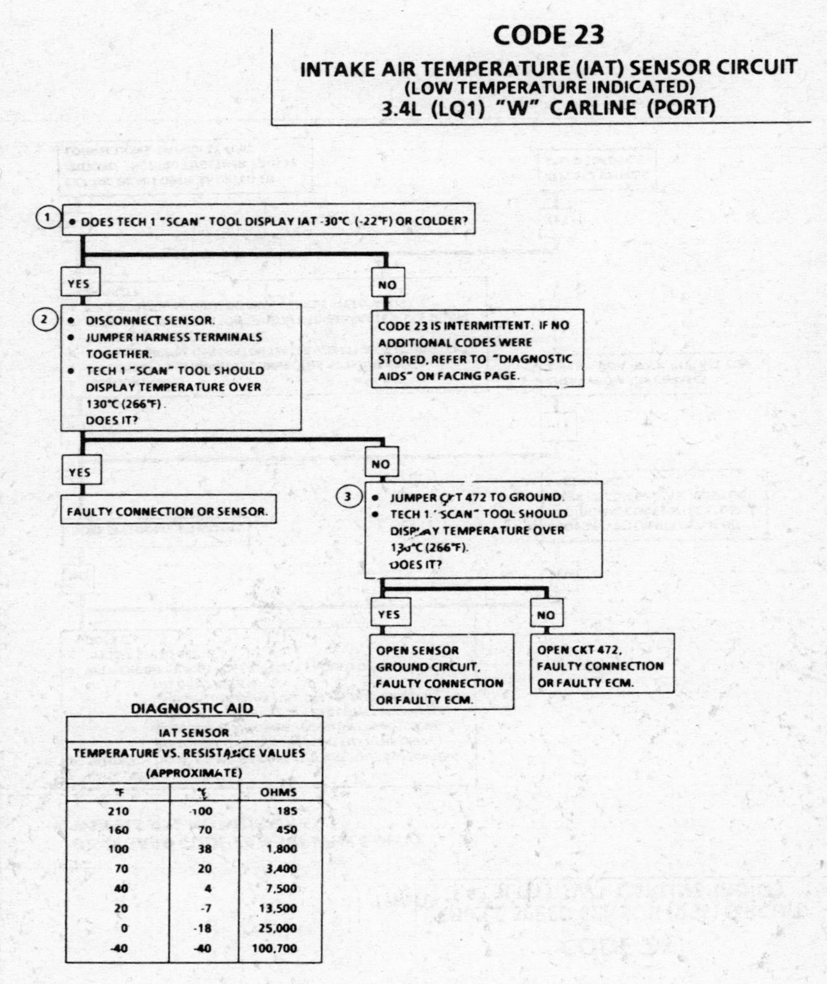
1
• DOES TECH 1 "SCAN" TOOL DISPLAY IAT -30°C (-22°F) OR COLDER?
YES
NO
2
• DISCONNECT SENSOR.
• JUMPER HARNESS TERMINALS TOGETHER.
• TECH 1 "SCAN" TOOL SHOULD DISPLAY TEMPERATURE OVER 130°C (266°F). DOES IT?
CODE 23 IS INTERMITTENT. IF NO ADDITIONAL CODES WERE STORED, REFER TO "DIAGNOSTIC AIDS" ON FACING PAGE.
YES
NO
FAULTY CONNECTION OR SENSOR.
3
• JUMPER CKT 472 TO GROUND.
• TECH 1 "SCAN" TOOL SHOULD DISPLAY TEMPERATURE OVER 130°C (266°F). DOES IT?
YES
NO
OPEN SENSOR GROUND CIRCUIT, FAULTY CONNECTION OR FAULTY ECM.
OPEN CKT 472, FAULTY CONNECTION OR FAULTY ECM.

DIAGNOSTIC AID

IAT SENSOR TEMPERATURE VS. RESISTANCE VALUES (APPROXIMATE)		
°F	°C	OHMS
210	100	185
160	70	450
100	38	1,800
70	20	3,400
40	4	7,500
20	-7	13,500
0	-18	25,000
-40	-40	100,700

CLEAR CODES AND CONFIRM "CLOSED LOOP" OPERATION AND NO "SERVICE ENGINE SOON" LIGHT.

DIAGNOSTIC CHARTS — 3.4L engine

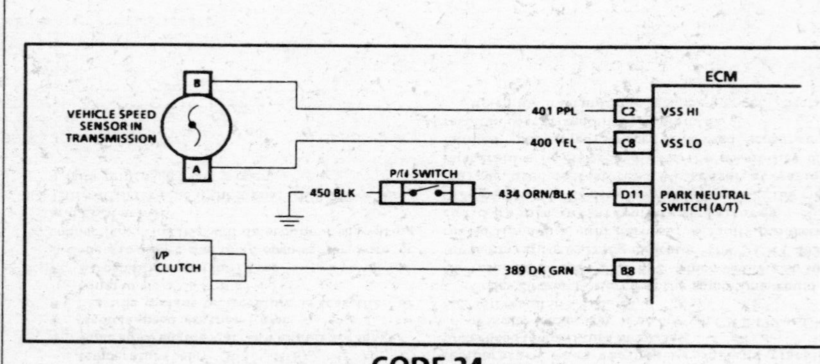
VEHICLE SPEED SENSOR IN TRANSMISSION
B
A
401 PPL
400 YEL
P/N SWITCH
450 BLK
434 ORN/BLK
I/P CLUTCH
389 DK GRN
ECM
C2
C8
D11
B8
VSS HI
VSS LO
PARK NEUTRAL SWITCH (A/T)

CODE 24

VEHICLE SPEED SENSOR (VSS) CIRCUIT 3.4L (LQ1) "W" CARLINE (PORT)

Circuit Description:

Vehicle speed information is provided to the ECM by the vehicle speed sensor which uses a Permanent Magnet (PM) generator and it is mounted in the transaxle. The PM generator produces a pulsing voltage whenever vehicle speed is over about 3 mph. The AC voltage level and the number of pulses increases with vehicle speed. The ECM then converts the pulsing voltage to mph which is used for calculations, and the mph can be displayed with a "Scan" tool. Output of the generator can also be seen by using a digital voltmeter on the AC scale while rotating the generator.

The function of VSS buffer used in past model years has been incorporated into the ECM. The ECM then supplies the necessary signal for the instrument panel (4000 pulses per mile) for operating the speedometer and the odometer. If the vehicle is equipped with cruise control, the ECM also provides a signal (2000 pulses per mile) to the cruise control module.

Disregard a Code 24 set when drive wheels are not turning.

Test Description: Number(s) below refer to circled number(s) on the diagnostic chart.

1. Code 24 will set if vehicle speed equals 0 mph when:
   - VSS indicates less than 2 mph.
   - MAP is less than 30 kPa.
   - Engine speed is between 2200 and 4400 rpm
   - TPS is less than 2%.
   - Not in park or neutral.
   - No Code 21, 22, 33 or 34.
   - All conditions met for 3 seconds.

   These conditions are met during a road load deceleration. Disregard Code 24 that sets when drive wheels are not turning.
   - The PM generator only produces a signal if drive wheels are turning greater than 3 mph.
2. If CKTs 400, 401 and 389 are OK, and if the speedometer works properly, Code 24 is being caused by a faulty ECM, faulty MEM-CAL or an incorrect MEM-CAL.

Diagnostic Aids:

"Scan" should indicate a vehicle speed whenever the drive wheels are turning greater than 3 mph.

A problem in CKT 389 will not affect the VSS input or the readings on a "Scan."

Check CKT 400 and CKT 401 for proper connections to be sure there clean and tight and the harness is routed correctly. Refer to "Intermittents" in "Symptoms," Section

(A/T) A faulty or misadjusted Park/Neutral (P/N) switch can result in a false Code 24. Use a "Scan" and check for proper signal while in overdrive (440-T4). Refer to CHART C-1A for P/N switch diagnosis check.

CODE 24

VEHICLE SPEED SENSOR (VSS) CIRCUIT 3.4L (LQ1) "W" CARLINE (PORT)

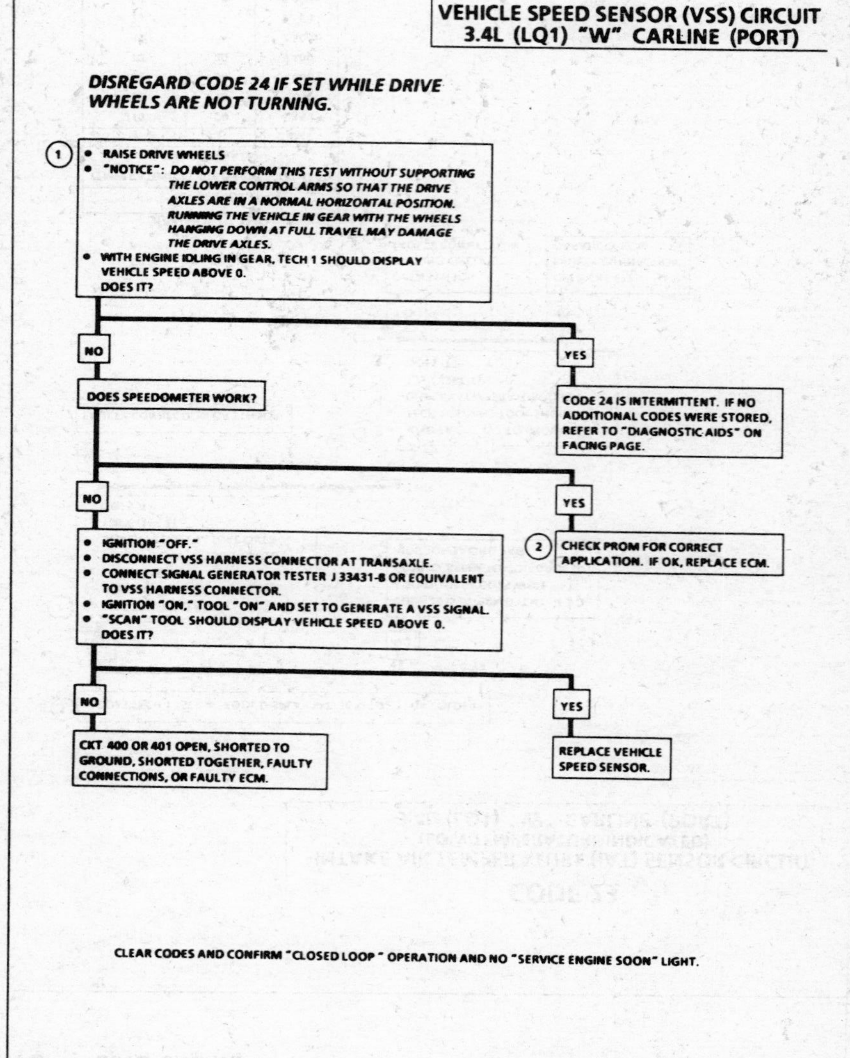
DISREGARD CODE 24 IF SET WHILE DRIVE WHEELS ARE NOT TURNING.
1
• RAISE DRIVE WHEELS
• "NOTICE": DO NOT PERFORM THIS TEST WITHOUT SUPPORTING THE LOWER CONTROL ARMS SO THAT THE DRIVE AXLES ARE IN A NORMAL HORIZONTAL POSITION. RUNNING THE VEHICLE IN GEAR WITH THE WHEELS HANGING DOWN AT FULL TRAVEL MAY DAMAGE THE DRIVE AXLES.
• WITH ENGINE IDLING IN GEAR, TECH 1 SHOULD DISPLAY VEHICLE SPEED ABOVE 0. DOES IT?
NO
YES
DOES SPEEDOMETER WORK?
CODE 24 IS INTERMITTENT. IF NO ADDITIONAL CODES WERE STORED, REFER TO "DIAGNOSTIC AIDS" ON FACING PAGE.
NO
YES
• IGNITION "OFF."
• DISCONNECT VSS HARNESS CONNECTOR AT TRANSAXLE.
• CONNECT SIGNAL GENERATOR TESTER J 33431-B OR EQUIVALENT TO VSS HARNESS CONNECTOR.
• IGNITION "ON," TOOL "ON" AND SET TO GENERATE A VSS SIGNAL.
• "SCAN" TOOL SHOULD DISPLAY VEHICLE SPEED ABOVE 0. DOES IT?
2
CHECK PROM FOR CORRECT APPLICATION. IF OK, REPLACE ECM.
NO
YES
CKT 400 OR 401 OPEN, SHORTED TO GROUND, SHORTED TOGETHER, FAULTY CONNECTIONS, OR FAULTY ECM.
REPLACE VEHICLE SPEED SENSOR.
CLEAR CODES AND CONFIRM "CLOSED LOOP" OPERATION AND NO "SERVICE ENGINE SOON" LIGHT.

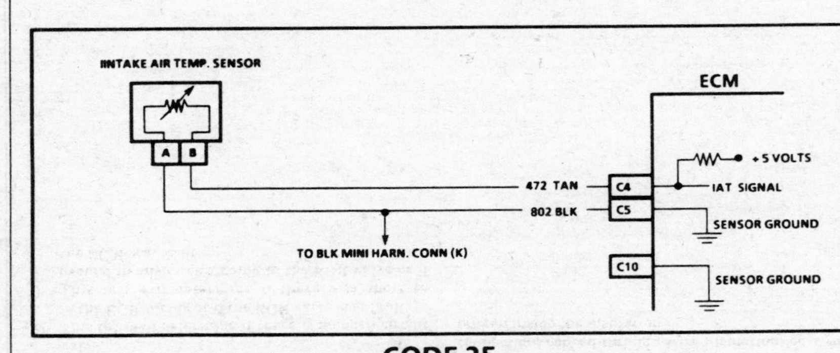
INTAKE AIR TEMP. SENSOR
A
B
ECM
+5 VOLTS
472 TAN
C4
IAT SIGNAL
802 BLK
C5
SENSOR GROUND
TO BLK MINI HARN. CONN (K)
C10
SENSOR GROUND

CODE 25

INTAKE AIR TEMPERATURE (IAT) SENSOR CIRCUIT
(HIGH TEMPERATURE INDICATED)
3.4L (LQ1) "W" CARLINE (PORT)

Circuit Description:

The Intake Air Temperature (IAT) sensor uses a thermistor to control the signal voltage to the ECM. The ECM applies a voltage (about 5 volts) on CKT 472 to the sensor. When the air is cold the sensor (thermistor) resistance is high, therefore the ECM will see a high signal voltage. If the air is warm the sensor resistance is low therefore the ECM will see a low voltage.

The IAT sensor is located in the air cleaner.

Test Description: Number(s) below refer to circled number(s) on the diagnostic chart.

1. Code 25 will set if:
   - A signal voltage indicates a Intake Air Temperature (IAT) greater than 135°C (293°F) for .2 seconds.
   - A vehicle speed over 1 mph is present.

   Due to the conditions necessary to set a Code 25 the "Service Engine Soon" light will remain "ON" while the signal is low and vehicle speed is present.

Diagnostic Aids:

A "Scan" tool reads temperature of the air entering the engine and should read close to ambient air temperature when engine is cold, and rises as underhood temperature increases.

A short to ground in CKT 472 will result in a Code 25.

The "Temperature to Resistance Values" scale at the right may be used to test the IAT sensor at various temperature levels to evaluate the possibility of a "shifted" (mis-scaled) sensor. A "slewed" sensor could result in poor driveability complaints.

Refer to "Intermittents" in "Symptoms," Section

CODE 25

INTAKE AIR TEMPERATURE (IAT) SENSOR CIRCUIT
(HIGH TEMPERATURE INDICATED)
3.4L (LQ1) "W" CARLINE (PORT)

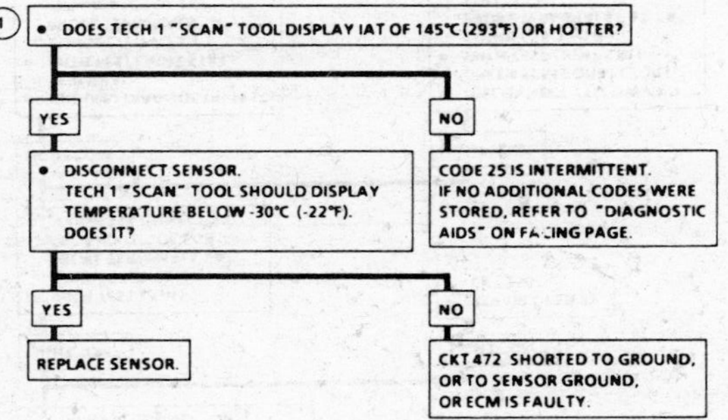
1
• DOES TECH 1 "SCAN" TOOL DISPLAY IAT OF 145°C (293°F) OR HOTTER?
YES
NO
• DISCONNECT SENSOR.
TECH 1 "SCAN" TOOL SHOULD DISPLAY TEMPERATURE BELOW -30°C (-22°F).
DOES IT?
CODE 25 IS INTERMITTENT.
IF NO ADDITIONAL CODES WERE STORED, REFER TO "DIAGNOSTIC AIDS" ON FACING PAGE.
YES
NO
REPLACE SENSOR.
CKT 472 SHORTED TO GROUND, OR TO SENSOR GROUND, OR ECM IS FAULTY.

DIAGNOSTIC AID

IAT SENSOR		
TEMPERATURE VS. RESISTANCE VALUES (APPROXIMATE)		
°F	°C	OHMS
210	100	185
160	70	450
100	38	1,800
70	20	3,400
40	4	7,500
20	-7	13,500
0	-18	25,000
-40	-40	100,700

CLEAR CODES AND CONFIRM "CLOSED LOOP" OPERATION AND NO "SERVICE ENGINE SOON" LIGHT.

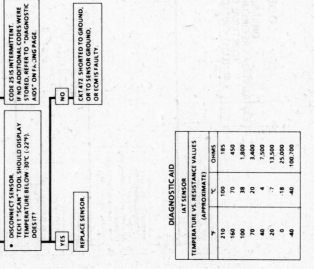

DIAGNOSTIC CHARTS — 3.4L engine

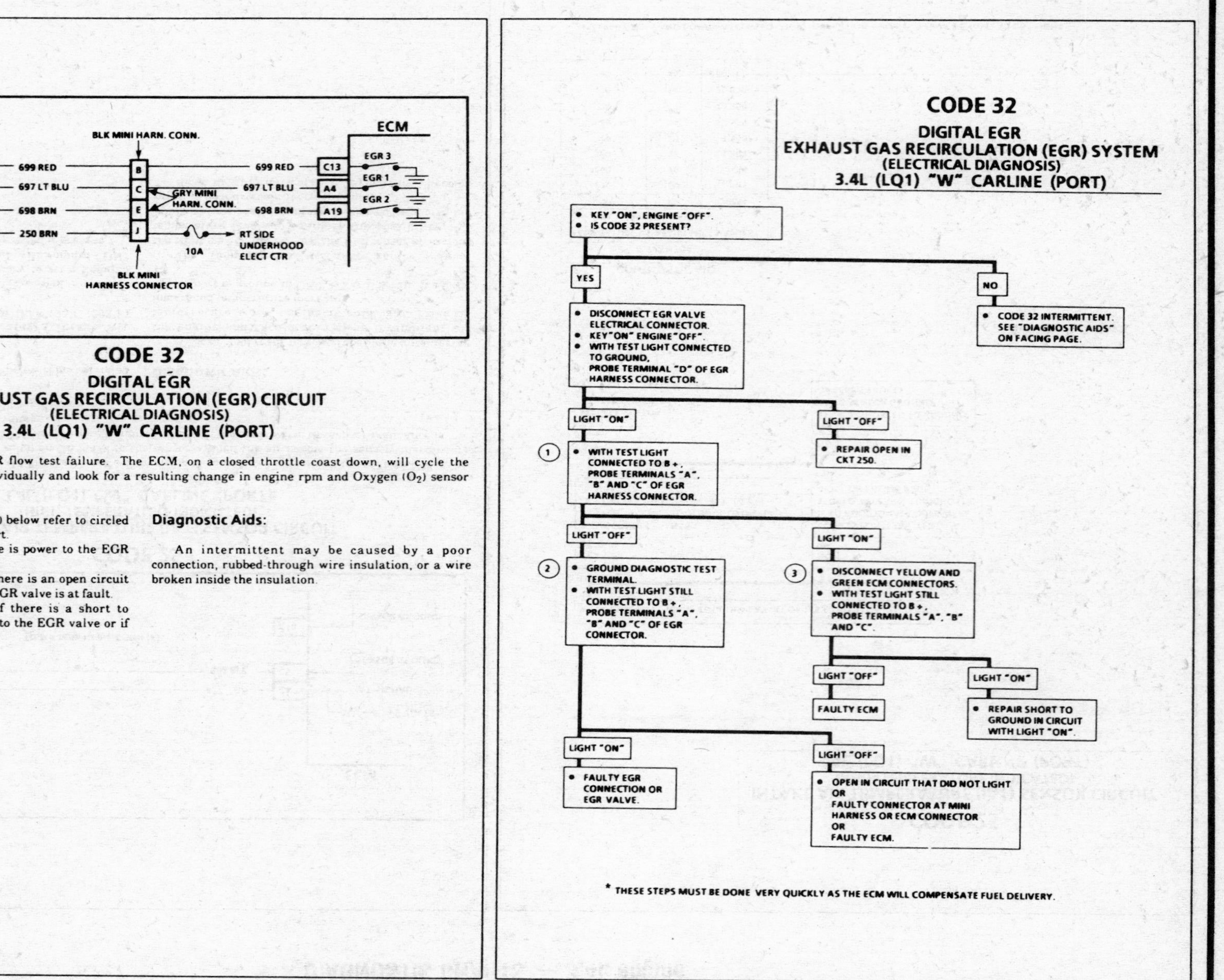
TOP VIEW OF EGR VALVE
A
C
B
D
699 RED
697 LT BLU
698 BRN
250 BRN
BLK MINI HARN. CONN.
B
C
E
J
GRY MINI HARN. CONN.
BLK MINI HARNESS CONNECTOR
10A
RT SIDE UNDERHOOD ELECT CTR
699 RED
697 LT BLU
698 BRN
C13
A4
A19
ECM
EGR 3
EGR 1
EGR 2
CODE 32
DIGITAL EGR
EXHAUST GAS RECIRCULATION (EGR) SYSTEM
(ELECTRICAL DIAGNOSIS)
3.4L (LQ1) "W" CARLINE (PORT)
• KEY "ON", ENGINE "OFF".
• IS CODE 32 PRESENT?
YES
NO
• CODE 32 INTERMITTENT. SEE "DIAGNOSTIC AIDS" ON FACING PAGE.
• DISCONNECT EGR VALVE ELECTRICAL CONNECTOR.
• KEY "ON" ENGINE "OFF".
• WITH TEST LIGHT CONNECTED TO GROUND, PROBE TERMINAL "D" OF EGR HARNESS CONNECTOR.
LIGHT "ON"
LIGHT "OFF"
• REPAIR OPEN IN CKT 250.
1
• WITH TEST LIGHT CONNECTED TO B+, PROBE TERMINALS "A", "B" AND "C" OF EGR HARNESS CONNECTOR.
LIGHT "OFF"
LIGHT "ON"
2
• GROUND DIAGNOSTIC TEST TERMINAL.
• WITH TEST LIGHT STILL CONNECTED TO B+, PROBE TERMINALS "A", "B" AND "C" OF EGR CONNECTOR.
3
• DISCONNECT YELLOW AND GREEN ECM CONNECTORS.
• WITH TEST LIGHT STILL CONNECTED TO B+, PROBE TERMINALS "A", "B" AND "C".
LIGHT "OFF"
LIGHT "ON"
FAULTY ECM
• REPAIR SHORT TO GROUND IN CIRCUIT WITH LIGHT "ON".
LIGHT "ON"
LIGHT "OFF"
• FAULTY EGR CONNECTION OR EGR VALVE.
• OPEN IN CIRCUIT THAT DID NOT LIGHT OR FAULTY CONNECTOR AT MINI HARNESS OR ECM CONNECTOR OR FAULTY ECM.
* THESE STEPS MUST BE DONE VERY QUICKLY AS THE ECM WILL COMPENSATE FUEL DELIVERY.

CODE 32
DIGITAL EGR
EXHAUST GAS RECIRCULATION (EGR) CIRCUIT
(ELECTRICAL DIAGNOSIS)
3.4L (LQ1) "W" CARLINE (PORT)

Circuit Description:

Code 32 represents an EGR flow test failure. The ECM, on a closed throttle coast down, will cycle the solenoids "ON" and "OFF" individually and look for a resulting change in engine rpm and Oxygen (O_2) sensor activity.

Test Description: Number(s) below refer to circled number(s) on the diagnostic chart.

1. This test determines if there is power to the EGR valve.
2. This test will determine if there is an open circuit in the EGR wiring or if the EGR valve is at fault.
3. This test will determine if there is a short to ground in any circuit going to the EGR valve or if the ECM is at fault.

Diagnostic Aids:

An intermittent may be caused by a poor connection, rubbed-through wire insulation, or a wire broken inside the insulation.

CODE 33

MANIFOLD ABSOLUTE PRESSURE (MAP) SENSOR CIRCUIT
(SIGNAL VOLTAGE HIGH - LOW VACUUM)
3.4L (LQ1) "W" CARLINE (PORT)

Circuit Description:

The Manifold Absolute Pressure (MAP) sensor responds to changes in manifold pressure (vacuum). The ECM receives this information as a signal voltage that will vary from about 1/1.5 volts at idle (high vacuum) to 4/4.5 volts at Wide Open Throttle (WOT) (low vacuum).

Test Description: Number(s) below refer to circled number(s) on the diagnostic chart.

1. Code 33 will set when:
   - No Code 21 or Code 22.
   - Engine running.
   - Manifold pressure greater than 74 kPa (A/C "OFF") 83.4 kPa (A/C "ON.")
   - Throttle angle less than 2%.
   - Conditions met for 4.8 seconds.

   Engine misfire or a low unstable idle may set Code 33.
2. With the MAP sensor disconnected, the ECM should see a low voltage if the ECM and wiring are OK.

Diagnostic Aids:

If idle is rough or unstable, refer to "Symptoms" in Section "6E3-B" for items which can cause an unstable idle.

An open in CKT 802 or the connection will result in a Code 33.

Ignition "ON" engine "OFF," voltages should be within the values shown in the table on the chart. Also CHART C-1D can be used to test the MAP sensor.

Refer to "Intermittents" in "Symptoms," Section

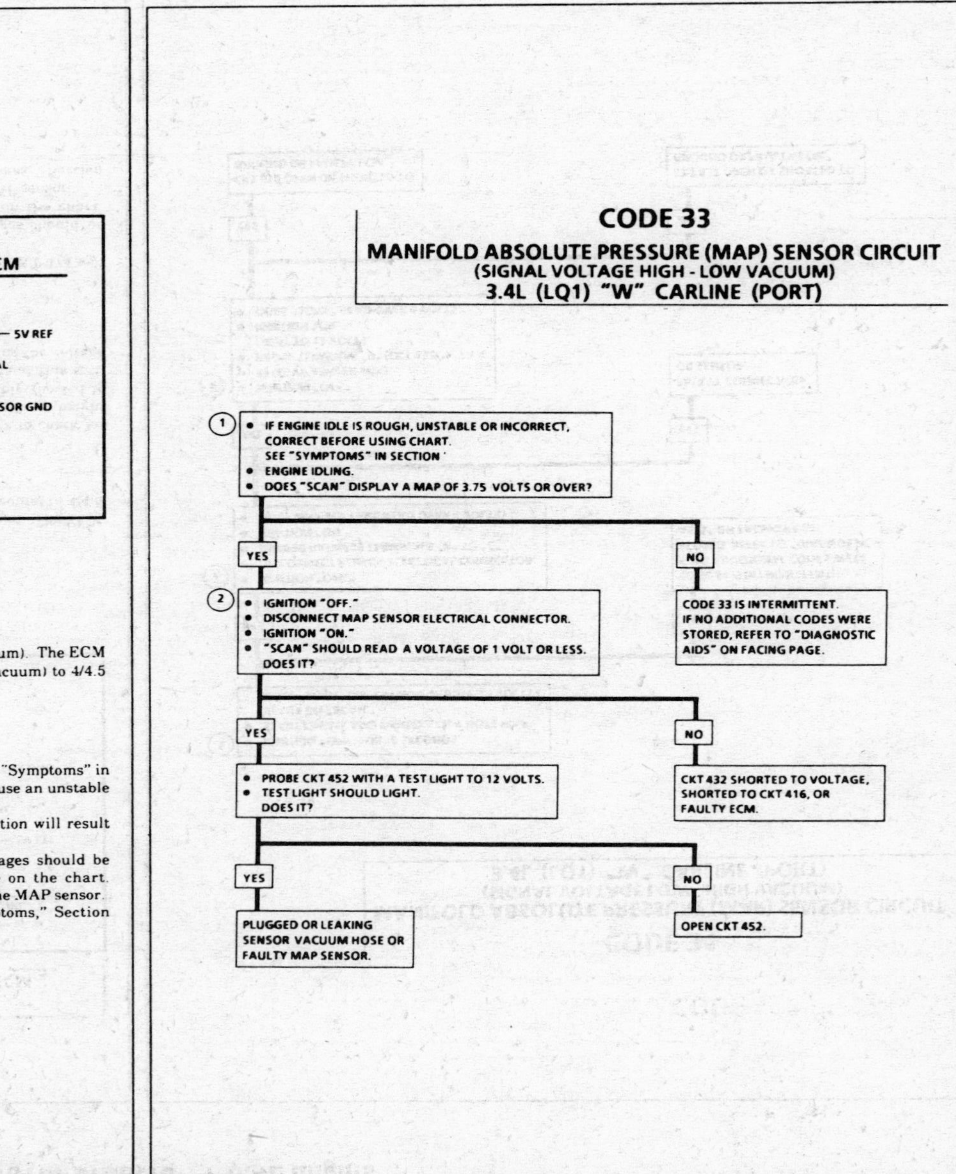

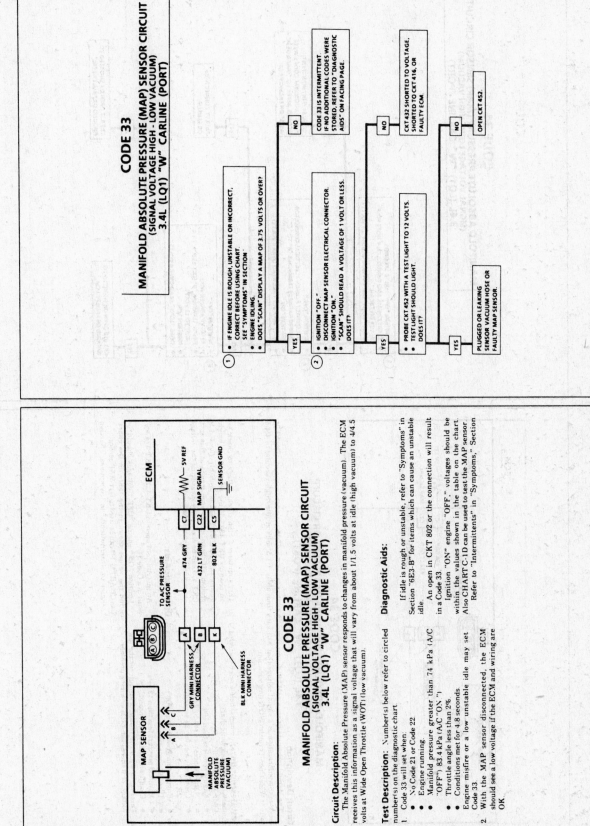

MAP SENSOR

A B C

MANIFOLD ABSOLUTE PRESSURE (VACUUM)

GRY MINI HARNESS CONNECTOR

BLK MINI HARNESS CONNECTOR

TO A/C PRESSURE SENSOR

A — 474 GRY — C7 — 5V REF

B — 432 LT GRN — C22 — MAP SIGNAL

K — 802 BLK — C5 — SENSOR GND

ECM

CODE 34

MANIFOLD ABSOLUTE PRESSURE (MAP) SENSOR CIRCUIT (SIGNAL VOLTAGE LOW - HIGH VACUUM) 3.4L (LQ1) "W" CARLINE (PORT)

Circuit Description:

The Manifold Absolute Pressure (MAP) sensor responds to changes in manifold pressure (vacuum). The ECM receives this information as a signal voltage that will vary from about 1/1.5 volts at idle (high vacuum) to 4/4.5 volts at Wide Open Throttle (WOT) (low vacuum).

Test Description: Number(s) below refer to circled number(s) on the diagnostic chart.

1. Code 34 will set if:
   - Engine rpm less than 700.
   - Manifold pressure reading less than 13 kPa.
   - Conditions met for 22 second.

   OR
   - Engine rpm greater than 700.
   - Throttle angle over 20%.
   - Manifold pressure less than 13 kPa.
   - Conditions met for 22 second.
2. This test to see if the sensor is at fault for the low voltage, or if there is an ECM or wiring problem.
3. This simulates a high signal voltage to check for an open in CKT 432. If the test light is bright during this test, CKT 432 is probably shorted to ground. If "Scan" reads over 4 volts at this test, CKT 474 can be checked by measuring the voltage at terminal "C" (should be 5 volts.)

Diagnostic Aids:

An intermittent open in CKT 432 or CKT 474 will result in a Code 34.

Ignition "ON" engine "OFF," voltages should be within the values shown in the table on the chart. Also CHART C-1D can be used to test MAP sensor.

Refer to "Intermittents" in "Symptoms," Section

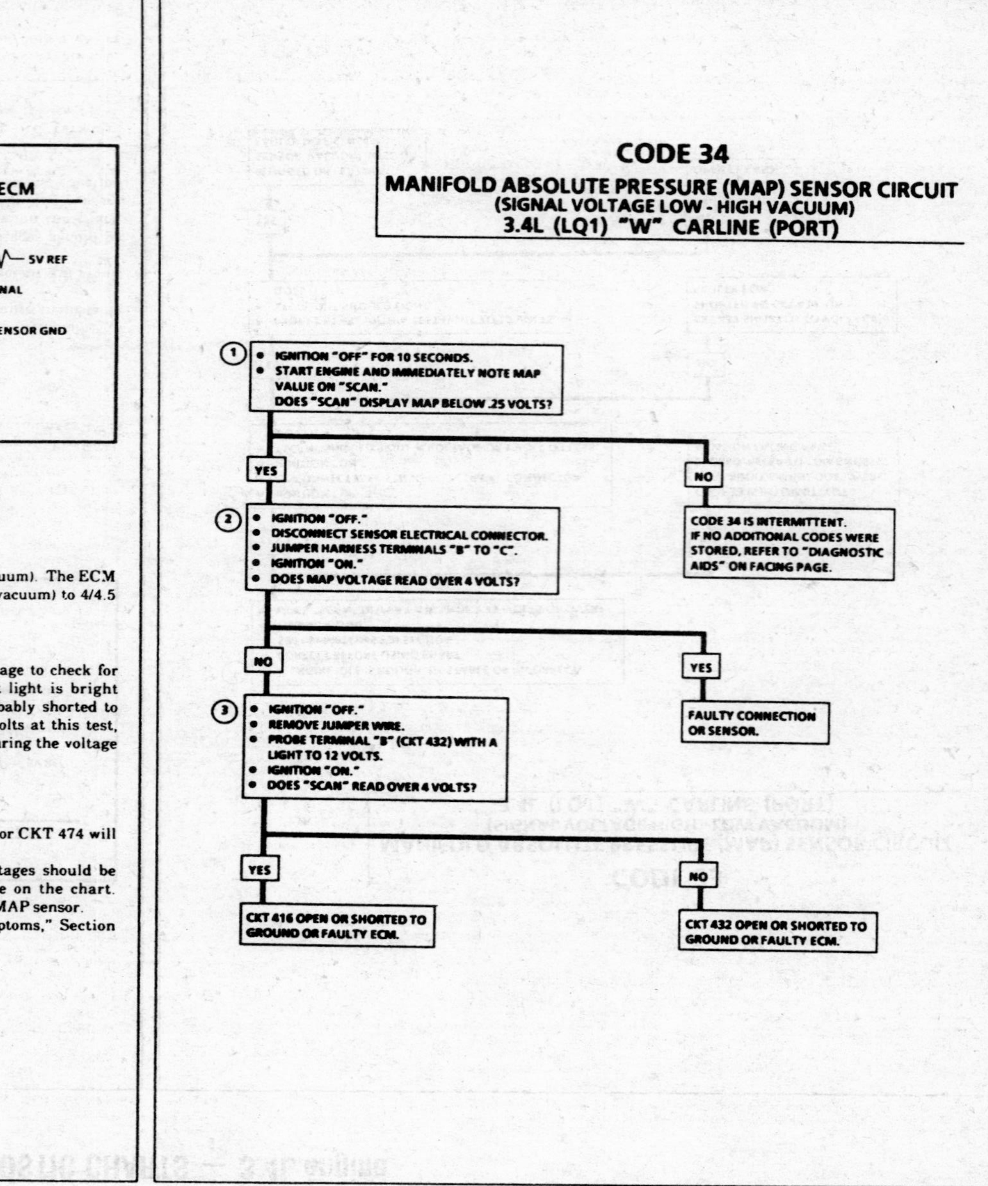

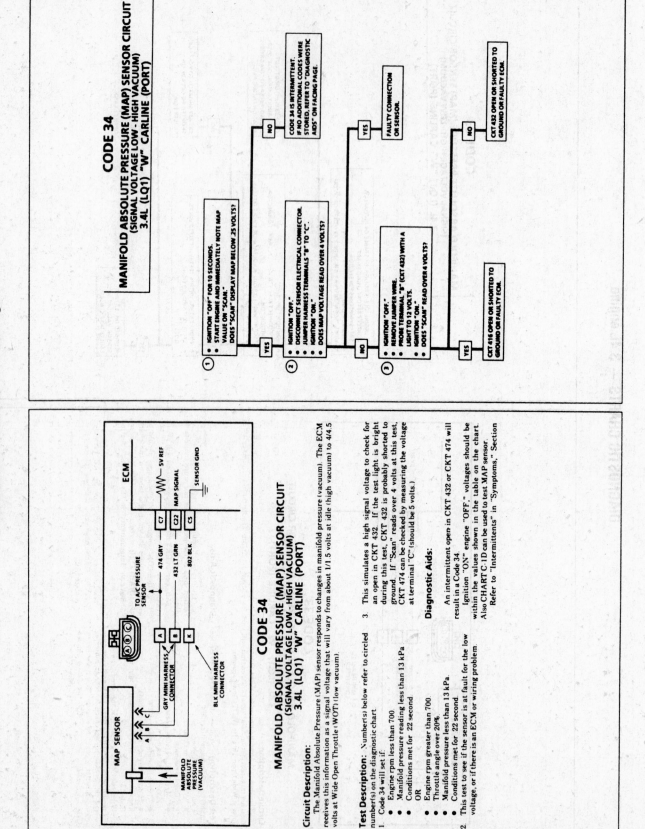

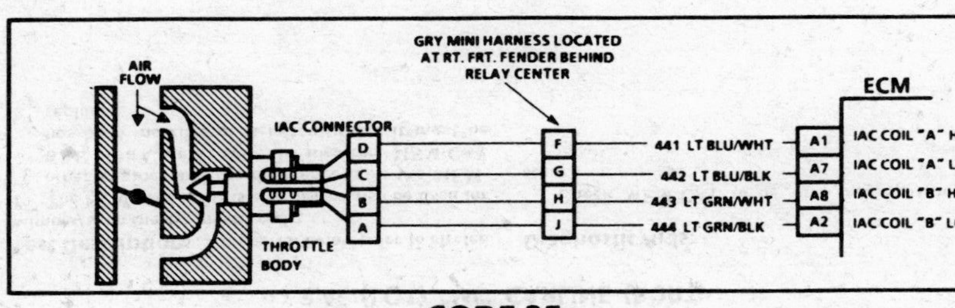
GRY MINI HARNESS LOCATED AT RT. FRT. FENDER BEHIND RELAY CENTER
AIR FLOW
IAC CONNECTOR
THROTTLE BODY
ECM
D
C
B
A
F
G
H
J
441 LT BLU/WHT
442 LT BLU/BLK
443 LT GRN/WHT
444 LT GRN/BLK
A1
A7
A8
A2
IAC COIL "A" HI
IAC COIL "A" LO
IAC COIL "B" HI
IAC COIL "B" LO

CODE 35

IDLE SPEED CONTROL (ISC) CIRCUIT 3.4L (LQ1) "W" CARLINE (PORT)

Circuit Description:

Code 35 will set when the closed throttle engine speed is 200 rpm above or below the desired (commanded) idle speed for 50 seconds. Review the "General Description" of the IAC operation in "Fuel Metering System" Section

Test Description: Number(s) below refer to circled number(s) on the diagnostic chart.

1. The Tech 1 rpm control mode is used to extend and retract the IAC valve. The valve should move smoothly within the specified range. If the idle speed is commanded (IAC extended) too low (below 700 rpm), the engine may stall. This may be normal and would not indicate a problem. Retracting the IAC beyond its controlled range (above 1500 rpm) will cause a delay before the rpm's start dropping. This too is normal.
2. This test uses the Tech 1 to command the IAC controlled idle speed. The ECM issues commands to obtain commended idle speed. The node lights each should flash red and green to indicate a good circuit as the ECM issues commands. While the sequence of color is not important if either light is "OFF" or does not flash red and green, check the circuits for faults, beginning with poor terminal contacts.

Diagnostic Aids:

A slow, unstable, or fast idle may be caused by a non-IAC system problem that cannot be overcome by the IAC valve. Out of control range IAC "Scan" tool counts will be above 60 if idle is too low, and zero counts if idle is too high. If idle speed is above 600-700 rpm in drive with an A/T, locate and correct vacuum leak. If rpm is below spec., check for foreign material around throttle plates. Refer to "Fuel Metering System," Section The following checks should be made to repair a non-IAC system problem:

- Vacuum Leak (High Idle)
  If idle is too high, stop the engine. Fully extend (low) IAC with tester. Start engine. If idle speed is above 800 rpm, locate and correct vacuum leak including PCV system. Also check for binding of throttle blade or linkage.
- System too lean (High Air/Fuel Ratio)
  The idle speed may be too high or too low. Engine speed may vary up and down and disconnecting the IAC valve does not help. Code 44 may be set. "Scan" O_2 voltage will be less than 300 mV (.3 volt). Check for low regulated fuel pressure, water in the fuel or a restricted injector.
- System too rich (Low Air/Fuel Ratio)
  The idle speed will be too low. "Scan" tool IAC counts will usually be above 80. System is obviously rich and may exhibit black smoke in exhaust. "Scan" too O_2 voltage will be fixed above 800 mV (.8 volt).
  Check for high fuel pressure, leaking or sticking injector. Silicone contaminated O_2 sensors "Scan" voltage will be slow to respond.
- Throttle Body
  Remove IAC valve and inspect bore for foreign material.
- IAC Valve Electrical Connections
  IAC valve connections should be carefully checked for proper contact.
- PCV Valve
  An incorrect or faulty PCV valve may result in an incorrect idle speed.
- Refer to "Rough, Unstable, Incorrect Idle or Stalling" in "Symptoms," Section
- If intermittent poor driveability or idle symptoms are resolved by disconnection the IAC, carefully recheck connections, valve terminal resistance, or replace IAC.
- A/C compressor or relay failure. See CHART C-10 if the A/C control relay drive circuit is shorted to ground or if the relay is faulty, an idle problem may exist.
- If above are all OK, refer to "Rough, Unstable, Incorrect Idle, or Stalling" in "Symptoms," Section

CODE 35

IDLE SPEED CONTROL (ISC) CIRCUIT 3.4L (LQ1) "W" CARLINE (PORT)

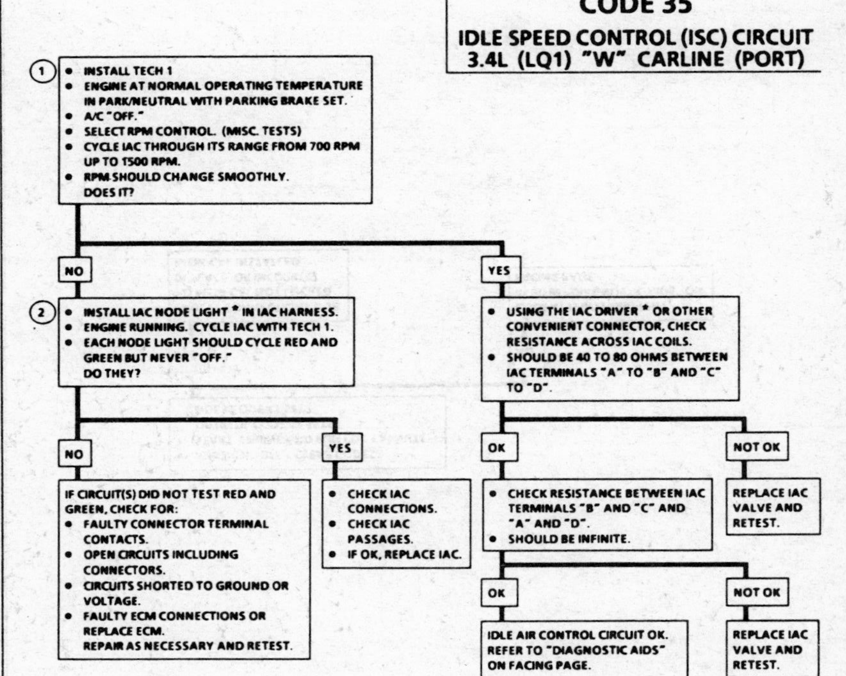
1
• INSTALL TECH 1
• ENGINE AT NORMAL OPERATING TEMPERATURE IN PARK/NEUTRAL WITH PARKING BRAKE SET.
• A/C "OFF."
• SELECT RPM CONTROL. (MISC. TESTS)
• CYCLE IAC THROUGH ITS RANGE FROM 700 RPM UP TO 1500 RPM.
• RPM SHOULD CHANGE SMOOTHLY.
DOES IT?
NO
YES
2
• INSTALL IAC NODE LIGHT * IN IAC HARNESS.
• ENGINE RUNNING. CYCLE IAC WITH TECH 1.
• EACH NODE LIGHT SHOULD CYCLE RED AND GREEN BUT NEVER "OFF."
DO THEY?
• USING THE IAC DRIVER * OR OTHER CONVENIENT CONNECTOR, CHECK RESISTANCE ACROSS IAC COILS.
• SHOULD BE 40 TO 80 OHMS BETWEEN IAC TERMINALS "A" TO "B" AND "C" TO "D".
NO
YES
OK
NOT OK
IF CIRCUIT(S) DID NOT TEST RED AND GREEN, CHECK FOR:
• FAULTY CONNECTOR TERMINAL CONTACTS.
• OPEN CIRCUITS INCLUDING CONNECTORS.
• CIRCUITS SHORTED TO GROUND OR VOLTAGE.
• FAULTY ECM CONNECTIONS OR REPLACE ECM.
REPAIR AS NECESSARY AND RETEST.
• CHECK IAC CONNECTIONS.
• CHECK IAC PASSAGES.
• IF OK, REPLACE IAC.
• CHECK RESISTANCE BETWEEN IAC TERMINALS "B" AND "C" AND "A" AND "D".
• SHOULD BE INFINITE.
REPLACE IAC VALVE AND RETEST.
OK
NOT OK
IDLE AIR CONTROL CIRCUIT OK. REFER TO "DIAGNOSTIC AIDS" ON FACING PAGE.
REPLACE IAC VALVE AND RETEST.

* IAC DRIVER AND NODE LIGHT REQUIRED KIT
222-L FROM: CONCEPT TECHNOLOGY, INC.
J 37027 FROM: KENT-MOORE, INC.

CLEAR CODES, CONFIRM "CLOSED LOOP" OPERATION, NO "SERVICE ENGINE SOON" LIGHT, PERFORM IAC RESET PROCEDURE PER APPLICABLE SERVICE MANUAL AND VERIFY CONTROLLED IDLE SPEED IS CORRECT.

MEM-CAL ACCESS COVER
GASKET
ECM
J4 J3 J2 J1

CODE 41
CYLINDER SELECT ERROR
(FAULTY OR INCORRECT MEM-CAL)
3.4L (LQ1) "W" CARLINE (PORT)

Test Description: Number(s) below refer to circled number(s) on the diagnostic chart.

1. The ECM used for this engine can also be used for other engines and the difference is in the MEM-CAL. If a Code 41 sets, the incorrect MEM-CAL has been installed or it is faulty and it must be replaced.

Diagnostic Aids:

Check MEM-CAL to be sure locking tabs are secure.

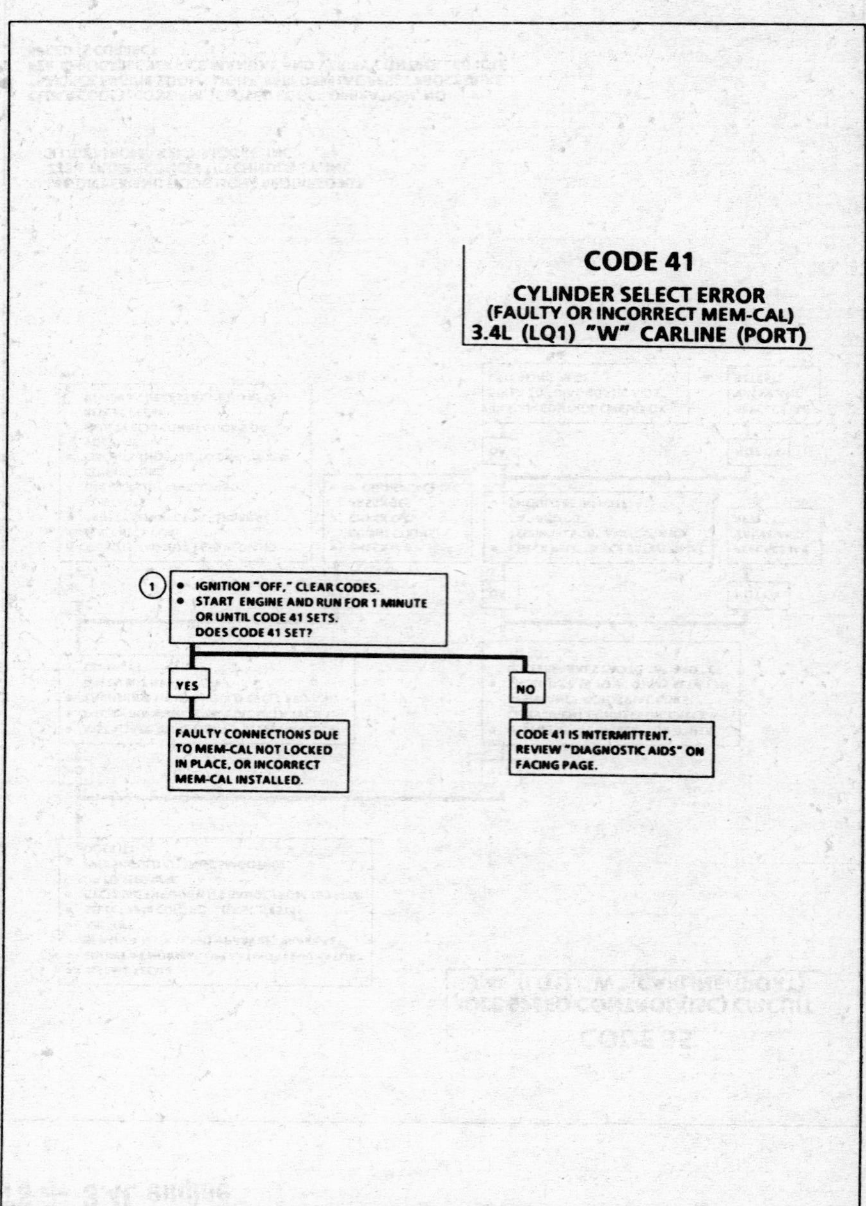
CODE 41
CYLINDER SELECT ERROR
(FAULTY OR INCORRECT MEM-CAL)
3.4L (LQ1) "W" CARLINE (PORT)
1
• IGNITION "OFF," CLEAR CODES.
• START ENGINE AND RUN FOR 1 MINUTE OR UNTIL CODE 41 SETS.
DOES CODE 41 SET?
YES
NO
FAULTY CONNECTIONS DUE TO MEM-CAL NOT LOCKED IN PLACE, OR INCORRECT MEM-CAL INSTALLED.
CODE 41 IS INTERMITTENT. REVIEW "DIAGNOSTIC AIDS" ON FACING PAGE.

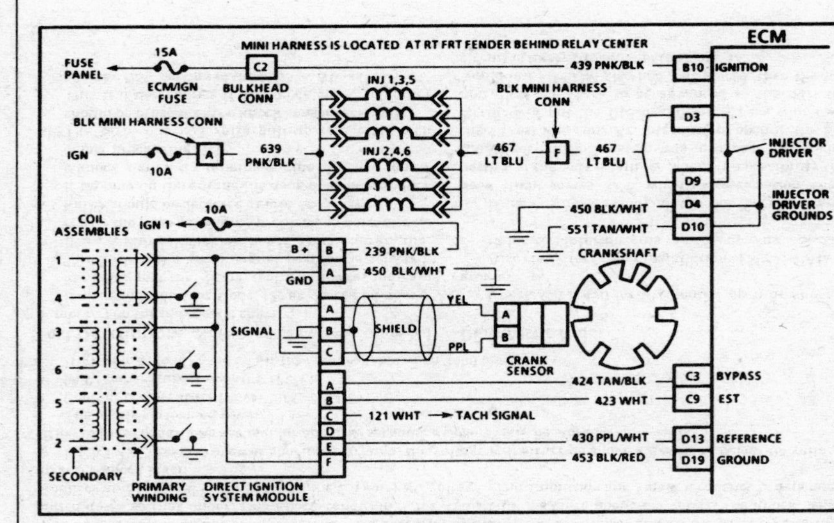

CODE 42

ELECTRONIC SPARK TIMING (EST) CIRCUIT 3.4L (LQ1) "W" CARLINE (PORT)

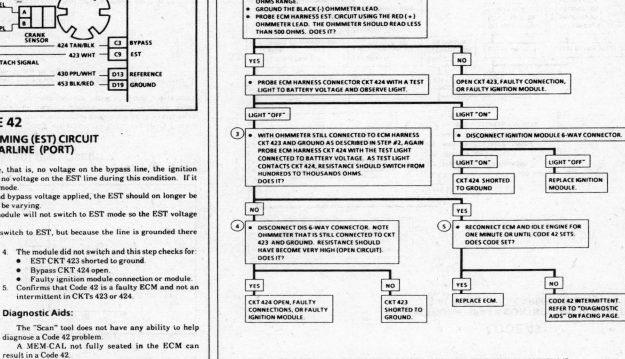

Circuit Description:

When the system is running on the ignition module, that is, no voltage on the bypass line, the ignition module grounds the EST signal. The ECM expects to see no voltage on the EST line during this condition. If it sees a voltage, it sets Code 42 and will not go into the EST mode.

When the rpm for EST is reached (about 400 rpm), and bypass voltage applied, the EST should on longer be grounded in the ignition module so the EST voltage should be varying.

If the bypass line is open or grounded, the ignition module will not switch to EST mode so the EST voltage will be low and Code 42 will be set.

If the EST line is grounded, the ignition module will switch to EST, but because the line is grounded there will be no EST signal. A Code 42 will be set.

Test Description: Number(s) below refer to circled number(s) on the diagnostic chart.

1. Code 42 means the ECM has seen an open or short to ground in the EST or bypass circuits. This test confirms Code 42 and that the fault causing the code is present.
2. Checks for a normal EST ground path through the ignition module. An EST CKT 423 shorted to ground will also read less than 500 ohms; however, this will be checked later.
3. As the test light voltage touches CKT 424, the module should switch causing the ohmmeter to "overrange" if the meter is in the 1000-2000 ohms position. Selecting the 10-20,000 ohms position will indicate above 5000 ohms. The important thing is that the module "switched."
4. The module did not switch and this step checks for:
   - EST CKT 423 shorted to ground.
   - Bypass CKT 424 open.
   - Faulty ignition module connection or module.
5. Confirms that Code 42 is a faulty ECM and not an intermittent in CKTs 423 or 424.

Diagnostic Aids:

The "Scan" tool does not have any ability to help diagnose a Code 42 problem.

A MEM-CAL not fully seated in the ECM can result in a Code 42.

Refer to "Intermittents" in "Symptoms," Section

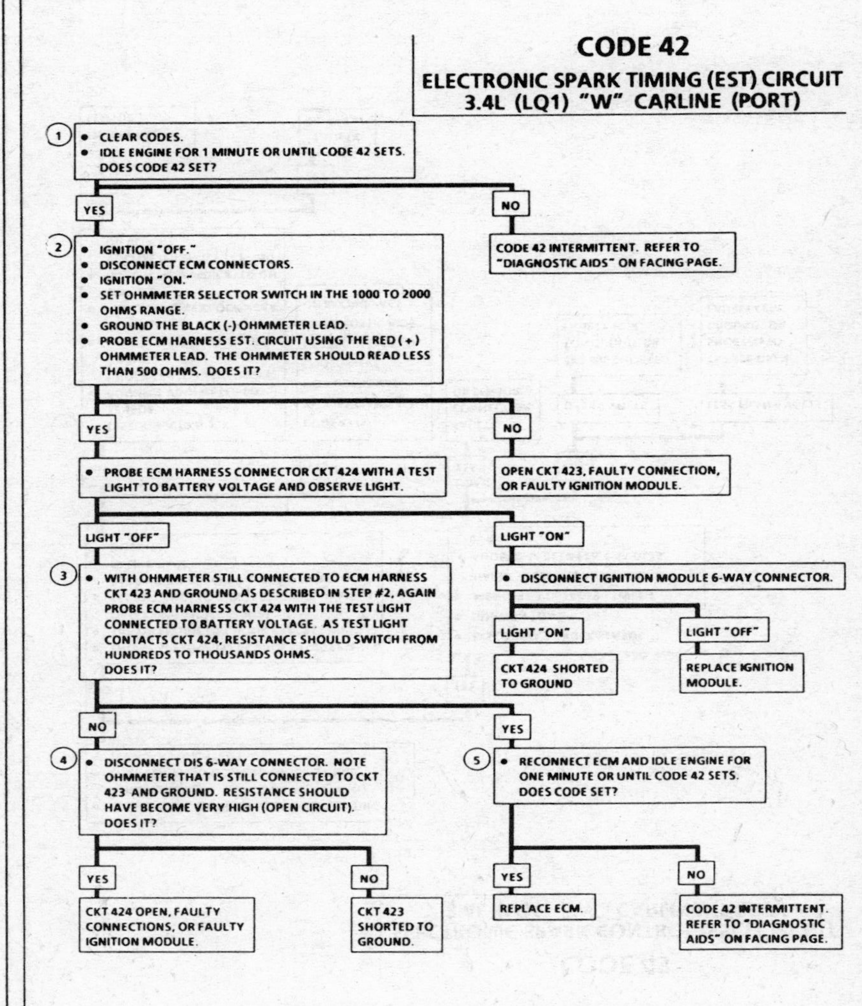

DIAGNOSTIC CHARTS — 3.4L engine

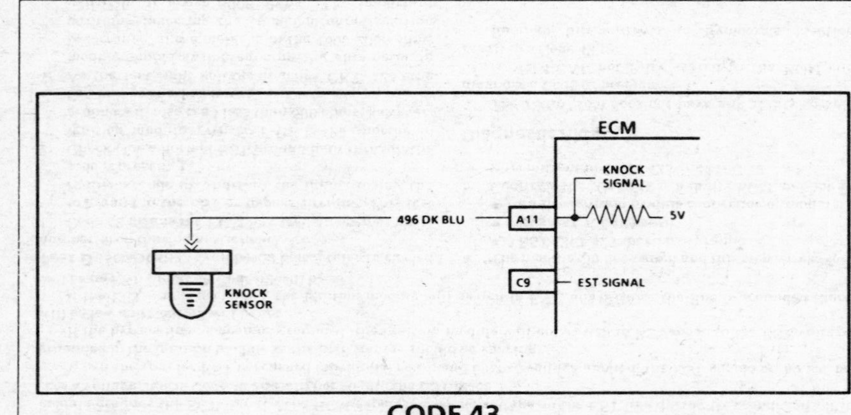
ECM
KNOCK SIGNAL
5V
496 DK BLU
A11
C9
EST SIGNAL
KNOCK SENSOR

CODE 43

ELECTRONIC SPARK CONTROL (ESC) CIRCUIT 3.4L (LQ1) "W" CARLINE (PORT)

Circuit Description:

The knock sensor is used to detect engine detonation and the ECM will retard the Electronic Spark Timing (EST) based on the signal being received. The circuitry within the knock sensor causes the ECM 5 volts to be pulled down so that under a no knock condition, CKT 496 would measure about 2.5 volts. The knock sensor produces an AC signal which rides on the 2.5 volts DC voltage. The amplitude and signal frequency is dependent upon the knock level.

If CKT 496 becomes open or shorted to ground, the voltage will either go above 4.8 volts or below .64 volts. If either of these conditions are met for about 10 seconds, a Code 43 will be stored.

The test is performed when:

- Coolant temperature is over 90°C (194°F).
- IAT temperature is over 0°C (32°F).
- High engine load based on air flow and rpm between 3400 and 4400.

Test Description: Number(s) below refer to circled number(s) on the diagnostic chart.

1. If the conditions for Code 43, as described above, are being met the "Scan" tool will always indicate "Yes" when the knock signal position is selected. If an audible knock is heard from the engine, repair the internal engine problem, as normally no knock should be detected at idle.
2. If tapping on the engine lift hook does not produce a knock signal, try tapping engine closer to sensor before proceeding.
3. The ECM has a 5 volts pull-up resistor which should be present at the knock sensor terminal.
4. This test determines if the knock sensor is faulty or if the ESC portion of the MEM-CAL is faulty.

Diagnostic Aids:

Check CKT 496 for a potential open or short to ground.

Also check for proper installation of MEM-CAL.

Refer to "Intermittents" in "Symptoms," Section

If the customer's complaint is the "Service Engine Soon" light comes "ON" when in acceleration, the B portion of the code is failing. There is a possibility that the direct ignition system was in bypass mode when the 43 test was run. An intermittent open in the EST circuit will put the DIS module in bypass which will not allow the spark to be advanced so the 43B test would fail. If ECM also had a 42 stored, then the EST circuit is likely the cause of the Code 43.

CODE 43

ELECTRONIC SPARK CONTROL (ESC) CIRCUIT 3.4L (LQ1) "W" CARLINE (PORT)

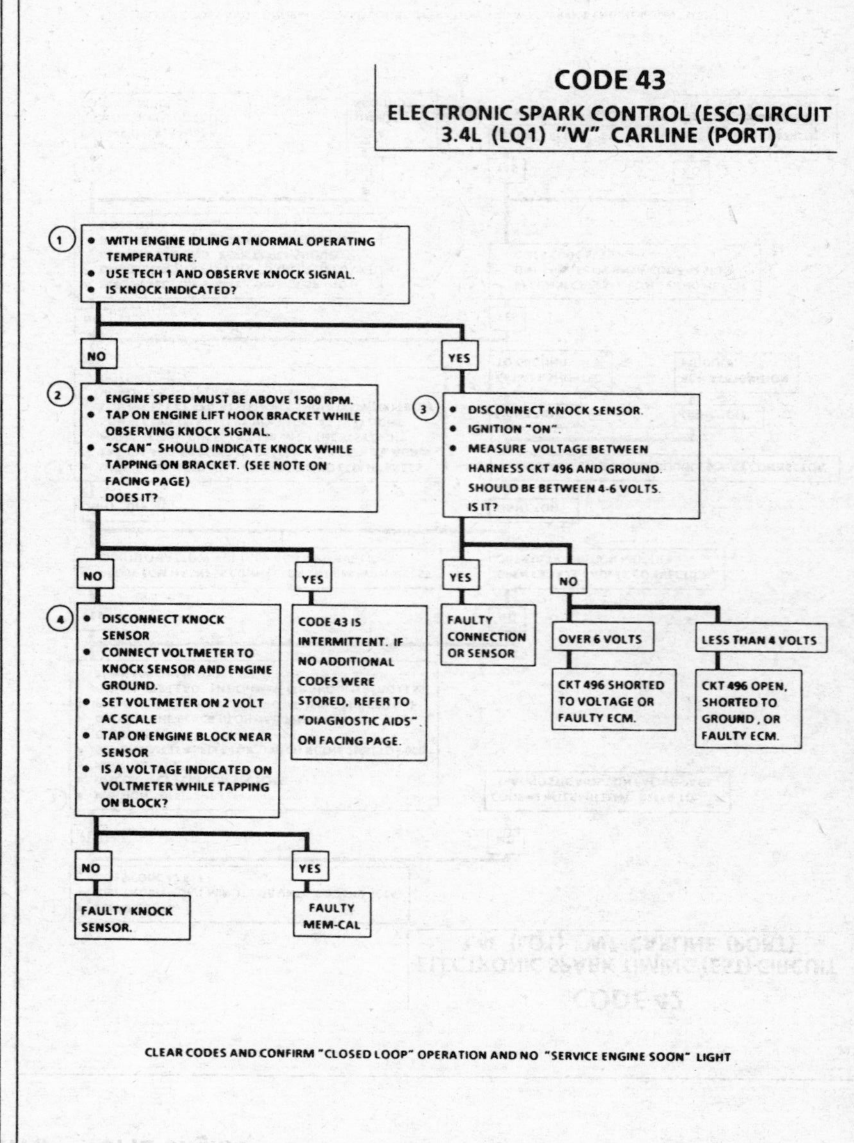
1
• WITH ENGINE IDLING AT NORMAL OPERATING TEMPERATURE.
• USE TECH 1 AND OBSERVE KNOCK SIGNAL.
• IS KNOCK INDICATED?
NO
YES
2
• ENGINE SPEED MUST BE ABOVE 1500 RPM.
• TAP ON ENGINE LIFT HOOK BRACKET WHILE OBSERVING KNOCK SIGNAL.
• "SCAN" SHOULD INDICATE KNOCK WHILE TAPPING ON BRACKET. (SEE NOTE ON FACING PAGE)
DOES IT?
3
• DISCONNECT KNOCK SENSOR.
• IGNITION "ON".
• MEASURE VOLTAGE BETWEEN HARNESS CKT 496 AND GROUND. SHOULD BE BETWEEN 4-6 VOLTS.
IS IT?
NO
YES
4
• DISCONNECT KNOCK SENSOR
• CONNECT VOLTMETER TO KNOCK SENSOR AND ENGINE GROUND.
• SET VOLTMETER ON 2 VOLT AC SCALE
• TAP ON ENGINE BLOCK NEAR SENSOR
• IS A VOLTAGE INDICATED ON VOLTMETER WHILE TAPPING ON BLOCK?
CODE 43 IS INTERMITTENT. IF NO ADDITIONAL CODES WERE STORED, REFER TO "DIAGNOSTIC AIDS" ON FACING PAGE.
YES
NO
FAULTY CONNECTION OR SENSOR
OVER 6 VOLTS
LESS THAN 4 VOLTS
CKT 496 SHORTED TO VOLTAGE OR FAULTY ECM.
CKT 496 OPEN, SHORTED TO GROUND, OR FAULTY ECM.
NO
YES
FAULTY KNOCK SENSOR.
FAULTY MEM-CAL
CLEAR CODES AND CONFIRM "CLOSED LOOP" OPERATION AND NO "SERVICE ENGINE SOON" LIGHT

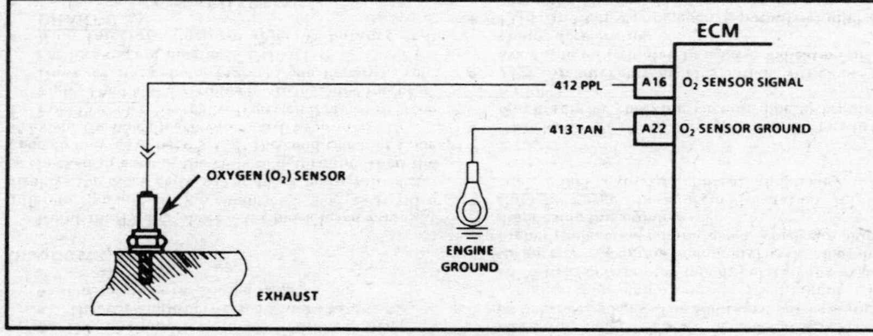
ECM
412 PPL
A16
O_2 SENSOR SIGNAL
413 TAN
A22
O_2 SENSOR GROUND
OXYGEN (O_2) SENSOR
ENGINE GROUND
EXHAUST

CODE 44

OXYGEN (O_2) SENSOR CIRCUIT
(LEAN EXHAUST INDICATED)
3.4L (LQ1) "W" CARLINE (PORT)

Circuit Description:

The ECM supplies a voltage of about .55 volt between terminals "A16" and "A22". (If measured with a 10 megohm digital voltmeter, this may read as low as .35 volt.) The Oxygen (O_2) sensor varies the voltage within a range of about 1 volt if the exhaust is rich, down through about .10 volt if exhaust is lean.

The sensor is like an open circuit and produces no voltage when it is below about 315°C (600°F). An open sensor circuit or cold sensor causes "Open Loop" operation.

Test Description: Number(s) below refer to circled number(s) on the diagnostic chart.

1. Code 44 will set if:
   - No Code 33 or Code 34.
   - Voltage on CKT 412 remains below .2 volt for 60 seconds or more.
   - The system is operating in "Closed Loop."

Diagnostic Aids:

Using the "Scan," observe the block learn values at different rpm and air flow conditions. The "Scan" also displays the block cells, so the block learn values can be checked in each of the cells to determine when the Code 44 may have been set. If the conditions for Code 44 exists the block learn values will be around 150.

- O_2 Sensor Wire Sensor pigtail may be mispositioned and contacting the exhaust manifold.
- Check for intermittent ground in wire between connector and sensor.
- Lean Injector(s) Perform injector balance test CHART C-2A.
- Fuel Contamination Water, even in small amounts, near the in-tank fuel pump inlet can be delivered to the injectors. The water causes a lean exhaust and can set a Code 44.
- Fuel Pressure System will be lean if pressure is too low. It may be necessary to monitor fuel pressure while driving the car at various road speeds and/or loads to confirm. See "Fuel System Diagnosis" CHART A-7.
- Exhaust Leaks If there is an exhaust leak, the engine can cause outside air to be pulled into the exhaust and past the sensor. Vacuum or crankcase leaks can cause a lean condition.
- If the above are OK, it is a faulty Oxygen (O_2) sensor.

CODE 44

OXYGEN (O_2) SENSOR CIRCUIT
(LEAN EXHAUST INDICATED)
3.4L (LQ1) "W" CARLINE (PORT)

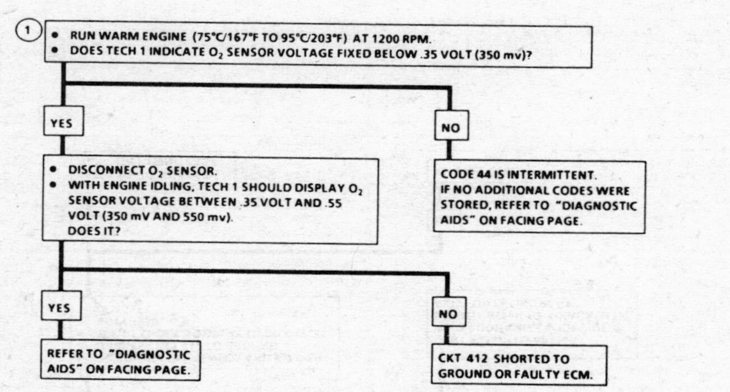
1
• RUN WARM ENGINE (75°C/167°F TO 95°C/203°F) AT 1200 RPM.
• DOES TECH 1 INDICATE O_2 SENSOR VOLTAGE FIXED BELOW .35 VOLT (350 mv)?
YES
NO
• DISCONNECT O_2 SENSOR.
• WITH ENGINE IDLING, TECH 1 SHOULD DISPLAY O_2 SENSOR VOLTAGE BETWEEN .35 VOLT AND .55 VOLT (350 mV AND 550 mv). DOES IT?
CODE 44 IS INTERMITTENT. IF NO ADDITIONAL CODES WERE STORED, REFER TO "DIAGNOSTIC AIDS" ON FACING PAGE.
YES
NO
REFER TO "DIAGNOSTIC AIDS" ON FACING PAGE.
CKT 412 SHORTED TO GROUND OR FAULTY ECM.

CLEAR CODES AND CONFIRM "CLOSED LOOP" OPERATION AND NO "SERVICE ENGINE SOON" LIGHT.

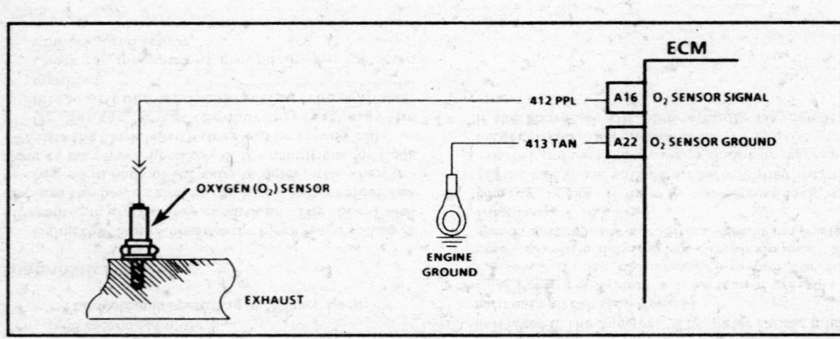
ECM
412 PPL
A16
O_2 SENSOR SIGNAL
413 TAN
A22
O_2 SENSOR GROUND
OXYGEN (O_2) SENSOR
ENGINE GROUND
EXHAUST

CODE 45

OXYGEN (O_2) SENSOR CIRCUIT
(RICH EXHAUST INDICATED)
3.4L (LQ1) "W" CARLINE (PORT)

Circuit Description:

The ECM supplies a voltage of about .55 volt between terminals "A16" and "A22". (If measured with a 10 megaohm digital voltmeter, this may read as low as .35 volt.) The Oxygen (O_2) sensor varies the voltage within a range of about 1 volt if the exhaust is rich, down through about .10 volt if exhaust is lean.

The sensor is like an open circuit and produces no voltage when it is below about 315°C (600°F). An open sensor circuit or cold sensor causes "Open Loop" operation.

Test Description: Number(s) below refer to circled number(s) on the diagnostic chart.

1. Code 45 will set if:
   - Voltage on CKT 412 remains above .7 volt for 50 seconds.
   - Engine time after start is 1 minute or more.
   - Throttle angle between 3% and 45%.
   - Operation is in "Closed Loop".

Diagnostic Aids:

Using the "Scan," observe the block learn values at different rpm and air flow conditions. The "Scan" also displays the block cells, so the block learn values can be checked in each of the cells to determine when the Code 45 may have been set. If the conditions for Code 45 exists, the block learn values will be around 115.

- Fuel Pressure. System will go rich if pressure is too high. The ECM can compensate for some increase. However, if it gets too high, a Code 45 may be set. See fuel system diagnosis CHART A-7.
- Rich Injector. Perform injector balance test CHART C-2A.
- Leaking Injector. See CHART A-7.
- Check for fuel contaminated oil.
- O_2 Sensor Contamination. Inspect Oxygen (O_2) sensor for silicone contamination from fuel, or use of improper RTV sealant. The sensor may have a white, powdery coating and result in a high but false signal voltage (rich exhaust indication). The ECM will then reduce the amount of fuel delivered to the engine, causing a severe surge driveability problem.
- HEI Shielding. An open ground CKT 453 (ignition system reflow) may result in EMI, or induced electrical "noise". The ECM looks at this "noise" as reference pulses. The additional pulses result in a higher than actual engine speed signal. The ECM then delivers too much fuel, causing system to go rich. Engine tachometer will also show higher than actual engine speed, which can help in diagnosing this problem.
- Canister Purge. Check for fuel saturation. If full of fuel, check canister control and hoses.
- Check for leaking fuel pressure regulator diaphragm by checking vacuum line to regulator for fuel.
- TPS. An intermittent TPS output will cause the system to go rich, due to a false indication of the engine accelerating.
- EGR. An EGR staying open (especially at idle) will cause the Oxygen (O_2) sensor to indicate a rich exhaust, and this could result in a Code 45.

CODE 45

OXYGEN (O_2) SENSOR CIRCUIT
(RICH EXHAUST INDICATED)
3.4L (LQ1) "W" CARLINE (PORT)

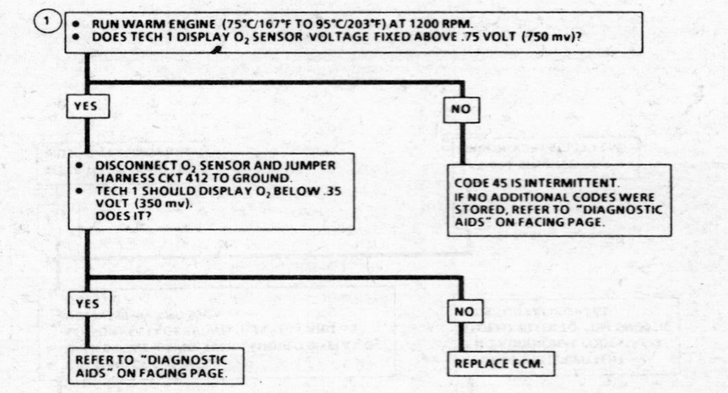
1
• RUN WARM ENGINE (75°C/167°F TO 95°C/203°F) AT 1200 RPM.
• DOES TECH 1 DISPLAY O_2 SENSOR VOLTAGE FIXED ABOVE .75 VOLT (750 mv)?
YES
NO
• DISCONNECT O_2 SENSOR AND JUMPER HARNESS CKT 412 TO GROUND.
• TECH 1 SHOULD DISPLAY O_2 BELOW .35 VOLT (350 mv).
DOES IT?
CODE 45 IS INTERMITTENT.
IF NO ADDITIONAL CODES WERE STORED, REFER TO "DIAGNOSTIC AIDS" ON FACING PAGE.
YES
NO
REFER TO "DIAGNOSTIC AIDS" ON FACING PAGE.
REPLACE ECM.

CLEAR CODES AND CONFIRM "CLOSED LOOP" OPERATION AND NO "SERVICE ENGINE SOON" LIGHT.

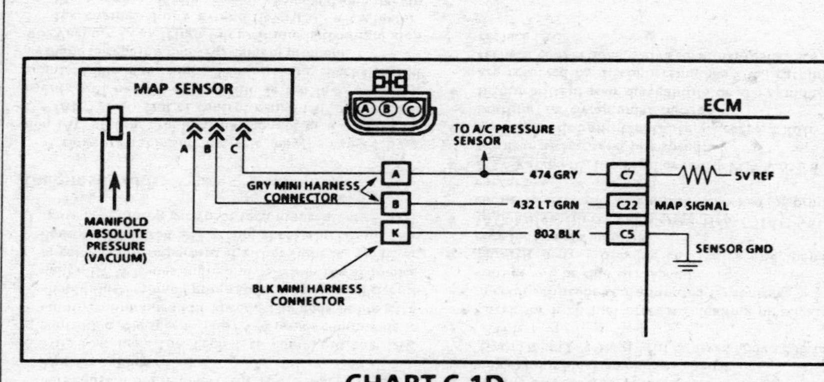
MAP SENSOR
ECM
TO A/C PRESSURE SENSOR
A B C
GRY MINI HARNESS CONNECTOR
474 GRY
C7
5V REF
432 LT GRN
C22
MAP SIGNAL
802 BLK
C5
SENSOR GND
MANIFOLD ABSOLUTE PRESSURE (VACUUM)
BLK MINI HARNESS CONNECTOR

CHART C-1D

MANIFOLD ABSOLUTE PRESSURE (MAP) OUTPUT CHECK 3.4L (LQ1) "W" CARLINE (PORT)

Circuit Description:

The Manifold Absolute Pressure (MAP) sensor measures manifold pressure (vacuum) and sends that signal to the ECM. The MAP sensor is mainly used for fuel calculation when the ECM is running in the throttle body backup mode. The MAP sensor is also used to determine the barometric pressure and to help calculate fuel delivery.

Test Description: Number(s) below refer to circled number(s) on the diagnostic chart.

1. Checks MAP sensor output voltage to the ECM. This voltage, without engine running, represents a barometer reading to the ECM.
2. Applying 34 kPa (10 inch Hg) vacuum to the MAP sensor should cause the voltage to be 1.2 volts less than the voltage at Step 1. Upon applying vacuum to the sensor, the change in voltage should be instantaneous. A slow voltage change indicates a faulty sensor.

   The engine must be running in this step or the "scanner" will not indicate a change in voltage. It is normal for the "Service Engine Soon" light to come "ON" and for the system to set a Code 33 during this step. Make sure the code is cleared when this test is completed.
3. Check vacuum hose to sensor for leaking or restriction. Be sure no other vacuum devices are connected to the MAP hose.
4. Disconnect sensor from bracket and twist sensor by hand (only) to check for intermittent connection. Output changes greater than .10 volt indicate a bad sensor. If OK, replace sensor.

CHART C-1D

MANIFOLD ABSOLUTE PRESSURE (MAP) OUTPUT CHECK 3.4L (LQ1) "W" CARLINE (PORT)

NOTE: THIS CHART ONLY APPLIES TO MAP SENSORS HAVING GREEN OR BLACK COLOR KEY INSERT (SEE BELOW).

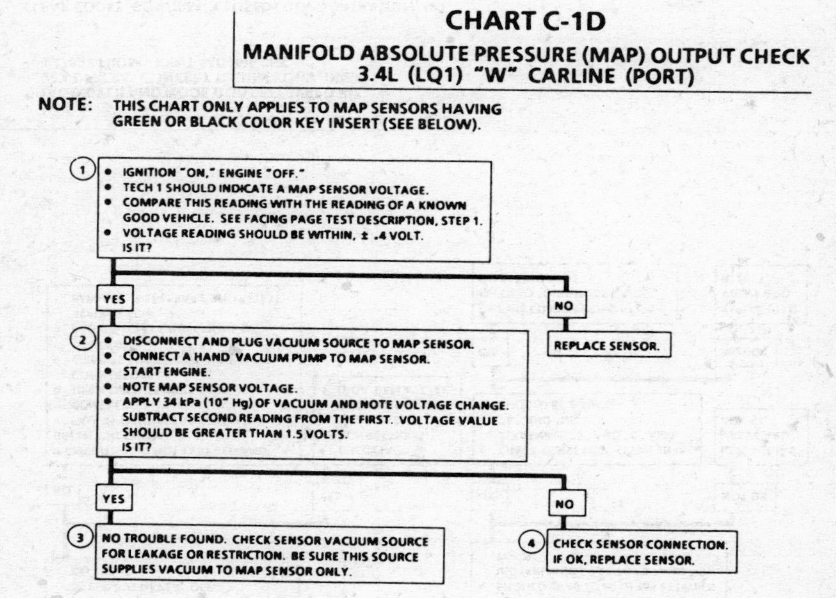
1
• IGNITION "ON," ENGINE "OFF."
• TECH 1 SHOULD INDICATE A MAP SENSOR VOLTAGE.
• COMPARE THIS READING WITH THE READING OF A KNOWN GOOD VEHICLE. SEE FACING PAGE TEST DESCRIPTION, STEP 1.
• VOLTAGE READING SHOULD BE WITHIN, ± .4 VOLT. IS IT?
YES
NO
REPLACE SENSOR.
2
• DISCONNECT AND PLUG VACUUM SOURCE TO MAP SENSOR.
• CONNECT A HAND VACUUM PUMP TO MAP SENSOR.
• START ENGINE.
• NOTE MAP SENSOR VOLTAGE.
• APPLY 34 kPa (10" Hg) OF VACUUM AND NOTE VOLTAGE CHANGE. SUBTRACT SECOND READING FROM THE FIRST. VOLTAGE VALUE SHOULD BE GREATER THAN 1.5 VOLTS. IS IT?
YES
NO
3
NO TROUBLE FOUND. CHECK SENSOR VACUUM SOURCE FOR LEAKAGE OR RESTRICTION. BE SURE THIS SOURCE SUPPLIES VACUUM TO MAP SENSOR ONLY.
4
CHECK SENSOR CONNECTION. IF OK, REPLACE SENSOR.

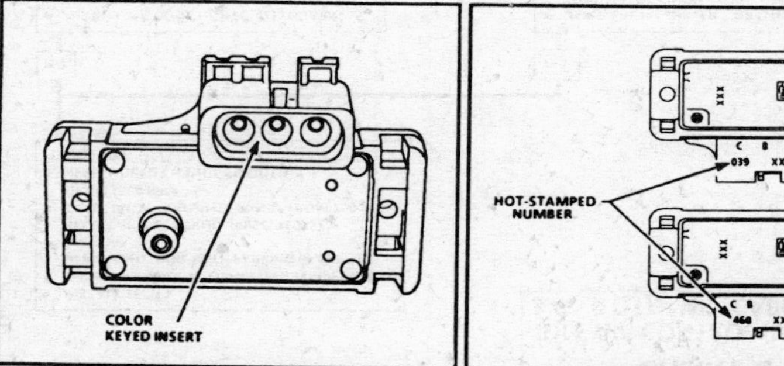
COLOR KEYED INSERT
HOT-STAMPED NUMBER
C B A
039 XXXX
466 XXXX
XXX

Figure 1 - Color Key Insert

Figure 2 - Hot-Stamped Number

"AFTER REPAIRS," CONFIRM "CLOSED LOOP" OPERATION AND NO "SERVICE ENGINE SOON" LIGHT.

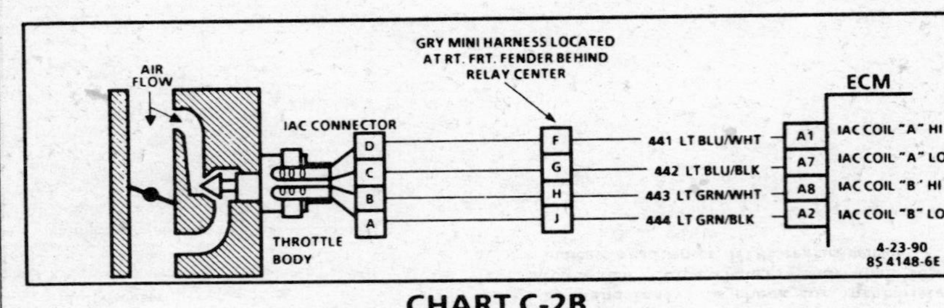
GRY MINI HARNESS LOCATED
AT RT. FRT. FENDER BEHIND
RELAY CENTER
AIR FLOW
IAC CONNECTOR
D
C
B
A
THROTTLE BODY
F
G
H
J
441 LT BLU/WHT
442 LT BLU/BLK
443 LT GRN/WHT
444 LT GRN/BLK
ECM
A1
A7
A8
A2
IAC COIL "A" HI
IAC COIL "A" LO
IAC COIL "B" HI
IAC COIL "B" LO
4-23-90
8S 4148-6E

CHART C-2B

IDLE AIR CONTROL (IAC) CIRCUIT 3.4L (LQ1) "W" CARLINE (PORT)

Circuit Description:

The ECM controls engine idle speed with the IAC valve. To increase idle speed, the ECM retracts the IAC valve pintle away from its seat, allowing more air to bypass the throttle bore. To decrease idle speed, it extends the IAC valve pintle towards its seat, reducing bypass air flow. A "Scan" tool will read the ECM commands to the IAC valve in counts. Higher the counts indicate more air bypass (higher idle). The lower the counts indicate less air is allowed to bypass (lower idle).

Test Description: Number(s) below refer to circled number(s) on the diagnostic chart.

1. The Tech I rpm control mode is used to extend and retract the IAC valve. The valve should move smoothly within the specified range. If the idle speed is commanded (IAC extended) too low (below 700 rpm), the engine may stall. This may be normal and would not indicate a problem. Retracting the IAC beyond its controlled range (above 1500 rpm) will cause a delay before the rpm's start dropping. This too is normal.
2. This test uses the Tech I to command the IAC controlled idle speed. The ECM issues commands to obtain commended idle speed. The node lights each should flash red and green to indicate a good circuit as the ECM issues commands. While the sequence of color is not important if either light is "OFF" or does not flash red and green, check the circuits for faults, beginning with poor terminal contacts.

Diagnostic Aids:

A slow, unstable, or fast idle may be caused by a non-IAC system problem that cannot be overcome by the IAC valve. Out of control range IAC "Scan" tool counts will be above 60 if idle is too low, and zero counts if idle is too high. The following checks should be made to repair a non-IAC system problem:

- Vacuum Leak (High Idle) - If idle is too high, stop the engine. Fully extend (low) IAC with tester. Start engine. If idle speed is above 800 rpm, locate and correct vacuum leak including PCV system. Also check for binding of throttle blade or linkage.
- System too lean (High Air/Fuel Ratio) - The idle speed may be too high or too low. Engine speed may vary up and down and disconnecting the IAC valve does not help. Code 44 may be set. "Scan" O_2 voltage will be less than 300 mV (.3 volt). Check for low regulated fuel pressure, water in the fuel or a restricted injector.
- System too rich (Low Air/Fuel Ratio) - The idle speed will be too low. "Scan" tool IAC counts will usually be above 80. System is obviously rich and may exhibit black smoke in exhaust.
  "Scan" tool O_2 voltage will be fixed above 800 mV (.8 volt).
  Check for high fuel pressure, leaking or sticking injector. Silicone contaminated O_2 sensors "Scan" voltage will be slow to respond.
- Throttle body. - Remove IAC valve and inspect bore for foreign material.
- IAC Valve Electrical Connections - IAC valve connections should be carefully checked for proper contact.
- PCV Valve - An incorrect or faulty PCV valve may result in an incorrect idle speed.
- Refer to "Rough, Unstable, Incorrect Idle or Stalling" in "Symptoms," Section
- If intermittent poor driveability or idle symptoms are resolved by disconnecting the IAC, carefully recheck connections, valve terminal resistance, or replace IAC.

CHART C-2B

IDLE AIR CONTROL (IAC) CIRCUIT 3.4L (LQ1) "W" CARLINE (PORT)

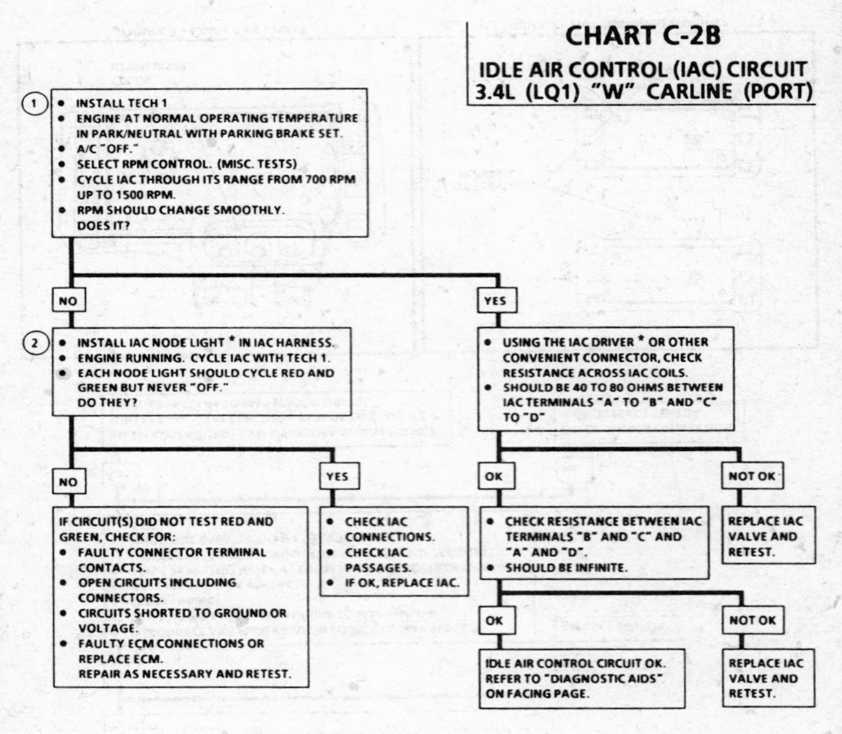
1
• INSTALL TECH 1
• ENGINE AT NORMAL OPERATING TEMPERATURE IN PARK/NEUTRAL WITH PARKING BRAKE SET.
• A/C "OFF."
• SELECT RPM CONTROL. (MISC. TESTS)
• CYCLE IAC THROUGH ITS RANGE FROM 700 RPM UP TO 1500 RPM.
• RPM SHOULD CHANGE SMOOTHLY.
DOES IT?
NO
YES
2
• INSTALL IAC NODE LIGHT * IN IAC HARNESS.
• ENGINE RUNNING. CYCLE IAC WITH TECH 1.
• EACH NODE LIGHT SHOULD CYCLE RED AND GREEN BUT NEVER "OFF."
DO THEY?
• USING THE IAC DRIVER * OR OTHER CONVENIENT CONNECTOR, CHECK RESISTANCE ACROSS IAC COILS.
• SHOULD BE 40 TO 80 OHMS BETWEEN IAC TERMINALS "A" TO "B" AND "C" TO "D"
NO
YES
OK
NOT OK
IF CIRCUIT(S) DID NOT TEST RED AND GREEN, CHECK FOR:
• FAULTY CONNECTOR TERMINAL CONTACTS.
• OPEN CIRCUITS INCLUDING CONNECTORS.
• CIRCUITS SHORTED TO GROUND OR VOLTAGE.
• FAULTY ECM CONNECTIONS OR REPLACE ECM.
REPAIR AS NECESSARY AND RETEST.
• CHECK IAC CONNECTIONS.
• CHECK IAC PASSAGES.
• IF OK, REPLACE IAC.
• CHECK RESISTANCE BETWEEN IAC TERMINALS "B" AND "C" AND "A" AND "D".
• SHOULD BE INFINITE.
REPLACE IAC VALVE AND RETEST.
OK
NOT OK
IDLE AIR CONTROL CIRCUIT OK. REFER TO "DIAGNOSTIC AIDS" ON FACING PAGE.
REPLACE IAC VALVE AND RETEST.
* IAC DRIVER AND NODE LIGHT REQUIRED KIT
222-L FROM: CONCEPT TECHNOLOGY, INC.
J 37027 FROM: KENT-MOORE, INC.
CLEAR CODES, CONFIRM "CLOSED LOOP" OPERATION, NO "SERVICE ENGINE SOON" LIGHT, PERFORM IAC RESET PROCEDURE PER APPLICABLE SERVICE MANUAL AND VERIFY CONTROLLED IDLE SPEED IS CORRECT.

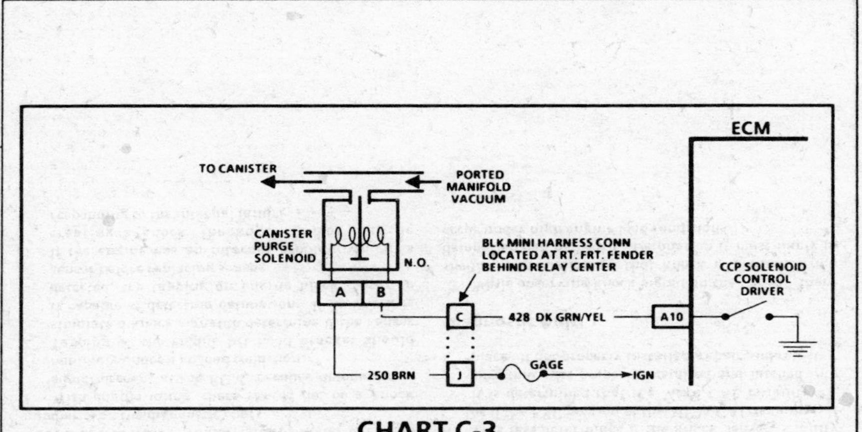
ECM
TO CANISTER
PORTED MANIFOLD VACUUM
CANISTER PURGE SOLENOID
N.O.
A
B
BLK MINI HARNESS CONN LOCATED AT RT. FRT. FENDER BEHIND RELAY CENTER
C
428 DK GRN/YEL
A10
CCP SOLENOID CONTROL DRIVER
250 BRN
J
GAGE
IGN

CHART C-3

CANISTER PURGE VALVE CHECK 3.4L (LQ1) "W" CARLINE (PORT)

Circuit Description:

Canister purge is controlled by a solenoid that allows manifold vacuum to purge the canister when de-energized. The ECM supplies a ground to energize the solenoid (purge "OFF.") The purge solenoid control by the ECM is pulse width modulated (turned "ON" and "OFF" several times a second). The duty cycle (pulse width) is determined by the amount of air flow, and the engine vacuum as determined by the MAP sensor input. The duty cycle is calculated by the ECM and the output commanded when the following conditions have been met:

- Engine run time after start more than 3 minutes.
- Coolant temperature above 80°C (176°F)
- Vehicle speed above 15 mph
- Throttle of idle (about 3%)

Also, if the diagnostic "test" terminal is grounded with the engine stopped, the purge solenoid is de-energized (purge "ON.")

Test Description: Number(s) below refer to circled number(s) on the diagnostic chart.

1. Checks to see if the solenoid is opened or closed. The solenoid is normally energized in this step; so it should be closed.
2. Checks for a complete circuit. Normally there is ignition voltage on CKT 250 and the ECM provides a ground on CKT 428.
3. Completes functional check by grounding "test" terminal. This should normally de-energize the solenoid opening the valve which should allow the vacuum to drop (purge "ON.")

CHART C-3

CANISTER PURGE VALVE CHECK 3.1L (LQ1) "W" CARLINE (PORT)

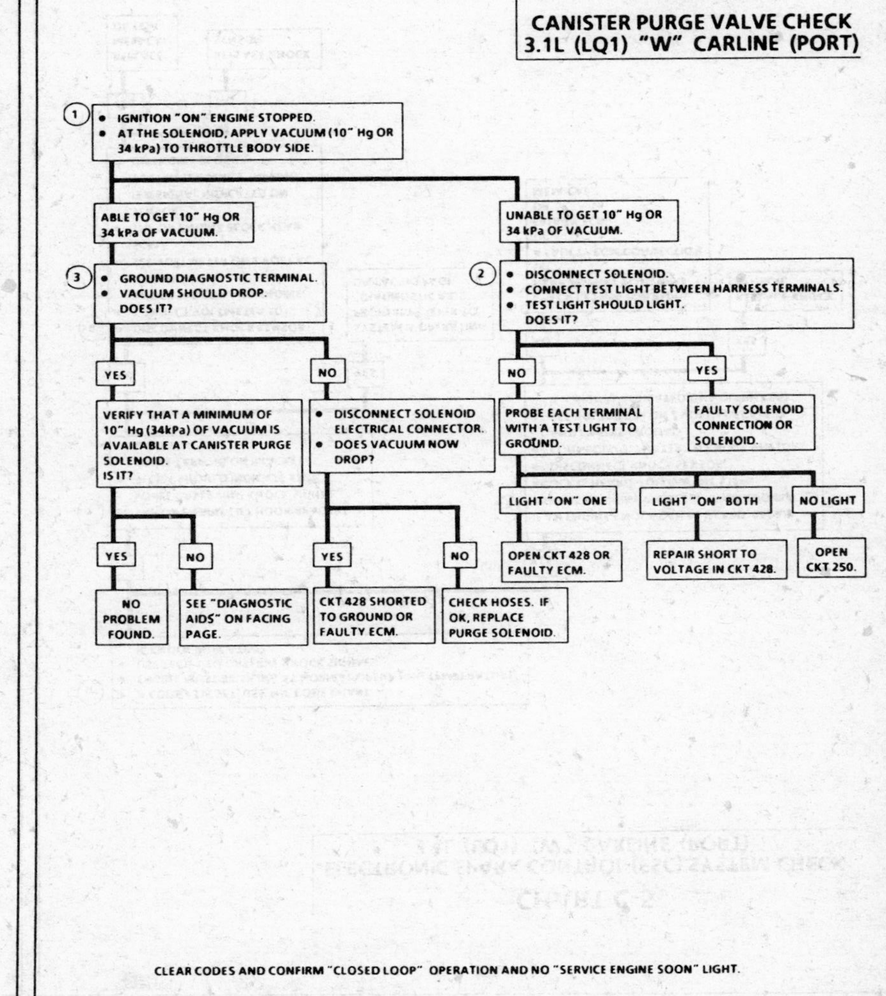
1
• IGNITION "ON" ENGINE STOPPED.
• AT THE SOLENOID, APPLY VACUUM (10" Hg OR 34 kPa) TO THROTTLE BODY SIDE.
ABLE TO GET 10" Hg OR 34 kPa OF VACUUM.
UNABLE TO GET 10" Hg OR 34 kPa OF VACUUM.
3
• GROUND DIAGNOSTIC TERMINAL.
• VACUUM SHOULD DROP.
DOES IT?
2
• DISCONNECT SOLENOID.
• CONNECT TEST LIGHT BETWEEN HARNESS TERMINALS.
• TEST LIGHT SHOULD LIGHT.
DOES IT?
YES
NO
NO
YES
VERIFY THAT A MINIMUM OF 10" Hg (34kPa) OF VACUUM IS AVAILABLE AT CANISTER PURGE SOLENOID.
IS IT?
• DISCONNECT SOLENOID ELECTRICAL CONNECTOR.
• DOES VACUUM NOW DROP?
PROBE EACH TERMINAL WITH A TEST LIGHT TO GROUND.
FAULTY SOLENOID CONNECTION OR SOLENOID.
LIGHT "ON" ONE
LIGHT "ON" BOTH
NO LIGHT
YES
NO
YES
NO
OPEN CKT 428 OR FAULTY ECM.
REPAIR SHORT TO VOLTAGE IN CKT 428.
OPEN CKT 250.
NO PROBLEM FOUND.
SEE "DIAGNOSTIC AIDS" ON FACING PAGE.
CKT 428 SHORTED TO GROUND OR FAULTY ECM.
CHECK HOSES. IF OK, REPLACE PURGE SOLENOID.
CLEAR CODES AND CONFIRM "CLOSED LOOP" OPERATION AND NO "SERVICE ENGINE SOON" LIGHT.

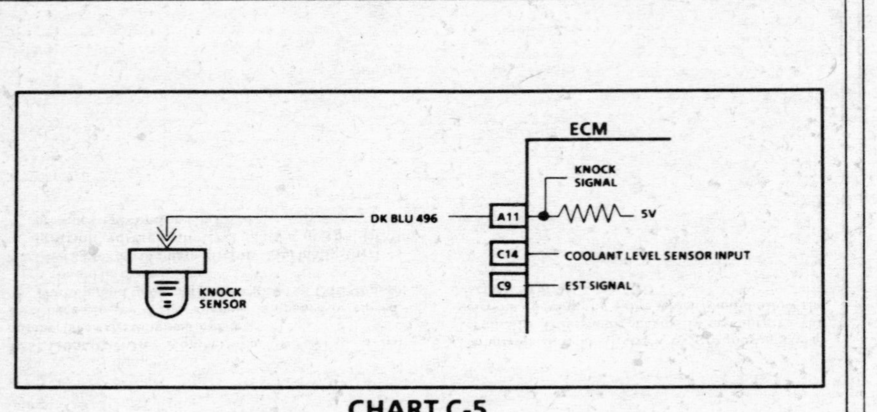
ECM
KNOCK SIGNAL
5V
DK BLU 496
A11
C14
COOLANT LEVEL SENSOR INPUT
C9
EST SIGNAL
KNOCK SENSOR

CHART C-5
ELECTRONIC SPARK CONTROL (ESC) SYSTEM CHECK 3.4L (LQ1) "W" CARLINE (PORT)

Circuit Description:

The knock sensor is used to detect engine detonation and the ECM will retard the electronic spark timing based on the signal being received. The circuitry, within the knock sensor, causes the ECM's 5 volts to be pulled down so that under a no knock condition, CKT 496 would measure about 2.5 volts. The knock sensor produces an AC signal which rides on the 2.5 volts DC voltage. The amplitude and frequency are dependent upon the knock level.

The MEM-CAL used with this engine, contains the functions which were part of remotely mounted ESC modules used on other GM vehicles. The ESC portion of the MEM-CAL, then sends a signal to other parts of the ECM which adjusts the spark timing to retard the spark and reduce the detonation.

Test Description: Number(s) below refer to circled number(s) on the diagnostic chart.

1. With engine idling, there should not be a knock signal present at the ECM, because detonation is not likely under a no load condition.
2. Tapping on the engine lift hood bracket should simulate a knock signal to determine if the sensor is capable of detecting detonation. If no knock is detected, try tapping on engine block closer to sensor before replacing sensor.
3. If the engine has an internal problem which is creating a knock, the knock sensor may be responding to the internal failure.
4. This test determines if the knock sensor is faulty or if the ESC portion of the MEM-CAL is faulty. If it is determined that the MEM-CAL is faulty, be sure that it is properly installed and latched into place. If not properly installed, repair and retest.

Diagnostic Aids:

While observing knock signal on the "Scan," there should be an indication that knock is present when detonation can be heard. Detonation is most likely to occur under high engine load conditions.

CHART C-5
ELECTRONIC SPARK CONTROL (ESC) SYSTEM CHECK 3.4L (LQ1) "W" CARLINE (PORT)

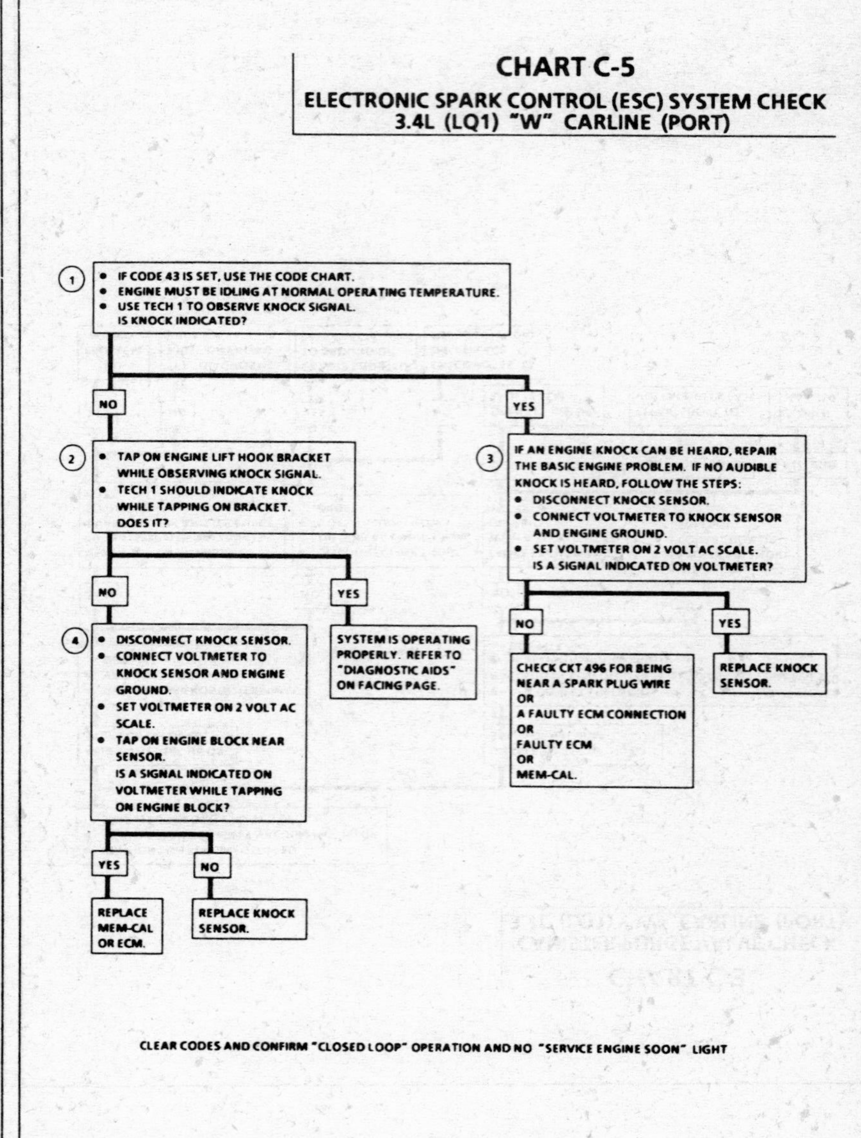
1
• IF CODE 43 IS SET, USE THE CODE CHART.
• ENGINE MUST BE IDLING AT NORMAL OPERATING TEMPERATURE.
• USE TECH 1 TO OBSERVE KNOCK SIGNAL.
IS KNOCK INDICATED?
NO
YES
2
• TAP ON ENGINE LIFT HOOK BRACKET WHILE OBSERVING KNOCK SIGNAL.
• TECH 1 SHOULD INDICATE KNOCK WHILE TAPPING ON BRACKET.
DOES IT?
3
IF AN ENGINE KNOCK CAN BE HEARD, REPAIR THE BASIC ENGINE PROBLEM. IF NO AUDIBLE KNOCK IS HEARD, FOLLOW THE STEPS:
• DISCONNECT KNOCK SENSOR.
• CONNECT VOLTMETER TO KNOCK SENSOR AND ENGINE GROUND.
• SET VOLTMETER ON 2 VOLT AC SCALE.
IS A SIGNAL INDICATED ON VOLTMETER?
NO
YES
4
• DISCONNECT KNOCK SENSOR.
• CONNECT VOLTMETER TO KNOCK SENSOR AND ENGINE GROUND.
• SET VOLTMETER ON 2 VOLT AC SCALE.
• TAP ON ENGINE BLOCK NEAR SENSOR.
IS A SIGNAL INDICATED ON VOLTMETER WHILE TAPPING ON ENGINE BLOCK?
SYSTEM IS OPERATING PROPERLY. REFER TO "DIAGNOSTIC AIDS" ON FACING PAGE.
NO
YES
CHECK CKT 496 FOR BEING NEAR A SPARK PLUG WIRE OR A FAULTY ECM CONNECTION OR FAULTY ECM OR MEM-CAL.
REPLACE KNOCK SENSOR.
YES
NO
REPLACE MEM-CAL OR ECM.
REPLACE KNOCK SENSOR.
CLEAR CODES AND CONFIRM "CLOSED LOOP" OPERATION AND NO "SERVICE ENGINE SOON" LIGHT

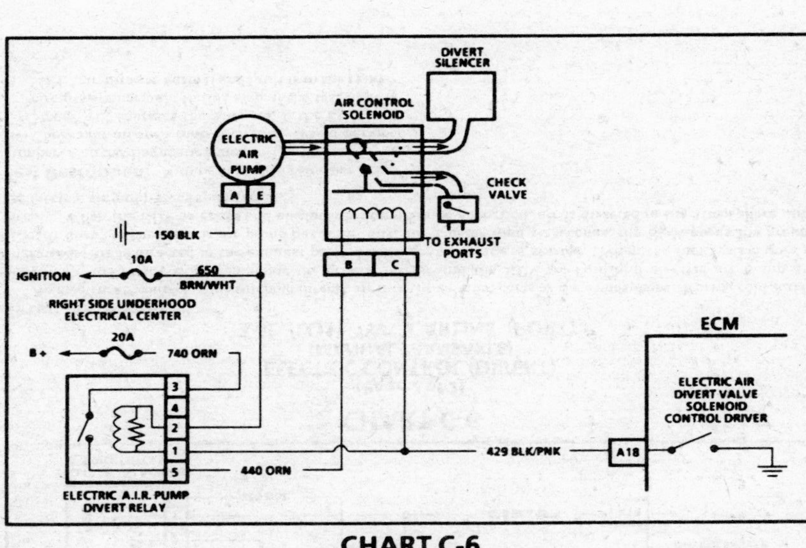

CHART C-6

(Page 1 of 2)
ELECTRIC CONTROL (DIVERT)
(MANUAL TRANSAXLE)
3.4L (LQ1) "W" CARLINE (PORT)

Circuit Description:

This system uses a single bed converter and air management is controlled by an air control valve (divert valve).

When grounded by the ECM, the solenoid causes the valve to direct air to the exhaust ports. When de-energized air diverts to the atmosphere. Air will go to the ports provided the valve has a ground to the ECM and good manifold vacuum

Test Description: Number(s) below refer to circled number(s) on the diagnostic chart.

1. This is a system performance test. When vehicle goes to "Closed Loop," air will switch from the ports to divert.
2. Tests for a grounded electric divert circuit. Normal system light will be "OFF."
3. Checks for an open control circuit. Grounding "test" terminal will energize the solenoid if ECM and circuits are normal. In this step, if test light is "ON," circuits are normal and faulty is in valve connections or valve.
4. Checks for an open control circuit, "Field Service Mode" will energize the solenoid, if the ECM and circuits are normal. In this step, if the test light is "ON," circuits are normal and fault is in the valve.

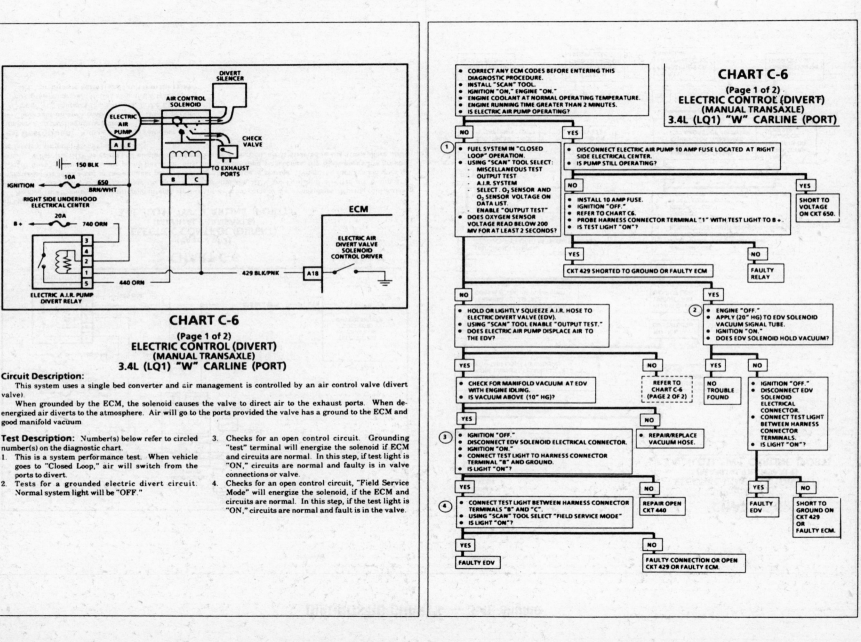

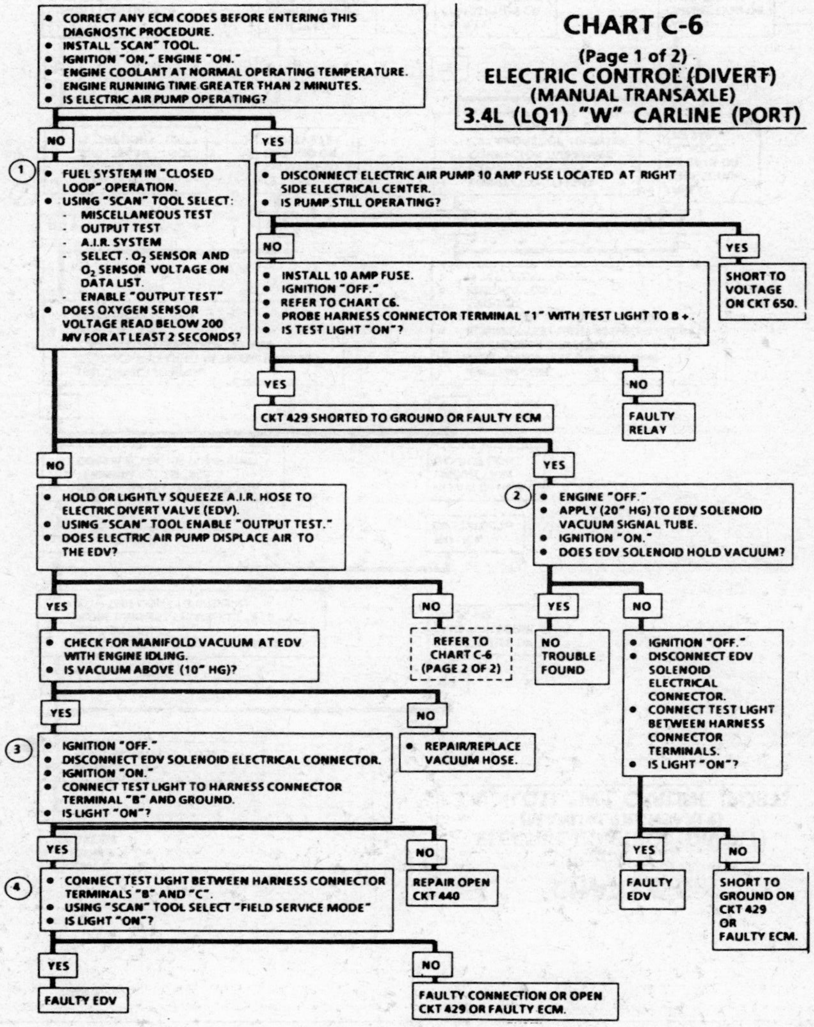

CHART C-6

(Page 1 of 2)
ELECTRIC CONTROL (DIVERT)
(MANUAL TRANSAXLE)
3.4L (LQ1) "W" CARLINE (PORT)

- CORRECT ANY ECM CODES BEFORE ENTERING THIS DIAGNOSTIC PROCEDURE.
- INSTALL "SCAN" TOOL.
- IGNITION "ON," ENGINE "ON."
- ENGINE COOLANT AT NORMAL OPERATING TEMPERATURE.
- ENGINE RUNNING TIME GREATER THAN 2 MINUTES.
- IS ELECTRIC AIR PUMP OPERATING?

YES:

- DISCONNECT ELECTRIC AIR PUMP 10 AMP FUSE LOCATED AT RIGHT SIDE ELECTRICAL CENTER.
- IS PUMP STILL OPERATING?

YES: SHORT TO VOLTAGE ON CKT 650.

NO:

- INSTALL 10 AMP FUSE.
- IGNITION "OFF."
- REFER TO CHART C6.
- PROBE HARNESS CONNECTOR TERMINAL "1" WITH TEST LIGHT TO B+.
- IS TEST LIGHT "ON"?

YES: CKT 429 SHORTED TO GROUND OR FAULTY ECM

NO: FAULTY RELAY

NO:

(1)
- FUEL SYSTEM IN "CLOSED LOOP" OPERATION.
- USING "SCAN" TOOL SELECT:
  - MISCELLANEOUS TEST
  - OUTPUT TEST
  - A.I.R. SYSTEM
  - SELECT O_2 SENSOR AND O_2 SENSOR VOLTAGE ON DATA LIST.
  - ENABLE "OUTPUT TEST"
- DOES OXYGEN SENSOR VOLTAGE READ BELOW 200 MV FOR AT LEAST 2 SECONDS?

YES:

(2)
- ENGINE "OFF."
- APPLY (20" HG) TO EDV SOLENOID VACUUM SIGNAL TUBE.
- IGNITION "ON."
- DOES EDV SOLENOID HOLD VACUUM?

YES: NO TROUBLE FOUND

NO:

- IGNITION "OFF."
- DISCONNECT EDV SOLENOID ELECTRICAL CONNECTOR.
- CONNECT TEST LIGHT BETWEEN HARNESS CONNECTOR TERMINALS.
- IS LIGHT "ON"?

YES: FAULTY EDV

NO: SHORT TO GROUND ON CKT 429 OR FAULTY ECM.

NO:

- HOLD OR LIGHTLY SQUEEZE A.I.R. HOSE TO ELECTRIC DIVERT VALVE (EDV).
- USING "SCAN" TOOL ENABLE "OUTPUT TEST."
- DOES ELECTRIC AIR PUMP DISPLACE AIR TO THE EDV?

NO: REFER TO CHART C-6 (PAGE 2 OF 2)

YES:

- CHECK FOR MANIFOLD VACUUM AT EDV WITH ENGINE IDLING.
- IS VACUUM ABOVE (10" HG)?

NO:
- REPAIR/REPLACE VACUUM HOSE.

YES:

(3)
- IGNITION "OFF."
- DISCONNECT EDV SOLENOID ELECTRICAL CONNECTOR.
- IGNITION "ON."
- CONNECT TEST LIGHT TO HARNESS CONNECTOR TERMINAL "B" AND GROUND.
- IS LIGHT "ON"?

NO: REPAIR OPEN CKT 440

YES:

(4)
- CONNECT TEST LIGHT BETWEEN HARNESS CONNECTOR TERMINALS "B" AND "C".
- USING "SCAN" TOOL SELECT "FIELD SERVICE MODE"
- IS LIGHT "ON"?

YES: FAULTY EDV

NO: FAULTY CONNECTION OR OPEN CKT 429 OR FAULTY ECM.

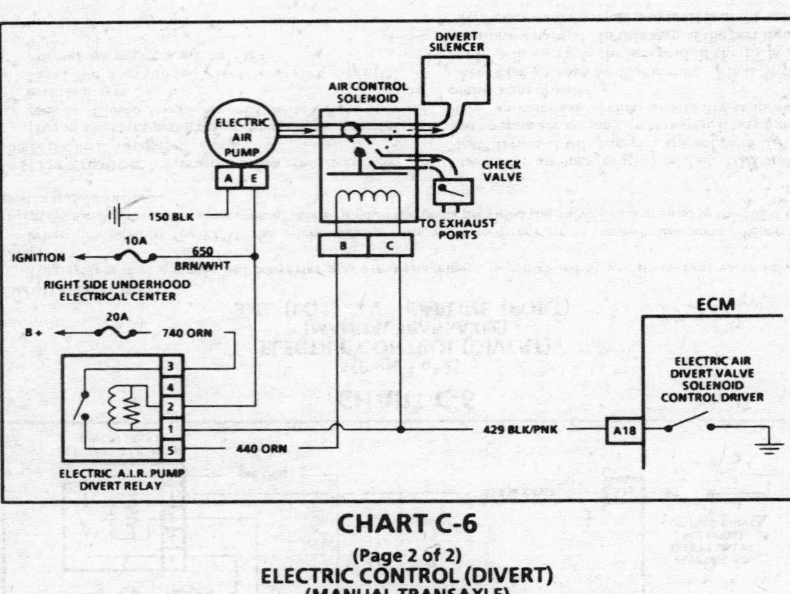
DIVERT SILENCER
AIR CONTROL SOLENOID
ELECTRIC AIR PUMP
A E
CHECK VALVE
TO EXHAUST PORTS
B C
150 BLK
10A
650
BRN/WHT
IGNITION
RIGHT SIDE UNDERHOOD ELECTRICAL CENTER
20A
B+
740 ORN
3
4
2
1
5
440 ORN
429 BLK/PNK
A18
ECM
ELECTRIC AIR DIVERT VALVE SOLENOID CONTROL DRIVER
ELECTRIC A.I.R. PUMP DIVERT RELAY

CHART C-6

(Page 2 of 2)

ELECTRIC CONTROL (DIVERT)

(MANUAL TRANSAXLE)

3.4L (LQ1) "W" CARLINE (PORT)

Circuit Description:

An electric air control valve solenoid directs air into the exhaust ports or the atmosphere. During cold starts, above 15°C (59°F) the ECM completes the ground circuit and the EDV solenoid and electric air pump are energized. Air is directed to the exhaust ports whenever the engine is started. When the fuel system goes to "Closed Loop" or the electric air pump has been "ON" for greater than 80 seconds, the ECM opens the ground circuit. When the EDV solenoid and electric air pump are de-energized, air is directed to the atmosphere until the electric air pump stops spinning.

Test Description: Number(s) below refer to circled number(s) on the diagnostic chart.

1. Checks for an open control circuit. "Field Service Mode" will energize the solenoid, if the ECM and circuits are normal. In this step, if the test light is "ON," circuits are normal and fault is in the relay.

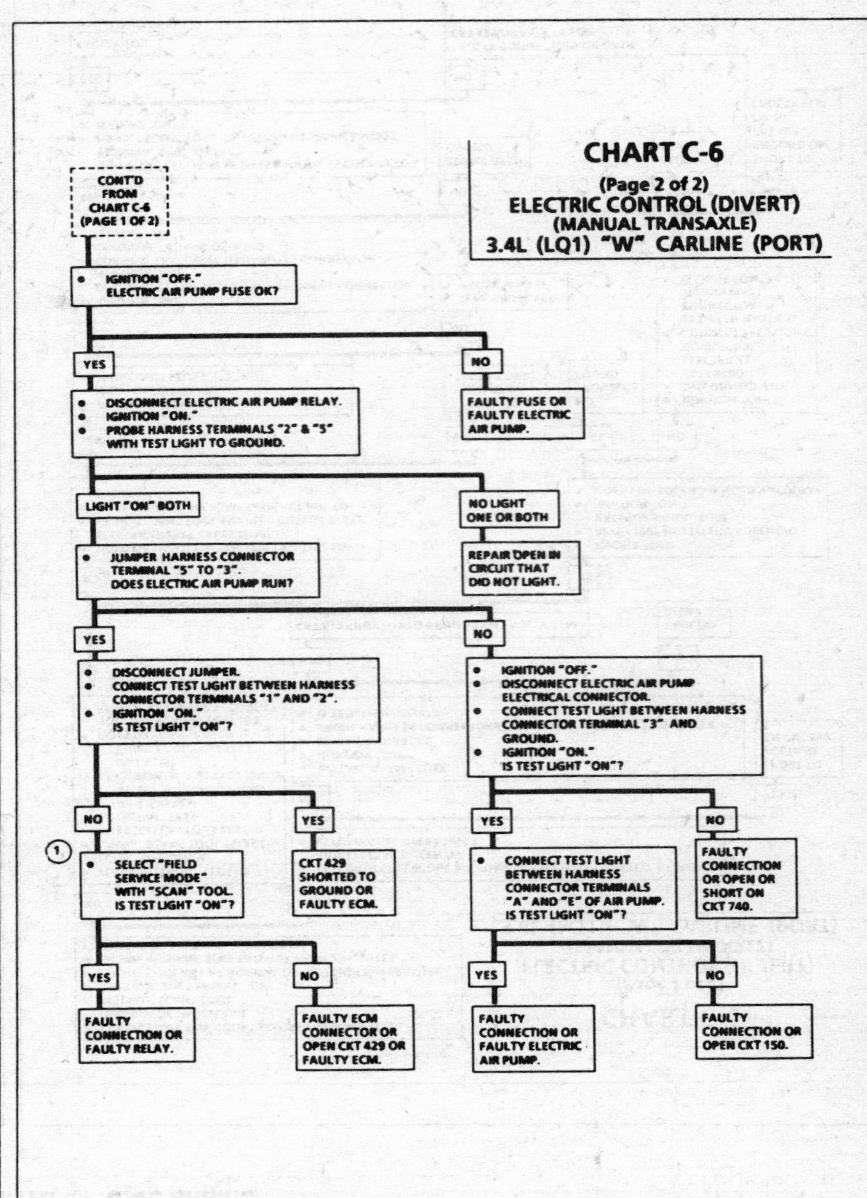
CHART C-6
(Page 2 of 2)
ELECTRIC CONTROL (DIVERT)
(MANUAL TRANSAXLE)
3.4L (LQ1) "W" CARLINE (PORT)
CONT'D FROM CHART C-6 (PAGE 1 OF 2)
• IGNITION "OFF."
ELECTRIC AIR PUMP FUSE OK?
YES
NO
FAULTY FUSE OR FAULTY ELECTRIC AIR PUMP.
• DISCONNECT ELECTRIC AIR PUMP RELAY.
• IGNITION "ON."
• PROBE HARNESS TERMINALS "2" & "5" WITH TEST LIGHT TO GROUND.
LIGHT "ON" BOTH
NO LIGHT ONE OR BOTH
REPAIR OPEN IN CIRCUIT THAT DID NOT LIGHT.
• JUMPER HARNESS CONNECTOR TERMINAL "5" TO "3".
DOES ELECTRIC AIR PUMP RUN?
YES
NO
• DISCONNECT JUMPER.
• CONNECT TEST LIGHT BETWEEN HARNESS CONNECTOR TERMINALS "1" AND "2".
• IGNITION "ON."
IS TEST LIGHT "ON"?
• IGNITION "OFF."
• DISCONNECT ELECTRIC AIR PUMP ELECTRICAL CONNECTOR.
• CONNECT TEST LIGHT BETWEEN HARNESS CONNECTOR TERMINAL "3" AND GROUND.
• IGNITION "ON."
IS TEST LIGHT "ON"?
NO
YES
YES
NO
1
• SELECT "FIELD SERVICE MODE" WITH "SCAN" TOOL.
IS TEST LIGHT "ON"?
CKT 429 SHORTED TO GROUND OR FAULTY ECM.
• CONNECT TEST LIGHT BETWEEN HARNESS CONNECTOR TERMINALS "A" AND "E" OF AIR PUMP.
IS TEST LIGHT "ON"?
FAULTY CONNECTION OR OPEN OR SHORT ON CKT 740.
YES
NO
YES
NO
FAULTY CONNECTION OR FAULTY RELAY.
FAULTY ECM CONNECTOR OR OPEN CKT 429 OR FAULTY ECM.
FAULTY CONNECTION OR FAULTY ELECTRIC AIR PUMP.
FAULTY CONNECTION OR OPEN CKT 150.

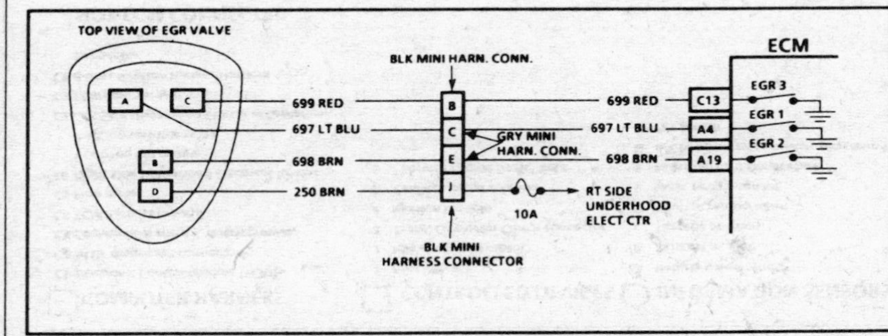

CHART C-7

EXHAUST GAS RECIRCULATION (EGR) FLOW CHECK 3.4L (LQ1) "W" CARLINE (PORT)

Circuit Description:

The digital (EGR) valve is designed to accurately supply EGR to an engine independent of intake manifold vacuum. The valve controls EGR flow from the exhaust to the intake manifold through three orifices which increment in size to produce seven combinations. When a solenoid is energized, the armature with attached shaft and swivel pintle is lifted opening the orifice.

The flow accuracy is dependent on metering orifice size only, which results in improved control.

Test Description: Number(s) below refer to circled number(s) on the diagnostic chart.

1. Codes should be diagnoses using appropriate chart before preparing a functional check.
2. This step activates each solenoid individually. As you energize #1 or #2 solenoid, the engine rpm should drop. #3 solenoid has the large port and may stall the engine when energized.

NOTE: If the digital EGR valve shows signs of excessive heat, a melted condition. Check the exhaust system for blockage (possibly a plugged converter) using the procedure found on CHART B1. If the exhaust system is restricted repair the cause, one of which might be an injector which is open due to one of the following:

a. stuck
b. grounded driver circuit
c. possibly defective ECM

If this condition is found, the oil should be checked for possible fuel contamination.

CHART C-7

EXHAUST GAS RECIRCULATION (EGR) FLOW CHECK 3.4L (LQ1) "W" CARLINE (PORT)

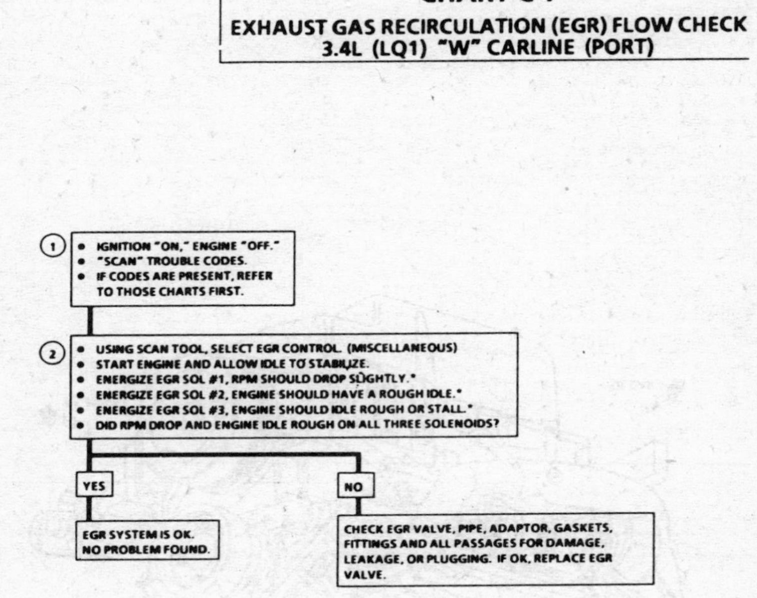

1
• IGNITION "ON," ENGINE "OFF."
• "SCAN" TROUBLE CODES.
• IF CODES ARE PRESENT, REFER TO THOSE CHARTS FIRST.
2
• USING SCAN TOOL, SELECT EGR CONTROL. (MISCELLANEOUS)
• START ENGINE AND ALLOW IDLE TO STABILIZE.
• ENERGIZE EGR SOL #1, RPM SHOULD DROP SLIGHTLY.*
• ENERGIZE EGR SOL #2, ENGINE SHOULD HAVE A ROUGH IDLE.*
• ENERGIZE EGR SOL #3, ENGINE SHOULD IDLE ROUGH OR STALL.*
• DID RPM DROP AND ENGINE IDLE ROUGH ON ALL THREE SOLENOIDS?
YES
NO
EGR SYSTEM IS OK. NO PROBLEM FOUND.
CHECK EGR VALVE, PIPE, ADAPTOR, GASKETS, FITTINGS AND ALL PASSAGES FOR DAMAGE, LEAKAGE, OR PLUGGING. IF OK, REPLACE EGR VALVE.
* THESE STEPS MUST BE DONE VERY QUICKLY, AS THE ECM WILL ADJUST THE IDLE AIR CONTROL VALVE TO CORRECT IDLE SPEED.

"AFTER REPAIRS," CONFIRM "CLOSED LOOP" OPERATION AND NO "SERVICE ENGINE SOON" LIGHT.

DIAGNOSTIC CHARTS — 3.8L engine

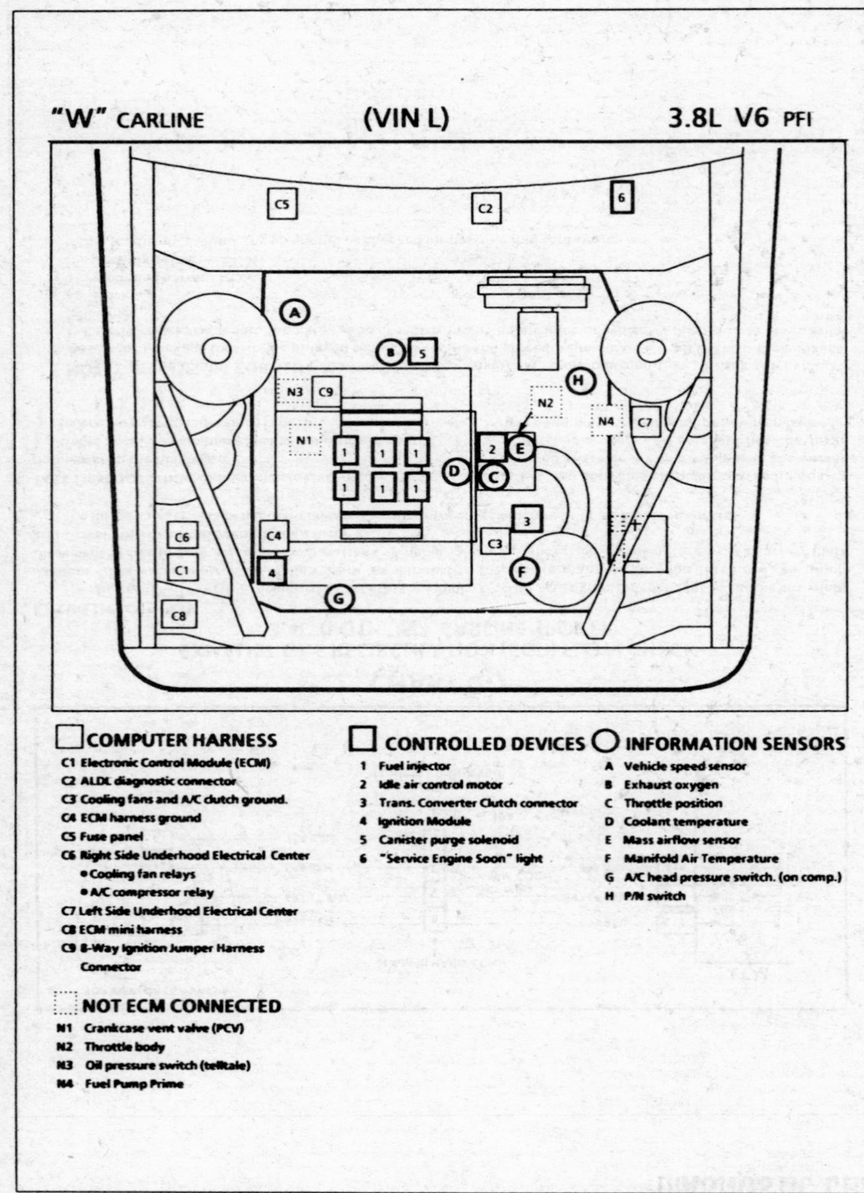
"W" CARLINE
(VIN L)
3.8L V6 PFI
COMPUTER HARNESS
C1 Electronic Control Module (ECM)
C2 ALDL diagnostic connector
C3 Cooling fans and A/C clutch ground.
C4 ECM harness ground
C5 Fuse panel
C6 Right Side Underhood Electrical Center
• Cooling fan relays
• A/C compressor relay
C7 Left Side Underhood Electrical Center
C8 ECM mini harness
C9 8-Way Ignition Jumper Harness Connector
NOT ECM CONNECTED
N1 Crankcase vent valve (PCV)
N2 Throttle body
N3 Oil pressure switch (telltale)
N4 Fuel Pump Prime
CONTROLLED DEVICES
1 Fuel injector
2 Idle air control motor
3 Trans. Converter Clutch connector
4 Ignition Module
5 Canister purge solenoid
6 "Service Engine Soon" light
INFORMATION SENSORS
A Vehicle speed sensor
B Exhaust oxygen
C Throttle position
D Coolant temperature
E Mass airflow sensor
F Manifold Air Temperature
G A/C head pressure switch. (on comp.)
H P/N switch

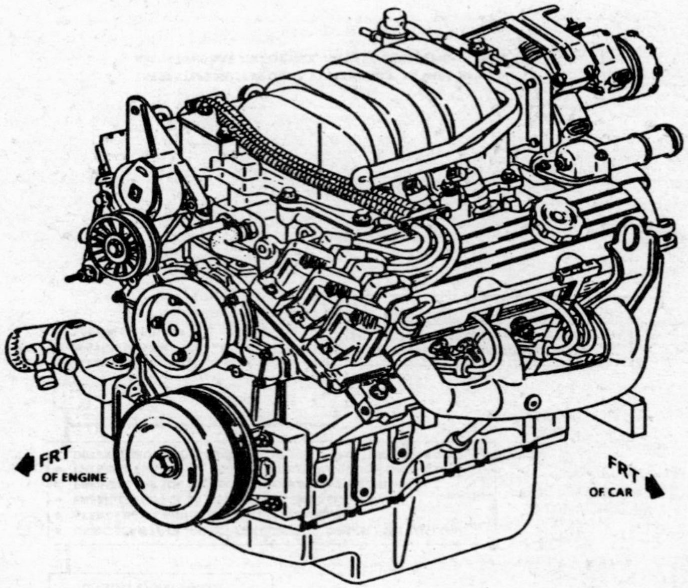

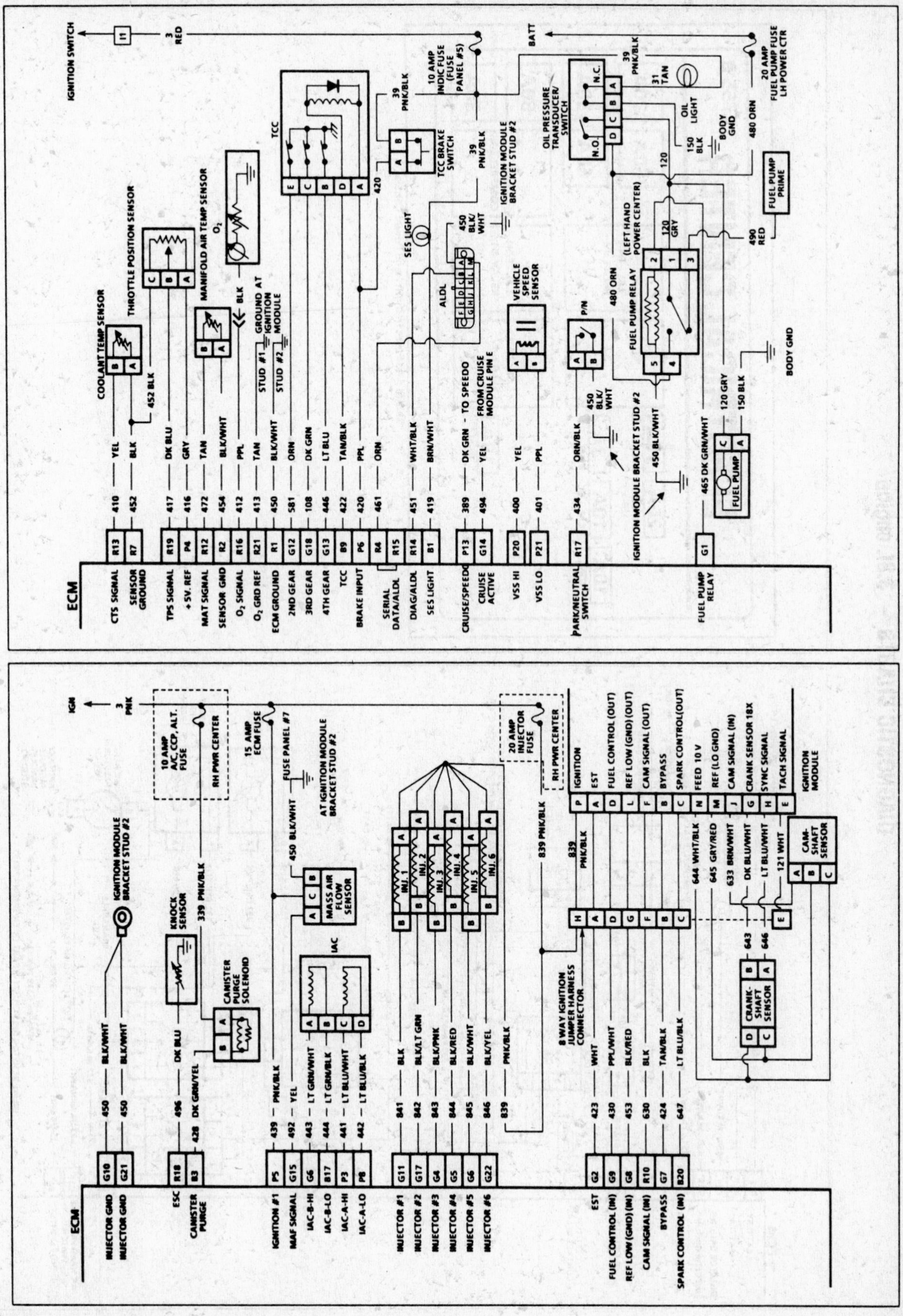

DIAGNOSTIC CHARTS — 3.8L engine

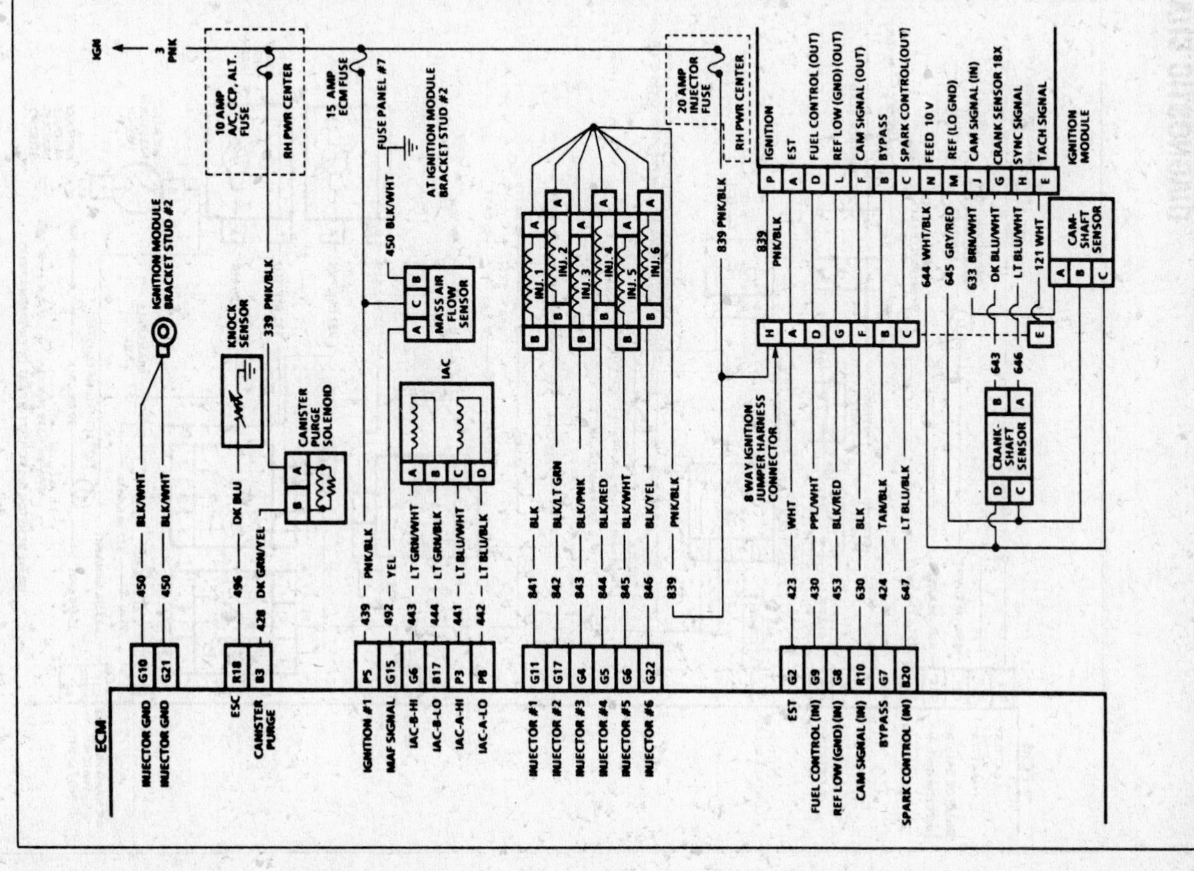

DIAGNOSTIC CHARTS — 3.8L engine

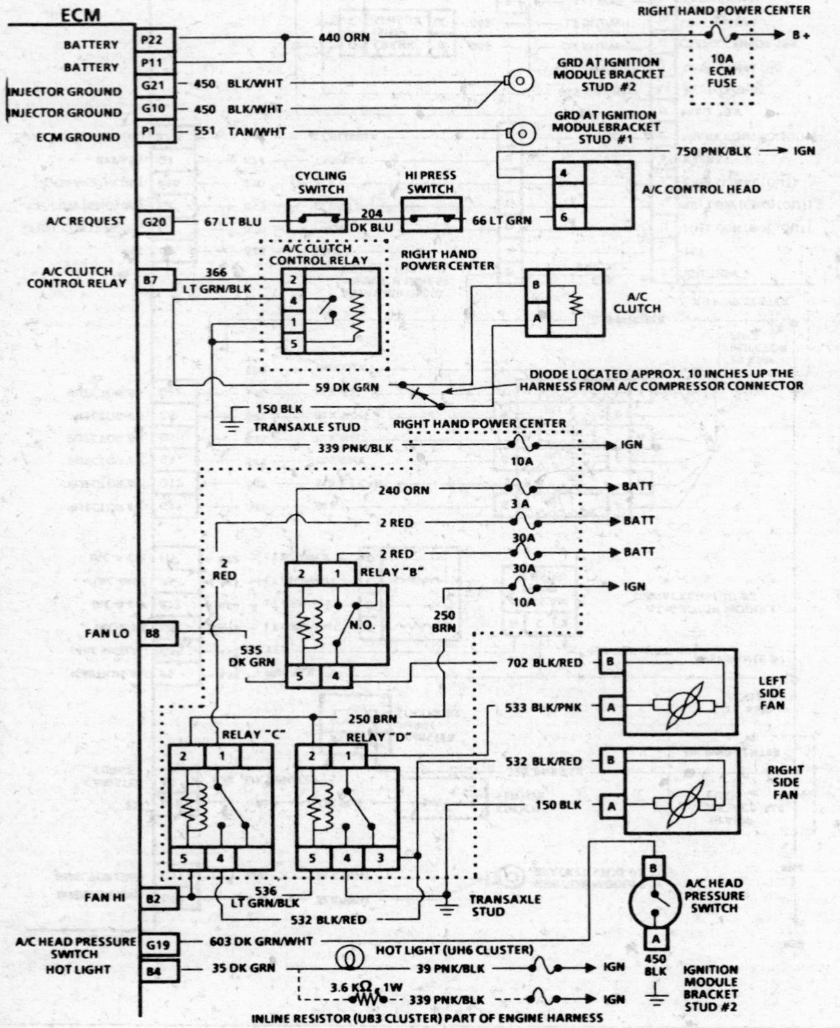

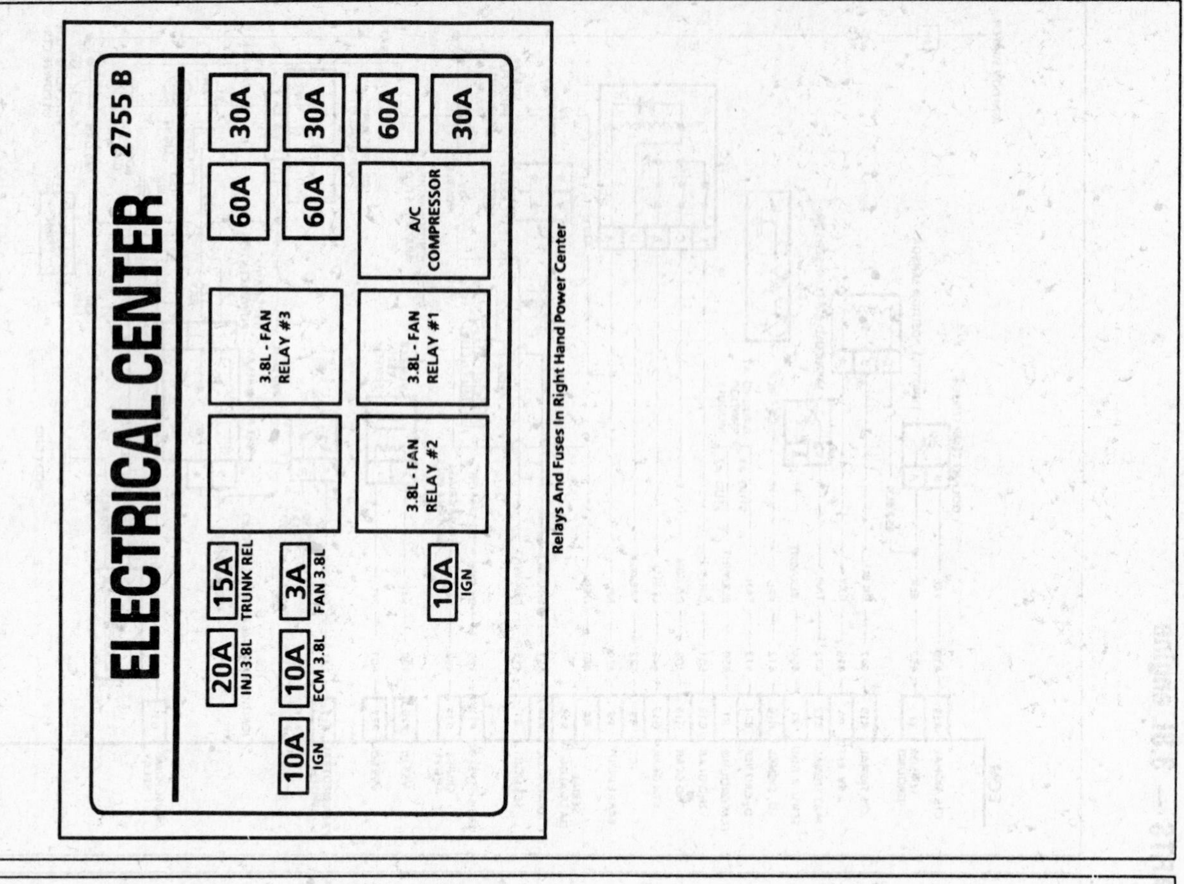

Relays And Fuses In Right Hand Power Center

ECM
BATTERY — P22 — 440 ORN
BATTERY — P11 — 450 BLK/WHT
INJECTOR GROUND — G21 — 450 BLK/WHT
INJECTOR GROUND — G10 — 551 TAN/WHT
ECM GROUND — P1
A/C REQUEST — G20 — 67 LT BLU
A/C CLUTCH CONTROL RELAY — B7 — 366 LT GRN/BLK
FAN LO — B8
FAN HI — B2
A/C HEAD PRESSURE SWITCH — G19 — 603 DK GRN/WHT
HOT LIGHT — B4 — 35 DK GRN

RIGHT HAND POWER CENTER
10A ECM FUSE
B+
GRD AT IGNITION MODULE BRACKET STUD #2
GRD AT IGNITION MODULEBRACKET STUD #1
750 PNK/BLK — IGN
A/C CONTROL HEAD
CYCLING SWITCH
204 DK BLU
HI PRESS SWITCH
66 LT GRN
A/C CLUTCH CONTROL RELAY
RIGHT HAND POWER CENTER
A/C CLUTCH
59 DK GRN
150 BLK
TRANSAXLE STUD
339 PNK/BLK
DIODE LOCATED APPROX. 10 INCHES UP THE HARNESS FROM A/C COMPRESSOR CONNECTOR
RIGHT HAND POWER CENTER
10A — IGN
240 ORN — 3A — BATT
2 RED — 30A — BATT
2 RED — 30A — BATT
10A — IGN
RELAY "B"
N.O.
250 BRN
702 BLK/RED
533 BLK/PNK
532 BLK/RED
150 BLK
535 DK GRN
250 BRN
RELAY "D"
2 RED
RELAY "C"
536 LT GRN/BLK
532 BLK/RED
TRANSAXLE STUD
LEFT SIDE FAN
RIGHT SIDE FAN
A/C HEAD PRESSURE SWITCH
450 BLK
IGNITION MODULE BRACKET STUD #2
HOT LIGHT (UH6 CLUSTER)
39 PNK/BLK — IGN
3.6 KΩ 1W — 339 PNK/BLK — IGN
INLINE RESISTOR (UB3 CLUSTER) PART OF ENGINE HARNESS

DIAGNOSTIC CHARTS — 3.8L engine

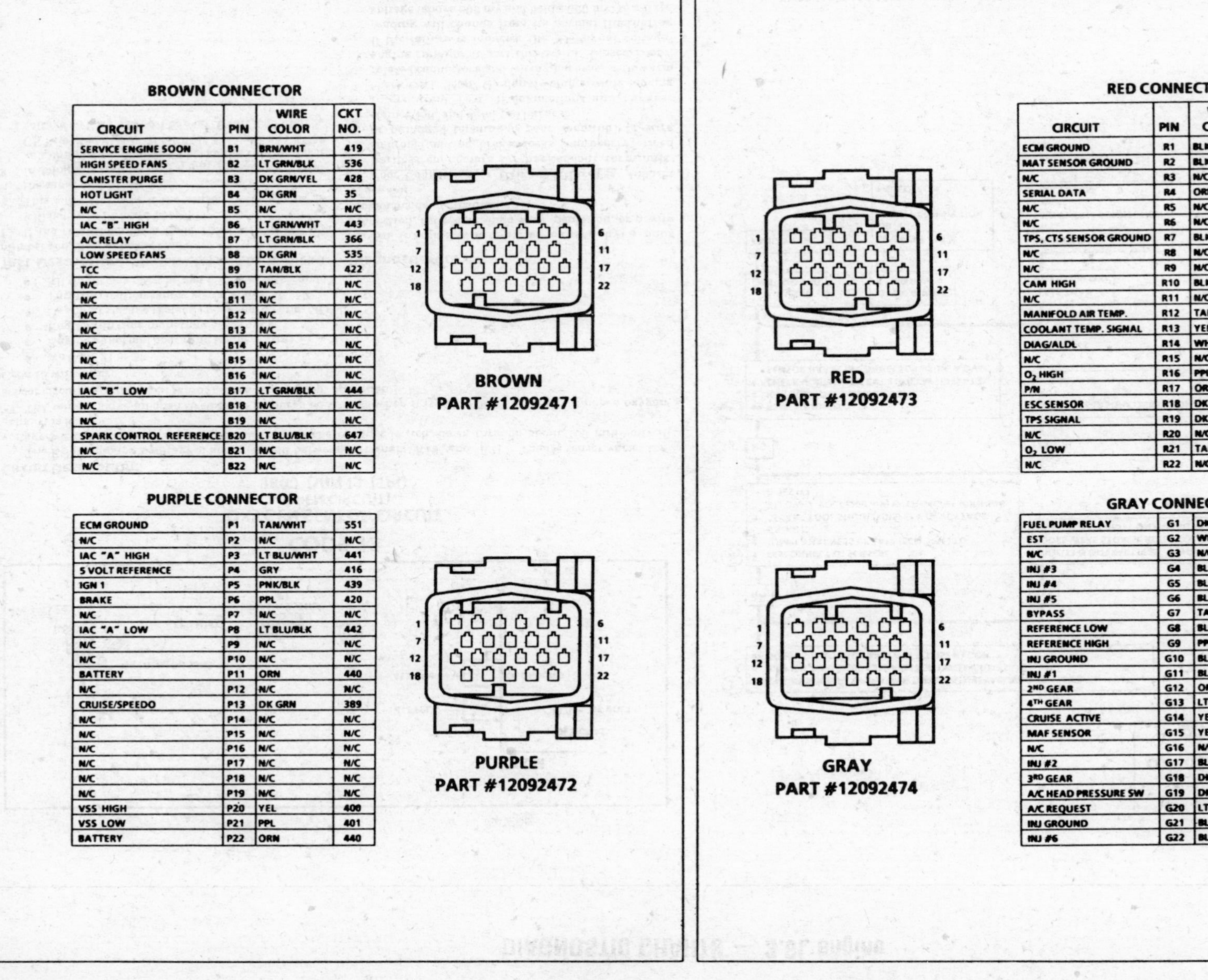

BROWN
PART #12092471

PURPLE
PART #12092472

RED
PART #12092473

GRAY
PART #12092474

BROWN CONNECTOR

CIRCUIT	PIN	WIRE COLOR	CKT NO.
SERVICE ENGINE SOON	B1	BRN/WHT	419
HIGH SPEED FANS	B2	LT GRN/BLK	536
CANISTER PURGE	B3	DK GRN/YEL	428
HOT LIGHT	B4	DK GRN	35
N/C	B5	N/C	N/C
IAC "B" HIGH	B6	LT GRN/WHT	443
A/C RELAY	B7	LT GRN/BLK	366
LOW SPEED FANS	B8	DK GRN	535
TCC	B9	TAN/BLK	422
N/C	B10	N/C	N/C
N/C	B11	N/C	N/C
N/C	B12	N/C	N/C
N/C	B13	N/C	N/C
N/C	B14	N/C	N/C
N/C	B15	N/C	N/C
N/C	B16	N/C	N/C
IAC "B" LOW	B17	LT GRN/BLK	444
N/C	B18	N/C	N/C
N/C	B19	N/C	N/C
SPARK CONTROL REFERENCE	B20	LT BLU/BLK	647
N/C	B21	N/C	N/C
N/C	B22	N/C	N/C

PURPLE CONNECTOR

CIRCUIT	PIN	WIRE COLOR	CKT NO.
ECM GROUND	P1	TAN/WHT	551
N/C	P2	N/C	N/C
IAC "A" HIGH	P3	LT BLU/WHT	441
5 VOLT REFERENCE	P4	GRY	416
IGN 1	P5	PNK/BLK	439
BRAKE	P6	PPL	420
N/C	P7	N/C	N/C
IAC "A" LOW	P8	LT BLU/BLK	442
N/C	P9	N/C	N/C
N/C	P10	N/C	N/C
BATTERY	P11	ORN	440
N/C	P12	N/C	N/C
CRUISE/SPEEDO	P13	DK GRN	389
N/C	P14	N/C	N/C
N/C	P15	N/C	N/C
N/C	P16	N/C	N/C
N/C	P17	N/C	N/C
N/C	P18	N/C	N/C
N/C	P19	N/C	N/C
VSS HIGH	P20	YEL	400
VSS LOW	P21	PPL	401
BATTERY	P22	ORN	440

RED CONNECTOR

CIRCUIT	PIN	WIRE COLOR	CKT NO
ECM GROUND	R1	BLK/WHT	450
MAT SENSOR GROUND	R2	BLK/WHT	454
N/C	R3	N/C	N/C
SERIAL DATA	R4	ORN	461
N/C	R5	N/C	N/C
N/C	R6	N/C	N/C
TPS, CTS SENSOR GROUND	R7	BLK	452
N/C	R8	N/C	N/C
N/C	R9	N/C	N/C
CAM HIGH	R10	BLK	630
N/C	R11	N/C	N/C
MANIFOLD AIR TEMP.	R12	TAN	472
COOLANT TEMP. SIGNAL	R13	YEL	410
DIAG/ALDL	R14	WHT/BLK	451
N/C	R15	N/C	N/C
O_2 HIGH	R16	PPL	412
P/N	R17	ORN/BLK	434
ESC SENSOR	R18	DK BLU	496
TPS SIGNAL	R19	DK BLU	417
N/C	R20	N/C	N/C
O_2 LOW	R21	TAN	413
N/C	R22	N/C	N/C

GRAY CONNECTOR

CIRCUIT	PIN	WIRE COLOR	CKT NO
FUEL PUMP RELAY	G1	DK GRN/WHT	465
EST	G2	WHT	423
N/C	G3	N/C	N/C
INJ #3	G4	BLK/PNK	843
INJ #4	G5	BLK/RED	844
INJ #5	G6	BLK/WHT	845
BYPASS	G7	TAN/BLK	424
REFERENCE LOW	G8	BLK/RED	453
REFERENCE HIGH	G9	PPL/WHT	430
INJ GROUND	G10	BLK/WHT	450
INJ #1	G11	BLK	841
2ND GEAR	G12	ORN	581
4TH GEAR	G13	LT BLU	446
CRUISE ACTIVE	G14	YEL	494
MAF SENSOR	G15	YEL	492
N/C	G16	N/C	N/C
INJ #2	G17	BLK/LT GRN	842
3RD GEAR	G18	DK GRN	108
A/C HEAD PRESSURE SW	G19	DK GRN/WHT	603
A/C REQUEST	G20	LT BLU	67
INJ GROUND	G21	BLK/WHT	450
INJ #6	G22	BLK/YEL	846

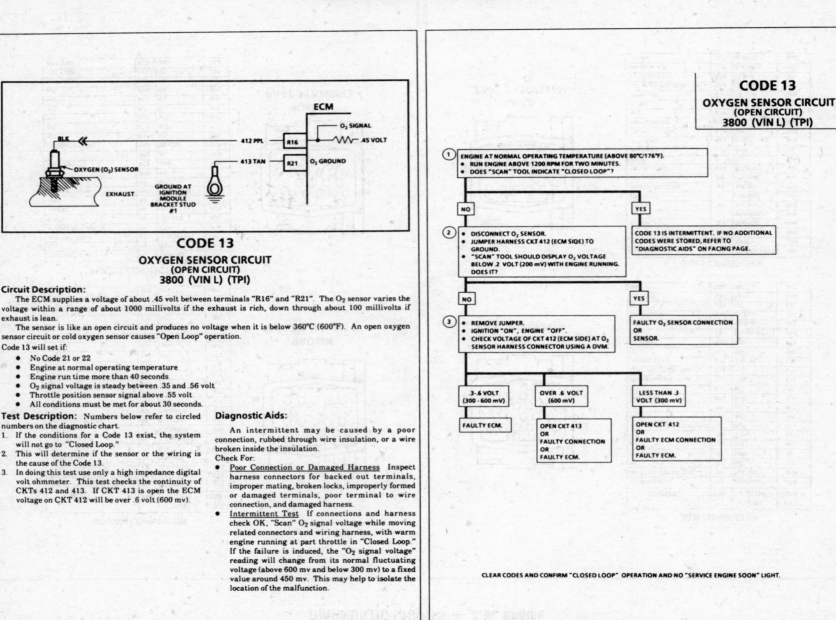

CODE 13

OXYGEN SENSOR CIRCUIT (OPEN CIRCUIT) 3800 (VIN L) (TPI)

Circuit Description:

The ECM supplies a voltage of about .45 volt between terminals "R16" and "R21". The O_2 sensor varies the voltage within a range of about 1000 millivolts if the exhaust is rich, down through about 100 millivolts if exhaust is lean.

The sensor is like an open circuit and produces no voltage when it is below 360°C (600°F). An open oxygen sensor circuit or cold oxygen sensor causes "Open Loop" operation.

Code 13 will set if:

- No Code 21 or 22
- Engine at normal operating temperature
- Engine run time more than 40 seconds
- O_2 signal voltage is steady between .35 and .56 volt
- Throttle position sensor signal above .55 volt
- All conditions must be met for about 30 seconds.

Test Description: Numbers below refer to circled numbers on the diagnostic chart.

1. If the conditions for a Code 13 exist, the system will not go to "Closed Loop."
2. This will determine if the sensor or the wiring is the cause of the Code 13.
3. In doing this test use only a high impedance digital volt ohmmeter. This test checks the continuity of CKTs 412 and 413. If CKT 413 is open the ECM voltage on CKT 412 will be over .6 volt (600 mv).

Diagnostic Aids:

An intermittent may be caused by a poor connection, rubbed through wire insulation, or a wire broken inside the insulation.

Check For:

- Poor Connection or Damaged Harness Inspect harness connectors for backed out terminals, improper mating, broken locks, improperly formed or damaged terminals, poor terminal to wire connection, and damaged harness.
- Intermittent Test If connections and harness check OK, "Scan" O_2 signal voltage while moving related connectors and wiring harness, with warm engine running at part throttle in "Closed Loop." If the failure is induced, the "O_2 signal voltage" reading will change from its normal fluctuating voltage (above 600 mv and below 300 mv) to a fixed value around 450 mv. This may help to isolate the location of the malfunction.

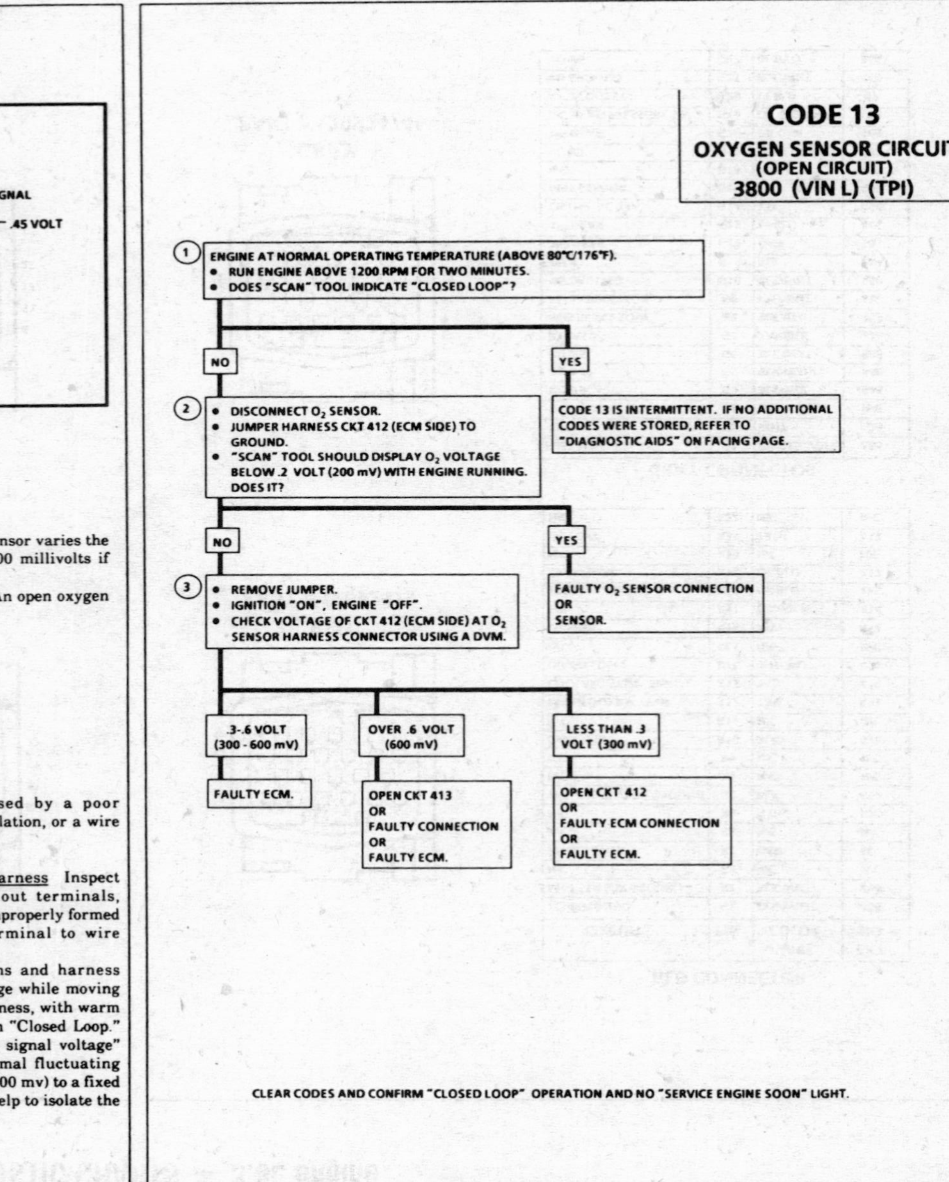

CODE 13
OXYGEN SENSOR CIRCUIT
(OPEN CIRCUIT)
3800 (VIN L) (TPI)
1 ENGINE AT NORMAL OPERATING TEMPERATURE (ABOVE 80°C/176°F).
• RUN ENGINE ABOVE 1200 RPM FOR TWO MINUTES.
• DOES "SCAN" TOOL INDICATE "CLOSED LOOP"?
NO
YES
CODE 13 IS INTERMITTENT. IF NO ADDITIONAL CODES WERE STORED, REFER TO "DIAGNOSTIC AIDS" ON FACING PAGE.
2 • DISCONNECT O2 SENSOR.
• JUMPER HARNESS CKT 412 (ECM SIDE) TO GROUND.
• "SCAN" TOOL SHOULD DISPLAY O2 VOLTAGE BELOW .2 VOLT (200 mV) WITH ENGINE RUNNING. DOES IT?
NO
YES
FAULTY O2 SENSOR CONNECTION OR SENSOR.
3 • REMOVE JUMPER.
• IGNITION "ON", ENGINE "OFF".
• CHECK VOLTAGE OF CKT 412 (ECM SIDE) AT O2 SENSOR HARNESS CONNECTOR USING A DVM.
.3-.6 VOLT (300 - 600 mV)
OVER .6 VOLT (600 mV)
LESS THAN .3 VOLT (300 mV)
FAULTY ECM.
OPEN CKT 413 OR FAULTY CONNECTION OR FAULTY ECM.
OPEN CKT 412 OR FAULTY ECM CONNECTION OR FAULTY ECM.
CLEAR CODES AND CONFIRM "CLOSED LOOP" OPERATION AND NO "SERVICE ENGINE SOON" LIGHT.

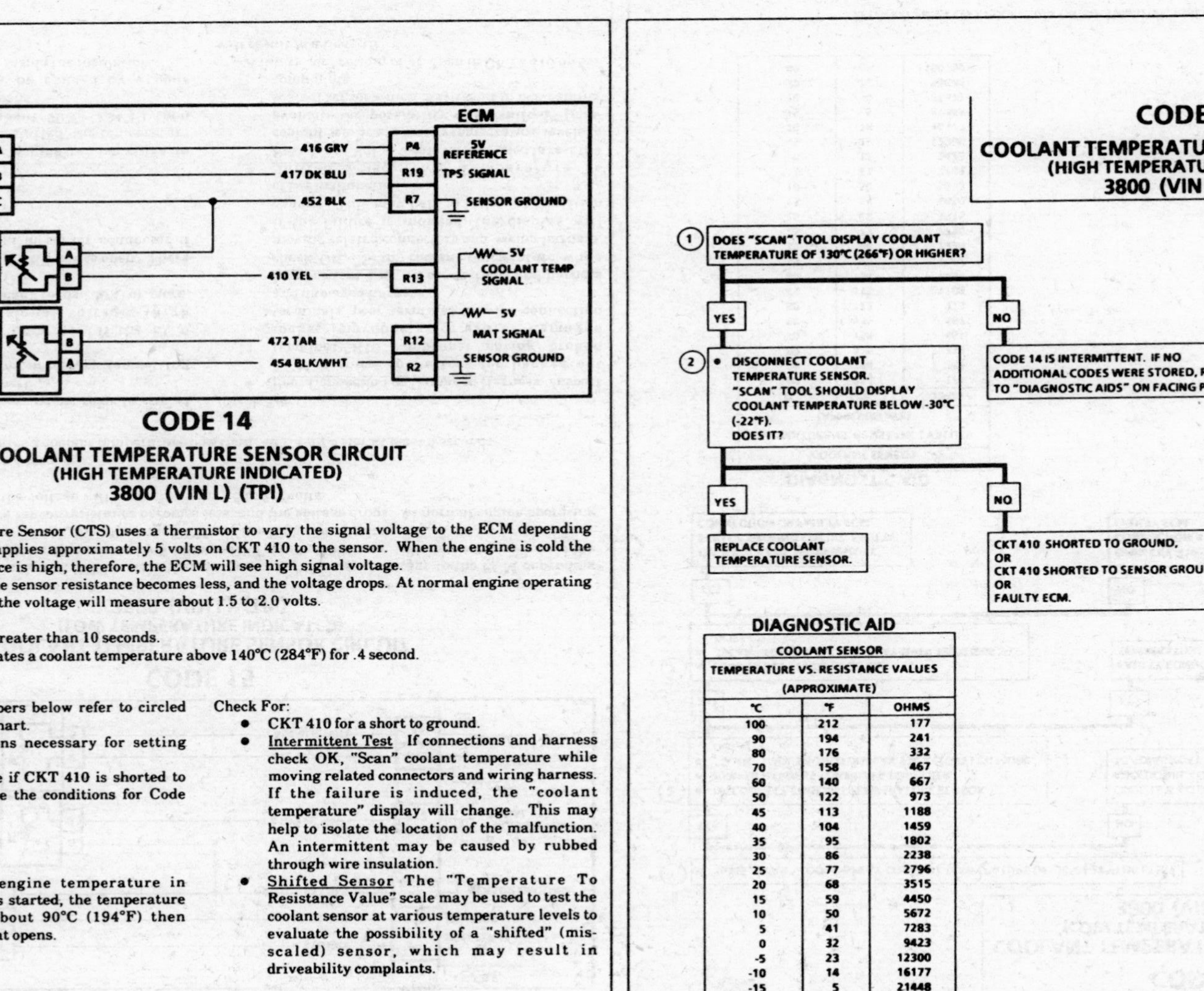
ECM
WOT
THROTTLE POSITION SENSOR
IDLE
A
B
C
416 GRY
417 DK BLU
452 BLK
P4
R19
R7
5V REFERENCE
TPS SIGNAL
SENSOR GROUND
COOLANT TEMPERATURE SENSOR
410 YEL
R13
5V
COOLANT TEMP SIGNAL
AIR TEMPERATURE SENSOR
472 TAN
454 BLK/WHT
R12
R2
5V
MAT SIGNAL
SENSOR GROUND
1 DOES "SCAN" TOOL DISPLAY COOLANT TEMPERATURE OF 130°C (266°F) OR HIGHER?
YES
NO
CODE 14 IS INTERMITTENT. IF NO ADDITIONAL CODES WERE STORED, REFER TO "DIAGNOSTIC AIDS" ON FACING PAGE.
2 • DISCONNECT COOLANT TEMPERATURE SENSOR. "SCAN" TOOL SHOULD DISPLAY COOLANT TEMPERATURE BELOW -30°C (-22°F). DOES IT?
YES
NO
REPLACE COOLANT TEMPERATURE SENSOR.
CKT 410 SHORTED TO GROUND, OR CKT 410 SHORTED TO SENSOR GROUND CIRCUIT OR FAULTY ECM.

CODE 14

COOLANT TEMPERATURE SENSOR CIRCUIT
(HIGH TEMPERATURE INDICATED)
3800 (VIN L) (TPI)

Circuit Description:

The Coolant Temperature Sensor (CTS) uses a thermistor to vary the signal voltage to the ECM depending on temperature. The ECM applies approximately 5 volts on CKT 410 to the sensor. When the engine is cold the sensor (thermistor) resistance is high, therefore, the ECM will see high signal voltage.

As the engine warms, the sensor resistance becomes less, and the voltage drops. At normal engine operating temperature (85°C to 95°C), the voltage will measure about 1.5 to 2.0 volts.

Code 14 will set if:

- Engine run time is greater than 10 seconds.
- Signal voltage indicates a coolant temperature above 140°C (284°F) for .4 second.

Test Description: Numbers below refer to circled numbers on the diagnostic chart.

1. Determines if conditions necessary for setting Code 14 exist.
2. This test will determine if CKT 410 is shorted to ground which will cause the conditions for Code 14.

Diagnostic Aids:

"Scan" tool displays engine temperature in degrees. After the engine is started, the temperature should rise steadily to about 90°C (194°F) then stabilize when the thermostat opens.

Check For:

- CKT 410 for a short to ground.
- Intermittent Test If connections and harness check OK, "Scan" coolant temperature while moving related connectors and wiring harness. If the failure is induced, the "coolant temperature" display will change. This may help to isolate the location of the malfunction. An intermittent may be caused by rubbed through wire insulation.
- Shifted Sensor The "Temperature To Resistance Value" scale may be used to test the coolant sensor at various temperature levels to evaluate the possibility of a "shifted" (mis-scaled) sensor, which may result in driveability complaints.

CODE 14

COOLANT TEMPERATURE SENSOR CIRCUIT
(HIGH TEMPERATURE INDICATED)
3800 (VIN L) (TPI)

DIAGNOSTIC AID

COOLANT SENSOR		
TEMPERATURE VS. RESISTANCE VALUES (APPROXIMATE)		
°C	°F	OHMS
100	212	177
90	194	241
80	176	332
70	158	467
60	140	667
50	122	973
45	113	1188
40	104	1459
35	95	1802
30	86	2238
25	77	2796
20	68	3515
15	59	4450
10	50	5672
5	41	7283
0	32	9423
-5	23	12300
-10	14	16177
-15	5	21448
-20	-4	28677
-30	-22	52684
-40	-40	100707

AFTER REPAIRS CLEAR CODES, RUN ENGINE 5 MINUTES, AND RECHECK FOR CODES.

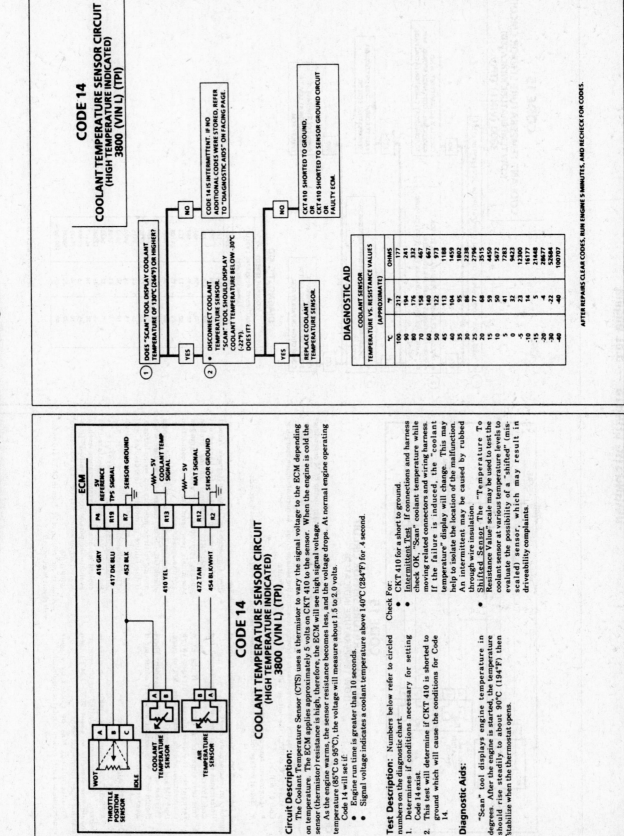

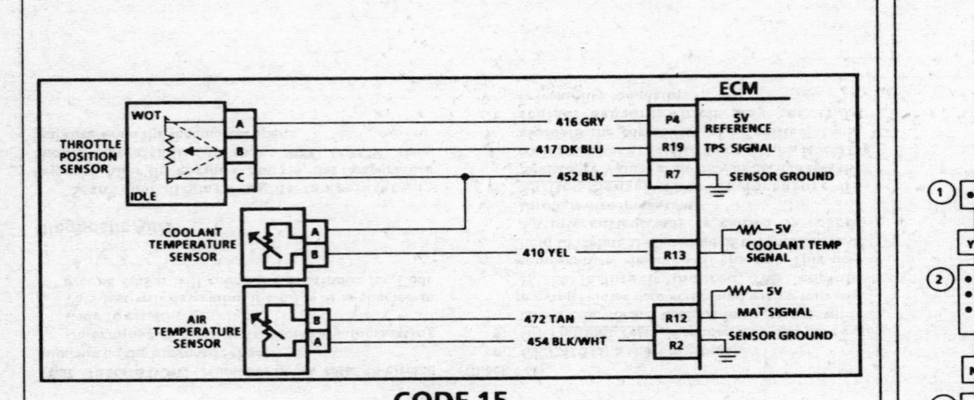

CODE 15

COOLANT TEMPERATURE SENSOR CIRCUIT
(LOW TEMPERATURE INDICATED)
3800 (VIN L) (TPI)

Circuit Description:

The Coolant Temperature Sensor (CTS) uses a thermistor to vary the signal voltage to the ECM depending on temperature. The ECM applies approximately 5 volts on CKT 410 to the sensor. When the engine is cold the sensor (thermistor) resistance is high, therefore, the ECM will see high signal voltage.

As the engine warms, the sensor resistance becomes less, and the voltage drops. At normal engine operating temperature (85°C to 95°C), the voltage will measure about 1.5 to 2.0 volts.

Code 15 will set if:

- Engine run time over 2 seconds.
- Signal voltage indicates a coolant temperature less than -40°C (-40°F) for at least 4 seconds.

Test Description: Numbers below refer to circled numbers on the diagnostic chart.

1. Determines if conditions necessary for setting Code 15 exist.
2. This test simulates a Code 14. If the ECM recognizes the low signal voltage, (high temperature) and the "Scan" reads 130°C or more, the ECM and wiring are OK.
3. This test will determine if CKT 410 is open. There should be 5 volts present at sensor connector if measured with a DVM.

Diagnostic Aids:

A "Scan" tool displays engine temperature in degrees. After the engine is started, the temperature should rise steadily to about 90°C (194°F) then stabilize when thermostat opens.

An intermittent may be caused by a poor connection, or a wire broken inside the insulation.

Check For:

- Poor Connection or Damaged Harness Inspect ECM harness connectors for backed out terminal "R13", improper mating, broken locks, improperly formed or damaged terminals, poor terminal to wire connection and damaged harness.
- Intermittent Test If connections and harness check OK, "Scan" coolant temperature while moving related connectors and wiring harness. If the failure is induced, the display will change. This may help to isolate the location of the malfunction.
- Shifted Sensor The "Temperature To Resistance Value" scale may be used to test the coolant sensor at various temperature levels to evaluate the possibility of a "shifted" (mis-scaled) sensor which may result in driveability complaints.

A faulty connection, or an open in CKTs 410 or 452 will result in a Code 15.

CODE 15

COOLANT TEMPERATURE SENSOR CIRCUIT
(LOW TEMPERATURE INDICATED)
3800 (VIN L) (TPI)

(1) • DOES "SCAN" TOOL DISPLAY COOLANT TEMPERATURE OF -30°C (-22°F) OR LESS?

YES → (2)

NO → CODE 15 IS INTERMITTENT. IF NO ADDITIONAL CODES WERE STORED, REFER TO "DIAGNOSTIC AIDS" ON FACING PAGE.

(2)
- DISCONNECT COOLANT TEMPERATURE SENSOR.
- JUMPER HARNESS TERMINALS TOGETHER.
- "SCAN" TOOL SHOULD DISPLAY 130°C (266°F) OR MORE. DOES IT?

NO → (3)

YES → FAULTY CONNECTION OR COOLANT TEMPERATURE SENSOR.

(3)
- JUMPER CKT 410 TO GROUND.
- "SCAN" TOOL SHOULD DISPLAY OVER 130°C (266 °F). DOES IT?

YES → OPEN COOLANT TEMPERATURE SENSOR GROUND CIRCUIT, FAULTY CONNECTION OR FAULTY ECM.

NO → OPEN CKT 410, FAULTY CONNECTION AT ECM, OR FAULTY ECM.

DIAGNOSTIC AID

COOLANT SENSOR
TEMPERATURE VS. RESISTANCE VALUES
(APPROXIMATE)

°C	°F	OHMS
100	212	177
90	194	241
80	176	332
70	158	467
60	140	667
50	122	973
45	113	1188
40	104	1459
35	95	1802
30	86	2238
25	77	2796
20	68	3515
15	59	4450
10	50	5672
5	41	7283
0	32	9423
-5	23	12300
-10	14	16177
-15	5	21448
-20	-4	28677
-30	-22	52684
-40	-40	100707

AFTER REPAIRS, CLEAR CODES, RUN ENGINE 5 MINUTES, AND RECHECK FOR CODES.

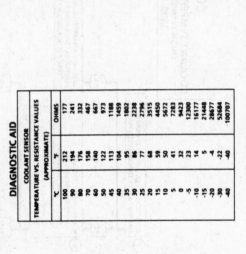

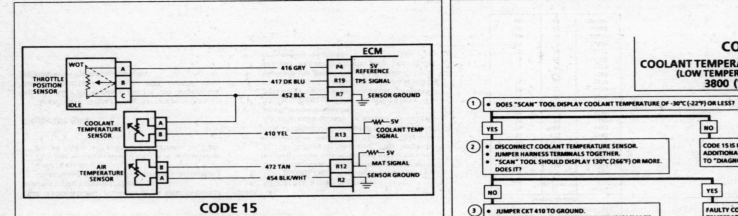

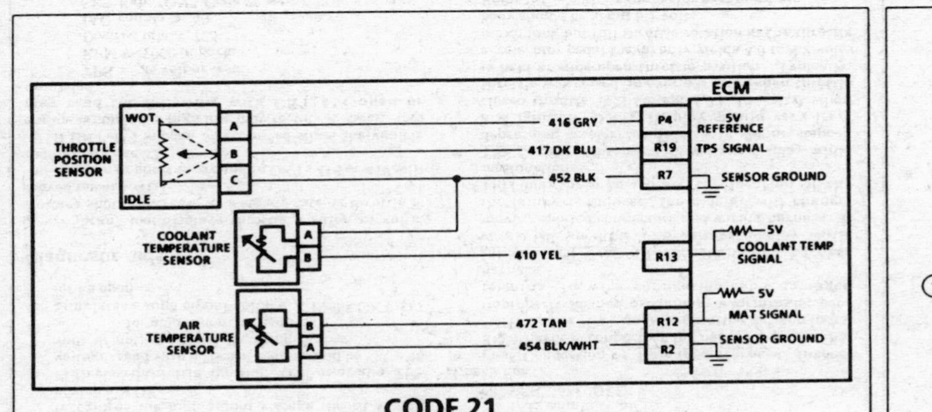

CODE 21

THROTTLE POSITION SENSOR (TPS) CIRCUIT (SIGNAL VOLTAGE HIGH) 3800 (VIN L) (TPI)

Circuit Description:

The Throttle Position Sensor (TPS) provides a voltage signal that changes relative to throttle blade angle. Signal voltage will vary from about .4 at idle to above 4 volts at Wide Open Throttle (WOT).

The TPS signal is one of the most important inputs used by the ECM for fuel control and for most of the ECM control outputs.

Code 21 will set if:

- TPS voltage is greater than 4.8 volts at any time.

OR

- Engine is running and air flow is less than 15 gm/sec.
- TPS signal voltage as read with a "Scan" tool is greater than .78 volt.
- Code 34 not present.
- All conditions met for 5 seconds.

Test Description: Numbers below refer to circled numbers on the diagnostic chart.

1. With closed throttle, ignition "ON," or at idle, TPS voltage should be .33-.46 volt. If not, see "Fuel Metering System, for adjustment procedures.
2. When the TPS sensor is disconnected, the TPS voltage should go low and a Code 22 will set. This test verifies the ECM and wiring are OK.
3. Probing CKT 452 with a test light checks the sensor ground CKT. A faulty sensor ground circuit will cause a Code 21.

Diagnostic Aids:

A "Scan" tool displays throttle position in volts. With closed throttle, ignition "ON" or at idle, voltage should be .33-.46 volt.

An open in CKT 452 will result in Codes 15 and 21.

Check For:

- Poor Connection or Damaged Harness Inspect ECM harness connectors for backed out terminal "R19", improper mating, broken locks, improperly formed or damaged terminals, poor terminal to wire connection, and damaged harness.
- Intermittent Test If connections and harness check OK, monitor TPS voltage while moving related connectors and wiring harness. If the failure is induced, the display will change. This may help to isolate the location of the malfunction.
- TPS Scaling Observe TPS voltage display while depressing accelerator pedal with engine stopped and ignition "ON." Display should vary from closed throttle TPS voltage when throttle was closed, to over 4.0 volts when throttle is held at wide open throttle position. Typically, accelerator pedal travel only yields 4.0 to 4.2 volts maximum, but full throttle rotation at the throttle body should be about 5.1 volts.

Connector Part Numbers:

TPS = 12015793
MAT = 12084247
CTS = 12078084

CODE 21

THROTTLE POSITION SENSOR (TPS) CIRCUIT (SIGNAL VOLTAGE HIGH) 3800 (VIN L) (TPI)

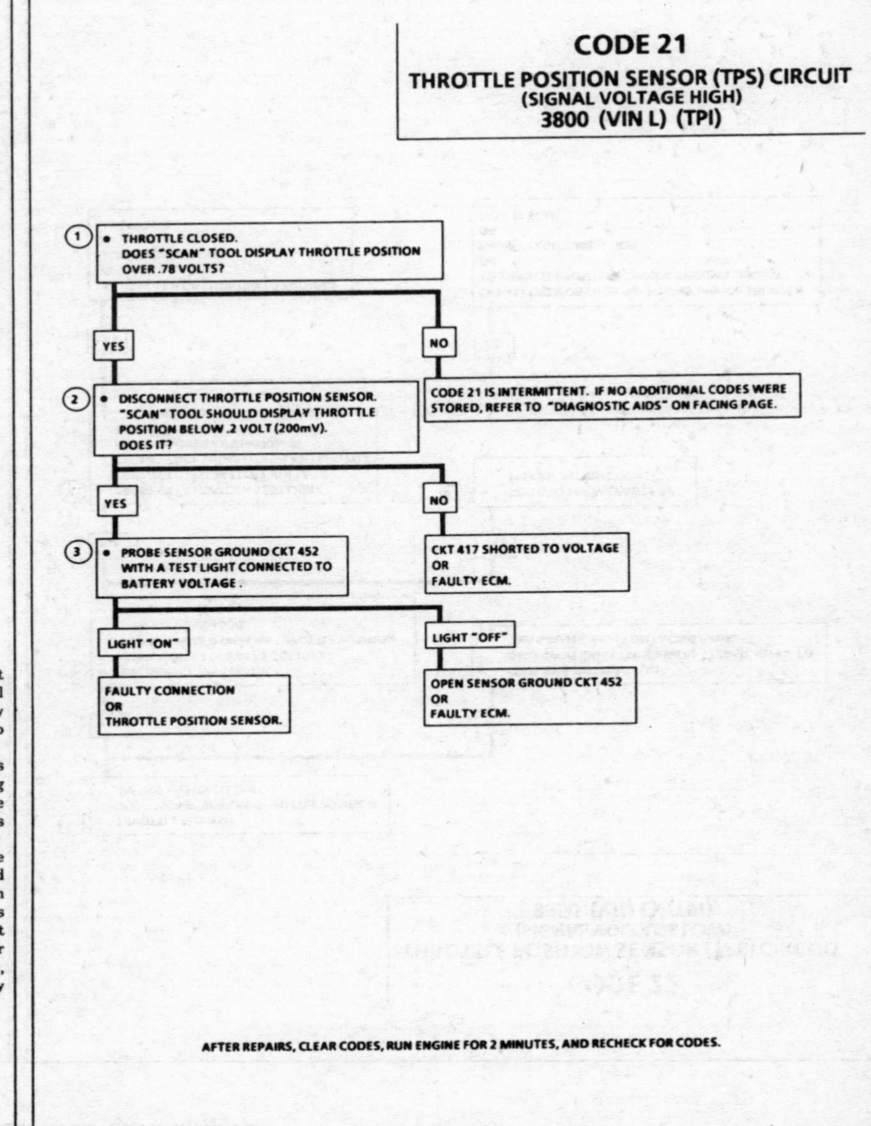

1
THROTTLE CLOSED.
DOES "SCAN" TOOL DISPLAY THROTTLE POSITION OVER .78 VOLTS?
YES
NO
CODE 21 IS INTERMITTENT. IF NO ADDITIONAL CODES WERE STORED, REFER TO "DIAGNOSTIC AIDS" ON FACING PAGE.
2
DISCONNECT THROTTLE POSITION SENSOR.
"SCAN" TOOL SHOULD DISPLAY THROTTLE POSITION BELOW .2 VOLT (200mV).
DOES IT?
YES
NO
CKT 417 SHORTED TO VOLTAGE
OR
FAULTY ECM.
3
PROBE SENSOR GROUND CKT 452 WITH A TEST LIGHT CONNECTED TO BATTERY VOLTAGE.
LIGHT "ON"
LIGHT "OFF"
FAULTY CONNECTION
OR
THROTTLE POSITION SENSOR.
OPEN SENSOR GROUND CKT 452
OR
FAULTY ECM.

AFTER REPAIRS, CLEAR CODES, RUN ENGINE FOR 2 MINUTES, AND RECHECK FOR CODES.

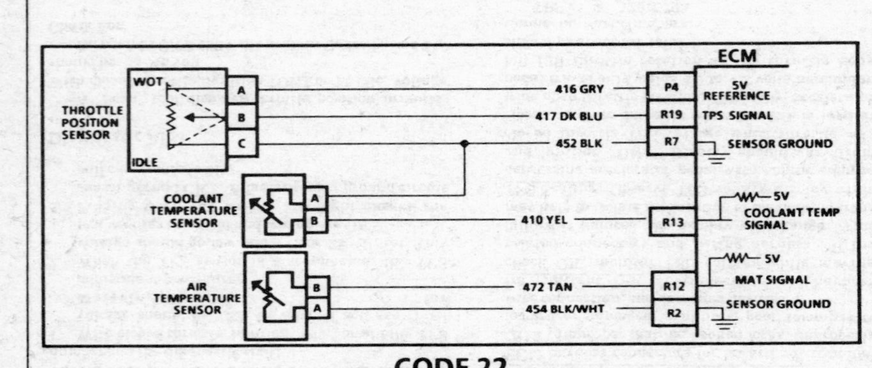

CODE 22

THROTTLE POSITION SENSOR (TPS) CIRCUIT (SIGNAL VOLTAGE LOW) 3800 (VIN L) (TPI)

Circuit Description:

The Throttle Position Sensor (TPS) provides a voltage signal that changes relative to throttle blade angle. Signal voltage will vary from about .4 volt at idle to above 4 volts at Wide Open Throttle (WOT).

The TPS signal is one of the most important inputs used by the ECM for fuel control and for most of the ECM control outputs.

Code 22 will set if:

- The ignition key is "ON"
- TPS signal voltage is less than .2 volt for 4 seconds.

Test Description: Numbers below refer to circled numbers on the diagnostic chart.

1. Determines if conditions necessary for setting Code 22 exist.
2. Simulates Code 21: (high voltage) If ECM recognizes the high signal voltage the ECM and wiring are OK.
3. With closed throttle, ignition "ON" or at idle, TPS voltage (read with a "Scan" tool) should be .33 - .46 volt. If not, see "Fuel Metering System," for adjustment procedures.
4. Simulates a high signal voltage. Checks CKT 417 for an open.

Diagnostic Aids:

A "Scan" tool displays throttle position in volts. Voltage should increase at a steady rate as throttle is moved toward WOT.

An open or short to ground in CKTs 416 or 417 will result in a Code 22.

If CKT 417 is open or grounded when the vehicle engine is started, a high idle may result. A "Scan" tool may read the following with CKT 417 open or grounded.

TPS = .04 volt or less
RPM > 1000 in park
Desired idle = 725
IAC counts > 40
SES light "ON" Code 22 set.

If the intermittent is repaired without cycling the key "OFF," the "Scan" may read the following.

TPS = .42 volt
RPM > 1500 in park
Desired idle = 725
IAC counts > 55
SES light "OFF"

Check For:

- Poor Connection or Damaged Harness Inspect ECM harness connectors for backed out terminal "R19" and/or "P4", improper mating, broken locks, improperly formed or damaged terminals, poor terminal to wire connection, and damaged harness.
- Intermittent Test If connections and harness check OK, monitor TPS voltage display while moving related connectors and wiring harness. If the failure is induced, the display will change. This may help to isolate the location of the malfunction.
- TPS Scaling Observe TPS voltage display while depressing accelerator pedal with engine stopped and ignition "ON". Display should vary from closed throttle TPS voltage (.33-.46 volts) when throttle was closed, to over 4.0 volts when throttle is held at wide open throttle position. Typically, accelerator pedal travel only yields 4.0 to 4.2 volts maximum, but full throttle rotation at the throttle body should be about 5.1 volts.

Refer to Code 21 for connector part numbers.

CODE 22

THROTTLE POSITION SENSOR (TPS) CIRCUIT (SIGNAL VOLTAGE LOW) 3800 (VIN L) (TPI)

(1) • THROTTLE CLOSED.
DOES "SCAN" DISPLAY THROTTLE POSITION .2V (200 mV) OR BELOW?

YES

(2) • DISCONNECT TPS SENSOR.
• JUMPER CKTS 416 & 417 TOGETHER.
"SCAN" SHOULD DISPLAY THROTTLE POSITION OVER 4.0 V (4000 mV).
DOES IT?

NO

• CODE 22 IS INTERMITTENT.
IF NO ADDITIONAL CODES WERE STORED, REFER TO "DIAGNOSTIC AIDS" ON FACING PAGE.

NO

(4) • PROBE CKT 417 WITH A TEST LIGHT CONNECTED TO BATTERY VOLTAGE.
"SCAN" TOOL SHOULD DISPLAY THROTTLE POSITION OVER 4.0V (4000 mV).
DOES IT?

YES

(3) • REFER TO FACING PAGE FOR SPECIFIC INSTRUCTIONS.

YES

CKT 416 OPEN OR SHORTED TO GROUND
OR
FAULTY CONNECTION
OR
FAULTY ECM.

NO

CKT 417 OPEN OR SHORTED TO GROUND, OR SHORTED TO THROTTLE POSITION SENSOR GROUND CIRCUIT
OR
FAULTY ECM CONNECTION
OR
FAULTY ECM.

***AFTER REPAIRS*, CLEAR CODES, RUN ENGINE FOR 2 MINUTES, AND RECHECK FOR CODES.**

THROTTLE POSITION SENSOR
WOT
IDLE
A B C
COOLANT TEMPERATURE SENSOR
AIR TEMPERATURE SENSOR
416 GRY
417 DK BLU
452 BLK
410 YEL
472 TAN
454 BLK/WHT
P4 R19 R7 R13 R12 R2
ECM
5V REFERENCE
TPS SIGNAL
SENSOR GROUND
5V
COOLANT TEMP SIGNAL
5V
MAT SIGNAL
SENSOR GROUND

CODE 23

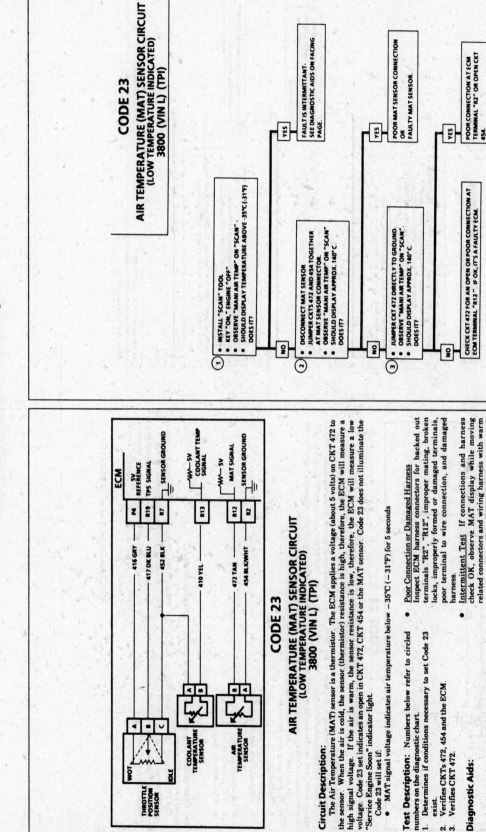

AIR TEMPERATURE (MAT) SENSOR CIRCUIT
(LOW TEMPERATURE INDICATED)
3800 (VIN L) (TPI)

Circuit Description:

The Air Temperature (MAT) sensor is a thermistor. The ECM applies a voltage (about 5 volts) on CKT 472 to the sensor. When the air is cold, the sensor (thermistor) resistance is high, therefore, the ECM will measure a high signal voltage. If the air is warm, the sensor resistance is low, therefore, the ECM will measure a low voltage. Code 23 set indicates an open in CKT 472, CKT 454 or the MAT sensor. Code 23 does not illuminate the "Service Engine Soon" indicator light.

Code 23 will set if:

- MAT signal voltage indicates air temperature below −35°C (−31°F) for 5 seconds

Test Description: Numbers below refer to circled numbers on the diagnostic chart.

1. Determines if conditions necessary to set Code 23 exist.
2. Verifies CKTs 472, 454 and the ECM.
3. Verifies CKT 472.

Diagnostic Aids:

An intermittent may be caused by a poor connection, or a wire broken inside the insulation. Check For:

- Poor Connection or Damaged Harness
  Inspect ECM harness connectors for backed out terminals "R2", "R12", improper mating, broken locks, improperly formed or damaged terminals, poor terminal to wire connection, and damaged harness.
- Intermittent Test If connections and harness check OK, observe MAT display while moving related connectors and wiring harness with warm engine running. If the failure is induced, the MAT display on "Scan" tool may change to a −40° temperature reading. This may help to isolate the location of the malfunction.
  Refer to Code 21 for connector part numbers.

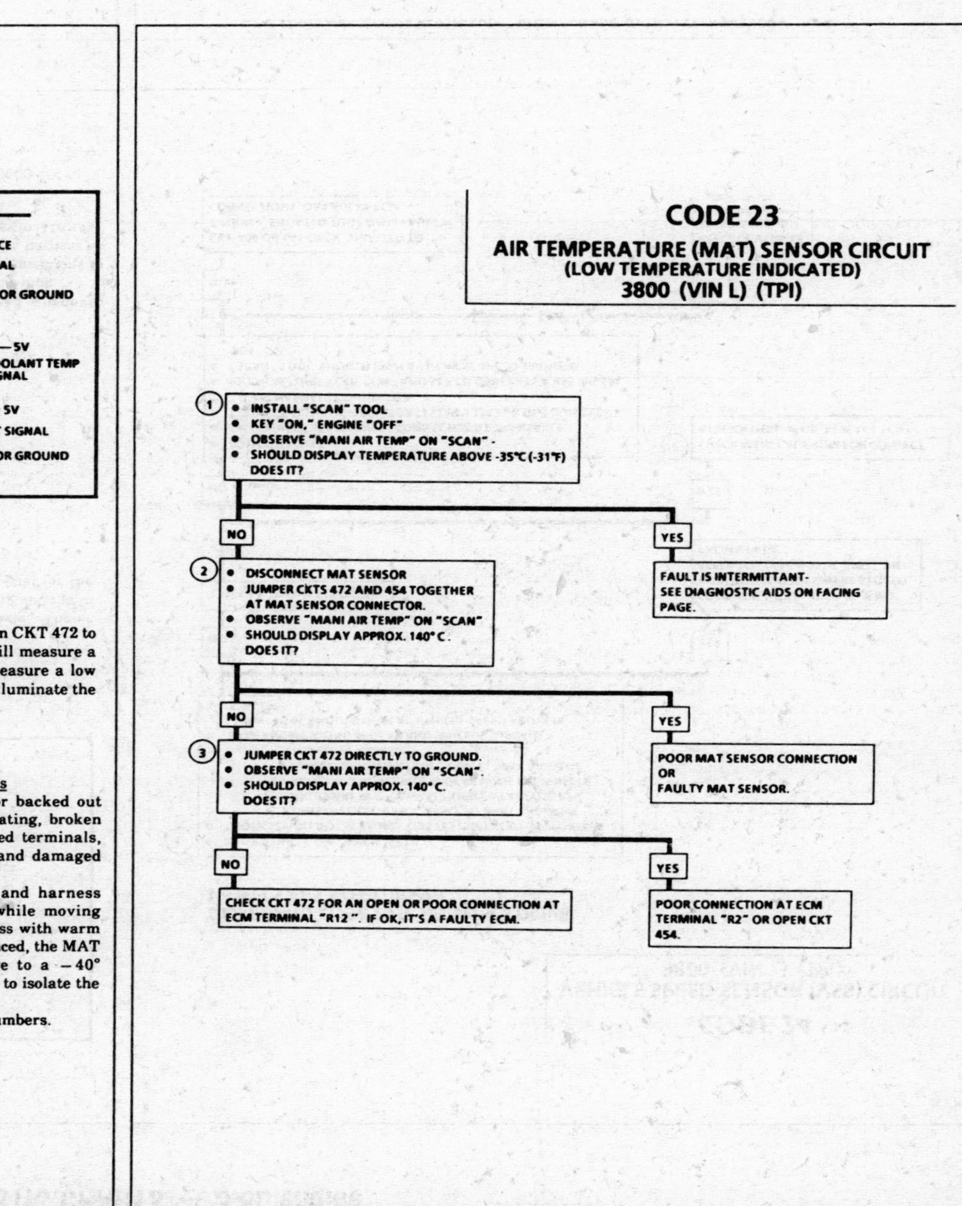

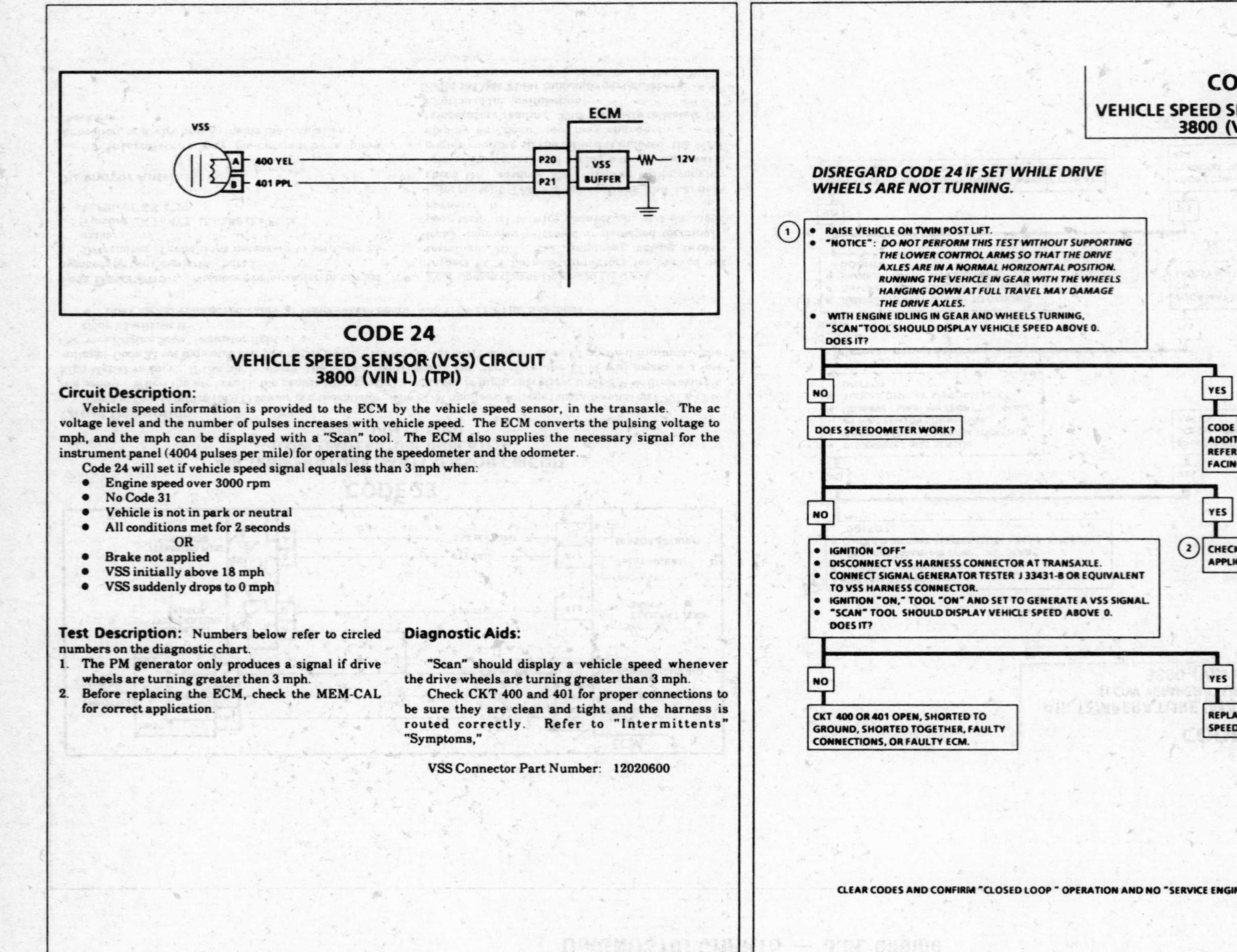

CODE 24

VEHICLE SPEED SENSOR (VSS) CIRCUIT 3800 (VIN L) (TPI)

Circuit Description:

Vehicle speed information is provided to the ECM by the vehicle speed sensor, in the transaxle. The ac voltage level and the number of pulses increases with vehicle speed. The ECM converts the pulsing voltage to mph, and the mph can be displayed with a "Scan" tool. The ECM also supplies the necessary signal for the instrument panel (4004 pulses per mile) for operating the speedometer and the odometer.

Code 24 will set if vehicle speed signal equals less than 3 mph when:

- Engine speed over 3000 rpm
- No Code 31
- Vehicle is not in park or neutral
- All conditions met for 2 seconds

OR

- Brake not applied
- VSS initially above 18 mph
- VSS suddenly drops to 0 mph

Test Description: Numbers below refer to circled numbers on the diagnostic chart.

1. The PM generator only produces a signal if drive wheels are turning greater then 3 mph.
2. Before replacing the ECM, check the MEM-CAL for correct application.

Diagnostic Aids:

"Scan" should display a vehicle speed whenever the drive wheels are turning greater than 3 mph.

Check CKT 400 and 401 for proper connections to be sure they are clean and tight and the harness is routed correctly. Refer to "Intermittents" "Symptoms,"

VSS Connector Part Number: 12020600

CODE 24

VEHICLE SPEED SENSOR (VSS) CIRCUIT 3800 (VIN L) (TPI)

DISREGARD CODE 24 IF SET WHILE DRIVE WHEELS ARE NOT TURNING.

(1)
- RAISE VEHICLE ON TWIN POST LIFT.
- "NOTICE": *DO NOT PERFORM THIS TEST WITHOUT SUPPORTING THE LOWER CONTROL ARMS SO THAT THE DRIVE AXLES ARE IN A NORMAL HORIZONTAL POSITION. RUNNING THE VEHICLE IN GEAR WITH THE WHEELS HANGING DOWN AT FULL TRAVEL MAY DAMAGE THE DRIVE AXLES.*
- WITH ENGINE IDLING IN GEAR AND WHEELS TURNING, "SCAN" TOOL SHOULD DISPLAY VEHICLE SPEED ABOVE 0. DOES IT?

YES: CODE 24 IS INTERMITTENT. IF NO ADDITIONAL CODES WERE STORED, REFER TO "DIAGNOSTIC AIDS" ON FACING PAGE.

NO: DOES SPEEDOMETER WORK?

YES: (2) CHECK MEM-CAL/PROM FOR CORRECT APPLICATION. IF OK, REPLACE ECM.

NO:
- IGNITION "OFF"
- DISCONNECT VSS HARNESS CONNECTOR AT TRANSAXLE.
- CONNECT SIGNAL GENERATOR TESTER J 33431-B OR EQUIVALENT TO VSS HARNESS CONNECTOR.
- IGNITION "ON," TOOL "ON" AND SET TO GENERATE A VSS SIGNAL.
- "SCAN" TOOL SHOULD DISPLAY VEHICLE SPEED ABOVE 0. DOES IT?

YES: REPLACE VEHICLE SPEED SENSOR.

NO: CKT 400 OR 401 OPEN, SHORTED TO GROUND, SHORTED TOGETHER, FAULTY CONNECTIONS, OR FAULTY ECM.

CLEAR CODES AND CONFIRM "CLOSED LOOP" OPERATION AND NO "SERVICE ENGINE SOON" LIGHT.

THROTTLE POSITION SENSOR — WOT — IDLE — A B C
COOLANT TEMPERATURE SENSOR — A B
AIR TEMPERATURE SENSOR — B A
416 GRY — P4 — 5V REFERENCE
417 DK BLU — R19 — TPS SIGNAL
452 BLK — R7 — SENSOR GROUND
410 YEL — R13 — 5V COOLANT TEMP SIGNAL
472 TAN — R12 — 5V MAT SIGNAL
454 BLK/WHT — R2 — SENSOR GROUND
ECM

CODE 25

AIR TEMPERATURE (MAT) SENSOR CIRCUIT
(HIGH TEMPERATURE INDICATED)
3800 (VIN L) (TPI)

Circuit Description:

The Air Temperature (MAT) sensor is a thermistor. The ECM applies a voltage (about 5 volts) on CKT 472 to the sensor. When air is cold, the sensor (thermistor) resistance is high, therefore, the ECM will measure a high signal voltage. If the air is warm, the sensor resistance is low, and the ECM will measure a low voltage. Code 25 will set indicates a short to ground in CKT 472 or a shorted MAT sensor. Code 25 does not illuminate the "Service Engine Soon" indicator light.

Code 25 will set if:

- MAT signal voltage indicates air temperature greater than 103°C (218°F).
- Vehicle speed is greater than 35 mph.
- Both of the above requirements are met for at least 5 seconds.

Test Description: Numbers below refer to the circled numbers on the diagnostic chart.

1. Determines if conditions necessary to set Code 25 exist.
2. With the MAT sensor disconnected, the "Scan" should read about -40°. If not, CKT 472 is grounded or the ECM at fault.

Diagnostic Aids:

An intermittent may be caused by a poor connection or rubbed through wire insulation.

Check For:

- Poor Connection or Damaged Harness Inspect ECM harness connectors for backed out terminals, improper mating, broken locks, improperly formed or damaged terminals, poor terminal to wire connection and damaged harness.
- Intermittent Test If connections and harness check OK, a digital voltmeter connected from affected terminal to ground while moving related connectors and wiring harness. If the failure is induced, the voltage reading will change.

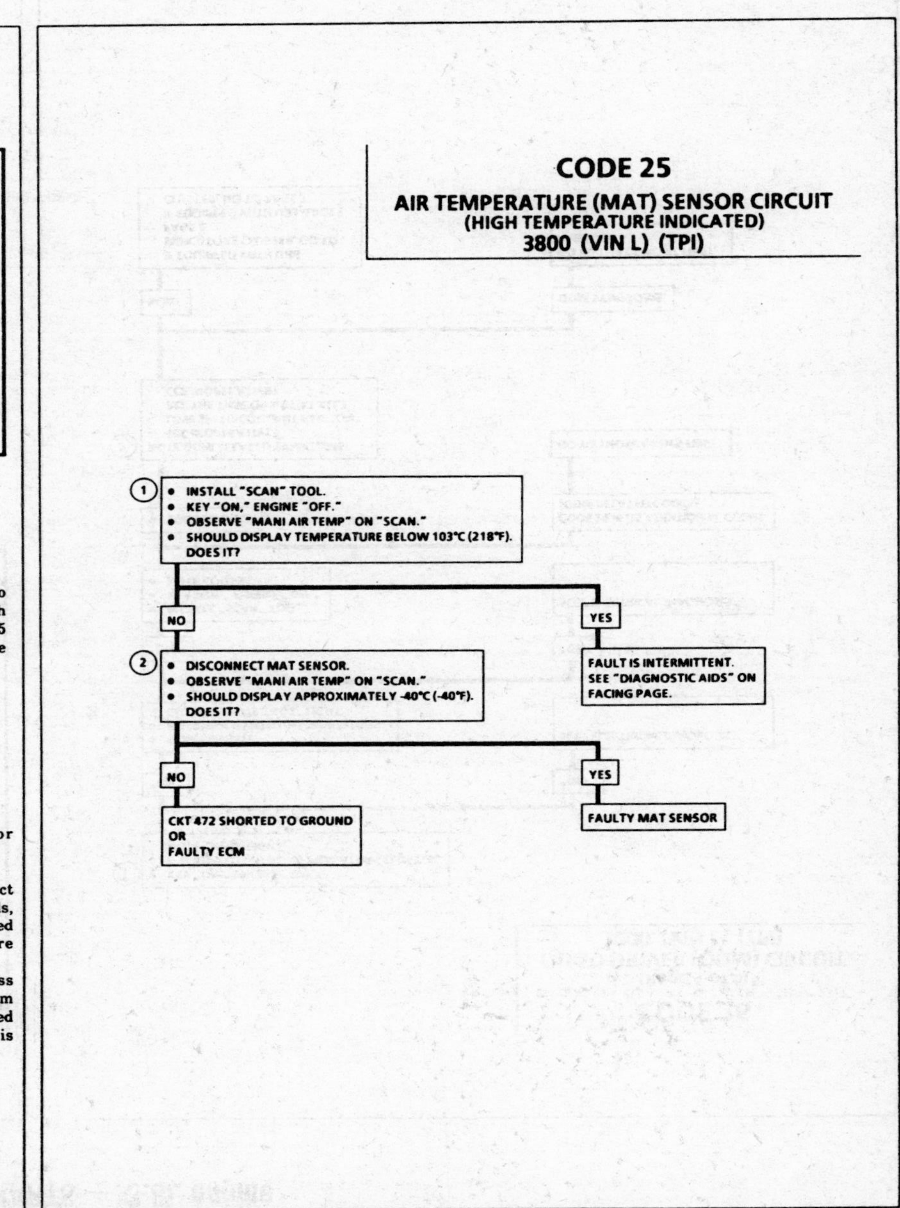
CODE 25
AIR TEMPERATURE (MAT) SENSOR CIRCUIT
(HIGH TEMPERATURE INDICATED)
3800 (VIN L) (TPI)
1
• INSTALL "SCAN" TOOL.
• KEY "ON," ENGINE "OFF."
• OBSERVE "MANI AIR TEMP" ON "SCAN."
• SHOULD DISPLAY TEMPERATURE BELOW 103°C (218°F).
DOES IT?
NO
YES
FAULT IS INTERMITTENT. SEE "DIAGNOSTIC AIDS" ON FACING PAGE.
2
• DISCONNECT MAT SENSOR.
• OBSERVE "MANI AIR TEMP" ON "SCAN."
• SHOULD DISPLAY APPROXIMATELY -40°C (-40°F).
DOES IT?
NO
YES
CKT 472 SHORTED TO GROUND OR FAULTY ECM
FAULTY MAT SENSOR

DIAGNOSTIC CHARTS — 3.8L engine

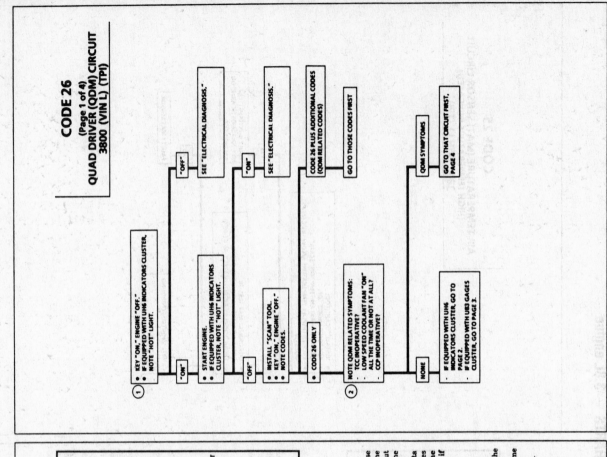

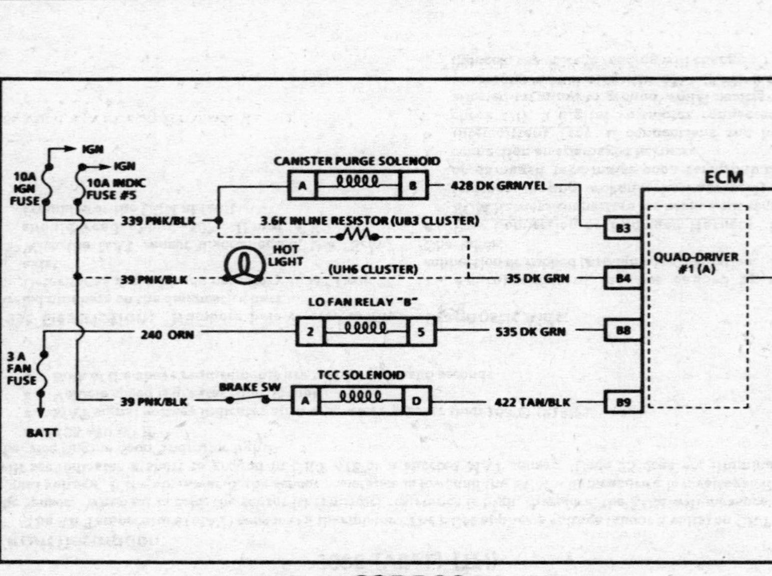

CODE 26
(Page 1 of 4)
QUAD-DRIVER (QDM) CIRCUIT
3800 (VIN L) (TPI)

Circuit Description:

The ECM is used to control several components such as those illustrated above. The ECM controls these devices through the use of a Quad-Driver Module (QDM). When the ECM is commanding a component "ON," the voltage potential of the output circuit will be "low" (near 0 volt). When the ECM is commanding the output circuit to a component "OFF," the voltage potential of the circuit will be "high." (Near battery voltage.) The primary function of the QDM is to supply the ground for the component being controlled.

Each QDM has a fault line which is monitored by the ECM. The fault line signal is available on the data stream for "Scan" tool test equipment. The ECM will compare the voltage at the QDM based on accepted values of the fault line. **If the QDM fault detection circuit senses a voltage other than the accepted value, the fault line will go from a "low" signal on the data stream to a "high" signal and a Code 26 will set if applicable.**

Test Description: Numbers below refer to circled numbers on the diagnostic chart.

1. The ECM does not know which controlled circuit caused the Code 26 so this chart will go through each of the circuits to determine which is at fault. On vehicles equipped with a UH6 cluster, this test checks the hot light driver and the hot light circuit.
2. QDM symptoms:
   - TCC - Inoperative - Code 39.
   - Hot Light (with UH6 cluster) - "ON" all the time/"OFF" during bulb check.
   - Coolant fans "ON" all the time or will not come "ON" at all.
   - Poor driveability due to 100% canister purge.

Connector Part Numbers:
CCP = 12015380
TCC = 12034342

CODE 26
(Page 1 of 4)
QUAD DRIVER (QDM) CIRCUIT
3800 (VIN L) (TPI)

(1)
- KEY "ON," ENGINE "OFF."
- IF EQUIPPED WITH UH6 INDICATORS CLUSTER, NOTE "HOT" LIGHT.

"ON"
- START ENGINE.
- IF EQUIPPED WITH UH6 INDICATORS CLUSTER, NOTE "HOT" LIGHT.

"OFF"
SEE "ELECTRICAL DIAGNOSIS."

(after START ENGINE:)

"OFF"
- INSTALL "SCAN" TOOL.
- KEY "ON," ENGINE "OFF."
- NOTE CODES.

"ON"
SEE "ELECTRICAL DIAGNOSIS."

(after NOTE CODES:)

- CODE 26 ONLY

CODE 26 PLUS ADDITIONAL CODES (QDM RELATED CODES)
GO TO THOSE CODES FIRST

(2)
NOTE QDM RELATED SYMPTOMS:
- TCC INOPERATIVE?
- LOW SPEED COOLANT FAN "ON" ALL THE TIME OR NOT AT ALL?
- CCP INOPERATIVE?

NONE
- IF EQUIPPED WITH UH6 INDICATORS CLUSTER, GO TO PAGE 2.
- IF EQUIPPED WITH UB3 GAGES CLUSTER, GO TO PAGE 3.

QDM SYMPTOMS
GO TO THAT CIRCUIT FIRST, PAGE 4

MAF SENSOR
C B A
15A ECM FUSE
PNK/BLK 439
FUSE BLOCK #7
BLK/WHT 450
492 YELLOW
G15
MAF SIGNAL
5 VOLT
ECM

CODE 34

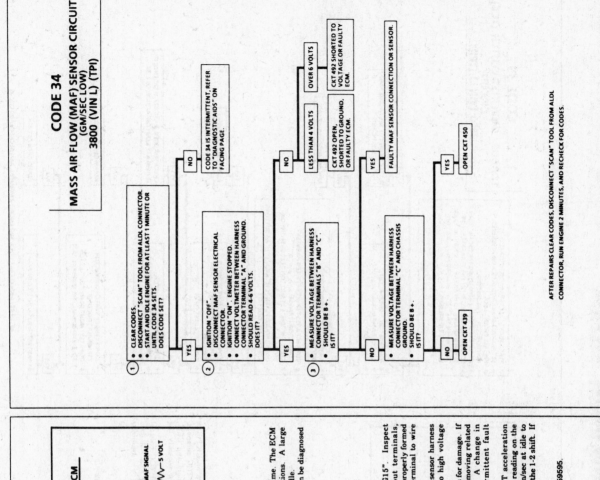

MASS AIR FLOW (MAF) SENSOR CIRCUIT
(GM/SEC LOW)
3800 (VIN L) (TPI)

Circuit Description:

The Mass Air Flow (MAF) sensor measures the flow of air which passes through it in a given time. The ECM uses this information to monitor the operating condition of the engine for fuel delivery calculations. A large quantity of air movement indicates acceleration, while a small quantity indicates deceleration or idle.

The MAF sensor produces a frequency signal which cannot be easily measured. The sensor can be diagnosed using the procedures on this chart.

Code 34 will set when of the following conditions exists:

- Engine running
- No MAF sensor signal
- Above conditions for over 4 seconds

Test Description: Numbers below refer to circled numbers on the diagnostic chart.

1. This step checks to see if ECM recognizes a problem.
2. A voltage reading at sensor harness connector terminal "A" of less than 4 or over 6 volts indicates a fault in CKT 492 or poor connection.
3. Verifies that both ignition voltage and a good ground circuit are available.

Diagnostic Aids:

An intermittent may be caused by a poor connection, mis-routed harness, rubbed through wire insulation, or a wire broken inside the insulation.

Check For:

- Poor connection at ECM pin "G15". Inspect harness connectors for backed out terminals, improper mating, broken locks, improperly formed or damaged terminals, and poor terminal to wire connection.
- Mis-routed Harness Inspect MAF sensor harness to insure that it is not too close to high voltage wires, such as spark plug leads.
- Damaged Harness Inspect harness for damage. If harness appears OK, "Scan" while moving related connectors and wiring harness. A change in display would indicate the intermittent fault location.
- Plugged Air Intake Filter A WOT acceleration from a stop should cause the MAF reading on the "Scan" to range from about 4-7 gm/sec at idle to 100 gm/sec or greater at the time of the 1-2 shift. If not, check for restriction.

MAF Connector Part Number: 12059595.

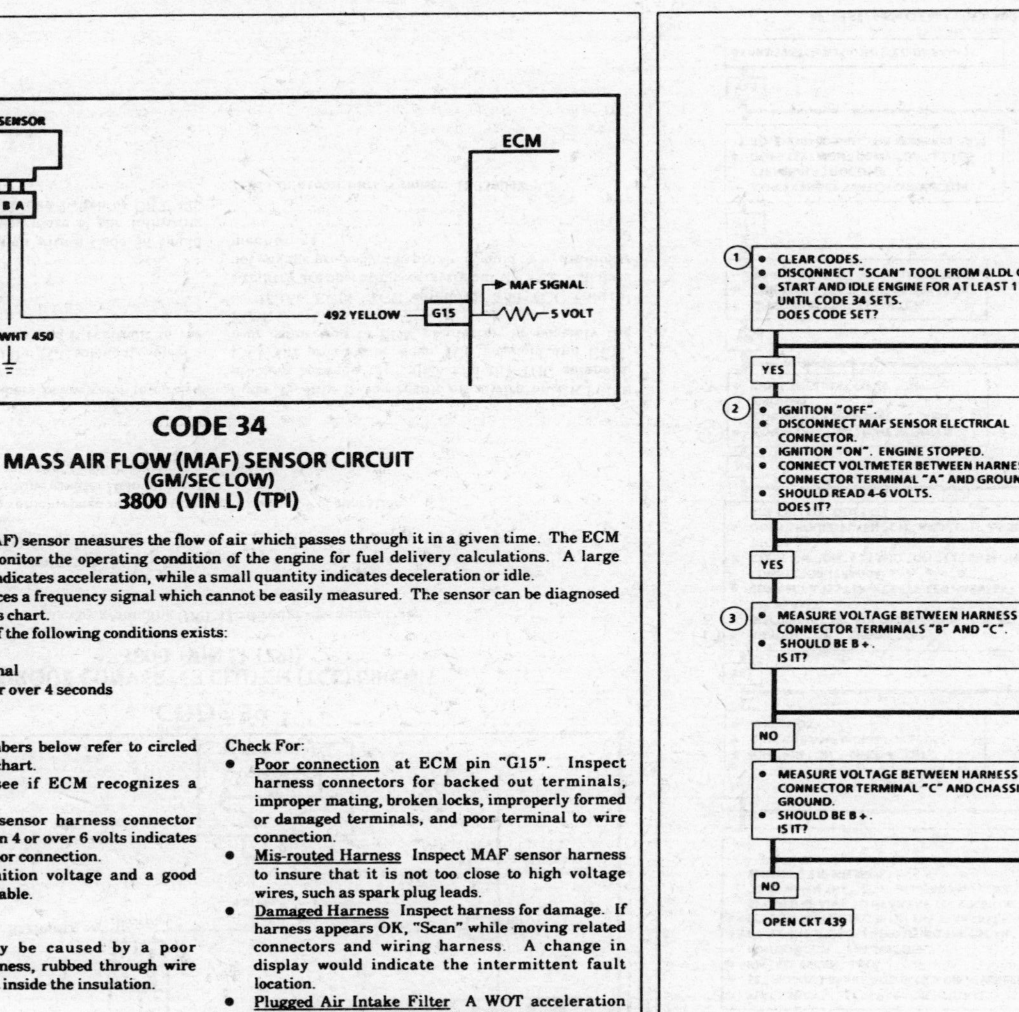

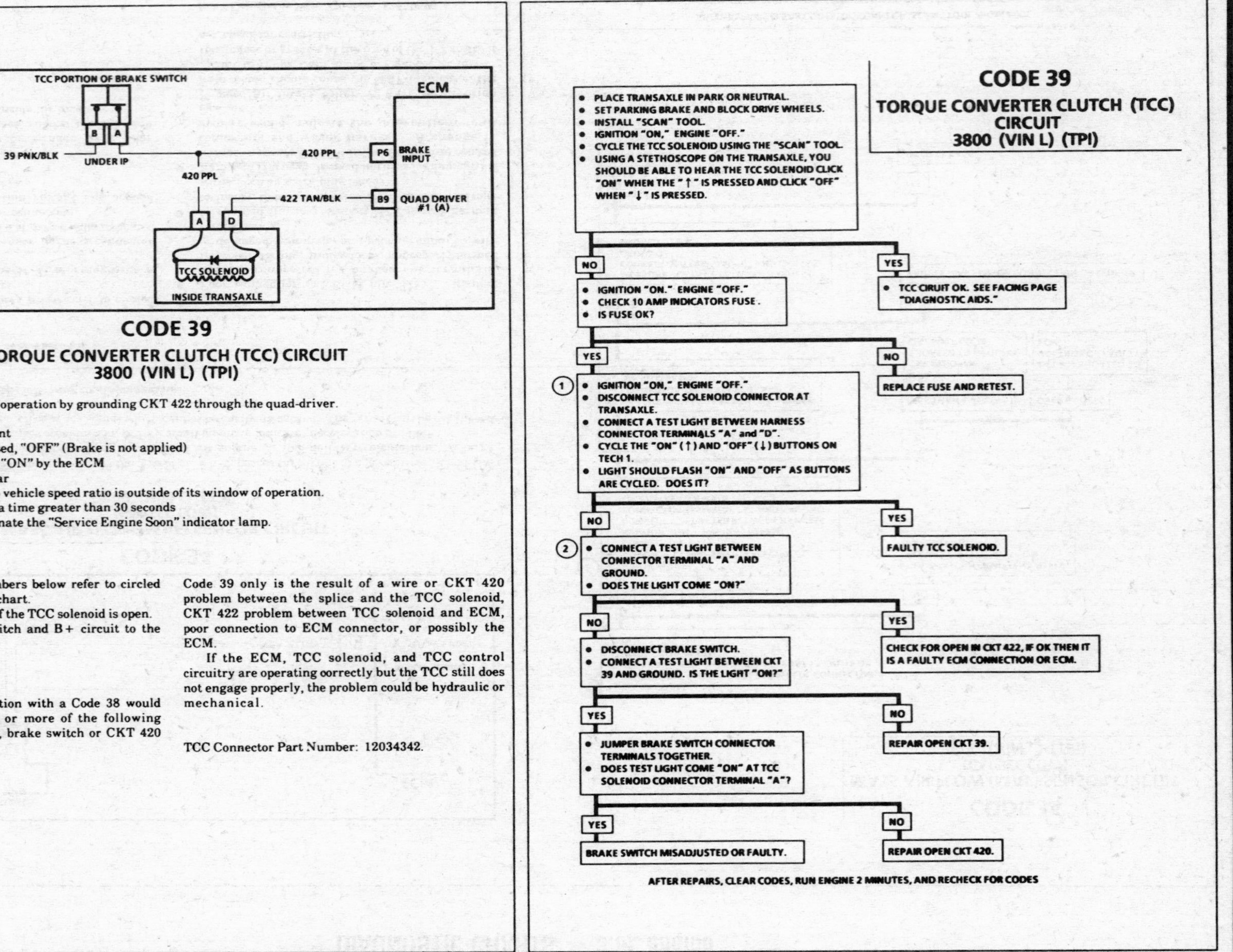

TCC PORTION OF BRAKE SWITCH
ECM
10 AMP INDICATORS FUSE
FUSE BLOCK #5
39 PNK/BLK
B
A
UNDER IP
420 PPL
P6
BRAKE INPUT
420 PPL
422 TAN/BLK
B9
QUAD DRIVER #1 (A)
A
D
TCC SOLENOID
INSIDE TRANSAXLE
CODE 39
TORQUE CONVERTER CLUTCH (TCC) CIRCUIT
3800 (VIN L) (TPI)
• PLACE TRANSAXLE IN PARK OR NEUTRAL.
• SET PARKING BRAKE AND BLOCK DRIVE WHEELS.
• INSTALL "SCAN" TOOL.
• IGNITION "ON," ENGINE "OFF."
• CYCLE THE TCC SOLENOID USING THE "SCAN" TOOL.
• USING A STETHOSCOPE ON THE TRANSAXLE, YOU SHOULD BE ABLE TO HEAR THE TCC SOLENOID CLICK "ON" WHEN THE "↑" IS PRESSED AND CLICK "OFF" WHEN "↓" IS PRESSED.
NO
YES
• TCC CIRUIT OK. SEE FACING PAGE "DIAGNOSTIC AIDS."
• IGNITION "ON." ENGINE "OFF."
• CHECK 10 AMP INDICATORS FUSE.
• IS FUSE OK?
YES
NO
REPLACE FUSE AND RETEST.
1
• IGNITION "ON," ENGINE "OFF."
• DISCONNECT TCC SOLENOID CONNECTOR AT TRANSAXLE.
• CONNECT A TEST LIGHT BETWEEN HARNESS CONNECTOR TERMINALS "A" and "D".
• CYCLE THE "ON" (↑) AND "OFF" (↓) BUTTONS ON TECH 1.
• LIGHT SHOULD FLASH "ON" AND "OFF" AS BUTTONS ARE CYCLED. DOES IT?
NO
YES
FAULTY TCC SOLENOID.
2
• CONNECT A TEST LIGHT BETWEEN CONNECTOR TERMINAL "A" AND GROUND.
• DOES THE LIGHT COME "ON?"
NO
YES
CHECK FOR OPEN IN CKT 422, IF OK THEN IT IS A FAULTY ECM CONNECTION OR ECM.
• DISCONNECT BRAKE SWITCH.
• CONNECT A TEST LIGHT BETWEEN CKT 39 AND GROUND. IS THE LIGHT "ON?"
YES
NO
REPAIR OPEN CKT 39.
• JUMPER BRAKE SWITCH CONNECTOR TERMINALS TOGETHER.
• DOES TEST LIGHT COME "ON" AT TCC SOLENOID CONNECTOR TERMINAL "A"?
YES
NO
BRAKE SWITCH MISADJUSTED OR FAULTY.
REPAIR OPEN CKT 420.
AFTER REPAIRS, CLEAR CODES, RUN ENGINE 2 MINUTES, AND RECHECK FOR CODES

CODE 39

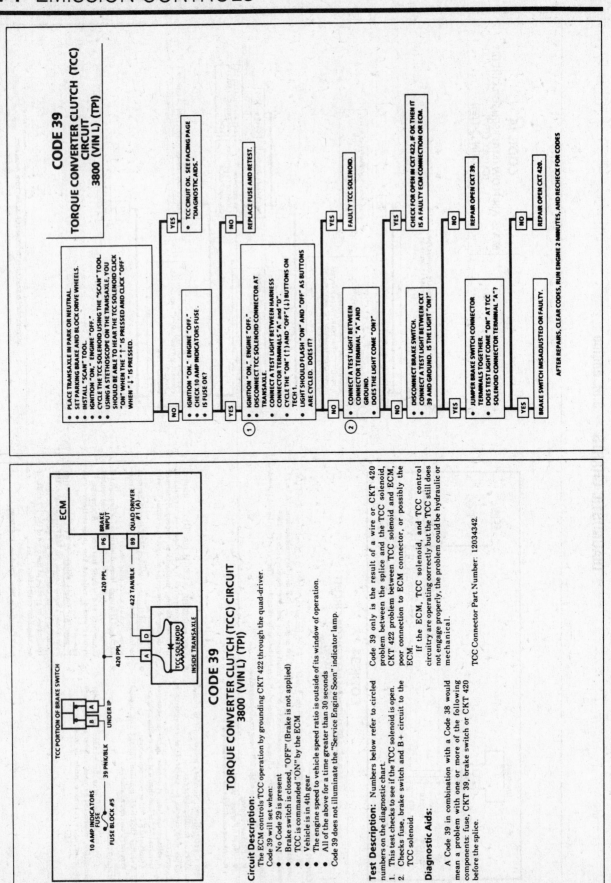

TORQUE CONVERTER CLUTCH (TCC) CIRCUIT 3800 (VIN L) (TPI)

Circuit Description:

The ECM controls TCC operation by grounding CKT 422 through the quad-driver.

Code 39 will set when:

- No Code 29 is present
- Brake switch is closed, "OFF" (Brake is not applied)
- TCC is commanded "ON" by the ECM
- Vehicle is in 4th gear
- The engine speed to vehicle speed ratio is outside of its window of operation.
- All of the above for a time greater than 30 seconds

Code 39 does not illuminate the "Service Engine Soon" indicator lamp.

Test Description: Numbers below refer to circled numbers on the diagnostic chart.

1. This test checks to see if the TCC solenoid is open.
2. Checks fuse, brake switch and B+ circuit to the TCC solenoid.

Diagnostic Aids:

A Code 39 in combination with a Code 38 would mean a problem with one or more of the following components: fuse, CKT 39, brake switch or CKT 420 before the splice.

Code 39 only is the result of a wire or CKT 420 problem between the splice and the TCC solenoid, CKT 422 problem between TCC solenoid and ECM, poor connection to ECM connector, or possibly the ECM.

If the ECM, TCC solenoid, and TCC control circuitry are operating correctly but the TCC still does not engage properly, the problem could be hydraulic or mechanical.

TCC Connector Part Number: 12034342.

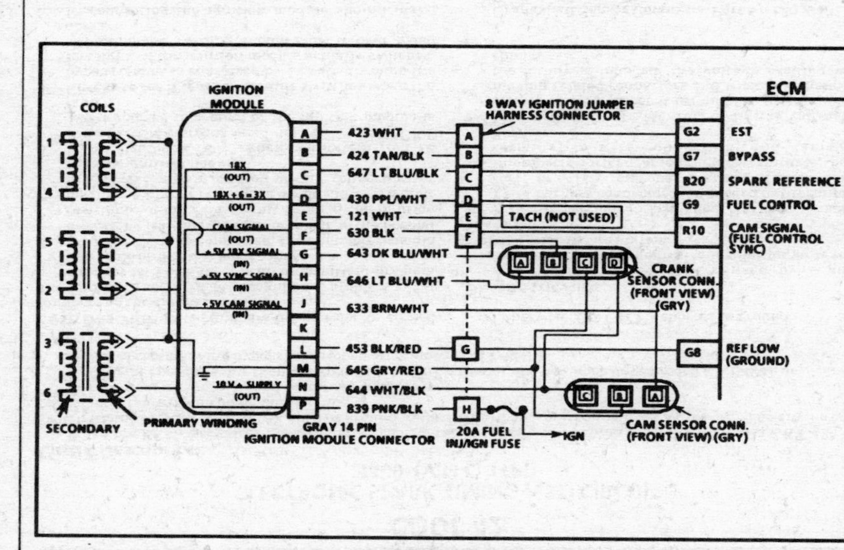

CODE 41

CAM SENSOR CIRCUIT 3800 (VIN L) (TPI)

Circuit Description:

The ECM uses the cam sensor to determine the position of the #1 piston during its power stroke. This signal is used by the ECM to calculate true Sequential Fuel Injection (SFI) mode of operation. A loss of this signal will set a Code 41. If the cam signal is lost while the engine is running the fuel injection system will shift to a calculated sequential fuel injection mode based on the last fuel injection pulse, and the engine will continue to run. The engine can be restarted and will run in the calculated sequential mode as long as the fault is present with a 1 in 6 chance of being correct.

Code 41 is set when the following conditions are met:

- Engine is running
- Cam sensor signal not received by ECM for 5 seconds.

Test Description: Numbers below refer to circled numbers on the diagnostic chart.

1. Checks to see if ECM recognizes a problem and sets Code 41.
2. This step verifies proper operation of CKTs 633, 644, and 645.
3. Step validates the integrity of CKT 630 from the ignition module to ECM.
4. If the camshaft gear magnet is interfacing with the cam sensor the voltage reading will be zero, bumping engine will cause the condition to go away.
5. If the voltage reading of CKT 630 is constantly varying and connection to terminal "R10" and the ignition jumper harness terminal "F" is good, the ECM is faulty.

Diagnostic Aids:

An intermittent may be caused by a poor connection, rubbed through wire insulation or a wire broken inside the insulation.

Check For:

- Poor Connection or Damaged Harness Inspect ECM harness connectors for backed out terminal "R10", improper mating, broken locks, improperly formed or damaged terminals, poor terminal to wire connection and damaged harness.
- Intermittent Test If connections and harness check OK, monitor a digital voltmeter connected from ECM terminal "R10" to ground while moving related connectors and wiring harness. If the failure is induced, the voltage reading will change. This may help to isolate the location of the malfunction.

Crankshaft Sensor Connector Part #: 12059401.
Camshaft Sensor Connector Part #: 12047911.
8 Way Connector Part #: 12047937

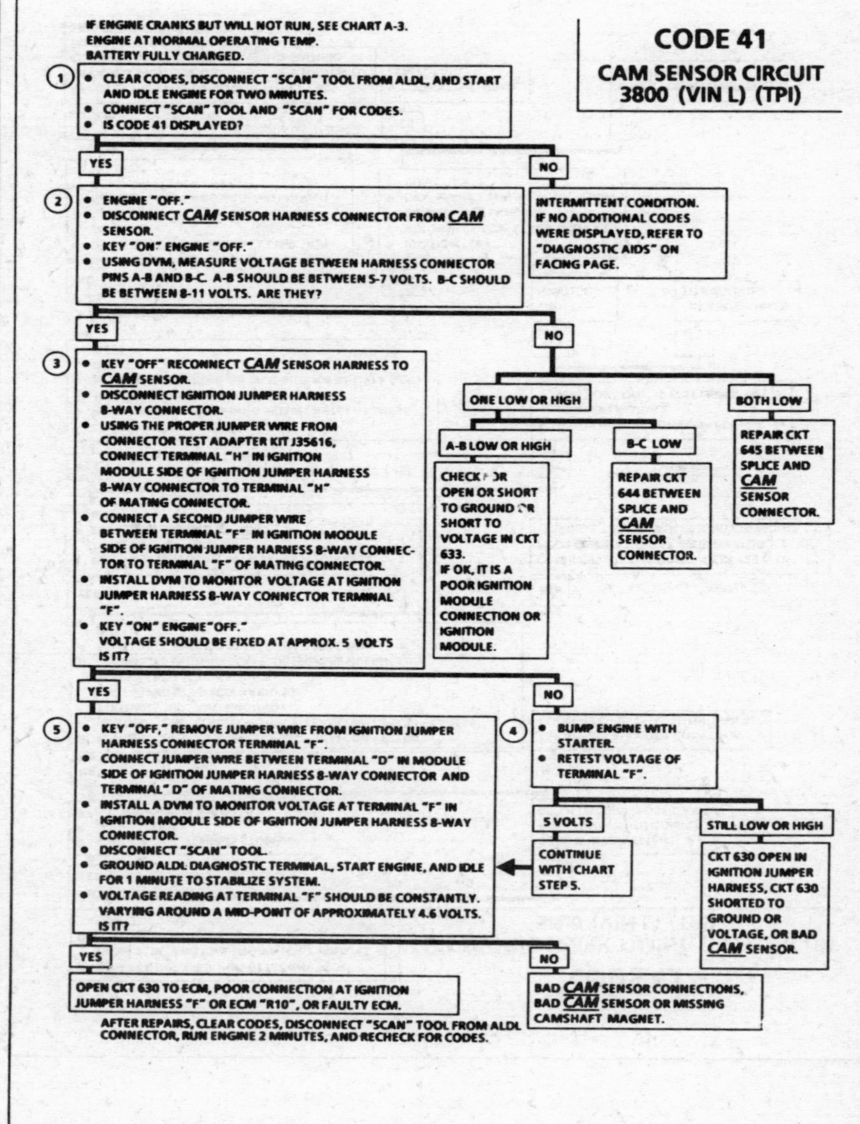

DIAGNOSTIC CHARTS — 3.8L engine

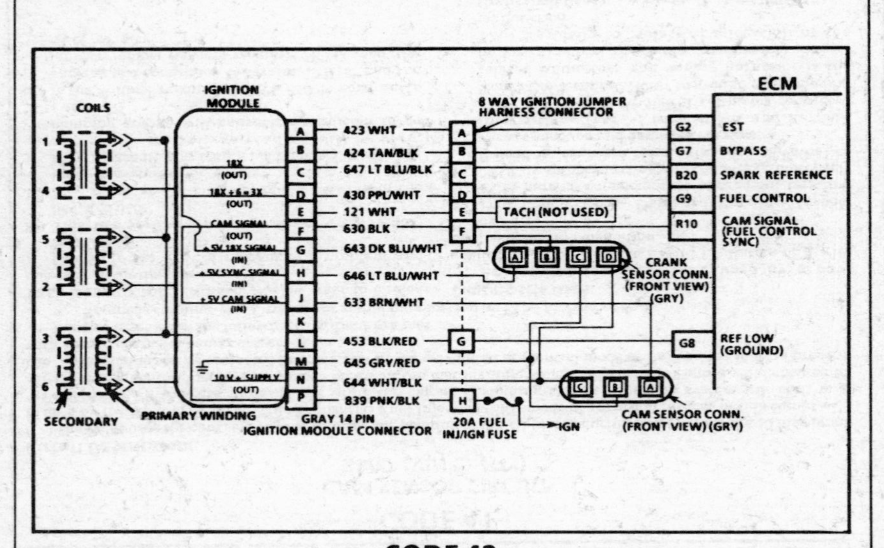

CODE 42

ELECTRONIC SPARK TIMING (EST) CIRCUIT 3800 (VIN L) (TPI)

Circuit Description:

When the ECM recognizes the second fuel control reference pulse, it applies a 5 volts to bypass CKT 424 to switch timing to ECM control. An open or ground in the EST or bypass circuit will set a Code 42. The engine can be restarted but will run on module timing.

To set a Code 42 the following conditions must be met:

- Engine speed greater than 600 rpm with no EST pulse for 400 ms (open or grounded CKT 423), or
- ECM commanding bypass mode (open or grounded CKT 424)

Test Description: Numbers below refer to circled numbers on the diagnostic chart.

1. Checks to see if ECM recognizes a problem. If it does not set Code 42, it is an intermittent problem and could be due to a loose connection.
2. With the ECM disconnected, the ohmmeter should be reading less than 200 ohms, which is the normal resistance of the EST circuit through the ignition module. A higher resistance would indicate a fault in CKT 423, a poor ignition module connection, or a faulty ignition module.
3. If test light was "ON" when connected from 12 volts to ECM harness terminal "G7", either CKT 424 is shorted to ground or the ignition module is faulty.
4. Checks to see if ignition module switches when the bypass circuit is energized by 12 volts through the test light. If the ignition module actually switches, the ohmmeter reading should shift to over 6,000 ohms.
5. Disconnecting the ignition module should make the ohmmeter read as if it were monitoring an open circuit (infinite reading).

Otherwise, CKT 423 is shorted to ground.

Diagnostic Aids:

An intermittent may be caused by a poor connection, rubbed through wire insulation, or a wire broken inside the insulation.

Check For:

- Poor Connection or Damaged Harness Inspect ECM harness connectors for backed out terminals "G7" or "G2", improper mating, broken locks, improperly formed or damaged terminals, poor terminal to wire connection, and damaged harness.
- Intermittent Test Monitor a digital voltmeter connected from affected terminal to ground while moving related connectors and wiring harness. If the failure is induced, the voltage reading will change.
-

Crankshaft Sensor Connector Part #: 12059401.
Camshaft Sensor Connector Part #: 12047911.
8 Way Connector Part #: 12047937.

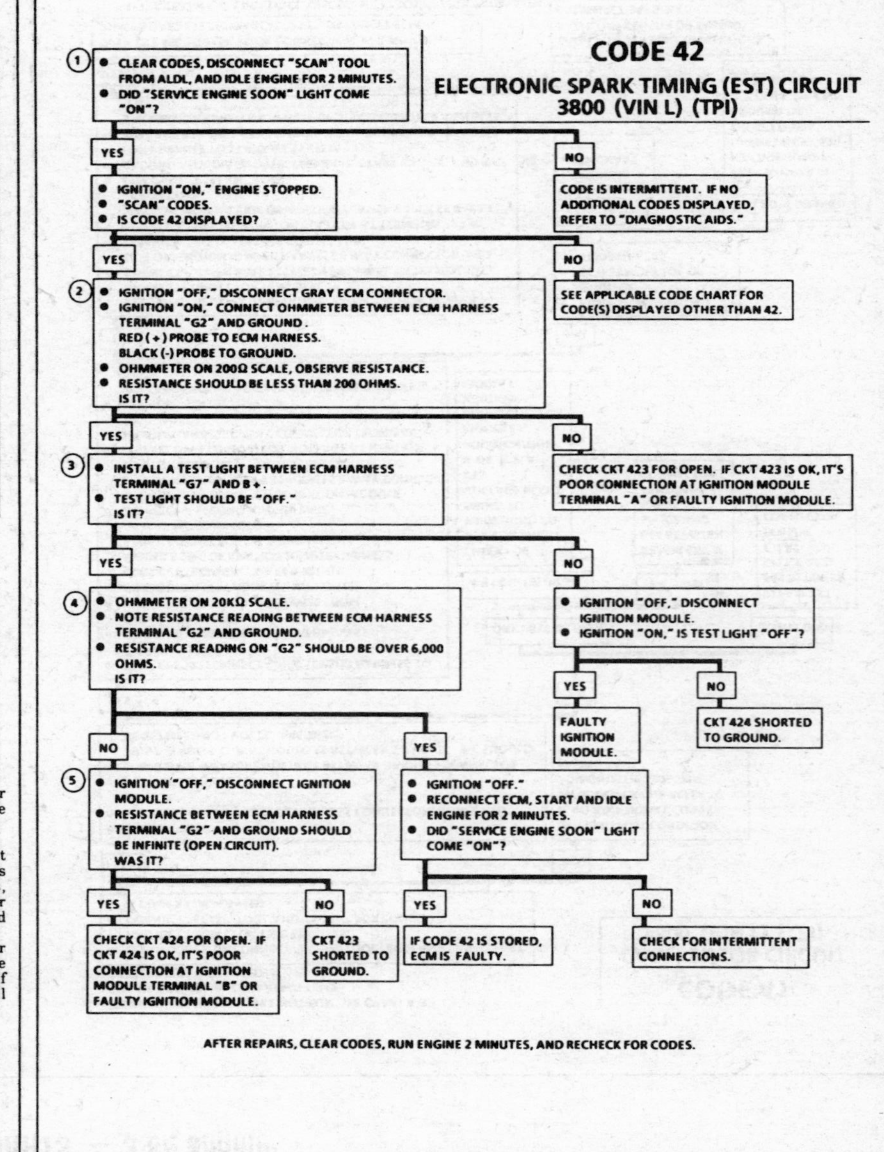

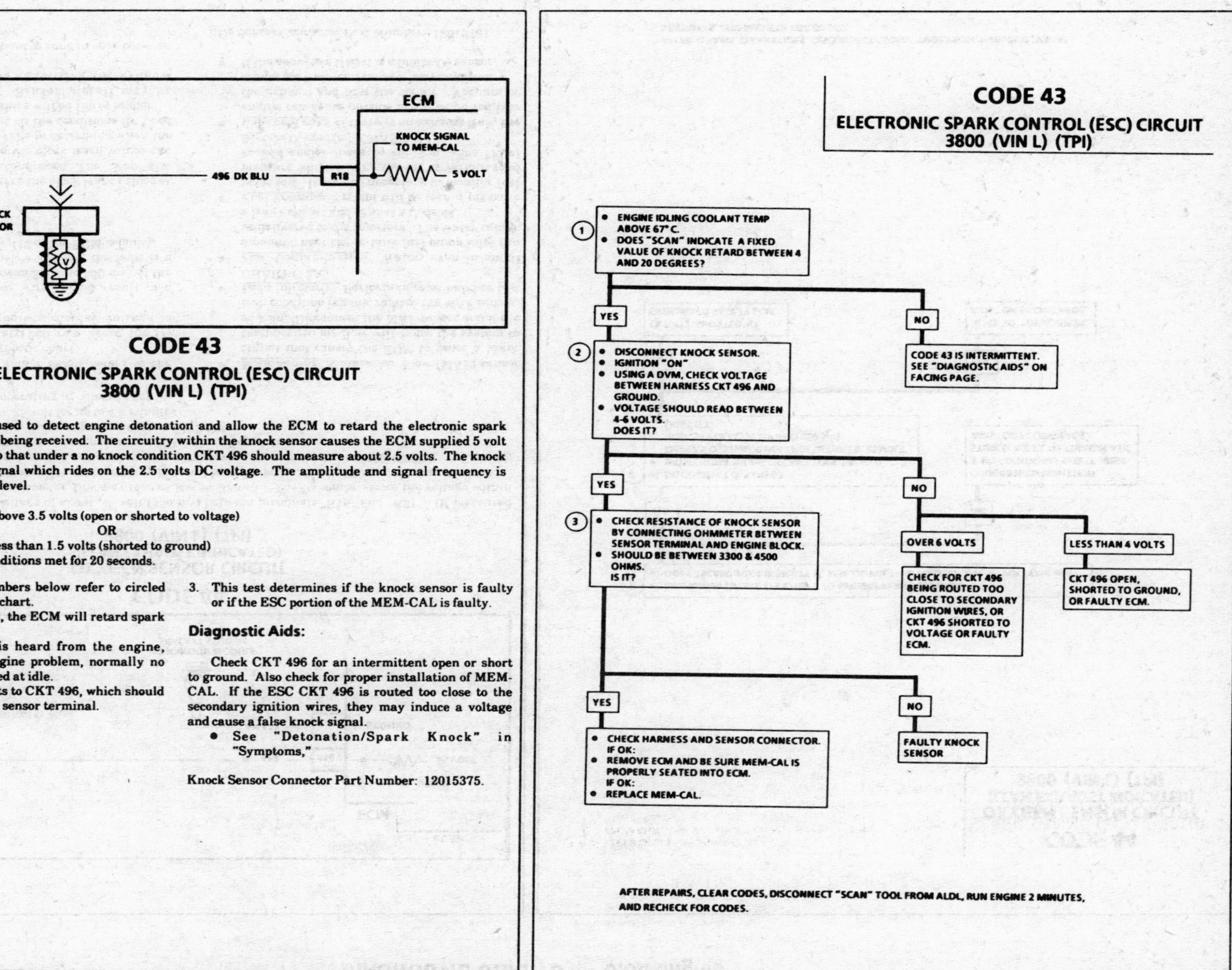
ECM
KNOCK SIGNAL TO MEM-CAL
496 DK BLU
R18
5 VOLT
KNOCK SENSOR
V
CODE 43
ELECTRONIC SPARK CONTROL (ESC) CIRCUIT
3800 (VIN L) (TPI)
1
• ENGINE IDLING COOLANT TEMP ABOVE 67° C.
• DOES "SCAN" INDICATE A FIXED VALUE OF KNOCK RETARD BETWEEN 4 AND 20 DEGREES?
YES
NO
CODE 43 IS INTERMITTENT. SEE "DIAGNOSTIC AIDS" ON FACING PAGE.
2
• DISCONNECT KNOCK SENSOR.
• IGNITION "ON"
• USING A DVM, CHECK VOLTAGE BETWEEN HARNESS CKT 496 AND GROUND.
• VOLTAGE SHOULD READ BETWEEN 4-6 VOLTS. DOES IT?
YES
NO
OVER 6 VOLTS
LESS THAN 4 VOLTS
CHECK FOR CKT 496 BEING ROUTED TOO CLOSE TO SECONDARY IGNITION WIRES, OR CKT 496 SHORTED TO VOLTAGE OR FAULTY ECM.
CKT 496 OPEN, SHORTED TO GROUND, OR FAULTY ECM.
3
• CHECK RESISTANCE OF KNOCK SENSOR BY CONNECTING OHMMETER BETWEEN SENSOR TERMINAL AND ENGINE BLOCK.
• SHOULD BE BETWEEN 3300 & 4500 OHMS. IS IT?
YES
NO
FAULTY KNOCK SENSOR
• CHECK HARNESS AND SENSOR CONNECTOR. IF OK:
• REMOVE ECM AND BE SURE MEM-CAL IS PROPERLY SEATED INTO ECM. IF OK:
• REPLACE MEM-CAL.
AFTER REPAIRS, CLEAR CODES, DISCONNECT "SCAN" TOOL FROM ALDL, RUN ENGINE 2 MINUTES, AND RECHECK FOR CODES.

CODE 43

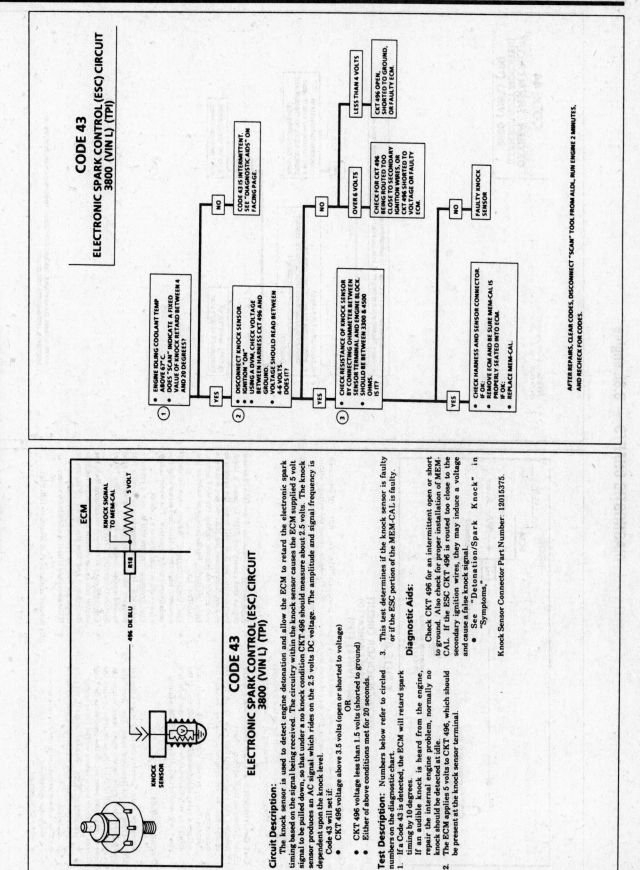

ELECTRONIC SPARK CONTROL (ESC) CIRCUIT 3800 (VIN L) (TPI)

Circuit Description:

The knock sensor is used to detect engine detonation and allow the ECM to retard the electronic spark timing based on the signal being received. The circuitry within the knock sensor causes the ECM supplied 5 volt signal to be pulled down, so that under a no knock condition CKT 496 should measure about 2.5 volts. The knock sensor produces an AC signal which rides on the 2.5 volts DC voltage. The amplitude and signal frequency is dependent upon the knock level.

Code 43 will set if:

- CKT 496 voltage above 3.5 volts (open or shorted to voltage)

OR

- CKT 496 voltage less than 1.5 volts (shorted to ground)
- Either of above conditions met for 20 seconds.

Test Description: Numbers below refer to circled numbers on the diagnostic chart.

1. If a Code 43 is detected, the ECM will retard spark timing by 10 degrees.
   If an audible knock is heard from the engine, repair the internal engine problem, normally no knock should be detected at idle.
2. The ECM applies 5 volts to CKT 496, which should be present at the knock sensor terminal.
3. This test determines if the knock sensor is faulty or if the ESC portion of the MEM-CAL is faulty.

Diagnostic Aids:

Check CKT 496 for an intermittent open or short to ground. Also check for proper installation of MEM-CAL. If the ESC CKT 496 is routed too close to the secondary ignition wires, they may induce a voltage and cause a false knock signal.

- See "Detonation/Spark Knock" in "Symptoms,"

Knock Sensor Connector Part Number: 12015375.

DIAGNOSTIC CHARTS — 3.8L engine

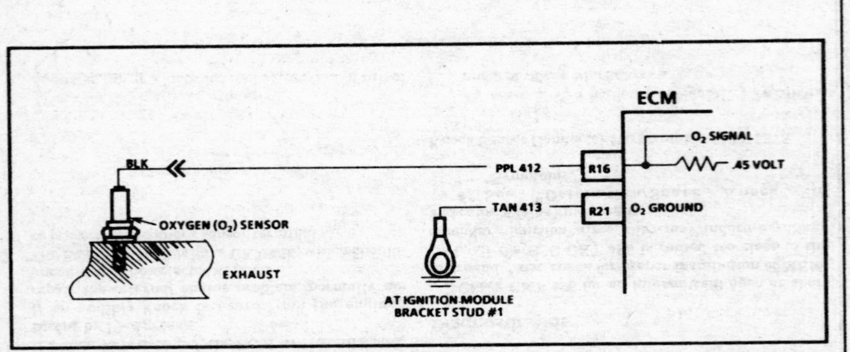

CODE 44
OXYGEN SENSOR CIRCUIT
(LEAN EXHAUST INDICATED)
3800 (VIN L) (TPI)

Circuit Description:

The ECM supplies a voltage of about .45 volt (450 mv) between terminals "R16" and "R21". (If measured with a 10 megaohm digital voltmeter, this may read as low as .32 volt.) The O_2 sensor varies the voltage within a range of about 1 volt, (1000 mv) if the exhaust is rich, down through about .10 volt (100 mv) if exhaust is lean.

The sensor is like an open circuit and produces no voltage when it is below about 360°C (600°F). A Code 44, Code 45, an open sensor circuit, or cold sensor causes "Open Loop" operation.

Code 44 is set when the O_2 sensor signal voltage on CKT 412:
- Remains below .25 volt for up to 4.5 minutes.
- The system is operating in "Closed Loop."

Test Description: Number below refers to the circled number on the diagnostic chart.
1. Running the engine at 1200 rpm keeps the O_2 sensor hot, so an accurate display voltage is maintained.
2. Opening the O_2 sensor wire should result in a voltage display of between 350 and 550 mv. If the display is still fixed below 350 mv, the fault is a short to ground in CKT 412 or the ECM is faulty.

Diagnostic Aids:

Using the "Scan," observe the block learn values at different rpm and air flow conditions. The "Scan" also displays the block cells, so the block learn values can be checked in each of the cells to determine when the Code 44 may have been set. If the conditions for Code 44 exist, the block learn values will be 150 or higher.
- O_2 Sensor Wire Sensor pigtail may be mispositioned and contacting the exhaust manifold.
- Check for intermittent ground in wire between connector and sensor.
- Poor ECM ground.
- MAF Sensor A Mass Air Flow (MAF) sensor output that causes the ECM to sense a lower than normal air flow will cause the system to go lean. Disconnect the MAF sensor and if the lean condition is gone, replace the MAF sensor.
- Lean Injector(s) Perform injector balance test CHART C-2A.
- Fuel Contamination Water, even in small amounts, near the in-tank fuel pump inlet can be delivered to the injectors. The water causes a lean exhaust and can set a Code 44.
- Fuel Pressure System will be lean if pressure is too low. It may be necessary to monitor fuel pressure while driving the car at various road speeds and/or loads to confirm. See "Fuel System Diagnosis," CHART A-7.
- Exhaust Leaks If there is an exhaust leak, the engine can cause outside air to be pulled into the exhaust and past the sensor. Vacuum or crankcase leaks can cause a lean condition.
- If the above are OK, it is a faulty O_2 sensor.

O_2 Sensor Connector Part Number: 12015791.

CODE 44
OXYGEN SENSOR CIRCUIT
(LEAN EXHAUST INDICATED)
3800 (VIN L) (TPI)

(1)
- RUN WARM ENGINE (75°C/167°F TO 95°C/203°F) AT 1200 RPM.
- DOES "SCAN" TOOL INDICATE O_2 SENSOR VOLTAGE FIXED BELOW .25 VOLT (250 mV)?

YES →

(2)
- DISCONNECT O_2 SENSOR.
- WITH ENGINE IDLING, "SCAN" TOOL SHOULD DISPLAY O_2 SENSOR VOLTAGE BETWEEN .35 VOLT AND .55 VOLT (350 mV AND 550 mV). DOES IT?

NO → CKT 412 SHORTED TO GROUND OR FAULTY ECM.

YES → REFER TO "DIAGNOSTIC AIDS" ON FACING PAGE.

NO (from 1) → CODE 44 IS INTERMITTENT. IF NO ADDITIONAL CODES WERE STORED, REFER TO "DIAGNOSTIC AIDS" ON FACING PAGE.

AFTER REPAIRS, CLEAR CODES, DISCONNECT "SCAN" TOOL FROM ALDL, RUN ENGINE 5 MINUTES, AND RECHECK FOR CODES.

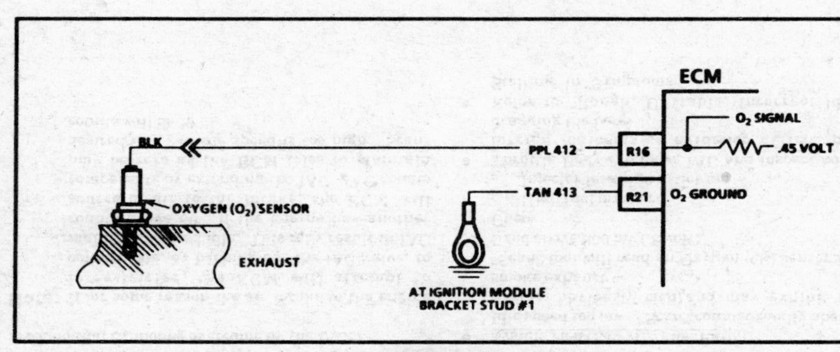
ECM
O₂ SIGNAL
.45 VOLT
BLK
PPL 412
R16
TAN 413
R21
O₂ GROUND
OXYGEN (O₂) SENSOR
EXHAUST
AT IGNITION MODULE BRACKET STUD #1

CODE 45

OXYGEN SENSOR CIRCUIT (RICH EXHAUST INDICATED) 3800 (VIN L) (TPI)

Circuit Description:

The ECM supplies a voltage of about .45 volt (450 mv) between terminals "R16" and "R21". (If measured with a 10 megaohm digital voltmeter, this may read as low as .32 volt.) The O_2 sensor varies the voltage within a range of about 1 volt (1000 mv) if the exhaust is rich, down through about .10 volt (100 mv) if exhaust is lean.

The sensor is like an open circuit and produces no voltage when it is below about 360°C (600°F). A Code 44, Code 45, an open sensor circuit or cold sensor causes "Open Loop" operation.

Code 45 is set when the O_2 sensor signal voltage or CKT 412:

- Remains above .75 volt for 2 minutes and in "Closed Loop"
- TPS voltage between .6 and 1.8 volts
- No Code 21 or Code 22

Test Description: Number below refers to the circled number on the diagnostic chart.

1. Checks to see if conditions are present to set Code 45.

Diagnostic Aids:

Check the following:

- <u>Fuel Pressure</u> System will go rich if pressure is too high. The ECM can compensate for some increase. However, if it gets too high, a Code 45 may be set. See "Fuel System Diagnosis," CHART A-7.
- <u>Rich Injector</u> Perform injector balance test CHART C-2A.
- <u>Leaking Injector</u> See CHART A-7.
- Check for fuel contaminated oil.
- <u>Canister Purge</u> Check for fuel saturation. If full of fuel, check canister control and hoses.
- <u>MAF Sensor</u> An output that causes the ECM to sense a higher than normal airflow can cause the system to go rich. Disconnecting the MAF sensor will allow the ECM to set a fixed value for the sensor. Substitute a different MAF sensor if the rich condition is gone while the sensor is disconnected.
- Check for leaking fuel pressure regulator diaphragm by checking vacuum line to regulator for fuel.
- <u>TPS</u> An intermittent TPS output will cause the system to go rich due to a false indication of the engine accelerating.
- False rich indication due to silicone contamination of the O_2 sensor. This will be indicated by a Code 45 accompanied by lean driveability conditions and a powdery white deposit on the sensor.

O_2 Sensor Connector Part Number: 12015791.

CODE 45

OXYGEN SENSOR CIRCUIT (RICH EXHAUST INDICATED) 3800 (VIN L) (TPI)

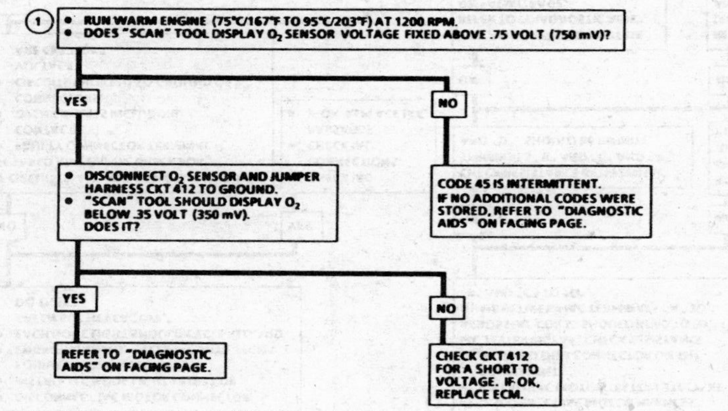
1
• RUN WARM ENGINE (75°C/167°F TO 95°C/203°F) AT 1200 RPM.
• DOES "SCAN" TOOL DISPLAY O₂ SENSOR VOLTAGE FIXED ABOVE .75 VOLT (750 mV)?
YES
NO
• DISCONNECT O₂ SENSOR AND JUMPER HARNESS CKT 412 TO GROUND.
• "SCAN" TOOL SHOULD DISPLAY O₂ BELOW .35 VOLT (350 mV). DOES IT?
CODE 45 IS INTERMITTENT. IF NO ADDITIONAL CODES WERE STORED, REFER TO "DIAGNOSTIC AIDS" ON FACING PAGE.
YES
NO
REFER TO "DIAGNOSTIC AIDS" ON FACING PAGE.
CHECK CKT 412 FOR A SHORT TO VOLTAGE. IF OK, REPLACE ECM.
CLEAR CODES, DISCONNECT "SCAN" TOOL FROM ALDL, START ENGINE AND CONFIRM "CLOSED LOOP" OPERATION AND NO "SERVICE ENGINE SOON" LIGHT.

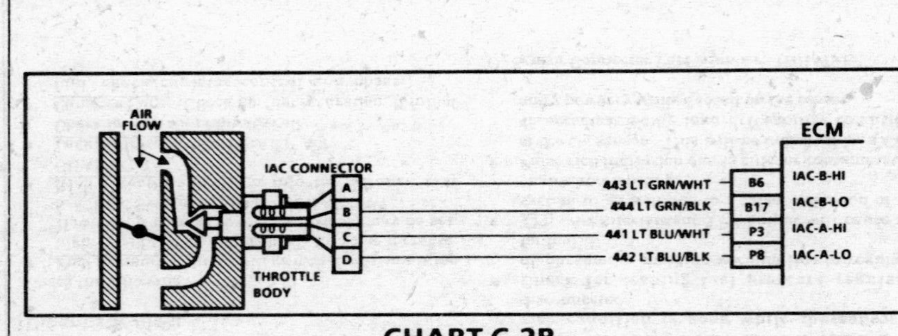

CHART C-2B

IDLE AIR CONTROL (IAC) VALVE CHECK 3800 (VIN L) (TPI)

Circuit Description:

The ECM controls idle rpm with the IAC valve. To increase idle rpm, the ECM retracts the IAC pintle from the seat, allowing more air to bypass the throttle plate. To decrease rpm, it extends the IAC pintle valve in towards the seat, reducing air flow through the IAC valve port in the throttle body. A "Scan" tool will read the ECM commands to the IAC valve in counts. The higher the counts, the more air allowed (higher idle). The lower the counts, the less air allowed (lower idle).

Test Description: Numbers below refer to circled numbers on the diagnostic chart.

1. The "Scan" tool is used to extend and retract the IAC valve. Valve movement is verified by an engine speed change.
2. This test checks all wires, connectors, and ECM.
3. This test check for shorted or open IAC valve coils.

Diagnostic Aids:

A slow, unstable idle may be caused by a system problem that cannot be overcome by the IAC.

Note: If for some reason the air intake to the engine is restricted, the ECM will attempt to compensate, by backing out the IAC valve, to maintain desired idle. This may result in IAC counts above 60. If the engine has another source of air to the intake, the ECM will compensate by extending the IAC - IAC counts may be zero as the ECM tries to maintain desired idle. If idle speed is too high, "Scan" counts will be "0".

- System lean (High Air/Fuel Ratio)
  Idle speed may be too high or too low. Engine speed may vary up and down, disconnecting IAC does not help. May set Code 44.
  "Scan" tool will read an Oxygen (O_2) sensor output less than 300 mv (.3 volt). Check for low regulated fuel pressure or water in fuel. A lean exhaust accompanied by an Oxygen (O_2) sensor output fixed above 800 mv (.8 volt) may be a contaminated sensor, usually caused by silicone. This may also set Code 45.
- System rich (Low Air/Fuel Ratio)
  Idle speed too low. "Scan" counts usually above 80. System obviously rich and may exhibit black smoke exhaust.
  "Scan" tool will read an Oxygen (O_2) sensor signal fixed above 800 mv (.8 volt).
  Check:
  - High fuel pressure
  - Injector leaking or sticking
- Throttle Body - Remove IAC and inspect bore for foreign material or evidence of IAC pintle dragging the bore.
- Refer to "Rough, Unstable, Incorrect Idle or Stalling" in "Symptoms,"

CHART C-2B

IDLE AIR CONTROL (IAC) VALVE CHECK 3800 (VIN L) (TPI)

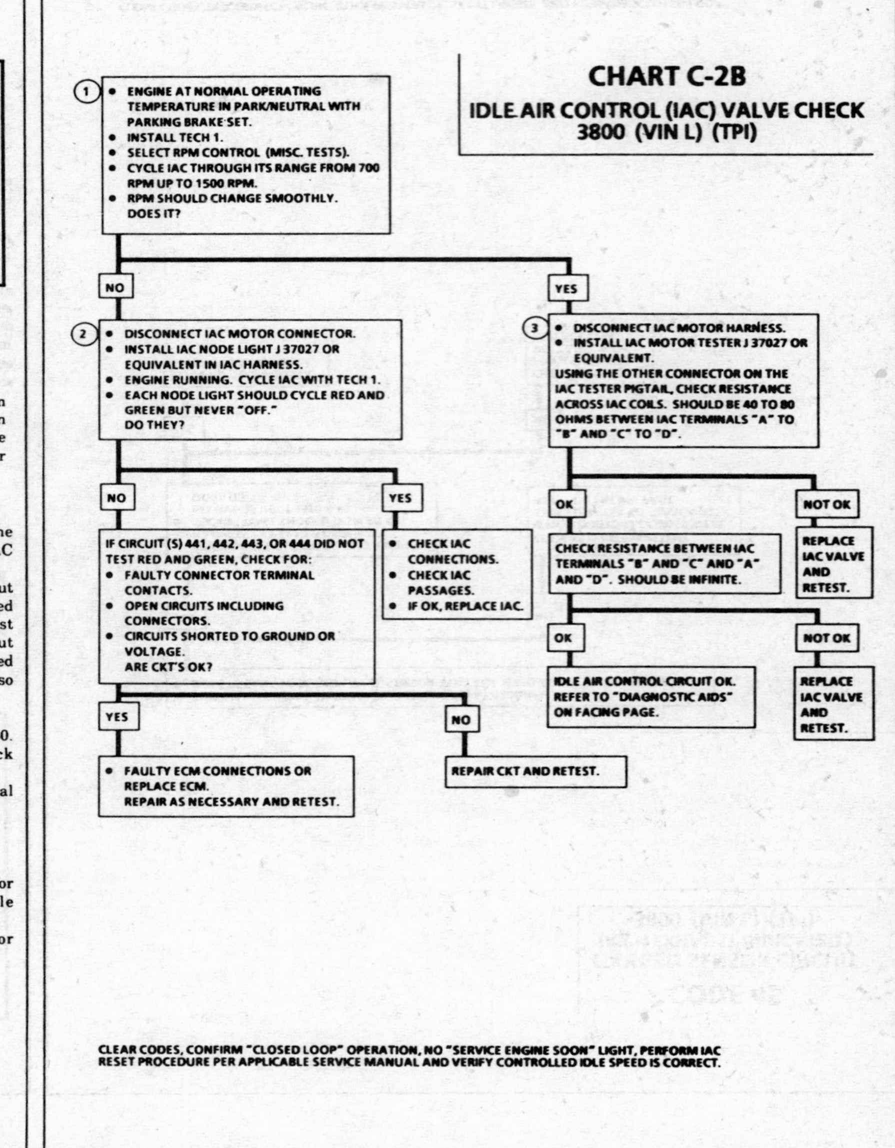

1
• ENGINE AT NORMAL OPERATING TEMPERATURE IN PARK/NEUTRAL WITH PARKING BRAKE SET.
• INSTALL TECH 1.
• SELECT RPM CONTROL (MISC. TESTS).
• CYCLE IAC THROUGH ITS RANGE FROM 700 RPM UP TO 1500 RPM.
• RPM SHOULD CHANGE SMOOTHLY. DOES IT?
NO
YES
2
• DISCONNECT IAC MOTOR CONNECTOR.
• INSTALL IAC NODE LIGHT J 37027 OR EQUIVALENT IN IAC HARNESS.
• ENGINE RUNNING. CYCLE IAC WITH TECH 1.
• EACH NODE LIGHT SHOULD CYCLE RED AND GREEN BUT NEVER "OFF." DO THEY?
3
• DISCONNECT IAC MOTOR HARNESS.
• INSTALL IAC MOTOR TESTER J 37027 OR EQUIVALENT.
USING THE OTHER CONNECTOR ON THE IAC TESTER PIGTAIL, CHECK RESISTANCE ACROSS IAC COILS. SHOULD BE 40 TO 80 OHMS BETWEEN IAC TERMINALS "A" TO "B" AND "C" TO "D".
NO
YES
IF CIRCUIT (S) 441, 442, 443, OR 444 DID NOT TEST RED AND GREEN, CHECK FOR:
• FAULTY CONNECTOR TERMINAL CONTACTS.
• OPEN CIRCUITS INCLUDING CONNECTORS.
• CIRCUITS SHORTED TO GROUND OR VOLTAGE.
ARE CKT'S OK?
• CHECK IAC CONNECTIONS.
• CHECK IAC PASSAGES.
• IF OK, REPLACE IAC.
OK
NOT OK
CHECK RESISTANCE BETWEEN IAC TERMINALS "B" AND "C" AND "A" AND "D". SHOULD BE INFINITE.
REPLACE IAC VALVE AND RETEST.
OK
NOT OK
IDLE AIR CONTROL CIRCUIT OK. REFER TO "DIAGNOSTIC AIDS" ON FACING PAGE.
REPLACE IAC VALVE AND RETEST.
YES
NO
• FAULTY ECM CONNECTIONS OR REPLACE ECM. REPAIR AS NECESSARY AND RETEST.
REPAIR CKT AND RETEST.
CLEAR CODES, CONFIRM "CLOSED LOOP" OPERATION, NO "SERVICE ENGINE SOON" LIGHT, PERFORM IAC RESET PROCEDURE PER APPLICABLE SERVICE MANUAL AND VERIFY CONTROLLED IDLE SPEED IS CORRECT.

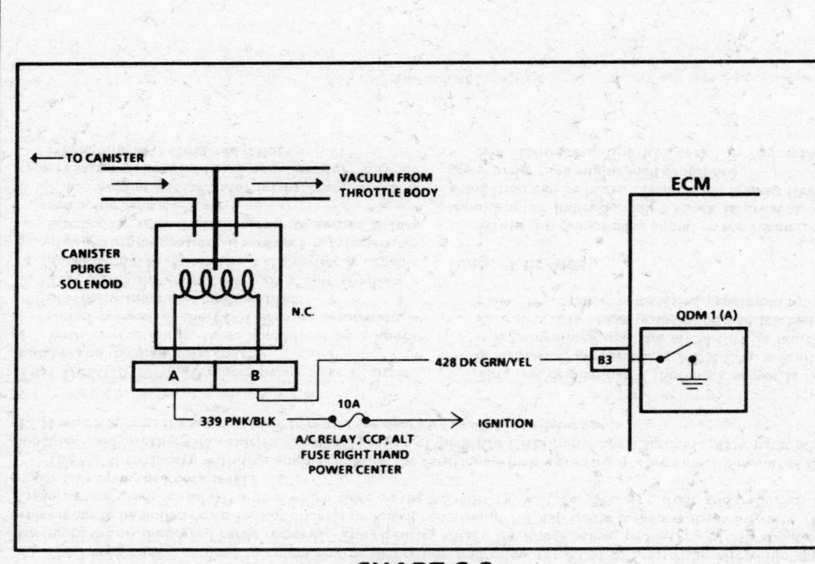

CHART C-3

CANISTER PURGE VALVE CHECK 3800 (VIN L) (TPI)

Circuit Description:

Canister purge is controlled by a solenoid that allows vacuum to purge the canister when energized. The ECM supplies a Pulse Width Modulated (PWM) ground to energize the solenoid (purge "ON").

If the diagnostic test terminal is grounded with the engine stopped or the following is met with the engine running the purge solenoid is energized (purge "ON").

- Engine run time after start more than 30 seconds
- Coolant temperature above 60°C (158°F)
- MAT sensor reading above 9.5°C (50°F)

Test Description: Numbers below refer to circled numbers on the diagnostic chart.

1. Checks to see if the solenoid is opened or closed. The solenoid is de-energized in this step, so it should be closed.
2. The "Scan" tool is used to cycle the CCP solenoid "ON" and "OFF" and check the operation of the solenoid.

CHART C-3

CANISTER PURGE VALVE CHECK 3800 (VIN L) (TPI)

(1)
- SET PARKING BRAKE AND BLOCK DRIVE WHEELS.
- CHECK VACUUM SOURCE. IF NO VACUUM, REPAIR CAUSE OF NO VACUUM. IF OK, CONTINUE WITH CHART.
- DISCONNECT THE CANISTER SIDE HOSE FROM THE PURGE SOLENOID AND CONNECT A VACUUM GAGE TO THE CANISTER SIDE OF THE SOLENOID.
- DISCONNECT ELECTRICAL CONNECTOR.
- WITH THE ENGINE IDLING NOTE VACUUM GAGE. SHOULD BE 0 VACUUM.

IS IT?

NO → REPLACE SOLENOID.

YES →

(2)
- INSTALL "SCAN" TOOL.
- RECONNECT SOLENOID CONNECTOR.
- UNDER MISC. TEST SELECT CCP CONTROL.
- CYCLE THE CCP SOLENOID "ON" AND "OFF." DOES THE VACUUM GO UP AND DOWN AS THE SOLENOID IS CYCLED "ON" AND "OFF"?

YES → CHECK CANISTER AND PURGE HOSE FOR DAMAGE. IF OK, NO PROBLEM FOUND.

NO →

- DISCONNECT CCP SOLENOID ELECTRICAL CONNECTER.
- KEY "ON" ENGINE "OFF."
- INSTALL A TEST LIGHT BETWEEN HARNESS TERMINAL "A" AND GROUND.

DOES THE LIGHT COME "ON"?

NO → REPAIR OPEN IN CKT 339.

YES →

- CONNECT A TEST LIGHT BETWEEN HARNESS CONNECTOR TERMINALS.

IS THE TEST LIGHT "ON"?

NO → CHECK FOR OPEN CKT 428. IF OK, LOOSE ECM CONNECTIONS OR FAULTY ECM.

YES → CHECK CKT 428 FOR A SHORT TO GROUND. IF IT'S OK REPLACE ECM.

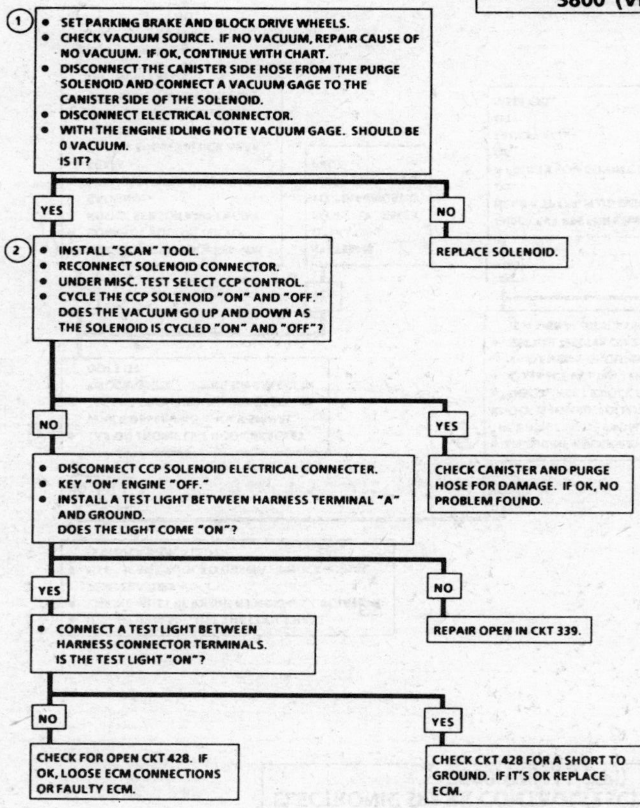

"AFTER REPAIRS, CLEAR CODES, RUN ENGINE 2 MINUTES, AND RECHECK FOR CODES."

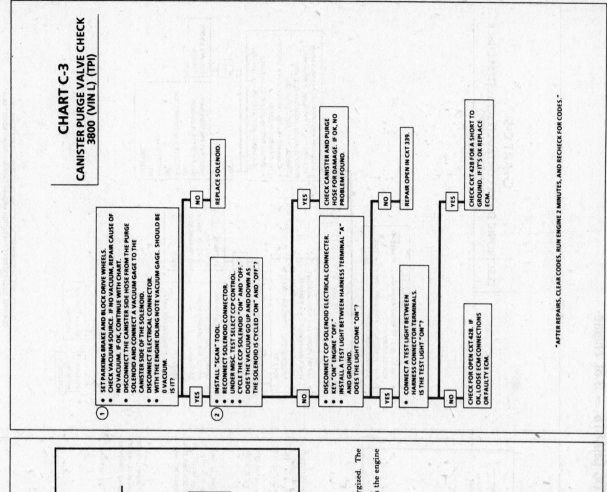

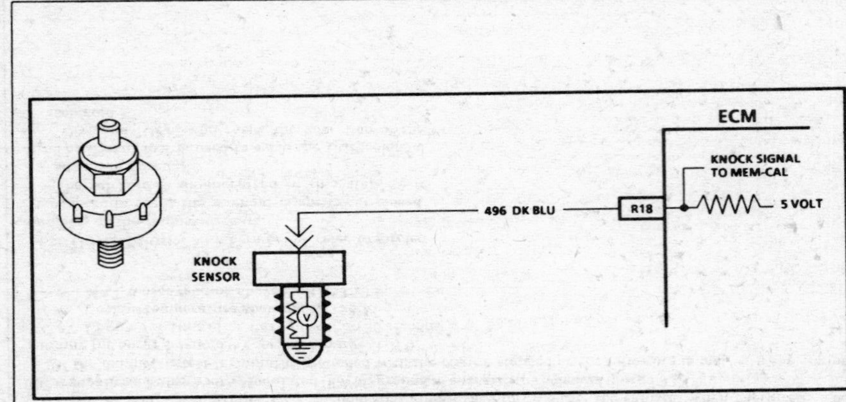
ECM
KNOCK SIGNAL TO MEM-CAL
496 DK BLU
R18
5 VOLT
KNOCK SENSOR

CHART C-5

ELECTRONIC SPARK CONTROL (ESC) SYSTEM CHECK 3800 (VIN L) (TPI)

Circuit Description:

The knock sensor is used to detect engine detonation and allow the ECM to retard the electronic spark timing based on the signal being received. The circuitry within the knock sensor causes the ECM's supplied 5 volt signal to be pulled down so that under a no knock condition, CKT 496 would measure about 2.5 volts. The knock sensor produces an AC signal which rides on the 2.5 volts DC voltage. The amplitude and frequency are dependent upon the knock level.

The MEM-CAL used with this engine contains the functions which were part of the remotely mounted ESC modules used on other GM vehicles. The ESC portion of the MEM-CAL then sends a signal to other parts of the ECM which adjusts the spark timing to retard the spark and reduce the detonation.

Test Description: Numbers below refer to circled numbers on the diagnostic chart.

1. With engine idling, there should not be a knock signal present at the ECM because detonation is not likely under a no load condition.
2. Tapping on the engine lift hook should simulate a knock signal to determine if the sensor is capable of detecting detonation. If no knock is detected, try tapping on engine block closer to sensor before replacing sensor.
3. If the engine has an internal problem which is creating a knock, the knock sensor may be responding to the internal failure.
4. This test determines if the knock sensor is faulty or if the ESC portion of the MEM-CAL is faulty. If it is determined that the MEM-CAL is faulty, be sure that it is properly installed and latched into place. If not properly installed, repair and retest.

Diagnostic Aids:

While observing knock signal on the "Scan," there should be an indication that knock is present when detonation can be heard. Detonation is most likely to occur under high engine load conditions.

- See "Detonation/Spark Knock" in "Symptoms,"

CHART C-5

ELECTRONIC SPARK CONTROL (ESC) SYSTEM CHECK 3800 (VIN L) (TPI)

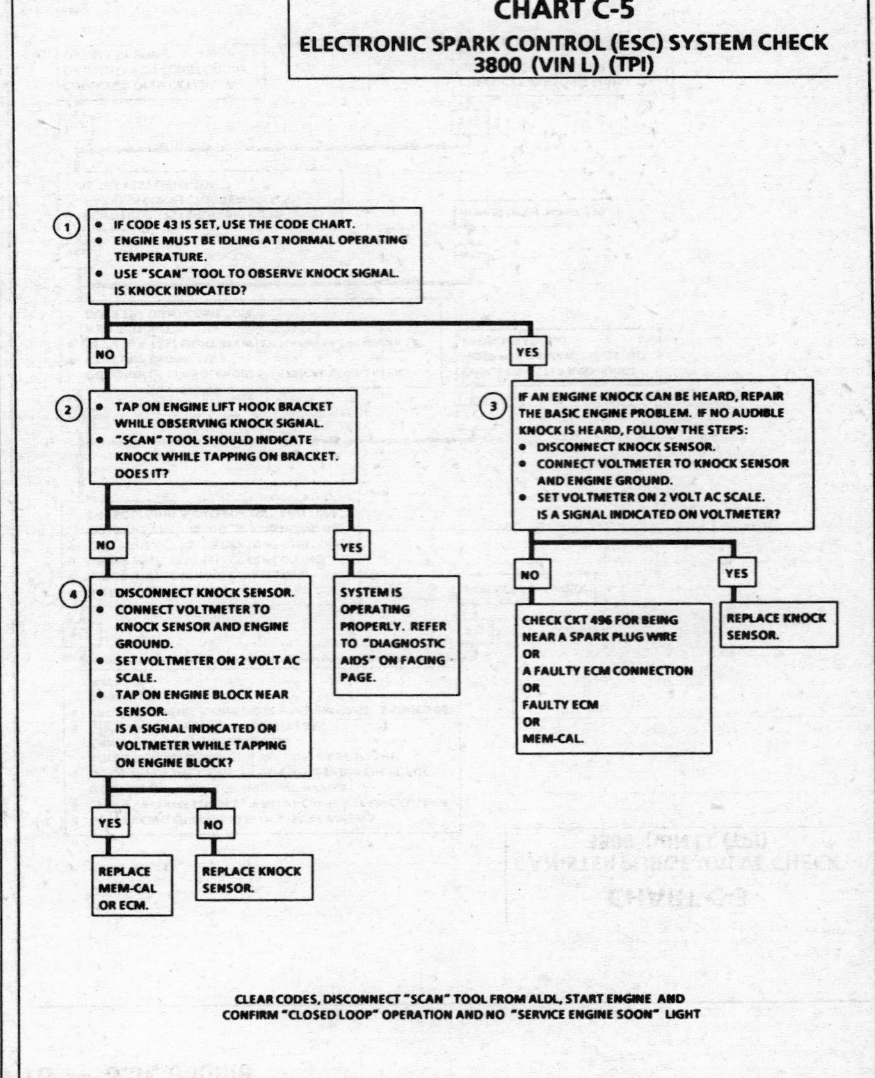
1
• IF CODE 43 IS SET, USE THE CODE CHART.
• ENGINE MUST BE IDLING AT NORMAL OPERATING TEMPERATURE.
• USE "SCAN" TOOL TO OBSERVE KNOCK SIGNAL.
IS KNOCK INDICATED?
NO
YES
2
• TAP ON ENGINE LIFT HOOK BRACKET WHILE OBSERVING KNOCK SIGNAL.
• "SCAN" TOOL SHOULD INDICATE KNOCK WHILE TAPPING ON BRACKET.
DOES IT?
3
IF AN ENGINE KNOCK CAN BE HEARD, REPAIR THE BASIC ENGINE PROBLEM. IF NO AUDIBLE KNOCK IS HEARD, FOLLOW THE STEPS:
• DISCONNECT KNOCK SENSOR.
• CONNECT VOLTMETER TO KNOCK SENSOR AND ENGINE GROUND.
• SET VOLTMETER ON 2 VOLT AC SCALE.
IS A SIGNAL INDICATED ON VOLTMETER?
NO
YES
4
• DISCONNECT KNOCK SENSOR.
• CONNECT VOLTMETER TO KNOCK SENSOR AND ENGINE GROUND.
• SET VOLTMETER ON 2 VOLT AC SCALE.
• TAP ON ENGINE BLOCK NEAR SENSOR.
IS A SIGNAL INDICATED ON VOLTMETER WHILE TAPPING ON ENGINE BLOCK?
SYSTEM IS OPERATING PROPERLY. REFER TO "DIAGNOSTIC AIDS" ON FACING PAGE.
NO
YES
CHECK CKT 496 FOR BEING NEAR A SPARK PLUG WIRE OR A FAULTY ECM CONNECTION OR FAULTY ECM OR MEM-CAL.
REPLACE KNOCK SENSOR.
YES
NO
REPLACE MEM-CAL OR ECM.
REPLACE KNOCK SENSOR.

CLEAR CODES, DISCONNECT "SCAN" TOOL FROM ALDL, START ENGINE AND CONFIRM "CLOSED LOOP" OPERATION AND NO "SERVICE ENGINE SOON" LIGHT

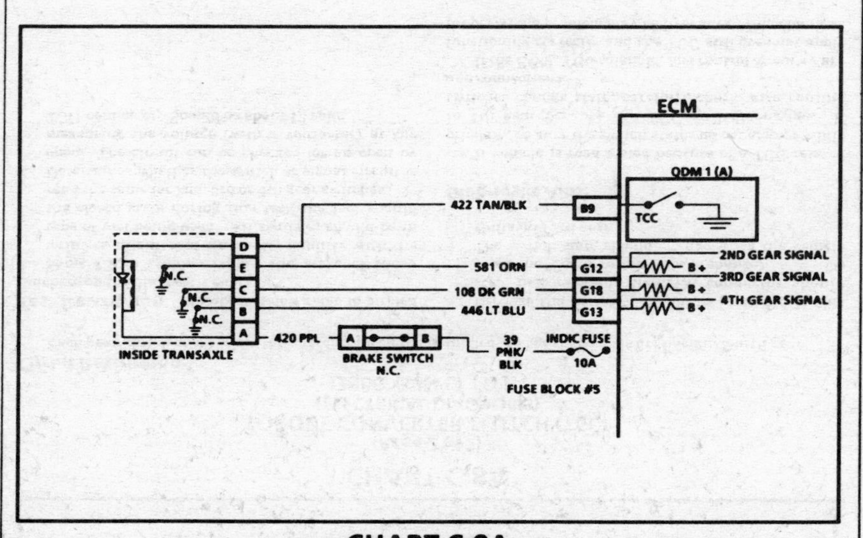
ECM
QDM 1 (A)
TCC
422 TAN/BLK
B9
581 ORN
108 DK GRN
446 LT BLU
G12
G18
G13
B+
2ND GEAR SIGNAL
3RD GEAR SIGNAL
4TH GEAR SIGNAL
D
E
C
B
A
N.C.
INSIDE TRANSAXLE
420 PPL
BRAKE SWITCH N.C.
39 PNK/BLK
INDIC FUSE
10A
FUSE BLOCK #5

CHART C-8A

(Page 1 of 2)
TORQUE CONVERTER CLUTCH (TCC)
(ELECTRICAL DIAGNOSIS)
3800 (VIN L) (TPI)

Circuit Description:

The purpose of the Torque Converter Clutch (TCC) feature is to eliminate the power loss of the torque converter when the vehicle is in a cruise condition. This allows the convenience of the automatic and the fuel economy of a manual transaxle. The heart of the system is a solenoid located inside the transaxle which is controlled by the ECM.

When the solenoid coil is activated ("ON"), the torque converter clutch is applied which results in a straight through mechanical coupling from the engine to the wheels. When the solenoid coil is deactivated ("OFF"), the torque converter clutch is released which allows the torque converter to operate in the conventional manner (fluidic coupling between engine and transaxle).

Each gear switch opens when the appropriate clutch is applied. All gear switches are open in fourth gear.

TCC will engage when:

- Engine warmed up.
- Vehicle speed above a calibrated value (about 40 mph 64 km/h).
- Throttle position sensor output not changing, indicating a steady road speed.
- Brake switch closed.
- 3rd or 4th gear switch open.

When operating in cruise control, the cruise active input to the ECM will allow TCC operation in 4th gear only.

Test Description: Numbers below refer to circled numbers on the diagnostic chart.

1. This test checks to see if the TCC solenoid is open.
2. Checks fuse, brake switch and CKTs 39 and 420 to the TCC solenoid.

Diagnostic Aids:

The "Scan" tool only indicates when the ECM has turned "ON" the TCC driver and this does not confirm that the TCC has engaged. To determine if TCC is functioning properly, road test the vehicle. Engine rpm should decrease when the "Scan" indicates the TCC driver has turned "ON."

CHART C-8A

(Page 1 of 2)
TORQUE CONVERTER CLUTCH (TCC)
(ELECTRICAL DIAGNOSIS)
3800 (VIN L) (TPI)

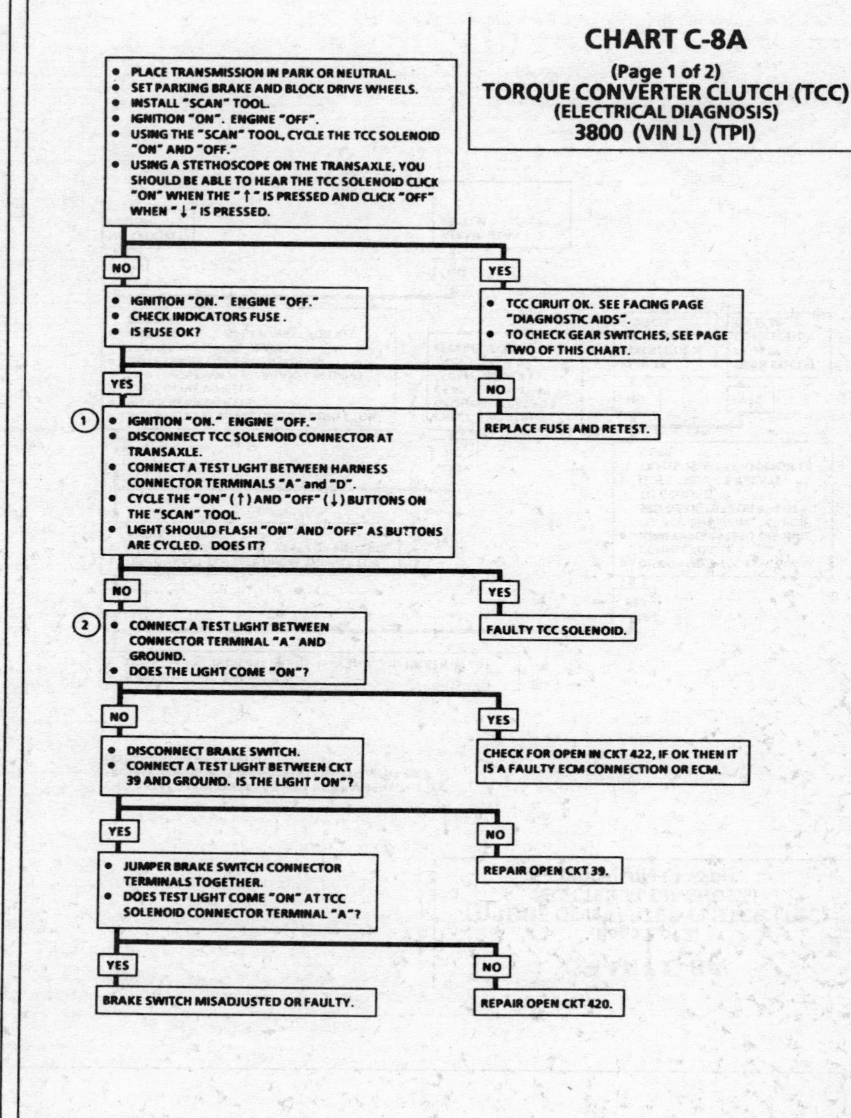
• PLACE TRANSMISSION IN PARK OR NEUTRAL.
• SET PARKING BRAKE AND BLOCK DRIVE WHEELS.
• INSTALL "SCAN" TOOL.
• IGNITION "ON". ENGINE "OFF".
• USING THE "SCAN" TOOL, CYCLE THE TCC SOLENOID "ON" AND "OFF."
• USING A STETHOSCOPE ON THE TRANSAXLE, YOU SHOULD BE ABLE TO HEAR THE TCC SOLENOID CLICK "ON" WHEN THE "↑" IS PRESSED AND CLICK "OFF" WHEN "↓" IS PRESSED.
NO
YES
• IGNITION "ON." ENGINE "OFF."
• CHECK INDICATORS FUSE.
• IS FUSE OK?
• TCC CIRUIT OK. SEE FACING PAGE "DIAGNOSTIC AIDS".
• TO CHECK GEAR SWITCHES, SEE PAGE TWO OF THIS CHART.
YES
NO
REPLACE FUSE AND RETEST.
1
• IGNITION "ON." ENGINE "OFF."
• DISCONNECT TCC SOLENOID CONNECTOR AT TRANSAXLE.
• CONNECT A TEST LIGHT BETWEEN HARNESS CONNECTOR TERMINALS "A" and "D".
• CYCLE THE "ON" (↑) AND "OFF" (↓) BUTTONS ON THE "SCAN" TOOL.
• LIGHT SHOULD FLASH "ON" AND "OFF" AS BUTTONS ARE CYCLED. DOES IT?
NO
YES
FAULTY TCC SOLENOID.
2
• CONNECT A TEST LIGHT BETWEEN CONNECTOR TERMINAL "A" AND GROUND.
• DOES THE LIGHT COME "ON"?
NO
YES
CHECK FOR OPEN IN CKT 422, IF OK THEN IT IS A FAULTY ECM CONNECTION OR ECM.
• DISCONNECT BRAKE SWITCH.
• CONNECT A TEST LIGHT BETWEEN CKT 39 AND GROUND. IS THE LIGHT "ON"?
YES
NO
REPAIR OPEN CKT 39.
• JUMPER BRAKE SWITCH CONNECTOR TERMINALS TOGETHER.
• DOES TEST LIGHT COME "ON" AT TCC SOLENOID CONNECTOR TERMINAL "A"?
YES
NO
BRAKE SWITCH MISADJUSTED OR FAULTY.
REPAIR OPEN CKT 420.

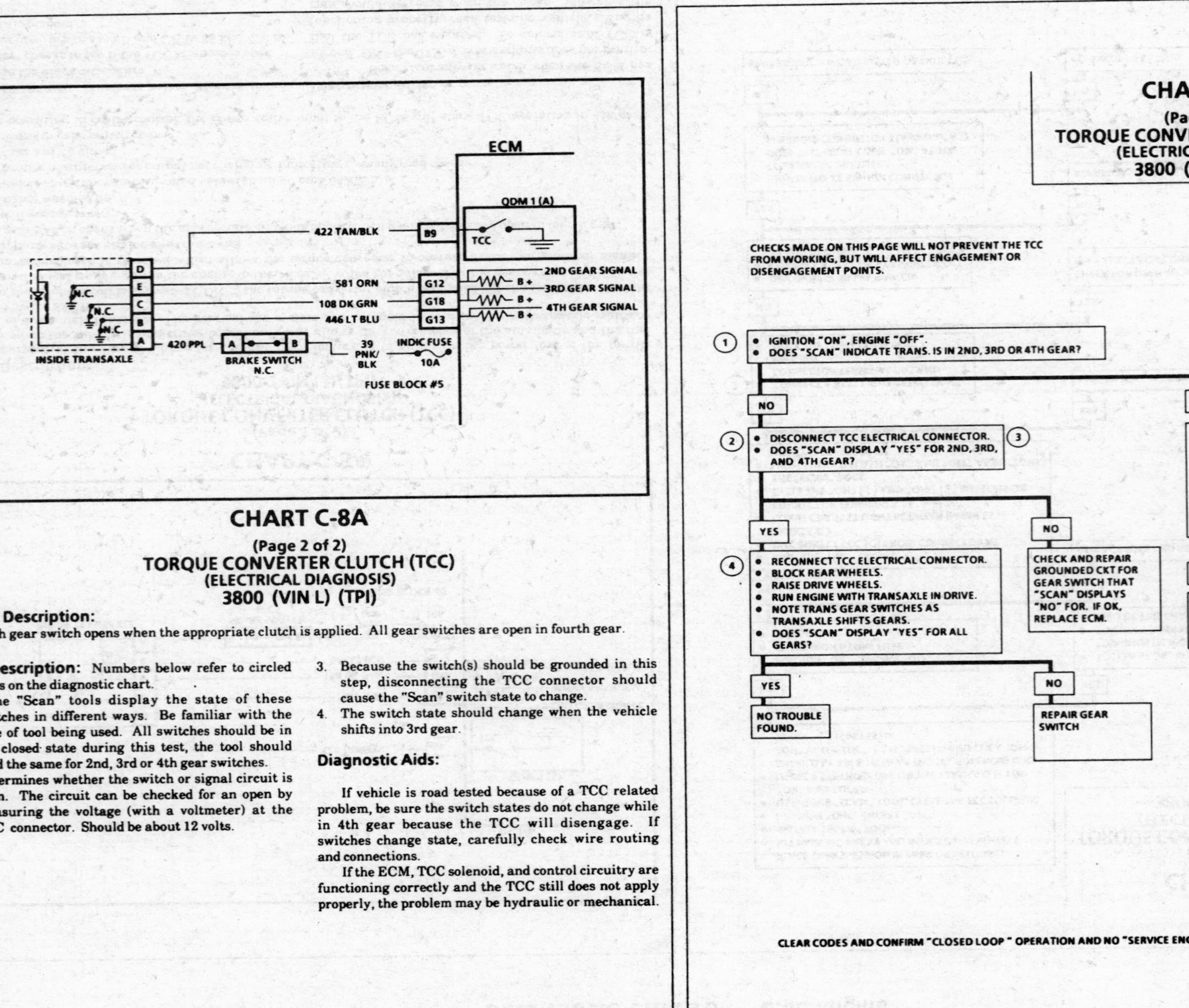

CHART C-8A

(Page 2 of 2)
TORQUE CONVERTER CLUTCH (TCC)
(ELECTRICAL DIAGNOSIS)
3800 (VIN L) (TPI)

Circuit Description:

Each gear switch opens when the appropriate clutch is applied. All gear switches are open in fourth gear.

Test Description: Numbers below refer to circled numbers on the diagnostic chart.

1. Some "Scan" tools display the state of these switches in different ways. Be familiar with the type of tool being used. All switches should be in the closed state during this test, the tool should read the same for 2nd, 3rd or 4th gear switches.
2. Determines whether the switch or signal circuit is open. The circuit can be checked for an open by measuring the voltage (with a voltmeter) at the TCC connector. Should be about 12 volts.
3. Because the switch(s) should be grounded in this step, disconnecting the TCC connector should cause the "Scan" switch state to change.
4. The switch state should change when the vehicle shifts into 3rd gear.

Diagnostic Aids:

If vehicle is road tested because of a TCC related problem, be sure the switch states do not change while in 4th gear because the TCC will disengage. If switches change state, carefully check wire routing and connections.

If the ECM, TCC solenoid, and control circuitry are functioning correctly and the TCC still does not apply properly, the problem may be hydraulic or mechanical.

CHART C-8A

(Page 2 of 2)
TORQUE CONVERTER CLUTCH (TCC)
(ELECTRICAL DIAGNOSIS)
3800 (VIN L) (TPI)

CHECKS MADE ON THIS PAGE WILL NOT PREVENT THE TCC FROM WORKING, BUT WILL AFFECT ENGAGEMENT OR DISENGAGEMENT POINTS.

(1)
- IGNITION "ON", ENGINE "OFF".
- DOES "SCAN" INDICATE TRANS. IS IN 2ND, 3RD OR 4TH GEAR?

NO →

(2)
- DISCONNECT TCC ELECTRICAL CONNECTOR. (3)
- DOES "SCAN" DISPLAY "YES" FOR 2ND, 3RD, AND 4TH GEAR?

YES →

(4)
- RECONNECT TCC ELECTRICAL CONNECTOR.
- BLOCK REAR WHEELS.
- RAISE DRIVE WHEELS.
- RUN ENGINE WITH TRANSAXLE IN DRIVE.
- NOTE TRANS GEAR SWITCHES AS TRANSAXLE SHIFTS GEARS.
- DOES "SCAN" DISPLAY "YES" FOR ALL GEARS?

YES → NO TROUBLE FOUND.

NO → REPAIR GEAR SWITCH

(2) NO → CHECK AND REPAIR GROUNDED CKT FOR GEAR SWITCH THAT "SCAN" DISPLAYS "NO" FOR. IF OK, REPLACE ECM.

(1) YES →
- DISCONNECT TCC ELECTRICAL CONNECTOR.
- JUMPER HARNESS TERMINAL "E" FOR 2ND GEAR, "C" FOR 3RD GEAR, "B" FOR 4TH GEAR TO GROUND.
- DOES "SCAN" INDICATE TRANS. IS IN THE APPLICABLE GEAR?

NO → FAULTY CONNECTION OR GEAR SWITCH.

YES → OPEN CIRCUIT, FAULTY CONNECTION OR ECM.

CLEAR CODES AND CONFIRM "CLOSED LOOP" OPERATION AND NO "SERVICE ENGINE SOON" LIGHT.

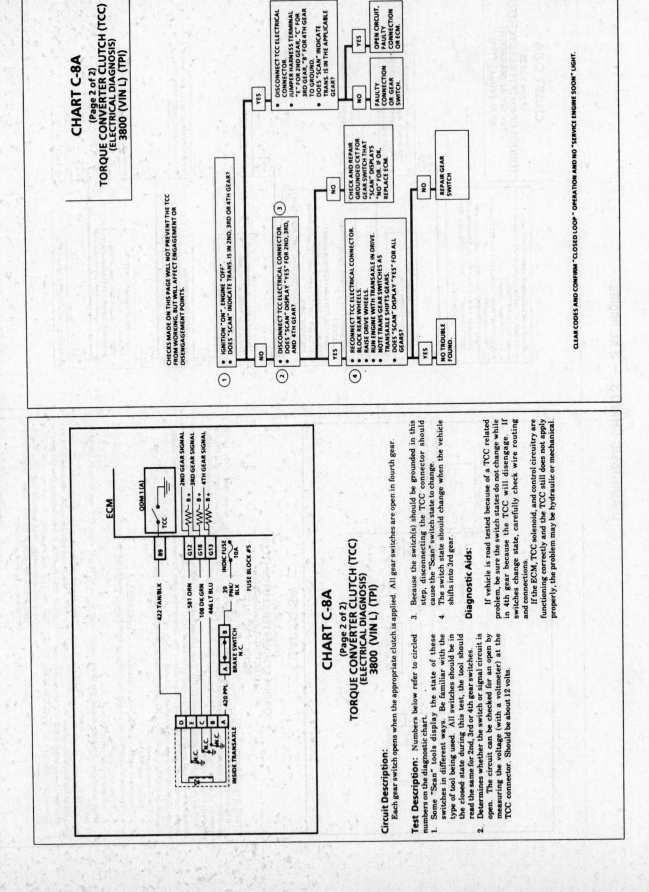

VEHICLE EMISSION CONTROL LABELS

➡ **Following is an assortment of representative vehicle emission control information labels. It is by no means a complete collection; only what was available at the time of publication was printed here.**

Always follow what is on your underhood sticker, as it is most likely the accurate label for that particular engine application.

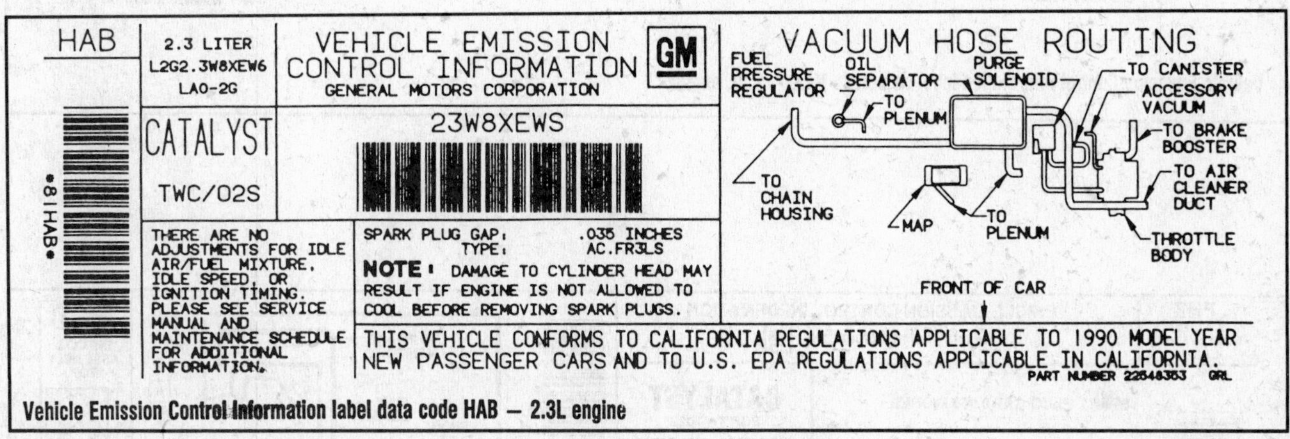

Vehicle Emission Control Information label data code HAB — 2.3L engine

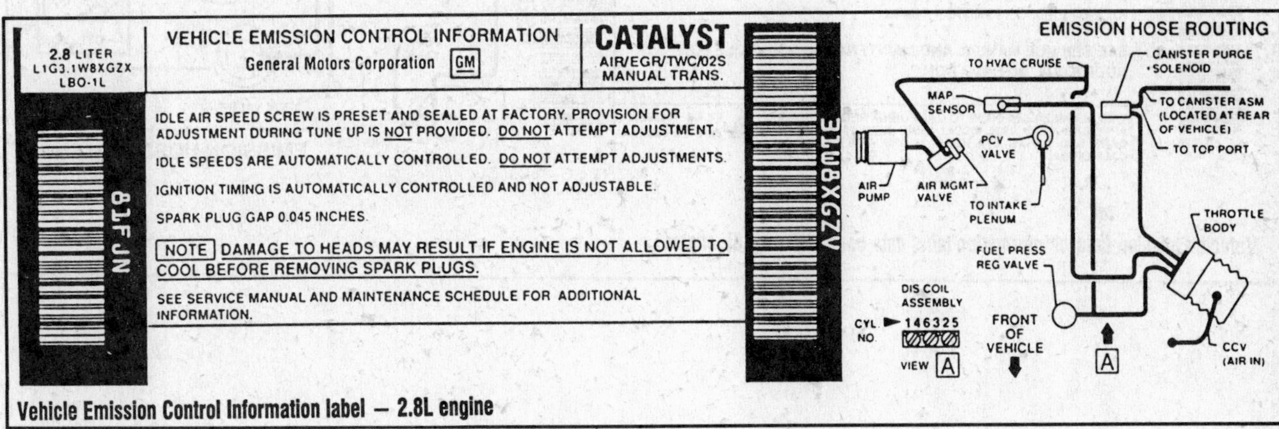

Vehicle Emission Control Information label — 2.8L engine

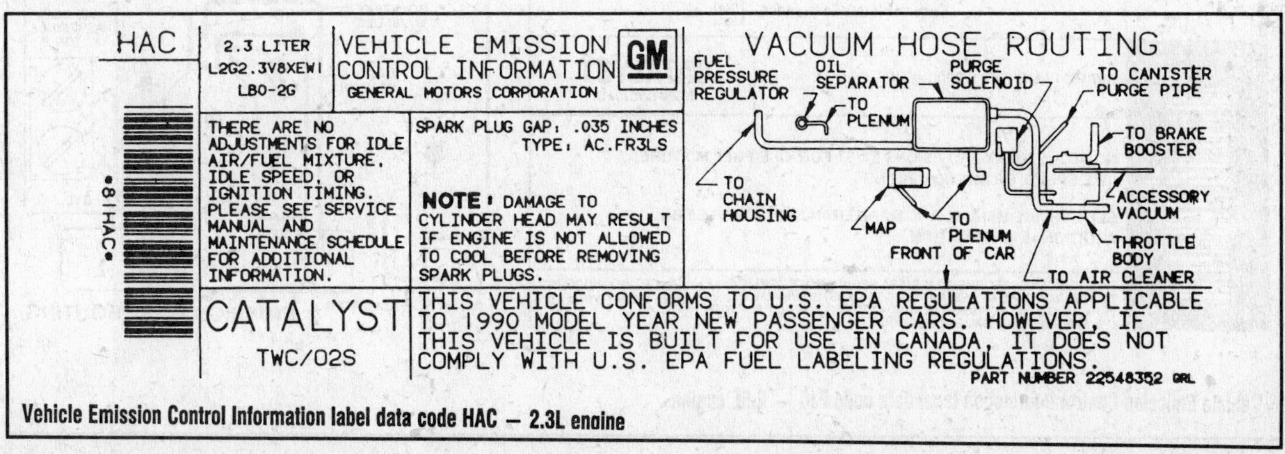

Vehicle Emission Control Information label data code HAC — 2.3L engine

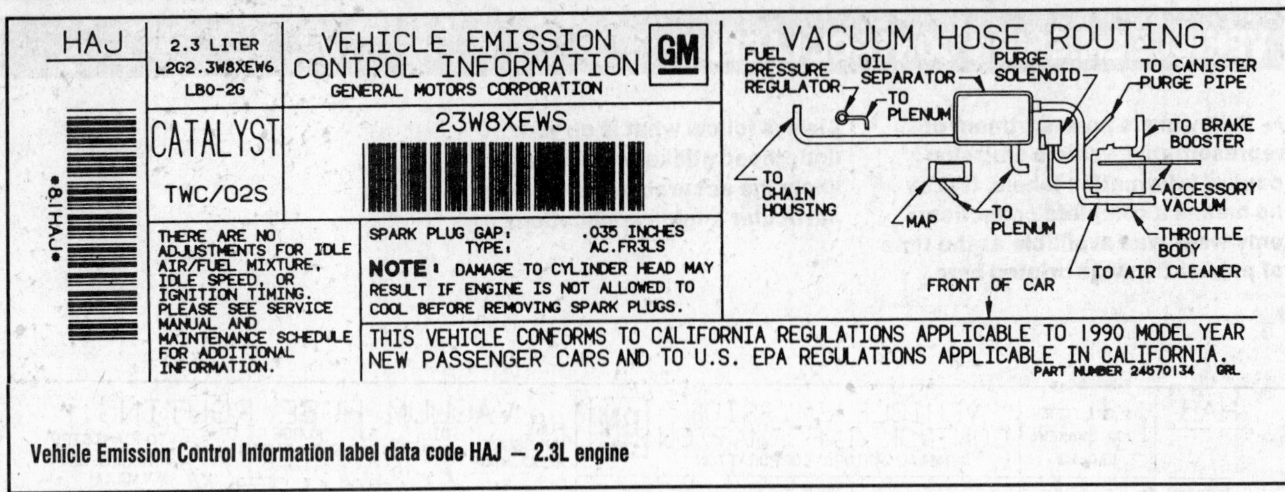

Vehicle Emission Control Information label data code HAJ — 2.3L engine

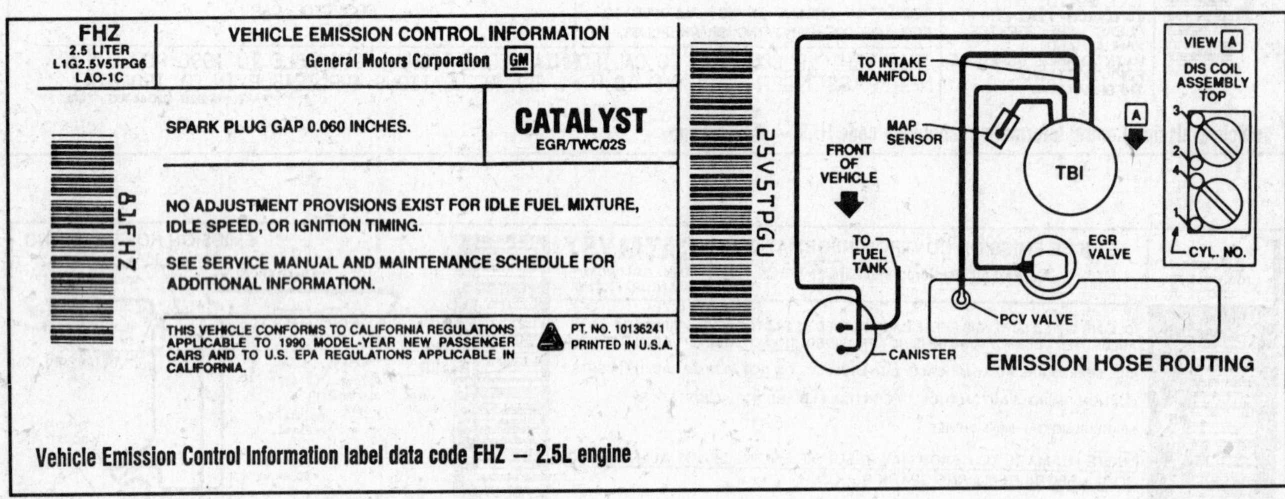

Vehicle Emission Control Information label data code FHZ — 2.5L engine

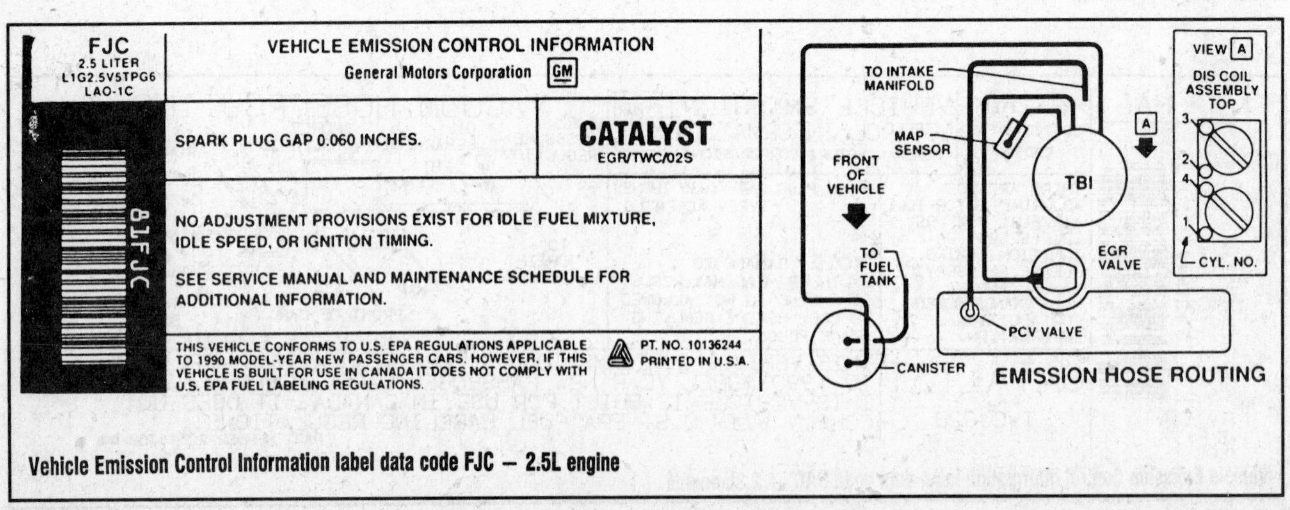

Vehicle Emission Control Information label data code FJC — 2.5L engine

JCA
3.8 LITER
M2G3.8V8XEB3
MBOP - 2D

VEHICLE EMISSION CONTROL INFORMATION
GENERAL MOTORS CORPORATION GM ®

CATALYST
EGR/02S/TWC

SPARK PLUG GAP: .060 inch

NO OTHER ADJUSTMENTS NEEDED.
SEE SERVICE MANUAL AND MAINTENANCE SCHEDULE
FOR ADDITIONAL INFORMATION.

THIS VEHICLE CONFORMS TO U.S. EPA REGULATIONS APPLICABLE TO 1991 MODEL-YEAR NEW PASSENGER CARS. HOWEVER, IF THIS VEHICLE IS BUILT FOR USE IN CANADA, IT DOES NOT COMPLY WITH U.S. EPA FUEL LABELING REGULATIONS.

 PT. NO. 24500192

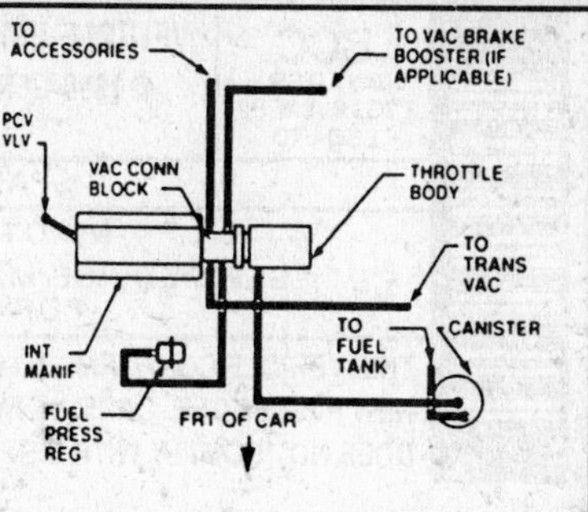

Vehicle Emission Control Information label data code JCA — 3.8L engine

JLE
3.8 LITER
M2G3.8V8JAW3
MBOP - 2F

VEHICLE EMISSION CONTROL INFORMATION
GENERAL MOTORS CORPORATION ® GM

CATALYST
02S/TWC

SPARK PLUG GAP: .060 inch

NO OTHER ADJUSTMENTS NEEDED.
SEE SERVICE MANUAL AND MAINTENANCE SCHEDULE
FOR ADDITIONAL INFORMATION.

THIS VEHICLE CONFORMS TO U.S. EPA REGULATIONS APPLICABLE TO 1991 MODEL-YEAR NEW PASSENGER CARS. HOWEVER, IF THIS VEHICLE IS BUILT FOR USE IN CANADA, IT DOES NOT COMPLY WITH U.S. EPA FUEL LABELING REGULATIONS.

 PT. NO. 24500199

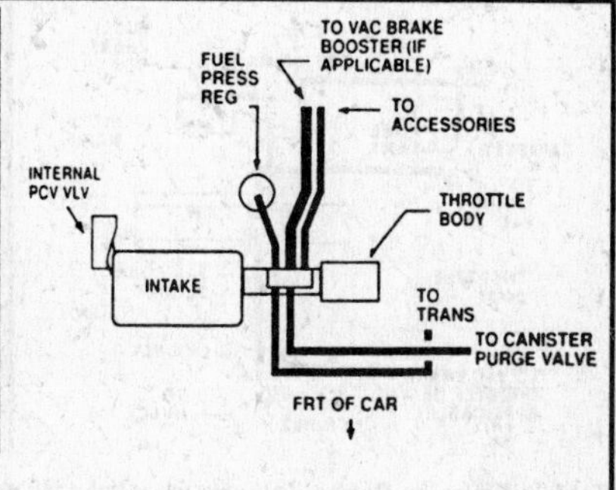

Vehicle Emission Control Information label data code JLE — 3.8L engine

JLL
3.8 LITER
M2G3.8W8JAW8
MBOP- 2C

VEHICLE EMISSION CONTROL INFORMATION
GENERAL MOTORS CORPORATION ® GM

CATALYST
02S/TWC

SPARK PLUG GAP: .060 inch

NO OTHER ADJUSTMENTS NEEDED.
SEE SERVICE MANUAL AND MAINTENANCE SCHEDULE FOR ADDITIONAL INFORMATION.

THIS VEHICLE CONFORMS TO CALIFORNIA REGULATIONS APPLICABLE TO 1991 MODEL-YEAR NEW PASSENGER CARS AND TO U.S. EPA REGULATIONS APPLICABLE IN CALIFORNIA.

 PT. NO. 24500201

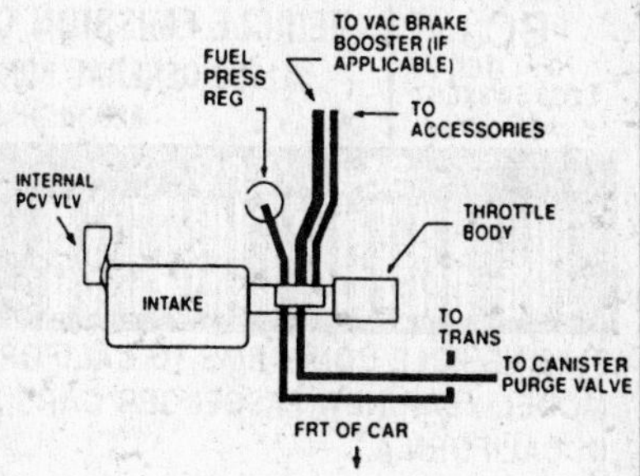

TO VAC BRAKE BOOSTER (IF APPLICABLE)
FUEL PRESS REG
TO ACCESSORIES
INTERNAL PCV VLV
THROTTLE BODY
INTAKE
TO TRANS
TO CANISTER PURGE VALVE
FRT OF CAR

Vehicle Emission Control Information label data code JLL — 3.8L engine

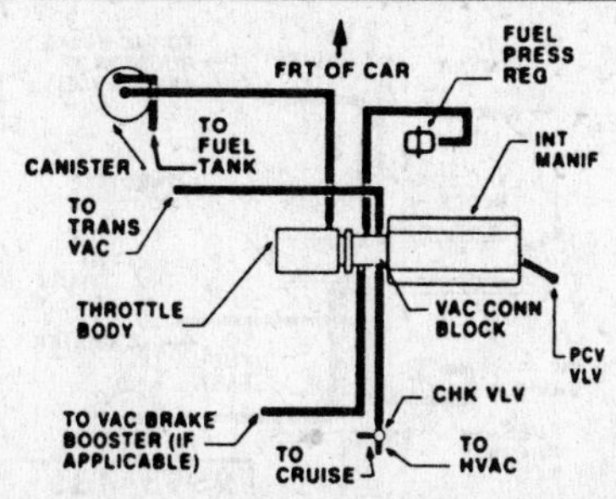

BCB
3.8 LITER
L2G3.8V8XEB2
LBO - 2D

VEHICLE EMISSION CONTROL INFORMATION
©1990 GENERAL MOTORS CORPORATION
ALL RIGHTS RESERVED GM

CATALYST
EGR/02S/TWC

SPARK PLUG GAP: .060 inch

NO OTHER ADJUSTMENTS NEEDED.
SEE SERVICE MANUAL AND MAINTENANCE SCHEDULE
FOR ADDITIONAL INFORMATION.

THIS VEHICLE CONFORMS TO U.S. EPA REGULATIONS APPLICABLE TO 1990 MODEL-YEAR NEW PASSENGER CARS. HOWEVER, IF THIS VEHICLE IS BUILT FOR USE IN CANADA, IT DOES NOT COMPLY WITH U.S. EPA FUEL LABELING REGULATIONS.

PRINTED IN U.S.A.

Vehicle Emission Control Information label data code BCB — 3.8L engine

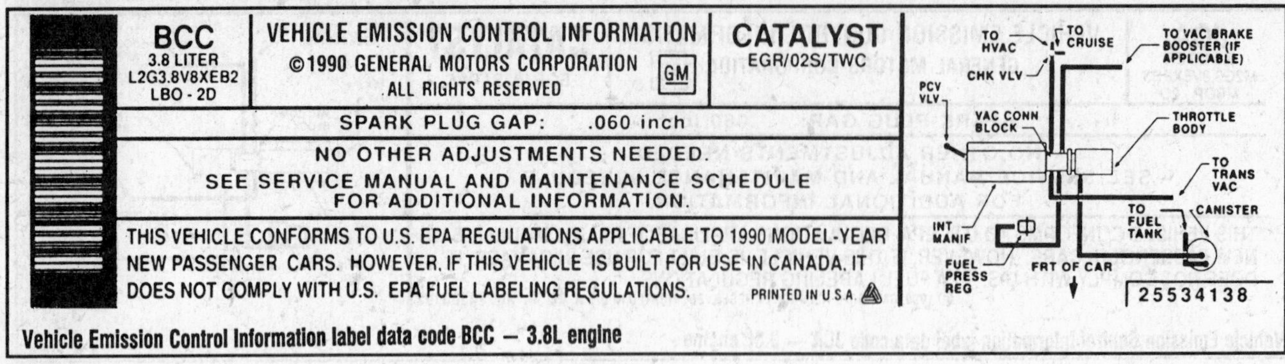

Vehicle Emission Control Information label data code BCC — 3.8L engine

Vehicle Emission Control Information label data code BCH — 3.8L engine

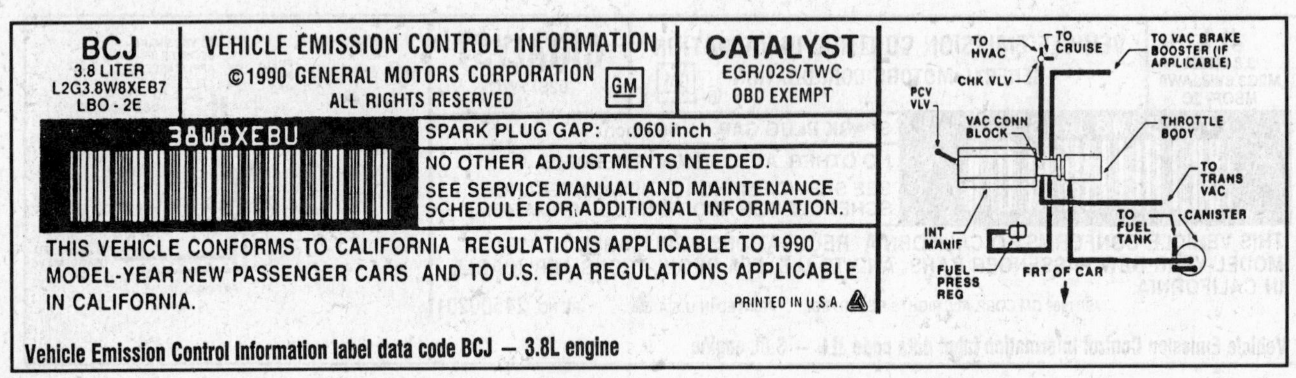

Vehicle Emission Control Information label data code BCJ — 3.8L engine

Vehicle Emission Control Information label data code BCK — 3.8L enginee

5

FUEL SYSTEM

THROTTLE BODY FUEL INJECTION SYSTEM 2.5L ENGINE

System Description

The electronic throttle body fuel injection system is a fuel metering system with the amount of fuel delivered by the throttle body injector(s) (TBI) determined by an electronic signal supplied by the Electronic Control Module (ECM). The ECM monitors various engine and vehicle conditions to calculate the fuel delivery time (pulse width) of the injector. The fuel pulse may be modified by the ECM to account for special operating conditions, such as cranking, cold starting, altitude, acceleration, and deceleration.

The Throttle Body Injection (TBI) system provides a means of fuel distribution for controlling exhaust emissions within legislated limits. The TBI system, by precisely controlling the air/fuel mixture under all operating conditions, provides as near as possible complete combustion.

This is accomplished by using an Electronic Control Module (ECM) (a small on-board microcomputer) that receives electrical inputs from various sensors about engine operating conditions. An oxygen sensor in the main exhaust stream functions to provide feedback information to the ECM as to the oxygen content, lean or rich, in the exhaust. The ECM uses this information from the oxygen sensor, and other sensors, to modify fuel delivery to achieve, as near as possible, an ideal air/fuel ratio of 14.7:1. This air/fuel ratio allows the 3-way catalytic converter to be more efficient in the conversion process of reducing exhaust emissions while at the same time providing acceptable levels of driveability and fuel economy.

The basic TBI model 700 is made up of 2 major casting assemblies: (1) a throttle body with a valve to control airflow and (2) a fuel body assembly with an integral pressure regulator and fuel injector to supply the required fuel. A device to control idle speed (IAC) and a device to provide information about throttle valve position (TPS) are included as part of the TBI unit.

Service Precautions

When working around any part of the fuel system, take precautionary steps to prevent fire and/or explosion:

- Disconnect negative terminal from battery (except when testing with battery voltage is required).
- When ever possible, use a flashlight instead of a drop light.
- Keep all open flame and smoking material out of the area.
- Use a shop cloth or similar to catch fuel when opening a fuel system.
- Relieve fuel system pressure before servicing.
- Use eye protection.
- Always keep a dry chemical (class B) fire extinguisher near the area.

Relieving Fuel System Pressure

1. Remove the fuel filler cap to relieve fuel tank vapor pressure.
2. From under the vehicle, disconnect the fuel pump electrical connector. It should be the only connector coming from the fuel tank.
3. Start the engine and run until the engine stalls. Engage the starter an additional 3 seconds to assure complete relief.
4. Install the fuel filler cap.
5. Disconnect the negative battery cable and continue with fuel system work.

Electric Fuel Pump

FUEL PRESSURE CHECK

1. Relieve the fuel pressure from the fuel system.
2. Turn the ignition **OFF**.
3. Uncouple the fuel supply flexible hose in the engine compartment and install fuel pressure gauge J29658/BT8205 or equivalent in the pressure line.
4. Be sure to tighten the fuel line to the gauge to ensure that there no leaks during testing.
5. Start the engine and observe the fuel pressure reading. The fuel pressure should be 26–32 psi (179–220 kPa).
6. Relieve the fuel pressure. Remove the fuel pressure gauge and reinstall the fuel line. Be sure to install a new O-ring on the fuel feed line.
7. Start the engine and check for fuel leaks.

REMOVAL & INSTALLATION

1. Disconnect the negative battery cable.
2. Relieve the fuel system pressure.
3. Raise and safely support the vehicle with jackstands.
4. Safely drain and remove the fuel tank assembly as outlined in the "Fuel tank" removal procedures in this Section.
5. Turn the fuel pump cam lock ring counterclockwise and lift the assembly out of the tank.
6. Remove the fuel pump from the level sensor unit as follows:
   a. Pull the pump up into the attaching hose or pulsator while pulling outward away from the bottom support.
   b. Take care to prevent damage to the rubber insulator and strainer during removal.
   c. When the pump assembly is clear of the bottom support, pull the pump out of the rubber connector for removal.

To install:

7. Replace any attaching hoses or rubber sound insulator that show signs of deterioration.
8. Push the fuel pump into the attaching hoses and install the pump/sensor assembly into the tank. Always use a new O-ring seal. Be careful not to fold over or twist the strainer when installing the sensor unit. Also, make sure the strainer does not block full travel of the float arm.
9. Install the cam lock and turn clockwise to lock.
10. Install the fuel tank as outlined in this Section.
11. Fill the tank with four gallons of gas and check for fuel leaks.

➧ SEE FIG. 1

Throttle Body

REMOVAL & INSTALLATION

1. Depressurize the fuel system. Raise the hood, install fender covers and remove the air cleaner assembly. Disconnect the negative battery cable.
2. Disconnect the electrical connectors for the idle speed control motor, the throttle position sensor, fuel injectors, EFE and any other

component necessary in order to remove the throttle body.

3. Remove the throttle return spring, cruise control, throttle linkage and downshift cable.

4. Disconnect all necessary vacuum lines, the fuel inlet line, fuel return line, brake booster line, MAP sensor hose and the AIR hose. Be sure to use a back-up wrench on all metal lines.

5. Remove the PCV, EVAP and/or EGR hoses from the front of the throttle body.

6. Remove the 3 throttle body mounting screws and remove the throttle body and gasket.

7. The installation is the reverse order of the removal procedure.

8. Torque the throttle body retaining screws to 18 ft. lbs. (24 Nm) and fuel lines to 20 ft. lbs. Always use new gaskets and O-rings.

9. Make certain cruise and shift cables do not hold the throttle above the idle stop. Reset the IAC by depressing the accelerator slightly, run engine for 3–4 seconds and turn ignition **OFF** for 10 seconds.

Fuel Meter Body Assembly

REMOVAL & INSTALLATION

1. Depressurize the fuel system. Raise the hood, install fender covers and remove the air cleaner assembly. Disconnect the negative battery cable.

2. Remove the electrical connector from the injector. Remove the grommet with wires from the fuel meter assembly.

3. Remove the fuel inlet and outlet lines and O-rings. Be sure to use a back-up wrench to keep the TBI nuts from turning. Be sure to discard the old O-rings.

4. Remove the TBI mounting hardware. Remove the 2 fuel meter body attaching screws.

5. Remove the fuel meter assembly from the throttle body and remove the fuel meter to throttle body gasket, discard the gasket.

6. Install the new throttle body to fuel meter body gasket. Match the cut portions in the gasket with the opening in the throttle body.

7. Install the fuel meter body assembly onto the throttle body assembly.

8. Install the fuel meter body to the throttle body attaching screw assemblies, precoated with a suitable thread sealer.

9. Torque the screw assemblies to 53 inch lbs. Install the fuel inlet and outlet nuts with new gaskets to the fuel meter body assembly. Torque the inlet and outlet nut to 20 ft. lbs. (27 Nm).

10. Install the fuel inlet and return lines and new O-rings. Be sure to use a back-up wrench to keep the TBI nuts from turning.

11. Install the grommet with wires to the fuel meter assembly. Connect the electrical connector to the injector.

12. With the engine **OFF** and the ignition **ON** check for fuel leaks.

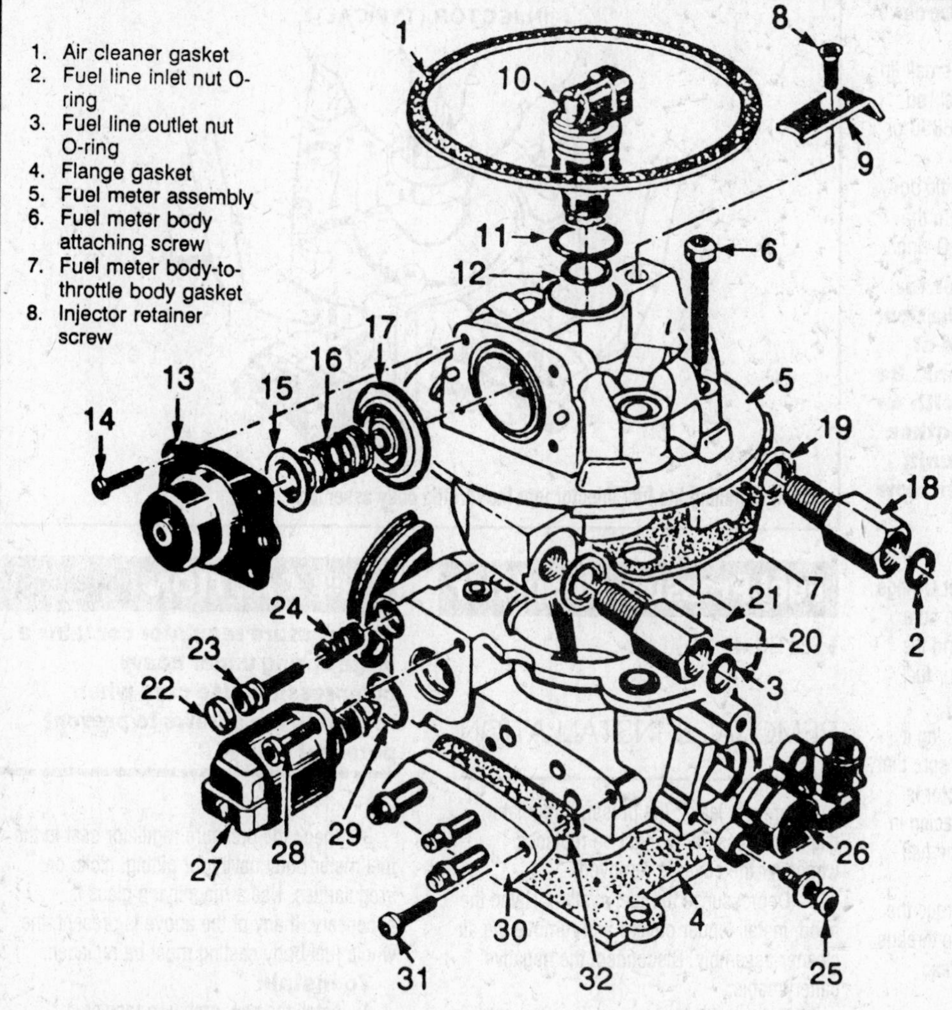

1. Air cleaner gasket
2. Fuel line inlet nut O-ring
3. Fuel line outlet nut O-ring
4. Flange gasket
5. Fuel meter assembly
6. Fuel meter body attaching screw
7. Fuel meter body-to-throttle body gasket
8. Injector retainer screw
9. Injector retainer
10. Fuel injector
11. Upper fuel injector O-ring
12. Lower fuel injector O-ring
13. Pressure regulator cover assembly
14. Pressure regulator attaching screw
15. Spring seat
16. Pressure regulator spring
17. Pressure regulator diaphragm assembly
18. Fuel inlet nut
19. Fuel nut seal
20. Fuel outlet nut
21. Throttle body assembly
22. Idle stop screw plug
23. Idle stop screw and washer assembly
24. Idle stop screw spring
25. Throttle Position Sensor (TPS)
26. TPS attaching screw and washer assembly
27. Idle air control valve
28. Idle air control attaching valve
29. Idle air control valve O-ring
30. Tube module assembly
31. Tube module assembly attaching screw
32. Tube module assembly gasket

Fig. 1 Exploded view of the TBI model 700 assembly

Fuel Injector

Use care in removing the injector to prevent damage to the electrical connector pins on top of the injector, the injector fuel filter and the nozzle. The fuel injector is serviced as a complete assembly only. The fuel injector is an electrical component and should not be immersed in any type of cleaner.

REMOVAL & INSTALLATION

➧ SEE FIGS. 2 AND 3

1. Depressurize the fuel system. Raise the hood, install fender covers and remove the air cleaner assembly. Disconnect the negative battery cable.
2. Disconnect electrical connector to injector by squeezing on tow tabs and pulling straight up.
3. Remove the injector retainer screw and retainer.
4. Use a suitable dowel rod and lay the dowel rod on top of the fuel meter body.
5. Insert a suitable pry tool into the small lip of the injector and pry against the dowel rod lifting the injector straight up. Tool J–26868 or equivalent can also be used.
6. Remove the injector from the throttle body Remove the upper and lower O-ring from the injector cavity. Be sure to discard both O-rings.

➡ Check the fuel injector filter for evidence of dirt and contamination. If present, check for presence of dirt in the fuel lines or fuel tank. Be sure to replace the injector with an identical part. Injectors from other models can fit in the TBI 700 unit, but are calibrated for different flow rates.

To install:

7. Lubricate the new upper and lower O-rings with automatic transmission fluid. Make sure that the upper O-ring is in the groove and the lower one is flush up against the injector fuel filter.
8. Install the injector assembly, pushing it straight into the fuel injector cavity. Be sure that the electrical connector end of the injector is parallel to the casting support rib and facing in the general direction of the cut-out in the fuel meter body for the wire grommet.
9. Install the injector retainer and torque the screw to 27 inch lbs. Be sure to coat the threads of the retainer screw with a suitable thread sealant.
10. With the engine **OFF** and the ignition **ON** check for fuel leaks.

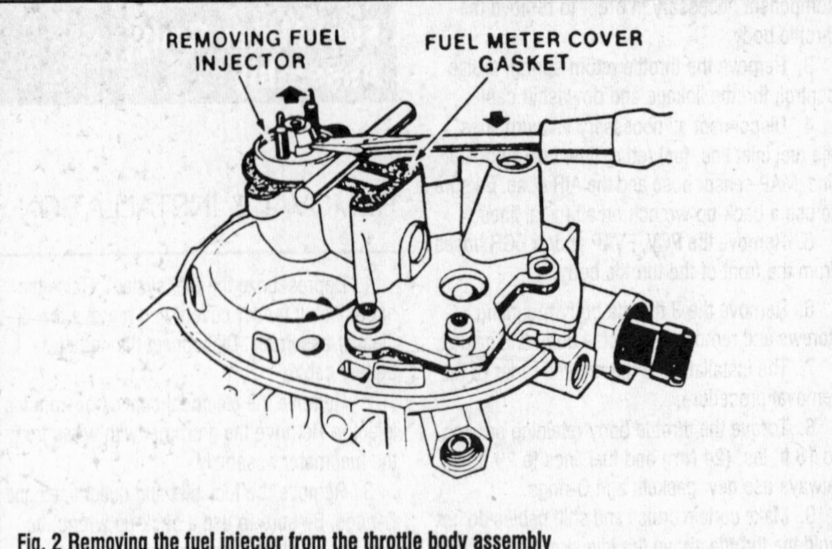

Fig. 2 Removing the fuel injector from the throttle body assembly

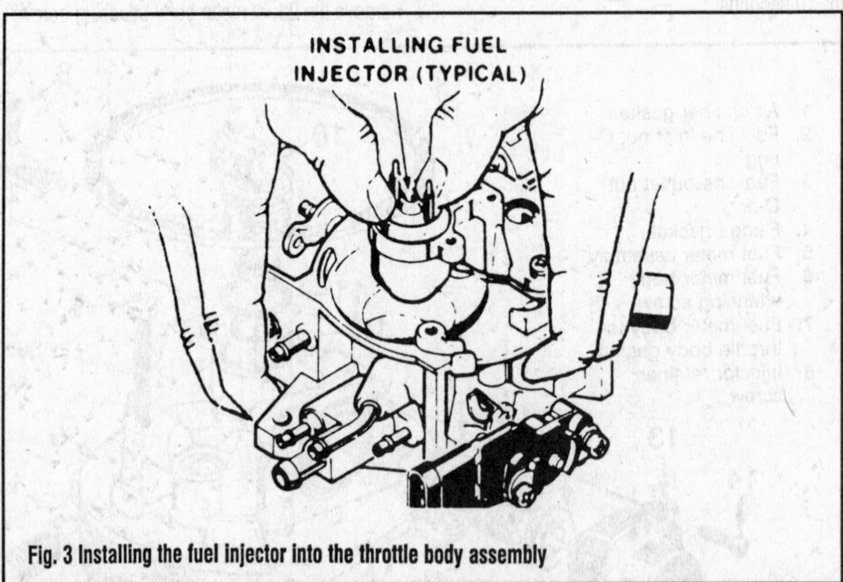

Fig. 3 Installing the fuel injector into the throttle body assembly

Fuel Pressure Regulator

➧ SEE FIG. 4

REMOVAL & INSTALLATION

To prevent leaks, the pressure regulator diaphragm assembly must be replaced whenever the cover is removed.

1. Depressurize the fuel system. Raise the hood, install fender covers and remove the air cleaner assembly. Disconnect the negative battery cable.
2. Remove the 4 pressure regulator retaining screws, while keeping the pressure regulator compressed.

✲✲ CAUTION

The pressure regulator contains a large spring under heavy compression. Use care when removing the screws to prevent personal injury.

3. Check the pressure regulator seat in the fuel meter body cavity for pitting, nicks or irregularities. Use a magnifying glass if necessary. If any of the above is present, the whole fuel body casting must be replaced.

To install:

4. Install the new pressure regulator diaphragm assembly making sure it is seated in the groove in the fuel meter body.

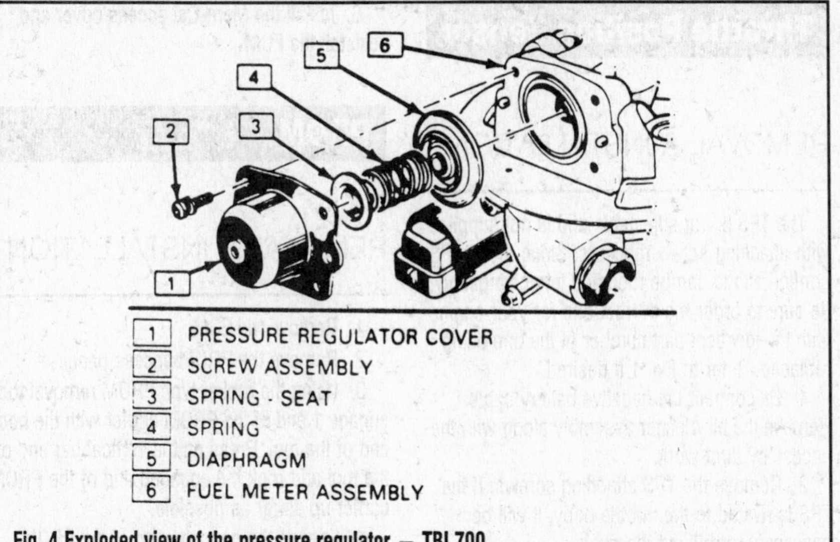

Fig. 4 Exploded view of the pressure regulator — TBI 700

5. Install the regulator spring seat and spring into the cover assembly.

6. Install the cover assembly over the diaphragm, while aligning the mounting holes. Be sure to use care while installing the pressure regulator to prevent misalignment of the diaphragm and possible leaks.

7. Coat the 4 regulator retaining bolts with a suitable thread sealer and torque the screws to 22 inch lbs. (2.5 Nm) .

8. With the engine **OFF** and the ignition **ON** check for fuel leaks.

Idle Air Control Valve

➧ SEE FIG. 5

REMOVAL & INSTALLATION

1. Remove the air cleaner.

2. Disconnect the electrical connection from the idle air control assembly.

3. Remove the idle air control assembly from the throttle body.

Clean the IAC valve O-ring sealing surface, pintle valve seat and air passage.

4. Use a suitable carburetor cleaner (be sure it is safe to use on systems equipped with a oxygen sensor) and a parts cleaning brush to remove the carbon deposits. Do not use a cleaner that contains methyl ethyl ketone. It is an extremely strong solvent and not necessary for this type of deposits. Shiny spots on the pintle or on the seat are normal and do not indicate a misalignment or a bent pintle shaft. If the air passage has heavy deposits, remove the throttle body for a complete cleaning.

➡ Before installing a new idle air control valve, measure the distance that the valve is extended. This measurement should be made from motor housing to end of the cone. The distance should be no greater than 1¹/₈ in. (28mm). If the cone is extended too far damage to the valve may result. The IAC valve pintle may also be retracted by using IAC/ISC Motor Tester J-37027/BT-8256K. It is recommended not to push or pull on the IAC pintle. The force required to move the pintle of a new valve should not cause damage. Do not soak the IAC valve in any liquid cleaner or solvent as damage may result.

5. Be sure to identify the replacement idle air control valve and replace with an identical part. The IAC valve pintle shape and diameter are designed for specific applications.

6. Install the new idle air control valve and torque the retaining screws to 27 inch lbs. (3 Nm) .

7. Reconnect all electrical connections.

8. The base idle will not be correct until the ECM resets the IAC.

Coolant Temperature Sensor

The coolant temperature sensor is located on the left side of the cylinder head. It may be necessary to drain some of the coolant from the coolant system.

REMOVAL & INSTALLATION

✻✻ CAUTION

When draining the coolant, keep in

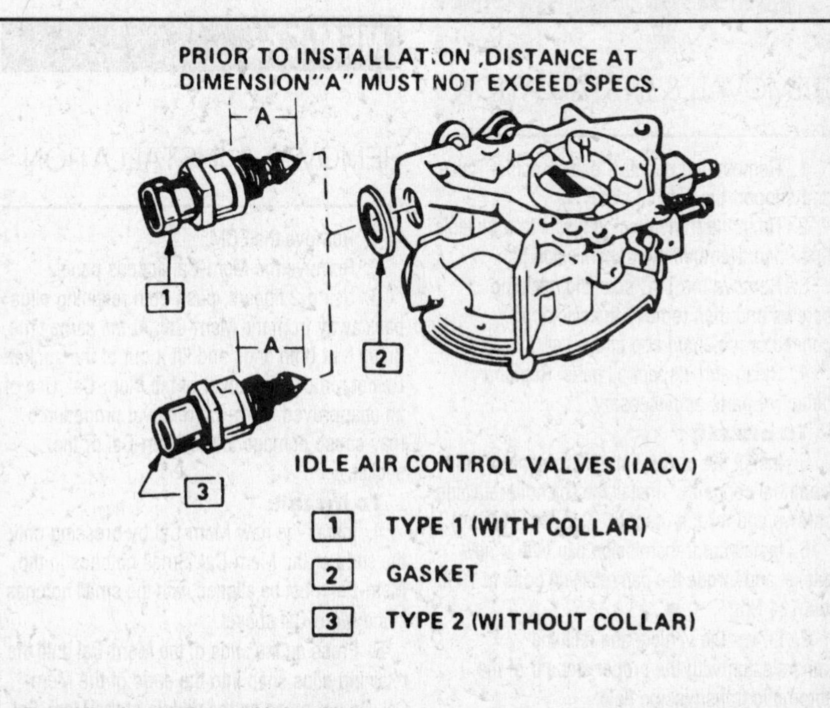

Fig. 5 Idle air control assembly installation

mind that cats and dogs are attracted by the ethylene glycol antifreeze, and are quite likely to drink any that is left in an uncovered container or in puddles on the ground. This will prove fatal in sufficient quantity. Always drain the coolant into a sealable container. Coolant should be reused unless it is contaminated or several years old.

1. Disconnect the negative battery cable and disconnect the electrical connector at the sensor.
2. Remove the threaded temperature sensor from the engine.
3. Check the sensor with the tip immersed in water at 50°F (15°C). The resistance across the terminals should approximately 5600Ω. Check Code 14 or 15 engine chart for specific resistance on vehicle being serviced. If not within specifications, replace the sensor.
4. Apply some pipe tape to the threaded sensor and install the sensor.
5. Fill the cooling system if any coolant was removed. Reconnect the sensor connector and the negative battery cable.

Torque Converter Clutch Solenoid

REMOVAL & INSTALLATION

1. Remove the negative battery cable. Raise and support the vehicle safely.
2. Drain the transmission fluid into a suitable drain pan. Remove the transmission pan.
3. Remove the TCC solenoid retaining screws and then remove the electrical connector, solenoid and check ball.
4. Clean and inspect all parts. Replace defective parts as necessary.

To install:

5. Install the check ball, TCC solenoid and electrical connector. Install the solenoid retaining screws and torque them to 10 ft. lbs. (14 Nm).
6. Install the transmission pan with a new gasket and torque the pan retaining bolts to 10 ft. lbs. (14 Nm).
7. Lower the vehicle and refill the transmission with the proper amount of the automatic transmission fluid.

Throttle Position Sensor

REMOVAL & INSTALLATION

The TPS is not adjustable and is not supplied with attaching screw retainers. Since these TPS configurations can be mounted interchangeably, be sure to order the correct one for your engine with the identical part number of the one being replaced. Refer to Fig. 1 if desired.

1. Disconnect the negative battery cable. Remove the air cleaner assembly along with the necessary duct work.
2. Remove the TPS attaching screws. If the TPS is riveted to the throttle body, it will be necessary to drill out the rivets.
3. Remove the TPS from the throttle body assembly.

➡ The throttle position sensor is an electrical component and should not be immersed in any type of liquid solvent or cleaner, as damage may result.

4. With the throttle valve closed, install the TPS onto the throttle shaft. Rotate the TPS counterclockwise to align the mounting holes. Install the retaining screws or rivets. Torque the retaining screws to 18 inch lbs. (2.0 Nm).
5. Install the air cleaner assembly and connect the negative battery cable.

MEM-CAL

REMOVAL & INSTALLATION

1. Remove the ECM.
2. Remove the Mem-Cal access panel.
3. Using 2 fingers, push both retaining clips back away from the Mem-Cal. At the same time, grasp it at both ends and lift it out of the socket. Do not remove the cover of the Mem-Cal. Use of an unapproved Mem-Cal removal procedures may cause damage to the Mem-Cal or the socket.

To install:

4. Install the new Mem-Cal by pressing only the ends of the Mem-Cal. Small notches in the Mem-Cal must be aligned with the small notches in the Mem-Cal socket.
5. Press on the ends of the Mem-Cal until the retaining clips snap into the ends of the Mem-Cal. Do not press on the middle of the Mem-Cal, only on the ends.
6. Install the Mem-Cal access cover and reinstall the ECM.

PROM

REMOVAL & INSTALLATION

1. Remove the ECM.
2. Remove the PROM access panel.
3. Using the rocker type PROM removal tool, engage 1 end of the PROM carrier with the hook end of the tool. Press on the vertical bar end of the tool and rock the engaged end of the PROM carrier up as far as possible.
4. Engage the opposite end of the PROM carrier in the same manner and rock this end up as far as possible.
5. Repeat this process until the PROM carrier and PROM are free of the PROM socket. The PROM carrier with PROM in it should lift off of the PROM socket easily.
6. The PROM carrier should only be removed by using the special PROM removal tool. Other methods could cause damage to the PROM or PROM socket.
7. Before installing a new PROM, be sure the new PROM part number is the same as the old one or the as the updated number per a service bulletin.

To install:

8. Install the PROM with the small notch of the carrier aligned with the small notch in the socket. Press on the PROM carrier until the PROM is firmly seated, do not press on the PROM itself only on the PROM carrier.
9. Install the PROM access cover and reinstall the ECM.

FUNCTIONAL CHECK

1. Turn the ignition switch to the **ON** position.
2. Enter the diagnostic mode.
3. Allow a Code 12 to flash 4 times to verify that no other codes are present. This indicates that the PROM is installed properly.
4. If trouble Code 51 occurs or if the SERVICE ENGINE SOON light in on constantly with no codes, the PROM is not fully seated, installed backwards, has bent pins or is defective.
5. If not fully seated press down firmly on the PROM carrier.
6. If installed backwards, replace the PROM.

➡ Any time the PROM is installed backwards and the ignition switch is turned ON, the PROM is destroyed.

7. If the pins are bent, remove the PROM straighten the pins and reinstall the PROM. If the bent pins break or crack during straightening, discard the PROM and replace with a new PROM.

➡ To prevent possible electrostatic discharge damage to the PROM or Cal-Pak, do not touch the component leads and do not remove the integrated circuit from the carrier.

MULTI-PORT FUEL INJECTION SYSTEM ENGINES

2.3L, 2.8L, 3.1L AND 3.4L

System Description

The Multi-Port Fuel Injection (MPI) system is controlled by an Electronic Control Module (ECM) which monitors engine operations and generates output signals to provide the correct air/fuel mixture, ignition timing and engine idle speed control. Input to the control unit is provided by an oxygen sensor, coolant temperature sensor, detonation sensor, hot film mass sensor and throttle position sensor. The ECM also receives information concerning engine rpm, road speed, transmission gear position, power steering and air conditioning.

The injectors are located, one at each intake port, rather than the single injector found on the throttle body system. The injectors are mounted on a fuel rail and are activated by a signal from the electronic control module. The injector is a solenoid-operated valve which remains open depending on the width of the electronic pulses (length of the signal) from the ECM; the longer the open time, the more fuel is injected. In this manner, the air/fuel mixture can be precisely controlled for maximum performance with minimum emissions.

Fuel is pumped from the tank by a high pressure fuel pump, located inside the fuel tank. It is a positive displacement roller vane pump. The impeller serves as a vapor separator and pre-charges the high pressure assembly. A pressure regulator maintains 28–36 psi (28–50 psi on turbocharged engines) in the fuel line to the injectors and the excess fuel is fed back to the tank. A fuel accumulator is used to dampen the hydraulic line hammer in the system created when all injectors open simultaneously.

The Mass Air Flow (MAF) Sensor is used to measure the mass of air that is drawn into the engine cylinders. It is located just ahead of the air throttle in the intake system and consists of a heated film which measures the mass of air, rather than just the volume. A resistor is used to measure the temperature of the film at 75° above ambient temperature. As the ambient (outside) air temperature rises, more energy is required to maintain the heated film at the higher temperature and the control unit used this difference in required energy to calculate the mass of the incoming air. The control unit uses this information to determine the duration of fuel injection pulse, timing and EGR.

The throttle body incorporates an Idle Air Control (IAC) that provides for a bypass channel through which air can flow. It consists of an orifice and pintle which is controlled by the ECM through a step motor. The IAC provides air flow for idle and allows additional air during cold start until the engine reaches operating temperature. As the engine temperature rises, the opening through which air passes is slowly closed.

The Throttle Position Sensor (TPS) provides the control unit with information on throttle position, in order to determine injector pulse width and hence correct mixture. The TPS is connected to the throttle shaft on the throttle body and consists of as potentiometer with on end connected to a 5 volt source from the ECM and the other to ground. A third wire is connected to the ECM to measure the voltage output from the TPS which changes as the throttle valve angle is changed (accelerator pedal moves). At the closed throttle position, the output is low (approximately 0.4 volts); as the throttle valve opens, the output increases to a maximum 5 volts at Wide Open Throttle (WOT). The TPS can be misadjusted open, shorted, or loose and if it is out of adjustment, the idle quality or WOT performance may be poor. A loose TPS can cause intermittent bursts of fuel from the injectors and an unstable idle because the ECM thinks the throttle is moving. This should cause a trouble code to be set. Once a trouble code is set, the ECM will use a preset value for TPS and some vehicle performance may return. A small amount of engine coolant is routed through the throttle assembly to prevent freezing inside the throttle bore during cold operation.

Service Precautions

When working around any part of the fuel system, take precautionary steps to prevent fire and/or explosion:

- Disconnect negative terminal from battery (except when testing with battery voltage is required).
- When ever possible, use a flashlight instead of a drop light.
- Keep all open flame and smoking material out of the area.
- Use a shop cloth or similar to catch fuel when opening a fuel system.
- Relieve fuel system pressure before servicing.
- Use eye protection.
- Always keep a dry chemical (class B) fire extinguisher near the area.

Relieving Fuel System Pressure

2.3L Engine

1. Remove the fuel filler cap to relieve fuel tank vapor pressure.
2. From under the vehicle, disconnect the fuel pump electrical connector. It should be the only connector coming from the fuel tank.
3. Start the engine and run until the engine stalls. Engage the starter an additional 3 seconds to assure complete relief.
4. Install the fuel filler cap.
5. Disconnect the negative battery cable and continue with fuel system work.

2.8L, 3.1L and 3.4L Engines

1. Disconnect the negative battery cable.
2. Loosen the fuel filler cap to relieve fuel tank vapor pressure.
3. Connect fuel pressure valve J 34730-1 or equivalent to the fuel pressure relief connection at the fuel rail.

4. Wrap a shop towel around the fittings while connecting the tool to prevent fuel spillage.
5. Install a bleed hose into an approved container and open the valve to bleed the system pressure.
6. Install the fuel filler cap.

Electric Fuel Pump

FUEL PRESSURE CHECK

1. Connect pressure gauge J-34730-1, or equivalent, to fuel pressure test point on the fuel rail. Wrap a rag around the pressure tap to absorb any leakage that may occur when installing the gauge.
2. Turn the ignition **ON** and check that pump pressure is 24–40 psi.
3. Start the engine and allow it to idle. The fuel pressure should drop to 28–32 psi due to the lower manifold pressure.

➡ The idle pressure will vary somewhat depending on barometric pressure. Check for a drop in pressure indicating regulator control, rather than specific values.

4. On turbocharged vehicles, use a low pressure air pump to apply air pressure to the regulator to simulate turbocharger boost pressure. Boost pressure should increase fuel pressure 1 lb. for every lb. of boost. Again, look for changes rather than specific pressures. The maximum fuel pressure should not exceed 46 psi.
5. If the fuel pressure drops, check the operation of the check valve, the pump coupling connection, fuel pressure regulator valve and the injectors. A restricted fuel line or filter may also cause a pressure drip. To check the fuel pump output, restrict the fuel return line and run 12 volts to the pump. The fuel pressure should rise to approximately 75 psi with the return line restricted.
6. Before attempting to remove or service any fuel system component, it is necessary to relieve the fuel system pressure.

REMOVAL & INSTALLATION

1. Disconnect the negative battery cable.
2. Relieve the fuel system pressure.
3. Raise and safely support the vehicle with jackstands.
4. Safely drain and remove the fuel tank assembly as outlined in the "Fuel tank" removal procedures in this Section.
5. Turn the fuel pump cam lock ring counterclockwise and lift the assembly out of the tank.
6. Remove the fuel pump from the level sensor unit as follows:
   a. Pull the pump up into the attaching hose or pulsator while pulling outward away from the bottom support.
   b. Take care to prevent damage to the rubber insulator and strainer during removal.
   c. When the pump assembly is clear of the bottom support, pull the pump out of the rubber connector for removal.

To install:

7. Replace any attaching hoses or rubber sound insulator that show signs of deterioration.
8. Push the fuel pump into the attaching hoses and install the pump/sensor assembly into the tank. Always use a new O-ring seal. Be careful not to fold over or twist the strainer when installing the sensor unit. Also, make sure the strainer does not block full travel of the float arm.
9. Install the cam lock and turn clockwise to lock.
10. Install the fuel tank as outlined in this Section.
11. Fill the tank with four gallons of gas and check for fuel leaks.

Throttle Body

➧ SEE FIGS. 6 AND 7

REMOVAL & INSTALLATION

✲✲ CAUTION

When draining the coolant, keep in mind that cats and dogs are attracted by the ethylene glycol antifreeze, and are quite likely to drink any that is left in an uncovered container or in puddles on the ground. This will prove fatal in sufficient quantity. Always drain the coolant into a sealable container. Coolant should be reused unless it is contaminated or several years old.

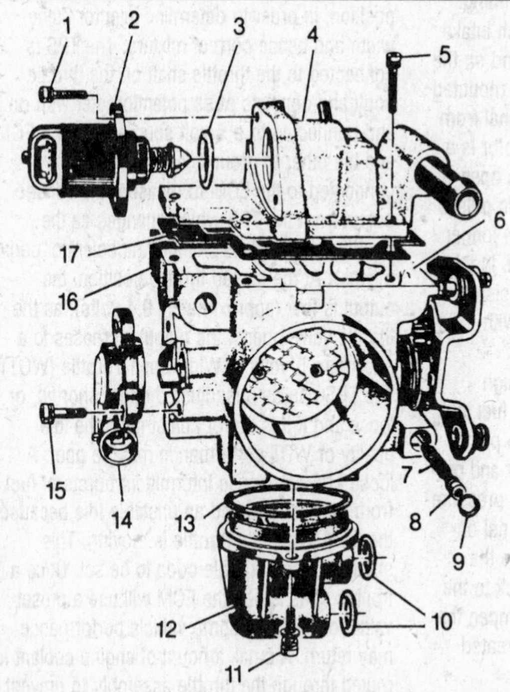

Fig. 6 Model B310 throttle body — 2.3L engine

2.3L Engine

1. Disconnect the negative battery cable. Drain the top half of the engine coolant into a suitable drain pan.
2. Remove the air inlet duct. Disconnect the idle air control valve and throttle position sensor connectors.
3. Remove and mark all necessary vacuum lines. Remove and plug the 2 coolant hoses.
4. Remove the throttle, T.V. and cruise control cables. Remove the power steering pump brace.
5. Remove the throttle body retaining bolts and then remove the throttle body assembly. Discard the flange gasket.
6. Installation is the reverse order of the removal procedure. Torque the retaining bolts to 20 ft. lbs. (27 Nm).
7. Refill the cooling system.

2.8L and 3.1L Engines

➡ **The 3.4L engine is equipped with an integrated throttle body/plenum assembly.**

1. Disconnect the negative battery cable. Drain the top half of the engine coolant into a suitable drain pan.
2. Remove the air inlet duct assembly. Disconnect the idle air control valve, throttle position sensor connectors and mass airflow sensor.
3. Remove and mark all necessary vacuum lines. Remove and plug the 2 coolant hoses.
4. Remove the 10mm screw holding the fuel lines to the throttle cable bracket. Remove the throttle, T.V. and cruise control cables. Remove the power steering pump brace.
5. Remove the throttle body retaining bolts and then remove the throttle body assembly. Discard the flange gasket.
6. Installation is the reverse order of the removal procedure. Torque the retaining bolts to 15 ft. lbs. (20 Nm).
7. Refill the cooling system.

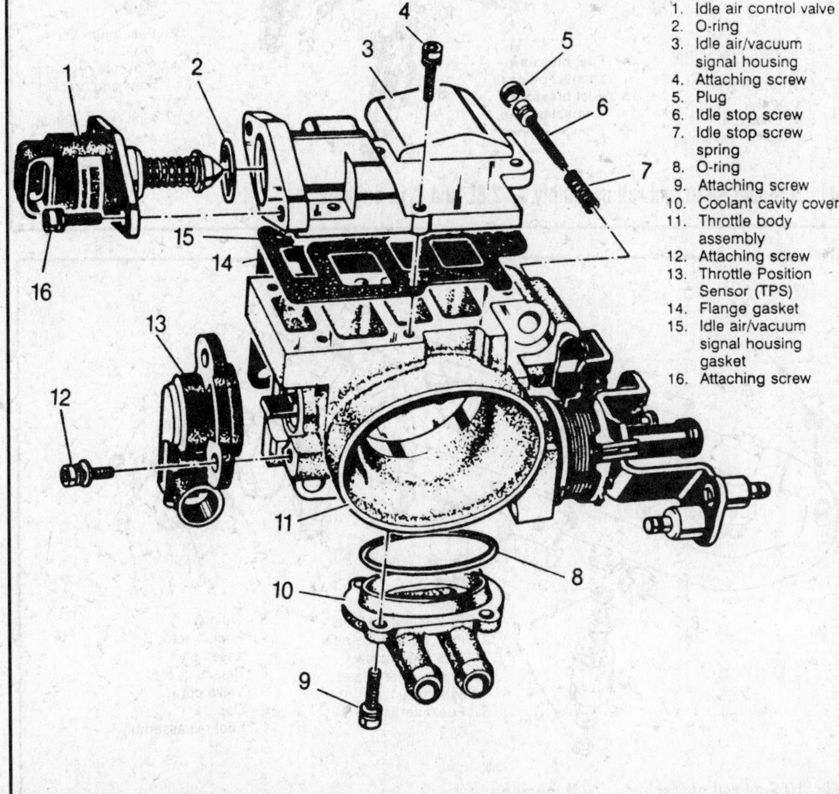

Fig. 7 Model B115 throttle body — 2.8L and 3.1L engines

Fuel Rail Assembly

➧ SEE FIGS. 8, 9 AND 10

When servicing the fuel rail assembly, be careful to prevent dirt and other contaminants from entering the fuel passages. Fittings should be capped and holes plugged during servicing. At any time the fuel system is opened for service, the O-ring seals and retainers used with related components should be replaced.

Before removing the fuel rail, the fuel rail assembly may be cleaned with a spray type cleaner, GM–30A or equivalent, following package instructions. Do not immerse fuel rails in liquid cleaning solvent. Be sure to always use new O-rings and seals when reinstalling the fuel rail assemblies.

There is an 8-digit number stamped on the under side of the fuel rail assembly on 4 cylinder engines and on the left hand fuel rail on dual rail assemblies (fueling even cylinders No. 2, 4, 6). Refer to this number if servicing or part replacement is required.

REMOVAL & INSTALLATION

2.3L Engine

1. Relieve fuel system pressure. Disconnect the negative battery cable.
2. Remove the crankcase ventilation oil/air separator and the canister purge solenoid.
3. Disconnect the fuel feed line and return line from the fuel rail assembly, be sure to use a backup wrench on the inlet fitting to prevent turning.
4. Remove the vacuum line at the pressure regulator. Remove the fuel rail assembly retaining bolts.
5. Push in the wire connector clip, while pulling the connector away from the injector.
6. Remove the fuel rail assembly and cover all openings with masking tape to prevent dirt entry.

➡ **If any injectors become separated from the fuel rail and remain in the intake manifold, both O-ring seals and injector retaining clip must be replaced. Use care in removing the fuel rail assembly, to prevent damage to the injector electrical connector terminals and the injector spray tips. When removed, support the fuel rail to avoid damaging its components. The fuel injector is serviced as a complete unit only. Since it is an electrical component, it should not be immersed in any type of cleaner.**

7. Be sure to lubricate all the O-rings and seals with clean engine oil. Carefully push the injectors into the cylinder head intake ports until the bolt holes on the fuel rail and manifold are aligned.
8. The remainder of the installation is the reverse order of the removal procedure.
9. Apply a coating of tread locking compound on the treads of the fittings. Torque the fuel rail retaining bolts to 19 ft. lbs. (26 Nm), the fuel feed line nut to 22 ft. lbs. (30 Nm) and the fuel pipe fittings to 20 ft. lbs. (26 Nm).

10. Energize the fuel pump and check for leaks.

2.8L, 3.1L, and 3.4L Engines

1. Disconnect the negative battery cable. Relieve fuel system pressure.
2. Remove the intake manifold plenum.
3. Disconnect the fuel feed line and return line from the fuel rail assembly, be sure to use a backup wrench on the inlet fitting to prevent turning.
4. Remove the vacuum line at the pressure regulator. Remove the fuel rail assembly retaining bolts.
5. Push in the wire connector clip, while pulling the connector away from the injector.
6. Remove the fuel rail assembly and cover all openings with masking tape to prevent dirt entry.

➡ If any injectors become separated from the fuel rail and remain in the intake manifold, both O-ring seals and injector retaining clip must be replaced. Use care in removing the fuel rail assembly, to prevent damage to the injector electrical connector terminals and the injector spray tips. When removed, support the fuel rail to avoid damaging its components. The fuel injector is serviced as a complete unit only. Since it is an electrical component, it should not be immersed in any type of cleaner.

7. Installation is the reverse order of the removal procedure. Be sure to lubricate all the O-rings and seals with clean engine oil. Carefully tilt the fuel rail assembly and push the injectors into the cylinder head intake ports until the bolt holes on the fuel rail and manifold are aligned. Perform the following torque specifications:

2.8L and 3.1L engines — Fuel rail retaining nuts to 88 inch lbs. (10 Nm).

2.8L and 3.1L engines — Fuel feed line nut to 17 ft. lbs. (23 Nm).

3.4L engine — Fuel rail retaining nuts to 88 inch lbs. (10 Nm).

3.4L engine — Fuel feed line nut to 22 ft. lbs. (30 Nm).

8. Connect the negative battery cable. Energize the fuel pump and check for leaks.

Fuel Injectors

➧ SEE FIG. 11

Use care in removing the fuel injectors to prevent damage to the electrical connector pins on the injector and the nozzle. The fuel injector is

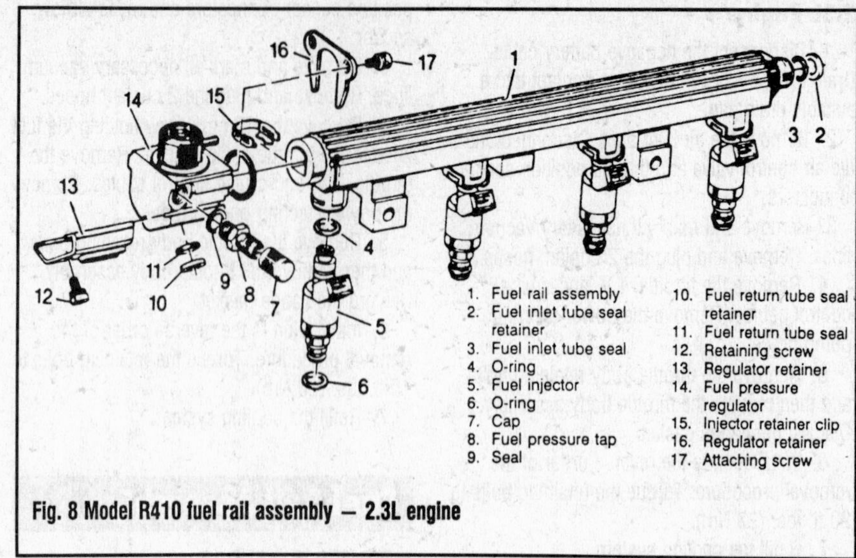

Fig. 8 Model R410 fuel rail assembly — 2.3L engine

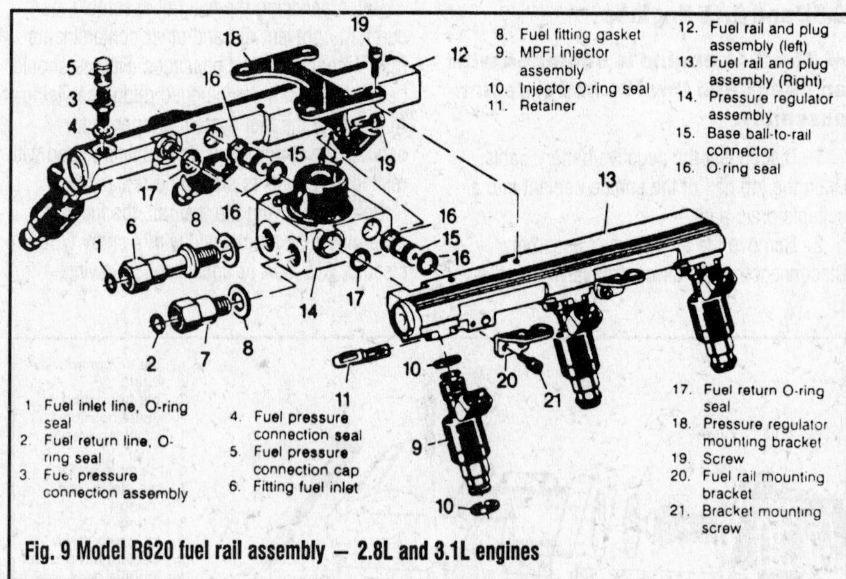

Fig. 9 Model R620 fuel rail assembly — 2.8L and 3.1L engines

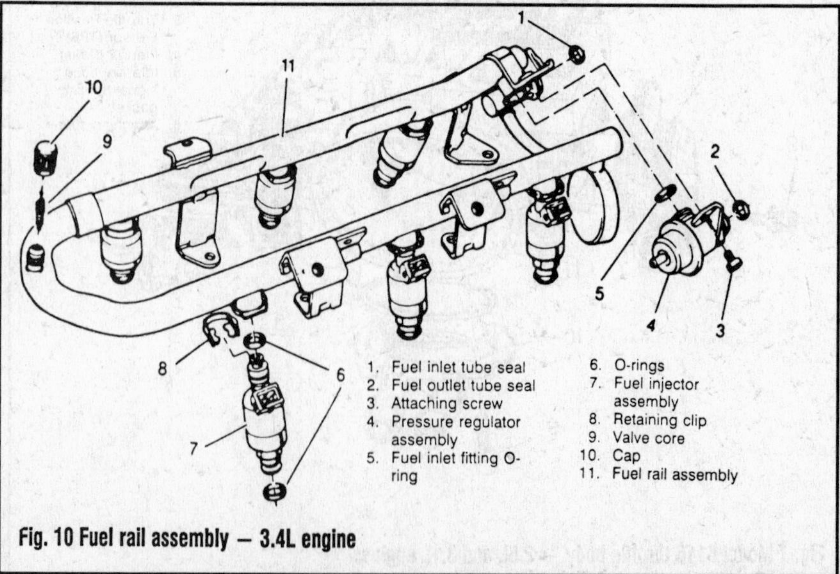

Fig. 10 Fuel rail assembly — 3.4L engine

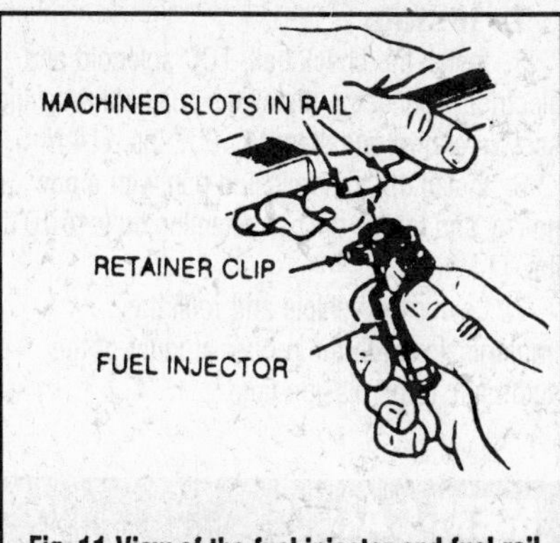

Fig. 11 View of the fuel injector and fuel rail

serviced as a complete assembly only and should not be immersed in any kind of cleaner. Support the fuel rail to avoid damaging other components while removing the injector. Be sure to note that different injectors are calibrated for different flow rates. When ordering new fuel injectors, be sure to order the identical part number that is inscribed on the bottom of the old injector.

REMOVAL & INSTALLATION

1. Relieve fuel system pressure. Disconnect the negative battery cable.
2. Disconnect the injector electrical connections.
3. Remove the fuel rail assembly.
4. Remove the injector retaining clip. Separate the injector from the fuel rail.
5. Remove both injector seals from the injector and discard.

To install:

6. Prior to installing the injectors, coat the new injector O-ring seals with clean engine oil. Install the seals on the injector assembly.
7. Use new injector retainer clips on the injector assembly. Position the open end of the clip facing the injector electrical connector.
8. Install the injector into the fuel rail injector socket with the electrical connectors facing outward. Push the injector in firmly until it engages with the retainer clip locking it in place.
9. Install the fuel rail and injector assembly. Install the intake manifold, if removed.
10. Connect the negative battery cable.
11. Turn the ignition switch ON and OFF to allow fuel pressure back into system. Check for leaks.

Fuel Pressure Regulator

➡ **On some applications, the pressure regulator and fuel rail are only available as an assembly. Check with your local parts retailer for parts availability and compatibility. Refer to the exploded views of the fuel rails.**

REMOVAL & INSTALLATION

1. Relieve fuel system pressure.
2. Disconnect the negative battery cable.
3. Disconnect the fuel feed line and return line from the fuel rail assembly, be sure to use a backup wrench on the inlet fitting to prevent turning.
4. Remove the fuel rail assembly from the engine.
5. With the fuel rail assembly removed from the engine, remove the pressure regulator mounting screw or retainer.
6. Remove the pressure regulator from the rail assembly by twisting back and forth while pulling apart.

To install:

7. Prior to assembling the pressure regulator to the fuel rail, lubricate the new rail-to-regulator O-ring seal with clean engine oil.
8. Place the O-ring on the pressure regulator and install the pressure regulator to the fuel rail.
9. Install the retainer or coat the regulator mounting screws with an approved tread locking compound and secure the pressure regulator in place. Torque the mounting screws to 102 inch lbs. (11.5 Nm).
10. Install the fuel rail assembly to the engine.
11. Connect the fuel feed line and return line to the fuel rail assembly, use a backup wrench on the inlet fitting to prevent turning.
12. Connect the negative battery cable.
13. Turn the ignition switch ON and OFF to allow fuel pressure back into system. Check for leaks.

Idle Air Control Valve

➧ SEE FIG. 12

REMOVAL & INSTALLATION

1. Disconnect the negative battery cable.
2. Disconnect electrical connector from idle air control valve.
3. Remove the screws retaining the idle air control valve. Remove the idle air control valve from mounting position.

To install:

4. Prior to installing the idle air control valve, measure the distance the valve plunger is extended. Measurement should be made from the edge of the valves mounting flange to the end of the cone. The distance should not exceed 1$^1/_8$ in. (28mm), or damage to the valve may occur when installed. If measuring distance is greater than specified above, press on the valve firmly to retract it, using a slight side to side motion to help it retract easier.
5. Use a new gasket and install the idle air control valve in mounting position.
6. Install the retaining screws. Torque the retaining screws to 27 inch lbs. (3 Nm). Connect the electrical connector.
7. The idle may be unstable for up to 7 minutes upon restarting while the ECM resets the IAC valve pintle to the correct position.

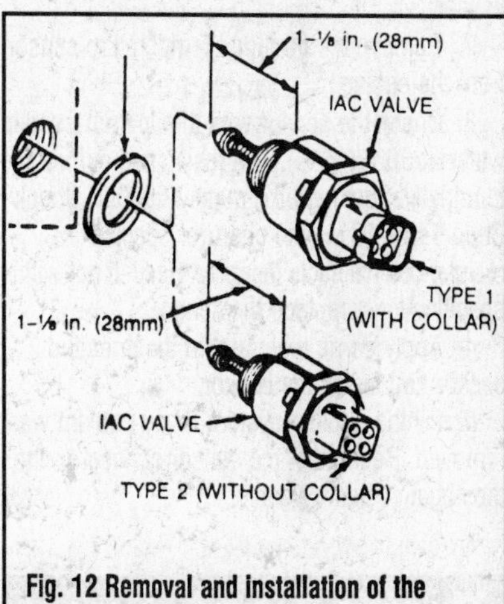

Fig. 12 Removal and installation of the Idle Air Control Valve (IAC)

Coolant Temperature Sensor

The coolant temperature sensor is located on the intake manifold water jacket or near (or on) the thermostat housing. It may be necessary to drain some of the coolant from the coolant system.

REMOVAL & INSTALLATION

✲✲ CAUTION

When draining the coolant, keep in mind that cats and dogs are attracted by the ethylene glycol antifreeze, and are quite likely to drink any that is left in an uncovered container or in puddles on the ground. This will prove fatal in sufficient quantity. Always drain the coolant into a sealable container. Coolant should be reused unless it is contaminated or several years old.

1. Disconnect the negative battery cable and disconnect the electrical connector at the sensor.
2. Remove the threaded temperature sensor from the engine.
3. Check the sensor with the tip immersed in water at 50°F (15°C). The resistance across the terminals should approximately 5600Ω. Check Code 14 or 15 engine chart for specific resistance on vehicle being serviced. If not within specifications, replace the sensor.
4. Apply some pipe tape to the threaded sensor and install the sensor.
5. Fill the cooling system if any coolant was removed. Reconnect the sensor connector and the negative battery cable.

Throttle Position Sensor

REMOVAL & INSTALLATION

1. Disconnect the electrical connector from the sensor. Refer to the throttle body exploded views for location of the TPS.
2. Remove the attaching screws, lock washers and retainers.
3. Remove the throttle position sensor. If necessary, remove the screw holding the actuator to the end of the throttle shaft.
4. With the throttle valve in the normal closed idle position, install the throttle position sensor on the throttle body assembly, making sure the sensor pickup lever is located above the tang on the throttle actuator lever.
5. Install the retainers, screws and lock washers using a thread locking compound.

TPS Output Check Test

WITH SCAN TOOL

1. Use a suitable scan tool to read the TPS voltage.
2. With the ignition switch **ON** and the engine **OFF**, the TPS voltage should be less, than 1.25 volts.
3. If the voltage reading is higher than specified, replace the throttle position sensor.

WITHOUT SCAN TOOL

1. Disconnect the TPS harness from the TPS.
2. Using suitable jumper wires, connect a digital voltmeter to terminals A and B on the TPS.
3. With the ignition **ON** and the engine running, the TPS voltage should be 0.450–1.25 volts at base idle to approximately 4.5 volts at wide open throttle.
4. If the reading on the TPS is out of specification, replace it.
5. Turn ignition **OFF**, remove jumper wires, then reconnect harness to throttle position switch.

Mass Air Flow Sensor

REMOVAL & INSTALLATION

1. Disconnect the negative battery cable.
2. Disconnect the electrical connector to the MAF sensor.
3. Remove the air cleaner and duct assembly. Remove the sensor retaining clamps and remove the sensor.
4. Installation is the reverse order of the removal procedure.

Torque Converter Clutch Solenoid

REMOVAL & INSTALLATION

1. Remove the negative battery cable. Raise and support the vehicle safely.
2. Drain the transmission fluid into a suitable drain pan. Remove the transmission pan.
3. Remove the TCC solenoid retaining screws and then remove the electrical connector, solenoid and check ball.
4. Clean and inspect all parts. Replace defective parts as necessary.

To install:

5. Install the check ball, TCC solenoid and electrical connector. Install the solenoid retaining screws and torque them to 10 ft. lbs. (14 Nm).
6. Install the transmission pan with a new gasket and torque the pan retaining bolts to 10 ft. lbs. (14 Nm).
7. Lower the vehicle and refill the transmission with the proper amount of the automatic transmission fluid.

MEM-CAL

REMOVAL & INSTALLATION

1. Remove the ECM.
2. Remove the Mem-Cal access panel.
3. Using 2 fingers, push both retaining clips back away from the Mem-Cal. At the same time grasp it at both ends and lift it out of the socket Do not remove the cover of the Mem-Cal. Use of an unapproved Mem-Cal removal procedures may cause damage to the Mem-Cal or the socket.

To install:

4. Install the new Mem-Cal by pressing only the ends of the Mem-Cal. Small notches in the Mem-Cal must be aligned with the small notches in the Mem-Cal socket.
5. Press on the ends of the Mem-Cal until the retaining clips snap into the ends of the Mem-Cal. Do not press on the middle of the Mem-Cal, only on the ends.
6. Install the Mem-Cal access cover and reinstall the ECM.

PROM

REMOVAL & INSTALLATION

1. Remove the ECM.
2. Remove the PROM access panel.
3. Using the rocker type PROM removal tool, engage 1 end of the PROM carrier with the hook end of the tool. Press on the vertical bar end of the tool and rock the engaged end of the PROM carrier up as far as possible.
4. Engage the opposite end of the PROM carrier in the same manner and rock this end up as far as possible.
5. Repeat this process until the PROM carrier and PROM are free of the PROM socket. The

PROM carrier with PROM in it should lift off of the PROM socket easily.

6. The PROM carrier should only be removed by using the special PROM removal tool. Other methods could cause damage to the PROM or PROM socket.

7. Before installing a new PROM, be sure the new PROM part number is the same as the old one or the as the updated number per a service bulletin.

To install:

8. Install the PROM with the small notch of the carrier aligned with the small notch in the socket. Press on the PROM carrier until the PROM is firmly seated, do not press on the PROM itself only on the PROM carrier.

9. Install the PROM access cover and reinstall the ECM.

FUNCTIONAL CHECK

1. Turn the ignition switch to the **ON** position.

2. Enter the diagnostic mode.

3. Allow a Code 12 to flash 4 times to verify that no other codes are present. This indicates that the PROM is installed properly.

4. If trouble Code 51 occurs or if the SERVICE ENGINE SOON light in on constantly with no codes, the PROM is not fully seated, installed backwards, has bent pins or is defective.

5. If not fully seated press down firmly on the PROM carrier.

6. If installed backwards, replace the PROM.

➡ Any time the PROM is installed backwards and the ignition switch is turned ON, the PROM is destroyed.

7. If the pins are bent, remove the PROM straighten the pins and reinstall the PROM. If the bent pins break or crack during straightening, discard the PROM and replace with a new PROM.

➡ To prevent possible electrostatic discharge damage to the PROM or Cal-Pak, do not touch the component leads and do not remove the integrated circuit from the carrier.

SEQUENTIAL PORT FUEL INJECTION 3.8L ENGINE

System Description

The Sequential Port Fuel Injection (SPFI) system is controlled by an Electronic Control Module (ECM) which monitors engine operations and generates output signals to provide the correct air/fuel mixture, ignition timing and engine idle speed control. Input to the control unit is provided by an oxygen sensor, coolant temperature sensor, detonation sensor, hot film air mass sensor and throttle position sensor. The ECM also receives information concerning engine rpm, road speed, transmission gear position, power steering and air conditioning.

With SPFI, metered fuel is timed and injected sequentially through the injectors into individual cylinder ports. Each cylinder receives 1 injection per working cycle (every 2 revolutions), just prior to the opening of the intake valve. In addition, on V6 engines, the SPFI system incorporates a Computer Controlled Coil Ignition (Cúl) system that uses an electronic coil module that replaced the conventional distributor and coil used on most engines. An Electronic Spark Control (ESC) is used to adjust the spark timing. On V8 engines, the conventional High Energy Ignition (HEI) system is used.

The injection system uses solenoid-type fuel injectors, 1 at each intake port, rather than the single injector found on the earlier throttle body system. The injectors are mounted on a fuel rail and are activated by a signal from the electronic control module. The injector is a solenoid-operated valve which remains open depending on the width of the electronic pulses (length of the signal) from the ECM; the longer the open time, the more fuel is injected. In this manner, the air/fuel mixture can be precisely controlled for maximum performance with minimum emissions.

Fuel is pumped from the tank by a high pressure fuel pump, located inside the fuel tank. It is a positive displacement roller vane pump. The impeller serves as a vapor separator and pre-charges the high pressure assembly. A pressure regulator maintains 34–47 psi (240–315 kPa) in the fuel line to the injectors and the excess fuel is fed back to the tank.

Engine idle is controlled by an Idle Air Control (IAC) valve, which provides a bypass channel through which air can flow. It consists of an orifice and pintle which is controlled by the ECM through a stepper motor. The IAC provides air flow for idle and allows additional air during cold start until the engine reaches operating temperature. As the engine temperature rises, the opening through which air passes is slowly closed.

Service Precautions

When working around any part of the fuel system, take precautionary steps to prevent fire and/or explosion:

• Disconnect negative terminal from battery (except when testing with battery voltage is required).

• When ever possible, use a flashlight instead of a drop light.

• Keep all open flame and smoking material out of the area.

• Use a shop cloth or similar to catch fuel when opening a fuel system.

• Relieve fuel system pressure before servicing.

• Use eye protection.

• Always keep a dry chemical (class B) fire extinguisher near the area.

Relieving Fuel System Pressure

1. Disconnect the negative battery cable.

2. Loosen the fuel filler cap to relieve fuel tank vapor pressure.

3. Connect fuel pressure valve J 34730-1 or equivalent to the fuel pressure relief connection at the fuel rail.

4. Wrap a shop towel around the fittings while connecting the tool to prevent fuel spillage.

5. Install a bleed hose into an approved container and open the valve to bleed the system pressure.

6. Install the fuel filler cap.

Electric Fuel Pump

FUEL PRESSURE CHECK

1. Connect pressure gauge J-34730–1, or equivalent, to fuel pressure test point on the fuel rail. Wrap a rag around the pressure tap to absorb any leakage that may occur when installing the gauge.

2. Turn the ignition **ON** and check that pump pressure is 24–40 psi.

3. Start the engine and allow it to idle. The fuel pressure should drop to 28–32 psi due to the lower manifold pressure.

➡ **The idle pressure will vary somewhat depending on barometric pressure. Check for a drop in pressure indicating regulator control, rather than specific values.**

4. If the fuel pressure drops, check the operation of the check valve, the pump coupling connection, fuel pressure regulator valve and the injectors. A restricted fuel line or filter may also cause a pressure drip. To check the fuel pump output, restrict the fuel return line and run 12 volts to the pump. The fuel pressure should rise to approximately 75 psi with the return line restricted.

5. Before attempting to remove or service any fuel system component, it is necessary to relieve the fuel system pressure.

REMOVAL & INSTALLATION

1. Disconnect the negative battery cable.
2. Relieve the fuel system pressure.
3. Raise and safely support the vehicle with jackstands.
4. Safely drain and remove the fuel tank assembly as outlined in the "Fuel tank" removal procedures in this Section.
5. Turn the fuel pump cam lock ring counterclockwise and lift the assembly out of the tank.
6. Remove the fuel pump from the level sensor unit as follows:
   a. Pull the pump up into the attaching hose or pulsator while pulling outward away from the bottom support.
   b. Take care to prevent damage to the rubber insulator and strainer during removal.
   c. When the pump assembly is clear of the bottom support, pull the pump out of the rubber connector for removal.

To install:

7. Replace any attaching hoses or rubber sound insulator that show signs of deterioration.
8. Push the fuel pump into the attaching hoses and install the pump/sensor assembly into the tank. Always use a new O-ring seal. Be careful not to fold over or twist the strainer when installing the sensor unit. Also, make sure the strainer does not block full travel of the float arm.
9. Install the cam lock and turn clockwise to lock.
10. Install the fuel tank as outlined in this Section.
11. Fill the tank with four gallons of gas and check for fuel leaks.

Throttle Body

➧ SEE FIG. 13

REMOVAL & INSTALLATION

1. Disconnect the negative battery cable. Drain the radiator coolant.
2. Remove the air inlet duct. The idle air control valve and throttle position sensor connectors.
3. Remove the throttle, throttle valve and cruise control cables.
4. Remove the throttle cable bracket.
5. Remove the throttle body retaining bolts and remove the throttle body from the intake manifold. Discard the flange gasket.
6. Installation is the reverse order of the removal procedure. Torque the retaining bolts to 11 ft. lbs (15 Nm).
7. Refill the cooling system.

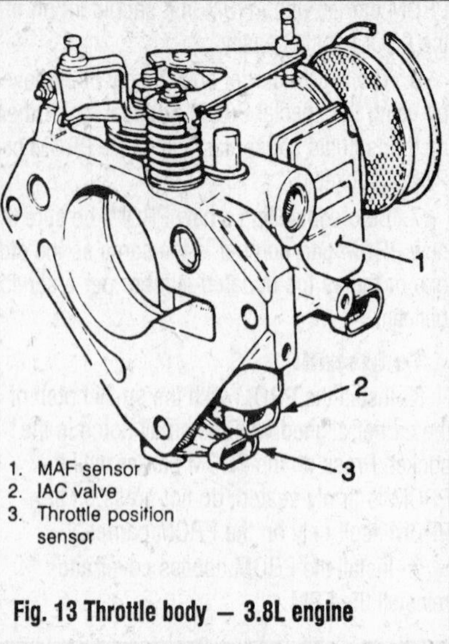

Fig. 13 Throttle body — 3.8L engine

Fuel Rail Assembly

When servicing the fuel rail assembly, be careful to prevent dirt and other contaminants from entering the fuel passages. Fittings should be capped and holes plugged during servicing. At any time the fuel system is opened for service, the O-ring seals and retainers used with related components should be replaced.

Before removing the fuel rail, the fuel rail assembly may be cleaned with a spray type cleaner, GM-30A or equivalent, following package instructions. Do not immerse fuel rails in liquid cleaning solvent. Be sure to always use new O-rings and seals when reinstalling the fuel rail assemblies.

There is an 8-digit number stamped on the under side of the fuel rail assembly on 4 cylinder engines and on the left hand fuel rail on dual rail assemblies (fueling even cylinders No. 2, 4, 6). Refer to this number if servicing or part replacement is required.

REMOVAL & INSTALLATION

1. Disconnect the negative battery cable. Relieve fuel system pressure.
2. Disconnect the fuel feed line and return line from the fuel rail assembly, be sure to use a backup wrench on the inlet fitting to prevent turning.
3. Remove the vacuum line at the pressure regulator. Remove the return line from pressure regulator.
4. Disconnect the electrical connectors from each fuel injector.
5. Remove the bolts retaining the fuel rail assembly to the intake manifold. Remove the fuel rail assembly and cover all openings with masking tape to prevent dirt entry.

➡ **If any injectors become separated from the fuel rail and remain in the intake manifold, both O-ring seals and injector retaining clip must be replaced. Use care in removing the fuel rail assembly, to prevent damage to the injector electrical connector terminals and the injector spray tips. When removed, support the fuel rail to avoid damaging its components. The fuel injector is serviced as a complete unit only. Since it is an electrical component, it should not be immersed in any type of cleaner.**

8. Installation is the reverse order of the removal procedure. Be sure to lubricate all the O-rings and seals with clean engine oil. Carefully push the injectors into the cylinder head intake ports until the bolt holes on the fuel rail and manifold are aligned. Apply a coating of tread locking compound on the treads of the fittings. Torque the fuel rail retaining bolts to 10 ft. lbs. (13 Nm). Energize the fuel pump and check for leaks.

Fuel Injectors

➧ SEE FIG. 14

REMOVAL & INSTALLATION

1. Relieve fuel system pressure.
2. Disconnect the negative battery cable.
3. Remove the injector electrical connections. Remove the fuel rail assembly.
4. Remove the injector retaining clip. Separate the injector from the fuel rail.
5. Remove both injector seals from the injector and discard.

To install:

6. Prior to installing the injectors, coat the new injector O-ring seals with clean engine oil. Install the seals on the injector assembly.
7. Use new injector retainer clips on the injector assembly. Position the open end of the clip facing the injector electrical connector.
8. Install the injector into the fuel rail injector socket with the electrical connectors facing outward. Push the injector in firmly until it engages with the retainer clip locking it in place.
9. Install the fuel rail and injector assembly.
10. Connect the negative battery cable.
11. Turn the ignition switch cf35 ON and cf35 OFF to allow fuel pressure back into system. Check for leaks.

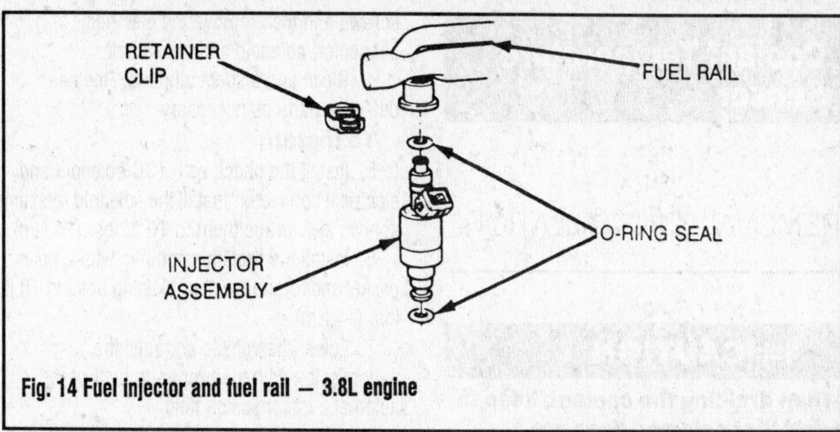

Fig. 14 Fuel injector and fuel rail — 3.8L engine

Fuel Pressure Regulator

➧ SEE FIG. 15

REMOVAL & INSTALLATION

1. Relieve fuel system pressure. Disconnect the negative battery cable.
2. Clean dirt and grease from the regulator retaining ring.
3. Disconnect the vacuum line from the regulator.
4. Remove the snapring from the regulator. Wrap a towel around the regulator to catch any fuel that may escape.
5. Lift and twist the regulator and remove it from the fuel rail assembly.
6. Cover all openings with masking tape to prevent dirt entry.

To install:

7. Install new O-ring seals onto the regulator. Prior to installing the regulator, lubricate the O-ring with engine oi.
8. Install the regulator into the regulator housing and install the snapring.
9. Connect the vacuum line to the regulator.
10. Connect the negative battery cable.
11. Turn the ignition switch cf35 ON and cf35 OFF to allow fuel pressure back into system. Check for leaks.

Idle Air Control (IAC) Valve

REMOVAL & INSTALLATION

1. Disconnect the negative battery cable.
2. Disconnect the connector from the IAC valve.
3. Remove the IAC attaching screws and remove the IAC.

➡ **Before installing the new IAC valve, measure the distance that the valve is extended. Measurement should be made from the motor housing to the end of the cone. Distance should be no greater than $1^1/_8$ in. (28mm). If the cone is extended too far, adjustment is required or damage may occur to the valve when installed.**

To install:

4. Use a new O-ring on the IAC and install the IAC.
5. Install the IAC attaching screws and tighten to 27 inch lbs. (3 Nm).
6. Connect the electrical connector to the IAC valve.
7. Start the engine and allow the engine to reach operating temperature.

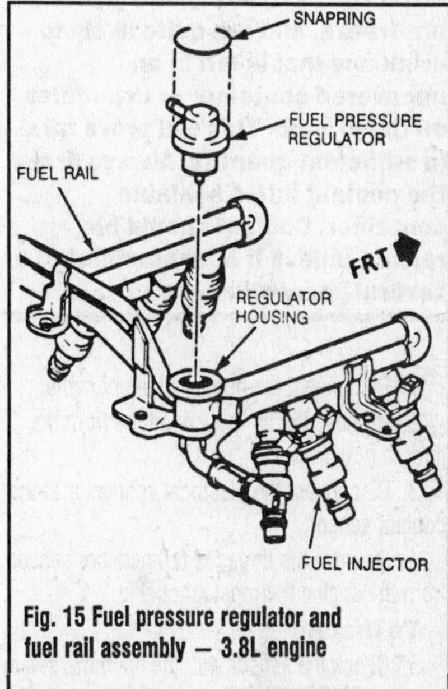

Fig. 15 Fuel pressure regulator and fuel rail assembly — 3.8L engine

8. The ECM will reset the IAC, whenever the ignition switch is turned **ON** and then **OFF**.

Camshaft Sensor

REMOVAL & INSTALLATION

1. Disconnect the negative battery cable.
2. Remove the serpentine drive belt and water pump drive pulley.
3. Disconnect the electrical connector at the sensor.
4. The cam sensor is located on the timing cover, behind the water pump, near the camshaft sprocket. Remove the cam sensor mounting bolt and remove the sensor from the engine.
5. Installation is the reverse order of the removal procedure.
6. Prior to installing the sensor, inspect the O-ring seal and replace as required.

Coolant Temperature Sensor

REMOVAL & INSTALLATION

✲✲ CAUTION

When draining the coolant, keep in mind that cats and dogs are attracted by the ethylene glycol antifreeze, and are quite likely to drink any that is left in an uncovered container or in puddles on the ground. This will prove fatal in sufficient quantity. Always drain the coolant into a sealable container. Coolant should be reused unless it is contaminated or several years old.

1. Disconnect the negative battery cable.
2. Remove the air induction tube from the throttle body.
3. Disconnect the electrical connector at the coolant sensor.
4. Remove the threaded temperature sensor from the engine thermostat housing.

To install:

5. Check the sensor with the tip immersed in water at 50°F (10°C). The resistance across the terminals should be 5670 ohms. If not within specifications, replace the sensor.
6. Apply a coating of an approved thread sealant on the threads of the temperature sensor. Install the sensor.
7. Reconnect the sensor connector and the negative battery cable.

Torque Converter Clutch Solenoid

REMOVAL & INSTALLATION

1. Remove the negative battery cable. Raise and support the vehicle safely.
2. Drain the transmission fluid into a suitable drain pan. Remove the transmission pan.
3. Remove the TCC solenoid retaining screws and then remove the electrical connector, solenoid and check ball.
4. Clean and inspect all parts. Replace defective parts as necessary.

To install:

5. Install the check ball, TCC solenoid and electrical connector. Install the solenoid retaining screws and torque them to 10 ft. lbs. (14 Nm).
6. Install the transmission pan with a new gasket and torque the pan retaining bolts to 10 ft. lbs. (14 Nm).
7. Lower the vehicle and refill the transmission with the proper amount of the automatic transmission fluid.

Throttle Position Sensor

REMOVAL & INSTALLATION

1. Disconnect the negative battery cable.
2. Disconnect the electrical connector from the from the TPS.
3. Remove the TPS attaching screws and remove the TPS.

To install:

4. Position the throttle valve in the normal closed idle position, install the TPS on the throttle body assembly, making sure the TPS pickup lever is located above the tang on the throttle actuator lever.
5. Install the TPS retainer and attaching screws using a thread locking compound on the screws. Loctite® 262 or equivalent should be used. Do not tighten the attaching screw until the TPS is adjusted.

TPS Adjustment

1. With the TPS attaching screws loose, install 3 jumper wires between TPS and harness connector.
2. With the ignition switch **ON**, use a digital voltmeter connected to terminals **B** and **C** and adjust TPS to obtain 0.40 ±0.05 volts.
3. Tighten the attaching screws, then recheck reading to insure the adjustment has not changed.

➡ If the TPS is being adjusted only, remove screws, add thread locking compound (Loctite® or equivalent), then reinstall the screws.

4. With the ignition switch **OFF**, remove the jumper wires and connect the harness to the TPS.

TPS Output Check Test

WITH SCAN TOOL

The following check should be performed only when the throttle body or TPS has been replaced.

1. Use a suitable scan tool to read the TPS voltage.
2. With the ignition switch **ON** and the engine **OFF**, the TPS voltage should be less, than 1.25 volts.
3. If the voltage reading is higher than specified, replace the throttle position sensor.

Knock Sensor

REMOVAL & INSTALLATION

1. Disconnect the negative battery cable.
2. Raise the vehicle and support it safely.
3. Disconnect the ESC wiring harness from the knock sensor.
4. Remove the knock sensor from the engine block.

To install:

➡ Do not apply thread sealant to sensor threads. Sensor is precoated at factory applying additional sealant will affect the sensors ability to detect detonation.

5. Install the knock sensor into the engine block.
6. Connect the electrical connector to the knock sensor.
7. Lower the vehicle. Connect the negative battery cable.

Mass Air Flow (MAF) Sensor

The Mass Air Flow Sensor is a part of the throttle body. Refer to the picture throttle body for location.

REMOVAL & INSTALLATION

1. Disconnect the negative battery cable.
2. Remove the fresh air duct from the throttle body and air cleaner assembly.
3. Disconnect the electrical connector to the MAF sensor.

4. Remove the sensor retaining screws and remove the sensor from the throttle body.

5. Installation is the reverse order of the removal procedure. Do not attempt to remove the gasket, it is not removable or serviced separately.

MEM-CAL

REMOVAL & INSTALLATION

1. Remove the ECM.
2. Remove the Mem-Cal access panel.
3. Using 2 fingers, push both retaining clips back away from the Mem-Cal. At the same time, grasp it at both ends and lift it out of the socket. Do not remove the cover of the Mem-Cal. Use of an unapproved Mem-Cal removal procedures may cause damage to the Mem-Cal or the socket.

To install:

4. Install the new Mem-Cal by pressing only the ends of the Mem-Cal. Small notches in the Mem-Cal must be aligned with the small notches in the Mem-Cal socket.
5. Press on the ends of the Mem-Cal until the retaining clips snap into the ends of the Mem-Cal. Do not press on the middle of the Mem-Cal, only on the ends.
6. Install the Mem-Cal access cover and reinstall the ECM.

PROM

REMOVAL & INSTALLATION

1. Remove the ECM.
2. Remove the PROM access panel.
3. Using the rocker type PROM removal tool, engage 1 end of the PROM carrier with the hook end of the tool. Press on the vertical bar end of the tool and rock the engaged end of the PROM carrier up as far as possible.
4. Engage the opposite end of the PROM carrier in the same manner and rock this end up as far as possible.
5. Repeat this process until the PROM carrier and PROM are free of the PROM socket. The PROM carrier with PROM in it should lift off of the PROM socket easily.
6. The PROM carrier should only be removed by using the special PROM removal tool. Other methods could cause damage to the PROM or PROM socket.
7. Before installing a new PROM, be sure the new PROM part number is the same as the old one or the as the updated number per a service bulletin.

To install:

8. Install the PROM with the small notch of the carrier aligned with the small notch in the socket. Press on the PROM carrier until the PROM is firmly seated, do not press on the PROM itself only on the PROM carrier.
9. Install the PROM access cover and reinstall the ECM.

FUNCTIONAL CHECK

1. Turn the ignition switch to the **ON** position.
2. Enter the diagnostic mode.
3. Allow a Code 12 to flash 4 times to verify that no other codes are present. This indicates that the PROM is installed properly.
4. If trouble Code 51 occurs or if the SERVICE ENGINE SOON light in on constantly with no codes, the PROM is not fully seated, installed backwards, has bent pins or is defective.
5. If not fully seated press down firmly on the PROM carrier.
6. If installed backwards, replace the PROM.

➡ **Any time the PROM is installed backwards and the ignition switch is turned ON, the PROM is destroyed.**

7. If the pins are bent, remove the PROM straighten the pins and reinstall the PROM. If the bent pins break or crack during straightening, discard the PROM and replace with a new PROM.

➡ **To prevent possible electrostatic discharge damage to the PROM or Cal-Pak, do not touch the component leads and do not remove the integrated circuit from the carrier.**

FUEL TANK

DRAINING

1. Disconnect the negative battery cable.

⁂ CAUTION

To reduce the risk of fire and personal injury, always keep a dry chemical (Class B) fire extinguisher near the work area.

2. Remove the fuel cap.
3. Raise the vehicle and support with jackstands.
4. Disconnect the filler vent hose from the tank.
5. Use a hand operated pump approved for gasoline to drain as much fuel as possible through the filler vent hose.
6. Reconnect the filler vent hose and tighten the clamp.
7. Install any removed lines, hoses and cap. Connect the negative battery cable.

REMOVAL & INSTALLATION

➧ SEE FIG. 16

1. Disconnect the negative battery cable.
2. Drain the fuel tank.
3. Remove the fuel filler door assembly and disconnect the screw retaining the filler pipe-to-body bracket.
4. Raise the vehicle and support with jackstands.
5. Disconnect the tank level sender lead connector.
6. Support the tank with a transmission jack or equivalent. Remove the two tank retaining straps.
7. Lower the tank far enough to disconnect the ground lead and fuel hoses from the pump assembly.
8. Remove the tank from the vehicle slowly to ensure all connections and hoses have been disconnected.
9. Remove the fuel pump/level sender assembly using a locking cam tool J-24187 or equivalent.

To install:

10. Using a new fuel pump O-ring gasket, install the pump/sender assembly into the tank.

**** CAUTION**

Do not twist the strainer when installing the pump/sender assembly. Make sure the strainer does not block the full travel of the float arm.

11. Place the tank on the jack.
12. Position the tank sound insulators in their original positions and raise the tank far enough to connect the electrical and hose connectors.
13. Raise the tank to the proper position and loosely install the retaining straps. Make sure the tank is in the proper position before tightening the retaining straps.
14. Torque the straps to 26 ft. lbs. (35 Nm).
15. Connect the grounding strap and negative battery cable.
16. With the engine OFF, turn the ignition key to the ON position and check for fuel leaks at the tank.

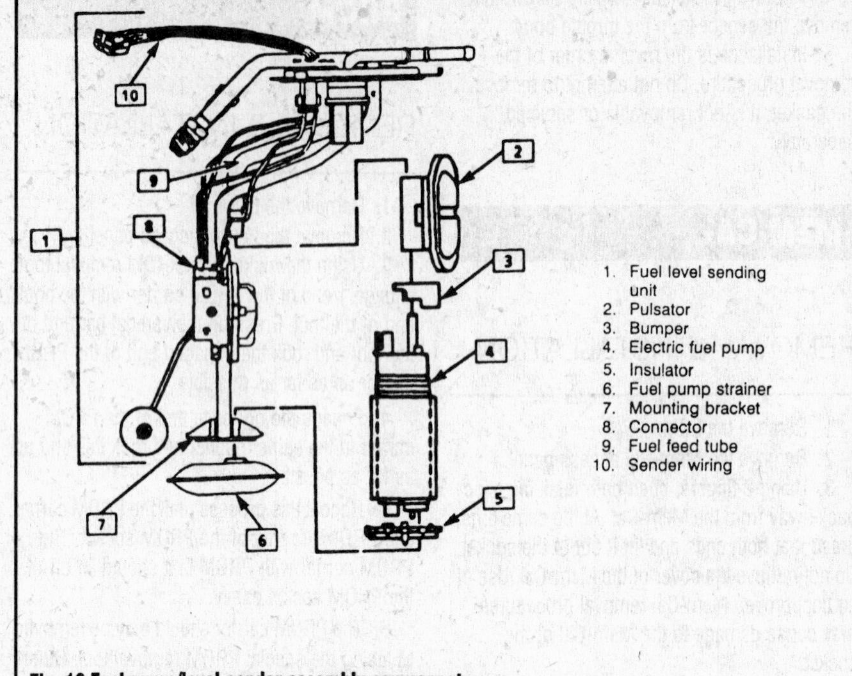

Fig. 16 Fuel pump/level sender assembly components

TORQUE SPECIFICATIONS

Component	U.S.	Metric
Fuel line fittings	20 ft. lbs.	26 Nm
Throttle body retaining screws		
2.5L engine	18 ft. lbs.	24 Nm
2.3L engine	20 ft. lbs.	27 Nm
2.8L and 3.1L engines	15 ft. lbs.	20 Nm
3.8L engine	11 ft. lbs.	15 Nm
Fuel meter assembly attaching screws 2.5L	53 inch lbs.	6 Nm
Injector retaining screw	27 inch lbs.	3 Nm
Fuel pressure regulator retaining screws		
2.5L engine	22 inch lbs.	2.5 Nm
2.8L, 3.1L and 3.4L engines	102 inch lbs.	11.5 Nm
3.8L engine	10 ft. lbs.	13 Nm
Idle air control valve retaining screw	27 inch lbs.	3 Nm
Coolant temperature sensor	22 ft. lbs.	30 Nm
TCC solenoid retaining screws	10 ft. lbs.	14 Nm
TPS retaining screws	18 inch lbs.	2 Nm
Fuel rail retaining bolts		
2.3L engine	19 ft. lbs.	26 Nm
2.8L, 3.1L and 3.4L engines	88 inch lbs.	10 Nm
Fuel feed line nut	22 ft. lbs.	30 Nm
Fuel tank straps	26 ft. lbs.	35 Nm

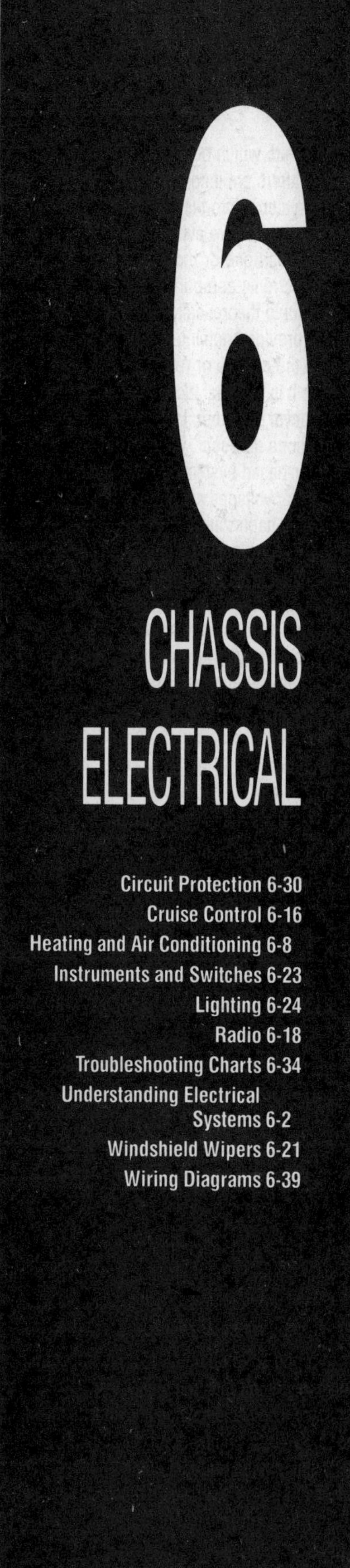

6 CHASSIS ELECTRICAL

UNDER-STANDING AND TROUBLE-SHOOTING ELECTRICAL SYSTEMS

At the rate which both import and domestic manufacturers are incorporating electronic control systems into their production lines, it won't be long before every new vehicle is equipped with one or more on-board computer. These electronic components (with no moving parts) should theoretically last the life of the vehicle, provided nothing external happens to damage the circuits or memory chips.

While it is true that electronic components should never wear out, in the real world, malfunctions do occur. It is also true that any computer-based system is extremely sensitive to electrical voltages and cannot tolerate careless or haphazard testing or service procedures. An inexperienced individual can literally do major damage looking for a minor problem by using the wrong kind of test equipment or connecting test leads or connectors with the ignition switch ON. When selecting test equipment, make sure the manufacturers instructions state that the tester is compatible with whatever type of electronic control system is being serviced. Read all instructions carefully and double check all test points before installing probes or making any test connections.

The following section outlines basic diagnosis techniques for dealing with computerized automotive control systems. Along with a general explanation of the various types of test equipment available to aid in servicing modern electronic automotive systems, basic repair techniques for wiring harnesses and connectors is given. Read the basic information before attempting any repairs or testing on any computerized system, to provide the background of information necessary to avoid the most common and obvious mistakes that can cost both time and money. Although the replacement and testing procedures are simple in themselves, the systems are not, and unless one has a thorough understanding of all components and their function within a particular computerized control system, the logical test sequence these systems demand cannot be followed. Minor malfunctions can make a big difference, so it is important to know how each component affects the operation of the overall electronic system to find the ultimate cause of a problem without replacing good components unnecessarily. It is not enough to use the correct test equipment; the test equipment must be used correctly.

Safety Precautions

** CAUTION

Whenever working on or around any computer based microprocessor control system, always observe these general precautions to prevent the possibility of personal injury or damage to electronic components.

- Never install or remove battery cables with the key ON or the engine running. Jumper cables should be connected with the key OFF to avoid power surges that can damage electronic control units. Engines equipped with computer controlled systems should avoid both giving and getting jump starts due to the possibility of serious damage to components from arcing in the engine compartment when connections are made with the ignition ON.
- Always remove the battery cables before charging the battery. Never use a high output charger on an installed battery or attempt to use any type of "hot shot" (24 volt) starting aid.
- Exercise care when inserting test probes into connectors to insure good connections without damaging the connector or spreading the pins. Always probe connectors from the rear (wire) side, NOT the pin side, to avoid accidental shorting of terminals during test procedures.
- Never remove or attach wiring harness connectors with the ignition switch ON, especially to an electronic control unit.
- Do not drop any components during service procedures and never apply 12 volts directly to any component (like a solenoid or relay) unless instructed specifically to do so. Some component electrical windings are designed to safely handle only 4 or 5 volts and can be destroyed in seconds if 12 volts are applied directly to the connector.
- Remove the electronic control unit if the vehicle is to be placed in an environment where temperatures exceed approximately 176°F (80°C), such as a paint spray booth or when arc or gas welding near the control unit location in the car.
- Disconnect the negative battery cable when are welding any part of the vehicle. The sudden surges of current may damage the electronic components.

ORGANIZED TROUBLESHOOTING

When diagnosing a specific problem, organized troubleshooting is a must. The complexity of a modern automobile demands that you approach any problem in a logical, organized manner. There are certain troubleshooting techniques that are standard:

1. Always check the fuses first. Establish when the problem occurs. Does the problem appear only under certain conditions? Were there any noises, odors, or other unusual symptoms?
2. Isolate the problem area. To do this, make some simple tests and observations; then eliminate the systems that are working properly. Check for obvious problems such as broken wires, dirty connections or split or disconnected vacuum hoses. Always check the obvious before assuming something complicated is the cause.
3. Test for problems systematically to determine the cause once the problem area is isolated. Are all the components functioning properly? Is there power going to electrical switches and motors? Is there vacuum at vacuum switches and/or actuators? Is there a mechanical problem such as bent linkage or loose mounting screws? Doing careful, systematic checks will often turn up most causes on the first inspection without wasting time checking components that have little or no relationship to the problem.
4. Test all repairs after the work is done to make sure that the problem is fixed. Some causes can be traced to more than one component, so a careful verification of repair work is important to pick up additional malfunctions that may cause a problem to reappear or a different problem to arise. A blown fuse, for example, is a simple problem that may require more than another fuse to repair. If you don't look for a problem that caused a fuse to blow, for example, a shorted wire may go undetected.

Experience has shown that most problems tend to be the result of a fairly simple and obvious cause, such as loose or corroded connectors or air leaks in the intake system; making careful inspection of components during testing essential to quick and accurate troubleshooting. Special, hand held computerized testers designed specifically for diagnosing the system are available from a variety of aftermarket sources, as well as from the vehicle manufacturer, but care should be taken that any test equipment being used is designed to diagnose that particular computer controlled system accurately without damaging the control unit (ECU) or components being tested.

Pinpointing the exact cause of trouble in an electrical system can sometimes only be accomplished by the use of special test equipment. The following describes commonly used test equipment and explains how to put it to best use in diagnosis. In addition to the information covered below, the manufacturer's instructions booklet provided with the tester should be read and clearly understood before attempting any test procedures.

TEST EQUIPMENT

Jumper Wires

Jumper wires are simple, yet extremely valuable, pieces of test equipment. Jumper wires are merely wires that are used to bypass sections of a circuit. The simplest type of jumper wire is merely a length of multistrand wire with an alligator clip at each end. Jumper wires are usually fabricated from lengths of standard automotive wire and whatever type of connector (alligator clip, spade connector or pin connector) that is required for the particular vehicle being tested. The well equipped tool box will have several different styles of jumper wires in several different lengths. Some jumper wires are made with three or more terminals coming from a common splice for special purpose testing. In cramped, hard-to-reach areas it is advisable to have insulated boots over the jumper wire terminals in order to prevent accidental grounding, sparks, and possible fire, especially when testing fuel system components.

Jumper wires are used primarily to locate open electrical circuits, on either the ground (-) side of the circuit or on the hot (+) side. If an electrical component fails to operate, connect the jumper wire between the component and a good ground. If the component operates only with the jumper installed, the ground circuit is open. If the ground circuit is good, but the component does not operate, the circuit between the power feed and component is open. You can sometimes connect the jumper wire directly from the battery to the hot terminal of the component, but first make sure the component uses 12 volts in operation. Some electrical components, such as fuel injectors, are designed to operate on about 4 volts and running 12 volts directly to the injector terminals can burn out the wiring. By inserting an inline fuse holder between a set of test leads, a fused jumper wire can be used for bypassing open circuits. Use a 5 amp fuse to provide protection against voltage spikes. When in doubt, use a voltmeter to check the voltage input to the component and measure how much voltage is being applied normally. By moving the jumper wire successively back from the lamp toward the power source, you can isolate the area of the circuit where the open is located. When the component stops functioning, or the power is cut off, the open is in the segment of wire between the jumper and the point previously tested.

Never use jumpers made from wire that is of lighter gauge than used in the circuit under test. If the jumper wire is of too small gauge, it may overheat and possibly melt. Never use jumpers to bypass high resistance loads (such as motors) in a circuit. Bypassing resistances, in effect, creates a short circuit which may, in turn, cause damage and fire. Never use a jumper for anything other than temporary bypassing of components in a circuit.

12 Volt Test Light

The 12 volt test light is used to check circuits and components while electrical current is flowing through them. It is used for voltage and ground tests. Twelve volt test lights come in different styles but all have three main parts; a ground clip, a probe, and a light. The most commonly used 12 volt test lights have pick-type probes. To use a 12 volt test light, connect the ground clip to a good ground and probe wherever necessary with the pick. The pick should be sharp so that it can penetrate wire insulation to make contact with the wire, without making a large hole in the insulation. The wraparound light is handy in hard to reach areas or where it is difficult to support a wire to push a probe pick into it. To use the wrap around light, hook the wire to probed with the hook and pull the trigger. A small pick will be forced through the wire insulation into the wire core.

Do not use a test light to probe electronic ignition spark plug or coil wires. Never use a pick-type test light to probe wiring on computer controlled systems unless specifically instructed to do so. Any wire insulation that is pierced by the test light probe should be taped and sealed with silicone after testing.

Like the jumper wire, the 12 volt test light is used to isolate opens in circuits. But, whereas the jumper wire is used to bypass the open to operate the load, the 12 volt test light is used to locate the presence of voltage in a circuit. If the test light glows, you know that there is power up to that point; if the 12 volt test light does not glow when its probe is inserted into the wire or connector, you know that there is an open circuit (no power). Move the test light in successive steps back toward the power source until the light in the handle does glow. When it does glow, the open is between the probe and point previously probed.

➡ The test light does not detect that 12 volts (or any particular amount of voltage) is present; it only detects that some voltage is present. It is advisable before using the test light to touch its terminals across the battery posts to make sure the light is operating properly.

Self-Powered Test Light

The self-powered test light usually contains a 1.5 volt penlight battery. One type of self-powered test light is similar in design to the 12 volt test light. This type has both the battery and the light in the handle and pick-type probe tip. The second type has the light toward the open tip, so that the light illuminates the contact point. The self-powered test light is dual purpose piece of test equipment. It can be used to test for either open or short circuits when power is isolated from the circuit (continuity test). A powered test light should not be used on any computer controlled system or component unless specifically instructed to do so. Many engine sensors can be destroyed by even this small amount of voltage applied directly to the terminals.

Open Circuit Testing

To use the self-powered test light to check for open circuits, first isolate the circuit from the vehicle's 12 volt power source by disconnecting the battery or wiring harness connector. Connect the test light ground clip to a good ground and probe sections of the circuit sequentially with the test light. (start from either end of the circuit). If the light is out, the open is between the probe and the circuit ground. If the light is on, the open is between the probe and end of the circuit toward the power source.

Short Circuit Testing

By isolating the circuit both from power and from ground, and using a self-powered test light, you can check for shorts to ground in the circuit. Isolate the circuit from power and ground. Connect the test light ground clip to a good ground and probe any easy-to-reach test point in the circuit. If the light comes on, there is a short somewhere in the circuit. To isolate the short, probe a test point at either end of the isolated circuit (the light should be on). Leave the test light probe connected and open connectors, switches, remove parts, etc., sequentially, until the light goes out. When the light goes out, the short is between the last circuit component opened and the previous circuit opened.

➡ The 1.5 volt battery in the test light does not provide much current. A weak battery may not provide enough power to illuminate the test light even when a complete circuit is made (especially if there are high resistances in the circuit). Always make sure that the test battery is strong. To check the battery, briefly touch the ground clip to the probe; if the light glows brightly the battery is strong enough for testing. Never use a selfpowered test light to perform checks for opens or shorts when power is applied to the electrical system under test. The 12 volt vehicle power will quickly burn out the 1.5 volt light bulb in the test light.

Voltmeter

A voltmeter is used to measure voltage at any point in a circuit, or to measure the voltage drop across any part of a circuit. It can also be used to check continuity in a wire or circuit by indicating current flow from one end to the other. Voltmeters usually have various scales on the meter dial and a selector switch to allow the selection of different voltages. The voltmeter has a positive and a negative lead. To avoid damage to the meter, always connect the negative lead to the negative (-) side of circuit (to ground or nearest the ground side of the circuit) and connect the positive lead to the positive (+) side of the circuit (to the power source or the nearest power source). Note that the negative voltmeter lead will always be black and that the positive voltmeter will always be some color other than black (usually red). Depending on how the voltmeter is connected into the circuit, it has several uses.

A voltmeter can be connected either in parallel or in series with a circuit and it has a very high resistance to current flow. When connected in parallel, only a small amount of current will flow through the voltmeter current path; the rest will flow through the normal circuit current path and the circuit will work normally. When the voltmeter is connected in series with a circuit, only a small amount of current can flow through the circuit. The circuit will not work properly, but the voltmeter reading will show if the circuit is complete or not.

Available Voltage Measurement

Set the voltmeter selector switch to the 20V position and connect the meter negative lead to the negative post of the battery. Connect the positive meter lead to the positive post of the battery and turn the ignition switch ON to provide a load. Read the voltage on the meter or digital display. A well charged battery should register over 12 volts. If the meter reads below 11.5 volts, the battery power may be insufficient to operate the electrical system properly. This test determines voltage available from the battery and should be the first step in any electrical trouble diagnosis procedure. Many electrical problems, especially on computer controlled systems, can be caused by a low state of charge in the battery. Excessive corrosion at the battery cable terminals can cause a poor contact that will prevent proper charging and full battery current flow.

Normal battery voltage is 12 volts when fully charged. When the battery is supplying current to one or more circuits it is said to be "under load". When everything is off the electrical system is under a "no-load" condition. A fully charged battery may show about 12.5 volts at no load; will drop to 12 volts under medium load; and will drop even lower under heavy load. If the battery is partially discharged the voltage decrease under heavy load may be excessive, even though the battery shows 12 volts or more at no load. When allowed to discharge further, the battery's available voltage under load will decrease more severely. For this reason, it is important that the battery be fully charged during all testing procedures to avoid errors in diagnosis and incorrect test results.

Voltage Drop

When current flows through a resistance, the voltage beyond the resistance is reduced (the larger the current, the greater the reduction in voltage). When no current is flowing, there is no voltage drop because there is no current flow. All points in the circuit which are connected to the power source are at the same voltage as the power source. The total voltage drop always equals the total source voltage. In a long circuit with many connectors, a series of small, unwanted voltage drops due to corrosion at the connectors can add up to a total loss of voltage which impairs the operation of the normal loads in the circuit.

INDIRECT COMPUTATION OF VOLTAGE DROPS

1. Set the voltmeter selector switch to the 20 volt position.
2. Connect the meter negative lead to a good ground.
3. Probe all resistances in the circuit with the positive meter lead.
4. Operate the circuit in all modes and observe the voltage readings.

DIRECT MEASUREMENT OF VOLTAGE DROPS

1. Set the voltmeter switch to the 20 volt position.
2. Connect the voltmeter negative lead to the ground side of the resistance load to be measured.
3. Connect the positive lead to the positive side of the resistance or load to be measured.
4. Read the voltage drop directly on the 20 volt scale.

Too high a voltage indicates too high a resistance. If, for example, a blower motor runs too slowly, you can determine if there is too high a resistance in the resistor pack. By taking voltage drop readings in all parts of the circuit, you can isolate the problem. Too low a voltage drop indicates too low a resistance. If, for example, a blower motor runs too fast in the MED and/or LOW position, the problem can be isolated in the resistor pack by taking voltage drop readings in all parts of the circuit to locate a possibly shorted resistor. The maximum allowable voltage drop under load is critical, especially if there is more than one high resistance problem in a circuit because all voltage drops are cumulative. A small drop is normal due to the resistance of the conductors.

HIGH RESISTANCE TESTING

1. Set the voltmeter selector switch to the 4 volt position.
2. Connect the voltmeter positive lead to the positive post of the battery.
3. Turn on the headlights and heater blower to provide a load.
4. Probe various points in the circuit with the negative voltmeter lead.
5. Read the voltage drop on the 4 volt scale. Some average maximum allowable voltage drops are:

FUSE PANEL—7 volts
IGNITION SWITCH—5 volts
HEADLIGHT SWITCH—7 volts
IGNITION COIL (+)—5 volts
ANY OTHER LOAD—1.3 volts

➡ Voltage drops are all measured while a load is operating; without current flow, there will be no voltage drop.

Ohmmeter

The ohmmeter is designed to read resistance (ohms) in a circuit or component. Although there are several different styles of ohmmeters, all will usually have a selector switch which permits the measurement of different ranges of resistance (usually the selector switch allows the multiplication of the meter reading by 10, 100, 1000 and 10,000). A calibration knob allows the meter to be set at zero for accurate measurement. Since all ohmmeters are powered by an internal battery (usually 9 volts), the ohmmeter can be used as a self-powered test light. When the ohmmeter is connected, current from the ohmmeter flows through the circuit or component being tested. Since the ohmmeter's internal resistance and voltage are known values, the amount of current flow through the meter depends on the resistance of the circuit or component being tested.

The ohmmeter can be used to perform continuity test for opens or shorts (either by observation of the meter needle or as a self-powered test light), and to read actual resistance in a circuit. It should be noted that the ohmmeter is used to check the resistance of a component or wire while there is no voltage applied to the circuit. Current flow from an outside voltage source (such as the vehicle battery) can damage the ohmmeter, so the circuit or component should be isolated from the vehicle electrical system before any testing is done. Since the ohmmeter uses its own voltage source, either lead can be connected to any test point.

➡ **When checking diodes or other solid state components, the ohmmeter leads can only be connected one way in order to measure current flow in a single direction. Make sure the positive (+) and negative (-) terminal connections are as described in the test procedures to verify the one-way diode operation.**

When using the meter for making continuity checks, do not be concerned with the actual resistance readings. Zero resistance, or any resistance readings, indicate continuity in the circuit. Infinite resistance indicates an open in the circuit. A high resistance reading where there should be none indicates a problem in the circuit. Checks for short circuits are made in the same manner as checks for open circuits except that the circuit must be isolated from both power and normal ground. Infinite resistance indicates no continuity to ground, while zero resistance indicates a dead short to ground.

RESISTANCE MEASUREMENT

The batteries in an ohmmeter will weaken with age and temperature, so the ohmmeter must be calibrated or "zeroed" before taking measurements. To zero the meter, place the selector switch in its lowest range and touch the two ohmmeter leads together. Turn the calibration knob until the meter needle is exactly on zero.

➡ **All analog (needle) type ohmmeters must be zeroed before use, but some digital ohmmeter models are automatically calibrated when the switch is turned on. Self calibrating digital ohmmeters do not have an adjusting knob, but its a good idea to check for a zero readout before use by touching the leads together. All computer controlled systems require the use of a digital ohmmeter with at least 10 Megohms impedance for testing. Before any test procedures are attempted, make sure the ohmmeter used is compatible with the electrical system or damage to the on-board computer could result.**

To measure resistance, first isolate the circuit from the vehicle power source by disconnecting the battery cables or the harness connector. Make sure the key is OFF when disconnecting any components or the battery. Where necessary, also isolate at least one side of the circuit to be checked to avoid reading parallel resistances. Parallel circuit resistances will always give a lower reading than the actual resistance of either of the branches. When measuring the resistance of parallel circuits, the total resistance will always be lower than the smallest resistance in the circuit. Connect the meter leads to both sides of the circuit (wire or component) and read the actual measured ohms on the meter scale. Make sure the selector switch is set to the proper ohm scale for the circuit being tested to avoid misreading the ohmmeter test value.

CAUTION

Never use an ohmmeter with power applied to the circuit. Like the self-powered test light, the ohmmeter is designed to operate on its own power supply. The normal 12 volt automotive electrical system current could damage the meter!

Ammeters

An ammeter measures the amount of current flowing through a circuit in units called amperes or amps. Amperes are units of electron flow which indicate how fast the electrons are flowing through the circuit. Since Ohms Law dictates that current flow in a circuit is equal to the circuit voltage divided by the total circuit resistance, increasing voltage also increases the current level (amps). Likewise, any decrease in resistance will increase the amount of amps in a circuit. At normal operating voltage, most circuits have a characteristic amount of amperes, called "current draw" which can be measured using an ammeter. By referring to a specified current draw rating, measuring the amperes, and comparing the two values, one can determine what is happening within the circuit to aid in diagnosis. An open circuit, for example, will not allow any current to flow so the ammeter reading will be zero. More current flows through a heavily loaded circuit or when the charging system is operating.

An ammeter is always connected in series with the circuit being tested. All of the current that normally flows through the circuit must also flow through the ammeter; if there is any other path for the current to follow, the ammeter reading will not be accurate. The ammeter itself has very little resistance to current flow and therefore will not affect the circuit, but it will measure current draw only when the circuit is closed and electricity is flowing. Excessive current draw can blow fuses and drain the battery, while a reduced current draw can cause motors to run slowly, lights to dim and other components to not operate properly. The ammeter can help diagnose these conditions by locating the cause of the high or low reading.

Multimeters

Different combinations of test meters can be built into a single unit designed for specific tests. Some of the more common combination test devices are known as Volt/Amp testers, Tach/Dwell meters, or Digital Multimeters. The Volt/Amp tester is used for charging system, starting system or battery tests and consists of a voltmeter, an ammeter and a variable resistance carbon pile. The voltmeter will usually have at least two ranges for use with 6, 12 and 24 volt systems. The ammeter also has more than one range for testing various levels of battery loads and starter current draw and the carbon pile can be adjusted to offer different amounts of resistance. The Volt/Amp tester has heavy leads to carry large amounts of current and many later models have an inductive ammeter pickup that clamps around the wire to simplify test connections. On some models, the ammeter also has a zero-center scale to allow testing of charging and starting systems without switching leads or polarity. A digital multimeter is a voltmeter, ammeter and ohmmeter combined in an instrument which gives a digital readout. These are often used when testing solid state circuits because of their high input impedance (usually 10 megohms or more).

The tach/dwell meter combines a tachometer and a dwell (cam angle) meter and is a specialized kind of voltmeter. The tachometer scale is marked to show engine speed in rpm and the dwell scale is marked to show degrees of distributor shaft rotation. In most electronic ignition systems, dwell is determined by the control unit, but the dwell meter can also be used to check the duty cycle (operation) of some electronic engine control systems. Some tach/ dwell meters are powered by an internal battery, while others take their power from the car battery in use. The battery powered testers usually require calibration much like an ohmmeter before testing.

Special Test Equipment

A variety of diagnostic tools are available to help troubleshoot and repair computerized engine control systems. The most sophisticated of these devices are the console type engine analyzers that usually occupy a garage service bay, but there are several types of aftermarket electronic testers available that will allow quick circuit tests of the engine control system by plugging directly into a special connector located in the engine compartment or under the dashboard. Several tool and equipment manufacturers offer simple, hand held testers that measure various circuit voltage levels on command to check all system components for proper operation. Although these testers usually cost about $300–500, consider that the average computer control unit (or ECM) can cost just as much and the money saved by not replacing perfectly good sensors or components in an attempt to correct a problem could justify the purchase price of a special diagnostic tester the first time it's used.

These computerized testers can allow quick and easy test measurements while the engine is operating or while the car is being driven. In addition, the on-board computer memory can be read to access any stored trouble codes; in effect allowing the computer to tell you where it hurts and aid trouble diagnosis by pinpointing exactly which circuit or component is malfunctioning. In the same manner, repairs can be tested to make sure the problem has been corrected. The biggest advantage these special testers have is their relatively easy hookups that minimize or eliminate the chances of making the wrong connections and getting false voltage readings or damaging the computer accidentally.

➡ **Remember, these testers check voltage levels in circuits; they don't detect mechanical problems or failed components if the circuit voltage falls within the preprogrammed limits stored in the tester PROM unit. Also, most of the hand held testers are designed to work only on one or two systems made by a specific manufacturer.**

A variety of aftermarket testers are available to help diagnose different computerized control systems. Owatonna Tool Company (OTC), for example, markets a device called the OTC Monitor which plugs directly into the assembly line diagnostic link (ALDL). The OTC tester makes diagnosis a simple matter of pressing the correct buttons and, by changing the internal PROM or inserting a different diagnosis cartridge, it will work on any model from full size to subcompact, over a wide range of years. An adapter is supplied with the tester to allow connection to all types of ALDL links, regardless of the number of pin terminals used. By inserting an updated PROM into the OTC tester, it can be easily updated to diagnose any new modifications of computerized control systems.

Wiring Harnesses

The average automobile contains about mile of wiring, with hundreds of individual connections. To protect the many wires from damage and to keep them from becoming a confusing tangle, they are organized into bundles, enclosed in plastic or taped together and called wire harnesses. Different wiring harnesses serve different parts of the vehicle. Individual wires are color coded to help trace them through a harness where sections are hidden from view.

A loose or corroded connection or a replacement wire that is too small for the circuit will add extra resistance and an additional voltage drop to the circuit. A ten percent voltage drop can result in slow or erratic motor operation, for example, even though the circuit is complete. Automotive wiring or circuit conductors can be in any one of three forms:

1. Single strand wire
2. Multistrand wire
3. Printed circuitry

Single strand wire has a solid metal core and is usually used inside such components as alternators, motors, relays and other devices. Multistrand wire has a core made of many small strands of wire twisted together into a single conductor. Most of the wiring in an automotive electrical system is made up of multistrand wire, either as a single conductor or grouped together in a harness. All wiring is color coded on the insulator, either as a solid color or as a colored wire with an identification stripe. A printed circuit is a thin film of copper or other conductor that is printed on an insulator backing. Occasionally, a printed circuit is sandwiched between two sheets of plastic for more protection and flexibility. A complete printed circuit, consisting of conductors, insulating material and connectors for lamps or other components is called a printed circuit board. Printed circuitry is used in place of individual wires or harnesses in places where space is limited, such as behind instrument panels.

Wire Gauge

Since computer controlled automotive electrical systems are very sensitive to changes in resistance, the selection of properly sized wires is critical when systems are repaired. The wire gauge number is an expression of the cross section area of the conductor. The most common system for expressing wire size is the American Wire Gauge (AWG) system.

Wire cross section area is measured in circular mils. A mil is $\frac{1}{1000}$ in. (0.001 in.) (0.0254mm); a circular mil is the area of a circle one mil in diameter. For example, a conductor $\frac{1}{4}$ in. in diameter is 0.250 in. or 6mm or 250 mils. The circular mil cross section area of the wire is 250^2 or 62,500 circular mils. Imported car models usually use metric wire gauge designations, which is simply the cross section area of the conductor in square millimeters (mm).

Gauge numbers are assigned to conductors of various cross section areas. As gauge number increases, area decreases and the conductor becomes smaller. A 5 gauge conductor is smaller than a 1 gauge conductor and a 10 gauge is smaller than a 5 gauge. As the cross section area of a conductor decreases, resistance increases and so does the gauge number. A conductor with a higher gauge number will carry less current than a conductor with a lower gauge number.

➡ **Gauge wire size refers to the size of the conductor, not the size of the complete wire. It is possible to have two wires of the same gauge with different diameters because one may have thicker insulation than the other.**

12 volt automotive electrical systems generally use 10, 12, 14, 16 and 18 gauge wire. Main power distribution circuits and larger accessories usually use 10 and 12 gauge wire. Battery cables are usually 4 or 6 gauge, although 1 and 2 gauge wires are occasionally used. Wire

length must also be considered when making repairs to a circuit. As conductor length increases, so does resistance. An 18 gauge wire, for example, can carry a 10 amp load for 10 feet without excessive voltage drop; however if a 15 foot wire is required for the same 10 amp load, it must be a 16 gauge wire.

An electrical schematic shows the electrical current paths when a circuit is operating properly. It is essential to understand how a circuit works before trying to figure out why it doesn't. Schematics break the entire electrical system down into individual circuits and show only one particular circuit. In a schematic, no attempt is made to represent wiring and components as they physically appear on the vehicle; switches and other components are shown as simply as possible. Face views of harness connectors show the cavity or terminal locations in all multi-pin connectors to help locate test points.

If you need to backprobe a connector while it is on the component, the order of the terminals must be mentally reversed. The wire color code can help in this situation, as well as a keyway, lock tab or other reference mark.

WIRING REPAIR

Soldering is a quick, efficient method of joining metals permanently. Everyone who has the occasion to make wiring repairs should know how to solder. Electrical connections that are soldered are far less likely to come apart and will conduct electricity much better than connections that are only "pig-tailed" together. The most popular (and preferred) method of soldering is with an electrical soldering gun. Soldering irons are available in many sizes and wattage ratings. Irons with higher wattage ratings deliver higher temperatures and recover lost heat faster. A small soldering iron rated for no more than 50 watts is recommended, especially on electrical systems where excess heat can damage the components being soldered.

There are three ingredients necessary for successful soldering; proper flux, good solder and sufficient heat. A soldering flux is necessary to clean the metal of tarnish, prepare it for soldering and to enable the solder to spread into tiny crevices. When soldering, always use a resin flux or resin core solder which is non-corrosive and will not attract moisture once the job is finished. Other types of flux (acid core) will leave a residue that will attract moisture and cause the wires to corrode. Tin is a unique metal with a low melting point. In a molten state, it dissolves and alloys easily with many metals. Solder is made by mixing tin with lead. The most common proportions are 40/60, 50/50 and 60/40, with the percentage of tin listed first. Low priced solders usually contain less tin, making them very difficult for a beginner to use because more heat is required to melt the solder. A common solder is 40/60 which is well suited for all-around general use, but 60/40 melts easier, has more tin for a better joint and is preferred for electrical work.

Soldering Techniques

Successful soldering requires that the metals to be joined be heated to a temperature that will melt the solder-usually 360–460°F (182–238°C). Contrary to popular belief, the purpose of the soldering iron is not to melt the solder itself, but to heat the parts being soldered to a temperature high enough to melt the solder when it is touched to the work. Melting flux-cored solder on the soldering iron will usually destroy the effectiveness of the flux.

➡ Soldering tips are made of copper for good heat conductivity, but must be "tinned" regularly for quick transference of heat to the project and to prevent the solder from sticking to the iron. To "tin" the iron, simply heat it and touch the flux-cored solder to the tip; the solder will flow over the hot tip. Wipe the excess off with a clean rag, but be careful as the iron will be hot.

After some use, the tip may become pitted. If so, simply dress the tip smooth with a smooth file and "tin" the tip again. An old saying holds that "metals well cleaned are half soldered." Flux-cored solder will remove oxides but rust, bits of insulation and oil or grease must be removed with a wire brush or emery cloth. For maximum strength in soldered parts, the joint must start off clean and tight. Weak joints will result in gaps too wide for the solder to bridge.

If a separate soldering flux is used, it should be brushed or swabbed on only those areas that are to be soldered. Most solders contain a core of flux and separate fluxing is unnecessary. Hold the work to be soldered firmly. It is best to solder on a wooden board, because a metal vise will only rob the piece to be soldered of heat and make it difficult to melt the solder. Hold the soldering tip with the broadest face against the work to be soldered. Apply solder under the tip close to the work, using enough solder to give a heavy film between the iron and the piece being soldered, while moving slowly and making sure the solder melts properly. Keep the work level or the solder will run to the lowest part and favor the thicker parts, because these require more heat to melt the solder. If the soldering tip overheats (the solder coating on the face of the tip burns up), it should be retinned. Once the soldering is completed, let the soldered joint stand until cool. Tape and seal all soldered wire splices after the repair has cooled.

Wire Harness and Connectors

The on-board computer (ECM) wire harness electrically connects the control unit to the various solenoids, switches and sensors used by the control system. Most connectors in the engine compartment or otherwise exposed to the elements are protected against moisture and dirt which could create oxidation and deposits on the terminals. This protection is important because of the very low voltage and current levels used by the computer and sensors. All connectors have a lock which secures the male and female terminals together, with a secondary lock holding the seal and terminal into the connector. Both terminal locks must be released when disconnecting ECM connectors.

These special connectors are weather-proof and all repairs require the use of a special terminal and the tool required to service it. This tool is used to remove the pin and sleeve terminals. If removal is attempted with an ordinary pick, there is a good chance that the terminal will be bent or deformed. Unlike standard blade type terminals, these terminals cannot be straightened once they are bent. Make certain that the connectors are properly seated and all of the sealing rings in place when connecting leads. On some models, a hinge-type flap provides a backup or secondary locking feature for the terminals. Most secondary locks are used to improve the connector reliability by retaining the terminals if the small terminal lock tangs are not positioned properly.

Molded-on connectors require complete replacement of the connection. This means splicing a new connector assembly into the harness. All splices in on-board computer systems should be soldered to insure proper contact. Use care when probing the connections or replacing terminals in them as it is possible to short between opposite terminals. If this happens to the wrong terminal pair, it is possible to damage certain components. Always use jumper wires between connectors for circuit checking and never probe through weatherproof seals.

Open circuits are often difficult to locate by sight because corrosion or terminal misalignment are hidden by the connectors. Merely wiggling a connector on a sensor or in the wiring harness may correct the open circuit condition. This should always be considered when an open circuit or a failed sensor is indicated. Intermittent problems may also be caused by oxidized or loose connections. When using a circuit tester for diagnosis, always probe connections from the wire side. Be careful not to damage sealed connectors with test probes.

All wiring harnesses should be replaced with identical parts, using the same gauge wire and connectors. When signal wires are spliced into a harness, use wire with high temperature insulation only. With the low voltage and current levels found in the system, it is important that the best possible connection at all wire splices be made by soldering the splices together. It is seldom necessary to replace a complete harness. If replacement is necessary, pay close attention to insure proper harness routing. Secure the harness with suitable plastic wire clamps to prevent vibrations from causing the harness to wear in spots or contact any hot components.

➡ **Weatherproof connectors cannot be replaced with standard connectors. Instructions are provided with replacement connector and terminal packages. Some wire harnesses have mounting indicators (usually pieces of colored tape) to mark where the harness is to be secured.**

In making wiring repairs, it's important that you always replace damaged wires with wires that are the same gauge as the wire being replaced. The heavier the wire, the smaller the gauge number. Wires are color-coded to aid in identification and whenever possible the same color coded wire should be used for replacement. A wire stripping and crimping tool is necessary to install solderless terminal connectors. Test all crimps by pulling on the wires; it should not be possible to pull the wires out of a good crimp.

Wires which are open, exposed or otherwise damaged are repaired by simple splicing. Where possible, if the wiring harness is accessible and the damaged place in the wire can be located, it is best to open the harness and check for all possible damage. In an inaccessible harness, the wire must be bypassed with a new insert, usually taped to the outside of the old harness.

When replacing fusible links, be sure to use fusible link wire, NOT ordinary automotive wire. Make sure the fusible segment is of the same gauge and construction as the one being replaced and double the stripped end when crimping the terminal connector for a good contact. The melted (open) fusible link segment of the wiring harness should be cut off as close to the harness as possible, then a new segment spliced in as described. In the case of a damaged fusible link that feeds two harness wires, the harness connections should be replaced with two fusible link wires so that each circuit will have its own separate protection.

➡ **Most of the problems caused in the wiring harness are due to bad ground connections. Always check all vehicle ground connections for corrosion or looseness before performing any power feed checks to eliminate the chance of a bad ground affecting the circuit.**

Repairing Hard Shell Connectors

Unlike molded connectors, the terminal contacts in hard shell connectors can be replaced. Weatherproof hard-shell connectors with the leads molded into the shell have non-replaceable terminal ends. Replacement usually involves the use of a special terminal removal tool that depress the locking tangs (barbs) on the connector terminal and allow the connector to be removed from the rear of the shell. The connector shell should be replaced if it shows any evidence of burning, melting, cracks, or breaks. Replace individual terminals that are burnt, corroded, distorted or loose.

➡ **The insulation crimp must be tight to prevent the insulation from sliding back on the wire when the wire is pulled. The insulation must be visibly compressed under the crimp tabs, and the ends of the crimp should be turned in for a firm grip on the insulation.**

The wire crimp must be made with all wire strands inside the crimp. The terminal must be fully compressed on the wire strands with the ends of the crimp tabs turned in to make a firm grip on the wire. Check all connections with an ohmmeter to insure a good contact. There should be no measurable resistance between the wire and the terminal when connected.

HEATING AND AIR CONDITIONING

➡ **Refer to Section 1 for proper discharging, evacuating and recharging procedures of the A/C system.**

Compressor

➧ SEE FIGS. 1–5

➡ **R-12 automotive refrigerants containing chlorofluorocarbon (CFC's) are tremendously hazardous to the earth's ozone layer in the upper atmosphere when released carelessly. Ozone filters out the harmful radiation from the sun that is known to cause skin cancer in humans. To protect our atmosphere and ourselves, an R-12 Recovery/Recycling machine that meets SAE standard J1991 and is UL approved, should be employed when discharging and/or charging the air conditioning system. If you don't own the proper equipment, DO NOT simply release the refrigerant into our atmosphere; instead take your car to an approved service station for repair. Also, if you leak check the system, do it with extra precision; after all, even the smallest leaks contribute to this serious atmospheric dilemma.**

REMOVAL & INSTALLATION

EXCEPT 3.4L ENGINE

1. Disconnect the negative battery cable.
2. Properly discharge the air conditioning system.
3. Remove the serpentine belt.
4. Remove the coolant recovery reservoir.
5. Disconnect the refrigerant hose assembly from the compressor. Discard the O-rings.

➡ **Cap the refrigerant lines when opening the system to prevent the entry of dirt and moisture and the loss of refrigerant lubricant.**

6. Disconnect the compressor clutch electrical connector.
7. Remove the compressor mounting bolts.
8. Remove the compressor.

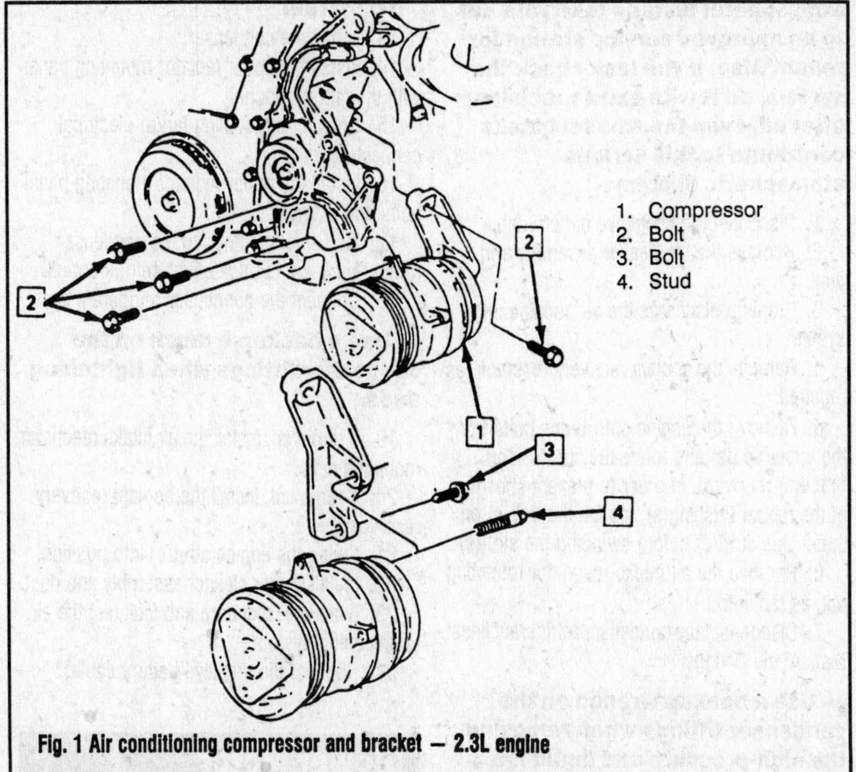

Fig. 1 Air conditioning compressor and bracket — 2.3L engine

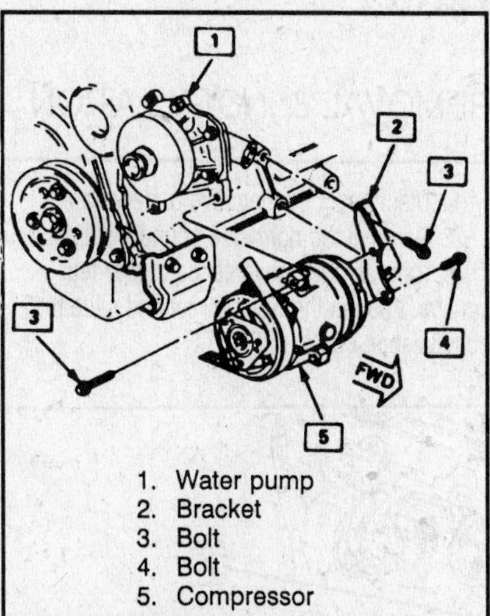

Fig. 2 Air conditioning compressor and bracket — 2.5L engine

9. Drain and measure the refrigerant oil from the compressor. Discard the old oil.

To install:

10. If the compressor is to be replaced, drain the oil from the new compressor and discard. Add new refrigerant oil equivalent to the amount drained from the old compressor.
11. Install the compressor and attaching bolts.
12. Install the compressor in the vehicle.
13. Install the compressor mounting bolts.
14. Connect the compressor clutch electrical connector.
15. Install new O-rings on the compressor refrigerant line fittings. Lubricate with refrigerant oil.
16. Connect the compressor refrigerant lines.
17. Install the coolant recovery reservoir.
18. Install the serpentine belt.
19. Evacuate, recharge and leak test the air conditioning system.
20. Connect the negative battery cable.

3.4L ENGINE

1. Disconnect the negative battery cable.
2. Remove the air cleaner assembly.
3. Properly discharge the air conditioning system.
4. Remove the coolant recovery reservoir.
5. Remove the serpentine belt.
6. Remove the engine torque strut.
7. Remove the engine torque strut bracket at the frame.
8. If equipped with manual transaxle, remove the engine torque strut bracket pencil brace.
9. Remove the right and left side cooling fan retaining bolts.
10. Remove the upper radiator mounting panel bolts and the panel.
11. Disconnect the cooling fan connectors.
12. Disconnect the refrigerant line manifold from the compressor. Discard the O-rings.

➡ Cap the refrigerant lines when opening the system to prevent the entry of dirt and moisture and the loss of refrigerant lubricant.

13. Disconnect the compressor electrical connector.
14. Remove the compressor retaining bolts.
15. Remove the compressor from the vehicle.
16. Drain and measure the refrigerant oil from the compressor. Discard the old oil.

To install:

17. If the compressor is to be replaced, drain the oil from the new compressor and discard. Add new refrigerant oil equivalent to the amount drained from the old compressor.
18. Install the compressor and attaching bolts.
19. Install the compressor in the vehicle.
20. Install the compressor retaining bolts.
21. Connect the compressor electrical connector.
22. Install new O-rings on the compressor refrigerant lines. Lubricate with refrigerant oil.
23. Connect the compressor manifold.

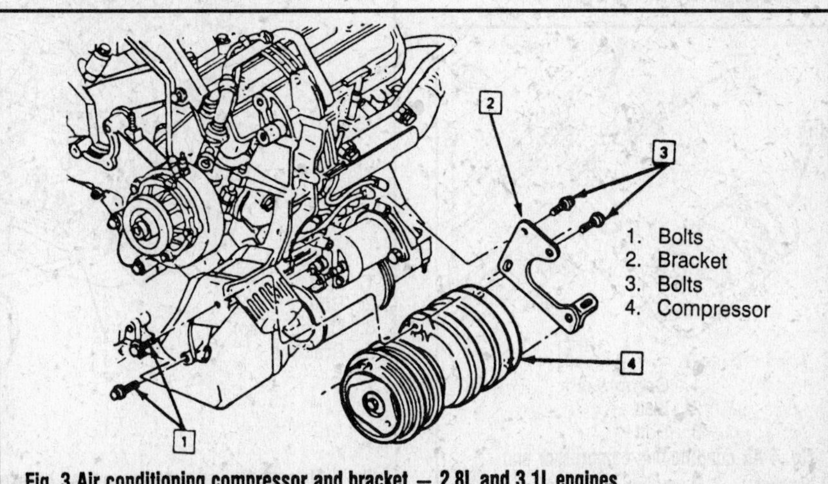

Fig. 3 Air conditioning compressor and bracket — 2.8L and 3.1L engines

24. Connect the cooling fan connectors.
25. Install the upper radiator mounting panel bolts and the panel.
26. Install the right and left side cooling fan retaining bolts.
27. If equipped with manual transaxle, install the engine torque strut bracket pencil brace.
28. Install the engine torque strut bracket at the frame.
29. Install the engine torque strut.
30. Install the serpentine belt.
31. Install the coolant recovery reservoir.
32. Evacuate, recharge and leak test the air conditioning system.
33. Install the air cleaner assembly.
34. Connect the negative battery cable.

Condenser

REMOVAL & INSTALLATION

➡ **R-12 automotive refrigerants containing chlorofluorocarbon (CFC's) are tremendously hazardous to the earth's ozone layer in the upper atmosphere when released carelessly. Ozone filters out the harmful radiation from the sun that is known to cause skin cancer in humans. To protect our atmosphere and ourselves, an R-12 Recovery/Recycling machine that meets SAE standard J1991 and is UL approved, should be employed when discharging and/or charging the air conditioning system. If you don't own the proper equipment, DO NOT simply release the refrigerant into our atmosphere; instead take your car to an approved service station for repair. Also, if you leak check the system, do it with extra precision; after all, even the smallest leaks contribute to this serious atmospheric dilemma.**

1. Disconnect the negative battery cable.
2. Remove the air cleaner assembly and duct.
3. Properly discharge the air conditioning system.
4. Remove the coolant recovery reservoir, as required.
5. Remove the engine strut brace bolts from the upper tie bar and rotate the strut(s) and brace(s) rearward. In order to prevent shearing of the rubber bushing(s), loosen the bolt(s) on the engine strut(s) before swinging the strut(s).
6. Remove the air intake resonator mounting nut, as required.
7. Disconnect the condenser refrigerant lines. Discard the O-rings.

➡ **Use a backup wrench on the condenser fittings when removing the high-pressure and liquid lines. Cap the refrigerant lines when opening the system to prevent the entry of dirt and moisture and the loss of refrigerant lubricant.**

8. Remove the upper radiator mounting panel bolts and clamps.
9. Disconnect the electrical connector from fan(s).
10. Remove the upper radiator mounting panel with the cooling fan(s) attached.
11. Tilt the radiator rearward.
12. Remove the condenser.

To install:

13. Install the condenser.
14. Install the upper radiator mounting panel with the fan(s) attached.
15. Connect the cooling fan(s) electrical connector(s).
16. Install the upper radiator mounting panel bolts and clamps.
17. Install new O-rings to the condenser refrigerant lines. Lubricate with refrigerant oil.
18. Connect the condenser refrigerant lines.

➡ **Use a backup wrench on the condenser fittings when tightening lines.**

19. If removed, install the air intake resonator mounting nut.
20. If removed, install the coolant recovery reservoir.
21. Swing the engine strut(s) into position.
22. Install the air cleaner assembly and duct.
23. Evacuate, recharge and leak test the air conditioning system.
24. Connect the negative battery cable.

Blower Motor

➧ SEE FIG. 6

REMOVAL & INSTALLATION

1. Disconnect the negative battery cable.
2. Remove the right side sound insulator.
3. Remove the convenience center rear screws. Loosen the front screw and slide the convenience center out.

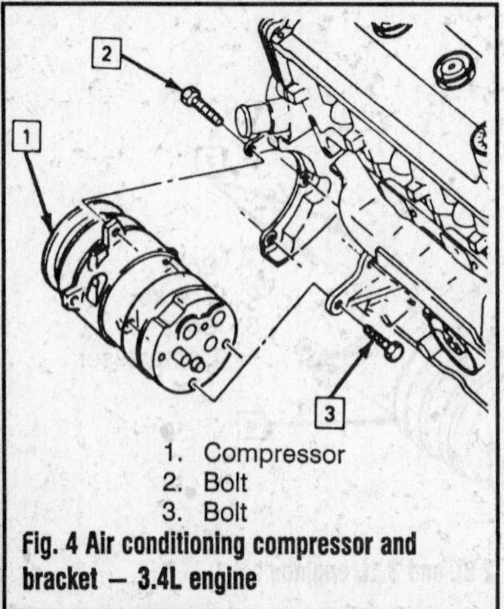

Fig. 4 Air conditioning compressor and bracket — 3.4L engine

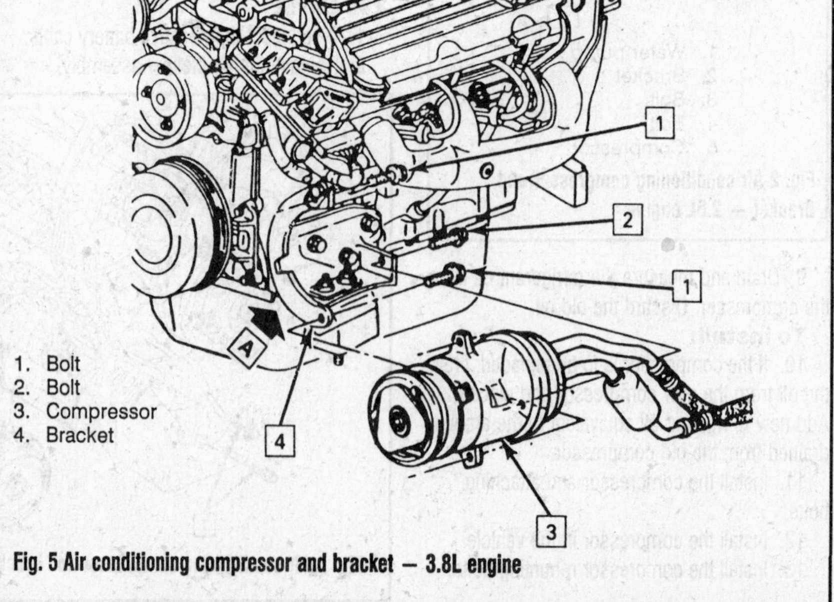

Fig. 5 Air conditioning compressor and bracket — 3.8L engine

4. Grasp the carpet at the top side of the cowl and pull forward.
5. Disconnect the blower motor electrical connection.
6. Disconnect the harness from the clip.
7. Remove the blower motor mounting screws.
8. Remove the blower motor.

To install:

9. Install the blower motor.
10. Connect the harness clip.
11. Connect the blower motor electrical connector.
12. Replace the carpet at the cowl.
13. Place the convenience center into position. Install the front and rear screws.
14. Install the right side lower insulator panel.
15. Connect the negative battery cable.

Heater Core

REMOVAL & INSTALLATION

1. Disconnect the negative battery cable.

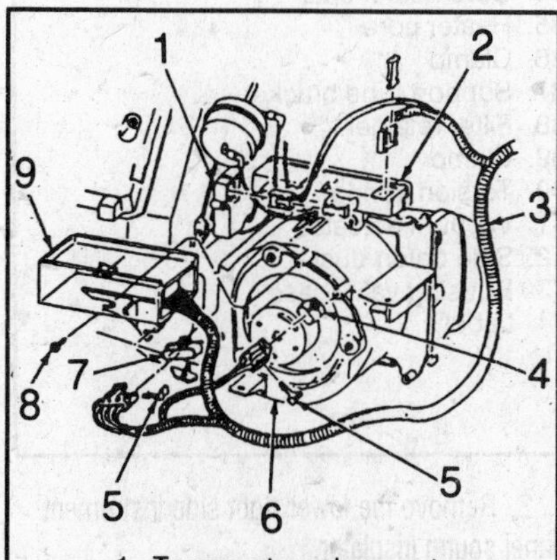

Fig. 6 Blower motor and related parts

✻✻ CAUTION

When draining the coolant, keep in mind that cats and dogs are attracted by the ethylene glycol antifreeze, and are quite likely to drink any that is left in an uncovered container or in puddles on the ground. This will prove fatal in sufficient quantity. Always drain the coolant into a sealable container. Coolant should be reused unless it is contaminated or several years old.

2. Drain the engine coolant into a clean container for reuse.
3. Remove the upper weatherstrip from the body.
4. Remove the upper secondary cowl.
5. Remove the lower secondary cowl upper nut.
6. Disconnect the heater hoses from the heater core.
7. Working inside the vehicle, remove the right and left side instrument panel sound insulators.
8. Remove the rear seat heater duct adapter.
9. Remove the lower heater duct.
10. Remove the heater core cover screws.
11. Remove the heater core cover.
12. Remove the heater core from the vehicle.

To install:

13. Install the heater core in the vehicle.
14. Install the heater core cover.
15. Install the heater core cover screws.
16. Install the lower heater duct.
17. Install the rear seat heater duct adapter.
18. Install the right and left side instrument panel sound insulators.
19. Working inside the engine compartment, connect the heater hoses to the heater core.
20. Install the lower secondary cowl upper nut.
21. Install the upper secondary cowl.
22. Install the upper weatherstrip from the body.
23. Connect the negative battery cable.
24. Fill cooling system and check for leaks. Start the engine and allow to come to normal operating temperature. Recheck for coolant leaks. Allow the engine to warm up sufficiently to confirm operation of cooling fan.

Evaporator Core

➧ SEE FIGS. 7 AND 8

REMOVAL & INSTALLATION

1. Disconnect the negative battery cable.

➡ R-12 automotive refrigerants containing chlorofluorocarbon (CFC's) are tremendously hazardous to the earth's ozone layer in the upper atmosphere when released carelessly. Ozone filters out the harmful radiation from the sun that is known to cause skin cancer in humans. To protect our atmosphere and ourselves, an R-12 Recovery/Recycling machine that meets SAE standard J1991 and is UL approved, should be employed when discharging and/or charging the air conditioning system. If you don't own the proper equipment, DO NOT simply release the refrigerant into our atmosphere; instead take your car to an approved service station for repair. Also, if you leak check the system, do it with extra precision; after all, even the smallest leaks contribute to this serious atmospheric dilemma.

2. Properly discharge the air conditioning system.

✻✻ CAUTION

When draining the coolant, keep in mind that cats and dogs are attracted by the ethylene glycol antifreeze, and are quite likely to drink any that is left in an uncovered container or in puddles on the ground. This will prove fatal in sufficient quantity. Always drain the coolant into a sealable container. Coolant should be reused unless it is contaminated or several years old.

3. Drain the cooling system.
4. Remove the upper weatherstrip from the body.
5. Remove the lower and upper secondary cowl panels.
6. Remove the evaporator core block connection at the cowl.
7. Remove the heater hoses and blow out the remaining coolant with shop air to prevent leakage into the passenger compartment when removing.
8. Remove the heater core cover and heater core.
9. Remove the evaporator core cover and evaporator.

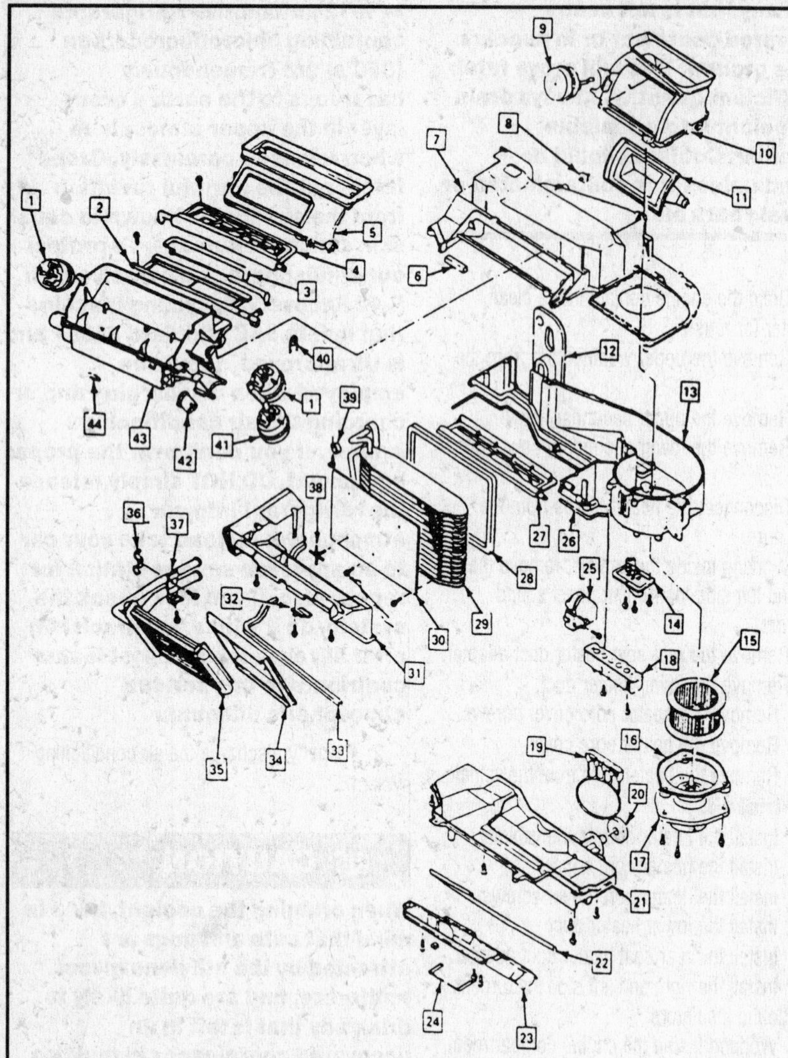

1. Vacuum actuator
2. Defroster valve
3. Inner and outer valve
4. Outer mode valve
5. Housing valce cover
6. Case seal
7. Upper and lower case
8. Case stud
9. Vacuum actuator
10. Air inlet case
11. Air inlet valve
12. Tube seal
13. Evaporator and blower lower case
14. Blower motor resistor
15. Blower motor fan
16. Gasket isolator
17. Fan and isolator motor
18. Vacuum electric solenoid
19. Vacuum harness
20. Drain seal
21. Core cover
22. Duct to core cover seal
23. Heater outlet duct
24. Duct seal
25. Electric actuator
26. Gasket
27. Temperature valve
28. Core evaporator seal
29. Evaporator core
30. Water core filter
31. Core shroud
32. Core heater clamp
33. Cover seal
34. Core heater seal
35. Heater core
36. Clamp
37. Support tube bracket
38. Filter retainer
39. Clamp
40. Torsion spring
41. Vacuum actuator
42. Side defog duct
43. Housing valve case
44. Label

Fig. 7 Exploded view of the evaporator case assembly

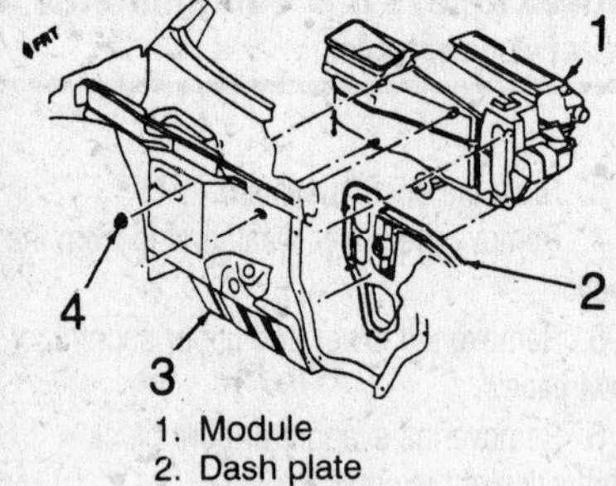

1. Module
2. Dash plate
3. Dash and toe panel
4. 89 inch lbs.

Fig. 8 Heater and air conditioning module-to-firewall mounting

To install:

10. Install the evaporator and core cover.
11. Install the heater core and cover.
12. Connect the heater hoses and tighten the clamps.
13. Install the evaporator core block connectors.
14. Install the lower and upper secondary cowl panels.
15. Fill the cooling system with the specified engine coolant and check for leaks.
16. Evacuate, recharge and leak test the air conditioning system.
17. Connect the negative battery cable.

Blower Resistor

REMOVAL & INSTALLATION

1. Disconnect the negative battery cable.
2. Remove the lower right side instrument panel sound insulator.
3. The blower resistor is located behind the right hand side of the instrument panel mounted in the heater-A/C plenum.
4. Remove the retaining screws and remove the resistor.
5. The installation is the reverse of the removal procedure.

Climate Control System Control Panel

SEE FIGS. 9–12

REMOVAL & INSTALLATION

Cutlass Supreme

1. Disconnect the negative battery cable.
2. Remove the cluster trim plate-to-dash securing screws.
3. Tilt the top of the cluster trim plate downward releasing the clips that mount the bottom of the plate to the dash and remove the trim plate.
4. Remove the screws securing the accessory trim plate-to-dash.
5. Tilt the top of the accessory trim plate downward releasing the clips that mount the bottom of the plate-to-dash.
6. Remove the control assembly from the dash and disconnect the electrical connectors.

To Install:

7. Install the control assembly and connect the electrical wiring-to-assembly.
8. Push the mounting clips into place, roll the top of the accessory trim plate upward into position and tighten screws.
9. Push the mounting clips into place, roll the top of the cluster trim plate upward into position and tighten the screws.
10. Connect the negative battery cable and check operation.

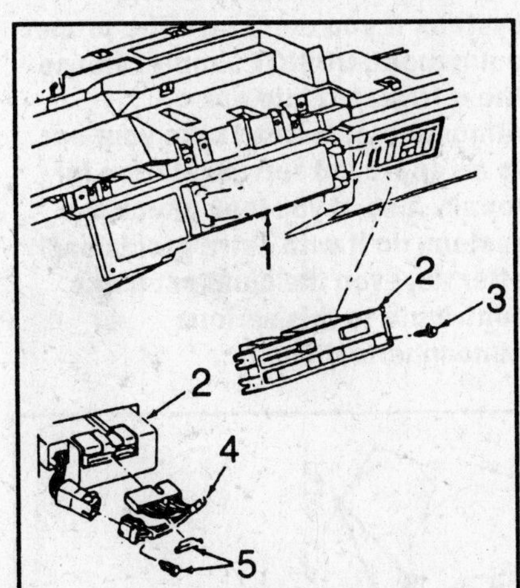

Fig. 9 A/C system control panel — Cutlass Supreme

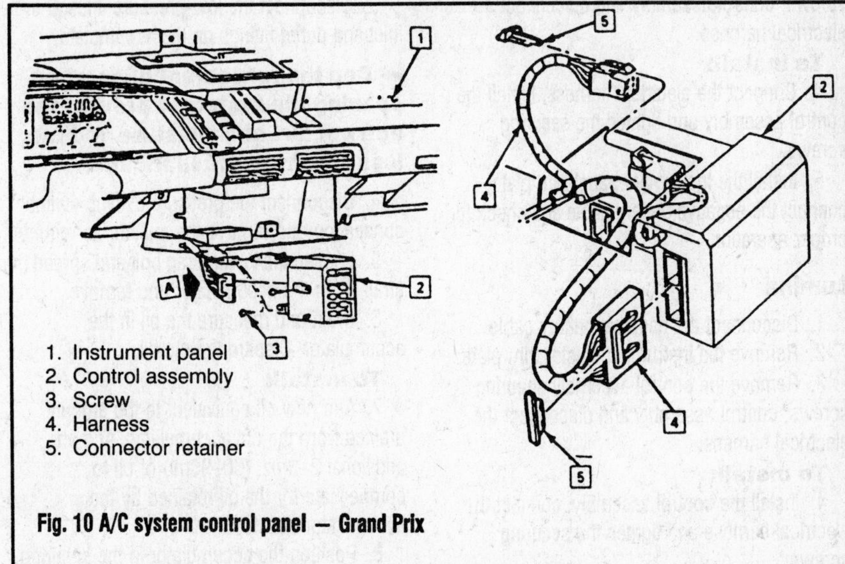

Fig. 10 A/C system control panel — Grand Prix

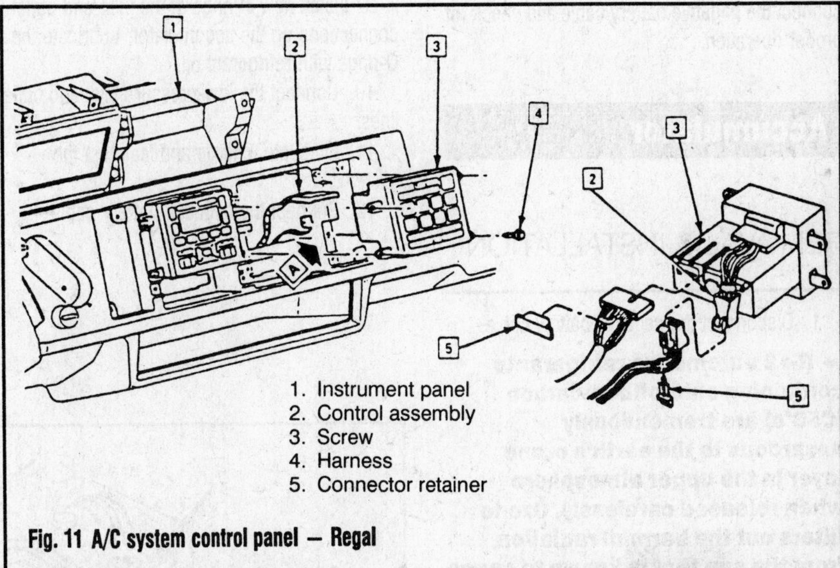

Fig. 11 A/C system control panel — Regal

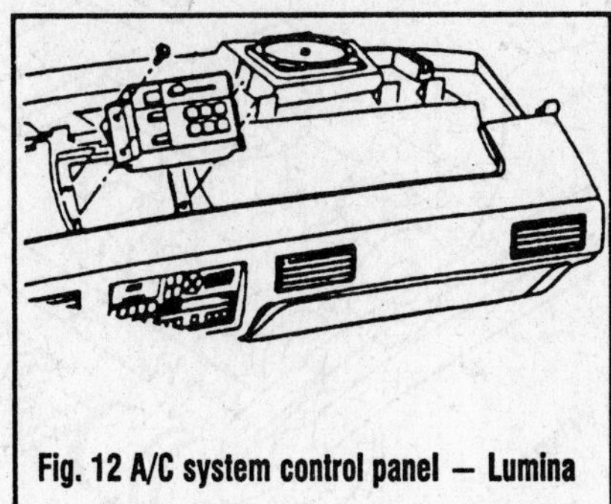
Fig. 12 A/C system control panel — Lumina

Grand Prix

1. Disconnect the negative battery cable.
2. Remove the lower left instrument panel pad.
3. Remove the control assembly trim plate.
4. Loosen the left securing screws, pull the assembly out and disconnect the electrical harness.

To Install:

5. Connect the electrical harness and position the control assembly into the screws. Tighten the securing screws.
6. Install the control trim panel, lower left instrument panel pad and connect the negative battery cable.

Regal

1. Disconnect the negative battery cable.
2. Remove the instrument panel trim plate.
3. Remove the control assembly securing

screws, control assembly and disconnect the electrical harness.

To install:

4. Connect the electrical harness, install the control assembly and tighten the securing screws.
5. Install the instrument panel trim plate, connect the negative battery cable and check for proper operation.

Lumina

1. Disconnect the negative battery cable.
2. Remove the instrument cluster trim plate.
3. Remove the control assembly securing screws, control assembly and disconnect the electrical harness.

To install:

4. Install the control assembly, connect the electrical harness and tighten the securing screws.
5. Install the instrument panel trim plate, connect the negative battery cable and check for proper operation.

Accumulator

REMOVAL & INSTALLATION

1. Disconnect the negative battery cable.

➡ R-12 automotive refrigerants containing chlorofluorocarbon (CFC's) are tremendously hazardous to the earth's ozone layer in the upper atmosphere when released carelessly. Ozone filters out the harmful radiation from the sun that is known to cause skin cancer in humans. To protect our atmosphere and ourselves, an R-12 Recovery/Recycling machine that meets SAE standard J1991 and is UL approved, should be employed when discharging and/or charging the air conditioning system. If you don't own the proper equipment, DO NOT simply release the refrigerant into our atmosphere; instead take your car to an approved service station for repair. Also, if you leak check the system, do it with extra precision; after all, even the smallest leaks contribute to this serious atmospheric dilemma.

2. Properly discharge the air conditioning system.
3. Disconnect the low-pressure lines at the inlet and outlet fittings on the accumulator.

➡ Cap the refrigerant lines when opening the system to prevent the entry of dirt and moisture and the loss of refrigerant lubricant.

4. Disconnect the pressure cycling switch connection and remove the switch, as required.
5. Loosen the lower strap bolt and spread the strap. Turn the accumulator and remove.
6. Drain and measure the oil in the accumulator. Discard the old oil.

To install:

7. Add new oil equivalent to the amount drained from the old accumulator. Add an additional 2–3 oz. (60–90ml) of oil to compensate for the oil retained by the accumulator dessicant.
8. Position the accumulator in the securing bracket and tighten the clamp bolt.
9. Install new O-rings at the inlet and outlet connections on the accumulator. Lubricate the O-rings with refrigerant oil.
10. Connect the low-pressure inlet and outlet lines.
11. Evacuate, charge and leak test the system.
12. Connect the negative battery cable.

Refrigerant Lines

➧ SEE FIG. 13

REMOVAL & INSTALLATION

1. Disconnect the negative battery cable.

➡ R-12 automotive refrigerants containing chlorofluorocarbon (CFC's) are tremendously hazardous to the earth's ozone layer in the upper atmosphere when released carelessly. Ozone filters out the harmful radiation from the sun that is known to cause skin cancer in humans. To protect our atmosphere and ourselves, an R-12 Recovery/Recycling machine that meets SAE standard J1991 and is UL approved, should be employed when discharging and/or charging the air conditioning system. If you don't own the proper equipment, DO NOT simply release the refrigerant into our atmosphere; instead take your car to an approved service station for repair. Also, if you leak check the system, do it with extra precision; after all, even the smallest leaks contribute to this serious atmospheric dilemma.

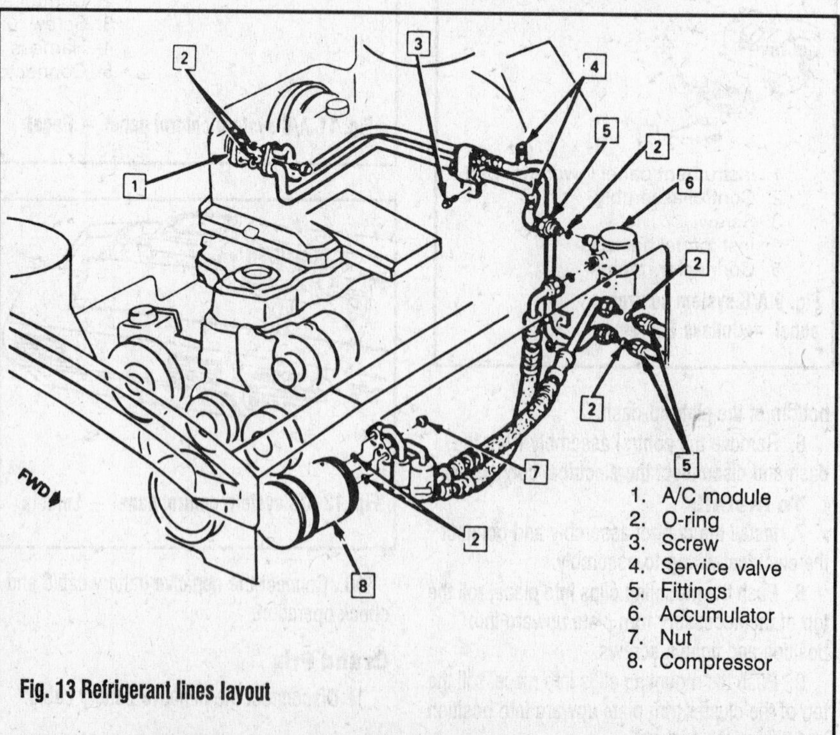

Fig. 13 Refrigerant lines layout

2. Properly discharge the air conditioning system.
3. Remove all items preventing access to any portion of the line, following the appropriate instructions elsewhere in this manual.
4. Remove the bolt or nut that attaches the line to the evaporator or condenser, or separate the taper fittings using a backup wrench.

➡ **Cap the refrigerant lines when opening the system to prevent the entry of dirt and moisture and the loss of refrigerant lubricant.**

5. Remove the retaining strap or bracket.
6. Remove the refrigerant line from the engine compartment and discard the O-rings.

To install:

7. Lubricate new O-rings with refrigerant oil and install to the line. Install the line to the air conditioning components and tighten the fitting, nut, or bolt.
8. Install all items that were removed during the removal procedure.
9. Evacuate, charge and leak test the system.
10. Connect the negative battery cable.

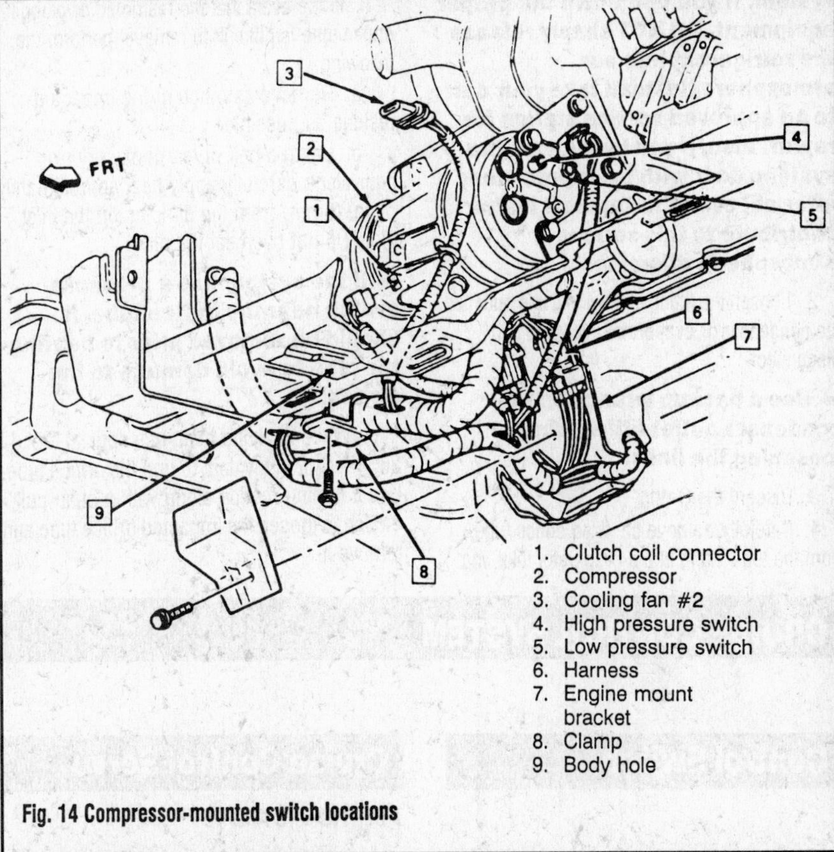

Fig. 14 Compressor-mounted switch locations

Vacuum Motors

REMOVAL & INSTALLATION

1. Disconnect the negative battery cable.
2. Remove the instrument panel, or portions thereof in order to gain access to the vacuum motor.
3. Disconnect the electrical connector and/or vacuum harness from the motor.
4. Remove the retaining screws and remove the motor from the vehicle.
5. The installation is the reverse of the removal procedure.
6. Connect the negative battery cable and check the system for proper operation.

High or Low Pressure Compressor Cutoff Switch

➧ SEE FIG. 14

REMOVAL & INSTALLATION

1. Disconnect the negative battery cable.

➡ **R-12 automotive refrigerants containing chlorofluorocarbon (CFC's) are tremendously hazardous to the earth's ozone layer in the upper atmosphere when released carelessly. Ozone filters out the harmful radiation from the sun that is known to cause skin cancer in humans. To protect our atmosphere and ourselves, an R-12 Recovery/Recycling machine that meets SAE standard J1991 and is UL approved, should be employed when discharging and/or charging the air conditioning system. If you don't own the proper equipment, DO NOT simply release the refrigerant into our atmosphere; instead take your car to an approved service station for repair. Also, if you leak check the system, do it with extra precision; after all, even the smallest leaks contribute to this serious atmospheric dilemma.**

2. Properly discharge the air conditioning system.
3. Disconnect the switch connector.
4. Remove the switch retaining ring and remove the switch from the compressor.
5. The installation is the reverse of the removal procedure.
6. Evacuate, charge and leak test the system.
7. Connect the negative battery cable.

Fixed Orifice Tube

REMOVAL & INSTALLATION

1. Disconnect the negative battery cable. Properly discharge the air conditioning system.

➡ **R-12 automotive refrigerants containing chlorofluorocarbon (CFC's) are tremendously hazardous to the earth's ozone layer in the upper atmosphere when released carelessly. Ozone filters out the harmful radiation from the sun that is known to cause skin cancer in humans. To protect our atmosphere and ourselves, an R-12 Recovery/Recycling machine that meets SAE standard J1991 and is UL approved, should be employed when discharging and/or charging the air conditioning**

system. If you don't own the proper equipment, DO NOT simply release the refrigerant into our atmosphere; instead take your car to an approved service station for repair. Also, if you leak check the system, do it with extra precision; after all, even the smallest leaks contribute to this serious atmospheric dilemma.

2. Loosen the fitting at the liquid line outlet on the condenser or evaporator inlet pipe and disconnect.

➡ **Use a backup wrench on the condenser outlet fitting when loosening the lines.**

3. Discard the O-ring.
4. Carefully, remove the fixed orifice tube from the tube fitting in the evaporator inlet line.
5. In the event that the restricted or plugged orifice tube is difficult to remove, perform the following:
   a. Remove as much of the impacted residue as possible.
   b. Using a hair dryer, epoxy drier or equivalent, carefully apply heat approximately 1/4 in. (6mm) from the dimples on the inlet pipe. Do not overheat the pipe.

➡ **If the system has a pressure switch near the orifice tube, it should be removed prior to heating the pipe to avoid damage to the switch.**

   c. While applying heat, use special tool J 26549–C or equivalent to grip the orifice tube. Use a turning motion along with a push-pull motion to loosen the impacted orifice tube and remove it.
6. Swab the inside of the evaporator inlet pipe with R-11 to remove any remaining residue.
7. Add 1 oz. of 525 viscosity refrigerant oil to the system.
8. Lubricate the new O-ring and orifice tube with refrigerant oil and insert into the inlet pipe.

➡ **Ensure that the new orifice tube is inserted in the inlet tube with the smaller screen end first.**

9. Connect the evaporator inlet pipe with the condenser outlet fitting.

➡ **Use a backup wrench on the condenser outlet fitting when tightening the lines.**

10. Evacuate, recharge and leak test the system.

CRUISE CONTROL SYSTEM

Control Switch

REMOVAL & INSTALLATION

1. Disconnect the negative battery terminal.
2. Disconnect cruise control switch connector at the base of steering column. It may be necessary to remove an under dash panel or trim piece for access.
3. Make sure lever is in **CENTER** or **OFF** position.
4. Pull lever straight out of retaining clip within the steering column.
5. Attach mechanic's wire or similar to the connector; gently pull the harness through the column, leaving the pull wire in place.

To install:

6. Place the transmission selector in **LOW** or **1**. Attach the mechanic's wire to the connector. Gently pull the harness into place, checking that the harness is completely clear of any moving or movable components such as tilt-column, telescoping column, brake pedal linkage, etc.
7. Position the lever and push it squarely into the retainer until it snaps in place.
8. Remove the mechanics' wire and connect the cruise control harness connector.
9. Reinstall any panels or insulation which were removed for access.
10. Connect the negative battery terminal.

Cruise Control Servo

➧ SEE FIGS. 15 AND 16

REMOVAL & INSTALLATION

1. Disconnect the negative battery cable.
2. Disconnect the 2 vacuum lines and one electrical connector at the servo.
3. Disconnect the cable.
4. Remove the retaining bolts and remove the servo.
5. The installation is the reverse of the removal procedure.
6. Connect the negative battery cable and check the cruise control system for proper operation.

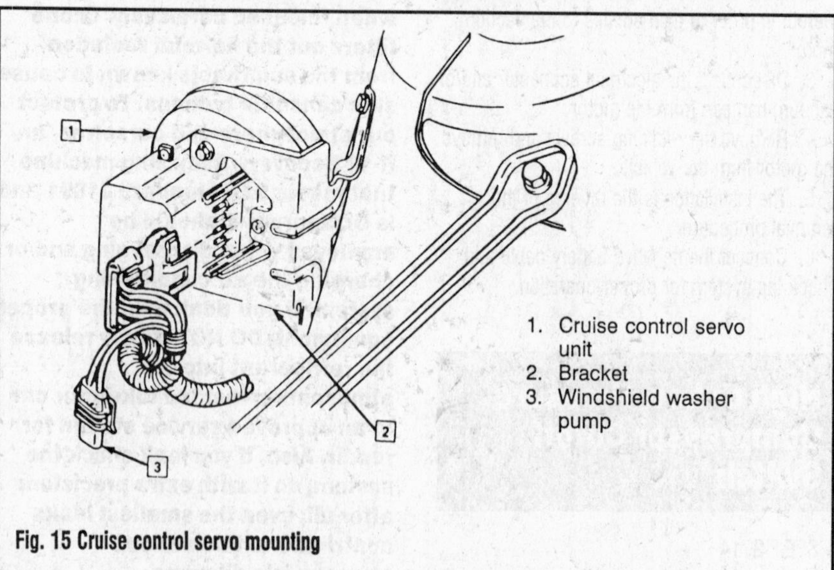

Fig. 15 Cruise control servo mounting

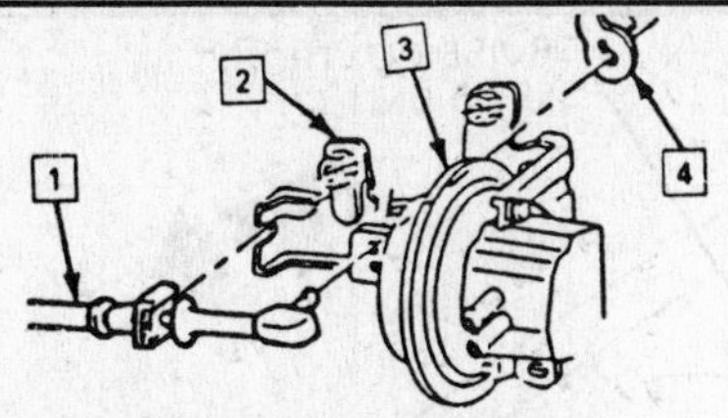

1. Cruise control cable
2. Bracket
3. Cruise control servo unit
4. Retainer

Fig. 16 Actuating cable-to-servo attachment

LINKAGE ADJUSTMENT

➡ Do not stretch cables or chains to make pins fit or holes align. This will prevent the engine from returning to idle.

1. Check that the cable is properly installed and that the throttle is closed to the idle position.
2. Pull the servo end of the cable toward the linkage bracket of the servo. Place the servo connector in one of the 6 holes in the bracket which allows the least amount of slack and does not move the throttle linkage.
3. Install the retainer clip. Check that the throttle linkage is still in the idle position.

Cruise Control Module

➧ SEE FIG. 17

REMOVAL & INSTALLATION

1. Disconnect the negative battery cable.
2. Remove the driver side sound insulation panel.
3. Disconnect the connector from the module, located on a bracket on the brake pedal bracket/column support.
4. Remove the retaining screw and remove the module.
5. The installation is the reverse of the removal procedure.
6. Connect the negative battery cable and check the cruise control system for proper operation.

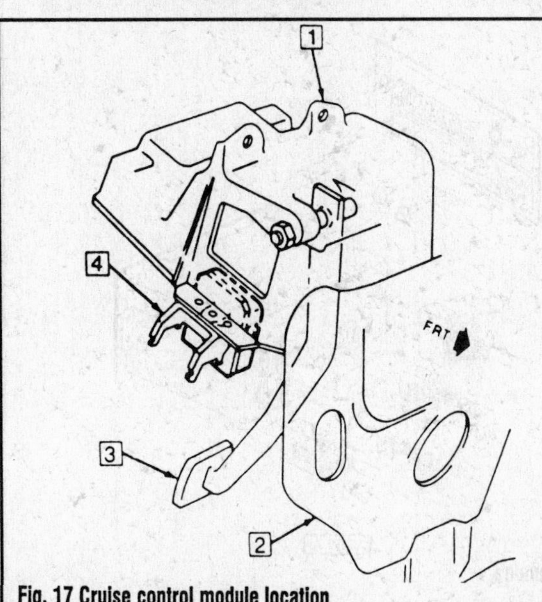

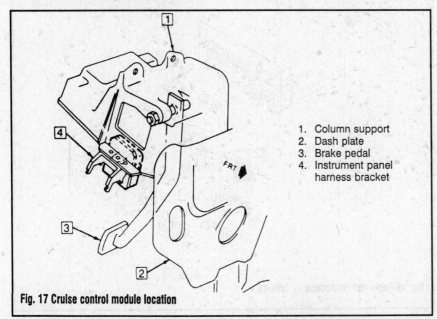

1. Column support
2. Dash plate
3. Brake pedal
4. Instrument panel harness bracket

Fig. 17 Cruise control module location

Vacuum Tank

➧ SEE FIG. 18

REMOVAL & INSTALLATION

1. Disconnect the negative battery cable.
2. Raise the car and support safely.
3. Disconnect the vacuum hoses from the tank.
4. Remove the retaining nuts and remove the tank.
5. The installation is the reverse of the removal procedure.
6. Connect the negative battery cable and check the cruise control system for proper operation.

Electric Brake Release Switch

REMOVAL & INSTALLATION

1. Disconnect the negative battery cable. At the brake switch, remove either the 2 electrical connectors or the electrical connector and the vacuum hose.
2. Remove the switch from the retainer.
3. Remove the tubular retainer from the brake pedal mounting bracket.

To install:

4. Install the tubular retainer to the brake pedal mounting bracket.
5. Press the brake pedal and install the release switch into the retainer until fully seated in the clips.
6. Connect the wiring and/or vacuum lines. Adjust the switch.

ADJUSTMENT

1. Depress the brake pedal and check that the release switch is fully seated in the clips.
2. Slowly pull the brake pedal back to the at-rest position; the switch and valve assembly will move within the clips to the adjusted position.
3. Measure pedal travel and check switch engagement. The electric brake release switch contacts must open at $^1/_8$–$^1/_2$ in. (3–13mm) of pedal travel when measured at the centerline of the pedal pad. The brake lights should illuminate after another $^3/_{16}$ in. (5mm) of travel. The vacuum release should engage at $^5/_8$–1 in. (16–25mm) of pedal travel.

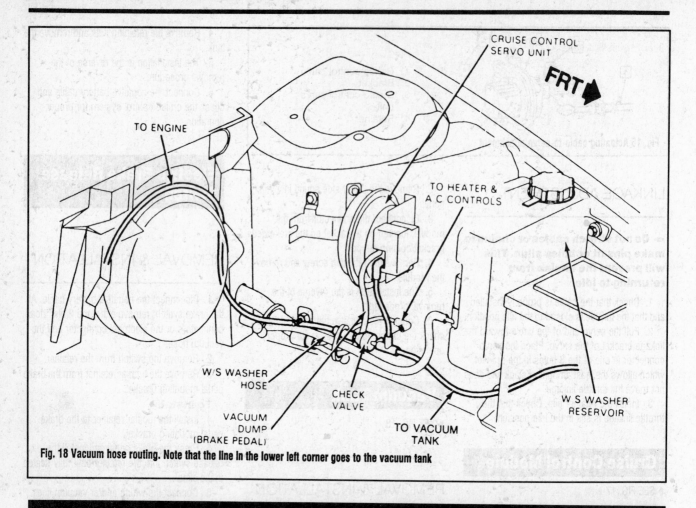

Fig. 18 Vacuum hose routing. Note that the line in the lower left corner goes to the vacuum tank

ENTERTAINMENT SYSTEMS

➧ SEE FIGS. 19–23

REMOVAL & INSTALLATION

Lumina

1. Disconnect the negative battery cable.
2. Remove the right instrument panel trim plate.
3. Remove the radio retaining bolts, disconnect electrical harness and remove the radio.

To install:

✲✲ CAUTION

When installing the radio, do not pinch the wires or a short circuit to ground may happen and damage the radio.

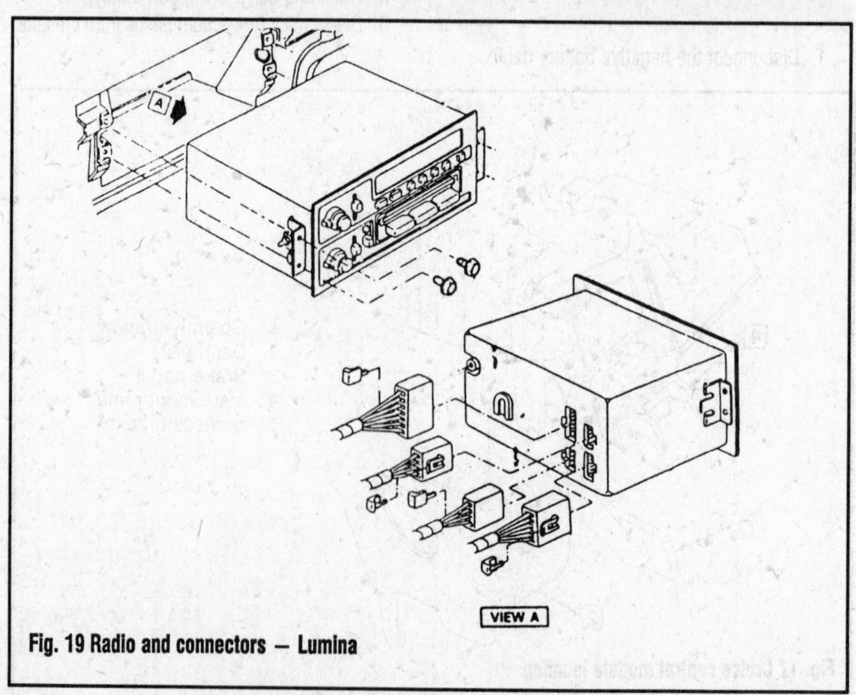

Fig. 19 Radio and connectors — Lumina

4. Connect the electrical harness to the back of the radio and tighten the retaining bolts.

5. Install the right side instrument panel trim plate and connect the negative battery cable.

Radio Controls

The Grand Prix, Cutlass Supreme and Regal are equipped with a remote radio receiver with the controls mounted in the instrument panel.

REMOVAL & INSTALLATION

Grand Prix, Cutlass Supreme and Regal

1. Disconnect the negative battery cable.
2. Remove the cluster trim plate.
3. Remove the control retaining bolts, disconnect the electrical harness and remove the radio controls.

To install:

CAUTION

When installing the radio controls, do not pinch the wires or a short circuit to ground may happen and damage the radio.

4. Connect the control electrical harness and tighten the control retaining bolts.
5. Install the cluster trim plate and reconnect the negative battery cable.

Radio Receiver

REMOVAL & INSTALLATION

1. Disconnect the negative battery cable.
2. Remove the right side sound insulator panel.
3. Remove the courtesy lamp and connector.
4. Remove the two receiver retaining bolts, disconnect the electrical harness and remove the receiver.

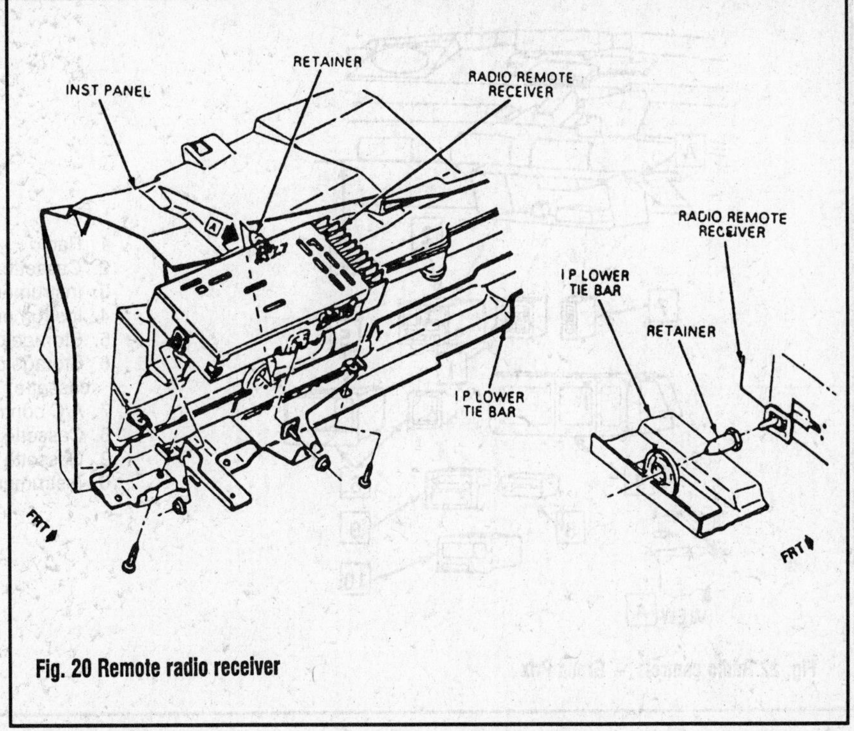

Fig. 20 Remote radio receiver

To install:

CAUTION

When installing the receiver assembly, do not pinch the wires or a short circuit to ground may happen and damage the radio.

5. Connect the electrical harness, antenna cable and tighten the receiver retaining bolts.
6. Install the courtesy lamp and bolt.
7. Install the right side sound insulator panel and connect the negative battery cable.

Cassette/Equalizer Compact Disc Player

REMOVAL & INSTALLATION

1. Disconnect the negative battery cable.
2. Remove the instrument panel accessory trim plate.
3. Remove the retaining bolts, pull unit out far enough to disconnect the electrical harness and remove the unit.

To install:

CAUTION

When installing the receiver assembly, do not pinch the wires or a short circuit to ground may happen and damage the radio.

4. Connect the electrical harness and tighten the unit retaining bolts.
5. Install the instrument panel accessory plate and connect the negative battery cable.

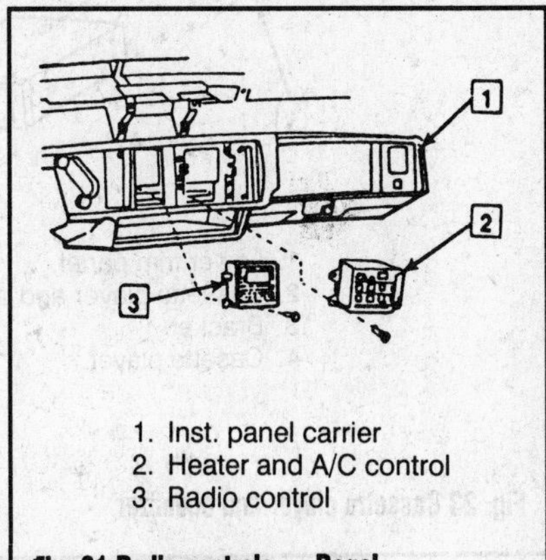

1. Inst. panel carrier
2. Heater and A/C control
3. Radio control

Fig. 21 Radio controls — Regal

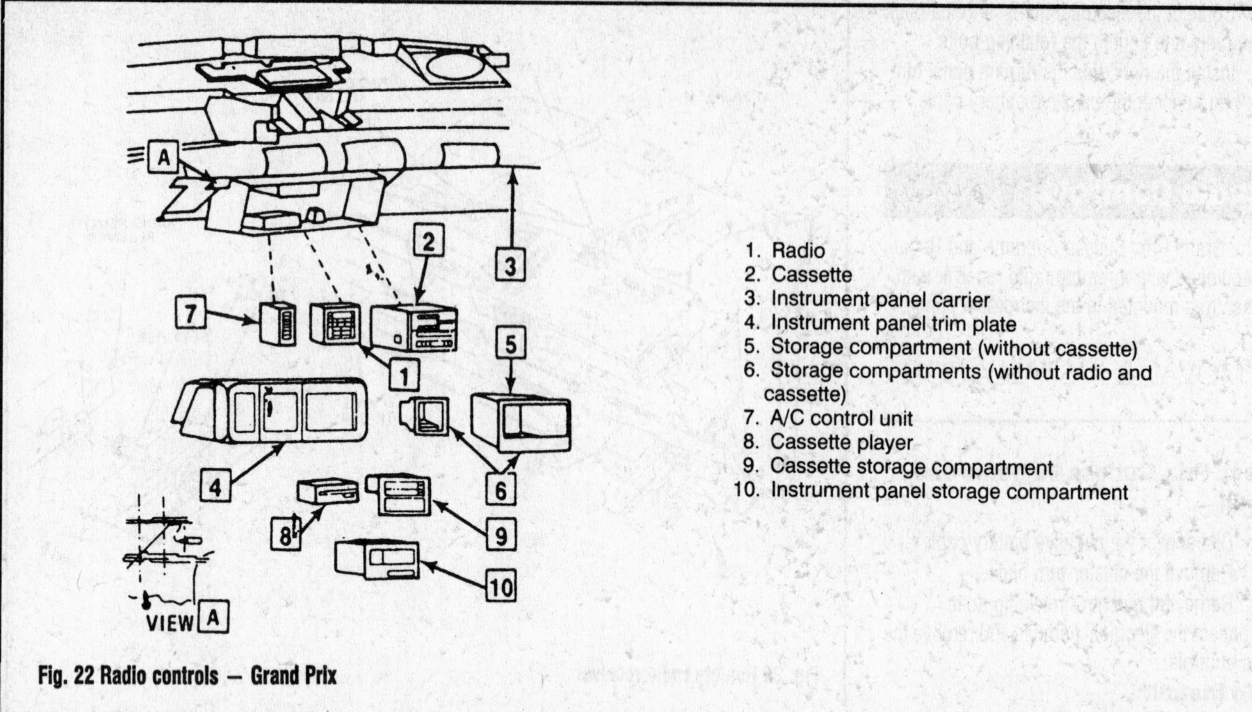

1. Radio
2. Cassette
3. Instrument panel carrier
4. Instrument panel trim plate
5. Storage compartment (without cassette)
6. Storage compartments (without radio and cassette)
7. A/C control unit
8. Cassette player
9. Cassette storage compartment
10. Instrument panel storage compartment

Fig. 22 Radio controls — Grand Prix

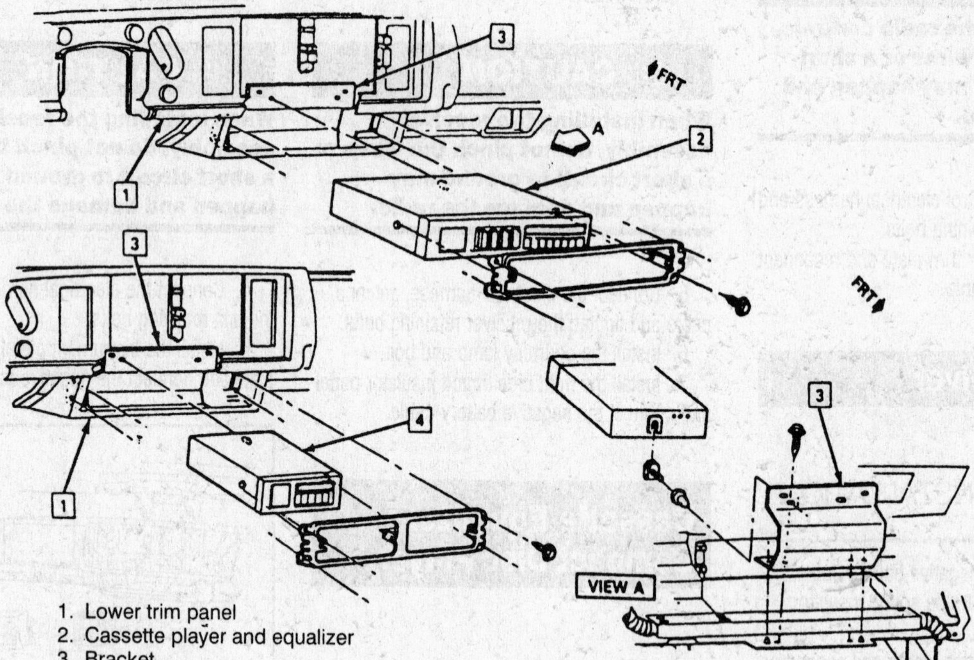

FRT
A
VIEW A

1. Lower trim panel
2. Cassette player and equalizer
3. Bracket
4. Casette player

Fig. 23 Cassette player and equalizer

WINDSHIELD WIPERS

Blade and Arm

➧ SEE FIG. 24

REMOVAL & INSTALLATION

1. Raise the hood and support.
2. Remove the protective cap and nut from the wiper arm.
3. Disconnect the washer hose from the arm.
4. Lift each wiper arm and insert a suitable pin or pop rivet completely through the two holes located next to the arm pivot.
5. Lift each arm off its transmission linkage shaft using a rocking motion.

To install:

6. Clean the metal shavings from the knurls of the shaft before installation.
7. Install the wiper arm onto the linkage shaft and adjust as follows.
   a. Right Arm: measure from the tip of the blade to the bottom edge of the glass. The measurement should be 9 in. (229mm).
   b. Left Arm: measure from the tip of the blade to the bottom edge of the glass. The measurement should be 2 in. (51mm).
8. Install the arm-to-shaft nut and torque to 25 ft. lbs. (34 Nm) and install the protective cap.
9. Connect the washer hose, close the hood and check for proper operation.

Wiper Module

➧ SEE FIGS. 25–28

REMOVAL & INSTALLATION

1. Raise the hood and support.
2. Remove the protective cap and nut from the wiper arm.
3. Disconnect the washer hose from the arm.
4. Lift each wiper arm and insert a suitable pin or pop rivet completely through the two holes located next to the arm pivot.
5. Lift each arm off its transmission linkage shaft using a rocking motion.
6. Remove the lower reveal molding screws, lower the hood and remove the lower reveal molding.

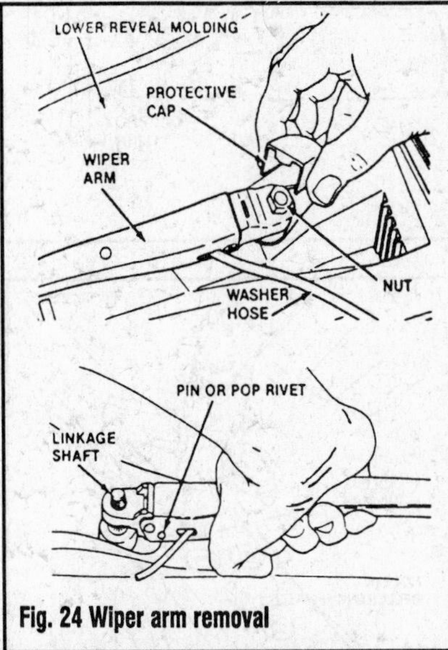

Fig. 24 Wiper arm removal

7. Remove the air inlet panel screws, underhood lamp switch and panel with the hood raised.
8. If the motor can run, place the crank arm in the inner wipe position as shown in the "Crank Arm Positioning" illustration in this section.
9. If the motor cannot run, rotate the motor crank arm to the inner wipe position by applying a channel lock pliers against the top edge of the crank arm and lower jaw against the crank arm nut and turn the motor to the correct position before disassembly.
10. Remove the three bellcrank housing screws and lower the linkage from the module.
11. Remove the module assembly from the vehicle.

To install:

12. Install the module assembly into the vehicle.
13. Install the three bellcrank housing screws after lowering the linkage into the module.
14. Install the air inlet panel, underhood lamp switch and tighten the panel screws.
15. Install the lower reveal molding, wiper arm and cap. Connect the washer hose.
16. Adjust the wiper arm positioning as outlined earlier in the "Wiper Arm" section. Check each operation for proper installation.

Wiper Linkage

REMOVAL & INSTALLATION

1. Disconnect the negative battery cable.
2. Remove the wiper arm and module as previously outlined in this section.
3. Remove the two linkage socket screws and disconnect the sockets from the link ball.
4. Remove the right and left bellcrank mounting screws and remove the linkage from the module.

To install:

5. Install the linkage to the module and tighten the bellcrank mounting screws. The motor crank arm MUST be in the inner wiper position at this point. Refer to the illustration.
6. Using a bolt or equivalent, line up the holes in the module and bellcrank as shown in the illustration.
7. Tighten the linkage socket screws while the alignment tool remains in place.
8. Install the module into the vehicle. Make sure the body seals are in the proper position.
9. Install the wiper arms and align the arms as outlined earlier in this section.
10. Connect the washer hose.
11. Run the wiper motor at HI and LO speeds with a wet and tacky windshield. Make sure the wiper parks properly.

Wiper Motor

REMOVAL & INSTALLATION

1. Disconnect the negative battery cable.

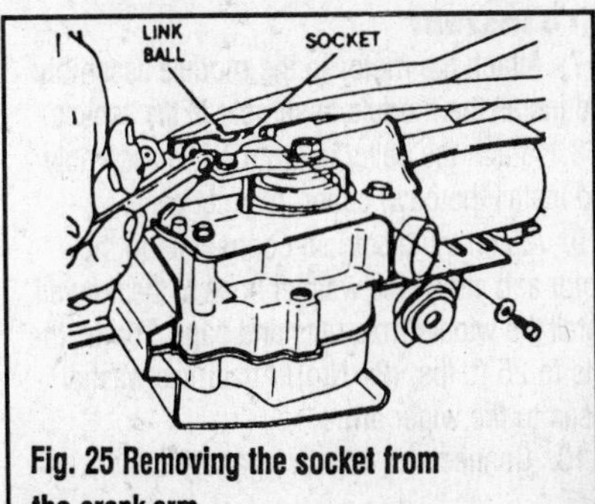

Fig. 25 Removing the socket from the crank arm

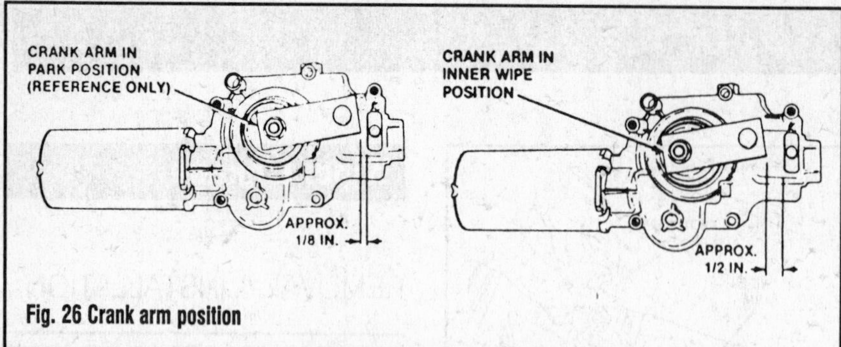

Fig. 26 Crank arm position

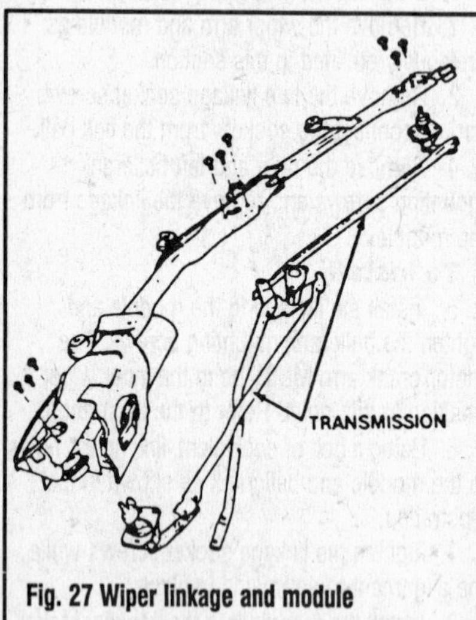

Fig. 27 Wiper linkage and module

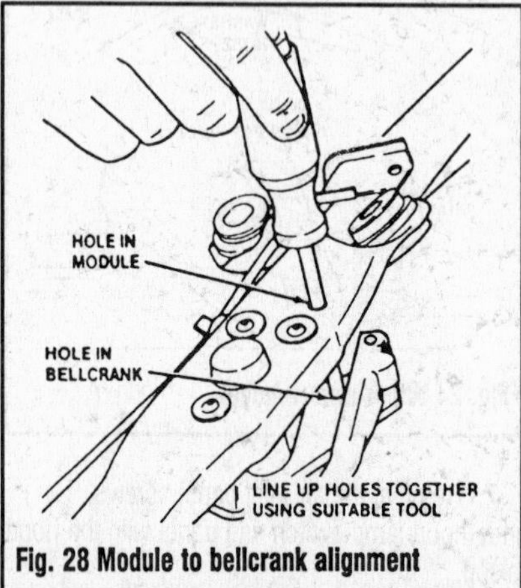

Fig. 28 Module to bellcrank alignment

2. Remove the washer hose, cap and retaining nut from each wiper arm. Remove the wiper arms from the vehicle.
3. Remove the screws retaining the cowl cover. Lower the hood partially and remove the cowl cover. Remove the air inlet panel.
4. Disconnect the wiring harness connectors at the wiper motor and the washer hose at the firewall.
5. Remove the 3 screws from the bellcrank housing and lower the wiper linkage.
6. Remove the wiper module assembly from the vehicle as outlined earlier. To remove the wiper motor from the module assembly, remove the 3 screw retaining the motor and remove the motor.

To install:

7. Attach the motor to the module assembly and install the module assembly in the vehicle.
8. Attach the bellcrank to module assembly and install the cowl cover, air inlet panel.
9. Attach the electrical connectors to the motor and attach the washer hose to the firewall. Install the wiper arms, nuts and caps. Torque the nuts to 25 ft. lbs. (34 Nm). Attach the washer hoses to the wiper arms.
10. Connect the negative battery cable.

Windshield Wiper Switch

REMOVAL & INSTALLATION

The wiper switch is controlled by the multi-function turn signal lever but the actual switch is located in the steering column.

1. Disconnect the negative battery cable.
2. Remove the steering wheel horn pad, wheel retaining nut and steering wheel.
3. Remove the turn signal canceling cam assembly.
4. Remove the hazard knob and position the turn signal lever so the housing cover screw can be removed through the opening in the switch. Remove the housing cover.
5. Remove the wire protector from the opening in the instrument panel bracket and separate the wires.
6. Disconnect the pivot and pulse switch connector. Remove the pivot switch connector and pivot switch.

To install:

7. Install the pivot and pulse switch assembly. Install the wiring protector around the instrument panel opening, covering all wires.
8. Install the steering column housing cover and torque the screws to 35 inch lbs. (4 Nm).
9. Install the hazard knob and lubricate the bottom side of the canceling cam with lithium grease.
10. Install the steering wheel and torque the shaft nut to 30 ft. lbs. (41 Nm).
11. Connect the negative battery cable and check steering column operations.

Washer Fluid Reservoir and Pump

➧ SEE FIG. 29

REMOVAL & INSTALLATION

1. Disconnect the negative battery cable.
2. Siphon the washer fluid from the reservoir.
3. Remove the reservoir mounting screws.
4. Disconnect the connector and washer hose.
5. Remove the assembly from the engine compartment and remove the pump from the reservoir.
6. The installation is the reverse of the removal procedure.
7. Connect the negative battery cable and check the washer for proper operation.

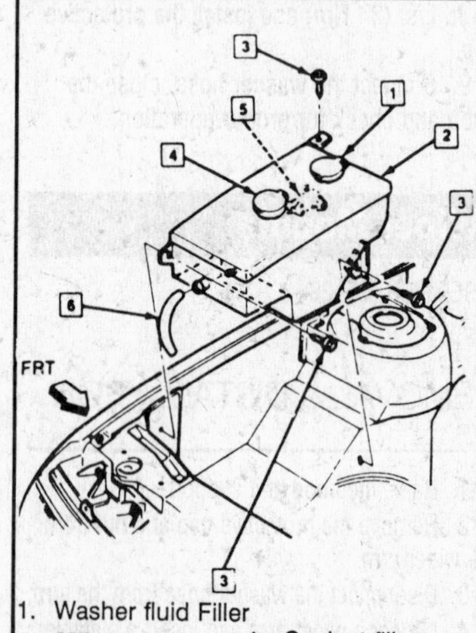

Fig. 29 View of the washer fluid reservoir and pump

INSTRUMENTS AND SWITCHES

➡ This section covers dash-mounted instruments only. Refer to sections 3 and/or 4 for sending unit and sensor service information and locations. Also, refer to section 10 for instrument panel and console service procedures and exploded views.

PRECAUTIONS

When handling a part that has an "ESD-sensitive" sticker warning of Electrostatic Discharge (it looks like a hand inside a black triangle with a white stripe through it), follow these guidelines to reduce any possible buildup of electrostatic charge:

- If replacing a part that has the sticker, do not open the package until just prior to installation. Before removing the part from its package, ground the package to a good ground on the car.
- Avoid touching the electrical terminals of the component.
- Always touch a good ground before handling a part with the sticker. This should be repeated while handling the part; do it more often when sliding across the seat, sitting from the standing position, or after walking.

Instrument Cluster

Individual gauges may not be replaceable on these clusters. If one has failed, cluster assembly replacement may be necessary, depending on application and parts availability.

Conventional speedometer cables are not used; the speedometer is a fully electronic unit.

REMOVAL & INSTALLATION

Cutlass Supreme

1. Disconnect the negative battery cable.
2. Remove the 5 screws retaining the cluster trim plate. Pull the bottom of the trim plate out and remove it from the vehicle.
3. Remove the screws retaining the instrument cluster and remove the cluster from the instrument panel. Disconnect the electrical connectors.

To install:

4. Install the cluster to the instrument panel. Connect the electrical leads.
5. Install the cluster trim panel. Connect the negative battery cable.

Grand Prix, Regal and Lumina

1. Disconnect the negative battery cable.
2. Remove the instrument panel pad from the vehicle.
3. Remove the cluster trim plate and the four screws retaining the instrument cluster. Pull the cluster forward, disconnect the electrical connectors, PRNDL cable and remove the cluster from the vehicle.

To install:

4. Install the cluster to the instrument panel. Connect the electrical leads and PRNDL cable.
5. Install the upper panel pad.
6. Install the cluster trim panel.
7. Connect the negative battery cable.

Headlight Switch

REMOVAL & INSTALLATION

Cutlass Supreme and 1991–92 Regal

1. Disconnect the negative battery cable.
2. Remove the 4 instrument cluster trim plate retaining screws and plate. Remove the air outlet trim plate.
3. Remove the 2 screws retaining the switch and remove the switch from the instrument panel.
4. Disconnect the electrical connector from the switch and remove the switch.

To install:

5. To install the switch, connect the electrical connector and install the switch in the instrument panel.
6. Install the air outlet and cluster trim plates.
7. Connect the negative battery cable.

Grand Prix and 1989–90 Regal

1. Disconnect the negative battery cable.
2. Remove the screw retaining the headlight switch to the instrument panel.
3. Pull the top of the switch out to release the lower retaining clips and remove it from the instrument panel.
4. Disconnect the electrical connector and remove the switch from the vehicle.

To install:

5. To install the switch, connect the electrical connector and install the switch in the instrument panel.
6. Connect the negative battery cable.

Lumina

1. Disconnect the negative battery cable.
2. Remove left instrument panel trim plate.
3. Remove retaining screws from switch and extract switch.
4. Disconnect the wire connectors.

To install:

5. To install switch, connect the electrical connector and install switch into dash.
6. Install screws and trim plate. Reconnect negative battery cable.

Rear Defogger Switch

The rear defogger switch is located in the Climate Control System Control Panel; refer to that section for service.

LIGHTING

Headlights

➧ SEE FIGS. 30–33

REMOVAL & INSTALLATION

Bulb

✻✻ CAUTION

Halogen bulbs contain gas under pressure. Handling the bulbs incorrectly could cause it to shatter into flying glass fragments. Do NOT leave the light switch ON. Always allow the bulb to cool before removal. Handle the bulb only by the base; avoid touching the glass itself.

1. Open the hood and support.
2. Remove the wire connector from the light bulb and turn the bulb out of the headlight assembly.
3. Install the bulb, connect the wiring and close the hood.

Light Assembly

1. Disconnect the negative battery cable.
2. Open the hood and support.
3. Remove the headlight cover assembly (Regal only).
4. Remove the headlight assembly screws, pull assembly forward, and turn the socket counterclockwise to remove.
5. Remove the bulb from the socket.

To install:

6. Turn the new bulb into the socket and the connect wire.
7. Install the assembly into position and tighten the retaining screws. Close the hood and connect the negative battery cable.

HEADLIGHT AIMING

Headlights should be checked for proper aim during your annual state inspection (each state has its own headlight aiming laws). If your state doesn't require state inspection, you should ideally have headlight aim checked annually, especially if you travel on rough road surfaces often. Headlights that are not aimed properly can create a dangerous situation by blinding oncoming drivers and by not illuminating the road properly for you. A universal do-it-yourself procedure that can be used in a pinch is given here, although it is not intended as the true method; expensive aiming tools are needed for that. If the headlights don't come close to straight ahead when aiming, something is probably broken; in fact, if they are so far off as to catch your attention in the first place, a crucial piece may have broken.

1. Park the car on a level surface, at least 15 ft. from a wall that is perpendicular to the ground surface. Make sure there is no excess weight in the trunk, unless you normally travel with that amount of weight in the car. Bounce the car a few times to settle the suspension.
2. Measure and record the distance from the ground to the center of each headlight lens.
3. Measure and record the distance between lens centers (from one side to the other side).
4. Turn the headlights on and adjust so the hot-spots (lit area of most concentrated intensity) are the same height from the ground and distance from each other that the lens centers were in Steps 2 and 3. Adjusting screws are located on the inner side (horizontal aim) and top (vertical aim)of the lens.
5. Adjust each headlight so the hot-spot drops about 1 in. (25mm).
6. Adjust each headlight so it points to the right about 1 in. (25mm) on the wall; this will prevent glare in an oncoming driver's eyes.
7. Take your car to a service station and see how good you did !

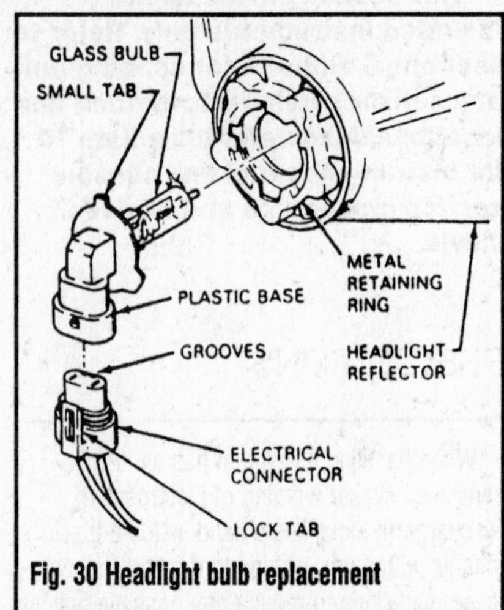

Fig. 30 Headlight bulb replacement

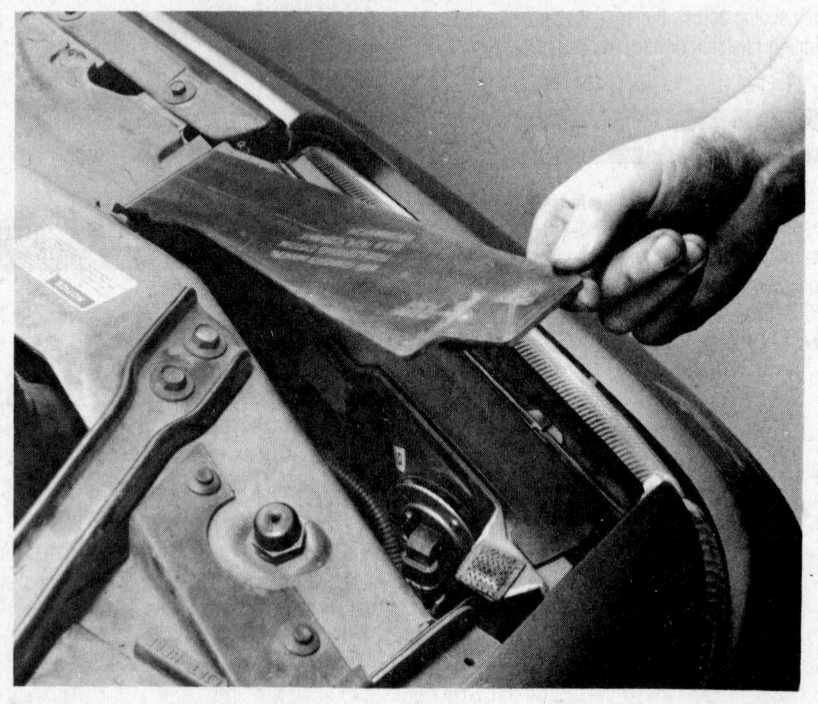

FIG. 30A. Lift up this plastic flap to expose the headlight bulb

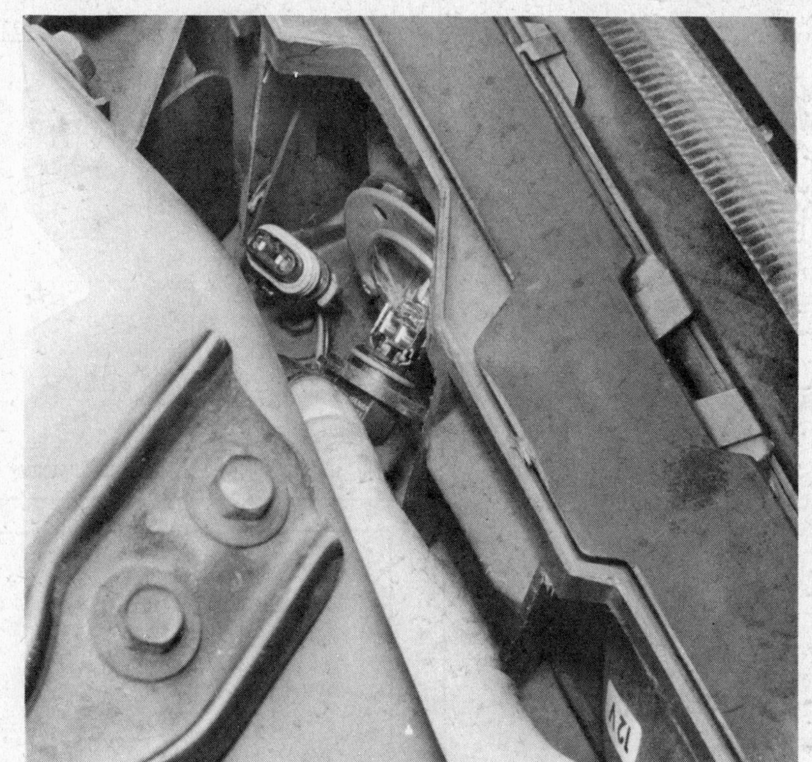

FIG. 30B. Unplug the connector and removing the headlight bulb from its socket

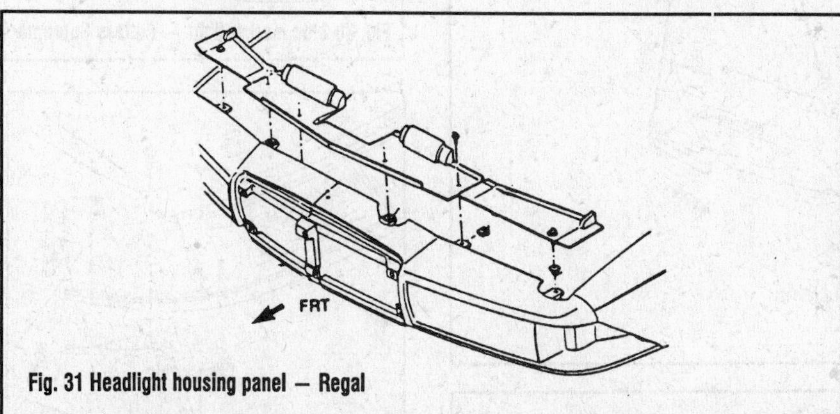

Fig. 31 Headlight housing panel — Regal

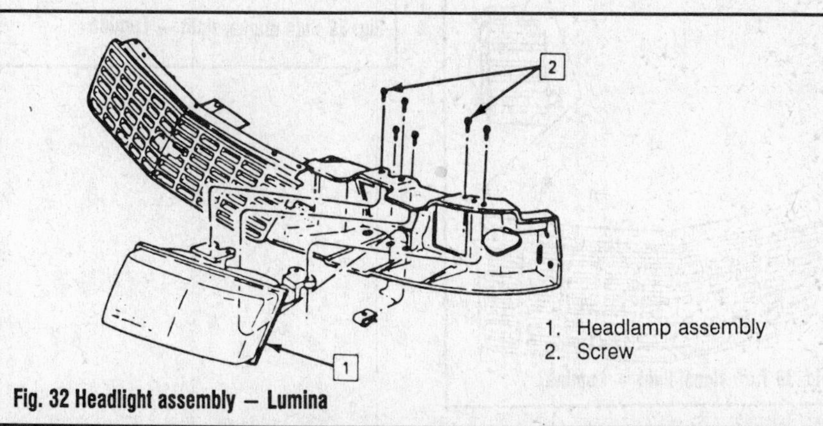

Fig. 32 Headlight assembly — Lumina

Signal and Marker Lights

REMOVAL & INSTALLATION

Front Turn Signal and Parking Lights

➧ SEE FIGS. 34–37

REMOVAL & INSTALLATION

LUMINA

1. Disconnect the negative battery cable.
2. Raise the hood and remove the grille assembly as outlined in Section 10.
3. Remove the retaining screw and turn signal assembly.
4. Install the signal assembly, retaining screws, grille and connect the negative battery cable.

REGAL

1. Disconnect the negative battery cable.
2. Raise the hood and support safely.
3. Remove the cover over the headlights by turning the knob and folding back.
4. Remove the three light housing nuts and remove the sockets from the housing.
5. Install the sockets, housing, three nuts and install the headlight cover.
6. Connect the negative battery cable and lower the hood.

GRAND PRIX AND CUTLASS SUPREME

1. Disconnect the negative battery cable.
2. Remove the two screws at the top of the assembly and pull the assembly forward.
3. Disconnect the electrical connector by opening the tab.
4. Remove the bulb and socket assembly.
5. Install the socket assembly, position the assembly into the housing and tighten the two retaining screws. Connect the negative battery cable.

Side Marker Lights

➧ SEE FIGS. 38 AND 39

1. Remove the light assembly retaining screws and light.
2. Remove the light socket from the assembly.
3. Install the socket, assembly and tighten the retaining screws.

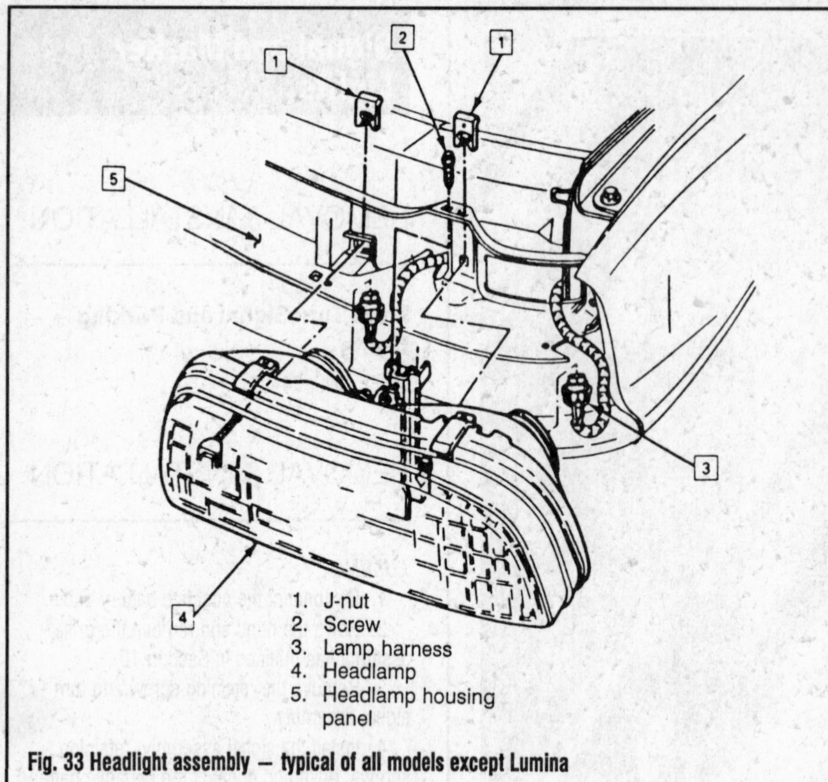

Fig. 33 Headlight assembly — typical of all models except Lumina

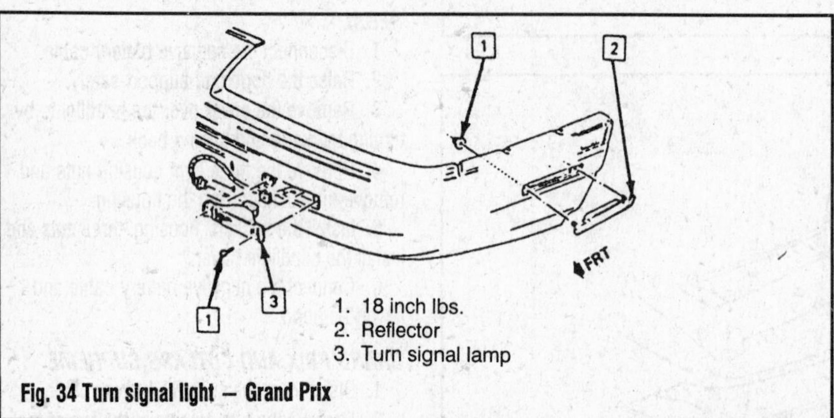

Fig. 34 Turn signal light — Grand Prix

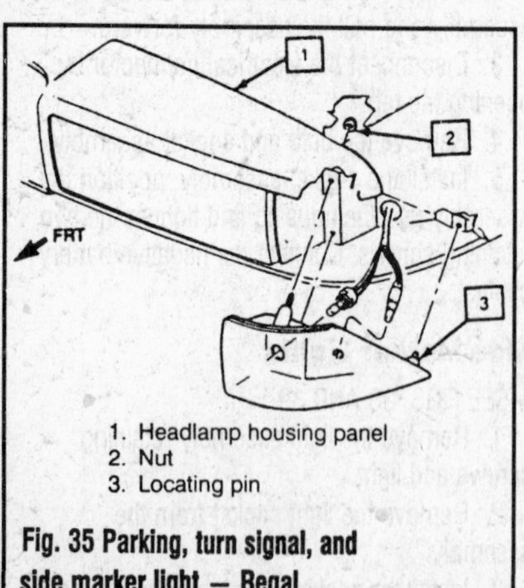

Fig. 35 Parking, turn signal, and side marker light — Regal

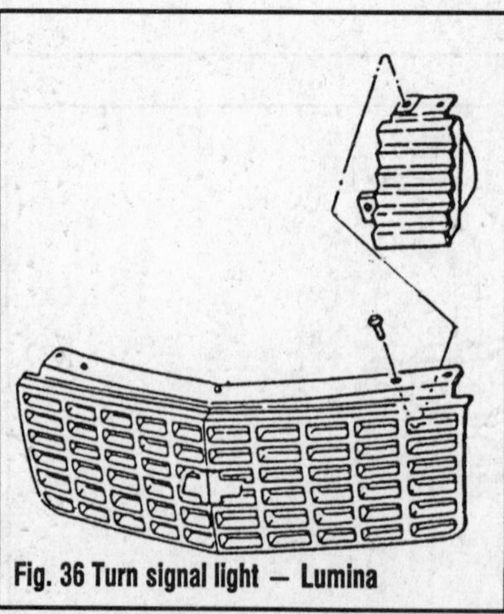

Fig. 36 Turn signal light — Lumina

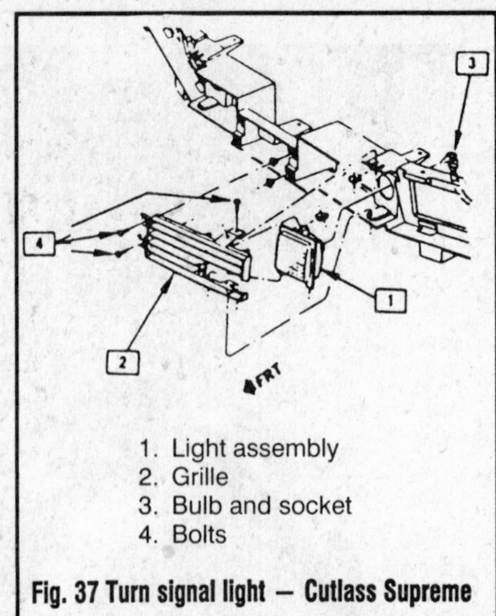

Fig. 37 Turn signal light — Cutlass Supreme

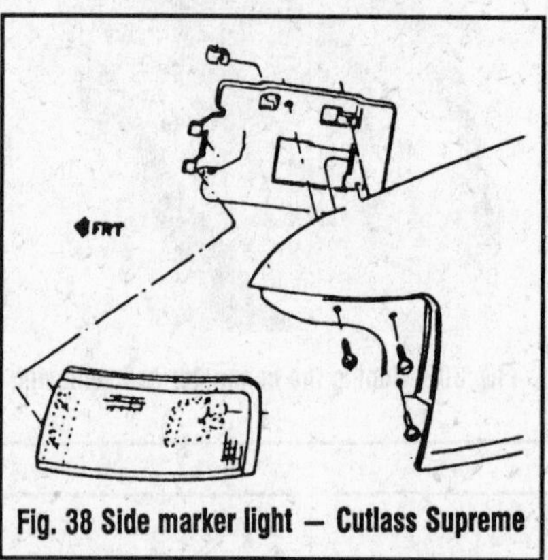

Fig. 38 Side marker light — Cutlass Supreme

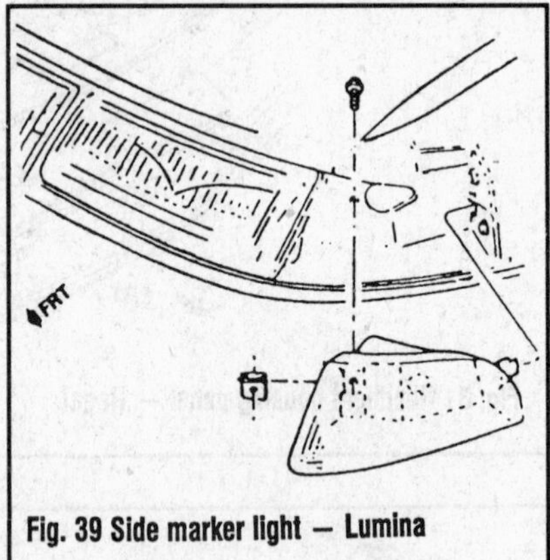

Fig. 39 Side marker light — Lumina

Rear Turn Signal/Brake/Reverse Lights

➧ SEE FIGS. 40–40B

➡ Take care to prevent water leaks if the sealing surfaces around the tail light assembly is disturbed. Damaged gaskets must be replaced by using body caulking compound or equivalent in the critical areas.

1. Disconnect the negative battery cable.
2. Open the rear luggage compartment.
3. Remove the three carpet retaining clips and fold the carpet forward.
4. Remove the bulb sockets from the light assembly.
5. Remove the light assembly retaining nuts and remove the assembly. If the light assembly does not come right out, it may be because the gasket is holding it in place. Pry very gently on all corners equally and push the assembly out of the rear light cavity. When the assembly starts to move, cut the gasket with a knife.

To install:

6. Install the light assembly with a new gasket and tighten the retaining nuts.
7. Install the light sockets into their proper location.
8. Install the carpeting and retaining clips.
9. Close the luggage compartment and connect the negative battery cable.

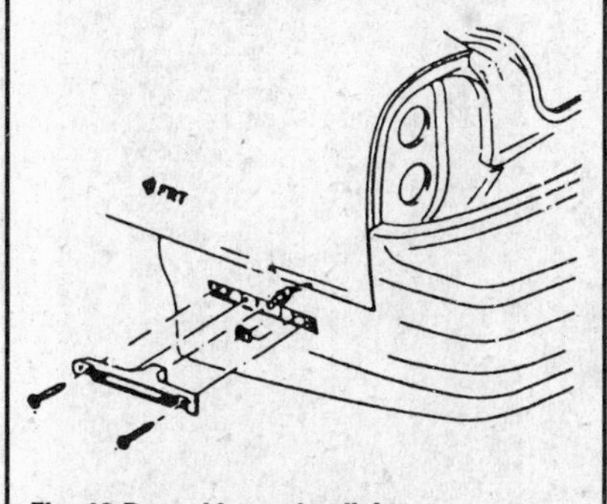

Fig. 40 Rear side marker light

Center High Mounted Brake Light

➧ SEE FIGS. 41 AND 42

1. Disconnect the negative battery cable.
2. Remove the lamp cover. It may be held on by screws or clips.
3. Disconnect the electric connector.
4. Remove the nuts or screws that retain the lamp assembly to the roof or window trim panel, and remove the bulb.

To install:

5. Install the bulb to the assembly.
6. Install the lamp assembly and connect the connector.
7. Install the lamp connector.
8. Connect the negative battery cable and check for proper operation.

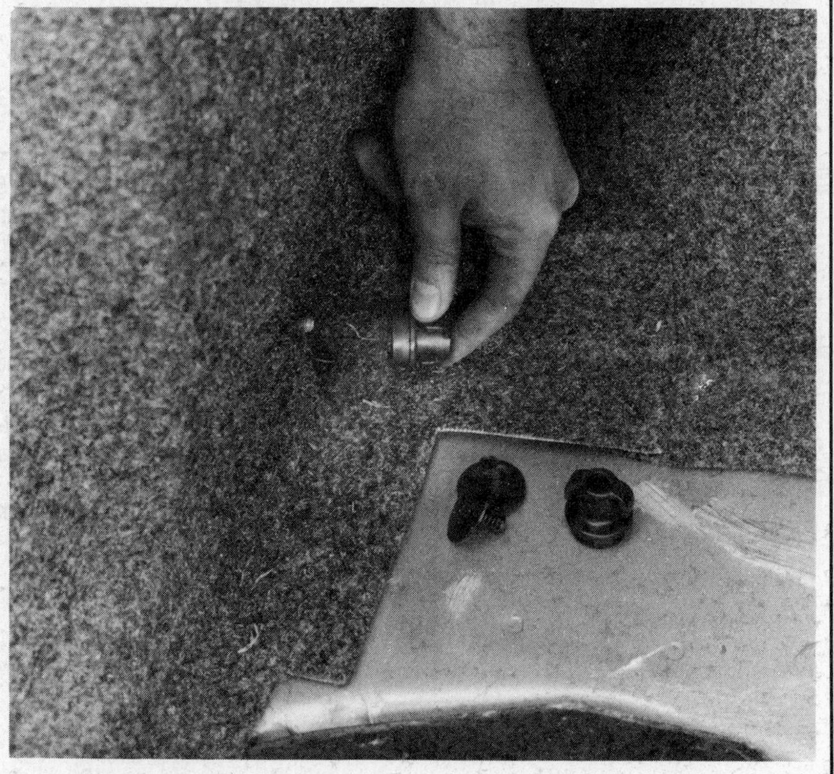

FIG. 40A. Remove these carpet retaining clips to expose the rear lamp assembly

Courtesy and Dome Light

➧ SEE FIG. 43

1. Disconnect the negative battery cable.
2. Remove the lamp lens from the housing by prying carefully. Press inward and down to disengage the retaining tabs. If the lens is cold, heat up the lens or interior of the car before prying the lens.
3. Remove the bulb from the terminal clips.
4. Remove the retaining nut(s), if equipped.
5. Remove the lamp assembly.

To install:

6. Install the lamp assembly.
7. Install the bulb to the clips.
8. Install the lens.

License Plate Lights

1. Disconnect the negative battery cable.
2. Remove the mounting screws and remove the lamp assembly..
3. Remove the socket from the lamp and remove the bulb from the socket.
4. The installation is the reverse of the removal procedure.

Fog Lights

REMOVAL & INSTALLATION

Grand Prix

1. Disconnect the negative battery cable.
2. Open the hood and remove the three

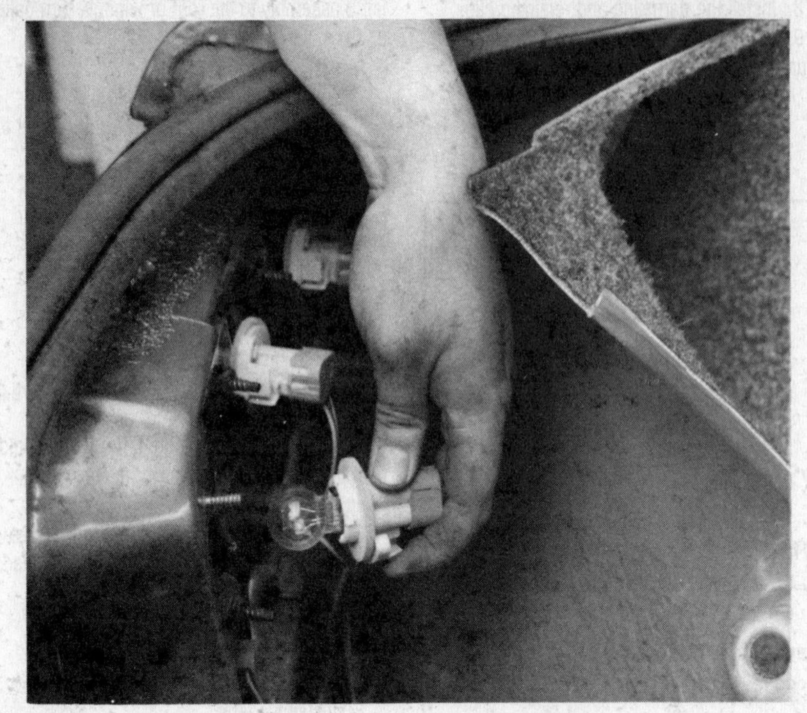

FIG. 40B. With the bulb sockets exposed, remove the faulty components

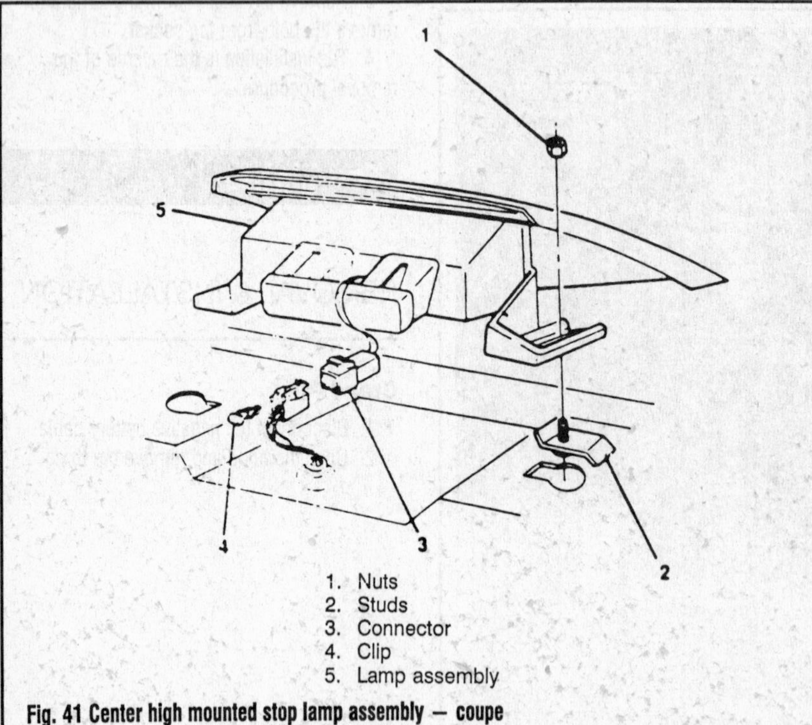

Fig. 41 Center high mounted stop lamp assembly — coupe

screws holding the cover over the rear of the lights.

3. Remove the one bolt holding the cover to the headlight housing panel.

4. Remove the cover by sliding it out from under the bolt.

5. Disconnect the light electrical connector.

6. Remove the bulb socket.

7. Remove the one bolt at the top rear of the assembly.

8. Remove the assembly from the vehicle, if replacing.

To install:

9. Install the light assembly making sure the guide pins on the bottom are aligned with the holes.

10. Install the one bolt, bulb/socket and electrical connector.

11. Install the cover under the bolt and tighten.

12. Install the three cover retaining screws, connect the negative battery cable and close the hood.

Lumina, Cutlass Supreme and Regal

1. Disconnect the negative battery cable and the fog light connector.

2. Remove the two retaining bolts under the front bumper.

3. Install the assembly, retaining bolts and connect the negative battery cable.

AIMING

1. Park the car on a level surface, at least 15 ft. from a wall that is perpendicular to the ground surface. Make sure there is no excess weight in the trunk, unless you normally travel with that amount of weight in the car. Bounce the car a few times to settle the suspension.

2. Measure and record the distance from the ground to the center of each fog light lens.

3. Turn the fog lights on and adjust so the hot-spots (lit area of most concentrated intensity) are 4 in. (102mm) below the height of the lenses. The ADJUSTING screw is located at the top right corner of the fog light.

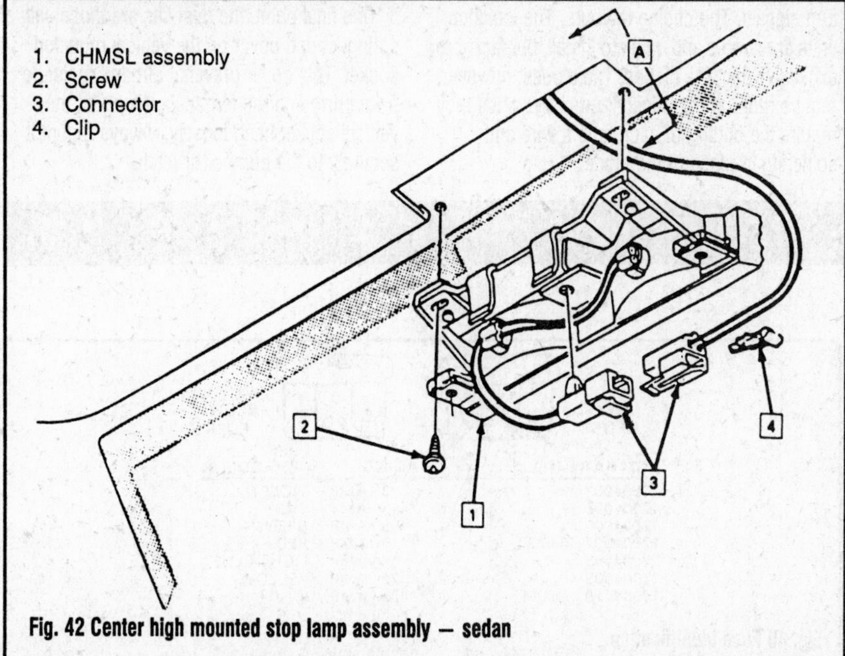

Fig. 42 Center high mounted stop lamp assembly — sedan

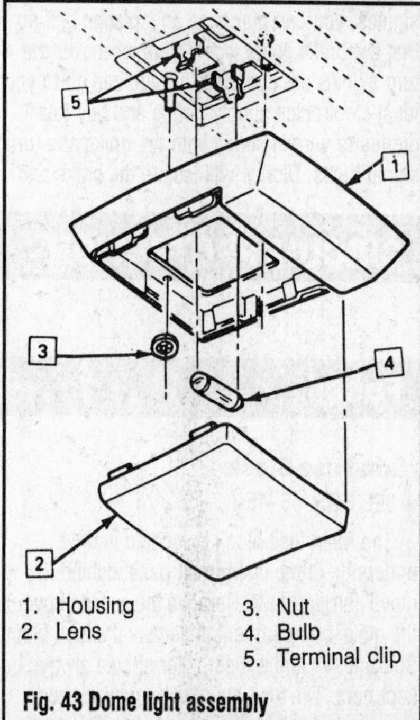

Fig. 43 Dome light assembly

TRAILER WIRING

Wiring the car for towing is fairly easy. There are a number of good wiring kits available and these should be used, rather than trying to design your own. All trailers will need brake lights and turn signals as well as tail lights and side marker lights. Most states require extra marker lights for overly wide trailers. Also, most states have recently required back-up lights for trailers, and most trailer manufacturers have been building trailers with back-up lights for several years.

Additionally, some Class I, most Class II and just about all Class III trailers will have electric brakes.

Add to this number an accessories wire, to operate trailer internal equipment or to charge the trailer's battery, and you can have as many as seven wires in the harness.

Determine the equipment on your trailer and buy the wiring kit necessary. The kit will contain all the wires needed, plus a plug adapter set which included the female plug, mounted on the bumper or hitch, and the male plug, wired into, or plugged into the trailer harness.

When installing the kit, follow the manufacturer's instructions. The color coding of the wires is standard throughout the industry.

One point to note: some domestic vehicles, and most imported vehicles, have separate turn signals. On most domestic vehicles, the brake lights and rear turn signals operate with the same bulb. For those vehicles with separate turn

REPLACEABLE LIGHT BULBS

Application	Number
EXTERIOR	
HEADLIGHT	
HIGH BEAM	9005
LOW BEAM	9006
FOG LAMP	H3
PARK/TURN	890
FRONT SIDE MARKER – COUPE	24
FRONT SIDE MARKER – SEDAN	24NA
BACKUP – COUPE	890
BACKUP – SEDAN	3057
HIGH LEVEL STOP – STANDARD	3155
HIGH LEVEL STOP – LUGGAGE RACK	891
DECK LID	920
LICENSE	194
REAR SIDE MARKER – COUPE	194
REAR SIDE MARKER – SEDAN	24
TAIL	194
TAIL/STOP/TURN	3057
INTERIOR	
ASHTRAY	194
COURTESY LAMP – QUARTER	212-2
CRUISE	PC161
DOME	212-2
DOME	561
GLOVEBOX	192
READING	24
READING LAMP	212-2

Fig. 44 Light bulb replacement information

signals, you can purchase an isolation unit so that the brake lights won't blink whenever the turn signals are operated, or, you can go to your local electronics supply house and buy four diodes to wire in series with the brake and turn signal bulbs. Diodes will isolate the brake and turn signals. The choice is yours. The isolation units are simple and quick to install, but far more expensive than the diodes. The diodes, however, require more work to install properly, since they require the cutting of each bulb's wire and soldering in place of the diode.

One final point, the best kits are those with a spring loaded cover on the vehicle mounted socket. This cover prevents dirt and moisture from corroding the terminals. Never let the vehicle socket hang loosely; always mount it securely to the bumper or hitch.

CIRCUIT PROTECTION

Fuses

Main Fuse Block

➧ SEE FIGS. 45–45A

The main fuse block is located in the underside of the instrument panel behind the glove compartment. Remove the access cover in the glove compartment to access the fuse block. Spare fuses and a fuse puller should always be kept here. The fuse block uses miniaturized fuses, designed for increased circuit protection and greater reliability. Various convenience connectors, which snap-lock into the fuse block, add to the serviceability of this unit. To remove a blown fuse, simply pull it from its terminals. When replacing fuses, only use the correct amperage replacement fuse. Each fuse has a number stamped on the top which indicates the amperage rating. Damage to the electrical system may result if the incorrect fuses are used.

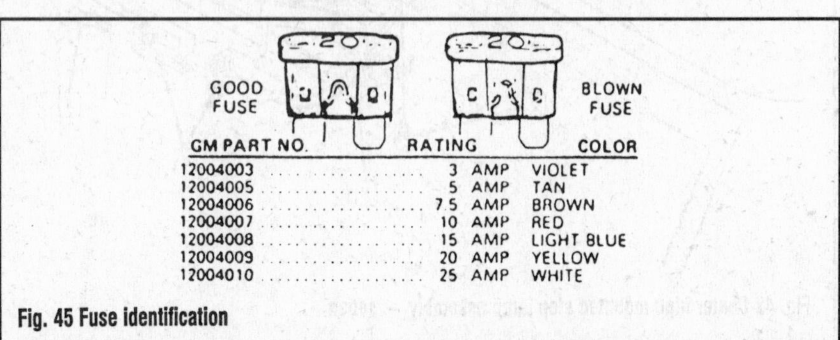

GM PART NO.	RATING	COLOR
12004003	3 AMP	VIOLET
12004005	5 AMP	TAN
12004006	7.5 AMP	BROWN
12004007	10 AMP	RED
12004008	15 AMP	LIGHT BLUE
12004009	20 AMP	YELLOW
12004010	25 AMP	WHITE

Fig. 45 Fuse identification

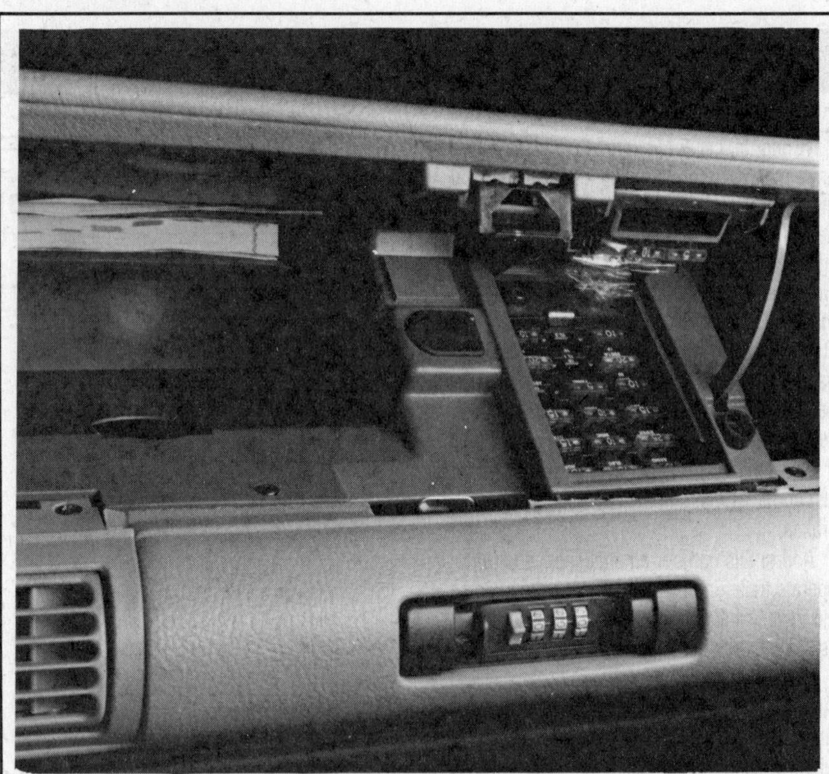

FIG. 45A. Access the fuses in the main fuse block through the glove box

Convenience Center

➧ SEE FIG. 46

The convenience center is located under the instrument panel, on the right side next to the fuse block. This unit houses circuit breakers, relays, chime module and hazard flasher.

Right Side Electrical Center

➧ SEE FIGS. 47–47A

The right side electrical center is located on the right side inner fender in the engine compartment. The center houses a variety of fuses, fusible links and relays, all of which are identified on the cover. The center can be serviced by removing the cover and remove the appropriate component.

Left Side Electrical Center

➧ SEE FIGS. 48–48A

The left side electrical center is located on the left inner fender behind the battery. The center houses the remote positive battery terminal, fuel pump relay and the ECM/fuel pump fuse. The remote positive battery terminal is used for jump starting only.

Forward Lamp Center

➧ SEE FIG. 49

The forward lamp center is located on the front right inner fender in front of the ECM unit. The center houses the fog light fuse, forward lamp relays and the horn relay.

Anti-Lock Brake (ABS) Electrical Center

➧ SEE FIG. 50

The ABS electrical center is used only with vehicles equipped with anti-lock brake systems. The center is located between the shock tower and the battery. The ABS center houses the ABS fuses, fusible cartridges, and relays.

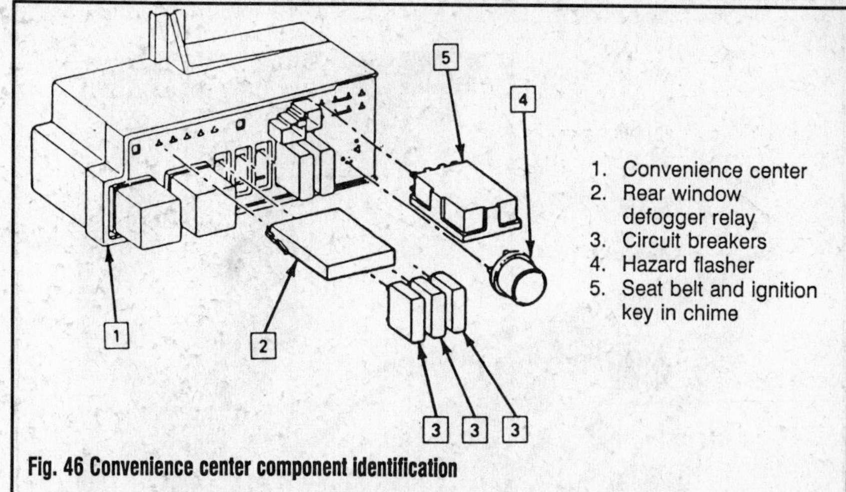

Fig. 46 Convenience center component identification

Fusible Links and Elements

Fusible links are sections of wire, with special insulation, designed to melt under electrical overload. Replacements are soldered in place of snapped links. The fusible links are located near the starter motor, and replaceable cartridges are in the right and left side electrical centers in the engine compartment. Refer to the wiring schematics included in this section for identification of fusible links.

Circuit Breakers

Various circuit breakers are used through out the electrical system. The breakers are designed to "trip" when an overload is placed on the system. The breaker automatically resets when the overload is removed. The breakers are located in the component center located behind the instrument panel.

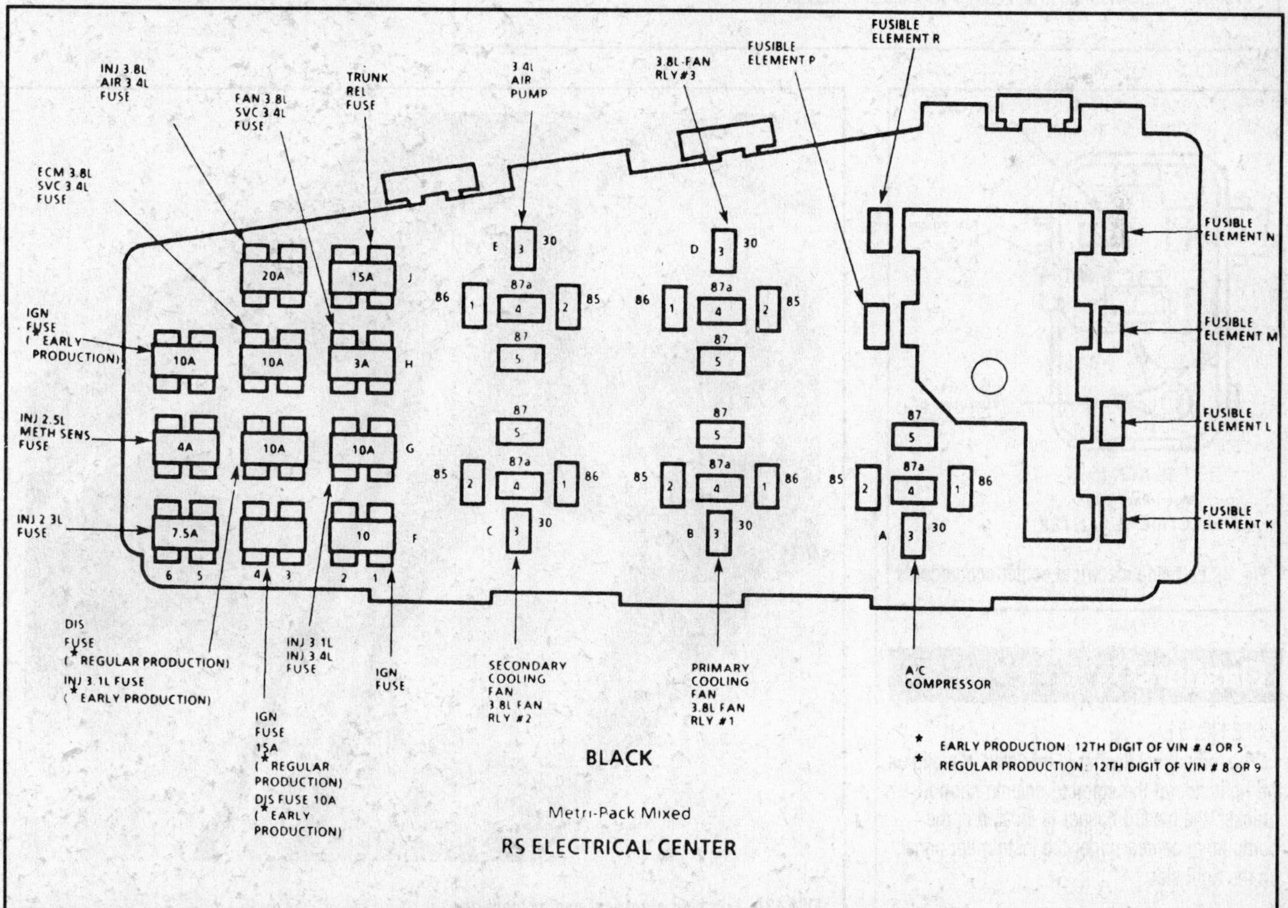

BLACK

Metri-Pack Mixed

RS ELECTRICAL CENTER

* EARLY PRODUCTION: 12TH DIGIT OF VIN # 4 OR 5
* REGULAR PRODUCTION: 12TH DIGIT OF VIN # 8 OR 9

Fig. 47 Right side electrical center component identification

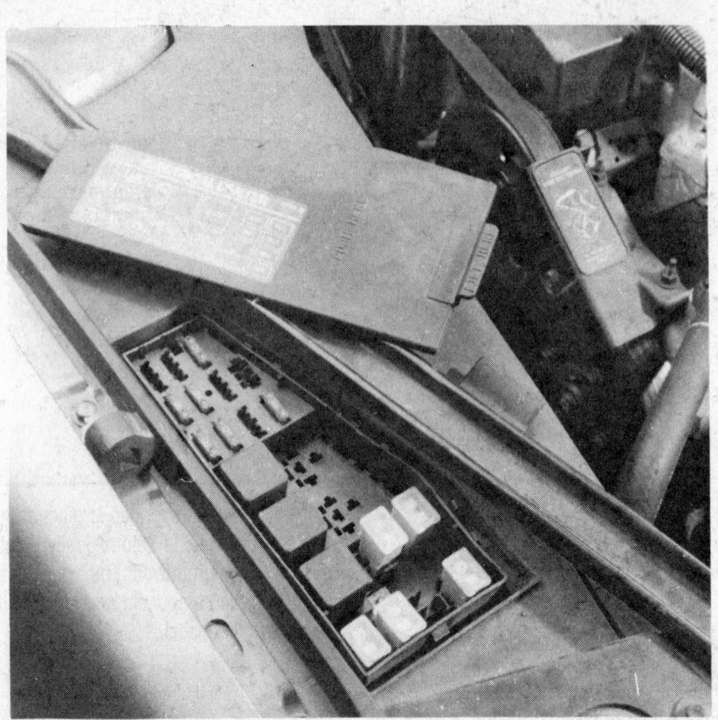

FIG. 47A. Right side electrical center with cover removed

Fuse Link

The fuse link is a short length of special, Hypalon (high temperature) insulated wire, integral with the engine compartment wiring harness and should not be confused with standard wire. It is several wire gauges smaller than the circuit which it protects. Under no circumstances should a fuse link replacement repair be made using a length of standard wire cut from bulk stock or from another wiring harness.

To repair any blown fuse link use the following procedure:

1. Determine which circuit is damaged, its location and the cause of the open fuse link. If the damaged fuse link is one of three fed by a common No. 10 or 12 gauge feed wire, determine the specific affected circuit.
2. Disconnect the negative battery cable.
3. Cut the damaged fuse link from the wiring harness and discard it. If the fuse link is one of three circuits fed by a single feed wire, cut it out of the harness at each splice end and discard it.
4. Identify and procure the proper fuse link and butt connectors for attaching the fuse link to the harness.

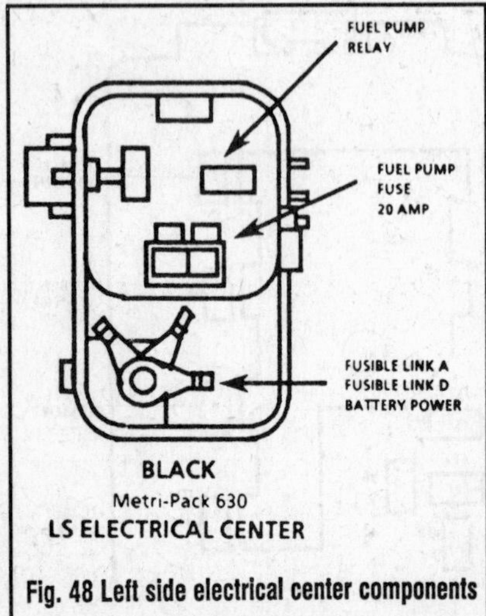

Fig. 48 Left side electrical center components

Flashers

➧ SEE FIG. 51

The turn signal flasher is mounted in a clip on the right side of the steering column support bracket. the hazard flasher is located in the component center, under the instrument panel, on the right side.

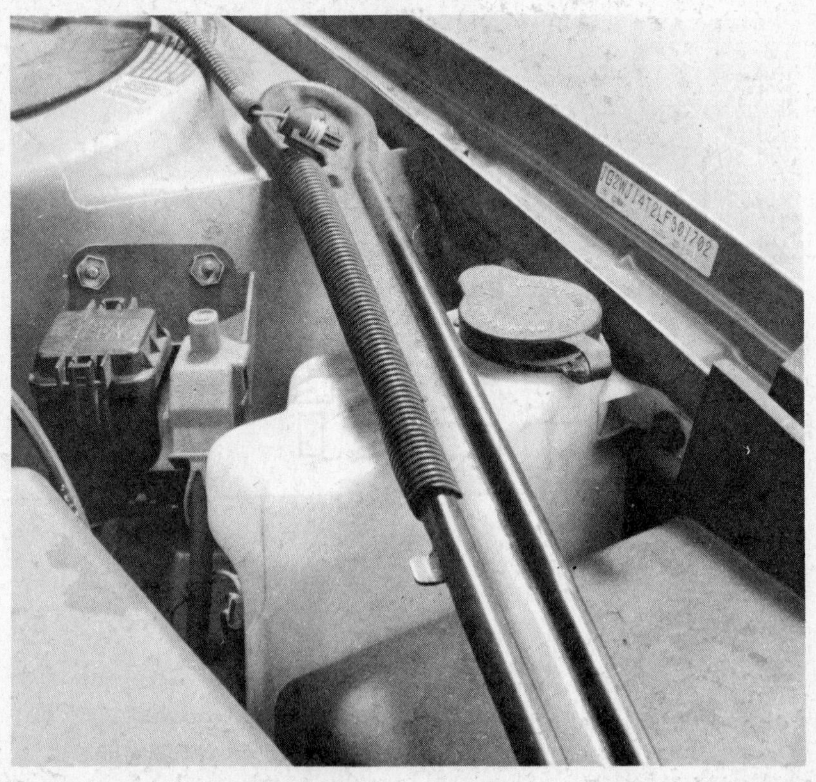

FIG. 48A. Left side electrical center location

5. To repair any fuse link in a 3-link group with one feed:

a. After cutting the open link out of the harness, cut each of the remaining undamaged fuse links close to the feed wire weld.

b. Strip approximately 1/2 in. (13mm) of insulation from the detached ends of the two good fuse links, Then insert two wire ends into one end of a butt connector and carefully push one stripped end of the replacement fuse link into the same end of the butt connector and crimp all three firmly together.

➡ Care must be taken when fitting the three fuse links into the butt connector as the internal diameter is a snug fit for three wires. Make sure to use a proper crimping tool. Pliers, side cutter, etc. will not apply the proper crimp to retain the wires and withstand a pull test.

c. After crimping the butt connector to the three fuse links, cut the weld portion from the feed wire and strip approximately 1/2 in. (13mm) of insulation from the cut end. Insert the stripped end into the open end of the butt connector and crimp very firmly.

d. To attach the remaining end of the replacement fuse link, strip approximately 1/2 in. (13mm) of insulation from the wire end of the circuit from which the blown fuse link was removed, and firmly crimp a butt connector or equivalent to the stripped wire. Then, insert the end of the replacement link into the other end of the butt connector and crimp firmly.

e. Using rosin core solder with a consistency of 60 percent tin and 40 percent lead, solder the connectors and the wires at the repairs and insulate with electrical tape.

6. To replace any fuse link on a single circuit in a harness, cut out the damaged portion, strip approximately 1/2 in. (13mm) of insulation from the two wire ends and attach the appropriate replacement fuse link to the stripped wire ends with two proper size butt connectors. Solder the connectors and wires and insulate with tape.

7. To repair any fuse link which has an eyelet terminal on one end such as the charging circuit, cut off the open fuse link behind the weld, strip approximately 1/2 in. (13mm) of insulation from the cut end and attach the appropriate new eyelet fuse link to the cut stripped wire with an appropriate size butt connector. Solder the connectors and wires at the repair and insulate with tape.

8. Connect the negative battery cable to the battery and test the system for proper operation.

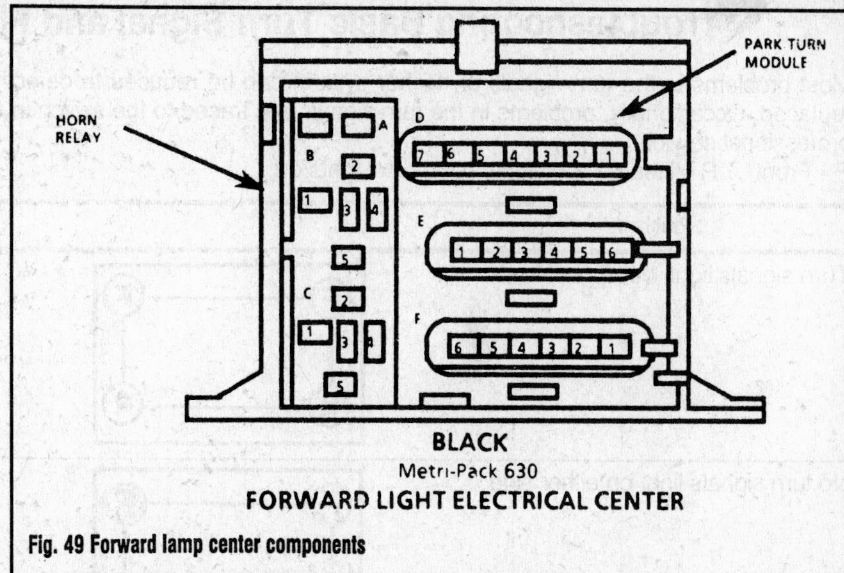

Fig. 49 Forward lamp center components

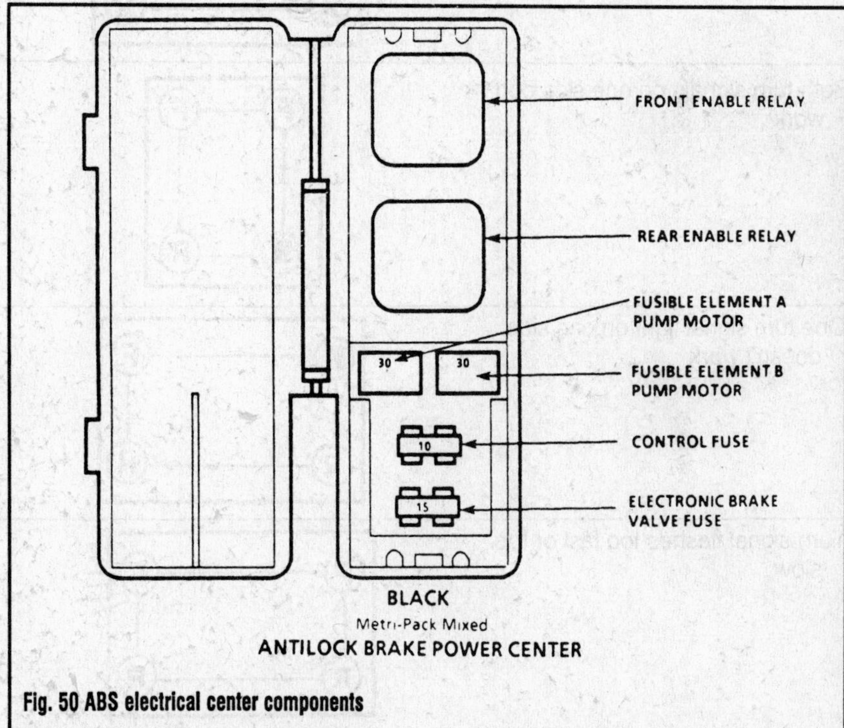

Fig. 50 ABS electrical center components

➡ Do not mistake a resistor wire for a fuse link. The resistor wire is generally longer and has print stating, "Resistor-don't cut or splice".

When attaching a single No. 16, 17, 18 or 20 gauge fuse link to a heavy gauge wire, always double the stripped wire end of the fuse link before inserting and crimping it into the butt connector for positive wire retention.

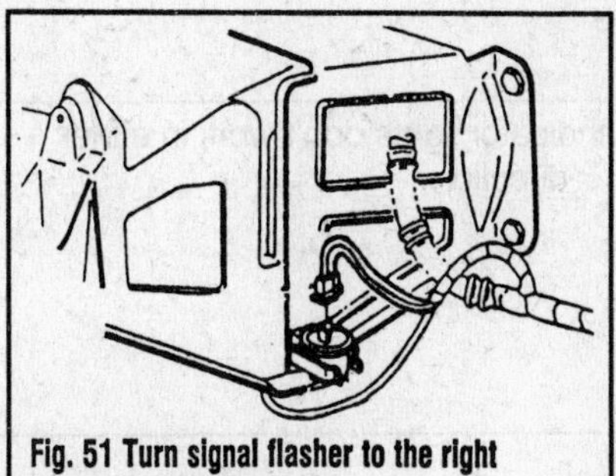

Fig. 51 Turn signal flasher to the right of the steering column

Troubleshooting Basic Turn Signal and Flasher Problems

Most problems in the turn signals or flasher system can be reduced to defective flashers or bulbs, which are easily replaced. Occasionally, problems in the turn signals are traced to the switch in the steering column, which will require professional service.

F = Front R = Rear ● = Lights off ○ = Lights on

Problem	Solution
Turn signals light, but do not flash	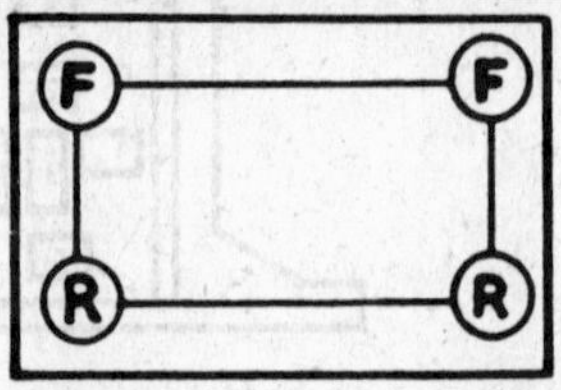 • Replace the flasher
No turn signals light on either side	 • Check the fuse. Replace if defective. • Check the flasher by substitution • Check for open circuit, short circuit or poor ground
Both turn signals on one side don't work	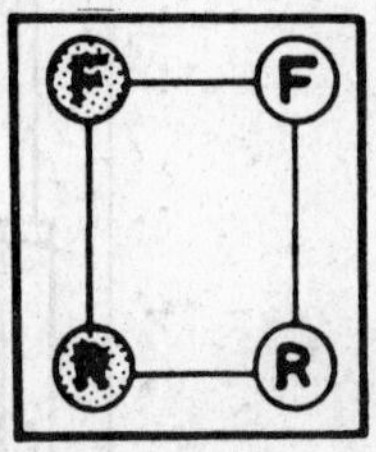 • Check for bad bulbs • Check for bad ground in both housings
One turn signal light on one side doesn't work	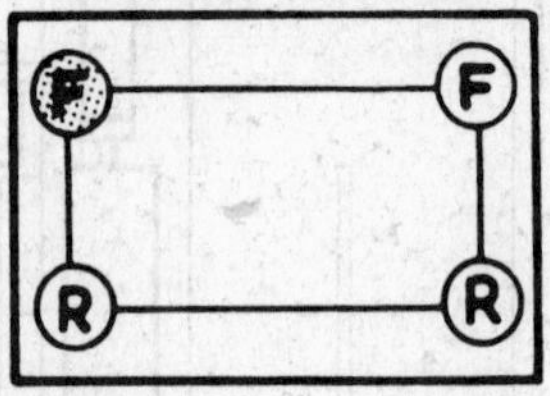 • Check and/or replace bulb • Check for corrosion in socket. Clean contacts. • Check for poor ground at socket
Turn signal flashes too fast or too slow	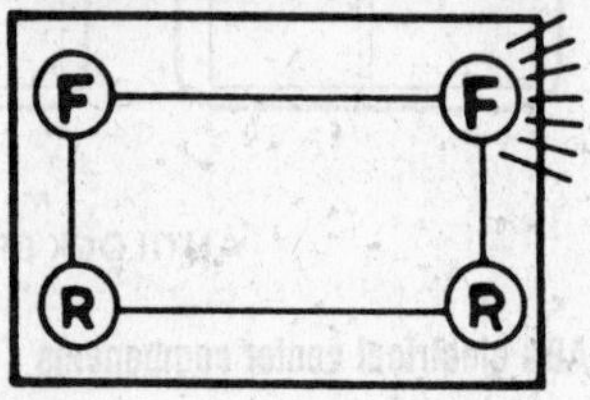 • Check any bulb on the side flashing too fast. A heavy-duty bulb is probably installed in place of a regular bulb. • Check the bulb flashing too slow. A standard bulb was probably installed in place of a heavy-duty bulb. • Check for loose connections or corrosion at the bulb socket
Indicator lights don't work in either direction	 • Check if the turn signals are working • Check the dash indicator lights • Check the flasher by substitution

Troubleshooting Basic Turn Signal and Flasher Problems

Most problems in the turn signals or flasher system can be reduced to defective flashers or bulbs, which are easily replaced. Occasionally, problems in the turn signals are traced to the switch in the steering column, which will require professional service.
F = Front R = Rear ● = Lights off ○ = Lights on

Problem	Solution
One indicator light doesn't light	• On systems with 1 dash indicator: See if the lights work on the same side. Often the filaments have been reversed in systems combining stoplights with taillights and turn signals. Check the flasher by substitution • On systems with 2 indicators: Check the bulbs on the same side Check the indicator light bulb Check the flasher by substitution

Troubleshooting Basic Lighting Problems

Problem	Cause	Solution
Lights		
One or more lights don't work, but others do	• Defective bulb(s) • Blown fuse(s) • Dirty fuse clips or light sockets • Poor ground circuit	• Replace bulb(s) • Replace fuse(s) • Clean connections • Run ground wire from light socket housing to car frame
Lights burn out quickly	• Incorrect voltage regulator setting or defective regulator • Poor battery/alternator connections	• Replace voltage regulator • Check battery/alternator connections
Lights go dim	• Low/discharged battery • Alternator not charging • Corroded sockets or connections • Low voltage output	• Check battery • Check drive belt tension; repair or replace alternator • Clean bulb and socket contacts and connections • Replace voltage regulator
Lights flicker	• Loose connection • Poor ground • Circuit breaker operating (short circuit)	• Tighten all connections • Run ground wire from light housing to car frame • Check connections and look for bare wires

Troubleshooting Basic Lighting Problems

Problem	Cause	Solution
Lights		
Lights "flare"—Some flare is normal on acceleration—if excessive, see "Lights Burn Out Quickly"	• High voltage setting	• Replace voltage regulator
Lights glare—approaching drivers are blinded	• Lights adjusted too high • Rear springs or shocks sagging • Rear tires soft	• Have headlights aimed • Check rear springs/shocks • Check/correct rear tire pressure
Turn Signals		
Turn signals don't work in either direction	• Blown fuse • Defective flasher • Loose connection	• Replace fuse • Replace flasher • Check/tighten all connections
Right (or left) turn signal only won't work	• Bulb burned out • Right (or left) indicator bulb burned out • Short circuit	• Replace bulb • Check/replace indicator bulb • Check/repair wiring
Flasher rate too slow or too fast	• Incorrect wattage bulb • Incorrect flasher	• Flasher bulb • Replace flasher (use a variable load flasher if you pull a trailer)
Indicator lights do not flash (burn steadily)	• Burned out bulb • Defective flasher	• Replace bulb • Replace flasher
Indicator lights do not light at all	• Burned out indicator bulb • Defective flasher	• Replace indicator bulb • Replace flasher

Troubleshooting Basic Dash Gauge Problems

Problem	Cause	Solution
Coolant Temperature Gauge		
Gauge reads erratically or not at all	• Loose or dirty connections • Defective sending unit • Defective gauge	• Clean/tighten connections • Bi-metal gauge: remove the wire from the sending unit. Ground the wire for an instant. If the gauge registers, replace the sending unit. • Magnetic gauge: disconnect the wire at the sending unit. With ignition ON gauge should register COLD. Ground the wire; gauge should register HOT.

Troubleshooting Basic Dash Gauge Problems

Problem	Cause	Solution
Ammeter Gauge—Turn Headlights ON (do not start engine). Note reaction		
Ammeter shows charge	• Connections reversed on gauge	• Reinstall connections
Ammeter shows discharge	• Ammeter is OK	• Nothing
Ammeter does not move	• Loose connections or faulty wiring	• Check/correct wiring
	• Defective gauge	• Replace gauge
Oil Pressure Gauge		
Gauge does not register or is inaccurate	• On mechanical gauge, Bourdon tube may be bent or kinked	• Check tube for kinks or bends preventing oil from reaching the gauge
	• Low oil pressure	• Remove sending unit. Idle the engine briefly. If no oil flows from sending unit hole, problem is in engine.
	• Defective gauge	• Remove the wire from the sending unit and ground it for an instant with the ignition ON. A good gauge will go to the top of the scale.
	• Defective wiring	• Check the wiring to the gauge. If it's OK and the gauge doesn't register when grounded, replace the gauge.
	• Defective sending unit	• If the wiring is OK and the gauge functions when grounded, replace the sending unit
All Gauges		
All gauges do not operate	• Blown fuse	• Replace fuse
	• Defective instrument regulator	• Replace instrument voltage regulator
All gauges read low or erratically	• Defective or dirty instrument voltage regulator	• Clean contacts or replace
All gauges pegged	• Loss of ground between instrument voltage regulator and car	• Check ground
	• Defective instrument regulator	• Replace regulator
Warning Lights		
Light(s) do not come on when ignition is ON, but engine is not started	• Defective bulb	• Replace bulb
	• Defective wire	• Check wire from light to sending unit
	• Defective sending unit	• Disconnect the wire from the sending unit and ground it. Replace the sending unit if the light comes on with the ignition ON.
Light comes on with engine running	• Problem in individual system	• Check system
	• Defective sending unit	• Check sending unit (see above)

Troubleshooting the Heater

Problem	Cause	Solution
Blower motor will not turn at any speed	• Blown fuse • Loose connection • Defective ground • Faulty switch • Faulty motor • Faulty resistor	• Replace fuse • Inspect and tighten • Clean and tighten • Replace switch • Replace motor • Replace resistor
Blower motor turns at one speed only	• Faulty switch • Faulty resistor	• Replace switch • Replace resistor
Blower motor turns but does not circulate air	• Intake blocked • Fan not secured to the motor shaft	• Clean intake • Tighten security
Heater will not heat	• Coolant does not reach proper temperature • Heater core blocked internally • Heater core air-bound • Blend-air door not in proper position	• Check and replace thermostat if necessary • Flush or replace core if necessary • Purge air from core • Adjust cable
Heater will not defrost	• Control cable adjustment incorrect • Defroster hose damaged	• Adjust control cable • Replace defroster hose

Troubleshooting Basic Windshield Wiper Problems

Problem	Cause	Solution
Electric Wipers		
Wipers do not operate— Wiper motor heats up or hums	• Internal motor defect • Bent or damaged linkage • Arms improperly installed on linking pivots	• Replace motor • Repair or replace linkage • Position linkage in park and reinstall wiper arms
Electric Wipers		
Wipers do not operate— No current to motor	• Fuse or circuit breaker blown • Loose, open or broken wiring • Defective switch • Defective or corroded terminals • No ground circuit for motor or switch	• Replace fuse or circuit breaker • Repair wiring and connections • Replace switch • Replace or clean terminals • Repair ground circuits
Wipers do not operate— Motor runs	• Linkage disconnected or broken	• Connect wiper linkage or replace broken linkage
Vacuum Wipers		
Wipers do not operate	• Control switch or cable inoperative • Loss of engine vacuum to wiper motor (broken hoses, low engine vacuum, defective vacuum/fuel pump) • Linkage broken or disconnected • Defective wiper motor	• Repair or replace switch or cable • Check vacuum lines, engine vacuum and fuel pump • Repair linkage • Replace wiper motor
Wipers stop on engine acceleration	• Leaking vacuum hoses • Dry windshield • Oversize wiper blades • Defective vacuum/fuel pump	• Repair or replace hoses • Wet windshield with washers • Replace with proper size wiper blades • Replace pump

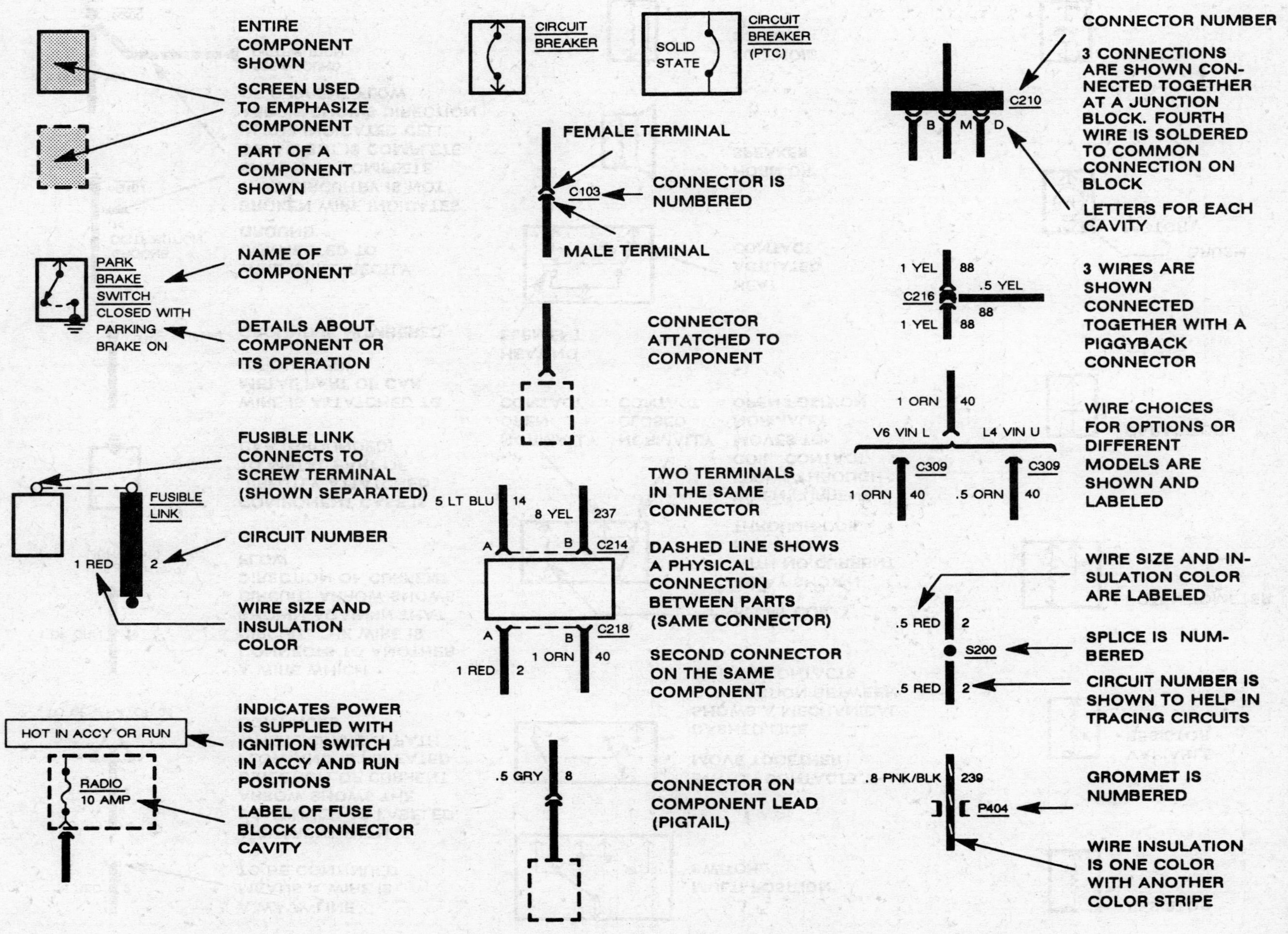

Symbols used in wiring schematics

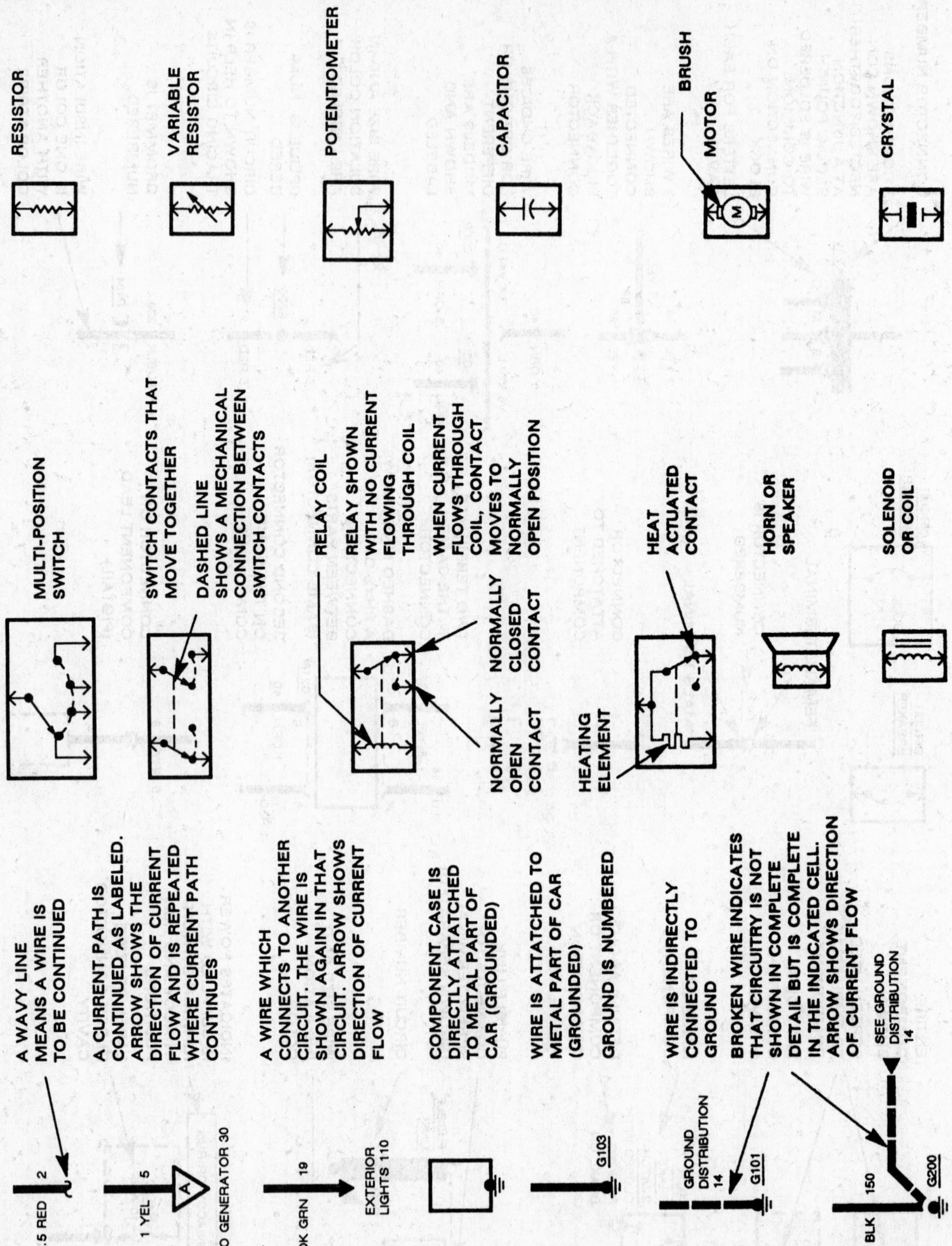

Symbols used in wiring schematics

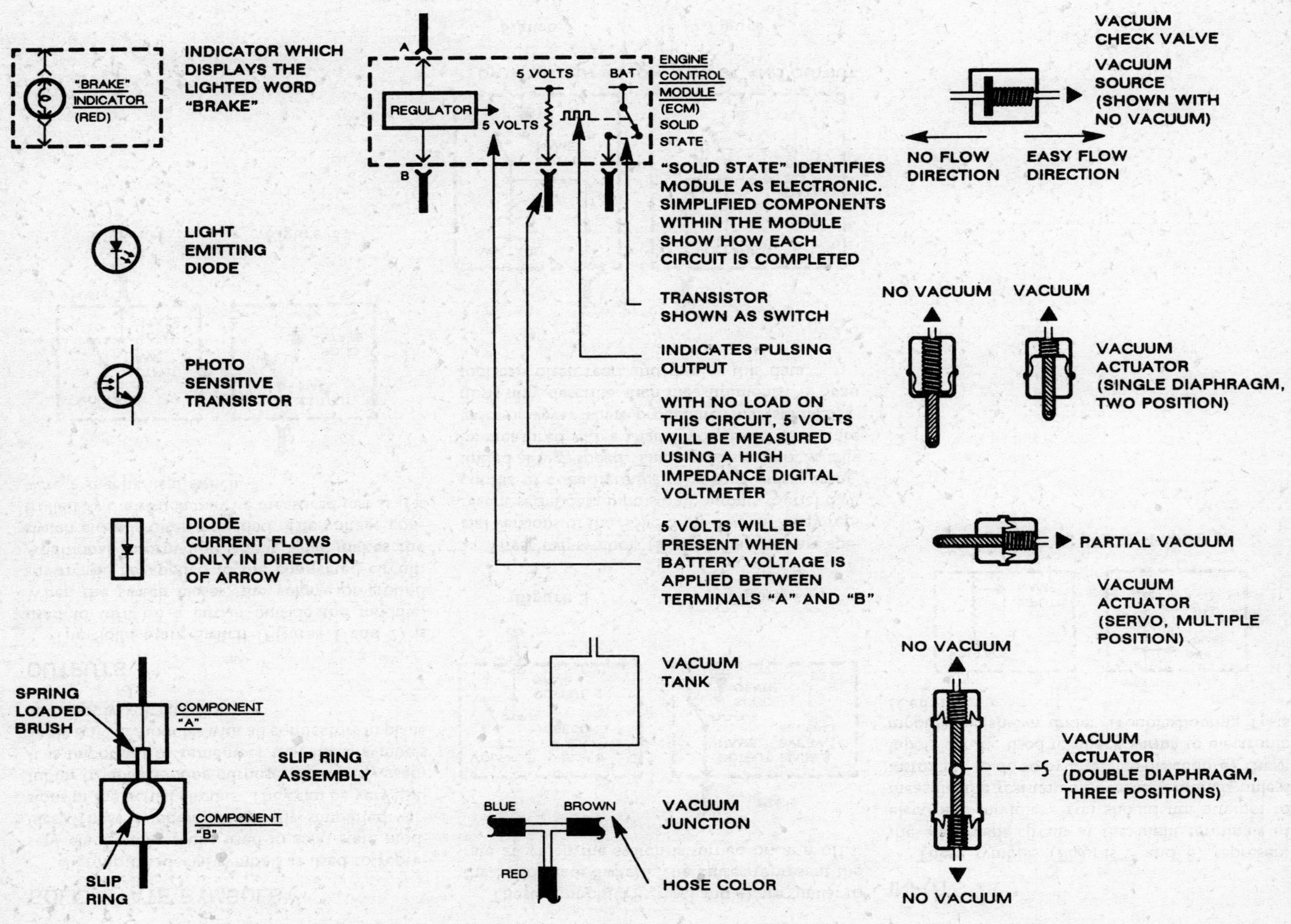
"BRAKE" INDICATOR (RED)
INDICATOR WHICH DISPLAYS THE LIGHTED WORD "BRAKE"
LIGHT EMITTING DIODE
PHOTO SENSITIVE TRANSISTOR
DIODE CURRENT FLOWS ONLY IN DIRECTION OF ARROW
SPRING LOADED BRUSH
COMPONENT "A"
SLIP RING ASSEMBLY
COMPONENT "B"
SLIP RING
A
REGULATOR
5 VOLTS
B
5 VOLTS
BAT
ENGINE CONTROL MODULE (ECM) SOLID STATE
"SOLID STATE" IDENTIFIES MODULE AS ELECTRONIC. SIMPLIFIED COMPONENTS WITHIN THE MODULE SHOW HOW EACH CIRCUIT IS COMPLETED
TRANSISTOR SHOWN AS SWITCH
INDICATES PULSING OUTPUT
WITH NO LOAD ON THIS CIRCUIT, 5 VOLTS WILL BE MEASURED USING A HIGH IMPEDANCE DIGITAL VOLTMETER
5 VOLTS WILL BE PRESENT WHEN BATTERY VOLTAGE IS APPLIED BETWEEN TERMINALS "A" AND "B"
VACUUM TANK
BLUE
BROWN
RED
VACUUM JUNCTION
HOSE COLOR
VACUUM CHECK VALVE
VACUUM SOURCE (SHOWN WITH NO VACUUM)
NO FLOW DIRECTION
EASY FLOW DIRECTION
NO VACUUM
VACUUM
VACUUM ACTUATOR (SINGLE DIAPHRAGM, TWO POSITION)
PARTIAL VACUUM
VACUUM ACTUATOR (SERVO, MULTIPLE POSITION)
NO VACUUM
VACUUM ACTUATOR (DOUBLE DIAPHRAGM, THREE POSITIONS)
NO VACUUM

Symbols used in wiring schematics

SOLID STATE SYMBOLS

A group of special symbols is used to represent electronic circuits used in solid state modules. These symbols are greatly simplified versions of the actual circuits. They can be very useful for troubleshooting purposes if properly used. It is important to remember that these symbols apply only to modules with all connectors in place and supply voltages on.

OUTPUTS

The Solid State Switch (Figures 1 and 2) is used to turn on a circuit outside the module. When the switch closes, the voltage or ground shown will be applied to the connected circuit. Additional information about what makes the switch close is often provided. The voltage controlled by the switch may be measured just as if it were a mechanical switch.

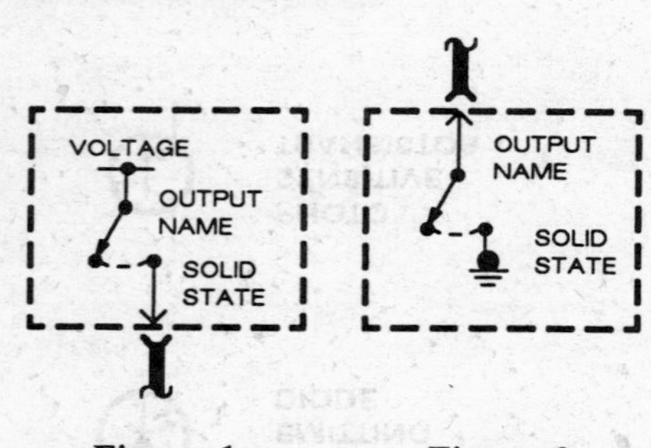

Figure 1 Figure 2

These symbols (Figures 3 and 4) are similar to the Solid State Switch. The pulses represent the rate at which the switch is turned on and off.

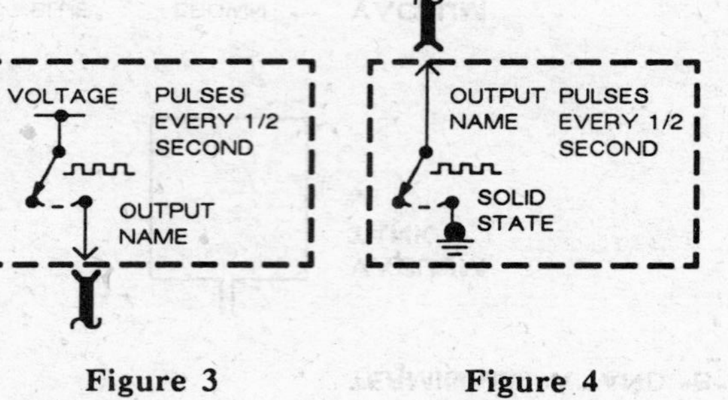

Figure 3 Figure 4

These two symbols (Figures 5 and 6) are special versions of the Solid State Switch. They represent serial data inputs and outputs. Serial data consits of coded groups of voltage pulses transmitted at high speed. These pulses cannot usually be measured with a Digital Voltmeter. There are cases however where procedures in System Diagnosis may describe such measurements. A Scan tool can often read and display this data.

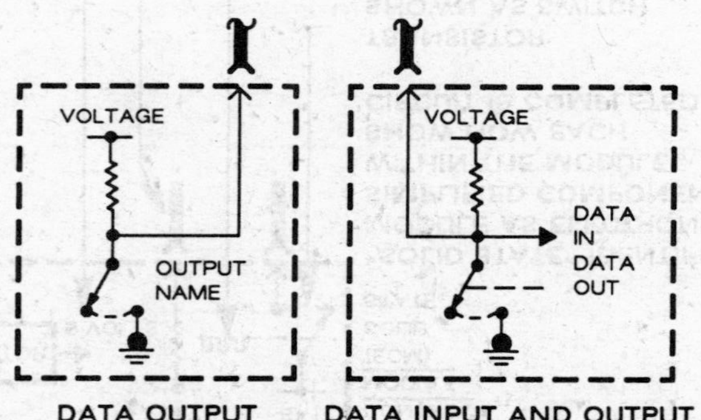

DATA OUTPUT DATA INPUT AND OUTPUT

Figure 5 Figure 6

INPUTS

These symbols (Figures 7 and 8) represent the equivalent circuit at the input terminals of electronic modules. You should not attempt to measure the resistance of these terminals unless instructed to do so by a service procedure. These inputs can be used to check wiring to electronic modules as shown under Troubleshooting Tests (Cell 4).

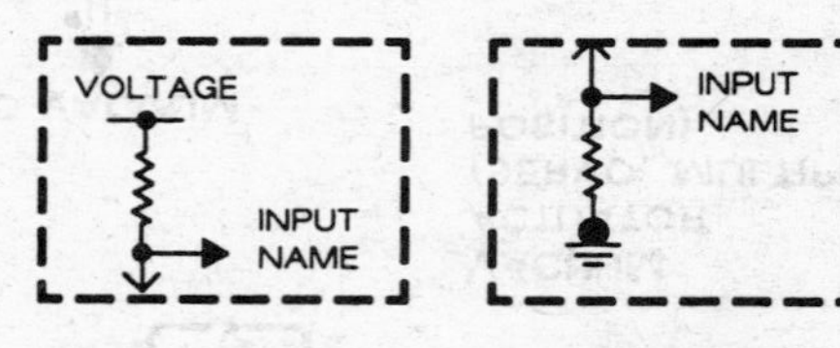

Figure 7 Figure 8

Symbols used in wiring schematics

ELECTROSTATIC DISCHARGE (ESD) SENSITIVE DEVICES

All ESD sensitive components contain Solid State circuits. The following information applies to all ESD sensitive devices. The ESD symbol (see Figure 1A) is used on schematics (see Figure 1B) to indicate which components are ESD sensitive.

Figure 1A - Electrostatic Discharge (ESD) Sensitive Device Symbol

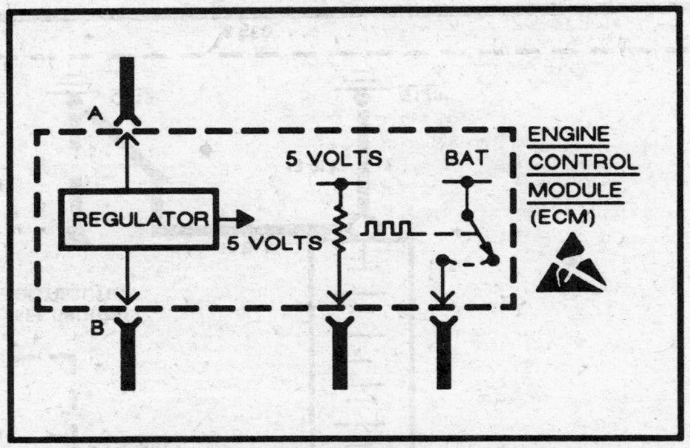

A
5 VOLTS
BAT
ENGINE CONTROL MODULE (ECM)
REGULATOR
5 VOLTS
B

Figure 1B - Component (on Schematic) Indicated as ESD Sensitive

Handling Procedures

When handling an electronic part that is ESD sensitive (see Figure 1A), the service technician should follow these guidelines to reduce any possible electrostatic charge build-up on the service technician's body and the electronic part in the dealership:

1. Always touch a known good ground before handling the part. This should be repeated while handling the part and more frequently after sliding across the seat, sitting down from a standing position or walking a distance.
2. Avoid touching electrical terminals of the part, unless so instructed by a written diagnostic procedure.
3. Do not open package of a new part until it is time to install the part.
4. Before removing the part from its package, ground the package to a known good ground on the car.

Measuring Procedures

1. Solid State circuits in electronic devices are shown greatly simplified.
2. Due to the simplification of the electronic devices on the schematics, resistance measurements could be misleading or could lead to electrostatic discharge.
3. Only measure the resistance at the terminals of these devices when instructed by a written diagnostic procedure.
4. When using a voltmeter, be sure to connect the ground lead first.

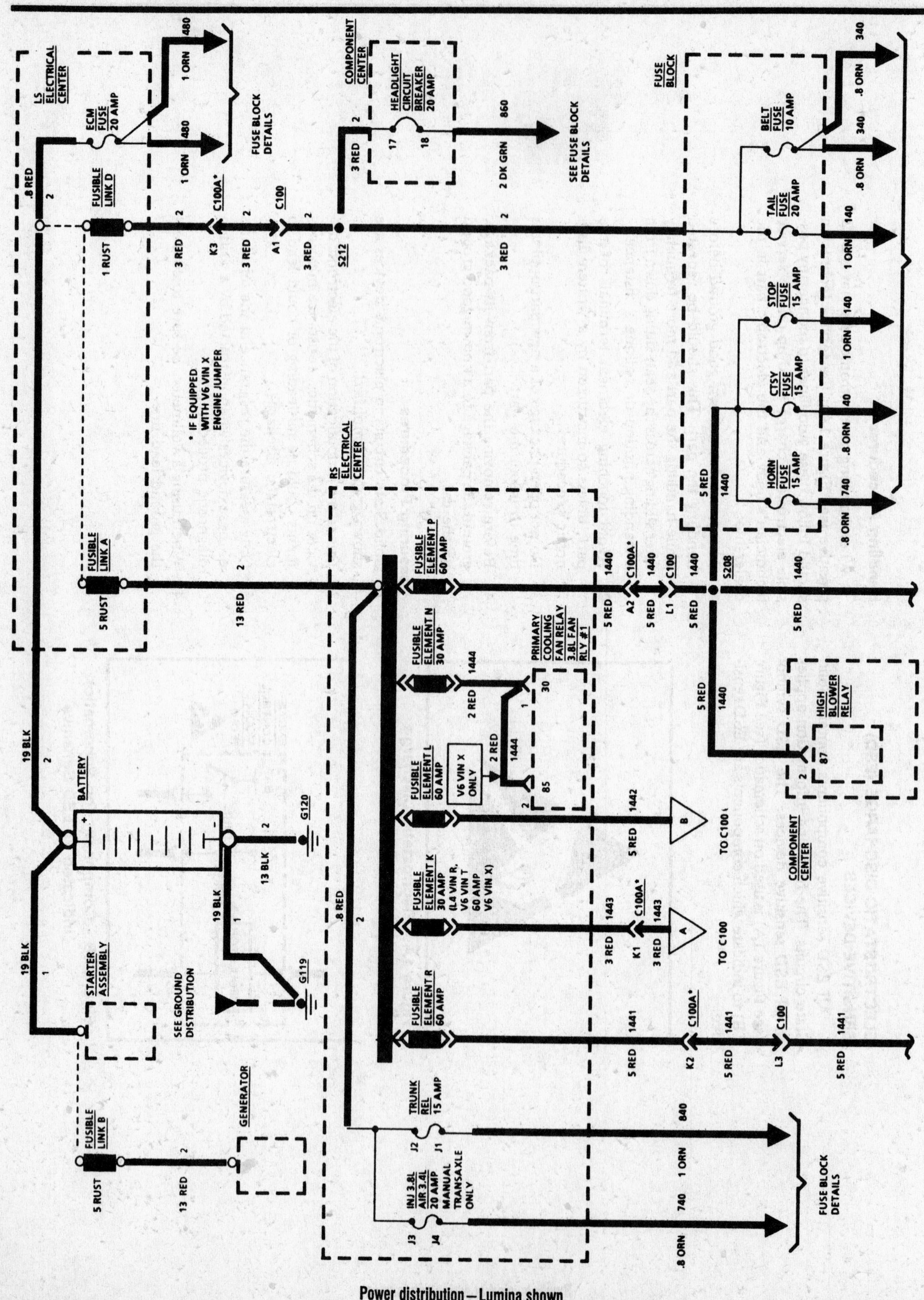

Power distribution—Lumina shown

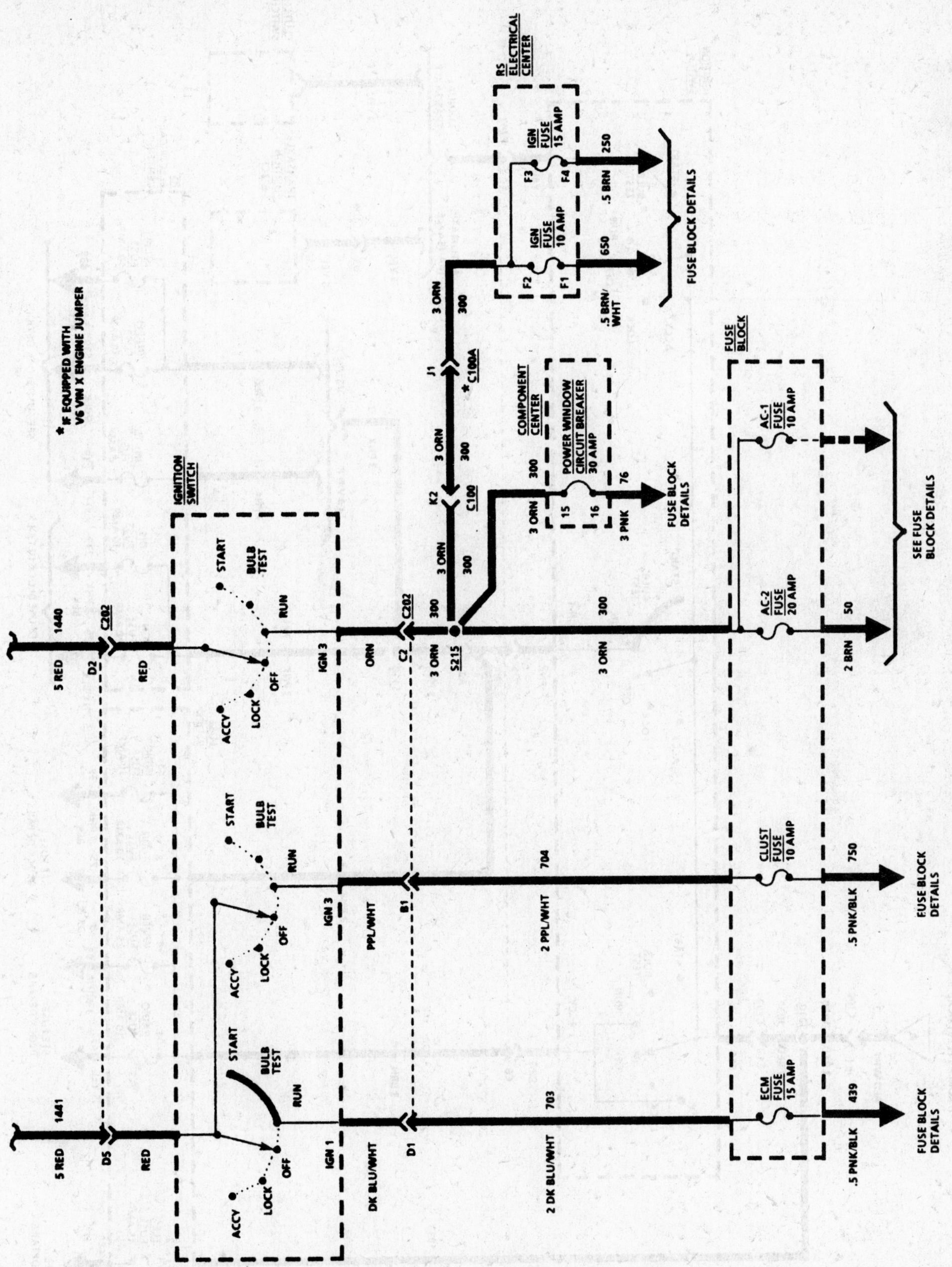

Power distribution—Lumina shown

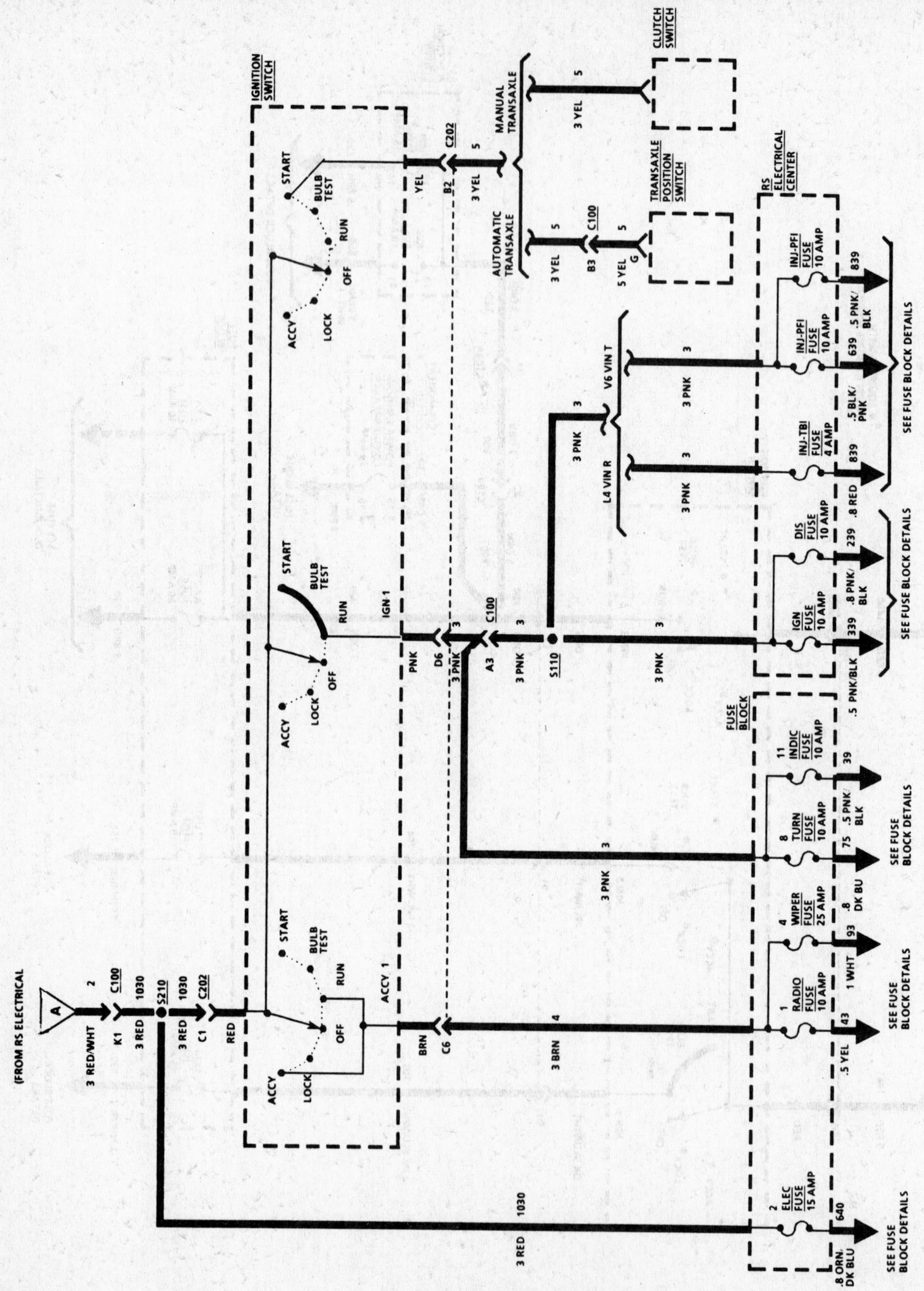

Power distribution—Lumina shown

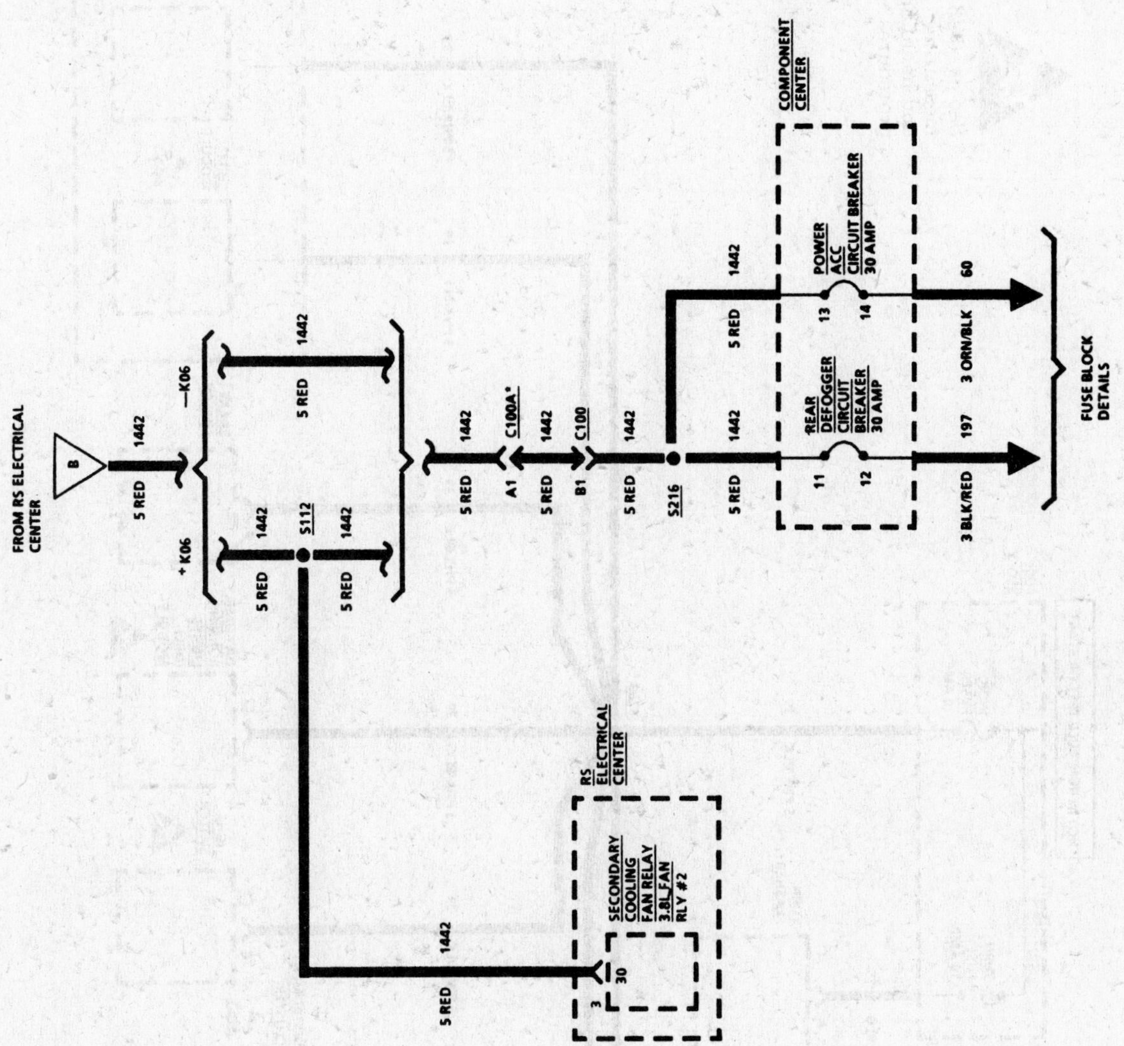

Power distribution—Lumina shown

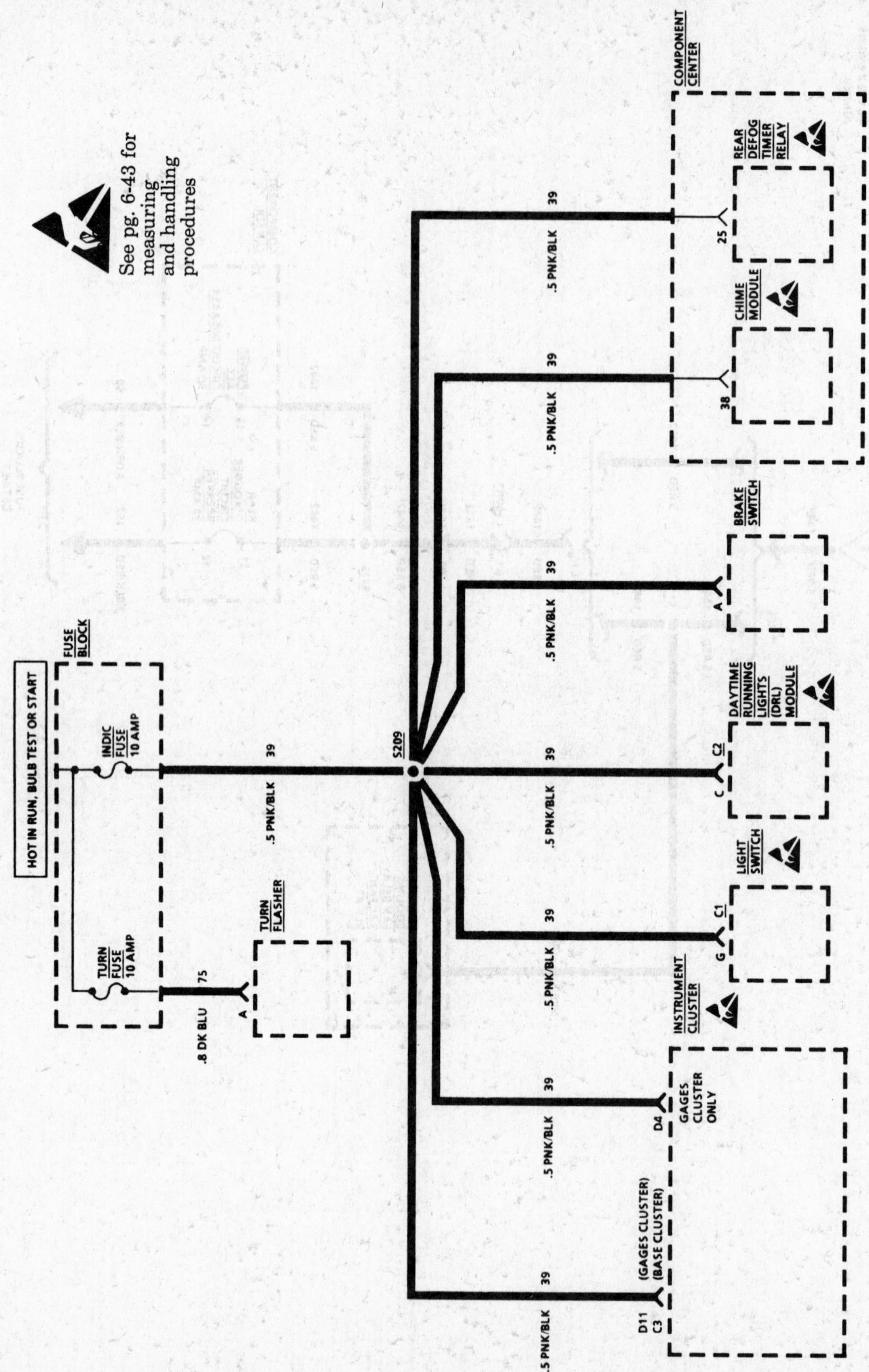

Fuse block details—Lumina shown

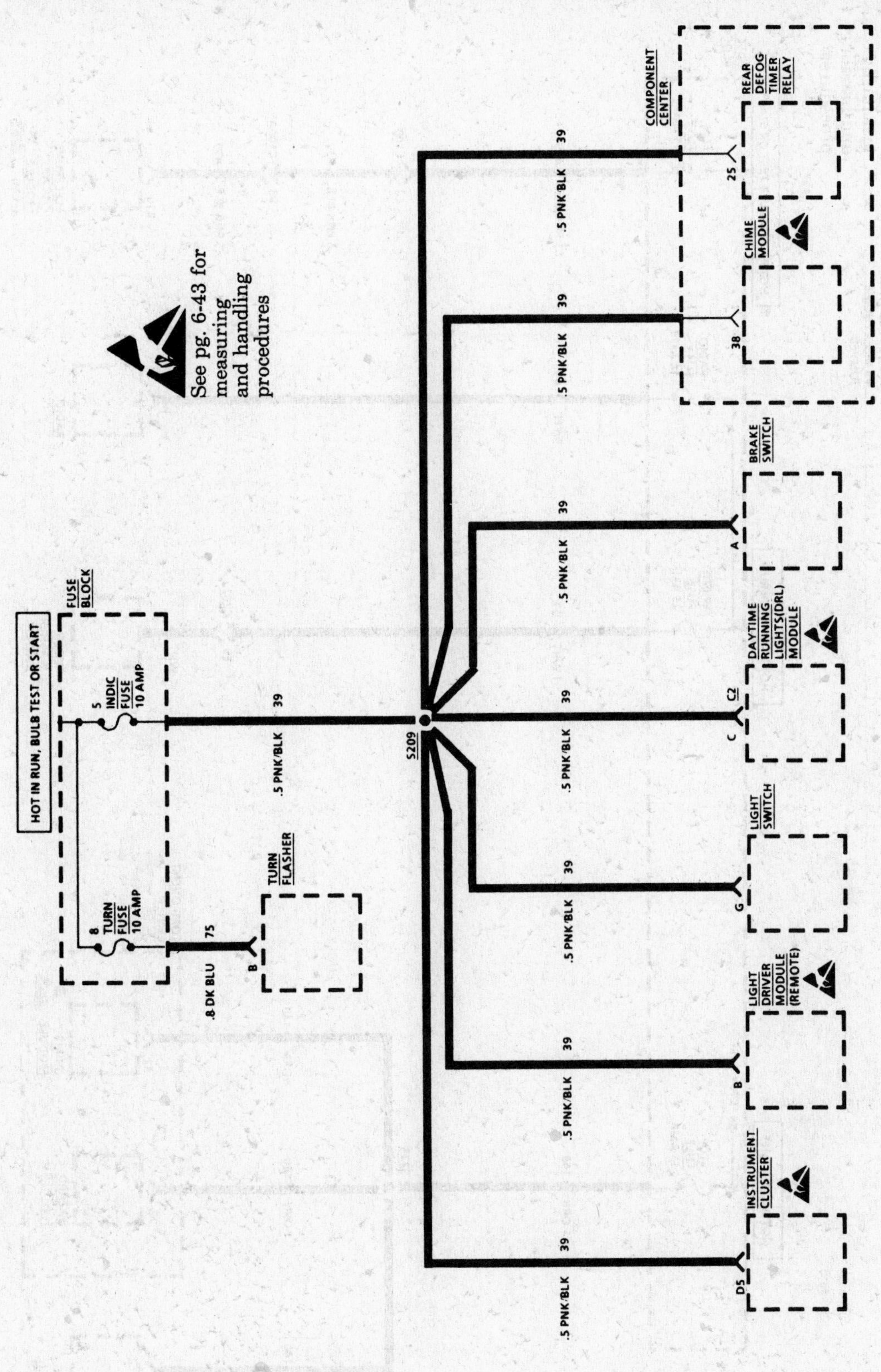

Fuse block details—Grand Prix shown

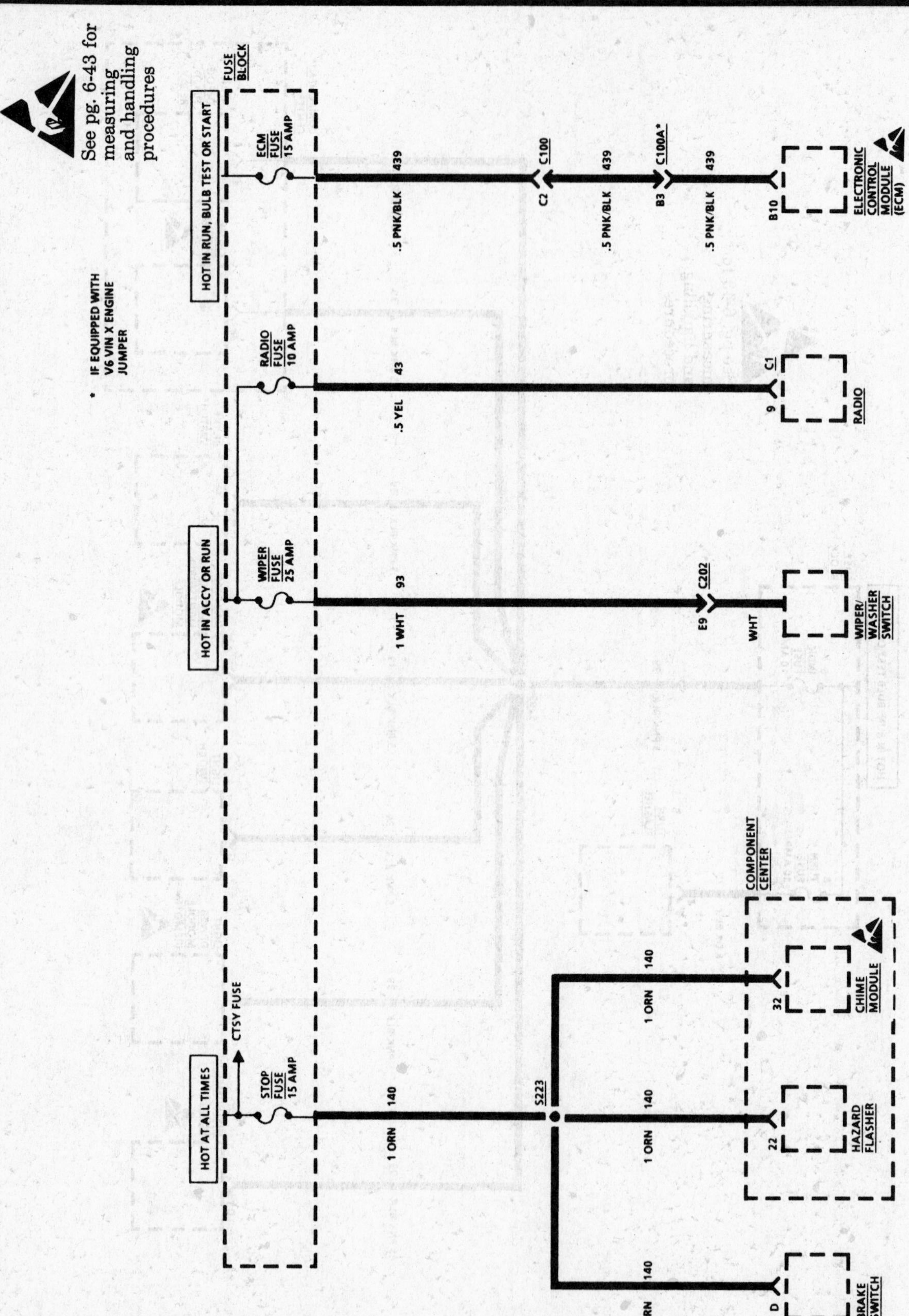

Fuse block details—Lumina shown

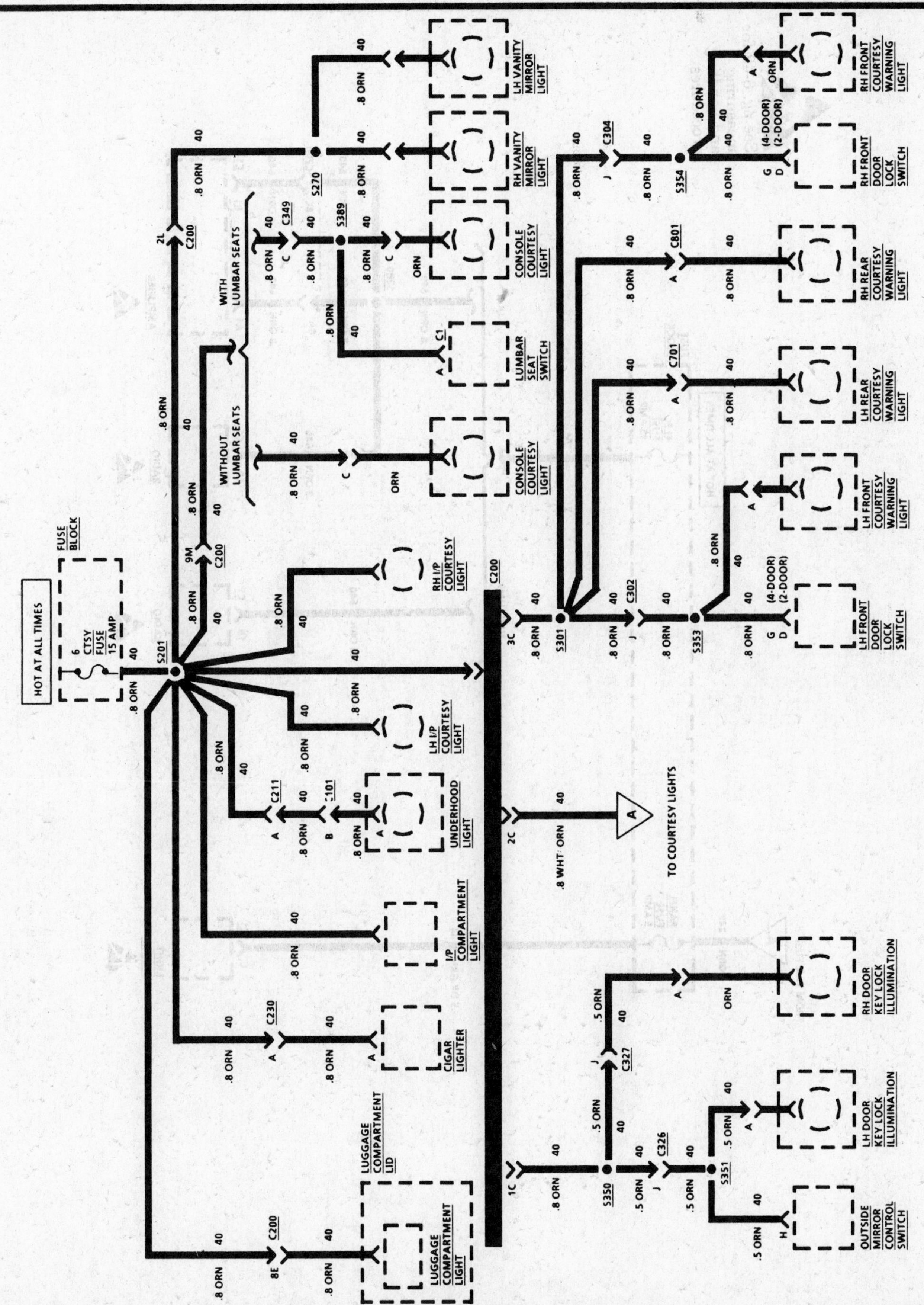

Fuse block details—Grand Prix shown

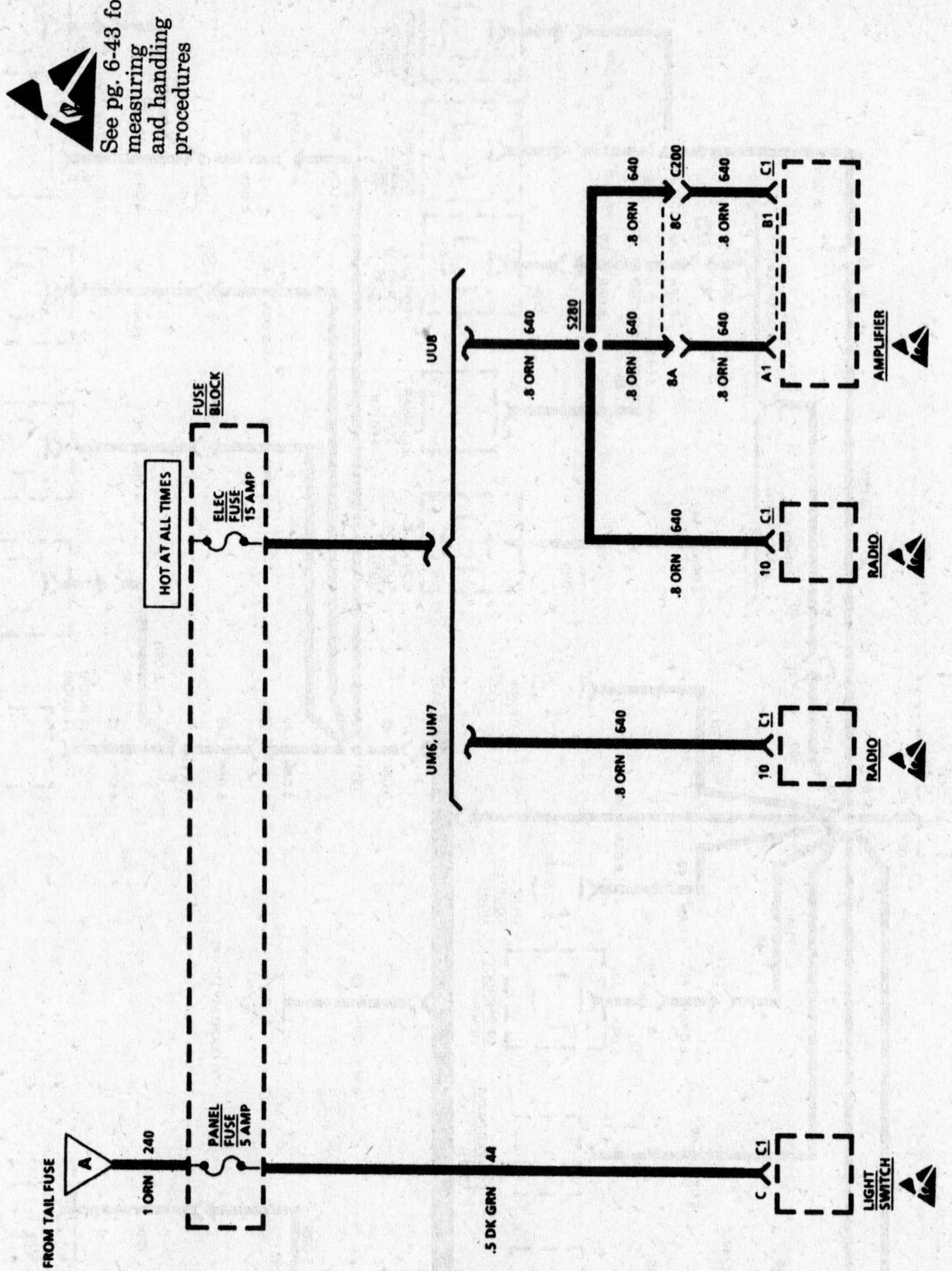

Fuse block details—Lumina shown

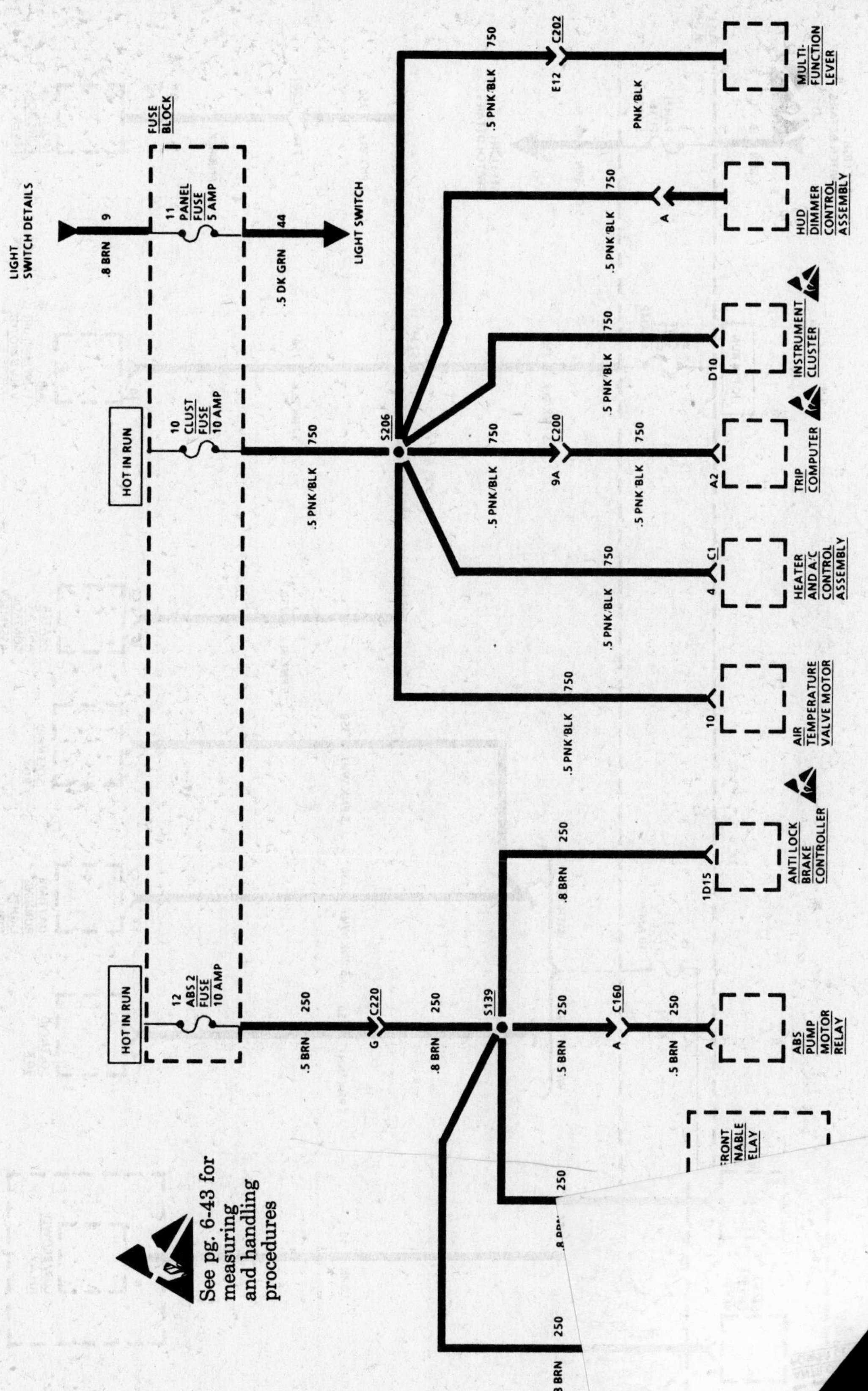

Fuse block details—Grand Prix shown

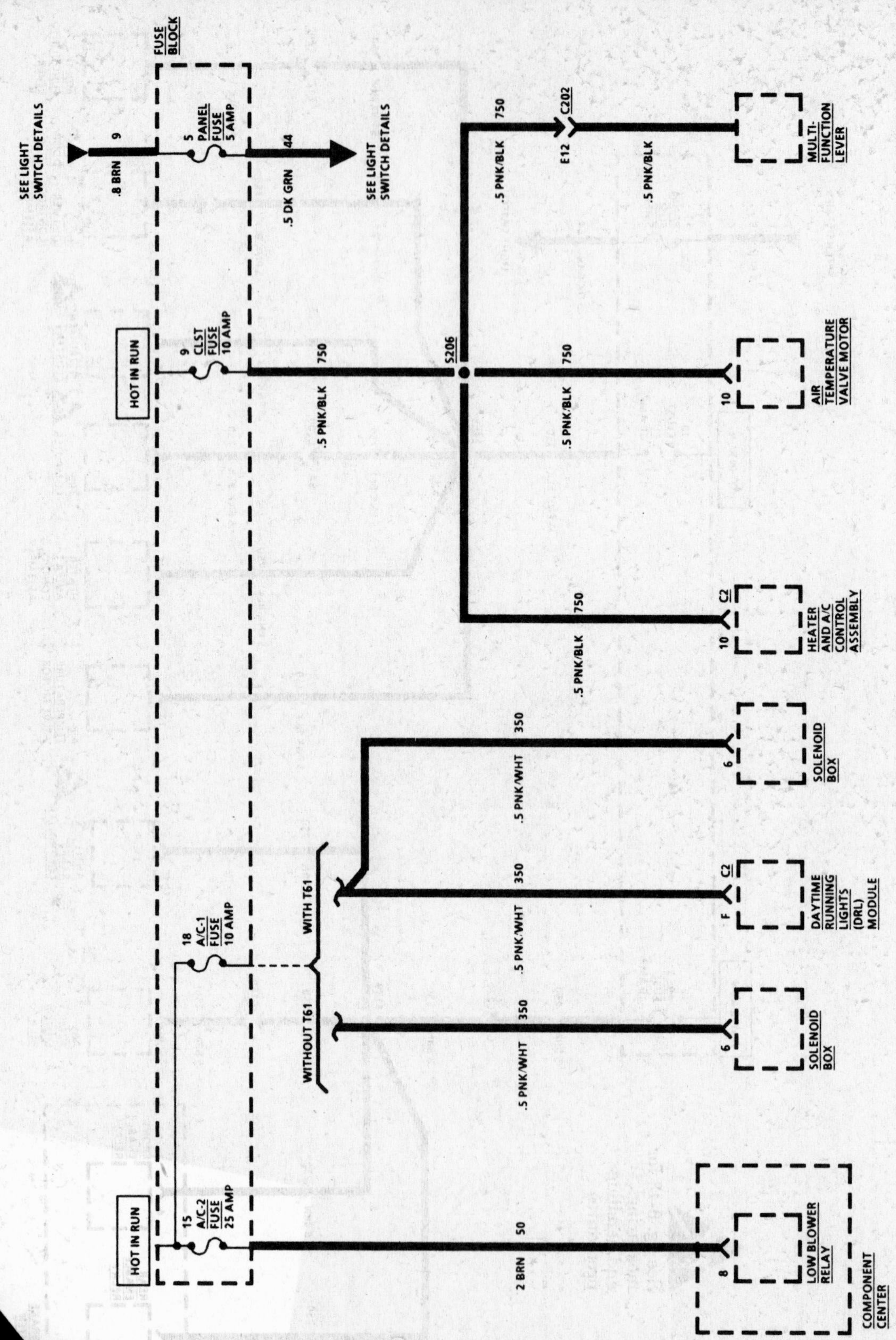

Fuse block details—Lumina shown

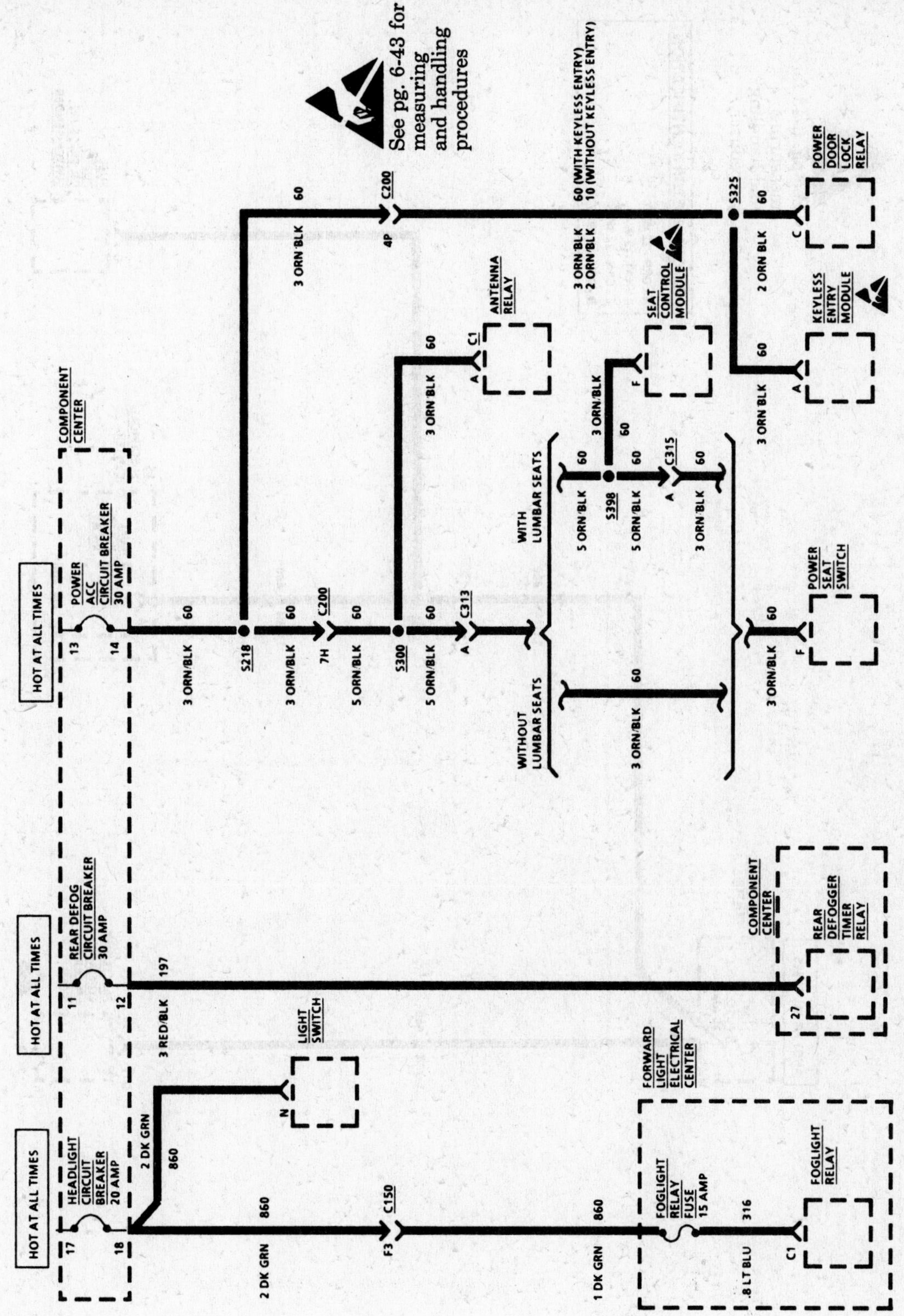

Component center—Grand Prix shown

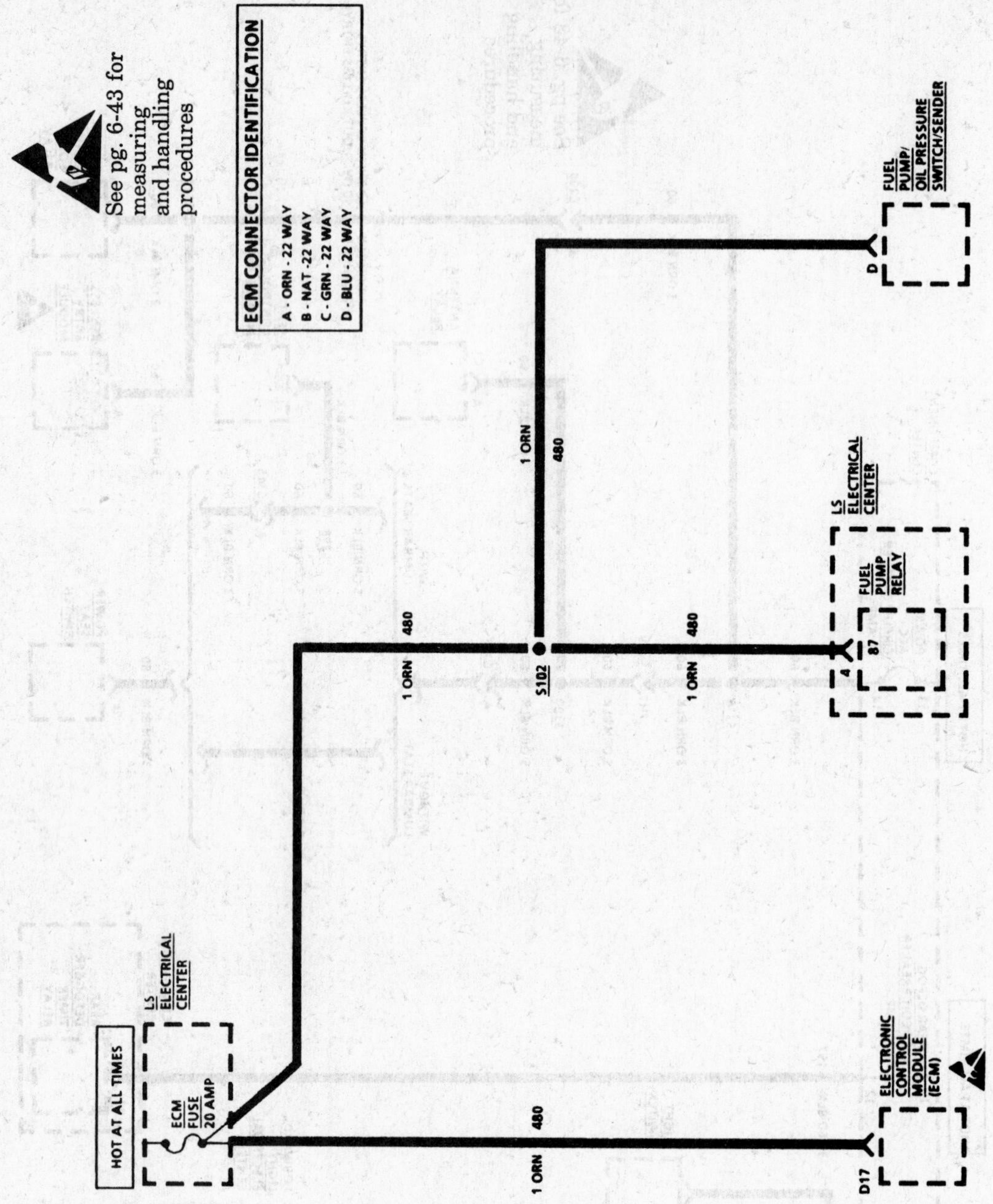

Left side electrical center—Lumina shown

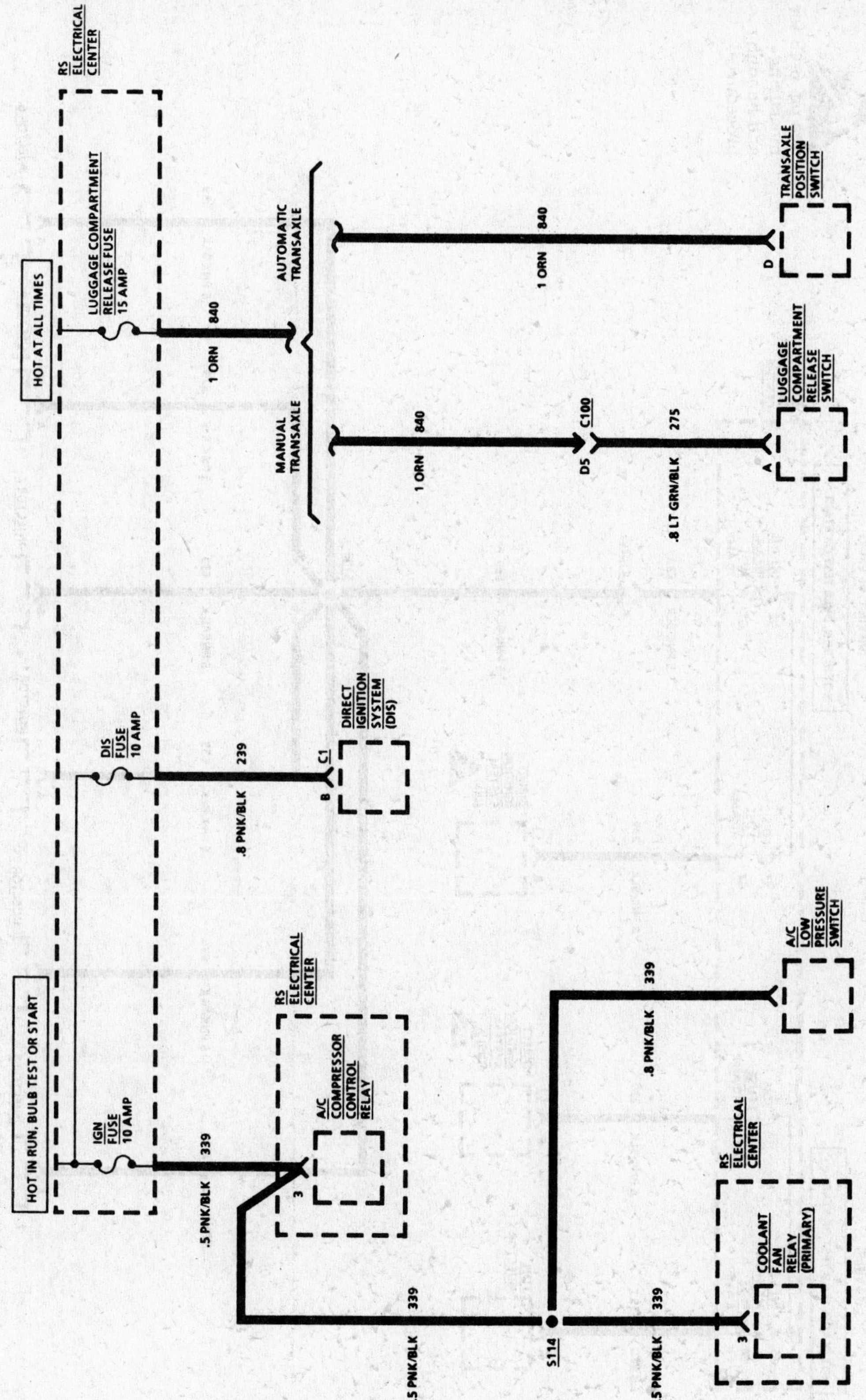

Right side electrical center—Lumina shown

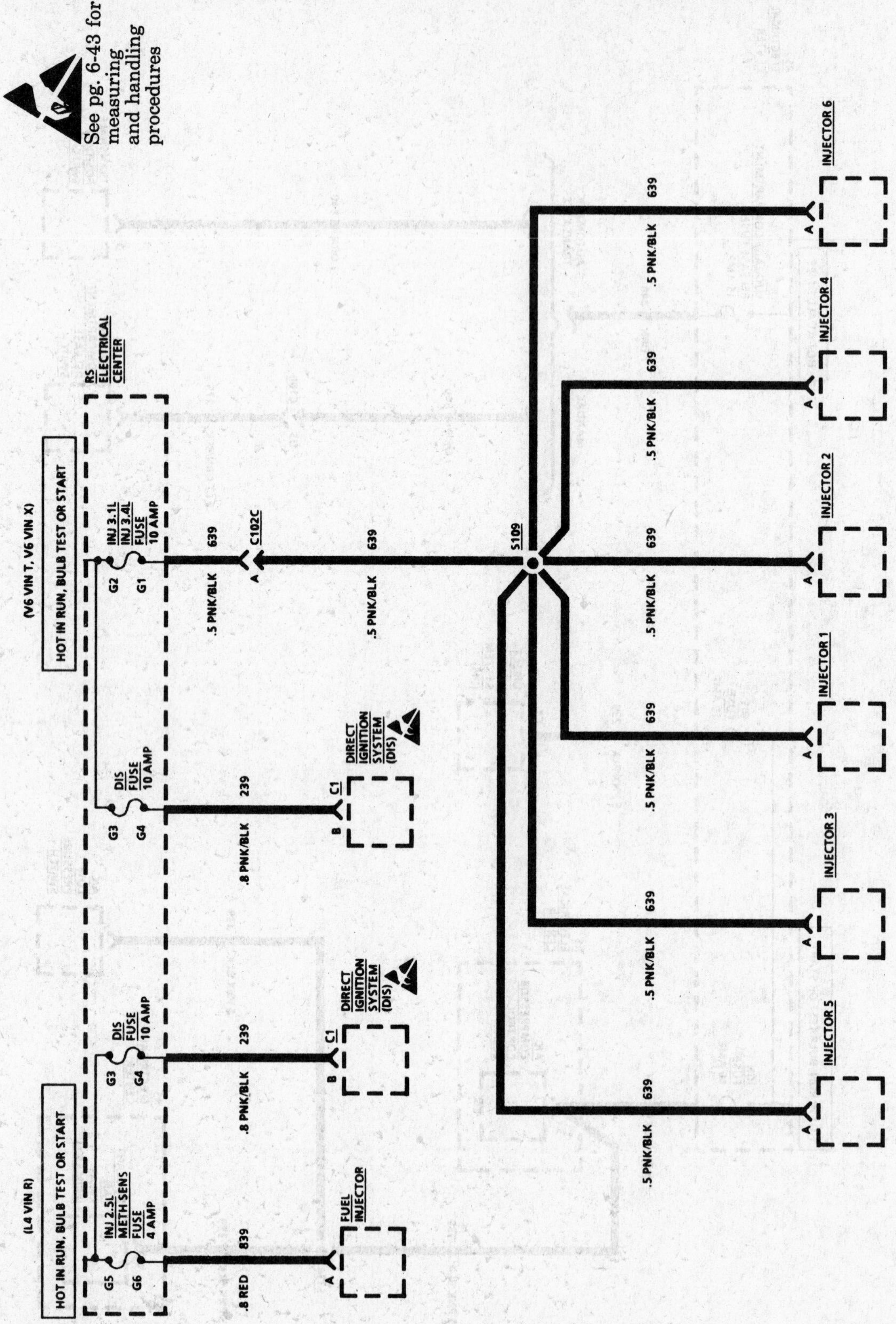

Right side electrical center—Lumina shown

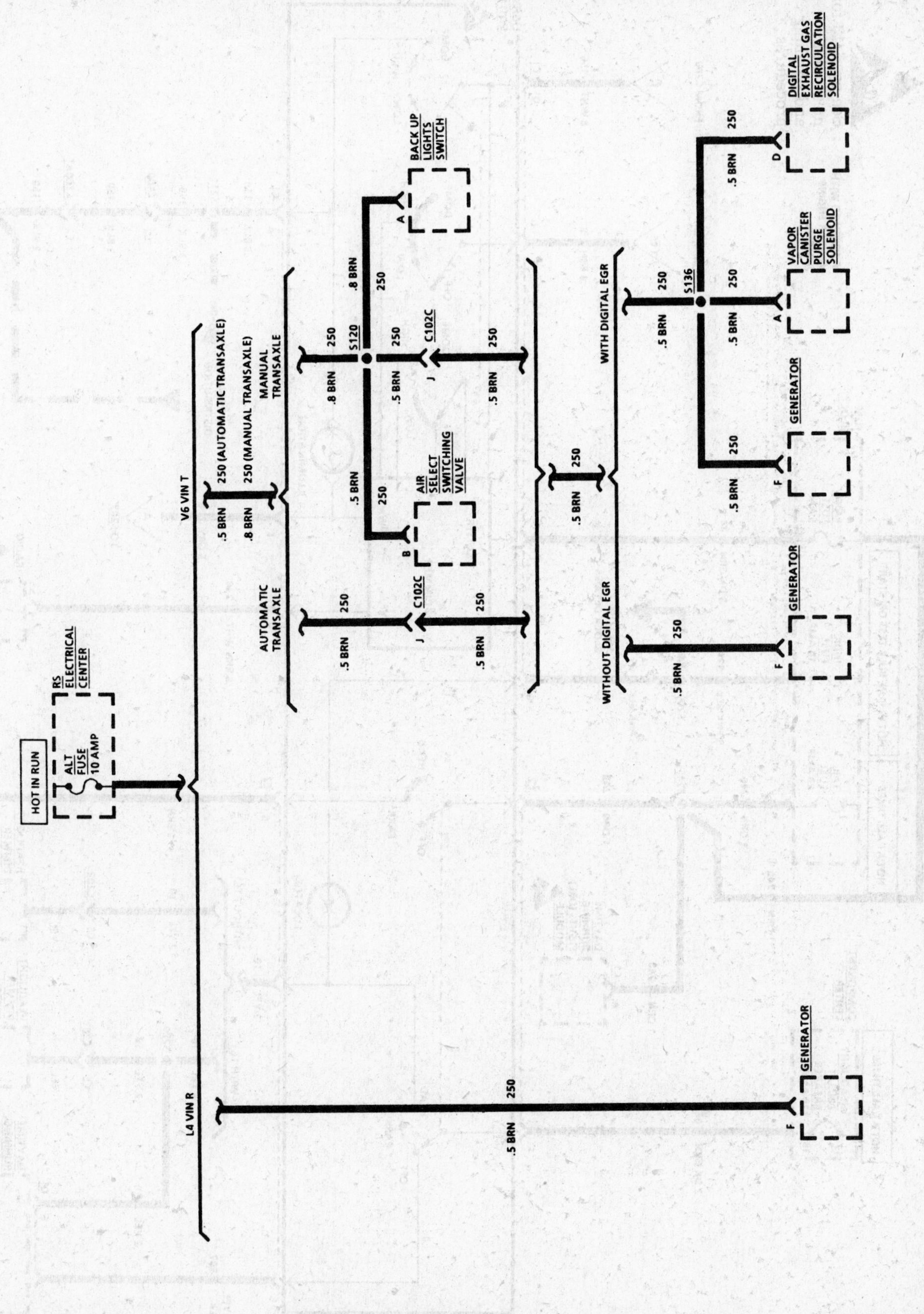

Right side electrical center—Lumina shown

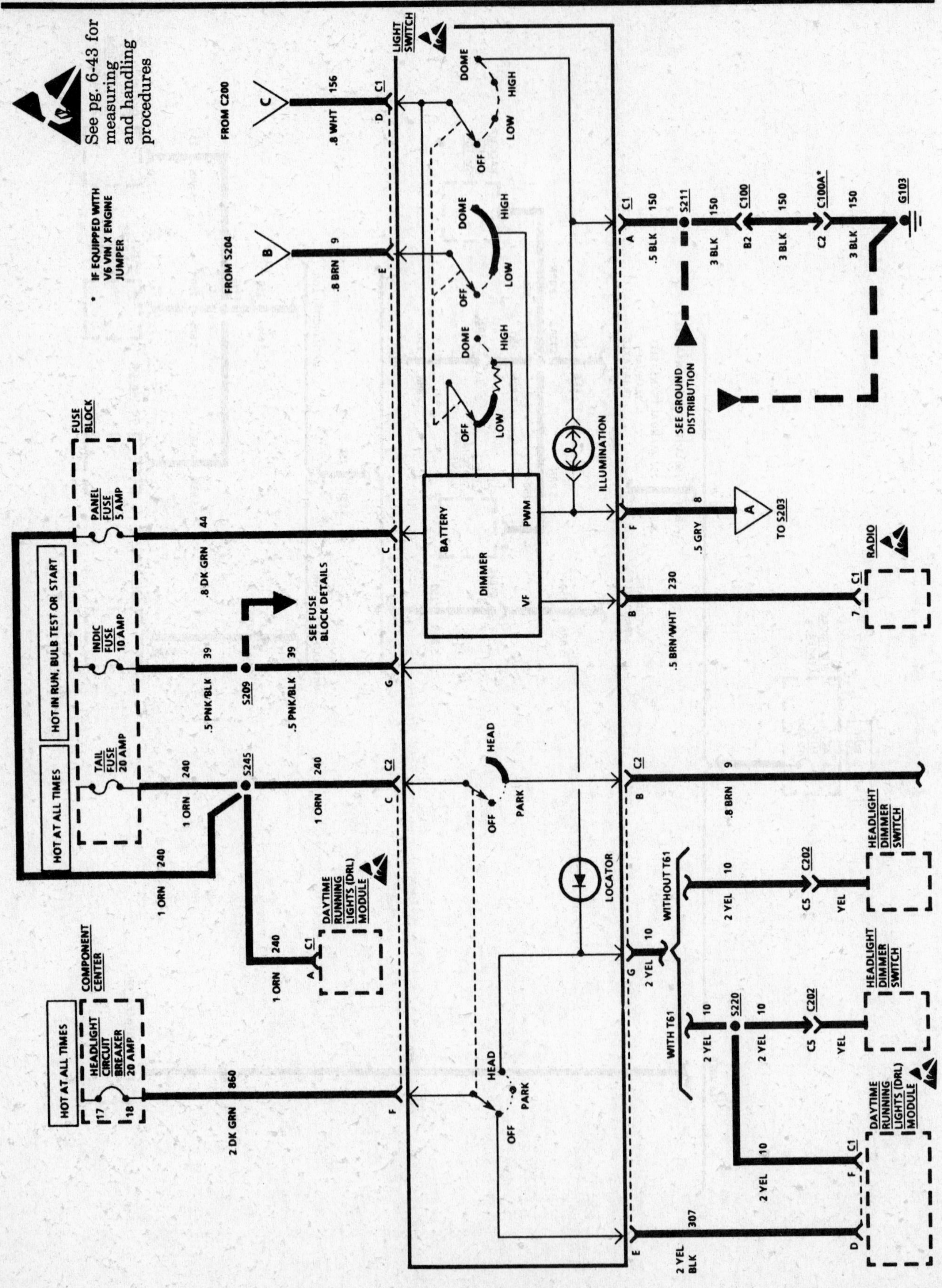

Light switch details—Lumina shown

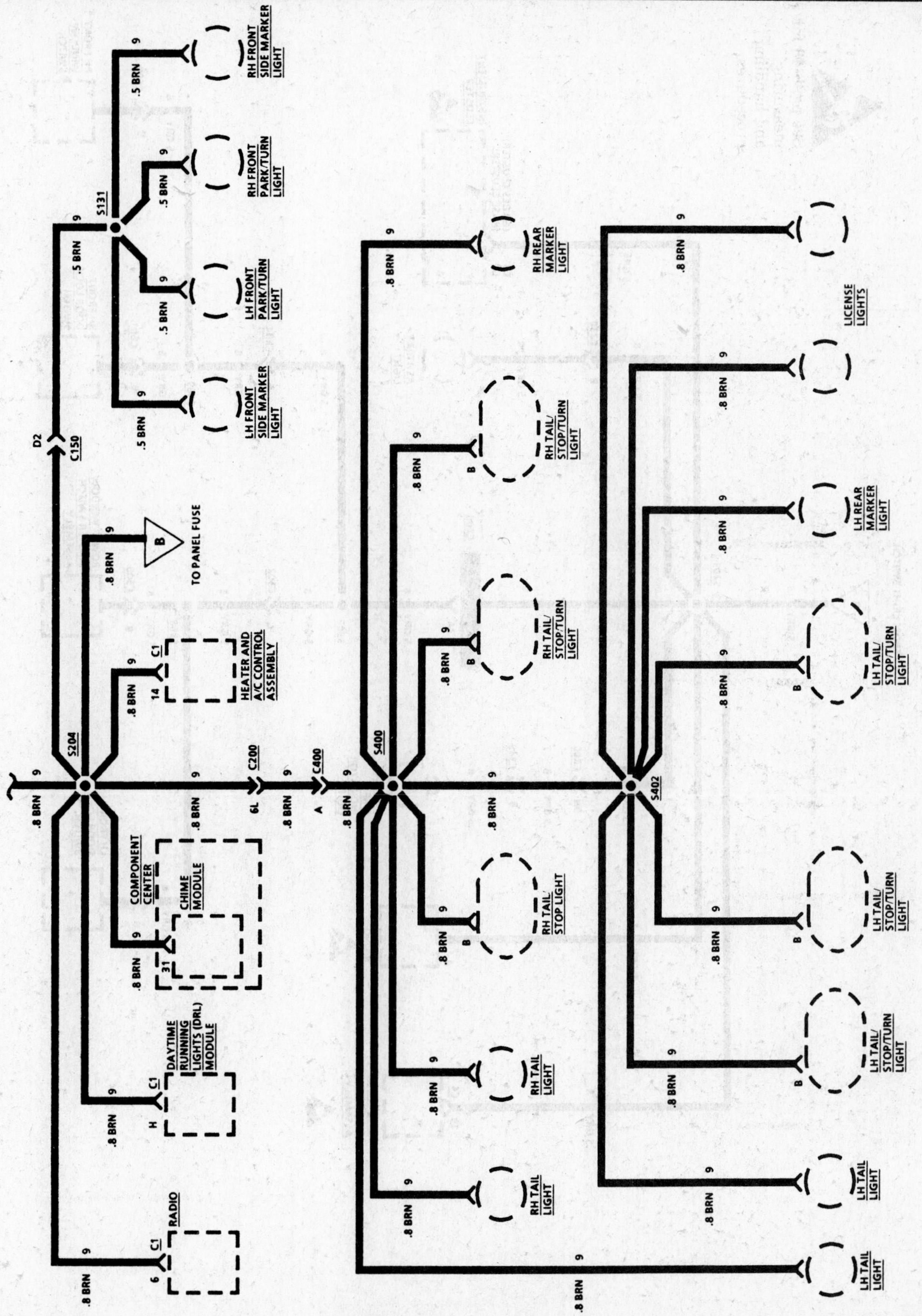

Light switch details—Lumina shown

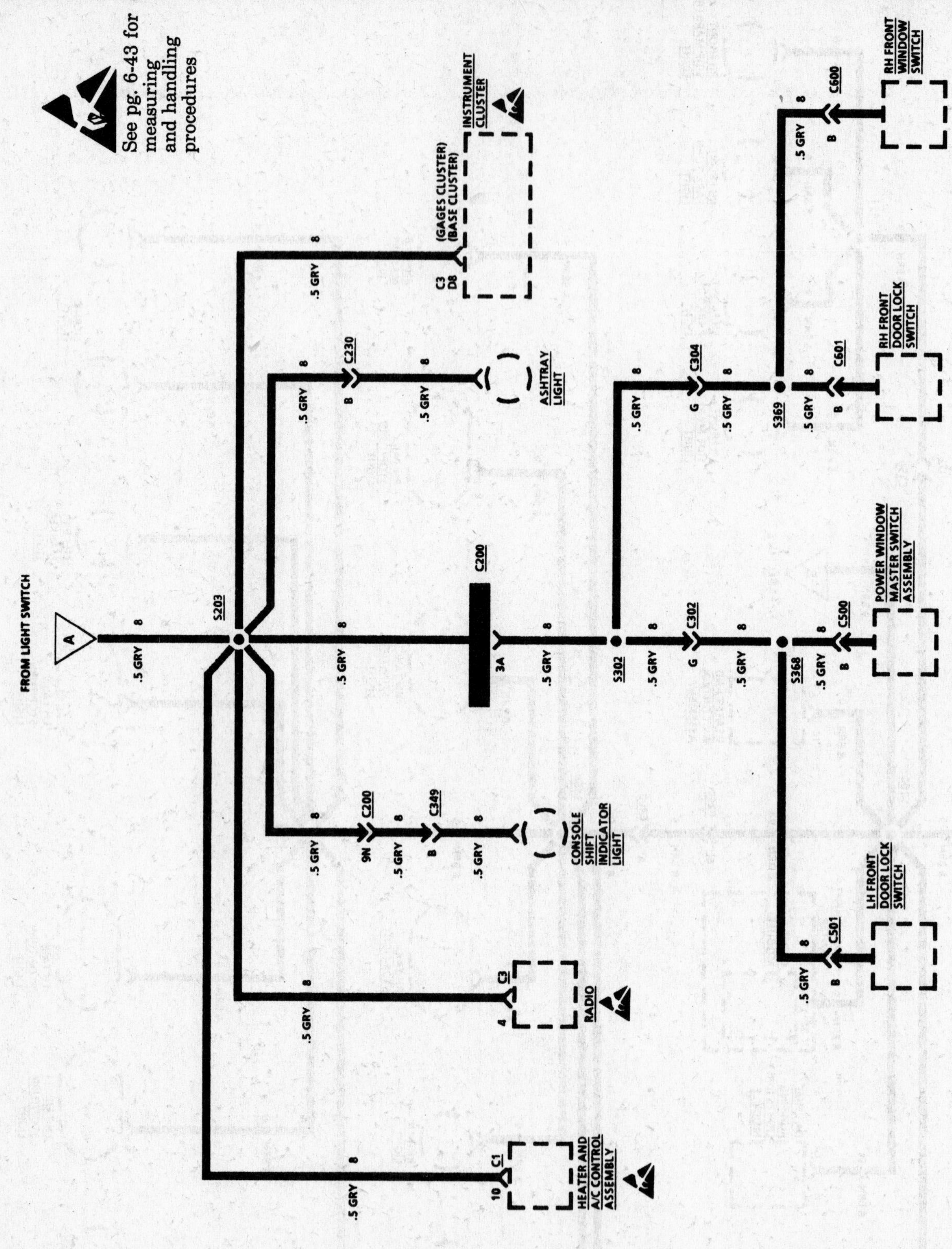

Light switch details—Lumina shown

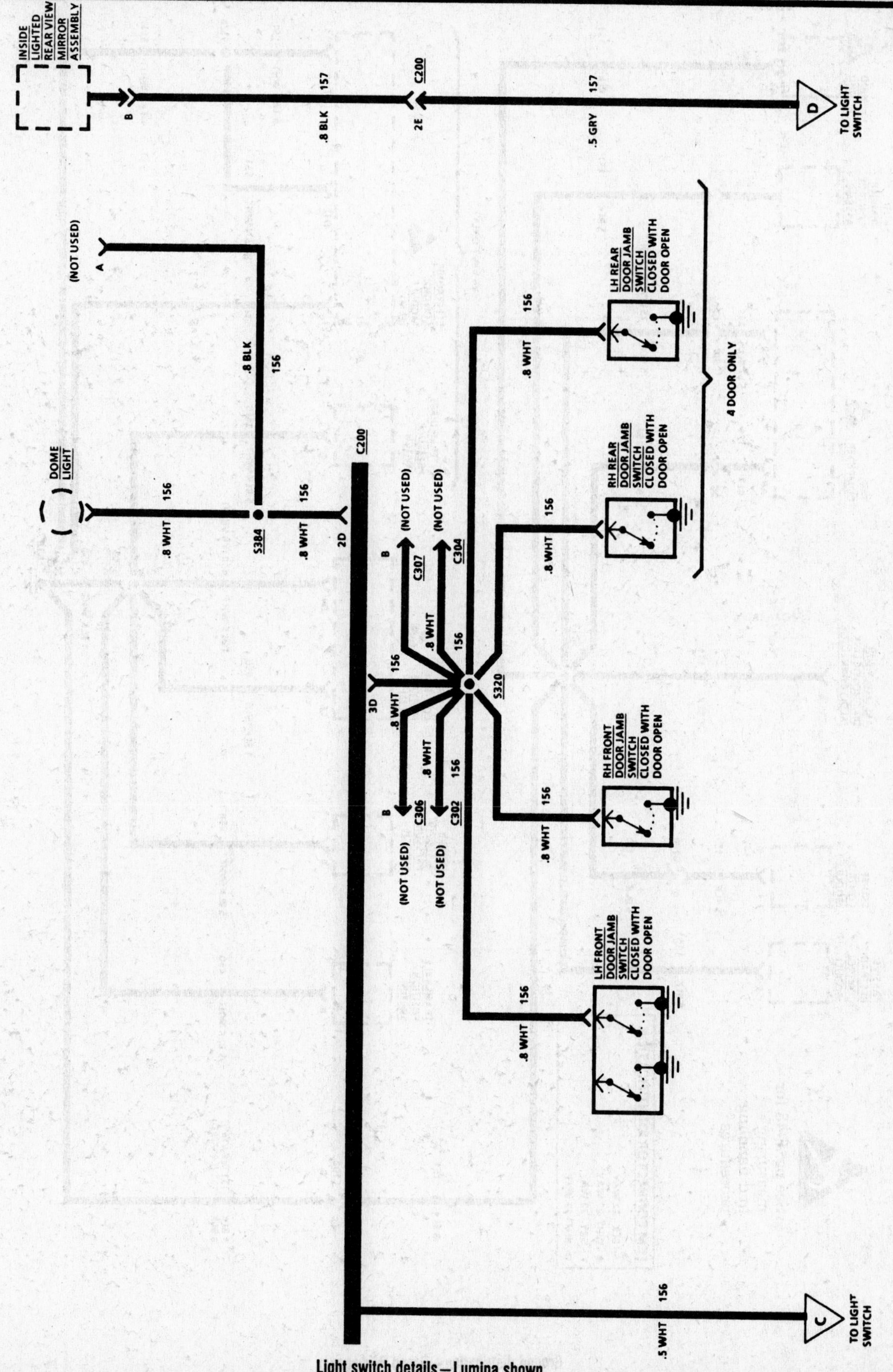

Light switch details—Lumina shown

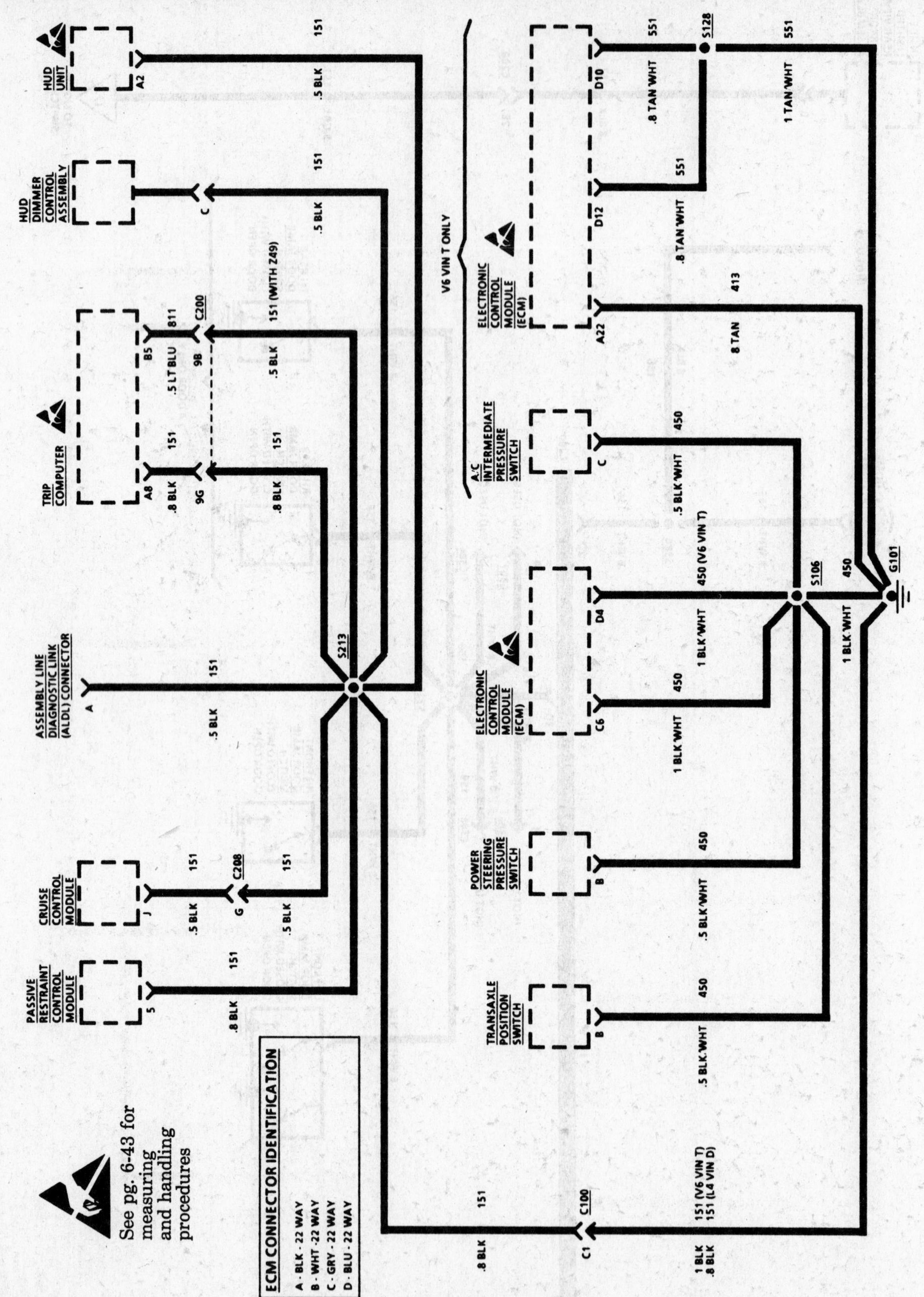
HUD UNIT
HUD DIMMER CONTROL ASSEMBLY
TRIP COMPUTER
ASSEMBLY LINE DIAGNOSTIC LINK (ALDL) CONNECTOR
CRUISE CONTROL MODULE
PASSIVE RESTRAINT CONTROL MODULE
ELECTRONIC CONTROL MODULE (ECM)
A/C INTERMEDIATE PRESSURE SWITCH
POWER STEERING PRESSURE SWITCH
TRANSAXLE POSITION SWITCH
V6 VIN T ONLY
S213
S106
S128
G101
C100
C200
C208
See pg. 6-43 for measuring and handling procedures
ECM CONNECTOR IDENTIFICATION
A - BLK - 22 WAY
B - WHT - 22 WAY
C - GRY - 22 WAY
D - BLU - 22 WAY

Ground distribution—Grand Prix shown

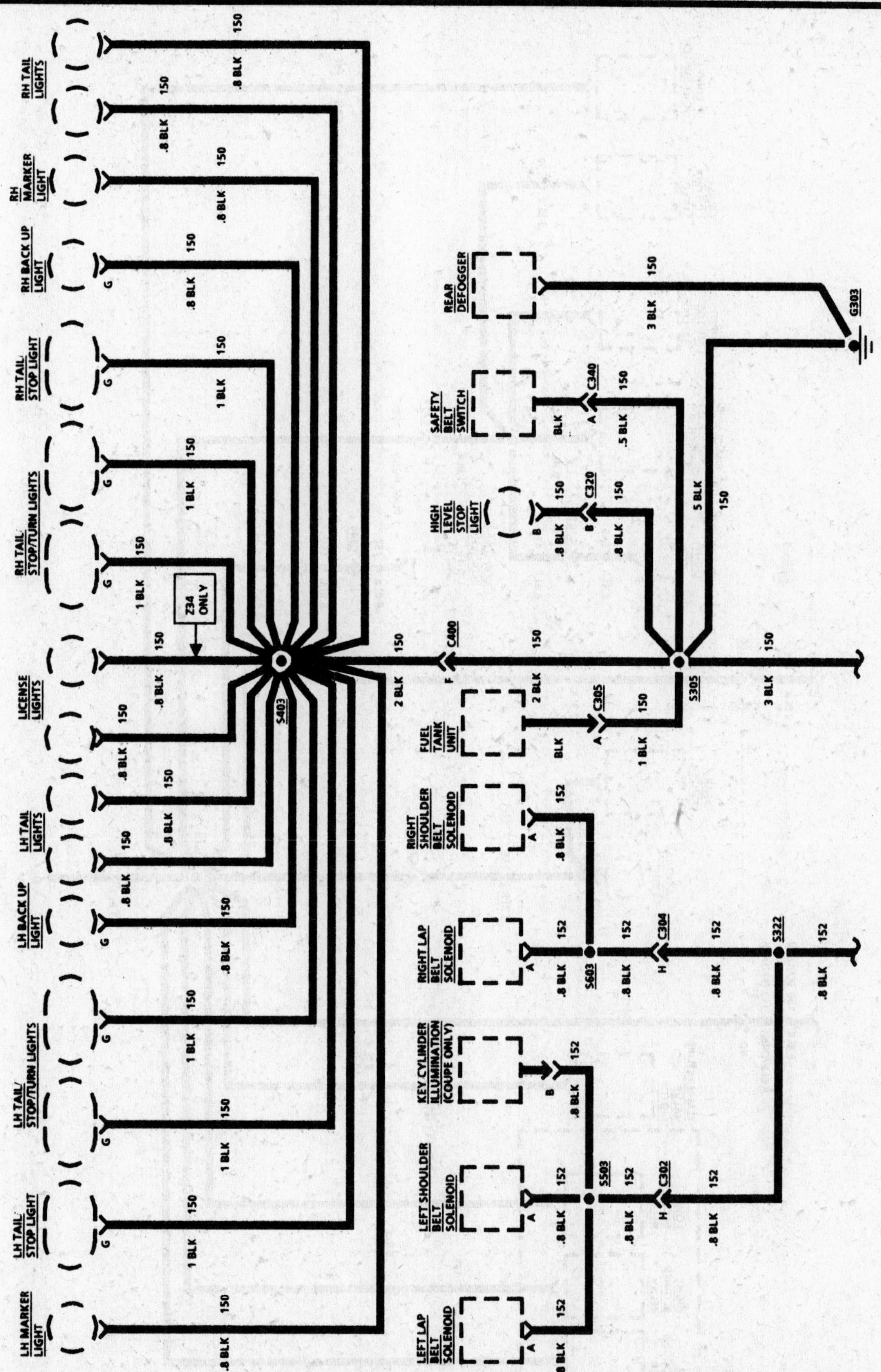

Ground distribution—Lumina shown

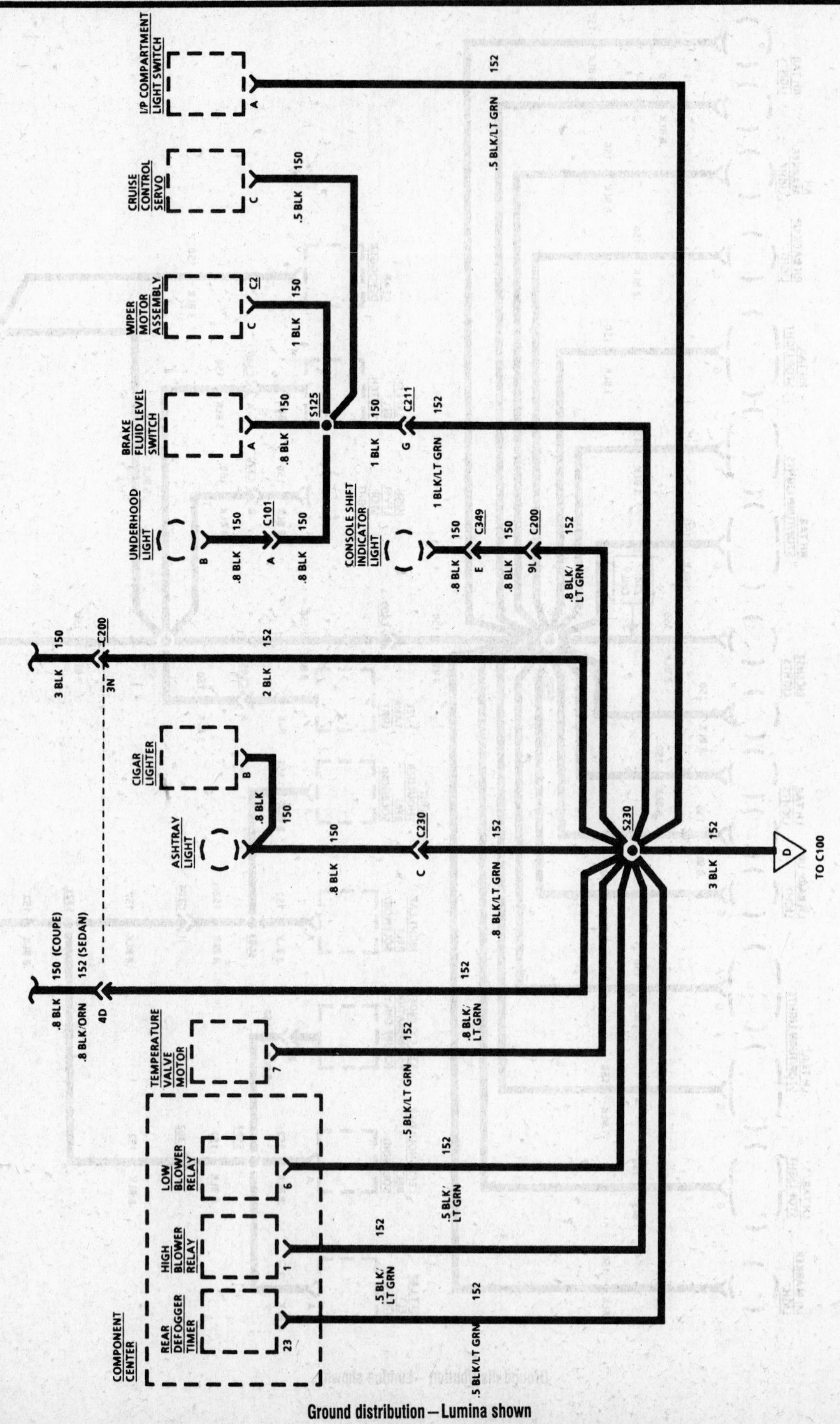

Ground distribution—Lumina shown

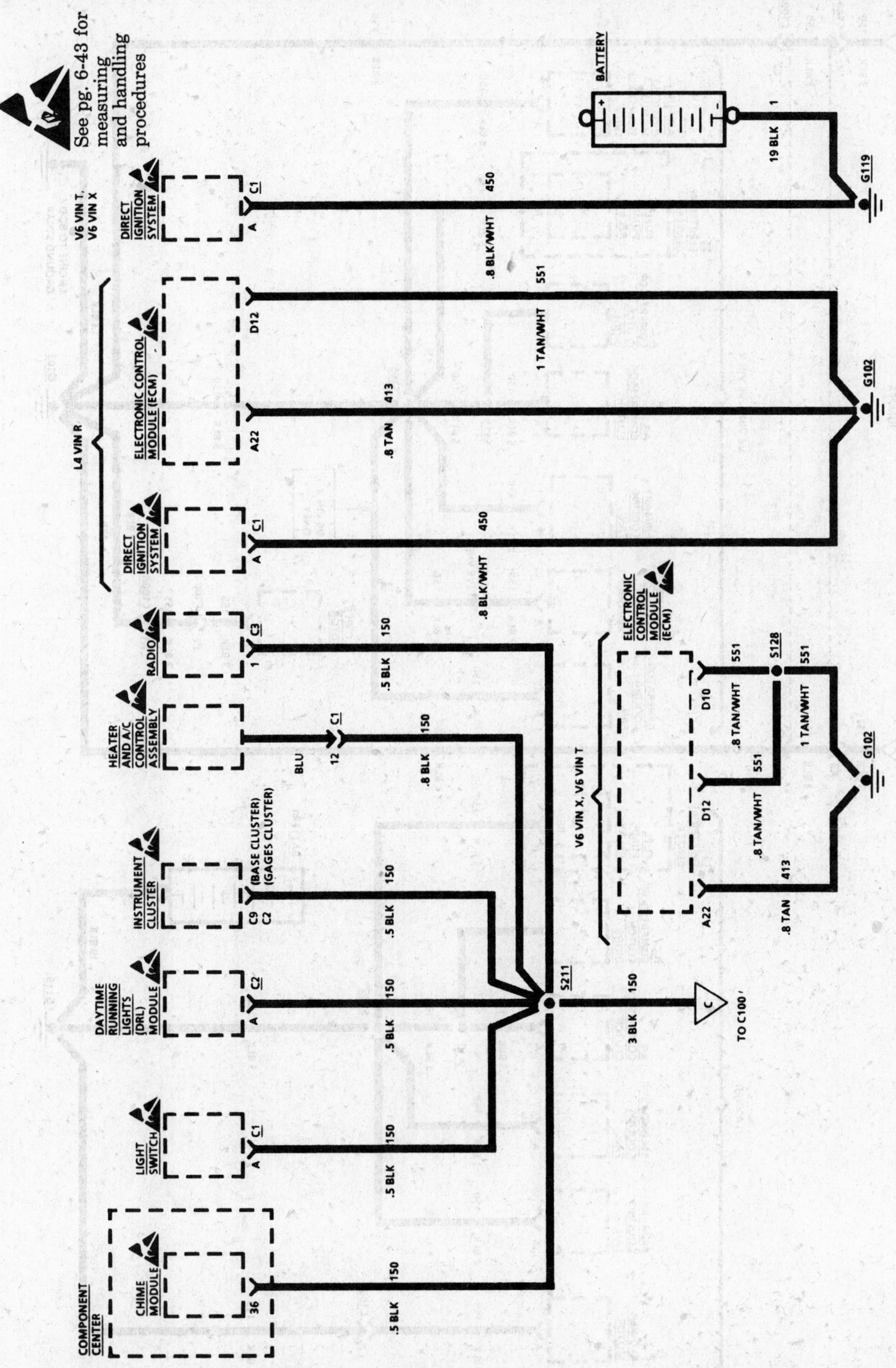

Ground distribution—Lumina shown

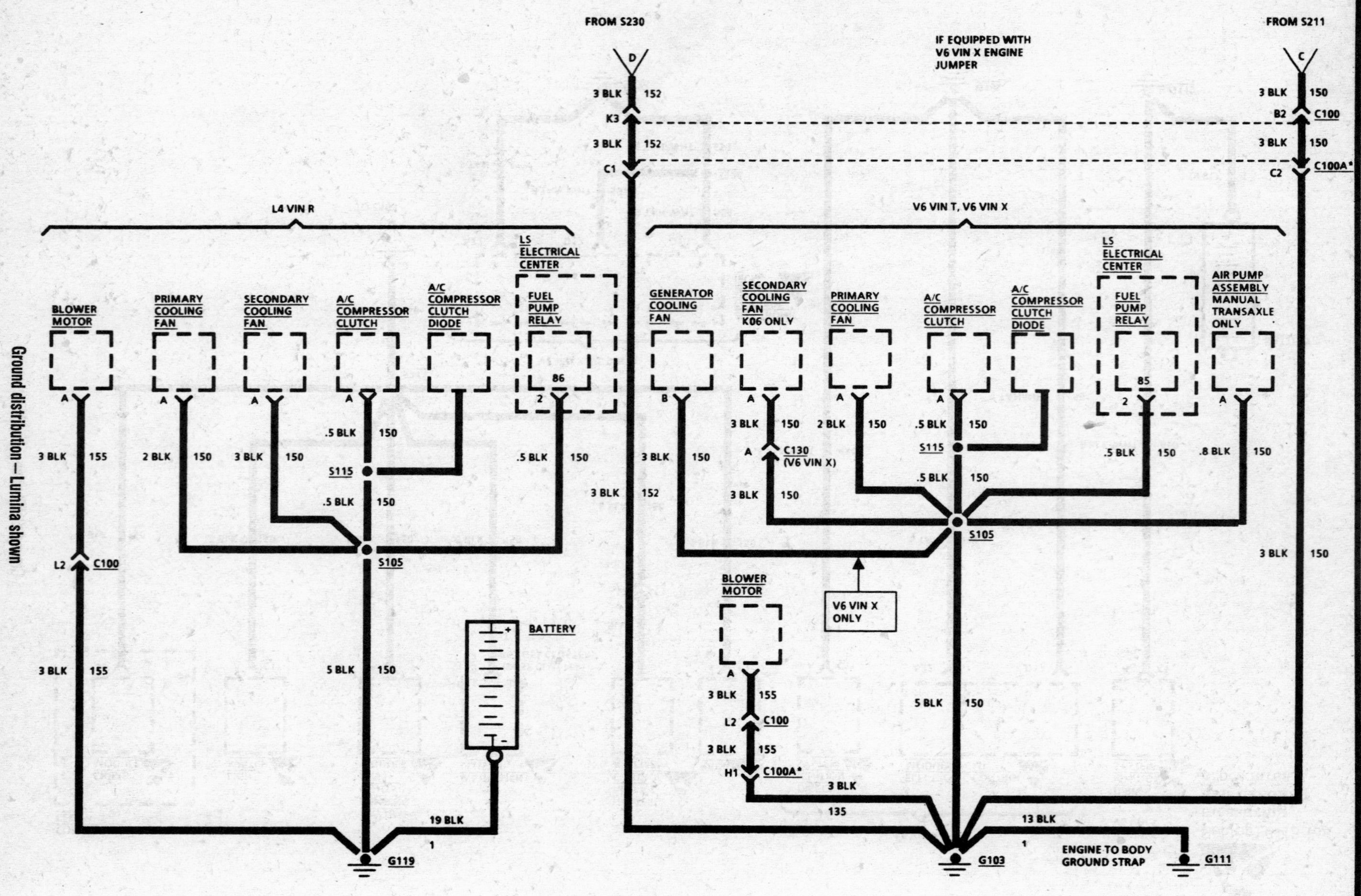

Ground distribution—Lumina shown

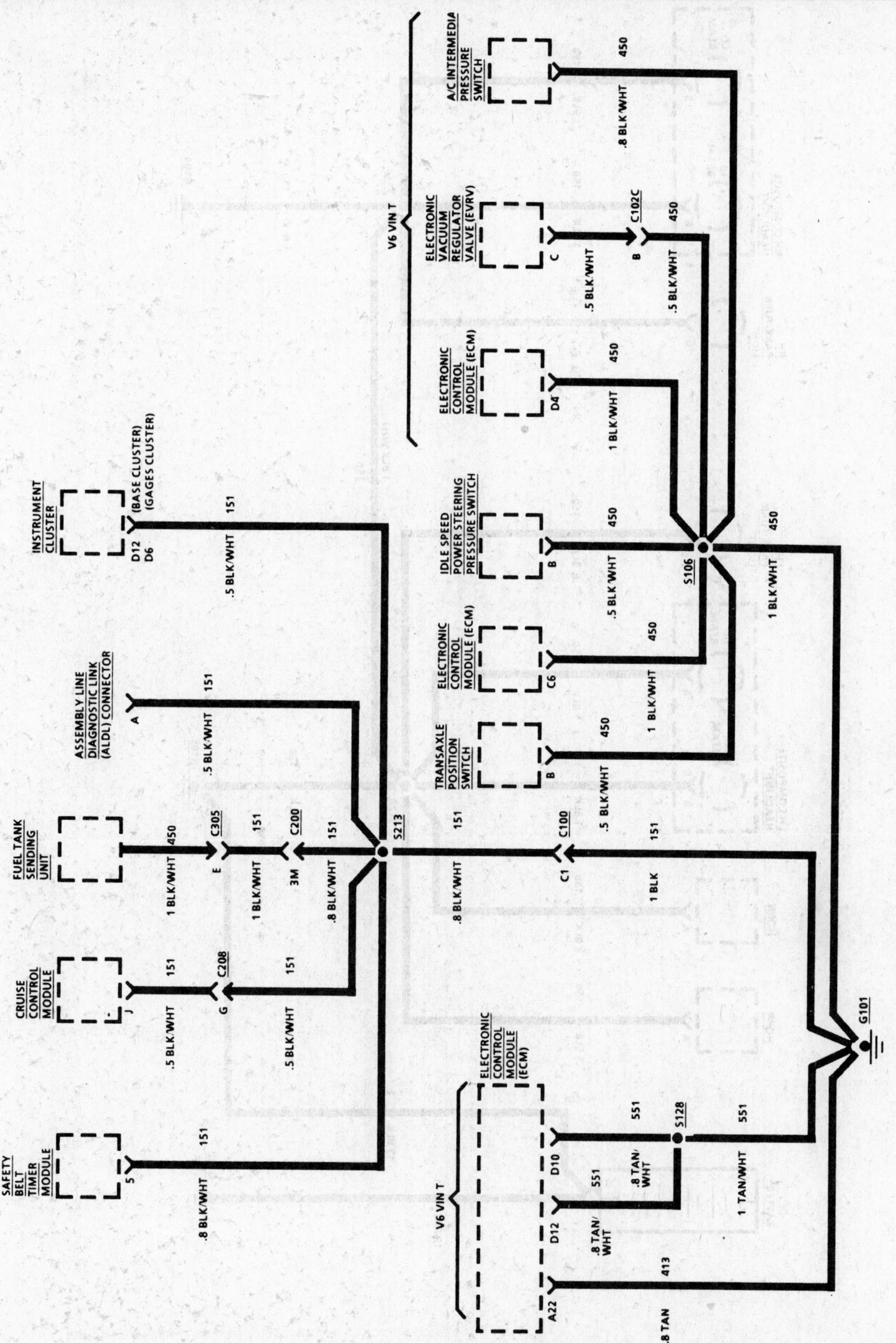

Ground distribution—Lumina shown

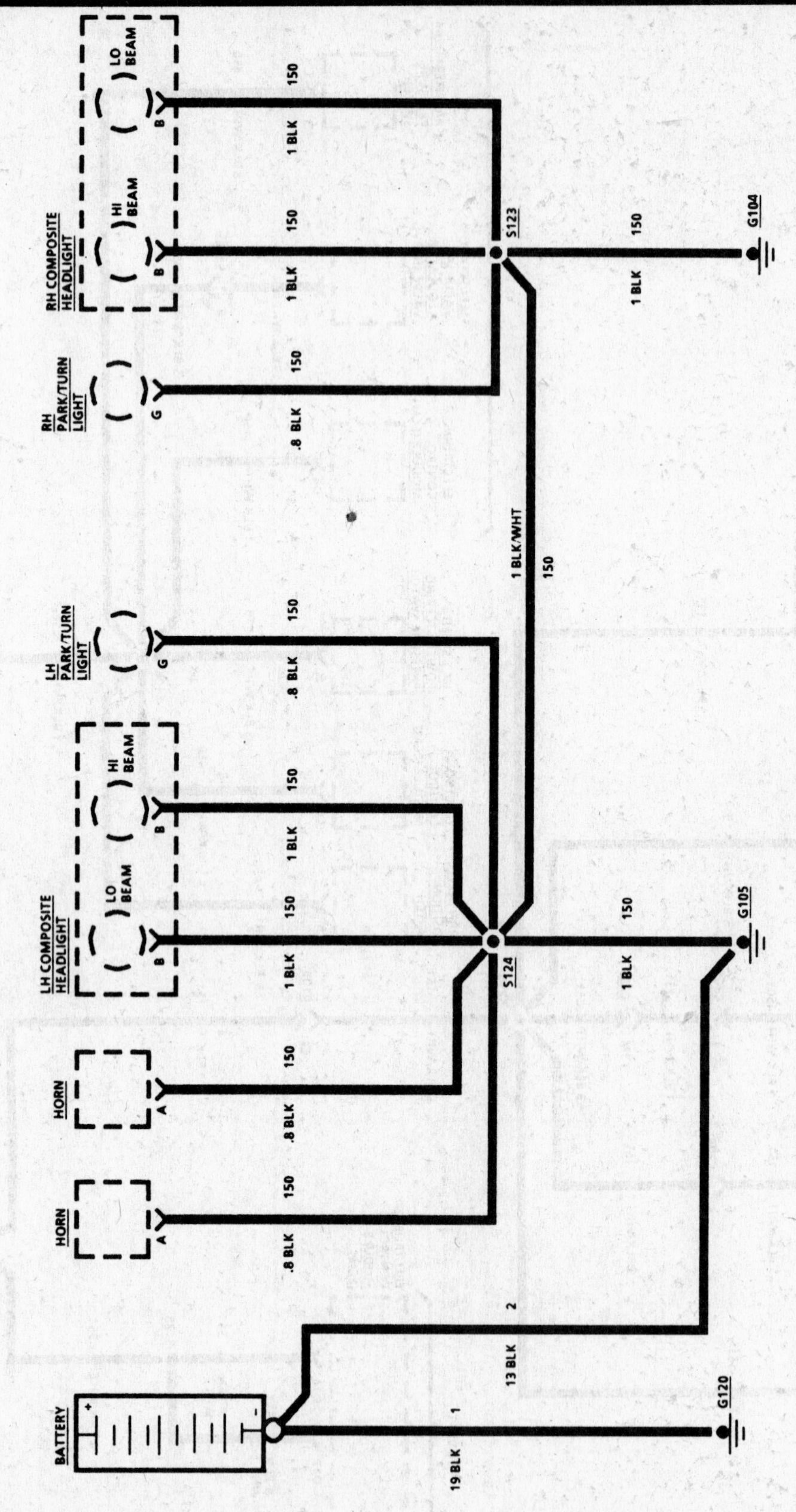

Ground distribution—Lumina shown

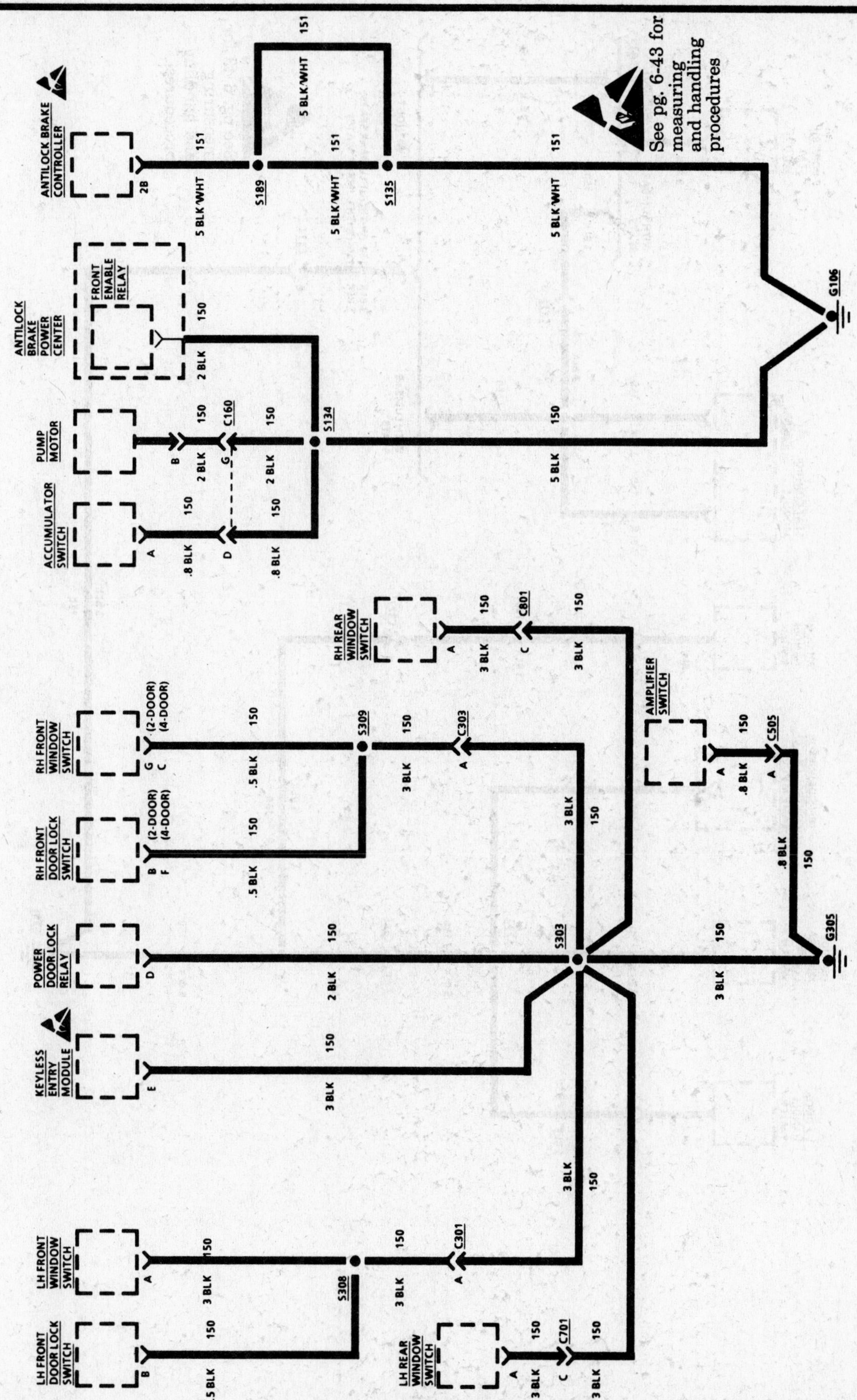

Ground distribution—Grand Prix shown

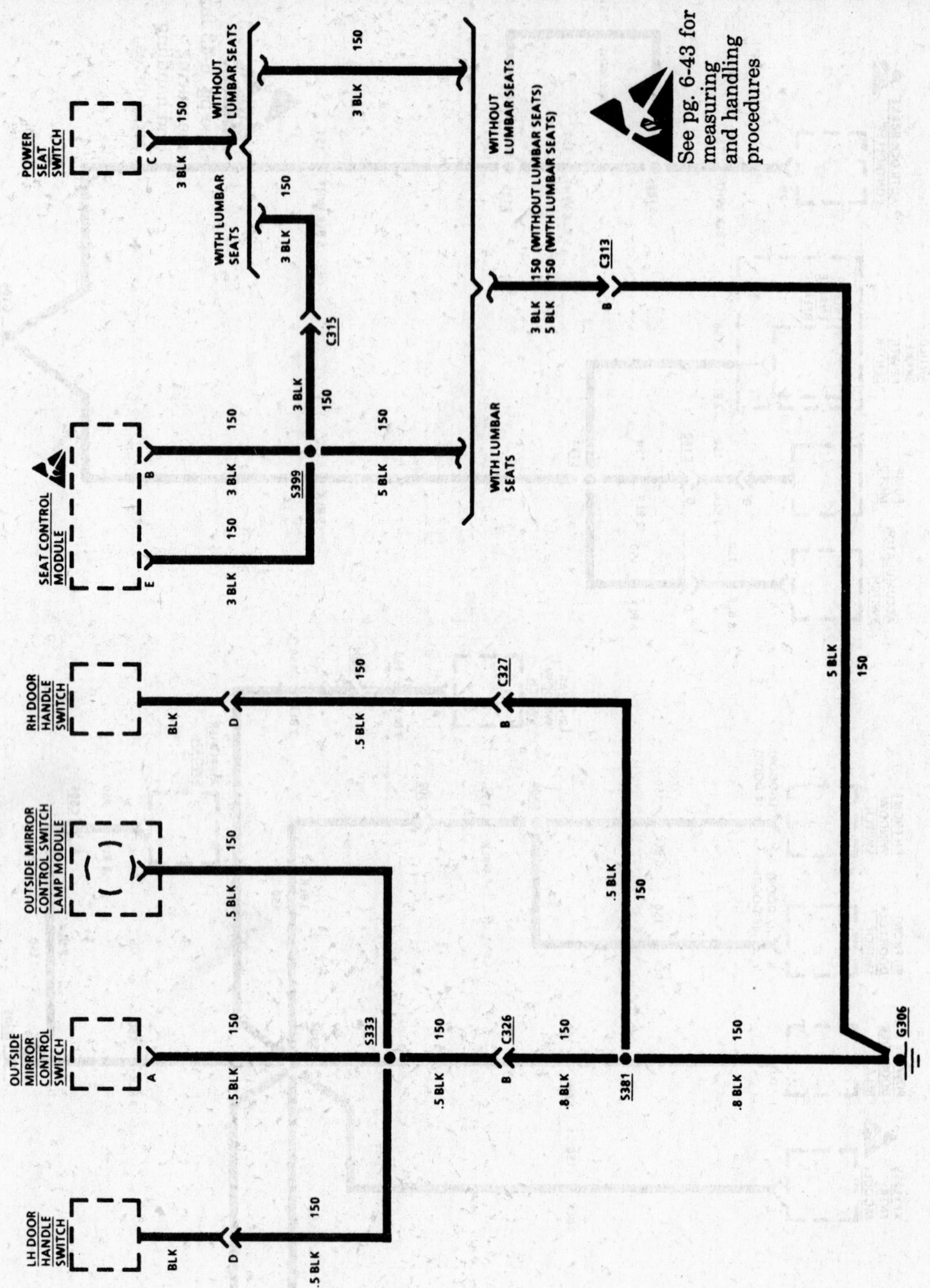

Ground distribution—Grand Prix shown

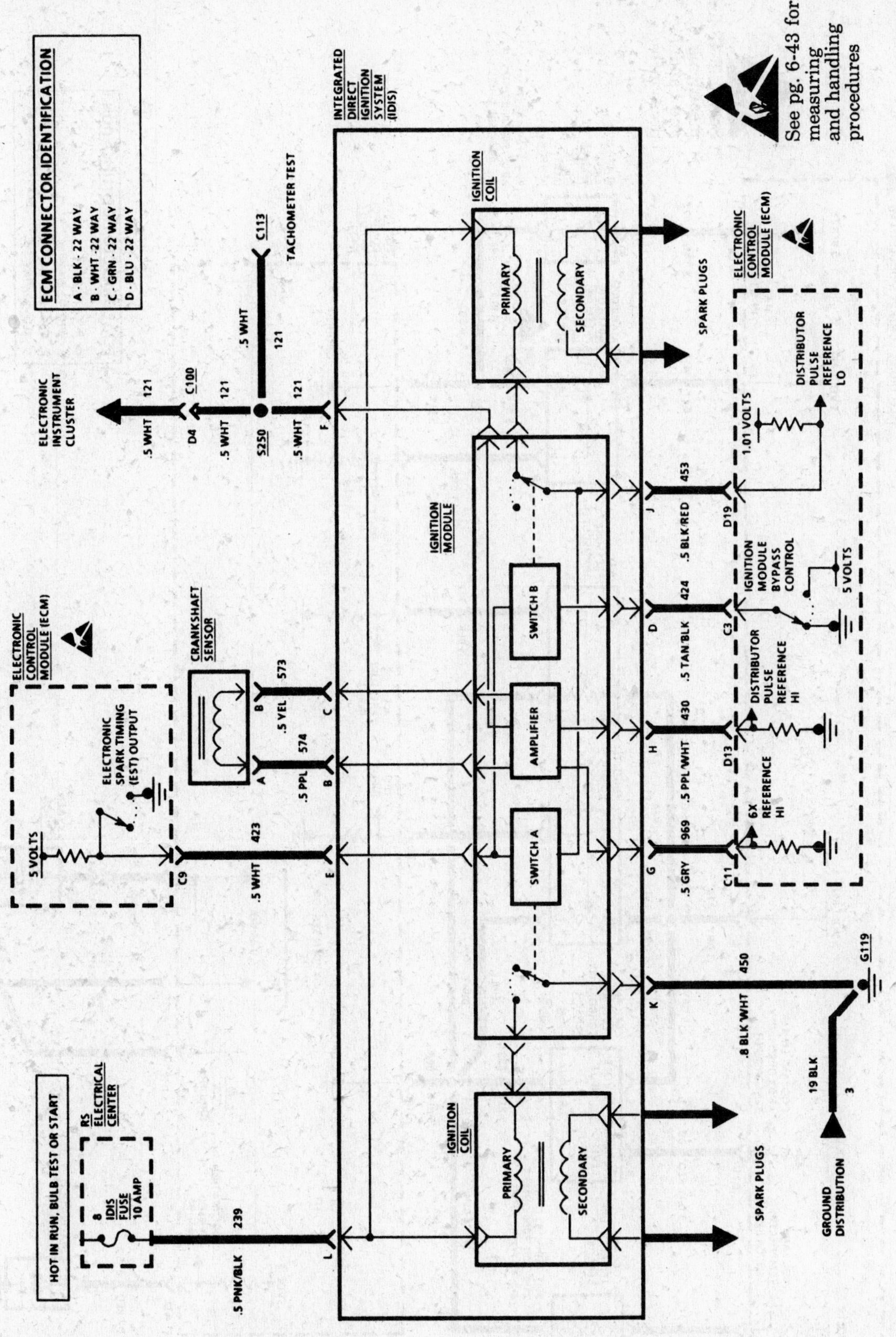

See pg. 6-43 for measuring and handling procedures

2.3L engine – Grand Prix shown

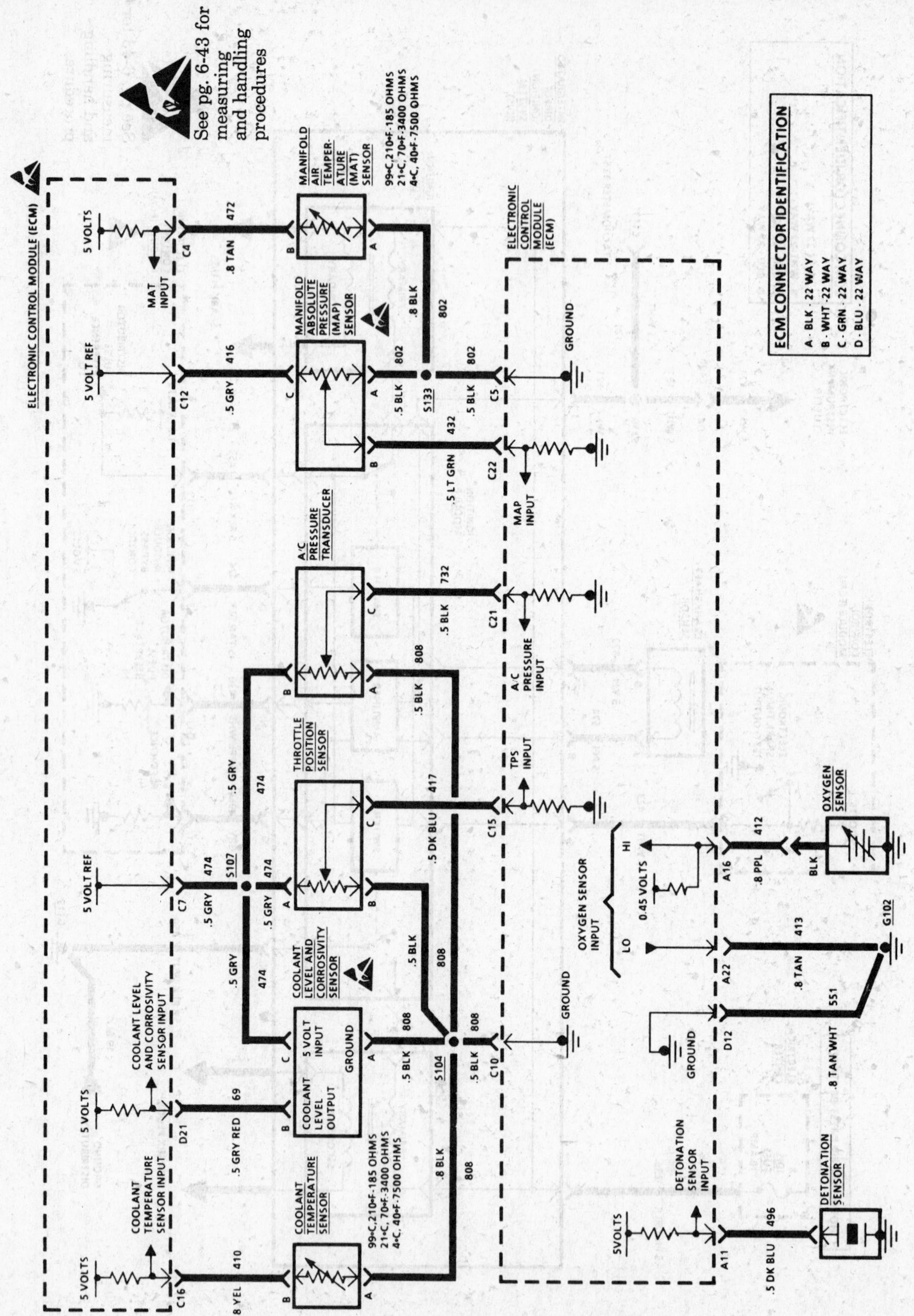

2.3L engine – Grand Prix shown

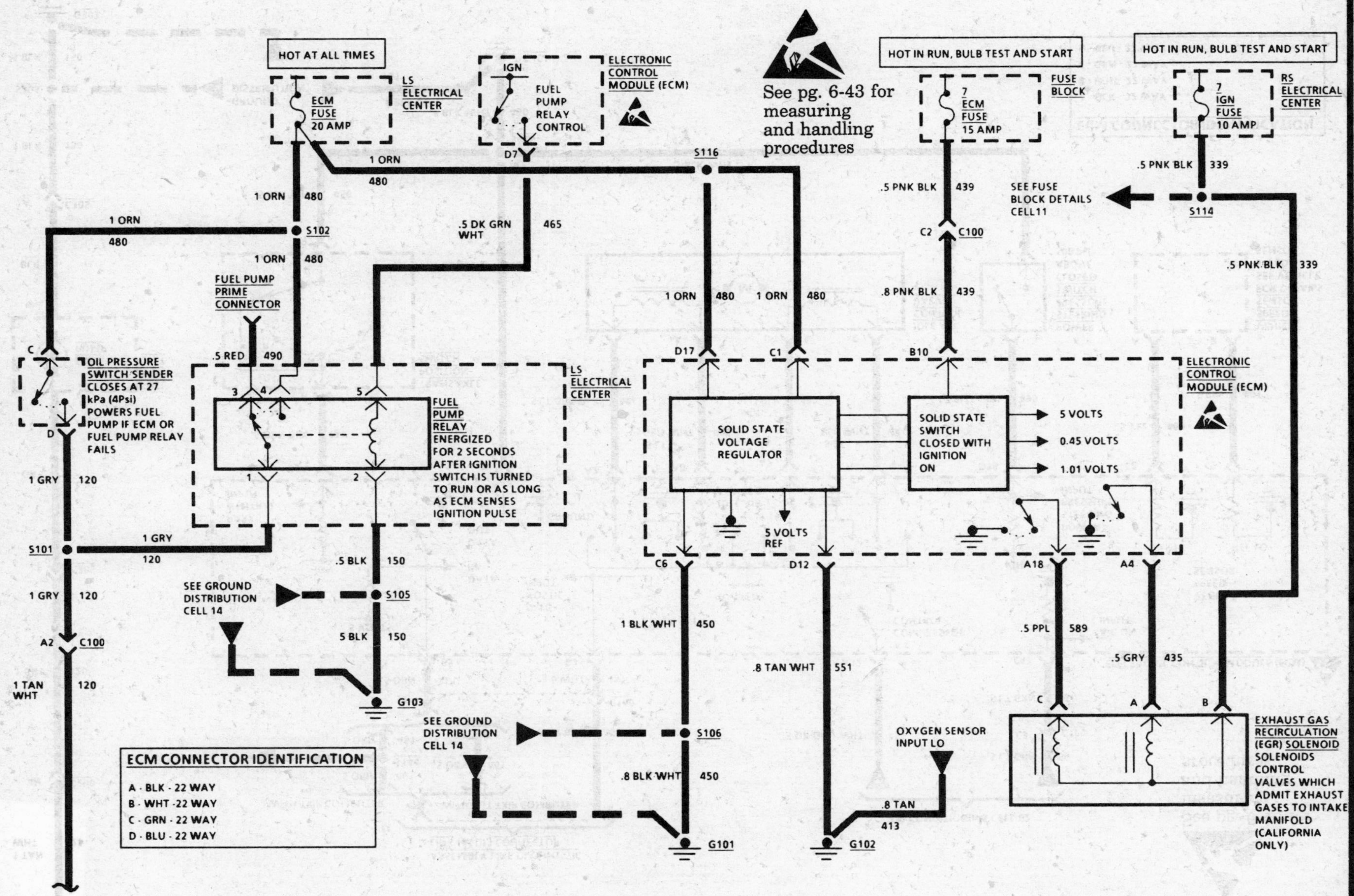

2.3L engine—Grand Prix shown

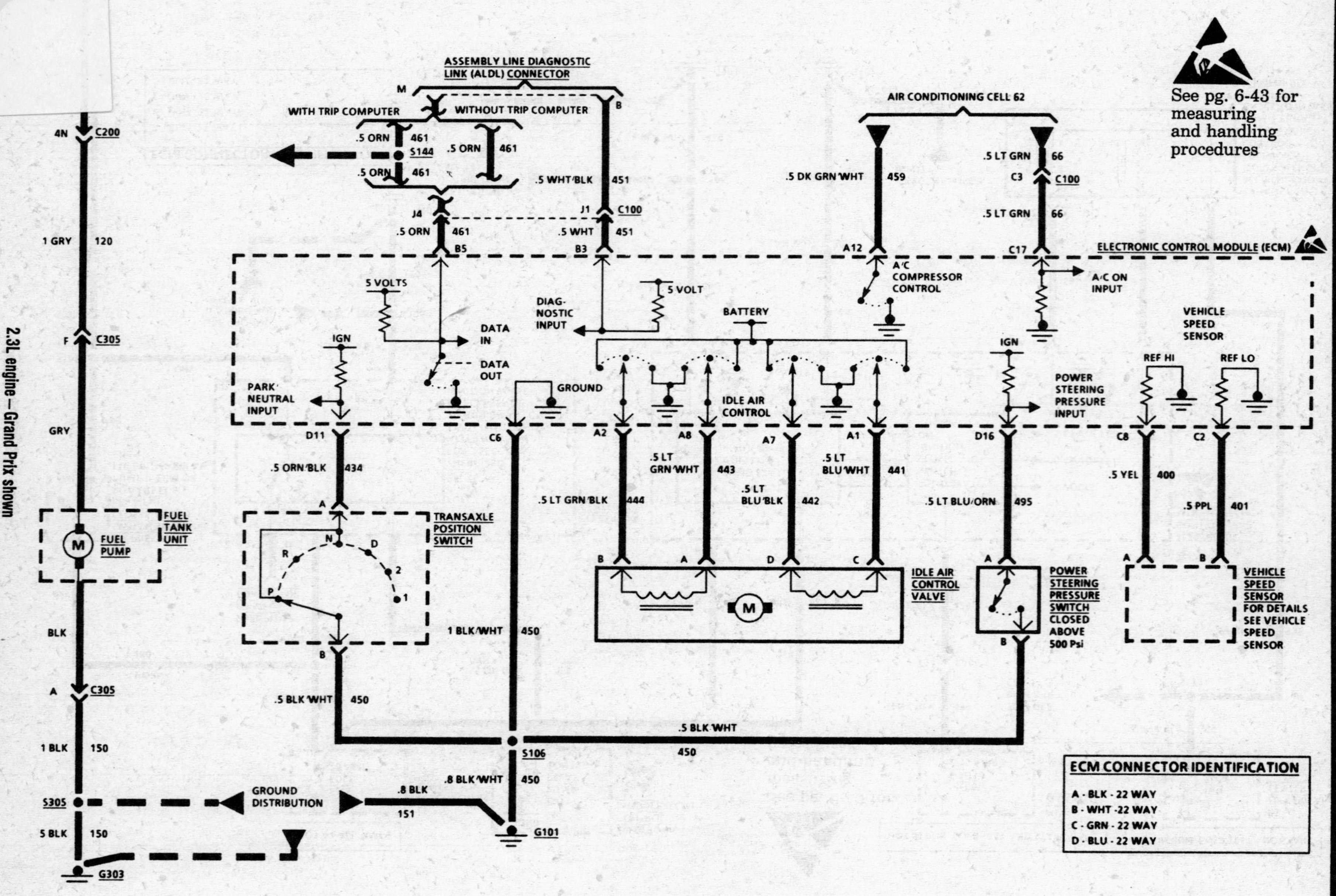

2.3L engine—Grand Prix shown

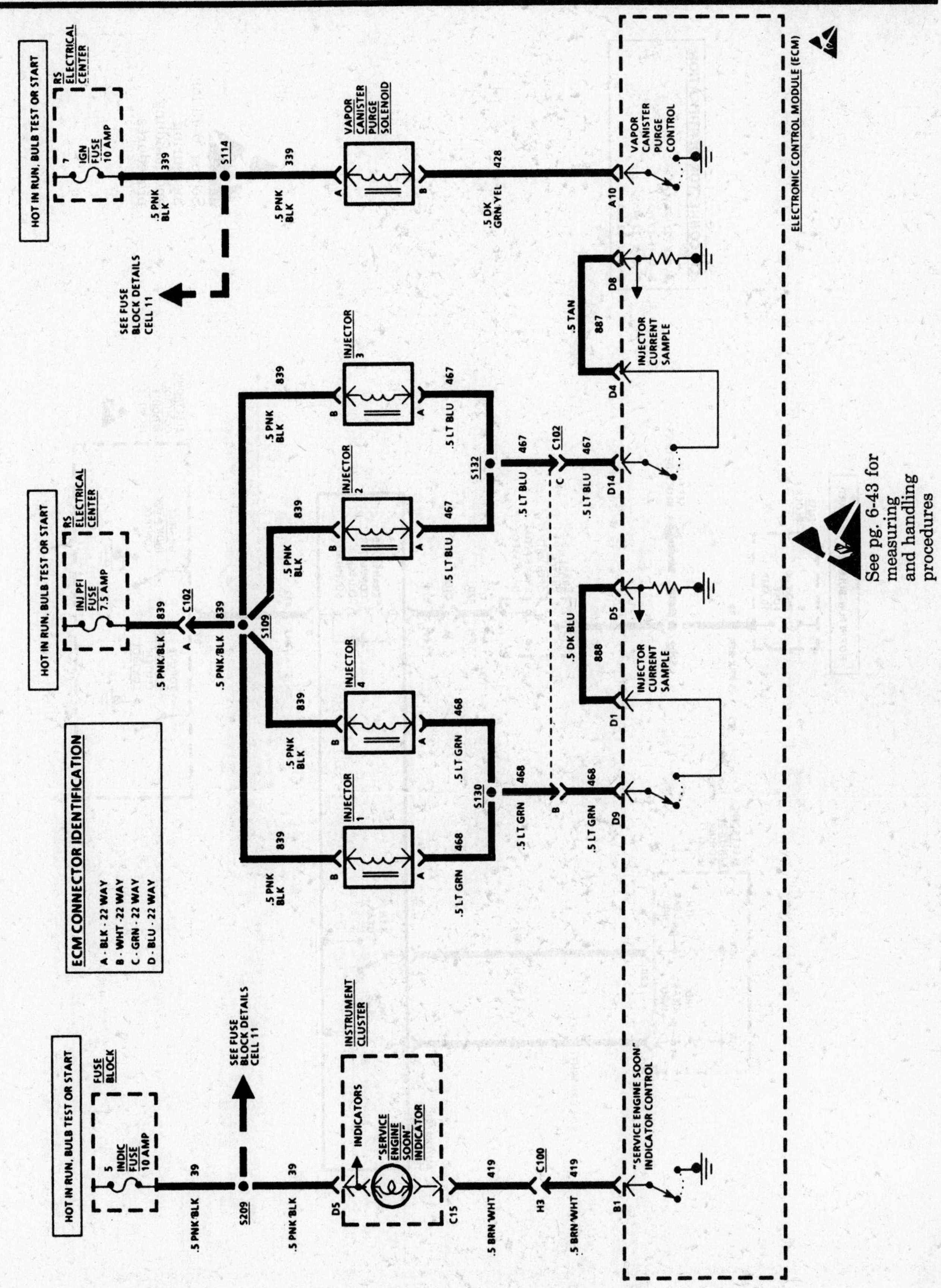

2.3L engine – Grand Prix shown

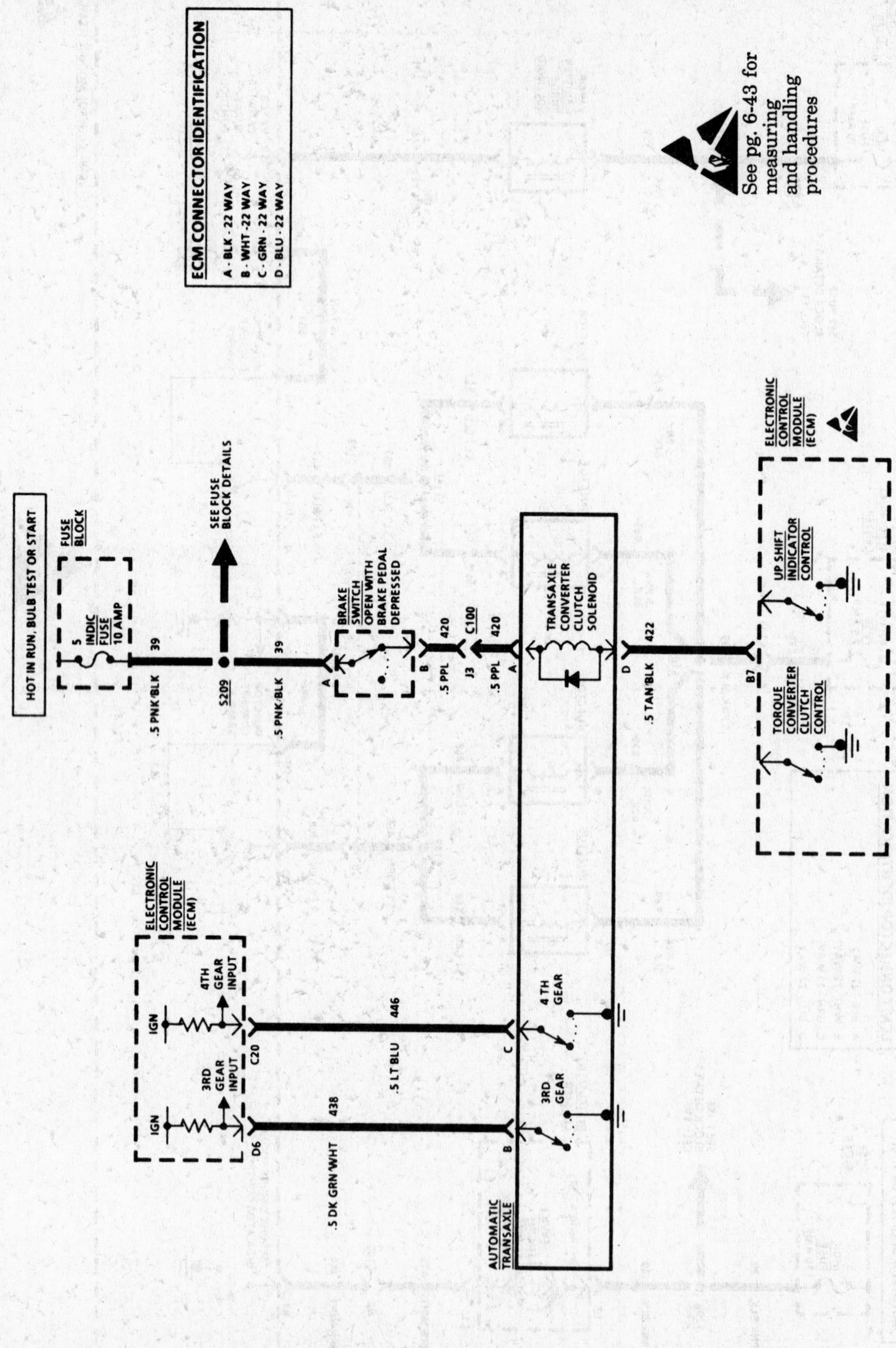

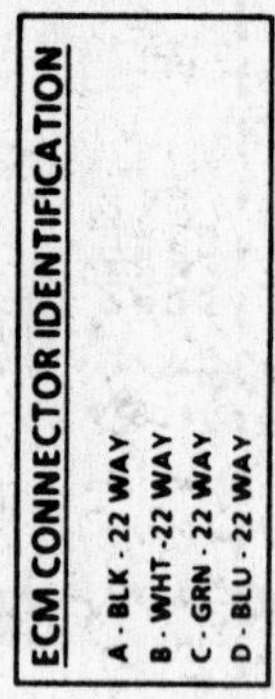

2.3L engine—Grand Prix shown

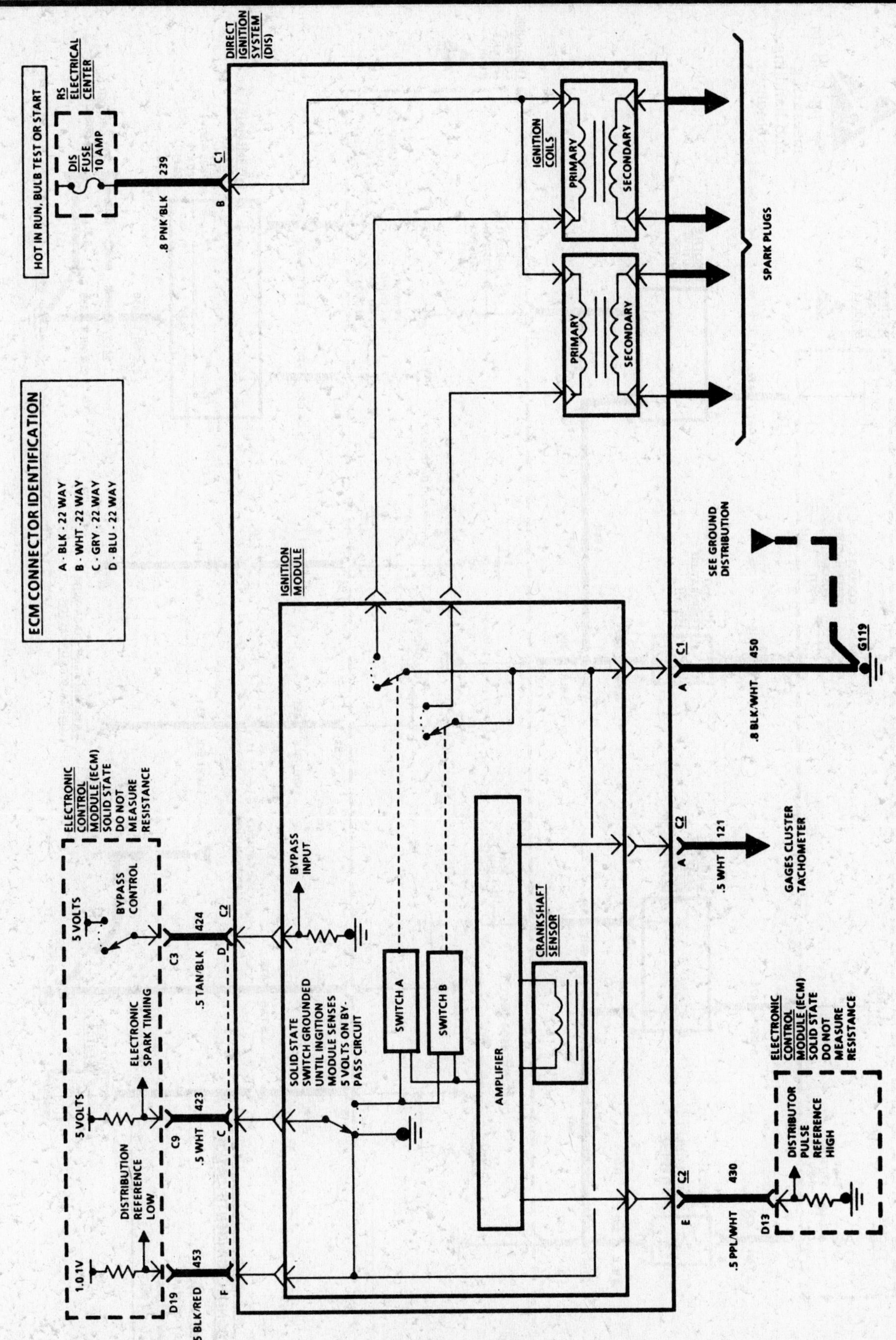

2.5L engine—Lumina shown

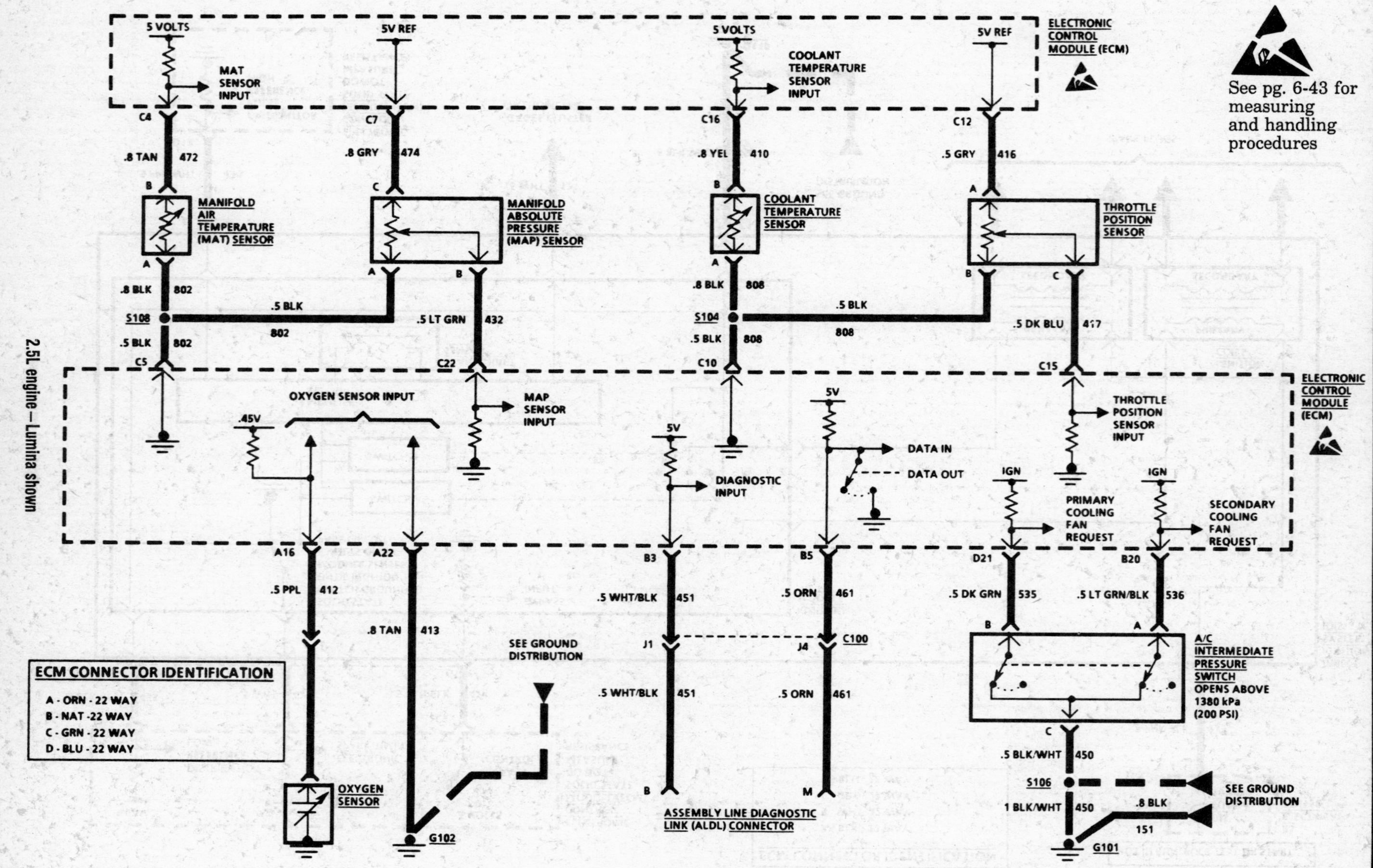

2.5L engine—Lumina shown

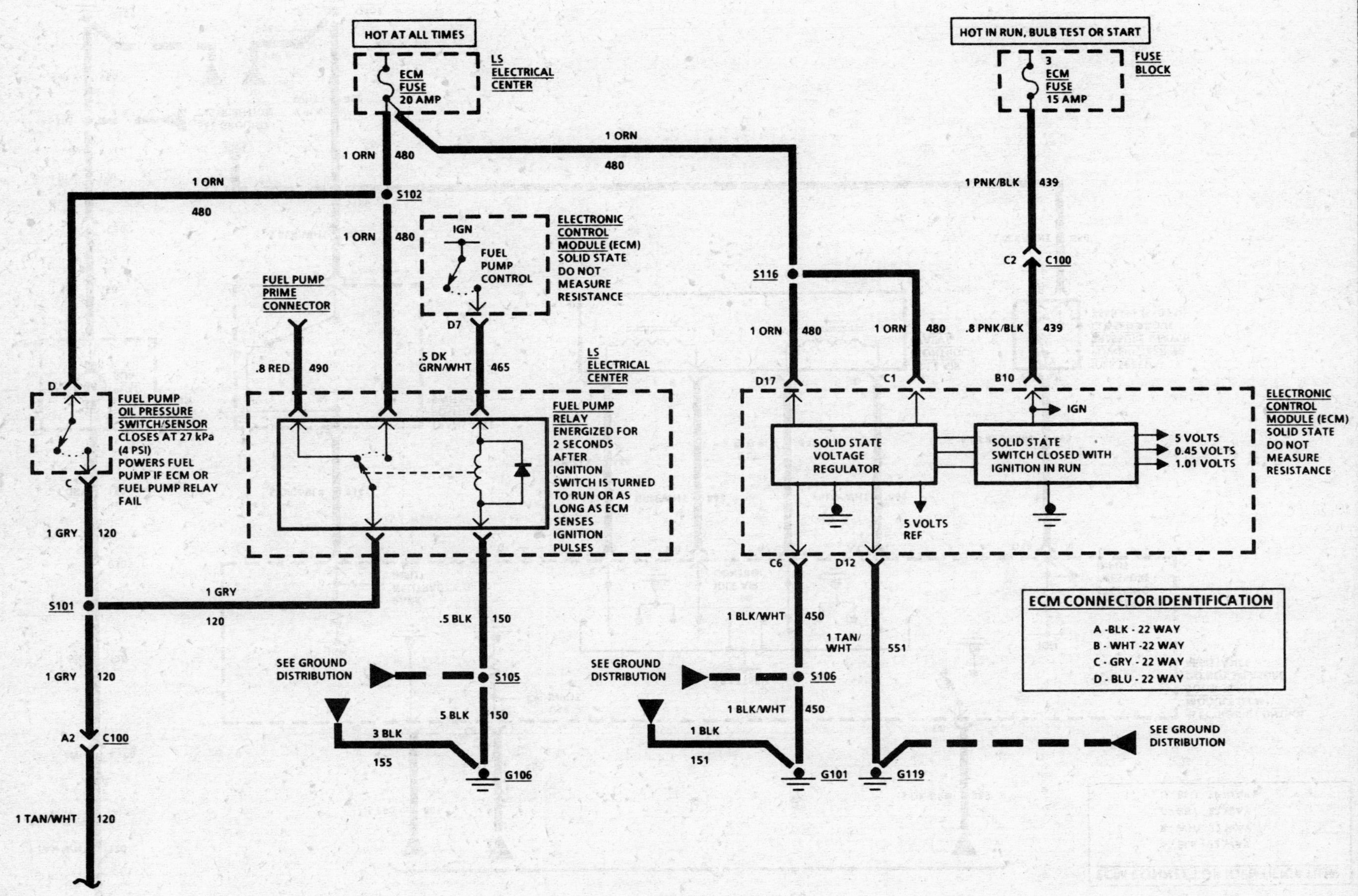

2.5L engine – Lumina shown

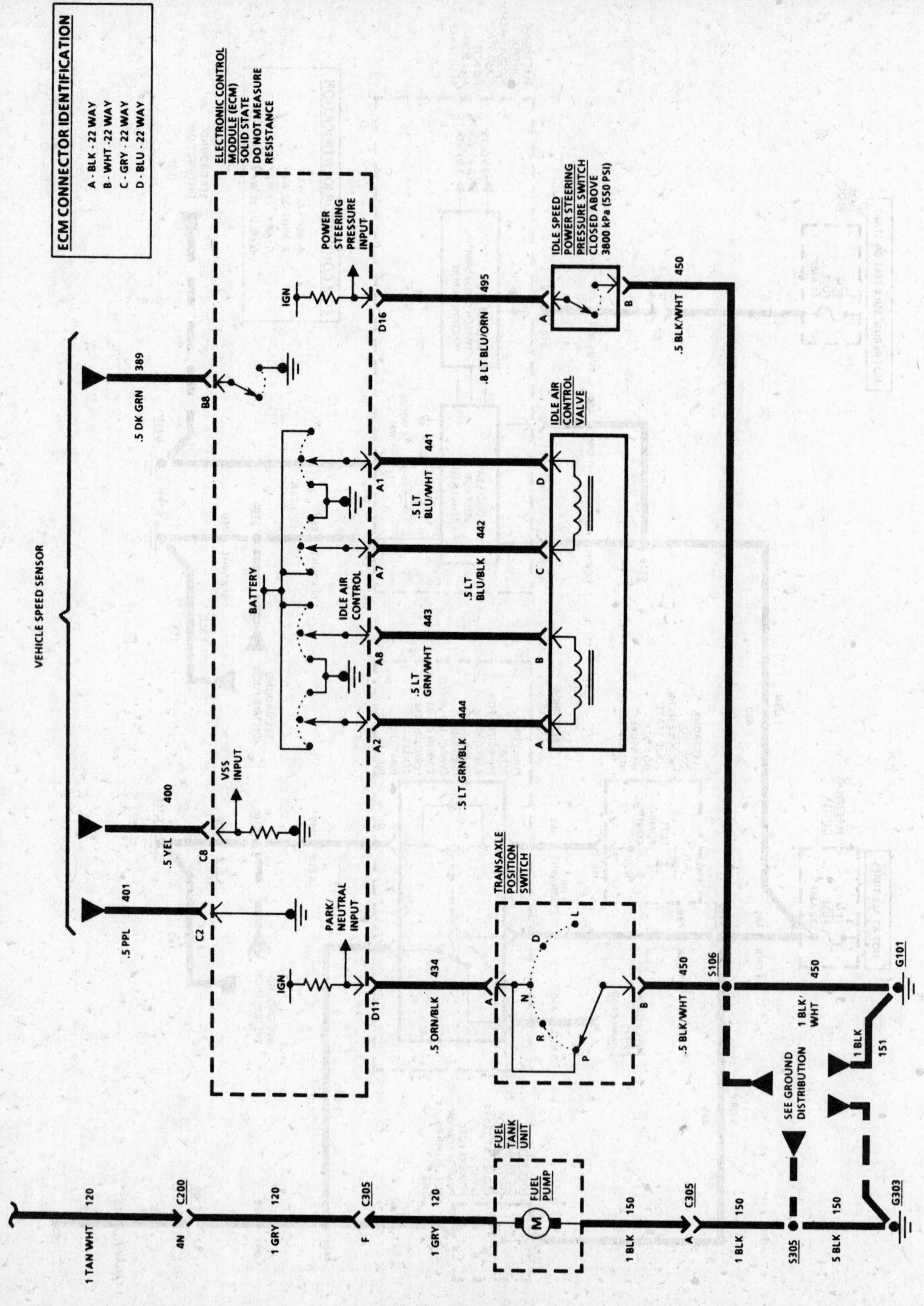

2.5L engine – Lumina shown

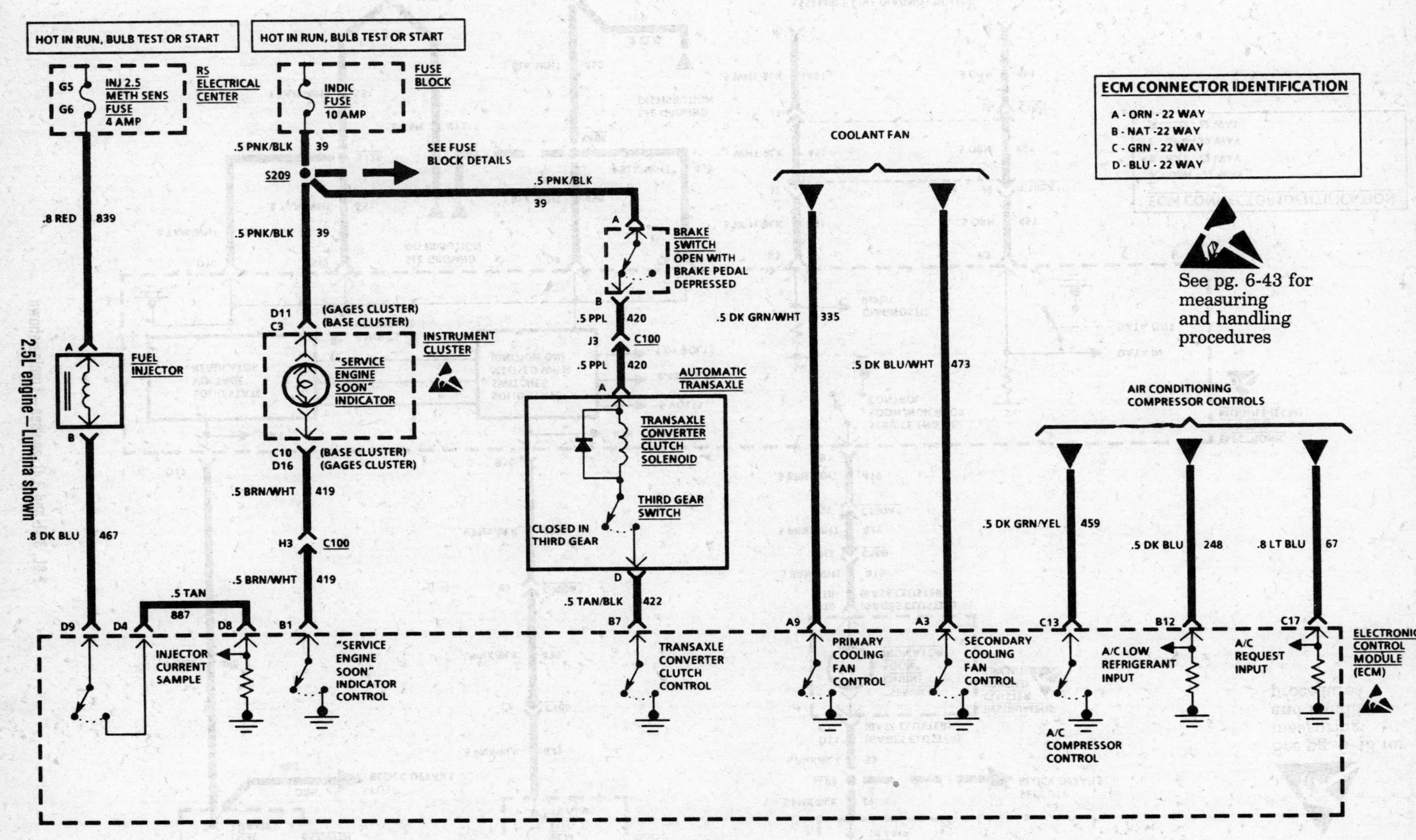

2.5L engine—Lumina shown

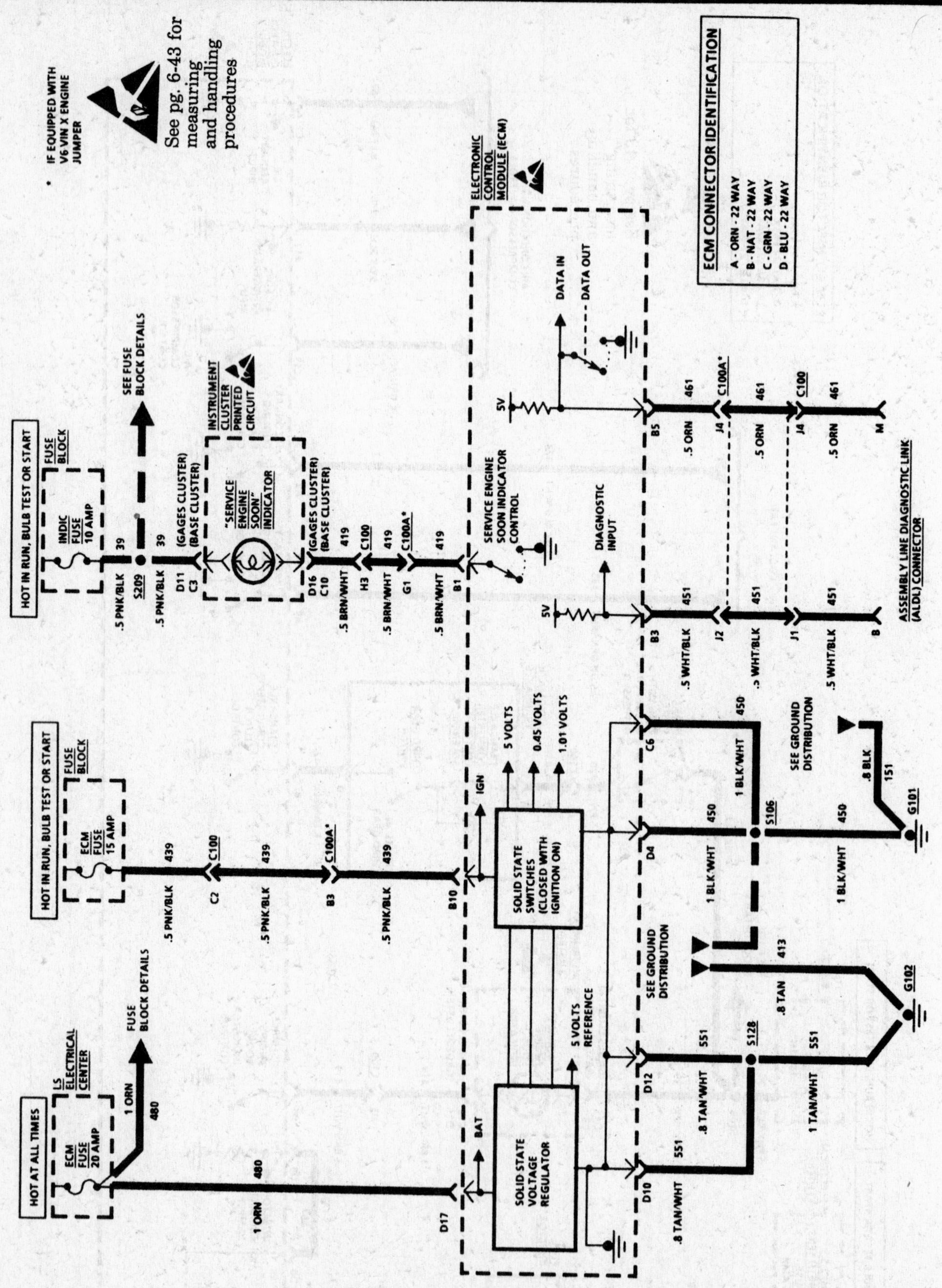

2.8L, 3.1L and 3.4L engines—Lumina shown

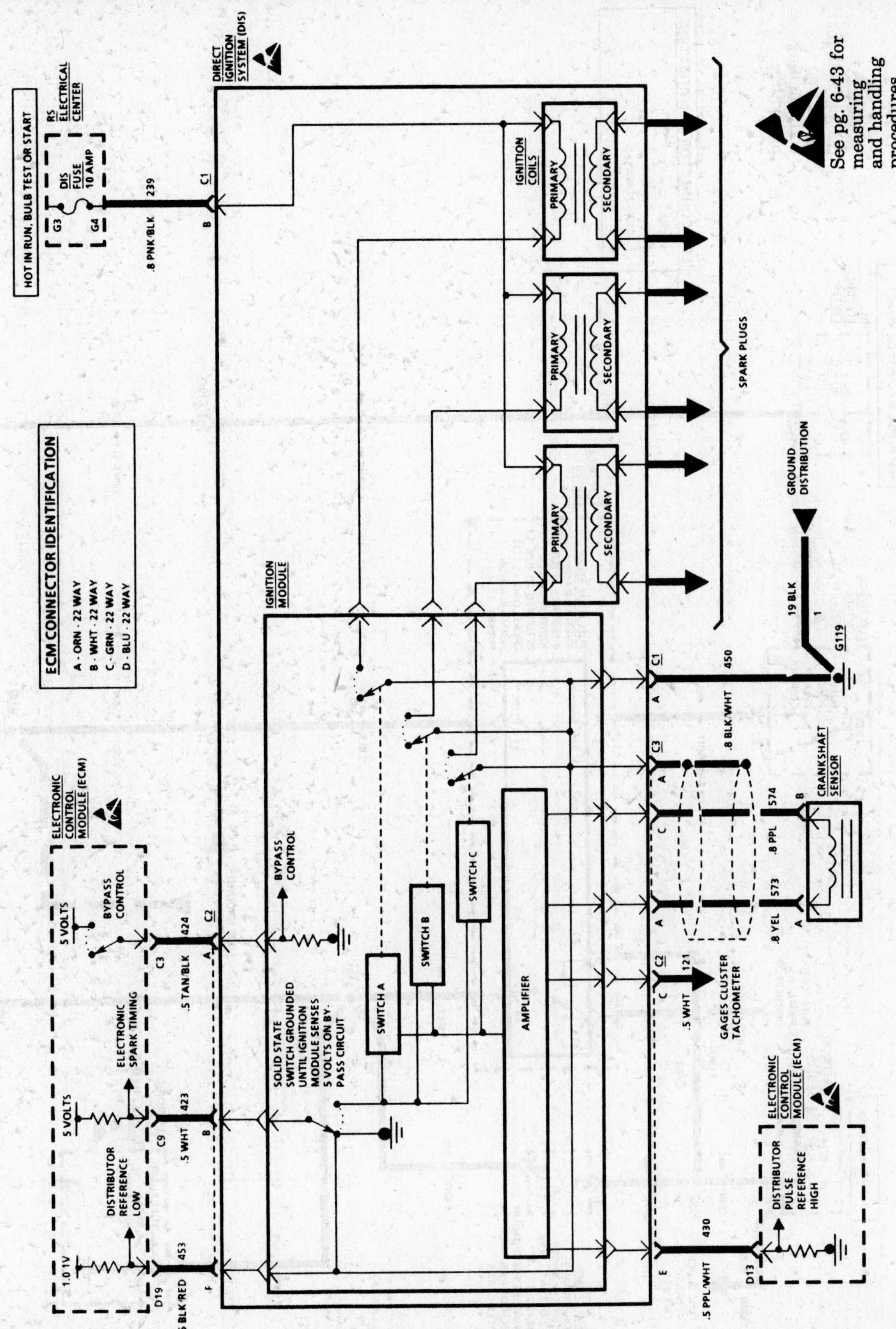

2.8L, 3.1L and 3.4L engines—Grand Prix shown

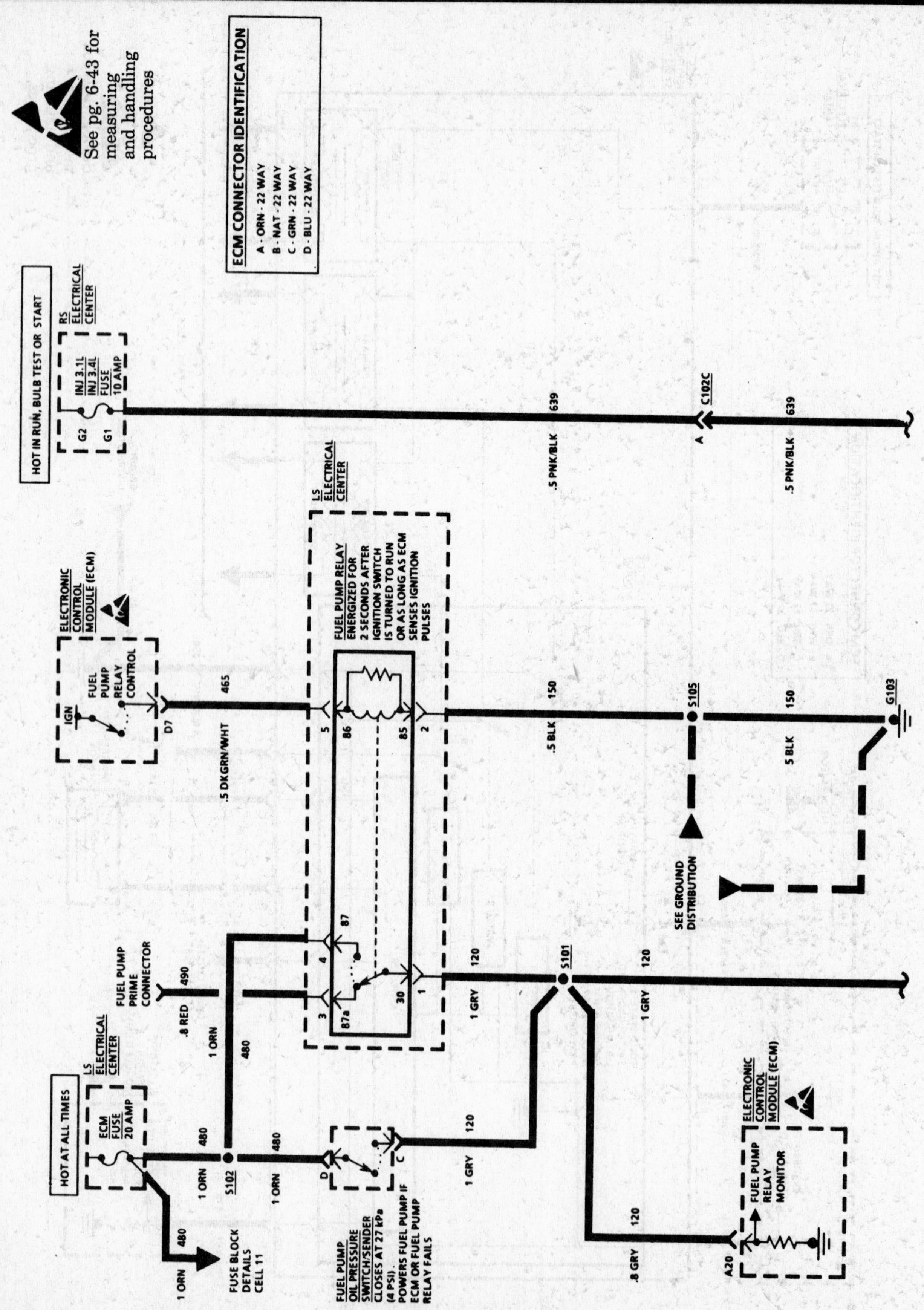

2.8L, 3.1L and 3.4L engines—Lumina shown

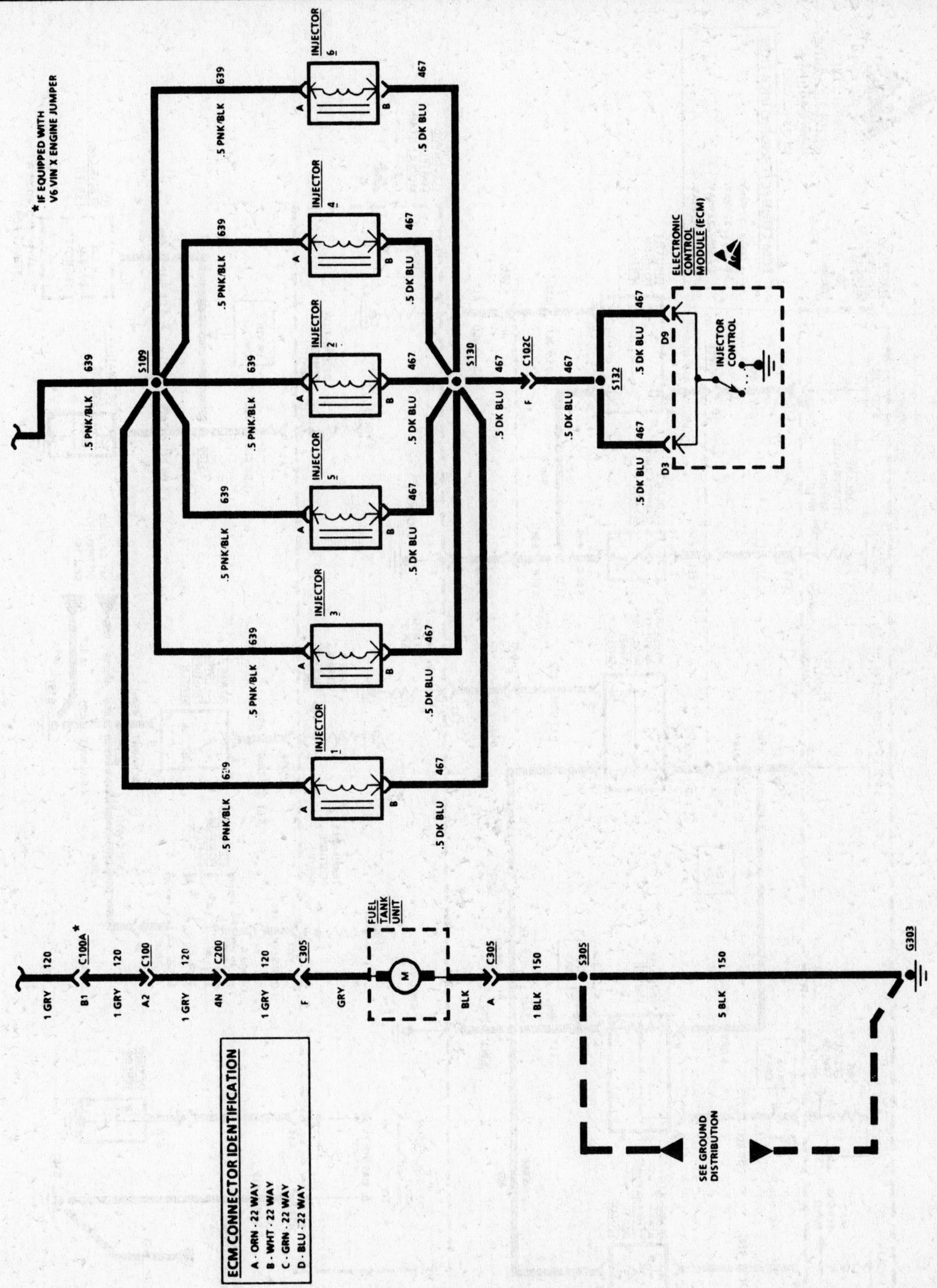

2.8L, 3.1L and 3.4L engines—Grand Prix shown

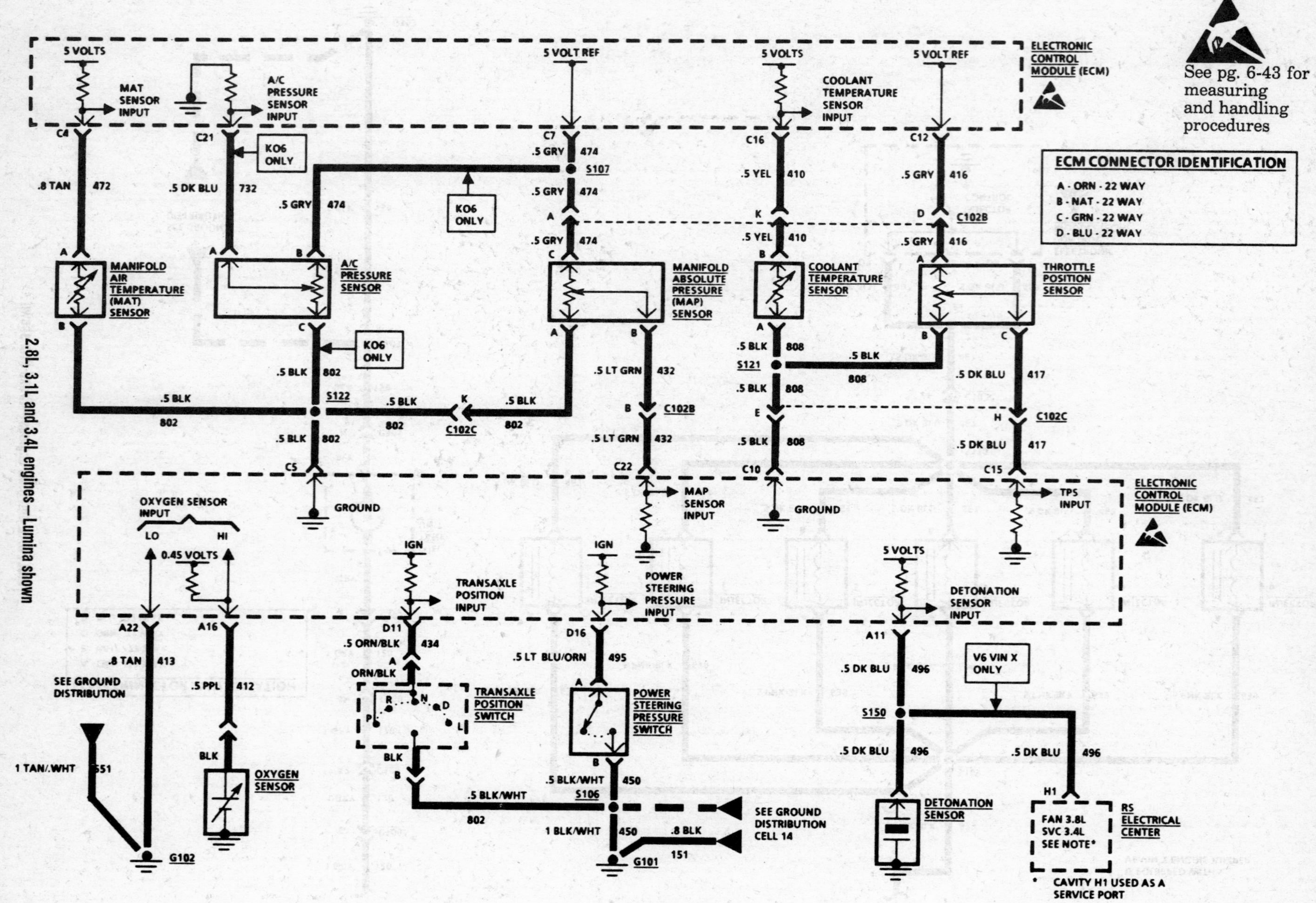

2.8L, 3.1L and 3.4L engines—Lumina shown

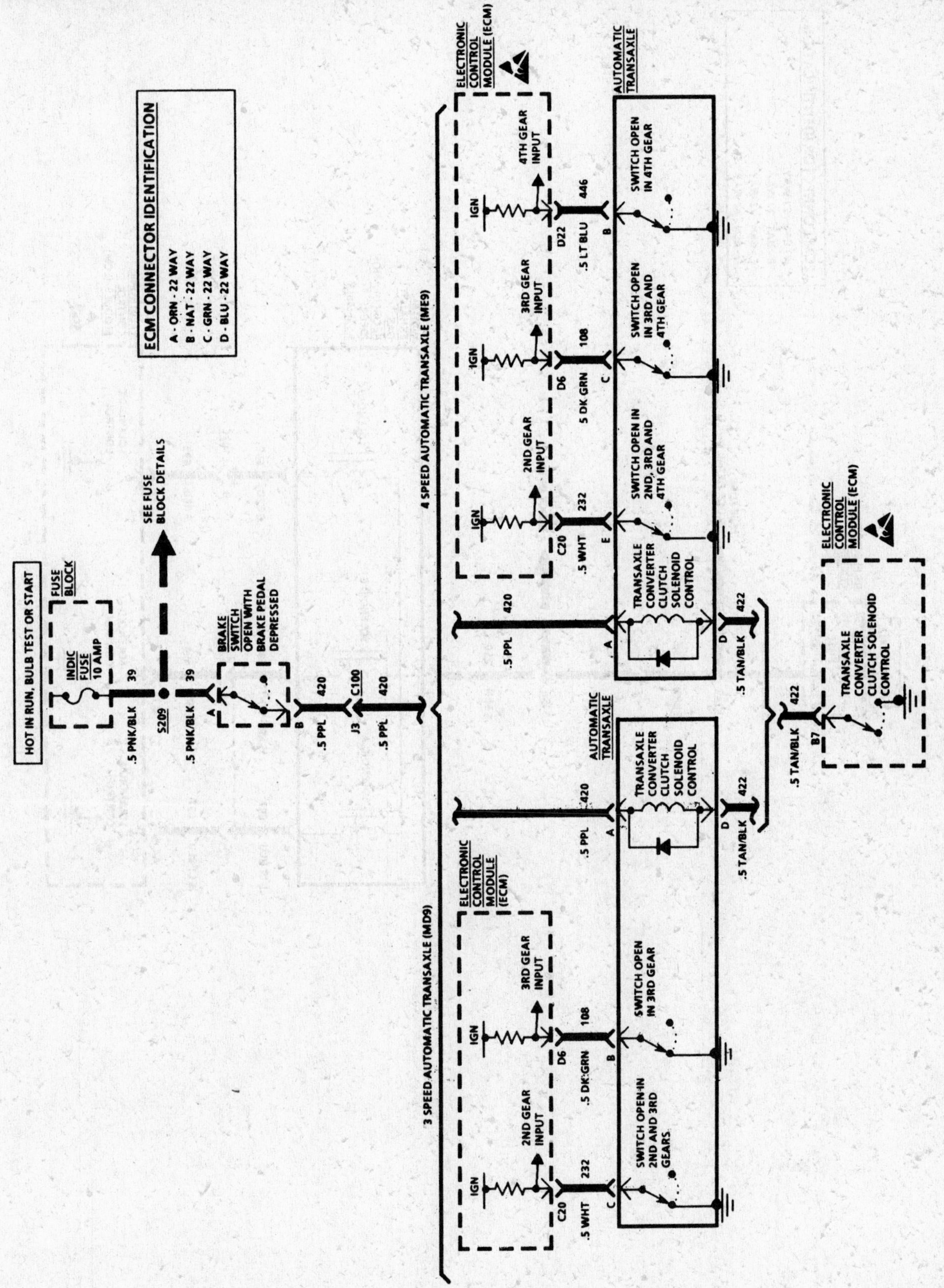

2.8L, 3.1L and 3.4L engines – Lumina shown

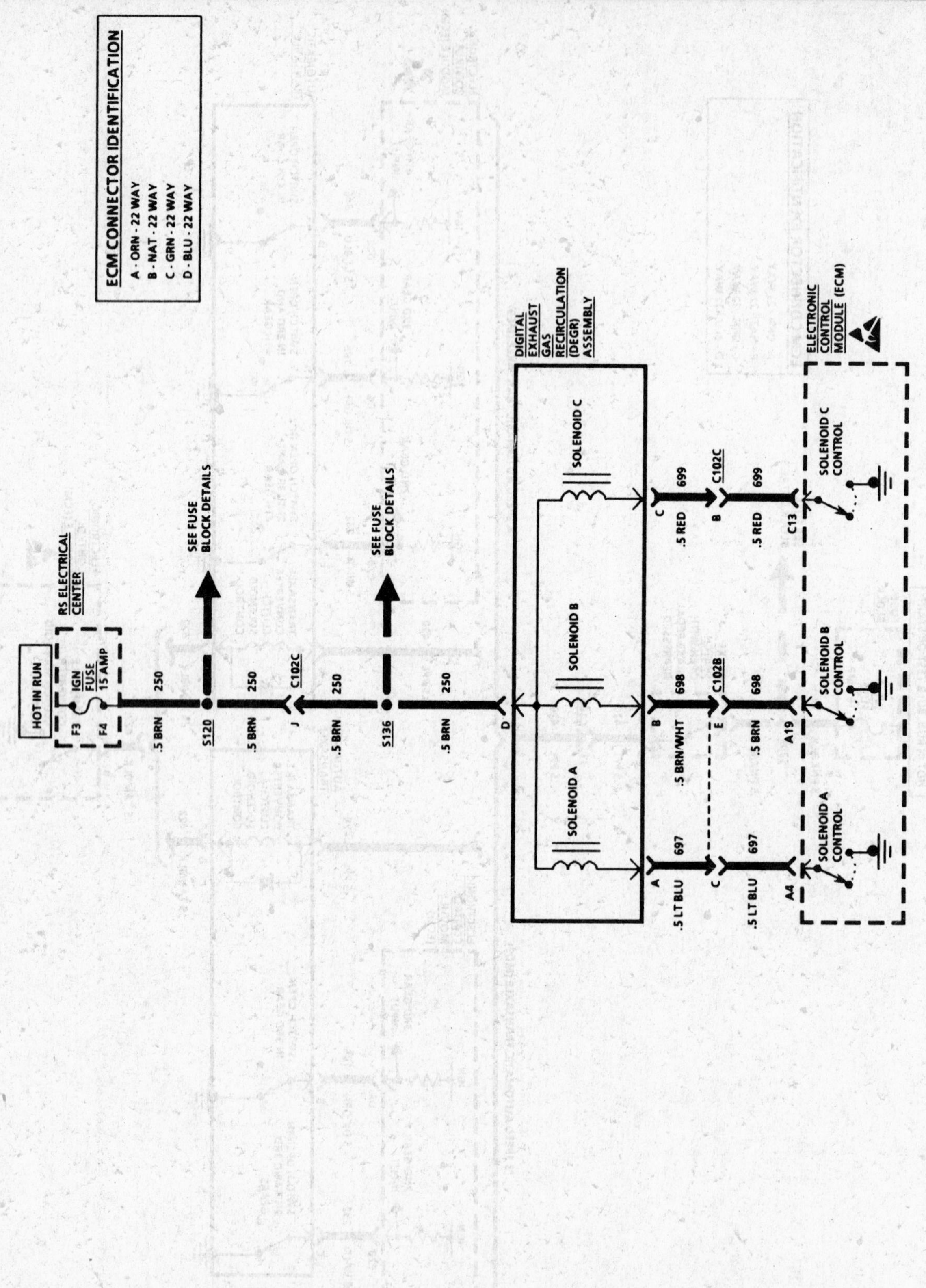

2.8L, 3.1L and 3.4L engines—Lumina shown

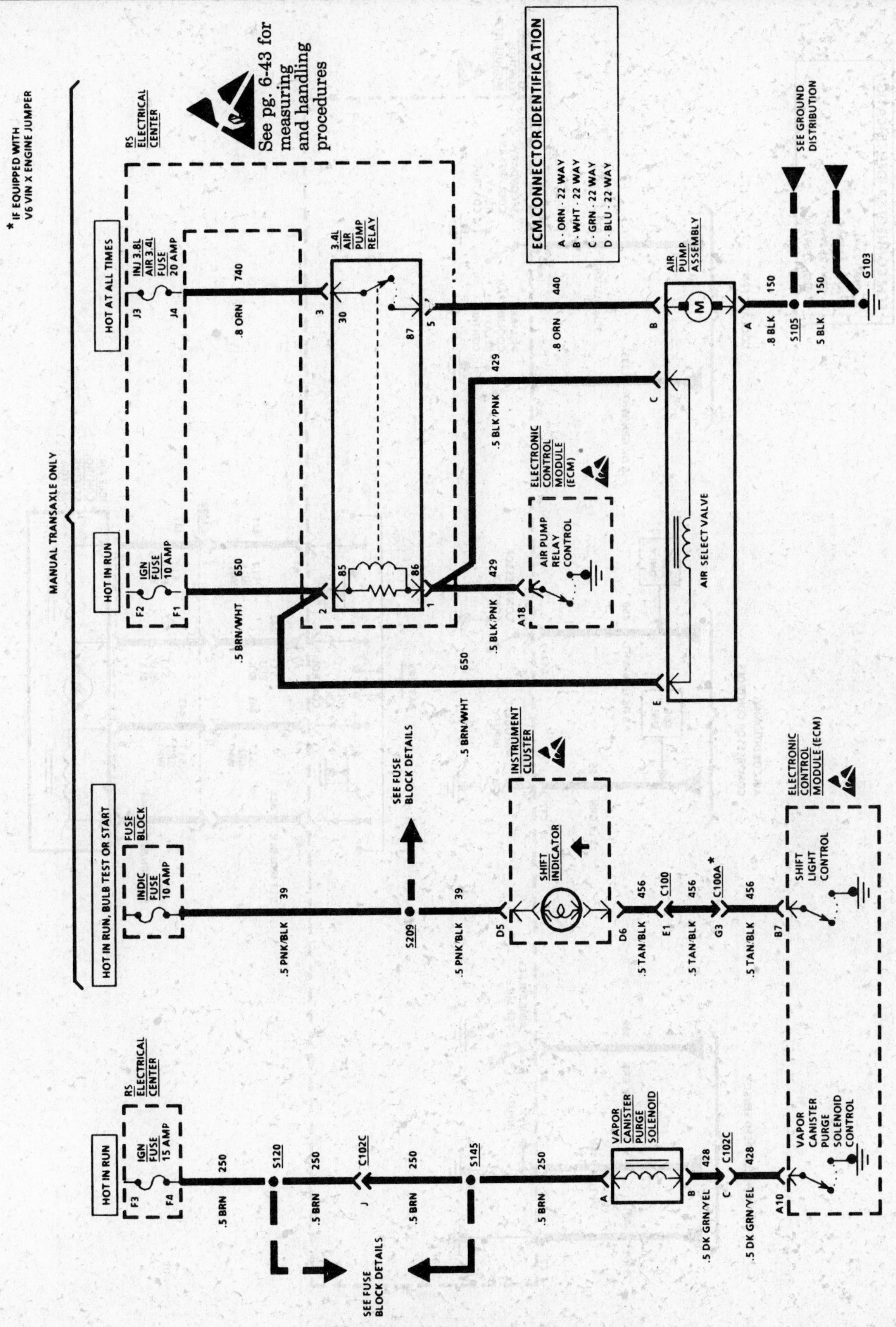

2.8L, 3.1L and 3.4L engines – Grand Prix shown

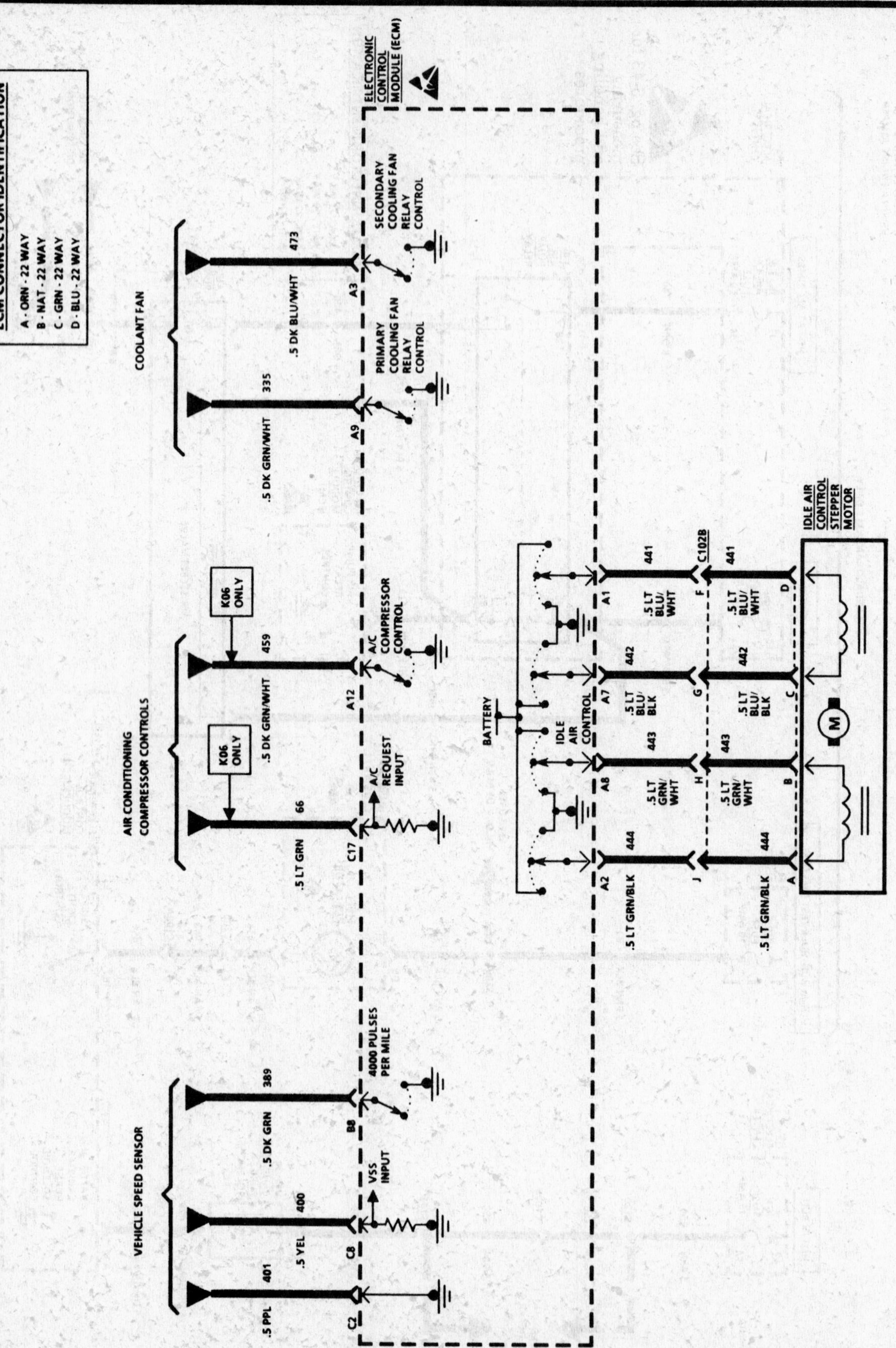

2.8L, 3.1L and 3.4L engines—Lumina shown

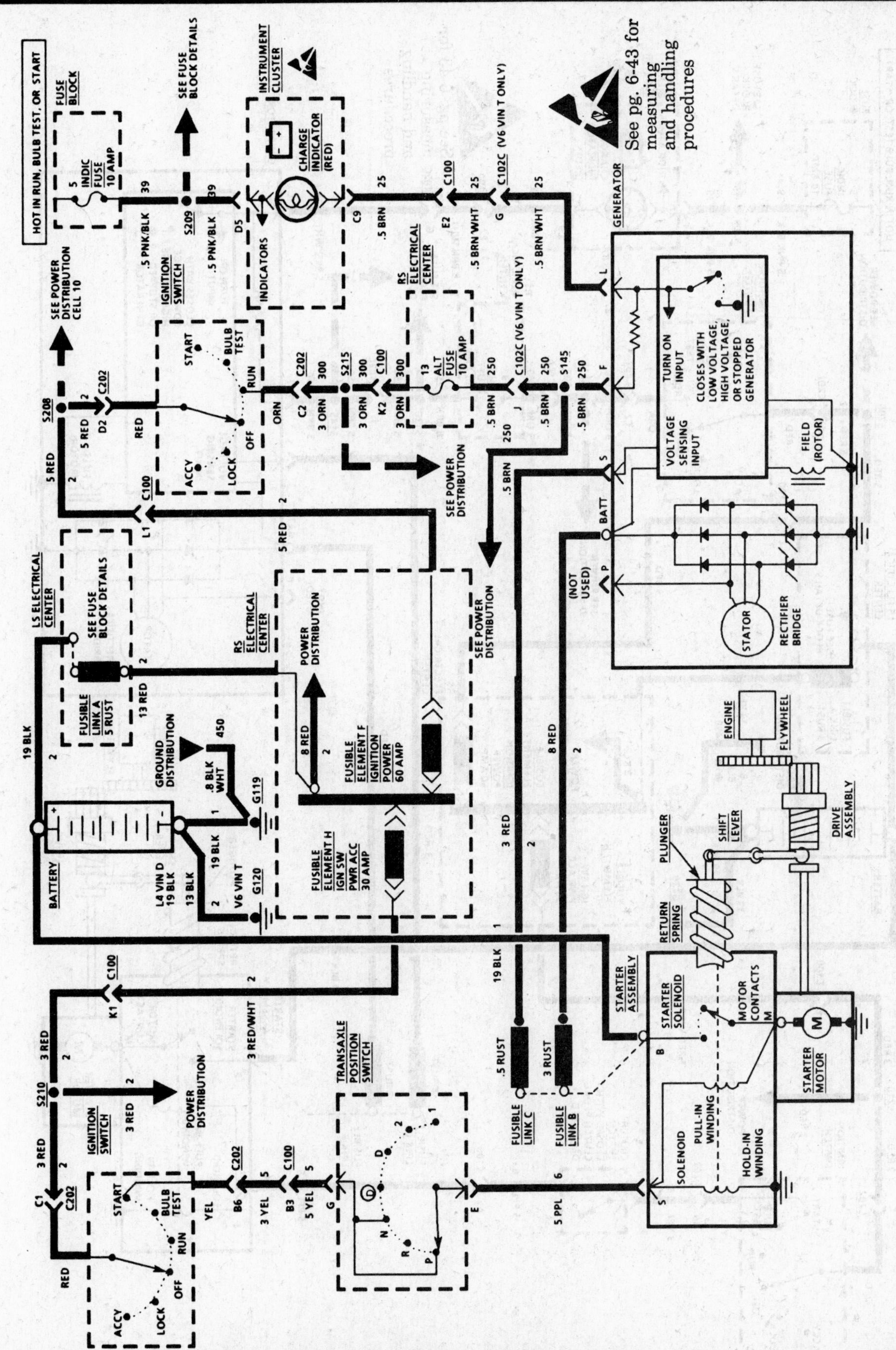

Starter and charging system with automatic transaxle – Grand Prix shown

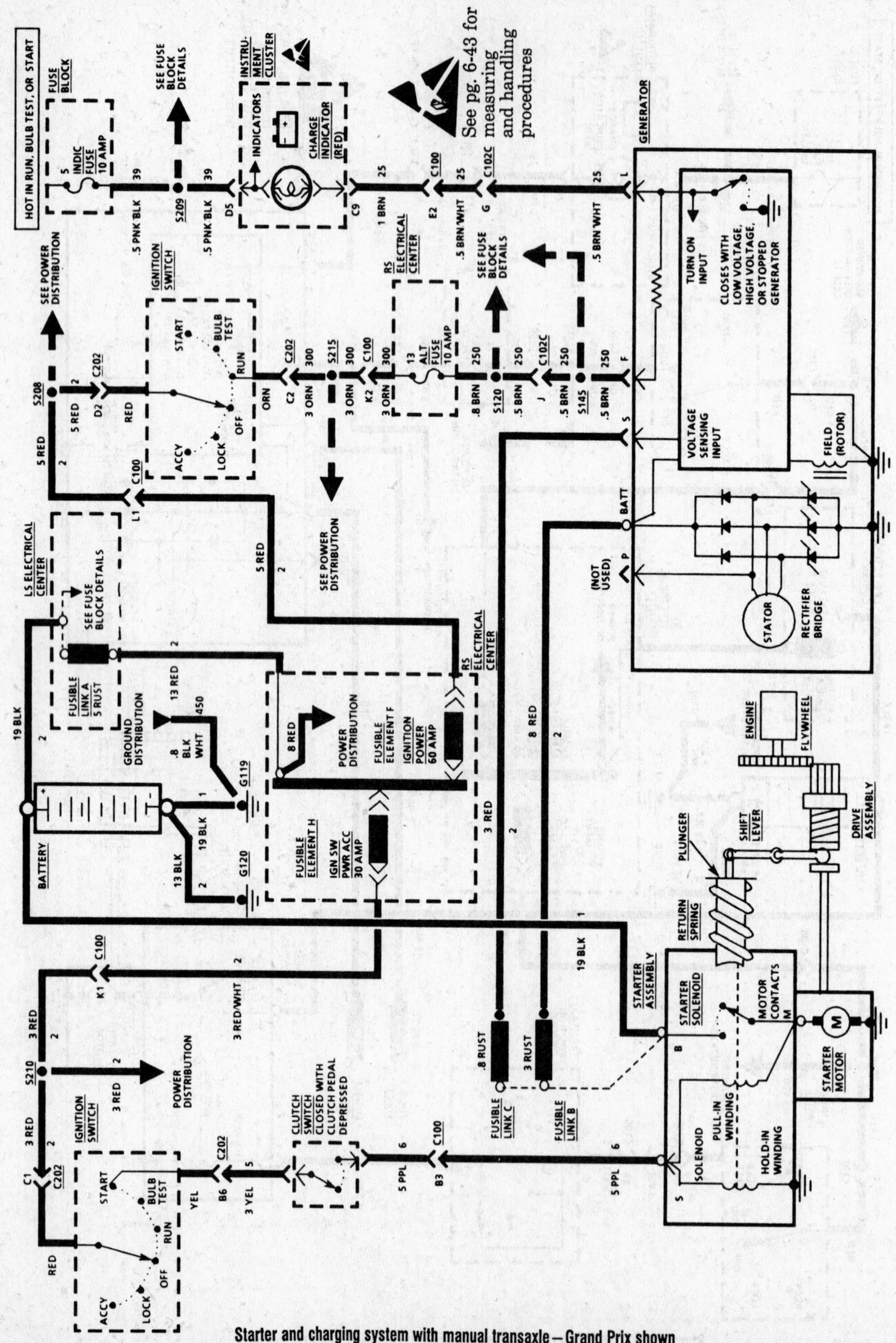

Starter and charging system with manual transaxle—Grand Prix shown

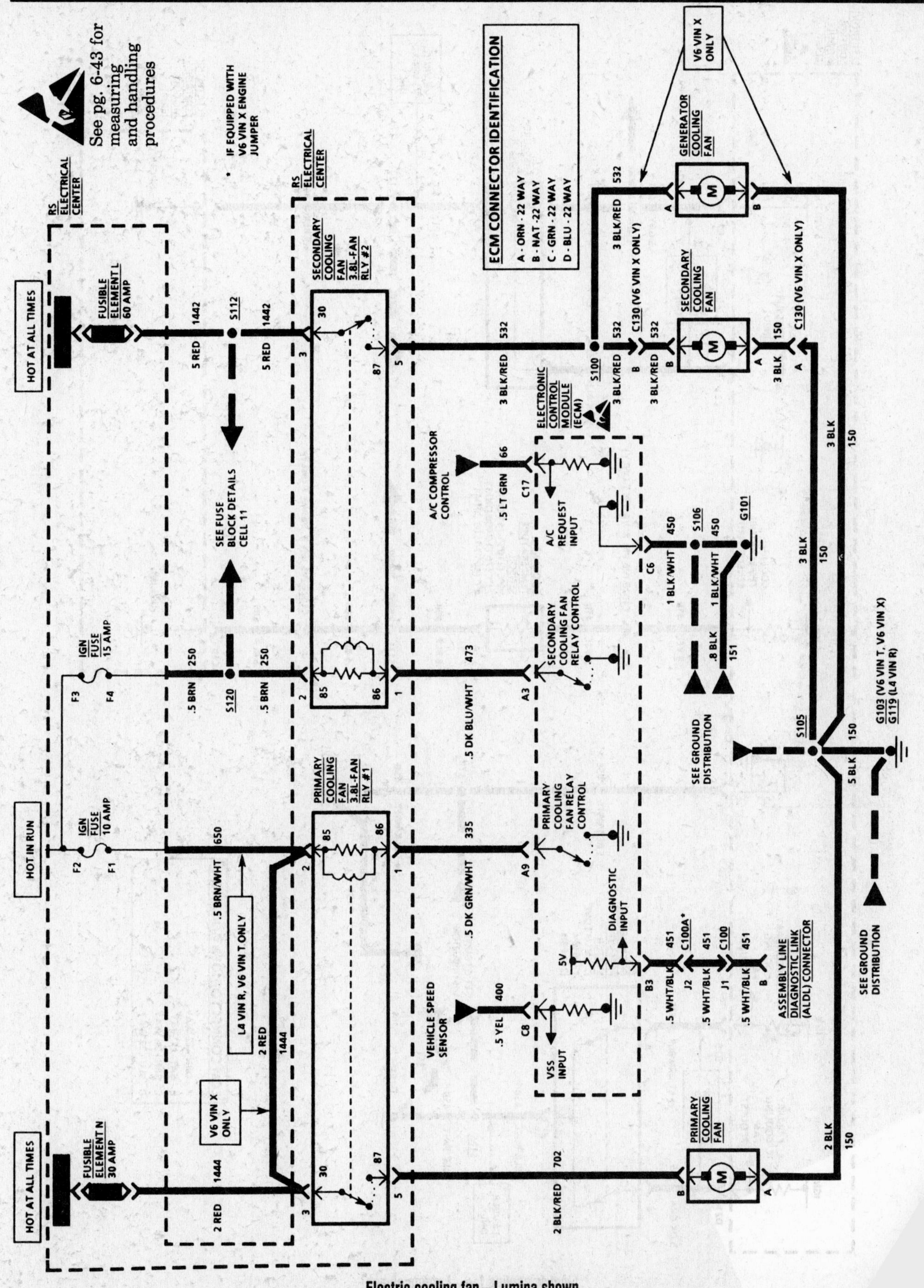

Electric cooling fan—Lumina shown

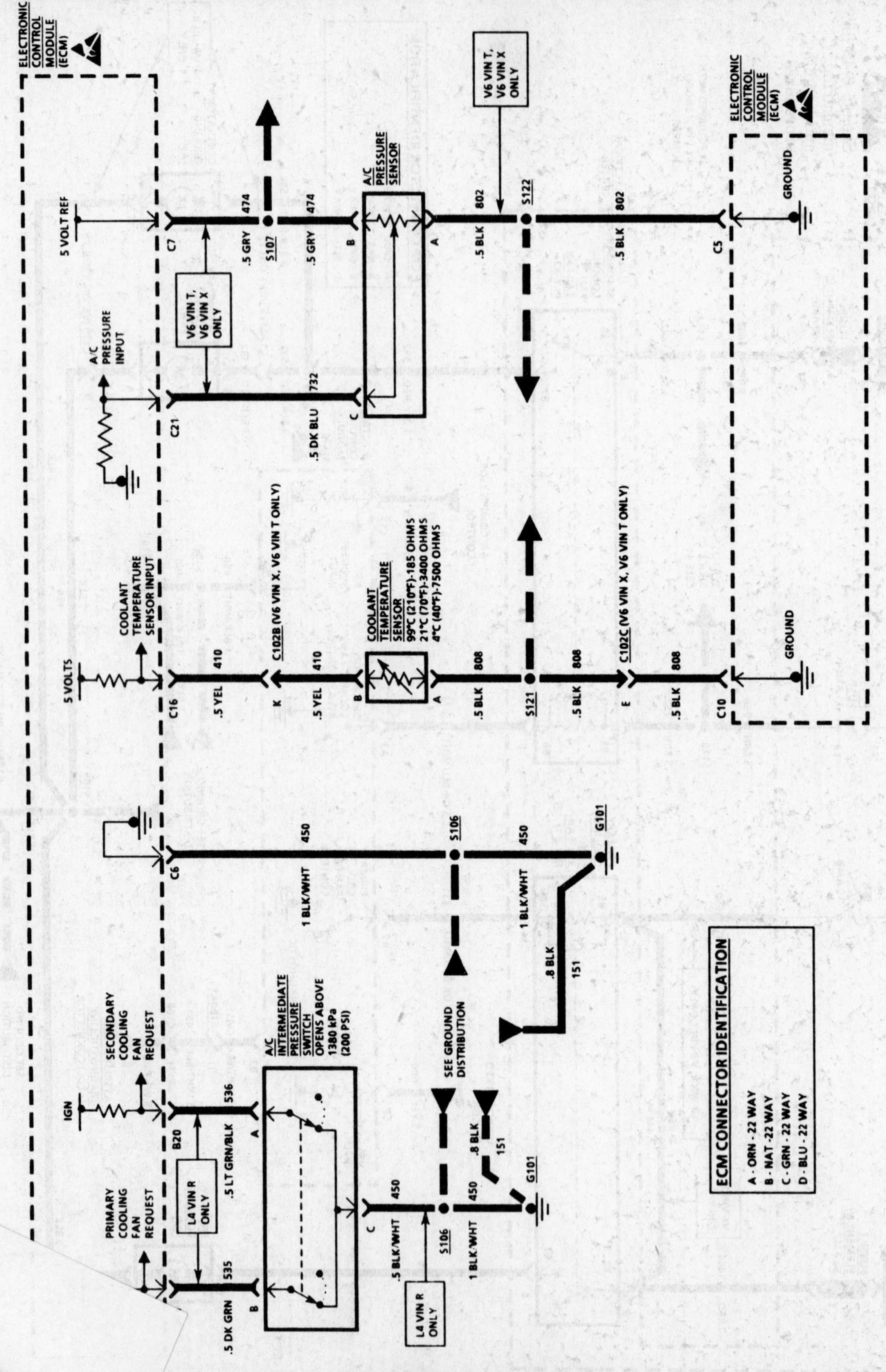

Electric cooling fan—Lumina shown

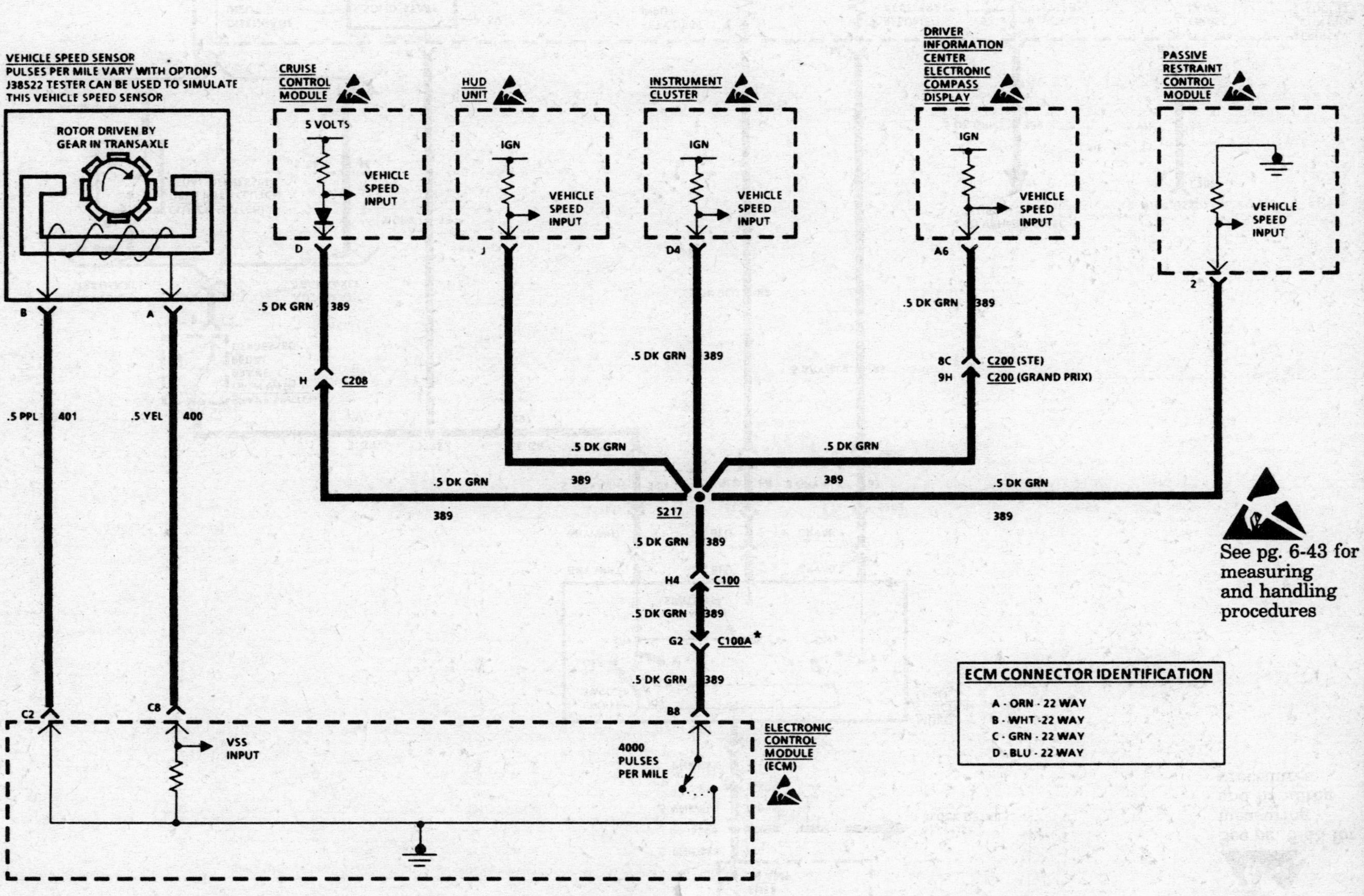
* IF EQUIPPED WITH V6 VIN X ENGINE JUMPER
VEHICLE SPEED SENSOR
PULSES PER MILE VARY WITH OPTIONS
J38522 TESTER CAN BE USED TO SIMULATE
THIS VEHICLE SPEED SENSOR
ROTOR DRIVEN BY GEAR IN TRANSAXLE
CRUISE CONTROL MODULE
5 VOLTS
VEHICLE SPEED INPUT
HUD UNIT
IGN
VEHICLE SPEED INPUT
INSTRUMENT CLUSTER
IGN
VEHICLE SPEED INPUT
DRIVER INFORMATION CENTER ELECTRONIC COMPASS DISPLAY
IGN
VEHICLE SPEED INPUT
PASSIVE RESTRAINT CONTROL MODULE
VEHICLE SPEED INPUT
D
J
D4
A6
2
B
A
.5 DK GRN 389
H C208
8C C200 (STE)
9H C200 (GRAND PRIX)
.5 PPL 401
.5 YEL 400
S217
H4 C100
G2 C100A *
B8
C2
C8
VSS INPUT
4000 PULSES PER MILE
ELECTRONIC CONTROL MODULE (ECM)
See pg. 6-43 for measuring and handling procedures
ECM CONNECTOR IDENTIFICATION
A - ORN - 22 WAY
B - WHT - 22 WAY
C - GRN - 22 WAY
D - BLU - 22 WAY

Vehicle speed sensor—Grand Prix shown

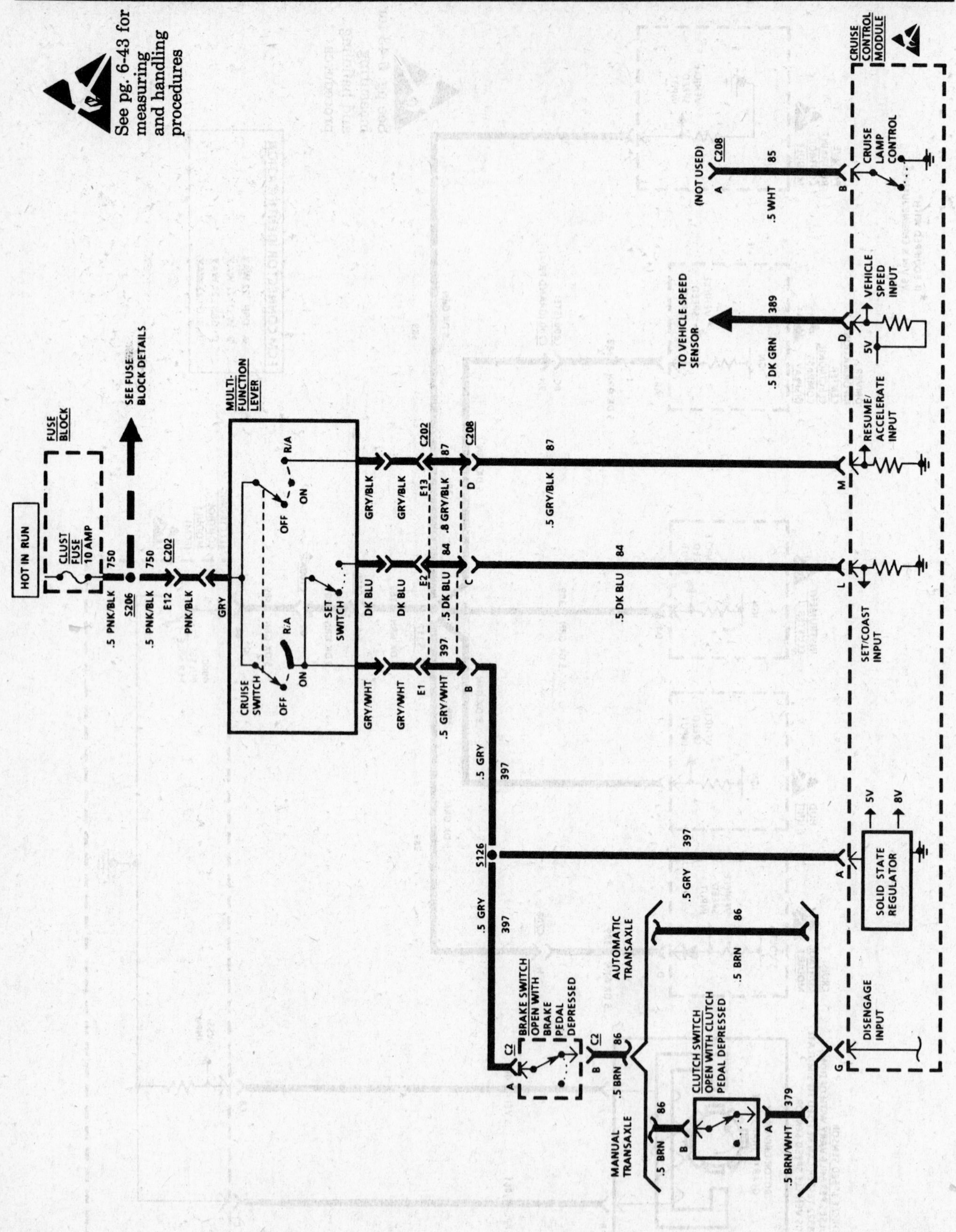

Cruise control—Lumina shown

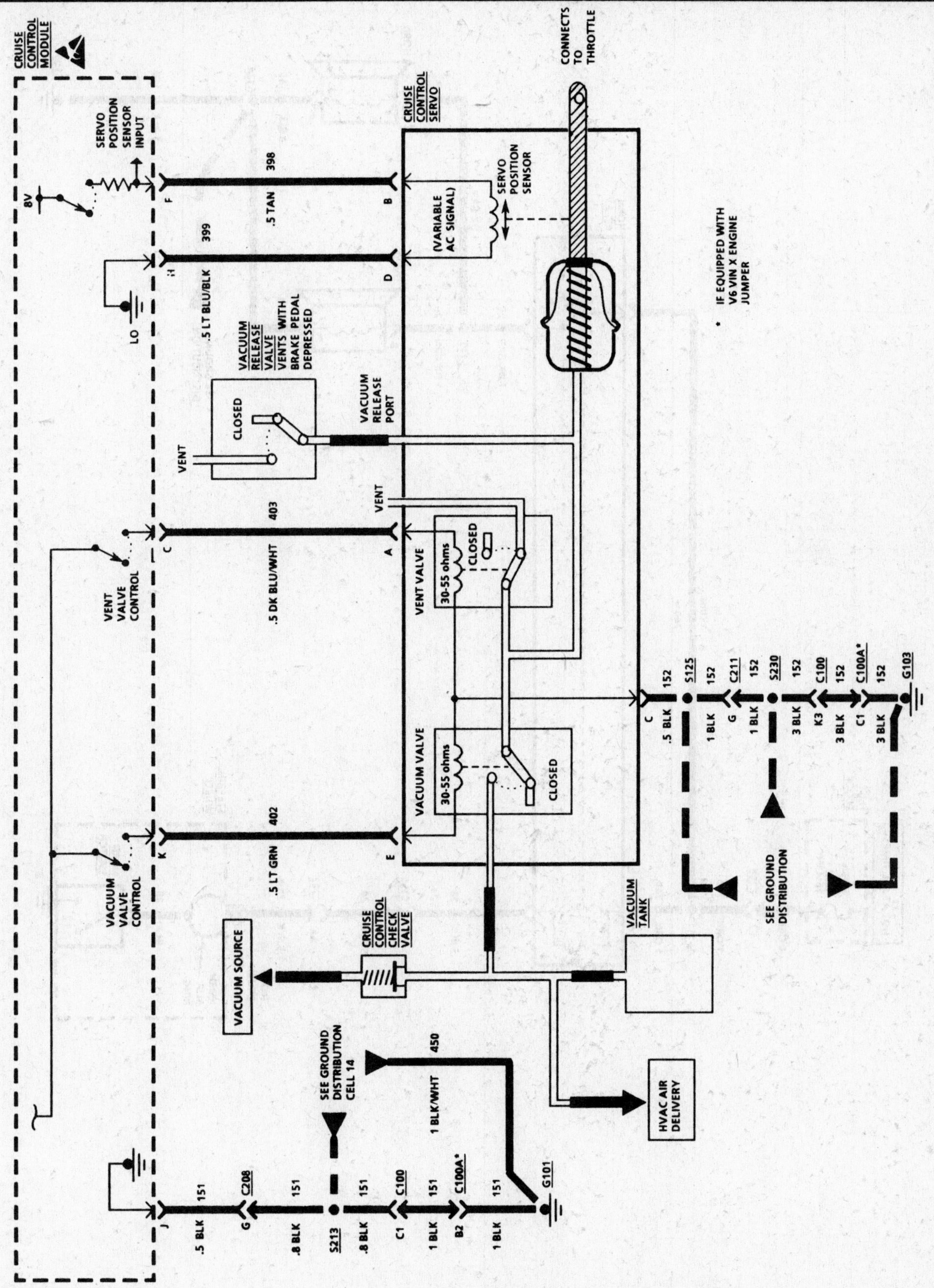

Cruise control—Lumina shown

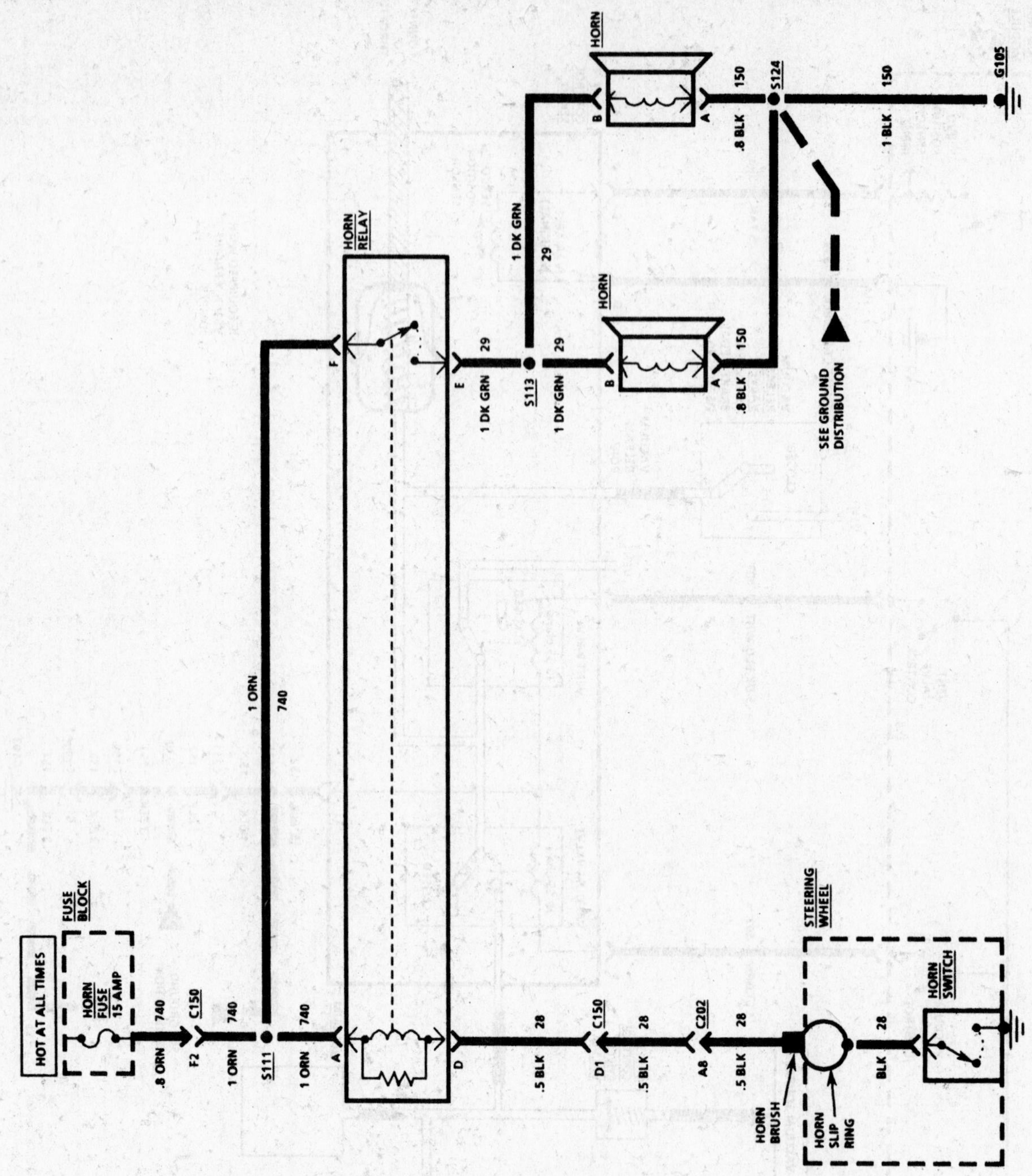

Horns — Lumina shown

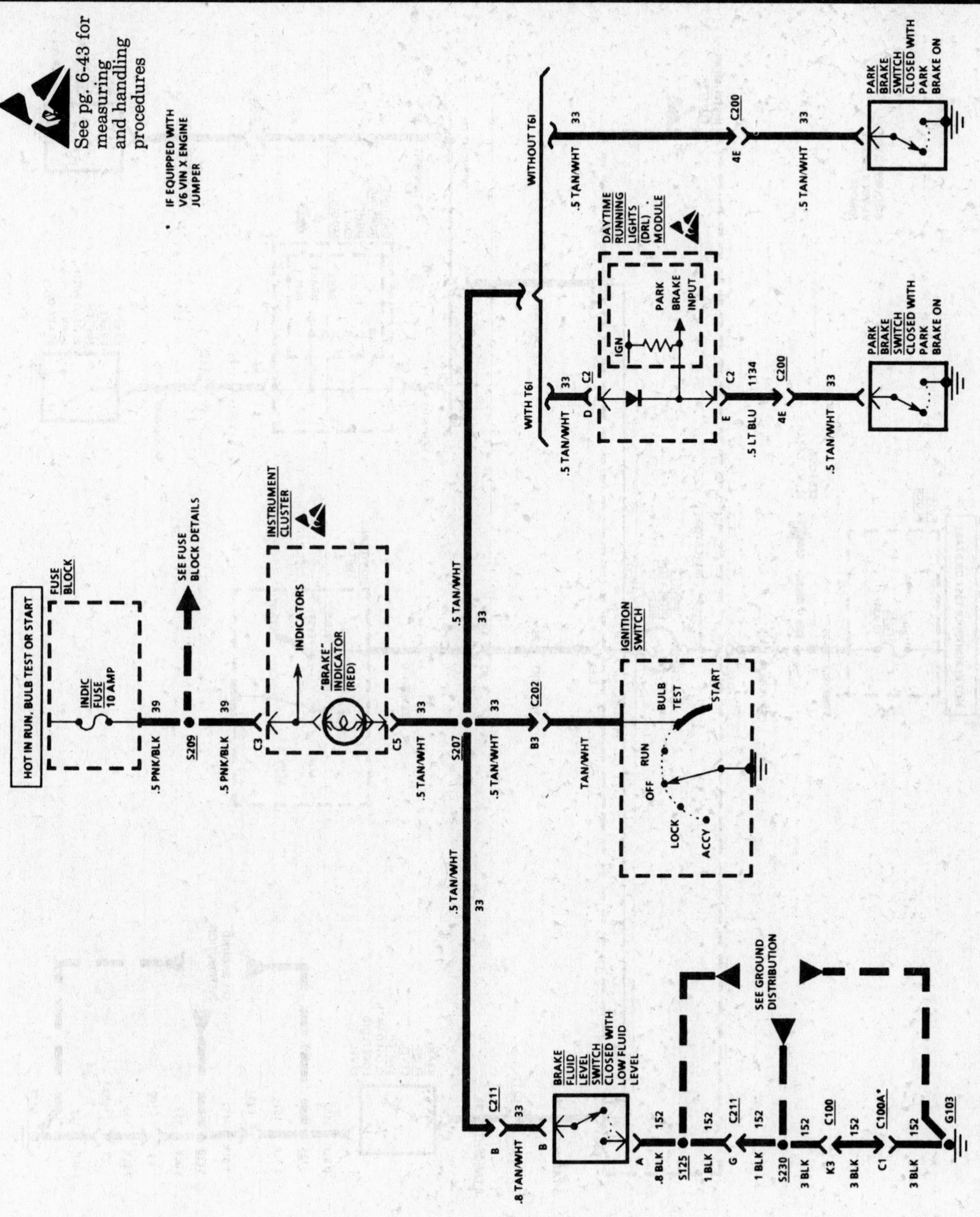

Brake warning system with base cluster—Lumina shown

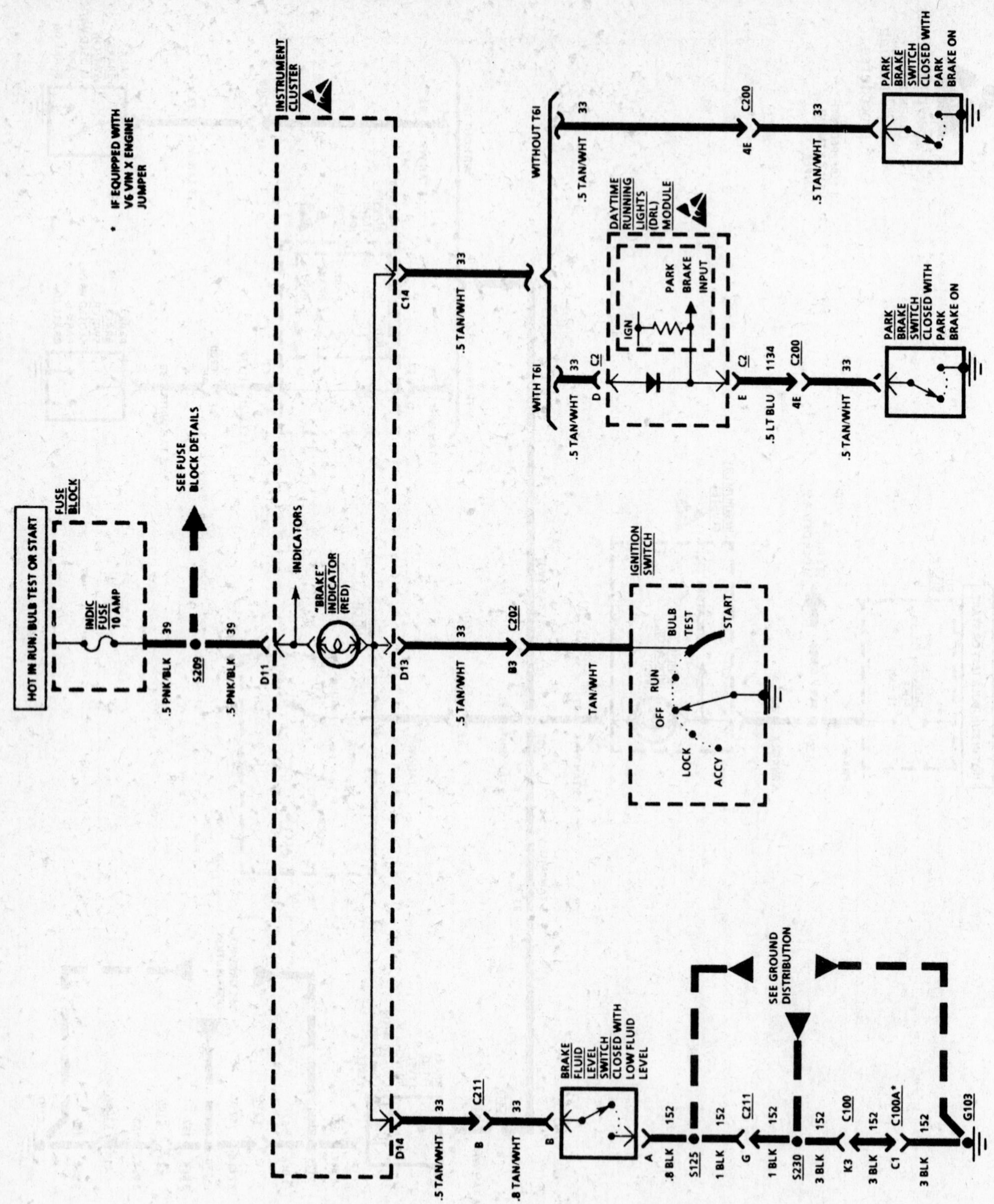

Brake warning system with gauges—Lumina shown

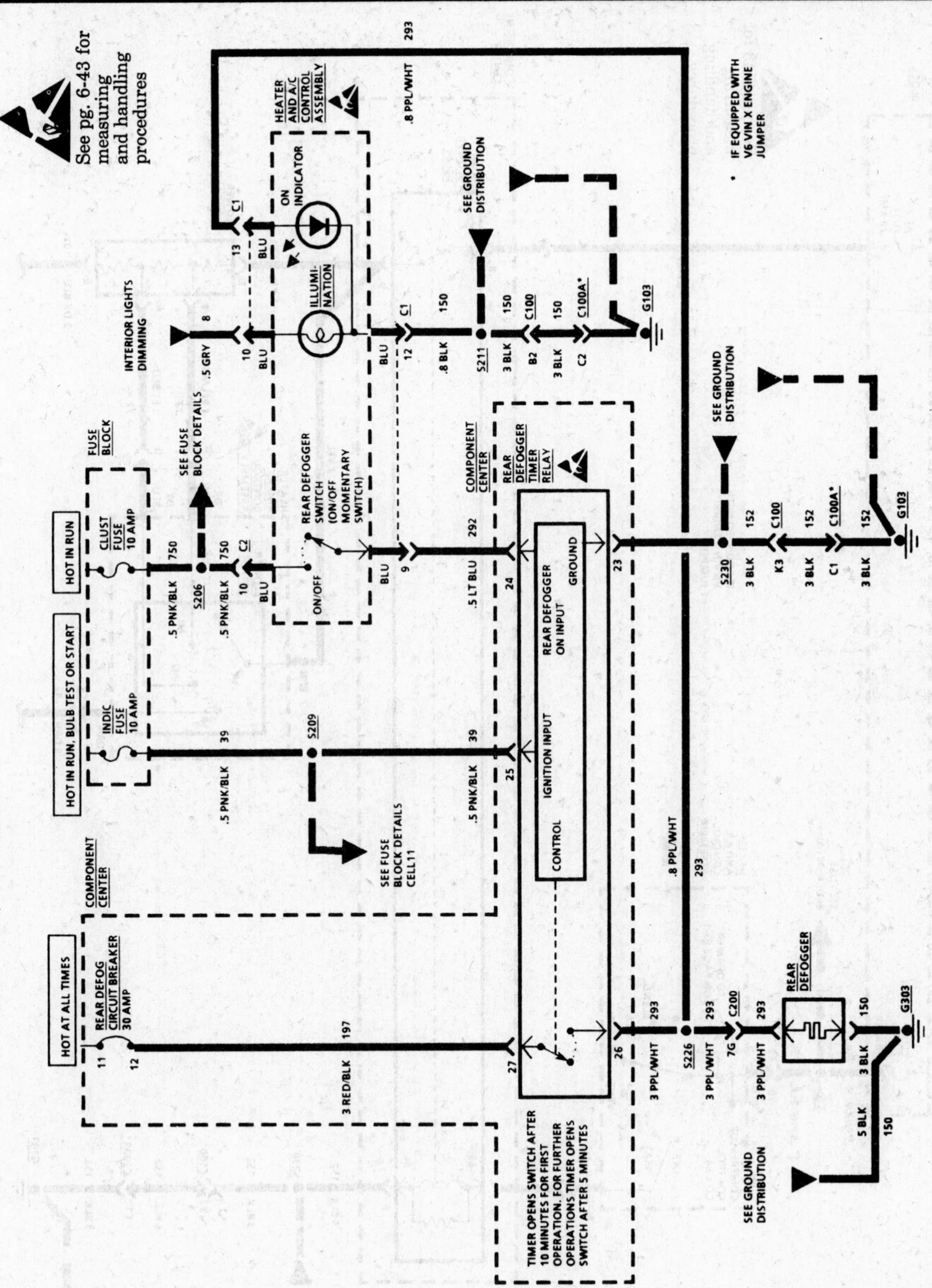

Rear defroster—Lumina shown

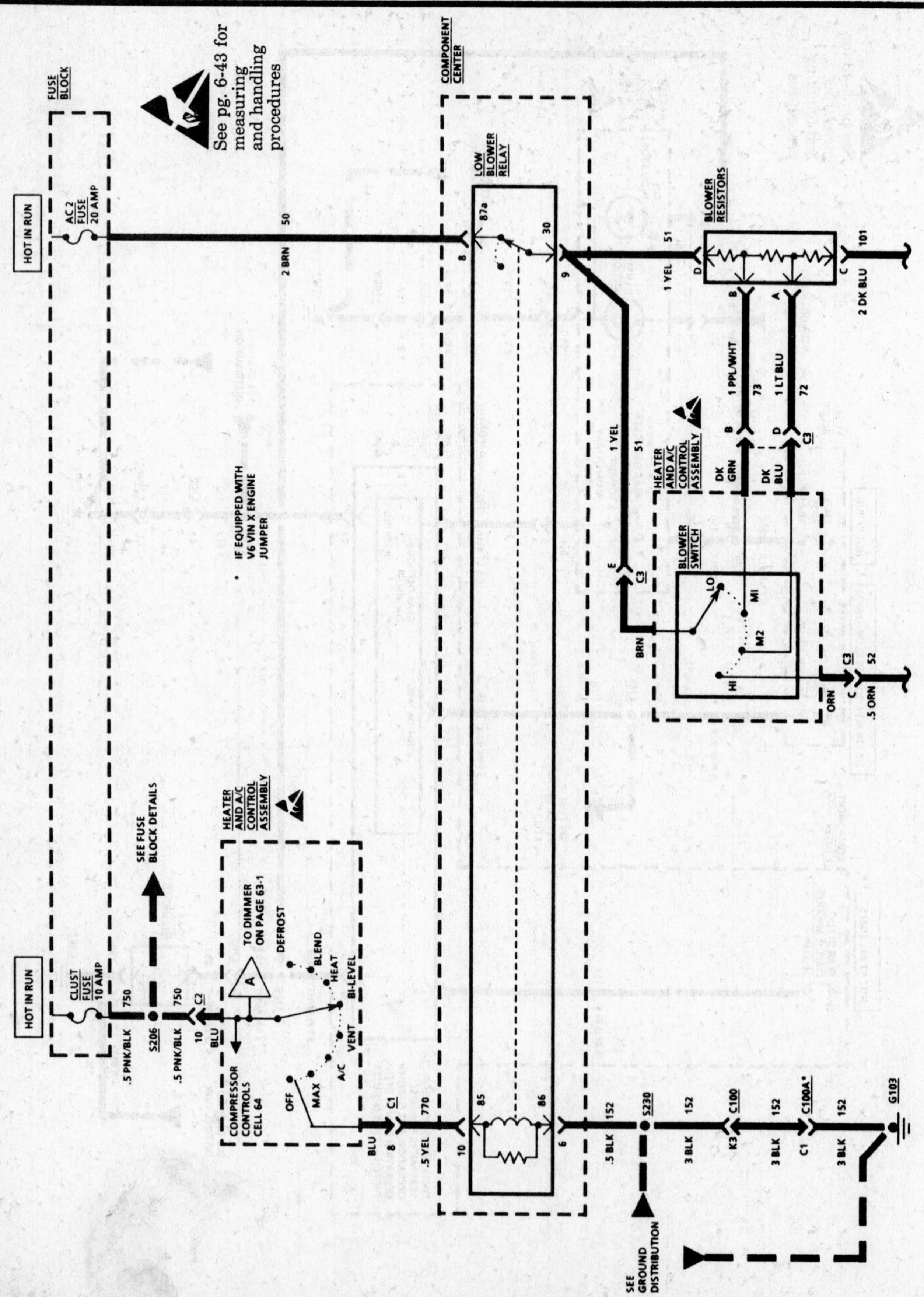

Air conditioning blower control—Lumina shown

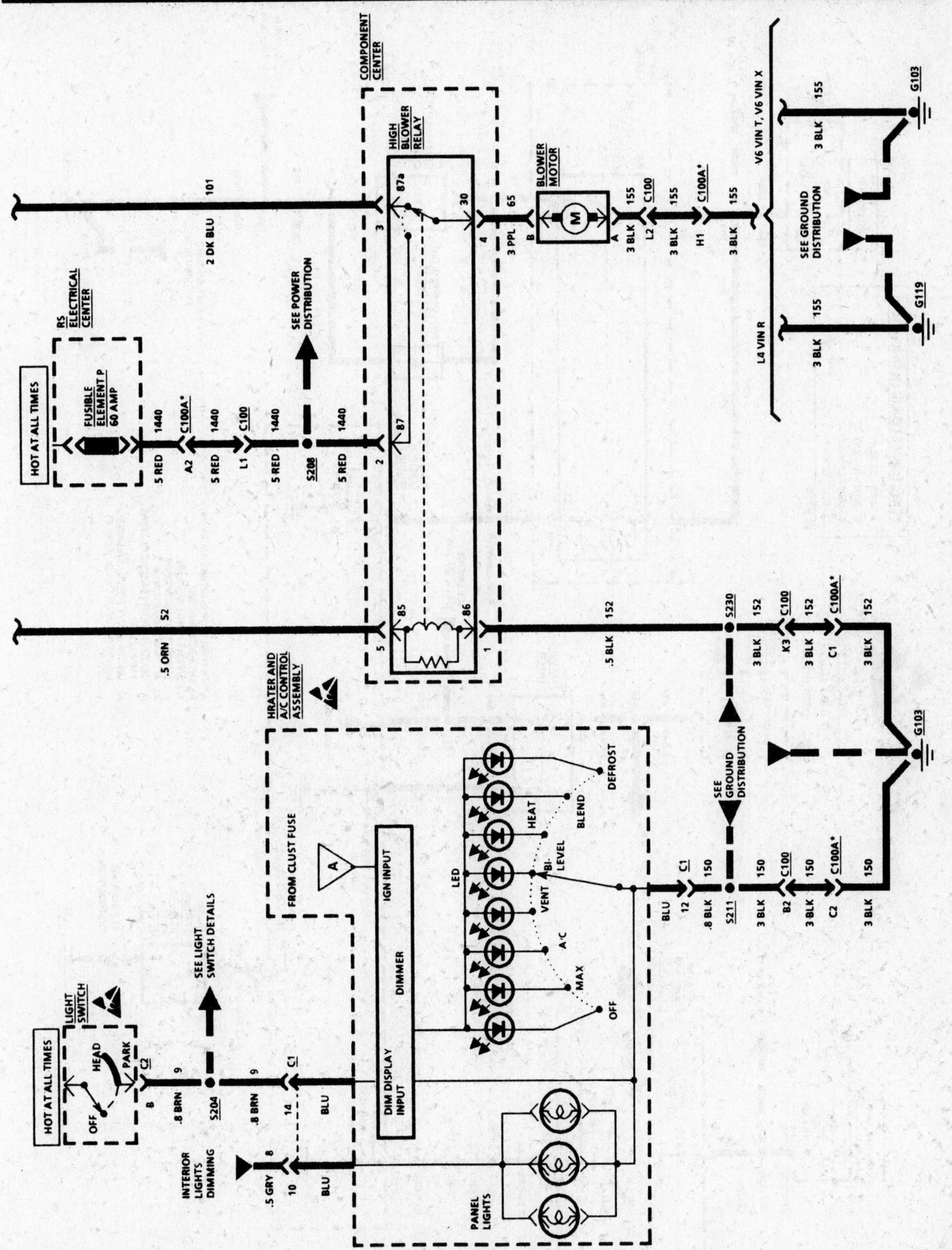

Air conditioning blower control—Lumina shown

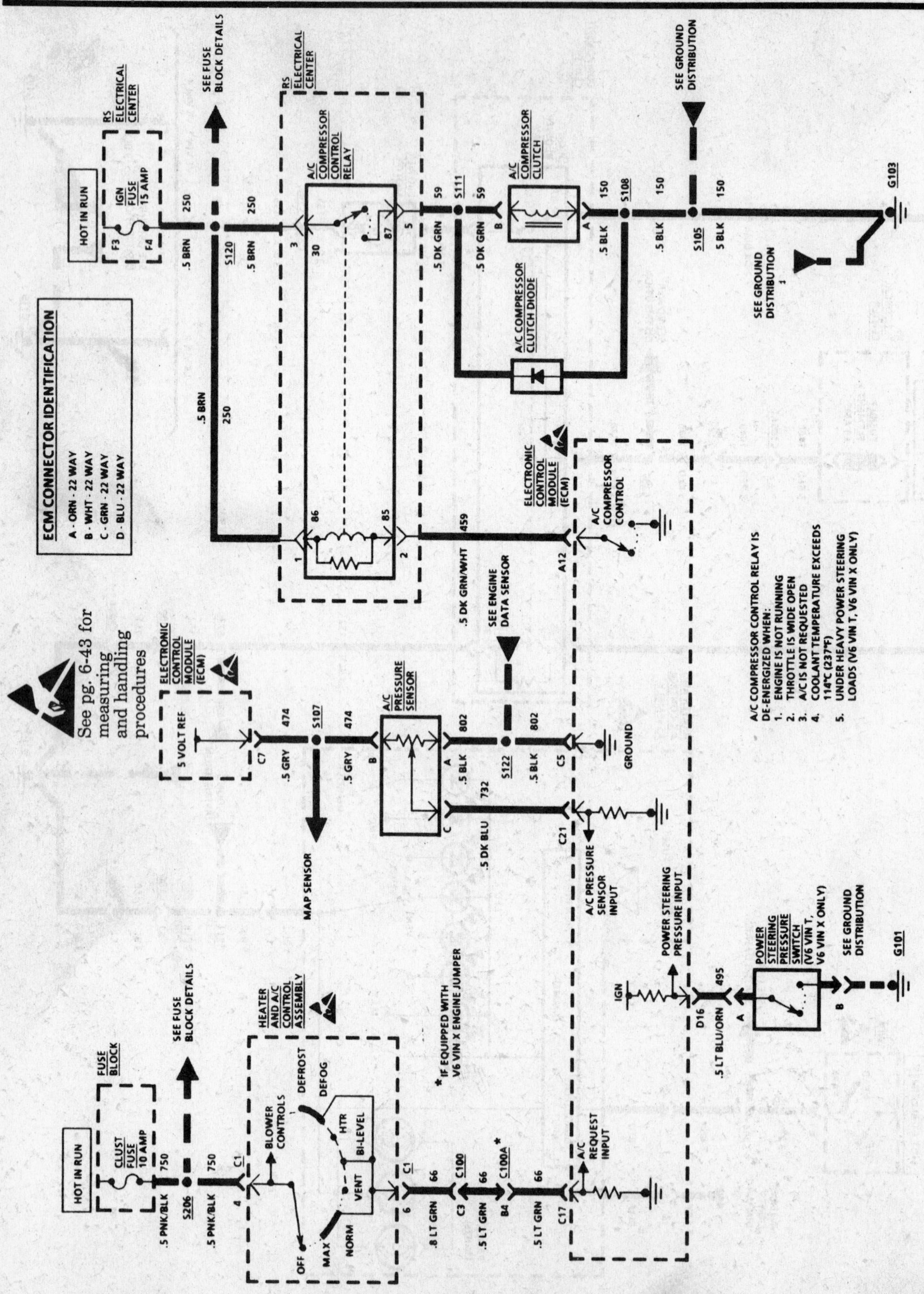

Air conditioning compressor control—Grand Prix shown

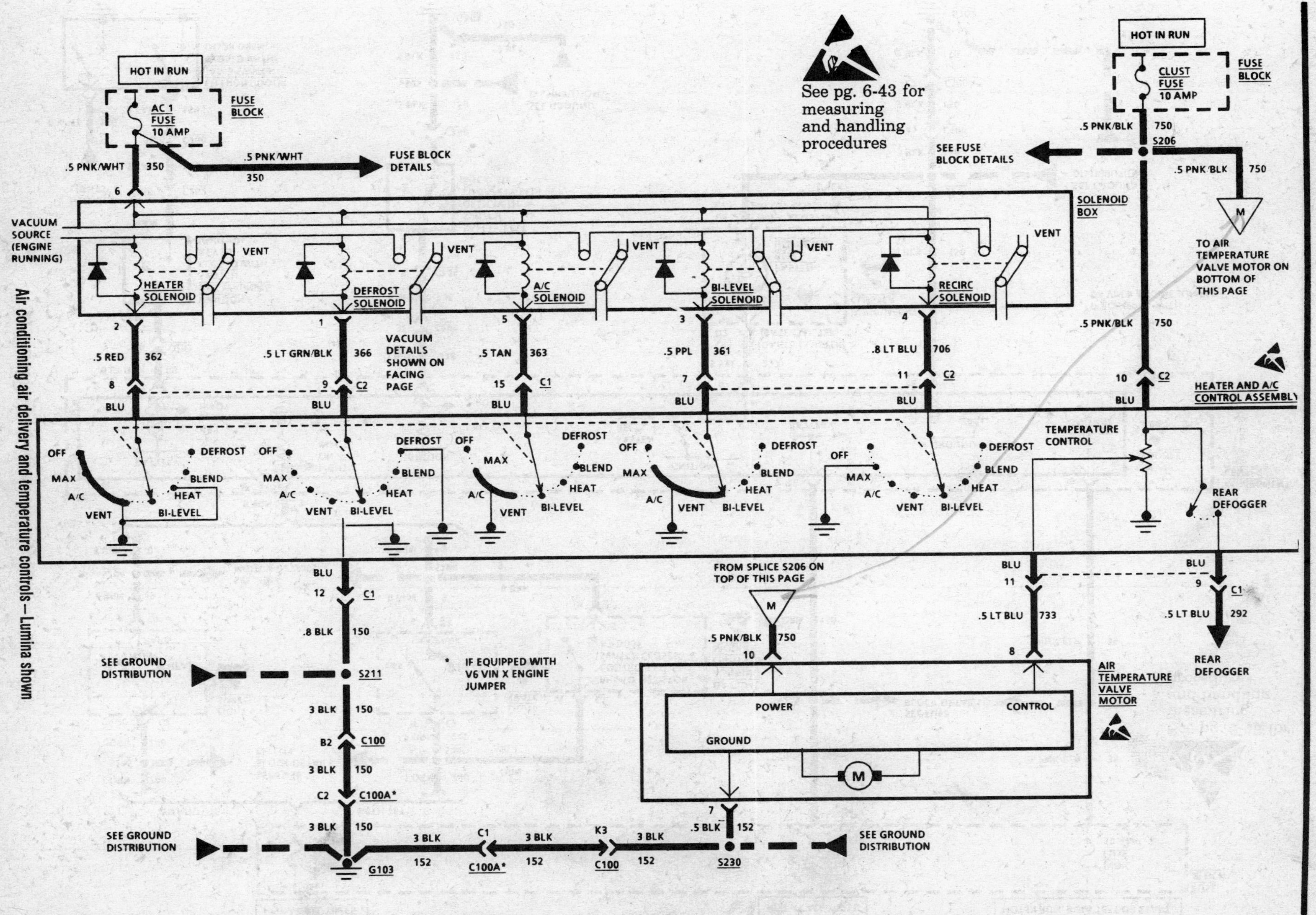

Air conditioning air delivery and temperature controls—Lumina shown

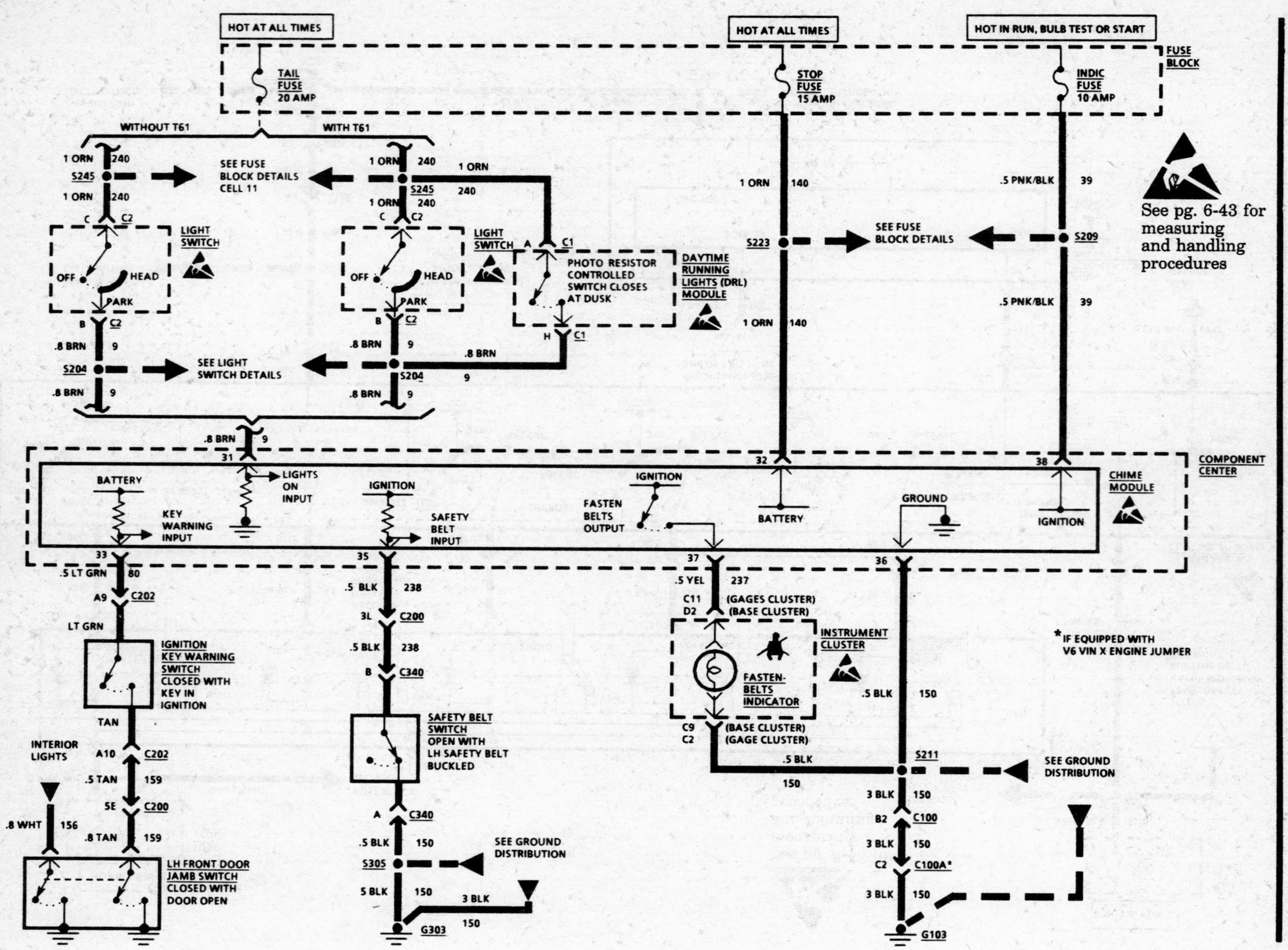

Warnings and alarms—Lumina shown

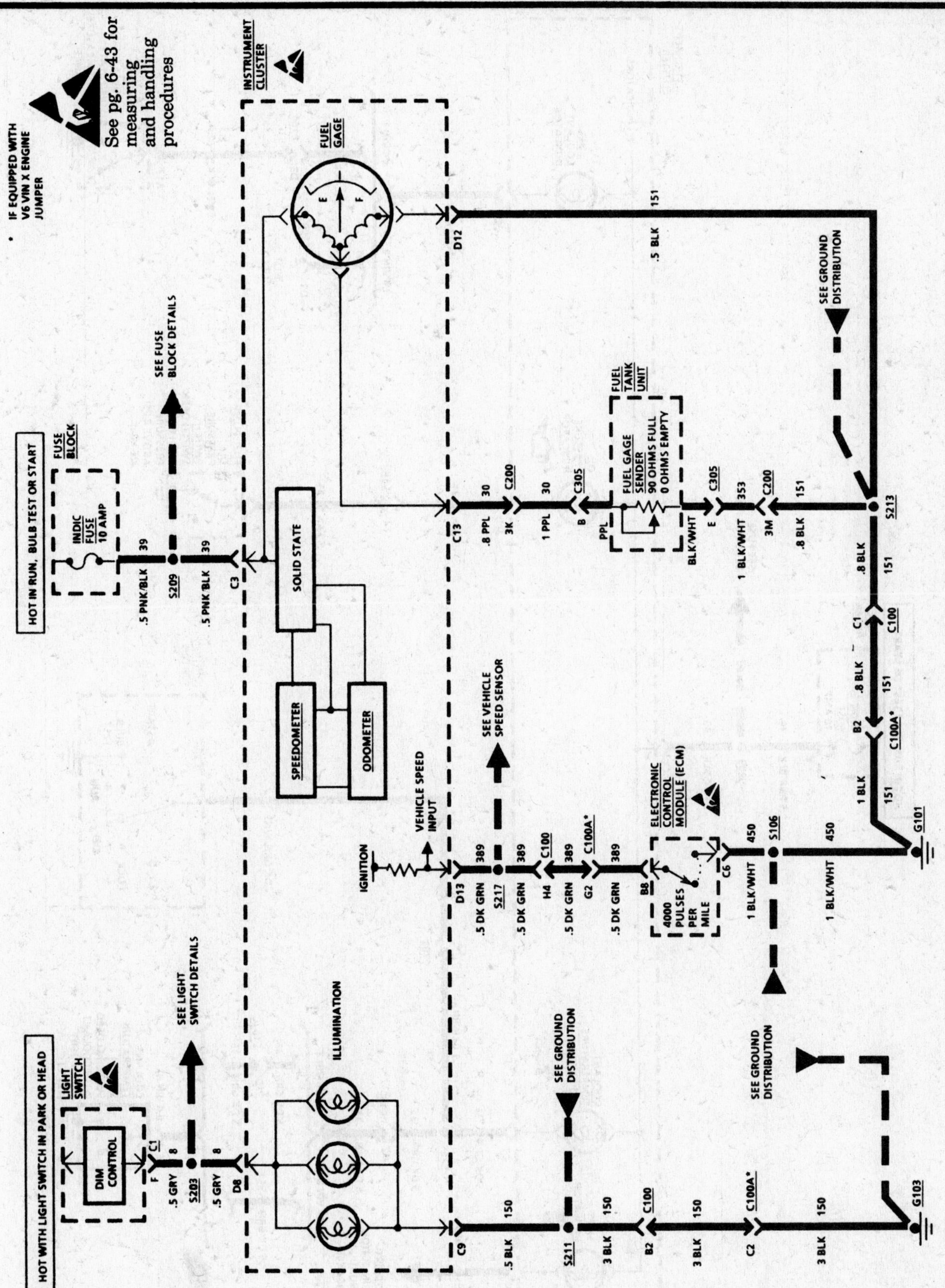

Base instrument cluster—Lumina shown

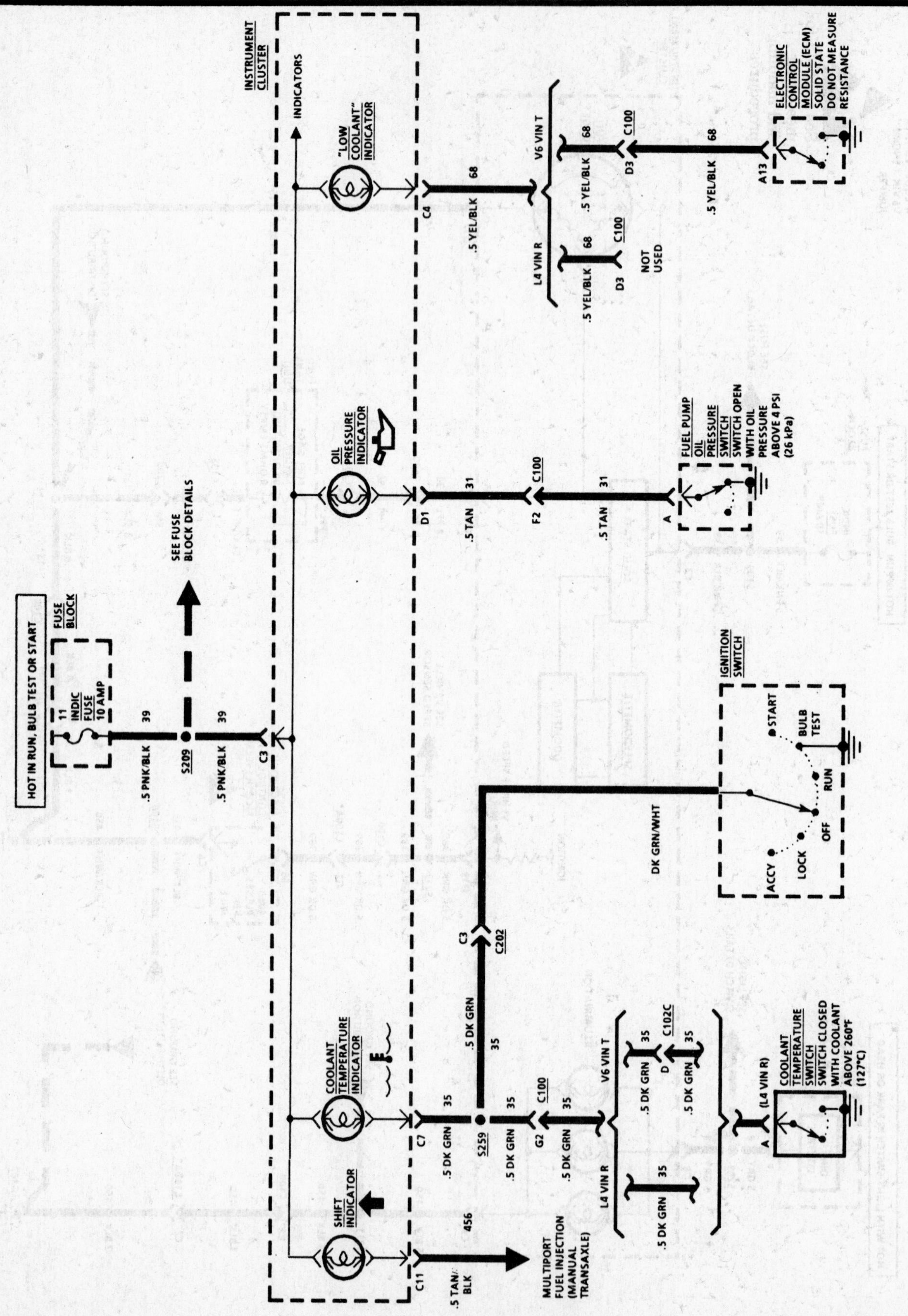

Base instrument cluster—Lumina shown

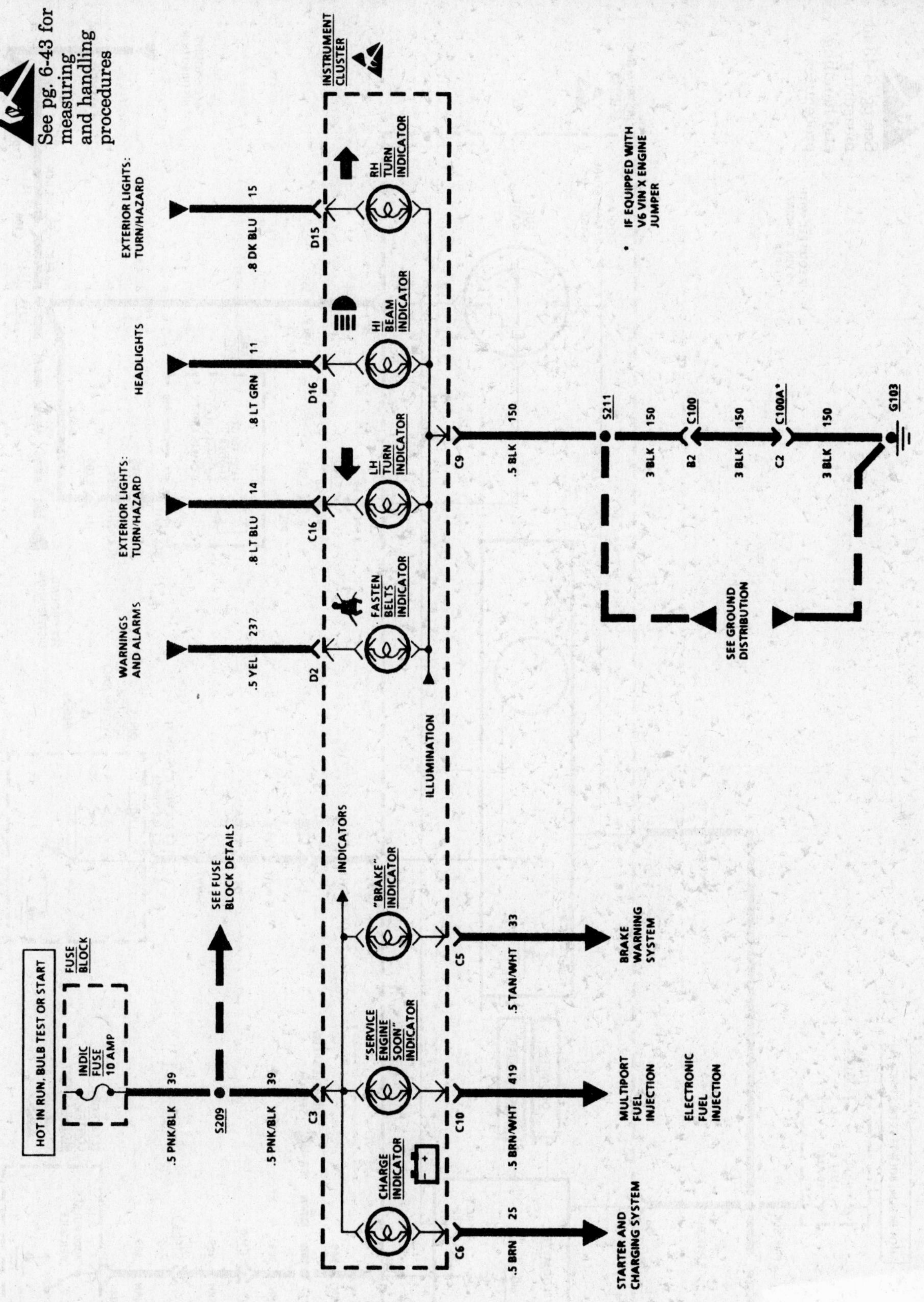

Base instrument cluster—Lumina shown

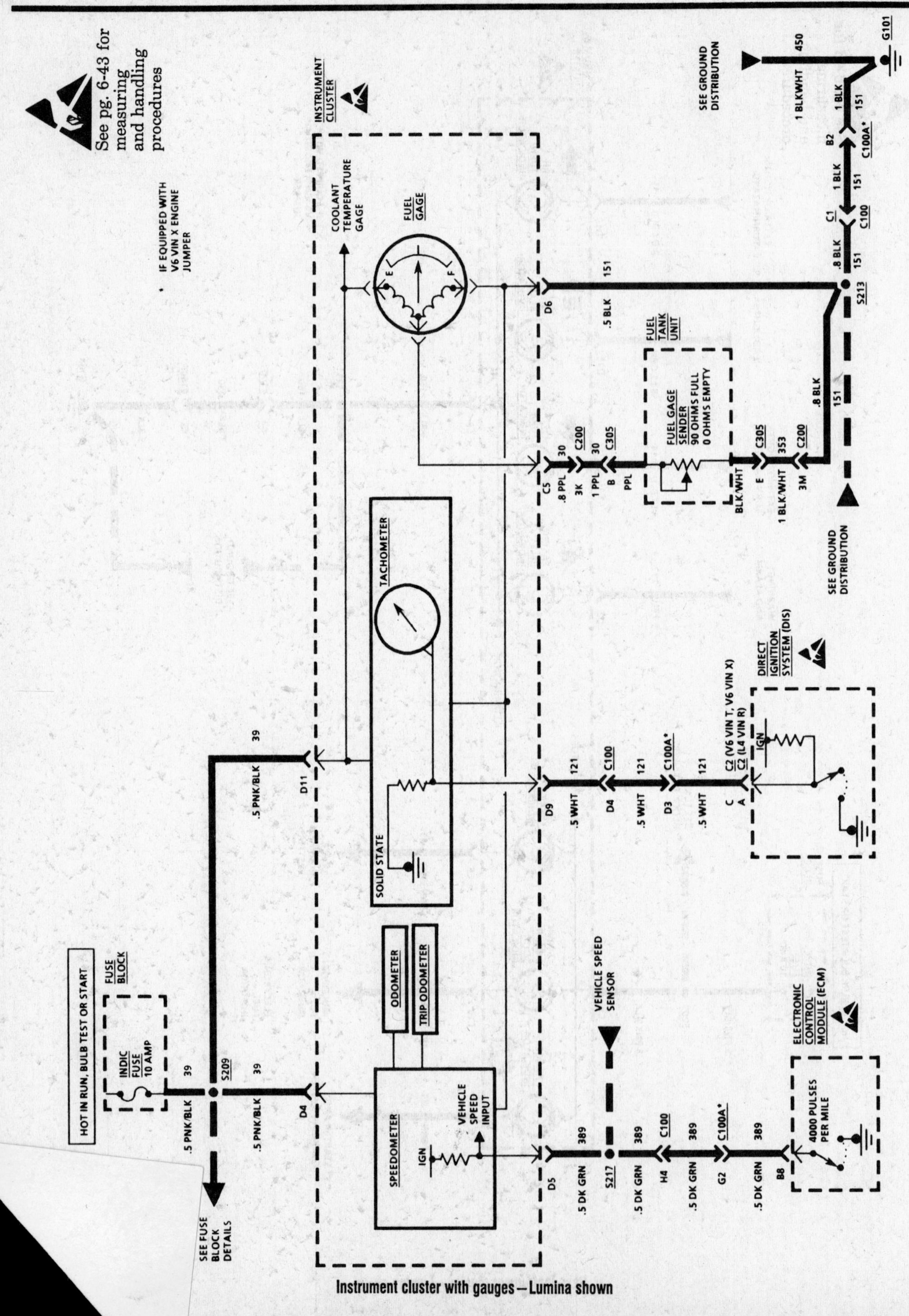

Instrument cluster with gauges—Lumina shown

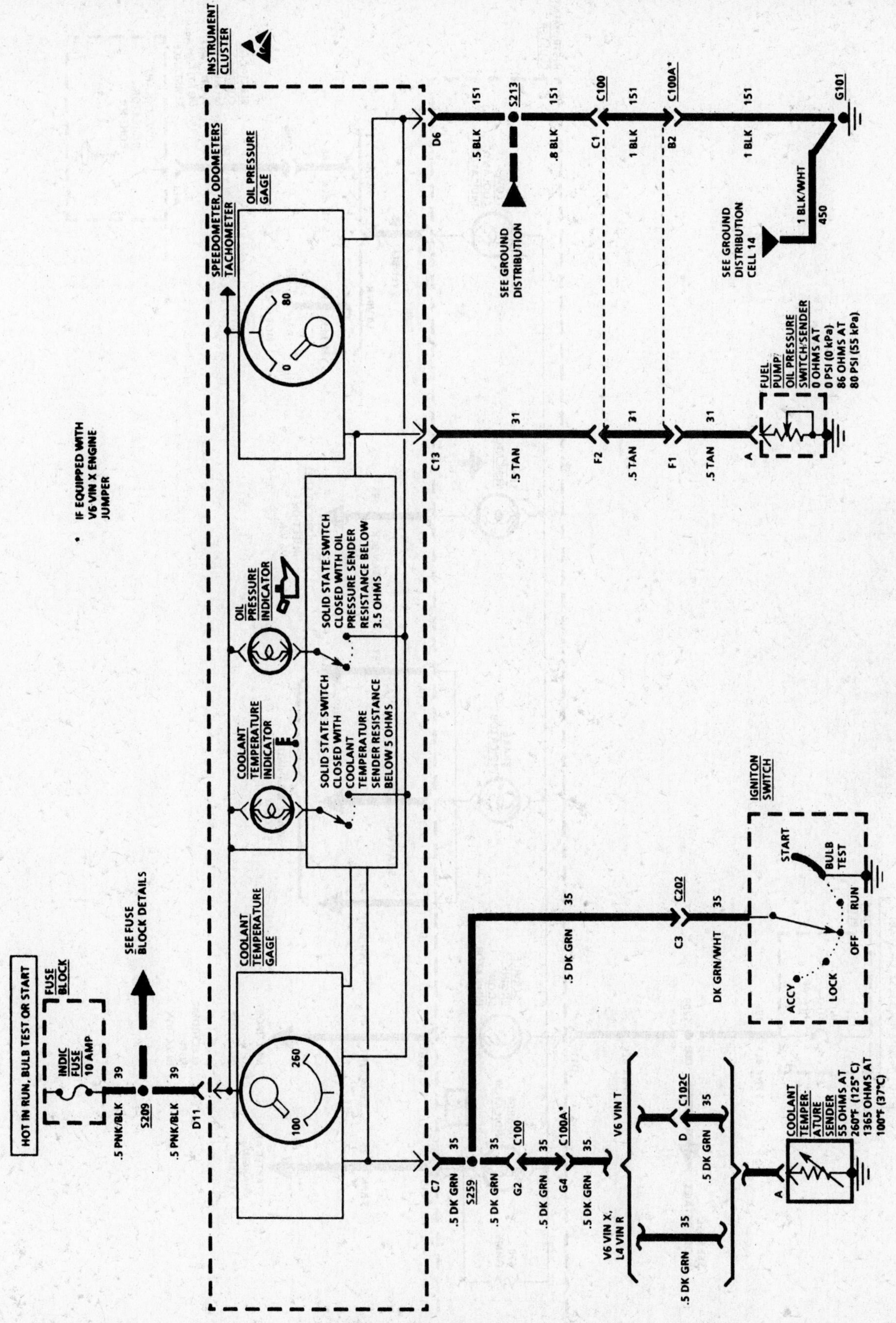

Instrument cluster with gauges—Lumina shown

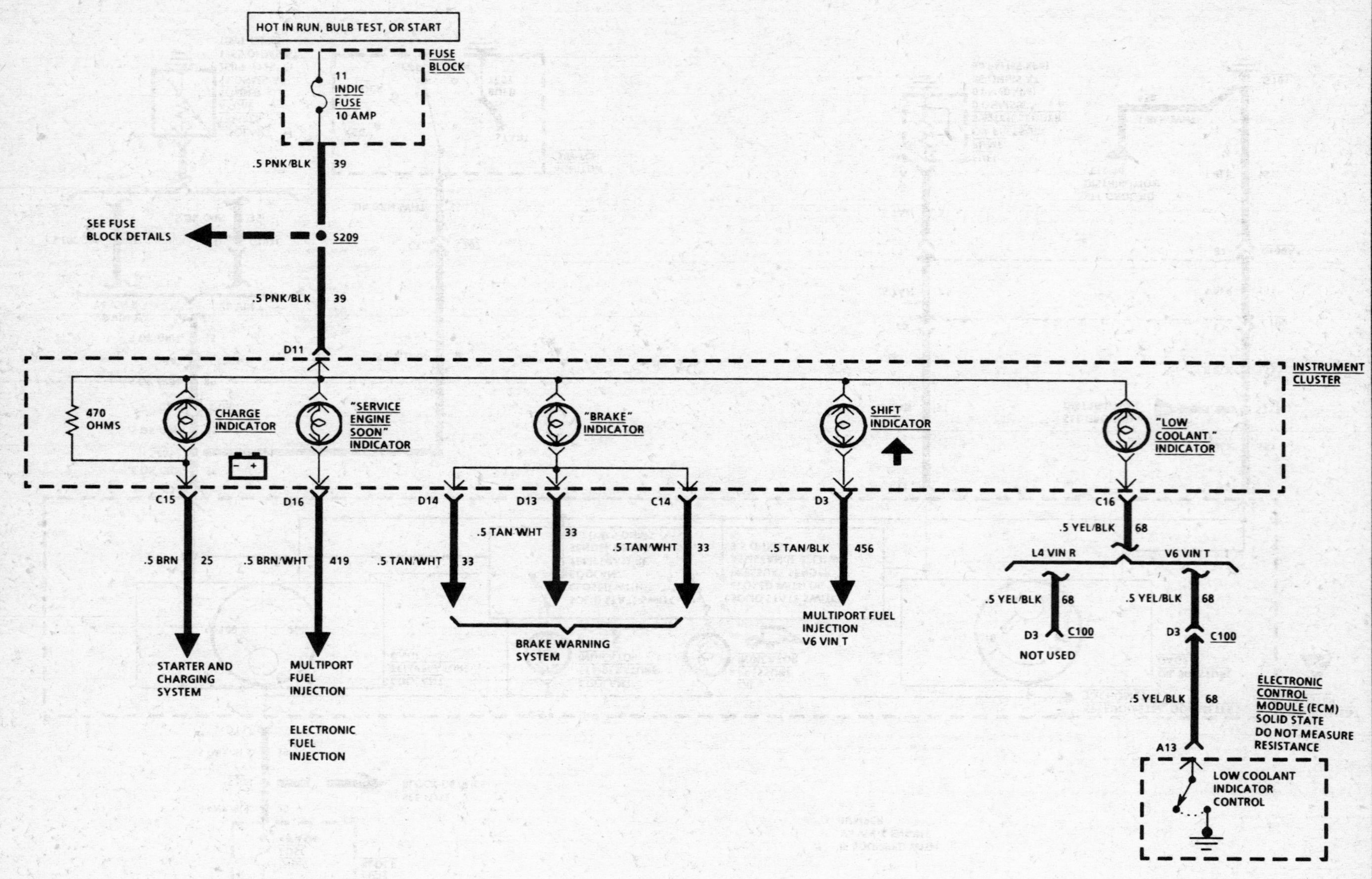

Instrument cluster indicators—Lumina shown

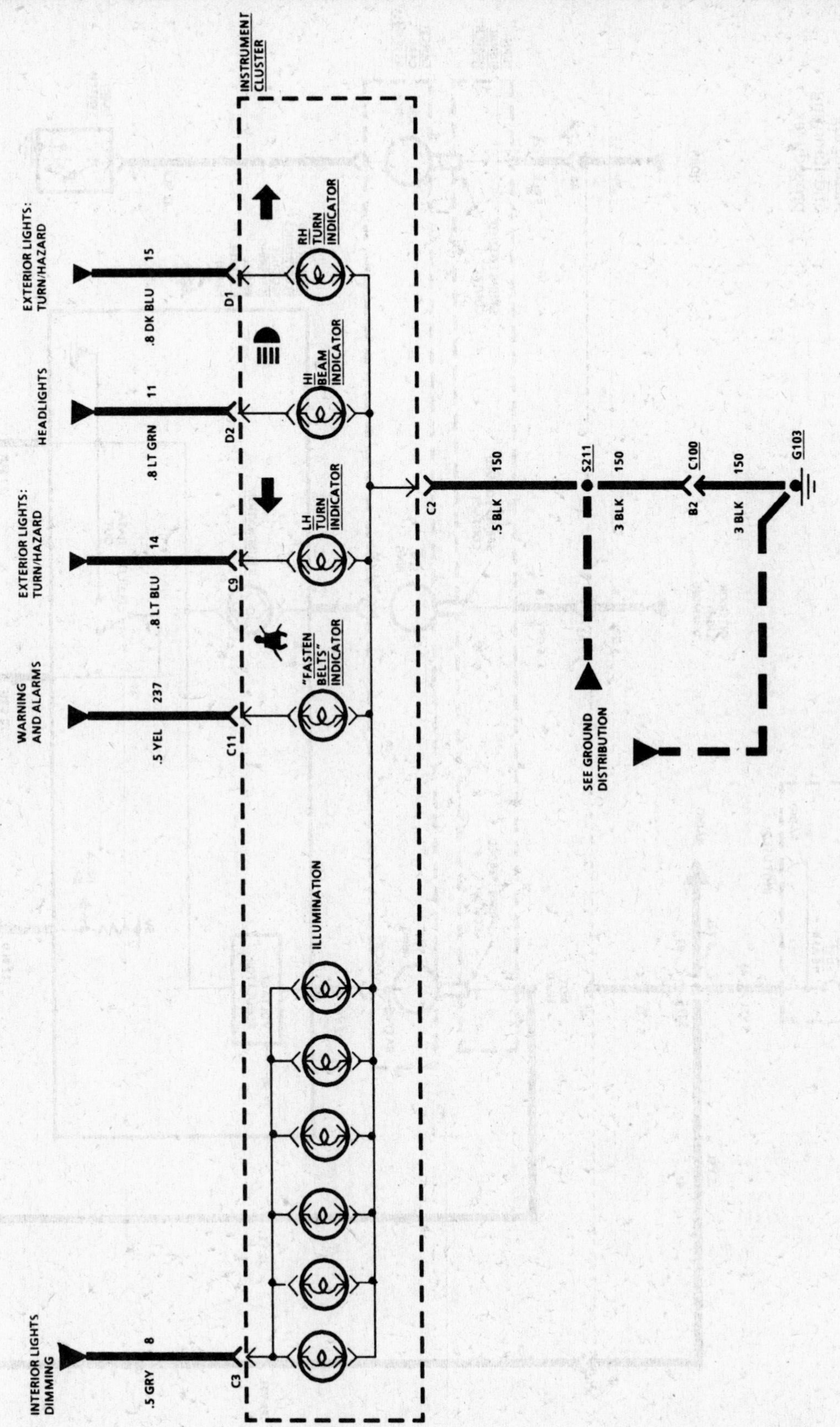

Instrument cluster indicators — Lumina shown

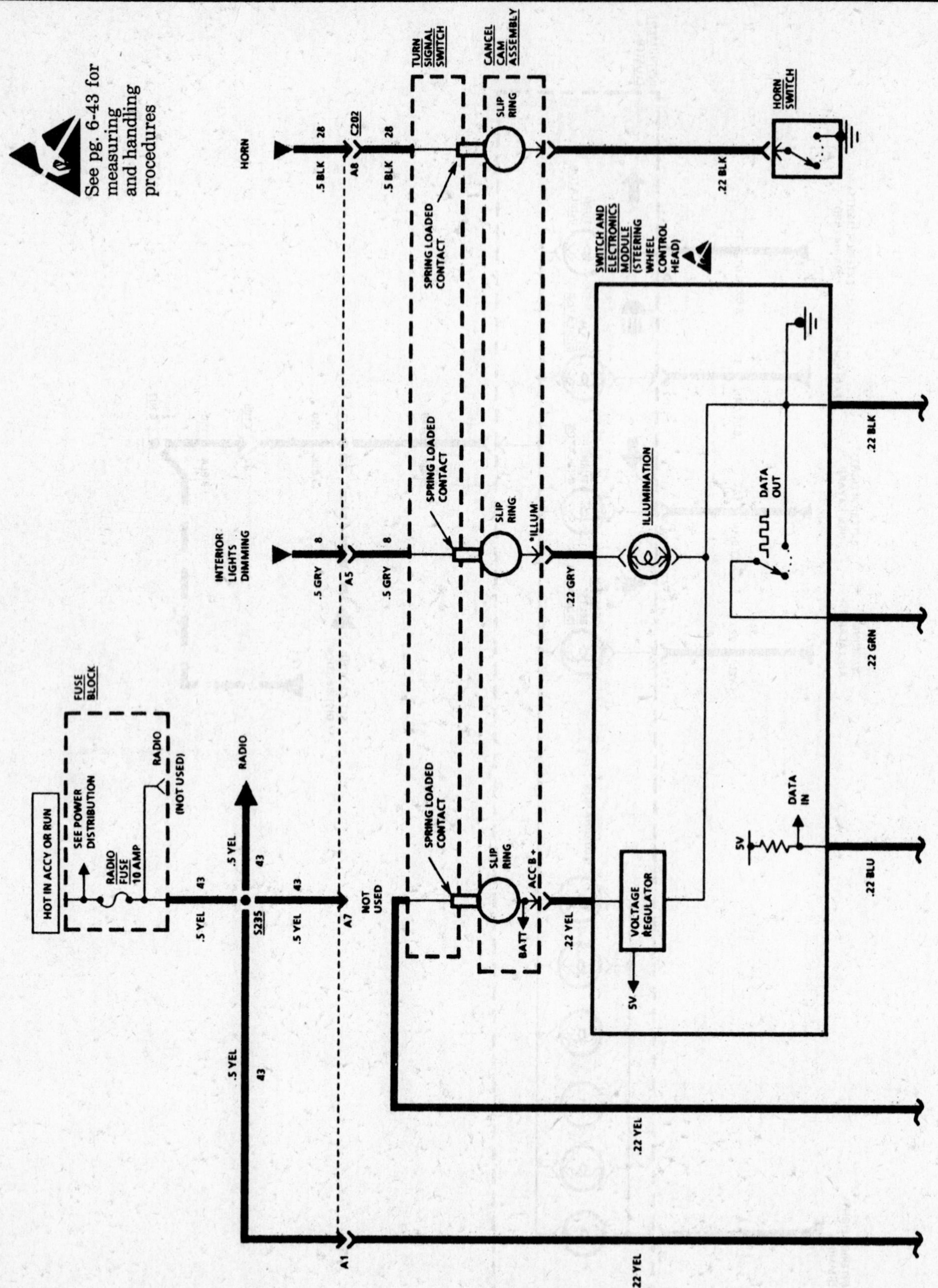

Steering wheel controls—Grand Prix shown

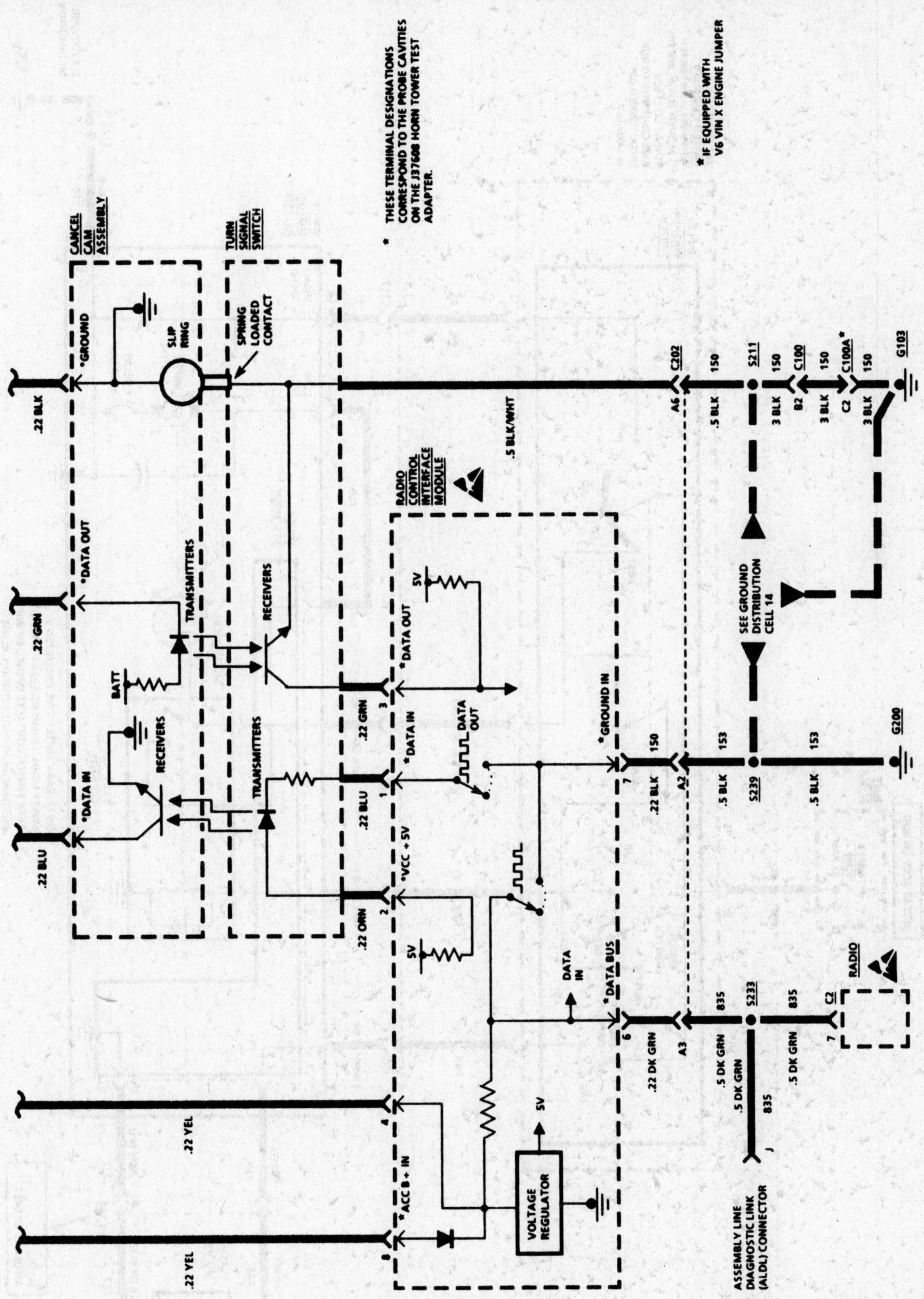

Steering wheel controls—Grand Prix shown

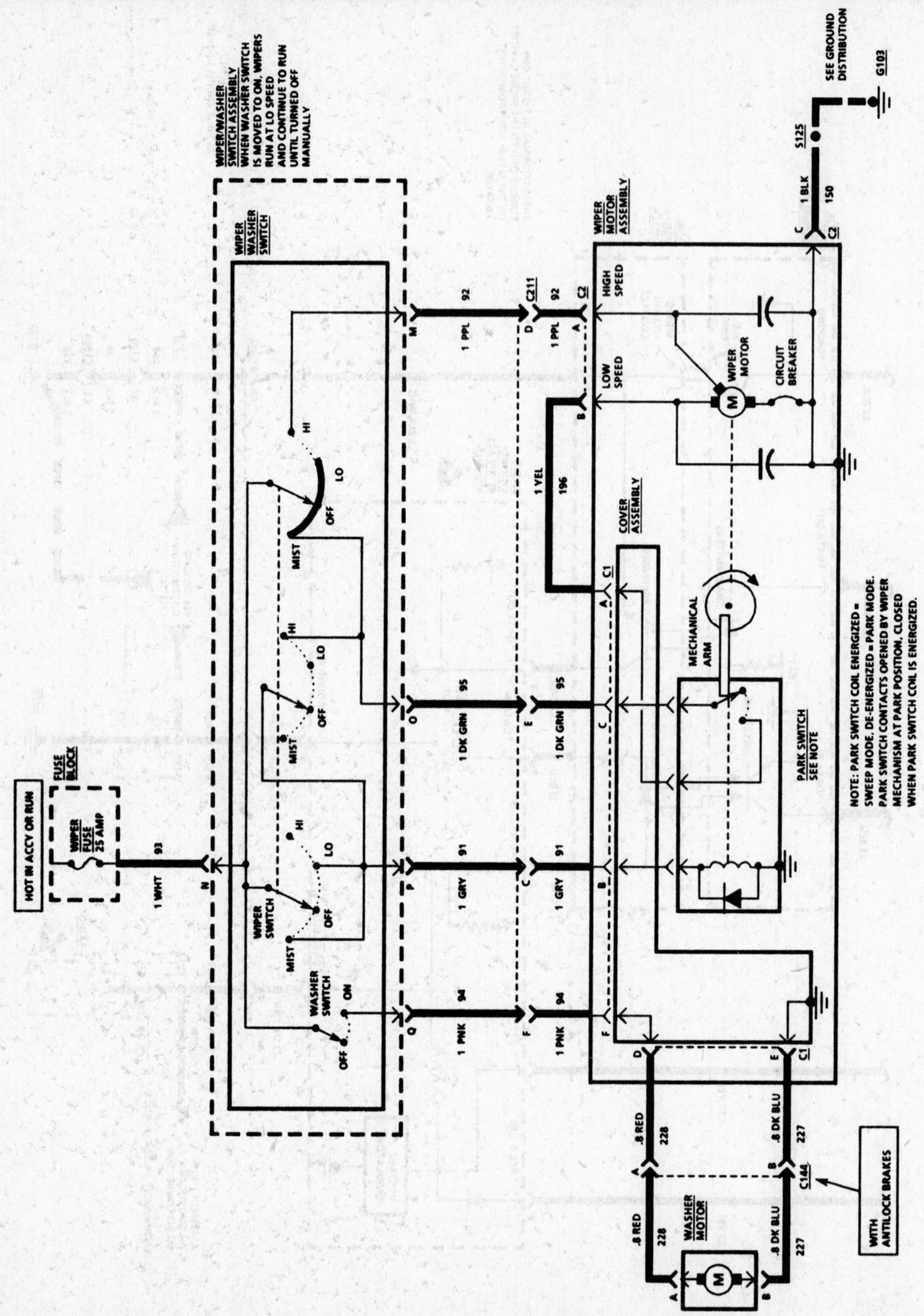

Wiper/washer system—Grand Prix shown

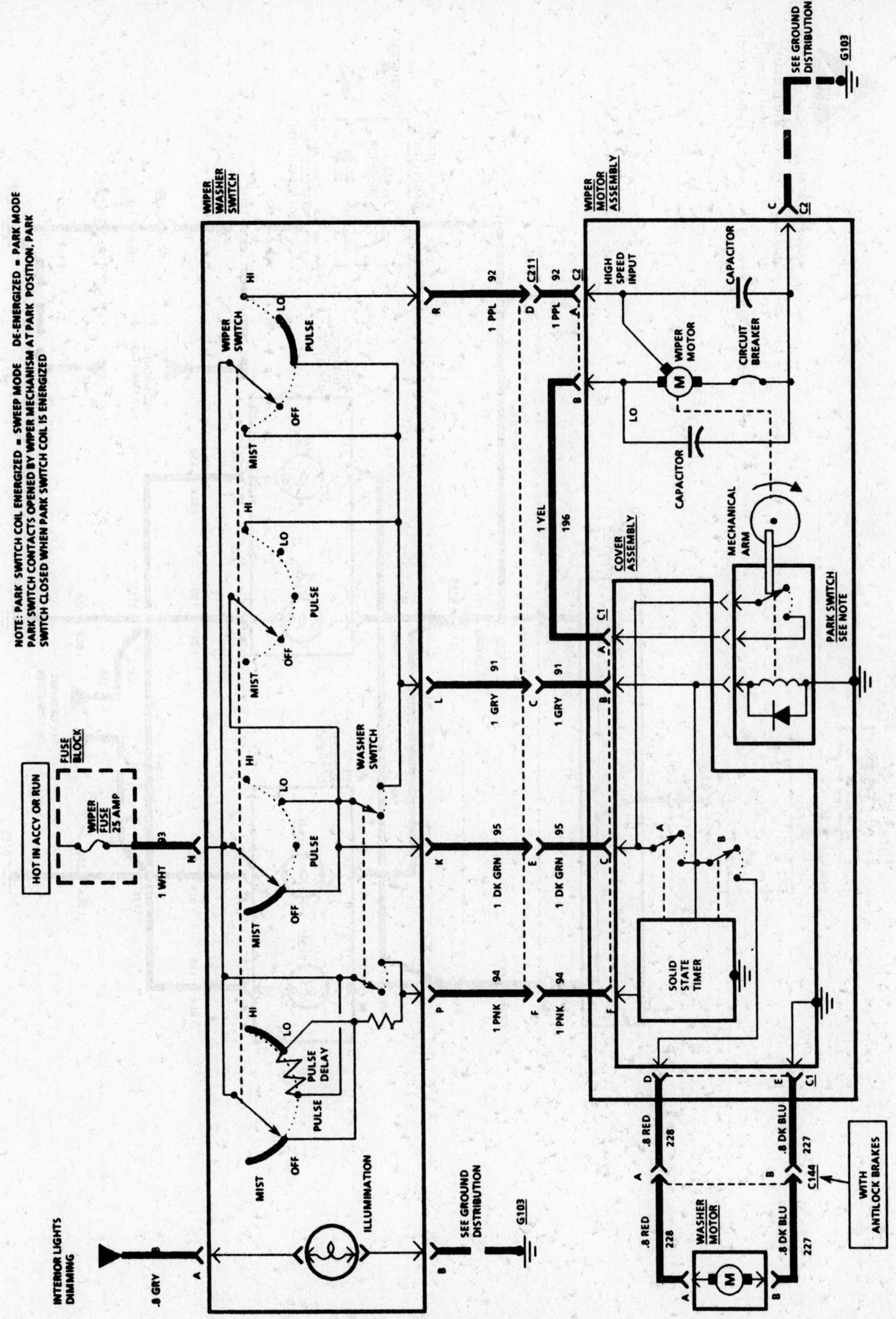

Intermittent wiper/washer system – Grand Prix shown

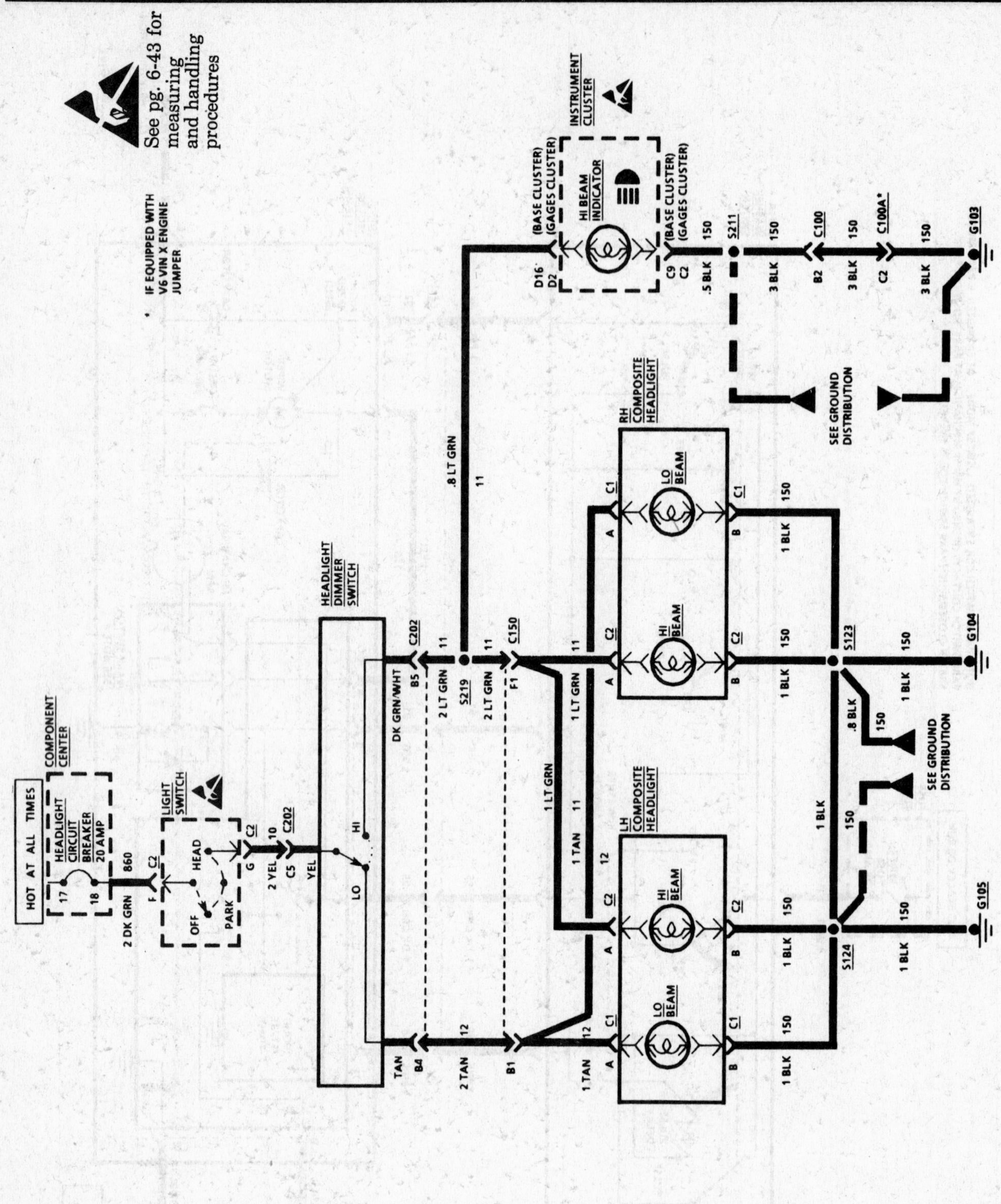

Headlights without Daytime Running Lights—Lumina shown

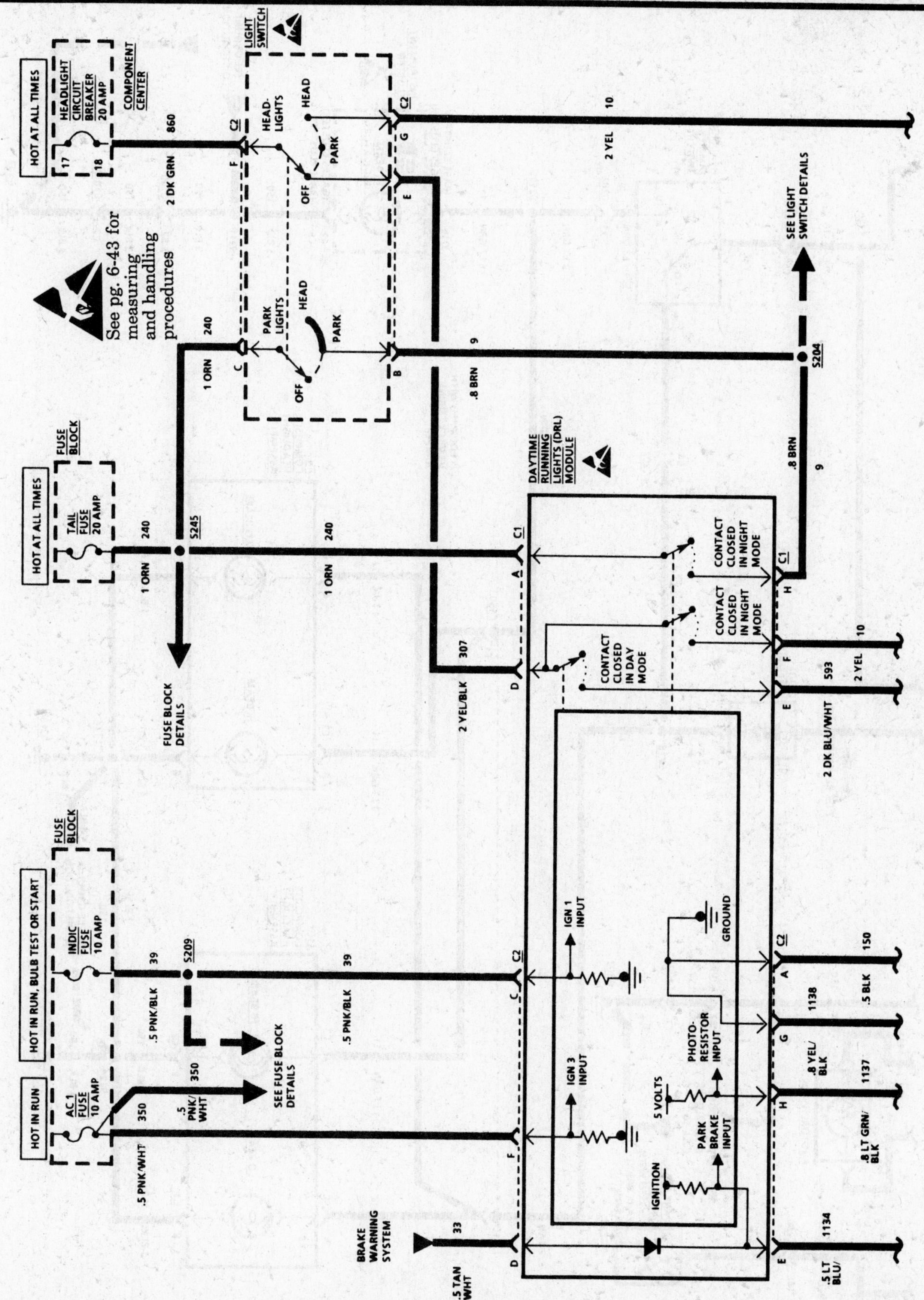

Headlights with Daytime Running Lights—Lumina shown

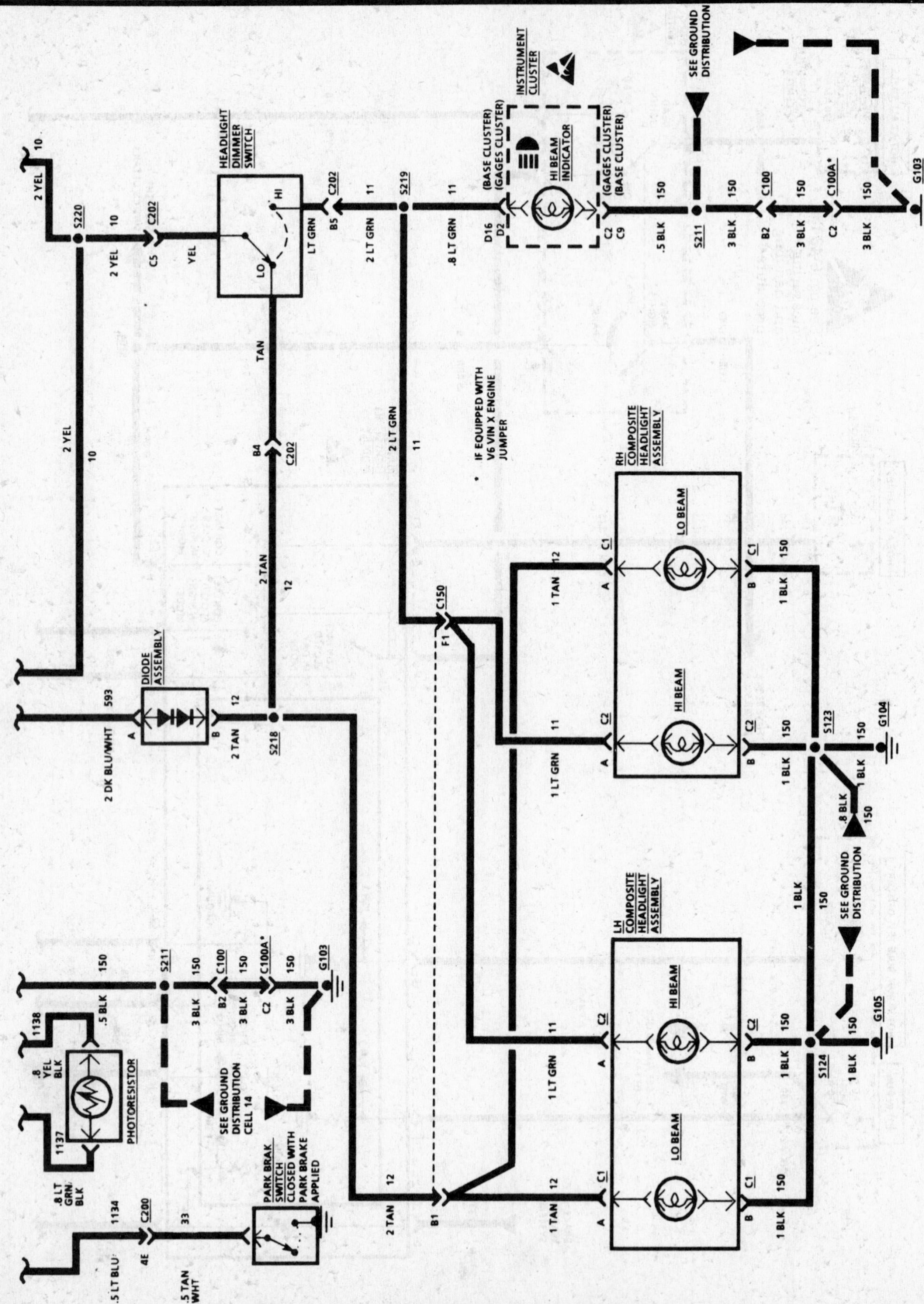

Headlights with Daytime Running Lights—Lumina shown

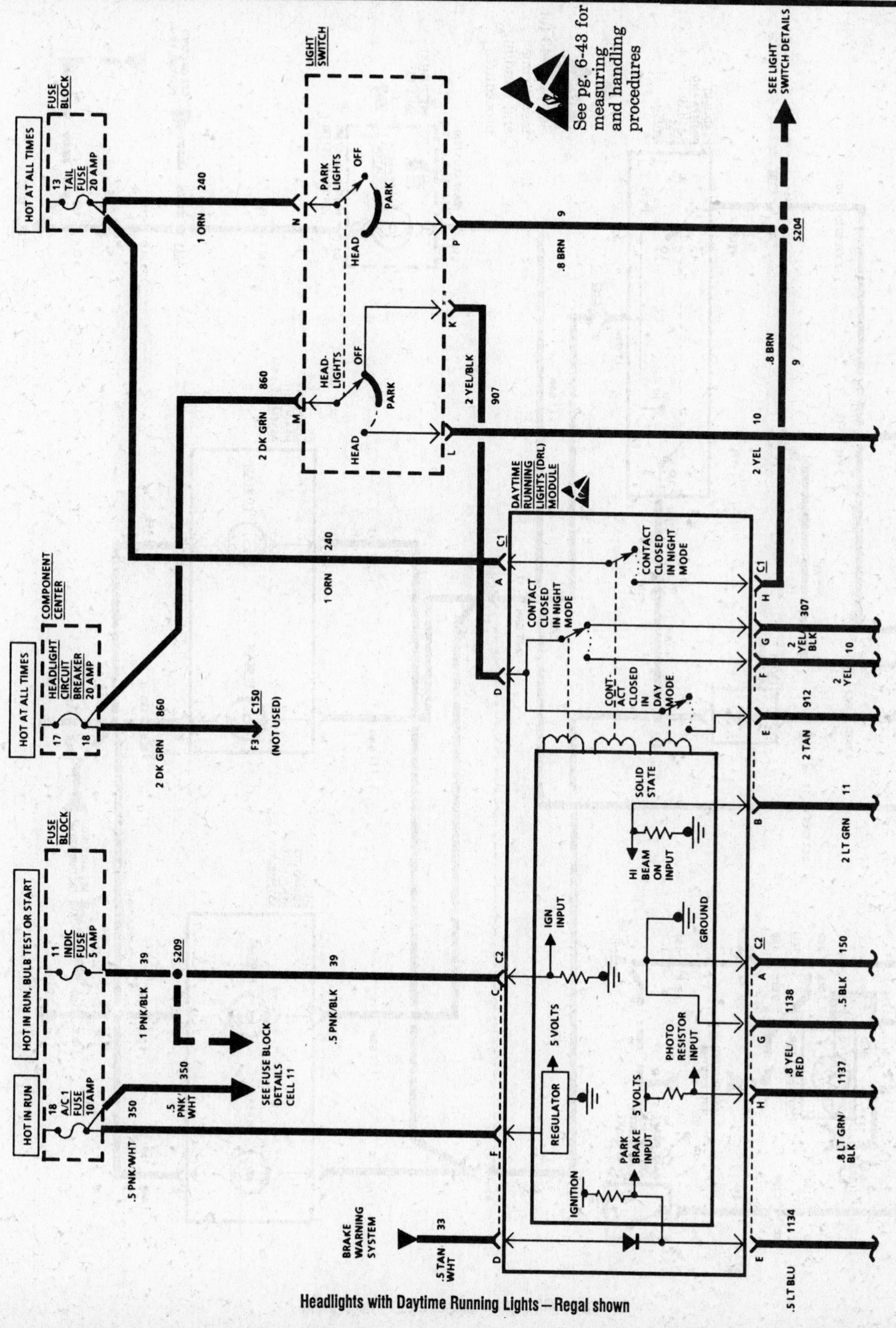

Headlights with Daytime Running Lights—Regal shown

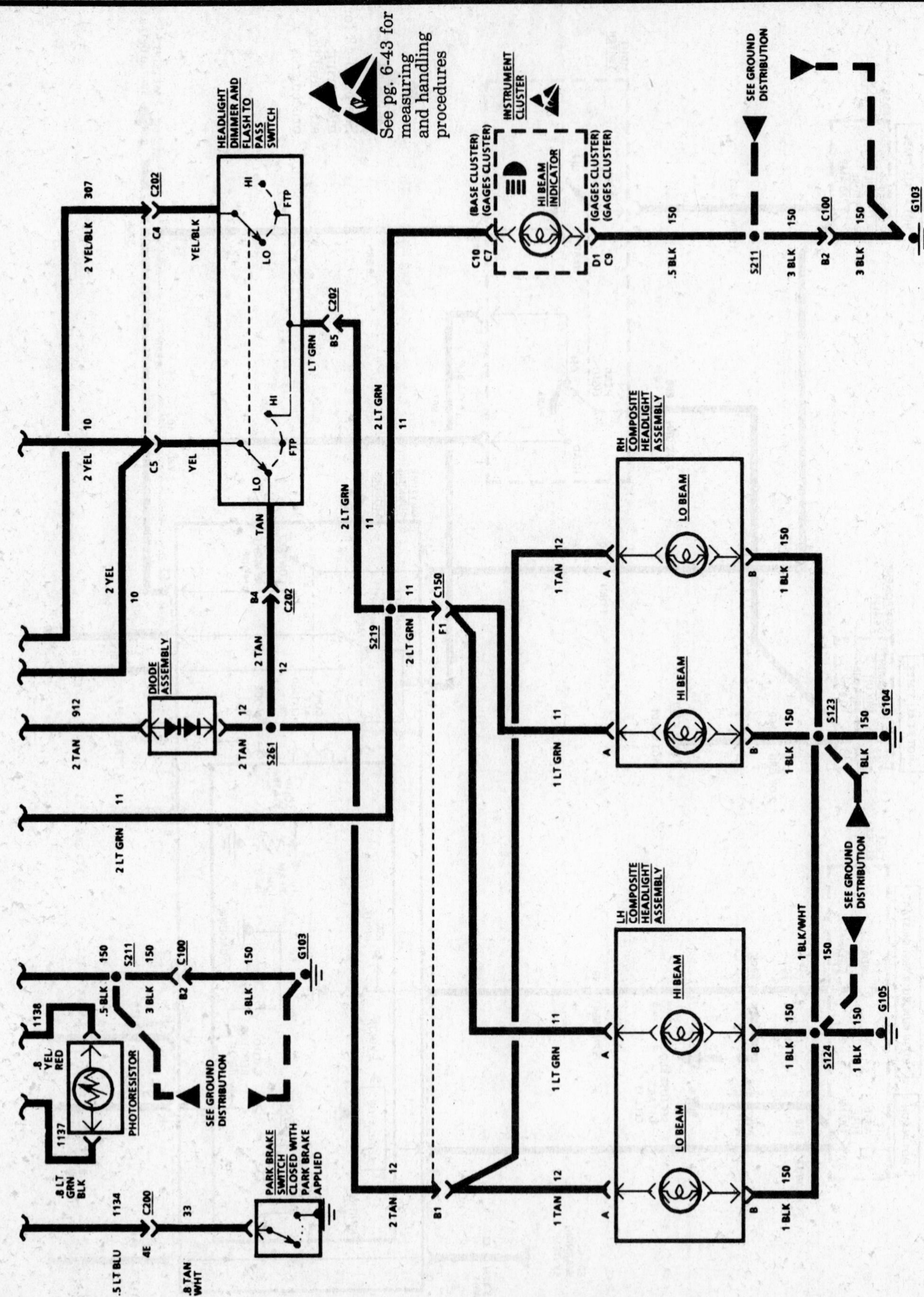

Headlights with Daytime Running Lights—Regal shown

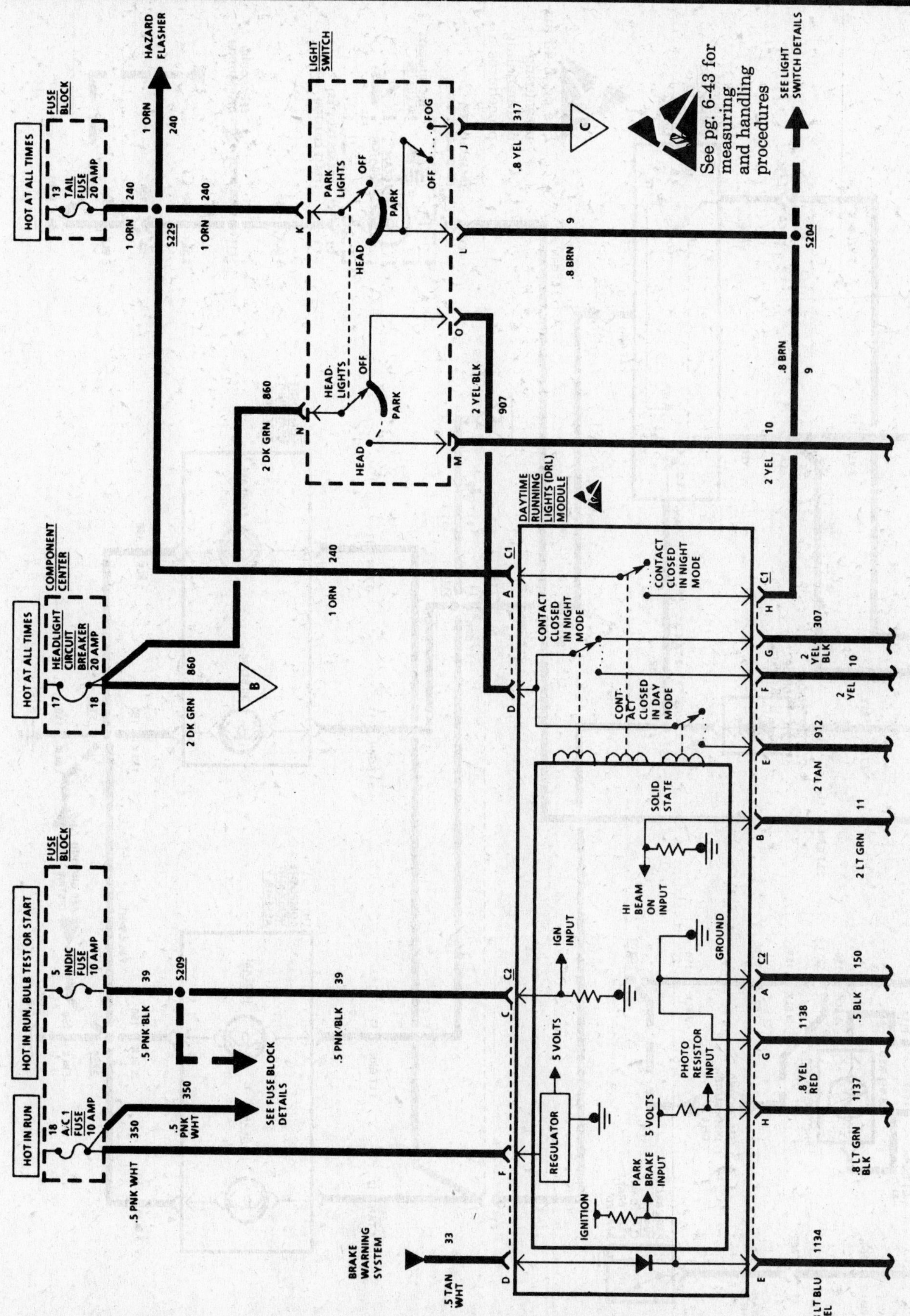

Headlights and fog lights with Daytime Running Lights – Grand Prix shown

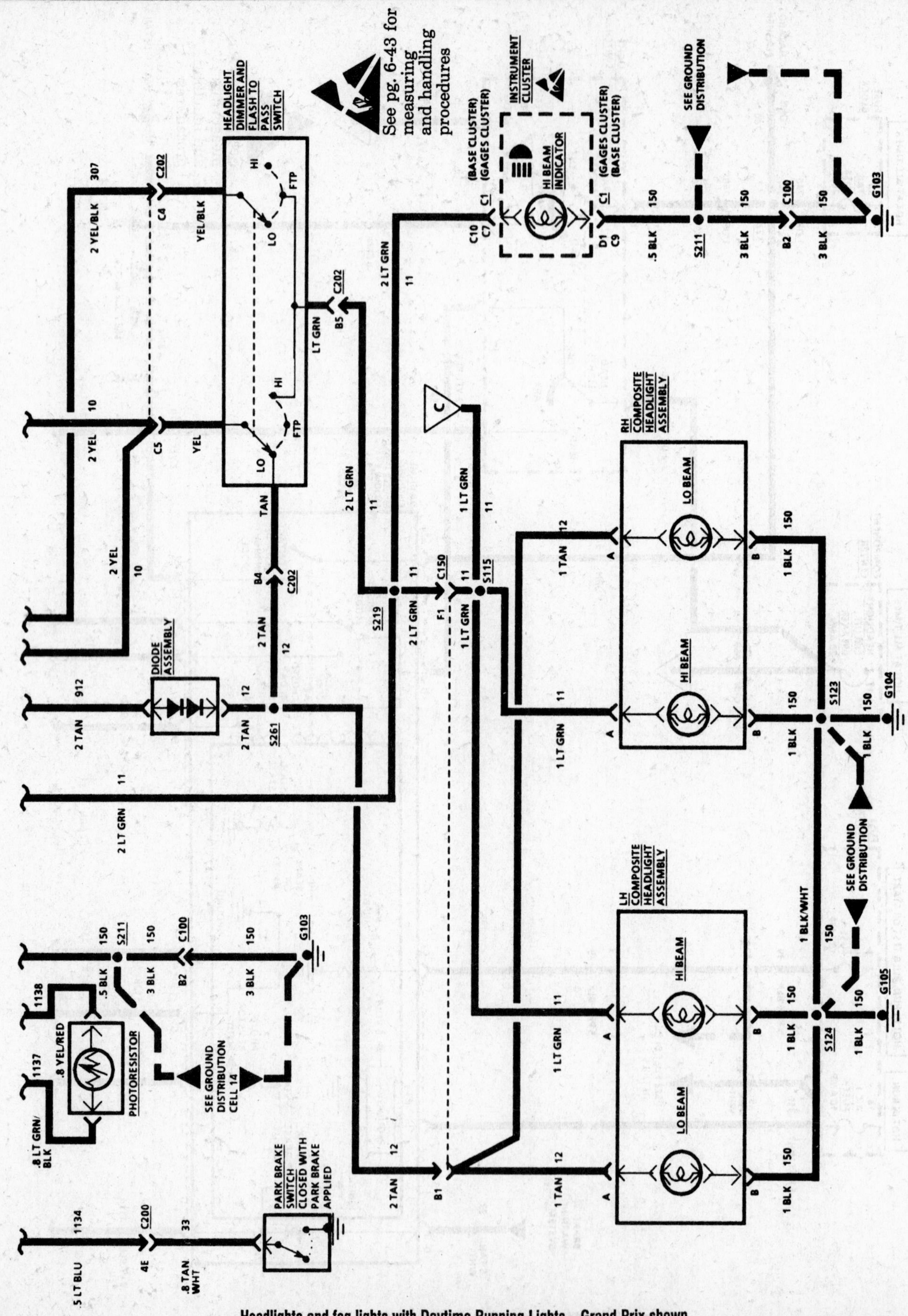

Headlights and fog lights with Daytime Running Lights—Grand Prix shown

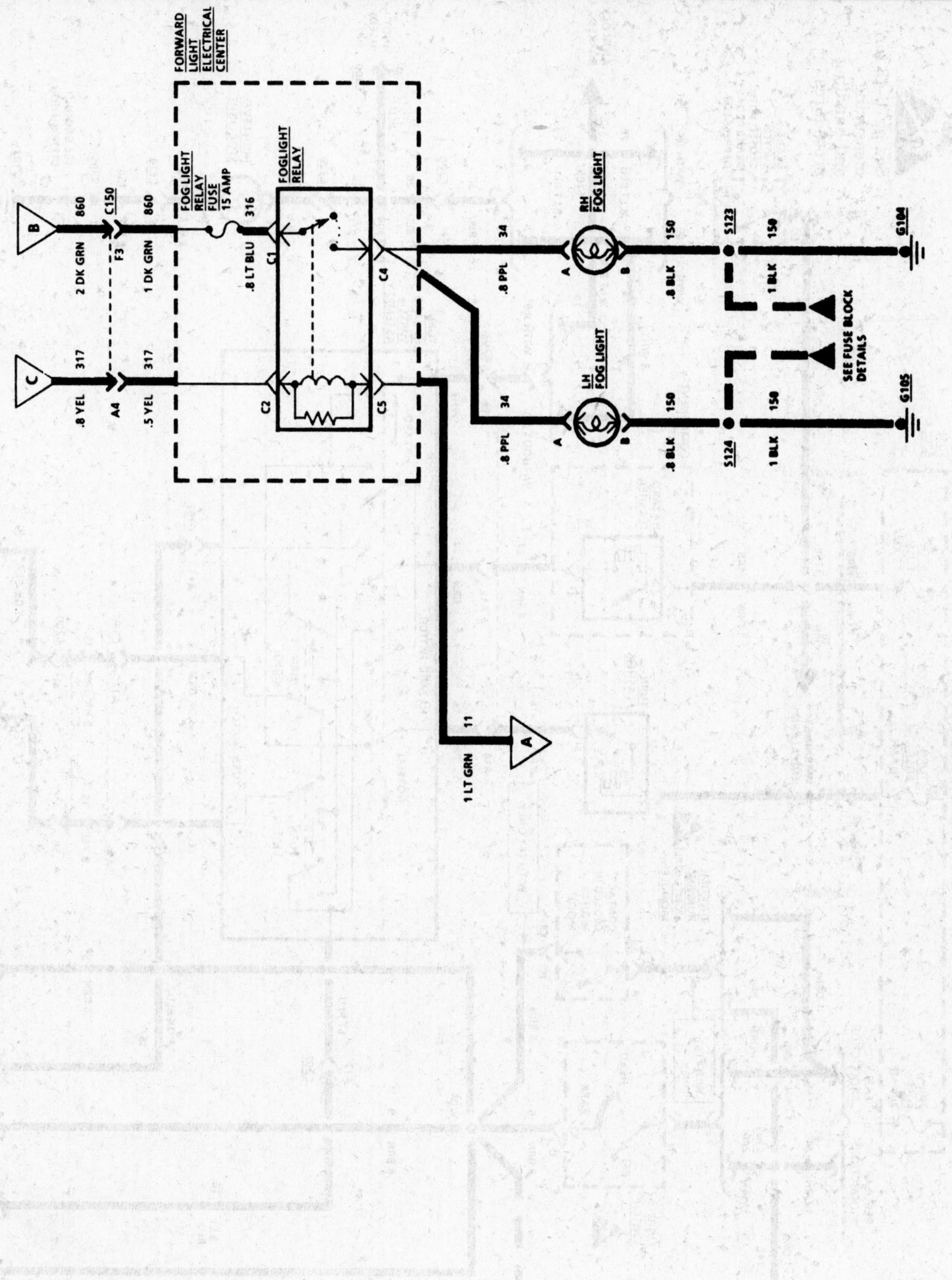

Headlights and fog lights with Daytime Running Lights—Grand Prix shown

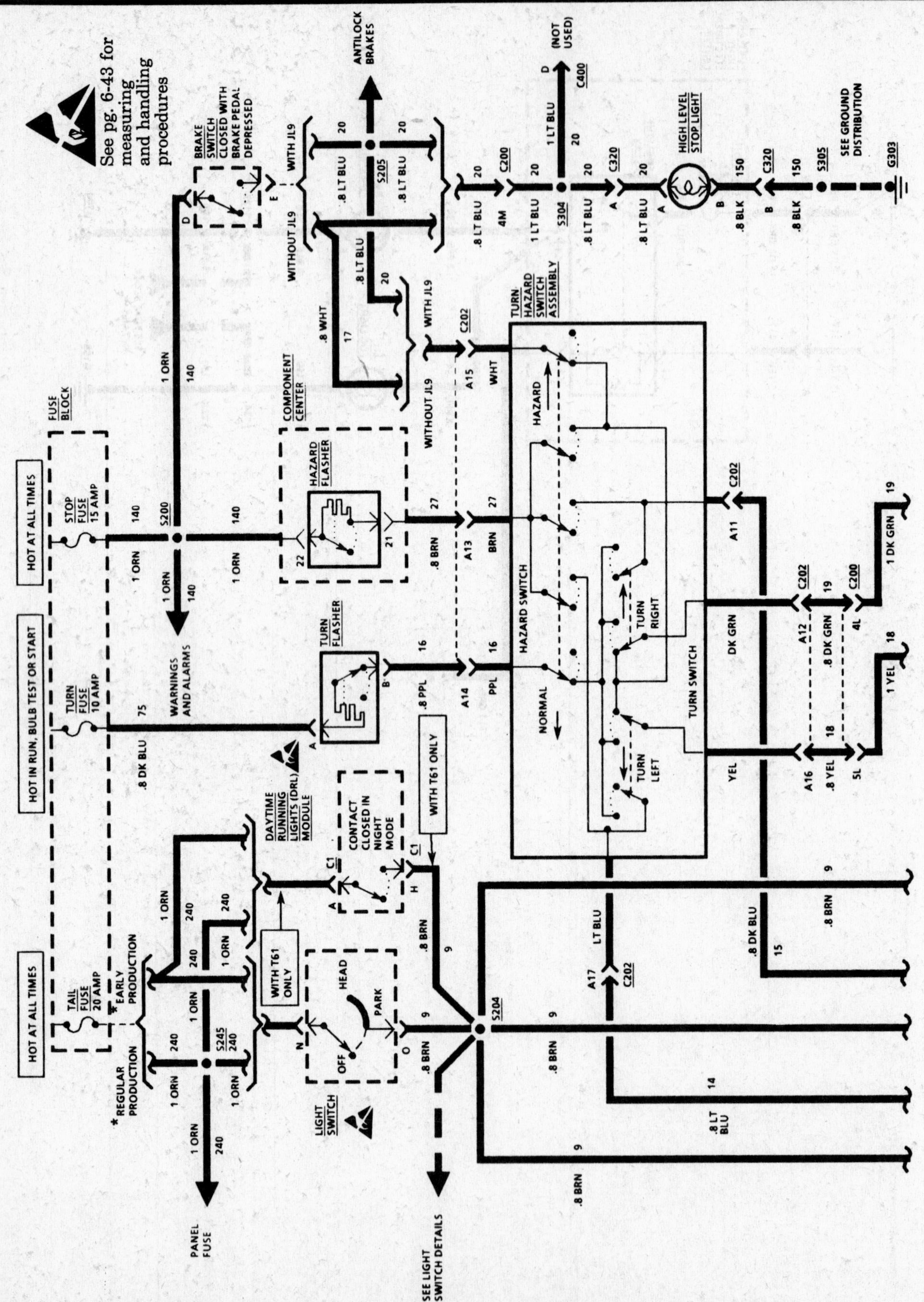

Turn/Hazard/Stop lamps—Regal shown

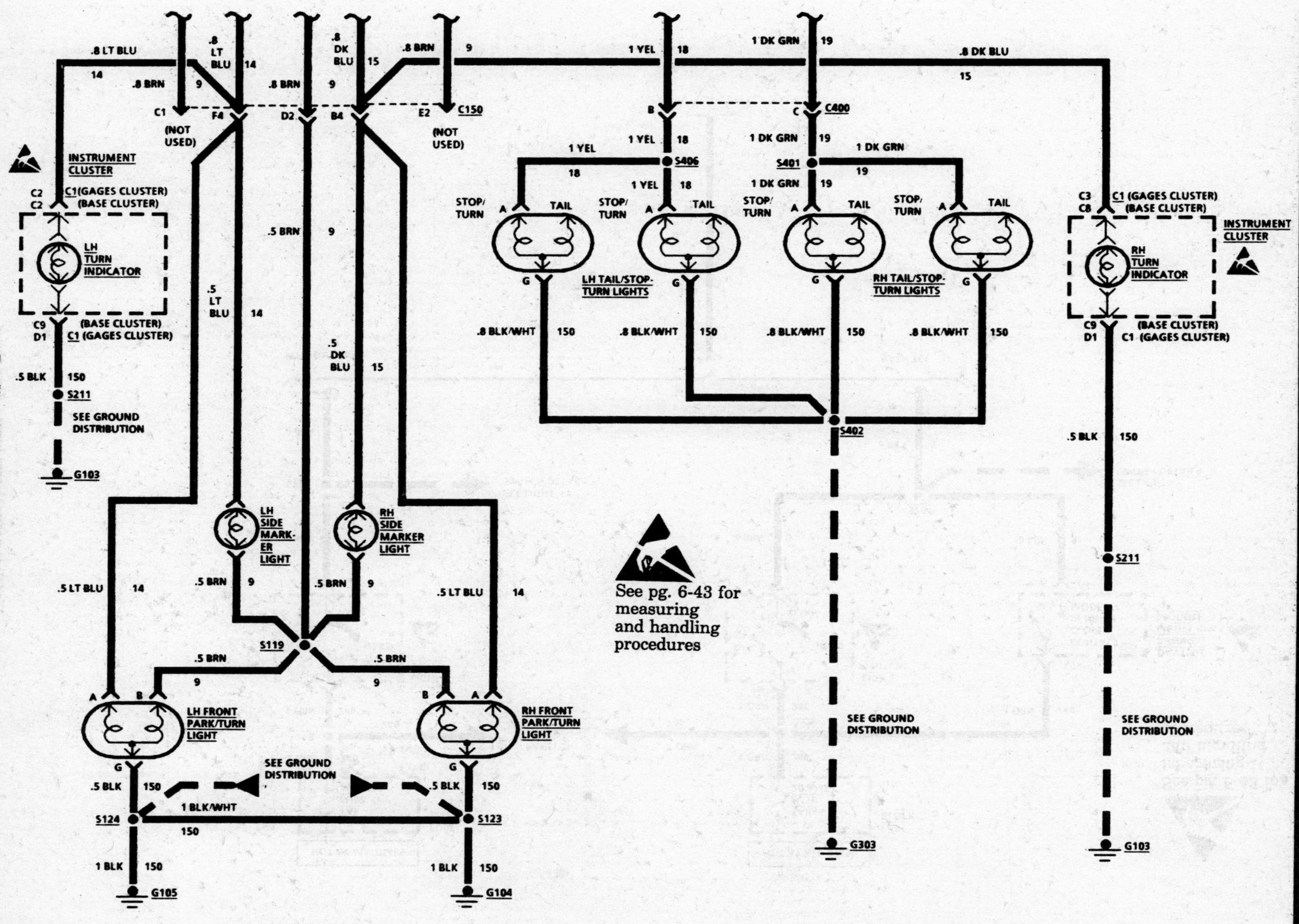

Turn/Hazard/Stop lamps—Regal shown

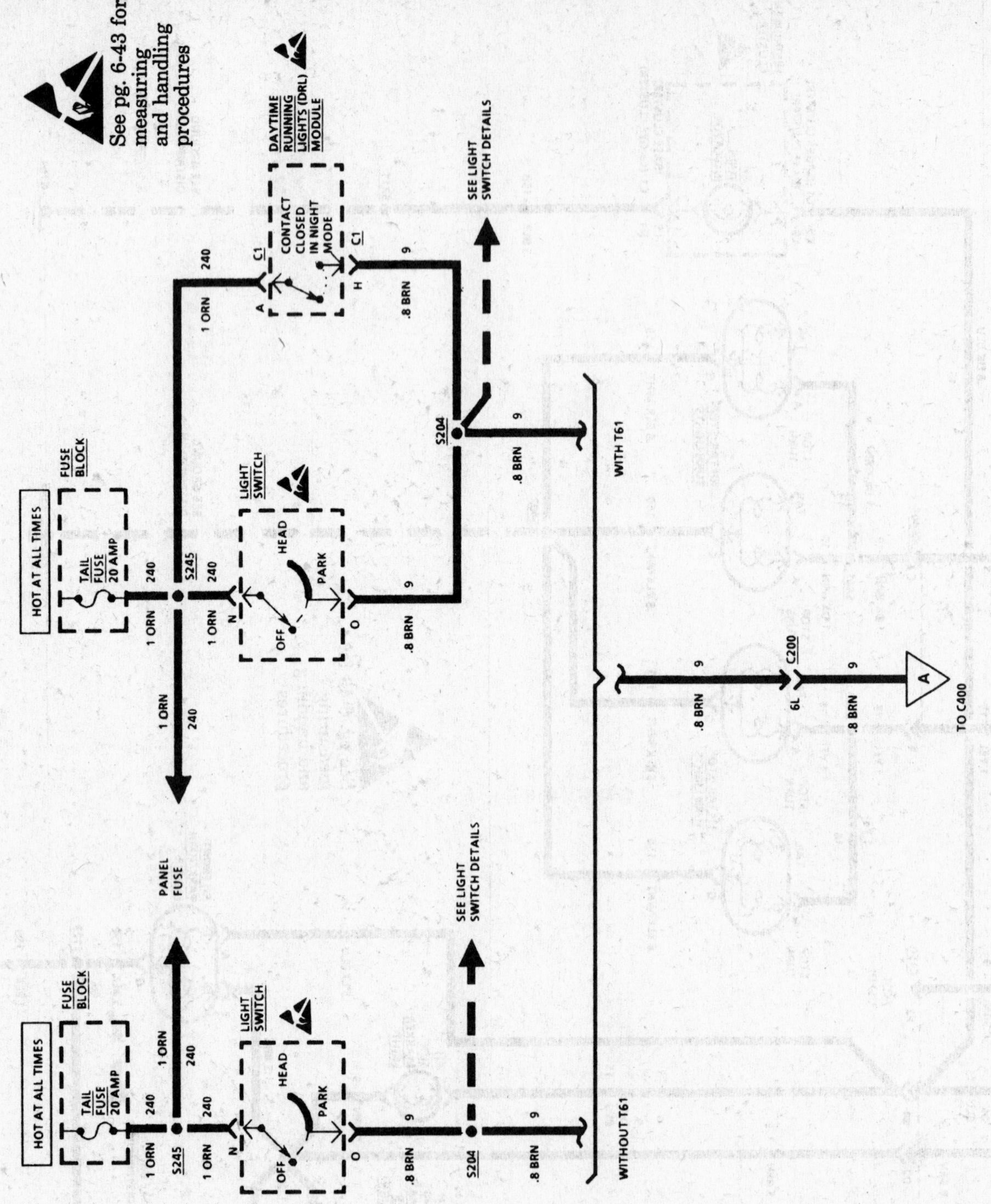

Tail/Rear marker/License lamps—Regal shown

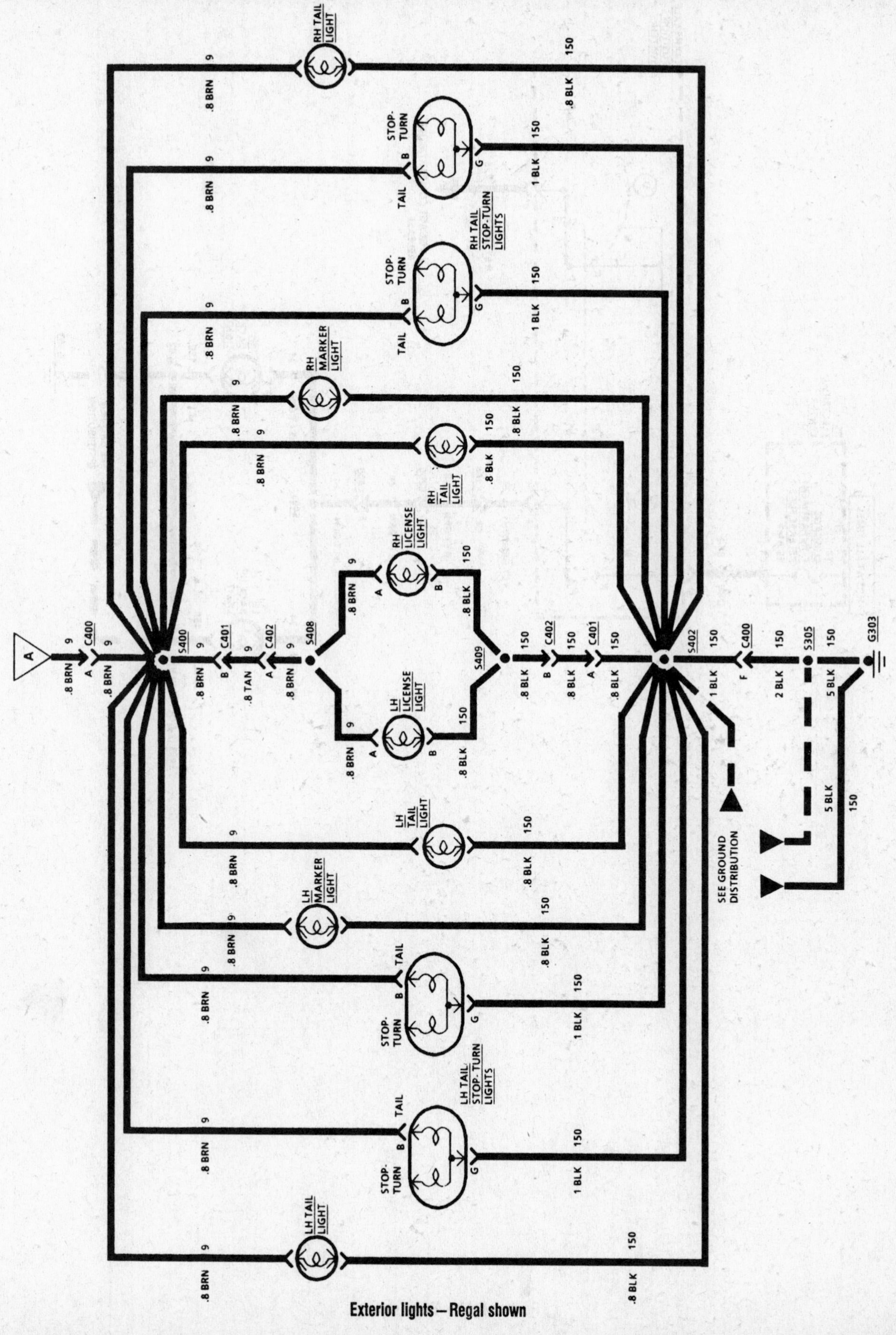

Exterior lights – Regal shown

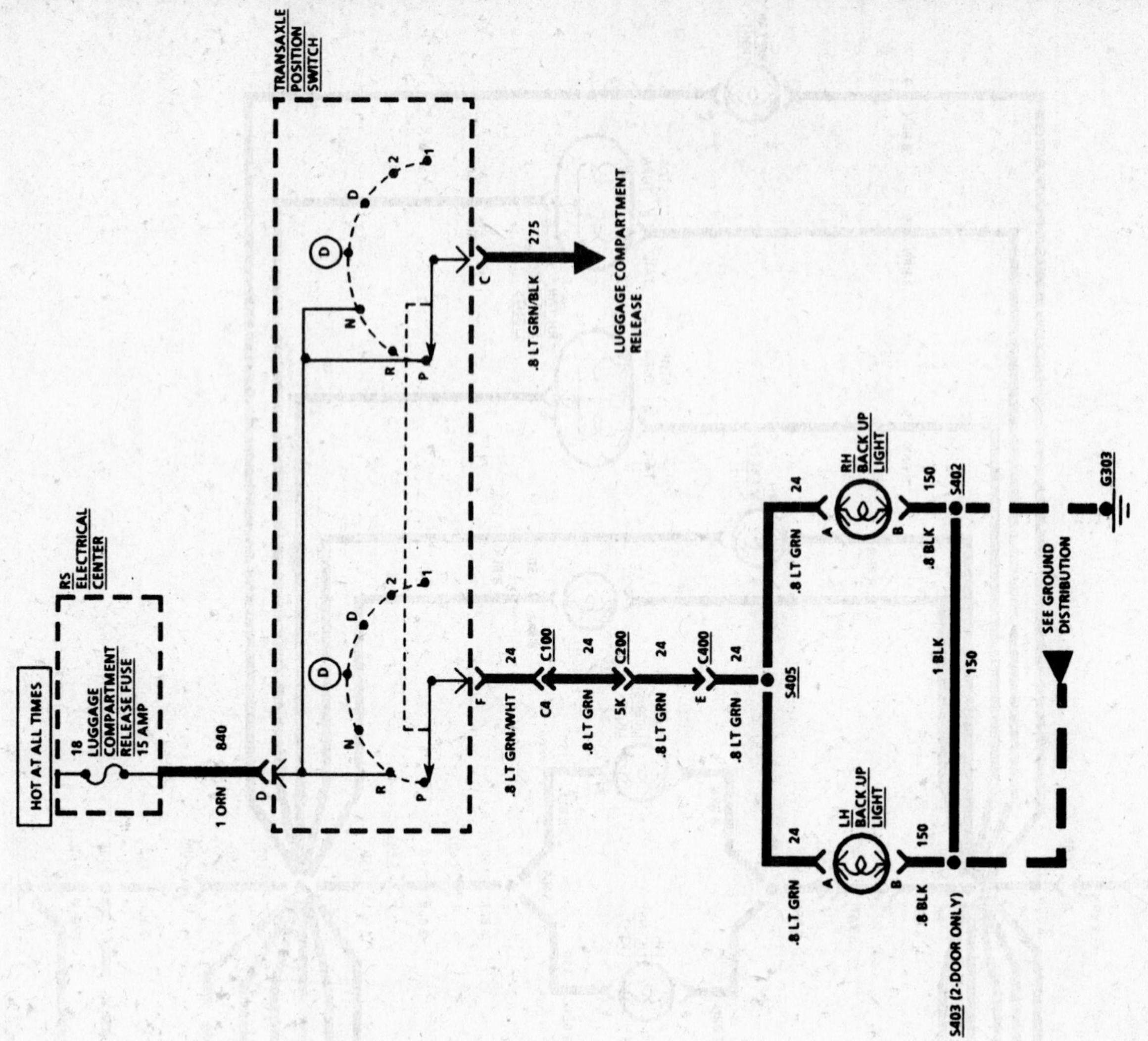

Reverse lights—Regal shown

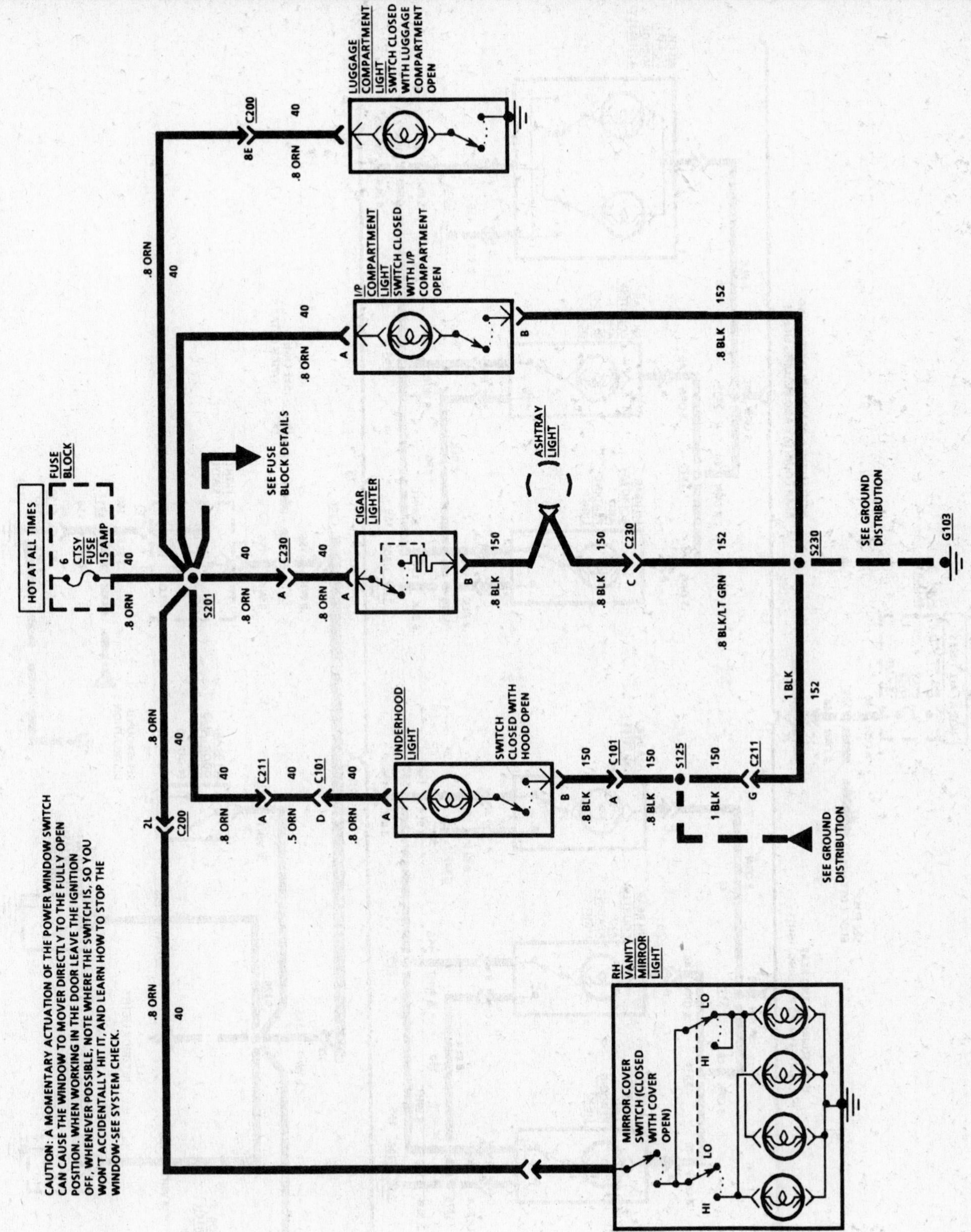

Interior lights—Regal shown

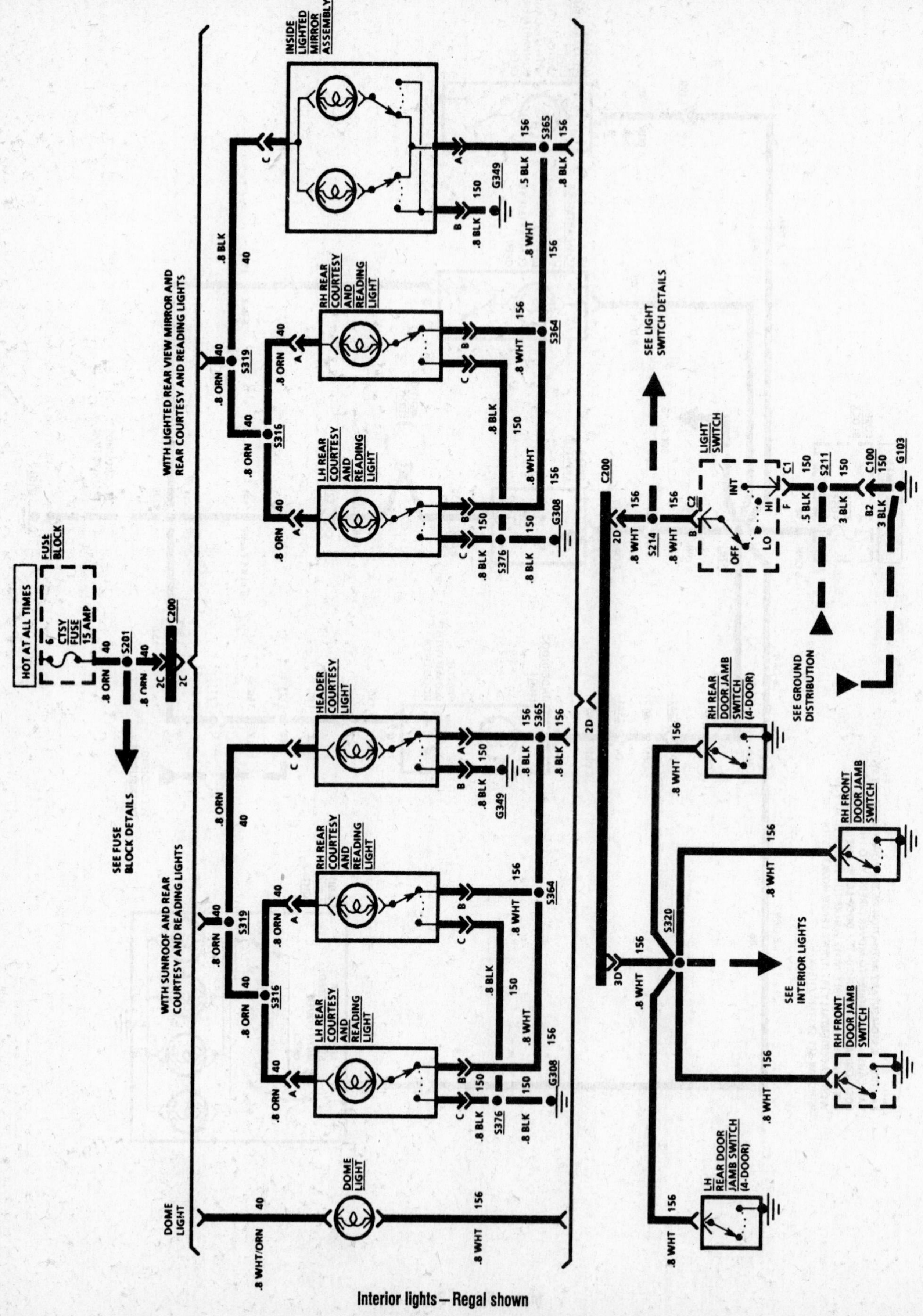

Interior lights—Regal shown

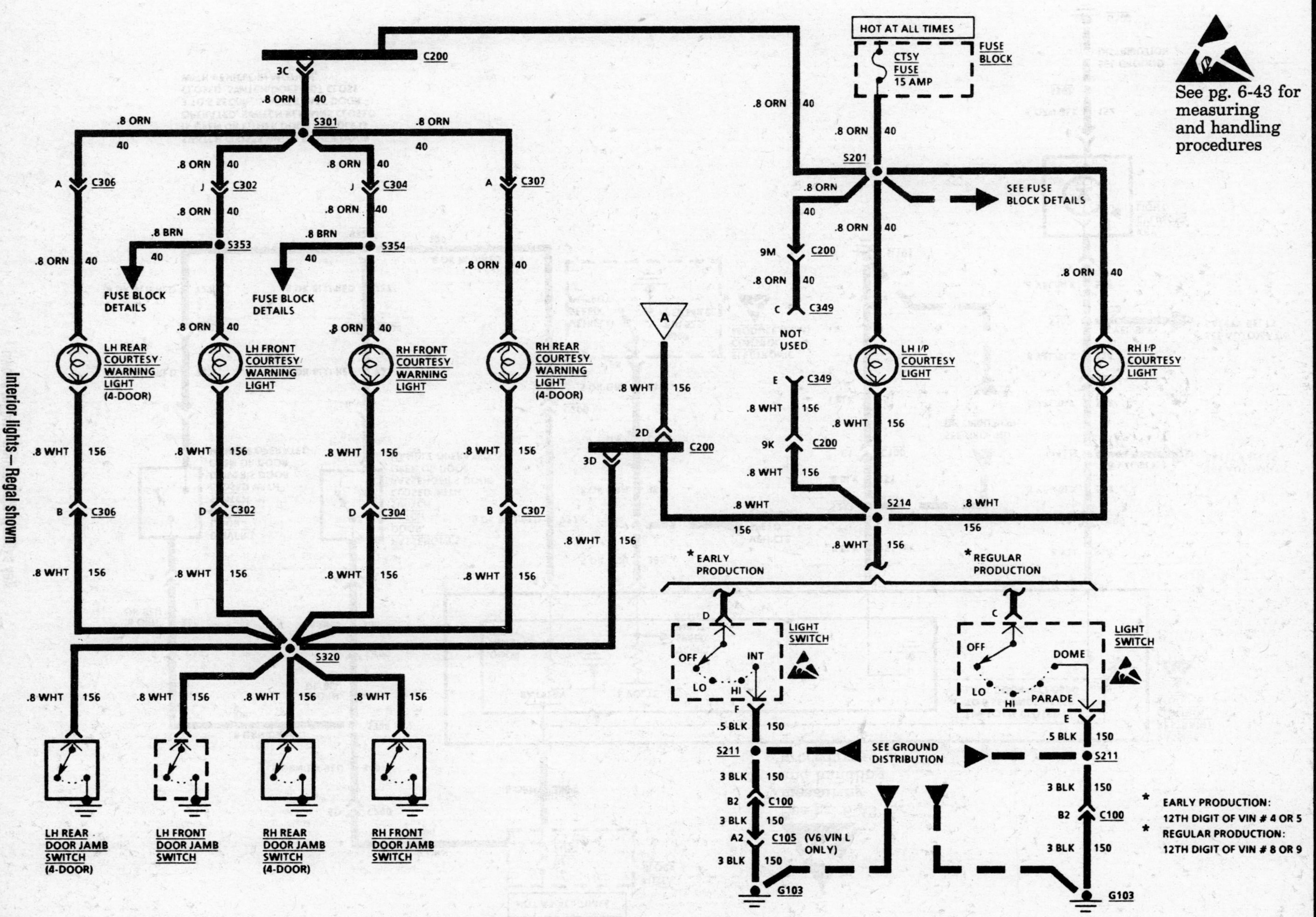

Interior lights—Regal shown

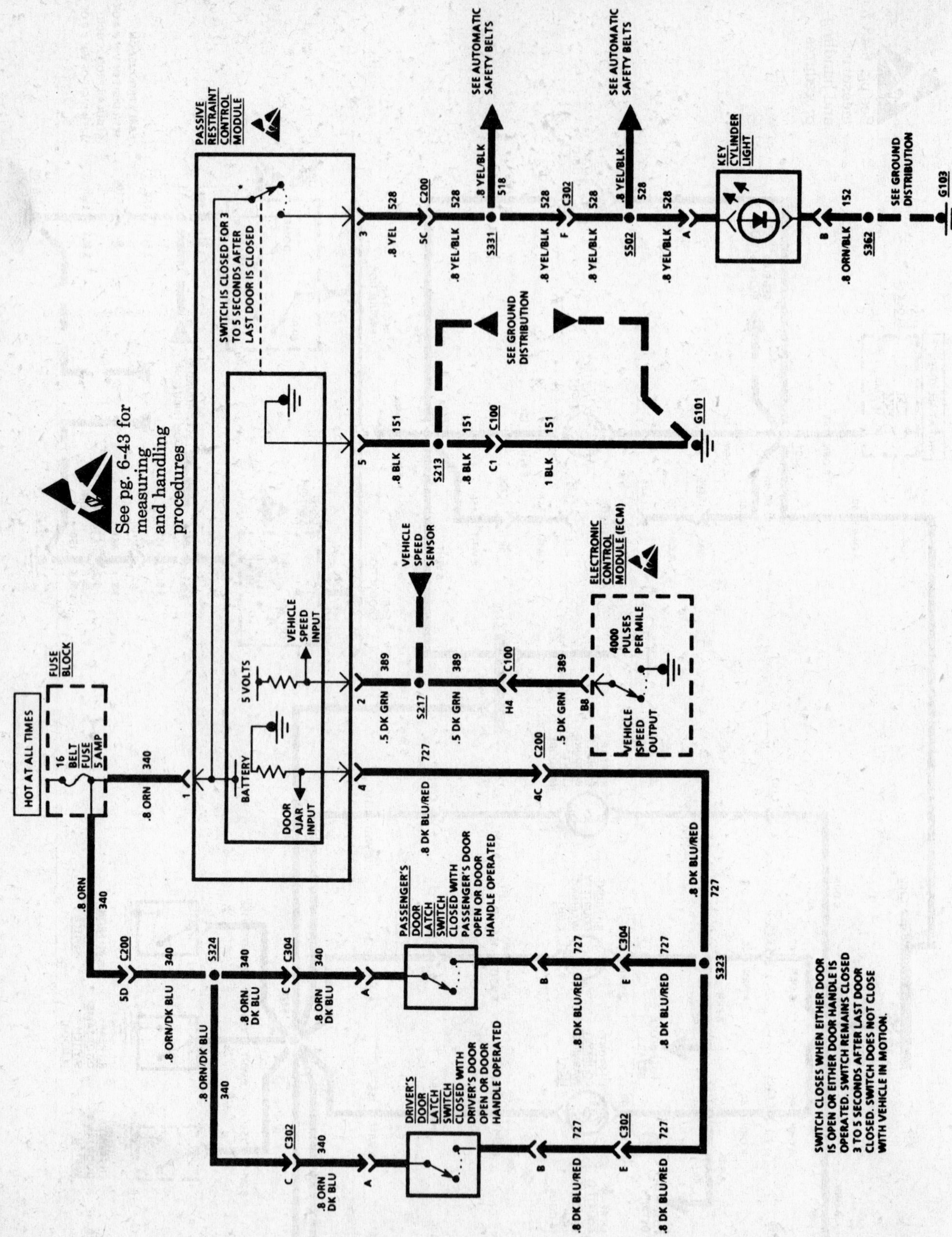

Key cylinder illumination—Regal shown

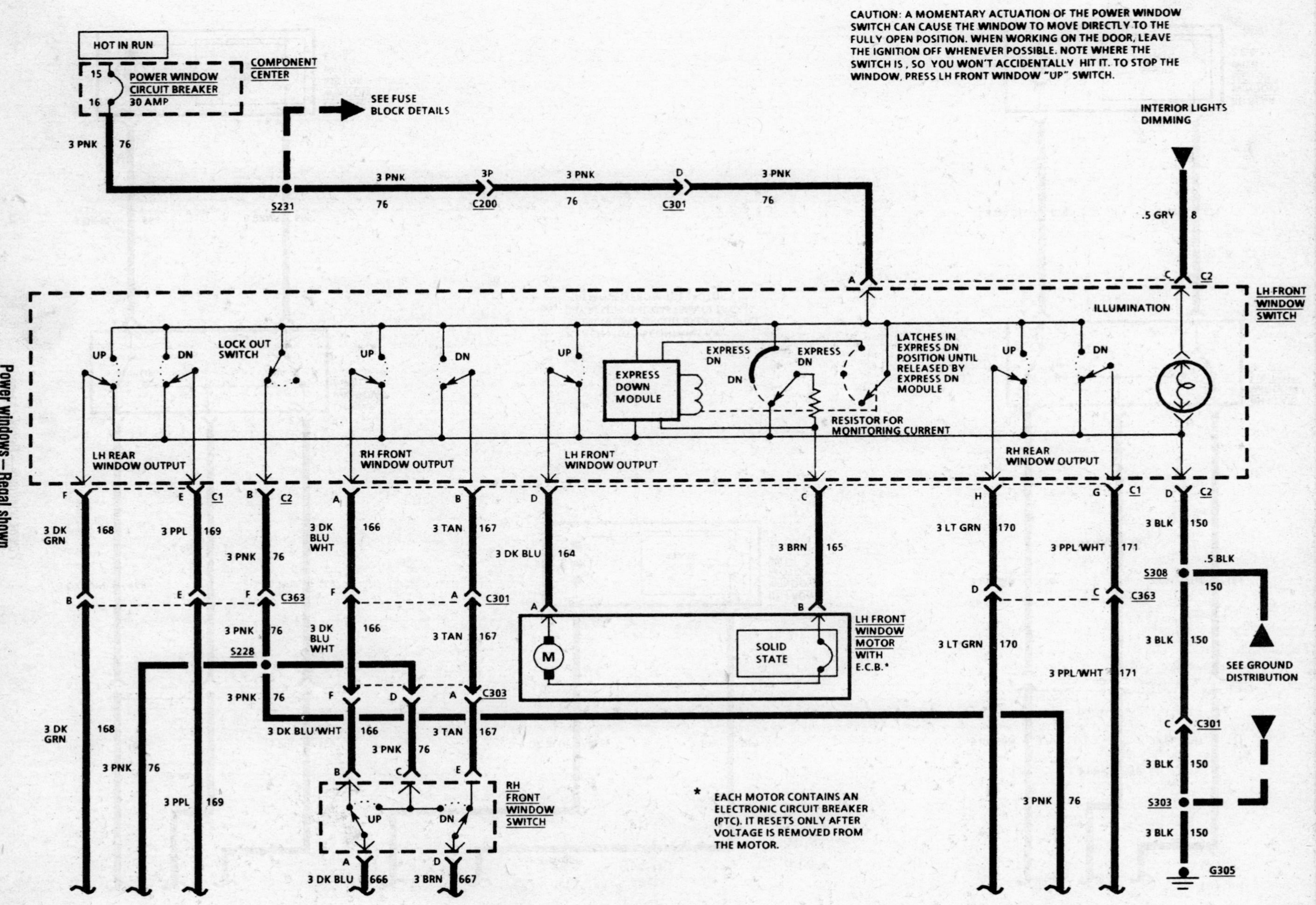

Power windows—Regal shown

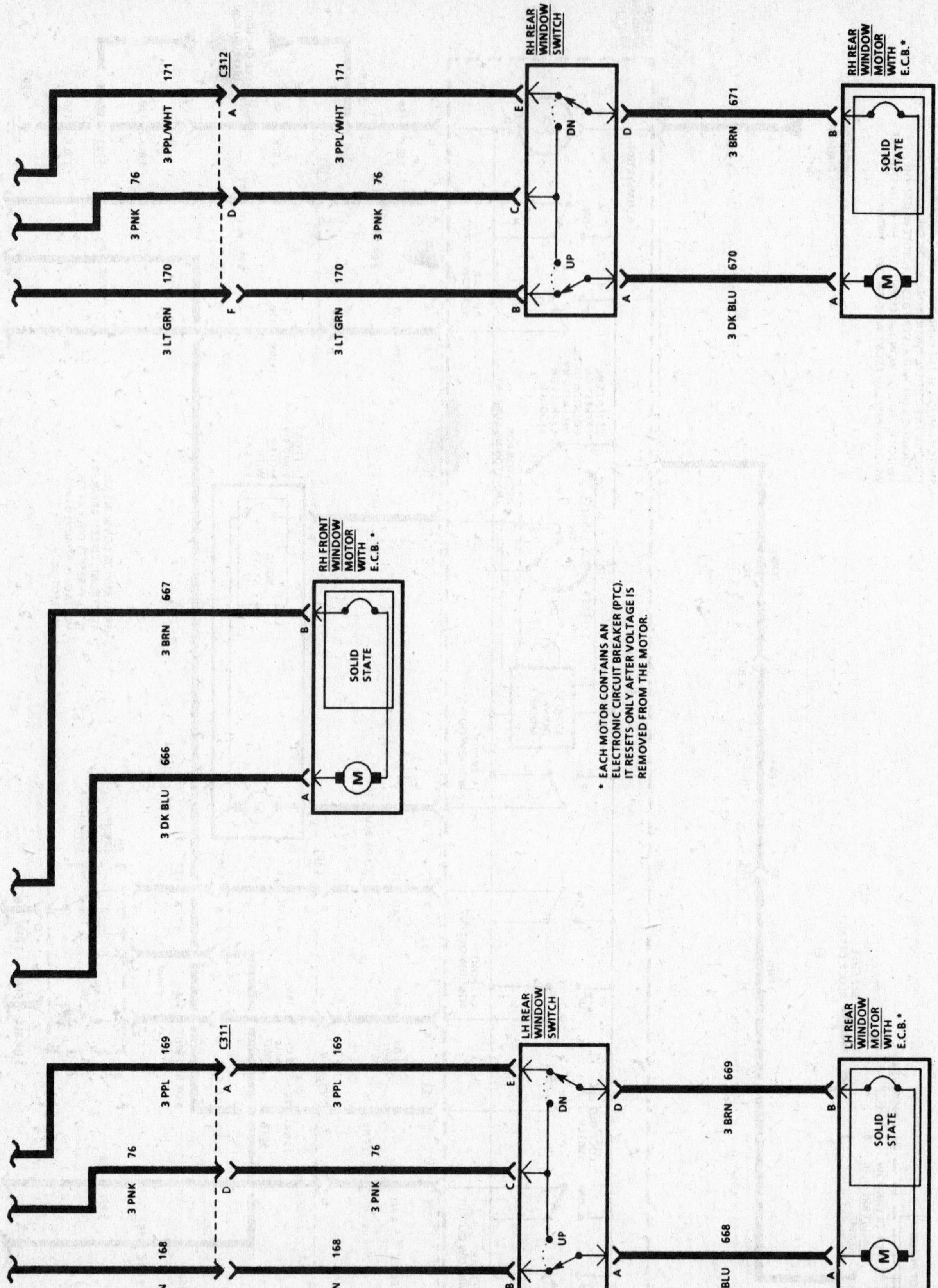

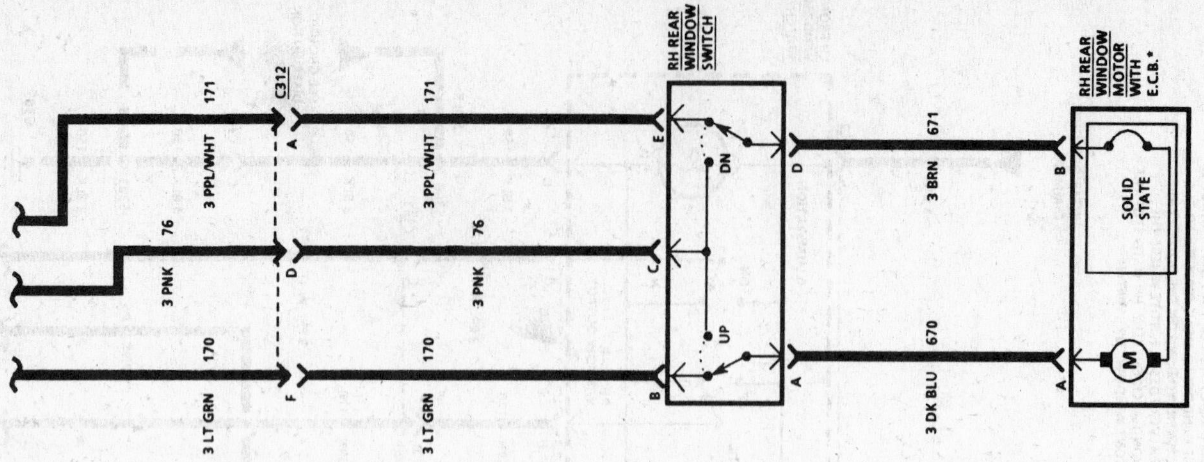

* EACH MOTOR CONTAINS AN ELECTRONIC CIRCUIT BREAKER (PTC). IT RESETS ONLY AFTER VOLTAGE IS REMOVED FROM THE MOTOR.

Power windows—Regal shown

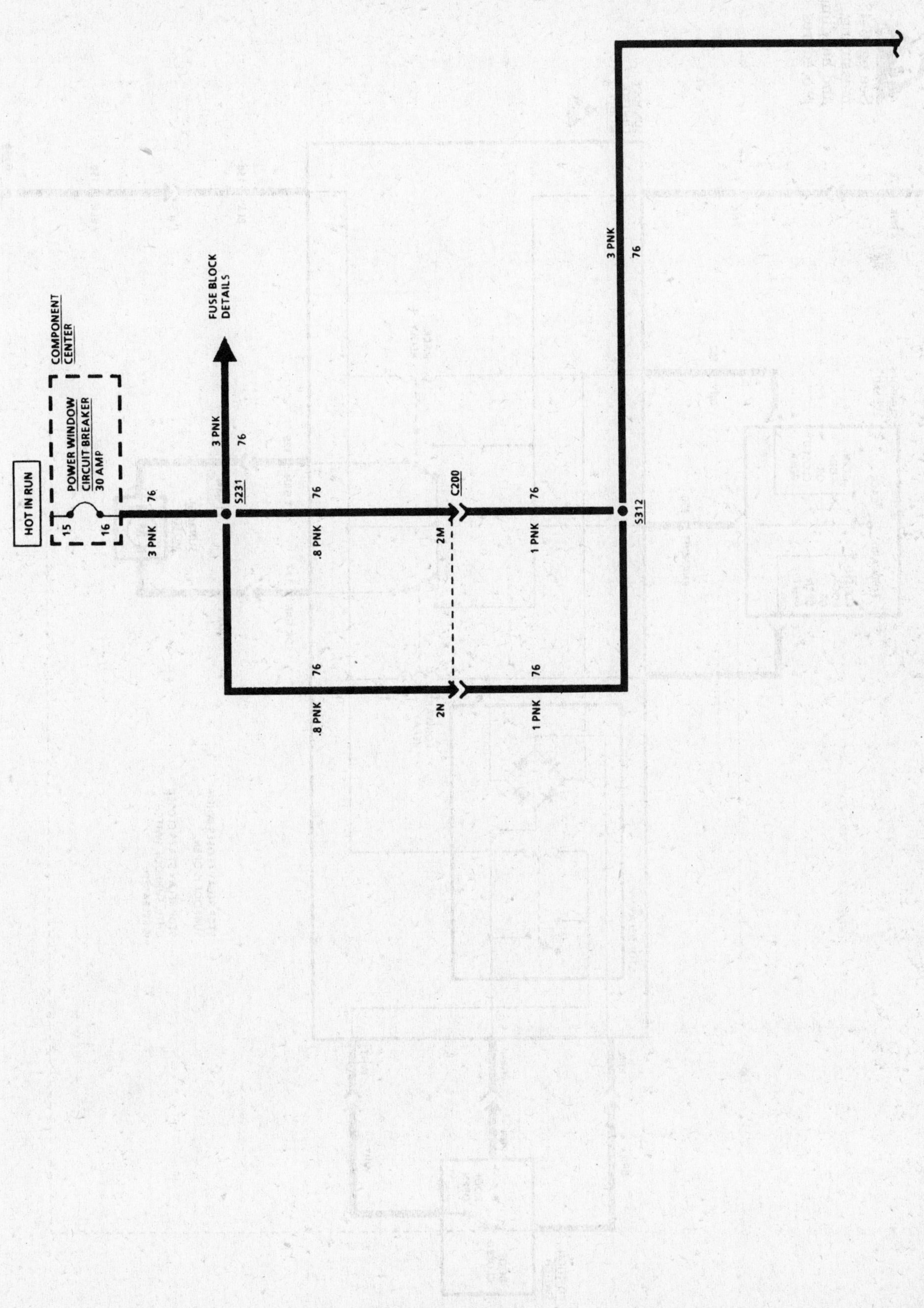

Sunroof—Regal shown

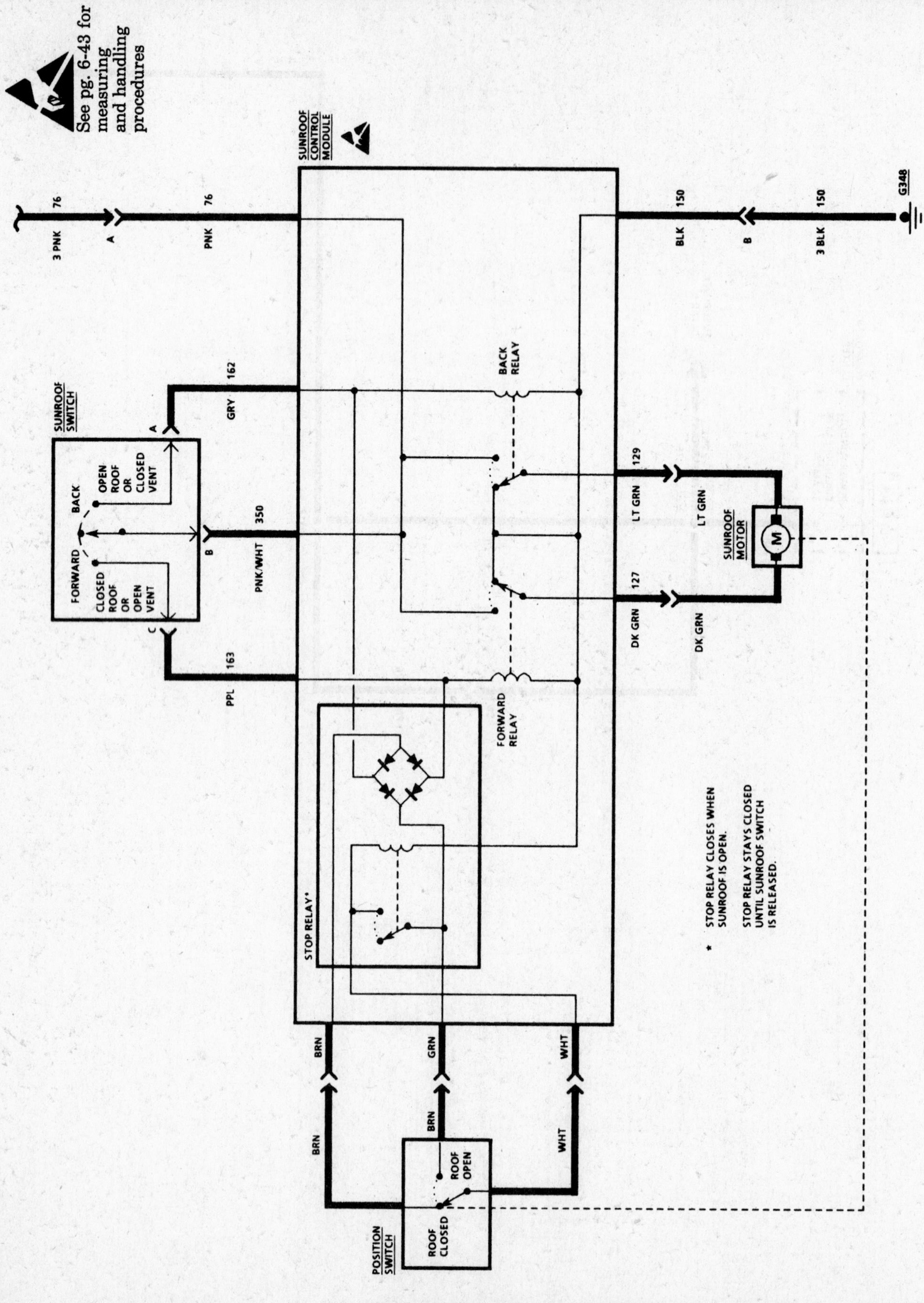

Sunroof – Regal shown

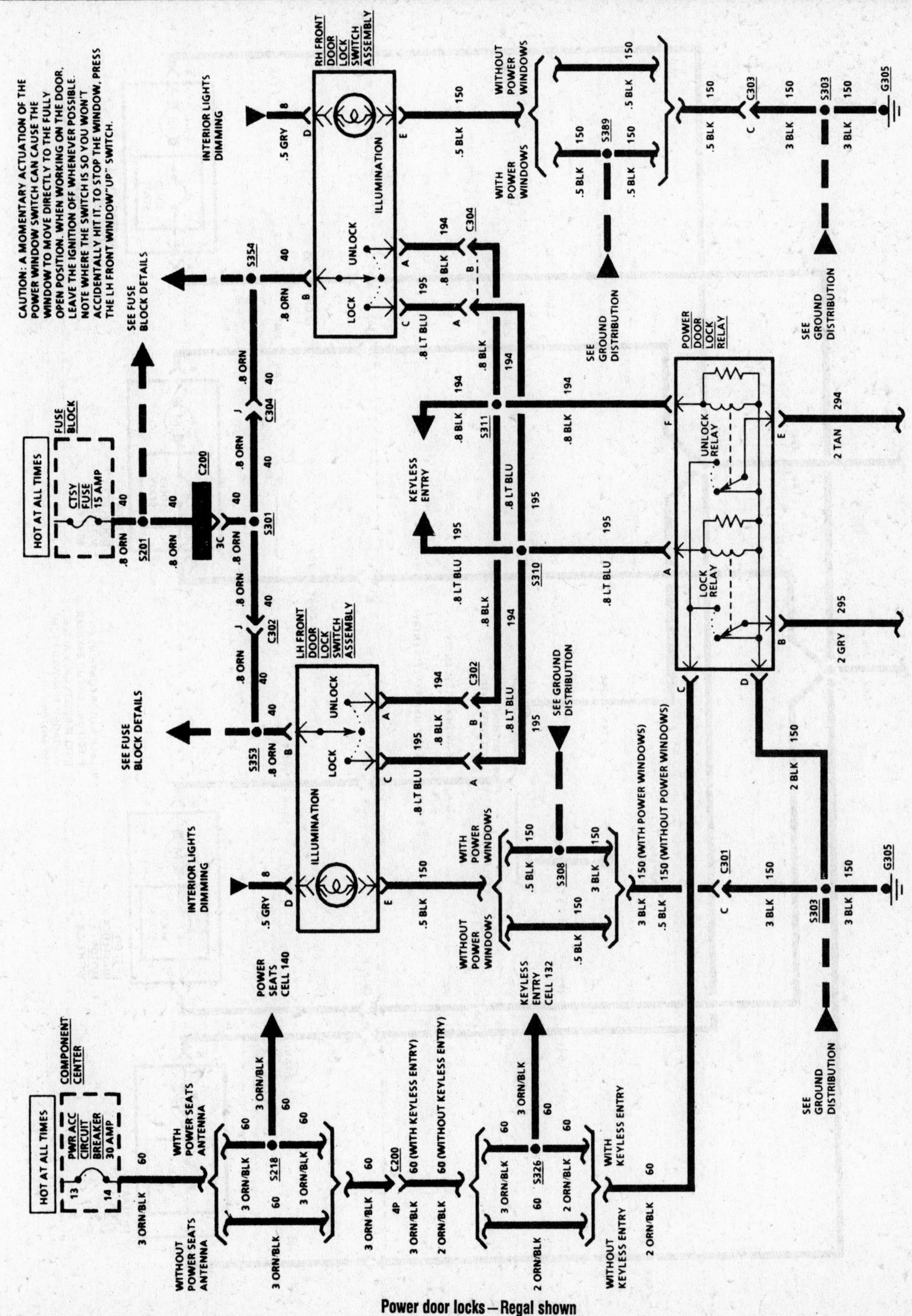

Power door locks—Regal shown

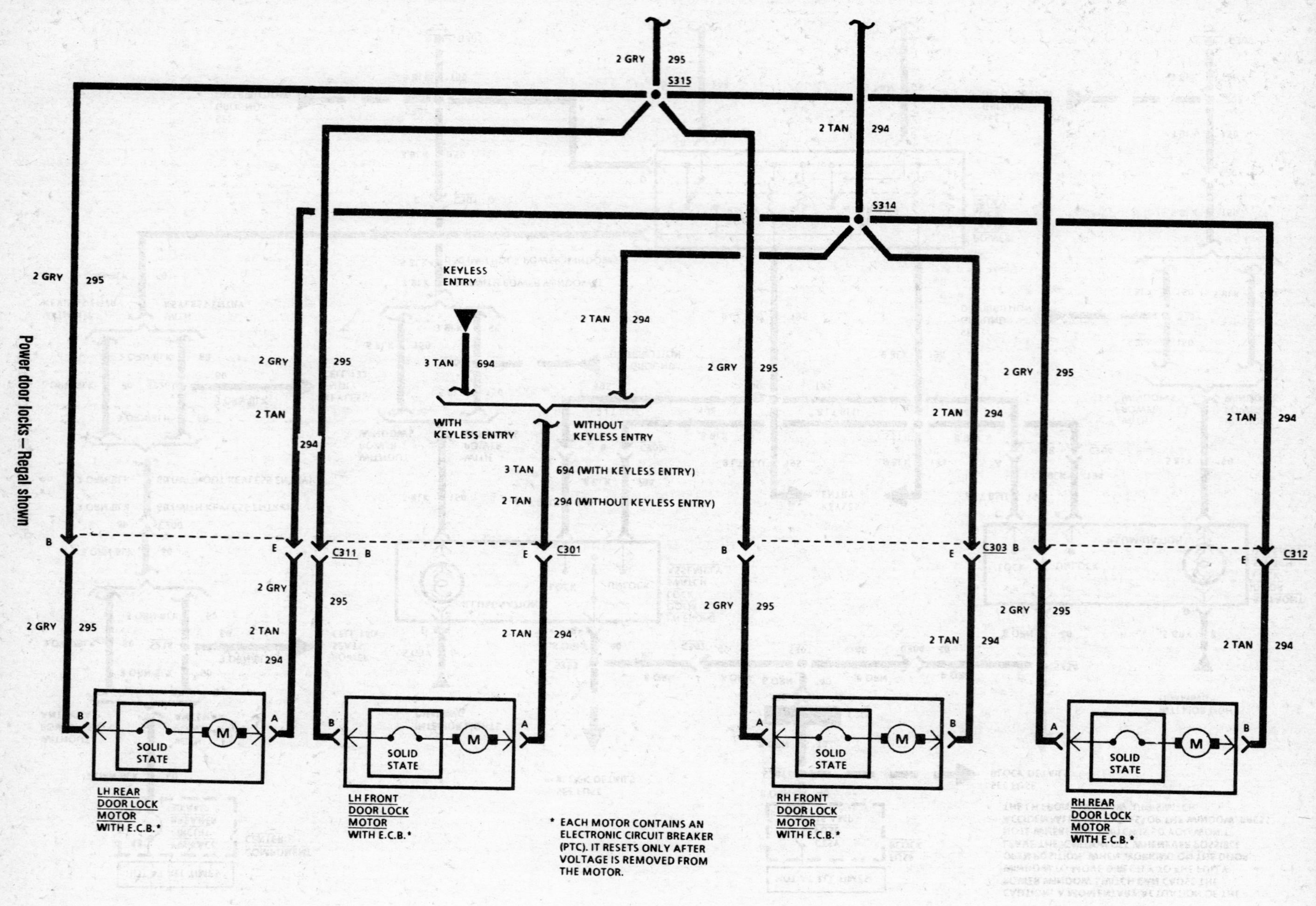

Power door locks—Regal shown

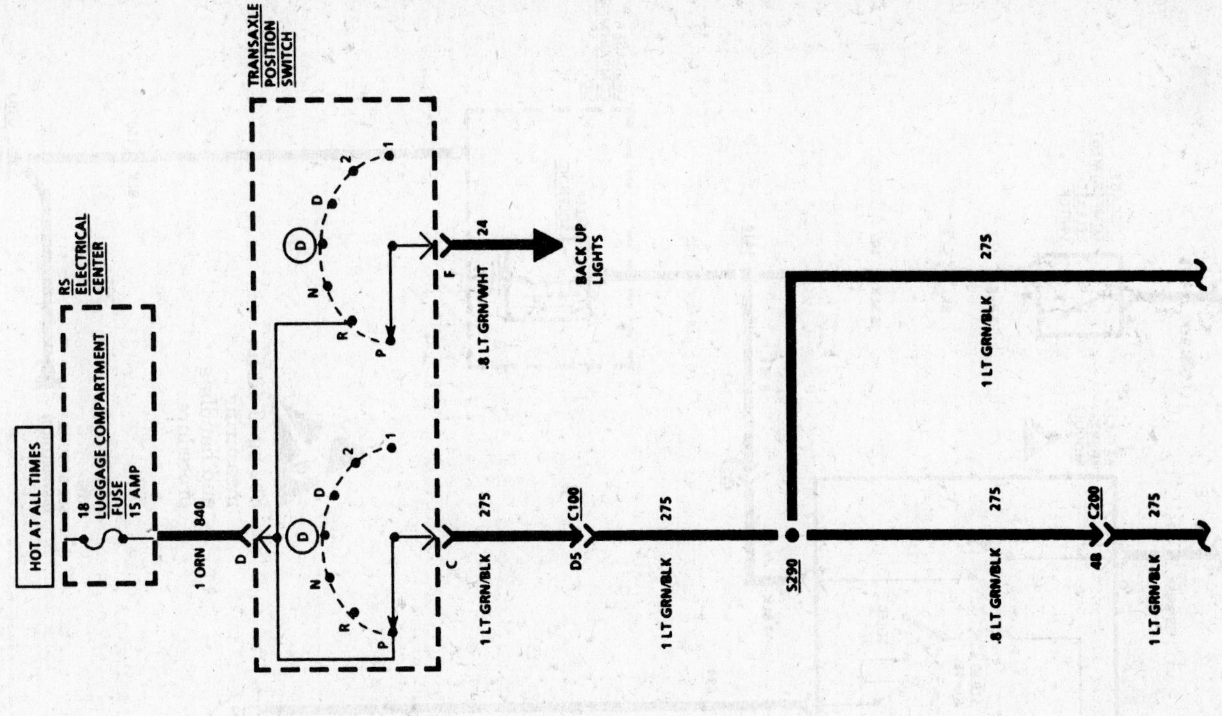

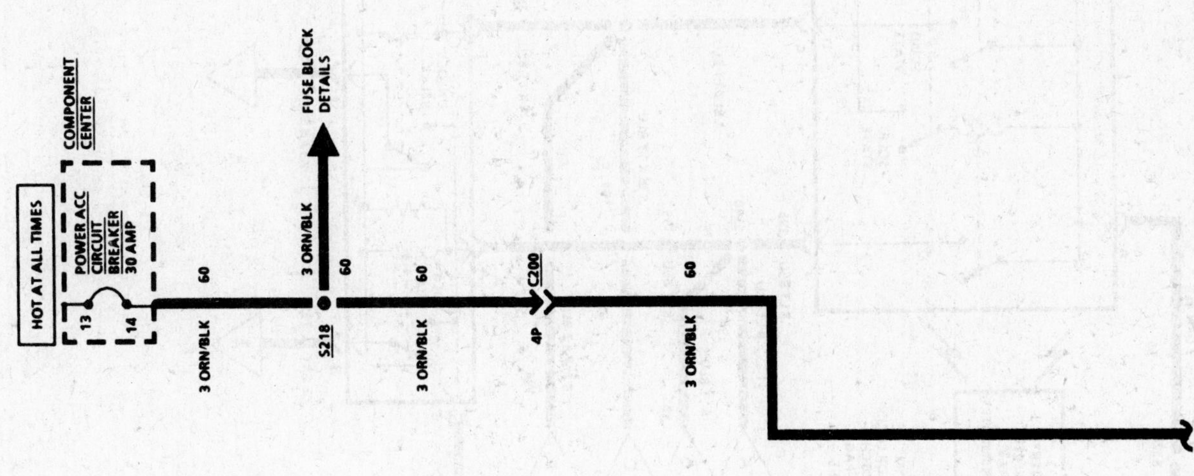

Keyless entry system—Regal shown

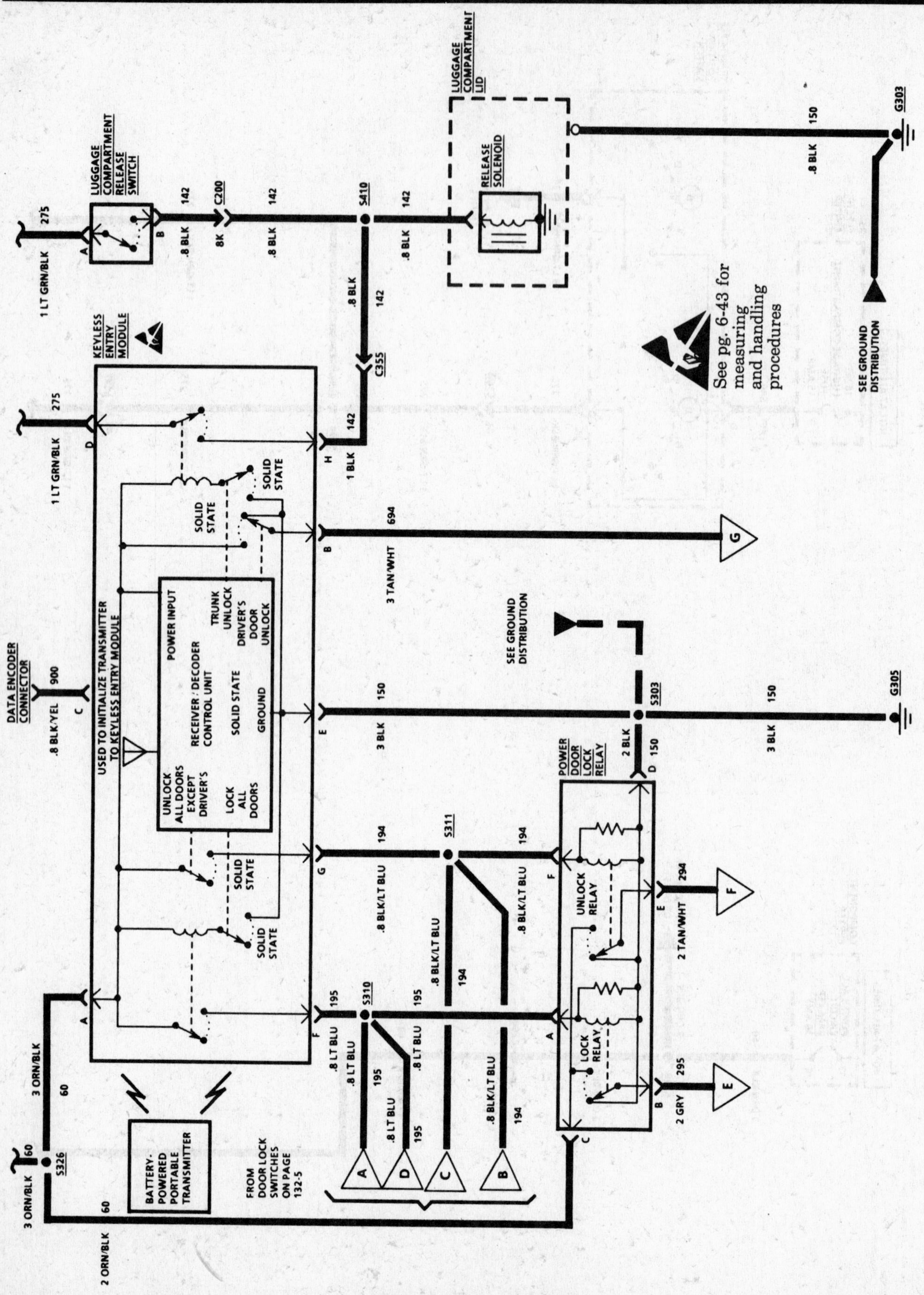

Keyless entry system—Regal shown

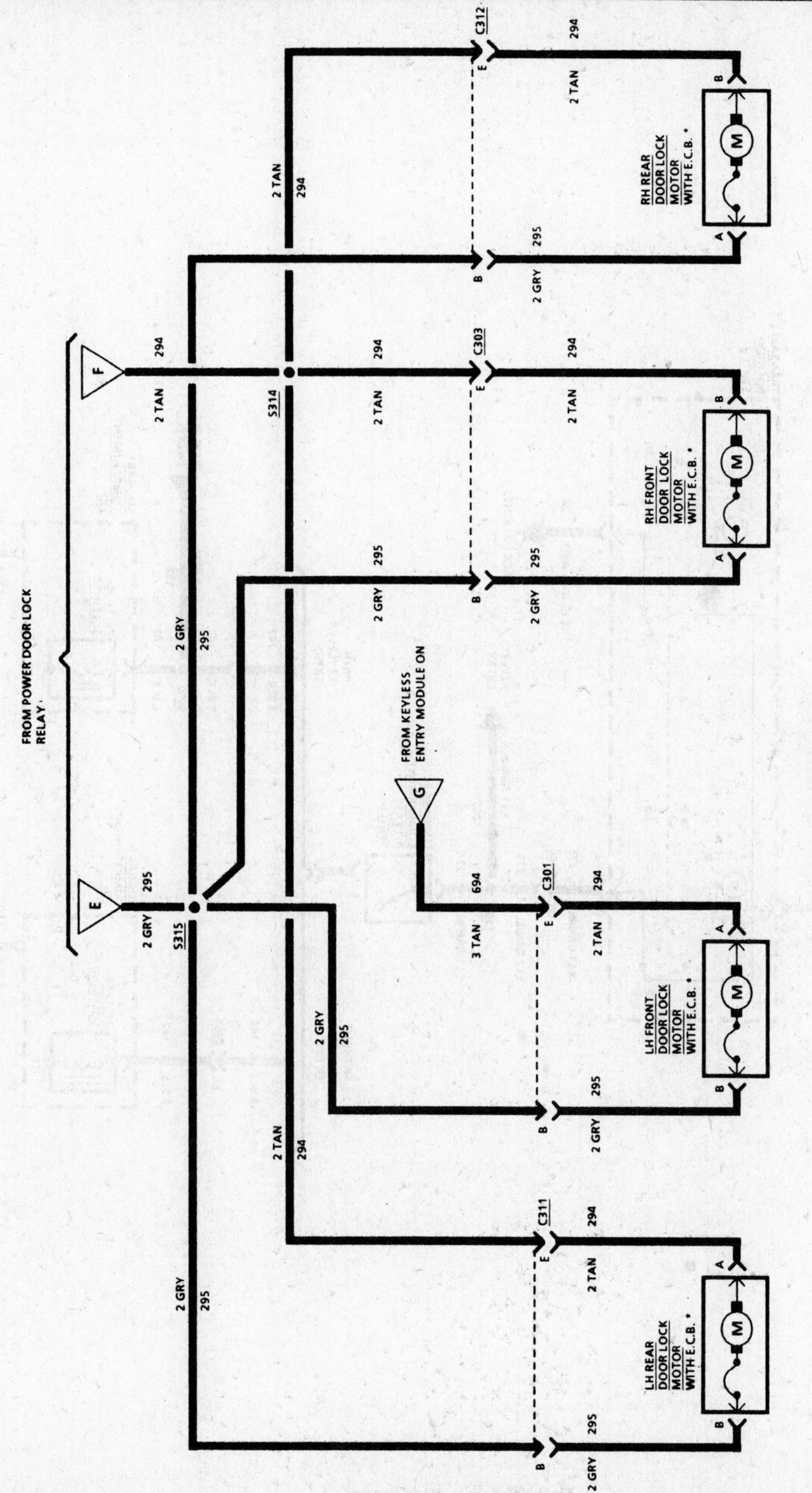

Keyless entry system — Regal shown

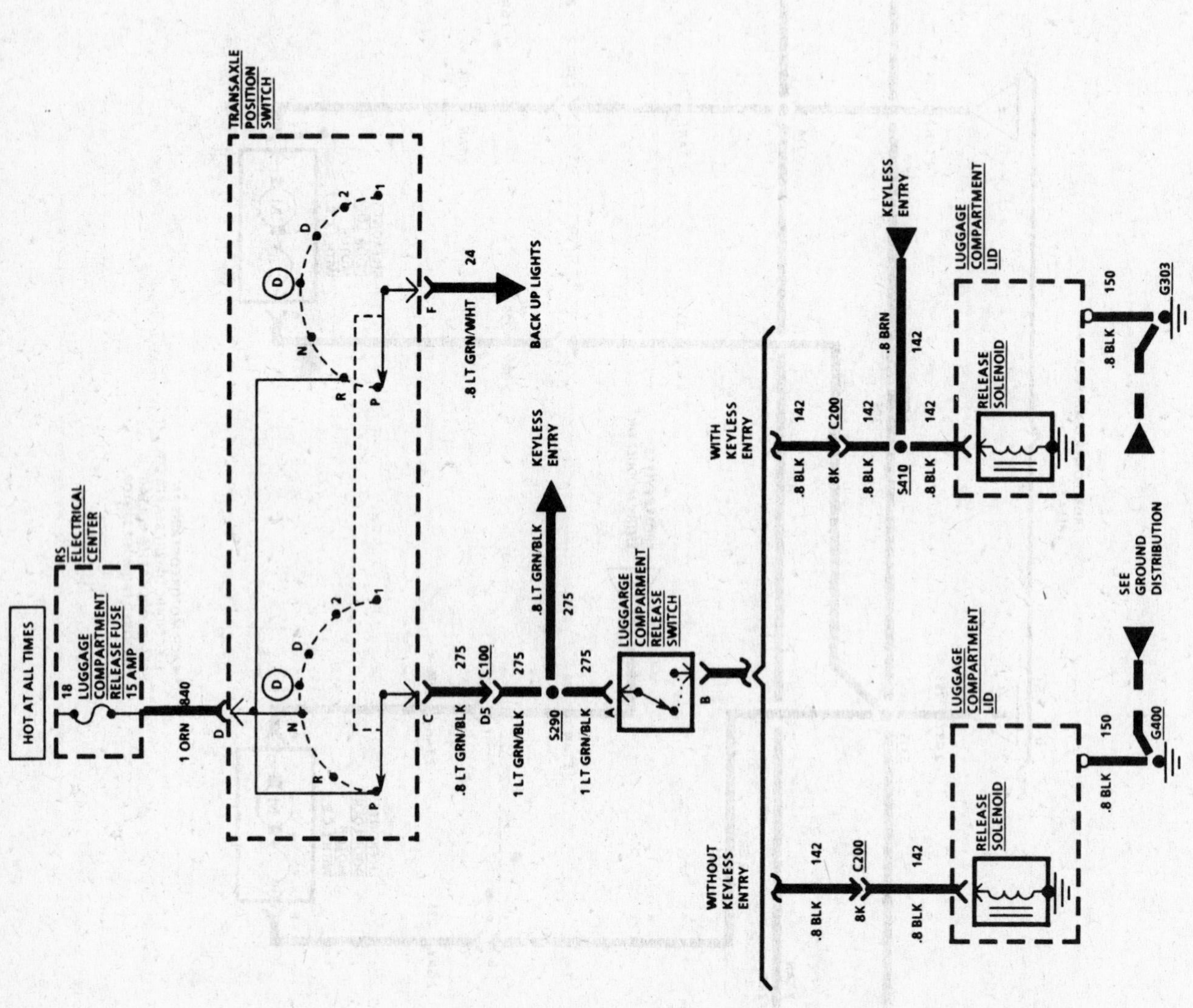

Trunk lid release – Regal shown

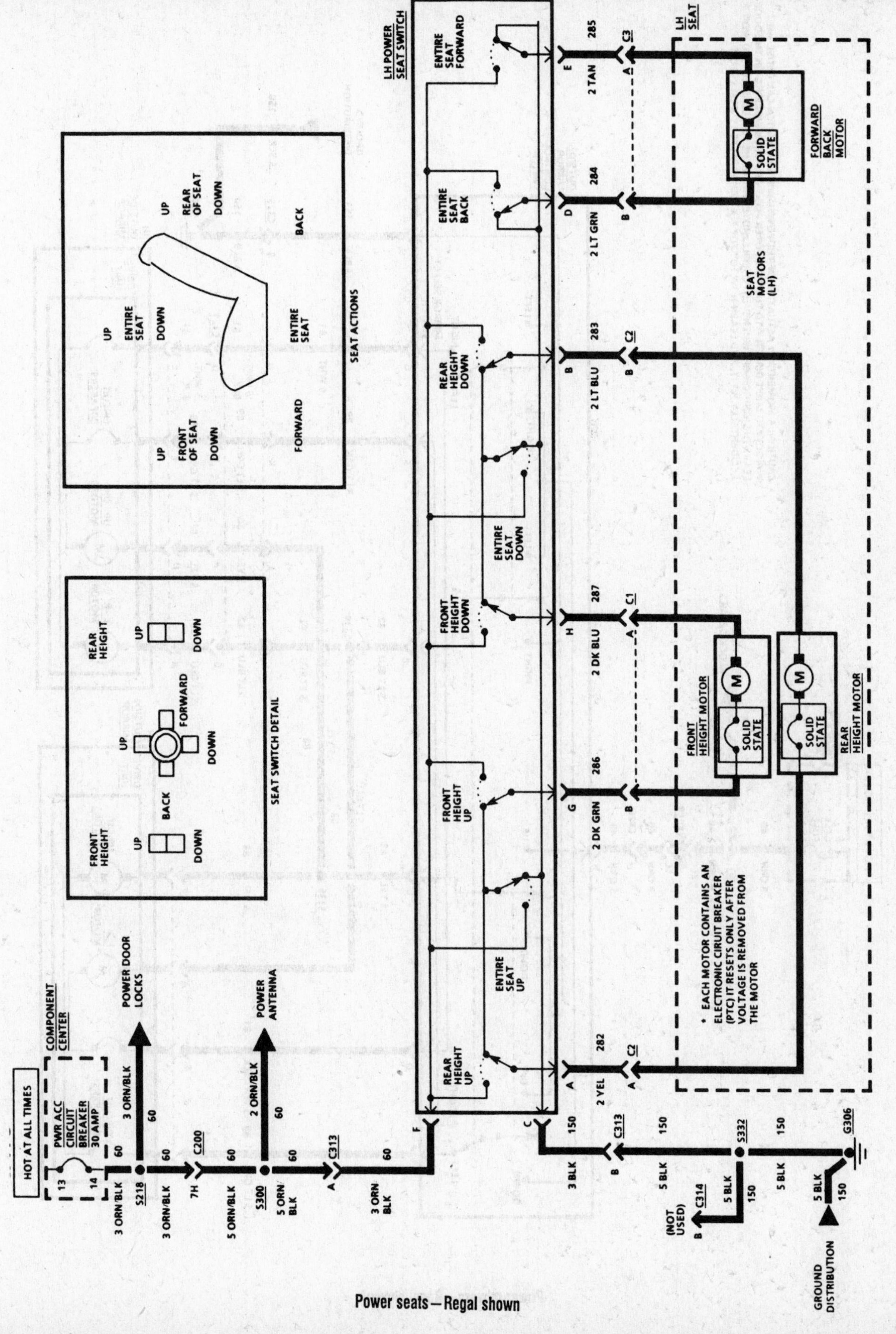

Power seats—Regal shown

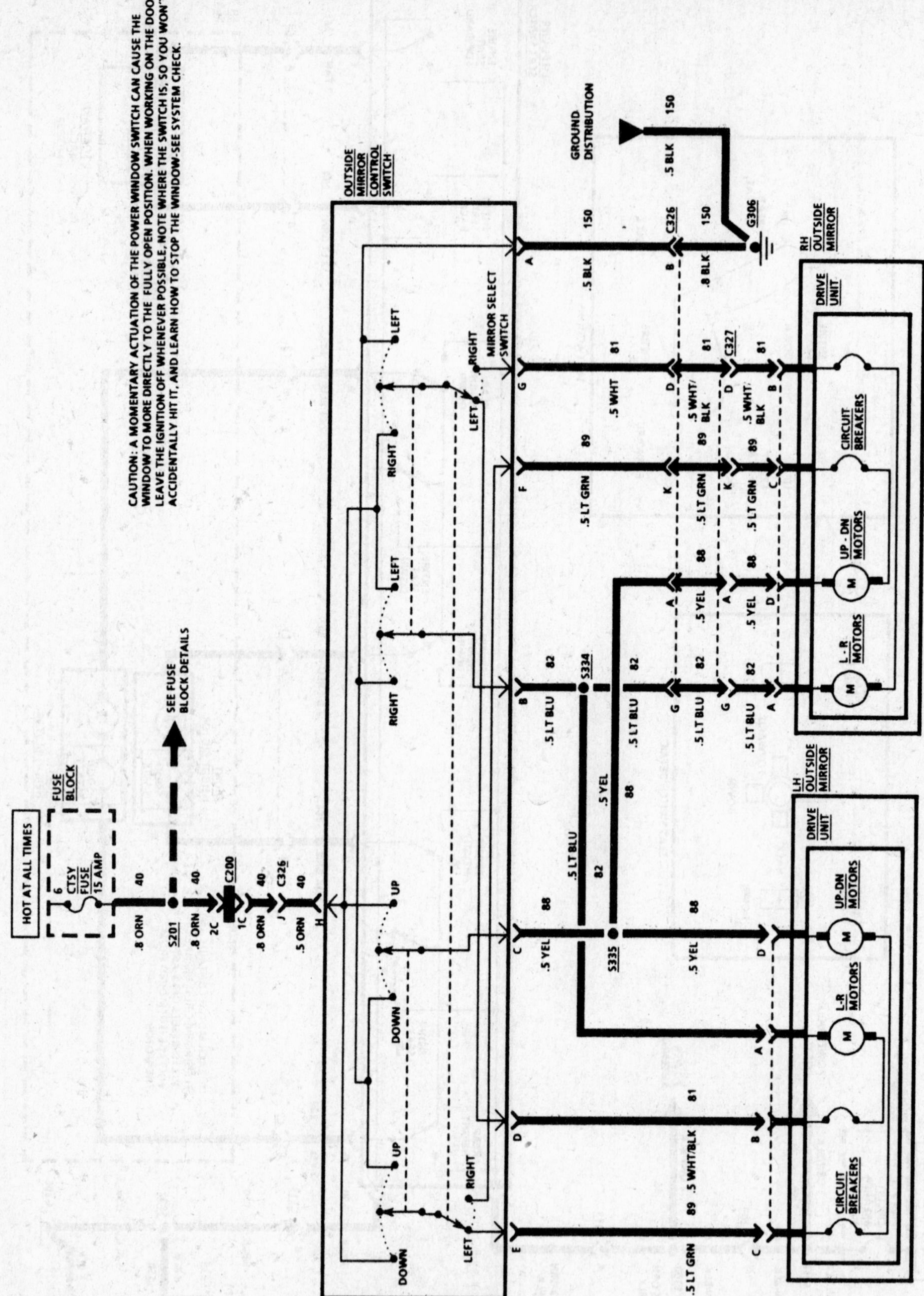

Power mirrors—Regal shown

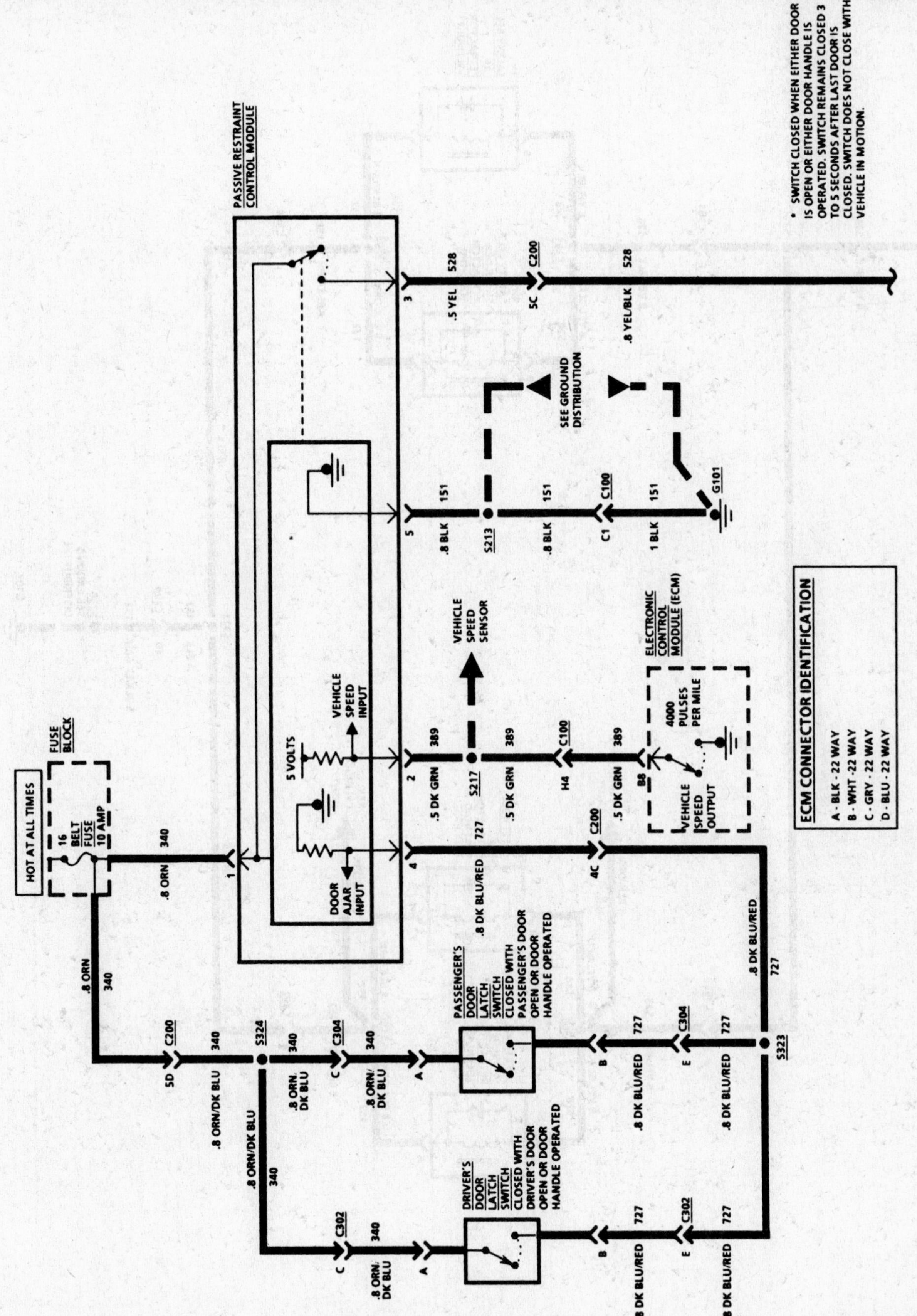

Automatic safety belts — Regal shown

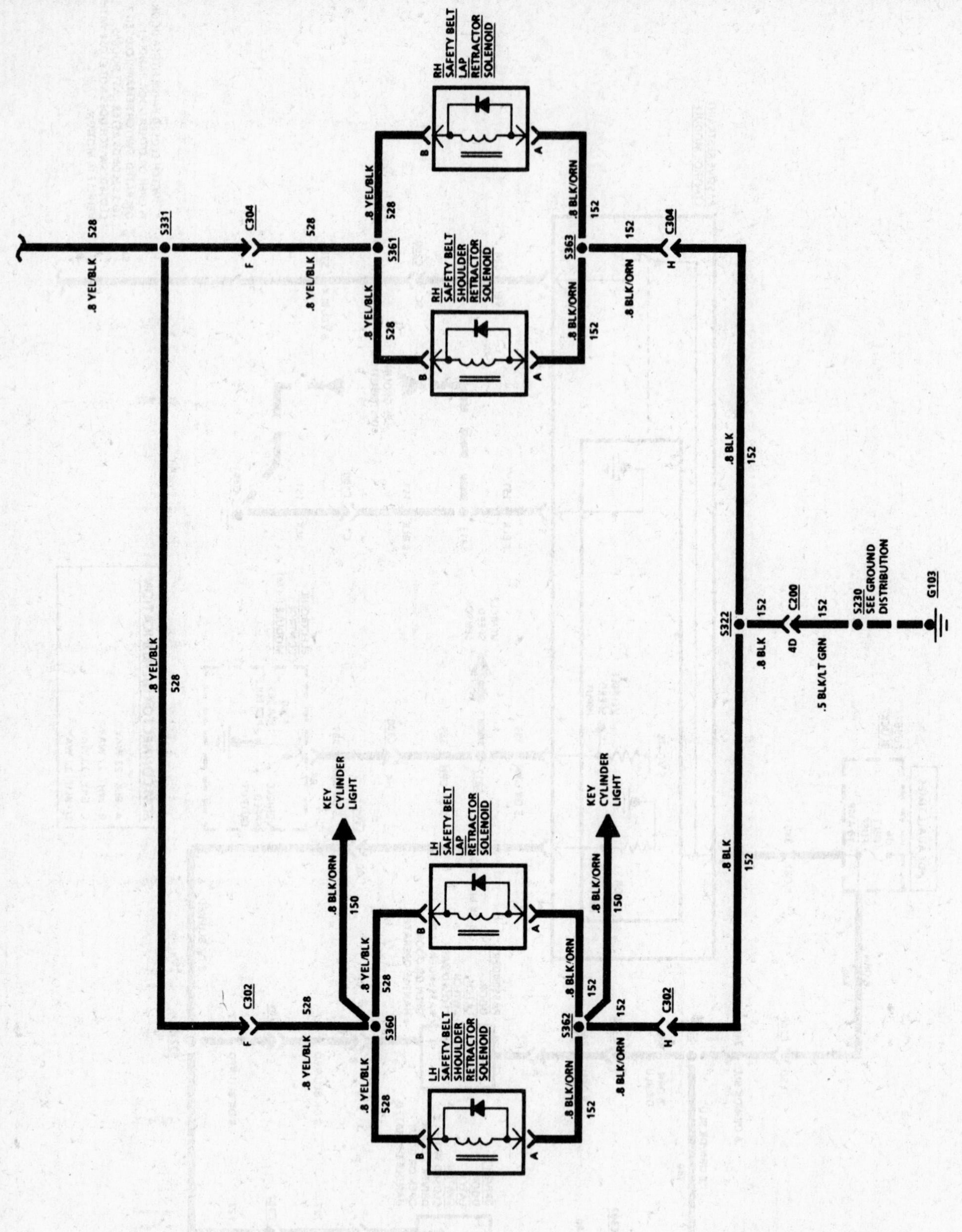

Automatic safety belts—Regal shown

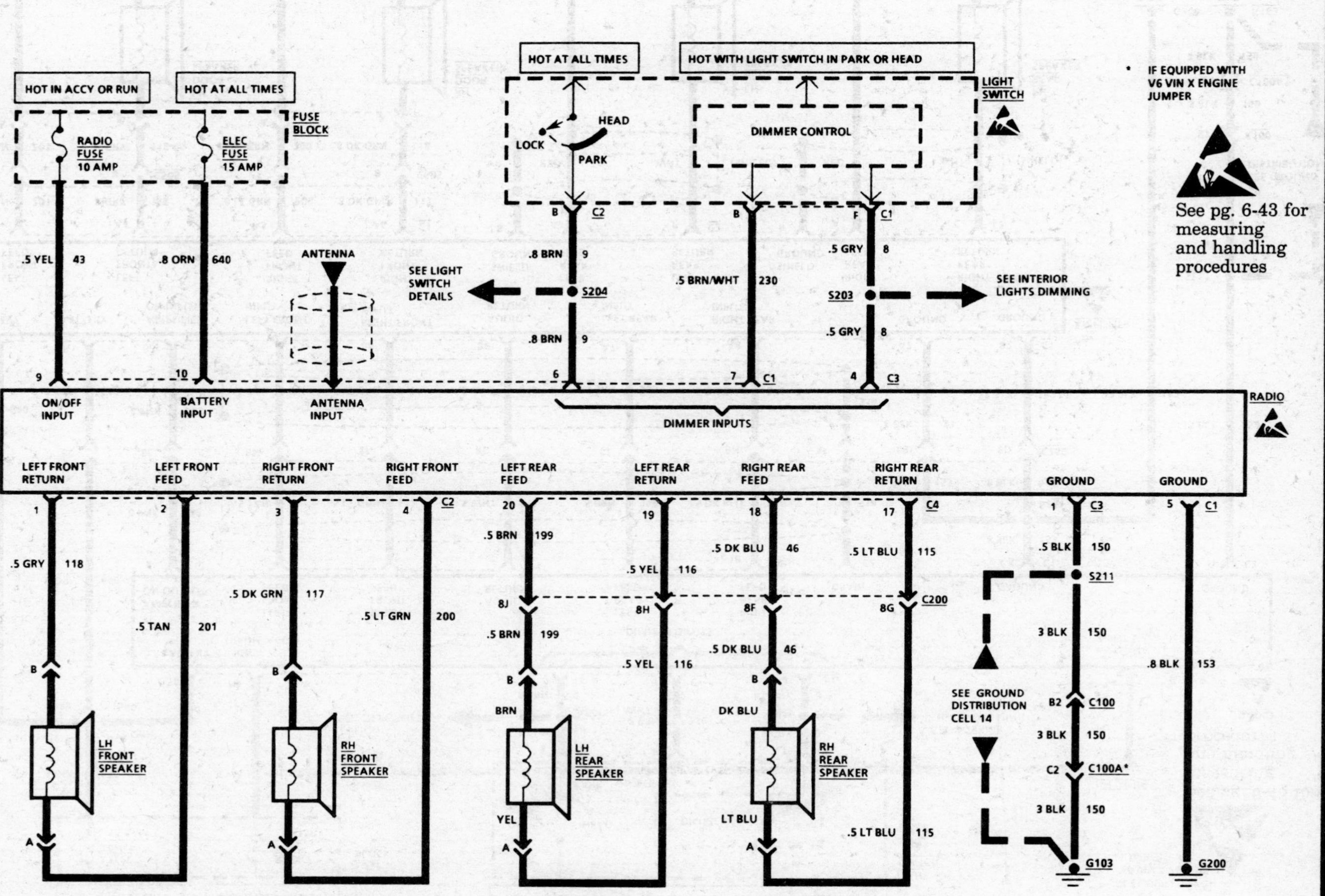

Base radio—Lumina shown

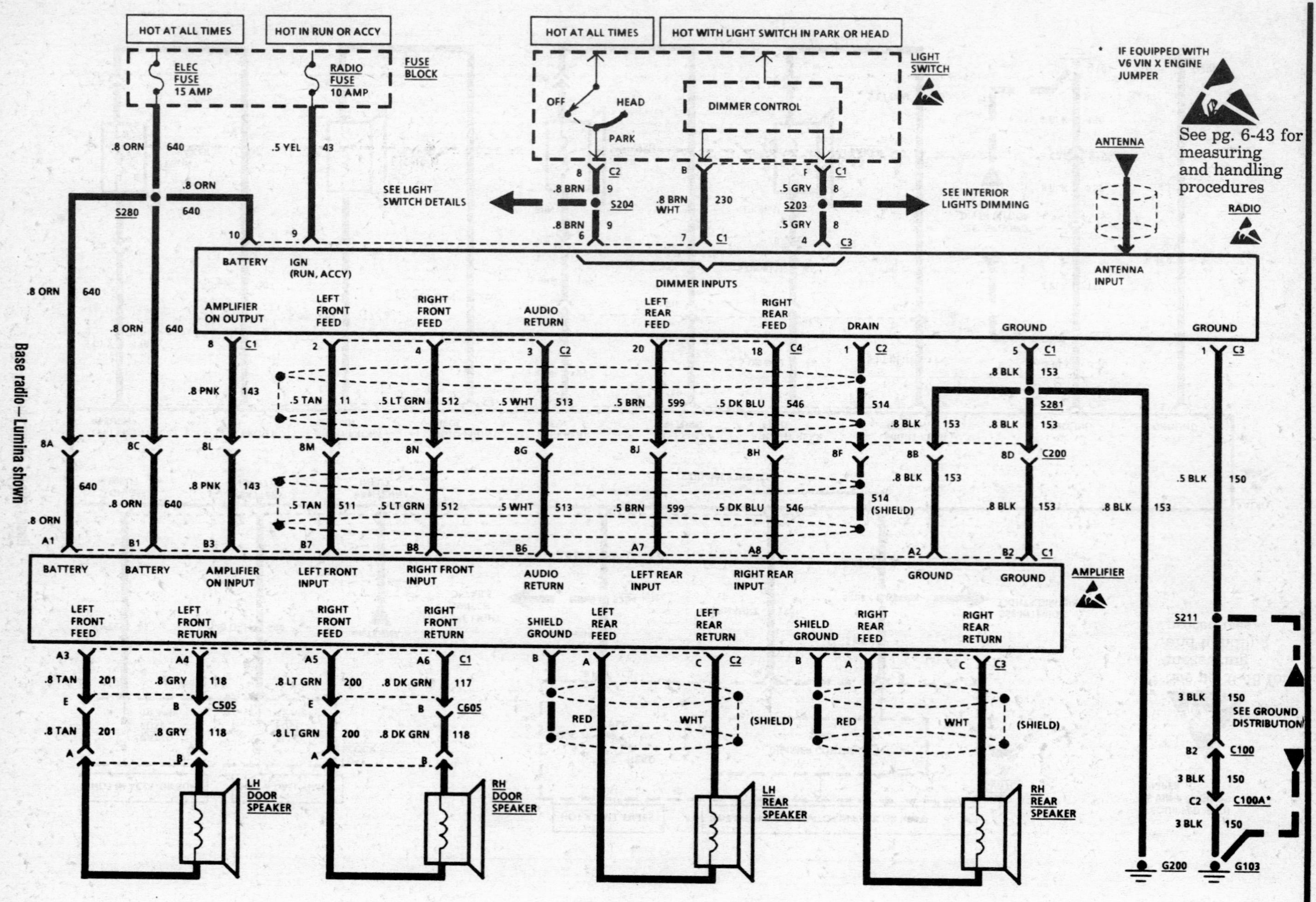

Base radio—Lumina shown

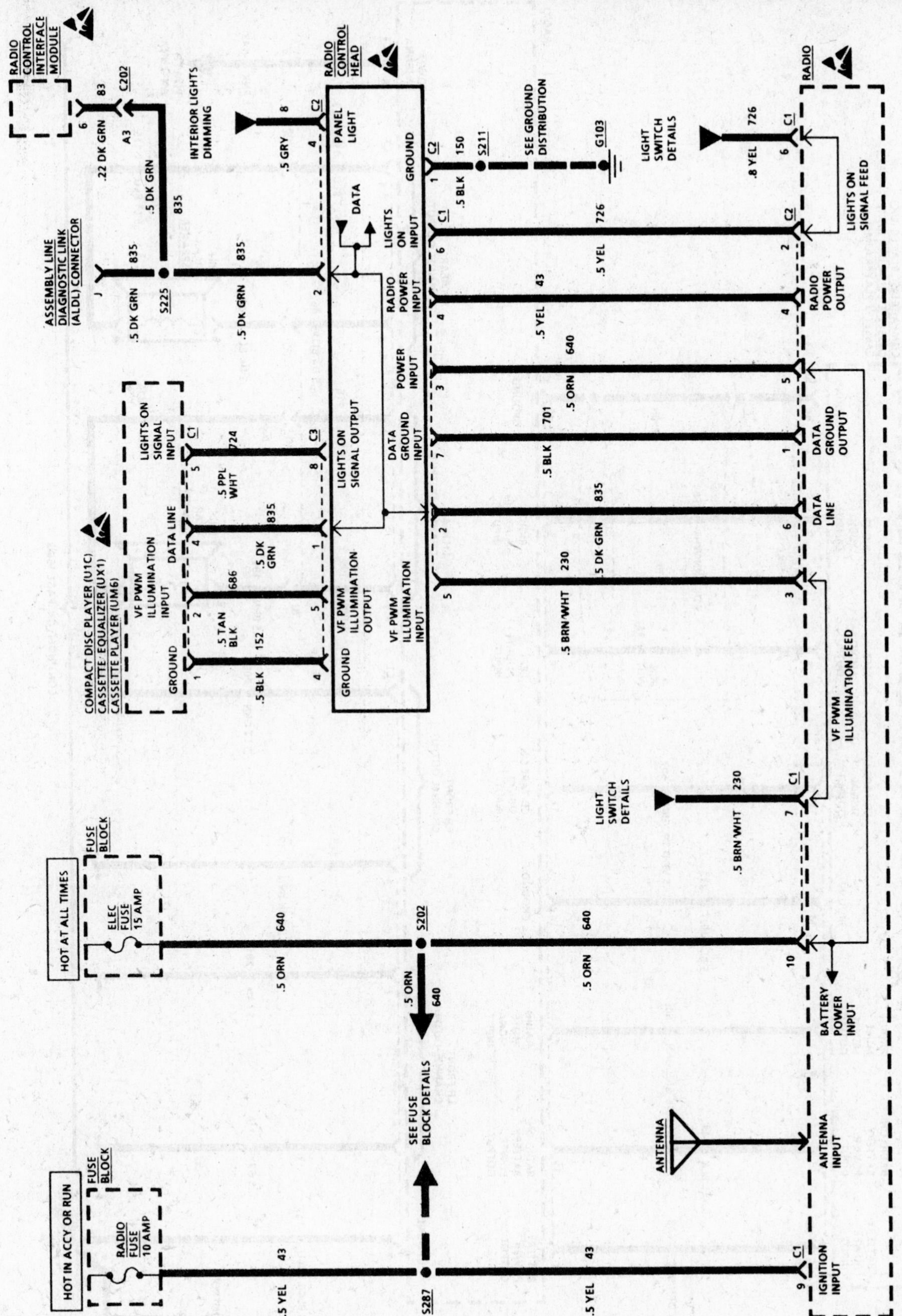

Radio with equalizer and compact disc player – Regal shown

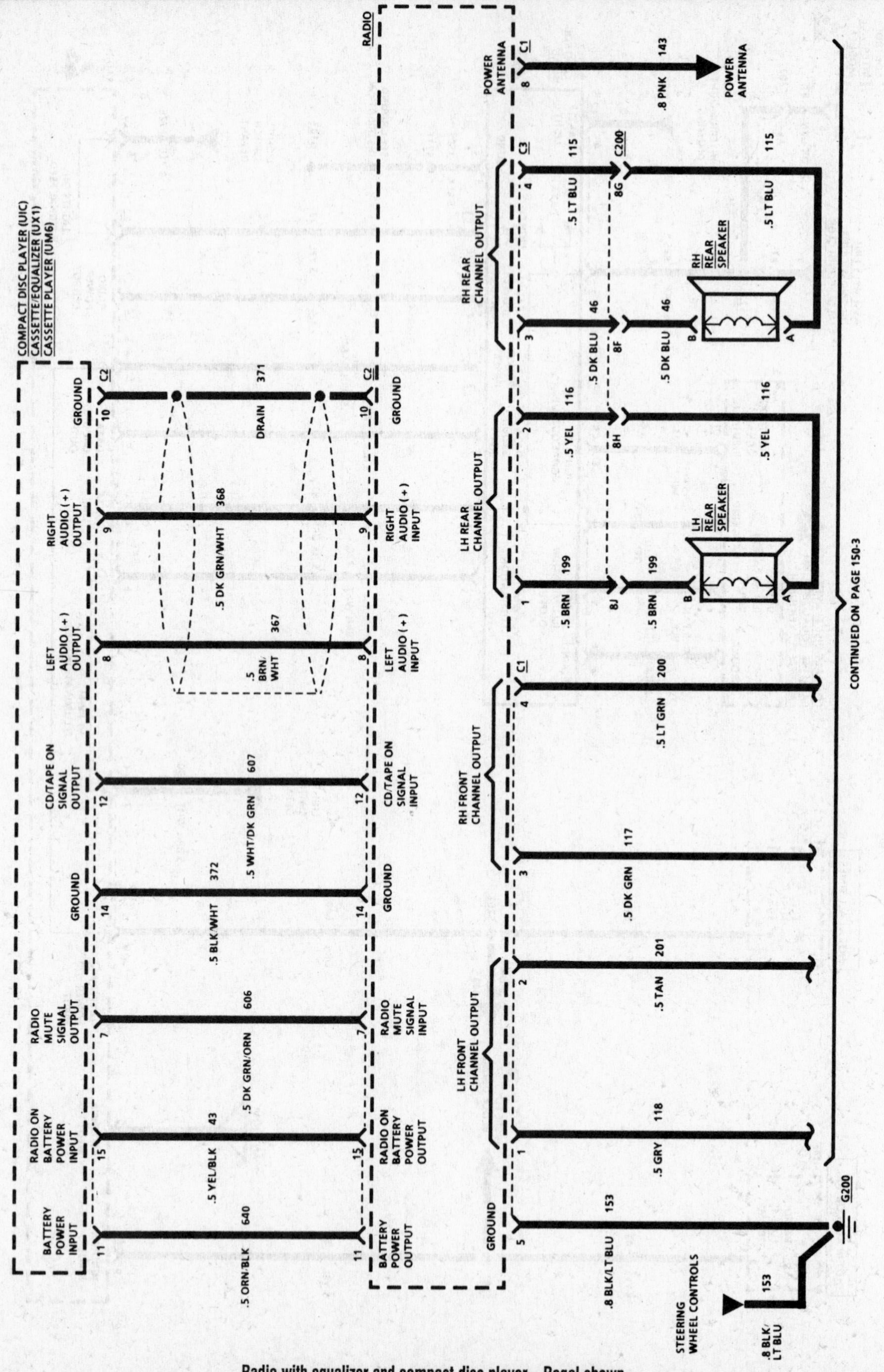

Radio with equalizer and compact disc player—Regal shown

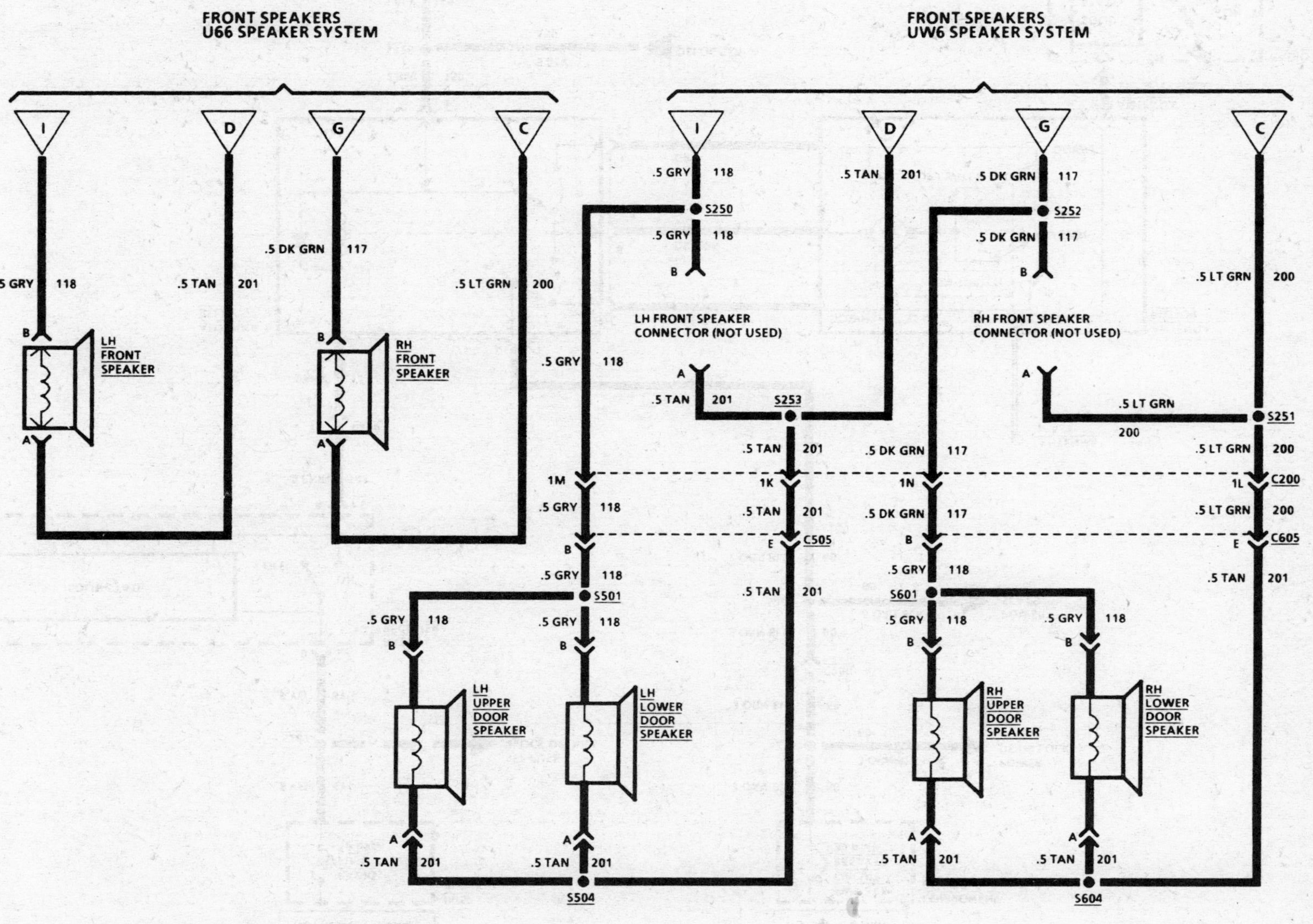

Radio with equalizer and compact disc player – Regal shown

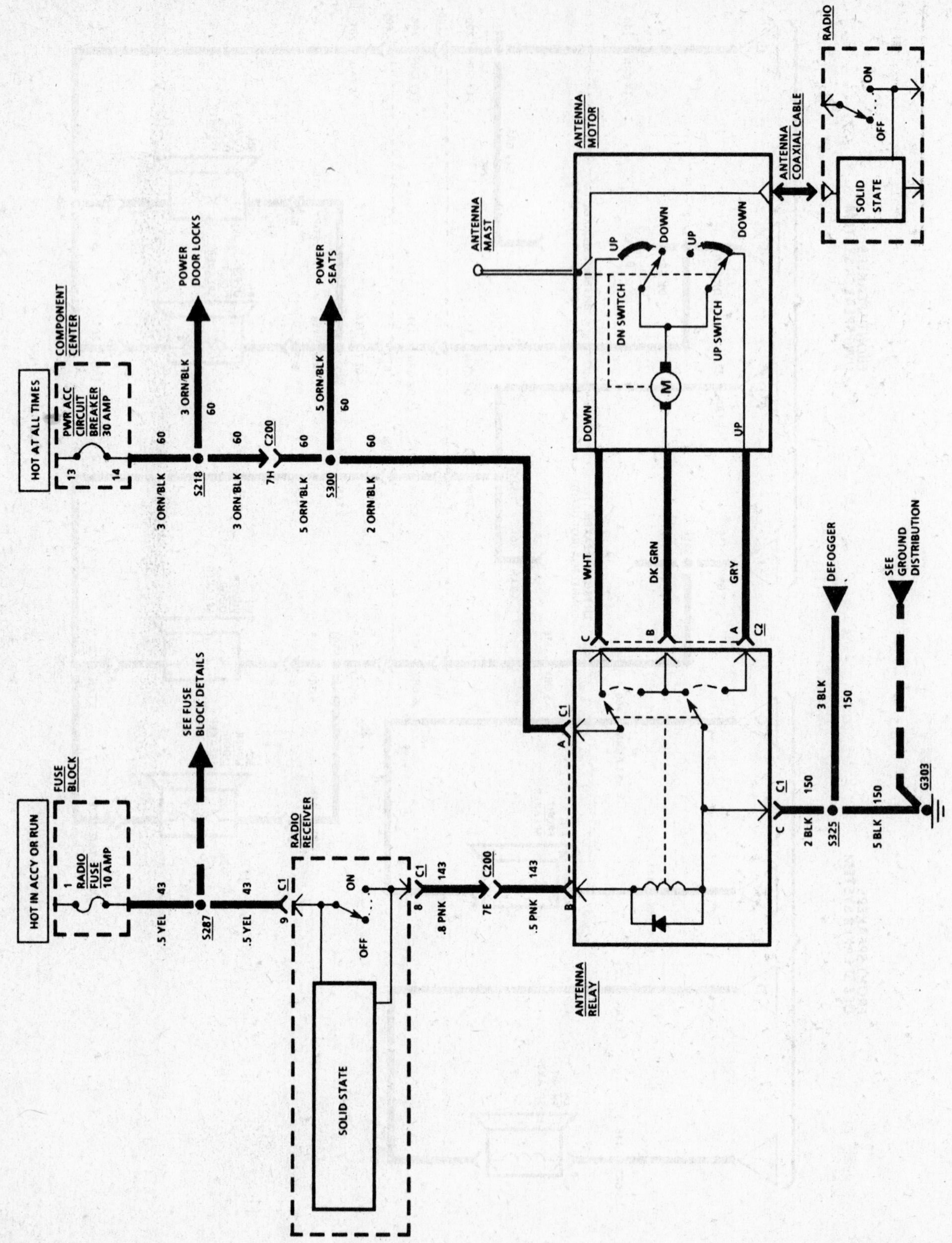

Power antenna—Regal shown

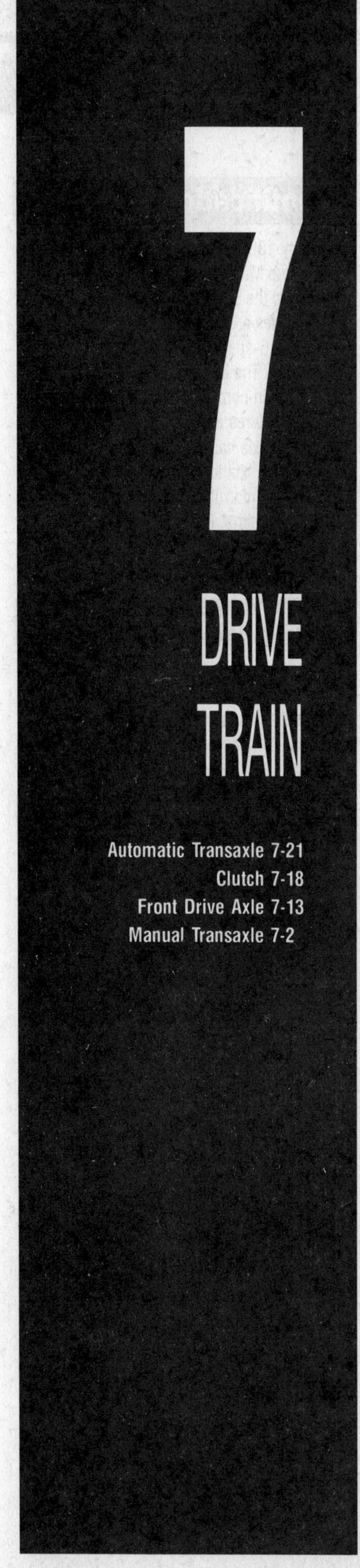

7 DRIVE TRAIN

MANUAL TRANSAXLE

Identification

In early 1990, General Motors changed the name of the Muncie HM-282 5-speed manual transaxle to the 5TM40. Only the name changed; the transaxles are identical. For 1991–92, the Getrag 284 5-speed transaxle is mated to the 3.4L engine. The Muncie and Getrag units are very similar in composition and their respective repair procedures are almost identical.

The transaxle has an identification tag and stamp on the exterior of the case. The identification information will assist in servicing and ordering parts. Refer to Section 1 for explanations of the tags' coding.

Adjustments

The shift linkage and cables are preset at the factory, requiring no adjustments. The clutch is a hydraulically-actuated system that is self-adjusting. No periodic adjustments are needed.

Reverse Light Switch

➧ SEE FIG. 1

REMOVAL & INSTALLATION

1. Disconnect the negative battery cable and remove the air cleaner assembly if necessary to gain access to the switch, which is located on top of the transaxle.
2. Disconnect the back-up light switch connector and remove the switch using the proper-size box wrench.
3. Apply thread locking compound to the switch threads when installing.
4. Connect the negative battery cable and make sure the reverse lights illuminate when in Reverse.

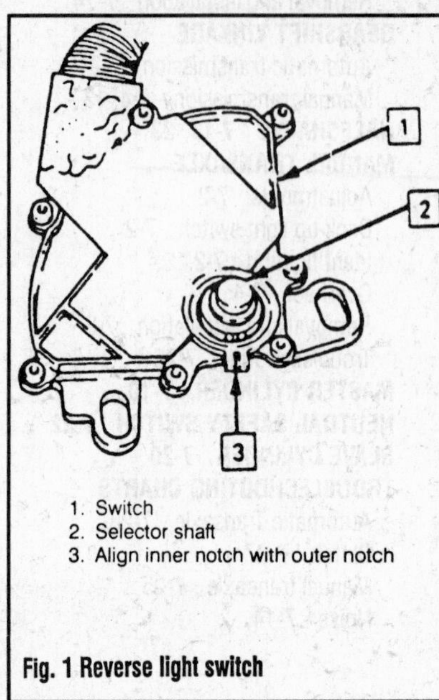

Fig. 1 Reverse light switch

Frame Assembly

➧ SEE FIGS. 2 AND 3

REMOVAL & INSTALLATION

1. Disconnect the negative battery cable and remove the air cleaner assembly.
2. Install the engine support fixture J28467–A.
3. Raise the vehicle and support with jackstands.
4. Position jackstands under the engine for support.
5. Remove the front wheel assemblies.
6. Disconnect the intermediate shaft from the steering gear stub shaft.
7. Remove the power steering hose bracket from the frame.
8. Remove the steering gear from the frame and support.

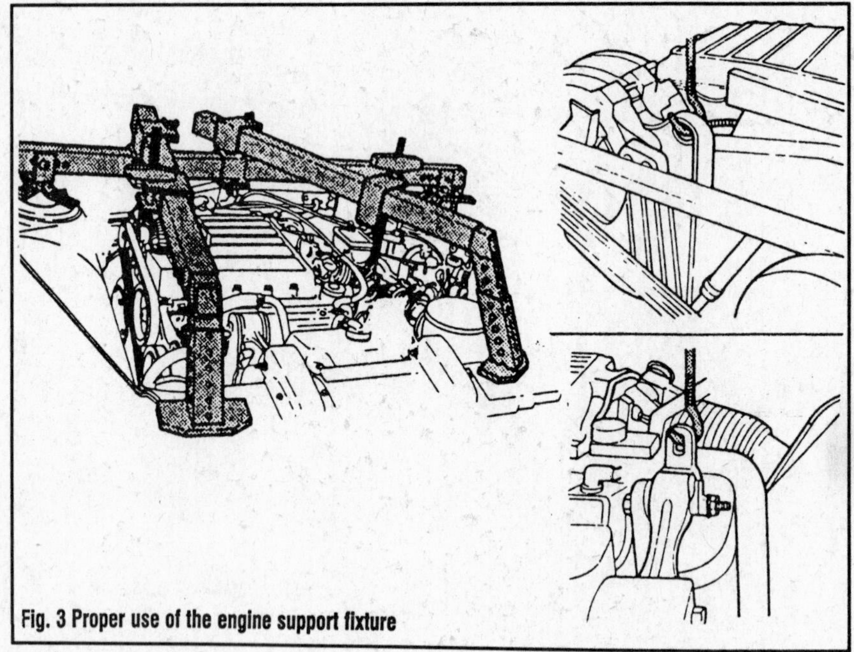

Fig. 3 Proper use of the engine support fixture

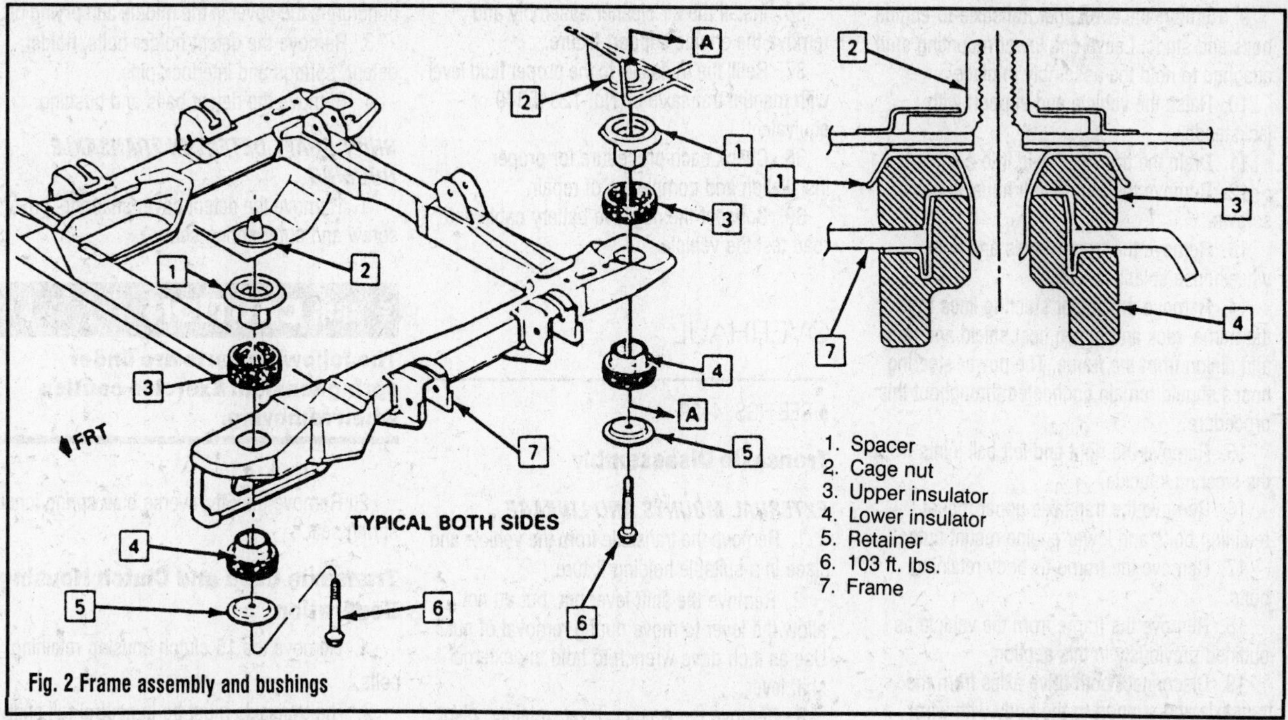

Fig. 2 Frame assembly and bushings

9. Remove the lower ball joints from the lower control arms.

10. Disconnect the engine and transaxle mounts.

11. Support the frame assembly and remove the frame-to-body mounting bolts.

12. Remove the frame assembly with the lower control arms and stabilizer shaft attached. Work the frame downward toward the rear of the vehicle.

13. Remove all loose frame hardware from the body.

To install:

14. Lubricate the frame insulators with rubber lubricant before installation.

15. Install the lower and upper insulators, retainers and spacers.

16. Install the transaxle mounting bracket, lower control arms and stabilizer shaft, if removed.

17. With an assistant, position the frame to the body, and hand tighten the retaining bolts.

18. Align the frame-to-body by inserting two 0.74 in. (19mm) × 8.0 in. (203mm) long pins in the alignment holes on the right side of the frame.

19. Torque the frame-to-body retaining bolts to 103 ft. lbs. (140 Nm).

20. Reconnect the engine and transaxle mounts.

21. Install the lower ball joints and steering gear.

22. Install the hoses and brackets.

23. Install the intermediate shaft-to-steering stub shaft.

24. Install the front wheels.

25. Lower the vehicle and remove the engine support fixture.

26. Install the air cleaner and connect the negative battery cable.

27. Have a qualified alignment technician check the front end alignment.

Transaxle Assembly

REMOVAL & INSTALLATION

➡ Before preforming any manual transaxle removal procedures, the clutch master cylinder pushrod MUST be disconnected from the clutch pedal and the connection in the hydraulic line must be separated using tool No. J-36221. Permanent damage may occur to the actuator if the clutch pedal is depressed while the system is not resisted by clutch loads. Also, the pushrod bushing should be replaced once it has been disconnected from the master cylinder.

1. Disconnect the negative battery cable and remove the air cleaner assembly.

2. Install the engine support fixture tool J28467-A along with the support leg.

3. Remove the clutch actuator from the transaxle.

4. Remove the electrical connectors from the back-up switch.

5. Remove the shift and selector cables from the transaxle case.

6. Re[illegible]ove the exhaust crossover pipe at the left exh[illegible]

7. [illegible] crossover.

8. [illegible] upwa[illegible] bolt[illegible]

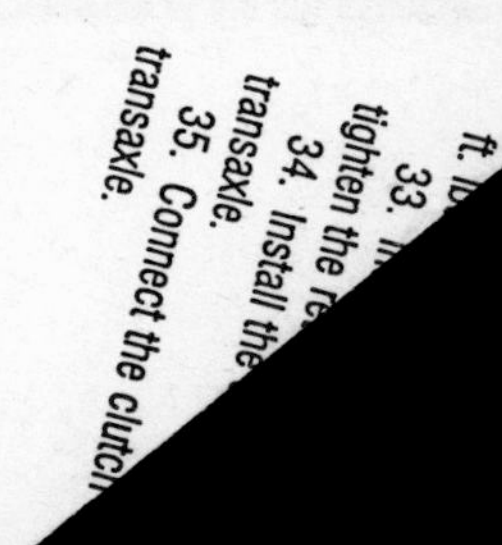

9. Remove the two upper transaxle-to-engine bolts and studs. Leave one lower mounting stud attached to hold the assembly in place.
10. Raise the vehicle and support with jackstands.
11. Drain the transaxle fluid into a pan.
12. Remove the four clutch housing cover screws.
13. Remove the front wheels and both wheelhouse splash shields.
14. Remove the power steering lines from the frame, rack and pinion heat shield and rack and pinion from the frame. The power steering hoses should remain connected throughout this procedure.
15. Remove the right and left ball joints from the steering knuckle.
16. Remove the transaxle upper mount retaining bolts and lower engine mount nuts.
17. Remove the frame-to-body retaining bolts.
18. Remove the frame from the vehicle as outlined previously in this section.
19. Disconnect both drive axles from the transaxle and support to the body with wire.
20. Remove the starter motor.
21. Securely support the transaxle case for removal.
22. Remove the remaining transaxle-to-engine retaining bolts and remove the transaxle by pulling it away from the engine.

To install:

23. Align the transaxle to the engine and work the input shaft through the clutch disc. Slide the assembly forward and install. Install the lower retaining bolts.
24. Install the starter motor and drive axles.
25. Install the frame assembly and retaining bolts as previously outlined in this section.
26. Install the engine mount retaining nuts and upper transaxle retaining bolt. Torque the transaxle-to-engine bolts to 55 ft. lbs. (75 Nm).
27. Install both ball joints to the steering knuckle.
28. Install the power steering assembly, heat shield and hose brackets.
29. Install the wheelhouse splash shields and front wheels.
30. Install the transaxle drain plug, clutch housing cover, then lower the vehicle.
31. Connect the reverse light switch and speed sensor wiring.
32. Install the two upper transaxle mounting bolts and studs. Torque the bolts and studs to 55 ...lbs. (75 Nm).
...nstall the crossover pipe, EGR pipe, and ...taining nuts.
... shift and select cables to the
... actuator to the

36. Install the air cleaner assembly and remove the engine support fixture.
37. Refill the transaxle to the proper fluid level with manual transaxle oil No. 12345349 or equivalent.
38. Check each procedure for proper installation and completion of repair.
39. Connect the negative battery cable and road test the vehicle.

OVERHAUL

➧ SEE FIGS. 4–29

Transaxle Disassembly

EXTERNAL MOUNTS AND LINKAGE

1. Remove the transaxle from the vehicle and place in a suitable holding fixture.
2. Remove the shift lever nut, but do not allow the lever to move during removal of nut. Use an inch drive wrench to hold the external shift lever.
3. Remove the washer, lever, retainer, pivot pin and pivot, bolts and bracket, fluid level indicator and the electronic speedometer retainer and assembly.

SHIFT RAIL DETENT IN CLUTCH HOUSING

1. Remove the clutch disengage bearing.
2. Remove the detent holder cover by puncturing the cover in the middle and prying off.
3. Remove the detent holder bolts, holder, detent, springs and interlock pins.
4. Remove the detent balls and bushing.

SHIFT SHAFT DETENT IN TRANSAXLE HOUSING

1. Remove the detent cover snapring, cover, screw and outer spring seat.

✻✻ CAUTION

The following parts are under spring tension. Exercise caution when removing.

2. Remove the 5th/reverse bias spring/inner spring seat.

Transaxle Case and Clutch Housing Separation

1. Remove the 15 clutch housing retaining bolts.
2. The transaxle must be in neutral (all shift rails protruding the same amount) with the clutch housing facing up. Remove the clutch housing by gently tapping the housing with a rubber hammer.
3. Remove the differential gear assembly, magnet and bearing.

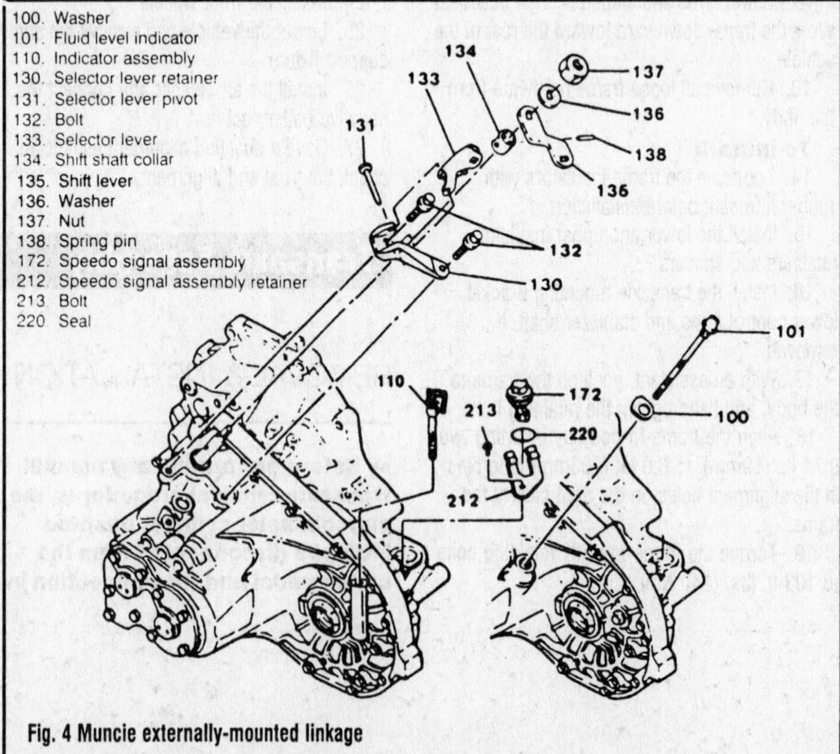

Fig. 4 Muncie externally-mounted linkage

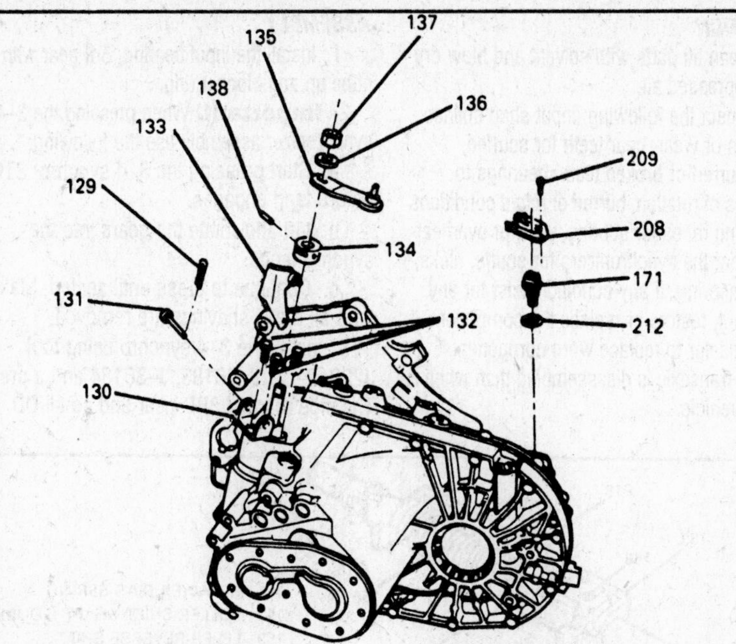

129 CLIP, RETAINER
130 PIN, SELECTOR LEVER PIVOT
131 RETAINER, SELECTOR LEVER
132 BOLTS
133 LEVER, SELECTOR
134 COLLAR, SHIFT SHAFT
135 LEVER, SHIFT
136 WASHER
137 NUT
138 PIN, SPRING
171 SPEED SENSOR ASSEMBLY
208 RETAINER, SPEED SENSOR ASSEMBLY
209 BOLT
212 SEAL

Fig. 5 Getrag externally-mounted linkage

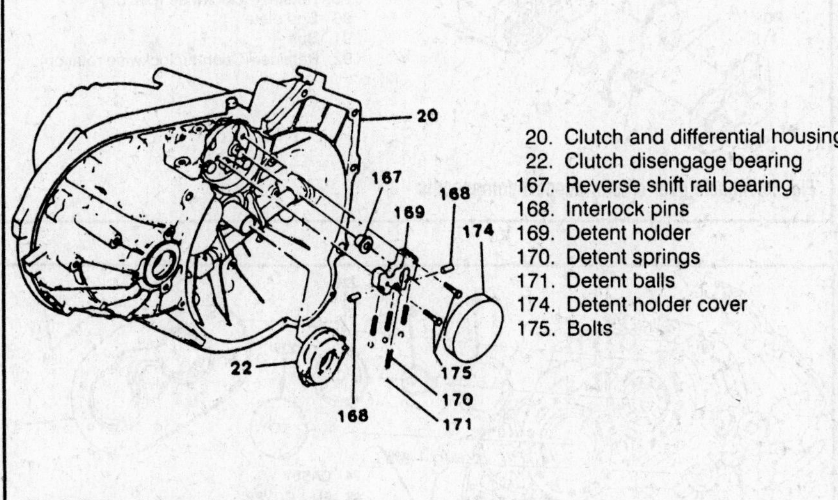

20. Clutch and differential housing
22. Clutch disengage bearing
167. Reverse shift rail bearing
168. Interlock pins
169. Detent holder
170. Detent springs
171. Detent balls
174. Detent holder cover
175. Bolts

Fig. 6 Shift rail detent in clutch housing

SHIFT SHAFT COMPONENTS

➡ **Do not bottom the pins out onto the case, and do not allow the pins to fall into the case when removing from the shafts.**

1. Remove the shift shaft pin using a punch.
2. Remove the shift shaft assembly consisting of the shaft, rollers, 1st/2nd bias spring and shift and reverse lever.

GEAR CLUSTER SUPPORT COMPONENTS

1. Engage the gear cluster in 4th and Reverse by pushing down on the gear rails.
2. Remove the nine bearing retainer cover bolts and cover. Remove the bearing oil delivery tubes if equipped.
3. Using tool J-36031, remove the bearing retainer Hex bolts and selective shim. Remove the reverse idler shaft retaining bolt.

GEAR CLUSTERS

1. Using tool J-36182-1 and J-36182I-2, position in a hydraulic press.
2. Position the transaxle case and gear cluster assembly in the press. Align the shift rail and shaft pilots to the fixture.
3. Position tool J-36185 on the shaft support bearings and pilots. Using the press, separate the shaft and gear clusters from the transaxle case.

GEAR CLUSTERS AND SHIFT RAILS

1. Remove the 1-2 shift rail assembly and lock pin.
2. Remove the 3-4 shift rail assembly.
3. Remove the 5th shift rail assembly and reverse assembly.
4. Remove the shift gate and disengage roller.

UNIT DISASSEMBLY AND REPAIR

Input Shaft

DISASSEMBLY

1. **Important!** Identify the blocker ring for the 3rd gear and 4th gear blocker ring. DO NOT MIX.
2. Remove the input shaft snapring before using the press.

➡ **The Getrag uses additional bearings and washers. Refer to the exploded view for reference.**

3. Remove 4th and 5th gears, bearings, race, blocker ring, synchronizer and gear using an arbor press.
4. Remove the 3rd gear bearing.

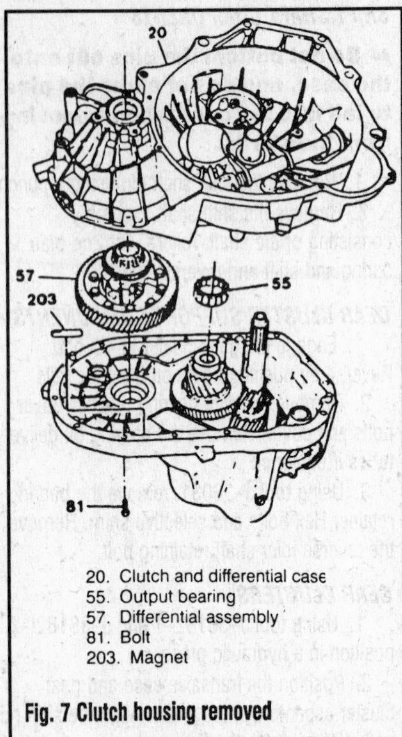

Fig. 7 Clutch housing removed

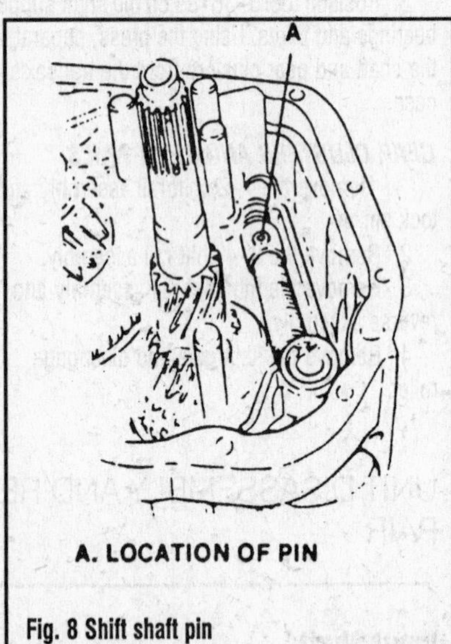

Fig. 8 Shift shaft pin

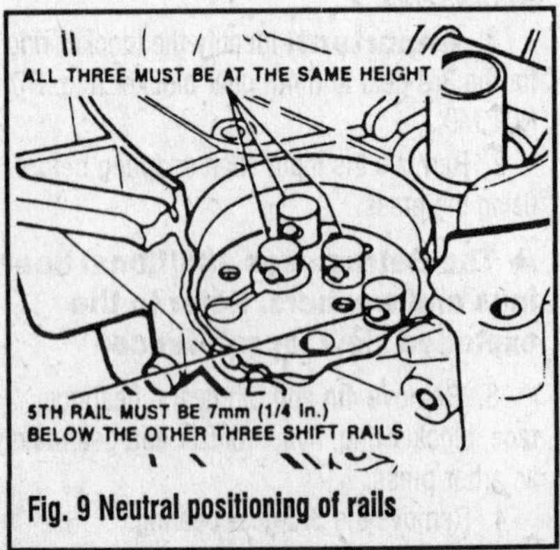

Fig. 9 Neutral positioning of rails

INSPECTION

1. Clean all parts with solvent and blow dry with compressed air.

2. Inspect the following: input shaft splines for cracks or wear, gear teeth for scuffed, nicked, burred or broken teeth, bearings for roughness of rotation, burred or pitted conditions and bearing races for scoring, wear or overheating. Inspect the synchronizers for scuffs, nicks, burrs or scoring. If any condition exist for any component, restore or replace the component. It is much easier to replace worn components while the transaxle is disassembled than when it is in the vehicle.

ASSEMBLY

1. Install the input bearing, 3rd gear with the cone up and blocker ring.

2. **Important!** When pressing the 3–4 synchronizer assembly use the following:

a. Start pressing the 3–4 synchro, STOP, before tang engages.

b. Lift and rotate the gears into the synchro tangs.

c. Continue to press until seated. Make sure all metal shavings are removed.

3. Install the 3–4 synchro using tool J22912–01, J-36183, J-36184 and a press. The side marked 3RD gear and small OD

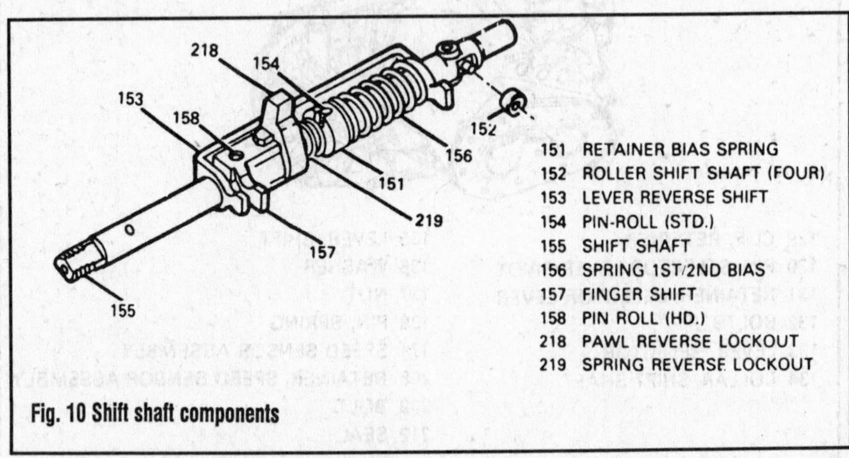

Fig. 10 Shift shaft components

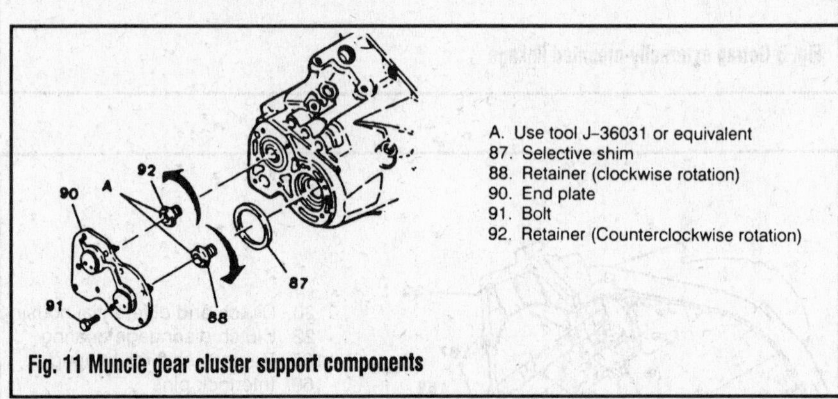

Fig. 11 Muncie gear cluster support components

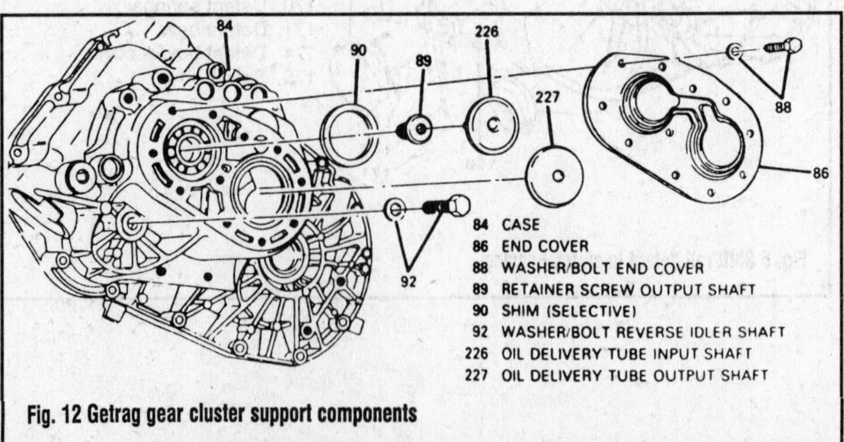

Fig. 12 Getrag gear cluster support components

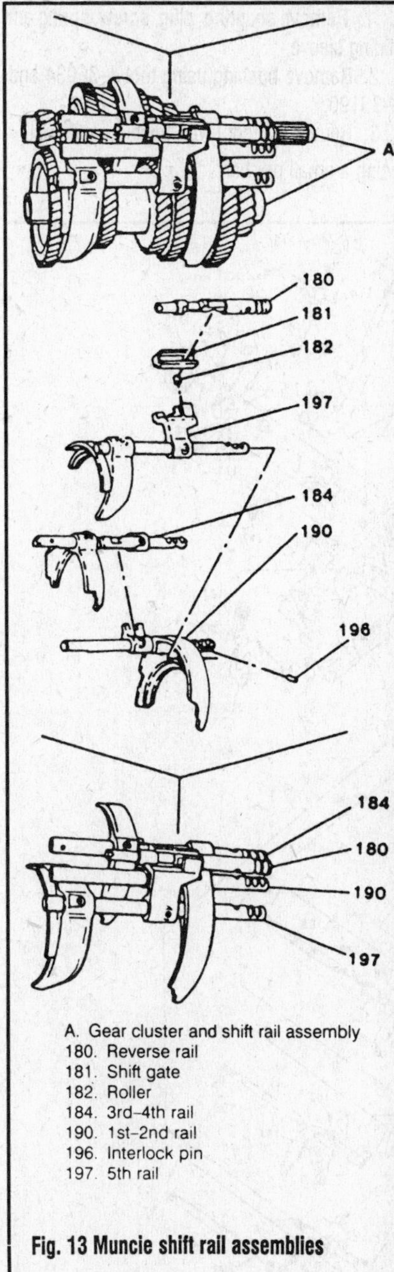

A. Gear cluster and shift rail assembly
180. Reverse rail
181. Shift gate
182. Roller
184. 3rd–4th rail
190. 1st–2nd rail
196. Interlock pin
197. 5th rail

Fig. 13 Muncie shift rail assemblies

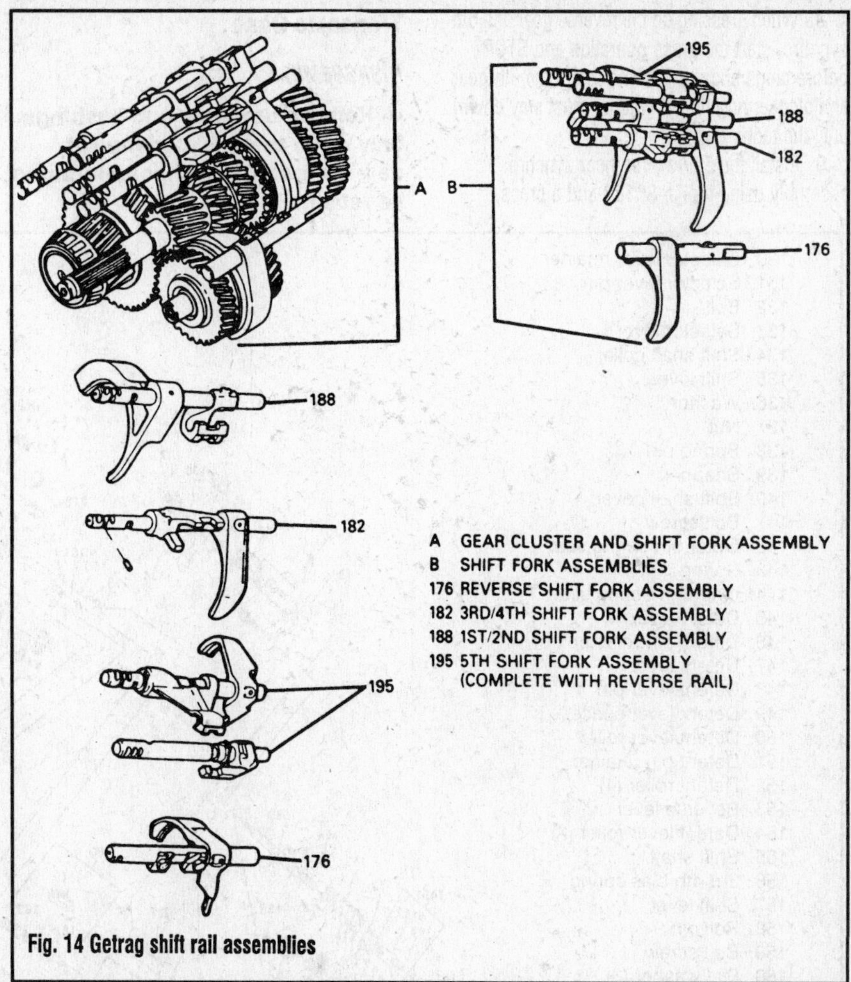

Fig. 14 Getrag shift rail assemblies

groove of the sleeve goes toward the 3rd gear.

4. Heat and install the bearing race and the bearing.

5. Install the blocker ring, then the 4th gear with the cone down. Heat the 5th gear and install using the press. The 5th gear should be flat side down.

6. Install the new snapring.

Output Shaft

DISASSEMBLY

1. **Important!** Identify the blocker ring for 5th gear, ring for 2nd gear and ring for 1st gear. DO NOT MIX.

2. Remove the 5th/reverse synchronizer assembly using tool J–22912–01 and a press.

➡ **The Getrag uses additional bearings and washers. Refer to the exploded view for reference.**

3. Remove the blocker ring, 5th gear, bearing, thrust washer and ball.

4. Remove the snapring.

5. Remove the 1st gear, bearing, caged thrust bearing and thrust washer using tool J36183 and a press. The 2nd gear, bearing, race, 1–2 synchro and blocker rings will press off with the 1st gear.

INSPECTION

1. Clean all parts with solvent and blow dry with compressed air.

2. Inspect the output shaft for spline wear, cracks or excessive wear, gear teeth for scuffed, nicked , burred or broken teeth and bearings for roughness, burred or pitted conditions. If scuffed, nicked, burred or scored conditions can not be removed with fine crocus cloth or soft stone, replace the component.

ASSEMBLY

1. Install the thrust washer with the chamfer down, caged thrust bearing with the needles down, 1st gear bearing, 1st gear with the cone up and the blocker ring.

2. When pressing the 1–2 synchronizer assembly, start the press operation and STOP before tangs engages. Lift and rotate gears to engage the blocker ring tangs. Continue to press until seated and make sure all metal shavings are removed.

3. Install the 1–2 synchro using tool J36183 and a press. The side marked "1ST" and small "OD" groove goes toward the 1st gear.

4. Heat and install the 2nd gear bearing race, bearing and 2nd gear with the cone down.

5. Heat and install the 3–4 gear cluster using tool J36183 and a press. Position the large OD gear down.

6. Install the new snapring, thrust washer positioning ball retained with petroleum jelly and the slotted thrust washer. Align the ID slot with ball.

7. Install the 5th gear bearing and the 5th gear with the cone up. Install the blocker ring.

8. When pressing on the reverse gear and 5th synchro, start the press operation and STOP before tangs engage. Lift and rotate the 5th gear and blocker ring (thrust washer must stay down) until the tangs engage.

9. Install the 5th/reverse gear synchro assembly using tool J-36183 and a press.

Transaxle Case

DISASSEMBLY

➡ **Remove bearings and bushings only when there is evidence of damage and the component cannot be reused.**

1. Remove snapring, plug, screw, spring and sliding sleeve.
2. Remove bushing using tool J-36034 and J-36190.
3. Remove detent lever, bushing and seal using a small pry bar.

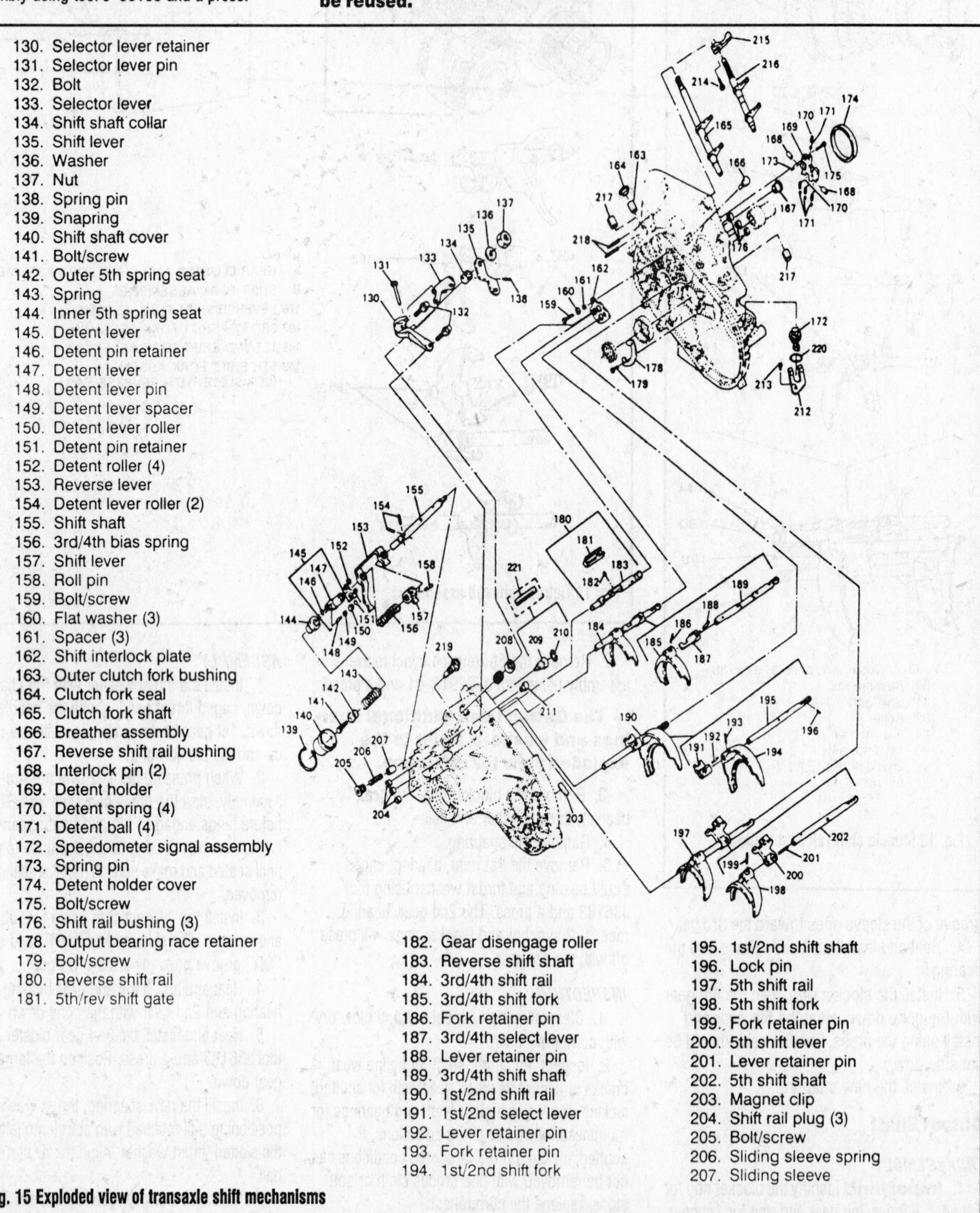

130. Selector lever retainer
131. Selector lever pin
132. Bolt
133. Selector lever
134. Shift shaft collar
135. Shift lever
136. Washer
137. Nut
138. Spring pin
139. Snapring
140. Shift shaft cover
141. Bolt/screw
142. Outer 5th spring seat
143. Spring
144. Inner 5th spring seat
145. Detent lever
146. Detent pin retainer
147. Detent lever
148. Detent lever pin
149. Detent lever spacer
150. Detent lever roller
151. Detent pin retainer
152. Detent roller (4)
153. Reverse lever
154. Detent lever roller (2)
155. Shift shaft
156. 3rd/4th bias spring
157. Shift lever
158. Roll pin
159. Bolt/screw
160. Flat washer (3)
161. Spacer (3)
162. Shift interlock plate
163. Outer clutch fork bushing
164. Clutch fork seal
165. Clutch fork shaft
166. Breather assembly
167. Reverse shift rail bushing
168. Interlock pin (2)
169. Detent holder
170. Detent spring (4)
171. Detent ball (4)
172. Speedometer signal assembly
173. Spring pin
174. Detent holder cover
175. Bolt/screw
176. Shift rail bushing (3)
178. Output bearing race retainer
179. Bolt/screw
180. Reverse shift rail
181. 5th/rev shift gate
182. Gear disengage roller
183. Reverse shift shaft
184. 3rd/4th shift rail
185. 3rd/4th shift fork
186. Fork retainer pin
187. 3rd/4th select lever
188. Lever retainer pin
189. 3rd/4th shift shaft
190. 1st/2nd shift rail
191. 1st/2nd select lever
192. Lever retainer pin
193. Fork retainer pin
194. 1st/2nd shift fork
195. 1st/2nd shift shaft
196. Lock pin
197. 5th shift rail
198. 5th shift fork
199. Fork retainer pin
200. 5th shift lever
201. Lever retainer pin
202. 5th shift shaft
203. Magnet clip
204. Shift rail plug (3)
205. Bolt/screw
206. Sliding sleeve spring
207. Sliding sleeve

Fig. 15 Exploded view of transaxle shift mechanisms

1. Input cluster shaft and gear assembly
2. Snapring
3. 5th input gear
4. 4th input gear
5. Cage bearing
6. Needle race
7. 4th blocker ring
8. 3rd/4th synchronizer assembly
9. 3rd/4th synchronizer sleeve
10. 3rd/4th synchronizer key (3)
11. 3rd/4th synchronizer ball (3)
12. 3rd/4th synchronizer spring (3)
13. 3rd/4th synchronizer hub clutch
14. 3rd blocker ring
15. 3rd input gear
16. Cage bearing (2)
17. Input shaft
18. Bolt
19. Reverse shift rail guide
20. Clutch and differential housing
21. Input shaft bearing/sleeve assembly
22. Clutch release bearing assembly
23. Driveshaft oil seal
24. Output cluster shaft and gear assembly
25. Reverse output/5th synchronizer assembly gear
26. Reverse gear
27. 5th synchronizer key (3)
28. 5th synchronizer ball (3)
29. 5th synchronizer spring (3)
30. 5th synchronizer sleeve
31. 5th gear blocker ring
32. 5th speed output bearing
33. 5th speed output bearing
34. Thrust washer positioner ball
35. Thrust washer
36. Snapring
37. 3rd/4th cluster gear
38. 2nd output gear
39. 2nd output bearing
40. 2nd output bearing race
41. 2nd gear blocker ring
42. 1st/2nd gear synchronizer assembly
43. 1st/2nd synchronizer sleeve
44. 1st/2nd synchronizer key (3)
45. 1st/2nd synchronizer ball (3)
46. 1st/2nd synchronizer spring (3)
47. 1st/2nd synchronizer hub
48. 1st gear blocker ring
49. 1st output gear
50. 1st output bearing
51. Thrust bearing
52. Thrust washer
53. Output shaft
54. Output shaft support bearing
55. Output bearing
56. Output bearing race
57. Gear and differential assembly
58. Differential assembly bearing
59. Differential bearing race
60. Differential bearing
61. Differential assembly case
62. Differential case
63. Differential cross pin
64. Pinion gear thrust washer
65. Side gear thrust washer
66. Differential side gear
67. Differential pinion gear
68. Pinion gear shaft bolt
69. Lock washer
70. Differential ring gear
71. Speedometer output gear (mechanical)
72. Speedometer output gear (electronic)
73. Differential selective shim
74. Differential assembly bearing
75. Differential bearing race
76. Differential bearing race
77. Differential ring bolt (10)
78. Pin (2)
79. Oil drain plug
80. Washer
81. Transaxle case bolt (15)
82. Washer
83. Plug
84.
85. Transaxle case
86. Output gear bearing
87. Output gear selective shim
88. Output gear bearing retainer
89. Oil slinger washer
90. Transaxle case end plate
91. Bolt (9)
92. Input gear bearing retainer
93. Input gear bearing
94. Reverse idler bolt
95. Detent lever bushing
96. Sliding sleeve bushing
97. Shift shaft needle bearing
98. Reverse rail bushing
99. Shift rail bushing (3)
100. Fluid level indicator washer
101. Fluid level indicator
102. Reverse idler shaft
103. Reverse idler gear
104. Reverse shift idler gear rail
105. Reverse idler gear assembly bracket
106. Reverse idler gear bracket ball
107. Reverse idler gear bracket spring
108. Reverse idler gear detent bracket sleeve
109. Reverse idler gear bracket

Fig. 16 Exploded view of the transaxle gears and case

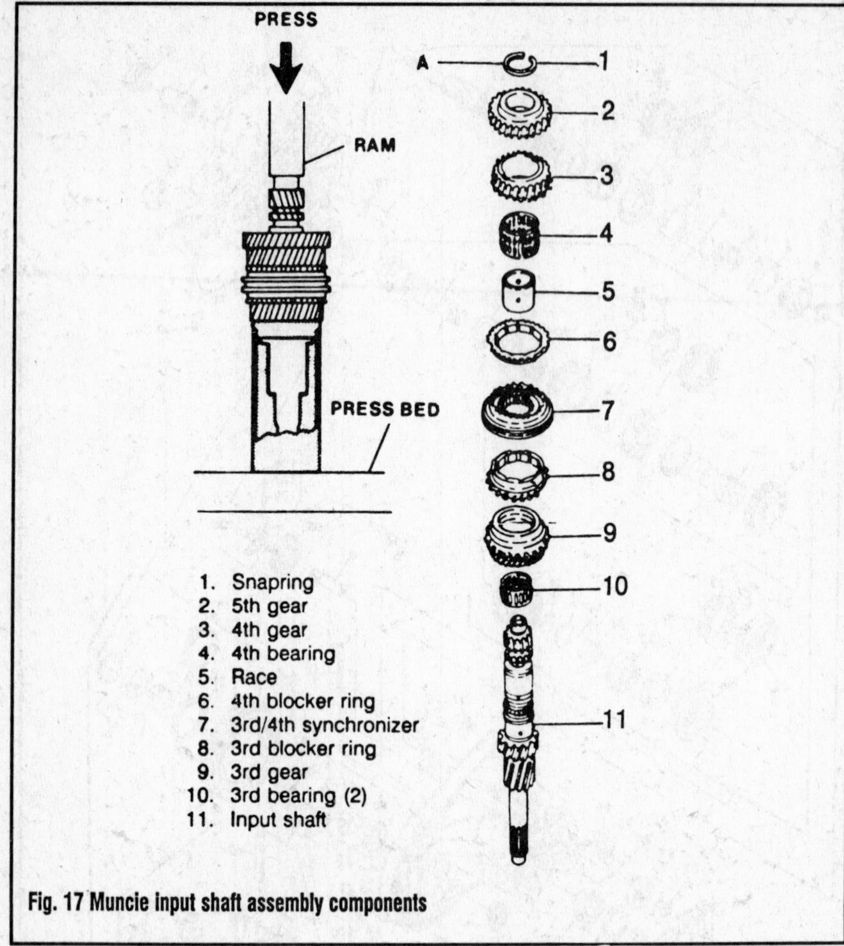

Fig. 17 Muncie input shaft assembly components

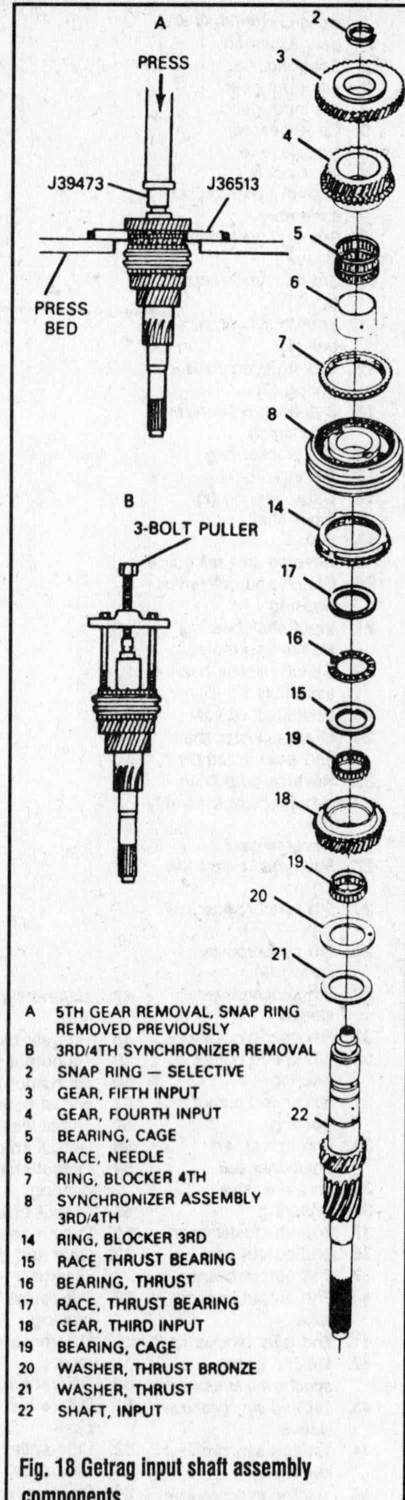

Fig. 18 Getrag input shaft assembly components

4. Remove the shift shaft seal using tool J36027.
5. Remove the axle seal, outer race, plugs, input shaft support bearing and the output shaft support bearing.
6. Remove the three shift rail bushing using tool J-36029, the reverse shift rail bushing by driving down and removing through the back-up light switch hole.

ASSEMBLY

1. Install the shift shaft bearing and seal using tool J-36189 and J-36190.
2. Install the three shift rail bushing using tool J-36029.
3. Install the reverse rail bushing using tool J-36030 and J-36190.
4. Install the differential carrier outer race, axle seal and plugs.
5. Install detent lever bushings, sliding sleeve bushing using tools J-36039 and J36034.
6. Install detent lever, sleeve, spring and screw tightened to 32 ft. lbs. (44 Nm).
7. Install plug, snapring and stud with the chamfer end out torqued to 15 ft. lbs. (21 Nm).

Synchronizers

DISASSEMBLY

1. Place 1–2, 3–4, and 5th–reverse synchronizers in a separate shop towel. Wrap the assemblies and press against the inner hub.
2. Clean with solvent and blow dry with compressed air.
3. Inspect assemblies for worn or broken gear teeth, worn or broken keys and distorted or cracked balls and springs. If scuffed, nicked or burred condition cannot be corrected with a soft stone or crocus cloth, replace the component.

ASSEMBLY

1. 1st–2nd gear synchro.
2. 3rd–4th gear synchro.
3. 5th gear synchro.

Differential Disassembly

1. Remove the side bearing using a tool No. J-22888 and a puller leg kit.
2. Remove the ten ring gear retaining bolts and gear.
3. Using a screwdriver, pry off the speedometer drive gear. Do NOT re-use the speedometer drive gear.
4. Drive out the lock and cross pin.
5. Remove the pinion gears and thrust washers. Remove the side gears and thrust washers.

Differential Assembly

➡ Before assembling the shafts, apply a coat of lubricant to the thrust washers, all gears, and washers.

1. Install the two side gears on the differential case together with the thrust washers.
2. Position the two thrust washers and pinion gears opposite of each other. Install them in their positions by turning the side gears.
3. Insert the cross pin and make sure the gear backlash is within the rated range of 0.02–0.08mm.
4. Install the lock pin and stake it when the correct backlash is achieved.
5. Heat the speed sensor rotor to about 203°F (95°C) with a hot oil dryer or in an oven. Install the gear on the differential.
6. Install the ring gear onto the differential case and install 10 new bolts. Torque the bolts to 73–79 ft. lbs. (98–107 Nm) in a diagonal sequence.
7. Install the side bearings on the differential case using an arbor press.

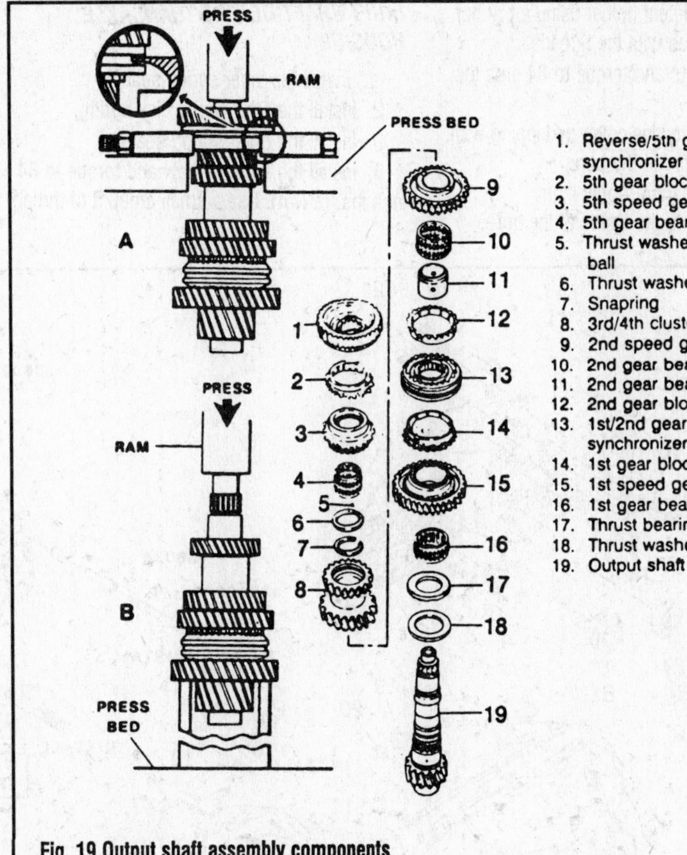

Fig. 19 Output shaft assembly components

Transaxle Assembly

GEAR/SHIFT RAIL ASSEMBLIES AND SUPPORT COMPONENTS

1. Position the gear cluster/shift rail assembly on tool J–36182–1 or equivalent. Align the shift rail and shaft pilots to the fixture.
2. Install the transaxle case. Align the bearing bores in the case with the shaft pilots.
3. Install the new output shaft bearing using tool J–35824 or equivalent and a hydraulic press.
4. Install the new input shaft bearing using tool J–35824 or equivalent and a hydraulic press. Push the rails to engage and hold the transaxle in 4th and reverse gear. The bearings must be seated.
5. Install the new input and output retainers using tool J–36031 or equivalent and torque to 50 ft. lbs. (70 Nm). Return the transaxle to **N**.

SHIFT SHAFT

1. Assemble the pins and rollers on the shift shaft. Retain with petroleum jelly.
2. Install the shift shaft assembly. Tap in with a light hammer and align the hole in the shaft with the hole in the shift lever.
3. Install the lever retainer pin using a $^3/_{16}$ in. (5mm) punch and a hammer. Install pin till it is even with the surface of the shift lever.

CLUTCH AND DIFFERENTIAL HOUSING

1. Apply sealant, part number 1052942 or equivalent, to the outside of the bolt hole pattern of the gear case flange.
2. Install the differential.
3. Install the output bearing noting the position of the cage. The small inner diameter of the bearing cage is toward the clutch housing.
4. Install the magnet.
5. Install the clutch housing.
6. Install the bolts and torque to 15 ft. lbs. (21 Nm).

OUTPUT SHAFT SUPPORT BEARING SELECTIVE SHIM PROCEDURE

➡ Be sure that the output bearing is seated in the bore by tapping the bearing into the case. Be sure that the bearing retainer is properly torqued. Selected shim can be 0.001 in. (0.025mm) above, or 0.004 in. (0.10mm) below the end plate mounting surface.

1. Using tool J–26900–19 metric dial depth gauge or equivalent, measure the distance between the end plate mounting surface and the outer race of the output shaft bearing.
2. Select the proper shim.

TRANSAXLE CASE END PLATE

1. Apply sealant, part number 1052942 or equivalent, to the outside of the end plate bolt hole pattern of the case.
2. Install the selective shim.
3. Install the oil shield.
4. Install the end cover plate.
5. Install the bolts and torque to 15 ft. lbs. (21 Nm).

SHIFT RAIL DETENT/CLUTCH AND DIFFERENTIAL HOUSING

1. Position the shift rails to expose the interlock notches in the **N** position.
2. Position the reverse shift rail to allow the detent ball to sit in the notch and on the reverse bushing.
3. Install the reverse bushing using a suitable socket.
4. Install the detent balls. Place them in the notched areas of the shift rails. Retain the ball positions with petroleum jelly.
5. Assemble the interlock pins and springs into the bores in the detent holder.
6. Install the detent holder and spring assembly. Position the detent balls over the springs using a small suitable tool. After all the detent balls are positioned over the springs, pry the reverse shift rail up to allow its detent ball to enter the spring pocket.

7. Position the detent holder using a pry bar to align the bolt holes with the threads.

8. Install the bolts and torque to 84 inch lbs. (9 Nm).

9. Install the protective cover by tapping with a hammer until seated in the bore.

10. Install the bearing. Apply high temperature grease to the inside of the bore.

SHIFT SHAFT DETENT/TRANSAXLE HOUSING

1. Install the inner spring seat.
2. Install the 5th/reverse bias spring.
3. Install the outer spring seat.
4. Install the spring screw and torque to 84 inch lbs. (9 Nm). Use a small amount of thread sealant, part number 11052624 or equivalent, to the screw.
5. Install the protective cover using a hammer. Position to below the snapring groove.
6. Install the snapring.

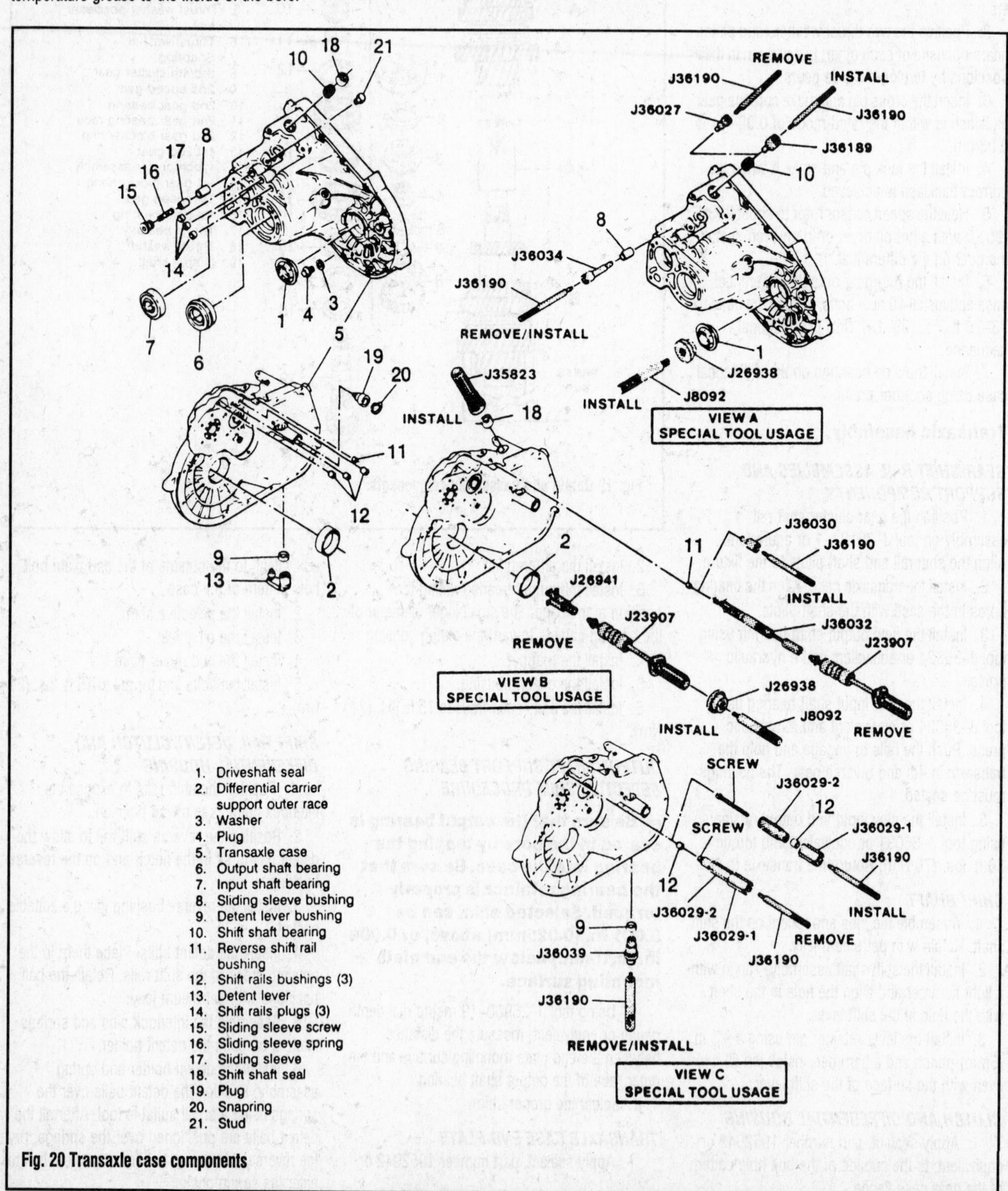

Fig. 20 Transaxle case components

EXTERNAL TRANSAXLE-MOUNTED LINKAGE

1. Install the bracket.
2. Install the bolts and torque to 17 ft. lbs. (23 Nm).
3. Install the collar and pin using a punch and a hammer.
4. Install the pivot.
5. Install a new pin.
6. Install the lever.
7. Install the washer and nut. Torque to 61 ft. lbs. (83 Nm). Do not allow the lever to move during installation of the nut.
8. Install the fluid level indicator and a new washer.
9. Install the electronic speedometer sensor assembly, retainer and bolt. Torque to 84 inch lbs. (9 Nm).

Halfshaft (Drive Axle)

The halfshaft assemblies used on these cars are flexible units consisting of an inner Tri-Pot joint and an outer Constant Velocity (CV) joint. The inner joint is completely flexible, capable of up and down, in and out movement. The outer joint is only capable of up and down movement.

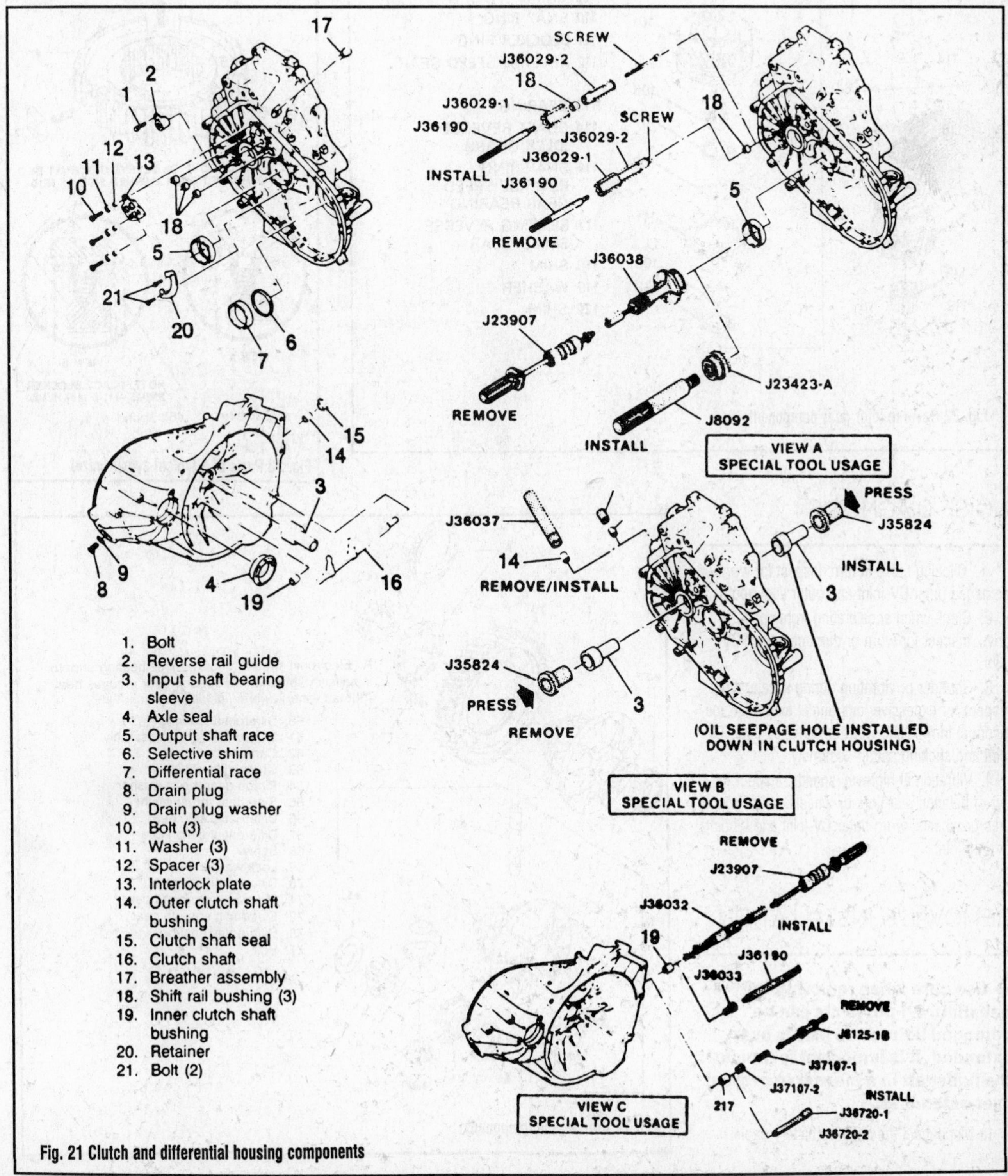

Fig. 21 Clutch and differential housing components

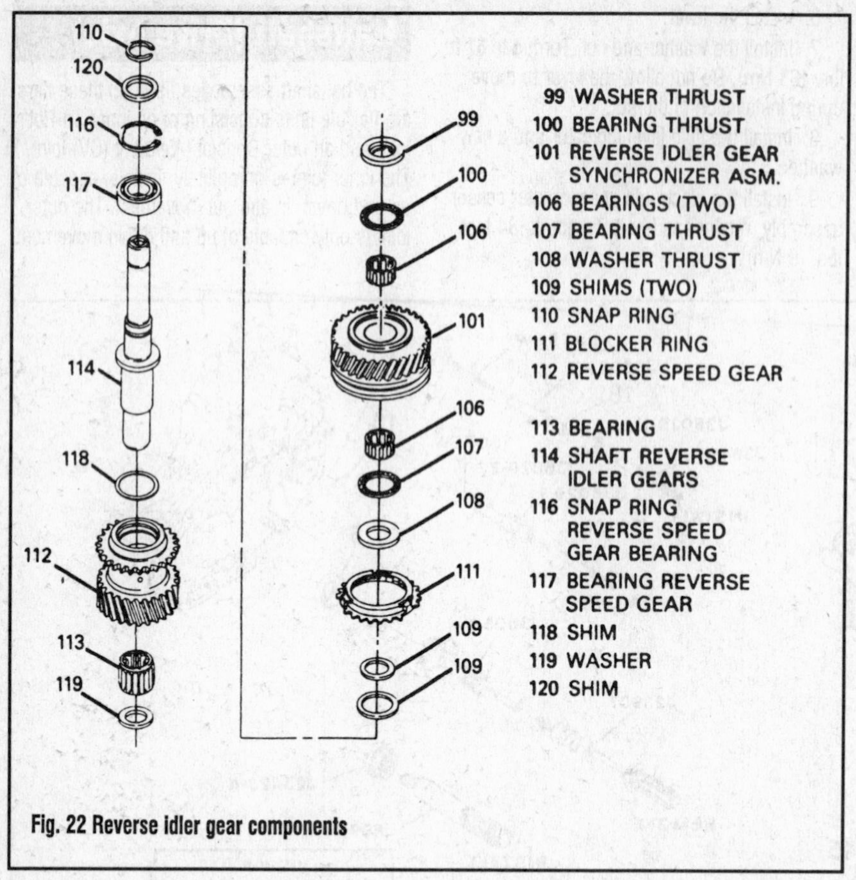

Fig. 22 Reverse idler gear components

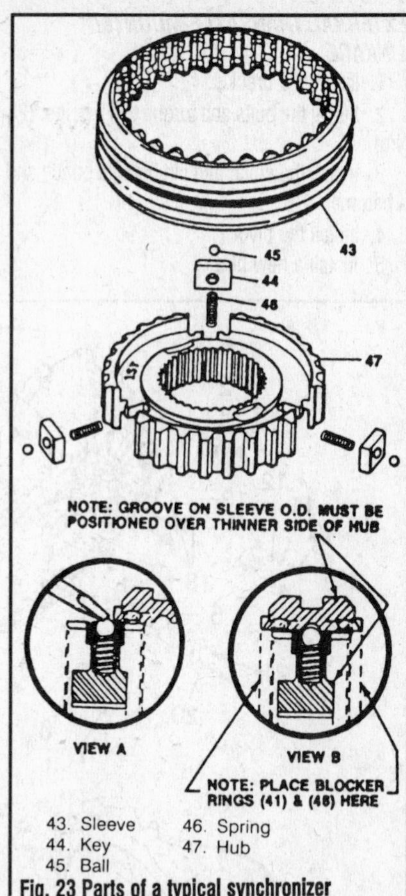

Fig. 23 Parts of a typical synchronizer

NOISE DIAGNOSIS

1. Clicking noise in turn: inspect for worn or damaged outer CV-joint and outer dust boots.
2. Clunk when accelerating from coast to drive: inspect for worn or damaged outer CV-joint.
3. Shudder or vibration during acceleration: inspect for excessive joint angle, excessive toe, incorrect trim height, worn or damaged outer CV-joint and sticking spider assembly.
4. Vibration at highway speeds: inspect for out of balance rear tires or wheels, out of round tires or wheels, worn outer CV-joint and binding or tight joint.

REMOVAL & INSTALLATION

➡ **Use care when removing the halfshaft. Tri-pot joints can be damaged if the drive axle is over-extended. It is important to handle the halfshaft in a manner to prevent over-extending.**

1. Disconnect the negative battery cable.

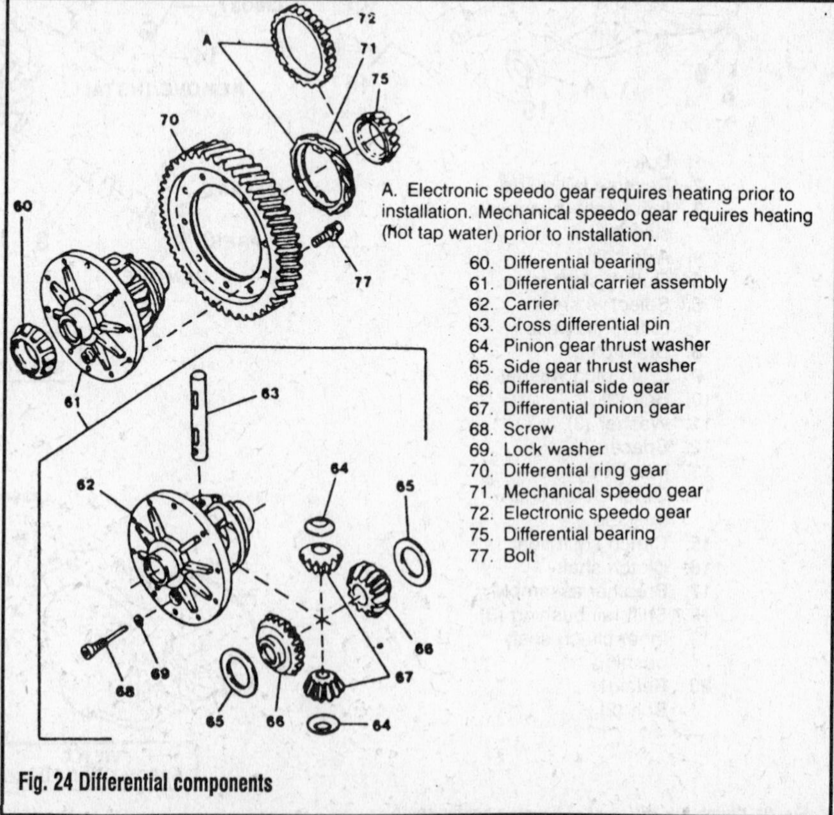

Fig. 24 Differential components

2. Raise the car and support with jackstands. Remove the wheel and tire.

3. Remove the brake calipers, bracket assemblies and hang out of the way with wire.

4. Remove the brake rotors.

5. Remove the four hub/bearing retaining bolts and hub.

6. Remove the ABS sensor mounting bolt and position the sensor out of the way, if equipped with ABS brakes.

7. Place a drain pan under the transaxle.

8. RIGHT using a axle shaft removing tool J–33008 or equivalent, separate the halfshaft from the transaxle.

9. LEFT using a suitable pry bar, separate the halfshaft from the transaxle. Pry on the frame and the groove provided on the inner joint.

10. Separate the halfshaft from the bearing assembly, if not removed.

To install:

11. Install the halfshaft/bearing assembly through the knuckle and into the transaxle until the retaining clip engages. Do NOT overextend the inner joint.

12. Install the ABS sensor.

13. Torque the bearing assembly retaining bolts to 52 ft. lbs. (70 Nm).

14. Remove the drain pan and install a new halfshaft nut and washer.

15. Install the rotor, brake caliper and wheels.

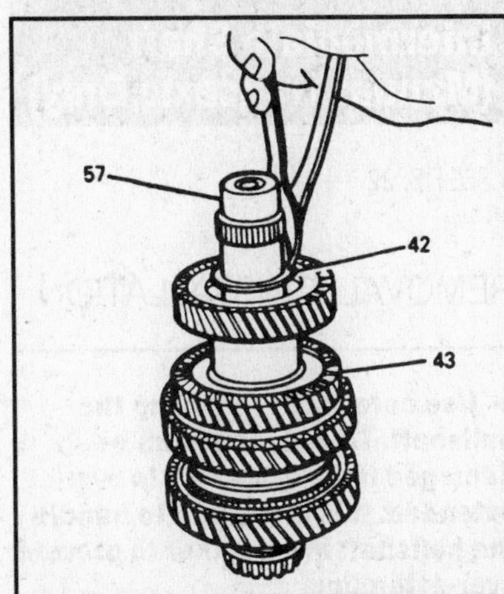

Part No. 42	
Millimeters	Inches
1.7	0.067
1.8	0.071
1.9	0.075
2.0	0.079

42 SNAP RING (SELECTIVE)
43 3RD/4TH CLUSTER GEAR
57 OUTPUT SHAFT

Fig. 25 3rd/4th cluster gear to output shaft snapring selection

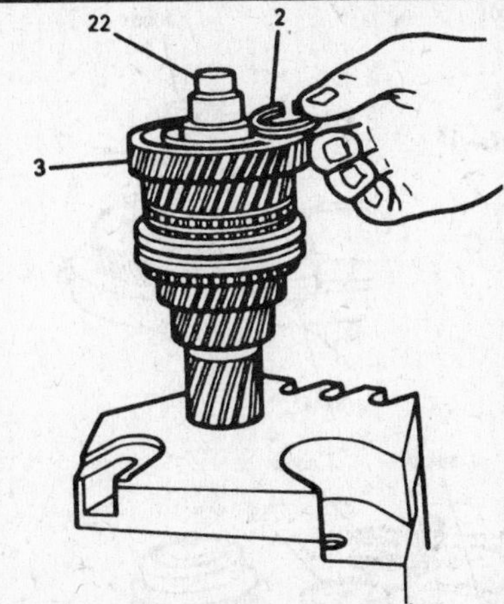

Part No. 2	
Millimeters	Inches
1.70	0.067
1.75	0.069
1.80	0.071
1.85	0.073
1.90	0.075
1.95	0.077
2.00	0.079

2 SNAP RING (SELECTIVE)
3 FIFTH INPUT GEAR
22 INPUT SHAFT

Fig. 26 5th gear to input shaft snapring selection

16. Lower the vehicle and torque the halfshaft axle nut to 184 ft. lbs. (250 Nm).

17. Add the necessary amount of transaxle fluid and connect the negative battery cable.

HALFSHAFT OVERHAUL

➧ SEE FIGS. 30 AND 31

Outer Joint Boot

1. Cut and remove the boot retaining clamps with wire cutters.

2. Remove the race retaining ring with snapring pliers. Remove the joint and boot assembly from the axle shaft. Refer to Step 1 of the CV-joint procedures.

3. Flush the grease from the joint and repack the boot with half of the grease provided with the new boot.

4. Install the new boot and clamps first. Second, install the joint and snap the race retaining ring into place. Put the remainder of the grease into the joint.

5. Using an axle seal clamp tool J–35910 and a torque wrench, torque the small clamp to 100 ft. lbs. (136 Nm). Torque the large clamp to 130 ft. lbs. (176 Nm).

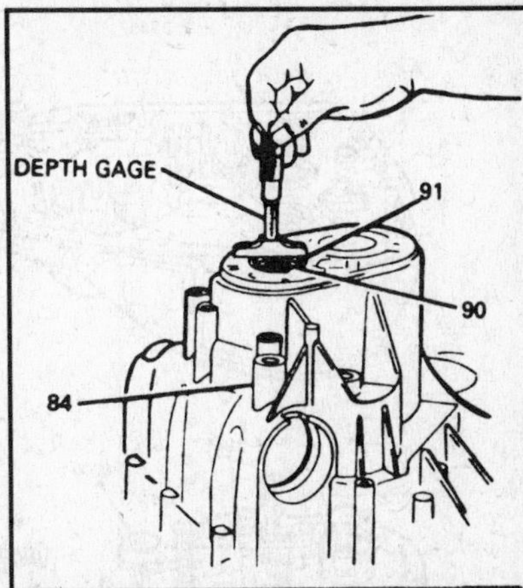

Part No. 121	
Millimeters	Inches
0.3	0.012
0.4	0.016
0.5	0.020

84 TRANSAXLE CASE
90 SPACER
91 BEARING, INPUT SHAFT
121 SHIM, REAR INPUT SHAFT BEARING (SELECTIVE)

Fig. 27 Rear input shaft bearing shim selection

Outer Joint Assembly

1. Remove the large boot clamp and joint assembly from the axle as previously mentioned. Clean out the grease from the joint to aid in disassembly.

2. Use a brass drift to gently tap on the cage until tilted enough to remove the first ball. Remove the other balls in a similar manner.

3. Pivot the cage and inner race at 90 to the center line of the outer race with the cage windows aligned with the lands of the outer race. Lift the cage out with the inner race. Refer to Step 2 of the CV-joint procedures.

4. Rotate the inner race up and out of the cage as in Step 2. Clean all parts with solvent and blow dry with compressed air.

To install:

5. Lightly coat the ball grooves with the provided CV grease.

6. Install the inner race into the cage, cage into the outer race and balls into the cage as removed.

7. Refill the joint with half the grease provided. Install the boot and clamps. Install the joint onto the axle. Fill the joint with the remaining grease and torque the clamps as in the previous procedure.

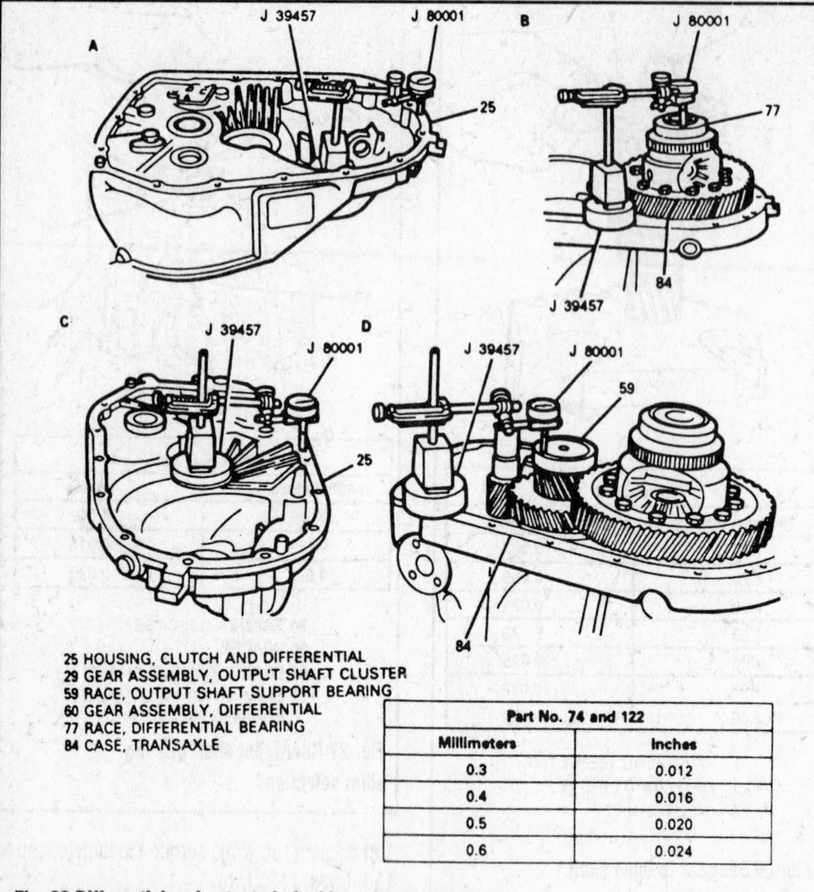

Part No. 74 and 122	
Millimeters	Inches
0.3	0.012
0.4	0.016
0.5	0.020
0.6	0.024

Fig. 28 Differential and output shaft shim selection procedure

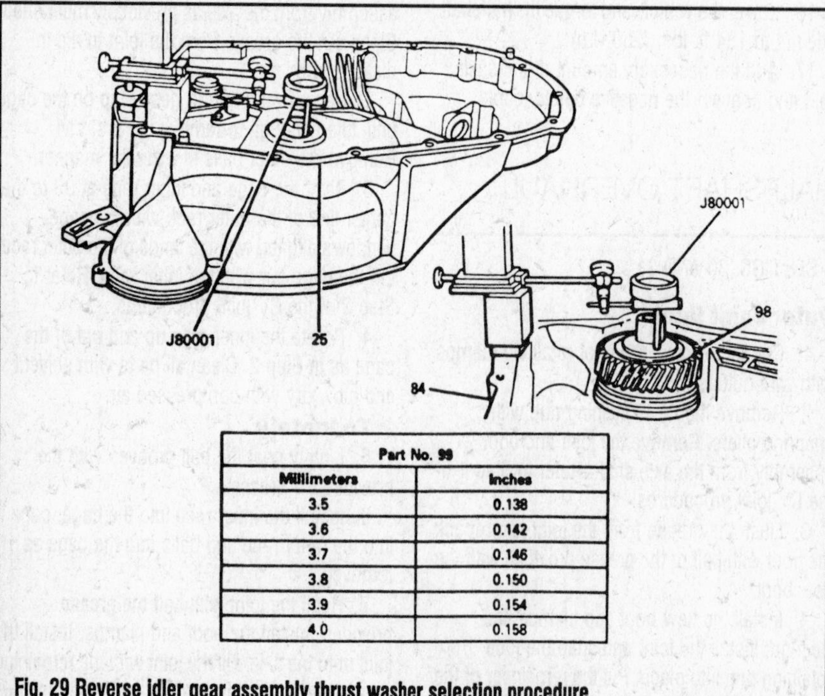

Part No. 98	
Millimeters	Inches
3.5	0.138
3.6	0.142
3.7	0.146
3.8	0.150
3.9	0.154
4.0	0.158

Fig. 29 Reverse idler gear assembly thrust washer selection procedure

Inner Tri-Pot Boot

1. Cut the clamps from the boot.
2. Remove the axle from the Tri-Pot housing as in Step 3.
3. Remove the spider assembly from the axle by removing the shaft retaining snaprings.
4. Clean all metal parts with solvent and blow dry with compressed air.

To install:

5. Refill the housing with half of the grease provided with the new boot. Install the boot and clamps first, then the spider and snapring assembly onto the axle.
6. Position the axle into the Tri-Pot housing. Install the remaining grease into the joint.
7. Using a seal clamp tool J-35910 or equivalent, torque the small clamp to 100 ft. lbs. (136 Nm) and torque the large clamp to 130 ft. lbs. (176 Nm) as in Step 3. Side cutters can be used the tighten the boot clamps, but care must be used so not to cut the new clamps.

Intermediate Shaft (Manual Transaxle Only)

➧ SEE FIG. 32

REMOVAL & INSTALLATION

➡ Use care when removing the halfshaft. Tri-pot joints can be damaged if the drive axle is over-extended. It is important to handle the halfshaft in a manner to prevent over-extending.

1. Disconnect the negative battery cable.
2. Raise the car and support with jackstands. Remove the right wheel and tire.
3. Position a drain pan under the transaxle.
4. Remove the right halfshaft assembly as previously outlined in this section.
5. Remove the housing-to-bracket bolts, bracket and housing-to-transaxle bolts.
6. Carefully disengage the intermediate axle shaft from the transaxle and remove the shaft.

To install:

7. Install the intermediate shaft into position and lock the shaft into the transaxle.
8. Install the housing-to-transaxle bolts and torque to 18 ft. lbs. (25 Nm).

9. Install the bracket-to-engine block bolts and torque to 37 ft. lbs. (50 Nm).

10. Install the housing-to-bracket bolts and torque to 37 ft. lbs. (50 Nm).

11. Coat the splines of the intermediate shaft with chassis grease and install the right halfshaft assembly as previously outlined in this section.

12. Install the front wheels.

13. Lower the vehicle and refill the transaxle to the proper level.

14. Connect the negative battery cable and recheck all procedures to ensure complete repair.

Intermediate Shaft Bearing

➧ SEE FIG. 33

REMOVAL & INSTALLATION

1. Remove the intermediate shaft from the vehicle as previously outlined.

2. Remove the seal, snapring and washer from the housing.

3. Press the spacer and bearing from the housing using a driver handle and bearing remover tools J-8592 and J-8810.

To install:

4. Press the bearing into the housing support, using a press and a bearing installer J36379 or equivalent.

5. Install the spacer, washer and snapring.

6. Install the seal into the housing using a seal installer tool J-23771 or equivalent.

7. Install the intermediate shaft into the vehicle.

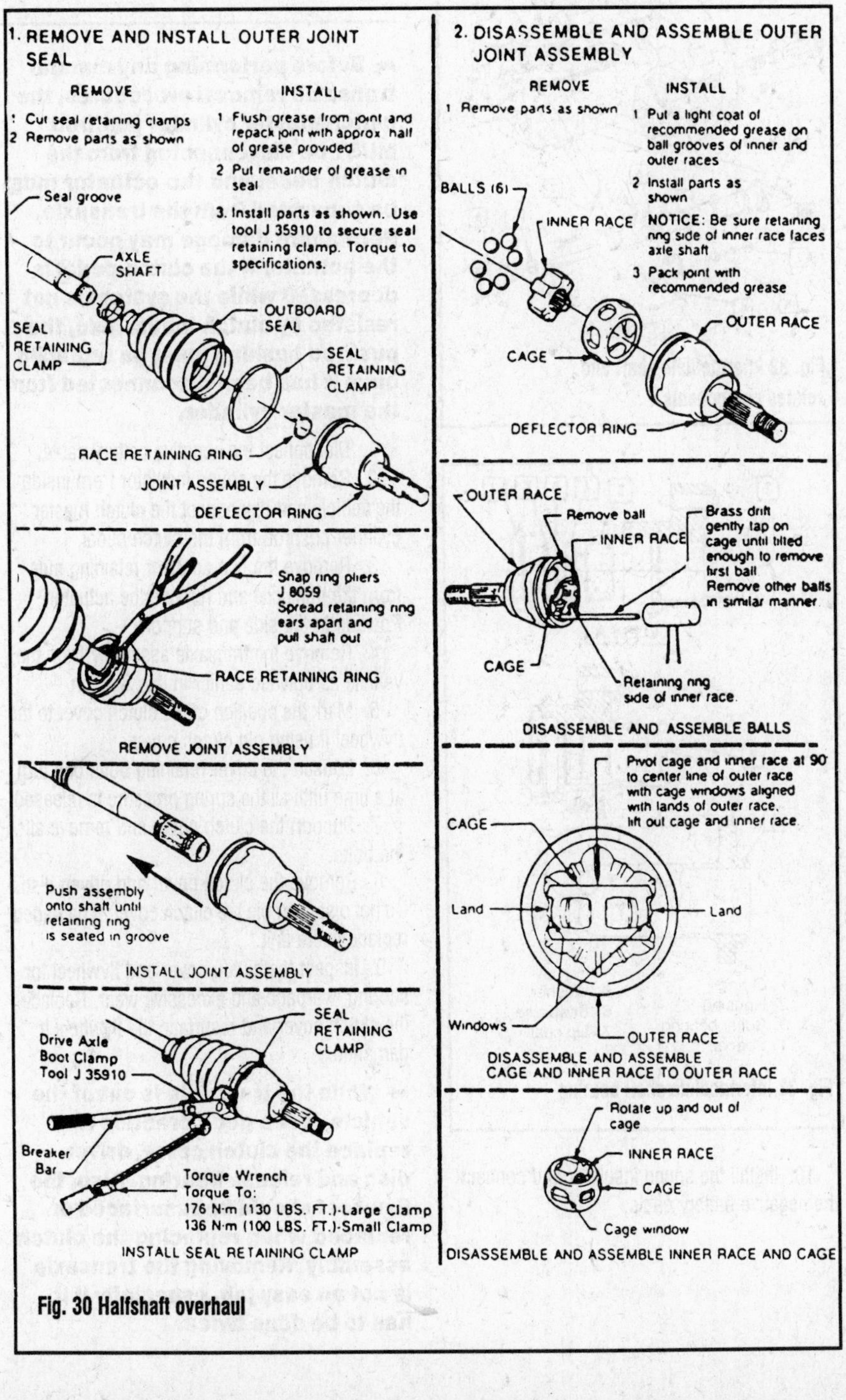

1. REMOVE AND INSTALL OUTER JOINT SEAL
REMOVE
1 Cut seal retaining clamps
2 Remove parts as shown
INSTALL
1 Flush grease from joint and repack joint with approx. half of grease provided
2 Put remainder of grease in seal
3. Install parts as shown. Use tool J 35910 to secure seal retaining clamp. Torque to specifications.
Seal groove
AXLE SHAFT
OUTBOARD SEAL
SEAL RETAINING CLAMP
SEAL RETAINING CLAMP
RACE RETAINING RING
JOINT ASSEMBLY
DEFLECTOR RING
Snap ring pliers J 8059
Spread retaining ring ears apart and pull shaft out
RACE RETAINING RING
REMOVE JOINT ASSEMBLY
Push assembly onto shaft until retaining ring is seated in groove
INSTALL JOINT ASSEMBLY
SEAL RETAINING CLAMP
Drive Axle Boot Clamp Tool J 35910
Breaker Bar
Torque Wrench
Torque To:
176 N·m (130 LBS. FT.)-Large Clamp
136 N·m (100 LBS. FT.)-Small Clamp
INSTALL SEAL RETAINING CLAMP
2. DISASSEMBLE AND ASSEMBLE OUTER JOINT ASSEMBLY
REMOVE
1 Remove parts as shown
INSTALL
1 Put a light coat of recommended grease on ball grooves of inner and outer races
2 Install parts as shown
NOTICE: Be sure retaining ring side of inner race faces axle shaft
3 Pack joint with recommended grease
BALLS (6)
INNER RACE
CAGE
OUTER RACE
DEFLECTOR RING
OUTER RACE
Remove ball
INNER RACE
Brass drift gently tap on cage until tilted enough to remove first ball
Remove other balls in similar manner
CAGE
Retaining ring side of inner race.
DISASSEMBLE AND ASSEMBLE BALLS
Pivot cage and inner race at 90° to center line of outer race with cage windows aligned with lands of outer race. lift out cage and inner race.
CAGE
Land
Land
Windows
OUTER RACE
DISASSEMBLE AND ASSEMBLE CAGE AND INNER RACE TO OUTER RACE
Rotate up and out of cage
INNER RACE
CAGE
Cage window
DISASSEMBLE AND ASSEMBLE INNER RACE AND CAGE

Fig. 30 Halfshaft overhaul

3. REMOVE AND INSTALL INNER TRI-POT SEAL
REMOVE
1. Cut seal retaining clamps
2. Remove parts as shown.
INSTALL
1. Flush grease from housing and repack housing with approx. half of grease furnished with new seal.
2. Put remainder of grease in seal.
3. Install parts as shown. Use tool J 35910 to secure seal retaining clamp. Torque to specifications.
SHAFT RETAINING RING
SPIDER ASSEMBLY
TRILOBAL TRI-POT BUSHING
TRI-POT HOUSING
AXLE
SPACER RING
TRI-POT JOINT SEAL
Seal groove
SEAL RETAINING CLAMP
SEAL RETAINING CLAMP
SEAL RETAINING CLAMPS
Side cutters
Drive Axle Boot Clamp Tool J 35910
SEAL RETAINING CLAMPS
Breaker Bar
Torque Wrench
Torque To:
176 N·m (130 LBS. FT.)-Large Clamp
136 N·m (100 LBS. FT.)-Small Clamp
REMOVE AND INSTALL SEAL RETAINING CLAMP
SPACER RING
Slide ring back on axle shaft
NOTICE: Be sure spacer ring is seated in groove at reassembly
SHAFT RETAINING RING
Remove from axle shaft then slide spider assembly off axle
SPIDER ASSEMBLY
SPACER RING
Snap ring pliers J-8059

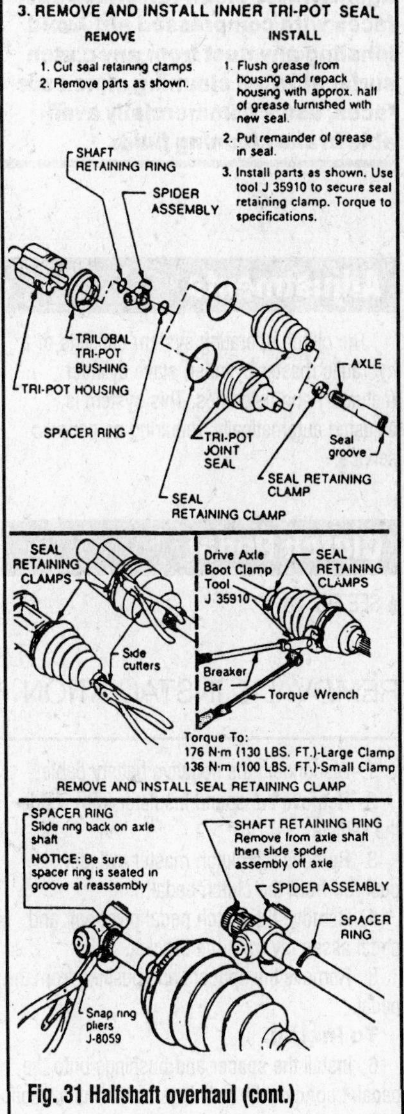

Fig. 31 Halfshaft overhaul (cont.)

CLUTCH

The clutch system consists of a driving member (flywheel and clutch cover), a driven member (clutch disc and input shaft) and a operating member (hydraulic system and release bearing).

CAUTION

The clutch driven disc contain asbestos, which has been determined to be a cancer causing agent. Never clean the clutch surfaces with compressed air! Avoid inhaling any dust from any clutch surface! When cleaning clutch surfaces, use a commercially available brake cleaning fluid.

Adjustments

The clutch operating system consists of a hydraulic master cylinder, slave cylinder (actuator) and fluid lines. This system is adjusted automatically, requiring no periodic service.

Clutch Pedal

➧ SEE FIG. 34

REMOVAL & INSTALLATION

1. Disconnect the negative battery cable.
2. Remove the sound insulator from inside the vehicle.
3. Remove the clutch master cylinder pushrod from the clutch pedal.
4. Remove the clutch pedal pivot bolt and pedal assembly from the bracket.
5. Remove the spacers and bushing from the pedal.

To install:

6. Install the spacer and bushings onto the pedal. Lubricate the bushings before installation.
7. Install the clutch pedal and pivot bolt. Torque the bolt and nut to 23 ft. lbs. (31 Nm).
8. Install a new pushrod bushing and lubricate.
9. Install the master cylinder pushrod in the clutch pedal pin groove.

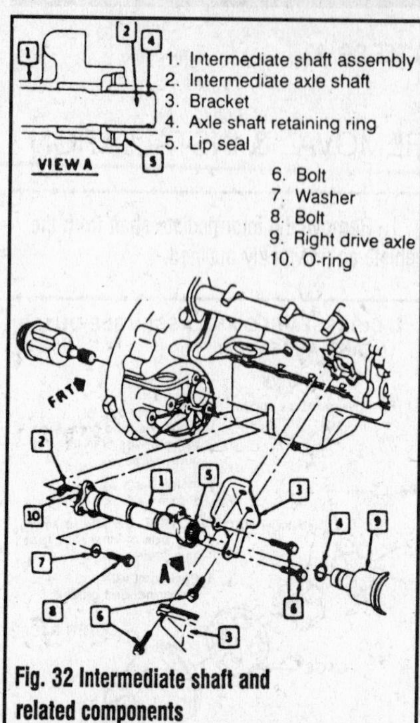

Fig. 32 Intermediate shaft and related components

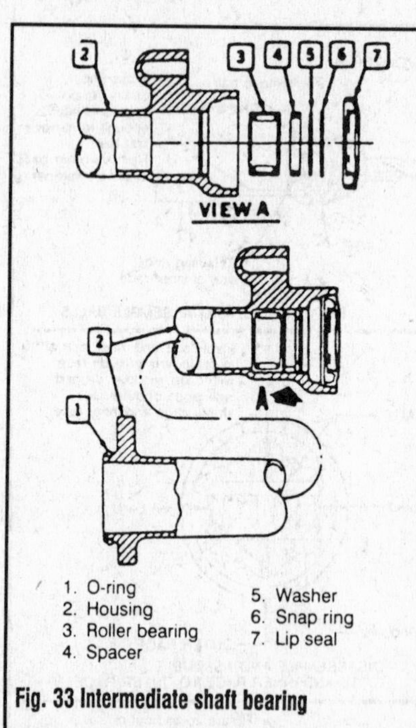

Fig. 33 Intermediate shaft bearing

10. Install the sound insulator and connect the negative battery cable.

Driven Disc and Pressure Plate

➧ SEE FIGS. 35 AND 36

REMOVAL & INSTALLATION

➡ Before performing any manual transaxle removal procedures, the clutch master cylinder pushrod MUST be disconnected from the clutch pedal and the actuator must be separated from the transaxle. Permanent damage may occur to the actuator if the clutch pedal is depressed while the system is not resisted by clutch loads. Also, the pushrod bushing must be replaced once it has been disconnected from the master cylinder.

1. Disconnect the negative battery cable.
2. Remove the sound insulator from inside the vehicle and disconnect the clutch master cylinder pushrod from the clutch pedal.
3. Remove the two actuator retaining nuts from the transaxle and remove the actuator. Position to the side and support.
4. Remove the transaxle assembly from the vehicle as outlined earlier in this Section.
5. Mark the position of the clutch cover to the flywheel if using old clutch cover.
6. Loosen the cover retaining bolts one turn at a time until all the spring pressure is released.
7. Support the clutch cover and remove all the bolts.
8. Remove the clutch cover and driven disc. Do not disassemble the clutch cover; if damaged replace entire unit.
9. Inspect the clutch cover and flywheel for scoring, warpage and excessive wear. Replace the clutch cover and resurface the flywheel if damaged.

➡ While the transaxle is out of the vehicle, it is a good practice to replace the clutch cover, driven disc and release bearing. Also, the flywheel should be resurfaced or replaced when replacing the clutch assembly. Removing the transaxle is not an easy job, especially if it has to be done twice.

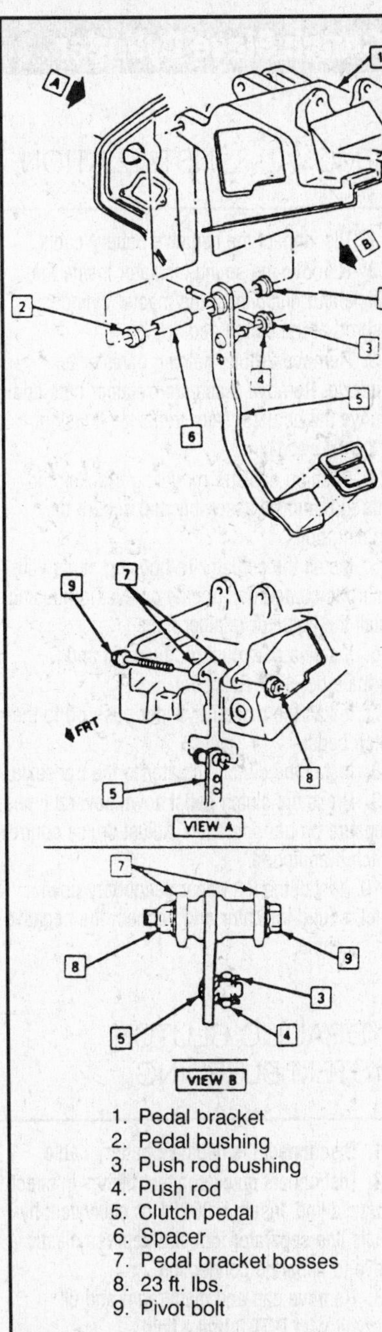

Fig. 34 Clutch pedal assembly

10. Clean the clutch cover and flywheel surfaces with solvent and low-grit sandpaper if installing the used parts.

To install:

11. Position the clutch disc and cover onto the flywheel mating surface. The raised hub and springs should face away from the flywheel. The disc may be marked "Flywheel Side", meaning the stamp faces the flywheel.

12. Loosely install the clutch cover retaining bolts. Do NOT tighten at this time.

13. Support the clutch disc using a clutch alignment tool J-35822 or equivalent. This tool is needed to align the clutch disc to the flywheel so when the transaxle is installed, the input splines will align with the flywheel pilot bearing.

14. With the clutch alignment tool installed, torque the clutch cover-to-flywheel bolts to 6 ft. lbs. (21 Nm). Remove the alignment tool.

15. Replace the release bearing if needed. Lightly lubricate the clutch fork ends which contact the bearing and the inner recess of the release bearing with chassis grease.

16. Make sure the release bearing and fork move freely on the fork shaft.

17. Tie the actuator lever to the studs to hold the release bearing in place.

✻✻ CAUTION

The clutch actuator lever must NOT move toward the flywheel until the transaxle is bolted to the engine.

18. Install the transaxle assembly.

19. Remove the actuator lever tie. Inspect the actuator pushrod for the bushing and replace if missing.

20. Install the actuator to the transaxle, making sure the bushing is centered in the pocket of the internal lever in the housing.

21. Install the actuator retaining nuts and tighten evenly to draw the actuator to the transaxle. Torque the nuts to 18 ft. lbs. (25 Nm).

22. Install a new bushing in the master cylinder pushrod and lubricate before installation.

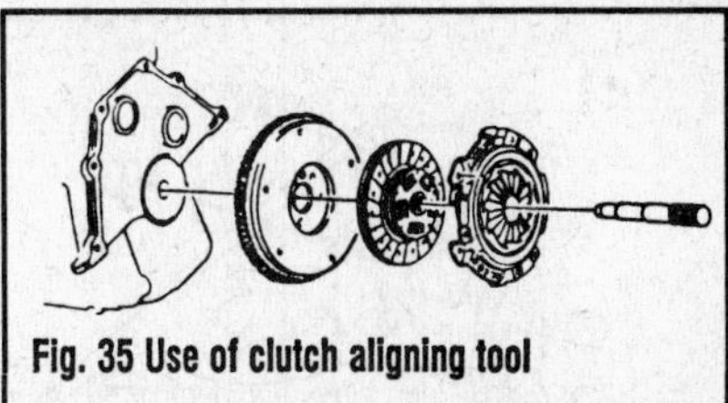
Fig. 35 Use of clutch aligning tool

23. Install the master cylinder pushrod to the clutch pedal.

24. Press the clutch pedal down several times to assure normal operation.

25. Install the sound insulator and negative battery cable.

Master Cylinder, Actuator and Reservoir

➧ SEE FIG. 37

REMOVAL & INSTALLATION

➡ **The factory hydraulic system is serviced as a single assembly. Replacement hydraulic assemblies are pre-filled with fluid and do not require bleeding. Individual components of the system are not available separately. Check with an aftermarket parts supplier to see if individual components can be purchased separately.**

1. Disconnect the negative battery cable.

2. Remove the sound insulator inside the vehicle and disconnect the master cylinder.

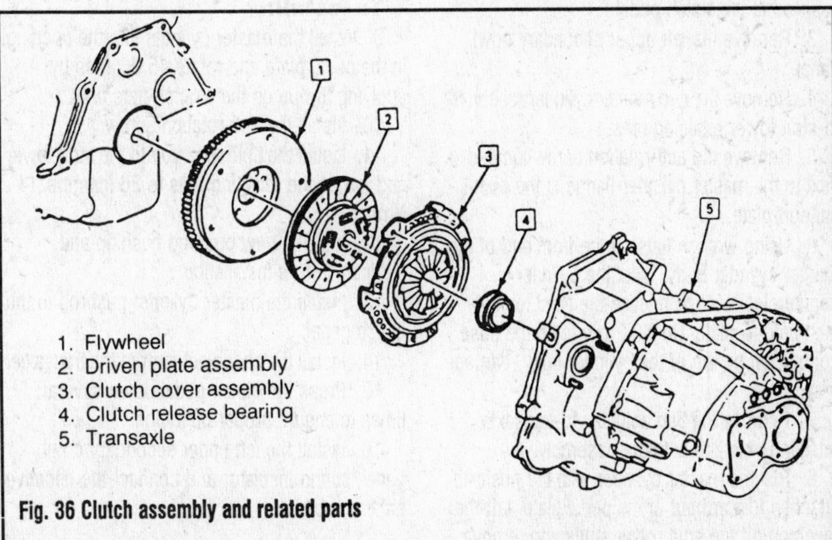

Fig. 36 Clutch assembly and related parts

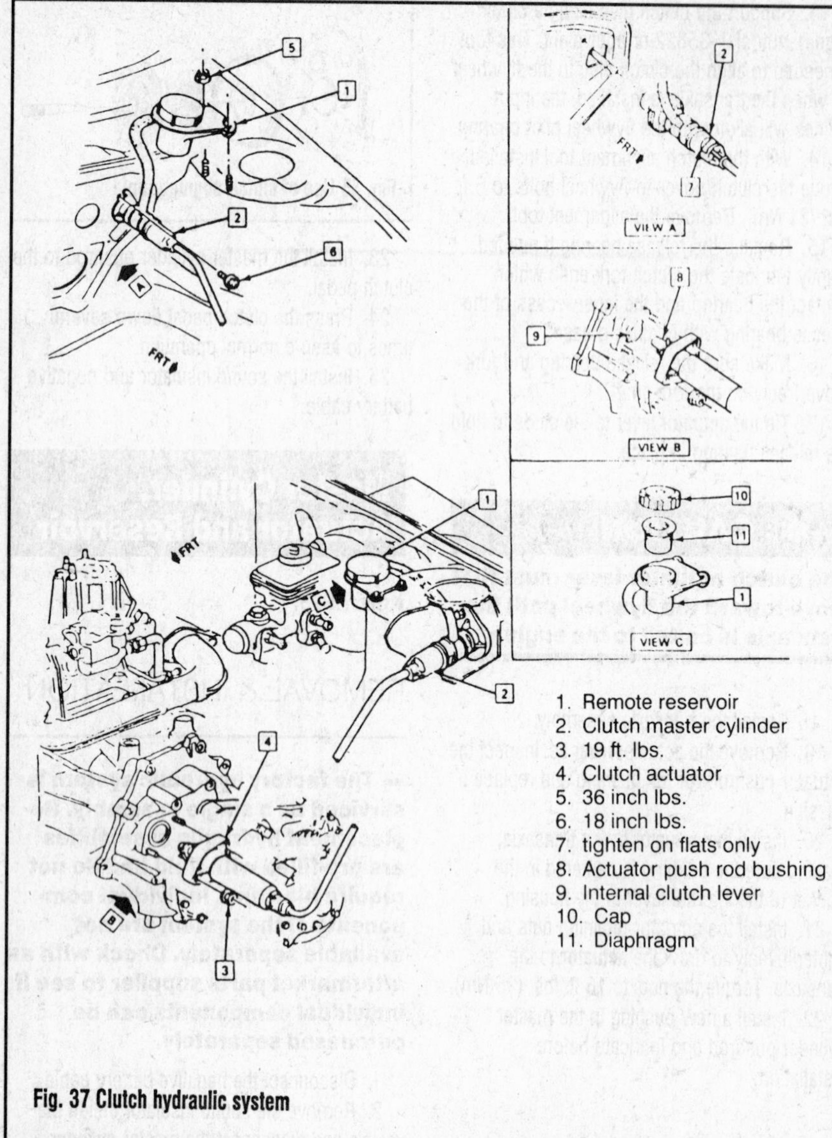

Fig. 37 Clutch hydraulic system

pushrod at the clutch pedal.

3. Remove the left upper secondary cowl panel.

4. Remove the two master cylinder reservoir-to-strut tower retaining nuts.

5. Remove the anti-rotation screw located next to the master cylinder flange at the pedal support plate.

6. Using wrench flats on the front end of the master cylinder body, twist the cylinder counterclockwise to release the twist lock attachment-to-plate. Do NOT torque on the hose connection on top of the cylinder body, damage may occur.

7. Remove the two actuator-to-transaxle retaining nuts and actuator assembly.

8. Pull the master cylinder with the pushrod attached forward out of the pedal plate. Lift the reservoir off the strut tower studs and remove the three components as a complete assembly.

To install:

9. Install the master cylinder into the opening in the pedal plate and rotate 45 degrees by applying torque on the wrench flats only.

10. Install the anti-rotation screw.

11. Install the fluid reservoir to the strut tower and torque the retaining nuts to 36 inch lbs. (4 Nm).

12. Install a new pushrod bushing and lubricate before installation.

13. Install the master cylinder pushrod to the clutch pedal.

14. Install the clutch actuator to the transaxle.

15. Press the clutch pedal down several times to ensure proper operation.

16. Install the left upper secondary cowl panel, sound insulator and connect the negative battery cable.

Clutch Slave Cylinder

REMOVAL & INSTALLATION

1. Disconnect the negative battery cable.

2. Remove the sound insulator inside the vehicle and disconnect the master cylinder pushrod at the clutch pedal.

3. Remove 2 bolts holding canister to transaxle. Remove 2 actuator retainer nuts and remove the actuator from transaxle housing.

To install:

4. Position canister mounting bracket and bolts to transaxle assembly and secure the retaining bolts.

5. Install the actuator-to-housing studs with pushrods centered in pocket of lever in housing. Install the actuator retainer nuts.

6. Install a new pushrod bushing and lubricate before installation.

7. Install the master cylinder pushrod to the clutch pedal.

8. Install the clutch actuator to the transaxle.

9. Press the clutch pedal down several times to ensure proper operation. Adjust cruise control switch if equipped.

10. Install the left upper secondary cowl panel, sound insulator and connect the negative battery cable.

HYDRAULIC CLUTCH SYSTEM BLEEDING

1. Disconnect the negative battery cable.

2. Disconnect quick connect fittings in clutch hydraulic line. Insert J–36221 or equivalent hydraulic line separator tool and depress plastic sleeve to separate connection.

3. Remove cap and diaphragm and fill reservoir with DOT 3 brake fluid.

4. Remove left hand upper secondary cowl.

5. Remove air from supply hose by squeezing it until no more air bubbles are seen ir reservoir.

6. Pump clutch pedal slowly until slight pressure is observed. Hold pressure on pedal and depress internal valve on quick connect fitting.

7. Repeat step 6 until pedal is firm and no bubbles are seen.

8. Reconnect clutch hydraulic line. Refill clutch system and replace reservoir cap. Reconnect battery cable.

AUTOMATIC TRANSAXLE

Identification

Refer to the "Engine and Transaxle" chart in Section 1 for powertrain combinations and identification plate locations and explanations.

On September 1, 1991, Hydra-matic changed the name designations of the THM 125C and THM 440–R4 automatic transaxle. The new name designations are Hydra-matic 3T40 and 4T60. Transaxles built between 1989–1990 will serve as transitional years in which a dual system, made up of the old designation and the new designation will be in effect.

Fluid Change

1. Raise the vehicle and support it safely with jackstands.
2. Disconnect the negative battery cable.
3. Remove the bottom pan bolts.
4. Loosen the rear bolts about four turns.
5. Carefully pry the oil pan loose and allow the fluid to drain.
6. Remove the remaining bolts, the pan, and the gasket or RTV sealant. Discard the old gasket.
7. Clean the pan with solvent and dry it thoroughly.
8. Remove the filter and O-ring seal.
9. Install a new transaxle filter and O-ring seal, locating the filter against the dipstick stop. Always replace the filter with a new one. Do not attempt to clean the old one!
10. Install a new gasket or RTV sealant. Thoroughly clean and dry all bolts and bolt holes. Install the pan and tighten the bolts in a crisscross manner, starting from the middle and working outward.
11. Lower the car and add about 4 quarts of Dexron II transmission fluid.
12. Start the engine and let it idle. Block the wheels and apply the parking brake.
13. At idle, move the shift lever through the ranges. With the lever in "PARK", check the fluid level and add as necessary.

➡ **Some transmission fluid currently being used may appear to be darker and have a strong odor. This is normal and not a sign of required maintenance or transmission failure.**

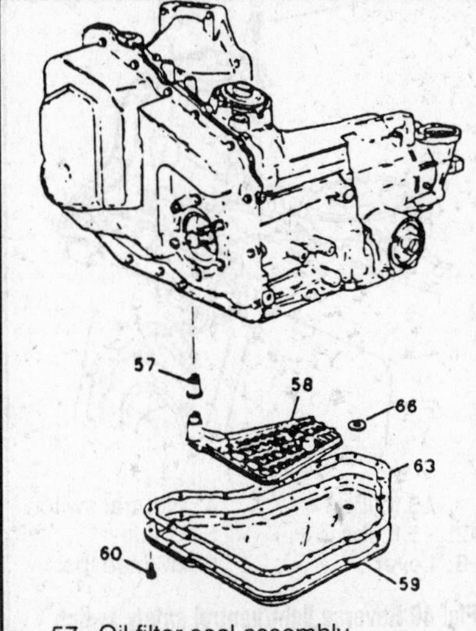

57. Oil filter seal assembly
58. Oil filter assembly
59. Transmission oil pan
60. Special screw (M8 x 1.25 x 16.0)
63. Pan gasket
66. Magnetic chip collector

Fig. 38 Fluid pan and filter assembly

Adjustments

CONTROL CABLE

1. Disconnect the negative battery cable.
2. Lift up the locking button at the transaxle and cable bracket.
3. Place the transaxle shift lever in the Neutral position. This position can be found by rotating the selector shaft/shift lever clockwise from Park through Reverse to Neutral.
4. Place the shift control inside the vehicle to the Neutral position.
5. Push down the locking button at the cable bracket and connect the negative battery cable.

PARK/LOCK CONTROL CABLE

1. Disconnect the negative battery cable.
2. With the shift lever in the Park position and the key in the Lock position, make sure that the shifter cannot be moved to another position. The key should be removable from the column.
3. With the key in the Run position and the shifter in the Neutral position, the key should NOT turn to the Lock position.
4. Adjust the cable by pulling up the cable connector lock at the shifter.
5. If the key cannot be removed in the Park position, snap the connector lock button to the up position and move the cable connector nose rearward until the key can be removed from the ignition.
6. Snap the lock button down and recheck operation and connect the negative battery cable.

THROTTLE VALVE (TV) CABLE

➧ SEE FIG. 39

1. Disconnect the negative battery cable.
2. Pull on the upper end of the TV cable. It should travel a short distance with light resistance caused by a small spring on the TV lever.
3. The cable should go to the zero position when the upper end of the cable is released.
4. Verify that the TV cable is installed properly in the throttle lever and the slider is in the non-adjusted position as shown in the illustration.

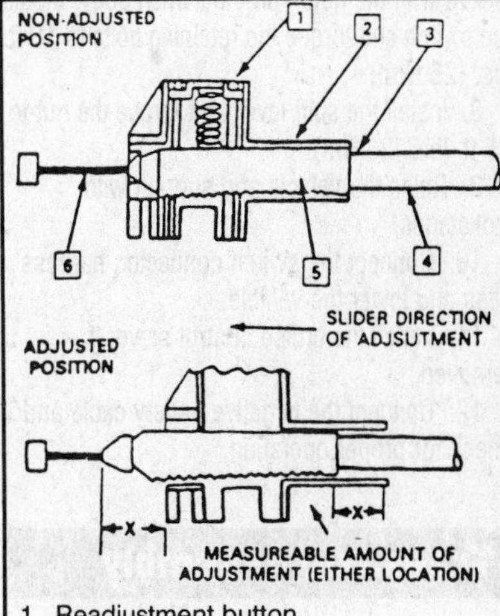

1. Readjustment button
2. Fitting
3. Slider against fitting; full non-adjusted position
4. Conduit
5. Slider
6. To throttle lever

Fig. 39 TV cable adjustment

5. With the engine NOT running, rotate the throttle lever to the full travel position (throttle body stop).

6. Depress and hold the adjustment button, pull the cable conduit out until the slider hits against the adjustment and release the button.

7. Repeat the adjustment.

Reverse light/Neutral Safety Switch

➧ SEE FIGS. 40 AND 41

REMOVAL & INSTALLATION

1. Disconnect the negative battery cable.
2. Place the transaxle in the NEUTRAL position.
3. Raise the vehicle and support with jackstands.
4. Disconnect the switch electrical connector and remove the retaining clips.
5. Lower the vehicle and remove the vacuum hoses and electrical connectors from the cruise control servo, if so equipped.
6. Remove the shift lever at the transaxle. Do NOT disconnect the lever from the cable. Remove the two retaining bolts and switch.

To install:

7. Align the notch (groove) on the inner sleeve with the notch on the switch body. Install the switch and torque the retaining bolts to 18 ft. lbs. (25 Nm).
8. Install the shift lever and torque the nut to 15 ft. lbs. (20 Nm).
9. Raise the vehicle and support with jackstands.
10. Connect the switch connector, harness clips and lower the vehicle.
11. Install the cruise control servo, if removed.
12. Connect the negative battery cable and check for proper operation.

Transaxle Assembly

REMOVAL & INSTALLATION

3-speed Unit

1. Disconnect the negative battery cable and remove the air cleaner assembly.

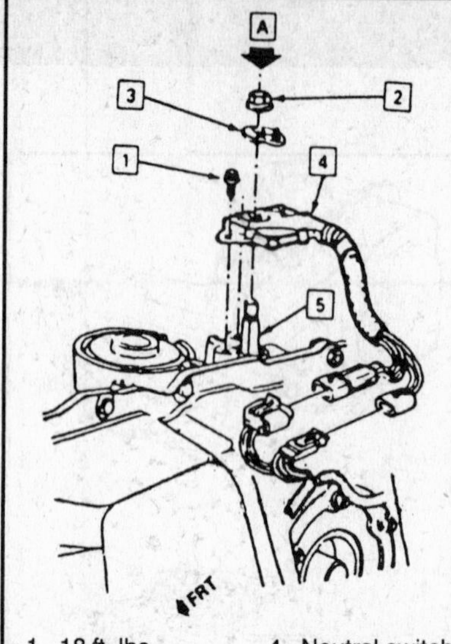

1. 18 ft. lbs.
2. 15 ft. lbs.
3. Lever
4. Neutral switch
5. Shaft
6. 80 inch lbs.

Fig. 40 Reverse light/neutral safety switch

2. Remove the shift control and throttle valve (TV) cables at the transaxle.
3. Remove the throttle cable bracket and brake booster hose.
4. Remove the engine torque struts, left torque strut bracket and oil cooler lines at the transaxle.
5. Install the engine support fixture tool J28467–A and J–36462.
6. Raise the vehicle and support with jackstands.
7. Remove the front wheels, splash shields, calipers and rotors. Support the caliper to the frame with wire.
8. Remove the front halfshafts (axle) assemblies as outlined in this Section.
9. Disconnect both ball joints and tie rod ends from the strut assemblies. For further assistance, refer to Section 8.
10. Remove the engine oil filter.
11. Remove the A/C compressor and support out of the way. Do NOT disconnect the refrigerant lines.
12. Remove the rack and pinion heat shield and electrical connector.
13. Remove the rack and pinion assembly and wire to the exhaust for support.
14. Remove the power steering hoses-bracket.
15. Remove the engine and transaxle mounts at the frame.
16. Support the frame with jackstands at each end, remove the frame bolts and frame. Refer to the "Frame" section in this Section.
17. Remove the torque converter cover and bolts.
18. Remove the starter bolts and support out of the way.
19. Remove the ground cable from the transaxle case.
20. Remove the fluid fill tube bolt and transaxle mount bracket.
21. Lower the vehicle.
22. Remove the fill tube.
23. Using the engine support fixture, lower the left side of the engine about 4 in. (102mm).
24. Raise the vehicle, support with jackstands and install a transaxle jack.
25. Remove the transaxle-to-engine bolts and transaxle.

To install:

26. The transaxle oil cooler lines should be flushed with a converter flush kit J–35944 or equivalent.
27. Lubricate the torque converter pilot hub with chassis grease. Make sure the torque converter is properly seated in the oil pump drive. Damage to the transaxle may occur if converter is not seated completely.
28. Position the transaxle into the vehicle and torque the transaxle-to-engine bolts to 55 ft. lbs. (75 Nm).
29. Install the transaxle mount bracket and lower the vehicle.
30. Using the engine support fixture, raise the engine into the proper position.
31. Install the fluid fill tube.
32. With an assistant, position and support the frame under the vehicle. Install the frame bolts and torque to 103 ft. lbs. (140 Nm).
33. Remove the frame supports and lower the vehicle.
34. Position the engine and transaxle into the frame mounts. Remove the engine support fixture.
35. Raise the vehicle, install the torque converter-to-flywheel bolts and torque to 44 ft. lbs. (60 Nm). Install the torque converter cover.
36. Install the starter motor and transaxle ground cable.
37. Install the ball joints and tie rods.
38. Install the halfshaft (axle) assemblies, rotors and calipers.
39. Install the rack and pinion, lines, and heat shields.
40. Install the A/C compressor.
41. Install the engine oil filter and refill to the proper level.
42. Lower the vehicle.
43. Install the throttle cable bracket, torque strut bracket and torque strut.
44. Install the transaxle oil cooler lines to the transaxle.
45. Install the shift control and TV cables.
46. Connect the negative battery cable, install

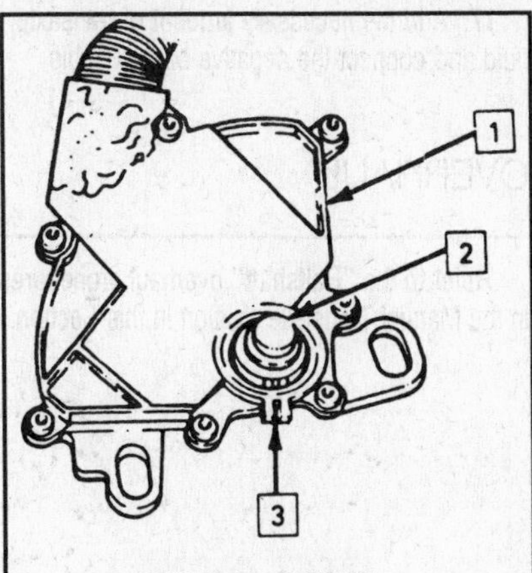

Fig. 41 Reverse light/neutral safety switch adjustment

the air cleaner and recheck each operation to ensure completion of repair.

47. Adjust the shift linkage and TV cable. Check the engine and transaxle oil levels.

48. Start the engine and check for fluid leaks.

4-Speed Units

1. Disconnect the negative battery cable and remove the air cleaner assembly.
2. Install the engine support fixture tool J28467–A and J–36462.
3. Remove the shift control and throttle valve (TV) cables at the transaxle.
4. Remove the throttle cable bracket and brake booster hose.
5. Remove the crossover pipe-to-left exhaust manifold, EGR tube at crossover and crossover-to-exhaust pipe bolts.
6. Loosen the crossover-to-right manifold and swing the crossover upward to gain clearance to the top bell housing bolts.
7. Remove the four upper bell housing bolts.
8. Remove the TCC electrical connector, neutral start switch electrical connector and vacuum modulator hose at the transaxle.
9. Raise the vehicle and support with jackstands.
10. Remove the vehicle speed sensor electrical connector.
11. Remove the front wheels, splash shields, calipers and rotors. Support the caliper to the frame with wire.
12. Remove the front halfshafts (axle) assemblies as outlined in this Section.
13. Disconnect both ball joints and tie rod ends from the strut assemblies. For further assistance, refer to Section 8.
14. Remove the rack and pinion heat shield and electrical connector.
15. Remove the rack and pinion assembly and wire to the exhaust for support.
16. Remove the power steering hoses, bracket, if so equipped.
17. Remove the engine and transaxle mounts at the frame.
18. Support the frame with jackstands at each end, remove the frame bolts and frame. Refer to the "Frame" section in this Section.
19. Remove the torque converter cover and bolts.
20. Remove the transaxle oil cooler lines , support bracket and torque converter cover.
21. Remove the starter bolts and support-out of the way.
22. Remove the ground cable from the transaxle case.
23. Support the transaxle with jackstands.
24. Remove the fluid fill tube bolt and transaxle mount bracket.
25. Remove the transaxle-to-engine bolts and transaxle.

To install:

26. The transaxle oil cooler lines should be flushed with a converter flush kit J–35944 or equivalent.
27. Lubricate the torque converter pilot hub with chassis grease.

⁂ CAUTION

Make sure the torque converter is properly seated in the oil pump drive. Damage to the transaxle may occur if converter is not seated completely.

28. Position the transaxle into the vehicle and torque the transaxle-to-engine bolts to 55 ft. lbs. (75 Nm).
29. Install the transaxle mount bracket.
30. Install the torque converter-to-flywheel bolts and torque to 44 ft. lbs. (60 Nm).
31. Install the starter motor, halfshafts (axles) and torque converter cover.
32. Connect the oil cooler lines and support bracket.
33. Install the frame assembly and retaining bolts. Torque the bolts to 103 ft. lbs. (140 Nm).
34. Install the lower engine mount retaining nuts and upper transaxle mount retaining nuts.
35. Install the ball joints-to-steering knuckle and rack and pinion assembly-to-frame.
36. Install the power steering heat shield and cooler lines-to-frame.
37. Install the wheel house splash shields.
38. Install the rotor, calipers and front wheels.
39. Install the vehicle speed sensor and lower the vehicle.
40. Connect the back-up/neutral switch.
41. Connect the modulator hose and TCC electrical connector.
42. Install the four upper bell housing bolts and torque to 55 ft. lbs. (75 Nm).
43. Install the crossover pipe to its proper position.
44. Install the crossover pipe-to-right and left manifolds.
45. Install the EGR tube-to-crossover.
46. Connect the TV and shift control cables.
47. Remove the engine support fixture J28467–A and J–36462.
48. Connect the negative battery cable and install the air cleaner.
49. Adjust the fluid level, TV and shift cables.
50. Recheck all procedures for completion of repair. Start the engine and check for fluid leaks.

Halfshafts

REMOVAL & INSTALLATION

➡ **Use care when removing the halfshaft. Tri-pot joints can be damaged if the drive axle is over-extended. It is important to handle the halfshaft in a manner to prevent over-extending.**

1. Disconnect the negative battery cable.
2. Raise the car and support with jackstands. Remove the wheel and tire.
3. Remove the brake calipers, bracket assemblies and hang out of the way with wire.
4. Remove the brake rotors.
5. Remove the four hub/bearing retaining bolts and hub.
6. Remove the ABS sensor mounting bolt and position the sensor out of the way, if equipped with ABS brakes.
7. Place a drain pan under the transaxle.
8. RIGHT using a axle shaft removing tool J–33008 or equivalent, separate the halfshaft from the transaxle.
9. LEFT using a suitable pry bar, separate the halfshaft from the transaxle. Pry on the frame and the groove provided on the inner joint.
10. Separate the halfshaft from the bearing assembly, if not removed.

To install:

11. Install the halfshaft/bearing assembly through the knuckle and into the transaxle until

the retaining clip engages. Do NOT overextend the inner joint.

12. Install the ABS sensor.

13. Torque the bearing assembly retaining bolts to 52 ft. lbs. (70 Nm).

14. Remove the drain pan and install a new halfshaft nut and washer.

15. Install the rotor, brake caliper and wheel assemblies.

16. Lower the vehicle and torque the halfshaft axle nut to 184 ft. lbs. (250 Nm).

17. Add the necessary amount of transaxle fluid and connect the negative battery cable.

OVERHAUL

Refer to the "Halfshaft" overhaul procedures in the Manual Transaxle section in this Section.

TORQUE SPECIFICATIONS

Component	U.S.	Metric
Frame-to-body retaining bolts	103 ft. lbs.	140 Nm
Manual transaxle-to-engine bolts	55 ft. lbs.	75 Nm
Detent lever retaining screw	32 ft. lbs.	44 Nm
Ring gear bolts	73–79 ft. lbs.	98–107 Nm
Input and output retainers	50 ft. lbs.	70 Nm
Clutch and differential housing bolts	15 ft. lbs.	21 Nm
Transaxle case end plate bolts	15 ft. lbs.	21 Nm
External transaxle-mounted linkage bracket bolts	17 ft. lbs.	23 Nm
Linkage lever retaining nut	61 ft. lbs.	83 Nm
Bearing assembly retaining bolts	52 ft. lbs.	70 Nm
Halfshaft axle end nut	184 ft. lbs.	250 Nm
Intermediate shaft housing-to-transaxle bolts	18 ft. lbs.	25 Nm
Intermediate shaft bracket-to-engine block bolts	37 ft. lbs.	50 Nm
Intermediate shaft housing-to-bracket bolts	37 ft. lbs.	50 Nm
Clutch pedal pivot bolt and nut	23 ft. lbs.	31 Nm
Clutch cover-to-flywheel bolts	6 ft. lbs.	21 Nm
Clutch actuator retaining nuts	18 ft. lbs.	25 Nm
Reverse light/neutral safety switch retaining bolts	18 ft. lbs.	25 Nm
Automatic transaxle shift lever nut	15 ft. lbs.	20 Nm
Automatic transaxle-to-engine bolts	55 ft. lbs.	75 Nm
Torque converter-to-flywheel bolts	44 ft. lbs.	60 Nm

Troubleshooting the Manual Transmission

Problem	Cause	Solution
Transmission shifts hard	• Clutch adjustment incorrect	• Adjust clutch
	• Clutch linkage or cable binding	• Lubricate or repair as necessary
	• Shift rail binding	• Check for mispositioned selector arm roll pin, loose cover bolts, worn shift rail bores, worn shift rail, distorted oil seal, or extension housing not aligned with case. Repair as necessary.
	• Internal bind in transmission caused by shift forks, selector plates, or synchronizer assemblies	• Remove, dissemble and inspect transmission. Replace worn or damaged components as necessary.
	• Clutch housing misalignment	• Check runout at rear face of clutch housing
	• Incorrect lubricant	• Drain and refill transmission
	• Block rings and/or cone seats worn	• Blocking ring to gear clutch tooth face clearance must be 0.030 inch or greater. If clearance is correct it may still be necessary to inspect blocking rings and cone seats for excessive wear. Repair as necessary.
Gear clash when shifting from one gear to another	• Clutch adjustment incorrect	• Adjust clutch
	• Clutch linkage or cable binding	• Lubricate or repair as necessary
	• Clutch housing misalignment	• Check runout at rear of clutch housing
	• Lubricant level low or incorrect lubricant	• Drain and refill transmission and check for lubricant leaks if level was low. Repair as necessary.
	• Gearshift components, or synchronizer assemblies worn or damaged	• Remove, disassemble and inspect transmission. Replace worn or damaged components as necessary.
Transmission noisy	• Lubricant level low or incorrect lubricant	• Drain and refill transmission. If lubricant level was low, check for leaks and repair as necessary.
	• Clutch housing-to-engine, or transmission-to-clutch housing bolts loose	• Check and correct bolt torque as necessary
	• Dirt, chips, foreign material in transmission	• Drain, flush, and refill transmission
	• Gearshift mechanism, transmission gears, or bearing components worn or damaged	• Remove, disassemble and inspect transmission. Replace worn or damaged components as necessary.
	• Clutch housing misalignment	• Check runout at rear face of clutch housing

Troubleshooting the Manual Transmission

Problem	Cause	Solution
Jumps out of gear	• Clutch housing misalignment	• Check runout at rear face of clutch housing
	• Gearshift lever loose	• Check lever for worn fork. Tighten loose attaching bolts.
	• Offset lever nylon insert worn or lever attaching nut loose	• Remove gearshift lever and check for loose offset lever nut or worn insert. Repair or replace as necessary.
	• Gearshift mechanism, shift forks, selector plates, interlock plate, selector arm, shift rail, detent plugs, springs or shift cover worn or damaged	• Remove, disassemble and inspect transmission cover assembly. Replace worn or damaged components as necessary.
	• Clutch shaft or roller bearings worn or damaged	• Replace clutch shaft or roller bearings as necessary
Jumps out of gear (cont.)	• Gear teeth worn or tapered, synchronizer assemblies worn or damaged, excessive end play caused by worn thrust washers or output shaft gears	• Remove, disassemble, and inspect transmission. Replace worn or damaged components as necessary.
	• Pilot bushing worn	• Replace pilot bushing
Will not shift into one gear	• Gearshift selector plates, interlock plate, or selector arm, worn, damaged, or incorrectly assembled	• Remove, disassemble, and inspect transmission cover assembly. Repair or replace components as necessary.
	• Shift rail detent plunger worn, spring broken, or plug loose	• Tighten plug or replace worn or damaged components as necessary
	• Gearshift lever worn or damaged	• Replace gearshift lever
	• Synchronizer sleeves or hubs, damaged or worn	• Remove, disassemble and inspect transmission. Replace worn or damaged components.
Locked in one gear—cannot be shifted out	• Shift rail(s) worn or broken, shifter fork bent, setscrew loose, center detent plug missing or worn	• Inspect and replace worn or damaged parts
	• Broken gear teeth on countershaft gear, clutch shaft, or reverse idler gear	• Inspect and replace damaged part
	Gearshift lever broken or worn, shift mechanism in cover incorrectly assembled or broken, worn damaged gear train components	• Disassemble transmission. Replace damaged parts or assemble correctly.

Troubleshooting Basic Clutch Problems

Problem	Cause
Excessive clutch noise	Throwout bearing noises are more audible at the lower end of pedal travel. The usual causes are: • Riding the clutch • Too little pedal free-play • Lack of bearing lubrication A bad clutch shaft pilot bearing will make a high pitched squeal, when the clutch is disengaged and the transmission is in gear or within the first 2″ of pedal travel. The bearing must be replaced. Noise from the clutch linkage is a clicking or snapping that can be heard or felt as the pedal is moved completely up or down. This usually requires lubrication. Transmitted engine noises are amplified by the clutch housing and heard in the passenger compartment. They are usually the result of insufficient pedal free-play and can be changed by manipulating the clutch pedal.
Clutch slips (the car does not move as it should when the clutch is engaged)	This is usually most noticeable when pulling away from a standing start. A severe test is to start the engine, apply the brakes, shift into high gear and SLOWLY release the clutch pedal. A healthy clutch will stall the engine. If it slips it may be due to: • A worn pressure plate or clutch plate • Oil soaked clutch plate • Insufficient pedal free-play
Clutch drags or fails to release	The clutch disc and some transmission gears spin briefly after clutch disengagement. Under normal conditions in average temperatures, 3 seconds is maximum spin-time. Failure to release properly can be caused by: • Too light transmission lubricant or low lubricant level • Improperly adjusted clutch linkage
Low clutch life	Low clutch life is usually a result of poor driving habits or heavy duty use. Riding the clutch, pulling heavy loads, holding the car on a grade with the clutch instead of the brakes and rapid clutch engagement all contribute to low clutch life.

Troubleshooting Basic Automatic Transmission Problems

Problem	Cause	Solution
Fluid leakage	• Defective pan gasket • Loose filler tube • Loose extension housing to transmission case • Converter housing area leakage	• Replace gasket or tighten pan bolts • Tighten tube nut • Tighten bolts • Have transmission checked professionally
Fluid flows out the oil filler tube	• High fluid level • Breather vent clogged • Clogged oil filter or screen • Internal fluid leakage	• Check and correct fluid level • Open breather vent • Replace filter or clean screen (change fluid also) • Have transmission checked professionally
Transmission overheats (this is usually accompanied by a strong burned odor to the fluid)	• Low fluid level • Fluid cooler lines clogged • Heavy pulling or hauling with insufficient cooling • Faulty oil pump, internal slippage	• Check and correct fluid level • Drain and refill transmission. If this doesn't cure the problem, have cooler lines cleared or replaced. • Install a transmission oil cooler • Have transmission checked professionally
Buzzing or whining noise	• Low fluid level • Defective torque converter, scored gears	• Check and correct fluid level • Have transmission checked professionally
No forward or reverse gears or slippage in one or more gears	• Low fluid level • Defective vacuum or linkage controls, internal clutch or band failure	• Check and correct fluid level • Have unit checked professionally
Delayed or erratic shift	• Low fluid level • Broken vacuum lines • Internal malfunction	• Check and correct fluid level • Repair or replace lines • Have transmission checked professionally

Lockup Torque Converter Service Diagnosis

Problem	Cause	Solution
No lockup	• Faulty oil pump • Sticking governor valve • Valve body malfunction (a) Stuck switch valve (b) Stuck lockup valve (c) Stuck fail-safe valve • Failed locking clutch • Leaking turbine hub seal • Faulty input shaft or seal ring	• Replace oil pump • Repair or replace as necessary • Repair or replace valve body or its internal components as necessary • Replace torque converter • Replace torque converter • Repair or replace as necessary
Will not unlock	• Sticking governor valve • Valve body malfunction (a) Stuck switch valve (b) Stuck lockup valve (c) Stuck fail-safe valve	• Repair or replace as necessary • Repair or replace valve body or its internal components as necessary
Stays locked up at too low a speed in direct	• Sticking governor valve • Valve body malfunction (a) Stuck switch valve (b) Stuck lockup valve (c) Stuck fail-safe valve	• Repair or replace as necessary • Repair or replace valve body or its internal components as necessary
Locks up or drags in low or second	• Faulty oil pump • Valve body malfunction (a) Stuck switch valve (b) Stuck fail-safe valve	• Replace oil pump • Repair or replace valve body or its internal components as necessary
Sluggish or stalls in reverse	• Faulty oil pump • Plugged cooler, cooler lines or fittings • Valve body malfunction (a) Stuck switch valve (b) Faulty input shaft or seal ring	• Replace oil pump as necessary • Flush or replace cooler and flush lines and fittings • Repair or replace valve body or its internal components as necessary
Loud chatter during lockup engagement (cold)	• Faulty torque converter • Failed locking clutch • Leaking turbine hub seal	• Replace torque converter • Replace torque converter • Replace torque converter
Vibration or shudder during lockup engagement	• Faulty oil pump • Valve body malfunction • Faulty torque converter • Engine needs tune-up	• Repair or replace oil pump as necessary • Repair or replace valve body or its internal components as necessary • Replace torque converter • Tune engine
Vibration after lockup engagement	• Faulty torque converter • Exhaust system strikes underbody • Engine needs tune-up • Throttle linkage misadjusted	• Replace torque converter • Align exhaust system • Tune engine • Adjust throttle linkage

Lockup Torque Converter Service Diagnosis

Problem	Cause	Solution
Vibration when revved in neutral	• Torque converter out of balance	• Replace torque converter
Overheating: oil blows out of dip stick tube or pump seal	• Plugged cooler, cooler lines or fittings • Stuck switch valve	• Flush or replace cooler and flush lines and fittings • Repair switch valve in valve body or replace valve body
Shudder after lockup engagement	• Faulty oil pump • Plugged cooler, cooler lines or fittings • Valve body malfunction • Faulty torque converter • Fail locking clutch • Exhaust system strikes underbody • Engine needs tune-up • Throttle linkage misadjusted	• Replace oil pump • Flush or replace cooler and flush lines and fittings • Repair or replace valve body or its internal components as necessary • Replace torque converter • Replace torque converter • Align exhaust system • Tune engine • Adjust throttle linkage

Transmission Fluid Indications

The appearance and odor of the transmission fluid can give valuable clues to the overall condition of the transmission. Always note the appearance of the fluid when you check the fluid level or change the fluid. Rub a small amount of fluid between your fingers to feel for grit and smell the fluid on the dipstick.

If the fluid appears:	It indicates:
Clear and red colored	• Normal operation
Discolored (extremely dark red or brownish) or smells burned	• Band or clutch pack failure, usually caused by an overheated transmission. Hauling very heavy loads with insufficient power or failure to change the fluid, often result in overheating. Do not confuse this appearance with newer fluids that have a darker red color and a strong odor (though not a burned odor).
Foamy or aerated (light in color and full of bubbles)	• The level is too high (gear train is churning oil) • An internal air leak (air is mixing with the fluid). Have the transmission checked professionally.
Solid residue in the fluid	• Defective bands, clutch pack or bearings. Bits of band material or metal abrasives are clinging to the dipstick. Have the transmission checked professionally.
Varnish coating on the dipstick	• The transmission fluid is overheating

SUSPENSION AND STEERING

WHEELS

Wheels

REMOVAL & INSTALLATION

1. Apply the parking brake. Remove the wheel cover or hub cap and loosen the lug nuts slightly.
2. Raise the vehicle and support safely.
3. Remove all wheel nuts.
4. Matchmark the wheel to the hub for proper installation.
5. Remove the tire and wheel assembly.

To install:

6. Thoroughly clean and dry the nuts, bolts, wheel, and mounting surfaces.
7. Lightly lubricate the lug studs. Wipe any excess to prevent spewing.
7. Install the wheel, aligning the marks.
8. Install the nuts and torque to 100 ft. lbs. (140 Nm).
9. Install the wheel cover and lower the vehicle.
10. Recheck the wheel nut torque.

INSPECTION

Check the wheel for damage, rust, corrosion. Scratches can be sanded and painted. Visibly bent wheels should be replaced. Check runout in all directions (up and down, in and out) using a dial indicator. For aluminum wheels, maximum runout is 0.030 in. (0.762mm) For steel wheels, the specification is 0.045 in. (1.143mm). If the wheel causes a vibration and tire balance does not solve the problem, replace the wheel.

Wheel Lug Studs

➧ SEE FIG. 1

REPLACEMENT

⁂ CAUTION

Brake-related work is necessary for the following procedure. Some brake pads contain asbestos, which has been determined to be a cancer-causing agent. Never clean the brake surfaces with compressed air! Avoid inhaling any dust from any brake surface! When cleaning brake surfaces, use a commercially available brake cleaning fluid.

1. Raise the vehicle and support safely.
2. Remove the wheel, brake caliper, bracket and rotor.
3. Cut about 1/2 in. (13mm) off of the outer end of the stud.
4. Position the stud at the 6 o'clock position. Use tool J 6627–A or equivalent to extract the stud from the hub. Do not hammer on the studs to remove, as this could damage the bearing.

To install:

5. Clean the hub and place the replacement stud in the hub.
6. Add enough washers to draw the stud into the hub.
7. Install the lug nut flat side to the washers and tighten until the stud head seats in the hub flange.

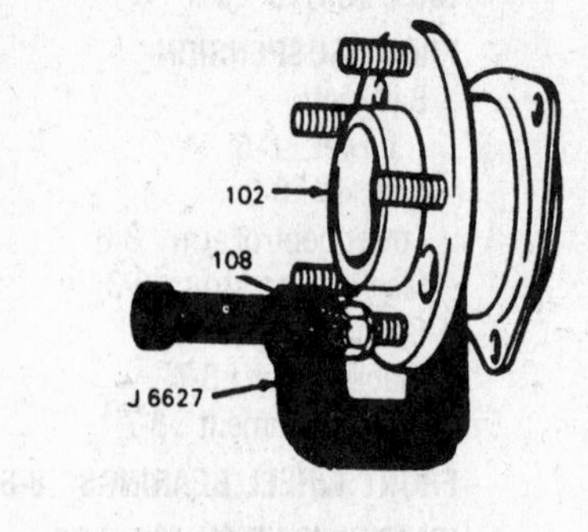

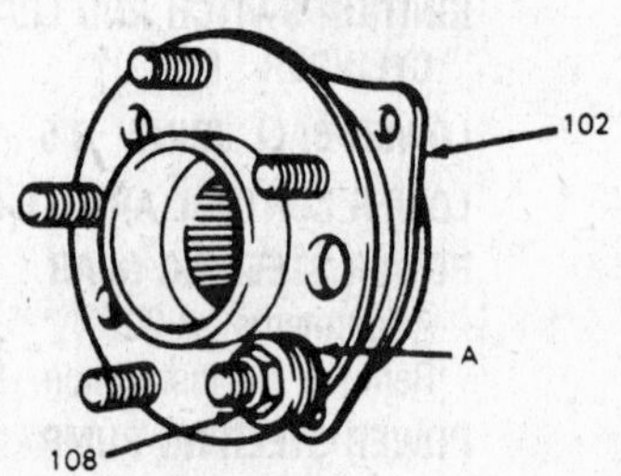

1. Hub/bearing assembly
2. Wheel lug stud
3. Washers

FIG. 1 Wheel lug stud removal using special tool

7. Remove the nut and washers.
8. Repeat for other studs as required.
9. Install the brake parts and wheel. Torque the lug nuts to 100 ft. lbs. (140 Nm).
10. Lower the vehicle and recheck the wheel nut torque.

FRONT SUSPENSION

⁂ CAUTION

Brake-related work is necessary for many of the following procedures. Some brake pads contain asbestos, which has been determined to be a cancer-causing agent. Never clean the brake surfaces with compressed air! Avoid inhaling any dust from any brake surface! When cleaning brake surfaces, use a commercially available brake cleaning fluid. Wear protective eye equipment when working on the suspension.

Strut Cartridge

➧ SEE FIGS. 2–4

REMOVAL & INSTALLATION

➡ During this procedure, the vehicle's weight is used used to

keep the coil spring from expanding. The front MacPherson strut assembly does NOT have to be removed from the vehicle to remove the strut cartridge.

1. Disconnect the negative battery cable.
2. Scribe the strut mount cover plate-to-body to ensure proper camber adjustment when installing.
3. Remove the three strut mount cover plate retaining nuts and cover.
4. Remove the strut shaft nut using a No. 50 Torx® bit.

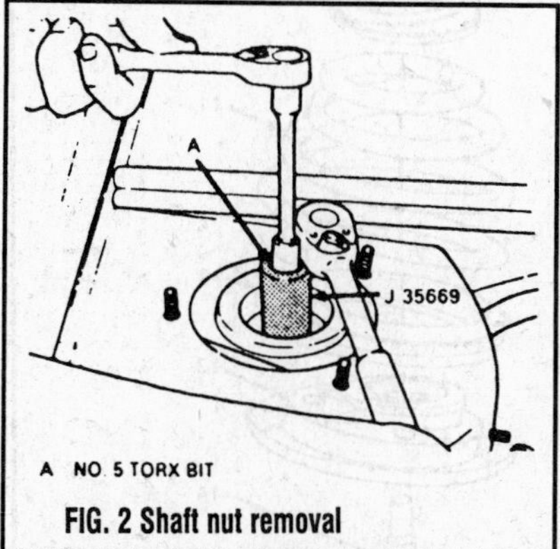

FIG. 2 Shaft nut removal

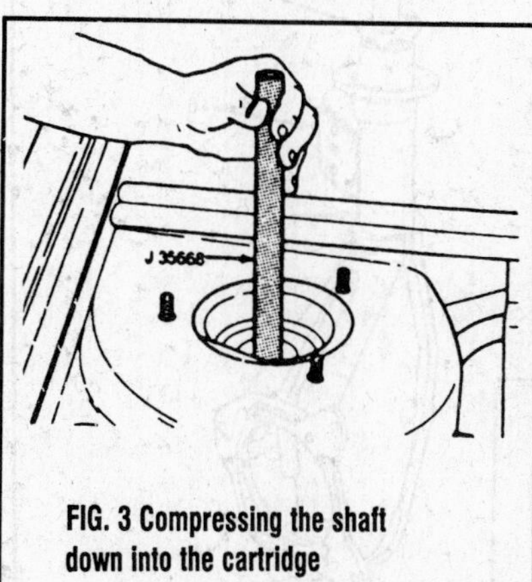

FIG. 3 Compressing the shaft down into the cartridge

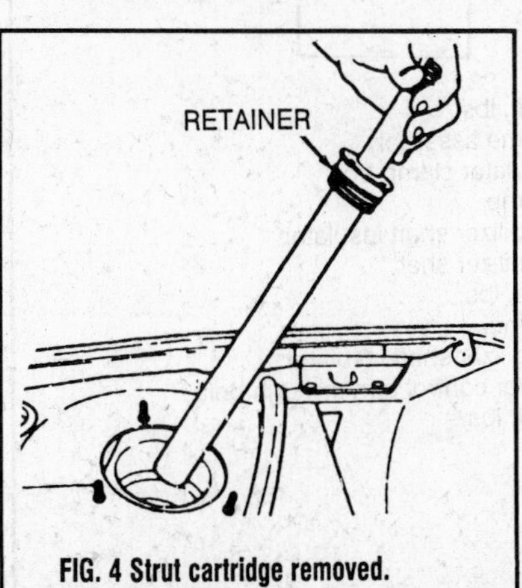

FIG. 4 Strut cartridge removed.

5. Remove the strut mount bushing by prying with a suitable pry bar.
6. Remove the jounce bumper retainer using a jounce bumper spanner wrench tool J35670. Remove the jounce bumper by attaching the strut extension rod J–35668. Compress the shaft down into the cartridge. Remove the extension rod and pull out the jounce bumper.
7. Remove the strut cartridge closure nut by attaching the strut extension rod and re-extending the shaft. Remove the extension rod and unscrew the closure nut using a strut cap nut wrench J–35671 or equivalent.
8. Remove the strut cartridge, then remove the oil from the strut tube using a suction device.

To install:

9. Install the self contained replacement cartridge using the strut cap nut wrench J–35671 or equivalent. The cartridge does not need oil added unless specified. If oil is not supplied with the cartridge, add the specified amount of hydraulic jack oil.
10. Install the jounce bumper and retainer.
11. Install the strut mount bushing. Use a soap solution to lubricate the bushing during installation.
12. Install the strut shaft nut and torque to 72 ft. lbs. (98 Nm).
13. Align the scribed marks from the strut cover-to-body. Install the strut cover plate and nuts. Torque the nuts to 17 ft. lbs. (24 Nm).
14. Connect the negative battery cable and check for proper suspension operation.

MacPherson Strut/ Knuckle Assembly

➧ SEE FIGS. 5–7

REMOVAL & INSTALLATION

✻✻ CAUTION

Do NOT remove the strut cartridge nut without compressing the coil spring first. This procedure MUST be followed because it keeps the coil spring compressed. Use care to support the strut assembly adequately because the coil spring is under heavy load; if released too quickly, serious personal injury could result. Never remove the center strut nut unless the spring is compressed with a MacPherson Strut Spring Compressor tool J-26584 or equivalent.

1. Disconnect the negative battery cable.
2. Loosen the cover plate bolts.
3. Loosen the wheel nuts. Raise and safely support the vehicle.
4. Remove the wheel assembly. Remove the brake caliper and bracket assembly; hang the caliper aside. DO NOT hang the caliper by the brake lines.
5. Remove the brake rotor. Remove the hub and bearing attaching bolts.
6. If equipped with ABS, remove the sensor and position aside. Remove the halfshaft. Remove the tie rod attaching nut, and separate the tie rod from the steering knuckle.
7. Remove the ball joint heat shield. Remove the lower ball joint attaching nut and separate the lower ball from the lower control arm.
8. Remove the hub and bearing attaching bolts and hub assembly.
9. Remove the cover plate bolts, and remove the strut from the vehicle.

To install:

10. Install the strut mount cover plate, tighten the nuts after lowering the vehicle. Install the lower ball joint and torque the nut to 15 ft. lbs. (20 Nm) plus at least an additional 90° (1½ flats) turn until the cotter pin hole is lined up. Install a new cotter pin and bend over. Install the heat shield.
11. Install the tie rod to the knuckle, install the nut and torque to 40 ft. lbs. (54 Nm). Install a new cotter pin and bend over.
12. Install the halfshaft and install the hub and bearing-to-knuckle attaching bolts. Tighten to 52 ft. lbs. (70 Nm). Install the ABS sensor if equipped.
13. Install the brake rotor and caliper assembly.
14. Install the wheel assembly, and tighten the wheel lug nuts.
15. Lower the vehicle, tighten the strut cover bolts to 18 ft. lbs. (24 Nm), and tighten the wheel nuts to 100 ft. lbs. (140 Nm).
16. Connect the negative battery cable.

OVERHAUL

✻✻ CAUTION

Do NOT remove the strut cartridge nut without compressing the coil spring first. This procedure MUST be followed because it keeps the coil spring compressed. Use care to support the strut assembly adequately because the coil spring is under heavy load; if released too quickly, serious personal injury could result. Never remove the

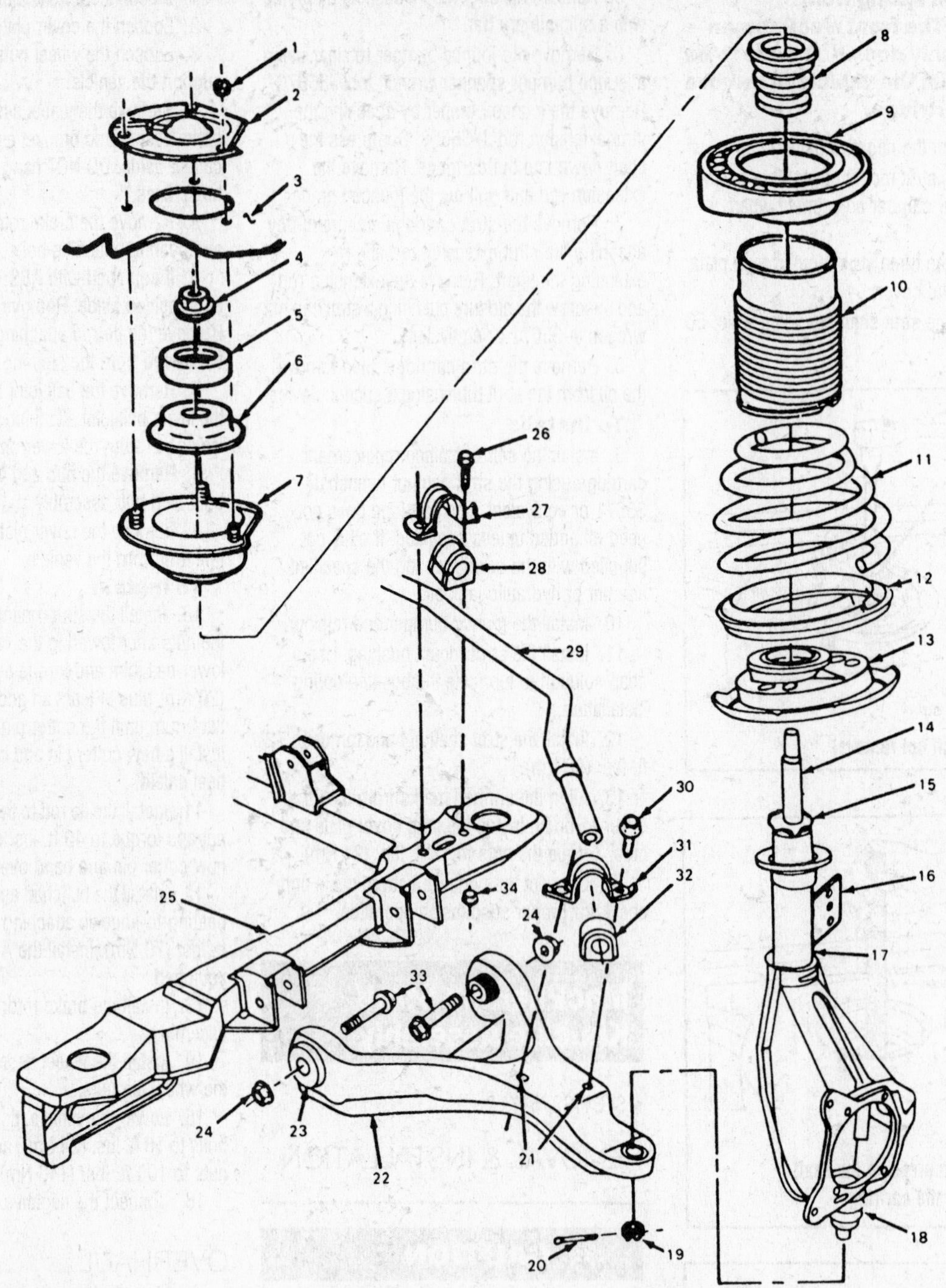

1. 17 ft. lbs.
2. Strut mount cover plate
3. Shock tower
4. 72 ft. lbs
5. Upper strut mount bushing
6. Bumper retainer
7. Strut mount
8. Bumper
9. Upper spring insulator
10. Dust shield
11. Spring
12. Lower spring insulator
13. Spring seat and bearing
14. Strut cartridge shaft
15. 82 ft. lbs.
16. Spring plate
17. Knuckle/strut assembly
18. Suspension ball joint
19. Castle nut
20. Cotter pin
21. Weld studs
22. Lower control arm
23. Lower control arm bushing
24. 72 ft. lbs.
25. Frame assembly
26. Insulator clamp bolt
27. Clamp
28. Stabilizer shaft insulator
29. Stabilizer shaft
30. 35 ft. lbs.
31. Clamp
32. Stabilizer shaft insulator
33. Lower control arm through bolt
34. 35 ft. lbs.

FIG. 5 Front suspension parts with exploded view of MacPherson strut

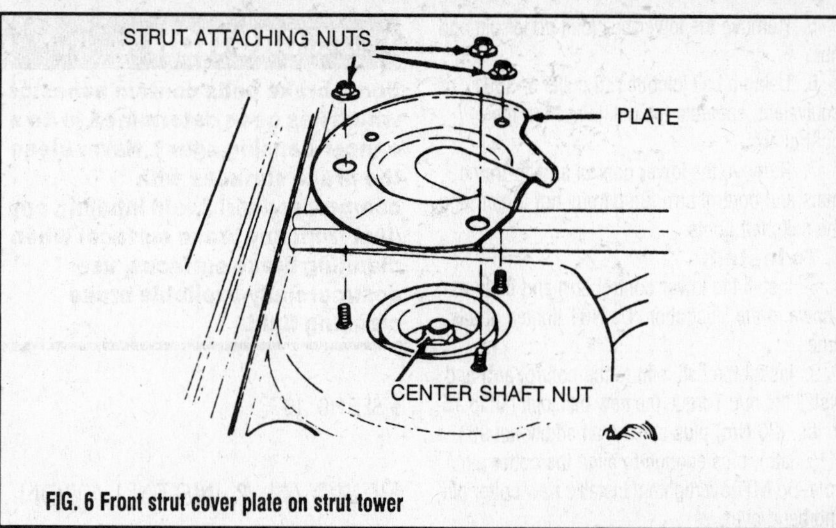

FIG. 6 Front strut cover plate on strut tower

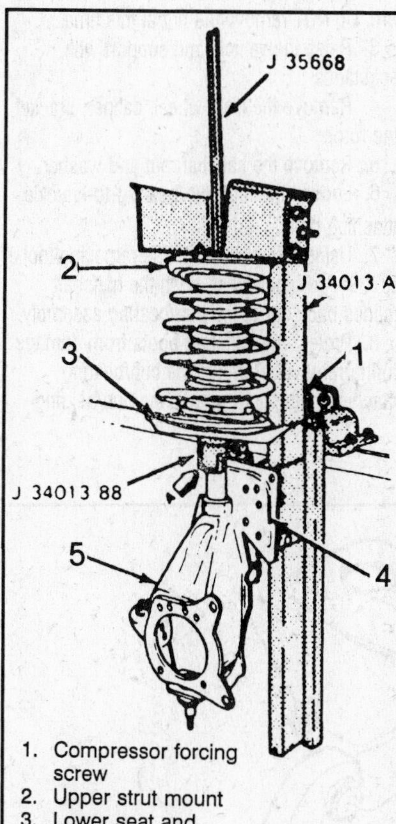

FIG. 7 Proper use of a MacPherson coil spring compressor

center strut nut unless the spring is compressed with a MacPherson Strut Spring Compressor tool J-26584 or equivalent.

Disassembly

1. Remove the MacPherson strut assembly as outlined in this section.
2. Mount the strut assembly in a strut compressing tool J–34013–A and J–34013–88. Compress the spring using the forcing screw. Release the spring tension enough to remove the spring insulator.
3. Using a Torx® bit and a strut shaft nut remover tool J–35669, remove the strut shaft nut. Make sure there is no spring tension on the shaft.
4. Release all spring tension and remove the coil spring and insulator. Remove any component needed to perform repair.

Assembly

1. Inspect all components for wear and damage.
2. Install the spring seat and bearing.
3. Install the lower spring insulator. The lower spring coil end must be visible between the step and the first retention tab of the insulator.
4. Install the spring, dust shield, and jounce bumper.
5. Install the upper spring insulator. The upper spring coil end must be between the step and location mark on the insulator.
6. Install the jounce bumper retainer-to-strut mount using a jounce bumper spanner tool J–35670 or equivalent.
7. Align the strut cartridge shaft with a strut extension rod tool J–35668.
8. Install the strut mount and the upper strut mount bushing.
9. Compress the strut assembly using the strut spring compressor tool J–34013–A and J34013–88.
10. Install the shaft nut using the strut rod installer and Torx® bit. Torque the shaft nut to 72 ft. lbs. (98 Nm).
11. Install the MacPherson strut assembly into the vehicle as outlined in this section.

Coil Spring

Refer to the MacPherson Strut Overhaul procedures for coil spring removal and installation.

Lower Ball Joint

➧ SEE FIG. 8

REMOVAL & INSTALLATION

1. Disconnect the negative battery cable.
2. Raise the vehicle and support with jackstands.
3. Remove the front wheels, ball joint heat shield and lower ball joint cotter pin.
4. Remove the ball joint nut.
5. Loosen, but do NOT remove the stabilizer shaft bushing assembly bolts.

➡ Do NOT damage the halfshaft boots when drilling out the ball joint rivets.

6. Remove the ball joint from the strut/knuckle assembly using a ball joint/tie rod puller J–35917 or equivalent.

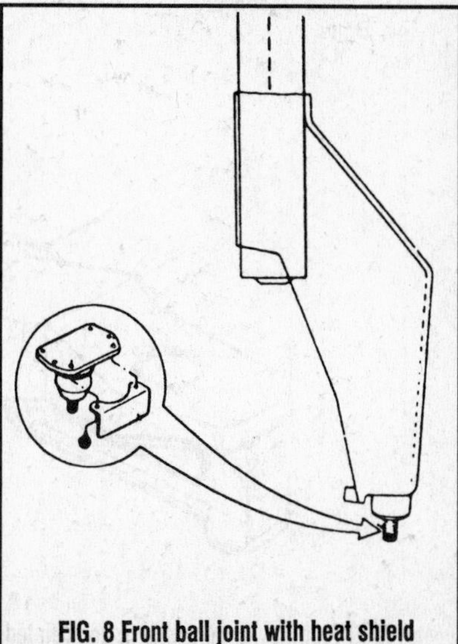

FIG. 8 Front ball joint with heat shield

7. Drill out the ball joint rivets and remove the ball joint from the knuckle. Refer to the instructions in the ball joint replacement kit.

To install:

8. Install the lower ball joint into the strut/knuckle assembly.
9. Install the four ball joint bolts and nuts in the kit and torque to specifications.
10. Install the ball joint-to-lower control arm. Install a new ball joint nut and torque to 15 ft. lbs. (20 Nm) plus at least an additional 90° (1½ flats), plus enough to align the cotter pin hole. Do NOT overtighten.
11. Install a new cotter pin and bend over.
12. Torque the stabilizer shaft bolts to 35 ft. lbs. (47 Nm).
13. Install the ball joint heat shield. Install the front wheels and lower the vehicle.
14. Connect the negative battery and check for proper suspension operation.

Lower Control Arm

➧ SEE FIG. 9

REMOVAL & INSTALLATION

1. Disconnect the negative battery cable.
2. Raise the vehicle and support with jackstands.
3. Remove the front wheels.
4. Remove the stabilizer shaft-to-lower control arm insulator bracket bolts.
5. Remove the lower ball joint cotter pin and nut.
6. Using a ball joint/tie rod puller J-35917 or equivalent, separate the ball joint from the control arm.
7. Remove the lower control arm-to-frame bolts and control arm. Be careful not to damage the halfshaft boots.

To install:

8. Install the lower control arm and bolts as shown in the illustration. Do NOT tighten at this time.
9. Install the ball joint to the control arm and install the nut. Torque the new ball joint nut to 15 ft. lbs. (20 Nm) plus at least an additional 90° (1½ flats), plus enough to align the cotter pin hole. Do NOT overtighten! Install a new cotter pin and bend over.
10. Torque the lower control arm-to-frame bolts to 56 ft. lbs. (75 Nm).
11. Install the stabilizer shaft-to-lower control arm bracket and torque to 35 ft. lbs. (47 Nm).
12. Install the front wheels and torque the lug nuts to 100 ft. lbs. (136 Nm).
13. Lower the vehicle and connect the negative battery cable.
14. Check for proper suspension operation before moving the vehicle.

Hub/Bearing Assembly

All "W" body cars are equipped with sealed hub and bearing assemblies. The hub and bearing assemblies are not serviceable. If the assembly is damaged, the complete unit must be replaced.

❊❊ CAUTION

Some brake pads contain asbestos, which has been determined to be a cancer-causing agent. Never clean the brake surfaces with compressed air! Avoid inhaling any dust from any brake surface! When cleaning brake surfaces, use commercially-available brake cleaning fluid.

➧ SEE FIG. 10

REMOVAL & INSTALLATION

1. Disconnect the negative battery cable.
2. Loosen the halfshaft nut and washer one turn. Do NOT remove the nut at this time.
3. Raise the vehicle and support with jackstands.
4. Remove the front wheel, caliper, bracket and rotor.
5. Remove the halfshaft nut and washer.
6. Loosen the four hub/bearing-to-knuckle attaching bolts.
7. Using a front hub spindle removing tool J 28733-A or equivalent, push the halfshaft splines back out of the hub/bearing assembly.
8. Protect the halfshaft boots from damage during removal. Remove the hub/bearing attaching bolts, and remove the hub/bearing.

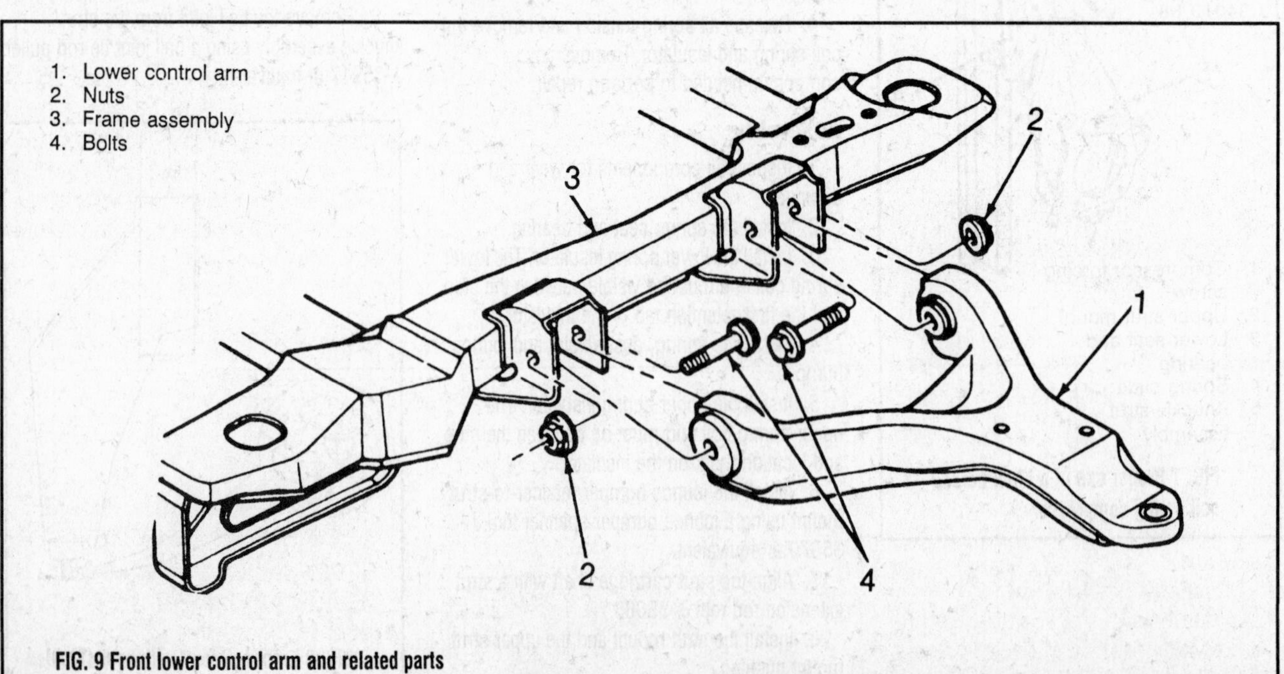

FIG. 9 Front lower control arm and related parts

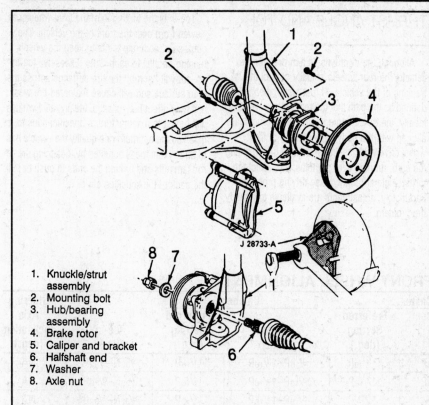

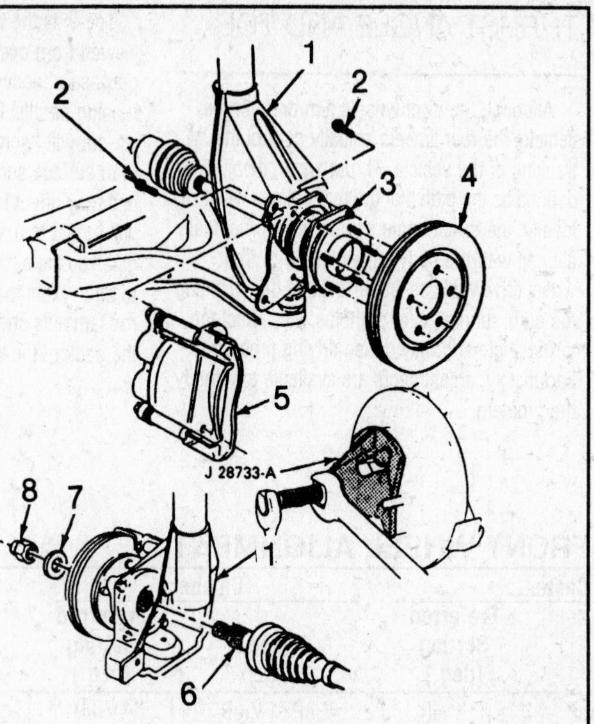

1. Knuckle/strut assembly
2. Mounting bolt
3. Hub/bearing assembly
4. Brake rotor
5. Caliper and bracket
6. Halfshaft end
7. Washer
8. Axle nut

FIG. 10 Front hub/bearing assembly and related parts

To Install:

9. Install the hub/bearing assembly onto the halfshaft splines. Install the four attaching bolts and torque to 52 ft. lbs. (70 Nm).
10. Install a new halfshaft nut and washer. Do NOT tighten the nut at this time.
11. Install the rotor, caliper and bracket.
12. Install the front wheel and torque the lug nuts to 100 ft. lbs. (135 Nm).
13. Lower the vehicle.
14. Torque the halfshaft end nut to 184 ft. lbs. (250 Nm). Connect the negative battery cable.

Stabilizer Shaft and Insulators

➧ SEE FIG. 5

REMOVAL & INSTALLATION

1. Disconnect the negative battery cable.
2. Raise the vehicle and support with jackstands.
3. Remove the front wheel.
4. Move the steering shaft dust seal for access to the pinch bolt. Refer to the "Rack and Pinion" section in this Section.
5. Remove the pinch bolt from the lower intermediate steering shaft.
6. Loosen all the stabilizer insulator clamp attaching nuts and bolts.
7. Place a jackstand under the center of the rear frame crossmember.
8. Loosen the two front frame-to-body bolts (four turns only).
9. Remove the two rear frame-to-body bolts and lower the rear of the frame just enough to gain access to remove the stabilizer shaft.
10. Remove the insulators and clamps from the frame and control arms. Pull the stabilizer shaft rearward, swing down and remove from the left side of the vehicle.

To Install:

11. Install the stabilizer shaft through the left side of the vehicle.
12. Coat the new insulators with rubber lubricant.
13. Loosely install the clamps to the control arms and clamps to the frame.
14. Raise the frame into position while guiding the steering gear into place.
15. Install new frame-to-body bolts and torque to 103 ft. lbs. (140 Nm).
16. Remove the frame jackstand.
17. Torque the stabilizer clamps-to-frame and control arms to 35 ft. lbs. (47 Nm).
18. Install the steering gear pinch bolt and dust seal.
19. Install the front wheels and torque the lug nuts to 100 ft. lbs. (136 Nm).
20. Check for completion of repair and lower the vehicle.
21. Connect the negative battery cable.

Front Wheel Alignment

The do-it-yourself mechanic should not attempt to perform any wheel alignment procedures. Highly specialized alignment tools are needed and making these adjustments blindly would most likely result in damage. The 4-wheel alignment should be performed by a certified alignment technician using the proper alignment tools. The following is informational only; procedures are not outlined.

CAMBER

Camber is an important alignment angle because it is both a tire wear angle and a directional control angle. Camber is the inward or outward tilt of the top of the tires when viewed from the front of the vehicle. If the center line of the tire is perfectly vertical, the tire is said to have zero (0) camber. If the top of the tire tilts outward, the tire has positive camber; if the top of the tire tilts inward, the tire has negative camber. Tire wear will logically follow these tilt angles. For instance, excessive negative camber will result in wear to the inner portion of the tread.

Another problem with inaccurate camber is that the vehicle will pull to the side with the most positive camber. The effect is similar to leaning to make a turn on a bicycle.

Camber is measured in degrees and the specification is determined by the R & D team according to the physical traits and properties of the vehicle. Adjustment is accomplished at the top of the strut tower where the plate bolts to the tower. "Pushing" the top of the strut out will increase the camber, and "pulling" it in will decrease the camber.

CASTER

Caster is the forward or rearward tilting of the steering axis (the center line is an imaginary line that passes through the upper mount and lower ball joint) from the vertical, as viewed from the side of the vehicle. Rearward tilt is positive caster, and forward tilt is negative caster. Zero (0) caster would indicate that the upper strut mount is directly above the lower ball joint.

Caster influences directional control, but is not a tire wearing angle. Caster also affects directional stability and steering effort. Caster angle is calculated to deliver the most desirable steering effort, normal wheel returning forces, and wheel pulling sensitivity. A vehicle will pull toward the side with the least amount of camber. Because of their naturally straight running characteristics, front wheel drive vehicle are not overly sensitive to caster, and accordingly, many (like these cars) do not have provisions for caster adjustment.

THRUST ANGLE AND TOE

Although the front wheels aim or steer the vehicle, the rear wheels actually control the tracking of the vehicle. Thrust angle, then, is defined as the path that the rear wheels will take. Ideally, the thrust angle should be geometrically aligned with the body centerline. With front wheel drive vehicles, imperfections due to hitting the curb, running over potholes, etc. affect the thrust angle and may cause driving problems. Fortunately, adjustments are available to remedy the problem.

Toe-in is the turning in of the front wheels, as viewed from over the front of the vehicle. The purpose of accurate toe is to keep the wheels running parallel to each other. Excessive toe-in or -out will "scrub" the tire surfaces across the road surface and will cause feathered tire wear and may affect fuel mileage. Ideally, all 4 wheels will be set to manufacturer's specifications to give you the optimum ride quality the vehicle has to offer. Front toe is adjusted by loosening the tie rod jam nuts and turning the ends to push or pull the back of the knuckles out or in.

FRONT WHEEL ALIGNMENT

		Caster		Camber			Steering
Year	Model	Range (deg.)	Preferred Setting (deg.)	Range (deg.)	Preferred Setting (deg.)	Toe-in (in.)	Axis Inclination (deg.)
1988-89	Cutlass Supreme	1 5/16P–2 5/16P	1 13/16P	3/16P–1 3/16P	11/16P	3/32N–3/32P	NA
	Grand Prix	1 5/16P–2 5/16P	1 13/16P	3/16P–1 3/16P	11/16P	3/32N–3/32P	NA
	Regal	1 1/2P–2 1/2P	2P	3/16P–1 3/16P	11/16P	3/32N–3/32P	NA
1990	Cutlass Supreme	1 1/2P–2 1/2P	2P	3/16P–1 3/16P	11/16P	3/32N–3/32P	NA
	Grand Prix	1 5/16P–2 5/16P	1 13/16P	3/16P–1 3/16P	11/16P	3/32N–3/32P	NA
	Regal	1 1/2P–2 1/2P	2P	3/16P–1 3/16P	11/16P	3/32N–3/32P	NA
	Lumina	1 1/2P–2 1/2P	2P	3/16P–1 3/8P	11/16P	3/32N–3/32P	NA
1991	Cutlass Supreme	1 1/2P–2 1/2P	2P	3/16P–1 3/16P	11/16P	3/32N–3/32P	NA
	Grand Prix	1 5/16P–2 5/16P	1 13/16P	3/16P–1 3/16P	11/16P	3/32N–3/32P	NA
	Regal	1 1/2P–2 1/2P	2P	3/16P–1 3/16P	11/16P	3/32N–3/32P	NA
	Lumina	1 1/2P–2 1/2P	2P	3/16P–1 3/8P	11/16P	3/32N–3/32P	NA
1992	Cutlass Supreme	1 1/2P–2 1/2P	2P	3/16P–1 3/16P	11/16P	3/32N–3/32P	NA
	Grand Prix	1 5/16P–2 5/16P	1 13/16P	3/16P–1 3/16P	11/16P	3/32N–3/32P	NA
	Regal	1 1/2P–2 1/2P	2P	3/16P–1 3/16P	11/16P	3/32N–3/32P	NA
	Lumina	1 1/2P–2 1/2P	2P	3/16P–1 3/8P	11/16P	3/32N–3/32P	NA

NA—Not adjustable
N—Negative
P—Positive

REAR SUSPENSION

The rear suspension features a lightweight composite fiberglass mono-leaf transverse spring. Each wheel is mounted to a tri-link independent suspension system. The three links consist of an inverted U-channel trailing arm and tubular front and rear rods.

Transverse Spring Assembly

SEE FIGS. 11 AND 12

REMOVAL & INSTALLATION

CAUTION

Do NOT disconnect any rear suspension components until the transverse spring has been compressed using a rear spring compressor tool J-35778 or equivalent. Failure to follow this

procedure may result in personal injury. Wear protective eye equipment when working on the suspension.

➡ **Do not use any corrosive cleaning agents, silicone lubricants, engine degreasers, solvents, etc. on or near the rear transverse fiberglass spring. These materials may cause spring strength depletion and consequent damage.**

1. Disconnect the negative battery cable.
2. Raise the vehicle and support with jackstands.
3. Remove the jack pad in the middle of the spring.
4. Remove the spring retention plates and the right trailing arm at the knuckle.
5. Separate the rear leaf spring compressor tool J–35778 from the center shank and hang the center shank of the tool at the spring center.

✲✲ CAUTION

Attach the center shank of the compressor from the front side of the vehicle only.

6. Install the compressor body to the center shank and spring. Center the spring on the rollers of the spring compressor only.
7. Fully compress the spring using the spring compressor tool J–35778.
8. Slide the spring to the left side. It may be necessary to pry the spring to the left using a pry bar against the right knuckle. When prying, do not damage any components.
9. Relax the spring to provide removal clearance from the right side, then remove the spring.

To install:

10. Using the spring compressor tool, compress the spring and install it through the left knuckle. Slide towards the left side as far as possible and raise the right side of the spring as far as possible.
11. Compress the spring fully and install it into right knuckle.

➡ **The rear spring retention plates are designed with tabs on one end. The tabs must be aligned with the support assembly to prevent damage to the fuel tank.**

12. Center the spring to align the holes for the spring retention plate bolts.
13. Install the spring retention plates and bolts. Do NOT tighten at this time.

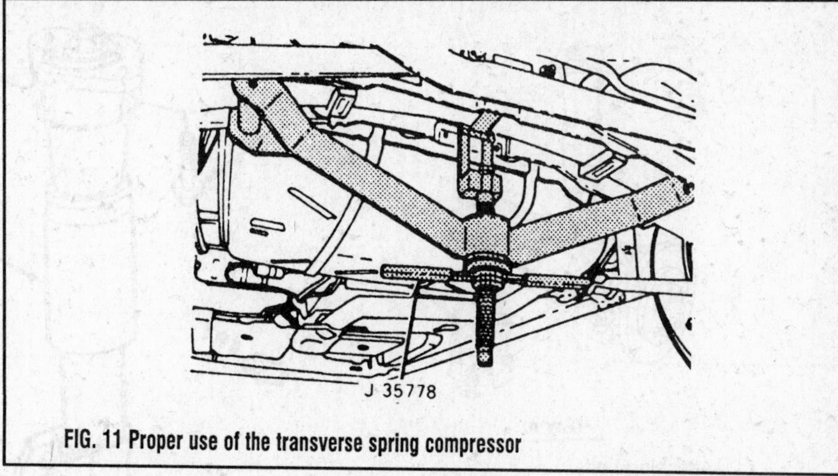

FIG. 11 Proper use of the transverse spring compressor

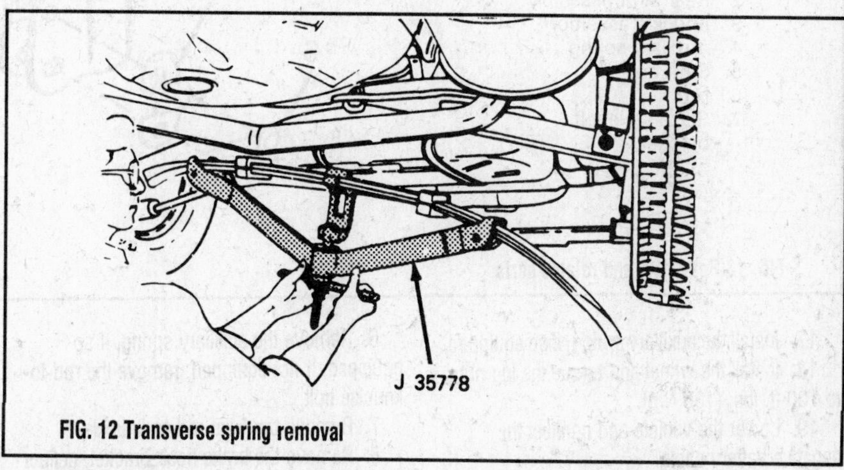

FIG. 12 Transverse spring removal

14. Position the trailing arm and install the bolt. Torque the bolt to 192 ft. lbs. (260 Nm).
15. Remove the spring compressor tool J35778.
16. Torque the spring retention plate bolts to 15 ft. lbs. (20 Nm).
17. Install the jack pads and torque the bolts to 18 ft. lbs. (25 Nm).
18. Install the wheels and torque the lug nuts to 100 ft. lbs. (136 Nm).
19. Lower the vehicle and connect the negative battery cable.

Rear Strut Assembly

➧ SEE FIG. 13

REMOVAL & INSTALLATION

1. Disconnect the negative battery cable.
2. Raise the vehicle and support with jackstands.
3. Remove the rear wheel assembly.
4. Scribe the strut-to-knuckle for proper installation.
5. Remove the auxiliary spring, if so equipped.
6. Remove the jack pad.
7. Install a rear leaf spring compressor tool J–35778 or equivalent. Refer the the "Transverse Spring Assembly" procedures in this section.
8. Fully compress the spring, but do NOT remove the retention plates or the spring.
9. Remove the two strut-to-body bolts.
10. Remove the brake hose from the strut.
11. Remove the strut and auxiliary spring upper bracket from the knuckle.

To install:

12. Position the strut to the body and knuckle bracket.
13. Install the strut-to-body bolts and torque to 34 ft. lbs. (46 Nm).
14. Install the strut-to-knuckle, align the scribe marks and torque the bolts to 133 ft. lbs. (180 Nm).
15. Install the brake hose bracket and remove the spring compressing tool.
16. Install the jack pad and torque the bolts to 18 ft. lbs. (25 Nm).

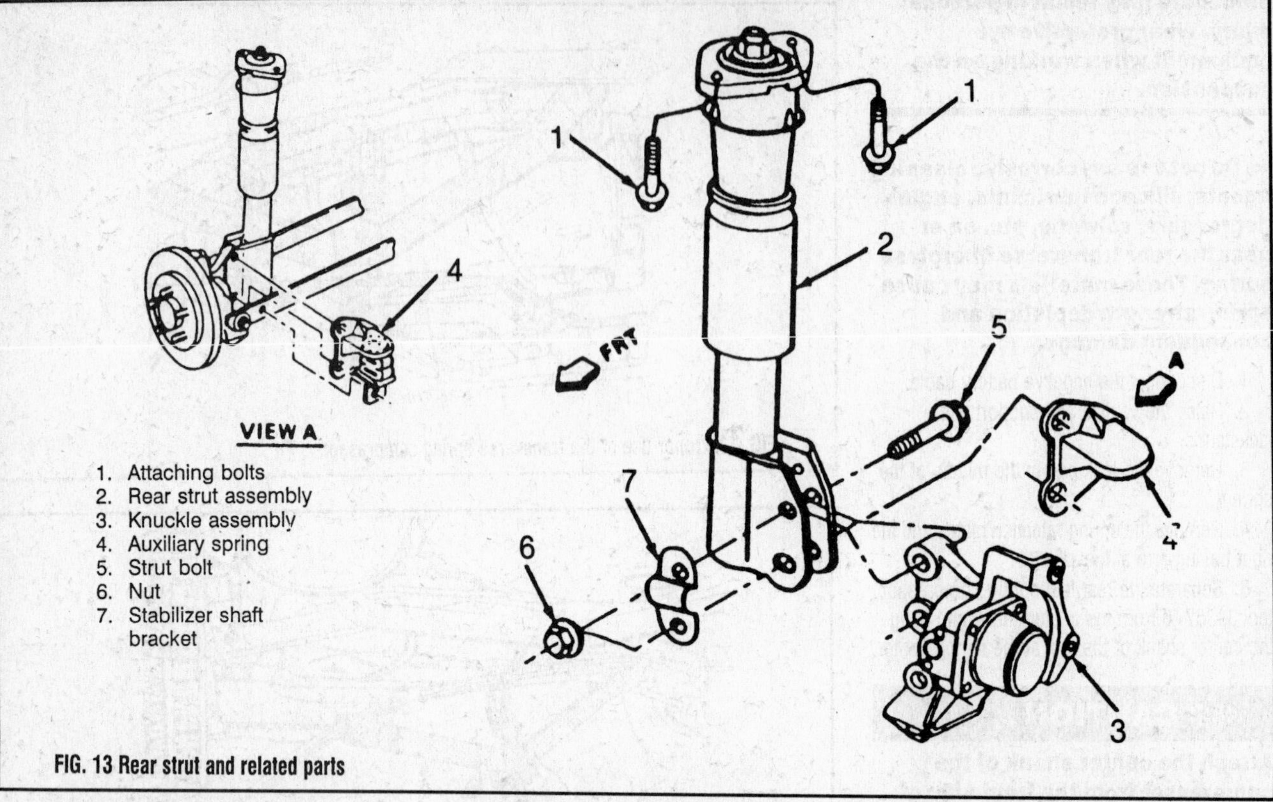

FIG. 13 Rear strut and related parts

17. Install the auxiliary spring, if so equipped.

18. Install the wheel and torque the lug nuts to 100 ft. lbs. (136 Nm).

19. Lower the vehicle and connect the negative battery cable.

OVERHAUL

The rear strut assembly is not serviceable. The assembly is replaced as a complete unit.

Rear Knuckle

➧ SEE FIG. 14

REMOVAL & INSTALLATION

1. Disconnect the negative battery cable.
2. Raise the vehicle and support with jackstands.
3. Remove the rear wheels and scribe the strut-to-knuckle.
4. Remove the jack pad and install the rear leaf spring compressor tool J-35778 as outlined in the "Transverse Spring Assembly" procedures in this Section.
5. Fully compress the spring but do not remove the spring or retention plates.
6. Remove the auxiliary spring, if so equipped. If not equipped, remove the rod-to-knuckle bolt.
7. Remove the front rod-to-knuckle.
8. Remove the brake hose bracket, caliper and rotor. Do not allow the caliper to hang by the brake hose.
9. Remove the hub and bearing assembly, trailing arm and the strut/upper auxiliary spring bracket from the knuckle. Remove the knuckle.

To install:

10. Install the knuckle and position it to the strut/upper auxiliary spring bracket.
11. Hand start the bolts, but do not tighten.
12. Install the front rod and trailing arm to the knuckle. Hand tighten the bolts.

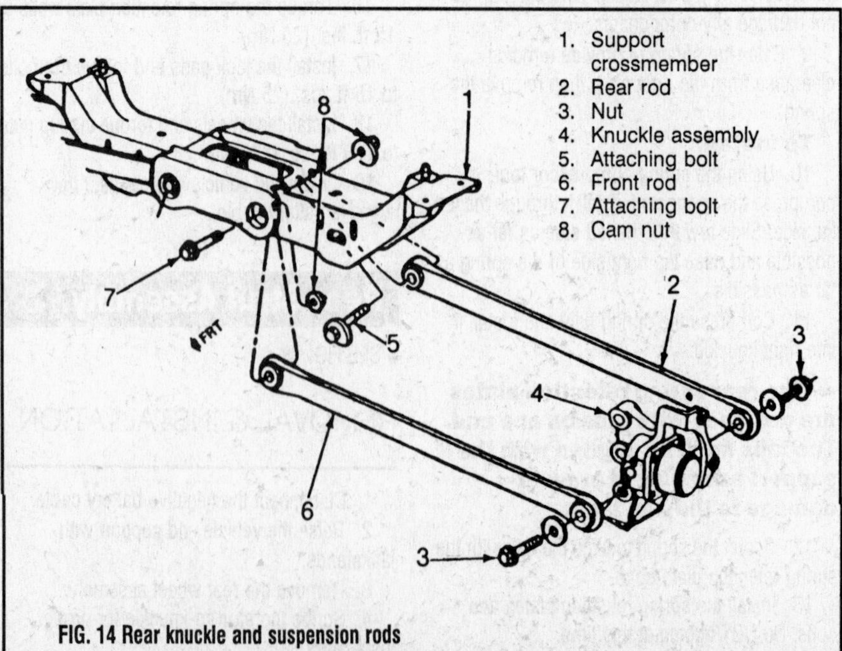

FIG. 14 Rear knuckle and suspension rods

13. Torque the trailing arm bolt and nut to 192 ft. lbs. (260 Nm).

14. Install the hub/bearing assembly and torque the bolts to 52 ft. lbs. (70 Nm).

15. Install the rotor and caliper.

16. Align the scribe marks to ensure proper alignment. Torque the strut-to-knuckle attaching bolts to 133 ft. lbs. (180 Nm).

17. Remove the rear leaf spring compressor.

18. Install the jack pad, auxiliary spring (if equipped) and rod-to-knuckle bolt. Apply thread locking compound to the knuckle bolts.

19. Torque the rod-to-knuckle bolts to 66 ft. lbs. (90 Nm) plus 90°.

20. Install the rear wheels and torque the lug nuts to 100 ft. lbs. (136 Nm).

21. Check for completion of repair, lower the vehicle and connect the negative battery cable.

Tri-Link Suspension Assembly

➧ SEE FIG. 15

REMOVAL & INSTALLATION

Trailing Arm

1. Raise the vehicle and support with jackstands.

2. Remove the trailing arm-to-knuckle nut and bolt.

3. Remove the trailing arm-to-body nut, bolt and the arm itself.

To install:

4. Install the trailing arm, bolts and nuts.

5. Torque the arm-to-knuckle bolt to 192 ft. lbs. (260 Nm) and the arm-to-body bolt to 48 ft. lbs. (65 Nm).

6. Lower the vehicle and recheck all repair procedures.

Rear Rod

1. Raise the vehicle and support with jackstands.

2. Remove the rear wheels.

3. Remove the auxiliary spring, if so equipped. If not equipped, remove the rod-to-knuckle bolt.

4. Remove the lower auxiliary spring bracket at the rod, if so equipped.

5. Scribe the toe adjusting cam, remove the rod-to-crossmember bolt and the rod itself.

To install:

6. Install the rod, push the bolt through the rod bushing and install the adjusting cam in its original location. Do not tighten at this time.

7. Install the lower auxiliary spring bracket-to-rod, if so equipped. Torque the nut to 133 ft. lbs. (180 Nm).

8. Install the rod-to-knuckle with thread locking compound. Do not tighten.

9. Install the rear wheels and lower the vehicle.

10. Torque the rod-to-knuckle bolt to 66 ft. lbs. (90 Nm) plus 90°. Torque the rod-to-crossmember bolt to 81 ft. lbs. (110 Nm) plus 60°.

11. Have a qualified alignment technician adjust the rear toe.

Front Rod

1. Raise the vehicle and support with jackstands.

2. Remove the rear wheels.

3. Remove the rod-to-knuckle bolt and exhaust pipe heat shield.

4. Lower and support the fuel tank just enough for access to the bolt at the frame.

5. Remove the rod-to-frame bolt and the rod itself.

To install:

6. Install the rod, bolts and nuts. Do not tighten at this time.

7. Apply thread locking compound to the rod-to-knuckle bolt.

8. Torque the rod-to-knuckle bolt to 66 ft. lbs. (90 Nm) plus 90°. Torque the rod-to-crossmember bolt to 81 ft. lbs. (110 Nm) plus 60°.

9. Reposition the fuel tank.

10. Install the exhaust pipe heat shield, rear wheels and lower the vehicle.

1. Rear strut
2. Attaching bolt
3. Auxiliary spring
4. Rear rod
5. Nut
6. Washer
7. Knuckle assembly
8. Nut
9. Washer
10. Bolt
11. Front rod
12. Stabilizer shaft bracket
13. Washer
14. Bolt
15. Trailing arm
16. Nut
17. Stabilizer shaft
18. Insulator

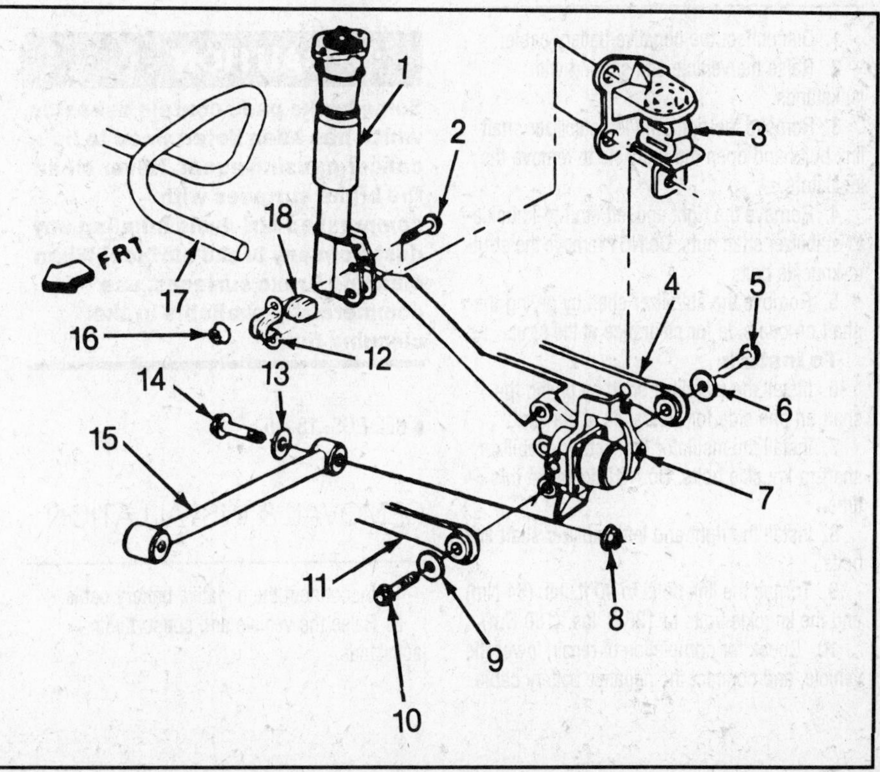

FIG. 15 Tri-Link suspension assembly

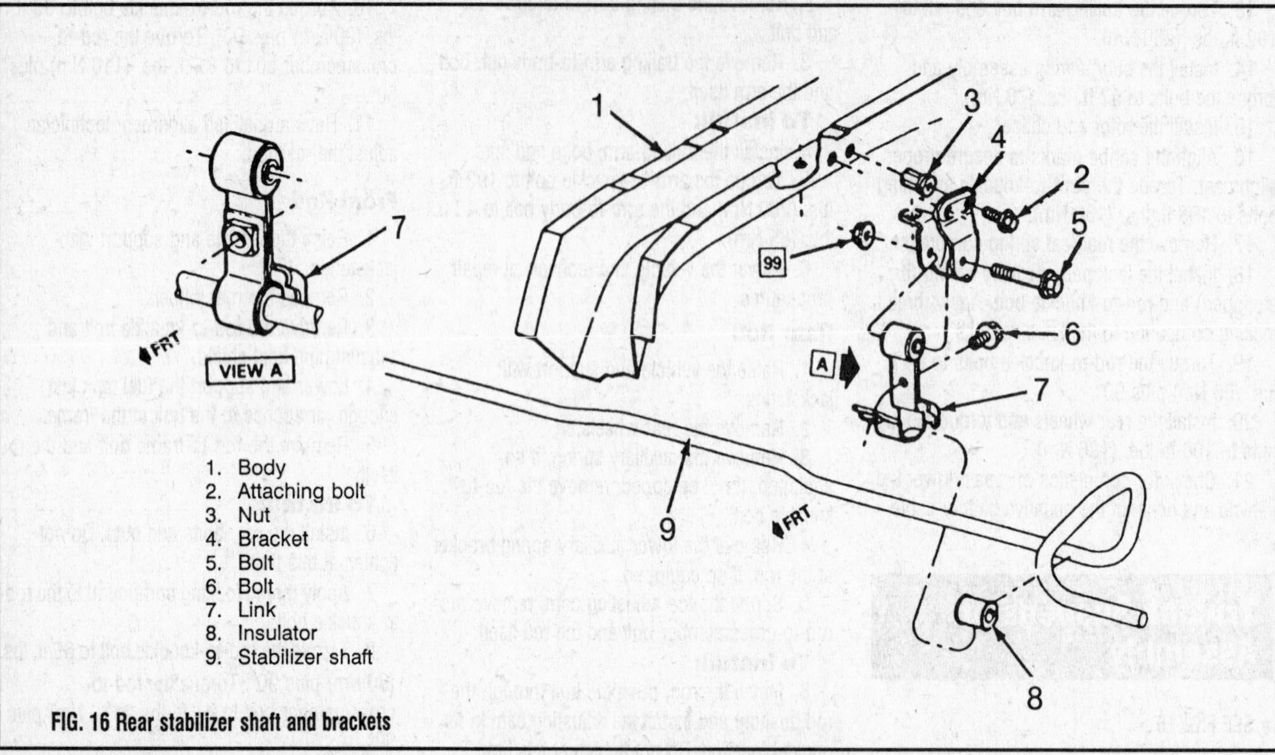

FIG. 16 Rear stabilizer shaft and brackets

Stabilizer Shaft

➧ SEE FIG. 16

REMOVAL & INSTALLATION

1. Disconnect the negative battery cable.
2. Raise the vehicle and support with jackstands.
3. Remove the right and left stabilizer shaft link bolts and open the brackets to remove the insulators.
4. Remove the right and left strut-to-knuckle-to-stabilizer shaft nuts. Do NOT remove the strut-to-knuckle bolts.
5. Remove the stabilizer shaft by prying the shaft on one side for clearance at the strut.

To install:

6. Install the stabilizer shaft by prying the shaft on one side for clearance at the strut.
7. Install the insulator brackets-to-stabilizer shaft-to-knuckle bolts. Do NOT tighten at this time.
8. Install the right and left stabilizer shaft link bolts.
9. Torque the link bolts to 40 ft. lbs. (54 Nm) and the knuckle bolts to 133 ft. lbs. (180 Nm).
10. Check for completion of repair, lower the vehicle, and connect the negative battery cable.

Hub/Bearing Assembly

All "W" body cars are equipped with sealed hub and bearing assemblies. The hub and bearing assemblies are not serviceable. If the assembly is damaged, the complete unit must be replaced.

✲✲ CAUTION

Some brake pads contain asbestos, which has been determined to be a cancer-causing agent. Never clean the brake surfaces with compressed air! Avoid inhaling any dust from any brake surface! When cleaning brake surfaces, use commercially-available brake cleaning fluid.

➧ SEE FIGS. 13–15

REMOVAL & INSTALLATION

1. Disconnect the negative battery cable.
2. Raise the vehicle and support with jackstands.
3. Remove the rear wheel, caliper, bracket and rotor.
4. Loosen the four hub/bearing-to-knuckle attaching bolts.
5. Remove the hub/bearing assembly.

To install:

6. Install the hub/bearing assembly onto the knuckle. Install the four attaching bolts and torque to 52 ft. lbs. (70 Nm).
7. Install the rotor, caliper and bracket.
8. Install the rear wheel and torque the lug nut to 100 ft. lbs. (135 Nm).
9. Lower the vehicle and connect the negative battery cable.

Rear Wheel Alignment

Refer to "Front Wheel Alignment" earlier in this Section for precautions and explanations of important alignment angles, which also pertain to the rear wheels. The following is in addition to that text, and is informational only.

Rear camber is accomplished by removing the rear strut and filing the lower mounting hole to an oblong shape. This will provide the movement needed for wheel tilt. Toe adjustment is accomplished by rotating a cam nut at the rear support rod.

REAR WHEEL ALIGNMENT SPECIFICATIONS

Year	Model	Camber (deg.) Range	Camber (deg.) Pref.	Toe-in (in.)
1988-89	Cutlass Supreme	0 to 1P	1/2P	7/64 out
	Grand Prix	0 to 1P	1/2P	7/64 out
	Regal	7/16N to 9/16P	1/16P	1/8 out
1990	Lumina	1/8N to 7/8P	3/8P	0
	Cutlass Supreme	5/64N to 7/64P	3/32P	7/64 out
	Grand Prix	0 to 1P	1/2P	7/64 out
	Regal	7/16N to 9/16P	1/16P	1/8 out
1991	Lumina	21/32N to 11/32P	5/32N	1/16 out
	Cutlass Supreme	11/16N to 5/16P	3/16N	1/16 out
	Grand Prix	3/8N to 5/8P	1/8	0
	Regal	7/16N to 9/16P	1/16P	1/8 out
1992	Lumina	①	②	1/16 out
	Cutlass Supreme	1/16P to 5/32P	3/32P	1/16 out
	Grand Prix	1/16N to 5/32P	3/32	1/16 out
	Regal	①	②	1/8 out

① With 14 in. tires: 9/32P to 3/8P
With 15 in. or 16 in. tires: 1/16P to 5/32P
② With 14 in. tires: 5/16P
With 15 in. or 16 in. tires: 3/32P

STEERING

The power rack and pinion steering system has a rotary control valve which directs hydraulic fluid coming from the steering pump to one side or the other side of the rack piston. The piston converts hydraulic pressure to linear force which moves the rack right or left. When power assist is not available, manual control is maintained; however, more steering effort is needed. A vane type steering pump provides hydraulic pressure for steering assist.

Steering Wheel

➧ SEE FIG. 17

REMOVAL & INSTALLATION

1. Disconnect the negative battery cable.
2. Remove the horn pad and retainer along with any other switches that are mounted to the steering wheel.
3. Disconnect the horn electrical lead from the canceling cam tower.
4. Turn the ignition switch to the ON position.

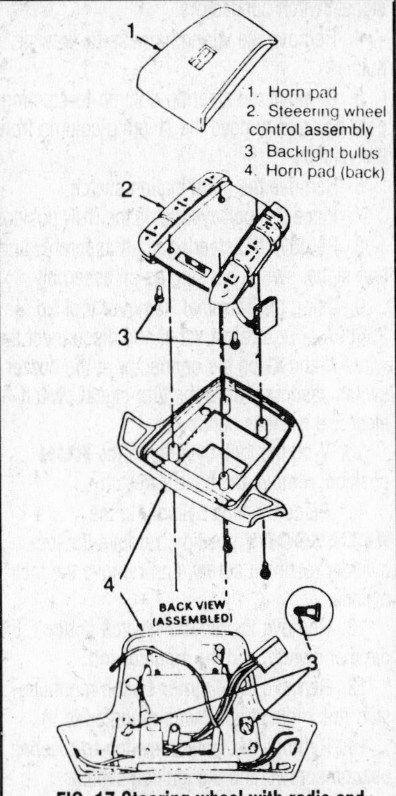

FIG. 17 Steering wheel with radio and temperature controls

5. Scribe an alignment mark on the steering wheel hub in line with the slash mark on the steering shaft.
6. Remove the steering shaft nut and install steering wheel puller J185903 or equivalent. Remove the steering wheel.

To install:

7. Align the matchmarks on the wheel hub and shaft and install the steering wheel. Tighten the steering wheel retaining nut to 30 ft. lbs. (41 Nm). Install the retainer
8. Connect the horn electrical lead and install the horn pad, etc.
9. Connect the negative battery cable.

Turn Signal Switch

➧ SEE FIG. 18

REMOVAL & INSTALLATION

➡ Tool No. J35689A or equivalent, is required to remove the terminals from the connector on the turn signal switch.

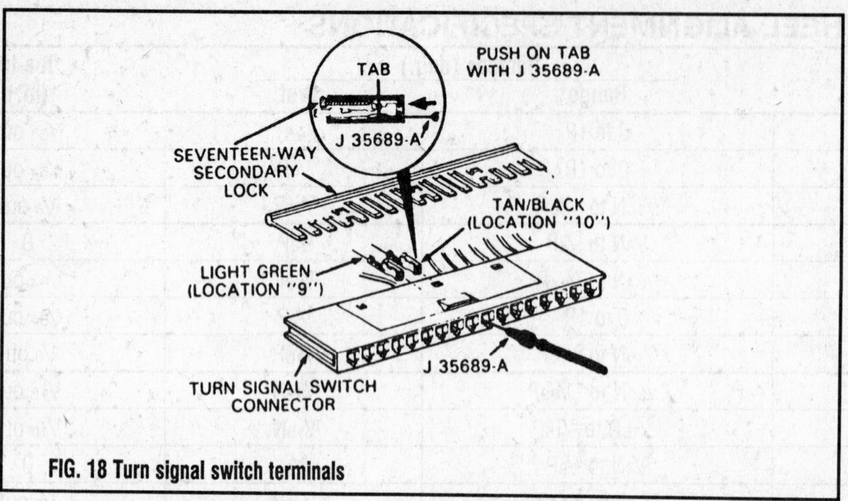

FIG. 18 Turn signal switch terminals

1. Remove the steering wheel.
2. Pull the turn signal canceling cam assembly from the steering shaft.
3. Remove the hazard warning knob-to-steering column screw and the knob.

➡ **Before removing the turn signal assembly, position the turn signal lever so the turn signal assembly to steering column screws can all be removed.**

4. Remove the column housing cover-to-column housing bowl screw and the cover. If equipped with cruise control, disconnect the cruise control electrical connector.
5. Remove the turn signal lever-to-pivot assembly screw and the lever; one screw is in the front and one is in the rear.
6. Using the terminal remover tool No. J 35689A or equivalent, label and disconnect the wires **F** and **G** on the connector at the buzzer switch assembly from the turn signal switch electrical harness connector.
7. Remove the turn signal switch-to-steering column screws and remove the switch.

To install:

8. Install the turn signal switch to the steering column, and tighten the turn signal switch-to-steering column screws.
9. Install the electrical connectors, and install the turn signal lever to the pivot assembly.
10. Install the hazard flasher knob. Install the canceling cam.
11. Install the steering wheel and column cover.
12. Connect the negative battery cable and check for proper operation.

Ignition Switch/Lock

➧ SEE FIGS. 19–21

REMOVAL & INSTALLATION

1. Disconnect the negative terminal from the battery. Remove the left side lower trim panel.
2. Remove the steering column-to-support screws and lower the steering column.
3. Disconnect the dimmer switch and turn signal switch connectors.
4. Remove the wiring harness-to-firewall nuts.
5. Remove the steering column-to-steering gear bolt and remove the steering column from the vehicle.
6. Remove the combination switch.
7. Place the lock cylinder in the RUN position.
8. Remove the steering shaft assembly and turn signal switch housing as an assembly.
9. Using the Terminal Remover tool No. J 35689A or equivalent, label and disconnect the wires **F** and **G** on the connector at the buzzer switch assembly from the turn signal switch electrical harness connector.
10. With the lock cylinder in the **RUN** position, remove the buzzer switch.
11. Place the lock cylinder in the **ACCESSORY** position, remove the lock cylinder retaining screw, and remove the lock cylinder.
12. Remove the dimmer switch nut/bolt, the dimmer switch, and the actuator rod.
13. Remove the dimmer switch mounting stud (the mounting nut was mounted to it).
14. Remove the ignition switch-to-steering column screws and the ignition switch.

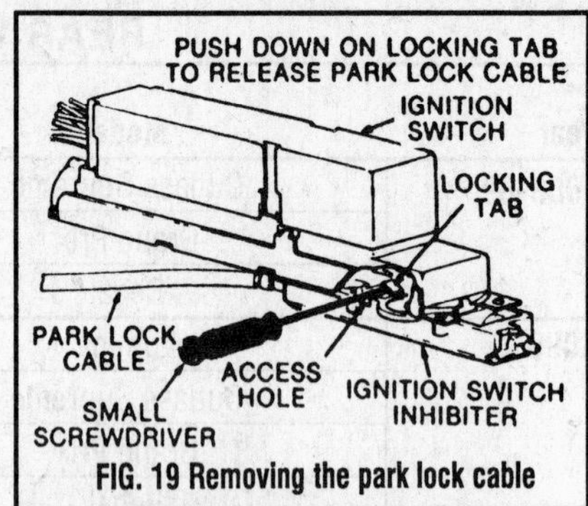

FIG. 19 Removing the park lock cable

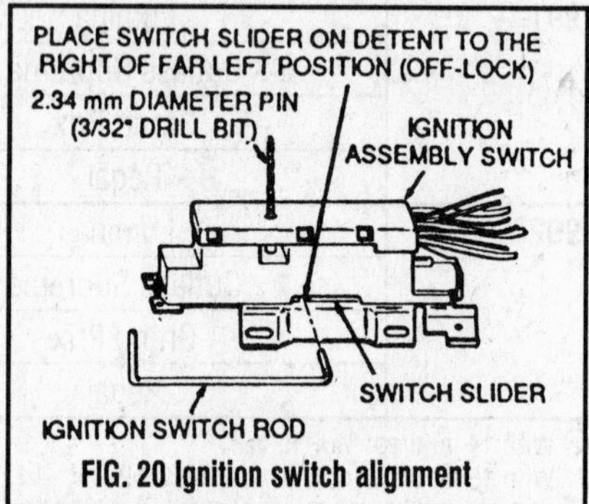

FIG. 20 Ignition switch alignment

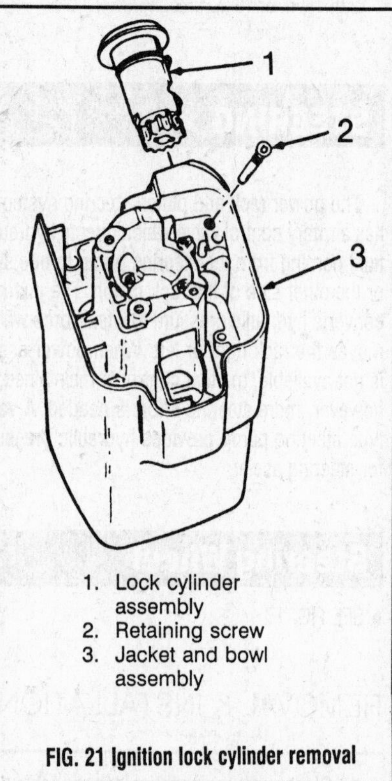

FIG. 21 Ignition lock cylinder removal

15. Remove the lock bolt screws and the lock bolt.
16. Remove the switch actuator rack and ignition switch.
17. Remove the steering shaft lock and spring.

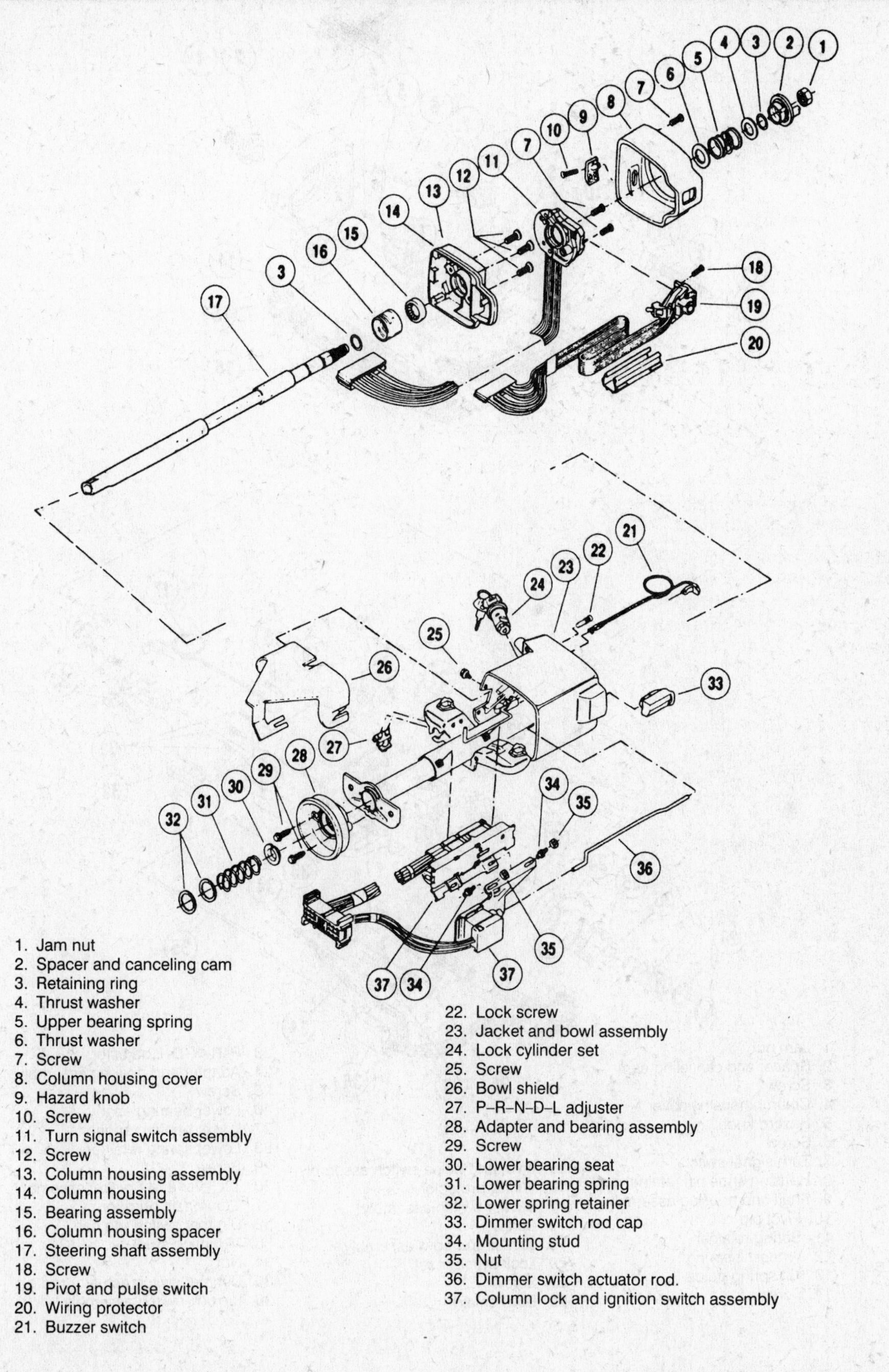
1. Jam nut
2. Spacer and canceling cam
3. Retaining ring
4. Thrust washer
5. Upper bearing spring
6. Thrust washer
7. Screw
8. Column housing cover
9. Hazard knob
10. Screw
11. Turn signal switch assembly
12. Screw
13. Column housing assembly
14. Column housing
15. Bearing assembly
16. Column housing spacer
17. Steering shaft assembly
18. Screw
19. Pivot and pulse switch
20. Wiring protector
21. Buzzer switch
22. Lock screw
23. Jacket and bowl assembly
24. Lock cylinder set
25. Screw
26. Bowl shield
27. P–R–N–D–L adjuster
28. Adapter and bearing assembly
29. Screw
30. Lower bearing seat
31. Lower bearing spring
32. Lower spring retainer
33. Dimmer switch rod cap
34. Mounting stud
35. Nut
36. Dimmer switch actuator rod.
37. Column lock and ignition switch assembly

FIG. 22 Exploded view of the standard steering column

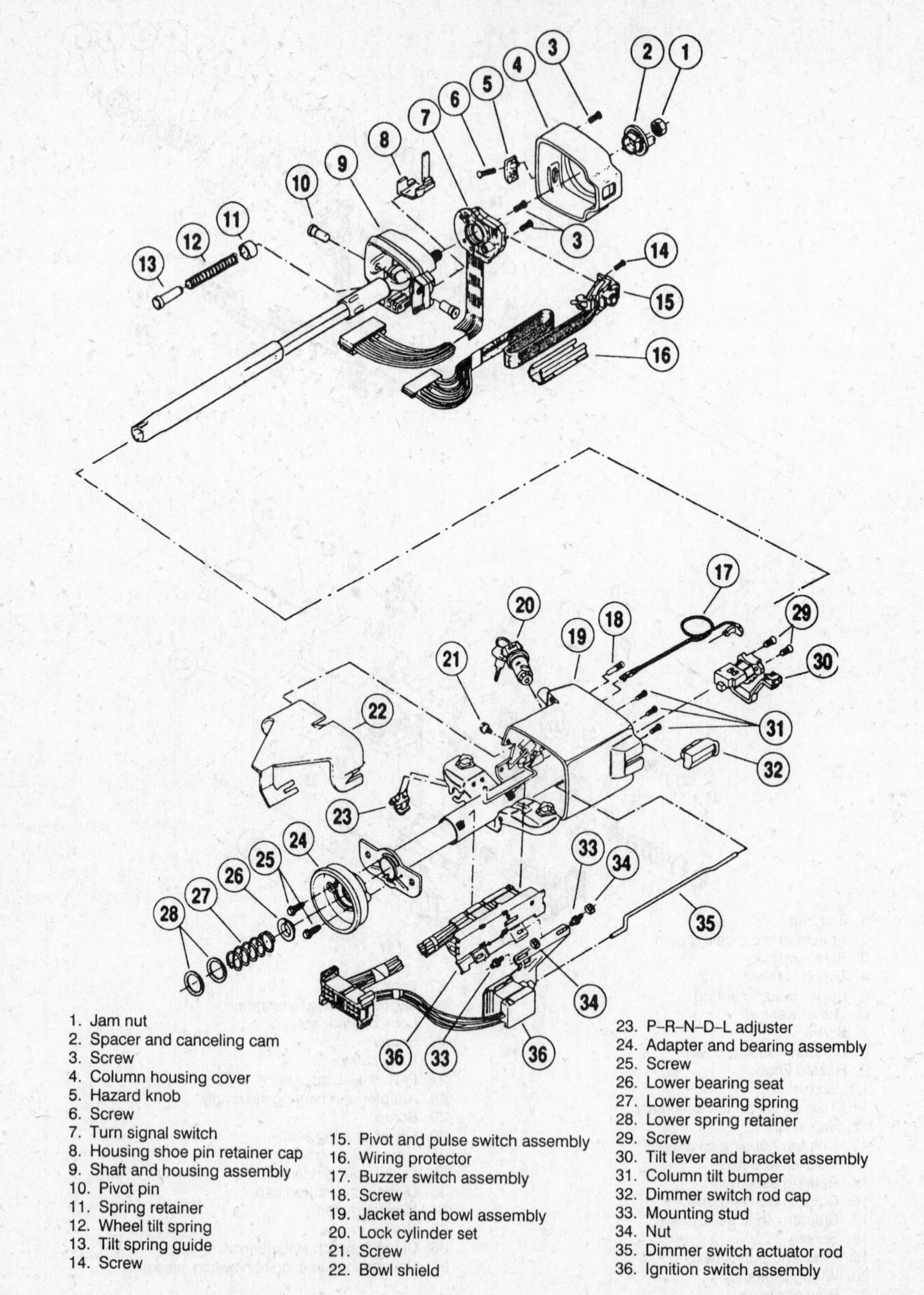
1. Jam nut
2. Spacer and canceling cam
3. Screw
4. Column housing cover
5. Hazard knob
6. Screw
7. Turn signal switch
8. Housing shoe pin retainer cap
9. Shaft and housing assembly
10. Pivot pin
11. Spring retainer
12. Wheel tilt spring
13. Tilt spring guide
14. Screw
15. Pivot and pulse switch assembly
16. Wiring protector
17. Buzzer switch assembly
18. Screw
19. Jacket and bowl assembly
20. Lock cylinder set
21. Screw
22. Bowl shield
23. P-R-N-D-L adjuster
24. Adapter and bearing assembly
25. Screw
26. Lower bearing seat
27. Lower bearing spring
28. Lower spring retainer
29. Screw
30. Tilt lever and bracket assembly
31. Column tilt bumper
32. Dimmer switch rod cap
33. Mounting stud
34. Nut
35. Dimmer switch actuator rod
36. Ignition switch assembly

FIG. 23 Exploded view of the tilt steering column

To install:

18. To install the lock bolt, lubricate it with lithium grease and install the lock bolt, spring and retaining plate.
19. Lubricate the teeth on the switch actuator rack, install the rack and the ignition switch through the opening in the steering bolt until it rests on the retaining plate.
20. Install the steering column lock cylinder set by holding the barrel of the lock cylinder, inserting the key and turning the key to the **ACCESSORY** position.
21. Install the lock set in the steering column while holding the rack against the lock plate.
22. Install the lock retaining screw. Insert the key in the lock cylinder and turn the lock cylinder to the **START** position and the rack will extend.
23. Center the slotted holes on the ignition switch mounting plate and install the ignition switch mounting screw and nut.
24. Install the dimmer switch and actuator rod into the center slot on the switch mounting plate.
25. Install the buzzer switch and turn the lock cylinder to the RUN position. Push the switch in until it is bottomed out with the plastic tab that covers the lock retaining screw.
26. Install the steering shaft and turn signal housing as an assembly.
27. Install the turn signal switch. Install the steering wheel to the column, and torque the steering shaft nut to 30 ft. lbs. (41 Nm).
28. Install the steering column in the vehicle. Connect all electrical leads. Install the lower trim panels.
29. Connect the negative battery cable and check for proper operation.

Steering Column

REMOVAL & INSTALLATION

1. Disconnect the negative battery cable.
2. Remove the lower left hand trim panel below the steering column.
3. Push the top of the intermediate shaft seal down for access to the intermediate shaft seal coupling.
4. Remove the intermediate shaft coupling pinch bolt.
5. Disconnect the shift indicator cable end and casing from the column. If the vehicle is equipped with park lock, disconnect the park lock cable from the column.
6. Disconnect the shift cable from the ball stud on the shift lever.
7. Remove the lower column bolts first and then remove the upper bolts. Lower the column to the seat.
8. Disconnect the electrical connectors, and remove the column from the vehicle.

To install:

9. Install the column into the vehicle and loosely install the column bolts. Install the intermediate shaft pinch bolt and tighten to 35 ft. lbs. (48 Nm).
10. Connect the electrical connector and all the shift cables. Connect the park lock cable, if equipped.
11. Tighten the steering column mounting bolts to 18 ft. lbs. (25 Nm).
12. Reposition the intermediate shaft seal and install the trim panel.
13. Connect the negative battery cable and check ALL steering column-mounted components for proper operation.

DISASSEMBLY

➧ SEE FIGS. 22 AND 23

Standard Column

1. Disconnect the negative battery cable.
2. Refer to "Turn Signal Switch" removal and remove all necessary components to remove the turn signal switch.
3. Remove the two lower spring retainers and discard them.
4. Remove the lower bearing spring and lower bearing seat.
5. Remove the adaptor screws, adaptor, and lower bearing assembly.
6. Place the lock cylinder in the **RUN** position.
7. Place the opening in retaining ring over the flat on the steering shaft. Remove the retaining ring with a small prying tool, and discard the ring.
8. Remove the thrust washer, upper bearing spring, and washer.
9. Remove the steering shaft from the lower end of the jacket and bowl assembly. Remove the housing screws.
10. Remove the steering column housing and housing spacer.
11. Remove the bearing using a drift and discard.
12. Remove the buzzer switch and lock cylinder.
13. Remove the rod cap from the dimmer switch rod, and remove the jacket and bowl assembly.

To install:

14. Install the rod cap into the jacket and bowl assembly.
15. Place the lock cylinder into the **OFF/LOCK** position and remove the key. Install the lock cylinder and lock retaining screw.
16. Insert the buzzer switch into its bore until bottomed with the plastic tab covering the retaining screw.
17. Lubricate the new bearing with lithium-based grease and press onto the housing using a $1^1/_2$ in. (38mm) socket until bottomed.
18. Install the housing spacer and steering column housing. Install the retaining screws.
19. Turn the lock cylinder to the **RUN** position and insert steering shaft into the lower end of the jacket and bowl assembly until the shaft rests against the bearing. The shaft will extend $2^1/_2$ in. (63.5mm) beyond the highest surface of the steering column housing when installed properly.
20. Install the thrust washer, upper bearing spring and thrust washer.
21. Install a new retaining ring onto the shaft until it seats in its groove.
22. Install the adaptor and lower bearing assembly. Install the adaptor screws.
23. Install the lower bearing seat and lower bearing spring.
24. Install two new lower spring retainers, compress the spring until the retainers are positioned 1.14 in. (29mm) from the lower end of the steering shaft.
25. Install the turn signal switch and all related parts.

Tilt Column

➡ Tilt wheel pivot pin removal tool J 21854-01 or equivalent will be needed to complete this procedure. Obtain this tool before attempting anything past Step 8 of the following procedure. Remove the two pivot pins in Step 9 using the aforementioned special tool only. Do not use screws to extract the pins! Follow the instructions furnished with the tool when using it.

1. Disconnect the negative battery cable.
2. Refer to "Turn Signal Switch" removal and remove all necessary components to remove the turn signal switch.
3. Place the tilt column in its highest position.
4. Insert a phillips head screwdriver into the square opening in the spring retainer, push down hard , and very carefully turn to the left to slowly release the retainer and wheel tilt spring.
5. Remove the spring retainer, tilt spring, and tilt spring guide.
6. Remove the two lower spring retainers and discard them.

7. Remove the lower bearing spring and lower bearing seat.

8. Remove the adaptor screws, adaptor, and lower bearing assembly.

9. Remove the two pivot pins using tool J 21854–01 or equivalent.

10. Place the lock cylinder in the **RUN** position.

11. Pull the tilt lever to release the shaft and housing assembly. Remove the shaft and housing assembly from the jacket and bowl assembly.

12. Place the lock cylinder into the **OFF/LOCK** position and remove the key. Remove the buzzer switch and lock cylinder.

13. Remove the column tilt bumpers.

14. Remove the tilt bracket screws, tilt lever and bracket assembly.

15. Remove the rod cap from the dimmer switch rod, and remove the jacket and bowl assembly.

To Install:

16. Install the rod cap into the jacket and bowl assembly.

17. Install the tilt lever and bracket assembly into the jacket and bowl assembly. Install the retaining screws.

18. Install the tilt bumpers until bottomed.

19. With the lock cylinder in the **OFF/LOCK** position and the key removed, install the lock cylinder and lock retaining screw.

20. Insert the buzzer switch into its bore until bottomed with the plastic tab covering the retaining screw.

21. Insert the key and place in the **RUN** position.

22. Install the shaft and housing assembly.

23. Lubricate the pivot pins with lithium-based grease, and install the pins in their bores until bottomed.

24. Place the tilt column in its highest position.

25. Lubricate the tilt spring guide with lithium-based grease, and install the guide into the tilt spring.

26. Make sure the recess in the spring guide engages around the locating tab in the jacket and bowl assembly. Insert the phillips head screwdriver into the square opening in the spring retainer, carefully push down, and turn to the right to lock in place.

27. Install the adaptor and lower bearing assembly. Install the retaining screws.

28. Install the lower bearing seat and lower bearing spring.

29. Install two new lower spring retainers, compress the spring until the retainers are positioned 1.14 in. (29mm) from the lower end of the steering shaft.

30. Install the turn signal switch and all related parts.

Steering Linkage

➧ SEE FIGS. 24 AND 25

REMOVAL & INSTALLATION

Outer Tie Rod Ends

1. Disconnect the negative battery cable.

2. Remove the cotter pin and hex slotted nut from the outer tie rod assembly.

3. Loosen the jam nut and remove the tie rod from the steering knuckle using a steering linkage removing tool J–35917 or equivalent.

4. Holding the inner tie rod stationary, count the amount of turns to remove the outer tie rod.

To install:

5. Lubricate the inner rod threads with anti-seize compound and install the outer tie rod the same amount of turns that it took to remove.

6. Install the outer tie rod-to-knuckle and install the slotted nut. Torque the nut to 40 ft. lbs. (54 Nm) and to 45 ft. lbs. (60 Nm) maximum to align the cotter pin slot. Do NOT back off to align the cotter pin.

7. Install a new cotter pin and bend over. Torque the jam nut to 50 ft. lbs. (70 Nm) and connect the negative battery cable.

8. Have a qualified alignment technician adjust the toe angle.

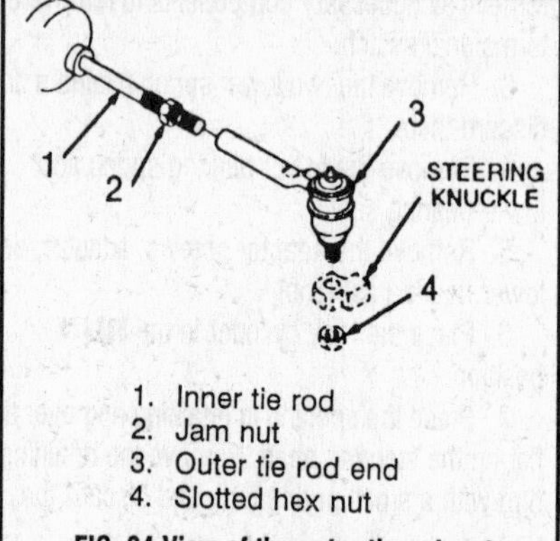

FIG. 24 View of the outer tie rod end

Inner Tie Rod

1. Disconnect the negative battery cable.

2. Remove the rack and pinion assembly from the vehicle as outlined in this Section.

3. Remove the outer tie rod end as previously outlined.

4. Remove the jam nut, boot clamps and boot. Use side cutters to cut the boot clamps.

5. Remove the shock dampener from the inner tie rod and slide back on the rack. Do not let the rack slide out of the rack housing while the tie rods are moved.

6. Place suitable wrenches on the flats of the rack and inner tie rod assemblies.

7. Rotate the housing counterclockwise until the inner rod separates from the rack.

To install:

8. Install the inner tie rod end onto the rack and torque to 70 ft. lbs. (95 Nm) with suitable wrenches.

9. Support the rack assembly in a vise.

10. Stake both sides of the inner tie rod housing to the flats on the rack.

11. Slide the shock dampener over the housing until it engages.

12. Install the boot and new boot clamps. Do NOT tighten the clamps at this time.

13. Apply grease to the inner tie rod, housing and boot.

14. Align the breather tube with the boot, making sure it is not twisted.

15. Crimp the boot clamps with a keystone clamp pliers tool J-22610 or equivalent.

16. Install the jam nut and outer tie rod end.

17. Install the rack and pinion assembly into the vehicle as outlined in this Section. Recheck each operation to ensure completion of repair. Make sure all fasteners have been torqued before moving the vehicle.

18. Have a qualified alignment technician adjust the front toe angle.

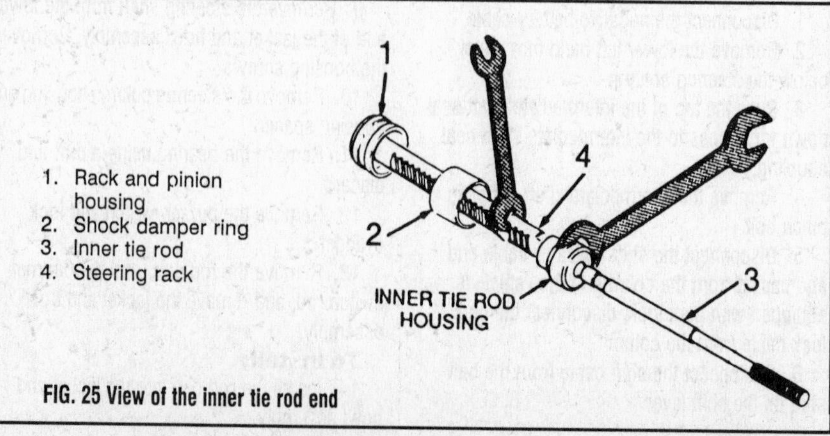

FIG. 25 View of the inner tie rod end

Power Rack and Pinion Steering Gear

➧ SEE FIG. 26

REMOVAL & INSTALLATION

1. Disconnect the negative battery cable.
2. Raise the vehicle and support with jackstands. Remove the front wheels.
3. Remove the intermediate shaft lower pinch bolt at the steering gear (end of the steering column shaft). Remove the intermediate shaft from the stub shaft.

✲✲ CAUTION

Failure to disconnect the intermediate shaft from the rack and pinion stub shaft may result in damage to the steering gear. This damage may cause a loss of steering control and may cause personal injury.

4. Remove both tie rod ends from the knuckle using a tie rod puller tool J–35917 or equivalent.
5. Support the vehicle body with jackstands so that the frame assembly can be lowered.

➡ **Do NOT lower the frame too far; engine components near the firewall may be damaged.**

6. Remove the rear frame bolts and lower the rear of the frame up to 5 in. (128mm).
7. Remove the heat shield, pipe retaining clip and the fluid pipes from the rack assembly. Use flare nut wrenches to remove the fluid pipes.
8. Remove the rack mounting bolts, nuts and rack assembly. Remove the rack assembly out through the left wheel opening.

To install:

9. Install the rack assembly through the left wheel opening.
10. Install the mounting bolts and nuts. Torque the bolts to 59 ft. lbs. (80 Nm).
11. Install the fluid pipes with new O-rings using flare nut wrenches.
12. Install the pipe retaining clips and heat shield.
13. Raise the frame and install the rear bolts. Torque the rear bolts to 103 ft. lbs. (140 Nm).
14. Install the tie rod ends, nut and cotter pin.

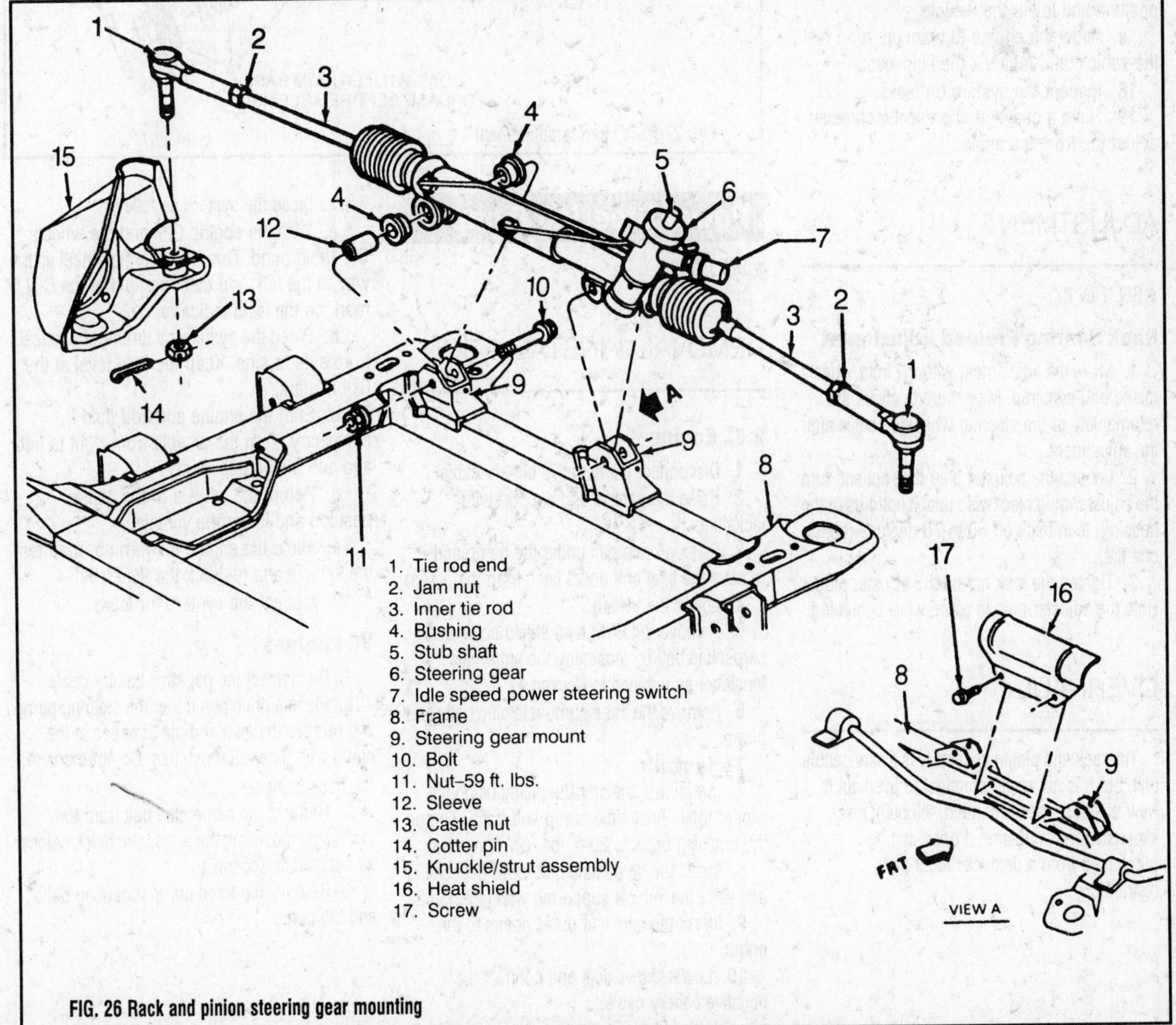

FIG. 26 Rack and pinion steering gear mounting

Torque the nuts to 40 ft. lbs. (54 Nm). Always use a new cotter pin.

15. Install the intermediate shaft-to-stub shaft. Torque the lower pinch bolt to 40 ft. lbs. (54 Nm).

16. Install the front wheels, lower the vehicle and fill the steering pump with GM steering fluid or its equivalent.

17. Bleed the power steering system as follows.

a. With the engine OFF and the wheels OFF the ground. Turn the steering wheel all the way to the left, add steering fluid to the COLD mark on the level indicator.

b. Bleed the system by turning the wheels from side to side. Keep the fluid level at the COLD mark.

c. Start the engine and add fluid if necessary. Turn the wheels from right to left and add fluid if necessary.

d. Return the wheels to the center position and lower the vehicle.

e. Allow the engine to warm up, road test the vehicle and recheck the fluid level.

18. Inspect the system for leaks.

19. Have a qualified alignment technician adjust the front toe angle.

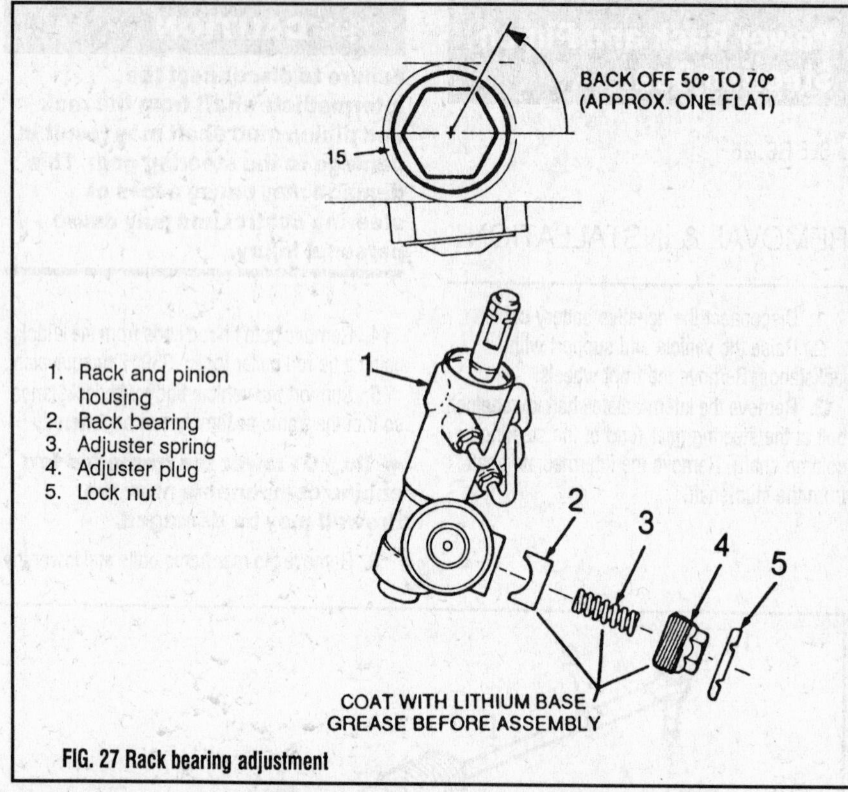

FIG. 27 Rack bearing adjustment

ADJUSTMENT

➧ SEE FIG. 27

Rack Bearing Preload Adjustment

1. Make the adjustment with the front wheels raised and centered. Make sure to check the returnability of the steering wheel to center after the adjustment.

2. Loosen the adjuster plug lock nut and turn the adjuster plug clockwise until it bottoms in the housing, then back off 50 to 70 degrees (about one flat).

3. Tighten the lock nut on the adjuster plug. Hold the adjuster plug in place while tightening.

OVERHAUL

The rack and pinion assembly is a serviceable unit, but it is not really practical to overhaul it. New units are recommended, although less expensive remanufactured ones can be purchased from a dealer or local parts distributor.

Power Steering Pump

➧ SEE FIG. 28

REMOVAL & INSTALLATION

2.5L Engine

1. Disconnect the negative battery cable.

2. Raise the vehicle and support with jackstands.

3. Place a drain pan under the pump and remove the inlet and outlet lines from the pump.

4. Lower the vehicle.

5. Remove the ECM heat shield cover and serpentine belt by loosening the automatic tensioner as outlined in Section 1.

6. Remove the three pump retaining bolts and pump.

To install:

7. If required, transfer the pulley using the proper tools. Install the pump and bolts. Torque the retaining bolts to 20 ft. lbs. (27 Nm).

8. Install the serpentine belt, ECM heat shield and raise the vehicle supported with jackstands.

9. Install the inlet and outlet hoses to the pump.

10. Lower the vehicle and connect the negative battery cable.

11. Bleed the system as follows.

a. With the engine OFF and the wheels OFF the ground. Turn the steering wheel all the way to the left, add steering fluid to the COLD mark on the level indicator.

b. Bleed the system by turning the wheels from side to side. Keep the fluid level at the COLD mark.

c. Start the engine and add fluid if necessary. Turn the wheels from right to left and add fluid if necessary.

d. Return the wheels to the center position and lower the vehicle.

e. Allow the engine to warm up, road test the vehicle and recheck the fluid level.

12. Inspect the system for leaks.

V6 Engines

1. Disconnect the negative battery cable.

2. Place a drain pan under the steering pump and remove the inlet and outlet hoses at the pump with flare nut wrenches. Do not damage the hose fittings.

3. Remove the serpentine belt from the pulleys by loosening the automatic belt tensioner as outlined in Section 1.

4. Remove the three pump mounting bolts and the pump.

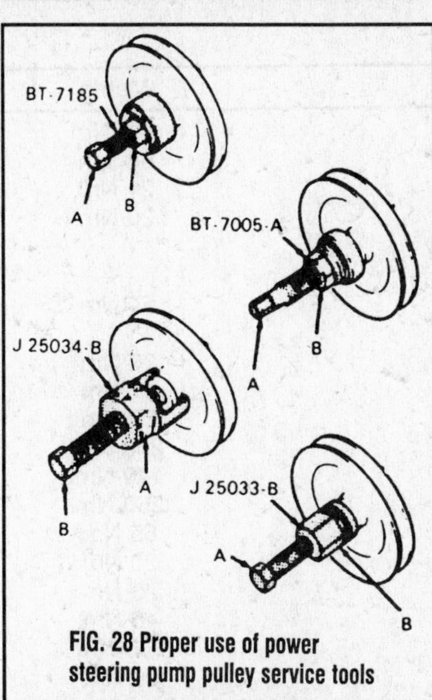

FIG. 28 Proper use of power steering pump pulley service tools

5. Remove the pump reservoir as follows.
 a. Using a suitable pry bar, remove the retaining clips from the reservoir.
 b. Separate the reservoir from the pump.
 c. Install the reservoir to the pump with a new O-ring seal and install the retaining clip. Make sure the tabs are fully engaged on the pump.
6. Remove the pump pulley using a power steering pump pulley removing tool J–25034–B or equivalent.

To install:

7. Install the reservoir and pulley to the pump.
8. Install the pump and retaining bolts. Torque the retaining bolts to 20 ft. lbs. (27 Nm).
9. Install the serpentine belt and ECM heat shield.
10. Install the inlet and outlet hoses using new O-rings, if so equipped.
11. Fill the reservoir with power steering fluid and connect the negative battery cable.
12. Bleed the system as follows.
 a. With the engine OFF and the wheels OFF the ground. Turn the steering wheel all the way to the left, add steering fluid to the COLD mark on the level indicator.
 b. Bleed the system by turning the wheels from side to side. Keep the fluid level at the COLD mark.
 c. Start the engine and add fluid if necessary. Turn the wheels from right to left and add fluid if necessary.
 d. Return the wheels to the center position and lower the vehicle.
 e. Allow the engine to warm up, road test the vehicle and recheck the fluid level.
13. Check the system for leaks, road test and recheck the fluid level.

OVERHAUL

The power steering pump assembly is a serviceable unit, but it is not really practical to overhaul it. New units are recommended, although less expensive remanufactured ones can be purchased from a dealer or local parts distributor.

Power Steering Hoses

REMOVAL & INSTALLATION

1. Disconnect the negative battery cable.
2. Raise the vehicle and support with jackstands.
3. Place a drain pan under the steering gear. Remove the inlet and outlet hoses from the steering gear using flare nut wrenches.
4. Remove the hose clamp from the frame.
5. Remove the inlet and outlet hoses from the steering pump.

To install:

6. Replace the O-rings if necessary.
7. Install the hoses-to-steering pump, do NOT tighten at this time.
8. Install the hoses-to-steering gear and tighten all fittings, using flare nut wrenches.
9. Install the hose clamp-to-frame and connect the negative battery cable.
10. Refill the pump reservoir with power steering fluid and bleed the system as follows.
 a. With the engine OFF and the wheels OFF the ground. Turn the steering wheel all the way to the left, add steering fluid to the COLD mark on the level indicator.
 b. Bleed the system by turning the wheels from side to side. Keep the fluid level at the COLD mark.
 c. Start the engine and add fluid if necessary. Turn the wheels from right to left and add fluid if necessary.
 d. Return the wheels to the center position and lower the vehicle.
 e. Allow the engine to warm up, road test the vehicle and recheck the fluid level.
11. Check the system for leaks, road test and recheck the fluid level.

TORQUE SPECIFICATIONS

Component	U.S.	Metric
Wheel nuts	100 ft. lbs.	140 Nm
MacPherson strut shaft nut	72 ft. lbs.	98 Nm
Strut cover plate nuts	18 ft. lbs.	24 Nm
Lower ball joint nut plus at least an additional 90° 1½ flats turn until the cotter pin hole is lined up	15 ft. lbs.	20 Nm
Tie rod nut	40 ft. lbs.	54 Nm
Hub/bearing assembly-to-knuckle attaching bolts	52 ft. lbs.	70 Nm
Stabilizer shaft attaching bolts	35 ft. lbs.	47 Nm
Lower control arm-to-frame bolts	56 ft. lbs.	75 Nm
Halfshaft end nut	184 ft. lbs.	250 Nm
Front crossmember-to-body bolts	103 ft. lbs.	140 Nm
Trailing arm-to-knuckle bolt	192 ft. lbs.	260 Nm
Trailing arm-to-body bolt	48 ft. lbs.	65 Nm
Spring retention plate bolts	15 ft. lbs.	20 Nm
Rear jack pad mounting bolts	18 ft. lbs.	25 Nm
Rear strut-to-body bolts	34 ft. lbs.	46 Nm
Rear strut-to-knuckle bolts	133 ft. lbs.	180 Nm
Rear rod-to-knuckle bolt plus 90°	66 ft. lbs.	90 Nm
Rear rod-to-crossmember bolt plus 60°	81 ft. lbs.	110 Nm
Lower auxiliary spring bracket-to-rod nut	133 ft. lbs.	180 Nm
Steering wheel retaining nut	30 ft. lbs.	41 Nm
Intermediate shaft pinch bolt	35 ft. lbs.	48 Nm
Steering column mounting bolts	18 ft. lbs.	25 Nm
Tie rod adjustment jam nut	50 ft. lbs.	70 Nm
Inner tie rod intalled to the rack	70 ft. lbs.	95 Nm
Steering rack mounting bolts	59 ft. lbs.	80 Nm
Power steering pump retaining bolts	20 ft. lbs.	27 Nm

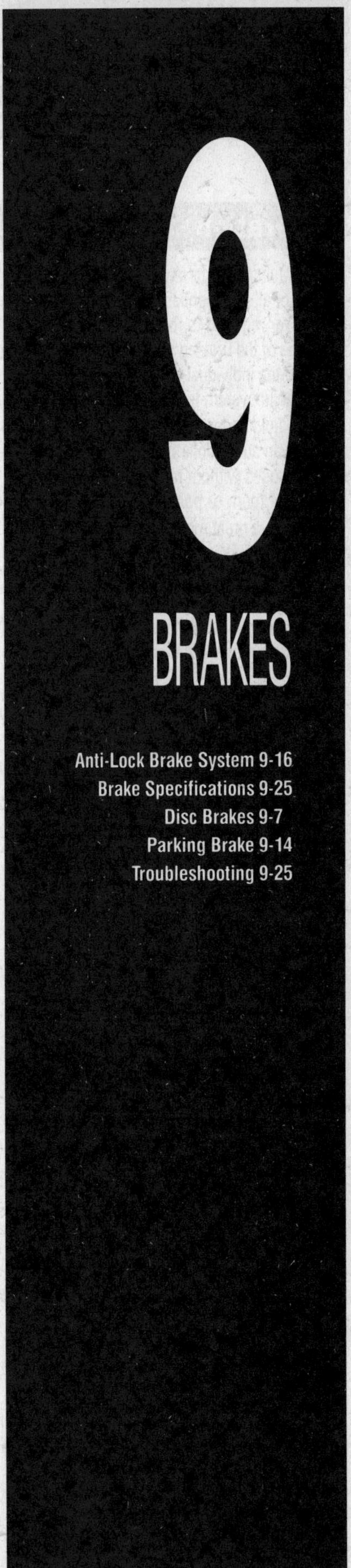

9
BRAKES
Anti-Lock Brake System 9-16
Brake Specifications 9-25
Disc Brakes 9-7
Parking Brake 9-14
Troubleshooting 9-25

STANDARD BRAKE SYSTEM

Operation

Hydraulic systems are used to actuate the brakes of all automobiles. The system transports the power required to force the frictional surfaces of the braking system together from the pedal to the individual brake units at each wheel. A hydraulic system is used for two reasons.

First, fluid under pressure can be carried to all parts of an automobile by small pipes and flexible hoses without taking up a significant amount of room or posing routing problems.

Second, a great mechanical advantage can be given to the brake pedal end of the system, and the foot pressure required to actuate the brakes can be reduced by making the surface area of the master cylinder pistons smaller than that of any of the pistons in the calipers.

The standard master cylinder consists of a fluid reservoir, double cylinder and piston assembly and internal proportioning valves. Double type master cylinders are designed to diagonally separate the left rear and right front from the right rear and left front braking systems hydraulically in case of a leak.

Steel lines carry the brake fluid to a point on the vehicle's frame near each of the vehicle's wheels. The fluid is then carried to the front and rear calipers by flexible tubes in order to allow for suspension and steering movements.

In disc brake systems, the pistons are part of the calipers. One or two pistons in each caliper is used to force the brake pads against the disc.

All pistons employ some type of seal, usually made of rubber, to prevent fluid leakage. A rubber dust boot seals the outer end of the cylinder against dust and dirt. The boot fits around the outer end of the piston on disc brake calipers.

The standard hydraulic system operates as follows: When at rest, the entire system, from the piston(s) in the master cylinder to those in the wheel calipers, is full of brake fluid. Upon application of the brake pedal, fluid trapped in front of the master cylinder piston(s) is forced through the lines to the wheel calipers. Here, it forces the pistons outward. The motion of the pistons is opposed by spring seals, in disc brakes.

Upon release of the brake pedal, a spring located inside the master cylinder immediately returns the master cylinder pistons to the normal position. The pistons contain check valves and the master cylinder has compensating ports drilled in it. These are uncovered as the pistons reach their normal position. The piston check valves allow fluid to flow toward the calipers as the pistons withdraw. Then, as the return springs force the brake pads into the released position, the excess fluid flows through the compensating ports into the reservoir. It is during the time the pedal is in the released position that any fluid that has leaked out of the system will be replaced through the compensating ports.

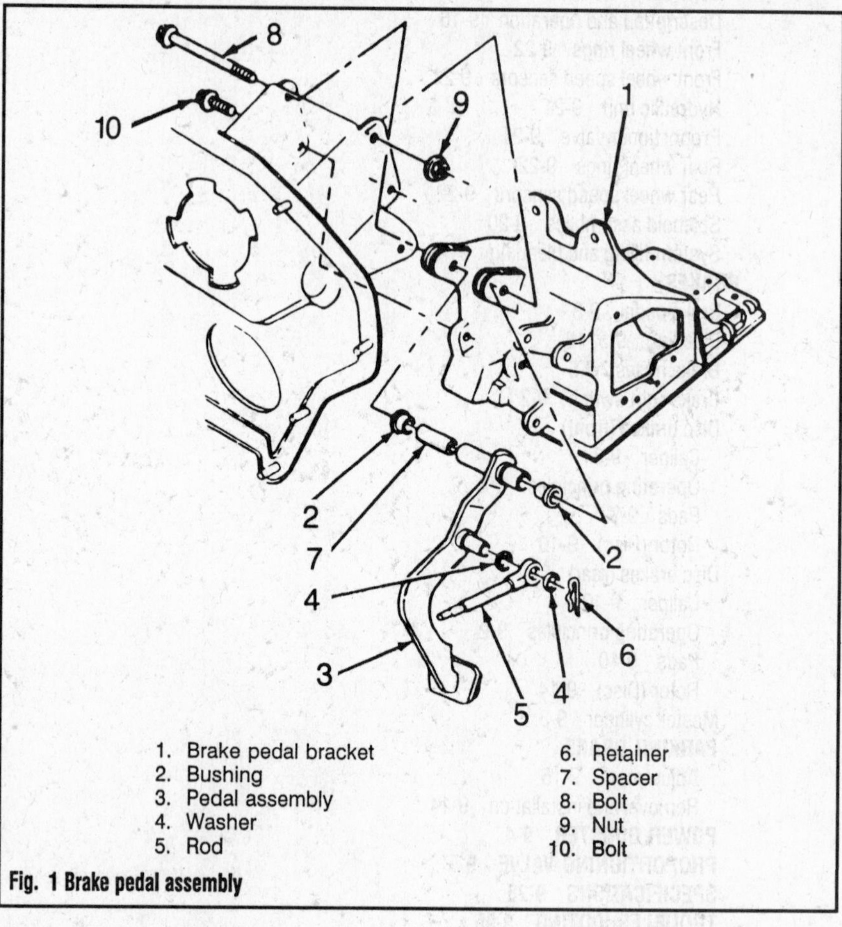

Fig. 1 Brake pedal assembly

Dual circuit master cylinders employ two pistons, located one behind the other, in the same cylinder. The primary piston is actuated directly by mechanical linkage from the brake pedal through the power booster. The secondary piston is actuated by fluid trapped between the two pistons. If a leak develops in front of the secondary piston, it moves forward until it bottoms against the front of the master cylinder, and the fluid trapped between the pistons will operate the rear brakes. If the rear brakes develop a leak, the primary piston will move forward until direct contact with the secondary piston takes place, and it will force the secondary piston to actuate the front brakes. In either case, the brake pedal moves farther when the brakes are applied, and less braking power is available.

All dual circuit systems use a switch to warn the driver when only half of the brake system is operational. This switch is located in a valve body which is mounted on the firewall or the frame below the master cylinder. A hydraulic piston receives pressure from both circuits, each circuit's pressure being applied to one end of the piston. When the pressures are in balance, the piston remains stationary. When one circuit has a leak, however, the greater pressure in that circuit during application of the brakes will push the piston to one side, closing the switch and activating the brake warning light.

In disc brake systems, the proportioning valves are designed to provide better front to rear braking balance with heavy application. The valve is used when more front apply force is needed to obtain normal braking pressure.

Warning lights may be tested by depressing the brake pedal and holding it while opening one of the wheel cylinder bleeder screws. If this does not cause the light to go on, substitute a new lamp, make continuity checks, and, finally, replace the switch as necessary.

The hydraulic system may be checked for leaks by applying pressure to the pedal gradually and steadily. If the pedal sinks very slowly to the floor, the system has a leak. This is not to be confused with a springy or spongy feel due to the compression of air within the lines. If the system leaks, there will be a gradual change in the position of the pedal with a constant pressure.

Check for leaks along all lines and at wheel cylinders. If no external leaks are apparent, the problem is inside the master cylinder.

Stoplamp Switch

REMOVAL & INSTALLATION

1. Disconnect the negative battery cable.
2. Remove the three fasteners from the left side insulator panel.
3. Slide the steering shaft protective cover towards the cowl.
4. Remove the vacuum hose at the cruise control cut off switch, if so equipped.
5. Remove the stoplamp switch-to-steering column bracket retaining pin.
6. Disconnect the electrical connector.
7. Push the switch arm to the left and towards the cowl to disconnect switch-to-pedal arm. Release the snap clip and remove the switch.

To install:

8. Install the switch and push up until it is seated into the top snap clip.
9. Install the electrical connectors.
10. Connect the switch to the pedal.
11. Install the switch-to-steering column retaining pin.
12. Install the vacuum hose if equipped with cruise control.
13. Install the steering shaft protective sleeve.
14. Adjust the stoplamp switch.
15. Install the left sound insulator, connect the negative battery cable and check switch operation.

Brake Pedal

➧ SEE FIG. 1

REMOVAL & INSTALLATION

1. Disconnect the negative battery cable.
2. Remove the driver's side sound insulator panel.
3. Remove the clevis pin, washer, rod, and spring washer from the pedal assembly.
4. Remove the stoplamp switch.
5. Remove the nut, bolt, bushings and sleeve from the pedal assembly.
6. Remove the brake pedal assembly from the pedal bracket.
7. Clean all parts and reverse the removal procedures to install. Lubricate all pivoting parts when installing.

Master Cylinder

➧ SEE FIGS. 2 AND 3

REMOVAL & INSTALLATION

➡ **Always use a proper size flare nut wrench when removing and installing the brake lines. Failure to use the proper wrench may cause damage to the line fittings.**

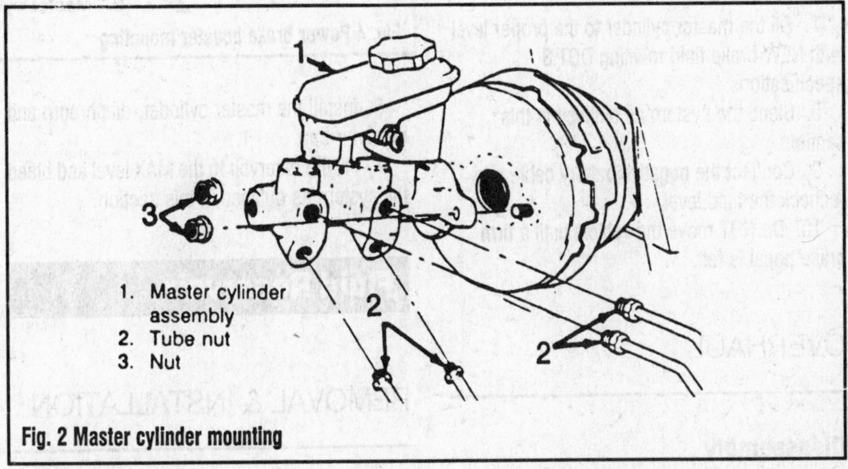

Fig. 2 Master cylinder mounting

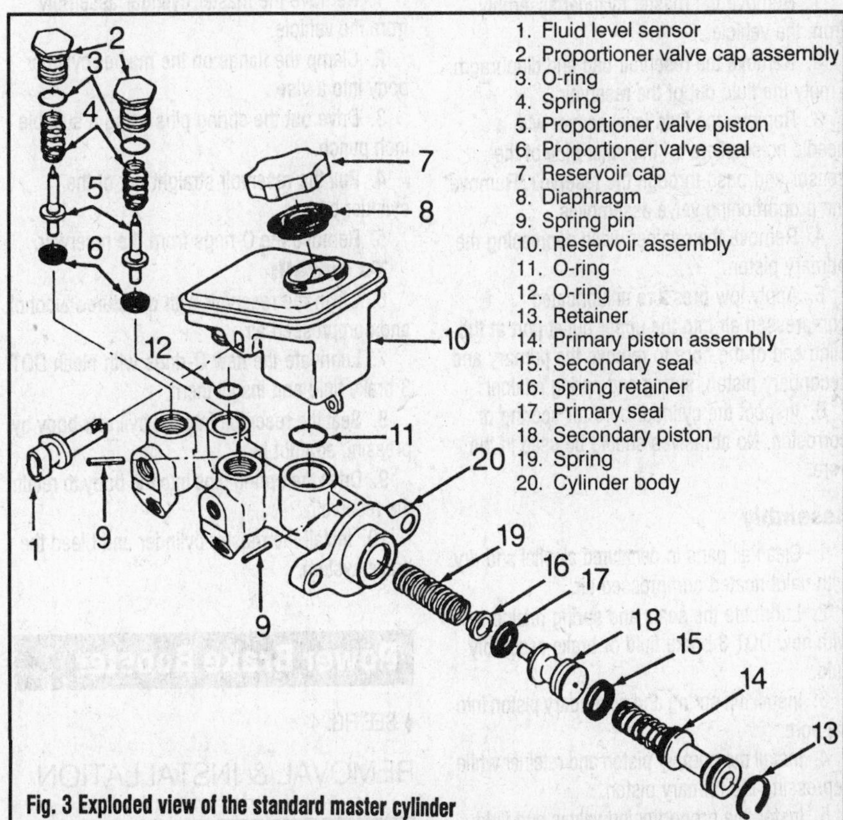

Fig. 3 Exploded view of the standard master cylinder

1. Disconnect the negative battery cable and fluid level sensor at the master cylinder.

2. Using a flare nut wrench, remove and plug the brake lines from the master cylinder. Plugging the lines will prevent fluid loss and contamination.

3. Remove the two master cylinder-to-brake power booster retaining nuts and remove the master cylinder.

To install:

4. Install the master cylinder and torque the retaining nuts to 20 ft. lbs. (27 Nm).

5. Connect the brake lines using a flare nut wrench.

6. Connect the fluid level sensor electrical wire.

7. Fill the master cylinder to the proper level with NEW brake fluid meeting DOT 3 specifications.

8. Bleed the system as outlined in this section.

9. Connect the negative battery cable and recheck the fluid level.

10. Do NOT move the vehicle until a firm brake pedal is felt.

OVERHAUL

Disassembly

1. Remove the master cylinder assembly from the vehicle.

2. Remove the reservoir cap and diaphragm. Empty the fluid out of the reservoir.

3. Remove the fluid level sensor with a needle noise pliers on the other side of the sensor and push through the reservoir. Remove the proportioning valve assemblies.

4. Remove the retainer while depressing the primary piston.

5. Apply low pressure unlubricated compressed air into the upper outlet port at the blind end of the bore to remove the primary and secondary piston, spring and spring retainer.

6. Inspect the cylinder bore for scoring or corrosion. No abrasives should be used in the bore.

Assembly

1. Clean all parts in denatured alcohol and dry with unlubricated compressed air.

2. Lubricate the seals and spring retainers with new DOT 3 brake fluid or brake assembly fluid.

3. Install the spring and secondary piston into the bore.

4. Install the primary piston and retainer while depressing the primary piston.

5. Install the proportioning valves and fluid level sensor.

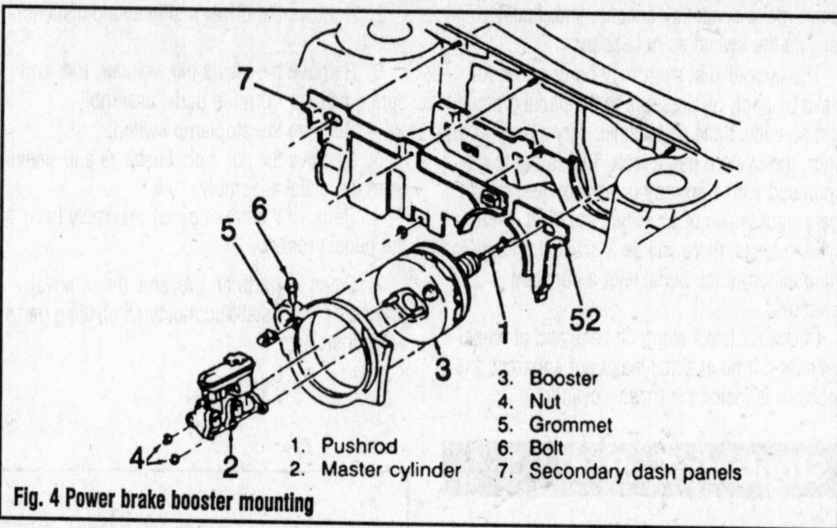

Fig. 4 Power brake booster mounting

6. Install the master cylinder, diaphragm and reservoir cap.

7. Fill the reservoir to the MAX level and bleed the system as outlined in this section.

Fluid Reservoir

REMOVAL & INSTALLATION

1. Remove the master cylinder assembly from the vehicle.

2. Clamp the flange on the master cylinder body into a vise.

3. Drive out the spring pins using a suitable inch punch.

4. Pull the reservoir straight out of the cylinder body.

5. Remove the O-rings from the reservoir.

To install:

6. Clean the reservoir with denatured alcohol and compressed air.

7. Lubricate the new O-rings with clean DOT 3 brake fluid and install them.

8. Seat the reservoir into the cylinder body by pressing straight in.

9. Drive the spring pins into the body to retain the reservoir.

10. Install the master cylinder and bleed the brake system.

Power Brake Booster

➧ SEE FIG. 4

REMOVAL & INSTALLATION

1. Disconnect the negative battery cable.

2. From inside the engine compartment, remove the panels around the booster assembly.

3. Remove the booster grommet bolt and grommet.

4. Remove the master cylinder from the power booster.

5. Scribe a mark on the front and rear booster covers in case the two covers get separated during removal.

➡ When disconnecting the pushrod from the brake pedal, the brake pedal must be kept stationary or damage to the brake switch may result.

6. Disconnect the brake pushrod from the brake pedal.

7. Unlock the booster from the front of the dash as follows.

a. Install a booster holding tool J-2280501 to the master cylinder mounting studs.

b. Torque the stud nuts to 28 ft. lbs. (38 Nm).

c. Use a suitable pry bar to pry the locking tab on the booster out of the locking notch on the mounting flange.

d. At the same time, turn the booster counterclockwise with a large wrench on the booster holding tool.

e. Do NOT attempt to remove the booster until the pushrod has been disconnected from the brake pedal.

To install:

8. Lubricate the inside and outside diameters of the grommet and front housing seal with silicone grease before installation.

9. Install the booster by turning the booster holding tool clockwise until the locking flanges are engaged. Make sure the locking tab is fully seated to prevent rotation of the booster.

10. Install the booster pushrod to the brake pedal.

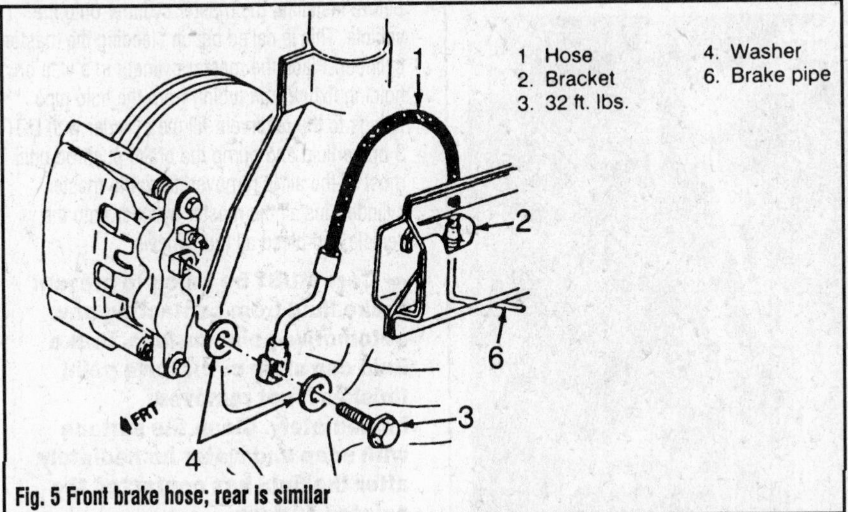

Fig. 5 Front brake hose; rear is similar

11. Install the master cylinder, booster grommet and secondary dash panel.

12. Connect the negative battery cable and bleed the system if the fluid pipes were disconnected from the master cylinder.

Proportioning Valves

REMOVAL & INSTALLATION

The proportioning valves are located in the master cylinder assembly. Refer to the "Master Cylinder" overhaul section and illustration in this Section for service procedures.

Brake Hoses

➧ SEE FIG. 5

REMOVAL & INSTALLATION

Front

1. Disconnect the negative battery cable.
2. Raise the vehicle and support with jackstands.
3. Remove the front wheel assembly.
4. Clean all dirt and foreign material from the brake hose and fitting.
5. Remove brake pipe from the brake hose at the bracket. Use flare nut and back-up wrenches to avoid fitting damage.
6. Remove the brake hose retainer at the mounting bracket.
7. Remove the hose from the bracket.
8. Remove the inlet fitting at the caliper, bolt and two copper washers.

To install:

9. Using new copper washers, install the inlet to the caliper. Torque the bolt to 30 ft. lbs. (40 Nm).
10. With the vehicle weight on the suspension, install the brake hose to the bracket and install the hose retainer. Make sure there are NO kinks in the hose.
11. Install the brake pipe to the hose and torque the fitting to 15 ft. lbs. (20 Nm).

✲✲ CAUTION

Make sure the hose is NOT kinked or touching any part of the frame or suspension after installation. These conditions may cause the hose to fail prematurely.

12. Check the hose after turning the steering wheel extreme right and then extreme left. If the hose is tight or touching anything, make the proper adjustments.
13. Install the wheel assembly.
14. Lower the vehicle and bleed the system as outlined in this Section.
15. Connect the negative battery cable and pump the brake pedal before moving the vehicle.

Rear

1. Disconnect the negative battery cable.
2. Raise the vehicle and support with jackstands.
3. Remove the rear wheel assembly.
4. Clean all dirt and foreign material from the brake hose and fitting.
5. Remove brake pipe from the brake hose at the bracket. Use flare nut and back-up wrenches to avoid fitting damage.
6. Remove the brake hose retainer at the mounting bracket.

7. Remove the hose from the bracket.
8. Remove the inlet fitting at the caliper, bolt and two copper washers.

To install:

9. Using new copper washers, install the inlet fitting to the caliper. Torque the bolt to 30 ft. lbs. (40 Nm).
10. With the vehicle weight on the suspension, install the brake hose to the bracket and install the hose retainer. Make sure there is NO kinks in the hose.
11. Install the brake pipe to the hose and torque the fitting to 15 ft. lbs. (20 Nm).

✲✲ CAUTION

Make sure the hose is NOT kinked or touching any part of the frame or suspension after installation. These conditions may cause the hose to fail prematurely.

12. Check the hose after turning the steering wheel extreme right and then extreme left. If the hose is tight or touching anything, make the proper adjustments.
13. Install the wheel assembly.
14. Lower the vehicle and bleed the system as outlined in this Section.
15. Connect the negative battery cable and pump the brake pedal before moving the vehicle.

Bleeding the Brake System

➡ The procedure for bleeding the ABS system differs from this one. Refer to the section on Bleeding under the "ANTI-LOCK BRAKING SYSTEM" head later in this section if working with ABS.

✲✲ CAUTION

The brake system MUST be bled after the hydraulic system has been serviced. Air enters the system when components are removed, and this air has to be removed to prevent a spongy pedal resulting in poor system performance.

➧ SEE FIGS. 5A–5B

The time required to bleed the system can be reduced by removing as much air as possible

FIG. 5A. Bleeding the front brakes

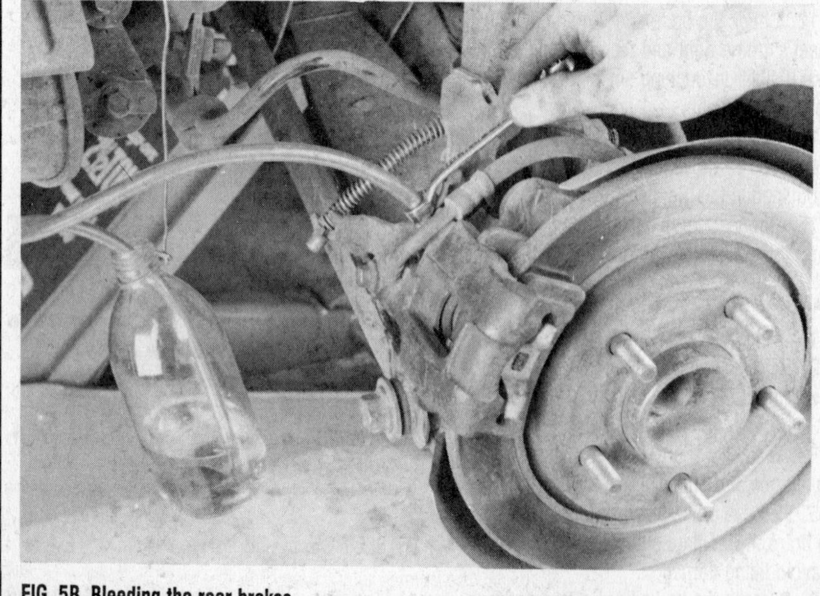
FIG. 5B. Bleeding the rear brakes

before installing the master cylinder onto the vehicle. This is called bench bleeding the master cylinder. Place the master cylinder in a vise or holding fixture, run tubing from the fluid pipe fittings to the reservoir, fill the cylinder with DOT 3 brake fluid and pump the brake pushrod until most of the air is removed from the master cylinder. Install the master cylinder onto the vehicle and bleed all four wheels.

➡ Care MUST be taken to prevent brake fluid from contacting any automotive paint surface. Brake fluid can stain or dissolve paint finishes if not removed immediately. Clean the surface with soap and water immediately after the fluid has contacted the painted surface.

1. Fill the master cylinder reservoir with brake fluid and keep the reservoir at least half full during the bleeding operation.
2. If the master cylinder has air in the bore, it must be removed before bleeding the calipers. Bleed the master cylinder as follows.
   a. Disconnect the forward brake pipe at the master cylinder.
   b. Fill the reservoir until fluid begins to flow from the forward pipe connector port.
   c. Reconnect the forward brake pipe and tighten.
   d. Depress the brake pedal slowly one time and hold. Loosen the forward brake pipe and purge the air from the bore. Tighten the brake pipe, wait 15 seconds and repeat until all air is removed.
   e. When the air is removed from the forward brake pipe, repeat the same procedures for the rear brake pipe.
3. Bleed the calipers in the following order, (right front, right rear, left rear, left front).
4. Install a box end wrench over the bleeder valve and connect a clear tube onto the valve. Place the other end of the tube into a container of new brake fluid. The end of the tube must be submerged in brake fluid.
5. Depress the brake pedal slowly one time and hold. Loosen the bleeder valve to purge the air from the caliper. Close the valve and release the pedal. Repeat the procedure until all air is removed from the brake fluid.
6. Do NOT pump the brake pedal rapidly; this causes the air to churn and make bleeding difficult.
7. After the calipers have been bled, check the brake pedal for sponginess and the BRAKE warning lamp for low fluid level.
8. Repeat the bleeding operation if a spongy pedal is felt.
9. Fill the reservoir to the MAX line.

FRONT DISC BRAKES

⁂ CAUTION

Some brake pads contain asbestos, which has been determined to be a cancer causing agent. Never clean the brake surfaces with compressed air! Avoid inhaling any dust from any brake surface! When cleaning brake surfaces, use a commercially available brake cleaning fluid.

Brake Pads

INSPECTION

The pad thickness should be inspected every time that the wheels are removed. Pad thickness can be checked by looking down through the inspection hole in the top of the caliper. If the thickness of the pad is worn to within 0.030 inch (0.76mm) (if the pads are the riveted type, be sure not to include the thickness of the rivets when measuring pad thickness), all the pads should be replaced. A thermal material is sandwiched between the lining and backing. Don't include this material when determining the lining thickness. This is the factory-recommended measurement. Your state's automobile inspection laws may be different.

⁂ CAUTION

Always replace all pads on both front wheels at the same time. Failure to do so will result in uneven braking action.

REMOVAL & INSTALLATION

➧ SEE FIGS. 6A–6E

1. Disconnect the negative battery cable.
2. Raise the vehicle and support with jackstands.
3. Remove the wheel and tire assembly.
4. Remove the two caliper mounting bolts. Remove the caliper and hang from the suspension with a piece of wire. Do not hang by the brake hose.
5. Using a suitable pry bar, lift up the outboard pad retaining spring so it will clear the center lug.
6. Remove the inboard pad by unsnapping the pad from the pistons.

To install:

7. Remove about 1/3 of the fluid from the brake reservoir with a syringe or equivalent.
8. Install the inboard pad to the caliper pistons. Bottom the pistons in the caliper bore using a C-clamp and the inboard brake pad.

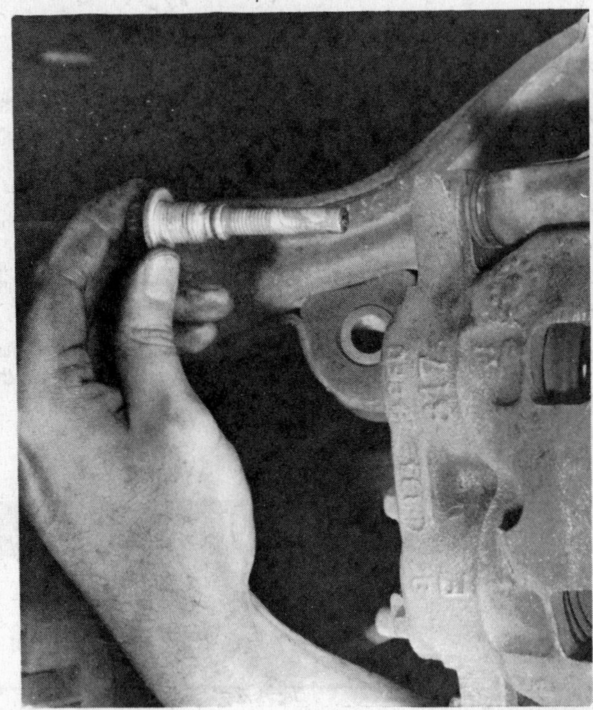

FIG. 6A. Removing or installing the top caliper mounting bolt

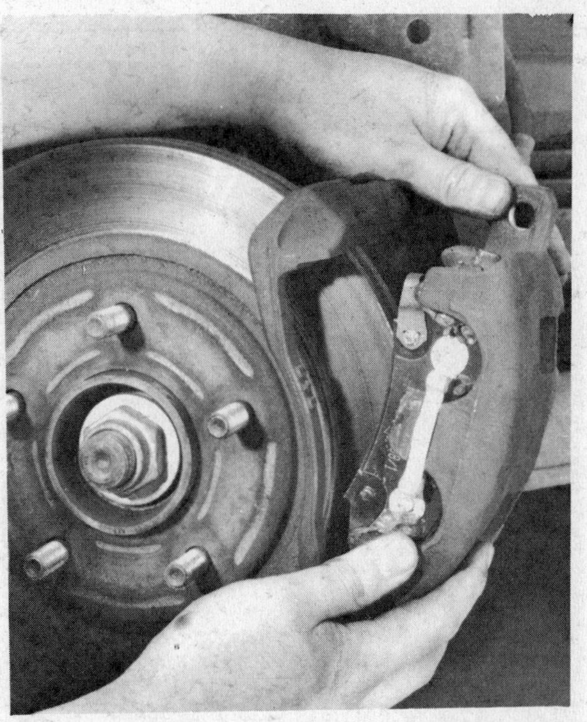

FIG. 6B. Remove or installing the front caliper from/to the adaptor

FIG. 6C. Prior to working on the pads, suspend the caliper with a wire to prevent damage to the brake hose

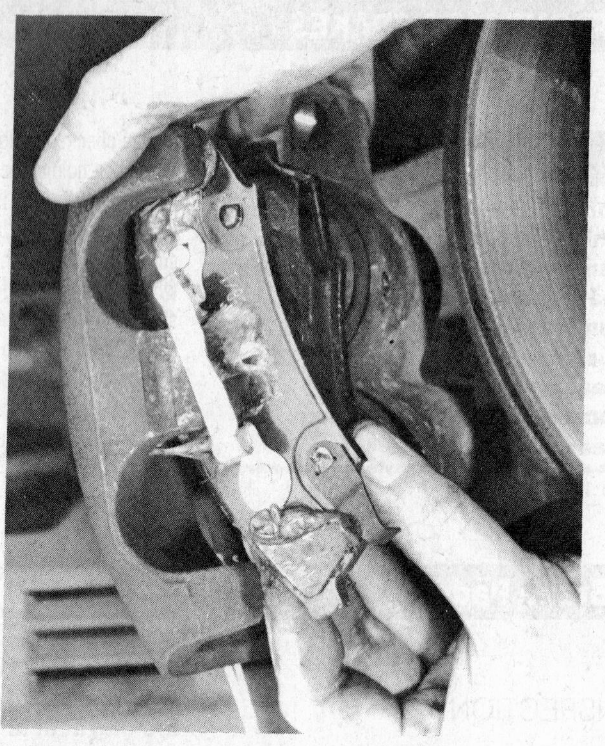

FIG. 6D. Removing or installing the outer pad

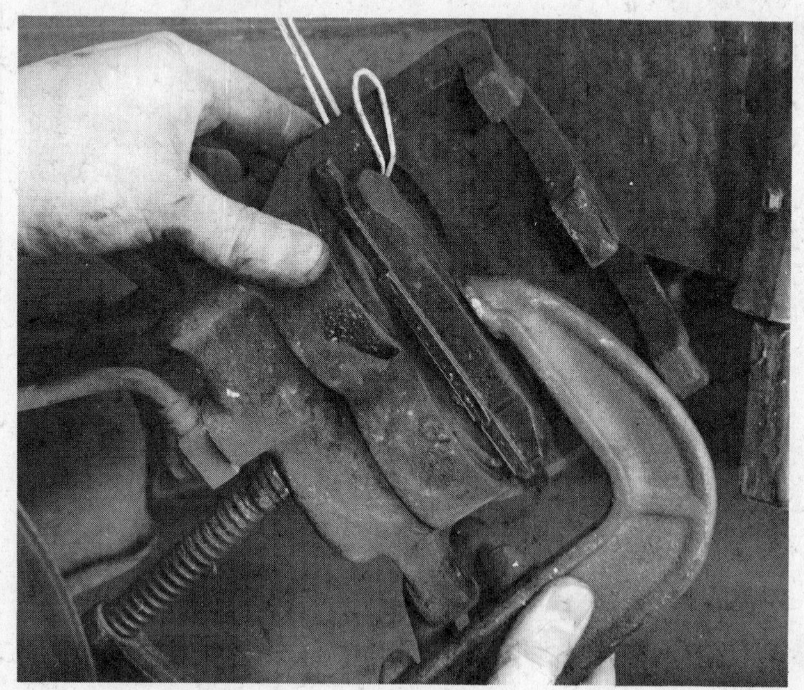

FIG. 6E. Bottoming the pistons in their bores using a C-clamp and the inner pad

9. Make sure both inboard pad tangs are inside the piston cavity.

10. Install the outboard pad by snapping the pad retainer spring over the housing center lug and into the housing slot.

11. Make sure both pads remain free of grease or oil. The wear sensor should be at the trailing edge of the pad during rotation.

12. Install the caliper assembly and wheels, and lower the vehicle.

13. Fill the master cylinder to the FULL mark and apply the brake pedal three times to seat the pads. Connect the negative battery cable.

Brake Caliper

➧ SEE FIGS. 6-8

REMOVAL & INSTALLATION

1. Remove of the brake fluid from the brake reservoir using a syringe or equivalent.

2. Raise the vehicle and support with jackstands.

3. Mark the relationship of the wheel to the hub and bearing assembly.

4. Remove the tire and wheel. Install two lug nuts to retain the rotor.
5. If the caliper is going to be removed, disconnect and plug the brake hose.
6. Remove the caliper mounting bolts and pull the caliper from the mounting bracket and rotor. Support the caliper with wire if not removing.

To install:

7. Inspect the bolt boots and support bushings for cuts or damage, replace if necessary.
8. Install the caliper over the rotor into the mounting bracket. Make sure the bolt boots are in place.
9. Lubricate the entire shaft of the mounting bolts and cavities with silicone grease.
10. Install the mounting bolts and torque to 79 ft. lbs. (107 Nm).
11. Install the brake hose, using new copper washers.
12. Remove the two wheel lugs, and install the wheels.
13. Lower the vehicle.
14. Fill the master cylinder and bleed the calipers as outlined in the "Brake System Bleeding" procedures in this Section.
15. Check for hydraulic leaks. Pump the brake pedal a few times before moving the vehicle.

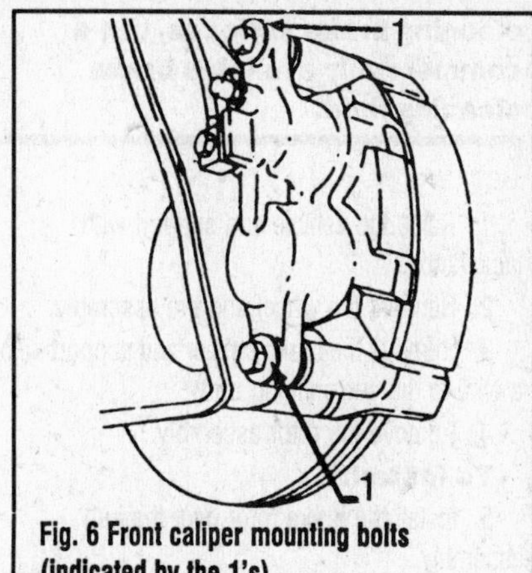

Fig. 6 Front caliper mounting bolts (indicated by the 1's)

Fig. 7 Compressing the dual caliper pistons

OVERHAUL

Disassembly

1. Remove the caliper assembly from the vehicle as outlined earlier in this Section.

**** CAUTION**

Do NOT place fingers in front of the pistons in an attempt to catch or protect them when applying compressed air. This could result in personal injury!

2. Remove the caliper pistons with compressed air applied into the caliper inlet hole.
3. If both pistons do not come out at the same time, use a piece of wood to back up the other piston until it starts moving.
4. Remove the boots with a non-metal prying tool.
5. Remove the piston seals using a seal pick.

Assembly

1. Carefully loosen the brake bleeder valve. If the valve breaks off, the caliper should be replaced.
2. Inspect the caliper bores, pistons and mounting threads for scoring or excessive wear.

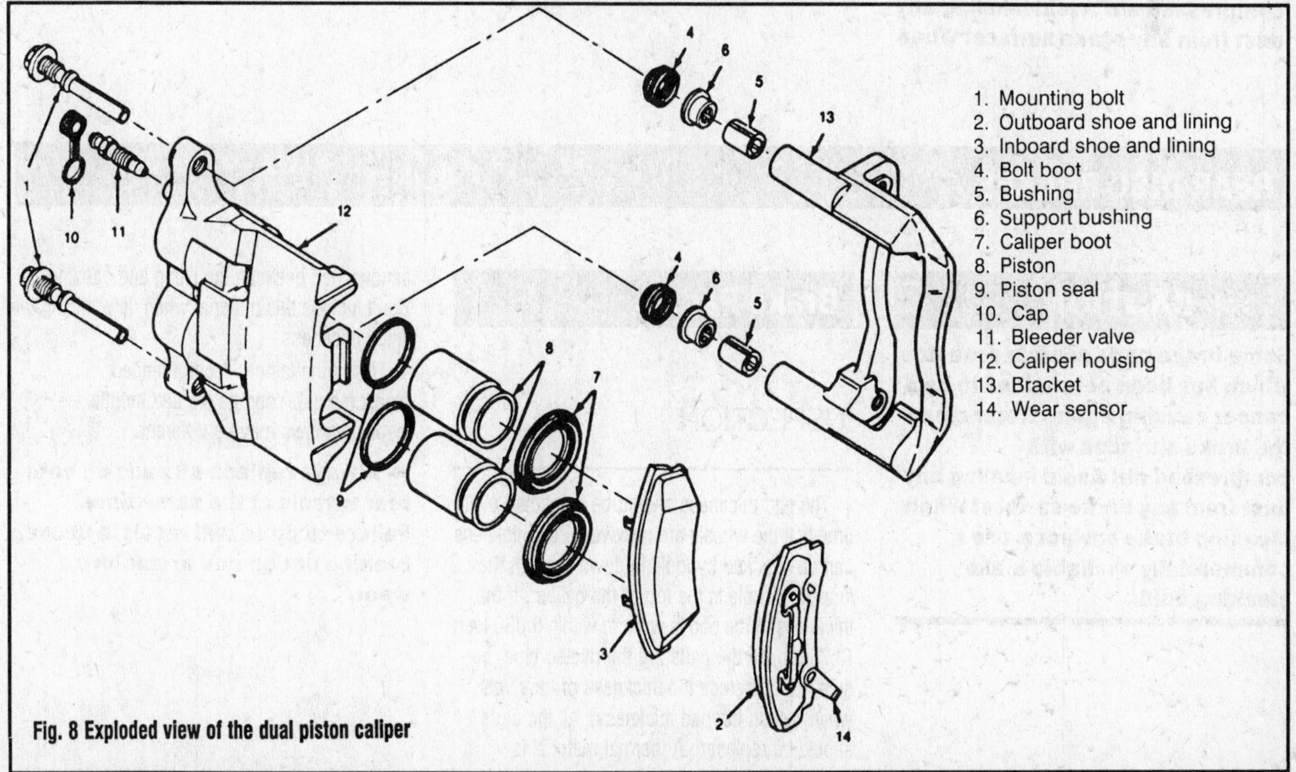

Fig. 8 Exploded view of the dual piston caliper

3. Use crocus cloth to polish out light corrosion from the piston and bore.
4. Clean all parts with denatured alcohol and dry with compressed air.
5. Lubricate and install the bleeder valve.
6. Lubricate the new piston seals and bore with clean brake fluid or brake assembly fluid.
7. Install the new seals and make sure they are not twisted.
8. Lubricate the piston bore.
9. Using the proper technique, use compressed air to install the pistons into the bore. Install the boots.
10. Install the caliper onto the vehicle.
11. Install the front wheel and bleed the brake system as outlined in the "Bleeding the Brake System" section in this Section.

Brake Rotor

REMOVAL & INSTALLATION

CAUTION

Some brake pads contain asbestos, which has been determined to be a cancer causing agent. Never clean the brake surfaces with compressed air! Avoid inhaling any dust from any brake surface! When cleaning brake surfaces, use a commercially available brake cleaning fluid.

1. Raise the vehicle and support with jackstands.
2. Remove the wheel and tire assembly.
3. Remove the brake caliper and support with a wire to the surrounding body.
4. Remove the rotor assembly.

To install:

5. Install the brake rotor over the hub assembly.
6. Install the brake caliper as outlined in this Section.
7. Install the wheel and tire assembly.
8. Lower the vehicle and pump the brake pedal before moving.

ROTOR INSPECTION

Thickness Variation Check

The thickness variation can be checked by measuring the thickness of the rotor at four or more points. All of the measurements must be made at the same distance from the edge of the rotor. A rotor the varies by more than 0.0005 inch (0.0127mm) can cause a pulsation in the brake pedal. If these measurement are excessive, the rotor should be refinished or replaced.

Lateral Runout Check

1. Remove the caliper and hang from the body with a piece of wire. Install two inverted lug nuts to retain the rotor.
2. Install a dial indicator to the steering knuckle so that the indicator button contacts the rotor about 1 in. (25mm) from the rotor edge.
3. Zero the dial indicator.
4. Move the rotor one complete revolution and observe the total indicated runout.
5. If the rotor runout exceeds 0.0015 inch (0.040mm) have the rotor refinished or replaced.

Refinishing Brake Rotors

All brake rotors have a minimum thickness dimension cast onto them. Do NOT use a brake rotor that will not meet minimum thickness specifications in the "Brake Specifications" chart at the end of this Section.

Accurate control of rotor tolerances is necessary for proper brake performance and safety. Machining of the rotor should be done by a qualified machine shop with the proper machining equipment.

The optimum speed for refinishing the rotor surface is a spindle speed of 200 rpm. Cross Feed for rough cutting should range from 0.006–0.010 in. (0.152–0.254mm) per revolution. The finish cuts should be made at crossfeeds no greater than 0.002 in. (0.05mm) per revolution.

REAR DISC BRAKES

CAUTION

Some brake pads contain asbestos, which has been determined to be a cancer causing agent. Never clean the brake surfaces with compressed air! Avoid inhaling any dust from any brake surface! When cleaning brake surfaces, use a commercially available brake cleaning fluid.

Brake Pads

INSPECTION

The pad thickness should be inspected every time that the wheels are removed. Pad thickness can be checked by looking down through the inspection hole in the top of the caliper. If the thickness of the pad is worn to within 0.030 inch (0.76mm) (if the pads are the riveted type, be sure not to include the thickness of the rivets when measuring pad thickness), all the pads should be replaced. A thermal material is sandwiched between the lining and backing. Don't include this material when determining the lining thickness.

This is the factory-recommended measurement. Your state's automobile inspection laws may be different.

➡ **Always replace all pads on both rear wheels at the same time. Failure to do so will result in uneven braking action and premature wear.**

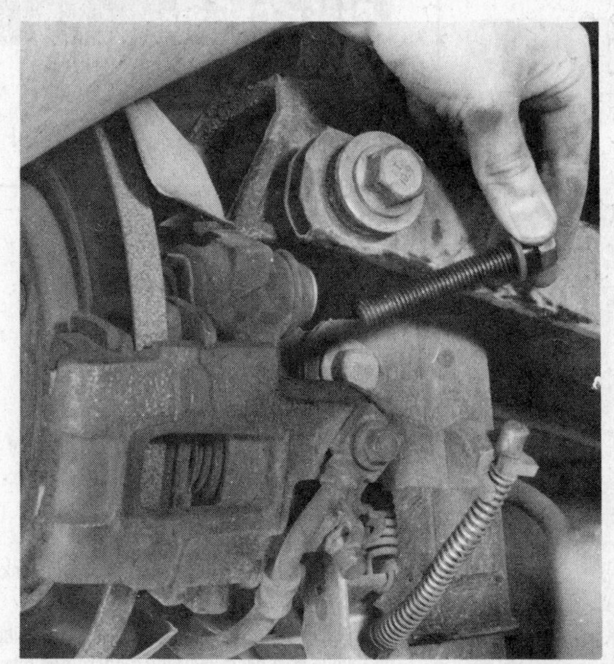

FIG. 9A. Removing or installing the top caliper mounting bolt

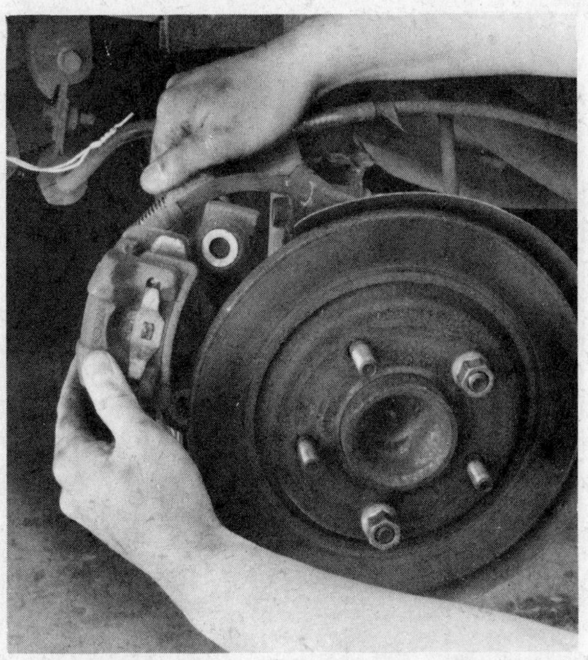

FIG. 9B. Remove or installing the rear caliper from/to the adaptor

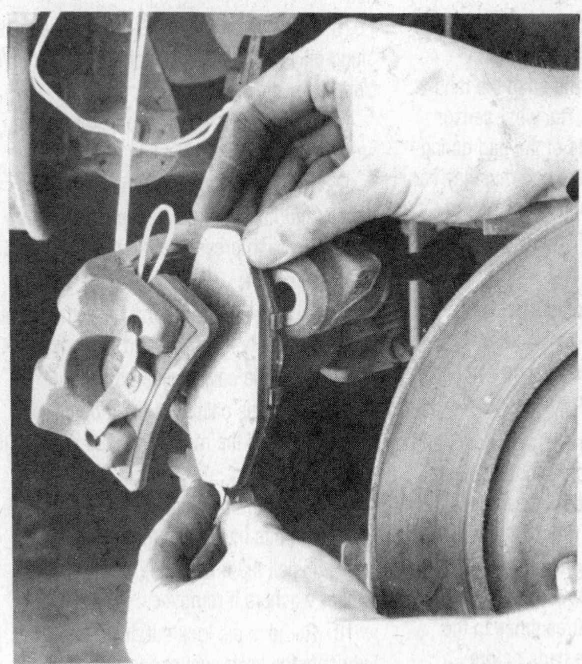

FIG. 9C. Prior to working on the pads, suspend the caliper with a wire to prevent damage to the brake hose. Inner pad service shown

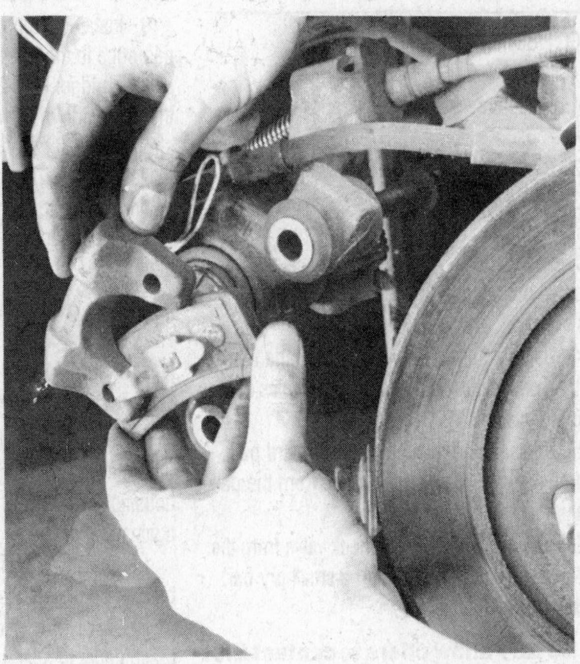

FIG. 9D. Removing or installing the outer pad from the retainer

FIG. 9E. Bottom the piston in its bore before installing the new pads

REMOVAL & INSTALLATION

➧ SEE FIGS. 9A–9E

1. Raise the vehicle and support with jackstands.
2. Remove the rear wheels assemblies.
3. Remove the rear caliper and hang by the suspension with a piece of wire to prevent brake hose damage. Refer to the "Front Caliper" removal procedures in this section for assistance.
4. Using a suitable pry bar, disengage the buttons on the outboard pad from the holes in the caliper housing.
5. Press in on the edge of the inboard pad and tilt outward to release the pad from the pad retainer.
6. Remove the two way check valve from the end of the caliper piston using a small pry bar.

To install:

➡ Do NOT allow pliers to contact the actuator screw. Protect the piston so the contact surface does not get damaged.

7. Bottom the piston into the caliper bore by positioning 12 in. (305mm) adjustable pliers over the caliper housing and piston surface.
8. Lubricate a new two way check valve and install it into the end of the piston.
9. Install the inboard brake pad. Engage the pad edge in the retainer tabs closest to the caliper bridge. Press down and snap the tabs at the open side of the caliper. The wear sensor should be at the leading edge of the pad during wheel rotation. The back of the pad must lay flat against the piston. The button on the back of the pad must engage the D-shaped notch in the piston.

➡ If the piston will not align or retract into the bore. Turn the piston clockwise using a piston turning tool J-7624 or equivalent.

10. Install the outboard brake pad. Snap the pad retainer spring into the slots in the caliper housing. The back of the pad must lay flat against the caliper.
11. Install the caliper onto the mounting bracket as outlined in this section.
12. Apply force at least three times to the brake pedal to seat the brake pads before moving the vehicle.
13. Install the rear wheels.
14. Lower the vehicle and check for fluid leaks.

Brake Caliper

➧ SEE FIG. 9

REMOVAL & INSTALLATION

1. Remove of the brake fluid from the reservoir with a syringe.
2. Raise the vehicle and support with jackstands.
3. Remove the rear wheel assembly and install two lug nuts to retain the rotor.
4. Remove the brake shield assembly.
5. Loosen the tension on the parking brake cable at the equalizer.
6. Remove the parking cable and return spring from the lever.
7. Hold the cable lever and remove the lock nut, lever and seal.
8. Push the piston into the caliper bore using two adjustable pliers over the inboard pad tabs.

➡ Do NOT allow pliers to contact the actuator screw. Protect the piston so the contact surface does not get damaged.

9. Reinstall the lever seal with the sealing bead against the caliper housing, lever and lock nut.
10. Remove and plug the brake hose inlet fitting only if the caliper is going to be removed from the vehicle.
11. Remove the bolt and bracket to gain access to the upper mounting bolt.
12. Remove the caliper mounting bolts, caliper and hang from the suspension with a piece of wire to prevent brake hose damage.

To install:

13. Inspect all brake parts for damage and deterioration. Replace any parts if necessary.
14. Push the caliper sleeves inward.
15. Install the caliper to the mounting bracket. Torque the mounting bolts to 92 ft. lbs. (125 Nm).
16. Install the bracket and bolt after the mounting bolts have been torqued.
17. Install the brake hose inlet with new copper washers if removed.
18. Remove the lock nut, lever and seal. Lubricate the lever seal and lever shift.
19. Install the seal and lever with the lever facing down.
20. Hold the lever back against the stop and torque the lock nut to 35 ft. lbs. (47 Nm).
21. Install the return spring and parking brake cable. Adjust the cable as outlined in the

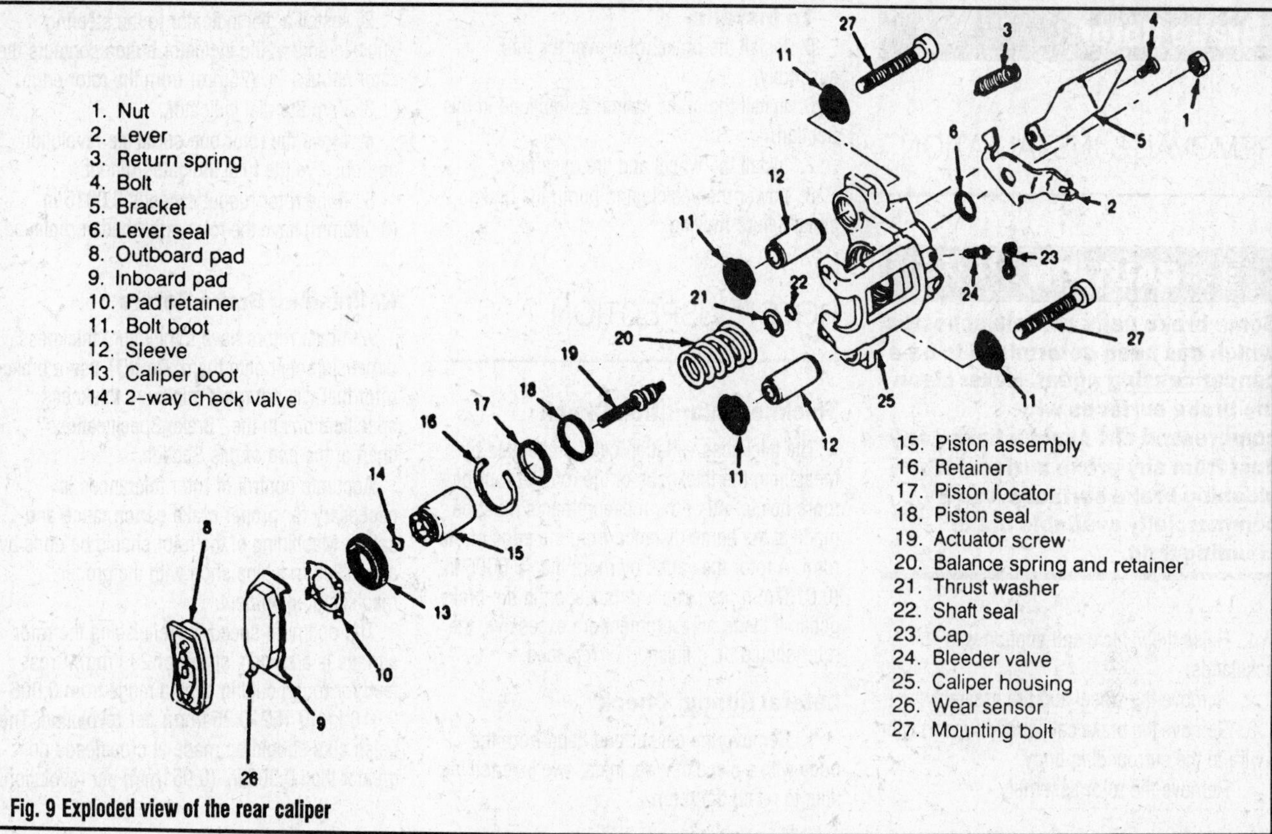

Fig. 9 Exploded view of the rear caliper

"Parking Brake Cable Adjustment" procedures in this Section.

22. Install the brake shield and rear wheel assembly.

23. Lower the vehicle.

24. Fill the brake reservoir with DOT 3 brake fluid.

25. Bleed the caliper if removed from the vehicle. Refer to the "Brake System Bleeding" procedures in this Section.

26. Inspect the brake system for fluid leaks.

27. Apply the brake pedal three times to seat the brake pads before moving the vehicle.

OVERHAUL

Disassembly

1. Remove the caliper assembly from the vehicle as previously outlined.

2. Remove the sleeve and bolt boots. Check the boots and bolts for damage and corrosion.

3. Remove the brake pad retainer from the end of the piston by rotating the retainer until the inside tabs line up with the notches in the piston.

4. Remove the lock nut, lever and seal from the caliper.

5. Remove the piston by using a wrench to rotate the actuator screw to work the piston out of the caliper bore.

6. Remove the balance spring and actuator screw.

7. Remove the shaft seal, thrust washer and boot.

8. Remove the retainer using ring pliers and a piston locator.

9. Remove the piston seal using a non-metallic seal pick.

10. Carefully remove the bleeder valve. If the valve breaks, the caliper should be replaced.

Assembly

1. Inspect all parts for damage and replace if necessary.

2. Clean all parts in denatured alcohol and dry with compressed air.

3. Install the bleeder valve.

4. Install the bracket and bolt.

5. Lubricate the new piston seals with clean brake fluid and install into the caliper bore. Make sure they are not twisted.

6. Lubricate the piston locating tool J36627, do NOT install the piston.

7. Install the thrust washer on the actuator screw with the copper side towards the piston.

8. Lubricate the shaft seal and install it on the actuator screw.

9. Install the actuator into the piston assembly.

10. Install the balance spring and retainer into the piston.

11. After all the components are lubricated and installed into the piston, install the piston into the bore. Push the piston into the bore so that the locator is past the retainer groove in the caliper bore.

12. Install the retainer using retainer ring pliers.

13. Install the boot onto the piston with the inside lip of the boot in the piston groove and the boot fold is towards the end of the piston. Push the piston to the bottom of the bore.

14. Lubricate and install the lever seal over the end of the actuator screw.

15. Install the lever and rotate away from the stop slightly. Hold the lever while torquing the lock nut to 32 ft. lbs. (44 Nm).

16. Install the pad retainer in the groove at the end of the piston.

17. Align the inside retainer tabs with the piston notches. Rotate the retainer so that the tabs enter the piston groove.

18. Lubricate with silicone grease and install the sleeve and bolt boots.

19. Install the caliper assembly and torque the retaining bolts to 92 ft. lbs. (125 Nm).

20. Bleed the brake system as outlined in this Section.

Brake Rotor

REMOVAL & INSTALLATION

**** CAUTION**

Some brake pads contain asbestos, which has been determined to be a cancer causing agent. Never clean the brake surfaces with compressed air! Avoid inhaling any dust from any brake surface! When cleaning brake surfaces, use a commercially available brake cleaning fluid.

1. Raise the vehicle and support with jackstands.
2. Remove the wheel and tire assembly.
3. Remove the brake caliper and support with a wire to the surrounding body.
4. Remove the rotor assembly.

To install:

5. Install the brake rotor over the hub assembly.
6. Install the brake caliper as outlined in this Section.
7. Install the wheel and tire assembly.
8. Lower the vehicle and pump the brake pedal before moving.

ROTOR INSPECTION

Thickness Variation Check

The thickness variation can be checked by measuring the thickness of the rotor at four or more points. All of the measurements must be made at the same distance from the edge of the rotor. A rotor the varies by more than 0.0005 in. (0.0127mm) can cause a pulsation in the brake pedal. If these measurement are excessive, the rotor should be refinished or replaced.

Lateral Runout Check

1. Remove the caliper and hang from the body with a piece of wire. Install two inverted lug nuts to retain the rotor.
2. Install a dial indicator to the steering knuckle so that the indicator button contacts the rotor about 1 in. (25mm) from the rotor edge.
3. Zero the dial indicator.
4. Move the rotor one complete revolution and observe the total indicated runout.
5. If the rotor runout exceeds 0.0015 in. (0.040mm) have the rotor refinished or replaced.

Refinishing Brake Rotors

All brake rotors have a minimum thickness dimension cast onto them. Do NOT use a brake rotor that will not meet minimum thickness specifications in the "Brake Specifications" chart at the end of this Section.

Accurate control of rotor tolerances is necessary for proper brake performance and safety. Machining of the rotor should be done by a qualified machine shop with the proper machining equipment.

The optimum speed for refinishing the rotor surface is a spindle speed of 200 rpm. Cross feed for rough cutting should range from 0.006–0.010 in. (0.152–0.254mm) per revolution. The finish cuts should be made at crossfeeds no greater than 0.002 in. (0.051mm) per revolution.

PARKING BRAKE

Cables

➧ SEE FIGS. 10 AND 11

REMOVAL & INSTALLATION

Front Cable

1. Raise the vehicle and support with jackstands.
2. Loosen the equalizer under the drivers side door.
3. Remove the front cable from the left rear cable at the retainer.
4. Remove the nut at the underbody bracket.
5. Remove the clip from underbody.
6. Lower the vehicle.
7. Remove the cable from the parking brake lever assembly using a brake cable release tool J-37043 or equivalent.

To install:

8. Install the cable to the parking brake lever assembly.
9. Raise the vehicle and support with jackstands.
10. Install the clip to the underbody and the nut at the underbody bracket.
11. Install the front cable to the left rear cable at the retainer.
12. Adjust the cable as outlined in this section.
13. Lower the vehicle and check operation.

Left Rear Cable

1. Raise the vehicle and support with jackstands.
2. Remove the spring from the equalizer under the drivers door and equalizer.
3. Remove the left rear cable from the front cable at the retainer.
4. Remove the cable retainer and cable from the caliper parking lever bracket using a cable release tool J-37043 or equivalent.

To install:

5. Install the cable to the bracket and cable support.
6. Install the cable to the brake lever and cable retainer.
7. Install the left rear cable to the front cable with the retainer.
8. Install the equalizer and spring.
9. Adjust the parking brake as outlined in this Section.
10. Lower the vehicle and check operation.

Right Rear Cable

1. Raise the vehicle and support with jackstands.

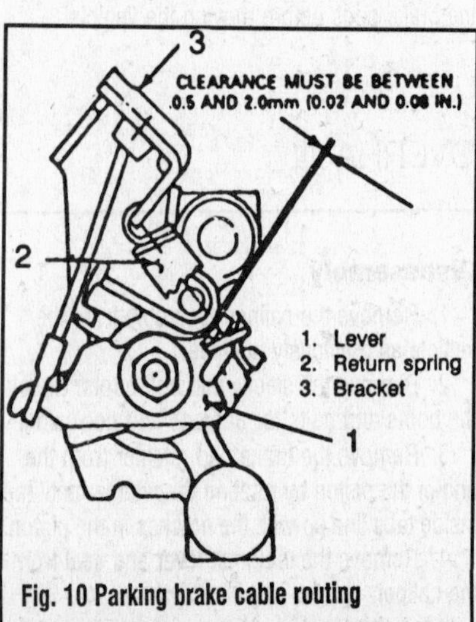

Fig. 10 Parking brake cable routing

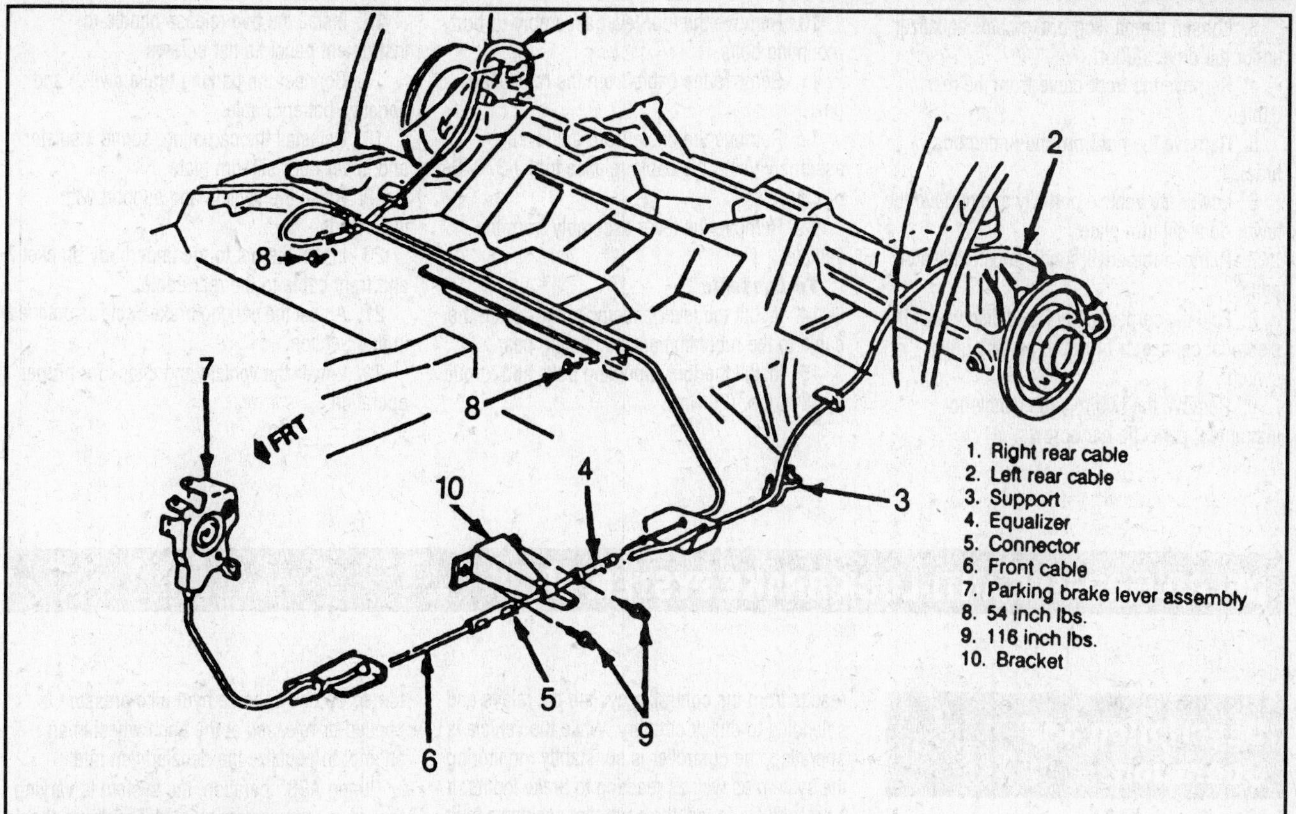

1. Right rear cable
2. Left rear cable
3. Support
4. Equalizer
5. Connector
6. Front cable
7. Parking brake lever assembly
8. 54 inch lbs.
9. 116 inch lbs.
10. Bracket

Fig. 11 Parking brake adjustment

2. Remove the spring from the equalizer under the drivers door and equalizer.

3. Remove the cable from the underbody bracket using a cable release tool J-37043 or equivalent.

4. Remove the bolts from the clips above the fuel tank.

5. Remove the cable retainer and cable from the caliper parking lever bracket using a cable release tool J-37043 or equivalent.

To install:

6. Position the cable above the fuel tank.

7. Install the cable to the bracket and cable support.

8. Install the cable to the brake lever and cable retainer.

9. Install the clips above the fuel tank.

10. Install the cable to the underbody brackets.

11. Install the equalizer and spring.

12. Adjust the parking brake as outlined in this Section.

13. Lower the vehicle and check operation.

PARKING BRAKE ADJUSTMENT

1. Apply the parking brake pedal three times with heavy force.

2. Do not apply the main brake pedal during this step. Fully apply and release the parking brake three times.

3. Raise the vehicle and support with jackstands.

4. Make sure the parking brake is fully released.

5. Remove the rear wheel assemblies and install two lug nuts to retain the rotors.

6. The parking brake levers at the calipers should be against the lever stop on the caliper housing. If not against the stops, check the cables for binding.

7. Tighten the parking brake cable at the adjuster until either the right or left lever reaches the dimensions shown in the "Cable Adjustment" illustration in this section.

8. Operate the parking brake several times to check adjustments. A firm pedal should be present.

9. Remove the two wheel lugs, install the rear wheels and lower the vehicle.

Parking Brake Lever Assembly

➧ SEE FIG. 12

REMOVAL & INSTALLATION

1. Disconnect the negative battery cable.

2. Raise the vehicle and support with jackstands.

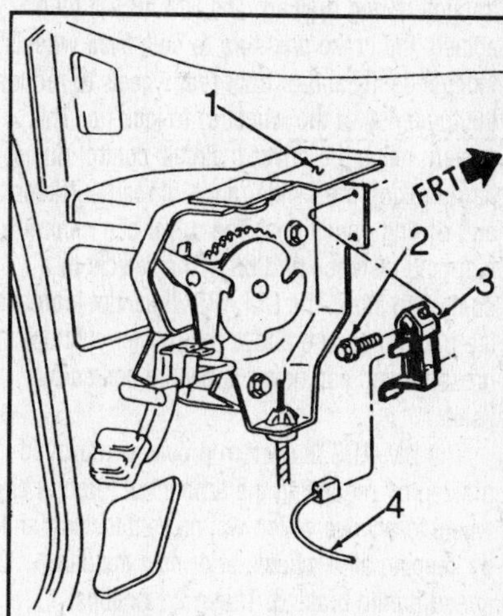

1. Parking brake lever assembly
2. Screw
3. Switch
4. Electrical harness

Fig. 12 Parking brake lever assembly

3. Loosen the parking brake cable equalizer under the drivers door.
4. Remove the front cable from the rear cable.
5. Remove the nut from the underbody bracket.
6. Lower the vehicle partially and remove the lower door sill trim plate.
7. Remove the drivers side sound insulator panel.
8. Fold the carpeting back and disconnect the electrical connector from the parking brake switch.
9. Remove the two release handle-to-instrument panel tie bar screws.
10. Remove the four lever assembly-to-body mounting bolts.
11. Remove the cable from the ratcheting gear.
12. Remove the cable from the lever assembly using the cable release tool J-37043 or equivalent.
13. Remove the lever assembly from the vehicle.

To install:

14. Install the lever assembly and attach the cable to the mounting and ratcheting gear.
15. Install the four mounting bolts and torque to 18 ft. lbs. (25 Nm).
16. Install the two release handle-to-instrument panel tie bar screws.
17. Connect the parking brake switch and negative battery cable.
18. Reinstall the carpeting, sound insulator and lower door sill trim plate.
19. Raise the vehicle and support with jackstands.
20. Install the nut to the underbody bracket and front cable to the rear cable.
21. Adjust the parking brake cable as outlined in this Section.
22. Lower the vehicle and check for proper operation.

DELCO MORAINE ANTI-LOCK BRAKE SYSTEM III

Description and Operation

➧ SEE FIG. 13

The Delco Moraine Anti-Lock Brake System (DM ABS-III) operates on all 4 wheels. The system is designed to reduce the tendency of 1 or more wheels to lock while braking. In most cases, the conventional power brake system of the vehicle performs the braking function; anti-lock braking occurs only when a combination of wheel speed sensors and a microprocessor determines a wheel (or wheels) is about to lose traction during braking. The DM ABS-III then adjusts the brake pressure to both front wheels independently and/or both rear wheels to reduce the tendency of the wheel(s) to lock-up. This system helps the driver maintain control during hard braking on a wide range of road surfaces and driving conditions. The driver can minimize stopping distance and bring the vehicle to a controlled stop. The DM ABS-III cannot increase the brake pressure above the master cylinder pressure and can never apply the brakes by itself.

The DM-ABS III system provides improved braking by regulating the amount of force at any wheel to a value which will prevent locking and by keeping all 4 wheels at or near the same speed during braking. These 2 functions combine to provide the driver with the shortest possible stop while maintaining control of the vehicle.

When the ignition switch is turned **ON**, the system enters its initial cycle. At this time, a clicking noise may be heard; this is normal and results from the controller cycling the relays and solenoids to check circuitry. While the vehicle is operating, the controller is constantly monitoring the system as well as reacting to brake inputs. If any faults are found, the controller assigns a fault code and stores the code for future retrieval. The amber warning light on the dash will be illuminated when a fault is detected.

The amber ABS dash light will inform the driver of system status. If the light is flashing, the controller has detected a fault but is still allowing the ABS system to operate. If the light is on constantly (no flash) the controller has detected a fault and disabled part or all of the ABS system. The front and rear wheel portions may be individually disabled by the controller. The amber warning light refers only to the ABS system; with ABS disabled, the vehicle will still have conventional braking capabilities if that system is not damaged.

➡ The red brake warning lamp can indicate conditions damaging to the ABS system, such as low fluid. If the red lamp is on with the amber lamp, attend to the conventional brake system before diagnosing ABS. The brake system must be operating properly before ABS diagnosis.

When the brake pedal is depressed, the controller is alerted that the brakes have been applied and monitors the speed of each wheel. If impending lock-up or uneven wheel speeds are detected, the controller cycles the solenoids on and off rapidly. This can occur independently on each front wheel or on the rear wheel which begins to lock first. When the solenoids are turned on or off, brake hydraulic pressure is applied or released at the each wheel in an attempt to equalize the deceleration rate.

During ABS operation, the system is varying the line pressures very quickly. The driver should not try to assist the system by pumping the brake pedal; hard, firm and continuous application is recommended for best ABS response. During ABS operation, the driver will feel a pulsing in the brake pedal as the line pressures change rapidly. Additionally, the clicking of the solenoids may be heard as well as momentary tire noise (screech or chirp). Both noises are normal for the system. Rapid speed change at a wheel may result in the wheel appearing to lock momentarily, resulting in road noise. Any wheel which locks and stays locked for more than 1 second is not normal; the system should be inspected immediately.

The DM ABS-III is designed only as a skid prevention system. It cannot operate properly if the base power brake system is defective. Dragging brakes, defective wheel bearings, etc. will not allow proper ABS operation.

SYSTEM COMPONENTS

Anti-lock Brake Controller

Located below the right front seat, the brake controller monitors the speed of each wheel to determine impending lock-up and, when necessary, activates the appropriate solenoid(s) to adjust brake pressures. The controller also monitors the complete system for malfunctions, provides diagnostic information and shuts the

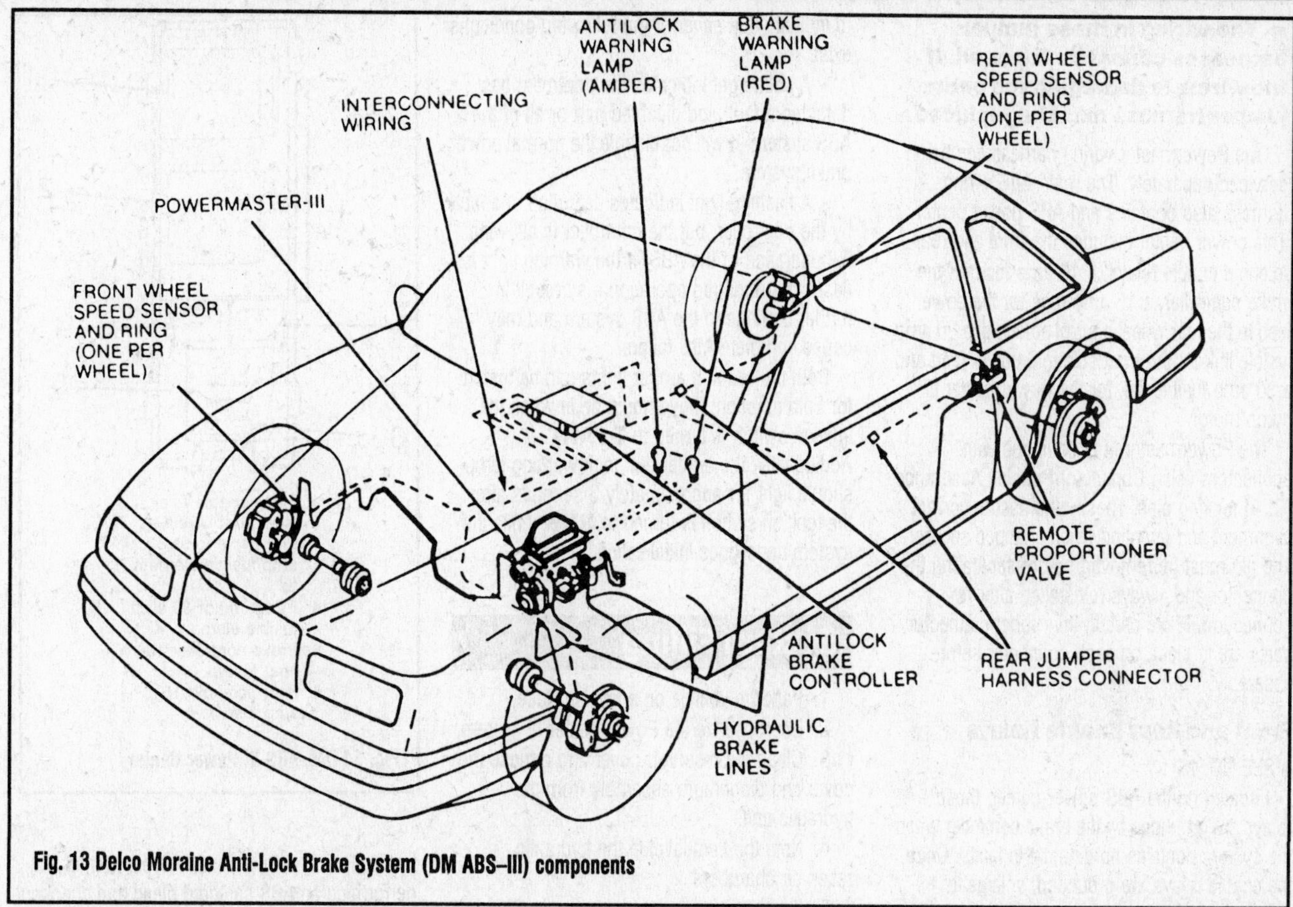

Fig. 13 Delco Moraine Anti-Lock Brake System (DM ABS–III) components

system down if a serious fault is detected. The control unit is not serviceable and must be replaced as a complete assembly.

Powermaster III Unit

The Powermaster III is an integral power booster and modulator designed to provide both normal power assist and anti-lock braking. Brake fluid pressure for both normal and ABS braking is created and maintained by a combination of an electric motor/pump and an accumulator. The accumulator is pre-charged to approximately 1200 psi (8274kpa) with nitrogen gas.

The electric pump maintains system pressure between 2200 psi (15,169kpa) and 2700 psi (18,616.5kpa). During an ABS stop, fluid to the wheel units is modulated by 3 solenoid assemblies. One solenoid is assigned to each front brake; both rear brakes are controlled by 1 solenoid.

Control Solenoids

Each solenoid assembly can apply, hold or release fluid pressure in the line it controls. The left and right front brakes can be controlled individually since each is controlled by its own solenoid. However, since there is a single solenoid for both rear brakes, they are modulated together when either rear wheel approaches lock-up. (Since the rear brake modulation is based on the lowest wheel speed, this type of system is known as a Select Low 3-channel System.) The solenoids are located on the Powermaster III and are controlled by electrical signals from the Brake Controller.

Wheel Speed Sensors

The wheel speed sensors generate an AC voltage as a magnetic toothed ring passes a stationary coil. The frequency of this voltage — which increases with wheel speed — is used by the Brake Controller to determine wheel speed. By comparing wheel speeds during braking, the Anti-lock Brake Controller determines impending wheel lock.

At the front, the speed sensor rings are located on the outer CV-joints, directly below the wheel speed sensor. No repair or air gap adjustment to the speed sensor units is possible or permissible.

The rear wheel speed sensors and rings are integral parts of the rear wheel hub and bearing assemblies. Each sensor and ring is self-contained and sealed from the environment. If a sensor or ring requires is damaged or malfunctioning, the entire rear hub and bearing assembly for that side must be replaced. No repair or air gap adjustment is possible or permissible.

Proportioning Valve

Proportional control of brake line pressure to the rear brakes takes place only after a preset input pressure has been reached. Above this preset pressure, the valve limits outlet pressure to the rear wheel brakes at a set percentage of the total system output. If malfunctioning, the proportioner valve must be replaced; the separate components of the valve cannot be serviced.

Interconnecting Wiring

The interconnecting wiring is made up of 3 specific harnesses:

- The main ABS harness
- The Powermaster III harness
- The rear harness from the controller to the rear wheel speed sensor jumper harness.

Two separate jumper harnesses extend from each rear wheel speed sensor to the rear harness through underbody connectors. Additionally, 2 separate jumper harnesses extend from each front wheel speed sensor to the main ABS wiring harness.

➡ The wiring in these jumper harnesses cannot be repaired. If the wiring is damaged, the entire jumper harness must be replaced.

The Powermaster wiring harness can be serviced separately. The main ABS wiring harness also contains and ABS power center. This power center includes the front and rear solenoid enable relays, a 10 amp fuse for the brake controller, a 15 amp fuse for the power feed to the rear wheel control solenoid, a 30 amp fusible link for the front solenoid power feed and a 30 amp fusible link for the Powermaster III pump motor.

The Powermaster III is equipped with connectors using Connector Position Assurance (CPA) locking pins. These pins assure correct alignment and retention when snapped securely. The pin must be removed before separating the connector and always reinstalled after re-connection. Make certain the rubber connector seals are in place on each connector before assembly.

Front and Rear Enable Relays

➧ SEE FIG. 14

Located on the ABS power center, these relays are grounded by the brake controller when the system contains no detectable faults. Once the enable relays are grounded, voltage is applied to the solenoids. If the brake controller detects a fault, loses power or loses ground, the controller de-energizes the ground to the front enable relay. The amber light on the dash will come on to indicate loss of ABS function. The controller may detect a fault in the rear circuits and disable only the rear; if this occurs the amber light will not come on.

Brake Switch

The brake pedal switch signals the brake controller that the brakes are in use. The switch must be functioning and properly adjusted for the ABS to perform correctly.

Brake Warning Indicator

The red brake warning lamp will light after the ignition switch is in the **RUN** position to indicate that any or all of the following conditions exist:

- Parking brake applied.
- Brake fluid level is low.
- Accumulator pressure is below 1800 psi (12,411kpa).

Each of these conditions can damage the brake and ABS systems or reduce there efficiency. If the red light remains on after starting, the vehicle should be checked as soon as possible.

The amber Anti-lock warning lamp will light after the ignition switch is in the **RUN** position to indicate that either of the following conditions exist:

- A solid light indicates the controller has detected a fault and disabled part or all of the ABS system. It will not disable the normal power brake system.
- A flashing light indicates detection of a fault by the controller, but the controller is allowing full operation of the ABS. If the warning light is flashing, prolonged operation may result in further damage to the ABS system and may cause complete ABS failure.

Both the red and amber lights can be tested for bulb function; they should be lit when the ignition switch is turned to **START**. Additionally, the amber anti-lock warning lamp should light for approximately 3 seconds after the ignition switch is turned to **RUN** while the system undergoes initialization.

System Filling

1. Park the vehicle on a level surface.
2. Depressurize the Powermaster III system.
3. Clean the reservoir cover and remove the cover and diaphragm assembly from the hydraulic unit.
4. Note the fluid level in the hydraulic reservoir chambers.
5. If any reservoir chamber is underfilled, look for signs of leakage. Make repairs as necessary. Fill the reservoir chambers with clean, DOT 3 brake fluid until the levels reach the full marks. Install the reservoir cover and diaphragm assembly.
6. If a reservoir chamber is over filled, correct the fluid level and install the cover and diaphragm assembly. Turn the ignition switch **ON** and allow the system to pressurize.
7. Again, depressurize the hydraulic unit and check the fluid level.

System Bleeding

➡ If the hydraulic unit has been replaced, or if air has entered the brake lines, the entire brake system – hydraulic unit, lines and calipers – must be bled at each wheel.

If only a hydraulic part of the hydraulic unit has been replaced (bleeder valve, tube and nut assembly, accumulator, reservoir, solenoid, or pressure switch), and no air has entered the brake lines, it may only be necessary to bleed the hydraulic unit by performing an ABS solenoid bleed and checkout test using a hand scanner tool or by bleeding the booster section of the hydraulic unit at its bleeder valves. Neither performing an ABS solenoid bleed and checkout test nor bleeding the hydraulic unit at its bleeder valves will remove air from the brake lines.

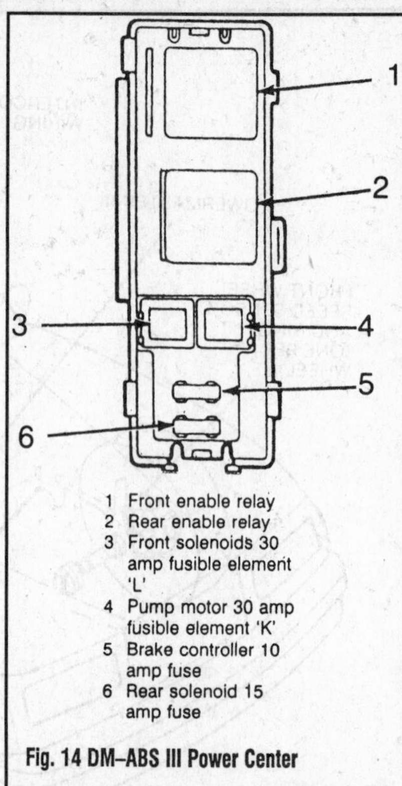

Fig. 14 DM–ABS III Power Center

Pressure Bleeding

➡ The pressure bleeding equipment must be of the diaphragm type. It must have a rubber diaphragm between the air supply and the brake fluid to prevent air, moisture and other contaminants from entering the hydraulic system. Use only DOT 3 brake fluid from a sealed container. Do not use any suspect or contaminated fluid. Do not use DOT 5 silicone fluid.

1. Depressurize the hydraulic unit before pressure bleeding.

➡ Make sure the vehicle ignition switch is OFF, unless otherwise noted. This will prevent the hydraulic unit pump from starting during the bleeding procedure.

2. Clean the reservoir cover and diaphragm assembly, then remove the cover.
3. Check the fluid level in both the reservoir sections and fill to the correct level using clean brake fluid, if necessary.
4. Install the bleeder adapter J–37115 or equivalent and secure with attachment cable.

Make sure attachment cable does not interfere with access to the bleeder valves on the hydraulic unit.

5. Attach the adapter to the pressure bleed equipment and charge to 5–10 psi (34.5–69kpa) for approximately 30 seconds. If no leaks exist, slowly increase the pressure to 30–35 psi (207–241kpa). 20–25 psi (138–241kpa) is acceptable but not preferred.

6. Bleed the adapter; place a rag over the valve to absorb vented fluid. Depress ball to open the bleeder valve; continue until fluid flows without air.

7. Raise and safely support the vehicle.

8. Bleed individual wheel brakes in this sequence: right rear, left rear, right front and left front.

a. Attach the bleeder hose to the bleeder valve and submerge the opposite end in a clean container partially filled with fresh brake fluid.

b. Slowly open the bleeder valve and allow the fluid to flow until no air is seen in the fluid.

c. Allow the brake fluid to flow for at least 20–30 seconds at each wheel when checking for trapped air.

d. To assist in freeing trapped air, tap lightly on the caliper castings with a rubber mallet.

e. Close the valve when the fluid begins to flow without any air bubbles.

9. Lower the vehicle.

10. Bleed the Powermaster III isolation valves.

a. Attach the bleeder hose to the bleeder valve on the inboard side of the Powermaster III and submerge the opposite end in a container partially filled with fresh brake fluid.

b. Slowly open the bleeder valve and allow the fluid to flow until no air is seen in the fluid.

d. Close the valve when the fluid begins to flow without any air bubbles.

e. Repeat the procedure on the outboard side of the bleeder valve.

11. Remove the bleeder adapter J–37115 from the hydraulic unit.

12. Check the fluid level in both the reservoir chambers. Using clean brake fluid, fill the reservoirs to the proper level, if necessary.

13. Replace the reservoir cover and snap all 4 cover tabs in place on the reservoir.

14. Apply brake pedal 3 times with sharp, jabbing applications.

15. Bleed the booster section of the Powermaster III.

a. If hand scanner 094–00101 is available connect it. Turn the ignition to **ON** and allow the pump to pressurize the accumulator. When the pump stops, use the scanner to perform the "Solenoid Bleed and Check Test".

b. If a hand scanner is not available, depress the brake pedal with moderate pressure and turn the key to **ON** without starting the motor for 3 seconds. Repeat this **OFF/ON** cycle 10 times to cycle the solenoids.

16. Bleed the accumulator. Do not check brake fluid level without depressurizing the Powermaster III; overfilling may result. After depressurizing, wait 2 minutes before checking level; this will allow air to clear from the brake fluid.

17. Turn the ignition to **ON**without starting the engine; allow the system to pressurize. Check brake pedal for correct feel and travel.

18. Road test the vehicle.

Manual Bleeding

1. Depressurize the hydraulic unit before pressure bleeding.

➡ **Make sure the vehicle ignition switch is OFF, unless otherwise noted. This will prevent the hydraulic unit pump from starting during the bleeding procedure.**

2. Clean the reservoir cover and diaphragm assembly; then remove the assembly.

3. Check the fluid level in both the reservoir sections and fill to the correct level using clean brake fluid, if necessary.

4. Raise the vehicle and support safely.

5. Bleed the right front wheel brake.

a. Attach a bleeder hose to the bleeder valve and submerge the opposite end in a clean container partially filled with brake fluid.

b. Open the bleeder valve.

c. Slowly depress the brake pedal.

d. To assist in freeing entrapped air, tap lightly on the caliper with a rubber mallet.

e. Close the valve and release the brake pedal.

f. Check the fluid level and add new brake fluid, if necessary.

6. Repeat Step 5 until the brake pedal feels firm at half travel and no air bubbles are observed in the bleeder hose.

7. Repeat Steps 5 and 6 on the left front wheel brake.

8. Turn the ignition switch **ON** and allow the pump motor to run. (Shut ignition switch **OFF** if the pump runs for more than 60 seconds; check the hydraulic system.)

9. Bleed the right rear wheel brake.

a. Attach a bleeder hose to the bleeder valve and submerge the opposite end in a clean container partially filled with brake fluid.

b. Open the bleeder valve.

c. With the ignition switch **ON**, slowly depress the brake pedal part way, until the brake fluid begins to flow from the bleeder hose. Hold for 15 seconds.

➡ **Do not fully depress the brake pedal.**

d. To assist in freeing entrapped air, tap lightly on the caliper castings with a rubber mallet.

e. Close the valve and release the brake pedal.

f. Repeat these Steps until no air bubbles are observed in the bleeder hose.

g. Check the fluid level and add new brake fluid, if necessary. Turn the ignition **OFF** and depressurize the hydraulic unit before checking the fluid level.

10. Repeat Steps 8 and 9 on the left rear wheel brake.

11. Lower the vehicle.

12. Bleed the Powermaster III isolation valves.

a. Attach the bleeder hose to the bleeder valve on the inboard side of the Powermaster III and submerge the opposite end in a container partially filled with fresh brake fluid.

b. Slowly open the bleeder valve and allow the fluid to flow until no air is seen in the fluid.

d. Close the valve when the fluid begins to flow without any air bubbles.

e. Repeat the procedure on the outboard side of the bleeder valve.

13. Bleed the hydraulic unit solenoids. This Step will insure that the brake pedal applies firmly and smoothly.

➡ **This Step can also be performed using a hand scanner.**

a. Apply moderate force on the brake pedal.

b. With the pedal applied, turn the ignition switch **ON** for 3 seconds, then turn **OFF**. Do this 10 times in succession to cycle the solenoids Do not start the engine.

14. Depressurize the hydraulic unit and wait 2 minutes for the air to clear from within the reservoir.

15. Bleed the hydraulic unit of air accumulated from the solenoids.

a. Attach the bleeder hose to the bleeder valve on the inboard side of the hydraulic unit and submerge the opposite end in a clean container partially filled with fresh brake fluid.

b. With the ignition switch **ON**, apply light force to the brake pedal.

c. With the pedal applied, slowly open the bleeder valve and allow the fluid to flow until no air is seen in the fluid.

d. Close the valve when the fluid begins to flow without any air bubbles.

e. Repeat the procedure on the outboard side of the hydraulic unit.

16. Turn the ignition switch **OFF**, depressurize the hydraulic unit.

17. Remove the reservoir cover and diaphragm assembly.

18. Check the fluid level in both reservoir sections. Using clean brake fluid, fill the reservoirs to their proper level, if necessary.

19. Install the reservoir cover and snap all 4 tabs in place on the reservoir.

20. Turn the ignition switch **ON** and allow the pump motor to run. Shut the ignition switch **OFF** if the pump motor runs for more than 60 seconds; check the hydraulic system.

21. Apply the brake pedal noting feel and travel. If feel is firm, smooth and without excess pedal travel, vehicle is ready for road testing. If pedal feel is soft, spongy or has excessive pedal travel re-bleed the front brakes. If conditions still exist, perform Preliminary Inspection. Depressurize Powermaster III and recheck fluid level.

Accumulator

➧ SEE FIG. 15

REMOVAL & INSTALLATION

➡ The accumulator is a nitrogen-charged pressure vessel which holds brake fluid under high pressure. It can not be repaired and must be serviced as an assembly.

1. Depressurize the Powermaster III completely.
2. Remove the air cleaner, duct and stud if present.
3. Remove the 30 amp fusible element K from the ABS power center.
4. Remove the accumulator by turning the hex nut on the end of the accumulator with a 17mm socket. Remove from the vehicle by sliding out from underneath the hydraulic unit, towards the left front wheel well.
5. Remove the O-ring from the accumulator.

To install:

6. Lightly lubricate a new O-ring with clean brake fluid and install on the accumulator.
7. Install the accumulator and torque to 24 ft. lbs. (33 Nm).
8. Install the 30 amp fusible element.
9. Install the air cleaner, duct and stud.
10. Bleed the system.

Solenoid Assemblies

➧ SEE FIG. 16

REMOVAL & INSTALLATION

➡ Wipe the reservoir cover assembly and surrounding area clean before removing. A clean work area is essential to completing this procedure without damaging the hydraulic unit.

1. Depressurize the Powermaster III.
2. Remove the reservoir cover assembly and reservoir assembly.
3. Disconnect the 3-pin electrical connector from the solenoid assembly.
4. Remove the screws attaching the solenoid assembly.
5. Remove the solenoid assembly. Make sure both lower solenoid O-rings (2 per solenoid) are removed from the hydraulic unit.

To install:

6. Install the solenoid assembly into position; make sure the lower solenoid O-rings are in place and in good condition before installing.
7. Install the screws holding the solenoid assembly and tighten to 45 inch lbs. (5 Nm).
8. Connect the electrical connector to the solenoid. Make sure all connector position assurance locking pins are installed.
9. Install the reservoir cover and reservoir assembly.
10. Bleed brake system.

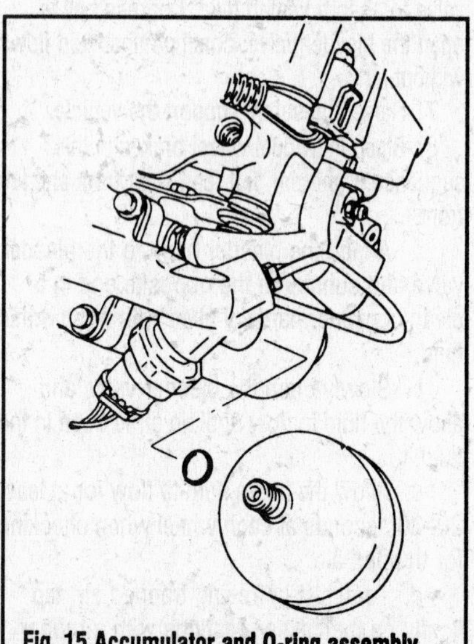

Fig. 15 Accumulator and O-ring assembly

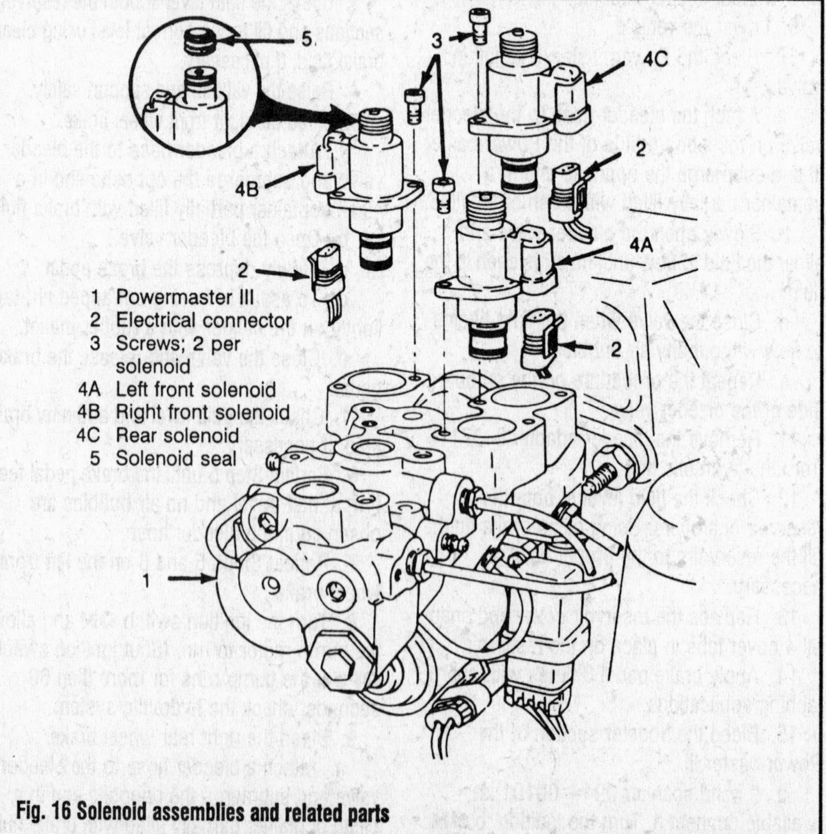

Fig. 16 Solenoid assemblies and related parts

Powermaster III (Hydraulic Unit)

SEE FIG. 17

REMOVAL & INSTALLATION

➡ Do not lift or pull the hydraulic unit using the hydraulic unit wiring harness.

1. Depressurize the Powermaster III completely.
2. Remove the 30 amp fusible element K from the ABS power center.
3. Disconnect the 7-pin vehicle electrical connector from the hydraulic unit harness.
4. Disconnect the vehicle 10-pin electrical connector from the hydraulic unit harness.
5. Disconnect the 2-pin connector from the fluid level sensor.
6. Disconnect the 3 brake pipes from the hydraulic unit. Plug the open lines to prevent fluid loss and contamination.
7. Inside the vehicle, remove the hair pin clip and pushrod from the brake pedal.
8. Remove the 2 attaching nuts from the cowl bracket studs.
9. Remove the hydraulic unit.

➡ To avoid damage to the protruding hydraulic unit parts, install unit on J-37116 (or equivalent) holding fixture.

To install:

10. Lightly lubricate the entire outer surface of the pushrod with silicone grease. Position the hydraulic unit in the vehicle. Guide the pushrod through the grommet.
11. Position the mounting bracket on the cowl bracket studs. Loosely install the attaching nuts.
12. Install the pushrod on the brake pedal mounting pin and install the hair pin clip.
13. Install the 2 attaching nuts. Torque the nuts to 20 ft. lbs. (27 Nm).
14. Install the 3 brake pipes to the hydraulic unit and torque to 15 ft. lbs. (17 Nm).
16. Connect the 3 electrical connectors to the hydraulic unit or its harness. Make sure all CPA locking pins are installed.
17. Install the 30 amp fusible element.
18. Adjust the brakelight switch.
19. Bleed the system thoroughly.

Proportioner Valve

REMOVAL & INSTALLATION

➡ The proportioner valve is not repairable; if any fault is present, it must be replaced as a complete assembly. The use of rubber hoses or hydraulic lines not specifically listed for use with DM ABS-III may lead to system problems requiring major repairs.

1. Depressurize the Powermaster III unit.
2. Raise and safely support vehicle.
3. Disconnect the input brake line (12mm) and the 2 output brake lines (10mm) from the proportioner valve.
4. Remove the proportioner valve.
5. When reinstalling, place the proportioner valve so that the rub pad is against vehicle body.
6. Connect the input and output brake lines to the valve. Tighten the nuts to 15 ft. lbs (17 Nm).
7. Lower the vehicle.
8. Bleed the system. Only the rear brake circuits require bleeding.

Front Wheel Speed Sensors

REMOVAL & INSTALLATION

1. Raise the vehicle and support it safely.
2. Disconnect the sensor connector from the wiring harness.
3. Remove the 2 front wheel speed sensor bolts and remove the connector bracket bolt.
4. Remove the front wheel speed sensor.

To install:

5. Install the front wheel speed sensor in place. Install the sensor retaining bolts and tighten the sensor retaining bolts (15mm) to 59 ft. lbs. (80 Nm). Tighten the connector bracket bolt.
6. Inspect for proper air gap between the sensor and the signal ring. While not adjustable, gap should be 0.019–0.068 in. (0.5–0.17mm). If the gap is not correct, the damaged or misaligned component must be corrected.
7. Connect the sensor connector to the wiring harness, making sure the CPA locking pin is in place.

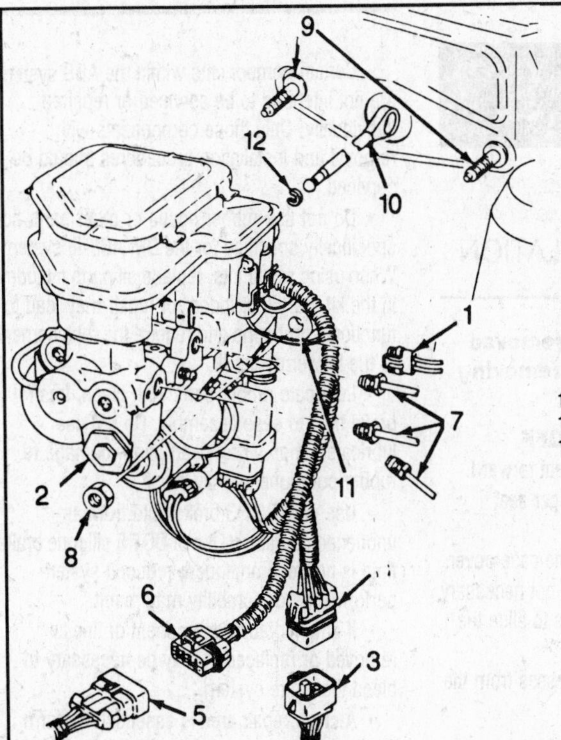

Fig. 17 Powermaster III hydraulic unit

8. Inspect and route the wiring to avoid contact with the suspension components.
9. Lower the vehicle.

Rear Wheel Speed Sensors

The rear wheel speed sensors are integral with the hub and bearing assemblies. Should a speed sensor require replacement, the entire hub and bearing assembly must be replaced.

Front Wheel Rings

The front wheel speed sensor rings are integral with the outer CV-joint housing. Should a front wheel speed sensor ring require replacement, the entire CV-joint must be replaced.

Rear Wheel Rings

The rear wheel speed sensors rings are integral with the hub and bearing assemblies. Should a ring require replacement, the entire hub and bearing assembly must be replaced.

Anti-Lock Brake Controller

REMOVAL & INSTALLATION

➡ **The controller can be removed from the vehicle without removing the front passenger seat.**

1. Turn the ignition switch to **OFF**.
2. Slide the front passenger seat forward.
3. If applicable, tip the passenger seat forward.
4. Remove the bolts holding the case cover.
5. Remove the controller. It is not necessary to remove the harness connectors to slide the controller out of the case.
6. Disconnect the wiring harnesses from the controller.

➡ **The anti-lock brake controller should be protected from extremes of temperature, shock or impact and the discharge of static electricity.**

To install:

7. Connect the wiring connectors to the controller. Make certain the CPA locking pins are correctly installed.
8. Install the controller into its case. Install the case cover and tighten the retaining bolts hand tight.
9. Return the front passenger seat to the correct position.

Diagnosis and Testing

SERVICE PRECAUTIONS

⁂ CAUTION

This brake system uses a hydraulic accumulator which, when fully charged, contains brake fluid at very high pressure. Before disconnecting any hydraulic lines, hoses or fittings be certain that the accumulator pressure is completely relieved. Failure to depressurize the accumulator may result in personal injury and/or vehicle damage.

- Certain components within the ABS system are not intended to be serviced or repaired individually. Only those components with removal and installation procedures should be serviced.
- Do not use rubber hoses or other parts not specifically specified for the DM ABS-III system. When using repair kits, replace all parts included in the kit. Partial or incorrect repair may lead to functional problems and require the replacement of the Powermaster III.
- Lubricate rubber parts with clean, fresh brake fluid to ease assembly. Do not use lubricated shop air to clean parts; damage to rubber components may result.
- Use only DOT 3 brake fluid from an unopened container. Use of DOT 5 silicone brake fluid is not recommended; reduced system performance or durability may result.
- If any hydraulic component or line is removed or replaced, it may be necessary to bleed the entire system.
- A clean repair area is essential. Perform repairs after components have been thoroughly cleaned; use only denatured alcohol to clean components. Do not allow ABS components to come into contact with any substance containing mineral oil; this includes used shop rags.
- Remove the lock pin before disconnecting CPA connectors at the Powermaster III.
- The Anti-lock brake controller is a microprocessor similar to other computer units in the vehicle. Insure that the ignition switch is **OFF** before removing or installing controller harnesses. Avoid static electricity discharge at or near the Controller.
- Fault codes stored within the system can only be read with a bi-directional scanner such as GM 9400100-A (Tech 1 Diagnostic Computer) or equivalent. Some scanners will require an additional cartridge (GM 9400008-A or equivalent) to read the system.
- The brake controller is equipped with on-board diagnostic programs beyond the setting of codes. Not all scanners are capable of using these other features. Consult the scanner manufacturer's manual for directions and capabilities.

PRE-DIAGNOSIS INSPECTION

A visual check of specific system components may reveal problems creating an apparent ABS malfunction. Performing this inspection may reveal a simple failure, thus eliminating extended diagnostic time. The steps should be performed in order.

1. Depressurize the Powermaster III.
2. Inspect the brake fluid level in the reservoir.
3. Inspect brake lines, hoses, Powermaster III and brake calipers for leakage.
4. Visually check brake lines and hoses for excessive wear, heat damage, punctures, contact with other parts, missing clips or holders, blockage or crimping.
5. Check the calipers and pins for rust or corrosion. Check for proper sliding action.
6. Check the caliper pistons for freedom of motion during application and release.
7. Inspect the front wheel speed sensors for proper mounting and connections.
8. Inspect the front speed sensor rings for broken teeth or poor mounting.
9. Measure front wheel speed sensor to ring air gap. Air gap is not adjustable but should be 0.019–0.068 in. (0.5–0.17mm).
10. Inspect rear wheel speed sensors for proper installation or damage. Inspect rear speed sensor wiring connections.
11. Brake pedal travel should not bottom near the floor after Powermaster III is depressurized.
12. Check for worn or missing isolator bushings on Powermaster III which may cause or amplify pump motor noise.

13. Inspect the high pressure line on Powermaster III which may be contacting other engine compartment components.

TROUBLE CODES

The Anti-lock Brake Controller contains diagnostic capabilities which can identify faults specifically including whether or not the fault is intermittent. The diagnostics must be read with a bi-directional scanner.

There are 58 possible 4-digit fault codes. The first 5 codes generated are stored in the order in which they occurred from least to most recent. Fault codes will not disappear when the ignition is turned off or the battery cable is disconnected. If no further fault codes occur within 50 driving cycles (Ignition switch **ON** and vehicle speed over 10 mph) the controller will clear the memory.

In order to access the trouble codes, connect a bi-directional scan tool to the ALDL connector and follow the scan tool manufacturer's instructions to read the codes. The ALDL connector is located behind the instrument panel to the right of the steering column.

A current code indicates that the malfunction occurred during the current ignition cycle. After all current codes have been displayed, the history codes will be displayed. History codes are malfunctions which do not currently exist, but could possibly aid in determining the cause of an intermittent condition.

After the trouble codes have been read, proceed to the appropriate trouble code diagnosis. The charts are located after the "Hydraulic Diagnosis" section.

➡ **Always turn the ignition switch OFF prior to initial troubleshooting to ensure all diagnostic data is preserved. If the ignition is not turned OFF prior to reading fault codes, any information stored for a fault in the last drive cycle will be lost.**

The hand scanner must be used to clear trouble codes from the memory after repairs are completed.

ADDITIONAL DIAGNOSTIC CAPABILITIES

➡ **Not all scanners can use the additional diagnostics within the controller. Consult tool manufacturer's instructions for correct application and use.**

ABS Data List – allows data parameters for many circuits to be monitored. This feature can be particularly helpful in tracking intermittent problems. **ABS Snapshot –** will store the ABS data list parameters for a period of time before, during and after a fault triggers a code. Snapshot may be set for a specific code, any ABS code or at operator's command. **Manual Relay and Solenoid Control –** allows the front and rear enable relays and the individual hold and release solenoids to be commanded ON or OFF. Feature will display actual output or voltage (HIGH or LOW) at that particular terminal on the controller. Solenoids can only be energized for about 40 seconds; they will then be turned off for purposes of cooling. **Enhanced Diagnostics –** used to determine if a trouble code is intermittent, identify how intermittent it is and give information regarding vehicle operating conditions when the most recent trouble code was set. The following data can be displayed:

- How often each of the 5 stored codes occurred. Example: A code which set once in the last 35 driving cycles might indicate a one-time occurrence such as a severe pot-hole.
- The speed the ABS controller sensed the vehicle travelling when the last fault occurred.
- State of the brake switch (ON, OFF or OPEN) at time of the last fault occurrence. Only the state of the switch is known; no information on braking or deceleration is given.
- Brake system fluid pressure.
- Whether or not brake pedal had been applied during this driving cycle. If no application is seen, fault may have been detected when ignition was turned **ON**.
- Whether or not ABS stop was in progress when fault occurred.
- How many drive cycles have occurred since last code was set.

INTERMITTENTS

The diagnostic procedures may or may not be helpful in determining the cause of intermittent problems in the system electrical components. In most cases, the fault must be present to locate the problem using the trouble trees.

Most intermittent problems are caused by faulty electrical connections or wiring. When an intermittent failure is encountered:

1. Check for history codes which may be stored in the anti-lock brake controller. If a history code is stored, this may indicate the circuitry which has the intermittent condition. Move the related connectors, harness and components in an effort to induce the failure.
2. Enter the Enhanced Diagnostic feature. This feature will help determine how intermittent the fault is and may help determine certain conditions that cause the fault.
3. Set the ABS snapshot to trigger on the intermittent trouble code and use the enhanced diagnostic feature to recreate the conditions that cause the intermittent code to set.
4. Check for poor mating of connector halves or terminals not fully seated in the connector body.
5. Inspect for improperly formed or damaged terminals. All connector terminals in a problem circuit should be carefully reformed to increase contact tension.
6. Check for poor terminal-to-wire connection. This requires removing the terminal from the connector body to inspect.

HYDRAULIC DIAGNOSIS

The Antilock Brake Controller must be scanned for trouble codes before attempting any of the following diagnostic procedures. The following tests should be used if directed here by a trouble tree or a system problem exists but no codes have been set.

If no codes have been set, the tests must be performed in the alphabetical order given. Always perform the pre-diagnosis inspection before any other testing is begun. If referred to hydraulic diagnosis from a trouble tree, perform the tests in numerical order for each test.

Test A – ABS System Functional Check

1. Properly connect hand scanner to ALDL connector.
2. An assistant must sit in the driver's seat and operate the brakes and hand scanner during testing.
3. Raise and safely support the vehicle.
4. Turn ignition switch **ON** and put transmission in **P**. Do not apply the brakes. Attempt to rotate each wheel by hand. If any wheel does not rotate, inspect for correct operation of parking brake or calipers.

➡ **The rear wheels should turn with little or no resistance. The front wheels will have some resistance caused by driveline and differential drag. This is normal. If the wheel can be turned with normal hand force, the condition is acceptable.**

5. Apply medium pressure to the brake pedal. Attempt to rotate each wheel again; no rotation should be possible.
6. If either of the front wheel rotate, replace the Powermaster III; the front master cylinder portion is malfunctioning. If either of the rear

wheels rotate, a Low or No Boost Pressure condition exists; refer to Test C.

7. Apply the service brakes with moderate effort and use the hand scanner to energize the hold and release solenoids for a specific wheel. Check the wheel for rotation. While some drag may be present due to residual line pressure, the wheel should rotate with hand force. Repeat this step for other wheels.

8. While the solenoids are energized, the brake pedal should not sink steadily to the floor, the pump should not run constantly or frequently, and the sound of fluid being forcefully sprayed in the reservoir should not be heard. If any of these conditions occur, check the wiring and connections to the appropriate solenoid. If any wires or connectors are found damaged, replace the Powermaster III wiring harness.

9. If the any condition in the previous step recurs after replacing the wiring harness, replace the Powermaster III unit.

Test B – ABS Hold Function Check

1. Properly connect hand scanner to ALDL connector.

2. An assistant must sit in the driver's seat and operate the brakes and hand scanner during testing.

3. Raise and safely support the vehicle.

4. Turn ignition switch **ON** and put transmission in **N**. Keep transmission in **N** throughout testing. Allow ABS unit to pressurize before proceeding.

5. Use the hand scanner to energize only the rear hold solenoid, then apply the brakes moderately.

6. Attempt to turn a rear wheel; it should turn freely for 6 or more seconds before the brakes apply.

7. While the solenoid is energized, the brake pedal should not sink steadily to the floor, the pump should not run constantly or frequently, and the sound of fluid being forcefully sprayed in the reservoir should not be heard.If any of these conditions occur, or if the brakes apply in 5 seconds or less, replace the rear solenoid assembly in the Powermaster III and retest the system. If similar conditions still exist, replace the Powermaster III unit.

8. Moderately apply the brakes and use the hand scanner to energize the hold function of 1 of the front wheels.

9. Attempt to turn the appropriate front wheel; it should turn freely for 6 or more seconds before the brakes apply.

10. While the solenoid is energized, the brake pedal should not sink steadily to the floor, the pump should not run constantly or frequently, and the sound of fluid being forcefully sprayed in the reservoir should not be heard. If any of these conditions occur, or if the brakes apply in 5 seconds or less, replace the proper solenoid assembly in the Powermaster III and retest the system. If similar conditions still exist, replace the Powermaster III unit.

11. Repeat the testing procedure for the other front wheel.

Test C – Low or No Boost Pressure Check

1. With ignition **OFF**, depressurize the Powermaster III unit completely.

2. Properly connect hand scanner to the ALDL connector.

3. Use the hand scanner to activate the pump. Note the total pump running time; this is the amount of time between ignition on and pump shut-off.

4. If the total time is 40 seconds or less, the Powermaster III is developing satisfactory boost pressure. If the running time is greater than 40 seconds, perform Test D.

5. Determine the pump off time by moderately applying the brakes and holding the brake pedal down. Use a stopwatch to measure the time between brake application and pump engagement.

➡ Some hand scanners can compute this time using the bleed-down check function.

6. If the pump off time is 50 seconds or less, a problem may exist within the Powermaster III. Refer to Test E. If the pump off time is greater than 50 seconds, the Powermaster III is holding boost pressure satisfactorily.

Test D – Pump Run Time Too Long

1. With ignition **OFF**, disconnect the wiring harness at pump connector. Turn the ignition switch **ON**.

2. Use a digital volt/ohmmeter (DVOM) to check voltage of Pin A to ground. If less than 12 volts, check the battery, charging system and non-ABS circuits for damage.

3. Turn the ignition switch to **OFF** and reconnect the pump harness to the connector. Depressurize the Powermaster III unit.

4. Remove the accumulator and install pressure gauge J-37118 or equivalent. Install the accumulator on the pressure gauge adapter.

5. Bleed the Powermaster III at the bleeder valves or use the hand scanner to perform ABS Solenoid Bleed and Checkout Test.

6. Observe the pressure gauge while turning ignition **ON**. The system should pressurize from 0–500 psi (0–3448kpa) or greater almost immediately after the ignition is switched on.

7. If the correct pressure is not reached, the accumulator is not holding sufficient precharge and must be replaced.

8. Allow the pump motor to run and and note the pressure at which it either stops or reaches the high-pressure limit. If the indicated pressure is greater than 2900 psi (19,995.5kpa), the pressure switch is faulty.

9. Using the hand scanner, monitor the pump state while applying the brakes slowly 1–3 times. Note the low pressure at which the pump engages. The pump should turn on at or above 2000 psi (13,790kpa). If it turns on at a lower pressure, the pressure valve must be replaced.

10. If the pressure switch functions properly, depressurize the Powermaster III completely. Remove the reservoir cover. Do not apply the brakes with the reservoir cover removed.

11. Visually check the pump outlet in the reservoir to be sure it is not clogged. If the outlet is clear, attach 1 end of a clear plastic hose over the relief valve in the reservoir.

12. Hold the other end of the tube pointed downward into the rear reservoir chamber. Turn the ignition switch **ON**.

13. If fluid flows through the tube into the reservoir, replace the relief valve. If fluid does not flow through the tube, replace the Powermaster III unit.

Test E – Pump Off Time Too Short

1. Turn the ignition switch to **OFF** and depressurize the Powermaster III unit.

2. Remove the accumulator and install pressure gauge J-37118 or equivalent. Install the accumulator on the pressure gauge adapter.

3. Bleed the Powermaster III at the bleeder valves or use the hand scanner to perform ABS Solenoid Bleed and Checkout Test.

4. Observe the pressure gauge while turning ignition **ON**. The system should pressurize from 0–500 psi (0–3448kpa) or greater almost immediately after the ignition is switched on.

5. If the correct pressure is not reached, the accumulator is not holding sufficient precharge and must be replaced.

6. Allow the system to pressurize until the pump shuts off. With the ignition still on, moderately apply and hold the brakes on. Measure the time between brake application and pump start-up.

7. If the pump off time is less than 50 seconds, check the accumulator precharge. If the accumulator precharge is less than 600 psi (4137kpa), replace the accumulator. If precharge is 600 psi (4137kpa) or greater and the pump off time is less than the correct value shown below, replace the Powermaster III unit.

Test F – External Leakage Check

1. Depressurize the Powermaster III unit.

2. Clean and remove the reservoir cover and diaphragm assembly. Inspect the fluid levels.

3. If the front chamber level is high, drain or siphon fluid to restore the correct level.

4. If the rear chamber level is too high, drain or siphon fluid to restore the correct level. High level in the rear chamber may be caused by filling the reservoir without depressurizing the system.

5. Clean and dry the Powermaster III unit so that any leaks or seepage may be easily detected. Install the reservoir cover and diaphragm.

6. turn the ignition **ON** and pump the brakes. Check for leaks on the Powermaster III and throughout the system, including lines, fittings and calipers.

7. Depressurize the Powermaster III, remove the cover and diaphragm and inspect the fluid levels. If the rear fluid level is too high, the Powermaster III must be replaced.

8. If the level in the front reservoir is too high:

a. Drain or siphon the brake fluid in the front reservoir to a point below the divider wall for the left front and right front circuits.

b. Install the reservoir cover and diaphragm. Turn the ignition switch **ON** and pump the brakes several times.

c. Depressurize the Powermaster III. Remove the reservoir cover and the diaphragm.

d. Note the level of fluid in the front reservoirs. If the fluid level has risen in either front chamber, the Powermaster III must be replaced. If the fluid level has dropped or remained constant, replace the reservoir, cover and diaphragm assembly.

BRAKE SPECIFICATIONS

All measurements in inches unless noted

Year	Model	Master Cylinder Bore	Brake Disc Original Thickness	Brake Disc Minimum Thickness	Brake Disc Maximum Runout	Minimum Lining Thickness Front	Minimum Lining Thickness Rear
1988-89	Cutlass Supreme	0.945	1.04 ②	0.972 ①	0.004	0.030	0.030
	Grand Prix	0.945	1.04 ②	0.972 ①	0.004	0.030	0.030
	Regal	0.945	1.04 ②	0.972 ①	0.004	0.030	0.030
	Lumina	0.945	1.04 ②	0.972 ①	0.004	0.030	0.030
1990	Cutlass Supreme	0.945	1.04 ②	0.972 ①	0.004	0.030	0.030
	Grand Prix	0.945	1.04 ②	0.972 ①	0.004	0.030	0.030
	Regal	0.945	1.04 ②	0.972 ①	0.004	0.030	0.030
	Lumina	0.945	1.04 ②	0.972 ①	0.004	0.030	0.030
1991	Cutlass Supreme	0.945	1.04 ②	0.972 ①	0.004	0.030	0.030
	Grand Prix	0.945	1.04 ②	0.972 ①	0.004	0.030	0.030
	Regal	0.945	1.04 ②	0.972 ①	0.004	0.030	0.030
	Lumina	0.945	1.04 ②	0.972 ①	0.004	0.030	0.030
1992	Cutlass Supreme	0.945	1.04 ②	0.972 ①	0.004	0.030	0.030
	Grand Prix	0.945	1.04 ②	0.972 ①	0.004	0.030	0.030
	Regal	0.945	1.04 ②	0.972 ①	0.004	0.030	0.030
	Lumina	0.945	1.04 ②	0.972 ①	0.004	0.030	0.030

① Rear rotor discard thickness 0.429
② Rear rotor original thickness 0.492

TORQUE SPECIFICATIONS

Component	U.S.	Metric
Master cylinder retaining nuts	20 ft. lbs.	27 Nm
Brake hose-to-caliper bolt	30 ft. lbs.	40 Nm
Brake pipe-to-hose fitting	15 ft. lbs.	20 Nm
Front caliper mounting bolts	79 ft. lbs.	107 Nm
Rear caliper mounting bolts	92 ft. lbs.	125 Nm
Parking brake lever locknut	32 ft. lbs.	44 Nm
Parking brake lever assembly mounting bolts	18 ft. lbs.	25 Nm
Accumulator hex nut	24 ft. lbs.	33 Nm
Solenoid assembly screws	45 inch lbs.	5 Nm
Powermaster III unit attaching nuts	20 ft. lbs.	27 Nm
ABS brake pipes	15 ft. lbs.	17 Nm
15mm front wheel speed sensor	59 ft. lbs.	80 Nm

ANTI–LOCK BRAKE SYSTEM DIAGNOSTICS CANNOT BE ENTERED

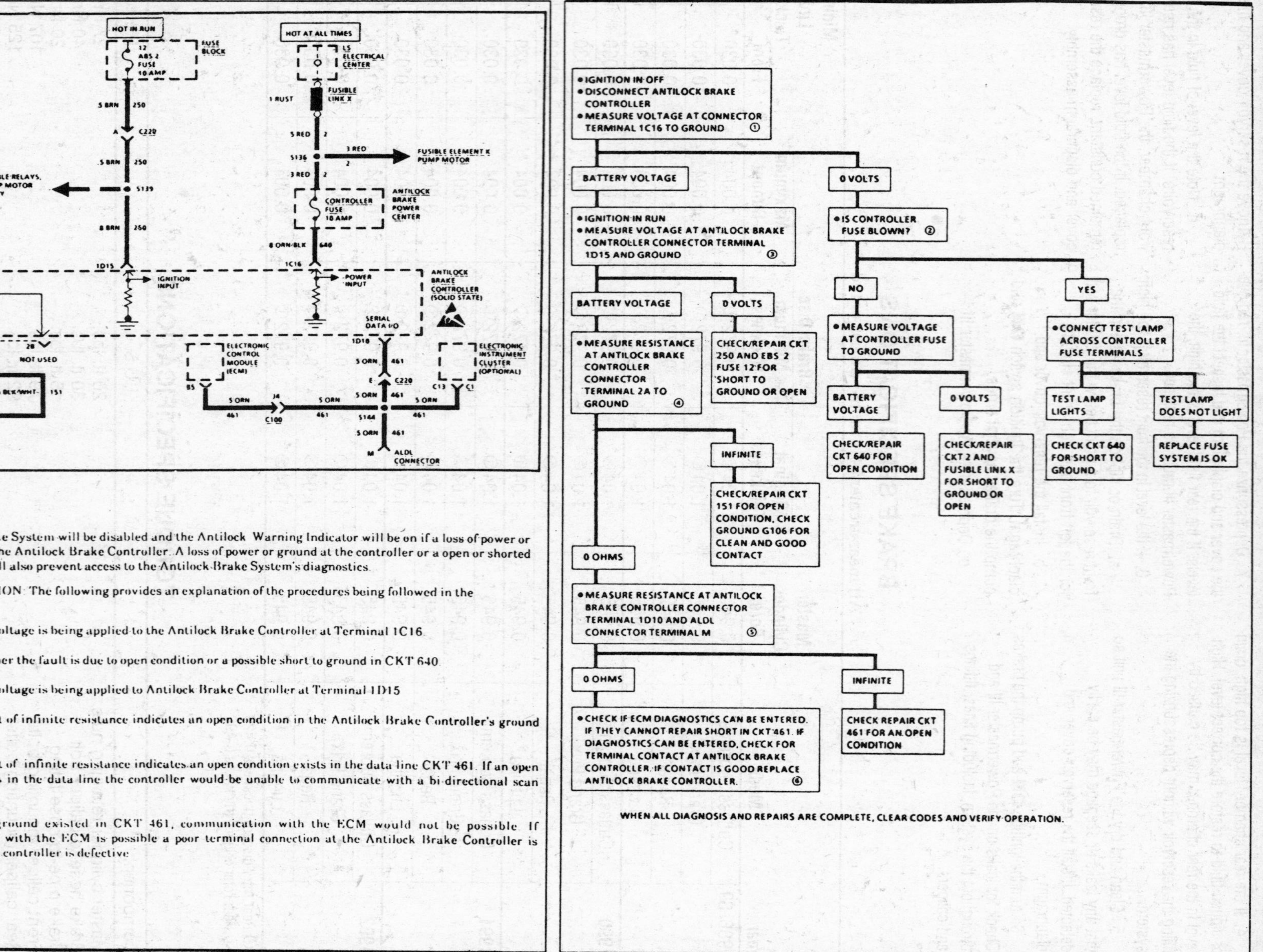

The Antilock Brake System will be disabled and the Antilock Warning Indicator will be on if a loss of power or ground occurs at the Antilock Brake Controller. A loss of power or ground at the controller or a open or shorted serial data line will also prevent access to the Antilock Brake System's diagnostics.

TEST DESCRIPTION: The following provides an explanation of the procedures being followed in the trouble tree.

① Determines if voltage is being applied to the Antilock Brake Controller at Terminal 1C16.

② Indicates whether the fault is due to open condition or a possible short to ground in CKT 640.

③ Determines if voltage is being applied to Antilock Brake Controller at Terminal 1D15.

④ A measurement of infinite resistance indicates an open condition in the Antilock Brake Controller's ground circuit.

⑤ A measurement of infinite resistance indicates an open condition exists in the data line CKT 461. If an open condition exists in the data line the controller would be unable to communicate with a bi-directional scan tool.

⑥ If a short to ground existed in CKT 461, communication with the ECM would not be possible. If communication with the ECM is possible a poor terminal connection at the Antilock Brake Controller is indicated or the controller is defective.

CODE A001 — ANTI-LOCK WARNING INDICATOR SHORTED TO GROUND

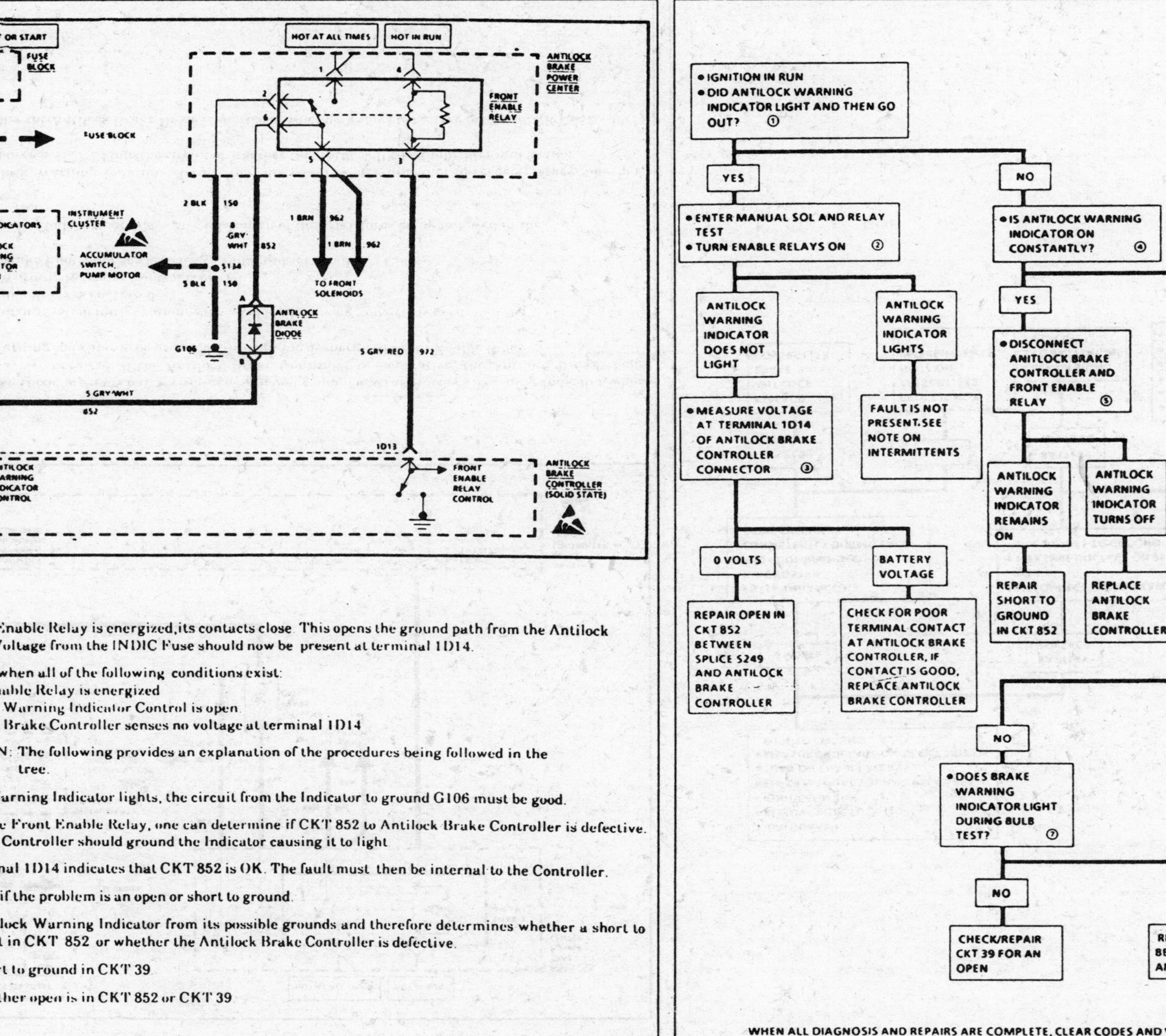

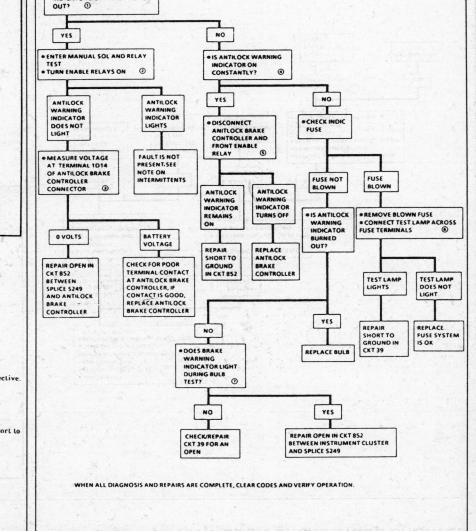

When the Front Enable Relay is energized, its contacts close. This opens the ground path from the Antilock Warning Indicator. Voltage from the INDIC Fuse should now be present at terminal 1D14.

CODE A001 will set when all of the following conditions exist:

- The Front Enable Relay is energized
- The Antilock Warning Indicator Control is open
- The Antilock Brake Controller senses no voltage at terminal 1D14

TEST DESCRIPTION: The following provides an explanation of the procedures being followed in the tree.

① If the Antilock Warning Indicator lights, the circuit from the Indicator to ground G106 must be good.

② By energizing the Front Enable Relay, one can determine if CKT 852 to Antilock Brake Controller is defective. In this mode, the Controller should ground the Indicator causing it to light

③ Voltage at terminal 1D14 indicates that CKT 852 is OK. The fault must then be internal to the Controller.

④ This determines if the problem is an open or short to ground.

⑤ Isolates the Antilock Warning Indicator from its possible grounds and therefore determines whether a short to ground is present in CKT 852 or whether the Antilock Brake Controller is defective.

⑥ Checks for a short to ground in CKT 39

⑦ Determines whether open is in CKT 852 or CKT 39

CODE A002 – ANTI-LOCK WARNING INDICATOR SHORTED TO BATTERY OR ANTI-LOCK BRAKE DIODE SHORTED

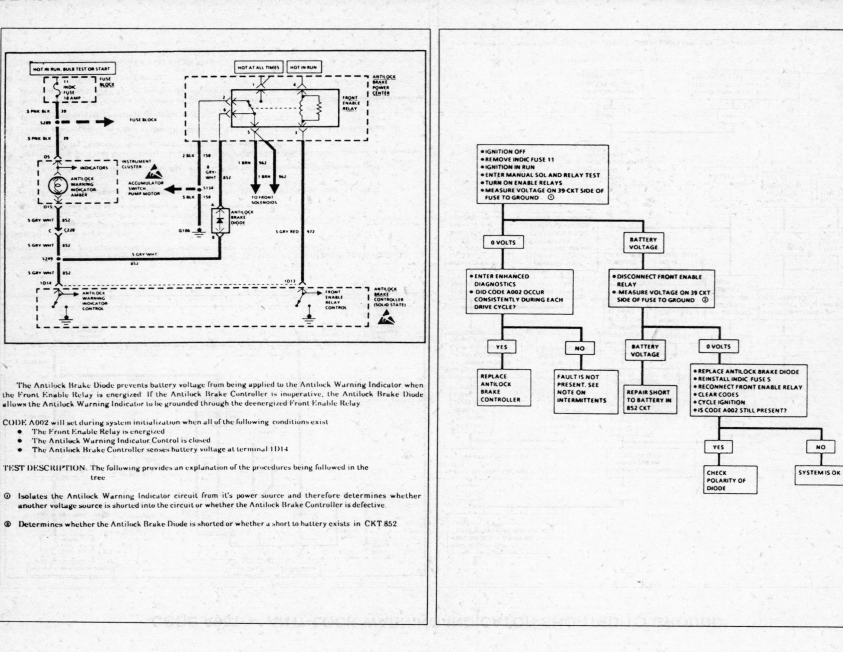

The Antilock Brake Diode prevents battery voltage from being applied to the Antilock Warning Indicator when the Front Enable Relay is energized. If the Antilock Brake Controller is inoperative, the Antilock Brake Diode allows the Antilock Warning Indicator to be grounded through the deenergized Front Enable Relay.

CODE A002 will set during system initialization when all of the following conditions exist

- The Front Enable Relay is energized
- The Antilock Warning Indicator Control is closed
- The Antilock Brake Controller senses battery voltage at terminal 1D14

TEST DESCRIPTION. The following provides an explanation of the procedures being followed in the tree

① Isolates the Antilock Warning Indicator circuit from it's power source and therefore determines whether another voltage source is shorted into the circuit or whether the Antilock Brake Controller is defective.

② Determines whether the Antilock Brake Diode is shorted or whether a short to battery exists in CKT 852.

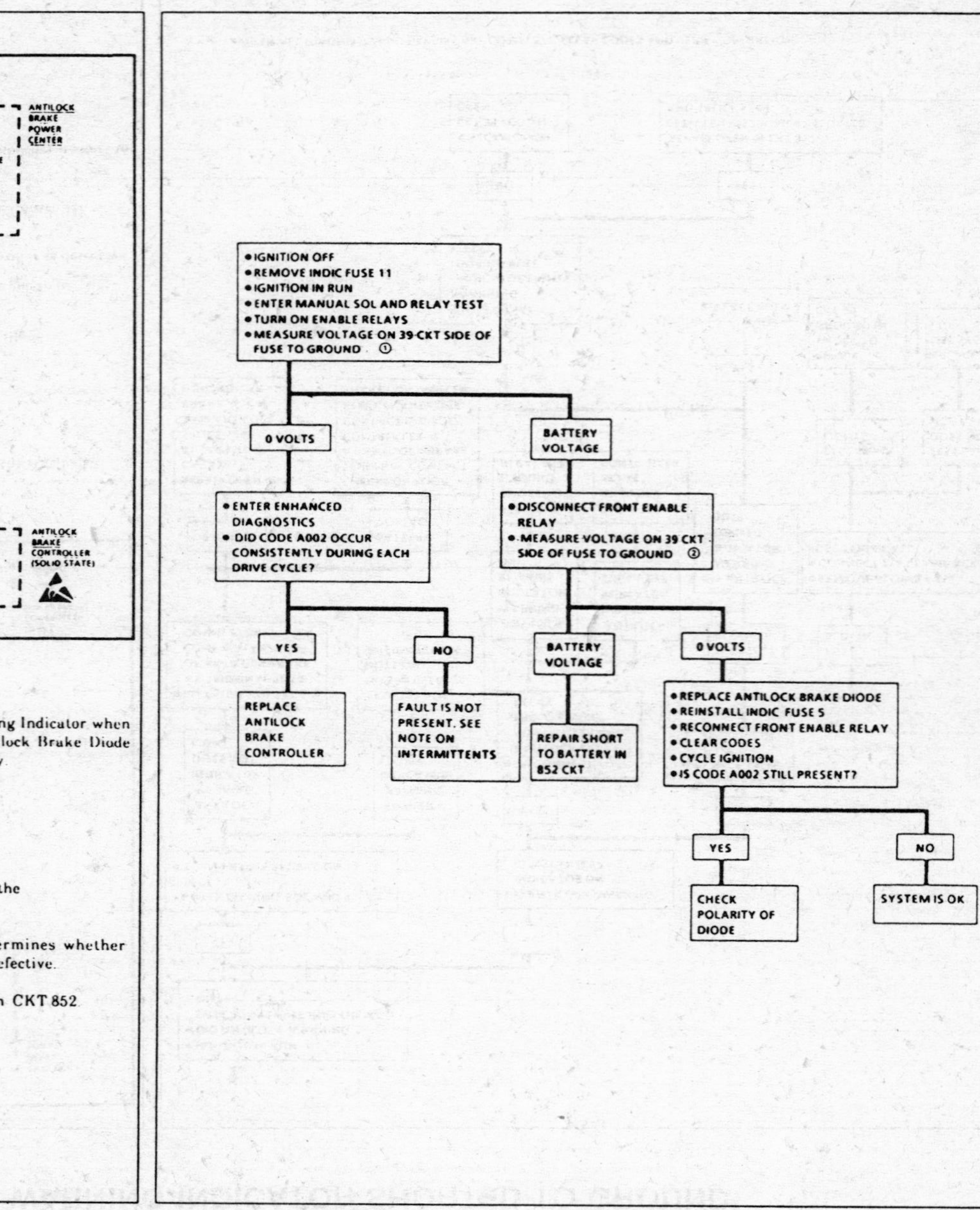

CODE A003 — ANTI-LOCK BRAKE DIODE OPEN OR GROUND OPEN

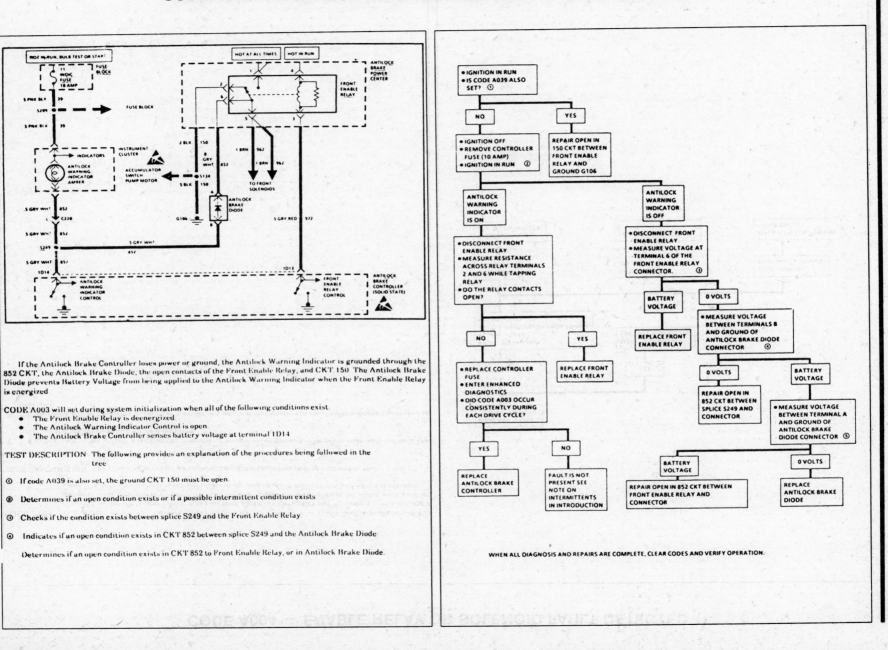

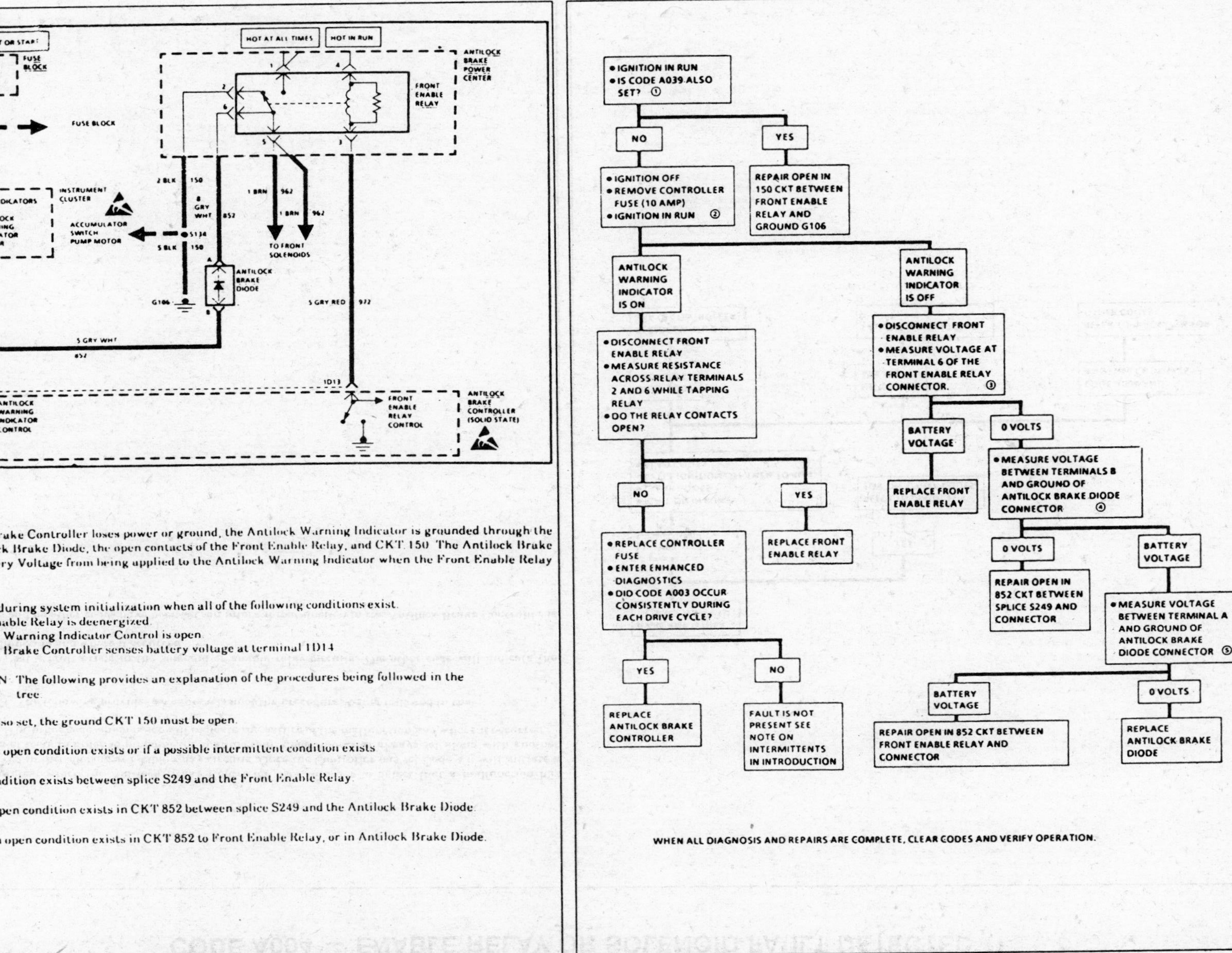

If the Antilock Brake Controller loses power or ground, the Antilock Warning Indicator is grounded through the 852 CKT, the Antilock Brake Diode, the open contacts of the Front Enable Relay, and CKT 150. The Antilock Brake Diode prevents Battery Voltage from being applied to the Antilock Warning Indicator when the Front Enable Relay is energized.

CODE A003 will set during system initialization when all of the following conditions exist.

- The Front Enable Relay is deenergized.
- The Antilock Warning Indicator Control is open.
- The Antilock Brake Controller senses battery voltage at terminal 1D14.

TEST DESCRIPTION: The following provides an explanation of the procedures being followed in the tree.

① If code A039 is also set, the ground CKT 150 must be open.

② Determines if an open condition exists or if a possible intermittent condition exists.

③ Checks if the condition exists between splice S249 and the Front Enable Relay.

④ Indicates if an open condition exists in CKT 852 between splice S249 and the Antilock Brake Diode.

⑤ Determines if an open condition exists in CKT 852 to Front Enable Relay, or in Antilock Brake Diode.

CODE A004 – ENABLE RELAY OR SOLENOID FAULT DETECTED

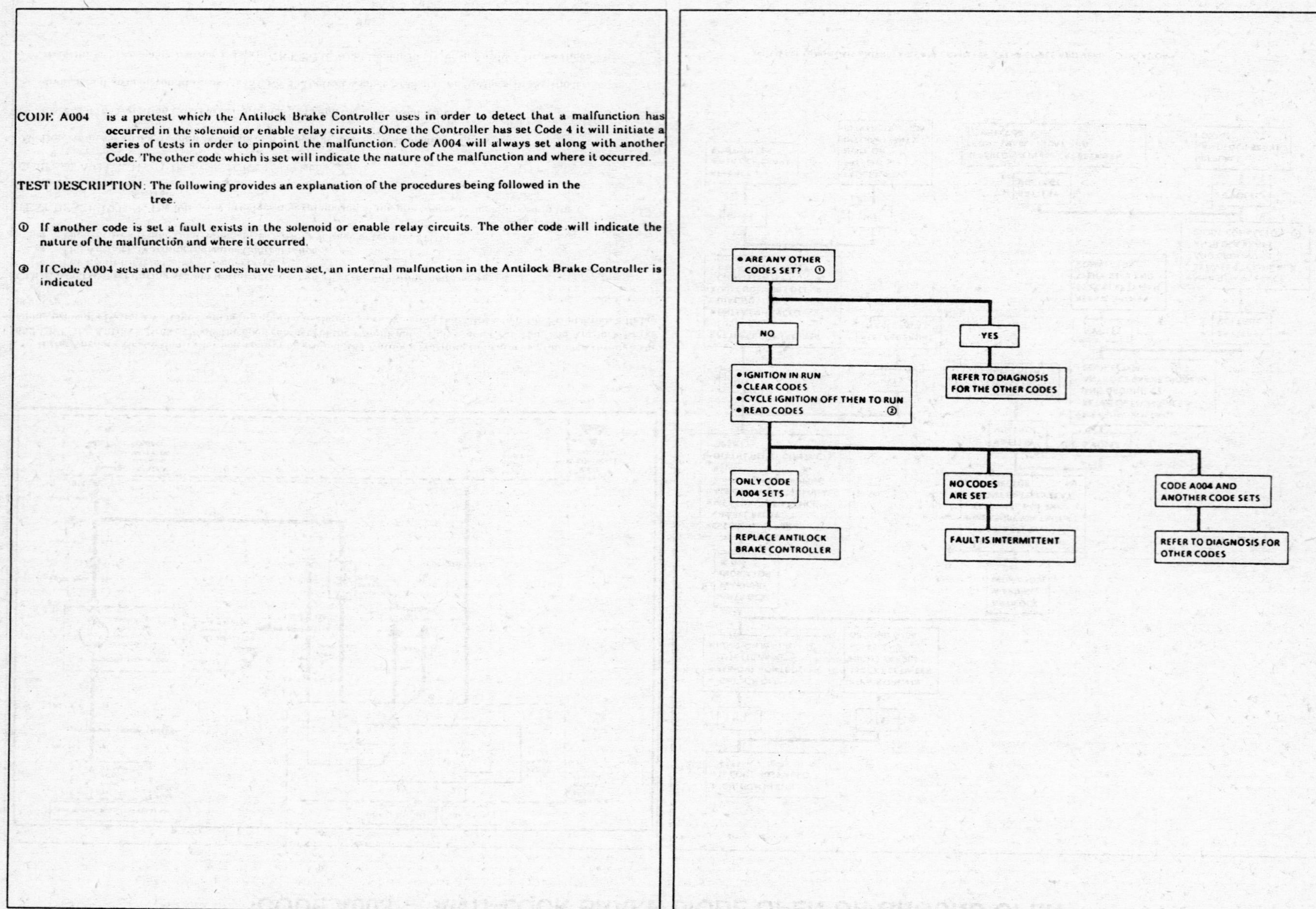

CODE A004 is a pretest which the Antilock Brake Controller uses in order to detect that a malfunction has occurred in the solenoid or enable relay circuits. Once the Controller has set Code 4 it will initiate a series of tests in order to pinpoint the malfunction. Code A004 will always set along with another Code. The other code which is set will indicate the nature of the malfunction and where it occurred.

TEST DESCRIPTION: The following provides an explanation of the procedures being followed in the tree.

① If another code is set a fault exists in the solenoid or enable relay circuits. The other code will indicate the nature of the malfunction and where it occurred.

② If Code A004 sets and no other codes have been set, an internal malfunction in the Antilock Brake Controller is indicated

CODE A005 — FRONT ENABLE RELAY COIL OPEN, CONTACT OPEN OR FUSE OPEN

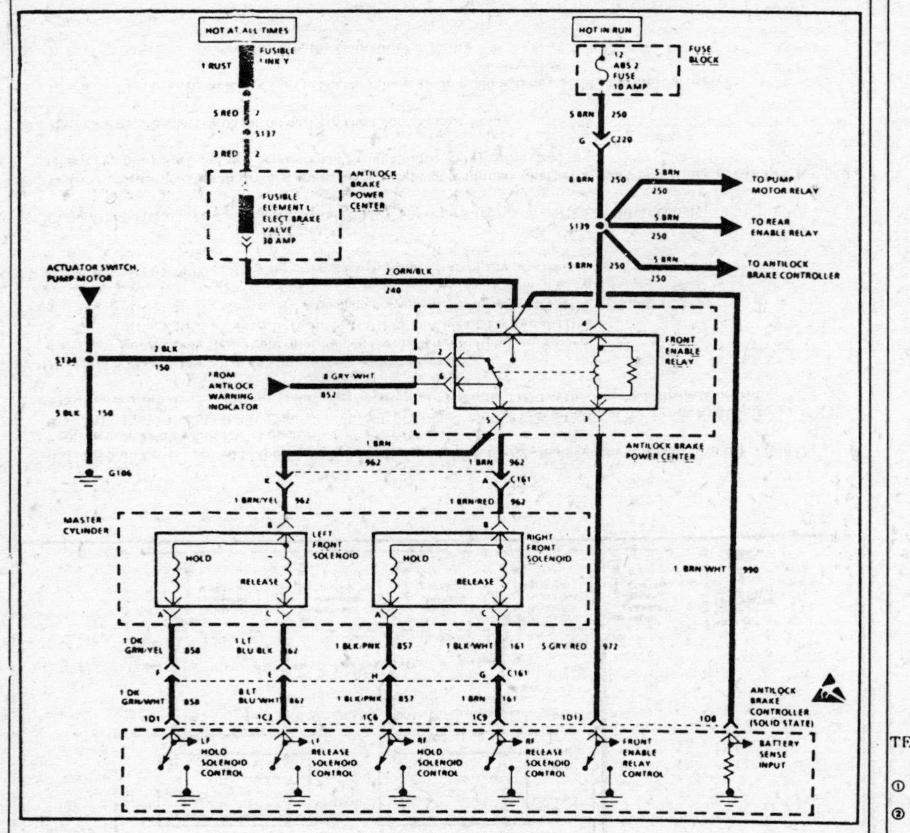

If the Ignition is in RUN and the Antilock Brake Controller does not detect any faults, the Controller will close the Front Enable Relay Control. This grounds the Front Enable Relay Coil and the Relay becomes energized. The contacts close, and voltage is applied from Fusible Element L to the Left Front Solenoid and the Right Front Solenoid. If the Controller is not closing any of the Solenoid Controls, the Controller will sense battery voltage at terminals 1D1, 1C3, 1C6, and 1C9.

CODE A005 will set when all of the following conditions exist.

- The Front Enable Relay Control is closed (Front Enable Relay energized)
- The Antilock Brake Controller senses no voltage at terminals 1D1, 1C3, 1C6 and 1C9

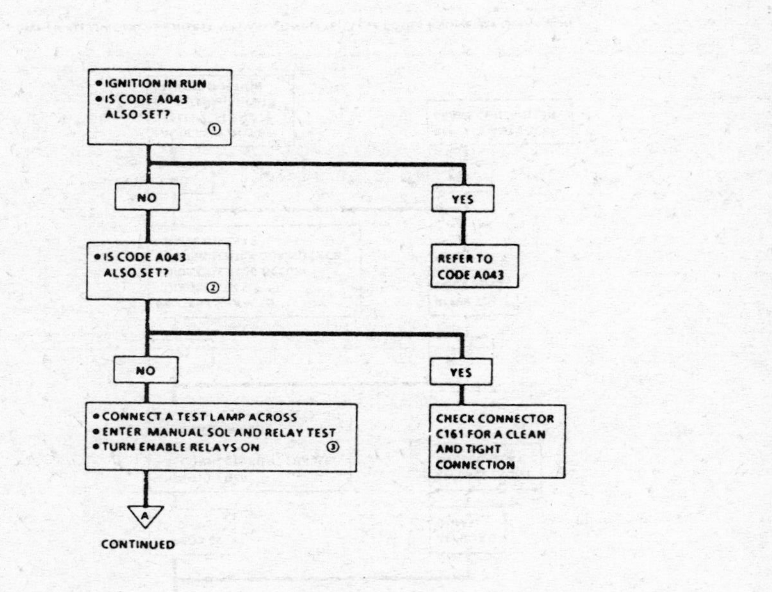

WHEN ALL DIAGNOSIS AND REPAIRS ARE COMPLETE, CLEAR CODES AND VERIFY OPERATION.

TEST DESCRIPTION: The following provides an explanation of the procedures being following in the trouble tree.

① If voltage is present at Front Enable Relay, but not at terminal 1D13, and open in CKT 972 is indicated.

② If Code A007 is also set, none of the solenoids are receiving voltage. This indicates a problem with connector C161.

③ If the test lamp lights, it shows that CKT 250, CKT 972, and the Antilock Brake Controller are good. This indicates that the fault is in the Front Enable Relay or connector, or the fault is intermittent.

④ This determines if Code A005 was set due to a hard failure or an intermittent condition.

⑤ If voltage is present at terminal 1D13, all external circuits must be good. this indicates an internal problem with the Controller.

⑥ If voltage is present at Front Enable Relay, but not at terminal 1D13, an open in CKT 972 is indicated.

CODE A006 – FRONT ENABLE RELAY COIL SHORTED TO BATTERY

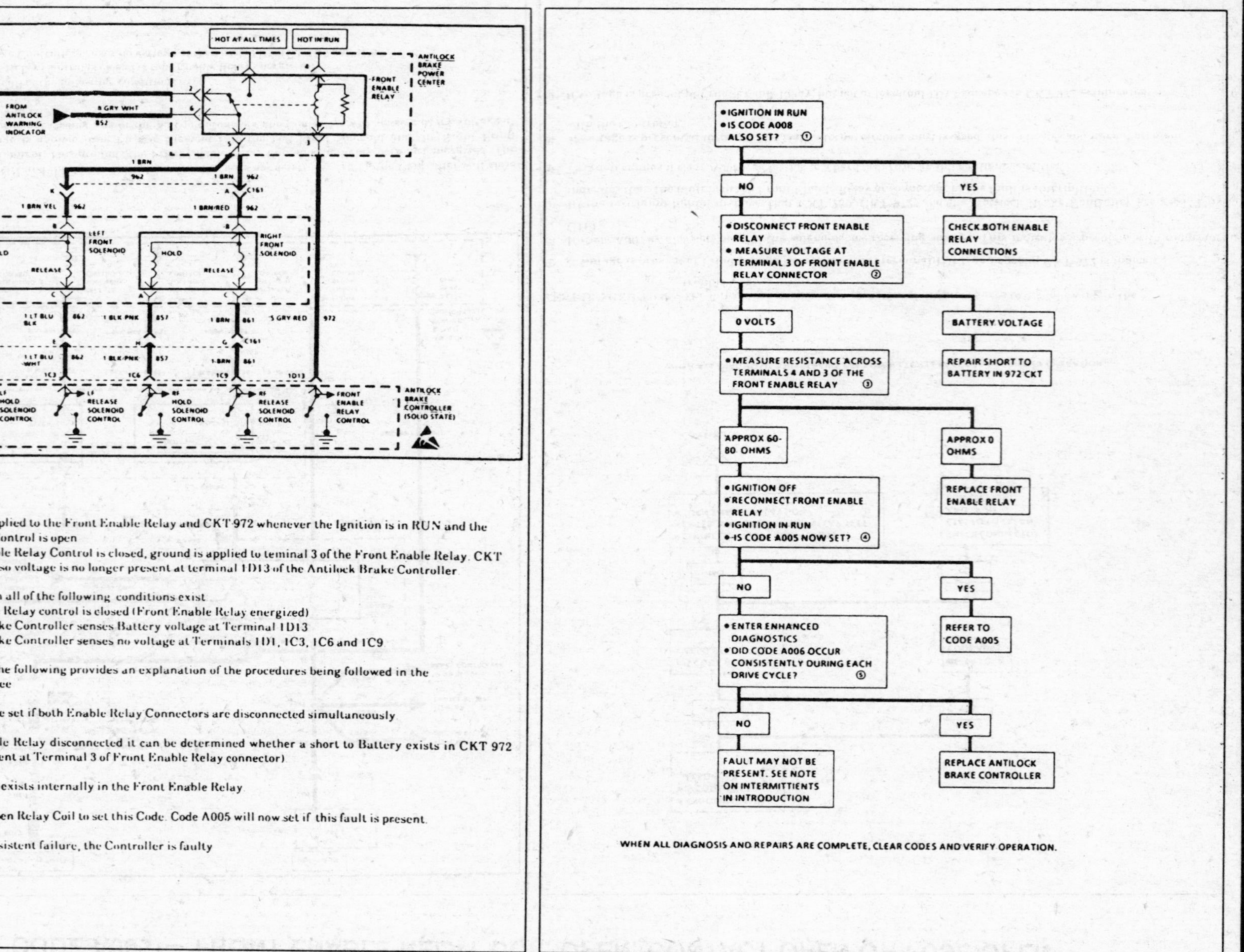

Battery Voltage is applied to the Front Enable Relay and CKT 972 whenever the Ignition is in RUN and the Front Enable Relay Control is open

When the Front Enable Relay Control is closed, ground is applied to teminal 3 of the Front Enable Relay. CKT 972 is now grounded, so voltage is no longer present at terminal 1D13 of the Antilock Brake Controller

CODE A006 will set when all of the following conditions exist

- The Front Enable Relay control is closed (Front Enable Relay energized)
- The Antilock Brake Controller senses Battery voltage at Terminal 1D13
- The Antilock Brake Controller senses no voltage at Terminals 1D1, 1C3, 1C6 and 1C9

TEST DESCRIPTION The following provides an explanation of the procedures being followed in the tree

① Code A008 will also be set if both Enable Relay Connectors are disconnected simultaneously

② With the Front Enable Relay disconnected it can be determined whether a short to Battery exists in CKT 972 (Battery voltage present at Terminal 3 of Front Enable Relay connector)

③ Determines if a short exists internally in the Front Enable Relay

④ It is possible for an open Relay Coil to set this Code. Code A005 will now set if this fault is present.

⑤ If Code A006 is a consistent failure, the Controller is faulty

CODE A007 — REAR ENABLE RELAY COIL OPEN, CONTACTS OPEN OR FUSE OPEN

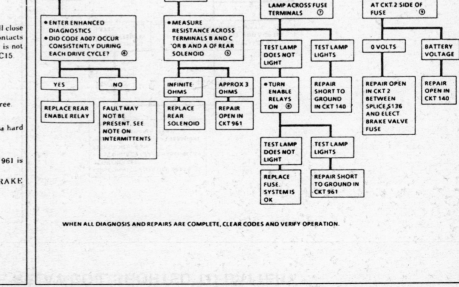

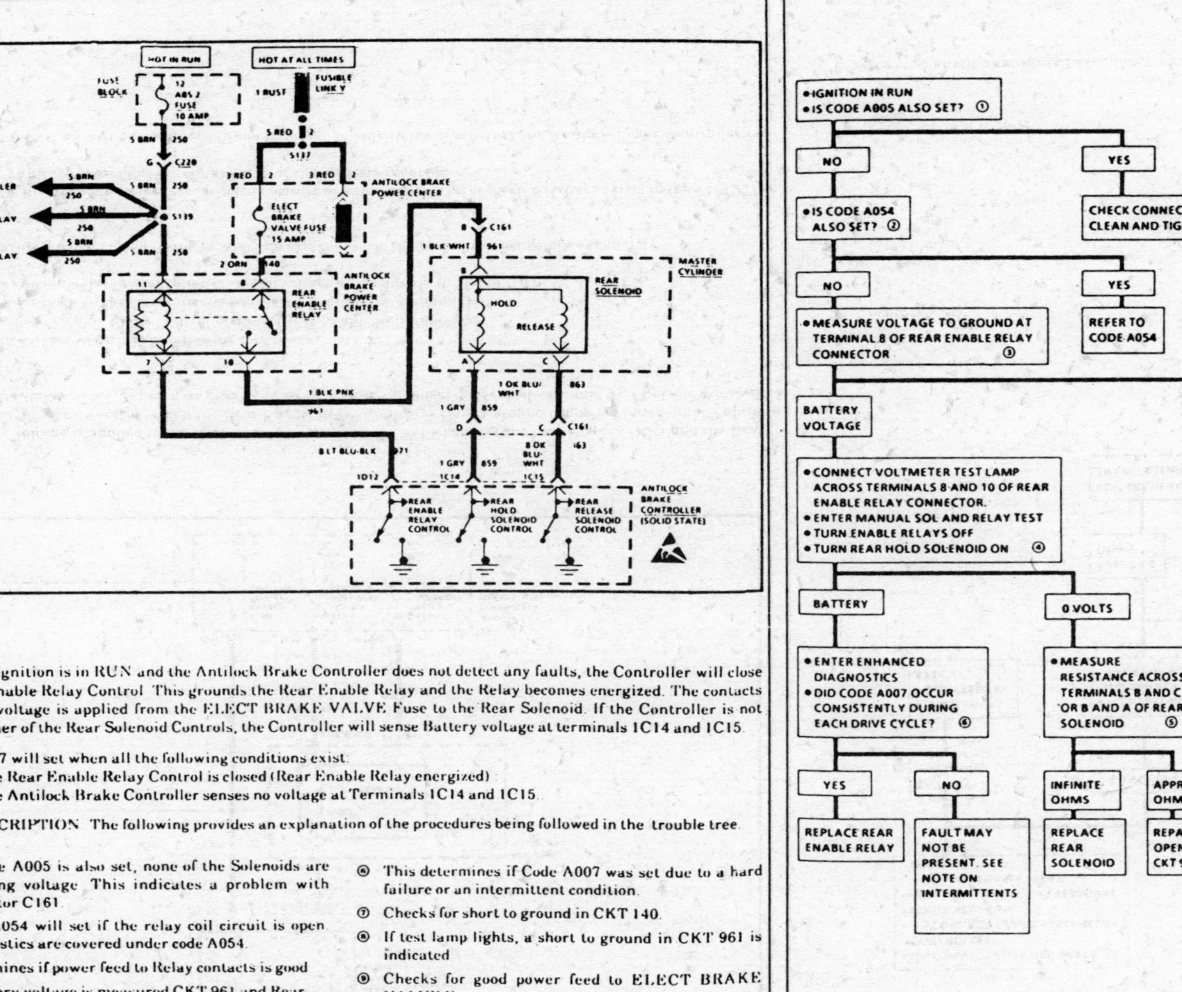

If the Ignition is in RUN and the Antilock Brake Controller does not detect any faults, the Controller will close the Rear Enable Relay Control. This grounds the Rear Enable Relay and the Relay becomes energized. The contacts close, and voltage is applied from the ELECT BRAKE VALVE Fuse to the Rear Solenoid. If the Controller is not closing either of the Rear Solenoid Controls, the Controller will sense Battery voltage at terminals 1C14 and 1C15.

CODE A007 will set when all the following conditions exist:

- The Rear Enable Relay Control is closed (Rear Enable Relay energized).
- The Antilock Brake Controller senses no voltage at Terminals 1C14 and 1C15.

TEST DESCRIPTION: The following provides an explanation of the procedures being followed in the trouble tree.

① If Code A005 is also set, none of the Solenoids are receiving voltage. This indicates a problem with connector C161.

② Code A054 will set if the relay coil circuit is open. Diagnostics are covered under code A054.

③ Determines if power feed to Relay contacts is good.

④ If Battery voltage is measured CKT 961 and Rear Solenoid are good.

⑤ Determines if open exists in Rear Solenoid or in CKT 961.

⑥ This determines if Code A007 was set due to a hard failure or an intermittent condition.

⑦ Checks for short to ground in CKT 140.

⑧ If test lamp lights, a short to ground in CKT 961 is indicated.

⑨ Checks for good power feed to ELECT BRAKE VALVE Fuse.

- • IGNITION IN RUN
  • IS CODE A005 ALSO SET? ①
  - YES → CHECK CONNECTOR C161 FOR A CLEAN AND TIGHT CONNECTION
  - NO → • IS CODE A054 ALSO SET? ②
    - YES → REFER TO CODE A054
    - NO → • MEASURE VOLTAGE TO GROUND AT TERMINAL 8 OF REAR ENABLE RELAY CONNECTOR ③
      - BATTERY VOLTAGE → • CONNECT VOLTMETER TEST LAMP ACROSS TERMINALS 8 AND 10 OF REAR ENABLE RELAY CONNECTOR. • ENTER MANUAL SOL AND RELAY TEST • TURN ENABLE RELAYS OFF • TURN REAR HOLD SOLENOID ON ④
        - BATTERY → • ENTER ENHANCED DIAGNOSTICS • DID CODE A007 OCCUR CONSISTENTLY DURING EACH DRIVE CYCLE? ⑥
          - YES → REPLACE REAR ENABLE RELAY
          - NO → FAULT MAY NOT BE PRESENT. SEE NOTE ON INTERMITTENTS
        - 0 VOLTS → • MEASURE RESISTANCE ACROSS TERMINALS B AND C OR B AND A OF REAR SOLENOID ⑤
          - INFINITE OHMS → REPLACE REAR SOLENOID
          - APPROX 3 OHMS → REPAIR OPEN IN CKT 961
      - 0 VOLTS → • CHECK ELECT BRAKE VALVE FUSE
        - FUSE BLOWN → • CONNECT TEST LAMP ACROSS FUSE TERMINALS ⑦
          - TEST LAMP DOES NOT LIGHT → • TURN ENABLE RELAYS ON ⑧
            - TEST LAMP DOES NOT LIGHT → REPLACE FUSE. SYSTEM IS OK
            - TEST LAMP LIGHTS → REPAIR SHORT TO GROUND IN CKT 961
          - TEST LAMP LIGHTS → REPAIR SHORT TO GROUND IN CKT 140
        - FUSE NOT BLOWN → • MEASURE VOLTAGE AT CKT 2 SIDE OF FUSE ⑨
          - 0 VOLTS → REPAIR OPEN IN CKT 2 BETWEEN SPLICE S136 AND ELECT BRAKE VALVE FUSE
          - BATTERY VOLTAGE → REPAIR OPEN IN CKT 140

WHEN ALL DIAGNOSIS AND REPAIRS ARE COMPLETE, CLEAR CODES AND VERIFY OPERATION.

CODE A008 — REAR ENABLE RELAY COIL SHORTED TO BATTERY

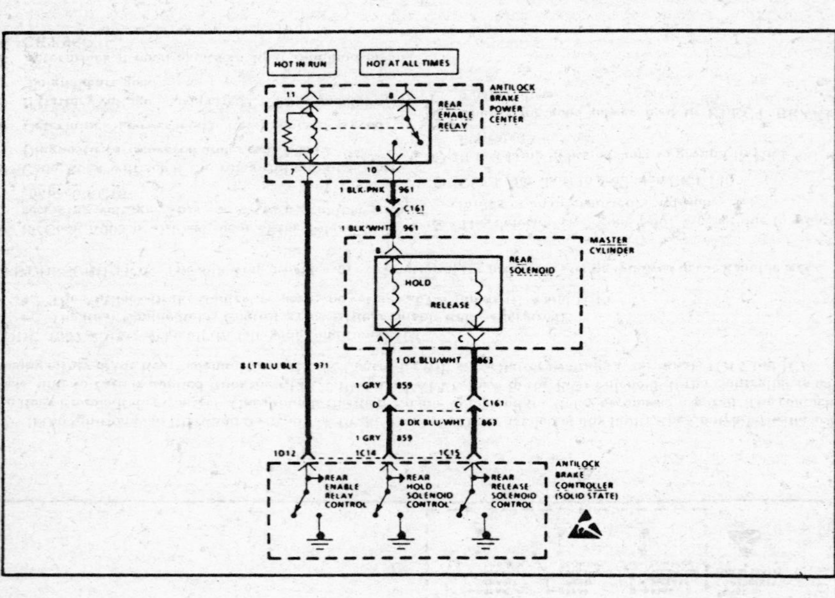

Battery voltage is applied to the Rear Enable Relay and CKT 971 whenever the Ignition is in RUN and the Rear Enable Relay Control is open. When the Rear Enable Relay Control is closed, ground is applied to terminal 7 of the Rear Enable Relay. CKT 971 is now grounded, so voltage is no longer present at terminal 1D12 of the Antilock Brake Controller.

CODE A008 will set when all the following conditions exist:

- The Rear Enable Relay Control is closed (Rear Enable Relay energized)
- The Antilock Brake Controller senses Battery voltage at Terminal 1D12
- The Antilock Brake Controller senses no voltage at Terminals 1C14 and 1C15.

TEST DESCRIPTION: The following provides an explanation of the procedures being followed in the tree.

① With the Rear Enable Relay disconnected it can be determined whether a short to Battery exists in the 971 CKT (Battery voltage present at Terminal 7 of Rear Enable Relay connector)

② Determines if a short exists internally in the Rear Enable Relay or whether the Antilock Brake Controller is defective.

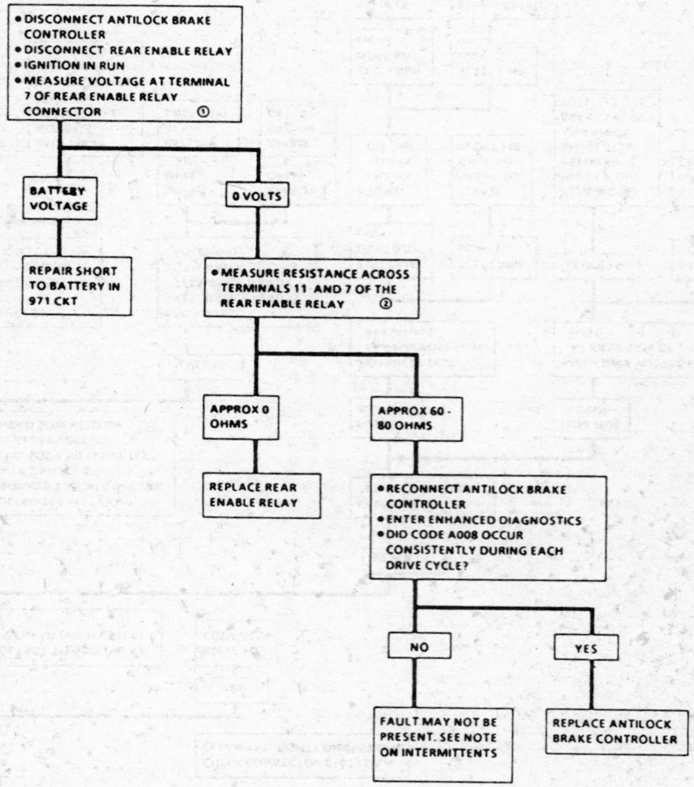

- DISCONNECT ANTILOCK BRAKE CONTROLLER
- DISCONNECT REAR ENABLE RELAY
- IGNITION IN RUN
- MEASURE VOLTAGE AT TERMINAL 7 OF REAR ENABLE RELAY CONNECTOR ①

BATTERY VOLTAGE → REPAIR SHORT TO BATTERY IN 971 CKT

0 VOLTS → • MEASURE RESISTANCE ACROSS TERMINALS 11 AND 7 OF THE REAR ENABLE RELAY ②

- APPROX 0 OHMS → REPLACE REAR ENABLE RELAY
- APPROX 60 - 80 OHMS →
  - RECONNECT ANTILOCK BRAKE CONTROLLER
  - ENTER ENHANCED DIAGNOSTICS
  - DID CODE A008 OCCUR CONSISTENTLY DURING EACH DRIVE CYCLE?

  NO → FAULT MAY NOT BE PRESENT. SEE NOTE ON INTERMITTENTS

  YES → REPLACE ANTILOCK BRAKE CONTROLLER

WHEN ALL DIAGNOSIS AND REPAIRS ARE COMPLETE, CLEAR CODES AND VERIFY OPERATION.

CODE A009 — RIGHT FRONT HOLD SOLENOID OPEN OR SHORTED TO GROUND

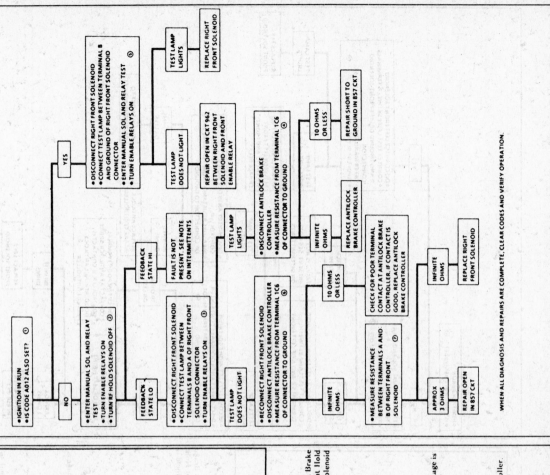

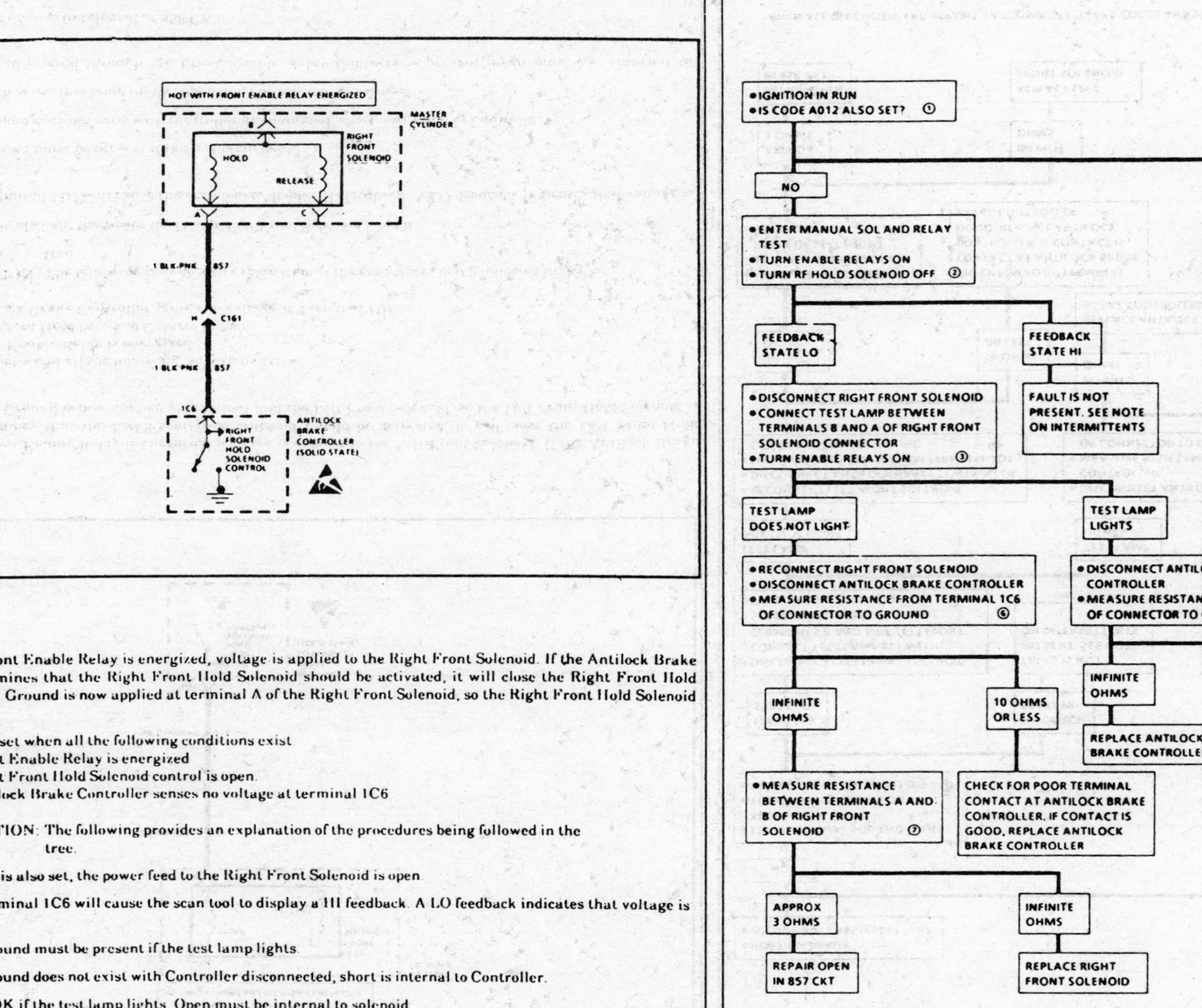

When the Front Enable Relay is energized, voltage is applied to the Right Front Solenoid. If the Antilock Brake Controller determines that the Right Front Hold Solenoid should be activated, it will close the Right Front Hold Solenoid Control. Ground is now applied at terminal A of the Right Front Solenoid, so the Right Front Hold Solenoid is on.

CODE A009 will set when all the following conditions exist

- The Front Enable Relay is energized
- The Right Front Hold Solenoid control is open
- The Antilock Brake Controller senses no voltage at terminal 1C6

TEST DESCRIPTION: The following provides an explanation of the procedures being followed in the tree.

① If Code A012 is also set, the power feed to the Right Front Solenoid is open.

② Voltge at terminal 1C6 will cause the scan tool to display a HI feedback. A LO feedback indicates that voltage is not present.

③ A short to ground must be present if the test lamp lights.

④ If short to ground does not exist with Controller disconnected, short is internal to Controller.

⑤ CKT 962 is OK if the test lamp lights. Open must be internal to solenoid

⑥ If continuity to ground through the Front Enable Relay contacts is present, open must be internal to Controller.

⑦ Determines if open is in Solenoid or 857 CKT.

CODE A010 – LEFT FRONT HOLD SOLENOID OPEN OR SHORTED TO GROUND

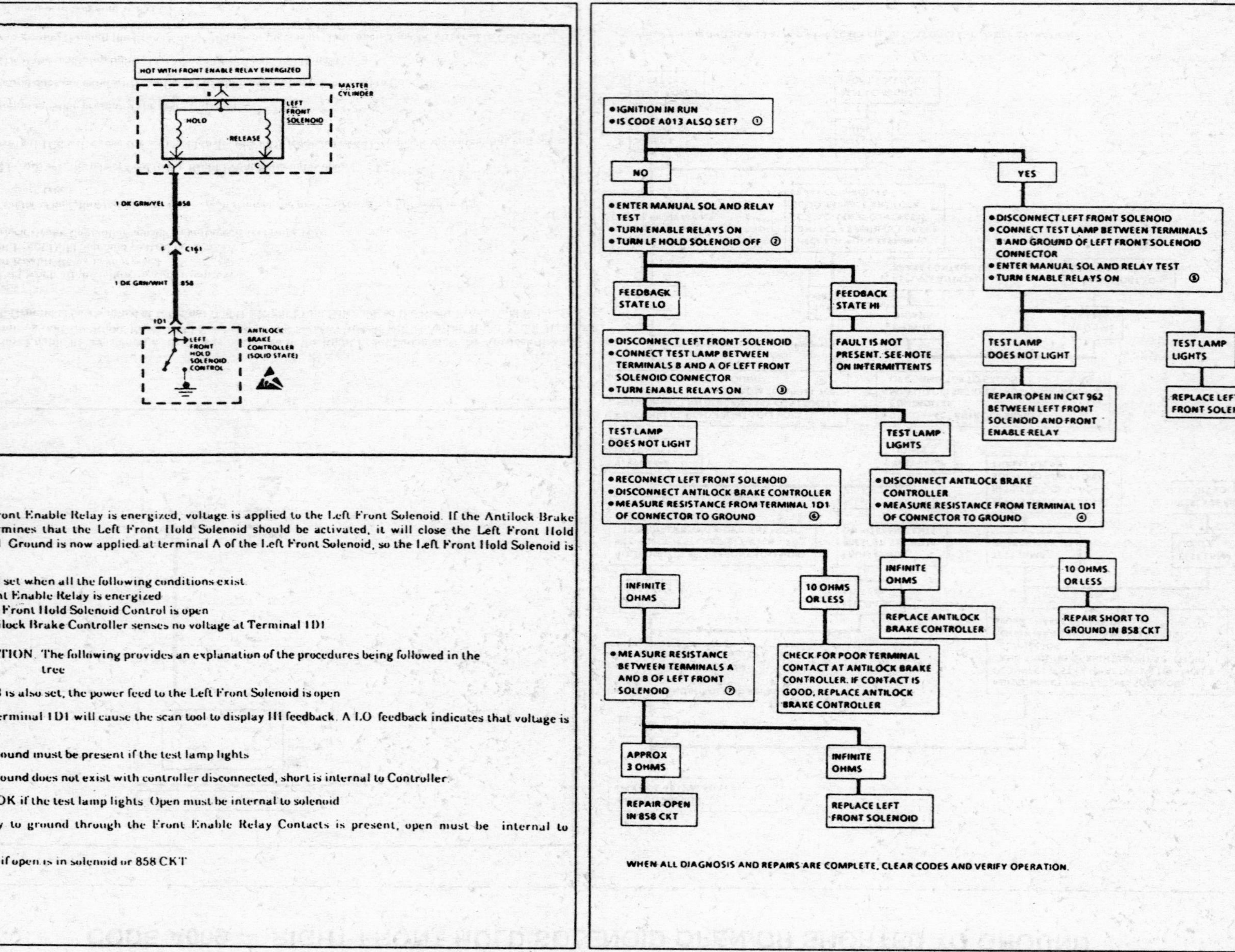
HOT WITH FRONT ENABLE RELAY ENERGIZED
MASTER CYLINDER
LEFT FRONT SOLENOID
HOLD
RELEASE
1 DK GRN/YEL 858
C161
1 DK GRN/WHT 858
1D1
LEFT FRONT HOLD SOLENOID CONTROL
ANTILOCK BRAKE CONTROLLER (SOLID STATE)
• IGNITION IN RUN
• IS CODE A013 ALSO SET? ①
NO
YES
• ENTER MANUAL SOL AND RELAY TEST
• TURN ENABLE RELAYS ON
• TURN LF HOLD SOLENOID OFF ②
FEEDBACK STATE LO
FEEDBACK STATE HI
FAULT IS NOT PRESENT. SEE NOTE ON INTERMITTENTS
• DISCONNECT LEFT FRONT SOLENOID
• CONNECT TEST LAMP BETWEEN TERMINALS B AND A OF LEFT FRONT SOLENOID CONNECTOR
• TURN ENABLE RELAYS ON ③
TEST LAMP DOES NOT LIGHT
TEST LAMP LIGHTS
• RECONNECT LEFT FRONT SOLENOID
• DISCONNECT ANTILOCK BRAKE CONTROLLER
• MEASURE RESISTANCE FROM TERMINAL 1D1 OF CONNECTOR TO GROUND ⑥
INFINITE OHMS
10 OHMS OR LESS
• MEASURE RESISTANCE BETWEEN TERMINALS A AND B OF LEFT FRONT SOLENOID ⑦
CHECK FOR POOR TERMINAL CONTACT AT ANTILOCK BRAKE CONTROLLER. IF CONTACT IS GOOD, REPLACE ANTILOCK BRAKE CONTROLLER
APPROX 3 OHMS
INFINITE OHMS
REPAIR OPEN IN 858 CKT
REPLACE LEFT FRONT SOLENOID
• DISCONNECT ANTILOCK BRAKE CONTROLLER
• MEASURE RESISTANCE FROM TERMINAL 1D1 OF CONNECTOR TO GROUND ④
INFINITE OHMS
10 OHMS OR LESS
REPLACE ANTILOCK BRAKE CONTROLLER
REPAIR SHORT TO GROUND IN 858 CKT
• DISCONNECT LEFT FRONT SOLENOID
• CONNECT TEST LAMP BETWEEN TERMINALS B AND GROUND OF LEFT FRONT SOLENOID CONNECTOR
• ENTER MANUAL SOL AND RELAY TEST
• TURN ENABLE RELAYS ON ⑤
TEST LAMP DOES NOT LIGHT
TEST LAMP LIGHTS
REPAIR OPEN IN CKT 962 BETWEEN LEFT FRONT SOLENOID AND FRONT ENABLE RELAY
REPLACE LEFT FRONT SOLENOID
WHEN ALL DIAGNOSIS AND REPAIRS ARE COMPLETE, CLEAR CODES AND VERIFY OPERATION.

When the Front Enable Relay is energized, voltage is applied to the Left Front Solenoid. If the Antilock Brake Controller determines that the Left Front Hold Solenoid should be activated, it will close the Left Front Hold Solenoid Control Ground is now applied at terminal A of the Left Front Solenoid, so the Left Front Hold Solenoid is on.

CODE A010 will set when all the following conditions exist

- The Front Enable Relay is energized
- The Left Front Hold Solenoid Control is open
- The Antilock Brake Controller senses no voltage at Terminal 1D1

TEST DESCRIPTION. The following provides an explanation of the procedures being followed in the tree

① If Code A013 is also set, the power feed to the Left Front Solenoid is open

② Voltage at terminal 1D1 will cause the scan tool to display HI feedback. A LO feedback indicates that voltage is not present

③ A short to ground must be present if the test lamp lights

④ If short to ground does not exist with controller disconnected, short is internal to Controller

⑤ CKT 962 is OK if the test lamp lights Open must be internal to solenoid

⑥ If continuity to ground through the Front Enable Relay Contacts is present, open must be internal to Controller

⑦ Determines if open is in solenoid or 858 CKT

CODE A011 — REAR HOLD SOLENOID OPEN OR SHORTED TO GROUND

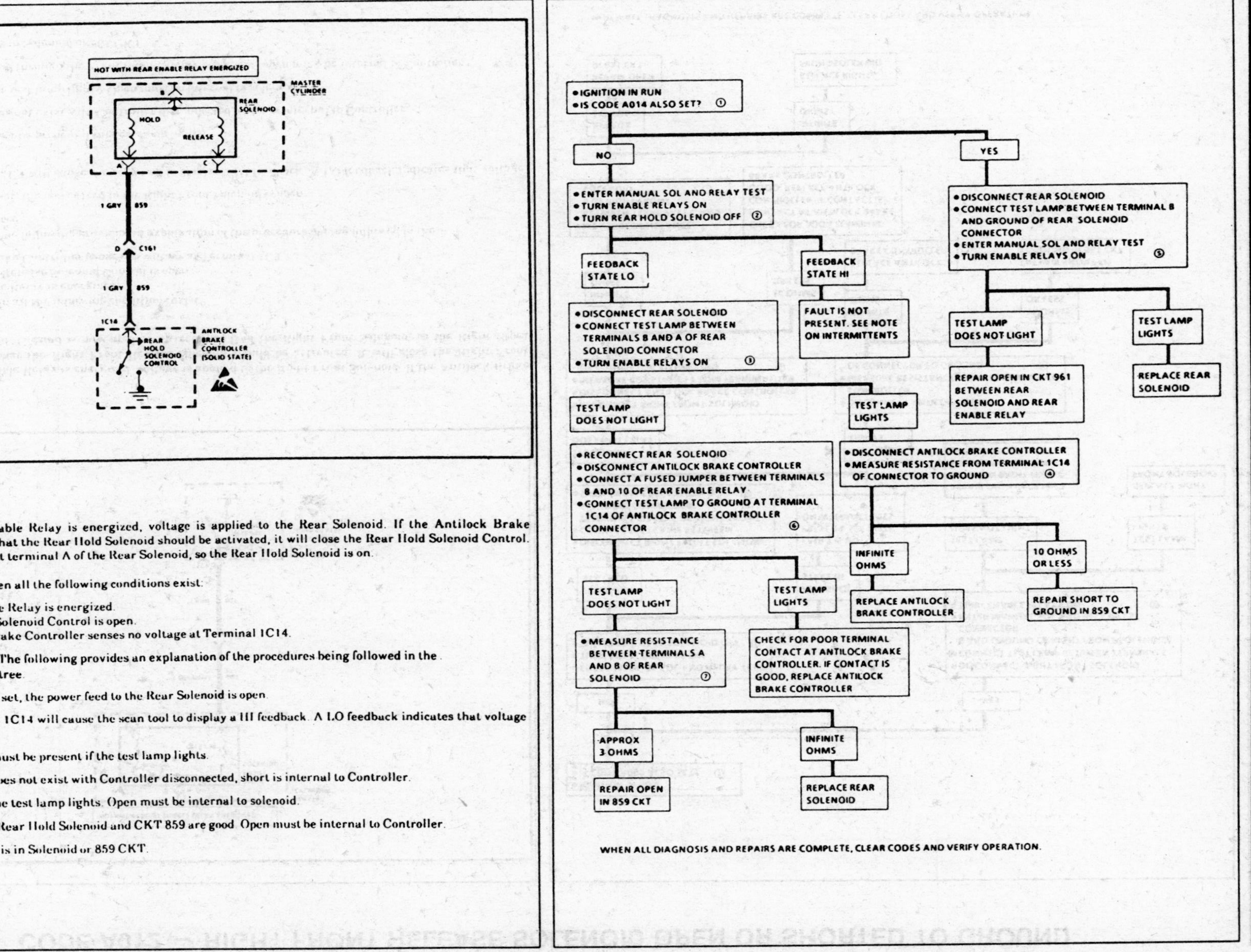
HOT WITH REAR ENABLE RELAY ENERGIZED
MASTER CYLINDER
REAR SOLENOID
HOLD
RELEASE
1 GRY 859
C161
1C14
REAR HOLD SOLENOID CONTROL
ANTILOCK BRAKE CONTROLLER (SOLID STATE)
• IGNITION IN RUN
• IS CODE A014 ALSO SET? ①
NO
YES
• ENTER MANUAL SOL AND RELAY TEST
• TURN ENABLE RELAYS ON
• TURN REAR HOLD SOLENOID OFF ②
FEEDBACK STATE LO
FEEDBACK STATE HI
FAULT IS NOT PRESENT. SEE NOTE ON INTERMITTENTS
• DISCONNECT REAR SOLENOID
• CONNECT TEST LAMP BETWEEN TERMINALS B AND A OF REAR SOLENOID CONNECTOR
• TURN ENABLE RELAYS ON ③
TEST LAMP DOES NOT LIGHT
TEST LAMP LIGHTS
• RECONNECT REAR SOLENOID
• DISCONNECT ANTILOCK BRAKE CONTROLLER
• CONNECT A FUSED JUMPER BETWEEN TERMINALS 8 AND 10 OF REAR ENABLE RELAY
• CONNECT TEST LAMP TO GROUND AT TERMINAL 1C14 OF ANTILOCK BRAKE CONTROLLER CONNECTOR ⑥
• DISCONNECT ANTILOCK BRAKE CONTROLLER
• MEASURE RESISTANCE FROM TERMINAL 1C14 OF CONNECTOR TO GROUND ④
INFINITE OHMS
10 OHMS OR LESS
REPLACE ANTILOCK BRAKE CONTROLLER
REPAIR SHORT TO GROUND IN 859 CKT
TEST LAMP DOES NOT LIGHT
TEST LAMP LIGHTS
• MEASURE RESISTANCE BETWEEN TERMINALS A AND B OF REAR SOLENOID ⑦
CHECK FOR POOR TERMINAL CONTACT AT ANTILOCK BRAKE CONTROLLER. IF CONTACT IS GOOD, REPLACE ANTILOCK BRAKE CONTROLLER
APPROX 3 OHMS
INFINITE OHMS
REPAIR OPEN IN 859 CKT
REPLACE REAR SOLENOID
• DISCONNECT REAR SOLENOID
• CONNECT TEST LAMP BETWEEN TERMINAL B AND GROUND OF REAR SOLENOID CONNECTOR
• ENTER MANUAL SOL AND RELAY TEST
• TURN ENABLE RELAYS ON ⑤
TEST LAMP DOES NOT LIGHT
TEST LAMP LIGHTS
REPAIR OPEN IN CKT 961 BETWEEN REAR SOLENOID AND REAR ENABLE RELAY
REPLACE REAR SOLENOID
WHEN ALL DIAGNOSIS AND REPAIRS ARE COMPLETE, CLEAR CODES AND VERIFY OPERATION.

When the Rear Enable Relay is energized, voltage is applied to the Rear Solenoid. If the Antilock Brake Controller determines that the Rear Hold Solenoid should be activated, it will close the Rear Hold Solenoid Control. Ground is now applied at terminal A of the Rear Solenoid, so the Rear Hold Solenoid is on.

CODE A011 will set when all the following conditions exist:

- The Rear Enable Relay is energized.
- The Rear Hold Solenoid Control is open.
- The Antilock Brake Controller senses no voltage at Terminal 1C14.

TEST DESCRIPTION: The following provides an explanation of the procedures being followed in the tree.

① If Code A014 is also set, the power feed to the Rear Solenoid is open.

② Voltage at terminal 1C14 will cause the scan tool to display a HI feedback. A LO feedback indicates that voltage is not present.

③ A short to ground must be present if the test lamp lights.

④ If short to ground does not exist with Controller disconnected, short is internal to Controller.

⑤ CKT 961 is OK if the test lamp lights. Open must be internal to solenoid.

⑥ If test lamp lights, Rear Hold Solenoid and CKT 859 are good. Open must be internal to Controller.

⑦ Determines if open is in Solenoid or 859 CKT.

CODE A012 — RIGHT FRONT RELEASE SOLENOID OPEN OR SHORTED TO GROUND

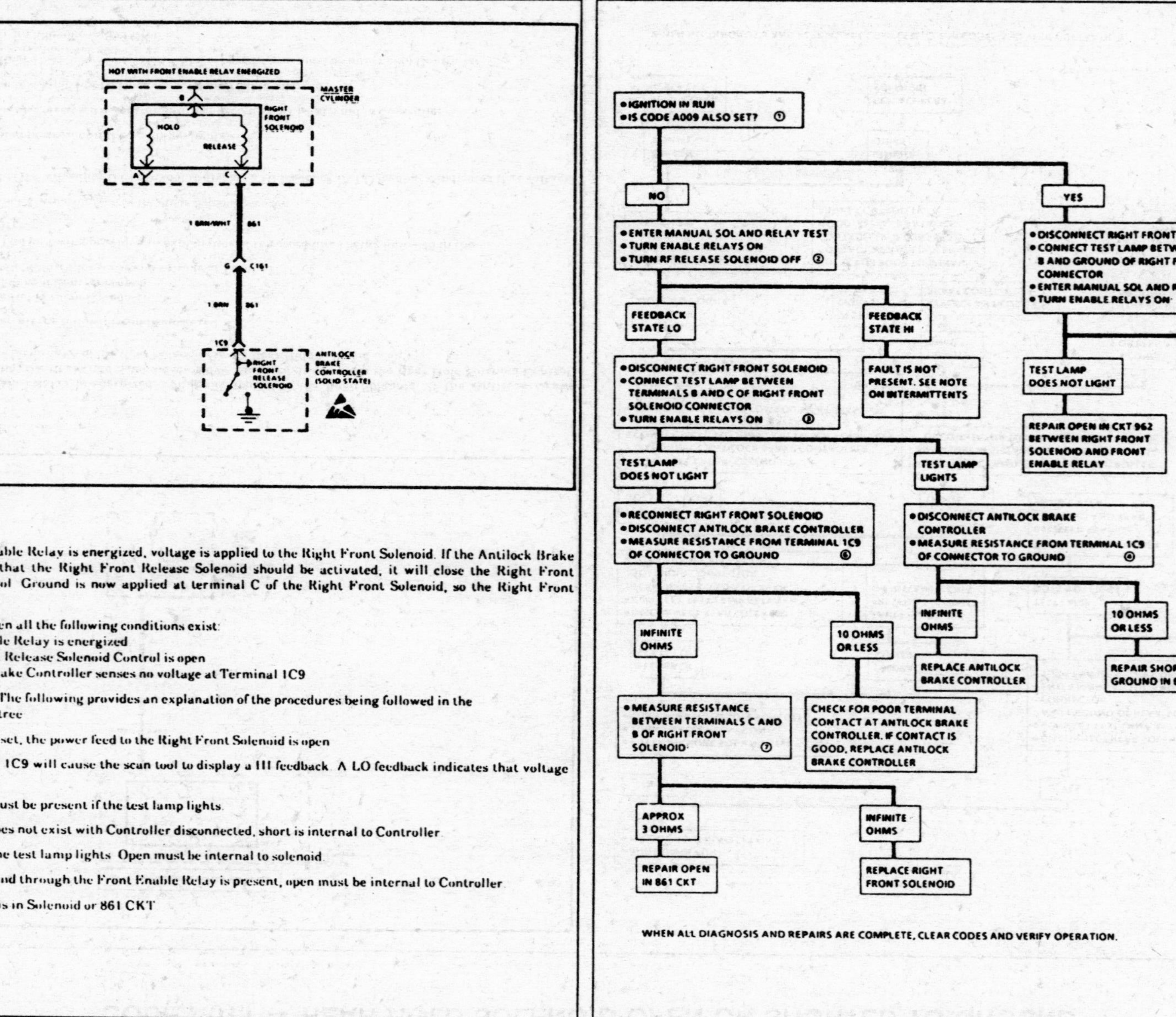
HOT WITH FRONT ENABLE RELAY ENERGIZED
MASTER CYLINDER
RIGHT FRONT SOLENOID
HOLD
RELEASE
1 BRN/WHT 861
C161
1 BRN 861
1C9
RIGHT FRONT RELEASE SOLENOID
ANTILOCK BRAKE CONTROLLER (SOLID STATE)
• IGNITION IN RUN
• IS CODE A009 ALSO SET? ①
NO
YES
• ENTER MANUAL SOL AND RELAY TEST
• TURN ENABLE RELAYS ON
• TURN RF RELEASE SOLENOID OFF ②
FEEDBACK STATE LO
FEEDBACK STATE HI
FAULT IS NOT PRESENT. SEE NOTE ON INTERMITTENTS
• DISCONNECT RIGHT FRONT SOLENOID
• CONNECT TEST LAMP BETWEEN TERMINALS B AND C OF RIGHT FRONT SOLENOID CONNECTOR
• TURN ENABLE RELAYS ON ③
TEST LAMP DOES NOT LIGHT
TEST LAMP LIGHTS
• RECONNECT RIGHT FRONT SOLENOID
• DISCONNECT ANTILOCK BRAKE CONTROLLER
• MEASURE RESISTANCE FROM TERMINAL 1C9 OF CONNECTOR TO GROUND ⑥
INFINITE OHMS
10 OHMS OR LESS
• MEASURE RESISTANCE BETWEEN TERMINALS C AND B OF RIGHT FRONT SOLENOID ⑦
CHECK FOR POOR TERMINAL CONTACT AT ANTILOCK BRAKE CONTROLLER. IF CONTACT IS GOOD, REPLACE ANTILOCK BRAKE CONTROLLER
APPROX 3 OHMS
INFINITE OHMS
REPAIR OPEN IN 861 CKT
REPLACE RIGHT FRONT SOLENOID
• DISCONNECT ANTILOCK BRAKE CONTROLLER
• MEASURE RESISTANCE FROM TERMINAL 1C9 OF CONNECTOR TO GROUND ④
INFINITE OHMS
10 OHMS OR LESS
REPLACE ANTILOCK BRAKE CONTROLLER
REPAIR SHORT TO GROUND IN 861 CKT
• DISCONNECT RIGHT FRONT SOLENOID
• CONNECT TEST LAMP BETWEEN TERMINALS B AND GROUND OF RIGHT FRONT SOLENOID CONNECTOR
• ENTER MANUAL SOL AND RELAY TEST
• TURN ENABLE RELAYS ON ⑤
TEST LAMP DOES NOT LIGHT
TEST LAMP LIGHTS
REPAIR OPEN IN CKT 962 BETWEEN RIGHT FRONT SOLENOID AND FRONT ENABLE RELAY
REPLACE RIGHT FRONT SOLENOID
WHEN ALL DIAGNOSIS AND REPAIRS ARE COMPLETE, CLEAR CODES AND VERIFY OPERATION.

When the Front Enable Relay is energized, voltage is applied to the Right Front Solenoid. If the Antilock Brake Controller determines that the Right Front Release Solenoid should be activated, it will close the Right Front Release Solenoid Control Ground is now applied at terminal C of the Right Front Solenoid, so the Right Front Release Solenoid is on

CODE A012 will set when all the following conditions exist:

- The Front Enable Relay is energized
- The Right Front Release Solenoid Control is open
- The Antilock Brake Controller senses no voltage at Terminal 1C9

TEST DESCRIPTION The following provides an explanation of the procedures being followed in the tree

① If Code A009 is also set, the power feed to the Right Front Solenoid is open

② Voltage at terminal 1C9 will cause the scan tool to display a HI feedback. A LO feedback indicates that voltage is not present

③ A short to ground must be present if the test lamp lights.

④ If short to ground does not exist with Controller disconnected, short is internal to Controller.

⑤ CKT 962 is OK, if the test lamp lights. Open must be internal to solenoid.

⑥ If continuity to ground through the Front Enable Relay is present, open must be internal to Controller.

⑦ Determines if open is in Solenoid or 861 CKT

CODE A013 – LEFT FRONT RELEASE SOLENOID OPEN OR SHORTED TO GROUND

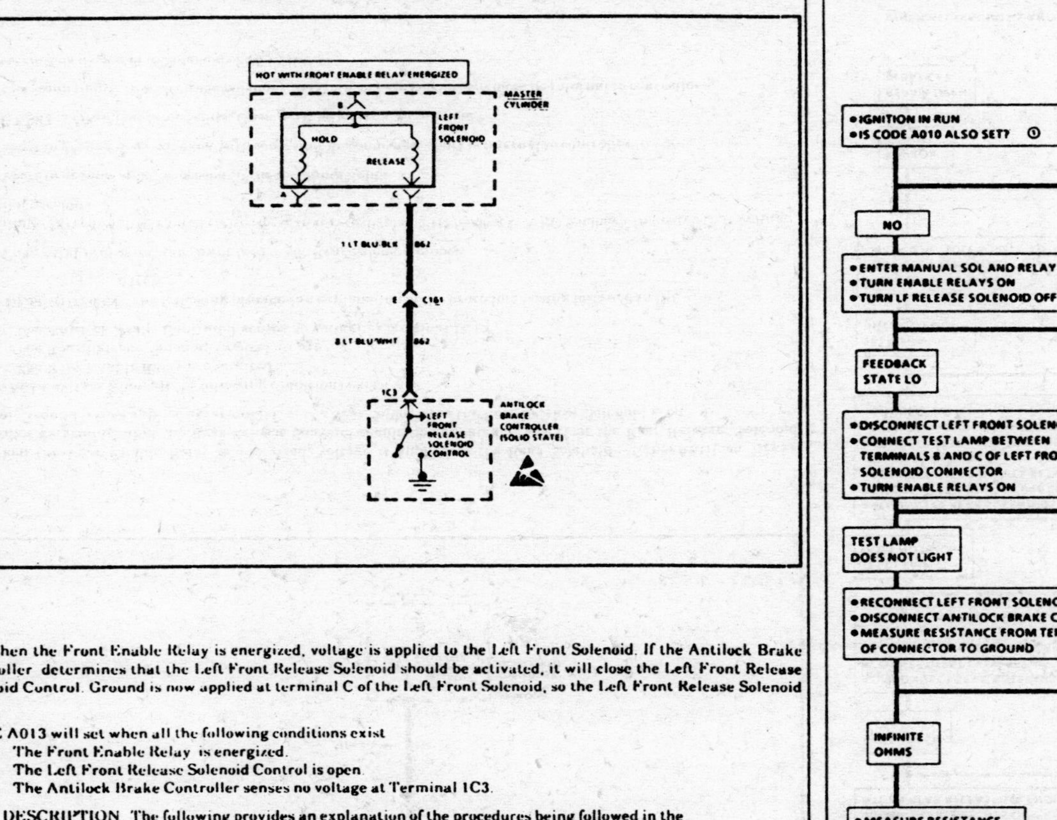

When the Front Enable Relay is energized, voltage is applied to the Left Front Solenoid. If the Antilock Brake Controller determines that the Left Front Release Solenoid should be activated, it will close the Left Front Release Solenoid Control. Ground is now applied at terminal C of the Left Front Solenoid, so the Left Front Release Solenoid is on.

CODE A013 will set when all the following conditions exist

- The Front Enable Relay is energized.
- The Left Front Release Solenoid Control is open.
- The Antilock Brake Controller senses no voltage at Terminal 1C3.

TEST DESCRIPTION The following provides an explanation of the procedures being followed in the tree

① If Code A010 is also set the power feed to the Left Front Solenoid is open.

② Voltage at terminal 1C3 will cause the scan tool to display a HI feedback. A LO feedback indicates that voltage is not present.

③ A short to ground must be present if the test lamp lights.

④ If short to ground does not exist with controller disconnected, short is internal to controller.

⑤ CKT 962 is OK if the test lamp lights. Open must be internal to solenoid.

⑥ If continuity to ground through the Front Enable Relay is present, open must be internal to Controller.

⑦ Determines if open is in solenoid or 862 CKT

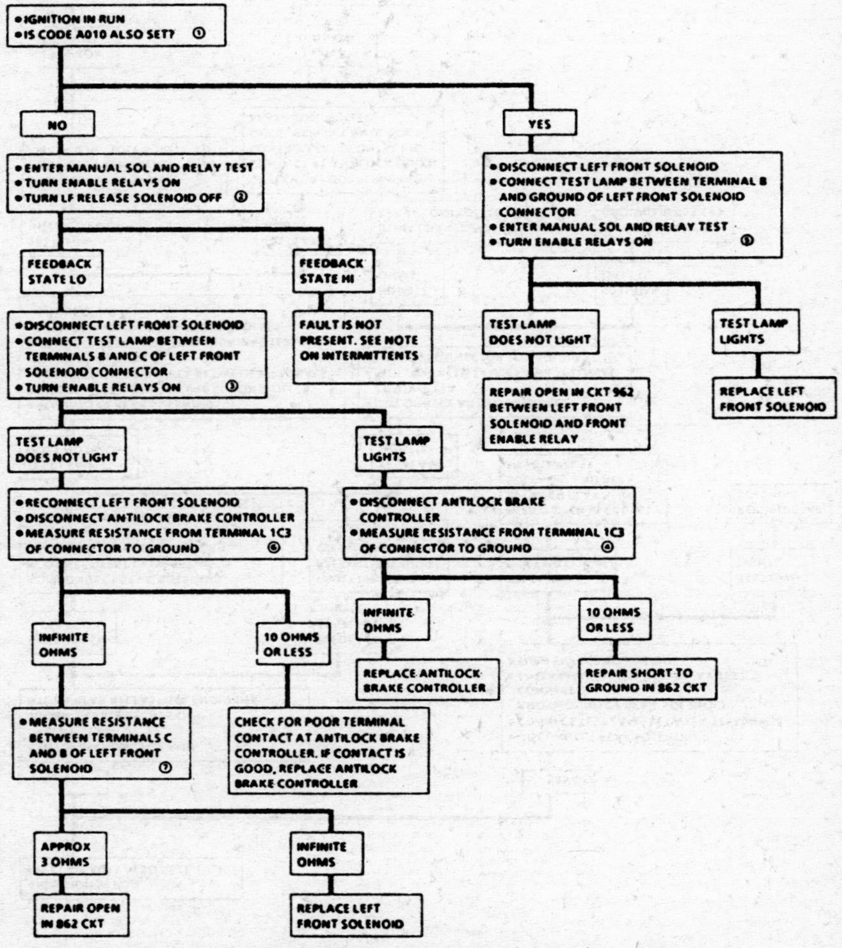

- IGNITION IN RUN
- IS CODE A010 ALSO SET? ①

NO

- ENTER MANUAL SOL AND RELAY TEST
- TURN ENABLE RELAYS ON
- TURN LF RELEASE SOLENOID OFF ②

FEEDBACK STATE LO

- DISCONNECT LEFT FRONT SOLENOID
- CONNECT TEST LAMP BETWEEN TERMINALS B AND C OF LEFT FRONT SOLENOID CONNECTOR
- TURN ENABLE RELAYS ON ③

TEST LAMP DOES NOT LIGHT

- RECONNECT LEFT FRONT SOLENOID
- DISCONNECT ANTILOCK BRAKE CONTROLLER
- MEASURE RESISTANCE FROM TERMINAL 1C3 OF CONNECTOR TO GROUND ⑥

INFINITE OHMS

- MEASURE RESISTANCE BETWEEN TERMINALS C AND B OF LEFT FRONT SOLENOID ⑦

APPROX 3 OHMS → REPAIR OPEN IN 862 CKT

INFINITE OHMS → REPLACE LEFT FRONT SOLENOID

10 OHMS OR LESS → CHECK FOR POOR TERMINAL CONTACT AT ANTILOCK BRAKE CONTROLLER. IF CONTACT IS GOOD, REPLACE ANTILOCK BRAKE CONTROLLER

TEST LAMP LIGHTS

- DISCONNECT ANTILOCK BRAKE CONTROLLER
- MEASURE RESISTANCE FROM TERMINAL 1C3 OF CONNECTOR TO GROUND ④

INFINITE OHMS → REPLACE ANTILOCK BRAKE CONTROLLER

10 OHMS OR LESS → REPAIR SHORT TO GROUND IN 862 CKT

FEEDBACK STATE HI → FAULT IS NOT PRESENT. SEE NOTE ON INTERMITTENTS

YES

- DISCONNECT LEFT FRONT SOLENOID
- CONNECT TEST LAMP BETWEEN TERMINAL B AND GROUND OF LEFT FRONT SOLENOID CONNECTOR
- ENTER MANUAL SOL AND RELAY TEST
- TURN ENABLE RELAYS ON ⑤

TEST LAMP DOES NOT LIGHT → REPAIR OPEN IN CKT 962 BETWEEN LEFT FRONT SOLENOID AND FRONT ENABLE RELAY

TEST LAMP LIGHTS → REPLACE LEFT FRONT SOLENOID

AN EXPLANATION OF EACH TEST PROCEDURE, REFERENCED BY A CIRCLED NUMBER, IS GIVEN ON THE FACING PAGE.

WHEN ALL DIAGNOSIS AND REPAIRS ARE COMPLETE, CLEAR CODES AND VERIFY OPERATION.

CODE A014 — REAR RELEASE SOLENOID OPEN OR SHORTED TO GROUND

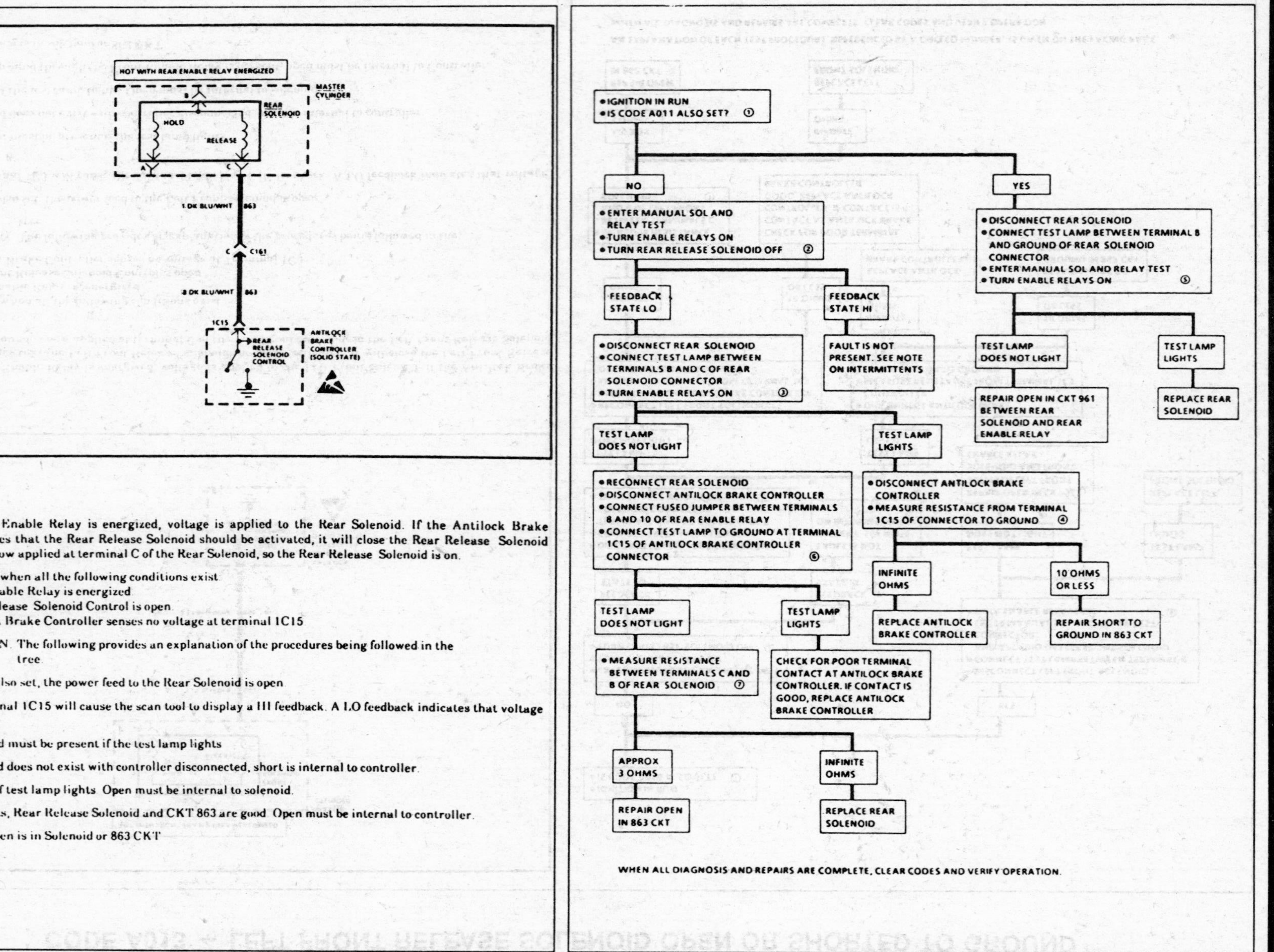

HOT WITH REAR ENABLE RELAY ENERGIZED
MASTER CYLINDER
REAR SOLENOID
HOLD
RELEASE
B
A
C
1 DK BLU/WHT 863
C161
.8 DK BLU/WHT 863
1C15
ANTILOCK BRAKE CONTROLLER (SOLID STATE)
REAR RELEASE SOLENOID CONTROL
• IGNITION IN RUN
• IS CODE A011 ALSO SET? ①
NO
YES
• ENTER MANUAL SOL AND RELAY TEST
• TURN ENABLE RELAYS ON
• TURN REAR RELEASE SOLENOID OFF ②
• DISCONNECT REAR SOLENOID
• CONNECT TEST LAMP BETWEEN TERMINAL B AND GROUND OF REAR SOLENOID CONNECTOR
• ENTER MANUAL SOL AND RELAY TEST
• TURN ENABLE RELAYS ON ⑤
FEEDBACK STATE LO
FEEDBACK STATE HI
• DISCONNECT REAR SOLENOID
• CONNECT TEST LAMP BETWEEN TERMINALS B AND C OF REAR SOLENOID CONNECTOR
• TURN ENABLE RELAYS ON ③
FAULT IS NOT PRESENT. SEE NOTE ON INTERMITTENTS
TEST LAMP DOES NOT LIGHT
TEST LAMP LIGHTS
REPAIR OPEN IN CKT 961 BETWEEN REAR SOLENOID AND REAR ENABLE RELAY
REPLACE REAR SOLENOID
TEST LAMP DOES NOT LIGHT
TEST LAMP LIGHTS
• RECONNECT REAR SOLENOID
• DISCONNECT ANTILOCK BRAKE CONTROLLER
• CONNECT FUSED JUMPER BETWEEN TERMINALS 8 AND 10 OF REAR ENABLE RELAY
• CONNECT TEST LAMP TO GROUND AT TERMINAL 1C15 OF ANTILOCK BRAKE CONTROLLER CONNECTOR ⑥
• DISCONNECT ANTILOCK BRAKE CONTROLLER
• MEASURE RESISTANCE FROM TERMINAL 1C15 OF CONNECTOR TO GROUND ④
INFINITE OHMS
10 OHMS OR LESS
REPLACE ANTILOCK BRAKE CONTROLLER
REPAIR SHORT TO GROUND IN 863 CKT
TEST LAMP DOES NOT LIGHT
TEST LAMP LIGHTS
• MEASURE RESISTANCE BETWEEN TERMINALS C AND B OF REAR SOLENOID ⑦
CHECK FOR POOR TERMINAL CONTACT AT ANTILOCK BRAKE CONTROLLER. IF CONTACT IS GOOD, REPLACE ANTILOCK BRAKE CONTROLLER
APPROX 3 OHMS
INFINITE OHMS
REPAIR OPEN IN 863 CKT
REPLACE REAR SOLENOID
WHEN ALL DIAGNOSIS AND REPAIRS ARE COMPLETE, CLEAR CODES AND VERIFY OPERATION.

When the Rear Enable Relay is energized, voltage is applied to the Rear Solenoid. If the Antilock Brake Controller determines that the Rear Release Solenoid should be activated, it will close the Rear Release Solenoid Control. Ground is now applied at terminal C of the Rear Solenoid, so the Rear Release Solenoid is on.

CODE A014 will set when all the following conditions exist

- The Rear Enable Relay is energized
- The Rear Release Solenoid Control is open.
- The Antilock Brake Controller senses no voltage at terminal 1C15

TEST DESCRIPTION. The following provides an explanation of the procedures being followed in the tree.

① If Code A011 is also set, the power feed to the Rear Solenoid is open

② Voltage at terminal 1C15 will cause the scan tool to display a HI feedback. A LO feedback indicates that voltage is not present.

③ A short to ground must be present if the test lamp lights

④ If short to ground does not exist with controller disconnected, short is internal to controller.

⑤ CKT 962 is OK if test lamp lights. Open must be internal to solenoid.

⑥ If test lamp lights, Rear Release Solenoid and CKT 863 are good. Open must be internal to controller.

⑦ Determines if open is in Solenoid or 863 CKT

CODE A015 — ONE OR MORE FRONT SOLENOIDS SHORTED

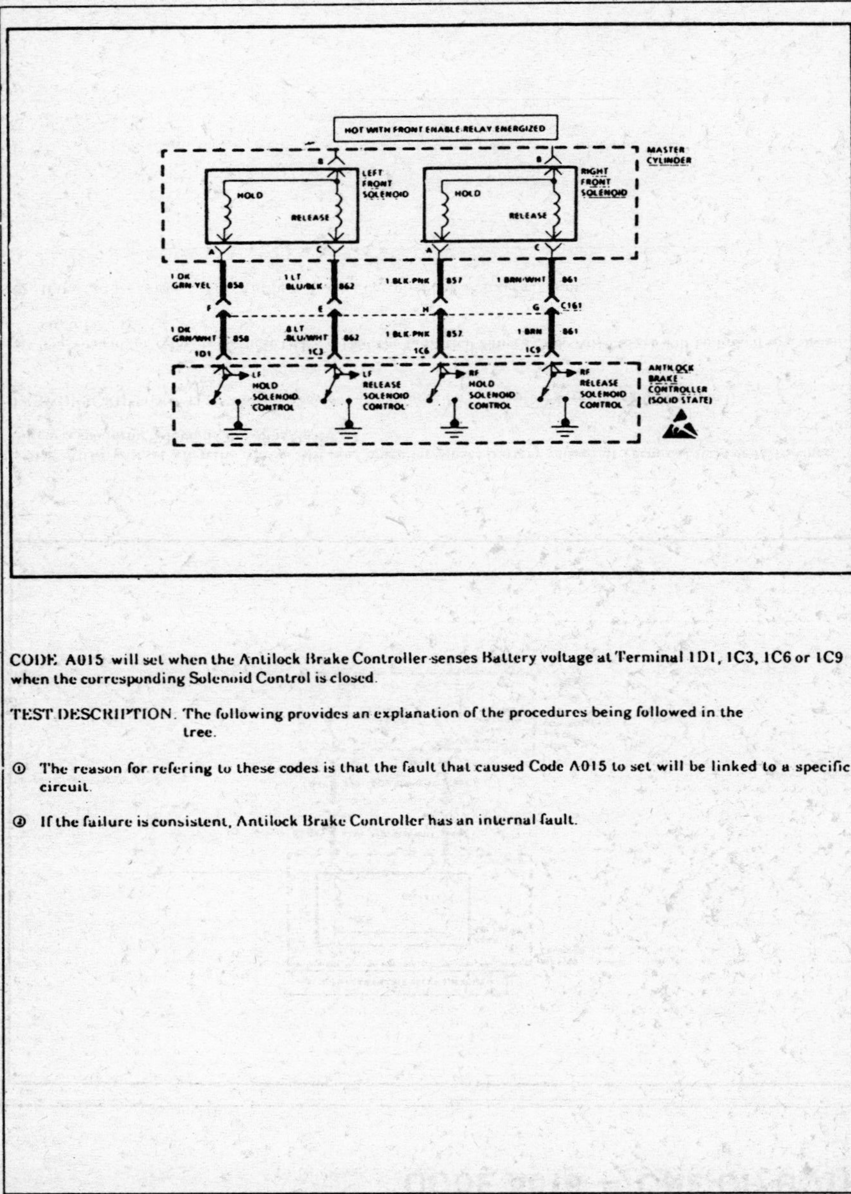

CODE A015 will set when the Antilock Brake Controller senses Battery voltage at Terminal 1D1, 1C3, 1C6 or 1C9 when the corresponding Solenoid Control is closed.

TEST DESCRIPTION. The following provides an explanation of the procedures being followed in the tree.

① The reason for refering to these codes is that the fault that caused Code A015 to set will be linked to a specific circuit.

② If the failure is consistent, Antilock Brake Controller has an internal fault.

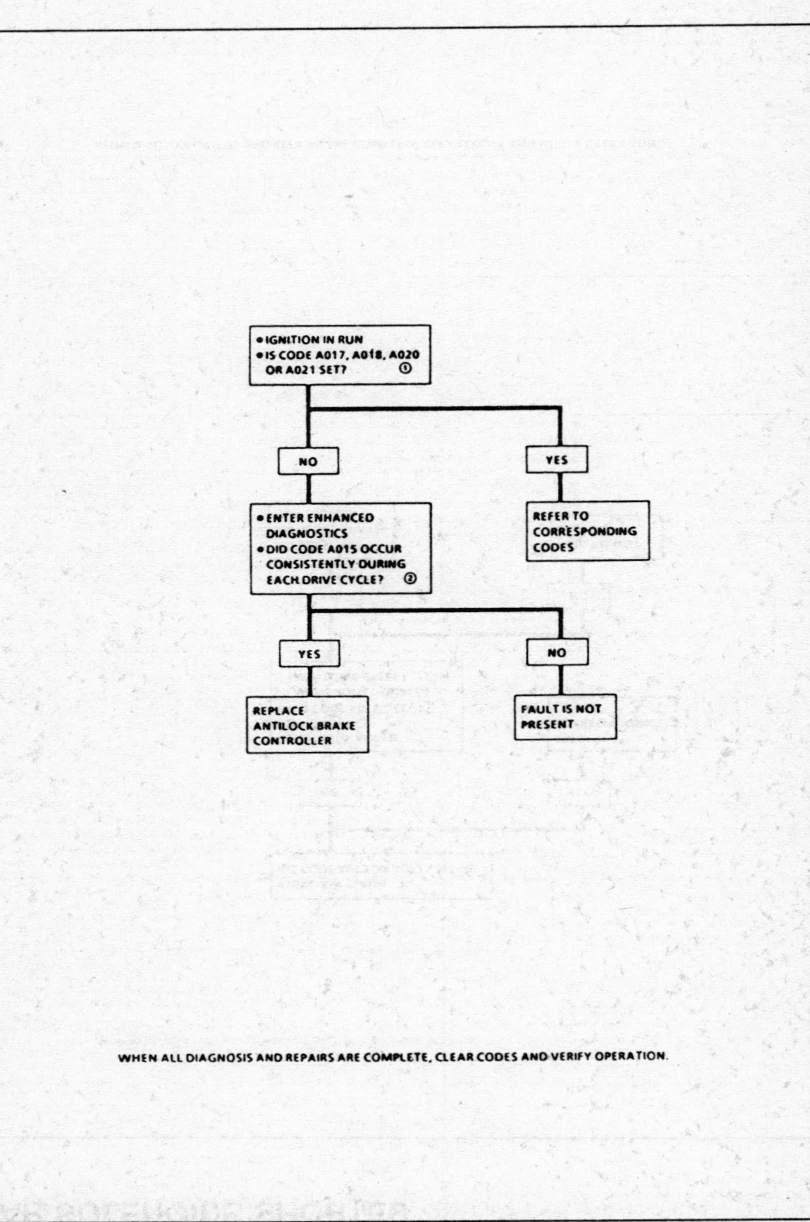

CODE A016 — ONE OR BOTH REAR SOLENOIDS SHORTED

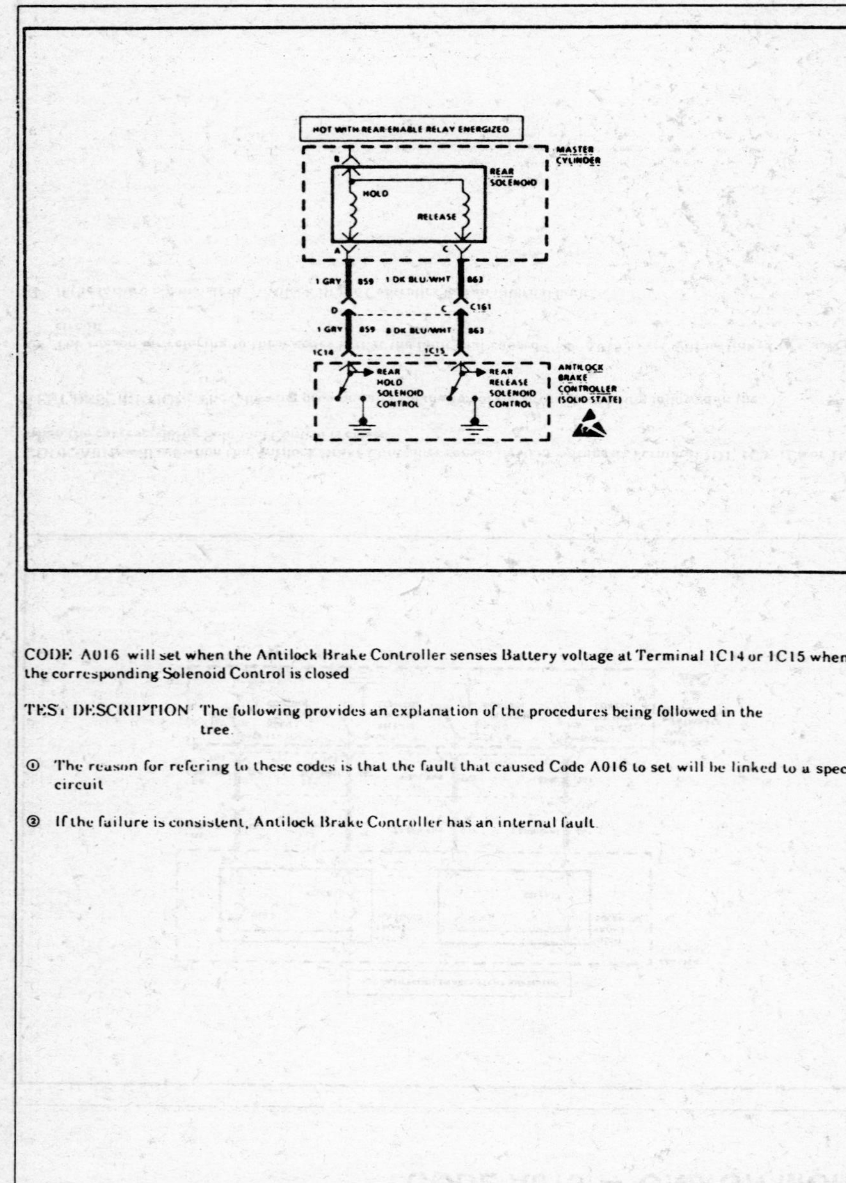

CODE A016 will set when the Antilock Brake Controller senses Battery voltage at Terminal 1C14 or 1C15 when the corresponding Solenoid Control is closed

TEST DESCRIPTION The following provides an explanation of the procedures being followed in the tree.

① The reason for refering to these codes is that the fault that caused Code A016 to set will be linked to a specific circuit

② If the failure is consistent, Antilock Brake Controller has an internal fault.

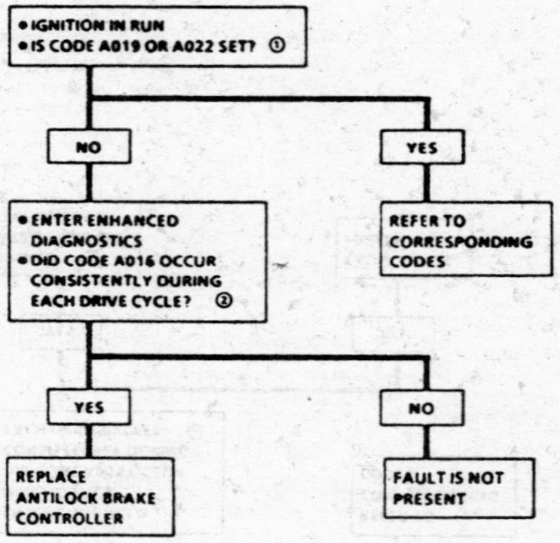

- IGNITION IN RUN
- IS CODE A019 OR A022 SET? ①

YES → REFER TO CORRESPONDING CODES

NO →

- ENTER ENHANCED DIAGNOSTICS
- DID CODE A016 OCCUR CONSISTENTLY DURING EACH DRIVE CYCLE? ②

YES → REPLACE ANTILOCK BRAKE CONTROLLER

NO → FAULT IS NOT PRESENT

WHEN ALL DIAGNOSIS AND REPAIRS ARE COMPLETE, CLEAR CODES AND VERIFY OPERATION.

CODE A017 – RIGHT FRONT HOLD SOLENOID SHORTED

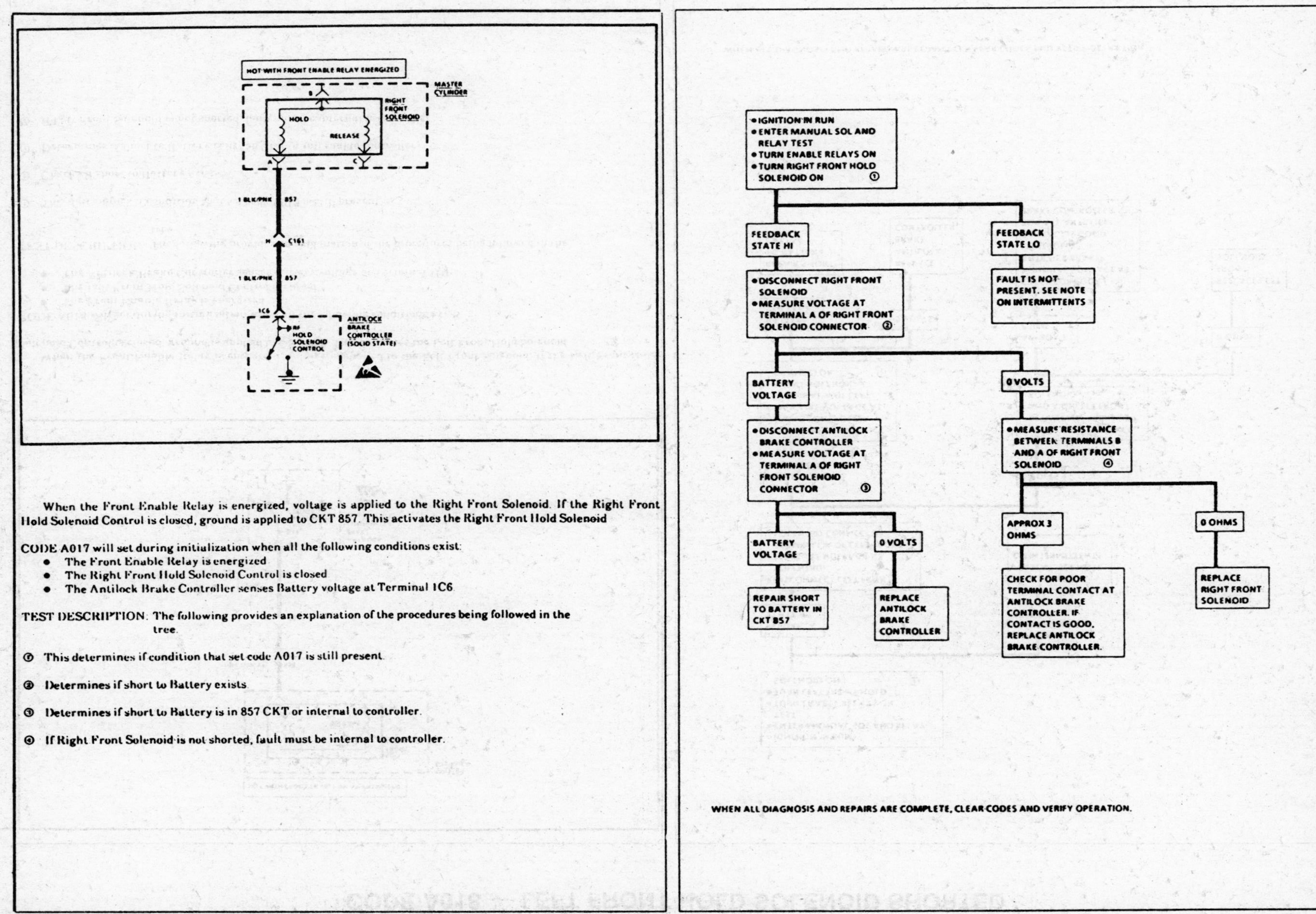

HOT WITH FRONT ENABLE RELAY ENERGIZED
MASTER CYLINDER
RIGHT FRONT SOLENOID
HOLD
RELEASE
1 BLK/PNK 857
C161
1 BLK/PNK 857
1C6
ANTILOCK BRAKE CONTROLLER (SOLID STATE)
RF HOLD SOLENOID CONTROL
• IGNITION IN RUN
• ENTER MANUAL SOL AND RELAY TEST
• TURN ENABLE RELAYS ON
• TURN RIGHT FRONT HOLD SOLENOID ON ①
FEEDBACK STATE HI
FEEDBACK STATE LO
FAULT IS NOT PRESENT. SEE NOTE ON INTERMITTENTS
• DISCONNECT RIGHT FRONT SOLENOID
• MEASURE VOLTAGE AT TERMINAL A OF RIGHT FRONT SOLENOID CONNECTOR ②
BATTERY VOLTAGE
0 VOLTS
• DISCONNECT ANTILOCK BRAKE CONTROLLER
• MEASURE VOLTAGE AT TERMINAL A OF RIGHT FRONT SOLENOID CONNECTOR ③
• MEASURE RESISTANCE BETWEEN TERMINALS B AND A OF RIGHT FRONT SOLENOID ④
BATTERY VOLTAGE
0 VOLTS
APPROX 3 OHMS
0 OHMS
REPAIR SHORT TO BATTERY IN CKT 857
REPLACE ANTILOCK BRAKE CONTROLLER
CHECK FOR POOR TERMINAL CONTACT AT ANTILOCK BRAKE CONTROLLER. IF CONTACT IS GOOD, REPLACE ANTILOCK BRAKE CONTROLLER.
REPLACE RIGHT FRONT SOLENOID
WHEN ALL DIAGNOSIS AND REPAIRS ARE COMPLETE, CLEAR CODES AND VERIFY OPERATION.

When the Front Enable Relay is energized, voltage is applied to the Right Front Solenoid. If the Right Front Hold Solenoid Control is closed, ground is applied to CKT 857. This activates the Right Front Hold Solenoid

CODE A017 will set during initialization when all the following conditions exist:

- The Front Enable Relay is energized
- The Right Front Hold Solenoid Control is closed
- The Antilock Brake Controller senses Battery voltage at Terminal 1C6

TEST DESCRIPTION: The following provides an explanation of the procedures being followed in the tree.

① This determines if condition that set code A017 is still present.

② Determines if short to Battery exists.

③ Determines if short to Battery is in 857 CKT or internal to controller.

④ If Right Front Solenoid is not shorted, fault must be internal to controller.

CODE A018 — LEFT FRONT HOLD SOLENOID SHORTED

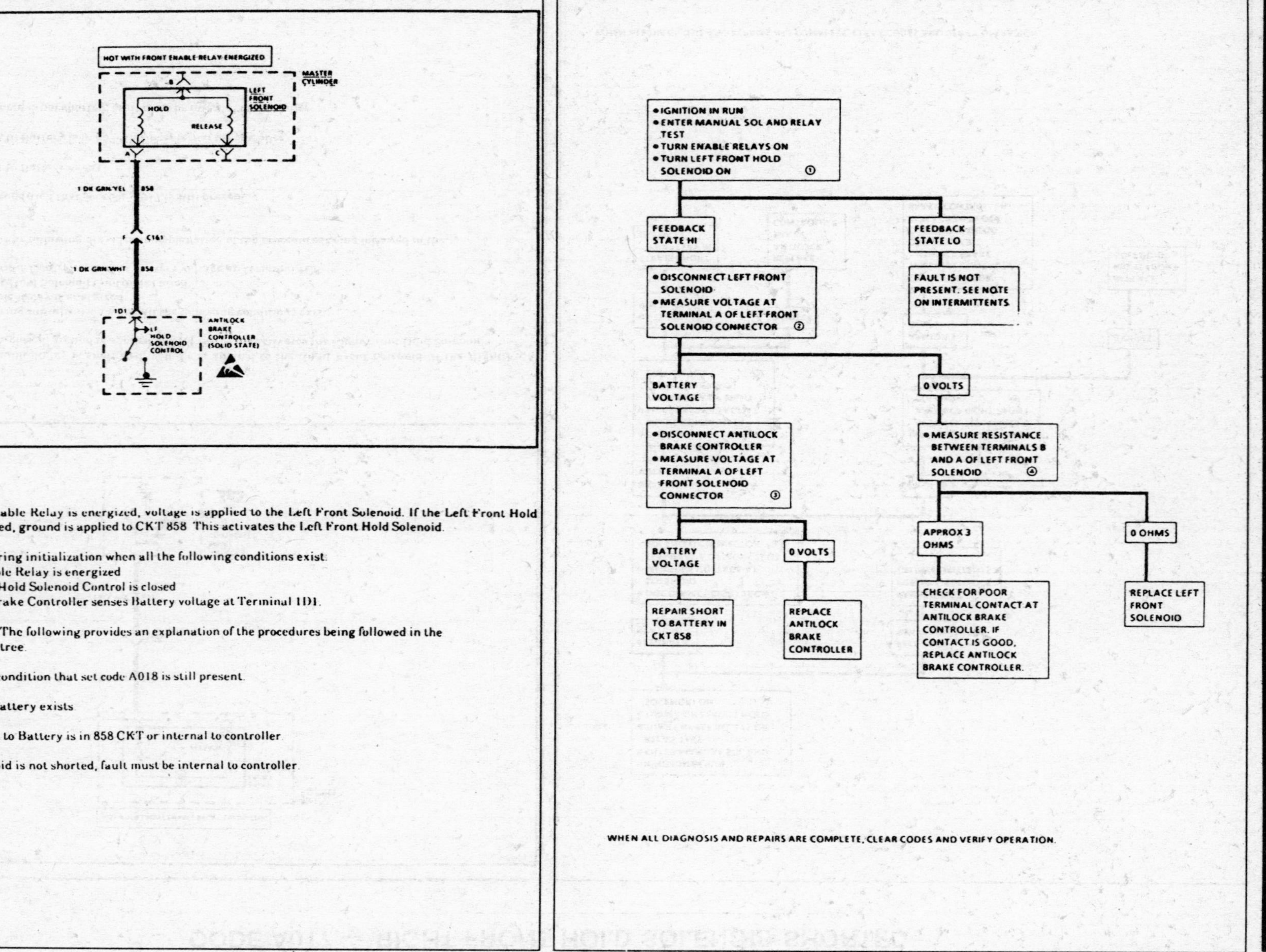

HOT WITH FRONT ENABLE RELAY ENERGIZED
MASTER CYLINDER
LEFT FRONT SOLENOID
HOLD
RELEASE
1 DK GRN/YEL 858
C161
1 DK GRN/WHT 858
1D1
LF HOLD SOLENOID CONTROL
ANTILOCK BRAKE CONTROLLER (SOLID STATE)
• IGNITION IN RUN
• ENTER MANUAL SOL AND RELAY TEST
• TURN ENABLE RELAYS ON
• TURN LEFT FRONT HOLD SOLENOID ON ①
FEEDBACK STATE HI
FEEDBACK STATE LO
FAULT IS NOT PRESENT. SEE NOTE ON INTERMITTENTS
• DISCONNECT LEFT FRONT SOLENOID
• MEASURE VOLTAGE AT TERMINAL A OF LEFT FRONT SOLENOID CONNECTOR ②
BATTERY VOLTAGE
0 VOLTS
• DISCONNECT ANTILOCK BRAKE CONTROLLER
• MEASURE VOLTAGE AT TERMINAL A OF LEFT FRONT SOLENOID CONNECTOR ③
• MEASURE RESISTANCE BETWEEN TERMINALS B AND A OF LEFT FRONT SOLENOID ④
BATTERY VOLTAGE
0 VOLTS
APPROX 3 OHMS
0 OHMS
REPAIR SHORT TO BATTERY IN CKT 858
REPLACE ANTILOCK BRAKE CONTROLLER
CHECK FOR POOR TERMINAL CONTACT AT ANTILOCK BRAKE CONTROLLER. IF CONTACT IS GOOD, REPLACE ANTILOCK BRAKE CONTROLLER.
REPLACE LEFT FRONT SOLENOID
WHEN ALL DIAGNOSIS AND REPAIRS ARE COMPLETE, CLEAR CODES AND VERIFY OPERATION.

When the Front Enable Relay is energized, voltage is applied to the Left Front Solenoid. If the Left Front Hold Solenoid Control is closed, ground is applied to CKT 858. This activates the Left Front Hold Solenoid.

CODE A018 will set during initialization when all the following conditions exist:

- The Front Enable Relay is energized
- The Left Front Hold Solenoid Control is closed
- The Antilock Brake Controller senses Battery voltage at Terminal 1D1.

TEST DESCRIPTION: The following provides an explanation of the procedures being followed in the tree.

① This determines if condition that set code A018 is still present.

② Checks if short to Battery exists

③ Determines if short to Battery is in 858 CKT or internal to controller

④ If Left Front Solenoid is not shorted, fault must be internal to controller.

CODE A019 — REAR HOLD SOLENOID SHORTED

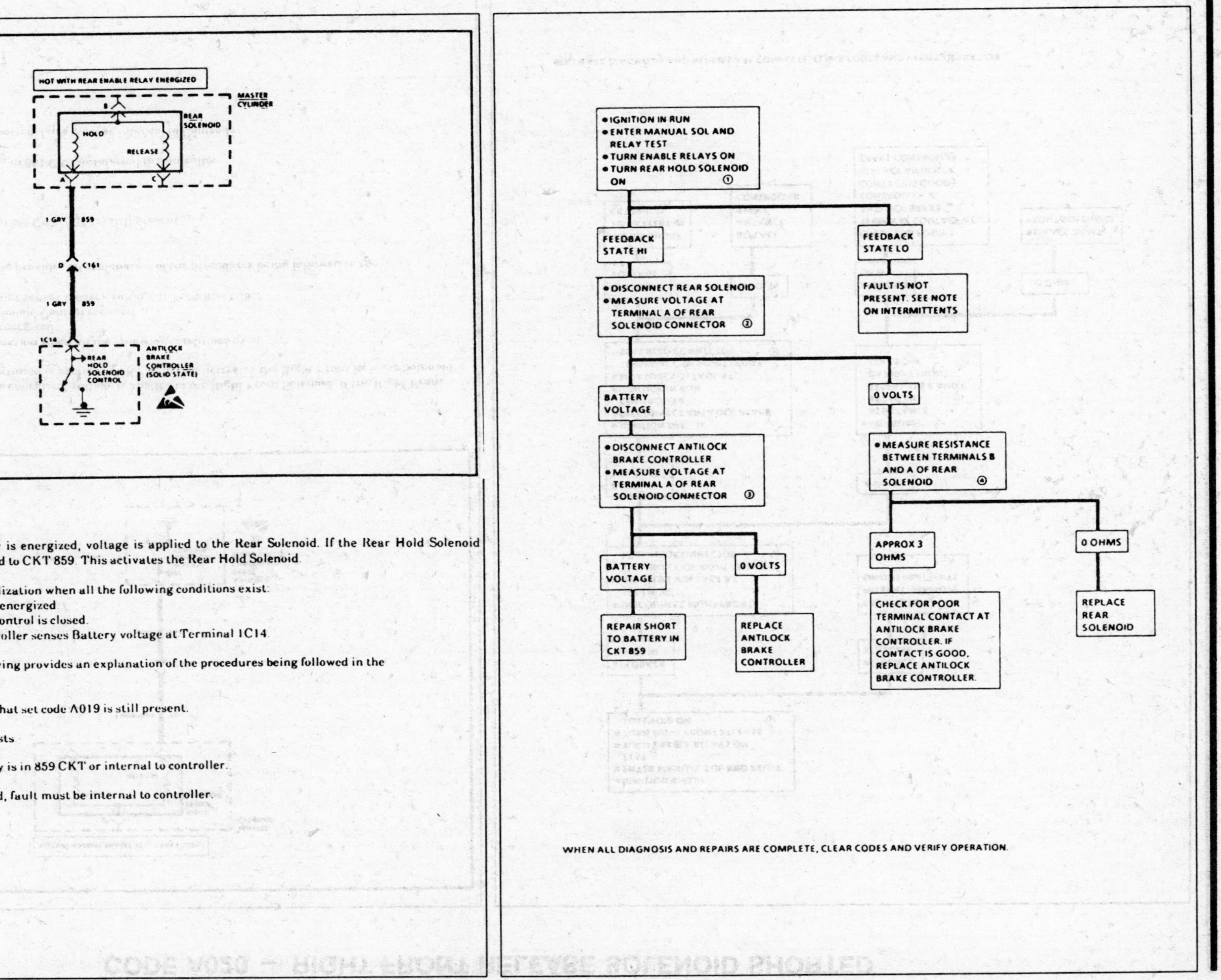
HOT WITH REAR ENABLE RELAY ENERGIZED
MASTER CYLINDER
REAR SOLENOID
HOLD
RELEASE
B
A
C
1 GRY 859
D C161
1 GRY 859
1C14
REAR HOLD SOLENOID CONTROL
ANTILOCK BRAKE CONTROLLER (SOLID STATE)
• IGNITION IN RUN
• ENTER MANUAL SOL AND RELAY TEST
• TURN ENABLE RELAYS ON
• TURN REAR HOLD SOLENOID ON ①
FEEDBACK STATE HI
FEEDBACK STATE LO
FAULT IS NOT PRESENT. SEE NOTE ON INTERMITTENTS
• DISCONNECT REAR SOLENOID
• MEASURE VOLTAGE AT TERMINAL A OF REAR SOLENOID CONNECTOR ②
BATTERY VOLTAGE
0 VOLTS
• DISCONNECT ANTILOCK BRAKE CONTROLLER
• MEASURE VOLTAGE AT TERMINAL A OF REAR SOLENOID CONNECTOR ③
• MEASURE RESISTANCE BETWEEN TERMINALS B AND A OF REAR SOLENOID ④
BATTERY VOLTAGE
0 VOLTS
REPAIR SHORT TO BATTERY IN CKT 859
REPLACE ANTILOCK BRAKE CONTROLLER
APPROX 3 OHMS
0 OHMS
CHECK FOR POOR TERMINAL CONTACT AT ANTILOCK BRAKE CONTROLLER. IF CONTACT IS GOOD, REPLACE ANTILOCK BRAKE CONTROLLER.
REPLACE REAR SOLENOID
WHEN ALL DIAGNOSIS AND REPAIRS ARE COMPLETE, CLEAR CODES AND VERIFY OPERATION.

When the Rear Enable Relay is energized, voltage is applied to the Rear Solenoid. If the Rear Hold Solenoid Control is closed, ground is applied to CKT 859. This activates the Rear Hold Solenoid.

CODE A019 will set during initialization when all the following conditions exist:

- The Rear Enable Relay is energized
- The Rear Hold Solenoid Control is closed.
- The Antilock Brake Controller senses Battery voltage at Terminal 1C14.

TEST DESCRIPTION The following provides an explanation of the procedures being followed in the tree.

① This determines if condition that set code A019 is still present.

② Checks if short to Battery exists.

③ Determines if short to Battery is in 859 CKT or internal to controller.

④ If Rear Solenoid is not shorted, fault must be internal to controller.

CODE A020 — RIGHT FRONT RELEASE SOLENOID SHORTED

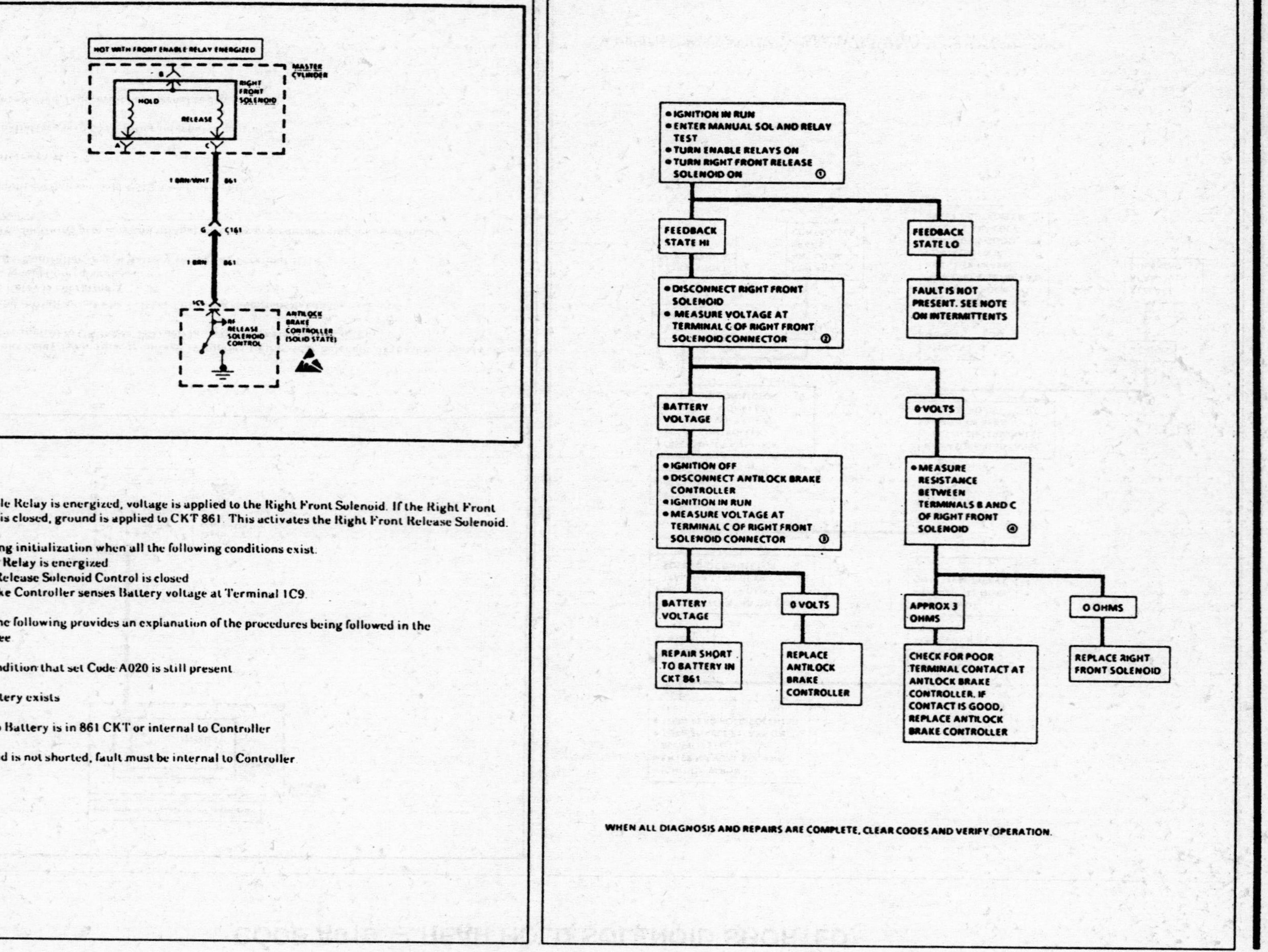
HOT WITH FRONT ENABLE RELAY ENERGIZED
MASTER CYLINDER
RIGHT FRONT SOLENOID
HOLD
RELEASE
B
A
C
1 BRN/WHT 861
G C161
1 BRN 861
1C9
RF RELEASE SOLENOID CONTROL
ANTILOCK BRAKE CONTROLLER (SOLID STATE)
• IGNITION IN RUN
• ENTER MANUAL SOL AND RELAY TEST
• TURN ENABLE RELAYS ON
• TURN RIGHT FRONT RELEASE SOLENOID ON ①
FEEDBACK STATE HI
FEEDBACK STATE LO
FAULT IS NOT PRESENT. SEE NOTE ON INTERMITTENTS
• DISCONNECT RIGHT FRONT SOLENOID
• MEASURE VOLTAGE AT TERMINAL C OF RIGHT FRONT SOLENOID CONNECTOR ②
BATTERY VOLTAGE
0 VOLTS
• IGNITION OFF
• DISCONNECT ANTILOCK BRAKE CONTROLLER
• IGNITION IN RUN
• MEASURE VOLTAGE AT TERMINAL C OF RIGHT FRONT SOLENOID CONNECTOR ③
• MEASURE RESISTANCE BETWEEN TERMINALS B AND C OF RIGHT FRONT SOLENOID ④
BATTERY VOLTAGE
0 VOLTS
APPROX 3 OHMS
0 OHMS
REPAIR SHORT TO BATTERY IN CKT 861
REPLACE ANTILOCK BRAKE CONTROLLER
CHECK FOR POOR TERMINAL CONTACT AT ANTILOCK BRAKE CONTROLLER. IF CONTACT IS GOOD, REPLACE ANTILOCK BRAKE CONTROLLER
REPLACE RIGHT FRONT SOLENOID
WHEN ALL DIAGNOSIS AND REPAIRS ARE COMPLETE, CLEAR CODES AND VERIFY OPERATION.

When the Front Enable Relay is energized, voltage is applied to the Right Front Solenoid. If the Right Front Release Solenoid Control is closed, ground is applied to CKT 861. This activates the Right Front Release Solenoid.

CODE A020 will set during initialization when all the following conditions exist.

- The Front Enable Relay is energized
- The Right Front Release Solenoid Control is closed
- The Antilock Brake Controller senses Battery voltage at Terminal 1C9.

TEST DESCRIPTION: The following provides an explanation of the procedures being followed in the tree

① This determines if condition that set Code A020 is still present.

② Checks if short to Battery exists

③ Determines if short to Battery is in 861 CKT or internal to Controller

④ If Right Front Solenoid is not shorted, fault must be internal to Controller

CODE A021 – LEFT FRONT RELEASE SOLENOID SHORTED

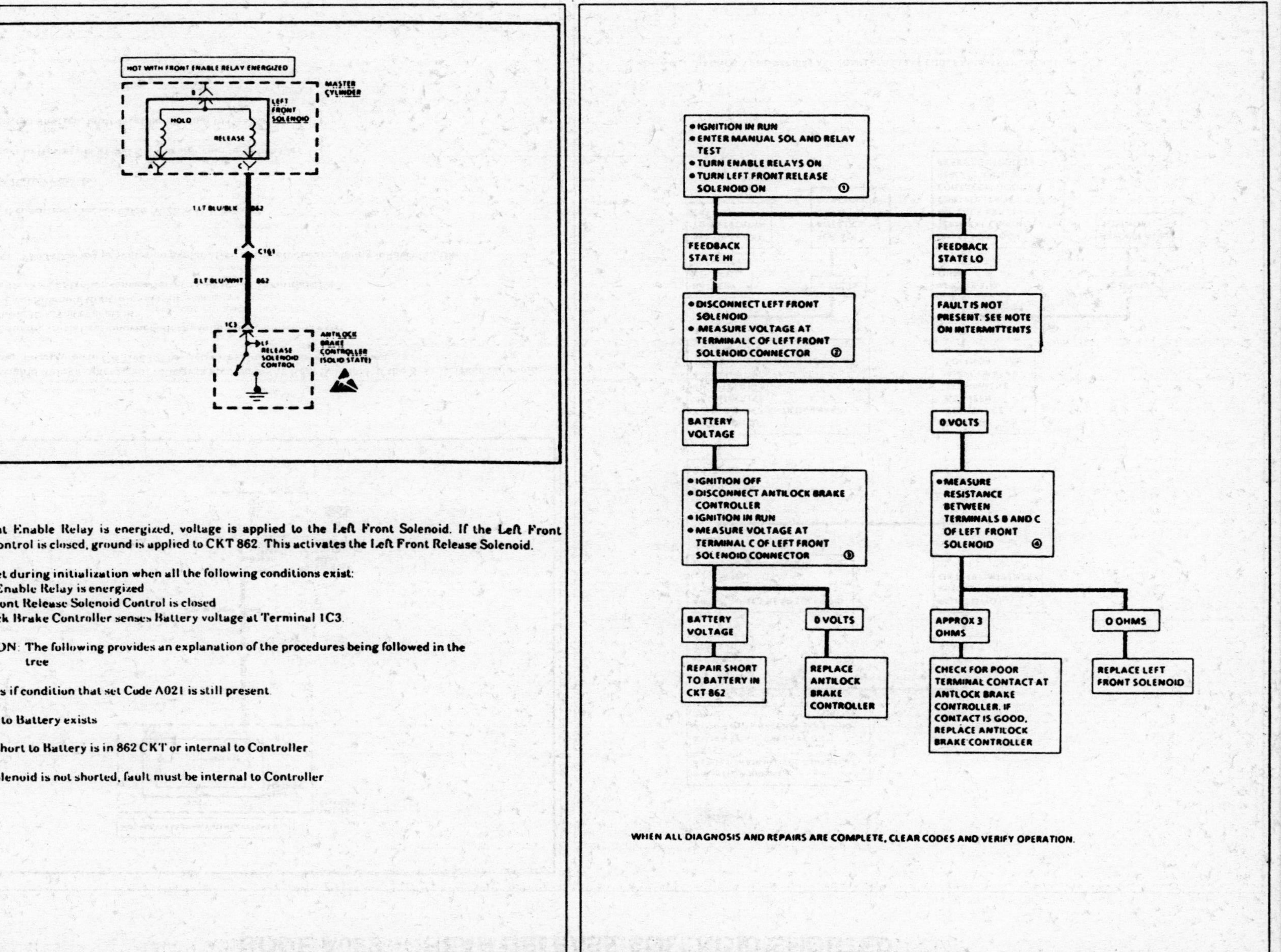
HOT WITH FRONT ENABLE RELAY ENERGIZED
MASTER CYLINDER
LEFT FRONT SOLENOID
HOLD
RELEASE
B
A
C
1 LT BLU/BLK 862
C181
E
LT BLU/WHT 862
1C3
LF RELEASE SOLENOID CONTROL
ANTILOCK BRAKE CONTROLLER (SOLID STATE)
• IGNITION IN RUN
• ENTER MANUAL SOL AND RELAY TEST
• TURN ENABLE RELAYS ON
• TURN LEFT FRONT RELEASE SOLENOID ON ①
FEEDBACK STATE HI
FEEDBACK STATE LO
• DISCONNECT LEFT FRONT SOLENOID
• MEASURE VOLTAGE AT TERMINAL C OF LEFT FRONT SOLENOID CONNECTOR ②
FAULT IS NOT PRESENT. SEE NOTE ON INTERMITTENTS
BATTERY VOLTAGE
0 VOLTS
• IGNITION OFF
• DISCONNECT ANTILOCK BRAKE CONTROLLER
• IGNITION IN RUN
• MEASURE VOLTAGE AT TERMINAL C OF LEFT FRONT SOLENOID CONNECTOR ③
• MEASURE RESISTANCE BETWEEN TERMINALS B AND C OF LEFT FRONT SOLENOID ④
BATTERY VOLTAGE
0 VOLTS
APPROX 3 OHMS
0 OHMS
REPAIR SHORT TO BATTERY IN CKT 862
REPLACE ANTILOCK BRAKE CONTROLLER
CHECK FOR POOR TERMINAL CONTACT AT ANTILOCK BRAKE CONTROLLER. IF CONTACT IS GOOD, REPLACE ANTILOCK BRAKE CONTROLLER
REPLACE LEFT FRONT SOLENOID
WHEN ALL DIAGNOSIS AND REPAIRS ARE COMPLETE, CLEAR CODES AND VERIFY OPERATION.

When the Front Enable Relay is energized, voltage is applied to the Left Front Solenoid. If the Left Front Release Solenoid Control is closed, ground is applied to CKT 862. This activates the Left Front Release Solenoid.

CODE A021 will set during initialization when all the following conditions exist:

- The Front Enable Relay is energized
- The Left Front Release Solenoid Control is closed
- The Antilock Brake Controller senses Battery voltage at Terminal 1C3.

TEST DESCRIPTION: The following provides an explanation of the procedures being followed in the tree

① This determines if condition that set Code A021 is still present.

② Checks if short to Battery exists

③ Determines if short to Battery is in 862 CKT or internal to Controller

④ If Left Front Solenoid is not shorted, fault must be internal to Controller

CODE A022 – REAR RELEASE SOLENOID SHORTED

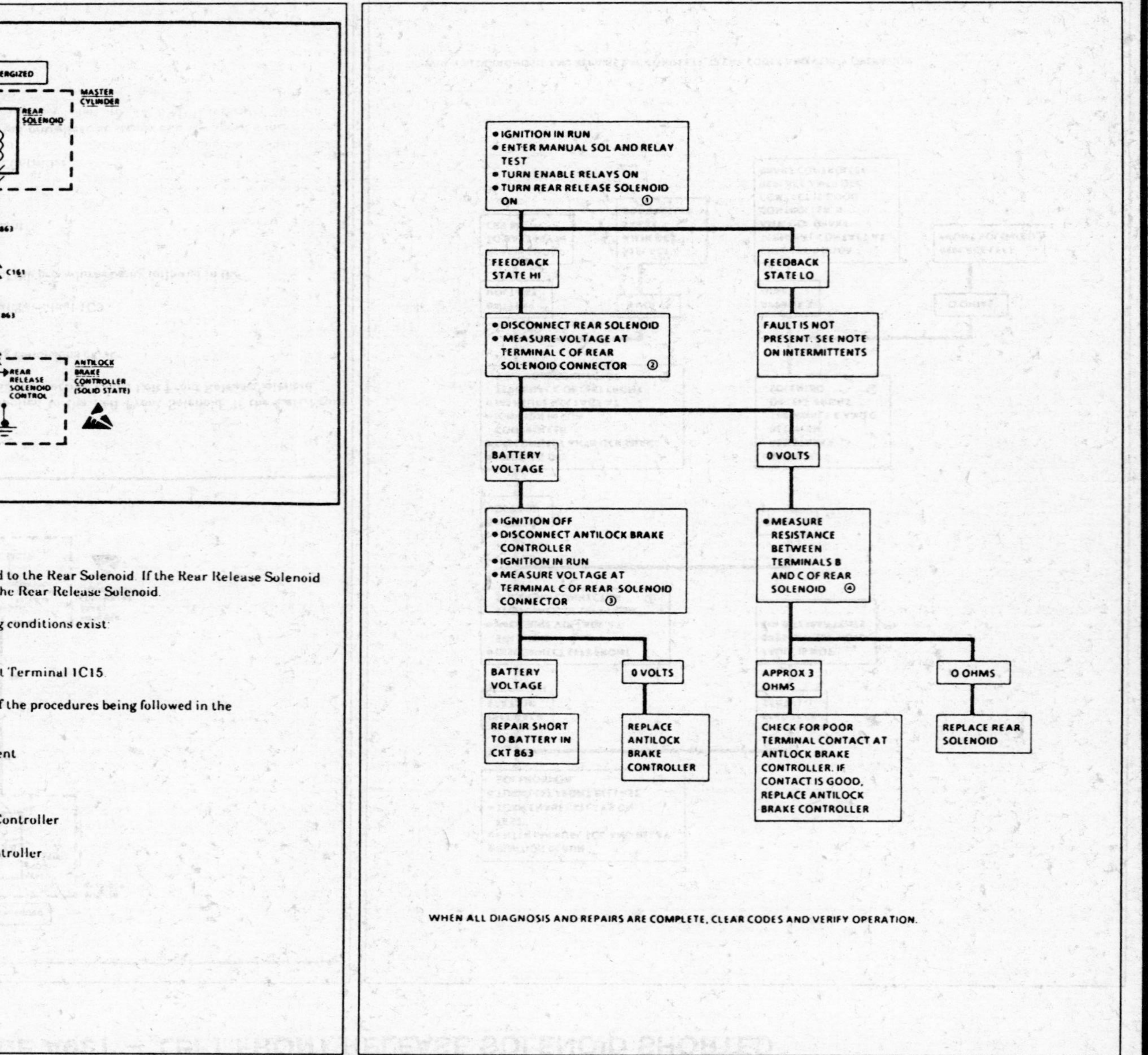
HOT WITH REAR ENABLE RELAY ENERGIZED
MASTER CYLINDER
REAR SOLENOID
HOLD
RELEASE
1 DK BLU/WHT 863
C161
.8 DK BLU/WHT 863
1C15
REAR RELEASE SOLENOID CONTROL
ANTILOCK BRAKE CONTROLLER (SOLID STATE)
• IGNITION IN RUN
• ENTER MANUAL SOL AND RELAY TEST
• TURN ENABLE RELAYS ON
• TURN REAR RELEASE SOLENOID ON ①
FEEDBACK STATE HI
FEEDBACK STATE LO
• DISCONNECT REAR SOLENOID
• MEASURE VOLTAGE AT TERMINAL C OF REAR SOLENOID CONNECTOR ②
FAULT IS NOT PRESENT. SEE NOTE ON INTERMITTENTS
BATTERY VOLTAGE
0 VOLTS
• IGNITION OFF
• DISCONNECT ANTILOCK BRAKE CONTROLLER
• IGNITION IN RUN
• MEASURE VOLTAGE AT TERMINAL C OF REAR SOLENOID CONNECTOR ③
• MEASURE RESISTANCE BETWEEN TERMINALS B AND C OF REAR SOLENOID ④
BATTERY VOLTAGE
0 VOLTS
APPROX 3 OHMS
0 OHMS
REPAIR SHORT TO BATTERY IN CKT 863
REPLACE ANTILOCK BRAKE CONTROLLER
CHECK FOR POOR TERMINAL CONTACT AT ANTLOCK BRAKE CONTROLLER. IF CONTACT IS GOOD, REPLACE ANTILOCK BRAKE CONTROLLER
REPLACE REAR SOLENOID
WHEN ALL DIAGNOSIS AND REPAIRS ARE COMPLETE, CLEAR CODES AND VERIFY OPERATION.

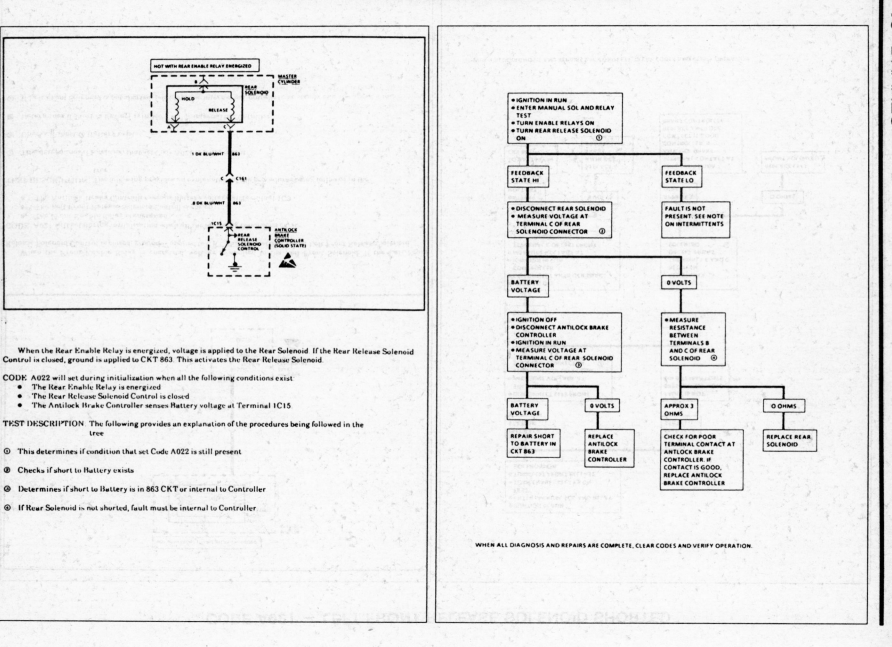

When the Rear Enable Relay is energized, voltage is applied to the Rear Solenoid. If the Rear Release Solenoid Control is closed, ground is applied to CKT 863. This activates the Rear Release Solenoid.

CODE A022 will set during initialization when all the following conditions exist:
- The Rear Enable Relay is energized
- The Rear Release Solenoid Control is closed
- The Antilock Brake Controller senses Battery voltage at Terminal 1C15.

TEST DESCRIPTION: The following provides an explanation of the procedures being followed in the tree

① This determines if condition that set Code A022 is still present

② Checks if short to Battery exists

③ Determines if short to Battery is in 863 CKT or internal to Controller

④ If Rear Solenoid is not shorted, fault must be internal to Controller

CODE A023 – RIGHT FRONT RELEASE SOLENOID ENERGIZED TOO LONG

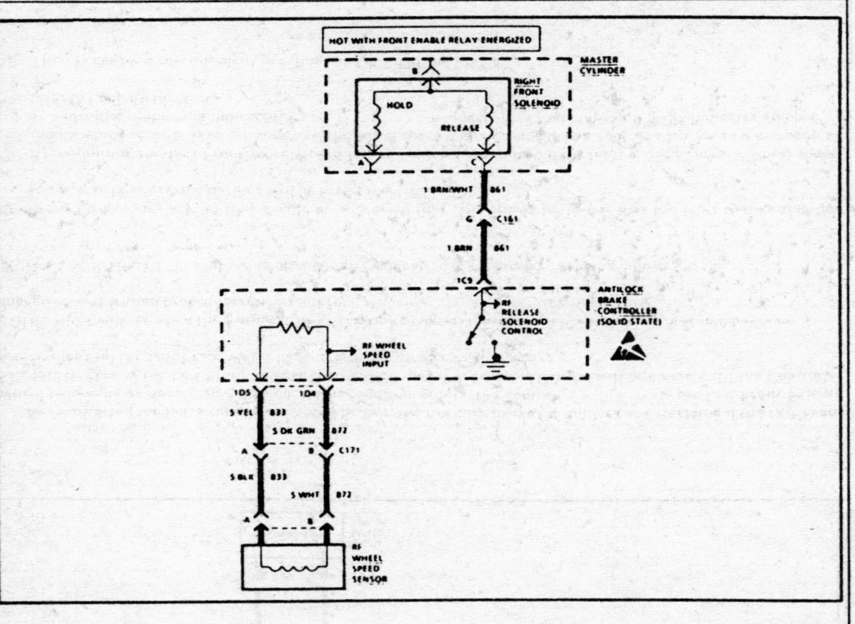
HOT WITH FRONT ENABLE RELAY ENERGIZED
MASTER CYLINDER
RIGHT FRONT SOLENOID
HOLD
RELEASE
1 BRN/WHT 861
C161
1 BRN 861
1C5
ANTILOCK BRAKE CONTROLLER (SOLID STATE)
RF RELEASE SOLENOID CONTROL
RF WHEEL SPEED INPUT
1D5
1D4
5 YEL 833
5 DK GRN 872
C171
5 BLK 833
5 WHT 872
RF WHEEL SPEED SENSOR

By monitoring the Right Front Wheel Speed Sensor, the Antilock Brake Controller can determine if the Right Front Wheel is locking up. If this condition occurs, the controller will activate the Right Front Release Solenoid by closing the Right Front Release Solenoid Control. The Solenoid Control will be closed until the Controller determines that the Right Front Wheel has increased to an acceptable speed.

CODE A023 will set when the Antilock Brake Controller senses that the Right Front Release Solenoid has been energized longer than proper operation requires.

TEST DESCRIPTION: The following provides an explanation of the procedures being followed in the tree.

① If any other codes are set they should be addressed first. The reason for this is that the fault that caused the solenoid to be energized too long will be better identified.

② By examining the Right Front Wheel Speed input, it can be determined if the fault is due to erratic wheel speed inputs which occur only at low speeds. If the wheel speed input is found to be steady at a low speed a mechanical or hydraulic problem is indicated. A wheel speed that stays at 0 MPH indicates an open – refer to Code A044.

③ This checks for a possible short to voltage on CKT 833 and CKT 872.

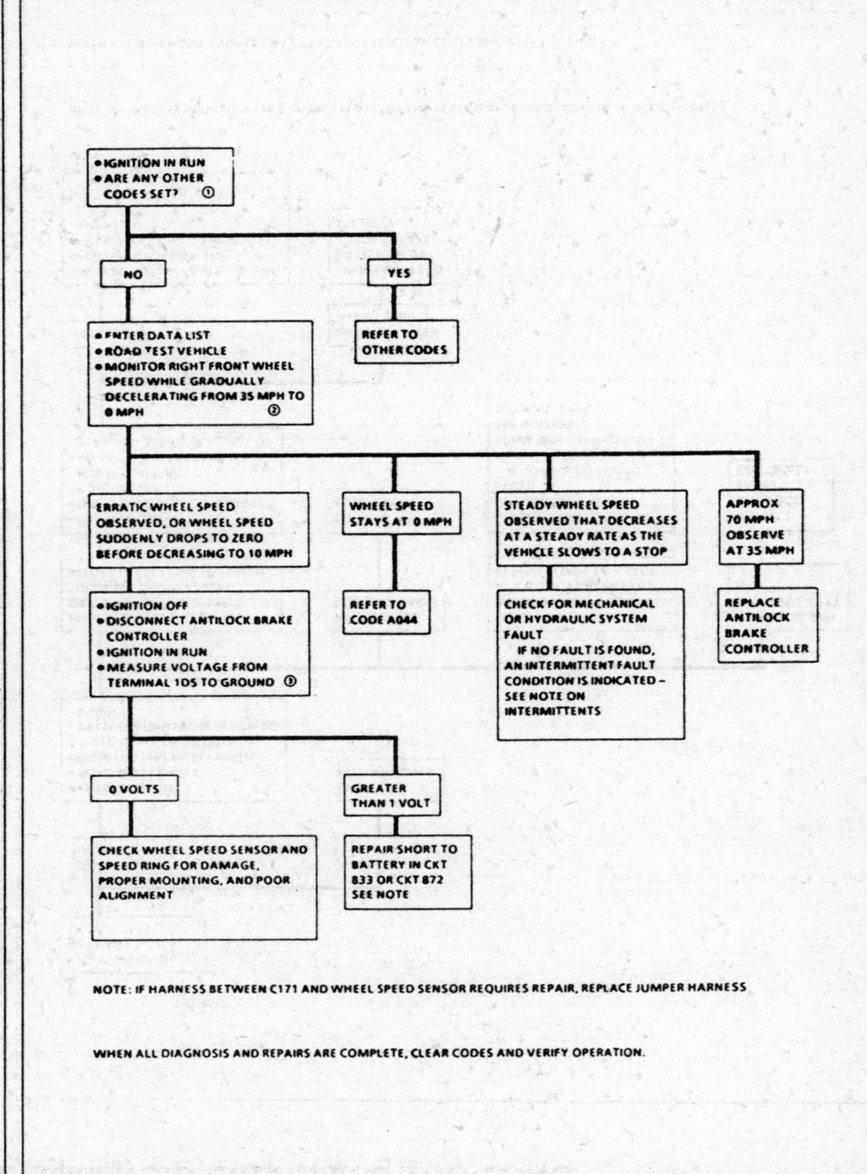
• IGNITION IN RUN
• ARE ANY OTHER CODES SET? ①
NO
YES
REFER TO OTHER CODES
• ENTER DATA LIST
• ROAD TEST VEHICLE
• MONITOR RIGHT FRONT WHEEL SPEED WHILE GRADUALLY DECELERATING FROM 35 MPH TO 0 MPH ②
ERRATIC WHEEL SPEED OBSERVED, OR WHEEL SPEED SUDDENLY DROPS TO ZERO BEFORE DECREASING TO 10 MPH
WHEEL SPEED STAYS AT 0 MPH
STEADY WHEEL SPEED OBSERVED THAT DECREASES AT A STEADY RATE AS THE VEHICLE SLOWS TO A STOP
APPROX 70 MPH OBSERVE AT 35 MPH
• IGNITION OFF
• DISCONNECT ANTILOCK BRAKE CONTROLLER
• IGNITION IN RUN
• MEASURE VOLTAGE FROM TERMINAL 1D5 TO GROUND ③
REFER TO CODE A044
CHECK FOR MECHANICAL OR HYDRAULIC SYSTEM FAULT
IF NO FAULT IS FOUND, AN INTERMITTENT FAULT CONDITION IS INDICATED – SEE NOTE ON INTERMITTENTS
REPLACE ANTILOCK BRAKE CONTROLLER
0 VOLTS
GREATER THAN 1 VOLT
CHECK WHEEL SPEED SENSOR AND SPEED RING FOR DAMAGE, PROPER MOUNTING, AND POOR ALIGNMENT
REPAIR SHORT TO BATTERY IN CKT 833 OR CKT 872 SEE NOTE
NOTE: IF HARNESS BETWEEN C171 AND WHEEL SPEED SENSOR REQUIRES REPAIR, REPLACE JUMPER HARNESS
WHEN ALL DIAGNOSIS AND REPAIRS ARE COMPLETE, CLEAR CODES AND VERIFY OPERATION.

CODE A024 – LEFT FRONT RELEASE SOLENOID ENERGIZED TOO LONG

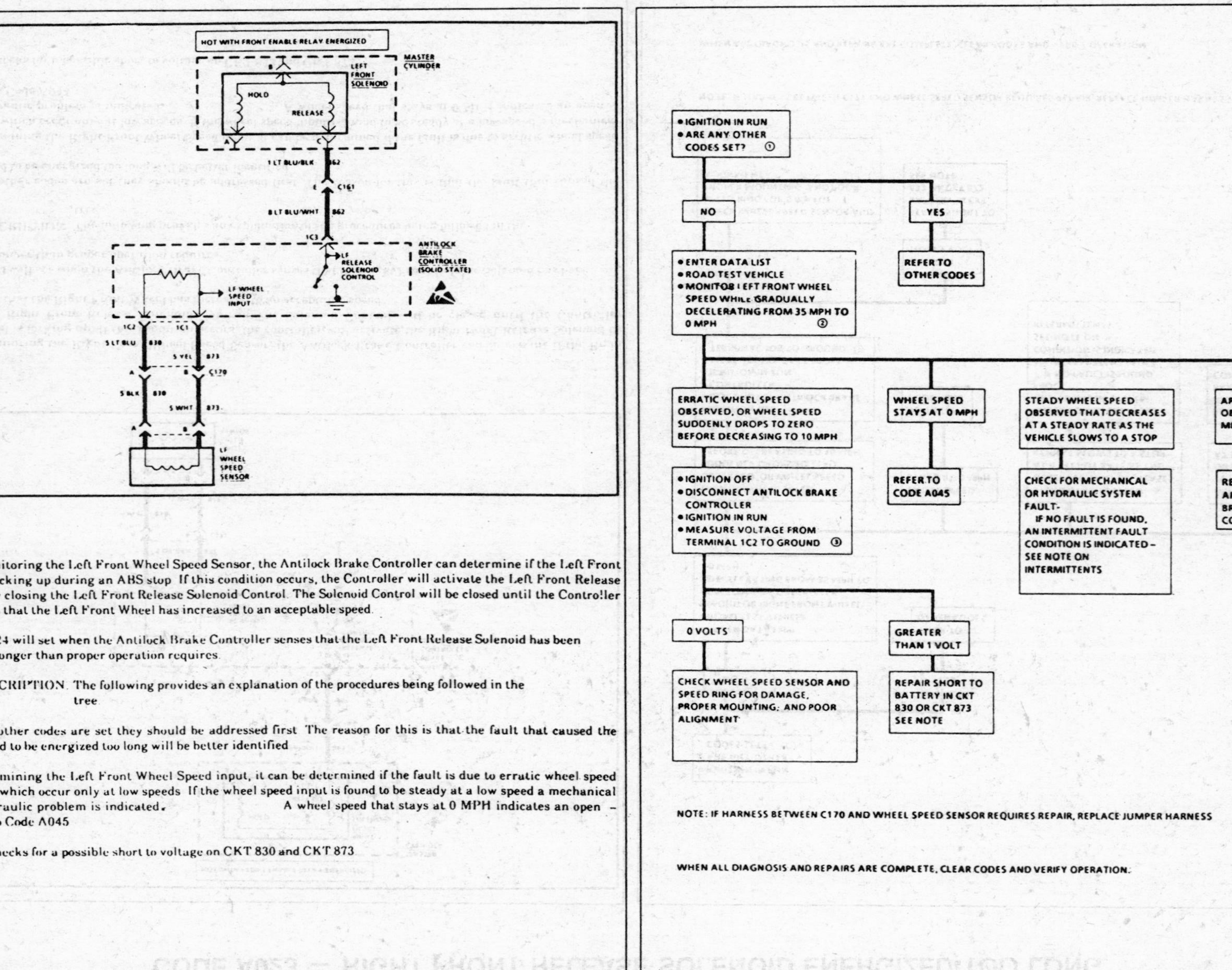

By monitoring the Left Front Wheel Speed Sensor, the Antilock Brake Controller can determine if the Left Front Wheel is locking up during an ABS stop. If this condition occurs, the Controller will activate the Left Front Release Solenoid by closing the Left Front Release Solenoid Control. The Solenoid Control will be closed until the Controller determines that the Left Front Wheel has increased to an acceptable speed.

CODE A024 will set when the Antilock Brake Controller senses that the Left Front Release Solenoid has been energized longer than proper operation requires.

TEST DESCRIPTION. The following provides an explanation of the procedures being followed in the tree.

① If any other codes are set they should be addressed first. The reason for this is that the fault that caused the solenoid to be energized too long will be better identified.

② By examining the Left Front Wheel Speed input, it can be determined if the fault is due to erratic wheel speed inputs which occur only at low speeds. If the wheel speed input is found to be steady at a low speed a mechanical or hydraulic problem is indicated. A wheel speed that stays at 0 MPH indicates an open – refer to Code A045.

③ This checks for a possible short to voltage on CKT 830 and CKT 873.

CODE A025 – REAR RELEASE SOLENOID ENERGIZED TOO LONG

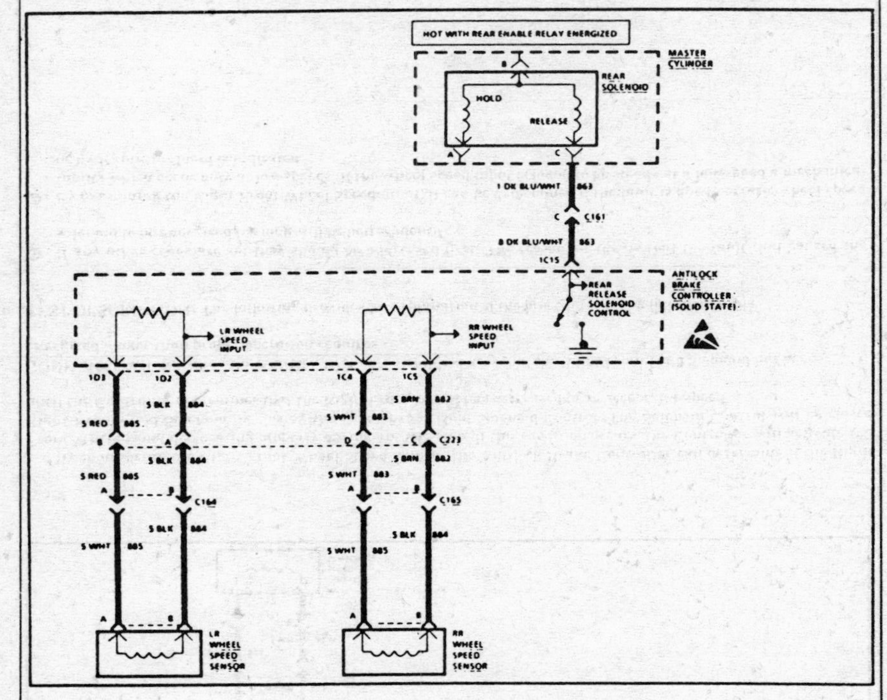
HOT WITH REAR ENABLE RELAY ENERGIZED
MASTER CYLINDER
REAR SOLENOID
HOLD
RELEASE
1 DK BLU/WHT 863
C161
8 DK BLU/WHT 863
1C15
ANTILOCK BRAKE CONTROLLER (SOLID STATE)
REAR RELEASE SOLENOID CONTROL
LR WHEEL SPEED INPUT
RR WHEEL SPEED INPUT
C223
C164
C165
5 RED 885
5 BLK 884
5 WHT 883
5 BRN 882
5 WHT 885
LR WHEEL SPEED SENSOR
RR WHEEL SPEED SENSOR

By monitoring the Rear Wheel Speed Sensors, the Antilock Brake Controller can determine if a rear wheel is locking up during an ABS stop. If the condition occurs, the Controller will activate the Rear Release Solenoid by closing the Rear Release Solenoid Control. The Solenoid Control will be closed until the Controller determines that both rear wheels have increased to acceptable speeds.

CODE A025 will set when the Antilock Brake Controller senses that the Rear Release Solenoid has been energized longer than proper operation requires

TEST DESCRIPTION: The following provides an explanation of the procedures being followed in the tree.

① If any other codes are set they should be addressed first. The reason for this is that the fault that caused the solenoid to be energized too long will be better identified.

② By examining the rear wheel speed inputs, it can be determined if the fault is due to erratic wheel speed inputs which occur only at low speeds. If the wheel speed input is found to be steady at low speed, a mechanical or hydraulic problem is indicated. A wheel speed that stays at 0 MPH indicates an open – refer to Code A046 or A047

③ This checks for a possible short to ground on the suspect Wheel Speed Sensor Circuit.

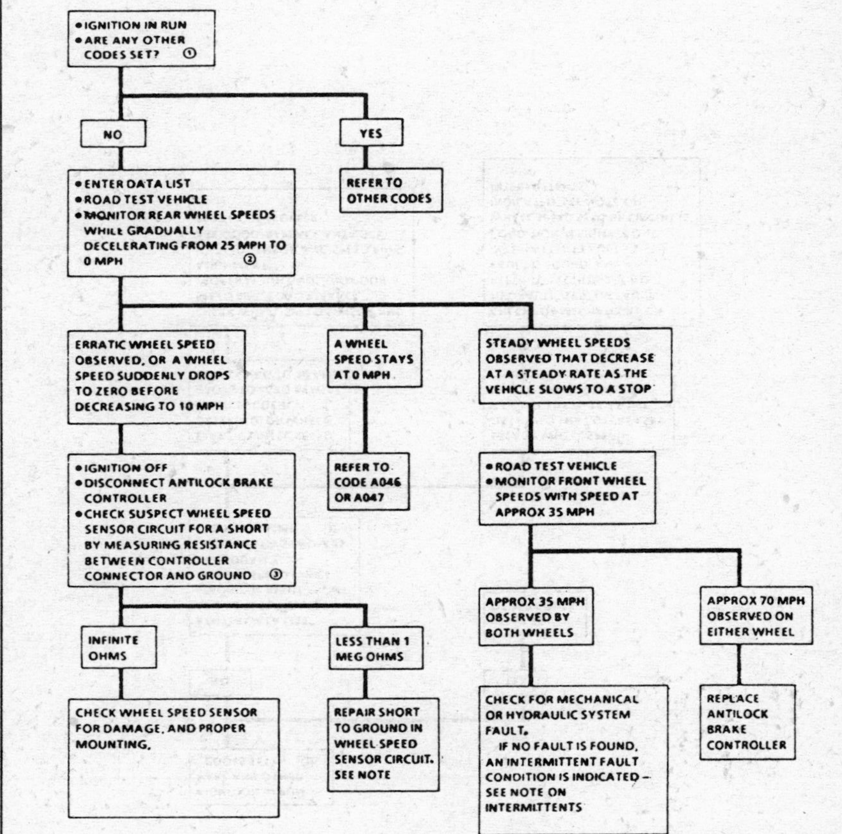
• IGNITION IN RUN
• ARE ANY OTHER CODES SET? ①
NO
YES
REFER TO OTHER CODES
• ENTER DATA LIST
• ROAD TEST VEHICLE
• MONITOR REAR WHEEL SPEEDS WHILE GRADUALLY DECELERATING FROM 25 MPH TO 0 MPH ②
ERRATIC WHEEL SPEED OBSERVED, OR A WHEEL SPEED SUDDENLY DROPS TO ZERO BEFORE DECREASING TO 10 MPH
A WHEEL SPEED STAYS AT 0 MPH
STEADY WHEEL SPEEDS OBSERVED THAT DECREASE AT A STEADY RATE AS THE VEHICLE SLOWS TO A STOP
• IGNITION OFF
• DISCONNECT ANTILOCK BRAKE CONTROLLER
• CHECK SUSPECT WHEEL SPEED SENSOR CIRCUIT FOR A SHORT BY MEASURING RESISTANCE BETWEEN CONTROLLER CONNECTOR AND GROUND ③
REFER TO CODE A046 OR A047
• ROAD TEST VEHICLE
• MONITOR FRONT WHEEL SPEEDS WITH SPEED AT APPROX 35 MPH
INFINITE OHMS
LESS THAN 1 MEG OHMS
APPROX 35 MPH OBSERVED BY BOTH WHEELS
APPROX 70 MPH OBSERVED ON EITHER WHEEL
CHECK WHEEL SPEED SENSOR FOR DAMAGE, AND PROPER MOUNTING.
REPAIR SHORT TO GROUND IN WHEEL SPEED SENSOR CIRCUIT. SEE NOTE
CHECK FOR MECHANICAL OR HYDRAULIC SYSTEM FAULT. IF NO FAULT IS FOUND, AN INTERMITTENT FAULT CONDITION IS INDICATED – SEE NOTE ON INTERMITTENTS
REPLACE ANTILOCK BRAKE CONTROLLER
NOTE: IF HARNESS BETWEEN C164 OR C165 AND WHEEL SPEED SENSOR REQUIRES REPAIR, REPLACE JUMPER HARNESS
WHEN ALL DIAGNOSIS AND REPAIRS ARE COMPLETE, CLEAR CODES AND VERIFY OPERATION.

CODE A026 — RIGHT FRONT HOLD SOLENOID ENERGIZED TOO LONG

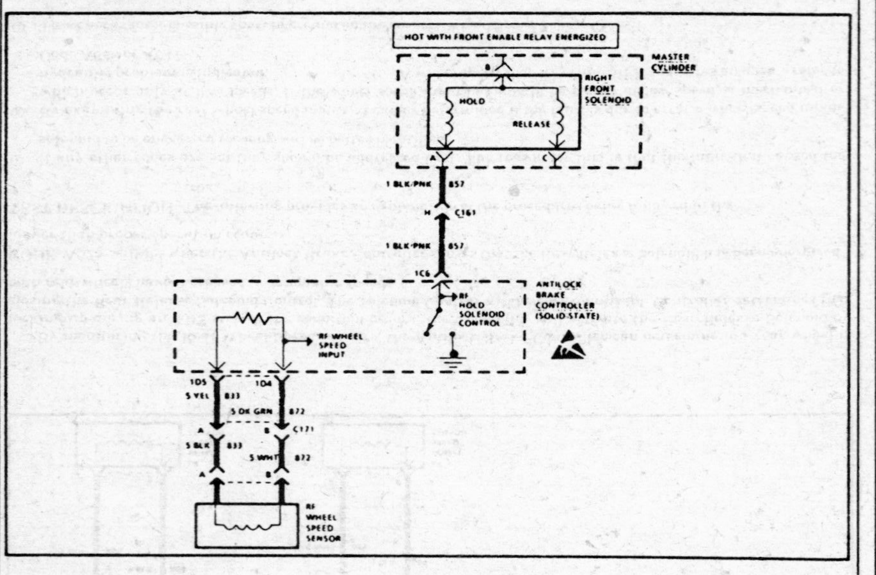

By monitoring the Right Front Wheel Speed Sensor, the Antilock Brake Controller can determine if the Right Front Wheel is not declerating properly during an ABS stop. If this condition occurs, the Controller will activate the Right Front Hold Solenoid by closing the Right Front Hold Solenoid Control. The Solenoid Control will be closed until the Controller determines that the Right Front Wheel has decreased to an acceptable speed.

CODE A026 will set when the Antilock Brake Controller senses that the Right Front Hold Solenoid has been energized longer than proper operation requires.

TEST DESCRIPTION: The following provides an explanation of the procedures being followed in the tree.

① If any other codes are set they should be addressed first. The reason for this is that the fault that caused the solenoid to be energized too long will be better identified.

② By examining the Right Front Wheel Speed input, it can be determined if the fault is due to erratic wheel speed inputs which occur only at low speeds. If the wheel speed input is found to be steady at a low speed a mechanical or hydraulic problem is indicated.

- IGNITION IN RUN
- ARE ANY OTHER CODES SET? ①

YES: REFER TO OTHER CODES

NO:

- ENTER DATA LIST
- ROAD TEST VEHICLE
- MONITOR RIGHT FRONT WHEEL SPEED WHILE GRADUALLY DECLERATING FROM 25 MPH TO 0 MPH ②

ERRATIC WHEEL SPEED OBSERVED, OR WHEEL SPEED SUDDENLY DROPS TO ZERO BEFORE DECREASING TO 10 MPH → CHECK WHEEL SPEED SENSOR AND SPEED RING FOR DAMAGE, PROPER MOUNTING, AND POOR ALIGNMENT. IF SPEED SENSOR AND SPEED RING ARE GOOD, REPLACE ANTILOCK BRAKE CONTROLLER

STEADY WHEEL SPEED OBSERVED THAT DECREASES AT A STEADY RATE AS THE WHEEL SLOWS TO A STOP → CHECK FOR MECHANICAL OR HYDRAULIC SYSTEM FAULT – REFER TO SECTION 5. IF NO FAULT IS FOUND, AN INTERMITTENT FAULT CONDITION IN RIGHT FRONT WHEEL SPEED SENSOR CIRCUIT IS INDICATED. SEE NOTE ON INTERMITTENTS

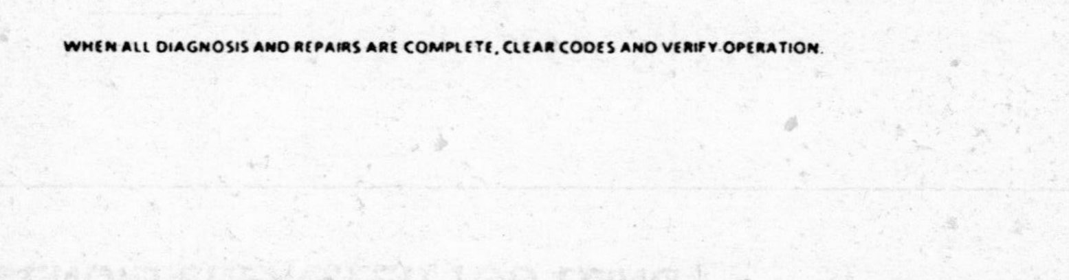

WHEN ALL DIAGNOSIS AND REPAIRS ARE COMPLETE, CLEAR CODES AND VERIFY OPERATION.

CODE A027 – LEFT FRONT HOLD SOLENOID ENERGIZED TOO LONG

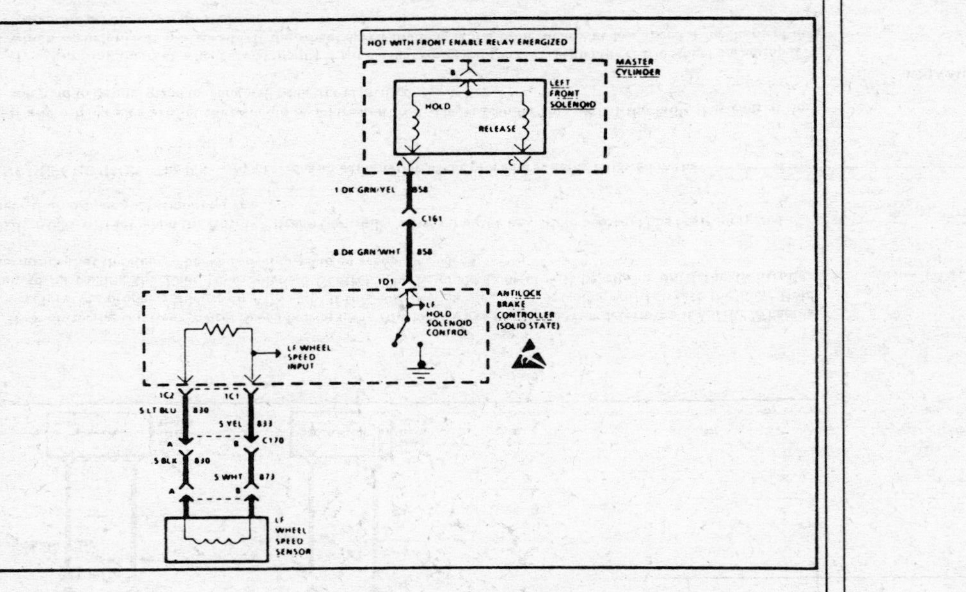
HOT WITH FRONT ENABLE RELAY ENERGIZED
MASTER CYLINDER
LEFT FRONT SOLENOID
HOLD
RELEASE
1 DK GRN/YEL 858
C161
.8 DK GRN/WHT 858
1D1
ANTILOCK BRAKE CONTROLLER (SOLID STATE)
LF HOLD SOLENOID CONTROL
LF WHEEL SPEED INPUT
1C2
1C1
.5 LT BLU 830
.5 YEL 833
C170
.5 BLK 830
.5 WHT 873
LF WHEEL SPEED SENSOR

By monitoring the Left Front Wheel Speed Sensor, the Antilock Brake Controller can determine if the Left Front Wheel is not decelerating properly during an ABS stop. If this condition occurs, the Controller will activate the Left Front Hold Solenoid by closing the Left Front Hold Solenoid Control. The Solenoid Control will be closed until the Controller determines that the Left Front Wheel has decreased to an acceptable speed.

CODE A027 will set when the Antilock Brake Controller senses that the Left Front Hold Solenoid has been energized longer than proper operation requires.

TEST DESCRIPTION: The following provides an explanation of the procedures being followed in the tree.

① If any other codes are set they should be addressed first. The reason for this is that the fault that caused the solenoid to be energized too long will be better identified.

② By examining the Left Front Wheel Speed input, it can be determined if the fault is due to erratic wheel speed inputs which occur only at low speeds. If the wheel speed input is found to be steady at a low speed a mechanical or hydraulic problem is indicated.

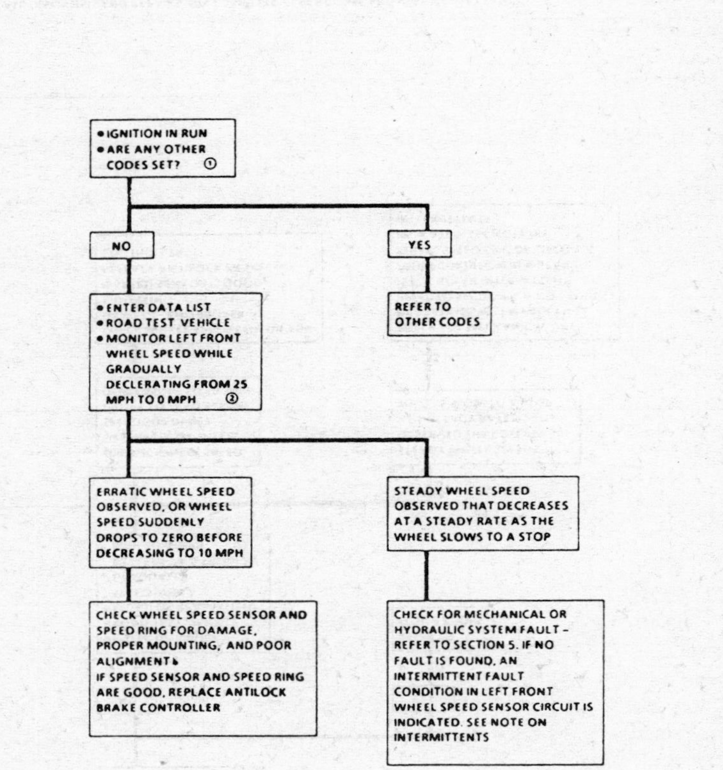
• IGNITION IN RUN
• ARE ANY OTHER CODES SET? ①
NO
YES
REFER TO OTHER CODES
• ENTER DATA LIST
• ROAD TEST VEHICLE
• MONITOR LEFT FRONT WHEEL SPEED WHILE GRADUALLY DECLERATING FROM 25 MPH TO 0 MPH ②
ERRATIC WHEEL SPEED OBSERVED, OR WHEEL SPEED SUDDENLY DROPS TO ZERO BEFORE DECREASING TO 10 MPH
STEADY WHEEL SPEED OBSERVED THAT DECREASES AT A STEADY RATE AS THE WHEEL SLOWS TO A STOP
CHECK WHEEL SPEED SENSOR AND SPEED RING FOR DAMAGE, PROPER MOUNTING, AND POOR ALIGNMENT.
IF SPEED SENSOR AND SPEED RING ARE GOOD, REPLACE ANTILOCK BRAKE CONTROLLER
CHECK FOR MECHANICAL OR HYDRAULIC SYSTEM FAULT – REFER TO SECTION 5. IF NO FAULT IS FOUND, AN INTERMITTENT FAULT CONDITION IN LEFT FRONT WHEEL SPEED SENSOR CIRCUIT IS INDICATED. SEE NOTE ON INTERMITTENTS

WHEN ALL DIAGNOSIS AND REPAIRS ARE COMPLETE, CLEAR CODES AND VERIFY OPERATION.

CODE A028 — REAR HOLD SOLENOID ENERGIZED TOO LONG

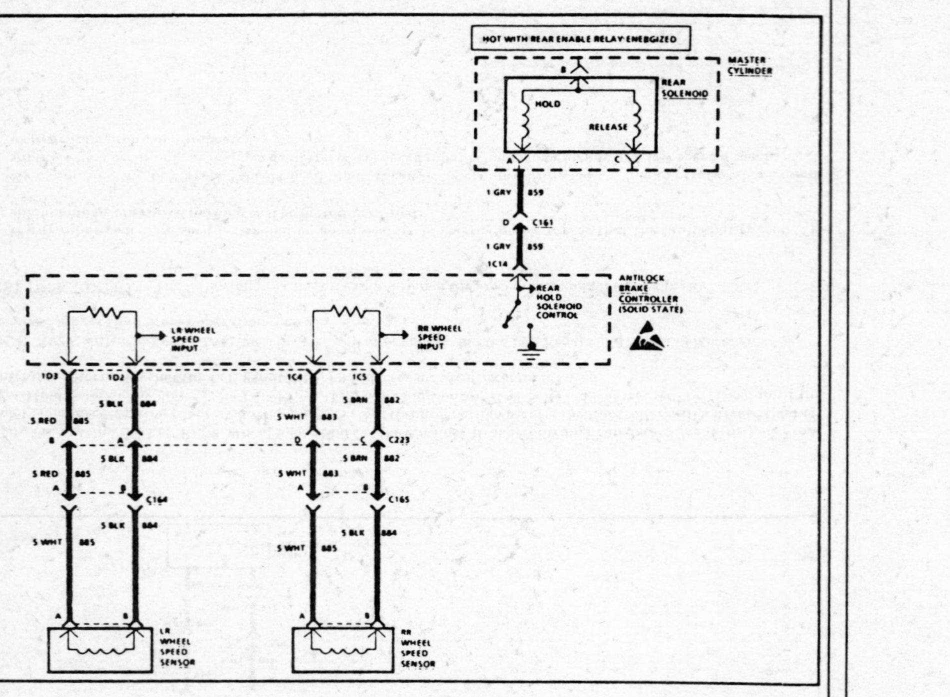

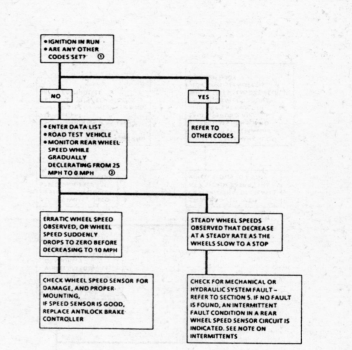

By monitoring the Rear Wheel Speed Sensors, the Antilock Brake Controller can determine if a Rear Wheel is not decelerating properly during an ABS stop. If this condition occurs, the Controller will activate the Rear Hold Solenoid by closing the Rear Hold Solenoid Control. The Solenoid Control will be closed until the Controller determines that the Rear Wheel has decreased to an acceptable speed.

CODE A028 will set when the Antilock Brake Controller senses that the Rear Hold Solenoid has been energized longer than proper operation requires.

TEST DESCRIPTION: The following provides an explanation of the procedures being followed in the tree.

① If any other codes are set they should be addressed first. The reason for this is that the fault that caused the solenoid to be energized too long will be better identified.

② By examining the rear wheel speed inputs, it can be determined if the fault is due to erratic wheel speed inputs which occur only at low speeds. If the wheel speed input is found to be steady at low speed a mechanical or hydraulic problem is indicated.

- IGNITION IN RUN
- ARE ANY OTHER CODES SET? ①

YES → REFER TO OTHER CODES

NO →

- ENTER DATA LIST
- ROAD TEST VEHICLE
- MONITOR REAR WHEEL SPEED WHILE GRADUALLY DECLERATING FROM 25 MPH TO 0 MPH ②

ERRATIC WHEEL SPEED OBSERVED, OR WHEEL SPEED SUDDENLY DROPS TO ZERO BEFORE DECREASING TO 10 MPH → CHECK WHEEL SPEED SENSOR FOR DAMAGE, AND PROPER MOUNTING. IF SPEED SENSOR IS GOOD, REPLACE ANTILOCK BRAKE CONTROLLER

STEADY WHEEL SPEEDS OBSERVED THAT DECREASE AT A STEADY RATE AS THE WHEELS SLOW TO A STOP → CHECK FOR MECHANICAL OR HYDRAULIC SYSTEM FAULT – REFER TO SECTION 5. IF NO FAULT IS FOUND, AN INTERMITTENT FAULT CONDITION IN A REAR WHEEL SPEED SENSOR CIRCUIT IS INDICATED. SEE NOTE ON INTERMITTENTS

WHEN ALL DIAGNOSIS AND REPAIRS ARE COMPLETE, CLEAR CODES AND VERIFY OPERATION.

CODE A030 – BOTH FRONT OR ONE FRONT AND ONE REAR WHEEL SPEED SENSOR OPEN OR SHORTED TO GROUND

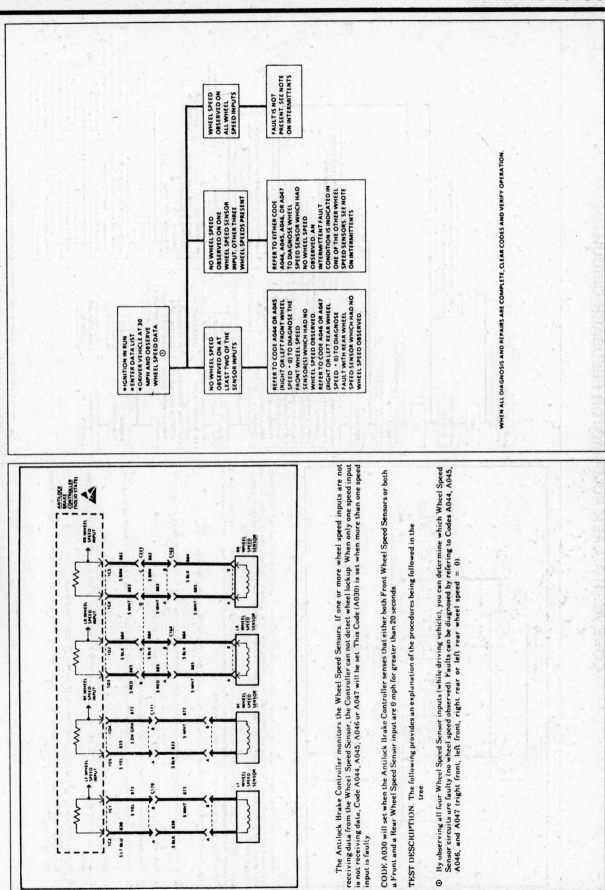

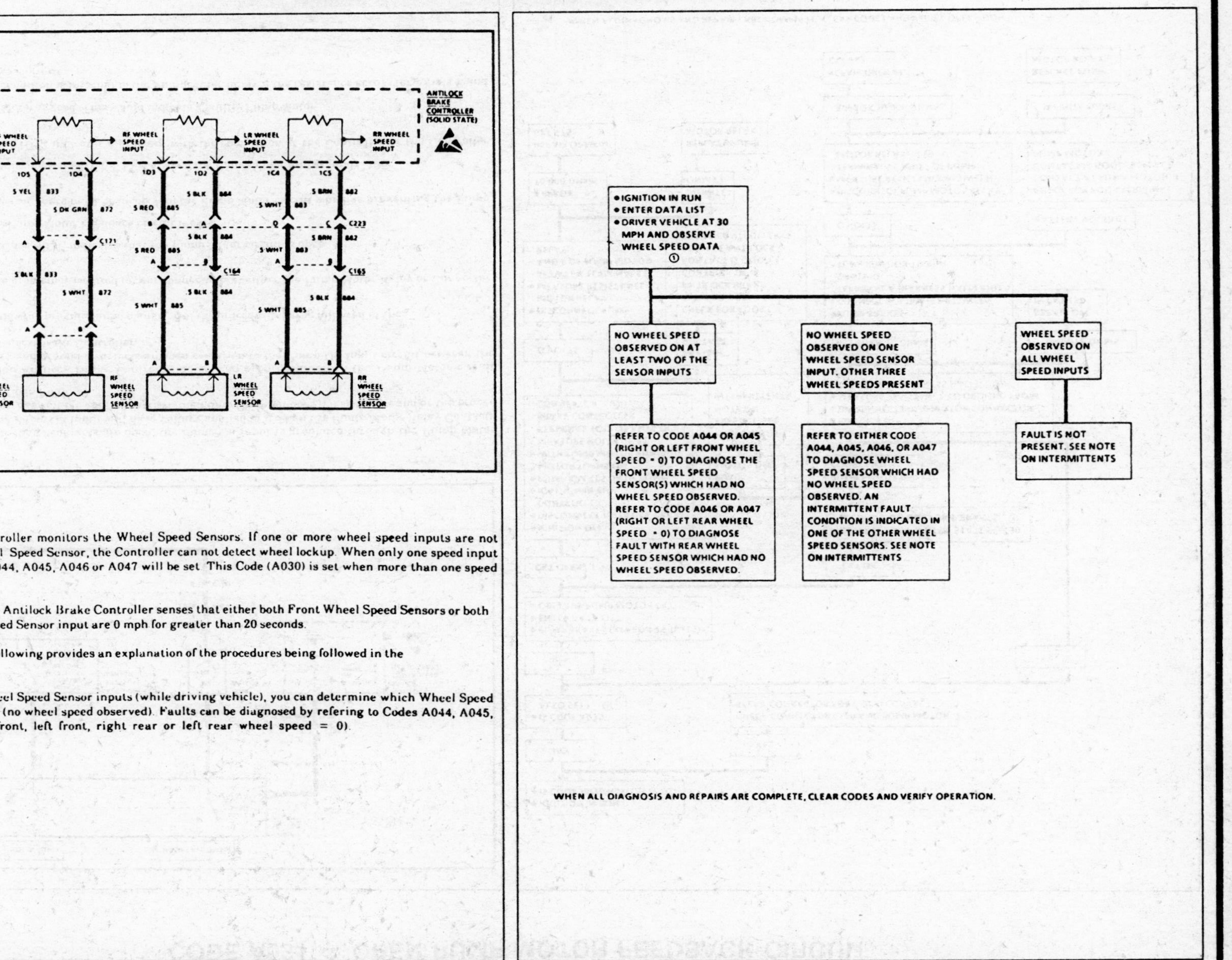
ANTILOCK BRAKE CONTROLLER (SOLID STATE)
LF WHEEL SPEED INPUT
RF WHEEL SPEED INPUT
LR WHEEL SPEED INPUT
RR WHEEL SPEED INPUT
LF WHEEL SPEED SENSOR
RF WHEEL SPEED SENSOR
LR WHEEL SPEED SENSOR
RR WHEEL SPEED SENSOR
• IGNITION IN RUN
• ENTER DATA LIST
• DRIVER VEHICLE AT 30 MPH AND OBSERVE WHEEL SPEED DATA ①
NO WHEEL SPEED OBSERVED ON AT LEAST TWO OF THE SENSOR INPUTS
NO WHEEL SPEED OBSERVED ON ONE WHEEL SPEED SENSOR INPUT. OTHER THREE WHEEL SPEEDS PRESENT
WHEEL SPEED OBSERVED ON ALL WHEEL SPEED INPUTS
REFER TO CODE A044 OR A045 (RIGHT OR LEFT FRONT WHEEL SPEED = 0) TO DIAGNOSE THE FRONT WHEEL SPEED SENSOR(S) WHICH HAD NO WHEEL SPEED OBSERVED. REFER TO CODE A046 OR A047 (RIGHT OR LEFT REAR WHEEL SPEED = 0) TO DIAGNOSE FAULT WITH REAR WHEEL SPEED SENSOR WHICH HAD NO WHEEL SPEED OBSERVED.
REFER TO EITHER CODE A044, A045, A046, OR A047 TO DIAGNOSE WHEEL SPEED SENSOR WHICH HAD NO WHEEL SPEED OBSERVED. AN INTERMITTENT FAULT CONDITION IS INDICATED IN ONE OF THE OTHER WHEEL SPEED SENSORS. SEE NOTE ON INTERMITTENTS
FAULT IS NOT PRESENT. SEE NOTE ON INTERMITTENTS
WHEN ALL DIAGNOSIS AND REPAIRS ARE COMPLETE, CLEAR CODES AND VERIFY OPERATION.

The Antilock Brake Controller monitors the Wheel Speed Sensors. If one or more wheel speed inputs are not receiving data from the Wheel Speed Sensor, the Controller can not detect wheel lockup. When only one speed input is not receiving data, Code A044, A045, A046 or A047 will be set. This Code (A030) is set when more than one speed input is faulty.

CODE A030 will set when the Antilock Brake Controller senses that either both Front Wheel Speed Sensors or both a Front and a Rear Wheel Speed Sensor input are 0 mph for greater than 20 seconds.

TEST DESCRIPTION. The following provides an explanation of the procedures being followed in the tree.

① By observing all four Wheel Speed Sensor inputs (while driving vehicle), you can determine which Wheel Speed Sensor circuits are faulty (no wheel speed observed). Faults can be diagnosed by refering to Codes A044, A045, A046, and A047 (right front, left front, right rear or left rear wheel speed = 0).

CODE A031 — OPEN PUMP MOTOR FEEDBACK CIRCUIT

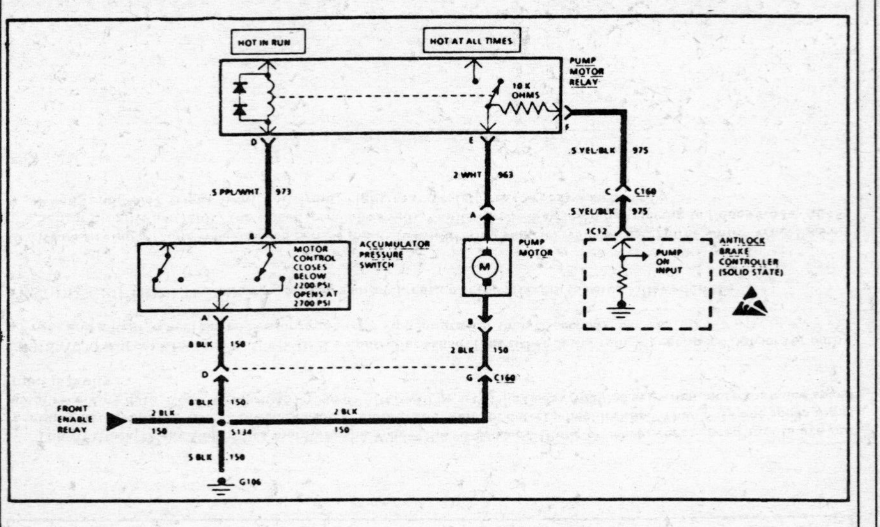

Whenever the Pump Motor Relay contacts are open, the Pump On Input is grounded through the Pump Motor Relay and the Pump Motor. The Pump On Input will have voltage applied to it when the Pump Motor Relay Contacts are closed (the Pump Motor also has voltage applied to it). If the Pump On Input does not sense ground or the proper voltage, the Controller will set Code A031.

CODE A031 will set when the Antilock Brake Controller detects an open condition in the Pump Motor circuit between the Pump Motor Relay and ground or detects an open condition in the Pump On Input circuit between the Pump Motor Relay and the Antilock Brake Controller.

TEST DESCRIPTION. The following provides an explanation of the procedures being followed in the tree.

① If Code A036 is also set, the problem is isolated to poor connections at either the Pump Motor Relay or Connector C160.

② Code A035, when set with Code A031, indicates that the Pump Motor circuit is open.

③ This step determines if the Pump Motor Feedback circuit is open.

④ If the Pump Motor is always on, there must be an open in the Pump Motor circuit which is preventing the Pump Motor from operating.

⑤ Determines if the open condition exists in CKT 150 between the Pump Motor and ground G106.

⑥ Battery voltage at terminal 1C12 indicates a problem with the connection at the Controller or the Controller itself.

⑦ Detects if circuit to Pump Motor is good. This would indicate a faulty Pump Motor.

⑧ Determines that the open condition is internal to the Pump Motor Relay if the resistance across terminals E and F of the Pump Motor Relay is infinite.

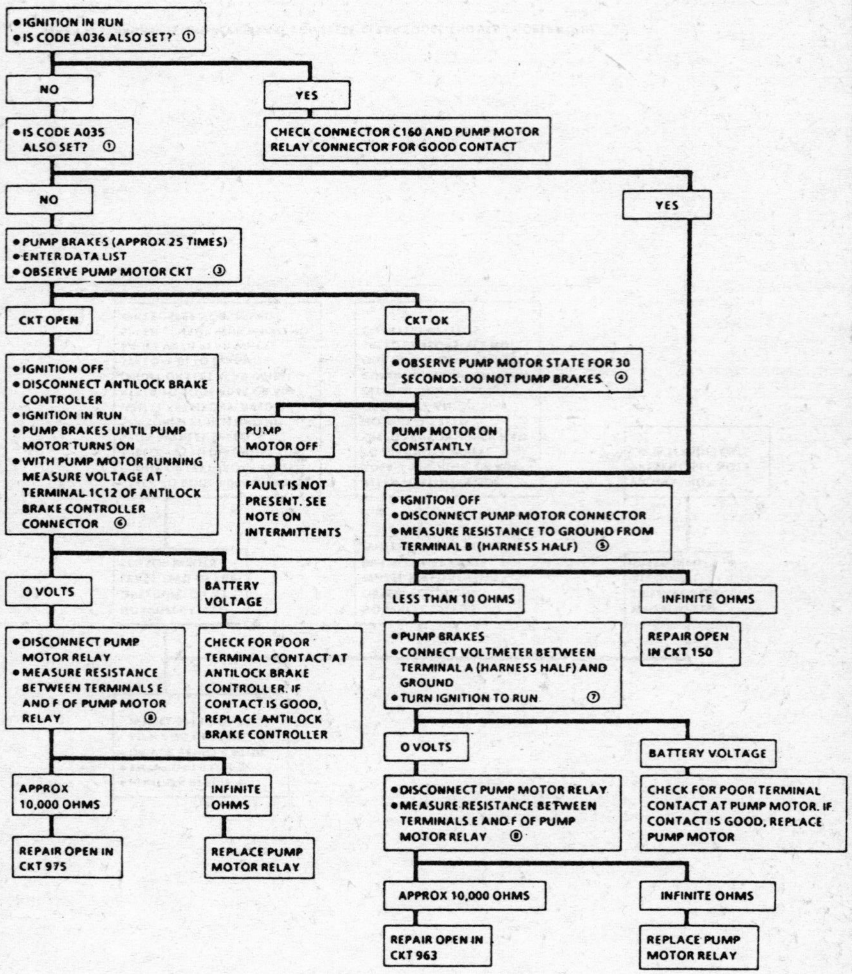

- • IGNITION IN RUN
  • IS CODE A036 ALSO SET? ①
  - YES → CHECK CONNECTOR C160 AND PUMP MOTOR RELAY CONNECTOR FOR GOOD CONTACT
  - NO → • IS CODE A035 ALSO SET? ②
    - YES → (go to • IGNITION OFF • DISCONNECT PUMP MOTOR CONNECTOR …)
    - NO → • PUMP BRAKES (APPROX 25 TIMES) • ENTER DATA LIST • OBSERVE PUMP MOTOR CKT ③
      - CKT OPEN → • IGNITION OFF • DISCONNECT ANTILOCK BRAKE CONTROLLER • IGNITION IN RUN • PUMP BRAKES UNTIL PUMP MOTOR TURNS ON • WITH PUMP MOTOR RUNNING MEASURE VOLTAGE AT TERMINAL 1C12 OF ANTILOCK BRAKE CONTROLLER CONNECTOR ⑥
        - 0 VOLTS → • DISCONNECT PUMP MOTOR RELAY • MEASURE RESISTANCE BETWEEN TERMINALS E AND F OF PUMP MOTOR RELAY ⑧
          - APPROX 10,000 OHMS → REPAIR OPEN IN CKT 975
          - INFINITE OHMS → REPLACE PUMP MOTOR RELAY
        - BATTERY VOLTAGE → CHECK FOR POOR TERMINAL CONTACT AT ANTILOCK BRAKE CONTROLLER. IF CONTACT IS GOOD, REPLACE ANTILOCK BRAKE CONTROLLER
      - CKT OK → • OBSERVE PUMP MOTOR STATE FOR 30 SECONDS. DO NOT PUMP BRAKES. ④
        - PUMP MOTOR OFF → FAULT IS NOT PRESENT. SEE NOTE ON INTERMITTENTS
        - PUMP MOTOR ON CONSTANTLY → • IGNITION OFF • DISCONNECT PUMP MOTOR CONNECTOR • MEASURE RESISTANCE TO GROUND FROM TERMINAL B (HARNESS HALF) ⑤
          - INFINITE OHMS → REPAIR OPEN IN CKT 150
          - LESS THAN 10 OHMS → • PUMP BRAKES • CONNECT VOLTMETER BETWEEN TERMINAL A (HARNESS HALF) AND GROUND • TURN IGNITION TO RUN ⑦
            - BATTERY VOLTAGE → CHECK FOR POOR TERMINAL CONTACT AT PUMP MOTOR. IF CONTACT IS GOOD, REPLACE PUMP MOTOR
            - 0 VOLTS → • DISCONNECT PUMP MOTOR RELAY • MEASURE RESISTANCE BETWEEN TERMINALS E AND F OF PUMP MOTOR RELAY ⑧
              - APPROX 10,000 OHMS → REPAIR OPEN IN CKT 963
              - INFINITE OHMS → REPLACE PUMP MOTOR RELAY

WHEN ALL DIAGNOSIS AND REPAIRS ARE COMPLETE, CLEAR CODES AND VERIFY OPERATION.

CODE A032 — OPEN BRAKE SWITCH OR HYDRAULIC LEAK

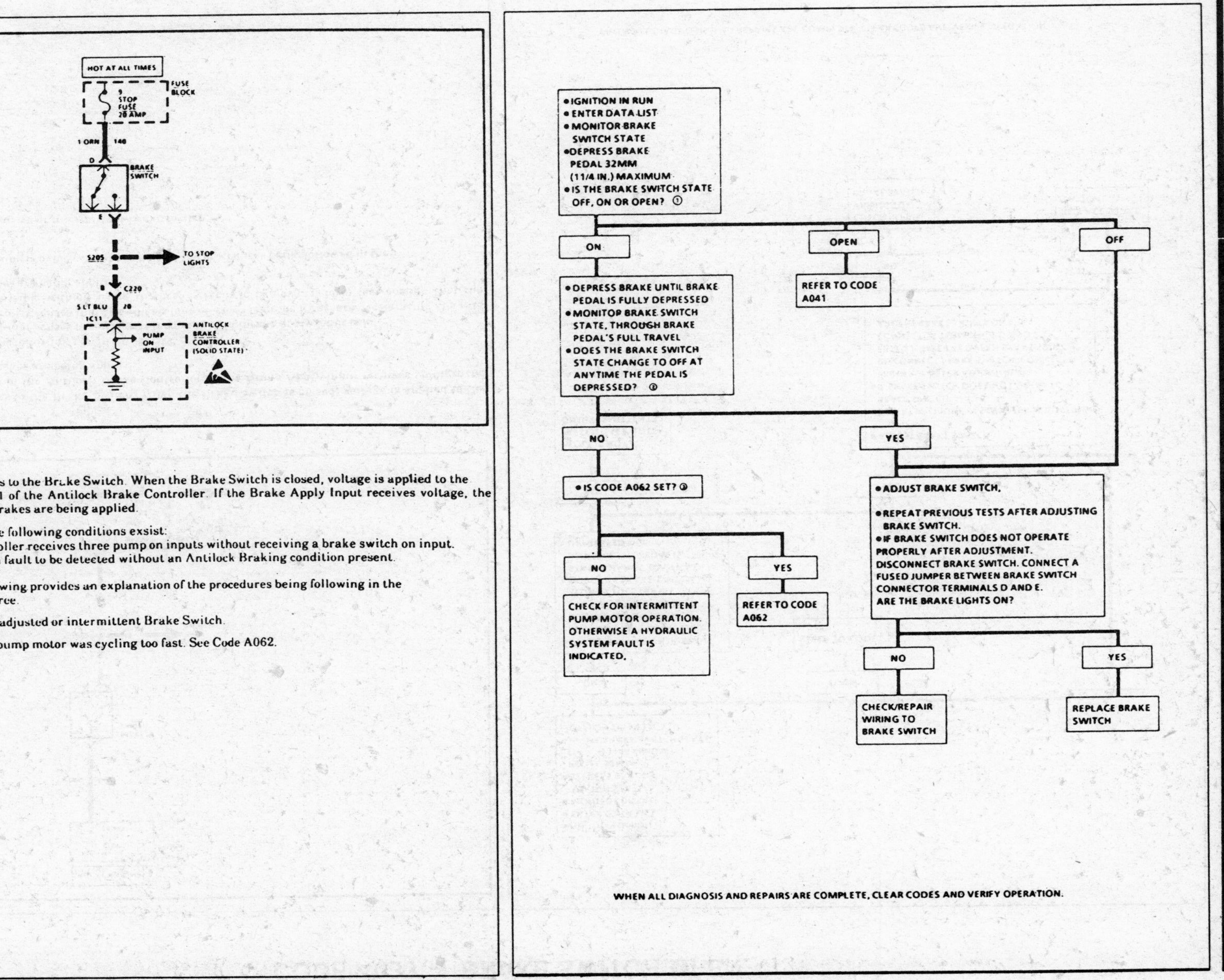
HOT AT ALL TIMES
FUSE BLOCK
9 STOP FUSE 20 AMP
1 ORN 140
D
BRAKE SWITCH
E
S205
TO STOP LIGHTS
B C220
5 LT BLU 20
1C11
PUMP ON INPUT
ANTILOCK BRAKE CONTROLLER (SOLID STATE)
• IGNITION IN RUN
• ENTER DATA LIST
• MONITOR BRAKE SWITCH STATE
• DEPRESS BRAKE PEDAL 32MM (11/4 IN.) MAXIMUM
• IS THE BRAKE SWITCH STATE OFF, ON OR OPEN? ①
ON
OPEN
OFF
REFER TO CODE A041
• DEPRESS BRAKE UNTIL BRAKE PEDAL IS FULLY DEPRESSED
• MONITOR BRAKE SWITCH STATE, THROUGH BRAKE PEDAL'S FULL TRAVEL
• DOES THE BRAKE SWITCH STATE CHANGE TO OFF AT ANYTIME THE PEDAL IS DEPRESSED? ②
NO
YES
• IS CODE A062 SET? ③
NO
YES
CHECK FOR INTERMITTENT PUMP MOTOR OPERATION. OTHERWISE A HYDRAULIC SYSTEM FAULT IS INDICATED.
REFER TO CODE A062
• ADJUST BRAKE SWITCH.
• REPEAT PREVIOUS TESTS AFTER ADJUSTING BRAKE SWITCH.
• IF BRAKE SWITCH DOES NOT OPERATE PROPERLY AFTER ADJUSTMENT. DISCONNECT BRAKE SWITCH. CONNECT A FUSED JUMPER BETWEEN BRAKE SWITCH CONNECTOR TERMINALS D AND E. ARE THE BRAKE LIGHTS ON?
NO
YES
CHECK/REPAIR WIRING TO BRAKE SWITCH
REPLACE BRAKE SWITCH
WHEN ALL DIAGNOSIS AND REPAIRS ARE COMPLETE, CLEAR CODES AND VERIFY OPERATION.

Voltage is applied at all times to the Brake Switch. When the Brake Switch is closed, voltage is applied to the Brake Lights and terminal 1C11 of the Antilock Brake Controller. If the Brake Apply Input receives voltage, the Controller determines that the brakes are being applied.

CODE A032 will set when all the following conditions exsist:

- The Antilock Brake Controller receives three pump on inputs without receiving a brake switch on input. This allows a brake switch fault to be detected without an Antilock Braking condition present.

TEST DESCRIPTION: The following provides an explanation of the procedures being following in the trouble tree.

① & ② Checks for a improperly adjusted or intermittent Brake Switch.

③ If Code A062 is also set, the pump motor was cycling too fast. See Code A062.

CODE A033 – BRAKE SWITCH OPEN

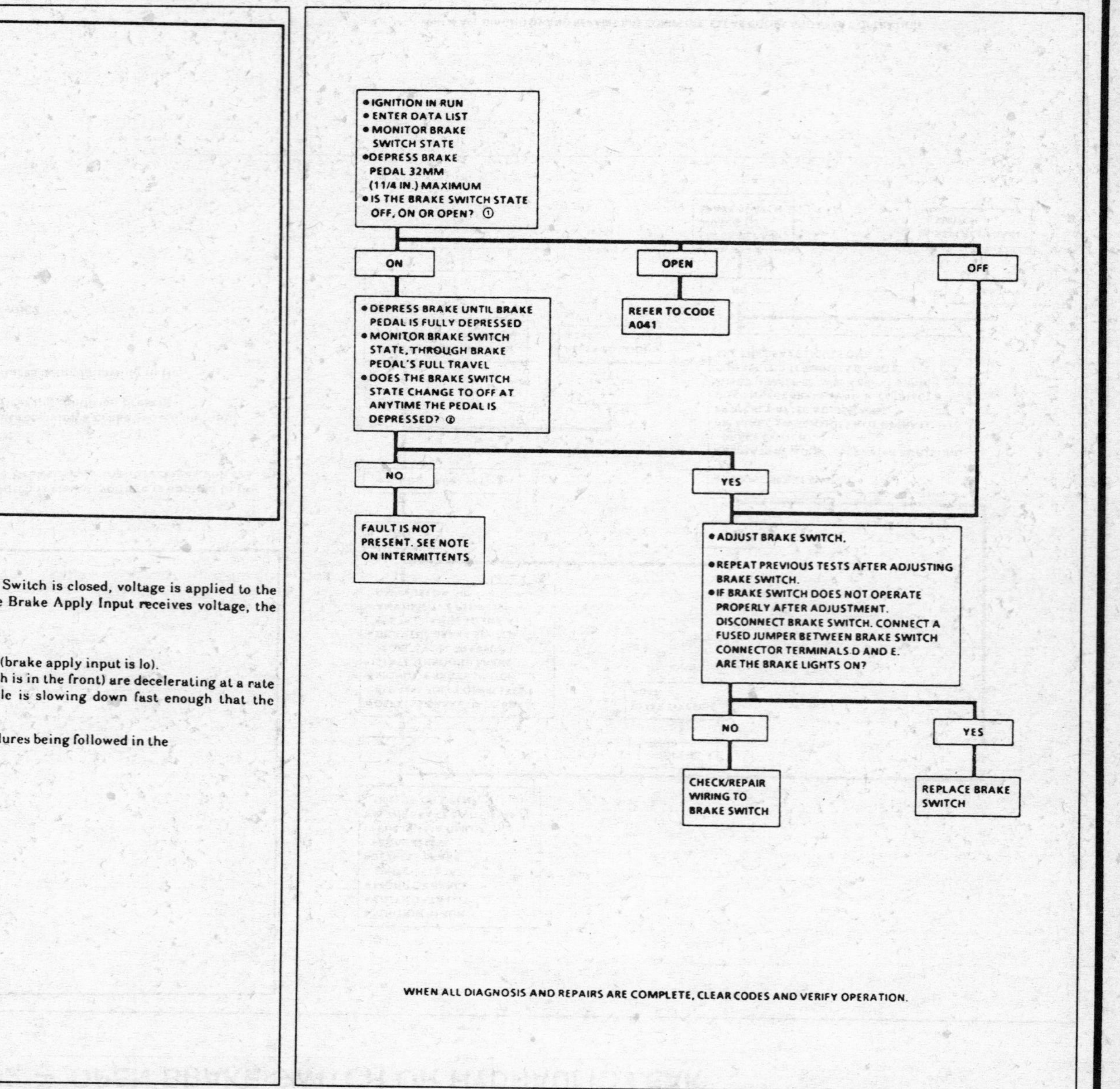

HOT AT ALL TIMES
9 STOP FUSE 20 AMP
FUSE BLOCK
1 ORN 140
D
BRAKE SWITCH
E
S205
TO STOP LIGHTS
B C220
S LT BLU 20
1C11
BRAKE APPLY INPUT
ANTILOCK BRAKE CONTROLLER (SOLID STATE)
• IGNITION IN RUN
• ENTER DATA LIST
• MONITOR BRAKE SWITCH STATE
• DEPRESS BRAKE PEDAL 32MM (11/4 IN.) MAXIMUM
• IS THE BRAKE SWITCH STATE OFF, ON OR OPEN? ①
ON
OPEN
OFF
REFER TO CODE A041
• DEPRESS BRAKE UNTIL BRAKE PEDAL IS FULLY DEPRESSED
• MONITOR BRAKE SWITCH STATE, THROUGH BRAKE PEDAL'S FULL TRAVEL
• DOES THE BRAKE SWITCH STATE CHANGE TO OFF AT ANYTIME THE PEDAL IS DEPRESSED? ②
NO
YES
FAULT IS NOT PRESENT. SEE NOTE ON INTERMITTENTS
• ADJUST BRAKE SWITCH.
• REPEAT PREVIOUS TESTS AFTER ADJUSTING BRAKE SWITCH.
• IF BRAKE SWITCH DOES NOT OPERATE PROPERLY AFTER ADJUSTMENT. DISCONNECT BRAKE SWITCH. CONNECT A FUSED JUMPER BETWEEN BRAKE SWITCH CONNECTOR TERMINALS D AND E. ARE THE BRAKE LIGHTS ON?
NO
YES
CHECK/REPAIR WIRING TO BRAKE SWITCH
REPLACE BRAKE SWITCH
WHEN ALL DIAGNOSIS AND REPAIRS ARE COMPLETE, CLEAR CODES AND VERIFY OPERATION.

Voltage is applied at all times to the Brake Switch. When the Brake Switch is closed, voltage is applied to the Brake Lights and terminal 1C11 of the Antilock Brake Controller. If the Brake Apply Input receives voltage, the Controller determines that the brakes are being applied.

CODE A033 will set when all of the following conditions exist:

- The Antilock Brake Controller senses no voltage at terminal 1C11 (brake apply input is lo).
- The Antilock Brake Controller senses that two wheels (one of which is in the front) are decelerating at a rate greater than normally possible without using the brakes (vehicle is slowing down fast enough that the controller knows the brakes are being applied).

TEST DESCRIPTION: The following provides an explanation of the procedures being followed in the tree

① & ② Checks for improperly adjusted or intermittent Brake Switch.

CODE A034 – BRAKE SWITCH SHORTED

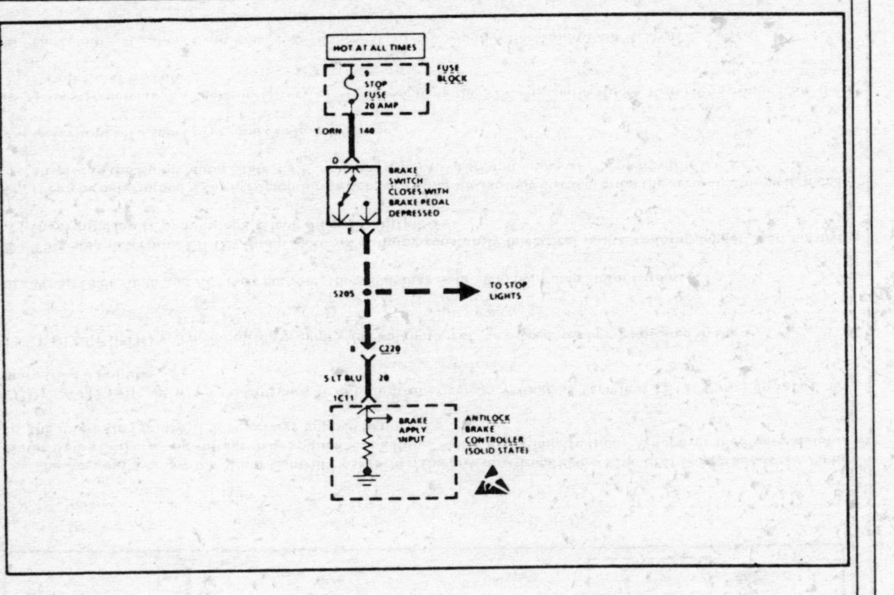

When the Brake Pedal is depressed, the Brake Switch closes. This applies voltage from the Stop Fuse to the Antilock Brake Controller and the brake lights. Before the Controller will initiate an Antilock Brake Stop, it must first sense voltage at the Brake Apply Input.

CODE A034 will set when all of the following conditions exist.

- The Antilock Brake Controller senses battery voltage at terminal 1C11 for a complete ignition cycle in which the vehicle speed surpasses 25 mph.
- The Antilock Brake Controller senses Battery voltage at terminal 1C11 during any following ignition cycle in which the vehicle speed surpasses 25 mph.

TEST DESCRIPTION: The following provides an explanation of the procedures being followed in the tree

① Confirms that a short exists in the circuit (brake lights on).

② Determines whether a short to Battery exists in the CKT 20, or whether the Brake Switch is shorted or maladjusted.

③ If Code A034 is a consistent failure, but CKTS and Brake Switch are good, the Antilock Brake Controller must have an internal fault.

④ This step verifies that the code is not about to become a current code by passing the second condition (see above).

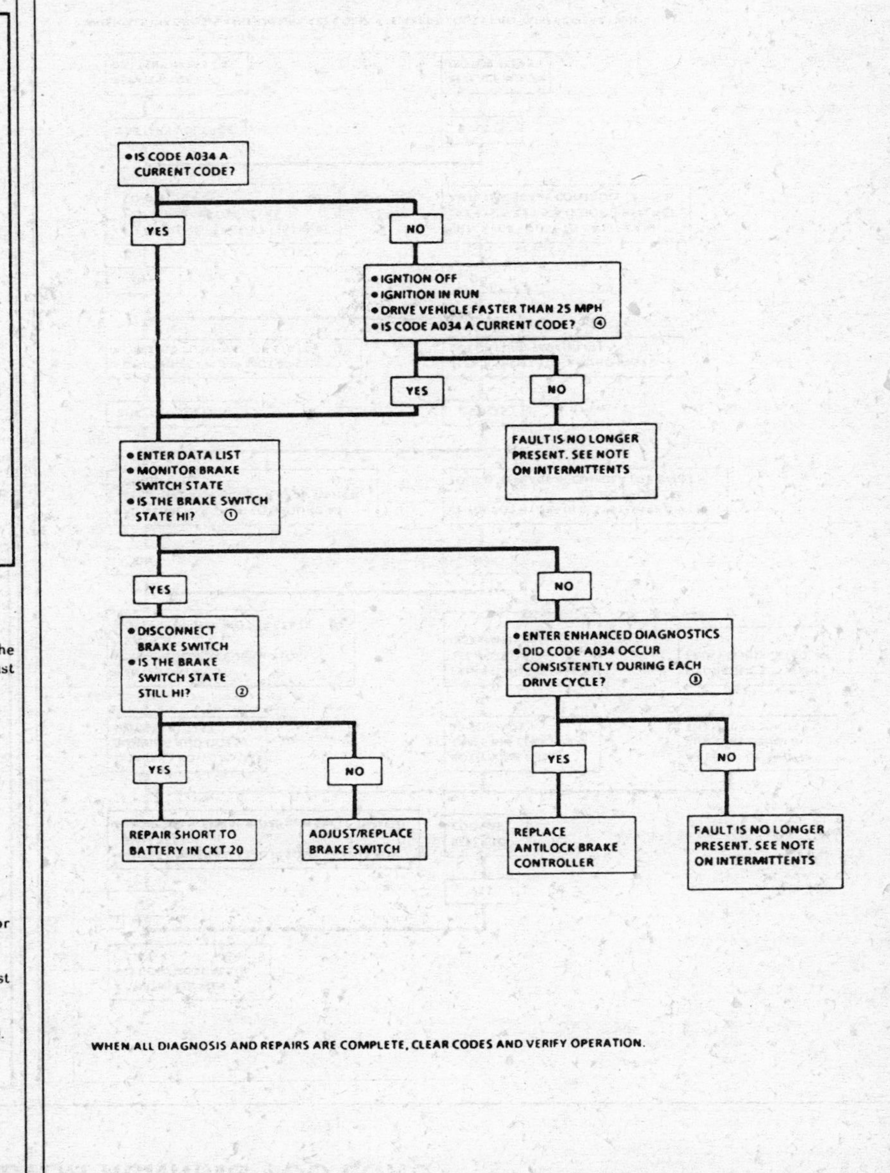

CODE A035 — PUMP MOTOR RUNNING TOO LONG

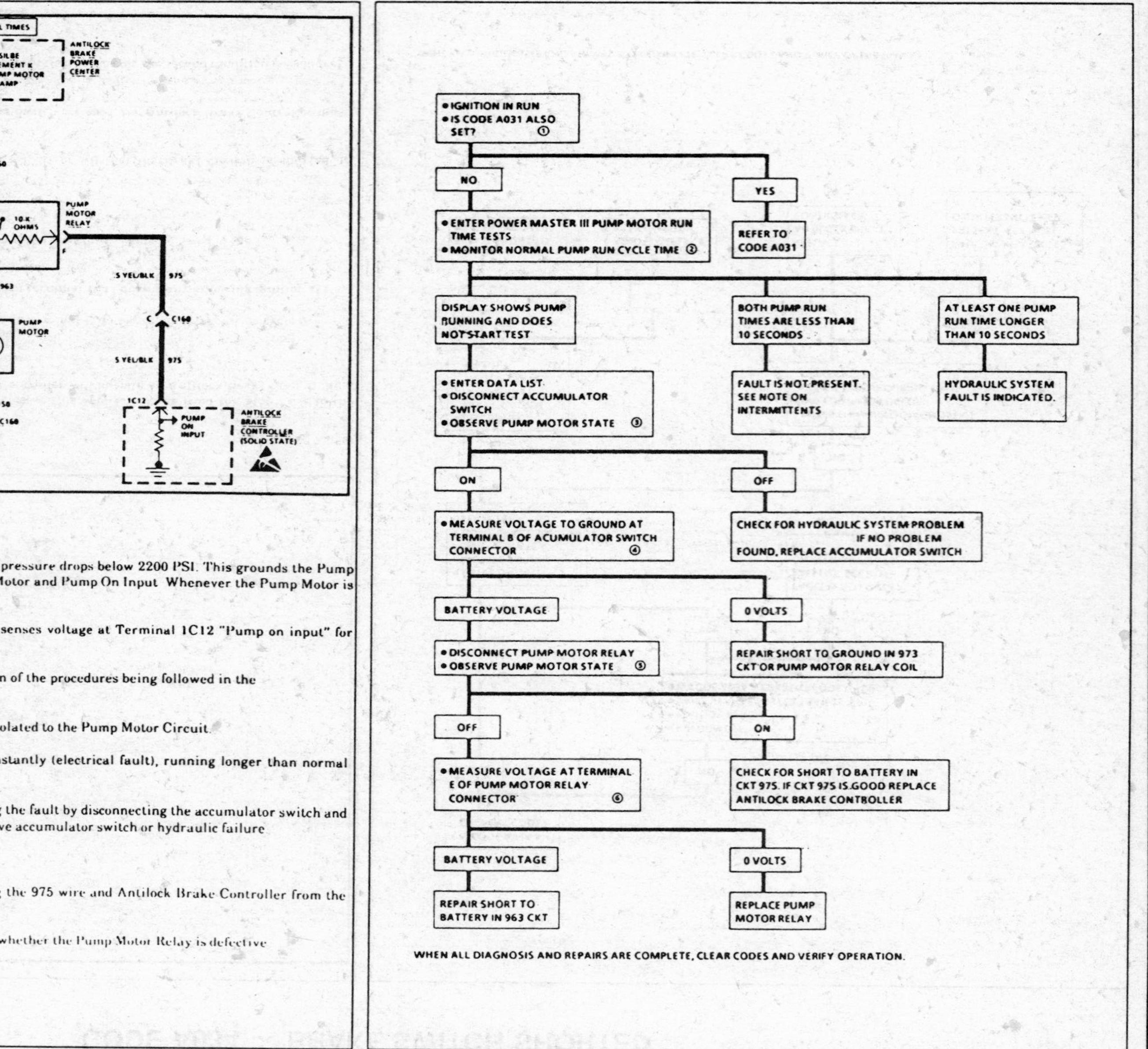

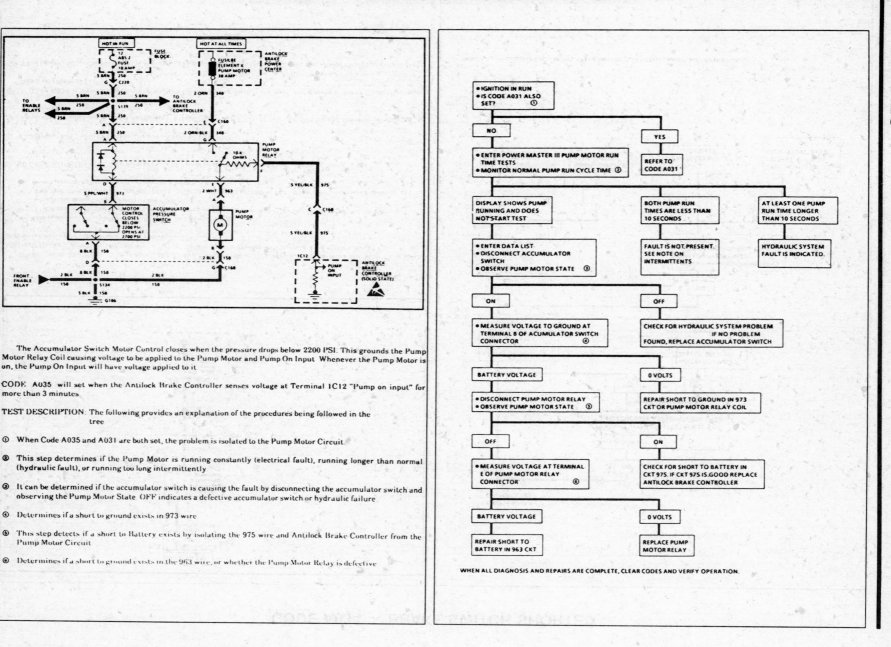

The Accumulator Switch Motor Control closes when the pressure drops below 2200 PSI. This grounds the Pump Motor Relay Coil causing voltage to be applied to the Pump Motor and Pump On Input. Whenever the Pump Motor is on, the Pump On Input will have voltage applied to it.

CODE A035 will set when the Antilock Brake Controller senses voltage at Terminal 1C12 "Pump on input" for more than 3 minutes.

TEST DESCRIPTION: The following provides an explanation of the procedures being followed in the tree.

① When Code A035 and A031 are both set, the problem is isolated to the Pump Motor Circuit.

② This step determines if the Pump Motor is running constantly (electrical fault), running longer than normal (hydraulic fault), or running too long intermittently.

③ It can be determined if the accumulator switch is causing the fault by disconnecting the accumulator switch and observing the Pump Motor State. OFF indicates a defective accumulator switch or hydraulic failure.

④ Determines if a short to ground exists in 973 wire.

⑤ This step detects if a short to Battery exists by isolating the 975 wire and Antilock Brake Controller from the Pump Motor Circuit.

⑥ Determines if a short to ground exists in the 963 wire, or whether the Pump Motor Relay is defective.

CODE A036 — PUMP MOTOR WILL NOT RUN

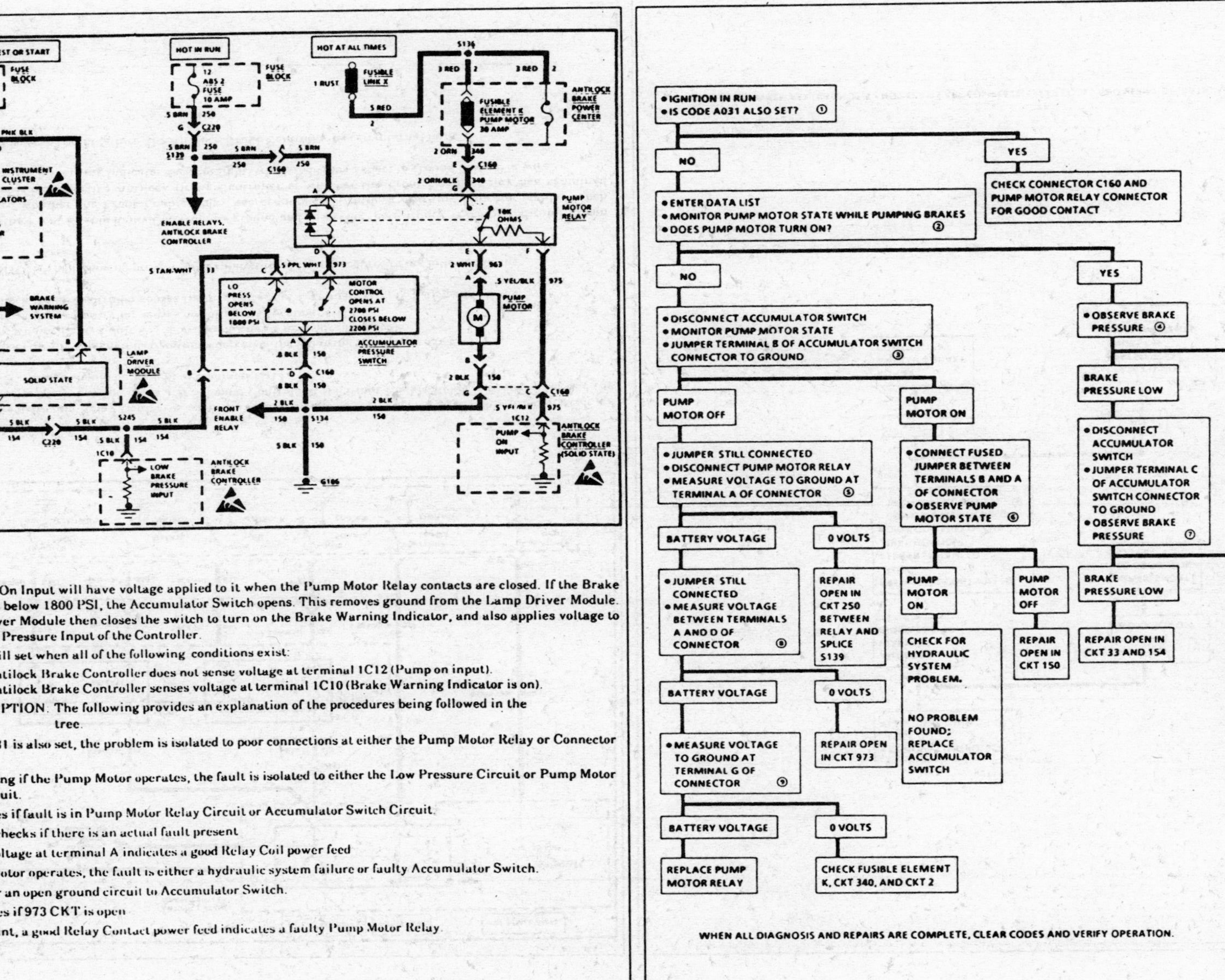

The Pump On Input will have voltage applied to it when the Pump Motor Relay contacts are closed. If the Brake Pressure drops below 1800 PSI, the Accumulator Switch opens. This removes ground from the Lamp Driver Module. The Lamp Driver Module then closes the switch to turn on the Brake Warning Indicator, and also applies voltage to the Low Brake Pressure Input of the Controller.

CODE A036 will set when all of the following conditions exist:

- The Antilock Brake Controller does not sense voltage at terminal 1C12 (Pump on input).
- The Antilock Brake Controller senses voltage at terminal 1C10 (Brake Warning Indicator is on).

TEST DESCRIPTION: The following provides an explanation of the procedures being followed in the tree.

① If code A031 is also set, the problem is isolated to poor connections at either the Pump Motor Relay or Connector C160.
② By observing if the Pump Motor operates, the fault is isolated to either the Low Pressure Circuit or Pump Motor Relay Circuit.
③ Determines if fault is in Pump Motor Relay Circuit or Accumulator Switch Circuit.
④ This step checks if there is an actual fault present.
⑤ Battery voltage at terminal A indicates a good Relay Coil power feed
⑥ If Pump Motor operates, the fault is either a hydraulic system failure or faulty Accumulator Switch.
⑦ Checks for an open ground circuit to Accumulator Switch.
⑧ Determines if 973 CKT is open.
⑨ At this point, a good Relay Contact power feed indicates a faulty Pump Motor Relay.

CODE A037 — FRONT ENABLE RELAY COIL SHORTED TO GROUND

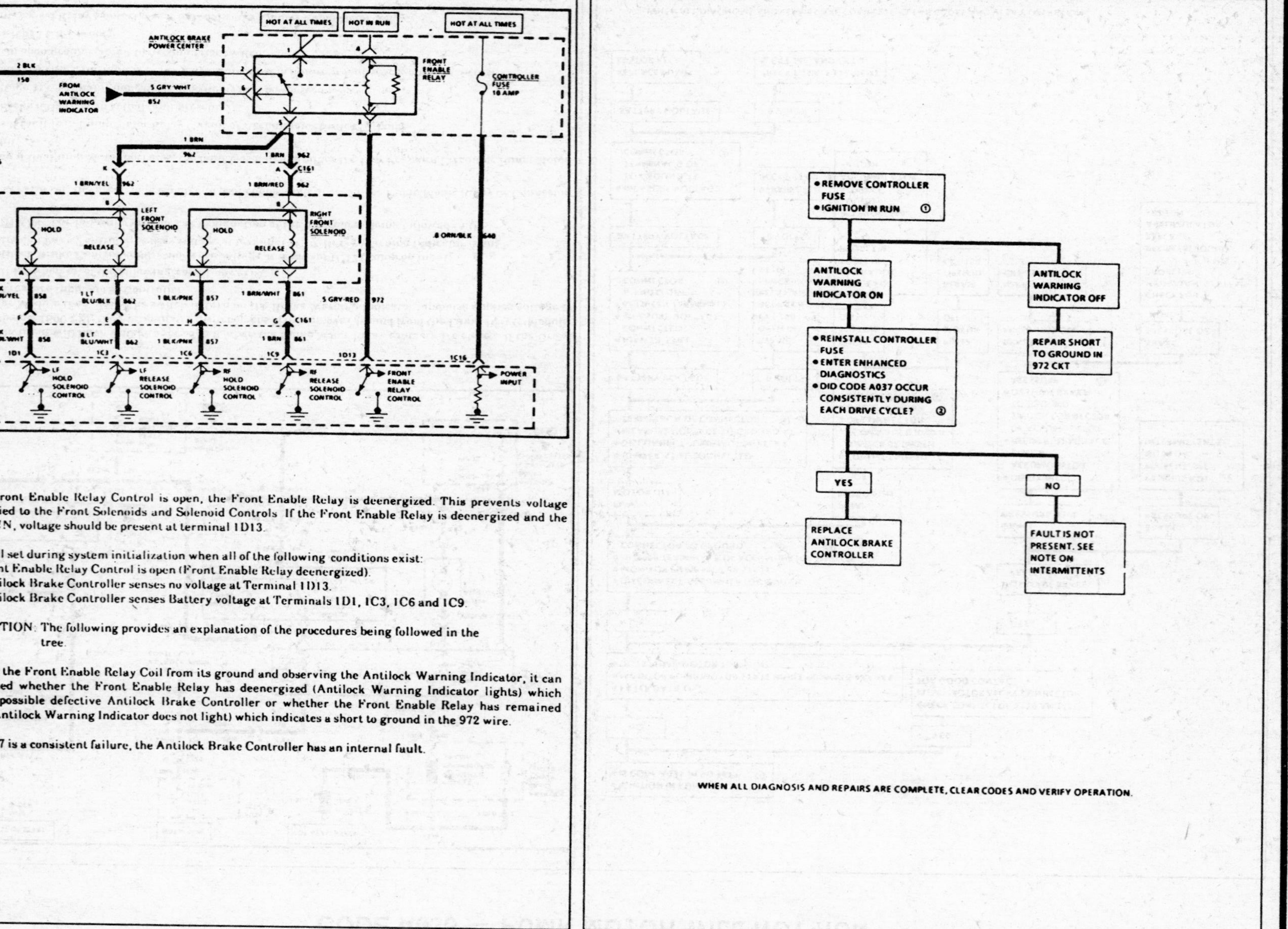

When the Front Enable Relay Control is open, the Front Enable Relay is deenergized. This prevents voltage from being applied to the Front Solenoids and Solenoid Controls. If the Front Enable Relay is deenergized and the Ignition is in RUN, voltage should be present at terminal 1D13.

CODE A037 will set during system initialization when all of the following conditions exist:

- The Front Enable Relay Control is open (Front Enable Relay deenergized).
- The Antilock Brake Controller senses no voltage at Terminal 1D13.
- The Antilock Brake Controller senses Battery voltage at Terminals 1D1, 1C3, 1C6 and 1C9.

TEST DESCRIPTION: The following provides an explanation of the procedures being followed in the tree.

① By isolating the Front Enable Relay Coil from its ground and observing the Antilock Warning Indicator, it can be determined whether the Front Enable Relay has deenergized (Antilock Warning Indicator lights) which indicates a possible defective Antilock Brake Controller or whether the Front Enable Relay has remained energized (Antilock Warning Indicator does not light) which indicates a short to ground in the 972 wire.

② If Code A037 is a consistent failure, the Antilock Brake Controller has an internal fault.

CODE A038 — REAR ENABLE RELAY COIL SHORTED TO GROUND

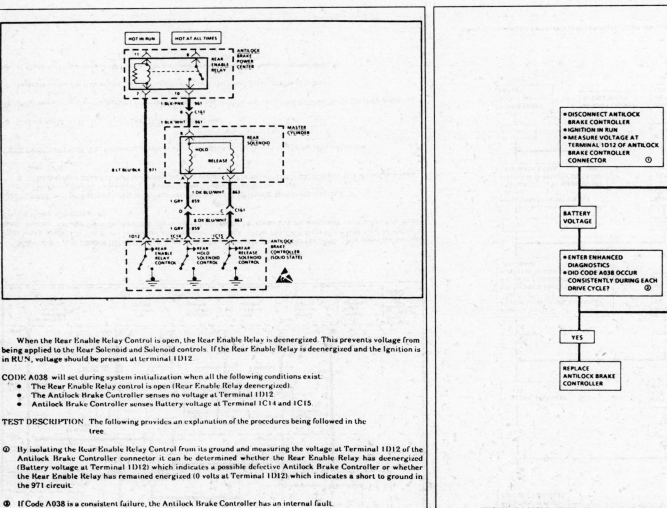

When the Rear Enable Relay Control is open, the Rear Enable Relay is deenergized. This prevents voltage from being applied to the Rear Solenoid and Solenoid controls. If the Rear Enable Relay is deenergized and the Ignition is in RUN, voltage should be present at terminal 1D12.

CODE A038 will set during system initialization when all the following conditions exist:

- The Rear Enable Relay control is open (Rear Enable Relay deenergized).
- The Antilock Brake Controller senses no voltage at Terminal 1D12.
- Antilock Brake Controller senses Battery voltage at Terminal 1C14 and 1C15.

TEST DESCRIPTION. The following provides an explanation of the procedures being followed in the tree.

① By isolating the Rear Enable Relay Control from its ground and measuring the voltage at Terminal 1D12 of the Antilock Brake Controller connector it can be determined whether the Rear Enable Relay has deenergized (Battery voltage at Terminal 1D12) which indicates a possible defective Antilock Brake Controller or whether the Rear Enable Relay has remained energized (0 volts at Terminal 1D12) which indicates a short to ground in the 971 circuit.

② If Code A038 is a consistent failure, the Antilock Brake Controller has an internal fault.

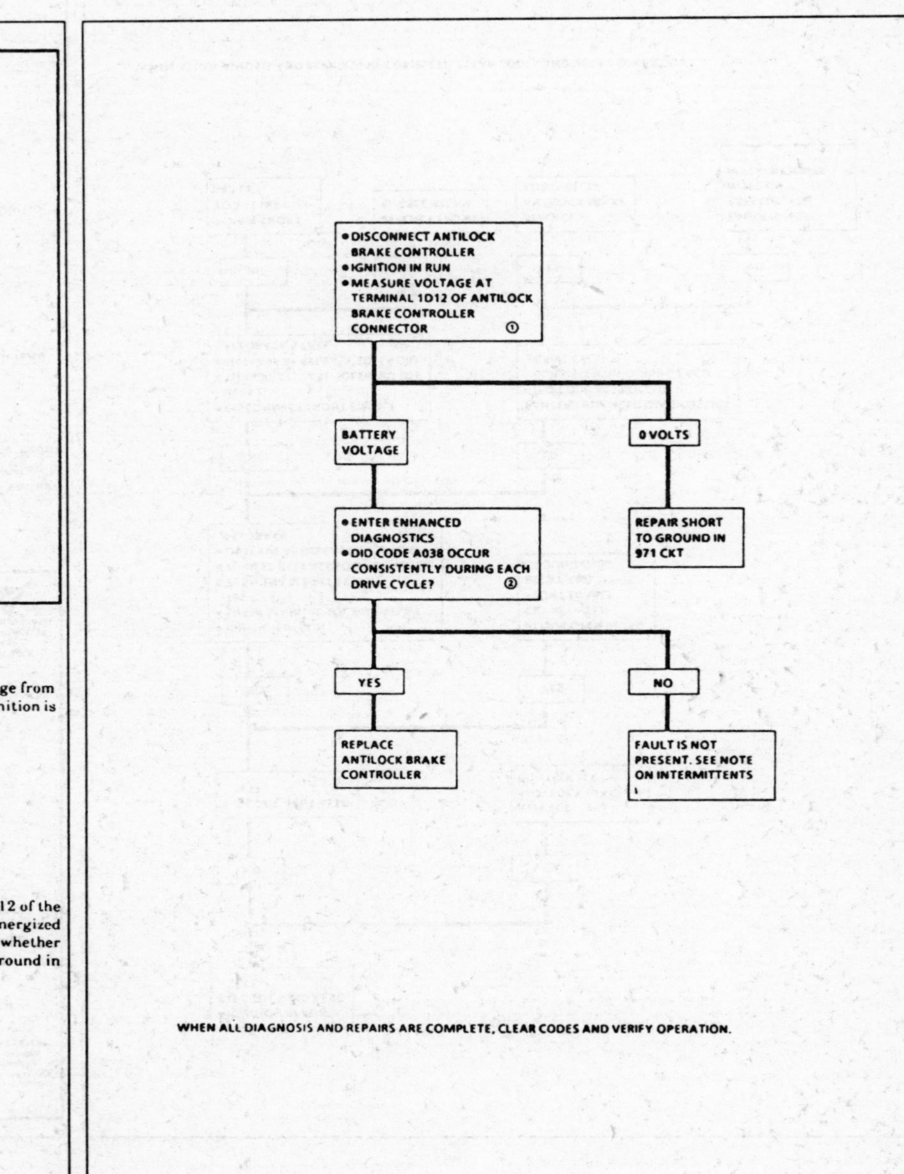

• DISCONNECT ANTILOCK BRAKE CONTROLLER
• IGNITION IN RUN
• MEASURE VOLTAGE AT TERMINAL 1D12 OF ANTILOCK BRAKE CONTROLLER CONNECTOR ①
BATTERY VOLTAGE
0 VOLTS
• ENTER ENHANCED DIAGNOSTICS
• DID CODE A038 OCCUR CONSISTENTLY DURING EACH DRIVE CYCLE? ②
REPAIR SHORT TO GROUND IN 971 CKT
YES
NO
REPLACE ANTILOCK BRAKE CONTROLLER
FAULT IS NOT PRESENT. SEE NOTE ON INTERMITTENTS
WHEN ALL DIAGNOSIS AND REPAIRS ARE COMPLETE, CLEAR CODES AND VERIFY OPERATION.

CODE A039 – FRONT ENABLE RELAY CONTACTS SHORTED TO BATTERY

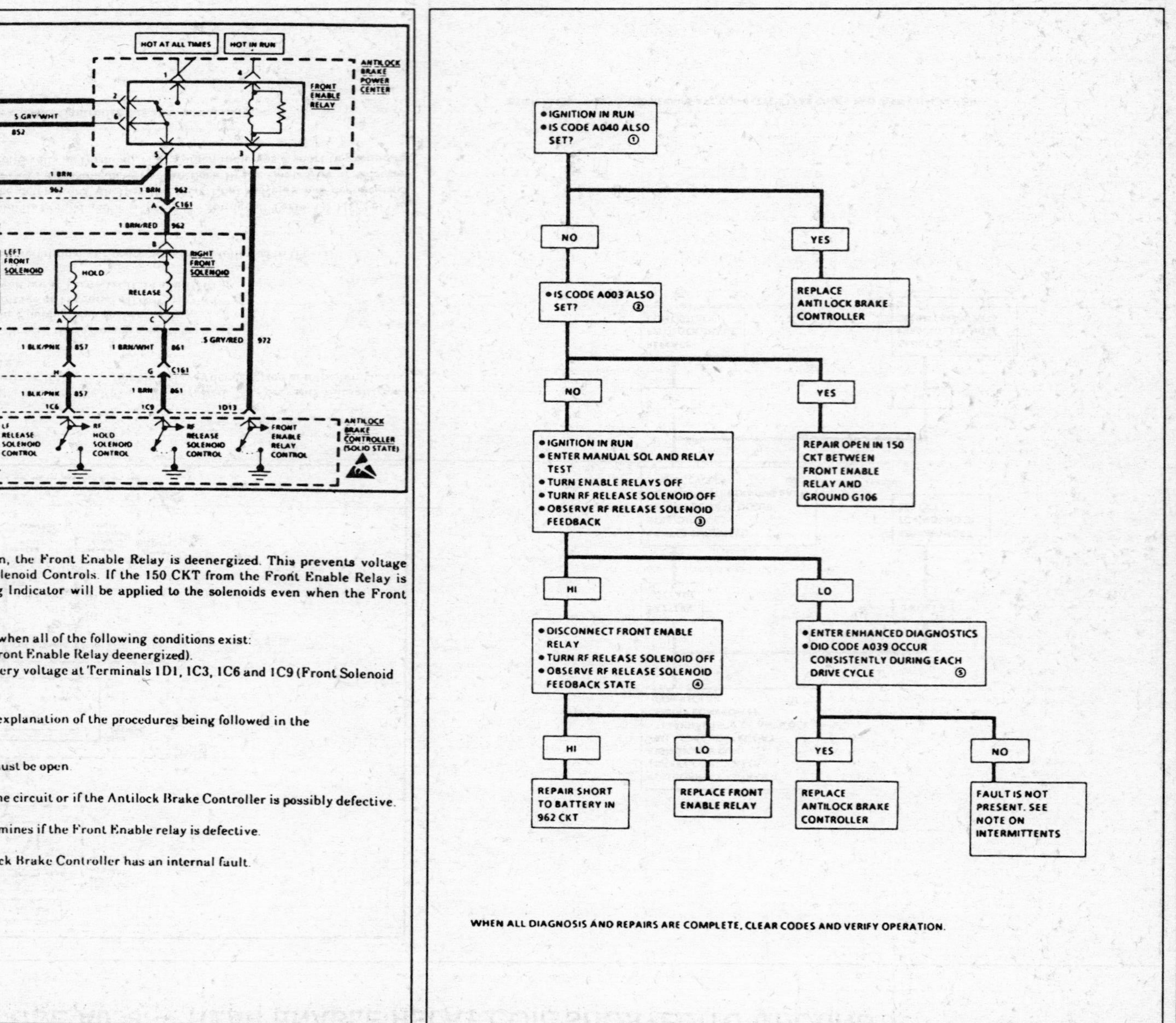

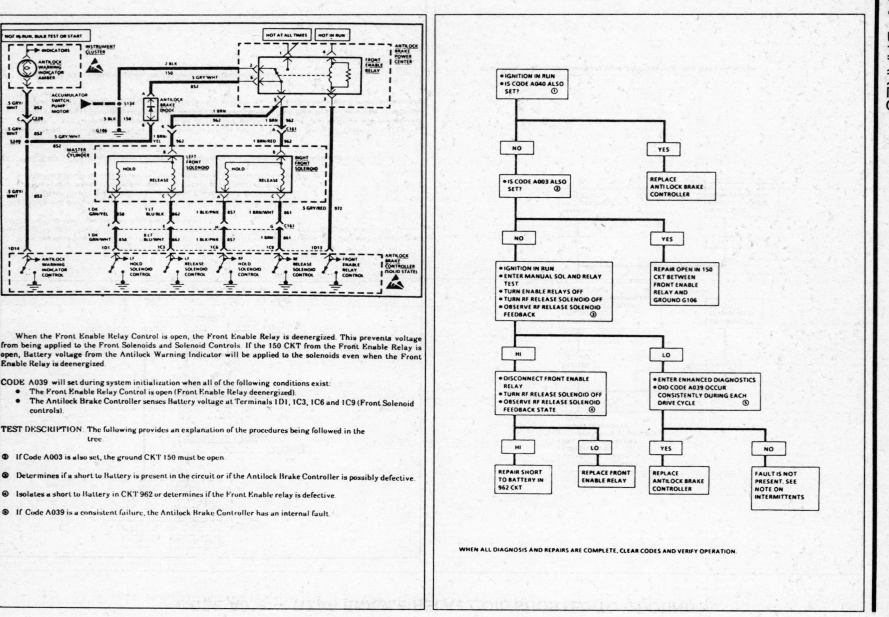

When the Front Enable Relay Control is open, the Front Enable Relay is deenergized. This prevents voltage from being applied to the Front Solenoids and Solenoid Controls. If the 150 CKT from the Front Enable Relay is open, Battery voltage from the Antilock Warning Indicator will be applied to the solenoids even when the Front Enable Relay is deenergized.

CODE A039 will set during system initialization when all of the following conditions exist:

- The Front Enable Relay Control is open (Front Enable Relay deenergized).
- The Antilock Brake Controller senses Battery voltage at Terminals 1D1, 1C3, 1C6 and 1C9 (Front Solenoid controls).

TEST DESCRIPTION. The following provides an explanation of the procedures being followed in the tree.

② If Code A003 is also set, the ground CKT 150 must be open.

③ Determines if a short to Battery is present in the circuit or if the Antilock Brake Controller is possibly defective.

④ Isolates a short to Battery in CKT 962 or determines if the Front Enable relay is defective.

⑤ If Code A039 is a consistent failure, the Antilock Brake Controller has an internal fault.

CODE A040 — REAR ENABLE RELAY CONTACTS SHORTED TO BATTERY

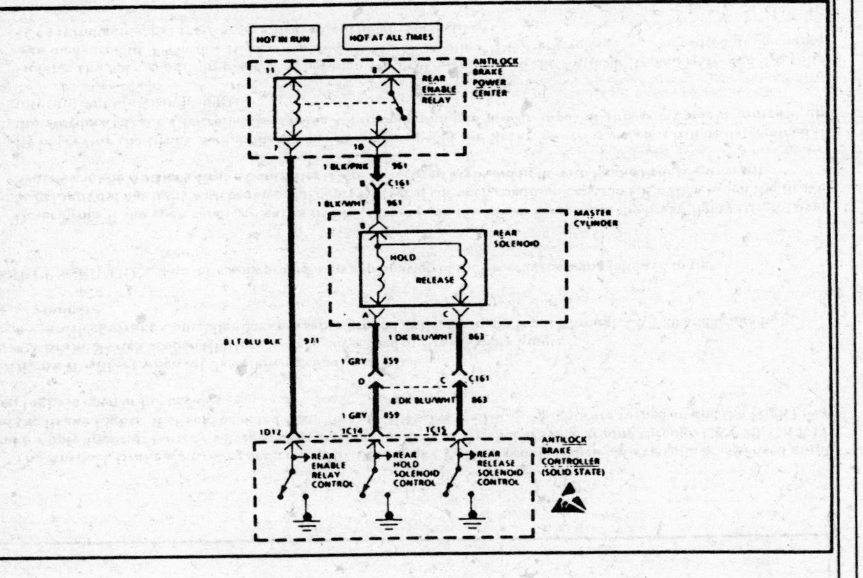

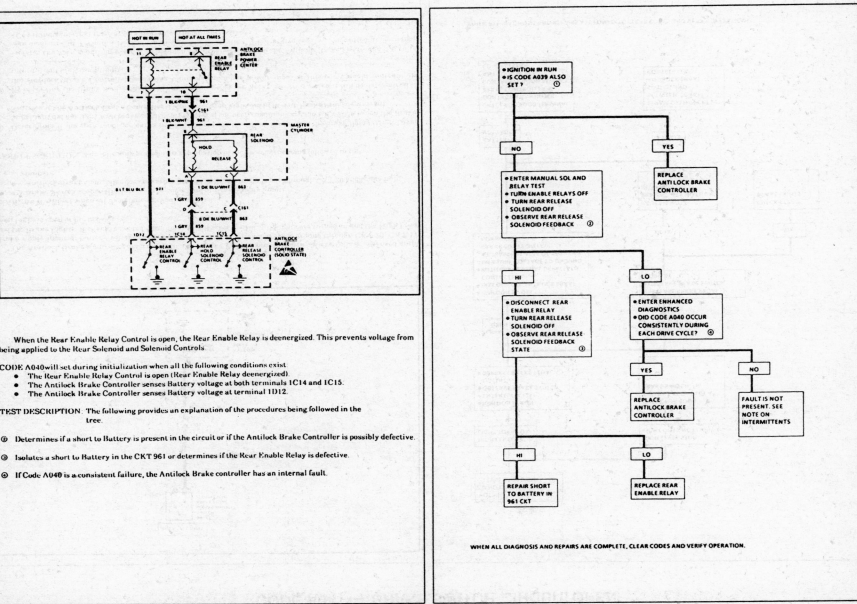

When the Rear Enable Relay Control is open, the Rear Enable Relay is deenergized. This prevents voltage from being applied to the Rear Solenoid and Solenoid Controls.

CODE A040 will set during initialization when all the following conditions exist:

- The Rear Enable Relay Control is open (Rear Enable Relay deenergized).
- The Antilock Brake Controller senses Battery voltage at both terminals 1C14 and 1C15.
- The Antilock Brake Controller senses Battery voltage at terminal 1D12.

TEST DESCRIPTION: The following provides an explanation of the procedures being followed in the tree.

② Determines if a short to Battery is present in the circuit or if the Antilock Brake Controller is possibly defective.

③ Isolates a short to Battery in the CKT 961 or determines if the Rear Enable Relay is defective.

④ If Code A040 is a consistent failure, the Antilock Brake controller has an internal fault.

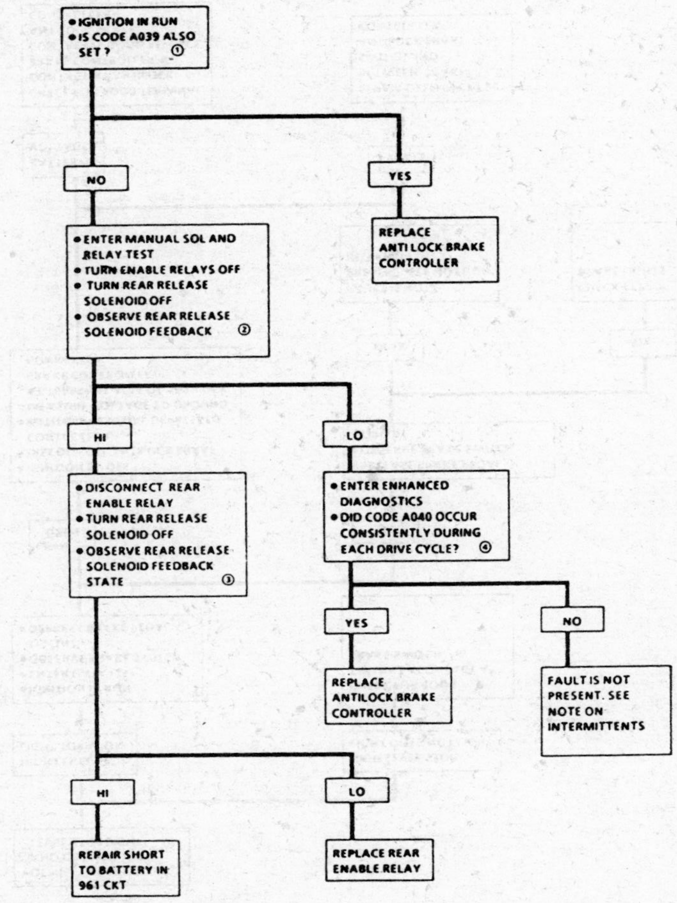

- IGNITION IN RUN
- IS CODE A039 ALSO SET? ①

YES → REPLACE ANTI LOCK BRAKE CONTROLLER

NO →

- ENTER MANUAL SOL AND RELAY TEST
- TURN ENABLE RELAYS OFF
- TURN REAR RELEASE SOLENOID OFF
- OBSERVE REAR RELEASE SOLENOID FEEDBACK ②

HI →

- DISCONNECT REAR ENABLE RELAY
- TURN REAR RELEASE SOLENOID OFF
- OBSERVE REAR RELEASE SOLENOID FEEDBACK STATE ③

HI → REPAIR SHORT TO BATTERY IN 961 CKT

LO → REPLACE REAR ENABLE RELAY

LO →

- ENTER ENHANCED DIAGNOSTICS
- DID CODE A040 OCCUR CONSISTENTLY DURING EACH DRIVE CYCLE? ④

YES → REPLACE ANTILOCK BRAKE CONTROLLER

NO → FAULT IS NOT PRESENT. SEE NOTE ON INTERMITTENTS

WHEN ALL DIAGNOSIS AND REPAIRS ARE COMPLETE, CLEAR CODES AND VERIFY OPERATION.

CODE A041 – BRAKE SWITCH CIRCUIT OPEN

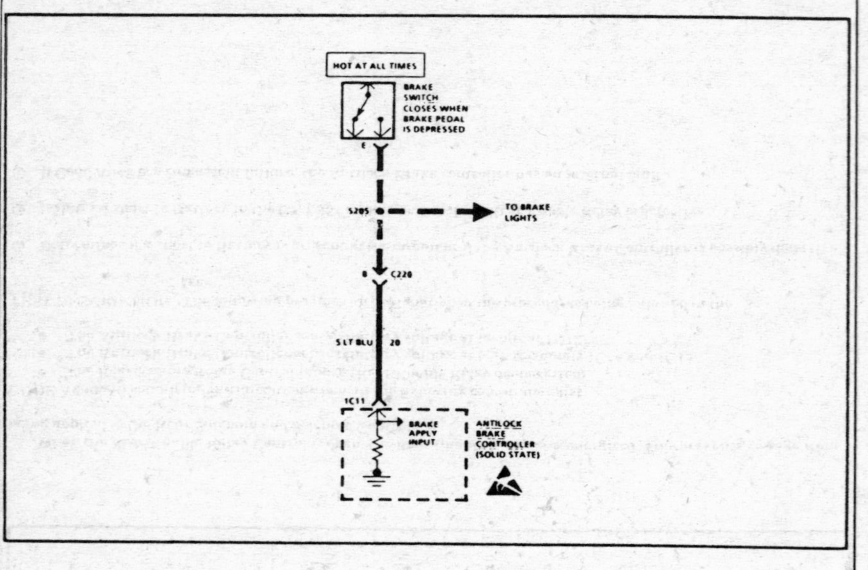
HOT AT ALL TIMES
BRAKE SWITCH CLOSES WHEN BRAKE PEDAL IS DEPRESSED
E
S205
TO BRAKE LIGHTS
B C220
SLT BLU 20
1C11
BRAKE APPLY INPUT
ANTILOCK BRAKE CONTROLLER (SOLID STATE)

The Antilock Brake Controller determines that the Brake Pedal is pressed when battery voltage is sensed at the Brake Apply Input. If battery voltage is not present, the Controller should sense ground through CKT 20, CKT 17, and the Brake Lights. It should be noted that this code will set if the Hazard Lights are turned on and the High Level Stop Light is open or burned out.

CODE A041 will set when all the following conditions exist:

- Brake Switch is open (Battery voltage not sensed at Brake Apply Input)
- Antilock Brake Controller does not sense ground at Brake Apply Input (through CKT 20 and brake light bulbs)

TEST DESCRIPTION: The following provides an explanation of the procedures being followed in the tree.

① Determines if the open condition exists in CKT 20 between the Brake Switch and the brake lights (High Level Stop Light did not light with brake pedal depressed) or if the open condition exists in CKT 20 between the Brake Switch and the Antilock Brake Controller (High Level Stop Light did light with Brake Pedal depressed).

② By observing the Brake Switch State when it is known that the Brake Switch is closed it can be determined if the Antilock Brake Controller is sensing the proper input (a proper input at this point would indicate an intermittent fault condition).

③ Isolates the open condition to CKT 20 between the Brake Switch and the Antilock Brake Controller if 0 volts was measured at Terminal 1C11 of Antilock Brake Controller. If Battery voltage was measured at Terminal 1C11 it indicates that the Antilock Brake Controller is defective.

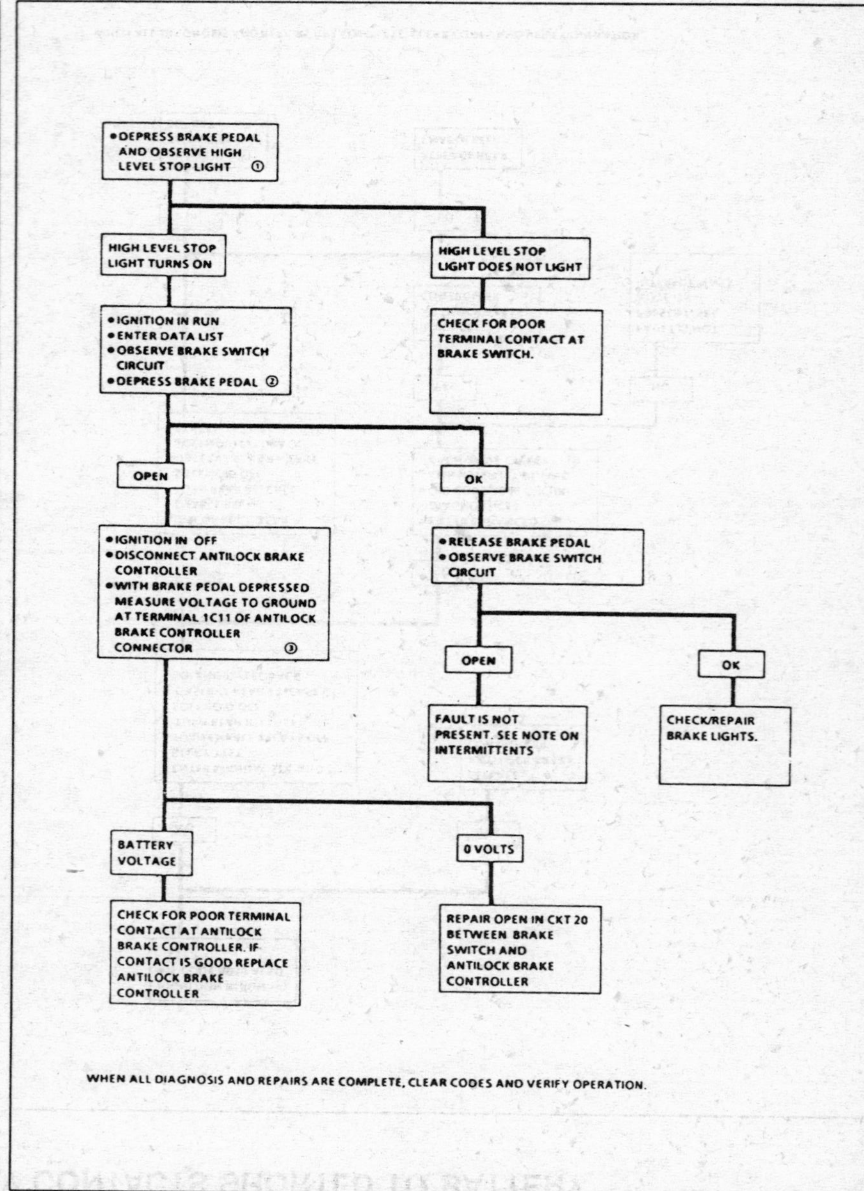
• DEPRESS BRAKE PEDAL AND OBSERVE HIGH LEVEL STOP LIGHT ①
HIGH LEVEL STOP LIGHT TURNS ON
HIGH LEVEL STOP LIGHT DOES NOT LIGHT
CHECK FOR POOR TERMINAL CONTACT AT BRAKE SWITCH.
• IGNITION IN RUN
• ENTER DATA LIST
• OBSERVE BRAKE SWITCH CIRCUIT
• DEPRESS BRAKE PEDAL ②
OPEN
OK
• IGNITION IN OFF
• DISCONNECT ANTILOCK BRAKE CONTROLLER
• WITH BRAKE PEDAL DEPRESSED MEASURE VOLTAGE TO GROUND AT TERMINAL 1C11 OF ANTILOCK BRAKE CONTROLLER CONNECTOR ③
• RELEASE BRAKE PEDAL
• OBSERVE BRAKE SWITCH CIRCUIT
OPEN
OK
FAULT IS NOT PRESENT. SEE NOTE ON INTERMITTENTS
CHECK/REPAIR BRAKE LIGHTS.
BATTERY VOLTAGE
0 VOLTS
CHECK FOR POOR TERMINAL CONTACT AT ANTILOCK BRAKE CONTROLLER. IF CONTACT IS GOOD REPLACE ANTILOCK BRAKE CONTROLLER
REPAIR OPEN IN CKT 20 BETWEEN BRAKE SWITCH AND ANTILOCK BRAKE CONTROLLER
WHEN ALL DIAGNOSIS AND REPAIRS ARE COMPLETE, CLEAR CODES AND VERIFY OPERATION.

CODE A042 — LOW BRAKE PRESSURE CIRCUIT OPEN

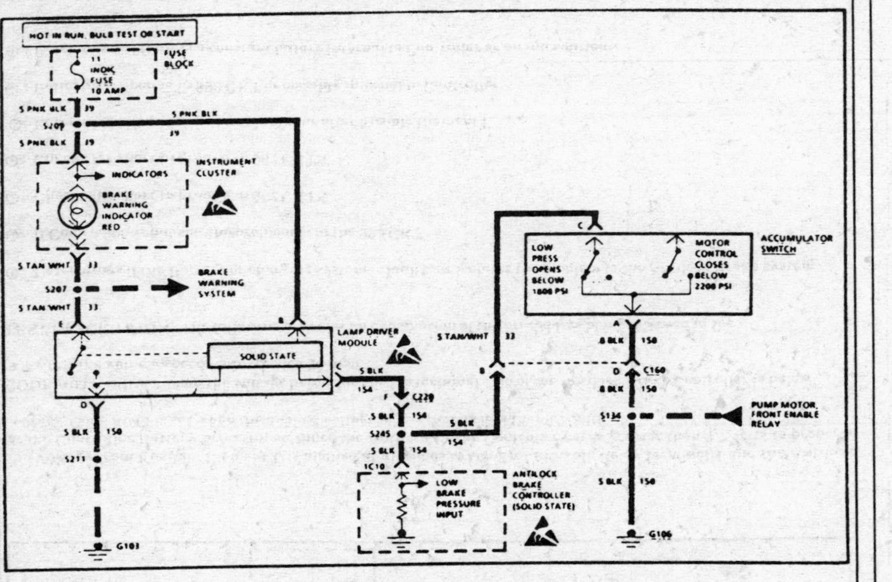

When the Low Pressure Switch in the Accumulator Switch is closed (pressure greater than approximately 1800 PSI), the Antilock Brake Controller senses ground at the Low Brake Pressure Input. If the Low Pressure Switch is open (pressure less than 1800 PSI) the Lamp Driver Module loses ground at terminal C. The Lamp Driver Module turns on the Brake Warning Indicator and applies voltage to the Low Brake Pressure Input. If the Controller does not sense ground or battery voltage at the Low Brake Pressure Input, it will set Code A042.

CODE A042 will set when the Antilock Brake Controller senses that an open condition exists in the 154 CKT between the Controller and the Lamp Driver Module.

TEST DESCRIPTION The following provides an explanation of the procedures being followed in the tree.

① If the Brake Warning Indicator lights constantly, there must be an open in the 154 CKT between the Lamp Driver Module and Splice S245.

② Determines if open condition is currently present.

③ Isolates the open condition to CKT 154 between splice S245 and the Antilock Brake Controller or determines a defective Antilock Brake Controller.

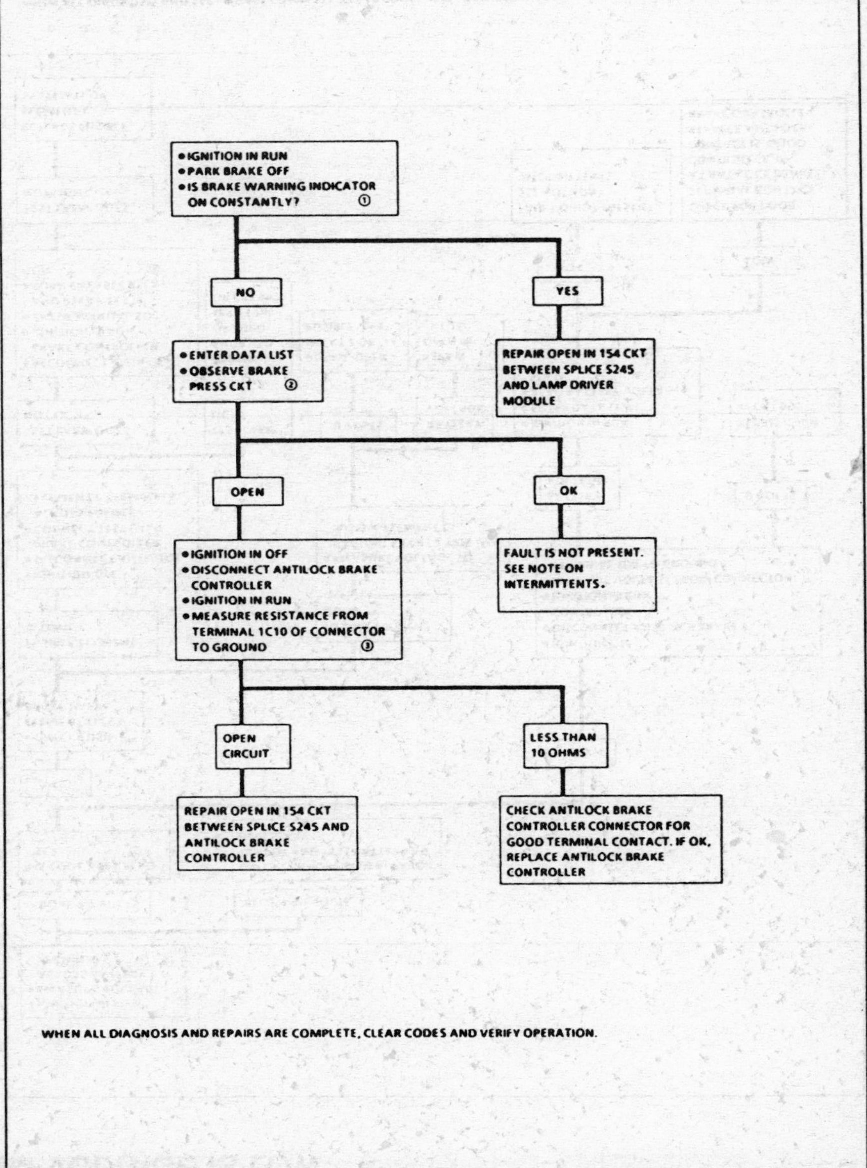

CODE A043 – SYSTEM VOLTAGE IS LOW

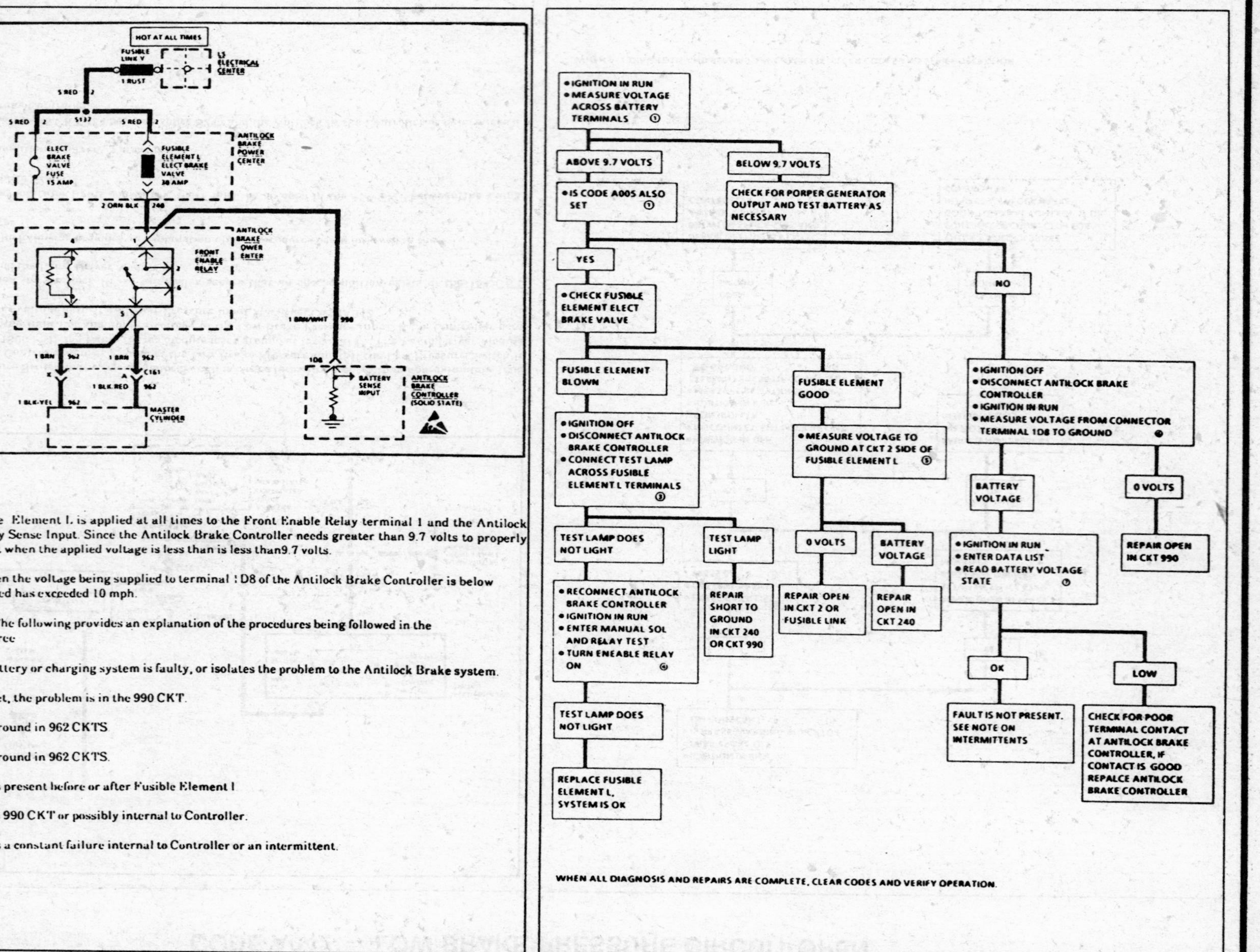

Voltage from Fusible Element L is applied at all times to the Front Enable Relay terminal 1 and the Antilock Brake Controller Battery Sense Input. Since the Antilock Brake Controller needs greater than 9.7 volts to properly operate, Code A043 is set when the applied voltage is less than is less than9.7 volts.

CODE A034 will set when the voltage being supplied to terminal 1D8 of the Antilock Brake Controller is below 9.7 volts and vehicle speed has exceeded 10 mph.

TEST DESCRIPTION: The following provides an explanation of the procedures being followed in the tree

① Determines if the Battery or charging system is faulty, or isolates the problem to the Antilock Brake system.

② If Code A005 is not set, the problem is in the 990 CKT.

③ Checks for short to ground in 962 CKTS.

④ Checks for short to ground in 962 CKTS.

⑤ Determines if open is present before or after Fusible Element L

⑥ Indicates if open is in 990 CKT or possibly internal to Controller.

⑦ Determines if fault is a constant failure internal to Controller or an intermittent.

CODE A044 – RIGHT FRONT WHEEL, SPEED ZERO

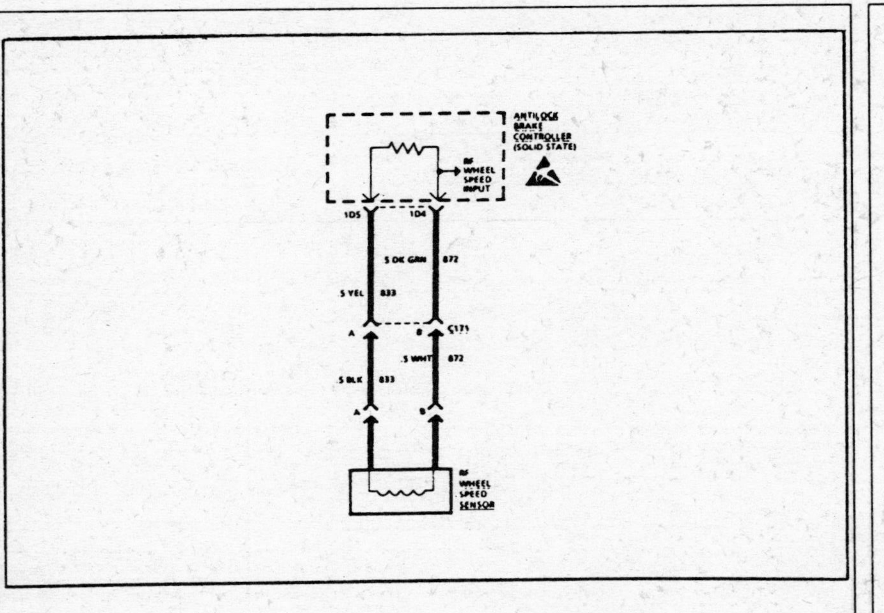
ANTILOCK BRAKE CONTROLLER (SOLID STATE)
RF WHEEL SPEED INPUT
105
104
.5 DK GRN 872
.5 YEL 833
A
B
C171
.5 WHT 872
.5 BLK 833
A
B
RF WHEEL SPEED SENSOR

The Wheel Speed Sensor generates a signal that indicates the speed of the wheel. Voltage pulses are produced as the magnetic teeth pass a coil. The frequency of this AC voltage is used by the Controller to determine how fast the wheel is turning. By comparing this wheel speed to the other wheel speeds, the Controller can detect if wheel lock-up is about to occur.

CODE A044 will set when all of the following conditions exist:

- The Antilock Brake Controller Senses the right front wheel speed to be 0 mph.
- The Antilock Brake Controller senses that the other three wheel speeds are greater than 5 mph and are operating correctly.

TEST DESCRIPTION. The following provides an explanation of the procedures being followed in the trouble tree.

① By observing the Right Front Wheel speed input, you can verify what type of input the controller is sensing. An unsteady or erratic wheel speed input indicates that a fault is present in the Wheel Speed Sensor or its related circuitry. If a steady wheel speed is observed, an intermittent fault condition is indicated.

② Indicates a defective Wheel Speed Sensor by isolating a short to ground internal to the sensor.

③ If resistance measured across the Wheel Speed Sensor is infinite, the fault is due to an open condition internal to the Speed Sensor

④ Determines a short to Battery is present in CKT 833 if Battery voltage is measured at Terminal A of the harness side of the Wheel Speed Sensor Connector

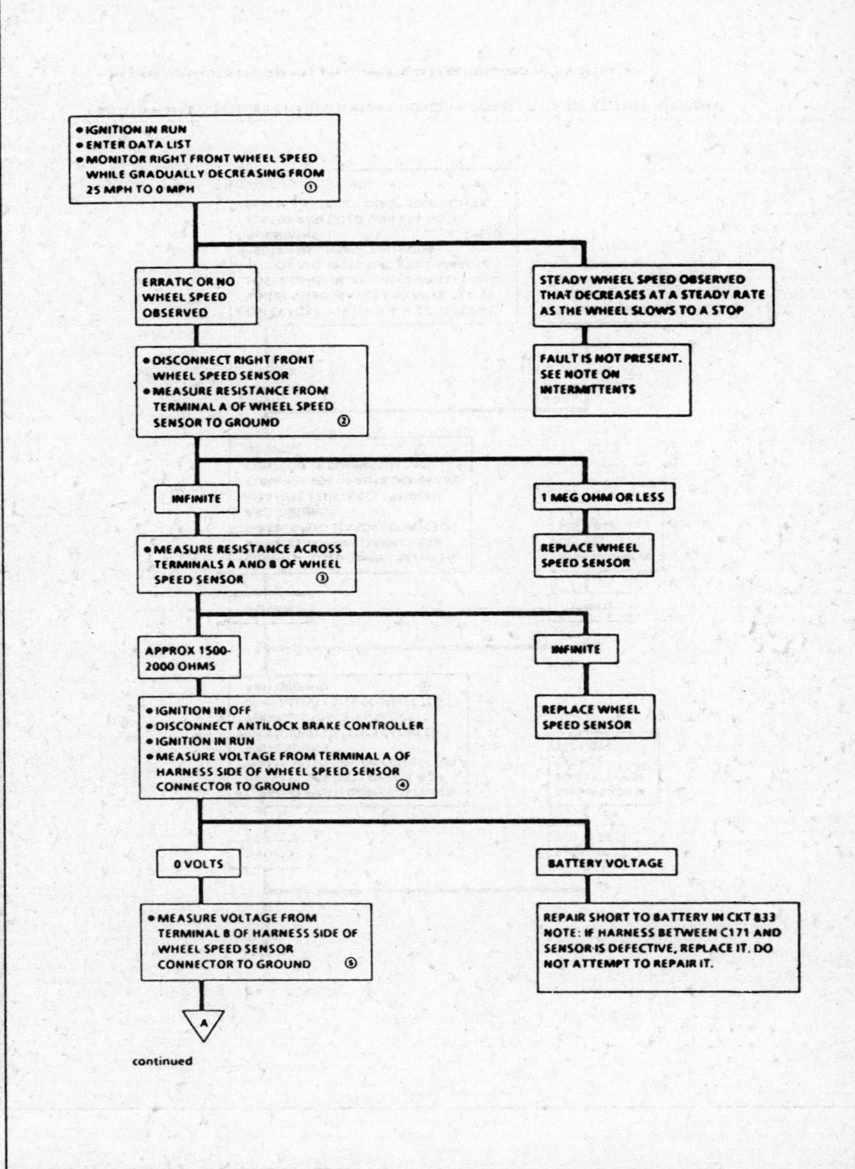
• IGNITION IN RUN
• ENTER DATA LIST
• MONITOR RIGHT FRONT WHEEL SPEED WHILE GRADUALLY DECREASING FROM 25 MPH TO 0 MPH ①
ERRATIC OR NO WHEEL SPEED OBSERVED
STEADY WHEEL SPEED OBSERVED THAT DECREASES AT A STEADY RATE AS THE WHEEL SLOWS TO A STOP
FAULT IS NOT PRESENT. SEE NOTE ON INTERMITTENTS
• DISCONNECT RIGHT FRONT WHEEL SPEED SENSOR
• MEASURE RESISTANCE FROM TERMINAL A OF WHEEL SPEED SENSOR TO GROUND ②
INFINITE
1 MEG OHM OR LESS
REPLACE WHEEL SPEED SENSOR
• MEASURE RESISTANCE ACROSS TERMINALS A AND B OF WHEEL SPEED SENSOR ③
APPROX 1500-2000 OHMS
INFINITE
REPLACE WHEEL SPEED SENSOR
• IGNITION IN OFF
• DISCONNECT ANTILOCK BRAKE CONTROLLER
• IGNITION IN RUN
• MEASURE VOLTAGE FROM TERMINAL A OF HARNESS SIDE OF WHEEL SPEED SENSOR CONNECTOR TO GROUND ④
0 VOLTS
BATTERY VOLTAGE
• MEASURE VOLTAGE FROM TERMINAL B OF HARNESS SIDE OF WHEEL SPEED SENSOR CONNECTOR TO GROUND ⑤
REPAIR SHORT TO BATTERY IN CKT 833
NOTE: IF HARNESS BETWEEN C171 AND SENSOR IS DEFECTIVE, REPLACE IT. DO NOT ATTEMPT TO REPAIR IT.
A

continued

CODE A044 – RIGHT FRONT WHEEL, SPEED ZERO

⑤ Determines a short to Battery is present in CKT 872 if Battery voltage is measured at Terminal B of the harness side of the Wheel Speed Sensor Connector.

⑥ With Terminal A of CKT 833 connected to ground, the resistance from Terminal 1D5 to ground should be zero. If infinite resistance is measured, an open condition is indicated in CKT 833.

⑦ With Terminal B of CKT 872 connected to ground, the resistance from Terminal 1D4 to ground should be zero. If infinite resistance is measured, an open condition is indicated in CKT 872.

⑧ At this point, all the connecting circuitry has tested good. The fault may be due to a poorly mated connector at the Wheel Speed Sensor or the Antilock Brake Controller. Other possible causes could be due to damage to the Speed Sensor or Speed Ring. Check for proper mounting,or poor alignment. If everything above tests good, replace the Antilock Brake Controller.

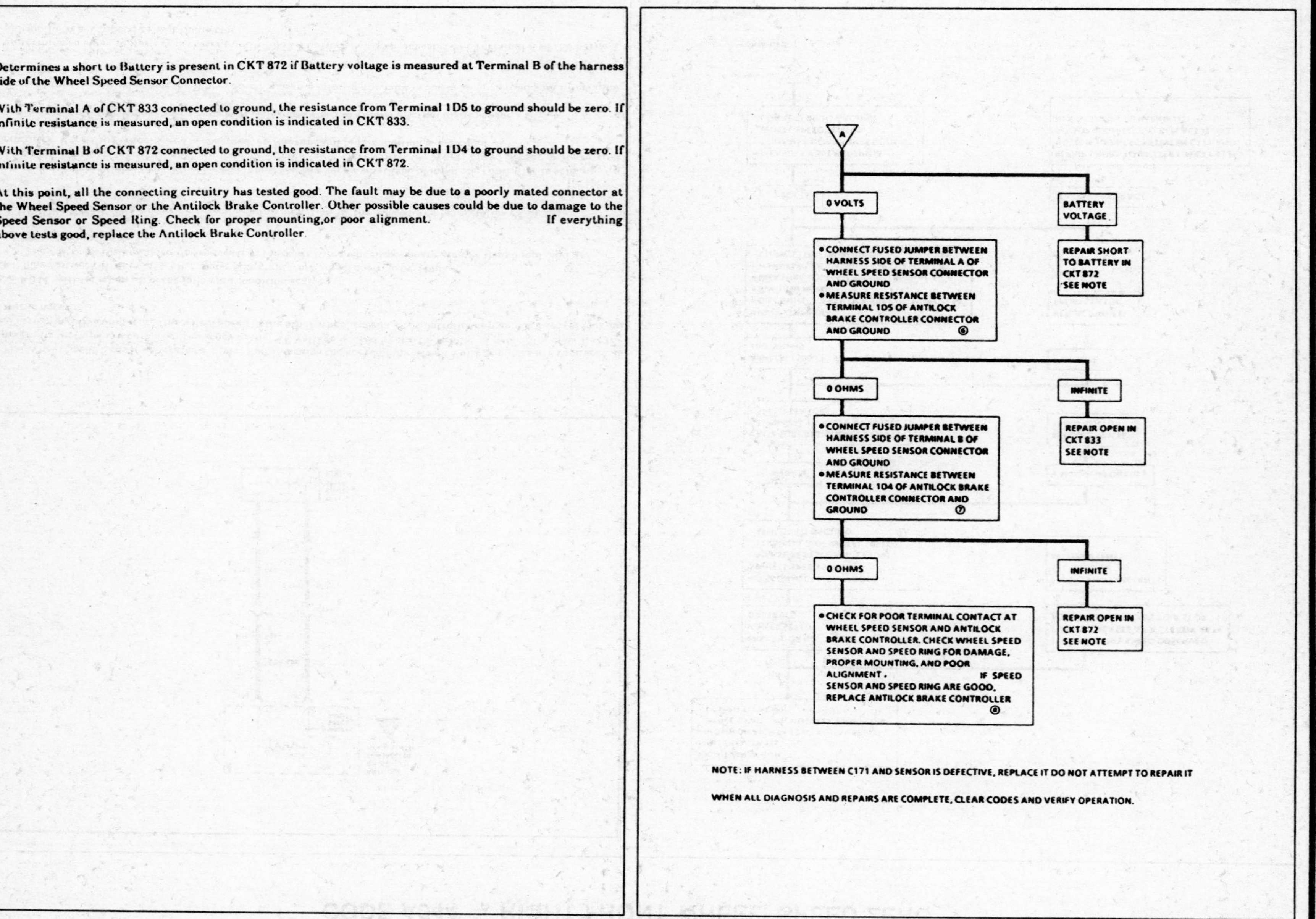
A
0 VOLTS
BATTERY VOLTAGE
• CONNECT FUSED JUMPER BETWEEN HARNESS SIDE OF TERMINAL A OF WHEEL SPEED SENSOR CONNECTOR AND GROUND
• MEASURE RESISTANCE BETWEEN TERMINAL 1D5 OF ANTILOCK BRAKE CONTROLLER CONNECTOR AND GROUND ⑥
REPAIR SHORT TO BATTERY IN CKT 872 SEE NOTE
0 OHMS
INFINITE
• CONNECT FUSED JUMPER BETWEEN HARNESS SIDE OF TERMINAL B OF WHEEL SPEED SENSOR CONNECTOR AND GROUND
• MEASURE RESISTANCE BETWEEN TERMINAL 1D4 OF ANTILOCK BRAKE CONTROLLER CONNECTOR AND GROUND ⑦
REPAIR OPEN IN CKT 833 SEE NOTE
0 OHMS
INFINITE
• CHECK FOR POOR TERMINAL CONTACT AT WHEEL SPEED SENSOR AND ANTILOCK BRAKE CONTROLLER. CHECK WHEEL SPEED SENSOR AND SPEED RING FOR DAMAGE, PROPER MOUNTING, AND POOR ALIGNMENT. IF SPEED SENSOR AND SPEED RING ARE GOOD, REPLACE ANTILOCK BRAKE CONTROLLER ⑧
REPAIR OPEN IN CKT 872 SEE NOTE
NOTE: IF HARNESS BETWEEN C171 AND SENSOR IS DEFECTIVE, REPLACE IT DO NOT ATTEMPT TO REPAIR IT
WHEN ALL DIAGNOSIS AND REPAIRS ARE COMPLETE, CLEAR CODES AND VERIFY OPERATION.

CODE A045 – LEFT FRONT WHEEL, SPEED ZERO

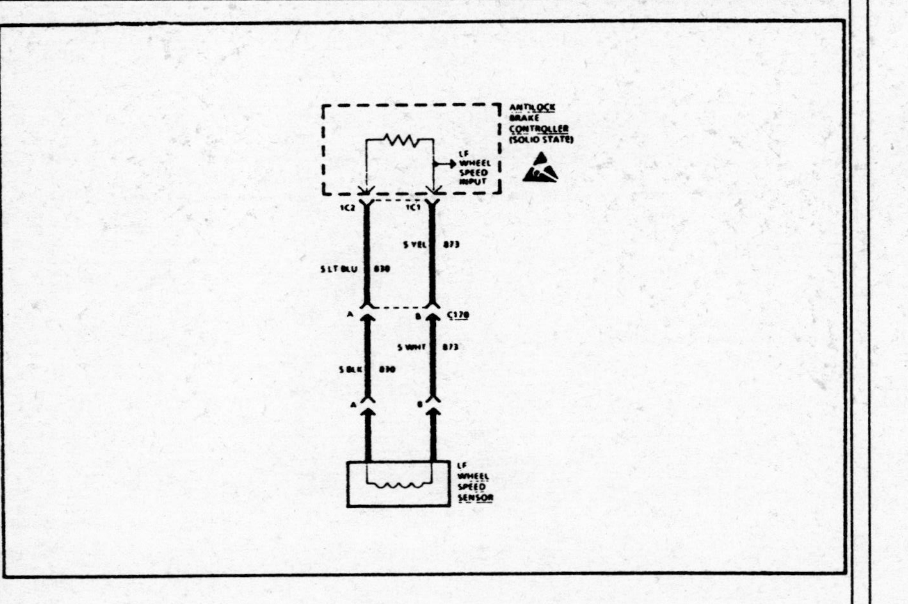

ANTILOCK BRAKE CONTROLLER (SOLID STATE)
LF WHEEL SPEED INPUT
1C2
1C1
5 YEL 873
5 LT BLU 830
A
B
C170
5 WHT 873
5 BLK 830
LF WHEEL SPEED SENSOR

The Wheel Speed Sensor generates a signal that indicates the speed of the wheel. Voltage pulses are produced as the magnetic teeth pass a coil. The frequency of this AC voltage is used by the Controller to determine how fast the wheel is turning. By comparing this wheel speed to the other wheel speeds, the Controller can detect if wheel lock-up is about to occur.

CODE A045 will set when all of the following conditions exist:

- The Antilock Brake Controller Senses the left front wheel speed to be 0 mph.
- The Antilock Brake Controller senses that the other three wheel speeds are greater than 5 mph and are operating correctly.

TEST DESCRIPTION: The following provides an explanation of the procedures being followed in the following trouble tree.

① By observing the Left Front Wheel speed input, you can verify what type of input the controller is sensing. An unsteady or erratic wheel speed input indicates that a fault is present in the Wheel Speed Sensor or its related circuitry. If a steady wheel speed is observed, an intermittent fault condition is indicated.

② Indicates a defective Wheel Speed Sensor by isolating a short to ground internal to the sensor.

③ If resistance measured across the Wheel Speed Sensor is infinite, the fault is due to an open condition internal to the Speed Sensor.

④ Determines a short to Battery is present in CKT 830 if Battery voltage is measured at Terminal A of the harness side of the Wheel Speed Sensor Connector.

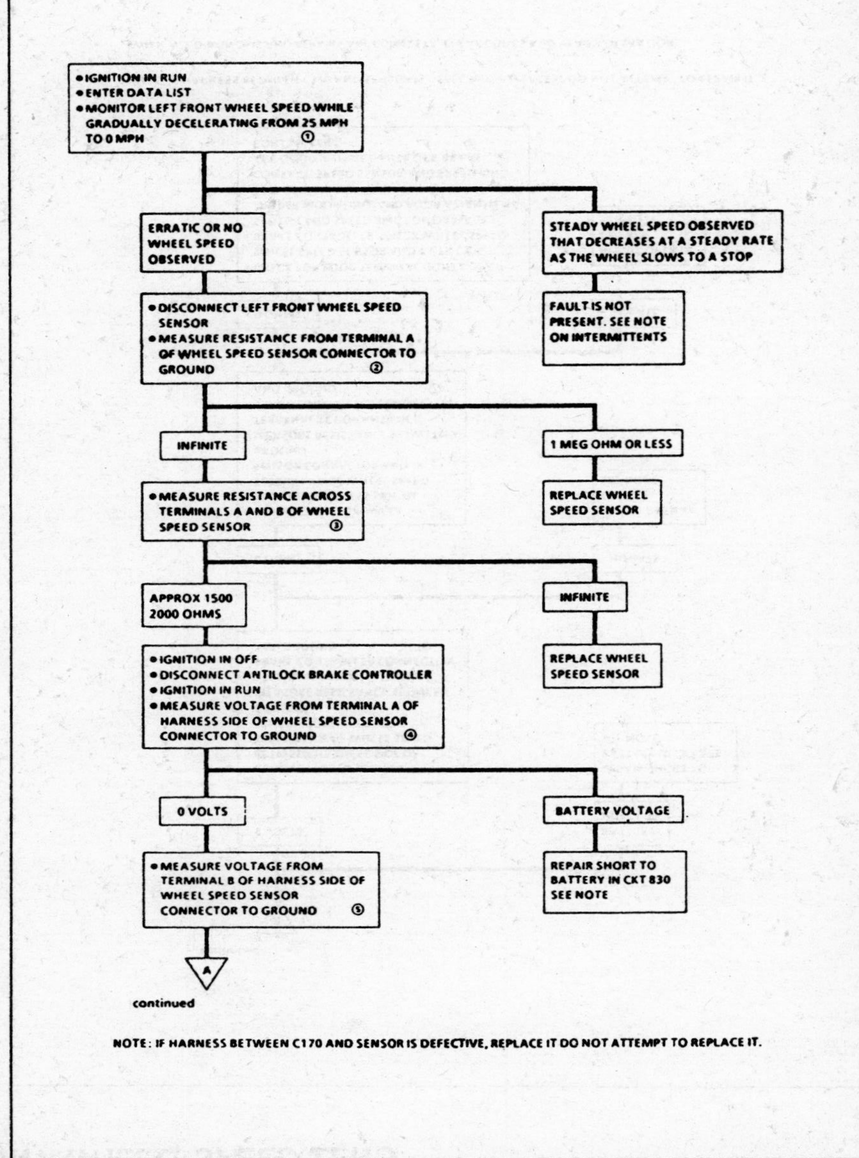

• IGNITION IN RUN
• ENTER DATA LIST
• MONITOR LEFT FRONT WHEEL SPEED WHILE GRADUALLY DECELERATING FROM 25 MPH TO 0 MPH ①
ERRATIC OR NO WHEEL SPEED OBSERVED
STEADY WHEEL SPEED OBSERVED THAT DECREASES AT A STEADY RATE AS THE WHEEL SLOWS TO A STOP
• DISCONNECT LEFT FRONT WHEEL SPEED SENSOR
• MEASURE RESISTANCE FROM TERMINAL A OF WHEEL SPEED SENSOR CONNECTOR TO GROUND ②
FAULT IS NOT PRESENT. SEE NOTE ON INTERMITTENTS
INFINITE
1 MEG OHM OR LESS
• MEASURE RESISTANCE ACROSS TERMINALS A AND B OF WHEEL SPEED SENSOR ③
REPLACE WHEEL SPEED SENSOR
APPROX 1500 2000 OHMS
INFINITE
• IGNITION IN OFF
• DISCONNECT ANTILOCK BRAKE CONTROLLER
• IGNITION IN RUN
• MEASURE VOLTAGE FROM TERMINAL A OF HARNESS SIDE OF WHEEL SPEED SENSOR CONNECTOR TO GROUND ④
REPLACE WHEEL SPEED SENSOR
0 VOLTS
BATTERY VOLTAGE
• MEASURE VOLTAGE FROM TERMINAL B OF HARNESS SIDE OF WHEEL SPEED SENSOR CONNECTOR TO GROUND ⑤
REPAIR SHORT TO BATTERY IN CKT 830 SEE NOTE
A
continued
NOTE: IF HARNESS BETWEEN C170 AND SENSOR IS DEFECTIVE, REPLACE IT DO NOT ATTEMPT TO REPLACE IT.

CODE A045 – LEFT FRONT WHEEL, SPEED ZERO

5. Determines a short to Battery is present in CKT 873 if Battery voltage is measured at Terminal B of the harness side of the Wheel Speed Sensor Connector.

6. With Terminal A of CKT 830 connected to ground, the resistance from Terminal 1C2 to ground should be zero. If infinite resistance is measured, an open condition is indicated in CKT 830.

7. With Terminal B of CKT 873 connected to ground, the resistance from Terminal 1C1 to ground should be zero. If infinite resistance is measured, an open condition is indicated in CKT 873.

8. At this point, all the connecting circuity has tested good. The fault may be due to a poorly mated connector at the Wheel Speed Sensor or the Antilock Brake Controller. Other possible cause could be due to damage to the Speed Sensor or Speed Ring. Check for proper mounting or poor alignment. If everthing above tests good, replace the Antilock Brake Contoller.

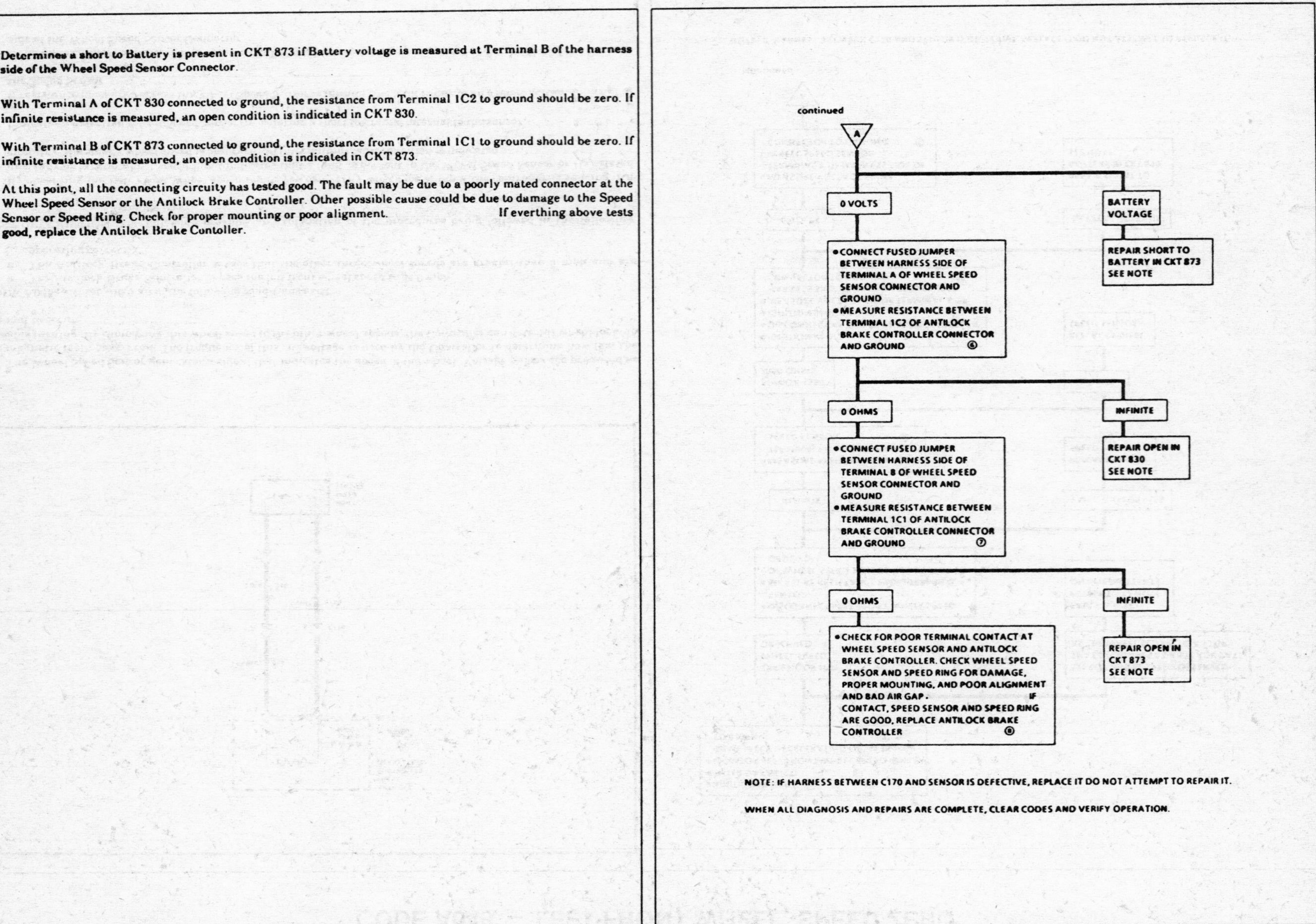
continued
A
0 VOLTS
BATTERY VOLTAGE
REPAIR SHORT TO BATTERY IN CKT 873 SEE NOTE
• CONNECT FUSED JUMPER BETWEEN HARNESS SIDE OF TERMINAL A OF WHEEL SPEED SENSOR CONNECTOR AND GROUND
• MEASURE RESISTANCE BETWEEN TERMINAL 1C2 OF ANTILOCK BRAKE CONTROLLER CONNECTOR AND GROUND ⑥
0 OHMS
INFINITE
REPAIR OPEN IN CKT 830 SEE NOTE
• CONNECT FUSED JUMPER BETWEEN HARNESS SIDE OF TERMINAL B OF WHEEL SPEED SENSOR CONNECTOR AND GROUND
• MEASURE RESISTANCE BETWEEN TERMINAL 1C1 OF ANTILOCK BRAKE CONTROLLER CONNECTOR AND GROUND ⑦
0 OHMS
INFINITE
REPAIR OPEN IN CKT 873 SEE NOTE
• CHECK FOR POOR TERMINAL CONTACT AT WHEEL SPEED SENSOR AND ANTILOCK BRAKE CONTROLLER. CHECK WHEEL SPEED SENSOR AND SPEED RING FOR DAMAGE, PROPER MOUNTING, AND POOR ALIGNMENT AND BAD AIR GAP. IF CONTACT, SPEED SENSOR AND SPEED RING ARE GOOD, REPLACE ANTILOCK BRAKE CONTROLLER ⑧
NOTE: IF HARNESS BETWEEN C170 AND SENSOR IS DEFECTIVE, REPLACE IT DO NOT ATTEMPT TO REPAIR IT.
WHEN ALL DIAGNOSIS AND REPAIRS ARE COMPLETE, CLEAR CODES AND VERIFY OPERATION.

CODE A046 – RIGHT REAR WHEEL, SPEED ZERO

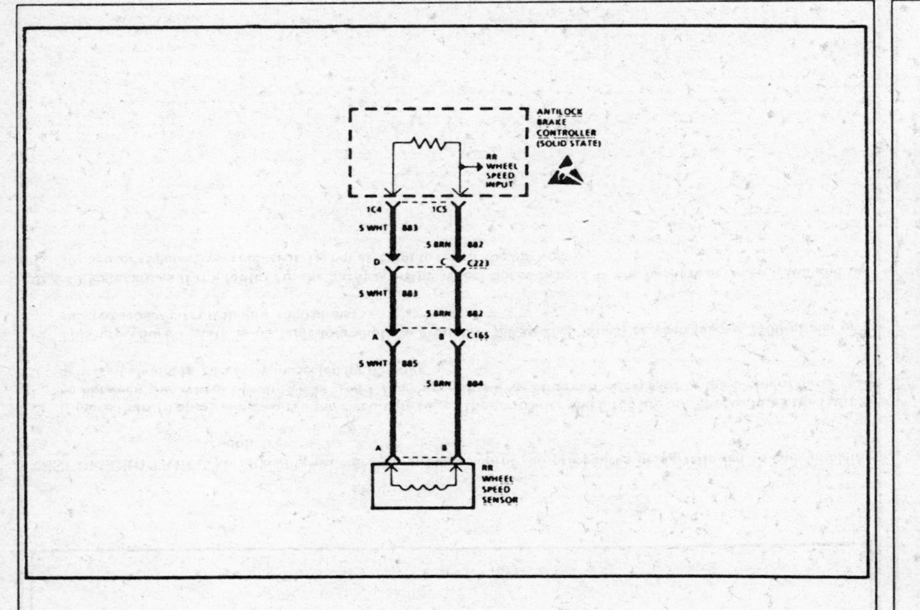

The Wheel Speed Sensor generates a signal that indicates the speed of the wheel. Voltage pulses are produced as the magnetic teeth pass the coil. The frequency of this AC voltage is used by the Controller to determine how fast the wheel is turning. By comparing this wheel speed to the other wheel speeds, the Controller can detect if wheel lock-up is about to occur.

CODE A046 will set when all of the following conditions exist:

- The Antilock Brake Controller senses the right rear wheel speed to be 0 mph.
- The Antilock Brake Controller senses that the other three wheel speeds are greater than 5 mph and are operating correctly.

TEST DESCRIPTION: The following provides an explanation of the procedures being followed in the trouble tree.

① Observation of erratic or no wheel speed input indicates the fault is present and is not intermittent.

② & ③ Step 2 determines if a sent to battery is the fault. If battery voltage is measured step 3 isolates the short to the harness or controller.

④ If 9000 to 15000 ohms was measured, its possibility of a open or short in the circuit between the antilock brake controller and connector C165 has been eliminated.

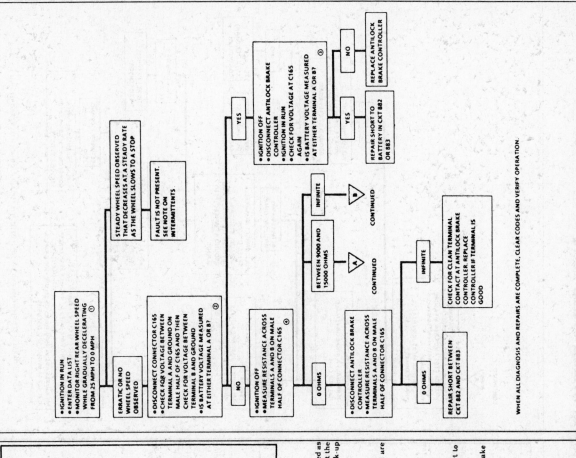

- IGNITION IN RUN
- ENTER DATA LIST
- MONITOR RIGHT REAR WHEEL SPEED WHILE GRADUALLY DECELERATING FROM 25 MPH TO 0 MPH ①

ERRATIC OR NO WHEEL SPEED OBSERVED

- DISCONNECT CONNECTOR C165
- CHECK FOR VOLTAGE BETWEEN TERMINAL A AND GROUND ON MALE HALF OF C165 AND THEN CHECK FOR VOLTAGE BETWEEN TERMINAL B AND GROUND
- IS BATTERY VOLTAGE MEASURED AT EITHER TERMINAL A OR B? ②

NO

- IGNITION OFF
- MEASURE RESISTANCE ACROSS TERMINALS A AND B ON MALE HALF OF CONNECTOR C165 ④

0 OHMS

- DISCONNECT ANTILOCK BRAKE CONTROLLER
- MEASURE RESISTANCE ACROSS TERMINALS A AND B ON MALE HALF OF CONNECTOR C165

0 OHMS → REPAIR SHORT BETWEEN CKT 882 AND CKT 883

INFINITE → CHECK FOR CLEAN TERMINAL CONTACT AT ANTILOCK BRAKE CONTROLLER. REPLACE CONTROLLER IF TERMINAL IS GOOD

BETWEEN 9000 AND 15000 OHMS → A CONTINUED

INFINITE → B CONTINUED

YES

- IGNITION OFF
- DISCONNECT ANTILOCK BRAKE CONTROLLER
- IGNITION IN RUN
- CHECK FOR VOLTAGE AT C165 AGAIN
- IS BATTERY VOLTAGE MEASURED AT EITHER TERMINAL A OR B? ③

YES → REPAIR SHORT TO BATTERY IN CKT 882 OR 883

NO → REPLACE ANTILOCK BRAKE CONTROLLER

STEADY WHEEL SPEED OBSERVED THAT DECREASES AT A STEADY RATE AS THE WHEEL SLOWS TO A STOP

FAULT IS NOT PRESENT. SEE NOTE ON INTERMITTENTS.

WHEN ALL DIAGNOSIS AND REPAIRS ARE COMPLETE, CLEAR CODES AND VERIFY OPERATION.

CODE A046 – RIGHT REAR WHEEL, SPEED ZERO

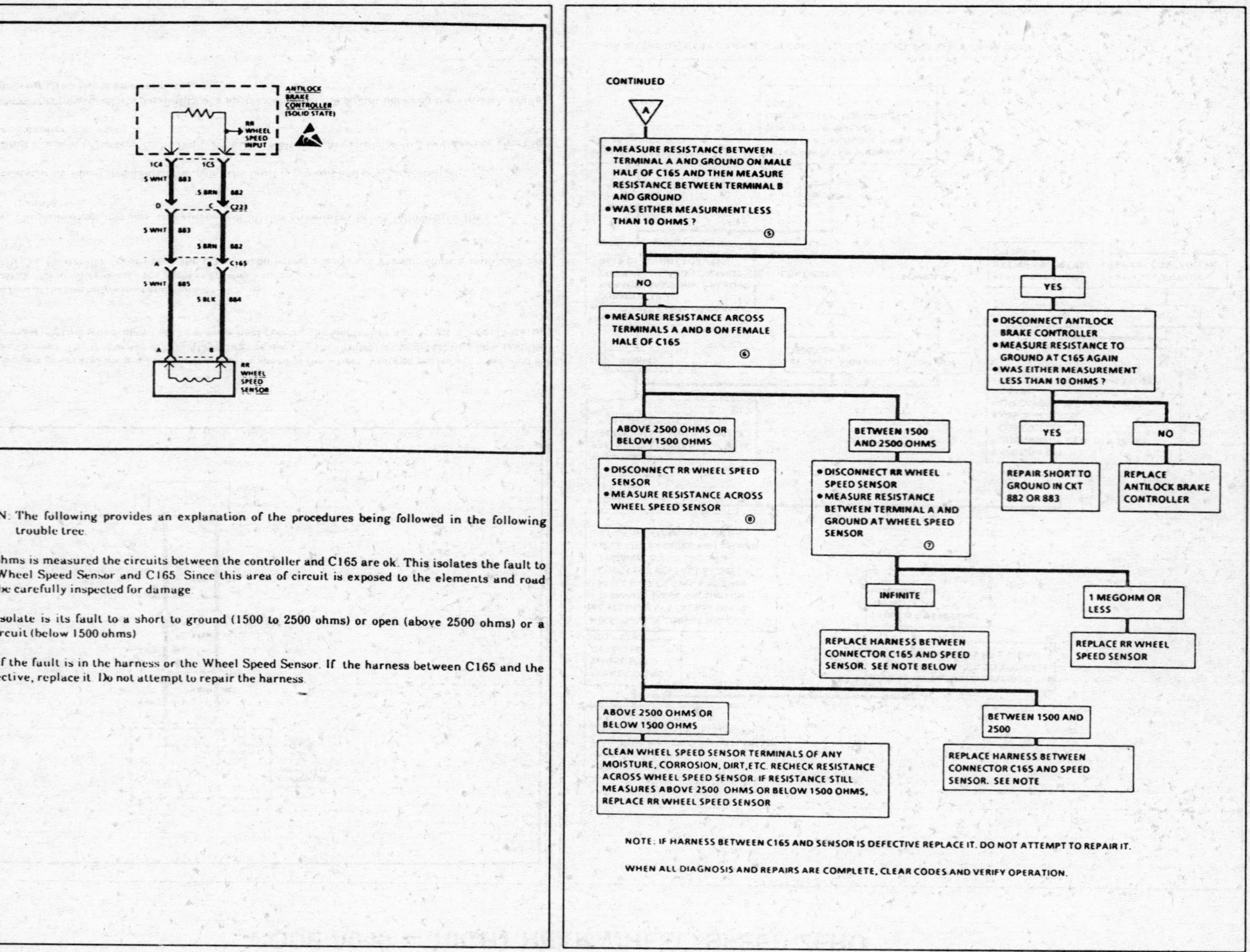
ANTILOCK BRAKE CONTROLLER (SOLID STATE)
RR WHEEL SPEED INPUT
1C4
1C5
5 WHT 883
5 BRN 882
D
C
C223
5 WHT 883
5 BRN 882
A
B
C165
5 WHT 885
5 BLK 884
A
B
RR WHEEL SPEED SENSOR
CONTINUED
A
• MEASURE RESISTANCE BETWEEN TERMINAL A AND GROUND ON MALE HALF OF C165 AND THEN MEASURE RESISTANCE BETWEEN TERMINAL B AND GROUND
• WAS EITHER MEASURMENT LESS THAN 10 OHMS ? ⑤
NO
YES
• MEASURE RESISTANCE ARCOSS TERMINALS A AND B ON FEMALE HALE OF C165 ⑥
• DISCONNECT ANTILOCK BRAKE CONTROLLER
• MEASURE RESISTANCE TO GROUND AT C165 AGAIN
• WAS EITHER MEASUREMENT LESS THAN 10 OHMS ?
ABOVE 2500 OHMS OR BELOW 1500 OHMS
BETWEEN 1500 AND 2500 OHMS
YES
NO
REPAIR SHORT TO GROUND IN CKT 882 OR 883
REPLACE ANTILOCK BRAKE CONTROLLER
• DISCONNECT RR WHEEL SPEED SENSOR
• MEASURE RESISTANCE ACROSS WHEEL SPEED SENSOR ⑧
• DISCONNECT RR WHEEL SPEED SENSOR
• MEASURE RESISTANCE BETWEEN TERMINAL A AND GROUND AT WHEEL SPEED SENSOR ⑦
INFINITE
1 MEGOHM OR LESS
REPLACE HARNESS BETWEEN CONNECTOR C165 AND SPEED SENSOR. SEE NOTE BELOW
REPLACE RR WHEEL SPEED SENSOR
ABOVE 2500 OHMS OR BELOW 1500 OHMS
BETWEEN 1500 AND 2500
CLEAN WHEEL SPEED SENSOR TERMINALS OF ANY MOISTURE, CORROSION, DIRT, ETC. RECHECK RESISTANCE ACROSS WHEEL SPEED SENSOR. IF RESISTANCE STILL MEASURES ABOVE 2500 OHMS OR BELOW 1500 OHMS, REPLACE RR WHEEL SPEED SENSOR
REPLACE HARNESS BETWEEN CONNECTOR C165 AND SPEED SENSOR. SEE NOTE
NOTE: IF HARNESS BETWEEN C165 AND SENSOR IS DEFECTIVE REPLACE IT. DO NOT ATTEMPT TO REPAIR IT.
WHEN ALL DIAGNOSIS AND REPAIRS ARE COMPLETE, CLEAR CODES AND VERIFY OPERATION.

TEST DESCRIPTION: The following provides an explanation of the procedures being followed in the following trouble tree.

⑤ If more than 10 ohms is measured the circuits between the controller and C165 are ok. This isolates the fault to be between the Wheel Speed Sensor and C165. Since this area of circuit is exposed to the elements and road debris, it should be carefully inspected for damage.

⑥ This procedure isolate is its fault to a short to ground (1500 to 2500 ohms) or open (above 2500 ohms) or a shorted sensor circuit (below 1500 ohms)

⑦ & ⑧ Determines if the fault is in the harness or the Wheel Speed Sensor. If the harness between C165 and the sensor is defective, replace it. Do not attempt to repair the harness.

CODE A046 – RIGHT REAR WHEEL, SPEED ZERO

ANTILOCK BRAKE CONTROLLER (SOLID STATE)
RR WHEEL SPEED INPUT
1C4
1C5
5 WHT 883
5 BRN 882
D
C
C223
5 WHT 883
5 BRN 882
A
B
C165
5 WHT 885
5 BLK 884
A
B
RR WHEEL SPEED SENSOR
4/29/88

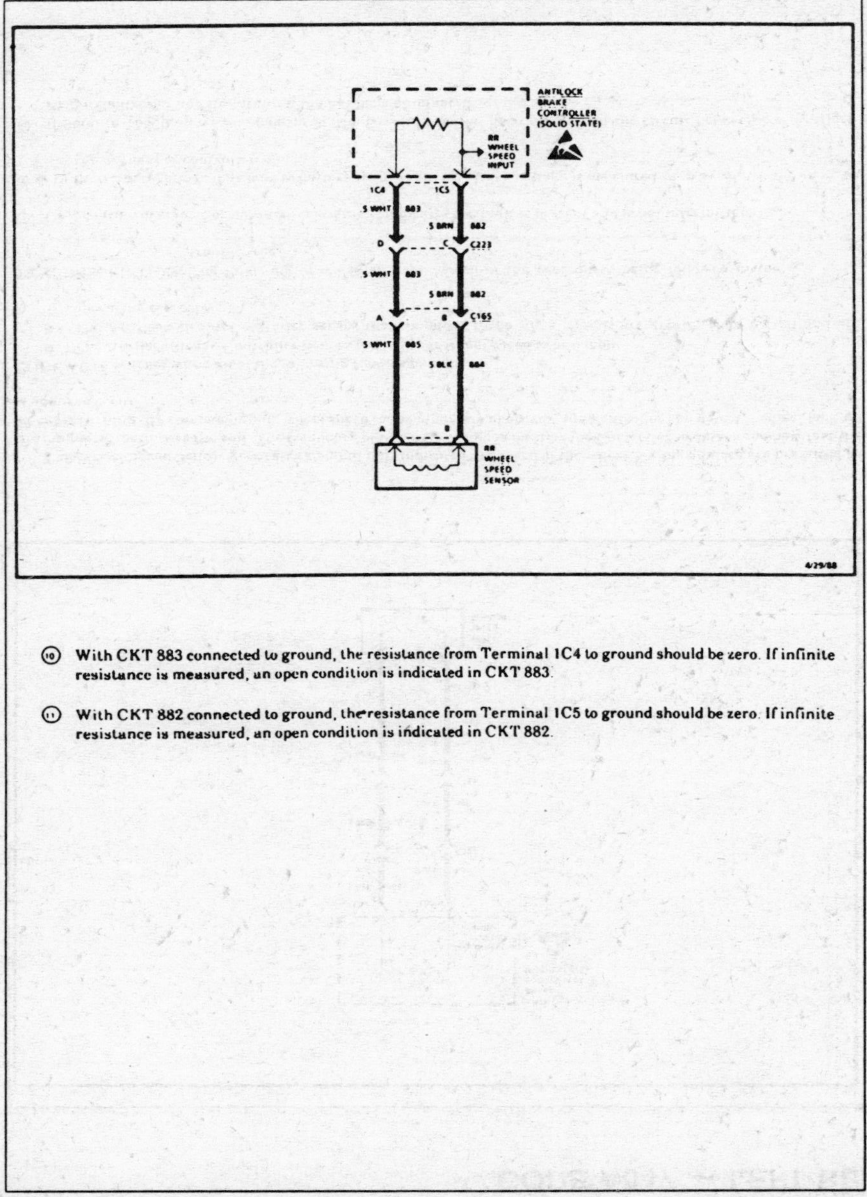

(10) With CKT 883 connected to ground, the resistance from Terminal 1C4 to ground should be zero. If infinite resistance is measured, an open condition is indicated in CKT 883.

(11) With CKT 882 connected to ground, the resistance from Terminal 1C5 to ground should be zero. If infinite resistance is measured, an open condition is indicated in CKT 882.

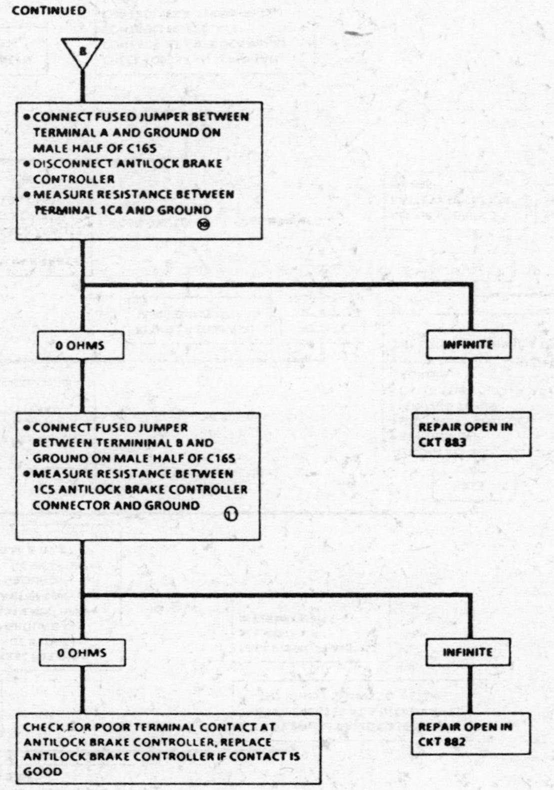

CONTINUED
B
• CONNECT FUSED JUMPER BETWEEN TERMINAL A AND GROUND ON MALE HALF OF C165
• DISCONNECT ANTILOCK BRAKE CONTROLLER
• MEASURE RESISTANCE BETWEEN TERMINAL 1C4 AND GROUND (10)
0 OHMS
INFINITE
REPAIR OPEN IN CKT 883
• CONNECT FUSED JUMPER BETWEEN TERMININAL B AND GROUND ON MALE HALF OF C165
• MEASURE RESISTANCE BETWEEN 1C5 ANTILOCK BRAKE CONTROLLER CONNECTOR AND GROUND (11)
0 OHMS
INFINITE
CHECK FOR POOR TERMINAL CONTACT AT ANTILOCK BRAKE CONTROLLER, REPLACE ANTILOCK BRAKE CONTROLLER IF CONTACT IS GOOD
REPAIR OPEN IN CKT 882

WHEN ALL DIAGNOSIS AND REPAIRS ARE COMPLETE, CLEAR CODES AND VERIFY OPERATION.

CODE A047 — LEFT REAR WHEEL, SPEED ZERO

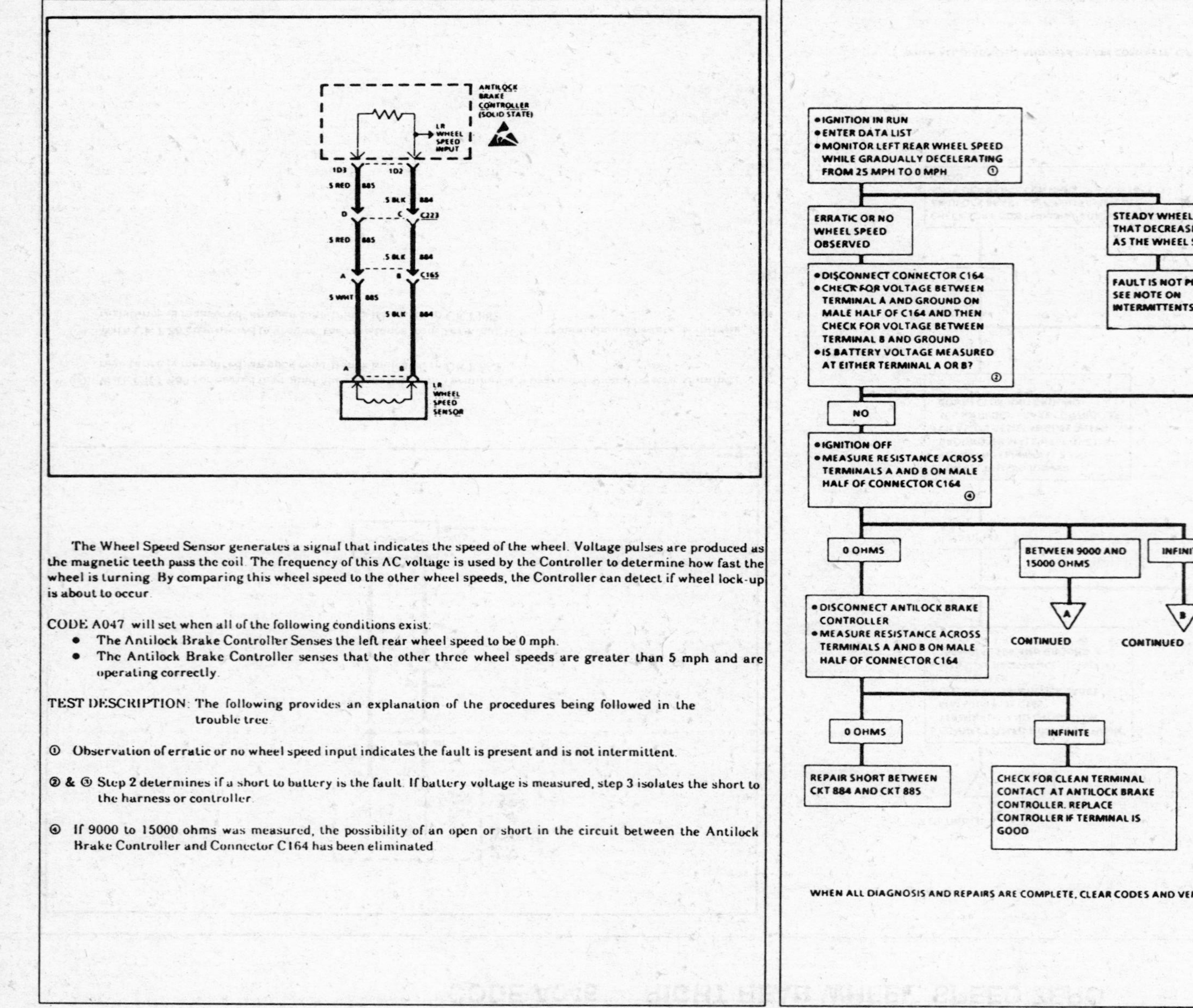
ANTILOCK BRAKE CONTROLLER (SOLID STATE)
LR WHEEL SPEED INPUT
1D3
1D2
5 RED 885
5 BLK 884
D
C
C223
5 RED 885
5 BLK 884
A
B
C165
5 WHT 885
5 BLK 884
A
B
LR WHEEL SPEED SENSOR
• IGNITION IN RUN
• ENTER DATA LIST
• MONITOR LEFT REAR WHEEL SPEED WHILE GRADUALLY DECELERATING FROM 25 MPH TO 0 MPH ①
ERRATIC OR NO WHEEL SPEED OBSERVED
STEADY WHEEL SPEED OBSERVED THAT DECREASES AT A STEADY RATE AS THE WHEEL SLOWS TO A STOP
FAULT IS NOT PRESENT. SEE NOTE ON INTERMITTENTS
• DISCONNECT CONNECTOR C164
• CHECK FOR VOLTAGE BETWEEN TERMINAL A AND GROUND ON MALE HALF OF C164 AND THEN CHECK FOR VOLTAGE BETWEEN TERMINAL B AND GROUND
• IS BATTERY VOLTAGE MEASURED AT EITHER TERMINAL A OR B? ②
NO
YES
• IGNITION OFF
• MEASURE RESISTANCE ACROSS TERMINALS A AND B ON MALE HALF OF CONNECTOR C164 ④
• IGNITION OFF
• DISCONNET ANTILOCK
• IGNITION IN RUN
• CHECK FOR VOLTAGE AT C164 AGAIN
• IS BATTERY VOLTAGE MEASURED AT EITHER TERMINAL A OR B? ③
0 OHMS
BETWEEN 9000 AND 15000 OHMS
INFINITE
A
CONTINUED
B
CONTINUED
YES
NO
REPAIR SHORT TO BATTERY IN CKT 884 OR 885
REPLACE ANTILOCK BRAKE CONTROLLER
• DISCONNECT ANTILOCK BRAKE CONTROLLER
• MEASURE RESISTANCE ACROSS TERMINALS A AND B ON MALE HALF OF CONNECTOR C164
0 OHMS
INFINITE
REPAIR SHORT BETWEEN CKT 884 AND CKT 885
CHECK FOR CLEAN TERMINAL CONTACT AT ANTILOCK BRAKE CONTROLLER. REPLACE CONTROLLER IF TERMINAL IS GOOD
WHEN ALL DIAGNOSIS AND REPAIRS ARE COMPLETE, CLEAR CODES AND VERIFY OPERATION.

The Wheel Speed Sensor generates a signal that indicates the speed of the wheel. Voltage pulses are produced as the magnetic teeth pass the coil. The frequency of this AC voltage is used by the Controller to determine how fast the wheel is turning. By comparing this wheel speed to the other wheel speeds, the Controller can detect if wheel lock-up is about to occur.

CODE A047 will set when all of the following conditions exist:

- The Antilock Brake Controller Senses the left rear wheel speed to be 0 mph.
- The Antilock Brake Controller senses that the other three wheel speeds are greater than 5 mph and are operating correctly.

TEST DESCRIPTION: The following provides an explanation of the procedures being followed in the trouble tree.

① Observation of erratic or no wheel speed input indicates the fault is present and is not intermittent.

② & ③ Step 2 determines if a short to battery is the fault. If battery voltage is measured, step 3 isolates the short to the harness or controller.

④ If 9000 to 15000 ohms was measured, the possibility of an open or short in the circuit between the Antilock Brake Controller and Connector C164 has been eliminated.

CODE A047 – LEFT REAR WHEEL, SPEED ZERO

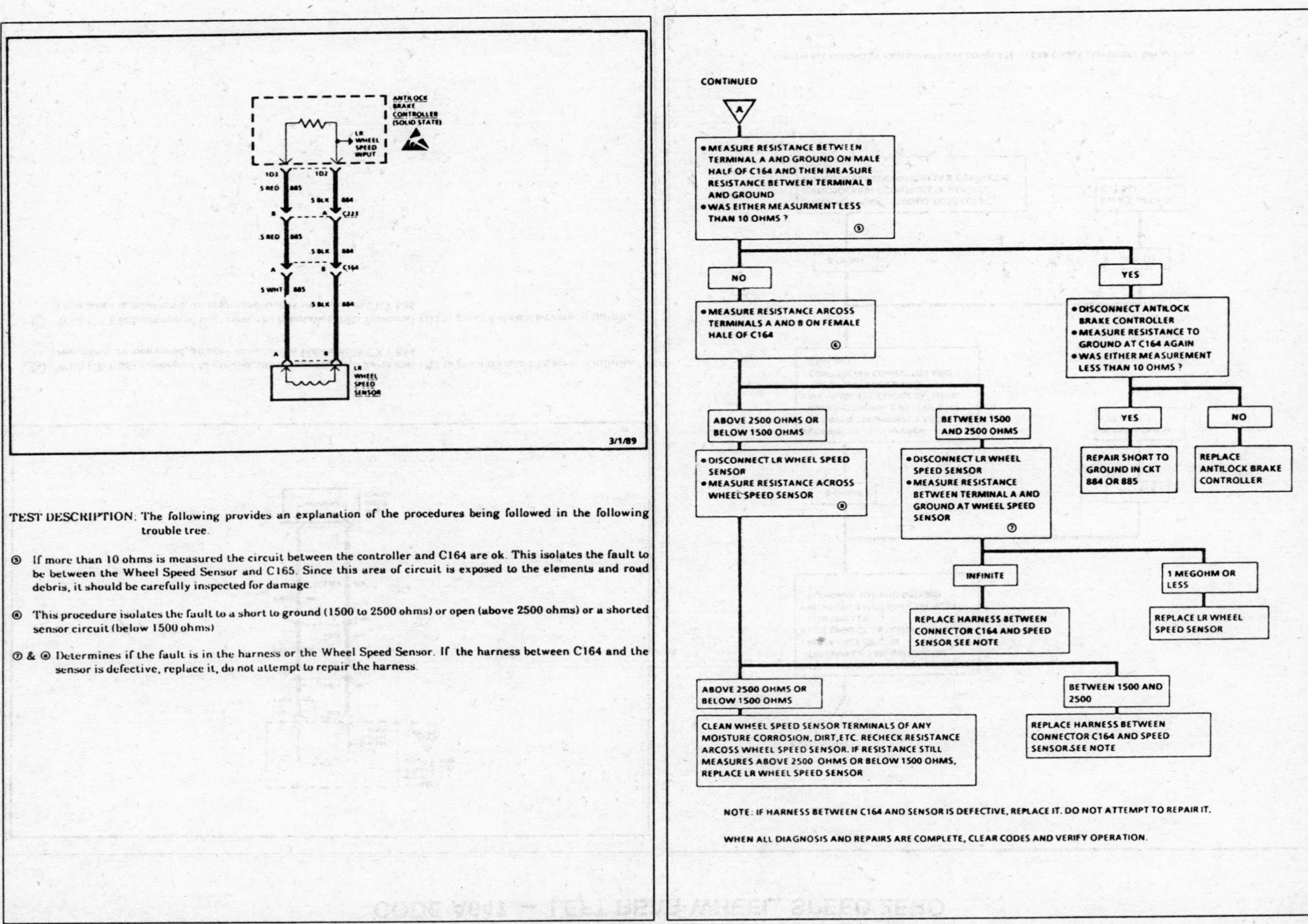
ANTILOCK BRAKE CONTROLLER (SOLID STATE)
LR WHEEL SPEED INPUT
1D3
1D2
5 RED 885
5 BLK 884
C223
C164
5 WHT 885
LR WHEEL SPEED SENSOR
3/1/89
CONTINUED
A
• MEASURE RESISTANCE BETWEEN TERMINAL A AND GROUND ON MALE HALF OF C164 AND THEN MEASURE RESISTANCE BETWEEN TERMINAL B AND GROUND
• WAS EITHER MEASURMENT LESS THAN 10 OHMS ? ⑤
NO
YES
• MEASURE RESISTANCE ARCOSS TERMINALS A AND B ON FEMALE HALF OF C164 ⑥
• DISCONNECT ANTILOCK BRAKE CONTROLLER
• MEASURE RESISTANCE TO GROUND AT C164 AGAIN
• WAS EITHER MEASUREMENT LESS THAN 10 OHMS ?
ABOVE 2500 OHMS OR BELOW 1500 OHMS
BETWEEN 1500 AND 2500 OHMS
YES
NO
REPAIR SHORT TO GROUND IN CKT 884 OR 885
REPLACE ANTILOCK BRAKE CONTROLLER
• DISCONNECT LR WHEEL SPEED SENSOR
• MEASURE RESISTANCE ACROSS WHEEL SPEED SENSOR ⑧
• DISCONNECT LR WHEEL SPEED SENSOR
• MEASURE RESISTANCE BETWEEN TERMINAL A AND GROUND AT WHEEL SPEED SENSOR ⑦
INFINITE
1 MEGOHM OR LESS
REPLACE HARNESS BETWEEN CONNECTOR C164 AND SPEED SENSOR SEE NOTE
REPLACE LR WHEEL SPEED SENSOR
ABOVE 2500 OHMS OR BELOW 1500 OHMS
BETWEEN 1500 AND 2500
CLEAN WHEEL SPEED SENSOR TERMINALS OF ANY MOISTURE CORROSION, DIRT, ETC. RECHECK RESISTANCE ARCOSS WHEEL SPEED SENSOR. IF RESISTANCE STILL MEASURES ABOVE 2500 OHMS OR BELOW 1500 OHMS, REPLACE LR WHEEL SPEED SENSOR
REPLACE HARNESS BETWEEN CONNECTOR C164 AND SPEED SENSOR.SEE NOTE
NOTE: IF HARNESS BETWEEN C164 AND SENSOR IS DEFECTIVE, REPLACE IT. DO NOT ATTEMPT TO REPAIR IT.
WHEN ALL DIAGNOSIS AND REPAIRS ARE COMPLETE, CLEAR CODES AND VERIFY OPERATION.

TEST DESCRIPTION: The following provides an explanation of the procedures being followed in the following trouble tree.

⑤ If more than 10 ohms is measured the circuit between the controller and C164 are ok. This isolates the fault to be between the Wheel Speed Sensor and C165. Since this area of circuit is exposed to the elements and road debris, it should be carefully inspected for damage.

⑥ This procedure isolates the fault to a short to ground (1500 to 2500 ohms) or open (above 2500 ohms) or a shorted sensor circuit (below 1500 ohms).

⑦ & ⑧ Determines if the fault is in the harness or the Wheel Speed Sensor. If the harness between C164 and the sensor is defective, replace it, do not attempt to repair the harness.

CODE A047 — LEFT REAR WHEEL, SPEED ZERO

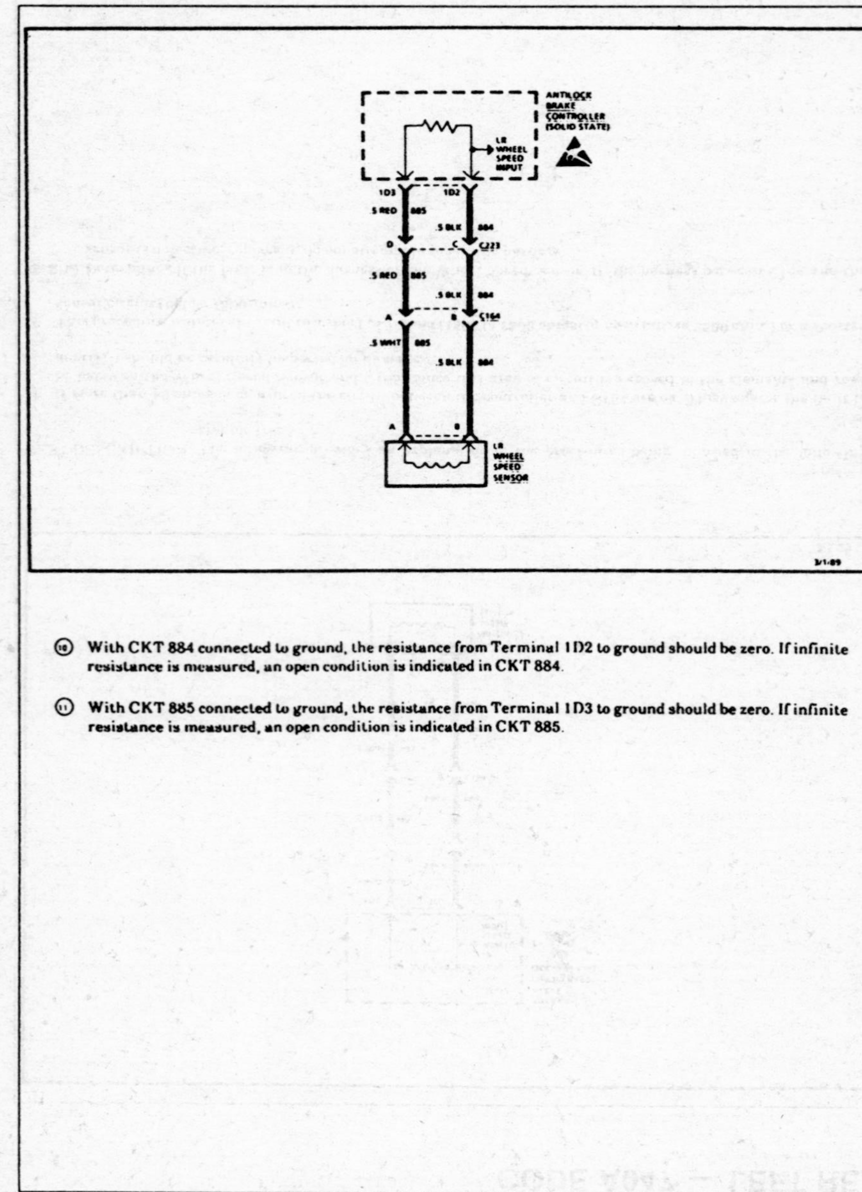

⑩ With CKT 884 connected to ground, the resistance from Terminal 1D2 to ground should be zero. If infinite resistance is measured, an open condition is indicated in CKT 884.

⑪ With CKT 885 connected to ground, the resistance from Terminal 1D3 to ground should be zero. If infinite resistance is measured, an open condition is indicated in CKT 885.

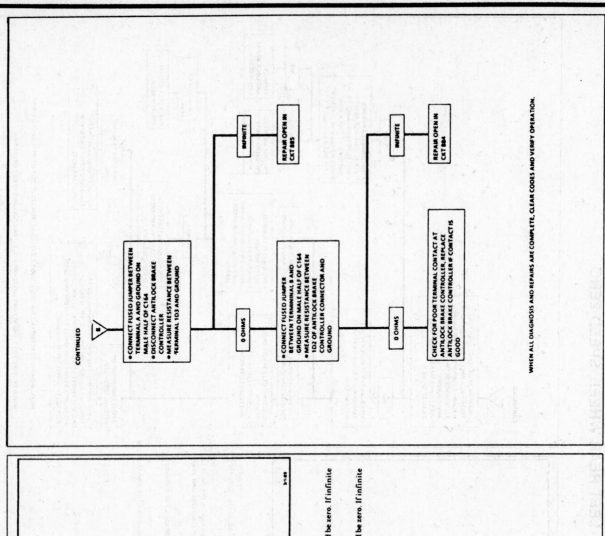

CONTINUED

(B)

- CONNECT FUSED JUMPER BETWEEN TERMINAL A AND GROUND ON MALE HALF OF C164
- DISCONNECT ANTILOCK BRAKE CONTROLLER
- MEASURE RESISTANCE BETWEEN TERMINAL 1D3 AND GROUND

0 OHMS →

- CONNECT FUSED JUMPER BETWEEN TERMININAL B AND GROUND ON MALE HALF OF C164
- MEASURE RESISTANCE BETWEEN 1D2 OF ANTILOCK BRAKE CONTROLLER CONNECTOR AND GROUND

INFINITE → REPAIR OPEN IN CKT 885

0 OHMS → CHECK FOR POOR TERMINAL CONTACT AT ANTILOCK BRAKE CONTROLLER, REPLACE ANTILOCK BRAKE CONTROLLER IF CONTACT IS GOOD

INFINITE → REPAIR OPEN IN CKT 884

WHEN ALL DIAGNOSIS AND REPAIRS ARE COMPLETE, CLEAR CODES AND VERIFY OPERATION.

CODE A048 — EXCESSIVE RIGHT FRONT WHEEL ACCELERATION

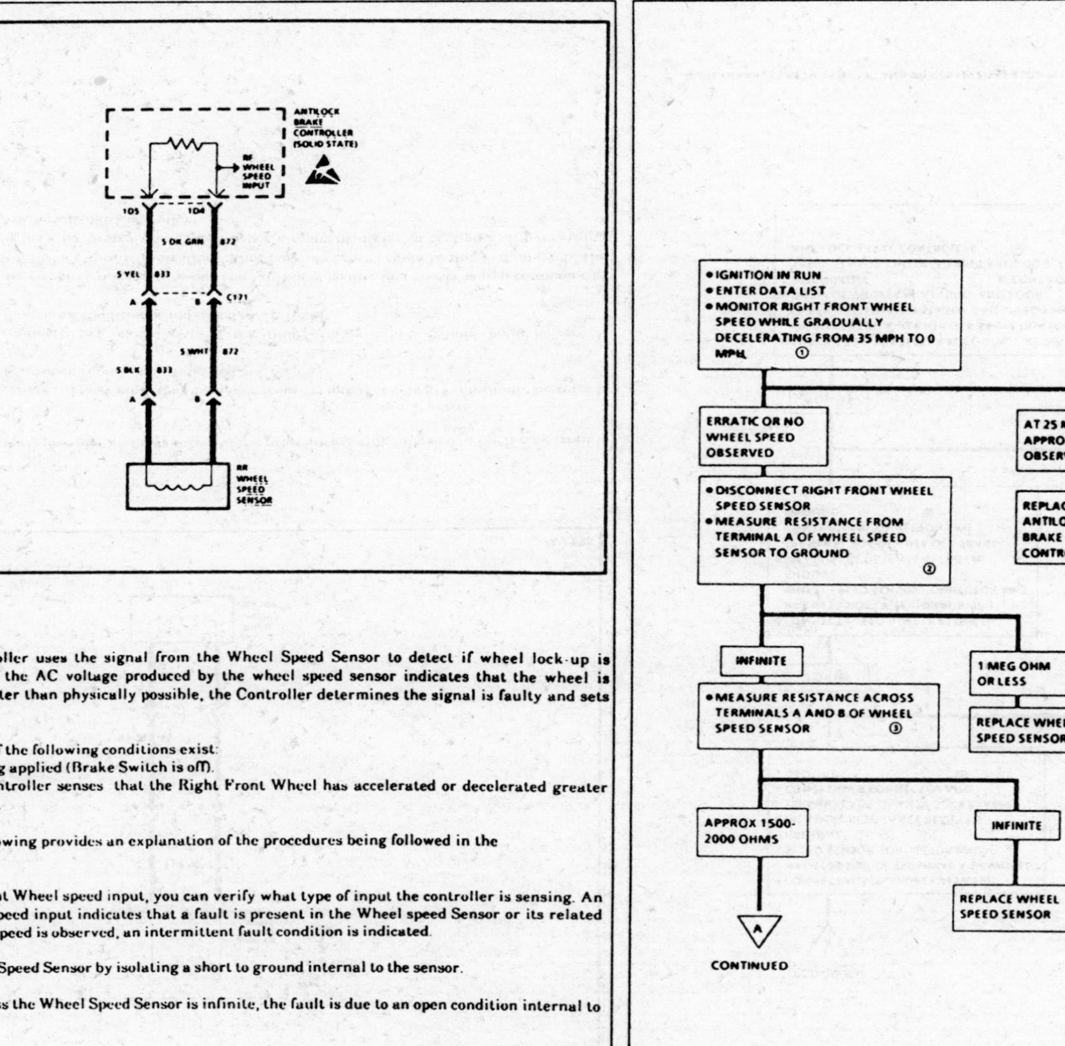
ANTILOCK BRAKE CONTROLLER (SOLID STATE)
RF WHEEL SPEED INPUT
105
104
5 DK GRN 872
5 YEL 833
A
B
C171
5 WHT 872
5 BLK 833
RR WHEEL SPEED SENSOR
• IGNITION IN RUN
• ENTER DATA LIST
• MONITOR RIGHT FRONT WHEEL SPEED WHILE GRADUALLY DECELERATING FROM 35 MPH TO 0 MPH ①
ERRATIC OR NO WHEEL SPEED OBSERVED
AT 25 MPH, APPROX 50 MPH OBSERVED.
STEADY WHEEL SPEED OBSERVED THAT DECREASES AT A STEADY RATE AS THE WHEEL SLOWS TO A STOP
• DISCONNECT RIGHT FRONT WHEEL SPEED SENSOR
• MEASURE RESISTANCE FROM TERMINAL A OF WHEEL SPEED SENSOR TO GROUND ②
REPLACE ANTILOCK BRAKE CONTROLLER
FAULT IS NOT PRESENT. SEE NOTE ON INTERMITTENTS
INFINITE
1 MEG OHM OR LESS
• MEASURE RESISTANCE ACROSS TERMINALS A AND B OF WHEEL SPEED SENSOR ③
REPLACE WHEEL SPEED SENSOR
APPROX 1500-2000 OHMS
INFINITE
REPLACE WHEEL SPEED SENSOR
A
CONTINUED

The Antilock Brake Controller uses the signal from the Wheel Speed Sensor to detect if wheel lock-up is impending. If the frequency of the AC voltage produced by the wheel speed sensor indicates that the wheel is accelerating or decelerating faster than physically possible, the Controller determines the signal is faulty and sets the code.

CODE A048 will set when all of the following conditions exist:

- The Brakes are not being applied (Brake Switch is off).
- The Antilock Brake Controller senses that the Right Front Wheel has accelerated or decelerated greater than physically possible.

TEST DESCRIPTION: The following provides an explanation of the procedures being followed in the tree.

① By observing the Right Front Wheel speed input, you can verify what type of input the controller is sensing. An unsteady or erratic wheel speed input indicates that a fault is present in the Wheel speed Sensor or its related circuitry. If a steady wheel speed is observed, an intermittent fault condition is indicated.

② Indicates a defective Wheel Speed Sensor by isolating a short to ground internal to the sensor.

③ If resistance measured across the Wheel Speed Sensor is infinite, the fault is due to an open condition internal to the Speed Sensor.

CODE A048 — EXCESSIVE RIGHT FRONT WHEEL ACCELERATION

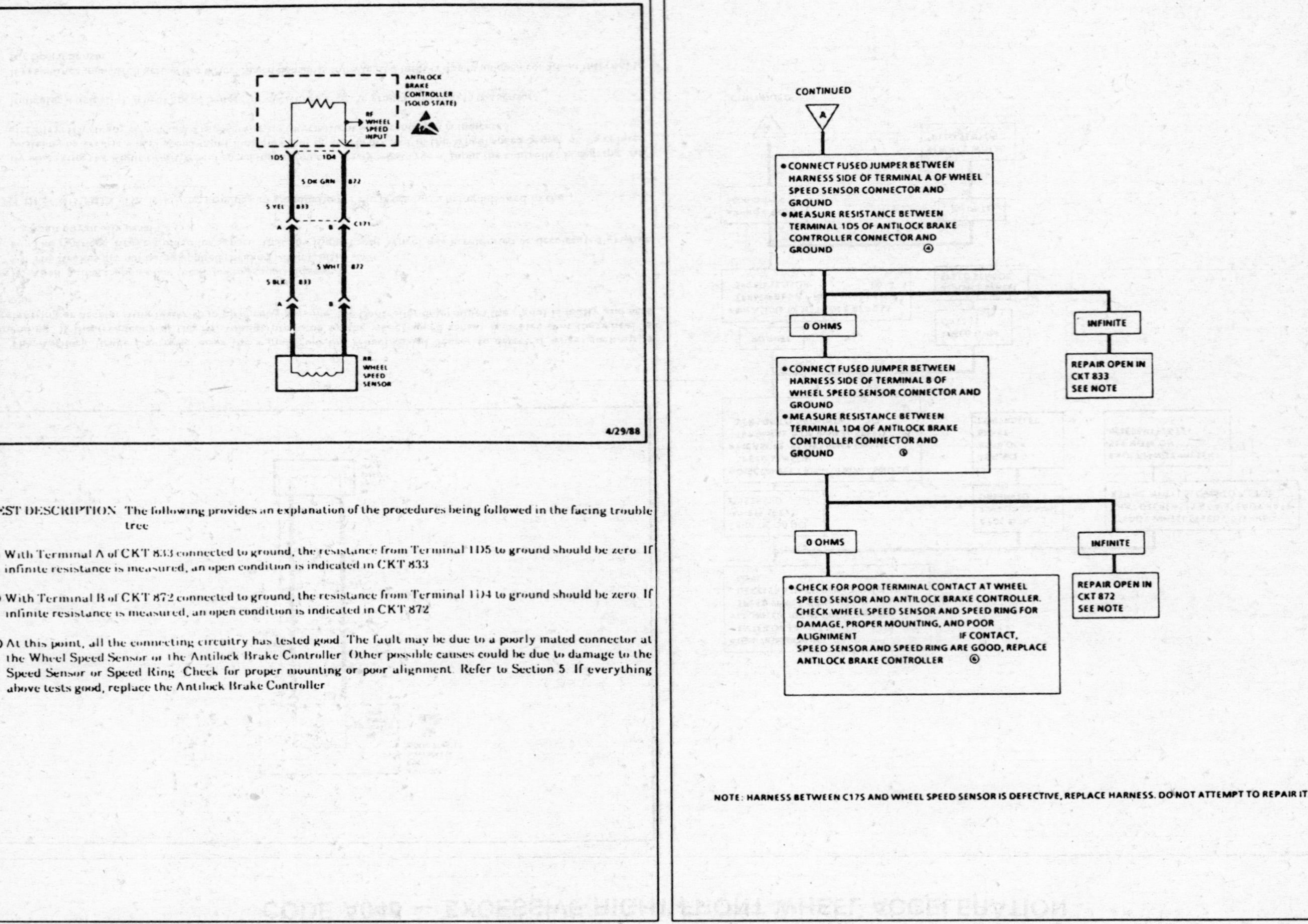
ANTILOCK BRAKE CONTROLLER (SOLID STATE)
RF WHEEL SPEED INPUT
1D5
1D4
5 DK GRN 872
5 YEL 833
A
B
C171
5 WHT 872
5 BLK 833
A
B
RR WHEEL SPEED SENSOR
4/29/88
CONTINUED
A
• CONNECT FUSED JUMPER BETWEEN HARNESS SIDE OF TERMINAL A OF WHEEL SPEED SENSOR CONNECTOR AND GROUND
• MEASURE RESISTANCE BETWEEN TERMINAL 1D5 OF ANTILOCK BRAKE CONTROLLER CONNECTOR AND GROUND ④
0 OHMS
INFINITE
REPAIR OPEN IN CKT 833 SEE NOTE
• CONNECT FUSED JUMPER BETWEEN HARNESS SIDE OF TERMINAL B OF WHEEL SPEED SENSOR CONNECTOR AND GROUND
• MEASURE RESISTANCE BETWEEN TERMINAL 1D4 OF ANTILOCK BRAKE CONTROLLER CONNECTOR AND GROUND ⑤
0 OHMS
INFINITE
REPAIR OPEN IN CKT 872 SEE NOTE
• CHECK FOR POOR TERMINAL CONTACT AT WHEEL SPEED SENSOR AND ANTILOCK BRAKE CONTROLLER. CHECK WHEEL SPEED SENSOR AND SPEED RING FOR DAMAGE, PROPER MOUNTING, AND POOR ALIGNMENT IF CONTACT, SPEED SENSOR AND SPEED RING ARE GOOD, REPLACE ANTILOCK BRAKE CONTROLLER ⑥
NOTE: HARNESS BETWEEN C175 AND WHEEL SPEED SENSOR IS DEFECTIVE, REPLACE HARNESS. DO NOT ATTEMPT TO REPAIR IT.

TEST DESCRIPTION The following provides an explanation of the procedures being followed in the facing trouble tree

④ With Terminal A of CKT 833 connected to ground, the resistance from Terminal 1D5 to ground should be zero If infinite resistance is measured, an open condition is indicated in CKT 833

⑤ With Terminal B of CKT 872 connected to ground, the resistance from Terminal 1D4 to ground should be zero If infinite resistance is measured, an open condition is indicated in CKT 872

⑥ At this point, all the connecting circuitry has tested good The fault may be due to a poorly mated connector at the Wheel Speed Sensor or the Antilock Brake Controller Other possible causes could be due to damage to the Speed Sensor or Speed Ring Check for proper mounting or poor alignment Refer to Section 5 If everything above tests good, replace the Antilock Brake Controller

CODE A049 – EXCESSIVE LEFT FRONT WHEEL ACCELERATION

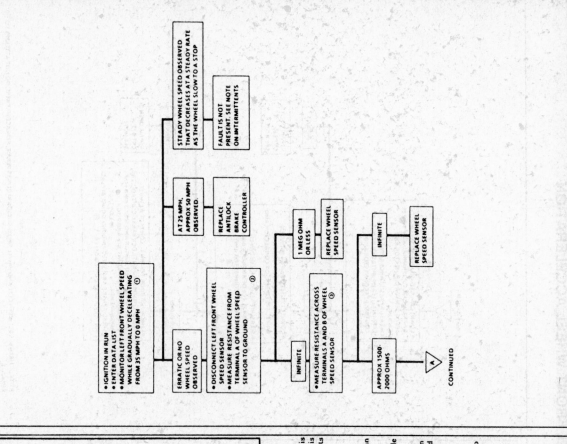

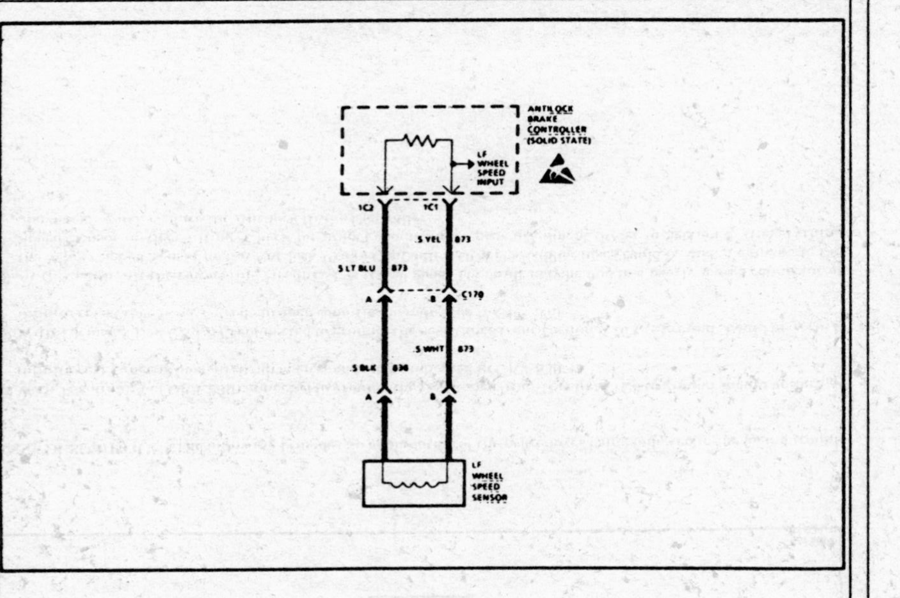

The Antilock Brake Controller uses the signal from the Wheel Speed Sensor to detect if wheel lock-up is impending. If the frequency of the AC voltage produced by the wheel speed sensor indicates that the wheel is accelerating or decelerating faster than physically possible, the Controller determines the signal is faulty and sets the code.

CODE A049 will set when all of the following conditions exist:

- The Brakes are not being applied (Brake Switch is off).
- The Antilock Brake Controller senses that the Left Front Wheel has accelerated or decelerated greater than physically possible.

TEST DESCRIPTION: The following provides an explanation of the procedures being followed in the facing trouble tree.

① By observing the Left Front Wheel speed input, you can verify what type of input the controller is sensing. An unsteady or erratic wheel speed input indicates that a fault is present in the Wheel Speed Sensor or its related circuitry. If a steady wheel speed is observed, an intermittent fault condition is indicated.

② Indicates a defective Wheel Speed Sensor by isolating a short to ground internal to the sensor.

③ If resistance measured across the Wheel Speed Sensor is infinite, the fault is due to an open condition internal to the Speed Sensor.

- IGNITION IN RUN
- ENTER DATA LIST
- MONITOR LEFT FRONT WHEEL SPEED WHILE GRADUALLY DECELERATING FROM 35 MPH TO 0 MPH ①

ERRATIC OR NO WHEEL SPEED OBSERVED

- DISCONNECT LEFT FRONT WHEEL SPEED SENSOR
- MEASURE RESISTANCE FROM TERMINAL A OF WHEEL SPEED SENSOR TO GROUND ②

INFINITE

- MEASURE RESISTANCE ACROSS TERMINALS A AND B OF WHEEL SPEED SENSOR ③

APPROX 1500-2000 OHMS

A CONTINUED

INFINITE

REPLACE WHEEL SPEED SENSOR

1 MEG OHM OR LESS

REPLACE WHEEL SPEED SENSOR

AT 25 MPH, APPROX 50 MPH OBSERVED.

REPLACE ANTILOCK BRAKE CONTROLLER

STEADY WHEEL SPEED OBSERVED THAT DECREASES AT A STEADY RATE AS THE WHEEL SLOW TO A STOP

FAULT IS NOT PRESENT. SEE NOTE ON INTERMITTENTS

CODE A049 – EXCESSIVE LEFT FRONT WHEEL ACCELERATION

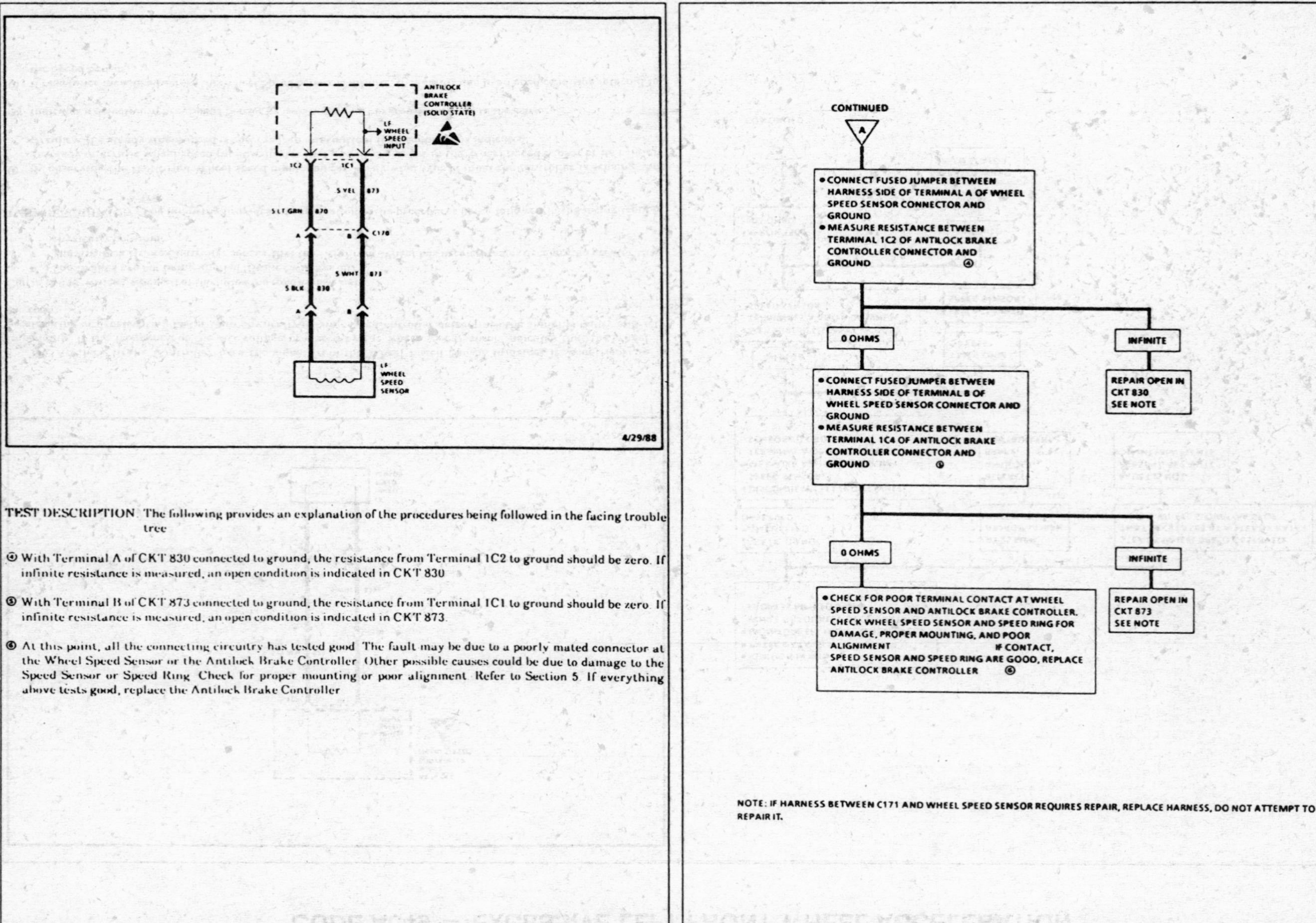
ANTILOCK BRAKE CONTROLLER (SOLID STATE)
LF WHEEL SPEED INPUT
1C2
1C1
5 YEL 873
5 LT GRN 870
C170
5 WHT 873
5 BLK 830
LF WHEEL SPEED SENSOR
4/29/88
CONTINUED
A
• CONNECT FUSED JUMPER BETWEEN HARNESS SIDE OF TERMINAL A OF WHEEL SPEED SENSOR CONNECTOR AND GROUND
• MEASURE RESISTANCE BETWEEN TERMINAL 1C2 OF ANTILOCK BRAKE CONTROLLER CONNECTOR AND GROUND ④
0 OHMS
INFINITE
REPAIR OPEN IN CKT 830 SEE NOTE
• CONNECT FUSED JUMPER BETWEEN HARNESS SIDE OF TERMINAL B OF WHEEL SPEED SENSOR CONNECTOR AND GROUND
• MEASURE RESISTANCE BETWEEN TERMINAL 1C4 OF ANTILOCK BRAKE CONTROLLER CONNECTOR AND GROUND ⑤
0 OHMS
INFINITE
REPAIR OPEN IN CKT 873 SEE NOTE
• CHECK FOR POOR TERMINAL CONTACT AT WHEEL SPEED SENSOR AND ANTILOCK BRAKE CONTROLLER. CHECK WHEEL SPEED SENSOR AND SPEED RING FOR DAMAGE, PROPER MOUNTING, AND POOR ALIGNMENT IF CONTACT, SPEED SENSOR AND SPEED RING ARE GOOD, REPLACE ANTILOCK BRAKE CONTROLLER ⑥
NOTE: IF HARNESS BETWEEN C171 AND WHEEL SPEED SENSOR REQUIRES REPAIR, REPLACE HARNESS, DO NOT ATTEMPT TO REPAIR IT.

TEST DESCRIPTION The following provides an explanation of the procedures being followed in the facing trouble tree

④ With Terminal A of CKT 830 connected to ground, the resistance from Terminal 1C2 to ground should be zero. If infinite resistance is measured, an open condition is indicated in CKT 830

⑤ With Terminal B of CKT 873 connected to ground, the resistance from Terminal 1C1 to ground should be zero. If infinite resistance is measured, an open condition is indicated in CKT 873.

⑥ At this point, all the connecting circuitry has tested good The fault may be due to a poorly mated connector at the Wheel Speed Sensor or the Antilock Brake Controller Other possible causes could be due to damage to the Speed Sensor or Speed Ring Check for proper mounting or poor alignment Refer to Section 5 If everything above tests good, replace the Antilock Brake Controller

CODE A050 – EXCESSIVE RIGHT REAR WHEEL ACCELERATION

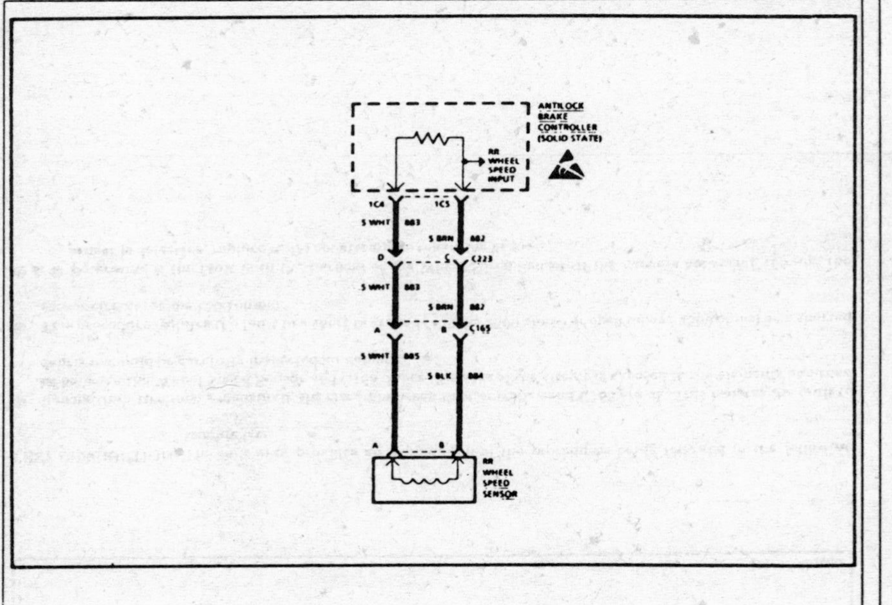
ANTILOCK BRAKE CONTROLLER (SOLID STATE)
RR WHEEL SPEED INPUT
1C4
1C5
5 WHT 883
5 BRN 882
D
C
C223
5 WHT 883
5 BRN 882
A
B
C165
5 WHT 885
5 BLK 884
A
B
RR WHEEL SPEED SENSOR

The Antilock Brake Controller uses the signal from the wheel speed sensor to detect if wheel lock-up is impending. If the frequency of the AC voltage produced by the wheel speed sensor indicates that the wheel is accelerating or decelerating faster than physically possible, the Controller determines the signal is faulty and sets the code.

CODE A050 will set when all of the following conditions exist:

- The Brakes are not being applied (Brake Switch is off)
- The Antilock Brake Controller senses that the Right Rear Wheel has accelerated or decelerated greater than physically possible.

TEST DESCRIPTION: The following provides an explanation of the procedures being followed in the trouble tree.

① Observation of erratic or no wheel speed input indicates the fault is present and is not intermittent.

②& ③ Step 2 determines if a short to battery is the fault. If battery voltage is measured, step 3 isolates the short to the harness or controller.

④ If 9000 to 15000 ohms is measured, the possibility of an open or short in the circuit between the Antilock Brake Controller and Connector C165 is eliminated

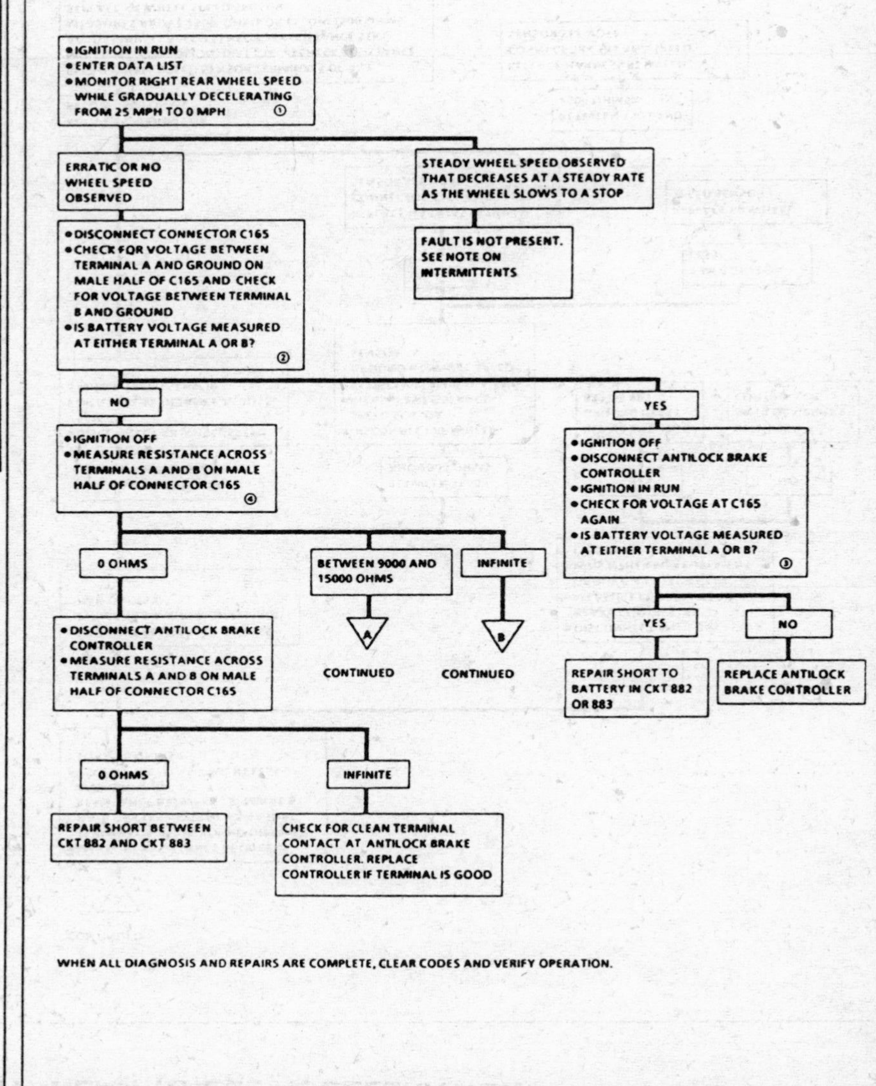
• IGNITION IN RUN
• ENTER DATA LIST
• MONITOR RIGHT REAR WHEEL SPEED WHILE GRADUALLY DECELERATING FROM 25 MPH TO 0 MPH ①
ERRATIC OR NO WHEEL SPEED OBSERVED
STEADY WHEEL SPEED OBSERVED THAT DECREASES AT A STEADY RATE AS THE WHEEL SLOWS TO A STOP
FAULT IS NOT PRESENT. SEE NOTE ON INTERMITTENTS
• DISCONNECT CONNECTOR C165
• CHECK FOR VOLTAGE BETWEEN TERMINAL A AND GROUND ON MALE HALF OF C165 AND CHECK FOR VOLTAGE BETWEEN TERMINAL B AND GROUND
• IS BATTERY VOLTAGE MEASURED AT EITHER TERMINAL A OR B? ②
NO
YES
• IGNITION OFF
• MEASURE RESISTANCE ACROSS TERMINALS A AND B ON MALE HALF OF CONNECTOR C165 ④
• IGNITION OFF
• DISCONNECT ANTILOCK BRAKE CONTROLLER
• IGNITION IN RUN
• CHECK FOR VOLTAGE AT C165 AGAIN
• IS BATTERY VOLTAGE MEASURED AT EITHER TERMINAL A OR B? ③
0 OHMS
BETWEEN 9000 AND 15000 OHMS
INFINITE
A
CONTINUED
B
CONTINUED
YES
NO
REPAIR SHORT TO BATTERY IN CKT 882 OR 883
REPLACE ANTILOCK BRAKE CONTROLLER
• DISCONNECT ANTILOCK BRAKE CONTROLLER
• MEASURE RESISTANCE ACROSS TERMINALS A AND B ON MALE HALF OF CONNECTOR C165
0 OHMS
INFINITE
REPAIR SHORT BETWEEN CKT 882 AND CKT 883
CHECK FOR CLEAN TERMINAL CONTACT AT ANTILOCK BRAKE CONTROLLER. REPLACE CONTROLLER IF TERMINAL IS GOOD
WHEN ALL DIAGNOSIS AND REPAIRS ARE COMPLETE, CLEAR CODES AND VERIFY OPERATION.

CODE A050 – EXCESSIVE RIGHT REAR WHEEL ACCELERATION

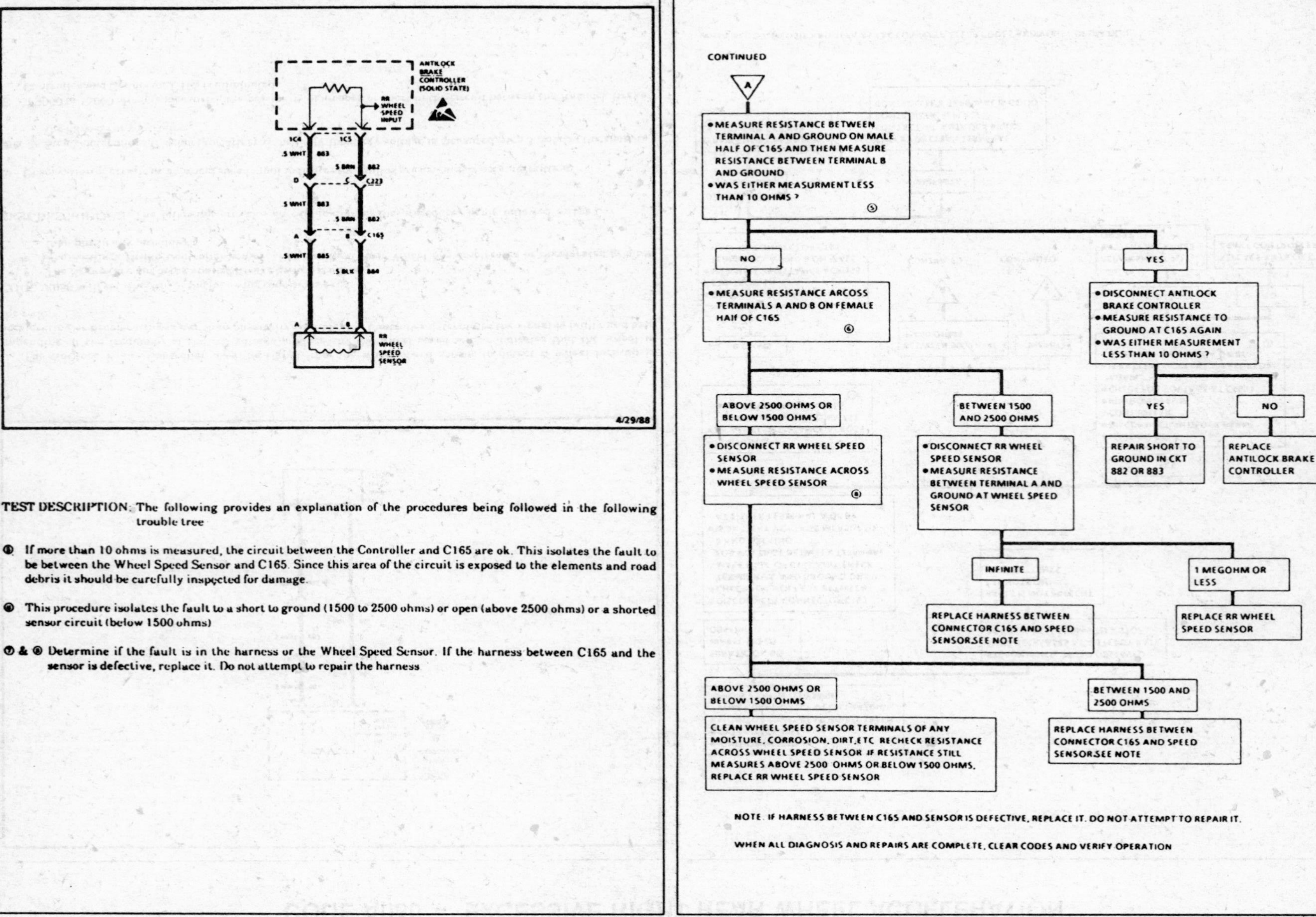

ANTILOCK BRAKE CONTROLLER (SOLID STATE)
RR WHEEL SPEED INPUT
1C4
1C5
.5 WHT 883
.5 BRN 882
D
C
C223
.5 WHT 883
.5 BRN 882
A
B
C165
.5 WHT 885
.5 BLK 884
A
B
RR WHEEL SPEED SENSOR
4/29/88
CONTINUED
A
• MEASURE RESISTANCE BETWEEN TERMINAL A AND GROUND ON MALE HALF OF C165 AND THEN MEASURE RESISTANCE BETWEEN TERMINAL B AND GROUND
• WAS EITHER MEASURMENT LESS THAN 10 OHMS ? ⑤
NO
YES
• MEASURE RESISTANCE ARCOSS TERMINALS A AND B ON FEMALE HAlf OF C165 ⑥
• DISCONNECT ANTILOCK BRAKE CONTROLLER
• MEASURE RESISTANCE TO GROUND AT C165 AGAIN
• WAS EITHER MEASUREMENT LESS THAN 10 OHMS ?
ABOVE 2500 OHMS OR BELOW 1500 OHMS
BETWEEN 1500 AND 2500 OHMS
YES
NO
• DISCONNECT RR WHEEL SPEED SENSOR
• MEASURE RESISTANCE ACROSS WHEEL SPEED SENSOR ⑧
• DISCONNECT RR WHEEL SPEED SENSOR
• MEASURE RESISTANCE BETWEEN TERMINAL A AND GROUND AT WHEEL SPEED SENSOR
REPAIR SHORT TO GROUND IN CKT 882 OR 883
REPLACE ANTILOCK BRAKE CONTROLLER
INFINITE
1 MEGOHM OR LESS
REPLACE HARNESS BETWEEN CONNECTOR C165 AND SPEED SENSOR.SEE NOTE
REPLACE RR WHEEL SPEED SENSOR
ABOVE 2500 OHMS OR BELOW 1500 OHMS
BETWEEN 1500 AND 2500 OHMS
CLEAN WHEEL SPEED SENSOR TERMINALS OF ANY MOISTURE, CORROSION, DIRT,ETC RECHECK RESISTANCE ACROSS WHEEL SPEED SENSOR IF RESISTANCE STILL MEASURES ABOVE 2500 OHMS OR BELOW 1500 OHMS, REPLACE RR WHEEL SPEED SENSOR
REPLACE HARNESS BETWEEN CONNECTOR C165 AND SPEED SENSOR.SEE NOTE
NOTE: IF HARNESS BETWEEN C165 AND SENSOR IS DEFECTIVE, REPLACE IT. DO NOT ATTEMPT TO REPAIR IT.
WHEN ALL DIAGNOSIS AND REPAIRS ARE COMPLETE, CLEAR CODES AND VERIFY OPERATION

TEST DESCRIPTION: The following provides an explanation of the procedures being followed in the following trouble tree

⑤ If more than 10 ohms is measured, the circuit between the Controller and C165 are ok. This isolates the fault to be between the Wheel Speed Sensor and C165. Since this area of the circuit is exposed to the elements and road debris it should be carefully inspected for damage.

⑥ This procedure isolates the fault to a short to ground (1500 to 2500 ohms) or open (above 2500 ohms) or a shorted sensor circuit (below 1500 ohms)

⑦ & ⑧ Determine if the fault is in the harness or the Wheel Speed Sensor. If the harness between C165 and the sensor is defective, replace it. Do not attempt to repair the harness

CODE A050 — EXCESSIVE RIGHT REAR WHEEL ACCELERATION

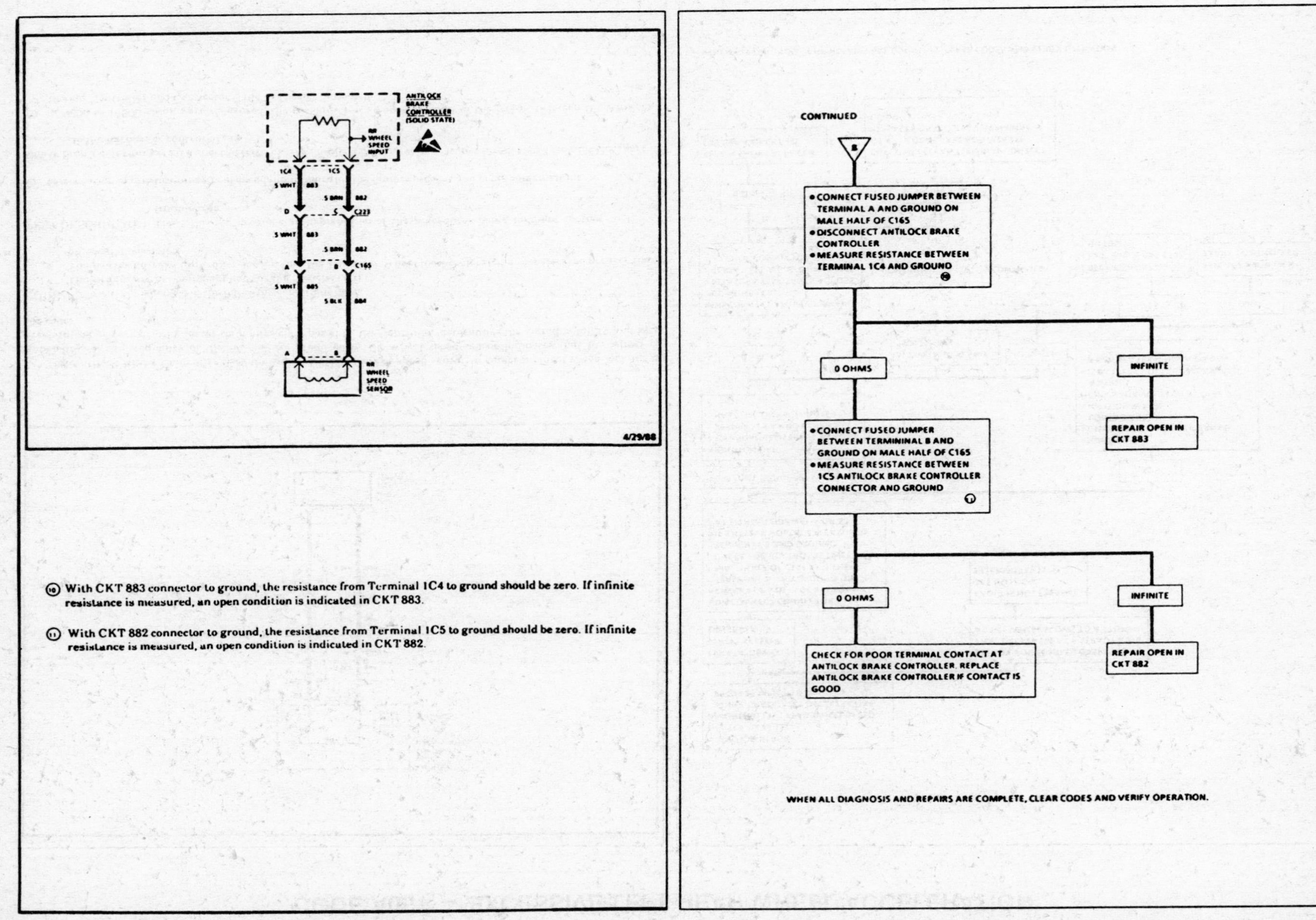
ANTILOCK BRAKE CONTROLLER (SOLID STATE)
RR WHEEL SPEED INPUT
1C4
1C5
5 WHT 883
5 BRN 882
C223
C165
5 WHT 885
5 BLK 884
RR WHEEL SPEED SENSOR
4/29/88
CONTINUED
B
• CONNECT FUSED JUMPER BETWEEN TERMINAL A AND GROUND ON MALE HALF OF C165
• DISCONNECT ANTILOCK BRAKE CONTROLLER
• MEASURE RESISTANCE BETWEEN TERMINAL 1C4 AND GROUND (10)
0 OHMS
INFINITE
REPAIR OPEN IN CKT 883
• CONNECT FUSED JUMPER BETWEEN TERMININAL B AND GROUND ON MALE HALF OF C165
• MEASURE RESISTANCE BETWEEN 1C5 ANTILOCK BRAKE CONTROLLER CONNECTOR AND GROUND (11)
0 OHMS
INFINITE
REPAIR OPEN IN CKT 882
CHECK FOR POOR TERMINAL CONTACT AT ANTILOCK BRAKE CONTROLLER. REPLACE ANTILOCK BRAKE CONTROLLER IF CONTACT IS GOOD
WHEN ALL DIAGNOSIS AND REPAIRS ARE COMPLETE, CLEAR CODES AND VERIFY OPERATION.

(10) With CKT 883 connector to ground, the resistance from Terminal 1C4 to ground should be zero. If infinite resistance is measured, an open condition is indicated in CKT 883.

(11) With CKT 882 connector to ground, the resistance from Terminal 1C5 to ground should be zero. If infinite resistance is measured, an open condition is indicated in CKT 882.

CODE A051 — EXCESSIVE LEFT REAR WHEEL ACCELERATION

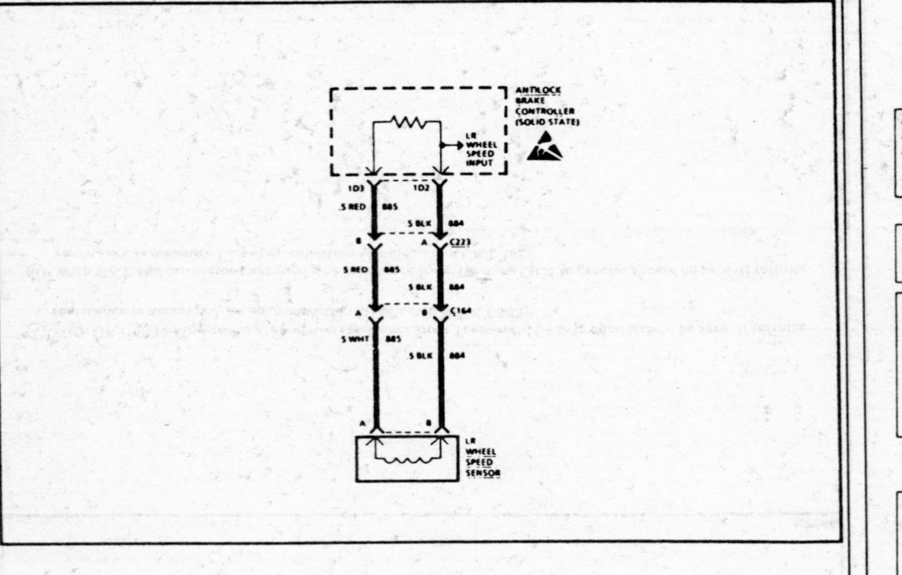
ANTILOCK BRAKE CONTROLLER (SOLID STATE)
LR WHEEL SPEED INPUT
1D3
1D2
.5 RED
885
.5 BLK
884
B
A
C223
.5 RED
885
.5 BLK
884
A
B
C164
.5 WHT
885
.5 BLK
884
A
B
LR WHEEL SPEED SENSOR

The Antilock Brake Controller uses the signal from the wheel speed sensor to detect if wheel speed lock-up is impending. If the frequency of the AC voltage produced by the wheel speed sensor indicates that the wheel is accelerating or decelerating faster than physically possible, the Controller determines the signal is faulty and sets the code.

CODE A051 will set when all of the following conditions exist:

- The Brakes are not being applied (Brake Switch is off).
- The Antilock Brake Controller senses that the Left Rear Wheel has accelerated or decelerated greater than physically possible.

TEST DESCRIPTION: The following provides an explanation of the procedures being followed in the trouble tree.

① Observation of erratic or no wheel speed input indicates the fault is present and is not intermettent.

②&③ Step 2 determines is if a short to Battery is the fault. If Battery voltage is measured, step 3 isolates the short to the harness or controller.

④ If 9000 to 15000 ohms were measured, the possibility of an open or short in the circuit between the Antilock Brakes Controller and Connector C164 has been eliminated.

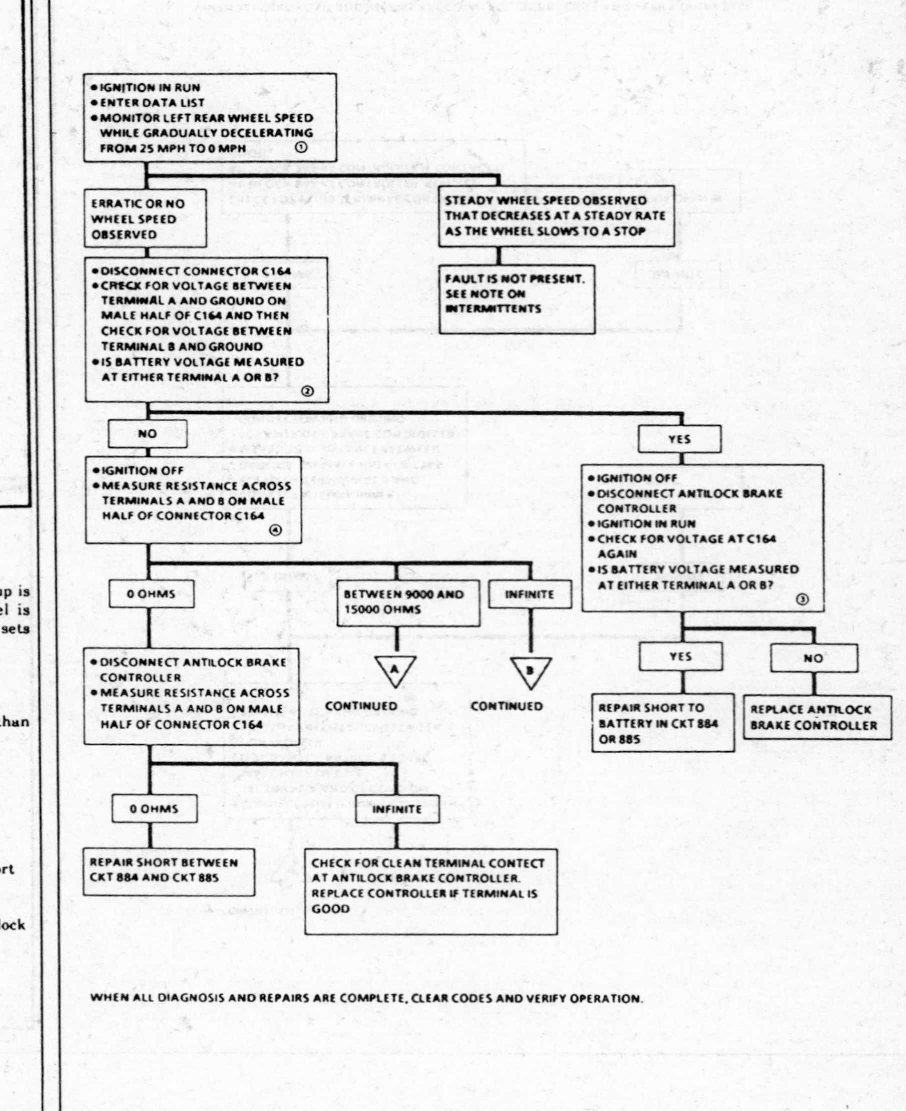
• IGNITION IN RUN
• ENTER DATA LIST
• MONITOR LEFT REAR WHEEL SPEED WHILE GRADUALLY DECELERATING FROM 25 MPH TO 0 MPH ①
ERRATIC OR NO WHEEL SPEED OBSERVED
STEADY WHEEL SPEED OBSERVED THAT DECREASES AT A STEADY RATE AS THE WHEEL SLOWS TO A STOP
FAULT IS NOT PRESENT. SEE NOTE ON INTERMITTENTS
• DISCONNECT CONNECTOR C164
• CHECK FOR VOLTAGE BETWEEN TERMINAL A AND GROUND ON MALE HALF OF C164 AND THEN CHECK FOR VOLTAGE BETWEEN TERMINAL B AND GROUND
• IS BATTERY VOLTAGE MEASURED AT EITHER TERMINAL A OR B? ②
NO
YES
• IGNITION OFF
• MEASURE RESISTANCE ACROSS TERMINALS A AND B ON MALE HALF OF CONNECTOR C164 ④
• IGNITION OFF
• DISCONNECT ANTILOCK BRAKE CONTROLLER
• IGNITION IN RUN
• CHECK FOR VOLTAGE AT C164 AGAIN
• IS BATTERY VOLTAGE MEASURED AT EITHER TERMINAL A OR B? ③
0 OHMS
BETWEEN 9000 AND 15000 OHMS
INFINITE
A
B
CONTINUED
CONTINUED
YES
NO
REPAIR SHORT TO BATTERY IN CKT 884 OR 885
REPLACE ANTILOCK BRAKE CONTROLLER
• DISCONNECT ANTILOCK BRAKE CONTROLLER
• MEASURE RESISTANCE ACROSS TERMINALS A AND B ON MALE HALF OF CONNECTOR C164
0 OHMS
INFINITE
REPAIR SHORT BETWEEN CKT 884 AND CKT 885
CHECK FOR CLEAN TERMINAL CONTECT AT ANTILOCK BRAKE CONTROLLER. REPLACE CONTROLLER IF TERMINAL IS GOOD
WHEN ALL DIAGNOSIS AND REPAIRS ARE COMPLETE, CLEAR CODES AND VERIFY OPERATION.

CODE A051 — EXCESSIVE LEFT REAR WHEEL ACCELERATION

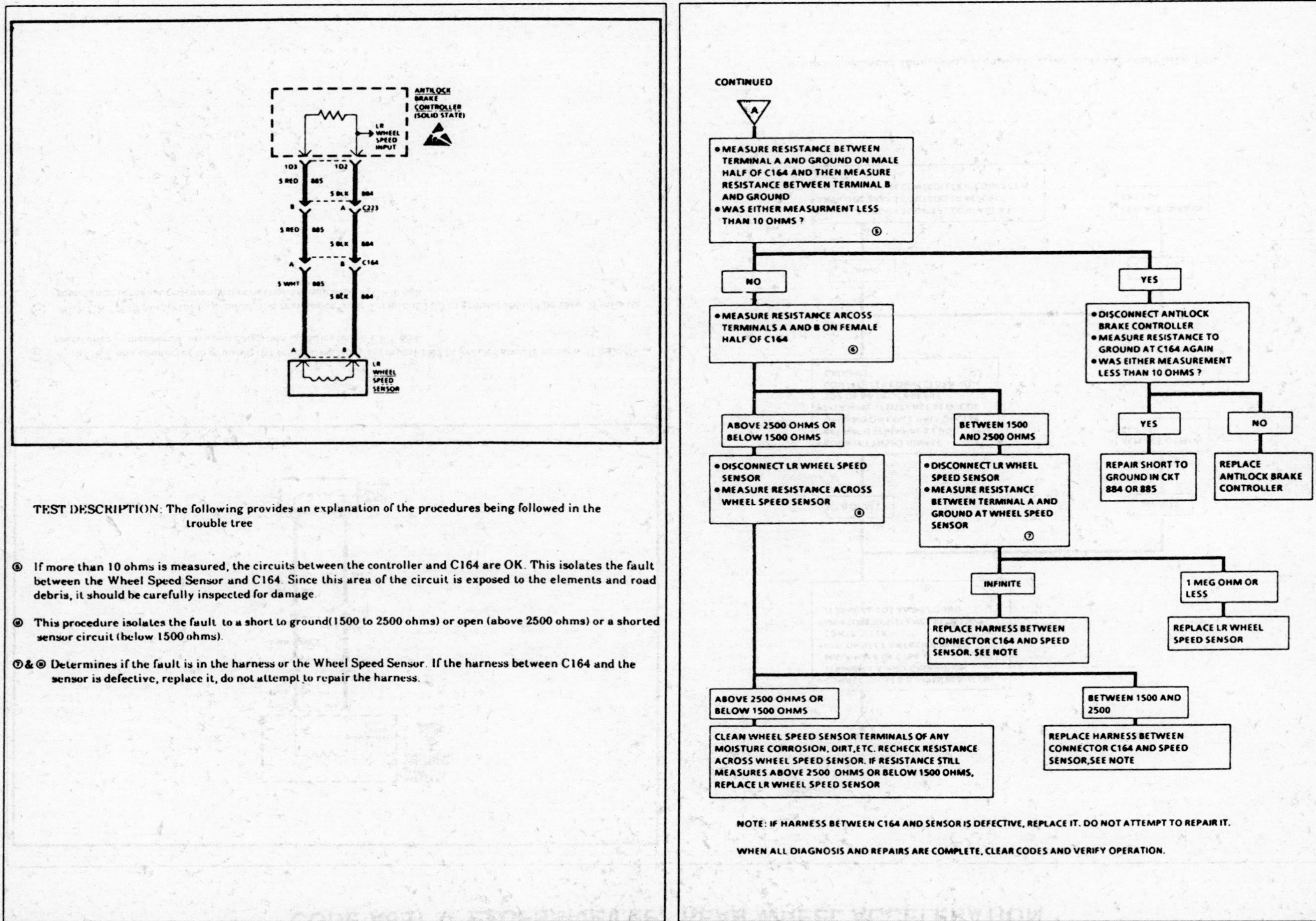
ANTILOCK BRAKE CONTROLLER (SOLID STATE)
LR WHEEL SPEED INPUT
103
102
5 RED
885
5 BLK
884
B
A
C223
5 RED
885
5 BLK
884
A
B
C164
5 WHT
885
5 BLK
884
A
B
LR WHEEL SPEED SENSOR
CONTINUED
A
• MEASURE RESISTANCE BETWEEN TERMINAL A AND GROUND ON MALE HALF OF C164 AND THEN MEASURE RESISTANCE BETWEEN TERMINAL B AND GROUND
• WAS EITHER MEASURMENT LESS THAN 10 OHMS ? ⑤
NO
YES
• MEASURE RESISTANCE ARCOSS TERMINALS A AND B ON FEMALE HALF OF C164 ⑥
• DISCONNECT ANTILOCK BRAKE CONTROLLER
• MEASURE RESISTANCE TO GROUND AT C164 AGAIN
• WAS EITHER MEASUREMENT LESS THAN 10 OHMS ?
ABOVE 2500 OHMS OR BELOW 1500 OHMS
BETWEEN 1500 AND 2500 OHMS
YES
NO
• DISCONNECT LR WHEEL SPEED SENSOR
• MEASURE RESISTANCE ACROSS WHEEL SPEED SENSOR ⑧
• DISCONNECT LR WHEEL SPEED SENSOR
• MEASURE RESISTANCE BETWEEN TERMINAL A AND GROUND AT WHEEL SPEED SENSOR ⑦
REPAIR SHORT TO GROUND IN CKT 884 OR 885
REPLACE ANTILOCK BRAKE CONTROLLER
INFINITE
1 MEG OHM OR LESS
REPLACE HARNESS BETWEEN CONNECTOR C164 AND SPEED SENSOR. SEE NOTE
REPLACE LR WHEEL SPEED SENSOR
ABOVE 2500 OHMS OR BELOW 1500 OHMS
BETWEEN 1500 AND 2500
CLEAN WHEEL SPEED SENSOR TERMINALS OF ANY MOISTURE CORROSION, DIRT, ETC. RECHECK RESISTANCE ACROSS WHEEL SPEED SENSOR. IF RESISTANCE STILL MEASURES ABOVE 2500 OHMS OR BELOW 1500 OHMS, REPLACE LR WHEEL SPEED SENSOR
REPLACE HARNESS BETWEEN CONNECTOR C164 AND SPEED SENSOR, SEE NOTE
NOTE: IF HARNESS BETWEEN C164 AND SENSOR IS DEFECTIVE, REPLACE IT. DO NOT ATTEMPT TO REPAIR IT.
WHEN ALL DIAGNOSIS AND REPAIRS ARE COMPLETE, CLEAR CODES AND VERIFY OPERATION.

TEST DESCRIPTION: The following provides an explanation of the procedures being followed in the trouble tree

⑤ If more than 10 ohms is measured, the circuits between the controller and C164 are OK. This isolates the fault between the Wheel Speed Sensor and C164. Since this area of the circuit is exposed to the elements and road debris, it should be carefully inspected for damage.

⑥ This procedure isolates the fault to a short to ground(1500 to 2500 ohms) or open (above 2500 ohms) or a shorted sensor circuit (below 1500 ohms).

⑦& ⑧ Determines if the fault is in the harness or the Wheel Speed Sensor. If the harness between C164 and the sensor is defective, replace it, do not attempt to repair the harness.

CODE A051 – EXCESSIVE LEFT REAR WHEEL ACCELERATION

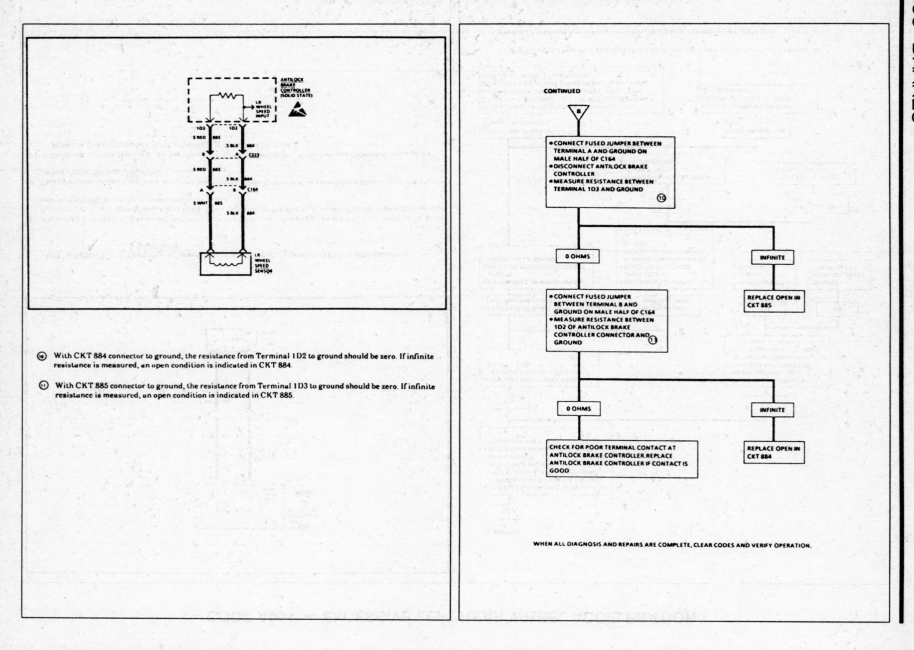

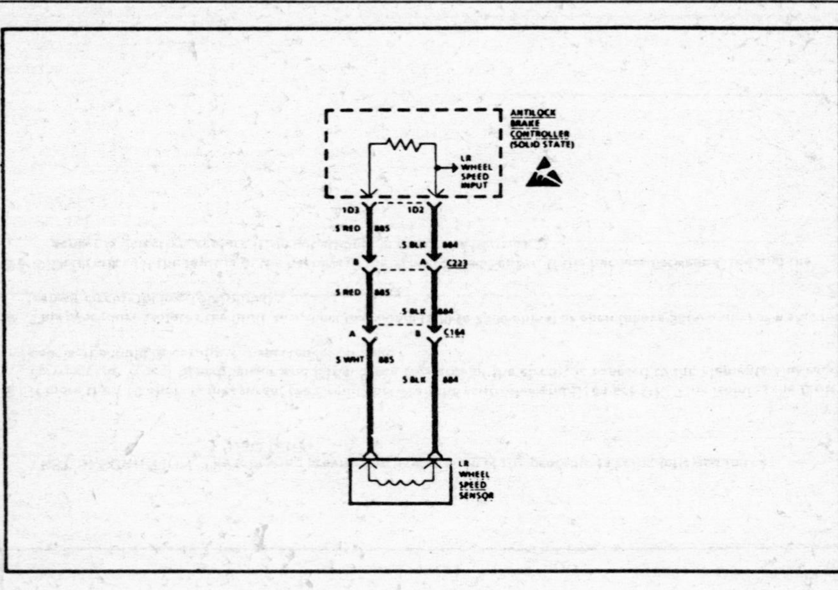

(10) With CKT 884 connector to ground, the resistance from Terminal 1D2 to ground should be zero. If infinite resistance is measured, an open condition is indicated in CKT 884.

(11) With CKT 885 connector to ground, the resistance from Terminal 1D3 to ground should be zero. If infinite resistance is measured, an open condition is indicated in CKT 885.

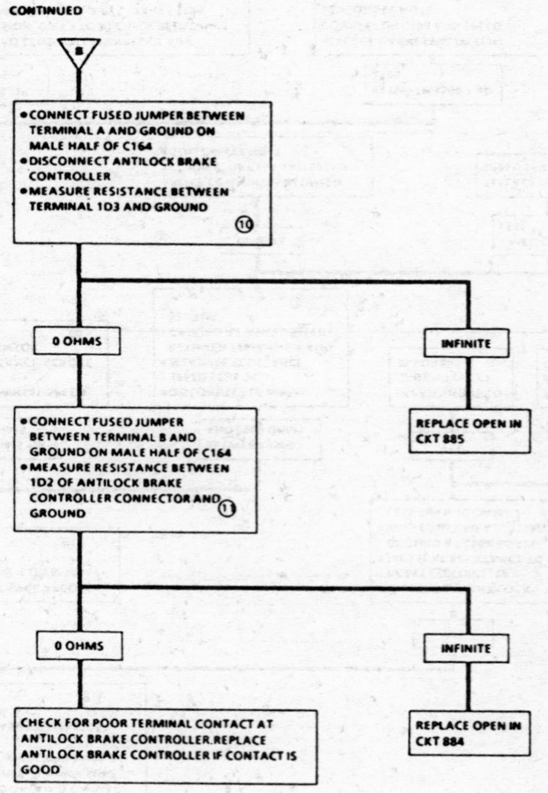

CONTINUED

B

- CONNECT FUSED JUMPER BETWEEN TERMINAL A AND GROUND ON MALE HALF OF C164
- DISCONNECT ANTILOCK BRAKE CONTROLLER
- MEASURE RESISTANCE BETWEEN TERMINAL 1D3 AND GROUND (10)

INFINITE → REPLACE OPEN IN CKT 885

0 OHMS →

- CONNECT FUSED JUMPER BETWEEN TERMINAL B AND GROUND ON MALE HALF OF C164
- MEASURE RESISTANCE BETWEEN 1D2 OF ANTILOCK BRAKE CONTROLLER CONNECTOR AND GROUND (11)

INFINITE → REPLACE OPEN IN CKT 884

0 OHMS → CHECK FOR POOR TERMINAL CONTACT AT ANTILOCK BRAKE CONTROLLER. REPLACE ANTILOCK BRAKE CONTROLLER IF CONTACT IS GOOD

WHEN ALL DIAGNOSIS AND REPAIRS ARE COMPLETE, CLEAR CODES AND VERIFY OPERATION.

CODES A052, A055 or A060 – INTERNAL CONTROLLER FAILURE

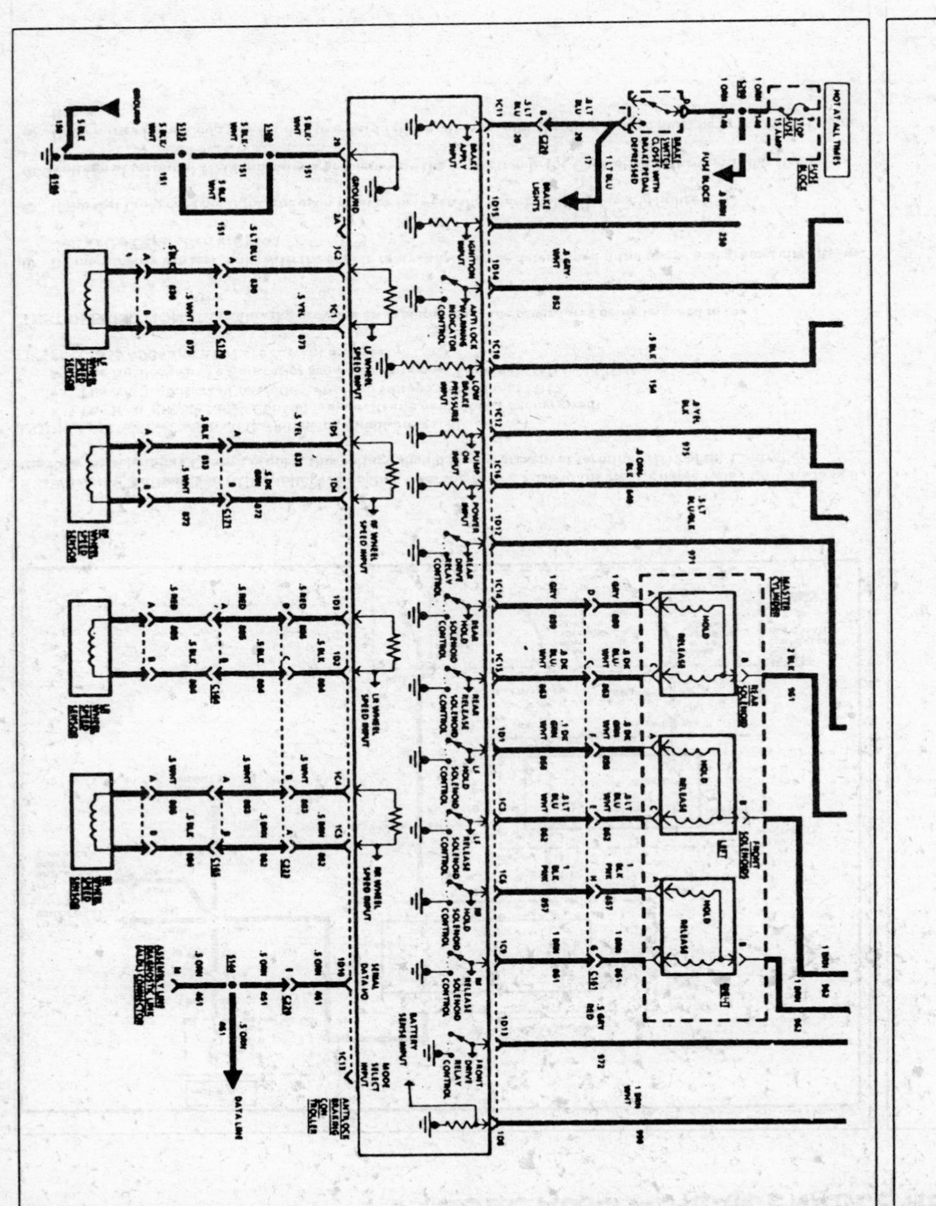

CODE A052

Antilock Brake Controller Calibration Error

CODE A052	will set when the Antilock Brake Controller detects a malfunction internal to itself. If this code is set, replace the Antilock Brake Controller.

CODE A055

Antilock Brake Controller internal voltage fault

CODE A055	will set when the Antilock Brake Controller detects a malfunction internal to itself. If this code is set, replace the Antilock Brake Controller.

CODE A060

Antilock Brake Controller internal fault

CODE A060	will set when the Antilock Brake Controller detects a malfunction internal to itself. If this code is set, replace the Antilock Brake Controller.

CODE A054 – REAR ENABLE RELAY COIL CIRCUIT OPEN

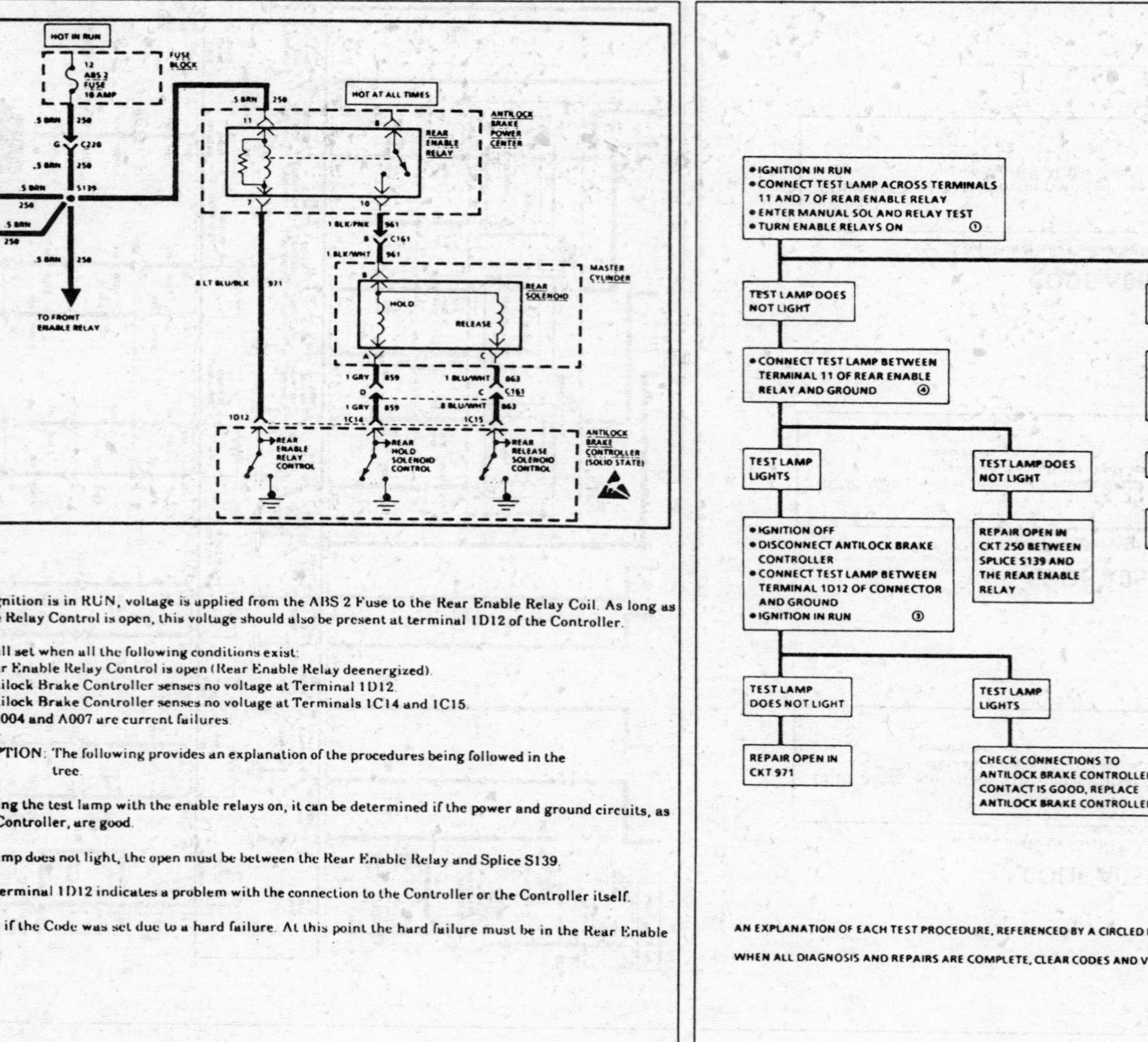

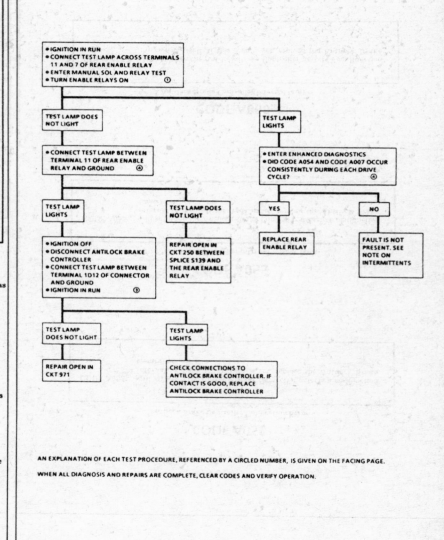

When the ignition is in RUN, voltage is applied from the ABS 2 Fuse to the Rear Enable Relay Coil. As long as the Rear Enable Relay Control is open, this voltage should also be present at terminal 1D12 of the Controller.

CODE A054 will set when all the following conditions exist:

- The Rear Enable Relay Control is open (Rear Enable Relay deenergized).
- The Antilock Brake Controller senses no voltage at Terminal 1D12.
- The Antilock Brake Controller senses no voltage at Terminals 1C14 and 1C15.
- Codes A004 and A007 are current failures.

TEST DESCRIPTION: The following provides an explanation of the procedures being followed in the tree.

① By monitoring the test lamp with the enable relays on, it can be determined if the power and ground circuits, as well as the Controller, are good.

② If the test lamp does not light, the open must be between the Rear Enable Relay and Splice S139.

③ Voltage at terminal 1D12 indicates a problem with the connection to the Controller or the Controller itself.

④ Determines if the Code was set due to a hard failure. At this point the hard failure must be in the Rear Enable Relay.

CODE A056 – OPEN BRAKE SWTICH OR HYDRAULIC LEAK

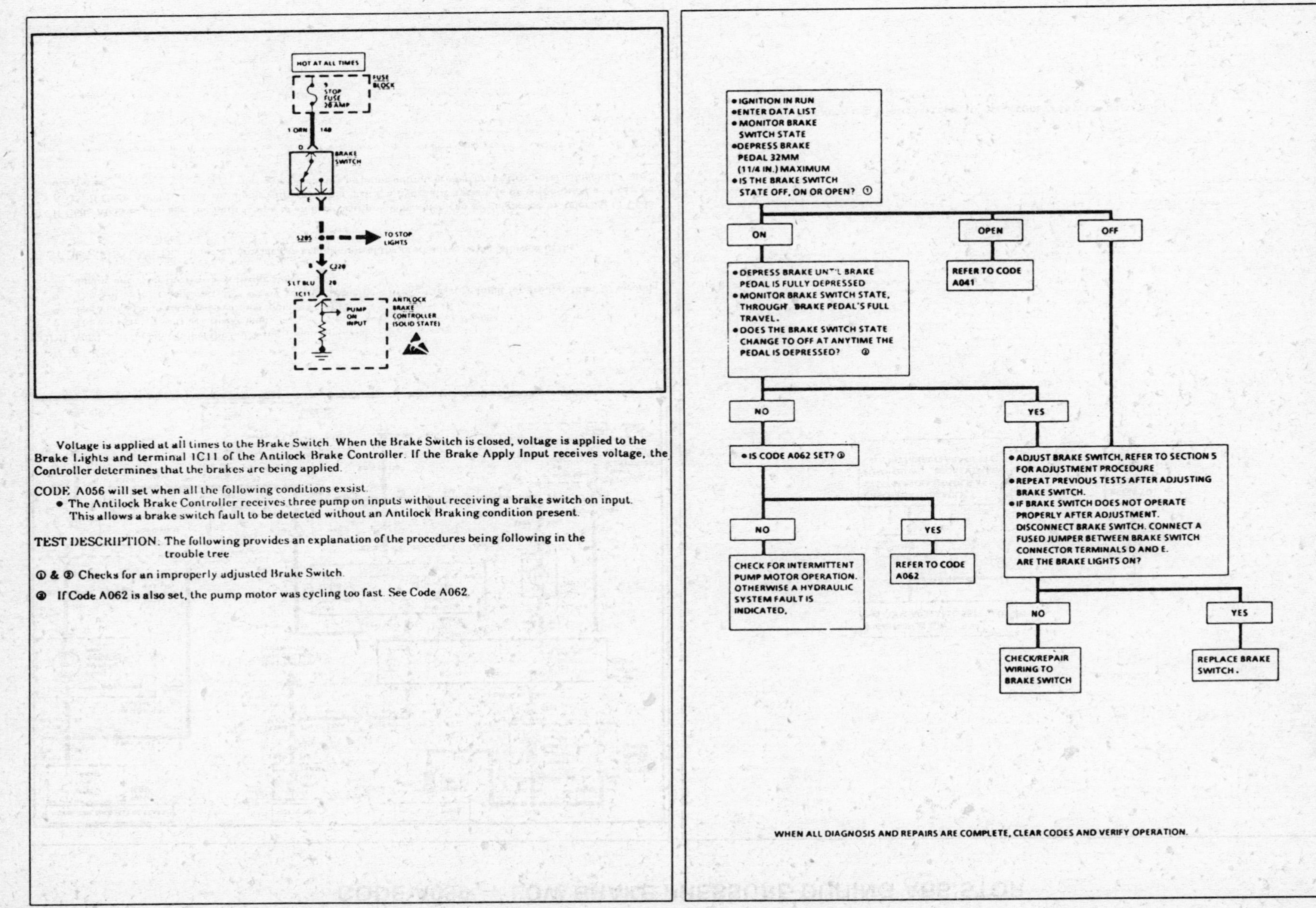
HOT AT ALL TIMES
FUSE BLOCK
9
STOP FUSE 20 AMP
1 ORN
140
D
BRAKE SWITCH
E
S205
TO STOP LIGHTS
B
C220
.5 LT BLU
20
1C11
PUMP ON INPUT
ANTILOCK BRAKE CONTROLLER (SOLID STATE)
• IGNITION IN RUN
• ENTER DATA LIST
• MONITOR BRAKE SWITCH STATE
• DEPRESS BRAKE PEDAL 32MM (11/4 IN.) MAXIMUM
• IS THE BRAKE SWITCH STATE OFF, ON OR OPEN? ①
ON
OPEN
OFF
REFER TO CODE A041
• DEPRESS BRAKE UNTIL BRAKE PEDAL IS FULLY DEPRESSED
• MONITOR BRAKE SWITCH STATE, THROUGH BRAKE PEDAL'S FULL TRAVEL.
• DOES THE BRAKE SWITCH STATE CHANGE TO OFF AT ANYTIME THE PEDAL IS DEPRESSED? ②
NO
YES
• IS CODE A062 SET? ③
NO
YES
CHECK FOR INTERMITTENT PUMP MOTOR OPERATION. OTHERWISE A HYDRAULIC SYSTEM FAULT IS INDICATED.
REFER TO CODE A062
• ADJUST BRAKE SWITCH, REFER TO SECTION 5 FOR ADJUSTMENT PROCEDURE
• REPEAT PREVIOUS TESTS AFTER ADJUSTING BRAKE SWITCH.
• IF BRAKE SWITCH DOES NOT OPERATE PROPERLY AFTER ADJUSTMENT. DISCONNECT BRAKE SWITCH. CONNECT A FUSED JUMPER BETWEEN BRAKE SWITCH CONNECTOR TERMINALS D AND E. ARE THE BRAKE LIGHTS ON?
NO
YES
CHECK/REPAIR WIRING TO BRAKE SWITCH
REPLACE BRAKE SWITCH.
WHEN ALL DIAGNOSIS AND REPAIRS ARE COMPLETE, CLEAR CODES AND VERIFY OPERATION.

Voltage is applied at all times to the Brake Switch. When the Brake Switch is closed, voltage is applied to the Brake Lights and terminal 1C11 of the Antilock Brake Controller. If the Brake Apply Input receives voltage, the Controller determines that the brakes are being applied.

CODE A056 will set when all the following conditions exsist.

- The Antilock Brake Controller receives three pump on inputs without receiving a brake switch on input. This allows a brake switch fault to be detected without an Antilock Braking condition present.

TEST DESCRIPTION: The following provides an explanation of the procedures being following in the trouble tree

① & ② Checks for an improperly adjusted Brake Switch.

③ If Code A062 is also set, the pump motor was cycling too fast. See Code A062.

CODE A059 – LOW BRAKE PRESSURE DURING ABS STOP

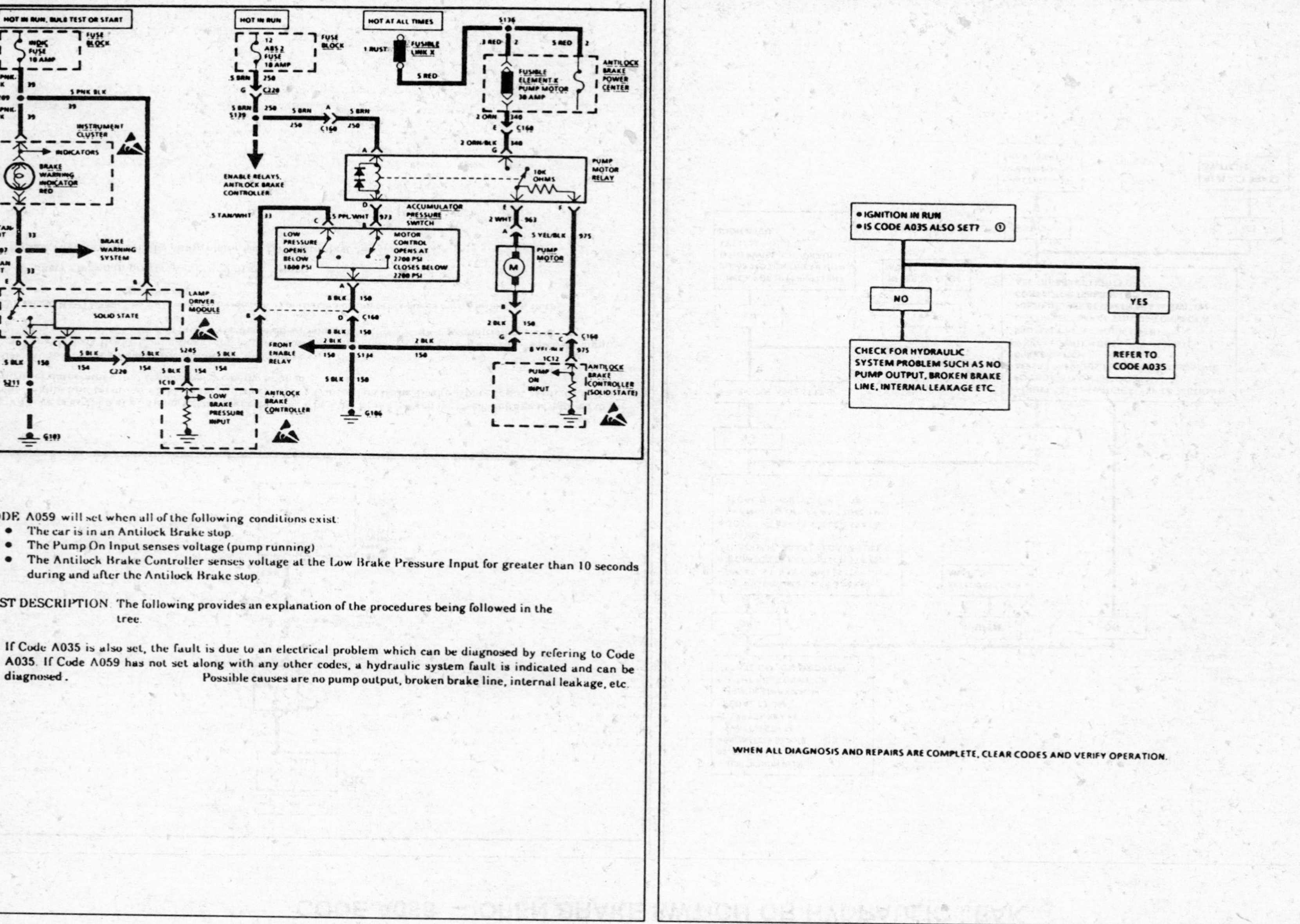

CODE A059 will set when all of the following conditions exist:

- The car is in an Antilock Brake stop.
- The Pump On Input senses voltage (pump running).
- The Antilock Brake Controller senses voltage at the Low Brake Pressure Input for greater than 10 seconds during and after the Antilock Brake stop.

TEST DESCRIPTION: The following provides an explanation of the procedures being followed in the tree.

① If Code A035 is also set, the fault is due to an electrical problem which can be diagnosed by refering to Code A035. If Code A059 has not set along with any other codes, a hydraulic system fault is indicated and can be diagnosed. Possible causes are no pump output, broken brake line, internal leakage, etc.

CODE A062 — LOW ACCUMULATOR PRECHARGE

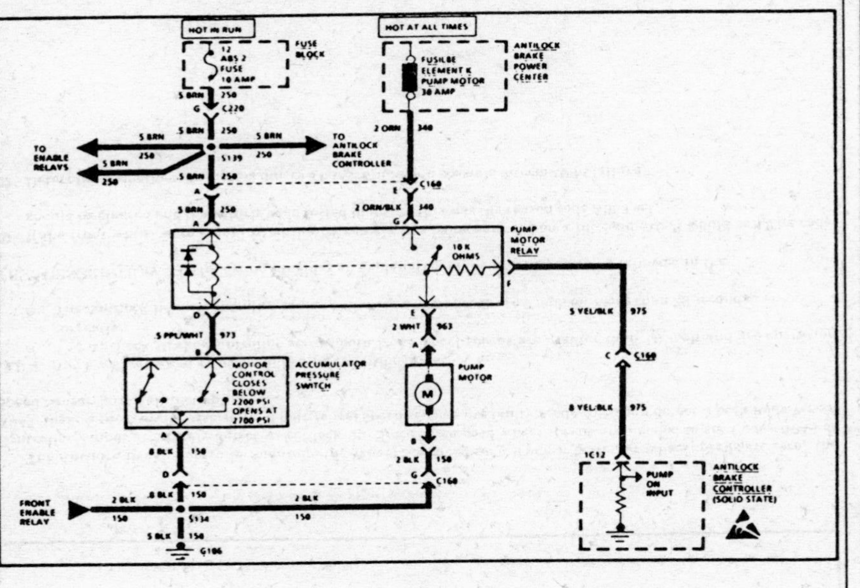

The Accumulator is precharged to approximately 1200 PSI with nitrogen gas. The Pump Motor maintains system pressure between 2200 PSI and approximately 2700 PSI. The Accumulator Switch Motor Control closes when the pressure drops below 2200 PSI. This grounds the Pump Motor Relay Coil causing voltage to be applied to the Pump Motor and Pump On Input. Whenever the Pump Motor is on, the Pump On Input will have voltage applied to it. The Pump Motor will run until system pressure is restored to approximately 2700 PSI.

CODE A062 will set when the Antilock Brake Controller detects short pump run times of less than 1.4 seconds in duration.

TEST DESCRIPTION: The following provides an explanation of the procedures being followed in the tree.

① If the pump run time from "OK pressure" to "pump off time" is less than six seconds a low accumulator precharge or poor accumulator switch point condition is indicated. Section 5 contains tests with a pressure gage which will isolate the problem further.

② If normal pump run cycle is less than 1.7 seconds a miscalibrated accumulator switch or low accumulator precharge is indicated. Section 5E contains tests with a pressure gage to check switch calibrations.

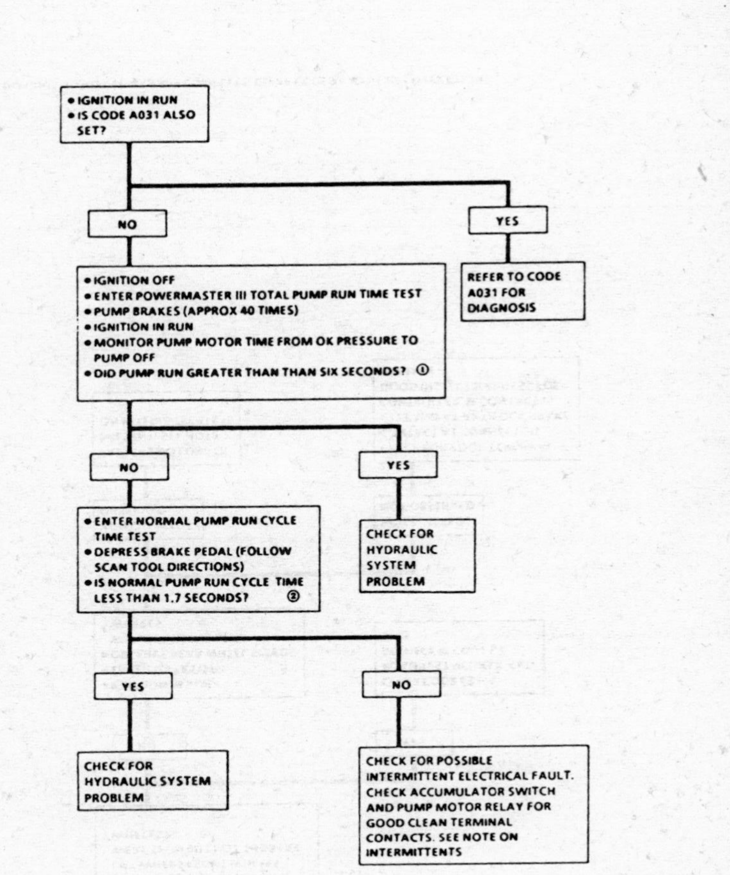

• IGNITION IN RUN
• IS CODE A031 ALSO SET?
NO
YES
REFER TO CODE A031 FOR DIAGNOSIS
• IGNITION OFF
• ENTER POWERMASTER III TOTAL PUMP RUN TIME TEST
• PUMP BRAKES (APPROX 40 TIMES)
• IGNITION IN RUN
• MONITOR PUMP MOTOR TIME FROM OK PRESSURE TO PUMP OFF
• DID PUMP RUN GREATER THAN THAN SIX SECONDS? ①
NO
YES
CHECK FOR HYDRAULIC SYSTEM PROBLEM
• ENTER NORMAL PUMP RUN CYCLE TIME TEST
• DEPRESS BRAKE PEDAL (FOLLOW SCAN TOOL DIRECTIONS)
• IS NORMAL PUMP RUN CYCLE TIME LESS THAN 1.7 SECONDS? ②
YES
NO
CHECK FOR HYDRAULIC SYSTEM PROBLEM
CHECK FOR POSSIBLE INTERMITTENT ELECTRICAL FAULT. CHECK ACCUMULATOR SWITCH AND PUMP MOTOR RELAY FOR GOOD CLEAN TERMINAL CONTACTS. SEE NOTE ON INTERMITTENTS

WHEN ALL DIAGNOSIS AND REPAIRS ARE COMPLETE, CLEAR CODES AND VERIFY OPERATION.

CODE A063 — BOTH REAR WHEEL SPEED SENSORS OPEN

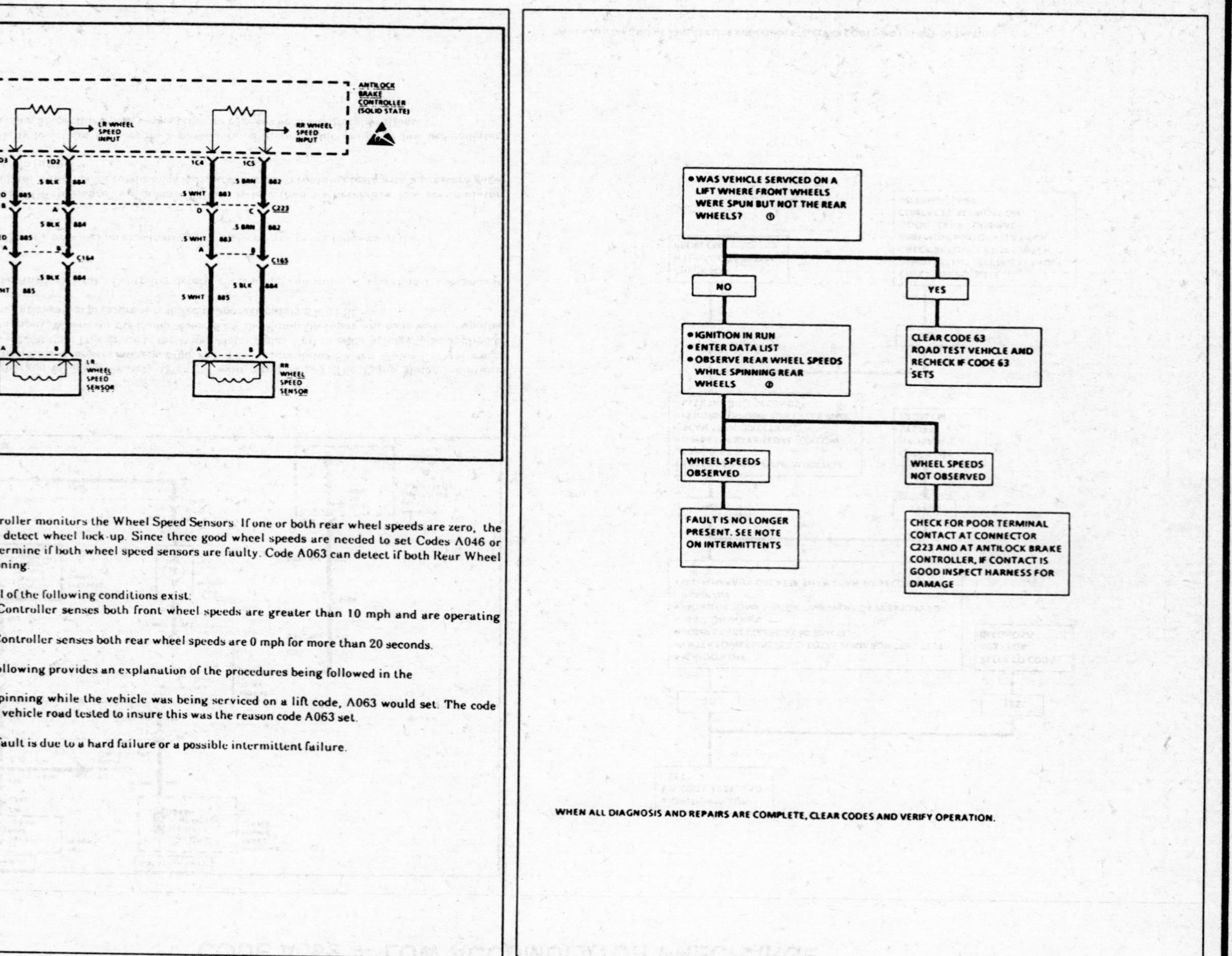

The Antilock Brake Controller monitors the Wheel Speed Sensors. If one or both rear wheel speeds are zero, the Controller cannot accurately detect wheel lock-up. Since three good wheel speeds are needed to set Codes A046 or A047, these Codes cannot determine if both wheel speed sensors are faulty. Code A063 can detect if both Rear Wheel Speed Sensors are malfunctioning.

CODE A063 will set when all of the following conditions exist:

- The Antilock Brake Controller senses both front wheel speeds are greater than 10 mph and are operating correctly.
- The Antilock Brake Controller senses both rear wheel speeds are 0 mph for more than 20 seconds.

TEST DESCRIPTION. The following provides an explanation of the procedures being followed in the tree.

① If the front wheel were spinning while the vehicle was being serviced on a lift code, A063 would set. The code should be cleared and the vehicle road tested to insure this was the reason code A063 set.

② Determines whether the fault is due to a hard failure or a possible intermittent failure.

Troubleshooting the Brake System

Problem	Cause	Solution
Low brake pedal (excessive pedal travel required for braking action.)	• Excessive clearance between rear linings and drums caused by inoperative automatic adjusters	• Make 10 to 15 alternate forward and reverse brake stops to adjust brakes. If brake pedal does not come up, repair or replace adjuster parts as necessary.
	• Worn rear brakelining	• Inspect and replace lining if worn beyond minimum thickness specification
	• Bent, distorted brakeshoes, front or rear	• Replace brakeshoes in axle sets
	• Air in hydraulic system	• Remove air from system. Refer to Brake Bleeding.
Low brake pedal (pedal may go to floor with steady pressure applied.)	• Fluid leak in hydraulic system	• Fill master cylinder to fill line; have helper apply brakes and check calipers, wheel cylinders, differential valve tubes, hoses and fittings for leaks. Repair or replace as necessary.
	• Air in hydraulic system	• Remove air from system. Refer to Brake Bleeding.
	• Incorrect or non-recommended brake fluid (fluid evaporates at below normal temp).	• Flush hydraulic system with clean brake fluid. Refill with correct-type fluid.
	• Master cylinder piston seals worn, or master cylinder bore is scored, worn or corroded	• Repair or replace master cylinder
Low brake pedal (pedal goes to floor on first application—o.k. on subsequent applications.)	• Disc brake pads sticking on abutment surfaces of anchor plate. Caused by a build-up of dirt, rust, or corrosion on abutment surfaces	• Clean abutment surfaces
Fading brake pedal (pedal height decreases with steady pressure applied.)	• Fluid leak in hydraulic system	• Fill master cylinder reservoirs to fill mark, have helper apply brakes, check calipers, wheel cylinders, differential valve, tubes, hoses, and fittings for fluid leaks. Repair or replace parts as necessary.
	• Master cylinder piston seals worn, or master cylinder bore is scored, worn or corroded	• Repair or replace master cylinder
Spongy brake pedal (pedal has abnormally soft, springy, spongy feel when depressed.)	• Air in hydraulic system	• Remove air from system. Refer to Brake Bleeding.
	• Brakeshoes bent or distorted	• Replace brakeshoes
	• Brakelining not yet seated with drums and rotors	• Burnish brakes
	• Rear drum brakes not properly adjusted	• Adjust brakes

Troubleshooting the Brake System (cont.)

Problem	Cause	Solution
Decreasing brake pedal travel (pedal travel required for braking action decreases and may be accompanied by a hard pedal.)	• Caliper or wheel cylinder pistons sticking or seized	• Repair or replace the calipers, or wheel cylinders
	• Master cylinder compensator ports blocked (preventing fluid return to reservoirs) or pistons sticking or seized in master cylinder bore	• Repair or replace the master cylinder
	• Power brake unit binding internally	• Test unit according to the following procedure: (a) Shift transmission into neutral and start engine (b) Increase engine speed to 1500 rpm, close throttle and fully depress brake pedal (c) Slow release brake pedal and stop engine (d) Have helper remove vacuum check valve and hose from power unit. Observe for backward movement of brake pedal. (e) If the pedal moves backward, the power unit has an internal bind—replace power unit
Grabbing brakes (severe reaction to brake pedal pressure.)	• Brakelining(s) contaminated by grease or brake fluid	• Determine and correct cause of contamination and replace brakeshoes in axle sets
	• Parking brake cables incorrectly adjusted or seized	• Adjust cables. Replace seized cables.
	• Incorrect brakelining or lining loose on brakeshoes	• Replace brakeshoes in axle sets
	• Caliper anchor plate bolts loose	• Tighten bolts
	• Rear brakeshoes binding on support plate ledges	• Clean and lubricate ledges. Replace support plate(s) if ledges are deeply grooved. Do not attempt to smooth ledges by grinding.
	• Incorrect or missing power brake reaction disc	• Install correct disc
	• Rear brake support plates loose	• Tighten mounting bolts
Chatter or shudder when brakes are applied (pedal pulsation and roughness may also occur.)	• Brakeshoes distorted, bent, contaminated, or worn	• Replace brakeshoes in axle sets
	• Caliper anchor plate or support plate loose	• Tighten mounting bolts
	• Excessive thickness variation of rotor(s)	• Refinish or replace rotors in axle sets
Noisy brakes (squealing, clicking, scraping sound when brakes are applied.)	• Bent, broken, distorted brakeshoes	• Replace brakeshoes in axle sets
	• Excessive rust on outer edge of rotor braking surface	• Remove rust

Troubleshooting the Brake System (cont.)

Problem	Cause	Solution
Hard brake pedal (excessive pedal pressure required to stop vehicle. May be accompanied by brake fade.)	• Loose or leaking power brake unit vacuum hose	• Tighten connections or replace leaking hose
	• Incorrect or poor quality brake-lining	• Replace with lining in axle sets
	• Bent, broken, distorted brakeshoes	• Replace brakeshoes
	• Calipers binding or dragging on mounting pins. Rear brakeshoes dragging on support plate.	• Replace mounting pins and bushings. Clean rust or burrs from rear brake support plate ledges and lubricate ledges with molydisulfide grease. **NOTE:** If ledges are deeply grooved or scored, do not attempt to sand or grind them smooth—replace support plate.
	• Caliper, wheel cylinder, or master cylinder pistons sticking or seized	• Repair or replace parts as necessary
	• Power brake unit vacuum check valve malfunction	• Test valve according to the following procedure: (a) Start engine, increase engine speed to 1500 rpm, close throttle and immediately stop engine (b) Wait at least 90 seconds then depress brake pedal (c) If brakes are not vacuum assisted for 2 or more applications, check valve is faulty
	• Power brake unit has internal bind	• Test unit according to the following procedure: (a) With engine stopped, apply brakes several times to exhaust all vacuum in system (b) Shift transmission into neutral, depress brake pedal and start engine (c) If pedal height decreases with foot pressure and less pressure is required to hold pedal in applied position, power unit vacuum system is operating normally. Test power unit. If power unit exhibits a bind condition, replace the power unit.
Hard brake pedal (excessive pedal pressure required to stop vehicle. May be accompanied by brake fade.)	• Master cylinder compensator ports (at bottom of reservoirs) blocked by dirt, scale, rust, or have small burrs (blocked ports prevent fluid return to reservoirs).	• Repair or replace master cylinder **CAUTION:** Do not attempt to clean blocked ports with wire, pencils, or similar implements. Use compressed air only.
	• Brake hoses, tubes, fittings clogged or restricted	• Use compressed air to check or unclog parts. Replace any damaged parts.
	• Brake fluid contaminated with improper fluids (motor oil, transmission fluid, causing rubber components to swell and stick in bores	• Replace all rubber components, combination valve and hoses. Flush entire brake system with DOT 3 brake fluid or equivalent.
	• Low engine vacuum	• Adjust or repair engine

Troubleshooting the Brake System (cont.)

Problem	Cause	Solution
Dragging brakes (slow or incomplete release of brakes)	• Brake pedal binding at pivot	• Loosen and lubricate
	• Power brake unit has internal bind	• Inspect for internal bind. Replace unit if internal bind exists.
	• Parking brake cables incorrrectly adjusted or seized	• Adjust cables. Replace seized cables.
	• Rear brakeshoe return springs weak or broken	• Replace return springs. Replace brakeshoe if necessary in axle sets.
	• Automatic adjusters malfunctioning	• Repair or replace adjuster parts as required
	• Caliper, wheel cylinder or master cylinder pistons sticking or seized	• Repair or replace parts as necessary
	• Master cylinder compensating ports blocked (fluid does not return to reservoirs).	• Use compressed air to clear ports. Do not use wire, pencils, or similar objects to open blocked ports.
Vehicle moves to one side when brakes are applied	• Incorrect front tire pressure	• Inflate to recommended cold (reduced load) inflation pressure
	• Worn or damaged wheel bearings	• Replace worn or damaged bearings
	• Brakelining on one side contaminated	• Determine and correct cause of contamination and replace brakelining in axle sets
	• Brakeshoes on one side bent, distorted, or lining loose on shoe	• Replace brakeshoes in axle sets
	• Support plate bent or loose on one side	• Tighten or replace support plate
	• Brakelining not yet seated with drums or rotors	• Burnish brakelining
	• Caliper anchor plate loose on one side	• Tighten anchor plate bolts
	• Caliper piston sticking or seized	• Repair or replace caliper
	• Brakelinings water soaked	• Drive vehicle with brakes lightly applied to dry linings
	• Loose suspension component attaching or mounting bolts	• Tighten suspension bolts. Replace worn suspension components.
	• Brake combination valve failure	• Replace combination valve
Noisy brakes (squealing, clicking, scraping sound when brakes are applied.) (cont.)	• Brakelining worn out—shoes contacting drum of rotor	• Replace brakeshoes and lining in axle sets. Refinish or replace drums or rotors.
	• Broken or loose holdown or return springs	• Replace parts as necessary
	• Rough or dry drum brake support plate ledges	• Lubricate support plate ledges
	• Cracked, grooved, or scored rotor(s) or drum(s)	• Replace rotor(s) or drum(s). Replace brakeshoes and lining in axle sets if necessary.
	• Incorrect brakelining and/or shoes (front or rear).	• Install specified shoe and lining assemblies
Pulsating brake pedal	• Out of round drums or excessive lateral runout in disc brake rotor(s)	• Refinish or replace drums, re-index rotors or replace

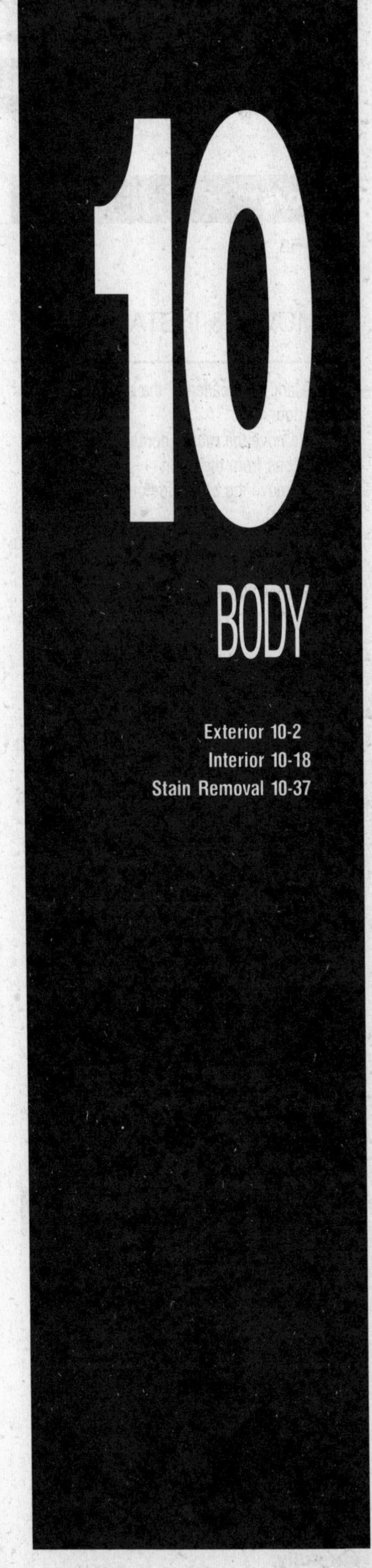
10
BODY
Exterior 10-2
Interior 10-18
Stain Removal 10-37

EXTERIOR

Doors

➧ SEE FIG. 1

REMOVAL & INSTALLATION

1. Mark the location of the door hinge straps on the door.
2. Remove the rubber conduit and electrical connections from the door.
3. Remove the body side check link screw (door slider).
4. With an assistant, support the door with a jack.
5. Remove the hinge pin bolts.
6. Remove the door from the hinges with an assistant.

To install:

7. Position the door over the hinges with an assistant and floor jack.
8. Apply Loctite® to the hinge bolts and install the door.
9. Make sure the door is in proper alignment with the frame and striker. If the door is not in alignment, refer to door alignment in this section.
10. Install the body side check link screw, electrical wiring and conduit, if so equipped.

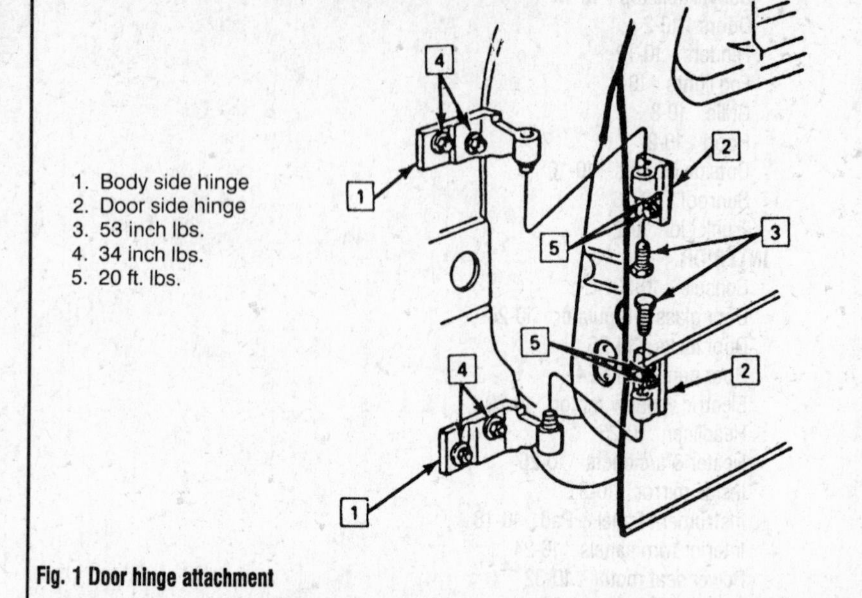

Fig. 1 Door hinge attachment

DOOR ALIGNMENT

Adjust the up and down, and in and out by loosening the four hinge-to-door retaining bolts and move to the desired position. An assistant is recommended to perform this procedure. Torque the bolts to 18 ft. lbs. (24 Nm).

Hood

REMOVAL & INSTALLATION

➥ Always remove the hood assembly with an assistant present. Cover the entire area with well padded blankets to prevent damage to the painted surfaces. The hood is heavy and may cause severe damage if not removed carefully.

1. Place covers over the front fenders and lower windshield to prevent damage.
2. Mark the hood hinge for proper installation.
3. With an assistant, remove the hinge-to-hood bolts and lift the hood clear of the vehicle.

To install:

4. Position the hood onto the hinges and loosely install the hinge bolts.
5. Align the hood to the body and torque the hinge bolts to 20 ft. lbs. (27 Nm).

Trunk Lid

➧ SEE FIG. 2

REMOVAL & INSTALLATION

➥ Always remove the trunk lid assembly with an assistant present. Cover the entire area with well-padded blankets to prevent damage to the painted surfaces. The trunk lid is heavy and may cause severe damage if not removed carefully.

1. Disconnect the negative battery cable and electrical connectors to the trunk lid, if so equipped.
2. Tie a string to the wire harness assembly and pull the wire out of the lid. Allow enough string so that when the lid is removed, the wire can be threaded through upon installation.
3. With an assistant, remove the four trunk lid retaining bolts and trunk lid.

To install:

4. With an assistant, install the trunk lid over the hinges.
5. Install the four retaining bolts and torque to 18 ft. lbs. (25 Nm).
6. Pull the string through the lid until the wire harness is through the inner lid. Reconnect the wiring harnesses, if so equipped.
7. Connect the negative battery cable.
8. Align the trunk lid by moving the lid to the proper position and tighten the hinge bolts.

Front Bumpers

➧ SEE FIGS. 3-10

REMOVAL & INSTALLATION

Cutlass Supreme

1. Disconnect the negative battery cable.
2. Raise the vehicle and support with jackstands.
3. Remove the air deflector.
4. Remove the fascia-to-wheelwell screws.
5. Remove the fascia-to-body retaining nuts.
6. Remove the upper and lower fascia-to-body retainers.

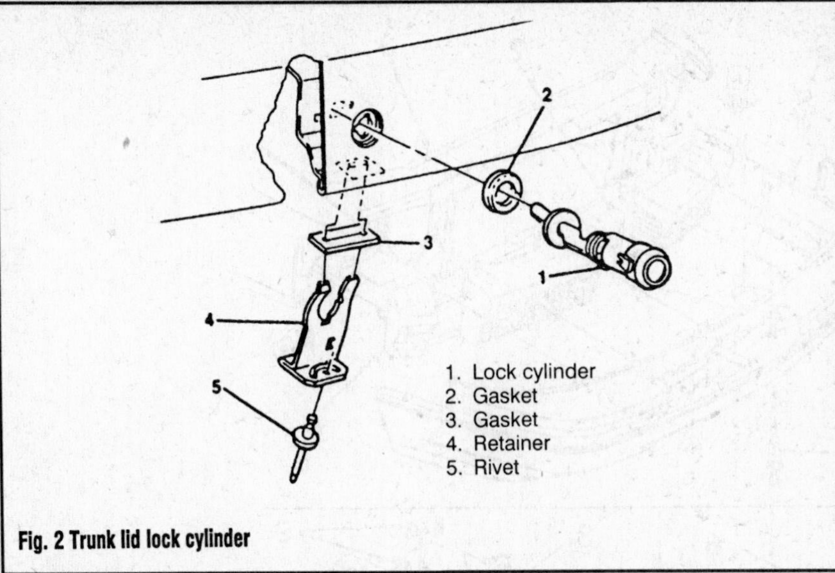

Fig. 2 Trunk lid lock cylinder

7. Remove the bumper-to-body retaining bolts.
8. Remove the bumper and fascia as an assembly.

To install:

9. Install the bumper assembly onto the vehicle.
10. Install bumper-to-body retaining bolts.
11. Install the upper and lower fascia-to-body retainers.
12. Install the fascia-to-body nuts.
13. Install the air deflector and connect the negative battery cable.

Regal

1. Disconnect the negative battery cable.
2. Raise the vehicle and support with jackstands.
3. Remove the chrome strip bracket, air deflector and center push retainers.
4. Remove the fascia-to-wheelwell screws.
5. Remove the upper and lower fascia-to-body retaining nuts (right and left).
6. Remove the bumper guards.
7. Remove the lower fascia-to-bumper nuts (center).
8. Unplug the top fascia retaining tabs.
9. Remove the bumper-to-body bolts and bumper assembly.

To install:

10. Install the bumper and fascia assembly.
11. Install the top fascia retaining tabs.
12. Install the bumper-to-body bolts.
13. Install the lower fascia-to-bumper nuts (center).
14. Install the bumper guards.
15. Install the upper and lower fascia-to-bumper nuts (right and left).
16. Install the fascia-to-wheelwell screws.
17. Install the center push retainers, air deflector, chrome strip bracket and connect the negative battery cable.

Lumina

1. Disconnect the negative battery cable.
2. Raise the vehicle and support with jackstands.
3. Remove the valance panels.
4. Remove the fascia-to-fender nuts.
5. Remove the bumper-to-body nuts.
6. Remove the assembly from the vehicle.

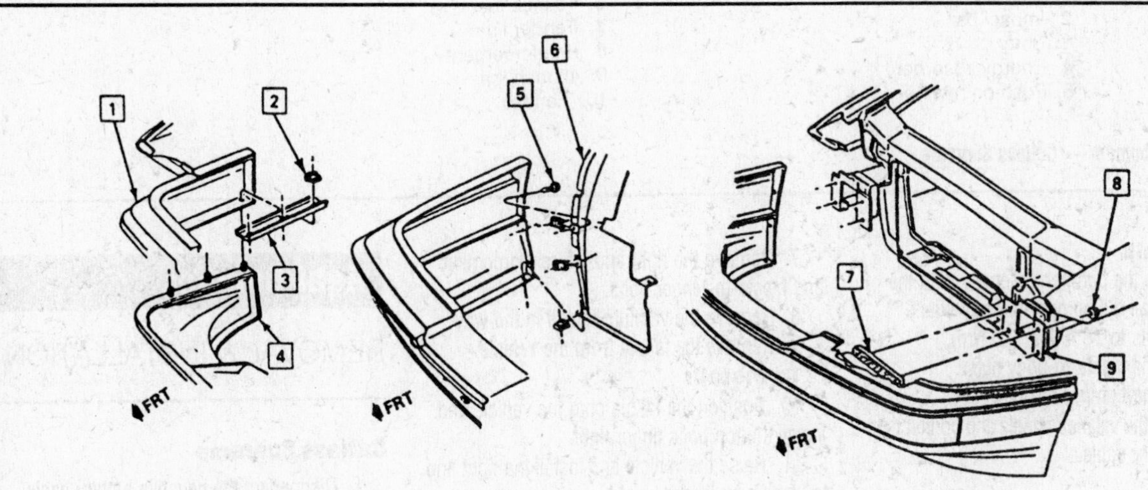

Fig. 3 Front bumper — Regal

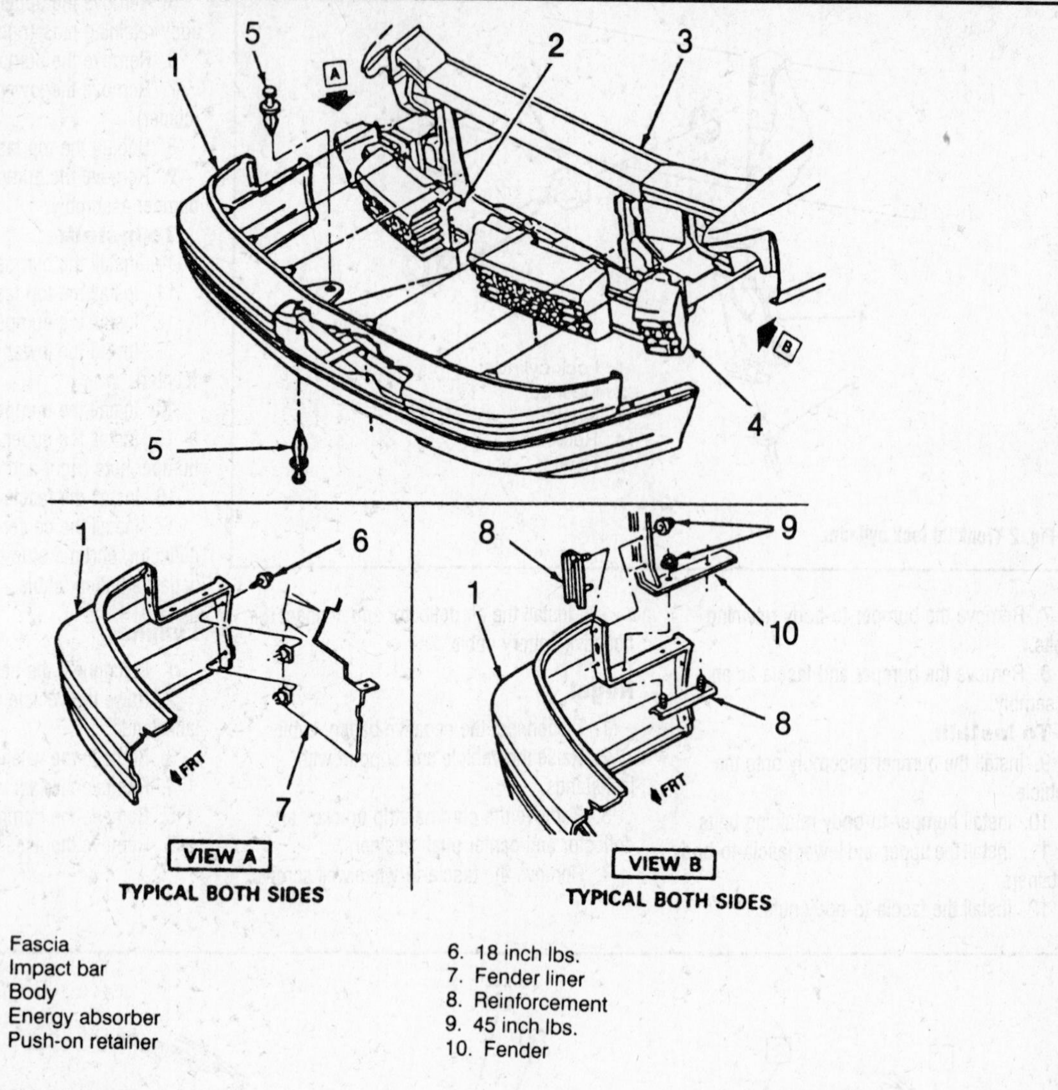

Fig. 4 Front bumper — Cutlass Supreme

To Install:

7. Position the bumper assembly onto the body and install the bumper-to-body nuts. Torque the nuts to 18 ft. lbs. (24 Nm).
8. Install the fascia-to-body nuts.
9. Install the bumper-to-body nuts.
10. Install the valance panels and connect the negative battery cable.

Grand Prix

1. Disconnect the negative battery cable.
2. Raise the hood and remove the top fascia bolts.
3. Raise the vehicle and support with jackstands.
4. Remove the turn signal lamps.
5. Remove the front valance-to-fascia bolts.
6. Remove the fender-to-fascia screws on both sides.
7. Remove the right and left reinforcement and fascia-to-fender bolts.
8. Remove the vacuum tank if in the way.
9. Remove the fascia from the vehicle.

To Install:

10. Position the fascia onto the vehicle and install the top bolts finger tight.
11. Raise the vehicle and install the right and left fascia-to-fender bolts.
12. Install the vacuum tank if removed.
13. Install the fender-to-fascia bolts on both sides.
14. Install the valance panel, turn signal lamps and lower the vehicle.
15. Tighten the top fascia bolts and connect the negative battery cable.

Rear Bumper

REMOVAL & INSTALLATION

Cutlass Supreme

1. Disconnect the negative battery cable.
2. Raise the vehicle and support with jackstands.
3. Remove the splash shield-to-upper and lower fascia screws.
4. From underneath the vehicle, remove the fascia-to-body nuts.
5. Remove the bumper-to-body nuts.
6. Disconnect the side marker lamp connections and lower the vehicle.
7. Remove the luggage compartment liner.

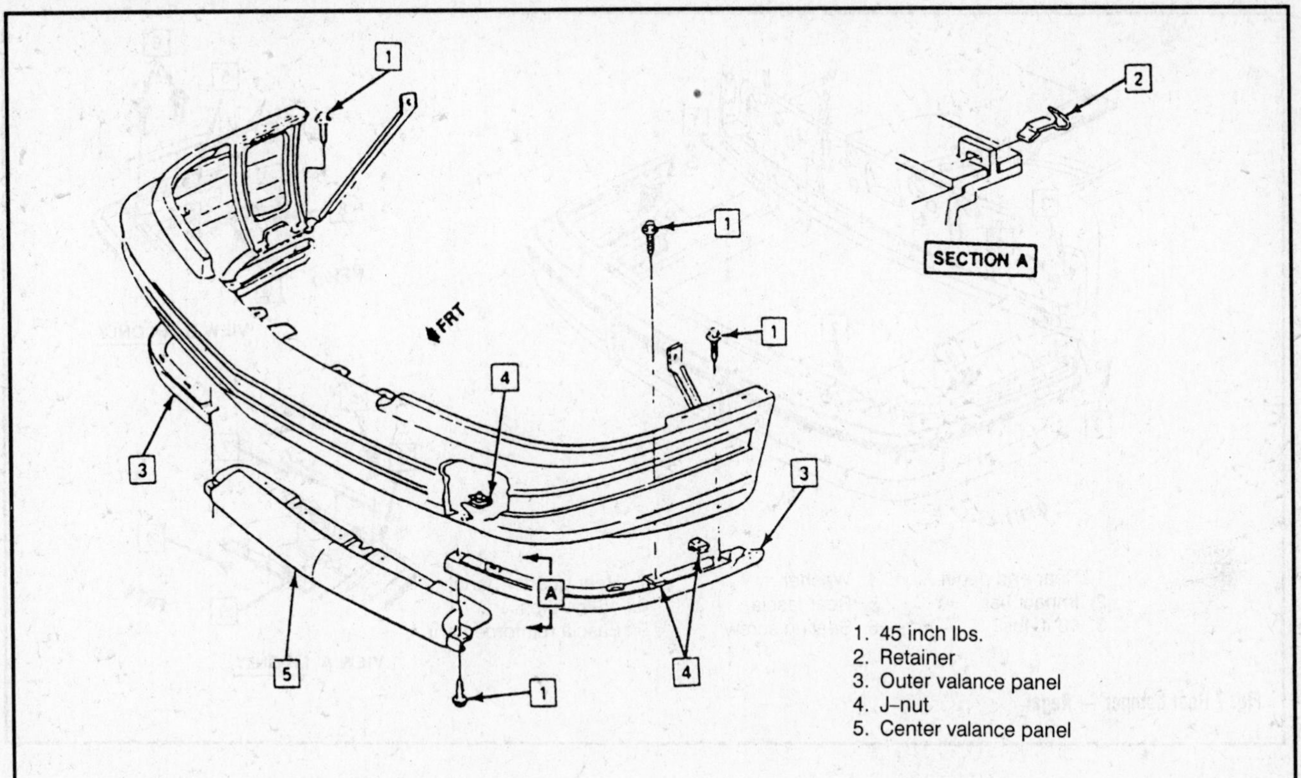

1
2
1
1
SECTION A
FRT
4
3
3
A
5
4
1
1. 45 inch lbs.
2. Retainer
3. Outer valance panel
4. J-nut
5. Center valance panel

Fig. 5 Front bumper — Lumina

1
A
B
2
3
4
1
5
FRT
6
6
FRT
1
VIEW A
FRT
1
6
VIEW B
1. Reinforcement
2. Body nut
3. Fender liner
4. 90 inch lbs.
5. Fender
6. Fascia

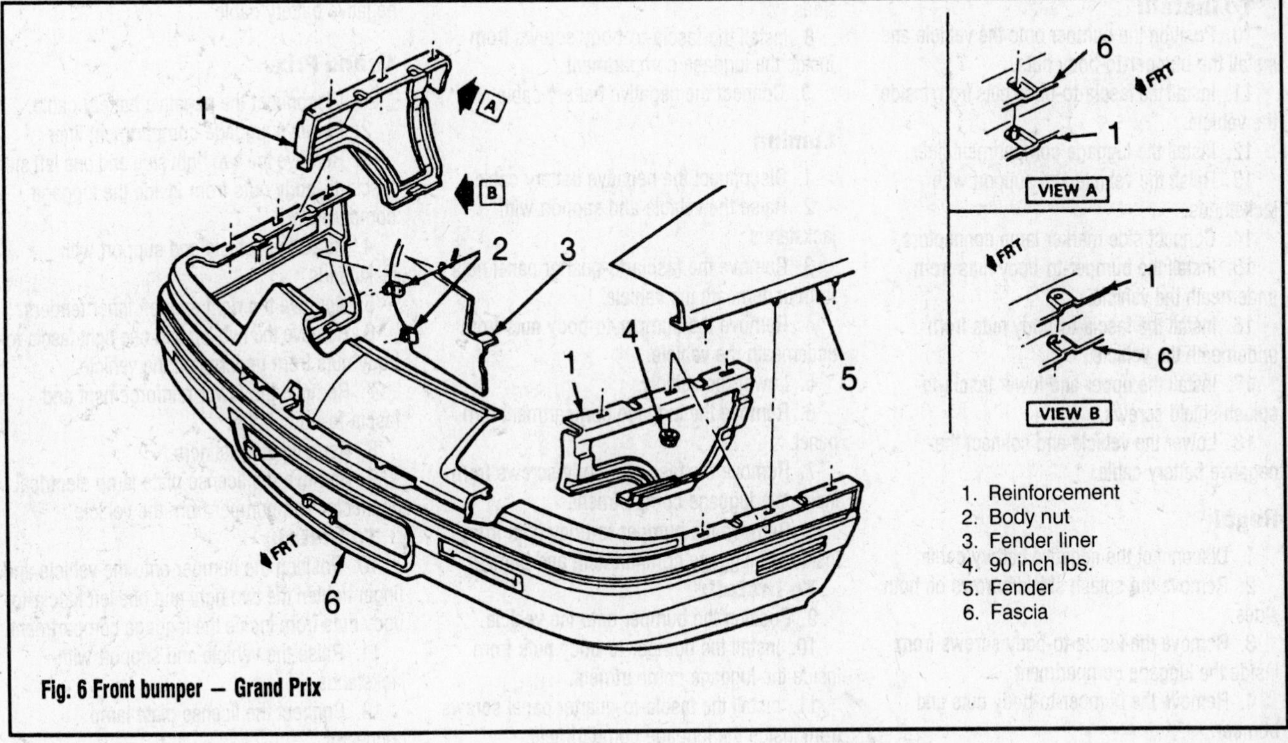

Fig. 6 Front bumper — Grand Prix

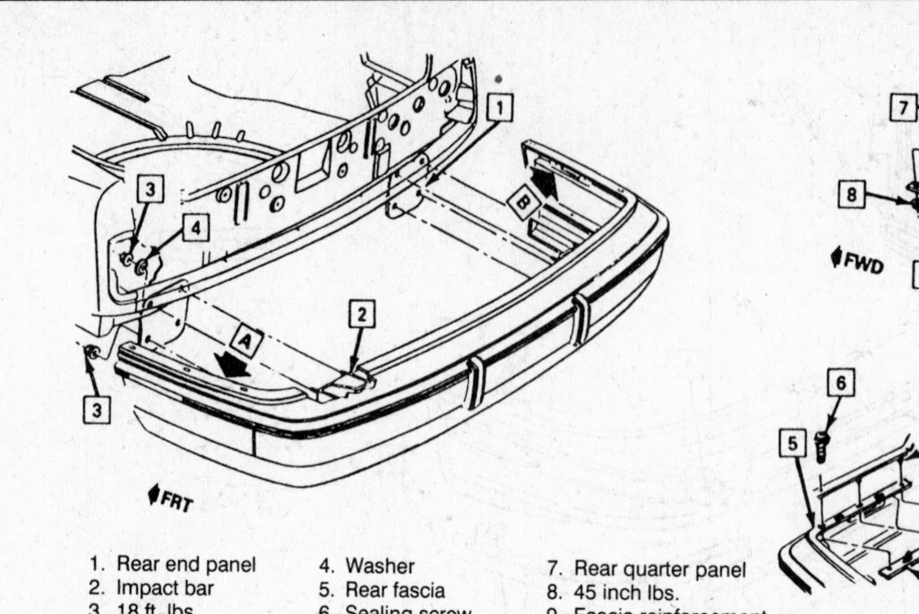

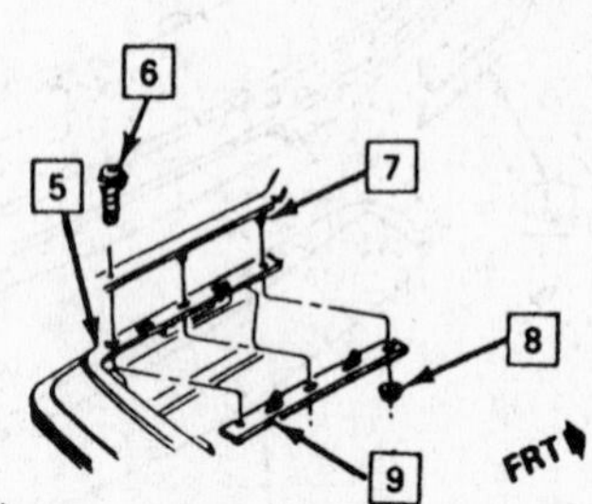

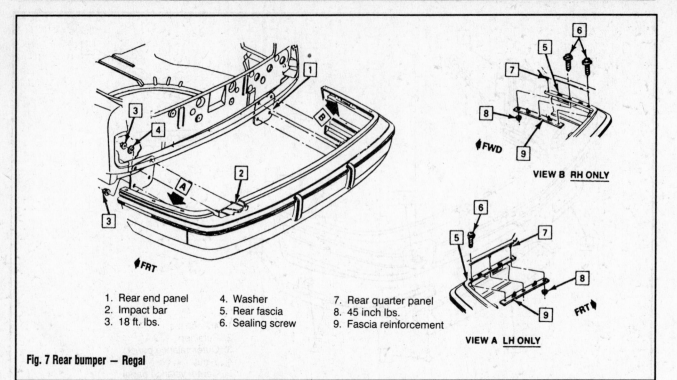

1. Rear end panel
2. Impact bar
3. 18 ft. lbs.
4. Washer
5. Rear fascia
6. Sealing screw
7. Rear quarter panel
8. 45 inch lbs.
9. Fascia reinforcement

Fig. 7 Rear bumper — Regal

8. From inside the luggage compartment, remove the fascia-to-body nuts and bumper-to-body nuts.
9. Remove the bumper assembly from the vehicle.

To Install:

10. Position the bumper onto the vehicle and install the bumper-to-body nuts.
11. Install the fascia-to-body nuts from inside the vehicle.
12. Install the luggage compartment liner.
13. Raise the vehicle and support with jackstands.
14. Connect side marker lamp connectors.
15. Install the bumper-to-body nuts from underneath the vehicle.
16. Install the fascia-to-body nuts from underneath the vehicle.
17. Install the upper and lower fascia-to-splash shield screws.
18. Lower the vehicle and connect the negative battery cable.

Regal

1. Disconnect the negative battery cable.
2. Remove the splash shield screws on both sides.
3. Remove the fascia-to-body screws from inside the luggage compartment.
4. Remove the bumper-to-body nuts and bumper.

To Install:

5. Install the fascia and bumper-to-body nuts.
6. Install the screws inside the luggage compartment.
7. Install the splash shield screws on both sides.
8. Install the fascia-to-body screws from inside the luggage compartment.
9. Connect the negative battery cable.

Lumina

1. Disconnect the negative battery cable.
2. Raise the vehicle and support with jackstands.
3. Remove the fascia-to-quarter panel nuts from underneath the vehicle.
4. Remove the bumper-to-body nuts from underneath the vehicle.
5. Lower the vehicle.
6. Remove the luggage compartment trim panel.
7. Remove the fascia-to-body screws from inside the luggage compartment.
8. Remove the bumper-to-body nuts from inside the luggage compartment and bumper.

To Install:

9. Position the bumper onto the vehicle.
10. Install the bumper-to-body nuts from inside the luggage compartment.
11. Install the fascia-to-quarter panel screws from inside the luggage compartment.
12. Install the luggage compartment trim panel.
13. Raise the vehicle and support with jackstands.
14. Install the bumper-to-body nuts from underneath the vehicle.
15. Lower the vehicle and connect the negative battery cable.

Grand Prix

1. Disconnect the negative battery cable.
2. Remove luggage compartment liner.
3. Remove the two right side and one left side fascia-to-body nuts from inside the luggage compartment.
4. Raise the vehicle and support with jackstands.
5. Remove the right and left inner fenders.
6. Remove the two left and one right fascia-to-body nuts from underneath the vehicle.
7. Remove the lower reinforcement and fascia-to-body bolts.
8. Remove the retainers.
9. Remove the license plate lamp electrical connector and bumper from the vehicle.

To Install:

10. Position the bumper onto the vehicle and finger tighten the two right and one left fascia-to-body nuts from inside the luggage compartment.
11. Raise the vehicle and support with jackstands.
12. Connect the license plate lamp connector.
13. Install the retainers.

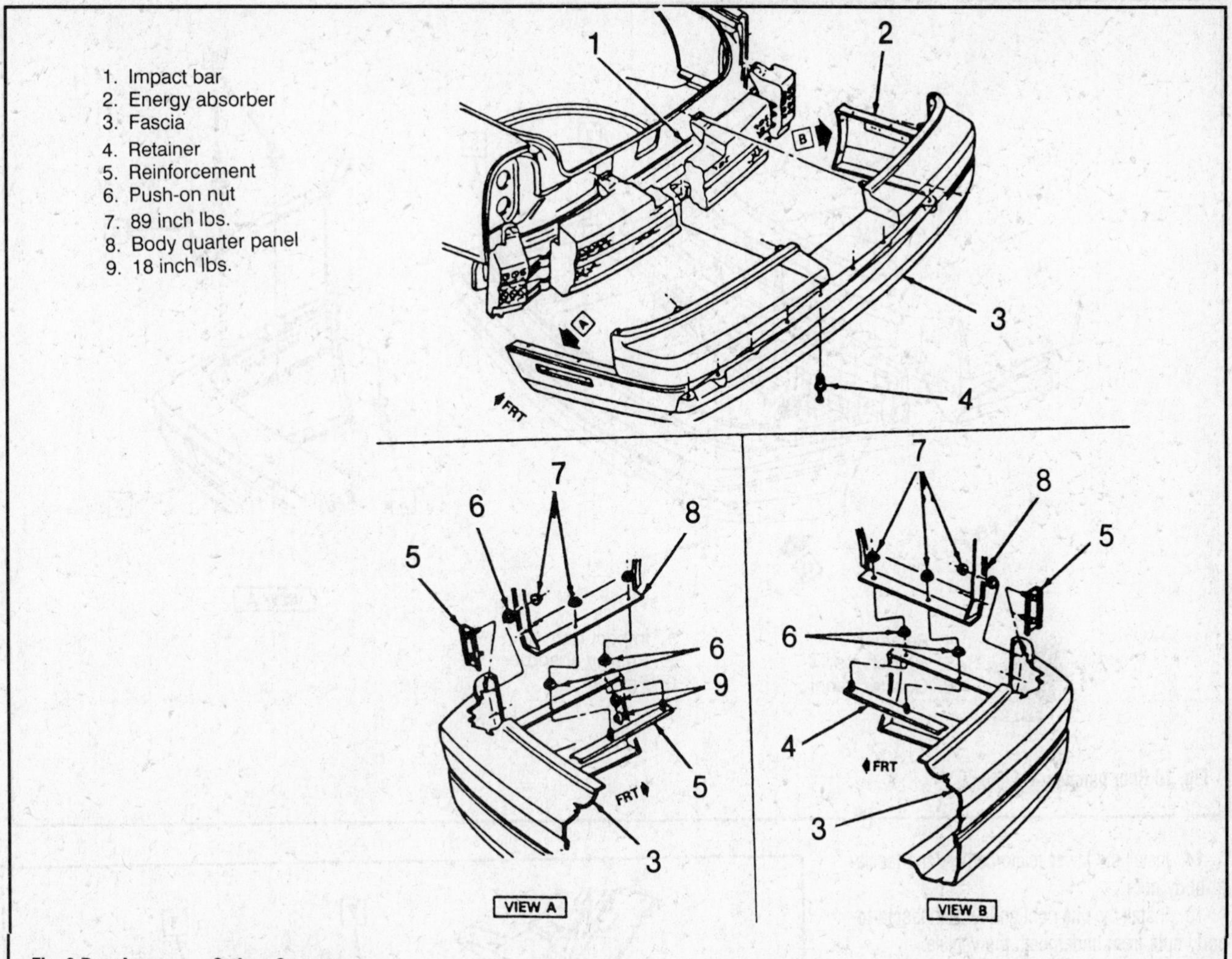

1. Impact bar
2. Energy absorber
3. Fascia
4. Retainer
5. Reinforcement
6. Push-on nut
7. 89 inch lbs.
8. Body quarter panel
9. 18 inch lbs.
FRT
VIEW A
VIEW B

Fig. 8 Rear bumper — Cutlass Supreme

FRT
1. Reinforcement
2. Fascia
3. Valance panel
4. 54 inch lbs.
5. Splash shield

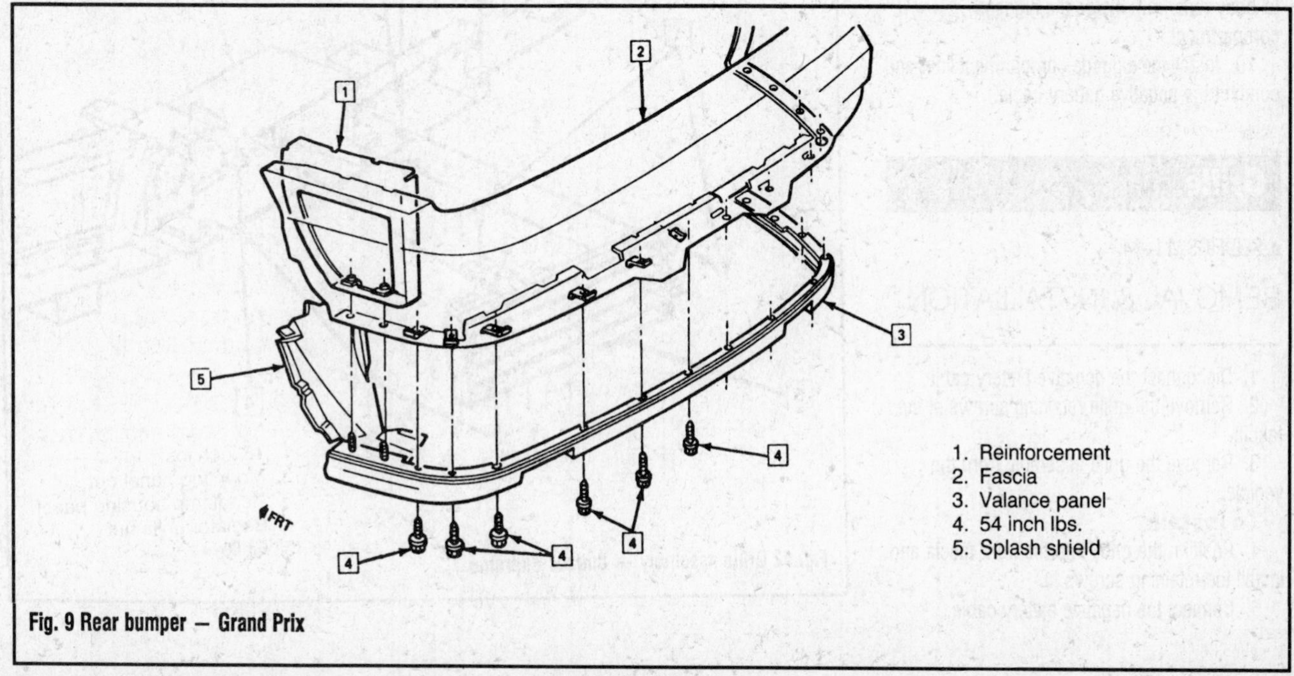

Fig. 9 Rear bumper — Grand Prix

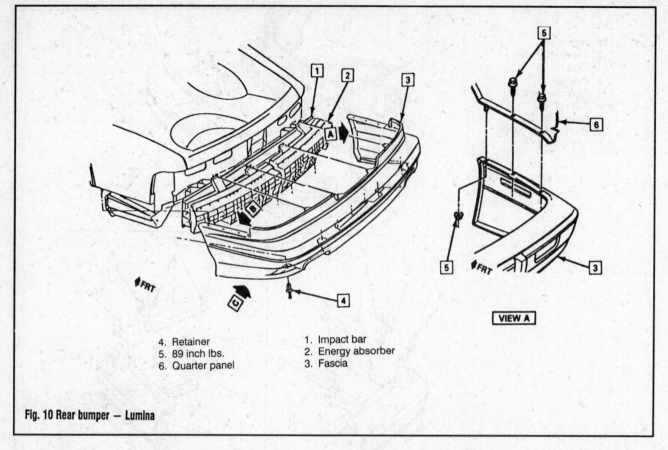

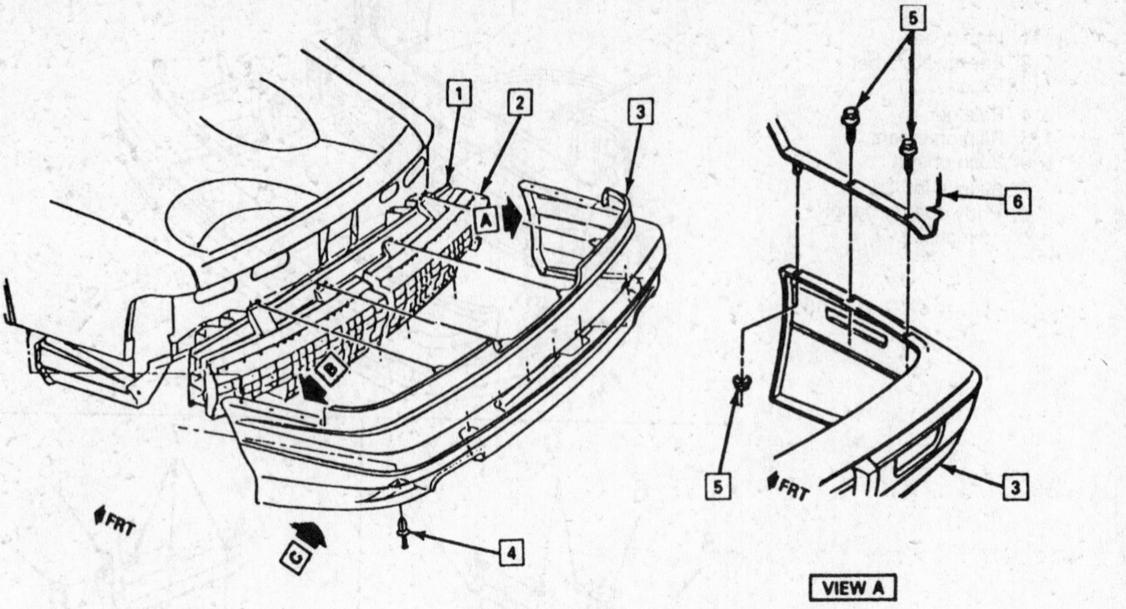

1
2
3
A
B
C
FRT
4
5
6
3
5
FRT
VIEW A
4. Retainer
5. 89 inch lbs.
6. Quarter panel
1. Impact bar
2. Energy absorber
3. Fascia

Fig. 10 Rear bumper — Lumina

14. Install the lower reinforcement and fascia-to-body nuts.

15. Install the one right and two left fascia-to-body nuts from underneath the vehicle.

16. Install the right and left fender liners.

17. Lower the vehicle.

18. Tighten the two right and one left fascia-to-body nuts from inside the luggage compartment.

19. Install the luggage compartment liner and connect the negative battery cable.

Grille

➧ SEE FIGS. 11–14

REMOVAL & INSTALLATION

1. Disconnect the negative battery cable.
2. Remove the grille retaining screws at the fascia.
3. Remove the grille assembly from the vehicle.

To Install:

4. Position the grille into the front fascia and install the retaining screws.
5. Connect the negative battery cable.

1
2
3
4
5
FRT
1. 18 inch lbs.
2. Mounting panel nut
3. Headlamp housing panel
4. Radiator grille nut
5. Grille

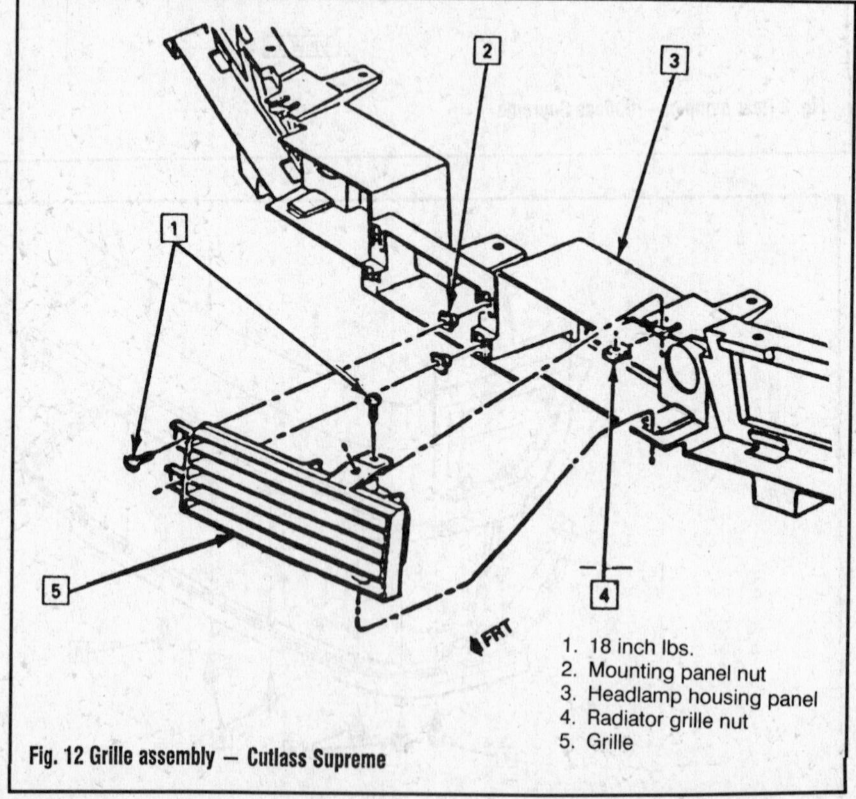

Fig. 12 Grille assembly — Cutlass Supreme

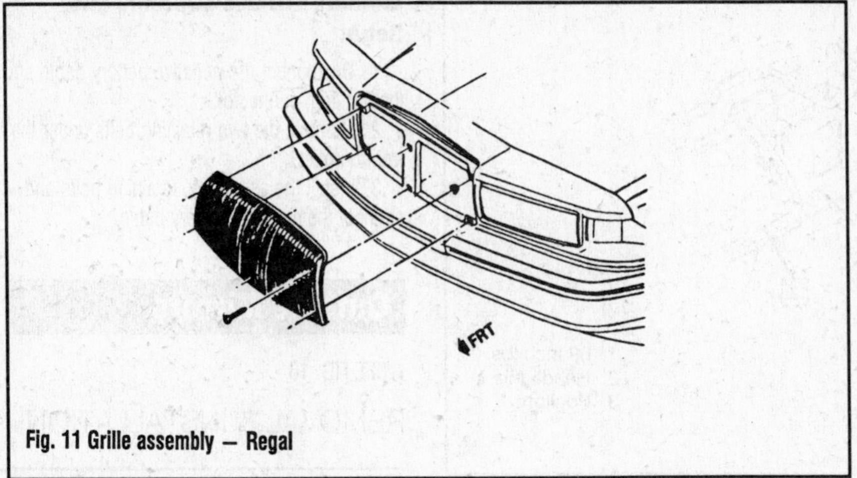

Fig. 11 Grille assembly — Regal

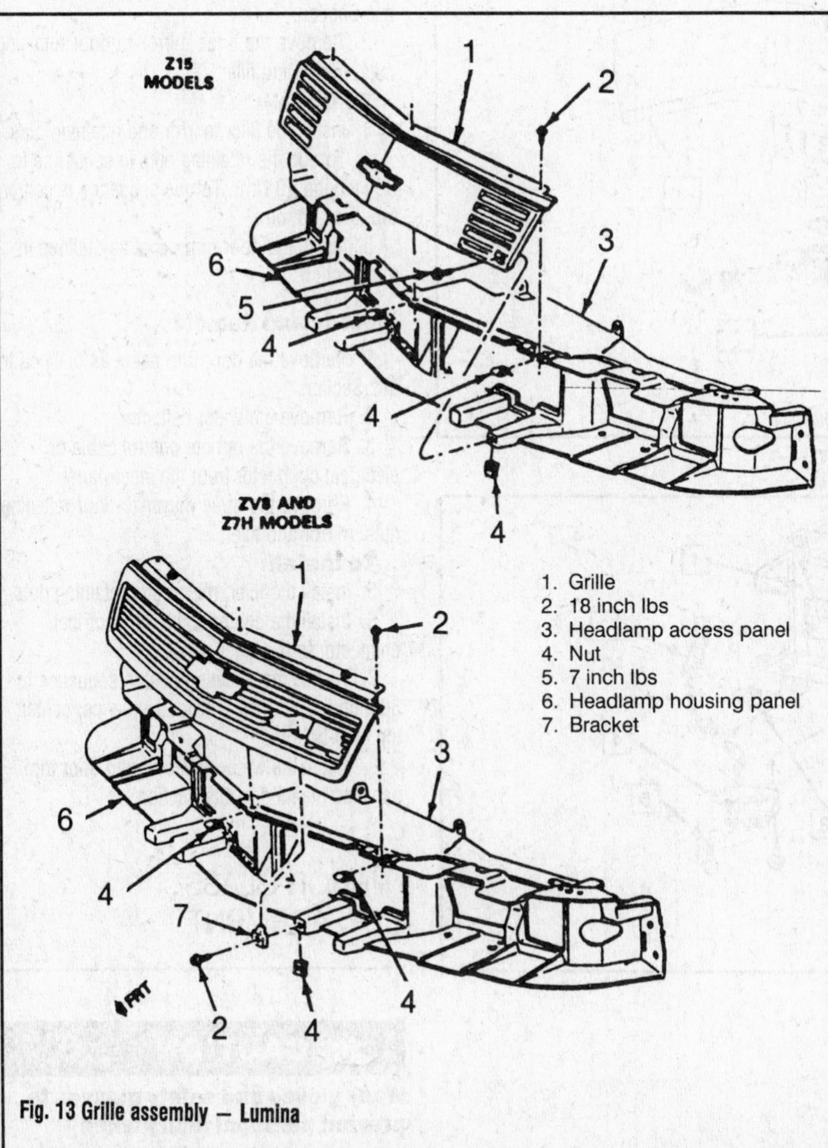

Fig. 13 Grille assembly — Lumina

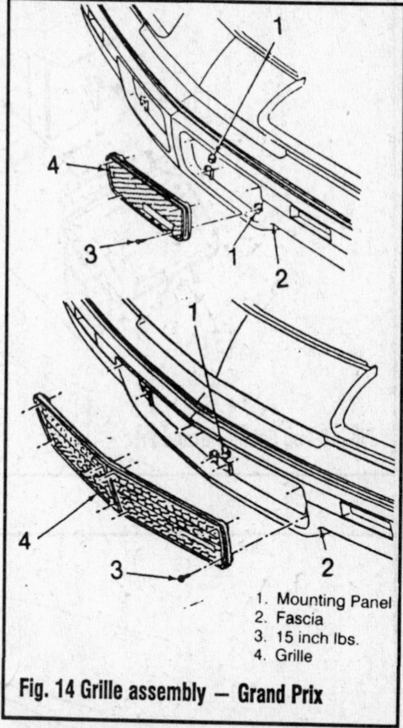

Fig. 14 Grille assembly — Grand Prix

Fog Lights

➧ SEE FIGS. 15–17

REMOVAL & INSTALLATION

Grand Prix

1. Disconnect the negative battery cable.
2. Open the hood and remove the three screws holding the cover over the rear of the lights.
3. Remove the one bolt holding the cover to the headlight housing panel.
4. Remove the cover by sliding it out from under the bolt.
5. Disconnect the light electrical connector.
6. Remove the bulb socket.
7. Remove the one bolt at the top rear of the assembly.
8. Remove the assembly from the vehicle, if replacing.

To Install:

9. Install the light assembly making sure the guide pins on the bottom are aligned with the holes.
10. Install the one bolt, bulb/socket and electrical connector.
11. Install the cover under the bolt and tighten.
12. Install the three cover retaining screws, connect the negative battery cable and close the hood.

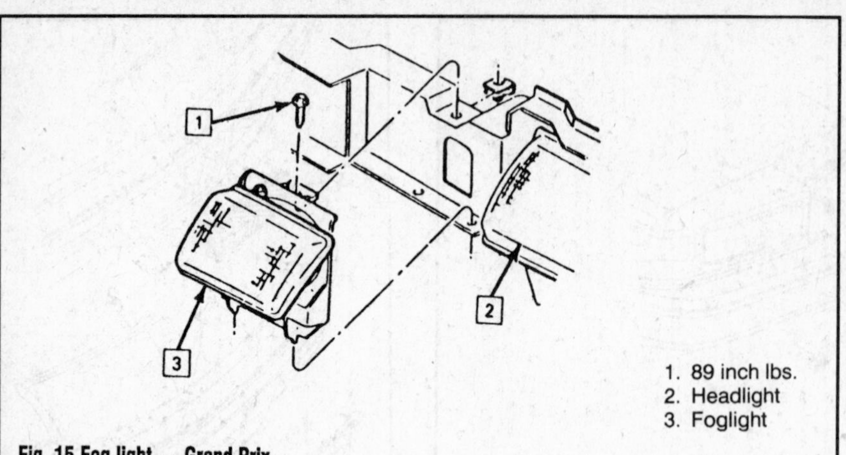

Fig. 15 Fog light — Grand Prix

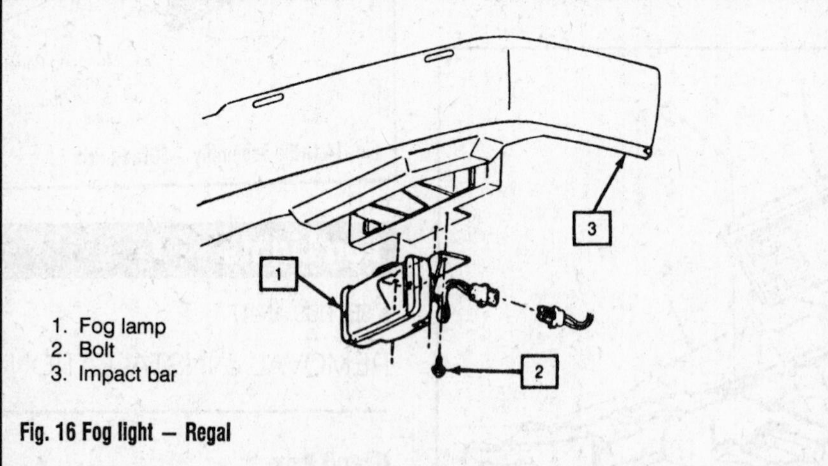

Fig. 16 Fog light — Regal

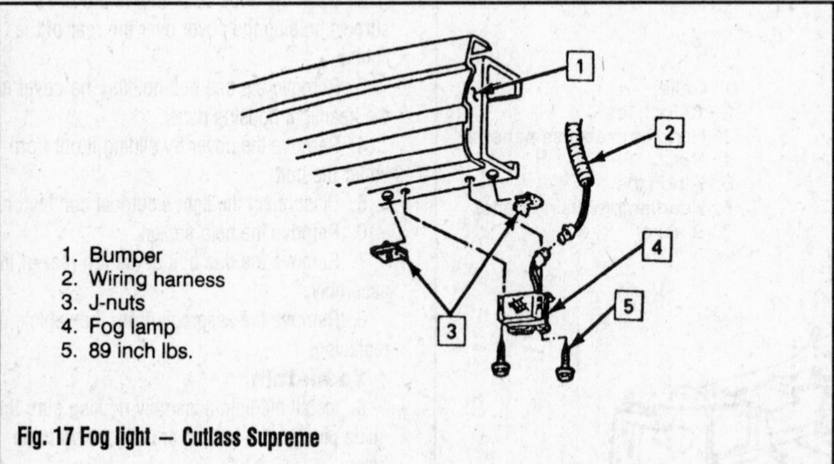

Fig. 17 Fog light — Cutlass Supreme

Lumina, Cutlass Supreme and Regal

1. Disconnect the negative battery cable and the fog light connector.
2. Remove the two retaining bolts under the front bumper.
3. Install the assembly, retaining bolts and connect the negative battery cable.

Outside Mirrors

➧ SEE FIG. 18

REMOVAL & INSTALLATION

Manual

1. Remove the door trim panel as outlined in this Section.
2. Remove the three mirror-to-door retaining nuts, mirror and filler.

To install:

3. Install the filler, mirror and retaining nuts.
4. Torque the retaining nuts in sequence to 80 inch lbs. (9 Nm). Torque sequence is center, top, then bottom.
5. Install the door trim panel as outlined in this Section.

Electric and Remote

1. Remove the door trim panel as outlined in this Section.
2. Remove the water deflector.
3. Remove the remote control cable or electrical connector from the inner panel.
4. Remove the three mirror-to-door retaining nuts, mirror and filler.

To install:

5. Install the filler, mirror and retaining nuts.
6. Install the control cable or electrical connector to the inner panel.
7. Torque the retaining nuts in sequence to 80 inch lbs. (9 Nm). Torque sequence; center, top then bottom.
8. Install the water deflector and door trim panel as outlined in this Section.

MIRROR GLASS REPLACEMENT

✲✲ CAUTION

Wear gloves and safety glasses to prevent personal injury when removing broken mirror glass.

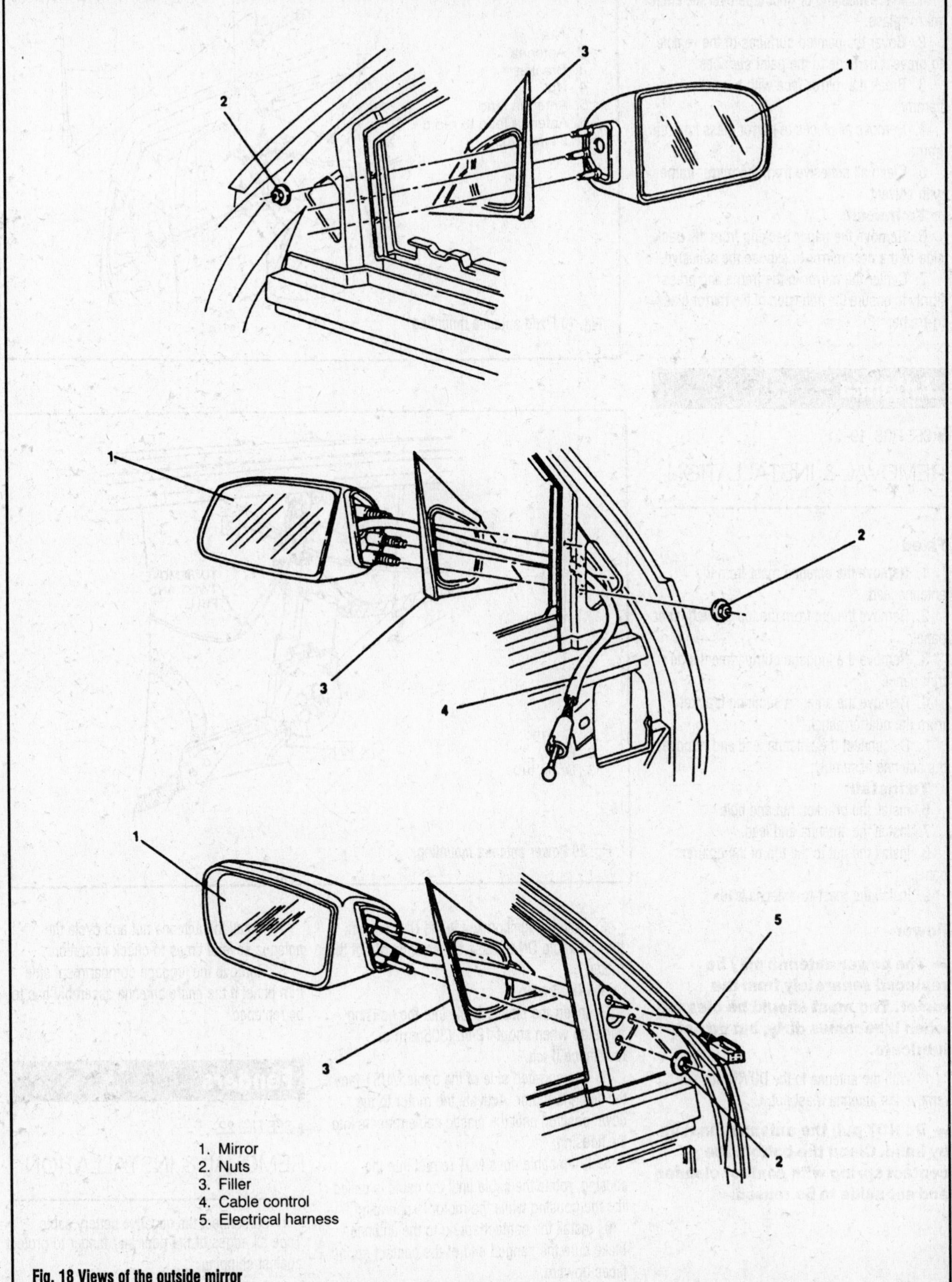

Fig. 18 Views of the outside mirror

1. Place masking or duct tape over the entire mirror glass.
2. Cover the painted surfaces of the vehicle to prevent damage to the paint surfaces.
3. Break the mirror face with a small hammer.
4. Remove all pieces of mirror glass from the frame.
5. Clean all adhesive from the mirror frame with solvent.

To install:

6. Remove the paper backing from the back side of the new mirror to expose the adhesive.
7. Center the mirror in the frame and press firmly to ensure the adhesion of the mirror glass-to-frame.

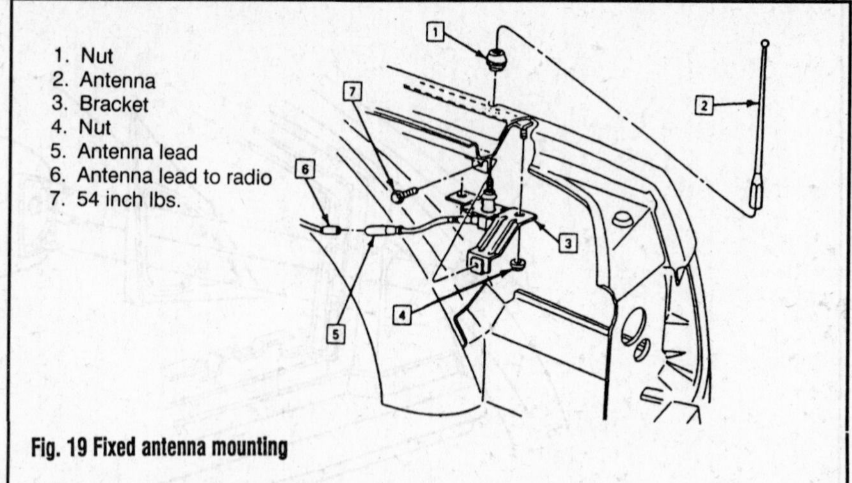

Fig. 19 Fixed antenna mounting

Antenna

SEE FIGS. 19–21

REMOVAL & INSTALLATION

Fixed

1. Remove the antenna mast from the antenna lead.
2. Remove the nut from the top of the quarter panel.
3. Remove the luggage compartment side trim panel.
4. Remove the antenna securing bracket from the quarter panel.
5. Disconnect the antenna lead and remove the antenna assembly.

To install:

6. Install the bracket, nut and bolt.
7. Install the antenna and lead.
8. Install the nut to the top of the quarter panel.
9. Install the mast-to-antenna lead.

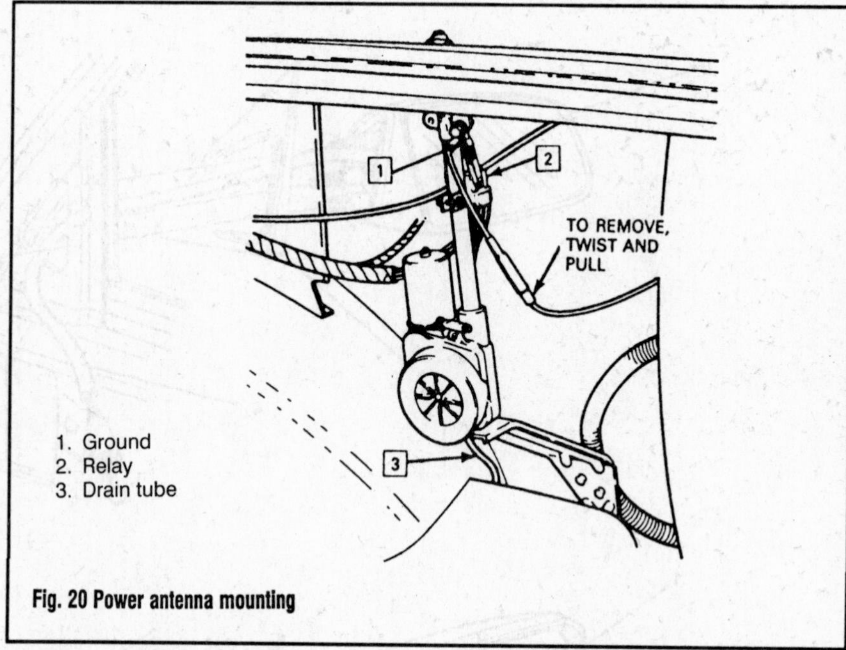

Fig. 20 Power antenna mounting

Power

➡ The power antenna may be replaced separately from the motor. The mast should be cleaned when it becomes dirty, but do not lubricate.

1. With the antenna in the DOWN position, remove the antenna mast nut.

➡ Do NOT pull the antenna mast up by hand. Clean the bottom the contact spring with contact cleaner and set aside to be reused.

2. With the ignition key in the ON position, turn the radio ON to raise the antenna out of the motor.

To install:

3. Insert the plastic cable into the housing and stop when about 12 in. (305mm) of resistance if felt.
4. The serrated side of the cable MUST face the antenna motor. Activate the motor to the down position until the plastic cable retracts into the housing.
5. If the cable does NOT retract into the housing, rotate the cable until the cable is pulled into the housing while the motor is operating.
6. Install the contact spring to the antenna. Make sure the flanged end of the contact spring faces upward.
7. Install the antenna nut and cycle the antenna several times to check operation.
8. Remove the luggage compartment side trim panel if the entire antenna assembly has to be replaced.

Fenders

SEE FIG. 22

REMOVAL & INSTALLATION

1. Disconnect the negative battery cable. Tape all edges of the door and fender to protect against chipping.

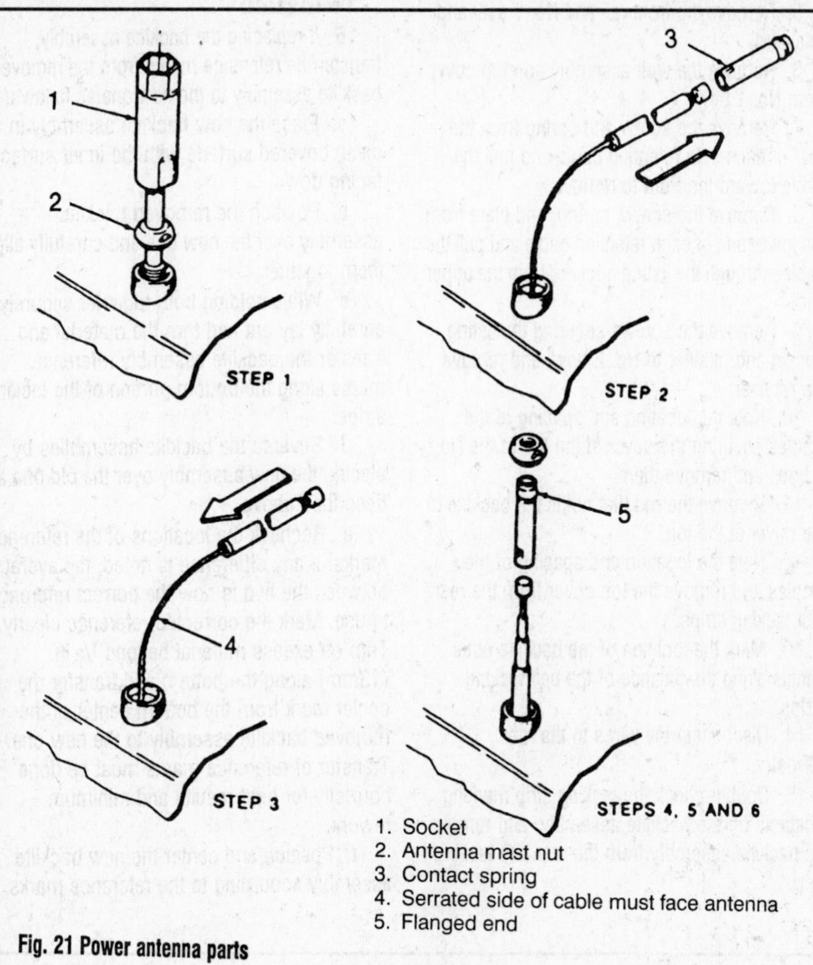

Fig. 21 Power antenna parts

2. Remove the header access panel.
3. On the right side, remove the engine compartment closeout panel.
4. Remove the front lower fender attaching bolts.
5. Remove the top fender attaching bolts.
6. Remove the front fender liner screws and liner nut from the weld stud.
7. Remove the fender liner from the wheelwell opening. If replacing the liner, remove the "J" nuts from the liner.
8. Remove the rocker panel.
9. Remove the upper rear and lower rear fender attaching bolts.
10. Remove the fender from the vehicle.

To install:

11. Install the fender to the vehicle, properly align, and install the lower rear and upper rear bolts. Realign and torque the lower bolts to 89 inch lbs. (10 Nm) and the upper bolt to 18 ft. lbs. (25 Nm).
12. Install the rocker panel.
13. Install the fender liner to the wheelwell.
14. Install the top fender bolts, but do not tighten them at this point.
15. Install the front lower fender bolts and torque to 89 inch lbs. (10 Nm).
16. Install the engine closeout panel (on the right side).
17. Install the header access panel.
18. Install the hood and align all body parts.
19. Connect the negative battery cable.

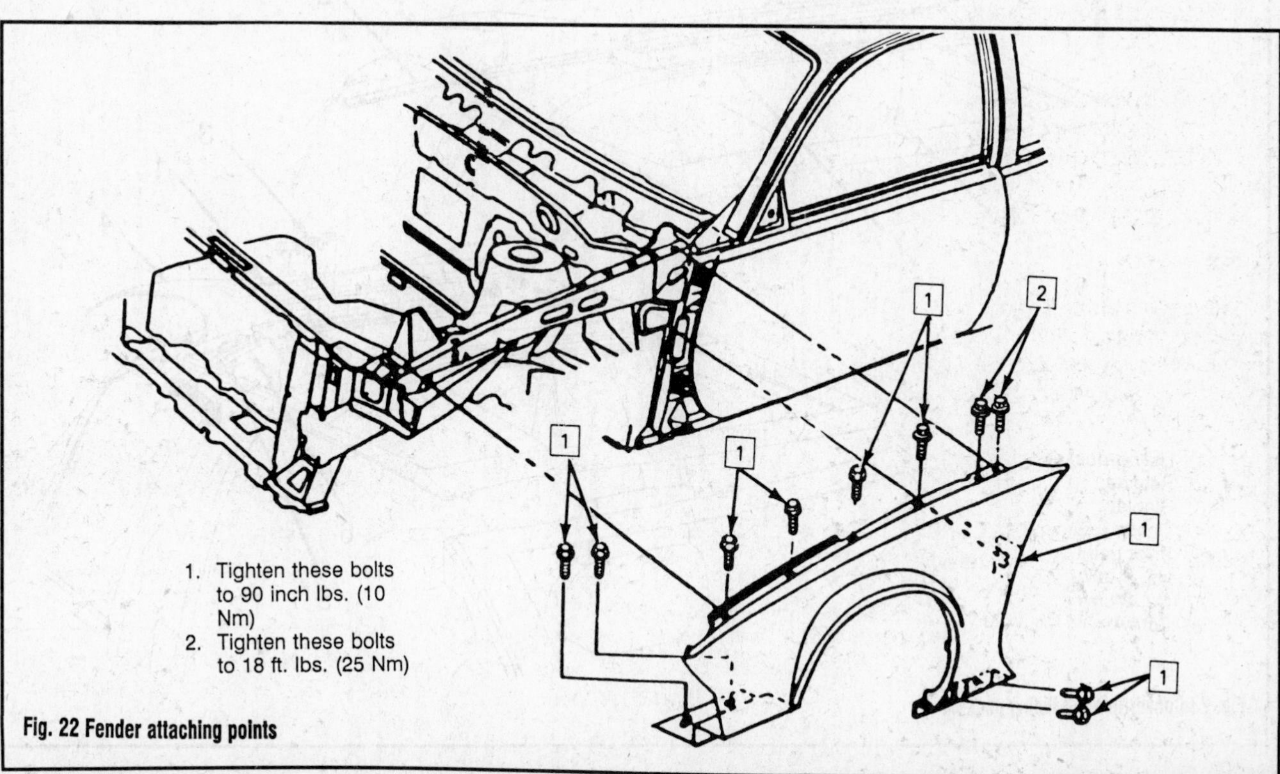

Fig. 22 Fender attaching points

Convertible Top Cover and Rear Window Assembly

➧ SEE FIGS. 23 AND 24

REMOVAL & INSTALLATION

➡ This is a fairly complicated procedure, and ultimate success depends largely on practice and skill. Hence, a professional convertible repair shop is the best place to take your car, should it need repair. But, if you want to attempt it yourself, here's the procedure.

1. Disconnect the negative battery cable.
2. Remove inner headliner by pulling loose all fastening tape strips from around all side windows, header, and rear, and screws in No. 4 bow.
3. Using a grease pencil, mark the locations of all attaching holes on the top cover material. Remove the quarter and rear belt moldings.
4. Cover all painted surfaces on the rear compartment lid and quarter panels.
5. Remove the front rail and No. 1 seal and retainers.
6. Remove the welt assembly and top cover from No. 1 bow.
7. Remove the screw and spring from the rear of each side retention cable and pull the cable toward the front to remove.
8. Remove the screw, spring, and plate from the lower end of each retention cable and pull the cables through the listing pockets from the upper end.
9. Remove the screws securing the listing pocket and retainer to No. 2 bow, and remove the retainer.
10. Note the location and spacing of the staples securing the cover at the top of the No. 3 bow, and remove them.
11. Remove the rod that holds the backlite to the cover at the top.
12. Note the location and spacing of the staples and remove the top cover from the rear belt tacking strips.
13. Mark the location of the backlite outer panels along the balance of the belt tacking strips.
14. Disconnect the wires to the rear defroster.
15. Double-check the tacking strip marking locations on the backlite assembly, and remove the backlite assembly from the rear belt tacking strip.

To Install:

16. If replacing the backlite assembly, transfer the reference marks from the removed backlite assembly to the new one as follows:
    a. Place the new backlite assembly in a clean covered surface with the inner surface facing down.
    b. Position the removed backlite assembly over the new one and carefully align them together.
    c. While holding both together securely, carefully lay out and trim the material and transfer the backlite assembly reference marks along the bottom portion of the tacking strips.
    d. Reverse the backlite assemblies by placing the new assembly over the old one as described above.
    e. Recheck the locations of the reference marks. If any difference is noted, the average between the two is now the correct reference to use. Mark the corrected reference clearly. Trim off excess material beyond 1/2 in. (13mm) along the bottom and transfer the center mark from the bottom center of the removed backlite assembly to the new one. Transfer of reference marks must be done correctly for best results and minimum rework.
    f. Position and center the new backlite assembly according to the reference marks.

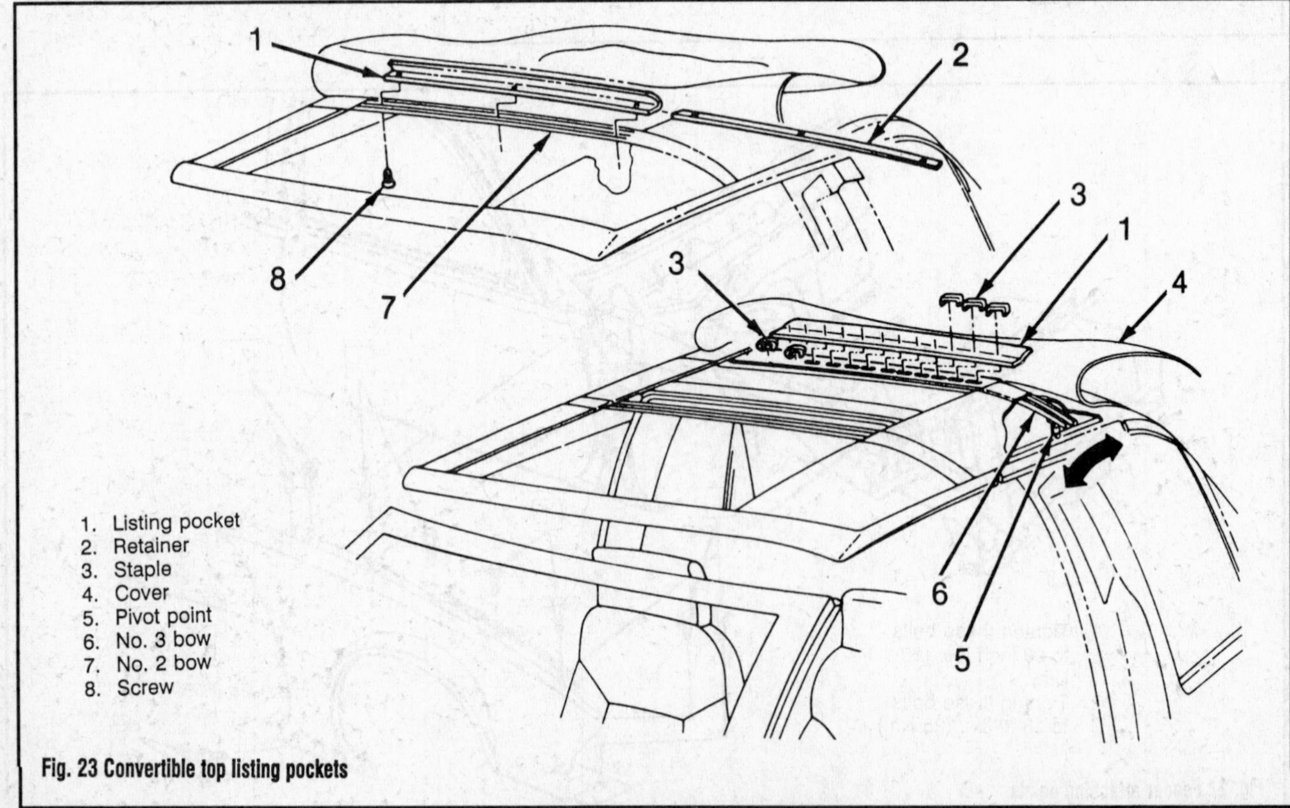

Fig. 23 Convertible top listing pockets

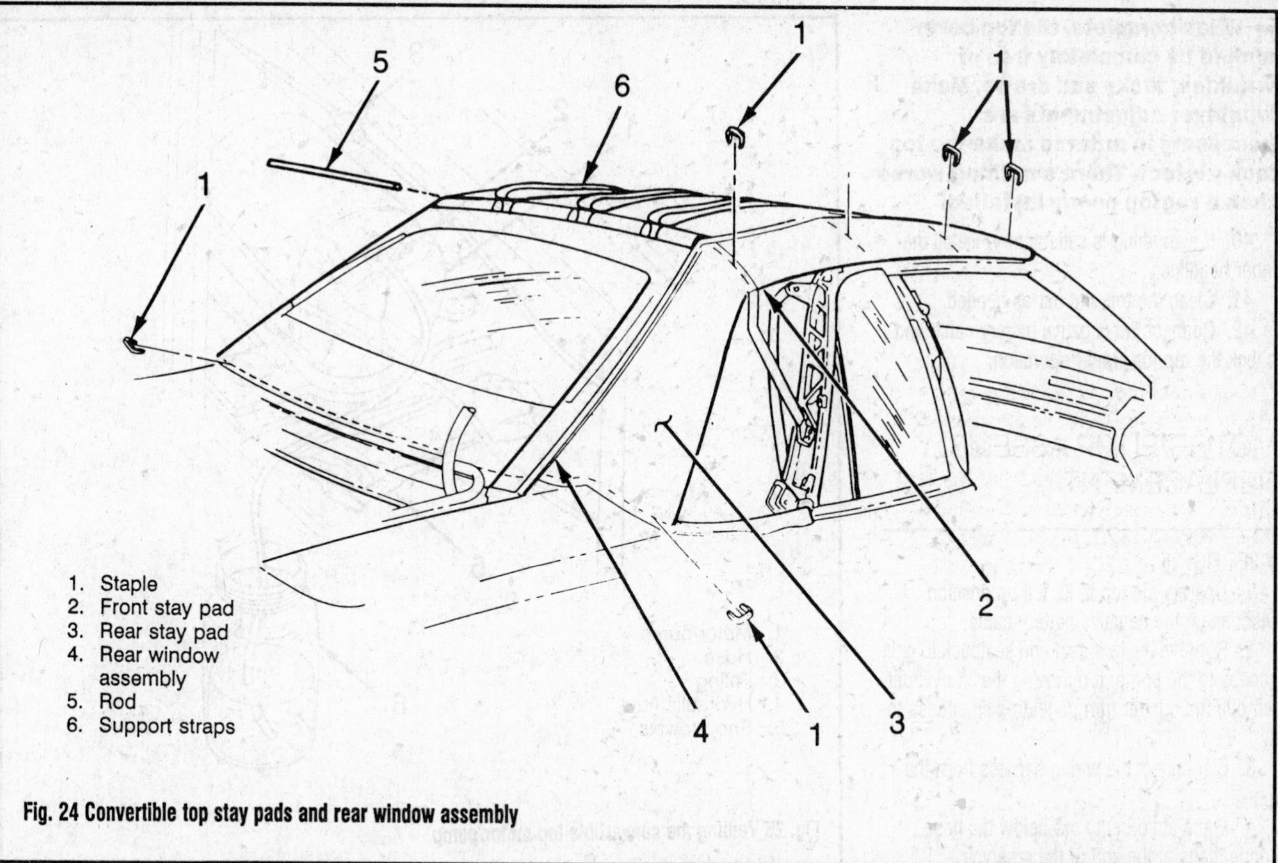

Fig. 24 Convertible top stay pads and rear window assembly

17. Install the backlite assembly to the backing strip using heavy duty $^3/_8$ in. staples. Apply downward pressure to the backlite assembly at each point of staple installation. Staple from the center to the ends.

18. After the backlite has been properly secured, trim off all excess material at the rear below the tacking strip.

19. Connect the rear defroster wires.

20. Transfer the reference marks from the old top cover to the new one as follows:

a. Place the new cover on a clean surface with the inner surface of the cover facing down.

b. Position the removed top cover over the new one.

c. Carefully align the backlite opening upper corners, rear quarter upper corners and rear quarter upper corners of both covers. Secure both covers together at these locations.

d. Transfer location marks for tacking strip.

e. Position the top cover over the top stack in the raised position. The cover may require some lateral stretching along the rear bow to achieve the proper fit of the quarter flaps to the rear side rails and to remove fullness from the top cover valance over the backlite.

21. Install the rod holding the backlite to the top cover; insert through the support strips.

22. Install the No. 2 bow top cover retainer into the new top cover listing pocket.

23. Install the side retention cables into the cover side rail listing pockets. If needed, a wire may assist you in pulling them through.

24. Install the Nos. 2 & 3 bow top cover listing pockets to their bows.

25. Raise the top slightly off of the windshield header.

26. Install the side retention cables to the springs and rear rails with the screws.

27. Install the rear retention cables into the rear listing pockets. Secure the lower ends of the the cables to the quarter belt line brackets with the screws.

28. Lock the top to the windshield header. Pull the top cover straight forward at seams to the desired top fullness, and align the center of the top cover with the center rivets in the No. 1 bow. While maintaining tension on the cover over the top of No. 1 bow, make a pencil mark on the cover outer surface along the forward edge of the No. 1 bow.

29. Raise the top off of the header to a comfortable working height.

30. Install the cover to No. 1 bow using staples after pulling $^1/_4$ in. (6mm) past the reference mark. Trim excess material.

31. Raise the top and lock to the windshield header. Check appearance of the top trim. If additional tension is needed, pull the cover further forward. Staple and recheck for satisfactory appearance.

32. Install the welt assembly to the No. 1 bow using staples.

33. Install the No. 1 bow seal retainer and front rail retainers.

34. Apply weatherstrip adhesive to the inner surface of the retainer. Attach the front rail and the No. 1 bow seal assembly to the front rail retainer and across No. 1 bow. Secure the seal to the bow with the attaching screws.

35. Install the top cover to the belt tacking strips starting at the rear and working rearward. Apply downward pressure to the top cover at each point of staple installation.

36. To prevent water leaks, cover all staples with preheated butyl tape, then heat the tape again to seal to the staples. Cover the butyl tape with duct tape.

37. Cut or pierce holes in the cover and along the backlite assembly along the tacking strip for belt molding attaching studs.

38. Install the rear belt and quarter belt moldings.

➡ **When complete, the top cover should be completely free of wrinkles, tucks and draws. Make whatever adjustments are necessary in order to make the top look perfect. There's nothing worse than a ragtop poorly installed!**

40. If everything is satisfactory, install the inner headliner.
41. Clean the top and car as needed.
42. Connect the negative battery cable and check the top for proper operation.

MOTOR/PUMP ASSEMBLY REPLACEMENT

➧ SEE FIG. 25

1. Operate the top to its full up position. Disconnect the negative battery cable.
2. Remove the rear seat and seatback to gain access to the pump. If removing the lift cylinder, remove the quarter trim panel to gain access to it.
3. Disconnect the wiring harness from the motor.
4. Place absorbent rags below the hose connections at the end of the reservoir.

✻✻ CAUTION

Failure to vent the unit prior to line disconnection may spew fluid into your face or on the cars painted surfaces.

5. Remove the fill plug slowly to vent the unit Then re-install the plug.
6. Disconnect the hydraulic lines and cap them.
7. Remove the mounting nuts and remove the motor/pump assembly.

To install:

8. Fill the reservoir with Dexron®II automatic transmission fluid.
9. Make sure that all threaded parts have thei sealing ring in place, and connect the hydraulic lines.
10. Connect the wiring harness.
11. Connect the negative battery cable and operate the top through several up and down cycles until movement is consistently smooth indicating that all air has been bled from the system.
12. Check all connections for leakage and recheck the fluid level by removing the full plug.
13. Install previously removed interior parts.

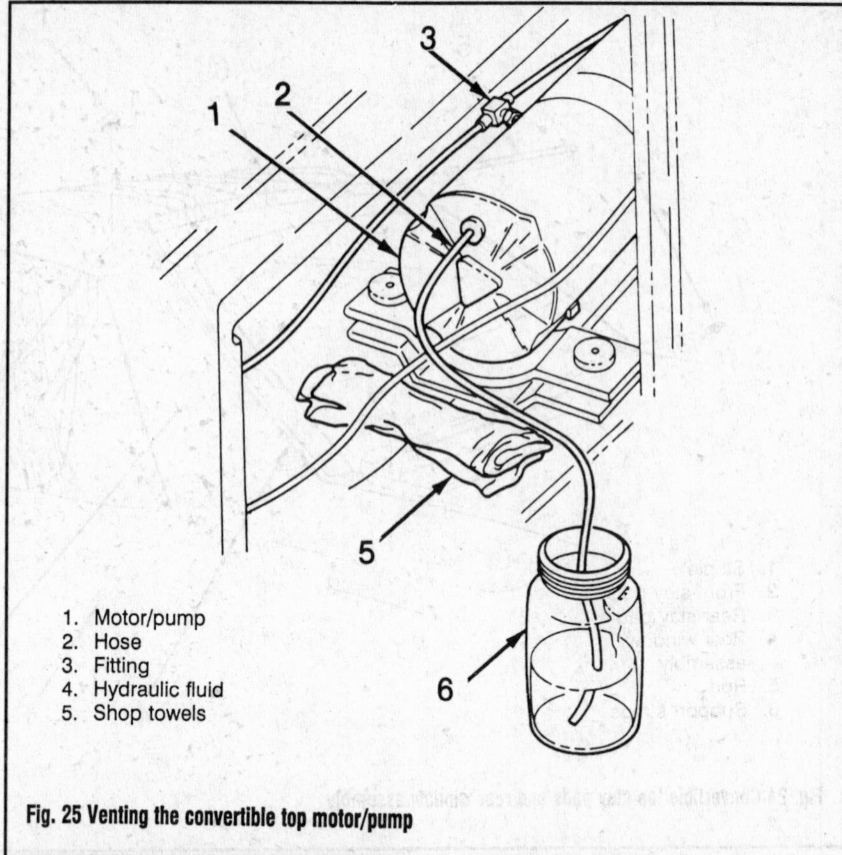

Fig. 25 Venting the convertible top motor/pump

Power Sunroof Assembly

➧ SEE FIG. 26

REMOVAL & INSTALLATION

1. Disconnect the negative battery cable.
2. Grasp the sunroof control switch and pull it straight downward. Remove the small nut and disconnect the connector from the switch.
3. Remove the sunshades, inside rearview mirror, passenger assist handle, dome lamp, and high level stoplamp.
4. Remove the headliner lace from the retainer around the sunroof opening. Withdraw the tucked headliner material.
5. Remove the windshield pillar and side roof rail garnish moldings.
6. Remove the upper quarter "sail" panels and loosen the upper trim at the door pillar.
7. Release the headliner hook and loop fasteners and lower by sliding the headliner to one side while at the same time lowering the opposite side from the center pillar trim. Recline the seatbacks and, with the aid of a helper, remove the headliner through the passenger door opening.
8. Remove the drain hoses.
9. Disconnect the connectors from the relay and harness assembly.
10. With the aid of a helper, remove the nuts securing the sunroof assembly to the roof, starting with the outer nuts and working your way inward. Lower and carefully remove the assembly through the passenger door opening.

To install:

11. Install the sunroof assembly to the roof, align, and install the securing nuts, starting from the center and working your way outward.
12. Connect the relay and harness.
13. Install the drain hoses and secure the hose clamps.
14. Carefully install the headliner to the roof panel. Engage the hook and loop fasteners.
15. Secure the upper trim at the door pillar.
16. Install the upper quarter "sail" panels.
17. Install the windshield pillar and side roof rail garnish moldings.
18. Tuck in the headliner material and connect the headliner lace to the retainer around the sunroof opening.
19. Install all remaining interior parts that were removed during the removal procedure.

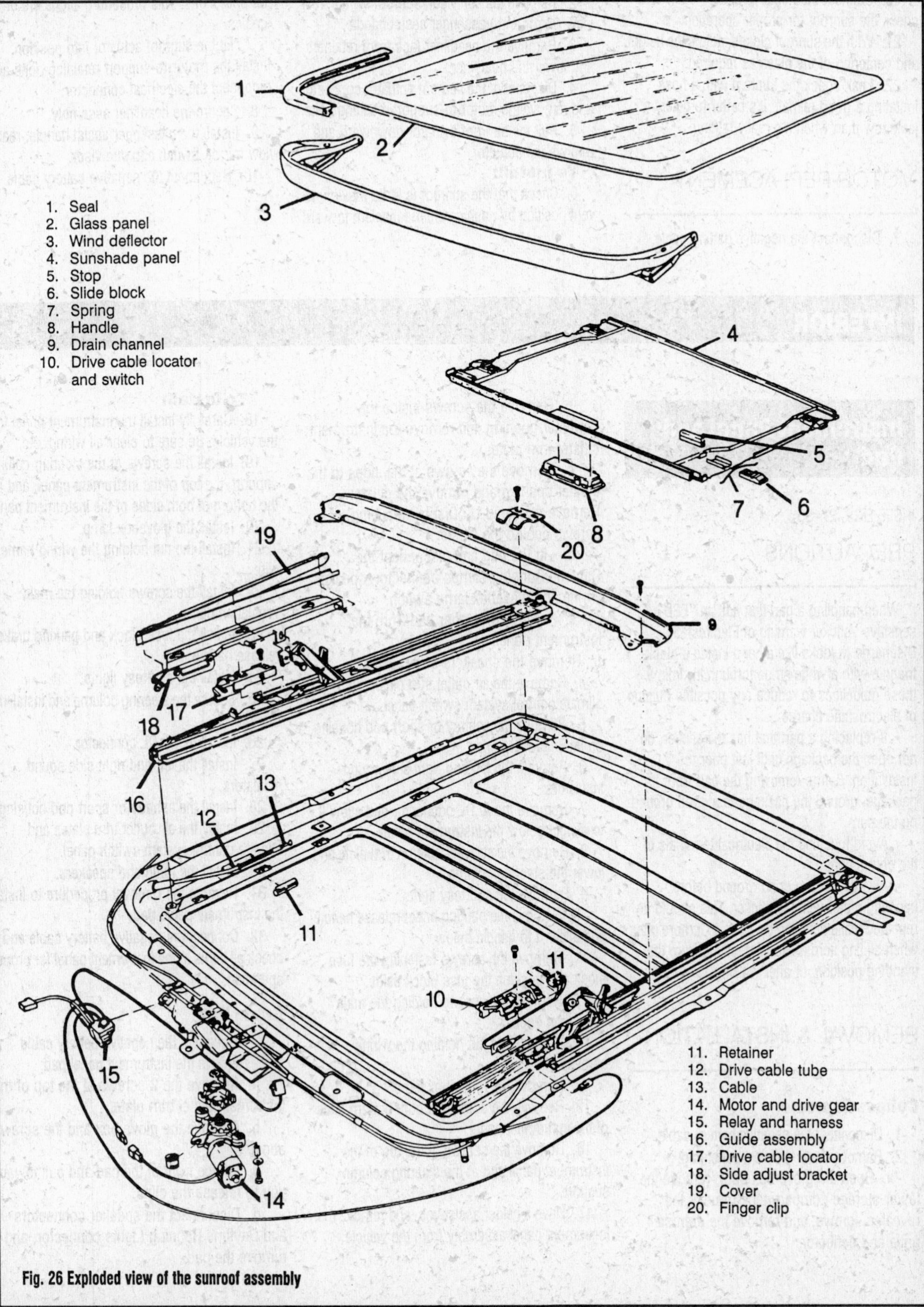

Fig. 26 Exploded view of the sunroof assembly

20. Connect the negative battery cable and check the sunroof for proper operation.

21. With the sunroof closed, adjust the height and centering of the glass as required.

22. Leak check the sunroof with a hose imitating a good rainfall. It's better to detect a leak now than when it's really raining.

MOTOR REPLACEMENT

1. Disconnect the negative battery cable.

2. Remove the sun visor, sunroof switch, rear view mirror and passenger assist handle.

3. Remove the headliner lace from retainers and lower the headliner.

4. Disconnect the sunroof actuator connector and remove the motor-to-support retaining bolts.

5. Pull the sunroof actuator downward and remove the actuator.

To install:

6. Check that the sunroof is at its maximum vent position by pushing the mechanism forward on both sides. This procedure aligns the drive cables.

7. Fit the sunroof actuator into position. Install the motor-to-support retaining bolts and reconnect the electrical connector.

8. Secure the headliner assembly.

9. Install the passenger assist handle, rear view mirror, switch and sun visor.

10. Reconnect the negative battery cable.

INTERIOR

Instrument Panel and Pad

➧ SEE FIGS. 27–30

PRECAUTIONS

When handling a part that has an "ESD-sensitive" sticker warning of Electrostatic Discharge (it looks like a hand inside a black triangle with a white stripe through it), follow these guidelines to reduce any possible buildup of electrostatic charge:

- If replacing a part that has the sticker, do not open the package until just prior to installation. Before removing the part from its package, ground the package to a good ground on the car.
- Avoid touching the electrical terminals of the component.
- Always touch a good ground before handling a part with the sticker. This should be repeated while handling the part; do it more often when sliding across the seat, sitting from the standing position, or after walking.

REMOVAL & INSTALLATION

Cutlass Supreme

1. Disconnect the negative battery cable.

2. Remove the instrument panel pad:

a. Open the glove box door, remove the lower storage compartment, remove the revealed screws, and remove the defroster grille and deflector.

b. Remove the screws inside the defroster opening and remove the instrument cluster trim plate.

c. Remove the screws at the sides of the cluster opening and remove the cluster. Remove the Head-Up Display retaining screws behind the cluster.

d. Lift the pad and disconnect the Daytime Running Lamps connector, speaker wiring and glovebox lamp switch.

e. Remove the upper pad from the instrument panel.

3. Remove the speakers and radio.

4. Remove the air outlet trim plates and climate control system switch panel.

5. Remove the ashtray or sport pod housing on International Series.

6. Remove the left and right side sound insulators.

7. Remove the ALDL connector and allow it to dangle below the instrument panel.

8. Remove the steering column trim plate and lower the steering column.

9. Remove the courtesy lights.

10. Remove the parking brake release handle and allow it to dangle below.

11. Remove the screws fastening the fuse block and position the fuse block aside.

12. Remove the screws holding the main ventilation duct.

13. Remove the nut holding the wiring harness clip.

14. Remove the glove box lamp.

15. Remove the screws at both bottom ends of the instrument panel.

16. Remove the screws at the top of the instrument panel and at the steering column support.

17. Have a helper assist you, and remove the instrument panel assembly from the vehicle.

To install:

18. Carefully install the instrument panel to the vehicle. Be sure to clear all wiring, etc.

19. Install the screws at the steering column support, the top of the instrument panel, and at the bottom of both sides of the instrument panel.

20. Install the glovebox lamp.

21. Install the nut holding the wiring harness clip.

22. Install the screws holding the main ventilation duct.

23. Install the fuse block and parking brake release handle.

24. Install the courtesy lights.

25. Secure the steering column and install the trim plate.

26. Install the ALDL connector.

27. Install the left and right side sound insulators.

28. Install the ashtray or sport pod housing.

29. Install the air outlet trim plates and climate control system switch panel.

30. Install the radio and speakers.

31. Reverse the removal procedure to install the instrument panel pad.

32. Connect the negative battery cable and check all items in the instrument panel for proper operation.

Grand Prix

1. Disconnect the negative battery cable.

2. Remove the instrument panel pad:

a. Remove the 2 screws at the top of the instrument panel trim plate.

b. Remove the glove box and the screw above it.

c. Lift the front of the pad and pull toward you to release the clips.

d. Disconnect the speaker connectors and Daytime Running Lights connector, and remove the pad.

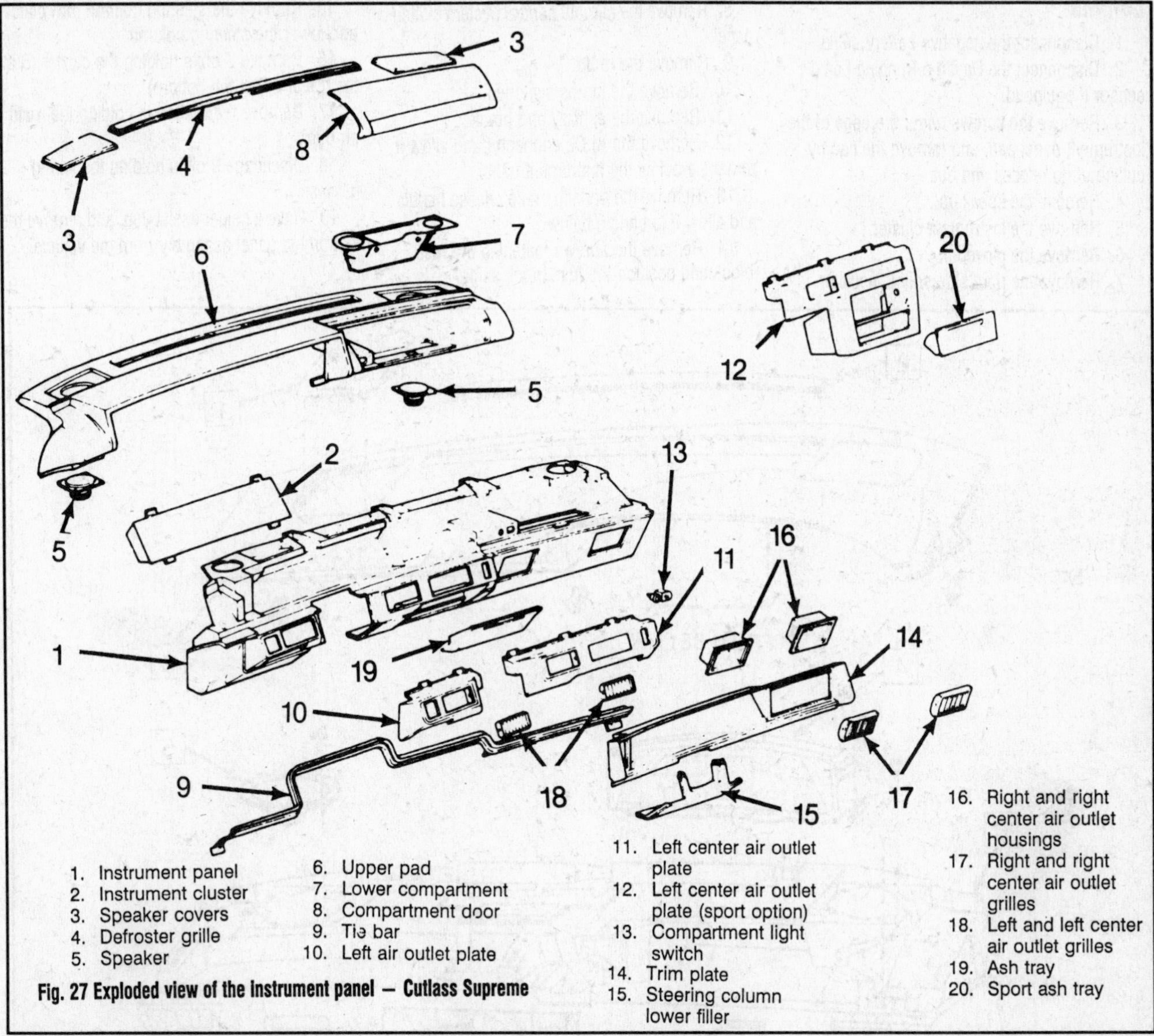

Fig. 27 Exploded view of the instrument panel — Cutlass Supreme

3. Remove the lights switches assembly and wiper/washer switch assembly.
4. Remove the instrument cluster trim plate.
5. Remove the parking brake release handle and allow it to dangle below.
6. Remove the ALDL connector and allow it to dangle below the instrument panel.
7. Remove the left and right side sound insulators.
8. Remove the steering column trim plate.
9. Lower the steering column.
10. Remove the screws fastening the fuse block and position the fuse block aside.
11. Disconnect the HVAC connector and remove the remote radio amplifier.
12. Remove the radio controls trim cover and climate control switch panel trim cover. Then remove the radio and climate control switch panel.
13. Remove the ashtray and cassette deck or compartment that replaces it if not equipped. Remove the remote radio receiver.
14. Remove the instrument cluster.
15. Remove both speakers.
16. Remove 7 screws holding ventilation duct to instrument panel.
17. Remove 3 nuts holding wiring harness carrier.
18. Have a helper assist you, and remove the instrument panel assembly from the vehicle.

To install:

19. Carefully install the instrument panel to the vehicle. Be sure to clear all wiring, etc.
20. Install the nuts holding wiring harness carrier.
21. Install the screws holding ventilation duct to instrument panel.
22. Install the speakers and instrument cluster. Install the remote radio receiver.
23. Install the ashtray and cassette deck or compartment.
24. Install the radio and climate control switch panel and trim covers.
25. Install the remote radio amplifier and connect the HVAC connector.
26. Secure the fuse block.
27. Secure the steering column and install the trim plate.
28. Install the left and right side sound insulators.
29. Install the ALDL connector.
30. Secure the parking brake release handle.
31. Install the instrument cluster trim plate.
32. Install the lights switches assembly and wiper/washer switch assembly.
33. Reverse the removal procedure to install the instrument panel pad.
34. Connect the negative battery cable and check all items in the instrument panel for proper operation.

Lumina

1. Disconnect the negative battery cable.
2. Disconnect the Daytime Running Lamp sensor if equipped.
3. Remove the screws under the edge of the instrument panel pad, and remove the pad by pulling up to release and out.
4. Remove the speakers.
5. Remove the instrument cluster.
6. Remove the glovebox.
7. Remove the right side sound insulator.
8. Remove the climate control system switch panel.
9. Remove the radio.
10. Remove the lamps switches.
11. Remove the ashtray and bracket.
12. Remove the ALDL connector and allow it to dangle below the instrument panel.
13. Remove the parking brake release handle and allow it to dangle below.
14. Remove the screws fastening the fuse block and position the fuse block aside.
15. Remove the steering column trim plate and lower the steering column.
16. Remove 7 bolts holding the carrier (5 at the top and 2 at the bottom).
17. Remove the 5 screws holding the main air duct.
18. Disengage 9 clips holding the wiring harness.
19. Have a helper assist you, and remove the instrument panel assembly from the vehicle.

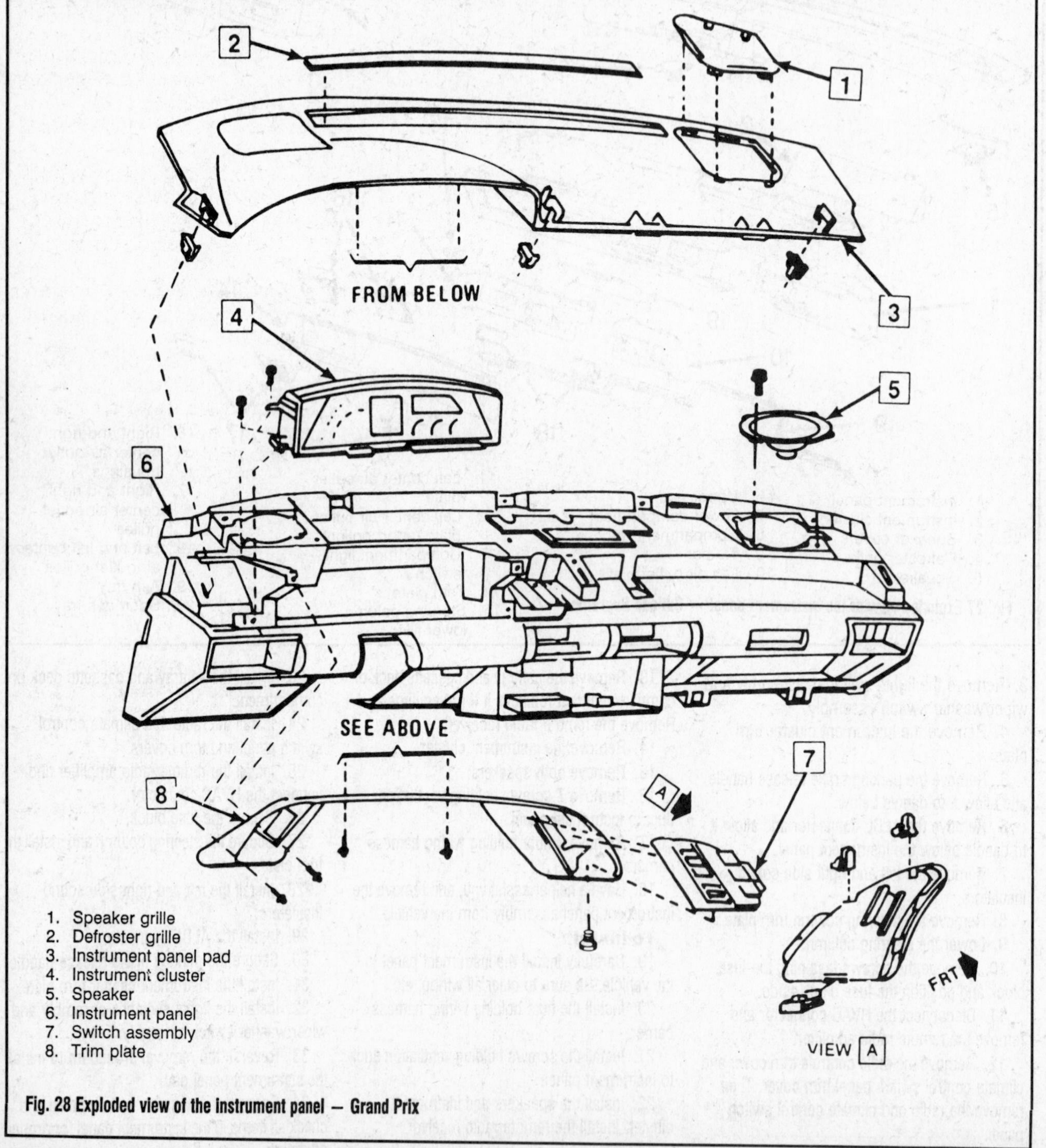

Fig. 28 Exploded view of the instrument panel — Grand Prix

To install:

20. Carefully install the instrument panel to the vehicle. Be sure to clear all wiring, etc.

21. Engage the clips holding the wiring harness.

22. Install the 5 screws holding the main air duct.

23. Install the bolts holding the carrier.

24. Secure the steering column and install the trim plate.

25. Secure the fuse block, parking brake release handle and ALDL connector.

26. Install the ashtray and bracket.

27. Install the lamps switches.

28. Install the radio.

29. Install the climate control system switch panel.

30. Install the right side sound insulator and glovebox.

31. Install the instrument cluster.

32. Install the speakers.

33. Install the instrument panel pad and screws.

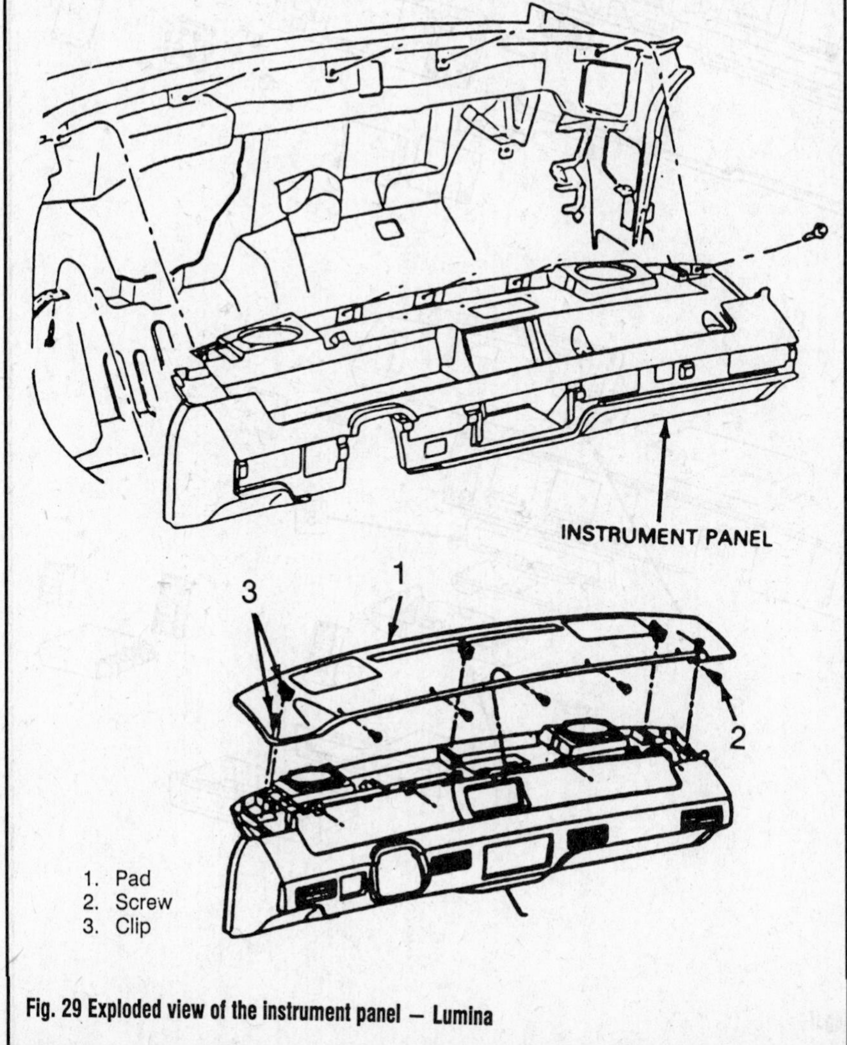

Fig. 29 Exploded view of the instrument panel — Lumina

34. Connect the Daytime Running Lamp sensor if equipped.

35. Connect the negative battery cable and check all items in the instrument panel for proper operation.

Regal

1. Disconnect the negative battery cable.
2. Remove the instrument panel pad:
   a. Carefully pry the speaker grilles and disconnect the Daytime Running Lamp sensor if equipped.
   b. Remove the screw under each speaker grille.
   c. Remove the screws at the lower edge of the instrument panel pad.
   d. Remove the pad by lifting the front and pulling toward you to release it.
3. Remove the speakers
4. Remove the instrument cluster.
5. Remove the glovebox.
6. Remove the right side sound insulator.
7. Remove the climate control system switch panel and sound system controls.
8. Remove the English/Metric switch.
9. Remove the lights switches.
10. Remove the cassette deck or compartment that replaces it if not equipped. Remove the ashtray and bracket.
11. Remove the ALDL connector and allow it to dangle below the instrument panel.
12. Remove the parking brake release handle and allow it to dangle below.
13. Remove the remote radio receiver.
14. Remove the steering column trim plate and lower the steering column.
15. Remove 7 bolts holding the carrier (5 at the top and 2 at the bottom). Remove the 2 bolts above the steering column.
16. Remove the 5 screws holding the main air duct.
17. Remove the 3 nuts holding the conduit. Two are above the glovebox and the other is through the cassette/compartment opening.
18. Disengage 9 clips holding the wiring harness.
19. Have a helper assist you, and remove the instrument panel assembly from the vehicle.

To install:

20. Carefully install the instrument panel to the vehicle. Be sure to clear all wiring, etc.

21. Engage the clips holding the wiring harness.

22. Install the 3 nuts holding the conduit.

23. Install the screws holding the main air duct.

24. Install the bolts holding the carrier.

25. Secure the steering column and install the trim plate.

26. Install the remote radio receiver.

27. Secure the fuse block, parking brake release handle and ALDL connector.

28. Install the ashtray and bracket.

29. Install the cassette deck or compartment.

30. Install the lights switches and English/ Metric switch.

31. Install the climate control system switch panel and sound system controls.

32. Install the right side sound insulator and glovebox.

33. Install the instrument cluster and speakers.

34. Reverse the removal procedure to install the instrument panel pad.

35. Connect the negative battery cable and check all items in the instrument panel for proper operation.

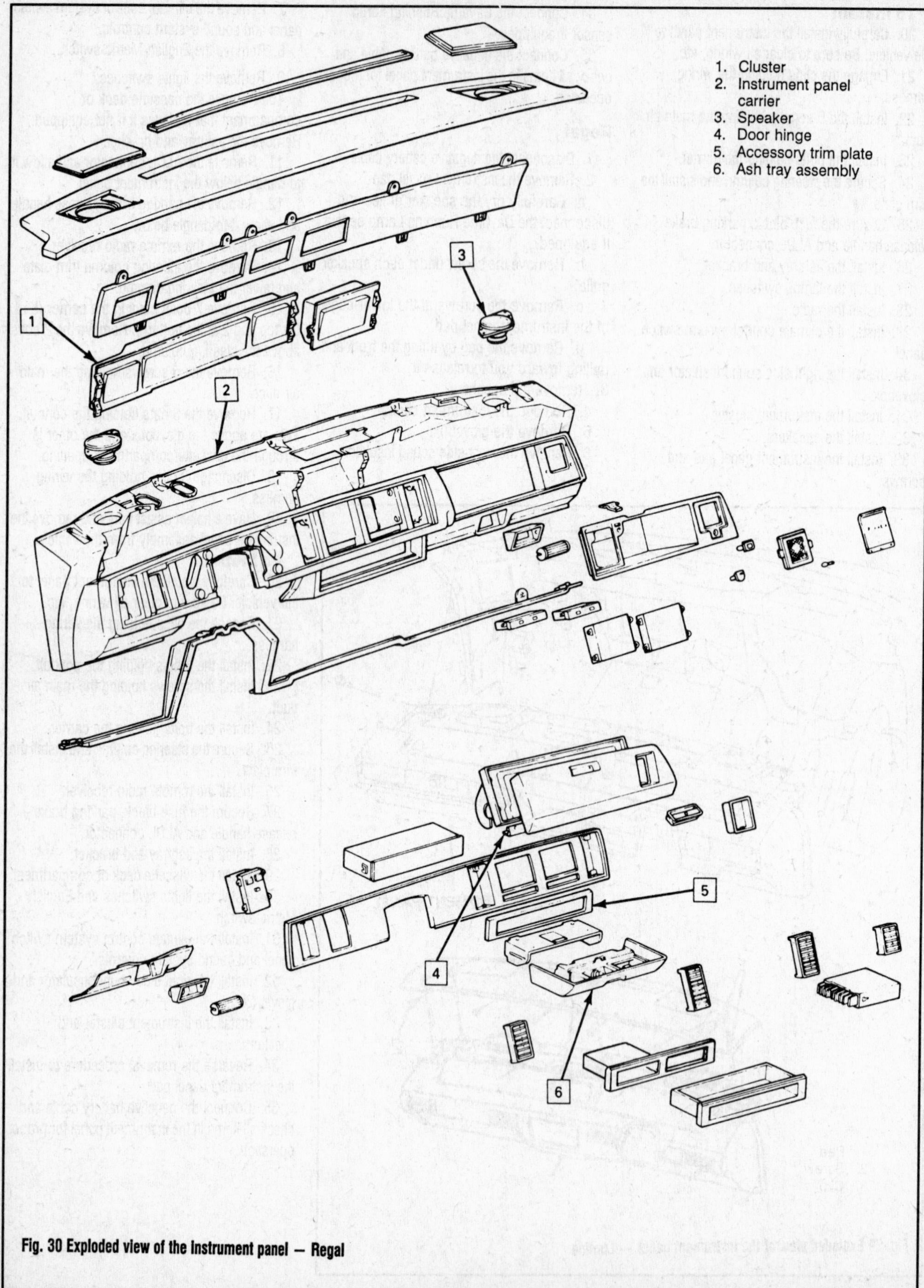

Fig. 30 Exploded view of the instrument panel — Regal

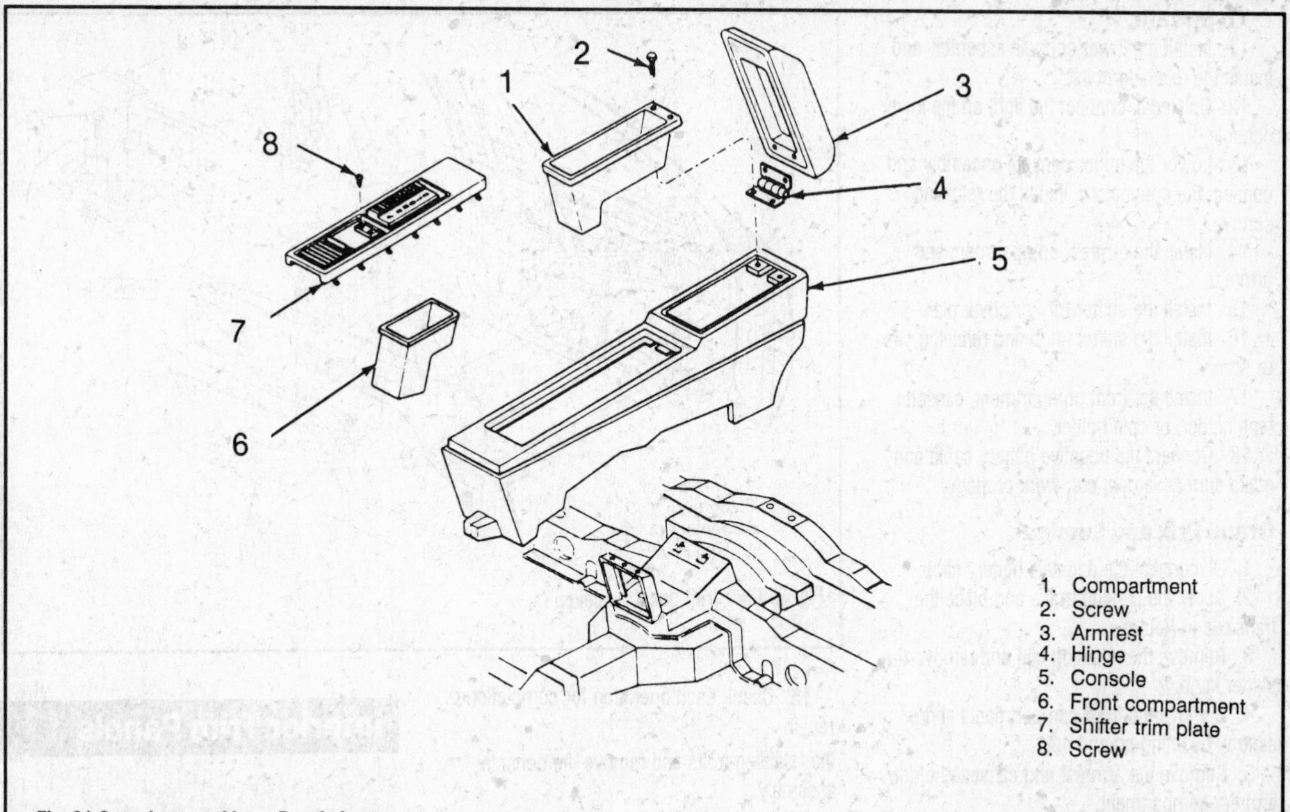

1. Compartment
2. Screw
3. Armrest
4. Hinge
5. Console
6. Front compartment
7. Shifter trim plate
8. Screw

Fig. 31 Console assembly — Regal shown

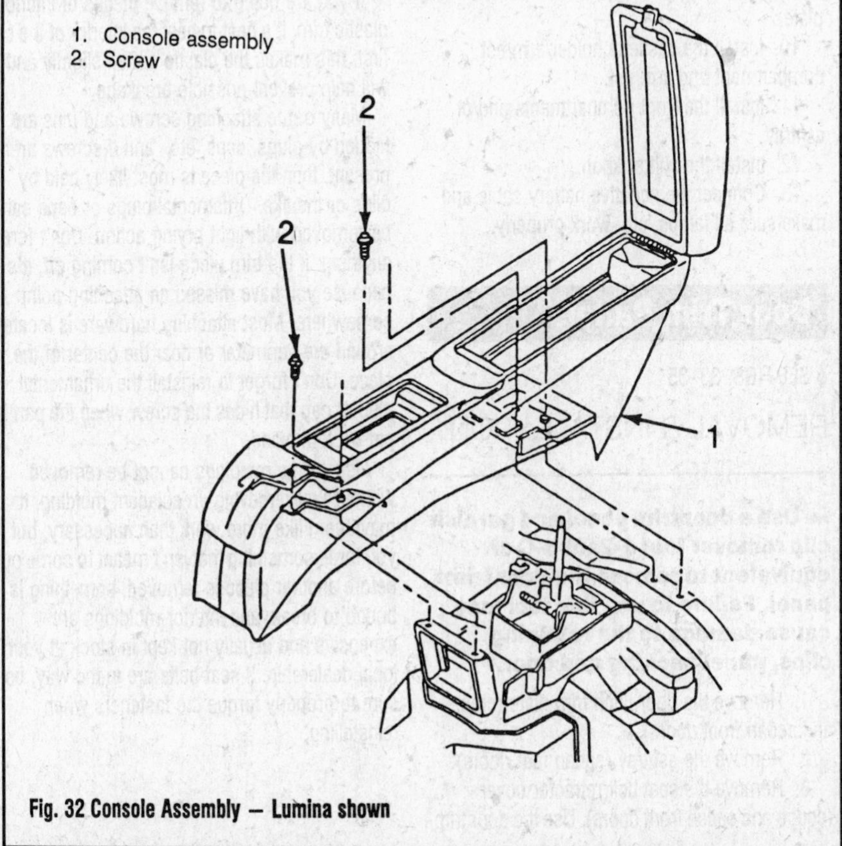

Fig. 32 Console Assembly — Lumina shown

Console

➧ SEE FIGS. 31 AND 32

REMOVAL & INSTALLATION

Cutlass Supreme and Regal

1. Disconnect the negative battery cable.
2. Apply the parking brake and place the transaxle in Neutral.
3. Remove the front compartment, cassette tape holder, or coin holder by lifting up and out.
4. On Regal, remove the retaining clip and remove the shifter knob. On Cutlass Supreme, remove the retaining screw and remove the shifter knob.
5. Remove the shifter trim or cover plate.
6. Remove the armrest and armrest compartment.
7. On Cutlass Supreme, disconnect the lamp at the light at the rear of the upper console.
8. Remove the upper console assembly slowly; disconnect any remaining connectors.
9. On Regal, disconnect the light on the lower console.
10. Remove the retaining bolts and remove the lower console assembly.

To install:

11. Install the lower console assembly and install the retaining bolts.

12. On Regal, connect the light on the lower console.

13. Lower the upper console assembly and connect the connectors. Install the retaining screws.

14. Install the armrest compartment and armrest.

15. Install the shifter trim or cover plate.

16. Install the shifter knob and retaining clip or screw.

17. Install the front compartment, cassette tape holder, or coin holder.

18.` Connect the negative battery cable and make sure all lamps, etc. work properly.

Grand Prix and Lumina

1. Disconnect the negative battery cable.

2. Apply the parking brake and place the transaxle in Neutral.

3. Remove the retaining clip and remove the shifter knob.

4. Remove the front compartments and/or ashtray by lifting up and out.

5. Remove the armrest and cassette holder/armrest compartment.

6. Remove the shifter trim or cover plate assembly. If equipped with trip calculator, lift the rear edge of the trim plate, then pull rear ward to release the clips at the front of the plate. Then remove the trip calculator.

7. Disconnect any remaining wiring, remove panel removing tool J-24595-C to release the clip retainers.

4. Remove the door lock trim plate and the power window switch, if so equipped.

5. Remove the window regulator handle by removing the inner retaining clip, if so equipped.

6. Remove the remote mirror control, if so equipped.

7. Remove the trim panel retaining screws.

8. Remove the door trim panel using the door trim panel removing tool J-24595-C or equivalent.

9. Disconnect all electrical and remote mirror controls.

To install:

10. Install the wiring harnesses through the openings in the panel, if so equipped.

11. Position the trim panel to the door and align the clips. Press the trim panel to the door until all the clips are fully engaged. Align all the holes before engaging the clips.

12. Install the screws, remote mirror control and inside door handle bezel, if so equipped.

13. Install the window regulator handle or power window switch.

14. Install the door trim plate, seat belt retractor cover or ashtray.

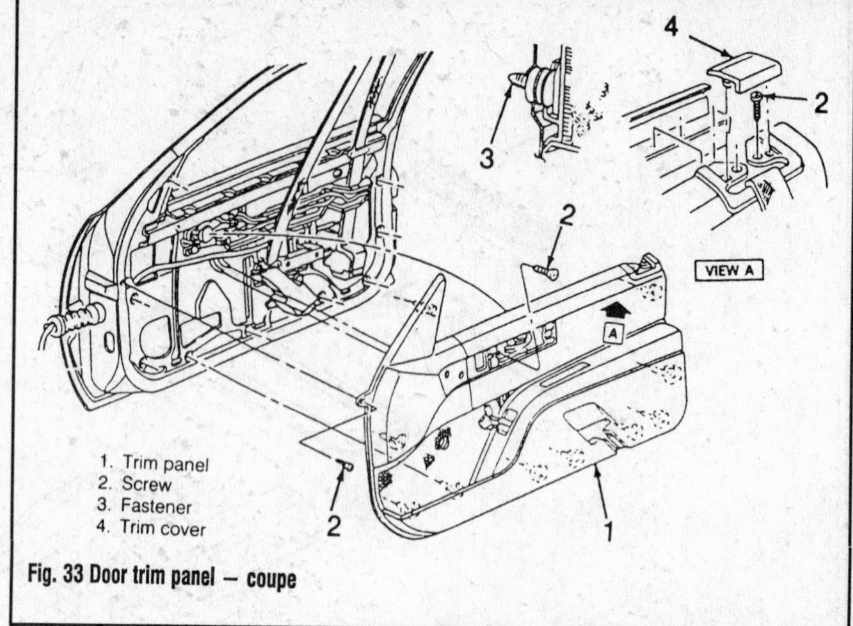

Fig. 33 Door trim panel — coupe

15. Check each operation for completion of repair.

the retaining bolts and remove the console assembly.

To install:

8. Lower the console assembly and connect the connectors. Install the retaining bolts.

9. Install the trip calculator and shifter trim or plate.

10. Install the cassette holder/armrest compartment and armrest.

11. Install the front compartments and/or ashtray

12. Install the shifter knob.

13. Connect the negative battery cable and make sure all lamps, etc. work properly.

Door Trim Panels

➧ SEE FIGS. 33-35

REMOVAL & INSTALLATION

➡ Use a door trim panel and garnish clip remover tool J-24595-C or equivalent to remove the door trim panel. Failure to use this tool may cause damage to the retaining clips, panel backing and door.

1. Remove the door latch trim plate (coupe and sedan front doors).

2. Remove the ashtray (sedan rear doors).

3. Remove the seat belt retractor cover (coupe and sedan front doors). Use the door trim

Interior Trim Panels

REMOVAL & INSTALLATION

If you are going to remove pieces of interior plastic trim, it's best to heat the interior of the car first; this makes the plastic soften slightly and will help prevent possible breakage.

Many of the attaching screws and pins are hidden by plugs, caps, etc., and if screws aren't present, then the piece is most likely held by clips or the like. Ornamental plugs or caps can be removed with light prying action. Don't force anything: if the trim piece isn't coming off, it's because you have missed an attaching point somewhere. Most attaching hardware is located around the perimeter or near the center of the piece. Don't forget to reinstall the ornamental plug or cap that hides the screw when the part is put back in place.

Also, some moldings cannot be removed without first removing an adjacent molding. It may seem like more work than necessary, but if you force something that isn't meant to come out before another piece is removed, something is bound to break, and interior moldings are expensive and usually not kept in stock at your local dealership. If seat belts are in the way, be sure to properly torque the fasteners when reinstalling.

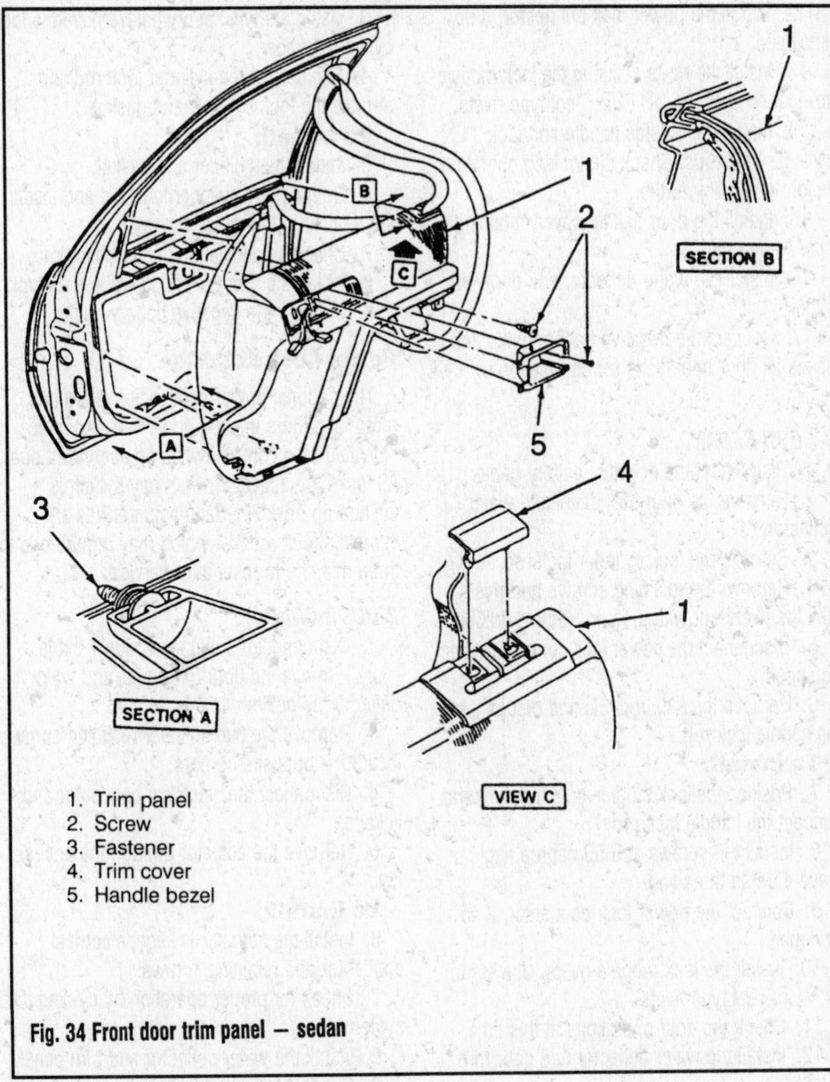

Fig. 34 Front door trim panel — sedan

Headliner

REMOVAL & INSTALLATION

1. Disconnect the negative battery cable.
2. Remove the retaining screws and remove the sun visors.
3. Carefully pry off the dome light lens and remove the revealed nuts to remove the assembly from the roof.
4. Remove the center high mounted stop lamp assembly.
5. Remove the windshield side upper garnish, upper quarter trim panels, and center pillar trim panels.
6. To remove the headliner, separate the hook and loop material until the entire headliner is loose. Then remove through the passenger door.

To install:

7. Load the headliner into the car. Be sure not to bend the preshaped headliner or it will permanently crease! Install the headliner by aligning the sun visor installation holes and engaging the front hook and loop material.
8. Engage the rear and center hook and loop fasteners.
9. Install the center pillar trim panels, upper quarter trim panels, and windshield side upper garnish.
10. Install the center high mounted stop lamp assembly.
11. Install the dome light assembly.
12. Install the sun visors.

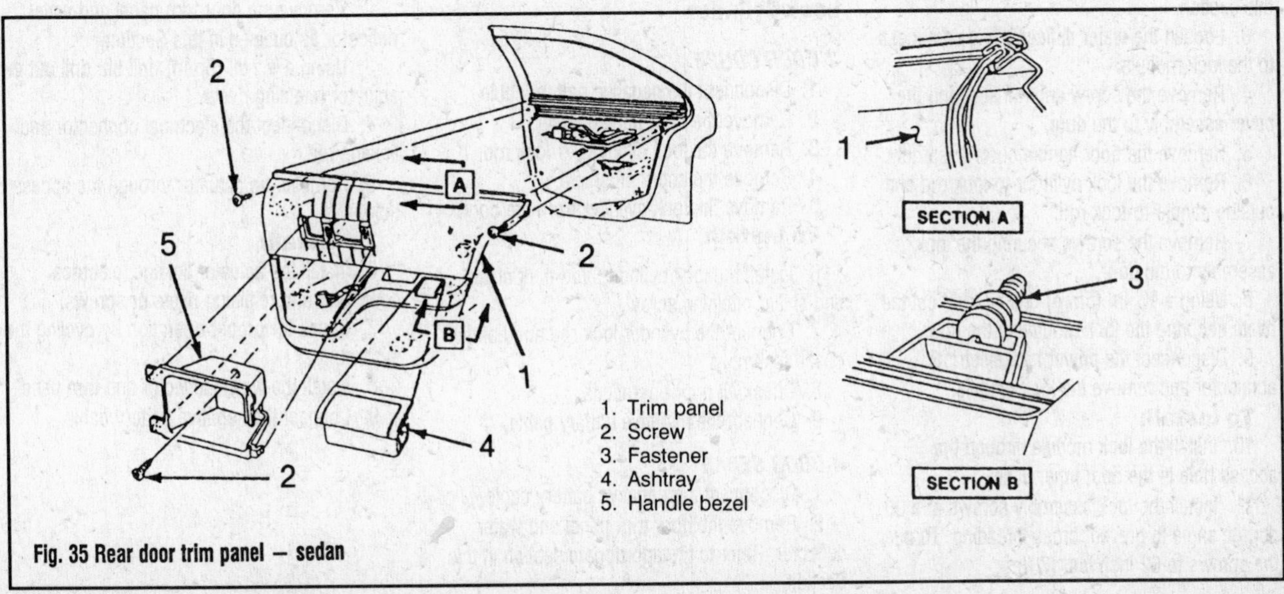

Fig. 35 Rear door trim panel — sedan

Heater/AC Ducts and Outlets

REMOVAL & INSTALLATION

Most outlets are held on by screws, some of which are hidden by other panels i.e. steering column trim panel, glove box door, or other accessory trim panels. If you have removed all visible screws and the outlet will not come out, start removing adjacent panels and look for hidden screws. Inspect the outlet carefully for retaining screws; if none are found, the outlet can most likely be pryed out of its opening. Either way, be sure to remove the outlet carefully as it probably has easily-broken tabs on it.

In order to remove any of the system's main duct work, the instrument panel must first be removed. Then remove the retaining screw(s) and remove the duct(s). Be sure to properly seal the duct when it is reinstalled.

Door Locks

➧ SEE FIGS. 36–39

REMOVAL & INSTALLATION

Lock Module

2-DOOR COUPE

1. Disconnect the negative battery cable.
2. Remove the door trim panel as outlined in this section.
3. Loosen the water deflector to gain access to the lock module.
4. Remove the screw and nut securing the cover assembly to the door.
5. Remove the door handle cover assembly.
6. Remove the lock cylinder-to-lock rod and outside handle-to-lock rod.
7. Remove the screws securing the lock assembly to the door.
8. Using a $^3/_{16}$ in. (5mm) drill bit, drill out the rivets securing the lock module to the door.
9. Disconnect the power lock electrical connector and remove the lock module.

To Install:

10. Install the lock module through the access hole in the door inner panel.
11. Install the lock assembly screws at a 90 degree angle to prevent cross threading. Torque the screws to 62 inch lbs. (7 Nm).
12. Install the power lock connector, if so equipped.
13. Install the rivets securing the lock module-to-door. Use $^3/_{16}$ in. × $^1/_4$ in. peel type rivets.
14. Install the outside handle and lock cylinder lock rods. Check the locking operation before going any further.
15. Install the door handle cover, retaining screws and nuts.
16. Install the water deflector and door trim panel.
17. Connect the negative battery cable and check all door operations for completion of repair.

4-DOOR SEDAN

1. Disconnect the negative battery cable.
2. Remove the door trim panel and water deflector.
3. Remove the lock cylinder lock rod.
4. Remove the retaining screws and rivets. Drill the rivets out with a $^3/_{16}$ in. (5mm) drill bit.
5. Disconnect the power lock connector, if so equipped.
6. Remove the lock module and disconnect the handle lock rod.

To Install:

7. Position the lock module onto the door and connect the handle lock rod.
8. Install the screws at a 90 degree angle to prevent cross threading.
9. Connect the power lock connector, if so equipped.
10. Install the lock module rivets. Use $^3/_{16}$ in. × $^1/_4$ in. peel type rivets.
11. Check the door operations at this time.
12. Install the water deflector and door trim panel.
13. Connect the negative battery cable and recheck door operations.

Lock Cylinder

2-DOOR COUPE

1. Disconnect the negative battery cable.
2. Remove the door handle cover.
3. Remove the lock cylinder-to-lock rod.
4. Remove the anti-theft shield.
5. Remove the lock cylinder from the door.

To Install:

6. Install the lock cylinder, anti-theft shield and shield retaining screw.
7. Connect the cylinder lock rod and handle cover assembly.
8. Check all door operations.
9. Connect the negative battery cable.

4-DOOR SEDAN

1. Disconnect the negative battery cable.
2. Remove the door trim panel and water deflector. Refer to the appropriate section in this Section.
3. Using a small flat pry bar, remove the lock cylinder retainer.
4. Disconnect the cylinder lock rod and remove the lock cylinder and gasket.

To Install:

5. Install the cylinder and gasket.
6. Connect the cylinder lock rod and install the retainer with a small flat pry bar.
7. Check all door operations at this time.
8. Install the trim panel and water deflector.
9. Connect the negative battery cable.

Power Lock Actuator

The optional power door lock system has motor actuators in each door. The system is activated by a control switch on each front door. All locks are activated when any switch is pushed up or down. Each actuator has an internal circuit breaker which may require one to three minutes to reset after service.

2-DOOR COUPE

1. Disconnect the negative battery cable.
2. Remove the door trim panel and water deflector as outlined in this Section.
3. Remove the two actuator retaining screws located at opposite corners.
4. Disconnect the electrical connector and linkage.
5. Remove the actuator through the access hole.

To Install:

6. Install the actuator linkage, electrical connector and retaining screws.
7. Check for proper operation by cycling the system.
8. Install the water deflector and trim panel.
9. Connect the negative battery cable.

4-DOOR SEDAN

1. Disconnect the negative battery cable.
2. Remove the door trim panel and water deflector as outlined in this Section.
3. Using a $^3/_{16}$ in. (5mm) drill bit, drill out the actuator retaining rivets.
4. Disconnect the electrical connector and linkage rod.
5. Remove the actuator through the access hole.

To Install:

6. Install the actuator linkage, electrical connector and retaining rivets or screws.
7. Check for proper operation by cycling the system.
8. Install the water deflector and trim panel.
9. Connect the negative battery cable.

1. Screws
2. Rivets
3. Connector
4. Lock module assembly
5. Rod
6. Rod
7. Retainer
8. Handle
9. Lock assembly
10. Screws
11. Actuator

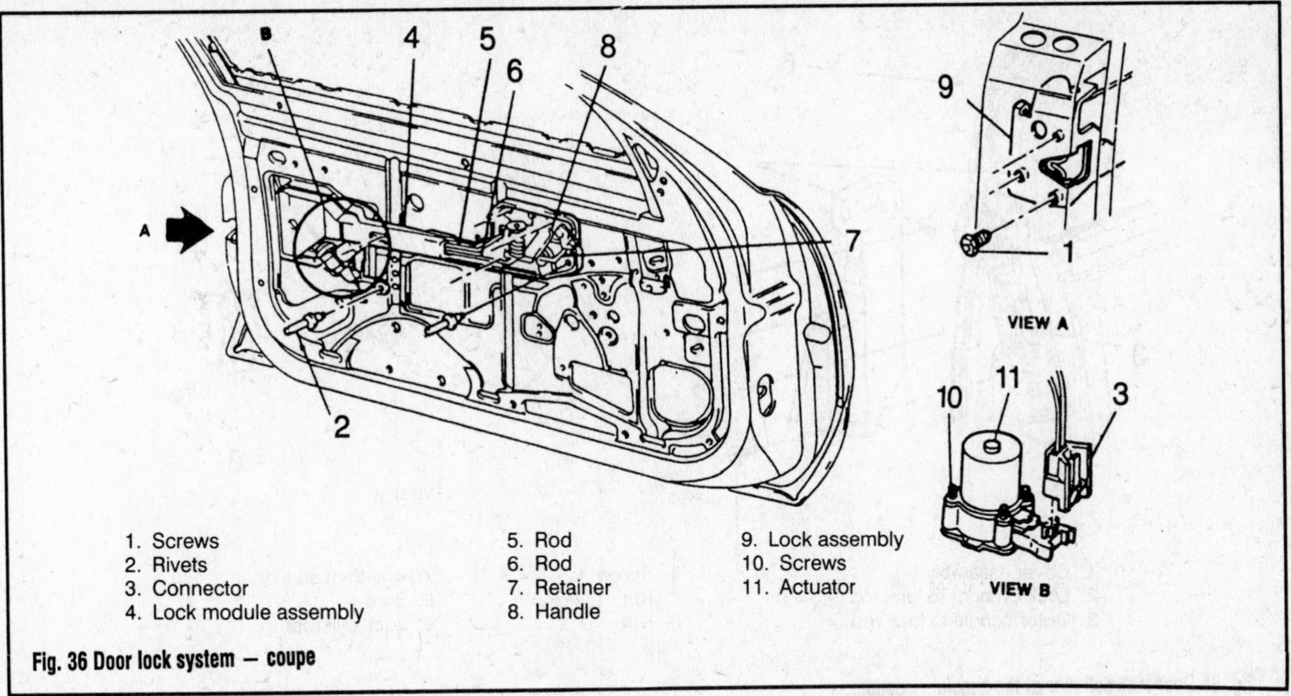

Fig. 36 Door lock system — coupe

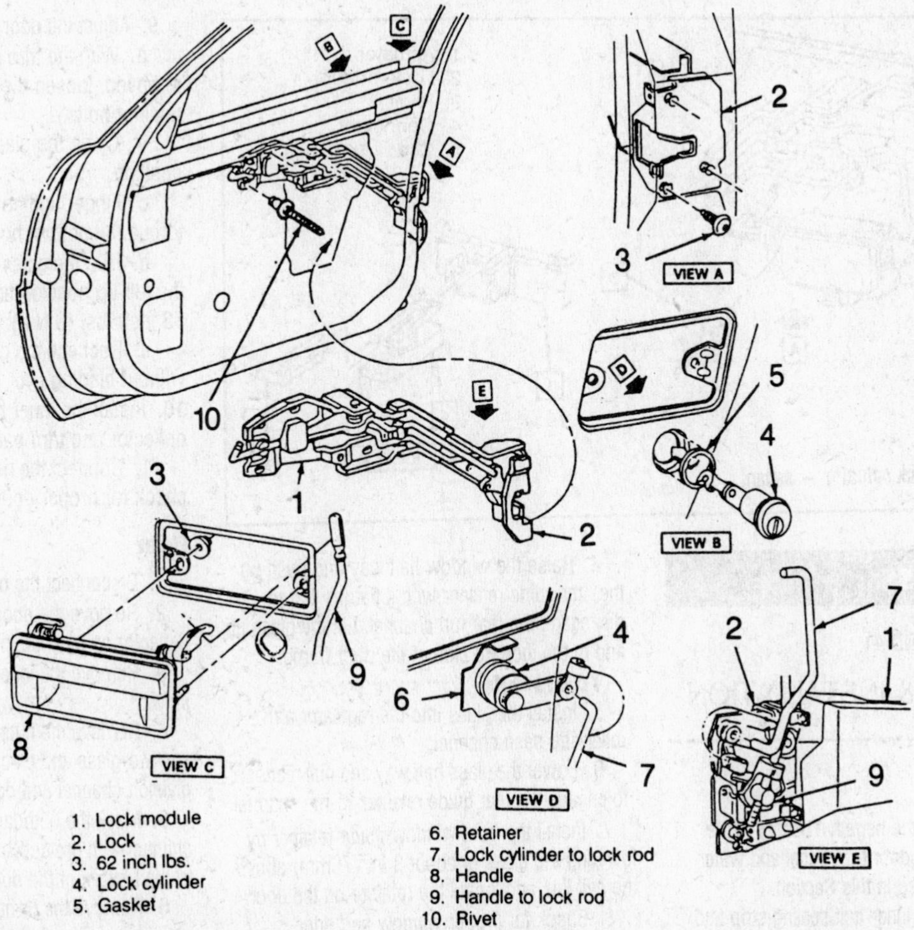

1. Lock module
2. Lock
3. 62 inch lbs.
4. Lock cylinder
5. Gasket
6. Retainer
7. Lock cylinder to lock rod
8. Handle
9. Handle to lock rod
10. Rivet

Fig. 37 Front door lock system — sedan; rear door similar

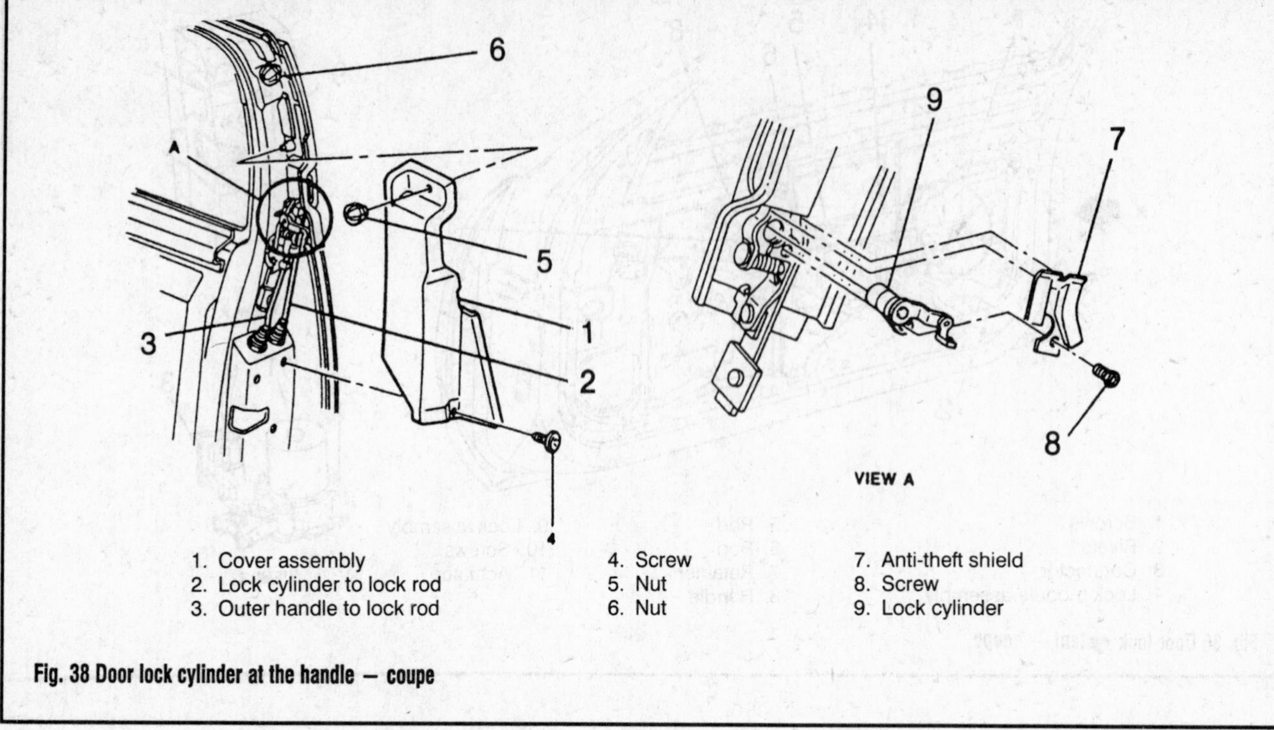

Fig. 38 Door lock cylinder at the handle — coupe

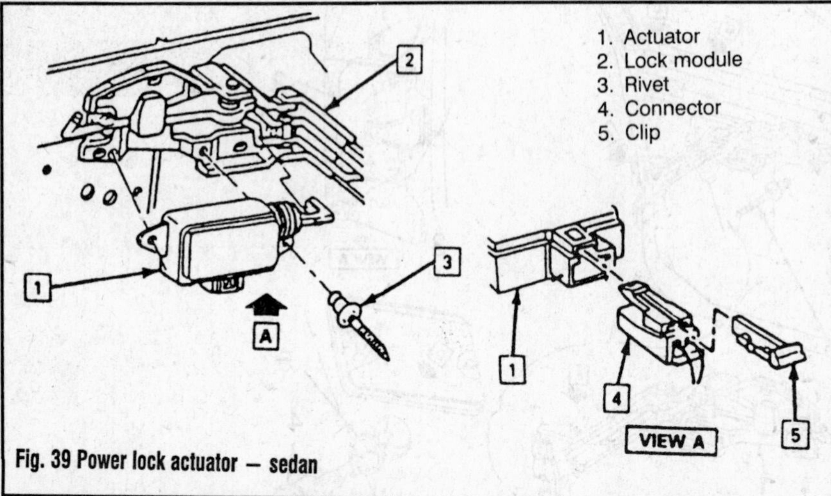

Fig. 39 Power lock actuator — sedan

Door Glass

➧ SEE FIGS. 40 AND 41

REMOVAL & INSTALLATION

Front

1. Disconnect the negative battery cable.
2. Remove the door trim panel and water deflector as outlined in this Section.
3. Remove the inner belt sealing strip and front window guide retainer.
4. Raise the window half way and push on the rear guide retainer with a flat pry bar to disengage the rear run channel. Lift the glass up and to the inboard side of the door frame.

To install:

5. Install the glass into the regulator arm roller and sash channel.
6. Lower the glass half way and pull rearward to engage the rear guide retainer-to-run channel.
7. Install the front window guide retainer by lowering the glass to about 3 in. (76mm) above the belt line and locate the retainer on the door.
8. Check for proper window and door operation at this time.
9. Adjust the door glass as follows.
   a. With the trim panel and water deflector removed, loosen the front window guide retainer bolts.
   b. Cycle the glass to the full DOWN position.
   c. Finger tighten the top retainer bolt and torque the bottom bolt to 53 inch lbs. (6 Nm).
   d. Run the glass up to 1 in. (25mm) from the full-up position and torque the top bolt to 53 inch lbs. (6 Nm).
   e. Recheck the glass for proper operation without binding.
10. Install the inner belt sealing strip, water deflector and trim panel.
11. Connect the negative battery cable and check for proper door operation.

Rear

1. Disconnect the negative battery cable.
2. Remove the door trim panel and water deflector as outlined in this Section.
3. Remove the inner and outer belt sealing strip.
4. Remove the nuts securing the regulator sash-to-glass and place a wedge between the division channel and door outer panel.
5. Mask the outboard side of the division channel with protective tape and lower the glass to the bottom of the door.
6. Remove the front portion of the glass channel from the front door frame.

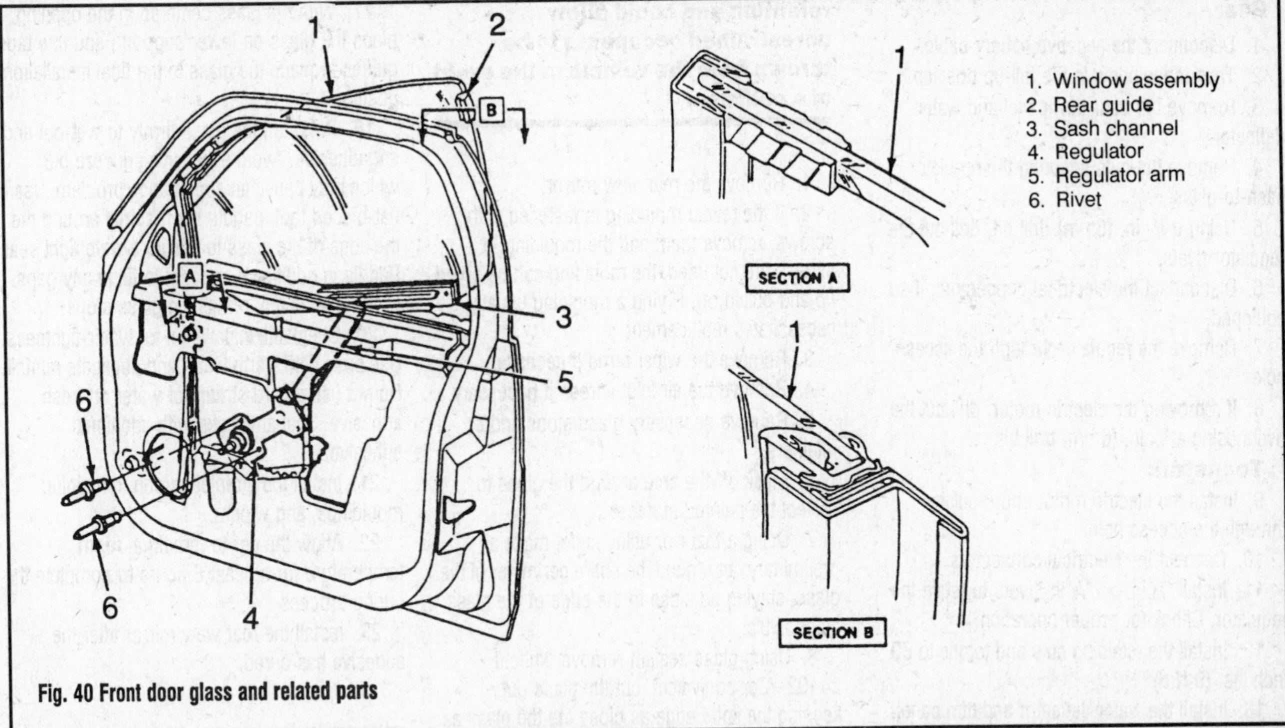

Fig. 40 Front door glass and related parts

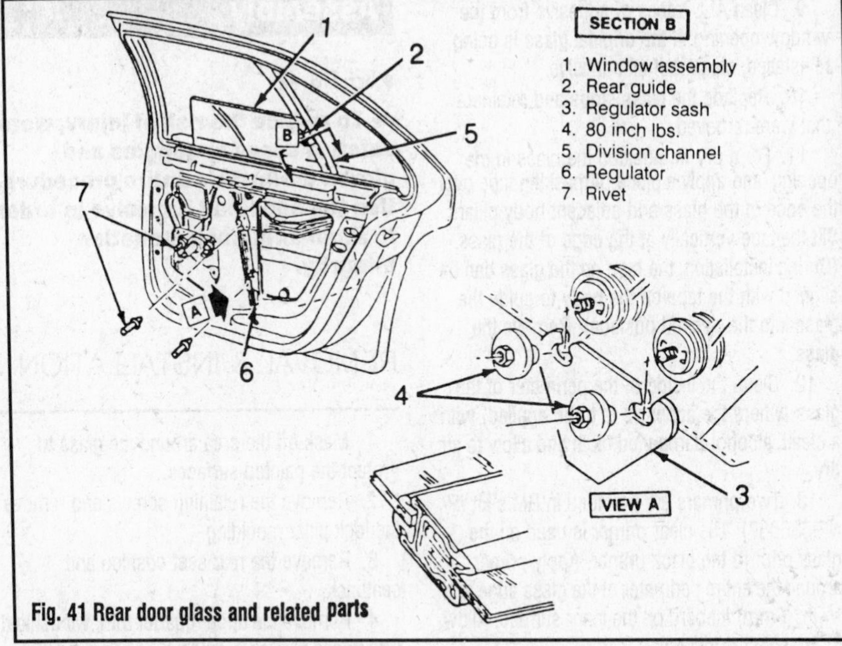

Fig. 41 Rear door glass and related parts

7. Make sure the glass is disengaged from the division channel and lift the glass upward and outboard of the door frame.

To install:

8. Install the glass to the door from the outboard side.
9. Install the front portion of the window channel-to-door frame by lowering the glass to the bottom.
10. Install the rear guide-to-division channel. Torque the nuts to 80 inch lbs. (9 Nm).
11. Remove the wedge and masking tape.
12. Check the window for proper operation.
13. Install the outer and inner belt sealing strips.
14. Install the water deflector and trim panel.
15. Connect the negative battery cable.

Window Regulator and Electric Motor

REMOVAL & INSTALLATION

Front

1. Disconnect the negative battery cable.
2. Tape the window in the full-up position.
3. Remove the door trim panel and water deflector.
4. Using a 1/4 in. (6mm) drill bit, drill out the regulator rivets.
5. Remove the regulator by disengaging the regulator arm from the sash channel.
6. Disconnect the electrical connectors, if so equipped.
7. If removing the electric motor, drill out the rivets using a 1/4 in. (6mm) drill bit.

To install:

8. Install the regulator through the access hole and attach the regulator arm-to-sash channel.
9. Connect the electrical connectors.
10. Install 1/4 in. × 1/2 in. rivets to retain the regulator. Check for proper operation.
11. Install the water deflector and trim panel.
12. Connect the negative battery cable and remove the tape.

Rear

1. Disconnect the negative battery cable.
2. Tape the window in the full-up position.
3. Remove the door trim panel and water deflector.
4. Remove the nuts securing the regulator sash-to-glass.
5. Using a $^1/_4$ in. (6mm) drill bit, drill out the regulator rivets.
6. Disconnect the electrical connectors, if so equipped.
7. Remove the regulator through the access hole.
8. If removing the electric motor, drill out the rivets using a $^1/_4$ in. (6mm) drill bit.

To install:

9. Install the electric motor and regulator through the access hole.
10. Connect the electrical connectors.
11. Install $^1/_4$ in. × $^1/_2$ in. rivets to retain the regulator. Check for proper operation.
12. Install the retaining nuts and torque to 80 inch lbs. (9 Nm).
13. Install the water deflector and trim panel.
14. Connect the negative battery cable and remove the tape.

Windshield or Rear Window

➡ **Stationary glass replacement is another of those items on a car that is best done by a professional. It is tough to accomplish satisfactory results in your backyard, and less than perfect results can be ultimately dangerous and can cause problems like water leaks, creaks and cracks. If you want to attempt it, follow the procedure exactly and work very carefully.**

REMOVAL & INSTALLATION

✲✲ CAUTION

To reduce the risk of injury, wear safety glasses or goggles and gloves during this entire procedure. Use the specified adhesive in order to attain original installation integrity. Use of anything else could result in poor window retention and could allow unrestrained occupants to be thrown from the vehicle in the event of a collision.

1. Remove the rear view mirror.
2. If the reveal moulding is fastened with screws, remove them and the moulding. If screws are not used, the moulding can be pryed up and pulled off. Prying a moulding usually necessitates replacement.
3. Remove the wiper arms if necessary.
4. Remove the air inlet screen if necessary.
5. Remove necessary glass stops and/or retainers.
6. Mask off the area around the glass to protect the painted surfaces.
7. Using a razor or utility knife, make a preliminary cut around the entire perimeter of the glass, staying as close to the edge of the glass as possible.
8. Using glass sealant remover knife J 24402–A or equivalent, cut the glass out, keeping the knife edge as close the the glass as possible. Remove the glass from the opening.

To install:

9. Clean ALL traces of adhesive from the window opening. If the original glass is being reinstalled, clean it of all adhesive.
10. Replace the glass stops and retainers that were removed.
11. For a dry fit, position the glass in the opening, and apply a piece of masking tape over the edge of the glass and adjacent body pillars. Slit the tape vertically at the edge of the glass. (During installation, the tape on the glass can be aligned with the tape on the body to guide the glass into the desired position). Remove the glass.
12. Clean the inside of the perimeter of the glass (where the adhesive is to be applied) with a clean, alcohol-dampened cloth and allow to air dry.
13. Two primers are provided in GM's kit (P/N 9636067). The clear primer is used on the glass prior to the black primer. Apply primer around the entire perimeter of the glass edge and $^1/_4$ in. (6mm) inboard on the inner surface. Allow to dry about 5 minutes.
14. Apply a smooth continuous bead of adhesive on the primed edge of the glass.
15. Install the reveal mounding with butyl tape on the top edge of the glass to retain the moulding.
16. With the aid of a helper, lift the windshield into the window opening or use suction cups to lift the backglass into its opening.
17. With the glass centered in the opening, place the glass on lower supports and use tape guides to place the glass in the final installation position.
18. Press on the glass firmly to wet-out and set adhesive. Avoid excessive squeeze out which may cause an appearance problem. Use a flat-bladed tool, paddle the material around the the edge of the glass to ensure a watertight seal. Paddle in additional material to fill in any gaps.
19. Install any remaining glass stops.
20. Check the installation for water-tightness. Use hose with warm water and duplicate rainfall. Do not use a hard stream of water on fresh adhesive. Seal any leaks with additional adhesive.
21. Install the air inlet screen, remaining mouldings, and wipers.
22. Allow the car to remain at room temperature for at least 6 hours to complete the curing process.
23. Install the rear view mirror after the adhesive has cured.

Quarter Window Assembly

➧ SEE FIG. 42

➡ **To reduce the risk of injury, wear safety glasses or goggles and gloves during this entire procedure. Use the specified adhesive in order to attain original installation integrity.**

REMOVAL & INSTALLATION

1. Mask off the area around the glass to protect the painted surfaces.
2. Remove the retaining screws and remove the lock pillar moulding.
3. Remove the rear seat cushion and seatback.
4. Remove the upper quarter trim, windshield trim upper garnish moulding, and lower quarter trim..
5. Using a curved blade tile knife or similar item, use multiple shallow cuts, and cut out the quarter window assembly out of its opening. Remove the window assembly.

To install:

6. Clean ALL traces of urethane from the pinch weld flange. To prevent corrosion, paint damage on the pinch weld by the knife must be covered with primer before installing the window.

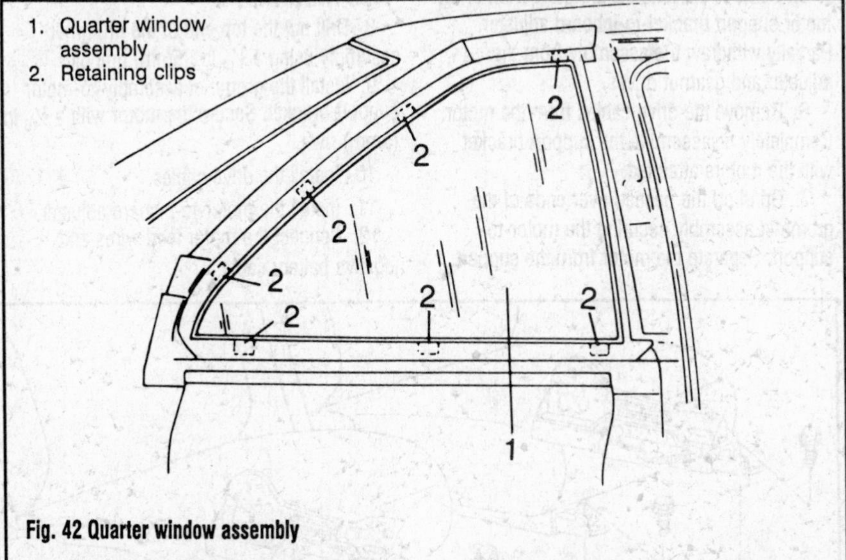

Fig. 42 Quarter window assembly

7. Two primers are provided in GM's kit (P/N 9636067). The clear primer is used prior to the black primer. Apply primer around the entire perimeter of the assembly. Allow to dry. Then apply the black primer over the clear primer and to the pinch weld flange. Allow to dry about 5 minutes.

8. Apply a smooth continuous $^3/_8$ in. (10mm) bead of urethane around the window assembly.

9. Install the quarter window assembly into the opening.

10. Install the retaining clips.

11. Check the installation for water-tightness. Use a hose with warm water and duplicate rainfall. Do not use a hard stream of water on fresh urethane. Seal any leaks with additional material.

12. Install all trim pieces and seat parts.

13. Allow the car to remain at room temperature for at least 6 hours to complete the curing process.

Inside Rear View Mirror

REMOVAL & INSTALLATION

The rearview mirror is attached to a support which is secured to the windshield glass. A service replacement windshield glass has the support bonded to the glass assembly. To install a detached mirror support or install a new part, use the following procedures to complete the service.

1. Locate the support position at the center of the glass 3 in. (76mm) from the top of the glass to the top of the support.

2. Circle the location on the outside of the glass with a wax pencil or crayon. Draw a large circle around the support circle.

3. Clean the area within the circle with household cleaner and dry with a clean towel. Repeat the procedures using rubbing alcohol.

4. Sand the bonding surface of the support with fine grit (320360) emery cloth or sandpaper. If the original support is being used, remove the old adhesive with rubbing alcohol and a clean towel.

5. Apply the adhesive as outlined in the kit instructions.

6. Position the support to the marked location with the rounded end UP.

CAUTION

Do NOT apply excessive pressure to the windshield glass. The glass may break, causing personal injury.

7. Press the support to the glass for 30–60 seconds. Excessive adhesive can be removed after five minutes with rubbing alcohol.

Seats

SEE FIGS. 43–47

REMOVAL & INSTALLATION

Front

1. Operate the seat to the full-forward position (full-forward and full-up if six way power seat).

2. Remove the track covers and front anchor bolts.

3. Operate the seat to the full-rearward position.

4. Remove the rear anchor bolts.

5. Disconnect the electrical connectors (six way power seats).

6. With an assistant, lift the seat out of the vehicle making sure the spacer washers remain in place.

Be careful not to damage the interior and painted surfaces when removing the seat assemblies.

To Install:

7. With an assistant, install the seat assembly into place and make sure the spacer washers are located between the floor pan and seat tracks.

8. Connect the electrical connectors (six way power seats).

9. Install the rear anchor bolts and torque to 15 ft. lbs. (20 Nm).

10. Operate the seat to the full-forward position.

11. Install the front anchor bolts and torque to 20 ft. lbs. (27 Nm).

12. Install the track covers and check for proper operation.

Rear

1. Remove the two bolts at the base of the seat bottom (one bolt for buckets).

2. Remove the seat bottom by lifting up and pulling out.

3. At the bottom of the seatback, remove the two or four anchor nuts.

4. Grasp the bottom of the seatback and swing upward to disengage the offsets on the upper frame bar. Then lift the seat and remove.

To Install:

5. Slide the seatback into place and make sure the offsets are engaged to the seatback.

6. Install the retaining nuts and torque to 20 ft. lbs. (27 Nm).

7. Install the seat bottom into position and torque the retaining bolts to 20 ft. lbs. (27 Nm).

Head Rest

REMOVAL & INSTALLATION

1. Fabricate a head rest removing tool as shown in the "Head Rest Removal" illustration in this section.

2. Raise the head rest to the full-up position.

3. Insert the spring clip release tool down into the left head rest shaft.

4. Push the head rest and tool down at the same time to disengage the detent from the tab.
5. Lift the head rest out after the detent has been released.

To Install:

6. Install the shafts into the guides.
7. Push the head rest into the full-down position.
8. Raise the head rest to ensure the detent is properly seated.

Power Seat Motors

The six-way power seat adjusters are actuated by three 12V, reversible permanent magnet motors with built in circuit breakers. The motors drive the front and rear vertical gearnuts and a horizontal actuator. When the adjusters are at their limit of travel, an overload relay provides stall torque so the motors are not overloaded. Each motor can be serviced as a separate unit.

REMOVAL & INSTALLATION

1. Disconnect the negative battery cable.
2. Remove the seat assembly from the vehicle as outlined in this Section.
3. Remove the adjuster assembly from the seat.
4. Remove the feed wires from the motor.
5. Remove the nuts securing the front of the motor support bracket-to-inboard adjuster. Partially withdraw the assembly from the adjuster and gearnut drives.
6. Remove the drive cables from the motor. Completely disassemble the support bracket with the motors attached.
7. Grind off the peened over ends of the grommet assembly securing the motor-to-support. Separate the motor from the support.

To Install:

8. Drill out the top end of the grommet assembly using a $^{3}/_{16}$ in. (5mm) drill bit.
9. Install the grommet assembly-to-motor support bracket. Secure the motor with a $^{3}/_{16}$ in. (5mm) rivet.
10. Install the drive cables.
11. Install the motor-to-inboard adjuster.
12. Connect the motor feed wires and negative battery cable.

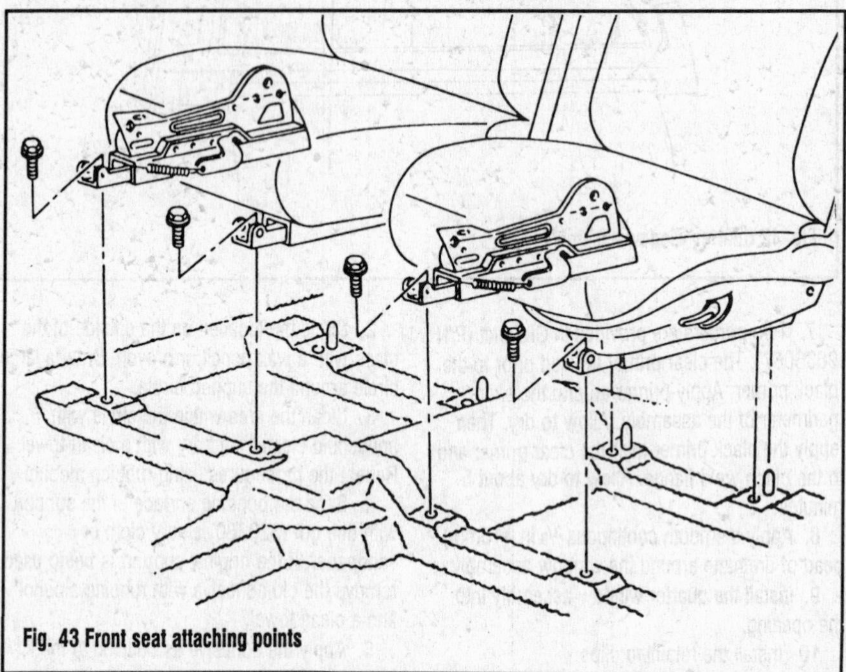

Fig. 43 Front seat attaching points

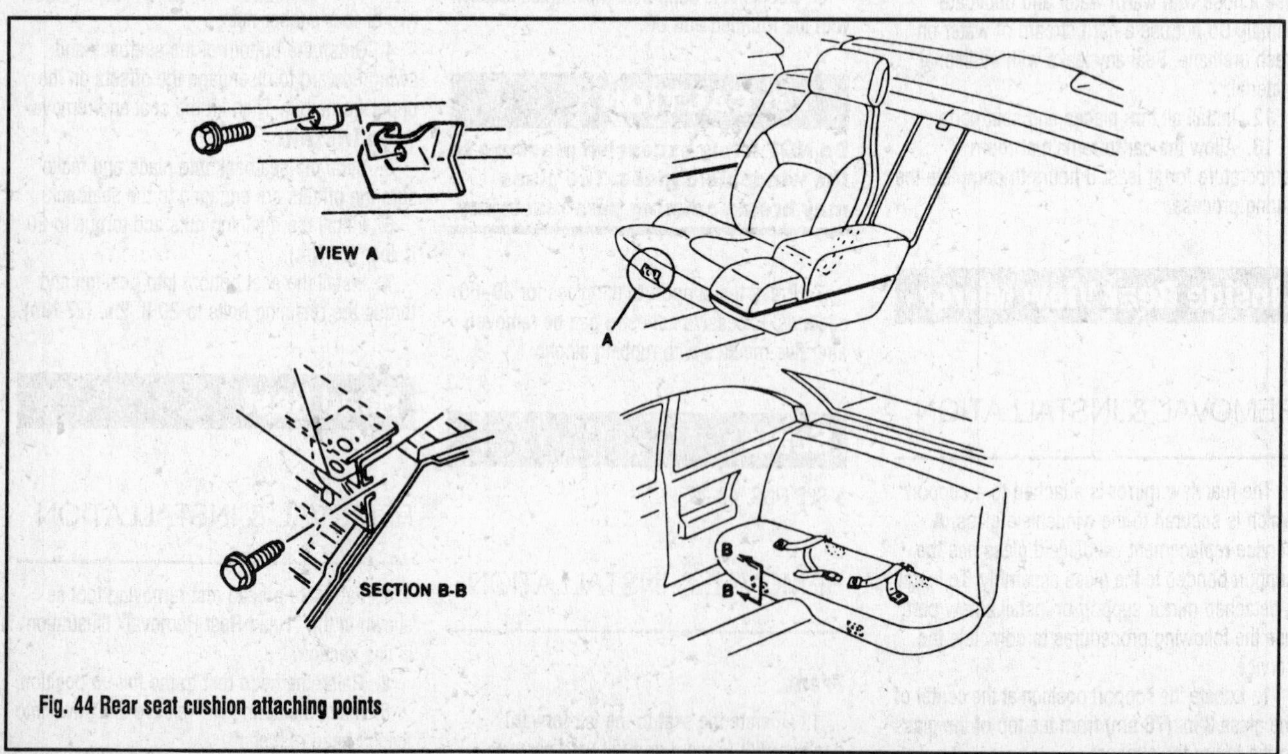

Fig. 44 Rear seat cushion attaching points

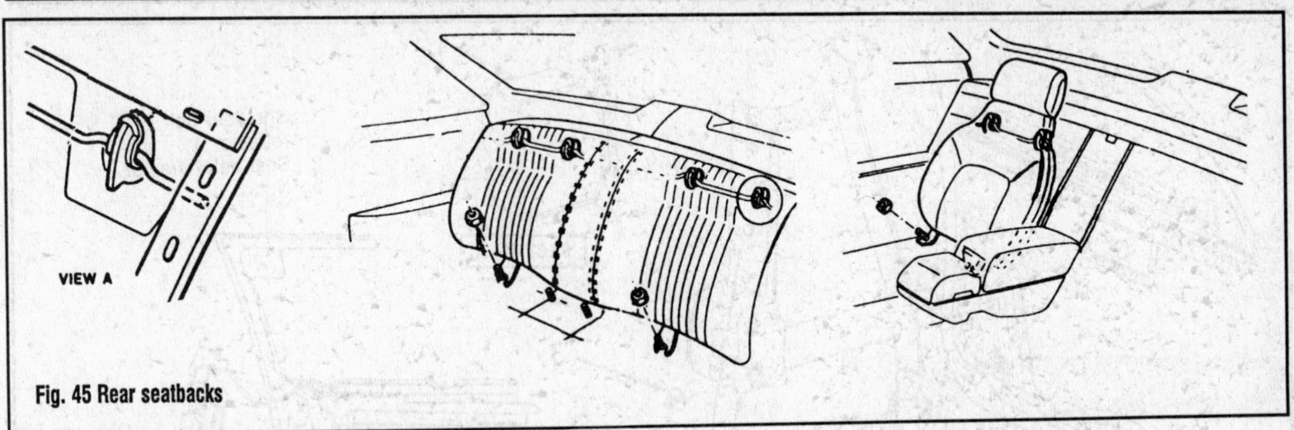

Fig. 45 Rear seatbacks

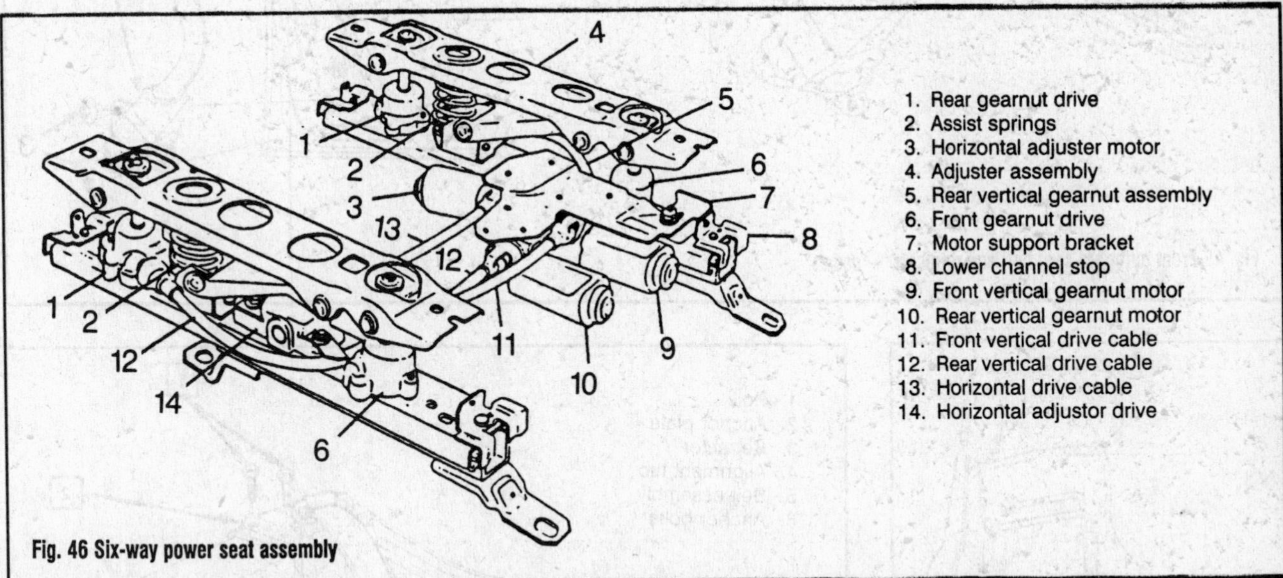

Fig. 46 Six-way power seat assembly

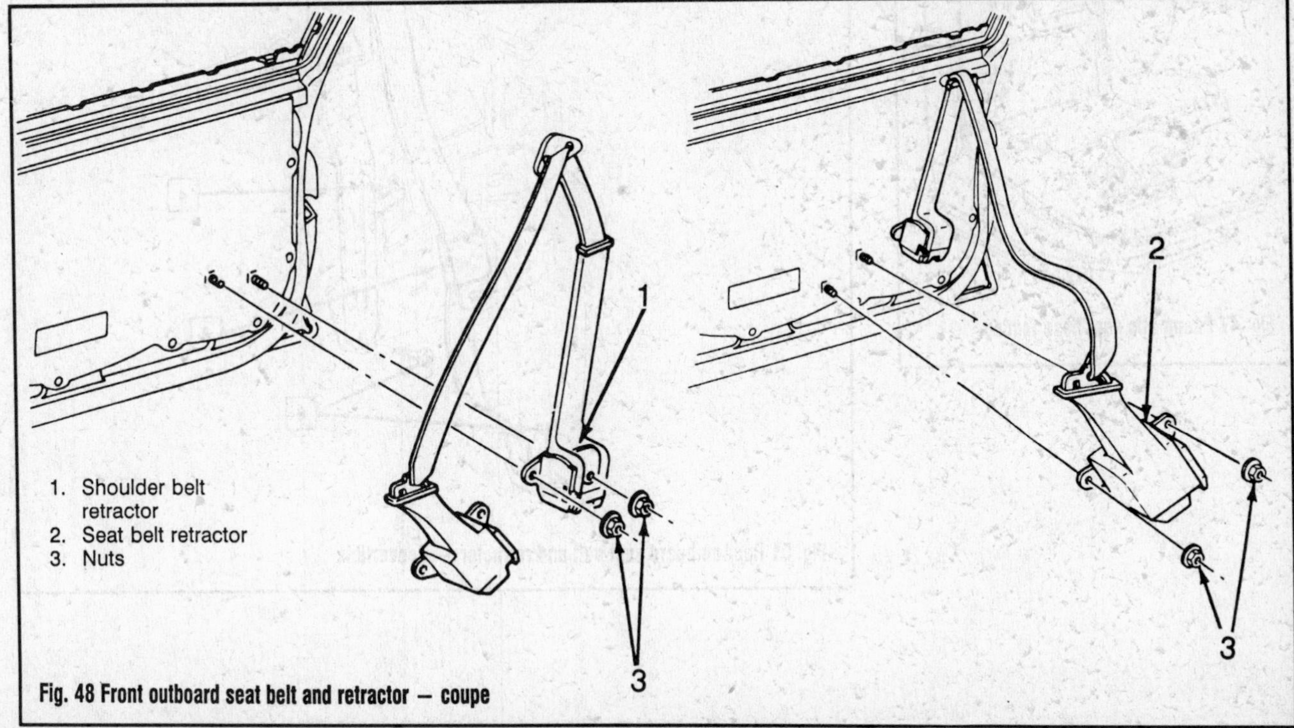

Fig. 48 Front outboard seat belt and retractor — coupe

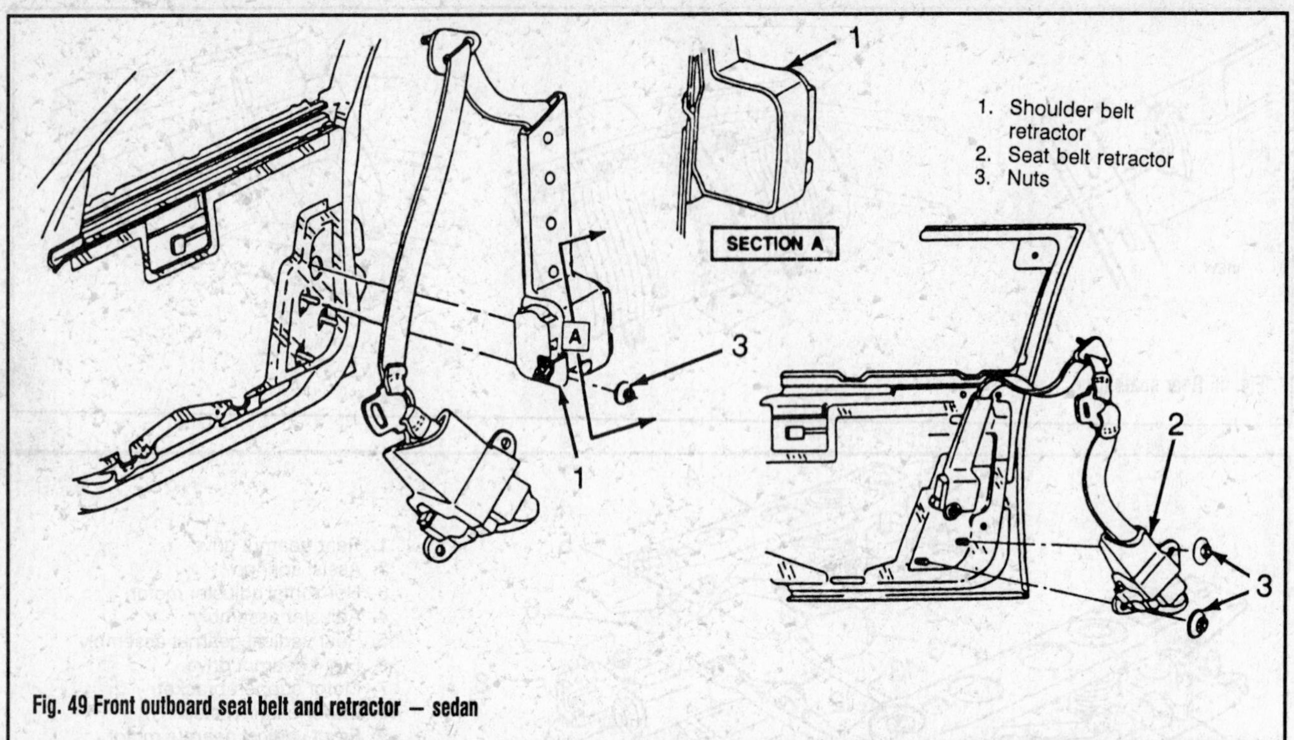

Fig. 49 Front outboard seat belt and retractor — sedan

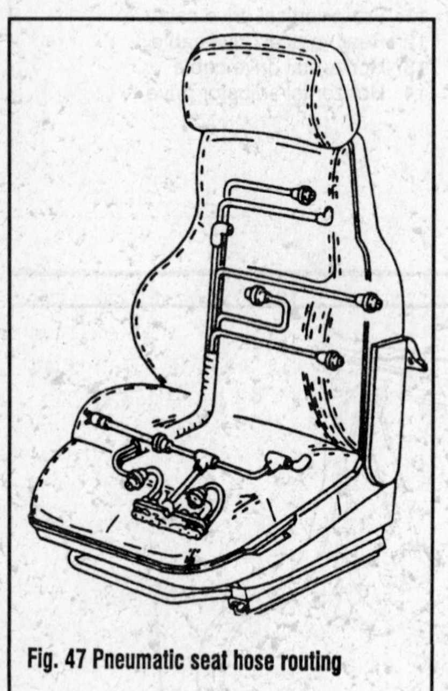

Fig. 47 Pneumatic seat hose routing

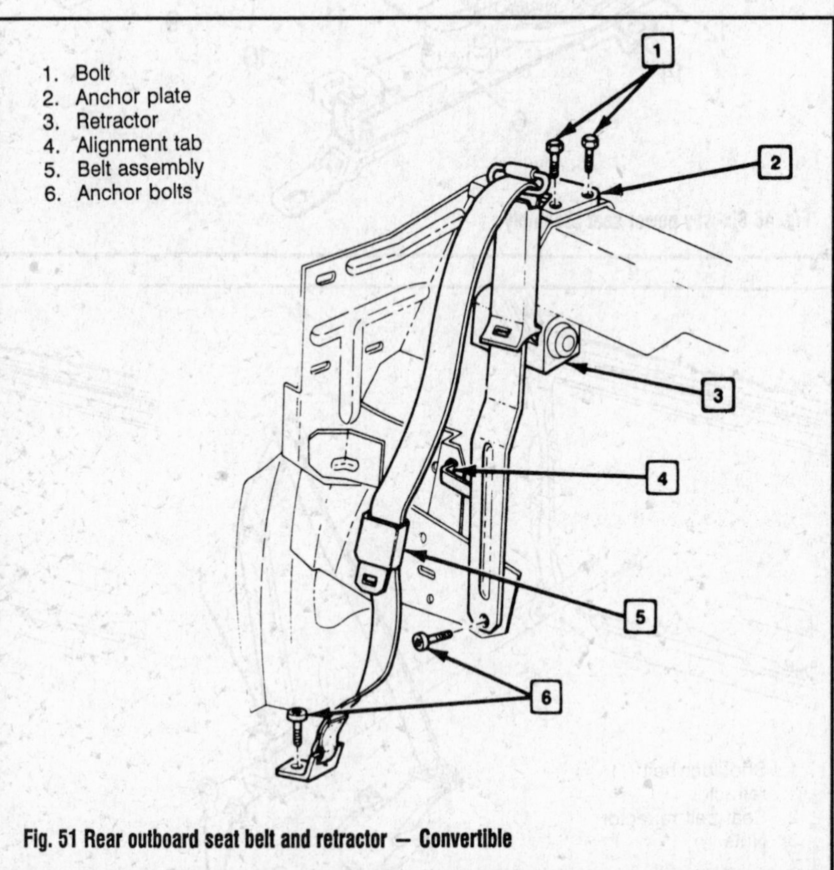

Fig. 51 Rear outboard seat belt and retractor — Convertible

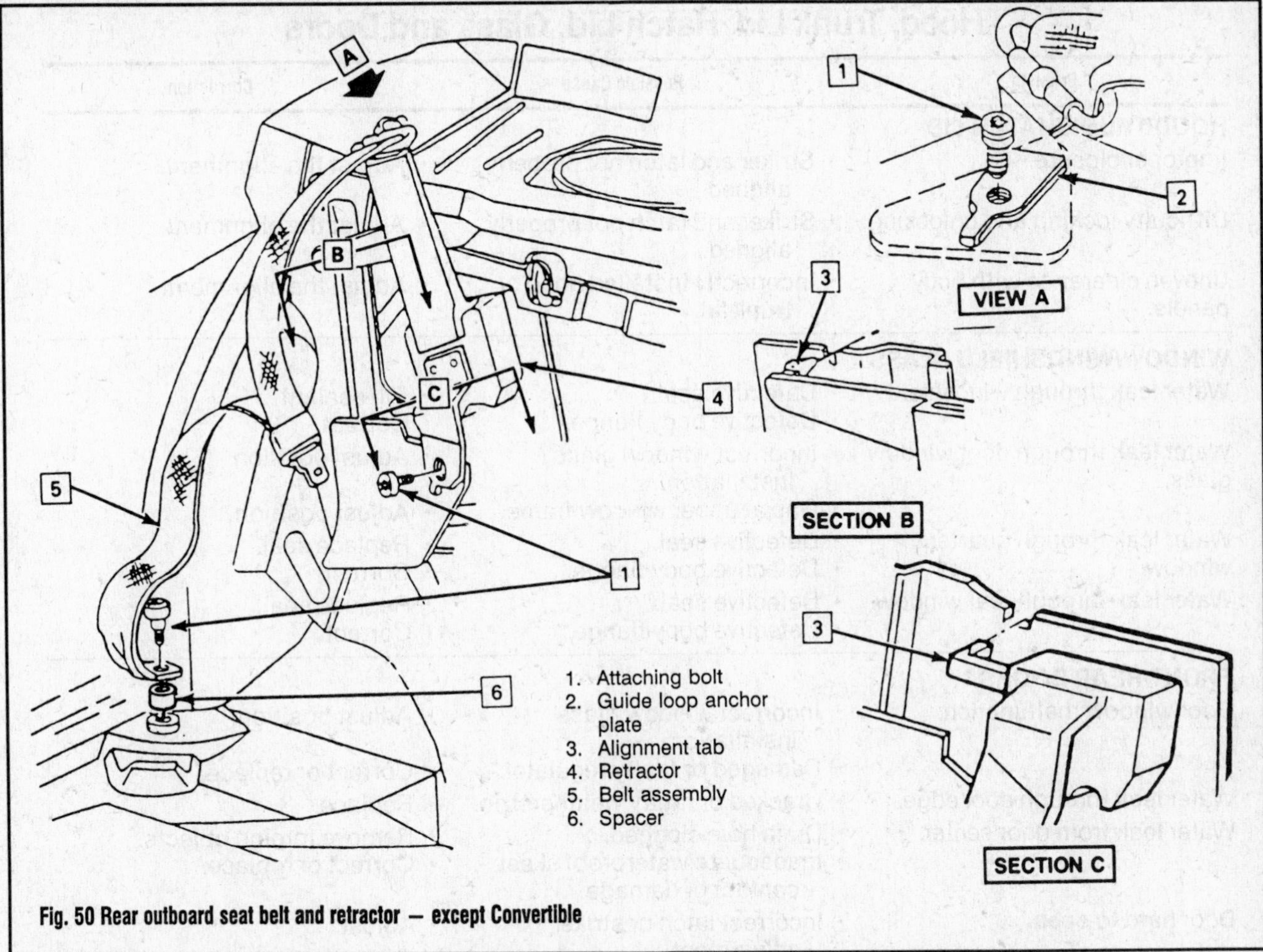

Fig. 50 Rear outboard seat belt and retractor — except Convertible

13. Install the adjuster assembly-to-seat bottom.

14. With an assistant, install the seat and check for proper operation.

Seat Belt Systems

➧ SEE FIGS. 48–51

REMOVAL & INSTALLATION

Front Outboard

1. Remove the 20 amp courtesy lamp fuse.
2. Remove the door trim panel.
3. Remove the screws securing the belt retainer to the door.
4. Disconnect the electrical connectors from the retractors.
5. Remove the retaining nuts from the retractor and remove the retractor.
6. Remove the shoulder belt retractor.
7. Pull back the water deflector and raise the window.
8. Remove the cover, nut, and washer from the upper guide loop and remove the upper guide loop.

To install:

9. Install the upper guide loop.
10. Install the washer and nut while holding the upper guide loop in place. Torque the nut to 21 ft. lbs. (28 Nm).
11. Install the cover and water deflector.
12. Install the shoulder belt retractor. Torque the nuts to 31 ft. lbs. (42 Nm).
13. Install the seat belt retractor. Torque the nuts to 31 ft. lbs. (42 Nm).
14. Connect the electrical connectors.
15. Install the belt retainer with the screws.
16. Install the trim panel and put the fuse back.

Center Belts

To remove the front center belts, simply pull them through the seat split and unbolt them from the floor. To remove the rear center belts, remove the rear seat cushion to reveal the bolts, and remove them. When installing, torque the bolts to 31 ft. lbs. (42 Nm).

Rear Outboard

1. Remove the rear seat cushion and seatback.
2. Remove the seat/window trim panel.
3. Remove the bolt securing the guide loop anchor plate using the proper Torx® socket.
4. Remove the bolts securing the belt assembly and retractor.
5. Remove the spacer if equipped, the retractor, and the belt assembly.

To install:

6. Install the belt assembly, retractor (be sure to seat the alignment tabs), and the spacer.
7. Install the retractor retaining bolt and torque to 31 ft. lbs. (42 Nm).
8. Install the guide loop anchor plate bolt and torque to 31 ft. lbs. (42 Nm).
9. Install the trim panel and seat parts.

Hood, Trunk Lid, Hatch Lid, Glass and Doors

Problem	Possible Cause	Correction
HOOD/TRUNK/HATCH LID		
Improper closure.	• Striker and latch not properly aligned.	• Adjust the alignment.
Difficulty locking and unlocking.	• Striker and latch not properly aligned.	• Adjust the alignment.
Uneven clearance with body panels.	• Incorrectly installed hood or trunk lid.	• Adjust the alignment.
WINDOW/WINDSHIELD GLASS		
Water leak through windshield	• Defective seal. • Defective body flange.	• Fill sealant • Correct.
Water leak through door window glass.	• Incorrect window glass installation. • Gap at upper window frame.	• Adjust position. • Adjust position.
Water leak through quarter window.	• Defective seal. • Defective body flange.	• Replace seal. • Correct.
Water leak through rear window.	• Defective seal. • Defective body flange.	• Replace seal. • Correct.
FRONT/REAR DOORS		
Door window malfunction.	• Incorrect window glass installation. • Damaged or faulty regulator.	• Adjust position. • Correct or replace.
Water leak through door edge.	• Cracked or faulty weatherstrip.	• Replace.
Water leak from door center.	• Drain hole clogged. • Inadequate waterproof skeet contact or damage.	• Remove foreign objects. • Correct or replace.
Door hard to open.	• Incorrect latch or striker adjustment.	• Adjust.
Door does not open or close completely.	• Incorrect door installation. • Defective door check strap. • Door check strap and hinge require grease.	• Adjust position. • Correct or replace. • Apply grease.
Uneven gap between door and body.	• Incorrect door installation.	• Adjust position.
Wind noise around door.	• Improperly installed weatherstrip. • Improper clearance between door glass and door weatherstrip. • Deformed door.	• Repair or replace. • Adjust. • Repair or replace.

How to Remove Stains from Fabric Interior

For best results, spots and stains should be removed as soon as possible. Never use gasoline, lacquer thinner, acetone, nail polish remover or bleach. Use a 3′ x 3″ piece of cheesecloth. Squeeze most of the liquid from the fabric and wipe the stained fabric from the outside of the stain toward the center with a lifting motion. Turn the cheesecloth as soon as one side becomes soiled. When using water to remove a stain, be sure to wash the entire section after the spot has been removed to avoid water stains. Encrusted spots can be broken up with a dull knife and vacuumed before removing the stain.

Type of Stain	How to Remove It
Surface spots	Brush the spots out with a small hand brush or use a commercial preparation such as K2R to lift the stain.
Mildew	Clean around the mildew with warm suds. Rinse in cold water and soak the mildew area in a solution of 1 part table salt and 2 parts water. Wash with upholstery cleaner.
Water stains	Water stains in fabric materials can be removed with a solution made from 1 cup of table salt dissolved in 1 quart of water. Vigorously scrub the solution into the stain and rinse with clear water. Water stains in nylon or other synthetic fabrics should be removed with a commercial type spot remover.
Chewing gum, tar, crayons, shoe polish (greasy stains)	Do not use a cleaner that will soften gum or tar. Harden the deposit with an ice cube and scrape away as much as possible with a dull knife. Moisten the remainder with cleaning fluid and scrub clean.
Ice cream, candy	Most candy has a sugar base and can be removed with a cloth wrung out in warm water. Oily candy, after cleaning with warm water, should be cleaned with upholstery cleaner. Rinse with warm water and clean the remainder with cleaning fluid.
Wine, alcohol, egg, milk, soft drink (non-greasy stains)	Do not use soap. Scrub the stain with a cloth wrung out in warm water. Remove the remainder with cleaning fluid.
Grease, oil, lipstick, butter and related stains	Use a spot remover to avoid leaving a ring. Work from the outisde of the stain to the center and dry with a clean cloth when the spot is gone.
Headliners (cloth)	Mix a solution of warm water and foam upholstery cleaner to give thick suds. Use only foam—liquid may streak or spot. Clean the entire headliner in one operation using a circular motion with a natural sponge.
Headliner (vinyl)	Use a vinyl cleaner with a sponge and wipe clean with a dry cloth.
Seats and door panels	Mix 1 pint upholstery cleaner in 1 gallon of water. Do not soak the fabric around the buttons.
Leather or vinyl fabric	Use a multi-purpose cleaner full strength and a stiff brush. Let stand 2 minutes and scrub thoroughly. Wipe with a clean, soft rag.
Nylon or synthetic fabrics	For normal stains, use the same procedures you would for washing cloth upholstery. If the fabric is extremely dirty, use a multi-purpose cleaner full strength with a stiff scrub brush. Scrub thoroughly in all directions and wipe with a cotton towel or soft rag.

TORQUE SPECIFICATIONS

Component	U.S.	Metric
Hinge-to-door retaining bolts	18 ft. lbs.	24 Nm
Hood-to-hinge bolts	20 ft. lbs.	27 Nm
Trunk lid retaining bolts	18 ft. lbs.	25 Nm
Bumper-to-body nuts	18 ft. lbs.	24 Nm
Outside Mirror retaining nuts	80 inch lbs.	9 Nm
Lower fender bolts	89 inch lbs.	10 Nm
Upper fender bolt	18 ft. lbs.	25 Nm
Lock module assembly screws	62 inch lbs.	7 Nm
Front window retainer bolts	53 inch lbs.	6 Nm
Rear window guide-to-division channel nuts	80 inch lbs.	9 Nm
Rear power window motor retaining nuts	80 inch lbs.	9 Nm
Rear anchor bolts for front seat	15 ft. lbs.	20 Nm
Front anchor bolts for front seat	20 ft. lbs.	27 Nm
Rear seat retaining nut or bolt	20 ft. lbs.	27 Nm
Front seat belt upper guide loop nut	21 ft. lbs.	28 Nm
All other seat-belt-related bolts	31 ft. lbs.	42 Nm

GLOSSARY

AIR/FUEL RATIO: The ratio of air to gasoline by weight in the fuel mixture drawn into the engine.

AIR INJECTION: One method of reducing harmful exhaust emissions by injecting air into each of the exhaust ports of an engine. The fresh air entering the hot exhaust manifold causes any remaining fuel to be burned before it can exit the tailpipe.

ALTERNATOR: A device used for converting mechanical energy into electrical energy.

AMMETER: An instrument, calibrated in amperes, used to measure the flow of an electrical current in a circuit. Ammeters are always connected in series with the circuit being tested.

AMPERE: The rate of flow of electrical current present when one volt of electrical pressure is applied against one ohm of electrical resistance.

ANALOG COMPUTER: Any microprocessor that uses similar (analogous) electrical signals to make its calculations.

ARMATURE: A laminated, soft iron core wrapped by a wire that converts electrical energy to mechanical energy as in a motor or relay. When rotated in a magnetic field, it changes mechanical energy into electrical energy as in a generator.

ATMOSPHERIC PRESSURE: The pressure on the Earth's surface caused by the weight of the air in the atmosphere. At sea level, this pressure is 14.7 psi at 32°F (101 kPa at 0°C).

ATOMIZATION: The breaking down of a liquid into a fine mist that can be suspended in air.

AXIAL PLAY: Movement parallel to a shaft or bearing bore.

BACKFIRE: The sudden combustion of gases in the intake or exhaust system that results in a loud explosion.

BACKLASH: The clearance or play between two parts, such as meshed gears.

BACKPRESSURE: Restrictions in the exhaust system that slow the exit of exhaust gases from the combustion chamber.

BAKELITE: A heat resistant, plastic insulator material commonly used in printed circuit boards and transistorized components.

BALL BEARING: A bearing made up of hardened inner and outer races between which hardened steel balls roll.

BALLAST RESISTOR: A resistor in the primary ignition circuit that lowers voltage after the engine is started to reduce wear on ignition components.

BEARING: A friction reducing, supportive device usually located between a stationary part and a moving part.

BIMETAL TEMPERATURE SENSOR: Any sensor or switch made of two dissimilar types of metal that bend when heated or cooled due to the different expansion rates of the alloys. These types of sensors usually function as an on/off switch.

BLOWBY: Combustion gases, composed of water vapor and unburned fuel, that leak past the piston rings into the crankcase during normal engine operation. These gases are removed by the PCV system to prevent the buildup of harmful acids in the crankcase.

BRAKE PAD: A brake shoe and lining assembly used with disc brakes.

BRAKE SHOE: The backing for the brake lining. The term is, however, usually applied to the assembly of the brake backing and lining.

BUSHING: A liner, usually removable, for a bearing; an anti-friction liner used in place of a bearing.

BYPASS: System used to bypass ballast resistor during engine cranking to increase voltage supplied to the coil.

CALIPER: A hydraulically activated device in a disc brake system, which is mounted straddling the brake rotor (disc). The caliper contains at least one piston and two brake pads. Hydraulic pressure on the piston(s) forces the pads against the rotor.

CAMSHAFT: A shaft in the engine on which are the lobes (cams) which operate the valves. The camshaft is driven by the crankshaft, via a belt, chain or gears, at one half the crankshaft speed.

CAPACITOR: A device which stores an electrical charge.

CARBON MONOXIDE (CO): A colorless, odorless gas given off as a normal byproduct of combustion. It is poisonous and extremely dangerous in confined areas, building up slowly to toxic levels without warning if adequate ventilation is not available.

CARBURETOR: A device, usually mounted on the intake manifold of an engine, which mixes the air and fuel in the proper proportion to allow even combustion.

CATALYTIC CONVERTER: A device installed in the exhaust system, like a muffler, that converts harmful byproducts of combustion into carbon dioxide and water vapor by means of a heat-producing chemical reaction.

CENTRIFUGAL ADVANCE: A mechanical method of advancing the spark timing by using fly weights in the distributor that react to centrifugal force generated by the distributor shaft rotation.

CHECK VALVE: Any one-way valve installed to permit the flow of air, fuel or vacuum in one direction only.

CHOKE: A device, usually a movable valve, placed in the intake path of a carburetor to restrict the flow of air.

CIRCUIT: Any unbroken path through which an electrical current can flow. Also used to describe fuel flow in some instances.

CIRCUIT BREAKER: A switch which protects an electrical circuit from overload by opening the circuit when the current flow exceeds a predetermined level. Some circuit breakers must be reset manually, while most reset automatically

COIL (IGNITION): A transformer in the ignition circuit which steps up the voltage provided to the spark plugs.

COMBINATION MANIFOLD: An assembly which includes both the intake and exhaust manifolds in one casting.

COMBINATION VALVE: A device used in some fuel systems that routes fuel vapors to a charcoal storage canister instead of venting them into the atmosphere. The valve relieves fuel tank pressure and allows fresh air into the tank as the fuel level drops to prevent a vapor lock situation.

COMPRESSION RATIO: The comparison of the total volume of the cylinder and combustion chamber with the piston at BDC and the piston at TDC.

CONDENSER: 1. An electrical device which acts to store an electrical charge, preventing voltage surges.
2. A radiator-like device in the air conditioning system in which refrigerant gas condenses into a liquid, giving off heat.

CONDUCTOR: Any material through which an electrical current can be transmitted easily.

CONTINUITY: Continuous or complete circuit. Can be checked with an ohmmeter.

COUNTERSHAFT: An intermediate shaft which is rotated by a mainshaft and transmits, in turn, that rotation to a working part.

CRANKCASE: The lower part of an engine in which the crankshaft and related parts operate.

CRANKSHAFT: The main driving shaft of an engine which receives reciprocating motion from the pistons and converts it to rotary motion.

CYLINDER: In an engine, the round hole in the engine block in which the piston(s) ride.

CYLINDER BLOCK: The main structural member of an engine in which is found the cylinders, crankshaft and other principal parts.

CYLINDER HEAD: The detachable portion of the engine, fastened, usually, to the top of the cylinder block, containing all or most of the combustion chambers. On overhead valve engines, it contains the valves and their operating parts. On overhead cam engines, it contains the camshaft as well.

DEAD CENTER: The extreme top or bottom of the piston stroke.

DETONATION: An unwanted explosion of the air/fuel mixture in the combustion chamber caused by excess heat and compression, advanced timing, or an overly lean mixture. Also referred to as "ping".

DIAPHRAGM: A thin, flexible wall separating two cavities, such as in a vacuum advance unit.

DIESELING: A condition in which hot spots in the combustion chamber cause the engine to run on after the key is turned off.

DIFFERENTIAL: A geared assembly which allows the transmission of motion between drive axles, giving one axle the ability to turn faster than the other.

DIODE: An electrical device that will allow current to flow in one direction only.

DISC BRAKE: A hydraulic braking assembly consisting of a brake disc, or rotor, mounted on an axle, and a caliper assembly containing, usually two brake pads which are activated by hydraulic pressure. The pads are forced against the sides of the disc, creating friction which slows the vehicle.

DISTRIBUTOR: A mechanically driven device on an engine which is responsible for electrically firing the spark plug at a predetermined point of the piston stroke.

DOWEL PIN: A pin, inserted in mating holes in two different parts allowing those parts to maintain a fixed relationship.

DRUM BRAKE: A braking system which consists of two brake shoes and one or two wheel cylinders, mounted on a fixed backing plate, and a brake drum, mounted on an axle, which revolves around the assembly. Hydraulic action applied to the wheel cylinders forces the shoes outward against the drum, creating friction, slowing the vehicle.

DWELL: The rate, measured in degrees of shaft rotation, at which an electrical circuit cycles on and off.

ELECTRONIC CONTROL UNIT (ECU): Ignition module, amplifier or igniter. See Module for definition.

ELECTRONIC IGNITION: A system in which the timing and firing of the spark plugs is controlled by an electronic control unit, usually called a module. These systems have no points or condenser.

ENDPLAY: The measured amount of axial movement in a shaft.

ENGINE: A device that converts heat into mechanical energy.

EXHAUST MANIFOLD: A set of cast passages or pipes which conduct exhaust gases from the engine.

FEELER GAUGE: A blade, usually metal, of precisely predetermined thickness, used to measure the clearance between two parts. These blades usually are available in sets of assorted thicknesses.

F-HEAD: An engine configuration in which the intake valves are in the cylinder head, while the camshaft and exhaust valves are located in the cylinder block. The camshaft operates the intake valves via lifters and pushrods, while it operates the exhaust valves directly.

FIRING ORDER: The order in which combustion occurs in the cylinders of an engine. Also the order in which spark is distributed to the plugs by the distributor.

FLATHEAD: An engine configuration in which the camshaft and all the valves are located in the cylinder block.

FLOODING: The presence of too much fuel in the intake manifold and combustion chamber which prevents the air/fuel mixture from firing, thereby causing a no-start situation.

FLYWHEEL: A disc shaped part bolted to the rear end of the crankshaft. Around the outer perimeter is affixed the ring gear. The starter drive engages the ring gear, turning the flywheel, which rotates the crankshaft, imparting the initial starting motion to the engine.

FOOT POUND (ft.lb. or sometimes, ft. lbs.): The amount of energy or work needed to raise an item weighing one pound, a distance of one foot.

FUSE: A protective device in a circuit which prevents circuit overload by breaking the circuit when a specific amperage is present. The device is constructed around a strip or wire of a lower amperage rating than the circuit it is designed to protect. When an amperage higher than that stamped on the fuse is present in the circuit, the strip or wire melts, opening the circuit.

GEAR RATIO: The ratio between the number of teeth on meshing gears.

GENERATOR: A device which converts mechanical energy into electrical energy.

HEAT RANGE: The measure of a spark plug's ability to dissipate heat from its firing end. The higher the heat range, the hotter the plug fires.

HUB: The center part of a wheel or gear.

HYDROCARBON (HC): Any chemical compound made up of hydrogen and carbon. A major pollutant formed by the engine as a byproduct of combustion.

HYDROMETER: An instrument used to measure the specific gravity of a solution.

INCH POUND (in.lb. or sometimes, in. lbs.): One twelfth of a foot pound.

INDUCTION: A means of transferring electrical energy in the form of a magnetic field. Principle used in the ignition coil to increase voltage.

INJECTION PUMP: A device, usually mechanically operated, which meters and delivers fuel under pressure to the fuel injector.

INJECTOR: A device which receives metered fuel under relatively low pressure and is activated to inject the fuel into the engine under relatively high pressure at a predetermined time.

INPUT SHAFT: The shaft to which torque is applied, usually carrying the driving gear or gears.

INTAKE MANIFOLD: A casting of passages or pipes used to conduct air or a fuel/air mixture to the cylinders.

JOURNAL: The bearing surface within which a shaft operates.

KEY: A small block usually fitted in a notch between a shaft and a hub to prevent slippage of the two parts.

MANIFOLD: A casting of passages or set of pipes which connect the cylinders to an inlet or outlet source.

MANIFOLD VACUUM: Low pressure in an engine intake manifold formed just below the throttle plates. Manifold vacuum is highest at idle and drops under acceleration.

MASTER CYLINDER: The primary fluid pressurizing device in a hydraulic system. In automotive use, it is found in brake and hydraulic clutch systems and is pedal activated, either directly or, in a power brake system, through the power booster.

MODULE: Electronic control unit, amplifier or igniter of solid state or integrated design which controls the current flow in the ignition primary circuit based on input from the pick- up coil. When the module opens the primary circuit, the high secondary voltage is induced in the coil.

NEEDLE BEARING: A bearing which consists of a number (usually a large number) of long, thin rollers.

OHM:(Ω) The unit used to measure the resistance of conductor to electrical flow. One ohm is the amount of resistance that limits current flow to one ampere in a circuit with one volt of pressure.

OHMMETER: An instrument used for measuring the resistance, in ohms, in an electrical circuit.

OUTPUT SHAFT: The shaft which transmits torque from a device, such as a transmission.

OVERDRIVE: A gear assembly which produces more shaft revolutions than that transmitted to it.

OVERHEAD CAMSHAFT (OHC): An engine configuration in which the camshaft is mounted on top of the cylinder head and operates the valves either directly or by means of rocker arms.

OVERHEAD VALVE (OHV): An engine configuration in which all of the valves are located in the cylinder head and the camshaft is located in the cylinder block. The camshaft operates the valves via lifters and pushrods.

OXIDES OF NITROGEN (NOx): Chemical compounds of nitrogen produced as a byproduct of combustion. They combine with hydrocarbons to produce smog.

OXYGEN SENSOR: Used with the feedback system to sense the presence of oxygen in the exhaust gas and signal the computer which can reference the voltage signal to an air/fuel ratio.

PINION: The smaller of two meshing gears.

PISTON RING: An open ended ring which fits into a groove on the outer diameter of the piston. Its chief function is to form a seal between the piston and cylinder wall. Most automotive pistons have three rings: two for compression sealing; one for oil sealing.

PRELOAD: A predetermined load placed on a bearing during assembly or by adjustment.

PRIMARY CIRCUIT: Is the low voltage side of the ignition system which consists of the ignition switch, ballast resistor or resistance wire, bypass, coil, electronic control unit and pick-up coil as well as the connecting wires and harnesses.

PRESS FIT: The mating of two parts under pressure, due to the inner diameter of one being smaller than the outer diameter of the other, or vice versa; an interference fit.

RACE: The surface on the inner or outer ring of a bearing on which the balls, needles or rollers move.

REGULATOR: A device which maintains the amperage and/or voltage levels of a circuit at predetermined values.

RELAY: A switch which automatically opens and/or closes a circuit.

RESISTANCE: The opposition to the flow of current through a circuit or electrical device, and is measured in ohms. Resistance is equal to the voltage divided by the amperage.

RESISTOR: A device, usually made of wire, which offers a preset amount of resistance in an electrical circuit.

RING GEAR: The name given to a ring-shaped gear attached to a differential case,or affixed to a flywheel or as part a planetary gear set.

ROLLER BEARING: A bearing made up of hardened inner and outer races between which hardened steel rollers move.

ROTOR: 1. The disc-shaped part of a disc brake assembly, upon which the brake pads bear; also called, brake disc.
2. The device mounted atop the distributor shaft, which passes current to the distributor cap tower contacts.

SECONDARY CIRCUIT: The high voltage side of the ignition system, usually above 20,000 volts. The secondary includes the ignition coil, coil wire, distributor cap and rotor, spark plug wires and spark plugs.

SENDING UNIT: A mechanical, electrical, hydraulic or electromagnetic device which transmits information to a gauge.

SENSOR: Any device designed to measure engine operating conditions or ambient pressures and temperatures. Usually electronic in nature and designed to send a voltage signal to an on-board computer, some sensors may operate as a simple on/off switch or they may provide a variable voltage signal (like a potentiometer) as conditions or measured parameters change.

SHIM: Spacers of precise, predetermined thickness used between parts to establish a proper working relationship.

SLAVE CYLINDER: In automotive use, a device in the hydraulic clutch system which is activated by hydraulic force, disengaging the clutch.

SOLENOID: A coil used to produce a magnetic field, the effect of which is to produce work.

SPARK PLUG: A device screwed into the combustion chamber of a spark ignition engine. The basic construction is a conductive core inside of a ceramic insulator, mounted in an outer conductive base. An electrical charge from the spark plug wire travels along the conductive core and jumps a preset air gap to a grounding point or points at the end of the conductive base. The resultant spark ignites the fuel/air mixture in the combustion chamber.

SPLINES: Ridges machined or cast onto the outer diameter of a shaft or inner diameter of a bore to enable parts to mate without rotation.

TACHOMETER: A device used to measure the rotary speed of an engine, shaft, gear, etc., usually in rotations per minute.

THERMOSTAT: A valve, located in the cooling system of an engine, which is closed when cold and opens gradually in response to engine heating, controlling the temperature of the coolant and rate of coolant flow.

TOP DEAD CENTER (TDC): The point at which the piston reaches the top of its travel on the compression stroke.

TORQUE: The twisting force applied to an object.

TORQUE CONVERTER: A turbine used to transmit power from a driving member to a driven member via hydraulic action, providing changes in drive ratio and torque. In automotive use, it links the driveplate at the rear of the engine to the automatic transmission.

TRANSDUCER: A device used to change a force into an electrical signal.

TRANSISTOR: A semi-conductor component which can be actuated by a small voltage to perform an electrical switching function.

TUNE-UP: A regular maintenance function, usually associated with the replacement and adjustment of parts and components in the electrical and fuel systems of a vehicle for the purpose of attaining optimum performance.

TURBOCHARGER: An exhaust driven pump which compresses intake air and forces it into the combustion chambers at higher than atmospheric pressures. The increased air pressure allows more fuel to be burned and results in increased horsepower being produced.

VACUUM ADVANCE: A device which advances the ignition timing in response to increased engine vacuum.

VACUUM GAUGE: An instrument used to measure the presence of vacuum in a chamber.

VALVE: A device which control the pressure, direction of flow or rate of flow of a liquid or gas.

VALVE CLEARANCE: The measured gap between the end of the valve stem and the rocker arm, cam lobe or follower that activates the valve.

VISCOSITY: The rating of a liquid's internal resistance to flow.

VOLTMETER: An instrument used for measuring electrical force in units called volts. Voltmeters are always connected parallel with the circuit being tested.

WHEEL CYLINDER: Found in the automotive drum brake assembly, it is a device, actuated by hydraulic pressure, which, through internal pistons, pushes the brake shoes outward against the drums.

MASTER
INDEX